AMG's COMPREHENSIVE DICTIONARY *of* OLD TESTAMENT WORDS

Based on the original work of

Warren Baker, D.R.E.
Eugene Carpenter, Ph.D.

The Complete Word Study Dictionary: Old Testament

E. Richard Pigeon, Ph.D.
Editor

Advancing the Ministries of the Gospel
AMG Publishers

God's Word to you is our highest calling.

AMG's COMPREHENSIVE DICTIONARY OF OLD TESTAMENT WORDS
E. Richard Pigeon
Editor

Published by AMG Publishers
6815 Shallowford Rd.
Chattanooga, Tennessee 37421

ISBN 978-1-61715-428-7
First printing date: April 2017

Cover design: Bright Boy Design, Chattanooga, Tennessee
Interior design: Scribe Inc.

Printed in China

Table of Contents

Foreword

AMG's Comprehensive Dictionary of Old Testament Words is essentially a reorganization of the material contained in the excellent Complete Word Study Dictionary: Old Testament (2003) by Warren Baker and Eugene Carpenter. The entries of the present book are now organized alphabetically by English words, rather than by Strong's codes and Hebrew words.

I have consulted five translations of the Old Testament in editing the original work of Baker and Carpenter: English Standard Version, King James Version, New American Standard Bible, New International Version, and New King James Version. Understandably, many entries are cross-references. Additions to the present work include etymological information on the Hebrew words from James Strong and expanded definition for a significant number of names of people and places. I have also indicated when all references are provided for an entry or a sub-entry, and the number of times the Hebrew words appear in the Old Testament. Finally, in Part II of this work, you will find a complete Hebrew-English lexicon that relates each Hebrew term to the entry of the corresponding English term in Part I.

I wish to express my gratitude to Mrs. Gretchen S. Lebrun and Dr. Rick Shepherd who have collaborated in the revision of the book. I thank Mr. Trevor Overcash, at AMG Publishers, who has collaborated in the production of this work.

It is my sincere desire, as previously stated in my Preface to the AMG's Comprehensive Dictionary of New Testament Words (2014), that you will find this Comprehensive Dictionary of Old Testament Words also useful when studying the word of God, teaching it, or serving the Lord.

E. Richard Pigeon
Gatineau (Quebec)
Canada
erpigeon@videotron.ca
September 2016

Preface to the Complete Word Study Dictionary: Old Testament

The Complete Word Study Dictionary: Old Testament is the final volume in AMG's Word Study Series. These Bible study tools are designed to make the original languages of the Bible accessible to every student of the Word of God. This lexicon is intended as a companion volume to *The Complete Word Study Old Testament,* which identifies the words of the Hebrew text of the Old Testament by the placement of Strong's numbers and grammatical codes over the English text. Together these two volumes represent the Old Testament portion of this series.

This book consists of two parts: The Complete Word Study Dictionary: Old Testament and The Complete Word Study Old Testament Concordance.

The Complete Word Study Dictionary: Old Testament offers definitions and explanations for every word used in the Hebrew Old Testament. Each entry is identified by a number from Strong's Dictionary of the Hebrew Bible, so that readers can make great use of the information that is given about each word, even if they have no working knowledge of the Hebrew language.

The Complete Word Study Old Testament Concordance is also coded to Strong's numbering system. This concordance details every occurrence of every Hebrew and Aramaic word in the Old Testament by book, chapter, and verse.

Books of the Bible

Old Testament Books

Genesis	Gen.
Exodus	Ex.
Leviticus	Lev.
Numbers	Num.
Deuteronomy	Deut.
Joshua	Josh.
Judges	Judg.
Ruth	Ruth
1 Samuel	1 Sam.
2 Samuel	2 Sam.
1 Kings	1 Kgs.
2 Kings	2 Kgs.
1 Chronicles	1 Chr.
2 Chronicles	2 Chr.
Ezra	Ezra
Nehemiah	Neh.
Esther	Esther
Job	Job
Psalms	Ps.
Proverbs	Prov.
Ecclesiastes	Eccl.
Song of Solomon	Song
Isaiah	Is.
Jeremiah	Jer.
Lamentations	Lam.
Ezekiel	Ezek.
Daniel	Dan.
Hosea	Hos.
Joel	Joel
Amos	Amos
Obadiah	Obad.
Jonah	Jon.
Micah	Mic.
Nahum	Nah.
Habakkuk	Hab.
Zephaniah	Zeph.
Haggai	Hag.
Zechariah	Zech.
Malachi	Mal.

New Testament Books

Matthew	Matt.
Mark	Mark
Luke	Luke
John	John
Acts	Acts
Romans	Rom.
1 Corinthians	1 Cor.
2 Corinthians	2 Cor.
Galatians	Gal.
Ephesians	Eph.
Philippians	Phil.
Colossians	Col.
1 Thessalonians	1 Thes.
2 Thessalonians	2 Thes.
1 Timothy	1 Tim.
2 Timothy	2 Tim.
Titus	Titus
Philemon	Phm.
Hebrews	Heb.
James	Jas.
1 Peter	1 Pet.
2 Peter	2 Pet.
1 John	1 John
2 John	2 John
3 John	3 John
Jude	Jude
Revelation	Rev.

Abbreviations and Symbols

act.	(active)
adj.	(adjective, adjectival)
adv.	(adverb, adverbial, adverbially)
art.	(article)
B.C.	(before Christ)
ca.	(circa)
cf.	(compare, comparison)
chap.	(chapter)
coll.	(collective)
comp.	(compare)
conj.	(conjunction, conjunctive)
contr.	(contracted, contraction)
demons.	(demonstrative)
denom.	(denominative)
deriv.	(derivative, derivation)
e.g.	(for example)
ESV	(English Standard Version)
etc.	(and so forth)
f.	(following)
ff.	(following in the plural)
fem.	(feminine)
fig.	(figuratively)
i.e.	(that is)
inf.	(infinitive)
intens.	(intensive)
interj.	(interjection)
interr.	(interrogative)
KJV	(King James Version)
lit.	(literally)
masc.	(masculine)
Mss.	(manuscripts)
NAS, NASB	(New American Standard Bible)
NIV	(New International Version)
NKJV	(New King James Version)
neg.	(negative)
part.	(participle, participial)
pass.	(passive)
patron.	(patronymic, patronymical, patronymically)
plur.	(plural)
prep.	(preposition, prepositional)
prim.	(primitive)
prob.	(probably)
pron.	(pronoun, pronominal)
Ref.	(reference)
Refs.	(references)
sing.	(singular)
syn.	(synonym)
v.	(verse)
¶	indicates that all references are provided
*	indicates that not all references are provided

Guide to the Transliteration of Hebrew Consonants

Consonant	Hebrew Name	Transliteration	Phonetic Sound	Example
א	Aleph	ʾ	Silent	similar to h in honor
בּ	Beth	*b*	b	as in boy
ב	Veth	*ḇ*	v	as in vat
גּ	Gimel	*g*	g	as in get
ג	Gimel	*g̱*	g	as in get
דּ	Daleth	*d*	d	as in do
ד	Daleth	*ḏ*	d	as in do
ה	Hê	*h*	h	as in hat
ו	Waw	*w*	w	as in wait
ז	Zayin	*z*	z	as in zip
ח	Cheth	*ḥ*	ch	similar to ch in the German *ach*
ט	Teth	*ṭ*	t	as in time
י	Yodh	*y*	y	as in you
כּ	Kaph	*k*	k	as in kit
כ	Chaph	*ḵ*	ch	similar to ch in the German *ach*
ל	Lamed	*l*	l	as in lit
מ	Mem	*m*	m	as in move
נ	Nun	*n*	n	as in not
ס	Samek	h	*s*	s as in see
ע	Ayin	ʿ	Silent	similar to h in honor
פּ	Pê	*p*	p	as in put
פ	Phê	*p̱*	f	as in phone
צ	Tsadde	*ṣ*	ts	as in wits
ק	Qoph	*q*	q	as in Qatar
ר	Resh	*r*	r	as in run
שׂ	Sin	*ś*	s	as in see
שׁ	Shin	*š*	sh	as in ship
תּ	Taw	*t*	t	as in time
ת	Thaw	*ṯ*	th	as in this

Guide to the Transliteration of Hebrew Vowels

Vowel	Hebrew Name	Position	Transliteration	Sound
ְ	Shewa (Silent)	מְ	*Not transliterated or pronounced*	
ְ	Shewa (Vocal)	מְ	^{e}	u as in but
ַ	Pathah	מַ	*a*	a as in lad
ֲ	Hateph Pathah	מֲ	^{a}	a as in lad
ָ	Qamets	מָ	*ā*	a as in car
ֳ	Hateph Qamets	מֳ	^{o}	a as in car
ֵי	Sere Yodh	מֵי	*êy*	ey as in prey
ֵ	Sere	מֵ	*ê*	ey as in prey
ֶ	Seghol	מֶ	*e*	e as in set
ֱ	Hateph Seghol	מֱ	^{e}	e as in set
ִי	Hiriq Yodh	מִי	*iy*	i as in machine
ִ	Hiriq	מִ	*i*	i as in pin
ָ	Qamets Qatan	מָ	*o*	o as in hop
ֹ	Holem	מֹ	*ō*	o as in go
וֹ	Holem Waw	מוֹ	*ô*	o as in go
ֻ	Qubbuts	מֻ	*u*	u as in put
וּ	Shureq	מוּ	*û*	u as in tune

Explanations of Entries

Part I – Entry for a Common Word

For each entry of an English O.T. word being defined in this Comprehensive Dictionary, information is provided about the Hebrew word translated: its English transliteration, the part of speech of the word (noun, verb, etc.), the Hebrew word with the corresponding Strong's number, as well as information on the etymology of the word. A definition of the Hebrew word and its corresponding English word follows. Verses where the word is found in the O.T. are paraphrased and/or references are provided. In a large number of entries, all references are given (indicated by the sign ¶). In a few entries, an * indicates that all references are not given. Very often, cross-references for the same English word are provided indicating where they will be found under other English words.

① English word
② Transliteration of Hebrew word
③ Hebrew word
④ Strong's number
⑤ Etymology
⑥ Part of speech of the word in Hebrew
⑦ Definition of Hebrew word
⑧ Biblical reference for each verse
⑨ Paraphrased verse(s)
⑩ Indication of the completeness of references provided
⑪ Cross-reference(s) for the English word leading to another entry

① ② ③ ④ ⑤

ARMY – [1] ***'alqûm*** [אַלְקוּם <510>; prob. from NO <408> and STAND, STAND UP <6965> (i.e., no uprising)] ▶

⑥ ⑦

a. A masculine noun describing troops, a band of soldiers, military levy. Ref.:

⑧ ⑨

Prov. 30:31. The presence of a royal army or troops causes the king to overflow with pride

⑩

(NASB, NIV, NKJV; see b.). ¶

b. Possibly a compound noun meaning no uprising or no adversary. Ref.: Prov. 30:31, KJV; see a. ¶

[2] ***ma'ărāh*** [fem. noun: מַעֲרָה <4630>; fem. of MEADOW <4629> (in the sense of an open spot)] ▶ **This word refers to a group of men prepared and ready to fight for their country or people.** Ref.: 1 Sam. 17:23; also translated rank, line. Some prefer to read this as a specific place or location. ¶

⑪

– [3] 1 Sam. 17:10, 45 ➔ ARRAY (noun) <4634> [4] Zech. 9:8 ➔ GARRISON <4675> [5] See CAMP <4264>.

Part I – Entry for a Name of Person or Place

For each entry of an English name of person or place used in the O.T., information is provided about the Hebrew name translated: its English transliteration, the gender of the name or place in Hebrew, the Hebrew name with the corresponding Strong's number, as well as the etymology and/or meaning of the name when known. Information on the person or place is then provided. Verses where the word is found in the O.T. are paraphrased and/or references are provided. All references are given, unless indicated by an asterisk.

① English name
② Transliteration of Hebrew name
③ Part of speech of the word in Hebrew
④ Hebrew name
⑤ Strong's number
⑥ Etymology and/or meaning
⑦ Definition of Hebrew word
⑧ Reference(s) for each verse
⑨ Indication of the completeness of references provided

① ② ③ ④ ⑤ ⑥
AZUBAH – ***'azûḇāh*** [fem. proper noun: עֲזוּבָה <5806>; the same as FORSAKEN PLACE <5805>]: forsaken, deserted ▶

⑦ ⑧ ⑨
a. The mother of Jehoshaphat. Refs.: 1 Kgs. 22:42; 2 Chr. 20:31. ¶
b. The wife of Caleb. Refs.: 1 Chr. 2:18, 19. ¶

Part I – Entry for Cross-References

Numerous cross-references of terms are provided and linked to definitions of common words and names of people and places. It is possible that you may not find an English word of interest in Part I. However, if you know the Hebrew term, you can find the cross-reference by consulting the Hebrew-English Lexicon in Part II.

① English term
② Reference(s)
③ Target entry
④ Corresponding Strong's number

① ② ③ ④
ATONE – Ps. 78:38; 79:9; Is. 6:7 ➔ COVER (verb) <3722>.

Part II – Hebrew-English Lexicon

Part II of this Comprehensive Dictionary provides a list of all O.T. terms and, for each one, its corresponding English common word or name of person or place. The Strong's number, the English transliteration, and the frequency is also given for each Hebrew term. Frequencies of some terms may vary from those indicated by other authors, given that different manuscripts may have been considered.

① Strong's number
② Hebrew term
③ Transliteration of Hebrew term
④ Target entry in Part I
⑤ Frequency of Hebrew term in the O.T.

① ② ③ ④ ⑤
<1> אָב ***'āḇ*** [FATHER] 1,215x
<2> אַב ***'aḇ*** [FATHER] 9x
<3> אֵב ***'ēḇ*** [GREENNESS] 2x
<4> אֵב ***'ēḇ*** [FRUIT] 3x

Part I

Dictionary of Old Testament Words

A

A ONE – ***'almōniy*** [masc. noun: אַלְמֹנִי <492>; from WIDOWHOOD <489> in the sense of concealment] ▶ **The word serves as an indefinite pronoun meaning so and so, such a one, friend. Its exact meaning is difficult to discern.** It indicates an unidentified relative (Ruth 4:1) but also a certain unknown place (such a place, certain place) (1 Sam. 21:2; 2 Kgs. 6:8). ¶

AARON – ***'ahᵃrôn*** [masc. proper noun: אַהֲרוֹן <175>; of uncertain deriv.] ▶ **Moses' older brother and the first high priest in Israel.** He was the third descendant of Levi (Ex. 6:16–20; 1 Chr. 6:1–3). He was three years older than Moses (Ex. 7:7). He played important roles in Israel: God used him to welcome and receive Moses back to Egypt (Ex. 4:27), and he served as Moses' spokesman at times (Ex. 4:16; 7:1). He performed, at Moses' bidding, several of the plagues (Ex. 7:9, 10); he was permitted to ascend Sinai and eat and drink in the presence of the Lord (Ex. 24:1–10); he was in charge of the people while Moses was on Sinai, but unfortunately, he succumbed to the desires and threats of the people, fashioned a golden calf, and proclaimed an illegal feast to Yahweh, the Lord (Exodus 32). He was strongly rebuked by Moses (Ex. 32:21–24). God, nevertheless, chose him as Israel's first high priest, an office passed on by divine order to his sons (Exodus 28). He became involved in murmuring against Moses as sole leader of the people for which he was rebuked (Numbers 12). He was divinely approved as Israel's high priest (Numbers 16, 17) when his rod budded and bore fruit while the other rods did not. This is noted in the New Testament (Heb. 9:4). He and Moses failed to trust God at a key juncture (Meribah) in Israel's wilderness wanderings and were forbidden to enter the Promised Land (Num. 20:12). His death is emphasized to honor him (Num. 20; 33:38, 39; Deut. 10:6). He was buried on Mount Hor. He had four sons through Elisheba, his wife, named Nadab, Abihu, Eleazar, and Ithamar (Ex. 6:23). The first two were killed because they offered illegal fire before the Lord's altar (Lev. 10:1–3). Eleazar succeeded Aaron (Num. 20:28; Deut. 10:6). The phrases "sons of Aaron" / "descendants of Aaron" are found regularly in the Old Testament (e.g., Josh. 21:4, 10; 1 Chr. 6:54). *

ABADDON – Prov. 27:20 ➔ DESTRUCTION <10>.

ABAGTHA – ***ᵃḇagṯā'*** [masc. proper noun: אֲבַגְתָא <5>; of foreign origin] ▶ **One of the eunuchs mentioned as servants of Xerxes (Ahasuerus).** Ref.: Esther 1:10. ¶

ABANA – ***ᵃḇānāh*** [proper noun: אֲבָנָה <71>; perhaps fem. of STONE <68>] ▶ **A river of Damascus.** Ref.: 2 Kgs. 5:12; also spelled Abanah. ¶

ABANDON – [1] Deut. 32:15; Ps. 27:9 ➔ FORSAKE <5203> [2] Lam. 2:7 ➔ RENOUNCE <5010>.

ABARIM – ***ʿᵃḇāriym*** [proper noun: עֲבָרִים <5682>; plur. of SIDE <5676>]: regions beyond ▶ **The Israelites stayed in that region in the wilderness.** Refs.: Num. 33:47, 48. The Lord told Moses to go up into the mountain of Abarim to see the Promised Land (Num. 27:12; Deut. 32:49; see 34:1). Other ref.: Jer. 22:20. ¶

ABATE – Esther 2:1; 7:10 ➔ SUBSIDE <7918>.

ABDA – ***'aḇdā'*** [masc. proper noun: עַבְדָּא <5653>; from SERVE <5647>]: servant (of God) ▶
a. The father of Adoniram. Ref.: 1 Kgs. 4:6. ¶
b. A Levite. Ref.: Neh. 11:17. ¶

ABDEEL – ***'aḇdᵉ'ēl*** [masc. proper noun: עַבְדְּאֵל <5655>; from SERVE <5647> and GOD <410>]: servant of God ▶ **The father of Shelemiah, an official under Jehoiakim who was to seize Baruch and Jeremiah.** Ref.: Jer. 36:26. ¶

ABDI – ***'aḇdiy*** [masc. proper noun: עַבְדִּי <5660>; from SERVE <5647>]: servant (of the Lord) ▶
a. A Levite. Refs.: 1 Chr. 6:44; 2 Chr. 29:12. ¶
b. A postexilic Jew. Ref.: Ezra 10:26. ¶

ABDIEL – ***'aḇdiy'ēl*** [masc. proper noun: עַבְדִּיאֵל <5661>; from ABDI <5660> and GOD <410>]: servant of God ▶ **A descendant of Gad.** Ref.: 1 Chr. 5:15. ¶

ABDON – [1] ***'aḇdôn*** [proper noun: עַבְדּוֹן <5658>; from SERVE <5647>]: servitude ▶
a. A Levitical city. Refs.: Josh. 21:30; 1 Chr. 6:74. ¶
b. A judge. Refs.: Judg. 12:13, 15. ¶
c. A Benjamite. Ref.: 1 Chr. 8:23. ¶
d. The son of Jeiel. Refs.: 1 Chr. 8:30; 9:36. ¶
e. The son of Micah. Ref.: 2 Chr. 34:20. ¶
– [2] Josh. 19:28 ➔ EBRON <5683>.

ABED-NEGO – [1] ***'ᵃḇeḏ nᵉḡô*** [masc. proper noun: עֲבֵד נְגוֹ <5664>; the same as <5665> below]: servant of Nego (a Babylonian god) ▶ **This name was given to Azariah, a youth from Judah exiled in Babylon with Daniel.** Ref.: Dan. 1:7. He showed himself faithful to his God (Daniel 3; see <5665> below). ¶
[2] ***'ᵃḇēḏ nᵉḡô'*** [Aramaic masc. proper noun: עֲבֵד נְגוֹא <5665>; of foreign origin] ▶ **This is the Aramaic name of Azariah.** It corresponds to the Hebrew name (see <5664> above). The meaning is the same. Refs.: Dan. 2:49; 3:12–14, 16, 19, 20, 22, 23, 26, 28–30. ¶

ABEL (person) – ***heḇel*** [masc. proper noun: הֶבֶל <1893>; the same as VANITY <1892>]: vanity ▶ **The second son of Adam and Eve who pleased God by his faith.** Refs.: Gen. 4:2, 4. He was slain by his brother Cain (Gen. 4:8, 9). Seth replaced him (Gen. 4:25). Fittingly, his name means "vanity, wind," depicting his ephemeral life (cf. Heb. 11:1–3). ¶

ABEL (place) – ***'āḇēl*** [proper noun: אָבֵל <59>; from PLAIN (noun) <58>]: meadow ▶ **The word is used of a stone and a city.**
a. A proper noun designating a great stone named Abel where the ark was temporarily. Ref.: 1 Sam. 6:18; "great stone of Abel" (KJV, NIV: "the large rock"; NASB: "the large stone"; the Masoretic text reads rather "the great, large meadows"). ¶
b. A proper noun designating a city that was known as a place where proper judgment was rendered. Refs.: 2 Sam. 20:14, 15, 18. Sheba fled there for protection but was executed instead (see 2 Sam. 20:22).

The word is used in several other proper compound place names as well: e.g., Abel Beth Maacah (1 Kgs. 15:20); Abel Keramim (Judg. 11:33); Abel Meholah (Judg. 7:22); Abel Mizraim (Gen. 50:11). ¶

ABEL BETH MAACAH – ***'āḇēl bêyṯ-mᵃ'aḵāh*** [proper noun: אָבֵל בֵּית־מַעֲכָה <62>; from PLAIN (noun) <58>, HOUSE <1004>, and MAACAH <4601>]: meadow of the house of oppression ▶ **A place in northern Israel.** Refs.: 2 Sam. 20:15; 1 Kgs. 15:20; 2 Kgs. 15:29. ¶

ABEL KERAMIM – [1] ***'āḇēl kᵉrāmiym*** [proper noun: אָבֵל כְּרָמִים <64>; from PLAIN (noun) <58> and the plur. of VINEYARD <3754>]: meadow of the vineyards ▶ **A place belonging to the Ammonites.** Ref.: Judg. 11:33. ¶
– [2] Judg. 11:33 ➔ PLAIN (noun) <58>.

ABEL MAIM – ***'āḇēl mayim*** [proper noun: אָבֵל מַיִם <66>; from PLAIN (noun) <58> and WATER <4325>]: meadow of waters ▶ **A place in northern Israel.** Ref.: 2 Chr. 16:4. ¶

ABEL MEHOLAH – ***'āḇēl mᵉḥôlāh*** [proper noun: אָבֵל מְחוֹלָה <65>; from PLAIN (noun) <58> and DANCING <4246>]: meadow of dancing ▶ **A place in Israel.** Refs.: Judg. 7:22; 1 Kgs. 4:12; 19:16. ¶

ABEL MIZRAIM – ***'āḇēl miṣrayim*** [proper noun: אָבֵל מִצְרַיִם <67>; from PLAIN (noun) <58> and MIZRAIM <4714>]: meadow of the mourning of the Egyptians ▶ **A place beyond the Jordan.** Ref.: Gen. 50:11. ¶

ABEL SHITTIM – ***'āḇêl haššiṭṭiym*** [proper noun: אָבֵל הַשִּׁטִּים <63>; from PLAIN (noun) <58> and the plur. of ACACIA <7848>]: meadow of the acacias ▶ **A place in the plains of Moab, the complete name of Shittim.** See SHITTIM <7851> a. (Num. 33:49). ¶

ABEZ – Josh. 19:20 ➔ EBEZ <77>.

ABHOR – [1] ***bāḥal*** [verb: בָּחַל <973>; a prim. root] ▶ **This verb means to detest greatly or to obtain by greed.** The first meaning of this word is to abhor and comes from a Syriac word meaning to be nauseated by or to experience disgust with; it is also translated to detest, to be weary, to grow weary. It is used only in Zechariah 11:8 to refer to the flock who abhorred the shepherd. The second meaning, to obtain by greed, comes from an Arabic word with a similar meaning. This word only appears in Proverbs 20:21. However, a textual problem exists, and some people read the verse with the Hebrew word *bāhal* <926>, meaning to be in haste; it is translated to get hastily, to gain hastily, to gain hurriedly. ¶
[2] ***gā'al*** [verb: גָּעַל <1602>; a prim. root] ▶ **This verb means to detest; it is also translated to loath, to lothe, to despise, to reject.** It is used in Leviticus 26:15, 43 to warn Israel not to abhor God's commandments. He would otherwise abhor them (Lev. 26:30), yet not to such an extent that He would destroy them completely (Lev. 26:44). This word also describes Israel as an unfaithful wife who loathes her husband (God) and her children (Ezek. 16:45). A bull that is not able to mate with a cow is said, literally, to cause loathing (Job 21:10: to fail, failure). In 2 Samuel 1:21, a shield that failed to protect its owner, Saul, was cast away as detested rather than being oiled; also translated to be defiled, to be despised. Other refs.: Lev. 26:11; Jer. 14:19. ¶
[3] ***zāham*** [verb: זָהַם <2092>; a prim. root] ▶ **This word describes the loathing toward food that a critically sick person may experience.** Ref.: Job 33:20. ¶
[4] ***tā'aḇ*** [verb: תָּאַב <8374>; a prim. root (prob. identical with LONG FOR <8373> through the idea of puffing disdainfully at)] ▶ **This word means to detest strongly; it is also translated to loathe.** This unquestionably strong term of detest is used only in Amos 6:8. The Lord employed it to convey His utter contempt for the pride of the people of Jacob. ¶
[5] ***ta'aḇ*** [verb: תָּעַב <8581>; a prim. root] ▶ **This word expresses a strongly detestable activity or the logical response to such an activity. It also means to be abhorrent, to do abominably.** It is associated with a severe sense of loathing (Deut. 23:7; 1 Chr. 21:6); the condition of sinful people (Job 15:16); the activity of idol worship (1 Kgs. 21:26); and the Lord's opposition to sin (Ps. 5:6). *
– [6] Lev. 20:23 ➔ LOATHE <6973> [7] Ps. 22:24 ➔ DETEST <8262> [8] Ps. 139:21 ➔ LOATHE <6962> [9] Lam. 2:7 ➔ RENOUNCE <5010> [10] Ezek. 16:5 ➔ LOATHING <1604>.

ABHORRENCE – ***deră'ôn, dêrā'ôn*** [masc. noun: דְּרָאוֹן, דֵּרָאוֹן <1860>; from an unused root (meaning to repulse)] ▶ **This word is related to an Arabic verb, which means to repel. Thus, the object of repulsion is an abhorrence.** It is used only twice in the Old Testament and in both cases speaks about the eternal abhorrence of those who rebelled against the Lord. The prophet Isaiah ended his message by declaring the abhorrence of wicked men in the eternal state (Is. 66:24; also translated abhorring, loathsome). Daniel, likewise, spoke about the everlasting abhorrence of the wicked who were resurrected (Dan. 12:2: contempt). ¶

ABHORRENT – [1] Ex. 5:21: to make abhorrent ➔ STINK <887> [2] Jer. 15:4 ➔ TERROR <2113>.

ABHORRING – Is. 66:24 ➔ ABHORRENCE <1860>.

ABI – ***'aḇiy*** [fem. proper noun: אֲבִי <21>; from FATHER <1>]: father, the Lord is father ▶ **The mother of Hezekiah, king of Israel.** Ref.: 2 Kgs. 18:2. ¶

ABI-ALBON – ***ᵃḇiy ʿalḇôn*** [masc. proper noun: אֲבִי עַלְבוֹן <45>; from FATHER <1> and an unused root of uncertain derivation]: father of strength ▶ **One of David's mighty men.** Ref.: 2 Sam. 23:31. ¶

ABI GIBEON – ***ᵃḇiy giḇʿôn*** [proper noun: אֲבִי גִּבְעוֹן <25>; from FATHER <1> and GIBEON <1391>]: father of height, father of hill ▶ **Main city of the Hivites, one of the peoples of Canaan.** Refs.: 1 Chr. 8:29; 9:35. ¶

ABIASAPH – ***ᵃḇiyʾāsāp̱*** [masc. proper noun: אֲבִיאָסָף <23>; from FATHER <1> and GATHER <622>]: father of gathering ▶ **One of the sons of Korah.** Ref.: Ex. 6:24. ¶

ABIATHAR – ***ʾeḇyāṯār*** [masc. proper noun: אֶבְיָתָר <54>; from FATHER <1> and REMAIN <3498>]: father of him that survived, father of abundance ▶ **A priest who survived Saul's slaughter of the priests at Nob.** Refs.: 1 Sam. 22:6–23. He was the son of Ahimelech, son of Ahitub, priest of Nob, in the days of Saul (1 Sam. 22:20). His father, Ahimelech, gave holy bread to David and his men to eat during David's flight from Saul (1 Sam. 22:1–9). Abiathar fled to David, who protected him, and he served, along with Zadok, as David's priest (cf. 2 Sam. 15:24; 17:15; 20:25). Abiathar rescued the holy ephod from Nob and used it during David's reign (1 Sam. 23:6, 9, 10). He helped take the ark to Jerusalem (1 Chr. 15:11–13). He, however, backed the wrong person, Adonijah, for king instead of Solomon after David's death (1 Kgs. 1:7, 19, 25). Under Solomon, Zadok was raised above Abiathar in the priesthood. Abiathar is mentioned by Jesus in Mark 2:25, 26 in a general sense as a representative of the priesthood. *

ABIB – ***ʾāḇiyḇ*** [proper noun: אָבִיב <24>; from an unused root (meaning to be tender)]: budding, green fruit ▶ **One of the months of the Jewish calendar.** Refs.: Ex. 13:4; 23:15; 34:18; Deut. 16:1. It became the month of Nisan after the captivity (Neh. 2:1; Esther 3:7). The Hebrew word also means ear, head; see EAR <24>. ¶

ABIDA – ***ᵃḇiyḏāʿ*** [masc. proper noun: אֲבִידָע <28>; from FATHER <1> and KNOW <3045>]: father of knowledge ▶ **Grandson of Abraham and Keturah.** Refs.: Gen. 25:4; 1 Chr. 1:33. ¶

ABIDAN – ***ʾaḇiyḏān*** [masc. proper noun: אֲבִידָן <27>; from FATHER <1> and JUDGE (verb) <1777>]: father of judgment ▶ **An Israelite of the tribe of Benjamin.** Refs.: Num. 1:11; 2:22; 7:60, 65; 10:24. ¶

ABIDE – See DWELL <3427>.

ABIEL – ***ᵃḇiyʾēl*** [masc. proper noun: אֲבִיאֵל <22>; from FATHER <1> and GOD <410>]: God is my father ▶
a. An Israelite of the tribe of Benjamin. Refs.: 1 Sam. 9:1; 14:51. ¶
b. One of David's mighty men. Ref.: 1 Chr. 11:32. ¶

ABIEZER – ***ᵃḇiyʿezer*** [masc. proper noun: אֲבִיעֶזֶר <44>; from FATHER <1> and EZER <5829>]: father of help ▶
a. An Israelite of the tribe of Manasseh. Refs.: Josh. 17:2; Judg. 6:34; 8:2; 1 Chr. 7:18. ¶
b. An Israelite of the tribe of Benjamin. Refs.: 2 Sam. 23:27; 1 Chr. 11:28; 27:12. ¶

ABIEZRITE – ***ᵃḇiy hāʿezriy*** [masc. proper noun: אֲבִי הָעֶזְרִי <33>; from ABIEZER <44> with the art. inserted]: father of the Ezrite ▶ **Gideon was a member of this family.** Refs.: Judg. 6:11, 24; 8:32. ¶

ABIGAIL – ***ᵃḇiygayil*** [fem. proper noun: אֲבִיגַיִל <26>; from FATHER <1> and JOY <1524>]: my father is glad, the father's joy ▶
a. She was a Carmelite (Alebite). Refs.: 2 Sam. 2:2; 3:3. She was the wife of Nabal, a foolish boorish man, who died because of his insolent anger and behavior (see 1 Sam. 25:25, 37, 38). Abigail was a beautiful and wise woman. She became one of David's

wives after Nabal's death (1 Sam. 27:3). David's second son, Daniel or Chileab, was by her (2 Sam. 3:3; 1 Chr. 3:1). *

b. Abigal, a proper noun, and shortened form of Abigail. Ref.: 2 Sam. 17:25. She was a sister of David and the mother of Amasa (1 Chr. 2:16, 17), sharing the same mother, a daughter of Nahash or Jesse (1 Chr. 2:13–17). Nahash in 2 Samuel 17:25 may be another name for Jesse, David's father (cf. Is. 11:10). Or possibly, the text is corrupt in this reading, a scribal error. ¶

ABIGAL – 2 Sam. 17:25; 1 Chr. 2:16, 17 ➔ ABIGAIL <26> b.

ABIHAIL – ***ᵃḇiyḥayil*** [masc. and fem. proper noun: אֲבִיחַיִל <32>; from FATHER <1> and STRENGTH <2428>]: father of might ▶

a. The father of Zuriel. Ref.: Num. 3:35. ¶

b. The wife of Abishur. Ref.: 1 Chr. 2:29. ¶

c. A son of Huri. Ref.: 1 Chr. 5:14. ¶

d. The mother-in-law of Rehoboam. Ref.: 2 Chr. 11:18. ¶

e. The father of Esther. Refs.: Esther 2:15; 9:29. ¶

ABIHU – ***ᵃḇiyhû'*** [masc. proper noun: אֲבִיהוּא <30>; from FATHER <1> and HE, SHE, IT <1931>]: he is my father ▶ **He was Aaron's second son.** Ref.: Ex. 6:23. He ate and drank in the presence of God (Ex. 24:1, 9) on Mount Sinai. He and his brother Nadab were later slain before the Lord because they offered "strange fire," "unholy, unapproved fire" (Lev. 10:1–8; cf. Num. 3:4; 26:61; 1 Chr. 24:2) at the Lord's altar. *

ABIHUD – ***ᵃḇiyhûḏ*** [masc. proper noun: אֲבִיהוּד <31>; from FATHER <1> and VIGOR <1935> (in the sense of authority, majesty)]: father of praise, father of honor ▶ **An Israelite of the tribe of Benjamin.** Ref.: 1 Chr. 8:3. ¶

ABIJAH – ***ᵃḇiyyāh, ᵃḇiyāhû*** [masc. and fem. proper noun: אֲבִיָּה, אֲבִיָּהוּ <29>; from FATHER <1> and LORD <3050>]: my father is the Lord ▶ **A name referring to several different Israelite men in the Old Testament and also to two Israelite women.**

a. It refers to Hezron's wife who bore him Ashur, the father of Tekoa. Ref.: 1 Chr. 2:24. ¶

b. A descendant of Aaron who served in the priestly services. Ref.: 1 Chr. 24:10. He is also called Abijam (1 Kgs. 14:31; 15:1, 7, 8). He reigned in Judah (913–910 B.C.) and found both censure (1 Kgs. 15:3) and praise from the biblical authors (2 Chr. 13:1–14:1). He won a decisive battle against Jeroboam (2 Chr. 13:19–22). ¶

c. The son of Becher who was the son of Benjamin. Refs.: 1 Chr. 7:6–8. ¶

d. The second son of Samuel bears this name. Ref.: 1 Sam. 8:2. He served as a judge at Beersheba but was corrupt (1 Sam. 8:1–3). Other ref.: 1 Chr. 6:28. ¶

e. The son of Jeroboam I, the apostate first king of Israel. Refs.: 1 Kgs. 14:1–18. He received a positive evaluation from the writer. ¶

f. Rehoboam's son by Maacah, daughter (granddaughter?) of Absalom. Refs.: 1 Chr. 3:10; 2 Chr. 11:20–14:1. Rehoboam chose him from among his sons to be king (2 Chr. 11:22). ¶

g. An Israelite who signed the covenant of renewal with Nehemiah after the return from the Babylonian captivity. Ref.: Neh. 10:7. He returned under Zerubbabel to Jerusalem (Neh. 12:1, 4, 17). ¶

h. The name of Hezekiah's mother. She was the daughter of Zechariah (2 Chr. 29:1). ¶

ABIJAM – ***ᵃḇiyyām*** [masc. proper noun: אֲבִיָּם <38>; from FATHER <1> and SEA <3220>]: father of the sea ▶ **Abijam was the son of Rehoboam and reigned in his place over Judah.** Refs.: 1 Kgs. 14:31; 15:1, 7, 8. ¶

ABIMAEL – ***ᵃḇiymā'ēl*** [masc. proper noun: אֲבִימָאֵל <39>; from FATHER <1> and an elsewhere unused (prob. foreign) word]: my father is God ▶ **The son of Joktan in Arabia.** Refs.: Gen. 10:28; 1 Chr. 1:22. ¶

ABIMELECH – ***ᵓᵃḇiymeleḵ*** [masc. proper noun: אֲבִימֶלֶךְ <40>; from FATHER <1> and KING <4428>]: father of the king ▶

a. It may refer to two different kings of the Philistines. In Genesis 20:1–18; 21:22–32, dealing with Abraham, and in Genesis 26:1–33, dealing with Isaac. But some scholars feel the term may be, not a proper noun, but a cognomen of Philistine kings in general. *

b. It refers to a son of Gideon born to a concubine from Shechem. Ref.: Judg. 8:31. He tried to establish a corrupt kingship in Israel but failed. He had slain seventy of his brothers and declared himself king. He died ignominiously as he was besieging a city called Thebez (Judges 9). Kingship was discredited for the time being. ¶

c. It refers to a son of Abiathar, a priest, if the Masoretic text is correct. Refs.: 2 Sam. 8:17; 1 Chr. 18:16. ¶

d. In the superscription to Psalm 34, the king of Gath is given the name Abimelech. This could be, however, a general term (see a. above) for a Philistine king. ¶

ABINADAB – ***ᵓᵃḇiynāḏāḇ*** [masc. proper noun: אֲבִינָדָב <41>; from FATHER <1> and GIVE WILLINGLY <5068>]: father of freedom ▶

a. A Levite. Refs.: 1 Sam. 7:1; 2 Sam. 6:3, 4; 1 Chr. 13:7. ¶

b. The second son of Jesse. Refs.: 1 Sam. 16:8; 17:13; 1 Kgs. 4:11; 1 Chr. 2:13. ¶

c. A son of King Saul. Refs.: 1 Sam. 31:2; 1 Chr. 8:33; 9:39; 10:2. ¶

ABINOAM – ***ᵓᵃḇiynōʿām*** [masc. proper noun: אֲבִינֹעַם <42>; from FATHER <1> and BEAUTY <5278>]: father of beauty ▶ **He is, based on context, the father of Barak from Kedesh in Naphtali, a city west of and slightly north of the southern tip of the Sea of Galilee.** Refs.: Judg. 4:6, 12; 5:1, 12. Barak is listed as a faithful hero in the New Testament (Heb. 11:32). ¶

ABIRAM – ***ᵓᵃḇiyrām*** [masc. proper noun: אֲבִירָם <48>; from FATHER <1> and EXALT <7311>]: father of exaltation ▶

a. One of the sons of Eliab, who, along with others, rebelled against Moses' leadership. Ref.: Num. 16. He was from the line of Reuben. *

b. He is the son of Hiel of Bethel who lost Abiram when he laid the foundations to build Jericho. Ref.: 1 Kgs. 16:34; in fulfillment of Josh. 6:26. He was evidently Hiel's firstborn son. ¶

ABISHAG – ***ᵓᵃḇiyšag*** [fem. proper noun: אֲבִישַׁג <49>; from FATHER <1> and ERR <7686>]: father of error ▶ **Abishag the Shunammite ministered to King David.** Refs.: 1 Kgs. 1:3, 15; 2:17, 21, 22. ¶

ABISHAI – ***ᵓᵃḇiyšay*** [masc. proper noun: אֲבִישַׁי <52>; from FATHER <1> and GIFT <7862>]: father of gift ▶ **Abishai was the son of David's sister Zeruiah.** Refs.: 1 Sam. 26:6; 2 Sam. 2:18. He was a brother to Joab and Asahel (1 Chr. 2:16; 11:20). He was loyal and faithful to David and a leader of his mighty men (2 Sam. 23:18), possibly the leader of the second group of three (2 Sam. 23:18). He quelled the rebellion of Sheba against David (2 Sam. 20:6). He took part in several important events (e.g., 2 Sam. 2:18; 3:30). He protected David often and slew the giant Philistine Ishbi-Benob (2 Sam. 21:15–17) when he threatened David. *

ABISHUA – ***ᵓᵃḇiyšûaʿ*** [masc. proper noun: אֲבִישׁוּעַ <50>; from FATHER <1> and HELP (noun) <7771>]: father of help ▶

a. Son of the priest Phinehas. Refs.: 1 Chr. 6:4, 5, 50; Ezra 7:5. ¶

b. An Israelite of the tribe of Benjamin. Ref.: 1 Chr. 8:4. ¶

ABISHUR – ***ᵓᵃḇiyšûr*** [masc. proper noun: אֲבִישׁוּר <51>; from FATHER <1> and WALL <7791>]: father of order, father of the wall ▶ **An Israelite of the tribe of Judah.** Refs.: 1 Chr. 2:28, 29. ¶

ABITAL – ***ᵓᵃḇiyṭal*** [fem. proper noun: אֲבִיטַל <37>; from FATHER <1> and DEW <2919>]: father of dew ▶ **Mother of the fifth son of David.** Refs.: 2 Sam. 3:4; 1 Chr. 3:3. ¶

ABITUB – ***ᵃḇiyṭûḇ*** [masc. proper noun: אֲבִיטוּב <36>; from FATHER <1> and GOODNESS <2898>]: father of goodness ▶ **An Israelite of the tribe of Benjamin.** Ref.: 1 Chr. 8:11. ¶

ABJECT – Ps. 35:15 ➔ ATTACKER <5222>.

ABLAZE – Dan. 7:9: all ablaze ➔ lit.: burning fire ➔ BURNING (verb) <1815>.

ABLE (BE) – **1** ***yāḵōl*** [verb: יָכֹל <3201>; a prim. root] ▶ **This word means to be capable, and also to prevail.** It indicates to have the ability or power to do or endure something: of God's ability (Num. 14:16; 2 Chr. 32:13, 15; Jer. 44:22) or a person's ability (Gen. 13:16); it is used of God not being able to stand Israel's false worship any longer (Is. 1:13); not being able to endure a prideful, arrogant person (Ps. 101:5). Negated, it takes on the meaning of being incapable of maintaining an attitude or state of condition (Hos. 8:5). It indicates the ability to cause something to happen, as when Balak hoped he would be able to defeat Israel and drive them out of the land (Num. 22:6, 11). It indicates the ability to render or not to render (if negated) judgment about an issue (Gen. 24:50). It may take on the inference of daring to do something, e.g., eating in a restricted area, which, when negated, means people dare not or are not allowed to eat (Deut. 12:17). It indicates being an overcomer, a victor, to prevail over something or someone (Gen. 30:8); Rachel prevailed (*yāḵōl*) over her sister. (See also Ps. 13:4; Is. 16:12.) In an intellectual discussion, it means to grasp or understand something (Job 31:23; Ps. 139:6), to attain a mastery of it. *

2 ***yᵉḵil*** [Aramaic verb: יְכִל <3202>; corresponding to <3201> above] ▶ **This word means to be capable, and also to prevail. It is usually followed by an infinitive to complete its meaning.** It is used with God as the subject who is able to shut the lions' mouths and deliver Daniel (Dan. 6:20), as well as his three Hebrew companions in the furnace (Dan. 3:17); it is used of wise men who, in context negated, are not able to interpret a dream (Dan. 2:10), i.e., they do not have the needed skills and wisdom to do so (Dan. 2:27). God was able to deliver in an unparalleled way (Dan. 3:29; 4:37). Daniel was able to reveal dreams and mysteries because of God's help (Dan. 2:47; 4:18; 5:16). The little horn was able to overcome, overpower the saints of the Most High (Dan. 7:21). Other ref.: Dan. 6:4. ¶

3 ***kᵉhal*** [Aramaic verb: כְּהַל <3546>; a root corresponding to <3201> above and CONTAIN <3557>] ▶ **This word refers to having a skill, ability, or knowledge enabling a person to accomplish something.** Daniel had the skill and the divine enablement to interpret dreams and mysteries (Dan. 2:26; 4:18), while Babylonian wise men did not (Dan. 5:8, 15). ¶

ABLE-BODIED MAN – 2 Sam. 24:9 ➔ VALIANT MAN <381>.

ABNER – ***ᵃḇnêr, ᵃḇiynêr*** [masc. proper noun: אַבְנֵר, אֲבִינֵר <74>; from FATHER <1> and LAMP <5216>]: father of light ▶ **Abner served as the captain of Saul's army and was Saul's cousin or uncle.** Refs.: 1 Chr. 8:33; 9:39. He continued to support the house of Saul after Saul's death (2 Sam. 3:1), supporting Eshbaal, man of Baal (1 Chr. 8:33); later, Ishbosheth, man of shame (2 Sam. 2:8–17), as king at a city named Mahanaim. Abner tried to come over to David's camp but was killed by Joab, David's captain (cf. 2 Sam. 2:18–3:38). David mourned Abner's death as a great man (2 Sam. 3:6–38, especially 2 Sam. 3:33, 34). *

ABODE – **1** ***ḥāṣiyr*** [masc. noun: חָצִיר <2681>; a collateral form of VILLAGE <2691>] ▶ **This word denotes a dwelling place; it is also translated court, courtyard, home.** It is used to depict Edom as a dwelling place, destroyed by the Lord, where the ostrich will live (Is. 34:13). ¶

2 ***sōḵ*** [masc. noun: סֹךְ <5520>; from COVER (verb) <5526> a. (in the sense of to hide)] ▶ **This word means a cover, a hiding place, a tent; it is also translated**

thicket, den, lair, covert, as well as shelter, pavilion, dwelling, tabernacle. It describes a place where a person can be undetected. It is employed figuratively of the places from which the wicked attack the righteous (Ps. 10:9). In a positive sense, it refers to the protective, shielding hiding place of God's tent, Tabernacle, presence (Ps. 27:5). It indicates the place where God dwells (Ps. 76:2; Jer. 25:38). ¶

ABOMINABLE – Ezek. 4:14 ➔ OFFENSIVE THING <6292>.

ABOMINABLE IMAGE – 1 Kgs. 15:13 ➔ IMAGE <4656>.

ABOMINABLE THING – [1] ***šeqeṣ*** [masc. noun: שֶׁקֶץ <8263>; from DETEST <8262>] ▶ **This word means a detestation, an abomination, and a detestable thing.** Chiefly, this Hebrew word marks those things that were ceremonially unclean and forbidden (Lev. 7:21). It is used of certain sea creatures (Lev. 11:10); birds of prey (Lev. 11:13 ff.); and various creeping things (Lev. 11:20, 23, 41, 42). *
– [2] Is. 65:4 ➔ OFFENSIVE THING <6292>.

ABOMINATION – [1] ***šiqqûṣ, šiqquṣ*** [masc. noun: שִׁקּוּץ, שִׁקֻּץ <8251>; from DETEST <8262>] ▶ **This Hebrew word also means a detestable thing, an idol. It identifies an object that is abhorrent or blasphemous.** It is used to denote filth (Nah. 3:6); forbidden food (Zech. 9:7); and a blasphemous activity (Dan. 9:27). Most often, it is used as a synonym for an idol or idolatry (Jer. 7:30; Hos. 9:10). *
[2] ***tô'ēḇāh, tō'ēḇāh*** [fem. noun: תּוֹעֵבָה, תֹּעֵבָה <8441>; fem. act. part. of ABHOR <8581>] ▶ **This word means something abhorrent. It is primarily understood in the context of the Law.** It identifies unclean food (Deut. 14:3); the activity of the idolater (Is. 41:24); the practice of child sacrifice (Deut. 12:31); intermarriage by the Israelites (Mal. 2:11); the religious activities of the wicked (Prov. 21:27); and homosexual behavior (Lev. 18:22). In a broader sense, the word is used to identify anything offensive (Prov. 8:7). *
– [3] Lev. 7:18; 19:7 ➔ OFFENSIVE THING <6292>.

ABOMINATION (BE AN, HAVE IN) – Lev. 11:11, 13 ➔ DETEST <8262>.

ABOUND – Dan. 4:1; 6:25 ➔ GROW <7680>.

ABOVE – [1] ***ma'al*** [adv. prep.: מַעַל <4605>; from OFFER <5927> (in the sense of to go up)] ▶ **This word means upward, high, over.** It is used to mean above, often with *min* (FROM <4480>) prefixed meaning from above (Ex. 20:4; Deut. 4:39; 5:8; Josh. 2:11; Job 3:4; 18:16; 1 Kgs. 7:3; 8:23; Prov. 8:28; Is. 6:2). It expresses the idea of on top of, above by adding l^{e} to the above phrase (Gen. 22:9; Ex. 28:27; 39:20; Lev. 11:21). It indicates something above another level or room (Jer. 35:4). It is used in a figurative sense of setting one's throne above another (Jer. 52:32). *
[2] **from above: *'al*** [masc. noun: עַל <5920>; properly, the top] ▶
a. This word means height, on high. It is used to point to a direction, toward a location (Gen. 27:39; 49:25); especially toward heaven, upward (Ps. 50:4). It refers to the exaltation of a person (2 Sam. 23:1); and turning upward to God (Hos. 7:16). ¶
b. A masculine proper noun meaning Most High. It is taken as a title, an appellative for God, the Most High by some translators (2 Sam. 23:1; Hos. 7:16; 11:7). ¶

ABRAHAM – ***'aḇrāhām*** [masc. proper noun: אַבְרָהָם <85>; contr. from FATHER <1> and an unused root (prob. meaning to be populous)]: father of a great multitude ▶ **This name was bestowed on Abram ("exalted father") after he received the promise of land and progeny from the Lord.** Refs.: Gen. 15:17–21; 17:5, 9, 15, 17, 18, 22–24, 26. His father was Terah in Ur (Gen. 11:26). The Lord appeared to him several times (Gen. 12:7; 17:1; 18:1). He received the promises of God (Gen. 12:1–3), the covenant (Gen. 15:6, 13–17), and the seal of the covenant of circumcision (Gen. 17:26). He was blessed by God (Gen. 12:1–3). Through him the nations would be blessed. He was born in Ur of the Chaldeans but moved at God's call to Haran in Mesopotamia (Gen. 11:26–32). He moved on to Canaan from Haran at God's call (Gen. 12:1, 4). His call and actions prefigured the Exodus event itself. He was the father of the nation of Israel both biologically and, more importantly, spiritually. His faith was especially highlighted when he was willing to sacrifice his son at the Lord's command (Gen. 22), expecting to receive him back (Gen. 22:18), if necessary.

The promise of land included the territory from the great Euphrates River to the River of Egypt, El-Arish, but this promise was not fulfilled until the time of Solomon and/or David. Abraham's promised son, Isaac, became the inheritor of the promises and covenants (Gen. 25:5), not any son from Keturah or Hagar (Gen. 25:1–18). The promises passed on to Jacob and his descendants.

The God of Abraham was the Lord, (Yahweh; Gen. 14:22), the High God, the Creator (Gen. 14:18–20), the God of Moses and Israel (Ex. 3:15; 6:3). In a religious and spiritually true sense, Israel, as well as Isaac, was the "seed of Abraham." Gentile Christians are considered the spiritual (faith) seed of Abraham in the New Testament (cf. Gal. 3:16, 29). Abraham is uniquely considered the "father" of three great religions: Judaism, Christianity, and Islam. He is referred to nearly two hundred times in the Koran. *

ABRAM – ***'aḇrām*** [masc. proper noun: אַבְרָם <87>; contr. from ABIRAM <48>]: exalted father ▶ **This name refers to the biological and spiritual father of Israel. Abram was born to Terah in Ur of the Chaldeans.** The name means "exalted father" but was changed to Abraham, "father of a great multitude" (Gen. 17:5, 9, 15, 17, 18). He is referred to as Abram in Genesis 12:1–17:5; 1 Chronicles 1:27; Nehemiah 9:7. He was seventy-five years old when God called him (Gen. 12:1–18). He was chosen by God (Neh. 9:7). See entry under ABRAHAM <85>. *

ABRONAH – ***'aḇrōnāh*** [proper noun: עַבְרֹנָה <5684>; fem. of EBRON <5683>] passage, region beyond ▶ **A place in the wilderness where the Israelites camped on their way to the Promised Land.** Refs.: Num. 33:34, 35. ¶

ABSALOM – ***'abiysālôm, 'aḇšālôm*** [masc. proper noun: אַבְשָׁלוֹם, אֲבִישָׁלוֹם <53>; from FATHER <1> and PEACE <7965>]: father of peace ▶ **A name designating two sons of David.**

a. This son was beloved by David and the people but seemingly for the wrong superficial reasons. While he was handsome and had beautiful hair, he was also violent, passionate, headstrong, and a self-seeking man who was born in Hebron (2 Sam. 3:3). He killed Amnon for raping his half-sister Tamar (2 Sam. 13:20–38). The story of Absalom stretches over chapters 13–20 of 2 Samuel (cf. also 1 Kgs. 1:6; 2:7, 28; 1 Chr. 3:2). He was exiled from Jerusalem for three years (2 Sam. 13:37, 38). Upon his return, after an indefinite period, he plotted to overthrow David, his father (2 Sam. 15–18), but was eventually defeated and judged by God. He died an ignominious death (2 Sam. 18:1–33). The third Psalm's superscription sets the psalm in the time when David fled from before Absalom. Absalom's tragic story illustrated well the curse the Lord placed on David's house because of David's affair with Bathsheba and his murder of her husband Uriah (2 Sam. 12:11, 12). *

b. A proper noun for David's third son by Maacah, daughter of Talmai, king of Geshur. This is another rendering of Absalom (1 Kgs. 15:2, 10). His mother is identified by referring to him as her son. *

ABSALOM'S MONUMENT – 2 Sam. 18:18 ➔ HAND <3027>.

ABSTAIN – Lev. 22:2; Zech. 7:3 ➔ SEPARATE <5144>.

ABUNDANCE – [1] ***ziyz*** [masc. coll. noun: זִיז <2123>; from an unused root apparently meaning to be conspicuous] ▶

This word indicates a plentiful amount of supply. It is used figuratively of the abundance of Jerusalem as re-created by the Lord. It is used in conjunction with glory (*kāḇôḏ* <3519>) to mean, literally, the abundance of Israel/Jerusalem's glory (Is. 66:11). The Hebrew word also means living creatures; see MOVING CREATURES <2123>. ¶

2 ***yiṯrāh*** [fem. noun: יִתְרָה <3502>; fem. of REMAINDER <3499>] ► **This word indicates wealth, riches.** It refers to the excess or savings which have been saved up (Is. 15:7; Jer. 48:36). ¶

3 ***maḵbiyr*** [masc. noun: מַכְבִּיר <4342>; transitive part. of MULTIPLY <3527>] ► **This word indicates a more than adequate amount of something.** God gives food in abundance (Job 36:31). ¶

4 ***ʿᵃṯereṯ*** [verb: עֲתֶרֶת <6283>; from MULTIPLY <6280>] ► **This word refers to a more than ample supply of something, more than what is sufficient.** God would reveal the abundance of peace and truth (Jer. 33:6). ¶

5 ***pissāh*** [fem. noun: פִּסָּה <6451>; from VANISH <6461> (prob. in the sense of to disperse)] ►

a. This word refers to a supply or a presence of something beyond what is needed, even an excess of something. Ref.: Ps. 72:16. ¶

b. This word indicates a handful of something. In its context it refers to the presence of a handful of corn, i.e., a significant presence of corn where it might least be expected, promising an abundance of God's blessings (Ps. 72:16). ¶

6 ***śoḇʿāh*** [fem. noun: שָׂבְעָה <7654>; fem. of FULL (noun) <7648>] ► **This word refers to the satisfaction provided by an abundance of food to eat.** Ref.: Is. 23:18. On the other hand, material goods do not give real satisfaction (Is. 55:2). It indicates that a satisfaction of greed cannot be attained (Is. 56:11). Israel had an insatiable desire for following foreign gods (Ezek. 16:28). Israel's failure to find their true satisfaction in God meant that they could not find satisfaction elsewhere (Hag. 1:6). Other ref.: Ezek. 39:19. ¶

7 ***šep̱aʿ*** [masc. noun: שֶׁפַע <8228>; from an unused root meaning to abound] ► **This word refers to the huge amount of food and wealth that lies potentially in the seas near Israel.** Ref.: Deut. 33:19. ¶

8 ***šip̱ʿāh*** [fem. noun: שִׁפְעָה <8229>; fem. of <8228> above] ► **This word also means a multitude, a company. It is used to refer to a large number or great amount of something.** It refers to a large company or group of people (2 Kgs. 9:17; NIV: troops); a great amount of water (Job 22:11; 38:34; ESV, NIV: flood); even a great number of camels (Is. 60:6; NIV: herds); or horses (Ezek. 26:10). ¶

– 9 Gen. 41:29–31, 34, 47, 53 → PLENTY <7647> 10 Prov. 21:5 → PROFIT (noun) <4195> 11 Is. 33:6 → TREASURE <2633> 12 Is. 33:23 → INCREASE (noun) <4766> 13 Is. 33:23 → PREY <5706> 14 Is. 47:9 → STRENGTH <6109>.

ABUNDANCE (IN) – Job 36:31 → MULTIPLY <3527>.

ABUNDANCE (PLACE OF) – Ps. 66:12 → OVERFLOW (noun) <7310>.

ABUNDANT – 1 Is. 33:23 → INCREASE (noun) <4766> 2 Jer. 33:6 → abundant peace → lit.: abundance of peace → ABUNDANCE <6283>.

ABUSE – Prov. 9:7 → DEFECT <3971>.

ACACIA – ***šiṭṭāh*** [fem. noun: שִׁטָּה <7848>; from the same as WHIP <7850> (in the sense of scourge, e.g., the scourging thorns of the acacia)] ► **This Hebrew word indicates acacia wood, an acacia tree; shittim wood. It may refer to several species of wood that grow in Israel. It may refer specifically to Acacia seyal Delile, a species fairly common in the Sinai Peninsula and Jordan Valley.** It was used in the construction of the Tabernacle furnishings and the ark of the covenant (Ex. 25:5, 10, 13, 23, 28; 26:15, 26, 32; 27:1, 6; 30:1, 5; 35:7, 24; 36:20, 31, 36; 37:1, 4, 10, 15, 25, 28; 38:1, 6; Deut. 10:3). God will restore this tree to a devastated Israel (Is. 41:19). The Valley of Shittim (Joel 3:18) refers to an area where acacia trees abounded. ¶

ACCAD – ***'akkaḏ*** [proper noun: אַכַּד <390>; from an unused root prob. meaning to strengthen]: fortress ▶ **One of the city of the kingdom of Nimrod in the land of Shinar.** Ref.: Gen. 10:10; also translated Akkad. ¶

ACCEPT – ***qāḇal*** [verb: קָבַל <6901>; a prim. root] ▶ **This word means to take something offered, as well as to receive, to undertake, to choose.** As a general term, it means to accept something: a gift (Esther 4:4); instruction (Prov. 19:20). It has the sense of willingly taking on a task (Esther 9:23); or setting up something (Esther 9:27). It is used of accepting what God brings on us (Job 2:10). It has the sense of compared to, to match, to be opposite and paired (Ex. 26:5; 36:12). *

ACCEPTABLE – Ezra 6:10 ➔ PLEASING <5208>.

ACCEPTABLE (BE) – [1] Dan. 4:27 ➔ GOOD (BE, SEEM, THINK) <8232> [2] Mal. 3:4 ➔ PLEASING (BE) <6149>.

ACCESS – ***mahl***^{e}***ḵiym*** [masc. plur. noun: מַהְלְכִים <4108>] ▶ **This word means entry, approach; it is also translated free access, places to walk.** It is the plural of *mah*^{a}*laḵ* [JOURNEY (noun) <4109>]. It refers figuratively to potential access before God given to the high priest Joshua if he walked in the Lord's paths (Zech. 3:7). ¶

ACCHO – See ACCO <5910>.

ACCIDENT – 1 Sam. 20:26 ➔ CHANCE <4745>.

ACCO – ***'akkô*** [proper noun: עַכּוֹ <5910>; apparently from an unused root meaning to hem in]: to hem in ▶ **Asher did not drive out its inhabitants.** Ref.: Judg. 1:31. ¶

ACCOMPLISH – [1] Ps. 57:2; 138:8 ➔ END (COME TO AN) <1584> [2] Lam. 2:17 ➔ CUT OFF <1214>.

ACCOUNT – [1] Ezra 4:21; Dan. 6:2 ➔ COMMAND (noun) <2941> [2] Eccl. 7:27 ➔ SCHEME (noun) <2808>.

ACCOUNT (OF NO) – Is. 41:24 ➔ NOTHING <659>.

ACCOUNT (ON) – Gen. 12:13; 30:27; 39:5; Deut. 1:37 ➔ BECAUSE <1558>.

ACCOUNT, FULL ACCOUNT – Esther 10:2 ➔ SUM, EXACT SUM <6575>.

ACCOUNTABLE – Ezra 4:21; Dan. 6:2 ➔ COMMAND (noun) <2941>.

ACCOUNTED (BE) – ***ḥ***^{a}***šaḇ*** [Aramaic verb: חֲשַׁב <2804>; corresponding to THINK <2803>] ▶ **This word refers to God's consideration or evaluation of something; it is also translated to be reputed, to be regarded.** The inhabitants of the earth are accounted as nothing by Him (Dan. 4:35), for His power and ability extend far beyond them. ¶

ACCUMULATE – [1] ***rāḵaš*** [verb: רָכַשׁ <7408>; a prim. root] ▶ **This word describes the process of acquiring property, especially through God's blessing, including all kinds of possessions; it is also translated to gather.** Refs.: Gen. 12:5; 31:18; 36:6; 46:6. ¶
– [2] 2 Kgs. 20:17; Is. 39:6 ➔ STORE (verb) <686>.

ACCUSATION – ***śiṭnāh*** [fem. noun: שִׂטְנָה <7855>; from ACCUSE <7853>] ▶ **The primary meaning of the Hebrew word is accusation, i.e., the fact of blaming or criticizing someone. This word also means opposition, hostility.** In Ezra, the word is used to depict the accusation which those who opposed the rebuilding of the city walls in Jerusalem brought before the king (Ezra 4:6). The subsequent letter stated that the Jews were a rebellious people and that if the completion of the city walls were allowed, they would not submit to the authority of Artaxerxes, king of Persia. This accusation resulted in stopping the building process (see Ezra 4:23). ¶

ACCUSATION (GROUND OF) – Dan. 6:4, 5 ➔ COMPLAINT (GROUND FOR) <5931>.

ACCUSATIONS (LODGE) – Ps. 38:20; 109:20 ➔ ACCUSE <7853>.

ACCUSE – 1 ***qᵉraṣ*** [Aramaic verb: קְרַץ <7170>; corresponding to DESTRUCTION <7171> in the sense of a bit ("to eat the morsels of" any one, i.e., chew him up (fig.) by slander)] ► **This word refers to bringing a formal charge or accusation against a person. It also means to denounce.** Refs.: Dan. 3:8; 6:24. Others considered this word a noun meaning piece. It is used in the plural form and means literally pieces, their pieces, since it has a suffix in Aramaic. The word *'kl,* to eat, precedes, rendering the idiomatic, they devoured (ate) his/their pieces (bone?); i.e., they maliciously accused them/Daniel. ¶

2 ***śāṭan*** [verb: שָׂטַן <7853>; a prim. root] ► **This word means to slander, and to harbor animosity toward someone; it is also translated to be an adversary, to oppose, to lodge accusations, to be an accuser, to act as an accuser, to resist.** The verb is used only six times and presents a negative attitude or bias against something. The psalmist complained about those who attacked or slandered him when he pursued what was good (Ps. 38:20); even accusing or attacking him in spite of his positive attitude toward them (Ps. 109:4). The psalmist asked for his accusers to be destroyed by shame (Ps. 71:13; 109:20, 29). Satan stood ready to accuse or to persecute Joshua, the high priest, in the postexilic community (Zech. 3:1). Also, see the noun *śāṭān* (ACCUSER <7854>). ¶

– 3 Prov. 30:10 ➔ SLANDER <3960> 4 Dan. 3:8; 6:24 ➔ EAT <399> b.

ACCUSER – 1 ***śāṭān*** [masc. noun: שָׂטָן <7854>; from ACCUSE <7853>] ► **This word means a slanderer, and also an adversary, Satan. It is used twenty-seven times. In Job it is found fourteen times meaning (the) Satan, the accuser.** Satan presented himself among the sons of God and roundly accused Job of not loving or serving God with integrity (Job 1:6, 7; 2:1, 2, 4, 7); all of these uses are in the prologue of the book (Job 1–2). In Zechariah, this noun is used three times with the verb to accuse (*śāṭan* [ACCUSE <7853>]). Satan stood ready to accuse the high priest Joshua (Zech. 3:1, 2). In 1 Chronicles 21:1, Satan was depicted as the one who motivated David insolently to take a census of Israel's army (cf. 2 Sam. 24:1).

The noun is used in a general sense to indicate any adversary or someone who hinders or opposes. The angel of the Lord opposed Balaam and his donkey on their way to curse Israel, acting in opposition (Num. 22:22, 32); the Philistines feared that David might act in opposition to them in battle (1 Sam. 29:4; 2 Sam. 19:22). In Solomon's day, the Lord had given him rest all around him (cf. 1 Kgs. 4:24); except for Rezon who reigned in Aram (1 Kgs. 11:14, 23, 25). The psalmist's enemies appointed an accuser to attack him, a person who was wicked (Ps. 109:6). *

– 2 Jer. 18:19 ➔ CONTENDS (ONE WHO) <3401>.

ACCUSER (BE AN, ACT AS AN) – Ps. 71:13; 109:4, 20 ➔ ACCUSE <7853>.

ACCUSTOMED – 1 ***limmûḏ, limmuḏ*** [masc. adj.: לִמּוּד, לִמֻּד <3928>; from LEARN <3925>] ► **This word means used to something, learned, practiced, an expert, one taught, a follower, a disciple.** It described those who habitually practice evil (Jer. 13:23). It was also employed to help portray Israel as a wild donkey in heat that was accustomed to life in the rugged wilderness (Jer. 2:24). The Lord gave the Suffering Servant a "tongue of the learned," i.e., the gift of inspirational and instructive speech and an ear that listens like those

being taught (Is. 50:4). Isaiah says that the children of the desolate woman or widow will be taught by the Lord Himself (Is. 54:13). The word is also used once to denote Isaiah's disciples (Is. 8:16). ¶
– [2] Num. 22:30 ➔ PROFITABLE (BE) <5532> a.

ACHAN – [1] ***'āḵān*** [masc. proper noun: עָכָן <5912>; from an unused root meaning to trouble]: pain ▶ **The name of the man who coveted and took things devoted to God.** His sin caused God's wrath to fall on Israel, since he broke the covenant (Josh. 22:20). He was discovered, judged, and executed in the Valley of Achor. See ACHOR <5911>. Other refs.: Josh. 7:1, 18–20, 24. ¶
– [2] 1 Chr. 2:7 ➔ ACHAR <5917>.

ACHAR – ***'āḵār*** [masc. proper noun: עָכָר <5917>; from TROUBLE (BRING) <5916>]: troublesome ▶ **He was known as "the troubler of Israel."** Ref.: 1 Chr. 2:7; ESV: Achan. See ACHAN <5912>. ¶

ACHBOR – ***'aḵbôr*** [masc. proper noun: עַכְבּוֹר <5907>; prob. from MOUSE <5909>]: mouse ▶
a. An Edomite. Refs.: Gen. 36:38, 39; 1 Chr. 1:49. ¶
b. Courier of Josiah. Refs.: 2 Kgs. 22:12, 14; Jer. 26:22; 36:12. ¶

ACHIEVEMENT – Eccl. 4:4 ➔ lit.: skill in work ➔ SKILL <3788>.

ACHISH – ***'āḵiyš*** [masc. proper noun: אָכִישׁ <397>; of uncertain deriv.]: object of fear ▶ **A Philistine king.** He was the king of Gath, son of Maoch (1 Sam. 27:2), to whom David fled when Saul was pursuing him (1 Sam. 21:10). David feigned madness, and Achish let him be (1 Sam. 21:12–14). Achish used David to carry out raids (1 Sam. 27:8–12), even making him his bodyguard (1 Sam. 28:2). However, the Philistine officers distrusted him and would not let David go with them on raids (1 Sam. 29:2–11). Achish was saddened by this turn of events. *

ACHMETHA – ***'aḥm'ṯa'*** [Aramaic proper noun: אַחְמְתָא <307>; of Persian deriv.]: citadel, place of horses ▶ **A citadel in the province of Media.** Ref.: Ezra 6:2; also written Ecbatana. ¶

ACHOR – ***'aḵôr*** [proper noun: עָכוֹר <5911>; from TROUBLE (BRING) <5916>]: pain, trouble ▶ **A valley in the Judean Desert and located between Judah and Benjamin.** Ref.: Josh. 15:7. It was traditionally near Jericho. Based on references in the prophets, the territory and valley were barren or wilderness (Is. 65:10; Hos. 2:15). Achan was executed there for his treason (Josh. 7:24–26); his name also means "pain." ¶

ACHSAH – ***'aḵsāh*** [fem. proper noun: עַכְסָה <5915>; fem. of ANKLET <5914>]: anklet ▶ **The only daughter of Caleb.** Refs.: Josh. 15:16, 17; Judg. 1:12, 13; 1 Chr. 2:49. ¶

ACHSHAPH – ***'aḵšāp̱*** [proper noun: אַכְשָׁף <407>; from WITCHCRAFT (PRACTICE) <3784>]: enchantment, dedicated ▶ **A royal city of Canaan.** Refs.: Josh. 11:1; 12:20; 19:25. ¶

ACHZIB – ***'aḵziyḇ*** [proper noun: אַכְזִיב <392>; from DECEPTIVE <391>]: lie, deceit ▶
a. A lowland in Judah. Refs.: Josh. 15:44; Mic. 1:14. ¶
b. A lowland in Asher. Refs.: Josh. 19:29; Judg. 1:31. ¶

ACQUAINT – Job 22:21 ➔ PROFITABLE (BE) <5532> a.

ACQUAINTANCE – ***makkār*** [masc. noun: מַכָּר <4378>; from DETERMINE <5234> (in the sense of to recognize)] ▶ **This word denotes a friend.** It indicates a person from whom something is officially received, such as a special levy for the repair of the Temple (2 Kgs. 12:5, 7; also translated constituency). For other translators, the word designates a person who collected a special levy of money for the repair of the Temple (2 Kgs. 12:5, 7: donor, treasurer). ¶

ACQUAINTED (BE, BE INTIMATELY) – Ps. 139:3 ➔ PROFITABLE (BE) <5532> a.

ACQUIRE – [1] ***qānāh*** [verb: קָנָה <7069>; a prim. root] ▶
a. This word means to buy, to purchase, to possess. It is used with God as its subject to mean His buying back His people, redeeming them (Ex. 15:16; Ps. 74:2; Is. 11:11); of God's creating the heavens and earth (Gen. 14:19); Israel (Deut. 32:6), but see b. below also. It is used figuratively of obtaining wisdom (Prov. 4:5, 7); or good counsel (Prov. 1:5). It describes buying, acquiring various things: it describes the acquisition of a son by birth (Gen. 4:1); of land or fields (Gen. 33:19); a servant (Gen. 39:1); of persons freeing, ransoming slaves (Neh. 5:8); of various riches (Eccl. 2:7). In its participial form, it may refer to an owner (Lev. 25:30). It is used of God's possessing wisdom in the creation (Prov. 8:22).
b. This word means to create, to bring forth. See also a. above. It is used of acquiring a child from God (Gen. 4:1); of God acquiring, creating the heavens and earth (Gen. 14:19); of His creation of Israel (Deut. 32:6); of forming a fetus in the womb (Ps. 139:13). It can be used of God's creation of wisdom (Prov. 8:22) (see a.). *
– [2] Gen. 12:5; 31:18; 36:6; 46:6 ➔ ACCUMULATE <7408> [3] Lev. 19:20 ➔ BETROTH <2778>.

ACT (noun) – Prov. 8:22 ➔ WORK <4659> a.

ACT (verb) – Num. 31:16 ➔ PROVIDE <4560>.

ACT PROMPTLY – 2 Sam. 5:24 ➔ MOVE <2782>.

ACTION – ***maʿălāl*** [masc. noun: מַעֲלָל <4611>; from DO <5953>] ▶ **This word usually refers to a deed, something done by someone.** It may be good (Prov. 20:11); or evil (Deut. 28:20; Judg. 2:19; 1 Sam. 25:3; Mic. 3:4). It is used of God's marvelous deeds to save His people (Ps. 77:11; 78:7) but also His works of judgment (Mic. 2:7). *

ACTIVE – Lev. 13:51, 52; 14:44 ➔ PAINFUL (BE) <3992>.

ACTIVITY – [1] Eccl. 5:3 ➔ TASK <6045> [2] Eccl. 9:10 ➔ SCHEME (noun) <2808>.

ACTUALLY – Gen. 20:12 ➔ INDEED <546>.

ADADAH – ***ʿaḏʿāḏāh*** [proper noun: עַדְעָדָה <5735>; from CONGREGATION <5712>]: festival ▶ **A city in the south of Judah.** Ref.: Josh. 15:22. ¶

ADAH – ***ʿāḏāh*** [fem. proper noun: עָדָה <5711>; from PASS OVER <5710>]: ornament ▶
a. The wife of Lamech. Refs.: Gen. 4:19, 20, 23. ¶
b. The wife of Esau. Refs.: Gen. 36:2, 4, 10, 12, 16. ¶

ADAIAH – ***ʿăḏāyāhû, ʿăḏāyāh*** [masc. proper noun: עֲדָיָהוּ, עֲדָיָה <5718>; from ADORN <5710> and LORD <3050>]: the Lord has adorned ▶
a. The father of Maaseiah. Ref.: 2 Chr. 23:1. ¶
b. Grandfather of Josiah. Ref.: 2 Kgs. 22:1. ¶
c. A Levite. Ref.: 1 Chr. 6:41. ¶
d. A Benjamite. Ref.: 1 Chr. 8:21. ¶
e. A priest. Refs.: 1 Chr. 9:12; Neh. 11:12. ¶
f. A son of Bani. Ref.: Ezra 10:29. ¶
g. A son of another Bani. Ref.: Ezra 10:39. ¶
h. A Judaite. Ref.: Neh. 11:5. ¶

ADALIA – ***'aḏalyā'*** [masc. proper noun: אֲדַלְיָא <118>; of Persian deriv.]: firm, determined ▶ **Name of one of the ten sons of Haman.** Ref.: Esther 9:8. ¶

ADAM – ***'āḏām*** [proper noun: אָדָם <121>; the same as MAN <120>]: earth, red ▶
a. Proper noun or name used of the first human in some cases. It also occurs as a common noun meaning humanity, humankind, etc., depending on its content. Here the discussion centers on its use

as a proper noun or name for the first man or humankind.

The word is used in 1 Chronicles 1:1 to refer to the first person and gives him the name Adam, since it stands at the head of a list of proper names. In Genesis 1–5, it is used as a proper name or noun depending on the context. In Genesis 4:25; 5:3–5, the word *'ăḏām* refers to a specific person and is a proper name. It seems best to render the Hebrew as "man," a proper noun, in Genesis 5:1, since it echoes Genesis 1:26–28. In all earlier references, it is best rendered as "the man," since it bears the Hebrew article (except for Gen. 1:26; 2:5, 20). The NIV renders the proper name "Adam" in Genesis 2:20 for the first time (Gen. 2:20; 3:17, 20, 21; 4:1, 25; 5:3–5). The translations do not agree in detail as to when to render the noun as a proper name or a proper noun ("the man") (NASB, proper name [Gen. 2:20; 3:17, 21; 4:25; 5:1, 3–5]).

The root or etymology of the word is uncertain, but the biblical author is clearly making a wordplay about Adam's being taken from the ground (cf. *'ăḏām*: ADAM <121>) to *ăḏāmāh*: GROUND <127>; see Genesis 2:7; 3:19). *

b. A proper noun referring to a small town along the east side of the Jordan River. It is the location of a mighty act of God when He stopped the flow of the Jordan so Israel could cross it in flood time (Josh. 3:16). ¶

ADAMAH – ***ăḏāmāh*** [proper noun: אֲדָמָה <128>; the same as GROUND <127>]: red earth, earthy ▶ **Name of a city of Naphtali.** Ref.: Josh. 19:36. ¶

ADAMANT – Ezek. 3:9; Zech. 7:12 → DIAMOND <8068>.

ADAMI – ***ăḏāmiy*** [proper noun: אֲדָמִי <129>; from GROUND <127>]: red earth, earthy ▶ **Name of a city of Naphtali.** Ref.: Josh. 19:33. ¶

ADAR – [1] ***ăḏār*** [proper noun: אֲדָר <143>; prob. of foreign deriv. (perhaps meaning fire)] ▶ **The twelfth month in the Hebrew calendar.** It is used in the Book of Esther (3:7, 13; 8:12; 9:1, 15, 17, 19, 21) only and corresponds to February-March. A second Adar month (an intercalary month) was added as necessary to make the seasons of the years uniform. It is the same as next sub-entry <144>. ¶

[2] ***ăḏār*** [Aramaic proper noun: אֲדָר <144>; corresponding to <143> above]: glorious ▶ **The Babylonian proper name used for the twelfth month in Israel's calendar.** Ref.: Ezra 6:15. It is the same as previous sub-entry <143>. ¶

ADBEEL – ***'aḏbe'ēl*** [masc. proper noun: אַדְבְּאֵל <110>; prob. from GRIEVE <109> (in the sense of chastisement) and GOD <410>]: chastised by God, servant of God ▶ **Name of one of the sons of Ishmael.** Refs.: Gen. 25:13; 1 Chr. 1:29. ¶

ADD – ***yesap̱*** [Aramaic verb: יְסַף <3255>; corresponding to CONTINUE <3254>] ▶ **This word means to join to something so that it is increased in quantity or quality.** In Daniel 4:36, it is used to indicate an increase in the influence, splendor, and respect of Nebuchadnezzar's rulership. ¶

ADDAN – ***'addān*** [proper noun: אַדָּן <135>; intens. from the same as BASE (noun) <134>]: powerful, calamity ▶ **Name of a Babylonian place.** Ref.: Ezra 2:59; in Neh. 7:61, it is spelled Addon. ¶

ADDAR – ***'addār*** [proper noun: אַדָּר <146>; intens. from GLORIOUS <142>]: glorious ▶

a. Name of a grandson of Benjamin. Ref.: 1 Chr. 8:3. ¶

b. A city in Judah. Ref.: Josh. 15:3. ¶

ADDER – [1] Gen. 49:17 → VIPER <8207> [2] Job 20:16; Is. 30:6; 59:5 → VIPER <660> [3] Ps. 140:3 → VIPER <5919> [4] Prov. 23:32; Is. 11:8; 14:29; 59:5; Jer. 8:17 → VIPER <6848> [5] See ASP <6620>.

ADDITION – 1 Kgs. 7:29, 30, 36 → WREATH <3914>.

ADDITION (IN) – Eccl. 12:9, 12 ➔ MORE, MORE THAN <3148>.

ADDON – [1] ***'addôn*** [masc. proper noun: אַדּוֹן <114>; prob. intens. for LORD <113>]: powerful, calamity ▶ **Name of a man who was possibly an Israelite.** Ref.: Neh. 7:61. ¶
– [2] Neh. 7:61 ➔ ADDAN <135>.

ADER – 1 Chr. 8:15 ➔ EDER <5738>.

ADHERE – ***deḇaq*** [Aramaic verb: דְּבַק <1693>; corresponding to JOIN <1692>] ▶ **This word means to cling to, to stay together, to stick together; it is also translated to cleave, to hold together, to remain united.** It indicates the ability to stick or adhere together. In its contextual usage, it is negated to describing iron and clay, representing diverse ethnic groups or peoples that cannot cling together (Dan. 2:43). ¶

ADIEL – ***ʿaḏiy'êl*** [masc. proper noun: עֲדִיאֵל <5717>; from ORNAMENT <5716> and GOD <410>]: ornament of God ▶
a. A Simeonite. Ref.: 1 Chr. 4:36. ¶
b. A priest. Ref.: 1 Chr. 9:12. ¶
c. The father of an officer under David. Ref.: 1 Chr. 27:25. ¶

ADIN – ***ʿāḏiyn*** [masc. proper noun: עָדִין <5720>; the same as PLEASURES (GIVEN TO) <5719>]: soft, delicate ▶
a. Ancestor of returning Jewish exiles. Refs.: Ezra 2:15; 8:6; Neh. 7:20. ¶
b. A chief of the people who signed the covenant of renewal with Nehemiah after the return from the Babylonian captivity. Ref.: Neh. 10:16. ¶

ADINA – ***ʿaḏiynā'*** [masc. proper noun: עֲדִינָא <5721>; from PLEASURES (GIVEN TO) <5719>]: slender, delicate ▶ **One of David's mighty men.** Ref.: 1 Chr. 11:42. ¶

ADINO THE EZNITE – ***ʿaḏiynô hāʿeṣniy*** [masc. proper noun: עֲדִינוֹ הָעֶצְנִי <5722>; prob. from PLEASURES (GIVEN TO) <5719>]: slender, delicate ▶ **He was one of David's mighty men.** Ref.: 2 Sam. 23:8. ¶

ADITHAIM – ***ʿaḏiyṯayim*** [proper noun: עֲדִיתַיִם <5723>; dual of a fem. of PREY <5706>]: double prey ▶ **A city of the tribe of Judah.** Ref.: Josh. 15:36. ¶

ADJURATION – Lev. 5:1 ➔ OATH <423>.

ADJURE – 1 Sam. 14:24 ➔ CURSE (verb) <422>.

ADLAI – ***ʿaḏlay*** [masc. proper noun: עַדְלַי <5724>; prob. from an unused root of uncertain meaning]: justice of the Lord ▶ **Father of Shaphat, who was over David's herds.** Ref.: 1 Chr. 27:29. ¶

ADMAH – ***'aḏmāh*** [proper noun: אַדְמָה <126>; contr. for GROUND <127>]: earthy ▶ **Name of a city near the Dead Sea destroyed with Sodom and Gomorrah.** Refs.: Gen. 10:19; 14:2, 8; Deut. 29:23; Hos. 11:8. ¶

ADMATHA – ***'aḏmāṯā'*** [masc. proper noun: אַדְמָתָא <133>; prob. of Persian deriv.]: brown, gift of God ▶ **Name of a prince from Persia and Media.** Ref.: Esther 1:14. ¶

ADMINISTRATION – Dan. 2:49; 3:12 ➔ WORK <5673>.

ADMINISTRATOR – [1] Is. 22:15 ➔ PROFITABLE (BE) <5532> b. [2] Dan. 3:2, 3, 37; 6:7 ➔ PREFECT <5460> [3] Dan. 6:2–4, 6:6, 7 ➔ COMMISSIONER <5632>.

ADMIRED – 2 Sam. 1:23 ➔ PLEASANT <5273> a.

ADMONISH – [1] ***yāsar, sārar*** [verb: יָסַר, סָרַר <3256>; a prim. root] ▶ **This word means to discipline, to chasten, to instruct, to teach, to punish. It is used with two general poles of meaning (chastening or instructing) that at times merge.** Both aspects are presented in Scripture in terms of God and humans. Others can instruct and teach (Job 4:3), as can the conscience (Ps. 16:7). Still others can discipline, but God

is the ultimate source of true instruction and chastening. He often chides toward an instructive end, especially for His covenant people (Lev. 26:18, 23; Jer. 46:28); wisdom presents the disciplined one as blessed, even though the process is painful (Ps. 94:12; 118:18). However, chastisement is not always presented as positive or instructive, for Rehoboam promised an evil chastening that eventually split the united kingdom (1 Kgs. 12:11, 14); and God's just, unremitted punishment would bring desolation (Jer. 6:8; 10:24). *
– [2] Eccl. 4:13; 12:12 ➔ WARN <2094>.

ADNA – *'adnā'* [masc. proper noun: עַדְנָא <5733>; from DELIGHT ONESELF <5727>]: pleasure ▶
a. The head of a priestly family. Ref.: Neh. 12:15. ¶
b. A postexilic Jew. Ref.: Ezra 10:30. ¶

ADNAH – *'adnāh* [masc. proper noun: עַדְנָה <5734>; from DELIGHT ONESELF <5727>]: pleasure ▶
a. A prince of Judah. Ref.: 2 Chr. 17:14. ¶
b. A Manassite. Ref.: 1 Chr. 12:20. ¶

ADONI-BEZEK – *'ᵃdōniy bezeq* [masc. proper noun: אֲדֹנִי בֶזֶק <137>; from LORD <113> and BEZEK <966>]: lord of Bezek (breach, flash) ▶ **Name of a Canaanite king.** He was an unjust king towards his conquered people and in the end received "poetic justice" for these misdeeds (Judg. 1:4–7). He was defeated by Simeonites and Judahites (Judg. 1:4) at Bezek. He was mutilated and brought to Jerusalem where he expired. Bezek was located northeast of Shechem (cf. 1 Sam. 11:8). ¶

ADONI-ZEDEK – *'ᵃdōniy ṣedeq* [masc. proper noun: אֲדֹנִי צֶדֶק <139>; from LORD <113> and RIGHTEOUSNESS <6664>]: my lord is righteous ▶ **Name of a Canaanite king.** Refs.: Josh. 10:1, 3. ¶

ADONIJAH – *'ᵃdōniyyah, 'ᵃdōniyyāhû* [masc. proper noun: אֲדֹנִיָּה, אדניהו <138>; from LORD <113> and LORD <3050>]: my lord is Yahweh ▶
a. Name of David's fourth son by Haggith. He tried unsuccessfully to take the throne upon David's imminent death (1 Kgs. 1:1–53; 2:13–25). Solomon offered to spare Adonijah if he showed loyalty to him, but Adonijah tried to get the inside track on Solomon again and was executed (1 Kgs. 2:13–25). *
b. A proper name of a Levite appointed by Jehoshaphat to teach the Book of the Law in all the towns of Judah. Refs.: 2 Chr. 17:7–9. ¶
c. An Israelite who signed the covenant of renewal with Nehemiah after the return from the Babylonian captivity. Ref.: Neh. 10:16. ¶

ADONIKAM – *'ᵃdōniyqām* [masc. proper noun: אֲדֹנִיקָם <140>; from LORD <113> and STAND <6965>]: my lord has risen ▶ **Name of an Israelite.** Refs.: Ezra 2:13; 8:13; Neh. 7:18. ¶

ADONIRAM – *'ᵃdōniyrām* [masc. proper noun: אֲדֹנִירָם <141>; from LORD <113> and EXALT <7311>]: my lord is exalted ▶ **Name of an Israelite who was in charge of forced labor under Solomon.** Refs.: 1 Kgs. 4:6; 5:14. ¶

ADORAIM – *'ᵃdôrayim* [proper noun: אֲדוֹרַיִם <115>; dual from GLORIOUS <142> (in the sense of eminence)]: double dwelling place, honor ▶ **Name of a place in Judah.** Ref.: 2 Chr. 11:9. ¶

ADORAM – *'ᵃdōrām* [masc. proper noun: אֲדֹרָם <151>; contr. for ADONIRAM <141>]: my lord is exalted ▶ **Name of an Israelite; he was in charge of the forced labor and was stoned by the ten tribes of Israel.** Refs.: 2 Sam. 20:24; 1 Kgs. 12:18. ¶

ADORN – [1] *'āḏāh* [verb: עָדָה <5710>; a prim. root] ▶ **This word means to ornament, to deck, to decorate.** It means to deck oneself in splendor, to dress to attract attention and respect, usually in a bad sense (Job 40:10; Is. 61:10; Jer. 4:30; Ezek. 16:11; Hos. 2:13). Other refs.: Jer. 31:4; Ezek. 16:13; 23:40. The Hebrew word also means

to pass over, to take off; see PASS OVER <5710>. ¶
– [2] Ps. 93:5 ➜ BEAUTIFUL (BE) <4998>.

ADORN ONESELF – Jer. 4:30; 10:4 ➜ BEAUTIFUL (BE, MAKE ONESELF) <3302>.

ADRAMMELECH – *'aḏrammelek* [masc. proper noun: אַדְרַמֶּלֶךְ <152>; from GLORIOUS <142> and KING <4428>]: splendor of the king ▶
a. The name designates an idol. Ref.: 2 Kgs. 17:31. ¶
b. It designates also a son of Sennacherib. Refs.: 2 Kgs. 19:37; Is. 37:38. ¶

ADRIEL – *'aḏriy'êl* [proper noun: עַדְרִיאֵל <5741>; from FLOCK <5739> and GOD <410>]: flock of God ▶ **Saul's daughter was given to him for a wife.** Refs.: 1 Sam. 18:19; 2 Sam. 21:8. ¶

ADULLAM – *'ḏullām* [proper noun: עֲדֻלָּם <5725>; prob. from the pass. part. of the same as ADLAI <5724>] ▶ **A town in the low-lying hills of the Shephelah that the Israelites conquered.** Ref.: Josh. 12:15. It was allotted to the tribe of Judah (Josh. 15:35). Later, David fled there to hide from Saul (1 Sam. 22:1; 2 Sam. 23:13). Assyria captured it (Mic. 1:15) much later. Exiles returning from the Babylonian captivity reestablished the city (Neh. 11:30). Other refs.: 1 Chr. 11:15; 2 Chr. 11:7. ¶

ADULLAMITE – *'ḏullāmiy* [proper noun: עֲדֻלָּמִי <5726>; patrial from ADULLAM <5725>] ▶ **This word is a gentilic/ethnic form that indicates an inhabitant of the city of Adullam.** Refs.: Gen. 38:1, 12, 20. ¶

ADULTERER – Lev. 20:10; Is. 57:3; etc. ➜ ADULTERY (COMMIT) <5003>.

ADULTERY – [1] *ni'up* [masc. noun: נִאֻף <5004>; from ADULTERY (COMMIT) <5003>] ▶ **This word is used in its plural form only. It is figurative of idolatrous worship.** Refs.: Jer. 13:27; Ezek. 23:43. ¶

[2] *na'ḥpûp* [masc. noun: נַאֲפוּף <5005>; from ADULTERY (COMMIT) <5003>] ▶ **This word describes the act of marital infidelity.** Ref.: Hos. 2:2. ¶

ADULTERY (COMMIT) – *nā'ap* [verb: נָאַף <5003>; a prim. root] ▶ **This verb is used of the physical act of marital infidelity.** Refs.: Ex. 20:14; Lev. 20:10; Prov. 6:32; Jer. 5:7; 7:9; 29:23; Hos. 4:2; Mal. 3:5. But often it is used of spiritual adultery as well; idolatry (Is. 57:3; Jer. 3:9; Ezek. 23:37). *

ADUMMIM – *'ḏummiym* [proper noun: אֲדֻמִּים <131>; plur. of ADAM <121>]: red lands ▶ **Name of a pass bordering Judah and Benjamin.** Refs.: Josh. 15:7; 18:17. ¶

ADVANCE QUICKLY – 2 Sam. 5:24 ➜ MOVE <2782>.

ADVANTAGE – [1] Job 35:3 ➜ PROFITABLE (BE) <5532> a. [2] Prov. 21:5; Eccl. 3:19 ➜ PROFIT (noun) <4195> [3] Eccl. 1:3; 5:9, 16; 10:11; 7:12; 10:10 ➜ PROFIT (noun) <3504> [4] Eccl. 5:11 ➜ SKILL <3788> [5] Eccl. 6:11 ➜ MORE, MORE THAN <3148>.

ADVANTAGE (TAKE) – Gen. 27:36 ➜ SUPPLANT <6117>.

ADVERSARY – [1] *qiym* [masc. noun: קִים <7009>; from STAND, STAND UP <6965> (in the sense of to rise against)] ▶
a. This word refers to those who rise up against someone, withstand someone, are hostile. Ref.: Job 22:20; also translated foe.
b. This word also means substance. It indicates an object, a force, or in a positive sense, an essence, the basis of something. Ref.: Job 22:20. ¶
– [2] 1 Sam. 1:6 ➜ TROUBLE (noun) <6869> b. [3] 1 Sam. 28:16; Ps. 139:20 ➜ ENEMY <6145> [4] Ps. 56:2; 92:11 ➜ ENEMY <8324> [5] Ps. 92:11 ➜ ENEMY <7790> [6] Jer. 18:19 ➜ CONTENDS (ONE WHO) <3401> [7] Dan. 4:19 ➜ ENEMY <6146> [8] See ACCUSER <7854>.

ADVERSARY (BE AN) – [1] Ex. 23:22 → BESIEGE <6696> b. [2] Ex. 23:22 → TROUBLED (BE) <6887> [3] Ps. 38:20; 71:13; 109:4, 20 → ACCUSE <7853>.

ADVICE – [1] ***mᵉlaḵ*** [Aramaic masc. noun: מְלַךְ <4431>; from a root corresponding to KING (BE) <4427> in the sense of consultation] ► **This word is used of instructions, exhortations, or counsel given to someone; it is also translated counsel.** Ref.: Dan. 4:27. ¶
– [2] 1 Sam. 25:33 → TASTE (noun) <2940> [3] Prov. 1:30 → COUNSEL (noun) <4156> [4] Prov. 12:5 → COUNSEL (noun) <8458>.

ADVISER – [1] 1 Kgs. 4:5 → FRIEND <7463> [2] Ezra 7:14, 15 → CONSULT TOGETHER <3272> [3] Dan. 3:2, 3 → COUNSELOR <148>.

ADVISER, PERSONAL ADVISER – Gen. 26:26 → FRIEND <4828>.

ADVISOR – Dan. 3:24, 27; 4:36; 6:7 → COUNSELOR <1907>.

ADVOCATE – ***śāhêḏ*** [masc. noun: שָׂהֵד <7717>; from an unused root meaning to testify] ► **This word refers to a reliable person who will argue for or support a plaintiff in a court case.** Ref.: Job 16:19; also translated evidence, record, he who testifies. ¶

AFFAIR – Prov. 31:27 → WAY <1979>.

AFFAIRS – Dan. 2:49; 3:12 → WORK <5673>.

AFFAIRS (TURN OF) – 2 Chr. 10:15 → EVENTS (TURN OF) <5252>.

AFFECTION (SET ONE'S) – Deut. 7:7 → DESIRE (verb) <2836>.

AFFLICT – [1] ***dāḥaq*** [verb: דָּחַק <1766>; a prim. root] ► **This word means to cause distress, to oppress, to jostle; it is also translated to harass, to vex.** It refers to military, economic, and political affliction (Judg. 2:18). It is used of warriors marching in disciplined array without crowding or jostling one another (Joel 2:8; also translated to push, to thrust). ¶
[2] ***yāḡāh, nûḡ*** [verb: יָגָה, נוּג <3013>; a prim. root] ► **A verb indicating to suffer, to grieve; it is also translated to bring affliction, to inflict, to cause grief, to bring grief.** It refers to the emotion and despair brought about by some act or condition, such as Jerusalem's misfortunes (Lam. 3:33). Compassion is the cure for this state of affliction from the Lord and comes from Him as well (Lam. 1:12; 3:32). The virgins or pure daughters of Zion were in a state of despair and mourning from the Lord (Lam. 1:4, 5). It seems to refer to the sufferer tormented by his useless comforters (Job 19:2: to torment, to vex). It describes the affliction on Israel, the distress and pain from her enemies (Is. 51:23: one who afflicts, tormentor). It indicates those who sorrow or grieve because of the failure to keep the appointed feasts of God's people (Zeph. 3:18: to sorrow, to grieve, to be sorrowful, to mourn). ¶
– [3] Gen. 12:17; 2 Kgs. 15:5 → TOUCH <5060> [4] 2 Chr. 21:18; 2 Sam. 12:15; Zech. 14:18 → SMITE <5062>.

AFFLICTED – [1] ***mās*** [adj.: מָס <4523>; from MELT <4549> (in the sense of to be broken down, to lose courage)] ► **This word means distressed, suffering; it is also translated despairing.** Its meaning in context is difficult to ascertain precisely but seems to describe an especially hopeless person, despondent to the point of giving up (Job 6:14). ¶
– [2] Prov. 26:28 → OPPRESSED <1790>.

AFFLICTED (BE) – ***'ānāh*** [verb: עָנָה <6031>; a prim. root] ► **This word indicates to be oppressed, to be humbled. It refers to being in a state of oppression.** It means to bow down, to humble oneself, to be humbled (Ex. 10:3; Is. 58:10). In some senses of the verb, it means to inflict oppression, to subdue, to humble someone: of Israel's oppression in Egypt (Gen. 15:13;

Ex. 1:11, 12); to deal with persons harshly, to oppress them (Gen. 16:6); to humiliate a woman (Deut. 21:14); to afflict, humble oneself (Gen. 16:9; Lev. 16:29; Ps. 132:1). It is used of raping a woman (Gen. 34:2). It is possible to humble oneself, to afflict oneself by fasting (Ezra 8:21; Dan. 10:12). The psalmist was often disciplined by affliction from God (Ps. 119:71); the Suffering Servant of Isaiah was afflicted by the Lord (Is. 53:4). *

AFFLICTION – 1 ***mû'āqāh*** [fem. noun: מוּעָקָה <4157>; from WEIGHTED DOWN (BE) <5781>] ► **This word indicates an oppressive burden (ESV: crushing burden).** It is used of God's judgments on His people, a hardship to them at the time (Ps. 66:11). ¶

2 ***'enûṯ*** [fem. noun: עֱנוּת <6039>; from AFFLICTED (BE) <6031>] ► **This word indicates the state of being oppressed in various ways, physically, mentally, or spiritually.** God cares for this condition in His people (Ps. 22:24; NIV: suffering). ¶

3 ***'oniy*** [masc. noun: עֳנִי <6040>; from AFFLICTED (BE) <6031>] ► **This word also means misery. It refers to a state of oppression or extreme discomfort, physically, mentally, or spiritually.** Hagar was abused and afflicted by Sarah (Gen. 16:11); Leah was not loved as was Rachel (Gen. 29:32); Jacob was abused and tricked by Laban (Gen. 31:42); Israel was under affliction by the Egyptians (Ex. 3:7, 17); childlessness was an affliction in the Old Testament (1 Sam. 1:11); political, economic, and military oppression are in the range of the word (2 Kgs. 14:26). Job's illness was a burdensome affliction (Job 10:15; 30:16). The psalmist was under attack from those who hated him (Ps. 9:13). Affliction is a disciplinary measure from God in some cases (Is. 48:10). *

– 4 1 Kgs. 8:38; 2 Chr. 6:29 → SORE (noun) <5061> 5 1 Kgs. 22:27; Is. 30:20 → OPPRESSION <3906>.

AFFLICTION (BRING) – Lam. 3:33 → AFFLICT <3013>.

AFFORD – Ps. 144:13 → OBTAIN <6329>.

AFLAME – Is. 13:8 → lit.: as flame → FLAME <3851>.

AFRAID – 1 ***yāḡôr*** [adj.: יָגוֹר <3016>; from AFRAID (BE) <3025>] ► **This word means feared, fearful, dreadful. It is translated to be afraid, to fear, to dread.** It indicates an attitude of great anxiety and apprehension towards certain persons, events, or things (Jer. 22:25), such as the dreaded Babylonians (Jer. 39:17). ¶

– 2 See FEARING <3373>.

AFRAID (BE) – 1 ***rāhāh*** [verb: רָהָה <7297>; a prim. root] ► **This word implies a fear that stems from uncertainty or a sense of being utterly alone.** It occurs only in Isaiah 44:8. In the text, the Lord offered His assurance that He was still living and was in control of all situations. ¶

2 ***yāḡōr*** [verb: יָגֹר <3025>; a prim. root] ► **This word means to be terrified; it is also translated to fear, to dread.** In comparison to the more common verb for fear, *yārê'* [FEAR (verb) <3372>], which often refers to a general sense of vulnerability (cf. Gen. 15:1), *yāḡōr* refers to fear of specific occurrences such as catching a disease (Deut. 28:60); being reproached or scorned (Ps. 119:39). It describes the fear of God in Deuteronomy 9:19 but focuses on the specific possibility of God destroying Israel. Other refs.: Job 3:25; 9:28. ¶

– 3 Job 32:6 → CRAWL <2119> 4 Ps. 18:4 → TREMBLING (COME) <2727> 5 Is. 8:12 → TREMBLE <6206> 6 Is. 57:1; Jer. 38:19; 42:16 → ANXIOUS (BE, BECOME) <1672> 7 Jer. 22:25; 39:17 → AFRAID <3016> 8 Dan. 11:30 → GRIEVED (BE) <3512> 9 Mal. 2:5 → DISMAYED (BE) <2865> 10 See FEAR (verb) <3372>.

AFRAID (MAKE) – 1 ***bālah*** [verb: בָּלַהּ <1089>; a prim. root, rather by transposition for TERRIFIED (BE) <926>] ► **This word means to terrify, to tremble, to frighten; to deter; it is also translated to trouble. It describes an attempt to keep someone from doing something.** The enemies of the Jews tried to keep the returned

exiles from rebuilding the Temple by diplomatic and threatening words and actions (Ezra 4:4). ¶
– [2] Dan. 4:5 → FEAR (verb) <1763>.

AFTER – ***'aḥ^a^rêy*** [Aramaic prep.: אַחֲרֵי <311>; corresponding to BEHIND <310>] ► **The word means the future.** Refs.: Dan. 2:29, 45. It also indicates the temporal sequence of kings and kingdoms (Dan. 7:24). Pronominal suffixes may be attached to it, e.g., *'aḥ^a^ray*, after me, etc. ¶

AFTERBIRTH – ***šilyāh*** [fem. noun: שִׁלְיָה <7988>; fem. from TAKE AWAY <7953>] ►
a. This word refers to the placenta, a temporary vascular organ developed during a mammal's gestation period to nourish the fetus and provide for the discharge of its wastes. Ref.: Deut. 28:57.
b. This word is taken by some translators to mean a young one or newly born infant. Ref.: KJV, Deut. 28:57. ¶

AGAG – ***^a^gag*** [masc. proper noun: אֲגַג <90>; of uncertain deriv. (comp. AGEE <89>)] ►
a. An Amalekite king. Ref.: Num. 24:7. The reference in Numbers 24:7 may be proleptic, or it may have been a common name among the Amalekites, the sworn enemies of the Israelites from the time Israel departed Egypt (see Ex. 17:8–16). ¶
b. Perhaps a title like "Pharaoh." The name refers to a specific king in Saul's day (1 Sam. 15:8, 33), who was slain by Samuel. Haman may have been a descendant of the Amalekites (Esther 3–5; 6:7; 8; 9). *

AGAGITE – ***^a^gāgiy*** [masc. proper noun: אֲגָגִי <91>; patrial or patron. from AGAG <90>] ► **Possibly a descendant of Agag.** Haman, an enemy of the Jews, was an Agagite (Esther 3:1, 10; 8:3, 5; 9:24). ¶

AGAIN – ***'ôḏ*** [adv.: עוֹד <5750>; from WITNESS (BEAR) <5749> (properly, iteration or continuance)] ► **This word means in addition, as well as, still, more, longer, also, yet. It indicates repetition and/or continuance of something.** It expresses the fact that something continues to happen (Gen. 18:22; 29:7; 46:29; 1 Kgs. 22:43). It can mean not yet used with *lô'* (2 Chr. 20:33; Jer. 40:5). It is used often in the phrase, still (*'ôḏ*) speaking (Gen. 29:9; 1 Kgs. 1:22, 42; 2 Kgs. 6:33; Esther 6:14). It indicates repetition or repeated action (Gen. 7:4; 8:10, 12; 2 Kgs. 6:33). The construction of *lô'. . . 'ôḏ* means no more (Gen. 17:5; Ex. 2:3; Josh. 5:1, 12). It indicates doing something once more, again (Gen. 4:25; 9:11; 18:29). It takes on the sense of still or more in some contexts (Gen. 19:12; Josh. 14:11; Ps. 139:18; Amos 6:10). It takes prefixes: *b^e^*, in the continuance of what is going on (Gen. 25:6; Deut. 31:27). It indicates time within which something will happen (Gen. 40:13, 19; Josh. 1:11; Is. 7:8). *

AGAINST – [1] ***mûl, mô'l, môl*** [verb: מוּל, מוֹאל, מוֹל <4136>; from CIRCUMCISE <4135> (in the sense of to cut short)] ► **This word means in front of, toward, opposite.** It indicates a position in front of something (2 Sam. 11:15); or indicates toward the front of (Lev. 5:8; 1 Sam. 17:30), turning toward another person. It has a nominal (noun) sense that indicates the front or opposite (Ex. 26:9; 1 Kgs. 7:5). It is combined with prepositions on the front of it to nuance its meaning. As a geographical term, it means opposite most often (Ex. 34:3). It means in the presence of someone, especially God (Ex. 18:19). It may indicate in the direction of south, north, etc. (1 Kgs. 7:39). *
– [2] Dan. 7:25 → CONCERNING <6655> [3] See WITH <854>.

AGATE – [1] ***kaḏkōḏ*** [masc. noun: כַּדְכֹּד <3539>; from the same as <3537> in the sense of striking fire from a metal forged (a sparkling gem)] ► **This word denotes a precious stone; it is also translated ruby.** It indicates the Lord will use precious stones to construct Zion's military defenses (Is. 54:12). Merchants used such stones to pay for various goods and services (Ezek. 27:16). ¶

2 *šᵉḇô* [fem. noun: שְׁבוֹ <7618>; from an unused root] ▶ **This word refers to a precious stone set in the breastpiece of judgment of the high priest.** Refs.: Ex. 28:19; 39:12. It was the middle stone in the third row of stones representing the twelve tribes of Israel. ¶

AGE – 1 ***śeyḇ*** [masc. noun: שֵׂיב <7869>; from GRAY (BE) <7867>] ▶ **This word means advanced stage of life.** In 1 Kings, Ahijah is described as being aged, and his eyesight has failed (1 Kgs. 14:4). The usage of this word for Ahijah designates his wisdom. To have a head of gray hair is to have a crown of wisdom. ¶
– 2 Job 11:17; Ps. 39:5 ➔ WORLD <2465> 3 Dan. 1:10 ➔ JOY <1524>.

AGE (FULL, OLD, RIPE OLD) – Job 5:26; 30:2 ➔ FULL VIGOR <3624>.

AGE (OLD) – Gen. 21:2, 7; 37:3; 44:20 ➔ OLD AGE <2208>.

AGE-OLD – Judg. 5:21 ➔ ANCIENT <6917>.

AGE, OLD AGE – 1 ***zōqen*** [masc. noun: זֹקֶן <2207>; from OLD (BE) <2204>] ▶ **This word means extremely advanced stage of life.** It is used only once in the Old Testament (Gen. 48:10), describing Jacob at the time he blessed Ephraim above Manasseh. By this time, he was well-advanced in years, so much so that his sight was extremely poor. ¶
– 2 Gen. 24:36; Ps. 71:9, 18; Is. 46:4 ➔ OLD AGE <2209>.

AGED – 1 ***yāšiyš*** [adj.: יָשִׁישׁ <3453>; from AGED <3486>] ▶ **This word is found only in Job and referred to people who had gray hair; they were considered old or elderly.** Refs.: Job 15:10; 32:6. It referred to a class of people, such as modern-day senior citizens (Job 12:12: KJV, ancient; 29:8). ¶
2 ***yāšēš*** [adj.: יָשֵׁשׁ <3486>; from an unused root meaning to blanch] ▶ **This word means elderly; it is also translated infirm, weak, stooped for age.** It is used only with the word *zāqên* (OLD, OLD MAN <2205>). When King Zedekiah rebelled, the Lord caused the king of the Chaldeans to destroy Jerusalem and all the people in it. The Chaldean king showed no mercy for any of the people, including the aged or old (2 Chr. 36:17). ¶

AGEE – ***'āgê'*** [masc. proper noun: אָגֵא <89>; of uncertain deriv. (comp. AGAG <90>)] ▶ **Name of an Israelite, father of Shammah.** Ref.: 2 Sam. 23:11. ¶

AGGRESSION – Is. 14:6 ➔ PERSECUTION <4783>.

AGGRESSIVE – Is. 18:2, 7 ➔ TREADING DOWN <4001>.

AGILE (MAKE) – ***pāzaz*** [verb: פָּזַז <6339>; a prim. root, identical with REFINED (BE) <6338>] ▶
a. This word is used figuratively to indicate the mental quickness of Joseph or his determination. He could prevail over his persecutors by being agile, able to move and surmount evil. Others translate this word as meaning to be strong. It is used to indicate the fortitude of Joseph in remaining firm and able before his enemies (Gen. 49:24). ¶
b. This word means to leap. It describes David's jumping and dancing before the Lord, an expression of great joy and delight before God (2 Sam. 6:16). ¶

AGONY – 1 2 Sam. 1:9 ➔ ANGUISH <7661> 2 Jer. 50:43; Mic. 4:9 ➔ PAIN (noun) <2427>.

AGREE – 1 ***zᵉman*** [Aramaic verb: זְמַן <2164>; corresponding to APPOINTED <2163>] ▶ **This word means to make arrangements together; it is also translated to conspire, to prepare.** Nebuchadnezzar believed that his wise men were conspiring together, which is why he insisted they tell him both his dream and its interpretation (Dan. 2:9). See the related Hebrew verb *zāman* (APPOINTED <2163>). ¶

– [2] Gen. 34:15, 22, 23; 2 Kgs. 12:8 → CONSENT <225> [3] Job 22:21 → PROFITABLE (BE) <5532> a. [4] Dan. 6:7 → CONSULT TOGETHER <3272>.

AGREEMENT – [1] Gen. 34:15: to enter into an agreement → CONSENT <225> [2] Num. 30:2–5, 7, 10–14 → PLEDGE (noun) <632> [3] Neh. 9:38: agreement, firm agreement, binding agreement → COVENANT <548> [4] Is. 28:18 → VISION <2380> [5] Dan. 6:6, 11, 15: to come by agreement → ASSEMBLE TOGETHER <7284>.

AGUR – ***'āḡûr*** [masc. proper noun: אָגוּר <94>; pass. part. of GATHER <103>]: who gathers ▶ **The words of Agur are recorded in Proverbs 30.** Ref.: Prov. 30:1. ¶

AH! – Jer. 4:10; Ezek. 4:14; etc. → ALAS! <162>.

AHA – ***he'āḥ*** [interj.: הֶאָח <1889>; from BEHOLD (interj.) <1887> and ALAS! <253>] ▶ **This word may express joy or satisfaction and comfort.** Ref.: Is. 44:16. The same can be expressed with an evil motive toward something (Ezek. 25:3). Figuratively, it expresses the satisfied neighing and anticipation of a warhorse toward a battle (Job 39:25). *

AHAB – ***'aḥ'āḇ*** [masc. proper noun: אַחְאָב <256>; from BROTHER <251> and FATHER <1>]: father's brother ▶
a. Name of an Israelite king, son of Omri, and the seventh king in Israel (ca. 874–852 B.C.). He was notoriously corrupt and infamous for marrying the Sidonian Princess Jezebel through whom idolatry and spiritual prostitution permeated Israel. The priests of Baal filled the land (1 Kgs. 18:19, 20). He worshiped the god Baal, setting up a temple for Baal in Samaria, his capital city (1 Kgs. 16:32). He set up Asherah poles representing the goddess of fertility Asherah, who was also the consort of El. Elijah called for a drought for over three years as a sign to Ahab (1 Kgs. 17:1; 18:5, 6; cf. Jas. 5:17, 18). The Lord also caused it to rain again as a sign to Ahab through Elijah (1 Kgs. 18:44–46). But the Lord also delivered Ahab in battle as a sign to him that the Lord desired to bless him (1 Kgs. 20:13) and to demonstrate who was the true Lord of the land. He fought many battles against the Syrians (1 Kgs. 22:1). But Ahab's corruption and rebellion were displayed even more openly when he had a fellow Israelite, Naboth, killed in order to get his vineyard (1 Kgs. 21:1–19). The Lord destroyed not only Ahab but his entire house (1 Kgs. 9:6–10). Both Ahab and his father Omri became bywords for evil and corruption among the prophets (Mic. 6:16). Ahab died at Ramoth-Gilead because he followed his false prophets (1 Kgs. 22:19–38). Ahaziah, his son, reigned after his death. *
b. The name of a false prophet, a son of Kolaiah. He was condemned by Jeremiah for prophesying in Yahweh's, the Lord's, name. Jeremiah predicted his death (Jer. 29:21, 22) at the hands of Babylonian forces. ¶

AHARAH – ***'aḥraḥ*** [masc. proper noun: אַחְרַח <315>; from BEHIND <310> and BROTHER <251>]: after his brother ▶ **A son of Benjamin.** Ref.: 1 Chr. 8:1. ¶

AHARHEL – ***'ᵃḥarḥêl*** [masc. proper noun: אֲחַרְחֵל <316>; from BEHIND <310> and WALL <2426>]: behind an entrenchment ▶ **An Israelite of the tribe of Judah.** Ref.: 1 Chr. 4:8. ¶

AHASBAI – ***'ᵃḥasbay*** [masc. proper noun: אֲחַסְבַּי <308>; of uncertain deriv.]: who possesses God ▶ **Father of Eliphelet who was one of David's mighty men.** Ref.: 2 Sam. 23:34. ¶

AHASUERUS – ***'ᵃḥašwêrôš*** [masc. proper noun: אֲחַשְׁוֵרוֹשׁ <325>; of Persian origin]: the chief of the governors, king ▶ **This noun designates a king of Persia, also Xerxes I (Greek, Aramaic), who reigned 485–465 B.C. He was involved in the great Battle of Salamis in Greece in 480 B.C.** In Ezra 4:6, he is an opponent to Israel's rebuilding the city walls. He is the king during the events in Esther (Esther 1:2; 6:2; etc.). Some scholars argue that in the Book of Esther the king may be Artaxerxes II (404–359 B.C.). He is mentioned as the father of Darius the Mede, who is still not fully identified, although he may be Cyrus (Dan. 9:1). *

AHAVA – ***'ah^{a}wā'*** [proper noun: אַהֲוָא <163>; prob. of foreign origin] ▶ **The name of a river of Babylonia.** Refs.: Ezra 8:15, 21, 31. ¶

AHAZ – ***'āḥāz*** [masc. proper noun: אָחָז <271>; from HOLD (TAKE) <270>]: he holds ▶
a. The name of a king of Judah who ruled 735–715 B.C. Ahaz is a shortened name for Jehoahaz. His reign lasted 17 years. He was the son of Jotham, who reigned before him. His most famous son was Hezekiah (2 Kgs. 15:38; 16:1, 2, 5, 7, 8). He did not follow the will of God as David had (2 Kgs. 16), but pursued the practices of the pagan nations (2 Kgs. 16:1–4). He was faithless at crucial times and did not trust the Lord to deliver him and Judah from their enemies (Is. 7:1–12), especially from Assyria. He brought in pagan altar styles into the Temple area (2 Kgs. 16:10–20). Isaiah prophesied during his reign (Is. 1:1; 14:28). *
b. The name of a Benjamite, a son of Micah. Ahaz fathered Jehoaddah (1 Chr. 8:35, 36) and was himself a great-grandson of King Saul (1 Chr. 9:39, 42). *

AHAZIAH – ***^{a}ḥazyāhû, ^{a}ḥazyāh*** [masc. proper noun: אֲחַזְיָהוּ, אֲחַזְיָה <274>; from HOLD (TAKE) <270> and LORD <3050>]: Yah (Lord) has seized ▶
a. The name of a king of Israel. He was Ahab's son and ruled in Samaria (1 Kgs. 22:51) while Jehoshaphat ruled in Judah. He reigned two years (853–852 B.C.) and did not follow the Lord. He served Baal-Zebub the Canaanite god (1 Kgs. 22:53), even inquiring of him for health reasons (2 Kgs. 1:2). Because he did this, the Lord caused his death as announced by Elijah (2 Kgs. 1:16, 17). *
b. The same name was borne by a king of Judah. Ahaziah, also Jehoahaz (2 Chr. 21:17), the son of Jehoram (2 Kgs. 8:24–26), son of Jehoshaphat (2 Kgs. 8:16). He was killed by Jehu (2 Kgs. 9:27–29) in fulfillment of Elijah's prophecies years earlier. He reigned less than one year (841 B.C.). His mother was the wicked Queen Athaliah, Ahab's daughter. *

AHBAN – ***'aḥbān*** [masc. proper noun: אַחְבָּן <257>; from BROTHER <251> and PERCEIVE <995>]: brother of understanding ▶ **An Israelite of the tribe of Judah.** Ref.: 1 Chr. 2:29. ¶

AHER – ***'aḥêr*** [masc. proper noun: אַחֵר <313>; the same as OTHER <312>]: another, who follows ▶ **An Israelite of the tribe of Benjamin.** Ref.: 1 Chr. 7:12. ¶

AHI – ***^{a}ḥiy*** [masc. proper noun: אֲחִי <277>; from BROTHER <251>]: brother ▶
a. An Israelite of the tribe of Gad. Ref.: 1 Chr. 5:15. ¶
b. An Israelite of the tribe of Asher. Ref.: 1 Chr. 7:34. ¶

AHIAM – ***^{a}ḥiy'ām*** [masc. proper noun: אֲחִיאָם <279>; from BROTHER <251> and MOTHER <517>]: brother of the mother ▶ **One of David's mighty men.** Refs.: 2 Sam. 23:33; 1 Chr. 11:35. ¶

AHIAN – ***'aḥyān*** [masc. proper noun: אַחְיָן <291>; from BROTHER <251>]: brotherly, brother of the day ▶ **An Israelite of the tribe of Manasseh.** Ref.: 1 Chr. 7:19. ¶

AHIEZER – ***^{a}ḥiy'ezer*** [masc. proper noun: אֲחִיעֶזֶר <295>; from BROTHER <251> and HELP (noun) <5828>]: brother of help ▶
a. The name of a man of the tribe of Dan. He helped produce a census of the tribes of Israel (Num. 1:12); he was son of Ammishaddai (Num. 2:25). He also presented the tribe's dedication offering of the Tabernacle (Num. 7:66, 71). He was in charge of the standard of the tribe as well (Num. 10:25). ¶

b. This other Ahiezer was a trained warrior who chose to support and help David, although he was related to Saul. Ref.: 1 Chr. 12:3. ¶

AHIHUD – [1] *ʼḥiyhûḏ* [masc. proper noun: אֲחִיהוּד <282>; from BROTHER <251> and VIGOR <1935> (in the sense of authority, majesty)]: brother of majesty ▶ **An Israelite of the tribe of Asher.** Ref.: Num. 34:27. ¶
[2] *ʼḥiyḥuḏ* [masc. proper noun: אֲחִיחֻד <284>; from BROTHER <251> and RIDDLE <2330>]: brother of mystery ▶ **An Israelite of the tribe of Benjamin.** Ref.: 1 Chr. 8:7. ¶

AHIJAH – *ʼḥiyyāh* [masc. proper noun: אֲחִיָּה <281>; from BROTHER <251> and LORD <3050>]: brother of Yah, Yah being a shortened form of Yahweh, Lord ▶ **This name was given to at least nine different individuals in the Old Testament. It refers to the following persons:**
a. A priest who served under Saul and "wore the ephod." He was from the line of high priests (1 Sam. 14:3). He was in charge of the ark of God (1 Sam. 14:18). ¶
b. An official under Saul who served as recorder or secretary. Ref.: 1 Kgs. 4:3. ¶
c. A prophet of Shiloh where the ark was. Ref.: 1 Kgs. 11:29. He announced the rending of the Southern Kingdom from Jeroboam (1 Kgs. 11:29–31; 12:15); Jeroboam's son Abijah's death (1 Kgs. 14:2, 4–6, 18); and the extinction of Jeroboam's house (1 Kgs. 14:6–16). His written words became a source of events under Solomon (2 Chr. 9:29). Other ref.: 2 Chr. 10:15. ¶
d. The father of King Baasha of Israel. Refs.: 1 Kgs. 15:27, 29, 33; 21:22; 2 Kgs. 9:9. He was of the tribe of Issachar. His son Baasha was a wicked king whose house was eradicated from Israel (1 Kgs. 16:1–7; 2 Kgs. 9:9, 10). ¶
e. He is listed as a grandson of Hezron. He was the son of Jerahmeel (1 Chr. 2:25). ¶
f. He is listed as a descendant of Saul, a son of Ehud. Ref.: 1 Chr. 8:7. ¶
g. The name is borne by one of David's mighty men. Ref.: 1 Chr. 11:36. He is called "the Pelonite." ¶
h. The name is borne by a Levite under David. He was in charge of Temple treasuries (1 Chr. 26:20). ¶
i. This Ahijah signed the covenant of renewal with Nehemiah after the return from the Babylonian captivity. Ref.: Neh. 10:26. ¶

AHIKAM – *ʼḥiyqām* [masc. proper noun: אֲחִיקָם <296>; from BROTHER <251> and STAND, STAND UP <6965>]: brother who has risen ▶ **A prince of Judah who protected Jeremiah from being put to death.** Refs.: 2 Kgs. 22:12, 14; 25:22; 2 Chr. 34:20; Jer. 26:24; 39:14; 40:5–7, 9, 11, 14, 16; 41:1, 2, 6, 10, 16, 18; 43:6. ¶

AHILUD – *ʼḥiylûḏ* [masc. proper noun: אֲחִילוּד <286>; from BROTHER <251> and BIRTH (GIVE) <3205>]: brother of a child ▶
a. The father of Jehoshaphat. Refs.: 2 Sam. 8:16; 20:24; 1 Kgs. 4:3; 1 Chr. 18:15. ¶
b. The father of Baana who was one of the governors of Solomon. Ref.: 1 Kgs. 4:12. Possibly that Ahilud was the father of both Jehoshaphat and Baana. ¶

AHIMAAZ – *ʼḥiyma'aṣ* [masc. proper noun: אֲחִימַעַץ <290>; from BROTHER <251> and the equivalent of MAAZ <4619>]: brother of wrath ▶
a. The name refers to a son of Zadok, a speedy messenger. Ref.: 2 Sam. 18:27. He helped carry the message of Absalom's defeat and demise to David (2 Sam. 18:19). *
b. It refers to Saul's father-in-law who was the father of Ahinoam, Saul's wife. Ref.: 1 Sam. 14:50. ¶
c. It refers to an officer who served under Solomon. Ref.: 1 Kgs. 4:15. He functioned as a district governor (1 Kgs. 4:7, 8) and married Solomon's daughter Basemath. ¶

AHIMAN – *ʼḥiyman*, *ʼḥiymān* [masc. proper noun: אֲחִימַן, אֲחִימָן <289>; from BROTHER <251> and FROM <4480>]: brother of a portion, i.e., a gift ▶
a. A son of Anak. Refs.: Num. 13:22; Josh. 15:14; Judg. 1:10. ¶

b. A Levite, gatekeeper of the house of God. Ref.: 1 Chr. 9:17. ¶

AHIMELECH – *ʾaḥiymeleḵ* [masc. proper noun: אֲחִימֶלֶךְ <288>; from BROTHER <251> and KING <4428>]: brother of the king ▶
a. He served as a priest in Saul's time. Refs.: 1 Sam. 21:1, 2, 8; 22:9, 11. He was the son of Ahitub. He was priest in Nob and gave David bread when he was fleeing from Saul. Saul had him executed for rebellion. *
b. The name refers to a Hittite who served under David before David was crowned king. Ref.: 1 Sam. 26:6. ¶
c. The name refers to the father of Abiathar. Refs.: 1 Sam. 22:20; 23:6; 30:7. But in 2 Samuel 8:17 it refers to Ahimelech as son of Abiathar. Generally, it is thought that 2 Samuel 8:17 features a copyist's error. ¶

AHIMOTH – *ʾaḥiymôṯ* [masc. proper noun: אֲחִימוֹת <287>; from BROTHER <251> and DIE <4191>]: brother of death ▶ **A Levite, son of Elkana.** Ref.: 1 Chr. 6:25. ¶

AHINADAB – *ʾaḥiynāḏāḇ* [masc. proper noun: אֲחִינָדָב <292>; from BROTHER <251> and GIVE WILLINGLY <5068>]: generous brother ▶ **An officer of Solomon at Mahanaim.** Ref.: 1 Kgs. 4:14. ¶

AHINOAM – *ʾaḥiynōʿam* [fem. proper noun: אֲחִינֹעַם <293>; from BROTHER <251> and BEAUTY <5278>]: pleasant brother ▶
a. The name of Saul's wife, daughter of Ahimaaz. Ref.: 1 Sam. 14:50. This is the only reference to any wife of Saul. ¶
b. It refers to one of David's wives, a Jezreelite. She was his first wife (1 Sam. 25:43) and bore his first son, Amnon (2 Sam. 3:2). *

AHIO – *ʾaḥyô* [masc. proper noun: אַחְיוֹ <283>; prolonged from BROTHER <251>]: brotherly ▶
a. The name of a son of Abinadab. Refs.: 2 Sam. 6:3, 4; 1 Chr. 13:7. ¶
b. An Israelite of the tribe of Benjamin. Ref.: 1 Chr. 8:14. ¶
c. A Gibeonite. Refs.: 1 Chr. 8:31; 9:37. ¶

AHIRA – *ʾaḥiyraʿ* [masc. proper noun: אֲחִירַע <299>; from BROTHER <251> and BAD <7451>]: brother of wrong ▶ **An Israelite of the tribe of Naphtali.** Refs.: Num. 1:15; 2:29; 7:78, 83; 10:27. ¶

AHIRAM – *ʾaḥiyrām* [masc. proper noun: אֲחִירָם <297>; from BROTHER <251> and EXALT <7311>]: brother of height, brother exalted ▶ **An Israelite of the tribe of Judah.** Ref.: Num. 26:38. ¶

AHIRAMITE – *ʾaḥirāmiy* [masc. proper noun: אֲחִירָמִי <298>; patron. from AHIRAM <297>] ▶ **A descendant of Ahiram.** Ref.: Num. 26:38. ¶

AHISAMACH – *ʾaḥiysāmāḵ* [masc. proper noun: אֲחִיסָמָךְ <294>; from BROTHER <251> and LAY ON <5564>]: brother of support ▶ **An Israelite of the tribe of Dan.** Refs.: Ex. 31:6; 35:34; 38:23. ¶

AHISHAHAR – *ʾaḥiyšaḥar* [masc. proper noun: אֲחִישַׁחַר <300>; from BROTHER <251> and DAWN <7837>]: brother of the dawn ▶ **An Israelite of the tribe of Benjamin.** Ref.: 1 Chr. 7:10. ¶

AHISHAR – *ʾaḥiyšār* [masc. proper noun: אֲחִישָׁר <301>; from BROTHER <251> and SING <7891>]: brother of the singer ▶ **An Israelite over the household of Solomon.** Ref.: 1 Kgs. 4:6. ¶

AHITHOPHEL – *ʾaḥiyṯōpel* [masc. proper noun: אֲחִיתֹפֶל <302>; from BROTHER <251> and FOOLISH <8602>]: brother of folly ▶ **He served as chief advisor and counselor to David but joined Absalom, forsaking David during Absalom's rebellion and conspiracy.** Ref.: 2 Sam. 15:12. He was from Gilon. The Lord confounded Ahithophel's counsel at David's request (2 Sam. 15:31, 34). Absalom turned against his advice and followed Hushai the Arkite's counsel (2 Sam. 17:5–22). Ahithophel, ashamed and threatened, committed suicide (2 Sam. 17:23). *

AHITUB – ***ᵃḥiyṭûḇ*** [masc. proper noun: אֲחִיטוּב <285>; from BROTHER <251> and GOODNESS <2898>]: brother of goodness ▶
a. A son of Phinehas. Refs.: 1 Sam. 14:3; 22:9, 11, 12, 20. ¶
b. The father of Zadok. Refs.: 2 Sam. 8:17; 1 Chr. 6:7, 8, 52; 1 Chr. 18:16. ¶
c. A priest. Refs.: 1 Chr. 6:11, 12; Ezra 7:2. ¶
d. Another priest. Refs.: 1 Chr. 9:11; Neh. 11:11. ¶

AHLAB – ***'aḥlāḇ*** [proper noun: אַחְלָב <303>; from the same root as FAT <2459>]: fertile ▶ **A place allotted to Asher (although the inhabitants were not dispossessed).** Ref.: Judg. 1:31. ¶

AHLAI – ***'aḥlay*** [masc. proper noun: אַחְלַי <304>; the same as WOULD THAT! <305>]: may God support! ▶
a. A son of Sheshan of the tribe of Judah. Ref.: 1 Chr. 2:31. This name refers most likely, however, to a daughter (see 1 Chr. 2:34). ¶
b. The father of one of David's mighty men. Ref.: 1 Chr. 11:41. ¶

AHOAH – ***ᵃḥôaḥ*** [masc. proper noun: אֲחוֹחַ <265>; by reduplication from BROTHER <251>]: brotherly, brother of the Lord ▶ **An Israelite of the tribe of Benjamin.** Ref.: 1 Chr. 8:4. ¶

AHOHITE – ***'aḥôḥiy*** [masc. proper noun: אֲחוֹחִי <266>; patron. from AHOAH <265>]: brotherhood ▶ **A descendant of Ahoah, an Israelite of the tribe of Benjamin.** Refs.: 2 Sam. 23:9, 28; 1 Chr. 11:12, 29; 27:4. ¶

AHUMAI – ***ᵃḥûmay*** [masc. proper noun: אֲחוּמַי <267>; perhaps from BROTHER <251> and WATER <4325>]: brother of waters ▶ **An Israelite of the tribe of Judah.** Ref.: 1 Chr. 4:2. ¶

AHUZZAM – ***ᵃḥuzzām*** [masc. proper noun: אֲחֻזָּם <275>; from HOLD (TAKE) <270>]: their possession ▶ **An Israelite of the tribe of Judah.** Ref.: 1 Chr. 4:6. ¶

AHUZZATH – ***ᵃḥuzzaṯ*** [masc. proper noun: אֲחֻזַּת <276>; a variation of POSSESSION <272>]: possession ▶ **An advisor of Abimelech.** Ref.: Gen. 26:26. ¶

AHZAI – ***'aḥzay*** [masc. proper noun: אַחְזַי <273>; from HOLD (TAKE) <270>]: possessor ▶ **An Israelite priest.** Ref.: Neh. 11:13. ¶

AI – ***'ay, 'ayya', 'ayyāṯ*** [proper noun: עַי, עַיָּא, עַיָּת <5857>; from RUINS <5856>]: heap, ruin ▶
a. It was located north, northeast of Jerusalem. There may have been at least one other Ai. See b. Abraham camped between Bethel and Ai (Gen. 12:8; 13:3). It was conquered by Joshua only after an initial failure because of Achan's sin in Israel (Josh. 7:1–8:29). Jericho and Ai became model signal victories for Israel (Josh. 9:3). Some former inhabitants of Ai returned from Babylonian exile (Ezra 2:8; Neh. 7:32). *
b. A city in the Transjordan territory in Moab. Ref.: Jer. 49:3. Its exact location is unclear. ¶

AIAH – ***'ayyāh*** [masc. proper noun: אַיָּה <345>; the same as FALCON <344>]: bird of prey, falcon ▶
a. A Horite, son of Zibeon. Refs.: Gen. 36:24; 1 Chr. 1:40. ¶
b. The father of Rizpah, Saul's concubine. Refs.: 2 Sam. 3:7; 21:8, 10, 11. ¶

AIJALON – ***'ayyālôn, 'ayālôn*** [proper noun: אַיָּלוֹן, אַיָּלֹן <357>; from DEER <354>]: deer field ▶
a. A city in the territory of Dan. Ref.: Josh. 19:42. However, it was not captured by Dan (Judg. 1:35). It was a Levitical city (Josh. 21:24), a place where both people of Benjamin and Ephraim lived. It was reinforced by Solomon's son Rehoboam (2 Chr. 11:10). Later, Philistines captured it (2 Chr. 28:18). *
b. A city in Zebulun. Ref.: Judg. 12:12. Elon, a judge, was buried in it. Its exact location is unclear. ¶

AIJELETH – Ps. 22 (title) ➔ DEER <365> b.

AIL – Job 16:3 ➔ GRIEVOUS <4834>.

AIN – ***'ayin*** [proper noun: עַיִן <5871>; the same as EYE (noun) <5869>]: fountain, eye ▶
a. A town on the northeast border of Canaan. Ref.: Num. 34:11. ¶
b. A town in the Negev of Judah. Refs.: Josh. 15:32; 19:7; 21:16; 1 Chr. 4:32. ¶

AKAN – [1] ***'ăqān*** [masc. proper noun: עֲקָן <6130>; from an unused root meaning to twist]: uncertain, tortuous ▶ **A descendant of Ezer.** Ref.: Gen. 36:27. ¶
– [2] 1 Chr. 1:42; Gen. 36:27 ➔ JAAKAN <3292>.

AKBOR – See ACHBOR <5907>.

AKKAD – Gen. 10:10 ➔ ACCAD <390>.

AKKUB – ***'aqqûḇ*** [masc. proper noun: עַקּוּב <6126>; from SUPPLANT <6117>]: crafty, insidious ▶
a. An Israelite of the tribe of Judah. Ref.: 1 Chr. 3:24. ¶
b. A gatekeeper in Solomon's time. Refs.: 1 Chr. 9:17; Ezra 2:42; Neh. 7:45. ¶
c. A gatekeeper in Nehemiah's time. Refs.: Neh. 11:19; 12:25. ¶
d. The head of a family of Temple servants. Ref.: Ezra 2:45. ¶
e. A Levite who helped Ezra expound the Law. Ref.: Neh. 8:7. ¶

AKRABBIM – [1] Num. 34:4; Josh. 15:3; Judg. 1:36 ➔ SCORPION PASS <4610> c. [2] Num. 34:4; Josh. 15:3; Judg. 1:36 ➔ SCORPION <6137> b.

AKSAH – See ACHSAH <5915>.

AL-TASHHETH – ***'al tašḥêṯ*** [masc. proper noun: אַל תַּשְׁחֵת <516>; from NO <408> and DESTROY <7843>]: Do Not Destroy ▶
a. This proper name is often interpreted as the title of a tune to which a particular Psalm was to be sung. See titles of Psalms 57–59; 75. ¶
b. Some translators interpret it as a tune title translated "Do Not Destroy," though some believe it should be understood as directions to preserve the Psalm and not a tune title. See beginning of Psalms 57–59; 75. ¶

ALABASTER – [1] 1 Chr. 29:2 ➔ MARBLE <7893> [2] Esther 1:6 ➔ PORPHYRY <923> [3] Song 5:15 ➔ LINEN, FINE LINEN <8336> b.

ALAMMELECH – ***'allammeleḵ*** [proper noun: אַלַּמֶּלֶךְ <487>; from OAK <427> and KING <4428>]: oak of the king ▶ **Village of the tribe of Asher.** Ref.: Josh. 19:26. ¶

ALAMOTH – ***'ălāmôṯ*** [fem. plur. noun: עֲלָמוֹת <5961>; plur. of YOUNG WOMAN <5959> (properly, girls)] ▶ **This word is a technical term used to indicate some aspect of a psalm, its tune; its formal genre, its presentation, e.g., set to a certain voice (soprano?).** Refs.: Ps. 46:1; 1 Chr. 15:20. It was a product of the sons of Korah. ¶

ALARM – Dan. 4:5, 19; 5:6, 9, 10; 7:15, 28 ➔ HASTE (BE IN) <927>.

ALARMED (BE) – Job 40:23 ➔ HURRY (verb) <2648>.

ALAS! – [1] ***'ăhāh*** [interj.: אֲהָהּ <162>; apparently a prim. word expressing pain exclamatorily] ▶ **This word is also usually rendered ah! or oh! indicating great emotion.** It usually indicates despair (Josh. 7:7; Judg. 11:35; Ezek. 11:13) but also a strong sense of marvel with fear (Judg. 6:22). It can indicate a feeling of inability (Jer. 1:6) or confusion (Jer. 4:10; Ezek. 4:14). It may introduce an announcement of the day of the Lord (Joel 1:15). *
[2] ***'āḥ*** [interj.: אָח <253>; a variation for <162> above] ▶ **This particle indicates pain or grief; it is also translated oh!, Look!** Refs.: Ezek. 6:11; 21:15. ¶
[3] ***hāh*** [interj.: הָהּ <1929>; a shortened form of <162> above] ▶ **A strong emotional interjection used to announce a coming**

day of horrific judgment on the ancient nation of Egypt and other nations of the world. Ref.: Ezek. 30:2. The Hebrew word is also translated Woe! ¶
4 ***hô*** [interj.: הוֹ <1930>; by permutation from ALAS! <1929>] ▶ **A strong emotional interjection.** It is repeated in Amos 5:16 for even more emphasis to announce the coming of the Lord's day of judgment. ¶
5 ***hôy*** [interj.: הוֹי <1945>; a prolonged form of <1930> above (akin to WOE <188>)] ▶ **This word also means ho! woe!** It is used in lamenting a person's death (1 Kgs. 13:30). It is used in prophetic announcements of judgment or threats (Is. 1:4, 24; Jer. 48:1; Ezek. 13:18; Amos 5:18). It is used to draw attention to an unexpected but momentous occasion (Is. 18:1) or to a hope-filled and joyous expectation (Zech. 2:6). *

ALEMETH – ***'ālemeṯ*** [proper noun: עָלֶמֶת <5964>; from HIDE <5956>]: covering ▶
a. Son of Becher. Ref.: 1 Chr. 7:8. ¶
b. Son of Jehoadah. Refs.: 1 Chr. 8:36; 9:42. ¶
c. A town in Benjamin, the same as Almon (ALMON <5960>). Ref.: 1 Chr. 6:60. ¶

ALGUM TREES – ***'algûmmiym*** [masc. plur. noun: אַלְגּוּמִּים <418>; by transposition for ALMUG <484>] ▶ **This word means and is also translated algum logs, algum timber.** These items were obtained by Solomon from Lebanon for use in constructing the Temple (2 Chr. 2:8; 9:10, 11). ¶

ALIAH – 1 Chr. 1:51 → ALVAH <5933> b.

ALIAN – 1 Chr. 1:40 → ALVAN <5935> b.

ALIEN – See STRANGER <1616>.

ALIENATED (BE) – 1 ***yāqa'*** [verb: יָקַע <3363>; a prim. root] ▶ **This word means to be estranged, to turn quickly, to turn away, to turn in disgust, to depart.** Refs.: Jer. 6:8; Ezek. 23:17, 18. Used of a bodily joint, it has the meaning of dislocation (Gen. 32:25: to dislocate, to put out of joint, to be wrenched). It has the sense of violent, total rejection, amounting to execution in Numbers 25:4 (to hang, to execute, to kill); however, it was accomplished. A similar meaning is suggested by the context in 2 Samuel 21:6, 9, 13. ¶
– 2 Ezek. 23:18, 22, 28 → DISGUSTED (BECOME) <5361>.

ALIGHT FROM – Josh. 15:18; Judg. 1:14 → GET OFF <6795>.

ALIVE – Dan. 4:17 → LIVING (adj.) <2417>.

ALL – 1 ***kōl*** [particle: כֹּל <3605>; from PERFECT (MAKE) <3634>] ▶ **This word means each, every, everything, the whole, entire. It has an inclusive meaning of entirely or every one of something. Its exact meaning must be discerned from its usage in its context.** Some representative samplings will help: With the definite article, it means the whole or everything of something (Eccl. 11:5); used before a definite noun, it expresses the whole of that noun, the whole earth (Gen. 9:19); whole people (Gen. 41:40). Used after a noun, it can refer to the whole or entirety of the preceding noun (2 Sam. 2:9); before a plural noun, it usually means all, all the nations (Is. 2:2); before a collective noun, it means all or every, all people (Gen. 7:21). Before a singular noun, it means every (Esther 3:8). Other nuances of its use can be discerned from studying its context closely. *
2 ***kōl*** [Aramaic particle: כֹּל <3606>; corresponding to <3605> above] ▶ **This word means every, any, entire.** Depending on the context: whole or all (Dan. 3:2, 3, 5); every, any (Dan. 6:7). It can mean the whole, everything (Dan. 2:40). It is used figuratively in phrases like all peace, security (Ezra 5:7). *

ALL AROUND – ***sāḇiyḇ*** [adv. or prep.: סָבִיב <5439>; from AROUND (GO, TURN) <5437>] ▶ **This word indicates surrounding, on every side.** It means round about, in the vicinity or area (Gen. 23:17; Ex. 19:12; 25:11; Judg. 20:29). It indicates something scattered or present all around a certain area (Ex. 16:13).

With *min* (FROM <4480>) on the front, it means from all around, from round about (Jer. 4:17; Is. 42:25; Ezek. 16:33, 37). It is repeated for emphasis (2 Chr. 4:3; Ezek. 8:10). In its plural form, it may take on the sense of the areas or parts around about (Jer. 49:5). In its singular and plural forms, it can take on the meaning of the circuit (of travel, area, etc.); the circuits (Ex. 7:24; 1 Chr. 11:8; Eccl. 1:6). *

ALLEGORY – [1] Ezek. 17:2 ➔ ENIGMA <2420> [2] Ezek. 17:2 ➔ to set forth an allegory ➔ to put forth a riddle ➔ RIDDLE <2330>.

ALLIANCE – Is. 30:1 ➔ COVERING <4541>.

ALLON – [1] ***'allôn*** [proper noun: אַלּוֹן <438>; the same as OAK <437>]: oak ▶
a. A city on the coast of Naphthali near Kadesh Naphtali. Ref.: Josh. 19:33; see OAK <437>. ¶
b. An Israelite of the tribe of Simeon. Ref.: 1 Chr. 4:37. ¶
– [2] Josh. 19:33 ➔ OAK <437>.

ALLON BACUTH – ***'allôn bāḵûṯ*** [proper noun: אַלּוֹן בָּכוּת <439>; from OAK <437> and a variation of MOURNING <1068>]: oak of weeping ▶ **A place near Bethel.** Deborah, the nurse of Rebekah, was buried there (Gen. 35:8). ¶

ALLOTMENT – ***t^{e}rûmiyyāh*** [fem. noun: תְּרוּמִיָּה <8642>; formed as OFFERING <8641>] ▶ **This word means an offering. It occurs only once in the Old Testament and is a slightly different form of the word *t^{e}rûmāh* (<8641>), meaning offering.** In Ezekiel 48:12 (KJV: oblation), it describes the allotment (*t^{e}rûmiyyāh*) of the allotment of land (*t^{e}rûmāh*) that will be given to the Levites. ¶

ALLOW – Gen. 31:28 ➔ FORSAKE <5203>.

ALLOWANCE – ***^{a}ruḥāh*** [fem. noun: אֲרֻחָה <737>; fem. pass. part. of TRAVEL <732> in the sense of appointing] ▶ **This word means an amount appointed; it is also translated allowance of food, ration, victuals, provisions.** It describes an allowance of food given to Jeremiah (Jer. 40:5) and to Jehoiachin while he was confined in Babylon (2 Kgs. 25:30; Jer. 52:34). The word describes a portion (dinner, dish, small serving) of vegetables as a modest meal (Prov. 15:17). ¶

ALLOWANCE OF FOOD – Jer. 40:5 ➔ ALLOWANCE <737>.

ALLOY – Is. 1:25 ➔ TIN <913>.

ALMIGHTY – ***šadday*** [masc. noun and name: שַׁדַּי <7706>; from BREAST <7699> (that which nurtures and sustains; cf. Is. 60:16; 66:11)] ▶ **This word, Shaddai or Almighty, occurs forty-eight times in the Hebrew Bible, thirty-one times in the book of Job. This is a name for the Lord—the Old Testament people of faith referring to Him as El Shaddai, God Almighty who nurtures, sustains, satisfies, and strengthens like a mother her child.** The term is found in the passages that report God's promises of fertility, land, and abundance to them, indicating that He, the Almighty, could fulfill His promises (Gen. 17:1; 28:3; 35:11). The Lord appeared to Abraham when he was ninety-nine years old and identified himself as El Shaddai, God Almighty (Gen. 17:1). All three patriarchs knew Him by this name (Gen. 28:1–3; 35:11); as did Joseph (Gen. 48:3; cf. Ex. 6:3); Ezekiel the prophet knew the tradition of Shaddai as well (Ezek. 10:5). Balaam, Naomi, the psalmist, Joel, and Isaiah employed the term Shaddai, Almighty (Num. 24:4; Ruth 1:20; Ps. 68:14; Is. 13:6; Joel 1:15). But it is especially Job who uses the term appropriately as a non-Israelite (Job 5:17; 13:3; 24:1; 37:23), since it is a universal term for God. It is always found in poetic sections of material. The book of Job also uses the name the Lord, Yahweh, twenty-seven times, and it is found all but five times in the prose sections (Job 1, 2; 42:7–17). *

ALMODAD – ***'almôḏāḏ*** [masc. proper noun: אַלְמוֹדָד <486>; prob. of foreign deriv.] ► **Descendant of Shem by Joktan.** Refs.: Gen. 10:26; 1 Chr. 1:20. ¶

ALMON – ***'almôn*** [proper noun: עַלְמוֹן <5960>; from HIDE <5956>]: hidden ► **One of the cities given to the Levites on the territory of Benjamin.** Ref.: Josh. 21:18. See also ALEMETH <5964> c. ¶

ALMON-DIBLATHAIM – ***'almon diḇlaṯāyᵉmāh*** [proper noun: עַלְמֹן דִּבְלָתָיְמָה <5963>; from the same as ALMON <5960> and the dual of FIGS (CAKE OF) <1690>]: something hidden toward Diblathaim (the two cakes of figs) ► **A place where the Israelites camped in the desert on their way to the Promised Land.** Refs.: Num. 33:46, 47. ¶

ALMOND (MADE LIKE, SHAPED LIKE) – ***šāqaḏ*** [verb: שָׁקַד <8246>; a denom. from ALMOND, ALMOND TREE <8247>] ► **This word indicates the almondlike forms of certain items used in the Tabernacle.** Refs.: Ex. 25:33, 34; 37:19, 20. ¶

ALMOND, ALMOND TREE – ***šāqêḏ*** [masc. noun: שָׁקֵד <8247>; from WATCH (verb) <8245>] ► **This word refers to the nutlike kernel of the fruit of a prunus tree and to the tree itself.** It is edible and was highly desired as food in ancient Israel (Gen. 43:11). Aaron's rod produced ripe almonds as a sign of his right to the high priesthood (Num. 17:8). The almond tree first bears blossoms (Eccl. 12:5). It is used in wordplay by Jeremiah, *šāqêḏ,* almond; *šōqêḏ,* to watch over (Jer. 1:11). ¶

ALMOND TREE – ***lûz*** [masc. noun: לוּז <3869>; prob. of foreign origin] ► **This word means an almond or prunus tree bearing a small peachlike fruit.** It is used of the material (poplar?) from which Jacob made some rods in a puzzling breeding process (Gen. 30:37; KJV: hazel tree). ¶

ALMUG – ***'almuggiym*** [masc. plur. noun: אַלְמֻגִּים <484>; prob. of foreign deriv. (used only in the plur.)] ► **These trees were imported from a distant land named Ophir.** The only usage is found in 1 Kings 10:11, 12. They are perhaps red sandalwood or Lebanese trees. ¶

ALOES – ***'ahāl*** [masc. noun: אֲהָל <174>; of foreign origin] ► **The word appears only in the plural, designating a resinous and aromatic wood.** These aloes were a feature of Jacob and Israel's land of inheritance, according to a prophecy by Balaam (Num. 24:6). Aloes were used to scent garments (Ps. 45:8). It is used metaphorically in Song of Solomon 4:14. Other ref.: Prov. 7:17. ¶

ALONE – [1] ***baḏ*** [adj. and masc. noun: בַּד <905>; from ALONE (BE) <909>] ► **This word means apart, besides. It has several basic uses.** With *lᵉ* prefixed, it means alone, by itself, apart from, such as five curtains alone (Ex. 26:9; 36:16); him alone (Judg. 7:5; see especially Zech. 12:12–14). This idea is also expressed by putting a suffix on the end of *baḏ* to express being alone (Gen. 2:18; 21:28; 32:16; 2 Sam. 10:8; Ps. 51:4). It limits an idea, such as "by You only" (Eccl. 7:29; Is. 26:13). Used with *min* <4480> after it, it means apart from, besides (Ex. 12:37; Num. 29:39; Deut. 3:5), as it does when *min* is prefixed to it (Gen. 26:1; 46:26; Lev. 9:17; 23:38). The Hebrew word also means a part or parts of something; see PART (noun) <905>. *

[2] ***bāḏāḏ*** [masc. noun: בָּדָד <910>; from ALONE (BE) <909>] ► **This word indicates isolation, aloneness, desolation. It describes a state of separation, of solitude.** A leper had to dwell outside the camp (Lev. 13:46) by himself. Any city could be isolated, cut off by itself (Is. 27:10); also translated desolate, solitary. It describes the status of Israel dwelling alone among the nations (Num. 23:9; also translated apart), separated unto the Lord religiously and physically (Deut. 33:28: alone, secure, secluded; cf. Jer. 49:31). The Lord's unique leadership of Israel is described by this word (Deut. 32:12; Ps. 4:8). It describes the isolation and loneliness of a person seemly cut

off from the Lord (Jer. 15:17). Other refs.: Lam. 1:1; 3:28; Mic. 7:14. ¶

[3] ***gap̱*** [masc. noun: גַּף <1610>] ▶ **This word is used to indicate a person's own body, a person alone, or by himself or herself (KJV).** Refs.: Ex. 21:3, 4. The Hebrew word also means high point; see HIGHEST <1610>. ¶

ALONE (BE) – ***bāḏaḏ*** [verb: בָּדַד <909>; a prim. root] ▶ **This word means to be isolated, lonely. It describes a state of isolation, of separation, loneliness.** Three subjects are mentioned: a straggling lone soldier of Assyria (Is. 14:31); Israel depicted as a wild donkey wandering alone (Hos. 8:9); and a lonely bird resembling a broken person before the Lord (Ps. 102:7). ¶

ALOUD – Mic. 4:9 ➔ NOISE <7452>.

ALREADY – ***k^{e}ḇār*** [adv.: כְּבָר <3528>; from MULTIPLY <3527>] ▶ **This word indicates long ago; it is also translated now.** Its use is consistent, indicating that something existed or happened already or long ago. There is really nothing new (Eccl. 1:10; 2:12; 3:15; 4:2; 6:10; 9:6, 7). It can refer to a time in the future when "already" something will happen or be forgotten (Eccl. 2:16). ¶

ALSO – [1] ***'ap̱*** [particle: אַף <637>; a prim. particle] ▶ **This Hebrew word means moreover, yea, indeed, even.** Its main meanings are also, even, or it notes emphasis (Gen. 40:16; Ps. 89:27); contrast (Ps. 44:9). It means yes when used with *kiy* (BECAUSE <3588>) to introduce a conditional sentence (yes, if . . . , Ezek. 14:21); really, when used before *kiy* to introduce a question (Gen. 3:1). It introduces clauses of time when used before *kiy*, e.g., Neh. 9:18, even if. *

[2] ***'ap̱*** [Aramaic conj.: אַף <638>; corresponding to <637> above] ▶ **This word indicates that something was said or done or not said or done.** Refs.: Ezra 5:10, 14; Dan. 6:22. It also indicates that something is to be continued or added to (Ezra 6:5). ¶

[3] ***gam*** [adv. conj.: גַּם <1571>; by contr. from an unused root meaning to gather] ▶ **This word means even, moreover, indeed, yea, as well as, both, though.** In different contexts, it can be translated in various ways: it ties things together, new and old (Song 7:13); includes other things or persons, such as a husband (Gen. 3:6); adds action (Gen. 3:22); intensifies, such as even a blameless nation (Gen. 20:4); indicates neither . . . nor (1 Sam. 28:20). It may stress a particular word with which it is used and mean even or else (Ex. 4:9; Num. 22:33; Prov. 14:13). It introduces a climax to a statement (Gen. 27:33) and means yes (KJV, yea). It expresses agreement in oneself with another, e.g., I also (Gen. 20:6; Josh. 24:18; Judg. 2:21). When used in pairs *gam. . . gam*, it also means . . . as or as . . . as (Jer. 2:36) or as . . . so (Is. 66:3, 4). It means though in some contexts: "They tried Me, though [*gam*] they had seen My work" (of judgment) (Ps. 95:9 NASB, cf. Ps. 129:2; Jer. 6:15; Ezek. 20:23). When used in the phrase *gam kiy* (BECAUSE <3588>), it is best rendered as yes, when, or even when (Prov. 22:6; Is. 1:15; Lam. 3:8; Hos. 8:10). *

ALTAR – [1] ***maḏbaḥ*** [Aramaic masc. noun: מַדְבַּח <4056>; from OFFER <1684>] ▶ **This word refers to a place at the Temple where sacrifices of all kinds were offered.** Ref.: Ezra 7:17. ¶

[2] ***mizbêaḥ*** [masc. noun: מִזְבֵּחַ <4196>; from OFFER <2076>] ▶ **This word means the place of sacrifice. The sacrificial system was at the focal point of the pre-Israelite and Israelite systems of worship since the sacrifice and subsequent meal were used to solemnize a covenant or treaty and to symbolize a positive relationship between the two parties.** Noah built an altar and offered sacrifices on exiting the ark (Gen. 8:20); the patriarchs built altars and sacrificed at various points along their journeys: Abram (Gen. 12:7, 8; 22:9); Isaac (Gen. 26:25); Jacob (Gen. 35:7); Moses (Ex. 24:4). At Mount Sinai, God commanded that the Israelites build the Tabernacle and include two altars: a bronze altar in the courtyard for the sacrificing of

animals (Ex. 27:1–8; 38:1–7) and a golden altar inside the Tabernacle for the burning of incense (Ex. 30:1–10; 37:25–29). Solomon (1 Kgs. 6:20, 22; 8:64) and Ezekiel (Ezek. 41:22; 43:13–17) followed a similar pattern. God also commanded that the altar for burnt offerings be made of earth or undressed stones because human working of the stones would defile it. Moreover, God commanded that the altar should have no steps so that human nakedness would not be exposed on it (Ex. 20:24–26). *

ALTAR HEARTH – 1 ***ᵃriy'êl, ᵃri'êl*** [masc. noun: אֲרִיאֵל, אֲרִאֵל <741>; either by transposition for ARIEL <739> or, more prob., an orthographical variation for <2025> below] ▶ **This word refers to the fire grate of the altar for the new Temple of Ezekiel's vision.** Refs.: Ezek. 43:15, 16; NIV, NASB, altar hearth; KJV, altar. ¶
2 ***har'êl*** [masc. noun: הַרְאֵל <2025>; from MOUNTAIN <2022> and GOD <410>] ▶ **This word depicts the altar fire grate for the burnt offering in Ezekiel's Temple vision.** Ref.: Ezek. 43:15. ¶

ALUSH – ***'ālûš*** [proper noun: אָלוּשׁ <442>; of uncertain deriv.] ▶ **A place in the desert where the Israelites camped.** Refs.: Num. 33:13, 14. ¶

ALVAH – ***'alwāh, 'alyāh*** [masc. proper noun: עַלְוָה, עַלְיָה <5933>; the same as INIQUITY <5932>]: injustice ▶
a. A chief descending from Esau. Refs.: Gen. 36:40; 1 Chr. 1:51. ¶
b. Aliah, different Hebrew spelling for the same as a. Ref.: 1 Chr. 1:51, KJV, NKJV, NASB. ¶

ALVAN – ***'alwān, 'alyān*** [masc. proper noun: עַלְוָן, עַלְיָן <5935>; from OFFER <5927>]: lofty ▶
a. A Horite, son of Shobal. Refs.: Gen. 36:23; 1 Chr. 1:40. ¶
b. Alian, another spelling for a. Ref.: 1 Chr. 1:40, KJV, NKJV, NASB. ¶

AMAD – ***'am'āḏ*** [proper noun: עַמְעָד <6008>; from PEOPLE <5971> and ETERNITY <5703>]: eternal people ▶ **A village on the border of Asher.** Ref.: Josh. 19:26. ¶

AMAL – ***'āmāl*** [masc. proper noun: עָמָל <6000>; from LABOR (noun) <5999>]: labor ▶ **An Israelite of the tribe of Asher.** Ref.: 1 Chr. 7:35. ¶

AMALEK – ***ᵃmālêq*** [proper masc. noun: עֲמָלֵק <6002>; prob. of foreign origin] ▶ **Amalek was the son of Esau's son Eliphaz and his concubine Timnah.** Hence, he was a grandson of Esau's wife Adah who was Canaanite and Hittite (Gen. 36:2, 10–12). His descendants became the Amalekites according to the biblical record. They were hostile toward Israel after the Exodus and threatened God's people through guerrilla warfare (Deut. 25:17–19). God placed a curse on them to exterminate them for attacking His people (Ex. 17:8–16). They ranged far and wide, but the Negev was a central location for them (Num. 13:29). God confirmed His intent to destroy them through Balaam's prophecy (Num. 24:20).

They teamed up with the Ammonites to attack Israel (Judg. 3:13) and with others (Judg. 7:12; Ps. 83:7). Saul defeated them but failed to destroy them (1 Sam. 14:48; 15:1–32; 28:18). David removed them as a national threat (1 Sam. 30; 2 Sam. 8:12). *

AMALEK, AMALEKITE – ***ᵃmālêqiy*** [proper noun: עֲמָלֵקִי <6003>; from AMALEK <6002>] ▶ **A descendant from Amalek.** Refs.: Gen. 14:7; Num. 14:25, 43, 45; Judg. 12:15; 1 Sam. 15:6, 15; 27:8; 30:1, 13; 2 Sam. 1:8, 13. It is used with *'iyš* (MAN <376>) to designate Amalekites (1 Sam. 30:13; 2 Sam. 1:8, 13). ¶

AMAM – ***ᵃmām*** [proper noun: אֲמָם <538>; from MOTHER <517>]: their mother; gathering, junction ▶ **A village of the South of Judah.** Ref.: Josh. 15:26. ¶

AMANA – ***ᵃmānāh*** [proper noun: אֲמָנָה <549>; the same as COVENANT <548>]: permanent, faithful ▶ **A region in Anti-Lebanon.** Ref.: Song 4:8. ¶

AMARIAH – ***ʾămaryāh, ʾămaryāhû*** [masc. proper noun: אֲמַרְיָה, אֲמַרְיָהוּ <568>; from SAY <559> and LORD <3050>]: the Lord has said, promised ▶
a. It refers to one of Aaron's descendants, a grandfather of Zadok, a high priest in Israel under David. Refs.: 1 Chr. 6:7, 52; Ezra 7:3. ¶
b. A son of Azariah in Aaron's line. His father served as a priest in Jerusalem in Solomon's Temple (1 Chr. 6:11). ¶
c. The second son of Hebron descended from Kohath. Refs.: 1 Chr. 23:19; 24:23. ¶
d. The name of a high priest who was over the Levites who were administering the Law of the Lord, in addition to his usual duties. Ref.: 2 Chr. 19:11. ¶
e. It refers to a Levite who assisted Kore in collecting gifts made to the Lord. Ref.: 2 Chr. 31:15. ¶
f. The name of a son of Binnui, an Israelite who intermarried with the people of the land in the time of Ezra. Ref.: Ezra 10:42. ¶
g. It refers to Amariah, a priest who returned under Nehemiah and who sealed Nehemiah's covenant to serve the Lord and keep the Law of God. Refs.: Neh. 10:3; 12:2, 13. ¶
h. A son of Shephatiah who resettled in Jerusalem under Nehemiah. He was of the line of Judah (Neh. 11:4). ¶
i. A son of Hezekiah who had a son, Gedaliah. He was an ancestor of Zephaniah (Zeph. 1:1). ¶

AMASA – ***ʿămāśā'*** [masc. proper noun: עֲמָשָׂא <6021>; from LOAD (verb) <6006>]: burden ▶
a. General of Absalom. Refs.: 2 Sam. 17:25; 19:13; 20:4, 5, 8–10, 12; 1 Kgs. 2:5, 32; 1 Chr. 2:17. ¶
b. Ephraimite prince. Ref.: 2 Chr. 28:12. ¶

AMASAI – ***ʿămāśay*** [masc. proper noun: עֲמָשַׂי <6022>; from LOAD (verb) <6006>]: burdensome ▶
a. An ancestor of Samuel. Refs.: 1 Chr. 6:25, 35. ¶
b. One of David's warriors. Ref.: 1 Chr. 12:18. ¶
c. A musician in David's day. Ref.: 1 Chr. 15:24. ¶
d. A Levite in Hezekiah's day. Ref.: 2 Chr. 29:12. ¶

AMASHAI – ***ʿămašsay*** [masc. proper noun: עֲמַשְׁסַי <6023>; from LOAD (verb) <6006>]: burdensome ▶ **A priest in the time of Nehemiah.** Ref.: Neh. 11:13. ¶

AMASIAH – ***ʿămasyāh*** [masc. proper noun: עֲמַסְיָה <6007>; from LOAD (verb) <6006> and LORD <3050>]: the Lord sustains ▶ **He was a volunteer for the service of the Lord and the commander of 200,000 mighty men of valor.** Ref.: 2 Chr. 17:16. ¶

AMASS – Eccl. 2:8 ➔ GATHER <3664>.

AMAZED (BE) – Ex. 15:1 ➔ TERRIFIED <926>.

AMAZEMENT – Dan. 3:24: in amazement ➔ lit.: was astonished ➔ ASTONISHED (BE) <8429>.

AMAZIAH – ***ʾămaṣyāh, ʾămaṣyāhû*** [masc. proper noun: אֲמַצְיָה, אֲמַצְיָהוּ <558>; from STRONG (BE) <553> and LORD <3050>]: the Lord strengthens ▶
a. He was the son of Joash, a Judean king. He warred against Jehoash of Israel (2 Kgs. 13:12). He reigned twenty-nine years. He served the Lord faithfully during his righteous long reign. He defeated the Edomites (2 Kgs. 14:7) but suffered defeat in Jerusalem at the hands of King Jehoash of Israel (2 Kgs. 14:11–20). His enemies assassinated him in Lachish (2 Kgs. 14:19, 20). *
b. It refers to an Amaziah of the Simeonites, who had a son, Joshah. Ref.: 1 Chr. 4:34. ¶
c. It refers to a son of Hilkiah of the Merarites who were part of the Temple musicians. Ref.: 1 Chr. 6:45. ¶
d. It indicates a priest of Bethel under King Jeroboam II in Israel who confronted Amos the prophet. Refs.: Amos 7:10, 12, 14. He was condemned by Amos. ¶

AMBASSADOR (BE) – ***ṣāyar*** [verb: צָיַר <6737>; a denom. from MESSENGER

<6735> in the sense of ambassador] ▶ **This word describes the behavior and implies the responsibilities that a faithful representative of a person or nation fulfills.** Ref.: Josh. 9:4. ¶

AMBER – ***ḥašmal, ḥašmalāh*** [masc. noun: חַשְׁמַל, חַשְׁמַלָה <2830>; of uncertain deriv.] ▶ **This word means a glowing substance.** It is used three times in the phrase *k^e'êyn ḥ^ašmal* meaning "like the glowing or gleaming of *ḥašmal*" (Ezek. 1:4, 27; 8:2). The word is uncertain in meaning but may mean metal (NIV, NASB, glowing metal; ESV, gleaming metal) or amber (KJV, NKJV). ¶

AMBUSH – 1 ***'ōreḇ*** [masc. noun: אֹרֶב <696>; the same as DEN <695>] ▶ **This word means ensnarement, surprise attack; it is also translated trap.** It is used figuratively to describe the harm and evil that wicked people plan for their own neighbor (Jer. 9:8); NKJV and KJV translate: to lie in wait, to lay his wait. It describes the political intrigue or plotting aimed against the king or by the king (Hos. 7:6, NKJV and KJV translate as a verb, *'āraḇ* <693>, to lie in wait, to plot). ¶
2 ***ma^arāḇ*** [masc. noun: מַאֲרָב <3993>; from WAIT (LIE IN) <693>] ▶ **See previous definition. This word is also translated hiding place, lying in wait, lurking places.** It is used of accosting persons secretly, lying hidden to destroy them (Josh. 8:9; 2 Chr. 13:13); sometimes, it refers to the place of ambush more directly (Judg. 9:35). It is used of the wicked sitting in places of ambush, waiting to ambush the innocent (Ps. 10:8). ¶
– 3 Ps. 10:8, 9; etc. ➔ HIDING PLACE <4565> 4 Obad. 1:7 ➔ TRAP <4204>.

AMBUSH (LIE IN, SET AN) – See WAIT (LIE IN) <693>.

AMEN – ***'āmên*** [adv.: אָמֵן <543>; from NURSE (verb) <539> (in the sense of being sure, secure)] ▶ **This word means verily or truly. It is used more often as the declaration, "I agree; may it be so." It comes from a root meaning to confirm, to support, to be faithful. The major idea behind this word is constancy and reliability.** It is used as a declaration to acknowledge affirmation of a statement (1 Kgs. 1:36); acceptance of a curse (Neh. 5:13); affirmation of a prophecy (Jer. 28:6). It is also used in response to worship and praise (1 Chr. 16:36; Neh. 8:6). *

AMERCE – Deut. 22:19 ➔ FINE (verb) <6064>.

AMETHYST – ***'aḥlāmāh*** [fem. noun: אַחְלָמָה <306>; perhaps from DREAM (verb) <2492> (and thus dream-stone)] ▶ **A semiprecious stone.** It was one of the stones mounted in the third row upon the breastpiece of the high priest (Ex. 28:19; 39:12). It is a jasper or amethyst stone. It had a tribal name engraved on it, so that the high priest represented that tribe before the Lord. ¶

AMI – ***'āmiy*** [masc. proper noun: אָמִי <532>; an abbreviation for AMON <526>]: increased ▶ **A descendant of those known as "the sons of Solomon's servants."** Ref.: Ezra 2:57; see verse 55. In Nehemiah 7:59, he is named Amon. ¶

AMIABLE – Ps. 84:1 ➔ BELOVED <3039>.

AMISS – ***šālûh*** [Aramaic fem. noun: שָׁלָה <7955>; from a root corresponding to NEGLIGENT (BE) <7952>] ▶ **This word refers to anything untoward or offensive.** It refers to anything spoken that is not fitting, that is derogatory toward the true God, since He is the God of great deliverance (Dan. 3:29). ¶

AMITTAI – ***^amittay*** [masc. proper noun: אֲמִתַּי <573>; from TRUTH <571>]: faithfulness, truth ▶ **Father of the prophet Jonah.** Refs.: 2 Kgs. 14:25; Jon. 1:1. ¶

AMMAH – ***'ammāh*** [proper noun: אַמָּה <522>; the same as CUBIT <520>]: cubit, beginning ▶

a. A hill near the Jordan Valley. Ref.: 2 Sam. 2:24. ¶
b. A feminine noun translated as a mother city. Ref.: 2 Sam. 8:1. ¶
c. A noun that is part of the name Metheg Ammah <4965>. Ref.: 2 Sam. 8:1. ¶

AMMICHUR – ***'ammiyḥûr*** [masc. proper noun: עַמִּיחוּר <5991>; from PEOPLE <5971> and WHITE <2353>]: people of majesty ▶ **Father of the king of Geshur to whom Absalom went after having killed Amnon.** Ref.: 2 Sam. 13:37; also written Ammihud. ¶

AMMIEL – ***'ammiy'el*** [masc. proper noun: עַמִּיאֵל <5988>; from PEOPLE <5971> and GOD <410>]: people of God ▶ **One of the twelve spies sent by Moses to explore the Promised Land.** Ref.: Num. 13:12. Other persons: 2 Sam. 9:4, 5; 17:27; 1 Chr. 3:5; 26:5. ¶

AMMIHUD – [1] ***'ammiyhûḏ*** [masc. proper noun: עַמִּיהוּד <5989>; from PEOPLE <5971> and VIGOR <1935> (also in the sense of authority, majesty)]: people of majesty ▶ **A descendant of Ephraim.** Refs.: Num. 1:10; 2:18; 7:48, 53; 10:22; 34:20, 28; 2 Sam. 13:37; 1 Chr. 7:26; 9:4. ¶
– [2] 2 Sam. 13:37 ➔ AMMICHUR <5991>.

AMMINADAB – ***'ammiynāḏaḇ*** [masc. proper noun: עַמִּינָדָב <5992>; from PEOPLE <5971> and GIVE WILLINGLY <5068>]: people of liberality ▶
a. A man of Judah, father-in-law of Aaron, and ancestor of David. Refs.: Ex. 6:23; Num. 1:7; Ruth 4:19, 20; 1 Chr. 2:10. ¶
b. A Levite of the family of Kohath. Refs.: 1 Chr. 15:10, 11. ¶
c. Another Levite of the family of Kohath. Ref.: 1 Chr. 6:22. ¶
d. Other refs.: Num. 2:3; 7:12, 17; 10:14. ¶

AMMINADIB – ***'ammiy nāḏiyḇ*** [proper noun: עַמִּי נָדִיב <5993>; from PEOPLE <5971> and WILLING <5081>]: generous people ▶ **This word could also mean and be translated "my noble people."** Ref.: Song 6:12. ¶

AMMISHADDAI – ***'ammiyšadday*** [masc. proper noun: עַמִּישַׁדָּי <5996>; from PEOPLE <5971> and ALMIGHTY <7706>]: people of the Almighty ▶ **His son Ahiezer was chief of the tribe of Dan.** Refs.: Num. 1:12; 2:25; 7:66, 71; 10:25. ¶

AMMIZABAD – ***'ammiyzaḇaḏ*** [masc. proper noun: עַמִּיזָבָד <5990>; from PEOPLE <5971> and ENDOW <2064> (in the sense of to give)]: people of the Giver ▶ **His son Benaiah was one of David's strong men.** Ref.: 1 Chr. 27:6. ¶

AMMON – ***'ammôn*** [proper noun: עַמּוֹן <5983>; from PEOPLE <5971>]: tribal (i.e., inbred) ▶ **This word designates a part of the inhabitants of Canaan whom Israel was to conquer and exterminate.** They were located east of the Jordan with a capital city at Rabbah. Their territory lay between the Arnon and Jabbok Rivers. Their origin was from the incestuous relationship between Lot and his younger daughter (Gen. 19:38). They were a powerful people (Num. 21:24), and Lot's descendants continued to control the land (Deut. 2:19, 37). Their land was allotted to Gad, but through the centuries, the Ammonites largely erased the Gadites from power (Judg. 13:10–25). They became hostile toward Israel (Judg. 3:13; 10:9, 10; 11:4–36) and posed a religious threat to Israel (Judg. 10:6–18). Saul subdued them (1 Sam. 14:47, 48), and David further subdued and controlled them (2 Sam. 8:12; 10; 11; 12; 17). Solomon succumbed to the lure of Molech, the god of Ammon (1 Kgs. 11:7, 8). Josiah cleansed the land of Judah from Ammonite shrines (2 Kgs. 23:13). As Judah became corrupt, the Ammonites continued to help in their destruction but as part of the Lord's judgment and discipline of His people (2 Kgs. 24:1–4). The nation was condemned by the prophets and Israel's God will judge and destroy them (Is. 11:14; Jer. 9:26; 49:1; Ezek. 25:2; Amos 1:13; Zeph. 2:8, 9). *

AMMONITE – ***'ammôniy*** [proper noun: עַמּוֹנִי <5984>; patron. from AMMON <5983>] ▶ **This word is the gentilic form or ethnic form of Ammon. It indicates a descendant of these people who accepted their culture.** See AMMON <5983>. Refs.: Deut. 2:20; 1 Sam. 11:1, 2; Ezra 9:1; Neh. 2:10, 19. *

AMMONITESS – ***'ammōniyṯ*** [proper noun: עַמֹּנִית <5985>; fem. of AMMONITE <5984>] ▶ **See AMMONITE <5984>.** Refs.: 1 Kgs. 14:21, 31; 2 Chr. 12:13; 24:29. ¶

AMNON – ***'amnôn, 'amiynôn*** [masc. proper noun: אַמְנוֹן, אֲמִינוֹן <550>; from NURSE (verb) <539> (in the sense of to support)]: supported, under the tutelage ▶
a. The name identifies David's firstborn son in Hebron. Ref.: 2 Sam. 3:2. He committed a grievous sin in Israel by raping his half-sister Tamar, sister of Absalom, his half-brother. Absalom killed him in revenge (2 Sam. 13:23–39). *
b. It refers to a son of Shimon in the descendants of the line of Judah. Ref.: 1 Chr. 4:20. ¶

AMOK – ***'āmôq*** [masc. proper noun: עָמוֹק <5987>; from DEEP, DEEP (BE) <6009>]: deep ▶ **A priest who returned from the Babylonian captivity with Zerubbabel.** Refs.: Neh. 12:7, 20. ¶

AMON – 1 ***'āmôn*** [masc. proper noun: אָמוֹן <526>; the same as MASTER WORKMAN <525>]: one who feeds, worker, artisan ▶
a. This noun refers to Amon, governor of Samaria. He imprisoned the prophet Micaiah at the word of King Ahab (1 Kgs. 22:26; 2 Chr. 18:25). ¶
b. It refers to a son of Manasseh, king of Judah, who took the throne at his father's death. Ref.: 2 Kgs. 21:18. He was assassinated after ruling two years. He was a wicked king like his father (2 Kgs. 21:20–22). Josiah, his famous righteous son, was made king in his place (2 Kgs. 21:24). *
c. He was descended in the line of Solomon's servants and one who returned from the Babylonian exile under Nehemiah. Ref.: Neh. 7:59. ¶
2 ***'āmôn, nō' 'āmôn*** [masc. proper noun: אָמוֹן, נֹא אָמוֹן <528>; of Egyptian deriv.] ▶ **This word means an artisan or a master craftsman. It is also a proper name of an Egyptian god.** Refs.: Jer. 46:25; Nah. 3:8. The Egyptian god was the local deity of Thebes but came to be the supreme god in Egypt. ¶
– 3 Neh. 7:59 ➔ AMI <532>.

AMONG – 1 See BETWEEN <996>, <997> 2 See WITH <854>.

AMORITE – ***'ᵉmōriy*** [masc. proper noun: אֱמֹרִי <567>; prob. patron. from an unused name derived from SAY <559> in the sense of publicity, i.e., prominence]: a sayer ▶ **A member of the people occupying the land of Canaan before its conquest by the Israelites.** Refs.: Gen. 10:16; 14:7, 13; 1 Sam. 7:14; 2 Sam. 21:2; 1 Kgs. 4:19; 9:20; 21:26; 2 Kgs. 21:11. *

AMOS – ***'āmôs*** [masc. proper noun: עָמוֹס <5986>; from LOAD (verb) <6006>]: burden, one who bears the burden ▶ **This word designates the prophet from Tekoa, south of Jerusalem, sent to prophesy to northern Israel.** Ref.: Amos 1:1. He was a dresser of sycamore trees. He had no official or political ties to prophecy or prophets at the idolatrous court (Amos 7:1–13). He acted purely at the Lord's calling (Amos 7:14, 15). He prophesied during the reigns of Uzziah in Judah (779–740 B.C.) and Jeroboam II in Samaria, Israel (783–743 B.C.). There was a devastating earthquake in his day. The Northern Kingdom's prosperity had reached a peak under Jeroboam II, but the poor were being crushed and were enslaved to sustain the wealth of the rich (Amos 4). Amos had a universal message and passion concerning personal and social righteousness (Amos 1–3; 5:24). He was, however, given a vision of a restored house of David (Amos 9:11–13). Other ref.: Amos 8:2. ¶

AMOUNT – Lev. 27:23 ➔ NUMBER (noun) <4373>.

AMOUNT (DETERMINE THE) – Ex. 12:4 ➔ COUNT (MAKE ONE'S) <3699>.

AMOUNT (EXACT) – Esther 4:7 ➔ SUM, EXACT SUM <6575>.

AMOZ – ***'āmôṣ*** [masc. proper noun: אָמוֹץ <531>; from STRONG (BE) <553>]: strong, courageous ▶ **Father of the prophet Isaiah.** Refs.: 2 Kgs. 19:2, 20; 20:1; 2 Chr. 26:22; 32:20, 32; Is. 1:1; 2:1; 13:1; 20:2; 37:2, 21; 38:1. ¶

AMRAM – [1] ***ʿamrām*** [masc. proper noun: עַמְרָם <6019>; from PEOPLE <5971> and RISE <7311>]: exalted people ▶
a. A Levite, son of Kohath, ancestor of Aaron and Moses. Refs.: Ex. 6:18, 20; Num. 3:19; 26:58, 59; 1 Chr. 6:2, 3, 18; 23:12, 13; 24:20. ¶
b. An Israelite who had married a foreign woman. Ref.: Ezra 10:34. ¶
– [2] 1 Chr. 1:41 ➔ HAMRAM <2566>.

AMRAMITE – ***ʿamrāmiy*** [proper noun: עַמְרָמִי <6020>; from AMRAM <6019>] ▶ **This word designates a descendant of Amram (<6019> a.).** Refs.: Num. 3:27; 1 Chr. 26:23. ¶

AMRAPHEL – ***'amrāpel*** [masc. proper noun: אַמְרָפֶל <569>; of uncertain (perhaps foreign) deriv.] ▶ **A king of Shinhar.** Refs.: Gen. 14:1, 9. ¶

AMZI – ***'amṣiy*** [masc. proper noun: אַמְצִי <557>; from STRONG (BE) <553>]: my strength ▶
a. A Levite, descendant of Merari. Ref.: 1 Chr. 6:46. ¶
b. A priest, son of Zechariah. Ref.: Neh. 11:12. ¶

ANAB – ***ʿanāb*** [proper noun: עֲנָב <6024>; from GRAPE <6025>]: grape-town ▶ **A city belonging to Judah in its hill country.** Refs.: Josh. 11:21; 15:50. ¶

ANAH – ***ʿanāh*** [proper noun: עֲנָה <6034>; prob. from ANSWER (verb) <6030>]: who answers ▶
a. Mother of Aholibamah and mother-in-law of Esau. Refs.: Gen. 36:2, 14, 18, 25. ¶
b. A descendant of Seir who found hot springs in the desert. Refs.: Gen. 36:24; 1 Chr. 1:40, 41. ¶
c. Another descendant of Seir. Refs.: Gen. 36:20, 29; 1 Chr. 1:38. ¶

ANAHARATH – ***'anāḥarāṯ*** [proper noun: אֲנָחֲרַת <588>; prob. from the same root as SNORTING <5170>]: groan, narrow path ▶ **A place in the valley of Jezreel, part of the territory of Issachar.** Ref.: Josh. 19:19. ¶

ANAIAH – ***ʿanāyāh*** [proper noun: עֲנָיָה <6043>; from ANSWER (verb) <6030>]: the Lord has answered ▶
a. A priest who stood beside Ezra when he read the book of the Law in Jerusalem. Ref.: Neh. 8:4. ¶
b. A chief of the people who signed the covenant of renewal with Nehemiah after the return from the Babylonian captivity. Ref.: Neh. 10:22. ¶

ANAK – ***ʿanāq*** [masc. proper noun: עֲנָק <6061>; from the same as CHAIN <6060>]: long-necked ▶ **His descendants, a people great and tall, lived in the land of Canaan.** Refs.: Num. 13:22, 28, 33; Deut. 9:2; Josh. 15:13, 14; 21:11; Judg. 1:20. ¶

ANAKIM – See ANAKITE <6062>.

ANAKITE – ***ʿanaqiy*** [proper noun: עֲנָקִי <6062>; from ANAK <6061>] ▶ **A descendant of Anak (<6061>).** Refs.: Deut. 1:28; 2:10, 11, 21; 9:2; Josh. 11:21, 22; 14:12, 15; in the plural: Anakim. ¶

ANAMIM – ***ʿanāmiym*** [proper noun: עֲנָמִים <6047>; as if plur. of some Egyptian word]: a fountain ▶ **An Egyptian tribe descending from Mizraim.** Refs.: Gen. 10:13; 1 Chr. 1:11. ¶

ANAMMELECH – ***ʿanammeleḵ*** [masc. proper noun: עֲנַמֶּלֶךְ <6048>; of foreign origin]: the god Anu is king ▶ **This word**

refers to a pagan god to whom the Sepharvites sacrificed their children by fire. Ref.: 2 Kgs. 17:31. These are said to be gods of the Sepharvites, a people otherwise unknown. ¶

ANAN – ***'ānān*** [masc. proper noun: עָנָן <6052>; the same as CLOUD <6051>]: cloud ▶ **A chief of the people who signed the covenant of renewal with Nehemiah after the return from the Babylonian captivity.** Ref.: Neh. 10:26. ¶

ANANI – ***'ănāniy*** [masc. proper noun: עֲנָנִי <6054>; from CLOUD <6051>]: cloudy ▶ **An Israelite of the tribe of Judah.** Ref.: 1 Chr. 3:24. ¶

ANANIAH – ***'ănāneyāh*** [proper noun: עֲנָנְיָה <6055>; from a Hebrew verb meaning to bring, see under WITCHCRAFT (PRACTICE) <6049>, and LORD <3050>]: the Lord has covered ▶
a. Grandfather of Azariah. Ref.: Neh. 3:23. ¶
b. A city in Nehemiah's day. Ref.: Neh. 11:32. ¶

ANATH – ***'ănāṯ*** [masc. proper noun: עֲנָת <6067>; from ANSWER (verb) <6030>]: answer, favor ▶ **Very little is known about Anath except that he was the father of the judge Shamgar.** Refs.: Judg. 3:31; 5:6. ¶

ANATHOTH – ***'ănāṯôṯ*** [proper noun: עֲנָתוֹת <6068>; from ANATH <6067>]: answers, favors ▶
a. A city of the tribe of Benjamin which became a Levitical city. Ref.: Josh. 21:18. Abiathar, one of David's priests, came from there. Some exiles who returned were from this city (Ezra 2:23). Jeremiah the prophet came from Anathoth (Jer. 1:1; 11:21, 23). It was to be judged severely (Is. 10:30). *
b. A grandson of Benjamin and son of Beker. Ref.: 1 Chr. 7:8. ¶
c. A chief of the people who signed the covenant of renewal with Nehemiah after the return from the Babylonian captivity. Ref.: Neh. 10:19. ¶

ANATHOTHITE – ***'anneṯôṯiy*** [proper noun: עַנְּתוֹתִי <6069>; from ANATHOTH <6068>] ▶ **An inhabitant of Anathoth (<6068> a.).** Refs.: 2 Sam. 23:27; 1 Chr. 11:28; 12:3; 27:12; Jer. 29:27. ¶

ANCESTRY – Ezek. 16:3; 29:14; 21:30 ➔ ORIGIN <4351>.

ANCIENT – [1] ***'attiyq*** [adj.: עַתִּיק <6267>; from MOVE <6275> (in the sense of to grow old)] ▶
a. This word is used to refer to historical, archival records, considered to be old and therefore accurate. Ref.: 1 Chr. 4:22. It has the sense of weaned or removed from the breast, gotten older (Is. 28:9). ¶
b. An adjective meaning taken, drawn from. It refers to a child just weaned from, taken from the breasts (Is. 28:9). ¶
[2] ***'attiyq*** [Aramaic adj.: עַתִּיק <6268>; corresponding to <6267> above] ▶ **This word is used in the phrase ancient, old, of days, i.e., old with reference to time; as old as the days that have been recorded.** Refs.: Dan. 7:9, 13, 22. ¶
[3] ***qeḏûmiym*** [masc. noun: קְדוּמִים <6917>; pass. part. of MEET <6923> (maybe in the sense of to come before)] ▶ **This word designates something of great age according to its usage, but its exact meaning is unknown.** Ref.: Judg. 5:21; also translated age-old. ¶
– [4] 1 Sam. 24:13 ➔ EASTERN <6931> b. [5] Job 12:12 ➔ AGED <3453> [6] Jer. 5:15 ➔ STRENGTH <386>.

ANEM – ***'ānêm*** [proper noun: עָנֵם <6046>; from the dual of EYE <5869>]: two fountains ▶ **A city of Issachar.** Ref.: 1 Chr. 6:73. ¶

ANER – ***'ānêr*** [proper noun: עָנֵר <6063>; prob. from BOY <5288>]: boy ▶
a. An ally of Abram Refs.: Gen. 14:13, 24. ¶
b. A city in Manasseh. Ref.: 1 Chr. 6:70. ¶

ANGEL – [1] ***mal'aḵ*** [Aramaic noun: מַלְאַךְ <4398>; corresponding to MESSENGER <4397>] ▶ **This word is a cognate of the**

Hebrew noun *mal'āk̲*: MESSENGER <4397>. Refs.: Dan. 3:28; 6:23. ¶
– 2 Ps. 78:25 → lit.: mighty one → MIGHTY <47> 3 See MESSENGER <4397>.

ANGELS – Ps. 68:17 → THOUSANDS (UPON, OF) <8136>.

ANGER (noun) – 1 ***ḥêmāh, ḥêmā'*** [fem. noun: חֵמָה, חֵמָא <2534>; from CONCEIVE <3179>] ▶ **This word means wrath, heat. It is also synonymous with the feminine noun meaning heat or rage. Figuratively, it can signify hot displeasure, indignation, poison, or rage.** This noun describes the great fury that the king of the North will execute in his utter destruction (Dan. 11:44); a person's burning anger (2 Sam. 11:20); and God's intense anger against Israel and those who practiced idolatry (2 Kgs. 22:17). *
2 ***ḥārôn*** [masc. noun: חָרוֹן <2740>; from ANGRY (GET) <2734>] ▶ **This word means displeasure, wrath, and also heat, fierceness.** It is used metaphorically of God's anger (2 Kgs. 23:26) in the phrase *ḥ^a^rôn 'ap̲* or its equivalent, meaning literally, "the heat of (one's) nose." But it is used of the Lord's anger always (Ex. 32:12; Num. 25:4; Deut. 13:17; Josh. 7:26; 1 Sam. 28:18; Ps. 2:5; Jer. 4:8, 26; 25:37; Hos. 11:9; Nah. 1:6). In some cases, *'ap̲* is left out (Ex. 15:7; Neh. 13:18; Ps. 88:16). The phrase *ḥ^a^rôn hayyônāh* in Jeremiah 25:38 may be the only time it does not refer to the Lord's anger. Instead, it may refer to the anger of the oppressing sword or an oppressor himself. But the Lord's anger is indirectly displayed through the oppressor. *
– 3 Dan. 3:13 → FURY <2528> 4 See NOSE <639>.

ANGER (PROVOKE TO) – ***kā'as*** [verb: כָּעַס <3707>; a prim. root] ▶ **This word means to incite to displeasure, irritation, wrath; it also means to be angry.** The causative sense of the verb occurs most often and frequently signifies idolatry provoking God to anger (cf. 1 Kgs. 14:9; Ps. 106:29; Ezek. 8:17). The result of provocation may be expressed as *'ap̲*, anger (NOSE <639>) (Deut. 9:18; 2 Kgs. 23:26; Jer. 7:20). In a noncausative sense, the verb means to be angry; people were warned not to become angry hastily (Eccl. 7:9); God says that after He punishes, He will not be angry (Ezek. 16:42). Three times it refers to the people's anger directed toward righteousness (2 Chr. 16:10; Neh. 4:1; Ps. 112:10). *

ANGER (verb) – ***r^e^gaz*** [Aramaic verb: רְגַז <7265>; corresponding to SHAKE <7264>] ▶ **This word means to irritate, to enrage; it is also translated to provoke to wrath. The term occurs only once in the entire Old Testament.** In a report written to King Darius, the elders of the Jews were quoted as conceding to the fact that the Babylonian exile and destruction of Solomon's Temple (ca. 586 B.C.) took place because their ancestors had angered the God of heaven (Ezra 5:12). ¶

ANGLE – Is. 19:8; Hab. 1:15 → HOOK <2443>.

ANGRY – 1 Kgs. 20:43; 21:4 → DISPLEASED <2198>.

ANGRY (BE) – 1 ***'ānap̲*** [verb: אָנַף <599>; a prim. root] ▶ **This word means to be enraged or to breathe through the nose. It derives its meaning from the heavy breathing and snorting typical of anger.** It is used solely in reference to God's anger or severe displeasure with His people: Moses (Deut. 1:37; 4:21); Aaron (Deut. 9:20); Solomon (1 Kgs. 11:9); and Israel (Deut. 9:8; 1 Kgs. 8:46; 2 Kgs. 17:18; Ps. 60:1; 79:5) all provoked this divine anger. In Psalm 2:12, this word is used in reference to the Messiah. Other refs.: 2 Chr. 6:36; Ezra 9:14; Ps. 85:5; Is. 12:1. ¶
2 ***b^e^nas*** [Aramaic verb: בְּנַס <1149>; of uncertain affinity] ▶ **This word means to be irritated. It is used often in the Aramaic translations but only once in the Hebrew Bible.** Daniel states that Nebuchadnezzar was angry because his diviners could not reveal to him his dream and its interpretation (Dan. 2:12). It is followed by

the phrase *qᵉṣap̱* (<7108>) *śaggiy'* (<7690)>, meaning he was very angry. ¶

3 ***qāṣap*** [verb: קָצַף <7107>; a prim. root] ▶ **This word means to provoke to anger. It refers to anger that arose because people failed to perform their duties properly.** Pharaoh was angry with his chief baker and his chief cupbearer (Gen. 40:2; 41:10); while Moses was angry with the people for hoarding manna (Ex. 16:20); Aaron's sons' apparent failure to follow rules of sacrifice (Lev. 10:16); and the captains' failure to finish off the enemy (Num. 31:14). King Ahasuerus was also angry with Vashti for failing to show off her beauty when summoned (Esther 1:12). The word often expressed an authority being angry with a subject but not always (2 Kgs. 13:19; Esther 2:21). Sometimes the anger was not justified (2 Kgs. 5:11; Jer. 37:15). The word could also refer to God being angry or provoked (Deut. 9:7, 8, 22; Zech. 1:2; 8:14); an anger that could be aroused by a corporate failure to keep troublemakers in line (Num. 16:22; Josh. 22:18). Isaiah 8:21 contains a reflexive form of the word, as if the anger was unable to find a reasonable object and thus caused the occult practitioners to fret themselves. *

4 ***qᵉṣap̱*** [Aramaic verb: קְצַף <7108>; corresponding to <7107> above] ▶ **This word corresponds to the Hebrew word *qāṣap̱* (<7107>) and refers to anger aroused by someone's failure to fulfill a duty properly.** It occurs only in Daniel 2:12 where Nebuchadnezzar became angry over the failure of the Babylonian wise men to tell him his dream with its interpretation. ¶

– 5 Ps. 95:10 ➔ LOATHE <6962> 6 See ANGER (PROVOKE TO) <3707> 7 See INDIGNANT (BE) <2194>.

ANGRY (BE, BECOME) – ***zā'ap̱*** [verb: זָעַף <2196>; a prim. root] ▶ **This word means to be dejected, to be enraged.** Its root idea is to storm, which is seen in the use of the related noun *zā'ap* [AGE (noun) <2197>] to describe the raging sea in Jonah 1:15 (to rage). The word describes an unsettled storm within a person that exhibits itself in either dejection or rage. The cupbearer and baker were dejected when they couldn't understand their dreams (Gen. 40:6; also translated to be sad, to be troubled). The guard thought that Daniel and his friends would look downcast if denied the king's food (Dan. 1:10: to be worse). King Uzziah was enraged when the priests attempted to remove him from the Temple (2 Chr. 26:19; also translated to become furious, to be wroth, to be enraged). Other ref.: Prov. 19:3. ¶

ANGRY (GET) – ***ḥārāh, nāḥār*** [verb: חָרָה, נָחַר <2734>; a prim. root; comp. BURN (verb) <2787>] ▶ **This word means to burn, to be kindled, to glow, to grow warm. Figuratively, it means to become angered or vexed.** Anger can be between two people: Potiphar's anger was kindled against Joseph when his wife accused Joseph of rape (Gen. 39:19). Anger can also be between God and a person: God's anger is against those who transgress His law (Josh. 23:16). This word can also describe a future event of one becoming angry (Is. 41:11). *

ANGUISH – 1 ***qôṣer*** [masc. noun: קוֹצֶר <7115>; from SHORTEN <7114> (e.g., in the sense of shortness of spirit)] ▶ **This word indicates despair, discouragement.** The word means literally short. In context it refers to a shortness of spirit, depression because of oppression (Ex. 6:9; also translated despondency, broken). ¶

2 ***šāḇaṣ*** [masc. noun: שָׁבָץ <7661>; from WEAVE <7660> (in the sense of to entangle)] ▶ **This word refers to a state of mind and the physical state of a person in deep pain and near death; it is also translated agony, throes of death.** Ref.: 2 Sam. 1:9. ¶

– 3 Ex. 15:14; Job 6:10; Ps. 48:6 ➔ PAIN (noun) <2427> 4 Deut. 28:65 ➔ DESPAIR (noun) <1671> 5 Job 15:24 ➔ DISTRESS (noun) <4691> 6 Ps. 31:10; 116:3 ➔ SORROW (noun) <3015> 7 Ps. 39:2; Is. 65:14 ➔ PAIN (noun) <3511> 8 Ps. 116:3 ➔ DISTRESS (noun) <4712> 9 Ps. 119:143 ➔ DISTRESS (noun) <4689> 10 Prov. 1:27; Is. 8:22; 30:6 ➔ DISTRESS (noun) <6695> b. 11 Is. 9:1 ➔

CONSTRAINT <4164> 12 Is. 21:3; Ezek. 30:4, 9; Nah. 2:10 ➔ PAIN (noun) <2479> 13 Ezek. 7:25 ➔ ANGUISH <7089> 14 Dan. 6:20 ➔ TROUBLED <6088>.

ANGUISH (BE) – Ps. 38:18 ➔ ANXIOUS (BE, BECOME) <1672>.

ANGUISHED – Dan. 6:20 ➔ TROUBLED <6088>.

ANIAM – ***ᵃniyʿām*** [masc. proper noun: אֲנִיעָם <593>; from LAMENT <578> and PEOPLE <5971>]: lamentation of (the) people ► **A son of Shemida, a descendant of Manasseh.** Ref.: 1 Chr. 7:19. ¶

ANIM – ***ʿāniym*** [proper noun: עֲנִים <6044>; from plur. of EYE <5869>]: fountains ► **A city that became part of the inheritance of the tribe of Judah.** Ref.: Josh. 15:50. ¶

ANIMAL – 1 ***bᵉhêmāh*** [fem. noun: בְּהֵמָה <929>; from an unused root (prob. meaning to be mute)] ► **This Hebrew word usually functions collectively, meaning animals, beasts, livestock, cattle.** It takes on the following meanings in context: animals or beasts in general (Ex. 9:9; 1 Kgs. 4:33); wild animals; beasts of the earth (Deut. 28:26; 32:24; 1 Sam. 17:44). Often it refers to cattle or livestock (NIV, NASB, Gen. 1:24–26; 2:20; 8:1; 47:18); beasts of burden (Gen. 34:23); or beasts for riding (Neh. 2:12, 14). * 2 ***bᵉʿiyr*** [masc. noun: בְּעִיר <1165>; from BURN (verb) <1197> (in the sense of eating)] ► **This word denotes cattle, livestock; beasts.** It refers to beasts of burden (Gen. 45:17); cattle (Ps. 78:48); and grazing animals (Ex. 22:5); to animals or domesticated beasts in general (Num. 20:4). The Lord provided water for the animals as well as for people in the desert (Num. 20:8, 11). ¶ 3 ***ḥay, ḥayyāh*** [fem. noun: חַי, חַיָּה <2416>; from LIVE <2421>] ► **This word means a living thing, a creature, a beast. The basic meaning is living things, but its most common translation is animals or beasts.** The word refers to all kinds of animals and beasts of the field or earth (Gen. 1:24, 25; 1 Sam. 17:46) and sometimes stands in parallel with birds of the air (Ezek. 29:5). The nations, such as Egypt, were referred to metaphorically as beasts (Ps. 68:30). Beasts were categorized in various ways: beasts of burden (Is. 46:1); land animals (Gen. 1:28; 8:19); cattle (Num. 35:3); sea creatures (Ps. 104:25); clean, edible creatures (Lev. 11:47; 14:4); unclean, nonedible creatures (Lev. 5:2); large and small creatures (Ps. 104:25).

Two further categories of animals are noted: wild animals or animals of prey and animal or beastlike beings. God made the wild animals of the field. Sometimes the Lord used wild beasts as instruments of His judgments (Ezek. 14:15; 33:27), but on other occasions He protected His people from ravenous beasts (Gen. 37:20; Lev. 26:6). At any rate, vicious beasts will not inhabit the land of the Lord's restored people (Is. 35:9). The bizarre living beings mentioned in Ezekiel 1:5, 13, 22; 3:13 were like birds and animals but were composite beings. They could not be described adequately by human language, for they also had the forms of humans, each with faces of a man, lion, ox, and eagle. However, they did not resemble flesh and blood in their appearance (Ezek. 1:13) and were tied to the movement of the Spirit (Ezek. 1:20). * – 4 Gen. 43:16 ➔ SLAUGHTER (noun) <2874>.

ANKLE – 1 ***ʾepes, ʾōphes*** [masc. noun: אֶפֶס, אֹפֶס <657>; from FAIL <656>] ► **A masculine noun indicating joints that connect the foot and the leg, or soles of the feet. It is used only in the dual, referring to two extremities.** In Ezekiel 47:3 it means, therefore, the soles of the feet or ankles. This Hebrew word also means ceasing, end, naught; see NOTHING <657>. ¶ – 2 2 Sam. 22:37; Ps. 18:36 ➔ FOOT <7166>.

ANKLE CHAIN – Is. 3:20 ➔ MARCHING <6807> b.

ANKLET – 1 ***ʿekes*** [masc. noun: עֶכֶס <5914>; from TINKLE <5913>] ► **This word describes a leg bracelet, an ornament**

worn around the ankle. A showy piece of jewelry worn by the rich and vain. The Lord would remove this vanity by His judgments (Is. 3:18); the word is also translated jingling anklet, tinkling ornament, bangle. The Hebrew word also means a fetter, a noose; see FETTER <5914>. ¶
– [2] Is. 3:20 ➔ MARCHING <6807> b.

ANNALS – 2 Chr. 13:22; 24:27 ➔ STORY <4097>.

ANNIHILATE – Dan. 7:26 ➔ CONSUME <8046>.

ANNOTATIONS – 2 Chr. 13:22; 24:27 ➔ STORY <4097>.

ANNOYANCE – Esther 7:4 ➔ LOSS <5143>.

ANNUL – Is. 28:18 ➔ COVER (verb) <3722>.

ANOINT – [1] ***māšaḥ*** [verb: מָשַׁח <4886>; a prim. root] ▶ **The most common usage of this verb is the ritual of divine installation of individuals into positions of leadership by pouring oil on their heads.** Most frequently, people were anointed for kingship: Saul (1 Sam. 10:1); David (1 Sam. 16:13); and Solomon (1 Kgs. 1:34). The word is also used of people anointed as priests (Ex. 28:41; Num. 35:25); and prophets (1 Kgs. 19:16; Is. 61:1). In its common usage, this verb can refer to the rubbing of a shield with oil (Is. 21:5); the painting of a house (Jer. 22:14); the anointing of an individual with ointments or lotions (Amos 6:6); the spreading of oil on wafers (Ex. 29:2). If the verb is used in association with a religious ceremony, it connotes the sanctification of things or people for divine service. Once the Tabernacle was erected, it and all its furnishings were anointed with oil to consecrate them (Ex. 40:9–11). *
[2] ***sûk*** [verb: סוּךְ <5480>; a prim. root] ▶ **This word means to pour upon.** Oil is frequently the substance used for anointing (Deut. 28:40; 2 Sam. 14:2; Ezek. 16:9; Mic. 6:15). This procedure could be performed on oneself (2 Sam. 12:20; Ruth 3:3; Dan. 10:3) as well as on another person (2 Chr. 28:15; Ezek. 16:9). In several instances, the absence of anointing oil among God's people is an indication of divine judgment (Deut. 28:40; Mic. 6:15). ¶

ANOINTED – [1] ***māšiyaḥ*** [masc. noun: מָשִׁיחַ <4899>; from ANOINT <4886>] ▶ **This word means one who has received an unction; see ANOINT.** Although it is a noun, it can function both as a substantive (1 Sam. 24:6, 10); or an adjective (Lev. 4:3, 5, 16). Since it refers to an individual who has been anointed by divine command (2 Sam. 1:14, 16), it can reference the high priest of Israel (Lev. 4:3, 5, 16; 6:22); however, it is usually reserved as a marker for kingship, primarily the kings of Israel (1 Sam. 26:9, 11, 16, 23). In this way, the patriarchs were regarded as God's anointed kings (1 Chr. 16:22; Ps. 105:15). One unique instance of this term is in reference to Cyrus the Persian, a non-Israelite who was regarded as God's anointed (Is. 45:1); therefore, one is forced to understand this characterization, not as a statement of the individual's inherent goodness and perfection, since Cyrus was a worshipper of pagan deities like Marduk. On the contrary, it is a statement of God's appointing or choosing an individual for a task. Furthermore, the concept of the *māšiyaḥ*, meaning Messiah, as a Savior is not fully developed in the Old Testament. The closest that one comes to this in the Old Testament is Daniel 9:25, 26. This concept is developed later, during the New Testament period, and fits better with the parallel Greek word *christos*. *
[2] ***mimšaḥ*** [masc. noun: מִמְשַׁח <4473>; from ANOINT <4886>, in the sense of expansion] ▶ **This word possibly means expansion, extension.** It occurs only in Ezekiel 28:14 and would, with this meaning, read "cherub of extension" (i.e., a cherub with wings outstretched). However, this definition is now seriously questioned, largely because the term derives from the verb *māšaḥ* (<4886>), meaning to anoint. The term more likely expresses the sense of

anointment or anointing. Taking the word this way, the phrase conveys the more satisfying expression "cherub of anointing," i.e., the anointed cherub. ¶

ANOINTING – ***mišḥāh, mošḥāh*** [fem. noun: מִשְׁחָה, מָשְׁחָה <4888>; from ANOINT <4886>] ► **This word refers to a priestly portion.** When used in reference to the anointing, *mišḥāh* is always used to modify *šemen* (<8081>), meaning olive oil (Ex. 37:29). At times, this phrase is further qualified by the addition of another modifier, like *qōḏeš* (<6944>), meaning holy (Ex. 30:31); *yehōwāh* (<3068>), the proper name of the God of Israel (Lev. 10:7); or *'elōhym* (<430>), meaning his God (Lev. 21:12). This "oil of anointing" was made from a combination of olive oil and spices (Ex. 30:25; 35:8, 28). It was then used to anoint someone or something and to consecrate the individual or item to God, such as the Aaronic priests (Ex. 29:7, 21; Lev. 8:2, 12, 30; 21:10); and the Tabernacle (Ex. 40:9; Lev. 8:10). It was also used in the customary ministrations of the Tabernacle (Ex. 31:11; 35:15; Num. 4:16). In addition, this term identified the portion of the sacrifices presented to God, then given to the priests (Lev. 7:35). *

ANOTHER – [1] ***'oḥoriy*** [Aramaic adj.: אָחֳרִי <317>; from AFTER <311>] ► **This word indicates a further or different kingdom arising after Babylon and subsequent kingdoms to that one.** Refs.: Dan. 2:39; 7:5, 6, 8. Finally, it indicates another or different (in kind?) horn, the little horn of Daniel (Dan. 7:20). ¶

[2] ***'oḥorān*** [Aramaic adj.: אָחֳרָן <321>; from AFTER <311>, the same as <317> above] ► **This word means other, something/somebody else.** It indicates someone with special dream interpretive powers (Dan. 2:11). It also means simply a different people (Dan. 2:44), different person (Dan. 5:17), other gods (Dan. 3:29), or a subsequent king or kingdom (Dan. 7:24). ¶

– [3] Esther 1:19; Zech. 11:9 ➔ NEIGHBOR <7468> [4] See OTHER <312>.

ANSWER (noun) – [1] ***ma'aneh*** [masc. noun: מַעֲנֶה <4617>; from ANSWER (verb) <6030> a.] ►

a. This word refers to something said or written as a retort or reply to assertions made. Refs.: Job 32:3, 5. A wise person responds with a gentle answer (Prov. 15:1); and an appropriate reply (Prov. 15:23). God is involved in the response of people (Prov. 16:1). Some cannot respond to verbal instructions alone (Prov. 29:19). It is used of God's reply or lack thereof (Mic. 3:7). ¶

b. This word means end, purpose. It indicates the ultimate goal and destiny of something or someone. The wicked person is made for the purpose or time of evil (Prov. 16:4). ¶

[2] ***piṯgām*** [Aramaic masc. noun: פִּתְגָם <6600>; corresponding to EDICT <6599>] ► **This word means an official written response; it is also translated reply, letter, report, decree; sentence, this word, this matter, decision.** It is related to the Hebrew word *piṯgām* (edict) and was used in Ezra to describe the written communication that was used between the kings, the Israelites, and their adversaries (Ezra 4:17; 5:7, 11; 6:11). In Daniel, this word described the affair surrounding the unwillingness of Shadrach, Meshach, and Abednego to bow to the golden image (Dan. 3:16); in addition to the matters contained in Nebuchadnezzar's dream (Dan. 4:17). ¶

– [3] Job 21:34; 34:36 ➔ RETURN (noun) <8666>.

ANSWER (verb) – [1] ***'ānāh, le'annôṯ*** [עָנָה, לַעֲנוֹת <6030>; a prim. root] ►

a. A verb meaning to give answer, i.e., to respond, to reply, to testify. It refers to responding, answering a person: of people responding (Gen. 18:27; 23:5); of God answering, responding by word or deed (1 Sam. 7:9; 14:37; 28:6, 15; 1 Kgs. 18:37); of a lover's response (Song 2:10; 5:6). It is often coupled with *'āmar*, they said: he answered (*'ānāh*) and said (*we'āmar*) (Ex. 4:1). It has the legal sense of witness to, about, against, to testify in some contexts (Gen. 30:33; Deut. 31:21; 2 Sam. 1:16). In its passive use, it

means to be given, provided with a response (Prov. 21:13; Ezek. 14:4, 7). *
b. A verb meaning to sing, to shout, to howl. It is used of singing joyously to the Lord and in praise of His Law (Ex. 15:21; 1 Sam. 18:7; Ezra 3:11; Ps. 119:172); or in a riotous, uncontrolled way (Ex. 32:18). It is used of a victory song or crying out in victory (Jer. 51:14). It is used figuratively of a rested Israel singing again (Hos. 2:15). It refers to the howling or crying out of animals (Is. 13:22). *
c. A proper noun meaning Leannoth; part of a song title Mahalath Leannoth. It is found in the title of Psalm 88. The title seems to refer to affliction. The psalm is a powerful plea for deliverance from death. *
2 ***ʿnāh*** [Aramaic verb: עֲנָה <6032>; corresponding to <6030> above] ▶ **The basic meaning of this word is to respond, to reply to something said or to a situation.** Refs.: Dan. 2:5, 7, 8, 15, 20; 3:9, 16; 4:19, 30. It is coupled with *'āmar*, to say: he answered and said (Dan. 2:5). *

ANT – ***nᵉmālāh*** [fem. noun: נְמָלָה <5244>; fem. from CUT DOWN <5243>] ▶ **This word refers to a small insect living in colonies.** It is used to set forth the ant as a model of wise living, wisdom (forethought), and industriousness. Refs.: Prov. 6:6; 30:25. ¶

ANTELOPE – ***tᵉ'ô*** [masc. noun: תְּאוֹ <8377>; from DRAW A LINE <8376> (in the case of the antelope, prob. from the white strip on the cheek)] ▶
a. This word means a large group of swift-running and sleek bovid ruminants, usually in wild herds in Africa or Asia. Ref.: Deut. 14:5. It was edible in Israel and could be caught in a net (Is. 51:20).
b. This word refers to a category of animal that includes cattle, buffalo, bison, yaks, and guar; it is also translated wild ox. It was considered edible in Israel and clean (Deut. 14:5). It would have been difficult to catch in a net (Is. 51:20). ¶

ANTIMONY – ***pûḵ*** [masc. noun: פּוּךְ <6320>; from an unused root meaning to paint] ▶ **A word referring to glistening stones used in decorations. It may denote antimony or turquoise.** It refers to the ornamental and decorative supplies David prepared for use in the Temple (1 Chr. 29:2). It is used in a figurative sense of God's adornment of a restored Zion (Is. 54:11). This word also means paint for the eyes; see MAKEUP <6320>. ¶

ANTIQUITY – Is. 23:7 ➔ FORMER TIME <6927>.

ANTOTHIJAH – ***'anṯōṯiyyāh*** [masc. proper noun: עַנְתֹתִיָּה <6070>; from the same as ANATHOTH <6068> and LORD <3050>]: answers of the Lord ▶ **An Israelite of the tribe of Benjamin.** Ref.: 1 Chr. 8:24. ¶

ANUB – ***'ānûḇ*** [masc. proper noun: עָנוּב <6036>; pass. part. from the same as GRAPE <6025>]: linked together ▶ **An Israelite of the tribe of Judah.** Ref.: 1 Chr. 4:8. ¶

ANXIETY – 1 ***dᵉ'āgāh*** [fem. noun: דְּאָגָה <1674>; from ANXIOUS (BE) <1672>] ▶ **This word refers to apprehension because of approaching trouble. It also means care.** In Joshua 22:24 (fear, concern), it refers to a concern that Israel might forget God and prompted the building of a memorial altar. Elsewhere, it refers to anxiety over running out of food or an anxiety caused by God's judgment (Ezek. 4:16; 12:18, 19). This anxiety was sometimes roused by bad news (Jer. 49:23) and sometimes relieved by good words (Prov. 12:25; also translated heaviness). ¶
2 ***śar'appiym*** [masc. noun: שַׂרְעַפִּים <8312>; from OPINION <5587>] ▶ **This word means a disquieting thought, an apprehensive feeling.** The psalmist rejoiced that the Lord calmed his inner anxieties (Ps. 94:19; ESV: care). This is the same word used by the psalmist when he asked God to search him and know his anxieties (Ps. 139:23). ¶

ANXIETY (BE FULL OF) – Ps. 38:18 ➔ ANXIOUS (BE, BECOME) <1672>.

ANXIOUS – Deut. 28:65: anxious mind ➔ lit.: trembling heart ➔ TREMBLING <7268>.

ANXIOUS (BE) – Dan. 7:15 ➔ GRIEVED (BE) <3735>.

ANXIOUS (BE, BECOME) – ***dā'ag*** [verb: דָּאַג <1672>; a prim. root] ▶ **This word describes uneasiness of mind as a result of the circumstances of life; it is also translated to worry, to be in anguish, to be sorry, to be full of anxiety, to be troubled, to be afraid, to dread.** It denotes the anxiety of Saul's father when Saul was away from home (1 Sam. 9:5; 10:2); the anxiety of David which resulted from his sin (Ps. 38:18); and the fear of famine (Jer. 42:16). On the other hand, Jeremiah described the righteous person as one who would not be anxious in drought (Jer. 17:8). This word is also used as a synonym for the Hebrew word *yārê'* <3372>, meaning to fear when speaking of the anxiety of King Zedekiah (Jer. 38:19) or fear in general (Is. 57:11). ¶

ANXIOUS THOUGHT – Ps. 94:19 ➔ ANXIETY <8312>.

ANYTHING – ***m^{e}'ûmāh, mûmāh*** [indefinite pron.: מְאוּמָה, מוּמָה <3972>; apparently a form of DEFECT <3971>] ▶ **This word is indefinite.** It may refer to anything at all (1 Kgs. 10:21) or to whatever the context demands, e.g., any possession (Jer. 39:10). Often it is negated and means "nothing at all" (Gen. 30:31; 39:6, 9; 40:15; 1 Sam. 12:4, 5). It is used adverbially at least once meaning "with respect to anything at all" (1 Sam. 21:2). *

APART – Num. 23:9 ➔ ALONE <910>.

APART (THAT IS SET) – Josh. 16:9 ➔ SEPARATE (adj.) <3995>.

APART FROM – ***bal^{a}ḏêy, bil^{a}ḏêy*** [particle: בַּלְעֲדֵי, בִּלְעֲדֵי <1107>; constructive plur. from NOT <1077> and ETERNITY <5703>] ▶ **This word means without, besides, except for.** It is used with pronominal suffixes to mean except for or without, e.g., without your (permission), *bil'ādeyḵā* (Gen. 41:44), referring to Joseph. It can mean apart from the person indicated by the attached suffix (Gen. 14:24; 41:16). With a prefixed *min* (<4480>), the word means except for someone or something (Num. 5:20; 2 Kgs. 18:25). Before a verb form, it may mean with respect to (what I see) (Job 34:32) in the sense of what I do not realize I see. *

APE – ***qôp̱*** [masc. noun: קוֹף <6971>; prob. of foreign origin] ▶ **This word refers to an exotic animal brought to Israel by ship from Tarshish (Spain or merely large merchant ships?).** Refs.: 1 Kgs. 10:22; 2 Chr. 9:21. This touch of vanity added to the splendor of Solomon's kingdom. ¶

APHARSATHCHITES – ***^{a}pars^{e}ḵāy, ^{a}parsaṯḵāy*** [Aramaic masc. plur. proper noun: אֲפַרְסְכָי, אֲפַרְסַתְכָי <671>; of foreign origin (only in the plur.)] ▶
a. A people settled in Samaria. Refs.: KJV, Ezra 4:9; 5:6; 6:6. ¶
b. An Aramaic masculine noun referring to officials, lesser governors. Refs.: NASB, NIV, Ezra 4:9; 5:6; 6:6. ¶

APHARSITES – ***^{a}pār^{e}sāy*** [proper noun: אֲפָרְסָי <670>; of foreign origin (only in the plur.)] ▶
a. Members of a tribe from Assyria. Ref.: Ezra 4:9, KJV. ¶
b. A reference to the people of Persia. Ref.: Ezra 4:9, NIV, NKJV. ¶
c. A reference to secretaries. Ref.: Ezra 4:9, NASB. ¶

APHEK – ***^{a}piyq, ^{a}pêq*** [proper noun: אֲפִיק, אֲפֵק <663>; from CONTROL (verb) <662> (in the sense of strength)]: strength, fortress ▶
a. It names a city allotted to the tribe of Asher. Ref.: Josh. 19:30. The tribe was not able to drive out the inhabitants of the city (Judg. 1:31) but intermingled with them. It is located southeast of Acco. ¶
b. It names a city on the border of the Amorites, Sidonian territory, located

southeast of Baal-gad in Lebanon. Ref.: Josh. 13:4. ¶
c. A city in the southeast area of Sharon country near the Jarkon River. Joshua executed its king (Josh. 12:18). Philistines gathered there for two major battles (1 Sam. 4:1; 29:1). It was located northeast of Joppa. Herod the Great built Antipatris, a fortress there in ca. 35 B.C. ¶
d. A city east of the Jordan where Israel and the Arameans battled. Refs.: 1 Kgs. 20:26, 30; 2 Kgs. 13:17. Ben-Hadad was defeated there. Some scholars place it east of Galilee. ¶

APHEKAH – ***^{a}pêqāh*** [proper noun: אֲפֵקָה <664>; fem. of APHEK <663>]: strength, fortress ▶ **City of Judah.** Ref.: Josh. 15:53. ¶

APHIAH – ***^{a}piyaḥ*** [masc. proper noun: אֲפִיחַ <647>; perhaps from BREATHE <6315>]: refreshed ▶ **An ancestor of King Saul.** Ref.: 1 Sam. 9:1. ¶

APHRAH (HOUSE OF) – Mic. 1:10 ➔ BETH OPHRAH <1036>.

APHSES – 1 Chr. 24:15 ➔ HAPPIZZEZ <6483>.

APOSTASY – Jer. 2:19; etc. ➔ TURNING AWAY <4878>.

APOTHECARY – Neh. 3:8 ➔ PERFUMER <7546>.

APPAIM – ***'appayim*** [masc. proper noun: אַפַּיִם <649>; dual of NOSE <639>]: nostrils ▶ **An Israelite of the tribe of Judah.** Refs.: 1 Chr. 2:30, 31. ¶

APPALLED (BE) – Dan. 4:19 ➔ ASTONISHED <8075>.

APPALLING THING – Jer. 18:13 ➔ HORRIBLE THING <8186>.

APPAREL – [1] Judg. 14:19 ➔ SPOIL (noun) <2488> [2] 1 Kgs. 10:5; 2 Chr. 9:4; Is. 63:3; Zeph. 1:8 ➔ CLOTHING <4403>.

APPAREL (CHANGEABLE SUIT OF) – Is. 3:22 ➔ FESTAL APPAREL <4254>.

APPEAR – [1] Song 4:1; 6:5 ➔ DESCEND <1570> [2] Dan. 5:5 ➔ TAKE OUT <5312>.

APPEAR (MADE) – Gen. 30:37 ➔ EXPOSING <4286>.

APPEARANCE – [1] ***rêw*** [Aramaic masc. noun: רֵו <7299>; from a root corresponding to SEE <7200>] ▶ **This word refers to the overall form and presentation of something, e.g., the statue in Nebuchadnezzar's vision.** Refs.: Dan. 2:31; 3:25. ¶
– [2] Lam. 4:7 ➔ COURTYARD <1508>.

APPEASE – [1] Gen. 32:20; Prov. 16:14 ➔ COVER (verb) <3722> [2] Esther 2:1; 7:10 ➔ SUBSIDE <7918>.

APPEASED (BE) – Prov. 6:35 ➔ WILLING (BE) <14>.

APPERTAIN – Jer. 10:7 ➔ DUE (BE THE) <2969>.

APPLE – [1] ***bāḇāh*** [fem. noun: בָּבָה <892>; fem. act. part. of an unused root meaning to hollow out] ▶ **This word indicates the pupil (*b^{e}ḇāḇaṯ*) of the eye.** It is used in a figurative sense to describe Israel as the Lord's most prized possession (Zech. 2:8) whom He will defend at all costs. ¶
– [2] Deut. 32:10; Ps. 17:8; Prov. 7:2 ➔ PUPIL <380>.

APPLE, APPLE TREE – ***tappûaḥ*** [masc. noun: תַּפּוּחַ <8598>; from BREATHE <5301> (in relation to the fragrance of an object)] ▶ **This word refers to a round, firm, fleshy, edible fruit grown on a tree in several colors, red, yellow, green, or to the tree itself.** It is used in a famous proverb (Prov. 25:11). The bridegroom is described as an apple tree among the trees of the forest (Song 2:3, 5). The smell of apples was considered refreshing and pleasant (Song 7:8). Other refs.: Song 8:5; Joel 1:12. ¶

APPLY – ***mārah̤*** [verb: מָרַח <4799>; a prim. root] ▶ **This word indicates placing something on a location or something else; a medicinal bandage on a sore or boil.** Ref.: Is. 38:21; KJV: to lay. ¶

APPOINT – [1] ***yā'ad*** [verb: יָעַד <3259>; a prim. root] ▶ **This word means to designate, and also to summon, to engage, to agree, to assemble.** It also means allotted or appointed time, such as the amount of time David appointed to Amasa to assemble the men of Judah (2 Sam. 20:5). This word can also take the meaning of appointing or designating someone to be married (Ex. 21:8, 9). Another meaning is to meet someone at an appointed time. Amos asked the question, How can two walk together unless they appoint a time at which to meet (Amos 3:3)? *

[2] ***m^{e}nā', m^{e}nāh*** [Aramaic verb: מְנָא, מְנָה <4483>; corresponding to COUNT <4487>] ▶ **This word means to set up, to install persons, to authorize them for a certain purpose.** Refs.: Ezra 7:25; Dan. 2:24, 49; 3:12. It has the sense of tested, tried, counted, a passive participle of the simple stem (peal stem) in Aramaic (Dan. 5:26: to number). ¶

[3] ***sāman*** [verb: סָמַן <5567>; a prim. root] ▶

a. The verb is used in a passive sense to indicate a place picked out, determined for planting something. Ref.: Is. 28:25. Its meaning is not entirely clear. ¶

b. A verb meaning to plot out. It is taken to mean an area of ground plotted out for something, prepared (Is. 28:25). ¶

– [4] Job 7:3; Jon. 1:17; 4:6–8 ➔ COUNT <4487> [5] Ps. 73:9 ➔ LAY, LAY CLAIM <8371> b.

APPOINTED – [1] ***zāman*** [verb: זְמַן <2163>; a prim. root] ▶ **This verb means to fix, to set a time.** In the book of Ezra, so many Israelites had violated the command not to marry foreign women that leaders had to set a fixed time for people to come by towns to repent (Ezra 10:14: appointed, set). In Nehemiah, the Levites, priests, and people worked out a time (by casting lots) for each family to contribute wood for the altar (Neh. 10:34: fixed, set, appointed). In the closing words of his book, Nehemiah reminded the Lord of his leadership in this matter (Neh. 13:31: appointed, designated). See the related Aramaic verb *z^{e}man* (AGREE <2164>). ¶

– [2] Lev. 16:21 ➔ READINESS (IN) <6261> [3] Num. 1:16; 16:2 ➔ CHOSEN <7148> [4] Josh. 20:9 ➔ DESIGNATED <4152> [5] Is. 30:32 ➔ FOUNDATION <4145>.

APPOINTED PLACE – Ezek. 43:21 ➔ APPOINTMENT <4662>.

APPOINTED TIME, APPOINTED PLACE – ***mô'ēd*** [masc. noun: מוֹעֵד <4150>; from APPOINT <3259>] ▶ **This word can signify a set occasion for meeting in general.** Refs.: Gen. 18:14; Ex. 13:10. It can also signify a specific appointed time, usually for a sacred feast or festival (Lev. 23:2, 4, 37, 44; Hos. 9:5; 12:9); the time of the birds' migration (Jer. 8:7); the time of wine (Hos. 2:9); the same time next year (Gen. 17:21). In addition to the concept of time, this word can also signify an appointed meeting place: "The mount of the congregation" identifies the meeting place of God or the gods (Is. 14:13), and "the house appointed for all living" identifies the meeting place of the dead—i.e., the netherworld (Job 30:23). Moreover, the term is used to distinguish those places where God's people were to focus on God and their relationship with Him, which would include: the tent of meeting (Ex. 33:7); the Temple (Lam. 2:6); the synagogue (Ps. 74:8). *

APPOINTED TIMES – ***mô'ād*** [masc. noun: מוֹעָד <4151>; from APPOINT <3259>] ▶ **This word describes the assigned rendezvous or postings for soldiers, often translated as ranks.** Ref.: Is. 14:31. ¶

APPOINTMENT – [1] ***mipqād*** [masc. noun: מִפְקָד <4662>; from ATTEND <6485>] ▶ **This word means selection, designation. It also means a mandate, a**

counting, a census; an appointed place. Ten men became assistant overseers for the management of offerings in the house of the Lord by the appointment of King Hezekiah (2 Chr. 31:13; also translated commandment). King David ordered Joab to take a census of the number of people under his rule (2 Sam. 24:9; 1 Chr. 21:5; also translated numbering). Twice the word functions to designate a location. In Ezekiel 43:21, the bull of the sin offering was to be burnt in the appointed place (also translated designated part) of the Temple precincts. In Nehemiah 3:31, the word was utilized (possibly as a proper name) to identify a particular gate in the city of Jerusalem, the "Inspection Gate"; see INSPECTION <4663>. ¶
– [2] Ezra 6:9 ➔ REQUEST <3983>.

APPORTION – Job 7:3 ➔ COUNT <4487>.

APPRISE – 1 Sam. 9:15; 20:2, 12 ➔ REVEAL <1540>.

APRON – Gen. 3:7 ➔ BELT <2290>.

AR – ***'ār*** [proper noun: עָר <6144>; the same as CITY <5892>]: city ▶ **One of the main cities of Moab.** Refs.: Num. 21:15, 28; Deut. 2:9, 18, 29; Is. 15:1. ¶

ARA – ***ʾărā'*** [masc. proper noun: אֲרָא <690>; prob. for LION <738>]: gathering, strong ▶ **An Israelite of the tribe of Asher.** Ref.: 1 Chr. 7:38. ¶

ARAB – ***ʾărāḇ*** [proper noun: אֲרָב <694>; from WAIT (LIE IN) <693>]: ambush ▶ **A village in the mountains of Judah.** Ref.: Josh. 15:52. ¶

ARABIA – ***ʿărāḇ, ʿărab*** [proper noun: עֲרָב, עֲרַב <6152>; from EVENING (BECOME) <6150> in the figurative sense of sterility] ▶ **This word seems to encompass the large Arabian peninsula at times.** It refers to traveling caravans through Israelite territory (1 Kgs. 10:15) and was a general term referring to the area from Aram (Syria) to the Arabian Desert (Ezek. 27:21). Solomon collected revenues from the people of the area. They lived and worked in a nomadic style of life, often in the desert (Is. 21:13). Even these people would taste the judgments of the Lord (Jer. 25:24). Other ref.: 2 Chr. 9:14. ¶

ARABIAN – ***'arḇiy, ʿărāḇiy*** [proper noun: עַרְבִי, עֲרָבִי <6163>; patrial from ARABIA <6152>] ▶ **An inhabitant of Arabia.** Refs.: 2 Chr. 17:11; 21:16; 22:1; 26:7; Neh. 2:19; 4:7; 6:1; Is. 13:20; Jer. 3:2. ¶

ARAD – ***ʿărād*** [masc. proper noun: עֲרָד <6166>; from an unused root meaning to sequester itself]: fugitive, wild donkey ▶
a. A Canaanite king. Ref.: Num. 21:1; 33. 40; Josh. 12. 14. ¶
b. A Canaanite city. Ref.: Judg. 1:16. ¶
c. Son of Beriah. Ref.: 1 Chr. 8:15. ¶

ARAH – [1] ***'āraḥ*** [masc. proper noun: אָרַח <733>; from TRAVEL <732>]: traveler ▶
a. A descendant of Asher. Ref.: 1 Chr. 7:39. ¶
b. Head of a family of which the members came back from Babylon. Refs.: Ezra 2:5; Neh. 6:18; 7:10. ¶
– [2] Josh. 13:4 ➔ MEARAH, ARAH <4631> b.

ARAM – ***ʾărām*** [proper noun: אֲרָם <758>; from the same as STRONGHOLD <759>]: high, exalted ▶ **Aram is another name for Syria, found often in the Old Testament as early as Abraham's journeys when he settled in Haran in Aram.** Refs.: Gen. 11:28–32. The name means "Aram of two rivers" in northern Mesopotamia. Balaam, the pagan soothsayer, came from Aram (Num. 23:7). It was often at war with Israel, even in the time of Judges (Judg. 3:10; 2 Sam. 8:5, 6). Israel fell prey to the religious intrigues of Syria's gods (Judg. 10:6). Aram's most famous city, its capital, was Damascus (2 Sam. 8:5, 6). Their soldiers were often mercenaries (2 Sam. 10:6, 7). The Arameans purchased war equipment from Israel in Solomon's day (1 Kgs. 10:29).

Israel's history was closely interwoven with the nation and territory of Aram (Saul, David, Solomon, and later kings, e.g., Ahab). The language of Aram, Aramaic, was at one time the lingua franca of the ancient Near East and left its impression in the Aramaisms of the Old Testament. Elisha the prophet was involved with the kings of Damascus, Hazael and Ben-Hadad (2 Kgs. 8:7–15). *

ARAM OF THE (TWO) RIVERS – ***ªram nahª-rayim*** [proper noun: אֲרַם נַהֲרַיִם <763>; from ARAM <758> and the dual of RIVER <5104>] ▶ **This word is equal to Mesopotamia ("between the rivers"). It is bounded by the upper Euphrates on its west and by the Tigris River on the east.** Abraham's servant sought a wife for Isaac there (Gen. 24:10), and Balaam came from the area (Deut. 23:4). It was a source of trouble later in the time of the judges and David (Judg. 3:8, 10; 1 Chr. 19:6; Ps. 60:1). ¶

ARAM-ZOBAH – ***ªram ṣôḇāh*** [proper noun: אֲרַם צוֹבָה <760>; from ARAM <758> and ZOBAH <6678>]: Aram: elevated; Zobah: empty ▶ **A powerful Aramean kingdom.** Ref.: Ps. 60 (title). ¶

ARAMAIC (IN) – ***ªrāmiyṯ*** [adv.: אֲרָמִית <762>; fem. of ARAMEAN <761>]: see ARAM ▶ **This word means: in the Aramean (Syriac) language.** Biblical Aramaic describes the language in Ezra 4:8–6:18; 7:12–26 and Daniel 2:4b-7:28, as well as a few words in Genesis 31:47 and Jeremiah 10:11. It was also spoken by Rabshakeh of Assyria and the leaders of Judah (2 Kgs. 18:26; Is. 36:11). Official letters were written in it (Ezra 4:7).

The language was named for the people from Aram who spoke it. The Arameans were an influential people but not fully understood yet. Many of the Elephantine Papyri and Dead Sea Scrolls were written in Aramaic. Termed Syriac in the KJV, it is a Semitic language like Hebrew and very similar to Hebrew. The language was at one time the lingua franca (cf. 2 Kgs. 18:26) of the ancient Near East. In a few cases, a few words called "Aramaisms" appear even in the New Testament (e.g., Mark 5:41; John 1:42; Act. 9:36, 40; 1 Cor. 16:22). ¶

ARAMEAN – [1] ***ªrammiy*** [masc. proper noun: אֲרַמִּי <761>; patrial from ARAM <758>]: see ARAM <758> ▶ **This word is a gentilic noun (with the ending *iy*) indicating a person from Syria or Aram.** It referred to an area between the Tigris and Euphrates Rivers (Gen. 25:9–20). Bethuel, Isaac's father-in-law, was an Aramean. Syrian refers to the same ethnic group. Laban was an Aramean as was Naaman (2 Kgs. 5:20). The origins of the Israelites were tied to them (Deut. 26:5). The Syrians and Israelites were often at war (2 Kgs. 9:15). Manasseh had a concubine from among the Arameans (1 Chr. 7:14). *
[2] ***ªrômiym*** [masc. proper noun: אֲרוֹמִים <726>; a clerical error for EDOMITE <130>] ▶ **Some ancient versions read Edomite and Syrian.** The Arameans came to Elath and lived there (2 Kgs. 16:6). ¶
– [3] 2 Chr. 22:5 ➔ SYRIAN <7421>.

ARAN – ***ªrān*** [masc. proper noun: אֲרָן <765>; from SHOUT (verb) <7442>]: wild goat, firmness ▶ **A descendant of Seir the Horite.** Refs.: Gen. 36:28; 1 Chr. 1:42. ¶

ARARAT – ***ªrāraṭ*** [proper noun: אֲרָרַט <780>; of foreign origin] ▶ **The name of the mountain range on which the ark of Noah rested after the flood.** Ref.: Gen. 8:4. It is used to indicate an area, "land of Ararat" (2 Kgs. 19:37; Is. 37:38). It is in modern Armenia in the area of Lake Van. Other ref.: Jer. 51:27. ¶

ARAUNAH – ***ªrawnāh*** [masc. proper noun: אֲרַוְנָה <728>; an orthographical variation of ARVADITE <721>]: the Lord is firm, cedar ▶ **The name of a Jebusite who owned a threshing floor or building.** Refs.: 2 Sam. 24:16, 18, 20–24. A destroying angel of pestilence struck Israel from there. David bought the threshing floor from Araunah to stop the Lord's pestilence and plague upon the land (2 Sam. 24:18–21) because of David's sin. ¶

ARBA – ***'arba'*** [masc. proper noun: אַרְבַּע <704>; the same as FOUR <702>]: square, strength of Baal ▶ **The father of Anak.** Refs.: Josh. 15:13; 21:11. He was the greatest man among the Anakim (see Josh. 14:15). He founded Kiriath-Arba which became known as Hebron (see Gen. 35:27). ¶

ARBATHITE – ***'arḇāṯiy*** [proper noun: עַרְבָתִי <6164>; from BETH ARABAH <1026>] ▶ **An inhabitant of Beth Arabah.** Refs.: 2 Sam. 23:31; 1 Chr. 11:32. ¶

ARBITE – ***'arbiy*** [masc. proper noun: אַרְבִּי <701>; patrial from ARAB <694>] ▶ **A native of Arab in Judah.** Ref.: 2 Sam. 23:35. ¶

ARCH – Ezek. 40:16, 21, 22; etc. ➔ VESTIBULE <361>.

ARCHER – 1 ***qaššāṯ*** [masc. noun: קַשָּׁת <7199>; intens. (as denom.) from BOW (noun) <7198>] ▶ **This word indicates a person trained in the use of a bow.** Specifically it refers to Hagar's son Ishmael who learned the skill of a bowman (Gen. 21:20). ¶

2 ***raḇ*** [masc. noun: רַב <7228>; contr. from SHOOT, SHOOT OUT <7232>] ▶ **This word is uncertain. It seems to mean bowmen or arrows.** Refs.: Job 16:13; Jer. 50:29. ¶

– 3 Judg. 5:11 ➔ DIVIDE <2686> b. 4 Jer. 4:29 ➔ THROW <7411>.

ARCHEVITE – ***'arkᵉwāy*** [proper noun: אַרְכְּוָי <756>; patrial from ERECH <751>]: length ▶ **A native of Erech.** Ref.: Ezra 4:9. ¶

ARCHITE, ARKITE – ***'arkiy*** [masc. proper noun: אַרְכִּי <757>; patrial from another place (pertaining to Joseph's descendants) of similar name with ERECH <751>]: fugitive ▶ **This word refers to a descendant of Ham in the line of Canaan who lived in Arqa.** It was located just north of modern Tripoli. It is mentioned in several ancient sources from Egypt and Assyria. Its modern archaeological tell is Tell Arqa in Syria. Joseph's allotment of land passed by it (Josh. 16:2). Hushai was a wise man serving David and was an Arkite (2 Sam. 15:32). *

ARCHIVE – 1 Ezra 4:15; 6:1 ➔ BOOK <5609> 2 Ezra 5:17; 6:1 ➔ TREASURE <1596>.

ARCHIVES – Ezra 4:15 ➔ lit.: the book of the records ➔ RECORD <1799>.

ARCHWAY – Ezek. 40:16, 21, 22; etc. ➔ VESTIBULE <361>.

ARCTURUS – Job 9:9; 38:32 ➔ BEAR (noun) <5906>.

ARD – ***'ard*** [masc. proper noun: אַרְדְּ <714>; from an unused root prob. meaning to wander]: fugitive ▶ **An Israelite of the tribe of Benjamin.** Refs.: Gen. 46:21; Num. 26:40. ¶

ARDITE – ***'ardiy*** [proper noun: אַרְדִּי <716>; patron. from ARD <714>]: fugitive ▶ **A descendant of Ard.** Ref.: Num. 26:40. ¶

ARDON – ***'ardôn*** [masc. proper noun: אַרְדּוֹן <715>; from the same as ARD <714>]: roaming ▶ **An Israelite of the tribe of Judah.** Ref.: 1 Chr. 2:18. ¶

ARELI – ***'ar'ēliy*** [proper noun: אַרְאֵלִי <692>; from VALIANT ONE <691>]: lion of God, valiant ▶

a. An Israelite, son of Gad. Refs.: Gen. 46:16; Num. 26:17. ¶

b. The family of the Arelites. Ref.: Num. 26:17. ¶

ARELITE – Num. 26:17 ➔ ARELI <692>.

ARGOB – ***'argōḇ*** [proper noun: אַרְגֹּב <709>; from the same as CLOD <7263>]: pile of stones, strong ▶

a. The name of an area in Basham, east of the Jordan, the land of King Og. Refs.: Deut. 3:4, 13, 14. Later, it was part of Solomon's lands (1 Kgs. 4:13). ¶

b. He was an administrator or official of Pekahiah, king of Israel who was assassinated by Pekah and his followers. Ref.: 2 Kgs. 15:25; so NIV, NASB; KJV seems to indicate that he was an officer to Pekah in the affair. ¶

ARGUMENTS (STRONG) – ***ʿaṣumôṯ*** [fem. plur. noun: עֲצֻמוֹת <6110>; fem. of MIGHTY <6099>] ▶ **This word points out strong reasons, rationales.** It refers to supposed proofs and arguments used in a legal case or debate (Is. 41:21; ESV: proofs). ¶

ARIDAI – ***ᵃriyḏay*** [masc. proper noun: אֲרִידַי <742>; of Persian origin]: great, brilliant ▶ **One of the sons of Haman, the enemy of the Jews at the time of Esther.** Ref.: Esther 9:9. ¶

ARIDATHA – ***ᵃriyḏāṯāʾ*** [masc. proper noun: אֲרִידָתָא <743>; of Persian origin]: noble by birth ▶ **One of the sons of Haman, the enemy of the Jews at the time of Esther.** Ref.: Esther 9:8. ¶

ARIEH – ***ʾaryêh*** [masc. proper noun: אַרְיֵה <745>; the same as LION <738>]: lion ▶ **This man was killed at the same time as King Pekahiah by Pekah.** Ref.: 2 Kgs. 15:25. ¶

ARIEL – [1] ***ᵃriyʾēl*** [masc. proper noun: אֲרִיאֵל <739>; from LION <738> and GOD <410>]: lion of God ▶

a. This word refers to Ariel of Moab, whose two sons were killed by one of David's mighty men. Refs.: 2 Sam. 23:20; 1 Chr. 11:22, NASB. The NKJV renders this as lion-like heroes.

b. It indicates a hero warrior, a man of courage. The NKJV renders this as lion-like heroes (cf. KJV, lionlike men), while the NIV renders it as best men (2 Sam. 23:20). ¶

[2] ***ᵃriyʾēl*** [masc. proper noun: אֲרִיאֵל <740>; the same as <739> above]: lion of God ▶

a. This word refers to a Jew in exile in Babylon, a leader of his community, who helped Ezra gather Levites to return to Jerusalem. Ref.: Ezra 8:16. ¶

b. The name was applied to Jerusalem as the chief stronghold and chosen place of the Lord. Refs.: Is. 29:1, 2, 7. ¶

ARIOCH – ***ʾaryôḵ*** [masc. proper noun: אַרְיוֹךְ <746>; of foreign origin] ▶

a. A king in Ellasar who warred with three other kings against five kings in the early days of Abraham. Refs.: Gen. 14:1, 9. The battle was in the Valley of Siddim (see Gen. 14:1–4). ¶

b. The name of a Babylonian officer at Nebuchadnezzar's palace in Babylon. Refs.: Dan. 2:14, 15, 24, 25. He was the overseer of the king's guard who would have been in charge of executing the wise men of Babylon (see Dan. 2:1–25). ¶

ARISAI – ***ᵃriysay*** [masc. proper noun: אֲרִיסַי <747>; of Persian origin]: like a lion ▶ **One of the sons of Haman, the enemy of the Jews at the time of Esther.** Ref.: Esther 9:9. ¶

ARISE – ***šôʾ, šôʾāh, šōʾāh*** [verb: שׁוֹא, שׁוֹאָה, שֹׁאָה <7721>; from an unused root (akin to CARRY <5375> and RAVAGE (noun) <7722>)] ▶ **This word means to lift up; it is also translated to rise, to mount up.** It is used in its infinitive construct form to indicate the rising of the waves of the sea before they fall (Ps. 89:9). ¶

ARK – [1] ***ʾārôn, ʾārōn*** [common noun: אָרוֹן, אָרֹן <727>; from PICK (verb) <717> (in the sense of gathering)] ▶ **This word means a box, a chest, a coffin. It is treated as masculine in some passages and as feminine in others.** It refers to the chest for collecting money offerings (2 Kgs. 12:9, 10); or the sarcophagus in which the mummy of Joseph was placed (Gen. 50:26). In a sacred or cultic context, the term identifies the ark of the covenant (Num. 10:33), which at one time contained the tablets of the law (Deut. 10:5); a copy of the Law which Moses had written (Deut. 31:26); a pot of manna (Ex. 16:33, 34); Aaron's rod (Num. 17:10). This word is often used with another word to denote the ark of the covenant: "the ark of the LORD your God"

(Josh. 4:5); "the ark of God" (1 Sam. 3:3); "the ark of the God of Israel" (1 Sam. 5:7); "the holy ark" (2 Chr. 35:3). *
2 ***têḇāh*** [fem. noun: תֵּבָה <8392>; perhaps of foreign deriv.] ▶ **This word is used to depict Noah' vessel and Moses' basket.** Refs.: Gen. 6:14–16; 9:10, 18; Ex. 2:3, 5. In both cases, persons were rescued from water. *

ARKITE – ***'arqiy*** [proper noun: עַרְקִי <6208>; uncertain etymology] ▶ **A tribe whose ancestor was Canaan or an inhabitant of Erek or Arqa.** Refs.: Gen. 10:17; 1 Chr. 1:15. ¶

ARM – 1 ***'ezrôa'*** [fem. noun: אֶזְרוֹעַ <248>; a variation for <2220> below] ▶ **Upper limb of the body, connecting the shoulder and hand.** This word refers to the Lord's outstretched arm (Jer. 32:21), and to Job's pitiful plea concerning his condition and his feeble arm (Job 31:22). ¶
2 ***d^erā'*** [Aramaic fem. noun: דְּרָע <1872>; corresponding to <2220> below] ▶ **This word designates the silver upper limbs on the statue of Nebuchadnezzar's dream.** Ref.: Dan. 2:32. ¶
3 ***z^erôa', z^erōa'*** [fem. noun: זְרוֹעַ, זְרֹעַ <2220>; from SOW <2232>] ▶ **See <248> above. This word also refers to power, strength, might.** It indicates the arm of a person (Judg. 15:14; 16:12; 2 Sam. 1:10). It is used figuratively often of the Lord's arm: the Lord's arms guided and led Ephraim (Hos. 11:3). The arm often stood for the strength or power of humans or God: of God (2 Sam. 22:35; Ps. 18:34); of people (Job 26:2). Its most significant theological use is to depict the Lord's arm, His strength and power as His instruments of deliverance or even judgment; an arm stretched out (Ex. 15:16; Deut. 4:34; 5:15; 26:8; Ps. 136:12; Jer. 21:5; Ezek. 20:33, 34). But His outstretched arm and great power were forces that created the heavens and the earth (Jer. 27:5). As a good shepherd, His strong arm cares for His sheep (Is. 40:11). The arm became a symbol of might and power of human (1 Sam. 2:31) or divine strength (Ps. 71:18). It stands for the military forces of the king of the South in Daniel 11:15 and of the king of the North (Dan. 11:31). It clearly refers to the shoulder of a sacrificial ram as well (Num. 6:19). *
– 4 Ps. 65:6 → GIRD <247>.

ARMED – Josh. 1:14; 4:12; Judg. 7:11 → BATTLE (EQUIPPED FOR, ARRAYED FOR) <2571>.

ARMED (FULLY) – Ezek. 38:4 → SPLENDIDLY <4358>.

ARMLET – 1 ***'eṣ'āḏāh*** [fem. noun: אֶצְעָדָה <685>; a variation from MARCHING <6807>] ▶ **This word refers to a narrow band worn on the arm; it is also translated bracelet, chain.** This item is mentioned as booty found after Israel defeated Midian and was presented to the high priest (Num. 31:50). It may refer to a "pace chain," a chain between the ankles. Elsewhere it refers to an armlet (2 Sam. 1:10) that clasped the upper arm. ¶
– 2 Is. 3:20 → MARCHING <6807> b.

ARMONI – ***'armōniy*** [masc. proper noun: אַרְמֹנִי <764>; from STRONGHOLD <759> (i.e., palace)]: belonging to the palace ▶ **One of the sons of Saul who was put to death by the Gibeonites.** Ref.: 2 Sam. 21:8. ¶

ARMOR – 1 ***zōnôṯ*** [fem. noun: זֹנוֹת <2185>; regarded by some as if from WELL-FED <2109> or an unused root, and applied to military equipment] ▶
a. The word refers to military protective equipment. It is taken to mean Ahab's armor by some translators (1 Kgs. 22:38, KJV). ¶
b. The word also refers to a prostitute. It indicates the prostitutes who bathed at the pool of Samaria where Ahab's chariot was washed after he was slain (1 Kgs. 22:38, ESV, NASB, NIV, NKJV). ¶
2 ***siryôn*** [masc. noun: סִרְיֹן <5630>; for ARMOR <8302>] ▶ **It is part of a warrior's outfit, a heavy protective armor for defensive purposes. This word is also translated scale-armor, brigandines.** Refs.: Jer. 46:4; 51:3. ¶

[3] ***širyôn, širyān, širyāh*** [שִׁרְיוֹן, שִׁרְיָן, שִׁרְיָה <8302>; from LOOSE (LET) <8281> in the original sense of turning] ▶
a. A masculine noun indicating a protective covering to prevent injury to the body; a breastplate. It refers to scale armor worn as protective gear (1 Sam. 17:5, 38). It was still vulnerable at various points (1 Kgs. 22:34; 2 Chr. 18:33; 26:14). It may refer to a small version of this armor, a breastplate (Neh. 4:16). It is used as a figure of righteousness serving as a breastplate or scale armor (Is. 59:17).
b. A feminine noun referring to protective covering for the body. It is rendered as javelin (NASB, NIV) or habergeon (armor) (KJV). In all cases, it refers to the protective coverings of Leviathan (Job 41:26).
c. A masculine noun indicating a javelin. It is rendered as a javelin, a sharp throwing instrument or weapon (Job 41:26, NIV, NASB). See b. ¶
– [4] 1 Sam. 17:6 ➔ GREAVES <4697> [5] 1 Sam. 17:38, 39 ➔ CLOTHES <4055> [6] Job 41:13 ➔ BRIDLE <7448> b. [7] Is. 8:9: to strap on the armor ➔ GIRD <247>.

ARMOR (IN FULL) – Ezek. 23:12; 38:4 ➔ SPLENDIDLY <4358>.

ARMOR, ARMOUR – 2 Sam. 2:21 ➔ SPOIL (noun) <2488>.

ARMORY – Song 4:4 ➔ ROW OF STONES <8530>.

ARMOUR (WITH ALL SORTS OF) – Ezek. 38:4 ➔ SPLENDIDLY <4358>.

ARMPIT – Jer. 38:12 ➔ WRIST <679>.

ARMS – [1] Ps. 129:7 ➔ BOSOM <2683> [2] Ps. 129:7; Is. 49:22 ➔ BOSOM <2684>.

ARMY – [1] ***'alqûm*** [אַלְקוּם <510>; prob. from NO <408> and STAND, STAND UP <6965> (i.e., no uprising)] ▶
a. A masculine noun describing troops, a band of soldiers, military levy. Ref.: Prov. 30:31. The presence of a royal army or troops causes the king to overflow with pride (NASB, NIV, NKJV; see b.). ¶
b. Possibly a compound noun meaning no uprising or no adversary. Ref.: Prov. 30:31, KJV; see a. ¶
[2] ***ma'ᵃrāh*** [fem. noun: מַעֲרָה <4630>; fem. of MEADOW (place) <4629> (in the sense of an open spot)] ▶ **This word refers to a group of men prepared and ready to fight for their country or people.** Ref.: 1 Sam. 17:23; also translated rank, line. Some prefer to read this as a specific place or location. ¶
– [3] 1 Sam. 17:10, 45 ➔ ARRAY (noun) <4634> [4] Zech. 9:8 ➔ GARRISON <4675> [5] See CAMP <4264>.

ARNAN – ***'arnān*** [masc. proper noun: אַרְנָן <770>; prob. from the same as ARNON <769>]: agile, strong ▶ **An Israelite, probably a descendant of David.** Ref.: 1 Chr. 3:21. ¶

ARNON – ***'arnôn*** [proper noun: אַרְנוֹן <769>; from SHOUT (verb) <7442>]: tumultuous, impetuous ▶ **This word designates a river that bounded Moab on the north and the land of the Amorites on the south.** Refs.: Num. 21:13–15. It was a boundary of Reuben later in Israel's history. It flows west into the Dead Sea almost opposite Ein-Gedi. *

AROD – ***'ᵃrôḏ*** [masc. proper noun: אֲרוֹד <720>; an orthographical variation of ARVAD <719>]: fugitive, my posterity ▶ **One of the sons of Gad and founder of a family.** Refs.: Gen. 46:16 (spelled Arodi); Num. 26:17. ¶

ARODI – [1] ***'ᵃrôḏiy*** [masc. proper noun: אֲרוֹדִי <722>; patron. from ARVADITE <721>]: fugitive, my posterity ▶
a. A son of Gad. Ref.: Gen. 46:16. ¶
b. A son of Arod. Ref.: Num. 26:17. ¶
– [2] Gen. 46:16 ➔ AROD <720>.

AROER – ***'ᵃrô'ēr, 'ᵃrō'ēr, 'ar'ôr*** [proper noun: עֲרוֹעֵר, עֲרֹעֵר, עַרְעוֹר <6177>; the same as SHRUB <6176>]: nudity ▶
a. A city on the Arnon River in Transjordan. It was located near the Arnon Gorge (2 Kgs. 10:33). The river was the southern

border of Sihon's kingdom. The city was inherited by the tribe of Reuben (Josh. 12:2; 13:9, 16; 1 Chr. 5:8). The Gadites had helped construct the city (Num. 32:34). In the time of Jephthah, Israel had owned the city for three hundred years (Judg. 11:26). Jeremiah mentions the effect of God's judgments on its inhabitants (Jer. 48:19). *

b. A city near Rabbah. Ref.: Josh. 13:25. ¶

c. A city in southern Judah. Ref.: 1 Sam. 30:28. ¶

AROERITE – ***ᵃrō'ēriy*** [proper noun: עֲרֹעֵרִי <6200>; patron. from AROER <6177>] ▶ **An inhabitant of Aroer (<6177>).** Ref.: 1 Chr. 11:44. ¶

AROMATIC RESIN – Gen. 2:12; Num. 11:7 ➔ BDELLIUM <916>.

AROUND – ***mêsab̲, misbāh*** [masc. noun: מֵסַב, מְסִבָּה <4524>; from AROUND (GO) <5437>] ▶ **This word means the surrounding area.** It is used adverbially as well, meaning around about an object or all over it (1 Kgs. 6:29). It designates the surrounding territory of a city (2 Kgs. 23:5); with a suffix on the end (*mᵉsibbiy*), it means all around a person, surrounding him or her (Ps. 140:9); or around, surrounding it, i.e., a table (or couch) (Song 1:12). Other ref.: Job 37:12. ¶

AROUND (GO, TURN) – ***sāb̲ab̲*** [verb: סָבַב <5437>; a prim. root] ▶ **This word also means to surround; to turn back, to change.** It indicates a curving motion or an encircling motion of something, but it is used figuratively as well: to turn, to change direction (1 Sam. 15:12); to encircle or flow around about, throughout (Gen. 2:11, 13); to surround something (Gen. 19:4); to gather people around a central person or object (Gen. 37:7); to travel round about (Ex. 13:18). It indicates a surrounding setting prepared by a jeweler to receive jewels, etc. (Ex. 28:11). It refers to the motion of something that turns or moves about: a door (Prov. 26:14); the wind in its circuits (Eccl. 1:6). It is used metaphorically of a person's mind turning, its attention focusing (Eccl. 7:25); of Jerusalem opening like a door (Ezek. 26:2). It indicates the transforming of a matter, the changing of a matter (2 Sam. 14:20). It indicates the giving over, the turning over of something in its causative forms (1 Chr. 10:14); of changing a name (2 Kgs. 23:34); or of the features of a land being transformed, changed (Zech. 14:10). It describes boundaries that turn around (Num. 34:4, 5; Josh. 18:14). *

AROUSED (BE) – Hos. 11:8 ➔ YEARN <3648>.

ARPAD – ***'arpād̲*** [proper noun: אַרְפָּד <774>; from SPREAD, SPREAD OUT <7502>]: spread out ▶ **This word refers to a city in a province in northern Syria conquered by the Assyrians near Hamanth.** Refs.: 2 Kgs. 18:34; 19:13. It is Tell Eafad, north of modern Aleppo. It was judged severely by the Lord (Is. 10:9) and fell to Assyria. Other refs.: Is. 36:19; 37:13; Jer. 49:23. ¶

ARPHAXAD – ***'arpak̲šad̲*** [masc. proper noun: אַרְפַּכְשַׁד <775>; prob. of foreign origin] ▶ **One of the sons of Shem.** Refs.: Gen. 10:22, 24; 11:10–13; 1 Chr. 1:17, 18, 24. ¶

ARRANGE – 1 ***'ārak̲*** [verb: עָרַךְ <6186>; a prim. root] ▶ **This word means to set in order, to prepare. It is used of organizing or preparing something for various reasons.** As a technical military term, it means to prepare for battle, to get in battle array (Gen. 14:8); to be ready, to set up for battle (Jer. 6:23; Joel 2:5); to organize, to lay something out in order (Gen. 22:9; Lev. 24:8; Num. 23:4); to dress lamps, to care for them (Ex. 27:21); to arrange items on a table (Ex. 40:4, 23; Is. 21:5). It is used figuratively of the terrors or words of the Lord set out, prepared against someone (Job 6:4; 32:14); of preparing an argument or legal case (Job 13:18). It describes the presentation of prayer to the Lord (Ps. 5:3); of the Lord's preparation of a meal, a table for His children (Ps. 23:5; 78:19). It is used of Lady Wisdom's preparation of a table of wisdom

for those who seek her (Prov. 9:2). The word is used to describe what has been prepared by God for judgment, Topheth, a place of human sacrifice (Is. 30:33). The Hebrew word also means to value, to judge the quality; see VALUE (verb) <6186>. *
– 2 Eccl. 12:9 ➔ STRAIGHT (MAKE) <8626>.

ARRANGEMENT – 1 ***pᵉquddāh*** [fem. noun: פְּקֻדָּה <6486>; fem. pass. part. of ATTEND <6485>] ▶ **The root idea of this word is something that is attended to or set in order. This word also means an office, an officer, accounting.** The word signifies the arrangement of fighting men under an officer (2 Chr. 17:14), of priests or Levites in an order (1 Chr. 23:11; 24:19); or the arrangement of the Tabernacle and its contents (Num. 4:16). It signifies the office of one in charge of something (Ps. 109:8); and the officers themselves (2 Kgs. 11:18; Is. 60:17). Most often, the word means accounting and refers to a time of accounting when God attended to people's actions, usually to call them to account for their sins (Num. 16:29; Jer. 48:44). In Job 10:12, however, God's attention was for Job's good. *
2 ***tᵉḵûnāh*** [fem. noun: תְּכוּנָה <8498>; fem. pass. part. of WEIGH <8505> (in the sense of to be equal)] ▶
a. This word refers to a pattern and to a treasure. It refers to the layout and organization of the Temple envisioned by Ezekiel (43:11; KJV: fashion). With reference to plunder, it has the sense of a kind of merchandise or valuables (treasures) (Nah. 2:9; KJV: store).
b. This word also refers to a seat; a place of dwelling. It refers to the place or location established where someone is. In context, it depicts God's dwelling or location (Job 23:3). ¶

ARRAY (noun) – ***maᵃrāḵāh*** [fem. noun: מַעֲרָכָה <4634>; from PLAN (verb) <4633>] ▶ **This word means rank, an orderly formation, a battle line.** It is used of the ordered array of an army ready to fight (1 Sam. 4:2, 12, 16; 17:22). Sometimes it refers to the orderly battle itself (1 Sam. 17:20). It indicates the ranks or sections of an army (1 Sam. 17:10, 45), especially the ranks or battalions of the living God (1 Sam. 17:26, 36). It is used of an orderly array of various objects, e.g., lamps (Ex. 39:37; Lev. 24:6). *

ARRAY (verb) – Is. 61:10 ➔ COVER (verb) <3271>.

ARRIVE – See COME <857>.

ARROGANCE – 1 ***ʿāṯāq*** [adj.: עָתָק <6277>; from MOVE <6275> in the sense of license] ▶ **This Hebrew word means impudent and refers to pride, insolence.** It identifies an act and attitude of unwarranted or excessive pride, self-importance (1 Sam. 2:3; KJV: arrogancy). Or it means to speak against someone, especially a righteous person in a disrespectful or harmful way (Ps. 31:18: grievous things, insolent things, arrogantly, insolently). It describes pride as especially arrogant or insolent (Ps. 75:5: stiff, insolent, haughty, defiantly). Especially the arrogant wicked pour out insolent speech (Ps. 94:4: insolent things, arrogantly, hard things, arrogant words). ¶
– 2 1 Sam. 15:23 ➔ PRESS <6484> 3 2 Kgs. 19:28; Is. 37:29 ➔ EASE (AT) <7600> b. 4 Is. 2:17 ➔ LOFTINESS <1365> 5 Jer. 49:16; 50:31, 32; Ezek. 7:10; Obad. 1:3 ➔ PRIDE <2087>.

ARROGANCE (WITH) – Ps. 17:10 ➔ MAJESTY <1348>.

ARROGANCY – 1 Sam. 2:3 ➔ ARROGANCE <6277>.

ARROGANT – 1 Ps. 86:14; 119:21, 51, 69, 78, 85, 122; Prov. 21:24; Is. 13:11; Jer. 43:2; Mal. 3:15; 4:1 ➔ PROUD <2086> 2 Ps. 101:5; Prov. 16:5 ➔ PROUD <1362> 3 Ps. 123:4 ➔ EASE (AT) <7600> b. 4 Prov. 21:24; Hab. 2:5 ➔ HAUGHTY <3093> 5 Is. 2:11 ➔ LOFTINESS <1365> 6 Is. 33:19 ➔ FIERCE <3267>.

ARROGANT (BECOME) – Dan. 5:20 ➔ EXALT <7313>.

ARROGANT WORDS – Ps. 94:4 ➔ ARROGANCE <6277>.

ARROGANTLY – [1] Ps. 17:10 ➔ MAJESTY <1348> [2] Ps. 31:18; 94:4 ➔ ARROGANCE <6277>.

ARROW – [1] ***ḥēṣ*** [masc. noun: חֵץ <2671>; from DIVIDE <2686> b. (in the sense of to shoot arrows)] ▶ **This word denotes a hunting and military missile shot from a bow.** The Lord's arrows (Num. 24:8; Deut. 32:23, 42) were His judgments; or even His Messianic ruler sent by Him (Ps. 45:5). His arrow of deliverance for His people was like lightning (Zech. 9:14). The wickedness and harmful words of evil persons are described as arrows of violence (Ps. 11:2; 64:3; 91:5; Prov. 25:18). A fool's or demented person's words are described as arrows, firebrands, and even death (Prov. 26:18). Isaiah's Servant of the Lord is His choice arrow (Is. 49:2). Jeremiah describes himself as the target of the Lord's arrow of judgment (Lam. 3:12). *
[2] ***ḥēṣiy*** [masc. noun: חֵצִי <2678>; prolongation from ARROW <2671>] ▶ **This word indicates a piercing missile shot from a bow.** It was a sign to David (1 Sam. 20:36–38). It designates the slender shaft from Jehu's bow that killed Joram, king of Israel (2 Kgs. 9:24). ¶
– [3] Job 16:13 ➔ ARCHER <7228>.

ARTAXERXES – ***'artaḥšaśtā'*** [masc. proper noun: אַרְתַּחְשַׁשְׂתָּא <783>; of foreign origin] ▶ **This is the name of the Persian king, Artaxerxes I, who ruled 465–424 B.C.** Refs.: Ezra 4:7, 8. He stopped the work on Jerusalem's city walls (Ezra 4:18–23). Ezra returned to Jerusalem in his reign (Ezra 7:1–7) about 458 B.C. Under Ezra, Artaxerxes prospered Ezra's work and the Law of God (Ezra 7:13–28). He permitted Nehemiah to return to Jerusalem to build its walls (Neh. 2:1–10) and become governor there (Neh. 5:14). Nehemiah returned to Persia in ca. 433 B.C. for a while (Neh. 13:6). ¶

ARTICLE – [1] ***kᵉliy*** [masc. noun: כְּלִי <3627>; from FINISH <3615> (in the sense of something prepared)] ▶ **This word indicates a vessel, an instrument, a jewel. It has a broad inclusive sense and indicates useful objects of all kinds. The context must determine what object is indicated and for what task.** It refers to vessels, receptacles of all kinds (Gen. 31:37; Lev. 6:28; 11:32–34; 2 Sam. 17:28); for storing (Jer. 32:14). It indicates implements, ornaments, various kinds of equipment and utensils (Gen. 24:53; 27:3; 45:20; 49:5; 1 Sam. 8:12; 17:22; 2 Sam. 24:22; 2 Kgs. 23:4; Ezek. 40:42; Jon. 1:5). It even refers to articles of clothing or weapons (Deut. 22:5; 2 Kgs. 7:15). *
– [2] Ezra 5:14, 15; 6:5; 7:19 ➔ VESSEL <3984>.

ARTIFICER – Gen. 4:22 ➔ CRAFTSMAN <2794>.

ARTISAN – [1] 2 Kgs. 24:14, 16; Jer. 24:1; 29:2 ➔ SMITH <4525> [2] Jer. 52:15 ➔ CRAFTSMAN <527>.

ARTIST – ***'ommān*** [masc. noun: אָמָּן <542>; from NURSE (verb) <539> (in the sense of training)] ▶ **This word means an artificer, an expert artisan; it also indicates a craftsman. It is also translated skillful workman, cunning workman, master.** It indicates the person who produces a work of skill and beauty (Song 7:1). ¶

ARUBBOTH – ***ᵃrubbôṯ*** [proper noun: אֲרֻבּוֹת <700>; plur. of WINDOW <699>]: opening, lattices ▶ **A place situated probably in Judah.** Ref.: 1 Kgs. 4:10. ¶

ARUMAH – ***ᵃrûmāh*** [proper noun: אֲרוּמָה <725>; a variation of RUMAH <7316>]: heights ▶ **A village near Sichem.** Ref.: Judg. 9:41. ¶

ARVAD – ***'arwaḏ*** [proper noun: אַרְוַד <719>; prob. from RESTLESS (BE) <7300>]: place of the fugitives, wandering ▶ **A city of Phoenicia.** Refs.: Ezek. 27:8, 11. ¶

ARVADITE – ***'arwāḏiy*** [masc. proper noun: אַרְוָדִי <721>; patrial from ARVAD

<719>] ▶ **An inhabitant of Arvad.** Refs.: Gen. 10:18; 1 Chr. 1:16. ¶

ARZA – ***'arṣā'*** [masc. proper noun: אַרְצָא <777>; from EARTH <776>]: ground, firm ▶ **A palace administrator of King Elah at Tirzah.** Ref.: 1 Kgs. 16:9. ¶

ASA – ***'āsā'*** [masc. proper noun: אָסָא <609>; of uncertain deriv.]: one who heals ▶
a. The name of a good king in Judah. He was the third king in Judah after the monarchy. He was the grandson of Rehoboam. His mother (or grandmother) was Maacah (1 Kgs. 15:9, 10). He was evaluated as a good king who followed the Lord. He ruled forty-one years (910–869 B.C.) He did not remove the high places (1 Kgs. 15:9–14). He warred with Baasha, king of Israel, but overcame him by making a treaty with Ben-Hadad of Aram (1 Kgs. 15:18–22). He built fortifications in Judah (Jer. 41:9). He was diseased in his feet during his old age (1 Kgs. 15:23, 24). Jehoshaphat, his son, succeeded him. *
b. A Levite, a son of Elkanah, who returned from exile to Jerusalem. Ref.: 1 Chr. 9:16. ¶

ASAHEL – ***'ᵃśāh'êl*** [masc. proper noun: עֲשָׂהאֵל <6214>; from DO <6212> and GOD <410>]: God has made ▶
a. A son of Zeruiah, David's sister. He was killed by Abner, son of Ner, Saul's military commander (2 Sam. 2:8, 18–23). He was the brother of Joab, David's military commander. Joab killed Abner because of his murder of Asahel (2 Sam. 3:27, 30). He was one of David's mighty men (2 Sam. 23:24). *
b. The father of Jonathan who opposed Ezra's plans to deal with intermarriages. Ref.: Ezra 10:15. ¶
c. One of the men Jehoshaphat appointed to teach the Law of God throughout Judah. Ref.: 2 Chr. 17:8. ¶
d. A Levite whom Hezekiah appointed to oversee the collection of tithes in the Temple. Ref.: 2 Chr. 31:13. ¶

ASAIAH – ***'ᵃśāyāh*** [masc. proper noun: עֲשָׂיָה <6222>; from DO <6213> and LORD <3050>]: made by the Lord ▶
a. A prince of the tribe of Simeon. Ref.: 1 Chr. 4:36. ¶
b. A Levite, chief of a Merarite family, in the time of David. Refs.: 1 Chr. 6:30; 15:6, 11. ¶
c. A man of the tribe of Judah who returned to Jerusalem after the captivity. Ref.: 1 Chr. 9:5. ¶
d. A servant of King Josiah. He was sent to Huldah the prophetess to inquire of the Lord about the Book of the Law (2 Kgs. 22:12, 14; 2 Chr. 34:20). ¶

ASAPH – ***'āsāp̱*** [masc. proper noun: אָסָף <623>; from GATHER <622>]: gatherer, convener ▶
a. He was one of David's chief music leaders. Son of Berachiah (1 Chr. 6:39) and a Levite (1 Chr. 15:17). He sounded the bronze cymbals. He ministered before the ark of God (1 Chr. 16:5). His sons were appointed to various duties by David (1 Chr. 25:1). He composed many psalms (Ps. 50; 73–83). The singers at the Temple under Ezra were descendants of Asaph (Ezra 2:41). His descendants helped dedicate the new Temple (Ezra 3:10) and the wall (Neh. 12:35, 36). *
b. An Asaph was the father of King Hezekiah's secretary, Joah, an important official position. Refs.: 2 Kgs. 18:17, 18. *
c. Forefather of a Korahite who served as a gatekeeper. Ref.: 1 Chr. 26:1. ¶
d. It designates a person who cared for the Persian king's forests. He gave Nehemiah timber for work in Jerusalem (Neh. 2:8, 9). ¶
e. It refers to a Levite who lived in Jerusalem on the return from the Babylonian exile. Ref.: Neh. 11:17. ¶

ASAREL – ***'ᵃśar'êl*** [masc. proper noun: אֲשַׂרְאֵל <840>; by orthographical variation from BLESS <833> and GOD <410>]: kept by God ▶ **An Israelite of the tribe of Judah.** Ref.: 1 Chr. 4:16. ¶

ASARELAH – [1] ***'ᵃśar'êlāh*** [masc. proper noun: אֲשַׂרְאֵלָה <841>; from the same as ASAREL <840>]: right towards God ▶ **One of the sons of Asaph.** Ref.: 1 Chr. 25:2. ¶

– [2] 1 Chr. 25:2 ➔ JESHARELAH <3480>.

ASCEND – [1] ***nāsaq*** [verb: נָסַק <5266>; a prim. root] ▶ **This word means to go upward.** It is used figuratively of ascending to God in heaven to His abode (Ps. 139:8). ¶
– [2] Ps. 139:8 ➔ GO UP <5559> a.

ASCENT – [1] ***ma'leh*** [masc. noun: מַעֲלֶה <4608>; from OFFER <5927> (in the sense of to lift)] ▶
a. A masculine noun meaning a place by which one goes up. In general it refers to a gradual feature of the land, an upward grade, as well as an upward pathway or roadway. Refs.: Num. 34:4; Josh. 10:10; 15:3, 7; 18:17; Judg. 1:36; 8:13; Is. 15:5. It indicates a man-made way of ascent or stairway (Ezek. 40:31, 34, 37). It is used for a raised platform or podium (Neh. 9:4); or of the upper levels of structures (2 Chr. 32:33). ¶
b. A masculine proper noun meaning a place by which one goes up. This represents merely a capitalization of the noun ascent or pass to include it in the proper name of the Pass of Adummin. Refs.: Josh. 15:7; 18:17. Not all translators do this. ¶
[2] ***ma'lāh*** [fem. noun: מַעֲלָה <4609>; fem. of <4608> above (in the sense of to lift)] ▶
a. A word meaning a step, a degree; lit.: journey to a higher place. It is used of a step or stair (Ex. 20:26; 1 Kgs. 10:19, 20; 2 Kgs. 9:13; Neh. 3:15; 12:37), especially of steps in Ezekiel's Temple vision (Ezek. 40:6, etc.). Amos 9:6 uses the word figuratively to refer to upper levels, chambers, rooms in God's habitations. The word is used in Psalms 120–134 in the titles to designate these as Songs of Ascent, indicating the pilgrimage of persons up to the city of Jerusalem. It is used of the "going up" out of Babylonian captivity (Ezra 7:9). *
b. A word meaning thought. It refers to something that is rising or arising. In context with *rûḥakem*, thoughts or ideas, it means ascending spirits, ascending thoughts (Ezek. 11:5). *

ASENATH – ***'āsenat*** [fem. proper noun: אָסְנַת <621>; of Egyptian deriv.]: dedicated to Neith (an Egyptian goddess) ▶ **Wife of Joseph, mother of Manasseh and Ephraim.** Refs.: Gen. 41:45, 50; 46:20. ¶

ASH – ***'ōren*** [masc. noun: אֹרֶן <766>; from the same as ARAN <765> (in the sense of strength)] ▶ **This word refers to a tree; it is also translated fir, pine, cedar.** It is found only in Isaiah 44:14. The words depicting ancient trees in Scripture are difficult to decipher with certainty. ¶

ASH HEAP – ***'ašpōt̲, 'ašpôt̲*** [masc. noun: אַשְׁפֹּת, אַשְׁפּוֹת <830>; plur. of a noun of the same form as QUIVER <827>, from STICK OUT <8192> (in the sense of scraping)] ▶ **This word means a pile of rubbish or filth; it is also translated dung hill, refuse heap, dump.** It is used in poetry to describe the condition of the needy (poor) (1 Sam. 2:8; Ps. 113:7). It depicts, most likely, a dump or dung hill during the time of Jeremiah (Lam. 4:5). It describes the Refuse or Dung Gate during the time of Nehemiah (Neh. 2:13; 3:13, 14; 12:31). ¶

ASH PIT – Lam. 4:5 ➔ ASH HEAP <830>.

ASHAMED (BE) – [1] ***bôš*** [verb: בּוֹשׁ <954>; a prim. root] ▶ **This word means to be conscience-stricken, to be embarrassed, to be humiliated. It also means to act shamefully, or to put to shame.** It is both an external and a subjective experience, ranging from disgrace (Hos. 10:6) to guilt (Ezra 9:6). In Genesis 2:25, shame is related to the sexual nature of humans. Moreover, to act shamefully is equivalent to acting unwisely (Prov. 10:5; 14:35). To be ashamed is to experience distress, as farmers with no harvest (Jer. 14:4; Joel 1:11), but the blessing of God means that one will never be put to shame (Ps. 25:20; Joel 2:26, 27). *
[2] ***ḥāpêr*** [stative verb: חָפֵר <2659>; a prim. root] ▶ **This word refers to a state of embarrassment, humiliation. It also means to be disgraced.** Those who trust the

Lord and look to Him will not experience shame (Ps. 34:5). It is a state the righteous psalmist often calls down on his enemies (Ps. 35:4, 26; 40:14; 70:2; 71:24; 83:17). It often parallels Hebrew *bôš*, shame; to be ashamed. Those who worship idols or who are diviners will be caught in shame (Is. 1:29; Mic. 3:7). It is used figuratively of the moon being shamed (Is. 24:23); or of Lebanon being abashed (Is. 33:9). It is used of the shame of Israel that the Lord will remove (Is. 54:4) but also of the shame and humiliation of a wicked Jerusalem (Jer. 15:9). Wicked Babylon will be abashed, shamed (Jer. 50:12). It refers to caravans being put to a shameful disappointment (Job 6:20). It depicts the customary, shameful actions of an evil person (Prov. 13:5). Other ref.: Is. 33:9. ¶

3 ***kālam*** [verb: כָּלַם <3637>; a prim. root] ▶ **This word means to be humiliated. It describes also to be disgraced; to blush.** It refers to an act that humiliates a person (2 Sam. 10:5); or an abuse or attack of words (Job 11:3). A person's own character or behavior can cause shame (2 Sam. 19:3; Jer. 14:3). In some of its causative uses, it refers to disgracing or shaming someone (1 Sam. 20:34; 25:15; Prov. 28:7); or it may indicate the mistreatment of animals (1 Sam. 25:7). The Lord's help for His servant was enough to preserve him from disgrace or confusion (Is. 50:7). The word is used of a formal sentence and a time of social disgrace (Num. 12:14). In Judges 18:7, it takes on a sense of not lacking or being in want; it was a prosperous land in every way. *

ASHAN – ***'āšān*** [proper noun: עָשָׁן <6228>; the same as SMOKE (noun) <6227>]: smoke; anger ▶ **A city belonging to the tribe of Judah and given later to the tribe of Simeon.** Refs.: Josh. 15:42; 19:7; 1 Chr. 4:32; 6:59. ¶

ASHARELAH – 1 Chr. 25:2 ➔ JESHARELAH <3480>.

ASHBEA – ***'ašbêa'*** [masc. proper noun: אַשְׁבֵּעַ <791>; from SWEAR <7650>]: adjurer, man of Baal ▶ **An Israelite of the tribe of Judah.** Ref.: 1 Chr. 4:21. ¶

ASHBEL – ***'ašbêl*** [masc. proper noun: אַשְׁבֵּל <788>; prob. from the same as SKIRT <7640>]: vanity, man of Baal ▶ **Second son of Benjamin.** Refs.: Gen. 46:21; Num. 26:38; 1 Chr. 8:1. ¶

ASHBELITE – ***'ašbêliy*** [masc. proper noun: אַשְׁבֵּלִי <789>; patron. from ASHBEL <788>] ▶ **A descendant of Ashbel.** Ref.: Num. 26:38. ¶

ASHDOD – ***'ašdôḏ*** [proper noun: אַשְׁדּוֹד <795>; from DESTROY <7703>]: strong to oppress, fortress ▶ **A Philistine city.** Ref.: Josh. 11:22. Joshua fought against it as one of the five major Philistine cities (Gaza, Ashdod, Ashkelon, Gath, Ekron [Josh. 13:3]). The ark of God lodged there in Dagon's temple (1 Sam. 5:1–7) but was moved from there because of the Lord's curse on Ashdod (cf. 1 Sam. 5:3–12). The Assyrians conquered it under Sargon (Is. 20:1). God judged Ashdod harshly (Jer. 25:20; Amos 1:8; Zeph. 2:4; Zech. 9:6). *

ASHDOD (LANGUAGE OF) – ***'ašdôḏiyṯ*** [proper noun: אַשְׁדּוֹדִית <797>; fem. of ASHDODITE <796>] ▶ **This word refers to the local speech (or dialect) current in the city of Ashdod on the shore of the Mediterranean Sea.** Israelites, through improper marriages with these people, were speaking this language (Neh. 13:24). ¶

ASHDODITE – ***'ašdôḏiy*** [masc. proper noun: אַשְׁדּוֹדִי <796>; patrial from ASHDOD <795>] ▶ **An inhabitant of Ashdod or someone native from this city.** Refs.: Josh. 13:3; 1 Sam. 5:3, 6; Neh. 4:7; 13:23. ¶

ASHDOTHPISGAH – ***'ašdôṯ happisgāh*** [proper noun: אַשְׁדוֹת הַפִּסְגָּה <798>; from the plur. of SLOPE <794> and PISGAH <6449> with the art. interposed]: ravines of the Pisgah ▶ **A place east of the Jordan.** Refs.: Deut. 3:17; Josh. 12:3; 13:20. ¶

ASHER – ***'āšêr*** [masc. proper noun: אָשֵׁר <836>; from BLESS <833>]: happy, blessed ▶

a. The name of Leah's second son to Jacob through Zilpah. He then had four sons and a daughter (Gen. 46:17; Num. 26:46; 1 Chr. 7:30–40). Jacob blessed Asher and his posterity (Gen. 49:20). *
b. The name is applied to the tribe of Asher in Israel, descended from the son of Jacob (see a.). There were five chief families in Asher (Num. 26:44 ff.). Moses blessed the tribe before his demise (Deut. 33:24). The territory of Asher was bounded on the east by the Mediterranean Sea, and much of its land lay in the Plain of Acco. It reached from Mount Carmel on the south to the Litani River in the north. It was bounded by Manasseh (south), Zebulun (southeast), Naphtali (east), Aram/Lebanon (north). In Ezekiel's vision, Asher is named as bordering Dan (Ezek. 48:2, 3, 34), and the New Jerusalem features a western gate bearing Asher's name. The tribe failed to conquer all of its territory (Judg. 1:31, 32). Unfortunately, Asher did not aid Deborah and Barak (Judg. 5:17). They did fight against the Midianites under Gideon (Judg. 6:35; 7:33). Anna, the prophetess in the New Testament, was from this tribe (Luke 2:36). *

ASHERAH – ***ªšērāh, ªšêyrāh*** [fem. noun: אֲשֵׁרָה, אֲשֵׁירָה <842>; from BLESS <833>] ▶ **This word signifies the Canaanite fertility goddess believed to be the consort of Baal.** Because of this association, the worship of Baal and Asherah was often linked together (Judg. 3:7; 1 Kgs. 18:19; 2 Kgs. 23:4). The noun is most often used for a carved wooden image of the goddess instead of a proper name (Judg. 6:26; 1 Kgs. 14:15). This image was frequently associated with high places and fresh (i.e., green) trees—the latter contributing to the misleading translations of the Septuagint and Vulgate that the word denoted "groves" (Deut. 12:3; 1 Kgs. 14:23; Jer. 17:2). The Israelites were commanded by God to cut down and burn the images (Ex. 34:13; Deut. 12:3), and occasionally the Israelites took steps to eliminate them (1 Kgs. 15:13; 2 Kgs. 23:4, 6, 7). Nevertheless, throughout much of Israel's preexilic history, false worship was a problem, even to the extent that Asherah's image was erected in God's Temple itself (2 Kgs. 21:7; Is. 27:9). *

ASHERITE – ***'āšēriy*** [masc. proper noun: אָשֵׁרִי <843>; patron. from ASHER <836>] ▶ **An Israelite of the tribe of Asher.** Ref.: Judg. 1:32. ¶

ASHEROTH – See ASHERAH <842>.

ASHES – [1] ***'ēper*** [masc. noun: אֵפֶר <665>; from an unused root meaning to bestrew] ▶ **This word means the residue left after burning; it also means soil, dust.** It describes loose soil or dirt put on a person's head to indicate mourning (2 Sam. 13:19; Ezek. 27:30). It is used in the phrase sackcloth and ashes (*saq wā'ēpek*, Is. 58:5; Jon. 3:6). It describes the wicked figuratively as ashes under the feet of the righteous (Ezek. 28:18; Mal. 4:3). Humans are mere dust and ashes (Gen. 18:27). It is used to describe the ashes of the red heifer (Num. 19:9, 10) used in a cleansing ritual. *
[2] ***piyaḥ*** [masc. noun: פִּיחַ <6368>; from BREATHE <6315> (in the sense of something easily puffed away)] ▶ **This word indicates the black carbon particles and other substances left after something has burned; it is also translated soot.** Refs.: Ex. 9:8, 10. Ashes include white or grayish materials left after combustion. ¶
– [3] 1 Kgs. 20:38, 41 ➔ BANDAGE <666> [4] Amos 2:1 ➔ PLASTER (noun) <7875> [5] See FATNESS <1880>.

ASHHUR – ***'ašḥûr*** [masc. proper noun: אַשְׁחוּר <806>; prob. from BLACK (BE) <7835>]: darkness, black ▶ **An Israelite, son of Hezron.** Refs.: 1 Chr. 2:24; 4:5. ¶

ASHIMA – ***ªšiymā'*** [masc. proper noun: אֲשִׁימָא <807>; of foreign origin] ▶ **This is the name of a god(s) set up and worshiped in the deserted land of Samaria.** Ref.: 2 Kgs. 17:30. The people who worshiped this deity came from Hamath and had been resettled in Samaria by the Assyrians. ¶

ASHKELON – ***'ašqᵉlôn*** [proper noun: אַשְׁקְלוֹן <831>; prob. from WEIGH <8254>

in the sense of weighing place (i.e., mart)]: weighing place ▶ **The city was taken by the Judahites in the time of the judges.** Ref.: Judg. 1:18. It was one of the five famous Philistine cities (Judg. 1:18; 14:19). Samson visited the city in anger (Judg. 14:19). It is mentioned in the story of the capture of the ark by the Philistines (1 Sam. 6:17, 18) and in David's lament for Saul. It was an object of God's wrath (Jer. 25:20). *

ASHKELONITE – ***'ešqᵉlôniy*** [masc. proper noun: אֶשְׁקְלוֹנִי <832>; patrial from ASHKELON <831>] ▶ **An inhabitant of Ashkelon.** Ref.: Josh. 13:3. ¶

ASHKENAZ – ***'aškᵉnaz*** [masc. proper noun: אַשְׁכְּנַז <813>; of foreign origin] ▶
a. The name refers to a descendant of Japheth through Gomer. Ref.: Gen. 10:3. Japheth was the third son of Noah (Gen. 10:1). ¶
b. It refers to a people from the north, in this case, from the area north of Babylon on the Euphrates. It probably refers to the Scythians mentioned by the Greek historian Herodotus. Jeremiah calls them to war against and to destroy Babylon (Jer. 51:27). ¶

ASHNAH – ***'ašnāh*** [proper noun: אַשְׁנָה <823>; prob. a variation for JESHANAH <3466>]: hard, fortification ▶
a. A city in Judah. Ref.: Josh. 15:33. ¶
b. Another city in Judah. Ref.: Josh. 15:43. ¶

ASHPENAZ – ***'ašpᵉnaz*** [masc. proper noun: אַשְׁפְּנַז <828>; of foreign origin] ▶ **The chief of the king's eunuchs in Babylon.** Ref.: Dan. 1:3. ¶

ASHTAROTH – ***'aštārôṯ*** [fem. proper noun: עַשְׁתָּרוֹת <6252>; plur. of FLOCKS <6251>] ▶
a. A Canaanite false goddess; the word is also translated Ashtoreth. This was a pagan Canaanite goddess of love, war, and fertility, also called Astarte. Israel often apostatized from the Lord and worshiped her (Judg. 2:13; 10:6; 1 Sam. 7:3, 4; 12:10; 31:10). See Ashtoreth <6253>. ¶
b. A city in Manasseh, the same as *'aštᵉroṯ qarnayim* (Ashteroth Karnaim <6255>). It was the capital city of Og, king of Bashan, and was given to the tribe of Manasseh (Deut. 1:4; Josh. 9:10; 12:4; 13:12, 31; 1 Chr. 6:71). It was located west of the Sea of Galilee. ¶

ASHTERATHITE – ***'aštᵉrāṯiy*** [proper noun: עַשְׁתְּרָתִי <6254>; patrial from ASHTAROTH <6252>] ▶ **An inhabitant of a city in Manasseh (see ASHTAROTH <6252> b.).** Ref.: 1 Chr. 11:44. ¶

ASHTEROTH KARNAIM – ***'aštᵉrōṯ qarnayim*** [proper noun: עַשְׁתְּרֹת קַרְנַיִם <6255>; from ASHTAROTH <6252> and the dual of HORN <7161>]: Ashtaroth of (the) double horns ▶ **A city in Manasseh; same as Ashtaroth (<6252> b.).** Ref.: Gen. 14:5. ¶

ASHTORETH – [1] ***'aštōreṯ*** [fem. proper noun: עַשְׁתֹּרֶת <6253>; prob. for FLOCKS <6251>] ▶ **A Phoenician goddess. A pagan Canaanite goddess (see ASHTAROTH <6252>) of love, war, fertility.** She was worshiped especially by the Sidonians (1 Kgs. 11:5, 33; 2 Kgs. 23:13). ¶
– [2] Judg. 2:13; 10:6; 1 Sam. 7:3, 4; 12:10; 31:10 ➔ ASHTAROTH <6252> a.

ASHURBANIPAL – Ezra 4:10 ➔ OSNAPPAR <620>.

ASHURITES – ***ᵃšuriym*** [masc. plur. proper noun: אֲשֻׁרִים <839>; contr. from BOX TREE <8391>] ▶ **The word is taken as a proper noun indicating the Ashurites, a people not mentioned elsewhere.** Ref.: Ezek. 27:6, KJV, NKJV. The NASB, NIV prefer to translate it as boxwood, cypress wood respectively. ¶

ASHVATH – ***'ašwāṯ*** [masc. proper noun: עַשְׁוָת <6220>; from WROUGHT <6219>]: shining ▶ **A descendant of Abraham through Asher.** Ref.: 1 Chr. 7:33. ¶

ASIDE (GO) – 1 Kgs. 18:27 ➔ DROSS <5509>.

ASIDE (GO, TURN) – ***śāṭāh*** [verb: שָׂטָה <7847>; a prim. root] ▶ **This word means to go away, to go astray.** It means to turn aside from expected behavior or faithfulness, as when a person commits adultery, resulting in a woman's defilement (Num. 5:12, 19, 20, 29). It refers to a man's refusing to be enamored of a prostitute, not going astray after her (Prov. 7:25). It is used of turning away from walking with the wicked (Prov. 4:15). ¶

ASIDE (THAT IS SET) – Josh. 16:9 ➔ SEPARATE (adj.) <3995>.

ASIEL – ***ʿaśiy'ēl*** [masc. proper noun: עֲשִׂיאֵל <6221>; from DO <6213> and GOD <410>]: made by God ▶ **A descendant of Abraham through Simeon.** Ref.: 1 Chr. 4:35. ¶

ASK – [1] ***šā'al*** [verb: שָׁאַל <7592>; a prim. root] ▶ **This word means to enquire, to request. One could appeal to another person or even God for something.** Refs.: 1 Sam. 23:2; Ps. 122:6; 137:3; Eccl. 7:10. People sometimes sought information by asking Urim and Thummim (Num. 27:21), or an occult wooden object (Ezek. 21:21; Hos. 4:12). Asking could be done as a begging request or a stern demand (1 Kgs. 2:16; Job 38:3; Ps. 109:10; Mic. 7:3). The Hebrew expression of asking about someone's peace is similar to the English expression, "How are you?" (Gen. 43:27; Judg. 18:15; Jer. 15:5). Very rarely, the term could refer to borrowing or lending. But this is certainly not the meaning when the people of Israel asked goods from the Egyptians they plundered (Ex. 3:22; 22:14; 1 Sam. 1:28; 2:20; 2 Kgs. 4:3; 6:5). *

[2] ***še'ēl*** [Aramaic verb: שְׁאֵל <7593>; corresponding to <7592> above] ▶ **This word means to demand, to require.** Tattenai, the governor of the province beyond the river, asked the elders of the returned Jews for their names and for the name of the one who authorized their rebuilding of the Temple in Jerusalem (Ezra 5:9, 10). Later on, King Artaxerxes decreed that the treasurers in that same province had to provide whatever Ezra asked of them so that the priestly ministry at the newly rebuilt Temple could be maintained (Ezra 7:21; cf. Dan. 2:10, 11, 27). ¶

– [3] Is. 21:12 ➔ BOIL (verb) <1158> [4] Dan. 6:11 ➔ MERCY (SHOW, ASK FOR) <2604>.

ASLEEP – 1 Sam. 26:7, 12; 1 Kgs. 3:20; 18:27; Song 7:9 ➔ SLEEPING <3463>.

ASLEEP (BE, FALL) – ***rāḏam*** [verb: רָדַם <7290>; a prim. root] ▶ **This word refers to being in a state of deep sleep from exhaustion.** Ref.: Judg. 4:21. It indicates a state of stupor or confusion (Ps. 76:6). It describes a deep sleep or trance of a prophet (Dan. 8:18; 10:9). Other refs.: Prov. 10:5; Jon. 1:5, 6. ¶

ASNAH – ***'asnāh*** [masc. proper noun: אַסְנָה <619>; of uncertain deriv.]: bramble ▶ **One of the Nethinim of which some of the descendants came back from the Babylonian exile.** Ref.: Ezra 2:50. ¶

ASNAPPER – Ezra 4:10 ➔ OSNAPPAR <620>.

ASP – [1] ***peṯen*** [masc. noun: פֶּתֶן <6620>; from an unused root meaning to twist] ▶ **This word refers to a venomous snake; it is also translated cobra, serpent, adder, snake.** It refers to a deadly poisonous snake of Asia and Africa with loose skin around its neck close to its head (Deut. 32:33). Its venom is used to depict the character of the wicked (Job 20:14, 16; Ps. 58:4). The one who trusts God need not fear the poison of the cobra (Ps. 91:13). In the Messianic Age, the cobra will be tame (Is. 11:8). ¶

– [2] Ps. 140:3 ➔ VIPER <5919>.

ASPATHA – ***'aspāṯā'*** [masc. proper noun: אַסְפָּתָא <630>; of Persian deriv.]: drawn from the horse ▶ **One of the sons of Haman.** Ref.: Esther 9:7. ¶

ASPHALT – Gen. 11:3; 14:10; Ex. 2:3 ➔ TAR <2564>.

ASRIEL – ***'aśriy'ēl*** [masc. proper noun: אַשְׂרִיאֵל <844>; an orthographical variation for ASAREL <840>]: dedicated by God ► **An Israelite of the tribe of Manasseh.** Refs.: Num. 26:31; Josh. 17:2; 1 Chr. 7:14. ¶

ASRIELITE – ***'aśri'êliy*** [masc. proper noun: אַשְׂרִאֵלִי <845>; patron. from ASRIEL <844>] ► **A descendant of Asriel.** Ref.: Num. 26:31. ¶

ASS – [1] Gen. 32:15; Job 11:12; etc. ➔ DONKEY <5895> [2] See DONKEY <2543>.

ASS (SHE) – See DONKEY <860>.

ASS (WILD) – See DONKEY (WILD) <6501>.

ASSAIL – [1] Ps. 55:3 ➔ HATE <7852> [2] Ps. 62:3 ➔ ATTACK (verb) <2050>.

ASSAILANT – Ps. 35:15 ➔ ATTACKER <5222>.

ASSAULT (noun) – Deut. 17:8; 21:5 ➔ SORE (noun) <5061>.

ASSAULT (verb) – [1] Esther 7:8 ➔ SUBDUE <3533> [2] Esther 8:11 ➔ BESIEGE <6696> b. [3] Ps. 62:3 ➔ ATTACK (verb) <2050>.

ASSAULTS (DREADFUL) – Ps. 88:16 ➔ TERRORS <1161>.

ASSAYER – [1] ***bāḥôn*** [masc. noun: בָּחוֹן <969>; from TEST <974>] ►
a. This word refers to someone who evaluates and sizes up something; it is also translated tester. Jeremiah was called to be an assayer of the Lord's people (Jer. 6:27). ¶
b. This word means tower or fortification. It is used figuratively of Jeremiah among God's disobedient people (Jer. 6:27). As a tower or a fortification, he would examine them to see if they would turn to the Lord (ESV, NKJV, NASB; NIV, a tester of metals). ¶
– [2] Jer. 6:27 ➔ FORTIFICATION <4013> b, c.

ASSEMBLE – [1] ***qāhal*** [verb: קָהַל <6950>; a prim. root] ► **This word means to gather. It is closely connected with that of *qāhāl* (ASSEMBLY <6951>), a Hebrew noun meaning a convocation, a congregation, or an assembly. It indicates an assembling together for a convocation or as a congregation, often for religious purposes.** The word is used in reference to the act of congregating to fulfill a chiefly religious end (Josh. 18:1); of assembling for battle (Judg. 20:1; 2 Sam. 20:14); and of summoning to an appointed religious assembly (Deut. 31:28). *
[2] ***qālāh*** [verb: קָלָה <7035>; from <6950> above] ► **This word is used only once in the Old Testament and means to gather together.** It occurs in 2 Samuel 20:14 where Joab assembled the people. ¶
– [3] 1 Chr. 22:2; Esther 4:16 ➔ GATHER <3664> [4] Jer. 5:7 ➔ GATHER <1413> [5] Dan. 3:2, 3 ➔ GATHER <3673> [6] Joel 3:11 ➔ HASTEN <5789>.

ASSEMBLE TOGETHER – ***r^egaš*** [Aramaic verb: רְגַשׁ <7284>; corresponding to RAGE (verb) <7283>] ► **This word means to gather in a throng, to be turbulent, to be in tumult.** Occurring only in Daniel, this word describes the gathering of the men who conspired against the prophet (Dan. 6:6, 11, 15); it is also translated to come by agreement. ¶

ASSEMBLY – [1] ***'^asuppah*** [fem. noun: אֲסֻפָּה <627>; fem. of STOREHOUSE <624>] ► **This word means a gathering, a council. It comes from a root meaning to gather.** Although there are many usages of the different forms of the root, this particular word is used only once in the Hebrew Bible, and the usage is plural instead of singular. It is used with the word for master and can be translated as "the gathering of masters"; "the council of scholars"; or "the collected sayings of scholars" (Eccl. 12:11). ¶
[2] ***'aṣārāh, '^aṣereṯ*** [fem. sing. noun: עֲצָרָה, עֲצֶרֶת <6116>; from RESTRAIN <6113>] ► **This use of assembly (or gathering) usually has some religious or cultic connection;**

thus, it is often translated solemn assembly. These assemblies may be according to God's Law, such as the Feast of Passover (Deut. 16:8); or the all-day gathering at the end of the Feast of Booths in Nehemiah 8:18. But other assemblies were for the worship of other gods (2 Kgs. 10:20); or were detestable to God because of Israel's wickedness (Is. 1:13; Amos 5:21). Other refs.: Lev. 23:26; Num. 29:35; 2 Chr. 7:9; Jer. 9:2; Joel 1:14; 2:15. ¶

3 ***miqrā'*** [masc. noun: מִקְרָא <4744>; from CALL <7121>] ► **This word means a convocation, reading, a public meeting, and a calling together. It usually refers to a convocation for religious purposes.** The Passover included a holy convocation on the first and seventh days (Ex. 12:16); other festivals also included the gathering of the people (Num. 28:18, 25, 26; 29:1, 7, 12). This word can also mean reading in the sense of a public reading or that which is read in such a meeting. For example, Ezra read the Law of God to a gathering of the Israelites, explaining so the people could understand (Neh. 8:8). Other refs.: Lev. 23:2–4, 7, 8, 21, 24, 27, 35–37; Num. 10:2; Is. 1:3; 4:5. ¶

4 ***qāhāl*** [masc. noun: קָהָל <6951>; from ASSEMBLE <6950>] ► **This word means also a community, a congregation, a crowd, a company, a throng, a mob. It describes various gatherings and groups of people called together.** It can describe a gathering called for evil purposes—such as the deceitful assembly of the brothers Simeon and Levi to plan violence against the city of Shechem (Gen. 49:6; Ezek. 23:47). The man of God abhors the gathering of evildoers (Ps. 26:5); but he should proclaim the Lord's name in the worshiping congregation (Ps. 22:22). An assembly for war or a group of soldiers was common in the Old Testament (Num. 22:4; Judg. 20:2; 1 Sam. 17:47); the various groups of exiles that traveled from Babylon to Jerusalem were a renewed community (Ezra 2:64; Neh. 7:66; Jer. 31:8). Many assemblies were convened for holy religious purposes: the congregation of Israel gathered at Sinai to hear the Lord's words (Deut. 9:10); many feasts and holy convocations called for worship and fasting as noted by the author of Chronicles (2 Chr. 20:5; 30:25).

The word describes Israel as a congregation, an organized community. Israel was the Lord's community (Num. 16:3; 20:4). The word also describes the gathering of Israel before King Solomon when he dedicated the Temple (1 Kgs. 8:14); the high priest atoned for the whole community of Israel on the Day of Atonement (Lev. 16:17; Deut. 31:30). The word designates the community restored in Jerusalem after the Babylonian exile (Ezra 10:8, 12, 14); the gathering of the congregation of Israel when they killed the Passover lambs (Ex. 12:6).

The word refers to gatherings of any assembled multitude: an assembly of nations (Gen. 35:11); or of peoples (Gen. 28:3), such as Abraham's descendants were to comprise. It refers to a great mass of people as mentioned by Balak, king of Moab (Num. 22:4). *

5 ***qᵉhillāh*** [fem. noun: קְהִלָּה <6952>; from ASSEMBLE <6950>] ► **This word expresses the gathering of a collection of people, such as the congregation of Jacob referred to by Moses in his blessing of the tribes.** Ref.: Deut. 33:4. It can also describe the gathering of people for legal action (Neh. 5:7; NIV: meeting). ¶

– 6 Ps. 7:7; 82:1; etc. ➔ CONGREGATION <5712> 7 Ps. 26:12 ➔ CONGREGATION <4721>.

ASSHUR – ***'aššûr*** [proper noun: אַשּׁוּר <804>; apparently from BLESS <833> (in the sense of successful)] ►

a. The name of a second son of Shem who began the ancient line from which the Assyrians came, with their capital at Asshur. Refs.: Gen. 10:22; 1 Chr. 1:17. ¶

b. An ancient name for Assyria. It is found in Genesis 2:14. The Tigris River ran by its capital city Asshur. Nimrod is connected with the land in Genesis 10:11 where he built Nineveh, a later capital of Assyria. Asshur (Assyria) is mentioned by Balaam in his final prophecies (Num. 24:22, 24). Assyria/Asshur became a byword for violence and political terror tactics. It conquered and ruled by fear and brutality. Assyria took Northern Israel (Samaria) captive in 722 B.C. In ca. 701 B.C., Sennacherib, the king of Assyria, threatened to besiege and destroy Jerusalem in Hezekiah's reign and during the time of Isaiah the prophet (Is. 36, 37). God delivered the city. Jonah preached repentance to the great city of Nineveh, and the Assyrians repented and experienced the Lord's grace (see Jon. 3:4–4:11). On the other hand, later the prophet Nahum preached the destruction of the city and rejoiced over its fall, as did the rest of the ancient Near East (Nah. 1–3). Nineveh and the remnants of the Assyrian Empire fell in 612 B.C. *

ASSHURITE – ***'aššûriy*** [proper noun: אַשּׁוּרִי <805>; from a patrial word of the same form as ASSHUR <804>] ▶ **An inhabitant of Asshur.** Refs.: Gen. 25:3; 2 Sam. 2:9. ¶

ASSIGN – [1] Lev. 19:20 ➔ BETROTH <2778> [2] Job 7:3 ➔ COUNT <4487>.

ASSIR – ***'assiyr*** [masc. proper noun: אַסִּיר <617>; the same as PRISONERS <616>]: prisoner ▶
a. A son of Korah. Ref.: Ex. 6:24. ¶
b. A son of Ebiasaph. Refs.: 1 Chr. 6:22, 23, 1 Chr. 6:37. ¶
c. A son of Jeconiah. Ref.: 1 Chr. 3:17. ¶

ASSOCIATE – [1] Ezra 4:7 ➔ COMPANION <3674> [2] Ezra 4:9, 17, 23; 5:3, 6; 6:6, 13 ➔ COMPANION <3675> [3] Dan. 7:20 ➔ FELLOW <2273>.

ASSOCIATE WITH – See FEED (verb) <7462> b.

ASSUAGE – Gen. 8:1 ➔ SUBSIDE <7918>.

ASSURANCE – [1] 1 Sam. 17:18 ➔ PLEDGE (noun) <6161> [2] See SECURITY <983>.

ASSURED – Dan. 4:26 ➔ ENDURING <7011>.

ASSURED (BE) – Is. 46:8 ➔ SHOW YOURSELVES MEN <377>.

ASTONISHED (BE) – [1] ***dāham*** [verb: דָּהַם <1724>; a prim. root (comp. WASH <1740>)] ▶ **This word means to be surprised, bewildered, dismayed; it is also translated to be taken by surprise, to be confused.** It is used to describe God's seeming behavior and attitude toward Judah during a time of drought (Jer. 14:9). ¶
[2] ***šᵉmam*** [Aramaic verb: שְׁמַם <8075>; corresponding to DESTROYED (BE) <8074> (in the second meaning of to be appalled or astonished)] ▶ **This word means to be taken by surprise, dumbfounded at something, as well as amazed.** Ref.: Dan. 4:19; also translated to be appalled, to be dismayed, to be greatly perplexed. ¶
[3] ***tᵉwah*** [Aramaic verb: תְּוַהּ <8429>; corresponding to <8539> below] ▶ **This word indicates a state of wonderment and amazement at something or someone or at an extraordinary event or condition.** Ref.: Dan. 3:24; also translated to be astounded. ¶
[4] ***tāmah*** [verb: תָּמַהּ <8539>; a prim. root] ▶ **This word means to be amazed, to be astounded, as well as to be shocked, stunned at something.** Joseph's brothers were astonished at the situation they found themselves in (Gen. 43:33). It is used figuratively of the pillars of heaven being amazed, shocked (Job 26:11). Kings of the nations stand amazed at the splendor of Zion (Ps. 48:5). It carries the sense of being surprised at something unexpected (Eccl. 5:8). God's judgments cause astonishment and disbelief among those He destroys (Is. 13:8; Jer. 4:9; Hab. 1:5). It indicates amazement at God's vision of judgment (Is. 29:9; NASB: wait). ¶
– [5] Dan. 5:9 ➔ PERPLEXED <7672>.

ASTONISHMENT – [1] Deut. 28:28; Zech. 12:4 ➔ CONFUSION <8541> [2] Ps. 60:3 ➔ STAGGER (THAT MAKES) <8653> [3] Ezek. 4:16; 12:19 ➔ HORROR <8078> [4] Ezek. 5:15 ➔ DESOLATION <4923>.

ASTOUNDED – Dan. 3:24 ➔ ASTONISHED (BE) <8429>.

ASTRAY (GO) – [1] Num. 5:12, 19, 20, 29; Prov. 7:25 → ASIDE (GO, TURN) <7847> [2] Ps. 40:4 → TURN ASIDE <7750>.

ASTRAY (LEAD) – Ezek. 13:10 → SEDUCE <2937>.

ASTROLOGER – [1] ***hāḇar*** [verb: הָבַר <1895>; a prim. root of uncertain (perhaps foreign) deriv.] ▶ **This Hebrew verb literally indicates: divider of heaven. They prophesied by or evaluated the stars.** Ref.: Is. 47:13; ESV: those who divide the heavens. ¶
– [2] Dan. 2:2; 5:11 → ENCHANTER <825> [3] Dan. 2:10, 27; 4:7; 5:7, 11, 15 → ENCHANTER <826> [4] Dan. 2:27; 4:7; 5:7, 11 → CUT (verb) <1505>.

ASWAN – Is. 49:12 → SINIM <5515> b.

ATAD – Gen. 50:10, 11 → BRAMBLE <329> b.

ATARAH – ***ʿᵃṭārāh*** [fem. proper noun: עֲטָרָה <5851>; the same as CROWN (noun) <5850>]: crown ▶ **A wife of Jerahmeel and mother of Onam.** Ref.: 1 Chr. 2:26. ¶

ATAROTH – ***ʿᵃṭārôṯ, ʿᵃṭārōṯ*** [proper noun: עֲטָרוֹת, עֲטָרֹת <5852>; plur. of CROWN (noun) <5850>]: crowns ▶
a. A town east of Jordan. Refs.: Num. 32:3, 34. ¶
b. A town on the southwest border of Ephraim. Ref.: Josh. 16:2. ¶
c. A town in northeast Ephraim. Ref.: Josh. 16:7. ¶
d. A town in Judah. Ref.: 1 Chr. 2:54. ¶

ATAROTH-ADDAR – ***ʿaṭrôṯ ʾaddār*** [proper noun: עַטְרוֹת אַדָּר <5853>; from the same as ATAROTH <5852> and ADDAR <146>]: crowns of Addar ▶ **City on the border of the tribes of Benjamin and Ephraim.** Refs.: Josh. 16:5; 18:13. ¶

ATER – ***ʾāṭêr*** [masc. proper noun: אָטֵר <333>; from CLOSE <332>]: closed, maimed ▶
a. Descendants from this man came back from the Babylonian captivity. Refs.: Ezra 2:16; Neh. 7:21. ¶
b. A gatekeeper. Refs.: Ezra 2:42; Neh. 7:45. ¶
c. Another Israelite who signed the covenant of renewal with Nehemiah after the return from the Babylonian captivity. Ref.: Neh. 10:17. ¶

ATHACH – ***ʿᵃṯāḵ*** [proper noun: עֲתָךְ <6269>; from an unused root meaning to sojourn, to lodge]: lodging place, inn ▶ **A town in Judah.** Ref.: 1 Sam. 30:30. ¶

ATHAIAH – ***ʿᵃṯāyāh*** [masc. proper noun: עֲתָיָה <6265>; from SUSTAIN <5790> and LORD <3050>]: the Lord has helped ▶ **An Israelite of the tribe of Judah who dwelt in Jerusalem after his return from the Babylonian captivity.** Ref.: Neh. 11:4. ¶

ATHALIAH – ***ʿᵃṯalyāh, ʿᵃṯalyāhû*** [fem. and masc. proper noun: עֲתַלְיָה, עֲתַלְיָהוּ <6271>; from the same as ATHLAI <6270> and LORD <3050>]: afflicted by the Lord ▶
a. The daughter of King Ahab of northern Israel and granddaughter of Omri. She was the mother of Ahaziah king of Judah. She was wicked and tried to destroy the royal family of Judah (2 Kgs. 11:1–3). Joash, of the royal line, was shielded from her plans and kept hidden for six years. Jehoiada the priest then proclaimed Joash king. Athaliah was killed (2 Kgs. 11:9–16). *
b. A Benjamite. Ref.: 1 Chr. 8:26. ¶
c. A descendant of Elam. Ref.: Ezra 8:7. ¶

ATHARIM – Num. 21:1 → SPIES <871> b.

ATHLAI – ***ʿaṯlāy*** [masc. proper noun: עַתְלָי <6270>; from an unused root meaning to compress]: afflicted by the Lord ▶ **An Israelite who had married a foreign woman.** Ref.: Ezra 10:28. ¶

ATONE – Ps. 78:38; 79:9; Is. 6:7 → COVER (verb) <3722>.

ATONEMENT – ***kippuriym*** [masc. plur. noun: כִּפֻּרִים <3725>; from COVER (verb)

<3722>] ▶ **This word also means the act of reconciliation, the Day of Atonement.** It is used five times to indicate the act or process of reconciliation: a young bull was sacrificed each day for seven days during the ordination ceremony of Aaron and his sons to make atonement (Ex. 29:36). Once a year, the blood of a sin offering was used to make atonement on the horns of the altar of incense located in front of the Holy of Holies (Ex. 30:10). Ransom money of a half-shekel was used to effect atonement or reconciliation for male Israelites who were at least twenty years old (Ex. 30:16). The money was then used to service the Tent of Meeting.

When a person had wronged the Lord or another person, a ram was presented to the priest, along with proper restitution (Num. 5:8); a sin offering for atonement was presented yearly on the Day of Atonement (Num. 29:11). Three times the noun is used to indicate the Day of Atonement itself (Lev. 23:27, 28; 25:9). ¶

ATONEMENT (MAKE) – Ex. 32:30; Ps. 79:9; Ezek. 45:17 ➔ COVER (verb) <3722>.

ATROTH-BETH-JOAB – ***'aṭrôṯ-bêṯ-yô'āḇ*** [proper noun: עַטְרוֹת בֵּית יוֹאָב <5854>; from the same as ATAROTH <5852> and HOUSE <1004> and JOAB <3097>]: crowns of the house of Joab ▶ **A town in the territory of Judah.** Ref.: 1 Chr. 2:54. ¶

ATROTH-SHOPHAN – ***'aṭrôṯ šôpān*** [proper noun: עַטְרוֹת שׁוֹפָן <5855>; from the same as ATAROTH <5852> and a name otherwise unused (being from the same as TREASURE <8226>)]: crowns of Shophan ▶ **A city rebuilt by the Gadites.** Ref.: Num. 32:35. ¶

ATTACHED (BE) – 2 Chr. 3:12 ➔ JOINING <1695>.

ATTACK (noun) – Job 15:24 ➔ BATTLE <3593>.

ATTACK (verb) – [1] ***gûḏ*** [verb: גּוּד <1464>; a prim. root; akin to GREAT (BECOME) <1431>] ▶ **This word means to cause harm using violence; it is also translated to raid, to tramp upon, to overcome.** It is used to describe an enemy's attack on Gad and the response of Gad in return (Gen. 49:19) with a wordplay on the letter *gimel* (ג). It describes Babylon's coming invasion of Judah (Hab. 3:16). ¶

[2] ***haṯaṯ, hûṯ*** [verb: הָתַת, הוּת <2050>; a prim. root] ▶

a. This word means to assault, assail, topple. It indicates an attack mode, attitude, or actions against persons in order to injure them (Ps. 62:3). ¶

b. A verb meaning to imagine mischief, to scheme. It indicates a scheming attitude toward persons to bring them down (Ps. 62:3, KJV). ¶

[3] ***zānaḇ*** [verb: זָנַב <2179>; a prim. root meaning to wag] ▶ **This word means to smite the rear, to cut off stragglers, to destroy the rearguard.** It refers to Amalek's action in cutting off or destroying the Israelites in the rear during their trek out of Egypt (Deut. 25:18). At Joshua's command, Israel used this guerrilla warfare tactic to attack the armies of five great kings (Josh. 10:19). ¶

– [4] Esther 8:11 ➔ BESIEGE <6696> b. [5] Job 19:3 ➔ WRONG (verb) <1970> a. [6] Dan. 11:40 ➔ GORE <5055>.

ATTACKER – ***nêḵeh*** [adj.: נֵכֶה <5222>; from STRIKE <5221>] ▶ **This word refers to smiting, assailing.** It is related to the root of the verb *nāḵāh*, to smite, strike. It refers to hitting, smiting someone physically or with words (Ps. 35:15; also translated smiter, wretch, assailant, abject). ¶

ATTAI – ***'attay*** [masc. proper noun: עַתַּי <6262>; from READINESS (IN) <6261>]: timely, opportune ▶

a. A son of Jarha and descendant of Judah. Refs.: 1 Chr. 2:35, 36. ¶

b. One of David's warriors. Ref.: 1 Chr. 12:11. ¶

c. Son of Rehoboam. Ref.: 2 Chr. 11:20. ¶

ATTAIN – Job 20:18 ➔ what one has attained ➔ FRUIT OF ONE'S TOIL <3022>.

ATTEND – 1 ***pāqaḏ*** [verb: פָּקַד <6485>; a prim. root] ► **This word has various meaning; among others: to take note of, to look after, to visit, to search out.** It refers to someone (usually God) paying attention to persons, either to do them good (Gen. 50:24, 25; Ex. 3:16; 1 Sam. 2:21; Jer. 23:2); or to bring punishment or harm (Ex. 20:5; Is. 10:12; Jer. 23:2). The word also means, usually in a causative form, to appoint over or to commit to, i.e., to cause people to attend to something placed under their care (Gen. 39:4, 5; Josh. 10:18; Is. 62:6). The passive causative form means to deposit, i.e., to cause something to be attended to (Lev. 6:4). The word also means to number or to be numbered, which is an activity requiring attention. This meaning occurs over ninety times in the book of Numbers. The word can also mean (usually in a passive form) lacking or missing, as if a quantity was numbered less than an original amount (Judg. 21:3; 1 Sam. 20:18; 1 Kgs. 20:39). *
– 2 Dan. 7:10 ➔ SERVE <8120>.

ATTENDANCE – ***ma***^{a}***mād*** [masc. noun: מַעֲמָד <4612>; from STAND <5975>] ► **This word designates an office, a position, a place, a station, a duty.** It is used of the placement and service of a group of people, e.g., attendants or entertainers (1 Kgs. 10:5; 2 Chr. 9:4; 35:15). It is used of positions held by a group of people (1 Chr. 23:28); or a single individual (Is. 22:19). ¶

ATTENTION – ***qešeḇ*** [masc. noun: קֶשֶׁב <7182>; from LISTEN <7181>] ► **This word indicates attentiveness, response.** It means to focus on something, to pay attention, to watch closely (1 Kgs. 18:29; Is. 21:7). It can have the sense of simply any response or movement (2 Kgs. 4:31). ¶

ATTENTION (PAY) – Jer. 13:15 ➔ EAR (GIVE) <238>.

ATTENTIVE – ***qaššāḇ, qaššuḇ*** [adj.: קַשָּׁב, קַשֻּׁב <7183>; from LISTEN <7181>] ►
a. This word means for someone to be responsive, caring, especially of God's care and attention to His people through hearing their prayers. Refs.: Neh. 1:6, 11. ¶
b. This word refers to God's response figuratively to the prayers of His people. Ref.: 2 Chr. 6:40. He does so through both His ears and His eyes (2 Chr. 7:15; Ps. 130:2). ¶

ATTIRE – 1 ***qiššuriym*** [masc. plur. noun: קִשֻּׁרִים <7196>; from BIND <7194>] ► **This word indicates headbands, sashes, apparel.** It refers to the wedding dress worn at a woman's marriage ceremony (Jer. 2:32). God's coming judgments would violently remove all these luxury items from among His people (Is. 3:20). ¶
– 2 1 Kgs. 10:5; 2 Chr. 9:4 ➔ CLOTHING <4403> 3 Prov. 7:10 ➔ GARMENT <7897> 4 Is. 23:18 ➔ COVERING <4374> 5 Ezek. 23:15 ➔ dyed attire ➔ FLOWING TURBAN <2871>.

ATTIRED (BE) – Lev. 16:4 ➔ WEAR <6801>.

ATTRACTED (BE) – Deut. 21:11 ➔ DESIRE (verb) <2836>.

AUL – Ex. 21:6; Deut. 15:17 ➔ AWL <4836>.

AUNT – Lev. 18:14 ➔ FATHER'S SISTER <1733>.

AUTHORITATIVE – Eccl. 8:4 ➔ POWER <7983>.

AUTHORITY – 1 ***mōšel*** [masc. noun: מֹשֶׁל <4915>; from RULE (verb) <4910>] ► **This word means rule; it is also translated dominion, power.** The number in Strong's is associated with two words. The first comes from the verb *māšal* (PROVERB <4911>), meaning to represent or to be like, and is found only in Job 41:33 (like, equal), where it means "likeness." The second comes from the verb *māšal* [RULE (verb) <4910>] meaning to rule or to govern. This word is found in Daniel 11:4 and Zechariah 9:10, where it describes the dominion of Alexander and the coming Messiah. ¶

[2] ***tōqep̱*** [masc. noun: תֹּקֶף <8633>; from PREVAIL <8630>] ► **This word refers to strength, power, might.** It indicates the legal and royal authority exercised by people in governmental positions (Esther 9:29); especially the authority wielded by a king (Esther 10:2; Dan. 11:17). ¶
– [3] Eccl. 8:8 ➔ POWER <7983> [4] Dan. 11:3, 5 ➔ DOMINION <4474> [5] See VIGOR <1935>.

AUTHORIZED – Ezra 3:7 ➔ PERMISSION <7558>.

AVA – See AVVA <5755>.

AVAN – Ezek. 30:17 ➔ ON <204>.

AVEN – ***'āwen*** [proper noun: אָוֶן <206>; the same as NOTHINGNESS <205>]: nothingness, vanity ►
a. Another name for the city of On. Ref.: Ezek. 30:17; see ON <204>. ¶
b. The shortened form of Beth-Aven. Ref.: Hos. 10:8; see BETH-AVEN <1007>. ¶
c. A town in the kingdom of Damascus. Ref.: Amos 1:5. ¶

AVENGE, AVENGED (BE) – Lev. 26:25; Deut. 32:35; Judg. 16:28; etc. ➔ VENGEANCE <5357>.

AVITE – ***'awwiy*** [proper noun: עַוִּי <5757>; patrial from AVVA <5755>] ►
a. One of a group placed in Israel after the Assyrian deportation. Ref.: 2 Kgs. 17:31. ¶
b. A member of one of the original Canaanite nations. Refs.: Deut. 2:23; Josh. 13:3. ¶

AVITH – ***ʿᵃwiyṯ*** [proper noun: עֲוִית <5762>; as if plur. of AI <5857>]: ruins ► **The city of Hadad, the son of Bedad, an Edomite king.** Refs.: Gen. 36:35; 1 Chr. 1:46. ¶

AVOID – Prov. 20:3 ➔ LOSS OF TIME <7674>.

AVVA – ***'awwā', 'iwwāh*** [proper noun: עַוָּא, עִוָּה <5755>; for RUIN (noun) <5754>]: ruin ► **People from this city in Assyria, among others, were brought to occupy the cities of Samaria.** Refs.: 2 Kgs. 17:24; 18:34; 19:13; Is. 37:13; this name is also spelled Ava, Ivvah. ¶

AVVIM – ***'awwiym*** [proper noun: עַוִּים <5761>; plur. of AVITE <5757>] ► **A city in Benjamin.** Ref.: Josh. 18:23. ¶

AWAKE – [1] ***'ûr*** [verb: עוּר <5782>; a primitive root (rather identical with UNCOVER <5783> through the idea of opening the eyes)] ► **This word means to stir, to arouse, to awaken. It is used of raising something or someone to action, of agitating someone, of motivating him or her.** It is used of stirring oneself to action (Judg. 5:12; Ps. 57:8); especially of the Lord's arousing Himself or His arm (Ps. 7:6; 59:4; Is. 51:9). In its passive use, it means to be stirred up (Jer. 6:22; 25:32; Zech. 4:1). It means to rouse someone to action (Zech. 9:13); to use a weapon (2 Sam. 23:18); to stir up a nest of young birds (a figure of the Lord toward His people) (Deut. 32:11). *
[2] ***qûṣ, qiyṣ*** [verb: קוּץ, קִיץ <6974>; a prim. root (identical with SUMMER (verb) <6972> through the idea of abruptness in starting up from sleep)] ► **This word means to wake up, to arouse.** It means to arouse a person from sleep or to awake from sleep (1 Sam. 26:12; 2 Kgs. 4:31; Job 14:12). To awake and find oneself safe is considered a work of the Lord on behalf of His servants (Ps. 3:5). It may have the sense of act, doing something (Ps. 35:23). It depicts resurrection and is contained in some of the key references to this reality in the Old Testament (Is. 26:19; Dan. 12:2). It is used as an imperative call to Awake, meaning to become aware of a situation and to act accordingly (Joel 1:5). It is used mockingly of the lifeless, eternal sleep of idols (Hab. 2:19). *

AWAKEN – ***yāqaṣ*** [verb: יָקַץ <3364>; a prim. root] ► **This word indicates to emerge from sleep, to wake up.** It refers to regaining consciousness after sleeping off a drunken stupor (Gen. 9:24); or to awaken from sleep (Gen. 28:16; 41:4, 7, 21; Judg. 16:14, 20); Elijah used it mockingly of the Canaanite god Baal who had perhaps been asleep (1 Kgs. 18:27). It is used in a figurative sense of the Lord as He begins to act (Ps. 78:65). It refers figuratively and literally to one's enemies or creditors beginning to attack (Hab. 2:7). ¶

AWAY – Ezra 6:6 ➔ FAR <7352>.

AWE – Jer. 2:19 ➔ DREAD (noun) <6345>.

AWE (STAND IN) – Mal. 2:5 ➔ DISMAYED (BE) <2865>.

AWEL-MARDUK – 2 Kgs. 25:27; Jer. 52:31 ➔ EVIL-MERODACH <192>.

AWESOME – [1] Song 6:4, 10 ➔ TERRIBLE <366> [2] Dan. 2:31 ➔ FEAR (verb) <1763>.

AWL – ***marṣêaʿ*** [masc. noun: מַרְצֵעַ <4836>; from PIERCE <7527>] ► **This word describes an instrument for piercing.** It is used of boring a hole in a servant's ear as a mark of ownership (Ex. 21:6; Deut. 15:17; KJV: aul). ¶

AWNING – Ezek. 27:7 ➔ COVERING <4374>.

AX – [1] ***kaššiyl*** [masc. noun: כַּשִּׁיל <3781>; from FALL (verb) <3782>] ► **This word refers to a tool for cutting; it is also translated hatchet.** It was a weapon or tool used by the enemy to destroy much of the carved art work in the Solomonic Temple (Ps. 74:6). ¶

[2] ***magzêrāh*** [fem. noun: מַגְזֵרָה <4037>; from CUT (verb) <1504>] ► **This word is used of an iron implement.** It was used by the prisoners of war which David and Joab took of the Ammonites (2 Sam. 12:31). ¶

[3] ***qardōm*** [masc. noun: קַרְדֹּם <7134>; perhaps from MEET <6923> in the sense of striking upon] ► **This word refers to a tool with a sharp edge used to cut down trees and large shrubs, to chop wood, etc.** Refs.: Judg. 9:48; 1 Sam. 13:20, 21; Jer. 46:22. It is used in a simile of the devastation of Israel's enemies (Ps. 74:5; Jer. 46:22). ¶

AX, AXE – [1] ***garzen*** [masc. noun: גַּרְזֶן <1631>; from CUT OFF (BE) <1629>] ► **This word indicates a tool with a handle and an iron head, used to cut wood or to quarry stones.** Refs.: Deut. 19:5; 20:19; 1 Kgs. 6:7. Isaiah used it to refer to the king of Assyria as God's ax used to humble His people (Is. 10:15). ¶

– [2] Jer. 10:3 ➔ CUTTING TOOL <4621>.

AZALIAH – ***ᵃṣalyāhû*** [masc. proper noun: אֲצַלְיָהוּ <683>; from RESERVE (verb) <680> and LORD <3050> prolonged]: set aside for God, God is noble ► **Father of Shaphan the scribe who was sent to repair the house of the Lord.** Refs.: 2 Kgs. 22:3; 2 Chr. 34:8. ¶

AZANIAH – ***ᵃzanyāh*** [masc. proper noun: אֲזַנְיָה <245>; from EAR (GIVE) <238> and LORD <3050>]: heard by the Lord ► **Name of a Levite.** His son Jeshua signed the covenant of renewal with Nehemiah after the return from the Babylonian captivity (Neh. 10:9). ¶

AZAREL, AZAREEL – ***ᵃzar'ēl*** [masc. proper noun: עֲזַרְאֵל <5832>; from HELP (verb) <5826> and GOD <410>]: God has helped ►

a. A Benjamite warrior. Ref.: 1 Chr. 12:6. ¶

b. A Levite. Ref.: 1 Chr. 25:18. ¶

c. A Danite leader. Ref.: 1 Chr. 27:22. ¶

d. A postexilic Jew. Ref.: Ezra 10:41. ¶

e. A priest. Ref.: Neh. 11:13. ¶

f. Another priest. Ref.: Neh. 12:36. ¶

AZARIAH – [1] ***ᵃzaryāh, ᵃzaryāhû*** [masc. proper noun: עֲזַרְיָה, עֲזַרְיָהוּ <5838>; from HELP (verb) <5826> and LORD <3050>]: the Lord has helped ►

a. The son of Ethan, a man from Judah. Ref.: 1 Chr. 2:8. ¶

b. The son of Jehu. He was from Judah. Ref.: 1 Chr. 2:39. ¶

c. The son of Zephaniah. He shared in the responsibility of the Temple music (1 Chr. 6:36). ¶
d. The son of Zadok the priest. He was one of Solomon's chief administrators (1 Kgs. 4:2). ¶
e. Son of Nathan. He was the district official in charge of the officers (1 Kgs. 4:5). ¶
f. Son of Obed. He encouraged King Asa in his reforms (2 Chr. 15:1). ¶
g. Son of Ahimaaz of the tribe of Levi. Ref.: 1 Chr. 6:9. ¶
h. Two sons of Jehoshaphat, the brother of King Jehoram. Ref.: 2 Chr. 21:2. ¶
i. Another name for Uzziah. Ref.: 2 Kgs. 14:21.
j. Son of Jehoram. He was a commander of a unit of 100 men. He and others made a covenant with the king at the Temple of God (2 Chr. 23:1). ¶
k. Son of Obed. When they came to Jerusalem, the whole assembly made a covenant with the king in the Temple. He commanded a 100-man unit (2 Chr. 23:1–3). ¶
l. Son of Johanan. He was a priest in Solomon's home in Jerusalem (1 Chr. 6:10, 11). ¶
m. A king of Judah also called Uzziah and son of Amaziah. He was sixteen when he began to reign and reigned fifty-two years (792–740 B.C.). Ref.: 2 Kgs. 14:21. His mother Jecoliah was from Jerusalem. His reign was righteous except he did not take down the competing high places of worship (2 Kgs. 15:4). At his death, Isaiah received his call from God (Is. 6:1). He arrogantly and illegally tried to burn incense in the Temple, and the Lord smote him with leprosy. He then had to live in a separate house until his death. He reigned as coregent with Amaziah (792–767 B.C.) at the beginning of his reign; at the end of his reign, his son Jotham helped him govern. *
n. Chief priest. He and eighty priests opposed Uzziah the king for burning incense in the Temple. Only the priests were supposed to burn incense (2 Chr. 26:17, 20). ¶
o. Son of Johanan. He was one of the heads of the sons in Ephraim. He helped stop Israel from taking slaves in their fight against Judah (2 Chr. 28:12). ¶
p. A high priest of the house of God appointed by King Hezekiah. Refs.: 2 Chr. 31:10, 13. ¶
q. A Kohathite and son of Jehallelel. He was one of the priests that helped cleanse the Temple under King Hezekiah during the reform (2 Chr. 29:12). ¶
r. A Merarite. He was one of the priests that helped cleanse the Temple under King Hezekiah during the reform (2 Chr. 31:13). ¶
s. The son of Hilkiah who found the book of the Law in the Temple during the reign of Josiah. Azariah fathered Seraiah. Ezra was the son of Seraiah (Ezra 7:1). ¶
t. Enemy of Jeremiah. Son of Hoshaiah. Jeremiah, the prophet, advised the people not to leave Babylon to go to Egypt. Azariah was one of the arrogant men who accused Jeremiah of lying (Jer. 43:2). ¶
u. Hebrew name of Abednego, which a commander under King Nebuchadnezzar, changed from Azariah. Refs.: Dan. 1:6, 7, 11, 19. He was one of the three young men who were thrown into the furnace by Nebuchadnezzar. ¶
v. Son of Maaseiah. He helped do repairs during the restoration of the walls of Jerusalem (Neh. 3:23, 24). ¶
w. Postexilic Jew, possibly the same as v. Listed in the census of the first exiles returned to Jerusalem (Neh. 7:7). ¶
x. A Levite, possibly the same as v. He was in the assembly of men when Ezra read the Law (Neh. 8:7). ¶
y. A priest, possibly the same as v. His name was on the sealed document of the covenant (Neh. 10:2). ¶
z. Judaite prince, possibly the same as v. He was in one of the celebration chairs at the dedication of the wall of Jerusalem (Neh. 12:33). ¶
aa. Son of Meraioth. He went up to Jerusalem with Ezra from Babylon after the Temple was completed (Ezra 7:3). ¶
2 ***ʿzaryāh*** [masc. proper noun: עֲזַרְיָה <5839>; corresponding to <5838> above]: the Lord has helped ▶ **One of the three royal Hebrew boys taken into exile**

with Daniel. Ref.: Dan. 2:17. He was also known in Babylon as Abednego ("servant of Nego") (see Dan. 1:6, 7). ⁋

AZAZ – *'āzāz* [masc. proper noun: עֲזָז <5811>; from STRENGTHEN <5810>]: strong ▸ **A man of the tribe of Reuben.** Ref.: 1 Chr. 5:8. ⁋

AZAZEL – Lev. 16:8, 10, 26 → SCAPE-GOAT <5799>.

AZAZIAH – *"zazyāhû* [masc. proper noun: עֲזַזְיָהוּ <5812>; from STRENGTHEN <5810> and LORD <3050>]: the Lord has strengthened ▸
a. A Levite. Ref.: 1 Chr. 15:21. ⁋
b. Another Levite. Ref.: 2 Chr. 31:13. ⁋
c. A Benjamite. Ref.: 1 Chr. 27:20. ⁋

AZBUK – *'azbûq* [masc. proper noun: עַזְבּוּק <5802>; from STRONG <5794> and the root of EMPTY <950>]: strong devastation ▸ **Father of a certain Nehemiah who repaired the walls of Jerusalem.** Ref.: Neh. 3:16. ⁋

AZEKAH – *"zêqāh* [verb: עֲזֵקָה <5825>; from DIG <5823> (in the sense of preparing a plot of land for planting)]: tilled ▸ **This word designates a town in the Shephelah area allotted to Judah.** Refs.: Josh. 10:10, 11; 15:35. It was west of Gath and north of Maresheth-Gath. David's combat with Goliath was in its vicinity (1 Sam. 17:1). It became a strong military outpost (2 Chr. 11:9). Some exiles who returned from Babylon resettled in it (Neh. 11:30). Other ref.: Jer. 34:7. ⁋

AZEL – *'āṣêl, 'āṣal* [proper noun: אָצֵל <682>; from RESERVE (verb) <680>]: he has reserved ▸
a. A descendant of Jonathan, son of Saul. Refs.: 1 Chr. 8:37, 38; 9:43, 44. ⁋
b. A place in the vicinity of Jerusalem. Ref.: Zech. 14:5. ⁋

AZGAD – *'azgāḏ* [masc. proper noun: עַזְגָּד <5803>; from STRONG <5794> and FORTUNE <1409>]: Gad (or fortune) is strong ▸ **Members of his family came back from Babylon under Zerubbabel.** Refs.: Ezra 2:12; 8:12; Neh. 7:17; 10:15. ⁋

AZIEL – *'aziy'êl* [masc. proper noun: עֲזִיאֵל <5815>; from SAFETY (FLEE FOR) <5756> and GOD <410>]: to take refuge in God ▸ **A shortened form of Jaaziel <3268>.** Ref.: 1 Chr. 15:20. ⁋

AZIZA – *"ziyzā'* [masc. proper noun: עֲזִיזָא <5819>; from SAFETY (FLEE FOR) <5756>]: strong ▸ **An Israelite who had married a foreign woman.** Ref.: Ezra 10:27. ⁋

AZMAVETH – *'azmāweṯ* [proper noun: עַזְמָוֶת <5820>; from STRONG <5794> and DEATH <4194>]: death is strong ▸
a. One of David's mighty men. Refs.: 2 Sam. 23:31; 1 Chr. 11:33; 12:3. ⁋
b. The head of a family, possibly the same as a. Ref.: Ezra 2:24. ⁋
c. A village near Jerusalem. Ref.: Neh. 12:29. It is the same as Beth-Azmaveth <1041>. ⁋
d. An officer under David. Ref.: 1 Chr. 27:25. ⁋
e. A descendant of Micah. Refs.: 1 Chr. 8:36; 9:42. ⁋

AZMON – *'aṣmôn* [proper noun: עַצְמוֹן <6111>; from EZEM <6107>]: bone-like, strong ▸ **A place on the border of Judah's territory.** Refs.: Num. 34:4, 5; Josh. 15:4. ⁋

AZNOTH TABOR – *'aznôṯ tāḇôr* [proper noun: אַזְנוֹת תָּבוֹר <243>; from EAR (GIVE) <238> and TABOR <8396>]: summits of Tabor ▸ **A place on Naphtali's border.** Ref.: Josh. 19:34. ⁋

AZRIEL – *'azriy'êl* [masc. proper noun: עַזְרִיאֵל <5837>; from HELP (noun) <5828> and GOD <410>]: help of God ▸
a. A Manassite chief. Ref.: 1 Chr. 5:24. ⁋
b. A Naphtalite chief. Ref.: 1 Chr. 27:19. ⁋
c. A royal officer. Ref.: Jer. 36:26. ⁋

AZRIKAM – *'azriyqām* [masc. proper noun: עַזְרִיקָם <5840>; from HELP (noun)

<5828> and act. part. of STAND, STAND UP <6965>]: help against an enemy ▶
a. A descendant of David. Ref.: 1 Chr. 3:23. ¶
b. A prince of Judah. Ref.: 2 Chr. 28:7. ¶
c. A Benjamite. Refs.: 1 Chr. 8:38; 9:44. ¶
d. A Levite. Ref.: 1 Chr. 9:14; Neh. 11:15. ¶

AZUBAH – ***ʿ^{a}zûḇāh*** [fem. proper noun: עֲזוּבָה <5806>; the same as FORSAKEN PLACE <5805>]: forsaken, deserted ▶
a. The mother of Jehoshaphat. Refs.: 1 Kgs. 22:42; 2 Chr. 20:31. ¶
b. The wife of Caleb. Refs.: 1 Chr. 2:18, 19. ¶

AZZAN – ***ʿazzān*** [masc. proper noun: עַזָּן <5821>; from STRONG <5794>]: strong ▶ **Father of Paltiel, prince of the tribe of Issachar.** Ref.: Num. 34:26. ¶

AZZUR – ***ʿazzûr*** [masc. proper noun: עַזּוּר <5809>; from HELP (verb) <5826>]: one who helps ▶
a. The father of Hananiah. Ref.: Jer. 28:1. ¶
b. The father of Jaazaniah. Ref.: Ezek. 11:1. ¶
c. A chief of the people who signed the covenant of renewal with Nehemiah after the return from the Babylonian captivity. Ref.: Neh. 10:17. ¶

B

BAAL – [1] ***ba'al*** [proper noun: בַּעַל <1168>; the same as LORD <1167>]: lord ▶

a. This word names the Canaanite god Baal; lord. Used with the definite article, it means the god Baal served by the Canaanites and Philistines, but Israel was caught up in worshiping this pagan god, too (Judg. 2:11, 13; 6:25, 28, 30; 1 Kgs. 18:18, 19, 21; 19:18; 2 Kgs. 3:2; 10:18–23; Hos. 2:8). It occurs in the plural, indicating the many manifestations of pagan polytheism (Judg. 2:11; 1 Sam. 7:4; 12:10; 1 Kgs. 18:18; Jer. 2:23; Hos. 11:2). It is used without the definite article as a name indicating, e.g., high places of Baal (Num. 22:41; NIV renders as Bamoth Baal). In construct with a following word, *ba'al b^{e}riyṯ*, it means lord of the covenant (Judg. 8:33; 9:4). *

b. A proper noun naming a city, Baal. It denoted a border city of the tribe of Simeon (NIV renders as Baalath with a note; 1 Chr. 4:33). ¶

c. A masculine proper name, Baal. The name describes the immediate son of Reaiah but a descendant of Reuben, the firstborn of Jacob (1 Chr. 5:5). ¶

d. A masculine proper name found as a descendant of Benjamin. Ref.: 1 Chr. 8:30. He was from the line that produced King Saul (1 Chr. 9:36). ¶

– [2] Num. 25:3 → LORD <1167>.

BAAL-BERITH – ***ba'al b^{e}riyṯ*** [masc. proper noun: בַּעַל בְּרִית <1170>; from BAAL <1168> and COVENANT <1285>]: lord of the covenant ▶ **This word refers to a Canaanite god.** Refs.: Judg. 8:33; 9:4; cf. Judg. 9:46. He had his own temple in Shechem (Judg. 9:4). After Gideon's deliverance and death, Israel again worshiped the baals, lords of the land, specifically setting up Baal-Berith as their chief god. ¶

BAAL-GAD – ***ba'al gāḏ*** [proper noun: בַּעַל גָּד <1171>; from BAAL <1168> and FORTUNE <1409>]: lord of fortune ▶ **A place at the feet of Mount Hermon.** Refs.: Josh. 11:17; 12:7; 13:5. ¶

BAAL-HAMON – ***ba'al hāmôn*** [proper noun: בַּעַל הָמוֹן <1174>; from LORD <1167> and MULTITUDE <1995>]: lord of a multitude ▶ **A place where Solomon had a vineyard.** Ref.: Song 8:11. ¶

BAAL-HANAN – ***ba'al ḥānān*** [masc. proper noun: בַּעַל חָנָן <1177>; from LORD <1167> and GRACIOUS (BE) <2603>]: lord of compassion ▶

a. A king of Edom. Refs.: Gen. 36:38, 39; 1 Chr. 1:49, 50. ¶

b. A Gederite who was in charge of the olive and sycamore trees under King David. Ref.: 1 Chr. 27:28. ¶

BAAL-HAZOR – ***ba'al ḥāṣôr*** [proper noun: בַּעַל חָצוֹר <1178>; from LORD <1167> and a modification of VILLAGE <2691>]: lord of a village ▶ **A place beside Ephraim where Absalom killed his brother Amnon.** Ref.: 2 Sam. 13:23. ¶

BAAL-HERMON – ***ba'al ḥermôn*** [proper noun: בַּעַל חֶרְמוֹן <1179>; from LORD <1167> and HERMON <2768>]: lord of the summit ▶ **A mountain at the east of the Jordan, indicating the north-west limit of Manasseh's territory.** Refs.: Judg. 3:3; 1 Chr. 5:23. ¶

BAAL-MEON – ***ba'al m^{e}'ôn*** [proper noun: בַּעַל מְעוֹן <1186>; from BAAL <1168> and HABITATION <4583>]: lord of the habitation ▶ **City of Moab which was assigned to the tribe of Reuben who rebuilt it.** Refs.: Num. 32:38; 1 Chr. 5:8; Ezek. 25:9. ¶

BAAL-PEOR – ***ba'al p^{e}'ôr*** [masc. proper noun: בַּעַל פְּעוֹר <1187>; from BAAL <1168> and PEOR <6465>]: lord of the breach ▶ **This word is translated as a place name and as the name of an idol. It is rendered as a proper name Baalpeor (KJV) or as Baal of Peor (NIV, NKJV, NASB), stressing the location of this god's habitation (evidently a Moabite mountain).** Peor was one of the places from which Balaam blessed Israel (Num. 23:28). Baal-Peor became a byword for shame. See Hosea 9:10, where the word is identified with shame. This word is also found in Numbers 25:3, 5; Deuteronomy 4:3; Psalm 106:28. ¶

BAAL-PERAZIM – ***baʿal pᵉrāṣiym*** [proper noun: בַּעַל פְּרָצִים <1188>; from LORD <1167> and BREACH <6556>]: lord of the breaches ▶ **A place where David defeated the Philistines.** Refs.: 2 Sam. 5:20; 1 Chr. 14:11. See also PERAZIM <6559>. ¶

BAAL-SHALISHAH – ***baʿal šālišāh*** [proper noun: בַּעַל שָׁלִשָׁה <1190>; from BAAL <1168> and SHALISHAH <8031>]: lord of Shalishah, or of the third ▶ **A village from which was brought to Elisha bread of the firstfruits, loaves of barley, and fresh ears of grain.** Ref.: 2 Kgs. 4:42. ¶

BAAL-TAMAR – ***baʿal tāmār*** [proper noun: בַּעַל תָּמָר <1193>; from LORD <1167> and PALM TREE <8558>]: lord of the palm trees ▶ **A place of the tribe of Benjamin where the Israelites set themselves in array before attacking Gibeah.** Ref.: Judg. 20:33. ¶

BAAL-ZEBUB – ***baʿal zᵉḇûḇ*** [masc. proper noun: בַּעַל זְבוּב <1176>; from BAAL <1168> and FLY (noun) <2070>]: lord of flies ▶ **A Philistine god of the city of Ekron consulted by Ahaziah, king of Israel.** Refs.: 2 Kgs. 1:2, 3, 6, 16. ¶

BAAL-ZEPHON – ***baʿal ṣᵉpôn, baʿal ṣᵉpōn*** [proper noun: בַּעַל צְפֹן, בַּעַל צְפוֹן <1189>; from BAAL <1168> and NORTH <6828> (in the sense of cold)]: lord of the north ▶ **A place which was in front of the Israelites when they were camping before Pihahiroth, between Migdol and the sea, just before crossing it.** Refs.: Ex. 14:2, 9; Num. 33:7. ¶

BAALAH – ***baʿᵃlāh*** [proper noun: בַּעֲלָה <1173>; the same as MISTRESS <1172>]: mistress ▶ **A city in Judah.** Refs.: Josh. 15:9–11, 29; 2 Sam. 6:2; 1 Chr. 13:6. ¶

BAALATH – ***baʿᵃlāṯ*** [proper noun: בַּעֲלָת <1191>; a modification of MISTRESS <1172>]: mistress ▶ **A village of the tribe of Dan which was fortified later by Solomon.** Refs.: Josh. 19:44; 1 Kgs. 9:18; 2 Chr. 8:6. ¶

BAALATH-BEER – ***baʿᵃlaṯ bᵉʾēr*** [proper noun: בַּעֲלַת בְּאֵר <1192>; from MISTRESS <1172> and WELL (noun) <875>]: mistress of the well ▶ **A town on the border of the tribe of Simeon.** Ref.: Josh. 19:8. ¶

BAALE-BAMOTH – ***baʿᵃlêy bāmôṯ*** [masc. noun: בַּעֲלֵי בָמוֹת <1181>; from the plur. of BAAL <1168> and the plur. of HIGH PLACE <1116>]: lords of high places ▶ **This word is used to denote dominant heights; it is a place where Balak took Balaam to curse the Israelites for him.** Ref.: Num. 22:41. The ESV and the NIV have Bamoth-Baal. ¶

BAALE-JUDAH – ***baʿᵃlêy yᵉhûḏāh*** [proper noun: בַּעֲלֵי יְהוּדָה <1184>; from the plur. of LORD <1167> and JUDAH <3063>]: Judah (praise) ▶ **Another name for BAALAH <1173>.** Ref.: 2 Sam. 6:2. ¶

BAALI – ***baʿᵃliy*** [masc. proper noun: בַּעֲלִי <1180>; from LORD <1167> with a pron. suffix]: my master ▶ **This word is found in Hosea 2:16.** Some translations interpret it as the words "my master." ¶

BAALIS – ***baʿᵃliys*** [masc. proper noun: בַּעֲלִיס <1185>; prob. from a deriv. of ENJOY <5965> a.]: lord of exultation ▶ **A king of the Ammonites.** Ref.: Jer. 40:14. ¶

BAANA – ***baʿᵃnāʾ*** [masc. proper noun: בַּעֲנָא <1195>; the same as BAANAH <1196>]: in affliction ▶

a. One of Solomon's governors over one of his twelve districts. He had to supply provisions for the king for one month (1 Kgs. 4:12). ¶

b. Another of Solomon's governors and possibly the son of one of David's

wise men. Refs.: 1 Kgs. 4:16; cf. 2 Sam. 15:31–37. ¶
c. The father of Zadok, who helped repair the Fish Gate after the captives returned from the Babylonian exile. Ref.: Neh. 3:4. ¶

BAANAH – ***ba'ᵃnāh*** [masc. proper noun: בַּעֲנָה <1196>; from a deriv. of AFFLICTED (BE) <6031> with prep. prefix]: in affliction ►
a. He served as the commander of Saul's son Ish-bosheth who tried to seize the throne after Saul died. He was assassinated (2 Sam. 4:2, 5, 6, 9). ¶
b. The father of Heleb. He was a Netophathite (2 Sam. 23:29; 1 Chr. 11:30). ¶
c. A Jew of some standing, he was a leader with whom many exiles returned from Babylon. Refs.: Ezra 2:2; Neh. 7:7. ¶
d. He is listed as a leader of the people who sealed the covenant of Nehemiah to serve the Lord faithfully. Ref.: Neh. 10:27. ¶

BAARA – ***ba'ᵃrā'*** [fem. proper noun: בַּעֲרָא <1199>; from SENSELESS <1198>]: brutish, which burns ► **One of the wives of Shaharaim.** Ref.: 1 Chr. 8:8. ¶

BAASEIAH – ***ba'ᵃśêyāh*** [masc. proper noun: בַּעֲשֵׂיָה <1202>; from DO <6213> and LORD <3050> with a prep. prefix]: in the work of the Lord ► **A Levite, ancestor of Asaph the music leader.** Ref.: 1 Chr. 6:40. ¶

BAASHA – ***ba'šā'*** [masc. proper noun: בַּעְשָׁא <1201>; from an unused root meaning to stink]: temerity ► **A king of northern Israel (908–886 B.C.) who gained the kingship by assassinating Jeroboam II's son. He reigned in Tirzah.** He exterminated the dynasty of Jeroboam (1 Kgs. 16:3–8). He was a thorn in Judah's flesh during his reign. He is roundly condemned as a wicked king (1 Kgs. 15:33) who continued the evil policies and practices of Jeroboam I. God sent Jehu as a prophet who announced the eradication of Baasha's house from Israel (1 Kgs. 16:1–7; 21:22). *

BABBLE – Job 11:3 → TALK (EMPTY, IDLE) <907>.

BABBLER – Is. 44:25 → TALK (EMPTY, IDLE) <907>.

BABEL – [1] ***bāḇel*** [proper noun: בָּבֶל <894>; from MIX <1101>]: confusion ► **This word designates also Babylon, the name of the foreign power most often mentioned in the Old Testament.** Its beginnings go back to Nimrod, "a mighty warrior" and hunter but also a founder of cities and city-states (Gen. 10:8–12). At Babel the languages of the world became mixed and separated (Gen. 11:9), and their great towers (ziggurats) were built to approach the gods as humankind deemed necessary. God stopped the building of these "towers of hubris" (Gen. 11:5–8), where humankind tried to gather together as one (Gen. 11:1, 2). It was a part of the Assyrian Empire for a while (2 Kgs. 17:24, 30). The neo-Babylonian Empire, founded by Nabopolassar (626 B.C.), is often mentioned in the prophets (Isaiah, Jeremiah, Ezekiel, Daniel, Micah, Zechariah). Its greatest king, Nebuchadnezzar, ruled nearly 43 years and is the topic of much of the Book of Daniel (Dan. 1:1; 2–4). The Babylonians under Nebuchadnezzar destroyed Jerusalem and took Judah into exile in 587/6 B.C. (2 Kgs. 25:1–28; Jer. 52:3–34). Isaiah the prophet especially denounced the idolatry of Babylon (Is. 40–66). Israel was first deported to Babylon in 606 B.C. for seventy years in fulfillment of both the prophet Moses' and Jeremiah's prophecies (Deut. 28; Jer. 25:1–14). They returned in 536 B.C. under Cyrus, king of Persia (2 Chr. 36:20–23; Ezr. 1:1–3; Zech. 2:7). *
[2] ***bāḇel*** [Aramaic proper noun: בָּבֶל <895>; corresponding to <894> above]: confusion ► **This word refers to the city or nation of Babylon.** The Aramaic word is found only in Ezra and Daniel. See BABEL <894>. The references are to the neo-Babylonian Empire (ca. 626–586 B.C.). *

BABES – Is. 3:4 → CAPRICIOUS CHILDREN <8586>.

BABOON – 1 Kgs. 10:22; 2 Chr. 9:21 ➔ PEACOCK <8500> b.

BABY AT THE BREAST – Is. 49:15 ➔ NURSING CHILD <5764>.

BABYLON – See BABEL <894>, <895>.

BABYLONIAN – [1] ***bāḇelāy*** [Aramaic proper noun: בָּבְלָי <896>; patrial from BABEL <895>] ▶ **An inhabitant of Babylon.** Ref.: Ezra 4:9. ¶
– [2] See CHALDEAN <3778>, <3779>.

BACA – ***bāḵā'*** [proper noun: בָּכָא <1056>; from WEEP <1058>]: tears ▶ **Probably a valley in Israel and/or figuratively: a valley of weeping.** Ref.: Ps. 84:6. ¶

BACK – [1] ***'āḥôr*** [masc. noun: אָחוֹר <268>] ▶ **This work can in general refer to the hinder part or rear side of something.** Of a dwelling (Ex. 26:12, Tabernacle) or of God (Ex. 33:23). It indicates direction, such as before, behind, backward (Gen. 49:17; Ezek. 2:10), or westward (Is. 9:11, 12). Temporally, it can refer to the future (Is. 42:23) or mean finally, holding back to the last (Prov. 29:11). It is used metaphorically, causing wise men to fail or to turn back (Is. 44:25). *
[2] ***gaḇ*** [masc. noun: גַּב <1354>; from an unused root meaning to hollow or curve] ▶ **This word also means a convex surface, a mound.** The term designates the back of humans (Ps. 129:3) or cherubim (Ezek. 10:12). It denotes a mound used as a forbidden religious high place, a place of worship (Ezek. 16:24, 31, 39). It may be used as a technical term for the height of an altar (Ezek. 43:13, NIV, KJV) or its base molding (NASB). It refers to the thick part or protrusion of a shield (Job 15:26; cf. NIV, NASB, KJV [boss or knob of a shield], NKJV). It describes the eyebrows (Lev. 14:9) or even the rim of a wheel (1 Kgs. 7:33; Ezek. 1:18). Other ref.: Job 13:12 (defense, body). ¶
[3] ***gaḇ*** [Aramaic masc. noun: גַּב <1355>; corresponding to <1354> above] ▶ **This word refers to the backside of a leopard; it occurs once in one of Daniel's visions.** Strangely, four wings were attached to it (Dan. 7:6). ¶
[4] ***gaw*** [masc. noun: גַּו <1458>; another form for BACK <1460>] ▶ **This word refers to the rear portion of someone's body, between the neck and the pelvis, but is used with the verb to cast away, forming idioms that mean to cast behind one's back, i.e., to forget, to ignore, to reject.** The idiom indicates rejecting the Lord (1 Kgs. 14:9; Ezek. 23:35) or His laws (Neh. 9:26). ¶
[5] ***gêw*** [masc. noun: גֵּו <1460>; from RISE <1342> (corresponding to <1354> above)] ▶ **This word depicts the rear portion of a person's body, between the neck and the pelvis.** A fool's back is for lashes or a rod (Prov. 10:13; 19:29; 26:3) so that he might learn wisdom. In a figure of speech, the Lord casts the sins of repentant persons behind His back (Is. 38:17). Walking on someone's back means to humiliate and denigrate him or her (Is. 51:23). Other ref.: Is. 50:6. The Hebrew word also means a community of persons (Job 30:5); see COMMUNITY <1460>. ¶
[6] ***gêwāh*** [fem. noun: גֵּוָה <1465>; fem. of BACK <1460>] ▶ **This word describes the rear portion of the human body between the neck and the pelvis; it is also translated body.** In biblical usage, it refers to the back of the wicked person being pierced by an arrow (Job 20:25). ¶
– [7] 1 Kgs. 18:37 ➔ BACKWARD <322> [8] Ps. 38:7 ➔ LOINS <3689> [9] Song 3:10 ➔ SUPPORT (noun) <7507> [10] Is. 30:6 ➔ HUMP <1707> [11] Jer. 2:27; 18:17; 32:33; etc. ➔ NECK <6202> [12] Joel 2:20 ➔ END <5490>.

BACKBONE – ***'āṣeh*** [masc. noun: עָצֶה <6096>; from WINK <6095>] ▶ **This word refers to the spine or tailbone of an animal where the fat tail was located and had to be removed.** Ref.: Lev. 3:9. ¶

BACKSLIDING – [1] ***šôḇāḇ*** [adj.: שׁוֹבָב <7726>; from TURN <7725>] ▶ **This word means turning back or away; it also means faithless, apostate.** It refers to a

people who are always turning away from the Lord, leaving their God, acting unfaithfully towards Him and His laws (Is. 57:17; Jer. 3:14, 22). ¶
[2] ***šôḇēḇ*** [adj.: שׁוֹבָב <7728>; from TURN <7725>] ▶ **This word means apostate; it is also translated unfaithful, faithless.** It refers to a person who is constantly turning aside, away from a set path, acting as an apostate, as Israel and Judah always did (Jer. 31:22; 49:4). It refers to a person of an alien faith, not of Israel's faith or possibly those in Israel who have turned from Israel's God denying their own faith (Mic. 2:4; also translated traitor, turncoat, turning away). ¶
– [3] Jer. 2:19; etc. ➔ TURNING AWAY <4878>.

BACKWARD – ***ᵃḥōranniyṯ*** [adv.: אֲחֹרַנִּית <322>; prolonged from BACK <268>] ▶ **This word indicates motion away from one's front.** Refs.: 2 Kgs. 20:10, 11. It may be walking backward (Gen. 9:23); or falling backward (1 Sam. 4:18). It is used figuratively to describe a heart turning back to the Lord (1 Kgs. 18:37). Other ref.: Is. 38:8. ¶

BAD – [1] ***ra', rā'āh*** [adj.: רַע, רָעָה <7451>; from BAD (BE) <7489>] ▶ **The basic meaning of this word refers to evil, considered in 10 or more aspects that vary according to context. It means evil in a moral and ethical sense.** It is used to describe, along with good, the entire spectrum of good and evil; hence, it depicts evil in an absolute, negative sense, as when it describes the tree of the knowledge of good and evil (Gen. 2:9; 3:5, 22). It was necessary for a wise king to be able to discern the evil or the good in the actions of his people (Eccl. 12:14); men and women are characterized as evil (1 Sam. 30:22; Esther 7:6; Jer. 2:33). The human heart is evil all day long (Gen. 6:5) from childhood (Gen. 8:21); yet the people of God are to purge evil from among them (Deut. 17:7). The Lord is the final arbiter of whether something was good or evil; if something was evil in the eyes of the Lord, there is no further court of appeals (Deut. 9:18; 1 Kgs. 14:22). The day of the Lord's judgment is called an evil day, a day of reckoning and condemnation (Amos 6:3). Jacob would have undergone grave evil (i.e., pain, misery, and ultimate disaster) if he had lost Benjamin (Gen. 44:34). The word can refer to circumstances as evil, as when the Israelite foremen were placed in a grave situation (Ex. 5:19; 2 Kgs. 14:10).

The word takes on the aspect of something disagreeable, unwholesome, or harmful. Jacob evaluated his life as evil and destructive (Gen. 47:9; Num. 20:5); and the Israelites considered the wilderness as a threatening, terrifying place. The Canaanite women were evil in the eyes of Isaac (i.e., displeasing [Gen. 28:8]). The rabble's cry within Israel for meat was displeasing in the eyes of Moses (Num. 11:10). This word describes the vicious animal that killed Joseph, so Jacob thought (Gen. 37:33). The despondent countenances of persons can be described by this word; the baker's and the butler's faces were downcast because of their dreams (Gen. 40:7). It can also describe one who is heavy in heart (Prov. 25:20).

In a literal sense, the word depicts something that is of poor quality or even ugly in appearance. The weak, lean cows of Pharaoh's dream were decrepit, ugly-looking (Gen. 41:3, 20, 27); poisonous drinking water was described as bad (2 Kgs. 2:19; 4:41). From these observations, it is clear that the word can be used to attribute a negative aspect to nearly anything.

Used as a noun, the word indicates realities that are inherently evil, wicked, or bad; the psalmist feared no evil (Ps. 23:4). The noun also depicts people of wickedness, i.e., wicked people. Aaron characterized the people of Israel as inherently wicked in order to clear himself (Ex. 32:22). Calamities, failures, and miseries are all connotations of this word when it is used as a noun. *
– [2] Ezra 4:12 ➔ WICKED <873> [3] Prov. 25:19 ➔ BROKEN <7465> [4] Jer. 29:17 ➔ VILE <8182>.

BAD (BE) – ***rā'a'*** [verb: רָעַע <7489>; a prim. root] ▶ **This word means to do wrong.**

It indicates breaking, in contrast to the word *tāmam* (<8552>), which means to be whole. For example, tree branches that break are bad (Jer. 11:16). The word also refers to moral evil: an eye could be evil, i.e., covetous (Deut. 15:9); or a person could do evil (Gen. 44:5; Prov. 4:16; Jer. 4:22). The word also refers to physical evil: God harmed or punished those who provoked Him (Zech. 8:14); and Laban would have hurt Jacob without God's prevention (Gen. 31:7). In addition, the word expresses sadness and describes the face or heart as being bad (1 Sam. 1:8; Neh. 2:3). The causative participle signifies an evildoer (Ps. 37:1; Is. 9:17). The idiomatic phrase, to be evil in someone's eyes, means to displease (Gen. 48:17; 2 Sam. 11:25; Jon. 4:1). *

BADGER – 1 ***šāpān*** [masc. noun: שָׁפָן <8227>; from TREASURE <8226> (in the sense of something hidden)] ▶ **This word could refer to a rabbit or a badger (i.e., a burrowing mammal of the weasel family); it also means a coney.** It refers to a kind of rabbit, a pika, a hyrax (Lev. 11:5; Deut. 14:7; Ps. 104:18; Prov. 30:26); or a rock badger (NASB, shaphan). For another meaning of the Hebrew word, see SHAPHAN <8227>. *

2 ***tāḥaš*** [masc. noun: תַּחַשׁ <8476>; prob. of foreign deriv.] ▶ **This word refers to an unknown animal or the skin of some unknown animal. The renderings most common are: badger (KJV, NKJV); porpoise (NASB); goatskin (ESV).** The dugong, a large tropical sirenian mammal that inhabits the shores of the Indian Ocean, has also been suggested. Its skin was used in the construction of the covering of the Tabernacle and for making fine shoes and sandals (Ezek. 16:10). All refs.: Ex. 25:5; 26:14; 35:7, 23; 36:19; 39:34; Num. 4:6, 8, 10, 11, 12, 14, 25; Ezek. 16:10. ¶

BAFFLE – ***ᵃnas*** [Aramaic verb: אֲנַס <598>; corresponding to COMPEL <597>] ▶ **This word means to perplex; it is also translated to be difficult, to trouble.** It depicts the inability to solve a mystery or puzzling thing, such as the imagery in a dream (Dan. 4:9). ¶

BAFFLED (BE) – Dan. 5:9 ➔ PERPLEXED <7672>.

BAG – 1 ***ḥāriyṭ*** [masc. noun: חָרִיט <2754>; from the same as GRAVING TOOL <2747> (in the sense of something cut out or hollow)] ▶ **It was a flexible container capable of carrying money, up to a talent of silver weighing about 75 pounds.** Ref.: 2 Kgs. 5:23. Hence it could be called a "money purse" (Is. 3:22; also translated crisping pin, handbag, purse). ¶

2 ***kiys*** [masc. noun: כִּיס <3599>; a form of CUP <3563>] ▶ **This word refers to a container; it is also translated a purse.** A container of leather or cloth for holding various items: stone weights (Deut. 25:13; Prov. 16:11; Mic. 6:11); gold (Is. 46:6). It is used figuratively of fate or destiny (parallel to lot) (Prov. 1:14). For its possible use in Proverbs 23:31, see CUP <3563>. Most scholars prefer to read *kôs* as cup. ¶

3 ***mešek*** [masc. noun: מֶשֶׁךְ <4901>; from PULL <4900>] ▶

a. A word indicating a price, preciousness, an acquisition. It refers to a container, a pouch for seed (Ps. 126:6: precious); and to the acquiring of or the preciousness and unlimited value of wisdom (Job 28:18: price). ¶

b. This word refers to a container, a pouch, or a sack for seed used by a sower. Ref.: Ps. 126:6. ¶

c. A masculine noun referring to a trail, sowing. It refers to the trail of seeds or the path left from sowing seeds (Ps. 126:6). ¶

4 ***ṣᵉrôr*** [masc. noun: צְרוֹר <6872>; from FLOW OVER <6887> (prob. in the sense of to engulf, to shut up)] ▶

a. A word indicating a sack, a bundle, a pouch, a purse. It describes a relatively large cloth bag used to carry a variety of items while traveling (Gen. 42:35; Prov. 7:20). It is used figuratively of a bundle holding persons' lives in security (1 Sam. 25:29); and of transgressors sealed in a bag by God (Job 14:17). It signifies a small leather container of cosmetics (Song 1:13) or money (Hag. 1:6).

b. A word referring to a pebble, a piece of grain. It refers to a relatively small stone

left in a city, possibly a small building stone (2 Sam. 17:13). It is understood as grain in Amos 9:9 by some translators (NASB, grain; KJV, corn). A pebble or a tiny stone is also possible.
c. A masculine proper noun. Zeror is one of the ancestors of Saul, Israel's first king. He was Saul's great-grandfather (1 Sam. 9:1). *

BAGPIPE – ***sûmpônyāh*** [Aramaic fem. noun: סוּמְפּוֹנְיָה <5481>; of Greek origin] ▶ **This word refers to a musical instrument; it is also translated dulcimer, pipe and even "in harmony," a musical term.** It refers to one of the ensemble of musical instruments gathered to celebrate the dedication of Nebuchadnezzar's golden statue (Dan. 3:5, 7, 10, 15). As its renderings indicate, its meaning is disputed. ¶

BAHARUMITE – ***bahᵃrûmiy*** [proper noun: בַּחֲרוּמִי <978>; patrial from BAHURIM <980> (by transposition)] ▶ **Inhabitant of Baharum.** Ref.: 1 Chr. 11:33; see BARHUMITE <1273>. ¶

BAHURIM – ***baḥûriym, baḥuriym*** [proper noun: בַּחֻרִים, בַּחוּרִים <980>; masc. plur. of YOUNG MAN <970>]: young men ▶ **A village near the Mount of Olives.** Refs.: 2 Sam. 3:16; 16:5; 17:18; 19:16; 1 Kgs. 2:8. ¶

BAJITH – ***bayit*** [proper noun: בַּיִת <1006>; the same as HOUSE <1004>]: house ▶ **City or temple in Moab.** Ref.: Is. 15:2; also translated temple. ¶

BAKBAKKAR – ***baqbaqqar*** [masc. proper noun: בַּקְבַּקַּר <1230>; reduplicated from SEEK <1239>]: who searches with diligence ▶ **An Israelite of the tribe of Levi.** Ref.: 1 Chr. 9:15. ¶

BAKBUK – ***baqbûq*** [masc. proper noun: בַּקְבּוּק <1227>; the same as JAR <1228>]: bottle, jar ▶ **Members of his family came back from the Babylonian captivity.** Refs.: Ezra 2:51; Neh. 7:53. ¶

BAKBUKIA – ***baqbuqyāh*** [masc. proper noun: בַּקְבֻּקְיָה <1229>; from JAR <1228> and LORD <3050>]: emptied by the Lord ▶ **A Levite of Jerusalem mentioned after the exile.** Refs.: Neh. 11:17; 12:9, 25. ¶

BAKE – 1 ***'āpāh*** [verb: אָפָה <644>; a prim. root] ▶ **This word refers to the preparation of items of food by combining and heating ingredients.** Especially unleavened bread (Gen. 19:3; Ex. 12:39); but it also refers to whatever needed to be prepared over fire (Ex. 16:23). The participle of the verb always means baker (Gen. 40:1, 2, 5, 16; 41:10; Jer. 37:21; Hos. 7:4). In its passive form, it means to be baked (Lev. 6:17; 7:9; 23:17). *
2 ***'ûg*** [verb: עוּג <5746>; a prim. root] ▶ **This word refers to cooking a cake or bread on hot stones or over a fire.** Ref.: Ezek. 4:12. ¶
– 3 Dan. 4:22, 36; 5:18, 19 ➔ STIRRED <7246>.

BAKED – 1 ***maᵃpeh*** [masc. noun: מַאֲפֶה <3989>; from BAKE <644>] ▶ **This word refers to something that has been prepared in an oven (*tannûr*).** Ref.: Lev. 2:4; KJV: baken. ¶
2 ***tuppiyniym*** [masc. plur. noun: תֻּפִינִים <8601>; from BAKE <644>] ▶ **This word indicates portions of grain cooked by dry heat on a griddle (baked pieces).** They were presented to the Lord at the installation of Aaron and his sons as priests. Others translate this word as meaning broken pieces. This translation emphasizes the fact that the grain offering baked on a griddle is broken up into smaller portions (Lev. 6:21). ¶
– 3 Dan. 2:41: baked clay ➔ lit.: potter's clay ➔ POTTER <6353>.

BAKED (SOMETHING) – 1 Kgs. 17:12 ➔ BREAD <4580>.

BAKED ON COALS, HOT COALS, HOT STONES – ***reṣep*** [masc. noun: רֶצֶף <7529>; from FLASH (noun) (in the sense of burning coal) <7565>] ▶ **This word is**

used in its plural form to define cakes cooked on hot coals (*'ugaṯ rᵉṣāp̱îm*). Ref.: 1 Kgs. 19:6, cf. Is. 6:6. ❡

BAKEN – Lev. 2:4 ➔ BAKED <3989>.

BAKER – Gen. 40:1, 2, 5, 16; 41:10; Jer. 37:21; Hos. 7:4 ➔ BAKE <644>.

BALAAM – See BILEAM <1109>.

BALADAN – ***balᵃḏān*** [masc. proper noun: בַּלְאֲדָן <1081>; from BEL <1078> and LORD <113> (contr.)]: Baal (is his) lord ▶ **A Babylonian prince, father of Merodach-Baladan.** Refs.: 2 Kgs. 20:12; Is. 39:1. ❡

BALAH – ***bālāh*** [proper noun: בָּלָה <1088>; fem. of OLD <1087>]: old, worn out ▶ **A city in the southern part of Judah.** Ref.: Josh. 19:3. ❡

BALAK – ***bālāq*** [masc. proper noun: בָּלָק <1111>; from WASTE (MAKE) <1110>]: waster, empty ▶ **The name of the king of Moab who hired Bileam (Balaam) to curse Israel.** He tried to work with the leaders of the Midianites to destroy Israel (Num. 22:4–7). His people were in fact cursed by Israel's God (cf. Gen. 12:1–3). He was unable to curse the people whom God had blessed (Josh. 24:9; Mic. 6:5). *

BALANCE – 1 ***peles*** [masc. noun: פֶּלֶס <6425>; from WEIGH, WEIGH OUT <6424>] ▶ **This word means a device used for weighing; it is also translated scale, weight.** It refers to a balance or the indicator on a scale or balance (Prov. 16:11; Is. 40:12). In context it is used to show the immensity of God and His power as He weighs even the mountains. God's scales and balances are always just and accurate. ❡

– 2 Num. 3:46, 48, 49 ➔ LEFT, LEFT OVER <5736>.

BALANCED (BE) – Job 37:16 ➔ BALANCING <4657>.

BALANCES – 1 Lev. 19:36; Jer. 32:10; etc. ➔ BALANCE <3976> 2 Dan. 5:27 ➔ SCALES <3977>.

BALANCING – ***mip̱lāś*** [masc. noun: מִפְלָשׂ <4657>; from an unused root meaning to balance] ▶ **This word denotes hanging, hovering.** It is used to describe the floating, hanging in balance of a cloud as a wonder of God (Job 37:16). Some suggest the layering of clouds is in mind (NASB). ❡

BALD – 1 ***gibbêaḥ*** [adj.: גִּבֵּחַ <1371>; from an unused root meaning to be high (in the forehead)] ▶ **This word describes a person's head from which all hair has fallen out.** Ref.: Lev. 13:41. This unnatural condition did not make a person unclean according to the Law. ❡

2 ***gabbaḥaṯ*** [fem. noun: גַּבַּחַת <1372>; from the same as BALD <1371>] ▶ **This word depicts a forehead lacking hair, forehead; barrenness.** It refers to the baldness of one's forehead, bald at the front (Lev. 13:42, 43). And it indicates a bare spot on something, i.e., a garment, etc. (Lev. 13:55); it is translated without, on the front. ❡

3 ***qêrêaḥ*** [adj.: קֵרֵחַ <7142>; from SHAVE THE HEAD <7139>] ▶ **This word refers to a condition in which a man loses his hair.** Ref.: Lev. 13:40. He is still considered ritually clean. Elisha, a great prophet, was naturally bald (2 Kgs. 2:23; also translated baldhead, baldy). ❡

BALD (MAKE) – Lev. 21:5; Jer. 16:6; Ezek. 27:31; 29:18 ➔ SHAVE THE HEAD <7139>.

BALD HEAD – ***qārḥaṯ*** [fem. noun: קָרַחַת <7146>; from SHAVE THE HEAD <7139>] ▶ **This word refers to an area that has become bare on the back or crown of a person's head; hence, figuratively to a bare spot or an area eaten away or deteriorating in a piece of clothing.** Refs.: Lev. 13:42, 43. In Lev. 13:55 the word is translated bareness, rot, damage. ❡

BALDHEAD – 2 Kgs. 2:23 ➔ BALD <7142>.

BALDNESS – 1 ***qorḥāh, qorḥā'*** [fem. noun: קָרְחָה, קָרְחָא <7144>; from SHAVE THE HEAD <7139>] ▶ **This word refers to having no hair on a shorn head. It also means a shaved head.** It was a practice forbidden to priests in Israel (Lev. 21:5). It was a practice forbidden to the children of the Lord as a sign for the sake of the dead (Deut. 14:1). It is used poetically as the opposite of hair styles that displayed the beauty of one's hair (Is. 3:24). It could be a sign of mourning (Is. 15:2; 22:12; Mic. 1:16); or of devastation (Jer. 47:5; 48:37; Amos 8:10). Other refs.: Ezek. 7:18; 27:31. ¶
– 2 Lev. 13:41 ➔ lit.: bald ➔ BALD <1371>.

BALDY – 2 Kgs. 2:23 ➔ BALD <7142>.

BALL – ***dûr*** [masc. noun: דּוּר <1754>; from DWELL <1752>] ▶ **This word indicates a heap, pile, something balled up.** It is used figuratively to describe Israel's being rolled tightly like a ball and cast away (Is. 22:18) into exile. It is used of piling wood or bones for fuel under a cooking pot (Ezek. 24:5; KJV, burn; NKJV, pile). Other ref.: Is. 29:3. ¶

BALM – ***ṣ°riy, ṣᵉriy*** [masc. noun: צֳרִי, צְרִי <6875>; from an unused root meaning to crack (as by pressure)] ▶ **This word indicates an aromatic gum resin from certain trees and plants. It can be used as a cosmetic or as a medicine.** It was a much desired item of trade in the ancient Middle East (Gen. 37:25; 43:11; Ezek. 27:17). Its medicinal use is stressed in some passages, especially the balm available in Gilead (Jer. 8:22; 46:11; 51:8). ¶

BALSAM – Song 5:1 ➔ SPICE <1313>.

BALSAM TREE – ***bāḵā'*** [masc. noun: בָּכָא <1057>; the same as BACA <1056>] ▶ **This word indicates baka shrubs; it is also translated mulberry tree, poplar tree.** It refers to valley shrubs or balsam trees in the tops of which the Lord made the presence of His military forces known (2 Sam. 5:23, 24; 1 Chr. 14:14, 15). Balsam trees yield an aromatic resinous substance. ¶

BAMAH – ***bāmāh*** [proper noun: בָּמָה <1117>; the same as HIGH PLACE <1116> (see also BAMOTH <1120>)]: high place ▶ **A high place in Israel where the Israelites worshipped idols.** Ref.: Ezek. 20:29. ¶

BAMOTH – ***bāmôṯ, bāmôṯ ba'al*** [proper noun בָּמוֹת, בָּמוֹת בַּעַל <1120>; plur. of HIGH PLACE <1116>]: high places ▶
a. A place in the country of Moab. Refs.: Num. 21:19, 20. ¶
b. Balak brought Balaam up to Bamoth Baal (the high places of Baal). Refs.: Num. 22:41; Josh. 13:17. ¶

BAMOTH-BAAL – Num. 22:41 ➔ BAALE-BAMOTH <1181>.

BAN – 2 Chr. 26:21 ➔ GORE <5055>.

BAND (noun) – 1 ***gᵉḏûḏ*** [masc. noun: גְּדוּד <1416>; from GATHER <1413>] ▶ **This word is used to indicate a marauding company, a raiding party, or a group that makes inroads into enemy territory; it is also translated a troop.** It sometimes refers to Israel's military (2 Sam. 4:2; 2 Chr. 22:1), but more often, it refers to the marauding enemies of Israel (Gen. 49:19; 1 Sam. 30:8, 15, 23; 1 Kgs. 11:24; 2 Kgs. 5:2; 6:23; 24:2). In some instances, these marauding bands operate independently and are thus labeled as troops of robbers (Hos. 6:9; 7:1). By extension, the word sometimes refers to the actual raid itself (2 Sam. 3:22). On other occasions, it indicates the army in general (Job 29:25) or some division of troops within the army (1 Chr. 7:4; 2 Chr. 25:9, 10, 13; 26:11; Mic. 5:1). It is used figuratively for God's chastisements (Job 19:12) and His attacking forces (Job 25:3). *
2 **skillfully woven, intricately woven, artistic sash:** ***ḥēšeḇ*** [masc. noun: חֵשֶׁב <2805>; from THINK <2803> (in the sense of inventing something artistic)] ▶ **This word means waistband, a skillfully woven waistband; it is also translated curious girdle.** It describes the band or girdle on the ephod of the priest (Ex. 28:27, 28) used to secure it to him (Lev. 8:7) in a

way that it would not come loose or fall off. Other refs.: Ex. 28:8; 29:5; 39:5, 20, 21. ¶
– 3 2 Sam. 2:25; Is. 58:6 → BUNCH <92> 4 Job 38:31 → CORD <4189> 5 Job 39:5; etc. → BOND <4147> b. 6 Prov. 30:27 → to go forth by bands → DIVIDE <2686> a. 7 Is. 28:22; 52:2; etc. → BOND <4147> a. 8 Is. 58:6; Ps. 73:4 → BOND <2784> 9 Dan. 4:15, 23 → IMPRISONMENT <613> 10 Hos. 6:9 → COMPANY <2267>.

BAND (verb) – Ps. 94:21 → GATHER <1413>.

BANDAGE – 1 ***ᵃpēr*** [masc. noun: אֲפֵר <666>; from the same as ASHES <665> (in the sense of covering)] ► **This word means a piece of cloth wrapped around the head (as to cover a wound and/or for disguise); it is also translated headband (KJV translates the word ashes).** It describes something placed over a person's eyes in order to disguise him or her (1 Kgs. 20:38, 41). ¶
2 ***ḥittûl*** [masc. noun: חִתּוּל <2848>; from SWADDLE <2853>] ► **This word means a dressing for setting broken bones; it is also translated splint, roller.** It is used figuratively of binding up the power, the "arm" of Pharaoh militarily and politically (Ezek. 30:21), especially significant since Pharaoh's arm represented his military power and political might. ¶

BANDIT – Prov. 23:28 → ROBBER <2863>.

BANDS – 1 Judg. 15:14; Eccl. 7:26 → BOND <612> 2 Ezek. 12:14; 17:21; 38:6, 9, 22; 39:4 → TROOPS <102>.

BANGLE – Is. 3:18 → ANKLET <5914>.

BANI – ***bāniy*** [masc. proper noun: בָּנִי <1137>; from BUILD <1129>]: built, posterity ►
a. One of David's mighty men. Ref.: 2 Sam. 23:36. ¶
b. An Aaronite. Ref.: 1 Chr. 6:46. ¶
c. A descendant of Pharez. Refs.: 1 Chr. 9:4; Ezra 2:10; 10:29, 34. ¶
d. A son of Bani. Ref.: Ezra 10:38. ¶
e. A Levite. Refs.: Neh. 3:17; 8:7; 9:4, 5; 10:13, 14; 11:22. ¶

BANISHED – Is. 11:12 → DRIVE <1760>.

BANISHMENT – ***šᵉrōšû*** [Aramaic fem. noun: שְׁרֹשׁוּ <8332>; from a root corresponding to ROOT (TAKE) <8327> (in its pass. sense of to be uprooted)] ► **This word indicates the ejection of a person from a social or political community.** In context it does so because of a failure to observe the Mosaic covenant (Ezra 7:26). ¶

BANISHMENT (CAUSE OF) – Lam. 2:14 → MISLEADING <4065>.

BANK – 1 ***gāḏāh*** [fem. noun: גָּדָה <1415>; from an unused root (meaning to cut off)] ► **This word indicates the edge of a river.** It refers to the banks of the Jordan River when Israel entered the land of Canaan (Josh. 3:15; 4:18) and at other times when it was in a flood stage (1 Chr. 12:15). It is used to refer to the banks of the Euphrates River in a figurative sense (Is. 8:7). ¶
2 ***giḏyāh*** [fem. noun: גִּדְיָה <1428>; the same as BANK <1415>] ► **This word refers to the shores of the Jordan River at flood time.** Ref.: 1 Chr. 12:15. It is used figuratively of the banks of the Euphrates overflowing with the attacking Assyrians as they inundate Israel and Judah (Is. 8:7). ¶

BANNER – 1 ***degel*** [masc. noun: דֶּגֶל <1714>; from BANNERS (SET UP, LIFT UP) <1713>] ► **This word denotes a flag, sign, standard.** It depicted banners or standards to identify the various tribes of Israel (Num. 1:52; 2:2). It represented the tribe to which a group belonged (Num. 2:3, 10; also translated division). It depicted the attitude and intent of the lover toward his bride (Song 2:4). Other refs.: Num. 2:17, 18, 25, 31, 34; 10:14, 18, 22, 25. ¶
2 ***nês*** [masc. proper noun: נֵס <5251>; from SPARKLE <5264>] ► **This word refers to a symbol or sign.** It represents a cause, a person, God: a standard, a representation

of the Lord (Ex. 17:15); and the name of an altar dedicated to the Lord. It indicates a pole on which to display something (Num. 21:8, 9). It signifies a sign representing Zion (Is. 31:9; Jer. 4:6; also translated ensign, signal); or a tragedy that could serve as a *nês*, a warning or a sign (Num. 26:10). It indicates a flag or a symbol to rally around (Ex. 17:15; Is. 18:3). The Root of Jesse will stand as an ensign, a signal for the people (Is. 11:10). *
– [3] Song 6:4, 10 → with banners → set up with banners → BANNERS (SET UP, LIFT UP) <1713>.

BANNER (LIFT LIKE A) – Zech. 9:16 → SPARKLE <5264> b.

BANNER (SERVE AS A) – Ezek. 27:7 → SPREADING <4666>.

BANNERS (SET UP, LIFT UP) – ***dāgal*** [verb: דָּגַל <1713>; a prim. root] ▶ **This word means to carry a flag, a standard, an ensign; to distinguish.** It indicates the display of a symbol of loyalty and commitment to the Lord for His victories (Ps. 20:5). Its display showed the strength and dazzling glory of an army (Song 6:4, 10) arrayed in its orderly troops. It is used to describe the appearance of the beloved, distinguished among all others (Song 5:10); it is translated chief, chiefest, outstanding, distinguished. ¶

BANQUET – [1] ***kêrāh*** [fem. noun: כֵּרָה <3740>; from BUY <3739>] ▶ **This word indicates a feast or meal.** It refers to a great meal or feast and is used with its related verb for emphasis (2 Kgs. 6:23): "And he prepared a feast for them, a great feast." It describes the giving of a feast (*kêrāh*) to certain persons (2 Kgs. 6:23). Some scholars find the word in Job 41:6 and translate accordingly. ¶
[2] ***mištê'*** [Aramaic masc. noun: מִשְׁתֵּא <4961>; corresponding to FEAST <4960>] ▶ **This word denotes a feast.** It refers to a large spread of food or a place of celebration with eating and drinking (Dan. 5:10; ESV: banqueting). ¶
– [3] Dan. 5:1 → FEAST <3900> [4] Amos 6:7 → BANQUETING <4797>.

BANQUET (MAKE) – Job 41:6 → BUY <3739>.

BANQUETING – [1] ***mirzaḥ*** [masc. noun: מִרְזַח <4797>; from an unused root meaning to scream (e.g., a cry of joy, a cry of revelry)] ▶ **This word means an occasion of luxurious eating, drinking, and merriments; it is also translated banquet, feasting, revelry.** It refers to a meal; an extravagant festive banquet (Amos 6:7). ¶
– [2] Dan. 5:10 → BANQUET <4961>.

BAR – [1] ***bᵉriyaḥ*** [masc. noun: בְּרִיחַ <1280>; from FLEE <1272>] ▶ **This word denotes a crossbeam, bolt, gate; a noble (person).** It refers to wooden crossbars used to join wooden frames in the Tabernacle, gates, and doors (Ex. 26:26–29; Judg. 16:3; 1 Sam. 23:7). It refers to eerie features of the depths of the sea, the underworld (Jon. 2:6), and the unseen bolts or restraints God put on the activity of the sea (Job 38:10). Also in a figurative use, it refers to bars of distress, stress (Ps. 107:16), which are broken by the Lord. *
[2] ***māṭiyl*** [masc. noun: מְטִיל <4300>; from CAST <2904> in the sense of hammering out] ▶ **This word points to a long piece of metal, a rod.** It indicates strong, powerful limbs in a figurative description of Behemoth (Job 40:18). ¶
– [3] Num. 4:10, 12 → POLE <4132> [4] Ps. 68:30 → PIECE <7518> [5] Jer. 28:13 → YOKE <4133>.

BARACHEL – ***barak'ēl*** [masc. proper noun: בַּרַכְאֵל <1292>; from BLESS <1288> and GOD <410>]: God has blessed ▶ **The father of Elihu, one of Job's friend.** Refs.: Job 32:2, 6. ¶

BARAK – ***bārāq*** [masc. proper noun: בָּרָק <1301>; the same as LIGHTNING <1300>]: lightning flash ▶ **Barak helped Deborah call together Israel's tribes to war against Sisera. His father was Abinoam.** He refused to act alone, which prompted the Lord to deliver Israel from Sisera by the hand of a woman (Judg. 4:9; 5:24–27), Jael, wife of Heber the Kenite.

Barak and Deborah together composed and sang the "Song of Deborah" (Judg. 5:1). Other refs.: Judg. 4:6, 8, 10, 12, 14–16, 22; 5:12, 15. ¶

BARB – ***śēḵ*** [masc. noun: שֵׂךְ <7899>; from COVER (verb) <5526> in the sense of HEDGE (MAKE A) <7753>] ▶ **This word refers to a short needle-like stem or branch without leaves that can easily puncture a person's eye.** Ref.: Num. 33:55; also translated prick, irritant. ¶

BARBED IRON – Job 41:7 ➔ HARPOON <7905>.

BARBER – ***gallāḇ*** [masc. noun: גַּלָּב <1532>; from an unused root meaning to shave] ▶ **This word is used once to depict a person who cuts hair, normally with a razor.** Ref.: Ezek. 5:1. ¶

BARE (adj.) – 1 Is. 13:2 ➔ STICK OUT <8192> 2 Is. 47:2 ➔ STRIP <2834> 3 Ezek. 16:7; Hab. 3:9 ➔ NAKEDNESS <6181>.

BARE (MAKE) – 1 Is. 47:2; 52:10 ➔ STRIP <2834> 2 Jer. 13:22 ➔ VIOLENCE (DO) <2554> 3 Hab. 3:9 ➔ UNCOVER <5783>.

BARE (noun) – 1 ***ṣᵉḥiyaḥ*** [masc. noun: צְחִיחַ <6706>; from WHITER <6705>] ▶ **This word refers to a place dried up by the sun; an exposed place.** It describes totally bare places on tops of rocks (Ezek. 24:7, 8; 26:4, 14). It indicates open, vulnerable places along a wall that has been damaged badly (Neh. 4:13: higher place, open place, exposed place, opening). ¶

2 ***šᵉpiy*** [masc. noun: שְׁפִי <8205>; from STICK OUT <8192>] ▶ **This word carries the idea of a barren or smooth place.** It is used to describe dry places where God will open rivers (Is. 41:18); and infertile places where God will create pastures (Is. 49:9). The donkeys could not find grass in such places (Jer. 14:6). The barren place was where Balaam went to meet God (Num. 23:3); and where Israel was to lament their destruction (Jer. 7:29). At times, it could describe the bare hills (Jer. 3:2, 21) from which the dry winds originated in the barren wilderness (Jer. 4:11; 12:12). ¶

BAREFOOT – 1 ***yāḥēp̱*** [adj.: יָחֵף <3182>; from an unused root meaning to take off the shoes] ▶ **This word describes something or someone as wearing nothing in the feet; it is also translated unshod.** It indicates the absence of shoes or footwear (2 Sam. 15:30; Jer. 2:25). In David's case, it also implied mourning and depression, as well as in the case of Isaiah whose nakedness and bare feet were a sign of the destruction about to come on Jerusalem (Is. 20:2–4). It signifies licentiousness in Jeremiah's usage (Jer. 2:25). ¶

– 2 Job 12:17, 19; Mic. 1:8 ➔ STRIPPED <7758>.

BARGAIN – Job 6:27; 41:6 ➔ BUY <3739>.

BARHUMITE – ***barḥumiy*** [masc. proper noun: בַּרְחֻמִי <1273>; by transposition for BAHARUMITE <978>]: chosen, beloved ▶ **A transposed form of BAHARUMITE <978>.** Ref.: 2 Sam. 23:31. ¶

BARIAH – ***bāriyaḥ*** [masc. proper noun: בָּרִיחַ <1282>; the same as FLEEING <1281>]: fugitive ▶ **An Israelite, son of Shemaiah.** Ref.: 1 Chr. 3:22. ¶

BARK – 1 ***nāḇaḥ*** [verb: נָבַח <5024>; a prim. root] ▶ **This word refers to a sharp, abrupt sound made by a dog; the naturally expected ability of a dog to make these sounds.** Ref.: Is. 56:10. ¶

– 2 Ex. 11:7 ➔ MOVE <2782>.

BARKOS – ***barqôs*** [masc. proper noun: בַּרְקוֹס <1302>; of uncertain deriv.]: son who follows his father ▶ **Some members of his family came back from the Babylonian captivity.** Refs.: Ezra 2:53; Neh. 7:55. ¶

BARLEY – ***śᵉʿōrāh*** [fem. noun: שְׂעֹרָה <8184>; from SWEEP AWAY <8175> in the sense of roughness] ▶ **This word indicates a cereal grass with heavy, dense spikes of flowers, giving a bearded appearance.** It is also used in making malt. It was a major food crop in Israel and Philistia. Egypt's barley was ruined in the seventh plague (Ex. 9:31). Barley harvest was a time of rejoicing (2 Sam. 21:9). There was barley grain and barley flour (Deut. 8:8; 1 Kgs. 4:28; 2 Kgs. 4:42). It was also used as food for horses (1 Kgs. 4:28). *

BARN – 1 ***'āsām*** [masc. noun: אָסָם <618>; from an unused root meaning to heap together, a storehouse (only in the plur.)] ▶ **This word means a place for laying up and preserving produce; it is also translated storehouse. It refers to those buildings where the Lord gave His blessing on stored produce.** Ref.: Deut. 28:8. Barns full of plenty were a result of honoring the Lord with one's wealth (Prov. 3:10). ¶
2 ***māzû*** [masc. noun: מָזוּ <4200>; prob. from an unused root meaning to gather in] ▶ **It was a place where grain was stored that was used in preparing all kinds of foods, a garner.** Ref.: Ps. 144:13; also translated granary. ¶
– 3 Jer. 50:26 ➔ GRANARY <3965> 4 Joel 1:17 ➔ GRANARY <4460> 5 Hag. 2:19 ➔ FEAR (noun) <4035>.

BARN OWL – Lev. 11:18 ➔ WHITE OWL <8580> a.

BARREL – 1 Kgs. 17:12; 18:33 ➔ JAR <3537>.

BARREN – 1 ***'āqār*** [adj.: עָקָר <6135>; from HAMSTRING <6131> b. (sterile, as if extirpated in the generative organs)] ▶ **This word means childless. It refers to the state of not being fertile, not being able to become pregnant.** God is often mentioned as the one who brought about this condition and/or the one who overcomes it. Sarah, Rebekah, Rachel, the mother of Samson, and Hannah are chief examples of this situation (Gen. 11:30; 25:21; 29:31; Judg. 13:2, 3; 1 Sam. 2:5). It is used figuratively of Zion's not having borne the spiritual children of God as the Lord had hoped (Is. 54:1). *
– 2 Job 3:7; 15:34; Is. 49:21 ➔ SOLITARY <1565> 3 Prov. 30:16 ➔ OPPRESSION <6115> 4 Song 4:2; 6:6 ➔ BEREAVED <7909>.

BARREN LAND – Job 39:6 ➔ BARRENNESS <4420>.

BARRENNESS – ***m^elêḥāh*** [fem. noun: מְלֵחָה <4420>; from SEASON (verb) <4414> (in its denom. sense)] ▶ **This word refers to unfruitfulness, also to saltiness.** It indicates the barren, open desert as a home for the wild donkey (Job 39:6: salt land, barren land, salt flats). It indicates that a land is not fruitful (Ps. 107:34; also translated, salt waste, salty waste); and harbors little, if any, life (Jer. 17:6: salt). ¶

BARTER – Job 6:27; 41:6 ➔ BUY <3739>.

BARUCH – ***bārûḵ*** [masc. proper noun: בָּרוּךְ <1263>; pass. part. from BLESS <1288>]: blessed, happy ▶
a. The faithful scribe and friend of Jeremiah. He was the son of Neriah (Jer. 51:59) and brother to Seriah (Jer. 32:12; 51:59). He recorded Jeremiah's prophecies twice and also read them to the people (Jer. 36:4–32). He and Jeremiah were both forcefully taken to Egypt (Jer. 43:4–7). According to tradition, they died in Egypt. He was so well respected as a scribe that later apocalypses were given his name (e.g., The Apocalypse of Baruch). *
b. The name refers to a priest, a son of Zabbai. He helped Nehemiah rebuild the Jerusalem wall and supported the renewal covenant (Neh. 3:20; 10:6). ¶
c. It denotes the father of Maaseiah. Ref.: Neh. 11:5. He was son of Col-Hozeh, son of Hazaiah. ¶

BARZILLAI – ***barzillay*** [masc. proper noun: בַּרְזִלַּי <1271>; from IRON <1270>]: made of iron ▶
a. A man from Gilead. Refs.: 2 Sam. 17:27; 19:32–40). He was a faithful follower of David (1 Kgs. 2:7). ¶

b. It denotes a priest. Refs.: Ezra 2:61; Neh. 7:63. He married a daughter of Barzillai and had, evidently, taken on the name. ¶
c. It refers to a Meholathite. Ref.: 2 Sam. 21:8. His son married Saul's daughter Merab, who bore five sons to him. ¶

BASE (adj.) – Is. 3:5 ➔ DESPISED (BE) <7034>.

BASE (noun) – [1] ***'eḏen*** [masc. noun: אֶדֶן <134>; from the same as LORD <113> (in the sense of strength)] ▶ **This word indicates a pedestal or socket.** It was a term used of the construction of various parts of the Tabernacle in Exodus; e.g., these sockets served as holders and as a foundation for the hollow boards used to construct the Tabernacle (Ex. 26:19, 21, 25; 35:11; Num. 3:36, 37). It describes the bases of the earth (Job 38:6; also translated foundations, footings). And it describes the legs of the lover, set like pillars upon pedestals of gold, in Song of Solomon 5:15. *
[2] ***meḵunāh*** [fem. noun: מְכֻנָה <4369>; the same as STAND <4350>] ▶ **This word means a pedestal.** It refers to a stand or platform on which to live or stand (Zech. 5:11; also translated place). ¶
– [3] Ex. 25:31 ➔ THIGH <3409> [4] Ex. 29:12; Lev. 4:7, 18, 25, 30, 34; etc. ➔ FOUNDATION <3247> [5] Ex. 30:18, 28; 31:9; Lev. 8:11; 1 Kgs. 7:29, 31; Is. 33:23 ➔ STAND (noun) <3653> [6] 2 Kgs. 16:17 ➔ PAVEMENT <4837> [7] Song 3:10 ➔ SUPPORT (noun) <7507> [8] Ezra 3:3; Zech. 5:11 ➔ STAND (noun) <4350> [9] Ezek. 43:13, 14, 17 ➔ BOSOM <2436>.

BASEST – Dan. 4:17 ➔ LOWLIEST <8215>.

BASHAN – ***bāšān*** [proper noun: בָּשָׁן <1316>; of uncertain deriv.]: wide, open country ▶ **The name of a region east of the Jordan River ruled by Og, king of Bashan.** It was east and north of the Sea of Galilee. The Lord gave it into the hands of Israel (Num. 21:33). It was given to Manasseh as an allotment (Num. 32:33). The Yarmuk River cut across it. Its fertile lands were legendary (Deut. 32:14; Ps. 22:12; Is. 2:13; Ezek. 39:18). Both David and Solomon were in charge of it (1 Kgs. 4:13, 19). It was seized by various foreign powers during the vicissitudes of Israel's history (cf. 2 Kgs. 10:33; 14:25). It was an object of prophetic judgment by Jeremiah (Jer. 22:20), but its return to Israel is a part of the future hope of the prophets (Jer. 50:19; Mic. 7:14). *

BASHEMATH, BASEMATH – ***bāśemaṯ*** [fem. proper noun: בָּשְׂמַת <1315>; fem. of SPICE <1314> (in the sense of fragrance, perfume)]: fragrance ▶
a. One of the wives of Esau, a daughter of a Hittite. Ref.: Gen. 26:34. ¶
b. One of the wives of Esau, a daughter of Ishmael. Refs.: Gen. 36:3, 4, 10, 13, 17. ¶
c. A daughter of Solomon. Ref.: 1 Kgs. 4:15. ¶

BASIN – [1] ***'aggān*** [masc. noun: אַגָּן <101>; prob. from PLAY (verb) <5059>] ▶ **The word designates a large, deep bowl.** Ref.: Ex. 24:6; also translated bason (KJV). It is also translated cup, goblet in Isaiah 22:24 and Song of Solomon 7:2. ¶
[2] ***'agarṭāl*** [masc. noun: אֲגַרְטָל <105>; of uncertain deriv.] ▶ **This word designates a large bowl; it is also translated platter, dish, charger.** It refers to the thirty gold basins and the one thousand silver basins returned to the Temple in Jerusalem during the time of Ezra (Ezra 1:9, 10). ¶
[3] ***kiyyôr*** [masc. noun: כִּיּוֹר <3595>; from the same as FURNACE <3564>] ▶ **This word refers to a bowl or laver for washing or cooking.** Refs.: Ex. 30:18; 31:9; 35:16; 38:8; Lev. 8:11; 1 Sam. 2:14; 1 Kgs. 7:30; Zech. 12:6). In 2 Chronicles 6:13, it refers to a platform (KJV: scaffold) on which King Solomon stood and knelt in order to pray. *
[4] ***mizrāq*** [masc. noun: מִזְרָק <4219>; from SPRINKLE <2236>] ▶ **This word refers to bowls of bronze used in the Tabernacle and then the Temple service by priests serving in the ritual sacrifices of Israel.** Refs.: Ex. 27:3; 38:3; 1 Kgs. 7:40. It indicates more generally a bowl for wine (Amos 6:6). They were also used to carry flour mixed with oil for offerings (Num.

7:13, 19, 25, 31). Basins of silver and gold were also used in the Temples (1 Kgs. 7:50; 2 Kgs. 12:13; Neh. 7:70). *
[5] ***sap̱*** [masc. noun: סַף <5592>; from DOORKEEPER (BE A) <5605> (in the original sense of containing)] ▶ **It was a bowl or a large hollow dish or cup used in rituals, cultic events.** Refs.: Ex. 12:22; 2 Sam. 17:28; 1 Kgs. 7:50. It was among the Temple furnishings and instruments (Jer. 52:19). It is used figuratively of a cup, Jerusalem, and its contents that will cause consternation to all the nations around her (Zech. 12:2). Other ref.: 2 Kgs. 2:13. The Hebrew word also means a threshold, a doorway; see THRESHOLD <5592>. *
– [6] 1 Kgs. 7:37–39 ➔ STAND (noun) <4350> [7] Ezra 1:10; 8:27 ➔ BOWL <3713>.

BASKET – [1] ***dûḏ*** [masc. noun: דּוּד <1731>; from the same as LOVER <1730>] ▶ **This word describes a deep, two-handled cooking pot.** Ref.: 1 Sam. 2:14: kettle. It was used as a container to carry the severed heads of Ahab's seventy sons (2 Kgs. 10:7). A basket for figs is pictured in Jeremiah's visions (Jer. 24:2). It indicates Egyptian baskets that Israelites were forced to use in slavery (Ps. 81:6; KJV: pot). It refers to pots or caldrons as well (2 Chr. 35:13: caldron, kettle; Job 41:20: pot). ¶
[2] ***ṭene'*** [masc. noun: טֶנֶא <2935>; from an unused root prob. meaning to weave] ▶ **This word is used to describe a container holding offerings from the ground of the Promised Land of Canaan.** Refs.: Deut. 26:2, 4. It is also used symbolically to represent the rich abundance of the ground (Deut. 28:5, 17). ¶
[3] ***kelûḇ*** [masc. noun: כְּלוּב <3619>; from the same as DOG <3611>] ▶ **This word refers to a wicker-work container for fruit seen in a prophetic vision.** Refs.: Amos 8:1, 2. It refers also to a cage but is used figuratively of Jerusalem as full of deceit as a cage full of birds (Jer. 5:27). ¶
[4] ***sal*** [masc. noun: סַל <5536>; from EXALT <5549> (in the sense of to build up)] ▶ **This word refers to a container for holding various food or sacrificial items.** Loaves of bread (Gen. 40:16–18); various meal offerings of bread (Ex. 29:3); unleavened bread as an offering (Lev. 8:2; Num. 6:15); meat (Judg. 6:19). Other refs.: Ex. 29:23, 32; Lev. 8:26, 31; Num. 6:17, 19. ¶
– [5] Ex. 2:3, 5 ➔ ARK <8392> [6] Jer. 6:9 ➔ BRANCH <5552> b. [7] Jer. 24:1 ➔ MANDRAKE <1736>.

BASON – [1] Ex. 24:6 ➔ BASIN <101> [2] 1 Chr. 28:17; Ezra 1:10; 8:27 ➔ BOWL <3713>.

BASTARD – Deut. 23:2; Zech. 9:6 ➔ FORBIDDEN UNION (ONE BORN OF) <4464>.

BAT – ***'aṭallēp̱*** [masc. noun: עֲטַלֵּף <5847>; of uncertain deriv.] ▶ **This word refers to a winged creature forbidden as food to the Israelites, a nocturnal flying animal considered unclean to Israel.** Refs.: Lev. 11:19; Deut. 14:18. Other ref.: Is. 2:20. ¶

BATH – [1] ***baṯ*** [common noun: בַּת <1324>; prob. from the same as DESOLATE <1327>] ▶ **This word denotes a liquid measure.** The bath equaled one-tenth of a homer or kor or about twenty-three liquid or twenty dry quarts (Ezek. 45:14). It is mentioned as a liquid measure of oil (Ezek. 45:14); wine (2 Chr. 2:10); and water (1 Kgs. 7:26). Some authorities think another bath existed equaling twice the capacity of the better-known bath. *
[2] ***baṯ*** [Aramaic masc. noun: בַּת <1325>; corresponding to <1324> above] ▶ **This is the same liquid measure discussed under BATH <1324>.** One hundred baths of wine would have equaled about 2,300 quarts or about six hundred gallons (Ezra 7:22). King Artaxerxes of Persia ordered this amount of wine to be supplied to Ezra as he requested. ¶

BATH RABBIM – ***baṯ rabbiym*** [proper noun: בַּת רַבִּים <1337>; from DAUGHTER <1323> and a masc. plur. from MANY <7227>]: daughter of many ▶ **One of the gates of Heshbon.** Ref.: Song 7:4. ¶

BATHSHEBA – ***baṯ-šeḇa'*** [fem. proper noun: בַּת־שֶׁבַע <1339>; from DAUGHTER

<1323> and SEVEN <7651> (in the sense of SWEAR <7650>)]: daughter of an oath ▶ **The name of one of David's wives with whom he had committed adultery (2 Sam. 11:1–5).** David murdered her husband Uriah (2 Sam. 11:1–12:24). Her father was Eliam (2 Sam. 11:3; cf. 1 Chr. 3:5). Her first son, the result of adultery with David, died. After marrying David, she bore him four more sons including Solomon (2 Sam. 12:24; 1 Chr. 3:5). She secured the ascension of her son Solomon to the throne (1 Kgs. 1:1–2:19). She is called Bathshua in 1 Chronicles 3:5. Other ref.: Ps. 51:1. ¶

BATHSHUA – ***bat̲ šûaʻ*** [fem. proper noun: בַּת שׁוּעַ <1340>; from DAUGHTER <1323> and RICH (noun) <7771> a.]: daughter of wealth; daughter of an oath ▶
a. Wife of Judah. Ref.: 1 Chr. 2:3. ¶
b. Alternate spelling for Bathsheba, the wife of David. Ref.: 1 Chr. 3:5. ¶

BATTEN OF THE LOOM – Judg. 16:14 ➔ PEG <3489>.

BATTER DOWN – Is. 22:5 ➔ DIG <6979> b.

BATTERING RAM – [1] ***qōb̲el, q^{e}b̲ōl*** [masc. noun: קֹבֶל, קְבֹל <6904>; from ACCEPT <6901> in the sense of confronting (as standing opposite in order to receive)] ▶
a. This word indicates an engine of war used to strike the walls and gates of cities to demolish them. Ref.: Ezek. 26:9.
b. This word is understood to refer to the battle or to war itself by some translators. The preceding word (*m^{e}ḥî*) is then taken to mean a blow, a striking (of an engine of war) (Ezek. 26:9).
c. This word means something in front. It refers to a physical presence in front of persons, in their presence, publicly (2 Kgs. 15:10). ¶
– [2] Ezek. 4:2 ➔ LAMB <3733>.

BATTLE – [1] ***kiyd̲ôr*** [masc. noun: כִּידוֹר <3593>; of uncertain deriv.] ▶ **This word refers to a hostile, offensive action taken against someone.** In the context, it denotes an attack against the wicked by a well-prepared king (Job 15:24). ¶
[2] ***q^{e}rāb̲*** [masc. noun: קְרָב <7128>; from COME NEAR <7126>] ▶ **This word refers to hostilities and also indicates a war.** It refers to a state of formally declared hostilities against a people (2 Sam. 17:11); a time for carrying out hostilities (Job 38:23). Other refs.: Ps. 55:18, 21; 68:30; 78:9; 144:1; Eccl. 9:18; Zech. 14:3. ¶
– [3] Is. 8:9: to prepare for battle ➔ GIRD <247> [4] Is. 9:5 ➔ BOOT <5430> [5] Dan. 11:40 ➔ to engage in battle ➔ GORE <5055> [6] See WAR <4421>.

BATTLE (EQUIPPED FOR, ARRAYED FOR) – ***ḥ^{a}mušiym*** [plur. adj.: חֲמֻשִׁים <2571>; pass. part. of the same as STOMACH <2570>] ▶ **This word means armed, arrayed for combat, in orderly array.** It describes the Israelites as they went forth from Egypt (Ex. 13:18); crossed the Jordan (Josh. 1:14; 4:12); and the army of the Midianites as they encamped against Israel (Judg. 7:11). ¶

BATTLE-AX – [1] Jer. 51:20 ➔ WAR CLUB <4661> [2] Ezek. 9:2 ➔ lit.: weapon for slaughter ➔ ARTICLE <3627>, SLAUGHTER <4660>.

BATTLE TOWER – Is. 29:3 ➔ FORTIFIED PLACE <4694>.

BATTLEMENT – [1] Deut. 22:8 ➔ PARAPET <4624> [2] Song 8:9 ➔ CAMP <2918>.

BATTLEMENTS – Jer. 5:10 ➔ BRANCHES <5189>.

BAVVAI – ***bawway*** [masc. proper noun: בַּוַּי <942>; prob. of Persian origin]: by the mercy of God ▶ **Repairs to the wall of Jerusalem were carried out under him.** Ref.: Neh. 3:18. ¶

BAY – Zech. 6:3, 7 ➔ STRONG <554>.

BAZLUTH – ***baṣlût̲*** [masc. proper noun: בַּצְלוּת <1213>; from the same as ONION <1211>]: nudity ▶ **Members of his family**

came back from the captivity. Refs.: Ezra 2:52; Neh. 7:54. ¶

BDELLIUM – ***b**^{e}**d̲ōlaḥ*** [masc. noun: בְּדֹלַח <916>; prob. from SEPARATE (verb) <914>] ▶ **This word describes a yellowish gum resin that may look like gold pearls in its hardened stage.** Refs.: Gen. 2:12; Num. 11:7. Manna is said to resemble this material in its appearance; it is also translated aromatic resin. ¶

BE – [1] ***h**^{a}**wāh*** [Aramaic verb: הֲוָה <1934>; corresponding to FALL (verb) <1933> b.] ▶ **This word means to exist, to come to pass, to take place.** It has the sense of to happen (Dan. 2:28), to take place, to exist, to be of a kingdom, wrath (Dan. 2:40, 43; 7:23; Ezra 7:23). It means to change or become (Dan. 2:35). It indicates the possession of something when used with the preposition *l*^{e}, to (Dan. 5:17, to yourself or for yourself), and it may indicate the actions or character of peoples or nations (Dan. 5:17). *

[2] ***hāyāh*** [verb: הָיָה <1961>; a prim. root (comp. FALL (verb) <1933>)] ▶ **This verb means to exist, to become, to happen, to come to pass, to be done. It is used over 3,500 times in the Old Testament. In the simple stem, the verb often means to become, to take place, to happen.** It indicates that something has occurred or come about, such as events that have turned out a certain way (1 Sam. 4:16); something has happened to someone, such as Moses (Ex. 32:1, 23; 2 Kgs. 7:20); or something has occurred just as God said it would (Gen. 1:7, 9). Often a special Hebrew construction using the imperfect form of the verb asserts that something came to pass (cf. Gen. 1:7, 9). Less often, the construction is used with the perfect form of the verb to refer to something coming to pass in the future (Is. 7:18, 21; Hos. 2:16).

The verb is used to describe something that comes into being or arises. For instance, a great cry arose in Egypt when the firstborn were killed in the tenth plague (Ex. 12:30; cf. Gen. 9:16; Mic. 7:4); and when God commanded light to appear, and it did (Gen. 1:3). It is used to join the subject and the complement(s) as in Genesis 1:2 where the earth was desolate and void (two masculine nouns in Hebrew), or to say Adam and Eve were naked (Gen. 2:25). With certain prepositions, it can mean to follow or to be in favor of someone (Ps. 124:1, 2). The verb is used with a variety of other words, normally prepositions, to express subtle differences in meaning, such as to be located somewhere (Ex. 1:5); to serve or function as something (e.g., gods [Ex. 20:3]); to become something or as something, as when a person becomes a living being (Gen. 2:7); to be with or by someone (Deut. 22:2); to be or come on someone or something (e.g., the fear of humans on the beasts [Gen. 9:2]); to express the idea of better than or a comparison (Ezek. 15:2), as in the idea of too small (Ex. 12:4). *

[3] ***yēš*** [semiverbal expression: יֵשׁ <3426>; perhaps from an unused root meaning to stand out, or exist] ▶ **This semiverb states that something exists.** It should be compared to *'êyn* that asserts that something does not exist (Gen. 24:23; Ruth 3:12; Prov. 11:24). *Yēš* may be translated there is, there are. In contexts that call for a past-tense translation, it may be rendered there was, there were. Followed by the preposition *l*^{e}, to, attached to an object, the phrase shows possession (Gen. 33:9). Pronouns can be affixed to *yēs*, such as in the expression "he is" *yēšnô*; "you are" *yēšk̲a* (Judg. 6:36). *Yēš* used with *l*^{e} attached to some nouns expresses possibility or ability (2 Chr. 25:9). Preceded by *'im* (WHEN <518>), if, the phrase translates as if . . . are, showing condition (Gen. 23:8). The interrogative *h*^{a} attached to the front of *yēš* indicates a question (Is. 44:8). It is used with adverbs to show various locations: here is (1 Sam. 21:8); under (1 Sam. 21:3). *

BEACON – Is. 30:17 ➔ FLAG <8650>.

BEAD – [1] Num. 31:50 ➔ NECKLACE <3558> [2] Song 1:11 ➔ STUD <5351>.

BEADS (STRING OF) – Song 1:10 ➔ STRING OF JEWELS <2737>.

BEALIAH – ***bᵉʿalyāh*** [masc. proper noun: בְּעַלְיָה <1183>; from LORD <1167> and LORD <3050>]: the Lord is master ▶ **A Benjamite warrior who came to David at Ziklag.** Ref.: 1 Chr. 12:5. ¶

BEALOTH – ***bᵉʿālôṯ*** [proper noun: בְּעָלוֹת <1175>; plur. of MISTRESS <1172>]: mistresses ▶ **A village in Judah.** Refs.: Josh. 15:24; 1 Chr. 4:33; 1 Kgs. 4:16. ¶

BEAM – 1 ***gêḇ*** [masc. noun: גֵּב <1356>; from PLOWMAN <1461> (in the sense of one who cuts out)] ▶ **This word describes a part of the covering structure of the Temple.** Ref.: 1 Kgs. 6:9. The beams were made of cedar. Others think it may be a technical architectural term. The Hebrew word also means a pool; see POOL (noun) <1356>. ¶
2 ***kāp̱iys*** [masc. noun: כָּפִיס <3714>; from an unused root meaning to connect] ▶ **This word refers to a wooden girder or support in a royal building; it is also translated rafter.** It is personified to speak out against the violence of the kings of Babylon toward many nations (Hab. 2:11). ¶
3 ***kᵉruṯôṯ*** [fem. plur. noun: כְּרֻתוֹת <3773>; pass. part. of CUT (verb) <3772>] ▶ **This word refers to trimmed timber.** It describes cedar beams hewn to size, cut, and placed in the structures of Solomon's Temple and his own palace (1 Kgs. 6:36; 7:2, 12). ¶
4 ***mānôr*** [masc. noun: מָנוֹר <4500>; from BREAK UP <5214>] ▶ **The frame of a weaver's loom, to which a spear and/or spear shaft is compared.** Refs.: 1 Sam. 17:7; 2 Sam. 21:19; 1 Chr. 11:23; 20:5; also translated rod. ¶
5 ***qôrāh*** [fem. noun: קוֹרָה <6982>; from DIG <6979> b. (in the sense of forming trenches as it were)] ▶ **This word means a timber, a rafter; it also means a pole, a roof.** It refers to weight-bearing beams used in the construction of a building (2 Kgs. 6:2, 5); they were overlaid with gold in the Temple (2 Chr. 3:7). This term may be used to refer to the entire house (Gen. 19:8). Beams of cedar or other expensive wood were highly prized for their beauty or ornamentation (Song 1:17). ¶
– 6 Num. 4:10, 12 ➔ POLE <4132> 7 Ezra 5:8; 6:11 ➔ TIMBER <636>.

BEAMS (LAY) – 2 Chr. 34:11; Neh. 2:8; 3:3, 6; Ps. 104:3 ➔ HAPPEN <7135> b.

BEANS – ***pôl*** [masc. noun: פּוֹל <6321>; from an unused root meaning to be thick] ▶ **This word refers to part of a supply of victuals David had gathered together.** It also probably refers to broad beans (2 Sam. 17:28; Ezek. 4:9). ¶

BEAR (noun) – 1 ***dōḇ, dôḇ*** [masc. noun: דֹּב, דּוֹב <1677>; from SPEAK <1680> (in the sense of to move slowly)] ▶ **This word refers to a heavy wild animal with thick fur and sharp claws, both male and female.** Refs.: 1 Sam. 17:34, 36, 37; 2 Kgs. 2:24; Prov. 17:12. A female is especially dangerous when bereaved of her cubs (2 Sam. 17:8; Hos. 13:8). It was compared to the lion in savagery (Amos 5:19). Yet in the messianic reign, the bear and cow will live together in peace (Is. 11:7). Other refs.: Prov. 28:15; Is. 59:11; Lam. 3:10. ¶
2 ***dōḇ*** [Aramaic masc. noun: דֹּב <1678>; corresponding to <1677> above] ▶ **This word depicts the Persian Empire as a bear (see previous sub-entry) in Daniel's night vision.** Ref.: Dan. 7:5. ¶
3 ***ʿayiš, ʿāš*** [masc. noun: עַיִשׁ, עָשׁ <5906>; from HASTEN <5789>] ▶ **This word refers to the constellation Arcturus, Ursa Major.** The orderliness and splendor of this constellation is the result of God's wondrous work (Job 9:9; 38:32). ¶

BEAR (verb) – 1 ***sāḇal*** [verb: סָבַל <5445>; a prim. root] ▶ **This word means to shoulder a load, to carry.** It means to bear, to endure, to carry something: to carry burdens of some kind as a slave or laborer (Gen. 49:15); mockingly, it refers to bearing idols (Is. 46:7); to the Suffering Servant's bearing of sorrows (Is. 53:4, 11); of the Lord's carrying His people (Is. 46:4); carrying iniquities or punishments (Lam. 5:7); to general exhaustion (Eccl. 12:5). It is used of a cow bearing or carrying its young (Ps. 144:14). ¶

– [2] Is. 63:9; Lam. 3:28 ➔ OFFER <5190> [3] Lam. 2:22 ➔ CARE FOR <2946> [4] Zeph. 1:11 ➔ WEIGH OUT <5187>.

BEAR ALONG – See BRING <2986>.

BEARD – [1] ***zāqān*** [fem. noun: זָקָן <2206>; from OLD (BE) <2204>] ▶ **This word is generally used of the hair that grows on a man's chin and lower cheeks.** Refs.: 1 Chr. 19:5; Is. 15:2. Once it refers to the mane of a lion (1 Sam. 17:35). In biblical times, to have one's beard shaved was humbling. When shaved by another, it was an act of humiliation (2 Sam. 10:4, 5; Is. 7:20), but when pulled on (Ezra 9:3) or shaved by oneself, it was usually a sign of repentance (Jer. 41:5; 48:37). The beard is mentioned in connection with infection (Lev. 13:29, 30) and was to be trimmed properly according to ceremonial requirements (Lev. 19:27; 21:5). Ezekiel shaved and divided up his beard as a sign against Jerusalem (Ezek. 5:1). *
[2] ***śāpām*** [masc. noun: שָׂפָם <8222>; from LIP <8193>] ▶ **This word means a man's facial hair, particularly that growing over the upper lip; it is also translated mustache.** The most basic understanding of this word is evident in 2 Samuel 19:24, where the text refers to the proper grooming of one's mustache or beard. By extension, this word is also used to imply the upper lip where a mustache grows (Lev. 13:45); and the mouth in general (Ezek. 24:17, 22; Mic. 3:7). ¶

BEAST – [1] ***ḥêywāh*** [Aramaic fem. noun: חֵיוָה <2423>; from LIVE <2418>] ▶ **This word refers in general to all animals of the field or earth.** Ref.: Dan. 2:38. In Nebuchadnezzar's dream in a singular collective form, it refers to beasts of the field living under the protection of the great tree (Dan. 4:12, 14–16). The hearts of beasts are differentiated from the hearts of humans (Dan. 5:21). The word is used to refer to the four beasts of Daniel's dream (Dan. 7:3, 5–7, 11, 12, 17, 19, 23). Other refs.: Dan. 4:21, 23, 25, 32. ¶
– [2] Gen. 45:17; Ex. 22:5; Num. 20:4, 8, 11 ➔ ANIMAL <1165> [3] Prov. 9:2 ➔ SLAUGHTER (noun) <2874> [4] See ANIMAL <929>.

BEAT – [1] ***dûḵ*** [verb: דּוּךְ <1743>; a prim. root] ▶ **This word describes the process of pounding or bruising manna in a mortar.** Ref.: Num. 11:8; also translated to crush. ¶
[2] ***dāqaq*** [verb: דָּקַק <1854>; a prim. root (comp. TREAD DOWN <1915>)] ▶ **This verb means to pulverize, to reduce to powder by crushing.** It is used figuratively of pulverizing or crushing one's enemies (2 Sam. 22:43) or even peoples and nations (Mic. 4:13). Israel, renewed by God, will pulverize the mountains, overcoming all obstacles (Is. 41:15). Literally, it indicates the crushing, grinding fine of various items: grain, corn (Is. 28:28); asherahs, pagan symbols (2 Kgs. 23:6, 15); incense (Ex. 30:36); the golden calf ground up by Moses' orders (Ex. 32:20). *
[3] ***rāqa'*** [verb: רָקַע <7554>; a prim. root] ▶ **This word also means to stamp, to stretch out.** The fundamental picture is that of a smith pounding a piece of metal that in turn causes the metal to spread out as it flattens. This word conveys the action of flattening metal for some specific use (Ex. 39:3); stamping one's foot on the ground as a symbol of displeasure (Ezek. 6:11); the laying out of the earth in creation (Is. 42:5); and the flattening of an enemy (2 Sam. 22:43). *
[4] ***šāḥaṭ*** [verb: שָׁחַט <7820>; a prim. root (identical with KILL <7819> through the idea of striking)] ▶ **This word is used in its passive participle to describe a shield of beaten gold, hammered into shape by skilled craftsmen; it is also translated to hammer.** Refs.: 1 Kgs. 10:16, 17; 2 Chr. 9:15, 16. ¶
[5] ***šāḥaq*** [verb: שָׁחַק <7833>; a prim. root] ▶ **This word also means to wear, to rub away, to grind, to reduce to fine particles, to pulverize. The primary usage of the verb is to reduce to fine particles or to rub away.** In Job, the word is used to describe water wearing away stones in conjunction with torrents washing away the soil. This definition was used as a simile for

Job's accusation that Yahweh was destroying a person's hope (Job 14:19). Yahweh uses the verb to dictate to Moses how a blend of incense was to be made (Ex. 30:36). This formula, which was placed in front of the Testimony in the Tent of Meeting, was to be regarded as holy and only meant for the Lord. Anyone who used it in another context would be cut off from His people. In a figurative sense, *šāḥaq* is used to describe David's victory over his enemies in which he beat them down like fine dust (2 Sam. 22:43, Ps. 18:42). ¶

– 6 Deut. 1:44; Is. 2:4; Mic. 4:3 ➔ CRUSH <3807> 7 Prov. 28:3 ➔ SWEEP <5502> 8 Song 5:2 ➔ DRIVE HARD <1849> 9 Nah. 2:7 ➔ TAMBOURINES (PLAYING, BEATING) <8608>.

BEAT, BEAT OFF – Deut. 24:20; Judg. 6:11; Ruth 2:17; Is. 27:12; 28:27 ➔ THRESH <2251>.

BEAT DOWN – Jer. 5:17; Mal. 1:4 ➔ DEMOLISH <7567>.

BEATEN – 1 ***kāṯiyṯ*** [adj.: כָּתִית <3795>; from CRUSH <3807>] ▶ **This word indicates the process of crushing or pounding something; it is also translated pressed.** It is used in combination with the Hebrew *šemen*, oil, to indicate an especially pure, beaten, costly olive oil for food preparation or for lamps (Ex. 27:20; 29:40; Lev. 24:2; Num. 28:5; 1 Kgs. 5:11). ¶

– 2 Lev. 2:14, 16 ➔ CRUSHED <1643>.

BEATEN (BE) – 1 Josh. 8:15 ➔ TOUCH <5060> 2 Is. 17:6; 24:13 ➔ SHAKING <5363>.

BEATEN, BEATEN WORK – Ex. 25:18, 31, 36; 37:17, 22; Num. 8:4; 10:2 ➔ HAMMERED, HAMMERED WORK <4749>.

BEATINGS – ***mah^{a}lumôṯ*** [fem. plur. noun: מַהֲלֻמוֹת <4112>; from SMITE <1986>] ▶ **This word depicts stripes, blows; it is also translated beating, strokes.** It refers to slaps or strong physical rebukes amounting to blows on the lips, mouths, or backs of fools to correct their insolent behavior (Prov. 18:6; 19:29). ¶

BEAUTIFICATION – ***mārûq*** [masc. noun: מָרוּק <4795>; from POLISH <4838> (in the sense of beautifying by polishing)] ▶ **This word means being cleansed and perfumed with various oils; it is also translated purification, beautifying, preparation, beauty treatment.** The one occurrence of this word is in the book of Esther and mentions the treatments the women underwent for a year prior to meeting King Ahasuerus (Esther 2:12). See the related Hebrew root *māraq* (POLISH <4838>). ¶

BEAUTIFUL – 1 ***yāp̱eh*** [adj.: יָפֶה <3303>; from BEAUTIFUL (BE) <3302>] ▶ **This word is used in many settings to describe the attractiveness of various things and persons.** Of women (Gen. 12:11, 14; 2 Sam. 13:1; Esther 2:7). It is used to indicate a healthy appearance (Gen. 41:2). It may be used to mean good-looking, handsome of young men or adult males (2 Sam. 14:25). It combines with the word for form (*tô'ar*) to mean beautiful of form, e.g., Joseph was "handsome of form" (Gen. 39:6). Jerusalem is said to be beautiful as to its location (*y^{e}p̱êh nôp̱*) (Ps. 48:2). A singer may have a beautiful voice (Ezek. 33:32). Trees (Ezek. 31:3) and nearly everything is said to be beautiful "in its time" (Eccl. 3:11). *

2 ***y^{e}p̱êyp̱iyyah*** [adj.: יְפֵיפִיָּה <3304>; from BEAUTIFUL (BE) <3302> by reduplication] ▶ **This word means well-favored; it is also translated pretty, very pretty, fair. It is applied in a metaphor to Egypt described as a cow.** This word indicates that Egypt is a handsome or pretty cow or heifer (Jer. 46:20). She will be destroyed by a horsefly, Babylon (Jer. 46:20). ¶

3 ***nā'weh*** [adj.: נָאוֶה <5000>; from BEAUTIFUL (BE) <4998> or HABITATION <5116>] ▶ **This word means well-becoming; it is also translated comely, becoming, fitting, seemly, suited, to befit, to become.** It depicts what is appropriate, in place: praise to the righteous person (Ps. 33:1); wise speech is not fitting for

a fool (Prov. 17:7; cf. Prov. 19:10; 26:1). It points out what is pleasant, lovely, beautiful: praises to God are pleasant (Ps. 147:1); a young woman is lovely (Song 1:5; 2:14; 4:3; 6:4). It can have a slightly negative sense from the context, meaning attractive, decorous (Jer. 6:2). ¶

[4] ***šapiyr*** [Aramaic adj.: שַׁפִּיר <8209>; intens. of a form corresponding to SAPHIR <8208>] ► **This word describes the splendor and attractiveness of the foliage of a great tree in its biblical context.** Refs.: Dan. 4:12, 21; also translated lovely, fair. ¶

[5] ***šeper*** [masc. noun: שֶׁפֶר <8233>; from BEAUTIFUL (BE) <8231>] ► **This word indicates goodness, beauty.** It indicates the attractiveness of something, such as beautiful, fitting, appropriate words (Gen. 49:21; KJV: goodly). ¶

– [6] Prov. 24:4 ➔ PLEASANT <5273> a.

BEAUTIFUL (BE) – [1] ***nā'āh*** [verb: נָאָה <4998>; a prim. root] ► **This word means to be suitable, to be pleasant; it is also translated lovely, comely.** It indicates that something is appropriate or in order: holiness is appropriate for the Lord's house (Ps. 93:5: to befit, to become, to adorn); the cheeks of the beloved are beautiful, lovely (Song 1:10); feet that bring good news of God's grace are beautiful (Is. 52:7). ¶

[2] ***šāpar*** [verb: שָׁפַר <8231>; a prim. root] ► **This word means to be good, delightful.** It is used figuratively to describe the splendor and pleasantness of having the Lord as one's lot in life (Ps. 16:6). ¶

BEAUTIFUL (BE, MAKE ONESELF) – ***yāpāh*** [verb: יָפָה <3302>; a prim. root] ► **This Hebrew word means and is also translated to be fair, handsome, excellent, delightful; to adorn oneself, to beautify oneself, to decorate, to deck, to be majestic.** It is a term of approbation and of descriptive power referring to the king of Israel. It indicates excellence and splendor in both an ethical and moral sense (Ps. 45:2). It is used to depict the beauty of love itself (Song 4:10); of the shoes and feet of the beloved (Song 7:1). It takes on the meaning of to adorn oneself or something in some contexts and usages (Jer. 4:30; 10:4; Ezek. 16:13). It is used to describe the political, military, and royal splendor of the nation of Assyria (Ezek. 31:7). Other ref.: Song 7:6. ¶

BEAUTIFY ONESELF – Jer. 4:30 ➔ BEAUTIFUL (BE, MAKE ONESELF) <3302>.

BEAUTIFYING – Esther 2:12 ➔ BEAUTIFICATION <4795>.

BEAUTY – [1] ***ypiy*** [masc. noun: יְפִי <3308>; from BEAUTIFUL (BE) <3302>] ► **This word is used to describe the pleasing and satisfying appearance of things or persons.** Of a woman (Esther 1:11); a person exuding royal splendor (Is. 33:17); of Zion (Ps. 50:2); of plants or trees (Ezek. 31:8); of Jerusalem (Ps. 45:11; Ezek. 16:14). It refers to the shining attraction or sparkle of jewels or precious stones (Zech. 9:17). Some beauty is to be resisted, such as the beauty or attraction of an adulteress (Prov. 6:25). Other refs.: Prov. 31:30; Is. 3:24; Lam. 2:15; Ezek. 16:15, 25; 27:3, 4, 11; 28:7, 12, 17. ¶

[2] ***nō'am*** [masc. noun: נֹעַם <5278>; from PLEASANT <5276>] ► **This word means pleasantness; it is also translated favor, pleasant, gracious.** It is used of something that can be seen or beheld, e.g., the beauty or splendor of the Lord (Ps. 27:4). It has the sense of approval of or delight in someone (Ps. 90:17). Words and wisdom both can be pleasant to a person (Prov. 3:17; 15:26; 16:24). It is used in a figurative way to name a shepherd's staff representing a people (Zech. 11:7, 10). ¶

[3] ***tiph'ārāh*** [fem. noun: תִּפְאָרָה <8597>; from GLORIFY <6286>] ► **This word means splendor, as well as glory, honor.** Isaiah used the word to denote the so-called beauty of finery that would be snatched away by the Lord (Is. 3:18). The word was used in a similar manner in Ezekiel to denote that which the people trusted in other than God, in addition to what would be stripped away (Ezek. 16:17; 23:26). The making of priestly garments and other

apparel brought glory to Aaron and his sons, giving them dignity and honor (Ex. 28:2, 40). Wisdom was portrayed as giving a garland of grace and a crown of splendor in Proverbs (Prov. 4:9); Zion was told that it will be a crown of splendor in the Lord's hand (Is. 62:3); and in the book of Jeremiah, the king and queen were told that the crowns would fall from their heads (Jer. 13:18). The word was used in Deuteronomy to describe how God would recognize His people (Deut. 26:19). In Lamentations, it was used in an opposite manner to describe the splendor of Israel that was thrown down from heaven to earth in the Lord's anger (Lam. 2:1). Deborah used the word to describe the honor or glory of a warrior which would not be Barak's because he handled the situation wrongly (Judg. 4:9). *
– [4] 1 Chr. 16:29; 2 Chr. 20:21; Ps. 29:2; 96:9 ➔ GLORY <1927> [5] Esther 2:3, 9, 12: beauty preparations, beauty treatments ➔ COSMETICS <8562> [6] Ezek. 32:19 ➔ PLEASANT <5276>.

BEAUTY OF THE FORM – Lam. 4:7 ➔ COURTYARD <1508>.

BEAUTY TREATMENT – Esther 2:12 ➔ BEAUTIFICATION <4795>.

BEBAI – ***bêḇay*** [masc. proper noun: בֵּבַי <893>; prob. of foreign origin] ▶ **An Israelite of whom members of his family came back from the Babylonian captivity.** Refs.: Ezra 2:11; 8:11; 10:28; Neh. 7:16; 10:15. ¶

BECAUSE – [1] ***'ôḏôṯ, 'ōḏôṯ*** [fem. noun: אוֹדוֹת, אֹדוֹת <182>; from the same as FIREBRAND <181>] ▶ **The Hebrew word is used only in the plural, meaning (be)cause, reason, on account of, concerning; hence, it functions often as a preposition or conjunctive adverb.** It means (be)cause in Genesis 21:11, 25; Numbers 12:1 and on account of in Genesis 26:32 and Exodus 18:8. Its meaning as cause or reason is seen emphatically in Jeremiah 3:8. *
[2] ***gālāl*** [masc. noun: גָּלָל <1558>; from ROLL (verb) <1556>] ▶ **This word is combined with the preposition b^e to mean on account of, for the sake of. It indicates why something is done.** God blessed the Egyptian Potiphar because of Joseph (Gen. 39:5). Things would go well for Abraham because of his wife Sarah (Gen. 12:13), and Laban was blessed because of Jacob (Gen. 30:27). God denied Moses entrance to the Promised Land because of his reaction to Israel's behavior (Deut. 1:37). *
[3] ***ya'an*** [conj.: יַעַן <3282>; from an unused root meaning to pay attention] ▶ **This word also means on account of, but is also used as a preposition, because of.** Used as a preposition, it is followed by either a noun (Ezek. 5:9) or infinitive (1 Kgs. 21:20; Amos 5:11). As a conjunction, it is used alone to mean because (1 Sam. 15:23; 1 Kgs. 14:13; Ezek. 34:21); with *ᵃšer* meaning because that (Deut. 1:36; Judg. 2:20); with *kî* to mean because, because that (1 Kgs. 13:21; 21:29; Is. 3:16). *
[4] ***kiy*** [demonstrative particle: כִּי <3588>; a prim. particle] ▶ **This word means for, that, when, whenever; indeed, even; if; even when, even though. It is used in various ways and must be translated accordingly. In every case, the context in which the word functions will be the key to translating correctly.** Here is a listing of the major ways it is used: as a conjunction meaning because (Gen. 3:14); for (Ps. 6:2, 5); that (Gen. 1:10; 1 Kgs. 21:15); as a conjunctive time or condition indicator, when or if (Gen. 4:12); in a clause of condition, it means if, in fact, or in case (Job 7:13); as a demonstrative particle translated as yes, indeed, surely (Gen. 18:20; 1 Sam. 14:44); truly, especially found in oaths (Gen. 42:16); used with *'im . . . kî . . .*, it means if . . . then (Is. 7:9); in combination with *kî 'az*, it is best rendered as then; *kî 'attāh* usually means for them (Job 3:13). After a negative clause, *kî* is best rendered as rather (Gen. 3:6; 17:5; 24:4); preceded by the negative *lō'*, it is "no, but . . ." In clauses that concede something, it has the sense of even though, although, even when (Eccl. 4:14). It is used to show comparison when used in the construction *kî . . . kên*, as . . . so (Is. 55:9). *

[5] ***ʿaḇûr*** [prep. or conj.: עֲבוּר <5668>; pass. part. of PASS THROUGH, PASS OVER <5674> (in the sense of to go beyond)] ▶ **This word serves as a preposition or conjunction.** Its basic meanings are as a preposition, because, for the sake of, on account of (Gen. 3:17; 8:21; 12:13, 16; Ex. 9:16; Mic. 2:10); as a conjunction, so that, in order that, with a following infinitive or imperfect form of the verb (Gen. 21:30; 27:4, 10; Ex. 9:14; 19:9; 2 Sam. 10:3; 12:21; Ps. 105:45). It indicates the price for something and is placed in front of that item (Amos 2:6). *

[6] ***ʿêqeḇ*** [masc. noun: עֵקֶב <6118>; from SUPPLANT <6117> in the sense of HEEL <6119> (i.e., fig. the last of anything; also on account of)] ▶ **This word gives an adverbial sense of consequence, on account of. It basically means end, the last reason for something.** It is used as a conjunction meaning because (Gen. 22:18; 26:5; Num. 14:24). It refers to a good result, a reward for something done (Ps. 19:11; Prov. 22:4). It refers to a goal, end, or purpose to something (Ps. 119:33); or the chronological end of a process (Ps. 119:112). *

BECHER – ***beḵer*** [masc. proper noun: בֶּכֶר <1071>; the same as CAMEL (YOUNG) <1070>]: young camel ▶
a. A son of Ephraim. Ref.: Num. 26:35. ¶
b. A son of Benjamin. Refs.: Gen. 46:21; 1 Chr. 7:6, 8. ¶

BECHERITE – ***baḵriy*** [masc. proper noun: בַּכְרִי <1076>; patron. from BECHER <1071>] ▶ **A descendant of Becher, a son of Ephraim.** Ref.: Num. 26:35. ¶

BECOME – [1] Ps. 93:5 → BEAUTIFUL (BE) <4998> [2] Prov. 17:7 → BEAUTIFUL <5000>.

BECOMING – Ps. 33:1; Prov. 17:7 → BEAUTIFUL <5000>.

BECORATH – ***beḵôraṯ*** [masc. proper noun: בְּכוֹרַת <1064>; fem. of BIRTHRIGHT <1062>]: firstborn ▶ **An Israelite of the tribe of Benjamin, ancestor of King Saul.** Ref.: 1 Sam. 9:1. ¶

BED – [1] ***yāṣûaʿ*** [noun: יָצוּעַ <3326>; pass. part. of SPREAD (verb) <3331>] ▶
a. A masculine noun referring to a couch where one retires for rest. It refers to a place for sleeping but also figuratively means the place where husband and wife have sexual intercourse for procreation. It stands parallel with a synonym, *miškāḇ*, bed, couch, in the previous line in Genesis 49:4 (cf. 1 Chr. 5:1). Sheol is considered a place of darkness where people may make their resting places or beds (Job 17:13). It is a place of rest and sleep (Ps. 63:6; 132:3). Its use in 1 Kings 6:5 seems to carry the sense of a side chamber in the Temple. But see b. below, for this may indicate that the word in Kings is a different root word altogether. ¶
b. A common noun referring to a wing of a building, a side chamber, a flat surface; it is also translated story, structure. Its use in 1 Kings 6:5, 10 carries the sense of a side room or chamber. Its use in 1 Kings 6:6 indicates that it may refer to a flat ledge or a ledge extending out from the wall upon which things, such as timbers, could be positioned. ¶

[2] ***miṭṭāh*** [fem. noun: מִטָּה <4296>; from STRETCH OUT <5186>] ▶ **This word refers to a place for sleeping, and also means a couch, a funeral bier.** It indicates a place for reclining, a couch, or a bed for sleep (2 Kgs. 4:10); for recovery from illness (Gen. 47:31); for the dead, a bier for carrying the dead in a funeral procession (2 Sam. 3:31); and a portable couch (1 Sam. 19:15; 2 Sam. 3:31; Esther 1:6). It describes a couch for resting on during the day (1 Sam. 28:23; 1 Kgs. 21:4). The beds or couches mentioned in Amos 6:4 and Esther 1:6 were ornate and probably used for reclining at feasts, among high society. It is used with *ḥeder* to express bedroom (*ḥahar hammiṭṭôt*) (2 Kgs. 11:2). *

[3] ***maṣṣāʿ*** [masc. noun: מַצָּע <4702>; from SPREAD <3331>] ▶ **This word depicts a place to rest, recline, and sleep in safety and satisfaction.** Ref.: Is. 28:20. ¶

[4] ***miškaḇ*** [Aramaic masc. noun: מִשְׁכַּב <4903>; corresponding to <4904> below] ▶ **This word indicates a place for sleeping,**

resting, a place where a person can dream. Refs.: Dan. 2:28, 29; 4:5, 10, 13; 7:1. ¶

5 ***miškāḇ*** [masc. noun: מִשְׁכָּב <4904>; from LIE DOWN <7901>] ▶ **This word refers to a place for resting, sleeping.** Refs.: Ex. 8:3; 1 Kgs. 1:47. It is used figuratively to refer to the act of intercourse (approved or unapproved) (Gen. 49:4); the place of lovers (Ezek. 23:17). It is used with several verbs: to set up a bed, to make a bed (Is. 57:7); to unroll quilts for a bed (Is. 57:8). The phrase *ḥaḏar miškāb* refers to a bedroom (Ex. 8:3; 2 Kgs. 6:12). It has the sense of lying, of a woman having sex with a man in the phrase *miškāb zāḵar* (Num. 31:17, 18). A noon nap or siesta is indicated in a *miškāb ṣohᵒrayim* (2 Sam. 4:5). It is used with the phrase *yāḏa' zāḵār* to indicate that one has had sexual intercourse (Judg. 21:11, 12). *

6 ***ᵃrûgāh*** [fem. noun: עֲרוּגָה <6170>; fem. pass. part. of PANT <6165> (in the sense of something piled up as if, fig., raised by mental aspiration)] ▶ **This word designates a patch of ground for a garden, a plot.** It refers to a cultivated bed of plants. It refers to a bed of balsam (Song 5:13; 6:2). It is used figuratively of the land, the country from which a nation would grow; here it refers to Jerusalem and Judah (Ezek. 17:7, 10; also translated furrow, garden terrace). ¶

7 ***'ereś*** [masc. noun: עֶרֶשׂ <6210>; from an unused root meaning perhaps to arch] ▶ **This word signifies a couch, a bedstead.** It refers to a place for resting, sleeping (Deut. 3:11); a place of comfort and refreshment (Job 7:13); but at times a place of sorrow and weeping (Ps. 6:6). The Lord is with those who are sick on their beds (Ps. 41:3). It refers to a couch of enticement prepared by a prostitute (Prov. 7:16); but a place of true love and pleasure to a bride and bridegroom (Song 1:16). Beds (<4296>) of ivory and couches (<6210>) were enjoyed by the rich (Amos 6:4). Other refs.: Ps. 132:3; Amos 3:12 (couch). ¶

BED (LAY AS A) – Is. 14:11 ➔ SPREAD (verb) <3331>.

BED (MAKE ONE'S) – Ps. 139:8 ➔ SPREAD (verb) <3331>.

BEDAD – ***bᵉḏaḏ*** [masc. proper noun: בְּדַד <911>; from ALONE (BE) <909>]: separation, solitary ▶ **Father of Hadad, who was king of Edom.** Refs.: Gen. 36:35; 1 Chr. 1:46. ¶

BEDAN – ***bᵉḏān*** [masc. proper noun: בְּדָן <917>; prob. shortened for ABDON <5658>]: big, son of judgment ▶
a. A judge in Israel mentioned with Samuel. Ref.: 1 Sam. 12:11. ¶
b. An Israelite of the tribe of Manasseh. Ref.: 1 Chr. 7:17. ¶

BEDECKED – Song 5:14 ➔ COVER (verb) <5968>.

BEDEIAH – ***bêḏᵉyāh*** [masc. proper noun: בֵּדְיָה <912>; prob. shortened for OBADIAH <5662>]: servant of the Lord ▶ **An Israelite whom Ezra persuaded to separate himself from his pagan wife.** Ref.: Ezra 10:35. ¶

BEDSTEAD – Deut. 3:11 ➔ BED <6210>.

BEE – ***dᵉḇôrāh*** [fem. noun: דְּבוֹרָה <1682>; from SPEAK <1696> (in the sense of orderly motion)] ▶ **This word refers to a swarm or colony of flying insects notable for their systematic instincts.** Ref.: Judg. 14:8. Bees pursuing someone is used to depict the pursuit of the Amorites after Israel (Deut. 1:44). The attack of the wicked on the psalmist is likened to bees attacking a person (Ps. 118:12). The Assyrian army is pictured as an attacking bee (Is. 7:18). ¶

BEELIADA – ***bᵉ'elyāḏā'*** [masc. proper noun: בְּעֶלְיָדָע <1182>; from BAAL <1168> (in the sense of lord) and KNOW <3045>]: the Lord knows ▶ **A son of King David born in Jerusalem.** Ref.: 1 Chr. 14:7. ¶

BEER (noun) – See STRONG DRINK <7941>.

BEER (proper noun) – ***bᵉ'ēr*** [proper noun: בְּאֵר <876>; the same as WELL (noun) <875>]: well ▶ **A place in the desert as well as one in Israel, remote from Shechem.** Refs.: Num. 21:16; Judg. 9:21. ¶

BEER-ELIM – ***bᵉ'êr 'êliym*** [proper noun: בְּאֵר אֵלִים <879>; from WELL (noun) <875> and the plur. of GOD <410>]: well of the oaks, well of the strong ones ▶ **A village in Moab.** Ref.: Is. 15:8. ¶

BEER-LAHAI-ROI – ***bᵉ'êr laḥay rō'iy*** [proper noun: בְּאֵר לַחַי רֹאִי <883>; from WELL (noun) <875> and ANIMAL <2416> (with prefix) and VISION <7203>]: well of the Living One who sees ▶ **A well in the desert between Kadesh and Bered.** The angel of the Lord appeared there to Hagar (Gen. 16:14). Isaac dwelt there (Gen. 25:11); see also Genesis 24:62. ¶

BEERA – ***bᵉ'êrā'*** [masc. proper noun: בְּאֵרָא <878>; from WELL (noun) <875>]: well ▶ **An Israelite of the tribe of Asher.** Ref.: 1 Chr. 7:37. ¶

BEERAH – ***bᵉ'êrāh*** [masc. proper noun: בְּאֵרָה <880>; the same as BEERA <878>]: well ▶ **A leader of the Reubenites who was carried away into exile by the king of Assyria.** Ref.: 1 Chr. 5:6. ¶

BEERI – ***bᵉ'êriy*** [masc. proper noun: בְּאֵרִי <882>; from WELL (noun) <875>]: well ▶
a. A Hittite, father of Judith who was a wife of Esau. Ref.: Gen. 26:34.
b. The father of the prophet Hosea. Ref.: Hos. 1:1. ¶

BEEROTH – ***'bᵉ'êrôṯ*** [proper noun: בְּאֵרוֹת <881>; fem. plur. of WELL (noun) <875>]: wells ▶ **A city of the Gibeonites.** Refs.: Deut. 10:6; Josh. 9:17; 18:25; 2 Sam. 4:2; Ezra 2:25; Neh. 7:29. ¶

BEEROTH BENE-JAAKAN – ***bᵉ'êrōṯ bᵉnêy yaᵃqān*** [proper noun: בְּאֵרֹת בְּנֵי־יַעֲקָן <885>; from the fem. plur. of WELL (noun) <875>, and the plur. contr. of SON <1121>, and JAAKAN <3292>]: wells of the sons of Jaakan ▶ **A phrase used in Deuteronomy 10:6 to describe a particular location.** It is interpreted differently in each translation: as the proper name Beeroth Bene-Jaakan (NASB, ESV); as the description of Beeroth of the children of Jaakan (KJV); as the description of the wells of the Jaakanites (NIV); and as the description of the wells of Bene Jaakan (NKJV). ¶

BEEROTHITE – ***bᵉ'êrōṯiy*** [masc. proper noun: בְּאֵרֹתִי <886>; patrial from BEEROTH <881>] ▶ **An inhabitant of Beeroth.** Refs.: 2 Sam. 4:2, 3, 5, 9; 23:27. ¶

BEERSHEBA – ***bᵉ'êr šeḇa'*** [proper noun: בְּאֵר שֶׁבַע <884>; from WELL (noun) <875> and SEVEN <7651> (in the sense of SWEAR <7650>)]: well of the oath ▶ **A well dug in the desert by Abraham.** Refs.: Gen. 21:14, 31–33; 22:19; 26:23, 33; 28:10; 46:1, 5; Neh. 11:27, 30; Amos 5:5; 8:14. *

BEESHTERAH – ***bᵉ'ešᵉrāh*** [proper noun: בְּעֶשְׁתְּרָה <1203>; from FLOCKS <6251> (as sing. of ASHTAROTH <6252>) with a prep. prefix]: house (or temple) of Ashtaroth ▶ **The same place as Ashtaroth.** Ref.: Josh. 21:27; see 1 Chr. 6:71. ¶

BEETLE – Lev. 11:22 ➔ CRICKET <2728>.

BEFALL – [1] ***'ānāh*** [verb: אָנָה <579>; a prim. root (perhaps rather identical with LAMENT <578> through the idea of contraction in anguish)] ▶ **This word means to meet, to seek occasion or allow to meet, to happen.** It describes any kind of event or occurrence of something in general (Ps. 91:10; also translated to overtake), such as evil befalling or not befalling someone (Prov. 12:21). It also indicates an occurrence or event that takes place occasioned by God (Ex. 21:13: to deliver, to fall). And it depicts an event or occasion brought about by a person (2 Kgs. 5:7: to seek a quarrel). ¶
– [2] 1 Sam. 20:26; Eccl. 3:19 ➔ CHANCE <4745>.

BEFIT – [1] Ps. 33:1 ➔ BEAUTIFUL <5000> [2] Ps. 93:5 ➔ BEAUTIFUL (BE) <4998>.

BEFORE – [1] ***tᵉrôm*** [conj.: טְרוֹם <2958>; a variation of <2962> below] ▶ **This word is an adverbial conjunction of time.** It indicates the time just before daylight when it was still too dark to recognize another person clearly (Ruth 3:14). ¶

2 ***ṭerem*** [adv. and adv. prep.: טֶרֶם <2962>; from an unused root apparently meaning to interrupt or suspend] ▶ **Used with verbs, this word often means not yet or prior to something else.** For instance when there was not yet a shrub in the field (Gen. 2:5). It indicates when Abraham's servant had not yet finished speaking (Gen. 24:15, 45). It means before in Genesis 27:4 and Exodus 12:34, e.g., before Isaac died. It indicates a time before morning (Is. 17:14). It indicates the time before God created the earth (Ps. 90:2). With the preposition *min* (FROM <4480>), it indicates a time before which or when certain things were happening (Gen. 27:33; Judg. 14:18; Hag. 2:15). *

3 ***negeḏ*** [prep.: נֶגֶד <5048>; from TELL <5046>] ▶ **This word indicates in front of, opposite, corresponding to.** It has a special sense to indicate Eve's likeness to Adam (Gen. 2:18, 20), with the preposition *k*ᵉ prefixed. Its usual meanings are easily discernible from context: before (Gen. 31:32); over against, opposite (Ex. 19:2); in front of (Josh. 6:5); against (Job 10:17); in front of spatially (2 Kgs. 1:13). The phrase *'ad-negeḏ* means up to, as far as a certain spot (Neh. 3:16); in the presence of someone (Ps. 116:14, 18). It is used with a preposition attached often: *l*ᵉ helps give the sense of in front of (Gen. 33:12; Num. 22:32); in the presence of (Hab. 1:3). It is used figuratively with *l*ᵉ to point out what ought to be observed (Ps. 18:22). Used with *min* <4480>, it has the sense of opposite from something (Gen. 21:16; 2 Kgs. 2:7); or implies spatial distance (Num. 2:2; Deut. 32:52; 2 Kgs. 2:15). *

4 ***qᵉḇêl*** [Aramaic conj.: קֳבֵל <6903>; corresponding to <6905> below] ▶ **This word also means because, inasmuch as.** It has the sense of, in front of, before spatially (Dan. 2:31; 3:3; 5:1); or opposite, over against (Dan. 5:5). It often means because, giving the reason for something (Dan. 5:10). It is used in combinations with *hên, dᵉnā, dî,* to render: if . . . then; just as (Ezra 4:16; 6:13). *Kol-qᵒḇel* means in view of, because of (Dan. 2:12, 24; 3:7, 8; 6:9). The phrase *kol-qᵒḇêl dᵉnā min-dî* can be rendered, for this reason, because, or just because (Dan. 3:22). *

5 ***qāḇāl*** [masc. noun: קָבָל <6905>; from ACCEPT <6901> in the sense of opposite (see BATTERING RAM <6904>)] ▶ **This word has the sense of something in front.** It seems to mean in front of, publicly (2 Kgs. 15:10). ¶

6 ***qᵒḏām*** [Aramaic prep.: קֳדָם <6925>; corresponding to EAST <6924> (in the sense of earlier)] ▶ **This word means in front, in the presence of.** It refers to being in front of spatially or temporally; in time (Ezra 4:18, 23; Dan. 2:9; 7:7). It has the sense of in God's judgment, before Him (Dan. 6:22). It means to be afraid of something from before one (*min* [FROM <4480>] *qᵒdāmôhî;* Dan. 7:8). It is used with words meaning to pray, to answer before (Dan. 2:10, 11, 27). It describes a decree going out from (before) a king (Dan. 2:6; 6:26). *

7 ***šilšôm, šilšōm*** [adv.: שִׁלְשׁוֹם, שִׁלְשֹׁם <8032>; from DIVIDE INTO THREE PARTS <8027>] ▶ **This word also indicates in times past, formerly. It is always found combined into an idiom with another word.** It literally means three days ago, the day before yesterday, but its meaning has become generalized as well to mean formerly, in time past (Gen. 31:2, 5; Deut. 4:42: *kiṯmôl šilšom*). In Exodus 4:10, the phase *gam miṯmôl gam miššilšōm* occurs, meaning literally, neither yesterday or the day before yesterday, which as an idiom means not recently or anytime before that. *

8 ***šām*** [adv.: שָׁם <8033>; a prim. particle] ▶ **This word means where, in that direction.** It indicates a place or the place where: there (Gen. 2:8, 12); where (Job 39:30); where, when preceded with the relative *ᵃšJer* (Gen. 2:11; Ex. 20:21); to where, thither after motion verbs (Deut. 1:37; Judg. 19:15). It often has a *he* (ה) on the end indicating motion there, to a place (Gen. 19:20; Deut. 1:38). With *min* (<4480>) on the front, it means from there (*miššām*) (Gen. 2:10; 11:8, 9; 12:8). It can express the source or origin of something, e.g., man from the ground (Gen. 3:23); Philistines

from . . . (Gen. 10:14; Judg. 19:18); a goat from the flock (Gen. 27:9). *

9 ***tᵉmôl, tᵉmōl*** [adv.: תְּמוֹל, תְּמֹל <8543>; prob. for YESTERDAY <865>] ▶ **This word means previously, yesterday.** It always refers to a previous time: recent, only yesterday (Job 8:9); yesterday (Ps. 90:4, *kᵉyôm 'eṯmôl*). It often used with *šilšōm, tᵉmôl šilšōm,* formerly or day before yesterday (Gen. 31:2, 5; Ex. 5:8; 1 Sam. 4:7). *Gam tᵉmôl gam hayyôm* means both yesterday and today (Ex. 5:14). *

– 10 2 Kgs. 15:10 ➔ BATTERING RAM <6904> c.

BEGIN – 1 ***yᵉsuḏ*** [masc. noun: יְסֻד <3246>; from FOUNDATION (LAY A) <3245>] ▶ **This word indicates a commencement.** It is used in Ezra 7:9 to describe the beginning of Israel's journey toward Jerusalem. Most translators prefer to read this word as *yissaḏ*, a perfect verbal form, and translate it as "he [Ezra] began" (NASB, NIV, KJV, NKJV, ESV). ¶

– 2 Deut. 1:5 ➔ CONTENT (BE) <2974>.

BEGINNING – 1 ***ri'šāh*** [fem. noun: רִאשָׁה <7221>; from the same as HEAD (noun) <7218>] ▶ **Ezekiel used the word to denote an earlier time (Ezek. 36:11).** He spoke figuratively, saying that the Lord would make the mountains of Israel more prosperous than before. The Lord would also increase the number of people and animals, who would in turn be fruitful and multiply. ¶

2 ***rê'šiyṯ*** [noun: רֵאשִׁית <7225>; from the same as HEAD (noun) <7218>] ▶ **This word means the start, and also the first, the chief, the best, the firstfruits. Occurring fifty-one times in the Old Testament, this term holds the honor of being the first word written in the entire Bible (Gen. 1:1).** Often, the term denotes the point in time or space at which something started, except when it specifies the point when time and space themselves were started (Is. 46:10). It conveys the beginning of strife (Prov. 17:14); of a ruler's reign (Jer. 26:1, 27:1; 28:1; 49:34); of a sin (Mic. 1:13); of a kingdom (Gen. 10:10); or of wisdom and knowledge (Ps. 111:10; Prov. 1:7). On other occasions, the term signifies the highest of anything, i.e., the best or most excellent, such as the choicest parts of offerings (1 Sam. 2:29); the best of the spoil (1 Sam. 15:21); or the finest in oils (Amos 6:6). Elsewhere, the word designates the earliest or first products or results of something. It refers many times to the first products of a harvest (Lev. 23:10; Deut. 18:4; Neh. 12:44); and sometimes to the first product, i.e., the firstborn of a father (Gen. 49:3; Deut. 21:17). Both this term and the noun *rō'š* [HEAD (noun) <7218>] are derived from the same unused verbal root. *

3 ***tᵉḥillāh*** [fem. noun: תְּחִלָּה <8462>; from PIERCE <2490> in the sense of opening] ▶ **This word may refer to the first time, the start, or the first place.** Refs.: Gen. 13:3; 41:21. It indicates the first time or start of a process (2 Kgs. 17:25). In battle it can refer to a first launched attack (2 Sam. 17:9). *

BEGUILE – 1 Gen. 3:13 ➔ DECEIVE <5377> 2 Gen. 29:25; Josh. 9:22 ➔ DECEIVE <7411> 3 Num. 25:18 ➔ DECEIVE <5230>.

BEHAVIOR – 1 Sam. 21:13; Ps. 34 title ➔ TASTE (noun) <2940>.

BEHEMOTH – ***bᵉhêmôṯ*** [masc. noun: בְּהֵמוֹת <930>; in form a plur. or ANIMAL <929>, but really a sing. of Egyptian deriv.] ▶ **This word refers to a very large animal.** In Job 40:15, it seems to refer to a hippopotamus or crocodile. Most translators transliterate the word as Behemoth. ¶

BEHIND – ***'aḥar*** [prep.: אַחַר <310>; from STAY (verb) <309>] ▶ **The word means after, afterwards.** The usage is quite uniform, varying slightly according to context. Used more adverbially, it can mean such things as behind someone or something (Gen. 22:13); afterwards or after that (an event) (Gen. 18:5). Used more specifically as a preposition, it means behind (Gen. 37:17); after, such as to pursue something literally or figuratively (Job 39:8); after in a temporal sense, such as when clouds return after the rain (Eccl. 12:2); or after talking ceases (Job 42:7). *

BEHOLD (interj.) – [1] *^{a}lû* [Aramaic interj.: אֱלוּ <431>; prob. prolonged from THESE <412>] ▶ **This word indicates surprise and amazement.** Refs.: Dan. 2:31; 4:10, 13; 7:8. It is sometimes left untranslated or implied in the structure of the translation (cf. NIV, NKJV, Dan. 7:8). ¶
[2] *^{a}rû* [Aramaic interj.: אֲרוּ <718>; prob. akin to <431> above] ▶ **This word describes an expression of emotional surprise and terror.** Refs.: Dan. 7:2, 5–7, 13 at the appearance of strange beasts and the Son of Man carried on clouds in a vision. ¶
[3] ***hê'*** [interj.: הֵא <1887>; a prim. particle] ▶ **This word also means there!, surely; it is also translated now, indeed.** It is used by Joseph to get people's attention as he begins to address them (Gen. 47:23). It means surely or therefore in Ezekiel 16:43 as the prophet asserts the consequences of the people's rebellion. ¶
[4] ***hā', hê'*** [Aramaic interj.: הָא, הֵא <1888>; corresponding to <1887> above] ▶
a. This word indicates surprise and amazement. It is used to direct attention to something: the fourth man in the fiery furnace (Dan. 3:25: Look!, Lo).
b. This word points out something evident and can make a comparison: even as. Ref.: Dan. 2:43; even as iron and clay do not mix, neither do the peoples of the fourth empire of Daniel. ¶
[5] ***hên*** [particle: הֵן <2005>; a prim. particle] ▶ **This word serves as a demonstrative interjection meaning look, since, and as a conditional conjunction meaning if.** It may point out and stress a following word or clause: behold or "Since you have given no offspring to me" (Gen. 15:3, NASB); behold [since] the man . . . (Gen. 3:22). It introduces a statement that lays the basis for a following assertion or plea (Is. 64:9) or indicates a strongly felt agreement, good, behold, followed by an assertion (Gen. 30:34). It also, in some contexts, introduces conditional sentences, meaning if (Ex. 4:1; Lev. 25:20; Job 40:23; Is. 54:15). *

[6] ***hinnêh*** [interj.: הִנֵּה <2009>; prolongation for <2005> above] ▶ **This word also means look, now; if. It is used often and expresses strong feelings, surprise, hope, expectation, certainty, thus giving vividness depending on its surrounding context.** Its main meanings can only be summarized briefly here: It stresses a following word referring to persons or things (Gen. 12:19; 15:17; 18:9). It is used to answer, with the first person suffix attached, when one is called (Gen. 22:1, 7; 27:1; Ex. 3:4; 1 Sam. 3:4). It is used of God's response (Is. 52:6; 58:9; 65:1). It indicates a call to realize something God or others have done (Gen. 1:29; 17:20). It is followed with a particle of entreaty *nā'* when a request is involved (Gen. 12:11; 16:2; 1 Kgs. 20:31). It can call attention to something about to happen, a future reference (Ex. 32:34; 34:10). It is used to announce the Lord's sending of a child as a sign (Is. 7:14). The word adds vividness and emotional involvement for the reader: "Behold, it was very good" (NASB) (Gen. 1:31; 6:12; 8:13; 18:2; 37:7; Amos 7:1; 8:1). Finally, it is used to introduce a formula of challenge (Jer. 21:13). In a few passages, it has the sense of if (Lev. 13:5, 6, 8; Deut. 13:14; 1 Sam. 20:12). *

BEHOLD (verb) – [1] ***ra^{a}wāh*** [verb inf.: רַאֲוָה <7207>; a prim. root] ▶ **This word means to look; it is also translated to see.** Appearing only once in the Old Testament, it alludes to looking on the outward appearance and fondly admiring an object (Eccl. 5:11). ¶
– [2] Job 39:29; Ps. 84:9; 102:19; 119:18 ➔ LOOK (verb) <5027>.

BEHOLDING – ***r^{e}'iyṯ, r^{e}'ûṯ*** [fem. noun: רְאִית, רְאוּת <7212>; from SEE <7200>] ▶ **This word means look, sight. It is used in regard to an owner looking on his goods.** The author of Ecclesiastes rhetorically inquired as to the good of increasing wealth and goods, if only for the owner merely to look on them (Eccl. 5:11). ¶

BEKA – ***beqa'*** [masc. noun: בֶּקַע <1235>; from DIVIDE <1234>] ▶ **This word**

refers to a weight equal to ten gerahs or 6.1 grams (.22 oz.). It is defined (Ex. 38:26) as half a shekel or the weight of a gold nose ring (Gen. 24:22). ¶

BEL – ***bêl*** [masc. proper noun: בֵּל <1078>; by contr. for BAAL <1168>]: lord, vanity ▶ **This word designates a Babylonian god whose name means lord.** Refs.: Is. 46:1; Jer. 50:2; 51:44. The Lord is bringing swift judgment on this false pagan god. ¶

BELA – ***bela'*** [proper noun: בֶּלַע <1106>; the same as DEVOURING <1105>]: consuming, destruction ▶
a. Another name for Zoar. Refs.: Gen. 14:2, 8. ¶
b. An Edomite king. Refs.: Gen. 36:32, 33; 46:21; 1 Chr. 1:43, 44. ¶
c. A son of Benjamin. Refs.: Num. 26:38, 40; 1 Chr. 7:6, 7; 8:1, 3. ¶
d. A son of Azaz. Ref.: 1 Chr. 5:8. ¶

BELAITE – ***bal'iy*** [masc. proper noun: בַּלְעִי <1108>; patron. from BELA <1106>] ▶ **A member of the family of Bela, a son of Benjamin.** Ref.: Num. 26:38. ¶

BELCH – Ps. 59:7 ➔ UTTER <5042>.

BELIEFS – Job 11:4 ➔ LEARNING <3948>.

BELIEVE – [1] Gen. 15:6; Ex. 4:5; etc. ➔ NURSE (verb) <539> [2] Dan. 6:23 ➔ TRUST (verb) <540>.

BELITTLE – Prov. 11:12 ➔ DESPISE <936>.

BELL – [1] ***meṣillāh*** [fem. noun: מְצִלָּה <4698>; from TINGLE <6750>] ▶ **This word refers to a tinkling ornament worn by horses for noise and beauty.** In context the phrase "Holy to the Lord" will be inscribed on these bells (Zech. 14:20). ¶
[2] ***pa'amôn*** [masc. noun: פַּעֲמוֹן <6472>; from TIME <6471>] ▶ **This word refers to small tinkling ornaments that were fastened to the lower fringe of the High Priest's robe to indicate his presence and movement.** Refs.: Ex. 28:33, 34; 39:25, 26. ¶

BELLOW – [1] Job 6:5 ➔ LOW <1600> [2] Ps. 59:7 ➔ UTTER <5042>.

BELLOWS – ***mappuaḥ*** [masc. noun: מַפֻּחַ <4647>; from BREATHE <5301>] ▶ **This word signifies a set of bags pressed to force air into a furnace, making it hotter.** It is used figuratively of God's attempts to refine and purify His people (Jer. 6:29). ¶

BELLY – [1] ***gāḥôn*** [masc. noun: גָּחוֹן <1512>; prob. from GUSH <1518>] ▶ **Twice this word refers to the ventral side of reptiles.** (1) The belly of the serpent who deceived Eve (Gen. 3:14); and (2) to anything that crawls or moves on its belly (Lev. 11:42). In the latter case, all these creatures were detestable to the Israelites and could not be eaten. ¶
[2] ***me'êh*** [Aramaic masc. noun: מְעֵה <4577>; corresponding to BOWELS <4578>] ▶ **This word refers to the abdominal area of a human figure; of a huge image with an abdomen of bronze.** Ref.: Dan. 2:32; ESV: middle. ¶
– [3] Num. 25:8 ➔ STOMACH <6896> [4] 2 Sam. 2:23; 3:27; 4:6; 20:10 ➔ STOMACH <2570> [5] Ps. 73:4 ➔ BODY <193> a. [6] Jer. 51:34 ➔ STOMACH <3770>.

BELONGINGS – Jer. 10:17 (noun) ➔ BUNDLE <3666>.

BELOVED – [1] ***yāḏiyḏ, yeḏiyḏôṯ*** [adj.: יָדִיד, יְדִידוֹת <3039>; from the same as LOVER <1730>] ▶ **This word is used mainly to describe a person who is dearly cherished. It is often used in poetry.** Moses called Benjamin the beloved of the Lord (Deut. 33:12). Another use is to describe the loveliness of the Tabernacle of the Lord (Ps. 84:1: lovely, amiable). A third use is its literal meaning, love. The psalmist calls his poem (Ps. 45) a song of love (also translated wedding song). Other refs.: Ps. 60:5; 108:6; 127:2; Is. 5:1; Jer. 11:15. ¶
– [2] See LOVER <1730>.

BELOVED, DEARLY BELOVED – ***yeḏiḏûṯ*** [fem. noun: יְדִדוּת <3033>; from BELOVED <3039>] ▶ **This word means**

also highly valued, darling one. It is derived from the word *yāḏiyḏ*, which has a similar meaning. The word occurs only in Jeremiah 12:7 where it describes Israel as beloved of God's soul but forsaken by Him and delivered to their enemies because they only pretended to return His love (Jer. 12:1, 2). ¶

BELOW – ***maṭṭāh*** [adv.: מַטָּה <4295>; from EYES (PUT OUT THE) <5786> with directive enclitic appended (in the sense of blinding someone)] ▶ **This word means beneath, downward, under.** Its meaning is quite uniform. It indicates below, beneath (Ex. 26:24; Deut. 28:43; Prov. 15:24). With *lᵉ* on the front, it may mean a downward direction (2 Kgs. 19:30). It is used with *lᵉ* followed by *min* (FROM <4480>) to mean less than iniquity (Ezra 9:13). God's grace exceeded Israel's iniquity. *

BELSHAZZAR – 1 ***bêlša'ṣṣar*** [masc. proper noun: בֵּלְשַׁאצַּר <1112>; of foreign origin (comp. BELTESHAZZAR <1095>)]: Bel (a god) protects the king ▶ **This is the name of King Belshazzar of Babylon (ca. 551 B.C.) who was the son of Nabonidus, the true king of Babylon.** Ref.: Dan. 8:1. He was killed when Persia under Cyrus took the city of Babylon in 538 B.C. He defiled the holy vessels of the Temple of the Lord (Dan. 5:1–4). In his third year, Daniel dreamed a dream that showed the rise and demise of Greece (goat) and Media-Persia (ram). In Belshazzar's first year (ca. 553 B.C.), Daniel had dreamed about the rise and fall of four mighty world empires followed by the establishment of the kingdom of God, which will be ruled by the Son of Man and last forever (Dan. 7:13–28). ¶
2 ***bêlša'ṣṣar*** [Aramaic masc. proper noun: בֵּלְשַׁאצַּר <1113>; corresponding to <1112> above] ▶ **This name corresponds to the Hebrew name in Daniel 8:1.** It is found in Daniel 5:1, 2, 9, 22, 29, 30; 7:1. ¶

BELT – 1 ***'êzôr*** [masc. noun: אֵזוֹר <232>; from CHAINS <246>] ▶ **The word means an article of dress bound around the body; it is also translated girdle, waistband, sash, loincloth, waistcloth.** It was the inner piece of clothing (2 Kgs. 1:8; Ezek. 23:15). It could be of skin or linen (Jer. 13:1). It was used figuratively of Israel and Judah's faithfulness to the Lord (Jer. 13:1, 2, 4, 6, 7, 10, 11) and of the Lord's authority over kings (Job 12:18). In Isaiah 11:5, it is a metaphor for righteousness. Other ref.: Is. 5:27. ¶
2 ***ḥᵃgôrāh, ḥᵃgōrāh*** [fem. noun: חֲגוֹרָה, חֲגֹרָה <2290>; from GIRD ONESELF <2296>] ▶ **This word refers to a band worn around the waist, a girdle, a loincloth, loin coverings.** It refers to a loincloth of fig leaves as the first covering of humankind (Gen. 3:7: covering, loincloth, apron). It was a regular feature of Israelite clothing (Is. 3:24; also translated girdle, sash). It was a valuable and desirable part of a soldier's military uniform (2 Sam. 18:11; also translated girdle). To stain or to put the blood of battle on one's belt was to be guilty of violent bloodshed (1 Kgs. 2:5; also translated girdle). To put on a military belt was to prepare for war (2 Kgs. 3:21). ¶
3 ***mêzaḥ*** [masc. noun: מֵזַח <4206>; from LOOSE (COME) <2118>] ▶
a. This word means a band worn around the body; it is also translated girdle, strength. It is used of a girdle worn next to the skin. It is used figuratively of a "belt of oppression," an allusion to the inability of the mighty to contend with the Lord (Job 12:21); and the binding effects of a life of cursing and evil behavior toward others (Ps. 109:19). It has the sense of a restraining force (Is. 23:10). ¶
b. A masculine noun referring to a dock, a harbor. It indicates a harbor or port for ships (Is. 23:10), something God was taking away from Tyre. ¶
– 4 1 Sam. 18:4; 2 Sam. 20:8; Prov. 31:24 ➔ GIRDED <2289> b. 5 Job 38:31 ➔ CORD <4189> 6 Is. 22:21 ➔ SASH <73>.

BELTESHAZZAR – 1 ***bêlṭᵉša'ṣṣar*** [masc. proper noun: בֵּלְטְשַׁאצַּר <1095>; of foreign deriv.]: Bel (Lord), protect (him or his life) ▶ **This was the Babylonian name given to Daniel by a chief official,**

while Daniel was captive in Babylon. Refs.: Dan. 1:7; 10:1. Daniel did not recognize this pagan god but served the Lord God. ¶

[2] ***bêlṭᵉša'ṣṣar*** [Aramaic masc. proper noun: בֵּלְטְשַׁאצַּר <1096>; corresponding to <1095> above] ▶ **The meaning of this name is the same as the previous one.** It occurs in the Aramaic portions of Daniel (2:26; 4:8, 9, 18, 19; 5:12). ¶

BEN – ***bên*** [masc. proper noun: בֵּן <1122>; the same as SON <1121>]: son ▶ **An Israelite from the tribe of Levi.** Ref.: 1 Chr. 15:18. ¶

BEN-ABINADAB – ***ben ᵃḇiynāḏāḇ*** [masc. proper noun: בֶּן־אֲבִינָדָב <1125>; from SON <1121> and ABINADAB <41>]: son of the father of liberty (or generosity) ▶ **A governor of Solomon over Israel.** He was married to Taphath, the daughter of Solomon (1 Kgs. 4:11). ¶

BEN-AMMI – ***ben-'ammiy*** [masc. proper noun: בֶּן־עַמִּי <1151>; from SON <1121> and PEOPLE <5971> with pron. suffix]: son of my people ▶ **A son of Lot; he is the father of the Ammonites.** Ref.: Gen. 19:38. ¶

BEN-DEKER – ***ben-deqer*** [masc. proper noun: בֶּן־דֶּקֶר <1128>; from SON <1121> and a deriv. of PIERCE <1856>]: son of piercing, son of the one who carries the spear ▶ **A governor of Solomon over Israel.** Ref.: 1 Kgs. 4:9. ¶

BEN-GEBER – ***ben-geḇer*** [masc. proper noun: בֶּן־גֶּבֶר <1127>; from SON <1121> and MAN <1397> (in the sense of being mighty)]: son of the hero ▶ **A governor of Solomon over Israel.** Ref.: 1 Kgs. 4:13. ¶

BEN-HADAD – ***ben hᵃḏaḏ*** [masc. proper noun: בֶּן־הֲדַד <1130>; from SON <1121> and HADAD <1908>]: son of the mighty one, of (the god) Hadad ▶

a. The name of an important king of Syria (Aram) in biblical history. He ruled from Damascus (1 Kgs. 15:18, 20). He was in league with King Asa in Judah against Baasha in Northern Israel. This person was Ben-Hadad I, son of Tabrimmon, son of Hezion, king of Aram. He ruled ca. 893–860 B.C. The references in 1 Kings. 20:1–33 are taken to refer to this individual. Ben-Hadad then fought also with Ahab who conquered him (1 Kgs. 20:1–34). But Ahab let Ben-Hadad go free instead of executing him as he should have (1 Kgs. 20:35–43). *

b. A second king, Ben-Hadad II, seems to have ruled Aram (Syria) about 860–843 B.C. Some scholars hold that Ben-Hadad I and II are the same person. More believe that the Ben-Hadad of 1 Kings 20:1–33 is a son or grandson of Hadad I. This Ben-Hadad was son of the king of Aram, Hazael, and succeeded him. He and his father Hazael are both condemned in Amos 1:4. *

BEN-HAIL – ***ben ḥayil*** [masc. proper noun: בֶּן חַיִל <1134>; from SON <1121> and STRENGTH <2428>]: son of strength ▶ **An official of Jehoshaphat whom he sent to teach in the cities of Judah.** Ref.: 2 Chr. 17:7. ¶

BEN-HANAN – ***ben-ḥānān*** [masc. proper noun: בֶּן־חָנָן <1135>; from SON <1121> and HANAN <2605>]: son, gift of grace ▶ **An Israelite of the tribe of Judah.** Ref.: 1 Chr. 4:20. ¶

BEN-HESED – ***ben-ḥeseḏ*** [masc. proper noun: בֶּן־חֶסֶד <1136>; from SON <1121> and MERCY <2617>]: son of kindness ▶ **A governor of Solomon over Israel.** Ref.: 1 Kgs. 4:10. ¶

BEN-HUR – ***ben ḥûr*** [masc. proper noun: בֶּן־חוּר <1133>; from SON <1121> and HUR <2354>]: son of Hur (whiteness) ▶ **A governor of Solomon over Israel, in the hill country of Ephraim.** Ref.: 1 Kgs. 4:8. ¶

BEN-ONI – ***ben 'ôniy*** [masc. proper noun: בֶּן־אוֹנִי <1126>; from SON <1121> and NOTHINGNESS <205> (in the sense of sorrow)]: son of my sorrow ▶ **The name**

given by Rachel to her younger son; Jacob changed his name to Benjamin. Ref.: Gen. 35:18. ¶

BEN-ZOHETH – ***ben zôḥêṯ*** [masc. proper noun: בֶּן־זוֹחֵת <1132>; from SON <1121> and ZOHETH <2105>]: son of the removal, strong ▶ **An Israelite from the tribe of Judah.** Ref.: 1 Chr. 4:20. ¶

BENAIAH – ***bᵉnāyāh, bᵉnāyāhû*** [masc. proper noun: בְּנָיָה, בְּנָיָהוּ <1141> from BUILD <1129> and LORD <3050>]: the Lord builds up ▶

a. The commander of David's bodyguard made up of foreigners. Refs.: 2 Sam. 8:18; 20:23. He was a mighty man among David's "thirty" elite warriors (2 Sam. 23:20–23; 1 Chr. 27:6). After David died, he helped install Solomon as king (1 Kgs. 1:1–2:46) and removed Joab (1 Kgs. 2:34–46). He became a leading official for Solomon (1 Kgs. 4:4). *

b. A soldier. Refs.: 2 Sam. 23:30; 1 Chr. 11:31; 27:14. ¶

c. An Israelite of the tribe of Simeon. Ref.: 1 Chr. 4:36. ¶

d. Another Beniah was a priest, evidently a gatekeeper from the Levites. Ref.: 1 Chr. 15:18. He was also a musician (1 Chr. 15:20, 24; 16:5, 6). ¶

e. He was the father of Jehoiada who succeeded Ahithophel, King David's counselor. Ref.: 1 Chr. 27:34. ¶

f. The grandfather of Jehaziel, a prophet who uttered some famous words to King Jehoshaphat. Refs.: 2 Chr. 20:13–17. They foretold his victory over Moab and Ammon. ¶

g. A Levite who was overseer during the renovation of the Temple under King Hezekiah. Ref.: 2 Chr. 31:13. ¶

h. An Israelite, evidently a priest, guilty of intermarrying among foreigners. Ref.: Ezra 10:25. ¶

i. Another Israelite who had married a foreigner in Ezra's time. Ref.: Ezra 10:30. ¶

j. Another Israelite who had married a foreigner in Ezra's time. Ref.: Ezra 10:35. ¶

k. Another Israelite who had married a foreigner in Ezra's time. Ref.: Ezra 10:43. ¶

l. The father of a corrupt leader of Israel named Pelatiah. Refs.: Ezek. 11:1, 13. He plotted evil and misled the people of Jerusalem. ¶

BEND – [1] ***kāpan*** [verb: כָּפַן <3719>; a prim. root] ▶ **This word refers to a vine putting forth roots as it seeks nourishment for growth.** Ref.: Ezek. 17:7; NIV: to send out. It is used figuratively of Israel's political overtures to Egypt for aid, an ill-fated move. ¶

[2] ***nāḥaṯ*** [verb: נָחַת <5181>; a prim. root] ▶ **This word also means to bring down, to descend.** It means to bend a strong bow for battle (2 Sam. 22:35; Ps. 18:34; KJV: to break), to pull it down. It has a general sense of to descend, to go down someplace (Job 21:13); to descend against someone in battle (Jer. 21:13; Joel 3:11: to come down). It depicts the penetration of something: the arrows of the Lord's rebukes penetrate (Ps. 38:2: to sink, to pierce, to stick fast; Prov. 17:10: to enter more, to go deeper, to impress). It seems to have the sense of leveling off, smoothing something in Psalm 65:10 (to settle, to level). ¶

[3] ***'āwaṯ*** [verb: עָוַת <5791>; a prim. root] ▶ **This word means to stoop, and also to make crooked, to be crooked. It is always used in the intensive stems with the meaning to deal crookedly, to subvert, or to pervert.** Except for Ecclesiastes 12:3, where it refers to the strong men bending themselves (i.e., bowing down, stooping), it is used figuratively of bending or perverting justice and righteousness. Bildad and Elihu told Job that God does not pervert justice (Job 8:3; 34:12); but Job thought God had been crooked with him (Job 19:6: to wrong, to overthrow, to put in the wrong). Other refs.: Ps. 119:78; 146:9; Eccl. 1:15; 7:13; Lam. 3:36; Amos 8:5. ¶

BEND DOWN – 1 Kgs. 18:42 ➔ STRETCH ONESELF <1457>.

BENE-BERAK – ***bᵉnêy ḇᵉraq*** [proper noun: בְּנֵי־בְרַק <1139>; from the plur. construction of SON <1121> and LIGHTNING <1300>]: sons of lightning ▶ **A city of the tribe of Dan.** Ref.: Josh. 19:45. ¶

BENE-JAAKAN – ***b***^{e}***nêy ya***^{ʿa}***qān*** [proper noun: בְּנֵי יַעֲקָן <1142>; from the plur. of SON <1121> and JAAKAN <3292>]: sons of Jaakan ▶ **A place in the desert where the Israelites camped.** Refs.: Num. 33:31, 32. ¶

BENEFIT – [1] ***tagmûl*** [masc. noun: תַּגְמוּל <8408>; from REWARD (verb) <1580>] ▶ **This word indicates things or conditions that improve the lot of persons, their health, their spiritual well-being, or their economic situations.** Ref.: Ps. 116:12; NIV: goodness. ¶
– [2] Eccl. 5:11 ➔ SKILL <3788>.

BENEFIT (BE OF) – Job 22:2 ➔ PROFITABLE (BE) <5532> a.

BENINU – ***b***^{e}***niynû*** [masc. proper noun: בְּנִינוּ <1148>; prob. from SON <1121>]: our son, posterity ▶ **A Levite who signed the covenant of renewal with Nehemiah after the return from the Babylonian captivity.** Ref.: Neh. 10:13. ¶

BENJAMIN – ***binyāmiyn*** [masc. proper noun: בִּנְיָמִין <1144>; from SON <1121> and RIGHT HAND <3225>]: son of my right hand ▶
a. He was the youngest of Jacob's sons. His mother Rachel died at his birth and called him Benoni, "son of my sorrow" (Gen. 35:18, 24). He was second only to Joseph in his father's affections. Jacob called him a wolf that tears his prey (Gen. 49:27); Moses called him loved by the Lord, one whom God protected (Deut. 33:12). He went to Egypt with his brothers (Ex. 1:3). *
b. The name of the tribe descended from Benjamin. It consisted of many descendants and families (Gen. 46:19, 21; cf. 1 Chr. 7:6). The tribe inhabited territory in the center of Israel, bounded by Ephraim (north), Dan (west), Judah (south). The territories of Gad and Reuben touched the northeast border of Benjamin. Its border actually extended south of Jerusalem (Josh. 18:11–28). Bethel, Mizpah, and Gibeon were located in its territory, although its borders shifted slightly from time to time. The judge Ehud, a left-handed man, was from Benjamin, as was Saul, Israel's first king (Judg. 3:15; 1 Sam. 9:1). The Benjamites were threatened as a tribe over a Levite's concubine who was raped and killed in Benjamite territory (Judg. 19–21). After the monarchy, Benjamin stayed tied to Judah (1 Kgs. 12:21, 23; 15:16–22). The tribe had a place in Ezekiel's new Temple vision (Ezek. 48:22–32). *
c. It refers to a son of Bilham, son of Jediael. Ref.: 1 Chr. 7:10. He was a head of a family in Benjamin. ¶
d. A son of Harim of the priestly line who had taken a foreign wife. Ref.: Ezra 10:32. *
e. It refers to one or possibly two gates in Jerusalem bearing this name. Ref.: Jer. 20:2; cf. Jer. 37:13; Zech. 14:10. Legal matters or business issues were often transacted at these places. *

BENJAMITE – [1] ***ben-y***^{e}***miyniy*** [masc. proper noun: בֶּן־יְמִינִי <1145>; patron. from BENJAMIN <1144>] ▶ **A gentilic noun indicating that a person was associated with or a part of the tribe of Benjamin (see BENJAMIN <1144>).** Ehud was a Benjamite (Judg. 3:15), and the people of Gibeah were Benjamites (Judg. 19:16). Saul, the first king in Israel, was a Benjamite (1 Sam. 9:21). Cush, a Benjamite, has a psalm dedicated to him (Ps. 7:1). *
– [2] 1 Sam. 9:1, 4; 2 Sam. 20:1; Esther 2:5 ➔ JAMINITE <3228>.

BENT (BE) – Hos. 11:7 ➔ HANG <8511>.

BENUMBED (BE) – Ps. 38:8 ➔ STUNNED (BECOME) <6313>.

BEON – ***b***^{e}***ʿōn*** [proper noun: בְּעֹן <1194>; prob. a contr. of BETH BAAL MEON <1010>]: house of habitation ▶ **The same as Baal-Meon <1186> (probably a contr. of the noun).** Ref.: Num. 32:3. ¶

BEOR – ***b***^{e}***ʿôr*** [masc. proper noun: בְּעוֹר <1160>; from BURN <1197> (in the sense of burning)]: lamp, shepherd ▶

a. The father of Balaam. Refs.: Num. 22:5; 24:3, 15; 31:8; Deut. 23:4; Josh. 13:22; 24:9; Mic. 6:5. ¶
b. The father of a king of Edom. Refs.: Gen. 36:32; 1 Chr. 1:43. ¶

BERA – ***bera'*** [masc. proper noun: בֶּרַע <1298>; of uncertain deriv.]: son of evil ► **A king of Sodom.** Ref.: Gen. 14:2. ¶

BERACAH – ***beᵉrāḵāh*** [proper noun: בְּרָכָה <1294>; the same as BLESSING <1293>]: blessing ►
a. A Benjamite who came to David at Ziklag. Ref.: 1 Chr. 12:3. ¶
b. A valley where the Israelites blessed the Lord after a great victory. Ref.: 2 Chr. 20:26. ¶

BERAIAH – ***bᵉrā'yāh*** [masc. proper noun: בְּרָאיָה <1256>; from CREATE <1254> and LORD <3050>]: the Lord has created ► **An Israelite of the tribe of Benjamin.** Ref.: 1 Chr. 8:21. ¶

BEREAVED – ***šakkûl, šᵉḵûlāh*** [adj.: שַׁכּוּל, שְׁכוּלָה <7909>; from DEPRIVED OF CHILDREN <7921>] ► **The word is used figuratively to describe the fierceness of David and his men by comparing them to a wild bear robbed of her cubs.** Ref.: 2 Sam. 17:8. In another analogy, the intensity of God's punishment is described as a bear robbed of her cubs. God would attack the Israelites for their sins and rip them open (Hos. 13:8). Proverbs used the same figurative language, stating that it is better to meet a bear robbed of her cubs than a fool in his folly (Prov. 17:12). In a different sense, Jeremiah used this word to describe a punishment in which wives would be made childless and widows (Jer. 18:21: bereaved of their children, childless). Other refs.: Song 4:2; 6:6 (barren). ¶

BEREAVEMENT – ***šikkuliym*** [masc. noun: שִׁכֻּלִים <7923>; plur. from DEPRIVED OF CHILDREN <7921>] ► **This word also means childlessness. It refers to the loss of living children, as well as the miscarrying of infants.** Ref.: Is. 49:20. ¶

BERECHIAH, BERKIAH – ***bereḵyah, bereḵyāhû*** [masc. proper noun: בֶּרֶכְיָה, בֶּרֶכְיָהוּ <1296>; from KNEE <1290> and LORD <3050>]: blessing of the Lord ►
a. The father of Zechariah. Refs.: Zech. 1:1, 7. ¶
b. An Israelite of the tribe of Ephraim. Ref.: 2 Chr. 28:12. ¶
c. The father of Asaph. Refs.: 1 Chr. 6:39; 15:17. ¶
d. A son of Zerubbabel. Ref.: 1 Chr. 3:20. ¶
e. A Levite. Refs.: 1 Chr. 9:16; 15:23. ¶
f. The father of Meshullam. Refs.: Neh. 3:4, 30; 6:18. ¶

BERED – ***bereḏ*** [proper noun: בֶּרֶד <1260>; from HAIL (verb) <1258>]: hail ►
a. A town not far from the well of Lahai Roi. Ref.: Gen. 16:14. ¶
b. An Israelite from the tribe of Ephraim. Ref.: 1 Chr. 7:20. ¶

BERI – ***bêriy*** [masc. proper noun: בֵּרִי <1275>; prob. by contr. from BEERI <882>]: man of the well ► **An Israelite of the tribe of Asher.** Ref.: 1 Chr. 7:36. ¶

BERIAH – ***bᵉriy'āh, bᵉri'āh*** [masc. proper noun: בְּרִיעָה, בְּרִעָה <1283>; apparently from the fem. of BAD <7451>]: in trouble, unhappy ►
a. A son of Asher. Refs.: Gen. 46:17; Num. 26:44, 45; 1 Chr. 7:30, 31; 23:10, 11. ¶
b. A son of Ephraim. Ref.: 1 Chr. 7:23. ¶
c. A Benjamite. Refs.: 1 Chr. 8:13, 16. ¶
d. A Levite. Refs.: 1 Chr. 23:10, 11. ¶

BERIITE – ***bᵉriy'iy*** [masc. proper noun: בְּרִיעִי <1284>; patron. from BERIAH <1283>] ► **This word indicates a nationality of Beriites or descendant of Beriah.** Ref.: Num. 26:44. ¶

BERITE – ***bêriy*** [proper noun: בֵּרִי <1276>; of uncertain deriv.]: well ► **Possibly a place in Israel.** Ref.: 2 Sam. 20:14. ¶

BERITH – ***bᵉriyṯ*** [masc. proper noun: בְּרִית <1286>; the same as COVENANT <1285>]: covenant ► **This was the name**

of a Canaanite god. It is combined with the term El, god, forming the name of a temple in Shechem, El-Berith, literally, the god of the covenant (Judg. 9:46). ¶

BERODACH-BALADAN – ***b^{e}rō'ḏaḵ bal^{a}ḏān*** [masc. proper noun: בְּרֹאדַךְ בַּלְאֲדָן <1255>; a variation of MERODACH-BALADAN <4757>]: slaughter, fearless ▶ **A Babylonian king.** Ref.: 2 Kgs. 20:12. ¶

BEROTHAH, BEROTHAI – ***bêrôṯāh, bêrōṯay*** [proper noun: בֵּרוֹתָה, בֵּרֹתַי <1268>; prob. from FIR <1266>]: fir, fir-like ▶ **A city between Damascus and Hamath.** Refs.: 2 Sam. 8:8; Ezek. 47:16. ¶

BEROTHITE – ***bêrōṯiy*** [masc. proper noun: בֵּרֹתִי <1307>; patrial from BEROTHAH <1268>] ▶ **A native or an inhabitant of Berothai.** Ref.: 1 Chr. 11:39. ¶

BERRY – ***gargêr*** [masc. noun: גַּרְגַּר <1620>; by reduplication from DRAG (verb) <1641>] ▶ **This word indicates the fruit of the olive tree; it is also translated olive.** It is used once in its plural form to refer to olives left on the top boughs of an olive tree representing Damascus (Is. 17:6). ¶

BERYL – [1] ***taršiyš*** [masc. noun: תַּרְשִׁישׁ <8658>; prob. of foreign deriv.] ▶

a. This word refers to a gemstone; it is also translated jewels, topaz. It was placed in the fourth row of the breastpiece of the high priest as one of the twelve stones representing the tribes of Israel. It is used to describe the beauty of the bridegroom (Song 5:14). The wheels in Ezekiel's vision are compared to it (Ezek. 1:16; 10:9). It was part of the covering of the king of Tyre (Satan?) in Eden (Ezek. 28:13). Other refs.: Ex. 28:20; 39:13; Dan. 10:6. ¶

b. A proper noun Tarshish: the name of the gemstone in a. above. The word is given as a proper noun to indicate from where the stone came. Tarshish may refer to an area in modern Spain, a place along the shores of the Mediterranean, or perhaps North Africa or Sicily. Its location is not certain.

– [2] Ex. 28:17; 39:10; Ezek. 28:13 ➔ EMERALD <1304>.

BESAI – ***bêsay*** [masc. proper noun: בֵּסַי <1153>; from TREAD DOWN <947>]: trampled ▶ **One of the Nethinim.** Refs.: Ezra 2:49; Neh. 7:52. ¶

BESIDE – ***'êṣel*** [masc. noun: אֵצֶל <681>; from RESERVE (verb) <680> (in the sense of joining)] ▶ **This word also means nearness, next to. It is used only as a preposition.** It functions in two ways: (1) to indicate proximity (Gen. 39:10, 15; 41:3) meaning beside something or in a certain locality (Deut. 11:30; 1 Kgs. 1:9; 4:12); (2) to indicate removal from proximity or location when used with *min* <4480>, from (1 Sam. 17:30; 20:41; 1 Kgs. 3:20; Ezek. 40:7). *

BESIDES – Eccl. 12:9 ➔ MORE, MORE THAN <3148>.

BESIEGE – [1] ***ṣûr*** [verb: צוּר <6696>; a prim. root] ▶

a. This word means to lay siege, to bind. It describes attaching a money bag to one's hand to transport it safely or to putting money into bags (Deut. 14:25; 2 Kgs. 5:23). It has the sense of gathering and agitating people to go against a city (Judg. 9:31); or of setting up siegeworks or fortress outposts against a city (Is. 29:3); of besieging a city, attacking it (1 Sam. 23:8; 2 Sam. 11:1; 1 Kgs. 15:27; 16:17; 2 Kgs. 5:23; Dan. 1:1). It is used figuratively of constructing a protective barrier around a young girl (Song 8:9). *

b. This word means to attack, to harass, to be an adversary. It refers to attacking persons, putting them under duress, opposing them. God would serve as an adversary against the enemies of His people (Ex. 23:22). It refers to harassing or oppressing a people or nation (Deut. 2:9, 19); or even to attacking them (Esther 8:11), in context with God's approval. *

– [2] Is. 29:2 ➔ OPPRESS <6693>.

BESODEIAH – ***b^{e}sôḏ^{e}yāh*** [masc. proper noun: בְּסוֹדְיָה <1152>; from COUNSEL <5475> and LORD <3050> with prep. prefix]: in the counsel of the Lord ▶ **Father of Meshullam who repaired the Old Gate.** Ref.: Neh. 3:6. ¶

BESOM – Is. 14:23 ➔ BROOM <4292>.

BESOR – ***b^{e}sôr*** [proper noun: בְּשׂוֹר <1308>; from NEWS (BRING) <1319>]: cheerful ▶ **A brook south of Ziklag.** Refs.: 1 Sam. 30:9, 10, 21. ¶

BEST – [1] ***mêyṭāḇ*** [masc. noun: מֵיטָב <4315>; from GOOD (BE) <3190>] ▶ **This word indicates what is superlative in quality or worth for various purposes.** The best of the land of Egypt (Gen. 47:6, 11); the best part of crops at harvest time (Ex. 22:5); the best of animals for sacrifice or food (1 Sam. 15:9, 15). ¶
– [2] 1 Kgs. 10:18 ➔ REFINED (BE) <6338>.

BEST (SEEM) – Ezra 7:18 ➔ GOOD (SEEM) <3191>.

BESTIR ONESELF – 2 Sam. 5:24 ➔ MOVE <2782>.

BESTOW – [1] Ps. 21:5 ➔ LIKE (BE, BECOME) <7737> b. [2] Prov. 4:9 ➔ DELIVER <4042>.

BETAH – ***beṭaḥ*** [proper noun: בֶּטַח <984>; the same as SECURITY <983>]: assurance, security ▶ **A city in Syria from which King David took a large amount of bronze.** Ref.: 2 Sam. 8:8. ¶

BETEN – ***beṭen*** [proper noun: בֶּטֶן <991>; the same as WOMB <990>]: womb ▶ **Village of the tribe of Asher.** Ref.: Josh. 19:25. ¶

BETH ANATH – ***bêyṯ ʿ^{a}nāṯ*** [proper noun: בֵּית עֲנָת <1043>; an orthographical variation from BETH ANOTH <1042>]: house of replies ▶ **A fortified city in the territory of Naphtali.** Refs.: Josh. 19:38; Judg. 1:33. ¶

BETH ANOTH – ***bêyṯ ʿ^{a}nôṯ*** [proper noun: בֵּית עֲנוֹת <1042>; from HOUSE <1004> and a plur. from ANSWER (verb) a. <6030>]: house of replies ▶ **A city in the hills of Judah.** Ref.: Josh. 15:59. ¶

BETH ARABAH – ***bêyṯ hāʿ^{a}rāḇāh*** [proper noun: בֵּית הָעֲרָבָה <1026>; from HOUSE <1004> and DESERT <6160> with the art. interposed]: house of the desert ▶ **A village of the desert of Judah on the border between Judah and Benjamin.** Refs.: Josh. 15:6, 61; 18:18, 22. ¶

BETH ARBEL – ***bêyṯ 'arbê'l*** [proper noun: בֵּית אַרְבֵּאל <1009>; from HOUSE <1004> and DEN <695> and GOD <410>]: house of God's court ▶ **A city in Israel, destroyed by Shalman.** Ref.: Hos. 10:14. ¶

BETH ASHTAROTH – ***bêyṯ ʿaštārôṯ*** [proper noun: בֵּית עַשְׁתָּרוֹת <1045>; from HOUSE <1004> and ASHTAROTH <6252>; comp. BEESHTERAH <1203>, ASHTAROTH <6252>]: house of Ashtaroth (a Canaanite goddess) ▶ **This word designates the temple of Ashtaroth.** Ref.: 1 Sam. 31:10. ¶

BETH AVEN – ***bêyṯ 'āwen*** [proper noun: בֵּית אָוֶן <1007>; from HOUSE <1004> and NOTHINGNESS <205>]: house of vanity, of nothingness, i.e., of idolatry ▶ **City of the tribe of Benjamin.** Refs.: Josh. 7:2; 18:12; 1 Sam. 13:5; 14:23. Hosea gives this name to Bethel which had become a center of idolatry (Hos. 4:15; 5:8; 10:5, 8). ¶

BETH AZMAVETH – ***bêyṯ ʿazmāweṯ*** [proper noun: בֵּית עַזְמָוֶת <1041>; from HOUSE <1004> and AZMAVETH <5820>]: house of Azmaveth (death is strong) ▶ **A village near Jerusalem; 42 of its inhabitants came back from the Babylonian captivity.** Ref.: Neh. 7:28. ¶

BETH BAAL MEON, BETH MEON – ***bêyṯ baʿal m^{e}ʿôn, bêyṯ m^{e}ʿôn*** [proper noun: בֵּית בַּעַל מְעוֹן, בֵּית מְעוֹן <1010>; from HOUSE <1004> and BAAL <1168> and HABITATION <4583>]: house of Baal of the habitation, house of habitation ▶ **A city assigned to the tribe of Reuben.** Refs.: Josh. 13:17; Jer. 48:23. ¶

BETH BARAH – ***bêyṯ bārāh*** [proper noun: בֵּית בָּרָה <1012>; prob. from HOUSE <1004> and FORD <5679>]: house of the ford ▶ **One of the main fords of the Jordan where Gideon stopped his enemies.** Ref.: Judg. 7:24. ¶

BETH BIRI – ***bêyṯ bir'iy*** [proper noun: בֵּית בִּרְאִי <1011>; from HOUSE <1004> and CREATE <1254>]: house of my creation ▶ **A city of the tribe of Simeon.** Ref.: 1 Chr. 4:31. ¶

BETH CAR – ***bêyṯ kār*** [proper noun: בֵּית כָּר <1033>; from HOUSE <1004> and LAMB <3733>]: house of pastures ▶ **A place where the Israelites pursued the Philistines after the battle of Ebenezer.** Ref.: 1 Sam. 7:11. ¶

BETH DAGON – ***bêyṯ-dāḡôn*** [proper noun: בֵּית־דָּגוֹן <1016>; from HOUSE <1004> and DAGON <1712>]: house of Dagon (a false god) ▶
a. A town in Judah. Ref.: Josh. 15:41. ¶
b. A town in Asher. Ref.: Josh. 19:27. ¶

BETH DIBLATHAIM – ***bêyṯ diḇlāṯayim*** [proper noun: בֵּית דִּבְלָתַיִם <1015>; from HOUSE <1004> and the dual of FIGS (CAKE OF) <1690>]: house of the fig cakes ▶ **A city of the Moabites.** Ref.: Jer. 48:22. ¶

BETH EDEN – ***bêyṯ 'eḏen*** [proper noun: בֵּית עֵדֶן <1040>; from HOUSE <1004> and DELIGHT <5730>]: house of delight ▶ **A place in Syria.** Ref.: Amos 1:5. ¶

BETH EKED – ***bêyṯ 'êqeḏ*** [proper noun: בֵּית עֵקֶד <1044>; from HOUSE <1004> and a deriv. of BIND <6123>]: house of binding ▶ **A place in northern Israel, between Jezreel and Samaria.** Refs.: 2 Kgs. 10:12, 14. ¶

BETH EMEK – ***bêyṯ hā'êmeq*** [proper noun: בֵּית הָעֵמֶק <1025>; from HOUSE <1004> and VALLEY <6010> with the art. interposed]: house of the valley ▶ **A place on the border of the tribe of Asher.** Ref.: Josh. 19:27. ¶

BETH EZEL – ***bêyṯ hā'êṣel*** [proper noun: בֵּית הָאֵצֶל <1018>; from HOUSE <1004> and BESIDE <681> with the art. interposed]: house of the neighborhood ▶ **A place in the south of Judah.** Ref.: Mic. 1:11. ¶

BETH GADER – ***bêyṯ-gāḏêr*** [proper noun: בֵּית־גָּדֵר <1013>; from HOUSE <1004> and WALL <1447>]: house of the walls ▶ **A city of the tribe of Judah.** Ref.: 1 Chr. 2:51. ¶

BETH GAMUL – ***bêyṯ gāmûl*** [proper noun: בֵּית גָּמוּל <1014>; from HOUSE <1004> and DESERVES (WHAT ONE) <1576>]: house of the reward, of the camel ▶ **A city of the Moabites.** Ref.: Jer. 48:23. ¶

BETH GILGAL – ***bêyṯ haggilgāl*** [proper noun: בֵּית הַגִּלְגָּל <1019>; from HOUSE <1004> and GILGAL <1537>]: house of Gilgal (rolling) ▶ **Probably the same place as Gilgal.** Ref.: Neh. 12:29. ¶

BETH HAKKEREM – ***bêyṯ hakkerem*** [proper noun: בֵּית הַכֶּרֶם <1021>; from HOUSE <1004> and VINEYARD <3754>]: house of the vineyard ▶ **A place in Judah.** Refs.: Neh. 3:14; Jer. 6:1. ¶

BETH HARAM – ***bêyṯ hārām*** [proper noun: בֵּית הָרָם <1027>; from HOUSE <1004> and EXALT <7311> with the art. interposed]: house of the heights ▶ **A city in the valley of the Jordan.** It was rebuilt by the descendants of Gad (Josh. 13:27; see Num. 32:36: Beth Haran). ¶

BETH HARAN – ***bêyṯ hārān*** [proper noun: בֵּית הָרָן <1028>; prob. for BETH-HARAM <1027>]: house of the heights ▶ **See BETH HARAM <1027>.** Ref.: Num. 32:36. ¶

BETH HOGLAH – ***bêyṯ ḥoglāh*** [proper noun: בֵּית חָגְלָה <1031>; from HOUSE <1004> and the same as HOGLAH <2295>]: house of the partridge ▶ **A village of the tribe of Benjamin.** Refs.: Josh. 15:6; 18:19, 21. ¶

BETH HORON – ***bêyṯ ḥôrôn*** [proper noun: בֵּית חוֹרוֹן <1032>; from HOUSE <1004> and HOLE <2356>]: house of the great cavern ▶ **Two adjoining cities of the tribe of Ephraim.** Refs.: Josh. 10:10, 11; 16:3, 5; 18:13, 14; 21:22; 1 Sam. 13:18; 1 Kgs. 9:17; 1 Chr. 6:68; 7:24; 2 Chr. 8:5; 25:13. ¶

BETH JESHIMOTH – ***bêyṯ hayešiymôṯ*** [proper noun: בֵּית הַיְשִׁימוֹת <1020>; from HOUSE <1004> and the plur. of DESOLATION <3451> with the art. interposed]: house of the deserts ▶ **This city was assigned to the tribe of Reuben but was in the hands of the Moabites at the time of Ezekiel.** Refs.: Num. 33:49; Josh. 12:3; 13:20; Ezek. 25:9. ¶

BETH LEBAOTH – ***bêyṯ lebā'ôṯ*** [proper noun: בֵּית לְבָאוֹת <1034>; from HOUSE <1004> and the plur. of LION, LIONESS <3833> (comp. LEBAOTH <3822>)]: house of lionesses ▶ **A city of the tribe of Simeon.** Ref.: Josh. 19:6. ¶

BETH MAACAH – ***bêyṯ maʿaḵāh*** [proper noun: בֵּית מַעֲכָה <1038>; from HOUSE <1004> and MAACAH <4601>]: house of oppression ▶ **A shortened form of Abel Beth Maacah.** Refs.: 2 Sam. 20:14, 15. ¶

BETH MARCABOTH – ***beyṯ hammarkāḇôṯ*** [proper noun: בֵּית הַמַּרְכָּבוֹת <1024>; from HOUSE <1004> and the plur. of CHARIOT <4818> (with or without the art. interposed)]: house of the chariots ▶ **A place in the tribe of Simeon.** Refs.: Josh. 19:5; 1 Chr. 4:31. ¶

BETH MILLO – ***bêyṯ millô'*** [proper noun: בֵּית מִלּוֹא <1037>; from HOUSE <1004> and MILLO <4407>]: house of the rampart ▶ **This word is a reference to two locations: one near Shechem and one in Jerusalem.** The location near Shechem is mentioned in Judges 9:6, 20 (Beth Millo, NASB, NIV; house of Millo, KJV). The citadel in Jerusalem is mentioned in 2 Kings 12:20 (house of Millo, NASB, KJV; Beth Millo, NIV). ¶

BETH NIMRAH – ***bêyṯ nimrāh*** [proper noun: בֵּית נִמְרָה <1039>; from HOUSE <1004> and the fem. of LEOPARD <5246> (comp. NIMRAH <5247>)]: house of the leopard ▶ **A city allocated to and rebuilt by the tribe of Gad.** Refs.: Num. 32:36; Josh. 13:27. ¶

BETH OPHRAH – ***beyṯ leʿap̱rāh*** [proper noun: בֵּית לְעַפְרָה <1036>; from HOUSE <1004> and the fem. of DUST <6083> (with prep. interposed)]: house to (i.e., of) dust ▶ **This phrase in Micah 1:10 is interpreted by some as the proper noun Beth Ophrah.** Others translate the phrase house of Aphrah (i.e., house of dust). ¶

BETH PAZZEZ – ***bêyṯ paṣṣêṣ*** [proper noun: בֵּית פַּצֵּץ <1048>; from HOUSE <1004> and a deriv. from SCATTER <6327>]: house of dispersion ▶ **A city in the territory of Issachar.** Ref.: Josh. 19:21. ¶

BETH PELET – ***bêyṯ peleṭ*** [proper noun: בֵּית פֶּלֶט <1046>; from HOUSE <1004> and REFUGEE <6412>]: house of escape ▶ **A city at the extreme south of Judah.** Refs.: Josh. 15:27; Neh. 11:26. ¶

BETH PEOR – ***bêyṯ peʿôr*** [proper noun: בֵּית פְּעוֹר <1047>; from HOUSE <1004> and PEOR <6465>]: house of Peor (a false god of Midian) ▶ **A city near Pisgah on the east side of the Jordan.** Moses was buried in the valley in the land of Moab opposite Beth Peor (Deut. 3:29; 4:46; 34:6; Josh. 13:20). ¶

BETH RAPHA – ***bêyṯ rāp̱ā'*** [masc. proper noun: בֵּית רָפָא <1051>; from HOUSE <1004> and REPHAIM <7497>]: house of the giant ▶ **An Israelite of the tribe of Judah, son of Eshton.** Ref.: 1 Chr. 4:12. ¶

BETH REHOB – ***bêyṯ r^{e}ḥôḇ*** [proper noun: בֵּית רְחוֹב <1050>; from HOUSE <1004> and STREET <7339>]: house of the widening ▶ **A city inhabited by the Syrians.** Refs.: Judg. 18:28; 2 Sam. 10:6. ¶

BETH SHEAN – ***bêyṯ š^e'ān, bêyṯ šān*** [proper noun: בֵּית שְׁאָן, בֵּית שָׁן <1052>; from HOUSE <1004> and EASE (BE AT) <7599>]: house of ease, of security ▶ **A city attributed to the tribe of Manasseh.** Refs.: Josh. 17:11, 16; Judg. 1:27; 1 Sam. 31:10, 12; 2 Sam. 21:12; 1 Kgs. 4:12; 1 Chr. 7:29. ¶

BETH SHEMESH – ***bêyṯ šemeš*** [proper noun: בֵּית שֶׁמֶשׁ <1053>; from HOUSE <1004> and SUN <8121>]: house of the sun ▶
a. A city in northwest Judah. Refs.: Josh. 15:10; 21:16; 1 Sam. 6:9, 12, 13, 15, 19, 20; 1 Kgs. 4:9; 14:11, 13; 1 Chr. 6:59; 2 Chr. 25:21, 23; 28:18. ¶
b. A city in Naphtali. Refs.: Josh. 19:38; Judg. 1:33. ¶
c. A city in Issachar. Ref.: Josh. 19:22. ¶
d. The Egyptian sacred city of On, also known as Heliopolis. Ref.: Jer. 43:13. ¶

BETH SHITTAH – ***bêyṯ haššiṭṭah*** [proper noun: בֵּית הַשִּׁטָּה <1029>; from HOUSE <1004> and ACACIA <7848> with the art. interposed]: house of the acacia ▶ **A place in Israel.** Ref.: Judg. 7:22. ¶

BETH TAPPUAH – ***bêyṯ tappûaḥ*** [proper noun: בֵּית תַּפּוּחַ <1054>; from HOUSE <1004> and APPLE, APPLE TREE <8598>]: house of the fruit trees ▶ **A city of the tribe of Judah.** Ref.: Josh. 15:53. ¶

BETH ZUR – ***bêyṯ ṣûr*** [proper noun: בֵּית צוּר <1049>; from HOUSE <1004> and ROCK <6697>]: house of the rock ▶ **A city of the tribe of Judah.** Refs.: Josh. 15:58; 1 Chr. 2:45; 2 Chr. 11:7; Neh. 3:16. ¶

BETHEL – ***bêyṯ-'êl*** [proper noun: בֵּית־אֵל <1008>; from HOUSE <1004> and GOD <410>]: house of God ▶
a. A town situated on the Ephraim-Benjamin border. It is about 15 miles north of Jerusalem. It is mentioned often in the Old Testament next, in fact, to Jerusalem. Its archeological name is Beit Beitin. Jacob also called it Luz (Judg. 1:22, 23). Abraham tented near it (Gen. 12:8; 13:3), and Jacob dreamed important dreams there (Gen. 28:19). It was given to the tribe of Benjamin (Josh. 12:16; 18:22). Jeroboam I built an altar there to a golden calf (1 Kgs. 12:29, 32, 33). It became a slanderous byword among some prophets (Jer. 48:13; Hos. 10:15; Amos 4:4; 5:5, 6). Amaziah, the priest of Bethel in Amos' day, was soundly rebuked by the prophet (Amos 7:10–17). Josiah finally destroyed its corrupt altar and place of worship (2 Kgs. 23:4–19). It was resettled in the time of the return from exile (2 Kgs. 17:28). *
b. A town in southern Judah near Beersheba and Ziklag. Ref.: 1 Sam. 30:27. ¶

BETHELITE – ***bêyṯ hā^{e}liy*** [masc. proper noun: בֵּית הָאֱלִי <1017>; patrial from BETHEL <1008> with the art. interposed] ▶ **An inhabitant of Bethel.** Ref.: 1 Kgs. 16:34. ¶

BETHER – ***beṯer*** [masc. proper noun: בֶּתֶר <1336>; the same as HALF <1335>]: separation, division ▶ **This word (Song 2:17, KJV, NKJV, NASB) would refer to a city added in the Septuagint (Josh. 15:59).** Some translators interpret this as a masculine noun meaning rugged or cleft (Song 2:17: NIV, ESV). ¶

BETHLEHEM – ***beyṯ leḥem*** [proper noun: בֵּית לֶחֶם <1035>; from HOUSE <1004> and BREAD <3899>]: house of bread ▶
a. A name applied to a village in Judea. It was formerly called Ephrath (Gen. 35:19). Rachel died and was buried there. Elimelech, husband of Naomi, lived there and left to take his family to Moab (Ruth 1:1, 2). Naomi returned there with Ruth (Ruth 1:19, 22). David's father and family lived in Bethlehem (1 Sam. 16:1–4; 17:11–15). The Philistines controlled the town at certain times (2 Sam. 23:13, 14). It was resettled on the return from the Babylonian captivity (Ezra 2:21; Neh. 7:26). The greatest honor

and prophecy referring to Bethlehem was given by Micah (Mic. 5:2) concerning the "ruler of Israel," whose origins were from ancient times. *
b. The name was borne by a city in Zebulun. Ref.: Josh. 19:15. An Israelite judge, Ibzan, came from this city (Judg. 12:8, 10). It is about seven miles west and north of Nazareth. ¶

BETHLEHEMITE – ***bêyṯ hallaḥmiy*** [proper noun: בֵּית הַלַּחְמִי <1022>; patrial from BETHLEHEM <1035> with the art. inserted] ▶ **An inhabitant or native of Bethlehem.** Refs.: 1 Sam. 16:1, 18; 17:58; 2 Sam. 21:19. ¶

BETHSHEMITE – ***bêyṯ haššimšiy*** [proper noun: בֵּית הַשִּׁמְשִׁי <1030>; patrial from BETH SHEMESH <1053> with the art. inserted] ▶ **A native of Bethshemesh.** The ark came in the field of Joshua the Bethshemite (1 Sam. 6:14, 18). ¶

BETHUEL – ***bᵉṯû'êl*** [proper noun: בְּתוּאֵל <1328>; apparently from the same as WASTELAND <1326> and GOD <410>]: destroyed of God ▶
a. He was the son of Nahor, brother of Abraham. He became the father of Rebekah, Isaac's wife. Isaac told Jacob to get a wife from the house of Bethuel (Gen. 28:1, 2). He was an ancestor of the Arameans (Gen. 22:22, 23; 24:15, 24). *
b. The name of a town that the sons of Shimei, a Simeonite, and his brothers inhabited. Refs.: 1 Chr. 4:27–30. ¶

BETHUL – ***bᵉṯûl*** [proper noun: בְּתוּל <1329>; for BETHUEL <1328>] ▶ **The name of a city which the tribe of Simeon had for inheritance.** Ref.: Josh. 19:4; the same as BETHUEL <1328> b. ¶

BETONIM – ***bᵉṭōniym*** [proper noun: בְּטֹנִים <993>; prob. plur. from PISTACHIO NUT <992>]: heights, pistachio nuts ▶ **City of the tribe of Gad.** Ref.: Josh. 13:26. ¶

BETROTH – [1] ***'āraś*** [verb: אָרַשׂ <781>; a prim. root] ▶ **This word means to pledge in marriage; it is also translated to espouse, to pledge, to engage.** It means to become engaged to, to marry a woman (Deut. 20:7). It was customary to pay a bride-price at the time of betrothal (Ex. 22:16; 1 Sam. 18:25; 2 Sam. 3:14). It was considered adultery and much more dangerous to seduce a betrothed woman than a virgin (Ex. 22:16; Deut. 22:23, 25, 27, 28). A betrothed woman was bound to marry the man she was engaged to (Deut. 28:30). The word was used figuratively to describe the Lord's betrothal of Israel to Himself (Hos. 2:19, 20). Therefore, the relationship with His people was one of personal intimacy at its deepest level. ¶
[2] ***ḥārap̱*** [verb: חָרַף <2778>; a prim. root] ▶ **The verb means to engage, to acquire.** In context it refers to a slave woman acquired legally for a man to marry (Lev. 19:20); also translated acquired, assigned, promised. The Hebrew word also has the meaning of to reproach, to winter; see REPROACH (verb) <2778> and WINTER (verb) <2778>. ¶

BETROTHAL – ***kᵉlûlāh*** [fem. noun: כְּלוּלָה <3623>; denom. pass. part. from BRIDE <3618>] ▶ **This word denotes espousal. It indicates a time of engagement.** It is used figuratively to refer to the time of Israel's engagement to the Lord in her youth (Jer. 2:2); also translated espousals, bride. ¶

BETTER (GET THE) – Ps. 89:22 ➔ DEBT (IN) <5378>.

BETTER (THE) – Eccl. 6:11 ➔ MORE, MORE THAN <3148>.

BETWEEN – [1] ***bayin*** [noun used as a prep.: בַּיִן <996>; properly, the constructive form of an otherwise unused noun from PERCEIVE <995>] ▶ **This word means among, in the midst.** It means literally between two things (Gen. 15:17). It is repeated later in a sentence with the two words meaning (between . . . and, *bayin . . . ûbayin*; Gen. 1:4, 6; Is. 59:2). It indicates that something is within a certain area (Prov. 26:13, in the open square, NASB). Preceded by *'el* and followed by *l^e*, it gives location among (Ezek. 10:2), or with *min* <4480> on the front, it indicates from between (Gen. 49:10). In Nehemiah 5:18, it means interval, marking a period of ten days. *

2 **bêyn** [Aramaic prep.: בֵּין <997>; corresponding to <996> above] ▶ **This word means in the space separating two or more objects; it is also translated among. It is used in two verses in the Old Testament.** It indicates position between teeth (Dan. 7:5). With respect to more than two items, it describes a position among them (Dan. 7:8), i.e., among the ten horns. ¶

BEVERAGE (BLENDED) – Song 7:2 ➔ WINE (MIXED, BLENDED) <4197>.

BEWAIL ONESELF – Jer. 4:31 ➔ BREATH (GASP FOR) <3306>.

BEWARE – Ezra 4:22 ➔ HEED (TAKE) <2095>.

BEWILDERED (BE) – 1 Ex. 14:3; Esther 3:15 ➔ WANDER <943> 2 Is. 21:3 ➔ INIQUITY (COMMIT) <5753>.

BEYOND – 1 **hāl^e'āh** [adv.: הָלְאָה <1973>; from the prim. form of the art. *hāl*] ▶ **This word indicates also yonder, away; to there; from that time on.** It is used mostly to indicate place or location: it means to get back, literally, to get out there (Gen. 19:9); an area beyond a certain location (Gen. 35:21; 1 Sam. 10:3; Amos 5:27); an indicator of general location (Num. 16:37; 32:19). It indicates time beyond a certain set point: from the eighth day on (Lev. 22:27); from then on, from that day on (1 Sam. 18:9; Is. 18:2, 7; Ezek. 39:22). *

– 2 Eccl. 12:12 ➔ MORE, MORE THAN <3148>.

BEWILDERMENT – Deut. 28:28; Zech. 12:4 ➔ CONFUSION <8541>.

BEZAI – **bêṣāy** [masc. proper noun: בֵּצָי <1209>; perhaps the same as BESAI <1153>]: trampled ▶ **Members of his family came back from Babylon with Zerubbabel.** Refs.: Ezra 2:17; Neh. 7:23; 10:18. ¶

BEZALEL – **b^eṣal'êl** [masc. proper noun: בְּצַלְאֵל <1212>; prob. from SHADOW <6738> and GOD <410> with a prep. prefix]: in *the* shadow (i.e., protection) of God ▶

a. An artisan of the tribe of Judah, called by God who had filled him with the Spirit, with ability and intelligence to do work related to the Tabernacle. Refs.: Ex. 31:2; 35:30; 36:1, 2; 37:1; 38:22; 1 Chr. 2:20; 2 Chr. 1:5. ¶

b. An Israelite whom Ezra persuaded to put away his foreign wife. Ref.: Ezra 10:30. ¶

BEZEK – **bezeq** [proper noun: בֶּזֶק <966>; from LIGHTNING <965>]: lightning ▶ **A place in Canaan; Israelites later rallied there under Saul.** Refs.: Judg. 1:4, 5; 1 Sam. 11:8. ¶

BEZER – **beṣer** [proper noun: בֶּצֶר <1221>; the same as GOLD <1220>]: gold ▶

a. A city in Reuben, given to the Levites as a city of refuge. Refs.: Deut. 4:43; Josh. 20:8; 21:36; 1 Chr. 6:78. ¶

b. An Israelite, descendant of Asher. Ref.: 1 Chr. 7:37. ¶

BICHRI – **biḵriy** [masc. proper noun: בִּכְרִי <1075>; from BORN FIRST (BE) <1069>]: youth, firstborn ▶ **A Benjamite, the father of Sheba who rebelled against David.** Refs.: 2 Sam. 20:1, 2, 6, 7, 10, 13, 21, 22. ¶

BIDKAR – **biḏqar** [masc. proper noun: בִּדְקַר <920>; prob. from PIERCE <1856> with a prep. prefix]: piercing ▶ **An Israelite, captain under the reign of Jehu.** Ref.: 2 Kgs. 9:25. ¶

BIER – 2 Sam. 3:31 ➔ BED <4296>.

BIGTHA – **bigṯā'** [masc. proper noun: בִּגְתָא <903>; of Persian deriv.]: gift of the providence ▶ **A chamberlain serving in the presence of Xerxes.** Ref.: Esther 1:10. ¶

BIGTHAN or BIGTHANA – ***bigṯān, bigṯānā'*** [masc. proper noun: בִּגְתָנָא, בִּגְתָן <904>; of similar deriv. to BIGTHA <903>]: gift of the providence ▶ **A chamberlain, keeper of the palace's door, who conspired against Xerxes.** Refs.: Esther 2:21; 6:2. ❡

BIGVAI – ***bigway*** [masc. proper noun: בִּגְוַי <902>; prob. of foreign origin]: happy, fortune ▶

a. One of the leaders who came back from Babylon with Zerubbabel. Refs.: Ezra 2:2, 14; 8:14; Neh. 7:7, 19. ❡

b. An Israelite who signed the covenant of renewal with Nehemiah after the return from the Babylonian captivity. Ref.: Neh. 10:16. ❡

BILDAD – ***bildaḏ*** [masc. proper noun: בִּלְדַּד <1085>; of uncertain deriv.]: son of dispute ▶ **A name of one of Job's supposed comforters.** It is possible that he may have descended from Shuah, a son of Abraham (see Gen. 25:2). He, along with Eliphaz and Zophar, persisted in condemning Job for his supposed sins. The Lord reprimanded them (Job 42:9). Their retribution argument was simply that since Job was suffering, he must have sinned. Other refs.: Job 2:11; 8:1; 18:1; 25:1. ❡

BILEAM – ***bil'ām*** [proper noun: בִּלְעָם <1109>; prob. from NOT <1077> and PEOPLE <5971>]: who destroys the people, who swallows ▶

a. The Mesopotamian seer, pagan prophet or soothsayer, that Balak, king of Moab, hired to curse Israel because he was afraid of what Israel might do to Moab. Refs.: Num. 22:5, 7–10). The name may mean something like "swallower of a nation" (Hebrew *bāla'*: SWALLOW <1104>), "to swallow, to devour, to engulf." The "*am*" on the end may be an adverb used to intensify the meaning or, *'am* <5971> may mean "people, nation." At any rate, Bileam (Balaam in Greek) attempted to curse Israel—an impossible thing according to the biblical writer who shows intricately and with great force how no one—not even a great false prophet—can put a curse on God's people (Josh. 24:9, 10). The Lord made Balaam to utter one of the greatest prophecies of the Old Testament. He predicted a "star" would come out of Jacob. He later tried to curse Israel, tempting them to commit spiritual and physical prostitution by following after Baal of Peor (Num. 22:6; 23:8; 31:8, 16). This name became a byword of evil, corruption, and false religion in the New Testament also (2 Pet. 2:15; Jude 11; Rev. 2:14). Moreover, one of his prophecies is preserved from about 750 B.C. witnessing to his fame in the ancient Near East. Micah recalls this incident (Mic. 6:5).

The Moabites are cursed because of this incident (Deut. 23:4, 5). God actually turned Balaam's curse into a blessing. The Israelites later executed Balaam (Josh. 13:22). *

b. The name of a city given to the Kohathites by the tribe of Ephraim. Ref.: 1 Chr. 6:70. ❡

BILGAH – ***bilgāh*** [masc. proper noun: בִּלְגָּה <1083>; from SMILE (verb) <1082>]: cheerful ▶

a. A priest descended from Aaron. Ref.: 1 Chr. 24:14. ❡

b. A priest who came up from the Babylonian captivity with Zerubbabel. Refs.: Neh. 12:5, 18. ❡

BILGAI – ***bilgay*** [masc. proper noun: בִּלְגַּי <1084>; from SMILE (verb) <1082>]: cheerful ▶ **A priest who signed the covenant of renewal with Nehemiah after the return from the Babylonian captivity.** Ref.: Neh. 10:8. ❡

BILHAH – ***bilhāh*** [proper noun: בִּלְהָה <1090>; from AFRAID (MAKE) <1089>]: shyness, tenderness ▶

a. This word refers to a handmaid of Rachel. She bore two sons, Dan and Naphtali (Gen. 35:25). Reuben committed a great sin against Jacob (Israel) by sleeping with Bilhah (Gen. 35:22). Dan and Naphtali had a total of five sons as well (Gen. 46:22–25). *

b. It refers to a town in which the sons of Shimei and his brothers lived. Ref.: 1 Chr. 4:29; see 27–33. ¶

BILHAN – ***bilhān*** [masc. proper noun: בִּלְהָן <1092>; from AFRAID (MAKE) <1089>]: tender, timid ▶
a. A son of Ezer. Refs.: Gen. 36:27; 1 Chr. 1:42. ¶
b. An Israelite of the tribe of Benjamin. Ref.: 1 Chr. 7:10. ¶

BILSHAN – ***bilšān*** [masc. proper noun: בִּלְשָׁן <1114>; of uncertain deriv.]: eloquent, who seeks ▶ **One of the leaders who came back from Babylon with Zerubbabel.** Refs.: Ezra 2:2; Neh. 7:7. ¶

BIMHAL – ***bimhāl*** [masc. proper noun: בִּמְהָל <1118>; prob. from MIX <4107> with prep. prefix]: son of mixture, corrupted ▶ **An Israelite of the tribe of Asher.** Ref.: 1 Chr. 7:33. ¶

BIN – 1 Kgs. 17:12 ➔ JAR <3537>.

BIND – 1 ***'ālam*** [verb: אָלַם <481>; a prim. root] ▶
a. This word is used in an agricultural setting of tying up bundles of grain as pictured in Joseph's dream. Ref.: Gen. 37:7. ¶
b. A word meaning to be tongue-tied, to be speechless. It describes being speechless from awe or fright; the servant of the Lord was silent, speechless like a lamb before its shearers (Is. 53:7); Daniel was speechless in the presence of an awesome divine being (Dan. 10:15). It is used of a tongue or lips that have been put to silence (Ps. 31:18; 39:9; Ezek. 3:26) and lips that are wisely quiet before the wicked (Ps. 39:2). Other refs.: Ezek. 24:27; 33:22. ¶
2 ***'āsar*** [verb: אָסַר <631>; a prim. root] ▶ **This word means to tie up, as well as to obligate, to imprison, to hold captive.** It has several areas of meaning. It describes tying up or binding animals (Gen. 49:11; 1 Sam. 6:7; 2 Kgs. 7:10; Ps. 118:27). It refers to binding with a cord or fetters, such as the binding of Simeon (Gen. 42:24), Samson (Judg. 15:10; 16:5–8), and Zedekiah (2 Kgs. 25:7). Used figuratively, it means to bind or punish someone (a fool) with discipline or to exercise authority over someone (Ps. 105:22). The beauty of a woman's hair can hold a king captive (Song 7:5). It means to fasten or to gird on something, such as a waistcloth (Neh. 4:18; Job 12:18). As a military term, it means to begin the battle, to attack, to set the battle (1 Kgs. 20:14; 2 Chr. 13:3). Used as a technical legal term, it means to bind oneself to a vow of abstention (Num. 30:2–11), using its cognate noun *'issār* [PLEDGE (noun) <632>] after it (cf. NIV, to obligate). In its passive uses, it means to be bound, taken prisoner, or be imprisoned (Gen. 42:19; Judg. 16:6, 10; Is. 22:3). *
3 ***ḥāḇaš*** [verb: חָבַשׁ <2280>; a prim. root] ▶ **This word is used primarily to describe tightly fastening or wrapping one object with another.** It is frequently used of saddling a donkey (Gen. 22:3; Judg. 19:10; 1 Kgs. 2:40) but can be used to describe the binding of caps on the priests' heads (Ex. 29:9; Lev. 8:13); the tying of garments and carpets in a roll (Ezek. 27:24); the wrapping of weeds around Jonah's head (Jon. 2:5); God stopping the floods (Job 28:11). This word is often used to describe binding wounds (both physical and spiritual) with the result that healing occurs (Is. 61:1; Ezek. 30:21; Hos. 6:1). In a few cases, this binding may refer to one's ability to control (or rule) another (Job 34:17; 40:13). *
4 ***kᵉpaṯ*** [Aramaic verb: כְּפַת <3729>; a root of uncertain correspondence] ▶ **This word is used of the process of fastening, tying up securely, the three Hebrew youth cast into a fiery furnace.** It is used in its active form, to bind (Dan. 3:20); in its passive form, to be bound (Dan. 3:21); or bound (Dan. 3:23, 24). ¶
5 ***'ānaḏ*** [verb: עָנַד <6029>; a prim. root] ▶ **This word refers to fastening something to oneself in a public and conspicuous place and manner.** Ref.: Job 31:36; NIV: to put on. The word is used especially so of the binding and being aware of the guidance of one's parents (Prov. 6:21). ¶

[6] *'āqaḏ* [verb: עָקַד <6123>; a prim. root] ▶ **This word means to tie up someone, especially for a specific purpose.** Abraham bound Isaac to sacrifice him (Gen. 22:9). ¶
[7] *qāšar* [verb: קָשַׁר <7194>; a prim. root] ▶ **This word means to tie, to fasten, and also to conspire.** It refers literally to binding or tying something up (Gen. 38:28; Josh. 2:18, 21; Jer. 51:63); figuratively attaching or fastening something on (Is. 49:18); controlling, binding the Pleiades constellation (Job 38:31). It is used of connecting a wall together (Neh. 4:6, 8). It has many figurative uses: it is used of Jacob's soul being bound up with Benjamin (Gen. 44:30); of Jonathan's soul being bound to David's soul (1 Sam. 18:1); of forming a conspiracy together, forming an alliance against someone (1 Kgs. 15:27; 16:20; 2 Kgs. 9:14). It is used to indicate the binding of religious, moral, spiritual, and eternal teachings or concepts to oneself (Deut. 6:8; 11:18; Prov. 3:3; 6:21; 7:3). *
[8] *rāḵas* [verb: רָכַס <7405>; a prim. root] ▶ **This word means to attach; it is also translated to join, to tie.** It refers to joining things together; in context it refers to doing so by woven cords (Ex. 28:28; 39:21). ¶
[9] *rāṯaq* [verb: רָתַק <7576>; a prim. root] ▶ **This word means to tie up, to fasten securely.** It is negated and used figuratively of the unbinding and undoing of the cord of life (silver cord) (Eccl. 12:6: to break, to snap, to severe). It is used literally of prisoners of war being bound, fettered with chains or ropes (Nah. 3:10). ¶
[10] *śāqaḏ* [verb: שָׂקַד <8244>; a prim. root] ▶ **This word describes figuratively persons' transgressions being tied, secured, fastened to their necks, like a yoke.** Ref.: Lam. 1:14. ¶
– [11] Ex. 26:17; 36:22 ➔ PARALLEL (SET) <7947> [12] Lev. 8:7 ➔ GIRD <640> [13] Job 16:8 ➔ SHRIVEL <7059> b. [14] Job 30:18 ➔ GIRD <247> [15] Mic. 1:13 ➔ HARNESS <7573>.

BINDER – [1] 2 Chr. 34:11 ➔ FITTING <4226> [2] Ps. 129:7 ➔ SLAVE (TREAT AS A) <6014>.

BINDING – Judg. 15:14 ➔ BOND <612>.

BINDING OBLIGATION – Num. 30:2–5, 7, 10–14 ➔ PLEDGE (noun) <632>.

BINEA – ***bin'ā'*** [masc. proper noun: בִּנְעָא <1150>; of uncertain deriv.]: gushing, which (who) roams ▶ **An Israelite, descendant of Jonathan, the son of Saul.** Refs.: 1 Chr. 8:37; 9:43. ¶

BINNUI – ***binnûy*** [masc. proper noun: בִּנּוּי <1131>; from BUILD <1129>]: building, of the family ▶
a. The father of Noadiah. Ref.: Ezra 8:33. ¶
b. A son of Pahath-moab. Ref.: Ezra 10:30. ¶
c. A son of Bani. Ref.: Ezra 10:38. ¶
d. A Levite who came back from Babylon with Zerubbabel. Refs.: Neh. 3:24; 10:9; 12:8. ¶
e. The head of a family. Ref.: Neh. 7:15. ¶

BIRD – [1] ***'ôp̱*** [coll. masc. noun: עוֹף <5775>; from FLY (verb) <5774>] ▶ **This word means a flying creature.** It refers to winged birds or insects: birds (Gen. 1:20, 22) of all kinds, including carrion birds, birds that serve as scavengers (1 Sam. 17:44, 46); for food (Ps. 78:27); for offerings (Gen. 8:20; Lev. 1:14). It is also used of insects, clean or unclean (Lev. 11:20, 21: Deut. 14:19). *
[2] ***'ôp̱*** [Aramaic masc. noun: עוֹף <5776>; corresponding to <5775> above] ▶ **This word refers to a living thing with wings and feathers that normally can fly.** Daniel 2:38 refers to birds of the sky, heavens. Daniel saw a vision of a leopard that had bird wings on its back (Dan. 7:6). ¶
[3] ***ṣippôr*** [common noun: צִפּוֹר <6833>; from DEPART <6852> (in the sense of hopping in the case of a little bird)] ▶ **This word means a fowl, an egg-laying creature with a beak, wings, and feathers.** Used in a collective sense, it refers to birds (Gen. 7:14; 15:10; Ps. 11:1); or it can refer to one bird (Deut. 14:11; Hos. 11:11; Amos 3:5). Ezekiel depicts birds of prey of every kind (Ezek. 39:4). *

[4] *ṣippar* [Aramaic masc. noun: צִפַּר <6853>; corresponding to <6833> above] ▶ **This word refers to a fowl, an egg-laying creature with a beak, wings, and feathers.** In a figurative sense, it describes the people who found shelter in the kingdom of Babylon, the great tree of the king's dream (Dan. 4:12, 14, 21). It is also used to describe Nebuchadnezzar's appearance when he was driven away as a madman (Dan. 4:33). ¶

BIRD CATCHER – Hos. 9:8 ➔ FOWLER <3352>.

BIRD OF PREY – ***'ayiṭ*** [coll. masc. noun: עַיִט <5861>; from RUSH GREEDILY <5860>] ▶ **This word means a predatory bird; it is also translated vulture, fowl, ravenous bird, carrion bird, predatory bird. It is used of birds that eat carrion, previously dead animals.** These birds capture and eat other animals (Gen. 15:11; Job 28:7; Is. 18:6; 46:11; Ezek. 39:4). It is used figuratively of Judah's enemies (Jer. 12:9); or of an enemy invader (Is. 46:11). ¶

BIRSHA – ***birša'*** [masc. proper noun: בִּרְשַׁע <1306>; prob. from WICKEDNESS <1562> with prep. prefix]: son of wickedness ▶ **A king of Gomorrah.** Ref.: Gen. 14:2. ¶

BIRTH – [1] ***mašbêr*** [masc. noun: מַשְׁבֵּר <4866>; from BREAK <7665> (in the sense of to bring to birth)] ▶ **This word describes the opening of a womb; it is also translated point of birth, moment of birth.** It is used metaphorically of giving birth to spiritual as well as physical children (Hos. 13:13: breaking forth, opening). Used with *bô'* (COME <935>) and *'ad* (UNTIL <5704) meaning to come to the point of birth (2 Kgs. 19:3; Is. 37:3). ¶
– [2] 2 Kgs. 19:3; Is. 37:3; Hos. 9:11 ➔ BIRTH (GIVE) <3205> b. [3] Ezek. 16:3 ➔ ORIGIN <4351> [4] Ezek. 16:4 ➔ KINDRED <4138>.

BIRTH (GIVE) – ***yālad, lêdāh*** [verb and fem. noun: יָלַד, לֵדָה <3205>; a prim. root] ▶

a. A verb meaning to bring forth (children, young), to beget, to deliver. It is commonly used of women bearing children (Gen. 3:16) as well as animals who brought forth young (Gen. 30:39). In the case of birds, it may refer to the laying or production of eggs (Jer. 17:11). In a more general sense, it is used of men becoming the father of children (Gen. 4:18). It is used in figurative expressions: evil people bring forth iniquity (Job 15:35); Moses is said to beget, bear, conceive the people of Israel (Num. 11:12); God begets Israel (Deut. 32:18); a day brings forth many things (Prov. 27:1). In a passive use of the verb, it may refer to one's birthday, literally, "the day of her birth" (Hos. 2:5).

In certain forms of the verb, it means to help bring to birth, to serve as midwife (Ex. 1:16). In other forms of the verb, it takes on a causal sense, such as causing someone to give birth, as God causes His people to come to birth (Is. 66:9). The wicked in Israel are said to conceive, to bring forth iniquity (Is. 59:4). In Numbers 1:18, it takes on the meaning of having one's name put into a genealogical record. *
b. A feminine noun referring to childbirth, delivery. It indicates the time of or the process of childbirth (2 Kgs. 19:3); it is used of the failure of Israel to be fruitful when her time had come (Is. 37:3). Hosea stresses Israel's failure to become that nation God was looking for on the day of her birth (Hos. 9:11). The pangs of childbirth are employed in a simile to illustrate the pain of Israel's being thrust into exile (Jer. 13:21: labor, childbirth, travail). ¶

BIRTHRIGHT – ***b*ᵉ*ḵôrāh, b*ᵉ*ḵōrāh*** [fem. noun: בְּכֹרָה, בְּכוֹרָה <1062>; fem. of FIRSTBORN <1060>] ▶ **This word means firstborn, right of firstborn.** The firstborn son was a symbol and proof of the strength and virility of his father (Deut. 21:17). The word refers to the rights and privileges of the firstborn (Gen. 25:31–34; 43:33). This right could be sold or forfeited through deception (Gen. 27:36) or grave sin (1 Chr. 5:1, 2). The word also means firstborn in some contexts (Gen. 4:4; Deut. 12:6; Neh. 10:36). Other refs.: Deut. 12:17; 14:23. ¶

BIRTHSTOOL – Ex. 1:16 ➔ WHEEL <70>.

BIRZAITH – ***birzāwiṯ*** [masc. proper noun: בִּרְזָוִת <1269>; prob. fem. plur. from an unused root (apparently meaning to pierce]: holes ▶ **An Israelite from the tribe of Asher.** Ref.: 1 Chr. 7:31. ¶

BISHLAM – ***bišlām*** [masc. proper noun: בִּשְׁלָם <1312>; of foreign deriv.]: in peace ▶ **A Persian man who, with his companions, wrote to Artaxerxes complaining that the Jews were rebuilding Jerusalem.** Ref.: Ezra 4:7. ¶

BIT – [1] 2 Kgs. 19:28; Ps. 32:9; Is. 37:29 ➔ BRIDLE <4964> [2] Job 30:11 ➔ BRIDLE <7448> a. [3] Amos 6:11 ➔ BREACH <1233> [4] Amos 6:11 ➔ DEW <7447> b.

BITE – ***nāšaḵ*** [verb: נָשַׁךְ <5391>; a prim. root] ▶

a. This word refers to the sinking of a snake's fangs as it strikes. It is used figuratively of the character of Dan, one of the twelve tribal ancestors of Israel (Gen. 49:17); and of serpent bites in general (Num. 21:6, 8, 9; Eccl. 10:8, 11; Amos 5:19; 9:3). It describes the bite of an alcoholic beverage like wine (Prov. 23:32); and of the enemies the Lord sent against His people (Jer. 8:17). False prophets are described as biting at what is available to them (Mic. 3:5). ¶

b. This word also means to lend or borrow at interest. It is used to describe a loan given with the expectation of receiving back the principal plus an amount on top of that, interest. This was forbidden in Israel (Deut. 23:19, 20). The word means creditors in its participial plural form (Hab. 2:7; also translated to bite). ¶

BITHIAH – ***biṯyāh*** [fem. proper noun: בִּתְיָה <1332>; from DAUGHTER <1323> and LORD <3050>]: daughter (in the sense of worshipper) of the Lord ▶ **Daughter of the Pharaoh and wife of Mered, an Israelite of the tribe of Judah.** Ref.: 1 Chr. 4:18. ¶

BITHRON – ***biṯrôn*** [proper noun: בִּתְרוֹן <1338>; from DIVIDE <1334> (with the art.)]: great division, divided place ▶ **A gorge in the Jordan valley.** Ref.: 2 Sam. 2:29. This word is translated morning in some versions. ¶

BITING FLY – Jer. 46:20 ➔ DESTRUCTION <7171>.

BITTER – [1] ***m^{e}riyriy*** [adj.: מְרִירִי <4815>; from BITTER (BE, MAKE) <4843>] ▶ **This word indicates the harsh, mortal, caustic aspect of something; threatening.** In context it identifies Israel's destruction as bitter, hard to swallow (Deut. 32:24; ESV: poisonous; NIV: deadly). ¶

– [2] Gen. 26:35 ➔ GRIEF <4786> [3] 1 Kgs. 2:8 ➔ GRIEVOUS <4834>.

BITTER (BE, MAKE) – ***mārar*** [verb: מָרַר <4843>; a prim. root] ▶ **This word means to afflict, to grieve.** It has the sense of harshness, embitterment, offensiveness, affliction: of a physical attack on someone (Gen. 49:23; Dan. 8:7; 11:11); of backbreaking, debilitating work (Ex. 1:14; 23:21); of the effect of calamities in life (Ruth 1:13, 20; 1 Sam. 30:6; 2 Kgs. 4:27; Job 27:2; Is. 38:17; Lam. 1:4; Zech. 12:10); especially of the bitterness engendered by God's judgments on His people (Is. 22:4; 24:9). ¶

BITTER FOOD – Jer. 9:15; 23:15 ➔ WORMWOOD <3939>.

BITTER FRUIT, BITTER POISON – Deut. 29:18 ➔ WORMWOOD <3939>.

BITTER GRIEF – ***m^{e}riyrûṯ*** [fem. noun: מְרִירוּת <4814>; from BITTER (BE) <4843>] ▶ **This word points to strife, sharp anguish.** It is used of extreme grief, a wounded spirit of disappointment and anger, especially over the coming defeat of Jerusalem (Ezek. 21:6; also translated bitterness). ¶

BITTER, BITTER HERB – ***mārōr*** [masc. noun: מָרֹר <4844>; from BITTER (BE) <4843>] ▶ **This word describes the**

sharp, biting taste of different things. Of bitter herbs (Ex. 12:8; Num. 9:11); of unpleasant sour grapes (Deut. 32:32); of a bitter drink (Lam. 3:15). It is used figuratively of harsh, cutting, stinging words that create suffering in another person (Job 13:26). ¶

BITTER, BITTERLY – 1 ***nihyāh*** [fem. noun: נִהְיָה <5093>; fem. of WAILING <5092>] ▶ **This word indicates dolefulness, bitterness.** It refers to a formal expression of despair and hopelessness over a calamity (Mic. 2:4; also translated doleful, mournful). ¶
2 ***tamrûr*** [masc. noun: תַּמְרוּר <8563>; from BITTER (BE, MAKE) <4843>] ▶ **This Hebrew word indicates bitterness. It refers to something that is difficult to endure, harsh, sharp, cutting, unpleasant.** It refers to a bitter mourning for God's people (Jer. 6:26; 31:15), to anger that is aggravated by bitterness and caustic hatred (Hos. 12:14). ¶

BITTER, BITTERLY, BITTERNESS – ***mar, mār*** [masc. adj.: מַר, מָר <4751>; from BITTER (BE) <4843>] ▶ **These words refer to resentment, unpleasantness, something difficult to accept. The feminine form is** *mārāh*. As is common with Hebrew adjectives, it can modify a noun (Ex. 15:23), or it can be a substantive, functioning alone as the noun bitterness (Is. 38:15, 17). This word can also operate as an adverb, meaning bitterly (Is. 33:7; Ezek. 27:30). Used literally, it may modify water (Ex. 15:23) and food (Prov. 27:7). The Hebrew word can also be used to describe the results of continued fighting (2 Sam. 2:26). It can be used metaphorically to modify a cry or mourning (Gen. 27:34; Esther 4:1; Ezek. 27:30); to represent a characteristic of death (1 Sam. 15:32); or to describe a person as hot-tempered (Judg. 18:25); discontented (1 Sam. 22:2); provoked (2 Sam. 17:8); anguished (Ezek. 27:31); or ruthless (Hab. 1:6). One instance of this word that deserves special attention is the "bitter water," that determined the legal status of a woman accused of infidelity (Num. 5:18, 19, 23, 24, 27). This was holy water that was combined with dust from the Tabernacle floor and ink (see Num. 5:17, 23) and then was ingested by the accused. This water was literally "bitter" and would produce "bitterness" or punishment if the woman were guilty. *

BITTERN – Is. 14:23; 34:11; Zeph. 2:14 ➔ PORCUPINE <7090> c.

BITTERNESS – 1 ***memer*** [masc. noun: מֶמֶר <4470>; from an unused root meaning to grieve] ▶ **This word indicates something difficult to process, harsh; the opposite of pleasantness.** A foolish son is bitterness to his mother (Prov. 17:25), i.e., causes her grief or sharp sorrow. ¶
2 ***mamrōr*** [masc. noun: מַמְרֹר <4472>; from BITTER (BE) <4843>] ▶ **This word means severe distress; it is also translated misery. It is akin to a feeling of despair, hopelessness, revulsion, revolt.** It is something Job had because of his calamity (Job 9:18). ¶
3 ***morrah*** [fem. noun: מֹרָה <4787>; a form of GRIEF <4786>] ▶ **This word indicates a strong emotional response of disappointment, a feeling of being betrayed in one's soul.** Ref.: Prov. 14:10. ¶
– 4 Gen. 26:35; Prov. 14:10 ➔ GRIEF <4786> 5 Deut. 29:18; etc. ➔ POISON (noun) <7219> 6 Deut. 32:32; Lam. 3:15 ➔ BITTER, BITTER HERB <4842> 7 Lam. 3:19; Amos 5:7; 6:12 ➔ WORMWOOD <3939> 8 Ezek. 21:6 ➔ BITTER GRIEF <4814>.

BITUMEN – Gen. 11:3; 14:10; Ex. 2:3 ➔ TAR <2564>.

BIZIOTHIAH – ***bizyôṯyāh*** [proper noun: בִּזְיוֹתְיָה <964>; from DESPISE <959> and LORD <3050>]: despised by the Lord ▶ **A southernmost city of the tribe of Judah.** Ref.: Josh. 15:28. ¶

BIZTHA – ***bizzeṯā'*** [masc. proper noun: בִּזְּתָא <968>; of Persian origin]: sterile, eunuch ▶ **A chamberlain serving in the presence of Xerxes.** Ref.: Esther 1:10. ¶

BLACK – [1] ***šāḥōr*** [adj.: שָׁחֹר <7838>; from BLACK (BE) <7835>] ► **This word refers to the very darkest color. It is used to describe a hair growing in an infected area of the skin that indicates that the disease may be serious and the person is quarantined.** Refs.: Lev. 13:31, 37. Black or dark skin and black hair locks were considered beautiful (Song 1:5; 5:11). It describes a set of horses on one of the chariots which Zechariah saw in a vision (Zech. 6:2, 6). ¶
– [2] Gen. 30:32, 33, 35, 40 ➔ DARK-COLORED <2345> [3] Song 1:6 ➔ DARK <7840>.

BLACK (BE) – Lam. 5:10 ➔ YEARN <3648>.

BLACK (BE, GROW, TURN) – ***šāḥar*** [verb: שָׁחַר <7835>; a prim. root (identical with SEEK DILIGENTLY <7836> through the idea of the duskiness of early dawn)] ► **This word refers to the darkening of a person's skin because of illness, disease, some kind of skin disease.** Ref.: Job 30:30. ¶

BLACK CUMMIN – Is. 28:25, 27 ➔ DILL <7100>.

BLACK MARBLE – Esther 1:6 ➔ PRECIOUS STONE <5508> b.

BLACKNESS – [1] ***kimriyr*** [masc. noun: כִּמְרִיר <3650>; reduplication from YEARN <3648>] ► **This word refers to a darkening of something to hide it or swallow it up.** Ref.: Job 3:5. ¶
[2] ***pā'rûr*** [masc. noun: פָּארוּר <6289>; from GLORIFY <6286>] ► **The meaning of this word is assumed to be in dread or fear; however, it is uncertain.** It occurs two times, each with the verb *qāḇaṣ* (<6908>), meaning to gather. From the context, it is clear that the term is a negative one. In Joel 2:6 (to gather blackness; other translations: to grow pale, to turn pale, to be drained of color), the context is a warning against the Day of the Lord, when an imposing army will invade, and people will be struck with great fear. In Nahum 2:10 (same translations as in Joel 2:6), the context is a prophecy of judgment against and the impending doom of Nineveh, which was like a lion's den, a place of safety and sanctuary (yet no fear) but would soon be a place of destruction and devastation. ¶
[3] ***qaḏrûṯ*** [fem. noun: קַדְרוּת <6940>; from DARK (BE) <6937>] ► **This word describes the ability of God to clothe the heavens with extreme darkness (i.e., make them dark).** It is used only once in the Old Testament (Isaiah 50:3). ¶

BLADE – Judg. 3:22 ➔ FLAME <3851>.

BLAMELESS – Dan. 6:22 ➔ INNOCENCE <2136>.

BLAMELESS (BE) – Ps. 51:4 ➔ PURE (BE) <2135>.

BLANKET – ***śemiyḵāh*** [fem. noun: שְׂמִיכָה <8063>; from LAY ON <5564>] ► **This word also indicates a mantle, a covering.** It describes a loose, sleeveless coat but also anything that serves to cloak, envelop, or conceal, such as a cloak, a rug, a blanket, or a covering (Judg. 4:18). It refers to something used to hide or cover Sisera (Judg. 4:18). The context does not fix the meaning of the word exactly nor do its root letters. ¶

BLASPHEME – ***gāḏap̱*** [verb: גָּדַף <1442>; a prim. root] ► **This verb means to criticize in an abusive or angrily insulting manner; it is also translated to reproach, to bring reproach, to revile.** It describes the conscious verbal abuse of a person or God (Num. 15:30; 2 Kgs. 19:6, 22; Ps. 44:16; Is. 37:6, 23; Ezek. 20:27). Punishment for this sin was possible death or at least being cut off from the community of God's people. ¶

BLASPHEMY – 2 Kgs. 19:3; Neh. 9:18, 26; Is. 37:3 ➔ DISGRACE (noun) <5007>.

BLASTED – [1] Gen. 41:6, 23, 27 ➔ SCORCHED <7710> [2] Is. 37:27 ➔ SCORCHED <7709>.

BLASTING – Deut. 28:22; 1 Kgs. 8:37; 2 Chr. 6:28; Amos 4:9; Hag. 2:17 ➔ SCORCHED <7711> b.

BLAZING (noun) – Is. 10:16 ➔ BURNING (noun) <3350>.

BLAZING (verb) – Dan. 3:6, 11, 15, 17, 20, 21, 23, 26 ➔ BURNING (verb) <3345>.

BLEATING – Judg. 5:16 ➔ PIPING <8292>.

BLEMISH – [1] Lev. 21:17, 18, 21, 23; 22:20, 21, 25; 24:19, 20; Num. 19:2; Deut. 15:21; 17:1; 32:5; 2 Sam. 14:25; Song 4:7; Dan. 1:4 ➔ DEFECT <3971> [2] Lev. 21:20 ➔ DEFECT <8400> [3] Lev. 22:25 ➔ MARRED <4893> b.

BLEND (noun and verb) – Ex. 30:25 ➔ MIXTURE <4842>.

BLESS – [1] ***'āšar*** [verb: אָשַׁר <833>; a prim. root] ▶ **This word means to go straight, to go on, to advance forward, to be called blessed, or to be made happy.** Of blessing or happiness, this verb is primarily used causatively: to call one blessed (Ps. 72:17); to pronounce happiness (Gen. 30:13); to be made happy or blessed (Prov. 3:18). Used figuratively, it means to follow a straight path in understanding (Prov. 9:6) or in one's heart (Prov. 23:19). When it is used intensively, it means going straight or advancing (Prov. 4:14). *

[2] ***bāraḵ*** [verb: בָּרַךְ <1288>; a prim. root] ▶ **This word also means to kneel, to salute, to greet. It derives from the noun knee and perhaps suggests the bending of the knee in blessing. Its derived meaning is to invoke favor on someone or something, to cause to prosper, to praise.** The verb is used when blessing God (Gen. 9:26) or people (Num. 24:9). God used this verb when He blessed Abraham in the Abrahamic covenant (Gen. 12:3). It is used intensively when God blesses people or people bless each other (Josh. 17:14). When it is used reflexively, it describes a person blessing or congratulating himself (Deut. 29:19). Other meanings are to bend the knee (2 Chr. 6:13); and to greet someone with a salutation or friendliness (1 Sam. 25:14). *

[3] ***b^eraḵ*** [Aramaic verb: בְּרַךְ <1289>; corresponding to <1288> above] ▶
a. See definition in previous sub-entry; this word also means to praise. It describes Daniel's and Nebuchadnezzar's reverent verbal response to God who had helped them (Dan. 2:19, 20; 3:28; 4:34) in special ways. ¶
b. See definition in previous sub-entry; this word also means to kneel. It describes Daniel's practice of kneeling while he prayed to his God three times daily facing Jerusalem (Dan. 6:10). ¶

BLESSED – ***'ešer*** [masc. noun: אֶשֶׁר <835>; from BLESS <833>] ▶ **This Hebrew word means a person's state of bliss. It is always used to refer to people and is never used of God.** It is almost exclusively poetic and usually exclamatory, "O the bliss of . . ." In Proverbs, this blissfulness is frequently connected with wisdom (Prov. 3:13; 8:32, 34). This term is also used to describe a person or nation who enjoys a relationship with God (Deut. 33:29; Job 5:17; Ps. 33:12; 146:5). In some contexts, the word does not seem to have any religious significance (1 Kgs. 10:8; Prov. 14:21; Eccl. 10:17), and at least in one context, it has no religious significance (Ps. 137:8, 9). *

BLESSING – ***b^erāḵāh*** [fem. noun: בְּרָכָה <1293>; from BLESS <1288>] ▶ **The general idea of this word is one of good favor bestowed on another.** This may be expressed in the giving of a tangible gift (Gen. 33:11; 1 Sam. 25:27) or in the pronouncing of a verbal blessing (Gen. 27:36; 49:28). Most often, however, this word speaks of God's favor on the righteous (Gen. 12:2; Mal. 3:10). It is related to the common verb *bāraḵ* (<1288>), meaning to bless and is often used to contrast God's blessing and His curse. *

BLIGHT – Deut. 28:22; 1 Kgs. 8:37; 2 Chr. 6:28; Amos 4:9; Hag. 2:17 ➔ SCORCHED <7711> b.

BLIGHTED – [1] Gen. 41:6, 23, 27 ➔ SCORCHED <7710> [2] Is. 37:27 ➔ SCORCHED <7709>.

BLIND (adj.) – [1] ***'iwwêr*** [adj.: עִוֵּר <5787>; intens. from EYES (PUT OUT THE) <5786>] ▶ **This word refers to an inability to see, having one's eyes put out.** God is the ultimate cause of blindness (Ex. 4:11). Figuratively, it describes a person who lives in a state of darkness (Deut. 28:29). Blindness was a defect in an animal, disqualifying it from being sacrificed (Deut. 15:21). It describes spiritual dullness, blindness (Is. 42:18, 19; 43:8). *
– [2] Lev. 22:22 ➔ BLINDNESS <5788>.

BLIND (verb) – Ex. 23:8; Deut. 16:19; 2 Kgs. 25:7; Jer. 39:7; 52:11 ➔ EYES (PUT OUT THE) <5786>.

BLINDED (BE) – [1] ***šā'a'*** [verb: שָׁעַע <8173>; a prim. root] ▶
a. This word is used of making persons' eyes dim, to blur their sight or deprive them of vision in a figurative sense. Refs.: Is. 6:10; 29:9. ¶
b. This word means to take delight in; to fondle. It refers to taking joy or enjoyment in something (Ps. 94:19), especially God's laws (Ps. 119:16, 47, 40). It describes exceptional delights in the Messianic Kingdom (Is. 11:8) in a figurative sense (Is. 66:12). ¶
c. This word means to cry out. Some translators render this word as from a root meaning to cry out (Is. 29:9, KJV). ¶
– [2] Zech. 11:17 ➔ DIM (BE) <3543> a.

BLINDNESS – [1] ***sanwêriym*** [masc. plur. noun: סַנְוֵרִים <5575>; of uncertain deriv.] ▶ **This word indicates sudden loss of vision.** It refers to an inability to find one's way, inability to see properly (Gen. 19:11); it may be figurative as well as literal (2 Kgs. 6:18). ¶
[2] ***'iwwārôn, 'awweret*** [noun: עִוָּרוֹן, עַוֶּרֶת <5788>; from BLIND (adj.) <5787>] ▶
a. An abstract masculine noun meaning lack of vision. It is used especially in regard to the absence of spiritual and religious perception. Ref.: Deut. 28:28. It is used figuratively of horses being blind, i.e., the power and might of the nations (Zech. 12:4). ¶
b. A feminine noun meaning lack of vision. It refers to a defect in the sight of a sacrificial animal that rendered it unfit for sacrifice. Ref.: Lev. 22:22: blind. ¶

BLOCK (noun) – Is. 44:19 ➔ FOOD <944>.

BLOCK (verb) – [1] Ezek. 39:11 ➔ MUZZLE (verb) <2629> [2] Hos. 2:6 ➔ HEDGE (MAKE A, PUT A) <7753>.

BLOOD – [1] ***dām*** [masc. noun: דָּם <1818>; from STAND STILL <1826>; comp. RUDDY (BE) <119>, i.e., to be red] ▶ **This word means the red liquid in the circulatory system of either humans or animals. It is commonly used with the verb *šāpak* <8210> meaning to shed.** Figuratively, it signifies violence and violent individuals: man of blood (2 Sam. 16:8); house of blood (2 Sam. 21:1); in wait for blood (Prov. 1:11); shedder of blood (Ezek. 18:10). Blood also carries religious significance, having a major role in sacrificial rituals. The metaphor "blood of grapes" is used for wine (Gen. 49:11). *
[2] ***nêṣaḥ*** [masc. noun: נֵצַח <5332>; prob. identical with FOREVER <5331> through the idea of brilliancy of color] ▶ **This word means grape juice.** It occurs only in Isaiah 63:3, 6; it is also translated lifeblood. In this passage, God's treading of grapes is a picture of His judgment of Israel's enemies, particularly Edom (cf. Is. 63:1). Grape juice, as elsewhere in the Old Testament (cf. Deut. 32:14) and the New Testament, is a symbol of blood. In Isaiah 63, God returned from judgment with His garments stained with blood like the garments of a grape treader are stained with juice. ¶

BLOODSHED – ***miśpāḥ*** [masc. noun: מִשְׂפָּח <4939>; from JOIN <5596> (in the sense of to scrape out, to smite with the scab)] ▶ **This word refers to slaughter; it is also translated oppression.** It depicts social injustice or bloodshed for many in Israel, i.e., the putting to death of those not deserving to die (Is. 5:7). ¶

BLOODSHOT – Prov. 23:29 ➔ REDNESS <2448>.

BLOOM (IN) – Ex. 9:31 ➔ BUD (IN) <1392>.

BLOSSOM (noun) – 1 Gen. 40:10 ➔ FLOWER <5322> 2 Job 15:33 ➔ FLOWER <5328> 3 Song 6:11 ➔ GREENNESS <3>.

BLOSSOM (IN) – Song 2:13, 15; 7:12 ➔ GRAPE (TENDER) <5563>.

BLOSSOM (verb) – 1 ***ṣûṣ*** [verb: צוּץ <6692>; a prim. root (in the sense of to twinkle)] ▶
a. This word refers to the sprouting or budding of blooms or buds. It was miraculous in the case of Aaron's rod (Num. 17:8; Ezek. 7:10). It often has a figurative meaning. It refers to the multiplication of people, the flourishing of God's people in the time of the Messiah (Ps. 72:16; Is. 27:6). It indicates the temporary, fleeting flourishing of humankind in general (Ps. 90:6; 103:15); and the brief success of the wicked (Ps. 92:7). Other ref.: Ps. 132:18. ¶
b. This verb means to peek, to peer. It refers to a person taking a sensitive, inquisitive look at someone or something, often through some obstacle (Song 2:9; also translated to gaze, to look). ¶
– 2 Eccl. 12:5 ➔ SPARKLE <5340>.

BLOT – Job 31:7; Prov. 9:7 ➔ DEFECT <3971>.

BLOW (noun) – 1 ***meḥiy*** [masc. noun: מְחִי <4239>; from WIPE, WIPE OUT <4229>] ▶ **This word refers to a stroke delivered by a battering ram.** It refers to the shock and impact of a battering ram against the walls of a city or anything else (Ezek. 26:9). ¶
2 ***makkāh*** [fem. noun: מַכָּה <4347>; (plur. only) from STRIKE <5221>] ▶ **This word means a stroke. When it carries this literal sense, often a weapon (sword, rod, whip) functions as the instrument by which the impact is delivered.** The individual judged to be in the wrong in a legal case could receive as punishment a beating of up to forty blows or lashes (Deut. 25:3). In accordance with the royal edict decreed in the name of Xerxes, King of Persia, the Jews struck down their enemies with the blow of the sword (Esther 9:5). The Lord declared to Israel and Judah that He had dealt them a mighty blow because their guilt was so great (Jer. 30:14). Elsewhere, the term signifies the result of a blow: a wound. King Joram rested in Jezreel to recover from wounds incurred in battle against the Arameans (2 Kgs. 9:15). In another battle, King Ahab died of a wound, having been pierced by an arrow (1 Kgs. 22:35; cf. Is. 1:6; Jer. 6:7; 30:17; Mic. 1:9). In other passages, the word described calamities inflicted by God: affliction, misery, and plague. The Lord solemnly warned Israel that failing to diligently obey His commands would result in His overwhelming them with severe and lasting afflictions (Deut. 28:59, 61). The Philistines remembered that the "gods" of the Hebrews struck the Egyptians with all kinds of miseries (1 Sam. 4:8; cf. Jer. 10:19, 49:17). Finally, the term can convey the sense of defeat or slaughter. Joshua and his fighting men handed the Amorites a great defeat at Gibeon (Josh. 10:10; cf. v. 20). Samson took revenge on the Philistines, killing many in a terrible slaughter because they had burned his wife and father-in-law (Judg. 15:8; cf. Judg. 11:33; 1 Sam. 4:10; 14:14). *
– 3 Job 36:18 ➔ SUFFICIENCY <5607> c. 4 Ps. 39:10 ➔ OPPOSITION <8409> 5 Ps. 147:18; Is. 40:7 ➔ DRIVE <5380> 6 Prov. 6:33 ➔ SORE (noun) <5061> 7 Prov. 20:30 ➔ BRUISE (noun) <2250> 8 Is. 30:26 ➔ STROKE <4270> 9 Is. 30:32 ➔ FORD <4569>.

BLOW (verb) – 1 ***nāšap̱*** [verb: נָשַׁף <5398>; a prim. root] ▶ **This word describes God's bringing a great wind against the waters of the Red Sea to destroy the Egyptians.** Ref.: Ex. 15:10. It is used figuratively of God's removal of the rulers and judges of the world by merely blowing on them to wilt them (Is. 40:24). ¶
2 ***tāqa'*** [verb: תָּקַע <8628>; a prim. root] ▶ **This word means to thrust, to fasten, to**

clap. The basic idea of this word is to thrust or to burst, such as the wind blowing away locusts (Ex. 10:19); the thrusting of a spear through a body (2 Sam. 18:14); or the driving of a nail into the ground to secure an object, such as a tent (Gen. 31:25; Judg. 4:21; Jer. 6:3). At times, this word has the connotation of fastening as a pin fastens hair (Judg. 16:14); a nail fastens to a secure place (Is. 22:23, 25); or the fastening of Saul's body to the wall of the city of Beth-shan and his head to the wall of a pagan temple (1 Sam. 31:10; 1 Chr. 10:10). When describing hands, it can denote the clapping of hands in victory (Ps. 47:1; Nah. 3:19); or the clasping of hands in an agreement (Job 17:3; Prov. 11:15; 17:18). In the majority of usages, it refers to the blowing of trumpets (Num. 10:3–8; Josh. 6:8, 9; Judg. 7:18–20; Joel 2:15). *

– [3] Job 20:26; Is. 54:16; Ezek. 22:20, 21; Hag. 1:9 ➔ BREATHE <5301>.

BLOW AWAY – Ps. 1:4; 68:2; Is. 19:7 ➔ DRIVE AWAY <5086>.

BLOW FIERCELY – Jer. 6:29 ➔ BURN (verb) <2787>.

BLOWS – Prov. 18:6; 19:29 ➔ BEATINGS <4112>.

BLUE – ***t**^{e}**ḵêleṯ*** [fem. noun: תְּכֵלֶת <8504>; prob. from ONYCHA <7827>] ▶ **This word also means violet. It refers to the hue of certain highly colorful wool materials used in the Tabernacle.** Ref.: Ex. 25:4. Some translators render it as purple. It was used in various things of the Tabernacle: hangings, an ephod (Ex. 26:1; 28:5, 6; 28:33; 35:25); Temple hangings (2 Chr. 2:7, 14). It was employed in cords, loops, rings (Ex. 26:4; 28:28, 31, 37); palace curtains (Esther 1:6). More generally, it refers to fabrics (Jer. 10:9; Ezek. 23:6). It was a valuable trade item (Ezek. 27:7). *

BLUENESS – Prov. 20:30 ➔ BRUISE (noun) <2250>.

BLUNT (BE) – ***qāhāh*** [verb: קָהָה <6949>; a prim. root] ▶

a. This word means for a cutting tool to be unsharpened, to have a dull edge or point. Ref.: Eccl. 10:10.

b. This word also means to be set on edge. Literally, it refers to one's teeth being dull, blunted (an image for mouths puckering at the unpleasant taste of sour grapes). The assertion of the proverb, "and the children's teeth are set on edge" (Jer. 31:29, 30; Ezek. 18:2), refers to the wrongly supposed effect of the father's sins on the children. ¶

BLUSTERING – Job 8:2 ➔ MIGHTY <3524>.

BOAR – Ps. 80:13 ➔ PIG <2386>.

BOARD – [1] ***lûaḥ*** [masc. noun: לוּחַ <3871>; from a prim. root] ▶ **This word refers to a tablet, a slab of stone, a plank or long, flat piece of timber.** It is used to indicate planks or boards of an altar or frame structure (Ex. 27:8); a ship (Ezek. 27:5); a wooden panel (1 Kgs. 7:36; Song 8:9). It indicates metal plates on slabs (1 Kgs. 7:36). Smaller tablets were often used for writing materials or for carving inscriptions (Hab. 2:2). It is used several times of stone tablets (Ex. 24:12; 31:18; 32:16; 34:1, 4; Deut. 5:22; 1 Kgs. 8:9), indicating the tablets containing the Ten Commandments, the tablets of the testimony (Ex. 31:18), tablets of the covenant (Deut. 9:9). It is used in a figurative sense of the tablet of the heart (Prov. 3:3; 7:3; Jer. 17:1). *

[2] ***qereš*** [masc. noun: קֶרֶשׁ <7175>; from an unused root meaning to split off] ▶ **This word refers to the planks and long, flat pieces of acacia wood prepared for the Tabernacle.** Refs.: Ex. 26:15–23, 25–29; 35:11; 36:20–28, 30–34; 39:33; 40:18). It has the sense of an inlaid floor, a deck with boards, planks (Ezek. 27:6). Some scholars prefer to translate this word as frame or panel in some references. Its exact technical meaning still eludes us at this time. *

[3] 1 Kgs. 6:9 ➔ RANK <7713> b.

BOAST (noun) – Job 11:3; Is. 16:6; Jer. 48:30; 50:36 ➔ TALK (EMPTY, IDLE) <907>.

BOAST (verb) – 1 ***yāmar*** [verb: יָמַר <3235>; a prim. root] ▶
a. This word is used of glorying in something, being rightly proud in the case of enjoying the benefits and blessings on God's people. Ref.: Is. 61:6. ¶
b. This verb means to change, to replace. It refers to replacing something with something else, even changing gods, a major sin of Israel. Ref.: Jer. 2:11. ¶
– 2 See PRAISE (verb) <1984>.

BOASTER – Is. 44:25 ➔ TALK (EMPTY, IDLE) <907>.

BOASTING – Job 11:3; Is. 16:6; Jer. 48:30; 50:36 ➔ TALK (EMPTY, IDLE) <907>.

BOAT – 1 Is. 33:21 ➔ FLEET OF SHIPS <590> 2 See SHIP <591>.

BOAZ – ***bōʿaz*** [masc. proper noun: בֹּעַז <1162>; from an unused root of uncertain meaning]: in him is strength ▶
a. Boaz was a kinsman redeemer for Naomi and became the second husband of Ruth. His name may mean quickness, swiftness, or literally, in him, strength (*b^e^* plus *ʿaz*). He and Ruth bore Obed, grandfather of David (Ruth 4:13, 21). *
b. This word serves as the name for the north column of two pillars constructed at the porch of Solomon's Temple. Refs.: 1 Kgs. 7:21; 2 Chr. 3:17. ¶

BOCHERU – ***bōḵ^e^rû*** [masc. proper noun: בֹּכְרוּ <1074>; from BORN FIRST (BE) <1069>]: firstborn ▶ **A descendant of Jonathan, the son of Saul.** Refs.: 1 Chr. 8:38; 9:44. ¶

BOCHIM – ***bōḵiym*** [proper noun: בֹּכִים <1066>; plur. act. part. of WEEP <1058>]: those who weep ▶ **A place close to Gilgal.** The Israelites shed tears of repentance there after the angel of the Lord had spoken to them since they had disobeyed the commandments of God (Judg. 2:1, 5). ¶

BODY – 1 ***ʾûl*** [masc. noun: אוּל <193>; from an unused root meaning to twist, i.e., (by implication) be strong] ▶
a. This word means the physical human form. It also means belly or strength. Ref.: Psalm 73:4 (NASB: their body* is fat, *footnote: or belly; KJV: their strength is firm). It is a begrudging assertion of the health and wealth of the arrogant persons the psalmist encounters. ¶
b. This noun also indicates a mighty person, leader, or noble. Ref.: 2 Kings 24:15; also translated leading man, chief man, prominent people. ¶
2 ***g^e^wiyyāh*** [fem. noun: גְּוִיָּה <1472>; prolonged for BACK <1465>] ▶ **This word designates most often a corpse, a carcass.** It is used to depict a dead body, either a human, such as Saul (1 Sam. 31:10, 12), or an animal, such as Samson's lion (Judg. 14:8, 9). In the Bible, this word is used to describe the slaughter of a nation as dead bodies are scattered everywhere (Ps. 110:6; Nah. 3:3). Sometimes it refers to live bodies. But in these cases, the idea of defeat or humiliation is present (Gen. 47:18; Neh. 9:37). When the experience is visionary, however, the word depicts live beings with no humiliation implied (Ezek. 1:11, 23; Dan. 10:6). ¶
3 ***gûp̱āh*** [fem. noun: גּוּפָה <1480>; from SHUT <1479>] ▶ **This word means mortal remains, corpse. It appears only twice in the Old Testament and in the same verse.** First Chronicles 10:12 describes Saul's and his sons' dead bodies. It has a similar meaning to <1472> above as is demonstrated when that word is used in a parallel passage, 1 Samuel 31:12. ¶
4 ***g^e^šēm*** [Aramaic masc. noun: גְּשֵׁם <1655>; apparently the same as RAIN (verb) <1653>] ▶ **This word is found only in the book of Daniel. When Shadrach, Meshach, and Abednego emerged from the fiery furnace, it was used to describe their physical persons, unscathed by fire.** Ref.: Dan. 3:27. This term was also used to describe the nature of Nebuchadnezzar's being when he was turned into a beast (Dan. 5:21). Other refs.: Dan. 3:28 (also translated life); 4:33; 7:11. ¶
5 ***niḏneh*** [Aramaic masc. noun: נִדְנֶה <5085>; from the same as SHEATH <5084>] ▶ **This word means sheath for a**

sword. It is used only in the book of Daniel, where it figuratively described the relationship between Daniel's spiritual and physical being. His spirit was within his body in the same way as a sword fits into its sheath (Dan. 7:15). ¶
[6] ***ᵃṭiyn*** [masc. noun: עֲטִין <5845>; from an unused root apparently meaning to contain] ▶ **The meaning of this word is uncertain.** It may mean a body (NIV, Job 21:24). Others suggest breasts (KJV), sides (NASB), pails (NKJV, ESV). ¶
[7] ***qōḇāh*** [fem. noun: קֳבָה <6897>; from CURSE (verb) <6895> (which is from a root meaning to scoop out; thus a cavity)] ▶ **Some translators render this as belly, referring to the internal aspect of the body.** Ref.: Num. 25:8. See also STOMACH <6896>. ¶
– [8] Gen. 15:4 ➔ BOWELS <4578> [9] Num. 25:8 ➔ STOMACH <6896> [10] Deut. 21:23; Josh. 8:29; Is. 5:25 ➔ body, dead body ➔ CORPSE <5038> [11] Job 13:12 ➔ BACK <1354> [12] Job 20:23 ➔ ENTRAILS <3894> [13] Prov. 3:8 ➔ NAVEL <8270>.

BODYGUARD – [1] Gen. 37:36; 39:1; 40:3, 4; 41:10, 12; etc. ➔ GUARD, IMPERIAL GUARD <2876> [2] 1 Sam. 22:14; 2 Sam. 23:23; 1 Chr. 11:25 ➔ GUARD <4928> [3] Dan. 2:14 ➔ GUARD <2877>.

BOG – Ps. 40:2 ➔ MUD <2916>.

BOHAN – ***bōhan*** [masc. proper noun: בֹּהַן <932>; an orthographical variation of THUMB <931>]: thumb ▶ **An Israelite, son of Reuben.** Refs.: Josh. 15:6; 18:17. ¶

BOIL (noun) – [1] ***ᵃḇaʻbuʻōt*** [fem. noun: אֲבַעְבֻּעֹת <76>; (by reduplication) from an unused root (meaning to belch forth)] ▶ **The word indicates a festering boil or skin eruption, possibly blisters.** It refers specifically to the boils that broke out on people and beasts in the sixth plague (Ex. 9:9, 10). ¶
[2] ***šᵉḥiyn*** [masc. noun: שְׁחִין <7822>; from an unused root prob. meaning to burn] ▶ **This word refers to a serious skin disease and irritation with festering sores in it.** Refs.: Ex. 9:9–11; Deut. 28:27, 35, as in the sixth plague on Egypt. Some skin diseases were more serious than others (Lev. 13:18–20, 23). Hezekiah's boil was healed (2 Kgs. 20:7; Is. 38:21). Job suffered from this malady brought on by Satan (Job 2:7). ¶

BOIL (verb) – [1] ***bāʻāh*** [verb: בָּעָה <1158>; a prim. root] ▶ **This word means to cause to swell or to boil up. It also means to seek, to ask, to request.** It describes a swelling of water (Is. 64:2); or a rising of desire or interest (Is. 21:12: to inquire, to ask). In the latter interpretation, the verb is also used in the passive form, to be searched (out), with the implication of being ransacked or plundered. This meaning is evident by the context and by the synonymous parallelism in the following verse, "But how Esau will be ransacked, his hidden treasures pillaged!" (Obad. 1:6, NIV). Other ref.: Is. 30:13 (to swell, to bulge). ¶
[2] ***rāṯaḥ*** [verb: רָתַח <7570>; a prim. root] ▶ **This word means to be agitated and, figuratively, to seethe.** It refers to the great agitation and churning of the waters of the sea (Job 41:31); or the bubbling motion of hot water in a pot (Ezek. 24:5). Used of a person's inner emotional turmoil, it means to seethe, to be agitated, to be upset (Job 30:27). ¶

BOILED – ***bāšēl*** [adj.: בָּשֵׁל <1311>; from COOK (verb) <1310>] ▶ **This word means immersed in a liquid heated to the point of forming bubbles; it is also translated sodden.** Combined with the verb, to boil, this cognate adjective emphasizes that the Passover lamb must not be boiled (Ex. 12:9). It can refer to a boiled part of a ram (Num. 6:19). ¶

BOILING – [1] ***reṯaḥ*** [masc. noun: רֶתַח <7571>; from BOIL (verb) <7570>] ▶ **This noun combines with the cognate verb BOIL <7570>, serving as its object.** The expression becomes emphatic, literally: to boil vigorously its boiling (Ezek. 24:5). It has a feminine suffix attached to it. ¶
– [2] Job 41:20; Jer. 1:13 ➔ BREATHE <5301>.

BOILING PLACES – Ezek. 46:23 → HEARTHS <4018>.

BOLD – Prov. 7:13 → STRENGTHEN <5810>.

BOLD (BE) – Gen. 18:27 → CONTENT (BE) <2974>.

BOLD (BE, MAKE) – ***rāhab*** [verb: רָהַב <7292>; a prim. root] ▶ **This word indicates making a person courageous, brave, strong.** Ref.: Ps. 138:3; also translated to strengthen, to embolden. It has the sense of attempting to win back friends, pleading with them boldly (Prov. 6:3: to make sure, to plead, to plead urgently, to give no rest). It refers to the strong power of the bridegroom's eyes on his bride; they overwhelm her (Song 6:5: to overcome, to confuse, to overwhelm). It takes on a negative sense in Isaiah 3:5: to storm against, to rise against, to act proudly, to be insolent. ¶

BOLD-FACED – Ezek. 16:30 → BRAZEN <7986>.

BOLLED – Ex. 9:31 → BUD (IN) <1392>.

BOLSTER – 1 Sam. 19:13; 26:7, 11, 12 → HEAD (noun) <4763> b.

BOLT – [1] ***man'ûl, man'ul*** [masc. noun: מַנְעוּל, מַנְעֻל <4514>; from LOCK (verb) <5274>] ▶ **This word denotes part of a mechanism for securing a door; possibly a moveable crossbar or a socket. Its exact meaning is not known for sure.** It refers to an apparatus used to lock a gate (Neh. 3:3, 6, 13–15) or of a house or room (Song 5:5). ¶
– [2] 2 Sam. 13:17, 18 → LOCK (verb) <5274>.

BOND – [1] ***'êsûr*** [masc. noun: אֵסוּר <612>; from BIND <631>] ▶ **This word is used in the plural. It means restraints that hold someone captive; it is also translated bindings, bands, fetters, chains, prison.** They were used to bind Samson's hands and, evidently, were quite strong (Judg. 15:14). It refers figuratively to hands that are like chains or fetters (Eccl. 7:26). A house of binding means a prison (Jer. 37:15). ¶
[2] ***ḥarṣubbāh*** [fem. noun: חַרְצֻבָּה <2784>; of uncertain deriv.] ▶ **This word means fetter, chain, pain, torments.** It refers to unjust, wicked bonds or chains in a figurative sense, usually indicating social, economic, or political oppression (Is. 58:6; KJV, band). It indicates the pains or torments that often accompany death but which the wicked seem to be free of (Ps. 73:4: band, pain, pang, struggle). ¶
[3] ***môsêr, môsêrāh*** [masc. noun: מוֹסֵר, מוֹסֵרָה <4147>; from ADMONISH <3256> (in the sense of to chasten)] ▶
a. This word indicates a band, a chain, a fetter. It is used figuratively of the hold of death on a person (Ps. 116:16). It indicates the political and military bonds holding Jerusalem and God's people but also the chains of restraint the Lord puts on them because of their sin and rebellion (Is. 28:22; 52:2). ¶
b. A masculine noun indicating a band, a chain, a fetter. It is used mostly in a figurative sense: the freedom from bonds given to the wild animals (Job 39:5; also translated rope); of political and military oppression and control (Ps. 2:3; Ps. 107:14; Jer. 27:2) from which God can free His people (Jer. 2:20; 30:8; Nah. 1:13). But it also refers to Israel's breaking away from God's bonds on them (Jer. 5:5). ¶
[4] ***māsōreṯ*** [fem. noun: מָסֹרֶת <4562>; from BIND <631>] ▶ **This word indicates bringing persons into covenantal agreements, stipulations, making them partners in a covenant.** Ref.: Ezek. 20:37. ¶
– [5] Num. 30:2–5, 7, 10–14 → PLEDGE (noun) <632> [6] Is. 58:6 → BUNCH <92>.

BONDAGE – ***'aḇduṯ*** [fem. noun: עַבְדֻת <5659>] ▶ **This word means servitude; it is also translated slavery. It is derived from the word *'āḇaḏ* (<5647>), meaning to serve. It occurs three times in the Hebrew Bible.** In Ezra 9:8, 9, it refers twice to the bondage of the Hebrews under Babylon, a bondage where God revived them a little by allowing them to rebuild the wall and the Temple. In Nehemiah 9:17, it refers to severe bondage in Egypt (see Neh. 9:9), to which some rebellious Hebrews wanted to return. ¶

BONDAGE (BRING INTO) – Neh. 5:5 ➔ SUBDUE <3533>.

BONE – 1 ***gerem*** [masc. noun: גֶּרֶם <1634>; from BREAK <1633>] ► **This word indicates one of the hard parts of the skeletal system; it also means strength.** It depicts animals as strong, a strong or rawboned donkey (Gen. 49:14), used to symbolize Issachar. It depicts the strength or bones of Behemoth (Job 40:18). It is used figuratively of one's strength or bones being dried up by a despondent spirit (Prov. 17:22). A soft answer can soften a person's harsh disposition (Prov. 25:15). The word seems to refer to the bare steps or top steps of a stair, possibly referring to their hardness (2 Kgs. 9:13). ¶

2 ***gᵉram*** [Aramaic masc. noun: גְּרַם <1635>; corresponding to <1634> above] ► **This word indicates the hard skeletal parts of people who were thrown into the den of lions; those parts were crushed before the people hit the bottom of the den.** Ref.: Dan. 6:24. ¶

3 ***'eṣem*** [fem. sing. noun: עֶצֶם <6106>; from MIGHTY (BE) <6105> (in the sense of to be strong)] ► **This word also means substance, self.** The first use of the term in the Bible is in Genesis when Adam proclaimed Eve was bone of his bones (Gen. 2:23). This phrase is echoed later as an idiom of close relationship (Judg. 9:2; 2 Sam. 19:13). The word can also be employed for animal bones (Ex. 12:46; Num. 9:12; Job 40:18). Speaking figuratively, Jeremiah said that the Word of God was like fire shut in his bones (Jer. 20:9). *'Eṣem* can also denote identity, as in the phrase *bᵉ'eṣem hayyôm hazzeh*, (in this very day; Ex. 12:17). A similar construction is seen in Exodus 24:10 (the sky itself). *

BONNET – 1 Ex. 28:40; 29:9; 39:28; Lev. 8:13 ➔ CAP <4021> 2 Is. 3:20; Ezek. 44:18 ➔ TURBAN <6287>.

BOOK – 1 ***sᵉp̱ar*** [Aramaic masc. noun: סְפַר <5609>; from a root corresponding to NUMBER (verb) <5608>] ► **The word refers to the Pentateuch (book of Moses), i.e., the first five books of the Bible.** They were used to instruct the priests and Levites in their duties (Ezra 6:18). It refers to books of national records that rulers in Babylon could check regarding Israeli-Babylonian relations (Ezra 4:15). It also refers to books that the Ancient of Days will use to judge in favor of His saints against the boastful little horn (Dan. 7:10, cf. Dan. 7:21 ff.). The word is translated archives in the plural and used together with the word for house to signify library, as a house of books, in Ezra 6:1 (KJV: rolls). ¶

2 ***sêp̱er, sip̱rāh*** [masc. noun: סֵפֶר, סִפְרָה <5612>; from NUMBER (verb) <5608>] ► **This word means a document, a writing, a scroll.** Borrowed from an Assyrian word meaning missive or message, this word can refer to a letter (2 Sam. 11:14, 15; 1 Kgs. 21:8, 9, 11; 2 Kgs. 10:1, 2, 6, 7; Jer. 29:1); a divorce certificate (Deut. 24:1, 3; Is. 50:1; Jer. 3:8); a proof of purchase deed (Jer. 32:10–12, 14, 16); a book in which things were written for a need in the future (Ex. 17:14; 1 Sam. 10:25; Is. 30:8); a book of laws (Ex. 24:7; Deut. 30:10; Josh. 1:8; Neh. 8:1, 3; 13:1); a genealogical record (Gen. 5:1; Neh. 7:5); writing and language (Dan. 1:4, 17). *

BOOT – ***sᵉ'ôn*** [masc. noun: סְאוֹן <5430>; from WARRIOR <5431>] ► **In context this word refers to military footwear worn by the soldiers of the mighty Assyrian army, probably made of leather.** Ref.: Is. 9:5. Some authorities suggest sandal as a translation. The word was formerly taken to mean battle by earlier translators (Is. 9:5, KJV; NKJV, boot, sandal in note). ¶

BOOTH – 1 ***sukkāh*** [fem. sing. noun: סֻכָּה <5521>; from ABODE <5520>] ► **This word is used for temporary shelters.** They were used to cover animals (Gen. 33:17); warriors (2 Sam. 11:11); and the prophet Jonah (Jon. 4:5). It is used poetically to refer to the clouds (Job 36:29;

Ps. 18:11). A specialized usage is employed for booths constructed for the fall harvest festival (Lev. 23:42, 43). The festival was known as the *ḥag̱ hassuk̲k̲ôṯ* (FEAST <2282>), the Feast of Booths (Deut. 16:13, 16). This was to remind the Israelites that they lived in booths when the Lord brought them up from Egypt (Lev. 23:43). *
– [2] Lam. 2:6 ➔ TABERNACLE <7900>.

BOOTY – [1] Num. 31:11, 12, 26, 27, 32 ➔ PREY <4455> [2] Prov. 12:12 ➔ NET <4685> [3] See PLUNDER (noun) <957>.

BOR-ASHAN – 1 Sam. 30:30 ➔ CORASHAN <3565>.

BORDER – [1] ***gᵉḇûl*** [masc. noun: גְּבוּל <1366>; from BOUNDS (SET) <1379>] ▶ **This word designates a boundary, or territory; barrier, wall.** It is used to point out the limits or boundaries of territories (1 Sam. 13:18) or borderland of geographical areas (Ps. 78:54). It may refer to the territory enclosed (Gen. 47:21; Ex. 8:2; Deut. 19:3; Josh. 13:26). It depicts the limits God set for various aspects of His creation (Ps. 104:9) but also the man-made boundary markers set by people (Deut. 19:14; Prov. 22:28) that were to be respected. As a technical architectural term, it refers to lattice work, a barrier, or a wall (Ezek. 40:12) and also to some kind of border work (Ezek. 43:13, 17, 20). Figuratively, it is used to refer to a territory, a border of darkness, or holiness (Ps. 78:54; Mal. 1:4). *
[2] ***gᵉḇûlāh*** [fem. noun: גְּבוּלָה <1367>; fem. of BORDER <1366>] ▶ **This word indicates a territory or a boundary.** It describes the fixed limits the Lord has set for the entire earth, including its seasonal variations (Ps. 74:17). It depicts the fixed boundaries of the various nations and boundaries set by God (Is. 10:13) or a certain territory or area around a city (Num. 32:33). It denotes the boundary lines set up to define an area (Num. 34:2, 12) and sections or rows within a garden for planting various crops (Is. 28:25). *
[3] ***yarḵāh, yᵉrēḵāh*** [fem. noun: יַרְכָה, יְרֵכָה <3411>; fem. of THIGH <3409>] ▶ **This word refers also to a remote area, the highest part, the far end. It refers to something toward the back or side, distant, far away.** It refers to the part of Zebulun most distant from Jerusalem, toward the Mediterranean Sea and north (Gen. 49:13). It refers to the back or rear of a tent or building (Ex. 26:22, 23). It indicates the part of a mountain farthest away (Judg. 19:1, 18; 2 Kgs. 19:23); of the farthest part of the earth (Jer. 6:22; 25:32); of the northern territories (Is. 14:13). It refers to the remotest parts of the pit in Sheol, its most remote areas (Is. 14:15). It refers to the rear of an inner room, such as the Most Holy Place (1 Kgs. 6:16); the inner recesses of the hold of a ship (Jon. 1:5); a cave (1 Sam. 24:3); or a house (Amos 6:10). *
[4] ***tôṣā'āh, tōṣā'āh*** [fem. noun: תּוֹצָאָה, תֹּצָאָה <8444>; from GO OUT <3318>] ▶ **This word also means an extremity, an end point.** It refers to the end point or extreme reach of a border or borders, or border extremities (Num. 34:4, 5, 8, 9, 12; Josh. 15:4, 7; 1 Chr. 5:16). It may have the sense of issues surrounding death or escapes, releases from death (Ps. 68:20) that are from the Lord. From the heart go forth issues of life (Prov. 4:23). It refers literally to exits from a city (Ezek. 48:30). *
– [5] Josh. 11:2; 12:23 ➔ SIEVE <5299> b. [6] Josh. 13:2 ➔ REGION <1552> [7] See MOLDING <2213>.

BORE – Ex. 21:6 ➔ PIERCE <7527>.

BORN – [1] ***yillôḏ*** [adj.: יִלּוֹד <3209>; pass. from BIRTH (GIVE) <3205>] ▶ **This word designates what is given birth.** It refers to the baby or child who has been or will be born (Ex. 1:22). The context of the word indicates: where certain persons were born (Josh. 5:5; 2 Sam. 5:14; Jer. 16:3); to whom certain persons were born (2 Sam. 12:14). ¶
– [2] Gen. 14:14; 17:12, 13, 23, 27; Lev. 22:11; Jer. 2:14 ➔ DESCENDANT <3211> [3] Ex. 12:19, 48, 49; Lev. 19:34; Josh. 8:33; Ezek. 47:22 ➔ NATIVE <249>.

BORN HEALTHY – Lam. 2:20 ➔ CARED FOR (ONES) <2949>.

BORROW – 1 ***lāwāh*** [verb: לָוָה <3867>; a prim. root] ▶ **This word has the sense of to ask for something as well as to lend something according to context.** Ref.: Deut. 28:12. Money is loaned out (Ex. 22:25) or borrowed (Neh. 5:4). The wicked person borrows but does not pay back (Ps. 37:21); the righteous person both gives and lends to help others (Ps. 37:26; 112:5). Being generous to the poor is equivalent to lending to the Lord (Prov. 19:17). Borrowing can lead to enslavement (Prov. 22:7). God's judgments will encompass both borrower and lender (Is. 24:2). Other ref.: Deut. 28:44. The word also means to attach oneself to someone or something; see JOIN <3867>. ¶
– 2 Deut. 15:6 ➔ LEND <5670>.

BOSOM – 1 ***ḥêyq, ḥêq*** [masc. noun: חֵיק, חֵק <2436>; from an unused root, apparently meaning to enclose] ▶
a. This word indicates the upper part of a person's body where loved objects and persons are embraced. Ref.: 1 Kgs. 3:20. Persons can be clasped with hands or arms: one's wife or concubine (Gen. 16:5; Deut. 28:54); one's husband, literally the man of her bosom (*ḥ*^e^*yqāh*) (Deut. 28:56). The Lord carries His people, His flock in His bosom (Is. 40:11). The person, animal, or object that is held in one's bosom is cherished greatly. An adulteress is not allowed into this sacred arena of personal relationship (Prov. 5:20). What is attached to one's bosom affects a person deeply (Prov. 6:27). Fools permit anger to lie in their bosoms (Eccl. 7:9). The Lord repays the sins of the fathers into the bosoms of their children (Jer. 32:18). Those who are untrustworthy should not be trusted even if they are our cherished friends or companions (Mic. 7:5). In a more literal sense, the word refers to a fold in a garment just above the belt where one's hand can be held (Ex. 4:6, 7). *
b. This word is also used to indicate the hollow or bottom of a chariot. Ref.: 1 Kgs. 22:35: midst, floor, bottom. It can also indicate a channel or trough running around an altar (Ezek. 43:13, 14, 17: bottom, base, gutter). ¶
2 ***ḥêṣen*** [masc. noun: חֵצֶן <2683>; from an unused root meaning to hold firmly] ▶ **This word refers to either the grasp of one's arms or an open space in a garment for gathering something.** Ref.: Ps. 129:7: bosom, arms. ¶
3 ***ḥōṣen*** [masc. noun: חֹצֶן <2684>; a collateral form of <2683> above and meaning the same] ▶ **This word refers also to part of a garment covering the chest or lap, the front folds in one's robe.** It indicates the enclosing space between one's arms and breast when embracing something or someone or the part of a garment covering the bosom area of one's body (Neh. 5:13; Is. 49:22). ¶
4 ***ṣallaḥaṯ*** [fem. noun: צַלַּחַת <6747>] ▶ **This word indicates a person's body around the chest area.** Refs.: Prov. 19:24; 26:15. The Hebrew word is also translated pan, bowl; see DISH <6747>. ¶
– 5 Job 31:33 ➔ HEART <2243> 6 Ezek. 23:3, 8, 21 ➔ BREAST <1717>.

BOTTLE – 1 ***nō'ḏ, n*^e^*'ôḏ*** [masc. noun: נֹאד, נֹאוד <4997>; from an unused root of uncertain signification] ▶ **This word points to a wineskin. It was used of a container made of animal skin prepared so it would not leak.** It was used to hold wine (Josh. 9:4, 13; 1 Sam. 16:20); or milk (Judg. 4:19). It is used figuratively of a container for tears (Ps. 56:8) or of a wineskin in the smoke, image of a spirit withered by sorrow (Ps. 119:83). ¶
– 2 Job 32:19 ➔ MEDIUM <178> b. 3 1 Sam. 1:24; 10:3; 25:18; 2 Sam. 16:1; Job 38:37; Jer. 13:12; 48:12 ➔ SKIN BOTTLE <5035> 4 Jer. 19:1, 10 ➔ JAR <1228> 5 Hab. 2:15 ➔ WATERSKIN <2573>.

BOTTOM – 1 ***'ar'iy*** [Aramaic fem. noun: אַרְעִי <773>; fem. of EARTH <772>] ▶ **This word means the base; it is also translated floor.** It indicates the lowest area of a den of lions, evidently recessed in the ground (Dan. 6:24). ¶
– 2 Ex. 29:12; Lev. 4:7, 18, 25, 30, 34; etc. ➔ FOUNDATION <3247> 3 1 Kgs. 22:35; Ezek. 43:13, 14, 17 ➔ BOSOM <2436> 4 Song 3:10 ➔ SUPPORT (noun) <7507> 5 Amos 9:3 ➔ FLOOR <7172> 6 Zech. 1:8 ➔ RAVINE <4699>.

BOTTOMS – Jon. 2:6 ➔ FORM (noun) <7095>.

BOUGH – 1 **uppermost bough, topmost bough, highest bough:** ***'āmiyr*** [masc. noun: אָמִיר <534>; apparently from SAY <559> (in the sense of self-exaltation)] ▶ **This word means the summit (of a tree); it is also translated topmost branches.** It describes Damascus in a simile as like an olive tree with a few olives left in its topmost branches (Is. 17:6, 9). ¶
2 ***se'appāh*** [fem. noun: סְעַפָּה <5589>; fem. of BRANCH <5585>] ▶ **This word refers to the incomparable branches of a tree that are large enough for birds to nest in.** Refs.: Ezek. 31:6, 8. They are part of a figurative depiction of the Assyrian Empire. ¶
3 ***sar'appāh*** [fem. noun: סַרְעַפָּה <5634>; fem. of BOUGH <5589>] ▶ **This word is used of the branches of a tree where birds would nest, find shelter, usually a main branch.** Ref.: Ezek. 31:5. ¶
– 4 Judg. 9:48, 49 ➔ BRANCH <7754> 5 Is. 10:33 ➔ BRANCH <6288> b. 6 Is. 17:9 ➔ FOREST <2793> 7 Ezek. 17:6 ➔ BRANCH <6288> a.

BOUGH (THICK) – ***'abōt*** [common noun: עֲבוֹת <5688>; the same as LEAFY <5687> (something intertwined)] ▶ **This word indicates a branch, thick foliage, cloud.** The word is taken by some translators to mean boughs or thick foliage for use in worshiping the Lord (Ps. 118:27; NIV: boughs; others: cord). It is used in a figurative way to describe aspects of God's people Israel (Ezek. 19:11); or of Assyria (Ezek. 31:3). It has the meaning of clouds (NASB, ESV) or foliage (NIV) in Ezekiel 31:10, 14. The Hebrew word also means a rope, a cord, a line; see ROPE. ¶

BOUGHS – Song 7:8 ➔ FRUIT <5577>.

BOUGHT – Gen. 17:12, 13, 23, 27; Ex. 12:44 ➔ PURCHASE (noun) <4736>.

BOUNDARY – Job 26:10 ➔ END <8503>.

BOUNDING – Nah. 3:2 ➔ DANCE (verb) <7540>.

BOUNDS (SET) – ***gābal*** [verb: גָּבַל <1379>; a prim. root] ▶ **This verb means to mark off boundaries, to establish limits.** It describes the process of setting bounds around something or making a boundary (Ex. 19:12, 23; Deut. 19:14); or it depicts something that bounds or limits an area, such as the Jordan, which served to bound the territory of Benjamin on the east (Josh. 18:20). Used with the preposition *be*, it means to border on some other area or land (Zech. 9:2). ¶

BOW (noun) – ***qešet*** [fem. noun: קֶשֶׁת <7198>; from HARD (BE) <7185> in the original sense of bending] ▶ **This word refers to one of the most common weapons of war in antiquity, a curved piece of resilient wood bent by a string for propelling an arrow.** Refs.: Gen. 48:22; Josh. 24:12; Hos. 2:18. A bowshot was the distance covered by an arrow shot from a bow (Gen. 21:16). The bow and arrow was commonly used for hunting (Gen. 27:3). The phrase *ben-qešet*, son of a bow referred to an arrow, a useless weapon against Leviathan (Job 41:28). Judah is described as the Lord's bow (Zech. 9:13). The phrase *rišpê-qāšet* means the flaming of the bow, its arrows (Ps. 76:3). Hosea speaks of a bow of deception, one that misses its goal, when referring to his people Israel (Hos. 7:16). Job speaks of a bow (20:24). Isaiah 21:17 refers to bowmen, literally, the number of the bows. Men with the bow refers to archers, bowmen (1 Sam. 31:3). This word also indicates a rainbow. It is used figuratively of God's bow, the rainbow set for all time in the heavens (Gen. 9:13, 14, 16). *

BOW (EXPERT WITH THE) – Gen. 21:20 ➔ ARCHER <7199>.

BOW, BOWSTRING – Ps. 21:12 ➔ STRING <4340>.

BOW (verb) – ***kāra'*** [verb: כָּרַע <3766>; a prim. root] ▶ **The word signifies the crouching of a lion before going to sleep.** Refs.: Gen. 49:9; Num. 24:9. Also the bowing of an animal (Job 39:3); or a woman in order to give birth (1 Sam. 4:19); the bowing down of a man over a woman in sexual intercourse (adulterous, in this case) (Job 31:10); the yielding of knees from weakness, sometimes after one has been wounded (Judg. 5:27; 2 Kgs. 9:24); the bowing of knees under a heavy burden (Is. 10:4; 46:2); the bowing of knees in submission or subjugation (Esther 3:2, 5; Is. 45:23); bowing in repentance (Ezra 9:5); to worship a false god (1 Kgs. 19:18); or the true God (2 Chr. 29:29; Ps. 95:6). *

BOW, BOW DOWN – ***kāp̱ap̱*** [verb: כָּפַף <3721>; a prim. root] ▶ **This word is used in a religious sense of humbling oneself.** Refs.: Is. 58:5; Mic. 6:6. It is also used with reference to being defeated or oppressed by one's enemies (Ps. 57:6). It is used in a general sense of those who are in distress or have fallen for various reasons (Ps. 145:14; 146:8). The Lord helps them. ¶

BOW DOWN – 1 ***qāḏaḏ*** [verb: קָדַד <6915>; a prim. root] ▶ **This word means to incline one's head in reverence and worship.** Ref.: Gen. 24:26. It is always followed by the verb to worship, *ḥāwāh*. It means to bow down, to kneel; *ḥāwāh* must be interpreted according to whom or what is being reverenced, God, a person, etc. Israel bowed and worshiped God for His deliverance (Ex. 4:31). *

2 ***šûaḥ, šiyaḥ*** [verb: שׁוּחַ, שִׂיחַ <7743>; a prim. root] ▶

a. This word is used of something descending, going lower. It is also translated to sink down, to bring down, to lead down, to incline. One's soul into the dust (Ps. 44:25); the house of a prostitute to death (Prov. 2:18); one's soul bending down within a person, an onset of despair (Lam. 3:20; also translated to be humbled, to be downcast).

b. A verb meaning to be downcast. It refers often to the despair of one's soul, one's life that has sunk into the ground in utter hopelessness (Ps. 44:25). ¶

3 ***shâchâh*** [verb: שָׁחָה <7812>; a prim. root] ▶ **This word also means to prostrate oneself, to crouch, to fall down, to humbly beseech, to do reverence, to worship. The primary meaning of the word is to stoop, translated to bow down. The first time the word "worship" is used (Gen. 22:5), it is a translation of this word.** This verb is used to indicate bowing before a monarch or a superior and paying homage to him or her (Gen. 43:28). In contexts such as Genesis 24:26, *šāḥaḥ* (BOW DOWN <7817>) is used to indicate bowing down in worship to Yahweh. The psalmists used this word to describe all the earth bowing down in worship to God as a response to His great power (Ps. 66:4); or bowing down in worship and kneeling before the Lord (Ps. 95:6). This act of worship is given to God because He deserves it and because those that are speaking are people of His pasture.

The word is also used by Joseph when he described the sheaves of his brothers and parents bowing down to his sheaf after it stood upright in a dream that he had (Gen. 37:7). Gideon also interacted with a dream through which God spoke. When he overheard a man telling his friend a dream that the man had and its interpretation, he worshiped God (Judg. 7:15).

Joshua instructed the people of Israel not to associate with the nations remaining around them and not to bow down to or serve any of their gods. He instructed Israel to hold fast to the true God, Yahweh (Josh. 23:7). In Zephaniah, the word is also used for worship. When Yahweh destroys all the gods of the land, the nations on every shore will worship Him (Zeph. 2:11). *

4 ***šāḥaḥ*** [verb: שָׁחַח <7817>; a prim. root] ▶ **This word means to stoop, to crouch, to sink low.** It is used in a literal sense of a crouching lion (Job 38:40); knocking down a fortified wall (Is. 25:12); defeating a powerful enemy (Is. 26:5); as well as of God's bringing down and chastising His own people (Is. 29:4). It depicts a crumbling hill or mountain (Hab. 3:6). It is used figuratively more often of the wicked crouching to do harm (Ps. 10:10); of bowing down in humility (Is. 2:11, 17); or servitude (Is. 60:14). It is used to picture the sinking of a person's soul and life

(Lam. 3:20). It can have the sense of being subdued, crouched down in submission (Job 9:13). It depicts evil, wicked persons (Prov. 14:19). It signifies a sound that is low, hardly discernible (Eccl. 12:4). *
– [5] Deut. 33:3 ➔ SIT DOWN <8497> a. [6] 1 Kgs. 18:42 ➔ STRETCH ONESELF <1457> Eccl. 12:3 ➔ BEND <5791> [7] Is. 44:15, 17, 19; 46:6 ➔ FALL DOWN <5456> [8] Jer. 2:20 ➔ LIE DOWN <6808>.

BOW THE KNEE – ***’aḇrêḵ*** [verb: אַבְרֵךְ <86>; prob. an Egyptian word that may mean father of the king, tender father, attention!, or rejoice!] ▶ **This word is a sign of honor.** It occurs only in Genesis 41:43. It may possibly correspond to a Hebrew verb of four letters in an imperative form meaning to bow the knee. It designates the homage to be paid toward Joseph in Egypt. ¶

BOWED DOWN (BE) – Is. 21:3 ➔ INIQUITY (COMMIT) <5753>.

BOWED DOWN (WHO IS) – Is. 51:14 ➔ CAPTIVE EXILE <6808>.

BOWELS – [1] ***mê‘eh*** [masc. noun: מֵעֶה <4578>; from an unused root prob. meaning to be soft] ▶ **This word means intestines, belly, womb, sexual organs, sympathy; it is also translated: entrails, inward parts, stomach, body, inner parts, heart. It refers to internal organs.** When Joab stabbed Amasa, his entrails fell onto the ground (2 Sam. 20:10); the digestive tract; when a woman was suspected of infidelity, she was made to take an oath cursing the water that entered her stomach (Num. 5:22); and the sexual organs; God promised Abram that he would bear a son from his own loins (Gen. 15:4). It can also be used figuratively to mean the seat of emotions or heart (Is. 16:11). *
– [2] Judg. 3:22 ➔ DUNG <6574>.

BOWL – [1] ***gōl*** [masc. noun: גֹּל <1531>; from ROLL (verb) <1556>] ▶ **This word indicates a container for oil.** Ref.: Zech. 4:2. So it may indicate the bowl of a lamp positioned at the top of a lampstand. NASB and NIV have *gullāh* (<1543> below). ¶
[2] ***gullāh*** [fem. noun: גֻּלָּה <1543>; fem. from ROLL (verb) <1556>] ▶ **This word indicates a round-shaped golden container symbolizing life.** Ref.: Eccl. 12:6. It depicts two carved decorative bowls or horizontal projections on the tops of the pillar capitals in Solomon's Temple (1 Kgs. 7:41, 42; 2 Chr. 4:12, 13; also translated globe, pommel). It indicates a bowl for holding lamp oil (Zech. 4:2). It also means a spring (Josh. 15:19; Judg. 1:15); see SPRING <1543>. ¶
[3] ***kᵉp̄ôr*** [masc. noun: כְּפוֹר <3713>; from COVER (verb) <3722>] ▶ **This word refers to a vessel; it is also translated basin, bason, dish.** It refers to a small bowl made of silver or gold for use in the Temple of Ezra's day (Ezra 1:10; 8:27) or the Solomonic Temple (1 Chr. 28:17). The Hebrew word also means hoar frost; see FROST <3713>. ¶
[4] ***mᵉnaqqiyṯ*** [fem. plur. noun: מְנַקִּית <4518>; from FREE (BE) <5352> (in the sense of to be emptied)] ▶ **This word refers to some of the holy vessels used around the table of showbread to pour drink offerings.** They were made of gold (Ex. 25:29; 37:16). Other refs.: Num. 4:7; Jer. 52:19 (also translated cups). ¶
[5] ***sêp̄el*** [masc. noun: סֵפֶל <5602>] ▶ **This word indicates a basin, a dish.** It refers to a small container for milk or water (Judg. 5:25; 6:38). ¶
[6] ***ṣᵉlōḥiyṯ*** [fem. noun: צְלֹחִית <6746>; from RUSH (verb) <6743> (something prolonged or tall)] ▶ **This word is also translated jar, cruse.** It describes a dish or a deep, hollow container for holding salt or other similar substances (2 Kgs. 2:20). ¶
– [7] Gen. 44:2, 12, 16, 17; Ex. 25:31, 33, 34; 37:17, 19, 20 ➔ CUP <1375> [8] Ex. 24:6 ➔ BASIN <101> [9] 2 Sam. 17:28; 1 Kgs. 7:50; etc. ➔ BASIN <5592> [10] 1 Kgs. 17:12 ➔ JAR <3537> [11] Prov. 19:24 ➔ DISH <6747> [12] See BASIN <4219>.

BOWMAN – Jer. 4:29 ➔ THROW <7411>.

BOWSHOT – ***ṭāḥāh*** [verb: טָחָה <2909>; a prim. root] ▶ **This word refers to drawing**

a bow, or being far away as an arrow projected from a bow. It indicates Hagar's being distant enough not to hear or witness the death of her child (Gen. 21:16). The exact distance is, of course, not certain. ¶

BOX – [1] 1 Sam. 6:8, 11, 15 → CHEST <712> [2] 2 Kgs. 9:1, 3 → FLASK <6378>.

BOX TREE – [1] ***te'aššûr*** [masc. noun: תְּאַשּׁוּר <8391>; from BLESS <833> (in the sense of to go straight, to advance forward)] ▶ **This word is also translated pine (ESV), cypress (NASB, NIV).** It refers to a cypress tree or its wood. It is a huge evergreen, cone-bearing tree of the cypress family. It was highly desired in the construction of buildings (Is. 41:19). They were the glory and pride of Lebanon (Is. 60:13). ¶
– [2] Is. 41:19; 60:13 → PINE <8410>.

BOXWOOD – Ezek. 27:6 → ASHURITES <839>.

BOY – [1] ***na'ar*** [masc. noun: נַעַר <5288>; from SHAKE <5287> (in the sense of to be active)] ▶ **This word refers to a young person, as well as a young man, a servant.** It is used of a young person, a boy (Gen. 19:4); one old enough to serve in battle or as a personal private force (Gen. 14:24; 1 Sam. 21:2; 30:13, 17); or as a helper in the army (1 Sam. 14:1). It is used regularly to refer to a young male servant (Gen. 18:7; 22:3); or an attendant to the king (Esther 2:2). It is written *na'râ* (GIRL <5291>) several times but should be read as *na'rāh*, girl, young girl (see Gen. 24:14). Its plural form *ne'ārîm* may include both male and female persons (Ruth 2:21; Job 1:19). A young man, a lad, a young boy was not capable of ruling a land (Eccl. 10:16). It figuratively describes Israel in its formative early years (Hos. 11:1). *
– [2] 1 Sam. 17:56; 20:22 → YOUNG MAN <5958>.

BOZEZ – ***bôṣêṣ*** [proper noun: בּוֹצֵץ <949>; from the same as FINE LINEN <948>]: height ▶ **A sharp rock near Michmash.** Ref.: 1 Sam. 14:4. ¶

BOZKATH – ***boṣqaṯ*** [proper noun: בָּצְקַת <1218>; from SWELL <1216>]: height ▶ **A city of the extreme south of Judah.** Ref.: Josh. 15:39. The grandmother of Josiah was from there (2 Kgs. 22:1). ¶

BOZRAH – [1] ***boṣrāh*** [proper noun: בָּצְרָה <1224>; the same as FOLD (noun) <1223>] ▶
a. The mountainous capital city of Edom. The name means "fortress." It was where the major caravan highways of Edom ran (Gen. 36:33) and where early kings of Edom reigned. It lay south, southeast of the Salt Sea (Dead Sea). The prophets mention it in prophecies of judgment (Is. 34:6; 63:1; Jer. 49:1, 13, 22; Amos 1:12). Other ref.: 1 Chr. 1:44. ¶
b. It refers also to a city in Moab. Ref.: Jer. 48:24. It is mentioned in a prophecy of judgment. It may be the same as Bezer. ¶
– [2] Mic. 2:12 → FOLD (noun) <1223>.

BRACELET – [1] ***ṣāmiyḏ*** [masc. noun: צָמִיד <6781>; from JOIN <6775>] ▶ **This word indicates an ornament fastened on a woman's wrist or lower arm.** It was sometimes given as a gift (Gen. 24:22, 30, 47) to persons or to the Lord (Num. 31:50) for use in the Lord's service. It was used as an ornament of beauty (Ezek. 16:11; 23:42). Other ref.: Num. 19:15. ¶
[2] ***šêrāh*** [fem. noun: שֵׁרָה <8285>; from ENEMY <8324> in its original sense of pressing] ▶ **This word refers to a chain-like ornament for the wrist or lower arm, an item of luxury.** The Lord will destroy them when He brings judgment on Zion (Is. 3:19). ¶
– [3] Ex. 35:22 → HOOK <2397> [4] Ex. 35:22 → NECKLACE <3558> [5] 2 Sam. 1:10 → ARMLET <685>.

BRAID – Judg. 16:13, 19 → LOCK (noun) <4253>.

BRAIDED – ***migbālôṯ*** [fem. plur. noun: מִגְבָּלוֹת <4020>; from BOUNDS (SET) <1379>] ▶ **This word means intertwined; it is also translated twisted, wreathen.** It refers to hammered, twisted chains like cords to be placed on gold filigree settings (Ex. 28:14). ¶

BRAMBLE – 1 ***'āṭāḏ*** [masc. noun: אָטָד <329>; from an unused root (prob. meaning to pierce or make fast)] ▶
a. This thorny shrub or thornbush was considered one of the lowliest of trees. It is referred to in Jotham's fable (Judg. 9:14, 15). It was a scraggly bush that produced nothing of value—an apt figure to represent Abimelech. Other ref.: Ps. 58:9 (thorn). ¶
b. Atad: threshing floor in Transjordan; another name for *'āḇēl miṣrayim* (ABEL MIZRAIM <67>). Refs.: Gen. 50:10, 11. ¶
– 2 Song 2:2 ➔ THORN <2336>.

BRANCH – 1 ***dāliyṯ*** [fem. noun: דָּלִית <1808>; from DRAW <1802> (in the sense of to hang down)] ▶ **This word refers to a bough and also indicates foliage.** It refers to the branches of an olive tree (Jer. 11:16); of various vines (Ezek. 17:6, 7; 19:11); and to cedar trees (Ezek. 17:23; 31:7, 9, 12). ¶
2 ***zᵉmôrāh*** [fem. noun: זְמוֹרָה <2156>; from PRUNE <2168>] ▶ **This word refers particularly to the woody stem of a vine, to a slip, cutting, or shoot of a vine, also to a bough of a tree.** Refs.: Num. 13:23; Ezek. 15:2. It was used in pagan cult practices and was placed on or near the nose (Ezek. 8:17); also translated twig. It indicates vine slips (Is. 17:10; also translated seedling, vine-branch, vine) or branches (Nah. 2:2: vine branch, vine). ¶
3 ***zāmiyr*** [masc. noun: זָמִיר <2159>; from PRUNE <2168>] ▶ **Preceded by *'ēṯ*, time, this word describes this as the time of (pruning) branches.** It was a joyous spring event (Song 2:12). It is also translated singing (see SONG <2158>). ¶
4 ***kippāh*** [fem. noun: כִּפָּה <3712>; fem. of HAND <3709>] ▶ **This word refers to a palm frond, a crowning bough in general; a shoot, a sprout.** It is used to designate palm fronds used to celebrate at the Feast of Tabernacles (see Lev. 23:40). It is used of fresh, sprouting branches (Job 15:32) as well as more developed palm branches (Is. 9:14; 19:15) but with reference to the leaders of Israel. ¶
5 ***nêṣer*** [masc. noun: נֵצֶר <5342>; from KEEP <5341> in the sense of greenness as a striking color] ▶ **This word indicates literally a shoot, a branch of a plant but is used figuratively of the Lord's servant, the Branch, who will rule in the messianic kingdom.** He comes from the roots of the family of Jesse (Is. 11:1), the chosen royal line in Israel. It refers to Israel as a whole as God's branch in a restored state (Is. 60:21). It indicates a person as part of a family line (Is. 14:9); as a descendant in particular (Dan. 11:7). ¶
6 ***salsillāh*** [fem. noun: סַלְסִלָּה <5552>; from VALUE (verb) <5541> (in the original sense of to hang up)] ▶
a. This word refers to vine tendrils or small branches that bear grapes. Ref.: Jer. 6:9. In judgment God would, figuratively, glean these tendrils. ¶
b. This word was taken by older translations to refer to a basket into which grapes were dropped. Ref.: Jer. 6:9. ¶
7 ***sa'iyp*** [masc. noun: סָעִיף <5585>; from LOP, LOP OFF <5586> (in relation to the top)] ▶ **This word also means a bough.** It is used of the strong, green branches of an olive tree (Is. 17:6). Figuratively, it depicts the "branches" of a city, forsaken like the desert (Is. 27:10). The Hebrew word also means a fissure, a crack; see CLEFT <5585>. ¶
8 ***ᵃnap*** [Aramaic masc. noun: עֲנַף <6056>; corresponding to <6057> below] ▶ **This word refers to a bough of a tree.** It depicts, in Nebuchadnezzar's vision, the branches of a great symbolic tree (Dan. 4:12, 14, 21), the tree signifying Babylon and its king. ¶
9 ***'ānāp*** [masc. noun: עָנָף <6057>; from an unused root meaning to cover] ▶ **This word designates the bough of a tree.** In Leviticus 23:40, it refers to palm branches; in Psalm 80:10, it indicates the branches or boughs of a cedar tree; various branches in Ezekiel (Ezek. 17:8, 23; 36:8). It is used figuratively of the Assyrian Empire (Ezek. 31:3); and of the seed of the wicked (Mal. 4:1). ¶
10 ***pō'rāh, pu'rāh*** [fem. noun: פֹּארָה, פֻּארָה <6288>; from GLORIFY <6286>]
a. This word refers to boughs of a tree sent out to expand its influence. It functions

in a figurative sense in a parable in Ezekiel (Ezek. 17:6; also translated shoot, sprig, bough) of Assyria's growth and expansion (Ezek. 31:5, 6, 8, 12, 13). ¶

b. This word is used figuratively of the boughs or branches of Assyria. Ref.: Is. 10:33. ¶

[11] ***ṣemaḥ*** [masc. noun: צֶמַח <6780>; from GROW <6779>] ▶ **This word means a growth, a crop.** It refers to what grows on the ground, domesticated or wild (Gen. 19:25; Ps. 65:10; Is. 61:11). It is used especially of the restored fertility of God's land and people (Is. 4:2). It is used figuratively of a descendant, a Branch, of David (Jer. 23:5; 33:15; Zech. 3:8; 6:12); of Jerusalem (Ezek. 16:7). It refers to grain on the stalks (Hos. 8:7). *

[12] ***śôḵ, śôḵāh*** [masc. noun: שׂוֹךְ, שׂוֹכָה <7754>; from HEDGE (MAKE A) <7753>] ▶

a. This word refers to a bough of a tree; also translated bundle, bundle of brushwood. In context a bough is cut off and used to make a fire (Judg. 9:48).

b. This word has the same meaning as a., a bough cut from a tree to burn. Ref.: Judg. 9:49. ¶

[13] ***śāriyg*** [masc. noun: שָׂרִיג <8299>; from KNIT TOGETHER (BE) <8276> (in the sense of to be entwined)] ▶ **This word refers to woody stems, shoots, tendrils of a vine plant.** Refs.: Gen. 40:10, 12, but it is used in a figurative sense of days. It is used literally in Joel 1:7. ¶

– [14] Gen. 30:37–39, 41; Jer. 1:11 ➔ STICK <4731> [15] Job 8:16; 14:7 (tender branch); 15:30; Hos. 14:6 ➔ SHOOT (noun) <3127> [16] Job 14:9; 18:16; etc. ➔ HARVEST <7105> b. [17] Is. 16:8 ➔ PLANT (CHOICE, PRINCIPAL) <8291> [18] Is. 16:8 ➔ SHOOT (noun) <7976> [19] Is. 25:5 ➔ SONG <2158> [20] Ezek. 31:5 ➔ BOUGH <5634> [21] Zech. 4:12 ➔ GRAIN (HEAD OF, EAR OF) <7641>.

BRANCH (THICK) – Ezek. 19:11; 31:3 ➔ BOUGH (THICK).

BRANCHES – [1] ***nᵉṭiyšôṯ*** [fem. plur. noun: נְטִישׁוֹת <5189>; from FORSAKE <5203> (maybe in the sense of to disperse)] ▶ **This word means tendrils.** It refers to fresh branches or shoots of vines (Is. 18:5; also translated spreading branches). It is used figuratively and literally of Jerusalem (Jer. 5:10; KJV: battlements); and of Moab (Jer. 48:32; KJV, NKJV: plants) whom God will judge. ¶

[2] ***ʿᵒp̱a'yim*** [masc. plur. noun: עֳפָאִים <6073>; from an unused root meaning to cover] ▶ **This word refers to extensions, boughs of a tree, as a part of God's created world.** Ref.: Ps. 104:12. ¶

– [3] Song 7:8 ➔ FRUIT <5577>.

BRANCHES (FULL OF) – ***ʿānēp̱*** [adj.: עָנֵף <6058>; from the same as <6057>] ▶ **This word refers to an abundance of boughs put forth by a well-watered tree.** Ref.: Ezek. 19:10. ¶

BRAND – [1] Judg. 15:5 ➔ TORCH <3940> [2] Is. 50:11 ➔ FIREBRAND <2131> a. [3] Amos 4:11; Zech. 3:2 ➔ FIREBRAND <181>.

BRANDING – ***kiy*** [masc. noun: כִּי <3587>; from BURN (verb) <3554>] ▶ **This word denotes a scar or mark from burning.** It is used in a figurative way to mean disfigurement or scarring as opposed to beauty (Is. 3:24; KJV: burning). ¶

BRANDISH – [1] ***rāʿal*** [verb: רָעַל <7477>; a prim. root] ▶ **This word refers to waving, shaking, exhibiting one's sword in a threatening way.** It is a part of God's judgment upon the Assyrian capital (Nah. 2:3). ¶

– [2] Ezek. 32:10 ➔ FLY (verb) <5774> b.

BRASS – [1] Lev. 26:19; Job 40:18; Is. 48:4; etc. ➔ BRONZE <5154> [2] Job 6:12 ➔ BRONZE <5153> [3] Dan. 2:32, 35, 39; etc. ➔ BRONZE <5174>.

BRAVE – [1] ***'ammiyṣ, 'ammiṣ*** [adj.: אַמִּיץ, אַמִּץ <533>; from STRONG (BE) <553>] ▶ **This word signifies firm, powerful; together with *lēḇ* <3820> it is also translated courageous, stout of heart. It also means mighty, strong.** It is used to describe brave warriors (Amos 2:16) but also to depict the strength of God and His might (Job 9:4, 19; Is. 40:26), as well as His means of bringing judgment on peoples (Is. 28:2). It is used metaphorically to describe the strength or effectiveness of conspiracy (2 Sam. 15:12). ¶

[2] ***gibbôr, gibbōr*** [adj.: גִּבּוֹר, גִּבֹּר <1368>; intens. from the same as MAN <1397>] ▶ **This word also means strong, mighty.** It refers to God Himself as *'el gibbôr*, usually rendered as the Mighty God (Is. 10:21; Jer. 32:18). It is used to describe the Child born to rule and govern God's kingdom as Mighty God (Is. 9:6). The Lord is depicted as a mighty one for His people Israel, mighty to save (Deut. 10:17; Ps. 24:8; Zeph. 3:17). Angels are depicted as mighty in strength (Ps. 103:20). It describes the might and power of the messianic King (Ps. 45:3).

It means manly, strong, vigorous, and was a term of approbation (Gen. 10:8, 9; 1 Sam. 14:52; Ps. 112:2). It could be used of animals, such as a lion (Prov. 30:30), the mightiest beast. It refers regularly to warriors, heroes, champions in battle (1 Sam. 17:51; 2 Sam. 20:7; 2 Kgs. 24:16; Is. 21:17). It could be used in a bad sense to denote heroes at drinking wine (Is. 5:22). *

BRAVE MAN – Is. 33:7 ➔ VALIANT ONE <691>.

BRAY – [1] ***nāhaq*** [verb: נָהַק <5101>; a prim. root] ▶ **This word refers to uttering the harsh, grating cry of a donkey.** It is used of a loud, shrill sound of a wild ass or a donkey (Job 6:5); and of the despairing cries of persons existing as social outcasts (Job 30:7). ¶
– [2] Prov. 27:22 ➔ GRIND <3806>.

BRAZEN – [1] ***šalleṭeṯ*** [adj.: שַׁלֶּטֶת <7986>; from RULE OVER <7980>] ▶ **This word means impudent, domineering; it is also translated bold-faced, imperious.** It indicates an arrogant, insolent attitude of persons who care nothing about what others think of them (Ezek. 16:30). ¶
– [2] Prov. 7:13 ➔ STRENGTHEN <5810>.

BRAZIER – ***'aḥ*** [fem. noun: אָח <254>; of uncertain deriv.] ▶ **This word indicates a firepot of metal or clay.** Refs.: Jer. 36:22, 23; also translated hearth. This brazier was located in Jehoiakim's winter house where he burned the first draft of Jeremiah's prophecies. ¶

BREACH – [1] ***bāqiya'*** [masc. noun: בָּקִיעַ <1233>; from DIVIDE <1234>] ▶ **This word means a small fragment or break.** It refers to a crack or hole in the wall (Is. 22:9; also translated damage) of the City of David as a future prophetic picture of the fall of that city. It refers to the fragments (pieces, clefts, bits) of the small houses that will be left after the Lord judges His people Israel (Amos 6:11). ¶

[2] ***pereṣ*** [masc. noun: פֶּרֶץ <6556>; from BREAK OUT, BREAK DOWN <6555>] ▶ **This word indicates a gap, a break.** It refers to a rupture, a tear, a breaking up or shattering of something: a breach created in a wall of an enemy (2 Sam. 5:20); the breaking or rupture occurring in the process of childbirth (Gen. 38:29). It is used figuratively of separation created between persons or groups (Judg. 21:15). It refers to death, the ultimate breach in the fabric of life (Ps. 144:14); the death of newborn calves at birth and to an outbreaking of God's anger (2 Sam. 6:8). It is used figuratively of breaches in the walls of Israel, that is the failures of God's people to follow Him, misled by false prophets (Ezek. 13:5). *
– [3] Judg. 5:17 ➔ LANDING <4664> [4] 2 Kgs. 12:5–8, 12; 22:5 ➔ DAMAGE (noun) <919> [5] Prov. 17:14 ➔ OPEN <6362> [6] Amos 6:11 ➔ DEW <7447> c.

BREACH OF PROMISE – Num. 14:34 ➔ OPPOSITION <8569>.

BREAD – [1] ***leḥem*** [masc. noun: לֶחֶם <3899>; from EAT <3898>] ▶ **This word refers in a general sense to anything God has approved of for nourishment for humans or animals.** Refs.: Gen. 3:19; 25:34; Ps. 147:9. It often indicates grain which was used for preparing bread (Is.

28:28). The manna was bread from the Lord, heavenly bread (Ex. 16:4, 8, 12, 15; Neh. 9:15; Ps. 105:40). Bread was set on the table of showbread in the Tabernacle and termed the "bread of the presence" (Ex. 25:30). Some bread was used as a wave offering to the Lord (Lev. 23:17). Baked from the produce of the early harvest, this word indicates the "bread of the first fruits" (2 Kgs. 4:42). It was used in figurative language to indicate the bread of affliction or adversity (Deut. 16:3; Is. 30:20) or the bread of tears (Ps. 80:5). *

2 ***mā'ôg*** [masc. noun: מָעוֹג <4580>; from BAKE <5746>] ▶ **This word refers to a staple food available to even a poor person.** Ref.: 1 Kgs. 17:12; also translated cake, something baked. It is possibly used to stand for a whole meal, a banquet feast (Ps. 35:16), although its use in this verse is not clear. ¶

– 3 Gen. 40:16 ➔ WHITE, WHITE BREAD <2751> 4 2 Sam. 13:6, 8, 10 ➔ CAKE <3834>.

BREAD (MAKE) – 2 Sam. 13:6, 8 ➔ HEART (RAVISH THE) <3823>.

BREAD, LOAF OF BREAD – Gen. 18:6; Ex. 12:39; Num. 11:8; 1 Kgs. 17:13; 19:6; Ezek. 4:12 ➔ CAKE <5692>.

BREADTH – 1 ***merḥāḇ*** [masc. noun: מֶרְחָב <4800>; from ENLARGE <7337>] ▶ **This word refers to a large space, a spacious place. It indicates broadness, wideness.** In context it indicates the length and breadth of the earth; throughout the land (Hab. 1:6). It is used metaphorically to depict an open, free area; space; free from oppression and enemies (2 Sam. 22:20; Ps. 18:19: large, broad, spacious *place*); a blessed situation in life (Ps. 31:8; 118:5: wide, broad, spacious, large place). It is used of a big field (Hos. 4:16: large place, open country, large field, broad pasture, meadow). ¶

2 ***rōḥaḇ*** [masc. noun: רֹחַב <7341>; from ENLARGE <7337>] ▶ **This word means the distance between the two sides of something; it is also translated width.** It indicates the width of various objects: of the ark (Gen. 6:15); of land (Gen. 13:17); of the ark of the covenant (Ex. 25:10, 17, 23); of a bed (Deut. 3:11). It is used figuratively of great wisdom, breadth of mind (1 Kgs. 4:29); the Temple (2 Chr. 3:3). It refers to a great breadth or stretch of waters (Job 37:10). It is used often to depict the breadth of various parts of Ezekiel's Temple (Ezek. 40:5–7, 11, 13, 19–21; 41:1–5, etc.). It is used to refer to the width of a reconstructed Jerusalem (Zech. 2:2); and the width of a strange flying scroll (Zech. 5:2). *

– 3 Ezra 6:3; Dan. 3:1 ➔ WIDTH <6613>
4 Job 38:18 ➔ BROAD PLACE <7338>.

BREAK – 1 ***gāram*** [verb: גָּרַם <1633>; a prim. root] ▶

a. This word means to crush, to gnaw, to crush (bones), to chew. It describes Israel's action of crushing the bones of her enemies as she came out of Egypt (Num. 24:8). It is used figuratively to depict Judah gnawing the cup of judgment the Lord poured out on her (Ezek. 23:34). Some translators prefer to render it as to let something be left over (Zeph. 3:3, NIV, NASB, NKJV, ESV). ¶

b. A verb meaning to leave. It indicates letting something be left over (Zeph. 3:3). Others prefer to translate it as to gnaw (KJV). ¶

2 ***gāras*** [verb: גָּרַס <1638>; a prim. root] ▶ **This word means to be crushed, to be consumed, to be broken.** The soul wastes away or is crushed from longing after the Lord's ordinances (Ps. 119:20). It is used of teeth broken from grinding under the stress of God's judgments (Lam. 3:16) and oppression. ¶

3 ***nāp̱aṣ*** [verb: נָפַץ <5310>; a prim. root] ▶

a. This word means to shatter, to smash, to slay. It describes the action of shattering or breaking something: pitchers (Judg. 7:19; Jer. 22:28; 48:12); ashlar stones crushed, pulverized into powder (Is. 27:9); possibly breaking into smaller pieces timber, which has been loaded on rafts or bound together as rafts (1 Kgs. 5:9; see also b.); figuratively, of defeating the power of nations as pottery is broken (Ps. 2:9; Jer. 50:20–23); of breaking the political and military might of God's holy people (Dan. 12:7); of slaying infants by crushing their skulls (Ps. 137:9; Jer. 13:14). Used of persons, the word can indicate their dispersal, scattering (Is. 11:12). ¶

b. This word also means to spread out, to disperse, to scatter. It is used in ways similar to a. It indicates the dispersal of peoples across the earth (Gen. 9:19; also translated to overspread); of persons drifting away because of losing interest (1 Sam. 13:11); of dispersing timber that has been loaded on rafts or bound together as rafts, or possibly breaking timber into smaller pieces (1 Kgs. 5:9: to discharge, to break up, to break apart, to separate). See a. also. ¶

[4] ***nāṯas*** [verb: נָתַס <5420>; a prim. root] ▶ **This word means to shatter, to knock apart, to destroy.** It is used figuratively of breaking up, of complicating, or of destroying one's way of life (Job 30:13; KJV: to mar). ¶

[5] ***nāṯa'*** [verb: נָתַע <5421>; for DESTROY <5422>] ▶ **This word means to crush, to shatter, to crack; to defeat.** It occurs in an idiomatic phrase, the teeth of young lions are shattered (Job 4:10); i.e., they are defeated, rendered helpless. The reference is to the wicked depicted as young lions. ¶

[6] ***nāṯaq*** [verb: נָתַק <5423>; a prim. root] ▶ **This word also means to tear away, to pull away, to pull up, to draw away, to lift up, to remove.** It means to break or snap a rope or cord (Judg. 16:9; Eccl. 4:12), the cord standing symbolically for ties of friendship in Ecclesiastes. It is used of drawing out an army from an area to deceive the soldiers (Josh. 8:6, 16; Judg. 20:32); of something that has been mutilated or damaged by tearing (Lev. 22:24). It is used of the soles of feet lifted up onto dry ground when walking out of the River Jordan (Josh. 4:18). In a figurative sense, it describes plans or counsels being ruined, torn apart (Job 17:11); or of political or military control being broken (Ps. 2:3; Nah. 1:13). It is used (in a comparison to separating out impurities in a smelting process) of the wicked who are not removed (Jer. 6:29). It is used in an allegory of pulling up the roots of a plant or tree (Ezek. 17:9). *

[7] ***pārar*** [verb: פָּרַר <6565>; a prim. root] ▶ **This word means to divide, to frustrate. It is often used in conjunction with a covenant, i.e., to not respect such an agreement.** The Lord warned the Israelites what would happen if they broke the covenant with Him (Lev. 26:15); and pledged to them that He would not break it (Lev. 26:44). Asa, king of Judah, asked the king of Aram to break a covenant Aram had made with Israel (1 Kgs. 15:19). This word is also used to refer to the frustration of plans, as the enemies of Israel did to the Israelites trying to rebuild the Temple (Ezra 4:5). However, the Lord's purposes cannot be frustrated (Is. 14:27). *

[8] ***pāṯaṯ*** [verb: פָּתַת <6626>; a prim. root] ▶ **This word means to divide (into parts), to crumble, to part (in pieces).** It describes the breaking up or crumbling of a fried fine-meal offering. Oil was poured on it (Lev. 2:6). ¶

[9] ***rāṣaṣ*** [verb: רָצַץ <7533>; a prim. root] ▶ **This word means to push, to crush; to oppress; to struggle together.** It is used of infants tussling while still in the womb, pushing on each other, struggling together (Gen. 25:22). It describes one nation crushing, oppressing another nation as part of God's judgments (Deut. 28:33; Judg. 10:8). It refers to physically crushing something, e.g., a person's head (Judg. 9:53); or other physical objects (2 Kgs. 23:12). It is used of oppressing, treating another person unfairly or violently in any way, even unknowingly (1 Sam. 12:3, 4). It describes the crushing of Leviathan's head, the monster's head (Ps. 74:14). Its use in Ecclesiastes 12:6 is figurative, breaking the golden bowl of life, dying. Egypt is figuratively described as a crushed reed (Is. 36:6). It describes the breaking or ripping open of a person's hands or shoulders, again applied in a figurative sense to nations (Ezek. 29:7). Crushed by judgment from God describes the state of a nation receiving God's devastating blows (Hos. 5:11). The fat cows of Bashan (a figure of rich, effeminate noblemen or of wealthy,

heartless women) are described as crushing the needy to meet their cravings for luxury (Amos 4:1). *

[10] ***šāḇar*** [verb: שָׁבַר <7665>; a prim. root] ▶ **This word means to burst, to smash, to smash into pieces, to shatter, to tear down, to bring to birth. The word is most often used to express bursting or smashing.** Other meanings include God's actions against stubborn pride (Lev. 26:19); or a metaphor for deliverance expressed figuratively by the breaking of a yoke (Jer. 28:2). In a figurative sense, the word describes the breaking of Pharaoh's arms (Ezek. 30:21, 22). It also depicts the literal smashing or shattering of the tablets of the commandments (Ex. 32:19). Further expressions of the word can mean to bring to the moment of birth (Is. 66:9); to break down or destroy a people (Is. 14:25); to break objects of material quality (Gen. 19:9; Lev. 6:28; Jer. 49:35). *

– [11] 2 Sam. 22:35; Ps. 18:34 ➔ BEND <5181> [12] Job 24:16 ➔ DIG <2864> [13] Job 31:39 ➔ BREATHE <5301> [14] Job 39:15 ➔ THRESH <1758> [15] Ps. 38:8; 44:19; 51:8, 17 ➔ CRUSH <1794> [16] Ps. 60:2 ➔ TEAR OPEN <6480> [17] Eccl. 12:6 ➔ BIND <7576> [18] Song 2:17; 4:6 ➔ BREATHE <6315> [19] Is. 59:5 ➔ CRUSH <2115> [20] Jer. 16:7 ➔ DIVIDE <6536> [21] Ezek. 17:19 ➔ NOTHING (BRING TO) <6329> [22] Joel 2:7 ➔ SWERVE <5670> [23] Mic. 3:3 ➔ BREAK FORTH <6476> b. [24] See DIVIDE <1234>.

BREAK (UTTERLY) – Jer. 51:58 ➔ STRIP <6209> a.

BREAK AWAY, BREAK OFF – ***pᵉraq*** [Aramaic verb: פְּרַק <6562>; corresponding to BREAK OFF <6561>] ▶ **This word means to separate oneself, to renounce.** It means to tear oneself away from something, to break off from it, in context from the practice of wicked oppression of certain classes of society (Dan. 4:27). ¶

BREAK DOWN – [1] Num. 24:17; Is. 22:5 ➔ DIG <6979> b. [2] Hos. 10:2 ➔ NECK (BREAK THE) <6202>.

BREAK FORTH – [1] ***pāṣaḥ*** [verb: פָּצַח <6476>; a prim. root] ▶

a. This word means to burst out in singing. It means to make a loud noise, to shout forth. It is used of the people of the earth bursting forth in jubilation (Is. 14:7); of the mountains or nature breaking out in joy after holding in their excitement (Is. 44:23; 49:13; 52:9; 55:12). Other refs.: Ps. 98:4 (to make a joyful noise, to shout joyfully); Is. 54:1. ¶

b. This word means to crush. It refers to shattering or crushing something. In context the "bones" of God's people are shattered (Mic. 3:3). ¶

– [2] Job 38:8; Ezek. 32:2 ➔ GUSH <1518> [3] Dan. 7:2 ➔ STIR UP <1519>.

BREAK IN PIECES – ***rᵉʿaʿ*** [Aramaic verb: רְעַע <7490>; corresponding to BAD (BE) <7489>] ▶ **This word also means to shatter, to crush. The term occurs only twice in the Old Testament; both are located within the same passage in the book of Daniel.** In interpreting King Nebuchadnezzar's dream, Daniel declared that the fourth kingdom, represented by the legs of iron and feet of iron mixed with clay of the statue, would be as strong as iron and would break the previously mentioned kingdoms into pieces (Dan. 2:40). This term is closely related to the Hebrew verb *rāʿaʿ* (<7489>), to be bad. ¶

BREAK INTO PIECES – See CRUSH <1855>.

BREAK OF DAY – Dan. 6:19 ➔ at break of day ➔ very early in the morning ➔ MORNING <5053>.

BREAK LOOSE – Jer. 2:23 ➔ TRAVERSE <8308>.

BREAK OFF – [1] ***pāraq*** [verb: פָּרַק <6561>; a prim. root] ▶ **This word means to remove, to tear off, to rescue. It carries with it the feeling and implication of violent actions.** It is used in a figurative sense of breaking a yoke of oppression (Gen. 27:40); of roughly removing

gold ornaments from someone (Ex. 32:2, 3, 24). It describes tearing apart rocks violently (1 Kgs. 19:11); in a figurative sense, the wicked ripping apart the souls (lives) of the righteous (Ps. 7:2). It describes the way Israel had been ripped and torn apart by her enemies (Ezek. 19:12). *
– [2] Ps. 89:33 ➔ NOTHING (BRING TO) <6329>.

BREAK OUT – [1] ***gāla'*** [verb: גָּלַע <1566>; a prim. root] ▶ **This word means to expose, to burst forth, to meddle with, to be obstinate; it is also translated to start, to quarrel.** It expresses quarreling and being obstinate by insisting on having one's own way (Prov. 17:14; 20:3). It indicates separating oneself from others to seek one's own wishes (Prov. 18:1: to quarrel against, to rage against, to break out against, to start quarrels against, to intermeddle). ¶
[2] ***pāraḥ*** [verb: פָּרַח <6524>; a prim. root] ▶
a. This word means to blossom, to flourish, to erupt. It is used of vine blossoms or other blossoming plants coming out, opening up (Gen. 40:10; Song 6:11; 7:12; Hab. 3:17); or fresh green shoots or sprigs growing from a stump (Job 14:9). It is used of all kinds of sores or boils breaking out on a person's skin (Ex. 9:9, 10; Lev. 13:12, 20, 25). It is used of the divinely guarded sprouting of wooden rods (Num. 17:5). Figuratively, it indicates the increase and prospering of the righteous (Ps. 72:7; Prov. 11:28; 14:11); or of evil, arrogance coming to fruition (Ezek. 7:10; Hos. 10:4). *
b. This verb also means to fly. It is used of things which fly. It refers most likely to birds in Ezekiel 13:20. The phrase *lᵉp̱orḥôṯ* is difficult, but in context, as if birds (flying things), is a probable translation. Souls, lives were being hunted as if they were birds (flying creatures). ¶
[3] ***śāṯar*** [verb: שָׂתַר <8368>; a prim. root] ▶ **This word refers to skin eruptions of some kind, possibly boils, tumors, etc. that burst out and appear quickly on one's skin.** Ref.: 1 Sam. 5:9. ¶
– [4] Judg. 20:33 ➔ GUSH <1518> [5] Ps. 78:21 ➔ KINDLE <5400>.

BREAK OUT, BREAK DOWN – ***pāraṣ*** [verb: פָּרַץ <6555>; a prim. root] ▶ **This word means to burst forth.** It indicates the powerful multiplication and spreading of something in all directions (Gen. 28:14), especially the spread of God's people so they would be a blessing to all peoples according to the promises to Abraham. It describes the growth of the families of God's people (Gen. 30:30, 43); especially of the twelve tribes in Egypt (Ex. 1:12). It is used of making a breach, a bursting, an urging of a person to do something, of something going forth or out: a birth, breaching the womb (Gen. 38:29); of a breaking out of God's wrath against a person or people (Ex. 19:22, 24; 2 Sam. 5:20; 6:8); of breaching a wall (2 Kgs. 14:13); of broken walls that have been crumbled, breached (Neh. 2:13); of tearing down, demolishing a wall (Is. 5:5). It refers to breaching the earth, drilling a mine shaft, a hole into it (Job 28:4). It takes on the sense of urging or pushing someone (2 Kgs. 5:23). God's plagues broke forth in judgment (Ps. 106:29). Wine vats or containers are described as bursting forth, breaking out with new wine (Prov. 3:10). ¶

BREAK THROUGH – See PULL DOWN <2040>.

BREAK UP – ***niyr*** [verb: נִיר <5214>; a root probably identical with that of LAMP <5216>), through the idea of the gleam of a fresh furrow] ▶ **This word is used in an agricultural sense of plowing untilled ground.** In context it is used of Israel's repentance and returning to God (Jer. 4:3; Hos. 10:12). ¶

BREAKING – [1] ***reṣaḥ*** [masc. noun: רֶצַח <7524>; from KILL <7523>] ▶ **This word indicates slaughtering; shattering. It indicates a violent smiting, a crushing of a person's bones.** In context it is used figuratively of the impact the enemies' words have on the psalmist emotionally and spiritually (Ps. 42:10); it is also translated sword, deadly wound, mortal agony. Other ref.: Ezek. 21:22 (slaughter, murder). ¶

– [2] Ezek. 21:6 ➔ DESTRUCTION <7670>.

BREAKING IN – ***maḥteret̲*** [fem. noun: מַחְתֶּרֶת <4290>; from DIG <2864> (in the sense of to break)] ▶ **This word designates a burglary, a forced entry; it is also translated breaking up (KJV), secret search (KJV and NKJV).** It is used of the act of a burglar or thief who would attempt to gain entrance into a house to steal or to loot it (Ex. 22:2; Jer. 2:34). ¶

BREAKING UP – Ex. 22:2 ➔ BREAKING IN <4290>.

BREAST – [1] ***dad̲*** [masc. noun: דַּד <1717>; apparently from the same as LOVER <1730>] ▶ **This word refers to the organ in which mammary glands are located; it also denotes a nipple.** It refers to a wife's breasts (Prov. 5:19), which are to satisfy her husband alone. It is used figuratively to describe the breasts of Israel pictured as a young girl (Ezek. 23:3, 8, 21) in her early prostitution among the nations; it is also translated bosom, teats. ¶

[2] ***ḥāzeh*** [masc. noun: חָזֶה <2373>; from SEE <2372>] ▶ **This word refers to a brisket. It is a technical priestly and sacrificial term denoting the front part of a sacrificial animal.** It was used as a wave offering and in the installation of the priests (Ex. 29:26, 27; Lev. 8:29); in the offering of peace or well-being (Lev. 7:30; 9:20, 21); as part of Hazabite or Nazirite offering (Num. 6:20). It was required of Aaron and his sons (Lev. 7:31, 34; 10:14, 15; Num. 18:18). ¶

[3] ***šad̲, šōd̲*** [masc. noun: שַׁד, שֹׁד <7699>] ▶ **a. This word is used of the milk-producing organs of both women and animals that nurture newborns; the chest area of men or women.** Ref.: Gen. 49:25. Fertile breasts are a blessing from God. The breasts sustain a child at birth (Job 3:12; 24:9; Ps. 22:9; Song 8:1; Is. 28:9). The breasts are used to depict tender loving care in an amorous setting (Song 1:13); and are depictions of beauty (Song 4:5; 7:3; 8:8, 10). The beating of one's breasts, male or female, was a sign of despair (Is. 32:12; Ezek. 23:34). For a mother to withhold her breasts from her baby, which even a mother jackal does not do, is a sign of cruelty (Lam. 4:3). The development of breasts is a sign of maturing (Ezek. 16:7). The breasts of wanton young women are mentioned figuratively in the Lord's reproach of Samaria and Jerusalem for their alliance with Egypt (Ezek. 23:3, 21).

b. This word is also used as a metaphor taken from a newborn child drawing nourishment from a nursing mother. It is used figuratively of the "breasts" of royalty or kings (Is. 60:16); and of the breasts of Jerusalem satisfying her children (Is. 66:11). *

– [4] Dan. 2:32 ➔ CHEST <2306> [5] Hos. 13:8 ➔ CAUL <5458>.

BREASTPIECE – ***ḥōšen*** [masc. noun: חֹשֶׁן <2833>; from an unused root prob. meaning to contain or sparkle] ▶ **This word is also translated breastplate. It was a pouch or a bag worn by the high priest, and it was highly decorative, made by a skilled workman. It was similar to the ephod in construction and featured gold, blue, purple, scarlet material, and fine twined linen. It was bound to the ephod.** It also bore stones representing the tribes of Israel. It carried within it the Urim and Thummin and was worn over Aaron's heart (Ex. 28:15, 22–24, 26, 28–30; Lev. 8:8). Other refs.: Ex. 25:7; 28:4; 29:5; 35:9, 27; 39:8, 9, 15–17, 19, 21. ¶

BREASTPLATE – Ex. 28:15, 22–24, 26, 28–30; Lev. 8:8; etc. ➔ BREASTPIECE <2833>.

BREASTS – Job 21:24 ➔ BODY <5845>.

BREATH – [1] ***nepeš*** [fem. noun: נֶפֶשׁ <5315>; from REST (verb) <5314>] ▶ **This word refers to that which inhales and exhales. It also means the inner being with its thoughts and emotions. It is used 753 times in the Old Testament and has a broad range of meanings.** Most of its uses fall into these categories: breath, literally or figuratively (Jer. 15:9); the inner being with its thoughts and emotions (Judg. 10:16;

Prov. 14:10; Ezek. 25:6); and by extension, the whole person (Gen. 12:5; Lev. 4:2; Ezek. 18:4). Moreover, the term can cover the animating force of a person or his or her dead body (Lev. 21:11; Num. 6:6; Jer. 2:34). It is even applied to animals in a number of the above senses: the breath (Job 41:21); the inner being (Jer. 2:24); the whole creature (Gen. 1:20); and the animating force (Lev. 17:11). When this word is applied to a person, it doesn't refer to a specific part of a human being. The Scriptures view a person as a composite whole, fully relating to God and not divided in any way (Deut. 6:5; cf. 1 Thes. 5:23). *

[2] ***nišmāh*** [Aramaic fem. noun: נִשְׁמָה <5396>; corresponding to <5397> below] ▶ **This word indicates the spirit that animates and makes a person alive; it is also translated life, life-breath.** God holds our breath in His hands (Dan. 5:23). ¶

[3] ***n^e^šāmāh*** [fem. noun: נְשָׁמָה <5397>; from GASP <5395>] ▶ **This word refers to a blowing, respiration; it also means wind, spirit. Its meaning is parallel to *nep̱eš* (<5315>) above and *rûaḥ* (SPIRIT <7307>).** It refers to the breath of God as a destructive wind that kills and clears the foundations of the earth (2 Sam. 22:16; Job 4:9); a stream of brimstone that kindles a fire (Is. 30:33); a freezing wind that produces frost (Job 37:10); the source of life that vitalizes humanity (Job 33:4). The breath of humans is recognized as the source and center of life (1 Kgs. 17:17; Job 27:3). It is also understood that such breath originates with God, and He can withhold it, thereby withholding life from humanity (Gen. 2:7; Job 34:14; Is. 42:5). Therefore, people's breath is a symbol of their weakness and frailty (Is. 2:22). Since breath is the source of life, by extension, this word is also used to represent life and anything that is alive (Deut. 20:16; Josh. 10:40; 11:11, 14; Is. 57:16). Like *nep̱eš* (BREATH <5315>), this word also connotes the human mind or intellect (Prov. 20:27). *

– [4] See SPIRIT <7307>.

BREATH (GASP FOR) – ***yāp̱aḥ*** [verb: יָפַח <3306>; a prim. root] ▶ **This word means to inhale and exhale with difficulty, to struggle for air.** It is used in a metaphor to personify the last efforts of labored breathing by Jerusalem, the daughter of Zion, before her enemies (Jer. 4:31; also translated to bewail oneself). ¶

BREATH OUT – ***yāp̱êaḥ*** [adj.: יָפֵחַ <3307>; from BREATH (GASP FOR) <3306>] ▶ **This word indicates snorting, exhaling.** It is used figuratively to indicate the breathing out violence (*ḥāmāṣ*) against the psalmist by his enemies (Ps. 27:12; also translated spouting). ¶

BREATHE – [1] ***nāp̱aḥ*** [verb: נָפַח <5301>; a prim. root] ▶ **This word means to exhale, to expel air, to blow.** In a figurative sense it is used of God blowing the breath of life into Adam (Gen. 2:7). It refers to a fire that is not blown, meaning not fanned to expand it (Job 20:26). It means to harm or to cause failure, perhaps death (Job 31:39; the expression "to breathe one's last" is also translated "to lose one's life," "to break one's spirit"). It is used of blowing something like smoke (Job 41:20: seething, boiling); of a blacksmith's use of something like bellows to heat up his coals (Is. 54:16; Ezek. 22:20, 21: to blow). It depicts the rising steam of a bubbling pot (Jer. 1:13: seething, boiling). It is used of the four winds blowing to create life (Ezek. 37:9). It is used of either blowing on an offering or sniffing it in disdain (Mal. 1:13: to sneer, to sniff, to snuff, to snort); or of something being swept away by the Lord (Hag. 1:9: to blow, to blow away). Other ref.: Jer. 15:9. ¶

[2] ***pûaḥ*** [verb: פּוּחַ <6315>; a prim. root] ▶ **The word is only used in poetic contexts in the Hebrew Bible and means to blow.** In the Song of Songs, the expression until the day breathes refers to the early morning when shadows flee (Song 2:17; 4:6; also translated to break); and the north wind is told to blow on the garden (Song 4:16). But just as often, the word implies a negative connotation, such as to snort at an enemy (Ps. 10:5; also translated to sneer, to puff); to incite a city (Prov. 29:8); or the Lord to blow out His anger (Ezek. 21:31). In a

unique usage, Proverbs uses the verb to refer to speaking lies (Prov. 6:19; 14:5, 25; 19:5, 9); but once for speaking truth (Prov. 12:17). Other ref.: Hab. 2:3. ¶

BREATHING – Lam. 3:56 ➔ RELIEF <7309>.

BREATHING ONE'S LAST – Job 11:20 ➔ lit.: breathing out life ➔ BREATHING OUT <4646>.

BREATHING OUT – ***mappāḥ*** [masc. noun: מַפָּח <4646>; from BREATHE <5301>] ► **This word means exhaling (of life), expiring; it comes from the verb *nāp̱aḥ* (<5301>), meaning to breathe or to blow, and occurs only once in the Old Testament.** In Job 11:20, this word describes the soul that expires. ¶

BREED – [1] Gen. 30:38, 39, 41; 31:10 ➔ CONCEIVE <3179> [2] Ex. 16:20 ➔ EXALTED <7426> b.

BREEDING – Zeph. 2:9 ➔ POSSESSED <4476>.

BRIAR – Mic. 7:4 ➔ BRIER <2312>.

BRIBE (noun) – [1] ***šōḥaḏ*** [masc. noun: שֹׁחַד <7810>; from REWARD (GIVE A) <7809>] ► **This word refers to what is given in a situation to influence persons to act or think in a way they would not normally do. It also refers to a reward, a gift.** It was often given to pervert justice and to blind the judgment of even good persons (Ex. 23:8; Deut. 16:19). God does not take bribes (Deut. 10:17). The person who took a bribe was cursed by God (Deut. 27:25). The perversion of justice through bribes was a major downfall of Israel (1 Sam. 8:3). A bribe could consist of a major political gift or present to another king or nation, a glorified bribe (1 Kgs. 15:19). *
– [2] Mic. 7:3 ➔ RECOMPENSE (noun) <7966> [3] See RANSOM (noun) <3724>.

BRIBE (verb) – Ezek. 16:33 ➔ REWARD (GIVE A) <7809>.

BRICK – ***lᵉḇênāh*** [fem. noun: לְבֵנָה <3843>; from BRICK (MAKE) <3835>] ► **This was a major man-made building material, evidently dried, not fired.** Refs.: Gen. 11:3; Ex. 1:14; 5:7, 8, 16, 18, 19; 24:10. The Israelites used such brick in forbidden rites on which to burn incense (Is. 65:3). It was used as material to write or draw on (Ezek. 4:1), as Ezekiel did. Other ref.: Is. 9:10. ¶

BRICK (MAKE) – ***lāḇên*** [verb: לָבֵן <3835>; a prim. root] ► **This word is used of the entire process of molding small rectangular blocks for various construction projects both at Babel and in Egypt.** Refs.: Gen. 11:3; Ex. 5:7, 14. The Hebrew word also means to make white, to make spotless; see WHITE (MAKE) <3835>. ¶

BRICK COURTYARD, BRICK PAVEMENT, BRICK TERRACE – Jer. 43:9 ➔ BRICK KILN <4404>.

BRICK KILN – ***malbên*** [masc. noun: מַלְבֵּן <4404>; from BRICK (MAKE) <3835> denom.] ► **The Hebrew word refers to a mold for making small rectangular building blocks; it is also translated brick work, brickmaking, brick mold.** It designates a mold for setting bricks (2 Sam. 12:31; Nah. 3:14). It is used of the brick floor in Pharaoh's palace in Egypt (Jer. 43:9; also translated brick terrace, brick courtyard, brick pavement). ¶

BRICK MOLD – Nah. 3:14 ➔ BRICK KILN <4404>.

BRICK WORK – 2 Sam. 12:31; Nah. 3:14 ➔ BRICK KILN <4404>.

BRICKMAKING – 2 Sam. 12:31 ➔ BRICK KILN <4404>.

BRIDAL PAYMENT – Gen. 34:12; Ex. 22:17; 1 Sam. 18:25 ➔ DOWRY <4119>.

BRIDE – ***kallāh*** [fem. noun: כַּלָּה <3618>; from PERFECT (MAKE) <3634>] ► **This word refers to a spouse (as perfect), usually just before or after her marriage;**

it refers also to a daughter-in-law. In the biblical world, it refers to a woman under the authority of her father, then of her husband and father-in-law. It indicates specifically a young daughter-in-law (Gen. 11:31; Hos. 4:13, 14); a young married woman, a bride (Is. 49:18). *

BRIDE-PRICE – Gen. 34:12; Ex. 22:17; 1 Sam. 18:25 ➔ DOWRY <4119>.

BRIDE-PRICE (PAY, GIVE) – Ex. 22:16 ➔ ENDOW <4117>.

BRIDEGROOM – Ex. 4:25, 26; Ps. 19:5; Is. 61:10; 62:5; Jer. 7:34; 16:9; 25:10; 33:11; Joel 2:16 ➔ SON-IN-LAW <2860>.

BRIDLE – [1] ***meṯeg*** [masc. noun: מֶתֶג <4964>; from an unused root meaning to curb] ▶ **This word denotes an instrument used to control an animal, especially a horse, camel, etc.** Ref.: Prov. 26:3. The phrase *meṯeg h*^{a}*'mmāh* means to take control (2 Sam. 8:1; see METHEG AMMAH <4965>). It is used figuratively of the Lord bridling the king of Assyria (2 Kgs. 19:28; Is. 37:29); it is also translated bit. Persons were not made to be bridled (Ps. 32:9: bit). ¶

[2] ***resen*** [masc. noun: רֶסֶן <7448>; from an unused root meaning to curb] ▶

a. This word indicates control exercised over something, someone, or a behavioral pattern; it is also translated restraint. Ref.: Job 30:11. It may indicate the means used to restrain something (Job 41:13), e.g., a bridle (Ps. 32:9). It is used figuratively of God's leading the nations with a bridle (Is. 30:28).

b. A masculine noun meaning mail, armor. It refers to a protective covering of some kind, mail, armor, a flexible body armor. In context it refers to the natural protective covering of Leviathan (Job 41:13). ¶

– [3] Ps. 39:1 ➔ MUZZLE (noun) <4269>.

BRIER – [1] ***ḥēḏeq*** [masc. noun: חֵדֶק <2312>; from an unused root meaning to sting] ▶ **This word refers to prickly plants, thorns and the nightshade of the Jordan Valley, an unpleasant, undesirable plant.** It is used in a simile to represent derisively the best leader Israel has (Mic. 7:4). In a proverb, it indicates the way of the lazy, i.e., they cannot bring themselves to traverse the road they need to in order to succeed (Prov. 15:19: thorn). ¶

[2] ***sārāḇ*** [masc. noun: סָרָב <5621>; from an unused root meaning to sting] ▶ **This word refers to a nettle-like shrub with prickly leaves and heads with prickly stickers.** Ref.: Ezek. 2:6; NASB: thistle. In context it describes bothersome, troublesome people of Israel. ¶

[3] ***sirpaḏ*** [masc. noun: סִרְפַּד <5636>; from BURN (verb) <5635>] ▶ **This word refers to a shrub with prickly, spiny stems or leaves, possibly a prickly type of weed.** Their presence indicates a forsaken, uncared for area (Is. 55:13; NASB: nettle). ¶

[4] ***šāmiyr*** [masc. noun: שָׁמִיר <8068>; from KEEP <8104> in the original sense of pricking] ▶ **This word refers to prickly, scrambling plants or shrubs, always an unwanted feature of plants growing wild.** Refs.: Is. 5:6; 7:23–25; 32:13. It is said that wickedness consumes even briers and thorns in its destructive capacity (Is. 9:18). Other refs.: Is. 10:17; 27:4. For another meaning of the Hebrew word, see DIAMOND <8068>. ¶

– [5] Job 31:40 ➔ THORN <2336>.

BRIERS – ***barqᵉniym*** [masc. plur. noun: בַּרְקֳנִים <1303>; from LIGHTNING <1300>] ▶ **This word denotes the wild desert prickly plants used by Gideon to punish the kings of Midian after catching them.** Refs.: Judg. 8:7, 16. ¶

BRIGANDINES – Jer. 46:4; 51:3 ➔ ARMOR <5630>.

BRIGHT – [1] ***bāhiyr*** [adj.: בָּהִיר <925>; from an unused root (meaning to be bright)] ▶ **This word describes the exceeding brilliance of the sun right after the wind has cleared the skies following a storm.** This is an example of one of God's marvels in the created order (Job 37:21). ¶

– [2] 2 Chr. 4:16 ➔ POLISH <4838> [3] Song 5:14 ➔ POLISHED <6247> [4] Song 6:10 ➔ PURE <1249> [5] Ezek. 1:13 ➔ BRIGHTNESS <5051> [6] Ezek. 27:19 ➔ WROUGHT <6219> [7] Nah. 3:3 ➔ FLAME <3851>.

BRIGHT (BE) – [1] Job 25:5 ➔ SHINE <166> [2] Lam. 4:7 ➔ PURE (BE) <2141>.

BRIGHTEN – Ezra 9:8; Eccl. 8:1 ➔ LIGHT (GIVE) <215>.

BRIGHTNESS – [1] ***zōhar*** [masc. noun: זֹהַר <2096>; from WARN <2094> (in the sense of to shine)] ▶ **This word refers to the appearance of a being like a man whom Ezekiel saw in a vision.** From his loins and up, he was clothed in brightness (Ezek. 8:2). It also describes figuratively the resurrected righteous who will shine like the brightness of the heavens (stars) (Dan. 12:3). ¶

[2] ***ziyw*** [Aramaic masc. noun: זִיו <2122>; corresponding to ZIV <2099>] ▶ **This word means radiancy; it is also translated splendor, dazzling.** It is used to indicate the brightness or splendor of a huge metallic statue in Daniel 2:31 as well as the glory, splendor, and impressiveness of the city of Babylon (Dan. 4:36). It describes a fresh-looking complexion or cheerful expression of a person's face that changes or pales under terrifying circumstances (Dan. 5:6, 9, 10; 7:28); the word is translated face, countenance, color. ¶

[3] ***nōgah*** [fem. noun: נֹגַהּ <5051>; from LIGHTEN <5050>] ▶ **This word indicates the illumination of some light source; it is also translated bright, flash, glow, light, lightning, radiance, shining, splendor, sunshine.** Such light sources are: God's brightness (2 Sam. 22:13; Ps. 18:12; Is. 60:3; Hab. 3:4, 11); the light at dawn from the sun and from the moon at night (2 Sam. 23:4; Prov. 4:18; in a simile, Is. 60:19); light from a great blazing fire (Is. 4:5); moral and ethical understanding in the Lord's ways (Is. 50:10); the light and brightness of righteousness (Is. 62:1); light from God's glory (Ezek. 1:4, 13, 27, 28; 10:4). Other refs.: Joel 2:10; 3:15; Amos 5:20. ¶

[4] ***nᵉgōhāh*** [fem. noun: נְגֹהָה <5054>; from <5051> above] ▶ **The word is used of times of blessing, prosperity, and good news; a message or event of hope amid a setting of gloom and despair.** Ref.: Is. 59:9. ¶

– [5] Job 31:26 ➔ PRECIOUS <3368> [6] Ezek. 28:7, 17 ➔ SPLENDOR <3314>.

BRIGHTNESS (HAVE) – Job 25:5 ➔ SHINE <166>.

BRIMSTONE – ***gopriyṯ*** [fem. noun: גָּפְרִית <1614>; prob. fem. from GOPHER <1613>] ▶ **This word refers to an inflammable mineral substance; it is also translated sulfur.** It indicates brimstone as a part of the judgment on Sodom and Gomorrah (Gen. 19:24). In a figurative sense, it refers to God's judgment on a wicked person (Ps. 11:6; Ezek. 38:22). The breath of God is depicted as brimstone setting Topheth, a pagan place of worship, on fire (Is. 30:33). Other refs.: Deut. 29:23; Job 18:15; Is. 34:9. ¶

BRING – [1] ***gûz*** [verb: גּוּז <1468>] ▶ **This verb speaks of wind transporting quails over the land from the sea.** Ref.: Num. 11:31; also translated to drive. The Hebrew word also means to pass away (Ps. 90:10); see CUT OFF <1468>. ¶

[2] ***yāḇal*** [verb: יָבַל <2986>; a prim. root] ▶ **This word means to convey; it is also translated to carry, to bear along.** It is used of bringing or transporting items for various uses: as gifts (Ps. 68:29; 76:11); as booty (Hos. 10:6); as taxes or tribute (Zeph. 3:10). It indicates things brought by others: gifts (Is. 18:7); sacrifices (Is. 53:7); a bride in marriage (Ps. 45:14). It is used of the returning exiles from Babylonian captivity led by the Lord to Jerusalem (Is. 55:12; Jer. 31:9). In a figurative sense, it denotes being carried or led from womb to tomb (Job 10:19; 21:32) and depicts evil people being led to judgment (Job 21:30). *

[3] ***yᵉḇal*** [Aramaic verb: יְבַל <2987>; corresponding to <2986> above] ▶ **This word means to convey; it is also translated to carry.** It means to transfer or transport something from one place to another, e.g.,

the gold and silver utensils of the Temple from Babylon to Jerusalem (Ezra 5:14; 6:5), as well as silver and gold for monetary use (Ezra 7:15). ¶
– 4 Ps. 22:15 ➔ ESTABLISH <8239> 5 See COME <935>.

BRING, BRING BACK – Ezra 6:5 ➔ GO <1946>.

BRING, BRING DOWN – 2 Sam. 15:14 ➔ DRIVE <5080> b.

BRING DOWN – 1 ***n^{e}ḥêṯ*** [Aramaic verb: נְחַת <5182>; corresponding to BEND <5181>] ▶ **This word indicates to descend. It also means to deposit something at a location.** It is used of putting down, depositing the vessels of the Temple in their proper places (Ezra 5:15; 6:5; also translated to carry, to place). It is used of something being permanently stored away (Ezra 6:1: to store, to lay up). In Daniel the word is used to indicate descending, coming down (Dan. 4:13, 23); and of putting down, removing someone from the throne (Dan. 5:20: to depose). ¶
– 2 Ps. 44:25 ➔ BOW DOWN <7743> a. 3 Prov. 14:32 ➔ DRIVE <1760>.

BRING FORTH – 1 Gen. 1:11 ➔ PRODUCE (verb) <1876> 2 Job 39:3 ➔ CUT (verb) <6398> 3 Ps. 71:6 ➔ TAKE, TAKE OUT <1491> 4 Prov. 10:31 ➔ INCREASE (verb) <5107>.

BRING LOW – 1 ***dālal*** [verb: דָּלַל <1809>; a prim. root (comp. to DRAW <1802>)] ▶
a. This word means to hang low, languish, become thin, to not be equal. It denotes being or becoming small, of no importance: the Midianites humbled Israel (Judg. 6:6; also translated to be impoverished) through military defeats; the psalmist is spiritually depleted because of the fall of Jerusalem (Ps. 79:8; also translated to be in need). The simple are brought low, but the Lord rescues them (Ps. 116:6; 142:6). It depicts a lame person's legs (Prov. 26:7) or the leanness of Israel's condition (Is. 17:4; also translated to waste away). It pictures the low water level of streams or the languishing of hope before one's eyes (Job 28:4; Is. 38:14). Other ref.: Is. 19:6 (to by emptied, to thin out, to diminish, to dwindle). ¶
b. A verb meaning to dangle, to hang, to swing, to sway. It refers to the way men hunt for metals in far recesses of the earth (Job 28:4) or to the way the shafts they sink seem to hang or dangle in the earth. ¶
2 ***māḵaḵ*** [verb: מָכַךְ <4355>; a prim. root] ▶ **This word means to be made low, to sag, to decay.** It is used figuratively of sinking into wickedness and iniquity (Ps. 106:43; also translated to sink down, to waste away), as Israel often did. It is used of sagging or bent rafters or roofs (Eccl. 10:18; also translated to sink in). It is used to describe in a metaphor the fall or failure of persons in life (Job 24:24). ¶
3 ***ṣā'ar*** [verb: צָעַר <6819>; a prim. root] ▶ **This word means for a person to be or become insignificant, trifling, small.** Refs.: Job 14:21; Jer. 30:19; also translated to be disdained. It refers to insignificant persons or little ones without great worth or influence (Zech. 13:7). ¶

BRING OUT – Ps. 22:9 ➔ GUSH <1518>.

BRING OVER – ***g^{e}lāh, g^{e}lā'*** [Aramaic verb: גְּלָה, גְּלָא <1541>; corresponding to REVEAL <1540>] ▶ **This word is used of those who were deported to Babylonia.** Refs.: Ezra 4:10; 5:12; also translated to carry away (into exile), to deport. It has also the meaning of to uncover (Dan. 2:22, 28–30, 47); see REVEAL <1541>. ¶

BRING UP – Esther 2:20 ➔ CARE (UNDER THE) <545>.

BRING UP DELICATELY – Prov. 29:21 ➔ PAMPER <6445>.

BRISTLE UP – Job 4:15 ➔ STAND UP <5568>.

BRISTLING – ***sāmār*** [adj.: סָמָר <5569>; from STAND UP <5568>] ▶

a. This word refers to something that is standing straight up, firmly, in a threatening way, such as locusts. Ref.: Jer. 51:27; also translated rough, bristly. ¶
b. An adjective indicating swarming. It refers to a great number of something covering an area, coming in droves; it was used of locusts (Jer. 51:27: swarm). ¶

BRISTLY – Jer. 51:27 ➔ BRISTLING <5569> a.

BRITTLE (BE) – ***tᵉḇar*** [Aramaic verb: תְּבַר <8406>; corresponding to BREAK <7665>] ▶ **This word refers to something that crumbles, comes apart easily.** Ref.: Dan. 2:42; also translated to be fragile, to be broken. ¶

BROAD – 1 ***rāḥāḇ*** [adj.: רָחָב <7342>; from ENLARGE <7337>] ▶ **This word means wide, spacious, large.** It indicates that something is wide, broad: land (Ex. 3:8; Is. 22:18); a wall (Jer. 51:58). It refers to the broad freedom or openness of God's Law or to walking in it (Ps. 119:45). It indicates the size of something, e.g., land (Gen. 34:21); or to the spaciousness, extent of a land (Judg. 18:10). The inclusiveness of God's moral laws, their broadness is noted by the psalmist (Ps. 119:96). Followed by heart, the phrase refers to an arrogant heart or attitude (Ps. 101:5). An arrogant person is broad of soul (Prov. 28:25). It figuratively indicates a cup of punishment as being deep and wide (Ezek. 23:32). *
– 2 Num. 16:38 ➔ HAMMERED <7555> 3 2 Sam. 22:20; Ps. 18:19; 31:8; 118:5 ➔ BREADTH <4800>.

BROAD PASTURE – Hos. 4:16 ➔ BREADTH <4800>.

BROAD PLACE – ***rāḥaḇ*** [masc. noun: רַחַב <7338>; from ENLARGE <7337>] ▶ **This word means width, wide place; it is also translated spacious place, breadth, expanse, vast expanse.** Refs.: Job 36:16; 38:18. ¶

BROIDERED – Ex. 28:4 ➔ WOVEN <8665>.

BROKEN – 1 ***rō'āh*** [adj.: רֹעָה <7465>; for EVIL <7455>] ▶ **This word's meaning extends beyond something being merely fractured.** Used of a tooth, it seems to mean a bad or infected tooth in parallel with a weak or broken, unstable foot (Prov. 25:19). ¶
– 2 Ex. 6:9 ➔ ANGUISH <7115> 3 Lev. 6:21 ➔ BAKED <8601> b. 4 Lev. 21:20 ➔ CRUSHED <4790> 5 1 Sam. 2:4 ➔ DREAD (noun and adj.) <2844> b. 6 Ps. 109:16 ➔ GRIEVED (BE) <3512> 7 Prov. 15:13; 17:22; 18:14 ➔ CRUSHED <5218> a. 8 Is. 59:5 ➔ CRUSHED <2116> 9 Ezek. 21:6: broken heart ➔ lit.: the breaking of the heart ➔ DESTRUCTION <7670>.

BROKEN (BE) – 1 Job 7:5 ➔ MOMENT (BE FOR A) <7280> d. 2 Dan. 2:42 ➔ BRITTLE (BE) <8406>.

BROKEN IN PIECES – ***šᵉḇaḇiym*** [masc. plur. noun: שְׁבָבִים <7616>; from FOUL <7515> (in the sense of to trample down)] ▶ **This word refers to the shattered bits or fragments of something.** In context it refers to the shattered fragments of the golden calf of Samaria, an idol (Hos. 8:6). ¶

BRONZE – 1 ***nāḥûš*** [adj.: נָחוּשׁ <5153>; apparently pass. part. of DIVINATION (PRACTICE) <5172>] ▶ **This word describes a fairly strong metal made of tin or copper and used to forge weapons, among other things.** Ref.: Job 6:12; KJV: brass. ¶
2 ***nᵉḥûšāh*** [fem. noun: נְחוּשָׁה <5154>; fem. of BRONZE <5153>] ▶ **This word (KJV: brass) refers to a strong metal of copper and tin used literally to give the sense of hardness, unyieldingness, strength, firmness.** Refs.: Lev. 26:19; Job 40:18; Is. 48:4, a bronze forehead. Various things were made of bronze: bows (2 Sam. 22:35; Job 20:24; Ps. 18:34); doors (Is. 45:2). It also refers to copper, since bronze is man-made (Job 28:2). It is used in a figurative sense of bronze hoops (Mic. 4:13). Other ref.: Job 41:27. ¶

3 ***nᵉḥāš*** [Aramaic masc. noun: נְחָשׁ <5174>; corresponding to <5154> above] ▶ **This word is also translated brass. It was a highly valued metal alloy of copper and tin.** In Daniel it is featured in a statue (Dan. 2:32, 35, 39, 45); as part of the material of a band around a tree stump (Dan. 4:15, 23); as the material of bronze idols (Dan. 5:4, 23); a bronze claw on the fourth beast of Daniel's vision (Dan. 7:19). ¶
– 4 Gen. 4:22; 2 Sam. 8:10; etc. ➔ COPPER <5178>.

BROOCH – Ex. 35:22 ➔ HOOK <2397>.

BROOD – 1 ***pirḥāḥ*** [fem. noun: פִּרְחָח <6526>; from BREAK OUT <6524>] ▶ **This word refers also to a tribe, a gang of young people. Its meaning is not certain.** The translation brood is in line with the negative mood of the passive (Job 30:12; also translated youth, rabble, tribe). ¶
2 ***tarbûṯ*** [fem. noun: תַּרְבּוּת <8635>; from MANY (BE, BECOME) <7235>] ▶ **This word means offspring, a generation.** It refers to a group of persons, in context a group of evil or sinful people; hence, the NASB and other versions use the term brood (Num. 32:14). Literally, it is a generation, a group of sinful people (*tarbûṯ ᵃnāšîm ḥaṭṭā'îm*) (KJV, increase, but see PROFIT (noun) <8636>). ¶

BROOK – 1 ***miyḵāl*** [masc. noun: מִיכָל <4323>; apparently the same as ABLE (BE) <3201>] ▶ **This word refers to a small stream easily crossed and smaller than a river.** Ref.: 2 Sam. 17:20. ¶
– 2 Ezek. 47:19; 48:2; etc. ➔ WADI <5158>.

BROOM – ***maṭᵃṭê'*** [masc. noun: מַטְאֲטֵא <4292>; apparently a denom. from MUD <2916>] ▶ **This word refers to a sweeping tool for cleaning up.** It is used in an expression in which God will "sweep" away Babylon with His "broom" of destruction (Is. 14:23; KJV: besom). ¶

BROOM TREE, BROOM BUSH – ***reṯem, rōṯem*** [masc. noun: רֹתֶם ,רֶתֶם <7574>; from HARNESS <7573>] ▶ **This word refers to a tree or a large shrub of a genus of evergreen shrubs or trees of the cypress family; it is also translated juniper, juniper tree.** Refs.: 1 Kgs. 19:4, 5. It also indicates a broom tree, a flowering shrub of the pea family featuring abundant yellow flowers and long stiff fibers (Job 30:4). It could provide dried fuel for a fire (Ps. 120:4). ¶

BROTH – 1 ***māraq*** [masc. noun: מָרָק <4839>; from POLISH <4838> (as if a rinsing)] ▶ **This word describes a thin, clear soup made by boiling meat or other ingredients in water.** Refs.: Judg. 6:19, 20; Is. 65:4. ¶
2 ***pārāq*** [masc. noun: פָּרָק <6564>; from BREAK OFF <6561> (in the sense of crumbed meat in the case of soup)] ▶ **It is a thin, clear soup made by boiling meat and then removing the meat.** Israel made broth from unclean meats and ate it in pagan religious rituals (Is. 65:4). ¶

BROTHER – 1 ***'āḥ*** [masc. noun: אָח <251>; a prim. word] ▶ **The word is used not only of those with common parents but also of those with common ancestors.** Thus, the descendants of Israel are brothers (Lev. 19:17; 25:46), as are two nations with common ancestors (Amos 1:11, Obad. 1:10, 12). It further describes a close friend outside the immediate physical family (2 Sam. 1:26). *
2 ***'aḥ*** [Aramaic masc. noun: אַח <252>; corresponding to <251> above] ▶ **The word occurs only once and is the equivalent of the Hebrew word above.** Ref.: Ezra 7:18. ¶

BROTHER'S WIDOW – Deut. 25:9 ➔ BROTHER'S WIFE <2994>.

BROTHER'S WIFE – ***yᵉḇāmāh*** [fem. noun: יְבָמָה <2994>; fem. part. of MARRY <2992>] ▶ **This word indicates a sister-in-law; it is also translated brother's widow. It indicates the spouse of a deceased brother.** The living brother is then to take this sister-in-law, the deceased brother's wife, to impregnate her so that offspring will be produced (Deut. 25:7, 9). This term is also applied to Ruth, a Moabite, who became an Israelite by choice (Ruth 1:15: sister-in-law). Boaz raised up seed to her deceased Israelite husband and contributed to the line of David. ¶

BROTHERHOOD – ***'aḥ^{a}wāh*** [noun: אַחֲוָה <264>; from BROTHER <251>] ▶ **This word signifies the unity between Judah and Israel whose common ancestor is Jacob.** It is used only in Zechariah 11:14 (also translated family bond). The brotherhood is symbolically broken by Zechariah's breaking his staff. ¶

BROUGHT OUT – 1 Kgs. 10:28 ➔ GOING OUT, GOING FORTH <4161>.

BROUGHT UP – Esther 2:20 ➔ CARE (UNDER THE) <545>.

BROWN – [1] Gen. 30:32, 33, 35, 40 ➔ DARK-COLORED <2345> [2] Zech. 1:8 ➔ SORREL <8320> a.

BRUISE (noun) – ***ḥabbûrāh, ḥabburāh, ḥ^{a}ḇurāh*** [fem. noun: חַבּוּרָה, חַבֻּרָה, חֲבֻרָה <2250>; from JOIN TOGETHER <2266>] ▶ **This word denotes a contusion, a wound, an injury.** It refers to some kind of an injury received by Lamech from a young man (Gen. 4:23: striking, injuring, hurting, hurt). The Suffering Servant of Isaiah undergoes mistreatment indicated by this word (Is. 53:5: wound, stripe, scourging). Certain wounds, blows, or stripes that wound or cut will purge evil from a person (Prov. 20:30: blow, stripe, blueness). It is used figuratively of emotional or spiritual wounds (Ps. 38:5: wound); of those same wounds on a national scale in Judah (Is. 1:6). In a legal case, a wound was to be paid back by a corresponding wound or injury (Ex. 21:25). ¶

BRUISE (verb) – [1] ***šûp̱*** [verb: שׁוּף <7779>; a prim. root] ▶
a. This verb means to hurt, to crush. A verb used twice, once referring to the attack of the serpent and once of the seed of the woman (Gen. 3:15). It may be translated as crush in Job 9:17 to describe God's supposed attack on Job. It also has the sense of to engulf, to hide, to cover (Ps. 139:11). See b.
b. A verb meaning to strike, to snap at. It is used of the attack of the serpent and the response of the seed of the woman (Gen. 3:15). The verb is rendered figuratively as follows by the various translations: KJV, bruise . . . bruise; NIV, crush . . . strike; NASB, bruise . . . bruise; NKJV, bruise . . . bruise.
c. A verb meaning to cover, to envelop, to overwhelm, to hide. It is used of darkness engulfing or hiding a person from God (Ps. 139:11). ¶
– [2] Song 5:7 ➔ WOUND (verb) <6481>.

BRUSH – Job 30:4 ➔ BUSH <7880>.

BRUSHWOOD – ***h^{a}māsiym*** [masc. noun: הֲמָסִים <2003>; from an unused root apparently meaning to crackle] ▶ **This word refers to an easily kindled wood used to start a fire.** Ref.: Is. 64:2; also translated twigs. ¶

BRUTE – Prov. 30:2 ➔ FOOLISH <1198>.

BRUTISH – Ps. 49:10; 73:22; 92:6; Prov. 12:1; 30:2 ➔ FOOLISH <1198>.

BUBASTIS – Ezek. 30:17 ➔ PI-BESETH <6364>.

BUBBLING – Prov. 18:4 ➔ to bubble ➔ UTTER <5042>.

BUCKET – ***d^{e}liy*** [masc. noun: דְּלִי <1805>]; from DRAW <1802> ▶ **This word is used of an ancient leather pail or a vessel used for scooping and pouring water.** Refs.: Num. 24:7; Is. 40:15. ¶

BUCKLER – ***sōḥêrāh*** [fem. noun: סֹחֵרָה <5507>; properly act. part. fem. of MERCHANT <5503> (in the sense of something surrounding a person)] ▶ **This word refers to a small shield, a defensive weapon used to ward off the attacks and blows of an enemy.** It is used figuratively of God's faithfulness to His people as their shield or protection (Ps. 91:4; also translated bulwark, rampart). ¶

BUD (noun) – Ex. 25:31, 33–36; 37:17, 19–22 ➔ BULB <3730>.

BUD (IN) – ***gib̲'ōl*** [masc. noun: גִּבְעֹל <1392>; prolonged from CUP <1375>] ▶ **This word refers to the crop status of flax; it is also translated in bloom, bolled.** It was in bloom and therefore destroyed during the seventh plague of hail (Ex. 9:31). ¶

BUD (verb) – 1 ***nûṣ*** [verb: נוּץ <5132>; a prim. root] ▶ **This word means to bloom or to blossom.** It is a reference to beauty and splendor engendering love in this context (Song 6:11; 7:12; KJV: to flourish). The Hebrew word also means to depart from an area; see FLEE, FLEE AWAY <5132>. ¶
– 2 Song 6:11; 7:12 ➔ SPARKLE <5340>.

BUDS – 1 Kgs. 6:18; 7:24 ➔ GOURDS <6497>.

BUILD – 1 ***b***^{e}***nāh, b***^{e}***nā'*** [Aramaic verb: בְּנָה, בְּנָא <1124>; corresponding to <1129> below] ▶ **This word means to erect, to construct, to reconstruct.** It is used to describe the building of a city (Ezra 4:12, 13, 16, 21; Dan. 4:30) or the Temple, the house of God (Ezra 5:2–4; 6:3, 7). *
2 ***bānāh*** [verb: בָּנָה <1129>; a prim. root] ▶ **This word means to erect, to construct, to reconstruct. It is used literally to describe the construction of many things.** The main areas of its use are: to build a city (Gen. 11:4), house (Gen. 33:17). It describes the construction of the Temple of the Lord on earth (1 Kgs. 3:1; 5:18; 6:2; Ps. 78:69), as well as Jerusalem (Ps. 147:2). With a following *mâṣôr*, fortification, it means to build fortified cities (2 Chr. 11:5); to fortify (1 Kgs. 15:22; 16:24). It has the sense of rebuilding something (Josh. 6:26; Amos 9:14). With a following *b*^{e} preposition, it means build at or work on (Neh. 4:10, 17; Zech. 6:15).

It is used in a figurative sense: Eve is built from Adam's rib, not created separately (Gen. 2:22); used with a following *bayit l*^{e}, house to, it gives the idea of building a family (Deut. 25:9; Jer. 24:6) or making it possible for one to live on in descendants (Gen. 16:2; Jer. 12:16); it depicts wisdom building her house (Prov. 9:1). It is used to describe the building up of the lovingkindness of the Lord (Ps. 89:2). The Lord built His sanctuary not only on earth but truly in the heavens (Amos 9:6).

Nearly all these meanings and uses are also expressed in the passive use of the verb. The Jews who returned from exile were built up, established (Jer. 12:16; cf. Mal. 3:15). The Lord's lovingkindness will be established (Ps. 89:2, noted above). The throne or dynasty of King David is described as being established or built up using this word as was Israel herself after returning from exile (Ps. 89:4; Jer. 24:6; 31:4; 33:7). *
3 ***gāḏar*** [verb: גָּדַר <1443>; a prim. root] ▶ **This word indicates to close off, to wall up.** It is used figuratively of false prophets failing to erect a wall of stones of truth and justice to stand in the day of battle (Ezek. 13:5; 22:30) around Israel. It describes, again figuratively, the Lord's action to wall up or repair the breeches in the Davidic dynasty of kings (Amos 9:11). In its participial form, it denotes a mason, one who works with stones (2 Kgs. 12:12). Used ironically, it describes the Lord's activity in building a wall against His unfaithful people (Hos. 2:6), much as He did, seemingly, against Job (Job 19:8). *

BUILDING – 1 ***binyāh*** [fem. noun: בִּנְיָה <1140>; fem. from BUILD <1129>] ▶ **This word is a general term used to describe the Temple structure itself apart from the Temple inclusive of the court area.** Ref.: Ezek. 41:13. ¶
2 ***binyān*** [masc. noun: בִּנְיָן <1146>; from BUILD <1129>] ▶ **This word is used to refer to the Temple of Ezekiel's vision.** Refs.: Ezek. 40:5; 42:1, 5, 10. It refers to the back building of the complex as the whole (Ezek. 41:12, 15). ¶
3 ***binyān*** [Aramaic masc. noun: בִּנְיָן <1147>; corresponding to <1146> above] ▶ **This word is identical to its Hebrew**

counterpart above. It refers to the Temple that was to be built by the returned exiles (Ezra 5:4). ¶
– [4] Eccl. 10:18 → RAFTER <4746>.

BUILDINGS – Ezek. 40:2 → STRUCTURE <4011>.

BUKKI – ***buqqiy*** [masc. proper noun: בֻּקִּי <1231>; from EMPTY (MAKE) <1238>]: emptying ▶
a. An Israelite of the tribe of Dan. Ref.: Num. 34:22. ¶
b. A descendant of Aaron. Refs.: 1 Chr. 6:5, 51; Ezra 7:4. ¶

BUKKIAH – ***buqqiyyāhû*** [masc. proper noun: בֻּקִּיָּהוּ <1232>; from EMPTY (MAKE) <1238> and LORD <3050>]: emptied by the Lord ▶ **A Levite serving in the sanctuary.** Refs.: 1 Chr. 25:4, 13. ¶

BUL – ***bûl*** [masc. proper noun: בּוּל <945>; the same as FOOD <944> (in the sense of rain)]: who changes, god of the rain ▶ **This word designates the eighth month of the eleventh year of Solomon's reign, which would be 959 B.C.** In this month, the Temple was finished (1 Kgs. 6:38). ¶

BULB – ***kaptôr, kaptōr*** [masc. noun: כַּפְתּוֹר, כַּפְתֹּר <3730>; prob. from an unused root meaning to encircle] ▶ **This word indicates a bulge, or an ornamentation on a column; it is also translated knob, knop, bud, calyx.** A knobby decoration on a lampstand (Ex. 25:31, 33–36; 37:17, 19–22) is rendered bud(s) by some translators. It is used of the top part of a pillar or its decoration (Amos 9:1: lintel of the door, capital, top of the pillar, doorpost). It is a sign of desolation and desertion of a city when owls rest on the tops of its ornamental columns (Zeph. 2:14). ¶

BULGE – Is. 30:13 → BOIL (verb) <1158>.

BULL – ***tôr*** [Aramaic masc. noun: תּוֹר <8450>; corresponding (by permutation) to OX <7794>] ▶ **This word means a male bovine animal; it is also translated ox, bullock.** It was a favored animal for sacrifice in Israel (Ezra 6:9, 17; 7:17). Nebuchadnezzar's disease made his mind and lifestyle like that of cattle (*tôr*) (Dan. 4:25, 32, 33; 5:21). ¶

BULL, YOUNG BULL – ***par, pār*** [masc. noun: פַּר, פָּר <6499>; from BREAK <6565> (apparently as breaking forth in wild strength, or perhaps as dividing the hoof, in the case of a bull)] ▶ **This word refers often to young bullocks, a major source of food, sacrificial animals, and wealth in the ancient Near East.** Refs.: Gen. 32:15; Ex. 24:5; 29:1; Lev. 4:3; Num. 7:88. This term was used in peace offerings or offerings of well-being, burnt offerings (Judg. 6:25); sin offerings (Ezek. 43:19). Figuratively, it depicts leaders (Is. 34:7; Jer. 50:27; Ezek. 39:18). It is found in a powerful figurative expression, standing for the fruit of or the offering of our lips (Hos. 14:2; *pārîm śᵉpāṯênû*). *

BULLOCK – See BULL <8450>.

BULRUSH – [1] ***gōme'*** [masc. noun: גֹּמֶא <1573>; from DRINK (verb) <1572>] ▶ **This word refers to a strong, absorbent marsh plant; it is also translated papyrus, wicker, reed, rush.** It indicates the material of the basket into which Moses was placed (Ex. 2:3). It is also the material of which sailing vessels were made (Is. 18:2). It is grown in marshy land (Job 8:11) and is a sign of rich, fertile earth (Is. 35:7). ¶
– [2] Is. 9:14; 19:15; 58:5 → ROPE <100>.

BULRUSHES – ***'ārôṯ*** [fem. plur. noun: עָרוֹת <6169>; fem. from EMPTY (verb) <6168> (in the sense of a naked, or level plot)] ▶ **This word refers to plants; it is also translated papyrus, paper reeds.** It refers to marsh plants or to any plant growing in or around water that looks like a bulrush (Is. 19:7). The Nile River was famous for these plants. ¶

BULWARK – [1] Ps. 48:13 → RAMPART <2430> [2] Ps. 91:4 → BUCKLER <5507> [3] Eccl. 9:14 → NET <4685> [4] Jer. 50:15 → FOUNDATION <803>.

BUNAH – ***bûnāh*** [masc. proper noun: בּוּנָה <946>; from PERCEIVE <995>]: discretion, prudence ▶ **An Israelite of the tribe of Judah.** Ref.: 1 Chr. 2:25. ¶

BUNCH – [1] ***ᵃguddāh*** [fem. noun: אֲגֻדָּה <92>; fem. pass. part. of an unused root (meaning to bind)] ▶ **This word designates a group, or a bundle.** It refers to a bunch of hyssop (Ex. 12:22) but also to a group or band of men (2 Sam. 2:25; also translated unit, troop). In its figurative or metaphorical usage, it refers to wickedness as bands or bonds (Is. 58:6; also translated chains). In Amos 9:6, it refers to the structures or strata fitted together like a vault, layers, or strata (NASB, NKJV); it is also translated troop, vaulted dome, foundation. ¶
– [2] Is. 30:6 ➔ HUMP <1707>.

BUNDLE – [1] ***kin'āh*** [fem. noun: כִּנְעָה <3666>; from SUBDUE <3665> in the sense of folding (comp. GATHER <3664>)] ▶ **This word refers to a piece of luggage, a bag, or a folded and bound package or the materials in such a carrying bag.** Ref.: Jer. 10:17; also translated wares, belongings. ¶
[2] ***ṣeḇeṯ*** [masc. noun: צֶבֶת <6653>; from an unused root apparently meaning to grip] ▶ **This word indicates a handful.** It refers to a small bundle of grain, placed together from which some may be pulled out (Ruth 2:16). ¶
– [3] Judg. 9:48, 49 ➔ BRANCH <7754>.

BUNNI – ***bûnniy*** [masc. proper noun: בֻּנִּי <1138>; from BUILD <1129>]: understanding ▶
a. A Levite who lived before the exile. Ref.: Neh. 11:15. ¶
b. A Levite, contemporary of Nehemiah. Ref.: Neh. 9:4. ¶
c. A leader in Israel, who signed the covenant of renewal with Nehemiah after the return from the Babylonian captivity. Ref.: Neh. 10:15. ¶

BURDEN – [1] ***yᵉhāḇ*** [masc. noun: יְהָב <3053>; from GIVE <3051>] ▶ **This word indicates one's lot or portion in life which is to be cast on the Lord.** Ref.: Ps. 55:22; also translated cares. The word means literally "what is given." ¶
[2] ***maśśā'*** [masc. noun: מַשָּׂא <4853>; from CARRY <5375>] ▶ **This word means a weight that is carried; it is also translated load. By extension, it means a burden in the form of a prophetic utterance or oracle. It is derived from the verb *nāśā'* meaning to lift, to bear, to carry.** When used to express a burden or load, it is commonly used to describe that which is placed on the backs of pack animals, like donkeys (Ex. 23:5); mules (2 Kgs. 5:17); or camels (2 Kgs. 8:9). Another common usage is in designating what parts of the Tabernacle the sons of Kohath, Gershon, and Merari were to carry (Num. 4:15, 19, 24, 27, 31, 32, 47, 49). In Ezekiel 24:25, that whereupon one has set one's mind, *maśśā' napšām* (BREATH <5315>), is used to mean the desires of the heart and that to which persons lift up their souls. By extension, this term is also applied to certain divine oracles that were negative proclamations. Isaiah used this formula to pronounce judgments against the nations of Babylon (Is. 13:1); Philistia (Is. 14:28); Moab (Is. 15:1); Damascus (Is. 17:1); Egypt (Is. 19:1); the desert of the sea (Is. 21:1); Dumah (Is. 21:11); Arabia (Is. 21:13); the Valley of Vision (Is. 22:1); Tyre (Is. 23:1). Other prophets used the same formula to pronounce judgments on Nineveh (Nah. 1:1); Judah (Hab. 1:1); Damascus (Zech. 9:1); Jerusalem (Zech. 12:1); Israel (Mal. 1:1). This formula was also employed to prophesy threats or judgments on individuals (2 Kgs. 9:25; 2 Chr. 24:27; Prov. 30:1; 31:1). *
[3] ***mišpᵉṯayim*** [dual masc. noun: מִשְׁפְּתַיִם <4942>; from STICK OUT <8192>] ▶
a. This word could also refer to a saddlebag. Some understand it to refer to two saddlebags on a pack animal (Gen. 49:14). Others translate it as sheepfolds, sheep pens. Other less likely words have been suggested. See b. ¶
b. A dual masculine noun referring to campfires or sheepfolds. Ref.: Judg. 5:16. See comments to a. above. ¶
[4] ***nêṭel*** [masc. noun: נֵטֶל <5192>; corresponding to OFFER <5190> (in the sense

of to take up, to lift up)] ► **This word indicates that something is hard to lift, weighty compared to other things its size and volume.** It describes sand as being heavy (Prov. 27:3). ¶
[5] ***sêḇel*** [masc. noun: סֵבֶל <5447>; from BEAR (verb) <5445>] ► **This word means work, forced labor.** It refers to labor, work, burdens borne by Israel in Egypt under taskmasters (Ps. 81:6); forced state labor (1 Kgs. 11:28). It refers to the loads themselves that were carried (Neh. 4:17; NIV: materials). ¶
[6] ***sōḇel*** [masc. noun: סֹבֶל <5448>; from BEAR (verb) <5445>] ► **This word refers to a load, a heavy weight, that a worker had to carry, often placed there by oppressors.** God would remove these burdens (Is 9:4; 10:27; 14:25). ¶
[7] ***seḇālāh*** [fem. noun: סְבָלָה <5450>; from BURDEN <5447>] ► **This word means compulsory service, wearisome and laborious service; it is also translated hard labor, forced labor, heavy burden.** It refers to the forced heavy labor that Israel was subjected to in Egypt (Ex. 1:11; 2:11; 5:4, 5; 6:6, 7). ¶
– [8] 2 Chr. 6:29 → SORE (noun) <5061> [9] Ps. 66:11 → AFFLICTION <4157> [10] Eccl. 1:13 → TASK <6045> [11] Is. 1:14 → LOAD (noun) <2960> [12] Is. 30:27 → SMOKE <4858> b. [13] Zeph. 3:18 → GIFT <4864> [14] Mal. 1:13 → WEARINESS <4972> [15] Mal. 1:13 → HARDSHIP <8513>.

BURDEN-BEARER – ***sabbāl*** [masc. noun: סַבָּל <5449>; from BEAR (verb) <5445>] ► **This word means a porter; it is also translated carrier, transporter, laborer.** It refers to those persons responsible for transporting or moving construction materials as needed (1 Kgs. 5:15; 2 Chr. 2:2, 18; 34:13; Neh. 4:10). ¶

BURDENSOME – Zech. 12:3 → HEAVY, VERY HEAVY <4614>.

BURDENSOME (BE) – Is. 15:4 → TREMBLE <3415>.

BURIAL, BURIAL PLACE – ***qeḇûrāh, qeburāh*** [fem. noun: קְבוּרָה, קְבֻרָה <6900>] ► **This word is the passive participle of *qāḇar* (<6912>), meaning to bury, to inter a dead body.** The word can signify various types of graves: the dignified grave of a king (2 Kgs. 21:26; 23:30); the unknown burial place of Moses (Deut. 34:6). Jehoiakim was to be buried with the burial of a donkey, referring to either the place or manner of his sepulture (Jer. 22:19). Burial was important to the Hebrews of the Old Testament; the lack of a grave was considered a tragedy, the sign of an unwanted life that was best forgotten (Eccl. 6:3; Is. 14:20). The meaning is similar to that of the word *qeḇer* [GRAVE (noun) <6913>]. *

BURN (noun) – [1] ***kewiyyāh*** [verb: כְּוִיָּה <3555>; from BURN (verb) <3554>] ► **This word refers to skin damage or scars received from burning.** In the Mosaic Law, the person who inflicted such an injury on another person could only be repaid with the same punishment; poetic justice (Ex. 21:25; KJV: burning). ¶
[2] ***miḵwāh*** [fem. noun: מִכְוָה <4348>; from BURN (verb) <3554>] ► **This word refers to an area in a person's skin damaged by fire that could lead to a serious skin disease.** Refs.: Lev. 13:24, 25, 28; KJV: burning. ¶
– [3] Is. 33:12; Jer. 34:5 → BURNING (noun) <4955> [4] Ezek. 24:5 → BALL <1754>.

BURN (verb) – [1] ***bā'ar*** [verb: בָּעַר <1197>; a prim. root] ►
a. A word meaning to devour (especially by fire), to consume. The verb indicates the process of combustion. It describes the burning of fire itself (Jer. 20:9) or of various objects: a burning bush (Ex. 3:2, 3); burning wood (Ps. 83:14). It is used figuratively of the Lord's anger burning and consuming Jacob and Israel (Is. 6:13; 30:27; 42:25) and the wicked (Ps. 106:18; Jer. 44:6). It describes wickedness consuming persons like a fire (Is. 9:18).

In some contexts, it means to cause a fire or consume something, such as a field or olive trees (Ex. 22:6) or to burn something to ashes (Nah. 2:13).

b. A word meaning to remove, to graze, to ruin. It depicts cattle feeding or grazing in a field (Ex. 22:5) or an enemy of Israel being ruined or consumed (Num. 24:22). It describes dung being consumed or perhaps swept away (NASB; cf. NIV, burns; KJV, take away; 1 Kgs. 14:10). In certain contexts, it is best translated as remove, get rid of something, root out (Deut. 13:5; 2 Kgs. 23:34). *

c. A word meaning to be stupid, brutish. This root denotes being deluded, stupid for worshiping idols (Jer. 10:8), being without common religious sense (Jer. 10:8, 14) and led astray. *

[2] ***dālaq*** [verb: דָּלַק <1814>; a prim. root] ▶ **This word indicates to consume by fire, and also to pursue hotly.** It means to set on fire (Obad. 1:18: to burn, to kindle, to set on fire), to kindle a fire (Ezek. 24:10: kindle). It depicts fiery weapons, such as arrows (Ps. 7:13: fiery shaft, flaming), or other kinds of dangers, such as burning lips that tell tales (Prov. 26:23: burning, fervent). It indicates literal physical pursuit (Gen. 31:36: to pursue, to hunt down; 1 Sam. 17:53: to chase). It is used of the wicked pursuing the righteous (Ps. 10:2: to hotly pursue, to hunt down), sometimes in judgment from God (Lam. 4:19: to pursue, to chase). It also describes those who are addicted to wine (Is. 5:11: to inflame) pursuing it early in the morning. ¶

[3] ***ḥārar*** [verb: חָרַר <2787>; a prim. root] ▶ **This word means to be hot, to be scorched.** Jerusalem is scorched under the figurative caldron that Ezekiel saw (Ezek. 24:11; also translated to glow). It also describes the physical burning Job felt in his bones (Job 30:30). Figuratively, Jeremiah refers to Babylon as burning the bellows of Jerusalem (Jer. 6:29; also translated the bellows blow fiercely). This word can also connote an angry person kindling strife (Prov. 26:21). Other refs.: Ps. 69:3; 102:3; Is. 24:6; Ezek. 15:4, 5; 24:10. ¶

[4] ***yāṣaṯ*** [verb: יָצַת <3341>; a prim. root] ▶ **This word means to burn up, to consume something when used "with fire" (*bā'ēš*).** Thorns burn in a fire (Is. 33:12); a city burns (Jer. 49:2); the gates of Babylon burned (Jer. 51:58). It is used figuratively of evil or wickedness which burn as fire (Is. 9:18) as well as of God's own anger igniting and breaking out like fire (2 Kgs. 22:13, 17). In its passive uses, it means to be burned up as were the gates of Jerusalem (Neh. 1:3; 2:17). It takes on the meaning of to cause or set on fire in some usages and contexts (2 Sam. 14:30, 31). *

[5] ***yāqaḏ*** [verb: יָקַד <3344>; a prim. root] ▶ **This word means to consume by fire, and also to set fire.** It is used in a powerful metaphor of God's anger; a fire is kindled, burning in His anger (Deut. 32:22; Jer. 15:14; 17:4); the Lord will burn up the glory of the Assyrian king and nation (Is. 10:16). It describes a fire that burns in the Lord's nostrils—the offensive nature of His rebellious people (Is. 65:5). It is used literally of fire burning on the altar of sacrifice (Lev. 6:9, 12, 13); and fire in general (Is. 30:14). ¶

[6] ***kāwāh*** [verb: כָּוָה <3554>; a prim. root] ▶ **This word refers to something being seared from heat or fire.** It is used of a person's feet who walks on hot coals (Prov. 6:28); it is also translated to sear, to scorch. On the other hand, it is used in a metaphor to depict the people of God not being charred or singed by fire, for He would deliver them (Is. 43:2; NASB: to scorch). ¶

[7] ***lāhaṭ*** [verb: לָהַט <3857>; a prim. root] ▶ **a. A verb meaning to lick up in a blaze, to set fire on, to consume with fire.** It indicates devouring or scorching something by fire or flame (Deut. 32:22); or war (Is. 42:25). In its intensive stem, it also means to light or kindle coals (Job 41:21); or to set ablaze God's enemies (Mal. 4:1). In its participial form with *'ēš*, it depicts the Lord's minister as a burning fire (Ps. 104:4). It is used figuratively of the enemies of the righteous, those who breathe out fire (Ps. 57:4). The Lord Himself may consume the enemies of His people like a fire (Ps. 83:14; 106:18). Other refs.: Ps. 97:3; Joel 1:19; 2:3. ¶

b. A verb meaning to swallow, to devour. It is used in its participial form figuratively to describe the enemies of the righteous who devour them (Ps. 57:4). See a. also. ¶

[8] ***sārap̱*** [verb: סָרַף <5635>; a prim. root] ▶ **This word is a variant spelling of <8313> below.** It has traditionally been taken to mean to burn in context with a suffix, "he that burns him" (KJV, NIV, Amos 6:10). Some recent translations suggest reading it as to dig for, referring to a grave-digger or undertaker (NASB and others). ¶

[9] ***ṣûṯ*** [verb: צוּת <6702>; a prim. root] ▶ **This word means to set on fire.** It means to ignite, to burn up something that is in the way, an obstacle (Is. 27:4). ¶

[10] ***ṣāraḇ*** [verb: צָרַב <6866>; a prim. root] ▶ **This word means to set on fire; it is also translated to scorch.** It indicates igniting or kindling a fire. It is used figuratively of God's destruction of the Negev (Ezek. 20:47). ¶

[11] ***qāṭar*** [verb: קָטַר <6999>; a prim. root; identical with JOINED (BE) <7000> through the idea of fumigation in a close place and perhaps thus driving out the occupants] ▶ **This word means to produce smoke.** Often smoke is made by burning incense, but every major offering may also be associated with this word (Ex. 30:7; Lev. 1:9; 2:2; 3:5; 4:10; 7:5). One unusual use of this term describes Solomon's carriage as perfumed with myrrh and incense (Song 3:6). Many times this verb is used of improper worship directed either to the true God or to false gods (1 Kgs. 12:33; 2 Chr. 26:16, 18, 19; Jer. 48:35). In the Old Testament, the burning of incense was restricted to the Aaronic priesthood (Num. 16:40; 2 Chr. 26:16, 18, 19). In the New Testament, Zacharias, a priest and the father of John the Baptist, burned incense; and prayers of saints are compared to burning incense (cf. Luke 1:10, 11; Rev. 5:8; 8:3, 4). *

[12] ***śārap̱*** [verb: שָׂרַף <8313>; a prim. root] ▶ **Most often, this word is used to mean to absorb (devour) with fire, to destroy, or to consume. It is normally used to refer to sacrifices.** Many sacrificial laws prescribed specific ways for offerings to be burnt (Ex. 29:14). Burning could also be a form of punishment, as in the story of Achan (Josh. 7:25). Buildings and cities were other common objects of burning: men of Ephraim threatened to burn down Jephthah's house with fire (Judg. 12:1). Less frequently, this word refers to the process of firing bricks (Gen. 11:3). *

– [13] Ex. 30:1 ➔ BURNING (PLACE FOR) <4729> [14] Job 18:5 ➔ to stop burning ➔ to stop shining ➔ LIGHTEN <5050> [15] Ps. 18:28 ➔ LIGHT (GIVE) <215> [16] Song 1:6 ➔ SEE <7805> b. [17] Is. 9:19 ➔ SCORCH <6272> [18] Ezek. 39:9 ➔ KINDLE <5400>.

BURNING (adj. and noun) – ***ṣārāḇ, ṣāreḇeṯ*** [צָרָב, צָרֶבֶת <6867>; from BURN (verb) <6866>] ▶

a. An adjective referring to a conflagration, a scorching. It indicates an area of the skin that has been burned literally or by disease; a scorched area (Lev. 13:23, 28). **b. A feminine noun indicating a scab, a scar, an inflammation.** Some analyze this as a noun rather than a feminine participle of a. above. The meaning is the same. ¶

BURNING (noun) – [1] ***yᵉqêḏāh*** [Aramaic act. fem. noun: יְקֵדָה <3346>; from BURNING (verb) <3345>] ▶ **This word refers to the blazing of the fire in Daniel's vision.** Ref.: Dan. 7:11; the fourth beast is destroyed then by burning. ¶

[2] ***yᵉqôḏ, yᵉqōḏ*** [act. masc. noun: יְקוֹד, יְקֹד <3350>; from BURN (verb) <3344>] ▶ **This word refers to a conflagration.** In Isaiah its only use is a fire kindled like a blazing flame (Is. 10:16). It is probably being used both figuratively and literally of God's judgment on Assyria. ¶

[3] ***miśrāp̄āh*** [fem. noun: מִשְׂרָפָה <4955>; from BURN <8313>] ▶ **This word indicates the process of consuming by fire.** It refers to a burning of lime, meaning that an object was completely burned to ashes (Is. 33:12). It is used of the burning of spices at the burial of the rebellious king Zedekiah (Jer. 34:5). ¶

[4] ***śᵉrêp̄āh*** [fem. noun: שְׂרֵפָה <8316>; from BURN (verb) <8313>] ▶ **The connotation of this word is that of being thoroughly consumed with fire.** It is used to refer to kiln-fired brick (Gen. 11:3); a destructive flame (Amos 4:11); a burn-out mountain, i.e., an inactive volcano (Jer.

51:25); divine judgment (Lev. 10:6); and the burning of the red heifer (Num. 19:6). This word vividly portrays the state of the Temple during the Babylonian captivity (Is. 64:11). *
– [5] Ex. 21:25 ➔ BURN (noun) <3554> [6] Lev. 6:9 ➔ HEARTH <4169> [7] Lev. 13:24, 25, 28 ➔ BURN (noun) <4348> [8] Deut. 29:24 ➔ FIERCE <2750> [9] Ps. 11:6 ➔ BURNING HEAT <2152> [10] Prov. 26:23 ➔ BURN (verb) <1814> [11] Is. 3:24 ➔ BRANDING <3587> [12] Is. 33:14 ➔ HEARTH <4168>.

BURNING (verb) – [1] **to burn:** ***d*^{e}*laq*** [Aramaic verb: דְּלַק <1815>; corresponding to BURN (verb) <1814>] ▶ **This verb is used once in a participial form to describe the wheels of God's chariot throne as blazing fire.** Ref.: Dan. 7:9. ¶
[2] ***y*^{e}*qaḏ*** [Aramaic verb: יְקַד <3345>; corresponding to BURN (verb) <3344>] ▶ **All the references are found in Daniel in the story of the three Hebrew men in the furnace of blazing fire.** Refs.: Dan. 3:6, 11, 15, 17, 20, 21, 23, 26. The verb is always in an active participial form. ¶
– [3] Ps. 38:7 ➔ ROAST <7033> b.

BURNING (DIMLY, FAINTLY) – Is. 42:3 ➔ DARK <3544>.

BURNING (EXTREME, SEVERE) – Deut. 28:22 ➔ HEAT (FIERY, SCORCHING) <2746>.

BURNING (PLACE FOR) – ***miqṭār*** [masc. noun: מִקְטָר <4729>; from BURN <6999>] ▶ **This word refers to a location or spot for burning something, e.g., an altar on which to burn incense.** Ref.: Ex. 30:1. ¶

BURNING AGUE – Lev. 26:16 ➔ FEVER <6920>.

BURNING HEAT – [1] ***zal'āp̱āh*** [fem. noun: זַלְעָפָה <2152>; from ANGRY (BE) <2196>] ▶ **This word occurs only three times in the Old Testament. In two of the locations, the literal usage of this word is implied.** In Lamentations 5:10, Jeremiah explains the hunger pangs as the burning heat of famine; the word is also translated fever, feverish, terrible. In Psalm 11:6, David describes how God will pour out His wrath with this burning heat, along with fire and brimstone; the word is translated burning, horrible, scorching. In Psalm 119:53, the psalmist speaks figuratively about his righteous, burning zeal on account of those who forsake God's law; the word is translated indignation, burning indignation, hot indignation, horror. ¶
– [2] Hos. 13:5 ➔ DROUGHT <8514>.

BURNING LAMP, BURNING LIGHT – Job 41:19 ➔ TORCH <3940>.

BURNING SAND – ***šārāḇ*** [masc. noun: שָׁרָב <8273>; from an unused root meaning to glare] ▶ **This word refers to scorched ground; scorching heat.** It indicates something dried out, singed, darkened by heat from the sun (Is. 35:7; 49:10). ¶

BURNING STICK – Amos 4:11; Zech. 3:2 ➔ FIREBRAND <181>.

BURNISHED (adj.) – ***qālal*** [adj.: קָלָל <7044>; from SLIGHT (BE) <7043>] ▶ **This word means made smooth and bright by rubbing; it is also translated polished.** It refers to a metal that has been buffed or burnished to make it gleam (Ezek. 1:7; Dan. 10:6). ¶

BURNISHED (verb) – 2 Chr. 4:16 ➔ POLISH <4838>.

BURNT – Deut. 32:24 ➔ WASTED <4198>.

BURNT OFFERING – [1] ***'ᵃlāh*** [Aramaic fem. noun: עֲלָה <5928>; corresponding to <5930> below] ▶ **This word means a whole holocaust. It parallels the Hebrew word *'ōlāh* below.** It is used only by Ezra in reference to the daily burnt sacrifices required under the Law (Ezra 6:9). ¶
[2] ***'ōlāh*** [fem. noun: עֹלָה <5930>; fem. act. part. of OFFER <5927>] ▶ **This word**

means a whole holocaust, that which goes up. The primary discussion of this offering is found in Leviticus 1; 6:9, 10, 12. The noun is a feminine participial form of the verb meaning to go up, to ascend. The offering was voluntary. The Israelites understood the animal or fowl that was being sacrificed as a gift to God and thus ascending to God as smoke from the altar (Lev. 1:9), hence its name. The sacrifice was a pleasing odor acceptable to the Lord (Lev. 1:9). Those presenting the animal laid hands on the sacrifice—possibly to indicate ownership or to indicate that the animal was a substitute for themselves (Lev. 1:4). The blood of the sacrifice was sprinkled against the altar (Lev. 1:6). The offering and its ritual properly carried out atoned for the offerers, and they became acceptable before the Lord.

The total burning of the sacrifice indicates the total consecration of the presenter to the Lord. The animals that could be offered were bulls, sheep, rams, or male birds (Lev. 1:3, 10, 14). The ashes of the offering remained on the altar overnight. The priest removed them and deposited them in an approved location (Lev. 6:9, 10).

The burnt offerings were presented often in conjunction with the peace and grain offerings (Josh. 8:31; Judg. 6:26; 1 Kgs. 3:4; 8:64). The burnt offerings, along with other offerings, were employed in the various feasts, festivals, and celebrations recorded in the prophetic books. Often, however, the burnt offerings were condemned as useless because the Israelites didn't have their hearts right before God (Jer. 6:20; 7:21). Ezekiel foresaw renewed burnt offerings in a new Temple (Ezek. 40:38, 39). When Israel returned from exile, burnt offerings, along with others, were once again presented to the Lord (Ezra 3:2; 8:35). David's observation was correct and to the point, for he noted that whole burnt offerings did not satisfy or delight the Lord. Only an offering of a broken spirit and humble heart could do that (Ps. 51:16). Only then could acceptable sacrifices be given to the Lord (Ps. 51:19; 66:13). *

BURST – See DIVIDE <1234>.

BURSTING – Is. 30:14 ➔ FRAGMENT <4386>.

BURY – ***qāḇar*** [verb: קָבַר <6912>; a prim. root] ▶ **The word often refers to the placing of a dead body in a cave or a stone sepulcher rather than directly into the ground.** Refs.: Gen. 23:4; 50:13; 2 Sam. 21:14; 1 Kgs. 13:31; cf. Is. 22:16. Abraham stated that one goal of burial was to get the dead out of sight (Gen. 23:4). Dead bodies were seen as polluting the land until they were buried (Ezek. 39:11–14). It was also a reproach to the dead to be buried in a foreign place or not to be buried at all (Gen. 47:29, 30; 50:5; cf. 50:24–26; Jer. 20:6). Bones were sometimes specifically mentioned as the object of burial (Josh. 24:32; 1 Sam. 31:13; 1 Kgs. 13:31). Buried persons were said to sleep or be buried with their fathers, and they were often placed in the same tomb (Gen. 47:30; 50:13; Judg. 16:31; 2 Sam. 2:32; 17:23). *

BUSH – [1] ***s^{e}neh*** [masc. noun: סְנֶה <5572>; from an unused root meaning to prick] ▶ **This word indicates a desert shrub, a thorny shrub.** God spoke to Moses from one of these shrubs as it was ablaze with fire (Ex. 3:2–4; Deut. 33:16). ¶

[2] ***śiyaḥ*** [masc. noun: שִׂיחַ <7880>; from TELL <7878> (in the sense of to utter or put forth)] ▶ **This word means a shoot, brush, a plant, a shrub.** The most common usage of this word is a shrub or brush. It is used to denote that when the Lord made the heavens and earth, no shrub of the field had yet appeared nor had any plant sprung up (Gen. 2:5). *S:iyaḥ* designates the bushes under which Hagar placed Ishmael to die (Gen. 21:15). The two were dying due to lack of water, and therefore Hagar placed Ishmael underneath bushes, walked out of sight, still in hearing distance, and sat down. She did not want to watch her son die. In his discourse, Job designated the brush as the place where fathers of the sons who mocked him gathered salt herbs (Job 30:4). The bushes were also the place in which these fathers brayed (Job 30:7). ¶

– [3] Is. 7:19 ➔ PASTURE <5097> [4] Jer. 17:6 ➔ SHRUB <6199> [5] Jer. 17:6; 48:6 ➔ SHRUB <6176>.

BUSHY – Song 5:11 ➔ WAVY <8534> a.

BUSINESS – [1] 1 Kgs. 10:15 ➔ WARES <4536> [2] Eccl. 1:13; 2:26; 3:10; 4:8; 5:3; 8:16 ➔ TASK <6045>.

BUSY – 1 Kgs. 18:27 ➔ RELIEVE ONESELF <7873>.

BUSY (BE) – 1 Kgs. 18:27 ➔ DROSS <5509>.

BUT – [1] ***'ûlām*** [conjunctive adv.: אוּלָם <199>; apparently a variation of PERHAPS <194>] ▶ **This Hebrew word means on the contrary; it is also translated however, though, nevertheless.** It is rendered quite uniformly as a strong adversative (Gen. 28:19; Ex. 9:16; Num. 14:21; Job 1:11; Mic. 3:8). *
– [2] See NEVERTHELESS <1297>.

BUTLER – Gen. 40:1, 2, 5, 9, 13, 20, 21, 23; 41:9 ➔ CUPBEARER <4945>.

BUTT – [1] Ex. 21:35 ➔ SMITE <5062> [2] Ezek. 34:21; Dan. 8:4 ➔ GORE <5055>.

BUTTER – [1] ***ḥem'āh, ḥêmāh*** [fem. noun: חֶמְאָה, חֵמָה <2529>; from the same root as WALL <2346>] ▶ **This word refers to curdled milk that is much like butter.** Refs.: Gen. 18:8; 2 Sam. 17:29. It was often produced by churning milk to make butter (Prov. 30:33). It was a staple of the diet of Israelites and their neighbors (Deut. 32:14), even from infancy (Is. 7:15; 22). It could be served in high style in luxurious dishes (Judg. 5:25). It is used figuratively to describe the beauty and bounty of nature (Job 20:17) or a pleasant and unhindered state of life (Job 29:6). ¶
[2] ***maḥ^{a}mā'ōṯ*** [fem. plur. noun: מַחֲמָאֹת <4260>; a denom. from BUTTER <2529>] ▶ **This word indicates something curd-like (i.e., smooth and unctuous) used as a metaphor for treacherous speech.** It was smoother than butter or speech from a mouth smeared or smoothed with butter (Ps. 55:21). ¶

BUTTOCKS – [1] ***šêṯ*** [masc. noun: שֵׁת <8351>; from PUT <7896> (in the sense of to sit)] ▶
a. This word refers to the upper part of one's thigh or lower buttocks; it is also translated hip. Refs.: NASB, ESV, NIV: 2 Sam. 10:4; Is. 20:4. Some translations derive the word in these verses from <8357>; see below. *
b. This word means a foundation. It refers to the base supporting structure of something. In context it refers to the necessary moral and ethical foundations of righteousness, i.e., God's will, Law, covenant, etc. (Ps. 11:3). ¶
[2] ***šêṯāh*** [masc. noun: שֵׁתָה <8357>; from PUT <7896> (in the sense of to sit)] ▶ **This word refers to the upper part of persons' hips or the lower part of their buttocks.** Refs.: KJV, NKJV: 2 Sam. 10:4; Is. 20:4. Some translations derive the word in these verses from <8351>; see above. In context the exposure of the buttocks brought great shame and humiliation on the king's servants. In the ancient Near East, such public exposure was a sign of humility and shame, especially to the king's messengers. ¶
– [3] 1 Chr. 19:4 ➔ HIP <4667>.

BUTTRESS – Neh. 3:19, 20, 24, 25 ➔ CORNER (noun) <4740>.

BUY – [1] ***kārāh*** [verb: כָּרָה <3739>; usually assigned as a prim. root, but prob. only a special application of DIG <3738> (through the common idea of planning implied in a bargain)] ▶
a. A verb meaning to purchase, to bargain for, to barter for. It indicates getting something by barter, trade, or purchase (e.g., water) (Deut. 2:6). Persons, friends were not to be bartered over (Job 6:27); humans did not have the power to barter or bargain over Leviathan (Job 41:6; NIV, NASB, ESV). It is, however, used of Hosea's purchase of his wife (Hos. 3:2). ¶
b. It also indicates the giving of a feast or a banquet. Ref.: 2 Kgs. 6:23: to prepare; Job 41:6. ¶

2 *qᵉnā'* [Aramaic verb: קְנָא <7066>; corresponding to ACQUIRE <7069>] ▶ **This word refers to the acquisition of something by purchase, in context, with money.** Ref.: Ezra 7:17. ¶
3 *šāḇar* [verb: שָׁבַר <7666>; denom. from GRAIN <7668> (to deal in grain)] ▶ **This word means to acquire something by an exchange of money, land, or another object.** Refs.: Gen. 41:57; Deut. 2:6; Is. 55:1. It also means to sell, to let someone buy something, e.g., grain (Gen. 41:56; Deut. 2:28; Prov. 11:26; Amos 8:5). *
– 4 Job 28:16, 19 ➔ VALUE (verb) <5541>.

BUZ – ***bûz*** [masc. proper noun: בּוּז <938>; the same as CONTEMPT <937>]: contempt ▶ **a. The second son of Nahor and a tribe descending from him.** Refs.: Gen. 22:21; Jer. 25:23. ¶
b. An Israelite of the tribe of Gad. Ref.: 1 Chr. 5:14. ¶

BUZI – ***bûziy*** [masc. proper noun: בּוּזִי <941>; the same as BUZITE <940>]: contempt ▶ **A descendant of Buz, father of the prophet and priest Ezekiel.** Ref.: Ezek. 1:3. ¶

BUZITE – ***bûziy*** [masc. proper noun: בּוּזִי <940>; patron. from BUZ <938>] ▶ **A member of the tribe of Buz.** Refs.: Job 32:2, 6. ¶

BUZZARD – Lev. 11:13; Deut. 14:12 ➔ VULTURE (BLACK) <5822>.

BYWAY – 1 Judg. 5:6 ➔ CROOKED <6128> 2 Judg. 5:6 ➔ PATH <734>.

BYWORD – 1 ***mᵉšōl*** [masc. proper noun: מְשֹׁל <4914>; from PROVERB <4911>] ▶ **This word means a mocking proverb, an object of scorn.** It is used of Job's designation as a byword or object of ridicule (Job 17:6). ¶
2 ***šᵉniynāh*** [fem. noun: שְׁנִינָה <8148>; from SHARPEN <8150>] ▶ **This word also indicates a taunt. It refers to a scornful or jeering put-down.** Israel would become a taunt before the nations because of her rebelliousness and disobedience (Deut. 28:37; NIV: object of ridicule); especially in exile (1 Kgs. 9:7; Jer. 24:9). The Temple itself would become a byword (2 Chr. 7:20). ¶

C

CAB – 2 Kgs. 6:25 ➔ KAB <6894>.

CABBON – ***kabbôn*** [proper noun: כַּבּוֹן <3522>; from an unused root meaning to heap up]: hilly ▶ **A town in the plain of Judah.** Ref.: Josh. 15:40. ¶

CABIN – Jer. 37:16 ➔ CELL <2588>.

CABUL – ***kāḇûl*** [proper noun: כָּבוּל <3521>; from the same as FETTERS <3525> in the sense of limitation]: limitation, binding ▶ **A city of Asher.** Refs.: Josh. 19:27; 1 Kgs. 9:13. ¶

CAGE – [1] ***sûḡar*** [masc. noun: סוּגַר <5474>; from CLOSE <5462>] ▶ **This word describes a box-like enclosed structure for confining something.** Ref.: Ezek. 19:9; KJV: ward. ¶
– [2] Jer. 5:27 ➔ BASKET <3619>.

CAIN – ***qayin*** [masc. noun: קַיִן <7014>; the same as SPEAR, SPEARHEAD <7013> (with a play upon the affinity to ACQUIRE <7069>)]: acquisition ▶
a. A masculine proper noun designating the first person born of Eve and first son of Adam. His name means "acquired" of the Lord (Gen. 4:1–3). Unfortunately, he fostered an attitude of anger toward his brother Abel which made his offering unacceptable to God (Gen. 4:5–7; Heb. 11:4). He directed this anger toward Abel and killed him (4:8). As his punishment, he became a wandering outcast, but God mercifully "marked" him in some way to protect him from would-be avengers of blood (4:10–16). The Lord somehow cursed the land for Cain and his descendants, which may have driven Cain to build a city (4:17) in the land of Nod (4:16). He had several sons, one of whom began the practice of bigamy (4:19–22). More violence and killing was spread by Lamech (4:23, 24).
b. A proper noun designating Kain, a city in Judah. Ref.: Num. 24:22.
c. A proper noun designating a Kenite. Refs.: Num. 24:22; Judg. 4:11. *

CAINAN – See KENAN <7017>.

CAKE – [1] ***ḥallāh*** [fem. noun: חַלָּה <2471>; from PIERCE <2490>] ▶ **This word indicates baked flour-based food, also a wafer, a ring-shaped bread.** It refers to bread used in offerings, leavened (2 Sam. 6:19) or unleavened (Ex. 29:2; Lev. 8:26). It refers to the twelve cakes in the Holy Place made of fine wheat flour (Lev. 24:5). *
[2] ***kawwān*** [masc. noun: כַּוָּן <3561>; from SET UP <3559>] ▶ **This word indicates a sacrificial baked flour-based food.** These were small wafer-like cakes baked by the women of Israel in honor of the pagan Queen of Heaven (Jer. 7:18; 44:19). ¶
[3] ***leḇiḇāh*** [fem. noun: לְבִבָה <3834>; from HEART (RAVISH THE) <3823> (in the sense of making bread or a cake that was kneaded and baked)] ▶ **A favorite food from kneaded dough baked for a time of celebrating.** Refs.: 2 Sam. 13:6, 8, 10; also translated bread. ¶
[4] ***'ugāh*** [fem. noun: עֻגָה <5692>; from BAKE <5746>] ▶ **This word refers to a mass made from bread dough and usually baked on hot stones.** Refs.: Gen. 18:6; 1 Kgs. 17:13; 19:6. Figuratively, it describes northern Israel (Hos. 7:8; NIV: loaf). Other refs.: Ex. 12:39; Num. 11:8; Ezek. 4:12. ¶
[5] ***pannag*** [noun: פַּנַּג <6436>; of uncertain deriv.] ▶
a. A masculine noun meaning a baked flour-based food, a confection. It refers to one of the items in a list of goods traded among Tyre, Israel, and Judah (Ezek. 27:17). Its exact meaning is uncertain.
b. A proper noun Pannag. It is taken as a specific food item by some translators (KJV) (Ezek. 27:17; NKJV: millet; ESV: meal; NIV: confections). ¶
[6] ***ṣelûl, ṣeliyl*** [masc. noun: צְלוּל, צְלִיל <6742>; from SINK <6749> in the sense of rolling] ▶ **This word indicates a round loaf of bread.** It describes in a dream a loaf of (barley?) bread. The bread was round and shaped like a dish (Judg. 7:13). ¶

– [7] Gen. 40:16 → WHITE, WHITE BREAD <2751> [8] 1 Kgs. 14:3 → MOLDY <5350> [9] 1 Kgs. 17:12 → BREAD <4580>.

CAKE BAKED – ***lāšāḏ*** [masc. noun: לָשָׁד <3955>; from an unused root of uncertain meaning] ▶ **This word denotes freshness, moisture, vitality; cake(s).** It refers to a cake baked with oil (Num. 11:8). Its meaning is difficult to decipher in context (NIV, something; KJV, fresh; NASB, ESV, cake; NKJV, pastry). Other ref.: Ps. 32:4 (vitality, strength, moisture). ¶

CAKES (MAKE) – 2 Sam. 13:6, 8 → HEART (RAVISH THE) <3823>.

CALAH – ***kelaḥ*** [proper noun: כֶּלַח <3625>; the same as VIGOR <3624>]: completion, vigor ▶ **One of the most ancient cities of Assyria.** Refs.: Gen. 10:11, 12. ¶

CALAMITY – [1] ***'êyḏ*** [masc. noun: אֵיד <343>; from the same as FIREBRAND <181> (in the sense of bending down)] ▶ **This word means disaster, destruction.** It refers to a time of trouble when a person is in special need of help (Prov. 27:10); a calamity so severe that men and women should not rejoice or take selfish advantage of those whom the disaster renders helpless before God (Job 31:23; Prov. 17:5; Obad. 1:13). The calamity may result from a deliberate violation of principles (Prov. 1:26) or a more explicit judgment of God (Jer. 18:17). It may even befall a righteous person (2 Sam. 22:19; Ps. 18:18). *

– [2] Gen. 42:4, 38; 44:29 → HARM (noun) <611> [3] Job 6:21 → TERROR <2866> [4] Job 9:23 → TRIAL <4531> [5] Job 18:12: calamity is hungry for him → other translations: his strength is famished → STRENGTH <202> [6] Job 21:17 → ROPE <2256> [7] Prov. 22:8 → NOTHINGNESS <205> [8] Prov. 24:22 → DISASTER <6365> [9] Is. 47:11; Ezek. 7:26 → DISASTER <1943> [10] Is. 65:23 → TERROR <928>.

CALCOL – ***kalkōl*** [masc. proper noun: כַּלְכֹּל <3633>; from CONTAIN <3557>]: food, sustenance ▶ **One of the three sons of Mahol, who were wise.** Refs.: 1 Kgs. 4:31; 1 Chr. 2:6. ¶

CALCULATE – Prov. 23:7 → THINK <8176>.

CALDRON – [1] 2 Chr. 35:13 → BASKET <1731> [2] Job 41:20 → lit.: burning rushes → ROPE <100>.

CALEB – ***kālêḇ*** [masc. proper noun: כָּלֵב <3612>; perhaps a form of DOG <3611>, or else from the same root in the sense of forcible]: dog, capable ▶ **One of the twelve spies sent to check out the land of Canaan. He was the son of Jephunneh, a leader in Judah.** He counseled Israel to go up and take the land, as did Joshua (Num. 14:6–38). He helped conquer the Promised Land; he was from the line of Judah and fathered three sons (1 Chr. 4:15, 16). Hebron was allotted to Caleb (Josh. 14:6–9). His own testimony was that he had faithfully followed the Lord (Josh. 14:8). He inherited his land at the ripe age of eighty-five but still finished driving Anakites out of the land. According to Joshua, Jephunneh's father was a Kenizzite (Josh. 14:14). *

CALEB-EPHRATAH – ***kālêḇ 'eprāṯāh*** [proper noun: כָּלֵב אֶפְרָתָה <3613>; from *kālêḇ* (CALEB <3612>) and *'eprāṯāh* (EPHRATH <672>)] ▶ **A place where Hezron died.** Ref.: 1 Chr. 2:24. ¶

CALEBITE – ***kālibbiy*** [masc. proper noun: כָּלִבִּי <3614>; patron. for CALEB <3612>] ▶ **A member of the house of Caleb; Nabal was a Calebite.** Ref.: 1 Sam. 25:3. ¶

CALF – ***'êgel*** [common noun: עֵגֶל <5695>; from the same as CIRCULAR <5696> (as frisking round in the case of a calf)] ▶ **This word refers to a young cow or bull, a valuable property in ancient Israel.** It was a symbol of power and fertility; Israel fell into idolatry by creating images of calves (Ex. 32:4, 8, 19; Deut. 9:16); two calf images were set up in northern Israel (1 Kgs. 12:28, 32; 2 Kgs. 10:29). It is used in figurative language of mountains leaping for joy like calves (Ps. 29:6). Fatted, grain-fed calves were eaten and used in sacrifices and rituals (1 Sam. 28:24). The word was employed in figurative speech (Jer. 46:21; Mal. 4:2). *

CALKER – Ezek. 27:27 ➔ lit.: repairer of seams ➔ DAMAGE (noun) <919>.

CALL – ***qārā'*** [verb: קָרָא <7121>; a prim. root (rather identical with MEET (verb) <7122>)] ▶ **This word means to declare, to summon, to invite, to read, to be called, to be invoked, to be named. The verb means to call or to summon, but its context and surrounding grammatical setting determine the various shades of meaning given to the word.** Abraham called on the name of the Lord (Gen. 4:26; 12:8); the Lord called to Adam (Gen. 3:9; Ex. 3:4). With the Hebrew preposition meaning to, the verb means to name. Adam named all the animals and birds and his wife Eve (Gen. 2:20; 3:20); and God named the light day (Gen. 1:5). The word may introduce a long message, as in Exodus 34:6, that gives the moral and ethical definition of God. It can also mean to summon, such as when God summoned Bezalel to build the Tabernacle (Ex. 31:2).

In certain contexts, the verb has the sense of proclaiming or announcing. Jezebel urged Ahab to proclaim a holy day of fasting so Naboth could be killed (1 Kgs. 21:9); the Servant of Isaiah proclaimed freedom for the captives and prisoners (Is. 61:1). The word may mean simply to call out or cry out, as Potiphar's wife said she did (Gen. 39:15; 1 Kgs. 18:27, 28).

The word means to read aloud from a scroll or a book: the king of Israel was to read aloud from a copy of the Law (Deut. 17:19); just as Moses read the Book of the Covenant to all Israel at Sinai (Ex. 24:7). Baruch read the scroll of Jeremiah to the people (Jer. 36:6, 8).

In the passive stem, the word means to be called or summoned: Esther was called by name (Esther 2:14); in the book of Esther, the secretaries who were to carry out the king's orders were summoned (Esther 3:12; Is. 31:4). News that was delivered was called out or reported (Jer. 4:20). In Nehemiah's reform, the Book of Moses was read aloud in the audience of the people (Neh. 13:1). Also, Adam called his wife, i.e., named her, woman (Gen. 2:23). The word takes on the nuance of to be reckoned or called. Genesis 21:12 describes how Abraham's seed would be reckoned by the Lord through Isaac. *

CALL OUT – Dan. 6:20 ➔ CRY OUT <2200>.

CALLED – Num. 1:16; 26:9 ➔ CHOSEN <7148>.

CALLOUS (BE) – Ps. 119:70 ➔ FAT (BE) <2954>.

CALM – [1] Neh. 8:11 ➔ SILENCE!, KEEP SILENCE! <2013> [2] Ps. 107:29 ➔ STILL <1827>.

CALM (BE, BECOME) – Jon. 1:11, 12 ➔ QUIET (BE) <8367>.

CALM (GROW) – Ps. 107:30 ➔ QUIET (BE) <8367>.

CALMNESS – ***marpē'*** [masc. noun: מַרְפֵּא <4832>; from HEAL <7495> (in the sense of placidity)] ▶ **This word refers to a state of security, stability, relaxation. It also indicates peace.** A heart of peace is said to be a source of life for the body (Prov. 14:30: sound, tranquil, at peace). It has the sense of keeping calm amid tension and anger (Eccl. 10:4; also translated composure, conciliation, yielding). The Hebrew word also means health, healing; see REMEDY <4832>. ¶

CALNEH, CALNO – ***kalneh, kalnēh, kalnô*** [proper noun: כַּלְנֵה, כַּלְנֵה, כַּלְנוֹ <3641>; of foreign deriv.] ▶ **A city founded by Nimrod.** Refs.: Gen. 10:10; Is. 10:9; Amos 6:2. ¶

CALYX – Ex. 25:31, 33–36; 37:17, 19–22 ➔ BULB <3730>.

CAMEL – 1 ***gāmāl*** [masc. noun: גָּמָל <1581>; apparently from REWARD (verb) <1580>] ▶ **This animal was fitted to travel in desert areas.** It was a property of great value (Gen. 12:16; 24:10; Ex. 9:3; Judg. 7:12; 1 Sam. 15:3); used as a beast of burden (Gen. 24; 37:25; 1 Kgs. 10:2; Is. 30:6); and for riding (Gen. 31:17, 34; 1 Sam. 30:17). However, it was forbidden as food (Lev. 11:4; Deut. 14:7). *

2 ***kirkārāh*** [fem. noun: כִּרְכָּרָה <3753>; from DANCE (verb) <3769> (in the sense of a rapid motion as if dancing)] ▶ **An animal used for swift transportation in the time of Isaiah.** Ref.: Is. 66:20; other translations: swift beast, dromedary. It will be used as one means to gather together the nations to Jerusalem to see the glory of the Lord. ¶

– 3 1 Kgs. 4:28 ➔ HORSE <7409> b.

CAMEL (YOUNG) – 1 ***bêḵer*** [masc. noun: בֵּכֶר <1070>; from BORN FIRST (BE) <1069> (in the sense of youth)] ▶ **These camels were beasts of burden that could cross the deserts quickly.** The word depicts young camels bringing goods and products to a glorified Zion (Is. 60:6; also translated dromedary) from Midian and Ephah. ¶

2 ***biḵrāh*** [fem. noun: בִּכְרָה <1072>; fem. of CAMEL (YOUNG) <1070>] ▶ **This word describes a swift, young she-camel confused and running here and there.** Israel had been doing just that (Jer. 2:23; also translated dromedary). ¶

CAMP – 1 ***ṭiyrāh*** [fem. noun: טִירָה <2918>; fem. of (an equivalent to) ROW (noun) <2905>] ▶ **This word indicates a surrounding enclosure of some kind, such as a circular encampment or surrounding villages occupying an area. It also translated settlement, castle, fort, encampment, palace, battlement, tower, dwelling, habitation, place.** Ishmael's clans lived in such camps or villages (Gen. 25:16), probably with small stone walls. So did the Midianites and others (Num. 31:10; Ezek. 25:4). It denotes a row of stones or masonry around a court or its walls (Ezek. 46:23: row, ledge); or a battlement constructed around or on a wall (Song 8:9). Other refs.: 1 Chr. 6:54; Ps. 69:25. ¶

2 ***maḥ^{a}neh*** [masc. noun: מַחֲנֶה <4264>; from ENCAMP <2583>] ▶ **This word means a multitude, and also an army, a company.** The basic idea of this word is that of a multitude of people who have gathered together (Ezek. 1:24). This word is often used within the context of travel, like the wandering Israelites (Ex. 14:19, 20; Num. 4:5); or within the context of war (1 Sam. 17:1; 2 Kgs. 6:24; 19:35). This word is most often used of Israel but is also used to describe foreign nations (Josh. 10:5; Judg. 7:8–11, 13–15; 1 Sam. 29:1); or even God's encampment (Gen. 32:2; 1 Chr. 12:22). *

3 ***taḥ^{a}nāh*** [fem. noun: תַּחֲנָה <8466>; from ENCAMP <2583>] ▶ **This word refers to the place where a group of people set up temporary living headquarters.** Usually, it refers to a military encampment that would also post sentries, etc. (2 Kgs. 6:8). ¶

CAMP, CIRCLE OF THE CAMP – 1 Sam. 17:20; 26:5, 7 ➔ ENCAMPMENT <4570> a.

CAMPFIRE – Ps. 68:13 ➔ HOOK <8240> b.

CANAAN – ***k^{e}na'an*** [proper noun: כְּנַעַן <3667>; from SUBDUE <3665>]: land of purple; other possible meanings: humiliated, lowland, merchant ▶

a. Canaan was the son of Ham, Noah's second son. He is listed third (1 Chr. 1:13) or fourth (Gen. 10:6; 1 Chr. 1:8). Noah cursed him because of his father's sin and placed him under both Shem and Japheth (Gen. 9:18, 25–27). His basic social picture was one of servitude to others.

b. See a. above. The name Canaan means "land of purple" and refers to the land or people of Canaan. The Greek word Phoenicia also means the same. But this traditional explanation of the name has been strongly challenged. Canaan manufactured and exported a purple dye. The land later was called Palestine (also translated Palestina, Philistia) because of the

Philistines who immigrated there (part of the "sea peoples"). The language of Canaan was Semitic, and Hebrew is closely tied to it. This territory was inhabited by the descendants of Ham's son Canaan (Gen. 10:6–19). The Promised Land to Israel was essentially this land and its inhabitants which God would deliver to His chosen people, Israel, according to His promises to Abraham (Gen. 11:31; 12:5; 17:8; Ex. 3:16, 17). Canaan became the burial place of the patriarchs (Gen. 23:19). The Canaanites were off-limits for the Hebrews and Israelites—even in the time of the patriarchs (Gen. 28:1, 6).

The geographical and climatic features of the land were and are far ranging. It stretched from Kadesh Barnea in the south to Lebo Hamath in the north. Bordered on the west by the Great Sea, it reached to beyond the Jordan on the east, beyond the Dead Sea, and east of Damascus in the north (Gen. 15:17–21; Num. 34:2–29). Ezekiel mentions it without naming its extent in his Temple vision (Ezek. 47:13–48:29).
c. The name and even the word Canaan became synonymous with merchant, tradesman in certain historical and textual contexts. Canaan was the trade center for many nations in the Middle East. The city of Tyre was an import/export center (Is. 23:8), but the word could in this usage refer to other nations who were merchants or tradesmen, e.g., Babylon (Ezek. 16:29; 17:4). *

CANAANITE – ***k^{e}na^{ʿa}niy*** [masc. proper noun: כְּנַעֲנִי <3669>; patrial from CANAAN <3667>] ▶ **This word refers to a person of Canaan.** Refs.: Gen. 12:6; 38:2. With the definite article in front, it means the Canaanite (Num. 21:1; 33:40). The Hebrew word also means a merchant, a trader; see MERCHANT <3669>. *

CANAL – ***'ûḇāl, 'uḇāl*** [masc. noun: אוּבָל, אֻבָל <180>; from BRING <2986> (in the sense of STREAM <2988>)] ▶ **The word refers to a waterway in Susa, one of the capital cities of Persia.** Refs.: Dan. 8:2, 3, 6; also translated river. ¶

CANCEL – Is. 28:18 ➔ COVER (verb) <3722>.

CANCELING – Deut. 15:1, 2, 9; 31:10 ➔ REMISSION <8059>.

CANDLESTICK – Dan. 5:5 ➔ LAMPSTAND <5043>.

CANE – Zech. 8:4 ➔ SUPPORT (noun) <4938> a.

CANKERWORM – Joel 1:4; 2:25; Nah. 3:15, 16 ➔ LOCUST (YOUNG, CRAWLING) <3218>.

CANNEH – ***kanneh*** [proper noun: כַּנֵּה <3656>; for CALNEH <3641>] ▶ **A place in Mesopotamia.** Ref.: Ezek. 27:23. ¶

CANOPY – [1] ***'āḇ, 'ōḇ*** [masc. noun: עָב, עֹב <5646>; from an unused root meaning to cover] ▶
a. This word indicates an overhang, thick planks. Its technical meaning is not known for sure. Suggestions are as indicated: a canopy, a threshold (1 Kgs. 7:6; Ezek. 41:25, 26). ¶
b. This word also means a threshold, an overhanging roof. Refs.: 1 Kgs. 7:6; Ezek. 41:25, 26. It was a structure in front of certain other features of the king's palace. ¶
[2] ***šap̱riyr*** [masc. noun: שַׁפְרִיר <8237>; from BEAUTIFUL (BE) <8231>] ▶ **This word may refer to a tapestry, or other ornament, above a throne; it is also translated pavilion.** It refers to a covering structure of some kind placed in context over a specific set of stones in Egypt, indicating ownership and rulership in that spot (Jer. 43:10). ¶
– [3] 2 Kgs. 16:18 ➔ COVERED WAY <4329> [4] Is. 4:5 ➔ CHAMBER <2646> [5] Is. 40:22 ➔ CURTAIN <1852>.

CAP – [1] ***migḇā'āh*** [fem. noun: מִגְבָּעָה <4021>; from the same as HILL <1389>] ▶ **This word denotes a turban, a headband.** It indicates special high caps that Aaron's sons wore when performing priestly duties (Ex. 28:40; 29:9; 39:28; Lev. 8:13); it is also

translated hat, bonnet. They were made of fine linen to project beauty and splendor in honor of God. ¶
– [2] Dan. 3:21 ➔ HAT <3737>.

CAPACITY – 1 Chr. 23:29 ➔ MEASURE (noun) <4884>.

CAPE – Is. 3:22 ➔ MANTLE <4595>.

CAPER – Is. 13:21 ➔ DANCE (verb) <7540>.

CAPERBERRY – Eccl. 12:5 ➔ DESIRE (noun) <35>.

CAPHTOR – ***kaptôr, kaptōr*** [proper noun: כַּפְתּוֹר, כַּפְתֹּר <3731>; apparently the same as BULB <3730>]: crowning ▶ **The original seat of the Philistines, maybe the island of Crete.** Refs.: Deut. 2:23; Jer. 47:4; Amos 9:7. ¶

CAPHTORIM – See CAPHTORITE <3732>.

CAPHTORITE – ***kaptōriy*** [proper noun: כַּפְתֹּרִי <3732>; patrial from CAPHTOR <3731>] ▶ **A tribe descending from the Egyptians.** Refs.: Gen. 10:14; Deut. 2:23; 1 Chr. 1:12. ¶

CAPITAL – [1] ***kōteret*** [fem. noun: כֹּתֶרֶת <3805>; act. part. of CROWN (noun) <3803>] ▶ **This word indicates the crown of a pillar.** It is an ancient, technical architectural term describing the decorative top or top piece of a column or pillar (1 Kgs. 7:16–20, 31, 41, 42; KJV: chapiter). Sometimes it was made of bronze (2 Kgs. 25:17; Jer. 52:22). Other refs.: 2 Chr. 4:12, 13. ¶
[2] ***ṣepet*** [fem. noun: צֶפֶת <6858>; from an unused root meaning to encircle] ▶ **This word refers to a capital of a pillar.** It indicates the top part of a column or pilaster as opposed to the shaft and base sections (2 Chr. 3:15; KJV: chapiter). ¶
– [3] Amos 9:1; Zeph. 2:14 ➔ BULB <3730>.

CAPRICIOUS CHILDREN – ***taʿᵃlûliym*** [masc. plur. noun: תַּעֲלוּלִים <8586>; from DO <5953> b. (in the sense of to act childishly)] ▶ **This word defines children, God's mockingly appointed rulers of His people, as indecisive or as making decisions without reason, on a whim.** Ref.: Is. 3:4; also translated children, infants, babes. In a different context, its negative connotations give it the meaning of punishments (Is. 66:4; also translated delusions, harsh treatment). ¶

CAPSTONE – Zech. 4:7 ➔ TOP <7222>.

CAPTAIN – [1] ***kāriy*** [noun: כָּרִי <3746>; perhaps an abridged plur. of LAMB <3733> in the sense of leader (of the flock)] ▶ **This word means a military order, the Carites.** Under Benaiah (2 Sam. 20:23), the Kerethites or Cherethites, along with the Pelethites, remained loyal to David and Solomon when Adonijah attempted to become king. Joab, the commander of David's army, however, supported Adonijah (cf. 1 Kgs. 1:18, 19).

The Karites or Carites again supported a king against treachery when they helped overthrow Athaliah and installed Joash as king (2 Kgs. 11:19). It is possible that the Pelethites in 2 Kings were a different group of Pelethites because the spelling of the Hebrew word is slightly different than in other references. What is clear is this term designates a special military unit. Other ref.: 2 Kgs. 11:4. ¶
[2] ***qāṣiyn*** [masc. noun: קָצִין <7101>; from CUT OFF <7096> in the sense of determining] ▶ **The root meaning of this word is one who decides. It is also translated commander, chief, leader.** Sometimes the word indicates military leadership (Josh. 10:24; Judg. 11:6, 11; cf. Judg. 11:9; Dan. 11:18), but it can signify a nonmilitary authority (Is. 3:6, 7). A captain could be chosen by men (Judg. 11:6; Is. 3:6); but he was ultimately appointed by God (Judg. 11:11; cf. Judg. 2:16, 18; 11:29). Captains were sometimes subordinate to a higher human authority (Josh. 10:24; Dan. 11:18); but not always (Judg. 11:6, 11; cf. Judg. 12:7, 8). They had responsibility before God for the moral state of their followers (Is.

1:10; Mic. 3:1, 9); but their subordinates also had responsibility to influence their rulers positively (Prov. 25:15). Other refs.: Prov. 6:7; Is. 22:23. ¶
– 3 Jer. 51:27; Nah. 3:17 ➔ MARSHAL <2951> 4 Jon. 1:6 ➔ SAILOR <2259> 5 See LEADER <5057>.

CAPTIVE – 1 See CAPTIVITY <1473> 2 See PRISONER <615>, PRISONERS <616>.

CAPTIVE (TAKE) – ***šāḇāh*** [verb: שָׁבָה <7617>; a prim. root] ▶ **The main idea behind this word is that of being taken prisoner as a spoil of war or other military raid. It also means to lead into captivity.** It signified the fate that befell Lot at the hands of Chedorlaomer and his compatriots (Gen. 14:14); the threat that hung over the heads of any rebellious people (1 Kgs. 8:46); and forced enslavement by a foreign military power (2 Kgs. 5:2). *

CAPTIVE EXILE – ***ṣā'āh*** [verb: צָעָה <6808>; a prim. root] ▶ **This Hebrew verb means to imprison, to take captive.** It depicts a person imprisoned, kept in confinement and in chains (Is. 51:14; also translated exile, who is bowed down, cowering prisoner). ¶

CAPTIVES – 1 ***šiḇyāh*** [fem. noun: שִׁבְיָה <7633>; from CAPTIVE (TAKE) <7617>] ▶ **This word always describes those who had been defeated in war and were taken prisoner into a foreign land.** It was also used to describe the captives taken in victory by Israel (Deut. 21:11); as well as those taken in defeat from Israel by a foreign nation (2 Chr. 28:11, 13–15; Neh. 4:4). *
– 2 Ps. 126:1 ➔ CAPTIVITY <7870> 3 Is. 20:4; 45:13; Jer. 24:5; 28:4 ➔ CAPTIVITY <1546> 4 Dan. 2:25; 5:13; 6:13 ➔ CAPTIVITY <1547>.

CAPTIVITY – 1 ***gôlāh, gōlāh*** [fem. noun: גּוֹלָה, גֹּלָה <1473>; act. part. fem. of REVEAL <1540> (in the sense of to go into exile)] ▶ **This word refers to deprivation of liberty. It also means exile, captives, exiles.** It most often refers to the Babylonian captivity and its captives (2 Kgs. 24:16; Ezek. 1:1) but is also used of the Assyrian captivity (1 Chr. 5:22) and even of the exiles of foreign nations (Jer. 48:7, 11; Amos 1:15). The phrase, children of the captivity, occurs in Ezra and describes those who returned from the captivity in Babylon (Ezra 4:1; 6:19, 20; 10:7, 16). *
2 ***gālûṯ*** [fem. sing. noun: גָּלוּת <1546>; fem. from REVEAL <1540> (in the sense of to go into exile)] ▶ **This word refers to deprivation of liberty. It also means exile, captives, exiles.** It is used with the meaning of exiles in the prophetic messages concerning the prisoners of the king of Assyria (Is. 20:4); those exiles whom the Lord will free (Is. 45:13); and those whom God would protect (Jer. 24:5; 28:4). It is also used to refer to Jehoiachin's captivity (2 Kgs. 25:27; Ezek. 1:2), and the exile of the Israelites as a whole (Ezek. 33:21). It comes from the Hebrew root *gālāh* <1540>: to uncover; see REVEAL <1540>. *
3 ***gālû*** [Aramaic fem. sing. noun: גָּלוּ <1547>; corresponding to <1546> above] ▶ **This word refers to deprivation of liberty, exile; it is also translated exiles, captives.** In Aramaic, it is commonly used in the phrase, sons of captivity. In the book of Ezra, the word refers to the exiles who celebrated when the Temple was rebuilt after King Darius' decree (Ezra 6:16); it is also translated exiles for sons of the captivity. In the book of Daniel, it refers to Daniel's captivity (Dan. 2:25; 5:13; 6:13). ¶
4 ***ṭalṭêlāh*** [fem. noun: טַלְטֵלָה <2925>; from CAST (verb) <2904>] ▶ **This word indicates a deprivation of liberty, a hurling.** It describes figuratively the casting down of a ruler, Shebna, from power and authority (Is. 22:17). ¶
5 ***šiyḇāh*** [fem. noun: שִׁיבָה <7870>; by permutation from TURN <7725>] ▶ **This word indicates a condition of confinement and subjection to others.** In context captivity refers to the seventy-year exile of Israel in Babylon (Ps. 126:1); the word is also translated captives, fortunes. ¶
– 6 Ps. 144:14 ➔ GO OUT <3318> 7 Obad. 1:12 ➔ DISASTER <5235>.

CAPTIVITY, CAPTIVES – [1] ***šeḇûṯ, šeḇiyṯ*** [fem. noun: שְׁבוּת, שְׁבִית <7622>; from CAPTIVE (TAKE) <7617>] ► **This word conveys either a state of exile, such as being taken for a spoil of war, or the subjects of such deprivation of liberty.** The chief use was in declaring the liberating power of the Lord in releasing His people from such banishment (Deut. 30:3; Jer. 33:7; Hos. 6:11). Interestingly, when Job's fortunes were restored, he was said to have been freed from captivity (Job 42:10). *

[2] ***šeḇiy*** [masc. noun: שְׁבִי <7628>; from CAPTIVE (TAKE) <7617>] ► **This word was normally used to describe those captured in war and taken back to the conquering country.** Refs.: Num. 21:1; Ezra 3:8; Neh. 1:2. It could describe anything captured, such as booty (Num. 31:26); or horses (Amos 4:10). The word could also be used to describe prisoners in a dungeon (Ex. 12:29). *

CAPTURE (noun) – ***leḵeḏ*** [masc. noun: לֶכֶד <3921>; from CAPTURE (verb) <3920>] ► **This word means a taking, a seizure.** It is used figuratively of a person's being caught in the wicked's intrigues and attacks (Prov. 3:26: from being taken, caught, snared). ¶

CAPTURE (verb) – ***lāḵaḏ*** [verb: לָכַד <3920>; a prim. root] ► **This word means to take, to seize.** It indicates taking possession of, capturing, or catching various things: a city (Num. 21:32); a land (Josh. 10:42); captives of all social ranks in war (Judg. 7:25; 2 Sam. 8:4); foxes (Judg. 15:4); a river ford in the sense of seizing and occupying it (Judg. 3:28); as well as the waters of a river (Judg. 7:24, 25). It has the sense of the Lord choosing or picking something (Josh. 7:14–18); or seizing control of the government reins of a kingdom (1 Sam. 14:47), often by force (Dan. 11:15, 18). It is used figuratively in metaphors: of a sinner being seized in the snares of a wicked woman (Eccl. 7:26); of persons ensnared by the words of their own mouths (Prov. 6:2). It is used to indicate the "seizing" of water as it turns to ice and hardens (Job 38:30); of being seized by "cords of affliction" (Job 36:8). It is used of one thing interlocking with another (Job 41:17). *

CARAVAN – [1] ***'ōreḥāh*** [fem. noun: אֹרְחָה <736>; fem. act. part. of TRAVEL <732>] ► **This word means a traveling group; it is also translated company, traveling company.** It refers to a group of Ishmaelites, merchants, taking their wares to Egypt (Gen. 37:25). Merchant caravans of an Arabian Dedanite tribe are depicted in Isaiah 21:13, that will be attacked by both the Assyrians and Babylonians (cf. Ezek. 27:20; 38:13). ¶

– [2] Job 6:19 → WAY <1979>.

CARAVANS – Job 6:19 → PATH <734>.

CARAWAY – Is. 28:25, 27 → DILL <7100>.

CARBUNCLE – [1] Ex. 28:17; 39:10; Ezek. 28:13 → EMERALD <1304> [2] Is. 54:12 → CRYSTAL <688>.

CARCAS – ***karkas*** [masc. proper noun: כַּרְכַּס <3752>; of Persian origin]: severe ► **One of the seven chamberlains, or eunuchs, of king Ahasuerus.** Ref.: Esther 1:10. ¶

CARCASS – [1] ***rāmûṯ*** [fem. noun: רָמוּת <7419>; from EXALT <7311> (in the sense of to breed worms)] ►

a. This word indicates remains, refuse. It refers to the remains of rotting and decaying corpses of Pharaoh and the Egyptians (Ezek. 32:5).

b. Some translators render this word, less likely, as height (KJV). ¶

– [2] Gen. 15:11; etc. → CORPSE <6297> [3] Lev. 5:2; Deut. 14:8; Is. 5:25 → CORPSE <5038> [4] Judg. 14:8 → FALL (noun) <4658> [5] Judg. 14:8, 9 → BODY <1472>.

CARCHEMISH – ***karkemiyš*** [proper noun: כַּרְכְּמִישׁ <3751>; of foreign deriv.]: stronghold of Kemosh ► **A fortified city in Upper Mesopotamia where Babylon**

defeated Pharaoh Neco, king of Egypt. Babylon became the new superpower of the Middle East in 605 B.C. (2 Chr. 35:20, 21) and ruled over Syro-Palestine (Jer. 46:1, 2). Other ref.: Is. 10:9. ¶

CARE – 1 Ezra 5:8: with great care ➔ DILIGENTLY <629> 2 Ps. 94:19 ➔ ANXIETY <8312>.

CARE (TAKE) – 1 1 Kgs. 1:2 ➔ PROFITABLE (BE) <5532> a. 2 Ezra 4:22 ➔ HEED (TAKE) <2095>.

CARE (UNDER THE) – ***'omnāh*** [fem. noun: אָמְנָה <545>; fem. of TRUTH <544> (in the specific sense of training)] ► **This word means rearing up or bringing up.** It describes the care and rearing one receives under another's watchful eye, such as Esther received from Mordecai (Esther 2:20). ¶

CARE FOR – 1 ***ṭāpaḥ*** [verb: טָפַח <2946>; a prim. root] ► **This word means to handle solicitously; it is also translated to swaddle, to bear, to hold.** Ref.: Lam. 2:22. The Hebrew word also means to stretch, to spread out; see SPREAD OUT <2946>. ¶
– 2 Is. 34:15 ➔ GATHER <1716> 3 Ezek. 34:12 ➔ SEEK <1243>.

CARED FOR (ONES) – ***ṭippuḥiym*** [masc. plur. noun: טִפֻּחִים <2949>; from SPREAD OUT <2946>] ► **This word refers to children receiving tender attention.** Possibly it refers to children of such a quality, e.g., born healthy (NASB); or of a tiny size (KJV: of a span long). Ref.: Lam. 2:20 (NIV, ESV; NKJV: to cuddle). ¶

CAREFUL (BE) – 1 Lev. 22:2 ➔ SEPARATE <5144> 2 Ezra 4:22 ➔ HEED (TAKE) <2095> 3 Jer. 17:8 ➔ ANXIOUS (BE, BECOME) <1672> 4 Dan. 3:16 ➔ NEED (verb and noun) <2818>.

CARES – 1 Ps. 55:22 ➔ BURDEN <3053> 2 Eccl. 5:3 ➔ TASK <6045>.

CARESSES – Prov. 7:18 ➔ LOVE (noun) <159>.

CARITE – 2 Kgs. 11:4, 9 ➔ CAPTAIN <3746>.

CARKAS – See CARCAS <3752>.

CARMEL – 1 ***karmel*** [proper noun: כַּרְמֶל <3760>; the same as FIELD (FERTILE) <3759>]: fruitful land; the word is sometimes translated as "vineyard of God" (VINEYARD <3754> plus GOD <410>) ►
a. It is a high mountain protruding out from the Mediterranean coastline in northern Israel in Manasseh. By extension it refers to the range of hills in this territory as well. It was the place where Elijah defeated the prophets of Baal and restored Yahweh, the Lord, as God in Israel (1 Kgs. 18:19–42). It was known for its beauty (Song 7:5) and prominent position in the land. Its "withering" or "blossoming" tended to be used as a sign of blessing or judgment from the Lord (Amos 1:2; 9:3; Mic. 7:14, NIV, "fertile pasturelands"). In some places, it is translated as "fertile land" (esp. NIV, Is. 16:10) or "fruitful place" (KJV, Jer. 2:7; 4:26). *
b. A city near Hebron. Refs.: Josh. 15:55; 1 Sam. 15:12; 25:2, 5, 7, 40. ¶
– 2 2 Chr. 26:10; 2 Kgs. 19:23; Is. 37:24 ➔ FIELD (FERTILE, FRUITFUL, PLENTIFUL) <3759> a.

CARMELITE – ***karmᵉliy*** [masc. proper noun: כַּרְמְלִי <3761>; patron. from CARMEL <3760>] ► **Inhabitant of the city of Carmel.** Refs.: 1 Sam. 30:5; 2 Sam. 2:2; 3:3; 23:35; 1 Chr. 11:37. ¶

CARMELITESS – ***karmᵉliyṯ*** [fem. proper noun: כַּרְמְלִית <3762>; fem. of CARMELITE <3761>] ► **Abigail was a Carmelitess, i.e., an inhabitant of the city of Carmel.** Refs.: 1 Sam. 27:3; 1 Chr. 3:1. ¶

CARMI – ***karmiy*** [masc. proper noun: כַּרְמִי <3756>; from VINEYARD <3754>]: vinedresser ►
a. Son of Reuben. Refs.: Gen. 46:9; Ex. 6:14; Num. 26:6; 1 Chr. 5:3. ¶
b. A Judaite, father of Achan. Refs.: Josh. 7:1, 18; 1 Chr. 2:7; 4:1. ¶

CARMITE – ***karmiy*** [masc. proper noun: כַּרְמִי <3757>; patron. from CARMI <3756>] ▶ **Member of a family descending from Carmi.** Ref.: Num. 26:6. ¶

CARNELIAN – Ex. 28:17; 39:10 ➔ SARDIUS <124>.

CARPET – Ezek. 27:24 ➔ TREASURE <1595>.

CARRIAGE – 1 ***'appiryôn*** [masc. noun: אַפִּרְיוֹן <668>; prob. of Egyptian deriv.] ▶ **The word describes the palanquin or sedan chair in which Solomon rode on his wedding day.** Ref.: Song 3:9; also translated chariot, sedan chair, palanquin. ¶
2 ***n^eśû'āh*** [fem. noun: נְשׂוּאָה <5385>; from CARRY <5375>] ▶ **This word refers to what is borne or carried about.** It refers, in context, satirically, to idols that were carried about by beasts of burden, idols that were stupid, immobile gods (Is. 46:1). ¶
– 3 Judg. 18:21 ➔ GLORIOUS <3520> b.

CARRIED (WHAT IS) – Is. 46:1 ➔ CARRIAGE <5385>.

CARRIER – 1 Kgs. 5:15; 2 Chr. 2:2, 18 ➔ BURDEN-BEARER <5449>.

CARRIERS (BE, SERVE AS) – Ezek. 27:25 ➔ JOURNEY (verb) <7788>.

CARRION BIRD – Ezek. 39:4 ➔ BIRD OF PREY <5861>.

CARRION VULTURE – ***rāḥām, rāḥāmāh*** [masc. noun: רָחָם, רָחָמָה <7360>; from COMPASSION (HAVE) <7355>] ▶ **The exact identification of these birds is difficult. It refers to an unclean bird that was forbidden to Israel as food.** It fed upon, among other things, other animals, fish, carcasses dead or alive (Lev. 11:18; Deut. 14:17; also translated gier eagle, osprey). ¶

CARRY – 1 ***nāśā'*** [verb: נָשָׂא <5375>; a prim. root] ▶ **This verb also means to lift, to take away. It is used almost six hundred times in the Hebrew Bible and covers three distinct semantic ranges.** The first range is to lift, which occurs in both literal (Gen. 7:17; 29:1; Ezek. 10:16) and figurative statements: to lift the hand in taking an oath (Deut. 32:40); in combat (2 Sam. 18:28); as a sign (Is. 49:22); in retribution (Ps. 10:12). Other figurative statements include the lifting of: the head (Gen. 40:13); the face (2 Sam. 2:22); the eyes (Gen. 13:10); the voice (1 Sam. 30:4). It is also important to note that a person can take up or induce iniquity by a number of actions (Ex. 28:43; Lev. 19:17; 22:9; Num. 18:32). The second semantic category is to bear or to carry and is used especially in reference to the bearing of guilt or punishment of sin (Gen. 4:13; Lev. 5:1). This flows easily then into the concept of the representative or substitutionary bearing of one person's guilt by another (Lev. 10:17; 16:22). The final category is to take away. It can be used in the simple sense of taking something (Gen. 27:3); to take a wife or to get married (Ruth 1:4); to take away guilt or to forgive (Gen. 50:17); to take away or to destroy (Job 32:22). *
– 2 Ezra 5:15 ➔ BRING DOWN <5182> 3 Prov. 6:27 ➔ TAKE <2846> 4 Dan. 2:35 ➔ INSURRECTION (MAKE) <5376> 5 See BRING <2986>, <2987>.

CARRY AWAY – 1 Ezra 5:12 ➔ BRING OVER <1541> 2 Ps. 90:5 ➔ POUR OUT <2229>.

CARRY OUT – Lam. 2:17 ➔ CUT OFF <1214>.

CARRY UP – 1 Dan. 3:22 ➔ GO UP <5559> b. 2 Dan. 3:22 ➔ TAKE UP <5267>.

CARSHENA – ***karš^enā'*** [masc. proper noun: כַּרְשְׁנָא <3771>; of foreign origin]: illustrious ▶ **One of the seven princes of Persia and Media next to King Ahasuerus.** Ref.: Esther 1:14. ¶

CART – Gen. 45:19, 21; etc. ➔ WAGON <5699>.

CARVE – [1] ***ḥāqāh*** [verb: חָקָה <2707>; a prim. root] ▶ **This word also means to cut, to engrave, to portray.** It is used of a process of cutting or carving on wood or stone all kinds of religious art work (1 Kgs. 6:35: carved work, engraved work, carvings), especially on or in the Temple. It describes symbols and items that had been engraved on the walls of the Temple illegally as well (Ezek. 8:10; also translated to portrait, to pourtray, to engrave), including engravings of Babylonians (Ezek. 23:14: to portrait, to pourtray). It is used figuratively of the Lord's engraving, setting a limit, for the life of a person to follow (Job 13:27: to set a limit, to set a print, to put marks). ¶
[2] ***qāla'*** [verb: קָלַע <7049>; a prim. root] ▶ **This word describes the skilled sculptures and cuttings of Israel's craftsmen, especially in the Temple.** Refs.: 1 Kgs. 6:29, 32, 35. For another meaning of the Hebrew word, see SLING (verb) <7049>. ¶
– [3] Ps. 144:12 ➔ CUT (verb) <2404> [4] Hab. 2:18 ➔ CUT (verb) <6458>.

CARVED – [1] 1 Kgs. 6:18, 29, 32 ➔ CARVING <4734> [2] Prov. 7:16 ➔ COLORED <2405> [3] Song 5:14 ➔ POLISHED <6247>.

CARVED WORK – 1 Kgs. 6:35 ➔ CARVE <2707>.

CARVED, CARVED IMAGE – Lev. 26:1; Num. 33:52; Ezek. 8:12 ➔ PICTURE <4906>.

CARVING – [1] ***miqla'aṯ*** [fem. noun: מִקְלַעַת <4734>; from CARVE <7049>] ▶ **This word designates something sculpted or engraved.** It indicates something that has been cut out, whittled, such as flowers, cherubim, palm trees, etc. (1 Kgs. 6:18, 29, 32; 7:31). It could be made of wood, stone, or metal. ¶
– [2] 1 Kgs. 6:35 ➔ CARVE <2707>.

CASIPHIA – ***kāsipyā'*** [proper noun: כָּסִפְיָא <3703>; perhaps from SILVER <3701>]: silvery ▶ **A place on the way between Babylon and Jerusalem.** Ref.: Ezra 8:17. ¶

CASLUHIM – ***kasluḥiym*** [proper noun: כַּסְלֻחִים <3695>; a plur. prob. of foreign deriv.] ▶ **A people probably descending from the Egyptians and from whom the Philistines came.** Refs.: Gen. 10:14; 1 Chr. 1:12. ¶

CASLUHITES – Gen. 10:14; 1 Chr. 1:12 ➔ CASLUHIM <3695>.

CASSIA – [1] ***qiddāh*** [fem. noun: קִדָּה <6916>; from BOW DOWN <6915>] ▶ **This was a fine spice (cassia beds) used to make the anointing oil in the Tabernacle.** Ref.: Ex. 30:24. It was used in international trade in Tyre (Ezek. 27:19). ¶
[2] ***qᵉṣiy'āh*** [fem. noun: קְצִיעָה <7102>; from SCRAPE <7106> (in the sense of removing unwanted features of something)] ▶ **This word refers to a spice made from the bark of a tree of the laurel family of plants.** A coarse variety of cinnamon was obtained by grinding the bark (Ps. 45:8). ¶

CAST (noun) – [1] ***mûṣāq*** [masc. noun: מוּצָק <4165>; from EARRINGS <5694> (in the sense of adornment for people)] ▶ **This word refers to a casting, cast metal, a hard mass.** It is used of artistic metal products, indicating they were cast molten bronze (1 Kgs. 7:16, 23, 33, 37; 2 Chr. 4:2; Job 37:18; 38:38). ¶
– [2] Is. 22:18 ➔ TOSS (noun) <6802>.

CAST (verb) – [1] ***ṭûl*** [verb: טוּל <2904>; a prim. root] ▶ **This word describes hurling, throwing.** It refers to a physical casting of Israel into exile (Jer. 22:28) but also figuratively of a person's being hurled headlong or violently into consternation (Ps. 37:24). It describes one's fate being cast into one's lap (Prov. 16:33); being overwhelmed or overawed emotionally from something (Job 41:9). *
– [2] Ex. 15:4; Josh. 18:6 ➔ SHOOT (verb) <3384> [3] 2 Sam. 16:13 ➔ FLING <6080> [4] 1 Kgs. 7:24; Job 41:23 ➔ POUR, POUR OUT <3332> [5] 1 Kgs. 7:24: when it was cast ➔ lit.: in its casting ➔ CASTING <3333> [6] Job 16:11 ➔ TURN OVER <3399> [7] Ps. 89:44 ➔ DELIVER OVER

<4048> [8] Dan. 3:6, 11, 15, 20, 21, 24; 6:7, 12, 16, 24 ➔ THROW <7412>.

CAST (WHEN IT WAS) – 2 Chr. 4:3 ➔ PIPE <4166>.

CAST AWAY – [1] 2 Sam. 1:21 ➔ ABHOR <1602> [2] Prov. 10:3 ➔ PUSH <1920>.

CAST CLOUT – Jer. 38:11, 12 ➔ RAG <5499>.

CAST DOWN – [1] Ps. 36:12 ➔ DRIVE <1760> [2] Ps. 42:5, 6, 11; 43:5 ➔ BOW DOWN <7743> b. [3] Dan. 7:9 ➔ THROW <7412>.

CAST FORTH – Ps. 144:6 ➔ FLASH FORTH <1299>.

CAST LEAVES – Is. 6:13 ➔ FELLING <7995> b.

CAST LOTS – ***yāḏaḏ*** [verb: יָדַד <3032>; a prim. root] ▶ **This word indicates the tossing of some object or objects to gain an answer or direction in a matter.** Ref.: Joel 3:3. Even foreign nations cast lots to determine how to divide up Jerusalem (Obad. 1:11) and also concerning the great city of Nineveh (Nah. 3:10). ¶

CAST METAL – Ex. 34:17; Lev. 19:4; Deut. 27:15 ➔ COVERING <4541>.

CAST OFF (BE) – Mic. 4:7 ➔ DRIVEN AWAY (BE) <1972>.

CAST ONESELF DOWN – 1 Kgs. 18:42 ➔ STRETCH ONESELF <1457>.

CAST OUT – [1] ***gāraš*** [verb: גָּרַשׁ <1644>; a prim. root] ▶ **With God as subject, the verb depicts God driving or banishing Adam and Eve from the Garden of Eden and driving Cain from His presence.** Refs.: Gen. 3:24; 4:14; Jon. 2:4. The Lord caused Pharaoh to literally drive out the Israelites from Egypt (Ex. 6:1; 12:39) as Pharaoh had earlier forced Moses and Aaron from his presence (Ex. 10:11). It is used of persons driving out others from a location or activity (Ex. 2:17). It is used in the general sense of banishing outcasts from society (Job 30:5). In its figurative usage, it indicates divorcing one's wife (Lev. 21:7). It describes the sea or a river as driven and tossed (Is. 57:20; Amos 8:8). *

– [2] Deut. 6:19; 9:4 ➔ PUSH <1920> [3] Deut. 7:1, 22 ➔ REMOVE <5394> [4] Is. 66:5 ➔ DRIVE <5077> [5] Jer. 6:7 ➔ DIG <6979> c. [6] Jer. 51:34 ➔ WASH <1740>.

CAST OUT (ONE) – Is. 58:7 ➔ WANDERING <4788>.

CASTANETS – ***mᵉnaʿanʿiym*** [masc. plur. noun: מְנַעַנְעִים <4517>; from WANDER <5128> (in the sense of to shake)] ▶

a. This word points out a musical rattle; castanets or sistrum. It indicates a small percussion instrument that rattles, a sistrum or castanets (NASB, NIV, NKJV, ESV) (2 Sam. 6:5). ¶

b. A masculine plural noun referring to a musical horn. It is taken as a small horn, a cornet by earlier translators (2 Sam. 6:5; KJV: cornets). ¶

CASTING – ***yᵉṣuqāh*** [fem. noun: יְצֻקָה <3333>; fem. pass. part. of POUR, POUR OUT <3332>] ▶ **This word indicates the molding of metal.** It refers to something formed into a particular shape or form by pressing or pouring it into a mold (1 Kgs. 7:24; lit.: in its casting). ¶

CASTING DOWN – [1] ***yešaḥ*** [masc. noun: יֶשַׁח <3445>; from an unused root meaning to gape (as the empty stomach)] ▶ **This word denotes emptiness; dung (?). It is a strong word used to illustrate the corrupt, immoral condition of God's people because of their failure to be His moral, ethical, just people.** Their excrement will be among them (Mic. 6:14; KJV, casting down; NASB, vileness; NIV, empty; NKJV, ESV, hunger). The exact meaning is not yet clear, but its sense is evident in the context. ¶

– [2] Job 6:21 ➔ TERROR <2866>.

CASTLE – [1] Gen. 25:16; Num. 31:10; 1 Chr. 6:54 ➔ CAMP <2918> [2] 2 Chr. 17:12; 27:4 ➔ FORTRESS <1003>.

CATASTROPHE – Gen. 19:29 ➔ OVERTHROW (noun) <2018>.

CATCH (noun) – Prov. 12:12 ➔ NET <4685>.

CATCH (verb) – [1] ***ḥāṭap̱*** [verb: חָטַף <2414>; a prim. root] ▶ **This word means to take (by force); it is also translated to seize, to snatch.** It describes seizing upon or catching a person in a physical sense (Judg. 21:21). It is used in a more figurative sense of entrapping, catching poor, weak, helpless persons (Ps. 10:9). In the immediate context, it refers to entrapping or seizing such people for oppressive purposes (Ps. 10:9). ¶
[2] ***ḥālaṯ*** [verb: חָלַט <2480>; a prim. root] ▶ **This word means to pick up, to take as valid.** It indicates an attitude and response toward something said (1 Kgs. 20:33), a catching of the significance of something; the word is also translated to take up, to pick up, to grasp. ¶
[3] ***tāp̱aś*** [verb: תָּפַשׂ <8610>; a prim. root] ▶ **This word means to lay hold of, to seize; to capture; to wield.** It basically means to seize, to get possession of, to catch in its active usages: to grab hold of something, e.g., a garment (Gen. 39:12); to catch and hold a lizard (Prov. 30:28); to capture or to seize a person (1 Sam. 23:26). It has the sense figuratively of holding on to someone or something for support, e. g., Egypt (Ezek. 29:7). In a general sense, it may describe living in or occupying a hill, an area, or a location (Jer. 49:16). It takes on the sense of holding or wielding a tool or a weapon in a skillful way (Ezek. 21:11; Amos 2:15). By extension, it takes on a figurative sense of handling the Law skillfully or planning strategy in warfare (Num. 31:27: Jer. 34:3). In a passive sense, it means to be seized (Jer. 38:23; 50:24). *
– [4] Gen. 22:13 ➔ HOLD (TAKE) <270> [5] Jer. 16:16 ➔ FISH (verb) <1770> [6] Hab. 1:15 ➔ DRAG (verb) <1641>.

CATERPILLAR – [1] ***ḥāsiyl*** [masc. noun: חָסִיל <2625>; from CONSUME <2628>] ▶ **This word identifies also a grasshopper, a locust. It seems to identify a special stage in the development of these insects.** In each case, the insect is associated with God's judgment on Israel (1 Kgs. 8:37 and 2 Chr. 6:28; Ps. 78:46; Is. 33:4; Joel 1:4; 2:25). ¶
– [2] Amos 4:9 ➔ LOCUST <1501>.

CATERPILLER – [1] 1 Kgs. 8:37; 2 Chr. 6:28; Ps. 78:46; Is. 33:4: Joel 1:4; 2:25 ➔ CATERPILLAR <2625> [2] Ps. 105:34 ➔ LOCUST (YOUNG, CRAWLING) <3218>.

CATTLE – [1] Gen. 4:20; 47:6; etc. ➔ LIVESTOCK <4735> [2] Deut. 7:13; 28:4, 18, 51; Ps. 8:7 ➔ HERD <504> [3] Ps. 78:48; Num. 20:4, 8 ➔ ANIMAL <1165> [4] See ANIMAL <929>.

CAUGHT (FROM BEING) – Prov. 3:26 ➔ CAPTURE (noun) <3921>.

CAUL – [1] ***s^e^gôr*** [masc. noun: סְגוֹר <5458>; from CLOSE <5462>] ▶ **This word refers to an enclosure, a chest.** It refers to the part of the body enclosing the heart, the chest cavity (Hos. 13:8). The literal expression "the caul of their heart" (KJV) is translated "rib cage," "breast," "chest." The Hebrew word also means fine gold; see GOLD <5458>. ¶
– [2] Ex. 29:13, 22; Lev. 3:4; etc. ➔ LOBE (LONG, FATTY) <3508>.

CAULDRON – ***qallaḥaṯ*** [fem. noun: קַלַּחַת <7037>; apparently a form for DISH <6747>] ▶ **This word indicates a large kettle or pot.** Sacrificial meat was boiled in a cauldron (1 Sam. 2:14). It is employed in a simile in which the meat in the cauldron was the oppressed people of God (Mic. 3:3). ¶

CAULKER – Ezek. 27:27 ➔ lit.: repairer of seams ➔ DAMAGE (noun) <919>.

CAUSE – [1] ***diḇrāh*** [fem. noun: דִּבְרָה <1700>; fem. of WORD <1697>] ▶ **This**

word means one's case, and also end, regard, manner. In the book of Job, Eliphaz used it to describe how he was laying down his cause before God (Job 5:8). This word is also used in the Psalms when it describes the priest who would exercise his duties in the manner (or: order) of Melchizedek (Ps. 110:4). Sometimes, it is translated much more briefly than it reads in the original language, as the literal translation in Ecclesiastes would read, "concerning the condition (or: estate) of mankind," while the NIV translates it "as for men" (Eccl. 3:18). It can also mean for this reason or because (Eccl. 7:14; 8:2). ¶
– [2] 2 Chr. 10:15 ➔ EVENTS (TURN OF) <5252>.

CAUTIOUSLY – 1 Sam. 15:32 ➔ CHAIN <4574> a.

CAVE – [1] ***kārāh*** [fem. noun: כָּרָה <3741>; fem. of LAMB <3733>] ▶ **This word is also translated shelter, cottage, meadow, well.** It is used only once in Zephaniah 2:6. The ancient text of this passage is difficult to decipher. It has been traditionally rendered as cottages (KJV), but more recent translations give different interpretations, Kerethites (NIV, see KERETHITE <3774>), pastures (NASB; NKJV). ¶
[2] ***meḥillāh*** [fem. noun: מְחִלָּה <4247>; from PIERCE <2490>] ▶ **This word indicates a hole, a cavern.** A hollow or open hole in the ground where one can reasonably seek safety (Is. 2:19), especially during a time of God's judgment. ¶
[3] ***me'ārāh*** [fem. noun: מְעָרָה <4631>; from UNCOVER <5783>] ▶
a. This word refers to a naturally occurring place of retreat or even a place to live. Refs.: Gen. 19:30; 1 Sam. 24:3; 1 Kgs. 19:13. It is also a lair or den for animals (Is. 32:14). Caves served as burial places and were valuable property (Gen. 23:9, 11, 17, 19, 20; 49:29). *
b. This word indicates a wasteland, bare ground. A bare field or area of land that was deserted, uninhabited (Is. 32:14). ¶
– [4] Judg. 15:8, 11 ➔ CLEFT <5585> [5] 2 Sam. 17:9 ➔ PIT <6354> [6] Job 30; Nah. 2:12 ➔ HOLE <2356> [7] Is. 42:22 ➔ HOLE <2352>.

CAVERN – Is. 2:21 ➔ CLEFT <5366>.

CEASE – [1] ***bāṭal*** [verb: בָּטַל <988>; a prim. root] ▶ **This word also means to stand idle, to be inactive.** It describes the inactivity of either the decaying teeth of an elderly person or, literally, those who grind grain using millstones (Eccl. 12:3). It is likely that the writer wants our minds to move back and forth between literal and figurative images in his poetry. ¶
[2] ***beṭêl*** [Aramaic verb: בְּטֵל <989>; corresponding to <988> above] ▶ **This word also means to cause to be inactive, to stop, to discontinue; to delay, to hinder.** It refers to the cessation of work on the Temple of the Lord in the days of Artaxerxes and Darius, kings of Persia (Ezra 4:21, 23, 24; 5:5). The word means more properly delay in Ezra 6:8. ¶
[3] ***dāmāh*** [verb: דָּמָה <1820>; a prim. root] ▶ **This verb means to stop, to cause to perish, to be silent, to destroy.** It is used in reference to beasts that die (Ps. 49:12: to perish); a prophet who feels undone when he sees the Lord (Is. 6:5); Zion's destruction (Jer. 6:2); eyes that weep without ceasing (Lam. 3:49); the destruction of people who have no knowledge (Hos. 4:6); the destruction of merchants (Zeph. 1:11); the destruction of the nation of Edom (Obad. 1:5). *
[4] ***ḥādal*** [verb: חָדַל <2308>; a prim. root] ▶ **This word is used of the cessation or stopping of various things.** For example, worry (1 Sam. 9:5); childbearing (Gen. 18:11); natural phenomena, thunder, etc. (Ex. 9:29, 33, 34); the presence of the poor among Israel (Deut. 15:11); travel on highways; the peasantry (Judg. 5:6, 7); relationships with Job even by his family members (Job 19:14); the Lord's judgments on Israel (Amos 7:5). The word is used to urge Israel to cease to do evil (Is. 1:16). Jeremiah uses it to tell the Israelites to not come, to cease from coming to Babylon with him (Jer. 40:4). It can mean to leave someone alone (Ex. 14:12) or something, such as the pursuit of wealth (Prov. 23:4). In certain

contexts, it means to make up one's mind and act or else (Zech. 11:12). *

5 ***rāpāh*** [verb: רָפָה <7503>; a prim. root] ▶ **This word means to become slack, to relax, to desist, to become discouraged, to become disheartened, to become weak, to become feeble, to let drop, to discourage, to leave alone, to let go, to forsake, to abandon, to be lazy.** The word occurs forty-five times, often with the word *yāḏ* (<3027>), meaning hand, forming an idiomatic phrase that requires careful translation within the context of a particular passage. For example, when Ish-Bosheth, Saul's son, heard that Abner had died, his hands became feeble, i.e., his courage failed him (2 Sam. 4:1; cf. 2 Chr. 15:7; Is. 13:7; Jer. 6:24, 50:43; Ezek. 7:17; 21:7). The term was also employed to signify the act of ceasing from something (Judg. 8:3; 2 Sam. 24:16; Neh. 6:9; Ps. 37:8); of leaving someone alone (Ex. 4:26; Deut. 9:14; Judg. 11:37; Job 7:19); of letting go (Job 27:6; Prov. 4:13; Song 3:4); and of abandoning or forsaking someone (Deut. 4:31; 31:6, 8; Josh. 1:5; 10:6; Ps. 138:8). On rare occasions, the term conveyed a state of laziness or complacency (Ex. 5:8, 17; Josh. 18:3; Prov. 18:9). *

– 6 1 Sam. 10:2 ➔ FORSAKE <5203> 7 Ps. 77:2 ➔ STUNNED (BECOME) <6313> 8 Ps. 77:8 ➔ FAIL <656> 9 Prov. 20:3 ➔ LOSS OF TIME <7674> 10 Prov. 26:20 ➔ QUIET (BE) <8367> 11 Is. 33:1 ➔ END (MAKE AN) <5239>.

CEASE (MAKE TO) – Num. 17:5 ➔ SUBSIDE <7918>.

CEDAR – 1 Is. 44:14 ➔ ASH <766> 2 Ezek. 27:24: made of cedar ➔ bound with cords ➔ CORD <729>.

CEDAR, CEDAR TREE – ***'erez*** [masc. noun: אֶרֶז <730>; from CORD <729>] ▶ **It is a species of tree from Lebanon, evidently a cedar, a tall evergreen tree. Some feel that the word refers to a fir tree, since the cedar has a trunk too short for large construction work.** This word occurs quite often (Lev. 14:4, 6; Num. 19:6; Judg. 9:15; 1 Kgs. 4:33). It was considered a tall, stately tree (Judg. 9:15; 2 Kgs. 14:9; Amos 2:9). Solomon contrasted it with the smallest of plants (1 Kgs. 4:33). It was considered prime construction material (2 Sam. 7:2, 7; Ezra 3:7; Job 40:17; Song 8:9). It is used to depict the strong but devastated Davidic dynasty in a powerful allegory (Ezek. 17:3). *

CEDAR WORK, BEAM OF CEDAR – ***'arzāh*** [fem. noun: אַרְזָה <731>; fem. of CEDAR, CEDAR TREE <730>] ▶ **This word describes the cedar (a tall evergreen tree) construction or furnishings found in the Assyrian palace at Nineveh.** Ref.: Zeph. 2:14. It was laid bare because of God's destruction of the city. Cedar work was a regular feature of royal buildings or furnishings. ¶

CEILED – Ezek. 41:16 ➔ PANELED <7824>.

CEILING – ***sippun*** [masc. noun: סִפֻּן <5604>; from COVER (verb) <5603>] ▶ **This word refers to the top inside covering of the Solomonic Temple.** Ref.: 1 Kgs. 6:15. ¶

CELEBRATE THE RULE – Ps. 2:11 ➔ REJOICE <1523>.

CELL – ***ḥānûṯ*** [fem. noun: חָנוּת <2588>; from ENCAMP <2583>] ▶ **This word also refers to a vaulted room, a cellar.** It refers to a dungeon or a vaulted cell in a house in which Jeremiah was imprisoned (Jer. 37:16; KJV: cabin). ¶

CELLAR – 1 Sam. 13:6 ➔ STRONGHOLD <6877> a.

CENSER – 1 ***maḥtāh*** [fem. noun: מַחְתָּה <4289>; the same as RUIN (noun) <4288> in the sense of removal] ▶ **This word means a snuffholder, a firepan; a bucket, a pan, a small pan.** It was a gold or bronze container used to carry ashes and burned coals (1 Kgs. 7:50); or to carry coals in an offering of incense, a censer (Lev. 10:1;

16:12). It also describes a can of gold used as a lampstand accessory (Ex. 25:38) or snuffholder. It refers to bronze utensils or firepans (Ex. 27:3). *
[2] ***miqṯereṯ*** [fem. noun: מִקְטֶרֶת <4730>; from BURNING (PLACE FOR) <4729>] ▶ **It was an instrument for holding and burning incense to create a pleasant-smelling aroma.** Refs.: 2 Chr. 26:19; Ezek. 8:11. ¶
– [3] Ezra 1:9 ➔ KNIFE <4252>.

CENSUS – ***s*ᵉ*pār*** [masc. noun: סְפָר <5610>; from NUMBER (verb) <5608>] ▶ **This word refers to counting up, numbering something or a population of people.** Solomon recorded the total number of aliens in Israel (2 Chr. 2:17). ¶

CENTER – ***ṭabbûr*** [masc. noun: טַבּוּר <2872>; from an unused root meaning to pile up] ▶ **This word means summit; it is also translated highest part, middle, central, midst.** It is used figuratively of the center of the land which may be thought of in Israel as the highest part of the hill country, the center of the land and earth (Judg. 9:37; Ezek. 38:12). ¶

CENTRAL – Judg. 9:37 ➔ CENTER <2872>.

CERAMIC – Dan. 2:41, 43 ➔ MIRY <2917>.

CERTAIN – [1] ***yaṣṣiyḇ*** [Aramaic adj.: יַצִּיב <3330>; from TRUTH <3321>] ▶ **This word refers to something as true, reliable.** It is used of an interpretation of a dream or vision's being true, sure (Dan. 2:45; 7:16: also translated truth, meaning, exact meaning), or to an attitude or knowledge that is certain (Dan. 2:8; 3:24; 6:12; also translated certainty, certainly, to stand, to stand fast). ¶
– [2] 1 Sam. 21:2 ➔ A ONE <492>.

CERTAIN ONE – [1] ***palmôniy*** [pron.: פַּלְמוֹנִי <6422>; prob. for CERTAIN ONE <6423>] ▶ **This word means so-and-so; it is also translated one, particular one.** It is used as a definite pronoun to point out a particular person or speaker (Dan. 8:13). ¶
[2] ***pᵉlōniy*** [pron.: פְּלֹנִי <6423>; from DISTINCTION (MAKE) <6395>] ▶ **This word means a specific person, place.** It is a definite pronoun used to indicate and identify a certain person (Ruth 4:1; also translated such a one, friend); or place (1 Sam. 21:2; 2 Kgs. 6:8). ¶

CERTAINTY – [1] Prov. 22:21 ➔ TRUTH <7189> [2] Dan. 2:8 ➔ CERTAIN <3330>.

CERTAINLY – Dan. 3:24 ➔ CERTAIN <3330>.

CERTIFICATE – Deut. 24:1, 3; etc. ➔ BOOK <5612>.

CHAFF – [1] ***mappāl*** [masc. noun: מַפָּל <4651>; from FALL (verb) <5307>] ▶ **This word indicates fallen parts, sweeping; folds.** It is used to indicate the sweepings, grains, and partial chaff left of wheat or grain (Amos 8:6; KJV, NASB: refuse). It is used of the excess skin and folds of a Leviathan, possibly crocodile (Job 41:23; KJV: flakes). ¶
[2] ***mōts*** [masc. noun: מֹץ <4671>; from OPPRESSOR <4160> (in the sense of pressed out)] ▶ **This word refers to the fine pieces of grain, husks of wheat, grains in general, or fine-cut straw given to animals as fodder but figuratively indicating what is useless or worthless.** The wicked are compared to chaff that is easily blown away (Job 21:18; Ps. 1:4); nations under God's judgments are like chaff (Is. 17:13; 29:5; 41:15; Hos. 13:3). It is used to indicate the swift passage of time, as it passes away quickly like chaff (Zeph. 2:2). Other ref.: Ps. 35:5. ¶
[3] ***'ûr*** [Aramaic verb: עוּר <5784>; no information on root] ▶ **This word refers to the husks of wheat or various grains removed in the threshing process, as well as other impurities, etc.** Ref.: Dan. 2:35. ¶
– [4] Ex. 15:7; Mal. 4:1; etc. ➔ STUBBLE <7179> [5] Is. 5:24; 33:11 ➔ GRASS (DRY) <2842>.

CHAIN – [1] ***ᵃzēq*** [masc. noun: אָזֵק <246>; a variation for FIREBRAND <2131>] ▶ **This word is used in the plural form in the Old Testament. It means restraints, shackles.**

Jeremiah is freed from his chains (Jer. 40:1, 4) and permitted to go where he wishes. ¶
[2] ***hamniyḵ*** [Aramaic masc. noun: הַמְנִיךְ <2002>; of foreign origin] ▶ **This word refers to an ornament as a mark of distinction; it is also translated necklace.** It refers to the chain Daniel would receive if he sufficiently interpreted the writing on the wall (Dan. 5:7, 16, 29). ¶
[3] ***maʿadān, maʿadanāh, maʿadanniym*** [masc. proper noun: מַעֲדָן, מַעֲדַנָּה, מַעֲדַנִּים <4574>; from DELIGHT ONESELF <5727>] ▶
a. A feminine noun meaning delicacy, beauty, confidence. It is used to describe the chain or bands of the Pleiades constellation (Job 38:31; also translated cluster). It has the sense of cheerfulness or confidence in a person (1 Sam. 15:32: cheerfully, delicately, cautiously, in chains). ¶
b. A masculine plural noun indicating delicacies, delight. It is used of tasty food or special dishes often served at royal banquets (Gen. 49:20). It is used metaphorically of delight, making joyous, a renewal (Prov. 29:17). It refers to gourmet food or festive dishes (Lam. 4:5). ¶
[4] ***ʿanāq*** [masc. noun: עֲנָק <6060>; from a verb meaning to wear a necklace, see LIBERALLY (FURNISH, SUPPLY) <6059>] ▶ **This word indicates a necklace.** It is used figuratively of wearing parents' instructions around one's neck as a necklace or chain of remembrance (Prov. 1:9; also translated: ornament, pendant). It refers to a necklace worn as an ornament or jewelry (Song 4:9; also translated: link, strand, jewel). It was used of ornaments worn on animals, camels in particular (Judg. 8:26; also translated: neck band, collar). ¶
[5] ***rattôq*** [masc. noun: רַתּוֹק <7569>; from BIND <7576>] ▶ **This word refers to a flexible connection of a series of joined links.** Golden decorative chains were placed in the Temple sanctuary (1 Kgs. 6:21). It is used figuratively and literally of a chain by which the Lord will capture His own people (Ezek. 7:23). ¶
[6] ***rattiyqāh*** [fem. noun: רַתִּיקָה <7572>; from BIND <7576>] ▶ **This Hebrew word has the same meaning as <7569> above but is the preferred reading by some translators.** Ref.: 1 Kgs. 6:21. ¶
[7] ***reṯûqāh*** [fem. noun: רְתוּקָה <7577>; fem. pass. part. of BIND <7576>] ▶ **This word refers to decorative joined rings of silver made to lay over an idol.** Ref.: Is. 40:19. ¶
[8] ***šaršāh*** [fem. noun: שַׁרְשָׁה <8331>; from ROOT (TAKE) <8327> (in the sense of something rooted, i.e., linked)] ▶ **This word refers to an interlocking set of metal links or intertwined pieces of rope.** Ref.: Ex. 28:22. ¶
[9] ***šaršerāh*** [fem. noun: שַׁרְשְׁרָה <8333>; from ROOT (TAKE) <8327> (comp. <8331> above)] ▶ **This word indicates a set of interlocking or intertwined metal links.** In context chains of gold (Ex. 28:14); twisted chainwork (1 Kgs. 7:17); ornamental (2 Chr. 3:5, 16). Other ref.: Ex. 39:15. ¶
– [10] Gen. 41:42; 2 Chr. 3:16; Ezek. 16:11 ➔ NECKLACE <7242> [11] Num. 31:50 ➔ ARMLET <685> [12] Job 36:8; Ps. 149:8; Is. 45:14; Nah. 3:10 ➔ FIREBRAND <2131> b. [13] Ps. 116:16; Is. 28:22; 52:2 ➔ BOND <4147> a. [14] Is. 58:6 ➔ BOND <2784> [15] Is. 58:6 ➔ BUNCH <92> [16] Ezek. 19:4, 9 ➔ HOOK <2397>.

CHAIN (COMPASS ABOUT AS A) – Ps. 73:6 ➔ LIBERALLY (FURNISH, SUPPLY) <6059>.

CHAINS – [1] ***maʿadannôṯ*** [fem. plur. noun: מַעֲדַנּוֹת <4575>; by transposition from BIND <6029>] ▶
a. This word is used to describe the links or bands tying together the Pleiades constellation. Ref.: Job 38:31; also translated cluster. ¶
b. A feminine plural noun denoting sweet influences. It identifies the feeling created by viewing the Pleiades (Job 38:31). ¶
– [2] Ps. 68:6 ➔ PROSPERITY <3574> [3] Eccl. 7:26 ➔ BOND <612> [4] Is. 3:19 ➔ PENDANT <5188>.

CHAINS OF GOLD – Song 1:10 ➔ STRING OF JEWELS <2737>.

CHALCOL – 1 Kgs. 4:31 ➔ CALCOL <3633>.

CHALDEAN – 1 ***kasdāy*** [Aramaic masc. noun: כַּשְׂדָּי <3679>; for <3778> below] ► **This is a noun with a gentilic, ethnic ending indicating nationality.** It refers to Nebuchadnezzar, a Chaldean king of Babylon (Ezra 5:12). ¶

2 ***kaśdiym*** [proper noun: כַּשְׂדִּים <3778>] ►

a. The gentilic name of the inhabitants of a city (Babylon) and area (Babylonia) located in southern Mesopotamia on the Euphrates River. The city's ancient ruins are located ca. 50 miles south of modern Baghdad, Iraq. The term Chaldeans is also rendered as Babylonians in various translations (see e.g., 2 Kgs. 24:2 in NIV and textual note there). Isaiah called the people of Babylon Babylonians or Chaldeans (Is. 13:19). The city of Babylon and the subsequent kingdom of Babylon or Babylonia were founded by Nimrod, the famous descendant of Cush and his father Ham (Gen. 10:6–10). The land of Shinar (Gen. 11:1, 2) is the location where the Tower of Babel was constructed, and Daniel deftly places the exiles of Judah in the land of Shinar (Dan. 1:1–4). Abraham was called out from among the Chaldeans living in Ur (Gen. 11:31; 15:7). The neo-Babylonian Empire (626–539 B.C.) played a major role in the Old Testament, and its greatest ruler was a Chaldean king (Ezra 5:12). The nation and its people were subject to scathing invective prophecies from the Lord's messengers (e.g., Jer. 50:1–51:64). *

b. A technical use of the word Chaldeans (*kaśdiym* in Hebrew) refers to a group of priestly people who were given to the study of the heavenly bodies. Refs.: Dan. 2:2, 4. They were often consulted by kings and leaders for advice. Their presence in Babylonia in the time of Nebuchadnezzar is confirmed. ¶

c. A use of the word to refer to the nation or land of Chaldea, Babylon. Refs.: Jer. 50:10; 51:24, 35. *

3 ***kaśdāy*** [Aramaic proper noun: כַּשְׂדָּי <3779>; corresponding to <3778> above] ►

a. The gentilic name of the inhabitants of a city (Babylon) and area (Babylonia) located in southern Mesopotamia on the Euphrates River. Refs.: Dan. 2:5, 10; 3:8; 4:7; 5:7, 11, 30. ¶

b. A technical use of the word Chaldeans. It is the Aramaic word corresponding to <3778> b. above. See the comments there on Daniel 2:2.

CHALK – 1 ***gir*** [masc. noun: גִּר <1615>; perhaps from FURNACE <3564>] ► **This word means a powdery white rock; it is also translated lime.** It is used to define certain stones, stones of chalk, which could be pulverized rather easily (Is. 27:9). The stones were used to construct some altars. ¶

– 2 Is. 44:13 → MARKER <8279> c.

CHAMBER – 1 ***ḥuppāh*** [fem. noun: חֻפָּה <2646>; from COVER (verb) <2645>] ► **This word refers to a room, and also to a cover, a canopy.** It refers figuratively to the "bridal chamber" from which the sun comes forth (Ps. 19:5; cf. Joel 2:16: chamber, closet, dressing room, bridal chamber). It indicates a mighty, protective canopy over God's people (Is. 4:5: canopy, covering, defence). ¶

2 ***niškāh*** [fem. noun: נִשְׁכָּה <5393>; for ROOM <3957>] ► **This Hebrew word refers to a room, a cell; it is translated room, quarters, dwelling.** It refers to an area of a building prepared for habitation. In context an area such as this was repaired or restored (Neh. 3:30). It describes storage areas or chambers (Neh. 12:44); or an office area (Neh. 13:7). ¶

3 ***'illiy*** [Aramaic fem. noun: עִלִּי <5952>; from OFFER <5927>] ► **This word means an apartment on top of a roof; it is translated roof chamber, upper chamber, upper room, upstairs room.** It refers to a rooftop chamber on a house. It was used by Daniel for prayer daily (Dan. 6:10). These upper chambers were cool, especially at night. ¶

– 4 Num. 25:8 → TENT <6898>
5 1 Kgs. 6:5, 6, 10 → BED <3326> b.
6 Ps. 104:3, 13 → chamber, upper chamber → UPPER ROOM <5944>.

CHAMELEON – 1 Lev. 11:30 → LIZARD (MONITOR) <3581> 2 Lev. 11:30 → WHITE OWL <8580> b.

CHAMOIS – Deut. 14:5 ➔ MOUNTAIN SHEEP <2169>.

CHAMPION – ***bênayim*** [masc. dual noun: בֵּנַיִם <1143>; dual of BETWEEN <996> (i.e., man of the space between two armies)] ▶ **This word refers to a giant named Goliath, a Philistine warrior who was over nine feet tall.** He stepped forward as their hero, literally, the man of the space between the armies (*'îš bênayim*). He stood forth to represent them (1 Sam. 17:4, 23) as David represented Israel. ¶

CHANCE – 1 ***miqreh*** [masc. noun: מִקְרֶה <4745>; from HAPPEN <7136>] ▶ **This word refers to a fortunate or unfortunate event, a happening, a fate; it is translated by the verb to happen, to turn out, to befall as well as hap, accident, destiny.** It refers to something that occurs without human planning or intervention (Ruth 2:3; 1 Sam. 20:26); or (from the Philistine viewpoint) even God's intervention (1 Sam. 6:9). It is a feature of human life (Eccl. 2:14, 15; 3:19; 9:2, 3). ¶
– 2 Eccl. 9:11 ➔ OCCURRENCE <6294>.

CHANCELLOR – Ezra 4:8, 9, 17 ➔ COMMANDER <1169>.

CHANGE (noun) – 1 ***ḥ**ᵃ**liypāh*** [fem. noun: חֲלִיפָה <2487>; from PASS ON <2498>] ▶ **This word refers to something becoming different, a change of clothes, to renew.** It gives the idea of one thing following another, change upon change (1 Kgs. 5:14; Job 10:17). It indicates a new state reached, a changing (Job 14:14). God, however, does not change in His faithfulness and righteousness, His essence (Ps. 55:19). It was used to indicate changes of clothing (Gen. 45:22; Judg. 14:12, 13, 19; 2 Kgs. 5:5, 22, 23). ¶
2 ***p**ᵉ**ṣiyrāh*** [fem. noun: פְּצִירָה <6477>; from PRESS <6484>] ▶
a. This word means a sum required in exchange for service; it is also translated price. It indicates the cost for getting various agricultural tools sharpened (1 Sam. 13:21). ¶
b. A feminine noun indicating a file for sharpening. It indicates a file or a stone for sharpening various agricultural tools (1 Sam. 13:21). ¶

CHANGE (verb) – 1 ***ᵃdāh*** [Aramaic verb: עֲדָה <5709>; corresponding to PASS OVER <5710>] ▶ **This word means to pass away, to pass on. It also means to become different, to disappear.** It is used of times, seasons, and epochs of history coming and going, passing away (Dan. 2:21); of kingship passing from someone (Dan. 4:31; 5:20; 7:26). It is used of changing a document (Dan. 6:8, 12); or something/time being extended in other situations (Dan. 7:12, 14). It has the sense of passing on a smell or odor (in context) to something (Dan. 3:27). ¶
2 ***šānā'*** [verb: שְׁנָא <8132>; a prim. root] ▶
a. This word means to replace something with something else: clothes. Ref.: 2 Kgs. 25:29; also translated to put off, to put aside. It is used of a person's complexion changing (Eccl. 8:1). It is used metaphorically of pure gold that has changed, becoming dark (Lam. 4:1).
b. A verb meaning to become dull. It is used of fine gold changing, becoming dim and dull (Lam. 4:1, KJV). ¶
3 ***š**ᵉ**nā'*** [Aramaic verb: שְׁנָא <8133>; corresponding to <8132> above] ▶ **This word means to be different.** It refers to a difference that has become evident in something or persons; they have changed (Dan. 3:27; 5:6, 9; 6:17). It is used in an extreme case of a human heart changing into the heart of a beast (Dan. 4:16). It indicates that one thing is different from another (Dan. 7:3, 19, 23). God can change times and seasons (Dan. 2:21; 7:25). When used of decrees or orders, it means to alter, to violate them (Ezra 6:11; Dan. 3:28; 6:8, 15). It indicates a change of conditions or situations (Dan. 2:9); a change in facial expression (Dan. 3:19; 5:10; 7:28). *
4 ***šānāh*** [verb: שָׁנָה <8138>; a prim. root] ▶
a. The Hebrew word means to disguise, to be different. It means to become something different or to change an attitude or

character. God does not change ever (Mal. 3:6). For God's right hand to change means He would have to change His actions toward the righteous psalmist (Ps. 77:10). It can have the sense of different (Esther 1:7). In its intensive stem, it means to bring about change, to alter something: judgment (Prov. 31:5); clothes (Jer. 52:33); one's words (Ps. 89:34); one's political stance (Jer. 2:36); one's face or appearance (Job 14:20). In its reflexive sense, it means to change, to disguise oneself (1 Kgs. 14:2). Even David changed and disguised himself emotionally and outwardly to save himself (1 Sam. 21:13).
b. The Hebrew word means to repeat; to do again. It indicates doing something over a second time (1 Kgs. 18:34; Neh. 13:21; Job 29:22). God presented a dream to Joseph twice (Gen. 41:32); Abishai speaks of striking an enemy twice (1 Sam. 26:8); Amasa failed to strike a second time (2 Sam. 20:10). It can have the sense of repeating; repeating something that should be kept secret is evil (Prov. 17:9); and a fool repeats his errors (Prov. 26:11). *
– [5] Lev. 27:10, 33; Ps. 106:20; Jer. 2:11; etc. ➔ EXCHANGE (verb) <4171> [6] Num. 32:38 ➔ ENCLOSED <4142> [7] Jer. 2:11 ➔ BOAST <3225> b.

CHANNEL – [1] Prov. 21:1 ➔ STREAM (noun) <6388> [2] Zech. 4:2 ➔ PIPE <4166>.

CHANT – Amos 6:5 ➔ IMPROVISE <6527> a.

CHAPITER – [1] 1 Kgs. 7:16–20, 31, 41, 42; etc. ➔ CAPITAL <3805> [2] 2 Chr. 3:15 ➔ CAPITAL <6858>.

CHARASHIM – 1 Chr. 4:14 ➔ HARASHIM <2798>.

CHARCOAL – Prov. 26:21 ➔ COAL <6352>.

CHARGE (noun) – [1] Gen. 26:5; Deut. 11:1; Zech. 3:7 ➔ GUARD <4931> [2] Dan. 6:4, 5 ➔ COMPLAINT (GROUND FOR) <5931>.

CHARGE (BE IN) – Is. 22:15 ➔ PROFITABLE (BE) <5532> a.

CHARGE (verb) – [1] Neh. 5:7 ➔ DEBT (IN) <5378> [2] Prov. 28:15 ➔ RUSH (verb) <8264> a. [3] Dan. 8:4 ➔ GORE <5055> [4] Hab. 1:8 ➔ FROLIC <6335> a.

CHARGE OUT – Judg. 20:33 ➔ GUSH <1518>.

CHARGER – Ezra 1:9 ➔ BASIN <105>.

CHARGES (GROUND FOR) – Dan. 6:4, 5 ➔ COMPLAINT (GROUND FOR) <5931>.

CHARGES AGAINST (BRING) – Dan. 3:8 ➔ ACCUSE <7170>.

CHARIOT – [1] ***hōṣen*** [masc. noun: הֹצֶן <2021>; from an unused root meaning apparently to be sharp or strong] ▶ **This word possibly means arms or war; it is also translated weapon. See definition in next sub-entry.** It describes the chariots (or the weapons) that were a part of the Babylonian army coming against Judah (Ezek. 23:24). ¶
[2] ***merkāḇāh*** [fem. noun: מֶרְכָּבָה <4818>; fem. of SADDLE <4817>] ▶ **This word refers to something ridden, for riding and is used of a two-wheeled vehicle, drawn by horses and normally used in war.** Its uses include a war chariot (Ex. 14:25; 15:4); a chariot used by the state in its processions or for travel in general (Gen. 41:43; 46:29; Is. 22:18). It was a symbol of military might and war (Is. 2:7). It is used figuratively of the vehicles of war used by the Lord (Is. 66:15; Hab. 3:8). Israel constructed some idolatrous "chariots of the sun" (2 Kgs. 23:11). *
[3] ***reḵeḇ*** [masc. noun: רֶכֶב <7393>; from RIDE <7392>] ▶ **This word refers to a group of chariots (see definition in previous sub-entry) as a collective noun.** Refs.: Gen. 50:9; Ex. 14:6, 7, 9, 17, 18, 23, 26, 28). But it can refer to a single chariot (1 Kgs. 22:35). It was a major engine of war in the ancient world, but God could overthrow all of them (Ex. 15:19). It could be a symbol

of royal authority (1 Kgs. 1:5); special storage cities were used to house them (1 Kgs. 9:19). It describes a caravan or a line of donkeys or camels, probably a supply train for an army (Is. 21:7). The Hebrew word also means a millstone; see MILLSTONE (UPPER) <7393>. *

[4] ***rᵉḵûḇ*** [masc. noun: רְכוּב <7398>; from pass. part. of RIDE <7392>] ▶ **This word indicates the means of transport that the clouds provide for the Lord.** Ref.: Ps. 104:3. ¶

– [5] 1 Kgs. 4:26 ➔ SADDLE <4817> [6] Song 3:9 ➔ CARRIAGE <668> [7] Is. 66:20 ➔ COVERED <6632> b. [8] Ezek. 23:24; 26:10 ➔ WHEEL <1534> [9] Ezek. 27:20 ➔ SADDLE <7396> b.

CHARM – [1] ***laḥaš*** [masc. noun: לַחַשׁ <3908>; from WHISPER (verb) <3907>] ▶ **This word means whispering, enchantment, and superstitious ornaments. The action of whispering, with the connotations of casting a spell, is the basis for this word.** It is used in the Hebrew to signify charms or amulets worn by women (Is. 3:20; KJV: earrings); the charming of a snake (Eccl. 10:11: enchantment, to be charmed; Jer. 8:17: charm, to be charmed); one who crafts clever words so as to enchant (Is. 3:3; also translated enchanter, orator); a prayer whispered in a time of sudden distress (Is. 26:16). ¶

– [2] Song 7:6 ➔ DELIGHT (noun) <8588> [3] Is. 47:11 ➔ SEEK DILIGENTLY <7836> b. [4] Nah. 3:4 ➔ SORCERY <3785>.

CHARMED (BE) – Eccl. 10:11 ➔ CHARM <3908>.

CHARMING – [1] Ps. 58:5 ➔ COMPANY <2267> [2] Song 1:16 ➔ PLEASANT <5273> a.

CHASE – [1] 1 Sam. 17:53; Lam. 4:19 ➔ BURN (verb) <1814> [2] Ps. 35:5 ➔ DRIVE <1760>.

CHASING – [1] Eccl. 1:14; 2:11, 17, 26; 4:4, 6; 6:9 ➔ STRIVING <7469> [2] Eccl. 1:17; 2:22; 4:16 ➔ STRIVING <7475>.

CHATTER – Is. 38:14 ➔ CHIRP <6850>.

CHEAT – [1] Gen. 27:36 ➔ SUPPLANT <6117> [2] Ex. 8:29 ➔ MOCK <2048> [3] Mal. 1:14 ➔ DECEIVE <5230>.

CHEATS (ONE WHO) – Ps. 49:5 ➔ HEEL <6120> b.

CHEBAR – ***kᵉḇār*** [proper noun: כְּבָר <3529>; the same as ALREADY <3528>]: length ▶ **This word designates a river, also spelled Kebar.** Evidently a man-made canal off of the Euphrates River in Babylon where Ezekiel saw several visions and heard the sound of the presence of the Lord's throne-chariot. The river was south of Babylon near another city, Nippur, east of the city of Babylon. Refs.: Ezek. 1:1, 3; 3:15, 23; 10:15, 20, 22; 43:3. ¶

CHECKERED – Ex. 28:4 ➔ WOVEN <8665>.

CHEDORLAOMER – ***kᵉḏārlāʿōmer*** [masc. proper noun: כְּדָרְלָעֹמֶר <3540>; of foreign origin]: a handful of sheaves ▶ **King of Elam in the time of Abraham.** Refs.: Gen. 14:1, 4, 5, 9, 17. ¶

CHEEK – [1] 1 Kgs. 22:24; Lam. 1:2; Hos. 11:4; etc. ➔ JAW <3895> [2] Song 4:3; 6:7 ➔ TEMPLE (of the head) <7541>.

CHEER (BE OF GOOD) – Job 9:27 ➔ SMILE (verb) <1082>.

CHEER (HAVE, FIND) – Job 10:20 ➔ SMILE (verb) <1082>.

CHEERFUL (BE) – Job 9:27 ➔ SMILE (verb) <1082>.

CHEERFUL (MAKE) – Zech. 9:17 ➔ INCREASE (verb) <5107>.

CHEERFULLY – 1 Sam. 15:32 ➔ CHAIN <4574> a.

CHEESE – [1] ***gᵉḇiynāh*** [fem. noun: גְּבִינָה <1385>; fem. from the same as HUNCHBACK <1384>] ▶ **This word is used**

figuratively of God curdling Job like cheese as a picture of suffering. Ref.: Job 10:10. ¶

2 ***ḥāriyṣ*** [masc. noun: חָרִיץ <2757>; from MOVE <2782> (in the sense of cutting)] ▶ **This word indicates a piece (of cheese), a slice.** It was a serving of cheese especially good for soldiers in combat or preparing for combat (1 Sam. 17:18). The Hebrew word is also translated pick, sharp instrument; see PICK <2757>. ¶

3 ***šāp̱āh, šᵉpôṯ*** [fem. noun: שָׁפָה, שְׁפוֹת <8194>; from STICK OUT <8192> in the sense of clarifying] ▶ **This word refers to goat's cheese most likely. It describes the coagulated part of milk from which cheese is made.** It was a food provided to David at a difficult time for him and his men (2 Sam. 17:29). ¶

CHELAL – ***kᵉlāl*** [masc. proper noun: כְּלָל <3636>; from PERFECT (MAKE) <3634>]: complete ▶ **Ezra convinced him to put away his foreign wife.** Ref.: Ezra 10:30. ¶

CHELLUH – ***kᵉlûhû*** [masc. proper noun: כְּלוּהוּ <3622>; from FINISH <3615>]: completed ▶ **Ezra convinced him to put away his foreign wife.** Ref.: Ezra 10:35. ¶

CHELUB – ***kᵉlûḇ*** [masc. proper noun: כְּלוּב <3620>; the same as BASKET <3619>]: basket, cage ▶
a. Father of Ezri. Ref.: 1 Chr. 27:26. ¶
b. Father of Mehir who was over the agricultural workers during the time of David. Ref.: 1 Chr. 4:11. ¶

CHELUBAI – ***kᵉlûḇāy*** [masc. proper noun: כְּלוּבָי <3621>; a form of CALEB <3612>]: a variant of Caleb ▶ **One of the three sons of Hezron.** Ref.: 1 Chr. 2:9. ¶

CHEMARIM – Zeph. 1:4 ➔ PRIEST <3649>.

CHEMOSH – ***kᵉmôš*** [masc. proper noun: כְּמוֹשׁ <3645>; from an unused root meaning to subdue]: one who subdues ▶ **It refers to the chief god of the Moabites.** Refs.: Num. 21:29; Judg. 11:24; 1 Kgs. 11:7, 33; 2 Kgs. 23:13; Jer. 48:7, 13, 46. The Moabites are his people (Num. 21:29). Judges 11:24 claims him as the god of the Ammonites, but the text probably has a serious error. ¶

CHENAANAH – ***kᵉnaᵃnāh*** [masc. proper noun: כְּנַעֲנָה <3668>; from CANAAN <3667> (see MERCHANT <3669>)]: merchant ▶
a. Father of the false prophet Zedekiah. Refs.: 1 Kgs. 22:11, 24; 2 Chr. 18:10, 23. ¶
b. A Benjamite of the family of Jediael. Ref.: 1 Chr. 7:10. ¶

CHENANI – ***kᵉnāniy*** [masc. proper noun: כְּנָנִי <3662>; from SHOOT UP <3661>]: planted ▶ **A Levite returning from the Babylonian captivity.** Ref.: Neh. 9:4. ¶

CHENANIAH – ***kᵉnanyāhû, kᵉnanyāh*** [masc. proper noun: כְּנַנְיָהוּ, כְּנַנְיָה <3663>; from SHOOT UP <3661> and LORD <3050>]: planted by the Lord
a. A Levite, leader of the singing in the time of David. Refs.: 1 Chr. 15:22, 27. ¶
b. An Izharite; him and his sons were appointed to external duties for Israel, as officers and judges. Ref.: 1 Chr. 26:29. ¶

CHEPHAR-AMMONI – ***kᵉp̱ar haʿammôniy*** [masc. noun: כְּפַר הָעַמּוֹנִי <3726>; from VILLAGE <3723> and AMMONITE <5884>, with the art. interposed]: village of the Ammonites ▶ **A city of the tribe of Benjamin.** Ref.: Josh. 18:24. ¶

CHEPHIRAH – ***kᵉpiyrāh*** [proper noun: כְּפִירָה <3716>; fem. of LION (YOUNG) <3715>]: lioness, the village ▶ **One of the four cities of the Gibeonites with whom Joshua had made a covenant.** It was attributed to the tribe of Benjamin (Josh. 9:17; 18:26; Ezra 2:25; Neh. 7:29). ¶

CHEPHIRIM – Neh. 6:2 ➔ LION (YOUNG) <3715> b., c.

CHERAN – ***kᵉrān*** [masc. proper noun: כְּרָן <3763>; of uncertain deriv.] ▶ **One of the**

sons of Dishon the Horite. Refs.: Gen. 36:26; 1 Chr. 1:41. ¶

CHERETHITES – See KERETHITES <3774>.

CHERISH – 1 Kgs. 1:2 ➔ PROFITABLE (BE) <5532> a.

CHERITH – ***kᵉriyṯ*** [proper noun: כְּרִית <3747>; from CUT (verb) <3772>]: cutting, separation ► **A brook east of the Jordan where the prophet Elijah stayed.** Refs.: 1 Kgs. 17:3, 5. ¶

CHERUB – ***kᵉrûḇ*** [proper noun: כְּרוּב <3743>; the same as CHERUB, CHERUBIM <3742>] ► **A place in Babylonia from which some persons returned to Judea with Zerubbabel.** They could not prove that they belonged to Israel (Ezra 2:59; Neh. 7:61). ¶

CHERUB, CHERUBIM – ***kᵉrûḇ*** [masc. noun: כְּרוּב <3742>; of uncertain deriv.] ► **This word means an angelic being. It is commonly translated as cherub (plur., cherubim).** The Bible provides scant details concerning the likeness of these winged creatures, except for the apocalyptic visions of Ezekiel in Ezekiel 10. However, current pictures of cherubim as chubby infants with wings or as feminine creatures find no scriptural basis. The Bible portrays cherubim as the guardians of the Garden of Eden (Gen. 3:24) and seemingly the glory of the Lord (cf. Ezek. 10:3, 4, 18–20); as flanking the throne of God (Ps. 99:1; cf. Is. 37:16; though these may be poetic references to the mercy seat in the Tabernacle [Num. 7:89]); as embroidered images on the tapestry of the Tabernacle (Ex. 26:1, 31); and as sculpted images arching above the mercy seat on the ark of the covenant (Ex. 25:18–20, 22; 1 Kgs. 6:23–28; 2 Chr. 3:10–13). Figuratively, the word is used to describe God's winged transport (2 Sam. 22:11; Ps. 18:10). Interestingly, Satan is described as being the anointed cherub (Ezek. 28:14) before he was cast out of heaven. *

CHESALON – ***kᵉsālôn*** [proper noun: כְּסָלוֹן <3693>; from FOOLISH (BE) <3688> (see CONFIDENCE <3690>)]: hope ► **A city on the border of Judah, on Mount Jearim.** Ref.: Josh. 15:10. ¶

CHESED – ***keśeḏ*** [masc. noun: כֶּשֶׂד <3777>; from an unused root of uncertain meaning] ► **Son of Nahor and Milcah.** Ref.: Gen. 22:22. ¶

CHESIL – ***kᵉsiyl*** [proper noun: כְּסִיל <3686>; the same as FOOL, FOOLISH <3684>]: constellation ► **A town in the extreme south of Palestine.** Ref.: Josh. 15:30. ¶

CHEST – 1 ***'argāz*** [masc. noun: אַרְגָּז <712>; perhaps from SHAKE <7264> (in the sense of being suspended)] ► **This word means a container; it is also translated box, coffer.** It refers to a container holding several gold mice and molds of the tumors the Philistines were suffering from (1 Sam. 6:8, 11, 15). ¶
2 ***ḥᵃḏêh*** [Aramaic masc. noun: חֲדֵה <2306>; corresponding to BREAST <2373>] ► **This word describes the breast portion of the great statue in Nebuchadnezzar's dream.** Ref.: Dan. 2:32. ¶
– 3 2 Kgs. 12:9, 10 ➔ ARK <727> 4 Ezek. 27:24 ➔ TREASURE <1595> 5 Hos. 13:8 ➔ CAUL <5458>.

CHESTNUT TREE – Gen. 30:37; Ezek. 31:8 ➔ PLANE TREE <6196>.

CHESULLOTH – ***kᵉsûllôṯ*** [proper noun: כְּסוּלּוֹת <3694>; fem. plur. of pass. part. of FOOLISH (BE) <3688>]: fattened ► **A city on the border of Issachar.** Ref.: Josh. 19:18. ¶

CHEW – 1 Lev. 11:7 ➔ DRAG (verb) <1641> 2 Ezek. 23:34 ➔ BREAK <1633> a.

CHEZIB – ***kᵉziyḇ*** [proper noun: כְּזִיב <3580>; from LIAR (BE A) <3576>]: lying, deceitful ► **A place where Shelah, the son of Judah, was born.** Ref.: Gen. 38:5. ¶

CHIDON – ***kiyḏōn*** [proper noun: כִּידֹן <3592>; the same as SPEAR <3591>]: spear, javelin ▶ **Name of the threshing floor where Uzzah was struck down by the Lord because he had put his hand on the ark.** Ref.: 1 Chr. 13:9. ¶

CHIEF – [1] Gen. 36:15 ➔ GENTLE <441> [2] Josh. 10:24; Judg. 11:6, 11; etc. ➔ CAPTAIN <7101> [3] 1 Sam. 21:7: chief of herdsmen, chief of shepherds ➔ MIGHTY <47> [4] Song 5:10 ➔ BANNERS (SET UP, LIFT UP) <1713>.

CHIEF MAN – [1] Ex. 24:11 ➔ NOBLE <678> [2] 2 Kgs. 24:15 ➔ BODY <193> b.

CHIEF MUSICIAN – Ps. 4–6, 8, 9; etc. ➔ OVERSEE <5329>.

CHIEF OFFICER – [1] 2 Kgs. 18:17; Jer. 39:3, 13 ➔ RAB-SARIS <7249> [2] See LEADER <5057>.

CHIEFEST – Song 5:10 ➔ BANNERS (SET UP, LIFT UP) <1713>.

CHILD – [1] ***wālāḏ*** [masc. noun: וָלָד <2056>; for CHILD <3206>] ▶ **This word is used to assert that Sarai had no child before Isaac; she was barren.** Ref.: Gen. 11:30. ¶

[2] ***ṭap*** [masc. sing. noun: טַף <2945>; from MINCE <2952> (perhaps referring to the tripping gait of children)] ▶ **This word means little one.** Though the term is sometimes used in a parallel construction with *bāniym* (plur. of SON <1121>; Deut. 1:39), elsewhere it often denotes younger children. It is distinguished from young men, virgins (Ezek. 9:6), and sons (2 Chr. 20:13, "children"). It is often used in the formulaic pattern "men, women, and children" (Deut. 2:34; 3:6; 31:12; Jer. 40:7; 43:6), meaning everyone. *

[3] ***yeleḏ*** [masc. noun: יֶלֶד <3206>; from BIRTH (GIVE) <3205>] ▶ **This word refers to a young man, an infant.** It is commonly used to refer to a male child (Gen. 4:23) or a child (Gen. 30:26). It is used of a miscarried baby (Ex. 21:22). Followed by *zᵉqûnîm*, old age, it means a child of one's old age (Gen. 44:20). However, it refers to young men as well (1 Kgs. 12:8, 10, 14). It is also used to refer to the young of animals (Job 38:41; 39:3; Is. 11:7). *

[4] ***'ôlêl, 'ôlāl*** [masc. noun: עוֹלֵל, עוֹלָל <5768>; from NURSE (verb) <5763>] ▶

a. A word meaning an infant. It refers to offspring, sons and daughters, still quite young and holding the promise of descendants. The destruction of children was especially devastating to a people (2 Kgs. 8:12; Lam. 2:11, 20). *

b. A word meaning an infant. See a. As noted in a., the destruction of infants was especially heinous and devastating to a people (Ps. 137:9; Jer. 6:11; 9:21; Lam. 1:5; 2:19; 4:4; Joel 2:16; Mic. 2:9; Nah. 3:10). ¶

– [5] Gen. 21:23 ➔ OFFSPRING <5209> [6] Num. 13:22, 28; Josh. 15:14; 1 Chr. 20:4 ➔ DESCENDANT <3211> [7] 2 Chr. 32:21 ➔ COMING FORTH <3329> [8] Prov. 29:21 ➔ YOUTH <5290>.

CHILD (WITH) – See PREGNANT <2030>.

CHILDBEARING – Gen. 3:16 ➔ CONCEPTION <2032>.

CHILDBIRTH – [1] Gen. 3:16 ➔ CONCEPTION <2032> [2] Jer. 13:21 ➔ BIRTH (GIVE) <3205> b.

CHILDHOOD – [1] Prov. 29:21 ➔ YOUTH <5290> [2] Eccl. 11:9, 10 ➔ YOUTH <3208>.

CHILDLESS – [1] ***'ăriyriy*** [adj.: עֲרִירִי <6185>; from STRIP <6209> a.] ▶ **This word describes Abraham, who had no offspring.** Refs.: Gen. 15:2; Jer. 22:30. It is used for either a man or a woman (Lev. 20:20, 21). ¶

– [2] Gen. 11:30; 25:21; etc. ➔ BARREN <6135> [3] Jer. 18:21 ➔ BEREAVED <7909>.

CHILDREN – [1] Gen. 48:6 ➔ KINDRED <4138> [2] Is. 3:4 ➔ CAPRICIOUS CHILDREN <8586>.

CHILEAB – ***kil'āḇ*** [masc. proper noun: כִּלְאָב <3609>; apparently from RESTRAIN

<3607> and FATHER <1>]: restraint of his father ▶ **Second son of David by Abigail.** Ref.: Sam. 3:3. ¶

CHILION – ***kilyôn*** [masc. proper noun: כִּלְיוֹן <3630>; a form of FAILING <3631>]: pining (comp. MAHLON <4248>) ▶ **Second son of Elimelech and Naomi, he was the husband of Orpah.** Refs.: Ruth 1:2, 5; 4:9. ¶

CHILMAD – ***kilmad̲*** [proper noun: כִּלְמַד <3638>; of foreign deriv.]: market-place ▶ **A place which traded with Tyre.** It is mentioned with Sheba and Asshur (Ezek. 27:23). ¶

CHIMHAM – ***kimhām, kimhān*** [proper noun: כִּמְהָם, כִּמְהָן <3643>; from FAINT FOR <3642>]: pining, great desire ▶ **Probably a son of Barzillai the Gileadite.** Refs.: 2 Sam. 19:37, 38, 40; Jer. 41:17. ¶

CHIMNEY – Hos. 13:3 ➔ WINDOW <699>.

CHINNERETH – ***kinnᵉrôt̲, kinneret̲*** [proper noun: כִּנְּרוֹת, כִּנֶּרֶת <3672>; respectively plur. and fem. sing. from the same as LYRE <3658>]: lyre ▶
a. A fortified city of Naphtali or the region around it. Refs.: Deut. 3:17; Josh. 19:35; 1 Kgs. 15:20. ¶
b. A lake. Refs.: Num. 34:11; Josh. 11:2; 12:3; 13:27. It was later called the lake of Gennesaret (Luke 5:1) or the Sea of Galilee (John 6:1). ¶

CHIRP – ***ṣāp̲ap̲*** [verb: צָפַף <6850>; a prim. root] ▶ **This word means to twitter; it is also translated to whisper, to peep.** It refers to imitative sounds made by a group of spiritualists to consult with various gods or spirits (Is. 8:19). The sound of birds chirping is used figuratively of peoples conquered by the Assyrians (Is. 10:14). It is used figuratively of persons whispering from their graves (Is. 29:4). It describes the senseless gibberish of a sick person (Is. 38:14; also translated to chatter, to twitter, to cry). ¶

CHISEL – [1] Ex. 34:1, 4; Deut. 10:1, 3; 1 Kgs. 5:18 ➔ CUT (verb) <6458> [2] Is. 44:13 ➔ PLANE <4741> [3] Jer. 10:3 ➔ CUTTING TOOL <4621>.

CHISLEU – Neh. 1:1; Zech. 7:1 ➔ CHISLEV <3691>.

CHISLEV – ***kislêw*** [proper noun: כִּסְלֵו <3691>; prob. of foreign origin] ▶ **This word is the name given to the ninth month of the year, equal to our November/December.** Refs.: Neh. 1:1; Zech. 7:1; also translated Chisleu, Kislev. ¶

CHISLON – ***kislôn*** [masc. proper noun: כִּסְלוֹן <3692>; from FOOLISH (BE) <3688> (see CONFIDENCE <3690>)]: confidence, hope ▶ **Father of Elidad, the tribal chief of Benjamin in the time of Moses.** Ref.: Num. 34:21. ¶

CHISLOTH TABOR – ***kislōt̲ tāb̲ōr*** [proper noun: כִּסְלֹת תָּבֹר <3696>; from the fem. plur. of LOINS <3689> and TABOR <8396>]: flanks of Tabor ▶ **A place near Mount Tabor, on the border of the territory of Zebulun.** Ref.: Josh. 19:12. ¶

CHITLISH – See KITHLISH <3798>.

CHIUN – ***kiyyûn*** [masc. proper noun: כִּיּוּן <3594>; from SET UP <3559>]: statue, maybe of Saturn ▶
a. A name given to images. Ref.: Amos 5:26, Kiyyun (KJV, NKJV, Chiun; NASB, Kiyyun); your images. See also b. below.
b. A word referring to a pillar, a pedestal. It is translated as a pedestal or pillar on which to set up idols (Amos 5:26, NIV) by some recent translations. ¶

CHOICE – [1] 1 Kgs. 4:23 ➔ FATTENED <75> [2] Song 6:9 ➔ PURE <1249> [3] Is. 23:18 ➔ FINE (adj.) <6266> a. [4] Ezek. 17:21 ➔ FUGITIVE <4015>.

CHOICE FOOD – Neh. 8:10 ➔ FATNESS <4924> b.

CHOICE GARMENT – ***mak̲lûl*** [masc. noun: מַכְלוּל <4360>; from PERFECT (MAKE) <3634>] ▶ **This word means**

perfection, beauty. It indicates fine clothes or garments, a type of merchandise desired by many peoples. It has in mind garments or clothing that was of fine quality, splendid, beautiful (Ezek. 27:24; also translated beautiful garment, choice item, all sorts of things). ¶

CHOICE, CHOICEST – 1 ***māḇḥôr*** [masc. noun: מָבְחוֹר <4004>; from CHOOSE <977>] ▶ **This word indicates the select, major, best.** It refers to the best-endowed cities, the most desirable to have (2 Kgs. 3:19) and to the most excellent cypress timber of Lebanon that the ravaging Assyrians cut down (2 Kgs. 19:23). ¶
2 ***miḇḥār*** [masc. noun: מִבְחָר <4005>; from CHOOSE <977>] ▶ **This word indicates what is the most desirable to have.** The best (Gen. 23:6; Is. 37:24; Jer. 22:7); elite men of rank, political, military troops, and officers (Ex. 15:4; Ezek. 23:7; Dan. 11:15); the animals of best quality for sacrifices (Deut. 12:11). The choice trees of Lebanon are personified to rejoice at the fall of Assyria (Ezek. 31:16). Other refs.: Is. 22:7; Jer. 48:15; Ezek. 24:4, 5. ¶
– 3 Job 22:25 ➔ STRENGTH <8443> d.

CHOIR DIRECTOR – Ps. 4–6, 8, 9; etc. ➔ OVERSEE <5329>.

CHOIRMASTER – Ps. 4–6, 8, 9; etc. ➔ OVERSEE <5329>.

CHOOSE – 1 ***bāḥar*** [verb: בָּחַר <977>; a prim. root] ▶ **This word means to make a decision, to select, to take a keen look at, to prove. It denotes a choice, which is based on a thorough examination of the situation and not an arbitrary whim.** Although this word rarely means to prove, it does communicate that sense in Isaiah 48:10, where it describes the way God tested Israel in order to make a careful choice: "I have tested you in the furnace of affliction." In most contexts, the word suggests the concept to choose or to select. It can designate human choice (Gen. 13:11; Deut. 30:19; Josh. 24:15; Judg. 10:14) or divine choice (Deut. 7:7; 1 Sam. 2:28; Neh. 9:7; Ps. 135:4); however, in either case, it generally has theological overtones. This word can also have the connotations to desire, to like, or to delight in. A good example is Isaiah 1:29, where the word is in synonymous parallelism with *ḥāmaḏ* [DESIRE (verb) <2530>], meaning to desire or take pleasure in. *
– 2 1 Sam. 17:8 ➔ EAT <1262>.

CHOP – Deut. 29:11; Jer. 46:22 ➔ CUT (verb) <2404>.

CHOP DOWN – ***gᵉḏaḏ*** [Aramaic verb: גְּדַד <1414>; corresponding to CUT (verb) <1413>] ▶ **This verb means to fell; it is also translated to cut down, to hew down.** It is used to indicate the act of cutting down the symbolic tree in Nebuchadnezzar's dream (Dan. 4:14, 23). ¶

CHOSEN – 1 ***bāḥiyr*** [adj.: בָּחִיר <972>; from CHOOSE <977>] ▶ **This word depicts a person selected by God, such as Saul.** Ref.: 2 Sam. 21:6. God chose Moses (Ps. 106:23) and David for specific purposes (Ps. 89:3). The Lord chose His special Servant (Is. 42:1). But God's people as a whole were His chosen as well (1 Chr. 16:13; Ps. 106:5; Is. 43:20; 65:9, 15, 22). As all of the above contexts indicate, a person chosen by God also had special blessings and promises from the Lord. Other refs.: Ps. 105:43; 106:23; Is. 45:4. ¶
2 ***qāriy'*** [adj.: קָרִיא <7148>; from CALL <7121>] ▶ **This word means appointed, called.** It indicates that a person has been appointed or summoned for something (Num. 1:16; 26:9). It has the sense of important, influential (Num. 16:2). ¶

CHOZEBA – 1 Chr. 4:22 ➔ COZEBA <3578>.

CHRONIC – Lev. 13:11 ➔ SLEEP (verb) <3462> b.

CHRYSOLITE – Ex. 28:17; 39:10; Ezek. 28:13 ➔ TOPAZ <6357>.

CHUB – ***kûḇ*** [proper noun: כּוּב <3552>; of foreign deriv.] ▶ **This word is possibly**

another spelling for *lûḇ* (Libya); see LUBIM <3864>. It is found in Ezekiel 30:5. ¶

CHUN – ***kûn*** [proper noun: כּוּן <3560>; prob. from SET UP <3559>]: established ▶ **A city of Hadadezer from which David took a large amount of bronze.** Ref.: 1 Chr. 18:8; also spelled Kun, Cun. ¶

CHURL – Is. 32:5, 7 ➔ SCOUNDREL <3596>.

CHURN – Ezek. 32:2 ➔ TROUBLE (verb) <1804>.

CHURN UP – 1 Job 26:12; Is. 51:15; Jer. 31:35 ➔ MOMENT (BE FOR A) <7280> b. 2 Dan. 7:2 ➔ STIR UP <1519>.

CHURNING – 1 ***miyṣ*** [masc. noun: מִיץ <4330>; from OPPRESSOR <4160>] ▶ **This word indicates a twisting, a stirring.** In context it refers to the process that produces butter from milk, i.e., churning, stirring (Prov. 30:33; also translated forcing, pressing), but the churning of wrath or anger creates dissension and strife. ¶
– 2 Hab. 3:15 ➔ HEAP (noun) <2563>.

CIELED – Jer. 22:14; Hag. 1:4 ➔ COVER (verb) <5603> a.

CINNAMON – ***qinnāmôn*** [masc. noun: קִנָּמוֹן <7076>; from an unused root (meaning to erect)] ▶ **This word refers to a pleasant-smelling, yellow-brown spice made from the dried inner bark of certain trees or shrubs.** Ref.: Ex. 30:23. It was used also as an aphrodisiac (Prov. 7:17; Song 4:14). ¶

CIRCLE – ***ḥûg*** [masc. noun: חוּג <2329>; from CIRCLE (INSCRIBE A) <2328>] ▶ **This word means and is also translated vault, circuit.** Figuratively, it refers to the "roof" or vault of the heavens which the Lord walks on or sits on (Job 22:14; Is. 40:22); the horizon or circular edge of the deep (*ḥûg 'al-p^enêy t^ehôm*) (Prov. 8:27) that God established at the time He created the earth. ¶

CIRCLE (INSCRIBE A) – ***ḥûg*** [verb: חוּג <2328>; a prim. root (comp. FEAST (HOLD A) <2287>) (in the sense of to reel)] ▶ **This word means to surround, encircle, trace a circle.** Ref.: Job 26:10; also translated to compass, to draw a circular horizon, to mark out the horizon, possibly as a boundary line of the earth. ¶

CIRCUIT – Job 22:14 ➔ CIRCLE <2329>.

CIRCULAR – ***'āgōl, 'āgôl*** [adj.: עָגֹל, עָגוֹל <5696>; from an unused root meaning to revolve] ▶ **This word refers to anything shaped like a circle, a sphere.** Refs.: 1 Kgs. 7:23, 35; 2 Chr. 4:2; round (1 Kgs. 7:31; 10:19). ¶

CIRCUMCISE – ***mûl*** [verb: מוּל <4135>; a prim. root] ▶ **This word means to remove the foreskin of somebody. It also means to cut short, to cut off.** Abraham was commanded to circumcise both himself and his offspring as a sign of the covenant made between him and God (Gen. 17:10–14). As a result, Abraham had his son Ishmael, all the male slaves in his house, and himself circumcised that same day (Gen. 17:23–27). Later, when Isaac was born, Abraham circumcised him as well (Gen. 21:4). Moses commanded the Israelites to circumcise their hearts, i.e., to remove the hardness and to love God (Deut. 10:16; cf. Deut. 30:6; Jer. 4:4). When used in its intensive form, the verb carries the meaning to cut down, as seen in Psalm 90:6: "In the morning it [the grass] flourisheth, and groweth up; in the evening it is cut down, and withereth" (KJV). Used in the causative sense, the verb gives the meaning to cut off, to destroy (Ps. 118:10–12; lit., "I will cause them to be cut off"). See also the related verbs *māhal* (MIX <4107>), *mālal* (to cut down <4448>), and *nāmal* (to cut down <5243>). *

CIRCUMCISED – Gen. 17:11 ➔ CUT DOWN <5243>.

CIRCUMCISION – ***mûlāh*** [fem. plur. noun: מוּלָה <4139>; from CIRCUMCISE <4135>] ▶ **This word means instances of**

the removal of the male's foreskin. The only undisputed occurrence of the term is found at the end of Exodus 4:26. ¶

CISTERN – [1] ***bôr*** [masc. noun: בּוֹר <953>; from DECLARE <952> (with the meaning of to bore into) in the sense of WELL (noun) <877>] ▶ **This word means a water tank, and also a pit, a well. It can refer to rock-hewn reservoirs or man-made wells.** When empty, such cisterns served as perfect prisons (i.e., Joseph [Gen. 37:20, 22, 24, 28, 29] and Jeremiah [Jer. 38:6, 7, 9–11, 13]). The semantic range extends to prisons in general. Joseph refers to Pharaoh's dungeon as *bôr* (Gen. 40:15). Figuratively, it carries positive and negative connotations. Positively, it can signify a man's wife (Prov. 5:15), and Sarah is the cistern of Israel (Is. 51:1). Negatively, it represents death (Prov. 28:17); Sheol (Ps. 30:3); exile (Zech. 9:11). *

[2] ***geḇe'*** [masc. noun: גֶּבֶא <1360>; from an unused root meaning prob. to collect] ▶ **This word refers to something from which water can be scooped or drawn, either a cistern or a naturally occurring marshy area.** Refs.: Is. 30:14; Ezek. 47:11; also translated pit, marsh. ¶

– [3] Jer. 2:13 ➔ WELL (noun) <877> [4] Jer. 14:3 ➔ POOL (noun) <1356>.

CITADEL – [1] ***biyrāh*** [Aramaic fem. noun: בִּירָה <1001>; corresponding to <1002> below] ▶ **This word means a castle; it is also translated palace, fortress.** It describes a fortified building (Ezra 6:2), which was situated in Ecbatana in the Median province of Persia. ¶

[2] ***biyrāh*** [fem. noun: בִּירָה <1002>; of foreign origin] ▶ **This word refers to the Temple built by Solomon.** Refs.: 1 Chr. 29:1, 19. It also depicts a fortified building or area (acropolis) (Neh. 7:2; Dan. 8:2). Or its main intent may be to designate a building as the capitol (Neh. 1:1), palace, or citadel of a city or nation (Esther 1:2, 5; 2:3, 5, 8). *

– [3] 2 Kgs. 5:24; Is. 32:14 ➔ HILL <6076> [4] Ps. 122:7; Amos 3:11 ➔ STRONGHOLD <759>.

CITY – [1] ***'iyr*** [fem. noun: עִיר <5892>; from AWAKE <5782> (in the sense of guarding or watching in the case of a place)] ▶ **It is a place, a large urban area, where a gathering of persons carry on life.** Ref.: Gen. 4:17. There are various cities: a city militarily protected, fortified (Josh. 19:29); small towns dependent on and closely connected to other cities (Josh. 13:17; Jer. 19:15); royal cities attached to the king (Josh. 10:2); country towns (1 Sam. 27:5). The Israelites built cities for storage and defense (Ex. 1:11; 1 Kgs. 9:19). The Lord had Israel set aside certain cities for refuge, asylum, and temporary safety (Num. 35:11; Josh. 20:2). The city of Jerusalem is uniquely termed the city of God (Ps. 46:4; 87:3). God looked for cities that were known for righteousness (Is. 1:26); truth (Zech. 8:3); holiness (Neh. 11:1, 18; Is. 48:2; 52:1). Unfortunately, Jerusalem became known as a city of oppression (Zeph. 3:1); the city of blood (Ezek. 22:2; 24:6); along with Nineveh (Nah. 3:1). Cities were special to God, for there His people lived. *

[2] ***qiryā', qiryāh*** [Aramaic fem. noun: קִרְיָא, קִרְיָה <7149>; corresponding to <7151> below] ▶ **This word refers to an urban area, e.g., in Samaria, where groups of people had settled.** Refs.: Ezra 4:10, 12, 13, 15, 16, 19, 21. ¶

[3] ***qiryāh*** [fem. noun: קִרְיָה <7151>; from HAPPEN <7136> b. in the sense of flooring] ▶ **This word refers to a large urban area or town, often Jerusalem as the central city of Judah.** Refs.: Num. 21:28; Deut. 2:36; 3:4. It is used also as part of the proper name of many cities: Kiriath-arba, city of Arba, Hebron (Josh. 15:13; 21:11). Jerusalem is called the city of the Great King (Ps. 48:2). The word is used in its construct form (*qiryaṯ*) with a following word, e.g., the city of his strength, his fortress, a figurative expression (Prov. 10:15). Other ref.: Jer. 49:25. *

[4] ***qereṯ*** [fem. noun: קֶרֶת <7176>; from HAPPEN <7136> b. in the sense of building] ▶ **This word uniformly indicates a town, a city, a village.** Refs.: Job 29:7; Prov. 8:3; 9:3, 14; 11:11. ¶

CITY OF PALMS – ***'iyr hat-tᵉmāriym*** [proper noun: עִיר הַתְּמָרִים <5899>; from CITY <5892> and the plur. of PALM TREE <8558>] ▶ **Another description and name for the city of Jericho.** See appropriate entries: *tāmār* (PALM TREE <8558>), ***'iyr*** (CITY <5892>).

CITY OF SALT – ***'iyr hammelaḥ*** [proper noun: עִיר הַמֶּלַח <5898>; from CITY <5892> and SALT <4417>] ▶ **A city in the wilderness given as inheritance to the tribe of Judah.** Ref.: Josh. 15:62. ¶

CLAIM – Ps. 73:9 ➔ LAY, LAY CLAIM <8371> c.

CLAMP – 1 Chr. 22:3 ➔ FITTING <4226>.

CLAN – [1] ***mišpāḥāh*** [fem. noun: מִשְׁפָּחָה <4940>; from STICK OUT <8192> (comp. MAID SERVANT <8198>)] ▶ **This word means an extended family, a tribe.** It is a group in which there is a close blood relationship. In a technical sense, a *mišpāḥāh* is the middle of the subdivisions of the Israelite peoples. The inhabitants of an individual household were identified as a *bayiṯ* (<1004>), meaning house. Several households together constituted a *mišpāḥāh* (Gen. 10:31, 32; Ex. 6:14, 15, 19, 25). Several families or clans together constituted a *šēḇeṭ* (<7626>) or *maṭṭeh* (<4294>), meaning tribe. This noun is also used in a less technical sense to indicate an entire people or nation (Ezek. 20:32; Mic. 2:3); an ethnic or racial group (Gen. 10:5; 12:3); a tribe (Josh. 7:17; Judg. 13:2; 18:2, 11). It occurs in the sense of a guild of scribes in one verse (1 Chr. 2:55) because the scribal profession was originally a hereditary position. It can also represent a species or kind of animal (Gen. 8:19); or a divine plague (Jer. 15:3). *
– [2] Judg. 6:15 ➔ THOUSAND <505>.

CLAP – [1] ***māḥā'*** [verb: מָחָא <4222>; a prim. root] ▶ **This word is used with** *yāḏ*, **hand, or** *kap̱*, **palm, hand, to mean strike the hands, to clap in joy.** Refs.: Ps. 98:8; Is. 55:12; Ezek. 25:6. It is used figuratively of nature or nations clapping their hands. ¶
– [2] Job 27:23; 34:37; Lam. 2:15 ➔ STRIKE <5606>.

CLARITY – Ex. 24:10 ➔ CLEARNESS <2892>.

CLASP – ***qeres*** [masc. noun: קֶרֶס <7165>; from STOOP <7164>] ▶ **This word refers to a hook, the instrument used to connect curtains, tent sections, the veil, etc., to each other in the Tabernacle.** They were made of gold or bronze (Ex. 26:6, 11, 33; 35:11; 36:13, 18; 39:33; KJV: tache). ¶

CLATTERING – Nah. 3:2 ➔ DANCE (verb) <7540>.

CLAW – Dan. 7:19 ➔ NAIL <2953>.

CLAY – [1] ***ḥᵃsap̱*** [Aramaic masc. noun: חֲסַף <2635>; from a root corresponding to that of FLAKE-LIKE THING <2636>] ▶ **The clay, which is heavy sticky earth, is described as mixed with iron in the feet of the statue in Nebuchadnezzar's vision.** It indicates weakness or instability (Dan. 2:33–35, 41–43, 45). ¶
[2] ***maᵃḇeh*** [masc. noun: מַעֲבֶה <4568>; from THICK (BE) <5666>] ▶ **This word refers to a type of thick soil used to make molds for casting various metal items.** Ref.: 1 Kgs. 7:46. Some suggest an ore foundry as a translation. ¶
[3] ***'āḇ*** [common noun: עָב <5645>] ▶ **This word refers to a thick earth suitable for casting metal in it.** Ref.: 2 Chr. 4:17. The Hebrew word has two other meanings; see THICK CLOUD <5645> and THICKET <5645>. ¶
– [4] Lev. 15:12; Jer. 19:1 ➔ EARTHENWARE <2789> [5] Job 10:9; 13:12; 38:14; Is. 29:16; 45:9; 64:8; Jer. 18:4, 6; etc. ➔ MIRE <2563> [6] Ps. 40:2; Is. 41:25; Nah. 3:14 ➔ MUD <2916> [7] Jer. 43:9 ➔ MORTAR <4423> [8] See GROUND <127>.

CLAY (THICK) – Hab. 2:6 ➔ PLEDGE (noun) <5671> b.

CLEAN (adj.) – [1] Job 11:4; Prov. 14:4 ➔ PURE <1249> [2] Job 33:9 ➔ INNOCENT

<2643> [3] Prov. 16:2 ➔ PURE <2134> [4] Is. 30:24 ➔ SALTED <2548> [5] See PURE <2889>.

CLEAN (BE) – Job 15:14; 25:4; Ps. 73:13; Prov. 20:9 ➔ PURE (BE) <2135>.

CLEAN (BE, MAKE) – [1] Job 9:30; 25:5 ➔ PURE (BE) <2141> [2] See PURE (BE, MAKE) <2891>.

CLEAN (verb) – Ezek. 16:4 ➔ CLEANSING <4935>.

CLEANNESS – [1] ***bōr*** [masc. noun: בֹּר <1252>; from PURIFY <1305>] ▶ **The word indicates purity, undefiled condition. Its connotation is a cleanness or pureness in the spiritual sense rather than the physical.** Note the synonymous parallelism between this Hebrew word and *ṣeḏeq* <6664>, which means righteousness as the basis for divine reward or recompense (2 Sam. 22:21, 25; Ps. 18:20, 24). It occurs only once by itself (2 Sam. 22:25). It usually occurs with *yāḏ* <3027>, meaning hand (2 Sam. 22:21; Ps. 18:20, 24), or *kap̱* <3709>, meaning palm (Job 9:30; 22:30). ¶ – [2] Amos 4:6 ➔ INNOCENCE <5356>.

CLEANSE – [1] Job 9:30 ➔ PURE (BE) <2141> [2] Ps. 73:13; 119:9 ➔ PURE (BE) <2135> [3] Is. 1:6 ➔ CRUSH <2115> [4] Ezek. 16:4 ➔ CLEANSING <4935>.

CLEANSE AWAY – Prov. 20:30 ➔ COSMETICS <8562>.

CLEANSING – [1] ***ṭāhᵒrāh*** [fem. noun: טָהֳרָה <2893>; fem. of CLEARNESS <2892>] ▶ **This word means purification, ceremonial purifying.** It refers to a ceremonial cleansing pronounced by a priest on one formerly unclean (Lev. 13:7). The cleansing from such things as leprosy (Lev. 14:2, 23, 32); issues relating to genital organs (Lev. 15:13); touching a dead body (Num. 6:9); and childbirth (Lev. 12:4, 5) required additional procedures such as washing clothes and bathing. The birth of a child rendered a woman unclean, remaining in the blood of her purification (i.e., extra bleeding in the days following childbirth) for a set time after which she brought a sacrifice to the priest (cf. Luke 2:24). Cleansing from leprosy involved an extensive ceremony (Lev. 14:1–32). These ceremonies promoted good hygiene, but in the days of Hezekiah, God pardoned those who were seeking Him but failed to maintain ceremonial cleanness (2 Chr. 30:19). Other refs.: 1 Chr. 23:28; Neh. 12:45; Ezek. 44:26). ¶
[2] ***mišʿiy*** [masc. noun: מִשְׁעִי <4935>; prob. from LOOK FOR FAVOR OR IN DISMAY <8159> (in the sense of to inspect)] ▶ **This word refers to wash, washing.** It indicates the act of cleaning up, bathing a newborn infant. Preceded by *lᵉ*, to, for, it means ready for or fit for cleansing, washing (Ezek. 16:4; also translated to clean, to cleanse, to supple). ¶

CLEAR – [1] ***mišqāʿ*** [masc. noun: מִשְׁקָע <4950>; from DIE DOWN <8257> (in the sense of to settle)] ▶ **This word describes water that is pure and clean enough to drink.** Sediments and impurities have settled out of it (Ezek. 34:18; KJV: deep). ¶ – [2] Ex. 27:20; Lev. 24:2 ➔ PURE <2134> [3] Song 6:10 ➔ PURE <1249>.

CLEAR (BE) – Ps. 51:4 ➔ PURE (BE) <2135>.

CLEAR (BE, MAKE) – ***pāraš*** [verb: פָּרַשׁ <6567>; a prim. root] ▶ **This word means to show, to distinguish; it is also translated to explain, to declare.** It means to explain, to interpret something: the Lord's command about an incident (Lev. 24:12; Num. 15:34; Neh. 8:8). The Hebrew word also means to sting, to scatter; see STING <6567> and SCATTER <6567>. ¶

CLEAR (MAKE) – ***pᵉraš*** [Aramaic verb: פְּרַשׁ <6568>; corresponding to CLEAR (BE, MAKE) <6567>] ▶ **This word means to translate and to explain the meaning of something, especially a foreign language spoken or written.** Ref.: Ezra 4:18; it is translated in English clearly, plainly. ¶

CLEAR AWAY – Deut. 7:1, 22 ➔ REMOVE <5394>.

CLEAR-SIGHTED – Ex. 23:8 ➔ SEEING <6493>.

CLEAR, CLEARLY – Is. 18:4; 32:4 ➔ DAZZLING <6703>.

CLEARED – Job 26:13 ➔ FAIR <8235>.

CLEARLY – Ezra 4:18 ➔ CLEAR (MAKE) <6568>.

CLEARNESS – ***ṭōhar, ṭ*ᵉ*hār*** [masc. noun: טֹהַר, טְהָר <2892>; from PURE (BE) <2891>] ▶ **This word means purity, pureness, clarity, luster. It is from a verb meaning to be pure or to be clean, both physically and ceremonially.** It is used to denote the lustrous quality of a clear sky (Ex. 24:10; also translated clarity); the glory of an individual (Ps. 89:44); and the purification cycle after childbirth (Lev. 12:4, 6: purification, purifying). ¶

CLEAVE – 1 Lev. 1:17 ➔ SPLIT <8156> 2 Deut. 4:4 ➔ JOINING <1695> 3 Job 38:25 ➔ DIVIDE <6385> 4 Lam. 4:8 ➔ SHRIVELED UP (BE) <6821> 5 Dan. 2:43 ➔ ADHERE <1693>.

CLEFT – 1 ***ḥāgāw, ḥāgû*** [verb: חָגָו, חָגוּ <2288>; from an unused root meaning to take refuge] ▶ **This word indicates a place of concealment, an indentation in a rock or rocky area.** It is a secret place away from crowds (Song 2:14) for two lovers. But also it is a strategic location for armies and one's enemies to hide and fight (Jer. 49:16; Obad. 1:3). ¶

2 ***nāqiyq*** [masc. noun: נָקִיק <5357>; from an unused root meaning to bore] ▶ **This word means a fissure; it is also translated hole, crevice.** It indicates a large crack creating an opening in a rock (Is. 7:19; Jer. 13:4; 16:16); but some prefer to understand the word as referring to a rock ledge (cf. NASB, Is. 7:19). ¶

3 ***n*ᵉ*qārāh*** [fem. noun: נְקָרָה <5366>; from GOUGE <5365>] ▶ **This word refers to a cavern.** It refers to a large fissure or crevice in a rock, large enough for people to hide in or take shelter in (Ex. 33:22; Is. 2:21). ¶

4 ***sa'iyp*** [masc. noun: סָעִיף <5585>; from LOP, LŌP OFF <5586> (in relation to the top)] ▶ **This word refers to a fissure, a crack; it is also translated clift, crag, top.** It refers to a large rock overhang or a crevice large enough to be used as a temporary lodging place (Judg. 15:8, 11); or as a place to seek refuge (Is. 2:21). It was also a place used for sacred sacrificial rites of a pagan nature (Is. 57:5). The Hebrew word also means a branch, a bough; see BRANCH <5585>. ¶

5 ***šesa'*** [masc. noun: שֶׁסַע <8157>; from SPLIT <8156>] ▶ **This word indicates dividedness.** It describes the separation, division in the hooves of certain animals edible in Israel (Lev. 11:3, 7, 26; Deut. 14:6). ¶

– 6 Job 30:6 ➔ CLIFF <6178> 7 Song 2:17 ➔ BETHER <1336> 8 Amos 6:11 ➔ BREACH <1233>.

CLEVERNESS – Is. 25:11 ➔ TRICKERY <698>.

CLIFF – 1 ***maḏrêgāh*** [fem. noun: מַדְרֵגָה <4095>; from an unused root meaning to step] ▶ **This word indicates a mountain pathway in widely diverse settings. It is also translated mountainside, stairs, steep pathway, steep place.** Refs.: Song 2:14; Ezek. 38:20. ¶

2 ***'ārûṣ*** [עָרוּץ <6178>; pass. part. of TREMBLE <6206> (in the sense of to fear)] ▶
a. A feminine noun meaning a chasm; it is also translated gully, cleft. It is variously translated as cliff (KJV), clefts (NKJV), dreadful (NASB), dry (NIV) (Job 30:6). Its exact meaning is not yet clear. See b., c. ¶
b. An adjective meaning dreadful. It refers to valleys not suitable for habitation (Job 30:6). See a., c. ¶
c. An adjective meaning dry. It refers to dry, temporary streambeds (Job 30:6; NIV). See a., b. ¶

CLIFT – 1 Ex. 33:22 ➔ CLEFT <5366> 2 Is. 57:5 ➔ CLEFT <5585>.

CLIMB – Song 2:8 ➔ LEAP <1801>.

CLING – [1] Lam. 4:8 ➔ SHRIVELED UP (BE) <6821> [2] See JOIN <1692>.

CLING TO – Job 24:8 ➔ EMBRACE <2263>.

CLOAK – [1] ***miṭpaḥaṯ*** [fem. noun: מִטְפַּחַת <4304>; from SPREAD OUT <2946>] ▶ **This word means a mantle, and also a veil.** It indicates a mantle for women to wear (Ruth 3:15; also translated shawl, vail, garment). It was a sign of wealthy society and an item listed with other items of fine clothing (Is. 3:22; also translated outer garment, wimple). ¶
– [2] Gen. 25:25; Josh. 7:21, 24; 1 Kgs. 19:13, 19; Zech. 13:4 ➔ GARMENT <155> [3] Judg. 3:16 ➔ CLOTHES <4055> [4] Song 5:7 ➔ VEIL <7289> [5] Dan. 3:21, 27 ➔ COAT (noun) <5622>.

CLOD – [1] ***megrāp̱āh*** [fem. noun: מֶגְרָפָה <4053>; from SWEEP AWAY <1640>] ▶ **This word is used of lumps of dirt in a tilled garden during a time of drought.** Ref.: Joel 1:17. As likely meanings, spade or hoe have been suggested. ¶
[2] ***regeḇ*** [masc. noun: רֶגֶב <7263>; from an unused root meaning to pile together] ▶ **This word means a clump of soil; it is also translated clod (or lump) of earth.** In Job 38:38, the phenomenon of dirt forming into clods is reckoned as a work of God. The clods of soil serve to cover the wicked dead (Job 21:33). ¶
– [3] Job 7:5 ➔ CRUST <1487>.

CLODS (BREAK THE) – Is. 28:24; Hos. 10:11 ➔ HARROW <7702>.

CLOSE – [1] ***'āṭar*** [verb: אָטַר <332>; a prim. root] ▶ **This word is also translated to shut.** It is used figuratively of a pit shutting its mouth (Ps. 69:15). ¶
[2] ***sāgar*** [verb: סָגַר <5462>; a prim. root] ▶ **The meaning of this word is uniformly to shut, to stop.** For examples: to close up a hole in one's flesh (Gen. 2:21); to shut, to close a door, etc. (Gen. 7:16; 19:6, 10); to shut, enclose something, e.g., Israel in the wilderness terrain (Ex. 14:3); to close the womb from being fertile (1 Sam. 1:5). In its passive uses, it means to be shut, shut up, closed (Num. 12:14, 15; Josh. 6:1; 1 Sam. 23:7; Neh. 13:19; Eccl. 12:4). In its intensive and causative stems, it means to enclose, to deliver over to someone or something (1 Sam. 17:46; 24:18); to give into another's authority or power (Deut. 23:15; 1 Sam. 23:11; Amos 1:6; Obad. 1:14). It is used of things tightly fitted together, closed in on each other (Job 41:15). The Hebrew word is also related to gold; see PURE <5462>. *
[3] ***sāḵar*** [verb: סָכַר <5534>; a prim. root] ▶ **This word means to stop up, to shut up.** It means to close up or shut off something: the deep springs of water and the heavy rain from the skies are pictured figuratively as being shut down, closed in order to stop the flood waters (Gen. 8:2). It is used of stopping a person's mouth, shutting him or her up (Ps. 63:11; NIV: to silence). The Hebrew word also means to hand over, to deliver; see GIVE OVER <5534>. ¶
[4] ***'āṣam*** [verb: עָצַם <6105>; a prim. root] ▶ **This word means to bind (the eyes) fast; it is also translated to shut, to seal.** It is used of the Lord's shutting the eyes of a rebellious people (Is. 29:10). It means to cover one's eyes or to refuse to approve or countenance what is evil in the Lord's eyes (Is. 33:15). The Hebrew word also means to be mighty, to be numerous; see MIGHTY (BE) <6105>. ¶
– [5] Prov. 17:28 ➔ STOP <331> [6] Is. 1:6 ➔ CRUSH <2115>.

CLOSE IN – [1] 1 Sam. 23:26 ➔ CROWN (noun and verb) <5849> b. [2] Jon. 2:5 ➔ SURROUND <661>.

CLOSE-KNIT (BE) – Job 40:17 ➔ KNIT TOGETHER (BE) <8276>.

CLOSE OVER – Lam. 3:54 ➔ FLOW OVER <6687>.

CLOSET – Joel 2:16 ➔ CHAMBER <2646>.

CLOTH (noun) – [1] Num. 4:6–9, 11–13 ➔ GARMENT <899> [2] Is. 21:5 ➔ RUG <6844> a.

CLOTH, TICK CLOTH – ***maḵbêr*** [masc. noun: מַכְבֵּר <4346>; from MULTIPLY <3527> in the sense of covering] ▶ **This word refers to a blanket, a mat, or possibly netting.** In its only use, it covers the face of a dying man (2 Kgs. 8:15). ¶

CLOTH (WORKER IN) – Is. 19:10 ➔ FOUNDATION <8356> c., d.

CLOTH (verb) – Ps. 65:6 ➔ GIRD <247>.

CLOTHE – [1] ***lāḇaš, lāḇêš*** [verb: לָבַשׁ, לָבֵשׁ <3847>; a prim. root] ▶ **This word means to wear, to dress, to put on clothing.** It is used of putting on any kind of clothing or garments: clothes (Gen. 3:21; 28:20); armor (1 Sam. 17:38; Is. 59:17); royal robes (1 Kgs. 22:10; Ezra 3:10; Esther 6:8); clothing in general (2 Sam. 13:18; Hag. 1:6). It is used figuratively in various ways: of the Lord or people being clothed with righteousness and other qualities (Ps. 93:1; 104:1; Is. 51:9; 59:17); of the Spirit of the Lord "clothing," coming upon a person (Judg. 6:34); of worms clothing a person (Job 7:5); terror also may clothe a person (Ezek. 7:27). *
[2] ***leḇaš*** [Aramaic verb: לְבַשׁ <3848>; corresponding to <3847> above] ▶ **This word refers to putting on clothes.** In context it refers to attiring someone with a royal, purple robe (Dan. 5:7, 16, 29), indicating kingly authority. ¶
– [3] Ps. 73:6 ➔ TURN (verb) <5848> a. [4] Is. 61:10 ➔ PRIEST (MINISTER AS, SERVE AS) <3547> [5] Zech. 3:3, 4 ➔ COVER (verb) <3722>.

CLOTHED WITH, CLOTHED IN (BE) – ***kirbêl*** [verb: כִּרְבֵּל <3736>; from the same as FETTERS <3525>] ▶ **This word is used only to indicate the royal and Levitical regalia King David wore when he prepared to move the ark of God.** Ref.: 1 Chr. 15:27. ¶

CLOTHES – [1] ***gelôm*** [masc. noun: גְּלוֹם <1545>; from ROLL (verb) <1563> (in the sense of to fold together)] ▶ **This word indicates what is worn on the body; it also means fabric, wrapping.** It refers to one of the many articles that Tyre traded among the merchants of the world (Ezek. 27:24). Combined with the word for blue (*teḵêleṯ*), it indicates a blue fabric or blue clothes. ¶
[2] ***maḏ*** [masc. noun: מַד <4055>; from MEASURE (verb) <4058> (in the sense of measuring the size of someone to make clothes)] ▶ **This word means a tunic, a robe; it is also translated cloak, raiment, clothing, armor, garment, coat.** It refers to garments in general: an outer garment (Judg. 3:16; 1 Sam. 4:12); a military uniform or attire (1 Sam. 17:38, 39; 2 Sam. 20:8); priestly garments (Lev. 6:10). It also has the meaning of apportionment or measure in some contexts (Job 11:9; Jer. 13:25). It is used figuratively of wearing cursing as a garment (Ps. 109:18). Other refs.: Judg. 5:10; 1 Sam. 18:4; 2 Sam. 21:20. ¶
[3] ***sûṯ*** [masc. noun: סוּת <5497>; prob. from the same root as VEIL <4533> (in the sense of a covering)] ▶ **This word refers to garments in general.** In context it hints of the royal or kingly clothing of a ruler (Gen. 49:11; also translated robes, vesture). ¶
– [4] Job 27:16; Ezek. 16:13; Zeph. 1:8 ➔ CLOTHING <4403> [5] Is. 23:18 ➔ COVERING <4374>.

CLOTHING – [1] ***leḇûš, leḇuš, lāḇûš, lāḇuš*** [noun and adj.: לְבוּשׁ, לְבֻשׁ, לָבוּשׁ, לָבֻשׁ <3830>; from CLOTHE <3847>] ▶
a. A masculine noun indicating things worn on the body, garments, dress. This word refers to clothing of men or women (Gen. 49:11; Ps. 45:13). It is used as a collective noun of clothes or dress for women or men (2 Kgs. 10:22; Is. 14:19). It includes clothing of various materials (Job 30:18; Ps. 35:13; Prov. 27:26); or styles (Esther 6:8). It is used in metaphorical language: clouds like garments covering the sea (Job 38:9); or the clothing of idols (Jer. 10:9). A man was to claim and protect his wife by covering her with his garment (Mal. 2:16).
b. An adjective meaning dressed, attired. It describes the state of a person wearing

garments as opposed to being naked. The household of a wise woman may be clothed luxuriously (Prov. 31:21). It is used of a warrior outfitted in his military dress (1 Sam. 17:5; Ezek. 38:4). It is used figuratively and literally of a person attired with the clothing of those slain by a sword (Is. 14:19). Even heavenly beings are dressed (Ezek. 9:2, 3, 11; 10:2, 6, 7; Dan. 10:5; 12:6, 7). Filthy garments may refer to a corrupt moral character (Zech. 3:3). Royal garments were often purple (Ezek. 23:6). *

2 ***lᵉḇûš*** [Aramaic masc. noun: לְבוּשׁ <3831>; corresponding to <3830> above] ▶ **This word means attire; it is also translated garment, vesture.** It refers to a complete set of clothing worn by the three Hebrews (Dan. 3:21). The regalia of the Ancient of Days was pure white indicating holiness and purity (Dan. 7:9). ¶

3 ***malbûš*** [masc. noun: מַלְבּוּשׁ <4403>; from CLOTHE <3847>] ▶ **This word means vesture; it is also translated robes, attire, apparel, clothes, dress, raiment, garment, vestment.** It always refers to some type of clothing: luxurious, costly garments understood figuratively of God's blessings on Jerusalem (1 Kgs. 10:5; 2 Chr. 9:4; Ezek. 16:13); foreign garments (Zeph. 1:8); working clothes as the blood-stained garments of the Lord as a warrior (Is. 63:3). These items could also be counted as wealth (Job 27:16). Other ref.: 2 Kgs. 10:22b. ¶

4 ***śalmāh*** [masc. noun: שַׂלְמָה <8008>; transposed for CLOTHING <8071> below] ▶ **This word refers to a cloak, clothes, a robe.** It refers to a major piece of clothing, a mantle, that was valuable and necessary in ancient Israel (Ex. 22:9); in a pledge, it could not be retained overnight (Ex. 22:26; Deut. 24:13). It could be a long, warm garment used as a blanket at night to keep warm. These garments did not wear out during Israel's stay in the wilderness (Deut. 29:5). It may refer to a covering for sheep (1 Kgs. 10:25). The Lord uses light as a cloak to cover Himself (Ps. 104:2). A cloak could be perfumed and spiced to make it smell amorous (Song 4:11). *

5 ***śimlāh*** [fem. noun: שִׂמְלָה <8071>; perhaps by permutation for the fem. of IDOL <5566> (through the idea of a cover assuming the shape of the object beneath)] ▶ **This word refers to a relatively large garment.** Either an external garment heavy enough to sleep in (Ex. 22:27) or a blanket large enough to cover a person lying on a bed (Gen. 9:23). A change of garments could indicate a new beginning or getting ready for travel (Gen. 35:2). It refers to clothes in general (Gen. 37:34; Deut. 22:5). *

6 ***tilbōšeṯ*** [fem. noun: תִּלְבֹּשֶׁת <8516>; from CLOTHE <3847>] ▶ **This word indicates in a figurative sense garments of revenge, clothing of revenge, clothing indicative of vengeance put on by God to effect justice and judgment on His people.** Ref.: Is. 59:17. ¶

– 7 Ex. 21:10; Deut. 22:12 ➔ COVERING <3682> 8 Judg. 3:16 ➔ CLOTHES <4055> 9 Is. 23:18 ➔ COVERING <4374>.

CLOUD – 1 ***ʿᵃnan*** [masc. sing. Aramaic noun: עֲנַן <6050>; corresponding to <6051> below] ▶ **A cloud is a mass appearing in the sky and may refer, figuratively, to an indication of majesty and honor. This word occurs only in Daniel 7:13 in the phrase, clouds of heaven.** In a night vision, Daniel saw the Son of Man coming with the clouds of heaven. This use of clouds in apocalyptic language is familiar to the writer of Revelation who echoes the same phrase, "Look, he is coming with the clouds" (Rev. 1:7). See the Hebrew cognate *ʿānān* (<6051>) below. ¶

2 ***ʿānān*** [masc. sing. noun: עָנָן <6051>; from an Hebrew word meaning to bring, see under WITCHCRAFT (PRACTICE) <6049>] ▶ **In the ancient world, clouds were often seen as the pedestal or shroud of the divine presence. This imagery is also present in the Hebrew Bible.** God preceded the Israelites through the wilderness in a pillar of cloud (Ex. 13:21, 22); and the same cloud rested over the Tabernacle (Ex. 33:10). The cloud was over Mount Sinai (Ex. 19:9); and entered the Temple in Jerusalem (1 Kgs. 8:10, 11). Clouds are typical of the apocalyptic language of the Day of God (Ezek. 30:3; Joel 2:2; Zeph.

1:15). Other poetic uses of cloud describe God's shelter (Is. 4:5); Israel's evaporating love (Hos. 6:4); the transient nature of life (Job 7:9); and the breadth of a great army (Ezek. 38:9). See the Aramaic *ᵃnan* (<6050> above). *

3 ***ᵃnānāh*** [fem. noun: עֲנָנָה <6053>; from <6051> above] ▶ **The context implies a thick cloud that obscures visibility, capable of hiding something.** Ref.: Job 3:5. ¶

4 ***ᵃriypiym*** [masc. noun: עֲרִיפִים <6183>; from DROP, DROP DOWN <6201>] ▶ **Isaiah used this word when he pronounced God's judgments on Israel by means of foreign nations.** He stated that the judgment would be so severe that there would be only darkness and distress; there would be no light, as when storm clouds block out the light (Is. 5:30; KJV: heavens). ¶

5 ***ᵃrāp̱el*** [masc. sing. noun: עֲרָפֶל <6205>; prob. from DROP, DROP DOWN <6201>] ▶ **A cloud enshrouded God.** Refs.: Ex. 20:21; Job 22:13. It also served as His pedestal (2 Sam. 22:10; Ps. 18:9). The term is used figuratively to depict a stormy sea that has clouds for a garment (Job 38:9). Prophetic pictures of God's judgment are filled with clouds, darkening the ominous Day of the Lord (Jer. 13:16; Ezek. 34:12; Joel 2:2; Zeph. 1:15). *

6 ***šaḥaq*** [masc. noun: שַׁחַק <7834>; from BEAT <7833> (in the sense of something beaten small, e.g., a powder; by analogy, a thin vapor)] ▶ **This word means a fine cloud, a thin cloud. The primary usage of the word denotes a cloud.** Often this word is used to depict a cloud or clouds (in the plural) in the sky (Job 35:5, Prov. 8:28). In Psalms, this word is used to describe the heavens (Ps. 36:5). In a metaphorical sense, Moses described God as riding on the heavens and clouds in His majesty to help His people (Deut. 33:26). Used in this sense, it denotes Yahweh as Ruler over the heavens and all that is in them. This word is used to depict dark rain clouds which form a canopy around Him (2 Sam. 22:12). The word can also be used to denote nations as fine dust (Is. 40:15). *

– 7 Judg. 20:38 ➔ GIFT <4864> 8 Ezek. 19:11; 31:3, 10, 14 ➔ BOUGH (THICK).

CLOUD (BRING A) – Gen. 9:14 ➔ WITCHCRAFT (PRACTICE) <6049>.

CLOUD (COVER WITH A) – ***'ûḇ*** [verb: עוּב <5743>; a prim. root] ▶ **This word is used of bringing a cloud over something or someone.** It is employed figuratively of God's anger toward Israel (Lam. 2:1). ¶

CLOUD (FLASHING, STORM, BRIGHT) – Zech. 10:1 ➔ THUNDERSTORM <2385>.

CLOUDBURST – ***nep̱eṣ*** [noun: נֶפֶץ <5311>; from BREAK <5310>] ▶ **This word indicates a driving storm; it is also translated scattering. It refers to a sudden falling of a heavy, pelting rain.** It is used of God's making His power and presence known in this case (Is. 30:30). ¶

CLOUDS – Ps. 148:8 ➔ SMOKE (noun) <7008>.

CLOUTED (BE) – Josh. 9:5 ➔ SPOTTED (BE) <2921>.

CLOVEN – See CLEFT <8157>.

CLUB – 1 ***tôṯāḥ*** [masc. noun: תּוֹתָח <8455>; from an unused root meaning to smite] ▶

a. This word indicates a wooden, metal, or stone weapon. It is shaped by a craftsman for use in war, hunting, or for attacking a foe (Job 41:29).

b. This word means a dart. It refers to a piece of wood or metal sharpened to penetrate an object, used often in battle and in hunting (Job 41:29). ¶

– 2 Ezek. 39:9 ➔ STICK <4731>.

CLUB, WAR CLUB – ***mep̱iyṣ*** [masc. noun: מֵפִיץ <4650>; from SCATTER <6327> b. (in the sense of to break into pieces)] ▶ **This word refers to a hammer-like tool that delivers jolting blows.** The impact of a false witness on a person is compared to it (Prov. 25:18). ¶

CLUSTER – 1 ***'eškôl, 'eškōl*** [masc. noun: אֶשְׁכֹּל, אֶשְׁכּוֹל <811>; prob. prolonged from

TESTICLE <810>] ▶ **This word indicates a bunch, a group of vegetation, often grapes.** It may refer to just the stalk of the vine (Gen. 40:10) or the entire cluster of grapes (Num. 13:23, 24; Song 7:8; Mic. 7:1). It also describes a group of henna blossoms (Song 1:14) as like the breasts of the bride (Song 7:7). A cluster could contain new wine (Is. 65:8). Other ref.: Deut. 32:32. ¶
– [2] Job 38:31 ➔ CHAIN <4574> a. [3] Job 38:31 ➔ CHAINS <4575> a.

CLUSTER OF DATES – Song 5:11 ➔ WAVY <8534> b.

CLUSTER (CHOICE) – Is. 16:8 ➔ PLANT (CHOICE, PRINCIPAL) <8291>.

COAL – [1] ***gaḥeleṯ*** [fem. noun: גַּחֶלֶת <1513>; from an unused root meaning to glow or kindle] ▶ **This word denotes burning coal, live coals. A coal is a black rock used as fuel.** It literally refers to coals of fire (Lev. 16:12; 2 Sam. 22:13; Prov. 6:28) used to burn up sacrifices or provide heat (Is. 47:14). It is often used figuratively to indicate hot coals that ignite wood as a quarrelsome person causes strife (Prov. 26:21); burning coals used to describe the living creatures in Ezekiel's vision (Ezek. 1:13); hot coal describes the male reproductive capacity (2 Sam. 14:7) or God's acts of judgment (Ps. 120:4). Burning coals stand for an act of kindness or warming one's enemy (Prov. 25:22; cf. Rom. 12:20). *
[2] ***peḥām*** [masc. noun: פֶּחָם <6352>; perhaps from an unused root prob. meaning to be black] ▶ **This word indicates pieces of coal, charcoal, i.e., black rocks used as fuel.** It refers to a porous form of carbon that is highly flammable (Prov. 26:21). It was used to heat ovens, furnaces, etc. (Is. 44:12; 54:16). ¶
– [3] Song 8:6 ➔ FLASH (noun) <7565> [4] Lam. 4:8 ➔ SOOT <7815>.

COAST – [1] ***ḥôp̱*** [masc. noun: חוֹף <2348>; from an unused root meaning to cover] ▶ **This word refers also to a shore, a haven.** It indicates a seashore (Gen. 49:13; Deut. 1:7; Josh. 9:1; Judg. 5:17; Ezek. 25:16); a harbor, port, or haven for ships (Gen. 49:13: haven). Other ref.: Jer. 47:7. ¶
– [2] Josh. 12:23 ➔ SIEVE <5299> b. [3] Joel 3:4 ➔ REGION <1552>.

COASTLAND – ***'iy*** [masc. noun: אִי <339>; from DESIRE (verb) <183> (properly a habitable spot, as desirable)] ▶ **This word means the region of the seashore, an island.** It depicts the Phoenicians as inhabiting a coastland (Is. 20:6; 23:2, 6). Distant islands or shores were designated by this word (Is. 40:15). In general, the islands, shores, and coastlands of the Mediterranean Sea are indicated. *

COAT (noun) – [1] ***kuttōneṯ*** [fem. noun: כֻּתֹּנֶת <3801>; from an unused root meaning to cover (comp. SHOULDER <3802>)] ▶ **This word refers to an inner, shirt-like garment covering the body; it is also translated robe, tunic.** It indicates a long undergarment with a collar cut out for one's head (Gen. 37:3); the main common garment worn by men or women (2 Sam. 15:32: robe, coat; Song 5:3: robe, coat, dress, garment). Priests wore a priestly tunic (Ex. 28:4; Lev. 16:4; Ezra 2:69; Neh. 7:70, 72. These garments could be of linen or skins (Gen. 3:21) and were sometimes embroidered (Ex. 28:4, 39). They were torn as a sign of grief and mourning (2 Sam. 15:32). Worn by kings or rulers, they indicated authority (Is. 22:21). *
[2] ***sarbāl*** [Aramaic masc. noun: סַרְבָּל <5622>; of uncertain deriv.] ▶ **This word refers to an article of Persian dress, either long, wide pantaloons covering the lower body or long, flowing mantles; it is also translated trousers, cloaks, robes.** It refers to a piece of the extensive outfits that the three Hebrew young men wore none of which was singed by fire (Dan. 3:21, 27). ¶
– [3] Ps. 109:18 ➔ CLOTHES <4055>.

COAT (verb) – [1] ***ḥāmar*** [verb: חָמַר <2560>; a prim. root] ▶ **This word means to cover something with bitumen.** It describes the process of waterproofing the basket which was placed in the Nile River

with the infant Moses inside it (Ex. 2:3: to daub, to cover, to coat). The Hebrew word also means to ferment, to make red; see RED (BE) <2560>. ¶
– [2] Deut. 27:2, 4 ➔ PLASTER (verb) <7874>.

COAT OF MAIL – ***taḥrā'*** [fem. noun: תַּחְרָא <8473>; from ANGRY (GET) <2734> in the original sense of HOLE <2352> or WHITE <2353>] ▶
a. This word is also translated habergeon. The exact meaning eludes us. It refers to protective gear worn by soldiers in battle. Others suggest a leather cuirass, a tight-fitting armor to protect one's front and back (Ex. 28:32; 39:23; ESV: garment).
b. This word could also means a collar. It refers to the edging around the neck of a shirt to keep it from tearing. Refs.: Ex. 28:32; 39:23. ¶

COATING – ***ṭiyaḥ*** [masc. noun: טִיחַ <2915>; from (the equivalent of) OVERLAY <2902>] ▶ **This word means a thin, covering layer (on a wall); it is also translated whitewash, plaster, daubing, mortar. It is used of the coating put on a wall to improve its appearance.** But in context, it is symbolic of Israel's feeble attempts to cover her true condition with lies and falsities used as "plaster" (Ezek. 13:12). ¶

COBRA – See ASP <6620>.

COCKATRICE – Prov. 23:32; Is. 11:8; 14:29; 59:5; Jer. 8:17 ➔ VIPER <6848>.

COCKLE – Job 31:40 ➔ STINKWEED <890>.

COFFER – 1 Sam. 6:8, 11, 15 ➔ CHEST <712>.

COFFIN – Gen. 50:26 ➔ ARK <727>.

COILING – Is. 27:1 ➔ TWISTING <6129>.

COL-HOZEH – ***kol-ḥōzeh*** [masc. proper noun: כָּל־חֹזֶה <3626>; from ALL <3605> and SEER <2374>]: seer of all ▶
a. Father of Shallum, maybe the same as the next one. Ref.: Neh. 3:15. ¶
b. A Judaite in the time of Nehemiah. Ref.: Neh. 11:5. ¶

COLD (adj.) – ***qar*** [adj.: קַר <7119>; contr. from an unused root meaning to chill] ▶ **This word also means cool; even-tempered.** Used in a simile, it refers to chilly or cold refreshing water that soothes the soul (Prov. 17:27; 25:25; Jer. 18:14). Cold water, especially cool spring water, was highly prized in Israel, in the hot ancient Near East. ¶

COLD (noun) – [1] ***qōr*** [masc. noun: קֹר <7120>; from COLD (adj.) <7119>] ▶ **This word refers to the low temperatures of winter, to a condition that is chilly, lacking adequate heat.** Ref.: Gen. 8:22. ¶
[2] ***qārāh*** [fem. noun: קָרָה <7135>; fem. of COLD (adj.) <7119>] ▶ **This word refers to a condition without sufficient heat or warmth.** Refs.: Job 24:7; 37:9. God creates the cold (Ps. 147:17). It is used to form similes for comparison (Prov. 25:20; Nah. 3:17). ¶
– [3] Gen. 31:40 ➔ ICE <7140> [4] Prov. 25:13 ➔ HOOK <6793> c.

COLLAR – [1] Ex. 28:32; 39:23 ➔ COAT OF MAIL <8473> b. [2] Judg. 8:26 ➔ CHAIN <6060>.

COLLARS – Judg. 8:26 ➔ PENDANT <5188>.

COLLEAGUE – [1] Ezra 4:7 ➔ COMPANION <3674> [2] Ezra 4:9, 17, 23; 5:3, 6; 6:6, 13 ➔ COMPANION <3675>.

COLLECT – [1] Deut. 24:10 ➔ LEND <5670> [2] Eccl. 2:8 ➔ GATHER <3664>.

COLLECTED SAYING – Eccl. 12:11 ➔ ASSEMBLY <627>.

COLLECTION – ***qibbûṣ*** [fem. noun: קִבּוּץ <6899>; from GATHER <6908>] ▶ **This word refers in context to a group, an assortment of some sort, probably**

of idols or divine objects. Ref.: Is. 57:13; KJV: companies. ¶

COLLIDE – Dan. 11:40 ➔ GORE <5055>.

COLLOPS OF FAT – Job 15:27 ➔ FAT (noun) <6371>.

COLONNADE – 1 Chr. 26:18 ➔ PRECINCTS <6503> a.

COLOR – [1] Ezek. 27:24: many colors ➔ MULTICOLORED <1264> [2] Dan. 5:6, 9, 10; 7:28 ➔ BRIGHTNESS <2122>.

COLOR (DRAINED OF) – Joel 2:6; Nah. 2:10 ➔ BLACKNESS <6289>.

COLORED – ***ḥ^aṭuḇôṯ*** [fem. plur. noun: חֲטֻבוֹת <2405>; fem. pass. part. of CUT (verb) <2404>] ▶ **This word indicates something tinted; colored embroidered fabric.** It most likely refers to the famous colored linens produced in Egypt (Prov. 7:16; KJV: carved) and considered a luxury item. ¶

COLORED MATERIAL – Ezek. 27:24 ➔ MULTICOLORED <1264>.

COLORFUL – Ezek. 16:165 ➔ SPOTTED (BE) <2921>.

COLORFUL GARMENT – Judg. 5:30 ➔ DYED WORK, DYED MATERIALS <6648>.

COLORS (FAIR) – Is. 54:11 ➔ ANTIMONY <6320>.

COLORS (OF MANY) – ***pas*** [adj.: פַּס <6446>; from VANISH <6461>] ▶
a. This word means richly ornamented, made with many tints; it is also translated ornate, varicolored. It is used in its plural form *passîm.* It modifies a tunic or a robe, indicating its many colors or its length (Gen. 37:3, 23, 32; 2 Sam. 13:18, 19); a highly esteemed garment. ¶
b. An adjective indicating something long-sleeved. It refers to a long-sleeved tunic or robe worn by the king's daughter (2 Sam. 13:18, 19); it was a highly esteemed garment. ¶

COLORS (VARIOUS, DIVERS) – Ezek. 16:16 ➔ SPOTTED (BE) <2921>.

COLUMN – [1] ***tiymārāh*** [fem. noun: תִּימָרָה <8490>; from the same as PALM TREE <8558> (i.e., an unused root meaning to erect)] ▶ **This word refers to a rising shaft (of smoke); it is also translated pillar.** It refers to the caravan or royal carriage of Solomon that appears like a column of smoke (Song 3:6). It refers to a display of God's wonders on the Day of the Lord, including a display of columns of smoke literally or in some figurative sense (Joel 2:30). ¶
– [2] Is. 9:18 ➔ MAJESTY <1348> [3] Zeph. 2:14 ➔ BULB <3730>.

COMBED – ***śāriyq*** [adj.: שָׂרִיק <8305>; from the same as VINE (CHOICE) <8321>] ▶ **This word refers to a fine quality of flax made in Egypt, referred to as carded flax.** It also means flax that has been combed out or brushed with a card (Is. 19:9). ¶

COME – [1] ***'āṯāh, 'āṯā'*** [verb: אָתָה, אָתָא <857>; a prim. root (collateral to CONSENT <225> contr.)] ▶ **This word means to arrive, to happen. It is found in various contexts.** It indicates people who come to the Lord (Jer. 3:22) but in general for whatever reason (Deut. 33:21; Is. 41:25). It also describes the coming of a certain time or activity, such as morning (Job 16:22; Is. 21:12); beasts (Is. 56:9); calamity (Prov. 1:27; Job 3:25). In its causative stem, it is used to bring something (Jer. 12:9; Is. 21:14). *
[2] ***'^aṯāh, '^aṯā'*** [Aramaic verb: אֲתָה, אֲתָא <858>; corresponding to <857> above] ▶ **This word means to arrive, to bring.** Its basic meaning is to come (Ezra 4:12; Dan. 3:2). It is used in an active causative sense to mean to bring someone or something (Dan. 3:13; 5:2, 3); and in a passive sense, these same objects are brought (Dan. 3:13; 6:17) into various settings. *

3 ***bô'*** [verb: בּוֹא <935>; a prim. root] ▶ **This word means to arrive, to go, to bring.** It is used often and takes on many nuances of meaning: concerning physical location, it means to go, to come, to bring to a location (Gen. 6:19; 12:11; Josh. 6:1; Judg. 18:18); to a group or person (Ex. 18:19; Esther 2:12). It is used with the preposition *'el* to mean to have intercourse (Gen. 6:4; 16:2; Deut. 22:13). It bears the meaning of coming or arriving (Gen. 19:22; Prov. 18:3) physically or temporally, such as harvest time (Lev. 25:22). It means to take place, to happen (1 Sam. 9:6). Used with the preposition *b*^{e} and others, it can take on the idea of having dealings with (Josh. 23:7; Ps. 26:4; Prov. 22:24). It has several idiomatic uses: followed by *b*^{e}*dāmiym*, it indicates involvement in bloodguilt (1 Sam. 25:26). With the word "after," it means to be in pursuit of someone or something (Ex. 14:17).

It is used in a causative way to bring something, e.g., an army (2 Sam. 5:1–3) from the battleground, to gather in something (2 Sam. 9:10). It is used idiomatically in several short phrases all headed by *hêbiy'*, to bring: to bring justice (Eccl. 11:9); to bring legal cases (Ex. 18:19); to take something away (*hêbiy* + *mê'aḥar*, Ps. 78:71); to apply one's heart (Prov. 23:12); to understand. In a passive sense, it means to be brought, to be offered or burned, to be put into (Gen. 33:11; 43:18; Lev. 6:30; Lev. 11:32). In its participial forms, the words may refer to the near future (2 Kgs. 20:17; Is. 39:6; Jer. 7:32) or to future things to come to pass (Is. 27:6; 41:22).
– 4 Ezra 5:5 ➔ GO <1946> 5 Zeph. 1:14 ➔ QUICK, QUICKLY <4118> a. 6 See GO <1980>.

COME (THAT SHALL) – Deut. 32:35 ➔ READY <6264> b.

COME DOWN – Dan. 4:13, 23 ➔ BRING DOWN <5182>.

COME FORTH – 1 Judg. 20:33; Ezek. 32:2 ➔ GUSH <1518> 2 Dan. 5:5 ➔ TAKE OUT <5312>.

COME NEAR – 1 ***nāḡaš*** [verb: נָגַשׁ <5066>; a prim. root] ▶ **This word means to approach, to draw near, to bring near, to be brought near.** In the simple form of the verb, it indicates coming near, as when Jacob went near to Isaac his father who reached out and touched him (Gen. 27:22); it simply describes approaching a person for whatever reason (Gen. 43:19; Ex. 19:15). It is used of priests approaching the Lord (Ezek. 44:13); or the altar to carry out their priestly duties (Ex. 28:43; 30:20); and of armies drawing near for engagement in battle (Judg. 20:23; 2 Sam. 10:13). The word asserts close proximity in all these cases and can even describe the closeness of the scales of a crocodile (Job 41:16).

In the reflexive form, it describes coming near. Deuteronomy 25:9 prescribed the action of a widow towards her brother-in-law who would not perform his Levitical duty toward her: She was to approach him, take off one of his sandals, and spit in his face (cf. Is. 45:20).

In the causative form, the verb means to bring near: a slave who decided to remain with his master perpetually was brought to the judges and to the doorpost so his ear could be bored with an awl (Ex. 21:6; 1 Sam. 15:32); sacrifices were brought near as well (1 Sam. 13:9; 14:34). In a metaphorical sense, the word is used to call for the presentation of legal argumentation (Is. 41:21). The passive use of this form describes what is offered or presented, once to indicate that Abner's feet were not brought near, i.e., they were not placed in chains (2 Sam. 3:34); and once to describe incense and pure offerings brought in the Lord's name (Mal. 1:11). *

2 ***qāraḇ*** [verb: קָרַב <7126>; a prim. root] ▶ **This word means to approach.** The basic concept is a close, spatial proximity of the subject and the object (Gen. 37:18; Deut. 4:11); although it is also possible for this word to introduce actual contact (Ezek. 37:7; cf. Ex. 14:20; Judg. 19:13). This verb is also used in a temporal context to indicate the imminence of some event (Gen. 27:41). This usage is common to communicate the impending doom of

God's judgment, like Moses' day of calamity and the prophet's day of the Lord (Lam. 4:18). This term has also developed several technical meanings. It can refer to armed conflict. Sometimes it is clarified by modifiers, such as to fight or unto battle (Deut. 20:10). Other times, this word alone carries the full verbal idea of entering into battle. Some of these instances are clear by context (Deut. 25:11; Josh. 8:5); however, there are others where this meaning may be missed (Deut. 2:37; Ps. 27:2; 91:10; 119:150; cf. Deut. 2:19). Another technical meaning refers to sexual relations (Gen. 20:4; Deut. 22:14; Is. 8:3). One other technical meaning refers to the protocol for presenting an offering to God (Ex. 29:4; Lev. 1:5, 13, 14; Num. 16:9). *

[3] ***qᵉrêḇ*** [Aramaic verb: קְרֵב <7127>; corresponding to <7126> above] ▶ **This word means to approach.** It is used as a technical term to describe bringing a sacrifice, offering something to God (Ezra 6:10, 17; 7:17). It means simply to step up for a purpose (Dan. 3:8; 6:12); to come near to something (Dan. 3:8, 26; 6:12, 20). It is used when formally presenting a person (Dan. 7:13); or when personally approaching a person (Dan. 7:16). ¶

COME OUT – Dan. 3:26; 7:10 ➔ TAKE OUT <5312>.

COME UP – Ezra 4:12; Dan. 2:29; 7:3, 8, 20 ➔ GO UP <5559> b.

COMELINESS – Is. 53:2 ➔ GLORY <1926>.

COMELY – [1] Job 41:12 ➔ GRACEFUL <2433> [2] Ps. 33:1; Song 1:5; 2:14; 4:3; 6:4; Jer. 6:2 ➔ BEAUTIFUL <5000>.

COMELY (BE) – Is. 52:7 ➔ BEAUTIFUL (BE) <4998>.

COMFORT (noun) – [1] ***neḥāmāh*** [fem. noun: נֶחָמָה <5165>; from SORRY (BE) <5162> (in the sense of to comfort, to console, to have compassion)] ▶ **This word means compassion, consolation, encouragement.** In Job 6:10, Job was comforted that in the midst of his trials, he did not deny the Holy One; the psalmist declared that his comfort in his affliction was God's Word, which revived him (Ps. 119:50). ¶

[2] ***niyḏ*** [masc. noun: נִיד <5205>; from FLEE <5110> (in the sense of to show sympathy; to move)] ▶

a. A word meaning encouragement; it is also translated solace. It refers to the attempt to comfort persons, to give them assurance of hope, to comfort through words of encouragement (Job 16:5). ¶

b. A masculine noun referring to moving. It refers to moving one's lips to speak words of encouragement (Job 16:5, KJV). ¶

– [3] Job 15:11; Ps. 94:19 ➔ CONSOLATION <8575> [4] Job 30:28 ➔ SUN <2535>.

COMFORT (TAKE) – Job 10:20 ➔ SMILE (verb) <1082>.

COMFORT (verb) – [1] ***niḥûm, niḥum*** [verb: נִחוּם, נִחֻם <5150>; from SORRY (BE) <5162> (in the sense of to comfort, to console, to have compassion)] ▶ **This word indicates a cessation of discomfort, distress, or sorrow.** Ref.: Is. 57:18. It has the sense of emotions and speaks of comfort, feelings of compassion (also translated that arise (Hos. 11:8: compassion, sympathy, repenting). It indicates words that bring comfort, refreshment, or a feeling of being comforted (Zech. 1:13). ¶

– [2] Gen. 18:5; Judg. 19:5 ➔ REFRESH <5582> [3] Gen. 37:35; etc. ➔ SORRY (BE) <5162> [4] Job 17:13 ➔ REFRESH <7502>.

COMFORT ONESELF – Job 9:27 ➔ SMILE (verb) <1082>.

COMFORTER – ***maḇliygiyṯ*** [fem. noun: מַבְלִיגִית <4010>; from SMILE (verb) <1082>] ▶ **This word indicates healing or encouraging for one in great sorrow or pain.** In context it is asserted to be impossible for Israel whose sorrow seems to be beyond comfort (Jer. 8:18). The text is difficult to decipher (cf. KJV, NASB, NIV, ESV for various options). ¶

COMING DOWN – 2 Kgs. 6:9 ➔ GOING DOWN <5185>.

COMING FORTH – [1] ***yāṣiy'*** [adj.: יָצִיא <3329>; from GO OUT <3318>] ▶ **This word indicates the feature of proceeding from, offspring, children.** It refers to one's own children or offspring, who have come forth, in this case, the children or offspring of Sennacherib (2 Chr. 32:21; also translated son). ¶
– [2] Mic. 5:2 ➔ GOING FORTH <4163>.

COMING IN – ***môḇā'*** [masc. noun: מוֹבָא <4126>; by transposition for ENTRANCE <3996>] ▶ **This word refers to an entrance, entering.** It refers to the act itself of coming in (2 Sam. 3:25). In Ezekiel 43:11, it refers to the entrances of the prophet's visionary Temple. ¶

COMMAND (noun) – [1] ***ṭa'am*** [Aramaic noun: טְעֵם <2941>; from EAT <2939> (i.e., as in TASTE (noun) <2940>, a judgment, a decree)] ▶ **This word means a decree, an order.** It is closely related to the Hebrew word of the same spelling *ṭa'am* (<TASTE 2940>) and is equivalent to the Aramaic noun *ṭᵉ'êm* (<DECREE (noun) 2942>). In Ezra 6:14, the word refers to a command (also translated decree, commandment) of God; and therefore some argue this vocalization is a theological scribal distinction to differentiate between it and *ṭᵉ'êm*. The determined use of *ṭaᵉmā'* in Ezra 5:5 (report, matter) could be declined from either *ṭa'am* or *ṭᵉ'êm*. Other refs.: Ezra: 4:21 (account, accountable); 7:23 (to be decreed, to be commanded, to be prescribed); Dan. 6:2 (account, accountable). ¶
[2] ***maᵃmar*** [masc. noun: מַאֲמַר <3982>; from SAY <559> (in the sense of to command)] ▶ **In all three of its instances in the Old Testament, this word refers to that which is spoken with authority.** It referred to the command of King Ahasuerus that Queen Vashti ignored (Esther 1:15). It described Mordecai's instructions to Esther to keep quiet about her nationality (Esther 2:20). Finally, it referred to Esther's edict about the establishment of the days of Purim (Esther 9:32). This word comes from the common verb *'āmar* (SAY <559>) which can be translated to command, depending on the context (2 Chr. 31:11; Esther 1:10). ¶
[3] ***miṣwāh*** [fem. noun: מִצְוָה <4687>; from COMMAND (verb) <6680>] ▶ **This word can apply to the edicts issued by a human being, most likely the king.** Refs.: 1 Kgs. 2:43; Esther 3:3; Prov. 6:20; Is. 36:21; Jer. 35:18. It can also relate to a general corpus of human precepts (Is. 29:13); or a body of teachings (Prov. 2:1; 3:1). On the other hand, this expression can reference God's commands. In the Pentateuch, this is its only usage. It does not refer to human commandments. In the singular, it may distinguish a certain commandment (1 Kgs. 13:21); yet it appears most frequently in the plural to designate the entire corpus of divine law and instruction (Gen. 26:5; Ex. 16:28; Deut. 6:2; 1 Kgs. 2:3). It is also important to note that, in the plural, this word often appears in synonymous parallelism with such words as *ḥuqqîm* (STATUTE <2706>; *mišpāṭ* (JUSTICE <4941>); *'êḏōṯ* (TESTIMONY <5715>); *tôrôṯ* (LAW <8451>). *
– [4] Ezra 6:14 ➔ DECREE (noun) <2942> [5] Dan. 4:17 ➔ REQUEST <3983> [6] Hos. 5:11 ➔ PRECEPT <6673> b.

COMMAND (verb) – ***ṣāwāh*** [verb: צָוָה <6680>; a prim. root] ▶ **This word means to order, to direct, to appoint, to charge; to be ordered, to be commanded. The word means to give an order or to command, to direct someone; it indicates commands given to people in various situations.** The Lord commanded Adam and Eve to eat from certain trees but to refrain from eating from the tree of the knowledge of good and evil (Gen. 2:16; 3:17). He ordered Moses hundreds of times to do or say certain things as He established Israel's worship, feasts, festivals, and rituals (Ex. 7:2; 16:34; Num. 15:23). Israel was to keep all the directives the Lord gave them (Deut. 4:2; 1 Kgs. 11:10). The Lord commanded His prophets to speak (Amos 6:11; Nah. 1:14; Zech. 1:6). People gave orders to others as well, as when Pharaoh ordered that all newborn Hebrew males should be drowned in the Nile River (Ex. 1:22). Deborah ordered Barak to defeat Sisera (Judg. 4:6). Abraham ordered his family to follow the ways of the Lord (Gen. 18:19). Kings commanded their people (1 Kgs. 5:17; Jer. 36:26). Priests in Israel gave directives to the people about what to do under certain circumstances (Lev. 9:6; cf. Lev. 13:58). A person who was chosen for a task or position was commanded concerning his responsibilities by the priestly authorities (Num. 27:19, 23). The word may mean to give directives or to set in order as when the Lord told Hezekiah to order—i.e., to set things in order, in his household, for he was about to die (2 Kgs. 20:1).

God commands not only people but creation: He created all things by His command (Ps. 33:9; 148:5); He commanded the clouds not to send their rain on a disobedient vineyard (i.e., Israel [Ps. 78:23; Is. 5:6]); He commands the entire heavenly realms (Is. 45:12). God commands historical processes; He will ultimately set up David, His ruler, as the one who commands (Is. 55:4). *

COMMANDED (BE) – Ezra 7:23 ➔ COMMAND (noun) <2941>.

COMMANDER – [1] ***b*****e*****'êl*** [Aramaic masc. noun: בְּעֵל <1169>; corresponding to LORD <1167>] ► **This word means lord, master, overlord, owner. It is also translated commanding officer, chancellor.** It is used in Ezra 4:8, 9, and 17 as an official title for Rehum, a Persian provincial officer, the "chancellor." It corresponds to the Hebrew word *ba'al* (LORD <1167>), which also means lord or owner but is used with broader variations in meaning ranging from man, ruler, owner, and husband to the description of false gods. ¶
– [2] Josh. 10:24; Judg. 11:6, 11; etc. ➔ CAPTAIN <7101> [3] Jer. 51:23; etc. ➔ RULER <5461> [4] Jer. 51:27 ➔ MARSHAL <2951> [5] Nah. 3:17 ➔ CROWNED ONE <4502> a. [6] See LEADER <5057>.

COMMANDING OFFICER – Ezra 4:8, 9, 17 ➔ COMMANDER <1169>.

COMMANDMENT – [1] 2 Chr. 31:13 ➔ APPOINTMENT <4662> [2] Ezra 6:14 ➔ COMMAND (noun) <2941> [3] Ezra 6:14 ➔ DECREE (noun) <2942> [4] Hos. 5:11 ➔ PRECEPT <6673> b. [5] See COMMAND (noun) <4687> [6] See PRECEPT <6490>.

COMMEMORATE – Judg. 11:40 ➔ RECOUNT <8567>.

COMMISSIONER – ***sāraḵ*** [Aramaic masc. noun: סָרַךְ <5632>; of foreign origin] ► **This word means a royal minister of superior rank; it is also translated governor, president, high official, administrator. A loanword from Persian for head or chief, this term appears in the Old Testament only in Daniel.** It is a title given to three high-ranking government officials, one of whom was Daniel (Dan. 6:2–4, 6:6, 7). Appointed by Darius the Mede, the three officials oversaw the work of 120 satraps, whose function may have been to collect taxes for the king from throughout the empire. ¶

COMMIT – [1] Num. 31:16 ➔ PROVIDE <4560> [2] Ps. 37:5; Prov. 16:3 ➔ ROLL (verb) <1556>.

COMMON – [1] ***ḥōl*** [masc. noun: חֹל <2455>; from PIERCE <2490> (in the sense of to defile, to profane)] ► **This word means what is unholy, not consecrated; it is also translated profane. It comes from the verb *ḥālal*, meaning to pollute or to profane and is always used in opposition to *qōḏeš*, meaning sacred or set apart.** The priests were to make a distinction between the sacred and the common (Lev. 10:10). David discussed with the priest the difference between the common bread and the set-apart bread (1 Sam. 21:4, 5). The priests would teach the difference between the sacred and the common (Ezek. 44:23)—a distinction the priests of Ezekiel's day failed to teach (Ezek. 22:26). The Temple, described by Ezekiel, had a wall separating the sacred and the common (Ezek. 42:20); there was to be a clear distinction between

the land holy to the Lord and the common land (Ezek. 48:15). ¶
– [2] Dan. 2:41, 43 ➔ MIRY <2917>.

COMMON-LAND – Num. 35:2–5, 7; Josh. 14:4; etc. ➔ PASTURELAND <4054>.

COMMOTION – Is. 22:2 ➔ STORM (noun) <8663>.

COMMUNITY – [1] ***gêw*** [masc. noun: גֵּו <1460>] ▶ **This word indicates the fellowship or the midst of a group of persons of common background from which the lowly in society are driven.** Ref.: Job 30:5; also translated among men, human company, human society. The Hebrew word also means the back of a person's body; see BACK <1460>. ¶
– [2] Ezek. 47:22: from the community of Israel ➔ lit.: a native of the land ➔ NATIVE <249>.

COMPANIES – Is. 57:13 ➔ COLLECTION <6899>.

COMPANION – [1] ***ḥaḇar*** [Aramaic masc. noun: חֲבַר <2269>; from a root corresponding to JOIN TOGETHER <2266>] ▶ **This word is also translated friend, fellow. It indicates persons joined in relationship as friends.** It describes the relationship between Daniel and his fellow exiles (Dan. 2:13, 17, 18). ¶
[2] ***ḥāḇêr*** [adj. and masc. noun: חָבֵר <2270>; from JOIN TOGETHER <2266>] ▶ **This word indicates friendship, association with, being friends with; united.** It indicates being joined together in various ways: as a helpful friend or companion (Eccl. 4:10: companion, fellow); with regard to a plan or campaign (Judg. 20:11); with respect to a certain group of people, good or bad in character (Ps. 45:7; 119:63; Prov. 28:24; Is. 1:23); through an association of certain groups or persons, especially the joining of Judah and Israel as companions (Ezek. 37:16, 19); with regard to religious affiliation, e.g., those who worship idols (Is. 44:11). Other refs.: Song 1:7; 8:13. ¶
[3] ***ḥabbār*** [masc. noun: חַבָּר <2271>; from JOIN TOGETHER <2266>] ▶ **This word indicates an associate, a partner, traders.** It refers to a person belonging to the same business or trade (Job 41:6). ¶
[4] ***ḥ***[a]***ḇereṯ*** [fem. noun: חֲבֶרֶת <2278>; fem. of <2270> above] ▶ **This word refers to a female partner by marriage covenant.** Ref.: Mal. 2:14; also translated partner. ¶
[5] ***k***[e]***nāṯ*** [masc. noun: כְּנָת <3674>; from FLATTER <3655> (in the sense of having the same title)] ▶ **This word refers to a colleague, an associate.** It refers to a person in a group of connected individuals or companions (Ezra 4:7). ¶
[6] ***k***[e]***nāṯ*** [Aramaic masc. noun: כְּנָת <3675>; corresponding to <3674> above] ▶ **This word denotes a colleague, an associate.** It refers to a group of persons sharing some common ties, whether political or otherwise (Ezra 4:9, 17, 23; 5:3, 6; 6:6, 13); in context, it always refers to political ties. ¶
– [7] Lev. 6:2 ➔ NEIGHBOR <5997> [8] Judg. 11:37, 38; Ps. 45:14 ➔ FRIEND <7464> [9] Judg. 14:11, 20; 15:2, 6 ➔ FRIEND <4828> [10] Dan. 7:20 ➔ FELLOW <2273>.

COMPANY – [1] ***ḥeḇer*** [masc. noun: חֶבֶר <2267>; from JOIN TOGETHER <2266>] ▶ **This word means a group, an association, a spell.** It is used to refer to a band of bad priests (Hos. 6:9); a house of association, namely, a house shared with an antagonistic woman (Prov. 21:9; 25:24); or a magical spell or incantation (Deut. 18:11; Ps. 58:5; Is. 47:9, 12). ¶
[2] ***ḥeḇrāh*** [fem. noun: חֶבְרָה <2274>; fem. of COMPANY <2267>] ▶ **This word refers to the fellowship, ties, or comradeship of persons who walk together in agreement.** Ref.: Job 34:8, indicating like-mindedness. Elihu used it derisively of Job. ¶
[3] ***lah***[a]***qāh*** [fem. noun: לַהֲקָה <3862>; prob. from an unused root meaning to gather] ▶ **This word refers to a group of persons with a common interest.** In this case, it indicates a group of prophets who were prophesying (1 Sam. 19:20). ¶
– [4] Gen. 37:25: company, traveling company ➔ CARAVAN <736> [5] 2 Kgs. 9:17

→ ABUNDANCE <8229> [6] Ps. 55:14 → THRONG (noun) <7285> [7] Ps. 68:27 → THRONG (noun) <7277> a.

COMPARABLE – Lam. 4:2 → WORTH THEIR WEIGHT <5537>.

COMPARABLE TO – Gen. 2:18, 20 → BEFORE <5048>.

COMPASS (noun) – [1] ***mᵉḥûgāh*** [fem. noun: מְחוּגָה <4230>; from CIRCLE (INSCRIBE A) <2328>] ▶ **This word refers to an instrument for making circles.** It refers to a craftsman's technical tool used in fine artwork (Is. 44:13). ¶
– [2] Ex. 27:5; 38:4 → LEDGE <3749>.

COMPASS (verb) – [1] 1 Sam. 23:26; Ps. 5:12 → CROWN (noun and verb) <5849> b. [2] 2 Sam. 22:5; Ps. 18:4; 40:12; 116:3; Jon. 2:5 → SURROUND <661> [3] Job 26:10 → CIRCLE (INSCRIBE A) <2328> [4] Ps. 139:3 → SCRUTINIZE <2219>.

COMPASSION – [1] ***ḥemlāh*** [fem. noun: חֶמְלָה <2551>; from PITY (HAVE) <2550>] ▶ **This word means solicitude shown in sparing someone from harm; it is also translated mercy, pity, merciful.** It describes the act of the angelic beings who led Lot and his family out of Sodom (Gen. 19:16). It is also used in Isaiah 63:9 when retelling God's deeds of the past. In light of His angel saving the people in Egypt, the text refers to God showing mercy on them. Therefore, in its two uses, it denotes God's compassion which spares one from destruction or similar dismal fates. ¶
[2] ***nōḥam*** [masc. noun: נֹחַם <5164>; from SORRY (BE) <5162> (in the sense of to comfort, to console, to have compassion)] ▶ **This word means sorrow, sympathy, merciful change of purpose; it is also translated repentance, pity.** It comes from the verb *nāḥam* (<5162>), meaning to be sorry or to repent, and occurs only once in the Old Testament. In Hosea 13:14, it described the compassion that God would not have toward sinful Ephraim. ¶
[3] ***raḥᵃmiyn*** [Aramaic masc. noun: רַחֲמִין <7359>; corresponding to WOMB <7356>] ▶ **This word refers to a central characteristic of God, His feeling of mercy, pity, and love toward His people.** Ref.: Dan. 2:18. ¶

COMPASSION (HAVE) – [1] ***rāḥam, ruḥāmāh*** [verb: רָחַם, רֻחָמָה <7355>; a prim. root] ▶ **This word means to have mercy, to find mercy. The word pictures a deep, kindly sympathy and sorrow felt for another who has been struck with affliction or misfortune, accompanied with a desire to relieve the suffering.** The word occurs forty-seven times in the Old Testament, with God being by far the most common subject and His afflicted people the object (Deut. 13:17; 2 Kgs. 13:23; Is. 14:1; 30:18; 60:10; Jer. 12:15; 31:20; Lam. 3:32). Though the Lord showed compassion, it was not because of any meritorious work the recipient had done; it was solely due to God's sovereign freedom to bestow it on whom He chose (Ex. 33:19; cf. Rom. 9:14–16). Two types of people God has sovereignly chosen to have mercy on include those who fear Him (Ps. 103:13); and those who confess and forsake their sin (Prov. 28:13). *
– [2] See PITY (HAVE, SHOW) <2550>.

COMPASSIONATE – [1] ***raḥûm*** [adj.: רַחוּם <7349>; from COMPASSION (HAVE) <7355>] ▶ **This word indicates a merciful and forgiving character and attitude. It is an important word defining the character of God, and every use is in reference to God.** It is part of the moral definition of God given in Exodus 34:6 (Deut. 4:31; Ps. 78:38; 86:15; 103:8). It is used in the phrase *ḥannûn wᵉraḥûm,* gracious and compassionate (2 Chr. 30:9; Neh. 9:17, 31; Ps. 111:4; 145:8; Joel 2:13; Jon. 4:2). Other ref.: Ps. 112:4. ¶
[2] ***raḥᵃmāniy*** [adj.: רַחֲמָנִי <7362>; from COMPASSION (HAVE) <7355>] ▶ **This word means characterized by pity.** It refers to persons who normally show great care and pity, concern for others, especially their children (Lam. 4:10; KJV: pitiful). ¶

COMPEL – [1] ***'ānas*** [verb: אָנַס <597>] ▶ **This word is also translated to be compulsory, to be compulsion.** It refers to the lack of a social or royal compulsion to do something (Esther 1:8). In Persia such a social or royal custom or decree compelling one to drink could not have been broken without serious consequences. The laws of the Medes and Persians could not be broken. ¶
– [2] 1 Sam. 13:12 ➔ CONTROL (verb) <662> [3] Job 32:18 ➔ OPPRESS <6693>.

COMPETE – ***taḥărāh*** [verb: תַּחֲרָה <8474>; from ANGRY (GET) <2734> through the idea of the heat of jealousy] ▶
a. This word means to contend, to challenge. In context it indicates competing against swift horses (Jer. 12:5). For Jeremiah 22:15, see b.
b. A verb meaning to close oneself in; derived also from ***ḥarāh*****.** It means to close oneself in cedar, with the connotation in order to compete with kings or to show oneself a king (Jer. 22:15). However NASB, ESV, and NIV translate the Hebrew word to compete, to have more and more. ¶

COMPILE – Prov. 25:1 ➔ MOVE <6275>.

COMPLACENCY – 2 Kgs. 19:28 ➔ EASE (AT) <7600> b.

COMPLACENT (BE) – Zeph. 1:12 ➔ CONGEAL <7087>.

COMPLAIN – [1] ***'ānan*** [verb: אָנַן <596>; a prim. root] ▶ **This word means to criticize, to find fault.** It describes the response of the people of Israel who found fault with the food supply they had in the wilderness (Num. 11:1). Complaining is ruled out because of humanity's sins (Lam. 3:39) in the case of the fall of Jerusalem to Babylon. ¶
– [2] Ex. 15:24; etc. ➔ MURMUR <3885> [3] Deut. 1:27; Ps. 106:25; Is. 29:24 ➔ MURMUR <7279>.

COMPLAINT – [1] ***śiyaḥ*** [masc. noun: שִׂיחַ <7879>; from TELL <7878>] ▶ **This word means primarily resentment, grievance. It also means contemplation, meditation, prayer, talk, utterance, babbling.** In Job's narrative, he stated that even his couch would not ease his complaint (Job 7:13); that even if he were to forget his complaint, he would still dread all of his sufferings (Job 9:27); and because he loathed his very life, he would give free reign to his complaint (Job 10:1). Elijah mocked the prophets of Baal, telling them to cry louder because their god might be deep in thought (1 Kgs. 18:27). The word is also used to denote Hannah's prayer containing words of great anguish (1 Sam. 1:16). The psalmist used the word to depict meditation that he hoped would be pleasing to the Lord (Ps. 104:34). *
– [2] Ex. 16:7–9, 12; Num. 14:27; 17:5, 10 ➔ GRUMBLING <8519>.

COMPLAINT (GROUND FOR) – ***'illāh*** [Aramaic fem. noun: עִלָּה <5931>; fem. from a root corresponding to OFFER <5927>] ▶ **This word indicates a basis for charges; it is also translated ground for charges, ground of accusation, charge, occasion.** It employs in a technical legal sense of a cause for allegation, a basis for accusing someone (Dan. 6:4, 5). ¶

COMPLETE (adj.) – [1] ***tāmiym*** [adj.: תָּמִים <8549>; from COMPLETE (BE) <8552>] ▶ **This word means blameless; full, whole.** In over half of its occurrences, it describes an animal to be sacrificed to the Lord, whether a ram, a bull, or a lamb (Ex. 29:1; Lev. 4:3; 14:10). With respect to time, the term is used to refer to a complete day, a complete seven Sabbaths (weeks), and a complete year (Lev. 23:15; 25:30; Josh. 10:13). When used in a moral sense, this word is linked with truth, virtue, uprightness, and righteousness (Josh. 24:14; Ps. 18:23; Prov. 2:21; 11:5). The term is used of one's relationship with another person (Judg. 9:19; Prov. 28:18; Amos 5:10); and of one's relationship with God (Gen. 17:1; Deut. 18:13; 2 Sam. 22:24, 26). Moreover, this word described the blamelessness of God's way, knowledge, and Law (2 Sam. 22:31; Job 37:16; Ps. 19:7). *
– [2] Ps. 139:22 ➔ END <8503>.

COMPLETE (BE) – ***tāmam*** [verb: תָּמַם <8552>; a prim. root] ▶ **This word means to finish, to conclude. At its root, it carries the connotation of finishing or bringing closure.** It is used to signify the concluding of an oration (Deut. 31:30); the completing of a building project (1 Kgs. 6:22); the exhausting of resources (Gen. 47:15; Lev. 26:20); the utter destruction of something (Num. 14:33); and the fulfilling of an established period of time (Deut. 34:8). *

COMPLETE (verb) – [1] ***šᵉlēm*** [Aramaic verb: שְׁלֵם <8000>; corresponding to COMPLETED (BE) <7999>] ▶ **This word refers to work being done, such as rebuilding the Temple in Jerusalem.** Ref.: Ezra 5:16. Closely related to this meaning is the secondary meaning, to make an end. In Daniel 5:26, this word is used to say that God would bring the days of Belshazzar's reign to an end. This word could also mean to restore in the sense of delivering something from captivity and returning it to the rightful owner. It was used when discussing the restoration of the Temple furnishings in Jerusalem (Ezra 7:19: to deliver). ¶
– [2] Ezra 6:15 ➔ FINISH <3319> [3] Is. 10:12 ➔ CUT OFF <1214>.

COMPLETED (BE) – ***šālam*** [verb: שָׁלַם <7999>; a prim. root] ▶ **The primary meaning of this word is to be safe or uninjured in mind or body.** Refs.: Job 8:6; 9:4. It is normally used when God is keeping His people safe. In its simple form, this verb also means to be completed or to be finished. This could refer to something concrete such as a building (1 Kgs. 7:51); or things more abstract, such as plans (Job 23:14). Other meanings of this verb include to be at peace with another person (Ps. 7:4); to make a treaty of peace (Josh. 11:19; Job 5:23); to pay, to give a reward (Ps. 62:12); to restore, repay, or make retribution (Ex. 21:36; Ps. 37:21). *

COMPLETENESS – ***tōm*** [masc. noun: תֹּם <8537>; from COMPLETE (BE) <8552>] ▶ **This word means fulness, integrity.** It is used in Job to describe how a man could die, i.e., in complete security (Job 21:23). When Absalom invited two hundred men from Jerusalem to his party, the word denoted that the men did not have any idea of what was about to happen (2 Sam. 15:11). In Genesis, Abimelech acted with a clear conscience after Abraham stated that Sarah was his sister (Gen. 20:5, 6). In a statement of wisdom, Proverbs uses the word to indicate that righteousness guards the person of integrity (Prov. 13:6); while the psalmist asks that his integrity and uprightness protect him because his hope is in the Lord (Ps. 25:21). *

COMPOSITION – Ex. 30:32, 37; Ezek. 45:11 ➔ PROPORTION <4971>.

COMPOSURE – Eccl. 10:4 ➔ CALMNESS <4832>.

COMPOUND (noun) – Ex. 30:25 ➔ MIXTURE <4842>.

COMPOUND (verb) – ***rāqaḥ*** [verb: רָקַח <7543>; a prim. root (in the sense of to perfume)] ▶ **This word means to mix perfume; to mix ointment.** It is used to describe an anointing oil, mixed or blended to produce a pleasant-smelling substance (Ex. 30:25). It describes the process of creating it as mixing and combining it (Ex. 30:33). It describes the process of combining ingredients to produce incense (Ex. 30:35). It describes the mixing of spices (1 Chr. 9:30; 2 Chr. 16:14). Its participial form *rōqê(a)ḥ* indicates a perfumer (Ex. 30:25; Eccl. 10:1). It describes the blending of spices in a boiling pot of food (Ezek. 24:10). ¶

COMPREHEND – Ps. 139:3 ➔ SCRUTINIZE <2219>.

COMPREHENSION – See UNDERSTANDING <998>.

COMPULSION (BE) – Esther 1:8 ➔ COMPEL <597>.

COMPULSORY (BE) – Esther 1:8 ➔ COMPEL <597>.

CONANIAH – ***kônanyāhû*** [masc. proper noun: כּוֹנַנְיָהוּ <3562>; from SET UP <3559> and LORD <3050>]: the Lord has established ▶
a. A Levite in charge of the contributions, the tithes and the dedicated things under the reign of Hezekiah. Refs.: 2 Chr. 31:12, 13. ¶
b. A chief of the Levites. Ref.: 2 Chr. 35:9. ¶

CONCEDE – Deut. 32:31 ➔ JUDGE (noun) <6414>.

CONCEIT – Prov. 18:11 ➔ PICTURE <4906>.

CONCEIVE – [1] ***hārāh*** [verb: הָרָה <2029>; a prim. root] ▶ **Literally, this word means for a woman to become pregnant.** Refs.: Gen. 16:4, 5; 19:36; 25:21; 38:18. It is often followed by the verb to bear, give birth, *wattahar wattêled*, she became pregnant and gave birth (Gen. 4:1, 17; 21:2; Ex. 2:2). It has several figurative or metaphorical uses: of Moses' conceiving Israel (Num. 11:12); of Israel's failed pregnancy (Is. 26:18); of Assyria's conception of chaff (Is. 33:11); of the godless who become pregnant with trouble and evil (Job 15:35; Ps. 7:14; Is. 59:4). *
[2] ***yāḥam*** [verb: יָחַם <3179>; a prim. root] ▶ **This word also means to be hot.** It indicates that an animal is in heat, in rut (Gen. 30:38, 39, 41; 31:10); also translated to mate, to breed, to be in heat. It describes the act of conception in sexual intimacy (Ps. 51:5). It refers to keeping one's body warm (1 Kgs. 1:1: get warm, keep warm, get heat; Eccl. 4:11: keep warm, have heat) or to heating something (Ezek. 24:11). ¶

CONCEPTION – ***hêrôn, hêrāyôn*** [masc. noun: הֵרוֹן, הֵרָיוֹן <2032>; from CONCEIVE <2029>] ▶ **This word refers to the pregnancy period and process of childbearing. It will be painful.** Ref.: Gen. 3:16; also translated childbearing, childbirth. It also marks the event of conception (Ruth 4:13). It is used figuratively of Ephraim conceiving children (Hos. 9:11). ¶

CONCERN – Josh. 22:24 ➔ ANXIETY <1674>.

CONCERNED (BE) – ***'āšat*** [verb: עֲשַׁת <6245>; a prim. root] ▶ **This word means to pay attention; it is also translated to think upon, to consider, to take notice, to give a thought.** It means to care for someone or something, especially regarding God in response to prayer (Jon. 1:6). The Hebrew word also means to shine, to excel; see SLEEK (BE) <6245>]. ¶

CONCERNING – ***ṣad*** [Aramaic masc. noun: צַד <6655>; corresponding to SIDE <6654>] ▶ **This word refers to a matter from whence, with respect to someone or something. It also indicates against.** In context with respect to Daniel, from the side of Daniel (Dan. 6:4). It has the sense of against in an accusatory way (Dan. 7:25). ¶

CONCILIATION – Eccl. 10:4 ➔ CALMNESS <4832>.

CONCLUDE – Eccl. 9:1 ➔ DECLARE <952>.

CONCUBINE – [1] ***lᵉḥênāh*** [Aramaic fem. noun: לְחֵנָה <3904>; from an unused root of uncertain meaning] ▶ **This word refers to secondary wives, a feature of royal, ancient Near-Eastern culture.** Refs.: Dan. 5:2, 3, 23. ¶
[2] ***piylegeš*** [fem. noun: פִּילֶגֶשׁ <6370>; of uncertain deriv.] ▶ **A concubine was a legitimate wife; however, she was of secondary rank.** This is evident by the references to the concubine as having a husband (Judg. 19:2); and that this man and her father are considered to be son-in-law (cf. Judg. 19:5) and father-in-law (cf. Judg. 19:4), respectively. But concubines were presented opposite the wives of higher rank (1 Kgs. 11:3; Song 6:8). The ability to have and to keep concubines was a sign of wealth, status, and often of royalty (1 Kgs. 11:3; Esther 2:14; Song 6:8). To sleep with a king's concubine would have indicated plans to usurp the throne (2 Sam. 3:7; 16:21, 22; cf. 1 Kgs. 2:21–24). *

[3] ***šiddāh*** [fem. noun: שִׁדָּה <7705>] ▶
a. This word refers to a member of a harem. It refers to secondary wives in polygamous societies (Eccl. 2:8). In Ecclesiastes, it constituted a part of the qoheleth's pursuit of total pleasure.
b. This word refers to a musical instrument. This is the rendering of the word in the KJV and NKJV (Eccl. 2:8). ¶

CONDEMN – Amos 2:8 ➔ FINE (verb) <6064>.

CONDITION – Eccl. 3:18 ➔ CAUSE <1700>.

CONDITION (ORIGINAL) – 2 Chr. 24:13 ➔ PROPORTION <4971>.

CONDITION (ORIGINAL, PROPER) – 2 Chr. 24:13 ➔ PROPORTION <4971>.

CONDUCT – Ps. 112:5 ➔ CONTAIN <3557>.

CONEY – See BADGER <8227>.

CONFECTION – Ex. 30:35 ➔ PERFUME <7545>.

CONFECTIONS – Ezek. 27:17 ➔ CAKE <6436> b.

CONFER – Judg. 19:30 ➔ COUNSEL (TAKE) <5779>.

CONFIDANT – 2 Sam. 15:37; 16:16 ➔ FRIEND <7463>.

CONFIDENCE – [1] ***biṭṭāḥôn*** [masc. noun: בִּטָּחוֹן <986>; from TRUST (verb) <982>] ▶ **This word means a belief or conviction that one can rely on someone or something; it is also translated trust, hope.** It is used to signify Hezekiah's trust in God when Jerusalem was under siege (2 Kgs. 18:19); or the hope that living people possess (Eccl. 9:4). Other ref.: Is. 36:4. ¶
[2] ***kislāh*** [fem. noun: כִּסְלָה <3690>; fem. of LOINS <3689>] ▶ **This word means self assurance, but also foolishness, stupidity.** The root idea of fatness (see *kāsal* [FOOLISH (BE) <3688>]) may have two implications. In Job 4:6, *kislāh* means the confidence of one who is fat and firm. Eliphaz cast doubt on Job's righteousness by asking why he was confused if he really feared God. In Psalm 85:8, on the other hand, God warned His restored people not to return to their former folly. In that verse, the word refers to sluggish foolishness that is no longer alive to the fear of God. ¶
– [3] Job 22:29 ➔ PRIDE <1466> [4] Is. 30:1 ➔ TRUST (noun) <985> [5] See TRUST (noun) <4009>.

CONFISCATION – ***ᵃnāš*** [Aramaic masc. noun: עֲנָשׁ <6065>; corresponding to FINE (noun) <6066>] ▶ **This word refers to the seizure of goods as a legal penalty for crimes.** Ref.: Ezra 7:26. ¶

CONFUSE – [1] ***hāmam*** [verb: הָמַם <2000>; a prim. root (comp. MURMUR <1949> and MURMUR <1993>)] ▶ **This word means to make a noise, to move noisily, to put into commotion.** When it means to move noisily, it often refers to the wheels of wagons or chariots (Is. 28:28). The idea of moving noisily or with commotion carries over into the idea of confusion: God confuses the Egyptians when they pursue Israel (Ex. 14:24); and He sends confusion to the nations before the Israelites go into Canaan (Josh. 10:10). *
– [2] Gen. 11:9 ➔ MIX <1101> [3] Song 6:5 ➔ BOLD (BE, MAKE) <7292>.

CONFUSED (BE) – Jer. 14:9 ➔ ASTONISHED (BE) <1724>.

CONFUSION – [1] ***mᵉhûmāh*** [fem. noun: מְהוּמָה <4103>; from STIR (verb) <1949>] ▶ **This word means panic, tumult, disturbance; it is also translated turmoil, defeat, destruction, vexation, unrest.** If the Israelites diligently observed God's covenant stipulations, He would throw the nations occupying Canaan into a great panic and give them over into the Israelites' hands (Deut. 7:23; also translated defeat, destruction). If, however, the

Israelites did not obey and thus forsook the Lord their God, this same panic would be sent upon them instead (Deut. 28:20; KJV: vexation). After the Philistines captured the ark of God and brought it to Gath (one of their five main cities), the Lord struck the people of that city with a great panic and severe tumors (1 Sam. 5:9, 11). Isaiah the prophet warned Jerusalem that a day of tumult, trampling, and confusion was at hand for it (Is. 22:5). The term also functions to describe daily life in certain geographical locations during troubled periods of time: Jerusalem (Ezek. 22:5); Israel and the surrounding lands (2 Chr. 15:5); and the mountains of Samaria (Amos 3:9). Once the word describes the trouble wealth brings to a household that does not fear the Lord (Prov. 15:16). Other refs.: 1 Sam. 14:20 (KJV: discomfiture); Ezek. 7:7; Zech. 14:13. ¶

[2] ***'iw'iym*** [masc. plur. noun: עִוְעִים <5773>; from INIQUITY (COMMIT) <5753> (also in the sense of distorting, perverting)] ▶ **This word refers to distortion, dizziness; it is also translated perverse. It is a collective plural noun indicating staggering, dizziness.** In context or figurative references, it describes a deluded and misled Egyptian people (Is. 19:14). ¶

[3] ***timmāhôn*** [masc. noun: תִּמָּהוֹן <8541>; from ASTONISHED (BE) <8539>] ▶ **This word means stupefaction; it is also translated bewilderment, astonishment, panic.** It refers to a curse that God will bring on a disobedient people of confusion, disorientation at what is happening (Deut. 28:28); even horses will be dazed (Zech. 12:4). ¶

– [4] Lev. 18:23; 20:12 ➔ PERVERSION <8397> [5] Neh. 4:8 ➔ ERROR <8442> [6] Ps. 60:3 ➔ STAGGER (THAT MAKES) <8653> [7] Is. 22:5; Mic. 7:4 ➔ PERPLEXITY <3998>.

CONFUSION (BE IN, BE THROWN IN) – Esther 3:15 ➔ WANDER <943>.

CONGEAL – ***qāpā'*** [verb: קָפָא <7087>; a prim. root] ▶ **This word means to curdle; to become settled, stagnant.** It refers to something standing still or slowing down its movement, becoming thick (Ex. 15:8). It is used figuratively of a person in great suffering being curdled, tossed about like hardening cream (Job 10:10). It depicts a dead or stagnant spirit in a person (Zeph. 1:12; also translated to be complacent). It means, used with reference to the heavenly bodies, to shrink, to lose brightness (Zech. 14:6). ¶

CONGREGATION – [1] ***maqhêl*** [fem. noun: מַקְהֵל <4721>; from ASSEMBLE <6950>] ▶ **This word refers to a public gathering; it is also translated assembly.** A group of people gathered together for a common purpose, especially for worshiping the Lord and God of Israel (Ps. 26:12; 68:26). ¶

[2] ***'êḏāh*** [fem. noun: עֵדָה <5712>; fem. of WITNESS <5707>] ▶ **This word means an assembly, a band, an entourage, a pack. It is modified to indicate various kinds of groups or communities.** It is used to describe a congregation of heavenly or human beings; an assembly of divine beings over which God presides (Ps. 82:1); a gathering of nations (Ps. 7:7); a community of the righteous (Ps. 1:5); a group of evildoers (Num. 26:9; Ps. 22:16); ruthless people (Ps. 86:14). It describes an entire circle of families and friends (Job 16:7).

Most often the word refers to Israel as a group in many settings. It describes all Israel gathered before Solomon (1 Kgs. 8:5; 12:20); or as a total community in general (Hos. 7:12); it refers to the community of Israel at the Exodus in phrases like the congregation of the Lord (Num. 27:17; 31:16; Josh. 22:16); the community of Israel (Ex. 12:3, 6; Num. 16:9); or the community of the sons of Israel (Ex. 16:1, 2; 17:1). At times leaders in Israel were described as the leaders or elders of the congregation (Ex. 16:22; Lev. 4:15; Num. 4:34).

The word is used to describe a swarm of bees (Judg. 14:8); and figuratively describes the people in Psalm 68:30 as bulls, evidently supporters of foreign nations. *

– [3] Deut. 33:4 ➔ ASSEMBLY <6952> [4] Ps. 58:1 ➔ OAK TREES <482>.

CONIAH – ***konyāhû*** [masc. proper noun: כָּנְיָהוּ <3659>; for JECONIAH <3204>] ▶ **A shortened form of *yᵉkonyāh* (JECONIAH <3204>).** Refs.: Jer. 22:24, 28; 37:1. ¶

CONJURE – Is. 47:11 ➔ SEEK DILIGENTLY <7836> b.

CONJURER – [1] Dan. 2:2; 5:11 ➔ ENCHANTER <825> [2] Dan. 2:10, 27; 4:7; 5:7, 11, 15 ➔ ENCHANTER <826>.

CONQUERED (BE) – Num. 24:18 ➔ lit.: be a possession ➔ POSSESSION <3424>.

CONQUERING – Is. 18:2, 7 ➔ TREADING DOWN <4001>.

CONSCIOUS – ***rā'eh*** [adj.: רָאֶה <7202>; from SEE <7200>] ▶ **This word means seeing.** It appears in Job 10:15 in an idiomatic use, meaning to be drenched or utterly covered with affliction. The connection with the root meaning stems from the visible signs of being afflicted. ¶

CONSECRATE – Hos. 9:10 ➔ SEPARATE <5144>.

CONSECRATION – [1] ***nêzer*** [masc. noun: נֵזֶר <5145>; from SEPARATE <5144>] ▶ **This word means an ordination.** This could be the consecration of the high priest (Lev. 21:12); or of a person taking a vow as a Nazirite (Num. 6:5, 7, 9, 12). This term is also used to identify a crown as the symbol of the wearer's consecration. This could be the king's crown (2 Sam. 1:10; 2 Kgs. 11:12); or the golden crown of the high priest (Ex. 29:6; 39:30). Jeremiah also used this term to refer to the hair of the personified Jerusalem (Jer. 7:29). The basis of this extension could be the connection between the Nazirite and his long, uncut hair as his symbol of consecration (Num. 6:5); or to the idea that a woman's long hair itself is her "crown of consecration." This would be similar to Paul's teaching in the New Testament (cf. 1 Cor. 11:15). *

– [2] Ex. 29:22; Lev. 7:37; 8:22 ➔ SETTING <4394>.

CONSENT – [1] ***'ûṯ*** [verb: אוּת <225>; a prim. root] ▶ **This word means to come to terms with another party; it is also translated to agree, to enter into an agreement.** It is used by Jacob's sons to lure the sons of Shechem to be circumcised (Gen. 34:15, 22, 23). And it indicates agreement or consent to something (2 Kgs. 12:8). ¶

– [2] Deut. 13:8; Judg. 11:17; Job 39:9; Prov. 1:10; Is. 1:19 ➔ WILLING (BE) <14>.

CONSIDER – [1] ***zāmam*** [verb: זָמַם <2161>; a prim. root] ▶ **This verb means to purpose, to devise. It derives its meaning from the idea of talking to oneself in a low voice, as if arriving at some conclusion.** It denotes the action of fixing thought on an object so as to acquire it (Prov. 31:16); devising a plan or an agenda (Lam. 2:17; Zech. 8:15); conceiving an idea (Gen. 11:6); and determining a course of action (Ps. 17:3). In an adverse sense, it also denotes the plotting of evil against another (Ps. 31:14; 37:12; Prov. 30:32). *

[2] ***pāsag*** [verb: פָּסַג <6448>; a prim. root] ▶ **This word means to go through, to view.** It has the sense of walking or passing through something to view it carefully, to appreciate it (Ps. 48:13). ¶

[3] ***sāḵal, sākhal*** [verb: שָׂכַל, שָׂכַל <7919>; a prim. root] ▶ **This word means to act with insight, to be prudent, to give insight, to teach, to prosper, to ponder, to understand, to act prudently, to act with devotion.** The primary meaning of the word is to be prudent. The word is used in Isaiah to denote what was hoped and expected of Israel, i.e., that they would consider and understand that the hand of the Lord had acted (Is. 41:20). The word is also used in Deuteronomy to denote a lack of understanding on the part of the people. If they were wise and would understand, they would know what their end would be (Deut. 32:29). Jeremiah used this word to denote wisdom in terms of insight and comprehension (Jer. 9:24). In a similar usage of the word, fools are to take heed and become wise (Ps. 94:8). The wisdom of comprehension will open their eyes to the

Lord, who sees and punishes wrong actions. In a confession of sins, the Holy Spirit is remembered as having been sent to instruct (Neh. 9:20); the prudent person keeps quiet in evil times (Amos 5:13); those who meditate on the Book of the Law day and night, being careful to do everything in it, will be prosperous and successful (Josh. 1:8). In the causative form, *śāḵal* denoted God's actions to Solomon if he observed what the Lord required and walked in His ways. If this pattern were followed, the Lord would prosper Solomon (1 Kgs. 2:3). *

4 ***śᵉḵal*** [Aramaic verb: שְׂכַל <7920>; corresponding to <7919> above] ▶ **This word means to attend (to something); it is also translated to contemplate, to think about.** The reflexive form of the word is used in Daniel to depict the state of mind that Daniel was in while he was shown the vision. While Daniel was contemplating the horns that he had previously seen, a smaller horn appeared and brought his attention back to the vision itself (Dan. 7:8). ¶

– 5 1 Sam. 16:7; Ps. 74:20; 119:6, 15 ➔ LOOK (verb) <5027> 6 Prov. 20:25 ➔ SEEK <1239> 7 Jon. 1:6 ➔ CONCERNED (BE) <6245>.

CONSOLATION – 1 ***tanḥûm*** [masc./fem. noun: תַּנְחוּם <8575>; from SORRY (BE) <5162>] ▶ **This word means comfort, commiseration.** It is used of God's words spoken to console Job in his suffering (Job 15:11). God's comforting of the psalmist delighted his soul (Ps. 94:19), i.e., God's efforts at ameliorating and helping His faithful followers. It is used figuratively of the comforting breasts of Jerusalem (Is. 66:11). In a time of God's judgments, consolations will be removed (Jer. 16:7). Other ref.: Job 21:2. ¶

– 2 Job 6:10 ➔ COMFORT (noun) <5165>.

CONSPICUOUS – Dan. 8:5 ➔ VISION <2380>.

CONSPIRACY – 1 ***qešer*** [masc. noun: קֶשֶׁר <7195>; from BIND <7194>] ▶ **This word means a plan to commit an act together; it is also translated a treason.** It refers to a binding together of persons for hostile reasons: Absalom against David (2 Sam. 15:12); Zimri's conspiracy (1 Kgs. 16:20), etc. Conspiracy could be good as well as bad (Is. 8:12). There were many conspiracies among the Israelites themselves (Jer. 11:9). Even certain prophets were guilty of conspiracy against God and the people (Ezek. 22:25). *

2 ***rōḵes*** [masc. noun: רֹכֶס <7407>; from BIND <7405> (as of something tied, e.g., meshes)] ▶

a. This word refers to intrigue, ruses, and plans to act against someone. Ref.: Ps. 31:20; also translated plot.

b. It also indicates pride. Some translate the word more generally of human self-honor and self-aggrandizement (Ps. 31:20). ¶

CONSPIRE – 1 Gen. 37:18; Ps. 105:25 ➔ DECEIVE <5230> 2 Dan. 2:9 ➔ AGREE <2164> 3 Mic. 7:3 ➔ WEAVE <5686>.

CONSTANT – 1 Prov. 19:13; 27:15 ➔ CONTINUAL (BE) <2956> 2 Prov. 27:15 ➔ CONTINUAL <5464>.

CONSTANTLY – Dan. 6:16, 20 ➔ CONTINUALLY <8411>.

CONSTELLATION – 1 ***kᵉsiyl*** [proper noun: כְּסִיל <3685>; the same as FOOL, FOOLISH <3684>] ▶ **This word refers especially to Orion.** It refers to the constellation or collection of stars and heavenly bodies (Amos 5:8; Job 9:9; 38:31), always with the purpose of pointing out the Lord as their creator and orchestrator. Other ref.: Is. 13:10. ¶

2 ***mazzāl*** [fem. noun: מַזָּל <4208>; apparently from FLOW <5140> in the sense of raining] ▶ **This word indicates the celestial signs in the firmament; it is also translated planet.** It refers to zodiacal signs in the heavens (2 Kgs. 23:5), often a temptation to Israel to worship them. ¶

– 3 Job 38:32 ➔ MAZZAROTH <4216>.

CONSTITUENCY – 2 Kgs. 12:5, 7 ➔ ACQUAINTANCE <4378>.

CONSTRAIN – Job 32:18 ➔ OPPRESS <6693>.

CONSTRAINT – ***mûṣāq, muṣaq*** [masc. noun: מוּצָק, מוּצַק <4164>; from POUR, POUR OUT <3332>] ▶ **This word means restriction, anguish; frozen (water).** It indicates that which hems a person in a physical or emotional way, creating compulsion or forced behavior (Job 36:16; also translated restraint, straitness, cramping, restriction), exactly what the Lord does not place on His people. It is used to indicate the solidification of water into ice, caused metaphorically by the breath of God (Job 37:10: to be frozen, to be straitened). It has the sense of hemmed in and hence in anguish or distress (Is. 9:1: anguish, vexation, distress). ¶

CONSULT TOGETHER – ***yᵉʿaṭ*** [Aramaic verb: יְעַט <3272>; corresponding to COUNSEL (verb) <3289>] ▶ **This word indicates to take counsel, to deliberate.** It refers to a ruse and evil plan formed in consultation by certain officials (Dan. 6:7; also translated to agree). In Ezra it refers to the seven officials who were chief advisors to the Persian king (Ezra 7:14, 15: counselors, advisers). ¶

CONSULTATION – Prov. 20:18 ➔ COUNSEL (noun) <8458>.

CONSUME – [1] ***ḥāsal*** [verb: חָסַל <2628>; a prim. root] ▶ **This word means to eat off; it is also translated to devour.** It is used to describe the destruction and consumption created by locusts (Deut. 28:38) as one of the covenant curses. ¶
[2] ***sûp̱*** [Aramaic verb: סוּף <5487>; corresponding to CONSUME, BE CONSUMED <5486>] ▶ **This word means to be fulfilled, to be ended, to end.** The word is used in Daniel 2:44 (also translated to put an end, to bring to an end) in connection with the divinely established kingdom that will never be destroyed and will bring all other kingdoms to an end. In Daniel 4:33, it referred to King Nebuchadnezzar, who finished speaking as God began to address him. ¶
[3] ***šᵉmaḏ*** [Aramaic verb: שְׁמַד <8046>; corresponding to DESTROYED (BE) <8045>] ▶ **This word is also translated to annihilate. It signifies more than simply ruining or destroying something but described a destruction that could not be reversed or fixed.** Its connotations go far beyond mere destruction to mean to consume, to destroy completely without hope of restoration. In Daniel 7:26, this verb was used to signify a total destruction of a ruler's power. This verb is used only to describe a final destruction. God is the power behind this ultimate destruction. ¶
– [4] Job 6:17; Ps. 118:12 ➔ EXTINGUISH <1846> [5] Ps. 6:7; 31:9, 10 ➔ WASTE AWAY <6244> [6] Ps. 39:11 ➔ MELT <4529> [7] Ps. 119:20 ➔ BREAK <1638> [8] Is. 64:7 ➔ MELT AWAY <4127>.

CONSUME AWAY – Ezek. 4:17; Zech. 14:12 ➔ WASTE AWAY <4743>.

CONSUME, BE CONSUMED – ***sûp̱*** [verb: סוּף <5486>; a prim. root] ▶ **This word means to come to an end, to cease, to terminate; it is also translated to meet one's end, to be demolished.** The Old Testament describes Purim as an annual observance whose celebration should not cease (Esther 9:28: to fail). The psalmist used the term to describe how quickly the prosperity enjoyed by the wicked is brought to an end (Ps. 73:19: utterly). Elsewhere, it is a general term that refers to the end of something as a result of God's judgment (Is. 66:17; Jer. 8:13: to gather, to take away, to snatch away; Zeph. 1:2, 3; also translated to remove, to sweep away). Other ref.: Amos 3:15. ¶

CONSUMED (BE) – Deut. 32:24 ➔ EAT <3898>.

CONSUMPTION – [1] ***šaḥep̱eṯ*** [fem. noun: שַׁחֶפֶת <7829>; from an unused root meaning to peel, i.e., emaciate] ▶ **This word is also translated wasting disease.** It refers to a disease that causes a person's body to waste away (Lev. 26:16; Deut. 28:22). It could be brought about by the Lord as a curse on a disobedient people. ¶
– [2] Is. 10:22 ➔ FAILING <3631>.

CONTAIN – ***kûl*** [verb: כּוּל <3557>; a prim. root] ▶ **This word indicates clasping or holding in something.** The heavens cannot contain God (1 Kgs. 8:27). It is used of attempting to hold in the knowledge or word of God in oneself (Jer. 20:9; KJV: to forbear). It is used of maintaining a supply of food or providing it in time of famine or difficult times (Gen. 45:11: to provide, to nourish; Neh. 9:21: to sustain, to provide). It means to sustain or make good, to maintain a course or business in a time of judgment (Ps. 112:5: to guide, to maintain, to conduct). In its passive uses, it means to be provided with something (1 Kgs. 20:27: to be provisioned, to be given with provisions). It is used to indicate the holding in or containing of something (1 Kgs. 7:26; Jer. 2:13). It is used literally of a cup containing something (Ezek. 23:32). It has the figurative sense of holding something within oneself, e.g., God's wrath held in by Jeremiah (Jer. 6:11); or enduring illness (Prov. 18:14: to sustain, to endure). In Ruth 4:15, the Lord is the sustainer (*kûn*) of a person in old age; also translated to sustain, nourisher. *

CONTEMN – [1] Ps. 107:11 ➔ LOOK (verb) <5027> [2] Song 8:7 ➔ DESPISE <936>.

CONTEMNED (BE) – Is. 16:14 ➔ DESPISED (BE) <7034>.

CONTEMPLATE – [1] Ps. 119:15 ➔ LOOK (verb) <5027> [2] Dan. 7:8 ➔ CONSIDER <7920>.

CONTEMPLATION – Ps. 32; 42; 44; 45; 52–55; 74; 78; 88; 89; 142 ➔ MASKIL <4905>.

CONTEMPT – [1] ***bûz*** [masc. noun: בּוּז <937>; from DESPISE <936>] ▶ **This word indicates also shame. Contempt is an attitude of disrespect and scorn toward persons.** Contempt may spring from pride or personal wickedness (Job 31:34; Ps. 123:3, 4; Prov. 18:3) but also from pride because of wealth (Job 12:5). It indicates persons who could become the object or laughingstock of contempt (Gen. 38:23). God pours out contempt on the objects of His judgments (Ps. 107:40). Other refs.: Job 12:21; Ps. 31:18; 119:22; Prov. 12:8 (despised). ¶
– [2] Esther 1:18 ➔ DISRESPECT <963> [3] Ezek. 36:5 ➔ MALICE <7589> [4] Dan. 12:2 ➔ ABHORRENCE <1860> [5] Mic. 7:6; Nah. 3:6 ➔ to treat with contempt ➔ FOOLISH (BE) <5034>.

CONTEMPT (BRING INTO) – Is. 16:14 ➔ DESPISED (BE) <7034>.

CONTEMPTIBLE – Dan. 11:21 ➔ DESPISE <959>.

CONTEMPTIBLE THING – Ezek. 35:12 ➔ DISGRACE (noun) <5007>.

CONTEMPTUOUSLY – Mic. 7:6 ➔ to treat contemptuously ➔ FOOLISH (BE) <5034>.

CONTEND – [1] ***maṣṣûṯ*** [fem. noun: מַצּוּת <4695>; from FIGHT (verb) <5327>] ▶ **This word signifies warfare, contention.** It refers to that which engenders hostility, fighting, quarreling (Is. 41:12; also translated to quarrel, to wage war). ¶
[2] ***'āśaq*** [verb: עָשַׂק <6229>; from MEET (verb) <6923>] ▶ **This word is also translated to quarrel, to strive, to dispute.** It means to argue with, to fight over something, to make claims and counterclaims (Gen. 26:20). ¶
– [3] Num. 26:9 ➔ FIGHT <5327> [4] Deut. 2:5, 9, 19, 24; Prov. 28:4; Jer. 50:24 ➔ STRIVE <1624> [5] Jer. 12:5 ➔ COMPETE <8474> a.

CONTENDS (ONE WHO) – [1] ***yissôr*** [masc. sing. noun: יִסּוֹר <3250>; from ADMONISH <3256>] ▶ **This word means one who reproves.** Its only occurrence is in Job 40:2. ¶
[2] ***yāriyḇ*** [masc. noun: יָרִיב <3401>; from STRIVE <7378>] ▶ **This word indicates an opponent, a contender. It refers to one's adversary in a legal way, a case, but in a more general way as well.** God

contends with and overcomes the adversaries of His people (Ps. 35:1: also translated to strive; Is. 49:25; Jer. 18:19: also translated opponent, adversary, accuser). ¶

CONTENT (BE) – [1] ***yā'al*** [verb: יָאַל <2974>; a prim. root (prob. rather the same as FOOLISHLY (BE, DO, ACT) <2973> through the idea of mental weakness)] ▶ **This word means to choose to do something. The focus of this verb is on the decision to act.** This concept is expressed on three levels. On the first level, the individual shows a willingness to act a certain way, to accept an invitation (Ex. 2:21; Josh. 7:7; Judg. 19:6). On the next level, the individual is more active and voluntarily decides to act a certain way (Gen. 18:27; Deut. 1:5); the word is translated to take upon oneself, to undertake, to be bold, to begin. On the final level, the individual is even more active and voluntarily decides to act a certain way with determination and resolve (to persist, to determine, to be determined: Josh. 17:12; Judg. 1:27, 35; Hos. 5:11). This verb provides strong support for the theological concept of human free will because humanity is permitted to decide to act a certain way. God, however, will hold humanity responsible for those decisions and actions. *
– [2] Prov. 6:35 ➔ WILLING (BE) <14>.

CONTENTION – Prov. 13:10; Is. 58:4 ➔ STRIFE <4683>.

CONTENTIONS – ***midyāniym*** [masc. plur. noun: מִדְיָנִים <4079>; a variation for STRIFE <4066>] ▶ **This word means brawlings; it is also translated quarrels, disputes.** Refs.: Prov. 18:18, 19; 19:13; 21:9, 19; 23:29; 25:24; 26:21; 27:15. ¶

CONTENTMENT – Job 36:11 ➔ PLEASANT <5273> a.

CONTENTS – Lev. 1:16 ➔ FEATHER <5133> b.

CONTINUAL – ***sagriyr*** [masc. noun: סַגְרִיר <5464>; prob. from CLOSE <5462> in the sense of sweeping away] ▶ **This word refers to a moderate constant rainfall that will not let up, putting everyone in a state of agitation and aggravation.** Ref.: Prov. 27:15; NASB: constant. ¶

CONTINUAL (BE) – ***ṭārad*** [verb: טָרַד <2956>; a prim. root] ▶ **This word means to be constant, continuous, no break, no let up.** It is used to describe the incessant, destructive behavior of a quarrelsome wife (Prov. 19:13). A "constant dripping of rain" is used to depict the contentious wife or woman as well (Prov. 27:15). ¶

CONTINUALLY – [1] ***tḏiyr, tḏiyrā'*** [Aramaic fem. noun: תְּדִיר, תְּדִירָא <8411>; from DWELL <1753>] ▶ **This Hebrew noun means continuance; it is also translated constantly.** It is used adverbially to describe a practice or an attitude that is done or held without fail (Dan. 6:16, 20). ¶
– [2] Prov. 6:21; etc. ➔ CONTINUITY <8548>.

CONTINUE – [1] ***yāsap*** [verb: יָסַף <3254>; a prim. root] ▶ **The word indicates continuing to do something, to do something repeatedly, to enhance, increase something, or to do something after a period of inactivity. It also means to increase, to do again.** Israel will revive and take root after being destroyed (Is. 10:20); Israel continued to sin over and over, adding (*yāsap*) to her sins, increasing them (Judg. 13:1; 1 Sam. 12:19; Is. 1:5); but her afflicted could increase or add to (*yāsap*) their joy or gladness in the Lord (Is. 29:19). The angel of the Lord did not again (*yāsap*) appear to Manoah after His second appearance (cf. Num. 11:25; Judg. 13:12). It indicates an addition to the number of persons or objects (Gen. 4:2; 38:26; 2 Sam. 24:3). The Lord added sons to Jacob and Rachel (Gen. 30:24); Solomon added to the tax burden of Israel (1 Kgs. 12:11). It indicates the continuation of a plan or process (Gen. 8:10), as when Noah again (*yāsap*) sent out a dove. Of course, when the verb is negated, it means to do something no more, no longer. Because of Cain's sin, the ground

would no longer yield its fruits abundantly to him (Gen. 4:12); it indicates something will not be done again (Ex. 11:6). It is used of human reactions and emotions. Joseph's brothers hated him still more (*yāsap̱*) (Gen. 37:5). Finally, it is found in an oath formula in which it is stated that God will do such and such "and still more" (1 Kgs. 2:23). *
2 ***nûn*** [verb: נוּן <5125>; a prim. root] ▶ **This word means to perpetuate; it is also translated to increase.** It indicates the propriety and strengthening of a person, e.g., the righteous king of God's people (Ps. 72:17). ¶

CONTINUE ON – Job 21:7 ➔ MOVE <6275>.

CONTINUING – Jer. 30:23 ➔ DRAG (verb) <1641>.

CONTINUITY – ***tāmiyḏ*** [masc. noun: תָּמִיד <8548>; from an unused root meaning to stretch] ▶ **This word commonly refers to actions concerning religious rituals. It is translated always, at all times, regularly.** God commanded that the Israelites always set showbread on a table in the Tabernacle (Ex. 25:30). Similarly, special bread was to be set on the table continually every Sabbath (Lev. 24:8). Mealtime could also be seen as following a set pattern: David commanded that Mephibosheth always eat with him (2 Sam. 9:7). In another light, the psalmist referred to God as One he could continually turn to in times of need (Ps. 71:3). *

CONTRARY – 1 Lev. 26:21, 23, 24, 27, 28, 40, 41 ➔ HOSTILITY <7147> 2 Ezek. 16:34 ➔ OPPOSITE (noun) <2016>.

CONTRARY (BE) – Num. 22:32 ➔ TURN OVER <3399>.

CONTRIBUTION – See OFFERING <8641>.

CONTRITE – 1 Ps. 34:18; Is. 57:15 ➔ CRUSHED <1793> 2 Is. 66:2 ➔ CRIPPLED <5223>.

CONTROL (BRING UNDER) – Josh. 18:1 ➔ SUBDUE <3533>.

CONTROL (verb) – 1 ***'āp̱aq*** [verb: אָפַק <662>; a prim. root] ▶ **This word means to maintain one's composure; it is also translated to refrain, to restrain, to withhold, to hold back; to force, to compel.** It depicts self-control (Gen. 43:31; 45:1; Esther 5:10). It means to make oneself do something (1 Sam. 13:12). It depicts the Lord's self-control (Is. 42:14; 63:15; 64:12). ¶
2 ***bālam*** [verb: בָּלַם <1102>; a prim. root] ▶ **This word means to restrain, to hold in, to curb. It is also translated to harness, to hold in check.** It means to curb the wild nature of a horse or mule with a bit or bridle (Ps. 32:9). A person should not need this kind of restraint. ¶
– 3 Prov. 25:28 ➔ SELF-CONTROL <4623>.

CONVOCATION – Ex. 12:16; Num. 28:18, 25, 26; etc. ➔ ASSEMBLY <4744>.

CONVULSED (BE) – Ezek. 27:35 ➔ IRRITATE <7481>.

COOK (noun) – 1 ***ṭabbāḥah*** [fem. noun: טַבָּחָה <2879>; fem. of GUARD, IMPERIAL GUARD <2876> (in the sense of cook)] ▶ **This word refers to a position of preparing food which, according to this verse, was assigned to daughters of Israel in the administration of the king of Israel.** This position was along with bakers and perfumers (1 Sam. 8:13). ¶
– 2 1 Sam. 9:23, 24 ➔ GUARD, IMPERIAL GUARD <2876>.

COOK (verb) – 1 ***bāšal*** [verb: בָּשַׁל <1310>; a prim. root] ▶ **This word means preparing food. It also means to boil, to roast; to ripen.** It indicates simply cooking without an object (Ezek. 24:5). It describes the preparation of various foods: to bake cakes or bread (2 Sam. 13:8), to cook or boil meat (Deut. 16:7; 1 Kgs. 19:21). In its passive use, it indicates something boiled (Ex. 12:9), a cooking method forbidden in

preparing the Passover lamb. It describes the ripening of grapes and fruit of the vine (Gen. 40:10). It is used in a figurative sense to indicate that the harvest, the nations of the world, are ripe and ready to be cut (Joel 3:13). *
– [2] Gen. 25:29 ➔ PROUDLY (DEAL) <2102>.

COOKING HEARTHS – Ezek. 46:23 ➔ HEARTHS <4018>.

COOL – Prov. 17:27; Jer. 18:14 ➔ COLD (adj.) <7119>.

COPING – 1 Kgs. 7:9 ➔ HANDBREATH <2947> c.

COPPER – ***nᵉḥōšeṯ*** [common noun: נְחֹשֶׁת <5178>; for BRONZE <5154>] ▶ **This word refers to a reddish brown metal; it is also translated bronze.** Copper is a metal occurring naturally (Deut. 8:9); bronze is a metal alloy of copper and tin. The meaning of this word depends on its use in context. It is found listed among other materials of the ancient world (Gen. 4:22; 2 Sam. 8:10). There were skilled craftsmen who worked in bronze (1 Kgs. 7:14) as a medium of construction, art, and ornamentation. Bronze made possible a better grade of all kinds of implements and tools of labor or war: weapons, pillars, columns, bases, stands, the great bronze sea of Solomon (Num. 16:39; 1 Sam. 17:5, 6; 2 Kgs. 25:13, 14). The word describes chains of copper or bronze (Judg. 16:21). It was considered a highly prized spoil of war (2 Sam. 8:8; Jer. 52:17, 20). It is used figuratively to indicate God's refusal to respond to His people (Deut. 28:23); and in visions of bronze mountains (Zech. 6:1). The Hebrew word also means lewdness, lust; see LUST (noun) <5178>. *

COPY (noun) – [1] ***paršeḡen, paṯšeḡen*** [masc. noun: פַּרְשֶׁגֶן, פַּתְשֶׁגֶן <6572>; of foreign origin] ▶
a. This word refers to a reproduction of a letter or other written document, hand-copied. Ref.: Ezra 7:11. ¶
b. It refers also to a duplicate reproduction of a royal edict or proclamation put into whatever language or dialect that was needed. Refs.: Esther 3:14; 4:8; 8:13. ¶
[2] ***paršeḡen*** [Aramaic masc. noun: פַּרְשֶׁגֶן <6573>; corresponding to <6572> above] ▶ **This word refers to a duplicate of a letter or other document produced for distribution as needed.** Refs.: Ezra 4:11, 23; 5:6. ¶

COPY (verb) – Prov. 25:1 ➔ MOVE <6275>.

COR – ***kōr*** [masc. noun: כֹּר <3734>; from the same as FURNACE <3564>] ▶
a. A measure of grain or oil. It was a standard ancient measure of capacity, whether wet or dry (1 Kgs. 5:11). It equaled one hundred gallons or about six bushels of dry measure or more. Other refs.: 1 Kgs. 4:22; 2 Chr. 2:10; 27:5; Ezek. 45:14. ¶
b. An Aramaic noun indicating a measure of grain. It was equal to six bushels of wheat (Ezra 7:22) and, in context, was a gift from the Persian king. ¶

CORAL – ***rā'môṯ*** [fem. plur. noun: רָאמוֹת <7215>; from RISE <7213>] ▶ **This word refers to a precious stone or some precious substance of great value to be compared to wisdom.** Ref.: Job 28:18. It was used on the international scene as a medium of exchange or trading (Ezek. 27:16). ¶

CORAL, CORALS – Lam. 4:7 ➔ JEWELS <6443>.

CORASHAN – ***kôr 'āšān*** [proper noun: כּוֹר עָשָׁן <3565>; from PIERCE <3564> and SMOKE (noun) <6227>]: smoking furnace ▶ **A variant spelling for Bor-ashan.** It is only found in 1 Samuel 30:30, KJV and NKJV. ¶

CORD – [1] **bound with cords, in sturdy woven cords, in tightly wound cords, with cords twisted: *'ārûz*** [adj.: אָרוּז <729>; a prim. root] ▶ **This word means made of cedar or possibly a twisted rope. It describes one among several luxury**

items that Tyre traded with the nations. It is translated as an adjective modifying chest, chests of cedar (KJV, Ezek. 27:24) but also as tightly wound cords (NASB) or twisted cords (NIV). ¶

2 ***môšᵉkāh*** [fem. noun: מוֹשְׁכָה <4189>; act. part. fem. of PULL <4900>] ▶ **This word means a tie; it is also translated band, belt.** It is used figuratively of the "cords" that bind the constellation Orion in place (Job 38:31), keeping it in its created fixed order. ¶

3 ***pāṯiyl*** [masc. noun: פָּתִיל <6616>; from WRESTLE <6617> (in the sense of to twine)] ▶ **This word refers to a rope or string made of various materials.** Refs.: Ex. 28:28, 37; 39:3, 21, 31; the word is also translated lace, thread, wire, strand. Such cords were used for beauty and ornamentation depending on their color and makeup (Num. 15:38). They could be used for mundane things (Num. 19:15; the word is translated fastened, tied down, bound); or to tie up prisoners (Judg. 16:9). Certain cords were used in building and architectural work (Ezek. 40:3). Other refs.: Gen. 38:18, 25. ¶

4 ***tiqwāh*** [fem. noun: תִּקְוָה <8615>; from WAIT FOR <6960> (with the root meaning of twisting or winding a strand of cord or rope)] ▶ **This word refers to a piece of rope or a lace made of bright red thread with a tinge of orange.** Rahab placed it in her window (Josh. 2:18, 21; KJV: line). For another meaning of the Hebrew word, see HOPE (noun) <8615>. ¶

– 5 Ex. 35:18; 39:40; Num. 3:26, 37; 4:26, 32; Jer. 10:20 ➔ STRING <4340> 6 Josh. 2:18; Eccl. 4:12 ➔ THREAD <2339> 7 Job 41:2 ➔ ROPE <100> 8 See ROPE <2256>.

CORIANDER – ***gaḏ*** [masc. noun: גַּד <1407>; from CUT (verb) <1413>] ▶ **This word refers to the seed of an aromatic plant.** It is used in a simile or comparison to describe what manna was like (Ex. 16:31; Num. 11:7). It is an Eurasian aromatic herb. This word refers to its seed as fruit. ¶

CORMORANT – 1 ***šālaḵ*** [masc. noun: שָׁלָךְ <7994>; from THROW <7993> (in the sense of casting oneself, e.g., into the sea in the case of the cormorant)] ▶ **This word refers to a type of large, voracious, pelican-like diving bird not to be eaten by Israel.** It was considered detestable and unclean (Lev. 11:17; Deut. 14:17; NKJV: fisher owl). ¶

– 2 Is. 34:11; Zeph. 2:14 ➔ PELICAN <6893>.

CORN – 1 ***dāgān*** [masc. noun: דָּגָן <1715>; from GROW <1711>] ▶ **This word refers to cereal grains, one of the three blessings of the Lord on His people, i.e., of wine, oil, and grain.** Refs.: Num. 18:12; Deut. 7:13; 11:14; 12:17; Joel 1:10; Hag. 1:11. It is used alone rarely (Neh. 5:2, 3, 10; Ezek. 36:29). It is used forty times, and it is clear that the Lord gave this grain as a blessing (Gen. 27:28, 37; Ps. 4:7; Is. 62:8; Hos. 2:9). The land of Canaan is termed a land of grain and new wine (Deut. 33:28). The word indicates the firstfruits of grain and corn offered to the priests (Num. 18:12; Deut. 18:4); as a tithe (Deut. 12:17; 14:23); or for both (Neh. 10:39) reasons. *

– 2 See GRAIN <1250>.

CORN (FRESH) – Lev. 2:14; 23:14; 2 Kgs. 4:42 ➔ FIELD (FERTILE, FRUITFUL, PLENTIFUL) <3759> b.

CORN (GROUND) – 2 Sam. 17:19 ➔ GRAIN <7383>.

CORN (OLD) – Josh. 5:11, 12 ➔ PRODUCE (noun) <5669>.

CORNER (noun) – 1 ***zāwiyṯ*** [fem. noun: זָוִית <2106>; apparently from the same root as ZIV <2099> (in the sense of prominence)] ▶ **This word indicates a pillar or cornerstone.** It indicates the corner of an altar (Zech. 9:15) and the pillars of a house (Ps. 144:12; also translated corner pillar, corner stone). ¶

2 ***miqṣôa'***, ***miqṣōa'*** [masc. noun: מִקְצוֹעַ, מִקְצֹעַ <4740>; from CORNER (verb) <7106> in the denom. sense of bending] ▶ **This word is used as an architectural term. It indicates a place where two or**

more sides meet in structures such as the Tabernacle, altar, or court. Refs.: Ex. 26:23, 24; 36:28, 29; Ezek. 41:22; 46:21, 22. It was used as part of certain locations in Jerusalem (2 Chr. 26:9; Neh. 3:19, 20, 24, 25: also translated buttress, turning). ¶
3 ***mequsʿāt*** [fem. noun: מְקֻצְעָת <4742>; from CORNER (verb) <7106> in the denom. sense of bending] ▶ **This word indicates a bending, an angle.** It describes the place where two boards come together, forming an angle (Ex. 26:23; 36:28). ¶
4 ***pê'āh*** [fem. noun: פֵּאָה <6285>; fem. of HERE <6311>] ▶ **This word refers to four conjunctions.** At the top of the table of showbread (Ex. 25:26) or on a bed (Amos 3:12). When used of a person's head, it designates its sides (Lev. 13:41). In some passages, it refers figuratively of the forehead of a people or nation (Num. 24:17). In context it may refer to the border or boundary of a territory, its side (Josh. 15:5; Num. 24:17). *
5 ***pên*** [Aramaic masc. noun: פֵּן <6434>; from an unused root meaning to turn] ▶ **This word indicates an angle, angle of a street.** It is used in the plural once with the article to modify gates, the corner gate (Zech. 14:10). It describes a street corner in some translations (Prov. 7:8). ¶
6 ***pinnāh*** [fem. noun: פִּנָּה <6438>; fem. of CORNER (noun) <6434>] ▶ **This word refers to a location where various surfaces or lines meet to form an angle.** It is used of the corners of a house (Job 1:19); a wall (Neh. 3:24); an altar (Ex. 27:2); a street (Prov. 7:8), etc. The phrase *'eḇen pinnāh* means cornerstone (Job 38:6). It combines with more words to indicate corner tower (Zeph. 1:16); corner gate (2 Kgs. 14:13). Figuratively, it designates a leader (Judg. 20:2; 1 Sam. 14:38; Is. 19:13; Zech. 10:4). *

CORNER (BE MOVED INTO A, BE REMOVED INTO A) – Is. 30:20 → HIDE (verb) <3670>.

CORNER (verb) – ***qāṣaʿ*** [verb: קָצַע <7106>; a prim. root] ▶ **This word means to form a bend, an angle or a joint.** It indicates the construction of boards or frames that meet to form a joint, corner, or point (Ex. 26:23; 36:28). It is used in a causative passive stem to refer to corners already formed (Ezek. 46:22). For another meaning of the Hebrew word, see SCRAPE <7106>. ¶

CORNER PILLAR, CORNER STONE – Ps. 144:12 → CORNER (noun) <2106>.

CORNETS – 2 Sam. 6:5 → CASTANETS <4517> b.

CORPSE – 1 ***neḇêlāh*** [fem. noun: נְבֵלָה <5038>; from WITHER <5034>] ▶ **It describes a body devoid of life.** I may be human (Josh. 8:29; Is. 5:25) or animal (Deut. 14:8). The Law clearly stated that contact with the carcass of a dead animal (Lev. 5:2) or with the body of a dead person (cf. Num. 19:11) would render an individual unclean. Also, it was possible for the land to be defiled by the presence of an unburied corpse (Deut. 21:23). Hence, Jeremiah used the word *neḇêlāh* for idols. Pagan idols were devoid of life just like corpses and were a source of defilement for the people, priests, and land. *
2 ***peger*** [masc. noun: פֶּגֶר <6297>; from EXHAUSTED (BE) <6296> (in the sense of to loose consciousness)] ▶ **This word can refer to the carcasses of animals (Gen. 15:11); however, it is usually used in connection with dead bodies of human beings.** Though this term can refer to a single body (Is. 14:19), it is usually found in the plural (Is. 34:3; Jer. 31:40; Ezek. 6:5). In several instances, the singular is used as a collective (1 Sam. 17:46; Amos 8:3; Nah. 3:3). One occurrence of this word is a metaphor for the lifelessness of idols (Lev. 26:30). *
– 3 Ps. 110:6; Nah. 3:3 → BODY <1472>.

CORRESPONDING TO – Gen. 2:18, 20 → BEFORE <5048>.

CORROSION – Ezek. 24:6, 11, 12 → SCUM <2457>.

CORRUPT (adj.) – 1 Prov. 6:12 → CROOKED <6143> 2 Jer. 2:21 → DEGENERATE <5494>.

CORRUPT (verb) – [1] ***šᵉḥaṯ*** [Aramaic verb: שְׁחַת <7844>; corresponding to DESTROY <7843>] ▶ **This word means perverted. It can also function as a noun, in which it designates fault.** The verb is used in Daniel to depict what the astrologers did to their words in an effort to gain more time from the king (Dan. 2:9). The inability of the astrologers and other wise men to interpret Nebuchadnezzar's dream set the stage for Daniel.

In Daniel 6:4, the word is used as a noun (fault) and designated the charge against Daniel. Since no fault could be found, the administrators and satraps persuaded King Darius to issue and enforce the decree that no one could pray to anyone or anything but him for a period of thirty days or be thrown into the den of lions. ¶
– [2] Dan. 11:32 ➔ DEFILED (BE) <2610>.

CORRUPT (BE) – [1] Ps. 38:5 ➔ WASTE AWAY <4743> [2] Ps. 73:8 ➔ SCOFF <4167>.

CORRUPT (BECOME) – ***'ālaḥ*** [verb: אָלַח <444>; a prim. root] ▶ **This word means to turn filthy morally. It describes humankind as turning filthy: as given to evil, or iniquity, as they are to drinking water.** This state of pollution is strong in the fool (Ps. 14:3) and the godless (Ps. 53:3), who are, in fact, in the same condition. Other ref.: Job 15:16. ¶

CORRUPTION – [1] Lev. 22:25 ➔ MARRED <4893> b. [2] 2 Kgs. 23:13; etc. ➔ DESTRUCTION <4889>.

CORRUPTLY (DEAL) – Is. 26:10 ➔ UNJUSTLY (DEAL) <5765>.

COSMETICS – ***tamrûq*** [masc. noun: תַּמְרוּק <8562>; from POLISH <4838> (in the sense of to beautify by polishing)] ▶ **This Hebrew word means scraping, rubbing, purifying. It carries the connotation of scraping away that which is impure or harmful.** This word appears three times in reference to ritual purification (Esther 2:3, 9, 12; also translated beauty preparations, beauty treatments, purification). Figuratively, it is used to imply a remedy for an illness (Prov. 20:30: to cleanse away, to scour away, to scrub away). ¶

COST – ***nipqāh*** [Aramaic fem. noun: נִפְקָה <5313>; from TAKE OUT <5312>] ▶ **This word refers to the amount of labor and materials expended for something, its value in monetary term.** Refs.: Ezra 6:4, 8; also translated expense. ¶

COSTLY – 1 Kgs. 5:17; 7:9–11; Dan. 11:38 ➔ PRECIOUS <3368>.

COSTLY (BE) – Ps. 49:8 ➔ PRECIOUS (BE) <3365>.

COSTLY GARMENTS, COSTLY FABRIC – Ezek. 16:10, 13 ➔ SILK <4897>.

COSTLY STONE – Esther 1:6 ➔ PRECIOUS STONE <5508> a.

COSTLY STONES – Prov. 20:15 ➔ JEWELS <6443>.

COSTLY THINGS – Jer. 20:5 ➔ HONOR (noun) <3366>.

COTTAGE – Zeph. 2:6 ➔ CAVE <3741>.

COUCH – [1] Gen. 49:4; 1 Chr. 5:1 ➔ BED <3326> [2] Prov. 7:16; Song 1:16; Amos 3:12; 6:4 ➔ BED <6210> [3] Song 1:12 ➔ AROUND <4524>.

COUCHING PLACE – Ezek. 25:5 ➔ RESTING PLACE <4769>.

COUNCIL – [1] Ps. 68:27 ➔ THRONG (noun) <7277> b. [2] Ps. 82:1 ➔ CONGREGATION <5712>.

COUNSEL (noun) – [1] ***mô'êṣāh*** [fem. noun: מוֹעֵצָה <4156>; from COUNSEL (verb) <3289>] ▶ **This word refers to advice given by wisdom personified.** Refs.: Prov. 22:20; see 1:30. The wicked fall from their own devices or counsel (Ps. 5:10;

NIV: intrigues). The context determines the nature of the counsel, e.g., created by a hard, stubborn heart (Ps. 81:12); or of an evil heart (Jer. 7:24). Other refs.: Hos. 11:6 (NIV: plan); Mic. 6:16 (NIV: tradition). ¶
[2] ***sôḏ*** [masc. noun: סוֹד <5475>; from FOUNDATION (LAY A) <3245> (in the sense for this Hebrew word to sit close together)] ► **Confidentiality is at the heart of this term. Among other meanings, it refers to consultation, secret, friendship.** According to Proverbs 25:9, information shared in confidence should remain confidential. Yet gossip makes it difficult to do this (Prov. 11:13; 20:19: secret). Elsewhere, this term reflects a more general meaning of counsel, which is viewed as essential to successful planning (Prov. 15:22). When it means counsel, this term suggests the idea of intimacy. For example, Job used this term to refer to his close friendship with God (Job 29:4); and with individuals he thought of as his close friends (Job 19:19). David used this term to describe one of his close friendships (Ps. 55:14). God establishes a close, intimate relationship with those who revere Him and walk uprightly (Ps. 25:14; Prov. 3:32). Sometimes, however, human relationships involve less than ideal associations (Gen. 49:6). Used in a negative sense, this term can denote evil plotting (Ps. 64:2; 83:3). *
[3] ***taḥbulāh*** [fem. noun: תַּחְבֻּלָה <8458>; from PLEDGE (TAKE AS A) <2254> as denom. from ROPE <2256> (this would indicate a steerage, as a management of ropes)] ► **This word means advice and is also translated guidance.** It is used of God's counsel and advice given to direct the behavior of even the clouds (Job 37:12). It refers to wise advice that a wise person seeks out (Prov. 1:5); without it, a person is at a loss to know what to do (Prov. 11:14); war was to be carried out by wise counsel (Prov. 20:18; 24:6). Counsel from a wicked person was considered destructive (Prov. 12:5; NIV: advice). ¶
– [4] Dan. 2:14 ➔ PRUDENCE <5843>.

COUNSEL (TAKE) – ***'ûṣ*** [verb: עוּץ <5779>; a prim. root] ► **This word means to devise a plan, to take advice, to confer.** It refers to the process of coming up with a response or a way to deal with a situation (Judg. 19:30). Plans that thwart God's will do not work (Is. 8:10). ¶

COUNSEL (verb) – ***yā'aṣ*** [verb: יָעַץ <3289>; a prim. root] ► **This word means to advise, to consult, to be advised, to deliberate, to conspire, to take counsel.** Jethro, Moses' father-in-law, advised Moses about how to judge the people of Israel (Ex. 18:19); and wise men, such as Hushai and Ahithophel, served as counselors to kings and other important people (2 Sam. 17:15; 1 Kgs. 12:9); as did prophets (Jer. 38:15). Many counselors help ensure that plans will succeed (Prov. 15:22); God counseled His servants (Ps. 16:7); the coming ruler of Israel will be the "Wonderful Counselor" (Is. 9:6). The verb also means to decide, to make plans or decisions. These plans can be for or against someone or something with God or a human as a subject of the sentence (Is. 7:5; 14:24; Jer. 49:20; Hab. 2:10), but God's plans will never fail (Is. 14:24).

In the passive, this verb means to permit oneself to be counseled-wisdom is gained by a person who acts in this manner (Prov. 13:10; cf. Prov. 1:5). More often, this stem expresses a reciprocal sense: Rehoboam consulted together with the elders (1 Kgs. 12:6); and the enemies of the psalmist conspired against him (Ps. 71:10). In the reflexive stem, it means to take counsel against as when the Lord's enemies conspired against His people (Ps. 83:3). *

COUNSELOR – [1] ***ᵃḏargāzêr*** [Aramaic masc. noun: אֲדַרְגָּזֵר <148>; from the same as THRESHING FLOOR <147> and CUT (verb) <1505>] ► **This word means a high-ranking justice; it is also translated adviser, judge. It is found only in the book of Daniel when Nebuchadnezzar erected his statue for all to bow down to.** He sent a decree to all the important people (i.e., satraps, administrators, counselors) to come for the dedication ceremony (Dan. 3:2, 3). ¶
[2] ***haddāḇar*** [Aramaic masc. noun: הַדָּבַר <1907>; prob. of foreign origin] ► **This**

word means a chief minister of the king; it is also translated advisor, high official. It refers to high-ranking officials of King Nebuchadnezzar who undoubtedly served as royal advisors and counselors as well (Dan. 3:24, 27; 4:36; 6:7). ¶
– [3] Is. 9:6 ➔ COUNSEL (verb) <3289> [4] Dan. 3:2, 3 ➔ JUDGE (noun) <1884>.

COUNSELOR, COUNSELLOR – Ezra 7:14, 15 ➔ CONSULT TOGETHER <3272>.

COUNT – [1] ***mānāh*** [verb: מָנָה <4487>; a prim. root] ► **This word means to tally, to number.** It means basically to count up, to tally for oneself or for someone else: to tally up the stars of heaven (Gen. 13:16); to record the bits of dust of Jacob (Num. 23:10); the number of persons in Israel and Judah (2 Sam. 24:1); or money (2 Kgs. 12:10). It takes on the sense of consigning or allotting something for some reason (Job 7:3; Dan. 1:5, 10, 11). It is used figuratively of the Lord's appointing or establishing kindness and truth (Ps. 61:7); and of persons numbering their days in order to be wise (Ps. 90:12). God has unlimited ability to reckon the stars and to keep track of each one (Ps. 147:4); and He appoints events and experiences for His people (Job 7:3: to appoint, to apportion, to assign; Jon. 1:17; 4:6–8: to appoint, to prepare, to provide). In its passive sense, it means to be counted (Gen. 13:16; 1 Kgs. 3:8; 8:5; Is. 53:12). Other refs.: 1 Kgs. 20:25; 1 Chr. 9:29; 21:1, 17; 27:24; 2 Chr. 5:6; Eccl. 1:15; Is. 65:12; Jer. 33:13. ¶
– [2] Lev. 19:23 ➔ NAKEDNESS (EXPOSE ONE'S) <6188>.

COUNT (MAKE ONE'S) – ***kāsas*** [verb: כָּסַס <3699>; a prim. root] ► **This word means to estimate, to determine.** It is used of figuring out, calculating, or determining something, e.g., the lamb needed for the Passover (Ex. 12:4; also translated to determine the amount, to divide). ¶

COUNTENANCE – [1] Ex. 23:3 ➔ HONOR (verb) <1921> [2] Dan. 5:6, 9, 10; 7:28 ➔ BRIGHTNESS <2122>.

COUNTRY – Ezek. 47:8 ➔ REGION <1552>.

COUPLED (BE) – Ex. 26:24; 36:29 ➔ DOUBLE (BE) <8382>.

COUPLING – [1] ***ḥōḇereṯ*** [fem. noun: חֹבֶרֶת <2279>; fem. act. part. of JOIN TOGETHER <2266>] ► **This word refers to a junction, a connecting thing, a curtain that joins another, draperies.** It indicates the outermost curtains of two sets of drapes where loops would be placed for joining (Ex. 26:4, 10; 36:17). ¶
– [2] 2 Chr. 34:11 ➔ FITTING <4226>.

COURAGEOUS – Amos 2:16 ➔ BRAVE <533>.

COURSE – [1] 1 Kgs. 6:36; 7:12 ➔ ROW (noun) <2905> [2] Ezra 6:18 ➔ GROUP <4255> [3] Jer. 8:6; 23:10 ➔ RUNNING <4794>.

COURSES OF STONES – Song 4:4 ➔ ROW OF STONES <8530>.

COURT – [1] ***tᵉra‘*** [Aramaic masc. noun: תְּרַע <8651>; corresponding to GATE <8179>] ► **This word means the sphere where a king's government is administered, but also a door.** It refers to a gate or door (Dan. 2:49), but it signifies the court of the king (*biṯra‘ malkā’*). It indicates the opening to the great blazing furnace of Babylon (Dan. 3:26; also translated mouth, door). ¶
– [2] Ex. 21:22 ➔ JUDGE (noun) <6414> [3] 2 Kgs. 23:11; 1 Chr. 26:18 ➔ PRECINCTS <6503> a. [4] 2 Chr. 4:9; 6:13 ➔ LEDGE <5835> [5] Is. 34:13 ➔ ABODE <2681> [6] See VILLAGE <2691>.

COURTYARD – [1] ***gizrāh*** [fem. noun: גִּזְרָה <1508>; fem. of PART (noun) <1506>] ► **This word designates a separate area, place, enclosure. It also refers to the form, figure of a person; it is translated appearance, polishing.** It indicates the courtyard of Ezekiel's visionary Temple (Ezek. 41:12–15; 42:1, 10, 13). Depicting

how something looks, it is used to describe the appearance or polishing of God's people before their corruption and judgment (Lam. 4:7). ¶
– [2] Is. 34:13 ➔ ABODE <2681> [3] See VILLAGE <2691>.

COVE – Judg. 5:17 ➔ LANDING <4664>.

COVENANT – [1] **sure covenant, firm covenant:** ***^{a}mānāh*** [fem. noun: אֲמָנָה <548>; fem. of AMEN <543>] ► **This word means agreement, faith, support; it is also translated firm agreement, binding agreement, certain portion, fixed provision, firm regulation.** It occurs in Nehemiah 9:38 and Nehemiah 11:23. In Nehemiah 9:38, it is the object of the verb *kāraṯ* (CUT <3772>), which is also used in the idiom "to make (lit., cut) a covenant," suggesting a possible semantic overlap. ¶
[2] ***b^{e}riyṯ*** [fem. noun: בְּרִית <1285>; from EAT <1262> (in the sense of cutting; like CREATE <1254>)] ► **This word means treaty, alliance, agreement. It is used many times in the Old Testament. Its basic uses are outlined here.** It describes covenants, or agreements between and among human beings: between Abraham and the Amorites, Abraham and the Philistines, Jacob and Laban, etc. (Gen. 14:13; 21:27, 32; 31:44). The nations were said to have made a covenant against Israel (Ps. 83:5). It is used figuratively to depict a covenant with death (Is. 28:15, 18) or with the stones of the field (Job 5:23). *

It denotes an alliance, ordinance, or agreement between persons. References to covenants between people included Abraham's military treaty with the Ammorites (Gen. 14:13); Jonathan and David's pledge of friendship (1 Sam. 18:3); David's covenant with Abner (2 Sam. 3:12); the covenant of marriage (Prov. 2:17). The word *b^{e}riyṯ* is often preceded by the verb *karaṯ* to express the technical idea of "cutting a covenant."

This word is used to describe God's making a covenant with humankind. It may be an alliance of friendship (Ps. 25:14). The covenants made between God and humans defined the basis of God's relationships in the Old Testament. They showed the strength of His divine promise from Adam all the way through to the exile and restoration. The word is employed many times: God's covenant with Noah (Gen. 9:11–13, 15–17; Is. 54:10) in the form of a promise; with Abraham, Isaac, and Jacob (Gen. 15:18; 17:2, 4, 7, 9–11, 13, 14, 19, 21; Ex. 2:24; Lev. 26:42) to increase their descendants, giving them Canaan and making them a blessing to the nations; with all Israel and Moses at Sinai (Ex. 19:5; 24:7, 8; 34:10; Deut. 29:1) with the stipulations of the Ten Commandments, including the guiding cases in the Book of the Covenant. The words of this covenant (*diḇrêy habb^{e}riyṯ*) were kept in the ark in the Holy of Holies (Ex. 34:28; 40:20). A covenant with Phinehas established an everlasting priesthood in Israel (Num. 25:12, 13). It is used to refer to the covenant established with David and his house (Ps. 89:3, 28; Jer. 33:21), an eternal covenant establishing David and his descendants as the inheritors of an everlasting kingdom. Jeremiah refers to a new covenant (Jer. 31:31) that God will establish in the future. The concept is personified in a person, a Servant who becomes the covenant of the people (Is. 42:6; Is. 49:8).

In addition to the verb *karaṯ* mentioned above, the verb *qûm* is employed with *b^{e}riyṯ* meaning to establish a covenant (Gen. 6:18; 9:9; Ex. 6:4) or to confirm a covenant (Lev. 26:9; Deut. 8:18). The word is used with *nāṯan*, to give, meaning to give or make a covenant (Gen. 17:2; Num. 25:12). Five other verbs are used in this way less often (Deut. 29:12; 2 Sam. 23:5; 2 Chr. 15:12; Ps. 50:16; 111:9; Ezek. 16:8). A covenant could be transgressed or violated (Deut. 17:2; Judg. 2:20), but the Lord never broke His covenants; He always remembered a covenant (Gen. 9:15, 16; Ex. 2:24; 6:5; Lev. 26:42). *

COVER (noun) – [1] Ex. 25:29; 37:16; Num. 4:7 ➔ JAR <7184> b. [2] Lev. 9:19; Is. 14:11; Ezek. 27:7 ➔ COVERING <4374> [3] Num. 4:14 ➔ COVERING

<3681> [4] 1 Sam. 19:13, 16 ➔ PILLOW <3523> [5] 2 Kgs. 8:15 ➔ CLOTH, TICK CLOTH <4346> [6] Amos 3:12 ➔ DAMASCUS <1833> b. [7] Zech. 5:7 ➔ ROUND (SOMETHING) <3603>.

COVER (TAKE) – Is. 10:31 ➔ SAFETY (FLEE FOR) <5756>.

COVER (verb) – [1] ***ḥāp̱āh*** [verb: חָפָה <2645>; a prim. root; comp. SECRETLY (DO) <2644>, COVER (verb) <2653>] ▶ **This word means to overlay, to superimpose.** It indicates the covering of someone or something: with a veil (2 Sam. 15:30; Esther 6:12; Jer. 14:3, 4), with something to hide a guilty person's face (Esther 7:8). Figuratively, it describes the security, success, and wealth of Israel at home (Ps. 68:13) with wings covered or sheathed (NIV) with silver. Used literally of metals, it means to overlay something (2 Chr. 3:5, 7–9; also translated to line, to panel). ¶

[2] ***ḥāp̱ap̱*** [verb: חָפַף <2653>; a prim. root (comp. <2645> above, BAREFOOT <3182>)] ▶ **This word indicates to enclose, to shield; it is also translated to shelter, to surround.** It means to protect and guard. The Lord protected or shielded Benjamin (Deut. 33:12). ¶

[3] ***ṭālal*** [verb: טָלַל <2926>; a prim. root] ▶ **This word means to cover something with a roof, to supply a roof.** It indicates the process of constructing a covering for the Fountain Gate in Jerusalem after the return of the exiles from Babylon (Neh. 3:15; also translated to roof). ¶

[4] ***yā'aṭ*** [verb: יָעַט <3271>; a prim. root] ▶ **This word indicates wrapping oneself with a garment.** Ref.: Is. 61:10; some relate this verb to *'āṭāh* (WRAP AROUND <5844> a.); also translated to wrap, to array. It is used figuratively to indicate the Lord covering a person with garments of salvation. ¶

[5] ***kāsāh*** [verb: כָּסָה <3680>; a prim. root] ▶ **This word also means to clothe, to conceal. The active meaning of this verb is to cover, to cover up, i.e., to put something over.** It is used in a literal sense to indicate that something is covering something else, as when the waters of the Red Sea covered the Egyptians or the cloud of God's glory covered Mount Sinai or the Tabernacle (Ex. 15:5; 24:15). In a metaphorical sense, the word describes shame covering the guilty (Ps. 69:7; Jer. 3:25; Hab. 2:17); the Israelites' covering the altar with tears (Mal. 2:13); and the concealing of Joseph's blood to hide his brothers' guilt and sin (Gen. 37:26). On the other hand, the psalmist found reconciliation with God by not concealing his sin but confessing it (Ps. 32:5; Prov. 10:11). The word sometimes means to cover oneself with clothing or sackcloth, to clothe oneself with something (Ezek. 16:18; Jon. 3:6).

The passive form of the verb means to be covered, such as when the mountains were covered by the waters of the great flood (Gen. 7:19; Ps. 80:10). The reflexive form is used to mean to cover oneself; e.g., when the people of Nineveh covered themselves in repentance at Jonah's preaching (Jon. 3:8). The word in Ecclesiastes 6:4 describes the name of a stillborn child covering itself in darkness. *

[6] ***kāp̱ar*** [verb: כָּפַר <3722>; a prim. root] ▶ **This word means to forgive, to expiate, to reconcile. It is of supreme theological importance in the Old Testament as it is central to an Old Testament understanding of the remission of sin.** At its most basic level, the word conveys the notion of covering but not in the sense of merely concealing. Rather, it suggests the imposing of something to change its appearance or nature. It is therefore employed to signify the cancellation or "writing over" of a contract (Is. 28:18: to annul, to cancel, to disannul); the appeasing of anger (Gen. 32:20; Prov. 16:14: to appease, to pacify); and the overlaying of wood with pitch so as to make it waterproof (Gen. 6:14). The word also communicates God's covering of sin (as on the Day of Atonement, called Yom Kippur or literally, «Day of Covering,» Lev. 16:30–34; 23:27, 28). Persons made reconciliation with God for their sins by imposing something that would appease the offended party (in this case the Lord) and cover the sinners with

righteousness (Ex. 32:30; Ezek. 45:17; cf. Dan. 9:24: to make atonement). In the Old Testament, the blood of sacrifices was most notably imposed (Ex. 30:10: to make atonement). By this imposition, sin was purged (Ps. 79:9: to forgive, to atone, to make atonement, to purge away; Is. 6:7: to purge, to forgive, to atone) and forgiven (Ps. 78:38: to forgive, to atone). The offenses were removed, leaving the sinners clothed in righteousness (cf. Zech. 3:3, 4: to clothe). Of course, the imposition of the blood of bulls and of goats could never fully cover our sin (see Heb. 10:4), but with the coming of Christ and the imposition of His shed blood, a perfect atonement was made (Rom. 5:9–11). *

[7] ***lā'aṭ*** [verb: לָאַט <3813>; a prim. root] ▶ **This word refers to shielding or hiding one's face as a gesture of sorrow and shock.** This is what King David did at the death of Absalom (2 Sam. 19:4). ¶

[8] ***sāḵaḵ, śāḵaḵ*** [verb: סָכַךְ, שָׂכַךְ <5526>; a prim. root (properly, to entwine as a screen)] ▶

a. This word means to hide something or to shield something. The mercy seat on the ark of the covenant was covered by the wings of cherubim (Ex. 25:20); God's hand covered and protected Moses (Ex. 33:22). It is used of separating off an area with a curtain or hanging (Ex. 40:3, 21). Figuratively, it shows God shielding those who trust Him (Ps. 5:11; 91:4); He covers Himself in anger (Lam. 3:43) or with a cloud (Lam. 3:44). *

b. This word also means to stir up, to excite; it is also translated to spur, to incite, to set. It means to rouse up, to spur on in the context of the Lord's action (Is. 9:11; 19:2). ¶

c. This word also means to knit together. It describes the Lord's activity in creating a child's fetus within the womb (Job 10:11; Ps. 139:13). ¶

[9] ***sāp̱an*** [verb: סָפַן <5603>; from an unused root meaning to depress] ▶

a. This word means to put panels over something else. It indicates covering or paneling a structure with some material (1 Kgs. 6:9; 7:3, 7), especially the Solomonic Temple and palace. This was considered a sinful, social luxury by later prophets (Jer. 22:14; Hag. 1:4; KJV: cieled). ¶

b. A verb meaning to reserve for resting. It refers to setting up or aside a section or portion of something for someone. In context it means to reserve something for a ruler (Deut. 33:21; also translated to keep, to be seated). ¶

c. A verb meaning to protect as a treasure. It indicates covering and hiding something as a valuable possession or resource, especially resources of the Promised Land of Canaan (Deut. 33:19). ¶

[10] ***'ālap̱*** [verb: עָלַף <5968>; a prim. root] ▶ **This word means in context to hide one's identity by wrapping oneself in something.** Ref.: Gen. 38:14. It also means simply to cast over and is used to describe the bridegroom's abdomen in an amorous way, meaning set, decorated, inlaid (Song 5:14; also translated overlaid, bedecked). The Hebrew word also means to grow weak; see FAINT (verb) <5968>. ¶

[11] ***qāram*** [verb: קָרַם <7159>; a prim. root] ▶ **This word is used figuratively of the Lord's putting skin over the desiccated bones of a destroyed Israel.** Refs.: Ezek. 37:6, 8. ¶

– [12] Ex. 2:3 ➔ COAT (verb) <2560> [13] Job 14:17 ➔ SMEAR <2950> [14] Ps. 5:12 ➔ CROWN (noun and verb) <5849> b. [15] Ps. 73:6 ➔ TURN (verb) <5848> a. [16] Ps. 139:11 ➔ BRUISE (verb) <7779> c. [17] Prov. 7:16 ➔ SPREAD (verb) <7234> [18] Is. 25:7; 30:1 ➔ SPREAD (verb) <5259> [19] Lam. 3:16 ➔ COWER (MAKE) <3728>.

COVER, ATONEMENT COVER – Ex. 25:17–22; Lev. 16:2; etc. ➔ MERCY SEAT <3727>.

COVERED – [1] ***ṣāḇ*** [masc. noun: צָב <6632>; from an unused root meaning to establish] ▶

a. This word, combined with *'ᵃg ālāh* <5699>, refers to a cart, a wagon with a top. It indicates a transportation vehicle, most probably a covered wagon or possibly a litter on which people are carried (Num. 7:3; Is. 66:20).

b. A noun meaning a litter. It refers to a basic framework built to carry a person or persons on it, a stretcher for carrying the sick (Is. 66:20; NIV: chariot).
c. A noun referring to a great lizard. It refers to a creature of the reptile family (Uromastix spinipes) (Lev. 11:29, NASB, NIV, ESV, NKJV). It was unclean, not edible by Israel.
d. A noun referring to a tortoise. It refers to a turtle that lives on land. It was not edible to Israel since it was considered unclean (Lev. 11:29, KJV). ¶
– 2 Ezek. 41:16 ➔ PANELED <7824>.

COVERED WAY – ***mûsak*** [masc. noun: מוּסַךְ <4329>; from COVER (verb) <5526> a.] ▶ **This word means a structure with something over it, a canopy; it is also translated covert, pavilion.** Its exact meaning is unknown, but it is an architectural term probably referring to a covering structure (2 Kgs. 16:18). ¶

COVERING – 1 ***kāsûy*** [masc. noun: כָּסוּי <3681>; pass. part. of COVER (verb) <3680>] ▶ **This word refers to something being used (e.g., a blanket) to conceal and protect objects; it is also translated cover.** It is used to describe a covering of animal skins used in the transporting of articles from the Tabernacle (Num. 4:6, 14). ¶
2 ***kᵉsûṯ*** [fem. noun: כְּסוּת <3682>; from COVER (verb) <3680>] ▶ **This is used figuratively of the "blanket" provided by the payment of an offense against someone.** Ref.: Gen. 20:16. It refers literally to clothing in general or a cloak (Ex. 21:10; 22:27; Deut. 22:12; Job 24:7; 31:19). It is used figuratively of God bringing dark clouds to cover the sky (Is. 50:3) and of His power to see destruction, since it cannot be covered from His eyes (Job 26:6). ¶
3 ***lôṭ*** [masc. noun: לוֹט <3875>; from WRAP <3874>] ▶ **This word means a wrapping; it is also translated shroud.** It indicates the inability of people to perceive God and His works clearly (Is. 25:7). In this verse, Isaiah uses the noun and verb forms together meaning the covering that covers or the shroud that enfolds. This is a reference to the power of Christ's redemptive work to destroy that covering and to open the eyes of the blind (see 2 Cor. 3:14–16; 4:4–6). ¶
4 ***mikseh*** [masc. noun: מִכְסֶה <4372>; from COVER (verb) <3680>] ▶ **This word refers to something used to shelter, protect, or enclose an object.** Such things are Noah's ark or the Tent of Meeting or Tabernacle (Gen. 8:13; Ex. 26:14; 35:11). The covering of the Tabernacle was made double of ram's skins and porpoise skins. *
5 ***mᵉkasseh*** [masc. noun: מְכַסֶּה <4374>; from COVER (verb) <3680>] ▶ **This word is used of the fatty tissue (omentum) covering the entrails of animals of sacrifice.** Ref.: Lev. 9:19. It is used metaphorically of worms crawling over a person in Sheol (Is. 14:11). It indicates the clothing or covering the Lord confiscated from Tyre for His people (Is. 23:18: clothing, clothes, attire; Ezek. 27:7: awning). ¶
6 ***mᵉsukāh*** [fem. noun: מְסֻכָה <4540>; from COVER (verb) <5526> a.] ▶ **This word indicates also an outward adornment.** It is used figuratively of the outward splendor and dress of the king of Tyre and, according to some exegetes, Satan in the Garden of Eden in a literal sense (Ezek. 28:13). ¶
7 ***massêkāh*** [fem. noun: מַסֵּכָה <4541>; from POUR OUT <5258>] ▶ **This word means a pouring over; it usually denotes an image, molten metal, an alliance.** When the word means a libation or drink offering, it is associated with sacrifices that seal a covenant relationship (Is. 25:7; 28:20; 30:1); however, the word usually signifies an image or molten metal. In those cases, the word identifies an idol, which has been formed from molten metal and has been poured into a cast. The worship of such images is clearly prohibited by God (Ex. 34:17; Lev. 19:4; Deut. 27:15). The Israelites were commanded to destroy any idols they discovered in Canaan (Num. 33:52). The prophets proclaimed the futility of all idols, including those described as *massêkāh* (Is. 42:17); and God would punish those who worshiped them (Hos. 13:2–3; Nah. 1:14; Hab. 2:18). In spite of all this,

the Israelites formed and worshiped idols, including molten idols like Aaron's golden calf (Ex. 32:4, 8; Deut. 9:16; Neh. 9:18); Micah's idols (Judg. 17:3, 4; 18:17, 18); and Jeroboam's idols (1 Kgs. 14:9; cf. 1 Kgs. 12:28–30). *

8 ***marbād*** [masc. noun: מַרְבַד <4765>; from SPREAD (verb) <7234>] ▶ **This word refers to something similar to an afghan or a decorative blanket or to clothing.** Refs.: Prov. 7:16; 31:22. It is also translated tapestry, covering of tapestry. ¶

9 ***sēter, sitrāh*** [masc. and fem. noun: סֵתֶר, סִתְרָה <5643>; from HIDE <5641>] ▶

a. A masculine noun meaning a hiding place, a secret. It is used as an adverb meaning secretly (Deut. 13:6); literally, in secret (Deut. 27:15, 24; 28:57; Jer. 37:17; 38:16; 40:15). It modifies other words: a secret matter, a matter/word of secrecy (Judg. 3:19). It is equated with darkness as the hiding place of God (Ps. 18:11); and of God as the hiding place, the refuge, of those who need help (Ps. 32:7; 61:4). *

b. A feminine noun indicating a hiding place, a shelter, protection. It is used mockingly of pagan gods being hiding places for their worshipers (Deut. 32:38). ¶

– 10 Gen. 3:7 ➔ BELT <2290> 11 Song 3:10 ➔ SADDLE <4817> 12 Is. 4:5 ➔ CHAMBER <2646>.

COVET – Deut. 5:21 ➔ DESIRE (verb) <183>.

COVERT – 1 2 Kgs. 16:18 ➔ COVERED WAY <4329> 2 Ps. 61:4 ➔ COVERING <5643> a. 3 Is. 4:6 ➔ SHELTER <4563> 4 Jer. 25:38 ➔ ABODE <5520>.

COVETOUSNESS – See PROFIT (noun) <1215>.

COW – ***pārāh*** [fem. noun: פָּרָה <6510>; fem. of BULL, YOUNG BULL <6499>] ▶ **This word refers to female cattle, including heifers and cows yielding milk.** Heifers are female cattle that have not yet borne a calf. Israel is likened to a stubborn heifer (Hos. 4:16). It is used derisively of the rich, narcissistic women of Bashan, "cows of Bashan" (Amos 4:1). *

COWER (MAKE) – ***kāpaš*** [verb: כָּפַשׁ <3728>; a prim. root] ▶ **This word means to bend, to trample down, to humiliate, to cover over.** This word is a primary root, but it is used only once in the Hebrew Bible. There the writer of Lamentations felt like he was trampled in the dust (Lam. 3:16). ¶

COWERING PRISONER – Is. 51:14 ➔ CAPTIVE EXILE <6808>.

COZBI – ***kozbiy*** [fem. proper noun: כָּזְבִּי <3579>; from LIAR (BE A) <3576>]: lying, deceitful ▶ **A Midianite woman who was killed with Zimri, a man of Israel, by Phineas on account of Peor.** Refs.: Num. 25:15, 18; see the entire chapter. ¶

COZEBA – ***kōzēba'*** [proper noun: כֹּזֵבָא <3578>; from LIAR (BE A) <3576>]: lying, deceitful ▶ **A town of Judah.** Ref.: 1 Chr. 4:22; also translated Chozeba, Kozeba. ¶

CRACKNEL – 1 Kgs. 14:3 ➔ MOLDY <5350>.

CRAFT – Is. 2:16 ➔ VESSEL <7914> b.

CRAFTILY – Ex. 21:14 ➔ PRUDENCE <6195>.

CRAFTILY (DEAL) – 1 Ps. 105:25 ➔ DECEIVE <5230> 2 Jer. 9:4 ➔ SUPPLANT <6117>.

CRAFTINESS – ***'ōrem*** [masc. noun: עֹרֶם <6193>; from CRAFTY (BE) <6191>] ▶ **This word means wiliness, cunningness. It is used only once in the Hebrew Bible, in the book of Job.** Eliphaz told Job that God catches the wise in their craftiness. He cannot be fooled (Job 5:13; NASB: shrewdness). ¶

CRAFTSMAN – 1 ***'āmôn*** [masc. noun: אָמוֹן <527>; a variation from MULTITUDE <1995>] ▶ **This word means either a skilled artisan or a throng of people.** In Proverbs 8:30, the sense is that of a master architect or artisan (see MASTER WORKMAN <525>). The other appearances in

Jeremiah 46:25 and 52:15 seem to designate a general multitude of people. ¶

[2] ***ḥōrēš*** [masc. noun: חֹרֵשׁ <2794>; act. part. of SILENT (BE) <2790> (in the sense of doing skill work)] ▶ **This word indicates a worker in bronze and iron.** Ref.: Gen. 4:22; KJV: artificer. Others understand this as referring to implements, instruments, or tools (NIV, NASB, ESV). ¶

[3] ***ḥārāš*** [masc. noun: חָרָשׁ <2796>; from SILENT (BE) <2790> (in the sense of doing skill work)] ▶ **This word also means artisan, engraver. It denotes a craftsman who is skilled in a given medium.** It appears in reference to one skilled in metalwork (1 Chr. 29:5; Hos. 13:2); one skilled in woodwork (1 Chr. 14:1; Is. 40:20); and one skilled in stonework (Ex. 28:11). More broadly, the term is applied to those who make their living by fashioning idols (Is. 45:16); or one highly skilled in his or her vocation (Ezek. 21:31). *

CRAFTY (BE) – [1] ***'āram*** [verb: עָרַם <6191>; a prim. root (properly, to be or make bare)] ▶ **This word means to be shrewd, to be subtle; it is also translated to be very cunning, to deal very subtilly (KJV), to become shrewd.** This verb has a neutral tone but can assume either a negative tone: crafty and tricky (1 Sam. 23:22; Ps. 83:3); or a positive tone: prudent and wise (Prov. 15:5; 19:25; also translated sensible). ¶

– [2] Gen. 3:1; Job 5:12; 15:5 ➔ PRUDENT <6175>.

CRAG – Is. 2:21 ➔ CLEFT <5585>.

CRAMPED (BE) – Job 20:22; Is. 49:19 ➔ DISTRESSED (BE) <3334>.

CRAMPING – Job 36:16 ➔ CONSTRAINT <4164>.

CRANE – [1] ***'āg̱ûr*** [masc. noun: עָגוּר <5693>; pass. part. (but with act. sense) of an unused root meaning to twitter] ▶ **This word refers to a kind of bird, a crane (i.e., a large, tall wading bird), a swallow, or a thrush.** It is used in a simile referring to the noise this bird makes, a twittering, troubling sound (Is. 38:14). The bird's observance of its appointed instincts are praised, compared to Israel's failure to observe her responsibilities to God (Jer. 8:7). ¶

– [2] Is. 38:14; Jer. 8:7 ➔ HORSE <5483> b.

CRASH – Is. 37:26 ➔ WASTE (LAY, LIE) <7582>.

CRASH (TERRIBLE) – Is. 10:33 ➔ TERROR <4637>.

CRASHING – Job 36:33 ➔ NOISE <7452>.

CRAVE – [1] ***'āḵap̱*** [verb: אָכַף <404>; a prim. root] ▶ **This word means to beg, to constrain; it is also translated to urge, to drive on.** It depicts the need, drive or urge to work that hunger creates in the laborer (Prov. 16:26). ¶

– [2] Mic. 7:1 ➔ DESIRE (verb) <183>.

CRAVING – Jer. 2:24 ➔ DESIRE (noun) <185>.

CRAWL – ***zāḥal*** [verb: זָחַל <2119>; a prim. root] ▶ **This verb means to move close to the ground. It also means to fear, to be afraid.** It can refer to the movement of a snake on the ground (Deut. 32:24: serpent, crawling thing, viper; Mic. 7:17: snake, worm, reptile, crawling thing, creature that crawls). It can also be a metaphor for an individual who is afraid or one who creeps forward slowly and cautiously (Job 32:6: to be afraid, to be timid, to be fearful). ¶

CRAWLING THING – Deut. 32:24; Mic. 7:17 ➔ CRAWL <2119>.

CREAM – See BUTTER <2529>.

CREATE – ***bārā'*** [verb: בָּרָא <1254>; a prim. root] ▶ **Only God is the subject of this verb meaning to make by producing something new, to cause to come into existence.** It is used for His creating: heaven and earth (Gen. 1:1); humanity (Gen. 1:27); the heavenly host (Is. 40:26);

the ends of the earth (Is. 40:28); north and south (Ps. 89:12); righteousness and salvation (Is. 45:8); evil (Is. 45:7). David asked God to "create" in him a clean heart (Ps. 51:10). Isaiah promised that God will create a new heaven and earth (Is. 65:17).

There are other roots that are spelled the same, but have different meanings. These include: to make fat (1 Sam. 2:29); to clear timber (Josh. 17:15, 18; Ezek. 23:47); and to choose (Ezek. 21:19, KJV). *

CREATURE – Is. 13:21: doleful creature, howling creature ➔ OWL <255>.

CREATURE (LIVING, MOVING) – ***šereṣ*** [masc. noun: שֶׁרֶץ <8318>; from MULTIPLY <8317>] ▶ **This word indicates a being that crawls or swarms; insects or small animals.** God created them in the beginning (Gen. 1:20); they also died in the great flood (Gen. 7:21). These teeming (NASB) creatures included fish and whatever may be in the rivers and seas (Lev. 11:10; Deut. 14:19). If they had no scales, they were detestable, unclean to Israel for food. *

CREDITOR – [1] Deut. 15:2 ➔ LOAN <4874> [2] 2 Kgs. 4:1; Ps. 109:11; Is. 24:2; 50:1 ➔ LEND <5383> [3] Hab. 2:7 ➔ BITE <5391> b.

CREEP – [1] ***rāmaś*** [verb: רָמַשׂ <7430>; a prim. root] ▶ **This word means to move lightly. It indicates locomotion or traveling by going slowly along the ground on hands and knees for a person by wiggling or crawling for animals, insects, etc.** God created all these living beings that creep, crawl, or wiggle in order to move (Gen. 1:21; 26, 28, 30; 7:8, 14, 21; 8:17, 19; 9:2; Lev. 11:44, 46). These kinds of creatures were detestable, so Israel could not eat them (Lev. 20:25). The word has the general sense of movement, whatever moves (Ps. 69:34) or prowls (Ps. 104:20). *
– [2] Lev. 11:29, 41; etc. ➔ MULTIPLY <8317> a.

CREEPING THING – ***remeś*** [masc. coll. noun: רֶמֶשׂ <7431>; from CREEP <7430>] ▶ **This word also means moving things. It describes a large category of living beings that God created. It does not include large animals or birds. It includes many small animals, reptiles, beings that crawl, creep, move randomly, etc., along the earth.** God created them (Gen. 1:24–26). The phrase from mankind (*'āḏām*) to animals (beasts, *bᵉhêmāh*) to creeping things (*remeś*) to fowl (*'ôp̱*) is inclusive of what God affected in the flood (Gen. 6:7; 6:20). It indicates the extent of Solomon's great knowledge of the world (1 Kgs. 4:33). This word also describes swarming things that inhabit the seas (Ps. 104:25). Even these became idols to Israel (Ezek. 8:10). But, in the time of restoration, even these beings will be regarded as important by God (Hos. 2:18). It is used in a simile comparing rebellious Israel to these creatures (Hab. 1:14). *

CRESCENT, CRESCENT ORNAMENT – Judg. 8:21, 26; Is. 3:18 ➔ ORNAMENT <7720>.

CREST – Esther 6:8 ➔ CROWN (noun) <3804>.

CREVICE – Is. 7:19; Jer. 13:4; 16:16 ➔ CLEFT <5357>.

CRIB – ***'ēḇûs*** [masc. noun: אֵבוּס <18>; from FATTENED <75>] ▶ **The word means a stall; it is also translated manger, trough.** It is associated with a donkey (Is. 1:3); oxen where it may mean a trough for feeding (Prov. 14:4); and the wild ox (Job 39:9). ¶

CRICKET – [1] ***ḥargōl*** [masc. noun: חַרְגֹּל <2728>; from TREMBLING (COME) <2727>] ▶ **This word refers to a leaping and chirping insect. It also refers to a locust.** It refers to a winged insect that was considered clean and therefore edible by God's holy people (Lev. 11:22; KJV: beetle). John the Baptist ate locusts and wild honey. ¶
– [2] Deut. 28:42 ➔ WHIRRING <6767> c.

CRIME – Dan. 6:22 ➔ WRONG (noun) <2248>.

CRIMSON – [1] ***karmiyl*** [masc. noun: כַּרְמִיל <3758>; prob. of foreign origin] ▶ **This word indicates a cherry red color.** It refers to a dye and items colored by it, such as cloth or fabric (2 Chr. 2:7, 14; 2 Chr. 3:14). It was among items gathered for use in Solomon's Temple. ¶

[2] ***tôlā', tôlê'āh, tôla'aṯ*** [masc. noun: תּוֹלָע, תּוֹלֵעָה, תּוֹלַעַת <8438>; from DEVOUR <3216>] ▶

a. This color refers to the deep red color of one's sins that stands out in a shocking way, drawing attention to its intensity. God can make sins white, cleanse them away (Is. 1:18). These colors also are associated with royalty, palatial living, etc. (Lam. 4:5: scarlet, purple).

b. A masculine noun meaning a worm. It refers to some kind of soft-bodied animal that lives underground, in water, or as a parasite, which was the case of worms that fed on manna, putrefying it (Ex. 16:20; NIV: maggot).

c. This word also means crimson (bright red), purple, scarlet. It refers to the colors attributed by scholars to expensive cloth materials or threads, ropes, chains, etc. of cloth, used in the materials found in the Tabernacle and its furnishings (Ex. 25:4; etc.; Num. 4:8). A scarlet string was involved in the ritual of cleansing a leper (Lev. 14:4, 6); a house (Lev. 14:49, 51, 52); and in the law of the red heifer (Num. 19:6).

d. This word refers to some parasitic worm or insect larvae that destroyed manna and vineyards. Refs.: Ex. 16:20; Deut. 28:39. A worm destroyed Jonah's favorite shade plant (Jon. 4:7). It is used to describe the low character and estate of a person as a worm (Job 25:6; Ps. 22:6; Is. 41:14). It is described figuratively as the bedding provided in Sheol (Is. 14:11); a permanent tormenting feature of Sheol (Is. 66:24).

e. A masculine noun referring to a string. It refers to a scarlet string (*š^{e}nî tôla'aṯ*) used in several cleansing rituals (Lev. 14:4, 6, 49, 51, 52). *

CRIMSON (STAINED) – Is. 63:1 ➔ LEAVENED (BE) <2556>.

CRIMSONED – Is. 63:1 ➔ LEAVENED (BE) <2556>.

CRIPPLED – ***nāḵeh*** [adj.: נָכֶה <5223>; no information on root] ▶ **This word means maimed and also means smitten. It refers to the result of a physical accident or attack.** In context Saul's son had been dropped as a child and the bones in his feet were broken as a result, and he was crippled (2 Sam. 4:4; 9:3: lame, disabled). It is used in the phrase *nāḵeh rû(a)ḥ*, smitten of spirit, humble (Is. 66:2: contrite). ¶

CRISPING PIN – Is. 3:22 ➔ money purse ➔ BAG <2754>.

CRITICIZE – Is. 29:24 ➔ MURMUR <7279>.

CROCODILE – Lev. 11:30 ➔ LIZARD (MONITOR) <3581>.

CROCUS – Is. 35:1 ➔ ROSE <2261>.

CROOKBACKT – Lev. 21:20 ➔ HUNCHBACK <1384>.

CROOKED – [1] ***h^{a}paḵpaḵ*** [adj.: הֲפַכְפַּךְ <2019>; by reduplication from TURN (verb) <2015>] ▶ **This word denotes something perverted, devious; it is also translated perverse, froward.** It describes the winding, crooked, serpentine path of a guilty person (Prov. 21:8). ¶

[2] ***^{a}qalqal*** [adj.: עֲקַלְקַל <6128>; from PERVERTED <6127>] ▶ **This word means roundabout, winding, twisted.** It is used of a twisting, turning detour taken in order to reach one's destination (Judg. 5:6: byway, roundabout way, winding path). It is used figuratively of the crooked, immoral ways of the wicked (Ps. 125:5: crooked way). ¶

[3] ***'iqq^{e}šûṯ*** [fem. noun: עִקְּשׁוּת <6143>; from PERVERSE <6141>] ▶ **This word means perversion, deceitfulness; it is also translated perversity, deceitful, forward, corrupt, perverse.** It is used to describe a mouth that speaks without integrity, that does not speak truth but rather deception

and immorality; a mark of an evil, worthless person (Prov. 4:24: perversity; 6:12). ¶
[4] ***pᵉṯaltōl*** [adj.: פְּתַלְתֹּל <6618>; from WRESTLE <6617> (in the sense of to be shrewd, to be cunning, to be devious)] ▶ **This word is used in a negative sense of being wickedly cunning, distorted, ingenuous, used of God's people in their rebellious ways.** Ref.: Deut. 32:5; ESV: twisted. ¶
– [5] Deut. 32:5; etc. ➔ PERVERSE <6141> [6] Job 26:13 ➔ FLEEING <1281> [7] Is. 27:1 ➔ TWISTING <6129> [8] Is. 40:4 ➔ DECEITFUL <6121>.

CROOKED (MAKE, BE) – ***ʿāqaš*** [verb: עָקַשׁ <6140>; a prim. root] ▶ **This word means to be twisted, to be perverse; to prove something perverted, distorted.** It refers to moral, ethical, social, and legal perversion. It is the opposite of *tām*, perfect, indicating that something is out of order, guilty, wrong, perverse (Job 9:20). It is the opposite of upright, straight, level, indicating that something is uneven, twisted (Prov. 10:9; Mic. 3:9). It refers to a person who leads a crooked life (Prov. 28:18; Is. 59:8). ¶

CROOKED PLACES, CROOKED THINGS – Is. 42:16 ➔ ROUGH PLACES <4625>.

CROOKEDNESS – ***selep̱*** [masc. noun: סֶלֶף <5558>; from OVERTHROW (verb) <5557> (in the sense of to distort)] ▶ **This word refers to a distorted and perverse way of life or character.** Refs.: Prov. 11:3; 15:4; also translated perversity, perverseness, perversion, duplicity. ¶

CROP – [1] ***leqeš*** [masc. noun: לֶקֶשׁ <3954>; from GLEAN <3953>] ▶ **This word indicates spring yield, a second yield; late grass.** It identifies a late, second spring crop, especially important for the grazing of animals (Amos 7:1; KJV, ESV: growth). ¶
[2] ***murʾāh*** [fem. noun: מֻרְאָה <4760>; apparently fem. pass. causative part. of SEE <7200>] ▶ **This word refers to a small sack-like expansion of a bird's gullet or possibly the entire stomach.** Ref.: Lev. 1:16. ¶
– [3] Lev. 26:4, 20; Judg. 6:4; Ps. 78:46; Ezek. 34:27; Hag. 1:10; Zech. 8:12 ➔ INCREASE (noun) <2981> [4] Deut. 22:9 ➔ HARVEST <4395>.

CROSSROAD – ***pereq*** [masc. noun: פֶּרֶק <6563>; from BREAK OFF <6561>] ▶ **This word indicates a fork in the way.** It refers to a place where roads meet and thus where many people will pass by (Obad. 1:14). The Hebrew word also means robbery, pillage; see PLUNDER (noun) <6563>. ¶

CROSSWAY – Obad. 1:14 ➔ CROSSROAD <6563>.

CROUCH – Ps. 10:10 ➔ CRUSH <1794>.

CROWD – Joel 2:8 ➔ AFFLICT <1766>.

CROWD AROUND – Dan. 3:27 ➔ GATHER <3673>.

CROWN (noun) – [1] ***keṯer*** [masc. noun: כֶּתֶר <3804>; from SURROUND <3803>] ▶ **An ornament worn on a king's head to symbolize his power and authority.** A crown, probably a high turban, befitted a Persian king or queen (Esther 1:11; 2:17). A decoration of some kind was placed on a royal horse to honor its rider (Esther 6:8; also translated crest). ¶
[2] ***ʿᵃṭārāh*** [fem. noun: עֲטָרָה <5850>; from CROWN (noun and verb) <5849>] ▶ **It was a circlet or headdress worn by a king to symbolize his power and authority.** Crowns were often made of silver or gold with jewels set in them (2 Sam. 12:30; Esther 8:15; Zech. 6:11, 14). It could be a garland or a wreath as well, symbolizing the same thing. It is used figuratively of honor (Job 19:9); of a wife of character (Prov. 12:4); of a crown granted by wisdom (Prov. 4:9); of a "crown" worn by the greatest drunkards of Ephraim (Is. 28:1). In a metaphor, it pictures Jerusalem as God's crown (Is. 62:3). In the greatest metaphor, God is described as the ultimate crown of His people (Is. 28:5). *

3 ***ṣᵉp̱iyrāh*** [fem. noun: צְפִירָה <6843>; fem. formed like MALE GOAT <6842>] ▶
a. It is an ornament formed and worn in a way to indicate authority. It is used figuratively of God's becoming the diadem, the crown of the returned remnant of His people (Is. 28:5).
b. This word means a turn of affairs and is translated doom. In context it has the sense of doom (crown of doom?) and destruction richly deserved by Israel (Ezek. 7:7, 10).
c. This word also indicates morning. It refers to the time of the judgment of God, the time He arrives, the morning of that day (Ezek. 7:7, 10). ¶
– 4 2 Sam. 1:10; 2 Kgs. 11:12; etc. ➔ CONSECRATION <5145> 5 See MOLDING <2213>.

CROWN (noun and verb) – ***'āṭar*** [verb: עָטַר <5849>; a prim. root] ▶
a. This word is used figuratively of God's investiture of humankind as the kings and rulers of His creation, reflecting His image. Ref.: Ps. 8:5. It is used figuratively of God's granting a bountiful crop for the year (Ps. 65:11); or crowning His people with spiritual blessings (Ps. 103:4). It depicts Tyre as a powerful merchant city, granting royal favors (crowns) to the nations (Is. 23:8). It describes the crowning of persons on their wedding day (Song 3:11). ¶
b. This word means to surround, to encompass. It means to encircle, to entrap by encircling an enemy (1 Sam. 23:26: to encircle, to surround, to compass, to close in). It means to abundantly bless people, to shower them with something; in context God's approval and blessing (Ps. 5:12: to surround, to compass, to cover). ¶

CROWN (verb) – Prov. 14:18 ➔ SURROUND <3803>.

CROWNED ONE – ***minnᵉzār*** [masc. noun: מִנְּזָר <4502>; from SEPARATE <5144> (in the sense of to consecrate)] ▶
a. This word denotes a consecrated one, an anointed one. It refers to a dedicated courtier or guardsman serving the king (Nah. 3:17; also translated prince, commander). ¶
b. For other translators, this word refers to a guardsman, a guard. It refers to dedicated courtiers at court serving the monarchy in some way (Nah. 3:17). ¶

CRUCIBLE – 1 ***maṣrēp̱*** [masc. noun: מַצְרֵף <4715>; from REFINE <6884>] ▶ **This word defines a refining pot (KJV: fining pot).** It indicates a metal pot in which the impurities of precious metals were separated out (Prov. 17:3; 27:21). ¶
– 2 Ps. 12:6 ➔ FURNACE <5948>.

CRUEL – 1 ***'aḵzār*** [adj.: אַכְזָר <393>; from an unused root (apparently meaning to act harshly)] ▶ **This word means harsh, deadly.** It refers to the deadly or cruel venom of cobras (Deut. 32:33). Job calls God's actions toward him cruel (Job 30:21; also translated ruthlessly), and God accuses His own people of being cruel (Lam. 4:3; also translated heartless). It is rendered fierce to describe Leviathan (Job 41:10). ¶
2 ***'aḵzāriy*** [adj.: אַכְזָרִי <394>; from <393> above] ▶ **This word describes brutal persons, who are often contrasted to the person who is merciful or righteous.** Refs.: Prov. 5:9; 11:17; 12:10; 17:11. It refers to the cruel day of the Lord (Is. 13:9) which features the savagery of the cruel warriors of Babylon (Jer. 6:23; 30:14; 50:42). ¶
3 ***'aḵzᵉriyyûṯ*** [fem. abstract noun: אַכְזְרִיּוּת <395>; from <394> above] ▶ **This word indicates harshness, fierceness.** It is used to describe wrath or anger (Prov. 27:4); it is also translated fierce. ¶
– 4 Ps. 71:4 ➔ LEAVENED (BE) <2556>.

CRUELLY (TREAT, DEAL) – Job 39:16 ➔ HARDEN <7188>.

CRUELTY – Ezek. 34:4 ➔ SEVERITY <6530>.

CRUMBLE – Lev. 2:6 ➔ BREAK <6626>.

CRUMBLED – Josh. 9:5, 12 ➔ MOLDY <5350>.

CRUMBLY – Josh. 9:5, 12 ➔ MOLDY <5350>.

CRUSE – [1] 1 Sam. 26:11, 12, 16; 1 Kgs. 17:12, 14, 16; 19:6 ➔ JAR <6835> [2] 1 Kgs. 14:3 ➔ JAR <1228> [3] 2 Kgs. 2:20 ➔ BOWL <6746>.

CRUSH – [1] ***dāḵā'*** [verb: דָּכָא <1792>; a prim. root (comp. <1794> below)] ▶ **This word means to beat down, to bruise, to oppress. The Hebrew word is often used in a poetic or figurative sense.** Eliphaz spoke of those who lived in houses of clay, whose foundations were crushed easily (Job 4:19). The psalmist prayed that the king would crush an oppressor (Ps. 72:4) and accused the wicked of crushing the Lord's people (Ps. 94:5). The wise man exhorted others not to crush the needy in court (Prov. 22:22). Isaiah said that it was the Lord's will to crush the Servant (Is. 53:10). Metaphorically, this word can also be used in the same way the English word *crushed* is used to mean dejected or sad (Is. 19:10). *

[2] ***dāḵāh*** [verb: דָּכָה <1794>; a prim. root (comp. OPPRESSED <1790>, CRUSH <1792> above)] ▶ **This verb means to break in pieces; to crouch.** It is most often used figuratively of persons crushed emotionally and spiritually by the wicked (Ps. 10:10; KJV, NASB, NKJV, crouches); of persons weighed down and broken by their guilt before the Lord (Ps. 38:8) or seemingly under His judgment (Ps. 44:19); of bones broken by the Lord's imposition of guilt for sins (Ps. 51:8); of a broken spirit as an acceptable sacrifice to God (Ps. 51:17). ¶

[3] ***dᵉqaq*** [Aramaic verb: דקק <1855>; corresponding to BEAT <1854>] ▶ **This verb indicates the process of breaking into pieces, squashing.** It indicates the crushing of various objects in the book of Daniel: the stone crushed the feet of the statue (Dan. 2:34, 35, 45); the fourth monstrous kingdom broke all other kingdoms into pieces (Dan. 2:40); the kingdom of God will crush and destroy all other kingdoms (Dan. 2:44); the bones of Daniel's accusers were crushed (Dan. 6:24); the fourth beast will trample and crush the remainder of the earth (Dan. 7:7, 19, 23). ¶

[4] ***zûr*** [verb: זוּר <2115>; a prim. root; comp. DISTRESS (noun) <6695>] ▶ **This word indicates pressing or squeezing something out.** Ref.: Judg. 6:38. It indicates even crushing an object, such as an egg (Job 39:15; Is. 59:5). In a different context, it has a positive meaning of dressing a wound (Is. 1:6: to close, to press out, to cleanse). ¶

[5] ***kāṯaṯ*** [verb: כָּתַת <3807>; a prim. root] ▶ **This term means to beat, to hammer.** It is used in reference to the destruction of the golden calf (Deut. 9:21); and in the eschatological hope of hammering swords into plowshares (Is. 2:4; Mic. 4:3). It can also be used figuratively for destroying an enemy (Deut. 1:44). *

[6] ***māḥaq*** [verb: מָחַק <4277>; a prim. root] ▶ **This word means to utterly destroy.** It is used only once in the Old Testament, where it is used as a near synonym with *māḥaṣ* (PIERCE <4272>), meaning to wound severely, to pierce through, or to shatter. It describes Jael's actions in destroying Sisera by driving a tent peg between his temples (Judg. 5:26; also translated to pierce, to smash). ¶

[7] ***mā'aḵ*** [verb: מָעַךְ <4600>; a prim. root] ▶ **This word means to squeeze, to press, to bruise.** It means to press, crush, jab at something: to thrust an object into the ground (1 Sam. 26:7); to crush something, ruin it (Lev. 22:24, crushed testicles); to fondle or press something; used figuratively of Israel's breasts being pressed, fondled in her youth by pagan suitors (Ezek. 23:3, 21). ¶

– [8] Num. 11:8 ➔ BEAT <1743> [9] Num. 22:25 ➔ OPPRESS <3905> [10] Deut. 23:1 ➔ CRUSHING <1795> [11] Deut. 23:1 ➔ WOUND (verb) <6481> [12] Judg. 10:8 ➔ SHATTER <7492> [13] 2 Kgs. 19:25; Is. 6:11; 37:26 ➔ WASTE (LAY, LIE) <7582> [14] Job 40:12 ➔ TREAD DOWN <1915> [15] Ps. 119:20 ➔ BREAK <1638> [16] Prov. 27:22 ➔ GRIND <3806> [17] Dan. 2:35 ➔ PIECES (BREAK TO, IN) <1751> [18] Mal. 1:4 ➔ DEMOLISH <7567>.

CRUSHED – [1] ***gereś*** [masc. noun: גֶּרֶשׂ <1643>; from an unused root meaning to husk] ▶ **This word denotes that which is beaten, grits.** It designates early ripened crushed grains of wheat used as a grain offering (Lev. 2:14, 16), which the priest offered. ¶
[2] ***dakkā'*** [adj.: דַּכָּא <1793>; from CRUSH <1792>] ▶ **This word means destruction, a crumbled substance, an object compressed into a powder, or pulverized dust.** Thus, by extension, *dakkā'* can mean humble or contrite. God is the healer and rescuer of one who is crushed in spirit (Ps. 34:18). He also lives with those whose spirits are contrite and humble (Is. 57:15). It comes from the Hebrew verb *dāḵā'* (CRUSH <1792>), meaning to crush or to beat to pieces. It is translated destruction, dust in Psalm 90:3. ¶
[3] **which is crushed, that is crushed:** ***zûreh*** [masc. noun: זוּרֶה <2116>; from CRUSH <2115>] ▶ **This word refers to something compressed (or broken) from which something else breaks forth.** Ref.: Is. 59:5. ¶
[4] ***mārôaḥ*** [adj.: מָרוֹחַ <4790>; from APPLY <4799> (in the sense of to rub)] ▶ **This word indicates something pounded or compressed. It is used of testicles that have been crushed.** Ref.: Lev. 21:20; also translated damaged, broken. ¶
[5] ***nāḵē', nāḵā'*** [adj.: נָכֵא, נָכָא <5218>; from DRIVE OUT <5217> (in the sense of to smite)] ▶
a. This word means broken, beaten, wounded. It describes the life, the vitality, the drive, the spirit of a person that has been oppressed, broken by a grieved heart. A spirit broken, crushed, renders a person hopeless (Prov. 15:13; 17:22; 18:14). ¶
b. This word means stricken, broken, beaten. It is used of persons left in utter despair from judgment on Moab; they are grieved from the calamity (Is. 16:7). ¶
– [6] Prov. 26:28 ➔ OPPRESSED <1790>.

CRUSHED (BE) – Amos 2:13 ➔ WEIGHTED DOWN (BE) <5781>.

CRUSHING – ***dakkāh*** [fem. noun: דַּכָּה <1795>; from CRUSH <1794> like CRUSHED <1793>] ▶ **This word denotes the squeezing of the testicles.** Ref.: Deut. 23:1; KJV, wounded in the stones. ¶

CRUST – ***gûš*** [masc. noun: גּוּשׁ <1487>; of uncertain deriv.] ▶ **This word means a mass of earth, a lump; it is also translated a clod, a scab.** It refers to a diseased formation (NASB, a crust of dirt), scab, or irritation on the skin (Job 7:5), which in Job's case is described as festering or broken (NASB, runs). ¶

CRY (noun) – [1] ***ze'āqāh*** [fem. noun: זְעָקָה <2201>; from CRY OUT <2199>] ▶ **This word indicates a shout, an outcry, a crying out.** It refers to a plaintive crying out for aid or help by those oppressed in Sodom and Gomorrah (Gen. 18:20); or a shouting or wailing by captains or pilots of merchant ships because of economic calamity (Ezek. 27:28). It indicates ineffective and hopeless shouting directed toward fools who will not learn (Eccl. 9:17). And in general, it indicates a cry of distress because of war, destruction, pestilence (Is. 15:5; Jer. 18:22; 20:16); or a cry coming from the poor (Prov. 21:13). *
[2] ***ṣ'wāḥāh*** [fem. noun: צְוָחָה <6682>; from SHOUT (verb) <6681>] ▶ **In context this word refers to a shout of despair because of calamities or disasters striking God's people as well as Egypt in judgment.** Refs.: Ps. 144:14; Is. 24:11; Jer. 14:2; 46:12. ¶
[3] ***ṣ'āqāh*** [fem. noun: צְעָקָה <6818>; from CRY OUT <6817>] ▶ **This word describes a call for help, a shout of wailing and despair.** It describes the cries of outrage regarding sin that went up against Sodom and Gomorrah (Gen. 18:21; 19:13); and the outcries of Israel because of her oppression in Egypt (Ex. 3:7, 9). It is used of a deep, despairing cry over calamity (Ex. 11:6). The godless also utter cries of dismay (Job 27:9). Cries of deep distress will be a feature of the Day of the Lord (Zeph. 1:10). *
[4] ***rinnāh*** [fem. noun: רִנָּה <7440>; from SHOUT (verb) <7442>] ▶ **This word indicates glad shouting, joyful singing,**

crying out. It refers to the utterance and sound of a shout, a cry. It may be a sound or a cry to the Lord in supplication (1 Kgs. 8:28; Jer. 7:16); a cry of warning or of instructions (1 Kgs. 22:36); a cry of joy at the destruction of the wicked (Prov. 11:10; Is. 14:7). The Lord Himself cries out over His people (Zeph. 3:17). *

5 ***šûaʿ, shûaʿ*** [masc. noun: שׁוּעַ, שׁוּעַ <7769>; from CRY (verb) <7768>] ▶
a. This word designates a call for help, an exclamatory plea. It indicates a cry for help to God or people (Job 30:24), especially God (Ps. 5:2). ¶
b. This word refers to riches, wealth. It indicates one's abundant resources, excessive possessions, money, etc., so extensive that one might be tempted to rely on them, rather than on God, for help or deliverance (Job 36:19; ESV: cry for help). ¶

6 ***šewaʿ*** [masc. noun: שֶׁוַע <7773>; from CRY (verb) <7768>] ▶ **This word refers to a shout for help, an exclamatory plea.** It is used to describe the psalmist's cry to God for help, protection, and deliverance from the wicked (Ps. 5:2). ¶

7 ***šawᵉʿāh*** [fem. noun: שַׁוְעָה <7775>; fem. of CRY (noun) <7773>] ▶ **This word describes a shout for help.** It is used of Israel's cry to God for deliverance from Egyptian bondage (Ex. 2:23); and for a person's crying out to God for help in various situations (1 Sam. 5:12; Ps. 18:6; 34:15; 102:1; Jer. 8:19; Lam. 3:56). *

CRY (RAISE A WAR, RAISE A BATTLE) – Is. 42:13 ➔ CRY (verb) <6873>.

CRY (verb) – 1 ***pāʿāh*** [verb: פָּעָה <6463>; a prim. root] ▶ **This word means to shout, to call out, to groan.** It describes the behavior and sounds uttered in the throes of a woman giving birth but in context is used of God's crying out as He brought judgment on His people (Is. 42:14). ¶

2 ***ṣāraḥ*** [verb: צָרַח <6873>; a prim. root (in the sense of to be clear, e.g., in tone, i.e., shrill)] ▶ **This word indicates a roar, war shout.** It refers to a cry of despair by a warrior of Nineveh (Zeph. 1:14). It refers to the Lord's utterance of a war cry of attack as He goes forth to battle (Is. 42:13: to roar, to shout aloud, to raise a war cry, to raise a battle cry). ¶

3 ***šāwaʿ*** [verb: שָׁוַע <7768>; a prim. root] ▶ **This word means to shout for help, to shout.** It indicates a cry for help or of despair in general (Job 19:7; Ps. 72:12); especially a cry to God (Job 36:13; Ps. 18:41; 119:147; Is. 58:9; Hab. 1:2). *

– 4 Is. 38:14 ➔ CHIRP <6850> 5 Ezek. 9:4; 24:17; 26:15 ➔ GROAN (verb) <602> 6 Dan. 3:4; 4:14; etc. ➔ READ <7123>.

CRY, CRY OUT – 1 ***yāḇaḇ*** [verb: יָבַב <2980>; a prim. root] ▶ **This word indicates a shout or expression of pain and sorrow from worry and anxiety; it is also translated to lament, to wail.** Sisera's mother expressed her anxiety in a lament (Judg. 5:28). ¶

CRY OUT – 1 ***zāʿaq*** [verb: זָעַק <2199>; a prim. root] ▶ **This word means to shout, to exclaim, to call.** The primary activity implied is that of crying out in pain or by reason of affliction (Ex. 2:23; Job 35:9; Jer. 25:34). The verb signifies the action of calling on the Lord in a time of need (Joel 1:14; Mic. 3:4); uttering sounds of sorrow, distress, or alarm (2 Sam. 13:19; Is. 26:17; Ezek. 11:13); entreating for some favor (2 Sam. 19:28); and issuing a summons for help (Judg. 12:2). By inference, it also implies assembling together as in response to a call (Judg. 6:34, 35; 1 Sam. 14:20); and the making of a proclamation by a herald (Jon. 3:7). *

2 ***zᵉʿaq*** [Aramaic verb: זְעַק <2200>; corresponding to <2199> above] ▶ **This word means to exclaim; it is also translated to call out.** It described an impassioned, urgent cry from King Darius to Daniel concerning Daniel's condition in the lion's den (Dan. 6:20). ¶

3 ***ṣāhal*** [verb: צָהַל <6670>; a prim. root] ▶ **This word means to shout; to neigh.** It refers to making a loud sound, usually of great delight and joy (Esther 8:15; Is. 12:6; 24:14; 54:1; Jer. 31:7; 50:11). It is used of a cry of fear once (Is. 10:30); and of the lustful neighing of a stallion smelling a

mare in heat (Jer. 5:8). The Hebrew word also means to shine, to glisten; see SHINE <6670>. ¶

4 ***ṣā'aq*** [verb: צָעַק <6817>; a prim. root] ► **This word means to summon. It refers to shouting, complaining loudly, to pleading for relief or justice, calling for help.** The earth, figuratively, cries out because of injustices done to it (Gen. 4:10). Cries are aimed primarily to God or His representative leaders (Ex. 5:8, 15; 8:12; 14:10, 15). It indicates being called together, summoned (2 Kgs. 3:21); or indicates the act of calling people together (1 Sam. 10:17). The Lord hears the cries of His people who plead their cause with Him (Ps. 34:17; 77:1; Is. 19:20). *

– 5 Joel 1:20 → PANT <6165>.

CRYING – 1 Job 39:7 → STORM (noun) <8663> 2 Is. 22:5 → RICH <7771> b. 3 Mal. 2:13: crying, crying out → GROANING <603>.

CRYSTAL – 1 ***'eqdāḥ*** [masc. noun: אֶקְדָּח <688>; from CASSIA <6916> (but with the Hebrew meaning of glow, sparkle)] ► **This word refers to a very hard and costly gem; it is also translated carbuncle, sparkling jewel.** It describes the material of the restored gates of Zion, gates of crystal, which the Lord will provide (Is. 54:12). ¶

2 ***gāḇiyš*** [masc. noun: גָּבִישׁ <1378>; from an unused root (prob. meaning to freeze)] ► **This word refers to a precious gem; it is also translated pearl, jasper, quartz.** It is a semiprecious stone mentioned in Job 28:18, where it is compared unfavorably with the value of wisdom. ¶

3 ***zᵉḵôḵiyṯ*** [fem. noun: זְכוֹכִית <2137>; from PURE (BE) <2135>] ► **This word means fine glass, transparent glass.** It refers to a luxurious and valuable glass mentioned along with gold (Job 28:17) but of less value than wisdom. ¶

– 4 Ezek. 1:22 → ICE <7140>.

CUB – 1 ***gûr*** [masc. noun: גּוּר <1482>; perhaps from SOJOURN <1481>] ► **This word designates a lion's young one; it is also translated whelp.** It refers to a young, aggressive offspring. It is used literally of the young of jackals (Lam. 4:3). It is employed figuratively to depict the ancestor and tribal character of Judah (Gen. 49:9); Dan (Deut. 33:22); in general of the Israelites (Ezek. 19:2, 3, 5). It refers to the Assyrian capital of Nineveh as the lair of a lioness' cub (Nah. 2:11). ¶

2 ***gôr*** [masc. noun: גּוֹר <1484>; a variation of <1482> above] ► **This word designates a lion's young one; it is also translated whelp.** It refers figuratively to Babylonians growling or yelling for food to devour (Jer. 51:38) and to the Assyrians as lion cubs fed by the Assyrian war machine of oppression (Nah. 2:12). ¶

CUBIT – 1 ***'ammāh*** [fem. noun: אַמָּה <520>; prolonged from MOTHER <517>] ► **The basic meaning of this measure is forearm.** It was used to indicate a part of a door or a pivot of doors (Is. 6:4). The phrase *'ammat 'iyš* was an ordinary cubit (Deut. 3:11; cf. Ezek. 40:5, 13–15 for a cubit one handbreath longer). The ordinary cubit was about 50 centimeters long, 18 inches, and the longer cubit in Ezekiel was about 58 centimeters long, 22 inches. The phrase *'êl-'ammāh* means exactly to the cubit (Gen. 6:16). *

2 ***'ammāh*** [Aramaic fem. noun: אַמָּה <521>; corresponding to <520> above] ► **The word is used four times in the Old Testament.** Refs.: Ezra 6:3; Dan. 3:1. Ezra gives the height and width of the Temple as sixty cubits. Ironically, the height of Nebuchadnezzar's image in Daniel was six cubits wide and sixty cubits high. ¶

3 ***gōmeḏ*** [masc. noun: גֹּמֶד <1574>; from an unused root apparently meaning to grasp] ► **It is the length attributed to a short sword (ca. 18–22 inches) that could be carried on one's thigh.** Ref.: Judg. 3:16. ¶

CUCKOW – Lev. 11:16; Deut. 14:15 → SEA GULL <7828>.

CUCUMBER – ***qiššu'āh*** [fem. noun: קִשֻּׁאָה <7180>; from an unused root (meaning to be hard)] ► **This word refers to**

an Egyptian family of cucumbers (long green vegetables), succulent, full of water. They were a favorite food of the Israelites in Egypt (Num. 11:5). ¶

CUCUMBER FIELD – ***miqšāh*** [fem. noun: מִקְשָׁה <4750>; denom. from CUCUMBER <7180>] ▶ **This word refers to an area of ground reserved for planting and harvesting cucumbers (long green vegetables) or melons.** Refs.: Is. 1:8; Jer. 10:5. The first reference is also translated garden of cucumbers. It plays a part in a famous metaphor of Israel and another one satirizing idolatry. ¶

CUCUMBERS (GARDEN OF) – Is. 1:8 ➔ CUCUMBER FIELD <4750>.

CUD – ***gêrāh*** [fem. noun: גֵּרָה <1625>; from DRAG (verb) <1641>] ▶ **This word refers to the regurgitated food of a ruminant that is then held in the mouth and chewed.** Refs.: Lev. 11:3–7, 26; Deut. 14:6–8. It is used only in a legal context to help define what animals were clean and, therefore, edible for God's people. ¶

CUDDLE – Lam. 2:20 ➔ CARED FOR (ONES) <2949>.

CULTIVATE – ***'āḏar*** [verb: עָדַר <5737>; a prim. root] ▶ **This word means to prepare the soil to grow crops; it is also translated to hoe, to dig.** It refers to taking care of a garden or vineyard by cultivating it (Is. 5:6; 7:25). It is used figuratively of God's cultivating, hoeing His people as a gardener (Is. 5:6). The Hebrew word also has other meanings; see LACK, LACKING (BE) <5737>, RANK (KEEP) <5737>. ¶

CUMBRANCE – Deut. 1:12 ➔ LOAD (noun) <2960>.

CUMIN, CUMMIN – ***kammōn*** [masc. noun: כַּמֹּן <3646>; from an unused root meaning to store up or preserve] ▶ **This word refers to a seed that is sown by farmers and produces a herb used in seasoning.** Refs.: Is. 28:25, 27. ¶

CUN – 1 Chr. 18:8 ➔ CHUN <3560>.

CUNNING – 1 ***'oqbāh*** [fem. noun: עָקְבָּה <6122>; fem. of an unused form from SUPPLANT <6117>] ▶ **This word indicates deceitfulness.** It refers to trickery, acting according to a ruse, with threatening cunningness and deceit (2 Kgs. 10:19; also translated subtilty, deceptively). ¶
– 2 Gen. 3:1 ➔ PRUDENT <6175> 3 1 Sam. 23:22; Ps. 83:3 ➔ CRAFTY (BE) <6191> 4 Ps. 58:5 ➔ CHARMING <2267> 5 Dan. 8:25 ➔ INTELLIGENCE <7922>.

CUP – 1 ***gāḇiya'*** [masc. noun: גָּבִיעַ <1375>; from an unused root (meaning to be convex)] ▶ **This word points to a bowl or drinking container.** Refs.: Gen. 44:2, 12, 16, 17. It also denotes the golden cups on the lampstand for the Tabernacle (Ex. 25:31, 33, 34; 37:17, 19, 20). It refers to a cup for wine (Jer. 35:5). ¶
2 ***kôs*** [fem. noun: כּוֹס <3563>; from an unused root meaning to hold together] ▶ **This word is used of small drinking containers or goblets in general made of ceramic, metal, or wood.** Refs.: Gen. 40:11; 1 Kgs. 7:26. It is used in figurative senses: the cup in the Lord's right hand, i.e., a cup of judgment (Hab. 2:16); a cup of deliverance or salvation (Ps. 116:13); a cup of drunkenness or of anger (poison?) (Is. 51:22); a cup full of judgments for the wicked (Ps. 11:6). The Hebrew word also means owl; see OWL, LITTLE OWL <3563>. *
– 3 Is. 22:24 ➔ BASIN <101> 4 Jer. 52:19 ➔ BOWL <4518>.

CUPBEARER – ***mašqeh*** [masc. noun: מַשְׁקֶה <4945>; from WATER (GIVE) <8248> (properly, causing to drink)] ▶ **This word indicates someone officially appointed to, among other duties, serve wine to the king.** Refs.: Gen. 40:1, 2, 5, 9, 13, 20, 21, 23; 41:9; also translated butler. Wine could also be served at official banquets (1 Kgs. 10:5; 2 Chr. 9:4; Neh. 1:11). The Hebrew word also means a liquid, a watering place; see DRINK (noun) <4945>. ¶

CURB – Ps. 32:9 ➔ CONTROL (verb) <1102>.

CURD – See BUTTER <2529>.

CURDLE – Job 10:10 ➔ CONGEAL <7087>.

CURE – ***gāhāh*** [verb: גָּהָה <1455>; a prim. root] ▶ **This word describes the process of recovery from a serious wound.** In context, it indicates the unsuccessful attempt to heal Ephraim's sickness of apostasy (Hos. 5:13). The Hebrew word is translated to cure by NASB and KJV; NKJV, ESV, and NIV translate it to heal. ¶

CURE (BEYOND) – Is. 17:11 ➔ SICK (BE) <605>.

CURED – Is. 30:24 ➔ SALTED <2548>.

CURSE (noun) – 1 ***m*ᵉ*'ērāh*** [fem. noun: מְאֵרָה <3994>; from CURSE (verb) <779>] ▶ **This word designates a malediction.** It refers to God's sending evil or destruction on His disobedient people (Deut. 28:20; Mal. 2:2; 3:9); or on the wicked in general (Prov. 3:33). A curse may befall those who do not help the poor (Prov. 28:27). ¶
2 ***q*ᵉ*lālāh*** [fem. noun: קְלָלָה <7045>; from SLIGHT (BE) <7043>] ▶ **This word comes from the verb *qālal* (<7043>), meaning to curse. It designates a malediction.** This noun describes the general speaking of ill-will against another (2 Sam. 16:12; Ps. 109:17, 18); as well as the official pronouncement on a person, as Jacob feared he would receive from Isaac (Gen. 27:12, 13); or on a nation, as Balaam gave to Moab (Deut. 23:5; Neh. 13:2). God's curse is on the disobedient (Deut. 11:28; 28:15; Jer. 44:8); while His blessing, *b*ᵉ*rāḵāh* (<1293>), is on the righteous (Deut. 11:26; 30:19). Jeremiah used several other words in close connection with this one to describe the undesirable nature of this word: reproach, proverb, taunt, curse, hissing, desolation, and imprecation (Jer. 24:9; 25:18; 42:18). *
3 ***ta*ᵃ*lāh*** [fem. noun: תַּאֲלָה <8381>; from CURSE (verb) <422>] ▶ **This word refers to a cause of evil, a judgment placed on someone.** Ref.: Lam. 3:65. ¶
– 4 Deut. 29:19; Neh. 10:29; etc. ➔ OATH <423> 5 Judg. 17:2: to utter a curse, to put a curse ➔ CURSE (verb) <422>.

CURSE (verb) – 1 ***'ālāh*** [verb: אָלָה <422>; a prim. root] ▶ **This word means to imprecate, to provoke evil consequences; it also means to put under oath.** It is used in many cases of persons bringing curses on themselves if they are guilty of doing wrong (Judg. 17:2; it is translated to curse, to utter a curse, to put a curse). Similarly, *'ālāh* is used to prove someone's guilt or innocence. The person is guilty if the curse occurs but is innocent if the curse does not occur (1 Kgs. 8:31; 2 Chr. 6:22; translated to take an oath, to swear an oath). In 1 Samuel 14:24, the word is used to put someone under an oath (also translated to place under, to bind, to lay an oath; to adjure). In Hosea, the word refers to a curse placed on a person who makes a covenant or treaty and does not keep his word (Hos. 10:4: to swear, to take oath). Other ref.: Hos. 4:2 (to swear, to curse). ¶
2 ***'ārar*** [verb: אָרַר <779>; a prim. root] ▶ **This word generally denotes to inflict evil consequences, to utter a malediction. There are at least five other Hebrew verbs with the same general meaning. This word, in a more specific sense, means to bind (with a spell); to hem in with obstacles; to render powerless to resist. It is sometimes used as an antonym of *bārak*: BLESS <1288>.** In Genesis 3, God places curses on the serpent, the woman, and the man for their sins in the Garden of Eden. To the serpent, God says, "Cursed are you more than all cattle, and more than every beast of the field" (Gen. 3:14: NASB), meaning that the serpent would be the lowest of all animals. Then to the man, God says, "Cursed is the ground because of you," meaning that he would have difficulties in producing food from the soil. In Numbers 22:6, King Balak of Moab asks Balaam to curse the Israelites. His desire is for the Israelites to be immobilized or rendered impotent so he can defeat them, his superior enemy. *

[3] ***qāḇaḇ*** [verb: קָבַב <6895>; a prim. root (lit., to scoop out)] ▶ **The general idea of this word is a pronouncement of bad fortune, reproach or ill favor on another.** This word is used often in the story of Balaam and Balak, where Balak repeatedly requested that Balaam pronounce a curse on Israel (Num. 22:11, 17; 23:13, 25, 27). Rather than a curse, Balaam pronounced a blessing on them (Num. 23:8, 11; 24:10). In other instances of this word, it describes cursing the Lord (Lev. 24:11); cursing the day of one's birth (Job 3:8); or cursing the home of the foolish (Job 5:3). It is used twice in the Proverbs in a general way (Prov. 11:26; 24:24) as an opposite to the word *beṛāḵāh* (<1293>), meaning blessing, and similar to the much more frequent word *qālal* (<7043>), meaning to curse. ¶

CURSING – Deut. 28:20 ➔ CURSE (noun) <3994>.

CURTAIN – [1] ***dōq*** [masc. noun: דֹּק <1852>; from BEAT <1854>] ▶ **This word is used to depict the heavens stretched out like a canopy or drape.** Ref.: Is. 40:22. ¶

[2] ***yeriy'āh*** [fem. noun: יְרִיעָה <3407>; from TREMBLE <3415>] ▶ **This word denotes also a hanging, a shelter.** It is used to refer to the fabrics of goat hair used in the Tabernacle (Ex. 26:7; Num. 4:25), as well as other types of material (Ex. 26:1–10; 36:8–17). It is used of the tent that enclosed the ark of the Lord before the Temple was built (2 Sam. 7:2; 1 Chr. 17:1). Heaven is compared to a curtain stretched out by the Lord (Ps. 104:2). Many beautiful curtains or hangings adorned Solomon's palace (Song 1:5). It is used literally, but with symbolic significance, of wealth and riches of a nation (Jer. 4:20) or its dwellings in general (Hab. 3:7). Other refs.: Ex. 26:12, 13; Is. 54:2; Jer. 10:20; 49:29. ¶

[3] ***māsāḵ*** [masc. noun: מָסָךְ <4539>; from COVER (verb) <5526> a.] ▶ **This word means a covering, a screen.** It designates a screen or hanging used in the Tabernacle at the gate of entrance to the court (Ex. 27:16; 35:17; 39:40; 40:8, etc.); at the entrance into the Holy Place (Ex. 26:36, 37; 36:37; 39:38; 40:28, etc.); at the dividing point between the Holy Place and Holy of Holies (Ex. 35:12; 39:34; Num. 4:5). It refers to a covering used to cover a well where a person could hide (2 Sam. 17:19). It is used in a figurative sense to refer to a cloud used to hide the Israelites from the Egyptians (Ps. 105:39). *

[4] ***qela'*** [masc. noun: קֶלַע <7050>] ▶ **This word also means a drape, a hanging.** It describes the many hangings that were used in the Tabernacle and its court (Ex. 27:9, 11, 12, 14, 15; 38:9; 39:40; Num. 3:26; 4:26). It refers to a thin wooden leaf or door panel (1 Kgs. 6:34). For another meaning of the Hebrew word, see SLING (noun) <7050>. *

– [5] See VEIL <6532>.

CURVE – ***ḥammûq*** [masc. noun: חַמּוּק <2542>; from WITHDRAW <2559> (in the sense of to turn)] ▶ **This word refers to the beautifully shaped hips of the beloved bride as viewed through the eyes of the bridegroom.** Ref.: Song 7:1. It is also translated joints, rounded, graceful. ¶

CUSH – ***Kûš*** [masc. proper noun: כּוּשׁ <3568>; prob. of foreign origin]: black ▶

a. The first son of Ham, Noah's second son. His descendants occupied the Upper Nile territory of Egypt far to the south. Cush had five sons. Cush in Genesis 10:8 is the father of a famous mighty warrior who is mentioned in extra-biblical texts also. Hence, Cushites could also be located in southeast Mesopotamia. Refs.: Gen. 10:6–8; 1 Chr. 1:8–10. ¶

b. Cush probably refers to the territory of southeast Mesopotamia, although the northern Upper Nile region is not impossible. Most often the term Cush seems to refer to the Upper Nile regions (Esther 1:1; Job 28:19; Ps. 68:31), north of Ethiopia. Tirhakah, a Cushite king of Egypt, reigned in the time of Hezekiah (2 Kgs. 19:9). *

c. It refers to a person descended from Benjamin named Cush. Ref.: Ps. 7:1. ¶

CUSHAN – ***kûšān*** [proper noun: כּוּשָׁן <3572>; perhaps from CUSH <3568>]: black ▶ **The tents of Cushan (probably**

Ethiopia) were under distress. Ref.: Hab. 3:7. ¶

CUSHAN-RISHATHAIM – ***kûšan riš'āṯayim*** [proper noun: כּוּשַׁן רִשְׁעָתַיִם <3573>; apparently from CUSHAN <3572> and the dual of WICKEDNESS <7564>]: Cushan of double wickedness ▶ **King of Mesopotamia; he dominated the Israelites during eight years, but Othniel prevailed over him.** Refs.: Judg. 3:8, 10. ¶

CUSHI – ***kûšiy*** [masc. proper noun: כּוּשִׁי <3570>; the same as CUSHITE, CUSHI <3569>]: black ▶
a. Great-grandfather of Jehudi. Ref.: Jer. 36:14. ¶
b. Father of Zephaniah. Ref.: Zeph. 1:1. ¶

CUSHITE – ***kûšiyṯ*** [fem. proper noun: כּוּשִׁית <3571>; fem. of CUSHITE, CUSH <3569>]: black ▶ **Moses had married a Cushite woman or Ethiopian woman.** Ref.: Num. 12:1. ¶

CUSHITE, CUSHI – ***kûšiy*** [masc. proper noun: כּוּשִׁי <3569>; patron. from CUSH <3568>]: black ▶
a. Cushite, a person descended from Cush. Refs.: Gen. 10:6–8. Moses took a Cushite (Ethiopian) woman as a wife (Num. 12:1), perhaps after Zipporah his first wife died (Ex. 21–22). Cushites served in David's army (2 Sam. 18:21–33). Some translations render the term "Ethiopian" (Jer. 13:23, NIV). The Cushite's skin was evidently black. A Cushite, Ebed-Melech, rescued Jeremiah from certain death (Jer. 38:7–13). The term Nubian, a southern territory in Egypt, is also used to render Cush/ite (Dan. 11:43). God considered them His people, for all peoples are His (Amos 9:7). But even the Cushites received prophetic rebuke (Zeph. 2:12). *
b. Cushi, the name of a Cushite who served in David's army and whom Joab used as a messenger to David. Ref.: 2 Sam. 18:32. *

CUSTODY – ***mišmār*** [masc. noun: מִשְׁמָר <4929>; from KEEP <8104> (in the sense of to watch, to guard)] ▶ **This word means the state of being kept under guard; it is also translated ward, confinement. It also refers to a guard, a prison.** It indicates the condition of being guarded, watched, controlled (Gen. 40:3, 4, 7; 41:10; 42:17, 19; Lev. 24:12; Num. 15:34). It describes a group of guards and their location (1 Chr. 26:16; Jer. 51:12). It is used of a group of watchmen or armed men that are established for some purpose (Neh. 4:9, 22, 23; 7:3; 12:24, 25; Ezek. 38:7). It has the sense of security or safety (Neh. 13:14: services, offices) or possibly services, indicating the objects of the guard duties performed by Nehemiah. It has the sense of to keep guard (Prov. 4:23). Other ref.: Job 7:12. ¶

CUSTOM – [1] ***hᵃlāḵ*** [Aramaic masc. noun: הֲלָךְ <1983>; from DRIP (noun) <1982> (in the sense of traveler, visitor)] ▶ **This word indicates a tribute, duties on goods, toll.** It indicates a toll or a tax paid by cities to their rulers (Ezra 4:13, 20). The priests, Levites, singers, doorkeepers, and other Temple personnel were not subject to this toll or tax (Ezra 7:24). ¶
[2] ***tôrāh*** [fem. noun: תּוֹרָה <8452>; prob. fem. of ESTATE <8448> (in the sense of standard)] ▶ **This word is understood to refer to the way or manner in which God had dealt with David and his family concerning kingship.** Ref.: 2 Sam. 7:19; see TURN (noun) d. ¶
– [3] 2 Sam. 7:19 ➔ TURN (noun) <8447> d. [4] Ruth 4:7 ➔ TESTIMONY <8584>.

CUSTOMARY IMPURITY – Lev. 12:2 ➔ MENSTRUATION <1738>.

CUT (noun) – [1] ***śereṭ, śāreṭeṯ*** [verb: שֶׂרֶט, שָׂרֶטֶת <8296>; from CUT (verb) <8296>] ▶ **This word refers to an incision on one's body.** It is an injury self-inflicted by cutting oneself, in context, for a religious reason, but this was forbidden in Israel (Lev. 19:28; 21:5). ¶
– [2] Jer. 48:37 ➔ GASH (noun) <1418>.

CUT (verb) – [1] ***gāḏaḏ*** [verb: גָּדַד <1413>; a prim. root; comp. ATTACK (verb)

<1464>] ► **In some cases, this word is used to describe incising the skin.** It could be in mourning (Jer. 16:6; 41:5; 47:5) or in pagan religious practices (1 Kgs. 18:28); it is also translated to gash. God prohibited such pagan rites (Deut. 14:1). This Hebrew verb also means to gather together: see GATHER <1413>. ¶

[2] ***gāzaz*** [verb: גָּזַז <1494>; a prim. root (akin to CUT OFF <1468>)] ► **This word indicates the trimming of someone's hair. It also means to shear.** Jeremiah cut his hair as a sign of mourning (Jer. 7:29) and as a sign of the Lord's rejection of His people. It means to shear sheep (Gen. 31:19), as well as to be cut off or shorn (Nah. 1:12; also translated to destroy) in a figurative sense as in the destruction of Nineveh. *

[3] ***gāzar*** [verb: גָּזַר <1504>; a prim. root] ► **This word means to cleave, to part, to fell; it is also translated to divide, to separate; to ban, to exclude; passive: to be lost, to perish; to decide.** The basic meaning of this word can be seen in Solomon's command to divide the baby in two pieces (1 Kgs. 3:25, 26); in the act of cutting down trees (2 Kgs. 6:4); or when God divided the Red Sea (Ps. 136:13). It also describes a person separated from God's Temple (2 Chr. 26:21); from God's caring hand (Ps. 88:5); or from life itself (Is. 53:8). So great may be the separation that destruction may occur (Lam. 3:54; Ezek. 37:11; Hab. 3:17). In a few instances, this word means to decree (Esther 2:1; Job 22:28). The meaning is related to the Hebrew idiom, to cut a covenant, which means to make a covenant. In that idiom, the synonym *kāraṯ* <3772>, meaning to cut, is used. Other ref.: Is. 9:20 (to eat, to devour). ¶

[4] ***g^{e}zar*** [Aramaic verb: גְּזַר <1505>; corresponding to <1504> above] ► **The word means to decide, to determine. The participle is used as a noun meaning soothsayer or astrologer.** The verb occurs in Daniel 2:34, 45 to describe a stone cut without hands—an image that symbolizes the kingdom of God. Apparently, the idea of future events being cut out led to the word being used to signify soothsayers (also translated astrologers, diviners) who could foretell the future (Dan. 2:27; 4:7; 5:7, 11). ¶

[5] ***ḥāṭaḇ*** [verb: חָטַב <2404>; a prim. root] ► **This word means to fell, to cleave (wood), to carve (stone); it is also translated to chop, to hew, hewer (one who hews), cutter (one who cuts).** It is used to indicate the cutting of firewood (Deut. 19:5; 29:11; Josh. 9:21, 23, 27; Jer. 46:22; Ezek. 39:10) or timber for construction purposes (2 Chr. 2:10). It takes on the nuance of forming or chiseling corner pillars (of stone) (Ps. 144:12; also translated to sculpture, to fashion, to polish, to carve). ¶

[6] ***ḥāṣaḇ, ḥāṣêḇ, ḥōṣêḇ*** [verb and masc. noun: חָצַב, חָצֵב, חֹצֵב <2672>; a prim. root] ► **a. A verb meaning to strike, to hew, to quarry, to chisel, to dig, to carve.** It is used of cutting out cisterns to hold water (Deut. 6:11; 2 Chr. 26:10; Neh. 9:25); or of digging out copper from the hills (Deut. 8:9). It describes the process of engraving a rock (Job 19:24); or of chopping or cutting wood with an ax (Is. 10:15). Tombs were cut or hewn out of rock (Is. 22:16). Metaphorically, it describes the Lord's voice hewing out flames of fire (Ps. 29:7); and of wisdom hewing out her seven pillars of wisdom (Prov. 9:1). Israel was the Lord's wine vat hewn out by Him (Is. 5:2). He hewed His people from a rock (Is. 51:1) but had been forced to hew them in pieces by the words of the prophets (Hos. 6:5). Other refs.: Is. 51:9; Jer. 2:13. ¶

b. A masculine noun denoting the person who quarries stones, a mason, a hewer of stone. It designates those who help construct projects by preparing cut or hewn stones as building material (1 Kgs. 5:15), especially in the construction of the Temple or in its repair (2 Kgs. 12:12; 1 Chr. 22:2, 15; 2 Chr. 2:2, 18; 24:12). They were used in the construction of the second Temple (Ezra 3:7). ¶

[7] ***kāraṯ*** [verb: כָּרַת <3772>; a prim. root] ► **This word means to chop down, to wipe out, to remove, to make a covenant.** It can mean literally to cut something down or off, as grapes (Num. 13:23, 24); or branches (Judg. 9:48, 49). It can also be used figuratively, as with people

(Jer. 11:19; 50:16). Another important use of this word is to make a covenant (lit., to cut a covenant), perhaps deriving from the practice of cutting an animal in two in the covenant ceremony. God made a covenant with Abraham (Gen. 15:18); Abraham made one with Abimelech (Gen. 21:27). Finally, this word can also mean to destroy, as in Micah's prophecy (Mic. 5:10). *

8 ***nāṯaḥ*** [verb: נָתַח <5408>; a prim. root] ▶ **This word means to separate (body parts), to divide into pieces.** It describes the cutting a sacrifice into pieces or parts for placement on the altar (Ex. 29:17; Lev. 1:6, 12; 8:20; 1 Kgs. 18:23, 33). It indicates the dismembering of a human body (Judg. 19:29; 20:6); as well as a yoke of oxen (1 Sam. 11:7). ¶

9 ***pālaḥ*** [verb: פָּלַח <6398>; a prim. root] ▶ **This word means to slice, to cleave, to plow, to pierce through.** It refers to cutting up or splitting up something, e.g., slicing a vegetable (2 Kgs. 4:39); piercing or splitting open someone's kidney or liver (Job 16:13; Prov. 7:23). It figuratively depicts the birth process, the parting of the womb (Job 39:3: to bring forth); and plowing the ground, breaking it open (Ps. 141:7). ¶

10 ***pāsal*** [verb: פָּסַל <6458>; a prim. root] ▶ **This word means to carve, to form by hewing; it is also translated to hew, to chisel. It is used most often in the context of cutting stone.** Moses cut two stone tablets so God could record His words on them (Ex. 34:1, 4; Deut. 10:1, 3); the builders cut stones in building the Temple (1 Kgs. 5:18); and an idol maker cut the material to create an idol (Hab. 2:18: to carve, to graven, to shape). See the related nouns *pᵉsiyl* (<6456>) and *pesel* (<6459>), meaning idol. ¶

11 ***śāraṭ*** [verb: שָׂרַט <8295>; a prim. root] ▶ **This word means to make incisions or to injure oneself.** It means to administer cuts on oneself. In context it describes a practice forbidden in Israel (Lev. 21:5). It also has the sense of injuring oneself through self-exertion, excessive straining at a task too big to handle (Zech. 12:3). ¶

– 12 Job 21:21: to cut off, in half, in the midst, to an end ➔ DIVIDE <2686> a. 13 Job 38:25 ➔ DIVIDE <6385>.

CUT AWAY – Is. 18:5 ➔ CUT DOWN <8456>.

CUT DOWN – 1 ***nāmal*** [noun: נָמַל <5243>; a prim. root] ▶ **This noun is assumed to be the root for the Hebrew word *nᵉmālāh* (<5244>), meaning ant (see Prov. 6:6; 30:25).** Scholars assume that the word means cut or circumcised (Gen. 17:11; Job 14:2; 18:16; 24:24; Ps. 37:2). ¶

2 ***nāqap*** [verb: נָקַף <5362>; a prim. root] ▶ **This word means to strike off, to strip away. It occurs twice in the Hebrew Bible.** It is used passively in Isaiah 10:34 where it referred to the stripping away the forest thicket, describing God's destruction of Lebanon with an ax. In Job 19:26, the word is employed figuratively to describe the effects of his disease on his skin; it is translated to destroy. The Hebrew word also means to go around, to surround; see SURROUND <5362>. ¶

3 ***tāzaz*** [verb: תָּזַז <8456>; a prim. root] ▶ **This word means to strike down, to snip off, to prune off; it is also translated to cut away, to lop off. It describes the cutting off of healthy, spreading branches before harvest time.** It is used figuratively of judging Ethiopia (Is. 18:5). ¶

– 4 Psalm 90:6 ➔ CIRCUMCISE <4135> 5 Is. 6:13 ➔ FELLING <7995> a. 6 Dan. 4:14, 23 ➔ CHOP DOWN <1414>.

CUT DOWN, OFF, IN PIECES – ***gāḏaʿ*** [verb: גָּדַע <1438>; a prim. root] ▶ **This word describes severing a hand or arm in the sense of severing one's family line or one's strength.** Refs.: 1 Sam. 2:31; Lam. 2:3. It is further used figuratively to describe the cutting off or shattering of two staffs representing Israel or Judah (Zech. 11:10, 14). It describes the cutting down of pagan idols or objects of worship called Asherim (Deut. 7:5; Ezek. 6:6) and depicts the cutting down of the morning star, Lucifer, symbolic for the king of Babylon (Is. 14:12). The horns or strength of the wicked are cut off (Ps. 75:10). *

CUT OFF – 1 ***bāṣaʿ*** [verb: בָּצַע <1214>; a prim. root] ▶ **This word means to remove**

something, to break in pieces; to gain by violence. Figuratively, it bears the sense of being destroyed or judged (Job 27:8; Is. 38:12; Jer. 51:13). In some cases, it is used to express the dispensing of the Lord's judgment (Is. 10:12: to perform, to complete, to finish; Lam. 2:17: to fulfill, to accomplish, to carry out). It also describes taking from someone out of greed (Prov. 1:19; Jer. 8:10; Ezek. 22:12). *

[2] ***gûz*** [verb: גּוּז <1468>; a prim. root; comp. CUT (verb) <1494>] ▶ **This word means to pass away.** It is used figuratively of life passing away (Ps. 90:10; also translated to be soon gone, to pass away). The Hebrew word also means to bring, to drive (Num. 11:31); see BRING <1468>. ¶

[3] ***kāḥad*** [verb: כָּחַד <3582>; a prim. root] ▶ **This word also means to hide, to conceal, to destroy.** It has the basic idea of hiding or destroying by various measures: by cutting off or destroying Pharaoh and his people in plagues (Ex. 9:15); or by the Lord's destroying angel (Ex. 23:23). It has the meaning to make something disappear, to destroy or to efface it, such as the dynasty of Jeroboam (1 Kgs. 13:34). It has the sense of hiding or not revealing something in Job 20:12 (Ps. 139:15; Hos. 5:3). In other contexts, it means for something to be hidden (2 Sam. 18:13; Ps. 69:5); or kept hidden (Gen. 47:18; 1 Sam. 3:17, 18; Ps. 78:4). It is used of persons being effaced, destroyed (Zech. 11:8, 9, 16) by the Lord, or even scattered. *

[4] ***qāsas*** [verb: קָסַס <7082>; a prim. root] ▶ **This word also means to strip off. It means to prune, to remove.** It is used with reference to cutting off the fruit of a tree but used figuratively of peoples or a nation (Ezek. 17:9). ¶

[5] ***qāṣāh*** [verb: קָצָה <7096>; a prim. root] ▶ **This word means to scrape, to reduce, to remove a portion of something.** It means to rub the surface of something with an edge or rough tool to clean it or to remove unwanted residue (Lev. 14:41, 43). It means to decrease something in size, to diminish it, e.g., of sections of a nation that fall to a foreign power (2 Kgs. 10:32). It is used in figurative expressions (Prov. 26:6). To cut off a nation is to destroy it; to take away its people and dominion (Hab. 2:10). ¶

[6] ***qāṣaṣ, qāṣûṣ*** [קָצַץ, קָצוּץ <7112>; a prim. root] ▶

a. A verb meaning to remove a layer of something, to amputate, to split in pieces. It refers to a process of cutting sheets of gold into thin strips to use in woven materials. It was carried out by skilled craftsmen (Ex. 39:3). The verb is used of severing or cutting off something: a human hand (Deut. 25:12); human toes, fingers (Judg. 1:6, 7); feet (2 Sam. 4:12). It is used of cutting inanimate objects (2 Kgs. 16:17).

b. A verb meaning to be at the end, the utmost. The same word is understood to refer to a spatial location: farthest places, corners (Jer. 9:26; 25:23; 49:32).

c. An adjective meaning distant. It is understood as an adjective rather than a verbal form by some scholars (Jer. 9:26; 25:23; 49:32). The form itself, however, is a simple passive participle. *

[7] ***qᵉṣaṣ*** [Aramaic verb: קְצַץ <7113>; corresponding to <7112> above] ▶ **This word means to chop off; it is also translated to lop off, to trim off.** It describes the act of cutting off or pruning branches of a tree (Dan. 4:14). ¶

– [8] Job 18:16; 24:24 ➔ CUT DOWN <5243> [9] Ps. 76:12 ➔ GATHER <1219> [10] Ps. 118:10–12 ➔ CIRCUMCISE <4135> [11] Is. 38:12 ➔ ROLL UP <7088>.

CUT OFF (BE) – [1] ***gāraz*** [verb: גָּרַז <1629>; a prim. root] ▶ **This word is used figuratively to mean separated from God and not able to enjoy His presence or benefits.** Ref.: Ps. 31:22. ¶

[2] ***qāṭat*** [verb: קָטַט <6990>; a prim. root] ▶

a. This word refers to severing something, stopping it, removing it. Ref.: Job 8:14; NASB, NIV, see b. Its subject is hope, confidence, trust that may be cut off.

b. A verb whose meaning is uncertain. It is translated to be fragile (Job 8:14; KJV, NKJV, see a.). ¶

CUT SHORT (BE) – Job 17:1 ➔ EXTINCT (BE) <2193>.

CUT TO PIECES – ***bāṯaq*** [verb: בָּתַק <1333>; a prim. root] ▶ **This word means to thrust through, to hack up, to slaughter.** It is also translated to hack to pieces. It describes a terrifying treatment of the inhabitants of Jerusalem because of their unfaithfulness toward the Lord and their lewdness with pagan nations (Ezek. 16:40). ¶

CUT, CUT DOWN, CUT OFF – ***qāṣaḇ*** [verb: קָצַב <7094>; a prim. root] ▶ **This word means to sever, to shear.** It means to sever something, to separate by slicing, breaking (2 Kgs. 6:6). It is used to depict the shearing of sheep, cutting off their wool (Song 4:2). ¶

CUT, CUT DOWN, CUT UP – ***kāsaḥ*** [verb: כָּסַח <3683>; a prim. root] ▶ **This word describes the severing of vines or thorns.** This symbolize God's people, Israel (Ps. 80:16), but also the nations that have risen against them (Is. 33:12). ¶

CUTHAH – ***kûṯ, kûṯāh*** [proper noun: כּוּת, כּוּתָה <3575>; of foreign origin] ▶ **A Babylonian city from which the king of Assyria brought colonists into Samaria.** Refs.: 2 Kgs. 17:24, 30. ¶

CUTTER – Josh. 9:21, 23, 2 ➔ lit.: one who cuts ➔ CUT (verb) <2404>.

CUTTING – 1 ***ḥ******ᵃrōšeṯ*** [fem. noun: חֲרֹשֶׁת <2799>; from SILENT (BE) <2790> (in the sense of doing skill work)] ▶ **This word denotes a skillful working.** Bezalel, the master architect of the Tabernacle, was given the ability to perform all kinds of craftsmanship (Ex. 31:5) and skilled work (Ex. 35:33) in order to furnish the Tabernacle with utensils and a decor of beauty and honor. ¶
– 2 Lev. 19:28; 21:5 ➔ CUT (noun) <8296> 3 Jer. 48:37 ➔ GASH (noun) <1418>.

CUTTING TOOL – ***maᵃṣāḏ*** [masc. noun: מַעֲצָד <4621>; from an unused root meaning to hew] ▶ **This word designates an ax, tongs, chisel.** It refers to an instrument for shaping a piece of wood into an idol, probably a wood-carving tool (Is. 44:12; Jer. 10:3). ¶

CYMBALS – 1 ***mᵉṣiltayim*** [dual fem. noun: מְצִלְתַּיִם <4700>; from TINGLE <6750>] ▶ **This word describes a musical instrument, one of the percussion instruments used in the Levitical choir and other musical groups of Levites in worship in Israel, especially at the Temple.** Refs.: 1 Chr. 13:8; 15:16, 19, 28; 16:5, 42; 25:1, 6; 2 Chr. 5:12, 13; 29:25; Ezra 3:10; Neh. 12:27). ¶
– 2 2 Sam. 6:5; Ps. 150:5 ➔ WHIRRING <6767> c.

CYPRESS – 1 ***bᵉrôš*** [masc. noun: בְּרוֹשׁ <1265>; of uncertain deriv.] ▶ **This word indicates a conifer, possibly fir wood, pinewood, a fir tree.** It is also translated fir, juniper. It refers to pine logs (NIV), cypress timber (NASB, NKJV), or fir timber (KJV, 1 Kgs. 5:8, 10; 6:15, 34). This wood was used in constructing the Temple, ships (Ezek. 27:5), and even musical instruments (2 Sam. 6:5). Used in a figurative sense, it refers to spear shafts (Nah. 2:3). It is not clear whether the word refers to cypress, fir wood, or timber. This wood became a symbol of stateliness, luxury (Ezek. 31:8), or productiveness (Hos. 14:8). In a time of war, this timber was often cut down (Zech. 11:2). It is personified in Isaiah (Is. 14:8), rejoicing over the fall of Assyria (Is. 37:24), that had devastated forests. When Israel is restored, this tree will be restored (Is. 41:19). *
2 ***tirzāh*** [fem. noun: תִּרְזָה <8645>; prob. from LEAN (GROW) <7329>] ▶ **This word indicates a choice, large conifer highly desirable for construction projects.** In context it was used to construct an idol (Is. 44:14). ¶
– 3 Song 1:17 ➔ FIR <1266> 4 Is. 41:19; 60:13 ➔ BOX TREE <8391>.

CYPRESS WOOD – 1 Gen. 6:14 ➔ GOPHER <1613> 2 Ezek. 27:6 ➔ ASHURITES <839>.

CYPRUS – See KITTIM <3794>.

CYRUS – [1] ***kôreš, kōreš*** [masc. proper noun: כּוֹרֶשׁ, כֹּרֶשׁ <3566>; from the Persian] ▶ **This word designates the great king of Persia who destroyed Babylon, Cyrus II (559–530 B.C.).** He was God's instrument both to judge Babylon and to force Israel from exile and to rebuild Jerusalem (2 Chr. 36:22, 23; Is. 44:28; 45:1). His heart was moved by God (Ezra 1:1, 2, 7, 8) to let Israel and other peoples return to their homelands. His decree fulfilled Jeremiah's prophecy about a return from exile. Daniel lived into his reign (Dan. 1:21; 10:1). Other refs.: Ezra 3:7; 4:3, 5. ¶

[2] ***kôreš*** [masc. proper noun: כּוֹרֶשׁ <3567>; corresponding to <3566> above] ▶ **This word designates the Aramaic name corresponding to the Hebrew name Cyrus (II).** See a. above. It is found only in Ezra 5:13, 14, 17; 6:3, 14; Dan. 6:28. ¶

D

DABBASHETH – Josh. 19:11 ➔ DABBESHETH <1708>.

DABBESHETH – ***dabbešeṯ*** [proper noun: דַּבֶּשֶׁת <1708>; the same as HUMP <1707>]: hump, height ▶ **A city on the border of Zebulun.** Ref.: Josh. 19:11. ¶

DABERATH – ***dāḇ***ᵉ***raṯ*** [proper noun: דָּבְרַת <1705>; from WORD <1697>; perhaps in the sense of WORD <1699>: a pastureland]: pasture ▶ **A city within the territory of Issachar.** Refs.: Josh. 19:12; 21:28; 1 Chr. 6:72. ¶

DAGON – ***dāḡôn*** [masc. proper noun: דָּגוֹן <1712>; from FISH (noun) <1709>]: fish *god* ▶ **This word refers to the god of the Philistine city of Gaza.** Ref.: Judg. 16:23. A temple or house was dedicated to him (1 Chr. 10:10), probably in Ashdod. Other verses clearly indicate Dagon as the god of Ashdod (1 Sam. 5:2–5). The Lord set Himself against Dagon (1 Sam. 5:7). ¶

DAINTIES – 1 Gen. 49:20 ➔ CHAIN <4574> b. 2 Ps. 141:4 ➔ DELICACIES <4516>.

DAINTY – Jer. 6:2 ➔ DELIGHT (HAVE, FIND, TAKE) <6026>.

DAINTY, DAINTY MEAT – Prov. 23:3, 6 ➔ DELICIOUS FOOD <4303>.

DALPHON – ***dalpôn*** [masc. proper noun: דַּלְפוֹן <1813>; from LEAK <1811>]: dripping ▶ **One of the sons of Haman.** Ref.: Esther 9:7. ¶

DAMAGE (noun) – 1 ***beḏeq*** [masc. noun: בֶּדֶק <919>; from REPAIR <918>] ▶ **This word means a crack or a leak; it is also translated breach, seam, calker, caulker.** The word describes a chink, crack, or rent in the Temple (2 Kgs. 12:5–8, 12; 22:5) that needed to be repaired. It describes a leak or seam in a ship (Ezek. 27:9, 27) that needed to be caulked or repaired. ¶

2 ***ḥ***ᵃ***ḇāl*** [Aramaic masc. noun: חֲבָל <2257>; from DESTROY <2255>] ▶ **This word refers to economic and physical harm; it is also translated threat, hurt, harm, injury, wound.** It refers to economic or financial damage (Ezra 4:22), specifically to King Artaxerxes. It refers to physical damage or injury by fire (Dan. 3:25) or by wild animals (Dan. 6:23). ¶

– 3 Esther 7:4 ➔ LOSS <5143> 4 Is. 22:9 ➔ BREACH <1233> 5 Dan. 6:2 ➔ DAMAGE (verb) <5142>.

DAMAGE (verb) – ***n***ᵉ***zaq*** [Aramaic verb: נְזַק <5142>; corresponding to the root of LOSS <5143>] ▶ **This word means to injure, to cause loss; it is also translated to impair, to suffer, to diminish, to endamage.** It indicates, in context, a monetary loss or reduction (Ezra 4:13, 15, 22; Dan. 6:2) in the royal treasuries of kings. The Hebrew word is also translated by various nouns and adjectives: hurtful, harmful, damaging, troublesome, hurt, detriment, damage, loss. ¶

DAMAGED – Lev. 21:20 ➔ CRUSHED <4790>.

DAMAGING – Ezra 4:15 ➔ DAMAGE (verb) <5142>.

DAMASCUS – 1 ***d***ᵉ***mešeq*** [proper noun: דְּמֶשֶׂק <1833>; by orthographical variation from <1834> below] ▶

a. A word referring to the city of Damascus. It is paralleled with Samaria as a place of self-indulgent luxury (Amos 3:12; KJV). ¶

b. It could refer also to a piece of cloth, a damask; it is translated by some edge, cover, part, fabric. It indicates one of the things the raiders of Samaria and Israel snatched away (Amos 3:12). ¶

2 ***dûmmešeq, dammešeq, darmešeq*** [proper noun: דּוּמֶּשֶׂק, דַּמֶּשֶׂק, דַּרְמֶשֶׂק <1834>; of foreign origin] ▶ **This word designates the ancient capital of an Aram kingdom (Syria) during ca. 900–700 B.C. At times**

it also refers to the greater area around Damascus or to an Aramean kingdom. David and Solomon captured and controlled the city for some time (2 Sam. 8:5, 6), but in general, the city was a hotbed of resistance and hostility toward Israel (1 Kgs. 11:24; 15:18; 20:34; Is. 7:8; 8:4). It is mentioned 43 times in the Old Testament and even 15 times in the New Testament. It is located northeast of the Sea of Galilee, east of the Anti-Lebanon Mountains. The Abana and Pharpar rivers ran into it (2 Kgs. 5:12).

It figures in the life of Abraham (Gen. 14:15; 15:2). Elijah anointed Hazael as king over Damascus (1 Kgs. 19:15). The prophets proclaimed oracles of judgment against it (Jer. 49:23–27; cf. Ezek. 17:18; Amos 3:15; 9:1). *

DAMSEL – [1] Gen. 34:4 ➔ GIRL <3207> [2] Judg. 5:30 ➔ WOMB <7361> [3] Ruth 2:5, 8, 22, 23 ➔ GIRL <5291> [4] Ps. 68:25 ➔ YOUNG WOMAN <5959>.

DAN – ***dān*** [masc. proper noun: דָּן <1835>; from JUDGE (verb) <1777>]: judge ▶
a. Dan was the fifth son of Jacob through Rachel's maidservant Bilhah. Refs.: Gen. 35:25; 46:23. He went to Egypt with his household (Ex. 1:4). Dan is pictured as a viper along the road (Gen. 49:17). The capital of the Danite territory was renamed as Dan (Josh. 19:47). Other refs.: Gen. 30:6; 49:10; Num. 26:42; 1 Chr. 2:2. ¶
b. The city of Leshem (Laish) conquered by the Danites but renamed Dan after their ancestor. Ref.: Josh. 19:47. The name is used proleptically in Genesis 14:14. It was located on the northern boundary of Israel. The phrase "Dan to Beersheba" was used to define the north-south limits of Israel (2 Sam. 3:10; 17:11; 24:2, etc.). The sound of Israel's threatening northern enemies were heard proverbially from the distant north of Dan (Jer. 4:15; 18:16). It was also the location of pagan worship in Israel where huge altars and pillars have been found (cf. Amos 8:14). Jeroboam I set up a golden calf at Dan. *
c. The name of the tribe of Dan or its territory. It was allotted land lying among the tribes of Ephraim, Benjamin, Judah, and Manasseh. Its western border was on the Mediterranean Sea (Josh. 19:40–48). Some of the tribe later moved to a new location because they were hard-pressed by the Philistines from the Mediterranean coast (Judg. 1:34; 18:1–30). Samson's exploits were in the older location of Dan (Judg. 13:25), as were Deborah's (Judg. 5:17). In Ezekiel's vision, the tribe of Dan is located in its northern territory (Ezek. 48:1–32). *

DAN JAAN – ***dān ya'an*** [proper noun: דָּן יַעַן <1842>; from DAN <1835> and (apparently) BECAUSE <3282>]: purposeful judgment ▶ **A place between Gilead and Sidon.** Ref.: 2 Sam. 24:6. ¶

DANCE (noun) – [1] Judg. 21:21; etc. ➔ DANCING <4246> [2] Ps. 149:3; 150:4; Jer. 31:4, 13; Lam. 5:15 ➔ DANCING <4234>.

DANCE (verb) – [1] ***dûṣ*** [verb: דּוּץ <1750>; a prim. root] ▶ **This word probably means to move quickly and suddenly; it is also translated to leap, to go.** It indicates the dance of astonishment and dismay that grips those who see the beast leviathan approach (Job 41:22; KJV, sorrow is turned into joy; other translations: sorrow dances/leaps/goes before him). ¶
[2] ***kārar*** [verb: כָּרַר <3769>; a prim. root] ▶ **This word is used of David's whirling, impassioned moving to music before the Lord when the ark was brought to Jerusalem.** Refs.: 2 Sam. 6:14, 16. ¶
[3] ***rāqaḏ*** [verb: רָקַד <7540>; a prim. root (properly to stamp)] ▶ **This word means moving in a quick and lively way; it is also translated to skip, to leap, to whirl.** It means to make merry visibly by bodily gestures: It describes King David's dancing before the Lord (1 Chr. 15:29). It describes the happy skipping and frolicking of young calves (Job 21:11). It is used figuratively of hills and Lebanon skipping before the Lord (Ps. 29:6; 114:4, 6). It is an activity that has its time and place (Eccl. 3:4); even for animals (Is. 13:21; also translated to caper, to frolic). It is used to describe the fast flight

of chariots and of beasts (or armies?) on the mountains (Joel 2:5; Nah. 3:2: jumping, bounding, jolting, clattering). ¶

DANCING – [1] ***māḥôl*** [masc. noun: מָחוֹל <4234>; from SHAKE <2342>] ▶ **This word means the action of moving rhythmically to music; it is also translated dance.** It is an activity of a physical expression of joy (Ps. 30:11; Jer. 31:4, 13; Lam. 5:15) and praise to the Lord (Ps. 149:3; 150:4), often accompanied by musical instruments (Ps. 149:3). ¶
[2] ***mᵉḥōlāh*** [fem. noun: מְחֹלָה <4246>; fem. of THOUGHT <4284> (in the sense of something invented)] ▶ **See previous definition for <4234>.** It is used of a joyous celebration featuring rhythmic bodily movements by groups or individuals (Judg. 21:21; 1 Sam. 18:6; 21:11; 29:5), especially in praise of the Lord (Ex. 15:20); but on any joyous occasion (Judg. 11:34; Song 6:13). Other ref.: Ex. 32:19. ¶

DANGER – Eccl. 12:5 ➔ TERROR <2849>.

DANIEL – [1] ***dāni'ēl, dāniyyê'l*** [masc. proper noun: דָּנִאֵל, דָּנִיֵּאל <1840>; from DAN <1835> and GOD <410>]: judgment of God or God is my judge ▶
a. The second son of David, born to Abigail, former wife of Nabal from Carmel. Ref.: 1 Chr. 3:1; see 1 Sam. 25. ¶
b. A descendant of Ithamar who was a family head who returned from the Babylonian exile under Ezra. He sealed Nehemiah's pact to serve the Lord (Ezra. 8:2; Neh. 10:6). ¶
c. Daniel, the prophet, exiled in ca. 605 B.C. to Babylon, where he remained into the reign of Cyrus of Persia (Dan. 10:1–3; ca. 535 B.C.). He refused to be absorbed into Babylonian culture. He was gifted to understand and interpret dreams and visions. He was faithful to the Law of Moses even in exile. He interpreted dreams and visions of pagan kings and himself (by the help of divine intermediaries) that reported the course of world history and the divine establishment of the kingdom of God. He died and awaits the resurrection to receive his own allotment and reward (Dan. 12:1–13). His wisdom was also proverbial because of the way he handled himself in the court of Nebuchadnezzar. *
d. The name may refer to the righteous Daniel mentioned in an ancient Ugaritic Epic of Aqhat (ca. 1450 B.C.). It is more likely that the prophet here refers to the biblical Daniel, since the other two persons are biblical characters and all three men were "delivered" from a crisis situation, as Daniel's name indicates. Refs.: Ezek. 14:14, 20; 28:3. ¶
[2] ***dāniyyê'l*** [Aramaic masc. proper noun: דָּנִיֵּאל <1841>; corresponding to <1840> above] ▶ **The Aramaic name for the Hebrew entry <1840> above.** *

DANITES – ***dāniy*** [masc. proper noun: דָּנִי <1839>; patron. from DAN <1835>] ▶ **The people belonging to the descendants of Dan; members of the tribe of Dan.** Samson and his parents were Danites living in the original territory allotted to Dan (Judg. 13:1, 2). Most of the original Danites moved north to a location near the sources of the Jordan and the city of Leshem (Laish) (Judg. 18:1–30). Refs.: Judges 13:2; 18:1, 11, 30; 1 Chr. 12:35. ¶

DANNAH – ***dannāh*** [proper noun: דַּנָּה <1837>; of uncertain deriv.]: judging, murmuring ▶ **A village in Judah.** Ref.: Josh. 15:49. ¶

DAPPLED – Zech. 6:3, 6 ➔ MOTTLED <1261>.

DARA – ***dāra'*** [masc. proper noun: דָּרַע <1873>] ▶ **A shortened form of *darda'* (DARDA <1862>).** Ref.: 1 Chr. 2:6. ¶

DARDA – ***darda'*** [masc. proper noun: דַּרְדַּע <1862>; apparently from MOTHER-OF-PEARL <1858> and KNOWLEDGE <1843>]: pearl of wisdom ▶ **An Israelite of the tribe of Judah; his wisdom was praised.** Refs.: 1 Kgs. 4:31; 1 Chr. 2:6: Dara. ¶

DARIC – [1] ***ᵃdarkōn*** [masc. noun: אֲדַרְכֹּן <150>; of Persian origin] ▶ **This word**

means monetary value and weight; it is also translated dram, drachma. It is used only in 1 Chronicles 29:7, where David collected money for the first Temple, and in Ezra 8:27, where it tells the weight of gold basins for use in the second Temple. The word may refer to the Greek *drachma*, which weighed 4.3 grams, or to the Persian *daric*, which weighed about twice as much. ¶
– [2] Ezra 2:69; Neh. 7:70–72 ➔ DRACHMA <1871>.

DARIUS – [1] ***dārᵉyāweš*** [masc. proper noun: דָּרְיָוֶשׁ <1867>; of Persian origin]: who holds, lord ▶
a. King of Persia and Babylon (521–486 B.C.). He supported the rebuilding of the Temple and Jerusalem. The Temple was completed in 516 B.C. Refs.: Ezra 4:5; Hag. 1:1, 15; 2:10; Zech. 1:1, 7; 7:1. ¶
b. Darius II, named Nothus, who ruled Persia and Babylon 423–408 B.C. He is called "the Persian" in Nehemiah 12:22. ¶
c. The name of the person who became ruler over Babylon. Refs.: Dan. 9:1; 11:1. The name may be a throne name for Cyrus or possibly someone that Cyrus placed over Babylon (e.g., Gubaru). ¶
– [2] ***dārᵉyāweš*** [Aramaic masc. proper noun: דָּרְיָוֶשׁ <1868>; corresponding to <1867> above]: who holds ▶
a. The Aramaic name for Darius Hystaspes. See entry DARIUS <1867> a. He ordered the Temple to be completed (Ezra 4:24; 5:5–7; 6:1, 12–15). ¶
b. The Aramaic name for Darius the Mede. See entry DARIUS <1867> b. Refs.: Dan. 5:31; 6:1, 6, 9, 25, 28. ¶

DARK – [1] **very dark, pitch-dark: *'āp̱ēl*** [adj.: אָפֵל <651>] ▶ **This word is related to *'ōp̱el* (DARKNESS <652>), which means somberness or gloom.** The only time it occurs in the Old Testament is in Amos 5:20, "Shall not the day of the LORD be darkness, and not light? even very dark, and no brightness in it?" (KJV). ¶
[2] ***kêheh*** [fem. adj.: כֵּהֶה <3544>; from DIM (BE) <3543>] ▶ **This Hebrew word means faint, dim, somber.** It is used of the fading or healing of a skin disease causing discoloration (Lev. 13:6, 21, 26, 28, 39, 56). It describes eyes becoming dull or weak (1 Sam. 3:2); and a faintly burning wick (Is. 42:3: smoking, dimly burning, faintly burning, smoldering). Isaiah uses it to describe a person's weak or fearful spirit (Is. 61:3: fainting, faint, heaviness, despair). ¶
[3] ***šᵉḥarḥōr*** [adj.: שְׁחַרְחֹר <7840>; from BLACK (BE) <7835>] ▶ **This word means black (of a tanned skin); it is also translated swarthy.** It refers to skin that is swarthy, darkened, in context because of the sun's rays (Song 1:6). ¶
– [4] Gen. 15:17 ➔ dark, very dark ➔ DARKNESS <5939> [5] 2 Sam. 22:12 ➔ MASS <2841> [6] Ps. 18:11 ➔ DARKNESS <2824>.

DARK (BE) – [1] ***qāḏar*** [verb: קָדַר <6937>; a prim. root] ▶ **This word can also mean to mourn in the sense of being dark, or somber, with sadness or gloom.** Refs.: Job 5:11; Ps. 35:14; Jer. 8:21. Sometimes the sky grew dark due to an actual storm (1 Kgs. 18:45). Other times, it was not a literal darkness, as when the prophet Ezekiel prophesied against Pharaoh, saying that the heavens would be darkened when God acted against him (Ezek. 32:7, 8). Another example of symbolism was when Micah warned the false prophets that dark days were coming for them due to a lack of revelation (Mic. 3:6). *
– [2] Ps. 139:12; Amos 5:8 ➔ DARKEN <2821>.

DARK (BE, GROW) – ***ṣālal*** [verb: צָלַל <6751>; a prim. root (identical with SINK <6749> through the idea of hovering over; comp. IMAGE <6754>)] ▶ **This word means to be marked by slight or lessening light, to shadow. It is used only twice in the Hebrew Old Testament.** Nehemiah spoke of the gates of Jerusalem growing dim (in other words, evening came, and it grew dark) (Neh. 13:19). Assyria was compared to a Lebanese cedar that had such long, thick branches that it darkened the forest (Ezek. 31:3: to shade, to shadow, to overshadow). ¶

DARK (GROW) – Is. 24:11 ➔ EVENING (BECOME) <6150>.

DARK REGION – Ps. 88:6 ➔ DARKNESS <4285>.

DARK SPEECH – Num. 12:8 ➔ ENIGMA <2420>.

DARK-COLORED – ***ḥûm*** [adj.: חוּם <2345>; from an unused root meaning to be warm] ▶ **The color indicated may be something between black and white. This word is also translated black, brown.** Refs.: Gen. 30:32, 33, 35, 40. ¶

DARK, DARK PLACE – Ps. 74:20; 88:6; 143:3; Is. 29:15; Lam. 3:6 ➔ DARKNESS <4285>.

DARKEN – 1 ***ḥāšak̲*** [verb: חָשַׁךְ <2821>; a prim. root] ▶ **This word means to be dark, to grow dim, to be black, to hide, to obscure. The primary meaning of the word is to withhold light, to cause something to reflect or receive little light.** It is used to describe God's bringing about nightfall (Amos 5:8: to be dark, to darken); the deterioration of sight (Lam. 5:17: to grow dim); the covering of the earth with insects so as to obscure the ground (Ex. 10:15); the sullying of wisdom by foolishness (Job 38:2: to darken, to obscure); the act of concealing from view (Ps. 139:12: to be dark, to hide). Poetically, the word denotes the change in one's countenance in response to abject fear or distress (Eccl. 12:3: to be darkened, to grow dim, to be dimmed). *

2 Song 1:6 ➔ SEE <7805> b. 3 Is. 9:19 ➔ SCORCH <6272> 4 Is. 24:11 ➔ EVENING (BECOME) <6150>.

DARKENED (BE) – Zech. 11:17 ➔ DIM (BE) <3543> a.

DARKER – ***ḥak̲liyliy*** [adj.: חַכְלִילִי <2447>; by reduplication from an unused root apparently meaning to be dark] ▶ **This word refers to Judah's eyes as dull, deep-toned from drinking wine.** Ref.: Gen. 49:12; also translated dull, red. Perhaps the phrase should be rendered darker than wine (*ḥak̲liyliy . . . miyyāyin*), but others prefer to read sparkling. ¶

DARKNESS – 1 ***'ōp̄el*** [masc. noun: אֹפֶל <652>; from the same as DARK <651>] ▶ **This word is used only in poetry to denote gloom, especially a thick obscurity.** Although the term can be used in reference to physical darkness (Job 28:3; Ps. 91:6), it is more often used in a figurative sense to designate things like obscurity (Job 3:6); death (Job 10:22); evil (Job 23:17; 30:26; Ps. 11:2). In Isaiah 29:18, the term has both a literal and a figurative meaning in reference to the blind. ¶

2 ***ᵃpēlāh*** [fem. noun: אֲפֵלָה <653>; fem. of DARK <651>] ▶ **This word means obscurity, gloominess.** It signifies physical darkness: the plague of darkness (Ex. 10:22); the naïve walking in darkness (Prov. 7:9); the darkness which causes people to stumble and grope (Prov. 4:19; Deut. 28:29). Metaphorically, it is used to describe the calamity and misfortune that comes to the wicked (Is. 8:22; Jer. 23:12) or the darkness of the day of the Lord (Joel 2:2; Zeph. 1:15). Other refs.: Is. 58:10; 59:9. ¶

3 ***ḥᵃšōk̲*** [Aramaic masc. noun: חֲשׁוֹךְ <2816>; from a root corresponding to DARKEN <2821>] ▶ **This word is used figuratively of obscurity as the place of mystery or ignorance.** But the God of Daniel knows it fully (Dan. 2:22). ¶

4 ***ḥōšek̲*** [masc. noun: חֹשֶׁךְ <2822>; from DARKEN <2821>] ▶ **As in English, the Hebrew word has many symbolic uses, e.g., disorder, confusion, obscurity, desperate situation.** In its first occurrence, it is associated with disorder (Gen. 1:2) and is distinguished and separated from light (Gen. 1:4). In subsequent uses, whether used in a physical or a symbolic sense, it describes confusion and uncertainty (Job 12:25; 37:19); evil done in secret (Job 24:16; Prov. 2:13; Ezek. 8:12); obscurity, vanity, things forgotten (Job 3:4; 10:21; Eccl. 6:4); death (1 Sam. 2:9; Ps. 88:12). Although God created darkness (Is. 45:7) and uses it to judge His enemies (Ex. 10:21,

22; figuratively, Ps. 35:6), He enlightens the darkness of His people (Is. 9:2); bringing them out of desperate situations (Ps. 107:10, 14; Micah 7:8); observing secret actions (Job 34:22; Ps. 139:11, 12); and giving insight and freedom (Is. 29:18; 42:7). *

5 ***ḥešḵaṯ*** [fem. noun: חֶשְׁכַת <2824>; from DARKEN <2821>] ▶ **This word means dark or obscure. It is the construct form of the word *ḥᵃšēḵāh* below.** The psalmist alone uses this word in reference to the "dark waters" surrounding the Lord's pavilion (Ps. 18:11). The vivid picture is that of the murky darkness of extremely deep water. This imagery suggests the mystical, almost ethereal, gulf between the supernatural presence of the Holy One of Israel and the natural order. ¶

6 ***ḥᵃšēyḵāh, ḥᵃšēḵāh*** [fem. noun: חֲשֵׁיכָה, חֲשֵׁכָה <2825>; from DARKEN <2821>] ▶ **This word is similar in meaning to *ḥōšeḵ* above.** It refers to the experience of Abraham when God revealed to him the coming slavery of his descendants (Gen. 15:12); to the failure of the wicked to see God's standards and that results in disorder for them (Ps. 82:5; Is. 8:22); to the darkness sometimes surrounding persons that requires them to trust in God (Is. 50:10); He can see through darkness as well as light (Ps. 139:12). Other refs.: 2 Sam. 22:12; Ps. 18:11. ¶

7 ***maᵃpēl*** [masc. noun: מַאֲפֵל <3990>; from the same as DARK <651>] ▶ **This word indicates the thick darkness, or obscurity, the Lord put between Israel and the Egyptians so they could not see each other.** Ref.: Josh. 24:7. ¶

8 ***ma'pēlyāh*** [fem. noun: מַאְפֵּלְיָה <3991>; prolonged fem. of <3990> above] ▶ **This word refers to thick darkness, great darkness, i.e., obscurity. It refers literally to a dense darkness.** It is used figuratively to refer to the judgments and "thick darkness" the Lord made the land of Israel to His people (Jer. 2:31). ¶

10 ***maḥšāḵ*** [masc. noun: מַחְשָׁךְ <4285>; from DARKEN <2821>] ▶ **This word means an obscure place, a hiding place, secrecy; it is also translated dark region. The primary meaning of this word is darkness that is both blinding and confining.** Poetically, it is used to draw an image of the darkness and inescapability of the grave (Ps. 88:6; Lam. 3:6). The range of meaning also extends to the unknown things the Lord makes plain (Is. 42:16); and the back alleys where deviant behavior abounds (Ps. 74:20). Other refs.: Ps. 88:18; 143:3; Is. 29:15. ¶

11 ***'êypāh*** [fem. noun: עֵיפָה <5890>; fem. from FLY (verb) <5774> (as if from covering or disappearing)] ▶ **This word appears only twice in the Old Testament. In both instances, the word implies the obscurity of night as opposed to the light of day.** Refs.: Job 10:22 and Amos 4:13. In Job, the word is used in parallel to the word *'ōpel* (<652> above), meaning spiritual gloom or despair. ¶

12 ***ᵃlāṭāh*** [fem. noun: עֲלָטָה <5939>; fem. from an unused root meaning to cover] ▶ **This word refers to blackness, nighttime; it is also translated twilight, dusk, dark, very dark.** It refers to a mysterious blackness and overshading brought on Abraham by God (Gen. 15:17). It is used of nighttime (Ezek. 12:6, 7); and has a symbolic significance for Israel (Ezek. 12:12). ¶

– 13 Job 11:17 ➔ DECEIVE <8591> b. 14 Is. 50:3 ➔ BLACKNESS <6940>.

DARKON – ***darqôn*** [masc. proper noun: דַּרְקוֹן <1874>; of uncertain deriv.] ▶ **His sons came back from the Babylonian captivity.** Refs.: Ezra 2:56; Neh. 7:58. ¶

DARLING – 1 Ps. 22:20; 35:17 ➔ ONLY <3173> 2 Song 1:9, 15; 2:2, 10, 13; 4:1, 7; 5:2; 6:4 ➔ LOVE (noun) <7474>.

DART – 1 ***massā'*** [masc. noun: מַסָּע <4551>; from SET OUT <5265> in the sense of projecting] ▶ **This word indicates a projectile used to kill an animal or person.** Ref.: Job 41:26. The Hebrew word also means a stone quarry; see QUARRY <4551>. ¶

– 2 Job 41:29 ➔ CLUB <8455>.

DASH – Ex. 15:6 ➔ SHATTER <7492>.

DASH IN PIECES – ***rāṭaš*** [verb: רָטַשׁ <7376>; a prim. root] ▶ **This word is used of striking something in order to**

kill or destroy it; throwing it about violently. Refs.: 2 Kgs. 8:12; Is. 13:16; Hos. 10:14; 13:16; Nah. 3:10. It refers especially to infants and mothers in a time of war. It is used of arrows striking the enemy and demolishing them (Is. 13:18). ¶

DASHING – Judg. 5:22 ➔ GALLOPING <1726>.

DATHAN – ***dāṯān*** [masc. proper noun: דָּתָן <1885>; of uncertain deriv.]: fountain ▶ **An Israelite, son of Eliab, of the tribe of Reuben. He took part in a rebellion against Moses, along with many others who challenged Moses' position "over them."** They were engulfed by an earthquake (Deut. 11:6; Ps. 106:17; see also Num. 16:32). Other refs.: Num. 16:1, 12, 24, 25, 27, 26:9. ¶

DAUB – Ex. 2:3 ➔ COAT (verb) <2560>.

DAUBING – Ezek. 13:12 ➔ COATING <2915>.

DAUGHTER – ***baṯ*** [fem. noun: בַּת <1323>; from BUILD <1129> (as fem. of SON <1121>)] ▶ **This word designates a female child.** Refs.: Gen. 30:21; 34:1; Ex. 1:16, 22; Lev. 12:6. Combined with the phrase the king, it refers to a princess (2 Kgs. 9:34; 2 Chr. 22:11; Dan. 11:6). Properly modified, it can refer to a daughter-in-law (Ruth 1:11–13); sister (Ezek. 22:11); half-sister (Gen. 20:12); cousin (Esther 2:7); or granddaughter (Gen. 46:7).

It is used to address a person politely (Ruth 3:10, 11). It is used to designate women in various ways: of a certain city, land, or nation (Judg. 21:21; Song 3:11; Is. 3:16, 17); figuratively, it refers to a city as a daughter, e.g., daughter of Zion (Is. 1:8; 10:32); villages may be referred to as daughters of a central city (Num. 21:25; Josh. 15:45). In more figurative uses, it depicts the character of a person when modified by the following words: daughter of a strange god (Mal. 2:11); or daughter of a troop, i.e., a city of troops or warriors (Mic. 5:1; cf. Eccl. 12:4). The phrase daughter (KJV, apple) of an eye is found (Lam. 2:18, NASB, NIV, NKJV), meaning the pupil of the eye. The leech has two daughters that are never satisfied (Prov. 30:15). In at least one place, it refers to branches of a vine that climb a wall (Gen. 49:22, literally, daughter of walking up a wall). *

DAUGHTER-IN-LAW – See BRIDE <3618>.

DAVID – ***dāwiḏ, dāwiyḏ*** [masc. proper noun: דָּוִד, דָּוִיד <1732>; from the same as LOVER <1730>]: beloved ▶ **This word designates David, the man of God and great warrior king of Israel, reigned 1010–970 B.C. He sired Solomon through Bathsheba, Uriah the Hittite's wife. His name may mean "beloved," coming from the root d-w-d, "to love."**

The Book of Ruth records his genealogy (Ruth 4:17–22) through Ruth, the Moabitess. God chose him to reign after rejecting Saul. He "read" David's heart, thus indicating that moral and character issues were involved in God's choice of kings to reign. Samuel anointed him to be king (1 Sam. 16:13–23). David's rise was meteoric and is recorded in 1 Samuel while the place of Samuel and the demise of Saul are interwoven with David's in the author's recounting of the story. Saul unsuccessfully tried to kill David numerous times (1 Sam. 18; 19; 23; 24; 26). David was forced to live as a desperado and fugitive among the Philistines (1 Sam. 27; 29). He destroyed the Amalekites, Israel's ancient enemy (Ex. 17:8–15; 17; 1 Sam. 30). He was crowned king at Hebron and reigned over Judah for seven years and six months. He moved to Jerusalem and reigned thirty-three years, a total reign of forty years (2 Sam. 5:1–5). He captured Jerusalem and set up the ark there (2 Sam. 5:6–6:23). God established an eternal covenant with David and his house (2 Sam. 7).

David's reign saw the fulfillment of the promises and covenants with the fathers, for Israel became a mighty nation in the ancient Near East and ruled over the nations (Gen. 12:1–3; 15:12–21). But David sinned by committing murder, adultery, and deceit with respect to Bathsheba. From this time on, the house of David suffered a traumatic decline (2 Sam. 11–20). He, however, subdued the Philistines (2 Sam. 21:15–22). He became the "sweet psalmist of Israel" (2 Sam. 22:1–51). Most of the psalms are attributed to David, including some in which he confesses his guilt (Ps. 32; 51). Before his death, he made preparation for his son Solomon to succeed him (1 Kgs. 1; 2) and to build the Temple (1 Chr. 23–29). *

DAWN (noun) – 1 ***šaḥar*** [masc. noun: שַׁחַר <7837>; from SEEK DILIGENTLY <7836> (properly, to dawn)] ▶ **This word indicates daybreak, morning, rising up.** It is used of the coming of daylight, as the morning (dawn) came up (Gen. 19:15; 32:24, 26). The word *'ālāh,* to go, to come up is used with this noun to indicate the rising or coming of dawn. The phrase *be'ap̱'appê-šāḥar* means at the breaking of dawn, literally, rays or blinking of dawn (Job 3:9). Psalm 22 (title) refers to a song entitled "Hind of the Dawn." The phrase "like the dawn" is used in a simile to refer to a bride or bridegroom's beauty (Song 6:10). God is the ultimate source and cause of the dawn (Amos 4:13). *

2 ***šeparpār*** [Aramaic masc. noun: שְׁפַרְפָּר <8238>; from BEAUTIFUL (BE) <8231>] ▶ **This word refers to the time of light breaking forth for a new day, very early in the morning.** Ref.: Dan. 6:19. ¶

– 3 Job 3:9: first rays of dawn ➔ lit.: the eyelids of the morning ➔ EYELID <6079> 4 Job 3:9; 7:4; Ps. 119:147 ➔ TWILIGHT <5399> 5 Ps. 110:3 ➔ MORNING <4891> 6 Prov. 4:18 ➔ light of dawn ➔ shining light ➔ BRIGHTNESS <5051> 7 Is. 26:19 ➔ LIGHT (noun) <219> 8 Dan. 6:19 ➔ at dawn, at the first light of dawn ➔ very early in the morning ➔ MORNING <5053>.

DAWN OF LIFE – Eccl. 11:10 ➔ YOUTH <7839>.

DAWN (verb) – Is. 9:2 ➔ LIGHTEN <5050>.

DAWNING – 1 Job 3:9 ➔ EYELID <6079> 2 Job 7:4; Is. 5:11 ➔ TWILIGHT <5399> 3 Is. 60:3 ➔ RISING <2225>.

DAY – 1 ***yôm*** [masc. noun: יוֹם <3117>; from an unused root meaning to be hot] ▶ **This Hebrew word also means time, year. It stands as the most basic conception of time in the Old Testament.** It designates such wide-ranging elements as the daylight hours from sunrise to sunset (Gen. 1:5; 1 Kgs. 19:4); a literal twenty-four hour cycle (Deut. 16:8; 2 Kgs. 25:30); a generic span of time (Gen. 26:8; Num. 20:15); a given point in time (Gen. 2:17; 47:29; Ezek. 33:12). In the plural, the word may also mean the span of life (Ps. 102:3) or a year (Lev. 25:29; 1 Sam. 27:7). The prophets often infuse the word with end-times meanings or connotations, using it in connection with a future period of consequential events, such as the "day of the LORD" (Jer. 46:10; Zech. 14:1) or simply, "that day" (Is. 19:23; Zech. 14:20, 21). *

2 ***yôm*** [Aramaic masc. noun: יוֹם <3118>; corresponding to <3117> above] ▶ **This word corresponds to the Hebrew noun of the same spelling and meaning.** It refers to a twenty-four hour period (in which Daniel prays three times) (Dan. 6:10, 13). In the plural, it describes a time period marked by a particular state of affairs as, e.g., the days of Nebuchadnezzar's madness (Dan. 4:34) or the days of Belshazzar's father (Dan. 5:11). The number of days may be specified; in the book of Daniel, only King Darius could legally be worshiped for thirty days (Dan. 6:7, 12). The word is used to refer to God as the Ancient of Days, emphasizing in human terms God's eternal existence (Dan. 7:9, 13, 22). *

DAY (BY) – ***yômām*** [adv.: יוֹמָם <3119>; from DAY <3117>] ▶ **This word is used to mean during the period illuminated by the sun, such as the cloud of the Lord that led the Israelites by day in the wilderness.** Refs.: Num. 10:34; Neh. 9:19. It is often also used in parallel to something occurring by night, such as the sun by day and the moon by night (Jer. 31:35). *

DAY APPOINTED – Prov. 7:20 ➔ FULL MOON <3677>.

DAY STAR – Is. 14:12 ➔ MORNING STAR <1966>.

DAYBREAK – See MORNING <1242>.

DAZZLING – 1 ***ṣaḥ*** [adj.: צַח <6703>; from WHITER <6705>] ▶ **This word refers to something clear, shimmering, radiant.** It refers to presenting clear and distinct ideas, without stuttering or hesitation (Is. 32:4; also translated plainly, clearly, distinctly); to the appearance of a bright heat behaving like flashes of rising light (Is. 18:4); probably in heat waves of a hot burning wind (Jer. 4:11: dry, hot, scorching). It refers to the impression of dazzling beauty radiating from a bride's face (Song 5:10; also translated white, radiant). ¶
– 2 Dan. 2:31 ➔ BRIGHTNESS <2122>.

DEAD – ***rāp̄ā'*** [masc. noun: רָפָא <7496>; from HEAL <7495> in the sense of CEASE <7503>] ▶ **This word means shades, departed spirits, deceased ones, dead ones.** The term always occurs in the plural form (*r^ep̄ā'iym*) and consistently denotes those who died and entered into a shadowy existence within *š^e'ôl* (7585) (Job 26:5; Prov. 9:18; Is. 14:9). Three times the word is employed in direct parallelism with the Hebrew term for dead ones (*mêṯiym,* from *mûṯ* [<4191>], to die) (Ps. 88:10; Is. 26:14, 19). "Shades" or deceased ones do not rise (Is. 26:14); but see v. 19. They reside in a place of darkness and oblivion (Ps. 88:10). They cannot praise God (Ps. 88:10). The smooth words of the adulteress bring her victims down to death, to the place of the shades, never to return (Prov. 21:16; cf. Prov. 2:16–19; 9:13–18). Yet even in the Old Testament, a confident resurrection hope was gloriously and joyously held out to those in Sheol who obeyed God while alive (Is. 26:19). ¶

DEAD, DEAD BODY – Ps. 110:6; Nah. 3:3 ➔ BODY <1472>.

DEADLY – 1 Deut. 32:24 ➔ BITTER <4815> 2 Deut. 32:33 ➔ CRUEL <393> 3 Ezek. 9:1 ➔ DESTROYING <4892> 4 Ezek. 9:2 ➔ SLAUGHTER (noun) <4660>.

DEADLY WOUND – Ps. 42:10 ➔ BREAKING <7524>.

DEAF – ***ḥērēš*** [adj.: חֵרֵשׁ <2795>; from SILENT (BE) <2790>] ▶ **This word means lacking the ability to hear.** Ref.: Ps. 38:13. God can make one deaf since He is the creator and ruler of life (Ex. 4:11). The deaf were not to be laughed at or cursed (Lev. 19:14). To stop one's ears is to refuse to hear instruction or change (Ps. 58:4). God's future blessings include causing the deaf to hear (Is. 29:18; 35:5). God encouraged the Israelites to hear His servant (Is. 42:18, 19) and his message (43:18). ¶

DEAL OUT – Ps. 58:2 ➔ WEIGH, WEIGH OUT <6424>.

DEAL VIOLENTLY – Deut. 24:7 ➔ SLAVE (TREAT AS A) <6014>.

DEAR – 1 ***yaqqiyr*** [adj.: יַקִּיר <3357>; from PRECIOUS (BE) <3365>] ▶ **This word refers to what is honored, precious.** Ephraim, northern Israel, is described as God's dear, precious son. God's heart desires, yearns for what is honorable to Him (Jer. 31:20). ¶
– 2 2 Sam. 1:26 ➔ PLEASANT <5276>.

DEARTH – Jer. 14:1 ➔ DROUGHT <1226>.

DEATH – 1 ***môṯ*** [Aramaic masc. noun: מוֹת <4193>; corresponding to <4194> below] ▶ **In writing a letter to Ezra the scribe, King Artaxerxes of Persia used this term to designate execution.** It was one of the viable means of punishment available to Ezra in dealing with those who refused to obey the Law of God and the law of the king in the newly resettled land of Israel (Ezra 7:26). The term is the equivalent of the Hebrew noun *māweṯ* (<4194> below). ¶

2 *māweṯ* [masc. noun: מָוֶת <4194>; from DIE <4191>] ▶ **The term signifies end of life occurring by both natural and violent means.** Natural: Gen. 27:7, 10; Num. 16:29; violent: Lev. 16:1; Judg. 16:30). In other texts, it designates the place where the dead dwell known as Sheol (*šᵉʼôl* <7585>; Job 28:22; Ps. 9:13; Prov. 7:27). Because death and disease are so intimately related and due to the context, the word suggests the intended meaning of deadly disease, plague, epidemic, or pestilence (Job 27:15; Jer. 15:2, 18:21, 43:11). Figuratively, the term expresses the idea of ruin and destruction, especially when contrasted with the desirable notions of life, prosperity, and happiness (Prov. 11:19; 12:28; cf. Ex. 10:17). *
3 ***māmôṯ*** [masc. noun: מָמוֹת <4463>; from DIE <4191>] ▶ **This word is found only in the plural, as an abstract noun referring to various violent forms of terminating life; it also means a fatal disease.** In context it refers to a group of fatal, deadly diseases brought on by the judgment of God (Jer. 16:4); or the ends of those who die in battle (Ezek. 28:8). ¶
4 ***tᵉmûṯāh*** [fem. noun: תְּמוּתָה <8546>; from DIE <4191>] ▶ **This word comes from the verb *mûṯ* (<4191>), meaning to die. In its only two occurrences in the Old Testament, it is used with *ben* <1121> to describe those who were appointed to and deserving to perish.** More literally, it was those who were "sons of death," i.e., appointed to death (Ps. 79:11; 102:20). ¶
– 5 Ps. 55:15 ➔ DESOLATION <3451>.

DEATH OF THE SON – Psalm 9, superscription ➔ MUTH-LABBEN <4192>.

DEBATE – Is. 58:4 ➔ CONTENTION <4683>.

DEBIR – ***dᵉḇiyr*** [proper noun: דְּבִיר <1688>; the same as MOST HOLY PLACE <1687>]: oracle, orator ▶
a. A city in southern Judah. Refs.: Josh. 10:38, 39; 11:21; 12:13; 15:15, 49; 21:15; Judg. 1:11; 1 Chr. 6:58. ¶
b. An Ammonite king. Ref.: Josh. 10:3. ¶
c. A city in Gad. Ref.: Josh. 13:26. ¶
d. A city located on the boundary of northern Judah. Ref.: Josh. 15:7. ¶

DEBORAH – ***dᵉḇôrāh*** [fem. proper noun: דְּבוֹרָה <1683>; the same as BEE <1682>]: bee ▶
a. A nurse to Rebekah, Isaac's wife. Ref.: Gen. 35:8. She died and was buried at Bethel. ¶
b. A prophetess and judge in Israel who led the Israelites to deliverance from the Canaanites and their king in Jabin, who reigned in Hazor. Her husband was named Lapidoth (Judg. 4:4). In those days, she judged Israel (Judg. 4:5). She accompanied, at his request, Barak into battle against Sisera and his armies. She and Barak composed a victory song (Judges 5) to celebrate the triumph. Other refs.: Judg. 4:9, 10, 14; 5:1, 7, 12, 15. ¶

DEBT – 1 ***nᵉšiy*** [masc. noun: נְשִׁי <5386>; from LEND <5383>] ▶ **This word refers to an amount of money or other goods owed to a person.** Ref.: 2 Kgs. 4:7. It was a problem of the poor especially, a burden that destroyed them. ¶
– 2 Neh. 10:31; Prov. 22:26 ➔ USURY <4855> 3 Prov. 22:26 ➔ LOAN <4859>.

DEBT (BE IN) – ***nāšā'*** [verb: נָשָׁא <5378>; a prim. root (perhaps identical with DECEIVE <5377>, through the idea of imposition)] ▶ **The Hebrew word indicates lending or interest, serving as a creditor.** It refers to one who has made a loan to another person (1 Sam. 22:2, "everyone that was in debt, lit.: every man who had a creditor [*nōšeʼ*]"). It means those who lend or charge excessive interest (Neh. 5:7: to exact, to charge; Ps. 89:22: to exact, to outwit, to get the better; NASB reads as deceive, but see note). God's justice makes level all the financial and social classes (Is. 24:2: debtor, giver of usury). Other ref.: 1 Kgs. 8:31. ¶

DEBTOR – 1 ***ḥôḇ*** [masc. noun: חוֹב <2326>; from ENDANGER <2325>] ▶ **This word means one who owes something to another; it also indicates a debt**

or a loan. A righteous man returns a pledge (*ḥᵃḇōlāh*) given to him as security for a debt. Ref.: Ezek. 18:7. ¶
– [2] Is. 24:2 → DEBT (IN) <5378>.

DECAY – [1] Job 21:20 → DESTRUCTION <3589> [2] Prov. 12:4; Hab. 3:16 → ROTTENNESS <7538> [3] Eccl. 10:18 → BRING LOW <4355> [4] Is. 5:24 → STENCH <4716> [5] Jer. 49:7 → VANISH <5628>.

DECEASED – Is. 26:14 → DEAD <7496>.

DECEIT – [1] ***mirmāh*** [fem. noun: מִרְמָה <4820>; from DECEIVE <7411>] ▶ **This word means fraud, guile. The term signifies the intentional misleading of someone else through distorting or withholding the truth.** Jacob stole Esau's blessing through deceit (Gen. 27:35; cf. Gen. 34:13). Deceit fills the heart of those who plan evil (Prov. 12:20; cf. Ps. 36:3; Prov. 12:5, 17; 14:8). David exhorted his children to keep their tongues from evil and their lips from words of deceit (Ps. 34:13). The Lord cannot tolerate deceitful weights (Mic. 6:11); and a false balance is an abomination to Him (Prov. 11:1). *
[2] ***rᵉmiyyāh*** [fem. noun: רְמִיָּה <7423>; from THROW <7411> (in the sense, fig., to delude or betray)] ▶
a. This word means deception, treachery, lie; it is also translated faulty. It refers to what is not truth, steadfastness, or correct. Job asks if one should speak deceit for God (Job 27:4) and said his own tongue would not utter deceit (Job 13:7; 27:4). A person free of deceit is blessed (Ps. 32:2). The tongue of the wicked produces deceit (Ps. 52:2; Mic. 6:12). The word indicates what is not reliable, e.g., a treacherous bow (Ps. 78:57; Hos. 7:16).
b. This word indicates laziness, negligence, sloth. It refers to loose character in the sense of slackness, laziness, lack of diligence or attention: a lazy, slothful, or negligent hand (Prov. 10:4; 12:24); a lazy person (Prov. 12:27; 19:15); negligent, inadequate action or work (Jer. 48:10). *
– [3] Ps. 55:11; 72:14 → OPPRESSION <8496> [4] Prov. 26:26 → DECEPTION <4860> [5] Is. 30:10 → ILLUSION <4123> [6] Is. 30:12 → PERVERSE <3868>.

DECEITFUL – [1] ***ʿāqōḇ*** [adj.: עָקֹב <6121>] ▶ **The Hebrew word has two adjectival meanings: insidious and steep, which are both derived from the verb *ʿāqaḇ* (SUPPLANT <6117>) and the noun *ʿāqēḇ* (HEEL <6119>).** As Jeremiah proclaimed God's efforts with sinful humanity, he also declared that the heart is more deceitful than anything (Jer. 17:9). The other instance is related to the word for footprint. To describe the wickedness of Gilead, the prophet called it a town of bloody footprints (Hos. 6:8). The second adjectival meaning is steep, hilly. Isaiah spoke of making a path for the exiles to return, making the hilly places like a plain (Is. 40:4: crooked, rough, uneven). This famous passage is appropriated in the Gospels to describe John the Baptist's preparation for Jesus' ministry. ¶
– [2] Prov. 4:24 → CROOKED <6143> [3] Prov. 17:4 → NOTHINGNESS <205> [4] Prov. 29:13 → OPPRESSION <8496> [5] Is. 30:9 → LYING <3586> [6] Jer. 15:18 → DECEPTIVE <391>.

DECEITFUL (BE) – Prov. 27:6 → MULTIPLY <6280>.

DECEITFUL MAN – Prov. 29:13 → OPPRESSOR <8501>.

DECEITFUL THING – Mic. 1:14 → DECEPTIVE <391>.

DECEITFULLY (DEAL) – ***bāgaḏ*** [verb: בָּגַד <898>; a prim. root] ▶ **This word means to act treacherously, to be traitorous, to act unfaithfully, to betray.** The verb connotes unfaithfulness in relationships like marriage (Ex. 21:8; Jer. 3:20; Mal. 2:14); Israel's covenant with the Lord (Ps. 78:57; 119:158); friendships (Job 6:15; Jer. 3:20; Mal. 2:10); leadership (Judg. 9:23). *

DECEITFULLY (DEAL, ACT) – Ex. 8:29 → MOCK <2048>.

DECEITFULNESS – ***tarmāh, tarmiyṯ*** [fem. noun: תָּרְמָה, תַּרְמִית <8649>; from THROW <7411>] ▶ **a. This word means to do something underhandedly, with evil or trickery in mind.** In context messengers delivered a report and information in order to accomplish a secret plan (Judg. 9:31).
b. This word also means deception; delusion. It refers to the actions and intentions of those who turn from God's true statutes and ordinances (Ps. 119:118); a feature of even God's people who turn from Him (Jer. 8:5). False prophets suffered the deception of their own hearts and minds (Jer. 14:14; 23:26). Israel will have her deceitful tongue removed in her time of restoration in the Day of the Lord (Zeph. 3:13). ¶

DECEIVE – [1] ***nāḵal*** [verb: נָכַל <5230>; a prim. root] ▶ **This word means to act craftily, to cheat.** It indicates a conscious plan to deceive someone, to plan something against (Gen. 37:18: to conspire, to plot); to intend to trick or deal cunningly with (Num. 25:18: to seduce, to beguile, to deceive). It describes the plans and actions to oppress Israel in deceitful ways (Ps. 105:25: to conspire, to deal craftily, to deal subtilly). It refers to the cheat or deceptive person himself (Mal. 1:14: cheat, deceiver, swindler). ¶
[2] ***nāšā'*** [verb: נָשָׁא <5377>; a prim. root] ▶ **This word means to use beguiling methods or trickery to accomplish something.** To deceive a person (Gen. 3:13; KJV: to beguile); to deceive people by political means or giving false hopes of deliverance (2 Kgs. 18:29; 19:10; 2 Chr. 32:15); death deceives persons, surprising them (Ps. 55:15); it describes the prophecies of false prophets (Jer. 29:8). It refers to those who deceive themselves (Jer. 37:9; 49:16; Obad. 1:3, 7); or are deceived (Is. 19:13). Jeremiah charges God with deceiving His people, of making false assertions of peace to a people marked by wickedness (Jer. 4:10). Other refs.: Is. 36:14; 37:10; Jer. 23:39. ¶
[3] ***rāmāh*** [verb: רָמָה <7411>; a prim. root] ▶ **This word means to lie, to deal craftily, to betray someone in a matter.** Refs.: Gen. 29:25; Josh. 9:22; also translated to beguile. It refers to covering for someone, pulling a trick (1 Sam. 19:17; 28:12; 2 Sam. 19:26). A certain crass, joking deception intended as humor is condemned (Prov. 26:19). Israel and her priests strayed from God and deceived Him (Lam. 1:19). Other ref.: 1 Chr. 12:17. For another meaning of the Hebrew word see THROW <7411>. ¶
[4] ***tā'a', t*ᵉ*'ûpāh*** [תָּעַע, תְּעוּפָה <8591>; a prim. root] ▶
a. A verb meaning to trick someone into believing something false about oneself or something. In this case, Jacob applies the word to himself (Gen. 27:12). It may mean in context to despise, to scoff, to pay no attention to someone, e.g., a prophet (2 Chr. 36:16; KJV: to misuse).
b. A feminine noun meaning darkness. It refers to the absence of light, in context the darkness of night (Job 11:17). The KJV, however, takes the word from *'up̱*, to shine; hence, it translates it as a shining forth of light. ¶
– [5] Gen. 31:7; Judg. 16:10, 13, 15; Jer. 9:5 ➔ MOCK <2048> [6] Lev. 19:11 ➔ FALSELY (DEAL) <8266> [7] Num. 25:18 ➔ TRICK <5231> [8] 2 Kgs. 4:28 ➔ EASE (BE AT) <7951> b. or NEGLIGENT (BE) <7952> [9] Ps. 89:22 ➔ DEBT (IN) <5378>.

DECEIVED – Is. 44:20 ➔ MOCK <2048>.

DECEIVER – [1] Gen. 27:12 ➔ DECEIVE <8591> a. [2] Ps. 49:5 ➔ HEEL <6120> b. [3] Mal. 1:14 ➔ DECEIVE <5230>.

DECEIVER (BE A) – Jer. 9:4 ➔ SUPPLANT <6117>.

DECEPTION – [1] ***maššā'ôn*** [masc. noun: מַשָּׁאוֹן <4860>; from DECEIVE <5377>] ▶ **This word indicates an attitude of lying, trickery, cover-up that camouflages hatred, its real cause.** Ref.: Prov. 26:26; also translated guile, deceit. ¶
– [2] Mic. 1:14 ➔ DECEPTIVE <391>.

DECEPTIVE – [1] ***'akzāḇ*** [adj.: אַכְזָב <391>; from LIAR (BE A) <3576>] ▶ **This word means lying, deceitful.** It indicates what is not expected, such as a stream that promises water but has none (Jer. 15:18); it is also translated unreliable, as a liar. It is used in a powerful wordplay depicting the city Aczib as a city of deception that will dry up (Mic. 1:14; also translated lie, deception, deceitful thing). ¶
– [2] Lam. 2:14 ➔ FOOLISH <8602> a.

DECEPTIVELY – 2 Kgs. 10:19 ➔ CUNNING <6122>.

DECIDE – [1] 1 Kgs. 20:40 ➔ MOVE <2782> [2] Esther 2:1; Job 22:28 ➔ CUT (verb) <1504>.

DECISION – [1] ***ḥārûṣ*** [adj.: חָרוּץ <2742>; pass. part. of MOVE <2782>] ▶ **This word is used in the phrase *'êmeq beḥārûṣ* to refer to "the valley of decision" by the prophet Joel.** Ref.: Joel 3:14. The nations will gather there for war and judgment. The Hebrew word also means DILIGENT, GOLD, MOAT; see these entries. ¶
[2] ***re'û, re'ûṯ*** [Aramaic fem. noun: רְעוּ, רְעוּת <7470>; corresponding to STRIVING <7469>] ▶ **This word refers to making a choice in a matter, making up one's mind; it is also translated will, pleasure.** It refers to the choice or conclusion itself (Ezra 5:17). It applies to the desires of persons or God, their desires in a matter (Ezra 7:18). ¶
[3] ***še'êlāh*** [Aramaic fem. noun: שְׁאֵלָה <7595>; from ASK <7592>] ▶ **This word denotes a question at law (i.e., a judicial decision or edict); it is also translated demand, verdict, sentence.** It occurs only in Daniel 4:17 and is derived from the verbal root *še'êl* (<7593>). It is also related to the Hebrew noun *še'êlāh* (<7596>). In Nebuchadnezzar's second dream, he witnessed an angelic watchman crying out and announcing the verdict concerning the greatest tree in all the earth. Daniel later interpreted the dream, declaring that the great tree represented Nebuchadnezzar himself (cf. Dan. 4:4–27). ¶
– [4] Job 31:11 ➔ JUDGMENT <6415> [5] Is. 28:7 ➔ JUDGMENT <6417> [6] Dan. 4:17 ➔ ANSWER (noun) <6600>.

DECK – [1] Job 40:10; Jer. 4:30; 31:4; Ezek. 16:11, 13; 23:40; Hos. 2:13 ➔ ADORN <5710> [2] Prov. 7:16 ➔ SPREAD (verb) <7234> [3] Jer. 10:4 ➔ BEAUTIFUL (BE, MAKE ONESELF) <3302>.

DECLARATION – [1] ***'aḥwāh*** [fem. noun: אַחֲוָה <262>; from SHOW <2331> (in the sense of INTERPRET <2324>)] ▶ **This word indicates speech, discourse.** It refers to the declaration of Job (Job 13:17); it is also translated "my words," "what I say." ¶
– [2] Esther 10:2 ➔ SUM, EXACT SUM <6575>.

DECLARE – [1] ***bûr*** [verb: בּוּר <952>; a prim. root] ▶ **This word means to make evident, to search out; it is also translated to explain, to examine, to conclude.** It is used to describe the process the preacher of Ecclesiastes (Eccl. 9:1) goes through in his efforts to expound on the puzzles, riddles, and mysteries of life that surround every person under the sun. ¶
[2] ***nā'am*** [verb: נָאַם <5001>; a prim. root] ▶ **This word means to murmur, to mutter, to whisper, to utter; it is also translated to say.** The term is used once to describe the occupation which the false prophets of Jeremiah's day habitually practiced (they declare . . .). They uttered false prophecies and claimed they were from the Lord, thus leading many people astray (Jer. 23:31a). ¶
[3] ***ne'um*** [masc. noun: נְאֻם <5002>; from DECLARE <5001>] ▶ **This word introduces an oracle, an utterance; a prophetic citing of God's speech; it is also translated to say.** It is used as an introduction to various utterances and means thus says the Lord, utterance of the Lord, etc. (Is. 14:22; 56:8; Ezek. 16:58; Hos. 2:13; Joel 2:12; Amos 2:11; Obad. 1:4). It is used outside of the prophetic books in the form usually, *ne'um-yhwh*, utterance of the Lord (Gen. 22:16; Num. 14:28; 24:3, 4, 15, 16;

1 Sam. 2:30; etc.). It is used of the utterances of people, but they were probably in a prophetic state, such as David (2 Sam. 23:1). It is used of the voice of conscience in Psalm 36:1 when sin is committed. The word occurs often at the end, less often in the middle, and once at the beginning of these utterances (Is. 54:17; 56:8; Amos 3:10). *
– [4] Num. 15:34 ➔ CLEAR (BE, MAKE) <6567> [5] Deut. 1:5 ➔ EXPLAIN <874> [6] Job 32:6, 10, 17 ➔ SHOW <2331>.

DECORATE – [1] Jer. 4:30; Ezek. 23:40 ➔ ADORN <5710> [2] Jer. 10:4 ➔ BEAUTIFUL (BE, MAKE ONESELF) <3302>.

DECORATED – Song 5:14 ➔ COVER (verb) <5968>.

DECREASE – [1] ***mā'aṭ*** [verb: מָעַט <4591>; a prim. root] ► **This word means to become small, to be small, to reduce.** It indicates something already relatively small, diminutive, such as a family (Ex. 12:4); a small quantity of something (Ex. 16:17); an amount less than a set standard or quantity (Ex. 30:15); the act of reducing something, such as a price or value (Lev. 25:16); or the number of things or persons (Lev. 26:22). It has the sense of getting a few or small amount of something (Num. 35:8; 2 Kgs. 4:3). *
– [2] See LACKING (BE) <2637>.

DECREE (noun) – [1] ***'ᵉsār*** [Aramaic masc. noun: אֱסָר <633>; corresponding to PLEDGE (noun) <632> in a legal sense] ► **This word means an interdiction, prohibition; it is also translated injunction.** It refers to a royal decree issued to stop a certain thing or activity, such as Daniel's faithful prayers to the Lord three times daily (Dan. 6:7–9, 12, 13, 15). ¶
[2] ***gᵉzērāh*** [Aramaic fem. noun: גְּזֵרָה <1510>; from CUT (verb) <1505> (as CUT (verb) <1504>)] ► **This word indicates an announcement or a sentence.** It denotes a formal decree or sentence issued by heavenly beings (Dan. 4:17, 24). It was later interpreted by Daniel. ¶
[3] ***ṭᵉ'êm*** [Aramaic masc. noun: טְעֵם <2942>; from EAT <2939>, and equivalent to COMMAND (noun) <2941>] ► **This word means taste, flavor; judgment, command, sentence, royal edict.** Belshazzar held a great feast and tasted wine from the consecrated vessels of God's Temple (Dan. 5:2: to taste). When used figuratively, the word has the meaning of judgment or discretion, such as Daniel's counsel and wisdom to Nebuchadnezzar's chief guard (Dan. 2:14: wisdom, discretion, discernment). This word is also used in relaying a command of God, such as the rebuilding of the Temple (Ezra 6:14: decree, command, commandment), or of a person, as in the decree to worship the golden image of Nebuchadnezzar (Dan. 3:10). *
– [4] 2 Sam. 7:19 ➔ TURN (noun) <8447> d. [5] Ezra 6:11 ➔ ANSWER (noun) <6600> [6] Ezra 6:14 ➔ COMMAND (noun) <2941> [7] Esther 1:20 ➔ EDICT <6599> [8] Is. 10:1 ➔ STATUTE <2711> [9] Jon. 3:7 ➔ TASTE (noun) <2940> [10] See LAW <1881>, <1882>.

DECREE (verb) – Esther 2:1; Job 22:28 ➔ CUT (verb) <1504>.

DECREED (BE) – [1] ***ḥāṯaḵ*** [verb: חָתַךְ <2852>; a prim. root] ► **This word means to be officially ordered; it is also translated to be determined.** It is used of the seventy weeks laid out for Daniel's people, a period during which God's will for them will be accomplished (Dan. 9:24) and God's sovereignty will be demonstrated. ¶
– [2] Ezra 7:23 ➔ COMMAND (noun) <2941>.

DEDAN – ***dᵉḏān, dᵉḏāneh, rōḏān*** [masc. proper noun: דְּדָן, דְּדָנֶה, רֹדָן <1719>; of uncertain deriv.]: low country, low ground ►
a. A great-grandson of Ham. Refs.: Gen. 10:7; 1 Chr. 1:9. ¶
b. A grandson of Abraham. Refs.: Gen. 25:3; 1 Chr. 1:32. ¶
c. A southern Arabian tribe. Refs.: Jer. 25:23; Ezek. 25:13; 27:15, 20; 38:13. ¶
d. A northern Arabian tribe, from an area near Edom. Ref.: Jer. 49:8. ¶

e. The city or island of Rhodes, after the spelling in the Septuagint. Ref.: Ezek. 27:15. ¶

DEDANITE, DEDANIM – ***dᵉḏāniy*** [proper noun: דְּדָנִי <1720>; plur. of DEDAN <1719> (as patrial)] ► **A descendant or an inhabitant of Dedan.** Ref.: Is. 21:13. ¶

DEDICATE – 1 ***ḥānaḵ*** [verb: חָנַךְ <2596>; a prim. root] ► **This word means to inaugurate, and also to train.** It is related to the dedication of a house or temple (Deut. 20:5; 1 Kgs. 8:63; 2 Chr. 7:5). It is used once for training a child (Prov. 22:6: to train, to start off). ¶
– 2 Num. 6:2, 5, 12 ➔ SEPARATE <5144>.

DEDICATION – 1 ***ḥᵃnukkāh*** [Aramaic fem. noun: חֲנֻכָּה <2597>; corresponding to <2598> below] ► **This word means consecration.** It is used in relation to the dedication of Nebuchadnezzar's image (Dan. 3:2, 3); and the dedication of the new Temple of God (Ezra 6:16, 17). ¶
2 ***ḥᵃnukkāh*** [fem. noun: חֲנֻכָּה <2598>; from DEDICATE <2596>] ► **This word means initiation, consecration; it also refers to a ceremony. It was used to show that something was officially in service.** The word describes the dedication of the wall of Jerusalem after it was rebuilt under Nehemiah (Neh. 12:27). It also refers to the dedication of David's house (Ps. 30:1; cf. Deut. 20:5). The word refers to an altar dedication in 2 Chronicles 7:9 and also in Numbers 7 where it appears to refer particularly to the offerings offered on the altar (Num. 7:10, 11, 84, 88). The word is best known in reference to the altar rededication described in the apocryphal books of Maccabees, which has since been celebrated as the Jewish festival, Hanukkah. ¶

DEED – 1 ***ʿᵃḇāḏ*** [masc. noun: עֲבָד <5652>; from SERVE <5647>] ► **This word refers to anything that is performed, done, made, carried out.** Ref.: Eccl. 9:1; also translated work. ¶
2 ***ʿᵃlilāh*** [fem. noun: עֲלִילָה <5949>; from DO <5953> in the sense of effecting (e.g., an exploit of God or a performance of man)] ► **This word indicates actions, shameful actions.** It refers to immoral actions or behavior (Deut. 22:14, 17); or of deeds in general of whatever kind (1 Sam. 2:3); especially those performed by the Lord (Ps. 9:11; 105:1; Is. 12:4). The prophet Ezekiel often refers to the evil deeds of people (Ezek. 14:22, 23; 20:43; 24:14; 36:17, 19); also note Zephaniah 3:11. *
3 ***ʿᵃliyliyyāh*** [fem. noun: עֲלִילִיָּה <5950>; from <5949> above] ► **This word means action.** The Lord is said to be mighty, great (*raḇ*) in deeds on behalf of His people (Jer. 32:19; KJV, NKJV: work). ¶
– 4 Job 34:25 ➔ WORK <4566> 5 Prov. 8:22 ➔ WORK <4659> a. 6 Jer. 32:10; etc. ➔ BOOK <5612>.

DEEP (adj.) – 1 ***ʿāmōq*** [adj.: עָמֹק <6013>; from DEEP, DEEP (BE) <6009>] ► **This word means profound, and also mysterious.** It is used of the limits of God in profundity; His limits exceed the depth of Sheol (Job 11:8); He brings the depths into light (Job 12:22: deep things, deeps, mysteries). It indicates the wisdom, the words, that people speak (Prov. 18:4); or what their hearts contemplate (Prov. 20:5). The prostitute is considered a dangerous and deep pit (Prov. 23:27). Even the past is depicted as extremely deep, difficult to find out (Eccl. 7:24; NIV: profound); the word is repeated for emphasis here, *wᵉʿāmôq ʿāmôq* (deep, very deep). It is used of a deep, wide cup of punishment from God (Ezek. 23:32). *
– 2 Prov. 20:20 ➔ PUPIL <380> 3 Is. 33:19 ➔ UNINTELLIGIBLE (adj.) <6012> 4 Dan. 2:22 ➔ PROFOUND <5994>.

DEEP PLACE – Ps. 95:4 ➔ DEPTH <4277>.

DEEP SLEEP – ***tardêmāh*** [fem. noun: תַּרְדֵּמָה <8639>; from ASLEEP (BE, FALL) <7290>] ► **This word refers to a deep unconscious state needed, usually, for rest.** God may bring it on in special circumstances (Gen. 2:21; 15:12; 1 Sam. 26:12). It is a common event in the middle of the night and may be accompanied by dreams naturally or from God (Job 4:13; 33:15). Laziness, a moral problem, can result in a person falling into this state (Prov. 19:15). It is used in a figurative sense of a moral and spiritual stupor (Is. 29:10). ¶

DEEP THINGS – Job 12:22 ➔ DEEP (adj.) <6013>.

DEEP (noun) – [1] ***ṣûlāh*** [fem. noun: צוּלָה <6683>; from an unused root meaning to sink] ▶ **This word designates the seabed; it is also translated watery deep.** It refers to the bottom of the sea, its great depths, and the water-soaked condition of its bottom as well (Is. 44:27). ¶
[2] ***tᵉhôm, tᵉhōm*** [masc. noun: תְּהוֹם, תְּהֹם <8415>; from STIR (verb) <1949>] ▶ **This word refers to depth, a deep place.** It indicates the deep, primeval ocean on earth as created by God (Gen. 1:2). It refers to the deepest parts of the earth in a figurative sense (Ps. 71:20); and to the depths of the oceans (Gen. 7:11). It is the opposite of the heavens (Gen. 8:2). It can refer to the deep parts of a sea or a large body of water (Ex. 15:5). It refers to deep waters that can be brought up (Gen. 49:25; Deut. 8:7). It refers to sea waters (Ezek. 26:19). *
– [3] Ps. 69:2, 14; Ezek. 27:34 ➔ DEPTHS <4615> [4] Prov. 25:3 ➔ DEPTH (noun) <6011>.

DEEP, DEEP (BE) – ***ʿāmaq*** [verb: עָמַק <6009>; a prim. root] ▶ **This word means down or far, to be down or far from the surface; it is also translated to be profound, depth, deeply, greatly.** It describes thoughts and ideas of God which are asserted to be deep, difficult to fathom (Ps. 92:5). It describes a valley of abominations (Topheth) made deep, both physically and figuratively (Is. 30:33). It is used of apostatizing from God greatly, deeply (Is. 31:6; Hos. 5:2; 9:9). Sin as corruption can be entered into deeply (Hos. 9:9). It refers to a sign from God which can be deep, profound, spanning the universe in its profundity (Is. 7:11). It refers to the most distant or deeply hidden places to hide (Jer. 49:8). Other refs.: Is. 29:15; Jer. 49:30. ¶

DEEPLY – Is. 29:15; 31:6; Hos. 5:2; 9:9 ➔ DEEP, DEEP (BE) <6009>.

DEEPS – Job 12:22 ➔ DEEP (adj.) <6013>.

DEER – [1] ***ʾayyāl*** [masc. noun: אַיָּל <354>; an intens. form of MIGHTY <352> (in the sense of ram)] ▶ **This word refers to an animal with antlers; it is also translated hart, gazelle, stag.** It was lawful for the Israelites to slay and eat (Deut. 12:15, 22; 14:5; 15:22; 1 Kgs. 4:23) this animal. In a beautiful simile, the deer longs for the water brooks as the human soul longs for God (Ps. 42:1). It refers to the beloved in Song of Solomon 2:9, 17; 8:14. Other refs.: Is. 35:6; Lam. 1:6. ¶
[2] ***ʾayyeleṯ*** [fem. noun: אַיֶּלֶת <365>; the same as DOE <355>] ▶
a. This word means a doe of a fallow deer; it is also translated hind. It is the feminine of *ʾayyāl* above. It is used metaphorically to refer to the wife of one's youth (Prov. 5:19). Other ref.: Jer. 14:5. ¶
b. A proper noun designating Aijeleth. It is used with *shachar* <7837> meaning hind of the morning. Ref.: Ps. 22 (title). ¶
– [3] Gen. 49:21; 2 Sam. 22:34; Job 39:1; Ps. 18:33; Hab. 3:19 ➔ DOE <355>.

DEFAMING – Jer. 20:10 ➔ REPORT (BAD) <1681>.

DEFEAT (noun) – [1] ***ḥᵃlûšāh*** [fem. noun: חֲלוּשָׁה <2476>; fem. pass. part. of LAY LOW <2522>] ▶ **This word refers to weakness, prostration.** It refers to the state or condition of one who has been defeated (Ex. 32:18; KJV: being overcome), of one who cries out because of defeat in battle. ¶
– [2] Deut. 7:23 ➔ CONFUSION <4103>.

DEFEAT (verb) – [1] Ex. 17:13 ➔ LAY LOW <2522> [2] Lev. 26:17; Num. 14:42; Deut. 28:7, 25; Judg. 20:35; 1 Sam. 4:10; 2 Sam. 18:7; 1 Kgs. 8:33; 2 Kgs. 14:12 ➔ SMITE <5062>.

DEFECT – [1] ***mûm, mʾûm, muʾwm*** [masc. noun: מוּם, מאוּם, מְאוּם <3971>; as if pass. part. from an unused root prob. meaning

to stain] ▶ **This word usually describes a physical characteristic that is an imperfection or a deformity; it is also translated blemish, spot, flaw, fault.** A man with any sort of blemish could not be a priest (Lev. 21:17, 18, 21, 23) nor could an animal which had a blemish be sacrificed (Lev. 22:20, 21; Num. 19:2; Deut. 17:1). The word is also used to describe an injury caused by another (Lev. 24:19, 20); also translated disfigurement, to injure, injury. On the other hand, the absence of any blemish was a sign of beauty (2 Sam. 14:25; Song 4:7) or potential (Dan. 1:4). In a figurative sense, the word is used to describe the effect of sin (Deut. 32:5; Job 11:15; 31:7) or insult (Prov. 9:7). Other refs.: Lev. 22:25; Deut. 15:21. ¶
2 ***tᵉḇallul*** [masc. noun: תְּבַלֻּל <8400>; from MIX <1101>] ▶ **This word means confusion, obscurity. It comes from the verb *bālal*, meaning to mix or to confuse, and is used only once in the Old Testament.** It is used to describe an obscurity or some sort of defect in the eye that would prohibit a man from being a priest (Lev. 21:20; KJV: blemish). ¶
– 3 Is. 31:6 ➔ REBELLION <5627>.

DEFENCE – Is. 4:5 ➔ CHAMBER <2646>.

DEFEND – ***gānan*** [verb: גָּנַן <1598>; a prim. root] ▶ **This verb means to shield, to protect.** It indicates the Lord's defense of Jerusalem from the Assyrians (2 Kgs. 19:34; 20:6; Is. 31:5; 37:35; 38:6; Zech. 12:8) and His people Judah and Ephraim in the day of judgment (Zech. 9:15). ¶

DEFENSE – 1 ***massāḥ*** [masc. noun: מַסָּח <4535>; from TEAR (verb) <5255> in the sense of staving off] ▶ **This word refers to a guard. It defines the purpose of the action of watching, keeping guard over something.** Ref.: 2 Kgs. 11:6. It is translated various ways: that it be not broken down, to guard the palace, to guard the Temple. ¶
– 2 Ex. 15:2; Ps. 118:14; Is. 12:2 ➔ SONG <2172> 3 Job 13:12 ➔ BACK <1354> 4 Job 22:25 ➔ GOLD <1220>.

DEFENSE (PLACE OF) – Is. 33:16 ➔ STRONGHOLD <4679>.

DEFER – Is. 48:9 ➔ PROLONG <748>.

DEFIANT – Prov. 7:11 ➔ REBELLIOUS <5637>.

DEFIANTLY – Ps. 75:5 ➔ ARROGANCE <6277>.

DEFICIENT – Dan. 5:27 ➔ WANTING <2627>.

DEFILE – 1 ***gā'al*** [verb: גָּאַל <1351>; a prim. root] ▶ **This verb means to pollute, to stain, to make impure, to be unclean.** It means to be defiled, as when one's hands are polluted by blood (Is. 59:3). God's garments are stained (*gā'al*) by blood from His judgments on nations (Is. 63:3). Daniel refused to defile himself with unclean food in Babylon (Dan. 1:8). The word is used in a technical sense to define those who were defiled or polluted so that they could not take part in the priesthood (Ezra 2:62; Neh. 7:64). Jerusalem itself became defiled by her rebellious actions (Zeph. 3:1). Defiling the Lord's altar was equivalent to defiling Him (Mal. 1:7, 12). Other ref.: Lam. 4:14. ¶
– 2 Neh. 13:29 ➔ DEFILEMENT <1352> 3 Song 5:3 ➔ SOIL <2936>.

DEFILED (BE) – 1 ***ḥānēp̱*** [verb: חָנֵף <2610>; a prim. root] ▶ **This verb means to be profane, to pollute, to corrupt. It most often appears in association with the defilement of the land, suggesting a tainting not by active commission but by passive contact with those committing sin.** It denotes the pollution of the land through the shedding of blood (Num. 35:33 twice); through divorce (Jer. 3:1, 2); and through breaking God's covenant (Is. 24:5). The prophets also used the term to define Zion's defilement by the Babylonians (Mic. 4:11) and Israel by idolatry (Jer. 3:9). Two notable exceptions to this linkage with the land further intensify the notion that the primary meaning is one of passive contamination. In Jeremiah, the Lord declared

that the prophets and the priests were corrupted, seemingly by their association with the people's sin (Jer. 23:11: to be godless, to be polluted, to be profane, to be ungodly). Likewise, Daniel uses the word in reference to the corruption that comes from association with a deceiver (Dan. 11:32: to corrupt, to seduce, to turn). Other ref.: Ps. 106:38 (to pollute, to desecrate). ¶
– [2] 2 Sam. 1:21 ➔ ABHOR <1602>.

DEFILEMENT – ***gō'al*** [masc. noun: גֹּאַל <1352>; from DEFILE <1351>] ▶ **This word designates pollution, desecration.** It refers to cultic defilement brought about through forbidden marriages with non-Israelites by priests of Israel (Neh. 13:29); it is translated by a verb: to defile, to desecrate. ¶

DEFORMED (BE) – [1] ***śāra'*** [verb: שָׂרַע <8311>; a prim. root] ▶ **This word means to extend, to stretch out. It refers to a malformed or overly long member of the body; it is also translated to be superfluous, a limb too long.** In context it refers most likely to a disfigured limb of a person (Lev. 21:18); or an overdeveloped or malformed member (Lev. 22:23). Other ref.: Is. 28:20. ¶
– [2] Lev. 22:23 ➔ STUNTED (BE) <7038>.

DEFY – 1 Kgs. 13:21, 26 ➔ REBELLIOUS (BE) <4784>.

DEGENERATE – ***sûr*** [masc. noun: סוּר <5494>; pass. part. of TURN ASIDE <5493>] ▶ **This word refers to the resulting state of something that has deteriorated, become foul-smelling, rotten.** Ref.: Jer. 2:21; NIV: corrupt. ¶

DEGRADED (BE) – Deut. 25:3; Is. 16:14 ➔ DESPISED (BE) <7034>.

DEHAVITES – ***dehāwê'*** [Aramaic proper noun: דֶּהָוֵא <1723>; of uncertain deriv.]: villagers ▶ **One of the clans brought from Assyria to Samaria to replace the Israelites deported.** Ref.: Ezra 4:9. ¶

DEJECTED (BE) – Gen. 40:6 ➔ ANGRY (BE, BECOME) <2196>.

DEJECTEDLY – 1 Kgs. 21:27 ➔ SLOWLY <328>.

DEKER – ***deqer*** [proper noun: דֶּקֶר <1857>; from PIERCE <1856>]: piercing ▶ **See BEN-DEKER <1128>.** Ref.: 1 Kgs. 4:9, KJV. ¶

DELAIAH – ***d^{e}lāyāh, d^{e}lāyāhû*** [masc. proper noun: דְּלָיָה, דְּלָיָהוּ <1806>; from DRAW <1802> and LORD <3050>]: delivered by the Lord ▶
a. Son of Elioenai. Ref.: 1 Chr. 3:24. ¶
b. A priest. Ref.: 1 Chr. 24:18. ¶
c. A royal officer. Refs.: Jer. 36:12, 25. ¶
d. A Jew. Refs.: Ezra 2:60; Neh. 7:62. ¶
e. Father of Shemaiah. Ref.: Neh. 6:10. ¶

DELAY (noun) – Ezra 6:8: without delay ➔ DILIGENTLY <629>.

DELAY (verb) – [1] ***yāḥar*** [verb: יָחַר <3186>; a prim. root] ▶ **This word means to act too late based on a previous plan of action, to be tardy.** Ref.: 2 Sam. 20:5; also translated to tarry, to take longer. ¶
– [2] Gen. 43:10; Ex. 12:39; Judg. 3:26; Ps. 119:60; Is. 29:9 ➔ LINGER <4102> [3] Ex. 22:29; Judg. 5:28; 2 Sam. 20:5 ➔ STAY (verb) <309> [4] Josh. 10:13: delayed going down ➔ lit.: did not hasten to go down ➔ HASTEN <213> [5] Ezra 6:8 ➔ CEASE <989> [6] Prov. 20:20 – Is. 48:9 ➔ PROLONG <748>.

DELICACIES – [1] ***man'ammiym*** [masc. plur. noun: מַנְעַמִּים <4516>; from PLEASANT <5276>] ▶ **This word refers to choice, luxurious portions of food but in context may refer to evil deeds of evil men as well.** Ref.: Ps. 141:4; KJV: dainties. ¶
– [2] Gen. 49:20; Lam. 4:5 ➔ CHAIN <4574> b. [3] Dan. 1:5, 8, 13, 15, 16; 11:26 ➔ FOOD, CHOICE FOOD <6598>.

DELICACY – [1] Prov. 23:3, 6 ➔ DELICIOUS FOOD <4303> [2] Jer. 51:34 ➔ DELIGHT (noun) <5730> a.

DELICATE – [1] *'ānōg* [adj.: עָנֹג <6028>; from DELIGHT (HAVE, FIND, TAKE) <6026>] ► **This word means refined, genteel; it is also translated sensitive, refined.** It refers to a refined, suave, fastidious, neat, clean person in formal dress and behavior (Deut. 28:54, 56); but also of Babylon in her era of splendor and riches (Is. 47:1). ¶
– [2] Deut. 28:56; Jer. 6:2 ➔ DELIGHT (HAVE, FIND, TAKE) <6026>.

DELICATELY – 1 Sam. 15:32 ➔ CHAIN <4574> a.

DELICATELY BRED – Jer. 6:2 ➔ DELIGHT (HAVE, FIND, TAKE) <6026>.

DELICIOUS – Prov. 9:17 ➔ PLEASANT <5276>.

DELICIOUS FOOD – *maṭ'ām* [masc. noun: מַטְעָם <4303>; from TASTE (verb) <2938>] ► **This word means tasty food, delicacy.** It indicates gourmet food, special tidbits, or delicacies (Prov. 23:3, 6; KJV: dainty, dainty meat); a specially prepared meal of tasty food (Gen. 27:4, 7, 9, 14, 17, 31; also translated savory food, savory dish, savoury meat). ¶

DELIGHT (noun) – [1] *maḥmāl* [masc. noun: מַחְמָל <4263>; from PITY (HAVE, SHOW) <2550>] ► **This word means an object of mercy.** It occurs only once in the Old Testament. In Ezekiel 24:21, this word is used to describe the compassion and delight that the Temple was to the Israelites; it is also translated that which one pities, yearning. In this section of Scripture, Ezekiel's desire and delight for his wife is compared to Israel's desire and delight for the Temple (see Ezek. 24:15–27). ¶
[2] *'ēḏen, 'eḏnāh* [עֵדֶן, עֶדְנָה <5730>; from DELIGHT ONESELF <5727>] ►
a. A masculine noun referring to a luxury, a pleasure. Used in the plural, it means luxury, luxurious things (2 Sam. 1:24; also translated luxuriously); figuratively, of the many splendid things and enjoyments God gives (Ps. 36:8). It depicts the many enjoyments and pleasurable delights Israel had enjoyed previously (Jer. 51:34: delicacy). ¶
b. A feminine noun indicating sexual delight, ecstasy. It refers to the enjoyment of intimate love with one's spouse which in context implies the ability to become pregnant (Gen. 18:12: pleasure). ¶
[3] *'ōneg* [masc. noun: עֹנֶג <6027>; from DELIGHT (HAVE, FIND, TAKE) <6026>] ► **This word means enjoyment, luxury.** The Sabbath was to be a delight, a time of enjoyment for Israel (Is. 58:13). The word is used to describe a palace of delight, luxury, and extravagance (Is. 13:22; luxurious, pleasant). ¶
[4] *ša'šu'iym* [masc. plur. noun: שַׁעֲשֻׁעִים <8191>; from BLINDED (BE) <8173> b. (in the sense of to take delight in)] ► **This word often describes the pleasure given to the one who follows God's teachings, laws, and testimonies.** Refs.: Ps. 119:24, 77, 92, 143, 174. Wisdom, in creation, was constantly God's delight (Prov. 8:30, 31). It is used figuratively in the phrase a delightful plant, a pleasant plant to refer to God's pleasure in the people of Judah (Is. 5:7); likewise Ephraim was God's pleasant child (Jer. 31:20), His dear son (KJV). ¶
[5] *ta'nûg* [masc. noun: תַּעֲנוּג <8588>; from DELIGHT (HAVE) <6026>] ► **This word also means a pleasure. It refers to pleasure surrounding a carefree life of luxury.** Such a situation is not appropriate for a fool (Prov. 19:10; also translated luxury). It refers to all possible delights and pleasures of people (Eccl. 2:8; Mic. 2:9). It describes an attractive and delightful bride (Song 7:6). It describes God's children as His delight and enjoyment (Mic. 1:16). ¶
– [6] Prov. 24:25 ➔ PLEASANT <5276> [7] Prov. 29:17 ➔ CHAIN <4574> b. [8] Is. 62:4 ➔ my delight is in her ➔ HEPHZIBAH <2657>.

DELIGHT (BE A) – Is. 65:18 ➔ REJOICE <1523>.

DELIGHT (HAVE, FIND, TAKE) – *'ānag* [verb: עָנַג <6026>; a prim. root] ► **This word means to rejoice and is translated as**

well to delight; it also means to be delicate. It is used of taking delight and pleasure in God (Job 22:26; Ps. 37:4; Is. 55:2). It has the sense of making merry, jesting at someone (Is. 58:14; NIV: to find joy). It is used figuratively of taking delight in a restored Jerusalem (Is. 66:11). It is used of being fastidious, pampering, feminine as a woman (Deut. 28:56: delicate, refined, sensitive; Jer. 6:2: delicate, dainty, delicately bred); of keeping oneself clean, neat. Other refs.: Job 27:10; Ps. 37:11; Is. 57:4 (to mock, to ridicule, to jest, to sport). ¶

DELIGHT (TAKE) – Jer. 9:24 ➔ DELIGHT (verb) <2654>.

DELIGHT (verb) – [1] ***ḥāp̱ēṣ, ḥāp̱aṣ*** [verb: חָפֵץ, חָפַץ <2654>; a prim. root] ▶ **The verb means to have pleasure, to favor, to like; it is also translated to take delight, to desire, to be pleased.** Shechem took delight in Dinah (Gen. 34:19); King Ahasuerus also took delight in Esther (Esther 2:14). This word describes Solomon's pleasure in building the Temple (1 Kgs. 9:1). The Lord is described as taking pleasure in His people Israel (Is. 62:4). He is also pleased with those who practice justice and righteousness (Jer. 9:24). *
– [2] Job 22:26; 27:10; Ps. 37:4, 11; Is. 55:2; 58:14; 66:11 ➔ DELIGHT (HAVE, FIND, TAKE) <6026> [3] Ps. 5:4; 35:27 ➔ PLEASURE IN (HAVE, TAKE) <2655> [4] Prov. 7:18 ➔ ENJOY <5965> a.

DELIGHT ONESELF – ***ʿāḏan*** [verb: עָדַן <5727>; a prim. root] ▶ **This word means to revel, to take pleasure in.** It refers to enjoying something, using it jubilantly to the full, perhaps in an excessive or inordinate manner (Neh. 9:25). ¶

DELIGHTED (BE) – Ex. 18:9 ➔ REJOICE <2302>.

DELIGHTFUL – [1] Ps. 16:6 ➔ BEAUTIFUL (BE) <8231> [2] Song 1:16 ➔ PLEASANT <5273> a. [3] Song 7:6 ➔ PLEASANT <5276> [4] Is. 17:10 ➔ PLEASANT <5282> [5] Mic. 2:9 ➔ DELIGHT (noun) <8588>.

DELIGHTFUL (BE) – Song 4:10 ➔ BEAUTIFUL (BE, MAKE ONESELF) <3302>.

DELILAH – ***d^{e}liylāh*** [fem. proper noun: דְּלִילָה <1807>; from BRING LOW <1809>]: languishing, pretty ▶ **She was the seductress of Samson. She was from the Valley of Sorek and may have been a Philistine.** Samson loved her (Judg. 16:4). For a high price paid to her by the Philistines, she agreed to find out why Samson had his strength and relayed her knowledge to the Philistines. The Philistines then captured Samson and put his eyes out. She showed great determination and self-control as she slowly urged Samson to tell her the secret to his great strength. Other refs.: Judg. 16:6, 10, 12, 13, 18. ¶

DELIVER – [1] ***māg̱an*** [verb: מָגַן <4042>; a denom. from SHIELD <4043> (an indication of some kind of protection)] ▶ **This word indicates to give over, to abandon; to present, to bestow.** It refers to God's giving over of Abram's enemies to him (Gen. 14:20); and of wisdom's presentation of a crown (Prov. 4:9). Hosea speaks of God's inability to give up or surrender Israel to her deserved fate because of His love for her (Hos. 11:8). ¶
[2] ***nāṣal*** [verb: נָצַל <5337>; a prim. root] ▶ **This word means to snatch away. Deliverance often indicated the power of one entity overcoming the power of another.** It was frequently expressed as deliverance from the hand (i.e., power) of another (Gen. 32:11; Hos. 2:10). Thus, idols (1 Sam. 12:21) and mere human might (Ps. 33:16) were belittled as unable to deliver. God was frequently honored as delivering His people, whether from earthly enemies (2 Sam. 22:1; Jer. 1:8); or from more abstract things like transgressions (Ps. 39:8); and death (Ps. 33:19; 56:13). The word also refers to the taking of objects from another's power and is thus translated to recover (Judg. 11:26; 1 Sam. 30:8); to strip (2 Chr. 20:25); or to spoil (Ex. 3:22; 12:36). In a special usage, the word signifies warriors delivering one's eyes, i.e., escaping from sight (2 Sam. 20:6).

In 2 Samuel 14:6, a participle referred to one who would separate two men fighting each other. In Psalm 119:43, the psalmist asked God not to take (or deliver) His word out of his mouth. *

[3] ***neṣal*** [Aramaic verb: נְצַל <5338>; corresponding to <5337> above] ▶ **This word means to liberate, to rescue.** In Daniel 3:29, it referred to God's deliverance of the three Hebrews from the fiery furnace, an action Nebuchadnezzar recognized as beyond any other so-called god. In Daniel 6:14, the word referred to Daniel's deliverance from the den of lions, a feat that Darius unsuccessfully attempted. Daniel 6:27 referred to God's successful deliverance of Daniel from the hand (i.e., power) of the lions. As with the Hebrew form, this word acknowledges God as the deliverer of those who trust in Him. ¶

[4] ***pāḏa'*** [verb: פְּדַע <6308>; a prim. root] ▶ **This word occurs only once, and the context requires that it carry a meaning like to redeem, to rescue.** The verse talks of delivering one from going down to the pit; it is also translated to spare. Ref.: Job 33:24. ¶

[5] ***pālaṯ*** [verb: פָּלַט <6403>; a prim. root] ▶ **This word means to escape, to cause to escape, to take to safety, to bring forth.** It can be used to depict a deliverer, one who helps to escape (2 Sam. 22:2). It describes deliverance or rescue from threatening situations (2 Sam. 22:44). It signifies survivors who have escaped, gotten away safely in time of danger (Ezek. 7:16). It means to give birth to a calf, to calve (Job 21:10). It means to be given a legal judgment of freedom, a clearance (Job 23:7). It describes the Lord's deliverance of the psalmist's life from oppressors (Ps. 17:13). In its causative usage, it means to take to safety, to deliver (Is. 5:29; Mic. 6:14). *

[6] ***šezaḇ, šêyziḇ*** [Aramaic verb: שְׁזַב, שֵׁיזִב <7804>; corresponding to LEAVE <5800>] ▶ **This word refers consistently to rescuing or saving a person from an impossible situation.** God or a person may be the subject who is set on rescuing someone (Dan. 3:15, 17, 28; 6:14; 16, 20, 27). ¶

– [7] Ex. 21:13 ➔ BEFALL <579> [8] Num. 31:5 ➔ PROVIDE <4560> [9] Ezra 7:19 ➔ COMPLETE (verb) <8000> [10] Ps. 63:10; Jer. 18:21; Ezek. 35:5 ➔ to deliver, to deliver up ➔ SPILL <5064> [11] Ps. 144:7, 10, 11 ➔ OPEN <6475> b. [12] Is. 19:4 ➔ GIVE OVER <5534> [13] Is. 50:2 ➔ REDEMPTION <6304> [14] See REDEEM <6299> [15] See SAVE <3467>.

DELIVER OVER – ***māḡar*** [verb: מָגַר <4048>; a prim. root] ▶ **This word means to cast before, to yield up, to throw.** In a participial form, the term is used once to describe the people and princes of Israel who were being thrown to the sword because they stubbornly refused to heed God's discipline (Ezek. 21:12). When used in its intensive form, the verb conveys the idea to cast down or to overthrow, as witnessed in Psalm 89:44: "You have made his splendor to cease and cast his throne to the ground" (NASB). See the verb *nāḡar* (SPILL <5064>). ¶

DELIVERANCE – [1] ***haṣṣālāh*** [fem. noun: הַצָּלָה <2020>; from DELIVER <5337>] ▶ **This word refers to the rescue of the Jews from Haman and his plots through Esther, the Jewish queen of Persia.** Ref.: Esther 4:14. ¶

[2] ***pelêyṭāh*** [fem. noun: פְּלֵיטָה <6413>; fem. of REFUGEE <6412>] ▶ **This word means something delivered, a remnant.** Jacob split his group into two camps so that if Esau attacked one, the other could escape (Gen. 32:8: to escape). Joseph told his brothers that God used what they meant for evil to be deliverance for them (Gen. 45:7; also translated survivors). Moses told Pharaoh that the locusts would eat whatever was left from the hail (Ex. 10:5: what has escaped, that which is escaped, what is left). The Israelites looked for wives for the Benjamites who were left (Judg. 21:17: survivors, them that be escaped). David had everyone flee, or no one would be safe from Absalom (2 Sam. 15:14: to escape). ¶

[3] ***tešû'āh*** [fem. noun: תְּשׁוּעָה <8668>; from CRY (verb) <7768> in the sense of SAVE <3467>] ▶ **This word means salvation, a victory, safety.** Typically, the term is used in the context of military conflict (Judg.

15:18; 1 Sam. 11:13; 1 Chr. 11:14). While victory was usually not obtained through human means (Ps. 33:17; 108:12; 146:3; Prov. 21:31), safety came through a multitude of counselors (Prov. 11:14; 24:6). Principally, however, deliverance was to be found only in God (2 Chr. 6:41; Ps. 119:81; 144:10). The deliverance of the Lord was on the minds of both Isaiah and Jeremiah during the troubled times in which they lived (Is. 45:17; 46:13; Jer. 3:23; Lam. 3:26). *
– 4 Ps. 32:7 ➔ ESCAPE <6405>.

DELIVERANCES – Ps. 68:20 ➔ SALVATION <4190>.

DELUDED – Is. 44:20 ➔ MOCK <2048>.

DELUSION – 1 Jer. 10:15; 51:18 ➔ MOCKERY <8595> 2 Lam. 2:14 ➔ MISLEADING <4065> 3 Zech. 10:2 ➔ NOTHINGNESS <205>.

DELUSIONS – Is. 66:4 ➔ CAPRICIOUS CHILDREN <8586>.

DEMAND – Dan. 4:17 ➔ DECISION <7595>.

DEMANDS (AGREE TO) – 1 Kgs. 20:8 ➔ lit.: to consent ➔ WILLING (BE) <14>.

DEMOLISH – 1 ***rāšaš*** [verb: רָשַׁשׁ <7567>; a prim. root] ► **This word means to damage, to ruin; it is also translated to beat down, to destroy, to impoverish, to shatter, to crush.** It indicates the destination or ruin of something: fortified cities or towers (Jer. 5:17); or even a people or nation that has been defeated and abused (Mal. 1:4). ¶
– 2 Hos. 10:2 ➔ NECK (BREAK THE) <6202>.

DEMOLISHED (BE) – Amos 3:15 ➔ CONSUME, BE CONSUMED <5486>.

DEMORALIZED (BE) – Is. 19:3 ➔ EMPTY (MAKE) <1238>.

DEMON – ***šēḏ*** [masc. noun: שֵׁד <7700>] ► **This Hebrew word means a demon, a devil, i.e., an evil spirit; NIV translates false god. The primary or typical translation of this noun is demon or demons.** This noun was used to describe the recipient of a sacrifice (i.e., a sacrifice that was not directed or given to God [Deut. 32:17]). Certain sacrifices in which sons and daughters were sacrificed were also directed toward demons (Ps. 106:37). This word is also used to designate the recipients of forbidden sacrifices. ¶

DEN – 1 ***'ereḇ*** [masc. noun: אֶרֶב <695>; from WAIT (LIE IN) <693>] ► **This word indicates the lair or home of the beast lying in wait, as directed by God.** Refs.: Job 37:8; 38:40. ¶
2 ***gōḇ*** [Aramaic masc. noun: גֹּב <1358>; from a root corresponding to PLOWMAN <1461> (in the sense of one who digs)] ► **This word means a lair, a pit.** It describes an enclosed area where lions were kept (Dan. 6:7, 12). The entrance to the den could be closed and sealed (Dan. 6:17). Other refs.: Dan. 6:16, 19, 20, 23, 24. ¶
3 ***me'ûrāh*** [fem. noun: מְאוּרָה <3975>; fem. pass. part. of LIGHT (GIVE) <215> (in the sense of an aperture)] ► **This word refers to the hole where a viper lives.** In context a child will not fear to put his or her hand on a viper's den (Is. 11:8; NIV: nest). ¶
4 ***minhārāh*** [fem. noun: מִנְהָרָה <4492>; from FLOW (verb) <5102>] ► **This word refers to naturally occurring holes in the mountains made suitable for living.** Ref.: Judg. 6:2; also translated shelter. ¶
– 5 Job 37:8; 38:40; Ps. 104:22; Song 4:8; Amos 3:4; Nah. 2:12 ➔ DWELLING PLACE <4585> 6 Ps. 10:9 ➔ ABODE <5520> 7 Is. 11:8 ➔ HOLE <2352> 8 Is. 32:14 ➔ CAVE <4631>.

DENOUNCE – Dan. 3:8 ➔ ACCUSE <7170>.

DENSE – 1 Is. 30:27 ➔ HEAVINESS <3514> 2 Zech. 11:2 ➔ THICK <1208> or VINTAGE <1210>.

DENY – ***kāḥaš*** [verb: כָּחַשׁ <3584>; a prim. root] ► **This word means to deal**

falsely about something or with someone, the opposite of being truthful, honest. It also means to lie, to cringe. It is used of denying or disavowing something (Gen. 18:15); of deceiving or lying to a person with respect to something (Lev. 6:2, 3; Josh. 24:27). It naturally takes on the meaning of concealing something (Josh. 7:11). False prophets were always deceiving themselves and others (1 Kgs. 13:18; Zech. 13:4). It means to deny someone wrongly (Job 31:28). It is used of wine failing, disappointing people (Hos. 9:2). It takes on the meaning of cringing or fawning before the Lord (Ps. 18:44). *

DEPART – [1] ***mûš*** [verb: מוּשׁ <4185>; a prim. root (perhaps rather the same as FEEL <4184> through the idea of receding by contact)] ▶ **This word indicates failing to be present, the withdrawing of persons or things.** Persons (Ex. 33:11); various things (Ex. 13:22; Josh. 1:8; Prov. 17:13; Is. 54:10); especially of God's Word, which will never depart from His people (Is. 59:21). It is used figuratively of (not) removing one's neck from God's judgment (Mic. 2:3); of not departing from God's commands (Job 23:12). The person who trusts God will not fail to produce fruit (Jer. 17:8). It is used derisively of idols who do not leave their place and cannot move (Is. 46:7). *
[2] ***ṣāpar*** [verb: צָפַר <6852>; a prim. root] ▶ **This word refers to persons' going away from a location, leaving it.** Ref.: Judg. 7:3. ¶
– [3] Prov. 3:21; 4:21 ➔ PERVERSE <3868> [4] Song 4:8 ➔ JOURNEY (verb) <7788> [5] Is. 59:13 ➔ depart, depart away ➔ MOVE <5253> [6] Jer. 6:8 ➔ ALIENATED (BE) <3363>.

DEPART (THOSE WHO) – Jer. 17:13 ➔ TURN AWAY (THOSE WHO) <3249>.

DEPORT – Ezra 4:10; 5:12 ➔ BRING OVER <1541>.

DEPOSE – [1] Is. 22:19 ➔ PUSH <1920> [2] Dan. 5:20 ➔ BRING DOWN <5182>.

DEPOSIT – [1] ***piqqāḏôn*** [masc. noun: פִּקָּדוֹן <6487>; from ATTEND <6485>] ▶ **The root idea of this word is that something is left under someone's care or attention. The word occurs three times in the Old Testament.** In Genesis 41:36, it referred to a store (also translated reserve) of food that Joseph advised Pharaoh to store up for the coming famine. In Leviticus 6:2, 4, the word signified any deposit left in someone's care. If the keeper of this deposit dealt dishonestly with it, he had to pay a 20 percent penalty in addition to the deposit. ¶
– [2] Ezra 5:15; 6:5 ➔ BRING DOWN <5182> [3] Ezek. 24:6, 11, 12 ➔ SCUM <2457>.

DEPRAVITY – Hos. 5:2 ➔ SLAUGHTER (noun) <7821>.

DEPRESSION – ***šᵉqaᵃrûrāh*** [fem. noun: שְׁקַעֲרוּרָה <8258>; from DIE DOWN, DIE OUT <8257>] ▶ **This word means the hollow streak of a branch.** It refers to a depression on the walls of a house in Israel indicating some kind of mold or fungus attack (Lev. 14:37). ¶

DEPRIVE – See LACKING (BE) <2637>.

DEPRIVED OF CHILDREN – ***šāḵōl*** [verb: שָׁכֹל <7921>; a prim. root] ▶ **This word means to be bereft of (children), without something.** See Gen. 27:45; 43:14; Lev. 26:22; 1 Sam. 15:33. It also means to miscarry (Ex. 23:26; Job 21:10). The sword and war bereaved parents of their children (Deut. 32:25). With reference to land, it can mean barren, unfruitful (2 Kgs. 2:19); with reference to vines, it refers to casting off, losing their fruit (Mal. 3:11). God Himself would bereave His people of their children as punishment for their rebellions (Jer. 15:7; Ezek. 5:17; Hos. 9:12, 14). *

DEPTH – [1] ***meḥqār*** [masc. noun: מֶחְקָר <4278>; from SEARCH (verb) <2713>] ▶ **This word has the sense of things to be searched out, explored; it is also translated deep place.** In context it is used with *'ereṣ* to mean like places of the earth to be explored, depths unknown (Ps. 95:4), too deep to know. ¶

2 ***m^eṣôlāh, m^eṣûlāh, m^eṣulāh*** [fem. noun: מְצוֹלָה, מְצוּלָה, מְצֻלָה <4688>; from the same as DEEP (noun) <6683>] ▶ **This word is used of the deep (profoundness), the depths of the Nile and of the sea.** Refs. (the Nile): Ex. 15:5; Neh. 9:11; Ps. 107:24; Zech. 10:11. Refs. (the sea): Jon. 2:3; Mic. 7:19. In the last reference, it is used figuratively of the place where God casts the sins of His people. It is a general term for the sea itself (Job 41:31); and figuratively of the place of the dead (Ps. 68:22); or a perilous and dangerous set of circumstances (Ps. 69:2, 15; 88:6). It refers to a deep depression in the land, a ravine, or a hollow (Zech. 1:8). ¶

3 ***'ōmeq*** [masc. noun: עֹמֶק <6011>; from DEEP, DEEP (BE) <6009>] ▶ **This word is used of the great depth (profoundness), the fathomless deeps of the earth.** Ref.: Prov. 25:3. ¶

– 4 Is. 7:11; 29:15; Jer. 49:8, 30 ➔ DEEP, DEEP (BE) <6009>.

DEPTH OF THE SEA – Is. 44:27 ➔ DEEP (noun) <6683>.

DEPTHS – ***ma'^amaqqiym*** [masc. plur. noun: מַעֲמַקִּים <4615>; from DEEP, DEEP (BE) <6009>] ▶ **This word describes profoundness (of waters).** It is used of the deep waters of the sea or other bodies of water (Ps. 69:2, 14; Ezek. 27:34). It is used figuratively and literally of the Lord's drying up the water of the Red Sea (Is. 51:10). It stands for the psalmist's trials and entanglements of oppression (Ps. 130:1). ¶

DEPUTY – 1 1 Kgs. 4:19 ➔ GARRISON <5333> 2 Jer. 51:28 ➔ RULER <5461>.

DERIDE – Prov. 11:12 ➔ DESPISE <936>.

DERISION – 1 ***qeles*** [masc. noun: קֶלֶס <7047>; from MOCK <7046>] ▶ **This word refers to shame, disgrace, discredit, disrespect for someone or something. It also means reproach.** Refs.: Ps. 44:13; 79:4. Prophets often suffered derision and reproach because of their messages and sometimes their aberrant behavior (Jer. 20:8; NIV: reproach). ¶

2 ***šimṣāh*** [fem. noun: שִׁמְצָה <8103>; fem. of WHISPER (noun) <8102>] ▶ **This word refers to an object of humor and ridicule or disrespect.** Ref.: Ex. 32:25; also translated shame, laughingstock. Israel became such an object because of her rebellion and debauched behavior. ¶

– 3 See SCORN (noun) <3933>.

DESCEND – 1 ***gālaš*** [verb: גָּלַשׁ <1570>; a prim. root] ▶ **This word means to go down; it is also translated to appear, to leap down.** It refers to goats coming down from Mount Gilead (Song 4:1; 6:5) which serve as a simile for the hair of the bride. ¶

– 2 Song 4:8 ➔ JOURNEY (verb) <7788> 3 Dan. 4:13, 23 ➔ BRING DOWN <5182>.

DESCENDANT – 1 ***yāliyḏ*** [masc. noun: יָלִיד <3211>; from BIRTH (GIVE) <3205>] ▶ **This word indicates progeny of, offspring. It designates one born.** It may refer to a slave born into a household (Gen. 14:14; 17:12, 13, 23, 27; Jer. 2:14) or to a slave purchased from outside a household (Lev. 22:11). It is better translated as sons or descendants of in some contexts: descendants of Anak, giants (Num. 13:22, 28; Josh. 15:14; 1 Chr. 20:4); sons or descendants of the giant Rapha (2 Sam. 21:16, 18). ¶

– 2 Gen. 21:23; Is. 14:22 ➔ OFFSPRING <5209> 3 Lev. 25:47 ➔ MEMBER <6133> 4 Job 5:25; 21:8; etc. ➔ OFFSPRING <6631>.

DESCENDANTS – 1 1 Sam. 2:33 ➔ INCREASE (noun) <4768> 2 See SEED <2233>.

DESCENDING – Is. 30:30 ➔ REST <5183>.

DESCENT – 1 ***môrāḏ*** [masc. noun: מוֹרָד <4174>; from GO DOWN <3381>] ▶ **This word designates a steep slope, the slope or decline of a mountain or hill.** Refs.: Josh. 7:5; 10:11; Jer. 48:5; Mic. 1:4.

In 1 Kings 7:29, it is used to describe the skilled, artistic work of part of Solomon's sea and the cast metal as a beveled (also translated plaited, hanging, thin, hammered) (work); some kind of work with a slant to it. ¶
[2] ***naḥaṯ*** [masc. noun: נַחַת <5183>; from BRING DOWN <5182>] ▶ **This word is used figuratively of the Lord's arm coming down in judgment.** Ref.: Is. 30:30; also translated descending. The Hebrew word also means calmness, quietness; see REST <5183>. ¶

DESECRATE – [1] Neh. 13:29 ➔ DEFILEMENT <1352> [2] Ps. 106:38 ➔ DEFILED (BE) <2610>.

DESERT (noun) – [1] ***miḏbār*** [masc. noun: מִדְבָּר <4057>; from SPEAK <1696> in the sense of driving (by implication, a desert)] ▶ **This word indicates a wilderness area, a wasteland, or a pasture used for animals in general.** Refs.: Gen. 37:22; Job 38:26; Jer. 23:10; Joel 2:22; in reference to specific areas, especially the great Sinai wilderness (Deut. 2:7). Several other specific wilderness areas are indicated: the wilderness of Shur (Ex. 15:22); of Qedesh (Ps. 29:8); of Beersheba (Gen. 21:14); of En Gedi (1 Sam. 24:1) and others. It is used figuratively of the Lord making Israel like a wilderness (Hos. 2:3); and of the Lord depicted as a possible wilderness to His people (Jer. 2:31). Some wilderness areas featured cities and villages (Josh. 15:61; Is. 42:11). The Hebrew word also refers to the mouth; see MOUTH <4057>. *
[2] ***ʿărāḇāh*** [fem. noun: 6160> עֲרָבָה; from EVENING (BECOME) <6150> (in the sense of sterility)] ▶ **This word means a desert plain, a steppe, a wilderness. This word designates a prominent geographic feature of the Middle East.** It is used to designate the arid plateau in south Judah (Is. 51:3; see also 1 Sam. 23:24); various portions of the Jordan River valley and the adjacent plains (Josh. 12:1; 2 Sam. 2:29); the desert area in northern Arabia (Deut. 1:1); and any generic land formation similar to these arid plateaus (Deut. 1:7; Is. 40:3). There is some uncertainty as to the use of this word in Psalm 68:4. Most translations render the word as heavens or clouds, rather than the more literal meaning, desert. *
– [3] Num. 21:20; 23:28 ➔ JESHIMON <3452> [4] Is. 25:5; 32:2 ➔ DRY PLACE <6724>.

DESERT (verb) – Deut. 32:18 ➔ UNMINDFUL (BE) <7876>.

DESERT TRIBES – Ps. 72:9 ➔ WILDERNESS <6728>.

DESERTED PLACE – Is. 17:9 ➔ FORSAKEN PLACE <5805>.

DESERVES (WHAT ONE) – ***gᵉmûl*** [masc. noun: גְּמוּל <1576>; from REWARD (verb) <1580>] ▶ **This word indicates recompense, benefits, something merited, dealings, doings.** It indicates the actions or dealings with others (Judg. 9:16), such as Jerubbaal. The dealing of a nation or what a person's hands return to him or her (Ps. 28:4; Prov. 12:14; Is. 3:11; Obad. 1:15). It indicates a deserved receipt for something, whether accepted or returned (Joel 3:4, 7), which the Lord (Ps. 28:4; Is. 35:4; 66:6) or a person may render. God's good deeds amount to benefits received from Him (Ps. 103:2). *

DESIGN – ***ṣûrāh*** [fem. noun: צוּרָה <6699>; fem. of ROCK <6697>] ▶ **This word refers to the planned construction patterns of a building, of Ezekiel's visionary Temple.** Ref.: Ezek. 43:11; also translated form. ¶

DESIGN (ORIGINAL) – 2 Chr. 24:13 ➔ PROPORTION <4971>.

DESIGNATED – [1] ***mûʿāḏāh*** [fem. noun: מוּעָדָה <4152>; from APPOINT <3259>] ▶ **This word indicates something allotted to or for a specific social purpose, e.g., the six cities of refuge in Israel.** Ref.: Josh. 20:9; also translated appointed. Literally, there were cities agreed upon, witnessed to as places of refuge. ¶
– [2] Neh. 13:31 ➔ APPOINTED <2163>.

DESIGNATED PART – Ezek. 43:21 ➔ APPOINTMENT <4662>.

DESIRE (noun) – [1] ***ᵃḇiyyônāh*** [fem. noun: אֲבִיּוֹנָה <35>; from WILLING (BE) <14> (in the sense of to desire)] ▶ **The word describes the failure of desire (possibly sexual craving) of an aging person.** Ref.: Eccl. 12:5. Some think the word is better translated to indicate the caperberry which had become an ineffective stimulate in old age. ¶

[2] ***'awwāh*** [fem. noun: אַוָּה <185>; from DESIRE (verb) <183>] ▶ **This word is translated to desire, to lust, to want, to please.** It refers to hunger for meat (Deut. 12:15, 20, 21), but it also indicates the desire of one's soul in general for something (1 Sam. 23:20). It refers to the mating desire of animals as well (Jer. 2:24: desire, passion, occasion, heat, craving), but in Jeremiah it is a symbol of Israel's lustful, uncontrolled behavior. It even refers to God's will or desire (Hos. 10:10). Other ref.: Deut. 18:6. ¶

[3] ***ᵃrešeṯ*** [fem. noun: אֲרֶשֶׁת <782>; from BETROTH <781> (in the sense of desiring to possess)] ▶ **This word means wish, request.** It describes the desire of the king to know the Lord through both the Lord's blessing and gift of life (Ps. 21:2). ¶

[4] ***ḥemdāh*** [fem. noun: חֶמְדָּה <2532>; fem. of PLEASANT <2531>] ▶ **This word indicates what is attractive and pleasant.** A person, Saul, and his house to serve as king in Israel (1 Sam. 9:20); a goddess beloved of women (Dan. 11:37). It is used to define and describe things as excellent: beautiful craft, ships (Is. 2:16); beautiful, pleasant houses (Ezek. 26:12); things of all nations (Hag. 2:7). *

[5] ***ḥêp̱eṣ*** [masc. noun: חֵפֶץ <2656>; from DELIGHT (verb) <2654>] ▶ **This word means delight, pleasure, matter. The root idea is to incline toward something.** The word signifies delight in or (in an unrealized sense) a desire for earthly goods, such as Solomon's desire for timber (1 Kgs. 5:8–10); a delight in fruitful land (Mal. 3:12); or the delight of hands in their labor (Prov. 31:13). The word also refers to people's delight in God's Law (Ps. 1:2); His works (Ps. 111:2); God's own delight in His works (Is. 46:10; 48:14); His lack of delight in foolish or disrespectful people (Eccl. 5:4; Mal. 1:10). Three times the word is used to liken a person or nation to an undesirable vessel (Jer. 22:28; 48:38; Hos. 8:8). In addition, the word is used in Ecclesiastes to refer to a matter without respect to its delightfulness (Eccl. 3:1, 17). *

[6] ***ḥêšeq*** [noun: חֵשֶׁק <2837>; from DESIRE (verb) <2836>] ▶ **This word means a thing wished for.** Three of its uses referred to Solomon's building projects. He was able to build the Temple and the other constructions that he desired (1 Kgs. 9:1, 19; 2 Chr. 8:6). Isaiah 21:4 implied that the prophet desired Babylon's destruction (the twilight I longed for, the night of my pleasure), but the passage goes on to say that what he desired was so horrific that it terrified him. ¶

[7] ***ma'way*** [masc. noun: מַאֲוַי <3970>; from DESIRE (verb) <183>] ▶ **In context this word refers to the attempts and plans of the wicked to exalt themselves by their plans. It is used in the plural construct form once.** Ref.: Ps. 140:8. ¶

[8] ***môrāš*** [masc. noun: מוֹרָשׁ <4180>] ▶ **This word means and is translated thought, wish.** It describes the wishes or longings of the heart (Job 17:11). The Hebrew word also means possession; see POSSESSION <4180>. ¶

[9] ***miš'ālāh*** [fem. noun: מִשְׁאָלָה <4862>; from ASK <7592>] ▶ **This word indicates a plea or solicitation for something.** In context it denotes a plea for victory over one's evil enemies (Ps. 20:5: petition, request). The Lord answers the desires, petitions of those who delightfully serve Him (Ps. 37:4). ¶

[10] ***taᵃwāh*** [fem. noun: תַּאֲוָה <8378>; from DESIRE (verb) <183> (abbreviated)] ▶ **This word means something enjoyable, bounty; craving, greed.** It indicates something that is attractive and delightful to the eyes, desirable (Gen. 3:6). It refers to the abundant fertility and produce of mountainous land (Gen. 49:26). It describes food that is choice (NIV, Gen. 49:26), dainty

(KJV), favored (NASB). It indicates the longings of a person's heart, its cravings (Ps. 10:3; 21:2); or the longings of a humble person (Ps. 10:17). It is the opposite of revulsion (Ps. 38:9). The righteous will have their desires realized (Prov. 10:24; 11:23). When a desire is realized, it invigorates a person (Prov. 13:12, 19). For the prophet, the Lord's name and the remembrance of His deeds are His desires (Is. 26:8). *

[11] ***t^{e}šûqāh*** [fem. noun תְּשׁוּקָה <8669>; from OVERFLOW <7783>] ▶ **This word means longing. It was used to describe the strong feelings of desire that one person had for another, but it was not always a healthy desire.** As part of the judgment after Adam and Eve's sin, God said that a woman would long for her husband (Gen. 3:16). People are not the only thing that can long: God told Cain that sin was lying at his door, desiring to enter (Gen. 4:7). Other ref.: Song 7:10. ¶

– [12] 1 Chr. 29:18 ➔ FORMED <3336> [13] Job 34:36: my desire is that ➔ OH, THAT <15> [14] Prov. 10:3; 11:6 ➔ DESTRUCTION <1942>.

DESIRE (HAVE A) – Deut. 21:11 ➔ DESIRE (verb) <2836>.

DESIRE (verb) – [1] ***'āwāh*** [verb: אָוָה <183>; a prim. root] ▶ **This word means to be inclined; it is also translated to covet, to crave, to be enthralled, to long, to yearn.** It is used to signify coveting, as in the tenth commandment (Deut. 5:21; but *ḥāmaḏ* [<2530> below] is used in Ex. 20:17). The word may also signify acceptable desires for objects such as food or beauty (Ps. 45:11; Mic. 7:1); as well as for righteousness and God (Is. 26:9; Mic. 7:1). Both God and humans can be the subject of this word (Ps. 132:13, 14). *

[2] ***ḥāmaḏ, ḥ^{a}mûḏāh, ḥ^{a}muḏāh*** [verb: חָמַד, חֲמוּדָה, חֲמֻדָה <2530>; a prim. root] ▶ **This verb also means to take pleasure in, to lust, to covet, to be desirable, to desire passionately.** The verb can mean to desire intensely even in its simple stem: the tenth commandment prohibits desiring to the point of coveting, such as a neighbor's house, wife, or other assets (Ex. 20:17; cf. Ex. 34:24). Israel was not to covet silver or gold (Deut. 7:25; Josh. 7:21) or the fields and lands of others (Mic. 2:2). Achan coveted certain valuables in Jericho (Josh. 7:21). The word can also express slight variations in its basic meaning: the mountains of Bashan, including Mount Hermon, looked in envy on the chosen mountains of Zion (Ps. 68:16); the simple fool delighted in his naïve, senseless way of life (Prov. 1:22); and a man was not to lust after the beauty of an adulterous woman (Prov. 6:25).

The word expresses the idea of finding pleasure in something as when Israel took pleasure in committing spiritual fornication among its sacred oaks (Is. 1:29). The passive participle of the simple stem indicates someone beloved or endearing (Is. 53:2) but has a negative meaning in Job 20:20, indicating excessive desiring or craving (cf. Ps. 39:11).

The passive stem indicates something that is worthy of being desired, desirable; the fruit of the tree of the knowledge of good and evil appeared inviting to make a person wise (Gen. 2:9; 3:6; Prov. 21:20) but proved to be destructive. The plural of this verbal stem expresses satisfaction or reward for keeping God's Law (Ps. 19:10). *

[3] ***ḥāšaq*** [verb: חָשַׁק <2836>; a prim. root] ▶ **This word means to be attached to, to love, to delight in, to bind.** Laws in Deuteronomy described the procedure for taking a slave woman to whom one has become attached as a wife (Deut. 21:11: to desire, to have a desire, to be attracted). Shechem's soul longed after and delighted in Dinah, who was an Israelite (Gen. 34:8: to long, to have one's heart set on). God's binding love for Israel is described as unmerited love (Deut. 7:7: to set one's love, to set one's affection). Isaiah describes the figurative way in which God's love for his soul delivered him by casting all his sins behind His back (Is. 38:17: in love, lovingly). *

– [4] Deut. 12:15, 20, 21 ➔ DESIRE (noun) <185> [5] 1 Kgs. 9:1 ➔ DELIGHT (verb) <2654> [6] Job 14:15 ➔ LONG FOR <3700> [7] Prov. 31:4 ➔ OR <176> b.

DESIRED (NOT) – Zeph. 2:1 ➔ LONG FOR <3700>.

DESOLATE – [1] ***battāh*** [fem. noun: בַּתָּה <1327>; fem. from an unused root (meaning to break in pieces)] ▶ **This word means deserted; it is also translated steep.** It describes the ravines or valleys as desolate or steep where the Assyrians will settle when they come to attack Israel (Is. 7:19). ¶
[2] ***meḇûqāh*** [fem. noun: מְבוּקָה <4003>; from the same as EMPTY <950>] ▶ **This word means void, emptiness.** It indicates the desolation and devastation of a city in time of war (Nah. 2:10; also translated desolation, plundered), along with several other terms close in meaning. ¶
[3] ***šāmêm*** [masc. adj.: שָׁמֵם <8076>; from DESTROYED (BE) <8074>] ▶ **This word means ruined, wasted, destroyed.** This adjective corresponds to the verb *šāmêm*, to be destroyed. It can be used to describe both land and objects that have been destroyed. The connotations here are of an extreme destruction that has lasting effects and causes all people to stand up and take notice of what has happened. When Jerusalem fell, the Temple was torn apart and utterly destroyed, and this adjective was used to describe the condition of the Temple (Dan. 9:17). In Jeremiah 12:11, it is also used to prophesy what the land would be like after the fall of Jerusalem. This adjective paints a picture of harsh destruction. In these contexts, this destruction is indicative of God's judgment on His people. ¶
– [4] Job 15:34; 30:3; Is. 49:21 ➔ SOLITARY <1565> [5] Ps. 25:16 ➔ ONLY <3173> [6] Is. 15:6; Jer. 48:34; Ezek. 6:14; 33:28, 29; 35:3 ➔ DESOLATION <4923> [7] Is. 27:10 ➔ ALONE <910> [8] Ezek. 26:19 ➔ WASTE (LAY) <2717> [9] Nah. 2:10 ➔ EMPTY (adj.) <950> [10] See DRY (adj.) <2720>.

DESOLATE (BE, BECOME) – ***yāšam*** [verb: יָשַׁם <3456>; a prim. root] ▶ **This word means to lie waste, to be deserted.** In most cases, the people affected were afraid famine would cause the land to lie waste. During the famine, the Egyptians asked Joseph to buy them and their land so they would not die and their land become desolate (Gen. 47:19). The Israelites were commanded to tell the people of Canaan that they were to soon experience the fear and trembling of the Lord that would cause them to leave their land (Ezek. 12:19; also translated to be stripped, to be emptied). Other refs.: Ezek. 6:6; 19:7. ¶

DESOLATE (MAKE) – Is. 24:1 ➔ WASTE (MAKE, BE, LAY) <1110>.

DESOLATE PLACES – ***'ašmān*** [masc. noun: אַשְׁמָן <820>; prob. from OIL <8081>] ▶ **This word is taken by some translators as a figurative description of uninhabited places where injustice is rampant.** Ref.: KJV, NKJV, Is. 59:10. See also VIGOROUS PEOPLE <820>. ¶

DESOLATION – [1] ***yešiymāh*** [fem. noun: יְשִׁימָה <3451>; from DESOLATE (BE) <3456>] ▶ **This word is translated death.** It occurs in Psalm 55:15 in an imprecatory sense, where desolation was to be the ultimate end of a wicked and false person. As such, it links with the developed wisdom theme of wickedness as consummating in nothingness. Here the word invoked the result of falsity and idolatry that the true believer would escape by steadfast loyalty to God (cf. Ps. 55:16, 17, 22). Ezekiel used the verb from which this word is derived (*yāšam*) several times in describing the habitation of Israel due to idolatry and unbelief (Ezek. 6:6; 12:19; 19:7). The one who would falsely break the covenant (Ps. 55:20, 21) could expect desolation—a message Ezekiel preached to the people of the covenant. ¶
[2] ***mešammāh*** [fem. noun: מְשַׁמָּה <4923>; from DESTROYED <8074>] ▶ **This word indicates waste, a state of isolation, desertion.** It describes part of the conditions created by God's judgments on various lands and cities (Is. 15:6; Jer. 48:34), including Jerusalem (Ezek. 5:15: astonishment, horror, object of horror; 6:14; 35:3). Other refs.: Ezek. 33:28, 29. ¶

[3] ***šimmāh, šᵉmāmāh*** [fem. sing. noun: שִׁמָּה, שְׁמָמָה <8077>; fem. of DESOLATE <8076>] ▶ **This noun means waste.** It can be used to refer to many things such as land, cities, or houses (Ex. 23:29; Lev. 26:33; Is. 1:7). Most often it is used in conjunction with a passage describing what did happen to the land of Israel after God judged His people and sent them into exile. This shows the totality of the destruction that Israel endured. Nothing was to be saved from this destruction. Fields and vineyards were turned into wastelands and desolate fields after God's judgment (Jer. 12:10). God allowed such desolation as a punishment for the sins of His people because they refused to repent. This punishment could even fall on people of other nations, such as the Edomites (Ezek. 33:28, 29; 35:3). *
– [4] Is. 34:11 ➔ VOID <922> [5] Lam. 3:47 ➔ DEVASTATION <7612> [6] Nah. 2:10 ➔ DESOLATE <4003>.

DESOLATIONS – Ps. 74:3 ➔ RUINS <4876>.

DESPAIR (noun) – [1] ***dᵉʾāḇôn*** [masc. noun: דְּאָבוֹן <1671>; from SORROW (verb) <1669>] ▶ **This word describes a great sorrow or anguish of soul (*nephesh*) or mind in God's people when He sends them into exile among the nations.** Ref.: Deut. 28:65; also translated sorrow, anguish, languishing, despairing. ¶
– [2] Job 9:23 ➔ TRIAL <4531> [3] Is. 61:3 ➔ DARK <3544> [4] Ezek. 4:16; 12:19 ➔ HORROR <8078>.

DESPAIR (BE IN) – [1] ***pûn*** [verb: פּוּן <6323>; a prim. root meaning to turn, i.e., to be perplexed] ▶ **This word refers to a state of great distraction or helplessness, hopelessness.** Ref.: Ps. 88:15; also translated to be distracted, to be overcome, to be helpless, to be distraught. In context it describes despair because of illness. ¶
– [2] Ps. 69:20 ➔ SICK (BE) <5136>.

DESPAIR (verb) – ***yāʾaš*** [verb: יָאַשׁ <2976>; a prim. root] ▶ **The word refers to hopelessness in the sense that one concludes that something desirable is out of reach and usually stops working toward it.** In 1 Samuel 27:1, David hoped Saul would despair (give up) of finding him when he fled to the Philistines. The word may refer to loss of hope in God or a false god (Is. 57:10; Jer. 2:25; 18:12). It may also refer, similarly, to a loss of meaning in life (Eccl. 2:20; cf. Phil. 1:21, 22). In Job 6:26, the word describes an emotional state of despair without immediately focusing on the cause of despair. In three passages, the word occurs in a passive sense as a statement or exclamation meaning "it is hopeless" (also translated: there is no hope, it is no use) (Is. 57:10; Jer. 2:25; 18:12). ¶

DESPAIRING – [1] Deut. 28:65 ➔ DESPAIR (noun) <1671> [2] Job 6:14 ➔ AFFLICTED <4523>.

DESPERATE – Is. 17:11 ➔ SICK (BE) <605>.

DESPERATELY – Is. 17:11: desperately wicked, desperately sick ➔ SICK (BE) <605>.

DESPISE – [1] ***bûz*** [verb: בּוּז <936>; a prim. root] ▶ **This word indicates scorn or disrespect for someone or something; it is also translated to scorn, to belittle, to deride, to contemn, to mock.** Fools especially despise or hold contempt for wisdom (Prov. 1:7; 23:9). Contempt may be aimed at persons (Prov. 6:30; 11:12), but a mother or father are never to be despised (Prov. 23:22; 30:17). God's word or instruction is not to be held in contempt (Prov. 13:13), and love is said to be beyond contempt (Song 8:1, 7). Other refs.: Prov. 14:21; Is. 37:22; Zech. 4:10. ¶
[2] ***bāzāh*** [verb: בָּזָה <959>; a prim. root] ▶ **This word means to hold in disdain, to hold in contempt, to disrespect.** It can mean to prefer something more than the thing despised, e.g., Esau's birthright (Gen. 25:34), or not to treat something with proper respect (Ezek. 16:59; 22:8; Mal. 1:6). The psalmist thanks the Lord for not despising a broken and humble heart (Ps.

51:17). The notorious Syrian king, Antiochus Epiphanes, a forerunner of the Antichrist, is depicted as a despicable person who scorns God Himself (Dan. 11:21); the word is also translated vile, contemptible. *
[3] ***šā'ṭ, šûṭ*** [verb: שְׁאָט, שׁוּט <7590>; for act. part. of TURN ASIDE <7750> (comp. MALICE <7589>)] ► **This word means to scorn, to malign.** It indicates a strong dislike for someone or a people, a loathing or total disrespect, a situation Israel would be free from when the Lord judges her enemies and restores her (Ezek. 16:57; 28:24, 26). ¶
– [4] Lev. 26:30; Jer. 14:19; Ezek. 16:45 ➔ ABHOR <1602> [5] Ps. 107:11; Prov. 1:30; Is. 5:24 ➔ SPURN <5006> [6] Is. 49:7 ➔ DESPISED <960> [7] Ezek. 16:5 ➔ LOATHING <1604> [8] See MOCK <3932>.

DESPISED – [1] ***bûzāh*** [fem. noun: בּוּזָה <939>; fem. pass. part. of DESPISE <936>] ► **This word indicates contempt, an attitude of scorn and disrespect.** The Jews had become an object of scorn from Sanballat and his followers during the time of Nehemiah (Neh. 4:4). ¶
[2] ***bāzōh*** [adj.: בָּזֹה <960>; from DESPISE <959>] ► **This word indicates something or someone scorned or disdained.** The Servant in Isaiah is described with this term (Is. 49:7); the NIV treats the word as a verb, to be despised. ¶
[3] ***nᵉmiḇzāh*** [adj.: נְמִבְזָה <5240>; from DESPISE <959>] ► **This word has the sense of useless, worthless, useless booty or spoil gained in war.** Ref.: 1 Sam. 15:9; KJV: vile. The KJV understands a strong sense of something corrupt or despicable. ¶
– [4] Prov. 12:8 ➔ CONTEMPT <937>.

DESPISED (BE) – [1] ***qālāh*** [verb: קָלָה <7034>; a prim. root] ► **This word means to be lightly esteemed, to be scorn, to be disrespected.** It means to be of little account or value, to be belittled, shamed (Deut. 25:3: to be degraded, to be humiliated, to seem vile). It describes dishonoring one's own parents, treating them lightly (Deut. 27:16: to dishonor, to set light). It indicates treating an important issue lightly (1 Sam. 18:23: to seem a little thing, to be trivial, to be a small matter, to be a light thing). It refers to a social view of someone as unimportant (Prov. 12:9: to be despised, to be lightly esteemed, to be slighted, to be a nobody); or inferior (Is. 3:5: inferior, base, despised, nobody). It describes an insignificant remnant, nation, or people (Is. 16:14: to be despised, to be degraded, to be contemned, to bring into contempt). ¶
– [2] 2 Sam. 1:21 ➔ ABHOR <1602>.

DESPITE, DESPITEFUL – Ezek. 25:6, 15; 36:5 ➔ MALICE <7589>.

DESPONDENCY – Ex. 6:9 ➔ ANGUISH <7115>.

DESPONDENT – Ps. 109:16 ➔ GRIEVED (BE) <3512>.

DESPONDENTLY – 1 Kgs. 21:27 ➔ SLOWLY <328>.

DESTINE – Ps. 49:14 ➔ LAY, LAY CLAIM <8371> b.

DESTINED (BE) – Job 15:28 ➔ READY (BE, MAKE, GET) <6257>.

DESTINY – [1] Eccl. 7:2 ➔ END <5490> [2] Eccl. 9:2, 3 ➔ CHANCE <4745> [3] Is. 65:11 ➔ NUMBER (noun) <4507> b.

DESTITUTE – [1] ***'ar'ār*** [adj.: עַרְעָר <6199>; from STRIP <6209>] ► **This word indicates a person who is poor, without money, house, or home.** Ref.: Ps. 102:17. The Hebrew word also means a bush, a shrub in Jeremiah 17:6; see SHRUB <6199>. ¶
– [2] Prov. 31:8 ➔ DESTRUCTION <2475>.

DESTROY – [1] ***ḥᵃḇal*** [Aramaic verb: חֲבַל <2255>; corresponding to PLEDGE (TAKE AS A) <2254> (in the sense of to destroy)] ► **This word means to demolish, to ruin, to hurt.** King Darius issued a decree that ended with a plea for God to overthrow anyone who tried to destroy the Temple (Ezra 6:12). The tree in Nebuchadnezzar's dream was cut down and destroyed (Dan. 4:23). Because the angel shut the lions' mouths, they did not hurt Daniel (Dan. 6:22). This word also refers to a kingdom that will never be destroyed. In the interpretation of one of Nebuchadnezzar's dreams, Daniel told of a kingdom that would never be destroyed (Dan. 2:44). King Darius praised God when Daniel was not eaten by lions, saying the kingdom of God would not be destroyed (Dan. 6:26). Once again, Daniel saw a kingdom like this in his dream of the four beasts (Dan. 7:14). ¶

2 ***ḥāram*** [verb: חָרַם <2763>; a prim. root] ▶ **This word means to annihilate, to doom, to devote.** This word is most commonly associated with the Israelites destroying the Canaanites upon their entry into the Promised Land (Deut. 7:2; Josh. 11:20). It indicates complete and utter destruction (Judg. 21:11; 1 Sam. 15:18); the severe judgment of God (Is. 11:15); the forfeiture of property (Ezra 10:8); being "accursed" or set apart for destruction (Josh. 6:18). This latter application, being set apart, accounts for what appears to be a contradictory element in the verb. It is also used to mean devotion or consecration to the Lord (Lev. 27:28, 29; Mic. 4:13). Just as something accursed is set apart for destruction, so something devoted to God is set apart for His use. *

3 ***nāṯaṣ*** [verb: נָתַץ <5422>; a prim. root] ▶ **The idea is the breaking down of a structure so that it can no longer support its own weight.** Most often the word signified the destruction of idolatrous religious structures such as the altars that Israel was commanded to tear down on entering the Promised Land (Deut. 7:5; 12:3; Judg. 2:2; 2 Chr. 31:1). The word also signified the destruction of buildings: a tower (Judg. 8:9, 17; Ezek. 26:9); a leprous house (Lev. 14:45); or an entire city (Judg. 9:45). In a spiritual sense, the word signified the tearing down of an individual (Ps. 52:5); or a nation (Jer. 18:7). In Psalm 58:6, the word signified breaking the teeth of fierce lions. *

4 ***sāp̄āh*** [verb: סָפָה <5595>; a prim. root] ▶ **This word means to scrape or sweep away, to perish, to be captured.** It refers to the destruction or sweeping away of people (Ps. 40:14); or a city (Gen. 18:23, 24); especially as the judgment of God. In Deuteronomy 29:19, the word refers to complete destruction: the destruction of the saturated with the dry. In Isaiah 13:15, it means captured as if swept up into another's possession. It is also used of the scraping away (i.e., shaving) of a beard (Is. 7:20). *

5 ***šāḏaḏ*** [verb: שָׁדַד <7703>; a prim. root] ▶ **This word means to be burly, to ravage, to oppress, to assault, to spoil, to lay waste, to devastate. The primary meaning of the verb is to devastate or to destroy.** It is used to describe the destruction of the unfaithful, an action taken due to their duplicity (Prov. 11:3). The verb is also used in Isaiah's prophecy against Moab to describe the action that would result on its cities (Is. 15:1). The actions of an outlaw or thief are depicted by the verb concerning a righteous person's house (Prov. 24:15). The word expresses God's judgment on Egypt and the overthrowing of its hordes (Ezek. 32:12). The verb is also used to describe the actions of subjects such as a lion, a wolf, or a leopard in the figurative sense as a response to the rebellions and backsliding of Jerusalem (Jer. 5:6). Jeremiah uses the word to describe the destruction of a tent and the barrenness when everything was taken away (Jer. 10:20). *

6 ***šāḥaṯ*** [verb: שָׁחַת <7843>; a prim. root] ▶ **This word means to spoil, to ruin, to pervert, to corrupt, to become corrupt, to wipe out.** The verb is used to denote the action(s) of the world (i.e., it is corrupt) and ultimately the reason for God's flooding it (Gen. 6:11, 12). However, even if total destruction meant to punish the evil of humans, God was sure to save a remnant and therefore keep His part of the covenant. This idea of a saved remnant is predominant throughout the rest of the Old Testament.

Another usage of the verb depicts disobedience to God's command to be fruitful and multiply by spoiling or wasting semen on the ground (Gen. 38:9). In this case, Onan's disobedience led to his death, for what he did was wicked in the eyes of Yahweh. The verb is also used to describe violating the covenant in terms of being corrupt (Mal. 2:8). As Lot looked over the valley of the Jordan, this word was used to depict what would happen to Sodom and Gomorrah in a future time because of their wickedness (Gen. 13:10). In the context of the plagues, the smearing of blood on the lintels and doorposts protected Israel from the destruction of their firstborn (Ex. 12:23). When the destroyer came, he would pass by those who had blood on the lintels and doorposts of their houses.

Jerusalem was saved from destruction in 2 Samuel when the Lord was grieved due to the calamity of His people (2 Sam. 24:16). This verb is used to denote the destruction of a slave's eye that allowed him to go free (Ex. 21:26). In Deuteronomy, God prohibited the destruction of fruit trees, for their fruit could be eaten (Deut. 20:19–20). He commanded this, for the trees were for the benefit of humans. He also prohibited the shaving (i.e., in terms of spoiling, destroying) of one's beard (Lev. 19:27). *

– [7] Num. 24:17 ➔ DIG <6979> b. [8] Num. 33:52; Deut. 12:2, 3 ➔ PERISH <6> [9] Deut. 1:44 ➔ CRUSH <3807> [10] Deut. 12:3; 1 Sam. 28:9; Ps. 9:16 ➔ ENSNARE <5367> [11] Ezra 5:12 ➔ HIDE <5642> [12] Ezra 6:12 ➔ OVERTHROW (verb) <4049> [13] Job 14:19 ➔ BEAT <7833> [14] Job 19:26 ➔ CUT DOWN <5362> [15] Ps. 91:6 ➔ WASTE, LAY WASTE <7736> [16] Prov. 15:25 ➔ TEAR <5255> [17] Prov. 21:7 ➔ DRAG (verb) <1641> [18] Is. 42:14 ➔ GASP <5395> [19] Jer. 5:17 ➔ DEMOLISH <7567> [20] Dan. 2:12, 18, 24; 7:11 ➔ PERISH <7> [21] Nah. 1:12 ➔ CUT (verb) <1494> [22] Zeph. 2:11 ➔ LEAN (GROW, BECOME, WAX) <7329> [23] See PULL DOWN <2040> [24] See TURN <2015>.

DESTROYED – [1] ***dumāh*** [fem. noun: דֻּמָה <1822>; from CEASE <1820>] ▶ **This word is of debated meaning. If it derives from *dāmāh* (<1820>), it would mean destroyed one; if from *dāmam* (STAND STILL <1826>), it would mean silent one.** It is used only in Ezekiel 27:32 where it describes the wealthy and beautiful seaport of Tyre as having sunk into the sea, a symbol of being overrun by foreign armies (cf. Ezek. 26:3–5). This judgment came on the people of Tyre because of their pride and because they rejoiced over the fall of Jerusalem (cf. Ezek. 26:2). The ruined city would be relatively silent (although fishermen would still spread their nets there), but in Ezekiel 27:32 "destroyed one" seems to fit the context better. ¶

– [2] Is. 49:19 ➔ DESTRUCTION <2035>.

DESTROYED (BE) – [1] ***ḥᵃraḇ*** [Aramaic verb: חֲרַב <2718>; a root corresponding to WASTE (LAY) <2717>] ▶ **This word means to be utterly devastated, to be laid waste.** The only occurrence of this verb is preserved in a letter sent to Artaxerxes concerning the rebuilding of Jerusalem (Ezra 4:15). Certain antagonists of the Jewish people desired to hinder the rebuilding of the city and called to mind that it was due to wickedness that Jerusalem was destroyed by the Babylonians (cf. Jer. 52:12–20). The result left the city in utter desolation and without defense (cf. Neh. 2:17; Jer. 9:11). ¶

[2] ***šāmaḏ*** [verb: שָׁמַד <8045>; a prim. root] ▶ **This word is not used in its simple form and is only used in the passive and causative stems of the verb. The primary passive meaning is to be destroyed, to be exterminated, or to be annihilated, referring to individual people, households, or nations.** Refs.: Gen. 34:30; Prov. 14:11; Ezek. 32:12. It can also signify the devastation of land and places (Hos. 10:8). The causative forms have the same root meanings as the passive forms. It can mean to annihilate, to exterminate people (Deut. 1:27, 2:22); or to destroy objects such as cities, fortresses, or idols (Is. 23:11; Mic. 5:14). The difference between these two verb forms lies in who is destroying and who is being destroyed. *

[3] ***šāmêm*** [verb: שָׁמֵם <8074>; a prim. root] ▶ **The desolation or destruction that this verb refers to can be used of people.** Refs.: 2 Sam. 13:20; Lam. 1:13, 16. It can also be used of places (Lev. 26:31, 32;

Is. 61:4; Ezek. 35:12). A second meaning of this verb, which is extremely common, is to be appalled or astonished and is used in the simple, passive, and passive causative stems (Job 18:20; Is. 52:14; Jer. 18:16). The connection between these two meanings is not entirely clear; yet they are both used with great frequency. When this verb is used in the second meaning, it often describes a person's reaction on seeing desolation and destruction. For example, in 1 Kings 9:8, the reaction of people to a destroyed land was described with this verb. A much less common use of this verb is in the reflexive stem. Here it meant to be disheartened or dismayed (Ps. 143:4). *

DESTROYER – 1 Ps. 17:4 ➔ VIOLENT <6530> 2 Joel 2:25 ➔ CATERPILLAR <2625>.

DESTROYING – 1 ***mašḥêṯ*** [fem. noun: מַשְׁחֵת <4892>; for DESTRUCTION <4889>] ▶ **This word indicates devastation, annihilation.** It refers to the devastation wrought by means of an instrument of destruction (*kᵉlîy mašḥêṯ*) (Ezek. 9:1; also translated deadly). ¶
– 2 Esther 9:5 ➔ DESTRUCTION <12>.

DESTRUCTION – 1 ***ᵃḇaddōh*** [fem. noun: אֲבַדֹּה <10>; the same as PROPERTY (LOST) <9>, miswritten for DESTRUCTION <11>] ▶ **This word refers to the place of the dead, indistinguishable in meaning from *ᵃḇaddôn*: <11> below.** This form occurs only in Proverbs 27:20 where, along with Sheol, it identifies death as a place that can always hold more just as the eyes of humans always want more. This word originally may have been *ᵃḇêḏāh*, see PROPERTY (LOST) <9>, or *ᵃḇaddôn*, see <11> below, but was changed in the transmission of the ancient manuscript. ¶
2 ***ᵃḇaddôn*** [fem. noun: אֲבַדּוֹן <11>; intens. from PERISH <6>] ▶ **The Hebrew word Abaddon means destruction, ruin (i.e., death). It may also mean a place of destruction. It is used in wisdom literature and connotes the abode of the dead.** It commonly forms a word pair with *šᵉʾāl* (Job 26:6; Prov. 15:11; 27:20) but is also linked with death (Job 28:22; 31:12) and the grave (Ps. 88:11). See the Hebrew verb *ʾāḇad* <6> under RUIN (noun) <8>. ¶
3 ***ʾaḇḏān*** [noun, prob. masc.: אַבְדָן <12>; from PERISH <6>] ▶ **This word means to kill, to exterminate; it is also translated destroying.** It occurs only in Esther 9:5 where the Jews striking their enemies with the sword results in slaughter and destruction (or: killing and destroying). A similar form, *ʾoḇḏān* (<13> below), occurs in Esther 8:6 in a similar context: the desire of the Jews' enemies to bring destruction on them. These two forms may be identical. ¶
4 ***ʾoḇḏān*** [masc. noun: אָבְדָן <13>; from PERISH <6>] ▶ **This term conveys the slaughter of the Jews.** Ref.: Esther 8:6. See the Hebrew verb *ʾāḇaḏ* under PERISH <6>. ¶
5 ***hawwāh*** [fem. noun: הַוָּה <1942>; from FALL (verb) <1933>] ▶ **This word usually describes an event associated with calamity, evil, or destruction; it is also translated desire.** It can speak of the wickedness of evildoers (Ps. 5:9); the devastation a foolish son could cause his father (Prov. 19:13); the destruction intended by the tongue (Ps. 38:12; 52:2); the calamities of life which require refuge in God for protection (Ps. 57:1). In several places, this word depicts the evil desires of the wicked that resulted in destruction: God would cast away the wicked person's desire (Prov. 10:3); the evil desires of transgressors would be their downfall (Prov. 11:6); and destruction awaited the ones who trust in their own desires (Ps. 52:7). *
6 ***hayyāh*** [fem. noun: הַיָּה <1962>; another form for DISASTER <1943>] ▶ **This word is a slightly different form of *hawwāh* (<1942>) above.** It occurs only once in the Old Testament (Job 6:2). ¶
7 ***hᵃriysûṯ*** [fem. noun: הֲרִיסוּת <2035>; from PULL DOWN <2040>] ▶ **This word indicates devastation, overthrow, ruins.** It denotes the land of Judah (land of destruction, destroyed land, devastated land, land laid wasted) and Israel destroyed by Babylon and Assyria (Is. 49:19) but which will again be free and full of people. ¶

8 ***heres*** [masc. noun: הֶרֶס <2041>; from PULL DOWN <2040>] ▶ **This word indicates one of five cities in Egypt where the language of Canaan will be spoken, the city of destruction.** Ref.: Is. 19:18; some ancient manuscripts read the city of the sun. ¶

9 ***ḥᵃlôp̱*** [masc. noun: חֲלוֹף <2475>; from PASS ON <2498>] ▶ **This word refers to persons in society who are unfortunate and need others to affirm and uphold their rights for them; it is also translated destitute, unfortunate.** Ref.: Prov. 31:8. ¶

10 ***kiyḏ*** [masc. noun: כִּיד <3589>; from a prim. root meaning to strike] ▶ **This word is of uncertain meaning. It comes from a primitive root word and most likely means a crushing, a calamity, or a misfortune.** Job responded to Zophar and lamented about the wicked. Job wished that the wicked would see God's wrath and their own destruction (Job 21:20; NASB: decay). ¶

11 ***kālāh*** [fem. noun: כָּלָה <3617>; from FINISH <3615>] ▶ **This word means completion, complete ruin, annihilation.** In the sense of completion, God told Moses that Pharaoh would let the Israelites go by driving them completely out of Egypt (Ex. 11:1). Complete destruction or annihilation was most often attributed to God. Isaiah prophesied that the Lord would make a determined end to Israel (Is. 10:23); Nahum spoke of God's judgment by which He made an utter end of His enemies (Nah. 1:8, 9). Destruction of such massive quantity is attributed to humans in Daniel's prophecy of Greece (Dan. 11:16; KJV: *kālāh*: FINISH <3615>). Other refs.: Gen. 18:21; 2 Chr. 12:12; Neh. 9:31; Is. 28:22; Jer. 4:27; 5:10, 18; 30:11; 46:28; Ezek. 11:13; 13:13; 20:17; Dan. 9:27; Zeph. 1:18. ¶

12 ***mašḥiyṯ*** [fem. noun: מַשְׁחִית <4889>; from DESTROY <7843>] ▶ **This word means corruption, ruin.** Refs.: Ex. 12:13; 2 Kgs. 23:13; 2 Chr. 20:23; 22:4; Prov. 18:9; 28:24; Is. 54:16; Jer. 5:26; 22:7; 51:1; Ezek. 9:6; 21:31; 25:15; Dan. 10:8. See also DESTROY <7843>. ¶

13 ***qeṭeḇ*** [masc. noun: קֶטֶב <6986>; from an unused root meaning to cut off] ▶ **This word is closely associated with the word *qōṭeḇ* (<6987> below). God is always connected with this concept of destruction or ruin.** It seems ironic that in two passages, God was the source of the destruction (Deut. 32:24; Is. 28:2), while in another passage, He was the salvation from the destruction (Ps. 91:6). On further reflection, though, it becomes evident that God is the source of this destruction, which was a means of divine retribution. The difference is that in Deuteronomy and Isaiah, God was brought His judgment on the wicked, but in Psalms, God preserved the righteous in the midst of His judgment on the wicked. The specific nature of the destruction is flexible. In each of the passages, it is set in a different context and is parallel with a different word: *rešep* (<7566>), meaning fire (Deut. 32:24); *deḇer* (<1698>), meaning plague or pestilence (Ps. 91:6); and *mayim* (<4325>), meaning water (Is. 28:2). ¶

14 ***qōṭeḇ*** [masc. noun: קֹטֶב <6987>; from the same as <6986> above] ▶ **This word is closely associated with the word *qeṭeḇ* (DESTRUCTION <6986>) and is connected with judgment.** It occurs only once where it refers to the judgment that God was going to bring against Samaria for its wickedness (Hos. 13:14). See the word *deḇer* (<1698>), meaning plague or pestilence, as in Psalm 91:6. Even though this word appears in the context of God's impending judgment for wickedness, the specific verse in which it appears is actually a vision of hope for a coming restoration. God is going to allow judgment for a time, but then He will remove it because, without His permission, death and Sheol have no power. ¶

15 ***qereṣ*** [masc. noun: קֶרֶץ <7171>; from WINK <7169> b. (in the sense of to compress)] ▶ **This word is found only in Jeremiah 46:20. Due to the immediate context of the passage, however, the more probable meaning is biter (i.e., a biting fly, such as a gadfly, a horsefly, or a mosquito).** Egypt was described as a beautiful heifer, but a biting fly from the north (i.e., Babylon) was being sent to punish her. ¶

[16] ***šēḇer*** [masc. noun: שֶׁבֶר <7667>; from BREAK <7665>] ▶ **This word means ruin, affliction, fracture, solution of a dream, breach.** This noun can be used to express the result from the breaking of a dream (i.e., its interpretation [Judg. 7:15]). Isaiah used this noun to express the possible result of sin by speaking metaphorically of the shattering of a wall (Is. 30:13). In Leviticus, this noun is used to designate a fracture of the foot or hand, indicating a cripple (Lev. 21:19). The noun can also be used to indicate the primary reason for suffering due to disobedience to God. *

[17] ***šiḇrôn*** [masc. noun: שִׁבָּרוֹן <7670>; from BREAK <7665>] ▶ **This word means rupture (i.e., a pang). It is used figuratively for ruin and breaking.** This noun was used figuratively in Jeremiah to describe emotional distress by way of broken loins (Jer. 17:18). It was used in reference to the coming exile, in which it would seem as if Israel had been cut off from the covenant of God, although God, being faithful and true, would provide a remnant or a branch of David. It was also used in Ezekiel as the reason for distress and sorrow (Ezek. 21:6). This reference was also for the coming exile of Israel, in which God would give the Israelites over to those they hated. ¶

[18] ***šōḏ, šôḏ*** [masc. noun: שֹׁד, שׁוֹד <7701>; from WASTE, LAY WASTE <7736>] ▶ **This word means violence, desolation, robbery, spoil, wasting. The primary meaning of this word is violence or destruction.** In Job, the noun is used to describe an object or idea of which not to fear (Job 5:21). The word is also used in Psalms to designate a reason for God's arising to protect the weak (Ps. 12:5). Isaiah used the noun to depict the reason that God weeps bitterly (i.e., the destruction of His people due to their sin [Is. 22:4]). This word was also used by Jeremiah and Amos to describe violence and havoc as social sins (Jer. 6:7; Amos 3:10). The primary meaning of destruction was used by Hosea to express God's reason for the coming destruction of a nation (Hos. 7:13). *

[19] ***taḇliyṯ*** [fem. noun: תַּבְלִית <8399>; from WEAR OUT <1086>] ▶ **In Isaiah, the word is used to denote the end result of the direction of the wrath of the Lord, i.e., the ruin of the Assyrians.** Ref.: Is. 10:25. Even though disobedient, Israel was still loved and protected by the Lord, who maintained a remnant. ¶

– [20] Deut. 7:23; 1 Sam. 5:9, 11 ➔ CONFUSION <4103> [21] Deut. 29:23 ➔ OVERTHROW (noun and verb) <4114> [22] 2 Chr. 22:7 ➔ DOWNFALL <8395> [23] Job 21:17 ➔ ROPE <2256> [24] Job 30:24; 31:29 ➔ DISASTER <6365> [25] Ps. 73:18 ➔ RUINS <4876> [26] Ps. 90:3 ➔ CRUSHED <1793> [27] Ps. 107:20 ➔ PIT <7825> [28] Prov. 10:14, 15, 29; 13:3; 18:7; 21:15 ➔ RUIN (noun) <4288> [29] Is. 10:22 ➔ FAILING <3631> [30] Lam. 1:7 ➔ DOWNFALL <4868> [31] Ezek. 7:25 ➔ ANGUISH <7089> [32] See DEVOTED THINGS <2764>.

DETACH – See SEPARATE (verb) <914>.

DETACHMENT – 1 Sam. 13:23 ➔ GARRISON <4673>.

DETECT – Job 39:29 ➔ LOOK (verb) <5027>.

DETERMINE – [1] ***nāḵar*** [verb: נָכַר <5234>; a prim. root] ▶ **This verb means to pretend, to consider carefully, to investigate, to acknowledge, to recognize, to make unrecognizable. It is used mainly in the causative stem to indicate the process of investigation, knowing something, or knowing how to do something.** Jacob told Laban to investigate to see if he could recognize his gods in any of Jacob's tents (Gen. 31:32); Tamar challenged Judah to investigate the seal and cord she had to see if he could recognize them (Gen. 38:25, 26). The Hebrew word is also used to indicate someone already known previously (1 Kgs. 18:7; 20:41). The word is found metaphorically meaning to acknowledge, to follow, or to refuse to do so: evildoers refused to acknowledge the light (God's laws) and did not walk according to God's laws (Job 24:13). When the word is used with an infinitive, it means to know how to do something or to know something so that a person acts in a certain way. Judeans, who had intermarried with foreigners, had children who did not know how to speak the language of Judah, which was Hebrew (Neh. 13:24).

Finally, in the reflexive stem, the word means to present oneself in such a way as to fool others (1 Kgs. 14:5, 6); or to hide one's identity, as Joseph hid his identity from his brothers (Gen. 42:7). In the case of children, they reflected their characters by their actions, revealing their essential dispositions (Prov. 20:11). *

– 2 Josh. 17:12; Judg. 1:27, 35 ➔ CONTENT (BE) <2974> 3 Job 14:5; Is. 10:23; 28:22; Dan. 9:27 ➔ MOVE <2782>.

DETERMINED (BE) – 1 Dan. 9:24 ➔ DECREED (BE) <2852> 2 Hos. 5:11 ➔ CONTENT (BE) <2974> 3 Hos. 11:7 ➔ HANG <8511>.

DETEST – 1 ***šāqaṣ*** [verb: שָׁקַץ <8262>; a prim. root] ▶ **The primary meaning of this word is to make or to consider something odious. It also means to make abominable.** It is used to describe the attitude the Israelites were to have toward a graven image or idol (Deut. 7:26); and certain nonkosher foods (Lev. 11:11, 13). If the Israelites failed to observe this command by partaking of unclean food, they would become detestable to the Lord (Lev. 20:25). On the other hand, the psalmist stated that this was never the Lord's attitude toward the cries of the afflicted (Ps. 22:24: to abhor, to scorn). Other ref.: Lev. 11:43. ¶

– 2 Lev. 20:23; Num. 21:5; Prov. 3:11 ➔ LOATHE <6973> 3 Zech. 11:8 ➔ ABHOR <973>.

DETESTABLE IDOL – See ABOMINATION.

DETESTABLE IMAGE – 2 Chr. 15:16 ➔ IMAGE <4656>.

DETESTABLE THING – See ABOMINATION.

DETRIMENT – Ezra 4:22 ➔ DAMAGE (verb) <5142>.

DEUEL – ***d*ᵉ*'û'ēl*** [masc. proper noun: דְּעוּאֵל <1845>; from KNOW <3045> and GOD <410>]: knowledge of God ▶ **An Israelite of the tribe of Gad.** Refs.: Num. 1:14; 2:14; 7:42, 47; 10:20. ¶

DEVASTATE – 1 Is. 6:11 ➔ WASTE (LAY, LIE) <7582> 2 Is. 37:18 ➔ WASTE (LAY) <2717> 3 Jer. 51:2; Nah. 2:2 ➔ EMPTY (MAKE) <1238>.

DEVASTATED – Is. 49:19 ➔ DESTRUCTION <2035>.

DEVASTATION – ***šē'ṯ*** [fem. noun: שֵׁאת <7612>; from WASTE (LAY, LIE) <7582>] ▶ **This word refers to desolation, ruin.** It refers to the devastation and ruin brought on Jerusalem by the exile of the people and the destruction of the entire city (Lam. 3:47). ¶

DEVIATE – Joel 2:7 ➔ SWERVE <5670>.

DEVICE – 1 ***zāmām*** [masc. noun: זָמָם <2162>; from CONSIDER <2161>] ▶ **This Hebrew word means plans. It occurs once in the Old Testament.** David uses this word as he pleads with the Lord to intercede in the plans of the wicked (Ps. 140:8); it is translated wicked device, evil device, wicked scheme, evil plot, plan. ¶

2 ***ḥiššāḇôn*** [fem. noun: חִשָּׁבוֹן <2810>; from THINK <2803>] ▶ **This word refers to one's plans or possibly evil inventions that persons have discovered and that do not necessarily foster uprightness.** Ref.: Eccl. 7:29; also translated scheme, invention. It is used of engines of war or skillful, ingenious military devices created by King Uzziah (2 Chr. 26:15; also translated machine, engine). ¶

– 3 Ps. 5:10; 81:12; Mic. 6:16 ➔ COUNSEL (noun) <4156> 4 Eccl. 9:10 ➔ SCHEME (noun) <2808> 5 Lam. 3:62 ➔ MEDITATION <1902>.

DEVIL – Deut. 32:17; Ps. 106:37 ➔ DEMON <7700>.

DEVIOUS – 1 Prov. 2:15; 3:32; 14:2 ➔ PERVERSE <3868> 2 Prov. 4:24 ➔ PERVERSITY <3891>.

DEVISE – ***bāḏā'*** [verb: בָּדָא <908>; a prim. root] ▶ **This word means to think something up, to make it up; it is also translated to make something up, to invent, to feign.** It is used twice in a negative sense. It describes the making of a new illegal feast by Jeroboam I in Northern Israel in the eighth month (1 Kgs. 12:33) and the creation of false accusations against the Jews by Nehemiah's enemies (Neh. 6:8). ¶

DEVOTE – [1] Lev. 27:28, 29; etc. ➔ DESTROY <2763> [2] Hos. 9:10 ➔ SEPARATE <5144>.

DEVOTED THINGS – ***ḥêrem*** [masc. noun: חֵרֶם <2764>; from DESTROY <2763> (in the sense of to devote)] ▶ **This word means things devoted to destruction, devotion, things under ban, cursed. The basic meaning of the word, to be set aside or devoted, is qualified in several ways. Things, including persons, were set aside or devoted to a special function or an area of service by a declaration of God or His servants.** The entire city of Jericho was a deadly threat to the formation of God's people and fell under a ban, except for Rahab and her family (Josh. 6:17, 18), and was set aside for destruction. A person could be set aside for destruction (1 Kgs. 20:42) as well as an entire people, such as Edom (Is. 34:5). The Lord set the Israelites apart for destruction when they turned to other gods (Deut. 13:17; Is. 43:28); the Israelites could not take idols of the conquered pagans into their houses, even when acquired in battle. These items were set aside for destruction only (Deut. 7:26). This term was the last word in the text of the Prophets (Mal. 4:6) and expressed a potential curse on the entire restored exilic community of Israel. Happily, the Lord also announced a time when the ban for destruction would be lifted from Jerusalem forever (Zech. 14:11).

Various items could become holy, i.e., devoted to cultic or holy use, as in the case of a field given to the Lord (Lev. 27:21); or the spoils of war could be set aside for religious use only (Num. 18:14; Josh. 6:18; 1 Sam. 15:21), including gold, silver, items of bronze or iron, and animals. These items, set aside exclusively to holy use, could not be used for everyday purposes, for to use such items in this way was a grave sin. Achan and others died for this offense (Josh. 7:1, 12, 15; 22:20). Other refs.: Lev. 27:28, 29; Josh. 7:11, 13; 1 Chr. 2:7; Ezek. 44:29. The Hebrew word also means fishnet, snare; see NET <2764>. *

DEVOTION – Job 15:4 ➔ MEDITATION <7881>.

DEVOTION TO BOOKS – Eccl. 12:12 ➔ STUDY (noun) <3854>.

DEVOUR – [1] ***yāla'*** [verb: יָלַע <3216>; a prim. root] ▶ **This Hebrew word is translated as to devour, to swallow in Proverbs 20:25 by some translators (KJV).** Others find the root of *lā'a'* to say rashly, to devote rashly, and translate it accordingly (ESV, NIV, NASB, NKJV). ¶
– [2] Deut. 28:38 ➔ CONSUME <2628> [3] Job 39:24 ➔ DRINK (verb) <1572> [4] Prov. 20:25 ➔ SWALLOW (verb) <3886> a. [5] Is. 9:20 ➔ CUT (verb) <1504> [6] Dan. 7:5, 7, 19, 23 ➔ EAT <399> a.

DEVOURS (THAT) – Ps. 52:4 ➔ DEVOURING <1105>.

DEVOURED (BE) – Deut. 32:24 ➔ EAT <3898>.

DEVOURING – ***bela'*** [masc. noun: בֶּלַע <1105>; from SWALLOW (verb) <1104>] ▶ **This word means what is swallowed or destroyed.** It is used only twice in the Old Testament. In Psalm 52:4, it speaks of "devouring words"; it is also translated harmful, that devour. In Jeremiah 51:44, the word is used of the things the god Bel has swallowed. In both cases, it connotes a destructive action. ¶

DEW – [1] ***ṭal*** [masc. noun: טַל <2919>; from COVER (verb) <2926> (as covering vegetation)] ▶ **This word means water droplets condensed on a cool surface. It indicates light rain, a mist.** It is used in a literal sense often of some formation or presence of winter: night mist (Ps. 110:3; Is. 18:4); light rain from the sky (Gen. 27:28); clouds bring it (Prov. 3:20); it collects on physical objects and the ground (Ex. 16:13, 14; Judg. 6:37–40); it can come in drops (Job 38:28); the Lord or His prophet may cause it (Gen. 27:28; 1 Kgs. 17:1). It is used often in a figurative way in a simile or a metaphor: it comes in a secretive way, quickly (2 Sam. 17:12); it describes pleasant speech that distills pleasantly (Deut. 32:2); it describes giving life (Ps. 133:3); the Lord's kindness is like dew (Is. 18:4; Hos. 14:5, 6); the remnant of Jacob will be refreshing to the nations like dew (Mic. 5:7). It depicts the faithfulness of Ephraim and Judah; it passes quickly like dew (Hos. 6:4). The faithful warriors, youth, of the Lord's chosen king are like dew to His reign (Ps. 110:3). *

2 ***ṭal*** [Aramaic masc. noun: טַל <2920>; the same as DEW <2919>] ▶ **This word refers to the early morning dew, a small collection of water on the surface of something, dew of heaven, of the fields, and of the pastures.** It describes the dew which collected on Nebuchadnezzar while he lived among the animals in the fields (Dan. 4:15, 23, 25, 4:33; 5:21). ¶

3 ***rāsiys*** [masc. noun: רָסִיס <7447>; from MOISTEN <7450>] ▶

a. This word indicates a drop (of dew); dampness. It refers to a light condensation of water on something or, in context, the source from which something has become wet (Song 5:2). For Amos 6:11, see b., c.

b. This word means a piece, a fragment. It refers to the small parts into which an object can be broken. In context, it indicates a house broken into pieces of rubble or debris (Amos 6:11).

c. This word means a breach, a breach in the walls. It refers to holes in the structure of a house; collapsed sections in its walls or roof (Amos 6:11). ¶

DIADEM – 1 Job 29:14 ➔ TURBAN <6797> b. 2 Ezek. 21:26 ➔ TURBAN <4701>.

DIAMOND – 1 ***yah^alōm, yāh^alōm*** [masc. noun: יַהֲלֹם, יָהֲלֹם <3095>; from SMITE <1986> (in the sense of hardness)] ▶ **This word refers to a precious stone, a hard colorless mineral; it is also translated emerald.** The identification of the various precious or semiprecious stones in the Old Testament is difficult. Refs.: Ex. 28:18; 39:11; Ezek. 28:13. Bible lexicons take a similar position on the meaning of this word. ¶

2 ***šāmiyr*** [masc. noun: שָׁמִיר <8068>; from KEEP <8104> in the original sense of pricking, also for the keenness for scratching] ▶ **This word refers to a precious stone with an extremely hard point.** Ref.: Jer. 17:1. It seems to refer to flint, an extremely strong and hard stone; in context it is used in a simile of Ezekiel's head being hard like flint (Ezek. 3:9: adamant, emery). It describes Israel's hearts, hardened like flint, toward God's words and laws (Zech. 7:12). See also BRIER <8068>. ¶

DIBLAH – ***diḇlāh*** [proper noun: דִּבְלָה <1689>; prob. an orthographical error for RIBLAH <7247>]: two cakes of figs ▶ **A place not identified and cited only in Ezekiel.** Ref.: Ezek. 6:14. ¶

DIBLAIM – ***diḇlayim*** [masc. proper noun: דִּבְלַיִם <1691>; dual from the masc. of FIGS (CAKE) <1690>]: cake of figs ▶ **This word designates the father of Gomer, the wife of the prophet Hosea.** Ref.: Hos. 1:3. ¶

DIBON – ***diyḇôn*** [proper noun: דִּיבֹן <1769>; from SORROW (CAUSE) <1727>]: wasting ▶

a. A city north of Arnon. Refs.: Num. 21:30; 32:3, 34; 33:45, 46; Josh. 13:9, 17; Is. 15:2; Jer. 48:18, 22. ¶

b. A village in Judah. Ref.: Neh. 11:25. ¶

DIBRI – ***diḇriy*** [masc. proper noun: דִּבְרִי <1704>; from WORD <1697>]: talkative, orator ▶ **An Israelite of the tribe of Dan.** Ref.: Lev. 24:11. ¶

DICTATES – Jer. 16:12; 18:12; etc. ➔ STUBBORNNESS <8307>.

DIE – 1 ***gāwa'*** [verb: גָּוַע <1478>; a prim. root] ▶ **This word is apparently from a**

root meaning to breathe out. It means to stop living. It describes the death of humans and animals in the flood (Gen. 6:17; 7:21). It is used in a repeated formula (along with *mûṯ* <4191>, meaning to die) to describe the death of the patriarchs and Ishmael (Gen. 25:8, 17; 35:29; 49:33). Sometimes the context of the word refers to the root meaning of breathing out (Job 34:14; Ps. 104:29). In Zechariah 13:8, the word is used to predict the deaths of two-thirds of the nation of Israel. *

2 ***mûṯ*** [verb: מוּת <4191>; a prim. root] ▶ **This word means to kill, to put to death, to execute. It occurs in the simple stem of the verb in 600 of its 809 occurrences, meaning to be dead or to die.** It indicates a natural death in peace at an old age, as in the case of Abraham (Gen. 25:8; Judg. 8:32). Dying, however, was not intended to be a natural aspect of being human. It came about through unbelief and rebellion against God (Gen. 3:4) so that Adam and Eve died. The word describes dying because of failure to pursue a moral life (Prov. 5:23; 10:21). It describes various kinds of death: at the hand of God—the Lord smote Nabal, and he died (1 Sam. 25:37); the execution of the offender in capital offense cases (Gen. 2:17; 20:7); the sons of Job from the violence of a mighty storm (Job 1:19); a murderer could be handed over to die at the hand of the avenger of blood (Deut. 19:12). The prophets declared that many people would die by the hand of the Lord when He would bring the sword, famine, and plagues upon them (Jer. 11:22; cf. Jer. 14:12). The present participle of this form may indicate someone who is dying (Gen. 20:3); dead or a corpse (Deut. 25:5; Is. 22:2). People could also be put to death by legal or human authority (Gen. 42:20; Ex. 10:28).

The word indicates the dying of various nonhuman, nonanimal entities. A nation could die, such as Moab, Ephraim, or Israel (Ezek. 18:31; Hos. 13:1; Amos 2:2). A more powerful use of the verb is its description of the death of wisdom (Job 12:2) or courage (1 Sam. 25:37). *

– 3 Num. 17:12 ➔ PERISH <6> 4 Ps. 79:11 ➔ DEATH <8546>.

DIE DOWN – Prov. 26:20 ➔ QUIET (BE) <8367>.

DIE DOWN, DIE OUT – ***šāqa'*** [verb: שָׁקַע <8257>; a prim. root] ▶ **This word means to stop existing, to sink down, to settle.** It is used to describe the dying out, the going out of a fire (Num. 11:2); or of water going down, receding (Ezek. 32:14; Amos 8:8; 9:5). It is used in its causative stem in a physical sense of holding something down (Job 41:1). It describes figuratively the demise or fall of an empire such as Babylon (Jer. 51:64). ¶

DIFFERENCE – Ex. 8:23 ➔ REDEMPTION <6304>.

DIFFERENCE (MAKE A) – Ex. 11:7 ➔ DISTINCTION (MAKE) <6395>.

DIFFERENT – Ezek. 16:34 ➔ OPPOSITE (noun) <2016>.

DIFFICULT – Dan. 2:11 ➔ NOBLE <3358>.

DIFFICULT (BE) – Dan. 4:9 ➔ BAFFLE <598>.

DIFFICULT PROBLEM – Dan. 5:12, 16 ➔ PROBLEM <7001>.

DIFFICULTY – ***kᵉḇēḏuṯ*** [fem. noun.: כְּבֵדֻת <3517>; fem. of HEAVY <3515>] ▶ **This word indicates heaviness, effort.** It describes the stiffness with which the chariot wheels of the Egyptians drove because of the Lord's intervention on behalf of Israel (Ex. 14:25: heavily, with difficulty). ¶

DIG – 1 ***ḥāpar*** [verb: חָפַר <2658>; a prim. root] ▶ **This word means to excavate, to search for.** It refers to digging in the ground for various reasons: to make wells (Gen. 21:30; 26:15, 18, 19, 21, 22, 32; Num. 21:18); to find water (Ex. 7:24). In a general sense, it means to dig a hole in the ground (Deut. 23:13; Jer. 13:7). It is used in the sense of to search out, spy out (Deut. 1:22; Josh. 2:2, 3; Job 3:21; 11:18). It describes digging a hole in a figurative sense (Ps. 7:15; cf. Eccl. 10:8). It is rendered as a mole or rodent (digging animals) in Isaiah 2:20 (NIV, KJV). Other refs.: Job 39:21, 29; Ps. 35:7. ¶

2 ***ḥāṯar*** [verb: חָתַר <2864>; a prim. root] ▶ **This word depicts the act of excavating or rowing.** It indicates the process of scooping out dirt, of digging through a wall (Job 24:16: to dig, to break; Ezek. 8:8; 12:7), in context into the walls of the Temple or a house. It is employed figuratively of digging one's way into Sheol (Amos 9:2). It is used of the paddling motion of rowing a boat (Jon. 1:13). Other refs.: Ezek. 12:5, 12. ¶

3 ***kārāh*** [verb: כָּרָה <3738>; a prim. root] ▶ **This word refers to excavating, cleaning out sufficient dirt and debris for various purposes.** A grave (Gen. 50:5); a well (Gen. 26:25); a pit (Ex. 21:33), etc. It is used in several idioms and figures of speech: wicked persons get into a helpless situation, pits, into which they fall (Ps. 7:15); persons lacking character create problems and situations that catch others (Prov. 16:27), but they themselves will fall into their own pits (Prov. 26:27). The Lord opens His servants' ears (digs their ears) so they can hear (Ps. 40:6). The Lord digs a pit to receive the wicked (Ps. 94:13). *

4 ***'āzaq*** [verb: עָזַק <5823>; a prim. root] ▶ **This word means to break the earth.** It refers to the preparation of a plot of land for planting (Is. 5:2; KJV: to fence). ¶

5 ***qûr*** [verb: קוּר <6979>; a prim. root] ▶ **a. This word refers to removing dirt methodically for some purpose.** It is used figuratively of the Lord's digging as a feature of His judgments on Egypt (2 Kgs. 19:24; Is. 37:25).

b. This word indicates to break down, to destroy. It means to destroy, to disable, to batter down. It is used in a future sense of a royal ruler of Israel breaking down the sins of Sheth (Num. 24:17); and of a similar future action of God in the time of Isaiah (Is. 22:5).

c. A verb meaning to cast out; to pour out. It is used of distributing, passing out, making evil available (Jer. 6:7). ¶

– 6 2 Kgs. 19:24; Is. 37:25; 51:1 ➔ GOUGE <5365> 7 Is. 5:6; 7:25 ➔ CULTIVATE <5737>.

DIG (SOMETHING TO) – Deut. 23:13 ➔ PEG <3489>.

DIG DOWN – Gen. 49:6 ➔ HAMSTRING <6131> b.

DIGNITY – 1 ***nᵉḏiyḇāh*** [fem. noun: נְדִיבָה <5082>; fem. of WILLING <5081>] ▶ **This word indicates honor, nobility, glory.** It indicates a positive, approving, willing spirit, a spirit of dignity (Ps. 51:12: willing, generous, free). It has the sense of honor, dignity concerning a person's character (Job 30:15; KJV: soul). It has the sense of high-class, noble, honorable aspirations of a person who is honorable (Is. 32:8: generous, noble, liberal). ¶

2 ***śᵉ'ēṯ*** [fem. noun: שְׂאֵת <7613>; from CARRY <5375> (in the sense of to lift)] ▶ **a. This word indicates honoring, elevation.** It refers in general to a lifting up of someone or something: of the dignity given to the firstborn (Gen. 49:3); of a high office or place in society (Ps. 62:4); of God's unsurpassed exaltedness (Job 13:11; 31:23); of Leviathan's stirring himself up (Job 41:25); of an approving, uplifting look, recognition (Gen. 4:7). Other ref.: Hab. 1:7.

b. This word indicates swelling. KJV translates rising. It is an expansion or enlargement of a person's flesh or skin because of an infection or irritation, a condition that was diagnosed by the priests (Lev. 13:2, 10, 19, 28, 43; 14:56). ¶

DIKLAH – ***diqlāh*** [proper noun: דִּקְלָה <1853>; of foreign origin]: palm tree ▶ **A region of Arabia.** Refs.: Gen. 10:27; 1 Chr. 1:21. ¶

DILEAN – ***dil'ān*** [proper noun: דִּלְעָן <1810>; of uncertain deriv.]: gourd ▶ **A city in the plain of Judah.** Ref.: Josh. 15:38. ¶

DILIGENCE – Ezra 5:8; 6:12, 13; 7:26: with diligence ➔ DILIGENTLY <629>.

DILIGENCE (WITH) – Ezra 7:23 ➔ DILIGENTLY <149>.

DILIGENT – [1] ***ḥārûṣ*** [adj.: חָרוּץ <2742>; pass. part. of MOVE <2782>] ▶ **This word means industrious, sharp.** It refers to diligent or industrious persons who therefore succeed (Prov. 10:4; 13:4; 21:5); and even supervise or rule (Prov. 12:24). Diligence is considered a precious or valuable possession (Prov. 12:27). It indicates a sharp threshing sledge or cart (Is. 28:27; 41:15; Amos 1:3). It is used in a comparison to describe aspects of Leviathan's underside (Job 41:30: threshing sledge, pointed things, pointed marks). The Hebrew word also means DECISION, GOLD, MOAT; see these entries. ¶
– [2] Prov. 22:29 ➔ SKILLED <4106>.

DILIGENT SEARCH – Ps. 64:6 ➔ PLAN (noun) <2665>.

DILIGENTLY – [1] ***'aḏrazdā'*** [Aramaic adv.: אַדְרַזְדָּא <149>; prob. of Persian origin] ▶ **This word indicates the zeal and diligence exercised in the construction of the new Temple.** It is used in Ezra 7:23; also translated with zeal, in full, with diligence. ¶
[2] ***'osparnā'*** [Aramaic adv.: אָסְפַּרְנָא <629>; of Persian deriv.] ▶ **This word indicates speed or industriousness; eagerly, exactly, with care.** It reflects the manner in which the new Temple in Jerusalem was being built in the time of Zerubbabel (538–516 B.C.). It describes the speed, diligence, and strictness with which the decrees of Darius and Artaxerxes designating payment for the Temple and its worship services were to be carried out (Ezra 5:8; 6:8, 6:12, 13; 7:17, 21, 26). ¶

DILL – ***qeṣaḥ*** [masc. noun: קֶצַח <7100>; from an unused root apparently meaning to incise (in the sense of something being pungent)] ▶ **This word refers to a plant used for seasoning; dill, caraway, fitch, black cummin.** It refers to a bitter herb that produces aromatic leaves and bears bitter seeds used as a seasoning to preserve and flavor various foods (Is. 28:25, 27). ¶

DILUTE – Is. 1:22 ➔ MIX <4107>.

DIM – 1 Sam. 3:2 ➔ DARK <3544>.

DIM (BE) – ***kāhāh*** [verb: כָּהָה <3543>; a prim. root] ▶
a. This word means to faint, to become expressionless. It is used of something becoming weak, unable to function or respond. Jacob's eyes were dim or expressionless, while Moses' eyes did not experience this diminution (to be undimmed, not to be weak) (Deut. 34:7). It describes infection or disease as fading, getting better (Lev. 13:6); and of the spirit fainting (Ezek. 21:7). It is used in an emphatic verbal construction to express a person's eyes being extremely weak or blind (Zech. 11:17: to be darkened, to be blinded). *
b. A verb meaning to rebuke, to correct a person. It is used of the failure of Eli to rebuke or correct his sons for their wicked behavior (1 Sam. 3:13; also translated to restrain). ¶

DIM (BE, GROW) – Ps. 88:9 ➔ SORROW (verb) <1669>.

DIM (BECOME, GROW) – ***'āmam*** [verb: עָמַם <6004>; a prim. root] ▶ **This word means to lose brightness, to be hidden.** It refers to lose the glowing shining feature of gold, etc. (Lam. 4:1). It has the sense of to be hard, difficult for someone to solve (Ezek. 28:3; NASB: to be a match); and the meaning of to equal, to compare to, to match (Ezek. 31:8; also translated to match, to rival). Some scholars consider the word in Ezekiel to be from a different root with the same spelling. ¶

DIM (GROW) – Eccl. 12:3; Lam. 5:17 ➔ DARKEN <2821>.

DIMENSION – Job 38:5 ➔ MEASUREMENT <4461>.

DIMINISH – Ezra 4:13 ➔ DAMAGE (verb) <5142>.

DIMMED (BE) – Eccl. 12:3 ➔ DARKEN <2821>.

DIMNAH – ***dimnāh*** [proper noun: דִּמְנָה <1829>; fem. from the same as DUNG <1828>]: dunghill ► **A city on the border of Zebulun which was given to the Levites.** Ref.: Josh. 21:35. ¶

DIMNESS – [1] ***mā'ûp̱*** [masc. noun: מָעוּף <4588>] ► **This word pictures a place of distress overhung with the gloom of anxiety and despair.** Ref.: Is. 8:22; also translated gloom. ¶
– [2] Is. 9:1 ➔ GLOOM <4155>.

DIMON – ***diymôn*** [proper noun: דִּימוֹן <1775>; perhaps from DIBON <1769>]: river bed ► **A place in Moab.** Ref.: Is. 15:9. ¶

DIMONAH – ***diymônāh*** [proper noun: דִּי־מוֹנָה <1776>; fem. of DIMON <1775>]: river bed ► **A city near Edom.** Ref.: Josh. 15:22. ¶

DINAH – ***diynāh*** [fem. proper noun: דִּינָה <1783>; fem. of JUDGMENT <1779>]: judgment, justice ► **The daughter of Jacob.** Her mother was Leah (Gen. 30:21). She was raped by Shechem, son of Hamor, a Hivite (Gen. 34:1–4). Her brothers, Simeon and Levi, avenged her and destroyed all the males of Shechem (Gen. 34:25–31). All refs.: Gen. 30:21; 34:1, 3, 5, 13, 25, 26; 46:15. ¶

DINAITES – ***diynāyê', dayyānayyā'*** [Aramaic masc. plural proper noun: דִּינָיֵא, דַּיָּנַיָּא <1784>; patrial from an uncertain prim. root] ►
a. One of the clans brought from Assyria to Samaria to replace the Israelites deported. Ref.: Ezra 4:9, KJV, NKJV. ¶
b. This word also means judges. Ref.: Ezra 4:9, ESV, NASB, NIV. ¶

DINHABAH – ***dinhāḇāh*** [proper noun: דִּנְהָבָה <1838>; of uncertain deriv.] ► **City of Bela, king of Edom.** Refs.: Gen. 36:32; 1 Chr. 1:43. ¶

DINNER – Prov. 15:17 ➔ ALLOWANCE <737>.

DIP – [1] ***ṭāḇal*** [verb: טָבַל <2881>; a prim. root] ► **The term means to plunge something briefly into blood or water. It is connected with ritual behavior.** The priest was to dip his fingers, a live bird, cedar wood, hyssop, and scarlet yarn into blood for various ceremonies (Lev. 4:6, 17; 9:9; 14:6, 51). The clean person was to dip hyssop in water and sprinkle it for purification on unclean persons or things (Num. 19:18). It is used intransitively with the preposition *b^e^* when Naaman dipped himself in the Jordan to be healed of leprosy (2 Kgs. 5:14). *
– [2] Is. 30:14:9 ➔ STRIP <2834>.

DIPHATH – Gen. 10:3; 1 Chr. 1:6 ➔ RIPHATH <7384>.

DIRECT – [1] Job 37:3 ➔ LOOSE (LET) <8281> [2] Eccl. 10:10 ➔ SUCCESS (BRING, GIVE) <3787>.

DIRECTLY – ***hāgiyn*** [adj.: הָגִין <1903>; of uncertain deriv.] ► **This word indicates appropriate, corresponding.** It is used to indicate the way directly before the wall in Ezekiel's description of his envisioned Temple (Ezek. 42:12; NASB, the way in front of the wall; NIV, corresponding wall). ¶

DIRECTOR OF MUSIC – Ps. 4–6, 8, 9; etc. ➔ OVERSEE <5329>.

DIRT – [1] Judg. 3:22 ➔ DUNG <6574> [2] 2 Sam. 22:43; Ps. 18:42; Is. 57:20; Zech. 9:3 ➔ MUD <2916> [3] See GROUND <127>.

DIRTY – Song 5:3 ➔ SOIL <2936>.

DISABLED – 2 Sam. 4:4; 9:3 ➔ CRIPPLED <5223>.

DISALLOW – Num. 30:5, 8, 11 ➔ FORBID <5106>.

DISANNUL – Is. 28:18 ➔ COVER (verb) <3722>.

DISAPPEAR – [1] Job 14:11 ➔ GO <235> [2] Ps. 12:1 ➔ VANISH <6461>.

DISASTER – [1] ***hōwāh*** [fem. noun: הֹוָה <1943>; another form of DESTRUCTION

<1942>] ▶ **The root idea of this word is a pit or chasm, a symbol of something destructive.** The word describes a disaster coming on Babylon that it will not be able to prevent with its occult practices (Is. 47:11; also translated trouble, calamity, mischief). The only other occurrence of this word describes a series of disasters (literally, disaster upon disaster) prophesied to come on Israel because of idolatry (Ezek. 7:26; also translated mischief, calamity). In this passage, there will be no escape although Israel will look for a prophetic vision. ¶

[2] ***neḵer, nōḵer*** [masc. noun: נֵכֶר, נֹכֶר <5235>; from DETERMINE <5234>] ▶ **The meaning of this word derives from the idea of strangeness (cf. *nēḵār* [FOREIGN <5236>]); a calamity interrupts the normal flow of life.** The word occurs in Job 31:3 (KJV: strange punishment) where it refers to calamity as the punishment of iniquity. In Obadiah 1:12 (misfortune, captivity, that he became a stranger), the word occurs along with words of similar meaning (cf. Obad. 1:13, 14), describing a time in which Judah met with calamity. ¶

[3] ***piyḏ*** [masc. noun: פִּיד <6365>; from an unused root prob. meaning to pierce] ▶ **This Hebrew word means and is also translated destruction, distress, ruin, extinction, misfortune, calamity.** It is used of divine judgment (Job 30:24; 31:29), as when the father encouraged his son to avoid the wicked and focus on God because God's judgment will eventually come on the wicked (Prov. 24:22). ¶

– [4] 1 Kgs. 5:4 ➔ lit.: evil occurrence ➔ OCCURRENCE <6294> [5] Job 9:23 ➔ WHIP <7752> [6] Prov. 17:5; Obad. 1:13; etc. ➔ CALAMITY <343>.

DISC – Zech. 5:7 ➔ ROUND (SOMETHING) <3603>.

DISCERN – [1] Ps. 139:3 ➔ SCRUTINIZE <2219> [2] See PERCEIVE <995>.

DISCERNING – [1] Ex. 23:8 ➔ SEEING <6493> [2] Dan. 2:21 ➔ UNDERSTANDING <999>.

DISCERNMENT – [1] Job 12:20; Ps. 119:66 ➔ TASTE (noun) <2940> [2] Dan. 2:14 ➔ DECREE (noun) <2942>.

DISCHARGE – [1] **having a discharge:** ***yabbeleṯ*** [adj. and noun: יַבֶּלֶת <2990>; from BRING <2986>] ▶

a. This adjective describes something as oozing, running, a discharging pus. It indicates a diseased condition of an animal. Animals described with running sores, and oozing pus were disqualified as sacrificial animals (Lev. 22:22; KJV, wen; NKJV, ulcer; NIV, warts; NASB, running sore). ¶

b. A feminine noun indicating something with warts (NIV, Lev. 22:22). These ancient terms used in the Bible to describe diseases of the skin are difficult to decipher (see a.). ¶

[2] ***mišlaḥaṯ*** [fem. noun: מִשְׁלַחַת <4917>; from LAY, PUT <4916>] ▶ **This word refers to a group sent out and the act of sending them as well; it is also translated release.** Refs.: Ps. 78:49; Eccl. 8:8. ¶

[3] ***ṣāp̄āh*** [fem. noun: צָפָה <6824>; from OVERLAY <6823> (in the sense of to cover, e.g., an inundation)] ▶

a. This word refers to the loss of blood in a time of calamity suffered by the people in Egypt. Ref.: Ezek. 32:6; also translated flow, flowing. It is used, however, in a figurative as well as literal sense.

b. A feminine noun meaning a swimming. It indicates a profuse, large discharge of blood in battle, used figuratively as well as literally (Ezek. 32:6). ¶

[4] ***zôḇ*** [masc. noun: זוֹב <2101>; for GUSH <2100>] ▶ **This word indicates a flow, an issue.** It is a discharge from a man or woman's genitals (Lev. 15:33; cf. Lev. 15:3, 19). The monthly discharge of a woman's menstrual period (Lev. 15:25, 26, 28, 30). Other refs.: Lev. 15:2, 13, 15. ¶

– [5] 1 Kgs. 5:9 ➔ BREAK <5310> b.

DISCIPLINE – Prov. 13:1, 24 ➔ INSTRUCTION <4148>.

DISCLOSE – 1 Sam. 20:2, 12, 13 ➔ REVEAL <1540>.

DISCOMFIT – Ex. 17:13 ➔ LAY LOW <2522>.

DISCOMFITURE – 1 Sam. 14:20 ➔ CONFUSION <4103>.

DISCOURAGE – Num. 32:7, 9 ➔ FORBID <5106>.

DISCOURAGEMENT – Ex. 6:9 ➔ ANGUISH <7115>.

DISCOVER – [1] Lev. 20:18, 19; Hab. 3:13 ➔ EMPTY (verb) <6168> [2] Ps. 29:9; Jer. 13:26 ➔ STRIP <2834>.

DISCRETION – [1] 1 Sam. 25:33; Prov. 11:22 ➔ TASTE (noun) <2940> [2] Dan. 2:14 ➔ DECREE (noun) <2942> [3] Dan. 2:14 ➔ PRUDENCE <5843>.

DISDAIN – [1] Ezek. 16:31 ➔ MOCK <7046> [2] Ezek. 25:6 ➔ MALICE <7589>.

DISDAINED (BE) – Jer. 30:19 ➔ BRING LOW <6819>.

DISEASE – [1] ***maḏweh*** [masc. noun: מַדְוֶה <4064>; from MENSTRUATION <1738> (in the sense of to be unwell)] ▶ **This word refers to the illnesses the Lord placed on the Egyptians in the plagues.** Refs.: Deut. 7:15; Deut. 28:60, specifically defined as harmful in context. ¶

[2] ***maḥªleh, maḥªlāh*** [מַחֲלֶה, מַחֲלָה <4245>; from SICK (BE) <2470>] ▶

a. A masculine noun referring to sickness. It refers to any type of sickness (Prov. 18:14). God brought a sickness upon Jehoram, king of Judah (2 Chr. 21:15). ¶

b. A feminine noun denoting a sickness. It indicates sickness in general but also the sickness in particular that God put on the Egyptians (Ex. 15:26). If Israel obeyed God, He would remove illness and disease from among them (Ex. 23:25). God would heal sickness already contracted if His people would repent (1 Kgs. 8:37; 2 Chr. 6:28). ¶

[3] ***maḥªlû*** [masc. noun: מַחֲלוּ <4251>; from SICK (BE) <2470>] ▶ **This word refers to some indeterminate sickness suffered by Joash, king of Judah.** Ref.: 2 Chr. 24:25; also translated sick, wounded. ¶

– [4] Deut. 29:22; 2 Chr. 21:19; Ps. 103:3; Jer. 14:18; 16:4 ➔ SICKNESS <8463> [5] Jer. 16:4 ➔ DISEASE <4463>.

DISEASE (BE AFFLICTED WITH A) – 2 Chr. 16:12 ➔ DISEASED (BE, BECOME) <2456>.

DISEASED (BE, BECOME) – ***ḥālā'*** [verb: חָלָא <2456>; a prim. root (comp. SICK (BE) <2470>)] ▶ **This word refers to the illness that King Asa contracted in his feet during his reign, crippling him.** Ref.: 2 Chr. 16:12; also translated to be afflicted with a disease. ¶

DISFIGURED – Is. 52:14 ➔ MARRED <4893> a.

DISFIGUREMENT – Lev. 24:19 ➔ DEFECT <3971>.

DISGRACE (noun) – [1] ***ne'āṣāh*** [fem. noun: נְאָצָה <5007>; from ADULTERY (COMMIT) <5003>] ▶

a. This word indicates shame; it is also translated blasphemy, rejection, reviling. It describes a situation that brings embarrassment or rejection because of failure (2 Kgs. 19:3; Is. 37:3).

b. It refers to blasphemy, aspersion; it is also translated a contemptible thing, provocation, reproach, reviling. It indicates a disrespecting rejection and harmful attack by words and deeds against someone, especially God or His laws (Neh. 9:18, 26); or His holy land (Ezek. 35:12). ¶

[2] ***qiyqāl>ôn*** [masc. noun: קִיקָלוֹן <7022>; from SHAME <7036>] ▶ **This word is the opposite of honor; it indicates shame, having one's character impugned, a feeling of being insignificant, a recognition of one's error or sin.** Ref.: Hab. 2:16; also translated shameful spewing, utter shame, utter disgrace. This disgrace is brought by the Lord and deserved by His shameful people. ¶

DISGRACE (verb) – Jer. 14:21 ➔ FOOLISH (BE) <5034>.

DISGRACEFUL THING – Gen. 34:7; Deut. 22:21; Josh. 7:15; Jer. 29:23 ➔ FOLLY <5039>.

DISGUISE ONESELF – 1 Kgs. 20:38 ➔ SEARCH FOR <2664>.

DISGUST (TURN IN) – Ezek. 23:18, 22, 28 ➔ DISGUSTED (BECOME) <5361>.

DISGUSTED (BE) – [1] Gen. 27:46 ➔ LOATHE <6973> [2] Ps. 119:158 ➔ LOATHE <6962>.

DISGUSTED (BECOME) – ***nāqa'*** [verb: נָקַע <5361>; a prim. root] ▶ **This word means to turn away in revulsion, to be alienated.** It means to turn from in disdain, in disgust, and with strong disapproval (Ezek. 23:18). Those who have turned away are in a state of alienation and hostility toward someone (Ezek. 23:22, 28). ¶

DISH – [1] ***ṣallaḥaṯ*** [fem. noun: צַלַּחַת <6747>; from RUSH (verb) <6743> (something advanced or deep)] ▶ **This word refers to a shallow plate or slab for eating off of.** A standard set of these were used to eat from (2 Kgs. 21:13). It also refers to serving pans (2 Chr. 35:13); and serving dishes (Prov. 19:24; also translated bowl). The Hebrew word is also translated bosom; see BOSOM <6747>. ¶
[2] ***qe'ārāh*** [fem. noun: קְעָרָה <7086>; prob. from TEAR <7167>] ▶ **This word indicates a plate.** It refers to one category of utensils prepared for use in the Tabernacle, especially on the table of showbread (Ex. 25:29; 37:16). It refers to silver dishes that were donated to the Lord as offerings for the altar (Num. 7:13, 19, 25, etc.). *
– [3] Judg. 5:25 ➔ BOWL <5602> [4] 1 Chr. 28:17 ➔ BOWL <3713> [5] Ezra 1:9 ➔ BASIN <105> [6] Prov. 15:17 ➔ ALLOWANCE <737>.

DISHAN – ***diyšān*** [masc. proper noun: דִּישָׁן <1789>; another form of DISHON <1787>]: antelope ▶ **An Edomite, the seventh son of Seir.** Refs.: Gen. 36:21, 28, 30; 1 Chr. 1:38, 42. ¶

DISHEARTEN – Ezek. 13:22 ➔ GRIEVED (BE) <3512>.

DISHEARTENED (BE) – [1] Jer. 49:23 ➔ MELT AWAY <4127> [2] Dan. 11:30 ➔ GRIEVED (BE) <3512>.

DISHON – ***diyšōn, dišôn, dišōn*** [masc. proper noun: דִּישׁוֹן, דִּשׁוֹן, דִּשֹׁן <1787>; the same as IBEX <1788>]: antelope ▶
a. The fifth son of Seir. Refs.: Gen. 36:21, 26, 30; 1 Chr. 1:38. ¶
b. Grandson of Seir. Refs.: Gen. 36:25; 1 Chr. 1:41. ¶

DISHONEST GAIN – See PROFIT (noun) <1215>.

DISHONOR (noun) – ***'arwāh*** [fem. noun: עַרְוָה <6173>; corresponding to NAKEDNESS <6172>] ▶ **This word refers to a show of disrespect or a loss of wealth and influence.** In context it refers to the loss of revenues from the province of Judah (Ezra 4:14). ¶

DISHONOR (verb) – [1] Deut. 27:16 ➔ DESPISED (BE) <7034> [2] Jer. 14:21; Mic. 7:6 ➔ FOOLISH (BE) <5034>.

DISLOCATED (BE) – Gen. 32:25 ➔ ALIENATED (BE) <3363>.

DISMAY – [1] Job 41:22 ➔ SORROW (noun) <1670> [2] Jer. 15:8 ➔ TERROR <928> [3] Jer. 48:39 ➔ RUIN (noun) <4288> [4] Ezek. 4:16; 12:19 ➔ HORROR <8078>.

DISMAYED – Jer. 46:5 ➔ DREAD (noun and adj.) <2844> b.

DISMAYED (BE) – [1] ***ḥāṯaṯ*** [verb: חָתַת <2865>; a prim. root] ▶ **This Hebrew word means to be shattered, to dismay, to shatter, to scare.** The base meaning is probably breaking or shattering like a bow (Jer. 51:56); or of the drought-cracked ground (Jer. 14:4). Figuratively, it refers to nations shattered by God (Is. 7:8). It is also used with an intensive and a causative meaning to scare, to terrify, or to dismay (Is. 30:31).

Job said that God terrified him with dreams (Job 7:14: to scare, to frighten). God's name can also cause dismay (Mal. 2:5: to stand in awe, to be reverent, to be afraid) where it is parallel to the word *yārê'* [FEAR (verb) <3372>]. *
– [2] Ex. 15:1 ➔ TERRIFIED <926> [3] Jer. 14:9 ➔ ASTONISHED (BE) <1724> [4] Dan. 4:19 ➔ ASTONISHED <8075>.

DISMAYING – Jer. 48:39 ➔ RUIN (noun) <4288>.

DISMOUNT – Josh. 15:18; Judg. 1:14 ➔ GET OFF <6795>.

DISOBEY – 1 Kgs. 13:21, 26 ➔ REBELLIOUS (BE) <4784>.

DISORDER – Job 10:22 ➔ lit.: without any order ➔ ORDER <5468>.

DISOWN – Lam. 2:7 ➔ FOOLISH (BE) <5034>.

DISPERSE – [1] Gen. 9:19 ➔ BREAK <5310> b. [2] 1 Sam. 14:16 ➔ MELT AWAY <4127> [3] Dan. 11:24 ➔ SCATTER <967>.

DISPERSION – ***tᵉp̂ôṣāh*** [fem. noun: תְּפוֹצָה <8600>; from SCATTER <6327>] ▶
a. This word indicates a spreading out or distribution of persons. In this case, the leaders of Israel, the shepherds, were dispersed among the nations (Jer. 25:34).
b. This word means a shattering. It refers to the destruction of and the breaking of the authority and power of the leaders, the shepherds of Israel (Jer. 25:34). ¶

DISPLEASED – ***zā'ēp̱*** [adj.: זָעֵף <2198>; from ANGRY (BE) <2196>] ▶ **This word means dejected; it is also translated vexed, angry. It is only used twice in the Old Testament.** In each instance, it describes the dejected attitude of King Ahab when the prophet told him bad news (1 Kgs. 20:43) and when Naboth refused to sell his vineyard to Ahab (1 Kgs. 21:4). See the related verb *zā'ap̱* [ANGRY (BE, BECOME) <2196>], meaning to be dejected and the related noun *za'ap̱* (RAGE <2197>), meaning raging. ¶

DISPLEASED (BE) – ***bᵉ'ēš*** [Aramaic verb: בְּאֵשׁ <888>; corresponding to STINK <887>] ▶ **This verb expresses a strong feeling of distress with oneself and external circumstances.** Ref.: Dan. 6:14; also translated to be distressed. ¶

DISPLEASURE – Num. 14:34 ➔ OPPOSITION <8569>.

DISPOSED (BE) – Num. 22:30 ➔ PROFITABLE (BE) <5532> a.

DISPOSSESSED (BE) – Num. 24:18 ➔ lit.: be a possession ➔ POSSESSION <3424>.

DISPOSSESSING – Ezek. 45:9 ➔ EVICTION <1646>.

DISPUTE – Prov. 18:19 ➔ STRIFE <4066>.

DISPUTES – Prov. 18:18; etc. ➔ CONTENTIONS <4079>.

DISRESPECT – ***bizzāyôn*** [masc. noun: בִּזָּיוֹן <963>; from DESPISE <959>] ▶ **This word means disregard, contempt.** It means a lack of respect or disrespect in the case of the women of Media and Persia (Esther 1:18; also translated contempt). ¶

DISSOLVE – [1] Job 30:22; Ps. 75:3; Is. 14:31; Nah. 2:6 ➔ MELT AWAY <4127> [2] Ps. 6:6 ➔ MELT <4529> [3] Is. 34:4; Zech. 14:12 ➔ WASTE AWAY <4743>.

DISTAFF – [1] ***kiyšôr*** [masc. noun: כִּישׁוֹר <3601>; from SUCCESS (BRING) <3787> (in the sense of to be straight)] ▶ **This is a small dish or wheel located at the bottom of a spindle to give it inertia as it spins.** Ref.: Prov. 31:19. ¶
– [2] 2 Sam. 3:29 ➔ SPINDLE <6418>.

DISTANCE – Gen. 32:16 ➔ SPACE <7305>.

DISTANCE (SOME, LITTLE) – ***kiḇrāh*** [fem. noun: כִּבְרָה <3530>; fem. of ALREADY

<3528>] ▶ **This word is used to refer to the length of a journey remaining that is a relatively short distance.** Refs.: Gen. 35:16; 48:7. It also refers to a relatively short distance already traversed by someone (2 Kgs. 5:19); KJV translates little way. ¶

DISTANT – Jer. 9:26; 25:23; 49:32 ➔ CUT OFF <7112> c.

DISTANT (BE EQUALLY) – Ex. 36:22 ➔ PARALLEL (SET) <7947>.

DISTIL – Job 36:28 ➔ DRIP (verb) <7491>.

DISTILL – Job 36:27 ➔ REFINE <2212>.

DISTINCT (BE) – Ex. 33:16 ➔ DISTINCTION (MAKE) <6395>.

DISTINCTION – Ex. 8:23 ➔ REDEMPTION <6304>.

DISTINCTION (MAKE) – ***pālāh*** [verb: פָּלָה <6395>; a prim. root] ▶ **This word means to be distinct, separate, set apart, to be different.** It describes the fact that Israel was to be a distinct or different people to God (Ex. 33:16: to be separate, to be distinguished, to be separated, to be distinct, to distinguish). It can take on the sense of being wonderful or amazingly constructed (Ps. 139:14: to be wonderfully made). It has a causative sense of making distinct or separate, making different (Ex. 8:22; 9:4; Ps. 4:3). Other refs.: Ex. 11:7 (also translated to make a difference); Ps. 17:7 (marvelous, wondrous). ¶

DISTINCTLY – Is. 32:4 ➔ DAZZLING <6703>.

DISTINGUISH – Ex. 33:16 ➔ DISTINCTION (MAKE) <6395>.

DISTINGUISH ONESELF – ***n^eṣaḥ*** [Aramaic verb: נְצַח <5330>; corresponding to OVERSEE <5329>] ▶ **This word means to show oneself a leader, to show one's skills and leadership ability.** Ref.: Dan. 6:3. ¶

DISTINGUISHED – Song 5:10 ➔ BANNERS (SET UP, LIFT UP) ➔ <1713>.

DISTORT – [1] Is. 24:1 ➔ INIQUITY (COMMIT) <5753> [2] Mic. 3:9 ➔ CROOKED (MAKE, BE) <6140>.

DISTORTED WITH FEAR (BE) – Ezek. 27:35 ➔ IRRITATE <7481>.

DISTORTION – Is. 19:14 ➔ CONFUSION <5773>.

DISTRACTED (BE) – Ps. 88:15 ➔ DESPAIR (BE IN) <6323>.

DISTRAUGHT (BE) – Ps. 88:15 ➔ DESPAIR (BE IN) <6323>.

DISTRESS (noun) – [1] ***māṣôq*** [masc. noun: מָצוֹק <4689>; from OPPRESS <6693>] ▶ **This word refers to hardships and anxiety.** Refs.: Deut. 28:53, 55, 57; Jer. 19:9; KJV: straitness. It is especially brought on from disobeying the Lord but also from general social and political conditions (1 Sam. 22:2). The psalmist suffered anguish, relieved only by following the Lord's delightful Law (Ps. 119:143). ¶
[2] ***m^eṣûqāh*** [fem. noun: מְצוּקָה <4691>; fem. of PILLAR <4690> (the root of this word has the sense of something narrow)] ▶ **This word identifies a state of despair, hopelessness and anxiety.** It depicts the life of the wicked as spent in despair and distress (Job 15:24: anguish); but of the troubles of the righteous as well (Ps. 25:17; 107:6, 13, 19, 28). It is a feature of the Day of the Lord, a day of terror and distress (Zeph. 1:15). ¶
[3] ***mêṣar*** [masc. noun: מֵצַר <4712>; from STOMACH <6896>] (in the sense of something internal, tight) ▶ **This word indicates an anguish, a pain.** It depicts the anxieties and hope of a person in the throes of death or a serious illness (Ps. 116:3; also translated pang, terror); and from threatening enemies (Ps. 118:5; also translated to be hard pressed). It describes the tension, hopelessness, and oppression of Israel in

exile in Babylon (Lam. 1:3; also translated straits). ¶

4 ***ṣôq, ṣûqāh*** [noun: צוֹק, צוּקָה <6695>; from OPPRESS <6693>] ▶

a. A masculine noun referring to anguish, times of trouble. It describes a condition of political, military, and religious oppression on God's people (Dan. 9:25: also translated troublesome, troublous, trouble). ¶

b. A feminine noun also indicating anguish, trouble. It describes a period of personal emotional, economic, or spiritual distress or anxiety that assails a person that only wisdom can deliver from (Prov. 1:27). It refers to a time of devastating judgment on the earth (Is. 8:22). It indicates the oppression and distress on travelers in the torrid heat and drought of the desert (Is. 30:6). ¶

– 5 Gen. 35:3; 42:21; etc. ➔ TROUBLE (noun) <6869> a. 6 Job 30:24 ➔ DISASTER <6365> 7 Ps. 39:2 ➔ PAIN (noun) <3511> 8 Is. 9:1 ➔ CONSTRAINT <4164> 9 Is. 21:15 ➔ HEAVINESS <3514>.

DISTRESS (BE IN) – Gen. 32:7; Judg. 2:15; 10:9; Job 20:22 ➔ DISTRESSED (BE).

DISTRESS (NOT BE IN) – Job 36:19 ➔ GOLD <1222>.

DISTRESS (verb) – Deut. 28:53, 55, 57; Is. 29:2, 7; Jer. 19:9 ➔ OPPRESS <6693>.

DISTRESSED (BE) – 1 ***yāṣar*** [verb: יָצַר <3334>; from the root of *ṣ^a^rar* [ENEMY (BE AN) <6887>] ▶ **This word means to be in a state of mental suffering, to be frustrated. It indicates a state of anxiety, fear, and frustration in many different situations.** E.g., Jacob at meeting Esau (Gen. 32:7). The Lord's judgment on an unfaithful people caused them to be in great distress (Judg. 2:15). War was a time of great distress as well (Judg. 10:9). Pressure and disapproval from others may cause a person to be distressed (1 Sam. 30:6); and failure to satisfy sexual desires may lead to frustration (2 Sam. 13:2; also translated to be frustrated, to be vexed, to be tormented, to be obsessed). To see one's plans thwarted may lead to a state of distress (Job 18:7: to be shortened, to be straitened, to be weakened). The evil person may experience frustration amid riches (Job 20:22; also translated to be cramped, to overtake, to be in straits). On the other hand, the person who follows wisdom is not ultimately distressed (Prov. 4:12: to hinder, to impede, to straiten, to hamper). Other ref.: Is. 49:19 (to be narrow, to be small, to be cramped. ¶

– 2 1 Sam. 13:6 ➔ OPPRESS <5065> 3 Is. 21:3 ➔ INIQUITY (COMMIT) <5753> 4 Dan. 6:14 ➔ DISPLEASED (BE) <888> 5 Dan. 7:15 ➔ GRIEVED (BE) <3735>.

DISTRESSED (BE GREATLY) – Ezra 10:9 ➔ TREMBLE <7460>.

DISTRIBUTE – Dan. 11:24 ➔ SCATTER <967>.

DISTRICT – 1 ***pelek̲*** [masc. noun: פֶּלֶךְ <6418>; from an unused root meaning to be round] ▶ **This word describes areas which certain men were appointed to oversee during the rebuilding of the walls of Jerusalem.** Refs.: Neh. 3:9, 12, 14–18; KJV: part. The Hebrew word also means a spindle, a crutch; see SPINDLE. <6418>. ¶

– 2 Josh. 13:2; Ezek. 47:8; Joel 3:4 ➔ REGION <1552> 3 1 Kgs. 20:14, 15; Ezra 5:8; etc. ➔ PROVINCE <4082>, PROVINCE <4083>.

DISTURBANCE – 1 2 Chr. 15:5 ➔ CONFUSION <4103> 2 Neh. 4:8 ➔ ERROR <8442>.

DISTURBED (BE) – Job 40:23 ➔ HURRY (verb) <2648>.

DITCH – 1 2 Kgs. 3:16 ➔ POOL (noun) <1356> 2 Prov. 23:27 ➔ PIT <7745> 3 Is. 22:11 ➔ RESERVOIR <4724>.

DIVERS COLOURS – Judg. 5:30 ➔ DYED WORK, DYED MATERIALS <6648>.

DIVERSION – Dan. 6:18 → ENTERTAINMENT <1761>.

DIVIDE – 1 ***bāzā'*** [verb: בָּזָא <958>; a prim. root] ▶ **This word means to cut through, to wash away.** It describes the effect of the Nile River of Egypt and its tributaries or sources in Ethiopia (Is. 18:2, 7); it is also translated to spoil (KJV). ¶

2 ***bāqa'*** [verb: בָּקַע <1234>; a prim. root] ▶ **This word means to split, to break open; to hatch, to break into, to burst open, to burst forth. It has the basic idea of something splitting or dividing with force.** Its main translations include the following: to split, e.g., the sea, especially the Red Sea, or wood (Ex. 14:16, 21; Neh. 9:11; Ps. 78:13; Eccl. 10:9); rip open bodies (2 Kgs. 2:24; 8:12; 15:16; Hos. 13:16; Amos 1:13); to hatch eggs (Is. 34:15; 59:5). It has the meaning of invade or break into (2 Sam. 23:16; 2 Chr. 21:17). It describes the dividing of the Mount of Olives with the Lord standing on it (Zech. 14:4). It describes the breaking or breaching of various other things: wineskins (Josh. 9:13; Job 32:19); light (Is. 58:8); tunnels or valleys (Judg. 15:19; Job. 28:10; Mic. 1:4). It describes a city being taken by storm or breached (Is. 7:6; Ezek. 26:10). *

3 ***bāṯar*** [verb: בָּתַר <1334>; a prim. root] ▶ **This word means to cut or separate into pieces.** It implies from its context that Abraham did not cut the dove and young pigeon in half during the covenantal ritual described in Genesis 15:10. ¶

4 ***ḥāṣāh*** [verb: חָצָה <2673>; a prim. root (comp. <2686> a. below)] ▶ **This verb means to split, to leave out half.** It is used of separating something or dividing things in half (Gen. 32:7; 33:1); or distributing something among many (Num. 31:27). It describes the dividing up of a nation (Dan. 11:4). It refers to arranging an army into groups for battle (Judg. 7:16; 9:43). Combined with the preposition *'aḏ*, it means to reach out to something, to extend to (Is. 30:28). It describes the parting of water before Elijah (2 Kgs. 2:8) and Elisha (2 Kgs. 2:14). Other refs.: Ex. 21:35; Num. 31:42; Job 41:6; Ps. 55:23; Ezek. 37:22. ¶

5 ***ḥāṣaṣ*** [verb: חָצַץ <2686>; a prim. root (comp. <2673> above)] ▶

a. This word indicates to split, to split into ranks; to cut off, to come to an end, to sing. It means to divide something or separate out something for a purpose (Judg. 5:11: NASB; KJV and others, see b.); or to arrange something into orderly fashion (Prov. 30:27: to go forth by bands, to advance in rank, to go out in ranks, to march in rank, to advance in ranks). It may have the meaning of dividing off, cutting off, or ending one's life (Job 21:21: to cut off, in half, in the midst, to an end). ¶

b. This word means to shoot an arrow. Some take this verb form in context, a masculine plural participle, to indicate those who shoot arrows (Judg. 5:11; KJV, NKJV), expert archers. The word is also translated musicians, singers, those who divide the flock. ¶

6 ***pālag*** [verb: פָּלַג <6385>; a prim. root] ▶ **This word means to split.** It is used in the passive form to refer to the earth being divided (Gen. 10:25). In the factitive form, it refers to making or dividing a watercourse or cleaving a channel (Job 38:25). The factitive form is also used metaphorically of the Lord to cause dissension, i.e., dividing their tongues (Ps. 55:9). Other ref.: 1 Chr. 1:19. ¶

7 ***pᵉlag*** [Aramaic verb: פְּלַג <6386>; corresponding to <6385> above] ▶ **This word means to split. It is used only once when Daniel was interpreting Nebuchadnezzar's dream.** The feet of the statue in the dream were composed partly of clay and partly of iron, representing the idea that the kingdom would be divided (Dan. 2:41). ¶

8 ***pāraḏ*** [verb: פָּרַד <6504>; a prim. root] ▶ **This word means to split, to separate, to disperse, to be separated, to be scattered.** It means to split into two or more parts or pieces: a river into four streams (Gen. 2:10); the earth into various areas of habitation based on languages (Gen. 10:5). It describes the process of the nations being separated out (Gen. 10:32; 25:23). It is used of persons parting, going separate ways (Gen. 13:9; Ruth 1:17). It has the sense of being separate from, not a part of, not mixing with (Esther 3:8). It

describes the separating out of things from each other (Gen. 30:40). It describes the enemies of the Lord being dispersed, scattered (Ps. 92:9). It is used figuratively of a person's bones being out of place, separated, out of joint from distress and oppression. *
[9] ***pāras*** [verb: פָּרַס <6536>; a prim. root] ▶ **This word means to part, to split.** It describes the split, the separated structural feature of the hoofs of certain animals; some animals were edible, some not edible by Israel (Lev. 11:3–7, 26; Deut. 14:6–8). It refers to the dividing of the hoof as well as the hoof itself (Ps. 69:31). It describes the sharing, the dividing of bread with those who need it (Is. 58:7); or to divide or solemnly break bread in the act of mourning (Jer. 16:7). ¶
[10] ***pāras, pᵉrês, ûparsiyn, parsiyn*** [פָּרַס, פְּרֵס, וּפַרְסִין פַּרְסִין <6537>; corresponding to <6536> above] ▶
a. **An Aramaic verb meaning to be split, to be broken in two.** It refers in its participial form to something divided, split up; in context Babylon (Dan. 5:28).
b. A masculine proper noun Peres. The word is set aside in quotations or put into capitals and treated in a special way by some translations since it was part of an original message that was being interpreted (Dan. 5:28).
c. A masculine plural proper noun in quotation. This is a special treatment of this word just as for Peres as noted in b.
d. A masculine plural proper noun Parsin; a proper noun in quotations, used with the conjunction *û* (and). It refers to something divided up, such as the Babylonian kingdom (Dan. 5:25). See b. also. ¶
– [11] Ex. 12:4 ➔ COUNT (MAKE ONE'S) <3699> [12] Lev. 11:3, 7, 26; Deut. 14:6, 7 ➔ SPLIT <8156> [13] Judg. 19:29 ➔ CUT (verb) <5408> [14] 1 Kgs. 3:25, 26; Ps. 136:13 ➔ CUT (verb) <1504> [15] See SEPARATE (verb) <914>.

DIVIDE INTO THREE PARTS – ***šālaš*** [verb: שָׁלַשׁ <8027>; a prim. root] ▶ **This word means to do a third time; to split into three parts; to be three years old.** It is used in its passive intensive stem to describe something that has reached three years of age (Gen. 15:9; 1 Sam. 1:24, in variant). It describes dividing land into three areas or sections (Deut. 19:3). It is used of staying three days in a location (1 Sam. 20:19); and of doing something three times or a third time (1 Kgs. 18:34). It describes something as having those features (Ezek. 42:6). Other ref.: Eccl. 4:12. ¶

DIVIDING – Dan. 7:25 ➔ HALF <6387>.

DIVINATION – [1] ***miqsām*** [masc. noun: מִקְסָם <4738>; from DIVINATION (PRACTICE) <7080>] ▶ **This word refers to discerning the future or other events by a pagan process of using various devices, such as animal organs, etc.** Refs.: Ezek. 12:24; 13:7. In Israel it was employed by false prophets. ¶
[2] ***qesem*** [masc. noun: קֶסֶם <7081>; from DIVINATION (PRACTICE) <7080>] ▶ **This word described the cultic practice of foreign nations that was prohibited in Israel.** Ref.: Deut. 18:10. It was considered a great sin (1 Sam. 15:23; 2 Kgs. 17:17). False prophets used divination to prophesy in God's name, but God identified them as false (Jer. 14:14; Ezek. 13:6); and pledged to remove such practices from Israel (Ezek. 13:23). Several verses give some insight into what this actual practice looked like: it was compared to a kingly sentence (Prov. 16:10); and was used to discern between two choices (Ezek. 21:21, 22). Other refs.: Num. 22:7; 23:23. ¶
– [3] Num. 23:23; 24:1 ➔ ENCHANTMENT <5173>.

DIVINATION (LEARN BY, USE FOR) – Gen. 30:27; 44:5, 15 ➔ DIVINATION (PRACTICE) <5172>.

DIVINATION (PRACTICE) – [1] ***naḥaš*** [verb: נָחַשׁ <5172>; a prim. root] ▶ **This word described the pagan practice of seeking knowledge through supernatural means; it is also translated to interpret omens, to use enchantment; it is used as noun: enchanter, enchantment, omens.** This practice was expressly forbidden in the Law of Moses (Lev. 19:26; Deut. 18:10); and was used as an indication that the kings of Israel and Judah were wicked (2 Kgs. 17:17; 21:6; 2 Chr. 33:6). In its other usages, Laban used divination to confirm that Jacob was a blessing to him (Gen. 30:27: to learn by divination, to learn by experience, to divine); Joseph claimed that a cup helped him practice divination (Gen. 44:5, 15; also translated to use for divination, to divine); and the Arameans took Ahab's words as an omen (1 Kgs. 20:33). ¶

2 ***qāsam*** [verb: קָסַם <7080>; a prim. root (properly, to distribute; i.e., to determine by lot or magical scroll)] ▶ **This word occurs most frequently in the prophetic books as God's prophets proclaimed the judgment this practice brings.** Refs.: Is. 3:2; Mic. 3:6, 7. God had earlier established that He would guide His people through true prophets, not through diviners (Deut. 18:10, 14). Thus, the falsity of divination is repeatedly pointed out by the prophets (Jer. 29:8; Ezek. 13:9; 22:28; Zech. 10:2). Nevertheless, divination was a problem for Israel as well as for other nations (1 Sam. 6:2; 28:8; 2 Kgs. 17:17). This Hebrew term is broad enough to encompass necromancy, augury, and visions (1 Sam. 28:8; Ezek. 21:21–29; Mic. 3:6, 7). Divination was quite profitable for some even in New Testament times (cf. Acts 16:16–18). *

DIVINE – Gen. 30:27; 44:5, 15 ➔ DIVINATION (PRACTICE) <5172>.

DIVINER – Dan. 2:27; 4:7; 5:7, 11 ➔ CUT (verb) <1505>.

DIVISION – 1 ***ḥᵃluqqāh*** [fem. noun: חֲלֻקָּה <2515>; from SMOOTH <2512>] ▶ **This word designates a portion, a section.** It designates a particular area or section of the Holy Place (2 Chr. 35:5). ¶

2 ***miplaggāh*** [fem. noun: מִפְלַגָּה <4653>; from DIVIDE <6385>] ▶ **This word means a group; it is also translated grouping, subdivision, section.** It could also come from the verb *pālāh* [DISTINCTION (MAKE) <6395>], meaning to separate, and occurs only once in the Old Testament. In 2 Chronicles 35:12, this word is used to describe the household divisions among the Levites. ¶

3 ***pᵉlaggāh*** [fem. noun: פְּלַגָּה <6390>] ▶ **This word is derived from the verb *pālag* (<6385>), whose basic idea is to divide.** In the extensive-factitive form, it can refer to making a watercourse (Judg. 5:15, 16). It can also denote a stream (Job 20:17; also translated river). See the words *nāhār* (<5104>), meaning river, and *naḥal* (<6391>), meaning a torrent or wadi. ¶

4 ***pᵉluggāh*** [fem. noun: פְּלֻגָּה <6391>; from DIVIDE <6385>] ▶ **This word means and is also translated section, grouping, group.** It can only be found in 2 Chronicles 35:5, where Josiah instructed the people of Israel to stand in the holy place by their family divisions. ¶

5 ***pᵉluggāh*** [Aramaic fem. noun: פְּלֻגָּה <6392>; corresponding to <6391> above] ▶ **Like the word *pᵉlag* (HALF <6387>), this noun is derived from the verb *pᵉlag* (<6386>), meaning to divide, and represented the results of that action: the production of parts or divisions.** Unlike *pᵉlag* (6387), this term seems to assume multiple divisions yielding several equal parts. It is only used once to refer to the apportionment of priests into the divisions that would share the responsibility for the restored Temple (Ezra 6:18). ¶

– 6 Ex. 8:23 ➔ REDEMPTION <6304> 7 Num. 12:3, 10 ➔ BANNER <1714> 8 Josh. 11:23; 12:7; etc. ➔ ESCAPE (noun) <4256> b. 9 Ezra 6:18 ➔ GROUP <4255>.

DIVORCE – ***kᵉriyṯûṯ*** [fem. noun: כְּרִיתוּת <3748>; from CUT (verb) <3772>] ▶ **If a man was to find that his wife was unfaithful or any uncleanness in her, he was able to write a certificate of divorce (an official ending of the union) that resulted in her expulsion from his house.** Ref.: Deut. 24:1. Metaphorically, the Lord asked where Israel's certificate of divorce was. She should have had one to act so loosely; i.e., following other gods (Is. 50:1; Jer. 3:8). Other ref.: Deut. 24:3. ¶

DIVORCEMENT – Deut. 24:1; etc. ➔ DIVORCE <3748>.

DIZAHAB – ***diy zāhāḇ*** [proper noun: דִּי זָהָב <1774>; as if from WHO <1768> and GOLD <2091>]: region of gold ► **A place near where Moses spoke his last words to Israel.** Ref.: Deut. 1:1. ¶

DIZZINESS – Is. 19:14 ➔ CONFUSION <5773>.

DO – [1] ***'ālal*** [verb: עָלַל <5953>; a prim. root] ►

a. This word means to deal with, to treat severely, to abuse; to glean. It basically means to treat harshly or deal severely with; to practice evil: to do evil deeds in general (Ps. 141:4); to do evil toward a person (Lam. 1:12, 22; 2:20; 3:51). It describes the Lord's dealings with Egypt to free the Israelites (Ex. 10:2; 1 Sam. 6:6). It is used of Balaam accusing his donkey of dealing treacherously with him (Num. 22:29). It describes the sexual abuse of a woman (Judg. 19:25). *

b. A verb meaning to act childishly, to play the child. It means to behave foolishly as a child without maturity or strength. It is used of the enemies of Israel to depict the hopeless state of Israel who is oppressed by children (Is. 3:12). ¶

c. A verb meaning to defile. It means to make something unclean or unholy, to desecrate it. It is used figuratively of Job defiling and shaming his horn, a figurative expression of destroying his hope, character, strength (Job 16:15). ¶

d. A verb meaning to thrust in, to bury, to insert. It indicates striking an object into something. In context it refers to sticking a "horn," one's hope, character, strength, into the ground, i.e., giving up (Job 16:15). ¶

[2] ***'āśāh*** [verb: עָשָׂה <6213>; a prim. root] ► **This word means to make, to accomplish, to complete.** This frequently used Hebrew verb conveys the central notion of performing an activity with a distinct purpose, a moral obligation, or a goal in view (cf. Gen. 11:6). Particularly, it was used in conjunction with God's commands (Deut. 16:12). It described the process of construction (Gen. 13:4; Job 9:9; Prov. 8:26); engaging in warfare (Josh. 11:18); the yielding of grain (Hos. 8:7); observing a religious ceremony (Ex. 31:16; Num. 9:4); and the completion of something (Ezra 10:3; Is. 46:10). Provocatively, the word appears twice in Ezekiel to imply the intimate action of caressing or fondling the female breast (Ezek. 23:3, 8). *

DO AGAIN – See CHANGE (verb) <8138> b.

DO NOT – ***'al*** [Aramaic adv.: אַל <409>; corresponding to NO <408>] ► **An adverb of prohibition also meaning let not.** It is used as a prohibition in Daniel (Dan. 2:24; 4:19; 5:10). ¶

DO NOT DESTROY – Ps. 57:1; 58:1; 59:1; 75:1 ➔ AL-TASHHETH <516>.

DO NOTHING – Is. 30:7 ➔ LOSS OF TIME <7674>.

DOCILE – Jer. 11:19 ➔ GENTLE <441>.

DOCTRINE – Deut. 32:2; Prov. 4:2; Job 11:4; Is. 29:24 ➔ LEARNING <3948>.

DOCUMENT – [1] Ezra 4:18, 23 ➔ LETTER <5407> [2] Ezra 6:1 ➔ TREASURE <1596> [3] Esther 3:14 ➔ WRITING <3791> [4] Dan. 6:8–10 ➔ WRITING <3792>.

DODAI – ***dôḏay*** [masc. proper noun: דּוֹדַי <1737>; formed like MANDRAKE <1736>]: loving ► **Probably the same as DODO <1734>.** Ref.: 1 Chr. 27:4. ¶

DODANIM – ***dōḏāniym, rōḏāniym*** [masc. plur. proper noun: דֹּדָנִים, רֹדָנִים <1721>; a plur. of uncertain deriv.]: leaders ► **The fourth son of Javan.**

a. Dodanim, following the spelling of the Hebrew text. Refs.: Gen. 10:4, ESV, NASB, KJV; 1 Chr. 1:7, KJV. ¶

b. Rodanim, following the spelling of the Septuagint. Refs.: Gen. 10:4, NIV; 1 Chr. 1:7, ESV, NASB, NIV. ¶

DODAVAHU, DODAVAH – ***dōḏāwāhû*** [masc. proper noun: דֹּדָוָהוּ <1735>; from LOVER <1730> and LORD <3050>]: beloved of the Lord ► **Father of a man named Eliezer who prophesized against Jehoshaphat.** Ref.: 2 Chr. 20:37. ¶

DODO – ***dôḏô*** [masc. proper noun: דּוֹדוֹ <1734>; from LOVER <1730>]: loving ►
a. Grandfather of Tola. Ref.: Judg. 10:1. ¶
b. The father of Eleazar. Refs.: 2 Sam. 23:9; 1 Chr. 11:12. See DODAI <1737>. ¶
c. The father of Elhanan. Refs.: 2 Sam. 23:24; 1 Chr. 11:26. ¶

DOE – [1] ***'ayyālāh*** [fem. noun: אַיָּלָה <355>; fem. of DEER <354>] ► **This word indicates female deer; it is also translated hind, deer.** It refers to the beloved in Song of Solomon 2:7; 3:5. Jacob prophesies that Naphtali is a deer let free (Gen. 49:21). The feet of the deer are used as a symbol of swiftness (2 Sam. 22:34; Ps. 18:33; Hab. 3:19). The birth period of the deer was a mystery (Job 39:1), one of the secrets of God. Other ref.: Ps. 29:9. ¶
[2] ***ya'ᵃlāh*** [fem. noun: יַעֲלָה <3280>; fem. of GOAT (WILD, MOUNTAIN) <3277>] ► **This word denotes a female deer, a mountain goat.** Its beauty and pleasantness is used in a simile referring to the breasts of one's wife (Prov. 5:19; KJV: roe). ¶
– [3] Ps. 22 (title) ➔ DEER <365> b. [4] Prov. 5:19; Jer. 14:5 ➔ DEER <365> a.

DOEG – ***dō'ēḡ, dô'ēḡ*** [masc. proper noun: דֹּאֵג, דּוֹאֵג <1673>; act. part. of ANXIOUS (BE) <1672>]: fearful, timid ► **One of Saul's servants who was an Edomite, Saul's chief herdsman.** Ref.: 1 Sam. 21:7. He informed on David to Saul about Ahimelech the priest at Nob (1 Sam. 22:9, 20) and subsequently slew all the priests and the inhabitants of Nob, both people and animals (1 Sam. 22:18). Other ref.: Ps. 52 (title). ¶

DOG – ***keleḇ*** [masc. noun: כֶּלֶב <3611>; from an unused root meaning to yelp, or else to attack] ► **This word refers to a large and varied group of canines, usually domesticated. It also means a male prostitute.** In various contexts, it refers to a watchdog (Is. 56:10, 11); a hunting dog (Ps. 22:16); a stray dog (1 Kgs. 14:11). The concept is used in figurative expressions of contempt: of a scorned person (1 Sam. 17:43); of abasing oneself (1 Sam. 24:14; 2 Sam. 3:8); of a male cult prostitute (Deut. 23:18). It was used in a mocking sense of a false sacrifice as if it were the sacrifice of a dog (Is. 66:3), a pagan practice. The manner in which a dog lapped its water is noted in Judges 7:5. Dogs ate up Jezebel's dead body as a sign of reprobation toward her (2 Kgs. 9:10, 36). Dogs were known to growl and be menacing in their demeanor (Ex. 11:7), but God protected His people from even this, figuratively, as they left Egypt. *

DOLEFUL – Mic. 2:4 ➔ BITTER, BITTERLY <5093>.

DOMINEER – See RULE OVER <7980>, <7981>.

DOMINION – [1] ***mimšāl*** [masc. noun: מִמְשָׁל <4474>; from RULE (verb) <4910>] ► **This word means sovereign authority, ruling power.** One in human form spoke with Daniel, telling him about a warrior king and an officer who would soon rule their respective kingdoms with great authority (Dan. 11:3, 5). In 1 Chronicles 26:6 (one who rules, ruler, leader), the word describes the sons of Shemaiah as those who exercised ruling authority in their ancestral homes because of their great capabilities. ¶
[2] ***memšālāh*** [fem. noun: מֶמְשָׁלָה <4475>; fem. of <4474> above] ► **This word means rule, authority, province, realm. Often this term denotes the ruling power which one in authority exercises over his domain or kingdom.** God made the sun to have authority over the day and the moon to have authority over the night (Gen. 1:16; Ps. 136:8). The Lord sent the prophet Isaiah to announce to Shebna that He was going to forcibly remove him from office and give his authority to Eliakim instead (Is. 22:21). In other places, the word refers to the territory over which one rules or governs.

Hezekiah showed his whole realm to the king of Babylon's messengers (2 Kgs. 20:13; cf. Ps. 103:22; 114:2). Once it refers collectively to an envoy of powerful ambassadors, such as rulers, princes, or chief officers (2 Chr. 32:9). This term is derived from the verb *māšal* [RULE (verb) <4910>]; see also the related word *mimšāl* (<4474> above). *

3 ***šoltān*** [Aramaic masc. noun: שָׁלְטָן <7985>; from RULE OVER <7981>] ▶ **This word means sovereignty, ruling.** Most frequently, this noun is used in conjunction with God, showing that He has dominion over everything that exists (Dan. 4:3, 34). His dominion is greater than that of a person's many ways, one being that it is an everlasting dominion that can never be destroyed (Dan. 7:14). This noun can also be used of kings (Dan. 4:22). It was used in Daniel's dream of the four beasts to describe the dominion they have (Dan. 7:6, 12, 26). God both gives and takes away the dominion of all human rulers. Much less frequently, this word can be used in the concrete sense of a physical kingdom (Dan 6:26). ¶

– 4 Job 38:33 ➔ RULE (noun) <4896> 5 Dan. 11:4; Zech. 9:10 ➔ AUTHORITY <4915>.

DOMINION (HAVE) – 1 1 Chr. 4:22; Is. 26:13 ➔ MARRY <1166> 2 See RULE OVER <7980>, <7981>.

DONKEY – 1 ***'āṯôn*** [fem. noun: אָתוֹן <860>; prob. from the same as STRENGTH <386> (in the sense of patience)] ▶ **This word indicates an animal which resembles a small horse; also a she ass.** This animal was a primary means of transportation of persons or products (Gen. 12:16; 45:23; Judg. 5:10) and was property that constituted wealth (Gen. 32:15; Job 1:3, 14; 42:12). The most famous she ass is the talking donkey of Balaam (Num. 22:21–23, 25, 27–30), mentioned fourteen times. *

2 ***ḥᵃmôr, ḥᵃmôrah*** [masc. and fem. noun: חֲמוֹר, חֲמוֹרָה <2543>; from RED (BE) <2560>] ▶ **This word is used ninety-seven times in the Old Testament and refers to a donkey or a male ass, a major beast of burden in Israel.** Refs.: Gen. 12:16; 22:3; 42:26, 27. It was considered valuable property (Gen. 24:35; Ex. 20:17; 21:33; Num. 16:15; Josh. 6:21). It was used for transportation (Ex. 4:20; 2 Sam. 16:2) and used in pairs sometimes (Judg. 19:3, 10; 2 Sam. 16:1). Issachar was said to be like a strong donkey (Gen. 49:14). An ox and donkey could not be harnessed together for plowing (Deut. 22:10), but either could be used in tilling fields (Is. 32:20). The statement "burial of an ass" is used figuratively of a dishonorable burial of a person (Jer. 22:19), e.g., King Jehoiakim. *

3 ***'ayir, 'iyr*** [masc. noun: עֲיִר, עַיִר <5895>; from AWAKE <5782> (in the sense or raising; i.e., bearing a burden)] ▶

a. This word refers to donkeys, beasts of burden. Refs.: Gen. 32:15; KJV: foals; Is. 30:6, 24. They were also used for human transportation (Judg. 10:4; 12:14). They were a part of a person's wealth (Job 11:12). The king of Zion would ride on a donkey (Zech. 9:9). ¶

b. This word is translated as foal in Genesis 49:11 (NASB, KJV); donkey (NIV, NKJV). A foal may be a young horse, a mule, or a donkey. The second line of Genesis 49:11 identifies the foal as a colt, not a filly. ¶

DONKEY (WILD) – ***pere'*** [common noun: פֶּרֶא <6501>; from FRUITFUL (BE) <6500> in the secondary sense of running wild] ▶ **This Hebrew word is generally taken to refer to a wild ass or donkey.** Refs.: Job 6:5; 11:12; 24:5; 39:5; Is. 32:14. Others suggest zebra. The Lord cares for these animals (Ps. 104:11); even in their lone wanderings (Hos. 8:9). It is used in a metaphor to describe the character of Ishmael and his descendants (Gen. 16:12). Elsewhere, it serves as a depiction of Judah (Jer. 14:6) or Israel (Hos. 8:9). ¶

DONNING – Is. 3:24 ➔ GIRDING <4228>.

DONOR – 2 Kgs. 12:5, 7 ➔ ACQUAINTANCE <4378>.

DOOM – 1 Deut. 32:35 ➔ lit.: thing that shall come ➔ READY <6264> b. 2 Ezek. 7:7, 10 ➔ CROWN (noun) <6843> b.

DOOR – [1] ***dāl, deleṯ*** [masc. noun: דַּל, דֶּלֶת <1817>; from DRAW <1802> b.] ▶ **This word is used figuratively in the Psalms to refer to the entrance of the psalmist's lips.** Ref.: Ps. 141:3. *
[2] ***peṯaḥ*** [masc. noun: פֶּתַח <6607>; from OPEN <6605>] ▶ **This word refers to an opening, an entrance, a doorway.** It refers to an unobstructed area providing entrance into an enclosure, a tent, a city, a house (Gen. 18:1; 19:6, 11; Num. 11:10; 1 Kgs. 17:10). It refers to the entrance itself in Genesis 4:7 in a figurative expression. It is used often of the door, the entrance into the sacred tent (Ex. 33:9, 10; Num. 12:5; 20:6); or Temple (1 Kgs. 6:33; Ezek. 8:16). It refers to the opening of a cave (1 Kgs. 19:13). Micah 7:5 refers to guarding the opening of one's mouth. It is used figuratively of the doorway of hope (Hos. 2:15). *
– [3] Dan. 3:26 ➔ COURT <8651>.

DOOR POST (UPPER) – Ex. 12:7, 22, 23 ➔ LINTEL <4947>.

DOORFRAME (TOP OF THE) – Ex. 12:7, 22, 23 ➔ LINTEL <4947>.

DOORKEEPER – ***tārā'*** [Aramaic masc. noun: תָּרָע <8652>; from COURT <8651>] ▶ **This word refers to a group of Levitical workers at the Temple area in charge of the menial tasks of keeping the gates and doors functioning and in order.** Ref.: Ezra 7:24; also translated gatekeeper, porter. These workers were exempted from taxes, tribute, or any other charges. ¶

DOORKEEPER (BE A) – ***sāp̱ap̱*** [verb: סָפַף <5605>; a prim. root] ▶ **This word means to stand guard at the threshold, to be on duty at a door.** It indicates a relatively low-level position at the door of the Temple (Ps. 84:10), as opposed to having full access to the Temple. ¶

DOORPOST – [1] ***'ayil*** [masc. noun: אַיִל <352>; from the same as BODY <193>] ▶ **The word indicates a gatepost or lintel.** It refers to doorposts (1 Kgs. 6:31). It is also translated side pillars (NASB, Ezek. 40:9, 10, 16). For other meanings of the Hebrew word, see RAM <352>, MIGHTY <352>, OAK <352>. *
[2] ***'ōmᵉnāh*** [fem. noun: אֹמְנָה <547>; fem. act. part. of TRUTH <544> (in the original sense of supporting)] ▶ **Solomon's Temple had pillars or doorposts overlaid with gold.** Ref.: 2 Kgs. 18:16. ¶
[3] ***mᵉzûzāh*** [fem. noun: מְזוּזָה <4201>; from the same as ABUNDANCE <2123> (which is from a root meaning conspicuous)] ▶ **This word means a gate, a post.** It was a feature of houses (Ex. 12:7; 21:6; Deut. 6:9; 11:20); of temples or sacred houses (1 Sam. 1:9; 1 Kgs. 6:33; Ezek. 41:21; 43:8; 45:19); of the gates of cities (Judg. 16:3). *
– [4] Amos 9:1 ➔ BULB <3730>.

DOPHKAH – ***dop̱qāh*** [proper noun: דָּפְקָה <1850>; from DRIVE HARD <1849>]: who knocks ▶ **A place where the Israelites camped between the Red Sea and Rephidim.** Refs.: Num. 33:12, 13. ¶

DOR – ***dō'r, dôr*** [proper noun: דֹּאר, דּוֹר <1756>; from GENERATION <1755>]: generation, dwelling ▶ **A city of the Canaanites on the Mediterranean.** Refs.: Josh. 11:2; 12:23; 17:11; Judg. 1:27; 1 Kgs. 4:11; 1 Chr. 7:29. ¶

DOTE – [1] Jer. 50:36 ➔ FOOLISHLY (BE, DO, ACT) <2973> [2] Ezek. 23:5, 7, 9, 12, 16, 20 ➔ LUST (verb) <5689>.

DOTHAN – ***dōṯān*** [proper noun: דֹּתָן <1886>; of uncertain deriv.]: two wells ▶ **A city not far from Shechem and Samaria.** Joseph found his brothers there (Gen. 37:17; 2 Kgs. 6:13). ¶

DOUBLE (noun) – ***mišneh*** [masc. noun: מִשְׁנֶה <4932>; from CHANGE <8138> b. (in the sense of to repeat, to do again)] ▶ **This word means a copy, a repetition; second, next in position or rank.** It is used to indicate a doubling of something, such as money (Gen. 43:12, 15); or food (Ex. 16:5, 22). It refers to a copy of something, e.g., the Law (Deut. 17:18; Josh. 8:32). Finally, it indicates position or rank: second rank

(Gen. 41:43; 2 Kgs. 23:4), second oldest (1 Sam. 8:2; 17:13). It may indicate a certain ranked part of several parts, e.g., the second district (2 Kgs. 22:14; Zeph. 1:10). *

DOUBLE (verb) – *kāp̱al* [verb: כָּפַל <3717>; a prim. root] ▶ **This word means to make twice as much something.** It is used of doubling over, folding something, such as a curtain (Ex. 26:9) or other piece of cloth (Ex. 28:16; 39:9). It is used of something being done twice, doubled (Ezek. 21:14). ¶

DOUBLE (BE) – *tā'am* [verb: תָּאַם <8382>; a prim. root] ▶ **This word means to be coupled, to be joined. The primary thrust of this word is that of joining in a matched pair.** It is used only in two contexts: to describe the action of linking two corners of a curtain together (Ex. 26:24; 36:29); and poetically, to describe the birthing of twins (Song 4:2; 6:6). ¶

DOUBLE EDGES – Is. 41:15 ➔ TWO-EDGED <6374>.

DOUBLE-EDGED – Ps. 149:6 ➔ TWO-EDGED <6374>.

DOUBLE-MINDED – *sêʿēp̱* [masc. noun: סֵעֵף <5588>; from LOP, LOP OFF <5586> (in the sense of divided)] ▶ **This word indicates indecision, vanity of thought.** It indicates a person who engages in doublethink, a process of illogical thought, perverse thinking that distorts and reverses the truth (Ps. 119:113; KJV: vain). ¶

DOUBLE, DOUBLED – *kep̱el* [masc. noun: כֶּפֶל <3718>; from DOUBLE (verb) <3717>] ▶ **This word refers to something with two aspects or divided.** Ref.: Job 41:13. It is used to indicate the complex double side of wisdom or its real extent (Job 11:6; KJV, NIV). Israel paid double for her sins (Is. 40:2). ¶

DOUBT – Dan. 5:12, 16 ➔ PROBLEM <7001>.

DOUGH – [1] ***bāṣēq*** [masc. noun: בָּצֵק <1217>; from SWELL <1216>] ▶ **This word describes non-fermented mixture of flour and water.** Refs.: Ex. 12:34, 39. It was demanded in the celebration of the Passover or dough made with no restrictive stipulations attached to its makeup (2 Sam. 13:8; Jer. 7:18; Hos. 7:4). It was used in both worshiping the Lord and, in times of rebellion, to present gifts to pagan deities, such as the queen of heaven (Jer. 7:18). ¶
[2] ***ʿᵃriysāh*** [fem. noun: עֲרִיסָה <6182>; from an unused root meaning to comminute, to reduce to small granules] ▶ **This word refers to some kind of dough or course meal from which cakes or bread was baked, especially as offerings; it is also translated ground meal.** Refs.: Num. 15:20, 21; Neh. 10:37; Ezek. 44:30. ¶

DOVE – [1] ***yônāh*** [fem. noun: יוֹנָה <3123>; prob. from the same as WINE <3196> (apparently from the warmth of their mating)] ▶ **This word denotes a bird, also a pigeon.** It was the bird used by Noah to test the conditions after the flood waters began to abate (Gen. 8:8–12). Its cooing sounds were compared to the moaning of a sick, suffering person (Is. 38:14; 59:11; Ezek. 7:16). Its wings would glisten as gold or appear as gilded with silver, a symbol of a woman dwelling at home in safety (Ps. 68:13). It was used as an endearing expression about one's beloved (Song 2:14; 4:1; 5:2, 12). It is used in many more figurative expressions: of Ephraim like a silly dove (Hos. 7:11); of the exiles eagerly returning as doves (Hos. 11:11); of ships with white sails (Is. 60:8) and many more. Dove's dung was a last resort as food in a time of famine (2 Kgs. 6:25). A young dove or pigeon could be offered to the Lord (Lev. 1:14; 5:7, 11; 12:6, 8; Num. 6:10). The psalmist wished he had wings as a dove by which to escape his troubles (Ps. 55:6). Other refs.: Lev. 14:22, 30; 15:14, 29; Ps. 56:1; Song 1:5; 6:9; Jer. 4:28; Nah. 2:7. ¶
– [2] Ps. 56:1: The Silent Dove in Distant Lands, A Dove on Distant Oaks, The Dove on Far-off Terebinths ➔ JONATH ELEM REHOKIM <3128> [3] See TURTLE-DOVE <8449>.

DOVE DROPPINGS – 2 Kgs. 6:2 ➔ DOVE'S DUNG <2755>.

DOVE'S DROPPINGS – 2 Kgs. 6:25 ➔ DOVE'S DUNG <1686>.

DOVE'S DUNG – [1] ***diḇyôniym*** [masc. plur. noun: דִּבְיוֹנִים <1686>] ▶
a. This word may be a combination of *diḇ* + *yônîm* (<3123>, doves) which means the waste or dung of pigeons. Ref.: 2 Kgs. 6:25; KJV, NASB; cf. NKJV, dove droppings; NIV, seed pods. Two quarts of this material sold at the outrageous price of five shekels during a time of siege. Such dung possibly was a substitute for salt. ¶
b. A masculine plural noun meaning seedpods. Some translators render this as seed pods (NIV), but others translate it as dove's dung (2 Kgs. 6:25; ESV, KJV, NASB, NKJV prefer dove's dung or droppings). This material sold for the outrageous price of five shekels for two quarts in a time of heavy siege. ¶
[2] ***ḥ^{a}rêy yôniym*** [masc. noun: חֲרֵי יוֹנִים <2755>; from the plur. of DUNG <2716> and the plur. of DOVE <3123>] ▶ **This word is used in the phrase *ḥ^{a}rêy yôniym*, literally meaning the "excrement of doves" or "dung(s) of doves." It was eaten in times of severe famine and was normally of little monetary value.** Its nutritional value was minimal (2 Kgs. 6:25); also translated dove droppings, seed pods. ¶
– [3] 2 Kgs. 6:25 ➔ DUNG <2716>.

DOWN (COME) – Jer. 21:13; Joel 3:11 ➔ BEND <5181>.

DOWN (GO) – Job 21:13 ➔ BEND <5181>.

DOWNCAST – Job 22:29 ➔ HUMBLE <7807>.

DOWNCAST (BE) – [1] Ps. 42:5, 6, 11; 43:5 ➔ BOW DOWN <7743> b. [2] Lam. 3:20 ➔ BOW DOWN <7743> a.

DOWNFALL – [1] ***mišbāṯ*** [masc. noun: מִשְׁבָּת <4868>; from REST (verb) <7673> (in the sense of to put away, to cease)] ▶ **This word means and is also translated destruction, ruin; KJV: sabbath, in the sense of cessation.** It indicates the destruction of a city to useless remains, used up; the ruin of Jerusalem, her reduction to nothing (Lam. 1:7). ¶
[2] ***t^{e}ḇûsāh*** [fem. noun: תְּבוּסָה <8395>; from TREAD DOWN <947>] ▶ **This means ruin, destruction.** It is used to depict God's judgment on Ahaziah and more generally the house of Ahab (2 Chr. 22:7). Jehu, God's chosen instrument, killed Ahaziah and Joram, the princes of Judah, in addition to the sons of Ahaziah's relatives. ¶
– [3] Prov. 14:28 ➔ RUIN (noun) <4288> [4] Prov. 29:16; Ezek. 32:10 ➔ FALL (noun) <4658>.

DOWNPOUR – Hab. 3:10 ➔ STORM (noun) <2230>.

DOWNTRODDEN – Ps. 74:21 ➔ OPPRESSED <1790>.

DOWRY – [1] ***mōhar*** [masc. noun: מֹהַר <4119>; from ENDOW <4117>] ▶ **This word refers to the purchase price of a wife; it is also translated bridal payment, bride-price.** It was paid to the wife's family in order to acquire a wife (Gen. 34:12; Ex. 22:17; 1 Sam. 18:25). ¶
– [2] Gen. 30:20 ➔ GIFT <2065> [3] 1 Kgs. 9:16 ➔ PARTING GIFT <7964>.

DOWRY (PAY) – Ex. 22:16 ➔ ENDOW <4117>.

DRACHMA – [1] ***dark^{e}māh*** [masc. noun: דַּרְכְּמָה <1871>; of Persian origin] ▶ **This word means weight, monetary value; it is also translated daric, dram. It may refer to the Greek drachma that weighed 4.3 grams or to the Persian daric that weighed about twice as much.** It occurs in Ezra 2:69 describing gold given toward Temple construction. In Nehemiah 7:70–72, it also refers to gold given toward the work of revitalizing Jerusalem. This word apparently has the same meaning as *^{a}ḏarkōn* (DARIC <150>) but may have a different origin. ¶
– [2] Ezra 8:27 ➔ DARIC <150>.

DRAG (noun) – Hab. 1:15, 16 ➔ NET (noun) <4365>.

DRAG (verb) – [1] **to drag away, to drag out:** ***gārar*** [verb: גָּרַר <1641>; a prim. root] ► **The idea of a noise made in the back of the throat seems to be the root idea so that this word is onomatopoetic like the English word gargle. It means to chew, to destroy, to catch, to saw.** It is used once to signify rumination, an essential mark of a ceremonially clean animal (Lev. 11:7: to chew). It described hostile forces dragging people away (Prov. 21:7: to drag away, to sweep away, to destroy) or catching them like fish in a net (Hab. 1:15: to drag out, to catch). It also signifies sawing, as dragging a saw over wood (1 Kgs. 7:9: to saw). Other ref.: Jer. 30:23 (continuing, sweeping, whirling). ¶
[2] ***sāḥaḇ*** [verb: סָחַב <5498>; a prim. root] ► **This word means and is also translated to pull, to draw.** It describes pulling down and removing the stones and other parts of a city to demolish it (2 Sam. 17:13). The activity of dogs pulling and dragging something to devour it is expressed with this word (Jer. 15:3; KJV, ESV: to tear); as well as the process of people dragging trash out to throw into a garbage heap (Jer. 22:19), a picture of the fate of Jehoiakim. It describes persons being dragged from their land (Jer. 49:20) as part of God's judgments (Jer. 50:45). ¶
– [3] Ezek. 39:2 ➔ DRIVE <8338> a.

DRAG OFF – Job 20:28 ➔ SPILL <5064>.

DRAGNET – Hab. 1:15, 16 ➔ NET (noun) <4365>.

DRAGON – [1] ***tānnāh*** [fem. noun: תַּנָּה <8568>; prob. fem. of JACKAL <8565>] ► **This Hebrew word is rendered as dragon by the KJV, referring to a lizard, a large serpent or snake, and other inhabitants of the wilderness.** Ref.: Mal. 1:3. This word is now understood to mean a serpent; a jackal, the old serpent (Satan), etc. See also JACKAL <8565>. ¶
– [2] Neh. 2:13 ➔ JACKAL <8565> [3] Ps. 44:19; 74:13; etc. ➔ SERPENT <8577>.

DRAGON'S SPRING – ***'êyn hattanniyn*** [proper noun: עֵין הַתַּנִּין <5886>; from EYE (noun) <5869> (in the sense of fountain) and JACKAL <8565>]; fountain of jackals ► **A source in Jerusalem between the Valley Gate and the Dung Gate.** Ref.: Neh. 2:13; also translated Serpent Well, Dragon's Well, Jackal Well. ¶

DRAGON'S WELL – Neh. 2:13 ➔ DRAGON'S SPRING <5886>.

DRAIN – ***māṣāh*** [verb: מָצָה <4680>; a prim. root] ► **This word signifies to drain out, to wring out. It has the basic sense of removing or forcing out moisture or liquid from something.** A wet fleece; a hide (Judg. 6:38); blood drained from the altar (Lev. 1:15; 5:9); water or wine consumed by people (Ps. 73:10; 75:8); figuratively, of draining, drinking from the cup of the Lord's anger (Is. 51:17; Ezek. 23:34; cf. Ps. 75:8). ¶

DRAINED – 2 Kgs. 19:26; Is. 37:27 ➔ SHORT <7116>.

DRAM – 1 Chr. 29:7; Ezra 8:27 ➔ DARIC <150>.

DRAUGHT HOUSE – 2 Kgs. 10:27 ➔ GOING FORTH <4163> or LATRINE <4280>.

DRAW – [1] ***dālāh*** [verb: דָּלָה <1802>; a prim. root (comp. BRING LOW <1809>)] ►
a. This word describes the act of removing water from a well. Refs.: Ex. 2:16, 19. It describes also metaphorically drawing out a wise plan from a person's heart like deep water (Prov. 20:5) or of the Lord's lifting up people beset by their enemies (Ps. 30:1). ¶
b. A verb meaning to hang down, dangle, hang limp. It describes the legs of a lame person which dangle or hang down uselessly (Prov. 26:7; KJV, are not equal). ¶
[2] ***māšāh*** [verb: מָשָׁה <4871>; a prim. root] ► **This word indicates the action of taking something out, pulling.** It is used to

form Moses' name and expresses the action of Pharaoh's daughter in pulling him from the Nile River (Ex. 2:10); and the action of Moses as he drew Israel out of Egypt. It is used figuratively of David being drawn from the waters of distress (2 Sam. 22:17; Ps. 18:16). ¶
3 ***šā'aḇ*** [verb: שָׁאַב <7579>; a prim. root] ▶ **This word means to draw out, to collect, to pull out something.** Ref.: Gen. 24:11. It is used often of drawing water (Gen. 24:13, 19, 20, 43–45). Drawing water was considered a low-ranking menial task (Deut. 29:11; Josh. 9:21, 23, 27; Ruth 2:9). It is used figuratively of drawing water from the springs of salvation and deliverance (Is. 12:3). *
– 4 2 Sam. 17:13; Jer. 22:19; 49:20 ➔ DRAG (verb) <5498> 5 Ezra 6:11 ➔ PULL <5256> 6 Hag. 2:16:9 ➔ STRIP <2834>.

DRAW A LINE – ***tā'āh*** [verb: תָּאָה <8376>; a prim. root] ▶ **This word is used figuratively of establishing a border to mark certain boundaries of territories.** Refs.: Num. 34:7, 8; also translated to mark out, to point out, to run a line. ¶

DRAW OUT – 1 ***ḥālaṣ*** [verb: חָלַץ <2502>; a prim. root] ▶ **This word means to prepare, to deliver, to equip for war.** The primary meaning of the word is that of strengthening or fortifying (Is. 58:11). It is used to convey the activity of drawing out, such as occurs in breast-feeding (Lam. 4:3); removing a shoe (Deut. 25:9, 10; Is. 20:2); dispatching to another location (Lev. 14:40, 43); withdrawing from a crowd (Hos. 5:6); removing or delivering from danger (2 Sam. 22:20; Ps. 6:4; 50:15). Significantly, this word conveys the notion of taking up arms for battle (Num. 31:3; 32:17) or preparing for a general state of military readiness (Josh. 4:13; 2 Chr. 17:18). *
2 ***šālap*** [verb: שָׁלַף <8025>; a prim. root] ▶ **This word means to take off, to grow up.** It refers to the act of unsheathing a sword, drawing it from its sheath (Num. 22:23, 31; Josh. 5:13), especially in a legal situation (Ruth 4:7, 8). It refers to the coming out or the germinating of grass (Ps. 129:6: to grow up). *
– 3 Is. 58:10 ➔ OBTAIN <6329>.

DRAWING NEAR – ***qārêḇ*** [adj.: קָרֵב <7131>; from COME NEAR <7126>] ▶ **This word means approaching.** It refers to something or someone who approaches, comes close to something or someone: those at the king's table (1 Kgs. 4:27); an advancing soldier (1 Sam. 17:41); those approaching to engage in battle (Deut. 20:3). Some persons were forbidden to come near to certain holy things (Num. 1:51; 3:10, 38; 17:13; 18:7). Only certain people could come near and serve at Ezekiel's Temple (Ezek. 40:46; 45:4). ¶

DRAWN FROM – Is. 28:9 ➔ ANCIENT <6267> b.

DREAD (noun) – 1 ***paḥaḏ*** [masc. sing. noun: פַּחַד <6343>; from DREAD (verb) <6342>] ▶ **This word means a great fear; it is also translated fear, terror.** This dread was often caused by the Lord (1 Sam. 11:7; Job 13:11; Is. 2:10, 19, 21). The dread could cause trembling (Job 13:11; Ps. 119:120). The noun often occurs in a cognate accusative construction (see *pāḥaḏ* <6342>) (Deut. 28:67; Job 3:25; Ps. 14:5). A unique use of the term is found in Genesis 31:42, often translated the Dread or Fear of Isaac, parallel to the God of Abraham. *
2 ***paḥdāh*** [fem. noun: פַּחְדָּה <6345>; fem. of DREAD (noun) <6343>] ▶ **This word means fear, religious awe.** It appears only in Jeremiah 2:19, where it refers to the proper respect and reverence due to the Lord, which is lacking when one forsakes God and His commands. ¶
– 3 Deut. 11:25 ➔ FEAR (noun) <4172> 4 Deut. 28:60; Ps. 119:39 ➔ AFRAID (BE) <3025> 5 Ezek. 4:16; 12:19 ➔ HORROR <8078> 6 Dan. 10:7 ➔ TREMBLING <2731>.

DREAD (BE IN) – Is. 8:12 ➔ TREMBLE <6206>.

DREAD (noun and adj.) – ***ḥaṯ*** [noun and adj.: חַת <2844>; from DISMAYED (BE) <2865>] ▶
a. A masculine noun denoting fear, filled with terror. It describes extreme dread and

fear the animals have of humans after the flood (Gen. 9:2; also translated terror). This emotion is unknown to Job's Leviathan (Job 41:33: fear). ¶
b. An adjective identifying something as broken, dismayed, terrified. It refers to bows of the mighty as broken (*ḥattîm*) (1 Sam. 2:4: broken, shattered) or to warriors of Egypt who are terrified (Jer. 46:5: dismayed, terrified), causing them to hesitate in fear or draw back. ¶

DREAD (verb) – [1] ***pāḥaḏ*** [verb: פָּחַד <6342>; a prim. root] ▶ **This word means to fear greatly; it also means to be in dread, to be in awe. This verb occurs in poetry.** Those who worship and trust God have no need to dread, but those who break the Law (Deut. 28:66); sinners in Zion (Is. 33:14); and worshipers of idols (Is. 44:11) have reason to fear. It often takes a cognate accusative. For a positive use, in the eschatological perspective of Isaiah 60:5, the term is best translated to be awed. *
– [2] Prov. 10:24 ➔ FEAR (noun) <4034> [3] Is. 8:12 ➔ TREMBLE <6206> [4] Is. 57:1; Jer. 42:16 ➔ ANXIOUS (BE, BECOME) <1672> [5] Jer. 22:25; 39:17 ➔ AFRAID <3016>.

DREADED – Hab. 1:7 ➔ TERRIBLE <366>.

DREADFUL – [1] Job 30:6 ➔ CLIFF <6178> [2] Dan. 7:7, 19 ➔ FEAR (verb) <1763>.

DREADFUL (SOMETHING) – Job 6:21 ➔ TERROR <2866>.

DREAM (noun) – [1] ***ḥ^{a}lôm*** [masc. noun: חֲלוֹם <2472>; from DREAM (verb) <2492>] ▶ **This word refers to the sensations or images passing through one's mind during sleep, usually during the night.** Refs.: Gen. 20:3; 31:11, 24; 1 Kgs. 3:5; Job 7:14; Is. 29:7. The Lord often caused dreams. The verb is often found with the noun (Gen. 37:5, 6). The phrase *ba'al ḥ^{a}lômôṯ* means "a lord of dreams," "dreamer," or one who could interpret dreams (Gen. 37:19). Dreams were often prophetic (Gen. 37:9; 40:5; Num. 12:6; Dan. 2:1–3). The Lord will cause old men to dream dreams in the latter days (Joel 2:28). God could give a person an understanding of dreams (Dan. 1:17). False prophets could generate dreams out of their own minds (Deut. 13:1, 3, 5; Jer. 23:27; 27:9; 29:8; Zech. 10:2). *
[2] ***ḥêlem*** [Aramaic masc. noun: חֵלֶם <2493>; from a root corresponding to DREAM (verb) <2492>] ▶ **This word refers to visions sent by God to Nebuchadnezzar and to Daniel.** Refs.: Dan. 2:4–7, 9, 26; 4:5–9; 7:1. These dreams could be interpreted (Dan. 5:12). Other refs.: Dan. 2:28, 36, 45; 4:18, 19. ¶

DREAM (verb) – [1] ***ḥālam*** [verb: חָלַם <2492>; a prim. root] ▶
a. This word describes the process of a person producing images or receiving images in a sleeping state. The images may be produced by God (Gen. 28:12; 37:5, 6, 9, 10; 40:5; 41:5, 11); or they may be produced by the persons' minds themselves (Deut. 13:1, 3), a feature of false prophecy (Jer. 23:25; 27:9). Dreams could be used as a contrast to reality (Ps. 126:1; Is. 29:8). Dreams would be a feature of God's pouring out His Spirit on persons (Joel 2:28). Other refs.: Gen. 40:8; 41:15; 42:9; Deut. 13:5; Judg. 7:13; Jer. 29:8; Dan. 2:1, 3. ¶
b. A verb indicating to become strong, powerful. It refers to strength gained through the natural maturation process (Job 39:4) or to restoration to health after sickness (Is. 38:16). ¶
– [2] Is. 56:10 ➔ SLEEP (verb) <1957>.

DREGS – [1] ***qubba'aṯ*** [fem. noun: קֻבַּעַת <6907>; from ROB <6906> (a goblet; as deep like a cover)] ▶ **This word refers to a goblet, a chalice.** It is used in a figurative sense to indicate a cup holding the judgments of God (Is. 51:17; 22). ¶
[2] ***šemer*** [masc. plur. noun: שֶׁמֶר <8105>; from KEEP <8104> (in the sense of to be preserved)] ▶ **This word may refer to dregs, i.e., to the particles of solid matter that settle to the bottom of a liquid, such**

as wine. Ref.: Ps. 75:8. Wine in such a condition can be termed unsettled, stagnant, disturbed and is so described in a simile of Moab (Jer. 48:11). In a more positive context, it indicates fine aged wine (Is. 25:6: aged wine, wine on the lees). Zephaniah speaks of those persons who are congealed on their dregs (Zeph. 1:12), who won't act, have no conviction, do nothing, and are "stagnant in spirit" (NASB). ¶

DRENCH – Ps. 6:6 → MELT <4529>.

DRENCHED (BE) – [1] Job 24:8 → WET (BE) <7372> [2] Dan. 4:15, 23, 25, 33; 5:21 → WET (BE) <6647>.

DRESS (noun) – [1] Ezek. 16:13 → CLOTHING <4403> [2] See CLOTHING <3830>.

DRESS (IN FULL) – Ezek. 23:12 → SPLENDIDLY <4358>.

DRESS (verb) – Jer. 1:17 → GIRD <247>.

DRESSED – [1] ***gāziyṯ*** [fem. noun: גָּזִית <1496>; from TAKE, TAKE OUT <1491>] ▶ **This word indicates a cut stone, hewn stone, smooth stone, ashlar.** A cut stone used in building the Solomonic Temple (1 Kgs. 5:17; 6:36) and Solomon's palace (1 Kgs. 7:9, 11, 12). It was used in houses constructed for the rich (Amos 5:11). Cut stones dressed out by men were not permitted in a stone altar (Ex. 20:25). But they were permissible in certain parts of Ezekiel's Temple and its supporting components (Ezek. 40:42). It is used figuratively to depict the Lord's hemming in of Jeremiah's ministry and life (Lam. 3:9). Other refs.: 1 Chr. 22:2; Is. 9:10. ¶
– [2] 2 Kgs. 12:12; 22:6; 2 Chr. 34:11 → HEWN <4274> [3] Prov. 7:10 → GARMENT <7897>.

DRESSER – ***bālas*** [verb: בָּלַס <1103>; a prim. root] ▶ **This word indicates to gather, to scratch open, to care for.** It describes the process of caring for, gathering, or growing sycamore figs; the process of scratching or slitting open a sycamore fruit to help it ripen (Amos 7:14). In its participial form (*bôles*), it indicates Amos as one who cared for sycamore fruit and carried out this procedure: a dresser, a tender, a grower, a gatherer. ¶

DRESSING ROOM – Joel 2:16 → CHAMBER <2646>.

DRIED UP – [1] Is. 5:13 → PARCHED <6704> [2] Is. 15:6; Jer. 48:34 → DESOLATION <4923>.

DRIED, DRY – ***yāḇêš*** [adj.: יָבֵשׁ <3002>; from DRY UP <3001>] ▶ **The Nazarite vow prohibited partaking of the fruit of the vine, including dried, i.e., dissicated grapes.** Ref.: Num. 6:3. The Israelites complained in the desert because they had no food like they did in Egypt; all they had to eat was manna, and their souls were dried up (Num. 11:6). A second use of dry is when it refers to chaff that breaks in pieces. It is used figuratively of Job, who was weary and worn out (Job 13:25). *

DRINK (noun) – [1] ***mašqeh*** [masc. noun: מַשְׁקֶה <4945>; from WATER (GIVE) <8248> (properly, causing to drink)] ▶ **This word indicates a liquid, a drinking vessel, a watering place.** It is used of land that receives abundant rain and is well-watered (Gen. 13:10). It refers to liquids (Lev. 11:34; Is. 32:6) and is used to define vessels as drinking or watering vessels (1 Kgs. 10:21; 2 Chr. 9:20). It is used of a watering place, a place where water may be drawn (Ezek. 45:15; also translated rich pasture, fat pasture, well-watered pasture). The Hebrew word also means someone appointed to serve wine; see CUPBEARER <4945>. ¶
[2] ***šiqquw*** [masc. noun: שִׁקּוּ <8249>; from WATER (GIVE) <8248>] ▶ **This word refers to a liquid served up to a person to drink.** Ref.: Ps. 102:9. ¶
[3] ***šiqqûy*** [masc. noun: שִׁקּוּי <8250>; from WATER (GIVE) <8248>] ▶ **This word means a liquid, and also moisture.** It refers to a liquid served up to drink (Ps.

102:9). It takes on the meaning of vigor, renewal, health to human bones (Prov. 3:8: strength, refreshment, marrow, nourishment). It indicates water, ill-gotten by prostitution (Hos. 2:5). ¶
– [4] Ezra 3:7; etc. ➔ FEAST <4960>
[5] Is. 1:22; Hos. 4:18; Nah. 1:10 ➔ WINE <5433>.

DRINK (verb) – [1] ***gāmā'*** [verb: גָּמָא <1572>; a prim. root] ▶ **This word means to let a person drink, i.e., swallow a liquid.** Ref.: Gen. 24:17. It is used figuratively of a galloping horse that is swallowing up the ground (Job 39:24; also translated to devour, to race over, to eat up). ¶
[2] ***šāṯāh*** [verb: שָׁתָה <8354>; intens. of WATER (GIVE) <8248>] ▶ **This word is used of swallowing any kind of liquid.** People drinking wine (Gen. 9:21); people and animals drinking water (Gen. 24:14, 18, 19, 22; 25:34). God does not drink the blood of goats (Ps. 50:13). It is used of a great apocalyptic end-time banquet where animals and birds will figuratively drink blood (Ezek. 39:17). It is used figuratively of a fool drinking violence (Prov. 4:17; 26:6). It refers to drinking wine in preparation for a joyous occasion (Song 5:1). It is used of drinking the cup of the Lord's wrath (Is. 51:17); and of Israel's successful destruction of its enemies (Num. 23:24). In its passive sense, it means to be drunk (Lev. 11:34). *
[3] ***šᵉṯāh*** [Aramaic verb: שְׁתָה <8355>; corresponding to <8354> above] ▶ **This word refers to the imbibing of wine at a royal banquet.** Refs.: Dan. 5:1–4, 23. ¶

DRINK DEEPLY – ***māṣaṣ*** [verb: מָצַץ <4711>; a prim. root] ▶ **This word means to milk out, to drain out, to nurse. It describes the nursing and feeding activity of a child or small animal.** It is used figuratively of God's people nursing at the bosom of a restored Jerusalem (Is. 66:11; NASB: to suck). ¶

DRINK OFFERING – [1] ***nāsiyḵ*** [masc. noun: נָסִיךְ <5257>; from POUR OUT <5258>] ▶ **This term refers to the pouring out of a libation.** Ref.: Deut. 32:38. Here God mockingly inquires about the whereabouts of the gods that drank the drink offerings of wine offered by their pagan worshipers. In Daniel 11:8, this term refers to metal idols, see METAL IMAGE <5257>. The Hebrew word also means prince, leader; see PRINCE <5257>. ¶
[2] ***nᵉsaḵ*** [Aramaic masc. noun: נְסַךְ <5261>; corresponding to <5262> below] ▶ **This word means libation.** Its only occurrence in the Hebrew Bible is in Ezra 7:17 where Artaxerxes provided offerings and sacrifices to be delivered for the Temple in Jerusalem. This term is related to the verb ***nᵉsaḵ*** (OFFER <5260), meaning to pour out. For the Hebrew cognate of this noun, see *neseḵ* (<5262> below). ¶
[3] ***nēseḵ, nêseḵ*** [masc. sing. noun: נֶסֶךְ, נֵסֶךְ <5262>; from POUR OUT <5258>] ▶ **This word means libation, molten image. The most common usage of the term referred to a liquid offering that was poured out: *nāsaḵ* (POUR OUT <5258>).** Refs.: Gen. 35:14; Lev. 23:37; Num. 15:5, 7, 10, 24. It is employed both for offerings made to *Yahweh* as well as to foreign deities (2 Kgs. 16:13; Is. 57:6). The term is also used for a molten image (i.e., a "poured out" thing) (Is. 41:29; 48:5; Jer. 10:14). *
– [4] Is. 65:11 ➔ MIXED WINE <4469>.

DRINK ONE'S FILL – ***rāwāh*** [verb: רָוָה <7301>; a prim. root] ▶ **This word means to give water, to drench.** It refers to giving someone a drink literally and figuratively (Ps. 36:8; 65:10). It means to drink all that one wants, to satisfy (Prov. 5:19; 7:18). It is used figuratively by the prophets of tears (Is. 16:9); of a sword's being sated, satisfied (Is. 34:5); of ground being soaked with blood (Is. 34:7); of God's being filled with fat sacrifices (Is. 43:24); of priests' souls being filled (Jer. 31:14). *

DRINKER – Prov. 23:20, 21 ➔ DRUNKARD <5433>.

DRINKING – [1] ***šᵉṯiyyāh*** [fem. noun: שְׁתִיָּה <8360>; fem. of DRUNKENNESS <8358>] ▶ **This word refers to the process and act of consuming a beverage, in**

this case wine at a royal banquet. Ref.: Esther 1:8. ¶
– 2 1 Kgs. 10:21; 2 Chr. 9:20 ➔ DRINK (noun) <4945>.

DRIP (noun) – ***hêleḵ*** [masc. noun: הֵלֶךְ <1982>; from GO <1980>] ▶ **This word means to go, to travel, to flow; traveler, visitor.** It refers to flowing honey that was running from trees (1 Sam. 14:26: to drop, to drip, to ooze out). It indicates a person who is on the road journeying (2 Sam. 12:4: traveler). ¶

DRIP (verb) – 1 ***rā'ap̱*** [verb: רָעַף <7491>; a prim. root] ▶ **This word means to overflow, to drip down (of rain); it is also translated to pour, to distil, to drop, to fall, to rain down, to drop down, to shower.** It refers to rain that falls slowly and drips down on humankind (Job 36:28). It is used figuratively of the Lord's ways and paths, which, if followed, drip and are rich with an abundance of good things (Ps. 65:11); even the dry pastures of the desert or wilderness (Ps. 65:12); even the whole creation drips down abundance on the earth (Is. 45:8). It is by God's wisdom that the dew of heaven is made to water, drip on the earth and humankind (Prov. 3:20). ¶
– 2 Judg. 5:4; Prov. 5:3; Song 5:5 ➔ DROP (verb) <5197>.

DRIP DOWN – Is. 45:8 ➔ DRIP (verb) <7491>.

DRIPPING – ***delep̱*** [masc. noun: דֶּלֶף <1811>; from LEAK <1811>] ▶ **The word is used for the constant dribbling of water on a rainy day.** It is depicted as similar to a quarrelsome woman or contentious wife. Refs.: Prov. 19:13; 27:15; KJV: dropping. ¶

DRIVE – 1 **drive away, on, down:** ***dāḥāh*** [verb: דָּחָה <1760>; a prim. root] ▶ **This word means to push back, to chase, to lean.** The psalmist cries for the Lord to defeat and frustrate his enemies (Ps. 35:5; 36:12: to cast down, to throw down, to thrust down). It describes evil persons as threatening or leaning walls (Ps. 62:3: tottering). Figuratively, it indicates pushing persons down, harming them (Ps. 118:13) with the intent to harm greatly (Ps. 140:4: to overthrow, to trip). It generally describes the defeat or thrusting down of wicked persons (Prov. 14:32; also translated to banish, to bring down) and false prophets (Jer. 23:12). The Lord cares for the outcasts, the dispersed or scattered of Israel (Is. 11:12; 56:8). Other ref.: Ps. 147:2. ¶
2 ***nāḏā', nāḏāh*** [verb: נָדָא, נָדָה <5077>; a prim. root] ▶ **This word signifies to separate, to drive away, to disaffect.** It means to push someone away from a course of action (2 Kgs. 17:21; NIV: to entice); or to shut out (Is. 66:5: to cast out, to exclude). It is used figuratively of shoving something into the future, of keeping it at bay, e.g., the Day of the Lord (Amos 6:3: to put far away, to put off, to put far off). ¶
3 ***nāḏaḥ*** [verb: נָדַח <5080>; a prim. root] ▶
a. A verb meaning to banish, to push away, to scatter. It is used in various ways to indicate the idea of forcefully removing, impelling, or driving out: of the dispersion, the scattering of Israel into exile (Deut. 30:1, 4; Jer. 40:12; 43:5; 46:28; Mic. 4:6); of driving out something in a figurative sense (Job 6:13); Zion herself was considered an outcast, one driven out (Jer. 30:17). It is used of cattle straying off (Deut. 22:1). It means to be impelled to do something, e.g., by the lure of idolatry and false gods (Deut. 4:19; 30:17); by the seduction of a harlot (Prov. 7:21). *
b. A verb meaning to wield, bring (against). It is used of wielding or swinging an ax against something, striking it (Deut. 19:5; 20:19), whether a person or a tree. It is used figuratively of bringing evil and destruction on something or someone (2 Sam. 15:14: to bring, to bring down). ¶
4 ***nāhag*** [verb: נָהַג <5090>; a prim. root] ▶
a. A word also signifying to guide. It has the sense of leading, guiding something willingly or by force. It is used of driving cattle or flocks (Gen. 31:18; Ex. 3:1; 2 Kgs. 4:24; Job 24:3); taking away persons who

go willingly or only with force (Gen. 31:26; Is. 20:4); leading people or animals along (2 Sam. 6:3; 1 Chr. 20:1; Ps. 48:14; Is. 11:6; 49:10; 60:11); of God's stirring up a great wind (Ex. 10:13); charioteers driving their chariots (Ex. 14:25). It is employed figuratively of a person's mind guiding him or her (Eccl. 2:3); and the tender actions of a bride leading her bridegroom (Song 8:2). *

b. A verb meaning to sob, to lament. Some translators find the sense of lamenting, sobbing in Nahum 2:7 (to moan), perhaps as a dove's voice. Meaning a. fits well here, however. ¶

[5] ***nāšaḇ*** [verb: נָשַׁב <5380>; a prim. root] ▶ **This word means to blow, to push away.** It is used of scaring off birds of prey that have alighted on a dead animal (Gen. 15:11); of wind driving water back or making it flow again (Ps. 147:18; NIV: to stir). It is used of a dry, hot wind blowing on the grass, killing it (Is. 40:7). ¶

[6] ***šāšā'*** [verb: שָׁשָׂא <8338>; a prim. root] ▶ **a. This word means to drag along.** It means to urge someone, to provide impetus for moving on. It is used figuratively of God's moving Gog toward Israel and destruction (Ezek. 39:2).

b. A verb indicating to leave a sixth part. It means to take or leave behind only one-sixth of something (Ezek. 39:2, KJV).

– [7] Num. 11:31 ➔ BRING <1468> [8] Prov. 28:3; Jer. 46:15 ➔ SWEEP <5502>.

DRIVE ASUNDER – Hab. 3:6 ➔ LEAP <5425>.

DRIVE AWAY – ***nāḏap̄*** [verb: נָדַף <5086>; a prim. root] ▶ **This word means to blow something about, away or to be blown away.** It is used figuratively of evil persons being blown away by the wind like chaff, having no roots or stability (Lev. 26:36: driven, shaken, windblown; Ps. 1:4). It is used most often in a passive sense of being driven away, blown away: persons by the sound of a falling leaf (Lev. 26:36); crops by bad weather (Is. 19:7); chaff blown in the wind, representing nations (Is. 41:2: driven, windblown); riches falsely gotten (Prov. 21:6: fleeting, tossed to and fro); a leaf driven in the wind (Job 13:25: driven, windblown); a person defeated and driven by God (Job 32:13: to thrust down, to vanquish, to refute). Other ref.: Ps. 68:2. ¶

DRIVE HARD – [1] ***dāp̄aq*** [verb: דָּפַק <1849>; a prim. root] ▶ **This verb refers to driving small cattle; it also means to knock on a door.** Ref.: Gen. 33:13; KJV: overdrive. It also refers to knocking, beating, or pounding on someone's door (Judg. 19:22; Song 5:2). ¶

– [2] Is. 58:3 ➔ OPPRESS <5065>.

DRIVE ON – Prov. 16:26 ➔ CRAVE <404>.

DRIVE OUT – [1] ***nāḵā'*** [verb: נָכָא <5217>; a prim. root] ▶ **This word refers to forcing someone out of society or the land in disdain.** Ref.: Job 30:8; also translated to be scourged, to be whipped out, to be vile. ¶

– [2] Deut. 7:1, 22; 2 Kgs. 16:6 ➔ REMOVE <5394> [3] Is. 27:8 ➔ REMOVE <1898> [4] See CAST OUT <1644>.

DRIVE, DRIVE AWAY – ***ṭ*****^e^*****raḏ*** [Aramaic verb: טְרַד <2957>; corresponding to CONTINUAL (BE) <2956>] ▶ **This word refers to chasing away.** It is used of the Lord's afflicting Nebuchadnezzar to remove him from human society because of his extreme pride in his great city, Babylon (Dan. 4:25, 32, 33; 5:21), which he claimed to have built. ¶

DRIVE, DRIVE OUT – Deut. 6:19; 9:4; Job 18:18; Is. 22:19; Jer. 46:15 ➔ PUSH <1920>.

DRIVEN – Lev. 26:36; Is. 13:25; 41:2 ➔ DRIVE AWAY <5086>.

DRIVEN AWAY (BE) – ***hālā'*** [verb: הָלָא <1972>; prob. denom. from BEYOND <1973>] ▶ **This word means to be carried away.** It is used in its passive sense to indicate those who have been carried away, gone into exile (Mic. 4:7); it is also translated to be cast off, outcast. ¶

DRIVER OF A CHARIOT – ***rakkāḇ*** [masc. noun: רַכָּב <7395>; from RIDE <7392>] ▶ **This word refers to a chariot driver, a horseman.** It refers to the driver of a chariot (1 Kgs. 22:34; 2 Chr. 18:33); or to a horseman, a person who rode horses for various purposes in the line of duty, often employed by the king (2 Kgs. 9:17). ¶

DRIVING – ***minhāg*** [masc. noun: מִנְהָג <4491>; from DRIVE <5090>] ▶ **This word refers to the way one handles a chariot, the way he maneuvers it as the driver.** Ref.: 2 Kgs. 9:20. ¶

DROMEDARY – [1] 1 Kgs. 4:28 ➔ HORSE <7409> b. [2] Esther 8:10 ➔ ROYAL STUD <7424> a. [3] Is. 60:6 ➔ CAMEL (YOUNG) <1070> [4] Is. 66:20 ➔ CAMEL <3753> [5] Jer. 2:23 ➔ CAMEL (YOUNG) <1072>.

DROP (noun) – [1] ***'egel*** [masc. noun: אֶגֶל <96>; from an unused root (meaning to flow down or together as drops)] ▶ **This word refers to drips of dew.** Ref.: Job 38:28. ¶

[2] ***mar*** [masc. noun: מַר <4752>; from BITTER (BE) <4843> in its original sense of distillation] ▶ **This word denotes a drop or particle of water.** It is used in a famous metaphor to illustrate the smallness of the nations compared to the Lord's might (Is. 40:15). ¶

– [3] 1 Sam. 14:26 ➔ DRIP (noun) <1982> [4] Job 36:27 ➔ STACTE <5198>.

DROP (verb) – ***nāṭap̱*** [verb: נָטַף <5197>; a prim. root] ▶ **This word means to fall, to drip, to flow.** It is used to describe rain (Judg. 5:4; Ps. 68:8); and words which are like rain (Job 29:22). Lips may drip with honey (Prov. 5:3); and hands may drip with myrrh (Song 5:5). This word can also be taken figuratively, meaning to prophesy (Ezek. 21:2; Amos 7:16: to preach). It is sometimes used to refer to false prophets (Mic. 2:6). *

DROP OFF – [1] Deut. 28:40 ➔ REMOVE <5394> [2] Job 15:33 ➔ VIOLENCE (DO) <2554>.

DROP THROUGH – Eccl. 10:18 ➔ LEAK <1811>.

DROP, DROP DOWN – [1] ***'ārap̱*** [verb: עָרַף <6201>; a prim. root] ▶ **This word means to fall, to fall down.** In Moses' final blessing of Israel, he says they would experience God's security and bounty where His heavens drop dew (Deut. 33:28). In Moses' final song, he prayed that his teaching would drop like rain on his listeners (Deut. 32:2). See the nominal form of this root, *ʿărāp̱el* (<6205>; NIV: to fall), which means cloud. ¶

– [2] Job 36:28; Ps. 65:11, 12; Prov. 3:20; Is. 45:8 ➔ DRIP (verb) <7491>.

DROPLET – ***śā'iyr*** [masc. noun: שָׂעִיר <8164>; formed the same as GOAT <8163>] ▶ **This word means a raindrop; it is also translated small rain, gentle rain, shower.** It describes small beads of water that collect on fresh grass as dew droplets or the same effect produced by a light rain (Deut. 32:2). ¶

DROPPING – Prov. 19:13; 27:15 ➔ DRIPPING <1812>.

DROSS – ***siyg, sûg*** [masc. noun: סִיג, סוּג <5509>; from TURN BACK <5472>] ▶ **This word is used metaphorically and euphemistically to mock the god who may be busy relieving himself.** The word suggests dross or waste, excrement (1 Kgs. 18:27: to relieve oneself, to be busy, to go aside). It clearly means waste, dross from metals in other passages (Ps. 119:119; Prov. 25:4). It describes impurity or a false covering hiding a wicked heart (Prov. 26:23). It is symbolic of moral and religious corruption and apostasy (Is. 1:22, 25; Ezek. 22:18, 19). ¶

DROUGHT – [1] ***baṣṣōreṯ*** [fem. noun: בַּצֹּרֶת <1226>; fem. intens. from GATHER <1219>] ▶ **This word describes a period when rain and, hence, food were scarce in Judah, a judgment on God's people. It is also translated dearth.** Ref.: Jer. 14:1. The person who trusts in the Lord need not fear a devastating year of drought (Jer. 17:8). ¶

2 ***ḥ^a^rāḇôn*** [masc. noun: חֲרָבוֹן <2725>; from WASTE (LAY) <2717>] ▶ **This word denotes dearth, and also heat, dry heat.** It is used of the heat of summer (*qayis*) which mercilessly drained or sapped one's strength (Ps. 32:4); also translated heat, fever heat. In the context, it is compared to David's guilt and conscience which sap his strength. ¶

3 ***tal'ûḇāh*** [fem. noun: תַּלְאוּבָה <8514>; from FLAME <3851>] ▶ **This word refers to a time when there is no rain and a resulting scarcity of water.** Ref.: Hos. 13:5; also translated great drought, burning heat. ¶

– 4 Gen. 31:40; Hag. 1:11 ➔ HEAT (noun) <2721> 5 Is. 58:11 ➔ SCORCHED PLACE <6710>.

DROWN – ***ṭāḇa'*** [verb: טָבַע <2883>; a prim. root] ▶ **This word also means to sink; to penetrate.** It refers to death by drowning (Ex. 15:4), sunk in the waters of the Red Sea. In general, it refers to something sunk in (*b^e^*): Jeremiah sunk into the mud of a cistern (Jer. 38:6); the gates of Jerusalem sunk into the ground (Lam. 2:9); a stone thrown by David pierced Goliath's forehead (1 Sam. 17:49). It describes a mass of something sinking together, such as mountains (Prov. 8:25: to be settled, to be shaped). It is used metaphorically of nations sinking down (Ps. 9:15; also translated to fall) because of their rebellions; an oppressed or distressed person "sinking into the mire" (Ps. 69:2, 14; Jer. 38:22); the foundations of the earth sunk into their bases (Job 38:6). ¶

DROWNED – Job 10:15 ➔ CONSCIOUS <7202>.

DROWSINESS – ***nûmāh*** [fem. noun: נוּמָה <5124>; from SLUMBER (verb) <5123>] ▶ **This word refers to a state of sleepiness as an expression of laziness, in context.** The glutton and drunkard will be overcome by drowsiness (Prov. 23:21; also translated slumber). ¶

DRUNK, DRUNKEN – ***šāḵur, šāḵar*** [שָׁכֻר, שָׁכַר <7937>; a prim. root] ▶

a. An adjective indicating a state of intoxication. In context, however, a cup of judgment and a ruling from God had intoxicated His people (Is. 51:21).

b. A verb meaning to become intoxicated. It refers to the act and process of a person's becoming inebriated, overcome with wine or strong drink (Gen. 9:21). It indicates drinking freely when preceded by *waṯāḥ,* to drink (Gen. 43:34). It is used in a figure of speech describing arrows being made drunken (causative) with blood in a vicious battle (Deut. 32:42; Is. 49:26; Jer. 48:26; 51:39, 57). It describes Hannah's condition: she appeared drunken (1 Sam. 1:14), a reflexive use of the verb. In its intensive stem, it describes making someone drunken (2 Sam. 11:13; Hab. 2:15). *

DRUNK, DRUNKEN, DRUNKARD – ***šikkôr, šikkor*** [adj.: שִׁכּוֹר, שִׁכֹּר <7910>; from DRUNK, DRUNKEN <7937>] ▶ **This word means to be inebriated, under the influence of wine or strong drink, out of control.** Refs.: 1 Sam. 1:13; 25:36; 1 Kgs. 16:9; 20:16; Job 12:25; Ps. 107:27. It may indicate the drunkard, the drunken person (Prov. 26:9; Joel 1:5). *

DRUNKARD – ***sāḇā'*** [verb: סָבָא <5433>; a prim. root] ▶ **This word means to imbibe, to carouse, to get drunk; it is also translated drinker.** It means to drink heavily, to drink hard: a drunkard (Deut. 21:20; Prov. 23:20, 21; Ezek. 23:42; Nah. 1:10); those who engage in drinking too much (Is. 56:12: to fill). ¶

DRUNKENNESS – 1 ***šikkārôn*** [abstract masc. noun: שִׁכָּרוֹן <7943>; from DRUNK, DRUNKEN <7937>] ▶ **This word refers to an intoxicated state brought on by strong drink or by the cup of God's wrath.** Refs.: Ezek. 23:33; 39:19. It refers to the state of confusion that God's judgments will bring on corrupt kings over His people (Jer. 13:13). ¶

2 ***š^e^ṯiy*** [masc. noun: שְׁתִי <8358>; from DRINK (verb) <8354>] ▶ **This word indicates that a person is satiated with drinking, fully drunk with wine, beer, or strong drink.** Ref.: Eccl. 10:17. ¶

– 3 Zech. 12:2 ➔ REELING <7478>.

DRY (adj.) – 1 ***ḥārêḇ*** [adj.: חָרֵב <2720>; from WASTE (LAY) <2717>] ▶ **This word means not wet, and also desolate, wasted.** Two connected ideas undergird the translation of this word. The first is the sense of dryness as opposed to wetness. In this line, it is used specifically of the grain offering (Lev. 7:10) or a morsel of food (Prov. 17:1). The second is the sense of desolation. In this way, it is used to describe the wasted condition of Jerusalem after the Babylonian captivity (Neh. 2:3); the emptiness of the land, which is comparable to the sparse population of the Garden of Eden (Ezek. 36:35); and the condition of the Temple in Haggai's day, as it still lay in ruins (Hag. 1:4, 9). Other refs.: Neh. 2:17; Jer. 33:10, 12; Ezek. 36:38. ¶
– 2 Job 30:6 ➔ CLIFF <6178> 3 Jer. 4:11 ➔ DAZZLING <6703>.

DRY (BE) – 1 Gen. 8:13 ➔ WASTE (LAY) <2717> 2 Judg. 6:37, 39, 40 ➔ HEAT (noun) <2721> 3 Jer. 2:25 ➔ THIRST <6773>.

DRY GRASS – Is. 5:24 ➔ GRASS (DRY) <2842>.

DRY LAND – Ps. 68:6 ➔ PARCHED LAND <6707>.

DRY LAND, DRY GROUND – 1 ***ḥārāḇāh*** [fem. noun: חָרָבָה <2724>; fem. of DRY (adj.) <2720>] ▶ **The central principle of this word is the lack of moisture.** It is used to refer to the habitable ground inundated by the flood (Gen. 7:22); dry waterbeds (Ezek. 30:12); and land in general (Hag. 2:6). Three times the word describes the condition of a path made in the miraculous parting of water: for Moses and Israel (Ex. 14:21); for Joshua and Israel (Josh. 3:17); and for Elijah and Elisha (2 Kgs. 2:8). Other ref.: Josh. 4:18. ¶
2 ***yabbāšāh*** [fem. noun: יַבָּשָׁה <3004>; from DRY UP <3001>] ▶ **This word can be an adjective as well. In all uses, it is contrasted with water.** It often describes land formerly covered with water, such as the land appearing on the third day of creation; the land on which the people of Israel crossed the Red Sea (Ex. 14:16, 22, 29; Ps. 66:6); and the land on which they crossed the Jordan (Josh. 4:22). It also describes land onto which water is poured both literally (Ex. 4:9) and as a figure of the Holy Spirit being poured on the descendants of Jacob (Is. 44:3). Other refs.: Gen. 1:9, 10; Ex. 15:19; Neh. 9:11; Jon. 1:9, 13; 2:10. ¶
3 ***yabbešeṯ*** [fem. noun: יַבֶּשֶׁת <3006>; a variation of <3004> above] ▶ **This word is apparently identical to *yabbāšāh* above. It occurs only twice.** In Exodus 4:9, it refers to land upon which water had been poured and subsequently had turned to blood. In Psalm 95:5, it refers to dry land (in contrast to the sea), which the Lord's hands formed. ¶

DRY PLACE – ***ṣāyôn*** [masc. noun: צָיוֹן <6724>; from the same as DRYNESS <6723>] ▶ **This word refers to a place of extremely dry or drought conditions; it is also translated desert.** Refs.: Is. 25:5; 32:2. ¶

DRY SCALL – Lev. 13:30–37; 14:54 ➔ SKIN DISEASE <5424>.

DRY (verb) – 1 ***ṣāmaq*** [verb: צָמַק <6784>; a prim. root] ▶ **This word means to dry up (of woman's breasts), i.e., to stop producing milk in this case.** It is used in a figurative expression of giving Israel dry breasts to feed from so they will starve (Hos. 9:14). ¶
– 2 Job 14:11 ➔ GO <235>.

DRY UP – 1 ***yāḇaš, yāḇêš*** [verb: יָבַשׁ, יָבֵשׁ <3001>; a prim. root] ▶ **This common intransitive verb refers to the dehydration and withering of plants, trees, grass, crops, and the earth itself after the flood.** Ref.: Gen. 8:14. It also occurs with an intensive and causative sense meaning to dry, to wither. *Yahweh* dried the waters, particularly the sea (Josh. 2:10; Ps. 74:15; Is. 42:15; Jer. 51:36; Nah. 1:4). It is used figuratively to denote God destroying Babylon (Ezek. 17:24). *
2 ***našaṯ*** [verb: נָשַׁת <5405>; a prim. root] ▶ **This word is used of something**

without sufficient moisture, not wet or damp. It means to be parched, and also to fail. It is used figuratively of God's drying up the seas and rivers in judgment (Is. 19:5); and of waters going away or being removed from their natural state (Jer. 18:14; ESV: to run dry). It depicts the oppressed in their abject state of need (Is. 41:17); but also the strength and vigor of strong persons failing, and they become exhausted (Jer. 51:30). ¶
– 3 Is. 33:9 ➔ MOURN <56>.

DRYNESS – ***ṣiyyāh*** [fem. noun: צִיָּה <6723>; from an unused root meaning to parch] ▶ **This word indicates parched land, desert.** It refers to a time of drought, a lack of rain for supplying water (Job 24:19); or to the infertile, dry ground itself (Job 30:3). The thirsting of the dry ground for water is compared to the longing of the soul for God (Ps. 63:1). It refers to the desert and wilderness wanderings of Israel after the Exodus (Ps. 78:17; 105:41). The Lord is able to transform a desert into a place of flowing waters and babbling springs (Ps. 107:35), even the dry land *'ereṣ ṣiyyāh* (Is. 41:18). But He can turn a city of splendor into a desiccated wilderness (Zeph. 2:13). *

DUE (BE THE) – ***yā'āh*** [verb: יָאָה <2969>; a prim. root] ▶ **This word indicates to pertain, to be fitting, to belong to. It is used to indicate what is appropriate and fitting toward a person or object.** All nations should reverence and fear God, for it is appropriate because of who He is (Jer. 10:7; KJV, to appertain). ¶

DUKE – Gen. 36:15 ➔ GENTLE <441>.

DULCIMER – Dan. 3:5, 7, 10, 15 ➔ BAGPIPE <5481>.

DULL – Gen. 49:12 ➔ DARKER <2447>.

DULL (BE) – Eccl. 10:10 ➔ BLUNT (BE) <6949> a.

DULLNESS – Lam. 3:65 ➔ SORROW (noun) <4044>.

DUMAH – ***dûmāh*** [masc. proper noun: דּוּמָה <1746>; the same as SILENCE (noun) <1745>]: silence ▶
a. The son of Ishmael. Refs.: Gen. 25:14; 1 Chr. 1:30. ¶
b. A city in Judah. Ref.: Josh. 15:52. ¶
c. A symbolic name of Edom, indicating death and destruction. Ref.: Is. 21:11. ¶

DUMB – 1 Ex. 4:11; Ps. 38:13; Prov. 31:8; Is. 35:6; 56:10; Hab. 2:18 ➔ MUTE <483>
2 Hab. 2:19 ➔ SILENCE (noun) <1748>.

DUMB (BE, BECOME) – Ps. 39:2, 9; Is. 53:7; Ezek. 3:26; Dan. 10:15 ➔ BIND <481>.

DUNG – 1 ***dōmen*** [masc. noun: דֹּמֶן <1828>; of uncertain deriv.] ▶ **This word is used to describe unburied corpses, lying on the ground as manure or refuse.** Refs.: 2 Kgs. 9:37; Ps. 83:10; Jer. 8:2; 9:22; 16:4; 25:33, i.e., used as a simile for bodies. ¶
2 ***gālāl*** [masc. noun: גָּלָל <1557>; from ROLL (verb) <1556> (in the sense of removing)] ▶ **This word means something to be removed; it is also translated refuse.** It means something to be swept away as the Lord would sweep away the corrupt house of Jeroboam (1 Kgs. 14:10). It further served as a simile for the sweeping away of Judah's flesh in the day of God's judgment (Zeph. 1:17). ¶
3 ***gêlel*** [masc. noun: גֵּלֶל <1561>; a variation of <1557> above] ▶ **This word means and is also translated excrement, refuse, waste.** It describes dung from a human, human dung to be used as fuel (Ezek. 4:12, 15) or to be discarded (Job 20:7). It is employed in a simile to describe human flesh poured out like dung (Zeph. 1:17). ¶
4 ***ḥere'*** [masc. noun: חֶרֶא <2716>; from an unused (and vulgar) root prob. meaning to evacuate the bowels] ▶ **This word indicates excrement; a dove's dung, dung.** It had some food value and was eaten in extreme cases but had almost no monetary value (2 Kgs. 6:25, *ḥ^arêy yôniym*); see DOVE'S DUNG <1686>. It also refers to human excrement (2 Kgs. 18:27; Is. 36:12); also translated waste. ¶

[5] ***pereš*** [masc. noun: פֶּרֶשׁ <6569>; from CLEAR (BE, MAKE) <6567> (in the sense of to eliminate)] ► **This word refers to the feces, excrement produced in an animal or human being; it is also translated offal, refuse, intestines.** Refs.: Ex. 29:14; Lev. 4:11; 8:17; 16:27; Num. 19:5. It is used in a devastating figure of speech against Israel representing the refuse or excrement of their festivals (Mal. 2:3). ¶

[6] ***parš***^{e}***ḏōnāh*** [masc. noun: פַּרְשְׁדֹנָה <6574>; perhaps by compounding CLEAR (BE, MAKE) <6567> and DIVIDE <6504> (in the sense of straddling); comp. SPREAD (verb) <6576>] ► **This word refers to refuse, intestines; it is also translated entrails, dirt, bowels.** It refers to the bowels or other internal intestines that would protrude from a gaping hole in the skin and muscles of the lower stomach area; or to the excrement or contents of the bowels (Judg. 3:22). ¶

[7] ***ṣ***^{e}***p̱iya‘*** [masc. noun: צְפִיעַ <6832>; from the same as VIPER <6848> (which is from a root meaning to extrude, as thrusting out the tongue, i.e., hissing)] ► **This word means manure.** It indicates cow's excrement (Ezek. 4:15). ¶

– [8] Ezek. 4:12 ➔ EXCREMENT <6627>.

DUNG GATE – Neh. 2:13; 3:13, 14; 12:31 ➔ ASH HEAP <830>.

DUNGEON – [1] Gen. 40:15 ➔ CISTERN <953> [2] Is. 42:7 ➔ PRISON <4525>.

DUNGHILL – [1] ***maḏmênāh*** [fem. noun: מַדְמֵנָה <4087>; fem. from the same as DUNG <1828>] ► **This word means animal excrement; it is also translated manure, manure pile, refuse heap.** It is used figuratively of Moab being trodden down by the Lord like straw trodden down into a manure pile (Is. 25:10). ¶

[2] ***n***^{e}***wālû, n***^{e}***wāliy*** [Aramaic fem. noun: נְוָלוּ, נְוָלִי <5122>; from an unused root prob. meaning to be foul] ► **This word refers to a useless pile of rubble; it is also translated refuse heap, ash heap, rubbish heap, pile of rubble, ruins.** It refers to a demolished house (Ezra 6:11; Dan. 2:5; 3:29). ¶

– [3] 1 Sam. 2:8; Ps. 113:7 ➔ ASH HEAP <830>.

DUPLICATE – Ezra 1:9 ➔ KNIFE <4252>.

DUPLICITY – Prov. 11:3 ➔ CROOKEDNESS <5558>.

DURA – ***dûrā’*** [proper noun: דּוּרָא <1757>; prob. from DWELL <1753>]: circle ► **A plain, in the province of Babylon.** Nebuchadnezzar set up his image of gold there (Dan. 3:1). ¶

DURABLE – [1] Prov. 8:18 ➔ ENDURING <6276> [2] Is. 23:18 ➔ FINE (adj.) <6266> b.

DUSK – [1] Job 24:15 ➔ TWILIGHT <5399> [2] Ezek. 12:6, 7, 12 ➔ DARKNESS <5939>.

DUST – [1] ***’āḇāq*** [masc. noun: אָבָק <80>; from the root of WRESTLE <79>] ► **This word means especially extremely fine, powdery particles in contrast to the coarser dust or *‘āp̱ār* below.** Ref.: Ex. 9:9. It is used to signify the dust easily driven by the wind (Is. 5:24) and dust raised by the hooves of galloping horses (Ezek. 26:10). As a metaphor, it signifies the notion of utter insignificance (Is. 29:5); conditions of drought (Deut. 28:24); and clouds as the dust of God's feet (Nah. 1:3). ¶

[2] ***‘āp̱ār*** [masc. noun: עָפָר <6083>; from FLING <6080>] ► **This word also means dry earth, loose dirt.** The primary meaning of this word is the dry, loose dirt or dust that covers the ground (Amos 2:7; Mic. 1:10). It is used to imply earth or soil (Job 5:6; 28:2); the original material used to form the first man (Gen. 2:7); the material used to plaster walls (Lev. 14:42); the remains of a destroyed city (Ezek. 26:4); and anything pulverized into powder (Deut. 9:21). Figuratively, it signifies abundance (Gen. 13:16); utter defeat (2 Kgs. 13:7); and humiliation (Job 16:15). *

– [3] Ps. 90:3 ➔ CRUSHED <1793>.

DUST (SMALL, FINE) – Is. 40:15 ➔ CLOUD <7834>.

DUTY – 1 Num. 3:7; 9:23; 2 Chr. 8:14 ➔ GUARD <4931> 2 1 Chr. 23:28 ➔ ATTENDANCE <4612>.

DUTY (GO OFF) – Ps. 22:7 ➔ OPEN <6362>.

DUTY OF A BROTHER-IN-LAW, DUTY OF THE HUSBAND'S BROTHER (PERFORM, FULFILL THE) – Gen. 38:8; Deut. 25:5, 7 ➔ MARRY <2992>.

DWELL – 1 ***dûr*** [verb: דּוּר <1752>; a prim. root] ► **This word is used once. It means to settle down and be at home in the tent of wickedness.** Ref.: Ps. 84:10. The psalmist rejects such a condition compared to standing in the presence of God. ¶
2 ***dûr*** [Aramaic verb: דּוּר <1753>; corresponding to <1752> above] ► **This word is a broad term describing the life and existence of living things in their appropriate habitats wherever they live: humankind, wild animals, fowl; it is also translated to live.** Refs.: Dan. 2:38; 4:1, 12, 21; 6:25. Other ref.: Dan. 4:35; the word is translated inhabitant. ¶
3 ***zāḇal*** [verb: זָבַל <2082>; a prim. root] ► **This word indicates treating someone with honor, respect.** In Leah's case, she hoped her husband would treat her with honor and would dwell with her as a result of God's honoring her with her sixth son, Zebulun (Gen. 30:20). ¶
4 ***yāšaḇ*** [verb: יָשַׁב <3427>; a prim. root] ► **This word also means to sit, to inhabit, to endure, to stay. Apparently, to sit is the root idea, and other meanings are derived from this.** The subject of the verb may be God, human, animal (Jer. 50:39), or inanimate matter. The word sometimes emphasizes the location of persons, whether they were sitting under a tree (Judg. 6:11; 1 Kgs. 19:4) or in a house (2 Kgs. 6:32). It could also reflect a person's position: one sat as a judge (Prov. 20:8; Is. 28:6); as a widow (Gen. 38:11); or on a throne as king (Ex. 12:29; 2 Kgs. 13:13). Sometimes it indicated one's companions; one sits with scoffers (Ps. 1:1); or with the elders of the land (Prov. 31:23). The word may signify "to dwell," either temporarily (Lev. 23:42) or in a permanent dwelling (Gen. 4:16; Zeph. 2:15). Sometimes the word means that an object or person stays in a limited area (Ex. 16:29); or abides for a period of time (Lev. 12:4, 5; 2 Sam. 6:11); or for eternity (Ps. 9:7; 102:12; 125:1). The years are even said to sit, i.e., to pass (1 Kgs. 22:1). *
5 ***šᵉḵan*** [verb: שְׁכַן <7932>]; corresponding to SETTLE DOWN <7931> ► **This word means to inhabit a certain place or location, to remain there permanently.** Ref.: Ezra 6:12; it is used of God's name dwelling in Jerusalem in His Temple. The beasts of Nebuchadnezzar's tree vision lived in safety under the limbs of the great tree (Dan. 4:21: to have one's habitation, to lodge, to have one's home, to live, to have nesting places). ¶
– 6 Gen. 26:3; 35:27; 1 Kgs. 17:20; Ps. 15:1; 61:4; etc. ➔ SOJOURN <1481> 7 Ezra 4:17 ➔ SIT <3488>.

DWELLING – 1 ***māḵôn*** [masc. noun: מָכוֹן <4349>; from SET UP <3559>] ►
a. This word indicates a solid support or structure that can serve as a habitation or as a foundation for something. It is used of a dwelling place, especially the Lord's, such as Mount Zion or Mount Sinai (Ex. 15:17); the Temple of Solomon (1 Kgs. 8:13); God's heavenly dwelling place (1 Kgs. 8:39, 43, 49; Ps. 33:14). It refers to the entire area of Mount Zion (Is. 4:5). It refers to the location of the Temple, the holy place (Dan. 8:11). Ezra 2:68 is rendered best as foundation or location. Other refs.: 2 Chr. 6:2, 30, 33, 39; Is. 18:4. ¶
b. This word means a foundation, a basis. It stands for a support for the Lord's throne of righteousness and justice (Ps. 89:14; 97:2; KJV: habitation). It is used of the foundation of the earth itself (Ps. 104:5). ¶
2 ***miškan*** [Aramaic masc. noun: מִשְׁכַּן <4907>; corresponding to TABERNACLE <4908>] ► **This word indicates a**

habitation, a place of dwelling. It refers to the House of God, the Temple, in Jerusalem. It has the sense of a temporary habitation (Ezra 7:15). ¶
3 ***nā'āh*** [fem. noun: נָאָה <4999>; from BEAUTIFUL (BE) <4998> (in the sense of to be comely, to be in order)] ► **This word means an abode, a residence, a habitation, a pasture, a meadow. It describes a place where humans permanently settle and live; or an area where flocks and herds graze, reside, lie down, and rest.** In His fierce anger for their iniquities, the Lord vented His wrath on Israel, destroying without mercy the dwellings found within its borders (Lam. 2:2; cf. Jer. 25:37). The Lord roars from Zion, and the pastures of the shepherds wither (Amos 1:2). Painting a picture of abundant provisions, the psalmist praises God for the overflowing pastures of the wilderness (Ps. 65:12; cf. the description of wilderness pastures in Jer. 9:10). The most famous use of the term comes in Psalm 23, where in vivid imagery the Lord is depicted as the great Shepherd who causes His sheep to lie down in green pastures (Ps. 23:2). Once it is used in conjunction with the term used for God, forming the phrase pastures of God. In the context, the phrase refers to the land of Israel and recalls the idea of the people of Israel as God's flock (Ps. 83:12). Other refs.: Ps. 74:20; Jer. 23:10; Joel 1:19, 20; 2:22. ¶
4 ***šēḵen*** [masc. noun: שֵׁכֶן <7933>; from SETTLE DOWN <7931>] ► **This word indicates a habitation; it is also translated dwelling place.** It is a noun indicating a temporary dwelling place, the Tabernacle in the wilderness (Deut. 12:5). ¶
– 5 Gen. 27:39 ➔ SEAT <4186> 6 Deut. 26:15; 2 Chr. 30:27; etc. ➔ HABITATION <4583> 7 Neh. 3:30 ➔ CHAMBER <5393> 8 Job 23:3 ➔ ARRANGEMENT <8498> b. or SEAT <8499> 9 Ps. 27:5 ➔ ABODE <5520> 10 Ps. 49:14 ➔ HABITATION <2073> 11 Ps. 69:25 ➔ CAMP <2918> 12 Jer. 21:13 ➔ DWELLING PLACE <4585> 13 Lam. 2:6 ➔ TABERNACLE <7900>.

DWELLING PLACE – 1 ***me'ônāh, me'ōnāh*** [fem. noun: מְעוֹנָה, מְעֹנָה <4585>; fem. of HABITATION <4583> and meaning the same] ► **This word describes a habitat for animals.** Refs.: Job 38:40; Ps. 104:22; Amos 3:4: den. It is used in a general figurative sense of God hunting for the habitations of people (Jer. 21:13: habitation, dwelling, refuge); and of the Lord's dwelling place in the Temple in Zion (Ps. 76:2). God is called the refuge or habitat for His own people (Deut. 33:27). Other refs.: Job 37:8; Song 4:8; Nah. 2:12. ¶
– 2 Gen. 49:5 ➔ SWORD <4380> 3 Num. 24:21; Ps. 132:13 ➔ SEAT <4186> 4 Deut. 12:5 ➔ DWELLING <7933> 5 Prov. 24:15 ➔ RESTING PLACE <7258>.

DWELLING, DWELLING PLACE – 1 ***meḏôr, meḏār*** [Aramaic masc. noun: מְדוֹר, מְדָר <4070>; from DWELL <1753>] ► **This word indicates a place where gods or people make their home, an appropriate abode.** Ref.: Dan. 2:11. In Nebuchadnezzar's case, he lived in the dwelling place of animals for a time (Dan. 4:25, 32; 5:21). ¶
– 2 Lev. 26:11; 1 Chr. 6:32; etc. ➔ TABERNACLE <4908>.

DYED – 1 Is. 63:1 ➔ LEAVENED (BE) <2556> 2 Ezek. 23:15 ➔ dyed attire ➔ FLOWING TURBAN <2871>.

DYED RED (BE) – Ex. 25:5; 26:14; 35:7 ➔ RUDDY (BE) <119>.

DYED WORK, DYED MATERIALS – ***ṣeḇa'*** [masc. noun: צֶבַע <6648>; from an unused root meaning to dip (into coloring fluid)] ► **This word refers to a colorful garment.** It is used to depict an item among the spoils of war when Deborah and Barak defeated Sisera (Judg. 5:30). ¶

DYING GASP (BECOMING) – Job 11:20 ➔ lit.: breathing out life ➔ BREATHING OUT <4646>.

E

EAGER (BE) – Ps. 17:12 ➔ LONG FOR <3700>.

EAGLE – [1] ***nᵉšar*** [Aramaic masc. noun: נְשַׁר <5403>; corresponding to <5404> below] ▶ **This word refers to a large, carnivorous bird of prey known for its long feathers, power, and keen eyesight.** It describes the hair of Nebuchadnezzar which had grown to look like the feathers of an eagle (Dan. 4:33). In his vision Daniel saw a lion having eagles' wings (Dan. 7:4). ¶
[2] ***nešer*** [masc. noun: נֶשֶׁר <5404>; from an unused root meaning to lacerate] ▶ **This word refers to a large, carnivorous bird of prey known for its long feathers, wings, speed, power in flight, and keen eyesight.** Refs.: 2 Sam. 1:23; Ps. 103:5; Is. 40:31. It serves in the famous "eagles' wings" passage as the bird on which the Lord brought Israel to Himself (Ex. 19:4). The eagle represents the Lord as He hovers over His people to care for them (Deut. 32:11). It was forbidden as food to Israel (Lev. 11:13; Deut. 14:12). It is employed figuratively as a bird of prey to represent the attack of Israel's enemies (Deut. 28:49; Job 9:26). God is the creator of the eagle (Job 39:27). *

EAR (noun) – [1] ***'āḇiyḇ*** [masc. noun: אָבִיב <24>; from an unused root (meaning to be tender)] ▶ **This word means the head of a cereal plant that contains the grains; it is also translated head.** It is used twice in the Old Testament meaning a fresh, ripe ear of barley (Ex. 9:31). As an offering, it could be roasted in fire and presented to the Lord (Lev. 2:14). The Hebrew word also means one of the months of the Jewish calendar; see ABIB <24>. ¶
[2] ***'ōzen*** [masc. noun: אֹזֶן <241>; from EAR (GIVE) <238>] ▶ **This word is often used metaphorically as an instrument of obedience and intellect.** Refs.: Job 12:11; 13:1; Prov. 18:15; 25:12; Eccl. 1:8. In Jeremiah 6:10, the disobedient or inattentive are said to have uncircumcised ears. The Hebrew idiom for revealing something or making one aware is to open the ears (Ruth 4:4; 1 Sam. 20:2, 12, 13; Is. 35:5). *
– [3] Deut. 23:25 ➔ KERNEL <4425>.

EAR (GIVE) – ***'āzan*** [verb: אָזַן <238>; a prim. root] ▶ **This word means to lend an ear, to listen, to hear. It is almost always found in poetic texts of the Old Testament and is often found in songs.** The Song of Moses begins with an exhortation for the heavens to lend its ear (Deut. 32:1); Jeremiah asked for the people of Israel to listen to his prophecy (Jer. 13:15; also translated to give heed, to pay attention). God's people commonly asked the Lord to listen to their prayers and petitions; this significant use is found many times throughout the Book of Psalms (Ps. 5:1; 77:1; 80:1). *

EAR (verb) – 1 Sam. 8:12 ➔ PLOWING <2758>.

EARING – Gen. 45:6; Ex. 34:21 ➔ PLOWING <2758>.

EARNINGS – ***'eṯnan*** [masc. noun: אֶתְנַן <868>; the same as PAY <866>] ▶ **The word indicates the gift or hire for a prostitute; it is also translated wages, hire, fee, payment, money.** It refers specifically to a prostitute's pay (Deut. 23:18). Moses often depicts Israel as playing the prostitute (Ezek. 16:31, 34, 41; Hos. 9:1). Tyre was considered a pagan city of prostitution among the nations (Is. 23:17, 18). The word refers to expensive idols of Samaria (Mic. 1:7) that led her into more prostitution. ¶

EARRING – Is. 3:20 ➔ CHARM <3908>.

EARRINGS – [1] ***'āgiyl*** [masc. noun: עָגִיל <5694>; from the same as CIRCULAR <5696>] ▶ **This word refers to jewelry or ornamentation worn by either men or women.** Refs.: Num. 31:50; Ezek. 16:12. ¶
– [2] Song 1:10 ➔ TURN (noun) <8447> b.

EARRINGS, DANGLING EARRINGS – Is. 3:19 ➔ PENDANT <5188>.

EARTH – [1] ^{a}***raʿ*** [Aramaic masc. noun: אֲרַע <772>; corresponding to <776> below] ▶ **Functioning as an adverb, this word also carries the idea of downward, below, or towards the earth.** This concept appears in Jeremiah 10:11 in conjunction with the phrase "under the heavens" to say that the gods who did not make heaven and earth will perish. It is also used to mean the realm where humans live (Dan. 2:35). The word also occurs twice in Daniel 2:39; in the first instance, it means inferior or less than, and in the second occurrence, it means earth. See the equivalent Hebrew noun *'ereṣ* (<776> below). *
[2] ***'ereṣ*** [fem. noun: אֶרֶץ <776>; from an unused root prob. meaning to be firm] ▶ **This word refers to our planet. It means the world, and also land. It is used almost 2,500 times in the Old Testament.** It refers to the whole earth under God's dominion (Gen. 1:1; 14:19; Ex. 9:29; Ps. 102:25; Prov. 8:31; Mic. 4:13). Since the earth was God's possession, He promised to give the land of Canaan to Abraham's descendants (Gen. 12:7; 15:7). The Promised Land was very important to Abraham's descendants and to the nation of Israel that possessed the land (Josh. 1:2, 4). Israel's identity was tied to the land because it signified the fulfillment of God's promise to Abraham. If the Israelites were disobedient, however, they would be cursed by losing the land (Lev. 26:32–34, 36, 38, 39; Deut. 28:63, 64; Jer. 7:7). *
[3] ^{a}***raq*** [Aramaic fem. noun: אֲרַק <778>; by transmutation for <772> above] ▶ **Related to the Hebrew word *'ereṣ* (<776> above), this word corresponds to the term planet.** It occurs only once in the Hebrew Bible in Jeremiah 10:11. The English word *earth* occurs twice in this verse, but it does not translate the same Aramaic word. The first is the Aramaic word being defined here; the second is the Aramaic noun ^{a}*raʿ* (<772> above). Both of these words mean world. ¶
[4] ***yabbešeṯ*** [Aramaic fem. noun: יַבֶּשֶׁת <3007>; corresponding to DRY GROUND <3006>] ▶ **This word suggests any patch of dry land on which a person can stand.** It appears only in Daniel 2:10. Thus, the word is taken to imply the whole planet or the entire world. ¶
– [5] See GROUND <127> [6] See WORLD <8398>.

EARTHENWARE – ***ḥereś*** [masc. noun: חֶרֶשׂ <2789>; a collateral form mediating between ITCH <2775> and SECRETLY <2791>] ▶ **This word also means clay pottery, and potsherd.** It signifies any vessel made from clay (Lev. 15:12; Jer. 19:1); the sharp fragments of broken pottery (Job 41:30: sharp potsherds, jagged potsherds); and the larger potsherd useful to scoop burning coals from a fire (Is. 30:14: shard, sherd); or to scrape boils (Job 2:8: potsherd, piece of broken pottery). Figuratively, David used the image of kiln-dried pottery to describe the depletion of his strength (Ps. 22:15). Other refs.: Lev. 6:28; 11:33; 14:5, 50; Num. 5:17; Prov. 26:23; Is. 45:9; Jer. 32:14; Lam. 4:2; Ezek. 23:34. ¶

EASE (AT) – [1] ***ša***^{a}***nān*** [adj.: שַׁאֲנָן <7600>; from EASE (BE AT) <7599>] ▶
a. This word means to be confortable, to be quiet, to be complacent. It refers to a condition of relative tranquillity, undisturbed security and safety, without worries (Job 12:5; 21:23). It refers to the lack of care and worry possessed by the fortunate members of a society who dwell in security (Ps. 123:4); a condition that can be considered dangerous, evil (Is. 32:9, 11, 18; Amos 6:1; Zech. 1:15). Jerusalem will attain this condition by the power of God (Is. 33:20). ¶
b. This Hebrew word means arrogant, proud, insolent. It refers to a condition that can easily arise from the situation depicted in a. It refers to the arrogance of the Assyrian king and nation (2 Kgs. 19:28; Is. 37:29). Some assign this meaning to the word in Psalm 123:4 rather than the meaning in a. ¶
[2] ***šal***^{a}***nan*** [adj.: שַׁלְאֲנָן <7946>; for <7600> above] ▶ **This word refers to a time and condition of safety, health, and strength in one's life, a time seemingly safe from all dangers.** Ref.: Job 21:23. ¶
[3] ***šālêw, šālêyw, š***^{e}***lêyw*** [adj.: שָׁלֵו, שָׁלֵיו, שְׁלֵיו <7961>; from EASE (BE AT) <7951>] ▶

This word means peaceable, prosperous, care-free. It refers to a state and attitude of being undisturbed or heedless. It describes a place to live found by some of Simeon's descendants, a place very peaceful, at ease (1 Chr. 4:40); or any nation dwelling in security (Jer. 49:31). It describes a person who is at ease, without worry or anxiety (Job 16:12). The evil person has no such state (Job 20:20). Psalm 73:12 gives a contrary view of the wicked. It refers to a luxuriously affected, carefree people (Ezek. 23:42). It takes on the sense of prosperity in a general sense (Zech. 7:7). Other ref.: Job 21:23. ¶

EASE (BE AT) – [1] ***šā'an*** [verb: שָׁאַן <7599>; a prim. root] ▶ **This word means to be secure, to be at rest.** It describes a state of security, peace, rest: for individuals at death (Job 3:18); for persons who find wisdom (Prov. 1:33); and for nations who live in security and safety (Jer. 48:11). It refers to the undisturbed condition of a restored Israel cared for by God (Jer. 30:10; 46:27). ¶

[2] ***šālāh, šālaw*** [verb: שָׁלָה, שָׁלֵו <7951>; a prim. root] ▶

a. This word also to be safe, to prosper. It indicates being in a state of peace, quiet, and safety, at ease (Job 3:26; 12:6; Jer. 12:1). It refers to a time of quiet and safety, of wholeness for Jerusalem (Ps. 122:6). It can also describe a state of prosperity for the enemies of Israel and Zion (Lam. 1:5). ¶

b. This word means to deceive; to be negligent. It may indicate a kind of evil deception (2 Kgs. 4:28); or a failure to be diligent, to be neglectful in what is important (2 Chr. 29:11). ¶

[3] ***š^elêh*** [Aramaic verb: שְׁלֵה <7954>; corresponding to <7951> above] ▶ **This word means to be in a state of safety, contentment, and security in one's domicile, with no external threats of war or revolution according to its contextual usage.** Ref.: Dan. 4:4; also translated to be safe, to be at home. ¶

EASING – Nah. 3:19 ➔ HEALING <3545>.

EAST – [1] ***mizrāḥ*** [masc. noun: מִזְרָח <4217>; from RISE UP <2224>] ▶ **This word shows the direction of the sunrise, eastward.** It combines with *šemeš* to indicate the direction east, *mizraḥ šemeš* (Num. 21:11; 1 Kgs. 7:25). It is used alone more often to mean east (Josh. 11:3; 1 Chr. 9:24; Neh. 12:37; Ps. 103:12). With the definite article and the preposition *l^e*, to, in front, it is rendered as in or toward the east (Neh. 3:26). With *l^e* following, it means to the east of, eastward (2 Chr. 5:12). With *min* (FROM <4480>) on the front, it means from the east (Is. 41:2; 43:5; Dan. 11:44). With a ה ָ, *āh,* directive attached, it means eastward (Num. 32:19). *

[2] ***qeḏem*** [masc. noun: קֶדֶם <6924>; from MEET (verb) <6923> (in the sense of the front, relatively the East)] ▶ **This word shows the direction of the sunrise. It also means earlier, formerly, long ago. It is used regularly to mean east or eastern.** The Lord planted the Garden of Eden in the east (Gen. 2:8; 3:24); Abraham traveled toward the eastern hills (Gen. 12:8; 13:11). The word describes the East as a place known for its wise men (Gen. 29:1; Judg. 6:3; 1 Kgs. 4:30); Job was the greatest among these people (Job 1:3). Isaiah, however, called the East a place of superstitions (Is. 2:6). One of Jeremiah's oracles was directed against the people of the East (Jer. 49:28); but not, according to Ezekiel, until the Lord gave Judah to one of the peoples of the East—Babylon (Ezek. 25:4, 10). The famous movement of the whole earth's population to the east to build the Tower of Babel in the plain of Shinar is toward the area of Babylon (Gen. 11:2).

The word is also used to refer to former times, times of old. It describes the works of God before the world was created (Prov. 8:22, 23). The psalmist implored the Lord to remember the people He purchased long before (Ps. 74:2; 77:11; 143:5); for He was the psalmist's King from old (Ps. 74:12). The psalmist of Psalm 78:2 uttered wisdom and parables as a wise man from ancient times. God planned the fall of Assryia long before it happened (Is. 37:26; Lam. 2:17). The word also refers to Tyre, describing it as an old, ancient city (Is. 23:7). In an important passage, Micah 5:2 describes the Lord's coming Ruler from Bethlehem whose origins were from eternity or from ancient days. This word describes the mountains and the heavens as old, of long ago (Deut. 33:15; Ps. 68:33; Is. 46:10).

A few times the word means front or in front. The Lord knows His people before and behind—thus, altogether (Ps. 139:5). The Lord spurred Rezin's foes against him (i.e., from the front) to confront him (Is. 9:12). *

[3] ***qiḏmāh*** [fem. noun: קִדְמָה <6926>; fem. of <6924> above] ▶ **This word indicates a direction to the east, eastward, toward the rising sun.** Refs.: Gen. 2:14; 4:16; 1 Sam. 13:5; Ezek. 39:11. ¶

– [4] Ps. 75:6 ➔ GOING OUT, GOING FORTH <4161>.

EAST, EAST WIND – ***qāḏiym*** [masc. noun: קָדִים <6921>; from MEET (verb) <6923> (the fore or front part)] ▶ **This word indicates literally a wind from the east that brings evil conditions.** Refs.: Gen. 41:6, 23; Ex. 10:13. With *āh* on the end, it means eastward, towards the east (Ezek. 11:1; 44:1; 47:1). It indicates a structural feature of something, an east side, the east (Ezek. 40:23, 44; 42:9, 16). The phrase *dereḵ haqqāḏiym* means toward the east (Ezek. 43:2). The word is used over fifty times in Ezekiel. *

EASTERN – [1] ***qaḏmôn*** [adj.: קַדְמוֹן <6930>; from MEET (verb) <6923> (in the sense of to do something before the sun rises)] ▶ **This word indicates that something lies in the direction of the east, toward the east.** Ref.: Ezek. 47:8. ¶

[2] ***qaḏmôniy, qaḏmōniy*** [adj.: קַדְמוֹנִי, קַדְמֹנִי <6931>; from EASTERN <6930> (in the sense of to come before)] ▶

a. This word indicates someone or something located in the east or connected with the eastern regions of the nations. The Temple had gates north, east, west, south (Ezek. 10:19; 11:1). It refers to a place of habitation, the East (Job 18:20). The eastern sea was the Dead Sea (Joel 2:20; Zech. 14:8). Other ref.: Ezek. 47:18. ¶

b. This word means former, previous. It is used as a noun to refer to the ancient ones, the ones who lived before (1 Sam. 24:13; Job 18:20 [KJV]). It refers to past days, former days (Ezek. 38:17; Mal. 3:4). Other ref.: Is. 43:18. ¶

EASY (THINK, REGARD AS) – ***hûn*** [verb.: הוּן <1951>; a prim. root] ▶ **This verb refers to something that is considered to be an effortless accomplished task.** A rebellious Israel thought that taking Canaan would be an easy task for them (Deut. 1:41; also translated to be ready). ¶

EAT – [1] ***'āḵal*** [verb: אָכַל <398>; a prim. root] ▶ **This word means to consume food; it also means to devour, to consume by fire.** It has many uses. It is used of humans most often (Gen. 3:6, 11, 18; Ex. 16:35; 34:15; Ruth 2:14). It also means to eat a meal (Gen. 43:25; Ex. 2:20). It is used frequently in a cultic setting. To eat before the Lord is mentioned in the context of offering sacrifice (Deut. 12:7). The burnt offering was consumed by fire into ashes (Lev. 6:10). It is used to describe the feeding of birds or animals and translated often as devour, eat, consume (Gen. 37:20, 33; 1 Kgs. 13:28; 14:11). It describes the feeding of locusts (Joel 1:4; 2:25); moths (Job 13:28); flies (Ps. 78:45); worms (Deut. 28:39).

It is regularly used in a metaphorical sense describing the activity of fire that consumes or devours (Lev. 6:10; Nah. 3:13). The Lord is pictured as a consuming fire of judgment (Deut. 4:24). It describes the action of a consuming sword (Deut. 32:42; 2 Sam. 2:26). It depicts the consuming oppression of the poor (Prov. 30:14; Hab. 3:14). The passive use of *'āḵal* means to be eaten, devoured (Ex. 12:46; Zech. 9:4), or consumed (Neh. 2:3, 13; Is. 1:20). A causal use of the verb means to cause to eat or feed (Ex. 16:32; Deut. 8:3, 16; 1 Kgs. 22:27).

The word is used in some idioms; one means to eat up space, i.e., to lay claim to space (Ezek. 42:5). It refers to the act of an adulterous woman with regard to the sex act (Prov. 30:20), to enjoy love. *

[2] ***ᵃkal*** [Aramaic verb: אֲכַל <399>; corresponding to <398> above] ▶
a. This word means to consume, to devour. It describes Nebuchadnezzar's devouring grass like an ox (Dan. 4:33) and the voracious acts of destruction enacted by the beasts of Daniel (Dan. 7:5, 7, 19, 23). ¶
b. Possibly another Aramaic verb meaning to accuse, to slander. The word is best translated as slander (Dan. 3:8; 6:24). It means literally "to eat their pieces" (Dan. 3:8) or "to eat/crush their bones" (Dan. 6:24). It is likely the same as a., but used in an idiomatic phrase. ¶
[3] ***bārāh*** [verb: בָּרָה <1262>; a prim. root] ▶
a. This word describes the intake of bread or food. Refs.: 2 Sam. 12:17; 13:6, 10. It describes also the act of causing someone to eat food (2 Sam. 3:35; 13:5), to feed or to give him or her food. It has a more violent meaning: to devour (Lam. 4:10: food) human flesh as a result of Israel's destruction and the resulting famine. ¶
b. A verb meaning to select, make a covenant, assign a task. In its sole usage, Goliath uses it to challenge Israel's army to select or chose a representative for themselves (1 Sam. 17:8: to choose). ¶
[4] ***ṭᵉʻēm*** [verb: טְעֵם <2939>; corresponding to TASTE (verb) <2938>] ▶ **This word means to feed, to cause to eat.** It is used of giving grass to Nebuchadnezzar to eat like a beast (Dan. 4:25, 32; 5:21) of the field in fulfillment of God's decreed judgment on him. ¶
[5] ***lāḥam*** [verb: לָחַם <3898>; a prim. root] ▶ **This word means to consume food, to taste.** It indicates taking food for nourishment (Prov. 23:1). It is used figuratively of eating the food or bread of wickedness (Prov. 4:17); or the food of wisdom (Prov. 9:5). It is used symbolically of fellowshipping with a person, "eating his food" (Ps. 141:4; Prov. 23:6). It is used of famine voraciously devouring people (Deut. 32:24: to be devoured, to be consumed). The Hebrew word is also translated to fight; see FIGHT <3898>. ¶
– [6] Is. 9:20 ➔ CUT (verb) <1504>.

EAT (LET) – Gen. 25:30 ➔ FEED (verb) <3938>.

EAT AWAY – Ps. 80:13 ➔ RAVAGE (verb) <3765>.

EAT UP – Job 39:24 ➔ DRINK (verb) <1572>.

EATING (BE) – Job 20:23 ➔ ENTRAILS <3894>.

EATING (WITHOUT) – Dan. 6:18 ➔ FAST (verb) <2908>.

EATING AWAY – ***pᵉḥeṯeṯ*** [fem. noun: פְּחֶתֶת <6356>; from the same as PIT <6354>] ▶ **This word means bored out, gradually damaged or destroyed.** It is used once to denote the condition of a decaying leprous garment (Lev. 13:55; KJV: fret inward). The image underlying the word is similar to that of a wormhole or spot eaten away by a moth. ¶

EAVE – 1 Kgs. 7:9 ➔ HANDBREATH <2947> c.

EBAL – [1] ***ʻêyḇāl*** [proper noun: עֵיבָל <5858>; from an unused root prob. meaning to be bald]: bare, stony ▶
a. A man from Edom. He was a son of Shobal who descended from Seir, the Horite (Gen. 36:23). ¶
b. The son of Joktan, a Semite. It also indicates a son of Seir (same as a.) (1 Chr. 1:20–22, 40). ¶
c. The mountain in the area of Shechem where, on entrance to Canaan, the Israelites proclaimed the curses written in the covenant of Sinai. Refs.: Deut. 11:29; 27:4, 13; Josh. 8:30, 33. Joshua built an altar there for this ceremonial ritual. ¶
– [2] 1 Chr. 1:22 ➔ OBAL <5745>.

EBED – ***ʻeḇeḏ*** [masc. proper noun: עֶבֶד <5651>; the same as SERVANT <5650>]: servant ▶
a. The father of Gaal. Refs.: Judg. 9:26, 28, 30, 31, 35. ¶
b. A companion of Ezra. Ref.: Ezra 8:6. ¶

EBED-MELECH – ***ʻeḇeḏ meleḵ*** [masc. proper noun: עֶבֶד מֶלֶךְ <5663>; from SERVANT <5650> and KING <4428>]: servant of a king ▶ **He was a Cushite official serving in the palace of Zedekiah.** He orchestrated the release and removal of Jeremiah from a cistern where he would have died (Jer. 38:7–12). He was, henceforth, protected by the Lord (Jer. 39:15–17). ¶

EBENEZER – ***'eben hā'êzer*** [proper noun: אֶבֶן הָעֵזֶר <72>; from STONE <68> and HELP (noun) <5828>]: stone of the help ▶

a. A city where Israel was ignominiously defeated by the Philistines twice. Refs.: 1 Sam. 4:1; 5:1. This could be where Samuel placed a stone to commemorate a later victory over the Philistines (see 1 Sam. 7:12). Its exact location is obscure, some placing it near Beth-Shemesh, others placing it about 10 to 12 miles east of Joppa.

b. A stone erected by Samuel to commemorate an Israelite victory over the Philistines, meaning "stone of (the) help." Ref.: 1 Sam. 7:12. ¶

EBER – ***'êber*** [masc. proper noun: עֵבֶר <5677>; the same as SIDE <5676>]: the region beyond ▶

a. A son of Shelah. Refs.: Gen. 10:21, 24, 25; 11:14–17; Num. 24:24; 1 Chr. 1:18, 19, 25. ¶

b. A Gadite chief. Ref.: 1 Chr. 5:13. ¶

c. A Benjamite. Ref.: 1 Chr. 8:12. ¶

d. Another Benjamite. Ref.: 1 Chr. 8:22. ¶

e. A priest. Ref.: Neh. 12:20. ¶

EBEZ – ***'ebeṣ*** [proper noun: אֶבֶץ <77>; from an unused root prob. meaning to gleam] ▶ **A place in Palestine.** Ref.: Josh. 19:20; it is also spelled Abez. ¶

EBIASAPH – ***'ebyāsāp*** [masc. proper noun: אֶבְיָסָף <43>; contr. from ABIASAPH <23>]: father of gathering ▶ **An Israelite of the tribe of Levi.** Refs.: 1 Chr. 6:23, 37; 9:19. ¶

EBONY – ***hobniym*** [masc. noun: הָבְנִים <1894>; only in plur., from an unused root meaning to be hard] ▶ **It was one of the mediums of payment from India for merchandise from Tyre.** Ref.: Ezek. 27:15. ¶

EBRON – ***'ebrōn*** [proper noun: עֶבְרֹן <5683>; from SIDE <5676>]: region beyond, passage ▶ **A city on the border of Asher.** Ref.: Josh. 19:28. ¶

EBRONAH – Num. 33:34, 35 ➔ ABRONAH <5684>.

ECBATANA – Ezra 6:2 ➔ ACHMETHA <307>.

ECZEMA – Lev. 13:39 ➔ SPOT (FRECKLED, WHITE) <933>.

EDEN – [1] ***'eden*** [proper noun: עֶדֶן <5729>; from DELIGHT ONESELF <5727>]: pleasure, delight ▶ **A town in Mesopotamia.** Refs.: 2 Kgs. 19:12; Is. 37:12; Ezek. 27:23. ¶

[2] ***'êden*** [proper noun: עֵדֶן <5731>; the same as DELIGHT (noun) <5730>]: delight ▶

a. The place where God placed Adam and Eve to live and where they rebelled against the Lord's words. Satan was permitted in the garden and fostered the rebellion of the first human pair. They were subsequently driven from the garden by God (Gen. 3:21–24). Ezekiel takes the event seriously and notes the presence of an archetype of the King of Tyre in the Garden of Eden (Ezek. 28:11–15). The precise location of the garden is not known, even though the Tigris and Euphrates Rivers were part of it. It became a symbol of beauty and fertility (Ezek. 31:9; Joel 2:3). Other refs.: Gen. 2:8, 10, 15; 3:23; 4:16; Is. 51:3; Ezek. 31:16, 18; 36:35. ¶

b. The name of a Levite who took part in Hezekiah's purification of the Temple and its service. Refs.: 2 Chr. 29:12; 31:15. ¶

EDER – [1] ***'eder*** [masc. proper noun: עֶדֶר <5738>; from RANK (KEEP) <5737> (in the sense of an arrangement)]: flock ▶ **A Benjamite.** Ref.: 1 Chr. 8:15; KJV: Ader. ¶

[2] ***'êder*** [proper noun: עֵדֶר <5740>; the same as FLOCK <5739>]: flock ▶

a. A Levite. Refs.: 1 Chr. 23:23; 24:30. ¶

b. A location in southern Judah. Ref.: Josh. 15:21. ¶

EDGE – [1] ***pêyāh*** [fem. noun: פֵּיָה <6366>; fem. of MOUTH <6310>] ▶ **This word**

refers to the edge or sharpened part of a sword blade. In context it refers to the edges on a double-edged sword (Judg. 3:16). ¶
– [2] Ps. 89:43 ➔ FLINT <6864> [3] Amos 3:12 ➔ DAMASCUS <1833> b.

EDGE (BE SET ON) – Jer. 31:29, 30; Ezek. 18:2 ➔ BLUNT (BE) <6949> b.

EDGE OF THE CITY (AT THE) – 2 Sam. 15:17 ➔ LAST HOUSE <1023>.

EDICT – [1] ***piṯgām*** [masc. noun: פִּתְגָם <6599>; of Persian origin] ▶ **This word means a command, an order; it is also translated decree. It is used only twice in the Old Testament.** In Esther 1:20, it describes a king's authoritative edict (or law) that could not be repealed (cf. Esther 1:19). In Ecclesiastes 8:11, it refers to a court sentence (or judgment) that should be executed against evil. ¶
– [2] Dan. 6:7, 15 ➔ STATUTE <7010> [3] See LAW <1881>, <1882>.

EDIT – Esther 3:14 ➔ WRITING <3791>.

EDOM – ***ᵉḏôm, ᵉḏōm*** [proper noun: אֱדוֹם, אֱדֹם <123>; from RED <122>]: red ▶
a. Another name for Esau. Refs.: Gen. 25:30; 36:1, 8, 19, 43. Edom was the firstborn or oldest son of Isaac and Rebekah but lost his birthright when he sold it to Jacob for a pot of "red stuff" (NASB) or "red stew" (Gen. 25:30, NIV). His name came from a root meaning "red" or "ruddy" (Gen. 25:24, 30). He was the twin brother of Jacob, son of Isaac. ¶
b. The name also describes the country or people of Edom, Esau's descendants. His descendants lived in Edom (the land) even in Jacob's day (Gen. 32:3; 36:6–43). They had kings before Israel had any kings (Gen. 36:31–39). The nation existed at the time of the Exodus. They refused to let Israel pass through their land (Num. 20:14–21) even though they were physically related to Israel. Obadiah prophesied against Edom for not helping Israel and for fostering Babylon's destruction of Jerusalem and Judah (Obad. 1:1; Ps. 137:7). David controlled the land in his reign (2 Sam. 8:13, 14), but there was tribal warfare against Edom often (1 Kgs. 11:14–16). Sometimes Israel and Edom fought as allies (2 Kgs. 3:4–27). Sela, capital city of Edom, ensconced high in the rocky crags of Edom, was captured in the time of Amaziah of Judah (2 Kgs. 14:7; 2 Chr. 25:11, 12). Edom's gods were largely gods or goddesses of fertility. The language of Edom was similar to Hebrew and Moabite. The area of Edom, on the southeast corner of the Dead Sea, featured a reddish sandstone. *

EDOMITE – [1] ***ᵉḏōmiy*** [proper noun: אֲדֹמִי <130>; patron. from EDOM <123>] ▶ **Name of a descendant of Edom.** Refs.: Deut. 23:7; 1 Sam. 21:7; 22:9, 18, 22; 1 Kgs. 11:1, 14, 17; 2 Kgs. 16:6; 2 Chr. 25:14; 28:17; Ps. 52:1. ¶
– [2] 2 Kgs. 16:6 ➔ ARAMEAN <726>.

EDREI – ***'eḏreʿiy*** [proper noun: אֶדְרֶעִי <154>; from the equivalent of FORCE (noun) <153>]: strong, land sown ▶ **Name of two places in Palestine.** Refs.: Num. 21:33; Deut. 1:4; 3:1, 10; Josh. 12:4; 13:12, 31; 19:37. ¶

EFFECT (MAKE OF NO) – Ps. 33:10 ➔ FORBID <5106>.

EFFORT – [1] Eccl. 5:3 ➔ TASK <6045> [2] Ezek. 24:12 ➔ TOIL (noun) <8383> a.

EFFORT (MAKE EVERY) – Dan. 6:14 ➔ LABOR (verb) <7712>.

EFFORTS – Job 36:19 ➔ FORCES <3981>.

EGG – [1] ***bêyṣāh*** [fem. noun: בֵּיצָה <1000>; from the same as FINE LINEN <948> (i.e., to be white)] ▶ **This word indicates the egg (the reproductive body) of a mother bird.** Ref.: Deut. 22:6. Also of a snake (Is. 59:5) an ostrich (Job 39:14). It refers to abandoned eggs (Is. 10:14) gathered by an arrogant Assyrian king. ¶
[2] ***ḥallāmûṯ*** [fem. noun: חַלָּמוּת <2495>; from DREAM (verb) <2492> (in the sense

of insipidity)] ▶ **This word is used once, and the attention is on the tasteless white of an egg.** Ref.: Job 6:6. ¶

EGLAH – ***'eglāh*** [fem. proper noun: עֶגְלָה <5698>; the same as HEIFER <5697>]: heifer ▶ **One of David's wives, the mother of Ithream.** Refs.: 2 Sam. 3:5; 1 Chr. 3:3. ¶

EGLAIM – ***'eglayim*** [proper noun: אֶגְלַיִם <97>; dual of DROP (noun) <96>]: two sources, two ponds ▶ **A place in Moab.** Ref.: Is. 15:8. ¶

EGLATH SHELISHIYAH – ***'eglaṯ šᵉlišiyyāh*** [proper noun: עֶגְלַת שְׁלִשִׁיָּה <5697>] ▶ **This was a city in Moab east of the southern half of the Dead Sea.** Refs.: Is. 15:5; Jer. 48:34; KJV, NKJV: an heifer of three years old. ¶

EGLON – ***'eglôn*** [proper. noun: עֶגְלוֹן <5700>; from CALF <5695>]: calf-like ▶
a. A village in the low-lying hills of the Shephelah. Its inhabitants tried to withstand the Israelites' moving into the land. It was given to Judah as an inheritance (Josh. 15:39). *
b. The name of a Moabite king who oppressed Israel for some time. Refs.: Judg. 3:12, 14, 15, 17. Ehud, a left-handed Israelite judge, assassinated him and freed Israel. ¶

EGYPT – See **MIZRAIM**.

EGYPTIAN – ***miṣriy*** [proper noun: מִצְרִי <4713>; from MIZRAIM <4714>] ▶ **An inhabitant of Egypt.** Refs.: Gen. 12:12, 14; 16:1, 3; 21:9; 25:12; 39:1, 2, 5; 43:32; Ex. 1:19; 2:11, 12, 14, 19; Lev. 24:10; Deut. 23:7; 26:6; Josh. 24:7; 1 Sam. 30:11, 13; 2 Sam. 23:21; 1 Chr. 2:34; 11:23; Ezra 9:1. ¶

EHI – ***'ēḥiy*** [masc. proper noun: אֵחִי <278>; prob. the same as AHI <277>]: my brother ▶ **One of the sons of Benjamin.** Ref.: Gen. 46:21. ¶

EHUD – 1 ***'ēhûḏ*** [masc. proper noun: אֵהוּד <164>; from the same as OHAD <161>]: united, strong ▶
a. Israel's second "judge" or deliverer listed in the Book of Judges. Refs.: Judg. 3:15, 16, 20, 21, 23, 26; 4:1. He freed Israel from the oppression of the Moabites for eighty years. He was a left-handed man, a fact that helped him carry out the assassination of Eglon, king of Moab. ¶
b. A descendant of Benjamin and son of Bilhan. Ref.: 1 Chr. 7:10. ¶
2 ***'ēḥûḏ*** [masc. proper noun: אֵחוּד <261>; from GO ONE WAY OR THE OTHER <258>]: united, strong ▶ **An Israelite of the tribe of Benjamin.** Ref.: 1 Chr. 8:6. ¶

EIGHT, EIGHTH – ***šᵉmōneh, šᵉmōnāh*** [fem. noun: שְׁמֹנֶה, שְׁמֹנָה <8083>; apparently from FAT, FATNESS <8082> through the idea of plumpness (in the case of the number eight, as if a surplus above the "perfect" seven)] ▶ **As a cardinal number, this word refers to eight of something and combines with other numbers to form larger numbers.** Refs.: Gen. 5:4; 17:12. It can be used to form an ordinal number (1 Kgs. 16:29; 2 Kgs. 15:8). *

EIGHTH – ***šᵉmiyniy*** [adj.: שְׁמִינִי <8066>; from EIGHT, EIGHTH <8083>] ▶ **This word is an ordinal number that points out the eighth of something in a series.** The eighth day (Ex. 22:30; Lev. 9:1); the eighth year (1 Kgs. 6:38); the eighth month (1 Kgs. 12:32). *

EIGHT-STRINGED HARP – Ps. 6 (title); 12 (title) ➔ SHEMINITH <8067>.

EIGHT-STRINGED LYRE – Ps. 6 (title); 12 (title) ➔ SHEMINITH <8067>.

EIGHTY, EIGHTIETH – ***šᵉmōniym, šᵉmôniym*** [plur. adj.: שְׁמֹנִים, שְׁמוֹנִים <8084>; multiple from EIGHT, EIGHTH <8083>] ▶ **As a cardinal number, this word refers to the eightieth item of something.** E.g., eighty-five years (Josh. 14:10). It combines to form other numbers (Gen. 5:25, 26, 28). It can be used as an ordinal number (1 Kgs. 6:1). *

EKER – ***'ēqer*** [masc. proper noun: עֵקֶר <6134>; from MEMBER <6133>]: root, offspring ▶ **An Israelite of the tribe of Judah.** Ref.: 1 Chr. 2:27. ¶

EKRON – ***'eqrôn*** [proper noun: עֶקְרוֹן <6138>; from HAMSTRING <6131> b. (in the sense of to pluck out, to root out)]: eradication, extermination ▶ **It was located on the coastal plain on the borders of Judah and Dan.** It was one of five Philistine cities (Josh. 13:3) and was allotted to Judah (Josh. 15:11, 45, 46). Judah initially captured the city (Judg. 1:18). The city would not let the captured ark of God be brought into it (1 Sam. 5:10–12). Its people played a prominent part in getting the ark returned to Israel (1 Sam. 5:11–6:21). It was one of the southernmost cities of the Philistines (1 Sam. 17:52). It, with many other cities, could taste God's judgments (Jer. 25:20). *

EKRONITE – ***'eqrôniy*** [proper noun: עֶקְרוֹנִי <6139>; patrial from EKKON <6138>] ▶ **An inhabitant of Ekron.** Refs.: Josh. 13:3; 1 Sam. 5:10. ¶

EL BETHEL – ***'ēl bêyṯ 'ēl*** [proper noun: אֵל בֵּית אֵל <416>; from GOD <410> and BETHEL <1008>]: the God of Bethel ▶ **A place where God revealed himself to Jacob.** Ref.: Gen. 35:7. ¶

EL ELOHE ISRAEL – ***'ēl *lōhey yisrā'ēl*** [proper noun: אֵל אֱלֹהֵי יִשְׂרָאֵל <415>; from GOD <410> and GOD <430> and ISRAEL <3478>]: the (true) God of Israel ▶ **This name is given to the Lord as the "God, the (true) God of Israel."** Jacob set up an altar to him at Shechem, thus identifying also with the God of his fathers (Gen. 33:20). ¶

EL PARAN – ***'êyl pā'rān*** [proper noun: אֵיל פָּארָן <364>; from OAK <352> and PARAN <6290>]: oak of Paran ▶ **A place which is near the wilderness.** Ref.: Gen. 14:6. ¶

ELA – ***'ēlā'*** [masc. proper noun: אֵלָא <414>; a variation of OAK <424>]: oak, strong ▶ **An Israelite of the tribe of Benjamin.** Ref.: 1 Kgs. 4:18. ¶

ELADAH – ***'el'āḏāh*** [masc. proper noun: אֶלְעָדָה <497>; from GOD <410> and ADORN <5710>]: decked by God ▶ **A descendant, maybe the son, of Ephraim.** Ref.: 1 Chr. 7:20. ¶

ELAH – ***'ēlāh*** [proper noun: אֵלָה <425>; the same as OAK <424>]: oak, terebinth ▶ **This name is given to five persons and one place in the Old Testament.**
a. It refers to the head of a clan in Edom. Refs.: Gen. 36:41; 1 Chr. 1:52. He was a descendant of Esau (Gen. 36:40). ¶
b. It refers to the valley where David slew Goliath. Refs.: 1 Sam. 17:2, 19; 21:9. It corresponds to Wadi es-Sant located 18 miles southwest of Jerusalem. Warring armies could speak to each other across the valley. ¶
c. It designates a son of Baasha, fourth king in Israel. Refs.: 1 Kgs. 16:6, 8, 13, 14. He reigned two years in Tirzah. He is condemned by the biblical writer and pictured as a corrupt, carousing king. Zimri assassinated him (1 Sam. 6:10). ¶
d. It refers to the father of Hoshea, Elah. Refs.: 2 Kgs. 15:30; 17:1; 18:1, 9. He was the last king in Israel and was a puppet king, most likely, to the great Assyrian King Tiglath-pileser III. He reigned 732–722 B.C. ¶
e. The name of a son of Caleb. He also bore a son named Kenaz (1 Chr. 4:15). ¶
f. He was the son of a Benjamite named Uzzi who was a leader or chief of an Israelite tribe. Ref.: 1 Chr. 9:8. He resettled in Judah after the Babylonian Exile (1 Chr. 9:1, 2). ¶

ELAM – ***'êylām*** [proper noun: עֵילָם <5867>; prob. from HIDE <5956>]: hidden ▶
a. A territory and country lying to the north and east of the modern Persian Gulf in the plain of Khuzistan. It had a king, Chedorlaomer, who tried to conquer Canaan (Gen. 14:1, 9). Their ancient ancestor was Shem (Gen. 10:22). Elam was an avenging arm of the Lord in some cases but the victim of enemies in others (Is. 11:11; 21:2; 22:6; Jer. 25:25; 49:34–39; Ezek. 32:24; Dan. 8:2). Other ref.: 1 Chr. 1:17. ¶

b. The head of a family who returned from exile under Zerubbabel. Refs.: Ezra 2:7; Neh. 7:12. ¶
c. Another head of a family who returned from exile under Zerubbabel. Refs.: Ezra 2:31; Neh. 7:34. ¶
d. The head of a family who returned from exile under Ezra. Refs.: Ezra 8:7; 10:2, 26. ¶
e. A leader in the returned Jewish community who signed and supported Nehemiah's covenant of renewal. Ref.: Neh. 10:14. ¶
f. A Benjamite, a son of Shashak. Ref.: 1 Chr. 8:24. ¶
g. A Levite from the family of the Korahites who served as a gatekeeper. Ref.: 1 Chr. 26:3. ¶
h. A priest who took part in the dedication of Nehemiah's wall, evidently in the musical component of the celebrations. Ref.: Neh. 12:42. ¶

ELAMITE – ***'êlmāy*** [proper noun: עֵלְמָי <5962>; patrial from a name corresponding to ELAM <5867>] ▶ **An inhabitant of Elam, a country east of Babylonia, north of the Persian Gulf.** Ref.: Ezra 4:9. ¶

ELATH – ***'êylat̲, 'êylôt̲*** [proper noun: אֵילַת, אֵילוֹת <359>; from OAK <352>]: plantation of palm trees, oaks ▶ **A city on the Red Sea.** Refs.: Deut. 2:8; 1 Kgs. 9:26; 2 Kgs. 14:22; 16:6; 2 Chr. 8:17; 26:2. ¶

ELDAAH – ***'eldā'āh*** [masc. proper noun: אֶלְדָּעָה <420>; from GOD <410> and KNOW <3045>]: the one whom God has called ▶ **A son of Midian.** Refs.: Gen. 25:4; 1 Chr. 1:33. ¶

ELDAD – ***'eldād̲*** [masc. proper noun: אֶלְדָּד <419>; from GOD <410> and LOVER <1730>]: the one whom God loves ▶ **An Israelite on whom the Spirit rested.** Refs.: Num. 11:26, 27. ¶

ELDER – [1] ***śiyb̲, śāb̲*** [Aramaic verb: שִׂיב, שָׂב <7868>; corresponding to GRAY (BE) <7867>] ▶ **This word means to become aged, to grow gray.** It is used in Ezra to denote those appointed as leaders over Israel (Ezra 5:5, 9). It is again used in Ezra to depict the elders of the Jews, in whom the responsibility for rebuilding the Temple lay, according to Darius (Ezra 6:7, 8, 14). ¶
– [2] See OLD, OLD MAN <2205>.

ELEAD – ***'el'ād̲*** [masc. proper noun: אֶלְעָד <496>; from GOD <410> and WITNESS (BEAR) <5749>]: God has testified ▶ **A descendant, maybe the son, of Ephraim.** Ref.: 1 Chr. 7:21. ¶

ELEALEH – ***'el'ālê'*** [proper noun: אֶלְעָלֵא <500>; from GOD <410> and OFFER <5927>]: God is going up, God is exalted ▶ **A city rebuilt by the Reubenites.** Refs.: Num. 32:3, 37; Is. 15:4; 16:9; Jer. 48:34. ¶

ELEASAH – ***'el'āśāh*** [masc. proper noun: אֶלְעָשָׂה <501>; from GOD <410> and DO <6213>]: the one that God has made ▶
a. A son of Helez. Refs.: 1 Chr. 2:39, 40. ¶
b. Son of Rapha. Refs.: 1 Chr. 8:37; 9:43. ¶
c. A descendant of Pashhur. Ref.: Ezra 10:22. ¶
d. Son of Shaphan. Ref.: Jer. 29:3. ¶

ELEAZAR – ***'el'āzār*** [masc. proper noun: אֶלְעָזָר <499>; from GOD <410> and HELP (verb) <5826>]: God has helped, God helps ▶
a. Most often, this name depicts Eleazar, the third son of Aaron who succeeded him as high priest. Refs.: Ex. 6:23, 25; 28:1; Lev. 10:6, 12, 16; Num. 20:25–28; Deut. 6:10. He succeeded Aaron because his older brothers Nadab and Abihu were slain by the Lord (Lev. 10:1, 2). He is often featured with Moses or Joshua or both (Num. 26:1; Josh. 14:1). He became an expert in administering the covenantal laws in ancient Israel (Num. 19:3). He, along with Joshua, allotted the land to the tribes (Josh. 14:1–5; 19:51). He gave new rulings for the people as new situations arose (Josh. 17:3–6). His son was Phinehas (Josh. 22:13). He accompanied Aaron to the top of Mount Hor where Aaron died (Num. 20:25, 26). He was buried in the area of Ephraim at Gibeah (Josh. 24:33). The term

"sons of Eleazar" is found in the postexilic era and describes a major part of the priesthood at that time (1 Chr. 24:1–6). *

b. A son of Abinadab who guarded the ark of the Lord. Ref.: 1 Sam. 7:1. ¶

c. One of the exclusive "three" mighty men of David who slew many Philistines. Refs.: 2 Sam. 23:9, 10. ¶

d. A Merarite, a family division of Levites. Refs.: 1 Chr. 23:21, 22; 24:28. He had only daughters. ¶

e. A priest, who served and ministered in the house of God. Ref.: Neh. 12:42. ¶

f. A priest, a son of Phinehas, who ministered in the rebuilt Temple in Ezra's day. Ref.: Ezra 8:33. ¶

g. An Israelite who had intermarried with a foreigner in Ezra's day. Ref.: Ezra 10:25. ¶

ELEGANT – Ezek. 23:41 ➔ GLORIOUS <3520> a.

ELEONITE – ***'êlôniy*** [proper noun: אֵלֹנִי <440>; patron. from ALLON <438>] ▶ **A descendant from Elon, the son of Zebulun.** Ref.: Num. 26:26. ¶

ELEPH – ***'elep̱*** [proper noun: אֶלֶף <507>; the same as THOUSAND <505>]: thousand, multitude; ox ▶ **A city of the people of Benjamin near Jerusalem.** Ref.: Josh. 18:28. ¶

ELEVATE – Dan. 5:19 ➔ EXALT <7313>.

ELEVATION – ***nôp̱*** [masc. noun: נוֹף <5131>; from SPRINKLE <5130> (in the sense of offering something by waving it)] ▶ **This word is used both literally and figuratively of the height and splendor of Mount Zion.** Ref.: Ps. 48:2; also translated situation, loftiness. ¶

ELEVEN – ***'aštêy*** [numerical form in a noun or adj. construction: עַשְׁתֵּי <6249>; apparently masc. plur. construction of POLISHED <6247>] ▶ **This is the form that combines with *'āśār* (TEN <6240>) to render eleven or eleventh.** Refs.: Ex. 26:7; 2 Kgs. 25:2. *

ELHANAN – ***'elḥānān*** [masc. proper noun: אֶלְחָנָן <445>; from GOD <410> and GRACIOUS (BE) <2603>]: God is gracious ▶

a. A son of Jair, possibly a Bethlehemite. Refs.: 2 Sam. 21:19; 1 Chr. 20:5. ¶

b. A Bethlehemite, one of David's mighty men. Refs.: 2 Sam. 23:24; 1 Chr. 11:26. ¶

ELI – ***'êliy*** [masc. proper noun: עֵלִי <5941>; from OFFER <5927>]: lofty ▶ **This word designates Eli, the high priest in the time of Samuel's youth at Shiloh.** Refs.: 1 Sam. 1:1–3. He did not control his sons who profaned the priesthood (2 Sam. 2:12–17). As a result, they were killed in a battle with the Philistines. Eli was warned to control his sons by a prophet, but to no avail (1 Sam. 2:27–33). Eli's house was cut off from Israel, and he died by falling backwards and breaking his neck when he heard of the fate of his sons.

Previously, he had dealt kindly with Hannah and prayed for her (1 Sam. 1:17). She dedicated her child, Samuel, to the Lord under Eli (1 Sam. 1:23–28). *

ELIAB – ***ᵉliy'āḇ*** [masc. proper noun: אֱלִיאָב <446>; from GOD <410> and FATHER <1>]: God is father ▶

a. It referred to a prince of the tribe of Zebulun at the time of the Exodus event. Ref.: Num. 1:9. His father was Helon. *

b. It depicts the father of Abiram and Dathan. They rebelled against Moses (Num. 16:12–14; 26:8–11) and were destroyed by the Lord. Eliab's father was Pallu (Num. 26:8). *

c. It denotes David's oldest brother. Ref.: 1 Sam. 16:6. He despised David at times and considered David self-centered and self-seeking (1 Sam. 17:28). He had a daughter, Abihail. One of Rehoboam's wives was her daughter (2 Chr. 11:18). *

d. A Kohathite bore the name. He was a descendant of Samuel (1 Chr. 6:27; cf. Eliel, 1 Chr. 6:34; Elihu, 1 Sam. 1:1). ¶

e. A Gadite bore the name. He was third in command of the Gadites who helped David during his flight from Saul (1 Chr. 12:8, 9). ¶

f. A Levitical singer bears the name. He was appointed as part of the worship leaders of the Levites (1 Chr. 15:18), playing the lyre (1 Chr. 15:20). *

ELIADA – ***'elyāḏā'*** [masc. proper noun: אֶלְיָדָע <450>; from GOD <410> and KNOW <3045>]: God knows ▶
a. A son of David. Refs.: 2 Sam. 5:16; 1 Chr. 3:8. ¶
b. A Benjamite chief. Ref.: 2 Chr. 17:17. ¶
c. An Aramite. Ref.: 1 Kgs. 11:23. ¶

ELIAHBA – ***'elyaḥbā'*** [masc. proper noun: אֶלְיַחְבָּא <455>; from GOD <410> and HIDE <2244>]: God hides, God protects ▶ **One of David's mighty men.** Refs.: 2 Sam. 23:32; 1 Chr. 11:33. ¶

ELIAKIM – ***'elyāqiym*** [masc. proper noun: אֶלְיָקִים <471>; from GOD <410> and STAND, STAND UP <6965>]: God establishes ▶
a. It refers to the son of Hilkiah who was the chief in charge of the king's palace under Hezekiah. He served as one of Hezekiah's messengers to King Sennacherib of Assyria and to Isaiah the prophet (2 Kgs. 18:18, 26, 37; 19:2; Is. 22:20; 36:3, 11, 22; 37:2). He was highly regarded by the Lord (Is. 22:20). ¶
b. It applies to a son of the great King Josiah. Refs.: 2 Kgs. 23:34; 2 Chr. 36:4. He was made king by Pharaoh Neco after Josiah's death. His name was changed to Jehoiakim. He became an evil king. ¶
c. It refers to a priest in the time of Nehemiah. Ref.: Neh. 12:41. He helped in the worship services at the Temple. ¶

ELIAM – ***ᵉliy'ām*** [masc. proper noun: אֱלִיעָם <463>; from GOD <410> and PEOPLE <5971>]: God of the people ▶
a. It describes the father of Bathsheba. Ref.: 2 Sam. 11:3. He is referred to as Ammiel also (1 Chr. 3:5, see AMMIEL <5988>) by simply reversing the beginning and end of the Hebrew word, possibly a scribal error. ¶
b. It also refers to one of David's thirty mighty men. Ref.: 2 Sam. 23:34. He was son of Ahithophel and possible the same person mentioned in a. ¶

ELIASAPH – ***'elyāsāp̱*** [masc. proper noun: אֶלְיָסָף <460>; from GOD <410> and CONTINUE <3254> (in the sense of to increase)]: God has gathered ▶
a. Chief of the tribe of Gad. Refs.: Num. 1:14; 2:14; 7:42, 47; 10:20. ¶
b. Chief of the families of the Gershonites. Ref.: Num. 3:24. ¶

ELIASHAMA – ***ᵉliyšāmā'*** [masc. proper noun: אֱלִישָׁמָע <476>; from GOD <410> and HEAR <8085>]: God hears, God has heard ▶
a. He was the leading commander of the tribe of Ephraim, son of Ammihud, grandson of Joshua. Refs.: Num. 1:10; 2:18; 1 Chr. 7:26. *
b. It refers to a son of David born in Jerusalem. Ref.: 2 Sam. 5:16. *
c. It refers to a different son with the same name born to David in Jerusalem (a few mss. read Elishua instead). Ref.: 1 Chr. 3:6. ¶
d. It indicates a scribe of Jehoiakim, in effect, an ancient term for a keeper of records (Jer. 36:12), an official under the king. He kept the scrolls (Jer. 36:20, 21). ¶
e. It refers to a person listed as one of the royal seed of David who hoped to become king after Gedaliah was assassinated. Refs.: 2 Kgs. 25:25; Jer. 41:1. ¶
f. It refers to a Judaite. Ref.: 1 Chr. 2:41. ¶
g. It refers to a priest under Jehoshaphat, king of Judah, who helped vigorously teach the Book of the Law to all of Judah. Ref.: 2 Chr. 17:8. ¶

ELIASHIB – ***'elyāšiyḇ*** [masc. proper noun: אֶלְיָשִׁיב <475>; from GOD <410> and TURN (verb) <7725>]: God will restore, God returns ▶
a. He was a son of Elioenai and, therefore, was listed in the royal line of David's descendants. Ref.: 1 Chr. 3:24. In 1 Chronicles 24:12, the name is listed as a priest, evidently not the same person. ¶
b. The person listed in 1 Chronicles 24:12. He was a priest or of the priestly line (see a.). ¶
c. It refers to a priest during the time of Nehemiah. Ref.: Ezra 10:6. He is high

priest finally under Nehemiah (Neh. 3:1, 20, 21). He sinned with respect to Moses' marriage laws with foreigners (Neh. 13:4, 5). He also had a grandson, Joiada, who married the daughter of Sanballat, a Horonite (Neh. 13:28). ¶
d. An Eliashib is mentioned as a singer from the Levites who had intermarried with a foreigner. Ref.: Ezra 10:24. ¶
e. An Israelite who had intermarried with a foreigner in Ezra's time. Ref.: Ezra 10:36. ¶
f. Another Israelite who had intermarried with a foreigner in Ezra's day. Ref.: Ezra 10:27. ¶

ELIATAH – ***liyyāṯah, *liy'āṯah*** [masc. proper noun: אֱלִיאָתָה, אֱלִיָּתָה <448>; from GOD <410> and CONSENT <225>]: God has come ▶ **A musician under the reign of David.** Refs.: 1 Chr. 25:4, 27. ¶

ELIDAD – ***liḏāḏ*** [masc. proper noun: אֱלִידָד <449>; from the same as ELDAD <419>]: whom God loves ▶ **A prince of the tribe of Benjamin.** Ref.: Num. 34:21. ¶

ELIEL – ***liy'ēl*** [masc. proper noun: אֱלִיאֵל <447>; from GOD <410> repeated]: God is God, my God is God ▶
a. He is listed as a Kohathite musician. Ref.: 1 Chr. 6:34. But see also Eliab (1 Chr. 6:27; 1 Sam. 1:1). ¶
b. He served as a family leader or head in Manasseh and was considered a famous man and great warrior. Ref.: 1 Chr. 5:24. ¶
c. It refers to Eliel, a leader and son of Shimei, a descendant of Saul of the tribe of Benjamin. Refs.: 1 Chr. 8:20, 21. ¶
d. It refers to a son of Shashak. Refs.: 1 Chr. 8:22, 25. He was also a leader in the tribe of Benjamin. ¶
e. He was one of the mighty men of David's army. Ref.: 1 Chr. 11:46. ¶
f. One of David's mighty men who did mighty deeds for the Lord and His chosen king. Ref.: 1 Chr. 11:47. ¶
g. He was one of the Gadite warriors who defected from Saul to David and served as leaders. Ref.: 1 Chr. 12:11. ¶
h. He is listed as the leader from Hebron, a descendant of Hebron, who helped David bring the ark to Jerusalem. Refs.: 1 Chr. 15:9, 11. ¶
i. It designates a Levite who helped supervise the preparations of the Temple to receive offerings to its renovation. Ref.: 2 Chr. 31:13. ¶

ELIENAI – ***liy'êynay*** [masc. proper noun: אֱלִיעֵינַי <462>; prob. contr. for ELIOENEAI <454>]: God, my eyes ▶ **An Israelite of the tribe of Benjamin.** Ref.: 1 Chr. 8:20. ¶

ELIEZER – ***liy'ezer*** [masc. proper noun: אֱלִיעֶזֶר <461>; from GOD <410> and HELP (noun) <5828>]: God helps ▶
a. It designates Abraham's slave born in his household. Ref.: Gen. 15:2. Hence, he was Abraham's potential heir. He may be mentioned in Genesis 24:2. Isaac, of course, became the true heir. ¶
b. One of Moses' sons. He is mentioned first in Exodus 18:4. He is quoted in Exodus 18:4 and listed in the genealogies of Chronicles (1 Chr. 23:15, 17; 26:25). ¶
c. It refers to a Benjamite, a son of Becher. Ref.: 1 Chr. 7:8. ¶
d. It identifies a Reubenite who was a son of Zichri. He was a leader in Reuben during David's reign (1 Chr. 27:16). ¶
e. It is applied to a prophet in the reign of Jehoshaphat in Judah. He condemned the building of ships by the king and told of their destruction (1 Chr. 20:35–37). ¶
f. It describes a priest who helped David bring the ark to Jerusalem from Obed-edom's home. Ref.: 1 Chr. 15:24. ¶
g. It describes a leader under Ezra who helped gather Levites for Temple worship. Ref.: Ezra 8:16. ¶
h. It refers to a priest under Ezra who had intermarried with foreign women. Ref.: Ezra 10:18. ¶
i. It describes a Levite who had intermarried with foreign women in Ezra's day. Ref.: Ezra 10:23. ¶
j. It refers to a son of Harim who had intermarried with foreign women in Ezra's day. Ref.: Ezra 10:31. ¶

ELIHOREPH – ***’ᵉliyḥōrep̱*** [masc. proper noun: אֱלִיחֹרֶף <456>; from GOD <410> and WINTER (noun) <2779>]: God of winter, God of the reward (harvest time) ▶ **One of Solomon’s scribes.** Ref.: 1 Kgs. 4:3. ¶

ELIHU – ***’ᵉliyhû, ’ᵉliyhû’*** [masc. proper noun: אֱלִיהוּ, אֱלִיהוּא <453>; from GOD <410> and HE, SHE, IT <1931>]: He is God ▶
a. Elihu is listed as the great-grandfather of Samuel. Ref.: 1 Sam. 1:1. He was an Ephramite. ¶
b. It depicts a military leader in Manasseh. He defected to David when David was fleeing from Saul. Ref.: 1 Chr. 12:20. ¶
c. It refers to the youngest speaker in the Book of Job. He supposedly speaks “on God’s behalf” angrily toward both Job and his other friends. Refs.: Job 32:2, 4–6; 34:1; 35:1; 36:1. Some of his insights are correct, as he stresses the majesty and sovereignty of God. ¶
d. It refers to a Kohathite. He was a gatekeeper and a leader in the service of the Temple. Ref.: 1 Chr. 26:7. ¶
e. He was an officer placed over the tribe of Judah. Ref.: 1 Chr. 27:18. He was also a brother of David. ¶

ELIJAH – ***’ēliyyāh, ’ēliyyāhû*** [masc. proper noun: אֵלִיָּה, אֵלִיָּהוּ <452>; from GOD <410> and LORD <3050>]: God is Lord ▶
a. The major person is Elijah the Tishbite who was called by God to fight for Yahweh and to eradicate Baalism from Israel. His ministry extended from the time of Ahab (874–853 B.C.) into Jehoram’s (2 Chr. 21:4–16). He became, in effect, the covenant prosecutor for the Lord. He challenged Ahab, Jezebel, and the prophets of Baal constantly to make them realize that the Lord is God.

The Lord cared for Elijah miraculously (1 Kgs. 17:1). Elijah called a famine on the land and announced its end (1 Kgs. 17:1, 2; 18:16–46). The Lord encouraged him in times of depression (1 Kgs. 19:1–18). Elijah called Elisha, his successor (1 Kgs. 19:19–21). He condemned Ahab’s seizing of Naboth’s vineyard (1 Kgs. 21:17, 20, 28). He was taken up into the sky by a whirlwind (2 Kgs. 2:11–14). His return or a prophet like him was foretold by Malachi (Mal. 4:5). *
b. This noun identifies a Benjamite, a son of Jeroham. Ref.: 1 Chr. 8:27. ¶
c. This noun refers to an infamous priest who intermarried with a foreign woman. Ref.: Ezra 10:21. He descended from Harim. ¶
d. This noun indicates another unfortunate priest who intermarried with a foreign woman. He descended from Elam (Ezra 10:26). ¶

ELIKA – ***’ᵉliyqā’*** [masc. proper noun: אֱלִיקָא <470>; from GOD <410> and VOMIT (verb) <6958>]: God rejects ▶ **One of David’s mighty men.** Ref.: 2 Sam. 23:25. ¶

ELIM – ***’êylim*** [proper noun: אֵילִם <362>; plur. of OAK <352>]: plantation of palm trees, oaks ▶ **After the crossing of the Red Sea, the Israelites encamped there by the water.** Refs.: Ex. 15:27; 16:1; Num. 33:9, 10. ¶

ELIMELECH – ***’ᵉliymeleḵ*** [masc. proper noun: אֱלִימֶלֶךְ <458>; from GOD <410> and KING <4428>]: God is king ▶ **Man from Bethlehem of Judah, husband of Naomi.** Refs.: Ruth 1:2, 3; 2:1, 3; 4:3, 9. ¶

ELIOENEAI – ***’elyᵉhô‘êynay, ’elyô‘êynay*** [masc. proper noun: אֶלְיְהוֹעֵינַי, אֶלְיוֹעֵינַי <454>; from TO <413> and LORD <3068> and EYE <5869>]: the Lord, my eyes ▶
a. He was a gatekeeper at the Temple from the family of Korah, son of Mechelemiah. Ref.: 1 Chr. 26:3. ¶
b. He was a family head or leader who returned from exile under Ezra during the reign of the Persian King Artaxerxes (458 B.C.). Ref.: Ezra 8:4. ¶
c. He was a person in the royal line of David, lived after the Exile, and was a son of Neariah. Refs.: 1 Chr. 3:23, 24. ¶
d. It refers to a son of Beker, a Benjamite. He was the leader of a family and/or a warrior (1 Chr. 7:8). ¶

e. It refers to a descendant of Simeon and Shimei, an important family line. Ref.: 1 Chr. 4:36. ¶

f. He was listed as one of the descendants of Pashur who intermarried with foreigners after the exile. Ref.: Ezra 10:22. ¶

g. He was listed as guilty of intermarriage with foreigners after the exile. He was a son of Zattu and in the priestly line. Ref.: Ezra 10:27. ¶

h. He was a priest who performed in the worship (choir?) at the second Temple under Nehemiah. Ref.: Neh. 12:41. ¶

ELIPHAL – ***ᵉliypāl*** [masc. proper noun: אֱלִיפָל <465>; from GOD <410> and PRAY <6419>]: God is judge ▶ **One of David's mighty men.** Ref.: 1 Chr. 11:35. ¶

ELIPHAZ – ***ᵉliypaz*** [masc. proper noun: אֱלִיפַז <464>; from GOD <410> and GOLD <6337>]: God is gold ▶

a. It refers to a son of Esau. He fathered five sons (Gen. 36:4, 10–12, 15, 16; 1 Chr. 1:35, 36) by his wife. He fathered a son by his concubine Tinna named Amalek (Gen. 36:12). ¶

b. He was one of the outspoken and maligners of Job under the claim of helping Job and representing God. Refs.: Job 2:11; 4:1; 15:1; 22:1. But God condemned him and his two friends and instructed Job to pray for them (Job 42:7–9). At times he could try to be kind (Job 14:12–21), but his "retribution theology" and conviction that Job had sinned controlled his words and actions. He made himself the measure of his theology. ¶

ELIPHELEH – 1 Chr. 15:18, 21 → ELIPHELEHU <466>.

ELIPHELEHU – ***ᵉliypᵉlêhû*** [masc. proper noun: אֱלִיפְלֵהוּ <466>; from GOD <410> and DISTINCTION (MAKE) <6395>]: God distinguishes ▶ **A Levite who was a singer and a harpist when the ark of God was brought back to Jerusalem.** Refs.: 1 Chr. 15:18, 21; also translated Elipheleh. ¶

ELIPHELET – ***ᵉliypeleṭ, ʾelpeleṭ*** [masc. proper noun: אֱלִיפֶלֶט, אֶלְפֶּלֶט <467>; from GOD <410> and ESCAPE (noun) <6405>]: God is deliverance ▶

a. A descendant, a son, of David. His mother is not given (1 Chr. 3:6). ¶

b. This is another son of David. His mother is not noted (2 Sam. 5:16; 1 Chr. 3:8; 14:5, 7). ¶

c. The name of a son of Ahasbai, who was himself a Maacathite. Ref.: 2 Sam. 23:34. ¶

d. He is listed as a family chief or head in Jerusalem over Benjamites. Ref.: 1 Chr. 8:39. ¶

e. He was a son of Adonikam. He returned as a family chief under Ezra (Ezra 8:13). ¶

f. He is listed as an Israelite who married a foreign woman. His father was Hashum (Ezra 10:33). ¶

ELISHA – ***ᵉliyšāʿ*** [masc. proper noun: אֱלִישָׁע <477>; contr. for ELISHUA <474>]: God is salvation ▶ **A great prophet of Israel who worked during the ninth century. We know little about his background.** At some point, he became God's prophet who completed and extended the work of Elijah, who anointed him as his successor (1 Kgs. 19:16). His call was to "put to death" the line of Ahab and Jezebel out of Israel (1 Kgs. 19:17, 19) by his prophetic, "dynamic" word. He was active for nearly fifty years under as many as six kings (Ahab, Ahaziah, Jehoram, Jehu, Jehoahaz, Jehoash). His father was Shaphat. He drove oxen as a living, among other things (1 Kgs. 19:19–21). He was mentioned by Elijah (2 Kgs. 2:1–5), whom Elisha saw go up to heaven in a whirlwind.

He and Elijah were God's prophets who fought against Baalism and restored the "Lord as God" in Israel. Elisha performed many miracles, purifying water (2 Kgs. 2:19–22); providing food and money for a widow (2 Kgs. 4:1–7); restoring the Shunammite's son to life (2 Kgs. 4:32–37); purifying food and feeding many persons miraculously (2 Kgs. 4:38–44). He instructed Naaman about how to be healed (2 Kgs. 5:1–14) and caused an axe head to float (2 Kgs. 6:1–7). He spoke God's prophetic words in the political arena to even pagan kings (2 Kgs. 8:7–15). He anointed Jehu as king who would destroy the line of Ahab (2 Kgs. 9:1–13). Jezebel, Ahab's family line, and the prophets and priests of Baal were killed according to Elisha's prophecy (2 Kgs. 9:30–37; 10). He died soon after counseling Jehoash, king of Israel, concerning his wars with Aram (2 Kgs. 13:10–20). Even his bones retained some kind of honor before the Lord. A dead man was revived by coming into contact with them (2 Kgs. 13:21). *

ELISHAH – ***ᵉliyšāh*** [masc. proper noun: אֱלִישָׁה <473>; prob. of foreign deriv.] ▶ **A son of Javan who was the son of Japheth.** Refs.: Gen. 10:4; 1 Chr. 1:7; Ezek. 27:7. ¶

ELISHAPHAT – ***ᵉliyšāp̄āṭ*** [masc. proper noun: אֱלִישָׁפָט <478>; from GOD <410> and JUDGE (verb) <8199>]: God who defends, who judges ▶ **A commander of a unit of a hundred with whom Jehoiada made a covenant.** Ref.: 2 Chr. 23:1. ¶

ELISHEBA – ***ᵉliyšeḇaʿ*** [fem. proper noun: אֱלִישֶׁבַע <472>; from GOD <410> and SEVEN <7651> (in the sense of SWEAR <7650>)]: God of the oath ▶ **Wife of Aaron and mother of Nadab, Abihu, Eleazar, and Ithamar.** Ref.: Ex. 6:23. ¶

ELISHUA – ***ᵉliyšûaʿ*** [masc. proper noun: אֱלִישׁוּעַ <474>; from GOD <410> and CRY (noun) <7769>]: God of supplication, God is salvation ▶ **Son of David, born in Jerusalem.** Refs.: 2 Sam. 5:15; 1 Chr. 14:5. ¶

ELIZAPHAN – ***ᵉliyṣāp̄ān, ʾelṣāp̄ān*** [masc. proper noun: אֱלִיצָפָן, אֶלְצָפָן <469>; from GOD <410> and HIDE <6845>]: God of treasure ▶
a. Chief of the Kohathites. Refs.: Ex. 6:22; Lev. 10:4; Num. 3:30; 1 Chr. 15:8; 2 Chr. 29:13. ¶
b. Chief of Zebulon. Ref.: Num. 34:25. ¶

ELIZUR – ***ᵉliyṣûr*** [masc. proper noun: אֱלִיצוּר <468>; from GOD <410> and ROCK <6697>]: God is a rock ▶ **A leader of the people of Reuben.** Refs.: Num. 1:5; 2:10; 7:30, 35; 10:18. ¶

ELKANAH – ***ʾelqānāh*** [masc. proper noun: אֶלְקָנָה <511>; from GOD <410> and ACQUIRE <7069>]: God has created ▶
a. It refers to a grandson of Korah in the genealogical line of Moses and Aaron. Refs.: Ex. 6:24; 1 Chr. 6:23. ¶
b. It refers to the patient and compassionate Elkanah, husband of Hannah, and father of Samuel. Refs.: 1 Chr. 6:27, 6:34. *
c. It indicates a descendant of Levi, a Levite. Refs.: 1 Chr. 6:25, 36. ¶
d. It refers to the father of Zophai, a Levite from the same line as c. Refs.: 1 Chr. 6:26, 35. ¶
e. It indicates another Levite who lived in Jerusalem. He had a son named Asa (1 Chr. 9:16). ¶
f. It refers to a warrior of David, from the Benjamites, a Korahite. Ref.: 1 Chr. 12:6. ¶
g. It refers to another Levite who served as a doorkeeper of the ark. Ref.: 1 Chr. 15:23. ¶
h. He was a powerful officer or commander of Ahaz. He was slain in battle by Israelites under King Pekah (2 Chr. 28:7). ¶

ELKOSHITE – ***ʾelqōšiy*** [proper noun: אֶלְקֹשִׁי <512>; patrial from a name of uncertain deriv.] ▶ **Nahum was an Elkoshite; nothing sure is known about the city of Elkosh.** Ref.: Nah. 1:1. ¶

ELLASAR – ***ʾellāsār*** [proper noun: אֶלָּסָר <495>; prob. of foreign deriv.] ▶ **A city of Babylonia where Arioch was the king.** Refs.: Gen. 14:1, 9. ¶

ELNAAM – ***ʾelnaʿam*** [masc. proper noun: אֶלְנַעַם <493>; from GOD <410> and PLEASANT <5276>]: God of delights ▶ **Father of two of David's mighty warriors.** Ref.: 1 Chr. 11:46. ¶

ELNATHAN – ***ʾelnāṯān*** [masc. proper noun: אֶלְנָתָן <494>; from GOD <410> and GIVE <5414>]: God gives ▶
a. The grandfather of Jehoiachin. Refs.: 2 Kgs. 24:8; Jer. 26:22; 36:12, 25. ¶
b. The name of three Levites. They are mentioned in Ezra 8:16. ¶

ELON – ***'ēlôn, 'ēylôn*** [masc. proper noun: אֵלוֹן, אֵילוֹן <356>; from MIGHTY, OAK <352>]: oak, strong ▶
a. The son of Zebulun, Leah's sixth son, in Paddan Aram. Ref.: Gen. 46:14. He headed up a family clan (Num. 26:26). ¶
b. The name of Esau's father-in-law. Ref.: Gen. 26:34. Elon was a Hittite, a fact that grieved Isaac and Rebekah (Gen. 36:2). ¶
c. A judge/deliverer in Israel raised up by the Lord to lead Israel for ten years. He was of the tribe of Zebulun (Judg. 12:11, 12). ¶
d. A town in the territory allotted to the tribe of Dan. Refs.: Josh. 19:43; 1 Kgs. 4:9. It was in the coastal area east of Joppa. ¶

ELON BETHHANAN – ***'ēylôn bêyt ḥānān*** [proper noun: אֵילוֹן בֵּית חָנָן <358>; from ELON <356>, HOUSE <356>, and GRACIOUS (BE) <2603>]: oak of the house of mercy ▶ **This word designates Elon Bethhanan, the full name for the city of Elon (<356>).** Ref.: 1 Kgs. 4:9. ¶

ELPAAL – ***'elpa'al*** [masc. proper noun: אֶלְפַּעַל <508>; from GOD <410> and MAKE <6466>]: God makes ▶ **An Israelite of the tribe of Benjamin, son of Shaharaim.** Refs.: 1 Chr. 8:11, 12, 18. ¶

ELTEKEH – ***'elt^{e}qê'*** [proper noun: אֶלְתְּקֵא <514>; of uncertain deriv.] ▶ **A city of the tribe of Dan given to the Levites.** Refs.: Josh. 19:44; 21:23. ¶

ELTEKON – ***'elt^{e}qōn*** [proper noun: אֶלְתְּקֹן <515>; from GOD <410> and STRAIGHT (MAKE) <8626>]: God is straight ▶ **A village of the hill country of Judah.** Ref.: Josh. 15:59. ¶

ELTOLAD – ***'eltôlad*** [proper noun: אֶל־תּוֹלָד <513>; maybe from GOD <410> and a masc. form of GENERATION <8435> (comp. TOLAD <8434>)]: God of the generations, race of God ▶ **A city of the Simeonites.** Refs.: Josh. 15:30; 19:4. ¶

ELUL – ***'^{e}lûl*** [proper noun: אֱלוּל <435>; prob. of foreign deriv.] ▶ **The sixth month in the Hebrew calendar.** Ref.: Neh. 6:15. ¶

ELUZAI – ***'el'ûzay*** [masc. proper noun: אֶלְעוּזַי <498>; from GOD <410> and SAFETY (FLEE FOR) <5756> (in the sense of STRENGTH <5797>)]: God is my strength ▶ **One of the mighty men of David.** Ref.: 1 Chr. 12:5. ¶

ELZABAD – ***'elzābād*** [masc. proper noun: אֶלְזָבָד <443>; from GOD <410> and ENDOW <2064>]: God has granted ▶
a. One of the Gadites who joined David. Ref.: 1 Chr. 12:12. ¶
b. A gatekeeper from the family of Obed-Edom. Ref.: 1 Chr. 26:7. ¶

EMBALM – ***ḥānaṭ, ḥ^{a}nuṭiym*** [verb: חָנַט, חֲנֻטִים <2590>; a prim. root] ▶ **This word refers to the Egyptian process of treating the bodies of deceased persons.** They used various chemicals (Gen. 50:2, 26) and ceremoniously and meticulously wrapped them in material. It is translated embalming in Genesis 50:3. The Hebrew word also means to ripen; see RIPEN <2590>. ¶

EMBALMING – Gen. 50:3 ➔ EMBALM <2590>.

EMBERS (GLOWING) – Ps. 102:3 ➔ HEARTH <4168>.

EMBITTERED (BE) – [1] Ps. 73:21 ➔ LEAVENED (BE) <2556> [2] Ps. 73:21 ➔ SHARPEN <8150>.

EMBOLDEN – [1] Job 16:3 ➔ GRIEVOUS <4834> [2] Ps. 138:3 ➔ BOLD (BE, MAKE) <7292>.

EMBRACE – ***ḥābaq*** [verb: חָבַק <2263>; a prim. root] ▶ **The most common meaning of this word is to hug someone in a show of affection.** Refs.: Gen. 29:13; 33:4; 48:10; Prov. 5:20; Song 2:6; 8:3. It is often accompanied with the verb to kiss. There is a proper time to embrace and a proper time not to embrace (Eccl. 3:5). It means to acquire or give birth to a son (2 Kgs. 4:16; also translated to hold); used figuratively, it refers to the oppressed who cling to or hug even rocks in search of a shelter (Job 24:8:

to embrace, to cling to, to hug, to huddle around; Lam. 4:5); and to the wise person's embracing wisdom (Prov. 4:8). It indicates the folding of one's hands (Eccl. 4:5, see FOLDING <2264>). ¶

EMBROIDERED WORK – ***riqmāh*** [fem. noun: רִקְמָה <7553>; from WEAVER <7551>] ▶ **This word refers to decorative needlework; stones of various colors.** It refers to colorful material embroidered on both sides (Judg. 5:30). It indicates decorative ornamental stones (1 Chr. 29:2). Embroidered garments were highly esteemed in royal circles (Ps. 45:14). The Lord, in figurative language, clothed Israel in her youth in embroidered cloth (Ezek. 16:10, 13, 18). It indicates an eagle's colorful array or plumage of many colors (Ezek. 17:3). *

EMEK-KEZIZ – Josh. 18:21 ➔ VALLEY <6010> b.

EMERALD – [1] ***bāreqet, bār^{e}qath*** [fem. noun: בָּרֶקֶת, בָּרְקַת <1304>; from LIGHTNING <1300>] ▶ **This Hebrew word refers to a semiprecious stone, either a beryl or an emerald; it is also translated beryl, carbuncle.** Refs.: Ex. 28:17; 39:10. It was possibly dark green in color. One of these stones was set in the first row of the breastpiece worn on the ephod by the high priest. It bore one of the names of the tribes of Israel. It was, according to Ezekiel, found in the Garden of Eden (Ezek. 28:13). ¶
– [2] Ex. 28:18; 39:11; Ezek. 27:16; 28:13 ➔ TURQUOISE <5306> [3] Ex. 28:18; 39:11; Ezek. 28:13 ➔ DIAMOND <3095>.

EMERGE – Dan. 5:5 ➔ TAKE OUT <5312>.

EMEROD – Deut. 28:27; 1 Sam. 5:6, 9, 12; 6:4, 5 ➔ HILL <6076>.

EMERODS – 1 Sam. 6:11, 17 ➔ TUMORS <2914>.

EMERY – Ezek. 3:9 ➔ DIAMOND <8068>.

EMIM, EMITES – ***'êymiym*** [masc. proper noun: אֵימִים <368>; plur. of TERROR <367>]: terrors ▶ **These people lived in Shaveh-kiriathaim.** Ref.: Gen. 14:5. They are described as an ancient people by the author of Deuteronomy. They no longer existed as a people in the author's day but had been great, numerous, and as tall as the giants, the Anakim. They were also known by some as Rephaim (Deut. 2:10, 11). ¶

EMINENT – Ezek. 17:22 ➔ LOFTY <8524>.

EMINENT (SOMETHING) – Ezek. 7:11 ➔ PREEMINENCE <5089> a.

EMISSION – [1] Lev. 15:16–18, 32; 22:4 ➔ LAYER <7902> b. [2] Ezek. 23:20 ➔ ISSUE <2231>.

EMMER – Ex. 9:32; Is. 28:25; Ezek. 4:9 ➔ SPELT <3698>.

EMPTIED – Nah. 2:10 ➔ EMPTY (adj.) <950>.

EMPTIED (BE) – Ezek. 12:19 ➔ DESOLATE (BE, BECOME) <3456>.

EMPTINESS – [1] ***riyq*** [masc. noun: רִיק <7385>; from EMPTY (verb) <7324>] ▶ **This word means uselessness, vanity, a delusion.** It is used with a prefixed *l^e* to mean, in vain, uselessly (Lev. 26:16, 20; Job 39:16). It stands for an imagined plot or plan that is a delusion, vain (Ps. 2:1); or something that is worthless (Ps. 4:2). It refers to professed help that is useless, vain before the Lord (Is. 30:7; Jer. 51:58; Hab. 2:13). Figuratively, it describes Israel being treated in judgment as an empty vessel (Jer. 51:34). *
[2] ***šāw'*** [masc. noun: שָׁוְא <7723>; from the same as RAVAGE (noun) <7722> in the sense of desolating] ▶ **This word means vanity, evil, ruin, uselessness, deception, worthless, without result, fraud, deceit. The primary meaning of the word is deceit, lie, or falsehood.** God used the word to indicate that He punished Judah in vain. The word is

used by the psalmist to state that all activities such as laboring, guarding, rising early, staying up late, and toiling for food were useless without God's assistance (Ps. 127:1, 2). In the Ten Commandments, the word is used to describe what is prohibited (Deut. 5:20). The word is used in Proverbs to indicate that which the author desires to be kept away from him: in this case, falsehood and lies (Prov. 30:8). Idols were declared worthless with the usage of the noun in Jeremiah (Jer. 18:15). These idols were those that led the people of God to forget Him. *
– [3] Is. 34:11 ➔ VOID <922>.

EMPTY (adj.) – [1] ***bûqāh*** [fem. noun: בּוּקָה <950>; fem. pass. part. of an unused root (meaning to be hollow)] ▶ **This word means deprived, lacking; it is also translated emptied, desolate, pillaged. It describes the state of Nineveh after God's judgment on it.** The city was bereft of inhabitants and joy (Nah. 2:10: she is emptied). ¶
[2] ***rêyq, rêq*** [adj.: רֵיק, רֵק <7386>; from EMPTY (verb) <7324>] ▶ **This word means worthless, vain, containing nothing.** It indicates something that has nothing in it, evacuated, e.g., a pit (Gen. 37:24); a pitcher (Judg. 7:16); vessels (2 Kgs. 4:3); a pot (Ezek. 24:11; see v. 6). It indicates that an animal is lean, skinny (Gen. 41:27). It indicates idle or trifling when describing what God's Word is not (Deut. 32:47). It describes people as worthless as to moral character (Judg. 9:4; 11:3; 2 Sam. 6:20; 2 Chr. 13:7). It is used in a parable to mean removed, taken away (Neh. 5:13). Used by itself, it means vain things (Prov. 12:11). It indicates being hungry, empty (Is. 29:8). ¶
– [3] Gen. 1:2; Jer. 4:23 ➔ VOID <922> [4] Prov. 14:4 ➔ PURE <1249> [5] Mic. 6:14 ➔ CASTING DOWN <3445>.

EMPTY (BECOME) – Jer. 2:5 ➔ VAIN (BECOME) <1891>.

EMPTY (MAKE), EMPTY (verb) – ***bāqaq*** [verb: בָּקַק <1238>; a prim. root] ▶ **a. This word means to lay waste, to devastate, to destroy.** It described the destroying of land (Is. 24:1, 3; Jer. 51:2), especially as an act of God. It has the meaning of to deflate or demoralize the spirit of someone (Is. 19:3: to fail, to be demoralized, to lose heart) or to break or make void someone's counsel (Jer. 19:7). Israel is described as an empty vine (Hos. 10:1, KJV; cf. NKJV), a vine laid waste. Other ref.: Nah. 2:2. ¶
b. A verb meaning to grow or be luxuriant. It is rendered with this meaning in Hosea 10:1 (NIV, NASB). ¶

EMPTY (verb) – [1] ***'ārāh*** [verb: עָרָה <6168>; a prim. root] ▶ **This word means to be bare, nude, uncover; it is also translated to expose, to uncover, to pour, to lay bare.** It means to employ something, to pour something out: water from a vessel (Gen. 24:20); items from a chest or container (2 Chr. 24:11); pouring out one's soul, life (Is. 53:12). It has the sense of something increasing, spreading out, permeating an area (Ps. 37:35: to spread); of emptying, tearing down, or razing (Ps. 137:7); of leaving someone without help, exposed to danger (Ps. 141:8). It indicates uncovering or making bare one's forehead (Is. 3:17; also translated to raze, to tear down). It means to prepare a weapon for use, to uncover it (Is. 22:6). It is used of not exposing a woman's menstrual flow for intercourse (Lev. 20:18, 19; KJV: to discover). It has the figurative sense of exposing oneself to destruction as a people, a nation (Lam. 4:21: to make oneself naked, to strip oneself bare, to be stripped naked); as well as God's work in opening up a city to destruction (Zeph. 2:14). It indicates killing someone (Hab. 3:13: to lay bare, to lay open, to discover, to strip). Other ref.: Is. 32:15. ¶
[2] ***rûq, riyq*** [verb: רוּק, רִיק <7324>; a prim. root] ▶ **This word means to pour out, to draw out.** It is used of Abraham drawing out, leading forth his military men (Gen. 14:4); or, more literally, it indicates emptying out one's sacks (Gen. 42:35). It means to draw a sword, to empty its sheath (Ex. 15:9; Lev. 26:33). It describes the emptying of the heavens, pouring down rain (Eccl. 11:3; Mal. 3:10). It is used metaphorically of Moab not being emptied out (Jer. 48:11).

To cause persons to be empty is to cause them to be unfed (Is. 32:6). *

EMPTY STOMACH – Amos 4:6 ➔ lit.: cleanness of teeth ➔ INNOCENCE <5356>.

EMPTY-HANDED – ***rêyqām*** [adv.: רֵיקָם <7387>; from EMPTY (adj.) <7386>] ▶ **This word is used most often to indicate that a person is without something—wealth, sacrifices, gifts, money, etc.** Refs.: Gen. 31:42; Ex. 3:21; 23:15; 34:20; Deut. 15:13; 16:16. It means essentially the same thing when translated empty, meaning without something (Ruth 1:21; 3:17). It indicates without a sacrifice accompanying the ark (1 Sam. 6:3). It indicates that many were slain by Saul's sword (it did not return unsatisfied) (2 Sam. 1:22; cf. Jer. 50:9). It refers to a condition of injustice (widows sent away empty-handed) (Job 22:9). It has the sense of robbing or abusing a friend (Ps. 7:4). It has the sense of needlessly or without reason (Ps. 25:3). God's Word never returns empty; it accomplishes its purpose (Is. 55:11). Other ref.: Jer. 14:3. ¶

EMPTY-HEADED – Job 11:12 ➔ HOLLOW (noun) <5014>.

EN-DOR – ***'êyn dō'r*** [proper noun: עֵין דֹּאר <5874>; from EYE (noun) <5869> (in the sense of fountain) and GENERATION <1755> (in the sense of habitation, dwelling)]: fountain of dwelling ▶ **A place possessed by Manasseh but in the territory of Issachar.** Saul consulted a woman who was a medium there. Refs.: Josh. 17:11; 1 Sam. 28:7; Ps. 83:10. ¶

EN-GANNIM – ***'êyn ganniym*** [proper noun: עֵין גַּנִּים <5873>; from EYE (noun) <5869> (in the sense of fountain) and GARDEN <1588>]: fountain of the gardens ▶

a. A city in the foothills of Judah. Ref.: Josh. 15:34. ¶

b. A city in Issachar. Refs.: Josh. 19:21; 21:29. ¶

EN-HADDAH – ***'êyn ḥaddāh*** [proper noun: עֵין חַדָּה <5876>; from EYE (noun) <5869> (in the sense of fountain) and the fem. of a deriv. from SHARPEN <2300>]: swift fountain ▶ **A city on the border of Issachar.** Ref.: Josh. 19:21. ¶

EN-HAKKORE – ***'êyn haqqôrê'*** [proper noun: עֵין הַקּוֹרֵא <5875>; from EYE (noun) <5869> (in the sense of fountain) and CALL <7121>]: spring of him who called ▶ **God created that spring in Lehi for Samson who called it that name.** Ref.: Judg. 15:19. ¶

EN-HAZOR – ***'êyn ḥāṣôr*** [proper noun: עֵין חָצוֹר <5877>; from EYE (noun) <5869> (in the sense of fountain) and the same as HAZOR <2674>]: fountain of the village ▶ **One of the fortified cities of Naphtali.** Ref.: Josh. 19:37. ¶

EN-MISHPAT – ***'êyn mišpāṭ*** [proper noun: עֵין מִשְׁפָּט <5880>; from EYE (noun) <5869> (in the sense of fountain) and JUSTICE <4941> (in the sense of judgment)]: fountain of judgment ▶ **Same place as Kadesh.** Ref.: Gen. 14:7. ¶

EN-RIMMON – ***'êyn rimmôn*** [proper noun: עֵין רִמּוֹן <5884>; from EYE (noun) <5869> (in the sense of fountain) and POMEGRANATE <7416>]: fountain of the pomegranate ▶ **A place in Judah inhabited by the Jews after the Babylonian captivity.** Ref.: Neh. 11:29. ¶

EN-ROGEL – ***'êyn rōgêl*** [proper noun: עֵין רֹגֵל <5883>; from EYE (noun) <5869> (in the sense of fountain) and the act. part. of WALK (TEACH TO) <7270>]: spring of (a) walker ▶ **A spring located south of Jerusalem.** Refs.: Josh. 15:7; 18:16. Adonijah, trying to usurp David's throne, was crowned king there prematurely (1 Kgs. 1:9). Other ref.: 2 Sam. 17:17. ¶

EN-SHEMESH – ***'êyn šemeš*** [proper noun: עֵין שֶׁמֶשׁ <5885>; from EYE (noun) <5869> (in the sense of fountain) and SUN <8121>]: fountain of the sun ▶ **A source and a city on the border between Judah and Benjamin.** Refs.: Josh. 15:7; 18:17. ¶

EN-TAPPUAH – ***'êyn tappûaḥ*** [proper noun: עֵין תַּפּוּחַ <5887>; from EYE (noun) <5869> (in the sense of fountain) and APPLE, APPLE TREE <8598>]: fountain of an apple ► **A town on the border of the tribe of Manasseh.** Ref.: Josh. 17:7. ¶

ENAM – ***'ênām*** [proper noun: עֵינָם <5879>; dual of EYE (noun) <5869> (in the sense of fountain)]: two springs, double fountain ► **A city in Judah.** Ref.: Josh. 15:34. ¶

ENAN – ***'êynān*** [masc. proper noun: עֵינָן <5881>; from EYE (noun) <5869>]: having eyes ► **Father of a prince of the tribe of Naphtali in the times of Moses.** Refs.: Num. 1:15; 2:29; 7:78, 83; 10:27. ¶

ENCAMP – ***ḥānāh*** [verb: חָנָה <2583>; a prim. root (comp. GRACIOUS (BE) <2603>)] ► **This verb refers to pitching a tent or setting up camp for various reasons.** To encamp in a particular location (Gen. 26:17; Ex. 14:2, 9); to encamp against an enemy (with prep. *'al*, against, 1 Sam. 11:1; with preposition *bᵉ*, against, Judg. 9:50). It is used of armies or persons (Josh. 4:19). It is used of the Lord's encamping around His people and Temple to protect them (Zech. 9:8); and in a simile of locusts "encamped" on a stone wall (NASB, settling; Nah. 3:17). Jerusalem is the city in which David set up his camp (Is. 29:1). It takes on the idea of the day drawing to an end (Judg. 19:9). *

ENCAMPMENT – [1] ***ma'gāl*** [masc. noun: מַעְגָּל <4570>; from the same as CIRCULAR <5696>] ►
a. This word means a campsite; it is also translated camp, circle of the camp, trench. Refs.: 1 Sam. 17:20; 26:5, 7. ¶
b. A masculine noun meaning track, course, path. Refs.: Ps. 17:5; 23:3; 65:11; 140:5; Prov. 2:9, 15, 18; 4:11, 26; 5:6, 21; Is. 26:7; 59:8. ¶
– [2] Gen. 25:16; Num. 31:10; Ezek. 25:4 → CAMP <2918> [3] Gen. 42:27; 43:21; Ex. 4:24 → LODGING <4411>.

ENCHANTER – [1] ***'aššāp̱*** [masc. noun: אַשָּׁף <825>; from an unused root (prob. meaning to lisp, i.e., practice enchantment)] ► **This word means sorcerers, conjurers of spirits, necromancers, or astrologers.** Found only in the plural, it is borrowed from the Aramaic language. It is found only in the book of Daniel in relation to wise men or diviners (Dan. 2:2; 5:11). ¶
[2] ***'āšap̱*** [Aramaic masc. noun: אָשַׁף <826>; corresponding to <825> above] ► **The word refers to occult knowledge, divination; it is also translated conjurer, astrologer. It is closely related to the Hebrew word *'aššāp̱* above.** This designation, in both the Aramaic and the Hebrew forms, appears only in the book of Daniel. Since no etymology is apparent, its meaning must be determined by its context. The word always occurs in a list with one to three or four other words, whose meanings clearly refer to people with occult knowledge in the practice of divination (Dan. 2:10, 27; 4:7; 5:7, 11, 15). ¶
– [3] Lev. 19:26 → DIVINATION (PRACTICE) <5172> [4] Is. 3:3 → CHARM <3908>.

ENCHANTMENT – [1] ***lāṭ*** [masc. noun: לָט <3909>; a form of SOFTLY <3814> or else part. from WRAP <3874>] ► **This word means secrecy, mystery, privacy. It conveys the sense of a secret known to only a select group or to something done in secrecy.** Three times the word is used in reference to the enchantments of the Egyptian sorcerers in Pharaoh's court (Ex. 7:22; 8:7, 18; also translated secret arts). Other occurrences signify an action done without another party's notice (Ruth 3:7: softly, secretly, quietly) or in private (1 Sam. 18:22: secretly, in private, privately; 24:4: secretly, privily, stealthily, unnoticed). ¶
[2] ***naḥaš*** [masc. noun: נַחַשׁ <5173>; from DIVINATION (PRACTICE) <5172>] ► **This word means and is also translated omen, divination, sorcery.** In both instances of this word, it is used within the context of Balaam and his prophecies. In one discourse, Balaam declared that there was no omen against Jacob (Num. 23:23); and in preparing for another discourse, he did not seek omens (Num. 24:1). ¶

– [3] Lev. 19:26; 2 Kgs. 17:17; 21:6; 2 Chr. 33:6 ➔ DIVINATION (PRACTICE) <5172> [4] Eccl. 10:11 ➔ CHARM <3908>.

ENCHANTMENT (USE) – Lev. 19:26 ➔ DIVINATION (PRACTICE) <5172>.

ENCHANTMENTS – Ex. 7:11 ➔ FLAMING <3858>.

ENCIRCLE – [1] ***sûg*** [verb: סוּג <5473>; a prim. root (prob. rather identical with TURN BACK <5472> through the idea of shrinking from a hedge)] ▶ **This word refers to surrounding something.** It is used in a figurative, amorous sense of a bride's belly being fenced in or surrounded by lilies (Song 7:2; also translated to fence, to set about). It describes the fencing in of garden plants (Is. 17:11; also translated to grow, to fence). ¶
– [2] 1 Sam. 23:26 ➔ CROWN (noun and verb) <5849> b.

ENCLOSE – Song 4:12 ➔ LOCK (verb) <5274>.

ENCLOSED – ***mûsabbôṯ*** [fem. plur. adj.: מוּסַבּוֹת <4142>; fem. of STRUCTURE <4141>] ▶ **This word is used of the surrounding filigree settings of gold encompassing two onyx stones.** Refs.: Ex. 28:11; 39:6, 13. It has the sense of changing around in Numbers 32:38 where names of cities are changed. It seems to mean surrounding or swinging in Ezekiel 41:24 (also translated turning) where the doors of the Temple nave are described. ¶

ENCLOSED (BE) – Ezek. 46:22 ➔ JOINED (BE) <7000>.

ENCLOSING – Ex. 28:20 ➔ SETTING <4396>.

ENCOMPASS – 2 Sam. 22:5; Ps. 18:4; 40:12; 116:3; Jon. 2:5 ➔ SURROUND <661>.

END – [1] ***gaḇluṯ*** [fem. noun: גַּבְלֻת <1383>; from BOUNDS (SET) <1379>] ▶ **This word designates a twisting, braiding.** It describes the way chains of pure gold were joined together or connected for stability and beauty as a part of the high priest's outfit (Ex. 28:22; 39:15). Some suggest that it means welded together. ¶
[2] ***sôp̱*** [masc. noun: סוֹף <5490>; from CONSUME, BE CONSUMED <5486>] ▶ **This word means conclusion, completion.** It refers to the physical rear or end of something (conclusion to life) (Eccl. 7:2; NIV: destiny); the summary or final purpose of the teachings of someone (Eccl. 12:13). It is used in the phrase *merō'š wᵉ'aḏ-sōp̱*, from beginning to end to mean all of it (Eccl. 3:11). Other refs.: 2 Chr. 20:16; Joel 2:20 (back, rear guard, hinder part, western ranks). ¶
[3] ***sōph*** [Aramaic masc. noun: סוֹף <5491>; corresponding to <5490> above] ▶ **This word refers in context to the extremity of the earth.** Refs.: Dan. 4:11, 22. It is used to mean unto the end *'aḏ-sōp̱ā'* with respect to the kingdom of Daniel's God: i.e., on to the end, forever (Dan. 6:26; 7:26). It refers to the conclusion of an event, a dream, and the recording of it (Dan. 7:28). ¶
[4] ***qêṣ*** [masc. noun: קֵץ <7093>; contr. from CUT OFF <7112>] ▶ **This word indicates a limit of time or space. It refers to the finish, a final point, a goal of time, a space, or a purpose.** It indicates a certain point reached in time (Gen. 4:3); the finish or demise of something, e.g., the human race (Gen. 6:13); the conclusion of a set period of time, e.g., forty days with the preposition *min* (<4480>) (Gen. 8:6; 16:3). There is an end of things, e.g., Israel (Amos 8:2). The final end of things as foretold by the prophets will be a time of the end (Ezek. 21:25, 29; Dan. 8:17; 11:35, 40; 12:4, 9; Hab. 2:3); of God's peace in His kingdom, there will be no end (Is. 9:7); of people's life-long labor, toil, there is no cessation (Eccl. 4:8). In a spatial sense, it refers to the most remote areas (2 Kgs. 19:23; Jer. 50:26). There is seemingly no end to the flow of people, their number or extent (Eccl. 4:16). In a figurative sense, it describes the end or limit of words (Job 16:3); the completion of perfection attained

in God's commandments (Ps. 119:96). The phrase *miqqêṣ yāmim layyāmîm* means at the end time of each year (2 Sam. 14:26). The word, with *min* (<4480>), followed by an infinitive of *hāyāh* is used to indicate the end of a set period of time (Esther 2:12). With the definite article attached, it combines with the two following words to mean at the end of days of two years, i.e., after two years (2 Chr. 21:19). It indicates the close of Israel's long period of oppression in Egypt, 430 years (2 Chr. 21:19). *

5 ***qāṣeh, qêṣeh*** [masc. noun: קָצֶה, קֵצֶה <7097>; from CUT OFF <7096> (comp. <7093> above)] ▶

a. This word means an extremity, a border, an edge. It refers to the conclusion of a period of time (Gen. 8:3; Deut. 14:28; 2 Sam. 24:8). It has the sense of a border, an extremity, an edge, an end in spatial references: the end of a shepherd's staff (Judg. 6:21); a rod (1 Sam. 14:27, 43); curtains (Ex. 26:5; 36:12); the edge of a field or valley (Gen. 23:9; Josh. 15:8); a border (Num. 20:16). It refers to the rural areas of a city (Josh. 4:19; 1 Sam. 9:27). In certain expressions, it means from (among) one's brothers, from among all of them (Gen. 47:2). The phrase *miqqāṣṣeh* has the sense of from everywhere, in its entirety (Gen. 19:4; cf. Jer. 51:31).

b. This word means a limit. It is used in negative expressions of the form *'ên qêṣeh,* often with *l*^{e} following, there is no end (to) . . . (Is. 2:7; Nah. 2:9). It indicates no limit or numbering of dead people (Nah. 3:3). It refers to the unlimited resources and power of Thebes in Egypt, without end (limits) (Nah. 3:9). *

6 ***qāṣāh*** [fem. noun: קָצָה <7098>; fem. of <7097> above] ▶ **This word indicates an edge, an extremity.** It refers to the outer extremities or outer extent of something: the ends of the mercy seat (Ex. 25:18, 19); the outer curtain of a set (Ex. 26:4); the corners of the bronze altar (Ex. 27:4); the ends of the ephod (Ex. 28:7); and breastpiece (Ex. 28:23–26). It has the sense of the whole, the extent of a number of people or group (Judg. 18:2; 1 Kgs. 12:31; 13:33; 2 Kgs. 17:32). It refers to the end of the wings, the wing tips of the cherubim in the Temple (1 Kgs. 6:24). It describes figuratively the mere fringes or periphery of God's ways (Job 26:14); and refers to the ends of the earth, the entire world as lying within God's purview (Job 28:24). It is used to refer to one end (of heaven) to the other, the entire heavens (Ps. 19:6; 65:8; Is. 41:5; Jer. 49:36). God created the ends of the earth, the entire world (Is. 40:28). God gathered Israel from the ends of the earth, the entire world (Is. 41:9). Jerusalem was totally corrupt, both ends and the middle of her (Ezek. 15:4). The term has the sense of many or all peoples (Hab. 2:10). *

7 ***qāṣû, qiṣwāh*** [masc. noun: קָצוּ, קִצְוָה <7099>; from CUT OFF <7096>] ▶ **This word means an extremity, a corner.** It refers to the ends of the ark in the Tabernacle (Ex. 37:8); of the bronze grating (Ex. 38:5); of the corners of the shoulder pieces (Ex. 39:4). It is used figuratively of the distant corners or ends of the earth (Ps. 48:10; 65:5; Is. 26:15). ¶

8 ***q***^{e}***ṣāṯ*** [fem. noun: קְצָת <7117>; from CUT OFF <7096>] ▶ **This word means a corner, a part.** It refers to the four ends or corners of the mercy seat (Ex. 38:5); the outer top edges of the ephod (Ex. 39:4); the outer reaches of the earth (Ps. 65:8). It indicates a portion or a part of some whole from among the leaders of Israel (Neh. 7:70); such as the Jewish exiles (Dan. 1:2, 5, 15, 18). ¶

9 ***q***^{e}***ṣāṯ*** [fem. noun: קְצָת <7118>; corresponding to <7117> above] ▶ **This word means a part.** It indicates a share or a part of a larger whole: a part or a share of a kingdom (Dan. 2:42). It indicates the conclusion of a period of time (Dan. 4:29, 34). ¶

10 ***taḵliyṯ*** [fem. noun: תַּכְלִית <8503>; from FINISH <3615>] ▶ **This word indicates a boundary, a limit.** It refers to a physical marker that delineates or sets a boundary (Neh. 3:21). It is used figuratively of the boundaries of the Almighty, which, of course, are unsearchable (Job 11:7). It figuratively points to God's setting a boundary for light and darkness (Job 26:10); and to the extreme limits of the psalmist's hatred for those who oppose God (Ps. 139:22:

perfect, utmost, complete). Other ref.: Job 28:3 (limit, recess, perfection. ¶
– [11] Job 18:2 ➔ SNARE (noun) <7078> b. [12] Is. 16:4; 29:20: to come to an end ➔ FAIL <656> [13] See LATTER TIME <319>.

END (BRING TO AN) – Dan. 5:26 ➔ COMPLETE (verb) <8000>.

END (COME TO AN) – ***gāmar*** [verb: גָּמַר <1584>; a prim. root] ▶ **This word means to complete, to perfect, to fail, to cease.** The root idea of it is to end. In three intransitive uses, the psalmist prayed for wickedness to end, cried out that the godly person fails, and asked if God's promise fails forever (Ps. 7:9; 12:1; 77:8). In two transitive uses, God is the subject. He will perfect that which concerns the psalmist and will complete (or perform) all things for him (Ps. 57:2: to perform, to accomplish, to fulfill; 138:8: to perfect, to accomplish). ¶

END (COME TO AN, HAVE AN, MEET ONE'S) – Is. 66:17; Amos 3:15 ➔ CONSUME, BE CONSUMED <5486>.

END (DREADFUL, HORRIBLE) – Ezek. 26:21; 27:36; 28:19 ➔ TERROR <1091>.

END (MAKE AN) – ***nālāh*** [verb: נָלָה <5239>; apparently a prim. root] ▶ **This word means to cease, to stop, to finish.** It means to stop, an activity or an attitude, to bring it to a close (Is. 33:1). ¶

END (MAKE AN, PUT AN) – Dan. 9:24 ➔ RESTRAIN <3607> b.

END (PUT AN, BRING TO AN) – Dan. 2:44 ➔ CONSUME <5487>.

END (PUT TO AN) – ***ṣāmaṯ*** [verb: צָמַת <6789>; a prim. root] ▶ **This word means to terminate, to destroy. It appears most often in the imprecatory psalms—i.e., the psalms that call down curses on one's enemies.** The word occurs within the context of putting an end to the wicked (Ps. 73:27; 101:8); or to one's enemies (2 Sam. 22:41; Ps. 54:5; 143:12). In both of these cases, this word alludes to the physical death of these people. But in other instances, this word describes the process of rendering powerless by putting persons in prison (Lam. 3:53); the drying up of riverbeds (Job 6:17); or the wearying of the psalmist (Ps. 119:139). *

ENDAMAGE – Ezra 4:13 ➔ DAMAGE (verb) <5142>.

ENDANGER – ***ḥûḇ*** [verb: חוּב <2325>; a prim. root] ▶ **This word also means to bring into danger, to forfeit one's head.** It means to make guilty before someone and, hence, endanger one's standing (Dan. 1:10). ¶

ENDANGERED (BE) – Eccl. 10:9 ➔ IMPOVERISHED (BE) <5533> b.

ENDOW – [1] ***zāḇaḏ*** [verb: זָבַד <2064>; a prim. root] ▶ **This word means to give; it is also translated to present, to endue.** It indicates giving or bestowing a gift on someone, as when God bestowed a child on Leah (Gen. 30:20). ¶
[2] ***māhar*** [verb: מָהַר <4117>; a prim. root (perhaps rather the same as HURRY <4116> through the idea of readiness in assent)] ▶ **This word indicates the giving of a dowry; it is also translated to pay the bride-price, to give the bride-price, to pay the dowry.** It means to get a wife by paying the *mōhar* (DOWRY <4119>), the marriage dowry; gifts to acquire one's wife (Ex. 22:16). ¶

ENDOWMENT – Gen. 30:20 ➔ GIFT <2065>.

ENDUE – Gen. 30:20 ➔ ENDOW <2064>.

ENDURE – Prov. 18:14 ➔ CONTAIN <3557>.

ENDURING – [1] ***'āṯēq*** [adj.: עָתֵק <6276>; from MOVE <6275> (in the sense of to grow old)] ▶ **This word signifies something that lasts, is durable, does not decay, fade away.** Ref.: Prov. 8:18. ¶

2 ***qayyām*** [Aramaic adj.: קַיָּם <7011>; from STAND, STAND UP <6966>] ▶ **This word indicates something assured, steadfast. It describes something that does not come to an end, deteriorate, or fall.** It depicts God's character and actions (Dan. 6:26). It indicates that a situation is certain, assured to someone (Dan. 4:26; also translated sure, confirmed). ¶

ENEGLAIM – ***'êyn 'eglayim*** [proper noun: עֵין עֶגְלַיִם <5882>; from EYE (noun) <5869> (in the sense of fountain) and the dual of CALF <5695>]: fountain of two calves ▶ **A place near the Dead See foretold by Ezekiel to be filled with fish.** Ref.: Ezek. 47:10. ¶

ENEMY – 1 ***'ôyêb*** [masc. noun: אֹיֵב <341>; act. part. of ENEMY (BE AN) <340>] ▶ **The use of this word is uniform, and it refers to all kinds of opponents.** A personal enemy (Ex. 23:4); a national enemy (Gen. 22:17); an enemy of God (Ps. 8:2). But God can become the declared enemy of a rebellious people (Is. 63:10). *

2 ***'ār*** [masc. noun: עָר <6145>; from AROUSE <5782> (to be watchful for mischief, e.g., a foe)] ▶ **This word refers to one who is hostile towards other persons, seeking to defeat them, to act against them.** Ref.: 1 Sam. 28:16; in context the Lord had become Saul's adversary and accuser. In other contexts, it refers to enemies, adversaries of the Lord (Ps. 139:20). ¶

3 ***'ār*** [Aramaic masc. noun: עָר <6146>; corresponding to <6145> above] ▶ **This word refers in context to those opposed to King Nebuchadnezzar, both in his kingdom and outside of it.** Ref.: Dan. 4:19. ¶

4 ***šûr*** [masc. noun: שׁוּר <7790>; from LOOK (verb) <7789>] ▶ **This word refers to adversaries or hostile persons who actively oppose a person.** Ref.: Ps. 92:11; also translated foe. ¶

5 ***šôrêr, šôrêr*** [masc. noun: שֹׁרֵר, שׁוֹרֵר <8324>; a prim. root] ▶ **This word refers to an adversary, a foe; a slanderer.** It refers to hostile persons who want to harm or destroy righteous persons (Ps. 5:8; 27:11; 54:5; 56:2). God gives deliverance over the psalmist's foes (Ps. 59:10); but the righteous can have a victorious attitude toward their foes (see Ps. 92:11). ¶

– 6 Gen. 14:20; Num. 10:9; etc. ➔ NARROWNESS <6862> b.

ENEMY (BE AN) – ***'āyab*** [verb: אָיַב <340>; a prim. root] ▶ **This verb means to be hostile, to be an opponent.** The Lord asserts that He will be an enemy to the enemy of His people, if His people serve Him (Ex. 23:22. ¶

ENFORCE – Dan. 6:7 ➔ STRONG (BE, BECOME, GROW) <8631>.

ENGAGE – Ex. 22:16; Deut. 20:7; etc. ➔ BETROTH <781>.

ENGEDI – ***'êyn gediy*** [proper noun: עֵין גֶּדִי <5872>; from EYE (noun) <5869> (in the sense of fountain) and KID <1423>]: fountain of the kid ▶ **A town inherited by the tribe of Judah.** Ref.: Josh. 15:62. It was located on the west side of the Dead Sea (Ezek. 47:10). David went there for water when fleeing Saul (1 Sam. 23:29; 24:1). It produced excellent vineyards (Song 1:14). Other ref.: 2 Chr. 20:2. ¶

ENGINE – 2 Chr. 26:15 ➔ DEVICE <2810>.

ENGINE OF WAR – Ezek. 26:9 ➔ BATTERING RAM <6904> b.

ENGRAVE – 1 ***ḥāqaq*** [verb: חָקַק <2710>; a prim. root] ▶ **This word means to cut, to inscribe, to decree.** The basic meaning, to cut, is used for cutting a tomb out of rock (Is. 22:16), but it is used more commonly of engraving or writing (Is. 30:8; Ezek. 4:1; 23:14). It is employed for decreeing (i.e., inscribing) a law (Is. 10:1); and the word statute (*ḥōq* <2706>) is derived from it. Figuratively, God is said to have inscribed a boundary over the deep at creation (Prov.

8:27). It also expresses the idea of a commander of decrees (Deut. 33:21; Judg. 5:9). *
[2] ***ḥāraṯ*** [verb: חָרַת <2801>; a prim. root] ▶ **This word indicates cutting or inscribing on stone tablets, the Ten Commandments.** Ref.: Ex. 32:16; KJV, to grave. Such engraving was a common means of communicating in the ancient world of Israel. ¶
– [3] Ezek. 8:10 ➔ CARVE <2707>.

ENGRAVED WORK – 1 Kgs. 6:35 ➔ CARVE <2707>.

ENGRAVED, ENGRAVED STONE – Lev. 26:1; Num. 33:52 ➔ PICTURE <4906>.

ENGRAVING – [1] ***pittûaḥ*** [masc. noun: פִּתּוּחַ <6603>; pass. part. of OPEN <6605>] ▶ **This word indicates a carving, an inscription.** It means to create an opening by carving or cutting a hole or channel in wood, stone, clay, etc. It refers to writing engraved on stones (Ex. 28:11, 21). It refers to the words "Holy to the Lord" engraved on a plate of pure gold (Ex. 28:36). It describes decorative engravings on the Temple walls (1 Kgs. 6:29). In a time of judgment, all of this was destroyed (Ps. 74:6). It describes a special inscription engraved on a special stone by the Lord (Zech. 3:9). *
– [2] 1 Kgs. 7:31 ➔ CARVING <4734>.

ENGULF – [1] Deut. 11:4 ➔ FLOW OVER <6687> [2] Jon. 2:5 ➔ SURROUND <661>.

ENIGMA – [1] ***ḥiyḏāh*** [fem. noun: חִידָה <2420>; from RIDDLE <2330>] ▶ **This word means a riddle, an allegory. The Greek root of this English term is used in various contexts by the Septuagint (the Greek translation of the Hebrew Old Testament) to translate the Hebrew word.** Nearly half of this noun's occurrences refer to Samson's "riddle" when he tested the wits of the Philistines at his wedding feast (Judg. 14:12–19). The term is connected with several different words from the wisdom tradition, most notably the word frequently translated "proverb" (Ps. 78:2: saying; Prov. 1:6: riddle, saying; cf. 2 Chr. 9:1: hard question, difficult question). The term is also associated with the prophetic tradition, where it was contrasted with clear speaking and compared with communication through more obscure means (Num. 12:8: dark saying, dark speech, riddle; Ezek. 17:2: riddle, allegory). Daniel prophesied of a future destructive king whose abilities include "understanding enigmas." A somewhat similar Aramaic expression is used of Daniel himself earlier in the book (cf. Dan. 5:12; 8:23). Other refs.: 1 Kgs. 10:1; Ps. 49:4; Hab. 2:6. ¶
– [2] Prov. 1:6 ➔ SAYING <4426> [3] Dan. 5:12 ➔ RIDDLE <280> [4] Dan. 5:12, 16 ➔ PROBLEM <7001>.

ENJOY – [1] ***'ālas, ne'lāsāh*** [עָלַס, נֶעֱלָסָה <5965>; a prim. root] ▶
a. This verb means to find delight and pleasure in something and to express it. Ref.: Job 20:18; also translated to get enjoyment, to rejoice. It describes the act of sexual intimacy (Prov. 7:18; also translated to delight, to solace). ¶
b. This verb means to flap joyously, to wave proudly. It describes the appearance and manner of something acting or responding in an apparently happy manner (Job 39:13). It personifies ostrich wings in context. ¶
c. A feminine noun indicating to be attractive, beautiful. This translation takes the form of *'ālas, ne'lāsāh* as a noun. It is probably a passive form of the verb *'ālas*. If taken as a noun, it means beautiful (Job 39:13; KJV: goodly). ¶
– [2] Ps. 37:11 ➔ DELIGHT (HAVE, FIND, TAKE) <6026>.

ENJOYMENT (GET) – Job 20:18 ➔ ENJOY <5965> a.

ENLARGE – [1] ***pāṯāh*** [verb: פָּתָה <6601>; a prim. root] ▶ **This word means to extend territory.** Noah used the term to bless Japheth (Gen. 9:27). The Hebrew word also means to entice, to deceive; see ENTICE <6601>. ¶

2 ***rāḥab̲*** [verb: רָחַב <7337>; a prim. root] ▶ **This word indicates to extend; to open wide.** It means to gain living space, territory (Gen. 26:22); especially as the work of the Lord (Ex. 34:24; Deut. 12:20; 19:8). The psalmists praise God for enlarging them, giving them strength (2 Sam. 22:37). It is used of giving a person space, relief in a time of danger (Ps. 4:1). It indicates the social advancement or space from giving a gift (Prov. 18:16). Amos condemns the violent acquisition of territory (Amos 1:13). *

ENLARGEMENT – Esther 4:14 ➔ SPACE <7305>.

ENLIGHTEN – 1 2 Sam. 22:29; Ps. 18:28 ➔ LIGHTEN <5050> 2 Ezra 9:8; Ps. 13:3; 77:18; 97:4 ➔ LIGHT (GIVE) <215>.

ENMITY – ***'êyb̲āh*** [fem. noun: אֵיבָה <342>; from ENEMY (BE AN) <340>] ▶ **This word means hostility, animosity, or ill will.** It is used to signify acrimony, as between the woman and the serpent (Gen. 3:15); malice that leads to violent acts against another (Num. 35:21, 22); and the lingering hatred between mortal enemies (Ezek. 25:15; 35:5). ¶

ENOCH – ***ḥ***^{a}***nôk̲*** [masc. proper noun: חֲנוֹךְ <2585>; from DEDICATE <2596>]: initiated, consecrated ▶

a. Cain's first son after whom he named the first city he built. Enoch bore Irad and was the ancestor of Lamech (Gen. 4:17, 18). ¶

b. The son of Jared in the line that led from Seth to Noah. Refs.: Gen. 5:18, 19, 21–24; 1 Chr. 1:3. Enoch walked with God and he was not, for God took him (Gen. 5:24; cf. Heb. 11:5). ¶

c. The son of Midian who was a descendant of Abraham through his second wife Keturah. Refs.: Gen. 25:4; 1 Chr. 1:33. ¶

d. A son of Reuben, his first of three. Refs.: Gen. 46:9; Ex. 6:14; Num. 26:5; 1 Chr. 1:33; 5:3. ¶

ENOSH – ***'***^{e}***nôš*** [masc. proper noun: אֱנוֹשׁ <583>; the same as MAN <582>]: mortal, weak ▶ **Son of Seth.** Refs.: Gen. 4:26; 5:6, 7, 9–11; 1 Chr. 1:1. ¶

ENOUGH – ***day*** [masc. noun: דַּי <1767>; of uncertain deriv.] ▶ **This word means as often as, sufficient, adequate.** It indicates a sufficient amount of something: enough materials to build the Tabernacle (Ex. 36:7); a sufficient amount for someone, e.g., enough honey for energy (Prov. 25:16); sufficient animals for a sacrifice (Lev. 5:7; 12:8); enough money to redeem some property (Lev. 25:26, 28). Combined with other words, it can have a negative meaning: until (*'ad̲*) there is no need (NASB, until it overflows) (Mal. 3:10); nothing (Jer. 51:58); or an overabundance (*min* <4480> + day; Ex. 36:5). It is found in several idiomatic constructions: with the preposition *b*^{e} plus trumpet, it indicates as often as the trumpet sounds (Job 39:25); with the preposition *k*^{e}, it means corresponding to or fitting for (Deut. 25:2). Other idioms are: as numerous as (Judg. 6:5); according to need, e.g., yearly (1 Sam. 7:16; 2 Kgs. 4:8). With *l*^{e} plus *mâ* (*l*^{e}*madday*), it indicates of sufficient number (2 Chr. 30:3) or sufficiently (KJV). *

ENQUIRE – Ezra 7:14 ➔ SEARCH (MAKE) <1240>.

ENRAGED (BE) – 2 Chr. 26:19 ➔ ANGRY (BE, BECOME) <2196>.

ENSIGN – Is. 11:10; 18:3; 31:9 ➔ BANNER <5251>.

ENSIGN (LIFT LIKE AN) – Zech. 9:16 ➔ SPARKLE <5264> b.

ENSLAVE – Neh. 5:5; Jer. 34:11, 16 ➔ SUBDUE <3533>.

ENSNARE – 1 ***nāqaš*** [verb: נָקַשׁ <5367>; a prim. root] ▶ **This word means to strike, to strike down, to knock, to bring down; it is also translated to snare, to destroy, to lay snares, to set traps.** It is associated

with hunting birds, and therefore it is often translated to ensnare. It occurs four times in the Hebrew Bible and is used with the connotation of a subject attempting to destroy the object. For instance, the witch of Endor asked why Saul was entrapping her (1 Sam. 28:9). Deuteronomy 12:30 warned of being ensnared by the worship of other gods. According to Psalm 109:11, a creditor could also strike down one's estate. Other refs.: Ps. 9:16; 38:12. ¶
– [2] Deut. 7:25 → SNARE, BE SNARED <3369> [3] Is. 29:21 → SNARE (LAY A) <6983>.

ENTANGLE – [1] Ps. 18:4; 116:3 → SURROUND <661> [2] Jer. 2:23 → TRAVERSE <8308>.

ENTANGLED (BE) – Ex. 14:3 → WANDER <943>.

ENTER – [1] ***ʿalal*** [Aramaic verb: עֲלַל <5954>; from DO <5953> d. (in the sense of thrusting oneself in)] ► **This word is used often of getting an audience with the king and coming into his presence.** Refs.: Dan. 2:16, 24, 25; 4:6, 7; 5:7, 8, 10. It is used of entering into an area, a location (Dan. 6:10). It is used of bringing in someone or of being brought in (Dan. 2:24, 25; 5:13, 15; 6:10). It is used of an impersonal subject being brought in (Dan. 6:18). *
– [2] Ezek. 21:14 → SURROUND <2314>.

ENTER MORE – Prov. 17:10 → BEND <5181>.

ENTERTAINMENT – ***daḥawāh*** [Aramaic fem. noun: דַּחֲוָה <1761>; from the equivalent of DRIVE <1760>] ► **This word means and is also translated diversion, instrument of music, musician.** It depicts either the lack of musical instruments, entertainers, or some other diversion for rest and relaxation (Dan. 6:18). It is uncertain. Some have suggested food, perfumes, or even concubines as its meaning. ¶

ENTHRALLED (BE) – Ps. 45:11 → DESIRE (verb) <183>.

ENTICE – [1] ***sûṯ*** [verb: סוּת <5496>; perhaps denom. from THORN <7898>] ► **This word means to incite, to mislead, to tempt.** It has the sense of stirring up persons with the intention to get them to deviate, to act with destructive, harmful purposes or results in mind; to incite people to be evil, to lead them astray (Deut. 13:6; 1 Sam. 26:19; 2 Sam. 24:1; 1 Kgs. 21:25; Is. 36:18). It is also used of getting a person to concede or agree to something in a neutral or positive sense (Josh. 15:18; Judg. 1:14; Job 36:16). *
[2] ***pāṯāh*** [verb: פָּתָה <6601>; a prim. root] ► **This word means to deceive, to persuade; to be gullible.** It describes persons who are simple, naïve, and overcome by vain things (Job 5:2). It depicts the seducing of persons sexually (Ex. 22:16); or enticing them into sin and transgression in general (Prov. 1:10; 16:29); slander or deception with one's lips (Prov. 20:19; 24:28). It is used of strongly persuading people (Prov. 25:15). It indicates persons' deception of themselves (Deut. 11:16; Hos. 7:11); or of their being enticed or deceived into something (Job 31:9, 27; Jer. 20:10). It has the sense of being overcome or prevailed on to do something for the Lord (Ezek. 14:9). The Hebrew word also means to enlarge, to extend; see ENLARGE <6601>. *

ENTICE – 2 Kgs. 17:21 → DRIVE <5077>.

ENTRAILS – [1] ***leḥûm*** [masc. noun: לְחוּם <3894>; pass. part. of EAT <3898>] ► **This word means bowels, intestines. It is of uncertain meaning, owing to its rare use in Scripture, but it is generally understood to mean the intestines or inward parts of the body.** Occurring only in Job 20:23 (to be eating, body) and Zephaniah 1:17 (flesh, entrails), the context is the outpouring of the Lord's wrath. In the latter text, the apocalyptic image is a most graphic picture of battle: "Their blood will be poured out like dust and their flesh [*lāḥûm,* inner parts] like dung" (NASB). ¶
– [2] Judg. 3:22 → DUNG <6574> [3] 2 Sam. 20:10 → BOWELS <4578>.

ENTRANCE – 1 ***bi'āh*** [fem. noun: בִּאָה <872>; from COME <935>] ▶ **This word means a way in; it is also translated entry.** It was an entryway large enough to have the image of jealousy placed in it (Ezek. 8:5). It stood in the northern entrance. ¶

2 ***yi'tôn,'iyṯôn*** [masc. noun: יְאתוֹן, אִיתוֹן <2978>; COME <857>] ▶ **This word is used to describe an opening to be used as a gateway in Ezekiel's new Temple.** Ref.: Ezek. 40:15. ¶

3 ***māḇô'*** [common noun: מָבוֹא <3996>; from COME <935>] ▶ **This word indicates a place of access, a way in; it also means the west, the going down of the sun.** It indicates an entrance, a gate into a city in general (Judg. 1:24, 25); or special entrances or gates, e.g., for horses (2 Kgs. 11:16). It depicts the entrances into Ezekiel's new Temple in his vision (Ezek. 42:9; 44:5; 46:19). In a broader usage, it refers to any access to something or to somewhere, such as Tyre as an "entrance" or place of access to the Great Sea (Ezek. 27:3). It is used in a general sense of persons coming, making their entrances (Ezek. 33:31). It is used in the idiom for the "setting of the sun" (Deut. 11:30; Mal. 1:11), a way of expressing "west" as well. *

4 ***m***^{e}***ḇô'āh*** [fem. noun: מְבוֹאָה <3997>; fem. of <3996> above] ▶ **This word means an access, a way to enter; it is also translated entry, gateway.** It is used to indicate the area of access to the Great Sea enjoyed by the city of Tyre (see also ENTRANCE <3996>) (Ezek. 27:3). ¶

– 5 Ps. 119:130 ➔ UNFOLDING <6608> 6 Ezek. 43:11 ➔ COMING IN <4126> 7 See DOOR <6607>.

ENTREAT – 1 ***ḥannôṯ*** [masc. noun: חַנּוֹת <2589>; from GRACIOUS (BE) <2603> (in the sense of prayer)] ▶ **This Hebrew word indicates entreaty, a plea for grace.** It may mean to plead, to entreat, to ask for grace (Job 19:17, KJV). Other translations: to be repulsive, to be loathsome, to be a stench. The Hebrew word is also translated to be gracious; see GRACIOUS (BE) <2589>. ¶

– 2 Ex. 8:8; etc. ➔ PRAY <6279>.

ENTRY – 1 Ezek. 8:5 ➔ ENTRANCE <872> 2 Ezek. 27:3 ➔ ENTRANCE <3997>.

ENTWINE – ***sāḇaḵ*** [verb: סָבַךְ <5440>; a prim. root] ▶ **This word means to wrap around, to intertwine, to become entangled.** It describes the way the roots of a plant or tree cling to and entangle themselves to a rock pile (Job 8:17; also translated to wrap around, to wrap about); or the way thorns become entangled (Nah. 1:10; also translated tangled, folden together). ¶

ENVOY – ***ḥašman*** [noun: חַשְׁמַן <2831>; from an unused root (prob. meaning firm or capacious in resources)] ▶ **This word occurs in the plural in Psalm 68:31. It possibly means ambassadors.** It is also translated princes, nobles, but its meaning and derivation are uncertain. ¶

ENVY (LOOK WITH, GAZE IN, FUME WITH) – ***rāṣaḏ*** [verb: רָצַד <7520>; a prim. root] ▶

a. This word indicates looking at persons, keeping a hostile or envious eye on them. In context it is used figuratively of the mountains of Bashan (Ps. 68:16).

b. A verb meaning to leap. In context this translation depicts the leaping of the high hills in expectation, yet they will not be God's chosen abode (Ps. 68:16). ¶

EPHAH (measurement) – ***'êyp̄āh, 'êp̄āh*** [fem. noun: אֵיפָה, אֵפָה <374>; of Egyptian deriv.] ▶ **An ephah was a dry measurement and equaled ten omers (Ex. 16:36). It equaled three-fifths of a bushel or in metric measure, twenty-two liters. The omer was two quarts or about two liters.** The ephah was a measure used often when preparing sacrificial offerings or foods (Lev. 5:11; 6:20; Num. 5:15; 28:5; Judg. 6:19; 1 Sam. 17:17). It is especially prominent in the sacrificial practices of the new Temple vision of Ezekiel (Ezek. 45:10, 11, 13, 24; 46:5, 7, 11, 14). Israel was to keep honest measures as a part of her righteousness. Micah observes that in her rebellious and unrighteous practices, Israel had shortened her ephah (Mic. 6:10). The business practices of God's people were to be based on true weights and measures in the marketplace. *

EPHAH (person) – ***‘êypāh*** [proper noun: עֵיפָה <5891>; the same as DARKNESS <5890>]: darkness ▶
a. Son of Midian. Refs.: Gen. 25:4; 1 Chr. 1:33; Is. 60:6. ¶
b. A Judaite. Ref.: 1 Chr. 2:47. ¶
c. A concubine of Caleb. Ref.: 1 Chr. 2:46. ¶

EPHAI – ***‘êypay*** [masc. proper noun: עֵיפַי <5778>; from BIRD <5775>]: birdlike ▶ **A Netophathite whose sons were left in Judah after the deportation to Babylon.** Ref.: Jer. 40:8. ¶

EPHER – ***‘êper*** [masc. proper noun: עֵפֶר <6081>; prob. a variation of YOUNG <6082>]: gazelle ▶
a. Son of Midian. Refs.: Gen. 25:4; 1 Chr. 1:33. ¶
b. Son of Ezra. Ref.: 1 Chr. 4:17. ¶
c. The head of a family sent into exile. Ref.: 1 Chr. 5:24. ¶

EPHES-DAMMIM – ***'epes dammiym*** [proper noun: אֶפֶס דַּמִּים <658>; from NOTHING <657> and the plur. of BLOOD <1818>]: end of the vines ▶ **A place inside Judah.** Ref.: 1 Sam. 17:1. ¶

EPHLAL – ***'eplāl*** [masc. proper noun: אֶפְלָל <654>; from PRAY <6419>]: intercession ▶ **An Israelite of the tribe of Judah.** Ref.: 1 Chr. 2:37. ¶

EPHOD (garment) – [1] ***^{a}puddāh*** [fem. noun: אֲפֻדָּה <642>; fem. of <646> below] ▶ **The word refers to the special composition of the garment the high priest wore which had the twelve stones representing the twelve tribes of Israel on it.** The waistband of the priest was to be made like the *^{a}puddāh* (Ex. 28:8; 39:5). It also refers to (molten) images covered with gold (Is. 30:22: ornament). ¶
[2] ***'êpôd, 'êpōd*** [masc. noun: אֵפוֹד, אֵפֹד <646>; prob. of foreign deriv.] ▶ **A garment worn around the high priest's upper body that featured twelve semiprecious and precious stones on the front, each one bearing the name of one of the tribes of Israel.** Refs.: Ex. 28:4, 6, 12, 15, 25–28. The breastplate bearing the stones was on the front of the ephod itself. The ephod was made by a skilled workman and had two shoulder pieces which were fastened together to hold it securely. It also bore two stones, one on each of its shoulders that represented the tribes of Israel. Each stone had six of the tribes of Israel engraved on it.

It represents idolatrous cultic objects made by Gideon and Micah (Judg. 8:27; 17:5) and later used to obtain decisions, probably incorrectly (1 Sam. 23:9). The object was probably a sacred robe with some metallic aspect to it. The word refers to a simple linen ephod as well (1 Sam. 2:18, 28). *

EPHOD (person) – ***'êpōd*** [masc. proper noun: אֵפֹד <641>; the same as EPHOD (garment) <646> shortened]: something that covers ▶ **Father of Hanniel, a leader of the tribe of Manasseh.** Ref.: Num. 34:23. ¶

EPHRAIM – ***'eprayim*** [proper noun: אֶפְרַיִם <669>; dual of a masc. form of EPHRATH <672>]: double fruit ▶
a. The second son of Joseph. The name is a dual form and indicates fruitfulness (Gen. 41:52). He was born in Egypt as was Manasseh (Gen. 46:20) by Asenath, the daughter of Potiphera, Priest of On (Heliopolis, "city of the sun"). Jacob recognized the two boys as his by adoption (Gen. 48:5). Jacob blessed Ephraim, the younger, ahead of Manasseh, the elder (Gen. 48:20). His descendants were numerous (Num. 26:28; 1 Chr. 7:20, 22). *
b. The name refers to the territory allotted to Ephraim (see a. above), the tribe formed by his descendants. The tribe became tens of thousands (Deut. 33:17). The location of the tribal land was in central Israel, bordered on the north by Manasseh, the west by Dan, the south by Dan-Benjamin, the east by Manasseh

(Josh. 16). The name "Ephraim" became synonymous for Northern Israel. Ephraim and the north broke away from Judah and the line of David after Solomon's death (1 Kgs. 12:12–19). The prophets saw a day when Ephraim would be reunited with David and Judah, one nation-Israel, again (Ezek. 37:15–17; Zech. 9:10, 13; 10:7). The Lord never cast off Ephraim fully, for he loved them (Hos. 11:8). *

EPHRAIMITE – ***'eprāṯiy*** [masc. proper noun: אֶפְרָתִי <673>; patrial from EPHRATH <672>] ▶ **A descendant of Ephraim.** Refs.: Judg. 12:5; 1 Sam. 1:1; 1 Kgs. 11:26. See also EPHRATHITE <673>. ¶

EPHRATH – ***'eprāṯ, 'eprāṯāh*** [proper noun: אֶפְרָת, אֶפְרָתָה <672>; from FRUITFUL (BE) <6509>]: fruitfulness ▶
a. The word is used as a name for Bethlehem in antiquity. Rachel was buried there (Gen. 35:16, 19; 48:7), and Naomi lived there (Ruth 4:11). David's father, Jesse, came from there (see 1 Sam. 17:12). It was the territory of David (Ps. 132:6). It was prophesied as the place from which the Ruler over Israel would come, whose origins were mysterious and from ancient times (Mic. 5:2). Other ref.: 1 Chr. 2:24. ¶
b. The word refers to the second wife of Caleb, son of Hezron. Refs.: 1 Chr. 2:19, 50; 4:4. ¶

EPHRATHITE – ***'eprāṯiy*** [masc. proper noun: אֶפְרָתִי <673>; patrial from EPHRATH <672>] ▶ **An inhabitant of Ephrath.** Refs.: Ruth 1:2; 1 Sam. 17:12. See also EPHRAIMITE <673>. ¶

EQUAL – Job 41:33 ➔ AUTHORITY <4915>.

EQUIP – Is. 45:5 ➔ GIRD <247>.

EQUIPMENT – ***'āzên*** [masc. noun: אָזֵן <240>; from EAR (GIVE) <238>] ▶ **This word indicates a weapon or tool.** A tent peg or spade was to be kept among a person's equipment in order to keep the Lord's camp holy and clean by covering up one's excrement (Deut. 23:13). ¶

EQUITY – [1] Eccl. 2:21 ➔ SKILL <3788> [2] Is. 59:14 ➔ RIGHT <5229>.

ER – ***'êr*** [masc. noun: עֵר <6147>; from AWAKE <5782>]: watchful ▶
a. Son of Judah. Refs.: Gen. 38:3, 6, 7; 46:12; Num. 26:19; 1 Chr. 2:3. ¶
b. Grandson of Judah. Ref.: 1 Chr. 4:21. ¶

ERAN – ***'êrān*** [masc. proper noun: עֵרָן <6197>; prob. from AROUSE <5782>]: watchful ▶ **The oldest son of Ephraim.** Ref.: Num. 26:36. ¶

ERANITE – ***'êrāniy*** [proper noun: עֵרָנִי <6198>; patron. from ERAN <6197>] ▶ **A descendant of Eran.** Ref.: Num. 26:36. ¶

ERECH – ***'ereḵ*** [proper noun: אֶרֶךְ <751>; from PROLONG <748>]: length ▶ **One of the city of the kingdom of Nimrod in the land of Shinar.** Ref.: Gen. 10:10. ¶

ERECT – Lev. 26:13 ➔ UPRIGHT <6968>.

ERI – ***'êriy*** [masc. proper noun: עֵרִי <6179>; from AWAKE <5782>]: watchful ▶ **One of the sons of Gad.** Refs.: Gen. 46:16; Num. 26:16. ¶

ERITE – ***'êriy*** [masc. proper noun: עֵרִי <6180>; patron. of ERI <6179>] ▶ **A descendant of Eri (<6179>).** Ref.: Num. 26:16. ¶

ERR – [1] ***šāgag*** [verb: שָׁגַג <7683>; a prim. root] ▶ **This word means to stray, to be deceived, to go astray, to sin ignorantly.** The primary meaning of this word is to commit an error, to sin inadvertently. In Leviticus, this word referred to the unintentional sin atoned for by the sacrifice of a ram, referred to as a guilt offering (Lev. 5:18). In addition to Leviticus, Numbers 15:28 also described the priestly function in atonement for one's unintentional sin. Recognition of sin may result from a realization or awareness of covenant violations due to the work of the human consciousness. The psalmist used this word to describe an action before he was afflicted (i.e., he went astray [Ps. 119:67]). This verb was also used to designate erring mentally on the part of self or another person (i.e., being the deceived or the deceiver [Job 12:16]). ¶

2 ***šag̱āh*** [verb: שָׁגָה <7686>; a prim. root] ▶ **This word also means to stray, to go astray, to deceive, to wander, to make a mistake, to reel. It is primarily used to express the idea of straying or wandering.** It is used frequently to describe a wandering or aimless flock, both figuratively and literally (Ezek. 34:6). Isaiah used this verb to suggest swerving, meandering, or reeling in drunkenness (Is. 28:7). At times, it could define intoxication, not only from wine or beer but also from love (Prov. 5:19, 20). This verb also depicts moral corruption (Prov. 5:23). Deuteronomy 27:18 describes it as a reason for being cursed (i.e., leading a blind man astray). Leviticus 4:13 indicates a sin of ignorance of which the person is still guilty and must provide an atonement when knowledge of the sin is known. The word also expresses a misleading mentally (i.e., being a deceiver or the deceived). The idea of atonement for sin, even of that which is an inadvertent or unintentional sin, is a prevalent thought found in Scripture (Ezek. 45:20). *

ERROR – 1 ***m^{e}šûg̱āh*** [fem. noun: מְשׁוּגָה <4879>; from an unused root meaning to stray] ▶ **This word identifies an offense, something wrongly done against another, especially against God.** Ref.: Job 19:4. ¶

2 ***š^{e}g̱āg̱āh*** [fem. noun: שְׁגָגָה <7684>; from ERR <7683>] ▶ **This word means mistake, inadvertent transgression, ignorance.** The primary meaning is an inadvertent error performed in the daily routine of life that ranged from a slip of the tongue (Eccl. 5:6) to accidental manslaughter (Num. 35:11, 15; Josh. 20:3, 9). When used with the word *ḥāṭā'* [SIN (verb) <2398>], it describes a procedure or policy used by priests for the guilt offering that atones for inadvertent sin (Lev. 4:2, 22, 27; 5:15, 18). Unatoned sin breaks the order and peace between God and people, even if unintentional, and an atonement has to be made. The noun also describes acts in which the sinner is conscious, yet the sinfulness of those acts becomes known after the act takes place. *

3 ***š^{e}giy'āh*** [fem. noun: שְׁגִיאָה <7691>; from ERR <7686>] ▶ **This word means a moral mistake.** As written in Psalm 19:12, the noun signifies an error or lapse that is hidden from the sight of others. The inclusion of this noun in the verse seems to indicate that only God can see or discern this type of error or moral mistake. In its plural absolute form, this noun indicates a willful sin (see Ps. 19:13). ¶

4 ***šal*** [masc. noun: שַׁל <7944>; from NEGLIGENT (BE) <7952> abbreviated] ▶ **This word means a sin; it is also translated irreverence, irreverent act.** This noun is used only once in the Old Testament in 2 Samuel 6:7, but from this usage, we can gain the insight that the error described by this word is a great one. The context is that of Uzzah, whom God struck down because he touched the ark: this error cost him his life. This word has strong connotations of a great sin or error deserving of death. ¶

5 ***tāh^{o}lāh*** [fem. noun: תָּהֳלָה <8417>; fem. of an unused root, apparently from PRAISE (verb) <1984>, meaning bluster] ▶ **This word indicates a deviation from perfection, a flaw of any kind.** Ref.: Job 4:18; KJV: folly. ¶

6 ***tō'āh*** [fem. noun: תּוֹעָה <8442>; fem. act. part. of WANDER <8582>] ▶ **This word means a disturbance, trouble. It is a strongly negative term indicating confusion, perversion.** It describes a confusion or disturbance raised among people by troublemakers (Neh. 4:8). It refers to erroneous and wrong words, ideas, and concepts (Is. 32:6). ¶

ERRORS – Jer. 10:15; 51:18 ➔ MOCKERY <8595>.

ERUPTION – 1 Lev. 13:2; 14:56 ➔ SCAB <5597> 2 Lev. 13:6–8 ➔ RASH <4556>.

ESARHADDON – *'ēsarḥaddôn* [masc. proper noun: אֵסַרְחַדּוֹן <634>; of foreign deriv.]: Ashur (the god) has given a brother ▶ **A great Assyrian king who succeeded Sennacherib who tried to destroy Jerusalem.** Ref.: 2 Kgs. 19:37. He reigned 681–669 B.C. Other refs.: Ezra 4:2; Is. 37:38. ¶

ESAU – *'ēśāw* [masc. proper noun: עֵשָׂו <6215>; apparently a form of the pass. part. of DO <6213> in the original sense of handling]: hairy ▶ **The elder twin brother of Jacob.** Refs.: Gen. 25:25–30. The Lord revealed the general outline of Esau's life to Rebekah before the twins were born (Gen. 25:23). The elder would serve the younger. Both would father a nation. Esau foolishly sold his birthright to Jacob for food (Gen. 25:30, 31). He received his secondary name, Edom, because of the "red stew" that he purchased from Jacob. Esau considered his birthright of little value (Gen. 25:34). He was the favored son of Isaac. He was a hairy man, and Jacob deceived him and received his blessing from Isaac on his deathbed (Gen. 27:1–33). But Isaac also gave Esau a secondary blessing (Gen. 27:39, 40). Esau and Jacob were reconciled after Jacob's long absence from his father's house (Gen. 33). Esau's descendants were numerous (Gen. 35:1–43). He went to the mountainous territory of Seir to settle (Gen. 36:8, 9). There he became the father of the Edomites after marrying Canaanite wives, Adah and Oholibamah (Gen. 36:2). *

ESCAPE (noun) – [1] ***maḥᵃlōqeṯ*** [fem. noun: מַחֲלֹקֶת <4256>; from SHARE (verb) <2505> (in the sense of dividing persons in groups)] ▶

a. This word means smoothness, slipperiness, a flight. It is used to define a rock where David escaped from Saul, "the rock of escape" (1 Sam. 23:28). ¶

b. A noun meaning a group, a division. It designates a part or division of people by tribes (Josh. 11:23; 12:7; 18:10); or by sons of Levi (1 Chr. 23:6); or Aaron (1 Chr. 24:1), etc. It indicates sections or portions of land as well (Neh. 11:36; Ezek. 48:29). *

[2] ***pālêṭ, pallêṭ*** [verb: פָּלֵט, פַּלֵּט <6405>; from DELIVER <6403>] ▶

a. This word means a person free from captivity, a refugee; those spared. It describes persons escaped, spared from destruction (Jer. 44:14); fugitives, those who have fled (Jer. 50:28; 51:50). ¶

b. This word means deliverance. It modifies songs as songs of escape, deliverance (Ps. 32:7). Psalm 56:7 seems to employ DELIVER <6403> as an imperative, cast out, separate out (KJV, escape). ¶

– [3] Ps. 55:8 ➔ SHELTER <4655>.

ESCAPE (verb) – [1] ***mālaṭ*** [verb: מָלַט <4422>; a prim. root] ▶ **This word means to break free from captivity, to be rescued (e.g., from death). The picture of escape is as sparks leaping out of the fire or like a bird escaping the fowlers.** Refs.: Job 41:19; Ps. 124:7. This word is usually used within the context of fleeing for one's life as Lot was urged to do (Gen. 19:17, 19, 20, 22); as David did from the hands of Saul (1 Sam. 19:10–12; 27:1); or as Zedekiah could not do when facing the Chaldeans (Jer. 32:4; 34:3). It is also used to describe rescue from death (Esther 4:13; Ps. 89:48; Amos 2:14, 15); calamity (Job 1:15–17, 19); or punishment (Prov. 11:21; 19:5; 28:26). In a few instances, the word is used to describe protection (Eccl. 9:15; Is. 31:5); in one instance, it means to give birth to a child (Is. 66:7). *

– [2] Prov. 4:21 ➔ PERVERSE <3868>.

ESCAPE, ESCAPED – Gen. 32:8; Ex. 10:5; Judg. 21:17; 2 Sam. 15:14 ➔ DELIVERANCE <6413>.

ESEK – *'ēśeq* [proper noun: עֵשֶׂק <6230>; from CONTEND <6229>]: contention, dispute ▶ **A well dug by Isaac's herdsmen.** The herdsmen of Gerar quarreled with them saying the water belonged to them (Gen. 26:20). ¶

ESH-BAAL – *'ešba'al* [masc. proper noun: אֶשְׁבַּעַל <792>; from MAN <376> and BAAL <1168>]: man of Baal ▶ **A son of King Saul.** Refs.: 1 Chr. 8:33; 9:39. ¶

ESHAN – ***’eš‘ān*** [proper noun: אֶשְׁעָן <824>; from LEAN <8172> (with the meaning of to rely, to support oneself)]: support, slope ▶ **A village in the hills of Judah.** Ref.: Josh. 15:52. ¶

ESHBAN – ***’ešbān*** [masc. proper noun: אֶשְׁבָּן <790>; prob. from the same as SHEBNA <7644>]: understanding man, vigorous ▶ **One of the sons of Dishon, a descendant of Seir the Horite.** Refs.: Gen. 36:26; 1 Chr. 1:41. ¶

ESHCOL – ***’eškōl, ’eškôl*** [masc. proper noun: אֶשְׁכֹּל, אֶשְׁכּוֹל <812>; the same as CLUSTER <811>]: cluster (of grapes) ▶
a. The name of an Amorite. Refs.: Gen. 14:13, 24. ¶
b. A valley in Palestine. Refs.: Num. 13:23, 24; 32:9; Deut. 1:24. ¶

ESHEK – ***‘êšeq*** [proper noun: עֵשֶׁק <6232>; from OPPRESS <6231>]: oppression, dispute ▶ **A Benjamite, descendant of King Saul.** Ref.: 1 Chr. 8:39. ¶

ESHTAOL – ***’eštā’ōl*** [proper noun: אֶשְׁתָּאוֹל <847>; prob. from ASK <7592>]: hollow ▶ **It is a part of Judah's inheritance according to clans.** It was located in the western lowlands of the Negev. It was later given to Dan (Josh. 15:33; 19:41; Judg. 18:2, 8, 11). Samson's relatives came from this area (Judg. 13:25; 16:31). ¶

ESHTAOLITE – ***’eštā’uliy*** [proper noun: אֶשְׁתָּאֻלִי <848>; patrial from ESHTAOL <847>] ▶ **An inhabitant of Eshtaol.** Ref.: 1 Chr. 2:53. ¶

ESHTEMOA – ***’ešt^{e}môa‘, ’ešt^{e}mōh*** [proper noun: אֶשְׁתְּמוֹעַ, אֶשְׁתְּמֹה <851>; from HEAR <8085> (in the sense of obedience)]: obedience ▶
a. A city in Judah. Refs.: Josh. 15:50; 21:14; 1 Sam. 30:28; 1 Chr. 6:57. ¶
b. An Israelite of the tribe of Judah. Refs.: 1 Chr. 4:17, 19. ¶

ESHTON – ***’eštôn*** [masc. proper noun: אֶשְׁתּוֹן <850>; prob. from the same as SHUNI <7764>]: rest ▶ **An Israelite of the tribe of Judah.** Refs.: 1 Chr. 4:11, 12. ¶

ESPOUSAL – Jer. 2:2 ➔ BETROTHAL <3623>.

ESPOUSALS – Song 3:11 ➔ WEDDING <2861>.

ESPOUSE – 2 Sam. 3:14 ➔ BETROTH <781>.

ESTABLISH – [1] ***šāpaṯ*** [verb: שָׁפַת <8239>; a prim. root] ▶ **This word means to ordain; to place in, to put on.** It means to move something to a certain spot, to put a pot on a stove (2 Kgs. 4:38; Ezek. 24:3). God places a person in the ground in the dust of death (Ps. 22:15: to bring, to lay). It is used figuratively also of God's establishing and creating peace for His people (Is. 26:12). ¶
– [2] Prov. 8:28 ➔ STRENGTHEN <5810>.

ESTABLISHED (BE) – ***t^{e}qan*** [Aramaic verb: תְּקַן <8627>; corresponding to STRAIGHT (MAKE) <8626>] ▶ **This word means to be set in order; it is also translated to be reestablished, to be restored. It means to set up or to put something in place, to make it firm.** It describes God's reestablishing, restoring, establishing King Nebuchadnezzar in his kingship after first laying a terrifying judgment on him (Dan. 4:36). ¶

ESTATE – [1] ***tôr*** [masc. noun: תּוֹר <8448>; prob. the same as TURN (noun) <8447>] ▶ **This word refers to the standard of a human against which God had measured and appointed David.** Ref.: KJV, 1 Chr. 17:17; see TURN (noun) d. ¶
– [2] 1 Chr. 17:17 ➔ TURN (noun) <8447> d. [3] Eccl. 3:18 ➔ CAUSE <1700>.

ESTEEM (noun) – Prov. 18:11 ➔ PICTURE <4906>.

ESTEEM (verb) – Deut. 32:15 ➔ to lightly esteem, to scornfully esteem ➔ FOOLISH (BE) <5034>.

ESTEEMED (BE HIGHLY) – 1 Sam. 18:30 ➔ PRECIOUS (BE) <3365>.

ESTHER – ***'estêr*** [fem. proper noun: אֶסְתֵּר <635>; of Persian deriv.]: star ▶ **The Jewish queen of Persia. She was raised up by God at the right time and place to bring deliverance to the Jews in Persia.** Refs.: Esther 4:12–14. An Amalekite, Haman, plotted to destroy God's chosen people, but Esther and Mordecai worked together to thwart the plan (Esther 3, 4). The Persian King Ahasuerus (Xerxes) reigned 486–465 B.C. Her request to slay the enemies of the Jews is not to be followed today, but God's great deliverance of the Jews is still celebrated in the Feast of Purim today (Esther 10:18–32). *

ETAM – ***'êyṭām*** [proper noun: עֵיטָם <5862>; from BIRD OF PREY <5861>]: lair of rapacious beasts ▶
a. A town located in Simeon's tribal territory. It was in the Shephelah area in the northwest Negev (1 Chr. 4:3, 32). ¶
b. A town near Bethlehem in Judah and rebuilt by Rehoboam. Ref.: 2 Chr. 11:6. It is south, southwest of Jerusalem about six miles. ¶
c. A rock formation or cave where Samson hid from the Philistines after he slew many of them. It was likely in Judah's western area (Judg. 15:8, 11). ¶

ETERNITY – ***'aḏ*** [noun: עַד <5703>; from PASS OVER <5710> (in the sense of to advance; by implication, duration)] ▶ **This word means perpetuity, continuity.** The word signifies God's dwelling place (Is. 57:15). It also refers to the continuance of a king on the throne (Ex. 15:18; 1 Chr. 28:9; Ps. 132:12; Prov. 29:14). The word can indicate continual joy (Ps. 61:8; Is. 65:18); or continual anger (Mic. 7:18; Amos 1:11). The word's references to mountains that would be shattered (Hab. 3:6); the sun and the moon (Ps. 148:6) may show that the word sometimes means less than eternity or only an apparent eternity. The word occurs with the word *'ôlām* (FOREVER <5769>) (Ps. 10:16; 45:6; Dan. 12:3) and sometimes with the word *neṣaḥ* (FOREVER <5331>) (Ps. 9:18; Amos 1:11). *

ETH-KAZIN – ***'ēṯ qāṣiyn*** [proper noun: עֵת קָצִין <6278>; from TIME <6256> and ENDURING <7011>]: time of a judge ▶ **A place on the boundary of Zebulun.** Ref.: Josh. 19:13. ¶

ETHAM – ***'ēṯām*** [proper noun: אֵתָם <864>; of Egyptian deriv.]: limit of dwellings ▶ **The Israelites camped there on the edge of the wilderness after leaving Egypt.** Refs.: Ex. 13:20; Num. 33:6–8. ¶

ETHAN – ***'êyṯān*** [masc. proper noun: אֵיתָן <387>; the same as STRENGTH <386>]: ancient, firm, permanent ▶
a. An Israelite of the tribe of Judah. Refs.: 1 Kgs. 4:31; 1 Chr. 2:6, 8; Ps. 89:1. ¶
b. A Levite from the family of Gershon. Ref.: 1 Chr. 6:42. ¶
c. A Levite from the family of Merari. Refs.: 1 Chr. 6:44; 15:17, 19. ¶

ETHANIM – ***'eṯāniym*** [proper noun: אֵיתָנִים <388>; plur. of STRENGTH <386>]: permanent, enduring ▶ **The seventh month in the Hebrew calendar (according to one commentator, so named because permanent streams still flowed).** Solomon dedicated the Temple during this month (1 Kgs. 8:2). It was later named Tishri (September-October). ¶

ETHBAAL – ***'eṯba'al*** [masc. proper noun: אֶתְבַּעַל <856>; from WITH <854> and BAAL <1168>]: with Baal ▶ **King of the Sidonians, father of Jezebel.** Ref.: 1 Kgs. 16:31. ¶

ETHER – ***'ēṯer*** [proper noun: עֶתֶר <6281>; from MULTIPLY <6280>]: abundance ▶ **A town in Judah that became part of the inheritance of Simeon.** Refs.: Josh. 15:42; 19:7. ¶

ETHIOPIAN – Num. 12:1 ➔ CUSHITE <3571>.

ETHNAN – ***'eṯnān*** [masc. proper noun: אֶתְנָן <869>; the same as EARNINGS <868>

in the sense of ETHNI <867>]: gift ▶ **An Israelite of the tribe of Judah.** Ref.: 1 Chr. 4:7. ¶

ETHNI – ***'etniy*** [masc. proper noun: אֶתְנִי <867>; perhaps from PAY <866>]: my gift, reward ▶ **A Levite, descendant of Gershon.** Ref.: 1 Chr. 6:41. ¶

EUNUCH – [1] ***sariys*** [masc. noun: סָרִיס <5631>; from an unused root meaning to castrate] ▶ **This word means a castrated man, and also a court official.** Derived from an Assyrian phrase meaning one who is the head or chief, this word can refer to someone with a high-ranking military or political status (Gen. 40:2, 7; 1 Sam. 8:15). Potiphar held an official post called the captain of the guard while working in the court of an Egyptian pharaoh (Gen. 37:36; 39:1). The term eunuch comes from the custom of placing castrated males in certain key government positions (2 Kgs. 20:18; Esther 2:3, 14, 15, 21; 4:4, 5; Is. 39:7). According to Mosaic Law, males who had defective genital organs would have been excluded from the worshiping community of Israel (cf. Lev. 21:20; Deut. 23:1). In 2 Kings 18:17, the term appears in a phrase that probably does not denote a eunuch but simply means an important government official (Jer. 39:3, 13). *

– [2] Lev. 21:20: is a eunuch ➔ lit.: has crushed testicles ➔ TESTICLE <810>.

EUNUCH (BE A) – Lev. 21:20 ➔ lit.: to have crushed testicles ➔ CRUSHED <4790>.

EUPHRATES – ***peraṯ*** [proper noun: פְּרָת <6578>; from an unused root meaning to break forth]: breaking forth, rushing ▶

a. The name refers to the Euphrates River, a major river ca. 1,800 miles long. The Hebrew name comes from the Akkadian, *purattu*. It and the Tigris encompass the area of Mesopotamia ("between the rivers"). It has shifted its riverbed several times through the millennia. It begins in modern eastern Turkey and flows through Syria and modern Iraq to the Persian Gulf. It and the Tigris meet shortly before emptying into the gulf. It has seen the rise and fall of villages, cities (e.g., Babylon, Carchemish), and great empires (Assyria, Mitanni, Babylon, Persia, etc.) over the years. It was one of the rivers in the Garden of Eden (Gen. 2:14). It was the northernmost boundary of the land God promised to Abraham (Gen. 15:8; Deut. 1:7). It is sometimes called the "great river" or "the River" (Gen. 31:21).

b. It seems to be the name of a city or geographical area. Refs.: Perath; Jer. 13:4–7, NIV. It could possibly refer to the Euphrates River (see a.). *

EVALUATION – ***'êreḵ*** [masc. noun: עֵרֶךְ <6187>; from VALUE (verb) <6186>] ▶ **This word means an estimation, a value, an arrangement in order.** It refers to a set order for something or what is to be placed into a set arrangement (Ex. 40:4, 23). It refers to the orderly construction or build of a body or its structure (Job 41:12). It is used of an evaluation or price, a value placed on something (Lev. 5:15, 18; 6:6; 27:2–8; Job 28:13). It refers to wages or keep, a maintenance for someone (Judg. 17:10); and to an assessment of money laid on someone (2 Kgs. 12:4). It indicates something equal to or like something or someone else (Ps. 55:13). *

EVE – ***ḥawwāh*** [fem. proper noun: חַוָּה <2332>; causatively from SHOW <2331>]: living, making alive ▶ **This word is the name of the first woman created by the Lord God.** Adam gave her the name Eve (Gen. 3:20). She was the wife of Adam (Gen. 4:1). In Genesis 2:23, she was designated as a woman (*'iššāh* <802>), a female being apart from the male being, Adam, both sharing common humanity. As her name indicates, she then gave birth to the human race (Gen. 4:1, 2). ¶

EVEN AS – [1] Dan. 2:43 ➔ BEHOLD (interj.) <1888> [2] Dan. 4:31 ➔ WHILE <5751>.

EVEN-TEMPERED – Prov. 17:27 ➔ COLD (adj.) <7119>.

EVENING – ***'ereḇ*** [masc. noun: עֶרֶב <6153>; from EVENING (BECOME) <6150>] ▶ **This word is used consistently to indicate the close of the day, nightfall, sunset.** The phrase *lip̱nôṯ-'areḇ*, literally, the turning of the evening, means towards evening (Gen. 24:63; Deut. 23:11). The term *bên hā'arbayim* means between the evening, that is at dusk or at twilight (Ex. 12:6; 16:12; 30:8). *Le'eṯ 'ereḇ* means at the time of sunset, evening (Gen. 8:11). The phrase *ṣillê 'ereḇ* means shadows of evening (Jer. 6:4). *

EVENING (BECOME) – ***'āraḇ*** [verb: עָרַב <6150>; a prim. root, identical with PLEDGE (BE A) through the idea of covering with a texture] ▶ **This word means to grow dark.** It refers to the close of the day, sunset, when it is becoming dark (Judg. 19:9). It has the meaning of doing something in the evening in its causative infinitive (1 Sam. 17:16). It is used figuratively of joy turning into or becoming subdued, silenced (Is. 24:11). ¶

EVENT – Eccl. 2:14; 9:2, 3 ➔ CHANCE <4745>.

EVENTS (TURN OF) – ***nesibbāh*** [fem. noun: נְסִבָּה <5252>; fem. pass. part. of AROUND (GO, TURN) <5437>] ▶ **This word refers to the way things turn out; they change quickly, often unexpectedly or surprisingly.** Ref.: 2 Chr. 10:15; also translated cause, turn of affairs. In context God is in charge of the turn of events. ¶

EVER-FLOWING – Ps. 74:15 ➔ STRENGTH <386>.

EVERLASTING – ***'ālam*** [Aramaic masc. noun: עָלַם <5957>; corresponding to FOREVER <5769>] ▶ **This word means perpetuity, antiquity.** It can mean a perpetual period in the future (Dan. 4:3; 7:27); or a period of distant antiquity (Ezra 4:15, 19). It can also represent a period of time with no limits, either past or present (Dan. 4:34). It can stand alone (Dan. 4:3) or with the following prepositions, where it acts more like an adverb: *min* (FROM <4481>) (Dan. 2:20); and *'aḏ* (UNTIL <5705>) (Dan. 2:20; 7:18). *

EVI – ***'ewiy*** [masc. proper noun: אֱוִי <189>; prob. from DESIRE (verb) <183>]: desire, lust ▶ **A Midianite king killed by the Israelites led by Moses.** Refs.: Num. 31:8; Josh. 13:21. ¶

EVICTION – ***gerušāh*** [fem. noun: גְּרֻשָׁה <1646>; fem. pass. part. of CAST OUT <1644>] ▶ **This word refers to the injustices, specifically expulsions, committed against Israel by their leaders.** Refs.: Ezek. 45:9; also translated expropriation, exaction, dispossessing. ¶

EVIDENCE – Job 16:19 ➔ ADVOCATE <7717>.

EVIL – 1 ***mêra'*** [masc. noun: מֵרַע <4827>; from BAD (BE) <7489>] ▶ **This word is used of political and military violence and intrigue.** Ref.: Dan. 11:27; KJV: mischief. ¶
2 ***rōa'*** [masc. noun: רֹעַ <7455>; from BAD (BE) <7489>] ▶ **This word means badness.** It is used to depict the quality of meat and produce (Gen. 41:19, Jer. 24:2, 3, 8). In Genesis, the word is used to describe cows, while in Jeremiah it describes figs. Eliab, David's oldest brother, describes David as conceited with a wicked heart, for he claims that David left the sheep only to come and watch the battle (1 Sam. 17:28). *Rōa'* is also used as a reason for punishment or for the wrath of God (i.e., for evil that had been done [Deut. 28:20; Is. 1:16; Jer. 4:4; 21:12]). This word is also used to denote sadness or sorrow (Eccl. 7:3). In Ecclesiastes, the author states that sorrow is better than laughter, for a sad face is good for the heart. *
– 3 Ezra 4:12 ➔ WICKED <873> 4 Ps. 10:7 ➔ NOTHINGNESS <205> 5 See BAD <7451> 6 See INIQUITY <5771>.

EVIL (GO ON DOING) – Is. 26:10 ➔ UNJUSTLY (DEAL) <5765>.

EVIL GOSSIP – Ezek. 36:3 ➔ REPORT (BAD) <1681>.

EVIL MAN – Job 18:21; Zeph. 3:5 ➔ WICKED <5767>.

EVIL REPORT – See REPORT (BAD) <1681>.

EVIL-MERODACH – ***ʾwiyl mᵉrōḏaḵ*** [masc. proper noun: אֱוִיל מְרֹדַךְ <192>; of Chaldean deriv. and prob. meaning soldier of Merodach] ▶ **A Babylonian king who released Jehoiachin king of Judah from prison.** Refs.: 2 Kgs. 25:27; Jer. 52:31; also translated Awel-Marduk. ¶

EWE – ***rāḥēl*** [fem. noun: רָחֵל <7353>; from an unused root meaning to journey] ▶ **This word refers to a female sheep.** Refs.: Gen. 31:38; 32:14. It is used in a simile comparing the bride's teeth to a flock of white, clean ewes (Song 6:6). In a more famous simile, the Lord's Suffering Servant is compared to a silent sheep before its shearers (Is. 53:7). ¶

EXACT – [1] 2 Kgs. 23:35; Is. 58:3 ➔ OPPRESS <5065> [2] Neh. 5:7; Ps. 89:22 ➔ DEBT (IN) <5378> [3] Neh. 5:10, 11 ➔ LEND <5383>.

EXACTION – Ezek. 45:9 ➔ EVICTION <1646>.

EXACTOR – Is. 60:17 ➔ OPPRESS <5065>.

EXALT – [1] ***sālal*** [verb: סָלַל <5549>; a prim. root] ▶ **This word means to raise up, to build up, to lift up.** It means to hold someone or something in a position of a high or excessively high reputation or worth: Pharaoh over God's people (Ex. 9:17). It also means to raise something up, for something to rise up: God's troops (Job 19:12); one's assailants (Job 30:12); a song of praise to God (Ps. 68:4); a person exalted by wisdom (Prov. 4:8); an upward path of life, a lifting up (Prov. 15:19; Jer. 18:15); a roadway for God's people (Is. 57:14). Other refs.: Is. 62:10; Jer. 50:26. ¶

[2] ***rûm*** [verb: רוּם <7311>; a prim. root] ▶ **This word means to lift up; to be elevated.** It indicates that something is literally raised up high (Gen. 7:17; Job 22:12); or indicates the act of raising, picking up something (Gen. 14:22; Ex. 14:16; Josh. 4:5; Ezek. 10:16); setting it up (Gen. 31:45; Ezra 9:9). It describes the process of something growing (Is. 1:2; Ezek. 31:4); or of persons being promoted, raised up in their positions (1 Sam. 2:7; 1 Kgs. 14:7). It is used often of God's being exalted (Ex. 15:2; 2 Sam. 22:47; Ps. 30:1; 99:2; 108:5; Is. 33:10). It describes the haughtiness and boastfulness of people: their hearts (Deut. 8:14); eyes (Ps. 18:27); attitudes, with an uplifted hand, arrogant (Job 38:15). The antichrist figure exalts and lifts up himself (Dan. 11:36). It describes the presentation of a sacrifice (Lev. 2:9). It can have the sense of removing something, abolishing it (Dan. 8:11). *

[3] ***rûm*** [Aramaic verb: רוּם <7313>; corresponding to <7311> above] ▶ **This word literally means to raise up; it is also translated to extol, to set up, to elevate.** Used of God, it means to exalt Him (Dan. 4:37). It refers to honoring or promoting a person (Dan. 5:19); it indicates a person's heart being lifted up, becoming arrogant (Dan. 5:20); or persons lifting themselves up against God (Dan. 5:23). ¶

– [4] Job 10:16 ➔ RISE <1342> [5] Job 36:24 ➔ GREAT (MAKE) <7679> [6] Prov. 25:6 ➔ HONOR (verb) <1921>.

EXALT ONESELF – ***miṯnaśśēʾ*** [masc. noun: מִתְנַשֵּׂא <4984>; from CARRY <5375> (in the sense of to lift)] ▶ **This word refers to a person who elevates himself or herself.** It means to show oneself as great, to lift up oneself for some purpose: Adonijah (1 Kgs. 1:5; NIV: to put oneself forward). It is used of the Lord's self-exaltation over everything (1 Chr. 29:11). ¶

EXALTATION – Job 22:29 ➔ PRIDE <1466>.

EXALTED – [1] ***rāmam*** [verb: רָמַם <7426>; a prim. root] ▶

a. This word means to be lifted up. It can have the sense of to rise up from (*min* <4480>), to get away from (Num. 16:45).

It has the meaning in context of something literally rising up (Ezek. 10:15, 17, 19). In other contexts, it is used figuratively of a person's exaltation or high standing in society (Job 24:24). It is used figuratively of the Lord's arising, acting (Is. 33:10).
b. This word means to be full; it is also translated to breed. It indicates that something is decaying, rotting. Rotting with worms (*tôlā'îm*) indicates something is full of, seething with worms (Ex. 16:20). In context it refers to manna rotting and being full of worms. ¶
[2] ***śaggiy'*** [adj.: שַׂגִּיא <7689>; from GREAT (MAKE) <7679>] ► **This word means and is also translated great, excellent.** It refers to such greatness and magnificence as to put someone in an exalted or highly uplifted state, especially God (Job 36:26; 37:23). ¶

EXALTED (BE) – [1] ***gāḇah*** [verb: גָּבַהּ <1361>; a prim. root] ► **This verb means to be high, to be elevated; to be arrogant.** It describes anything that is literally tall or high, such as a tree or vine (Ezek. 19:11); the heavens (Job 35:5; Ps. 103:11; Is. 55:9), people (1 Sam. 10:23). It is used figuratively to refer to persons or things of high or great dignity: God (Is. 5:16); God's ways (Is. 55:9); the Servant of the Lord will be high and exalted before Him (Is. 52:13); kings who are exalted by the Lord (Job 36:7). It refers to pride or being lofty, literally exalted in heart, in either a good sense (2 Chr. 17:6) or more often in a bad sense. One can be lofty or haughty (Ps. 131:1; Prov. 18:12). It has the same meaning without being combined with heart (Is. 3:16; Jer. 13:15; Ezek. 16:50). In certain uses of the word, it means to make high, raise up, or exalt various things: trees (Ezek. 17:24); a wall (2 Chr. 33:14); a gate (Prov. 17:19), especially to lift up the humble or lowly (Ezek. 21:26) according to God's judgments; flames or sparks of fire (Job 5:7). *
[2] ***śagaḇ*** [verb: שָׂגַב <7682>; a prim. root] ► **This word indicates to be raised; to be high; to defend.** It refers to physical size indicating great height: city walls (Deut. 2:36; Is. 30:13). In a figurative sense, it indicates a high, impregnable city or habitation (Is. 26:5); or God's exalted name or person (Job 36:22; Is. 12:4). Its figurative use is developed most fully: of high inaccessible knowledge (Ps. 139:6); of the security of God's high name (Prov. 18:10, 11). Trust in the Lord results in the exaltation of a person (Prov. 29:25). It refers to persons' advancement or promotion, setting them on high (Job 5:11); or of their being placed in a place of safety (Ps. 20:1; 59:1; 69:29). To know God's name leads to security (Ps. 91:14); and the Lord secures the poor and needy (Ps. 107:41). *

EXALTED (BE HIGHLY) – Ex. 15:1, 21 ➔ RISE <1342>.

EXAMINE – [1] Neh. 2:13, 15 ➔ INSPECT <7663> [2] Eccl. 9:1 ➔ DECLARE <952>.

EXCEEDING – Dan. 2:31; 3:22; 7:7, 19 ➔ EXCELLENT <3493>.

EXCEEDINGLY – Dan. 3:22; 7:7, 19 ➔ EXCELLENT <3493>.

EXCELLENCE – [1] Ps. 68:34 ➔ MAJESTY <1346> [2] Eccl. 7:12 ➔ PROFIT (noun) <3504>.

EXCELLENCY – [1] Deut. 33:26, 29; Ps. 68:34 ➔ MAJESTY <1346> [2] Job 20:6 ➔ LOFTINESS <7863> [3] Eccl. 7:12 ➔ PROFIT (noun) <3504>.

EXCELLENT – [1] ***yattiyr*** [Aramaic adj.: יַתִּיר <3493>; corresponding to JATTIR <3492>] ► **This word designates something outstanding. Its basic sense is excellence, superiority.** It refers to the splendor of the statue in Daniel 2:31 as extraordinary, outstanding. It has the sense of very or extremely (Dan. 3:22; 7:7, 19); surpassing, exceeding (Dan. 4:36); special or excellent (Dan. 5:12, 14). Daniel had an excellent spirit (Dan. 6:3) and possessed superb wisdom. ¶
– [2] Job 37:23 ➔ EXALTED <7689> [3] Ps. 8:1, 9 ➔ MIGHTY <117> [4] Ps. 36:7 ➔ PRECIOUS <3368> [5] Prov. 8:6 ➔ LEADER <5057>.

EXCELLENT (BE) – Ps. 45:2 ➔ BEAUTIFUL (BE, MAKE ONESELF) <3302>.

EXCELLENT THINGS – Is. 12:5 ➔ MAJESTY <1348>.

EXCELS (WHO) – Prov. 22:29 ➔ SKILLED <4106>.

EXCEPT – 1 ***zûlāh*** [fem. noun: זוּלָה <2108>; from LAVISH <2107> (properly scattering, i.e., removal)] ▶ **This word functions as a preposition or conjunction meaning also apart from, besides.** It regularly acts as a preposition meaning except, besides (Deut. 4:12; 1 Kgs. 3:18); preceded by a negative here, it translates as only, but (Ps. 18:31; Is. 45:21; Hos. 13:4). It functions as a conjunction, except that, in Joshua 11:13. *
– 2 Gen. 43:3; Num. 11:6; Is. 10:4 ➔ NOT <1115>.

EXCEPTIONAL – Dan. 6:3 ➔ EXCELLENT <3493>.

EXCESS – Ezek. 16:49 ➔ FULLNESS <7653>.

EXCHANGE (noun) – ***t^{e}mûrāh*** [fem. noun: תְּמוּרָה <8545>; from EXCHANGE <4171>] ▶ **This word usually refers to the trading of one item for another.** In Leviticus, it is used to give rules for the exchange of animals and land that were dedicated to the Lord (Lev. 27:10, 33). In Ruth, the word indicates the Israelite custom of exchanging items to confirm a vow (Ruth 4:7). In Job, this word describes financial transactions (Job 20:18; 28:17). This word may be translated recompense in Job 15:31, where it describes the natural result of a life trusting in vanity. ¶

EXCHANGE (verb) – ***mûr*** [verb: מוּר <4171>; a prim. root] ▶ **This word means to change, to replace.** It indicates replacing one thing with another (Lev. 27:10, 33; Ezek. 48:14; Mic. 2:4); or an actual turning of one thing into another (Ps. 46:2; Hos. 4:7). It is used of persons changing their attitudes or decisions (Ps. 15:4). The Israelites sinned gravely by replacing the Lord with an idol of an ox or calf (Ps. 106:20; Jer. 2:11). Not changing is to remain the same (Jer. 48:11). ¶

EXCLUDE – 1 2 Chr. 26:21 ➔ CUT (verb) <1504> 2 Is. 66:5 ➔ DRIVE <5077>.

EXCREMENT – 1 ***tṣêʼāh*** [fem. noun: צֵאָה <6627>; from GO OUT <3318>] ▶ **This word refers to what is passed out of the bowel, excreted; it is also translated refuse, dung, waste.** It was unclean and to be covered with dirt immediately (Deut. 23:13). Ezekiel was commanded to eat human dung to represent the uncleanness of Jerusalem and Judah; but the Lord relented from this harsh command (Ezek. 4:12). ¶
– 2 2 Kgs. 18:27; Is. 36:12 ➔ DUNG <2716> 3 Ezek. 4:12, 15 ➔ DUNG <1561>.

EXCUSE ME – ***biy*** [particle used as an interj.: בִּי <994>; perhaps from <1158> (in the sense of asking)] ▶ **This word also means please, oh. It is intended to express politeness, pardon, deep concern with great respect toward the one spoken to.** It is used in addressing noble men, such as Jacob, Joseph, Moses, Eli, Solomon (Gen. 43:20; 44:18; Num. 12:11; 1 Sam. 1:26; 1 Kgs. 3:17, 26); divine beings, the angel of the Lord (Judg. 6:13, 15); but most often the Lord (Ex. 4:10, 13; Josh. 7:8; Judg. 13:8). ¶

EXECUTE – Num. 25:4 ➔ ALIENATED (BE) <3363>.

EXEMPT – 1 1 Chr. 9:33 ➔ FREE <6359> 2 1 Chr. 9:33 ➔ OPEN <6362>.

EXERT ONESELF – Dan. 6:14 ➔ LABOR (verb) <7712>.

EXHAUSTED – 1 Gen. 25:29, 30 ➔ WEARY (adj.) <5889> 2 Judg. 8:15; 2 Sam. 16:2 ➔ WEARY (adj.) <3287>.

EXHAUSTED (BE) – [1] ***pāgar*** [verb: פָּגַר <6296>; a prim. root] ▶ **This word describes the extreme physical and mental tiredness of persons, especially when pursuing soldiers.** Refs.: 1 Sam. 30:10, 21; also translated to be faint, to be weary. ¶
– [2] Judg. 4:21; 1 Sam. 14:31; 2 Sam. 21:15 ➔ WEARY (BE) <5888> [3] Jer. 51:30 ➔ DRY UP <5405>.

EXILE – [1] Is. 51:14 ➔ CAPTIVE EXILE <6808> [2] Is. 56:8 ➔ DRIVE <1760> [3] See CAPTIVITY <1473>.

EXILE, EXILES – Is. 20:4; 45:13; Jer. 24:5; 28:4; 2 Kgs. 25:27; Ezek. 1:2; 33:21 ➔ CAPTIVITY <1546>.

EXILES – Dan. 2:25; 5:13; 6:13 ➔ CAPTIVITY <1547>.

EXIST – See BE <3426>.

EXIT – Ezek. 42:11 ➔ GOING OUT, GOING FORTH <4161>.

EXPANSE – ***rāqiya'*** [masc. noun: רָקִיעַ <7549>; from BEAT <7554> (in the sense of to stretch out)] ▶ **This word means the firmament, an extended surface. Literally, it refers to a great expanse and, in particular, the vault of the heavens above the earth.** It denotes the literal sky that stretches from horizon to horizon (Gen. 1:6–8); the heavens above that contain the sun, moon, and stars (Gen. 1:14); or any vaulted ceiling or expanse that stands above (Ezek. 10:1). By extension, the psalmist uses the word to refer to the infinite and sweeping power of the Lord (Ps. 150:1). *

EXPANSE, VAST EXPANSE – Job 38:18 ➔ BROAD PLACE <7338>.

EXPECTATION – [1] Job 41:9; Prov. 11:7 (ESV) ➔ HOPE (noun) <8431> [2] Is. 20:5, 6; Zech. 9:5 ➔ HOPE (noun) <4007>.

EXPEL – [1] Josh. 23:5 ➔ PUSH <1920> [2] Is. 27:8 ➔ REMOVE <1898>.

EXPENSE – Ezra 6:4, 8 ➔ COST <5313>.

EXPERIENCE (LEARN BY) – Gen. 30:27 ➔ DIVINATION (PRACTICE) <5172>.

EXPLAIN – [1] ***bā'ar*** [verb: בָּאַר <874>; a prim. root] ▶ **This word means to expose; it is also translated to declare, to expound, to write, to inscribe.** It is used to describe Moses' oral exposition of the Law given at Sinai (Deut. 1:5). It also indicates a written process of clarifying and recording a revelation from God (Deut. 27:8; Hab. 2:2). ¶
– [2] Num. 15:34 ➔ CLEAR (BE, MAKE) <6567> [3] Job 15:17 ➔ SHOW <2331> [4] Eccl. 9:1 ➔ DECLARE <952> [5] Dan. 5:12 ➔ EXPLANATION <263>.

EXPLANATION – [1] ***'aḥ^{a}wāyah*** [Aramaic fem. noun: אַחֲוָיָה <263>; corresponding to DECLARATION <262>] ▶ **This word refers to the elucidation of riddles or enigmas.** Ref.: Dan. 5:12; also translated showing, interpreting, to explain. ¶
– [2] Eccl. 7:25, 27 ➔ SCHEME (noun) <2808> [3] Eccl. 8:1 ➔ INTERPRETATION <6592>.

EXPLOIT – Is. 58:3 ➔ OPPRESS <5065>.

EXPOSE – [1] Lev. 20:18, 19; Zeph. 2:14 ➔ EMPTY (verb) <6168> [2] Jer. 13:22 ➔ VIOLENCE (DO) <2554>.

EXPOSED – Gen. 30:37 ➔ EXPOSING <4286>.

EXPOSING – ***maḥśōp̱*** [masc. noun: מַחְשֹׂף <4286>; from STRIP <2834>] ▶ **This word indicates laying bare, peeling.** It describes Jacob's carefully removing small strips of bark from fresh poplar rods or sticks (Gen. 30:37; also translated exposed, made appear). ¶

EXPOUND – Deut. 1:5 ➔ EXPLAIN <874>.

EXPRESSION – Is. 3:9 ➔ LOOK (noun) <1971>.

EXPROPRIATION – Ezek. 45:9 ➔ EVICTION <1646>.

EXTEND – [1] Gen. 9:27 ➔ ENLARGE <6601> [2] Esther 4:11; 5:2; 8:4 ➔ HOLD OUT <3447> [3] Is. 58:10 ➔ OBTAIN <6329>.

EXTENSION – Dan. 7:12 ➔ LENGTHENING <754>.

EXTINCT (BE) – [1] ***zā'ak*** [verb: זָעַךְ <2193>; a prim. root] ▶ **This word means to be put out, to be extinguished; it is also translated to be cut short.** It refers to the conclusion or ending of Job's life, his days, because of his calamities and illnesses (Job 17:1). ¶
– [2] Is. 43:17 ➔ EXTINGUISH <1846>.

EXTINCTION – Job 31:29 ➔ DISASTER <6365>.

EXTINGUISH – [1] ***dā'ak*** [verb: דָּעַךְ <1846>; a prim. root] ▶ **This verb means to end something; it is also translated to quench, to consume, to go out, to put out, to snuff out, to be extinct.** It is used in a simile to depict the enemies of the psalmist and the Lord extinguishing the wicked like a wick (Ps. 118:12; Is. 43:17) or in the natural course of their lives (Job 18:5, 6; 21:17; Prov. 13:9; 20:20; 24:20). It describes watercourses drying up or vanishing (Job 6:17; KJV: to be consumed). ¶
– [2] 2 Sam. 14:7; Is. 43:17 ➔ QUENCH <3518>.

EXTINGUISHED (BE) – Job 17:1 ➔ EXTINCT (BE) <2193>.

EXTOL – [1] Job 36:24 ➔ GREAT (MAKE) <7679> [2] Dan. 4:37 ➔ EXALT <7313>.

EXTORTION – [1] Prov. 28:8 ➔ PROFIT (noun) <8636> [2] Prov. 28:16 ➔ OPPRESSIONS <4642> [3] Jer. 22:17 ➔ VIOLENCE <4835> [4] Hab. 2:6 ➔ PLEDGE (noun) <5671> a.

EXTORTIONER – [1] Ps. 109:11 ➔ LEND <5383> [2] Is. 16:4 ➔ OPPRESSOR <4160>.

EXTRAORDINARY – Dan. 2:31; 5:12, 14; 6:3 ➔ EXCELLENT <3493>.

EXULT – [1] 1 Sam. 2:1; 1 Chr. 16:32; Ps. 5:11; 9:2; 25:2; 68:3 ➔ REJOICE <5970> [2] Job 6:10 ➔ REJOICE <5539> a. [3] Ps. 89:16; Is. 61:10 ➔ REJOICE <1523> [4] Is. 13:3 ➔ REJOICING <5947>.

EXULTATION – [1] Hos. 9:1 ➔ JOY <1524> [2] Hab. 3:14 ➔ REJOICING <5951>.

EXULTING – Job 20:5 ➔ JOYFUL SHOUT <7445>.

EYE (noun) – [1] ***'ayin, 'êynayim*** [fem. noun: עַיִן, עֵינַיִם <5869>; prob. a prim. word] ▶ **This Hebrew word also means a spring, a fountain. It is used to refer to either an aperture or a source.** It is used to signify the physical organ of sight (Prov. 20:12); the providential oversight of the Lord (Ps. 33:18); and a water well (Gen. 16:7; Ex. 15:27). By extension, it refers to being in the presence of another (Jer. 32:12); the visible surface of the earth (Num. 22:5); the human face (1 Kgs. 20:38; 2 Kgs. 9:30); and the general appearance of something (1 Sam. 16:7; Ezek. 1:4). In a figurative sense, the eye was seen as the avenue of temptation (Job 31:7); the scope of personal judgment or opinion (Judg. 17:6); and the source of self-assessment (Prov. 26:5). *
[2] ***'ayin*** [Aramaic masc. noun: עַיִן <5870>; corresponding to <5869> above] ▶ **This word refers to the organ of sight by which a person sees.** It is used figuratively of God's eye being on His people (Ezra 5:5), i.e., He watches them carefully, guarding them. To raise one's eyes heavenward toward God is to perform an act of humility and recognition of God as God (Dan. 4:34). The word is used in figurative, apocalyptic language to indicate that what is not human, a horn in appearance, is indeed a symbol for a person (Dan. 7:8, 20); the little horn had human-like eyes. ¶

EYE (KEEP A CLOSE) – 1 Sam. 18:9 ➔ EYE (verb) <5770>.

EYE (verb) – ***'āwan*** [verb: עָוַן <5770>; denom. from EYE (noun) <5869>] ▶ **This word indicates to look askance, to eye with suspicion.** It means to observe something with a critical and questioning attitude (1 Sam. 18:9). ¶

EYEBROW – Lev. 14:9 ➔ BACK <1354>.

EYELID – ***'ap'ap*** [masc. noun: עַפְעַף <6079>; from FLY (verb) <5774>] ▶
a. This word refers to the two coverings of flesh that open and close over a person's eyes. The interesting simile of Leviathan's eyelids mention the eyelids of the dawn (Job 41:18). The word refers to God's sight or watchful eyes (Ps. 11:4). Sleep is the function of closed eyelids (Ps. 132:4; Prov. 6:4). Eyelids can be used for flirtation or for enticement (Prov. 4:25; 6:25). They can give forth an attitude of arrogance (Prov. 30:13); or display sorrow and weeping (Jer. 9:18). Other ref.: Job 16:16. ¶
b. A masculine noun indicating the opening rays of the sun. In a metaphor, it is used of the "eyelid" of the sun beginning to open, the morning light breaking through (Job 3:9; also translated dawning). ¶

EYES – Ps. 119:6, 15 ➔ to have the eyes fixed ➔ LOOK (verb) <5027>.

EYES (PUT OUT THE) – ***'āwar*** [verb: עָוַר <5786>; a prim. root (rather denom. from SKIN <5785> through the idea of a film over the eyes)] ▶ **This Hebrew word is used of putting out persons' eyes, blinding them.** Refs.: 2 Kgs. 25:7; Jer. 39:7; 52:11. In a figurative sense, it indicates the blinding of officials' eyes to injustice by means of bribes (Ex. 23:8; Deut. 16:19). ¶

EZBAI – ***'ezbay*** [masc. proper noun: אֶזְבַּי <229>; prob. from HYSSOP <231>]: hyssop-like, which shines ▶ **Father of one of the mighty men of David.** Ref.: 1 Chr. 11:37. ¶

EZBON – ***'eṣbôn*** [masc. proper noun: אֶצְבּוֹן <675>; of uncertain deriv.]: splendor, honor ▶
a. A son of Gad. Ref.: Gen. 46:16. ¶
b. A grandson of Benjamin. Ref.: 1 Chr. 7:7. ¶

EZEKIEL – ***yᵉḥezqê'l*** [masc. proper noun: יְחֶזְקֵאל <3168>; from STRONG (BE) <2388> and GOD <410>]: God strengthens ▶
a. He was a priest and the son of Buzi. Ref.: Ezek. 1:3. He was exiled in Babylon in ca. 597 B.C. He was thirty years old when God called him to prophesy (ca. 593 B.C.). He himself became a sign to the people (Ezek. 24:24). He had a vision of the corruption of God's people and the Temple (Ezek. 8) and predicted the fall of Jerusalem to Babylon. He also envisioned the final defeat of Israel's enemies (Ezek. 37–39) and the establishment of a New Jerusalem and new Temple where God would dwell permanently (Ezek. 48:35). ¶
b. He was a head of a priestly line. Ref.: 1 Chr. 24:16. ¶

EZEL – ***'ezel*** [proper noun: אֶזֶל <237>; from GO <235>]: departure, separation ▶ **A memorial stone in Palestine.** Ref.: 1 Sam. 20:19. ¶

EZEM – ***'eṣem*** [proper noun: עֶצֶם <6107>; from the same as BONE <6106>]: bone ▶ **One of the cities that became part of the inheritance of Simeon.** Refs.: Josh. 15:29; 19:3; 1 Chr. 4:29. ¶

EZER – [1] ***'ēṣer*** [masc. proper noun: אֵצֶר <687>; from STORE (verb) <686>]: treasure ▶ **One of the chiefs of the Horites in the land of Edom.** Refs.: Gen. 36:21, 27, 30; 1 Chr. 1:38, 42. ¶
[2] ***'ezer*** [masc. proper noun: עֶזֶר <5827>; from HELP (verb) <5826>]: help ▶
a. An Ephraimite. Ref.: 1 Chr. 7:21. ¶
b. A priest. Ref.: Neh. 12:42. ¶
[3] ***'ēzer*** [masc. proper noun: עֵזֶר <5829>; the same as HELP (noun) <5828>]: help ▶
a. A builder of the wall. Ref.: Neh. 3:19. ¶
b. A Judaite. Ref.: 1 Chr. 4:4. ¶
c. One of David's mighty men. Ref.: 1 Chr. 12:9. ¶
d. A priest. Ref.: Neh. 12:42. ¶

EZION GEBER – ***'eṣyôn geḇer*** [proper noun: עֶצְיוֹן גֶּבֶר <6100>; from BACKBONE <6096> and MAN <1397>]: the backbone of a man ▶ **This was one of the sites where Israel encamped.** Refs.: Num. 33:35, 36. It was located in the northern part of the Gulf of Elath/Aquaba (1 Kgs. 9:26), and Solomon outfitted a fleet of commercial ships there. Jehosaphat did the same, but his ships were destroyed, evidently by a storm (1 Kgs. 22:48). Other refs.: Deut. 2:8; 2 Chr. 8:17; 20:36. ¶

EZNITE – ***'êṣen*** [proper noun: עֵצֶן <6112>; from an unused root meaning to be sharp or strong] ▶ **A designation given to Azino, one of David's strong men.** Ref.: 2 Sam. 23:8. ¶

EZRA – 1 ***'ezrā'*** [masc. proper noun: עֶזְרָא <5830>; a variation of HELP (noun) <5833>]: help, assistance ▶ **He was the scribe, mighty in the Law of Moses (Ezra 7:8–10), who returned from the exile (458 B.C.; Ezra 7:1–10) and helped establish the fledgling religious community on the basis of the Law of Moses.** He cleansed the priesthood (Ezra 9, 10) and read the Law at the Water Gate (Neh. 8:2–18; ca. 444 B.C.) to the residents of Jerusalem and the surrounding areas. He also celebrated with Nehemiah the dedication of the rebuilt wall of Jerusalem (Neh. 12:26–36). *

2 ***'ezrā'*** [masc. proper noun: עֶזְרָא <5831>; corresponding to <5830> above]: help, assistance ▶ **The Aramaic for the Hebrew scribe's name, Ezra.** It appears only in Aramaic portions of Ezra (Ezra 7:12, 21, 25). The meaning is the same in both languages. ¶

3 ***'ezrāh*** [masc. proper noun: עֶזְרָה <5834>; the same as HELP (noun) <5833>]: help, assistance ▶ **A descendant of Judah.** Ref.: 1 Chr. 4:17. ¶

EZRAHITE – ***'ezrāḥiy*** [masc. proper noun: אֶזְרָחִי <250>; patron. from ZERAH <2226>]: lifted ▶ **A descendant of Zerach of the tribe of Judah.** Refs.: 1 Kgs. 4:31; Ps. 88:1; 89:1. ¶

EZRI – ***'ezriy*** [masc. proper noun: עֶזְרִי <5836>; from HELP (noun) <5828>]: help (of God) ▶ **He was over those who did the work of the field for tilling the soil under the reign of David.** Ref.: 1 Chr. 27:26. ¶

F

FABRIC – [1] Judg. 16:13, 14 ➔ WEB <4545> [2] Ezek. 27:24 ➔ CLOTHES <1545> [3] Amos 3:12 ➔ DAMASCUS <1833> b.

FACE (noun) – [1] *ᵃnap̱* [Aramaic masc. noun: אֲנַף <600>; corresponding to NOSE <639> (only in the plur. as a sing.)] ▶ **This word means the front of the head, and also a facial expression.** It is used in a figurative expression to fall on one's face in obeisance (Dan. 2:46), to honor or worship. It also refers literally to a person's face (Dan. 3:19); it is also translated visage. ¶
[2] ***pāneh, pāniym*** [masc. plur. noun: פָּנֶה, פָּנִים <6440>; from TURN (verb) <6437>] ▶ **Although the literal meaning of face is possible (Gen. 43:31; Lev. 13:41; 1 Kgs. 19:13), most of the time this word occurs in a figurative, idiomatic phrase.** Face can be a substitute for the entire person (Ex. 33:14, 15); or it can be a reflection of the person's mood or attitude: defiant (Jer. 5:3); ruthless (Deut. 28:50); joyful (Job 29:24); humiliated (2 Sam. 19:5); terrified (Is. 13:8); displeased (Gen. 4:5). It is also used to indicate direction (Gen. 31:21); or purpose (Jer. 42:15, 17). This noun also designates the top or surface of something: the ground (Gen. 2:6; 4:14); a field (Is. 28:25); or water (Gen. 1:2). It also connotes the front of something, like a pot (Jer. 1:13); or an army (Joel 2:20). With various prepositions, *pānîm* takes on the nature of a particle and expresses such concepts as upon (Ex. 23:17; Lev. 14:53); before a place (Num. 8:22); before a time (Ezek. 42:12; Amos 1:1); in the presence of (Esther 1:10). *
– [3] Dan. 5:6, 9, 10; 7:28 ➔ BRIGHTNESS <2122>.

FACE (verb) – 1 Sam. 14:5 ➔ PILLAR <4690>.

FADE – [1] Lev. 13:6 ➔ DIM (BE) <3543> a. [2] Lev. 13:6, 21, 26, 28, 39, 56 ➔ DARK <3544> [3] 2 Sam. 22:46; Ps. 18:45; Is. 1:30; 24:4; 28:1; Jer. 8:13; Ezek. 47:12 ➔ WITHER <5034>.

FADE, FADE AWAY – Job 14:22; 18:16; Ps. 37:2 ➔ CUT DOWN <5243>.

FAIL – [1] ***'āpês*** [verb: אָפֵס <656>; a prim. root] ▶ **This word indicates coming to an end, being used up, gone.** It refers to a depletion of money (Gen. 47:15, 16) or the ending of God's promise (Ps. 77:8: to cease, to vanish). Or it can indicate the completion of the Lord's judgments (Is. 16:4; 29:20). ¶
– [2] Ezra 6:9 ➔ NEGLECT (noun) <7960> [3] Esther 9:28 ➔ CONSUME, BE CONSUMED <5486> [4] Job 14:11 ➔ GO <235> [5] Job 21:10 ➔ ABHOR <1602> [6] Ps. 6:7; Job 32:15 ➔ MOVE <6275> [7] Ps. 12:1 ➔ VANISH <6461> [8] Is. 19:3 ➔ EMPTY (MAKE) <1238> [9] Is. 19:5; 41:17; Jer. 51:30 ➔ DRY UP <5405> [10] Is. 59:15; Zeph. 3:5 ➔ LACK, LACKING (BE) <5737> [11] Joel 1:10, 12 ➔ LANGUISH <535>.

FAILING – ***killāyôn*** [masc. noun: כִּלָּיוֹן <3631>; from FINISH <3615>] ▶ **This word refers to a weakening or blurring of one's eyes.** In context it was one of the Lord's curses on a disobedient people in exile (Deut. 28:65; NIV: weary with longing). It is used of the destruction of many Israelites in judgments from the Lord (Is. 10:22; KJV: consumption). ¶

FAILURE – Job 21:10 ➔ ABHOR <1602>.

FAINT (adj.) – [1] ***dāweh*** [adj.: דָּוֶה <1739>; from MENSTRUATION <1738>] ▶ **An adjective referring to a woman's menstrual state, menstrual cloth.** The word describes the weakened state of the prophet Jeremiah because of the devastations of Jerusalem (Lam. 1:13), likewise concerning his faint heart (Lam. 5:17). It describes the menstrual flow which rendered a woman impure (Lev. 15:33: indisposed, sick, unwell, ill). Intercourse was considered unclean during the menstrual state or period (Lev.

20:18: during her sickness, having her sickness, during her menstrual period, during her monthly period, menstruous). It refers to an impure thing or cloth to be thrown away (Is. 30:22: unclean, impure, menstruous, menstrual). ¶
– 2 Ps. 6:2 ➔ WEAK (adj.) <536> 3 Is. 40:29 ➔ WEARY <3287> 4 Is. 61:3 ➔ DARK <3544> 5 Jer. 8:18; Lam. 1:22 ➔ SICK <1742>.

FAINT (BE) – 1 1 Sam. 30:10, 21 ➔ EXHAUSTED (BE) <6296> 2 Is. 15:4 ➔ TREMBLE <3415>.

FAINT (BE, BECOME, GROW, WAX) – 1 Sam. 14:28, 31; 2 Sam. 21:15; Jer. 4:31 ➔ WEARY (BE) <5888>.

FAINT (BE, MAKE) – ***rāḵaḵ*** [verb: רָכַךְ <7401>; a prim. root] ▶ **This word also means to be fainthearted or timid; to be tender, to be weak, to be soft.** It indicates that a person lacks resolve and needs to be strong in the face of danger (Deut. 20:3, 8; Is. 7:4; Jer. 51:46); it is also translated to be penitent, to be responsive. It refers, on the other hand, to a tenderness, a humility of heart, that is a strength before God (2 Kgs. 22:19; 2 Chr. 34:27). God can make a person weak of heart and frail (Job 23:16; KJV: to make soft). Soft words can be deceptive, however (Ps. 55:21; NIV: to be soothing). It refers to the healing of a bruise with oil but with reference to the healing of Israel's spiritual and moral corruption (Is. 1:6: to soften, to sooth, to mollify). *

FAINT (verb) – 1 ***yā'ēp̱*** [verb: יָעֵף <3286>; a prim. root] ▶
a. This word indicates exhaustion, fainting; fatigued, tired out. It is used in a famous assertion declaring that the Lord does not become tired or weary, while even youths do so (Is. 40:28, 30). Yet those who look to the Lord share in His inner spiritual strength and renewal (Is. 40:31). It is used of a strong iron worker who exhausts himself constructing a vain, useless idol (Is. 44:12; cf. Jer. 51:58, 64; Hab. 2:13). In context it depicts the tireless lust of a female donkey in heat (Jer. 2:24). It possibly describes Gabriel's weary flight to Daniel in prayer (Dan. 9:21; but see b. and WEARINESS <3288>. ¶
b. A verb meaning to move swiftly. It is employed in Daniel 9:21 to describe the swift flight of the angel Gabriel, according to more recent translations (see a., and Dan. 9:21). However, see WEARINESS <3288> also. ¶
2 ***'ālap̱*** [verb: עָלַף <5968>; a prim. root] ▶ **This word means to grow weak.** It also means to grow weary to the point of losing consciousness or despairing utterly (Is. 51:20); from thirst (Amos 8:13); or sunstroke (Jon. 4:8; also translated to grow faint, to become faint, to be faint). See also COVER (verb) <5968>. ¶
– 3 Gen. 47:13 ➔ LANGUISH <3856> 4 Jer. 45:3 ➔ WEARY (verb) <3021> 5 Ezek. 21:7 ➔ DIM (BE) <3543> a.

FAINT FOR – ***kāmah*** [verb: כָּמַהּ <3642>; a prim. root] ▶ **A word indicating to long for, to yearn for.** It is used with flesh as its subject to indicate the longing of the psalmist's flesh (body?) for the Lord (Ps. 63:1). ¶

FAINT, FAINT (GROW, BE) – Ps. 102:1; Is. 57:16 ➔ TURN (verb) <5848> b.

FAINTED – ***'ulpeh*** [masc. noun: עֻלְפֶּה <5969>; from COVER (verb) <5968>] ▶ **This word refers to something withered; it is also translated wilted.** It describes the wilting and drying up of trees because of a lack of water (Ezek. 31:15). ¶

FAINTHEARTED (BE) – 1 Deut. 20:3, 8; Is. 7:4; Jer. 51:46 ➔ FAINT (BE, MAKE) <7401> 2 Josh. 2:9, 24; Jer. 49:23 ➔ MELT AWAY <4127>.

FAINTING – Is. 61:3 ➔ DARK <3544>.

FAINTNESS – ***mōreḵ*** [masc. noun: מֹרֶךְ <4816>; perhaps from FAINT (BE) <7401>] ▶ **This word refers to weakness, fearfulness.** It refers to a shattered state of stability, a feeling of frailty, an emotion and state experienced by those God would drive into exile (Lev. 26:36). ¶

FAIR – [1] ***šiprāh*** [fem. noun: שִׁפְרָה <8235>; from BEAUTIFUL (BE) <8231>] ▶ **This word also indicates brightness, clearness.** It refers to making something appear clean, neat, clear (of visibility). God clears the skies with His breath (Job 26:13). ¶
– [2] Gen. 12:11, 14; 2 Sam. 13:1; Esther 2:7 ➔ BEAUTIFUL <3303> [3] Dan. 4:12, 21 ➔ BEAUTIFUL <8209>.

FAIR (BE, MAKE ONESELF) – Ps. 45:2; Song 4:10; 7:6; Jer. 4:30; Ezek. 31:7 ➔ BEAUTIFUL (BE, MAKE ONESELF) <3302>.

FAIRS – Ezek. 27:12, 14, 16, 19, 22, 27 ➔ WARES <5801>.

FAITH – Deut. 32:20; Is. 26:2 ➔ FAITHFUL <529>.

FAITH (BREAK) – Ex. 21:8 ➔ DECEITFULLY (DEAL) <898>.

FAITHFUL – [1] ***'ēmûn*** [masc. noun: אֵמוּן <529>; from NURSE (verb) <539>] ▶ **This word is translated as an adjective (faithful, honest, trustworthy) and as a noun (faith, faithfulness, truth).** It is used to signify the rare and beneficial quality of trustworthiness in an individual (Prov. 13:17; 14:5; 20:6); the character of a righteous nation (Is. 26:2); and in a negative sense, a fundamental lack of dependability or faithfulness (Deut. 32:20). ¶
[2] ***ḥāsiyḏ*** [adj.: חָסִיד <2623>; from MERCIFUL <2616>] ▶ **This word means kind, benevolent, merciful, pious. It carries the essential idea of the faithful kindness and piety that springs from mercy.** It is used of the Lord twice: once to convey His holiness in the sense that His works are beyond reproach (Ps. 145:17: gracious, kind, holy, faithful); and once to declare His tender mercy (Jer. 3:12: merciful, gracious, faithful). Other occurrences of this word usually refer to those who reflect the character of God in their actions or personality. The word denotes those who share a personal relationship with the Lord (1 Sam. 2:9; Ps. 4:3; 97:10; 116:15); the state of one who fully trusts in God (Ps. 86:2); and those who manifest the goodness or mercy of God in their conduct (2 Sam. 22:26; Ps. 12:1; Mic. 7:2). More importantly, though, it signifies the nature of those who are specifically set apart by God to be the examples and mediators of His goodness and fidelity. Priests (Deut. 33:8); prophets (Ps. 89:19); and the Messiah (Ps. 16:10) all bear this "holy" mark and function. *
– [3] Deut. 7:9 ➔ NURSE (verb) <539> [4] 2 Sam. 22:26b; Ps. 18:25b ➔ MERCIFUL <2616> [5] Dan. 6:4 ➔ TRUST (verb) <540>.

FAITHFULNESS – [1] Deut. 32:4; Ps. 33:4; 100:5; 119:90; etc. ➔ TRUTH <530> [2] Deut. 32:20 ➔ FAITHFUL <529> [3] Is. 25:1: perfect faithfulness ➔ faithfulness and truth ➔ TRUTH <544> [4] See MERCY <2617> [5] See TRUTH <571>.

FAITHLESS – [1] Jer. 3:14, 22 ➔ BACKSLIDING <7726> [2] Jer. 31:22; 49:4 ➔ BACKSLIDING <7728>.

FAITHLESS PEOPLE – Ps. 101:3 ➔ REVOLTER <7846> b.

FALCON – [1] ***'ayyāh*** [fem. noun: אַיָּה <344>; perhaps from WOE! (interj.) <337>] ▶ **A bird of prey; this word is also translated kite, black kite, vulture.** These birds cannot be eaten; they are unclean (Lev. 11:14; Deut. 14:13). They were known for their keen sight (Job 28:7). ¶
– [2] Deut. 14:13; Is. 34:15 ➔ VULTURE <1772>.

FALL (noun) – [1] ***kiššālôn*** [masc. noun: כִּשָּׁלוֹן <3783>; from FALL (verb) <3782>] ▶ **This word means literally an action that causes one to trip on something; it is also translated stumbling.** It is used in context of a moral or spiritual collapse or falling from pride and inflated self-worth (Prov. 16:18). ¶
[2] ***mappeleṯ*** [fem. noun: מַפֶּלֶת <4658>; from FALL (verb) <5307>] ▶ **This word means a carcass, a ruin, overthrow, downfall.** It described the physical carcass

of a dead animal (Judg. 14:8); and the practical ruin of the wicked (Prov. 29:16). It also described the overthrow of two nations: Tyre (Ezek. 26:15, 18; 27:27); and Egypt (Ezek. 31:13, 16; 32:10). ¶

FALL (verb) – [1] ***hāwāh*** [verb: הָוָה <1933>; a prim. root; comp. DESIRE (verb) <183> and BE <1961>] ▶
a. This word is used of falling snow commanded to descend by God. Ref.: Job 37:6. ¶
b. A verb meaning to be, become, come to pass. In its imperative or command form, it regularly means to become something or someone (Gen. 27:29; Neh. 6:6; Job 37:6; Is. 16:4); a master, a king, falling snow, a hiding place. It indicates being in a location or state (Eccl. 2:22; 11:3). ¶
[2] ***kāšal*** [verb: כָּשַׁל <3782>; a prim. root] ▶ **This word means to stumble, to stagger, to totter, to cause to stumble, to overthrow, to make weak.** It is used literally of individuals falling or figuratively of cities and nations falling (Is. 3:8; Hos. 14:1). People can fall by the sword (Dan. 11:33); or because of evil (Prov. 24:16); wickedness (Ezek. 33:12); and iniquity (Hos. 5:5). *
[3] ***nāp̱al*** [verb: נָפַל <5307>; a prim. root] ▶ **This common Hebrew verb also means to lie, to prostrate oneself, to overthrow. It carries many possible variations in meaning, much like the English verb to fall.** For instance, it can be used literally of someone or something falling down (Gen. 14:10; 1 Sam. 4:18; 17:49; 2 Kgs. 6:5); or into a pit (Ex. 21:33; Deut. 22:4). It is employed for inanimate objects like walls, towers, trees, and hailstones (1 Kgs. 20:30; Eccl. 11:3). It is used idiomatically for a violent death, especially in battle (Judg. 5:27; 1 Sam. 4:10; Amos 7:17); and for the overthrow of a city (Jer. 51:8). The word also describes those who fall prostrate before God or those in authority (Gen. 50:18; 2 Chr. 20:18). With the preposition *'al* (<5921>), meaning upon, it carries the meaning to attack (literally, to fall upon) (Job 1:19); to desert (to fall away) (2 Kgs. 25:11; Jer. 21:9); to be overcome by sleep or emotion (to fall into) (Gen. 4:5; 15:12; Josh. 2:9; 1 Sam. 17:32; Neh. 6:16). It is used to express the idea of being bedridden or debilitated (Ex. 21:18); to be overtaken (lit., to fall into the hands of) (Judg. 15:18; Lam. 1:7); and to be born (Is. 26:18). In its causative usage, it also takes the meaning to cast lots (Neh. 10:34; Is. 34:17). *
[4] ***nᵉp̱al*** [Aramaic verb: נְפַל <5308>; corresponding to <5307> above] ▶ **This word means to prostrate oneself, to die.** The verb is commonly used in reference to paying homage to a human being (Dan. 2:46); or to an image (Dan. 3:5–7). It is also used to denote a violent death (Dan. 7:20). It carries the meaning of responsibility in Ezra 7:20, where it referred to taking responsibility for carrying out the king's order. See the Hebrew word ***nāp̱al*** (<5307> above). *
– [5] Ex. 21:13 ➔ BEFALL <579> [6] Lev. 13:40, 41 ➔ PULL, PULL OUT <4803> [7] Deut. 32:2 ➔ DROP, DROP DOWN <6201> [8] Job 18:12; Ps. 38:17 ➔ STUMBLING <6761> [9] Job 36:28 ➔ DRIP (verb) <7491> [10] Ps. 9:15 ➔ DROWN <2883> [11] Ps. 63:10 ➔ SPILL <5064> [12] Prov. 10:8, 10; Hos. 4:14 ➔ RUIN (COME TO) <3831>.

FALL (LET) – Ruth 2:16 ➔ PLUNDER (verb) <7997> b.

FALL AWAY – Ps. 101:3 ➔ TURN ASIDE <7750>.

FALL AWAY (ONE WHO) – Ps. 101:3 ➔ REVOLTER <7846> b.

FALL, FALL DOWN – ***s̱ᵉgḇiḏ*** [Aramaic verb: סְגִד <5457>; corresponding to FALL DOWN <5456>] ▶ **This word means to worship, to bow, to lie in worship; it is also translated to prostrate.** It occurs in Daniel 2:46, referring to King Nebuchadnezzar's prostration before Daniel and his command that an offering and incense be offered to Daniel for interpreting his dream. The only other occurrences are the eleven uses in Daniel 3 (5–7, 10–12, 14, 15, 18, 28), referring to the worship of the gold image Nebuchadnezzar made. All these occurrences are accompanied by the words to fall (FALL (verb) <5308>) or to serve (SERVE <6399>). The three Hebrew officials appointed by Nebuchadnezzar at Daniel's recommendation refused to fall and worship this foreign god. Instead, they yielded their own bodies to God in the fiery furnace (Dan. 3:28; cf. Rom. 12:1). ¶

FALL DOWN – ***sāgaḏ*** [verb: סָגַד <5456>; a prim. root] ▶ **This word means to bow down, to lie down in worship.** The word occurs four times, only in Isaiah (Is. 44:15, 17, 19; 46:6). It refers to bowing or lying flat before a wooden or golden idol to worship, to pray, or to seek deliverance from it (Is. 44:17). Isaiah satirized those who lowered themselves in this way before an idol and did not recognize that an idol is only the work of human hands. ¶

FALLEN GRAPES – ***pereṭ*** [masc. coll. noun: פֶּרֶט <6528>; from IMPROVISE <6527> (in the sense of to scatter words)] ▶ **This word refers to edible fruits fallen on the ground in a natural way.** Ref.: Lev. 19:10. ¶

FALLING – Ps. 56:13; 116:8 ➔ STUMBLING <1762>.

FALLING (STOP) – Gen. 8:2 ➔ RESTRAIN <3607> a.

FALLOW GROUND – ***niyr*** [masc. noun: נִיר <5215>; from BREAK UP <5214>] ▶ **This word signifies untilled ground.** It indicates farming land, property owned that lies unplowed (Prov. 13:23; also translated unplowed field, tillage). In Proverbs 21:4, it is rendered as plowing (KJV, NKJV) and unplowed field (NIV) but as lamp by other translators (NASB, ESV). Used figuratively, it indicates the hardened, untilled attitudes of the people of Judah and Israel that needed to be changed and refreshed (Jer. 4:3; Hos. 10:12). ¶

FALLOWDEER – Deut. 14:5; 1 Kgs. 4:23 ➔ ROEBUCK <3180>.

FALSE – 1 Prov. 17:4 ➔ NOTHINGNESS <205> 2 Is. 30:9 ➔ LYING <3586>.

FALSE GOD – Deut. 32:17; Ps. 106:37 ➔ DEMON <7700>.

FALSE PROPHET – Is. 44:25 ➔ TALK (EMPTY, IDLE) <907>.

FALSE (BE) – Ps. 44:17 ➔ FALSELY (DEAL) <8266>.

FALSE (BECOME) – 2 Kgs. 17:15 ➔ VAIN (BECOME) <1891>.

FALSEHOOD – Ps. 5:6; etc. ➔ LIE (noun) <3577>.

FALSELY (DEAL) – ***šāqar*** [verb: שָׁקַר <8266>; a prim. root] ▶ **This word means to engage in deceit; it is also translated to deceive, to be false, to lie. The notion of a treacherous or deceptive activity forms the fundamental meaning of this word.** It is used to describe an agreement entered into with deceitful intentions (Gen. 21:23); outright lying (Lev. 19:11); and the violation of a covenant (Ps. 44:17). Scripture states clearly that such activity is the domain of humans, not of God (1 Sam. 15:29). Other refs.: Ps. 89:33: Is. 63:8. ¶

FAME – ***šōma'*** [masc. noun: שֹׁמַע <8089>; from HEAR <8085>] ▶ **This word refers to a report; a reputation, the renown.** It refers to a rumor or a report that indicates the fame of a person (Josh. 6:27; Esther 9:4). It refers to the fame or reputation of the Lord, Yahweh in Canaan (Josh. 9:9). It indicates an oral message or report (Jer. 6:24). ¶

FAMILIAR (BE) – Ps. 139:3 ➔ PROFITABLE (BE) <5532> a.

FAMILIAR SPIRIT – Lev. 19:31; 20:27; Deut. 18:10–12; 1 Sam. 28:7, 9; 2 Kgs. 21:6; 1 Chr. 10:13; 2 Chr. 33:6; Is. 8:19; 29:4: that has a familiar spirit ➔ who is a medium ➔ MEDIUM <178>.

FAMILIES (BY) – Neh. 7:5 ➔ by genealogy ➔ GENEALOGY <3188>.

FAMILY – Josh. 7:17; Judg. 13:2; etc. ➔ CLAN <4940>.

FAMILY BOND – Zech. 11:14 ➔ BROTHERHOOD <264>.

FAMINE – 1 ***kāpān*** [masc. noun: כָּפָן <3720>; from BEND <3719> (as making to stoop with emptiness and pain)] ▶ **This word means a lack of food; it is also translated hunger.** It describes a time of drought and a lack of crops (Job 5:22); or a general lack of food for persons (Job 30:3) in context because of their low social standing. ¶
2 ***rᵉʿāḇôn*** [masc. noun: רְעָבוֹן <7459>; from HUNGRY (BE) <7456>] ▶ **This word means lack of food, starving.** It is an abstract noun referring to a famine and its conditions in general, but with reference to households (Gen. 42:19, 33). Those who trust the Lord will have an abundance, even during a time of famine (Ps. 37:19). ¶
– 3 See HUNGER <7458>.

FAMISH – Zeph. 2:11 ➔ LEAN (GROW, BECOME, WAX) <7329>.

FAMISHED – 1 Gen. 25:29, 30 ➔ WEARY (adj.) <5889> 2 See HUNGRY <7457>.

FAMISHED (BE) – See HUNGRY (BE) <7456>.

FAMOUS – Num. 16:2; 26:9 ➔ CHOSEN <7148>.

FAN – Job 20:26; Is. 54:16 ➔ BREATHE <5301>.

FAN, WINNOWING FAN – ***mizreh*** [masc. noun: מִזְרֶה <4214>; from SCATTER <2219>] ▶ **This word indicates a pitchfork, a winnowing fork to remove chaff from grain.** It was a farming tool used to clean out the chaff and debris from grains (Is. 30:24). It is used figuratively of God's "winnowing fork" of judgment on His people (Jer. 15:7). ¶

FANCY – Dan. 4:5 ➔ THOUGHT <2031>.

FANGS – 1 ***maltāʿôṯ*** [fem. plur. noun: מַלְתָּעוֹת <4459>; transposition for JAWS <4973>] ▶ **This word means jaws, jaw teeth.** It refers to the location of the wicked's teeth in context, the jaw bones or in general the mouth (Ps. 58:6; KJV: great teeth). ¶
– 2 Job 29:17; Ps. 58:6; Prov. 30:14; Joel 1:6 ➔ JAWS <4973>.

FANTASY – Dan. 4:5 ➔ THOUGHT <2031>.

FAR – 1 ***merḥāq*** [masc. noun: מֶרְחָק <4801>; from FAR AWAY (BE) <7368>] ▶ **This word designates a distant spot, a place, a far-away place.** It indicates in context the last house, the distant house (2 Sam. 15:17: at the last house, at the outskirts, etc.). It indicates a great space; the distance between in a figurative sense (Ps. 138:6: off); as well as in a literal sense, i.e., a distant country (Prov. 25:25: far, distant; 31:14: afar; Is. 10:3: far, afar; 17:13: off). It is used in a general sense of all distant places of the earth (Is. 8:9; Ezek. 23:40; Zech. 10:9). It is used often of the enemies God is bringing from a distant country, i.e., Assyria, Babylon (Is. 13:5; Jer. 4:16; 5:15). *
2 ***rāḥiyq*** [Aramaic adj.: רַחִיק <7352>; corresponding to FAR OFF, FAR AWAY <7350>] ▶ **This word means at a distant place; it is also translated away.** It serves as a predicate adjective to describe persons who are to keep themselves far away from a certain place (Ezra 6:6). ¶
3 ***rāḥêq*** [adj.: רָחֵק <7369>; from FAR AWAY (BE) <7368>] ▶ **This word means far away, at a very distant place.** It indicates in context persons who have strayed from God, who have removed themselves from Him (Ps. 73:27). ¶

FAR AWAY (BE, BECOME) – ***rāḥaq*** [verb: רָחַק <7368>; a prim. root] ▶ **This word indicates that something is or becomes a long way off, distant, or it means to wander away from.** It indicates physical distance (Deut. 12:21; 14:24). Distant from is expressed by adding *min* (from) to the object. It refers to persons' distancing themselves from other persons emotionally and physically (Prov. 19:7); but especially to the Lord's distancing Himself or being distant from those who need Him (Ps. 22:11, 19; 35:22; 38:21). It also describes persons distancing themselves from God (Is. 29:13). Israel as a nation went far from God spiritually (Jer. 2:5). God's people were to distance themselves from cases or charges against the innocent (Ex. 23:7). It has the sense of God's expanding the borders, making distant the borders of His people (Is. 26:15; Mic. 7:11). In its intensive stem, it has a causative sense of sending someone or something away, spreading it, likewise in its causative stem itself: the Lord removes people (Job 19:13; Is. 6:12; Ezek. 43:9). It means to be gone, to be distant, to make distance between (Gen. 44:4; Josh. 8:4; Judg. 18:22). False prophets prophesied lies to remove the people from their land (Jer. 27:10). *

FAR BE IT – ***ḥāliylāh*** [adversative interj.: חָלִילָה <2486>; a directive from PIERCE <2490>] ▶ **This word strongly indicates that something should not be the case.** Used by itself, it negates something stated or asserted in the context (1 Sam. 14:45); with *min*, it means far be it from . . . , indicating the person who should not do such and such a thing, as slaying righteous persons along with the wicked (Gen. 18:25). It is used with an infinitive to indicate what should not be done, e.g., rebellion, etc. (Josh. 22:29); it is used to indicate that because of the Lord, something should not be done (1 Sam. 24:6; 26:11). *

FAR OFF, FAR AWAY – ***rāḥôq, rāḥōq*** [adj.: רָחוֹק, רָחֹק <7350>; from FAR AWAY (BE) <7368>] ▶ **This word means very distant.** It refers to a great spatial distance, something far away, e.g., land (Deut. 29:22; Josh. 9:6, 9; 1 Kgs. 8:41); but it is used of many things (Deut. 20:15; Joel 3:8). It indicates time far away, far off (Ezek. 12:27). It takes on the nature of a noun to mean distance (Josh. 3:4). It refers to the space between two points (Gen. 22:4). It refers to distant time, *mêrāḥôq*, long ago (Is. 22:11). *Lᵉmerāḥôq* means long ago, used of God's distant prophecies of what was to come (2 Kgs. 19:25; Is. 37:26). It describes figuratively God's being far from one's heart or mind (Jer. 12:2); and of a value being far above something else (Prov. 31:10). It may indicate an inability to do something; it is far from someone (Eccl. 7:24). *

FARMER – [1] ***'ikār*** [masc. noun: אִכָּר <406>; from an unused root meaning to dig] ▶ **This word means a farmworker; it is also translated plowman, husbandman.** The workers labored in the fields (2 Chr. 26:10; Jer. 14:4) as a regular feature of Israel's agricultural community (Jer. 31:24). The farmers would be an important group affected by the judgments of the Lord (Is. 61:5; Jer. 51:23; Joel 1:11; Amos 5:16). ¶ – [2] 2 Kgs. 25:12 ➔ PLOWMAN <1461>.

FARMER (AS) – 2 Kgs. 25:12; Jer. 52:16 ➔ PLOWMAN (BE) <3009>.

FARTHEST – Jer. 9:26; 25:23; 49:32 ➔ CUT OFF <7112> b.

FARTHEST CORNER – ***'āṣiyl*** [masc. noun: אָצִיל <678>; from RESERVE (verb) <680> (in its secondary sense of separation)] ▶ **This word designates also corner, chief.** It can indicate the sides or borders of the earth, thereby referring to its extremities or remotest countries (Is. 41:9). It can also be used figuratively to mean nobles (Ex. 24:11); see NOBLE <678>. ¶

FARTHEST REGION – Is. 41:9 ➔ FARTHEST CORNER <678>.

FASHION (noun) – Ezek. 43:11 ➔ ARRANGEMENT <8498> a.

FASHION (verb) – [1] Job 10:8 ➔ HURT <6087> [2] Ps. 144:12 ➔ CUT (verb) <2404>.

FASHIONED (BE) – Ps. 139:16 ➔ FORM (verb) <3335>.

FAST (noun) – See FASTING <6685>.

FAST (STAND) – Ps. 89:28 ➔ NURSE (verb) <539>.

FAST (verb) – 1 ***ṣûm*** [verb: צוּלָה <6684>; a prim. root (in the sense of to cover over, i.e., the mouth)] ▶ **This word means to abstain from food. It is ideally a form of worship and recognition of God.** It means to refrain from eating food for various reasons: as a sign of mourning and distress, seeking God's mercy (Judg. 20:26; 1 Sam. 7:6; 31:13; 2 Sam. 12:16). It is purportedly in some cases done also to please the Lord, but evidently not with purity of motive (Zech. 7:5). Fasting was a sign of mourning before God for the dead (1 Sam. 31:13). *
2 ***ṭᵉwāṯ*** [Aramaic adj.: טְוָת <2908>; from a root corresponding to SPIN <2901>] ▶ **This word indicates going without eating.** It describes Darius as he refrains from eating during the night, worrying about Daniel's safety (Dan. 6:18). ¶
– 3 Zech. 7:3 ➔ SEPARATE <5144>.

FASTEN – 1 Ex. 29:5 ➔ GIRD <640> 2 Judg. 4:21 ➔ GO THROUGH <6795>.

FASTENED TOGETHER (BE) – Lam. 1:14 ➔ KNIT TOGETHER (BE) <8276>.

FASTING – 1 ***ṣôm*** [masc. noun: צוֹם <6685>; from FAST (verb) <6684>] ▶ **This word refers to the act or time of abstaining from food, an act of worship in mourning, despairing while entreating God.** A fast itself (2 Sam. 12:16); a public fast (1 Kgs. 21:9, 12). Some fasts were observed regularly (Esther 9:31; Zech. 8:19). A fast could bring on weakness of body (Ps. 109:24). *
2 ***taᵃniyṯ*** [fem. noun: תַּעֲנִית <8589>; from HUMBLE <6031> (in the sense of afflicted)] ▶ **This word means abstaining from food; it is also translated humiliation, heaviness, self-abasement.** It refers to a period of humbling oneself in prayer and fasting as Ezra did for the sins of himself and his people (Ezra 9:5). ¶

FAT (adj.) – 1 ***bᵉriy*** [adj.: בְּרִי <1274>; from EAT <1262>] ▶ **This word is used to modify sheep as fat sheep as opposed to lean sheep.** Ref.: Ezek. 34:20. ¶
2 ***bāriy'*** [adj.: בָּרִיא <1277>; from CREATE <1254> (in the sense of EAT <1262>)] ▶ **This word denotes something as heavy, plump, healthy.** It refers to cattle (Gen. 41:4); persons (Judg. 3:17); food (Hab. 1:16); healthy (fat) of flesh (Ps. 73:4; Dan. 1:15) through eating the Jewish diet. *
3 ***dāšên*** [adj.: דָּשֵׁן <1879>; from FAT (MAKE) <1878>] ▶ **This word means juicy, healthy, prosperous, rich.** It indicates the rich and plenteous grain harvests which the Lord will grant to His people (Is. 30:23). It describes the fruitfulness of the righteous person as full of sap, fat, being healthy spiritually from God's blessings (Ps. 92:14; also translated fresh, full of sap). Finally, it denotes those who are healthy, prosperous, and who will serve the Lord (Ps. 22:29). ¶

FAT (BE) – ***ṭāpaš*** [verb: טָפַשׁ <2954>; a prim. root] ▶ **This word means to be insensitive, unfeeling.** It is used to depict a heart covered with fat, i.e., not sensitive, not delighting in the Law of the Lord (Ps. 119:70; NIV, to be callous). ¶

FAT (BE, BECOME) – ***šāman, šāmên*** [verb: שָׁמַן, שָׁמֵן <8080>; a prim. root] ▶ **This word describes the process of becoming fat or being fat, i.e., to become heavy.** Refs.: Deut. 32:15; Neh. 9:25; Jer. 5:28. It means figuratively in several of these references to become surfeited, self-satisfied, lazy (Neh. 9:25); insensitive to God's will and plans (Deut. 32:15). Israel's heart became "fat," unreceptive, insensitive (Is. 6:10). ¶

FAT (GROW) – Deut. 32:15 ➔ THICK (BE, GROW) <5666>.

FAT (MAKE, GROW) – ***dāšên*** [verb: דָּשֵׁן <1878>; a prim. root] ▶ **This word means, in a figurative sense, to anoint, to satisfy.** In Proverbs, it is used for one's bones growing fat (i.e., one being in good health) after receiving good news (Prov. 15:30). Conversely, when Israel came to the Promised

Land, she grew fat with the food of the pagan culture and turned away to other gods (Deut. 31:20). In Isaiah, the word is used to describe the ground being covered with the fat of animals (Is. 34:7). *

FAT (noun) – [1] ***ḥêleḇ*** [masc. noun: חֵלֶב <2459>; from an unused root meaning to be fat] ▶ **This word refers to the covering of the interior of a part of the body; it refers also to the best.** It refers to the covering of the interior of the body, of a person's belly, of a person's face (Ex. 29:13; Judg. 3:22; Job 15:27). It indicates the best or fatty portions of an offering (Gen. 4:4; Lev. 4:26) which were pleasing to the Lord. Fat was God's portion of an offering (1 Sam. 2:15, 16). It was not to be eaten by people (Lev. 3:17; 7:23–25). The "fat of the land" refers to the best part of the land (Gen. 45:18) and also indicates the products of the land: oil, wine, corn (Num. 18:12, 29, 30, 32). But a heart grown fat symbolizes a heart that has become insensitive to God (Ps. 17:10; 119:70). *

[2] ***piymāh*** [fem. noun: פִּימָה <6371>; prob. from an unused root meaning to be plump] ▶ **This word refers to bulges of fat.** It refers to an excess of facial tissue creating plumpness or corpulence in context, a mark of a wicked person's face according to Eliphaz (Job 15:27). ¶

– [3] Lev. 1:8, 12; 8:20 ➔ SUET <6309> [4] Neh. 8:10 ➔ FATNESS <4924> b. [5] Is. 17:4; Dan. 11:24 ➔ FATNESS <4924> a.

FAT ANIMAL, FAT BEAST, FAT ONE – ***mêaḥ*** [masc. noun: מֵחַ <4220>; from WIPE, WIPE OUT <4229> in the sense of greasing or making fat] ▶ **This word designates a fatling, a sheep raised for fattening.** Ref.: Ps. 66:15; also translated fattened animal. In Isaiah 5:17, it seems to stand for wealthy or rich people, "fat ones." ¶

FAT ONES – Is. 10:16 ➔ FATNESS <4924> a.

FAT TAIL – ***'alyāh*** [fem. noun: אַלְיָה <451>; from CURSE (verb) <422> (in the original sense of strength)] ▶ **This word describes the fat tail or rump of sheep.** This portion of a sheep was used in the cultic sites of Israel. This part of the animal, along with other items, was involved in the wave offering before the Lord (Ex. 29:22; Lev. 8:25), the peace offering (Lev. 3:9), and the trespass offering (Lev. 7:3). Other ref.: Lev. 9:19. ¶

FAT, FATLING, FATTENED – ***m*^{e}*riy'*** [masc. noun: מְרִיא <4806>; from LIFT ONESELF <4754> in the sense of grossness, through the idea of domineering (comp. LORD <4756>)] ▶ **This word refers to a fatted calf, a fattened animal.** It refers to cattle raised for eating and sacrifice, the best cattle, well-nourished (2 Sam. 6:13; 1 Kgs. 1:9, 19, 25; Is. 1:11; Ezek. 39:18; Amos 5:22). The calf will be at peace with animals of prey in the messianic kingdom (Is. 11:6). ¶

FAT, FATNESS – ***šāmên, šāmān*** [שָׁמֵן, שָׁמָן <8082>; from FAT (BE, BECOME) <8080>] ▶

a. A Hebrew adjective meaning fat, rich, plentiful; robust. It refers to excellent-tasting food, gourmet food (Gen. 49:20). It indicates land that is fat, fertile, filled with an abundance of produce (Num. 13:20; Neh. 9:25, 35; Is. 30:23; Ezek. 34:14). With reference to people, it means, strong, robust, healthy (Judg. 3:29). The KJV renders this word as fat, meaning unresponsive, self-absorbed (Is. 6:10). It describes captives of the nation Babylon as plentiful, many (Hab. 1:16). ¶

b. A masculine noun indicating richness (of earth). It refers to either the rich produce that the earth generates or the fertile, nutritious state of soil (Gen. 27:28). ¶

FAT, FATTED, FATTENED – ***marbêq*** [masc. noun: מַרְבֵּק <4770>; from an unused root meaning to tie up] ▶ **This word depicts an animal that has been nourished and enlarged for slaughter as food.** Refs.: 1 Sam. 28:24: fat, fatted, fattened. It is used figuratively of merchants grown rich through their sales and trading (Jer. 46:21:

fat, fatted, fattened). It also has the sense of the place from which the fattening took place, the stalls or place of feeding and care (Amos 6:4; Mal. 4:2). ¶

FATE – Eccl. 2:14, 15; 3:19; 9:2, 3 ➔ CHANCE <4745>.

FATHER – [1] ***'āḇ*** [masc. noun: אָב <1>; a prim. word] ▶ **This word means a man who is or who acts as parent. It means head of a household, ancestor, patron of a class; benevolence, respect, honor. It is primarily used to mean either a human or spiritual father.** There are numerous references to a father as a begetter or head of a household (Gen. 24:40; Josh. 14:1). When referring to an ancestor, this word can be collective; Naboth would not give up the inheritance of his fathers (1 Kgs. 21:3). One of the most important meanings is God as Father (Is. 63:16). It can also mean originator of a profession or class; Jabal was called the father of nomadic farmers (Gen. 4:20). A father is also one who bestows respect or honor (Judg. 17:10). *
[2] ***'aḇ*** [Aramaic masc. noun: אַב <2>; corresponding to <1> above] ▶ **See previous definition for the Hebrew cognate *'āḇ* <1>. This noun also means ancestor.** The primary meaning is a male biological parent (Dan. 5:11, 13). In the plural, its meaning is ancestors or forefathers (Ezra 4:15). *

FATHER-IN-LAW – [1] ***ḥām*** [masc. noun: חָם <2524>; from the same as WALL <2346>] ▶ **This word refers to a husband's father.** Judah was a father-in-law (Gen. 38:13, 25; 1 Sam. 4:19, 21). ¶
– [2] Ex. 3:1; 4:18; 18:1, 2, 5–8, 12, 14, 15, 17, 24, 27; Num. 10:29; Judg. 1:16; 4:11 ➔ MARRIAGE <2859> b.

FATHER'S SISTER – ***dôḏāh*** [fem. noun: דּוֹדָה <1733>; fem. of LOVER <1730> (in the secondary sense of uncle)] ▶ **This word designates Jochebed as Amram's father's sister aunt.** Ref.: Ex. 6:20. Elsewhere, it indicates the wife of a father's brother (Lev. 18:14: aunt; 20:20: uncle's wife). ¶

FATLING – Ps. 66:15 ➔ FAT ANIMAL, FAT BEAST, FAT ONE <4220>.

FATNESS – [1] ***dešen*** [masc. noun: דֶּשֶׁן <1880>; from FAT (MAKE) <1878>] ▶ **This word indicates the spiritual blessings of God as abundance (NASB and others), fatness (KJV), richest of food or fare (NIV) freely bestowed on His people who will respond.** Refs.: Ps. 36:8; 63:5; Is. 55:2. It indicates the fat of olives (Judg. 9:9). It refers to food and drink (Job 36:16; Jer. 31:14). It indicates the wood ashes and fat ashes mixed together from the altar (Lev. 1:16; 4:12; 1 Kgs. 13:3, 5; Jer. 31:40). Other refs.: Lev. 1:16; 6:10, 11; Ps. 65:11. ¶
[2] ***mišmān, mašmanniym*** [מִשְׁמָן, מַשְׁמַנִּים <4924>; from FAT (BE) <8080>] ▶
a. A masculine noun meaning and also translated richness, fertility, fat. It is used of the good, abundant produce of the land (Gen. 27:28, 39). It points out strong or influential persons (Ps. 78:31); even soldiers (Is. 10:16: fat ones, sturdy warriors, stout warriors). It indicates a sign of an abundance of health and wealth (Is. 17:4; Dan. 11:24). ¶
b. A masculine plural noun describing festive food. It indicates the best portions of food at a festive meal (Neh. 8:10: fat, choice food). ¶

FATNESS (COVERED WITH) – Deut. 32:15 ➔ OBESE (BE) <3780>.

FATTED – 1 Kgs. 4:23; Prov. 15:17 ➔ FATTENED <75>.

FATTENED – **to fatten: *'āḇas*** [verb: אָבַס <75>; a prim. root] ▶ **This word relates to an animal that has been fed to become overweight; it is also translated fatted, choice.** It is a plural passive participle in 1 Kings 4:23 and refers to fatted fowl. It is used in the same form in the singular to indicate a fatted ox or calf in Proverbs 15:17 (cf. NASB, NKJV). ¶

FATTENED ANIMAL – Ps. 66:15 ➔ FAT ANIMAL, FAT BEAST, FAT ONE <4220>.

FAULT – [1] Job 11:15 ➔ DEFECT <3971> [2] Job 33:10 ➔ OPPOSITION <8569> [3] Dan. 6:4 ➔ CORRUPT (verb) <7844>.

FAVOR (noun) – [1] ***ḥaniynāh*** [fem. noun: חֲנִינָה <2594>; from GRACIOUS (BE) <2603>] ▶ **This word indicates kindness, compassion, pity.** It refers to a favorable and beneficial attitude of persons toward someone (Jer. 16:13), in this case, the exiles of Israel. ¶
– [2] Ps. 90:17; Zech. 11:7, 10 ➔ BEAUTY <5278>.

FAVOR (verb) – See GRACIOUS (BE) <2603>.

FAVORITE – Song 6:9 ➔ PURE <1249>.

FAVORITISM (SHOW) – Ex. 23:3; Lev. 19:15 ➔ HONOR (verb) <1921>.

FEAR (noun) – [1] ***yir'āh*** [fem. noun: יִרְאָה <3374>; from FEARING <3373>] ▶ **The word usually refers to the respect, reverence of God and is viewed as a positive quality.** This fear acknowledges God's good intentions (Ex. 20:20). It will motivate and delight even the Messiah (Is. 11:2, 3). This fear is produced by God's Word (Ps. 119:38; Prov. 2:5) and makes a person receptive to wisdom and knowledge (Prov. 1:7; 9:10). It is even identified with wisdom (Job 28:28; Prov. 15:33). The fear of the Lord may be lost by despair of one's own situation (Job 6:14) or envy of a sinner's (Prov. 23:17). This fear restrains people from sin (Gen. 20:11; Ex. 20:20; Neh. 5:9); gives confidence (Job 4:6; Prov. 14:26); helps rulers and causes judges to act justly (2 Sam. 23:3; 2 Chr. 19:9; Neh. 5:15); results in good sleep (Prov. 19:23); with humility, leads to riches, honor, and life (Prov. 22:4). The word also refers to the fear of briers and thorns (Is. 7:25); and the fear of Israel that would fall on other nations (Deut. 2:25). *
[2] ***megôrāh*** [fem. noun: מְגוֹרָה <4034>; fem. of TERROR <4032>] ▶ **This word occurs only once in the Bible; it means terror, dread. It is also translated to fear, to dread.** Proverbs 10:24 contrasts the fate of the wicked with that of the righteous. The ones serving the Lord will get their hearts' desires, but the wicked will get their worst nightmares (i.e., judgment). ¶
[3] ***megûrāh*** [fem. noun: מְגוּרָה <4035>; fem. of TERROR <4032> or of SOJOURNING <4033>] ▶ **The use of this Hebrew word for fear (or terror) tends to imply the haunting apprehensions that one holds deep within.** The Lord's judgments bring people's worst fears to reality (Is. 66:4), while His love frees us from them (Ps. 34:4; cf. 1 John 4:18). Haggai, however, uses this word to signify a storage place or a barn (Hag. 2:19). The link between the divergent ideas comes from the root word *gûr* (SOJOURN <1481>), which carries the connotation of dwelling as well as fear. ¶
[4] ***mōrā'*** [masc. noun: מֹרָא <4172>; from FEAR (verb) <3372>] ▶ **This word means terror, dread, reverence. The primary concept underlying the meaning of this word is a sense of fear or awe that causes separation or brings respect.** It is used to denote the fear animals have for humans (Gen. 9:2); terror on the Canaanites as Israel entered the Promised Land (Deut. 11:25); the reverence due those in authority (Mal. 1:6; also translated honor); an object of reverence, which for Israel was to be God, *yehōwāh* (LORD <3068>), alone (Is. 8:12, 13); a spectacle or event that inspires awe or horror (Deut. 4:34; 34:12; Jer. 32:21). Other refs.: Deut. 26:8; Ps. 9:20; 76:11; Mal. 2:5. ¶
– [5] Ex. 15:16; 23:27; Josh. 2:9; Ezra 3:3; Job 9:34 ➔ TERROR <367> [6] Josh. 22:24 ➔ ANXIETY <1674> [7] Job 41:33 ➔ DREAD (noun and adj.) <2844> a. [8] Prov. 29:25 ➔ TREMBLING <2731> [9] Ps. 31:13; Is. 31:9; Jer. 6:25; etc. ➔ TERROR <4032> [10] Ps. 78:33 ➔ TERROR <928> [11] Eccl. 12:5 ➔ TERROR <2849> [12] Is. 14:3 ➔ TURMOIL <7267> [13] Is. 21:4 ➔ TREMBLING <6427> [14] Jer. 2:19 ➔ DREAD (noun) <6345> [15] Jer. 49:24 ➔ PANIC <7374> [16] See DREAD (noun) <6343>.

FEAR (verb) – [1] ***deḥal*** [Aramaic verb: דְּחַל <1763>; corresponding to CRAWL <2119>

(which also means to fear, to be afraid)] ▶ **The idea of this word is one of slinking or crawling, such as a serpent or a worm; to back away or tremble in fright.** People trembled before the greatness which God gave Nebuchadnezzar (Dan. 5:19). Darius turned this and focused on the Giver of the greatness, saying that people would tremble before God's awesome being (Dan. 6:26). Other refs.: Dan. 2:31 (terrible, awesome, frightening); 4:5 (to make afraid, to make fearful); 7:7 (dreadful, terrifying), 19 (dreadful, terrifying). ¶

2 ***yārê'*** [verb: יָרֵא <3372>; a prim. root] ▶ **This word means to respect, to reverence, to be afraid, to be awesome, to be feared, to make afraid, to frighten. The most common translations are to be afraid, to fear, to fear God.** "The fear of the LORD is the beginning of knowledge" is a famous use of the noun (Prov. 1:7); the famous narrative of the near sacrifice of Isaac proved to God that Abraham feared Him above all (Gen. 22:12); people who feared God were considered faithful and trustworthy for such fear constrained them to believe and act morally (Ex. 18:21). The midwives of Pharaoh feared God and did not kill the newborn Hebrew males (Ex. 1:17, 21). The fear of the Lord was closely tied to keeping God's decrees and laws (Deut. 6:2); people who fear God delight in hearing of His deeds for His people (Ps. 66:16). The God of Israel was an object of respectful fear (Lev. 19:30; 26:2) for Obadiah and Hezekiah (1 Kgs. 18:3, 12; Jer. 26:19). In addition, because Israel feared and worshiped other gods, they were destroyed by Assyria (Judg. 6:10; 2 Kgs. 17:7, 35). They were to worship and fear only the Lord their God (Josh. 24:14). Israel had an unnecessary and unhealthy fear of the nations of Canaan (Deut. 7:19). The verb describes the fear of men: Jacob feared Esau, his brother (Gen. 32:7); and the official in charge of Daniel feared the king (Dan. 1:10). In the sense of respectful fear, each person was to honor his mother and father (Lev. 19:3). As a stative verb, it describes a state of being or attitude, such as being afraid or fearful: a man afraid of war was to remove himself from the army of Israel (Deut. 20:3, 8; Judg. 7:3); as a result of rebellion, Adam and Eve were afraid before the Lord (Gen. 3:10).

In the passive form, the word expresses the idea of being feared, held in esteem: God was feared and awesome (Ex. 15:11; Ps. 130:4); His deeds were awe-inspiring (Deut. 10:21; 2 Sam. 7:23); the Cushites were an aggressive people feared by many (Is. 18:2); even the threatening desert area was considered fearful or dreadful (Deut. 8:15).

The factitive or intensive form means to frighten or to impart fear: the wise woman of Tekoa was frightened by the people (2 Sam. 14:15); and the governor of Samaria, Sanballat, attempted to frighten Nehemiah so that he would not rebuild the wall of Jerusalem (Neh. 6:9). *

– 3 Lev. 19:32 ➔ HONOR (verb) <1921> 4 Deut. 9:19; Ps. 119:39; Job 3:25; 9:28 ➔ AFRAID (BE) <3025> 5 Prov. 10:24 ➔ FEAR (noun) <4034> 6 Jer. 22:25; 39:17 ➔ AFRAID <3016>.

FEARFUL – Lev. 26:36: I will make their hearts so fearful (NIV) ➔ lit.: I will send faintness into their hearts ➔ FAINTNESS <4816>.

FEARFUL (BE) – Job 32:6 ➔ CRAWL <2119>.

FEARFUL (MAKE) – Dan. 4:5 ➔ FEAR (verb) <1763>.

FEARFULNESS – Is. 21:4 ➔ TREMBLING <6427>.

FEARING – ***yārê'*** [adj.: יָרֵא <3373>; from FEAR (verb) <3372>] ▶ **This word refers to a feeling of anxiety; it also means afraid.** The Hebrew word is used when the author of Genesis speaks of Abraham fearing God because he did not hold back his only son (Gen. 22:12). Jacob asked God to save him from Esau, because he was afraid that Esau would attack him (Gen. 32:11). Jethro told Moses to select as judges men who feared God (Ex. 18:21). Proverbs says that a woman who fears the Lord is to be praised (Prov. 31:30). Jeremiah told the Israelite army that God said not to fear the king of Babylon (Jer. 42:11). See the primary verb *yārê'* [FEAR (verb) <3372>]. *

FEAST – 1 ***ḥāg, ḥag*** [masc. noun: חָג, חַג <2282>; from FEAST (HOLD A) <2287>] ▶ **This word also means a festival. It is used numerous times throughout the Old Testament referring to the celebrations of the Hebrew religious calendar.** It is used of the major feasts, including the Feast of Unleavened Bread and the Passover Feast (Ex. 34:18, 25; Lev. 23:6; Deut. 16:16; Ezra 6:22); the Feast of Weeks (Deut. 16:16; 2 Chr. 8:13); and the Feast of Tabernacles (Lev. 23:34; Num. 29:12; Deut. 31:10; Zech. 14:16). It was used in the Temple dedication during Solomon's reign (1 Kgs. 8:2, 65). Evil King Jeroboam held a festival described in 1 Kings 12:32, 33. The prophets often used this word to describe the negligence of the people in keeping the feasts commanded by Mosaic Law (Is. 29:1; Amos 5:21; Mal. 2:3). *

2 ***leḥem*** [Aramaic masc. noun: לְחֶם <3900>; corresponding to BREAD <3899>] ▶ **The only usage of this word refers to a banquet held in a royal palace.** Ref.: Dan. 5:1. ¶

3 ***mišteh*** [masc. noun: מִשְׁתֶּה <4960>; from DRINK (verb) <8354>] ▶ **This word means a celebration, and also a drink.** In a few instances, this word referred specifically to drinks (Ezra 3:7; Dan. 1:5, 8, 10, 16), but it usually referred to feasts prepared for special occasions: hospitality (Gen. 19:3); the weaning of a child (Gen. 21:8); making peace (Gen. 26:30; 2 Sam. 3:20); a wedding (Gen. 29:22; Judg. 14:10, 12, 17; Esther 2:18); merriment (Esther 1:3; 9:17–19; Job 1:4, 5; Eccl. 7:2). A feast was indicative of blessing (Prov. 15:15; Is. 25:6). *

– 4 Ps. 35:16 ➔ BREAD <4580>.

FEAST (HOLD A) – ***ḥāgag*** [verb: חָגַג <2287>; a prim. root (comp. TERROR <2283>, CIRCLE (INSCRIBE A) <2328>)] ▶ **This word refers to wild and confused actions in a perilous situation like the behavior of a drunken person.** Ref.: Ps. 107:27. It is usually used in the context of rejoicing and describes festive attitudes and actions, often while on the way to worship or when celebrating a feast (Ps. 42:4; Nah. 1:15). In fact, the word indicates the holding or observing of a festival (Ex. 5:1; 12:14; 23:14; Lev. 23:39, 41; Num. 29:12; Deut. 16:15) to the Lord, such as the Passover or Feast of Booths (Zech. 14:16, 18, 19). It also is used to describe the festive dancing and celebrations of a victory over enemies in battle (1 Sam. 30:16). ¶

FEAST ON – Job 39:30 ➔ SUCK UP <5966>.

FEASTING – Amos 6:7 ➔ BANQUETING <4797>.

FEATHER – ***nôṣāh, nōṣāh*** [fem. noun: נוֹצָה, נֹצָה <5133>; fem. act. part. of FIGHT <5327> in the Hebraic particular sense of flying] ▶

a. Feathers are part of a bird plumage. This word refers to the tuft of feathers of a bird. They were to be removed during an offering (Lev. 1:16). It also refers to the plumage of an ostrich (Job 39:13); or eagle (Ezek. 17:3, 7). ¶

b. A feminine noun meaning contents. It refers to the contents of a bird's crop or stomach removed when it was being offered (Lev. 1:16). ¶

FEATHERS – Ps. 91:4 ➔ WINGS <84>.

FEATHERS (LONG) – Ezra 4:14 ➔ SLOW <750>.

FEATHERS (SPREAD ONE'S) – Job 39:18 ➔ others translations: to lift oneself on high ➔ LIFT ONESELF <4754>.

FEE – Deut. 23:18 ➔ EARNINGS <868>.

FEEBLE – 1 1 Sam. 2:5: to become feeble, to wax feeble ➔ LANGUISH <535> 2 Job 4:33; 35:3 ➔ WEAK (adj.) <7504> 3 Is. 16:14 ➔ lit.: not mighty ➔ MIGHTY <3524>.

FEEBLE (BE) – 1 ***ḥāšal*** [verb: חָשַׁל <2826>; a prim. root] ► **This word describes the Israelites' weakened state when Amalek attacked them from the rear in their desert wanderings shortly after escaping from Egypt.** Ref.: Deut. 25:18; also translated to straggle, to lag. ¶
– 2 Gen. 30:42 → TURN (verb) <5848>
b. 3 Ps. 38:8 → STUNNED (BECOME) <6313>.

FEEBLENESS – Jer. 47:3 → LIMPNESS <7510>.

FEED (noun) – Gen. 24:25, 32; 42:27; 43:24; Judg. 19:19 → FODDER <4554>.

FEED (verb) – 1 ***zûn*** [Aramaic verb: זוּן <2110>; corresponding to WELL-FED <2109>] ► **This word is used in a reflexive sense to depict animals and creatures of the world eating the fruit of a huge tree in Nebuchadnezzar's dream.** Ref.: Dan. 4:12. ¶
2 ***lā'aṭ*** [verb: לָעַט <3938>; a prim. root] ► **This word indicates to swallow greedily, to devour.** It indicates devouring greedily, voraciously. It is used of Esau's ill-fated eating some stew (Gen. 25:30; also translated to let eat, to let have). ¶
3 ***rā'āh*** [verb: רָעָה <7462>; a prim. root] ► **a. This word means to nourish, to tend; to be a shepherd.** It means in general to care for, to protect, to graze, to feed flocks and herds (Gen. 30:31, 36; 37:2; Ex. 3:1; 1 Sam. 17:15). In its participial form *rō'eh,* it can mean shepherd (Gen. 4:2); sheepherders (Gen. 29:9). Shepherds pasture, lead the sheep, flocks to eat (Job 24:2). It is used figuratively of God as the Shepherd of Jacob and his people (Gen. 48:15; Is. 40:11; Hos. 4:16). The king of Israel was to shepherd the people for God (2 Sam. 5:2; 7:7; Jer. 3:15). The masculine participle refers to the leaders of God's people (Jer. 2:8; 22:22; Ezek. 34:2, 3, 8, 10). God is pictured as the one who shepherds an individual soul, a person (Ps. 49:14). It is used figuratively to describe the lips of the wise as shepherding the people (Prov. 10:21). It is used figuratively of the land of Israel, the pastures of the shepherds mourn or dry up (Amos 1:2). It indicates the grazing, feeding of animals, flocks, herds, cattle (Gen. 41:2). Fools feed on folly, not wisdom (Prov. 15:14).
b. This word also means to associate with, to be a companion, to be a friend. It indicates a relationship of friendship between persons (Judg. 14:20); or to live in an area and develop associations with the people of the land (Ps. 37:3). It indicates a person who regularly associates with a group of persons, a companion, an associate, a friend, sharing common ideas and activities (Prov. 13:20; 22:24; 28:7; 29:3). *
– 4 Dan. 5:21 → EAT <2939>.

FEED WITH – Prov. 30:8 → TEAR <2963>.

FEEL – 1 ***yāmaš*** [verb: יָמַשׁ <3237>; a prim. root] ► **This word is used once of Samson, a blind man, asking to sense, to touch with his hands the pillars of a Philistine temple.** Ref.: Judg. 16:26. Some derive the word used here from the verb *mûš* (DEPART <4185>). ¶
2 ***mûš*** [verb: מוּשׁ <4184>; a prim. root] ► **This word has the sense of touching something with one's hands to identify it and locate it.** Refs.: Gen. 27:21; Judg. 16:26. This human experience is not realized by idols (Ps. 115:7; also translated to handle), although they have hands. ¶
3 ***māšaš*** [verb: מָשַׁשׁ <4959>; a prim. root] ► **This word means to touch, to grope.** It refers to feeling around, groping after something to identify it or to move around, such as Isaac did (Gen. 27:12, 22); or as the Egyptians did during the plague of darkness (Ex. 10:21). It has the sense of staggering, trying to find one's way in a figurative sense (Deut. 28:29; Job 12:25), especially of the wicked (Job 5:14). Other refs.: Gen. 31:34, 37 (also translated to search); Job 12:25. ¶

FEET – ***margᵉlôṯ*** [masc. plur. noun: מַרְגְּלוֹת <4772>; denom. from FOOT <7272>] ► **This word describes the place where one's feet rest or stand, the area immediately**

around them. Refs.: Ruth 3:4, 7, 8, 14; Dan. 10:6. ¶

FEIGN – Neh. 6:8 ➔ DEVISE <908>.

FELL – Is. 6:13 ➔ FELLING <7995> a.

FELLING – ***šalleḵeṯ*** [fem. noun: שַׁלֶּכֶת <7995>; from THROW <7993>] ▶
a. This word refers to the falling or cutting down of a tree. Ref.: Is. 6:13.
b. This word indicates a casting off of leaves. It refers to a tree's losing its leaves in the fall (Is. 6:13). ¶

FELLOW – [1] ***ḥaḇrāh*** [Aramaic fem. noun: חַבְרָה <2273>; fem. of COMPANION <2269>] ▶ **This word means and is also translated a companion, an associate.** It refers to the ten horns that arose long before the little horn of Daniel 7:20 but were still related to it in some way. ¶
– [2] See COMPANION <2269>, <2270>.

FEMALE – [1] ***neqēḇāh*** [fem. noun: נְקֵבָה <5347>; from PIERCE <5344>] ▶ **This word refers to a female woman.** Refs.: Gen. 1:27; 5:2; Lev. 12:5, 7; 15:33; 27:4–7; Num. 5:3; 31:15; Jer. 31:22. **It refers also to a female animal.** Refs.: Gen. 6:19; 7:3, 9, 16; Lev. 3:1, 6; 4:28, 32; 5:6. Other ref.: Deut. 4:16 (a carved image). ¶
– [2] See WOMAN <802>.

FEMALE GOAT – ***'êz*** [fem. noun: עֵז <5795>; from STRENGTHEN <5810>] ▶ **This word refers to an animal of the flock that was milked and eaten, as well as used in many sacrificial rituals.** It was valuable property, a part of a person's wealth (Gen. 15:9; 27:9, 16; Lev. 22:27). Goat's milk was a choice drink (Prov. 27:27). Goat's hair was used as a covering and for other items (Ex. 25:4; 1 Sam. 19:13, 16). The phrases *ṣeḇir hā'êz* and *śe'îr 'izzîm* refer to a buck or he goat (Gen. 37:31; Dan. 8:5, 8). *

FENCE – [1] Job 10:11 ➔ HEDGE (MAKE A, PUT A) <7753> [2] Song 7:2; Is. 17:11 ➔ ENCIRCLE <5473> [4] Is. 5:2 ➔ DIG <5823>.

FENCE IN – Is. 17:11 ➔ GROW <7735>.

FENCED – 2 Chr. 11:10; 12:4 ➔ FORTIFIED PLACE <4694>.

FENS – Job 40:21 ➔ MARSH <1207>.

FERRET – ***'anāqāh*** [fem. noun: אֲנָקָה <604>; the same as GROANING <603>] ▶ **The word is also translated gecko.** This small animal is classified as unclean, a swarming thing which the Israelites were not permitted to eat (Lev. 11:30; see v. 31). ¶

FERRYBOAT – 2 Sam. 19:18 ➔ FORD <5679>.

FERTILITY – Gen. 27:39 ➔ FATNESS <4924> a.

FERVENT – Prov. 26:23 ➔ BURN (verb) <1814>.

FESTAL APPAREL – ***maḥalāṣāh*** [fem. noun: מַחֲלָצָה <4254>; from DRAW OUT <2502> (in the sense of something easily drawn out)] ▶ **This word means a celebration robe, a fine garment.** It indicates finely woven, white clothing; festival clothing (Is. 3:22; also translated changeable suit of apparel, fine robe); festive robes. They were a sign of a time of rejoicing (Zech. 3:4: rich robe, festal robe, change of raiment, pure vestment, fine garment). ¶

FESTER – Ps. 38:5 ➔ WASTE AWAY <4743>.

FESTERING – Lev. 21:20; 22:22 ➔ SCAB <1618>.

FESTERING BOIL – Ex. 9:9, 10 ➔ BOIL (noun) <76>.

FESTIVAL – [1] Judg. 9:27 ➔ OFFERING OF PRAISE <1974> [2] See FEAST <2282>.

FETCH – Deut. 24:10 ➔ LEND <5670>.

FETTER – [1] ***'eḵes*** [masc. noun: עֶכֶס <5914>; from TINKLE <5913>] ▶ **This**

word indicates instruments for confining persons, for controlling them to lead them to danger, execution, etc. Ref.: Prov. 7:22; also translated noose, stocks. The Hebrew word also describes a leg bracelet, an anklet; see ANKLET <5914>. ¶
– [2] Job 36:8; Ps. 149:8; Is. 45:14; Nah. 3:10 ➔ FIREBRAND <2131> b. [3] Is. 28:22; etc. ➔ BOND <4147> a.

FETTERS – [1] ***keḇel*** [masc. noun: כֶּבֶל <3525>; from an unused root meaning to twine or braid together] ▶ **This word refers to something used to restrict the freedom of a person's feet in captivity; it is also translated shackles.** In one context, it refers to Joseph's imprisonment in Egypt (Ps. 105:18). It is also used in a more general sense of iron fetters placed on the kings of the nations (Ps. 149:8). ¶
– [2] Eccl. 7:26 ➔ BOND <612>.

FEVER – [1] ***qaddaḥaṯ*** [fem. noun: קַדַּחַת <6920>; from KINDLE <6919>] ▶ **This word means an unusual elevated body temperature. It was one of the pestilences or plagues the Lord would send on a disobedient people.** Refs.: Lev. 26:16; Deut. 28:22. ¶
– [2] Job 30:30 ➔ HEAT (noun) <2721> [3] Lam. 5:10 ➔ BURNING HEAT <2152>.

FEVER HEAT – Ps. 32:4 ➔ DROUGHT <2725>.

FEVERISH – Lam. 5:10 ➔ BURNING HEAT <2152>.

FEW – [1] 2 Chr. 24:24 ➔ LITTLE ONE <4705> [2] Is. 24:6 ➔ VERY <4213>.

FEW IN NUMBER – ***maṯ*** [masc. noun: מַת <4962>; from the same as WHEN <4970> (in the sense of how long; properly an adult, as of full length)] ▶ **This word is used to refer to a small number of persons.** It refers to a few men or people (Gen. 34:30; Deut. 4:27; 1 Chr. 16:19; Jer. 44:28); to men as opposed to women (Deut. 2:34; 3:6; Is. 3:25); to persons in general (Job 11:3, 11; 19:19). *

FICKLE – Zeph. 3:4 ➔ RECKLESS (BE) <6348>.

FIELD – [1] ***bar*** [Aramaic masc. noun: בַּר <1251>; corresponding to GRAIN <1250>] ▶ **This word describes the place where beasts live freely.** Refs.: Dan. 2:38; 4:12, 15, 21, 23, 25, 32. Nebuchadnezzar's kingdom, given to him by God, was figuratively referred to as the location for these fields. ¶
[2] ***yagêḇ*** [masc. noun: יָגֵב <3010>; from PLOWMAN (BE) <3009>] ▶ **This word indicates the areas of land to be plowed by the plowmen, plowed ground, or fields.** Ref.: Jer. 39:10. ¶
[3] ***śaḏay, śāḏeh*** [masc. noun: שָׂדַי, שָׂדֶה <7704>; from an unused root meaning to spread out] ▶ **This word also means open country, a domain, a plot (of land). The primary meaning of the word is a field, oftentimes defined more descriptively as an open field.** The noun is used to describe pastureland in which flocks of sheep were fed (Gen. 29:2). The word is also used to describe a field or a plot of land that was normally unfrequented and in which one could meditate without being disturbed (Gen. 24:63, 65). Another meaning of the word is a field in which a slain man was found (Deut. 21:1). The word is also used as a place opposite of the Tent of Meeting in which the Israelites had made sacrifices but were to no longer (Lev. 17:5). In Numbers, the noun is used to indicate a land or territory that belonged to a nation or tribe (Num. 21:20). *
[4] ***śᵉḏêmāh*** [fem. noun: שְׁדֵמָה <7709>; apparently from <7704> above] ▶ **In general a field was a place where a variety of produce from the soil was generated.** Ref.: Hab. 3:17. It refers to fields transformed into vineyards, but in context it is used figuratively of the fields of Gomorah that produced evil (Deut. 32:32). It refers to open land or areas in general (2 Kgs. 23:4; Is. 16:8; Jer. 31:40). For another meaning of the Hebrew word, see SCORCHED <7709>. ¶
[5] ***śᵉrêmāh*** [fem. noun: שְׁרֵמָה <8309>; prob. by an orthographical error for <7709> above] ▶ **This word refers to parts of the**

open country good for agriculture or grazing. Ref.: Jer. 31:40; NIV: terrace. ¶

FIELD (FERTILE, FRUITFUL, PLENTIFUL) – ***karmel*** [masc. noun: כַּרְמֶל <3759>; from VINEYARD <3754>] ▶
a. This word usually refers to an area of fertile ground set aside for growing fruit trees and vines. Refs.: 2 Chr. 26:10; Is. 10:18; 16:10; 29:17; 32:15, 16. It also denotes an area covered with a thick forest (2 Kgs. 19:23: fruitful *forest*, thickest *forest*, finest *of the forests*, *forest of his* Carmel; Is. 37:24). *
b. This word indicates new grain, fresh kernels. It refers to grain that is newly ripened and fresh (Lev. 2:14; 23:14; 2 Kgs. 4:42) and of new growth, often used in religious festivals. ¶

FIELD COMMANDER – 2 Kgs. 18:17, 19; etc. ➔ RABSHAKEH <7262>.

FIELDS (WORK THE) – 2 Kgs. 25:12; Jer. 52:16 ➔ PLOWMAN (BE) <3009>.

FIERCE – [1] ***ḥᵒriy*** [masc. noun: חֳרִי <2750>; from ANGRY (GET) <2734>] ▶ **This word means burning; it is also translated heat, great, hot. It is used to describe anger.** The word occurs with *'ap̱* (<639>) which primarily means nose, but in this case, it means anger as derived from the snorting of an angry person. The anger may be righteous anger, such as God's anger at Israel's unfaithfulness (Deut. 29:24; Lam. 2:3); Moses' anger aroused by Pharaoh's stubbornness (Ex. 11:8); and Jonathan's anger at Saul's outburst against David (1 Sam. 20:34). It may also be unrighteous anger, such as the anger of troops dismissed with pay because of God's word (2 Chr. 25:10); and the anger of the kings of Israel and Syria against Judah (Is. 7:4). In all cases, the heat of the anger is evident whether expressed by leaving the room or by attempting to put to death the object of anger (2 Chr. 25:10; cf. v. 13). ¶
[2] ***yā'az*** [verb: יָעַז <3267>; a prim. root] ▶ **This word indicates to be strong, insolent, arrogant.** It indicates an attitude or disposition of persons, such as insolent, fierce, resistant (Is. 33:19). ¶
– [3] Gen. 49:7 ➔ STRONG <5794> a. [4] Job 41:10 ➔ CRUEL <393> [5] Prov. 27:4 ➔ CRUEL <395> [6] Hab. 1:8 ➔ SHARPEN <2300>.

FIERCENESS – [1] Is. 42:25 ➔ STRENGTH <5807> [2] Jer. 49:16 ➔ TERROR <8606>.

FIERY – Dan. 3:6, 11; etc. ➔ FIRE <5135>.

FIERY LAW – [1] ***'ešdāṯ*** [fem. noun: אֶשְׁדָּת <799>] ▶ **To get this meaning, the word is considered a compound word made up of *'ēš*, fire, and *dāṯ*, law.** Ref.: Deut. 33:2, NKJV, KJV. The Hebrew word is also translated FLASHING LIGHTNING and SLOPE; see these entries. ¶
– [2] Deut. 33:2 ➔ SLOPE <794>.

FIERY SHAFT – Ps. 7:13 ➔ BURN (verb) <1814>.

FIFTH – [1] ***ḥᵃmiyšiy, ḥamiššiy*** [ordinal number: חֲמִישִׁי, חֲמִשִּׁי <2549>; ordinal from FIVE <2568>] ▶ **This word is used to designate the fifth item in a series.** A fifth son (Gen. 30:17); a fifth day (Gen. 1:23). It refers to an amount of something equaling a fifth of the whole, such as a fifth of harvested grain (Gen. 47:24; Lev. 5:16). It denotes the fifth time in a series (Neh. 6:5). It is used to indicate something that has five sides, is five-sided (1 Kgs. 6:31), a pentagon. *
[2] ***ḥōmeš*** [masc. noun: חֹמֶשׁ <2569>; from FIFTH (TAKE A) <2567>] ▶ **This word refers to one-fifth of produce.** It refers to one-fifth of the produce of the land of Egypt (Gen. 47:26) that was stored up for difficult times of famine. ¶

FIFTH (TAKE A) – ***ḥāmaš*** [verb: חָמַשׁ <2567>; a denom. from FIVE <2568>] ▶ **This word is used once in a factitive or intensive form meaning to take one-fifth, or levy one-fifth as a tax.** Ref.: Gen. 41:34. ¶

FIFTH RIB – 2 Sam. 2:23; 3:27; 4:6; 20:10 ➔ STOMACH <2570>.

FIFTY – ***ḥ^{a}miššiym*** [pluralized numerical adj.: חֲמִשִּׁים <2572>; multiple of FIVE <2568>] ▶ **This word is the pluralized form of five, *ḥomêš*, used to designate fifty of something.** It may be used in various ways: by itself meaning fifty of something (Ex. 18:21, 25); with other numbers (Ex. 30:23); without other numbers (Num. 31:30); preceded by a word in the construct meaning of, e.g., "in the year of fifty," fiftieth year (2 Kgs. 15:23). *

FIG, FIG TREE – ***t^{e}'ênāh*** [fem. noun: תְּאֵנָה <8384>; perhaps of foreign deriv.] ▶ **This word describes the leaves of a fig tree, a tree bearing a hollow, pear-shaped false fruit with sweet, pulpy flesh containing numerous tiny, seedlike true fruits.** The words may stand for the tree (2 Kgs. 18:31) or the fig (Num. 13:23). The first clothing for humans was made from the leaves of a fig tree (Gen. 3:7). Figs were a prized food in the Promised Land (Num. 13:23). To have a vine and a fig tree was an ideal in Israel historically and in a restored community (Zech. 3:10). *

FIG, GREEN FIG – ***pag*** [masc. noun: פַּג <6291>; from an unused root meaning to be torpid, i.e., crude] ▶ **This word refers to early sweet tasting fruits put forth in spring, according to its immediate context.** Ref.: Song 2:13. ¶

FIGHT – [1] ***lāḥam*** [verb: לָחַם <3898>; a prim. root] ▶ **This word means to do battle, to wage war. It is used nearly always in the niphal reciprocal stem of the verb.** It means to close quarters and to engage in battle or war with the Egyptians (Ex. 1:10); against Israel (Num. 21:1, 23, 26; 22:11; Josh. 9:2); Israel against its enemies (Josh. 10:29). It is used of the Lord's fighting against Israel's enemies (Ex. 14:14, 25; 17:9, 10; Josh. 10:14) on behalf of His people. Its object is indicated with various prepositions, *'et̲, 'im, 'al.* It can be used with *yahad̲* following, to indicate fighting with each other (1 Sam. 17:10). It is used in the simple stem of the verb a few times only in Psalms to mean to do, to make battle: In the imperative form, it directs the Lord to fight against one's enemies (Ps. 35:1); in its simplest meaning, it indicates to fight (Ps. 56:1, 2). The Hebrew word is also translated to eat, to taste; see EAT <3898>. *

[2] ***nāṣāh*** [verb: נָצָה <5327>; a prim. root] ▶ **This word means and is also translated to struggle, to strive.** It means to contend with violently, to quarrel, to come to blows, to men fighting (Ex. 2:13; 21:22; Deut. 25:11; Lev. 24:10; 2 Sam. 14:6); to disputes, challenges, accusations among people (Num. 26:9: to contend, to strive, to rebel); to battles, war (Ps. 60:1). The Hebrew word also means to be ruined; see RUIN (BE, LIE IN) <5327>. ¶

FIGS (CAKE, LUMP, POULTICE OF) – ***d^{e}b̲êlāh*** [fem. noun: דְּבֵלָה <1690>; from an unused root (akin to DWELL <2082>) prob. meaning to press together] ▶ **This word refers to a sweet tasting fruit cake, a lump of pressed fruits.** It describes figs that were pressed into the form of a cake (2 Kgs. 20:7). They were usually round or brick-shaped. It was used for food (1 Sam. 25:18; 30:12) and as an application for skin eruptions (Is. 38:21). Other ref.: 1 Chr. 12:40. ¶

FIGURE – [1] Deut. 4:16 ➔ IDOL <5566> [2] Prov. 1:6 ➔ SAYING <4426>.

FIGURED, FIGURED STONE – Lev. 26:1; Num. 33:52 ➔ PICTURE <4906>.

FILE – 1 Sam. 13:21 ➔ CHARGE (noun) <6477> b.

FILIGREE – [1] ***mišb^{e}ṣôt̲*** [fem. noun: מִשְׁבְּצוֹת <4865>; from WEAVE <7660>] ▶ **This word indicates filigree settings, a lace-like ornamental work of intertwined wire made of gold, silver, copper, or bronze to receive settings of precious jewels.** Refs.: Ex. 28:11, 13, 14, 25; 39:6, 13, 16, 18; KJV: ouches. It can be used of any fine work like this, e.g., of clothing (Ps. 45:13: woven, interwoven, wrought). ¶
– [2] Ex. 28:20; 39:13 ➔ SETTING <4396>.

FILL – [1] Is. 56:12 → DRUNKARD <5433> [2] See FULL (BE) <4390>.

FILL, FILLED (BE) – ***mᵉlā’*** [Aramaic verb: מְלָא <4391>; corresponding to FULL (BE) <4390>] ▶ **This word means to take up empty space, to make something full.** In the book of Daniel, a stone fills the whole earth in a figurative sense (Dan. 2:35). It is used of a person’s being full of anger (Dan. 3:19). ¶

FILLET – [1] ***ḥāšûq*** [masc. noun: חָשׁוּק <2838>; pass. part. of DESIRE (verb) <2836> (in the sense of being attached)] ▶ **This word indicates a band around the pillars of the Tabernacle courtyard.** Refs.: Ex. 27:10, 11; 36:38; 38:10–12, 17, 19. ¶
– [2] Jer. 52:2 → THREAD <2339>.

FILLY – Song 1:9 → MARE <5484>.

FILTH – [1] Gen. 6:16; Is. 4:4; 28:8 → FILTHINESS <6675> [2] Hos. 5:11 → PRECEPT <6673> b.

FILTHINESS – [1] ***ṣô’āh*** [fem. noun: צוֹאָה <6675>; fem. of FILTHY <6674>] ▶ **This word is used figuratively of moral, spiritual, or behavioral uncleanness.** Ref.: Prov. 30:12. It refers in some contexts to Israel’s filth, refuse, a term standing for the corruption and rebellion of the whole nation (Is. 4:4; 28:8). ¶
– [2] Ezek. 16:36 → LUST (noun) <5178> [3] See UNCLEANNESS <2932>.

FILTHY – [1] ***‘ēḏ, ‘iddāh*** [masc. noun: עֵד, עִדָּה <5708>; from an unused root meaning to set a period] ▶ **This word refers to uncleanness, menstruation. It indicates a woman’s menstrual period or cloth that was considered unclean.** In context it is used of God’s people whose righteousness has become as a filthy rag (Is. 64:6; ESV: polluted). ¶
[2] ***ṣô’, ṣô’iy*** [adj.: צוֹא, צוֹאִי <6674>; from an unused root meaning to issue] ▶ **This word refers to the high priest Joshua’s priestly garments smeared and soiled with refuse and excrement.** It represented the defilement of the priesthood that occurred in Israel (Zech. 3:3, 4). ¶
– [3] Is. 28:8 → FILTHINESS <6675> [4] Lam. 1:8 → UNCLEAN <5206> a. [5] Zeph. 3:1 → LIFT ONESELF <4754>.

FILTHY (BE) – ***mārā’*** [verb: מָרָא <4754>; a prim. root] ▶ **Early translators of Zephaniah 3:1 interpreted this verb as meaning to be unclean and unholy before God, used of a defiled Jerusalem.** More recent translators understand the Hebrew word in that verse actually means “to be rebellious” [see REBELLIOUS (BE) <4784>]. Ref.: Zeph. 3:1; KJV: filthy. In actual fact the Hebrew word <4754> *mara›* occurs only in Job 39:8, where it means to raise oneself up, to lift oneself up; see LIFT ONESELF <4754>. ¶

FILTHY (BECOME) – [1] Ps. 14:3; 53:3; Job 15:16 → CORRUPT (BECOME) <444> [2] Lam. 1:8 → GLUTTON (BE) <2151> a.

FIN – ***sᵉnappiyr*** [masc. noun: סְנַפִּיר <5579>; of uncertain deriv.] ▶ **An organ attached to the body of fishes, used for propulsion and steering.** It characterized a fish that was clean and edible to Israel (Lev. 11:9, 10, 12; Deut. 14:9, 10). ¶

FIND – ***māṣā’*** [verb: מָצָא <4672>; a prim. root] ▶ **This verb is employed in both the active and passive senses (to be found). In addition, it is also used in a causative sense, to cause to find. Finally, the word is employed in several idioms that carry special meanings.** It is used to indicate finding or seeking just about anything: water (Gen. 26:32; Ex. 15:22); a place, goal, or location (Gen. 8:9); a knowledge of the Lord (Prov. 2:5); the word of the Lord (Amos 8:12); or words of wisdom (Prov. 4:22). The word indicates coming on something (Gen. 44:8); of finding something (Job 11:7; Eccl. 3:11). Additional idiomatic phrases include finding heart, meaning to be able to do something (2 Sam. 7:27); finding the vigor (life) of one’s hand, renewing one's strength (Is. 57:10); to not be found, not to exist or be dead (Job 20:8). The meanings discussed are used in passive constructions as well. Persons being sought are found (Gen. 18:29, 30; Josh. 10:17); and crime or evil can be found out (Ex. 22:4; 1 Sam. 25:28); as can evildoers (Ex. 22:2, 7). The verb means to happen to be, literally to be found, in several passages (Deut. 17:2; 18:10; Jer. 5:26). Finally, in the passive usage of the verb, it means not sufficient for someone, as in Joshua 17:16 where the hill country was not found to be sufficient for the people of Joseph. In the stem indicating cause, the verb can mean to bring on someone their just desserts, i.e., to cause proper justice to find them (Job 34:11; cf. Job 37:13). In 2 Samuel 3:8, the verb indicates the deliverance of someone into the power of another person, i.e., to make someone be found in the hand of another, in this case in the hand of David. *

FINE (adj.) – 1 ***ṭāḇ*** [Aramaic masc. noun: טָב <2869>; from GLAD (BE) <2853> (the same as GOOD <2896>)] ▶ **This word denotes goodness, purity.** It is used to describe pure gold, "good gold," or fine gold (Dan. 2:32), an especially high quality sample of this metal. It refers to what is pleasing to someone, such as a matter or proposal to a king (Ezra 5:17: good). ¶

2 ***ʿāṯiyq*** [adj.: עָתִיק <6266>; from MOVE <6275> (in the sense of to grow old)] ▶
a. This word means choice, good-looking. It indicates clothing or garments of the finest material and craftsmanship (Is. 23:18). ¶
b. This word means durable. It is taken by some translators to indicate the quality or durability of the items mentioned (Is. 23:18). ¶
– 3 Ezra 8:27 ➔ SHINY <6668> 4 Is. 19:9 ➔ COMBED <8305>.

FINE (noun) – ***ʿōneš*** [masc. noun: עֹנֶשׁ <6066>; from FINE (verb) <6064>] ▶ **This word means a penalty, an indemnity; it is also translated tribute, levy, punishment.** The basic meaning of the word is a monetary obligation placed on one who violated the Law or was under subjugation to a higher authority. It was used to refer to the tribute forced on Jehoahaz by the Egyptian pharaoh (2 Kgs. 23:33); and the punishment facing unrestrained anger (Prov. 19:19). ¶

FINE (IMPOSE A) – Prov. 17:26 ➔ FINE (verb) <6064>.

FINE (verb) – ***ʿānaš*** [verb: עָנַשׁ <6064>; a prim. root] ▶ **This word means to exact an amount of money as a penalty; it is also translated to punish, to condemn, to impose a fine.** The primary meaning is the monetary assessment for a crime and is clearly seen in Deuteronomy 22:19 (KJV: to amerce) (see also Ex. 21:22). Similarly, Amos used the word to denote the condemnation that rests on those under punishment (Amos 2:8). In a practical sense, the writer of wisdom extolled the educational benefits of applying such a fine to the wicked (Prov. 21:11); but he expressly warned against punishing the righteous (Prov. 17:26). Other refs.: 2 Chr. 36:3; Prov. 22:3; 27:12. ¶

FINE CLOTHES, FINE CLOTHING – Is. 3:24 ➔ RICH ROBE <6614> a.

FINE FABRIC – Is. 19:9 ➔ WHITE CLOTH <2355>.

FINE FLOUR – ***sōleṯ*** [common noun: סֹלֶת <5560>; from an unused root meaning to strip] ▶ **This word is used of a grade of flour ground fine from the best part of the wheat grain.** Refs.: Gen. 18:6; Ex. 29:2, 40; also translated as wheat flour. It was used in sacrifices and was considered a food to be served as a luxury item or in the king's household (1 Kgs. 4:22; Ezek. 16:13, 19). *

FINE GARMENT – Prov. 31:24 ➔ LINEN GARMENT <5466>.

FINE LINEN – 1 ***bûṣ*** [masc. noun: בּוּץ <948>; from an unused root (of the same form) meaning to bleach, i.e., (intransitive)

to be white] ▶ **This was a nice, costly white linen.** It is used to describe a house where Egyptian linen workers plied their trade (1 Chr. 15:27). Some Temple workers were skilled in working with linen (2 Chr. 2:14); it was part of the Temple veil (2 Chr. 3:14). It was used to pay for Tyrian imports (Ezek. 27:16). *
– [2] Prov. 31:24; Is. 3:23 ➔ LINEN GARMENT <5466> [3] Is. 19:9 ➔ WHITE CLOTH <2355>.

FINE, FINEST – 1 Kgs. 10:18 ➔ REFINED (BE) <6338>.

FINELY WORKED – Ex. 31:10; 35:19; 39:1, 41 ➔ WOVEN <8278> a.

FINEST – [1] Job 28:15 ➔ PURE <5462> [2] Is. 17:10 ➔ PLEASANT <5282> [3] Is. 25:6 ➔ REFINE <2212>.

FINGER – [1] ***’eṣba‘*** [fem. noun: אֶצְבַּע <676>; from the same as DYED WORK <6648> (in the sense of grasping)] ▶ **This word designates either digits of the hand or the foot.** Refs.: Ex. 29:12; Lev. 4:6, 17; 2 Sam. 21:20; 1 Chr. 20:6. Various functions of the finger are noted. It was an instrument that could be used for good or evil: (1) The forefinger of a priest applied blood or oil in certain rituals (Lev. 4:6, 17, 25; 14:16, 27). (2) It was used figuratively to describe God's act of writing (Ex. 31:18) or intervention (Ex. 8:19). (3) Several fingers were a measure of thickness (Jer. 52:21). (4) Idols were produced by the work of human fingers (Is. 2:8). *
[2] ***’eṣba‘*** [Aramaic fem. noun: אֶצְבַּע <677>; corresponding to <676> above] ▶ **Used as an anthropomorphism, this word describes digits of the hand and foot on the great image of Daniel and of the mysterious hand that wrote on the wall of Belshazzar's palace.** Refs.: Dan. 2:41, 42; 5:5. ¶

FINING POT – Prov. 17:3; 27:21 ➔ CRUCIBLE <4715>.

FINISH – [1] ***yeṣa’*** [Aramaic verb: יְצָא <3319>; corresponding to GO OUT <3318>] ▶ **This word means to conclude, to end something; it is also translated to complete.** It is used of the conclusion of the construction of the Temple built by the returned exiles (Ezra 6:15). ¶
[2] ***kālāh*** [verb: כָּלָה <3615>; a prim. root] ▶ **This word means to complete, to accomplish, to end, to fail, to exhaust.** Its primary meaning is to consummate or to bring to completion. This occasionally occurs in a positive sense as in the awesome goodness of God's perfected and finished creation (Gen. 2:1, 2). It also represents the favorable conclusion of meaningful human labor as in building the Tabernacle (Ex. 39:32); or preparing tithes (Deut. 26:12). However, *kālāh* is more often used with a negative connotation. God threatened to consume human unbelief (as in completing the life span), a promise terribly fulfilled at Korah's rebellion (Num. 16:21). Also, Israel was to be God's vehicle in consuming or finishing the heathen nations in the land (Deut. 7:22), thus completing the ban. The verb also describes the transitory reality of fallen human nature. We finish our years like a sigh (Ps. 90:9), passing away like an exhausted cloud (Job 7:9). *
[3] ***kelal*** [Aramaic verb: כְּלַל <3635>; corresponding to PERFECT (MAKE) <3634>] ▶ **This word means to complete.** It described the completed Temple (Ezra 5:11). It also carries the meaning of to restore (Ezra 4:12, 13, 16; 5:3, 9). See the related Hebrew root *kālal* [PERFECT (MAKE) <3634>] and the related Hebrew adjective *kāliyl* (WHOLE <3632>). Other ref.: Ezra 6:14. ¶
– [4] Ezra 5:16; Dan. 5:26 ➔ COMPLETE (verb) <8000> [5] Is. 10:12 ➔ CUT OFF <1214> [6] Is. 33:1 ➔ END (MAKE AN) <5239>.

FIR – [1] ***berôṯ*** [masc. noun: בְּרוֹת <1266>; a variation of CYPRESS <1265>] ▶ **This word denotes an evergreen tree; also pine, juniper. It is also translated cypress.** It is building material in the house of the lover and the beloved (Song 1:17) because of its beauty and stateliness. It parallels in grandeur the splendid cedars. ¶
– [2] Is. 41:19; 60:13 ➔ PINE <8410> [3] Is. 44:14 ➔ ASH <766> [4] See CYPRESS <1265>.

FIRE – 1 ***'ûr*** [masc. noun: אוּר <217>; from LIGHT (GIVE) <215>] ▶ **This word refers to the destructive burning of God's judgment.** Ref.: Is. 31:9. It also refers to God's destruction of the wicked (Ezek. 5:2). In Isaiah 44:16 and Isaiah 47:14, the noun is used to speak of a form of idol worship. Other refs.: Is. 24:15; 50:11. ¶
2 ***'ēš*** [fem. noun: אֵשׁ <784>; a prim. word] ▶ **This word relates to the destructive burning of various things.** It refers to any fire that breaks out and burns up something, whether people, things, or animals (Ex. 22:6). Both idols and the golden calf were burned up by fire (Ex. 32:20; Deut. 7:5, 25; 12:3). It is used as a symbol for God (Gen. 15:17; Ex. 3:2; 13:21, 22; 19:18; Deut. 4:11). It describes the fire made for cooking, roasting, etc. (Ex. 12:8, 9; Lev. 2:14). It was used on the brazen altar to burn offerings (Lev. 1:7; 6:9). In some cases, it was fire from the Lord which consumed sacrifices (Lev. 9:24; 2 Chr. 7:1, 3). It was used to describe strange fire offered before the Lord *'ēš zorā*, referring to impure (*profane* or *strange*) fire, probably from a campfire nearby rather than from the brazen altar which held the altar coals for use at the Golden Altar of Incense (Num. 3:4; 26:61; see Lev. 10:1–3; 16:1, 12–13). It was used to depict lightning in the plagues in Egypt (Ex. 9:23, 24; cf. Ps. 18:13). The Lord's anger could be depicted as burning like fire (Ps. 89:46; Ezek. 22:31; 38:19). But great wickedness was also described as consuming like fire (Is. 9:18, 19). The word is used in various short phrases in connection with other words: It is used to depict a torch or flame of fire (Ex. 3:2; Dan. 10:6, *labbaṯ-'ēš*; Joel 2:5). With several other words, it means spark of fire (Job 18:5); oven of fire (Zech. 12:6); flame of or flaming fire (Ps. 104:4); tongue of fire (Is. 5:24) and a few other combinations. *
3 ***'eššā'*** [Aramaic fem. noun: אֶשָּׁא <785>; corresponding to <784> above] ▶ **See previous definition. This word is also translated flame.** It is found in only Daniel 7:11, where the fourth beast of Daniel is burned up by fire. ¶
4 ***'iššāh*** [fem. noun: אִשָּׁה <800>; from <784> above] ▶ **This fire consumes or burns up lead.** In this case, lead is part of the impurities being burned up to purge God's people, but the process goes on in vain (Jer. 6:29). ¶
5 ***be'ērāh*** [fem. sing. noun: בְּעֵרָה <1200>; from BURN (verb) <1197>] ▶ **The only occurrence of this word is in Exodus 22:6.** One starts a fire which burns grain and he must make restitution. ¶
6 ***nûr*** [Aramaic masc. noun: נוּר <5135>; from an unused root (corresponding to that of LAMP <5216> meaning to shine)] ▶ **This word (also translated fiery) refers to the flames and heat of the king's furnace into which the Hebrew young men were cast.** Refs.: Dan. 3:6, 11, 15, 17, 20–27. It also refers to the river of flames flowing from the throne of the Ancient of Days (Dan. 7:9, 10). ¶
– 7 Is. 27:11: to set on fire, to make a fire ➔ LIGHT (GIVE) <215>.

FIRE (MAKE A) – Is. 44:15 ➔ KINDLE <5400>.

FIRE (SET ON) – 1 2 Sam. 14:30, 31 ➔ BURN (verb) <3341> 2 Is. 27:4 ➔ BURN (verb) <6702> 3 Obad. 1:18 ➔ BURN (verb) <1814>.

FIREBRAND – 1 ***'ûḏ*** [masc. noun: אוּד <181>; from an unused root meaning to rake together] ▶ **This word refers to a piece of firewood; it is also translated stump of firebrand, stub of firewood, brand, burning stick.** The word is used metaphorically to refer to Rezin and Remaliah, two powerless, ineffective kings in Syria and Israel, respectively (Is. 7:4). In Amos it refers to Israel as a barely burning but faintly alive people whom God rescued (Amos 4:11; Zech. 3:2). ¶
2 ***zêq, ziyqāh*** [זֵק, זִיקָה <2131>; from LEAP <2187>] ▶
a. This feminine word refers to fiery missiles of some sort (possibly flaming arrows). Ref.: Prov. 26:18. They were used as defensive weapons as well (Is. 50:11); also translated brand, spark, torch. ¶
b. A masculine noun indicating a fetter, chain. It refers to the trials or possibly

literal chains that may confine even kings (Job 36:8; Ps. 149:8). Enemies and captives are bound by these chains (Is. 45:14; Nah. 3:10) in order to lead them away. ¶
– [3] Judg. 15:4 ➔ TORCH <3940>.

FIREPOT – Jer. 36:22, 23 ➔ BRAZIER <254>.

FIRM – [1] ***'azāḏ*** [Aramaic verb: אָזָד <230>; of uncertain deriv.] ▶ **This word means to be gone, to go forth, to promulgate.** Some would prefer to designate this an adjective or a noun (i.e., firm) in Daniel 2:5, 8. It designates the word or command that had gone forth from King Nebuchadnezzar. ¶
– [2] Is. 22:23 ➔ NURSE (verb) <539>.

FIRM (MAKE) – Dan. 6:7 ➔ STRONG (BE, BECOME, GROW) <8631>.

FIRM (STAND) – [1] Ps. 89:28 ➔ NURSE (verb) <539> [2] Is. 46:8 ➔ SHOW YOURSELVES MEN <377>.

FIRM PLACE – Ezra 9:8 ➔ PEG <3489>.

FIRMNESS – Dan. 2:41 ➔ STRENGTH <5326>.

FIRST – [1] ***qaḏmāy*** [Aramaic adj.: קַדְמָי <6933>; from a root corresponding to MEET (verb) <6923> (in the sense of to do something earlier)] ▶ **This word refers to the initial item(s) in a sequence of things but also to previous item(s) with respect to a later item mentioned.** Refs.: Dan. 7:4, 8, 24. ¶
[2] ***ri'šôn, ri'šōn*** [adj.: רִאשׁוֹן, רִאשֹׁן <7223>; from BEGINNING <7221>] ▶ **This term means former, foremost, earlier, head, chief.** It occurs 182 times and denotes that which comes first among given items, whether in place, rank, or order (Gen. 25:25, 32:17; 2 Kgs. 1:14) or (more frequently) in time. Moses had the Tabernacle set up in the first month, just as the Lord commanded (Ex. 40:2, 17; cf. Num. 9:5; Ezra 7:9; Ezek. 45:18, 21). Zechariah warned the exiles who returned to the Promised Land from the Babylonian captivity not to be like their ancestors who refused to listen to the former prophets (Zech. 1:4, 7:7, 12). The Lord declares Himself to be the first and the last, the Eternal One (Is. 44:6, 48:12). In later Hebrew, the word came to signify the highest in rank or authority (i.e., chief, head). The archangel Michael is portrayed as holding the rank of chief prince (Dan. 10:13; cf. 1 Chr. 18:17; Esther 1:14). This word is derived from the noun *rō'š* [HEAD (noun) <7218>]. *
[3] ***ri'šôniy*** [adj.: רִאשׁוֹנִי <7224>; from <7223> above] ▶ **This word means initial.** The word of the Lord concerning all the people of Judah came to Jeremiah in the first year of King Nebuchadnezzar's reign over all Babylon (Jer. 25:1). ¶

FIRST RIPE – ***bakkûrôṯ*** [fem. noun: בַּכֻּרוֹת <1073>; by orthographical variation from FIRST RIPE FRUIT <1063>] ▶ **This word stands for early ready to eat figs that are delightful.** Ref.: Jer. 24:2; also translated ripen early. They symbolize the captives of Judah in Babylonian exile. ¶

FIRST RIPE FRUIT, FIRST RIPE FIG – ***bikkûrāh*** [fem. noun: בִּכּוּרָה <1063>; fem. of FIRSTFRUITS <1061>] ▶ **This word refers to the early ready to eat figs that are picked quickly and eaten at once.** Ref.: Is. 28:4. It functions figuratively for the godly person who has perished from the land (Mic. 7:1) and as Israel when God first found her (Hos. 9:10) and was delighted in her. It symbolizes the exiles as good figs whom the Lord will watch over (Jer. 24:2) and Ephraim, Northern Israel, as a people who will soon disappear from the land like a fresh first-ripe fig (Is. 28:4) that is swallowed in a second once it is picked. ¶

FIRSTBORN – [1] ***b'ḵôr, b'ḵōr*** [masc. noun: בְּכוֹר, בְּכֹר <1060>; from BORN FIRST (BE) <1069>] ▶ **This word refers to the oldest offspring of animals as well as the oldest child of persons.** Refs.: Gen. 4:4; 25:13. The firstborn of sons in Israel were redeemed, not sacrificed (Num. 3:40–43; 18:15, 17). The firstborn of clean animals were sacrificed to the Lord (Deut. 12:6, 17), but the firstborn males of unclean animals could be redeemed (Num. 18:15). A donkey, though clean, was redeemed because of its use as a beast of burden (Ex. 13:13; 34:20). The word is used metaphorically to refer to Israel as the Lord's firstborn son (Ex. 4:22). In combination with the word death, it means firstborn of death (Job 18:13), indicating a most powerful attack of ill health and death on a person. This is the fate of the wicked. The firstborn son held special privileges called his birthright (Gen. 25:5, 6; 27:19–36; 43:33; Deut. 21:15–17). This special standing could be lost (Gen. 25:31–34). Esau is described as despising his birthright (Gen. 25:34) as the firstborn of Isaac. *

[2] ***bᵉḵiyrāh*** [fem. noun: בְּכִירָה <1067>; fem. from BORN FIRST (BE) <1069>] ▶ **This word indicates a daughter born first. It always describes firstborn women.** Merab was the firstborn of King Saul (1 Sam. 14:49). The firstborn of Lot bore the father of the Moabites (Gen. 19:31, 33, 34, 37). A firstborn daughter was the first one given in marriage (Gen. 29:26). ¶

– [3] See BIRTHRIGHT <1062>.

FIRSTBORN (BE) – ***bāḵar*** [verb: בָּכַר <1069>; a prim. root] ▶ **This word means to be born first, to have the birthright.** It means to recognize as firstborn (Deut. 21:16). It describes animals being born as firstlings or firstborn (Lev. 27:26). It depicts a woman who bears her first son (Jer. 4:31). It also describes fruitful trees bearing fruit every month (Ezek. 47:12). ¶

FIRSTFRUITS – ***bikkûriym*** [masc. plur. noun: בִּכּוּרִים <1061>; from BORN FIRST (BE) <1069>] ▶ **This word refers to the yearly first gathering of the ripened produce of the land in honor of the fact that both the land and its produce belonged to the Lord.** The produce was presented as part of the Feast of First fruits during the Week of the Feast of Unleavened Bread (Ex. 23:16, 19; Lev. 23:6, 10–14) to the Lord in its harvested state or, in the case of some items, when the product had been properly prepared. A later "day of the first fruits" or Pentecost is mentioned in Numbers 28:26 (see also Lev. 23:15–21). At this festival, "bread of the first fruits" was made from the newly harvested grain (Lev. 23:20). Firstfruits were a part of the grain offering ritual (Lev. 2:14; 23:17, 20) and a staple in the support of the priests (Ezek. 44:30). The word refers to Israel as the firstfruits of the Lord's harvest (Jer. 2:3). *

FISH (noun) – [1] ***dāḡ*** [masc. noun: דָּג <1709>; from GROW <1711>] ▶ **This word is used of fish in the sea (water vertebrates having gills), often occurring alongside birds of the heavens and beasts of the field.** Refs.: Gen. 9:2; Ps. 8:7, 8; Ezek. 38:20. It also signifies fish as food and thus gives the name fish gate to the gate where they were brought into Jerusalem to sell (2 Chr. 33:14; Neh. 3:3; Zeph. 1:10). Further, it describes fish as an object of study (1 Kgs. 4:33); as a symbol of defenselessness (Hab. 1:14); and as showing God's sovereign creative power (Job 12:8). *

[2] ***dāḡāh*** [fem. noun: דָּגָה <1710>; from <1709> above] ▶ **This word is identical in meaning to *dāḡ* above.** It can be found in the book of Jonah, where the fish was called a *dāḡ* (Jon. 1:17; 2:10) but was called a *dāḡāh* in Jonah 2:1. In all other instances, this word was used in the collective sense to refer to the fish at creation (Gen. 1:26, 28); the fish who died in the plague (Ex. 7:18, 21; Ps. 105:29); the fish eaten in Egypt (Num. 11:5); and the fish in the waters (Deut. 4:18; Ezek. 29:4, 5; 47:9, 10). ¶

FISH (verb) – ***diyg*** [verb: דִּיג <1770>; denom. from FISH (noun) <1709>] ▶ **This word means to catch fish, or people in the verse of interest.** It refers to a person who catches fish but is used figuratively of God sending fishermen to fish for His people in exile to bring them back (Jer. 16:16; also translated to catch). ¶

FISHER – [1] Is. 19:8; Jer. 16:16 ➔ FISHERMAN <1771> [2] Jer. 16:16; Ezek. 47:10 ➔ FISHERMAN <1728>.

FISHER OWL – Lev. 11:17; Deut. 14:17 ➔ CORMORANT <7994>.

FISHERMAN – [1] ***dawwāḡ*** [masc. noun: דַּוָּג <1728>; an orthographical variation of FISH (noun) <1709> as a denom. (<1771> below)] ▶ **This word is used figuratively to depict God's searching for His people wherever they may be to bring them back to their land.** Ref.: Jer. 16:16. Used literally, it describes those who will catch fish, even along the Dead Sea, when God restores His people and their land (Ezek. 47:10). ¶
[2] ***dayyāḡ*** [masc. noun: דַּיָּג <1771>; from FISH (verb) <1770>] ▶ **This word is used only in the plural of men who cast fish lines or spread nets to catch fish.** Ref.: Is. 19:8. These fish are for the exiles of Israel to bring them back to their homeland (Jer. 16:16; KJV: fisher). ¶

FISHHOOK – [1] ***dûḡāh*** [fem. noun: דּוּגָה <1729>; fem. from the same as FISHERMAN <1728>] ▶ **It was a hook usually used to snag fish.** It was also used to hook and lead away the rebellious and corrupt rich, sophisticated but oppressive women of Bashan (Amos 4:2). ¶
– [2] Job 41:1 ➔ HOOK <2443>.

FISHING NET – Hab. 1:15, 16 ➔ NET (noun) <4365>.

FISHNET – Ezek. 26:5, 14 ➔ NET <2764>.

FIST – [1] ***'egrōp̱*** [masc. noun: אֶגְרֹף <106>; from SWEEP AWAY <1640> (in the sense of grasping)] ▶ **The fist is used as a weapon and as a symbol of violence.** Refs.: Ex. 21:18; Is. 58:4. ¶
– [2] Prov. 30:4; Eccl. 4:6 ➔ HAND <2651>.

FIT – [1] Ex. 26:17; 36:22 ➔ PARALLEL (SET) <7947> [2] Lev. 16:21 ➔ READINESS (IN) <6261>.

FIT (MAKE) – Prov. 24:27 ➔ READY (BE, MAKE, GET) <6257>.

FIT FOR – Gen. 2:18, 20 ➔ BEFORE <5048>.

FIT OUT – Song 3:10 ➔ INLAY <7528>.

FITCH – Is. 28:25, 27 ➔ DILL <7100>.

FITCHES – Ezek. 4:9 ➔ SPELT <3698>.

FITLY – [1] ***'ōp̱en*** [masc. noun: אֹפֶן <655>; from an unused root meaning to revolve] ▶ **This word means right time, right circumstance.** It refers to the proper time for appropriate words to be used (Prov. 25:11). ¶
[2] ***millê'ṯ*** [fem. noun: מִלֵּאת <4402>; from FULL (BE) <4390>] ▶ **This word indicates fullness, appropriateness.** It is usually rendered as a setting, a mounting location in an appropriate setting; "eyes mounted like jewels" (Song 5:12, NIV). ¶

FITTING – [1] ***m^{e}ḥabb^{e}rāh*** [fem. noun: מְחַבְּרָה <4226>; from JOIN TOGETHER <2266>] ▶ **This word indicates a joint, a hinge, a post. It is a technical construction term for clamps or binders prepared to use on the doors of the Temple.** Some of iron (1 Chr. 22:3: joint, joining, clamp, fitting); others of wood (2 Chr. 34:11: coupling, binder, joist). ¶
– [2] Ezra 4:14 ➔ PROPER <749> [3] Ps. 33:1; Prov. 17:7; 19:10; 26:1 ➔ BEAUTIFUL <5000>.

FIVE – ***ḥāmêš, ḥ^{a}mis-]šāh*** [masc. and fem. noun: חָמֵשׁ, חֲמִשָּׁה <2568>; a prim. numeral] ▶ **This word can refer to five of nearly anything.** Five years (Gen. 5:6); five hands, meaning five times (Gen. 43:34). It combines with other numbers: e.g., *ḥ^{a}miššāh 'āśār*, fifteen (Hos. 3:2); when it is pluralized, *ḥ^{a}miššîm*, it means fifty (FIFTY <2572>). *

FIX SECURELY – Prov. 8:28 ➔ STRENGTHEN <5810>.

FIXED – Neh. 10:34 ➔ APPOINTED <2163>.

FLAG – [1] ***tōren*** [masc. noun: תֹּרֶן <8650>; prob. for ASH <766>] ▶ **This word refers to a piece of cloth used as an emblem. It also refers to a mast, a flagstaff. It indicates a beacon, a flag, a flagstaff or pole.** It

is used of the people of Israel, defeated and decimated until only their lonely ensign is left to represent them (Is. 30:17). It refers to the mast or flag representing Israel (Is. 33:23). It refers possibly to a ship's mast for Tyre, a merchant of the seas (Ezek. 27:5). ¶
2 Ex. 2:3, 5; Is. 19:6 ➔ REED <5488>
3 Job 8:11 ➔ MEADOW (plant) <260>.

FLAGON – Is. 22:24 ➔ SKIN BOTTLE <5035>.

FLAGSTAFF – Is. 30:17 ➔ FLAG <8650>.

FLAIL – Judg. 8:7 ➔ THRESH <1758>.

FLAKE-LIKE THING – ***ḥaspas*** [verb: חַסְפַּס <2636>; reduplicated from an unused root meaning apparently to peel] ▶ **This word means to be flaky, to be round; to be crisp.** It is used to help identify the nature of manna (Ex. 16:14; also translated round thing). ¶

FLAKES – Job 41:23 ➔ CHAFF <4651>.

FLAME – 1 ***labbāh*** [fem. noun: לַבָּה <3827>; for <3852> below] ▶ **This word refers to a fire's bright light and heat.** It is used with *'ēš* following to mean flame of fire (Ex. 3:2). ¶
2 ***lahab̲*** [masc. noun: לַהַב <3851>; from an unused root meaning to gleam] ▶ **See definition above for <3827>. This word also refers to the flashing blade of a spear or sword.** It is used to indicate a flash or flame of fire (Judg. 13:20; Is. 29:6). It is used in a figurative sense of faces of flame (*lahab̲*), faces red and hot with fear at God's judgments (Is. 13:8). It is used to refer to the flashing blade of a sword (Nah. 3:3: bright, flashing) or spear (Job 39:23: flashing, glittering). The Lord's judgments are described as a flame (*lahab̲*) of consuming fire (Is. 29:6; 30:30; 66:15). The hot breath of Leviathan is described as a flame (Job 41:21). It is used in a simile to describe the sound of a locust swarm as a flame of fire (Joel 2:5). Other ref.: Judg. 3:22 (blade). ¶
3 ***lehāb̲āh*** [fem. noun: לֶהָבָה <3852>; fem. of <3851> above and meaning the same] ▶ **This word regularly refers to a flashing flame of fire both literally and symbolically of destruction.** Refs.: Num. 21:28; Jer. 48:45. It is emphasized by the following word *šalheb̲et̲* in Ezekiel 20:47, a "burning flame," a metaphor of God's coming judgments. Followed or preceded by *'ēš* (fire), it indicates a flaming fire (Is. 4:5; Lam. 2:3); or a consuming tongue of fire (Is. 5:24). It is used to describe the flashing light and fire in a hailstorm (Ps. 105:32). The head or point of Goliath's spear is referred to by this word (1 Sam. 17:7). *
4 ***šᵉb̲iyb̲*** [Aramaic masc. noun: שְׁבִיב <7631>; corresponding to <7632> below] ▶ **This word refers to the visible aspect of a fire, the burning gases or vapors, the tongue of light arising from a fire.** Ref.: Dan. 3:22. It refers to blazing flames (of fire) (Dan. 7:9). In context it serves to emphasize the Lord as enthroned among blazing flames, expressing His purity, power, and splendor. ¶
5 ***šāb̲iyb̲*** [masc. noun: שָׁבִיב <7632>; from the same as BROKEN IN PIECES <7616> (as split into tongues in the case of flame)] ▶ **See definition above for <3827>. This word also refers to a spark.** It indicates in a figurative sense the life and vigor of the wicked that fades away (Job 18:5). ¶
6 ***šalheb̲et̲, šalheb̲et̲yāh*** [fem. noun: שַׁלְהֶבֶת, שַׁלְהֶבֶתְיָה <7957>; from the same as <3851> above] ▶
a. This word refers figuratively to a flame of fire that destroys the growth of the wicked. Ref.: Job 15:30. It is used figuratively of God's destruction of the area of the Negev with military might under the symbol of a flame (Ezek. 20:47). ¶
b. This word indicates a mighty flame. It means literally the flame of the Lord (Song 8:6), but Yah (Lord) on the end of the word could indicate a superlative flame, a vehement flame (KJV), a mighty flame (NIV), the flame of the Lord (NASB, ESV). ¶
– 7 Judg. 20:38 ➔ GIFT <4864> 8 Job 41:19 ➔ TORCH <3940> 9 Song 8:6 ➔ FLASH (noun) <7565> 10 Dan. 7:11 ➔ FIRE <785>.

FLAMING – 1 ***lahaṭ, lᵉhāṭiym*** [masc. noun: לַהַט, לְהָטִים <3858>; from BURN

(verb) <3857>] ▶ **This word means something producing flame.** It describes the "flaming sword" of the cherubim stationed at the east side of the Garden of Eden (Gen. 3:24). In the masc. plur., the word means sorceries (Ex. 7:11: secret arts, enchantments). ¶
– [2] Ps. 7:13 ➔ BURN (verb) <1814> [3] Ps. 76:3 ➔ FLASH (noun) <7565>.

FLAMING ARROW – Prov. 26:18 ➔ lit.: firebrand, arrow ➔ FIREBRAND <2131> a., ARROW <2671> a.

FLANKS – Lev. 3:4, 10, 15; 4:9; 7:4; Job 15:27 ➔ LOINS <3689>.

FLAP JOYOUSLY – Job 39:13 ➔ ENJOY <5965> b.

FLASH (noun) – [1] ***rešep̱*** [masc. noun: רֶשֶׁף <7565>; from BURN <8313>] ▶ **This word means a flame, a lightning bolt, a burning pestilence.** It refers to a burning, flaming of love (Song 8:6; KJV: coal); of flaming, burning arrows of war (Ps. 76:3: flashing, flaming). It refers to lightning (or thunderbolts) as a form of destruction (Ps. 78:48). It indicates a plague, one of God's curses on a disobedient Israel (Deut. 32:24); or to pestilence (Hab. 3:5), another of God's means of disciplining His people. Other ref.: Job 5:7 (spark). ¶
– [2] Hab. 3:11 ➔ BRIGHTNESS <5051>.

FLASH (verb) – [1] ***rāzam*** [verb: רָזַם <7335>; a prim. root] ▶ **This word means to blink the eyes, to wink.** It means to blink one's eyes in an arrogant manner. In context it implies an attitude of resistance or hostility (Job 15:12). ¶
– [2] Job 37:15 ➔ SHINE, SHINE FORTH <3313>.

FLASH, FLASH FORTH – Ps. 18:14 ➔ SHOOT, SHOOT OUT <7232>.

FLASH FORTH – [1] ***bāraq*** [verb: בָּרַק <1299>; a prim. root] ▶ **This word means to produce light suddenly; it is also translated to cast forth, to send forth.** It refers to a flash of lightning (Ps. 144:6). It is followed by its related noun, *bārāq*, lightning, literally, to flash lightning. ¶
– [2] Amos 5:9 ➔ SMILE (verb) <1082>.

FLASHING – [1] Job 39:23; Nah. 3:3 ➔ FLAME <3851> [2] Ps. 76:3 ➔ FLASH (noun) <7565>.

FLASHING LIGHTNING – [1] ***'ešdāṯ*** [fem. noun: אֵשְׁדָּת <799>; from FIRE <784> and LAW <1881>] ▶ **This Hebrew word refers to a flash of light in a storm; it is also translated flaming fire (ESV).** The scene at Sinai featured this phenomenon of nature at the appearance (theophany) of the Lord (Deut. 33:2). The Hebrew word is also translated FIERY LAW and SLOPE; see these entries. ¶
– [2] Deut. 33:2 ➔ SLOPE <794>.

FLASK – [1] ***paḵ*** [masc. noun: פַּךְ <6378>; from TRICKLE <6379>] ▶ **This was a small bottle-shaped container for holding liquids, especially oil for anointing kings, prophets, priests.** Refs.: 1 Sam. 10:1; 2 Kgs. 9:1, 3; the word is also translated vial, box in the KJV. ¶
– [2] Jer. 19:1, 10 ➔ JAR <1228>.

FLAT CAKES – 1 Chr. 9:31 ➔ PANS <2281>.

FLATTER – ***kānāh*** [verb: כָּנָה <3655>; a prim. root] ▶ **This word means to give a surname, a title of praise or honor.** It depicts the assigning of an honorary name to someone (Job 32:21, 22; also translated to use flattery, to give flattering titles, to be skilled in flattery); or persons calling themselves by names, e.g., Jacob (Is. 44:5: to name, to surname). It means to show intimate knowledge and supervision over people by calling them by name (Is. 45:4: to name, to surname). ¶

FLATTERING – [1] Ps. 12:2, 3; 73:18; Prov. 6:24 ➔ SMOOTH <2513> [2] See SMOOTH <2509>.

FLATTERING TITLES (GIVE) – Job 32:21, 22 ➔ FLATTER <3655>.

FLATTERY – 1 ***ḥᵃlaqqāh*** [fem. noun: חֲלַקָּה <2514>; fem. from SHARE (verb) <2505>] ▶ **This word indicates deceitful, smooth words employed by a deceitful king.** Ref.: Dan. 11:32. ¶
2 ***ḥᵃlaqlaqqôṯ*** [fem. plur. noun: חֲלַקְלַקּוֹת <2519>; by reduplication from SHARE (verb) <2505>] ▶ **This word indicates slipperiness, using compliments to obtain something.** It describes uncertain people on treacherous paths of false prophets (Jer. 23:12: slippery ways, slippery paths) and hated enemies (Ps. 35:6: slippery). In a political sense, it refers to seizing power by intrigue, flattery, and hypocrisy (Dan. 11:21, 34: intrigue, hypocrisy). ¶

FLATTERY (USE, BE SKILLED IN) – Job 32:21, 22 ➔ FLATTER <3655>.

FLAVOR – Job 6:6; Jer. 48:11 ➔ TASTE (noun) <2940>.

FLAVORLESS – Job 6:6 ➔ FOOLISH <8602> a.

FLAW – Song 4:7 ➔ DEFECT <3971>.

FLAWLESS – Job 11:4 ➔ PURE <2134>.

FLAX – 1 ***pištāh*** [fem. noun: פִּשְׁתָּה <6594>; fem. of LINEN <6593>] ▶ **This word refers to the fiber of a plant used to make linen, and also a wick.** It refers to flax in the field before harvesting, but ripe for harvest (Ex. 9:31). It indicates a lamp wick made of flax (Is. 42:3). It is used in a simile of the destruction of Babylon (Is. 43:17; KJV: tow). ¶
– 2 Judg. 16:9 ➔ TOW <5296> 3 See LINEN <6593>.

FLEA – ***par'ōš*** [masc. noun: פַּרְעֹשׁ <6550>; prob. from GO (LET) <6544> and MOTH <6211>] ▶ **This word refers to a small leaping and blood-sucking insect. It indicates insignificance.** David applies the word to himself twice in conversation with Saul (1 Sam. 24:14; 26:20) as well as the difficulty of finding a flea. ¶

FLEE – 1 ***bāraḥ*** [verb: בָּרַח <1272>; a prim. root] ▶ **This verb describes running away, to run away, to disappear rapidly.** It describes the passing of a bar through something (Ex. 26:28; 36:33). Literally, it describes the act of fleeing, eloping, sometimes from a place or person, as when Moses fled from Pharaoh (Ex. 2:15; 1 Sam. 19:12, 18; Jer. 4:29). Figuratively, it depicts days or humans fleeing away, disappearing like a shadow (Job 9:25; 14:2). It carries the idea of coming or going quickly in some contexts (Song 8:14) or of putting to flight (Neh. 13:28; Job 41:28; Prov. 19:26). *
2 ***nāḏaḏ*** [verb: נָדַד <5074>; a prim. root] ▶ **This word means to turn from, to take flight, to turn away from.** Refs.: Is. 10:31; Jer. 4:25; 9:10; Nah. 3:7, 17. It is used figuratively of sleep escaping a person (Gen. 31:40); and of persons straying from the Lord (Hos. 7:13). It has the sense of to thrust away, to drive out (2 Sam. 23:6; Job 18:18); to wander around (Job 15:23; Prov. 27:8; Hos. 9:17). It describes the movement of a bird's wings (Is. 10:14). It is used of the disappearance or vanishing of a dream (Job 20:8). In its passive use, it means to be put out, to be banished (Job 20:8). *
3 ***nᵉḏaḏ*** [Aramaic verb: נְדַד <5075>; corresponding to <5074> above] ▶ **This word means to go away, to take flight.** It is used figuratively of a person's sleep escaping him or her (Dan. 6:18). ¶
4 ***nûḏ*** [verb: נוּד <5110>; a prim. root] ▶ **This word also means to wander, to mourn.** It has the sense of aimless motion or actions. It refers to a person moving about aimlessly without a home (Gen. 4:12, 14: wanderer, vagabond); to birds, persons, flora, inanimate objects moving or shaking (1 Kgs. 14:15: to shake, to sway; Ps. 11:1; Is. 24:20: to totter, to sway; Jer. 18:16: to shake, to wag). It has the meaning of to drive away, to cause to wander in a figurative sense (Ps. 36:11). It takes on the sense of concern for people, sympathy, mourning for them (Job 2:11; 42:11; Ps. 69:20); but also to show disdain by shaking one's head (Is. 51:19; Jer. 48:27). It means to bemoan oneself, to grieve, in its reflexive usage (Jer. 31:18). It refers to making a person or a

people wander about, homeless (2 Kgs. 21:8). *
5 ***nûḏ*** [Aramaic verb: נוּד <5111>; corresponding to HABITATION <5116>] ▶ **This word has the sense of something going away, escaping.** It is used of animals fleeing from an area (Dan. 4:14; also translated to get away, to get out). ¶
6 ***nûs*** [verb: נוּס <5127>; a prim. root] ▶ **This word indicates the idea of escape, fleeing away, getting to a safe spot.** It is used of warriors fleeing in battle (Gen. 14:10); of people fleeing disaster of various kinds (Gen. 19:20; Judg. 7:21; Jer. 48:44; Zech. 2:6; 14:5). It is employed figuratively of seas, shadows, strength, etc., all disappearing or fleeing away (Deut. 34:7; Ps. 114:3, 5; Song 2:17). In its causative sense, it means to cause someone or something to flee, to put to flight (Ex. 9:20; Deut. 32:30; Judg. 1:6). It indicates the speedy and onrushing manner in which the Lord escorts in His Redeemer (Is. 59:19). *
– 7 Job 30:3 ➔ GNAW, GNAWING <6207> b. 8 Jer. 48:9 ➔ FLY (verb) <5323>.

FLEE, FLEE AWAY – ***nûṣ*** [verb: נוּץ <5132>; a prim. root] ▶ **This word refers to leaving an area or location.** The inhabitants of Jerusalem were ordered to flee away, to depart from places to which they had wandered in exile (Lam. 4:15; ESV: to become fugitive). The Hebrew word also refers to the blooms of a flowering plant; see BUD (verb) <5132>. ¶

FLEECE – 1 ***gizzāh*** [fem. noun: גִּזָּה <1492>; fem. from CUT (verb) <1494>] ▶ **This word indicates a piece of wool, a soft covering of wool.** Refs.: Judg. 6:37–40. Gideon used a fleece to determine the Lord's will in his life. ¶
– 2 Deut. 18:4; Job 31:20 ➔ SHEARING <1488>.

FLEEING – 1 ***bāriaḥ, bāriyaḥ*** [masc. noun: בָּרִחַ, בָּרִיחַ <1281>; from FLEE <1272>] ▶ **This word indicates one escaping, a fugitive; crooked.** It describes a serpent, *nahaš*, in Job 26:13 that is escaping or writhing; hence, it is probably best translated as a gliding serpent (NIV) or as a fleeing serpent (NASB, NKJV). The KJV translates the word as crooked, giving more attention to the deceitful character of the serpent. Other refs.: Is. 15:5; 27:1; 43:14. ¶
– 2 Lev. 26:36 ➔ FLIGHT <4499>.

FLEES (ONE WHO) – ***niys*** [masc. noun: נִיס <5211>; from FLEE <5127>] ▶ **This word refers to a person trying to escape from something, e.g., danger or terror.** Ref.: Jer. 48:44. ¶

FLEET OF SHIPS – ***ᵓniy*** [masc. noun: אֳנִי <590>; prob. from BEFALL <579> (in the sense of conveyance)] ▶ **This word means a group of naval ships; it is also translated ships, navy, navy of ships, galley, boat.** These could be of average size (1 Kgs. 9:26, 27) and designated as ships of Solomon. Or possibly they were larger, seagoing vessels bound for Tarshish (1 Kgs. 10:11, 22). Ships propelled by oars are designated in Isaiah 33:21 as galley ships. ¶

FLEETING – 1 Ps. 39:4 ➔ REJECTED <2310> 2 Prov. 21:6 ➔ DRIVE AWAY <5086>.

FLESH – 1 ***bāśār*** [masc. noun: בָּשָׂר <1320>; from NEWS (BRING) <1319> (from its freshness)] ▶ **The basic meaning of human skin is frequently observed in the Old Testament, especially in the literature concerning sacrificial practices (Lev. 7:17) and skin diseases (Lev. 13).** It is also used of the animal body (Gen. 41:2–4, 18, 19); the human body (Is. 10:18); the penis (Gen. 17:11, 13, 14, 23–25); blood relations (Gen. 2:23, 24; 29:14); and human frailty (Gen. 6:3; Job 10:4). This word is further used in the phrase *kōl* (<3605>) *bāśār*, meaning all flesh, to indicate all living beings (Gen. 6:17, 19; 7:21); animals (Gen. 7:15, 16; 8:17); humanity (Gen. 6:12, 13). *
2 ***bᵉśar*** [Aramaic masc. noun: בְּשַׂר <1321>; corresponding to <1320> above] ▶ **This word is found only in the book of Daniel and means living beings.** When used figuratively, it signifies all flesh or humankind

(Dan. 2:11) and all creatures (Dan. 4:12). It is also used in relation to the devouring of flesh in a literal sense (Dan. 7:5). ¶

3 ***šᵉʼēr*** [masc. noun: שְׁאֵר <7607>; from REMAIN <7604>] ▶ **This word also means food, meat, body, self, blood relative, blood kindred.** The word is roughly synonymous with the noun *bāśār* (<1320>) above, meaning flesh. The term connotes the meaty part of an animal which can be eaten: quail (Ps. 78:20, 27; cf. Num. 11:31); or food in general (Ex. 21:10). Frequently, on account of context, the term strongly implies the idea of close (blood) relative or kindred (Lev. 18:6, 12, 13, 17; 20:19; 21:2; 25:49; Num. 27:11). In two contexts, the word suggests the notion of physical strength (Ps. 73:26; Prov. 5:11); and in Micah 3:2, 3, it refers to the actual physical flesh of a human body. Other refs.: Prov. 11:17; Jer. 51:35. ¶

– 4 1 Sam. 25:11 ➔ SLAUGHTER (noun) <2878> 5 Prov. 3:8 ➔ NAVEL <8270> 6 Nah. 2:12 ➔ TORN (WHAT IS) <2966> 7 Zeph. 1:17 ➔ ENTRAILS <3894>.

FLESHHOOK – Ex. 27:3; Num. 4:14; etc. ➔ FORK <4207>.

FLIGHT – ***mᵉnûsāh, mᵉnusāh*** [fem. noun: מְנוּסָה, מְנֻסָה <4499>; fem. of REFUGE <4498>] ▶ **This word means a running away; it is also translated fleeing.** It is used of an attempted escape from an enemy by falling back in retreat or open flight (Is. 52:12). It is brought about by the Lord Himself when His people fail to obey Him (Lev. 26:36). ¶

FLIGHT (COME IN SWIFT) – Dan. 9:21 ➔ FAINT (verb) <3286>.

FLIGHT (TAKE) – 1 Job 39:26 ➔ FLY (verb) <82> 2 Ps. 104:7 ➔ HURRY (verb) <2648>.

FLING – ***ʻāp̱ar*** [verb: עָפַר <6080>; a prim. root meaning either to be gray or perhaps rather to pulverize] ▶ **This word literally means to sprinkle dust or dirt and conveys the image of a dusty garment whose appearance is gray; it is also translated to kick, to throw, to cast, to shower with.** It was used to describe the scornful action of Shimei as he threw dirt on David and his procession (2 Sam. 16:13). ¶

FLINT – 1 ***ḥallāmiyš*** [masc. noun: חַלָּמִישׁ <2496>; prob. from DREAM (verb) <2492> b. (in the sense of hardness)] ▶ **This word refers to a type of rock made of very hard form of quartz.** Ref.: Deut. 8:15. Both oil and water came from it (Deut. 32:13; Ps. 114:8). It is mined by men (Job 28:9). It is used in a simile indicating hardness or fairness and resolve (Is. 50:7). ¶

2 ***ṣōr*** [masc. noun: צֹר <6864>; from BESIEGE <6696> (in the sense of something pressed hard or to a point)] ▶ **This word refers to a flint knife, an edge; it is also translated flint knife, sharp stone, sharp. It refers to a variety of chert, a rock that produces sparks when struck with certain metals.** It forms a cutting tool with sharp edges (Ex. 4:25; Josh. 5:2, 3). In fact, it has the meaning of edge in some places: of a sword (Ps. 89:43). Some translators translate this word in Isaiah 5:28 as flint. It is used figuratively to refer to a forehead like flint, meaning a person with absolute determination (Ezek. 3:9). ¶

– 3 Is. 5:28 ➔ NARROWNESS <6862> c. 4 Zech. 7:12 ➔ DIAMOND <8068>.

FLINT KNIFE – Ex. 4:25 ➔ FLINT <6864>.

FLINTY – Deut. 8:15; 32:13; Job 28:9 ➔ flinty rock ➔ lit.: rock of flint ➔ FLINT <2496>.

FLIRT – Is. 3:16 ➔ WANTONLY (GLANCE) <8265>.

FLOAT – 1 2 Kgs. 6:6 ➔ FLOW OVER <6687> 2 2 Chr. 2:16 ➔ RAFT <7513>.

FLOATS – 1 Kgs. 5:9 ➔ RAFTS <1702>.

FLOCK – 1 ***ʻēḏer*** [masc. noun: עֵדֶר <5739>; from RANK (KEEP) <5737> (in

the sense of an arrangement] ► **This word is used of a group of animals, sheep, goats, cattle.** Refs.: Gen. 29:2, 3, 8; 30:40; 32:16, 19; Judg. 5:16; Song 4:1; 6:5. Figuratively, it describes Israel as the flock of God (Is. 40:11; Jer. 13:20; Zech. 10:3). It depicts the bride's hair like a flock of goats (Song 4:1). *
– [2] Num. 32:24; Ps. 8:7 ➔ SHEEP <6792>.

FLOCK (LITTLE, SMALL) – ***ḥāśip*** [masc. noun: חָשִׂף <2835>; from STRIP <2834> (in the sense of separated, hence a small company)] ► **This word is used as a description of Israel encamped for war against the Arameans.** Ref.: 1 Kgs. 20:27. Israel was a small army compared to the multitude of Arameans. ¶

FLOCKS – ***'ašterôṯ*** [fem. plur. noun: עַשְׁתְּרוֹת <6251>; prob. from RICH (BE) <6238>] ► **This word indicates lambs, young (sheep).** It is used of young sheep or goats of a flock (Deut. 7:13; 28:4, 18, 51), no more than three years old. In context these frail animals are blessed by God, a key to Israel's success. ¶

FLOGGING – Ps. 89:32 ➔ SORE (noun) <5061>.

FLOOD – [1] ***mabbûl*** [masc. noun: מַבּוּל <3999>; from BRING <2986> in the sense of flowing] ► **This word refers to both the great deluge on the earth (Gen. 6:17; Ps. 29:10) and to its sources from above and below as well (Gen. 7:6, 7, 10, 17; 9:11, 15, 28).** The flood marked a turning point in history (Gen. 10:1, 32; 11:10). God was entirely in charge of it (Ps. 29:10). ¶
[2] ***šeṭep*** [masc. noun: שֶׁטֶף <7858>; from WASH <7857>] ► **This word also means mighty waters, a torrent. Its primary usage is flood or deluge.** The noun is used figuratively to indicate coming judgment (Dan. 9:26; 11:22; Nah. 1:8). In Job, the Lord is depicted as being able to cut channels for torrents of rain (Job 38:25; also translated overflowing of water). The psalmist indicates that through prayer, one can avoid the mighty waters (Ps. 32:6; also translated rush, rising). The word is also used figuratively to depict the intensity of anger (Prov. 27:4: torrent, outrageous, overwhelming). ¶
– [3] Job 22:11; 38:34 ➔ ABUNDANCE <8229>.

FLOODGATE – Gen. 7:11; 8:2; 2 Kgs. 7:2, 19; Is. 24:18; Mal. 3:10 ➔ WINDOW <699>.

FLOOR – [1] ***qarqa'*** [masc. noun: קַרְקַע <7172>; from TEAR <7167>] ► **This word indicates the level area or bottom of a structure or even a ground of dirt in a tent.** Ref.: Num. 5:17. The Temple had cypress floorboards (1 Kgs. 6:15, 16, 30). Solomon's palace featured cedar flooring (1 Kgs. 7:7). It refers to the bottom of the sea once (Amos 9:3), stressing its depth. ¶
– [2] 1 Kgs. 22:35 ➔ BOSOM <2436>.

FLOUR – ***qemaḥ*** [masc. noun: קֶמַח <7058>; from an unused root prob. meaning to grind] ► **This word refers to finely ground grains of various kinds serving as food.** It is the basic ingredient of bread, etc. (Gen. 18:6); also translated as meal (Gen. 18:6; Num. 5:15). It was often served with a meat dish (Judg. 6:19). It could be rendered as grain (Hos. 8:7). *

FLOURISH – [1] Job 15:32 ➔ GREEN (BE) <7487> a. [2] Ps. 72:16; 90:6; 92:7; 103:15; 132:18 ➔ BLOSSOM (verb) <6692> a. [3] Eccl. 12:5; Song 6:11; 7:12 ➔ SPARKLE <5340> [4] Song 6:11; 7:12 ➔ BUD (verb) <5132> [5] Hos. 13:15 ➔ FRUITFUL (BE) <6500>.

FLOURISH (MAKE) – Zech. 9:17 ➔ INCREASE (verb) <5107>.

FLOURISHING – See GREEN <7488>.

FLOW (noun) – Ezek. 32:6 ➔ DISCHARGE <6824> a.

FLOW (verb) – [1] ***negaḏ*** [Aramaic verb: נְגַד <5047>; corresponding to TELL <5046>] ► **This word indicates the natural movement**

of water in a river, a stream, etc. It is used in a heavenly vision of fire flowing out from before the Ancient of Days (Dan. 7:10); it is also translated to issue forth. ¶

[2] ***nāhar*** [verb: נָהַר <5102>; a prim. root] ▶

a. This word describes the movement of something like the movement of a river or stream; it is also translated to stream. It describes the flow of people and nations (Is. 2:2; Jer. 51:44; Mic. 4:1); of wealth, abundance (Is. 60:5; KJV: to flow together). It describes a person glowing, beaming, radiant, overjoyed about something (Jer. 31:12; KJV: to flow together). ¶

b. A verb meaning to be radiant, to rejoice. It means to shine, to glow, to beam over deliverance from God (Ps. 34:5); the abundance of Zion (Is. 60:5; Jer. 31:12). ¶

[3] ***rûq, riyq*** [verb: רִיק ,רוּק <7325>; a prim. root] ▶ **This word describes the running discharge from an open sore, making a person unclean.** Ref.: Lev. 15:3. ¶

– [4] Job 20:28; Lam. 3:49 ➔ to flow, to flow away ➔ SPILL <5064> [5] Prov. 10:31 ➔ INCREASE (verb) <5107> [6] See GUSH <2100>.

FLOW (verb and noun) – ***nāzal, nōzêl*** [נֹזֵל ,נָזַל <5140>; a prim. root] ▶

a. A verb meaning to move freely, to pour down, to drop, to melt. It refers to flowing water (Ex. 15:8; Num. 24:7); or the droplets of dew that evaporate (Deut. 32:2). It is used of rain (Job 36:28; Is. 45:8); of running tears (Jer. 9:18). In its causative usage, it means to cause water to flow (Ps. 78:16; Is. 48:21). It is used figuratively of water from one's own cistern, one's own wife (Prov. 5:15). *

b. A masculine noun referring to brooks, streams. Some translators prefer these renderings of this fixed participial form of the verb in a.

FLOW DOWN – Is. 64:1, 3 ➔ GLUTTON (BE) <2151> b.

FLOW OVER – ***ṣûp*** [verb: צוּף <6687>; a prim. root] ▶ **This word means to pour over, to engulf; to float.** It refers to the waters of the Red Sea overflowing and encompassing the Egyptians (Deut. 11:4; also translated to overwhelm, to engulf); of an ax head made to float in water (2 Kgs. 6:6); in a figurative sense of enemies overwhelming, overflowing people (Lam. 3:54; also translated to close over). ¶

FLOWER – [1] ***nêṣ*** [masc. noun: נֵץ <5322>; from SPARKLE <5340> (in the sense of brilliancy)] ▶ **This word refers to the colored part of a plant; it also means blossom.** It indicates fragile buds that open into blossoms that speak of fruitfulness (Gen. 40:10). The appearance of their flowers indicates that spring has arrived (Song 2:12). The Hebrew word also refers to a bird of prey; see HAWK <5322>. ¶

[2] ***niṣṣāh*** [fem. noun: נִצָּה <5328>; fem. of <5322> above)] ▶ **This word refers to the petals that are put forth by a plant indicating fertility and displaying beauty.** Ref.: Is. 18:5. It is used in a figurative sense of the wicked being cut off like the blossoms of an olive tree dropping (Job 15:33). ¶

[3] ***niṣṣān*** [masc. noun: נִצָּן <5339>; from <5322> above] ▶ **This word refers to the colorful petals put forth by a plant, indicating beauty and fertility, a sign of spring.** Ref.: Song 2:12. ¶

[4] ***peraḥ*** [masc. noun: פֶּרַח <6525>; from BREAK OUT <6524>] ▶ **This word also means a bud, a blossom. It refers to the petals and other parts put forth by blooming plants.** It describes often the ornamental work found in the Tabernacle, Temple, or their decorative ornaments (Ex. 25:31, 33, 34; Num. 8:4; 1 Kgs. 7:26, 49). It refers figuratively to the splendor and glory of Israel (Is. 5:24); or other nations (Is. 18:5; Nah. 1:4). It indicates a literal blossom, a flower generated as a sign from God (Num. 17:8). *

[5] ***ṣiyṣ*** [masc. noun: צִיץ <6731>; from BLOSSOM (verb) <6692>] ▶

a. This word refers to the flowers, petals, or blossoms put forth by various things. Refs.: Num. 17:8 (almond rod); Job 14:2; Ps. 103:15; Is. 40:6–8 (carved ornamental flowers). The glory of Israel passed like a flower (Is. 28:1).

b. This word indicates the plate worn by the high priest in his turban bearing the inscription, "Holy unto the Lord." Ref.: Ex. 28:36.
c. This word is used in a personification of Moab's flying away and being destroyed by the Lord. Ref.: Jer. 48:9: wing.
d. This word means salt. It is used of putting salt on the land of Moab, which would effectively destroy its fertility forever (Jer. 48:9). *
[6] ***ṣiyṣāh*** [fem. noun: צִיצָה <6733>; fem. of <6731> above] ▶ **This word is used symbolically to depict the splendor and prosperity of Ephraim, northern Israel, in her heyday, the height of her glory.** Ref.: Is. 28:4. ¶
– [7] Job 8:12: in flower ➔ GREENNESS <3>.

FLOWING – [1] Ex. 30:23 ➔ FREEDOM <1865> b. [2] Deut. 21:4: flowing water, flowing stream ➔ STRENGTH <386> [3] Prov. 18:4; Eccl. 10:1 ➔ to flow ➔ UTTER <5042> [4] Ezek. 32:6 ➔ DISCHARGE <6824> a. [5] Amos 6:4 ➔ HANG <5628>.

FLOWING TURBAN – ***ṭ^{e}ḇûl*** [masc. noun: טְבוּל <2871>; pass. part. of DIP <2881> (in the sense of being dyed)] ▶ **This word describes a part of Chaldean dress which were on their heads.** Ref.: Ezek. 23:15; KJV, dyed attire. Hence it was a repulsive symbol to the prophet Ezekiel. ¶

FLUSHED (BE) – Job 16:16 ➔ RED (BE) <2560>.

FLUTE – [1] ***ḥāliyl*** [masc. noun: חָלִיל <2485>; from PIERCE <2490>] ▶ **This word denotes a wind instrument; it is also translated pipe.** It was used in performing laments (Jer. 48:36) or during a time of joy (1 Sam. 10:5; 1 Kgs. 1:40; Is. 5:12). It was used to create and accompany times of gladness (Is. 30:29). ¶
[2] ***mašrôqiy*** [Aramaic fem. noun: מַשְׁרוֹקִי <4953>; from a root corresponding to HISS <8319>] ▶ **This word refers to one of the woodwind instruments.** It was among the collection of musical instruments present at Nebuchadnezzar's dedication of his golden image or obelisk (Dan. 3:5, 7, 10, 15; ESV: pipe). ¶
[3] ***'ûgāḇ, 'ugāḇ*** [masc. noun: עוּגָב, עֻגָב <5748>; from LUST AFTER <5689> (in the original sense of breathing)] ▶ **This word refers to a musical instrument consisting of a long, slim tube with holes in it to finger while blowing over a specially placed opening; it is also translated pipe, organ.** Refs.: Gen. 4:21; Job 21:12; 30:31. It was used to worship the Lord (Ps. 150:4). ¶
– [4] Ps. 5:1 ➔ NEHILOTH <5155>.

FLUTTER – Deut. 32:11 ➔ HOVER <7363>.

FLY (noun) – [1] ***z^{e}ḇûḇ*** [masc. noun: זְבוּב <2070>; from an unused root (meaning to flit)] ▶ **This word is used figuratively to refer to the most remote fly (a two-winged insect) in Egypt, i.e., the forces and armies of Egypt.** Ref.: Is. 7:18. Its other use is with the word death or dead, flies of death, dead flies (Eccl. 10:1), which function as a concrete symbol of foolishness. ¶
– [2] Is. 51:6 ➔ GNAT <3654>.

FLY (verb) – [1] ***'āḇar*** [verb: אָבַר <82>; a prim. root] ▶ **This word means to move through the air; it is also translated to soar, to take flight.** It is found only in Job 39:26. The high flight of the hawk and its southward route are understood only by the Creator. The flight of the hawk is orchestrated by the Lord as indicated by the causal aspect of the verb form. ¶
[2] ***dā'āh*** [verb: דָּאָה <1675>; a prim. root] ▶ **This word indicates to move through the air fast, swiftly; to swoop.** It is used figuratively to depict a nation swooping down on another nation like a bird of prey (Deut. 28:49; Jer. 48:40) and to describe God who speeds on the wings of the wind (Ps. 18:10), sometimes in judgment (Jer. 49:22). ¶
[3] ***nāṣā'*** [verb: נָצָא <5323>; a prim. root] ▶ **This word means to disappear, to flee, to go away.** It is used of God's destruction of Moab by His judgments (Jer. 48:9). ¶

[4] ***'ûp*** [verb: עוּף <5774>; denom. from BIRD <5775>] ▶ **a. This word means to move through the air, and also to flutter, to flicker, to glow, to shine; to grow weary.** It indicates the act of flying, especially by birds (Gen. 1:20; Deut. 4:17); of a swallow in a figurative sense (Prov. 26:2). Heavenly beings fly (Is. 6:6). It is used of the Lord flying on the cherubim (2 Sam. 22:11; Ps. 18:10); arrows flying in their flight (Ps. 91:5); of a swift army swooping, flying (Is. 11:14). The Lord is likened to hovering (flying) birds over their young (Is. 31:5). To fly away may have the sense of to escape in certain contexts (Ps. 55:6); or the sense of dying (Ps. 90:10). It is used of the to and fro motion of a drawn sword blade (Ezek. 32:10), to brandish a sword. It is used figuratively of honor or glory flying away, disappearing (Hos. 9:11). *
b. The Hebrew word means to brandish. It pictures the to and fro threatening movements of a drawn sword (Ezek. 32:10). ¶
– [5] 1 Sam. 14:32; 15:19 ➔ RUSH GREEDILY <5860> b. [6] Ezek. 13:20 ➔ BREAK OUT <6524> b.

FLY (CAUSE TO) – Dan. 9:21 ➔ FAINT (verb) <3286>.

FOAL – Gen. 32:15; 49:11 ➔ DONKEY <5895>.

FOAM – Ps. 46:3; 75:8; Lam. 1:20; 2:11 ➔ RED (BE) <2560>.

FODDER – [1] ***b^eliyl*** [masc. noun: בְּלִיל <1098>; from MIX <1101>] ▶ **This word describes a mixed food or mash for cattle.** Refs.: Job 6:5; 24:6. It was considered a desirable food for oxen and donkeys (Is. 30:24); it is also translated provender. ¶
[2] ***mispô'*** [masc. noun: מִסְפּוֹא <4554>; from an unused root meaning to collect] ▶ **This word refers to animal food; it is also translated feed, provender.** It is used of food for animals, donkeys (Gen. 42:27; 43:24; Judg. 19:19) or camels (Gen. 24:25, 32). ¶

FOE – [1] Job 22:20 ➔ ADVERSARY <7009> a. [2] Ps. 5:8; 27:11; 54:5; 56:2; 92:11 ➔ ENEMY <8324> [3] Ps. 49:5 ➔ HEEL <6120> b. [4] Ps. 92:11 ➔ ENEMY <7790>.

FOIL – Ps. 33:10 ➔ NOTHING (BRING TO) <6329>.

FOLD (noun) – [1] ***boṣrāh*** [fem. noun: בָּצְרָה <1223>; fem. from GATHER <1219>] ▶ **This word refers to a pen for sheep.** Ref.: Mic. 2:12; also translated pen, Bozrah. ¶
[2] ***miḵlā'āh, miḵlāh*** [fem. noun: מִכְלָאָה, מִכְלָה <4356>; from RESTRAIN <3607> a.] ▶ **This word depicts an enclosure, a pen.** It indicates a closed structure or fencing to contain animals (Ps. 50:9; Hab. 3:17); a place where the great King David labored in his youth (Ps. 78:70). ¶
– [3] Neh. 5:13 ➔ BOSOM <2684> [4] Jer. 50:6 ➔ RESTING PLACE <7258> [5] Ezek. 25:5 ➔ RESTING PLACE <4769>.

FOLD (verb) – [1] ***ṣā'an*** [verb: צָעַן <6813>; a prim. root] ▶ **This word means to travel; to take down a tent for moving.** It indicates in context either moving a tent about, traveling with it, or the folding up and, hence, taking down of a tent to move it, to journey with it (Is. 33:20). ¶
– [2] Ps. 77:18 ➔ ROLL (verb) <1563> [3] Eccl. 4:5 ➔ EMBRACE <2263>.

FOLDEN TOGETHER – Nah. 1:10 ➔ ENTWINE <5440>.

FOLDING – [1] ***gāliyl*** [adj.: גָּלִיל <1550>; from ROLL (verb) <1556>] ▶ **This word indicates something shaped like a ring; turning in a circle; pivot.** It indicates a door that turns on the pivot of hinges (1 Kgs. 6:34); it is also translated that turned on pivots, that turned in sockings. It also means rod, ring (Esther 1:6; Song 5:14); see RING <1550>. ¶
[2] ***ḥibbuq*** [masc. noun: חִבֻּק <2264>; from EMBRACE <2263>] ▶ **This word indicates a folding of one's hands, i.e., bringing them together and crossing them.** It is referring to the fool's folding of his or

her hands as a symbol of slothfulness (Prov. 6:10; 24:33). ¶

FOLDS – Job 41:23 ➔ CHAFF <4651>.

FOLIAGE (THICK) – Ezek. 19:11; 31:3, 10, 14 ➔ BOUGH (THICK).

FOLLOW – Deut. 33:3 ➔ SIT DOWN <8497> b.

FOLLY – [1] ***'iwweleṯ*** [fem. noun: אִוֶּלֶת <200>; from the same as FOOLISH <191>] ► **This word means something irrational; it is also translated foolishness.** Folly is destructive to the psalmist (Ps. 38:5), and only God can discern our follies (Ps. 69:5). It is used twenty-two times in Proverbs chapters 5–27 (e.g., Prov. 5:23; 12:23; 27:22). *
[2] ***kᵉsiylûṯ*** [fem. noun: כְּסִילוּת <3687>; from FOOL, FOOLISH <3684>] ► **This word means foolishness, stupidity.** It occurs only in Proverbs 9:13, naming the woman of folly, a symbolic character who appealed to the evil desires of naive people in order to cause them to stray from right paths into paths that lead to death. ¶
[3] ***nᵉḇālāh*** [fem. noun: נְבָלָה <5039>; fem. of FOOLISH <5036>] ► **The word means a disgraceful act, an irrational act.** It refers to deeds that are especially serious, grave, sinful, arrogant: rape, harlotry (Gen. 34:7; Deut. 22:21); breaking of Israel's covenantal laws (Josh. 7:15); sodomy (Judg. 19:23, 24); offering incorrect or vain advice in an arrogant way (Job 42:8); foolish talk (Is. 9:17); spiritual adultery (Jer. 29:23). *
[4] ***seḵel*** [masc. noun: סֶכֶל <5529>; from FOOLISHLY (ACT, DO) <5528>] ► **This word also means lack of sense, foolishness. It is the opposite of wisdom.** It means to act without the fear of God, without knowledge, moral integrity, or reason (Eccl. 10:6). ¶
– [5] Job 4:18 ➔ ERROR <8417> [6] Job 23:13; 24:12 ➔ WRONGDOING <8604> [7] Job 35:15 ➔ TRANSGRESSION <6580> [8] Ps. 49:13; Eccl. 7:25 ➔ LOINS <3689> [9] Ps. 73:7 ➔ PICTURE <4906> [10] Ps. 85:8 ➔ CONFIDENCE <3690> [11] Eccl. 2:3, 12, 13; 10:1, 13 ➔ FOOLISHNESS <5531>.

FONDLE – Ezek. 23:3, 21 ➔ CRUSH <4600>.

FOOD – [1] ***'ᵃḵiylāh*** [fem. noun: אֲכִילָה <396>; fem. from EAT <398>] ► **This word refers to what Elijah ate or to the eating of a meal.** Ref.: 1 Kgs. 19:8; KJV: meat. ¶
[2] ***'ōḵel*** [masc. noun: אֹכֶל <400>; from EAT <398>] ► **This word means something to be eaten.** Its use is uniform, but it refers to food for all kinds of living things: humans (Gen. 14:11) and animals (Ps. 104:21, 27). The phrase *'āśa' 'ōkel* means to make food (Hab. 3:17). *'Ēṯ 'ōkel* indicates mealtime (Ruth 2:14). It refers to flesh (Ps. 78:18, 30; 104:21) as well as to the prey or food of eagles (Job 9:26; 39:29) or wild animals (Ps. 104:21). It is used to modify the store (food) cities where grain was kept (Gen. 41:35; 47:24). *
[3] ***'oḵlāh*** [fem. noun אָכְלָה <402>; fem. of UCAL <401>] ► **This word means that which is eaten.** Refs.: Gen. 9:3; Ex. 16:15; Lev. 25:6; Jer. 12:9; Ezek. 21:32). *
[4] ***bûl*** [masc. noun: בּוּל <944>; for INCREASE (noun) <2981>] ► **This word means and is also translated produce; block, stock.** It describes the sustenance produced on the mountains for Behemoth (Job 40:20). Speaking of idols, Isaiah refers to a block of wood (Is. 44:19; KJV: stock of a tree) and using this wood as part of the idol. ¶
[5] ***bārûṯ*** [fem. noun: בָּרוּת <1267>; from EAT <1262>] ► **This word means something to be eaten.** It is found only in Psalm 69:21. ¶
[6] ***biryāh*** [fem. noun: בִּרְיָה <1279>; fem. from EAT <1262>] ► **This word means something to be eaten, diet.** It refers to some kind of prepared food delivered to Amnon by Tamar (2 Sam. 13:5, 7, 10). ¶
[7] ***maᵃḵāl*** [masc. noun: מַאֲכָל <3978>; from FOOD <396>] ► **This word means something to be eaten; it is also translated meat. It is used to depict food for humans or animals.** Refs.: Gen. 6:21;

Deut. 28:26; Ps. 79:2; Prov. 6:8. God considered all fruit-producing trees as good (Gen. 2:9; Deut. 20:20). He created flocks of animals for food as well (Ps. 44:11). Used with the adjective *ta^{a}weh*, this word means special, best, or favorite food (Job 33:20). It is used figuratively of people as food for the Babylonians (Hab. 1:16). Its use encompasses honey (Judg. 14:14). *

8 ***māzôn*** [masc. noun: מָזוֹן <4202>; from WELL-FED <2109>] ▶ **This word is a general term covering a broad range of foodstuffs; it is also translated provision(s), sustenance, victual.** Refs.: Gen. 45:23; 2 Chr. 11:23. It is listed with grain (*bār*, grain; *leḥem*, bread or food). ¶

9 ***māzôn*** [Aramaic masc. noun: מָזוֹן <4203>; corresponding to <4202> above] ▶ **This word refers to what was eaten for sustenance by all the earth.** Refs.: Dan. 4:12, 21. ¶

10 ***makkōleṯ*** [fem. noun: מַכֹּלֶת <4361>; from EAT <398>] ▶ **This word indicates what is consume by humans.** In context it is food made from wheat (1 Kgs. 5:11). ¶

11 ***ṣayiḏ*** [masc. noun: צַיִד <6718>; from a form of HUNT <6679>] ▶

a. This word refers to hunting; what is caught in hunting; game, venison. It refers to tracking down, capturing, and killing game for food. It was an ancient occupation (Gen. 10:9; 25:27). It refers to the game caught and the hunt itself (Gen. 25:28; 27:3, 5, 7, 19, 25, 30, 31, 33; Lev. 17:13; Prov. 12:27). ¶

b. This word means provisions, nourishment. In its causative stem, the verb means to take for provisions, to prepare provisions (Josh. 9:5, 14); or to things loaded, loads, provisions (Neh. 13:15). It refers to food, nourishment for birds, animals supplied by God (Job 38:41). It is used of the provisions furnished by the Lord for His sanctuary, the Temple (Ps. 132:15). ¶

12 ***ṣêyḏāh*** [fem. noun: צֵידָה <6720>; fem. of FOOD <6718>] ▶ **This word refers also to nourishment, provisions, venison.** It describes the game that a hunter brings back and prepares as food. It describes various food provisions packed and taken along on a trip (Gen. 42:25; 45:21; Ex. 12:39). It is used of the miraculous provision God supplied to Israel in the desert (Ps. 78:25). *

– 13 Judg. 17:10 ➔ PRESERVATION OF LIFE <4241> 14 Job 24:5; Ps. 111:5; Prov. 31:15 ➔ PREY <2964> 15 Lam. 4:10 ➔ EAT <1262> 16 Mal. 1:12 ➔ FRUIT <5108> a.

FOOD, CHOICE FOOD – ***paṯbag*** [masc. noun: פַּתְבַּג <6598>; of Persian origin] ▶ **This word refers to fine food, tasty gourmet cuisine served at the royal palace in the Middle East; it is also translated delicacies, meat.** To eat of it was the privilege of a few and indicated a special friendship with the king and his government (Dan. 1:5, 8, 13, 15, 16; 11:26). ¶

FOOL – 1 ***sāḵāl*** [masc. noun: סָכָל <5530>; from FOOLISHLY (ACT, DO) <5528>] ▶ **This word refers to an unintelligent person; it is also translated foolish.** It refers to a person who acts without wisdom, moral integrity, fear of God or knowledge (Eccl. 2:19; 7:17; 10:3, 14); acting senselessly, without knowing God (Jer. 4:22; 5:21). ¶

– 2 2 Sam. 3:33; Ps. 14:1; Prov. 17:7, 21; Jer. 17:11 ➔ FOOLISH <5036> 3 Prov. 30:32 ➔ to play the fool ➔ FOOLISH (BE) <5034> 4 Eccl. 10:6: fools are put in ➔ lit.: folly is set in ➔ FOLLY <5529> 5 Jer. 4:22; Prov. 1:7; 7:22; 24:7; 29:9; Hos. 9:7; Is. 19:11; etc. ➔ FOOLISH <191>.

FOOL (BE, BECOME) – Is. 19:13; Jer. 50:36 ➔ FOOLISHLY (BE, DO, ACT) <2973>.

FOOL (MAKE) – Judg. 16:10, 13, 15 ➔ MOCK <2048>.

FOOL, FOOLISH – ***k^{e}siyl*** [masc. noun: כְּסִיל <3684>; from FOOLISH (BE) <3688>] ▶ **This word refers to one of several types of unintelligent persons in Scripture, especially in Proverbs.** Such persons are usually unable to deal with life in a successful, practical way (Eccl. 4:5, 13) and are lacking in religious or spiritual sympathies (Ps. 49:10; Prov. 1:22, 32). Fools do not understand issues (*lō'-yāḇîn*, Psalm 92:6), for they conduct their lives in a haze or darkness (Eccl. 2:14–16). Fools act rashly (Eccl. 5:1), and their laughter is senseless (Eccl. 7:6). As the proverb goes, they are always going to the left, not the right (Eccl. 10:2). Wise persons receive honor, but the *k^{e}siyl* only shame after shame (Prov. 3:35). These persons need understanding, literally *lêḇ*, hearts (Prov. 8:5). They are sources of despair to their parents (Prov. 10:1). *

FOOLISH – 1 ***^{e}wiyl*** [adj.: אֱוִיל <191>; from an unused root (meaning to be perverse)] ▶ **This word is used in the sense of one who hates wisdom and walks in irrationality, despising wisdom and morality; it is also translated fool.** The adjective is used in Jeremiah 4:22, depicting God's people as a whole, while in Hosea 9:7 God's foolish people call the prophet a fool. The word depicts a simpleton, fool thirteen times in Proverbs (e.g., Prov. 1:7; 7:22; 24:7; 29:9). The wise advisors of Pharaoh in Zoan are ironically called fools (Is. 19:11). *

2 ***^{e}wiliy*** [adj.: אֱוִלִי <196>; from FOOLISH <191>] ▶ **The word describes a shepherd who is not sensible.** Ref.: Zech. 11:15. He does not care for the sheep but rather destroys them. ¶

3 ***nāḇāl*** [adj. or noun: נָבָל <5036>; from FOOLISH (BE) <5034>] ▶ **An arrogant bore, dense morally, intellectually, and spiritually. As an adjective or noun, it means unintelligent, a fool.** It is used to describe a whole nation (Deut. 32:6); or persons individually (2 Sam. 3:33). Such persons cannot speak well or civilly to anyone (Prov. 17:7) and shame their parents (Prov. 17:21). They reject God (Ps. 14:1). The person who gets unjust wealth dies a fool in God's eyes (Jer. 17:11). He dies a shameful and disrespectful death (2 Sam. 3:33). The word is used as an adjective to describe false prophets (Ezek. 13:3). *

4 ***tāp̄êl*** [תָּפֵל <8602>; from an unused root meaning to smear] ▶

a. An adjective meaning unintelligent, tasteless. It indicates a flat, bland taste without seasoning (Job 6:6; also translated flavorless, unsavoury). Used to describe oracles, it takes on the sense of useless, misleading, even foolish (Lam. 2:14; also translated deceptive, worthless).

b. A masculine noun indicating whitewash. It refers to a cheap and deceptive paintlike liquid used to whiten and cover over the outside of unsightly walls (Ezek. 13:10). In its immediate context, it indicates the whitewash representing the misleading message of peace put forth by the prophets (Ezek. 13:10, 11, 14, 15; 22:28).

c. A masculine noun referring to untempered mortar. It refers to the lack of a process wherein mortar is both strengthened and beautified by giving it the proper hardness, smoothness, and consistency (KJV, NKJV, Ezek. 13:10, 11, 14, 15; 22:28). ¶

– 5 Ps. 73:22 ➔ FOOLISH <1198> 6 Prov. 9:13 ➔ FOLLY <3687> 7 Eccl. 2:19; 7:17; Jer. 4:22; 5:21 ➔ FOOL <5530>.

FOOLISH (BE) – 1 ***kāsal*** [verb: כָּסַל <3688>; a prim. root] ▶ **This word means to be unintelligent, to become stupid.** It occurs once as a verb in Jeremiah 10:8, referring to those taught by idols. ¶

2 ***nāḇêl*** [verb: נָבֵל <5034>; a prim. root] ▶ **The verb means to treat with contempt, to act disdainfully.** It is used of treating someone with disapproval or as unworthy (Deut. 32:15: to lightly esteem, to scornfully esteem, to scoff at, to reject; Jer. 14:21: to disgrace, to dishonor; Mic. 7:6: to dishonor, to treat contemptuously, to treat with contempt; Nah. 3:6: to make vile, to treat with contempt); or of acting in contempt toward something or in a foolish way (Prov. 30:32: to do foolishly, to play the fool). The verb also means to wither, to languish, to fade: see WITHER <5034>. ¶

– 3 Jer. 5:4 ➔ FOOLISHLY (BE, DO, ACT) <2973>.

FOOLISH CONFIDENCE – Ps. 49:13 ➔ LOINS <3689>.

FOOLISH THING (DO A) – Gen. 31:28; 1 Sam. 13:13; 1 Chr. 21:8; 2 Chr. 16:9 ➔ FOOLISHLY (ACT, DO) <5528>.

FOOLISHLY – [1] Job 1:22 ➔ WRONGDOING <8604> [2] Prov. 30:32 ➔ to do foolishly ➔ FOOLISH (BE) <5034> [3] Jer. 29:23 ➔ to act foolishly ➔ literally: to do folly ➔ FOLLY <5039>.

FOOLISHLY (ACT, DO) – ***sāḵal*** [verb: סָכַל <5528>; for FOOLISH (BE) <3688>] ▶ **This word refers to acting in an indefensible manner, without reason.** It can be in foolish haste (Gen. 31:28); especially in disobeying God's instructions (1 Sam. 13:13; 1 Chr. 21:8; 2 Chr. 16:9). In an idiom, it means to play the fool (1 Sam. 26:21). Other refs.: 2 Sam. 15:31; 24:10; Is. 44:25. ¶

FOOLISHLY (BE, DO, ACT) – ***yā'al*** [verb: יָאַל <2973>; a prim. root] ▶ **This word depicts an action, behavior, and attitude that are against what is considered wise, prudent, upright.** Miriam and Aaron murmured against Moses, which was shown to be a foolish act in the circumstances (Num. 12:11). It means in some contexts to act against God's people and the Lord's plan for them (Is. 19:13; also translated to become fools). It means to behave against the way of the Lord (Jer. 5:4; also translated to have no sense, to be foolish). It refers to Babylonian priests being made to appear foolish by the failure and falsity of their oracles (Jer. 50:36: to be fool, to become a fool, to dote). ¶

FOOLISHNESS – [1] ***siḵlûṯ, śiḵlûṯ*** [fem. noun: סִכְלוּת, שִׂכְלוּת <5531>; from FOOLISHLY (ACT, DO) <5528>] ▶ **This word means a way of life devoid of wisdom, God, self-understanding, or an understanding of others; it is also translated folly.** Refs.: Eccl. 1:17; 2:3, 12, 13. Wisdom exceeds folly, and evil is attached to folly (Eccl. 2:13; 7:25); foolishness and folly are corrupting (Eccl. 10:1, 13). ¶
– [2] Is. 9:17 ➔ FOLLY <5039> [3] Ps. 38:5; 69:5 ➔ FOLLY <200>.

FOOLISHNESS (TURN INTO, MAKE) – 2 Sam. 15:31 ➔ FOOLISHLY (ACT, DO) <5528>.

FOOT – [1] ***qarsōl*** [fem. noun: קַרְסֹל <7166>; from STOOP <7164>] ▶ **This word refers to the part of the leg in contact with the ground; it is also translated ankle.** It is used figuratively of the Lord's making His people safe and stable so their feet do not slide or slip (2 Sam. 22:37; Ps. 18:36). ¶
[2] ***reḡal*** [Aramaic fem. noun: רְגַל <7271>; corresponding to <7272> below] ▶ **Figuratively, this word describes the feet (the part of the leg below the ankle) of a giant statue or of terrifying animals.** Refs.: Dan. 2:33, 34, 41, 4; 7:4, 7, 19. They were all seen in dreams and visions by Daniel. ¶
[3] ***reḡel*** [fem. noun: רֶגֶל <7272>; corresponding to WALK (TEACH TO) <7270> (in the sense of to walk along)] ▶ **It is the common word for a literal foot (the part of the leg below the ankle), human or animal.** It is used figuratively, but has acquired many other uses. It is used of a human foot (Gen. 18:4; Ex. 3:5); a foot of an animal or bird (Gen. 8:9; Ezek. 29:11); with *kaḇ* preceding, it indicates the sole of a foot (Deut. 2:5; 11:24); in some places, it stands for the whole leg of a person (1 Sam. 17:6). It is used figuratively of God's foot (Ex. 24:10; 2 Sam. 22:10; Ps. 18:9); or the foot or feet of other heavenly beings (2 Chr. 3:13; Is. 6:2; Ezek. 1:7). It indicates figuratively the feet of furniture (Ex. 25:26; 37:13). With *be* attached, it means on one's feet, traveling on foot, journeying by walking (Num. 20:19; Deut. 2:28). With the verb *nāśa'*, to lift, it means to set out, to start out (Gen. 29:1). It is found once in the plural preceded by *šālōš*, three, meaning three times (Ex. 23:14). The term *mêsîḵ 'eṯ-regel* means to have a bowel movement (Judg. 3:24). The phrase *mê raglêhem* refers to urine, water of their privates (2 Kgs. 18:27). *
– [4] Ex. 30:18, 28; 31:9; Lev. 8:11 ➔ STAND (noun) <3653> [5] 2 Kgs. 19:24 ➔ TIME <6471>.

FOOT (ON) – ***ragliy*** [masc. noun: רַגְלִי <7273>; from FOOT <7272>] ▶ **This word refers to foot soldiers; footmen.** It refers simply to a person traveling on foot (Ex. 12:37); but more technically of foot soldiers

(Judg. 20:2; 2 Sam. 8:4; 1 Kgs. 20:29); infantry (Jer. 12:5). *

FOOTHOLD – ***moemāḏ*** [masc. noun: מַעֲמָד <4613>; from STAND <5975>] ▶ **This word refers to a place to stand.** It describes a grip or firm place to stand in order to be safe or secure (Ps. 69:2). ¶

FOOTING – Job 38:6; Song 5:15 ➔ BASE (noun) <134>.

FOOTPRINT – Hos. 6:8 ➔ DECEITFUL <6121>.

FOOTSTEP – ***miḏrāḵ*** [masc. noun: מִדְרָךְ <4096>; from TREAD <1869>] ▶ **This word indicates a treading place.** It is used to indicate a very small portion of land or territory, e.g., on Mount Seir (Deut. 2:5). ¶

FOOTSTOOL – [1] ***hadôm*** [masc. noun: הֲדֹם <1916>; from an unused root meaning to stamp upon] ▶ **This term is always used with the word for feet and means the resting place of one's feet.** It indicates the place where God is pleased to dwell and to rule (1 Chr. 28:2). Zion is depicted as His footstool (Lam. 2:1), as is the ark where worship takes place (Ps. 99:5; 132:7). The concept expands to include the entire earth as God's footstool (Is. 66:1). But it also is used to indicate rulership or victory over one's enemies, the wicked, as when God makes His enemies a footstool (Ps. 110:1). ¶
[2] ***keḇeš*** [masc. noun: כֶּבֶשׁ <3534>; from SUBDUE <3533>] ▶ **This word refers to a golden seat with no arms, a feature of Solomon's throne.** Ref.: 2 Chr. 9:18. ¶

FOR – [1] ***ba'aḏ*** [particle: בַּעַד <1157>; from UNTIL <5704> with prep. prefix] ▶ **This word also means through, behind. It has many nuanced meanings.** The basic renderings are: behind, as in shutting a door behind oneself (Gen. 7:16); surrounding one, shutting a person in (Ps. 3:3; 139:11; Jon. 2:6). Figuratively, it is used after a verb of shutting to indicate (*ba'aḏ*) the womb (Gen. 20:18). After the verb to pray, it indicates what is prayed for (Gen. 20:7). It indicates stand on behalf (*ba'aḏ*) of something or someone (2 Sam. 10:12). It is used to indicate looking through (*ba'aḏ*) something (Gen. 26:8) or to describe motion over something (2 Sam. 20:21). It is used to render the idiom this . . . for that, e.g., skin for (*ba'aḏ*) skin (Job 2:4). *
[2] ***lemô*** [particle: לְמוֹ <3926>; a prolonged and separable form of the prep. prefix] ▶ **This word also means at, over, in. It may be an expanded form of the preposition *le*, to.** It indicates in context purpose, "for" the sword (Job 27:14); it indicates why something is done, e.g., people waited for Job's counsel (Job 29:21). It has the sense of "in," lions "in their lair" (Job 38:40 NASB). In Job 40:4 it signifies Job's purpose of covering his mouth because he is unable to reply to God. ¶

FOR EVER – Lev. 25:23, 30 ➔ PERMANENTLY <6783>.

FORBEAR – Jer. 20:9 ➔ CONTAIN <3557>.

FORBID – ***nû'*** [verb: נוּא <5106>; a prim. root] ▶ **This word means not to allow, to discourage, to thwart.** Negated, it means not to permit something, to stop it: the performance of a vow to the Lord (Num. 30:5, 8, 11; also translated to disallow, to oppose, to overrule); an action that should be carried out, i.e., taking the Promised Land (Num. 32:7, 9); God thwarting the plans or designs of people (Ps. 33:10; also translated to frustrate, to make of no effect). It is used in a figurative, idiomatic expression meaning, "let it happen to me," literally, "let my head not refuse" (Ps. 141:5). ¶

FORBIDDEN MARRIAGE (ONE BORN OF) – Deut. 23:2 ➔ FORBIDDEN UNION (ONE BORN OF) <4464>.

FORBIDDEN UNION (ONE BORN OF) – ***mamzêr*** [masc. noun: מַמְזֵר <4464>; from an unused root meaning to alienate] ▶ **This word identifies an illegitimate child.** It specifies a person who does not have a proper pedigree or genealogy and was born out of wedlock (Deut. 23:2; also translated: one of illegitimate birth, one born of forbidden marriage, bastard). In Zechariah 9:6 (mongrel, mixed race, mixed people, bastard), it is best rendered as a reference to foreign or mongrel persons. ¶

FORCE (noun) – [1] ***'eḏrā'*** [Aramaic noun: אֶדְרָע <153>; an orthographical variation for ARM <1872>] ▶ **This word means strength, literally, arm.** It indicates the threatening way in which the Jews were forced to stop building the new house of God (Ezra 4:23) in the time of Zerubbabel. ¶
– [2] Job 36:19 ➔ FORCES <3981>.

FORCE (NATURAL) – Deut. 34:7 ➔ VIGOR <3893>.

FORCE (verb) – [1] Ex. 5:13 ➔ HASTEN <213> [2] Judg. 1:34 ➔ OPPRESS <3905> [3] 1 Sam. 13:12 ➔ CONTROL (verb) <662> [4] Esther 7:8 ➔ SUBDUE <3533>.

FORCED LABOR – [1] ***mas*** [masc. noun: מַס <4522>; from MELT <4549> (in the sense of to be broken down)] ▶ **This word designates compulsory labor, service, tribute.** It refers to labor forced on someone or service demanded, usually by the state (Gen. 49:15; Deut. 20:11; 1 Kgs. 5:14; Is. 31:8); usually overseen by a foreman or task-master (Ex. 1:11; 1 Kgs. 4:6, 12:18). A person not willing to work or a lazy person may be put to forced labor (Prov. 12:24). *
– [2] 1 Kgs. 11:28 ➔ BURDEN <5447>.

FORCEFUL – Job 6:25 ➔ GRIEVOUS <4834>.

FORCES – ***maʾămāṣ*** [masc. noun: מַאֲמָץ <3981>; from STRONG (BE) <553>] ▶ **This word indicates energies, effort; expenditures.** It refers to exertions or expenditures used to deliver a person from stress or distress but all in vain (Job 36:19; also translated force, efforts). ¶

FORCIBLE – Job 6:25 ➔ GRIEVOUS <4834>.

FORCING – Prov. 30:33 ➔ CHURNING <4330>.

FORD – [1] ***maʿăḇar, maʿbārāh*** [masc. noun: מַעֲבָר, מַעְבָּרָה <4569>; from PASS THROUGH. PASS OVER <5674>] ▶
a. A masculine noun meaning passing; it is also translated pass, passage. It is used to describe a spot on land or in a river where a crossing can be undertaken (Gen. 32:22; 1 Sam. 13:23). In Isaiah 30:32, it has the sense of a stroke or blow made with a stick or rod. ¶
b. A feminine noun indicating a crossing place or passage. It refers to a suitable place for passing over or through something: over a river (Josh. 2:7; Judg. 3:28; 12:5, 6; Jer. 51:32); over land by using a ravine (1 Sam. 14:4; Is. 10:29). Other ref.: Is. 16:2. ¶
[2] ***ʿăḇārāh*** [fem. noun: עֲבָרָה <5679>; from PASS THROUGH, PASS OVER <5674>] ▶ **This word refers to a shallow place in a river where it can be crossed most easily; it is also translated plain, ferryboat.** Refs.: 2 Sam. 15:28; 17:16; 19:18. ¶

FOREHEAD – [1] ***mēṣaḥ*** [masc. noun: מֵצַח <4696>; from an unused root meaning to be clear, i.e., conspicuous] ▶ **This word means the part of the head between the eyebrows and the front of a person's hairline.** Aaron wore a holy plate on his forehead (Ex. 28:38); Goliath was killed from a stone striking his forehead (1 Sam. 17:49); Uzziah had leprosy on his forehead (2 Chr. 26:19, 20). A "bronze forehead" was symbolic of determination or obstinacy in a good or bad sense (Is. 48:4); as is the phrase, strong, hard of forehead (Ezek. 3:7–9). A mark on the forehead served as an identifying symbol (Ezek. 9:4). Other ref.: Jer. 3:3. ¶
[2] ***pōṯ*** [masc. noun: פֹּת <6596>; from an unused root meaning to open] ▶ **This word may mean a forehead (see previous definition) or scalp.** This meaning would parallel the previous line of poetry speaking of the scalp or top (crown) of the heads of women in Judah (Is. 3:17). The Hebrew word also refers to the private parts of a

woman and to a door hinge; see SECRET PARTS <6596> and HINGE <6596>. ¶

FOREIGN – 1 ***nêkār*** [masc. noun: נֵכָר <5236>; from DETERMINE <5234>] ▶ **The word comes from a root meaning to scrutinize, perhaps drawing on the idea that people look closely at something foreign or strange. The word modifies other nouns to signify a foreigner or a foreign god.** Foreigners with their false gods posed a threat to Israel's service to the Lord (Deut. 32:12; Judg. 10:16; Mal. 2:11); sometimes even infiltrating the Temple service (Neh. 13:30; Ezek. 44:9). They also posed a physical threat at times (Ps. 144:7; Is. 62:8; Jer. 5:19). However, foreigners sometimes turned to Israel's God (Is. 56:3, 6). The word also refers (with other words) to foreign land (Ps. 137:4; Jer. 5:19); and a foreign power (Ps. 144:7). *
– 2 Is. 28:11 ➔ STAMMERING <3934>
3 Ezek. 3:5, 6 ➔ UNINTELLIGIBLE <6012>.

FORESKIN – ***'orlāh*** [fem. adj.: עָרְלָה <6190>; fem. of UNCIRCUMCISED <6189>] ▶ **The word means the prepuce, i.e., the skin covering the end of the penis.** Refs.: Gen. 17:11; 1 Sam. 18:25, 27. It could also represent the state of being uncircumcised (having a foreskin [Gen. 34:14]) or the act of circumcision (cutting off the foreskin [Ex. 4:25]). Like the word *'ārêl* (UNCIRCUMCISED <6189>), this term could be used figuratively to represent the impure nature of fruit trees (Lev. 19:23); or the human heart (Deut. 10:16; Jer. 4:4). *

FOREST – 1 ***ḥōreš, ḥōres*** [masc. noun and proper noun: חֹרֶשׁ, חֹרֶשׁ <2793>; from PLOW <2790>] ▶
a. This word depicts woods, a bough, a thicket. It refers to woodland or forest areas (2 Chr. 27:4; also translated wooded hills, wooded areas). It describes the beauty of Assyria in her early rise to power (Ezek. 31:3: forest, shroud). It is also sometimes described as an undesirable location as well (Is. 17:9: bough, place in the forest) and in certain contexts indicates a forested wilderness area (1 Sam. 23:15; KJV, wood; ESV, NASB, Horesh).
b. This word refers to Horesh. It was a specific stand of forest and a wilderness location where David hid from Saul (1 Sam. 23:15, 16, 18, 19; KJV, wood). ¶
2 ***ya'ar*** [יַעַר <3293>; from an unused root probably meaning to thicken with verdure] ▶
a. A masculine noun referring to woods; honeycomb. This word is used in contexts and texts where it means a forest, thicket, woods (2 Sam. 18:8; 1 Kgs. 7:2; Zech. 11:2). It depicts a man-made or humanly manicured natural park area (Eccl. 2:6). *
b. A masculine noun meaning honeycomb. The word has this sense in Song of Solomon 5:1. It refers to an item the lover has eaten within his garden of delight. ¶
c. A masculine proper noun meaning Jaar. It may refer to a city by this name, "city of forests," Kiriath Jearim, or simply the field of Jaar (ESV, NASB, NIV, Ps. 132:6). ¶
3 ***pardês*** [masc. noun: פַּרְדֵּס <6508>; of foreign origin] ▶ **This word indicates an area covered by trees; also a park, an orchard.** It refers to an area covered by trees and thick shrubbery (Neh. 2:8); if man-made, a place well-landscaped and manicured, a park for beauty and enjoyment (Eccl. 2:5). It describes the bride as a garden or orchard full of fruits (Song 4:13). ¶
– 4 2 Kgs. 19:23; Is. 37:24 ➔ fruitful *forest*, thickest *forest*, finest *of the forests*, *forest of his* Carmel ➔ FIELD (FERTILE, FRUITFUL, PLENTIFUL) <3759> a.
5 Ps. 29:9 ➔ HONEYCOMB <3295>.

FORESTS – Ezek. 34:25 ➔ WOODS <3264>.

FOREVER – 1 ***nêṣaḥ, neṣaḥ*** [noun: נֵצַח, נֶצַח <5331>; from OVERSEE <5329>] ▶ **This word means ever, always, perpetual.** It is used especially in prayers to ask whether God has forgotten His people forever (Ps. 13:1; 77:8; Jer. 15:18); and to affirm that He has not (Ps. 9:18; 103:9). With a negative, the word may be translated never (Ps. 10:11; Is. 13:20; Amos 8:7). The word also describes as perpetual (or appearing so to the writer) such things as ruins (Ps. 74:3); and pain (Jer. 15:18). In some passages, the word points to God's eternal nature (Ps. 68:16; Is. 25:8); and in 1 Chronicles 29:11, *nēṣaḥ* is among those attributes ascribed to God, namely, the kingdom, power, and glory. God even refers to Himself as the *nêṣaḥ* of Israel (1 Sam. 15:29), a usage that may indicate His glory (see *nāṣaḥ* [OVERSEE <5329>]). It also points to His eternal, truthful nature that is contrary to lying or changing. *

[2] ***'ôlām*** [masc. noun: עוֹלָם <5769>; from HIDE <5956>; properly, concealed, i.e., the vanishing point; generally, time out of mind (past or future), i.e., (practically) eternity] ▶ **This word means a very long time. It usually refers to looking forward but many times expresses the idea of looking backward.** It may cover a given person's lifetime (Ex. 21:6; 1 Sam. 1:22); a period of many generations (Josh. 24:2; Prov. 22:28); the time of the present created order (Deut. 33:15; Ps. 73:12); time beyond this temporal sphere, especially when used regarding God (Gen. 21:33; Ps. 90:2; Dan. 12:2, 7). The term also applies to many things associated with God, such as His decrees, His covenants, and the Messiah (Gen. 9:16; Ex. 12:14; Mic. 5:2). This word describes the span of time in which God is to be obeyed and praised (1 Chr. 16:36; Ps. 89:1; 119:112). In the age to come, there will be no need for sun or moon, for God Himself will be the everlasting light (Is. 60:19, 20; cf. Rev. 22:5).

[3] ***'êylôm*** [masc. noun: עֵילוֹם <5865>; for <5769> above] ▶ **This word designates eternity. It indicates an infinite stretch of time into the future.** God chose to put His name in the Temple forever (2 Chr. 33:7). ¶

FORFEIT – Dan. 1:10 ➔ ENDANGER <2325>.

FORGE – [1] Gen. 4:22 ➔ SHARPEN <3913> [2] Ps. 119:69 ➔ SMEAR <2950>.

FORGER – Gen. 4:22 ➔ SHARPEN <3913>.

FORGER (BE) – Job 13:4 ➔ SMEAR <2950>.

FORGET – [1] ***nāšāh*** [verb: נָשָׁה <5382>; a prim. root] ▶ **This word means to not call to mind or to not let something dominate one's thinking.** Ref.: Gen. 41:51. It is used of God forgetting and forgiving, not choosing to count sin against a person (Job 11:6). It indicates God causing an ostrich to forget, to not have wisdom at hand (Job 39:17). It is negated when it speaks of God forgetting His people (Is. 44:21); but it is affirmed when He temporarily rejects them (Jer. 23:39). It is negated to indicate that a person can no longer remember happiness because of present calamities (Lam. 3:17). ¶

[2] ***šāḵaḥ*** [verb: שָׁכַח <7911>; a prim. root] ▶ **This word indicates that something has been lost to memory, or a period of time has softened the memory of it.** Hatred (Gen. 27:45); forgetting a person or an event (Gen. 40:23); forgetting the days of much food, abundance (Gen. 41:30). It is an especially important word with respect to God and His people: God never forgets them (Is. 49:15); they are not to forget their God, His covenant, and His deeds (Deut. 4:9, 23, 31; 6:12; 8:11; 9:7; 25:19; 32:18). But God does not pass over, wink at, or forget the wickedness of His people (Lam. 5:20; Amos 8:7). Those who forget God wither away (Job 8:13), as well as all the nations who forget Him. The helpless must not be left alone (Ps. 10:12). God's Law must not be forgotten (Ps. 119:61, 83, 93). Wisdom's teachings are not to be forgotten (Prov. 3:1; 4:5). *

[3] ***šᵉḵaḥ*** [Aramaic verb: שְׁכַח <7912>; corresponding to <7911> above] ▶ **This word means to discover, to come up, to find someone or something.** Ref.: a person, Daniel (2:25). Negated it means not to find someone or something (Dan. 2:35); to discover wisdom in a person (Dan. 5:11, 12, 14); to discover, find by weighing, evaluating (Dan. 5:27); to discover, to find a name in a registry or archives (Ezra 4:15); as well as other facts (Ezra 4:15, 19). *

[4] ***šāḵēaḥ*** [adj.: שָׁכֵחַ <7913>; from <7911> above] ▶ **This word means not**

remembering, neglectful. The nations who turn from, forget, or neglect God will be put into Sheol, along with the wicked (Ps. 9:17); including God's own nation and people (Is. 65:11). ¶

FORGETFULNESS – ***nᵉšiyyāh*** [fem. noun: נְשִׁיָּה <5388>; from FORGET <5382>] ▶ **This word refers to a state in which nothing is remembered, there is no consciousness, memories have been blanked out.** In context it is the state of being dead and in the grave (Ps. 88:12; NIV: oblivion). ¶

FORGIVE – [1] ***sālaḥ*** [verb: סָלַח <5545>; a prim. root] ▶ **This word mean also to pardon, to spare; pass.: to be forgiven, to be pardoned.** The verb's subject is always God: He forgave the people of Israel after Moses interceded for them in the desert (Num. 14:20; Is. 55:7); Solomon prayed that the Lord would always hear and forgive His people (1 Kgs. 8:30, 39; Dan. 9:19; Amos 7:2). Some sins of Israel, however, were not forgiven. Jehoiachin had shed so much innocent blood that the Lord was not willing to forgive him (2 Kgs. 24:4; Lam. 3:42). The verb means to free from or release from something: the word describes the Lord pardoning or releasing a young woman from her vows in some instances (Num. 30:5, 8); the Lord will not forgive an Israelite who in his heart approves of his own rebellious actions and continues in them (Deut. 29:20). The Lord forgives wickedness if it is repented of (Ex. 34:9; Num. 14:19).

In the passive stem, the Hebrew word means to be forgiven; the people are forgiven (Lev. 4:20, 26; 5:10; 19:22) for their unintentional sins (Num. 15:25, 28) by turning away from them. *

– [2] Ps. 78:38; 79:9; Is. 6:7 ➔ COVER (verb) <3722>.

FORGIVE (READY TO) – [1] Neh. 9:17 ➔ FORGIVENESS <5545> [2] Ps. 86:5 ➔ FORGIVING <5546>.

FORGIVENESS – ***sᵉliyḥāh*** [fem. noun: סְלִיחָה <5547>; from FORGIVE <5545>] ▶ **This word means pardon, remission.** God is a forgiving God (Neh. 9:17; also translated ready to pardon, ready to forgive). He does not keep a record of sin, but with Him there is forgiveness (Ps. 130:4). Daniel also proclaimed that God is forgiving, even though the Hebrews had sinned greatly against Him (Dan. 9:9). See the related Hebrew root *sālaḥ* (FORGIVE <5545>) and the related Hebrew adjective *sallāḥ* (FORGIVING <5546>). ¶

FORGIVING – [1] ***sallāḥ*** [adj.: סַלָּח <5546>; from FORGIVE <5545>] ▶ **This word means ready to pardon; it is also translated ready to forgive.** It is used only once in the Bible in a verse that describes the love and mercy of God (Ps. 86:5). See the related Hebrew root *sālaḥ* (FORGIVE <5545>) and noun *sᵉliyḥāh* (FORGIVENESS <5547>). ¶

– [2] Neh. 9:17; Dan. 9:9 ➔ FORGIVENESS <5545>.

FORK – [1] ***mazlēg, mizlāgāh*** [common noun: מַזְלֵג, מִזְלָגָה <4207>; from an unused root meaning to draw up] ▶ **This word refers to a sacrificial utensil.** It functioned as a tool to grasp a sacrificial meat offering, a meat fork, possibly of three tines (Ex. 27:3; Num. 4:14; 1 Sam. 2:13, 14; 1 Chr. 28:17; 2 Chr. 4:16). Other ref.: Ex. 38:3. ¶

[2] ***qillᵉšôn*** [masc. noun: קִלְּשׁוֹן <7053>; from an unused root meaning to prick] ▶ **This word indicates a pitchfork, a pronged tool, possibly a three-pronged tool (trident?) for hoeing, loosening the ground.** Ref.: 1 Sam. 13:21. ¶

FORK, WINNOWING FORK – Jer. 15:7 ➔ FAN, WINNOWING FAN <4213>.

FORK OF THE ROAD – Obad. 1:14 ➔ CROSSROAD <6563>.

FORM (noun) – [1] ***ṣiyr*** [masc. noun: צִיר <6736>; the same as HINGE <6735> (a form of beauty as if pressed out)] ▶ **This word focuses on the physical appearance of an item.** That form and structure could be of the human body: the psalmist records how dead bodies decay in the grave (Ps. 49:14). That form and structure could also be that of an idol: Isaiah states that those who formed idols would be ashamed and confounded (Is. 45:16). ¶

2 ***qeṣeḇ*** [masc. noun: קֶצֶב <7095>; from CUT, CUT OFF, CUT DOWN <7094>] ▶ **This word refers to the structure or configuration of something, its basic pattern. It is also translated size, shape; moreover, it has the meaning of roots.** It is used in context of supporting stands or foundations and of the cherubim (1 Kgs. 6:25; 7:37). Other ref.: Jon. 2:6 (bottoms, roots, moorings). ¶

3 ***tō'ar*** [masc. noun: תֹּאַר <8389>; from OUTLINE (MAKE AN) <8388>] ▶ **This word means shape, appearance, beauty.** It refers to the contours and outward form of something, e.g., the body of a woman or a man (Gen. 29:17; 39:6; Deut. 21:11; 1 Sam. 16:18); of an animal's body, it means healthy, strong-looking (Gen. 41:18, 19). It is used in a stereotypical way, the form of the son of a king, a royal-looking person, a person with dignity (Judg. 8:18). It also refers to the shape of trees, plants, etc. (Jer. 11:16). *

– 4 Ezek. 43:11 ➔ DESIGN <6699> 5 Dan. 2:31; 3:25 ➔ APPEARANCE <7299>.

FORM (WITHOUT) – Gen. 1:2 ➔ FORMLESS <8414>.

FORM (verb) – 1 ***yāṣar*** [verb: יָצַר <3335>; prob. identical with DISTRESSED (BE) <3334> (through the squeezing into share) (comp. SPREAD (verb) <3331>)] ▶ **This word also means to fashion, to shape, to devise. Its primary meaning is derived from the idea of cutting or framing.** It is used of God's fashioning man from the dust of the ground (Gen. 2:7); God's creative works in nature (Ps. 95:5; Amos 4:13); and in the womb (Ps. 139:16: to be fashioned, to be ordained, to be formed; Jer. 1:5; cf. Zech. 2:1); the molding of clay (Is. 29:16; 45:9); the framing of seasons (Ps. 74:17); the forging of metal (Is. 44:12); the crafting of weapons (Is. 54:17); the making of plans (Ps. 94:20; Is. 46:11; Jer. 18:11). It also signifies a potter (1 Chr. 4:23; Ps. 2:9; Is. 41:25; Zech. 11:13; etc.); a sculptor (Is. 44:9); or the Creator (Is. 43:1; 44:2, 24). By extension, the word conveys the notion of predestination and election (2 Kgs. 19:25: to plan, to form; Is. 49:5: to form). *

– 2 Song 2:13 ➔ RIPEN <2590>.

FORM OUT – Job 33:6 ➔ WINK <7169> b.

FORMED – that which was formed, the thing formed, what was formed: *yêṣer* [masc. noun: יֵצֶר <3336>; from FORM (verb) <3335>] ▶ **This Hebrew word means form, framing, purpose, imagination.** One use of this word was to refer to a pottery vessel formed by a potter (i.e., that which was formed [Is. 29:16]). Another example of a formed object was a graven image (Hab. 2:18). The psalmist said that man was formed from the dust (Ps. 103:14). This word also carries the connotation of something thought of in the mind, such as wickedness in people's hearts (Gen. 6:5); or something treasured or stored in the heart (1 Chr. 29:18: intent, desire, imagination, purpose). Other refs.: Gen. 8:21; Deut. 31:21; 1 Chr. 28:9; Is. 26:3. ¶

FORMER – Is. 43:18; Ezek. 38:17; Mal. 3:4 ➔ EASTERN <6931> b.

FORMER STATE – Ezek. 16:55 ➔ FORMER TIME <6927>.

FORMER TIME – 1 ***qaḏmāh*** [fem. noun: קַדְמָה <6927>; from MEET (verb) <6923> (in the sense of to come before)] ▶ **This word means a beginning, a previous occasion, a former state.** In the oracle concerning Tyre, it was called the city of old (Is. 23:7: origin, antiquity). The Lord promised to restore Sodom, Samaria, and Jerusalem to what they were before in order to bring shame on Jerusalem (Ezek. 16:55). A prophecy to the mountains of Israel said that they would be populated as they were in the past (Ezek. 36:11). See the Hebrew noun *qeḏem* (EAST <6924>) and *qaḏmāh* below. Other ref.: Ps. 129:6. ¶

[2] ***qadmāh*** [Aramaic fem. noun: קַדְמָה <6928>] ▶ **This word corresponds to <6927> above.** When the elders of Judah were questioned about rebuilding the Temple, they answered that they were restoring something built long ago (Ezra 5:11). Even after the edict from King Darius, Daniel continued to pray as he had done before (Dan. 6:10). ¶

FORMLESS – ***tōhû*** [masc. noun: תֹּהוּ <8414>; from an unused root meaning to lie waste] ▶ **This Hebrew word means formlessness, confusion, disorder. The exact meaning of this term is difficult at best since its study is limited to its relatively few Old Testament occurrences.** It is used to describe primeval earth before the seven creative days (Gen. 1:2); a land reduced to primeval chaos and formlessness (Is. 34:11; 45:18; Jer. 4:23); a destroyed city (Is. 24:10); nothingness or empty space (Job 26:7); a barren wasteland (Deut. 32:10; Job 6:18; 12:24; Ps. 107:40); that which is vain and futile (1 Sam. 12:21; Is. 45:19; 49:4); like idolatry (Is. 41:29; 44:9); unfounded allegations (Is. 29:21; 59:4); the nations compared to God (Is. 40:17); or human rulers (Is. 40:23). Although it is impossible to grasp the full import of this word, it is obvious that it has a negative and disparaging tone. It represents chaos, confusion, and disorder, all things that are opposed to the organization, direction, and order that God has demonstrated. *

FORMULA – Ex. 30:32, 37; Ezek. 45:11 ➔ PROPORTION <4971>.

FORNICATION – ***zᵉnûṯ*** [fem. noun: זְנוּת <2184>; from PROSTITUTE (verb) <2181>] ▶ **In the literal sense, this word refers to sexual sin that violates the marriage covenant.** Ref.: Hos. 4:11. Most often, however, this word is figuratively applied to God's nation Israel for their wickedness (Hos. 6:10). This fornication is usually associated with the worship of other gods (Jer. 3:2, 9; 13:27; Ezek. 23:27), but it can describe outright rebellion (Num. 14:33) or general iniquities (Ezek. 43:7, 9). ¶

FORSAKE – ***nāṭaš*** [verb: נָטַשׁ <5203>; a prim. root] ▶ **This word means to leave alone, to abandon.** It occurs in relation to the land that should be unused ("forsaken") in the seventh year (Ex. 23:11: to lie fallow, to lie still, to lie unused); the Israelites who abandoned God (Deut. 32:15); Saul's father who forgot about the donkeys and began to worry about him (1 Sam. 10:2: to cease, to stop); David who left his flock with a shepherd (1 Sam. 17:20); the psalmist who pleaded with God not to turn from him (Ps. 27:9; also translated to reject). This word is used once to mean to not permit when Laban was not allowed to kiss his grandchildren good-bye (Gen. 31:28: to allow, to permit, to let, to suffer). *

FORSAKEN – [1] ***'almān*** [adj.: אַלְמָן <488>; prolonged from BIND <481> in the sense of bereavement] ▶ **This word means widowed.** It occurs only in Jeremiah 51:5, assuring Israel and Judah that, even in exile, they have not been forsaken by their God. Although this Hebrew word is similar to the Hebrew word for widow, the context of this verse does not support the idea that Israel is pictured as the wife of the Lord. ¶
– [2] Is. 17:9 ➔ FORSAKEN PLACE <5805>.

FORSAKEN PLACE – ***ʿᵃzûḇāh*** [fem. abstract noun: עֲזוּבָה <5805>; fem. pass. part. of LEAVE <5800>] ▶ **This word designates isolated, abandoned places after people have left them.** It refers to deserted locations (Is. 6:12) or to similar locations in a forest setting (Is. 17:9). Others take the word to refer to a state of forsakenness, loneliness (KJV: forsaking, forsaken). ¶

FORSAKING – Is. 6:12 ➔ FORSAKEN PLACE <5805>.

FORT – [1] Num. 31:10 ➔ CAMP <2918> [2] 2 Kgs. 25:1; Jer. 52:4; Ezek. 4:2; 17:17; 21:22; 26:8 ➔ SIEGE WORK <1785> [3] 2 Chr. 17:12; 27:4 ➔ FORTRESS <1003> [4] Is. 32:14 ➔ HILL <6076> [5] Nah. 2:1 ➔ FORTIFIED PLACE <4694>.

FORTH (PUT) – Song 2:13 ➔ RIPEN <2590>.

FORTHWITH – Ezra 6:8 ➔ DILIGENTLY <629>.

FORTIFICATION – [1] ***miḇṣār*** [masc. noun: מִבְצָר <4013>; from GATHER <1219> c. (in the sense of to strengthen or fortify)] ▶
a. This word is used of a building or set of structures designed for efficient military defenses. A fortified city (Num. 32:17, 36; 2 Kgs. 3:19; Is. 25:12); a strongly fortified city (Dan. 11:15); fortresses in general (Hos. 10:14; Amos 5:9); fortifications on a wall and including the wall (Is. 25:12); sound fortifications (Dan. 11:24, 39). It is used figuratively of Jeremiah as a fortified city to carry out his mission (Jer. 1:18; 6:27) (KJV; see b., c. also). *
b. A masculine noun indicating a tester of metals, an assayer. It is used figuratively of the prophet Jeremiah, the teacher of God's people (NASB; see a., c. also) (Jer. 6:27).
c. A masculine noun indicating ore, metal which is tested. Some translators give the meaning ore, metal, to the word in Jeremiah 6:27 (NIV; see a., b. also).
– [2] Lam. 2:5 ➔ STRONGHOLD <759>.

FORTIFIED PLACE – ***m^{e}ṣûrāh, m^{e}ṣurāh*** [fem. noun: מְצוּרָה, מְצֻרָה <4694>; fem. of SIEGE <4692>] ▶ **This word designates a stronghold, a fortress.** It indicated a fortified city or location: cities in Judah and Benjamin (2 Chr. 11:10, 11, 23; 12:4; 14:6; 21:3); battle engines or fortified towers (Is. 29:3: siege work, battle tower, fort); a fortified station or structure in a city (Nah. 2:1: fort, fortress, rampart, munition). ¶

FORTRESS – [1] ***biyrāniyyôṯ*** [fem. noun: בִּירָנִיּוֹת <1003>; from CITADEL <1002>] ▶ **This word refers to fortified places used to protect and defend a people or nation; it is also translated castle, fort.** Fortresses were constructed by Jehosaphat (2 Chr. 17:12) and Jotham (2 Chr. 27:4) respectively in Judah. ¶
– [2] 2 Sam. 22:2; Ps. 18:2; 31:2, 3; etc. ➔ STRONGHOLD <4686> [3] 2 Sam. 22:46; Ps. 18:45; Mic. 7:17 ➔ RIM <4526> [4] Is. 23:13 ➔ STRONGHOLD <759> [5] Dan. 11:38; Is. 23:11 ➔ STRONGHOLD <4581> a., b. [6] Nah. 2:1 ➔ FORTIFIED PLACE <4694> [7] Zech. 9:12 ➔ STRONGHOLD <1225> [8] See CITADEL <1001>, <1002>.

FORTUNE – [1] ***gaḏ*** [masc. proper noun: גַּד <1408>; a variation of <1409> below] ▶ **This word denotes a false god. It could refer to the planet Jupiter.** It refers to a deity named Gad but means fortune (Is. 65:11, ESV, NASB, NIV; KJV, troop; NKJV, Gad, meaning idolatrous practices). ¶
[2] ***gaḏ*** [masc. noun: גַּד <1409>; from ATTACK (verb) <1464> (in the sense of distributing)] ▶
a. This word indicates luck or chance and is therefore given by Leah as the name for her maid's son, Gad. Ref.: Gen. 30:11, NASB; NIV. Others prefer to render it as a troop (KJV, NKJV).
b. This word is translated as a troop often. Ref.: Gen. 30:11, KJV, NKJV. Others favor rendering it as good fortune (NASB, NIV). It is rendered as troop in Isaiah 65:11 (KJV); as fortune, a god, (NASB, NIV); or as Gad, meaning idolatrous practices (NKJV). A careful study of the context of its use is necessary to decide which rendering is most likely correct. ¶

FORTUNES – Ps. 126:1 ➔ CAPTIVITY <7870>.

FORTUNE-TELLER – Deut. 18:10, 14 ➔ WITCHCRAFT (PRACTICE) <6049>.

FORTY – See FOUR <702>.

FORTY, FORTIETH – ***ʾarbāʿiym*** [masc. noun: אַרְבָּעִים <705>; multiple of FOUR <702>] ▶ **This word is always in its absolute form.** Used alone it means forty of something (Gen. 7:17; Judg. 3:11; 1 Sam. 4:18; 1 Kgs. 19:8; Amos 2:10). It combines with other numbers to give the counting numbers, forty-one (1 Kgs. 14:21; 15:10), etc. With the preposition *b^e* added, it means fortieth, such as in the fortieth year (Deut. 1:3) or in the forty-first year (2 Chr. 16:13). *

FOUL – 1 *rāpaś* [verb: רָפַשׂ <7515>; a prim. root] ▶ **This word means to trample down, to foul water, or to make muddy by trampling.** It means to ruin something, to corrupt it by trampling on it, such as a spring of water, muddying the water (Prov. 25:26: murky, trampled, troubled, muddled). In context it refers to muddying waters by trampling violently in them, but it refers to the confusion and turmoil spread among the nations by Egypt (Ezek. 32:2; 34:18). ¶
– 2 Ex. 7:21; 16:20; Ps. 38:5: to become foul, to grow foul, to be foul ➔ STINK <887>.

FOUL (BE) – Job 16:16 ➔ RED (BE) <2560>.

FOUL (BECOME, TURN) – Is. 19:6 ➔ REJECT <2186> b.

FOUL SMELL, FOUL ODOR – *ṣaḥ^anāh* [fem. noun: צַחֲנָה <6709>; from an unused root meaning to putrefy] ▶ **This word describes the putrid smell of something rotting, decaying.** It is used both literally and figuratively of the foulness of a destroyed enemy army (Joel 2:20; also translated smell, ill savour). ¶

FOUNDATION – 1 *'ōš* [Aramaic masc. noun: אֹשׁ <787>; corresponding (by transposition and abbreviation) to <803> below] ▶ **This word refers to the building support being restored to Jerusalem during the time of Zerubbabel's return (536 B.C.) and later.** Ref.: Ezra 4:12. It refers also to the restoring of the foundations of the new Temple (Ezra 5:16; 6:3). ¶
2 *'āšyāh* [fem. noun: אָשְׁיָה <803>; fem. pass. part. from an unused root meaning to be found] ▶ **This word is used both literally and figuratively to depict the strong and mighty supports and pillars constructed in Babylon.** The Lord would destroy them (Jer. 50:15; also translated pillar, bulwark, tower). ¶
3 *'āšiyš* [masc. noun: אָשִׁישׁ <808>; from the same as FIRE <784> (comp. <803> above)] ▶
a. This word may refer to the bases of the city Kir-hareseth, a devastated city in Moab. Ref.: KJV, NKJV, Is. 16:7. See <803> above. ¶
b. It means sacrificial raisin cakes which were produced in Kir-hareseth, a devastated city of Moab. Ref.: NASB, Is. 16:7. It is considered to be related to *'ašiyšāh*. See RAISIN CAKES <809>. ¶
c. A masculine noun meaning men. It refers to the people destroyed by God's judgment on the city of Kir-hareseth, a city of Moab. Ref.: NIV, Is. 16:7. It is considered to be related to *'iyš*; see MAN <376>. ¶
4 *y^esôḏ* [noun: יְסוֹד <3247>; from FOUNDATION (LAY A) <3245>] ▶ **The word refers to a base on which people build structures.** It is used several times to refer to the base (KJV: bottom) of the sacrificial altar, where the blood of sacrifices was poured (Ex. 29:12; Lev. 4:7, 18, 25, 30, 34). The Gate of the Foundation, mentioned in 2 Chronicles 23:5, may have been named from its proximity to the altar. In reference to larger buildings, the word is usually used to express the extent of destruction which sometimes included razing a city down to its foundation (Ps. 137:7; Mic. 1:6) and sometimes even the destruction of the foundation itself (Lam. 4:11; Ezek. 30:4). Egypt's foundations appear to symbolize its dependence on other nations (see Ezek. 30:4, 5). Symbolically, the word refers to principles on which people build their lives, whether they be faulty (Job 4:19; 22:16) or sound (Prov. 10:25; cf. Matt. 7:24–27). Other refs.: Lev. 5:9; 8:15; 9:9; 2 Chr. 24:27; Ezek. 13:14; Hab. 3:13. ¶
5 *y^esûḏāh* [fem. noun: יְסוּדָה <3248>; fem. of BEGIN <3246>] ▶ **This word means base and occurs only in Psalm 87:1.** The words in Zechariah 4:9, 8:9, and 12:1, are forms of the verb *yāsaḏ* [FOUNDATION (LAY A) <3245>]; the words in Isaiah 28:16, although difficult to analyze, also do not appear to belong under this reference. In Psalm 87:1, the word refers to Jerusalem as God's foundation or base in the holy mountain; ESV and NIV translate by the corresponding verb: he founded, he has founded.

The psalm enlarges on this, saying that Jerusalem will be the place of His particular dwelling, the home of a large number of His people, and a source of blessing. ¶

[6] ***mûsāḏ*** [masc. sing. noun: מוּסָד <4143>; from FOUNDATION (LAY A) <3245>] ▶ **This word means laying of the base structure.** Its only occurrences are in Isaiah 28:16 and 2 Chronicles 8:16 that refer to the foundations of Zion and the Temple, respectively. ¶

[7] ***môsāḏ*** [masc. noun: מוֹסָד <4144>; from FOUNDATION (LAY A) <3245>] ▶ **This word indicates the base structure on which other things are built.** The foundations or bases of the earth and mountains (Deut. 32:22; Prov. 8:29; Is. 24:18; Jer. 31:37); it refers to the foundations of Israel's past, both symbolic and literal (Is. 58:12); the foundations of her cities, walls, etc. It is used symbolically of the foundations of the earth (2 Sam. 22:8, 16; Ps. 18:7, 15). Babylon's foundation stones would be removed by the Lord (Jer. 51:26). These foundations are personified by the prophets (Mic. 6:2). Other refs.: Ps. 82:5; Prov. 40:21. ¶

[8] ***mûsāḏāh*** [fem. noun: מוּסָדָה <4145>; fem. of <4143> above] ▶ **This word means base, and also appointment.** Ezekiel used this word to describe the foundation of the Temple in his vision (Ezek. 41:8). Isaiah used it to describe the appointed rod of punishment by which the Lord would smite Assyria (Is. 30:32). ¶

[9] ***môsāḏāh*** [fem. sing. noun: מוֹסָדָה <4146>; fem. of <4144> above] ▶ **This word always occurs in the plural.** It often refers to the foundation of the world (2 Sam. 22:16; Ps. 18:15) or to the base of a man-made construction, such as a building or wall (Jer. 51:26). *

[10] ***mᵉyussāḏāh*** [fem. noun: מְיֻסָּדָה <4328>; properly, fem. pass. part. of FOUNDATION (LAY A) <3245>] ▶ **This word is a construction term indicating the bases or underpinnings of a structure.** Ref.: Ezek. 41:8. In this case, it refers to the foundations of some side chambers or rooms of Ezekiel's visionary Temple. ¶

[11] ***massaḏ*** [masc. noun: מַסַּד <4527>; from FOUNDATION (LAY A) <3245>] ▶ **This word refers to the structural supporting base of a building.** Ref.: 1 Kgs. 7:9. ¶

[12] ***šāṯāh*** [masc. noun: שָׁתָה <8356>; from PUT <7896>] ▶

a. Figuratively, this word indicates the supporting structures of righteousness. Ref.: Ps. 11:3. It refers literally to great stone columns and pillars made in Egypt (Is. 19:10).

b. This word also indicates a purpose, a goal, i.e., the reason or rationale for doing something, why it is done. Ref.: Is. 19:10.

c. This word refers to a person who works with cloth. It refers to those who weave and spin yarns into various kinds of cloth (Is. 19:10). ¶

– [13] 1 Sam. 2:8 ➔ PILLAR <4690> [14] Job 38:6 ➔ BASE (noun) <134> [15] Ps. 11:3 ➔ BUTTOCKS <8351> b. [16] Ps. 89:14; 97:2; 104:5 ➔ DWELLING <4349> b. [17] Amos 9:6 ➔ BUNCH <92>.

FOUNDATION (LAY A) – ***yāsaḏ*** [verb: יָסַד <3245>; a prim. root] ▶ **This Hebrew verb means to establish, to found, to fix.** In a literal sense, this term can refer to laying the foundation of a building, primarily the Temple (1 Kgs. 5:17; 6:37; Ezra 3:11; Is. 44:28); or to laying the foundation of a city like Jericho (Josh. 6:26; 1 Kgs. 16:34); or Zion (Is. 14:32). In a metaphorical sense, it can allude to the founding of Egypt (Ex. 9:18); the earth (Is. 48:13). This word can also connote the appointment or ordination of an individual(s) to a task or position (1 Chr. 9:22; Esther 1:8). Probably one of the most noteworthy occurrences of this word is in Isaiah 28:16, where God declares that He will "lay in Zion for a foundation a stone, a tried stone, a precious corner stone, a sure foundation: he that believeth shall not make haste" (KJV). The New Testament writers announce that that stone is Jesus Christ (Rom. 9:33; 1 Pet. 2:6). *

FOUNTAIN – [1] ***ma'yān*** [masc. noun: מַעְיָן <4599>; from EYE <5869> (as a denom. in the sense of spring)] ▶ **This word refers to an underground source of water coming to the surface; it is also**

translated spring. Refs.: Gen. 7:11; 8:2; Lev. 11:36; 1 Kgs. 18:5. It is used figuratively as a symbol of sexual pleasure (Prov. 5:16); as a vibrant carrier of God's salvation (Is. 12:3); as a source of joy and gladness (Ps. 84:6; Hos. 13:15). It describes a spring that will flow from the house of God in a restored Israel or world (Joel 3:18). *

2 ***māqôr*** [masc. noun: מָקוֹר <4726>; from DIG <6979> a.] ▶ **See previous definition. This word also designates a spring, a flow; it is also translated well, wellspring.** It indicates a source of water (Hos. 13:15); the flow of blood during a woman's menstrual period (Lev. 12:7; KJV: issue; 20:18). It indicates the water sources of a river literally or in a figurative sense (Jer. 51:36; Zech. 13:1). It is used often figuratively as a source of tears (Jer. 9:1); a source of life (Ps. 36:9); the Lord is pictured as the fountain or life of Israel (Ps. 68:26; Jer. 2:13); a man's wife is a fountain (Prov. 5:18); the mouth of the righteous person is a spring of life (Prov. 10:11); the wise teaching of wisdom (Prov. 13:14; 18:4); the fear of the Lord is a fountain of life (Prov. 14:27); understanding is pictured as a fountain of life, a source of how to live (Prov. 16:22). Other refs.: Prov. 25:26; Jer. 17:13. ¶

– 3 Eccl. 12:6 ➔ SPRING <4002>.

FOUR – 1 ***'arba', 'arbā'āh*** [common noun: אַרְבַּע, אַרְבָּעָה <702>; from SQUARE (BE) <7251>] ▶ **The word is also used as an ordinal number, it means fourth.** Put into its plural form, *'arbā'îm*, it means forty; put into its dual form, *'arbā'ayîm*, fourfold. With the preposition *bᵉ* added to it, followed by the month, it means fourth (Zech. 1:7). *

2 ***'arba'*** [Aramaic common noun: אַרְבַּע <703>; corresponding to <702> above] ▶ **Followed by *mᵉ'āh*, hundred, this word means four hundred.** Ref.: Ezra 6:17. It is used in Daniel to describe four beasts, four winds, four wings (Dan. 7:2, 3, 6, 17), and four men (Dan. 3:25), one of whom was like a son of the gods. ¶

FOURFOLD – ***'arba'tayim*** [masc. noun: אַרְבַּעְתַּיִם <706>; dual of FOUR <702>] ▶ **This word is the dual form of *'arba'*, four.** It is found only once in 2 Samuel 12:6 where it describes fourfold restitution for a lamb. ¶

FOURTH – 1 ***rᵉḇiy'iy, rᵉḇi'iy*** [adj.: רְבִיעִי, רְבִעִי <7243>; from SQUARE (BE) <7251>] ▶ **This word also means a fourth part.** It is an ordinal number indicating the fourth item in a series (Gen. 1:19; 2:14; 15:16). It indicates a fourth of something, a fraction, e.g., one-fourth of a hin (Ex. 29:40; Lev. 23:13; Num. 15:4). It can stand at the end of a construct chain to refer to the fourth in a series (2 Kgs. 10:30). It means a square, foursquare in its feminine form (Ezek. 48:20). *

2 ***rᵉḇiy'iy, rᵉḇi'iy*** [adj.: רְבִיעִי, רְבִעִי <7244>; corresponding to <7243> above] ▶ **This word also means a fourth part.** It serves as an ordinal number indicating the fourth in a series (Dan. 2:40; 3:25; 7:7, 19, 23). ¶

3 ***reḇa'*** [masc. noun: רֶבַע <7253>; from SQUARE (BE) <7251>] ▶ **This word indicates a fourth part, a quarter; four sides.** It refers to a fraction or a portion of something; one-fourth of a hin of oil or wine (Ex. 29:40); one-fourth of a shekel (1 Sam. 9:8). It indicates that something has four sides (Ezek. 1:8, 17; 43:16, 17). It indicates four options, sides, etc. (Ezek. 10:11). ¶

4 ***ribbêa'*** [adj.: רִבֵּעַ <7256>; from SQUARE (BE) <7251>] ▶ **This word is employed as a noun to refer in context to the fourth generation(s).** Refs.: Ex. 20:5; 34:7; Num. 14:18; Deut. 5:9. ¶

FOURTH, FOURTH PART – ***rōḇa'*** [masc. noun: רֹבַע <7255>; from SQUARE (BE) <7251>] ▶ **This word means a quarter.** It is used to indicate a fraction or part of something, a fourth part (Num. 23:10; 2 Kgs. 6:25). ¶

FOWL – 1 **fatted, fattened, choice fowl: *barbur*** [masc. noun: בַּרְבֻּר <1257>; by reduplication from GRAIN <1250>] ▶ **This word describes one item on Solomon's luxurious menu of daily provisions, probably chicken.** Ref.: 1 Kgs. 4:23. ¶

– [2] Gen. 15:11; Job 28:7; Is. 18:6 ➔ BIRD OF PREY <5861>.

FOWLER – [1] ***yāqôš*** [masc. noun: יָקוֹשׁ <3352>; pass. part. of SNARE, BE SNARED <3369>] ▶ **This word indicates traps or snares that are waiting to attack or hinder someone or something, e.g., the prophet of God; it is also translated a bird catcher.** Ref.: Hos. 9:8. ¶

[2] ***yaqûš*** [masc. noun: יָקוּשׁ <3353>; pass. part. of SNARE, BE SNARED <3369>] ▶ **This word is slightly different in spelling from <3352> above. The basic lexical meaning is the same, but its context affects its sense in some cases.** It is used figuratively of the evil plans of one's enemies (Ps. 91:3; also translated trapper). It also refers to a bird trap in Proverbs 6:5 but is used to warn sons and daughters to avoid the subtle and dangerous snares of life by following wisdom. Evil persons lay snares to catch the unwary (Jer. 5:26; also translated snare, to snare). For Hosea 9:8, see <3352> above. ¶

FOX – ***šûʿāl*** [masc. noun: שׁוּעָל <7776>; from the same as HANDFUL <8168> (in the sense of burrower)] ▶ **This noun refers to a small, wild canine with a bushy tail. It was abundant in ancient Palestine. The word is also translated a jackal.** Samson caught three hundred of them and chastised the Philistines with them (Judg. 15:4). They were weak, but God's judgments would make wicked people prey to foxes (Ps. 63:10). They could be destructive to vineyards (Song 2:15); and they inhabited ruins (Lam. 5:18). Figuratively, Israel had driven out her prophets from God, so that they were forced to live in ruins and were ostracized like foxes (Ezek. 13:4). Other ref.: Neh. 4:3. ¶

FRAGILE (BE) – [1] Job 8:14 ➔ CUT OFF (BE) <6990> b. [2] Dan. 2:42 ➔ BRITTLE (BE) <8406>.

FRAGMENT – [1] ***meḵittāh*** [fem. noun: מְכִתָּה <4386>; from CRUSH <3807>] ▶ **This word means a bursting, a shattering.** It is used of the shattered pieces of a smashed potter's vessel (Is. 30:14). ¶

– [2] Amos 6:11 ➔ BREACH <1233> [3] Amos 6:11 ➔ DEW <7447> b.

FRAGRANCE – [1] Song 4:16 ➔ SPICE <1314> [2] Ezek. 8:11 ➔ WORSHIPPER <6282> b.

FRAGRANT – [1] Ex. 25:6; 30:7; etc. ➔ SWEET <5561> [2] Ezek. 8:11 ➔ WORSHIPPER <6282> b.

FRAIL – Ps. 39:4 ➔ REJECTED <2310>.

FRAME – [1] ***šālāḇ*** [masc. noun: שָׁלָב <7948>; from PARALLEL (SET) <7947>] ▶ **This word refers to part of the supporting structures (stands) for the great bronze sea of Solomon.** Refs.: 1 Kgs. 7:28, 29; also translated upright, ledge. ¶

[2] ***šeqep*** [masc. noun: שֶׁקֶף <8260>; from LOOK DOWN <8259>] ▶

a. This word refers to a squared structure. It indicates a frame with four equal sides. In context it refers to doorways and doorposts (1 Kgs. 7:5).

b. Earlier translators took this word to mean a window as a separate word. Ref.: 1 Kgs. 7:5. ¶

[3] ***šāqûp, šāqup*** [masc. noun: שָׁקוּף, שֶׁקֶף <8261>; pass. part. of LOOK DOWN <8259>] ▶

a. This word refers to squared structures. It is used to indicate window frames (1 Kgs. 6:4; 7:4).

b. The word is rendered as windows by many translators. Ref.: KJV, 1 Kgs. 6:4; clerestory windows: windows in the upper section of walls (NIV, 1 Kgs. 6:4; 7:4). ¶

– [4] Num. 4:10, 12 ➔ POLE <4132> [5] Ps. 139:15 ➔ STRENGTH <6108> [6] Ezek. 40:2 ➔ STRUCTURE <4011>.

FRAME (WHOLE) – Job 17:7: my whole frame (NIV) ➔ lit.: all my members ➔ MEMBERS.

FRAMED (THING) – Is. 29:16 ➔ FORMED <3336>.

FRANKINCENSE – See INCENSE <3828>.

FRAUD – Ps. 10:7 ➔ OPPRESSION <8496>.

FREE – 1 ***ḥop̱šiy*** [adj.: חָפְשִׁי <2670>; from FREE (BE) <2666>] ▶ **This word indicates liberty from slave responsibilities or duties.** A person could be free (*ḥop̱šiy*) from slavery (Ex. 21:2, 5, 26, 27; Deut. 15:12, 13, 18). It indicates exemption from certain things, such as taxes (1 Sam. 17:25); or to have oppression removed from someone (Is. 58:6), including slaves (Jer. 34:9–11, 14, 16). Other refs.: Job 3:19; 39:5; Ps. 88:5. ¶
2 ***pāṭiyr*** [adj.: פָּטִיר <6359>; from OPEN <6362>] ▶ **This word means liberated from, exempt from.** It means to not be busy or tied up with some task or job (1 Chr. 9:33). ¶
– 3 1 Chr. 9:33 ➔ OPEN <6362> 4 Ps. 51:12 ➔ DIGNITY <5082> 5 Ps. 118:5 ➔ lit.: in a large place ➔ BREADTH <4800>.

FREE (BE) – 1 ***ḥap̱aš*** [verb: חָפַשׁ <2666>; a prim. root] ▶ **The subject of this verb is a woman who has not been freed, according to certain legal stipulations. This word occurs once and is negated.** Ref.: Lev. 19:20. ¶
2 ***nāqāh*** [verb: נָקָה <5352>; a prim. root] ▶ **This verb also means to be clean, to be pure. Originally, it meant to be emptied; therefore, its most basic sentiment is to be poured out and can have a negative or positive connotation.** In the negative sense, it refers to a city which has been deserted, emptied of people (Is. 3:26). In the positive sense, it is used to connote freedom from the obligations of an oath (Gen. 24:8, 41); from guilt (Num. 5:31; Judg. 15:3; Jer. 2:35); and from punishment (Ex. 21:19; Num. 5:28; 1 Sam. 26:9). Regardless of whether the connotation is positive or negative, most occurrences of this verb have a moral or ethical implication. Aside from the passive or stative form, this verb also has a factitive form. (The factitive concept is to make something a certain state, in this instance, to make something clean or pure.) The factitive form has two aspects: (1) acquittal, the declaration of someone as innocent (Job 9:28; 10:14; Ps. 19:12); (2) leaving someone unpunished (Ex. 20:7; 34:7; Jer. 30:11). *

FREE (SET) – Ps. 105:20 ➔ LOOSE (LET) <5425>.

FREE SPACE – ***nûaḥ, munnāḥ*** [masc. noun: נוּחַ, מֻנָּח <5117>; a prim. root] ▶ **This word refers to an area left open between two walls or rooms.** Refs.: Ezek. 41:9, 11. The Hebrew word also means to rest, to pause; see REST (verb) <5117> a. ¶

FREED (BE) – Lev. 19:20 ➔ FREE (BE) <2666>.

FREEDOM – 1 ***d^erôr*** [masc. noun: דְּרוֹר <1865>; from an unused root (meaning to move rapidly)] ▶
a. This word denotes liberty, emancipation. It referred to the freedom proclaimed during the sabbatical year (Lev. 25:10; Jer. 34:8, 15, 17); also translated liberty, release. In a cynical, ironical use, the prophet proclaims that Israel's liberty would be destroyed by God's judgments (Ezek. 46:17). Other ref.: Is. 61:1. ¶
b. The Hebrew word means and is also translated pure, flowing, liquid. It describes literally myrrh of flowing in Exodus 30:23, liquid myrrh. ¶
2 ***ḥup̱šāh*** [fem. noun: חֻפְשָׁה <2668>; from FREE (BE) <2666>] ▶ **This word refers to a state of liberty granted to an ex-slave woman. It also means emancipation.** Ref.: Lev. 19:20. She had certain freedoms regarding sexual intercourse according to the Mosaic Law. ¶
– 3 Is. 61:1 ➔ OPENING OF THE PRISON <6495>.

FREELY – ***ḥinnām*** [adv.: חִנָּם <2600>; from GRACE <2580>] ▶ **The primary meaning of this Hebrew word is related to the English word *gratis*. It also means undeservedly, without cause, for no purpose, in vain.** It appears in connection with goods exchanged without monetary charge (2 Sam. 24:24); services rendered without pay (Jer. 22:13); innocence, as having no offense (1 Kgs. 2:31); food without restriction or limit (Num. 11:5); faith without rational justification (Job 1:9); hostility without provocation (Ps. 69:4); religious activities done in vain (Mal. 1:10). *

FREEWILL OFFERING – ***nᵉḏāḇāh*** [fem. noun: נְדָבָה <5071>; from GIVE WILLINGLY <5068>] ▶ **This word means willingness, a voluntary gift. As an adverb, it means willingly, freely, spontaneously, voluntarily. This term can denote that state of being which allows a person to offer a gift or a favor to someone else without any thought of return or payback. The favor is not given out of any obligation owed by the giver; rather, it is the result of an overflow from an abundance within the heart.** The Lord declares that He loves Israel freely because His anger has turned away from them (Hos. 14:4). The Hebrews were commanded to diligently perform the vows they freely uttered to the Lord (Deut. 23:23). Most often, however, the term is utilized to signify an offering, a gift, or a sacrifice given voluntarily, as opposed to one offered in dutiful fulfillment of an obligation or vow (Lev. 22:23). Many from the congregation of Israel whose hearts were willing gave of their possessions as freewill offerings for the building of the Tent of Meeting and its services (Ex. 35:29; 36:3; cf. Lev. 7:16; Ezra 1:4; 3:5; 8:28; 46:12; Amos 4:5). Once the word possibly functions to convey an abundance, i.e., of rain (Ps. 68:9). *

FRESH – 1 ***ṭāriy*** [adj.: טָרִי <2961>; from an unused root apparently meaning to be moist] ▶ **This word indicates the condition of a donkey's jawbone used by Samson to slay one thousand Philistines.** Ref.: Judg. 15:15; KJV, new. Used of wounds, it indicates they are raw or bleeding, tender, but Isaiah used it of the spiritual wounds of his people (Is. 1:6: putrefying, putrifying, open). ¶
– 2 Ps. 92:14 ➔ FAT (adj.) <1879>.

FRESH (BE, BECOME) – ***ruṭᵃpaš*** [verb: רֻטֲפַשׁ <7375>; a root compounded form LUSH <7373> and FAT (BE) <2954>] ▶ **This word indicates a renewal of health and vigor; it is also translated to be renewed.** It refers to a healthy suppleness to a young person's skin (Job 33:25). ¶

FRESH, FRESH-CUT – Gen. 30:37; Num. 6:3; Judg. 16:7, 8 ➔ GREEN <3892>.

FRET (MAKE) – 1 Sam. 1:6 ➔ IRRITATE <7481>.

FRET INWARD – Lev. 13:55 ➔ EATING AWAY <6356>.

FRETTING – Lev. 13:51, 52; 14:44 ➔ PAINFUL (BE) <3992>.

FRIEND – 1 ***mêrêaʿ*** [masc. noun: מֵרֵעַ <4828>; from FEED <7462> b. (in the sense of to associate with, to be a companion)] ▶ **This word refers to a person with a trusted relationship to another person, standing ready to help his or her companion even in an official capacity. It also indicates a companion.** Refs.: Gen. 26:26: also translated adviser, personal adviser; Job 6:14. A poor person has few loyal friends, if any at all (Prov. 19:7). It also, however, included persons newly and formally appointed as "friends" of someone to serve a social function (Judg. 14:11, 20; 15:2, 6). It refers to supports of a person, e.g., friends of Saul's house (2 Sam. 3:8). ¶
2 ***rêʿeh*** [masc. noun: רֵעֶה <7463>; from FEED (verb) <7462> b. (with the meaning to associate with, to be a friend) ▶ **This word means a friend (see definition of <4828> above) of the king as a personal advisor.** It refers in context to a person who has a personal and official attachment to another person and promotes his or her welfare and cause (2 Sam. 15:37; 16:16; NIV: confidant). It indicates someone who has shown support for another (1 Kgs. 4:5). ¶
3 ***rêʿāh*** [fem. noun: רֵעָה <7464>; fem. of PERSON (ANOTHER) <7453>] ▶ **This word refers to a female friend (see definition of <4828> above) with whom strong bonds have been established.** Refs.: Judg.

11:37, 38; also translated companion. It refers to those who officially accompany and wait on the king's daughter (Ps. 45:14: companion). ¶

– [4] Ruth 4:1 ➔ A ONE <492> [5] Ruth 4:1 ➔ CERTAIN ONE <6423> [6] Prov. 7:4 ➔ RELATIVE <4129> [7] Prov. 16:28: close, best, chief, intimate friend ➔ GENTLE <441> [8] See COMPANION <2269>, <2270>.

FRIGHTEN – Ezra 4:4 ➔ AFRAID (MAKE) <1089>.

FRIGHTENED (BE) – Job 40:23 ➔ HURRY (verb) <2648>.

FRIGHTENED (COME) – Ps. 18:4 ➔ TREMBLING (COME) <2727>.

FRIGHTENING – Dan. 2:31 ➔ FEAR (verb) <1763>.

FRINGE – [1] Num. 15:38, 39 ➔ TASSEL <6734> [2] Deut. 22:12 ➔ TASSEL <1434>.

FROG – ***ṣᵉpardêaʿ*** [masc. noun: צְפַרְדֵּעַ <6854>; from DEPART <6852> and a word elsewhere unused meaning a swamp] ▶ **This is a water creature that can spread disease if it dies on land and is not buried properly.** Its most notorious reference is in the second plague in Egypt (Ex. 8:2–9, 11–13). This event was so vital to Israel's history that the recounting was repeated (Ps. 78:45; 105:30). ¶

FROLIC – [1] ***pûš*** [verb: פּוּשׁ <6335>; a prim. root] ▶

a. This word means to leap, to spring about, to gallop. It describes the playful, skipping, happy behavior of a heifer (Jer. 50:11; Mal. 4:2); or the speedy gallop of warhorses (Hab. 1:8: to press, to gallop, to charge). ¶

b. A verb meaning to scatter; to spread out, to grow fat. It refers to the scattered people of Nineveh because of God's judgment on the city (Nah. 3:18); and to the military horsemen of Babylon spreading out as they attacked (Hab. 1:8). It means to grow up, to develop as calves fed on choice grain (Mal. 4:2). Other ref.: Jer. 50:11 (to grow fat). ¶

– [2] Is. 13:21 ➔ DANCE (verb) <7540>.

FROM – [1] ***lᵉwāṯ*** [Aramaic prep. art.: לְוָת <3890>; from a root corresponding to JOIN <3867>] ▶ **This word is used to indicate motion away from someone or something.** It may take suffixes on the end of it, "from you" *lᵉwāṯāḵ* (Ezra 4:12). ¶

[2] ***min, minniy, minnêy*** [prep.: מִן, מִנִּי, מִנֵּי <4480>; from PORTION <4482>] ▶ **This word is used to indicate out of, away from; more than: after, since; immediately; because of, since, so that; without; direction as southward, etc.). Its spelling varies according to its location and usage.** Its basic meaning is from, away from, out of. Its basic meanings only can be noted here, but its exact meaning is easily discerned from its context: (1) With verbs, it expresses separation spatially or figuratively (Ex. 19:14; Deut. 22:8; Josh. 10:7). It can be used with a verb not indicating separation, e.g., to stay away from strife (Prov. 20:3; Is. 14:19). (2) With the basic sense of out of, from (Gen. 3:22–24; 4:10; 34:26; Ex. 2:10; 8:9; Judg. 15:7; Ps. 40:2), it often indicates what something is made of or formed from (Gen. 2:19; Hos. 13:2). With a pronominal suffix meaning from it, it means of one piece with it (Ex. 25:19, 31). It indicates a cause for something, on account of, because (Ex. 2:23; 6:9; 1 Kgs. 14:4; Prov. 20:4; Is. 53:5). (3) It is used to mean something is a part of something else, a part or share of it (Gen. 6:19; 7:8; 39:11; Num. 16:2). It indicates some of in an indefinite sense (Ex. 16:27; Lev. 25:49; Ps. 137:3). When repeated it means some . . . others or its equivalent expression (1 Chr. 9:28, 29). (4) It is used to mark time: from, since (Deut. 9:24), from a certain day or time (Lev. 22:27; Num. 15:23; 1 Sam. 18:9). It is used in phrases to mean from ancient times, antiquity (Hab. 1:12); from of old (Is. 42:14). It indicates right after a certain time (Gen. 38:24; Josh. 23:1; Ezek. 38:8). (5) Paired with *ʿaḏ* (UNTIL <5704>) it usually means from . . . even to, as far as (Gen. 10:19; 15:18;

Ex. 11:7; Jer. 51:62). In a figurative sense, this same construction can mean e.g., from young . . . to old, both inclusive (Gen. 19:4; 1 Sam. 5:9; Jer. 6:13). (6) It may further indicate than, in comparisons (Lev. 21:10; Judg. 14:18). (7) Prefixed to an infinitive, it is often translated as from (Gen. 16:2); a few times as on account of or because (Deut. 7:7, 8); or temporally as since or after (Num. 24:23; Is. 44:7). (8) It is often attached to other words in compounds and is sometimes used in front of infinitives of verbs: e.g., with *ʿāḇaḏ* (SERVE <5647>) meaning from serving (Ex. 14:5); with *bālaʿ* (SWALLOW <1104>) meaning from destroying (Lam. 2:8). (9) It is used in front of a verb form once as a conjunction indicating a negative purpose, "that . . . not" (Deut. 33:11). Other uses almost always fall under one of the above categories. *

[3] ***min*** [Aramaic prep.: מִן <4481>; corresponding to <4480> above] ▶ **This word means out of, among, more than.** It means out of something, e.g., a threshing floor (Dan. 2:35) or from a specific area, e.g., a temple as a storage area (Dan. 5:2). It is used with *yaḏ*, hand, to give the figurative idea of from the power of (Dan. 3:15). It is used to express comparison meaning different from (Dan. 7:3) or more than (Dan. 2:30). It is used to express the idea of a part of something or some group, etc. (Dan. 2:33, 41; 5:13). With *wᵉʿaḏ* following it, it expresses the temporal idea of since (Dan. 2:20; Ezra 4:15; 5:16). Followed by *dî*, it functions as a conjunction expressing cause, because (Ezra 5:11). With a pronoun suffix, it means from me, from you, etc. (Dan. 2:5). It is used to express with, to point out an instrument or agent (Dan. 4:25). It expresses the idea of based on or according to, e.g., the word or command of God (Ezra 6:14). The expression *min-yaṣṣib* means truly, certainly (Dan. 2:8). It is used in the idiom *min-qᵉšōṭ dî* indicating in fact, surely (Dan. 2:47). Judgment is rendered idiomatically as judgment upon (from, *min*) him, her, etc. (Ezra 7:26). Something may be changed from (*min*) what it was (Dan. 4:13). *

FRONT (IN) – 2 Kgs. 15:10 ➔ BATTERING RAM <6904> c., BEFORE <6905>.

FRONT OF (IN) – [1] ***lip̄nāy*** [adv.: לִפְנֵי <3942>; from the prep. prefix (to or for) and FACE <6440>] ▶ **This word is used to indicate physical position, before something.** Ref.: 1 Kgs. 6:17, i.e., the nave in front of the inner Temple sanctuary. ¶

– [2] Ex. 14:2; Ezek. 46:9 ➔ OPPOSITE (adv.) <5226>.

FRONTALS – Deut. 6:8; 11:18 ➔ FRONTLETS <2903>.

FRONTLETS – ***ṭôṭāp̄ôṯ*** [fem. plur. noun: טוֹטָפוֹת <2903>; from an unused root meaning to go around or bind] ▶ **This word denotes phylacteries, headbands, symbols; it is also translated frontals.** They were worn around the forehead to carry select verses from Holy Scripture to remind Israel of the Lord's ways with them (Ex. 13:16; Deut. 6:8; 11:18), of His will for them. Originally, this word was probably used figuratively to indicate complete dedication to the Lord and His ways, but later it was taken literally to refer to actual physical objects, as described here. ¶

FROST – [1] ***ḥᵃnāmāl*** [masc. noun: חֲנָמָל <2602>; of uncertain deriv.] ▶ **This word refers to a devastating cold spell that created a heavy frost or hail that destroyed Israel's sycamore trees or vines.** Ref.: Ps. 78:47; also translated sleet. Others suggest "devastating flood" as its meaning. ¶

[2] ***kᵉpôr*** [masc. noun: כְּפוֹר <3713>; from COVER (verb) <3722>] ▶ **This word means hoarfrost. It refers to the thin flakes or wafers of manna which the Lord gave to Israel.** Ref.: Ex. 16:14. It was literally frost from heaven given by the Lord (Job 38:29; Ps. 147:16). The Hebrew word also means bowl, basin; see BOWL <3713>. ¶

– [3] Gen. 31:40; Job 37:10; Jer. 36:30 ➔ ICE <7140>.

FROWARD – [1] Ps. 101:4 ➔ PERVERSE <6141> [2] Prov. 2:15; 3:32 ➔ PERVERSE <3868> [3] Prov. 4:24; 6:12 ➔ CROOKED <6143> [4] Prov. 21:8 ➔ CROOKED <2019>.

FROWARD AND STRANGE – Prov. 21:8 ➔ GUILTY (noun) <2054>.

FROZEN (BE) – Job 37:10 ➔ CONSTRAINT <4164>.

FRUIT – [1] ***'ēḇ*** [Aramaic masc. noun: אֵב <4>; corresponding to GREENNESS <3>] ▶ **In its context in Daniel, the word means the edible part which the tree of Nebuchadnezzar's dream bore abundantly.** Refs.: Dan. 4:12, 14, 21. The tree most likely represents Nebuchadnezzar and the Babylonian Empire (626–538 B.C.). See the Hebrew cognate *'ēḇ*: GREENNESS <3>. ¶
[2] ***zimrāh*** [fem. noun: זִמְרָה <2173>; from PRUNE <2168>] ▶ **This word indicates choice product.** The best fruit or product of the land of Canaan (Gen. 43:11) was collected as a gift for Joseph and the Egyptians at Jacob's command. ¶
[3] ***nôḇ, niyḇ*** [masc. noun: נוֹב, נִיב <5108>; from INCREASE (verb) <5107>] ▶
a. This word is used figuratively of good things spoken by the lips, good news. Ref.: Is. 57:19; also translated praise. It is used of the fruit offered on the altar, which the Israelites decried as contemptible (Mal. 1:12; also translated food). ¶
b. A masculine noun meaning fruit. It is the same as a., but its spelling is different. It is not found in Malachi 1:12 in this form. See c.
c. A masculine noun meaning praise. This is understood by some as a different word from a. and b. indicating praise. It is used of praise offered in response to God's offer of peace (Is. 57:19). ¶
[4] ***sansinnāh*** [masc. noun: סַנְסִנָּה <5577>; from an unused root meaning to be pointed] ▶ **This word refers to a cluster of fruit, possibly a blossom cluster of dates; it is also translated boughs, branches.** Figuratively, it describes the breasts of the bride (Song 7:8). ¶
[5] ***p^eriy*** [masc. noun: פְּרִי <6529>; from FRUITFUL (BE) <6509>] ▶ **This word refers to what is naturally produced, the crop from trees, land.** Refs.: Gen. 1:11, 12, 29; 3:2, 3, 6; Ps. 107:34. It is used figuratively of one's offspring (Gen. 30:2); or the result of one's deeds or actions (Is. 3:10). Fruit trees (*'ēṣ p^erî*) were a feature of the Garden of Eden and of a man-made garden of beauty and delight (Eccl. 2:5). The bride admires the fruit of her bridegroom (Song 2:3). Abundant fruit will be a mark of a restored Jerusalem (Amos 9:14; Zech. 8:12; Mal. 3:11). *
[6] ***t^enûḇāh*** [fem. noun: תְּנוּבָה <8570>; from INCREASE <5107>] ▶ **This word refers to the produce of the land, the fields, the fruit trees that God blessed. It also indicates a crop.** Refs.: Deut. 32:13; Lam. 4:9; Ezek. 36:30. It refers to the fruit produced on a fig tree. It is employed in an interesting parable (Judg. 9:11). It is used beautifully in a figurative sense to refer to the moral, ethical, and religious fruit Israel will give to the whole earth (Is. 27:6). ¶
– [7] Deut. 11:17; Hab. 3:17; Hag. 1:10 ➔ INCREASE (noun) <2981> [8] Deut. 22:9 ➔ HARVEST <4395> [9] Song 6:11 ➔ GREENNESS <3> [10] Is. 5:2, 4: bad fruit ➔ WORTHLESS ONE <891>.

FRUIT (BEAR, BRING FORTH) – Ps. 92:14 ➔ INCREASE (verb) <5107>.

FRUIT OF ONE'S TOIL – ***yāḡā'*** [masc. noun: יָגָע <3022>; from WEARY (verb) <3021>] ▶ **This word refers to the product of labor, earnings; it is also translated that for which one labors, what one has attained, what one toils for.** It is used of the benefits, physical or immaterial, of one's toil (Job 20:18). The Lord drives the wicked person to return them. ¶

FRUITFUL (BE) – [1] ***pārā'*** [verb: פָּרָא <6500>; a prim. root] ▶ **This word means to bear much fruit, to be successful; it is also translated to flourish, to thrive.** It indicates the growth and prosperity of Israel (Ephraim), economically and politically, which God would cut short (Hos. 13:15). ¶
[2] ***pārāh*** [verb: פָּרָה <6509>; a prim. root] ▶ This word also means to flourish. **It indicates the multiplication and successful production of fruit, offspring, or flavors from living fruits, vegetables, animals, or human beings: human offspring.** Refs.:

Gen. 1:22, 28; 8:17; 9:1, 7; Deut. 29:18. It describes Israel as a nation (Ex. 1:7; 23:30; Ps. 105:24). It shows the root of Jesse bearing messianic fruit, descendants (Is. 11:1). In its causative uses, it has the sense of making fruitful (Gen. 17:6). *

FRUSTRATE – 1 Ps. 33:10 ➔ FORBID <5106> 2 Prov. 22:12 ➔ OVERTHROW (verb) <5557>.

FRUSTRATED (BE) – 2 Sam. 13:2 ➔ DISTRESSED (BE) <3334>.

FRUSTRATION – Deut. 28:20 ➔ REBUKE (noun) <4045>.

FUEL – ***maᵃḵōleṯ*** [fem. noun: מַאֲכֹלֶת <3980>; from EAT <398> (in the sense of something consumed by fire)] ► **This word refers to the clothing and shoes of warriors killed in battle to be used as combustible for the fire.** Ref.: Is. 9:5. It refers as well, in a figurative and literal sense, to the people of the land (Is. 9:19). ¶

FUGITIVE – 1 ***miḇrāḥ*** [masc. noun: מִבְרָח <4015>; from FLEE <1272>] ► **This word refers to a person who has escaped, a survivor.** In context the word refers to Israelites who have fled in every direction because of God's judgments (Ezek. 17:21). According to some Hebrew manuscripts, some translate by choice, pick. ¶
– 2 Gen. 4:12; 14 ➔ WANDER <5128>.

FUGITIVE (BECOME) – Lam. 4:15 ➔ FLEE, FLEE AWAY <5132>.

FULFILL – 1 Ps. 57:2 ➔ END (COME TO AN) <1584> 2 Lam. 2:17 ➔ CUT OFF <1214>.

FULFILLED (BE) – Dan. 4:33 ➔ CONSUME <5487>.

FULFILLMENT (RICH) – Ps. 66:12 ➔ OVERFLOW (noun) <7310>.

FULL (adj.) – 1 ***mālê'*** [adj.: מָלֵא <4392>; from FULL (BE) <4390>] ► **This word is used to qualify various items as complete, ripe, grown.** Ears of corn (Gen. 41:7, 22); vessels (2 Kgs. 4:4); a full (shiny or powerful) wind of judgment (figurative use) (Jer. 4:12); full or complete value or price (Gen. 23:9). A full woman is a pregnant woman (Eccl. 11:5). It is used in an idiomatic sense of a family: children, husband, wife (Ruth 1:21). Used in the absolute state with accompanying words, it means full of, strewn with (2 Kgs. 7:15); full of God's anger or wrath (Jer. 6:11). It may come after its accompanying word and still mean full of, e.g., full of shoutings (Is. 22:2). As a predicate adjective, it means full (Eccl. 1:7). It is used many more times in a figurative sense of being full of blessings (Deut. 33:23); wisdom (Deut. 34:9; Ezek. 28:12); justice (Is. 1:21); confusion (Is. 22:2); lies (Nah. 3:1). *
2 ***śaḇēa'*** [adj.: שָׂבֵעַ <7649>; from SATISFIED <7646>] ► **This word indicates fulness and also means satisfied, abounding.** It indicates fullness of life in years and in satisfaction (Gen. 25:8; 35:29; 1 Chr. 29:28; Job 42:17). It indicates a fullness or satisfaction of God's approval and favor (Deut. 33:23). It indicates a general prosperity, the possession of an abundance of wealth (1 Sam. 2:5). It refers to a satiation, an overabundance of disgrace, a consciousness of misery (Job 10:15). The general condition of humankind is a fullness of turmoil (Job 14:1). A fullness or sufficiency of sleep comes to those who fear God (Prov. 19:23). ¶

FULL (BE) – 1 ***mālê'*** [verb: מָלֵא <4390>; a prim. root] ► **This word also means to fill, to be complete, to fulfill, to finish, to satisfy. This word occurs 251 times in the Old Testament and functions both in a spatial and temporal sense.** Spatially, the term pictures the act of making that which was empty of a particular content no longer so. It can also express that state of being in which a certain container is holding to capacity a particular object or objects. God commanded the water creatures to fill the seas (Gen. 1:22); and humanity to fill the earth (Gen. 1:28). Elijah directed the people to fill four water jars; the trench was also filled (1 Kgs. 18:34, 35). The word can also function in an abstract way: Judah filled the land with violence (Ezek. 8:17; cf. Lev. 19:29; Jer. 51:5). Theologically, the glory of the Lord filled the Temple (1 Kgs. 8:10, 11; cf. Is. 6:1); and Jeremiah declared that God fills heaven and earth (Jer. 23:24). Temporally, the term refers to the completion of a specified segment of time. According to the Law, a woman who had given birth to a boy could not enter the sanctuary until the thirty-three days of her blood purification were completed (Lev. 12:4). The Lord promised to establish King David's kingdom after his days were fulfilled (i.e., he died: 2 Sam. 7:12; cf. Lam. 4:18).

A final important use of the word entails the keeping of a vow or promise. The Lord fulfilled His promise to David that his son would build a house for His name (2 Chr. 6:4, 15; cf. 2 Sam. 7:12; 1 Kgs. 2:27; 2 Chr. 36:21). *
– [2] Ex. 16:20 ➔ EXALTED <7426> b. [3] Job 10:15 ➔ WATERED <7302>.

FULL (IN) – Ezra 7:23 ➔ DILIGENTLY <149>.

FULL (noun) – [1] ***mlō', mlô', mlô*** [masc. noun: מְלֹא, מְלוֹא, מְלוֹ <4393>; from FULL (BE) <4390>] ▶ **This word refers to what fills, makes complete, fullness; abundance.** It depicts in general what fills something up or out: fullness of a hand, a handful, *mlo' kāp*, (1 Kgs. 17:12); an omerfull of manna (Ex. 16:33); a lap full or skirt full (2 Kgs. 4:39). It can be an added assertion meaning, and fullness (*ûmlō'ô*), e.g., of the seas and its fullness (Is. 42:10); the land or earth and its fullness (Deut. 33:16). It indicates the multitude or abundance of nations (Gen. 48:19); or a (large) band or troop of shepherds (Is. 31:4). In 1 Samuel 28:20, it has the sense of full length, full-standing height; the whole of Saul's huge bodily frame fell. *
[2] ***śōḇa'*** [masc. noun: שֹׂבַע <7648>; from SATISFIED <7646>] ▶ **This word indicates abundance, satisfaction, completeness.** It refers to a state of satiation, overfullness, being stuffed (Ex. 16:3; Lev. 25:19) but usually in a good sense. If Israel obeyed, they would enjoy God's blessing of fullness of food (Lev. 26:5; Deut. 23:24). It is used in a figurative sense of the fullness of joy (Ps. 16:11); and of the fullness of food that God gave the Israelites in the wilderness (Ps. 78:25). Righteous persons will have enough and more to meet their needs (Prov. 13:25). Other ref.: Ruth 2:18. ¶

FULL MOON – ***kese', keseh*** [masc. noun: כֶּסֶא, כֶּסֶה <3677>; apparently from COVER (verb) <3680>] ▶ **This word refers, based on context, to the time when the moon is full, the 15th day of the month.** Refs.: Ps. 81:3; Prov. 7:20; also translated time appointed, day appointed. ¶

FULL PRODUCE – Num. 18:27 ➔ HARVEST <4395>.

FULLNESS – [1] ***śiḇ'āh*** [fem. noun: שִׂבְעָה <7653>; fem. of PLENTY <7647>] ▶ **This word indicates an abundance of something, more than is necessary.** Ref.: Ezek. 16:49; ESV: excess. This abundance is to be shared. ¶
– [2] Num. 18:27 ➔ HARVEST <4395> [3] Ps. 16:11 ➔ FULL (noun) <7648>.

FURBISH – [1] Jer. 46:4 ➔ POLISH <4838> [2] Ezek. 21:9–11, 28 ➔ PULL, PULL OUT <4803>.

FURIOUS (BECOME) – 2 Chr. 26:19 ➔ ANGRY (BE, BECOME) <2196>.

FURIOUSLY – 2 Kgs. 9:20 ➔ MADNESS <7697>.

FURNACE – [1] ***'attûn*** [Aramaic masc. noun: אַתּוּן <861>; prob. from FIRE <784>] ▶ **This word designates the huge furnace (an enclosure where great heat is produced) into which the three Hebrew companions of Daniel were thrown.** Refs.: Dan. 3:6, 11, 15, 17, 19–23, 26. ¶
[2] ***kiḇšān*** [masc. noun: כִּבְשָׁן <3536>; from SUBDUE <3533> (in the sense of reducing something)] ▶ **This word refers to an**

enclosed space where some kind of fuel is burned, producing heat and smoke; it is also translated kiln. It is used in a simile to compare the smoke ascending from Sodom and Gomorrah and from Mount Sinai to that arising from a furnace (Gen. 19:28; Ex. 19:18). Moses and Aaron took handfuls of soot or ashes from a kiln or furnace and cast them into the air in the sixth plague (Ex. 9:8, 10). ¶

3 ***kûr*** [masc. noun: כּוּר <3564>; from an unused root meaning properly to dig through] ▶ **This word refers to a furnace or smelting pot literally but is also used in figurative language to depict human suffering in judgment or discipline. It also mean a forge, a smelting pot.** Egypt was the iron furnace (literally, furnace of iron) (Deut. 4:20; 1 Kgs. 8:51; Jer. 11:4). It is used in the phrase "furnace of affliction/oppression" (Is. 48:10). It is compared to the Lord who tests hearts, not gold or silver (Prov. 17:3; 27:21). Israel is compared to the dross or impurities in one of these smelting furnaces (Ezek. 22:18, 20, 22). The Hebrew word is also translated to pierce; see PIERCE <3564>. ¶

4 ***ʿ*liyl** [masc. noun: עֲלִיל <5948>; from DO <5953> in the sense of completing (prob. a crucible, as working over the metal)] ▶ **This word refers to a structure made for the production of heat or for purifying metals.** Ref.: Ps. 12:6; NIV: crucible. ¶

5 ***tannûr*** [masc. noun: תַּנּוּר <8574>; from HABITATION <5126>] ▶ **This word is used to describe various things.** A firepot (Gen. 15:17); an oven for baking bricks or food (Ex. 8:3); a furnace for producing heat that consumes what is in it. God's enemies will be consumed by fire as in an oven (Ps. 21:9). It is used as a symbol of God's avenging presence, His furnace (Is. 31:9). It describes Israel's adulterous lust for false and forbidden liaisons among the nations (Hos. 7:4, 6, 7). The Day of the Lord is described as burning like a furnace (Mal. 4:1, NASB). *

– 6 Ps. 102:3 ➔ HEARTH <4168>.

FURNISH – 1 Num. 31:5 ➔ PROVIDE <4560> 2 Ps. 144:13 ➔ OBTAIN <6329>.

FURROW – 1 ***geḏûḏ*** [masc. noun: גְּדוּד <1417>; from CUT (verb) <1413>] ▶ **This word means a trench in a field made by a plow; it is also translated ridge.** It depicts the furrows of fertile earth that God waters abundantly (Ps. 65:10), giving bountiful crops as a sign of His goodness. ¶

2 ***maʿ*nāh** [fem. noun: מַעֲנָה <4618>; from AFFLICTED (BE) (verb) <6031>, in the sense of depression or tilling] ▶ **This word refers to a plowed row, a place for a furrow.** It refers to the groove or path made by a plow for planting (1 Sam. 14:14). It is used figuratively of the stripes or wounds the wicked placed on the people of Zion (Ps. 129:3). ¶

3 ***telem*** [masc. noun: תֶּלֶם <8525>; from an unused root meaning to accumulate] ▶ **This word describes the indentation in the ground left by overturned clods of earth created in a field by plowing.** Job speaks figuratively of the furrows of the ground weeping (Job 31:38). The wild ox cannot be harnessed for plowing (Job 39:10, KJV, unicorn). God provides water for the plowed furrows (Ps. 65:10; also translated ridges). It is used figuratively by Hosea (10:4; 12:11). ¶

– 4 Ezek. 17:7, 10 ➔ BED <6170> 5 Hos. 10:10 ➔ MARITAL RIGHTS <5772> b.

FURTHER – 1 Ps. 140:8 ➔ OBTAIN <6329> 2 Eccl. 12:12 ➔ MORE, MORE THAN <3148>.

FURY – 1 ***ḥemā'*** [Aramaic fem. noun: חֱמָא <2528>; corresponding to ANGER (noun) <2534>] ▶ **This word indicates anger, rage; it is also translated wrath.** It indicates the angry response of a person who has been disobeyed, especially a king (Dan. 3:13, 19). ¶

2 ***maḏhêḇāh*** [fem. noun: מַדְהֵבָה <4062>; perhaps from the equivalent of GOLD <1722> (the Hebrew word also means raging, boisterous behavior)] ▶

a. This word refers to the violent speed and fierceness of a nation's military activities, such as Babylon's. Ref.: Is. 14:4. ¶

b. This word could mean golden city. Traditionally, it referred to Babylon as the golden city (KJV, NKJV, Is. 14:4). Various ancient manuscripts or translations suggest that the better translation is fury (see a.), but this is not certain. ¶

FUTILITY – ***'lûl*** [masc. noun: אֱלוּל <434>; for WORTHLESSNESS <457>] ▶ **This word means a worthless thing.** It designates the deceptive production of false prophets spinning out futile, worthless things, idolatries (NIV) (Jer. 14:14; it is also translated thing of nought). ¶

FUTURE (IN THE) – Gen. 30:33 → TOMORROW <4279>.

G

GAAL – ***ga‘al*** [masc. proper noun: גַּעַל <1603>; from ABHOR <1602>]: loathing, contempt ▶ **The son of Ebed who lived in Shechem.** Ref.: Judg. 9:26. He incited a conspiracy against Abimelech (Judg. 9:28, 29). He was, instead, driven out of Shechem (Judg. 9:41). Other refs.: Judg. 9:30, 31, 35–37, 39. ¶

GAASH – ***ga‘aš*** [proper noun: גַּעַשׁ <1608>; from SHAKE <1607>]: earthquake, shaking ▶ **Joshua was buried on the north of the mountain of Gaash.** Refs.: Josh. 24:30; Judg. 2:9; 2 Sam. 23:30; 1 Chr. 11:32. ¶

GABA – See GEBA <1387>.

GABBAI – ***gabbay*** [masc. proper noun: גַּבַּי <1373>; from the same as BACK <1354>]: my back; one who gathers, a tax collector ▶ **An Israelite of the tribe of Benjamin who agreed to settle in Jerusalem after the captivity.** Ref.: Neh. 11:8. ¶

GABRIEL – ***gaḇriy'êl*** [masc. proper noun: גַּבְרִיאֵל <1403>; from MAN <1397> and GOD <410>]: mighty man of God ▶ **An angel of high rank sent to the prophet Daniel.** He explained to him a vision and revealed to him the prophecy of the seventy weeks (Dan. 8:16; 9:21). ¶

GAD – [1] ***gāḏ*** [masc. proper noun: גָּד <1410>; from ATTACK (verb) <1464>]: good fortune; troop ▶

a. The seventh son of Jacob born through Zilpah, Leah's maidservant. Ref.: Gen. 30:11. *

b. The tribe of Gad, the descendants of Jacob's seventh son. He bore many sons himself (Gen. 46:16; 49:19; Ex. 1:4). Jacob prophesied that Gad would be a fighter and prevail against his troublesome opponents (Gen. 49:19). Moses' prophetic blessing echoes this (Deut. 33:20). This tribe, along with Manasseh and Reuben was allotted land on the east side of the Jordan (Transjordan). Its western border was the Jordan River from the southern tip of Galilee almost down to the northern tip of the Dead Sea. Manasseh bounded it on the north, Reuben on the south (Josh. 13:13–28). The vicissitudes of Gad's history saw the tribe and tribal territory change hands numerous times: (2 Sam. 23:31–24:5; 2 Kgs. 15:29; Jer. 49:1–7). Ezekiel's vision of a new Temple has a portion of land for Gad (Ezek. 48:27, 28, 34). *

c. A prophet who wrote records of David's reign that are now lost. Ref.: 1 Chr. 29:29. He spoke to David as a prophet several times during his prophetic activity (1 Sam. 22:5; 2 Sam. 24:11–19). He was also active in Temple worship administration (2 Chr. 29:25). *

– [2] Gen. 30:11 ➔ FORTUNE <1409> [3] Is. 65:11 ➔ FORTUNE <1408> or <1409>.

GAD ABOUT – Jer. 31:22 ➔ WITHDRAW <2559>.

GADDI – ***gaddiy*** [masc. proper noun: גַּדִּי <1426>; intens. for GADI <1424>]: my happiness ▶ **A spy of the tribe of Manasseh who explored Canaan.** Ref.: Num. 13:11. ¶

GADDIEL – ***gaddiy'êl*** [masc. proper noun: גַּדִּיאֵל <1427>; from FORTUNE <1409> and GOD <410>]: blessed of God ▶ **A spy of the tribe of Zebulun who explored Canaan.** Ref.: Num. 13:10. ¶

GADFLY – Jer. 46:20 ➔ DESTRUCTION <7171>.

GADI – ***gāḏiy*** [masc. proper noun: גָּדִי <1424>; from FORTUNE <1409>]: happy ▶ **The father of King Menahem who reigned over Israel.** Refs.: 2 Kgs. 15:14, 17. ¶

GADITE – [1] ***gāḏiy*** [proper noun: גָּדִי <1425>; patron. from GAD <1410>] ▶ **A descendant of Gad.** Refs.: Num. 34:14; Deut. 3:12, 16; 4:43; 29:8; Josh. 1:12; 12:6; 13:8; 22:1; 2 Sam. 23:36; 2 Kgs. 10:33; 1 Chr. 5:18, 26; 12:8, 37; 1 Chr. 26:32. ¶ – [2] 2 Sam. 23:36 ➔ HAGRITE <1905>.

GAHAM – ***gaḥam*** [masc. proper noun: גַּחַם <1514>; from an unused root meaning to burn] ▶ **Son of Nahor, Abraham's brother.** Ref.: Gen. 22:24. ¶

GAHAR – ***gaḥar*** [masc. proper noun: גַּחַר <1515>; from an unused root meaning to hide]: hidden ▶ **The sons of Gahar were Temple servants.** Refs.: Ezra 2:47; Neh. 7:49. ¶

GAIN (noun) – [1] Lev. 25:37 ➔ INCREASE (noun) <4768> [2] Prov. 3:14; 31:18; Is. 23:18 ➔ MERCHANDISE <5504> [3] See PROFIT (noun) <1215>.

GAIN (verb) – [1] ***zᵉḇan*** [Aramaic verb: זְבַן <2084>; corresponding to the root of ZEBINA <2081>] ▶ **This word is used of an attempt to delay something, to obtain additional time or stall for time.** Ref.: Dan. 2:8. ¶
– [2] Prov. 3:13 ➔ OBTAIN <6329>.

GAIN (verb and noun) – Eccl. 1:3; 2:13; 3:9; 5:9, 16 ➔ PROFIT (noun) <3504>.

GAINED (TO BE) – Eccl. 2:11 ➔ PROFIT (noun) <3504>.

GALAL – ***gālāl*** [masc. proper noun: גָּלָל <1559>; from ROLL (verb) <1556> in the sense of HUGE <1560>]: great, rolling ▶ **Name of two Levites.** Refs.: 1 Chr. 9:15; and 1 Chr. 9:16; Neh. 11:17. ¶

GALBANUM – ***ḥelbināh*** [fem. noun: חֶלְבְּנָה <2464>; from FAT (noun) <2459>] ▶ **This word refers to a kind of gum resin.** It is an unpleasant-smelling resin used in the preparation of Israel's incense (Ex. 30:34). ¶

GALE – Job 21:18 ➔ STORM (noun) <5492> a.

GALEED – ***gal'ēḏ*** [proper noun: גַּלְעֵד <1567>; from HEAP (noun) <1530> and WITNESS <5707>]: heap of witness ▶ **Name given by Jacob to the mound commemorating the covenant between himself and Laban.** Refs.: Gen. 31:47, 48. ¶

GALILEE – ***gāliyl, gāliylāh*** [proper noun: גָּלִיל, גְּלִילָה <1551>; the same as RING <1550>]: wheel, circle, circuit ▶ **This word designates a large mountainous territory or region in northern Israel. It is mentioned six times in the Old Testament and often in the New Testament. Upper and Lower Galilee were located northwest and west of the Sea of Galilee. The Plan of Acco bordered it on the Mediterranean Sea. The Jezreel Valley lay to its south.** Solomon gave twenty towns in Galilee to Hiram, king of Tyre, for the cedar, pine, and gold he had supplied to Israel (1 Kgs. 9:11). The Levitical city of Kedesh was in the area (Josh. 20:7; 21:32). It came under the control of Assyria during Tiglath-pileser's reign (2 Kgs. 15:29) in Assyria and during Pekah's reign in Israel (752–732 B.C.). Many Gentiles lived in the territory, giving rise to the term "Galilee of the Gentiles" (Is. 9:1). Jesus ministered much in this territory in and around the Sea of Galilee. Other ref.: 1 Chr. 6:76. ¶

GALL – [1] ***mᵉrērāh*** [fem. noun: מְרֵרָה <4845>; from BITTER (BE) <4843>] ▶ **This word indicates the bile, a liquid produced by the gallbladder.** Refs.: Job 16:13; 20:25 (also translated liver). ¶
[2] ***mᵉrōrāh*** [fem. noun: מְרֹרָה <4846>; from BITTER (BE) <4843>] ▶ **This word also refers to bile, liver, a bitter thing.** It is used of the gallbladder (Job 20:25); its bile (Job 20:14; also translated venom). It indicates words that create grief in another person (Job 13:26). It describes clusters of grapes as bitter in a figurative sense (Deut. 32:32). ¶
– [3] Deut. 29:18; etc. ➔ POISON (noun) <7219> [4] Prov. 5:4; Lam. 3:15 ➔ WORMWOOD <3939>.

GALLBLADDER – Job 20:25 ➔ GALL <4845>.

GALLERY – [1] ***'attûq, 'attiyq*** [masc. noun: אַתּוּק, אַתִּיק <862>; from BREAK <5423> in the sense of decreasing] ▶ **This architectural term could indicate a porch.** It may mean a passage or street as well (Ezek. 41:15, 16; 42:3, 5). ¶
– [2] Song 7:5 ➔ TROUGH <7298> c.

GALLEY – Is. 33:21 ➔ FLEET OF SHIPS <590>.

GALLIM – ***galliym*** [proper noun: גַּלִּים <1554>; plur. of HEAP (noun) <1530>]: heaps ▶ **A city north of Jerusalem.** Refs.: 1 Sam. 25:44; Is. 10:30. ¶

GALLOP – [1] ***dāhar*** [verb: דָּהַר <1725>; a prim. root] ▶ **This word means to rush at the fast gait of horse; it describes the panic of military horses during the destruction and confusion of Nineveh's defeat.** Ref.: Nah. 3:2: galloping, pransing. ¶
– [2] Hab. 1:8 ➔ FROLIC <6335> a.

GALLOPING – [1] ***dahᵃrāh*** [fem. noun: דַּהֲרָה <1726>; by reduplication from GALLOP <1725>] ▶ **This word refers to a horse's fast gait; it describes the behavior of the armies' horses who defeated Sisera in the time of Debora.** Ref.: Judg. 5:22; also translated dashing, pransing. ¶
– [2] Jer. 47:3 ➔ STAMPING <8161> [3] Nah. 3:2 ➔ GALLOP <1725>.

GAMALIEL – ***gamliy'ēl*** [masc. proper noun: גַּמְלִיאֵל <1583>; from REWARD (verb) <1580> and GOD <410>]: reward of God ▶ **The name of an assistant to Moses who helped number the people of Israel.** Ref.: Num. 1:10. He came from Manasseh, a tribe from Joseph (Num. 2:20; 7:54, 59; 10:23). ¶

GAME – [1] Job 24:5 ➔ PREY <2964> [2] See FOOD <6718> a.

GAMMAD – Ezek. 27:11: man of Gammad ➔ GAMMADIM <1575>.

GAMMADIM – ***gammāḏiym*** [masc. proper noun: גַּמָּדִים <1575>; from the same as CUBIT <1574>]: valorous ones ▶ **Citizens of the city of Gammad.** Ref.: Ezek. 27:11. ¶

GAMUL – ***gāmûl*** [masc. proper noun: גָּמוּל <1577>; pass. part. of REWARD (verb) <1580>]: weaned, rewarded ▶ **A descendant of Aaron.** Ref.: 1 Chr. 24:17. ¶

GAPE – Job 16:10 ➔ OPEN <6473>.

GARBAGE – Lam. 3:45 ➔ REFUSE (noun) <3973>.

GARDEN – [1] ***gan*** [masc. noun: גַּן <1588>; from DEFEND <1598> (in the sense of to surround)] ▶ **This word refers to a place of abundant trees, water, fruits, and vegetables—where conditions for life are maximized. It also means enclosure.** It is used to indicate the Garden of Eden (pleasure) where the first human pair was placed (Gen. 2:8–10, 15, 16; 3:1–3, 8, 10, 23, 24; Ezek. 36:35; Joel 2:3). It could be enclosed (Lam. 2:6). It is combined with Lord to designate the garden of the Lord (Gen. 13:10) and with God to refer to the garden of God (Ezek. 28:13). A garden could feature many things, however: vegetables (Deut. 11:10; 1 Kgs. 21:2); spices, fruits, plants (Song 4:16; 5:1; 6:2). Assyria is referred to figuratively as a garden that surpassed even the garden of God (Ezek. 31:8, 9). *
[2] ***gannāh*** [fem. noun: גַּנָּה <1593>; fem. of <1588> above] ▶ **This word refers to planted areas in general that are taken away in times of judgment but restored in times of blessing.** Refs.: Amos 4:9; 9:14. Gardens were places of idolatrous worship in Israel (Is. 1:29; 66:17). They are used figuratively to indicate Israel as blessed (Num. 24:6) or cursed (Is. 1:30). The Lord causes things to prosper and grow (Is. 61:11). The success of the wicked, short-lived, is depicted as a garden (Job 8:16). *
[3] ***ginnāṯ*** [fem. noun: גִּנַּת <1594>; another form for <1593> above] ▶ **This word is combined in its construct with the king's palace to designate the planted area of the king's palace.** Refs.: Esther 1:5; 7:7, 8. Royal banquets were regularly held there. It depicts an orchard (Song 6:11) or nut garden. ¶

GARDEN (FRUITFUL) – Is. 10:18 ➔ FIELD (FERTILE, FRUITFUL, PLENTIFUL) <3759> a.

GARDEN TERRACE – Ezek. 17:7, 10 ➔ BED <6170>.

GAREB – ***gārêḇ*** [proper noun: גָּרֵב <1619>; from the same as SCAB <1618>]: scabby ▶ **a. An Ithrite, one of the strong men of David.** Refs.: 2 Sam. 23:38; 1 Chr. 11:40. ¶ **b. A hill.** Ref.: Jer. 31:39. ¶

GARLAND – [1] ***liwyāh*** [fem. noun: לִוְיָה <3880>; from JOIN <3867>] ▶ **This word indicates, probably figuratively, a decorative headpiece; it is also translated wreath, ornament.** It was worn as a sign of approval and honor, gracing a person's features (Prov. 1:9) as a result of following wisdom and awarded by wisdom itself (Prov. 4:9). ¶
– [2] Is. 61:3, 10 ➔ TURBAN <6287>.

GARLIC – ***šûm*** [masc. noun: שׁוּם <7762>; from an unused root meaning to exhale] ▶ **This word refers to a strong-smelling condiment of the lily family.** It is mentioned as one of the delicacies that Israel enjoyed in Egypt (Num. 11:50). ¶

GARMENT – [1] ***'addereṯ*** [fem. noun: אַדֶּרֶת <155>; fem. of MIGHTY <117>] ▶ **This word indicates a cloak, robe, splendor, or glory.** It indicates a fur garment in Genesis 25:25 to describe Esau's appearance at birth and a prophet's hairy garment (Zech. 13:4). It refers to a beautiful robe (Josh. 7:21, 24) or mantle or an ordinary mantle or robe (1 Kgs. 19:13, 19). It depicts a splendid vine (Ezek. 17:8; also translated goodly, majestic, noble) or kingly robe (Jon. 3:6). In Zechariah 11:3, it is used figuratively to refer to the glory or wealth of the shepherds' flocks or pasturelands. *
[2] ***beḡeḏ*** [masc. noun: בֶּגֶד <899>; from DECEITFULLY (DEAL) <898>] ▶ **This word describes any type of clothing item.** Ref.: Ps. 45:8. But combined with an appropriate qualifying word, it depicts specialized clothing and cultic garments as well, such as a widow's garment or cultic garments (Ex. 28:2–4). It refers to a lap garment or apron used to hold various items placed in it (2 Kgs. 4:39). Hence, it can be translated as a "lap full" (*m^elō' ḇigḏô*). It also describes a cloth or wrapping for the Tabernacle furniture (Num. 4:6–9, 11–13) or even a bed (1 Sam. 19:13). The Hebrew word also means deceit, fraud; see TREACHEROUSNESS <899>. *
[3] ***maḏweh*** [masc. noun: מַדְוֶה <4063>; from an unused root meaning to stretch] ▶ **This word is used of the clothes worn by the servants of King David.** Evidently, they were long garments (2 Sam. 10:4; 1 Chr. 19:4). ¶
[4] ***ma'ᵃṭeh*** [masc. noun: מַעֲטֶה <4594>; from WRAP AROUND <5844>] ▶ **This word refers to a cloak or a cape, probably, according to the text, an allusion to a royal or stately symbol of recognition.** Ref.: Is. 61:3 (also translated mantle). It was to be granted to those who mourned for Zion. ¶
[5] ***šiyṯ*** [masc. noun: שִׁית <7897>; from PUT <7896>] ▶ **This word refers to a piece of clothing but in context describes figuratively the clothing of the wicked, which represents their characters.** Ref.: Ps. 73:6. It refers to the dress or clothing worn by a harlot (Prov. 7:10: attire, dressed). ¶
– [6] Ex. 28:32; 39:23 ➔ COAT OF MAIL <8473> a. [7] Lev. 6:10; 1 Sam. 17:38; 2 Sam. 20:8; Ps. 109:18 ➔ CLOTHES <4055> [8] 1 Sam. 19:13, 16 ➔ PILLOW <3523> [9] 2 Kgs. 10:22b; Job 27:16; Zeph. 1:8 ➔ CLOTHING <4403> [10] Esther 8:15 ➔ ROBE <8509> [11] Ezek. 27:24 ➔ beautiful garment, choice garment ➔ CHOICE GARMENT <4360> [12] Dan. 3:21; 7:9 ➔ CLOTHING <3831>.

GARMENT (FINE) – Zech. 3:4 ➔ FESTAL APPAREL <4254>.

GARMENT, OUTER GARMENT – Ruth 3:15; Is. 3:22 ➔ CLOAK <4304>.

GARMENTS – See CLOTHING <3830>.

GARMITE – ***garmiy*** [masc. proper noun: גַּרְמִי <1636>; from BONE <1634>] ▶ **This word designates Keilah the Garmite in a genealogical list.** Ref.: 1 Chr. 4:19. ¶

GARNER – Ps. 144:13 ➔ BARN <4200>.

GARRISON – [1] ***maṣṣāḇ*** [masc. noun: מַצָּב <4673>; from STAND <5324>] ▶ **This**

word identifies an outpost, station, a place of standing. It indicates an outpost or military station (1 Sam. 13:23; 14:1, 4, 6, 11, 15) or a hideout for brigands or other bands of soldiers, etc. It has the sense of firm ground on which to stand (Josh. 4:3, 9). It is used of an established position or office a person holds (Is. 22:19). Other ref.: 2 Sam. 23:14. ¶

2 ***maṣṣāḇāh, miṣṣāḇāh*** [fem. noun: מַצָּבָה, מִצָּבָה <4675>; fem. of <4673> above] ▶ **This word is used of a place where armed men were gathered for battle, an outpost, a place that was defensible.** Ref.: 1 Sam. 14:12. But, evidently, it is applied to attacking forces as well (Zech. 9:8: army, guard, to guard). ¶

3 ***nᵉṣiyḇ*** [masc. noun: נְצִיב <5333>; from STAND (verb) <5324>] ▶ **This word is used to describe a military post, a fortified location or building.** Refs.: 1 Sam. 10:5; 13:3, 4; NIV: outpost. It describes a governor (1 Kgs. 4:19; also translated deputy, officer). They were manned, and tribute was collected in some of them (2 Sam. 8:6, 14). It indicates a pillar of salt (Gen. 19:26). *

GASH (noun) – ***gᵉḏûḏāh*** [fem. noun: גְּדוּדָה <1418>; fem. pass. part. of CUT (verb) <1413>] ▶ **This word represents ritualistic incisions or cuts; it is also translated cut, cutting, and by the verb to slash.** They were inflicted on the hands of Moabites in their hopeless acts of lamentation and mourning, for they were suffering judgment from the Lord (Jer. 48:37). ¶

GASH (verb) – 1 Kgs. 18:28; Jer. 16:6; 41:5; 47:5 ➔ CUT (verb) <1413>.

GASHMU – Neh. 6:6 ➔ GESHEM <1654>.

GASP – ***nāšam*** [verb: נָשַׁם <5395>; a prim. root] ▶ **This word means to breathe heavily, to pant. This particular form of the word is used only once in the Bible and describes the deep breathing and quick breathing of a woman in labor.** God said that although He had been silent, He would cry out like a woman about to give birth (Is. 42:14; KJV: to destroy). See the related Aramaic noun *nišmā'* (BREATH <5396>) and Hebrew noun *nᵉšāmāh* (BREATH <5397>). ¶

GATAM – ***ga'tām*** [masc. proper noun: גַּעְתָּם <1609>; of uncertain deriv.]: thin, weak ▶ **A son of Eliphaz and chief of a tribe in the land of Edom.** Refs.: Gen. 36:11, 16; 1 Chr. 1:36. ¶

GATE – 1 ***ša'ar*** [masc. noun: שַׁעַר <8179>; from THINK <8176> in its original sense of to split or open] ▶ **This word means a door, an entrance; a city, a town. It indicates the main entrance to a city or building.** It can be used to stand for city or town itself (Ps. 87:2; Is. 14:31): the gate of a city, which was a favorite gathering place of people for various reasons (Gen. 19:1; Ruth 4:1, 10, 11); the entrance to a court area (Ex. 27:16); the entrance to a camp (Ex. 32:26). It may mean a canal or the entrance to a river (Nah. 2:6). It is used figuratively in a dream to refer to "the gate of heaven" (Gen. 28:17). Sheol has an entrance gate as well (Is. 38:10); as does death (Job 38:17). Jerusalem had many gates over its long history (2 Kgs. 14:13; Neh. 2:13; 8:16; Jer. 37:13; Zech. 14:10). Temples and palace gates are mentioned (2 Kgs. 9:31; Jer. 7:2). The word refers to a meeting area that was often near the gate (Deut. 21:19; 2 Sam. 23:15, 16; 2 Kgs. 7:1, 18). *

– 2 Dan. 2:49 ➔ COURT <8651>.

GATEHOUSE – 1 Chr. 26:15, 17 ➔ STOREHOUSE <624>.

GATEKEEPER – 1 ***šô'ēr, šō'ēr*** [masc. noun: שׁוֹעֵר, שֹׁעֵר <7778>]; act. part. of THINK <8176> (in the sense of to split, to open) (as denom. from GATE <8179>) ▶ **This word indicates a person in charge of a gate, operating it, monitoring its use and its users; it is also translated porter.** Refs.: 2 Kgs. 7:10, 11. It is used often of gatekeepers in the Temple area (1 Chr. 9:17, 18, 24); they numbered in the thousands (1 Chr. 23:5; 26:1; Ezra 2:42, 70; 7:7; Neh. 7:1, 45, 73). *

– 2 Ezra 7:24 ➔ DOORKEEPER <8652>.

GATEWAY – Ezek. 27:3 ➔ ENTRANCE <3997>.

GATH – ***gaṯ*** [proper noun: גַּת <1661>; the same as WINEPRESS <1660>]: winepress ▶ **This word designates one of the five chief cities of the Philistines.** Only Gath is said to have had a king (1 Sam. 21:10, 12). Goliath, the giant, was from Gath (1 Sam. 17:4; cf. 2 Sam. 21:20). It was located nearly due east of Ashdod on the coast and lay on a major international road running north-south. The ark of God was lodged there temporarily, but the inhabitants suffered plagues, and it was moved on to Ekron (1 Sam. 5:8; 6:17). David ruled over it during his monarchy. It was captured by the Syrians (2 Kgs. 12:17). *

GATH-HEPHER – ***gaṯ-haḥēp̱er, gittāh-ḥēp̱er*** [proper noun: גַּת־הַחֵפֶר, גִּתָּה־חֵפֶר <1662>; from WINEPRESS <1660> and DIG <2658> with the art. inserted]: winepress of the well ▶ **A city on the border of Zebulun, close to Bethlehem.** Ref.: Josh. 19:13. The prophet Jonah was born there (2 Kgs. 14:25). ¶

GATH-RIMMON – ***gaṯ-rimmôn*** [proper noun: גַּת־רִמּוֹן <1667>; from WINEPRESS <1660> and POMEGRANATE <7416>]: press of the pomegranate ▶
a. A city of the tribe of Dan given to the Levites. Refs.: Josh. 19:45; 21:24; 1 Chr. 6:69. ¶
b. A city of the tribe of Manasseh given to the Levites. Ref.: Josh. 21:25. ¶

GATHER – 1 ***'āg̱ar*** [verb: אָגַר <103>; a prim. root] ▶ **The word means to collect crops, to harvest.** Ref.: Deut. 28:39. In Proverbs, it is used to describe the ant who gathers in its harvest (Prov. 6:8) and the wise son who gathers in the crops during the summer (Prov. 10:5). ¶
2 ***'āsap̱*** [verb: אָסַף <622>; a prim. root] ▶ **This word means to collect, to take away, to harvest. Its meaning varies depending on the context.** It can mean to gather people for different purposes (Gen. 29:22; 42:17; Ex. 3:16; 4:29). It is used of a nation collecting armies for fighting (Num. 21:23; Judg. 11:20; 1 Sam. 17:1; 2 Sam. 10:17); and the Lord taking away Rachel's disgrace of childlessness (Gen. 30:23). Oftentimes it refers to gathering or harvesting food or gathering other objects, such as animals (Jer. 12:9); quail (Num. 11:32); eggs (Is. 10:14); money (2 Kgs. 22:4; 2 Chr. 24:11). The word also refers to death or burial, literally meaning to be gathered to one's people (Gen. 25:8, 17; 35:29; 49:29, 33); to be gathered to one's fathers (Judg. 2:10); or to be gathered to one's grave (2 Kgs. 22:20; 2 Chr. 34:28). *
3 ***bāṣar*** [verb: בָּצַר <1219>; a prim. root] ▶
a. This verb means to harvest. It refers to the process of harvesting grapes (Lev. 25:5, 11; Deut. 24:21). In its participial form, it indicates a grape harvester (Jer. 6:9; 49:9; Obad. 1:5) whose activity illustrates the extent of God's judgments on Israel or her enemies. ¶
b. This verb means to humble, to cut off. It describes the power and sovereignty of God over the princes or rulers of the earth (Ps. 76:12). ¶
c. A verb indicating to be inaccessible or make inaccessible, to be thwarted. It describes the possibility of something being done or accomplished or found out (Gen. 11:6). In its passive sense, it describes the impossibility of something being thwarted or frustrated, such as God's counsel or purpose (Job 42:2). Used as a noun, it refers to unattainable knowledge or things, great and mighty things (NASB, Jer. 33:3). It means to strengthen or fortify in the sense of making a city or wall inaccessible (Is. 22:10; Jer. 51:53). *
d. A verb meaning to test, to assay. It is used in an emphatic form of the verb to indicate a tester (Jer. 6:27). In context it depicts someone who will test (KJV, try) God's people using them as the ore. ¶
4 ***gāḏaḏ*** [verb: גָּדַד <1413>; a prim. root (comp. ATTACK (verb) <1464>)] ▶ **This word means to assemble together.** It is used for troops (Mic. 5:1; also translated to muster, to marshal) or a crowd (Jer. 5:7: to assemble, to troop, to throng). Other ref.:

Ps. 94:21 (to gather, to band). This Hebrew verb also means to cut, to gash: see CUT (verb) <1413>. ¶

[5] ***dāg̱ar*** [verb: דָּגַר <1716>; a prim. root] ▶ **This word means to assemble together, to care for.** It refers to snake eggs being cared for (Is. 34:15, NIV, NASB, after hatching; KJV, NKJV, gathered together [for care]). It refers to a partridge hatching eggs it did not lay (Jer. 17:11) (NIV, NASB; NKJV, broods; KJV, sitteth on). ¶

[6] ***kānas*** [verb: כָּנַס <3664>; a prim. root] ▶ **A word meaning to assemble, to collect.** David assembled foreigners to be stonecutters (1 Chr. 22:2). Esther instructed Mordecai to gather the Jews and fast (Esther 4:16). The Lord gathered the waters (Ps. 33:7). The writer of Ecclesiastes collected silver and gold for himself (Eccl. 2:8; also translated to amass); there is a time to gather stones (Eccl. 3:5). The Lord told Ezekiel that He would gather Jerusalem together for punishment (Ezek. 22:21). Other refs.: Neh. 12:44; Ps. 147:2; Eccl. 2:26; Is. 28:20 (to wrap oneself); Ezek. 39:28. ¶

[7] k^{e}***naš*** [Aramaic verb: כְּנַשׁ <3673>; corresponding to <3664> above] ▶ **This word means to assemble, to be assembled.** It occurs only in Daniel 3:2, 3, and Daniel 3:27. It referred to the assembling of Babylonian officials, initiated by Nebuchadnezzar, to dedicate and worship an image. The assembly was apparently a formal occasion with high officials standing before the image, a herald proclaiming the purpose of the assembly, and musicians playing various instruments. Those assembled saw the Hebrews who refused to obey sentenced to the fiery furnace and subsequently delivered from it. ¶

[8] ***lāqaṭ*** [verb: לָקַט <3950>; a prim. root] ▶ **This word means to collect, to glean. It occurs with various objects such as manna, lilies, firewood, and people.** Refs.: Ex. 16:4, 5; Judg. 11:3; Song 6:2; Jer. 7:18. However, by far it is used most often with food, including once with grapes (Lev. 19:10; Is. 17:5). Even animals are able to gather the food God graciously provides (Ps. 104:28). About half of the occurrences of this term relate to the provision of the Mosaic Law to take care of the needy by allowing them to glean the fields, a provision featured prominently in the story of Ruth (Lev. 19:9, 10; 23:22; Ruth 2:2, 3, 7, 8, 15–19, 23). Isaiah used this term in both a picture of judgment and of restoration for the nation of Israel (Is. 17:5; 27:12). *

[9] ***qāḇaṣ*** [verb: קָבַץ <6908>; a prim. root] ▶ **This word means to collect, to assemble.** The passive form is used to signify the gathering or assembling of people, especially for battle (Josh. 9:2; Neh. 4:20; Jer. 49:14); and for religious and national purposes (1 Chr. 11:1; Ezra 10:1, 7). The word in an active form often signifies the gathering of materials: food into storehouses (Gen. 41:35); sheaves (Mic. 4:12); money and wealth (2 Chr. 24:5; Prov. 28:8); lambs by a shepherd (Is. 13:14; 40:11; Jer. 23:3). The word also refers to God's gathering of nations for judgment in the end times (Is. 43:9; 66:18; Joel 3:2); and especially to the gathering of His scattered people, Israel (Ps. 106:47; Jer. 29:14; 31:10; Hos. 1:11). *

[10] ***qāšaš*** [verb: קָשַׁשׁ <7197>; a prim. root] ▶ **This word means to collect things; to assemble together.** It describes the Israelites' gathering together stubble to make bricks (Ex. 5:7, 12); pieces of wood or sticks (Num. 15:32, 33; 1 Kgs. 17:10, 12). It indicates people gathering themselves together (Zeph. 2:1). ¶

– [11] Gen. 12:5; 31:18; 36:6; 46:6 ➔ ACCUMULATE <7408> [12] Job 24:6 ➔ GLEAN <3953> [13] Song 5:1 ➔ PICK (verb) <717> [14] Jer. 8:13 ➔ CONSUME, BE CONSUMED <5486> [15] Ezek. 22:20a ➔ GATHERING <6910>.

GATHER TOGETHER – 2 Sam. 20:14 ➔ ASSEMBLE <7035>.

GATHER UP – 1 Kgs. 18:46: he gathered up his garments ➔ lit.: he girded up his loins ➔ GIRD UP <8151>.

GATHERED TOGETHER – Ex. 15:8 ➔ PILED UP <6192>.

GATHERED TOGETHER (BE) – ^{a}***sēp̄āh*** [fem. noun: אֲסֵפָה <626>; from GATHER

<622>] ▶ **This word means to be assembled, to be congregated.** This particular word occurs only in Isaiah 24:22, "And they will be gathered together, as prisoners are gathered in the pit" (NKJV); it is also translated they will be herded together. ¶

GATHERER – Amos 7:14 ➔ DRESSER <1103>.

GATHERING – 1 ***'ōsep*** [masc. noun: אֹסֶף <625>; from GATHER <622>] ▶ **This word means a collection, ingathering, harvest.** The Hebrew word especially refers to a harvest of summer fruits, as is depicted in Micah 7:1, "Gather the summer fruits" (NKJV). The prophet Isaiah is the other biblical author to use this term. In Isaiah 32:10, he states that the complacent people will be troubled and insecure because "the gathering will not come," but, then in Isaiah 33:4, the prophet uses the same word to refer to the Lord's spoil being collected like "the gathering of the caterpillar." ¶
2 ***qᵉbuṣāh*** [fem. noun: קְבֻצָה <6910>; fem. pass. part. of GATHER <6908>] ▶ **This word occurs only in Ezekiel 22:20 where it signifies the collection, heaping of metals into a furnace.** It is a picture of God gathering Israel to pour out His burning anger on them. ¶
– 3 2 Sam. 22:12 ➔ MASS <2841> 4 Gen. 49:10 ➔ OBEDIENCE <3349>.

GATHERS (ONE WHO) – Ps. 129:7 ➔ SLAVE (TREAT AS A) <6014>.

GAUDY – Ezek. 16:165 ➔ SPOTTED (BE) <2921>.

GAUNT – Gen. 41:19, 20, 27 ➔ LEAN (adj.) <7534>.

GAUNTNESS – Job 16:8 ➔ LIE (noun) <3585>.

GAZA – 1 ***'azzāh*** [proper noun: עַזָּה <5804>; fem. of STRONG <5794>]: strong ▶ **An important city in southwest Israel. It was near the coast and at the dividing line between Canaan and the area of the Sinai Desert.** The Philistines controlled it most of the time even though it was allotted to Judah (Josh. 10:41; 15:47; Judg. 1:18). It was often under the influence of Egypt or the current ruling power of Canaan since it was situated at several major trade routes.

It was initially inhabited by the Avvites, a people who preceded the Philistines (Gen. 10:19; Deut. 2:23), as well as the Anakites (Josh. 11:22). Samson visited the city and removed the doors of the city gate (Judg. 16:1–3) but was later taken there as a captive. He avenged himself on the Philistines who ruled the city (Judg. 16:21–31). The grain god Dagon was worshiped there. (Some also refer to Dagon as the fish god.) Later, it became part of the five-city coalition of Philistine cities (Ashdod, Gaza, Ashkelon, Gath, Ekron). It was the recognized southern extent of Philistine influence and power (2 Kgs. 18:8). The prophets spoke of God's judgment on the city often (Jer. 25:20; 47:1, 5; Amos 1:6, 7; Zeph. 2:4; Zech. 9:5). Other refs.: Judg. 6:4; 1 Sam. 6:17; 1 Kgs. 4:24; 1 Chr. 7:28. ¶
2 ***šā'āh*** [verb: שָׁאָה <7583>; a prim. root] ▶ **This word means to look at intently, to observe closely for some purpose.** Ref.: Gen. 24:21; also translated to wonder, to watch. ¶
– 3 Ps. 102:19 ➔ LOOK (verb) <5027> 4 Song 2:9 ➔ BLOSSOM (verb) <6692> b. 5 Song 2:9; Is. 14:16 ➔ LOOK (verb) <7688>.

GAZELLE – 1 ***ṣᵉbiyyāh*** [fem. noun: צְבִיָּה <6646>; fem. of GLORY <6643> (also meaning beauty, gazelle)] ▶ **This word refers to a female gazelle. This animal is a small, graceful antelope with lustrous eyes, fragile and endearing.** Refs.: Song 4:5; 7:3. It was used in a metaphor of love toward a bride. ¶
– 2 Deut. 12:15, 22; etc. ➔ GLORY <6643>.

GAZEZ – ***gāzēz*** [masc. proper noun: גָּזֵז <1495>; from CUT (verb) <1494>]: shearer ▶ **One of Caleb's sons.** Ref.: 1 Chr. 2:46. ¶

GAZITE, GAZATHITE – ***'azzāṯiy*** [masc. proper noun: עַזָּתִי <5841>; patrial from

GAZA <5804>] ▶ **An inhabitant of Gaza.** Refs.: Josh. 13:3; Judg. 16:2. ¶

GAZZAM – ***gazzām*** [masc. proper noun: גַּזָּם <1502>; from the same as LOCUST <1501>]: devourer ▶ **The sons of Gazzam were Temple servants.** Refs.: Ezra 2:48; Neh. 7:51. ¶

GEBA – ***geḇa'*** [proper noun: גֶּבַע <1387>; from the same as CUP <1375>]: height, hill ▶ **This word (Geba or Gaba) designates a town. It was allotted to Benjamin.** Ref.: Josh. 18:24. It was also appointed as a Levitical city (Josh. 21:17; 1 Chr. 6:60; 8:6). It was situated in northern Judah (2 Kgs. 23:8). The exiles from Babylon resettled the city (Ezra 2:26; Neh. 7:30; 11:31; 12:29). It was about six miles north of Jerusalem. Asa, king of Judah, fortified it. Judah was defined as "from Geba to Beersheba" (2 Kgs. 23:8). *

GEBAL – 1 ***geḇal*** [proper noun: גְּבַל <1380>; from BOUNDS (SET) <1379> (in the sense of a chain of hills)]: mountain ▶ **A city in Phoenicia.** Ref.: Ezek. 27:9. ¶
2 ***geḇāl*** [proper noun: גְּבָל <1381>; the same as <1380> above]: mountain ▶ **An area south of the Dead Sea.** Ref.: Ps. 83:7. ¶

GEBALITES – ***giḇliy*** [masc. proper noun: גִּבְלִי <1382>; patrial from GEBAL <1380>] ▶ **This word refers to the inhabitants of the city of Gebal, a city not yet conquered in Joshua's day.** Ref.: Josh. 13:5. They were skilled workers with wood and stone (1 Kgs. 5:18). ¶

GEBER – ***geḇer*** [masc. noun: גֶּבֶר <1398>; the same as MAN <1397>]: strong, man ▶ **A governor of Solomon over the land of Gilead.** Ref.: 1 Kgs. 4:19. ¶

GEBIM – ***gêḇiym*** [proper noun: גֵּבִים <1374>; plur. of POOL (noun) <1356>]: cisterns ▶ **A village north of Jerusalem.** Ref.: Is. 10:31. ¶

GECKO – Lev. 11:30 → FERRET <604>.

GEDALIAH – ***geḏalyāh, geḏalyāhû*** [masc. proper noun: גְּדַלְיָה, גְּדַלְיָהוּ <1436>; from GREAT (BECOME) <1431> and LORD <3050>]: great is the Lord, the Lord has magnified ▶
a. This name describes the son of Ahikam, whom Nebuchadnezzar appointed as his chief minister in Judea after the fall of Jerusalem (586/87 B.C.; 2 Kgs. 25:22). He was joined by other Israelites including Jeremiah (Jer. 40:5–9; 41:1–18; 43:6). This group remained supportive of the king of Babylon (Jer. 40:5–16). Gedaliah was assassinated by Ishmael (2 Kgs. 25:22–25; Jer. 41:1–4). The remnant fled to Egypt. Other ref.: Jer. 39:14. ¶
b. He was a son of Jeduthun and led in the Temple worship with others. Refs.: 1 Chr. 25:3, 9. ¶
c. A priest who had married a foreign woman in Ezra's day. Ref.: Ezra 10:18. ¶
d. The father of Cushi, the father of the prophet Zephaniah. Ref.: Zeph. 1:1. ¶
e. An official of Zedekiah who counseled the king to put Jeremiah to death. Refs.: Jer. 38:1, 4, 5. ¶

GEDER – ***geḏer*** [proper noun: גֶּדֶר <1445>; the same as WALL <1444>]: wall ▶ **A city at the extreme south of Judah.** Ref.: Josh. 12:13. ¶

GEDERAH – ***geḏêrāh*** [proper noun: גְּדֵרָה <1449>; the same as WALL <1448> (with the art.)]: wall, enclosure ▶ **It is one of the cities lying within the territory of Judah in the deep south near Edom.** Ref.: Josh. 15:36. ¶

GEDERATHITE – ***geḏêrāṯiy*** [masc. proper noun: גְּדֵרָתִי <1452>; patrial from GEDERAH <1449>]: wall, fence ▶ **An inhabitant of Gederah.** Ref.: 1 Chr. 12:4. ¶

GEDERITE – ***geḏêriy*** [masc. proper noun: גְּדֵרִי <1451>; patrial from GEDER <1445>] ▶ **An inhabitant of Geder.** Ref.: 1 Chr. 27:28. ¶

GEDEROTH – ***geḏêrôṯ*** [proper noun: גְּדֵרוֹת <1450>; plur. of WALL <1448>]: walls, enclosure (especially for flocks) ▶ **A city of the plain of Judah or near it.** Refs.: Josh. 15:41; 2 Chr. 28:18. ¶

GEDEROTHAIM – ***gᵉḏêrōṯayim*** [proper noun: גְּדֵרֹתַיִם <1453>; dual of WALL <1448>]: two walls, double enclosures ▶ **It is one of the cities lying within the territory of Judah in the deep south near Edom.** Ref.: Josh. 15:36. The Septuagint translates this word "and its livestock shelters." In this case, there would be fourteen cities named and not fifteen. (Ref.: Nouveau Dictionnaire Biblique) ¶

GEDOR – ***gᵉḏôr*** [proper noun: גְּדוֹר <1446>; from BUILD <1443>]: wall, fortress ▶
a. An Israelite of the tribe of Benjamin. Refs.: 1 Chr. 8:31; 9:37. ¶
b. A son of Penuel of the tribe of Judah. Ref.: 1 Chr. 4:4. ¶
c. A son of Jered of the tribe of Judah. Ref.: 1 Chr. 4:18. ¶
d. A city of Judah. Ref.: Josh. 15:58. ¶
e. A city of Benjamin. Ref.: 1 Chr. 12:7. ¶
f. A city apparently of Simeon. Ref.: 1 Chr. 4:39. ¶

GEHAZI – ***gêyḥᵃziy, gêḥᵃziy*** [masc. proper noun: גֵּחֲזִי, גֵּיחֲזִי <1522>; apparently from VALLEY <1516> and SEE <2372>]: valley of the vision ▶ **The name of Elisha's servant.** He laid Elisha's staff upon the Shunnamite's dead son to restore him to life (2 Kgs. 4:12, 14, 25, 27, 29, 31, 36) but in vain. He deceitfully took gifts for himself that Elisha had refused from Naaman (2 Kgs. 5:20, 21, 25). As a consequence to this, the leprosy of Naaman would cling to him and his descendants forever (see 2 Kgs. 5:25–27). He recounted the great things Elisha had done for the Shunnamite woman to a certain king (2 Kgs. 8:4, 5). ¶

GELILOT – ***gᵉliylôt*** [proper noun: גְּלִילוֹת <1553>; plur. of REGION <1552>]: circles ▶ **A place on Judah and Benjamin's border.** Refs.: Josh. 18:17; 22:10, 11. ¶

GEMALLI – ***gᵉmalliy*** [masc. proper noun: גְּמַלִּי <1582>; prob. from CAMEL <1581>]: camel driver ▶ **The father of Ammiel, a spy of the tribe of Dan who explored the Promised Land.** Ref.: Num. 13:12. ¶

GEMARIAH – ***gᵉmaryāh, gᵉmaryāhû*** [masc. proper noun: גְּמַרְיָהוּ, גְּמַרְיָה <1587>; from END (COME TO AN) <1584> and LORD <3050>]: the Lord has completed ▶
a. A son of Hilkiah whom the king of Judah sent to the king of Babylon. Ref.: Jer. 29:3. ¶
b. A son of Shaphan who urged the king not to burn the writings of Jeremiah. Refs.: Jer. 36:10–12, 25. ¶

GEMS (COLORFUL) – Is. 54:11 ➔ ANTIMONY <6320>.

GENEALOGICAL – Neh. 7:5 ➔ lit.: of the genealogy ➔ GENEALOGY <3188>.

GENEALOGY – [1] **to register by, to reckon by, to keep, to maintain, etc. genealogy: *yāḥaś*** [verb: יָחַשׂ <3187>; a prim. root] ▶ **This word indicates the keeping of a genealogical record (i.e., a record of family history); to be in a genealogical record. This was especially important in Israel because the Israelites were chosen as God's holy people.** Certain positions could be held only by proving one's ancestry. It indicates the inclusion of a person in a genealogy by establishing his or her descent (Ezra 2:62). It can be rendered "to have a genealogy" (1 Chr. 4:33, NASB; cf. KJV, These were . . . "their genealogies") or to be enrolled in a genealogy (1 Chr. 5:1, 17; 2 Chr. 12:15; Neh. 7:5). It indicates the place where enrollment took place (Neh. 7:64). *
[2] ***yaḥaś*** [masc. noun: יַחַשׂ <3188>; from GENEALOGY <3187>] ▶ **This word denotes a pedigree, a genealogical record or register of family history.** It is the official listing of those included in a particular line of descent. Israel kept these records meticulously (Neh. 7:5). ¶

GENERAL – Jer. 51:27; Nah. 3:17 ➔ MARSHAL <2951>.

GENERATION – [1] ***dôr*** [masc. noun: דּוֹר <1755>; from DWELL <1752>] ▶ **This**

word means a period of time, a posterity, an age, a time, a setting of life. In general, it indicates the time from birth to death; the time from one's birth to the birth of one's first child; the living adults of a certain time or place; a period as it is defined through major events, persons, behavior, and the spirit of the age. It also marks a duration of time. There is no agreed on length of time which may stretch from twenty to one hundred years, but the word is also used figuratively to mean an indefinite or unending length of time in the past or future. These basic observations can be illustrated from various passages and contexts: the generation of Noah was characterized by wickedness and violence, yet he was a righteous man in his generation (Gen. 7:1); Moses spoke of a crooked generation in his day and in the future (Deut. 32:5); however, the psalmist spoke of a generation of righteous people (Ps. 14:5) and a generation of people who seek the Lord (Ps. 24:6). These generations will be blessed by God (Ps. 112:2). Generations come and go without interruption (Eccl. 1:4).

Time can be measured by the passing of generations, as when the great deeds of the Lord are passed on from generation to generation, in effect forever (Ps. 145:4; Is. 34:17); God's throne lasts forever, from generation to generation (Lam. 5:19). Likewise, God's judgments can endure forever (Jer. 50:39). The closing of an era can be marked by the death of all the persons belonging to that generation (Ex. 1:6; Judg. 2:10), but persons can be taken from their own proper age, dwellings, or circles of existence, as Hezekiah nearly was (Ps. 102:24; Is. 38:12), and a subgroup, such as fighting men, can pass away from an era (Deut. 2:14). On the other hand, God's length of days spans all generations without end (Ps. 102:24).

The generation or generations mentioned may refer to the past, present, or future. Noah was perfect during the time of his contemporaries (Gen. 6:9); the generations extended into the future when God established His covenant with Abraham and all future generations (Gen. 17:7, 12; cf. Lev. 25:30) or when He gave His name as a memorial for all generations to come (Ex. 3:15). The word often refers to past generations, such as the generation of the fathers (Ps. 49:19; Is. 51:9). God's constancy again stands out, for His days span all past eras as well as all future generations (Ps. 102:24). Israel was encouraged in Moses' song to remember the past generations of old (Deut. 32:7) when God effected His foundational acts of deliverance for Israel and gave them the Law at Sinai. Present generations are to learn from past generations (Deut. 32:7) and can affect future generations by declaring the Lord's power (Ps. 71:18).

Certain generations were singled out for special note: the third and fourth generations of children are punished for the sins of their fathers (Ex. 20:5; 34:7); the infamous generation that wandered in the wilderness for forty years experienced God's judgments until everyone in that generation died (Ps. 95:10). Yet the love of God is not bound, for, in a figurative sense, it is passed on to thousands of generations (i.e., without limitation) forever and to every person (Ex. 20:6; 34:7). ¶

2 ***dār*** [Aramaic masc. noun: דָּר <1859>; corresponding to <1755> above] ▶ **This word is used in a phrase that is literally translated "with generation and generation," the idea referring to God's kingdom enduring from generation to generation, i.e., from one family cycle to the next.** Refs.: Dan. 4:3; 4:34. ¶

3 ***tôlêḏôṯ*** [fem. noun: תּוֹלְדוֹת <8435>; from BIRTH (GIVE) <3205>] ▶ **This key Hebrew word carries with it the notion of everything entailed in a person's life and that of his or her progeny, one's history.** Refs.: Gen. 5:1; 6:9. In the plural, it is used to denote the chronological procession of history as humans shape it. It refers to the successive generations in one family (Gen. 10:32); or a broader division by lineage (Num. 1:20 ff.). In Genesis 2:4, the word accounts for the history of the created world. *

GENEROUS – Ps. 51:12; Is. 32:8 ➔ DIGNITY <5082>.

GENITALS (MALE) – Deut. 25:11 ➔ PRIVATE PARTS <4016>.

GENTLE – [1] ***'allûp̱, 'allup̱*** [adj. or masc. noun: אַלּוּף, אַלֻּף <441>; from LEARN <502>] ► **This word means docile, tame; friend, intimate, chief, captain.** Even though the adjectival usage is rare, it is found in the well-known description, "Like a gentle (or docile) lamb to the slaughter" (Jer. 11:19). In the nominal form, this word connotes the closest of companions; such companions can be separated by a whisperer or gossiper (Prov. 16:28: close, best, chief, intimate friend). In another aspect, this term was used to describe a leader of a nation or group. Esau's descendants were listed as chiefs of Edom (Gen. 36:15); the word is also translated duke. *

[2] ***rak̠*** [adj.: רַךְ <7390>; from FAINT (BE, MAKE) <7401> (in the sense of to be tender, to be soft)] ► **This word means tender, weak, indecisive.** It describes a desirable quality of meat used for food (Gen. 18:7); but indicates frailty, weakness in a person (Gen. 33:13; 2 Sam. 3:39). Leah's eyes were weak, tender (Gen. 29:17). It describes a character, a way of life that reflects refinement (Deut. 28:54, 56). It is used to indicate a tongue that speaks with kind prudence (Prov. 25:15); that speaks softly, gently (Prov. 15:1). It indicates the way a mother sees her son as a tender, beloved child (Prov. 4:3). It indicates a soft or reconciling word (Job 41:3). It describes the tender green growth of new branches on a tree (Ezek. 17:22). *

– [3] Deut. 28:56 ➔ REFINEMENT <7391> [4] 2 Sam. 18:5: be gentle ➔ deal gently ➔ SLOWLY <328>.

GENTLENESS – 2 Sam. 22:36; Ps. 18:35 ➔ HUMILITY <6038>.

GENTLY – 2 Sam. 18:5; Job 15:11; Is. 8:6 ➔ SLOWLY <328>.

GENUBATH – ***gᵉnuḇaṯ*** [masc. proper noun: גְּנֻבַת <1592>; from STEAL <1589>]: theft ► **Son of Hadad, an Edomite prince, and the sister of the queen of Egypt.** Ref.: 1 Kgs. 11:20. ¶

GERA – ***gêrā'*** [masc. proper noun: גֵּרָא <1617>; perhaps from GERAH <1626>]: sojourner ► **The name of six Israelites or more from the tribe of Benjamin.** Refs.: Gen. 46:21; Judg. 3:15; 2 Sam. 16:5; 19:16, 18; 1 Kgs. 2:8; 1 Chr. 8:3, 5, 7). ¶

GERAH – ***gêrāh*** [fem. noun: גֵּרָה <1626>; from DRAG (verb) <1641> (as in CUD <1625>)] ► **This word denotes a small unit of weight. It indicates a unit of weight used as money.** The gerah was one-twentieth of a shekel (Ex. 30:13; Ezek. 45:12) as used in the sanctuary (Lev. 27:25; Num. 3:47; 18:16). It was 1/6000 of a talent and one tenth of a beka. Its modern equivalent is .5 - .6 gram or .02 ounce. ¶

GERAR – ***gᵉrār*** [proper noun: גְּרָר <1642>; prob. from DRAG (verb) <1641>]: stay, lodging place ► **This word designates a town near the Mediterranean coast, east of Gaza.** Abraham's and Isaac's encounters with two kings of the Philistines occurred in this area (Gen. 20:1, 2; 26:1, 6, 17, 20, 26). The famous "well of Isaac" was in this vicinity (Gen. 26:20, 26). It figures in a minor way in later Israelite history (2 Chr. 4:13, 14). Other ref.: Gen. 10:19. ¶

GERIZIM – ***gᵉriziym*** [proper noun: גְּרִזִּים <1630>; plur. of an unused root from CUT OFF (BE) <1629> (comp. GIRZITES <1511>)]: cutters, dry places ► **A mountain south, southeast of Shechem a short distance, and south of Mount Ebal.** Moses and later Joshua read out covenant blessings at a covenant renewal ceremony (Deut. 11:29; 27:12; Josh. 8:33) on this mountain. Jotham escaped to it, fleeing from Abimelech (Judg. 9:7). It became the favored place of worship for the Samaritans (John 4:20). ¶

GERSHOM – ***gêršôm, gêršōm*** [masc. proper noun: גֵּרְשׁוֹם, גֵּרְשֹׁם <1647>; for GERSHON <1648>]: stranger, banishment ►

a. A son of Moses. Refs.: Ex. 2:22; 18:3; 1 Chr. 23:15, 16; 26:24. ¶

b. The oldest son of Levi. Refs.: 1 Chr. 6:16, 17, 20, 43, 62, 71; 15:7. ¶

c. Son of Phinehas. Ref.: Ezra 8:2. ¶

d. The father of Jonathan. Ref.: Judg. 18:30. ¶

GERSHON – ***gêršôn*** [masc. proper noun: גֵּרְשׁוֹן <1648>; from CAST OUT <1644>]: banishment, expulsion, exile ▶ **The oldest son of Levi.** Refs.: Gen. 46:11; Ex. 6:16, 17; Num. 3:17, 18, 21, 25; 4:22, 38, 41; 7:7; 10:17; 26:57; Josh. 21:6, 27; 1 Chr. 6:1; 23:6. See also GERSHOM <1647> b. ¶

GERSHONITE – ***gêršunniy*** [masc. proper noun: גֵּרְשֻׁנִּי <1649>; patron. from GERSHON <1648>] ▶ **A child or a descendant of Gershon.** Refs.: Num. 3:21, 23, 24; 4:24, 27, 28; 26:57; Josh. 21:33; 1 Chr. 23:7; 26:21; 29:8; 2 Chr. 29:12. ¶

GERUTH – Jer. 41:17 ➔ HABITATION <1628>.

GESHAN – ***gêyšān*** [masc. proper noun: גֵּישָׁן <1529>; from the same as CRUST <1487>]: filthy ▶ **An Israelite of the tribe of Judah.** Ref.: 1 Chr. 2:47. ¶

GESHEM – ***gešem, gašmû*** [masc. proper noun: גֶּשֶׁם, גַּשְׁמוּ <1654>; the same as RAIN (verb) <1653>]: shower ▶ **An Arabian, adversary of the Jews after the return from captivity.** Refs.: Neh. 2:19; 6:1, 2, 6: Gashmu. ¶

GESHUR – ***gᵉšûr*** [proper noun: גְּשׁוּר <1650>; from an unused root (meaning to join)]: bridge ▶ **A district of Syria.** Refs.: Josh. 13:13; 2 Sam. 3:3; 13:37, 38; 14:23, 32; 15:8; 1 Chr. 2:23; 3:2. ¶

GESHURITE – ***gᵉšûriy*** [masc. proper noun: גְּשׁוּרִי <1651>; patrial from GESHUR <1650>] ▶
a. The inhabitants of Geshur. Refs.: Deut. 3:14; Josh. 12:5; 13:11, 13. ¶
b. A tribe of people near Philistia. Refs.: Josh. 13:2; 1 Sam. 27:8. ¶

GESTURE (verb) – Is. 33:15 ➔ SHAKE <5287>.

GET – **1** Deut. 24:10 ➔ LEND <5670> **2** Prov. 3:13 ➔ OBTAIN <6329>.

GET AWAY – Num. 16:45 ➔ EXALTED <7426> a.

GET AWAY, GET OUT – Dan. 4:14 ➔ FLEE <5110>.

GET OFF – ***ṣānaḥ*** [verb: צָנַח <6795>; a prim. root] ▶ **This word means to dismount an animal.** It is used of Achsah or Acsah, Caleb's daughter, getting down from her donkey (Josh. 15:18; Judg. 1:14); it is also translated to alight from, to light off, to dismount. The Hebrew word also means to go down; see GO THROUGH <6795>. ¶

GETHER – ***geṯer*** [masc. proper noun: גֶּתֶר <1666>; of uncertain deriv.]: fear, valley of trial ▶ **A descendant of Aram.** Refs.: Gen. 10:23; 1 Chr. 1:17. ¶

GEUEL – ***gᵉ'û'êl*** [masc. proper noun: גְּאוּאֵל <1345>; from RISE <1342> and GOD <410>]: majesty of God ▶ **A spy of the land of Canaan from the tribe of Gad.** Ref.: Num. 13:15. ¶

GEZER – ***gezer*** [proper noun: גֶּזֶר <1507>; the same as PART (noun) <1506>]: portion ▶ **A city located in the northern area of the Shephelah due east of Ashdod on the coast.** Refs.: Josh. 10:33; 12:12. It was given to Ephraim (Josh. 16:3) and became a Levitical city (Josh. 21:21; 1 Chr. 6:67). David pursued Philistines into Gezer. According to 1 Kings. 9:15–17, Pharaoh captured it and gave it to his daughter as a marriage dowry. *

GEZRITES – 1 Sam. 27:8 ➔ GIRZITES <1511>.

GIAH – ***giyaḥ*** [proper noun: גִּיחַ <1520>; from GUSH <1518>]: fountain, waterfall ▶ **A place near Gibeon in Benjamin.** Ref.: 2 Sam. 2:24. ¶

GIANTS – Gen. 6:4; Num. 13:33 ➔ NEPHILIM <5303>.

GIBBAR – ***gibbār*** [masc. proper noun: גִּבָּר <1402>; intens. of MAN <1399>]: powerful man, hero ▶ **An Israelite whose descendants came back from the Babylonian**

captivity with Zerubbabel. Ref.: Ezra 2:20. ¶

GIBBETHON – ***gibb^{e}ṯôn*** [proper noun: גִּבְּתוֹן <1405>; intens. from HILL <1389>]: high place ▶ **A city of Dan assigned to the Levites.** Refs.: Josh. 19:44; 21:23; 1 Kgs. 15:27; 16:15, 17. ¶

GIBEA – ***giḇ'ā'*** [masc. proper noun: גִּבְעָא <1388>; by permutation for HILL <1389>]: hill ▶ **A descendant of Caleb.** Ref.: 1 Chr. 2:49. ¶

GIBEAH – ***giḇ'āh*** [proper noun: גִּבְעָה <1390>; the same as HILL <1389>]: hill ▶
a. A city allotted to Judah located in the hills of Hebron. Ref.: Josh. 15:57. ¶
b. A location and/or city in the mountains of Ephraim. The name is translated "hill" in a few places. Eleazar, Aaron's son, was buried there (Josh. 24:33). Its exact location is not yet determined. ¶
c. A town allotted to Benjamin. Ref.: Josh. 18:28. The men of the city raped and killed a Levite's concubine, and the city was practically destroyed because of the act (Judg. 19:20). Isaiah refers to it, as does Hosea (Hos. 5:8; 9:9; 10:9), each time as an example of wickedness and a picture of the judgment of God on such behavior. However, it also served as the capital for Saul, Israel's first king (1 Sam. 10:10–26; 11:4). It is translated as "hill" (NASB) in 2 Samuel 6:3, 4 by some translations and not at all by the NIV in 2 Samuel 6:4. *

GIBEATH – ***giḇ'aṯ*** [proper noun: גִּבְעַת <1394>; from the same as CUP <1375>]: hill ▶ **A town of Benjamin.** Ref.: Josh. 18:28. ¶

GIBEATHITE – ***giḇ'āṯiy*** [masc. proper noun: גִּבְעָתִי <1395>; patrial from GIBEAH <1390>] ▶ **A native or an inhabitant of Gibeah.** Ref.: 1 Chr. 12:3. ¶

GIBEON – ***giḇ'ôn*** [proper noun: גִּבְעוֹן <1391>; from the same as GEBA <1387>]: height, hill ▶ **A mighty city inhabited by Hivites (Horites?) who deceived Joshua and Israel into making a treaty of peace with them.** Refs.: Josh. 9:1–27. It was a powerful city (Josh. 10:2), and the surrounding peoples attacked it because it had made a treaty with Israel. Joshua and Israel, however, later fought at Gibeon and defeated a powerful coalition of Canaanite kings. God mightily intervened, and the sun "stood still" over Gibeon until their enemies were defeated (Josh. 10:1–15). The city was given to the tribe of Benjamin but became a Levitical city (Josh. 18:25). Several momentous events occurred in the city (2 Sam. 2:12–24; 20:8; 21:1–11). People from the city helped rebuild Jerusalem's walls (Neh. 3:7; 7:25). Jeremiah cursed a false prophet from Gibeon (Jer. 28:1). It is located at El-Jib about 6 miles northwest of Jerusalem. *

GIBEONITE – ***giḇ'ôniy*** [masc. proper noun: גִּבְעוֹנִי <1393>; patrial from GIBEON <1391>] ▶ **An inhabitant of Gibeon.** Refs.: 2 Sam. 21:1–4, 9; 1 Chr. 12:4; Neh. 3:7. ¶

GIDDALTI – ***giddaltiy*** [masc. proper noun: גִּדַּלְתִּי <1437>; from GREAT (BECOME) <1431>]: I make great ▶ **A musician, under the reign of David, responsible for the music of the sanctuary.** Refs.: 1 Chr. 25:4, 29. ¶

GIDDEL – ***giddêl*** [masc. proper noun: גִּדֵּל <1435>; from GREAT (BECOME) <1431>]: who has become great ▶
a. The head of a family. Refs.: Ezra. 2:47; Neh. 7:49. ¶
b. A servant of Solomon. Refs.: Ezra 2:56; Neh. 7:58. ¶

GIDEON – ***giḏ'ôn*** [masc. proper noun: גִּדְעוֹן <1439>; from CUT DOWN <1438>]: smiter, hewer ▶ **An important judge who delivered the Israelites from the Midianites and a coalition of other peoples in his day.** He did this with a small handpicked group of soldiers (Judg. 7:1–8), singled out by the Lord (Judg. 6, 7). The Lord Himself sent fear into the camp of the Midianites (Judg. 7:13, 14). The Israelites sought to make him king after he had slain

Zebah and Zalmunna, princes of the Midianite coalition (Judg. 8:6–21). He refused the offer. He made a gold ephod, however, which was later worshiped foolishly by the Israelites (Judg. 8:25–27).

He was given the name Jerub-Baal which means "Let Baal contend/fight" because he had challenged the god Baal (Judg. 6:31, 22; 8:29–32). He had seventy sons. A son named Abimelech by a concubine arose after him to claim kingship for himself (Judg. 8:29–31). The Israelites soon began to go after Baal when Gideon died. *

GIDEONI – ***giḏʿōniy*** [masc. proper noun: גִּדְעֹנִי <1441>; from CUT DOWN <1438>]: one who cuts ▶ **An Israelite of the tribe of Benjamin.** Refs.: Num. 1:11; 2:22; 7:60, 65; 10:24. ¶

GIDOM – ***giḏʿōm*** [proper noun: גִּדְעֹם <1440>; from CUT DOWN <1438>]: extermination, desolation ▶ **A town apparently belonging to the tribe of Benjamin between Gibeah and the rock of Rimmon.** Ref.: Judg. 20:45. ¶

GIER EAGLE – Lev. 11:18; Deut. 14:17 → CARRION VULTURE <7360>.

GIFT – [1] ***'eškār*** [masc. noun: אֶשְׁכָּר <814>; from WAGES <7939>] ▶ **The word refers to valuable presents brought to Solomon from the kings of Sheba and Seba.** Ref.: Ps. 72:10. These items are also designated as payment(s) from Rhodes or Dedan to Tyre (Ezek. 27:15); the word is also translated present. ¶

[2] ***zeḇeḏ, zêḇeḏ*** [masc. noun: זֶבֶד, זֵבֶד <2065>; from ENDOW <2064>] ▶ **This word means and is also translated endowment, dowry.** In context it stands for the child given to Leah (Gen. 30:20). ¶

[3] ***minḥāh*** [fem. noun: מִנְחָה <4503>; from an unused root meaning to apportion, i.e., to bestow] ▶ **This word means a present, a tribute, an offering.** It is used to signify a gift as in the peace gifts that Jacob presented to Esau (Gen. 32:13). Secondly, it signifies a tribute. An example of the use of this word is Judges 3:15, where Ehud was sent from Israel to Moab on the pretense of bringing a tribute. Perhaps the most frequent use of this word is to denote a grain offering. Grain offerings were brought on pans, suggesting cakes (Lev. 2:5) and mixed with oil and other substances (Num. 6:15). *

[4] ***maś'êṯ*** [fem. noun: מַשְׂאֵת <4864>; from CARRY <5375>] ▶ **This word means an uprising, an utterance, a burden, a portion, a tribute, a reward.** The main use connotes something that rises or is lifted up, such as smoke in a smoke signal (Judg. 20:38: cloud, flame); or hands in a sacrifice of praise (Ps. 141:2: lifting up). Figuratively, a reproach could be lifted up as a burden (Zeph. 3:18: burden). This word can also depict a portion or a gift that is carried to someone, often from the table of nobility. For example, David sent a gift of food to Uriah's house (2 Sam. 11:8; also translated present); as part of the feast honoring Queen Esther, the king sent gifts to his subjects (Esther 2:18). *

[5] ***mattān*** [masc. noun: מַתָּן <4976>; from GIVE <5414>] ▶ **This word indicates what is given, a present.** Refs.: Gen. 34:12; Num. 18:11; Prov. 18:16; 19:6; 21:14. Gifts could be a means of attaining favor or of creating problems (Prov. 18:16; 19:6; 21:14). ¶

[6] ***mattᵉnāh*** [Aramaic fem. noun: מַתְּנָה <4978>; corresponding to <4979> below] ▶ **This word indicates what is given, a present.** Refs.: Dan. 2:6, 48; 5:17. It has the sense of a reward in context. ¶

[7] ***mattānāh*** [fem. noun: מַתָּנָה <4979>; from <4976> above] ▶ **This word refers to what is given for various reasons: compensation, offerings, bribe, etc.** As compensation or for support (Gen. 25:6; Esther 9:22; Ezek. 46:16, 17); as offerings, gifts, to the Lord (Ex. 28:38; Lev. 23:38; Num. 18:29; Ps. 68:18). Persons in Israel gave as they were able (Deut. 16:7). The Levites were called the Lord's gift to the priesthood (Num. 18:6, 7). This word has the sense of a bribe in the wisdom literature (Prov. 15:27; Eccl. 7:7). *

[8] ***mattaṯ, mattāṯ*** [fem. noun: מַתַּת, מַתָּת <4991>; from <4976> above abbreviated] ▶ **This word depicts what is given,**

a present. In some contexts, it has the sense of a reward or a gift of thanks (1 Kgs. 13:7). Usually, it indicates a gift only (Prov. 25:14); but it can be God's gifts of food, drink, and work (Eccl. 3:13; 5:19). The phrase *mattan yaḏ* means as much as is at hand or as much as a person can give (Ezek. 46:5, 11). ¶
9 ***nêḏeh*** [masc. noun: נֵדֶה <5078>; from DRIVE <5077> in the sense of freely flinging] ▶ **This word refers to something given for a favor or a bribe; or to attract a person to do something.** Ref.: Ezek. 16:33a. ¶
10 ***nāḏān*** [masc. noun: נָדָן <5083>; prob. from an unused root meaning to give] ▶ **In context this word refers to something given for sexual favors, but in a spiritual, religious sense.** It is a form of bribery (Ezek. 16:33; NKJV: payment). ¶
11 ***niśśê'ṯ*** [נִשֵּׂאת <5379>; pass. part. fem. of CARRY <5375>] ▶ **It refers to something given to persons freely, in context in the sense of political gifts or benefits.** Ref.: 2 Sam. 19:42. ¶
12 ***šay*** [masc. noun: שַׁי <7862>; prob. from LIKE (BE) <7737> b. (in the sense of to place, to grant)] ▶ **This word means and is also translated present, tribute.** It refers to something given freely to show friendship, appreciation, support, recognition, in this case because of the splendor of the Temple in Jerusalem (Ps. 68:29). Gifts may be given because of reverence to a person or holy fear (Ps. 76:11); or as an act of worship or homage (Is. 18:7). ¶
13 ***šalmon*** [masc. noun: שַׁלְמֹן <8021>; from COMPLETED (BE) <7999>] ▶ **This word is used only in its plural form of *šalmōniym*. It is not used to describe simple gifts or presents given out of goodwill but those given as bribes to try to sway persons in authority to do what the giver wants them to do.** Ref.: Is. 1:23; also translated reward. These bribes are accepted only by corrupt people and end up corrupting people even further. Those who are totally corrupt even seek out bribes. Along with these bribes went the idea of a lack of justice and righteousness as a result of God's will not being done in those matters. ¶
– 14 1 Sam. 9:7 ➔ PRESENT (noun) <8670>.

GIFT (MAKE A) – Job 6:22 ➔ REWARD (GIVE A) <7809>.

GIHON – ***giyḥôn*** [proper noun: גִּיחוֹן <1521>; from GUSH <1518>]: stream ▶
a. A river that flowed through Eden and on through the land of Cush. Ref.: Gen. 2:13. It possibly was located in southern Mesopotamia in antiquity. ¶
b. A spring on the eastern side of Mount Zion in the Kidron Valley. As Hezekiah anticipated the Assyrian army, he directed its water into the Pool of Siloam (2 Chr. 32:30) within the city. Other refs.: 1 Kgs. 1:33, 38, 45; 2 Chr. 33:14. ¶

GILALAI – ***gil^{a}lay*** [masc. proper noun: גִּלֲלַי <1562>; from DUNG <1561>]: dungy ▶ **An Israelite of the tribe of Levi.** Ref.: Neh. 12:36. ¶

GILBOA – ***gilbōa'*** [proper noun: גִּלְבֹּעַ <1533>; from WAVE <1530> and BOIL (verb) <1158>]: springing fountain, bubbling fountain ▶ **A mountain range located east of the Valley of Jezreel.** Ref.: 1 Sam. 28:4. Saul and his three sons were slain there by the Philistines (1 Sam. 31:8–10). It was in the territory of Issachar (2 Sam. 1:21). *

GILEAD – ***gil'āḏ*** [proper noun: גִּלְעָד <1568>; prob. from GALEED <1567>]: hill of testimony ▶
a. A term used generally to refer to a mountainous, rugged area east of the Jordan and south of the Yarmuk River. At times it reached as far south as the northern tip of the Dead Sea. In some cases, it is spoken of as if it extended south to the Arnon River. It reached eastward to the eastern desert area. Basham was to the north of it; the Jabbok River is in its central area. The tribe of Gad lived in its central territory; Manasseh (N) and Reuben (S) touched it on the north/south respectfully. The name Gilead could apply to all of the Transjordanian territory (Deut. 2:36; 34:1; Judg. 10:4–18; 11:5–29; 12:4–7; 20:1; Jer. 50:19). Each reference to Gilead must be studied in context to discern exactly what

area is being referred to. It was a place of great abundance and prosperity (Song 4:1; 6:5; Jer. 22:6; Zech. 10:10). The term "balm of Gilead" expressed its healthy and proverbial luxury and wealth (Jer. 8:22; 46:11). It was, at times, a place where rebellions and wars were rampant (1 Kgs. 22:1–4; 2 Kgs. 8:28). In the narrowest use of the word, it refers to a city (Hos. 6:8). *

b. It refers to a mountain west of the Jordan River. Ref.: Judg. 7:3. Some suggest the reference may be to Mount Gilboa. ¶

c. The name of Manasseh's grandson and son of Machir. Ref.: Num. 26:29, 30. He fathered the Gileadites (Josh. 17:1–6). The heads of this clan demanded a ruling about the inheritance laws for families that had daughters but no sons. *

d. The father of Jephthah, one of Israel's judges. Ref.: Judg. 11:1, 2. His mother was a prostitute. ¶

e. It refers to Gilead, a Gadite chief, who was the son of Michael. Ref.: 1 Chr. 5:14. ¶

GILEADITES – ***gil'ādiy*** [masc. proper noun: גִּלְעָדִי <1569>; patron. from GILEAD <1568>] ▶

a. A branch of the Manassites. Ref.: Num. 26:29. ¶

b. The inhabitants of Gilead. Refs.: Num. 26:29; Judg. 10:3; 11:1, 40; 12:7; 2 Sam. 17:27; 19:31; 1 Kgs. 2:7; 2 Kgs. 15:25; Ezra 2:61; Neh. 7:63. ¶

GILGAL – ***gilgāl*** [proper noun: גִּלְגָּל <1537>; the same as WHEEL <1536>]: wheel, rolling ▶

a. The place where Israel camped on entering Canaan. Refs.: Josh. 4; 5; 9; 10; 14. The name means circle or rolling (cf. Josh. 5:9). It was an important religious center for Israel during the times of Samuel and Saul (1 Sam. 7; 10; 11; 13; 15). Twelve stones were set up there for the twelve tribes (Josh. 4:20). A great ceremony of circumcision was celebrated there, as was a great Passover feast (Josh. 5:9, 10). It is mentioned 35 times in the Old Testament. It was a place condemned by the prophets for it fostered false worship of the Lord as did Bethel (Hos. 4:15; 9:15; Amos 4:4; 5:5). Jeroboam I had built golden calves at Gilgal and Bethel. Its exact location is uncertain, but it was possibly northeast of Jericho. *

b. The name of a city ruled by a king named Goyim. Ref.: Josh. 12:23. Its location is uncertain. ¶

c. Another city northeast of Judah, about 8 miles east of Jerusalem. Ref.: cf. Josh. 18:7. ¶

d. A city through which both Elijah and Elisha passed. Refs.: 2 Kgs. 2:1; 4:38. Its location is unknown. Elijah was shortly thereafter taken up to heaven. A famine occurred there in Elisha's day. ¶

e. A city near to Jerusalem in the time of Nehemiah. Ref.: Neh. 12:29. ¶

GILOH – ***gilōh*** [proper noun: גִּלֹה <1542>; from BRING OVER <1540> (in the sense of carrying away into exile)]: exile ▶ **City in the hill country that was given to the tribe of Judah as an inheritance.** Refs.: Josh. 15:51; 2 Sam. 15:12. ¶

GILONITE – ***giylōniy*** [masc. proper noun: גִּילֹנִי <1526>; patrial from GILOH <1542>] ▶ **Ahithophel the Gilonite was a counselor of David.** Refs.: 2 Sam. 15:12; 23:34. ¶

GIMZO – ***gimzô*** [proper noun: גִּמְזוֹ <1579>; of uncertain deriv.]: fertile in sycamores ▶ **A city in Judah which was invaded by the Philistines.** Ref.: 2 Chr. 28:18. ¶

GINATH – ***giynaṯ*** [proper noun: גִּינַת <1527>; of uncertain deriv.]: protection ▶ **Father of Tibni who followed half of the people of Israel.** Refs.: 1 Kgs. 16:21, 22. ¶

GINNETHON – ***ginnᵉṯôy, ginnᵉṯôn*** [masc. proper noun: גִּנְּתוֹן ,גִּנְּתוֹי <1599>; from DEFEND <1598>]: gardener ▶ **An Israelite priest who, with Nehemiah and others, sealed a pact of fidelity to the Lord.** Refs.: Neh. 10:6; 12:4, 16. ¶

GIRD – 1 ***'āzar*** [verb: אָזַר <247>; a prim. root] ▶ **This word means to fasten something on, to arm, to bind.** The soldier must put on his armor and gird up for battle (Jer. 1:17; also translated to prepare, to dress, to get ready). Elijah bound his leather girdle on his loins (2 Kgs. 1:8; also translated to wear). In his distress, Job asserts that his garment binds him (Job 30:18). The word is used metaphorically to describe the girding on of strength. The Lord is said to be girded with strength and might (Ps. 65:6; also translated to cloth, to arm), and He girds up the great Persian king to do His will (Is. 45:5: also translated to equip, to strengthen). Persons can gird themselves (Is. 8:9; also translated to strap on the armor, to prepare for battle) literally or figuratively. *

[2] ***'āpaḏ*** [verb: אָפַד <640>; a prim. root (rather a denom. from EPHOD (garment) <646>)] ▶ **This word indicates the fastening or tight wrapping of a band around a person; it is also translated to fasten, to bind, to tie**. Refs.: Ex. 29:5; Lev. 8:7. In these references, it indicates that the ephod would be firmly fastened to the high priest. ¶

GIRD ONESELF – ***ḥāgar*** [verb: חָגַר <2296>; a prim. root] ▶ **To gird oneself indicates to bind on one's person in preparation for a number of things.** To prepare for a journey (2 Kgs. 4:29); to prepare for war (1 Sam. 17:39) or violence (Judg. 3:16); to be capable of military service (2 Kgs. 3:21); lit., to put on a belt or to gird oneself with a belt or girdle for battle (1 Kgs. 20:11); to prepare for priestly service by girding on the priestly sash (Ex. 29:9). Other persons were girded accordingly: the priest, e.g., with an ephod (1 Sam. 2:18); or the petitioner or mourner in sackcloth (1 Kgs. 20:32; Is. 32:11; Joel 1:8). It is used symbolically of a king girding on his sword to gain victory for his people (Ps. 45:3) as he, ideally, rides forth girded in righteousness (Is. 11:5). The divine being of Daniel's vision wears a belt of pure gold (Dan. 10:5). The wise wife of Proverbs girds herself with strength (Prov. 31:17); and even the hills put on rejoicing as a belt when God blesses them (Ps. 65:12). *

GIRD UP – ***šānas*** [verb: שָׁנַס <8151>; a prim. root] ▶ **This word is used figuratively in the phrase "girded up his loins" to indicate preparing to run a race, readying oneself.** Ref.: 1 Kgs. 18:46. It would have involved, in Elijah's case, holding up or tucking in his cloak so that he could run speedily. ¶

GIRDED – ***ḥāgôr, ḥ*ᵃ*gôr*** [adj. and masc. noun: חָגוֹר, חֲגוֹר <2289>; from GIRD ONESELF <2296>] ▶

a. An adjective meaning wearing around. It was an impressive but arrogant and prideful feature of the loin section of a Babylonian officer's uniform (Ezek. 23:15; also translated wearing) that lured Israel to adulate them. ¶

b. A masculine noun indicating a sash, a belt, or a girdle. It was part of a military officer's uniform (1 Sam. 18:4; 2 Sam. 20:8). Other ref.: Prov. 31:24. ¶

GIRDING – ***maḥ*ᵃ*gōreṯ*** [fem. noun: מַחֲגֹרֶת <4228>; from GIRD ONESELF <2296>] ▶ **This word refers to a wrapping.** It refers to the putting on and wearing of sackcloth (Is. 3:24; also translated donning, skirt), a sign of grave mourning. ¶

GIRDLE – [1] Ex. 28:27, 28; etc. ➔ curious girdle ➔ BAND (noun) <2805> [2] Ex. 28:40; 29:9; Lev. 8:13; Is. 22:21 ➔ SASH <73> [3] 1 Sam. 18:4; 2 Sam. 20:8; Prov. 31:24 ➔ GIRDED <2289> b. [4] 2 Sam. 18:11; 1 Kgs. 2:5; Is. 3:24 ➔ BELT <2290> [5] 2 Kgs. 1:8; Jer. 13:1, 2, 4; Ezek. 23:15; etc. ➔ BELT <232> [6] Ps. 109:19 ➔ BELT <4206>.

GIRGASHITE, GIRGASITE – ***girgāšiy*** [masc. proper noun: גִּרְגָּשִׁי <1622>; patrial from an unused name (of uncertain deriv.)]: who dwells in clayey soil ▶ **One of the seven tribes in the land of Canaan of which the territory was given to Israel.** Refs.: Gen. 10:16; 15:21; Deut. 7:1; Josh. 3:10; 24:11; 1 Chr. 1:14; Neh. 9:8. ¶

GIRL – [1] ***yaldāh*** [fem. noun: יַלְדָּה <3207>; fem. of CHILD <3206>] ▶ **This word means a female child, and also a young woman.** It refers also to a marriageable young girl (Gen. 34:4; KJV: damsel) or one who becomes a slave or is sold into harlotry (Joel 3:3). Girls playing in the streets were a sign of joy in God's restored Zion (Zech. 8:5). ¶

[2] ***naʿărāh*** [fem. noun: נַעֲרָה <5291>; fem. of BOY <5288>] ▶ **This word also refers to a young woman, a maidservant.** It is used of a young girl (2 Kgs. 5:2); or young daughters (Job 41:5). It indicates a young girl who is marriageable (Gen. 24:14, 16, 28, 55, 57; Ex. 2:5; Prov. 9:3); and to those attending her (Gen. 24:61). It points out a virgin (Deut. 22:15, 16, 23, 29; Judg. 21:12; 1 Kgs. 1:2). It is used figuratively of the maidservants or attendants of wisdom personified (Prov. 9:3). It describes young female gleaners in the fields (Ruth 2:5, 8, 22, 23). *

– [3] Ex. 2:8 ➔ YOUNG WOMAN <5959> [4] Judg. 5:30 ➔ WOMB <7361>.

GIRZITES – ***gizriy*** [masc. proper noun: גִּזְרִי <1511>; patrial from Gezer <1507>] ▶ **David made a raid upon the Girzites.** Ref.: 1 Sam. 27:8; also translated Gezrites. See also GEZER. ¶

GISHPA, GISPA – ***gišpā'*** [masc. proper noun: גִּשְׁפָּא <1658>; of uncertain deriv.] ▶ **An Israelite who was in charge of the Temple servants in the time of Nehemiah.** Ref.: Neh. 11:21. ¶

GITTAIM – ***gittayim*** [proper noun: גִּתַּיִם <1664>; dual of WINEPRESS <1660>]: two winepresses ▶ **A region or a city of Benjamin.** Refs.: 2 Sam. 4:3; Neh. 11:33. ¶

GITTITE – ***gittiy*** [masc. proper noun: גִּתִּי <1663>; patrial from GATH <1661>] ▶ **A native or inhabitant of Gath.** Refs.: Josh. 13:3; 2 Sam. 6:10, 11; 15:18, 19, 22; 18:2; 21:19; 1 Chr. 13:13; 20:5. ¶

GITTITH – ***gittiyṯ*** [fem. noun: גִּתִּית <1665>; fem. of GITTITE <1663>] ▶ **A musical instrument or tune. It occurs in the titles or superscriptions to three psalms.** Refs.: Ps. 8; 81; 84. Some translations note that the word may refer to a musical or liturgical term (cf. NIV, ESV). ¶

GIVE – [1] ***yāhaḇ, haḇ*** [verb: יָהַב, הַב <3051>; a prim. root] ▶ **Verbs indicating to present or deliver something; to come, to pay attention.** The basic form of this verb is given as *yāhab* or *haḇ*, but its meaning and usage are not affected by this. It indicates the handing over or turning over of something to someone: one's wife (Gen. 29:21); a garment (Ruth 3:15); a price (Zech. 11:12). It takes on the meaning of give in its imperative form: to give lots; that is a decision from the Lord about what is to be done (1 Sam. 14:41). It means to set something or someone in a certain location (Deut. 1:13; 2 Sam. 11:15). It is used of attributing glory to the Lord (Ps. 29:1, 2) or greatness (Deut. 32:3). It has the idiomatic meaning of "Come, now!" in its imperative forms (*haḇ, hāḇāh*, Gen. 11:3; 38:16; Ex. 1:10).

[2] ***yᵉhaḇ*** [Aramaic verb: יְהַב <3052>; corresponding to <3051> above] ▶ **This word means to present or deliver something, to pay.** It is used of giving various things or of various things that are given in its possessive sense: gold and silver vessels are given to Sheshbazzar (Ezra 5:14; cf. Ezra 7:19), and materials for offerings are given (Ezra 6:9). God gave His disobedient people into the hands of Babylon (Ezra 5:12). It describes the laying of the Temple's foundation in Zerubbabel's day (Ezra 5:16) and the payment of money to cover the costs of building the Temple (Ezra 6:4, 8). The word also describes the Lord's impartations of wisdom to the wise (Dan. 2:21), especially to Daniel (Dan. 2:23). Various other items are given over: one's own body (Dan. 3:28); a change of disposition from human to beastly (Dan. 4:16); rewards (Dan. 5:17); kingship and its authority (Dan. 5:18). In a political and administrative setting, it refers to giving accountability to one's superiors (Dan. 6:2). In a legal sense, it is used of giving judgment (Dan. 7:22). It is used to depict the Lord's presentation of the sovereignty of the kingdom to the saints of the Most High God (Dan. 7:27). Most translators do not find this word in Numbers 21:14 but see WAHEB <2052> b. *

[3] ***nāthan*** [verb: נָתַן <5414>; a prim. root] ▶ **This word is used approximately**

two thousand times in the Old Testament; therefore, it is understandable that it should have a broad semantic range. However, it is possible to identify three general categories of semantic variation: **(1) To give**, whether it be the exchange of tangible property (Gen. 3:6; Ex. 5:18); the production of fruit (Ps. 1:3); the presentation of an offering to the Lord (Ex. 30:14); the passing on of knowledge and instruction (Prov. 9:9); the granting of permission (Gen. 20:6). Often, God provides either preservation (Lev. 26:4; Deut. 11:14, 15; Jer. 45:5); or plague (Ex. 9:23). **(2) This Hebrew word also means to put, to place, or something literally placed**: the luminaries in the sky (Gen. 1:17); God's bow in the clouds (Gen. 9:13); the ark on a cart (1 Sam. 6:8); the abomination in the Temple. It could also be something figuratively placed: an obstacle (Ezek. 3:20); God's Spirit (Is. 42:1); reproach (Jer. 23:40); curses (Deut. 30:7). **(3) The word can also mean to make or to constitute**, such as the prohibition against making incisions in one's flesh (Lev. 19:28); God making Abraham into a father of many nations (Gen. 17:5); or Solomon making silver as stones (1 Kgs. 10:27). *

[4] ***n^{e}ṯan*** [Aramaic verb: נְתַן <5415>; corresponding to <5414> above] ▶ **The basic meaning of this word, to give, is nuanced according to its context.** It means to pay tribute, taxes, etc. (Ezra 4:13); to furnish, supply, provide (Ezra 7:20); to get, permit, allow (Dan. 2:16); to bestow officially (Dan. 4:17, 25, 32). ¶

– [5] 2 Sam. 24:12 ➔ OFFER <5190> [6] Esther 9:19, 22 ➔ LAY, PUT <4916> a. [7] Eccl. 10:1 ➔ to give, to cause to give, to give off ➔ UTTER <5042>.

GIVE OVER – [1] ***sāḵar*** [verb: סָכַר <5534>; a prim. root] ▶ **This word means to surrender persons to someone or something, to deliver them for some purpose.** Ref.: Is. 19:4; also translated to give into, to hand over, to deliver. The Hebrew word also means to close, to shut up; see CLOSE <5534>. ¶

– [2] Ps. 63:10; Jer. 18:21; Ezek. 35:5 ➔ SPILL <5064>.

GIVE UP – [1] 1 Sam. 27:1 ➔ DESPAIR (verb) <2976> [2] Eccl. 3:6 ➔ PERISH <6> [3] Hos. 11:8 ➔ DELIVER <4042>.

GIVE WAY – Nah. 2:10 ➔ SMITE TOGETHER <6375>.

GIVE WILLINGLY – ***nāḏaḇ*** [verb: נָדַב <5068>; a prim. root] ▶ **This word described the free, voluntary desire of the heart to offer oneself or of one's resources to the service of the Lord.** It was used to describe the willing contributions that the people of Israel made to build the Tabernacle (Ex. 25:2; 35:21, 29); Solomon's Temple (1 Chr. 29:5, 6, 9, 14, 17); and Zerubbabel's Temple (Ezra 1:6; 2:68; 3:5). In a few other instances, it spoke of the willing sacrifice of service that Amaziah made (2 Chr. 17:16); the returning exiles made (Neh. 11:2); and Deborah commended (Judg. 5:2, 9). See the related noun *n^{e}ḏāḇāh* (FREEWILL OFFERING <5071>). ¶

GIZONITE – ***gizôniy*** [masc. proper noun: גִּזוֹנִי <1493>; patrial from the unused name of an otherwise unknown person or place] ▶ **A word qualifying Hashem who was one of David's mighty men.** Ref.: 1 Chr. 11:34. ¶

GLAD (BE) – [1] ***ṭ^{e}'ēḇ*** [Aramaic verb: טְאֵב <2868>; a prim. root] ▶ **This word describes an appreciative and joyful response at the outcome of an event.** This was the case of Daniel's preservation from a violent death (Dan. 6:23; also translated to be pleased). ¶

– [2] Prov. 24:17; Is. 9:3; 65:19 ➔ REJOICE <1523>.

GLAD (MAKE) – Ps. 21:6 ➔ REJOICE <2302>.

GLADNESS – [1] 1 Chr. 16:27 ➔ JOY <2304> [2] Ps. 65:12 ➔ JOY <1524>.

GLASS – Job 28:17 ➔ CRYSTAL <2137>.

GLEAN – ***lāqaš*** [verb: לָקַשׁ <3953>; a prim. root] ▶ **A Hebrew word of uncertain**

meaning, translated as to despoil, to take everything, to glean. Its only occurrence is in Job 24:6 (KJV: to gather). It is most likely the denominative verb of the noun *leqeš* (CROP <3954>), meaning spring crop or aftergrowth. ¶

GLEANING – [1] ***leqeṭ*** [masc. noun: לֶקֶט <3951>; from GATHER <3950>] ▶ **This word refers to the gatherings of a harvest, usually applied to the produce remaining in a field after the initial harvest.** Refs.: Lev. 19:9; 23:22. ¶
[2] ***'ōlēlôṯ*** [fem. plur. noun: עֹלֵלוֹת <5955>; fem. act. part. of DO <5953>] ▶ **This word indicates produce and things left over after a major harvest has taken place.** Ref.: Obad. 1:5. It refers to picking the leftovers of the grape harvest as well as other harvests (Judg. 8:2). It is used figuratively of the gleanings of persons and houses left in a city after God has gone over it in judgments (Is. 17:6). It is used of the grape pickers in Micah 7:1, fruit gatherers. Other refs.: Is. 24:13; Jer. 49:9. ¶

GLEDE – [1] Deut. 14:13 ➔ KITE <1676> [2] Deut. 14:13 ➔ RED KITE <7201>.

GLEN – Zech. 1:8 ➔ RAVINE <4699>.

GLIDING – Job 26:13 ➔ FLEEING <1281>.

GLISTEN – Ps. 104:15 ➔ SHINE <6670>.

GLISTENING – [1] 1 Chr. 29:2; Is. 54:11 ➔ ANTIMONY <6320> [2] Ps. 68:13 ➔ GREENISH <3422>.

GLITTERING – Job 39:23 ➔ FLAME <3851>.

GLOATING – Hab. 3:14 ➔ REJOICING <5951>.

GLOBE – 1 Kgs. 7:41, 42 ➔ BOWL <1543>.

GLOOM – [1] ***mû'āp̱*** [masc. noun: מוּעָף <4155>; from FLY <5774> (in the sense of something disappearing)] ▶ **This word means darkness. It indicates an absence of light or brightness and pictures a dismal condition.** It is used figuratively of the dimmed understanding of peoples (Is. 9:1; KJV: dimness). ¶
– [2] Is. 8:22 ➔ DIMNESS <4588> [3] Amos 5:20 ➔ DARK <651>.

GLORIFY – ***pā'ar*** [verb: פָּאַר <6286>; a prim. root] ▶ **In the factitive form, God brings beauty and glory to His chosen people (Ps. 149:4; Is. 55:5; 60:9); and to His Temple (Ezra 7:27; Is. 60:7). In the reflexive form, one beautifies and exalts one's self and not others.** Gideon is instructed to reduce the number of men in his army so the Israelites could not give themselves the glory for the victory that was to come (Judg. 7:2). In God's judgment against Assyria—a country that was merely an instrument in God's hand—Isaiah rhetorically asked whether the ax and the saw could take credit for the work accomplished through them (Is. 10:15). Obviously, the answer is no. In the same way, people should not take glory in what God is doing through their lives. In several passages, Isaiah also states that God brings glory to Himself by His actions through His people (Is. 44:23; 49:3; 60:21; 61:3). Other refs.: Ex. 8:9; Deut. 24:20; Is. 60:13. ¶

GLORIOUS – [1] **to be glorious: *'āḏar*** [verb: אָדַר <142>; a prim. root] ▶ **A verb meaning to magnify, glorify, or, in the passive sense, to be magnified.** Whereas the Hebrew noun *kāḇôḏ* (GLORY <3519>) pictures glory in terms of weight, this word pictures it in terms of size. The Hebrew word is used only three times in the Old Testament: to celebrate God's power and holiness after the deliverance of Israel from Egypt (Ex. 15:6, 11; also translated majestic); and to describe the Law given on Sinai as great and glorious (Is. 42:21; also translated honorable, honourable). ¶
[2] ***kāḇôḏ, kᵉḇûddāh*** [כָּבוֹד, כְּבוּדָּה <3520>; irregular pass. part. of HEAVY (BE) <3513> (in the sense of expressing the idea of enjoying honor or glory)] ▶
a. An adjective used in context to refer to the splendor of the king's daughter (Ps.

45:13). It includes her royal attire as well as a beautiful couch (Ezek. 23:41: stately, splendid, elegant). ¶
b. A feminine noun indicating abundance, possessions, riches. It is used as a collective noun referring to a group of valuables (Judg. 18:21: goods, valuables, possessions, carriage). ¶
– [3] Zech. 11:2 ➔ MIGHTY <117>.

GLORIOUS (BE) – Is. 63:1 ➔ HONOR (verb) <1921>.

GLORIOUS THINGS – Is. 12:5 ➔ MAJESTY <1348>.

GLORY – [1] ***heḏer*** [masc. noun: הֶדֶר <1925>; from HONOR (verb) <1921>] ▶ **This word means splendor, ornament.** It is used once in Daniel, where it speaks of the splendor of the kingdom (Dan. 11:20). This word is difficult to translate. It has been translated "the glory of the kingdom" (KJV), "royal splendor" (NIV), or a particular place, such as "the Jewel [the heart or gem] of his kingdom" (NASB). ¶
[2] ***hāḏār*** [masc. noun: הָדָר <1926>; from HONOR (verb) <1921>] ▶ **This word means splendor, majesty.** It describes the impressive character of God in 1 Chronicles 16:27 and His thunderous voice in Psalm 29:4. Isaiah describes sinners fleeing from the *hāḏār* of the Lord (Is. 2:10, 19). Often the Psalms use this word in conjunction with others to describe God's glory, splendor, and majesty (Ps. 96:6; 145:5). It also refers to the majesty of kings (Ps. 21:5; 45:3). Psalm 8:5 expresses the splendor of God's creation of humans in comparison to the rest of creation. In Isaiah's prophetic description of the Suffering Servant, he uses *hāḏār* to say that the Servant will have no splendor to attract people to Him (Is. 53:2). *
[3] ***hᵃḏārāh*** [fem. noun: הֲדָרָה <1927>; fem. of <1926> above] ▶ **In four of the five occurrences of this word, it occurs in the context of worshiping the Lord, "the beauty (*hᵃḏārāh*) of holiness" (KJV).** Refs.: 1 Chr. 16:29; 2 Chr. 20:21; Ps. 29:2; 96:9. The word also expresses the glory kings find in a multitude of people (Prov. 14:28). ¶
[4] ***kāḇôḏ, kāḇōḏ*** [masc. sing. noun.: כָּבוֹד, כָּבֹד <3519>; from HEAVY (BE) <3513> (in the pass. form, expressing the idea of enjoying honor or glory)] ▶ **This word means honor, majesty, wealth.** It is commonly used of God (Ex. 33:18; Ps. 72:19; Is. 3:8; Ezek. 1:28); humans (Gen. 45:13; Job 19:9; Ps. 8:5; 21:5); and objects (1 Sam. 2:8; Esther 1:4; Is. 10:18), particularly of the ark of the covenant (1 Sam. 4:21–22). *
[5] ***ṣᵉḇiy*** [masc. noun: צְבִי <6643>; from SWELL <6638> in the sense of prominence] ▶ **This word has essentially two meanings: something beautiful and a gazelle.** The first meaning describes something that is beautiful or glorious, such as the glorious land which God gave Israel that flowed with milk and honey (Ezek. 20:6, 15); or the beautiful flower of Ephraim (Is. 28:1). This word was normally used to depict the glory of a nation: Israel (2 Sam. 1:19); Babylon (Is. 13:19); Tyre (Is. 23:9); Ephraim (Is. 28:1, 4); a city (Ezek. 25:9); a mountain (Dan. 11:45); or a land in general (Dan. 8:9; 11:16, 41). In a few instances, it speaks of the Lord Himself (Is. 4:2; Is. 28:5). The second meaning of this word is a gazelle, which is described in the dietary laws of the Old Testament (Deut. 12:15, 22); used to describe the speed of a runner (2 Sam. 2:18; 1 Chr. 12:8; Prov. 6:5); and compared to a lover (Song 2:9, 17; 8:14). *
– [6] Ps. 89:44 ➔ CLEARNESS <2892> [7] Dan. 2:37; 4:30, 36; 5:18, 20; 7:14 ➔ HONOR (noun) <3367> [8] Zech. 11:3 ➔ GARMENT <155>.

GLOW (noun) – Is. 4:5 ➔ BRIGHTNESS <5051>.

GLOW (verb) – Ezek. 24:11 ➔ BURN (verb) <2787>.

GLOWING EMBERS – Ps. 102:3 ➔ HEARTH <4168>.

GLOWING WITH HEALTH – 1 Sam. 16:12; 17:42 ➔ RED <132>.

GLUTTON (BE) – ***zālal*** [verb: זָלַל <2151>; a prim. root (comp. LAVISH <2107>)] ▶

a. This word means to be greedy, also to be vile, frivolous, worthless; to despise. It describes an especially serious corruption of character in a worthless, gluttonous son (Deut. 21:20), closely akin to one who drinks too much (Prov. 23:20, 21). A good son avoids company with this vile, gluttonous person (Prov. 28:7; also translated to be riotous). It is the opposite of what is useful, valuable, and precious (Jer. 15:19: vile, worthless). It means to hold up to disdain, to despise (Lam. 1:8: to become vile, unclean, filthy; to be removed). ¶
b. This Hebrew word means and is translated to quake, to shake, to tremble. It refers poetically to the response of the mountains to God's descent upon them (Is. 64:1, 3; KJV, to flow down). ¶

GNASH – ***ḥāraq*** [verb: חָרַק <2786>; a prim. root] ▶ **This word indicates to grind the teeth at.** It is used figuratively of persons grinding or striking their teeth at someone in anger (Ps. 35:16; 37:12). The wicked gnash their teeth in despair at the success of the one who fears God (Ps. 112:10). Job complains that God has gnashed His teeth at him in his suffering (Job 16:9). The enemies responsible for the fall of Jerusalem, Zion, grind their teeth in disrespect at the Lord's city (Lam. 2:16). ¶

GNAT – ***kēn*** [masc. noun: כֵּן <3654>; from SHOOT UP <3861> in the sense of fastening] ▶ **This word means a small biting insect; it is also translated lice, fly.** It is used of the gnats or lice referred to in the third plague (Ex. 8:16–18; Ps. 105:31). Some translators find the word in Isaiah 51:6 (like flies, like gnats), but others prefer to read "in like manner." A few translators render the word as flies, a less likely translation. ¶

GNAW – Ezek. 23:34 ➔ BREAK <1633> a.

GNAW, GNAWING – ***'āraq*** [verb and masc. noun: עָרַק <6207>; a prim. root] ▶
a. A verb meaning to nibble, to chew on something incessantly to get food from it. Ref.: Job 30:3. It is used figuratively of pains that weaken, tear away at a person (Job 30:17).
b. A verb meaning to flee, to roam. A verb meaning to wander about aimlessly. It is used of outcasts of society wandering about searching for food (Job 30:3).
c. A masculine noun indicating that which is chewed; sinews. It refers to tendons or muscular power, strength, or a person's strength in spirit and soul. Job's strength was continually being worn away by his suffering (Job 30:17). ¶

GNAWING – Job 30:17 ➔ GNAW, GNAWING <6207> c.

GO – [1] ***'āzal*** [verb: אָזַל <235>; a prim. root] ▶ **This word means to disappear, to fail, to go away, to depart.** God helps His people when their strength is gone (Deut. 32:36). It describes food when it is all used up (1 Sam. 9:7; also translated to be spent). The word depicts the disappearance of water as it evaporates (Job 14:11; also translated to fail, to dry, to disappear) but also the simple departure of a person (Prov. 20:14). Other refs.: Jer. 2:36; Ezek. 27:19. ¶
[2] ***ᵃzal*** [Aramaic verb: אֲזַל <236>; the same as <235> above] ▶ **This word, meaning to depart, is found in the Aramaic portions of Ezra and Daniel.** It depicts persons traveling (Ezra 4:23; 5:8, 15) and describes persons walking from one place to another (Dan. 2:17, 24; 6:18, 19). ¶
[3] ***hûḵ*** [Aramaic verb: הוּךְ <1946>; corresponding to <1981> below] ▶ **This word, used causatively, refers to the coming, bringing or arrival of things and people.** Of a report (Ezra 5:5; also translated to come, to reach); to the taking of vessels to the Temple (Ezra 6:5; also translated to take back, to bring, to bring back); and to people going to Jerusalem (Ezra 7:13). ¶
[4] ***hālaḵ*** [verb: הָלַךְ <1980>; a prim. root (akin to <3212> below)] ▶ **This word means to move, to depart, to come, to walk. It carries with it the basic idea of movement.** The flowing of a river (Gen. 2:14); the descending of floods (Gen. 8:3); the crawling of beasts (Lev. 11:27); the slithering of snakes (Lev. 11:42); the blowing of

the wind (Eccl. 1:6); the tossing of the sea (Jon. 1:13). Since it is usually a person who is moving, it is frequently translated "walk" (Gen. 48:15; 2 Sam. 15:30). Like a similar verb *dāraḵ* (TREAD <1869>), this word is also used metaphorically to speak of the pathways (i.e., behavior) of one's life. A son could walk in (i.e., follow after) the ways of his father (2 Chr. 17:3) or not (1 Sam. 8:3). Israel was commanded to walk in the ways of the Lord (Deut. 28:9), but they often walked after other gods (2 Kgs. 13:11). *

5 ***hᵃlaḵ*** [Aramaic verb: הֲלַךְ <1981>; corresponding to <1980> above (comp. <1946> above)] ► **This verb means to walk, to travel, to journey.** It means simply to go, to journey (Ezra 7:13). It describes things brought or delivered to a location or person (Ezra 5:5; 6:5). It depicts a person walking about (Dan. 3:25; 4:29, 4:37). ¶

6 ***yālaḵ*** [verb: יָלַךְ <3212>; a prim. root (comp. <1980> above] ► **For this Hebrew word, see the discussion under <1980> above.**

– 7 Gen. 12:8 → MOVE <6275> 8 Is. 57:9 → JOURNEY (verb) <7788> 9 Mic. 4:10 → GUSH <1518> 10 See COME <935>.

GO (LET) – 1 ***pāra'*** [verb: פָּרַע <6544>; a prim. root] ► **This word means to let loose, to unbind.** Moses saw that Aaron had let the Israelites get out of hand when Moses was up on the mountain (Ex. 32:25). This word can also apply to hair, as with those who were commanded not to let their hair down from their turbans. This warning was given to Aaron concerning mourning (Lev. 10:6); and to high priests in general (Lev. 21:10). However, lepers were to let their hair down to call attention to their condition (Lev. 13:45). A possible unfaithful wife had her hair loosened by the priest in connection with the drinking of bitter water to see if she was guilty (Num. 5:18). This word can also mean to ignore (Prov. 1:25); to avoid (Prov. 4:15); or to lead (Judg. 5:2). *

– 2 Job 37:3 → LOOSE (LET) <8281>.

GO (TEACH TO) – Hos. 11:3 → WALK (TEACH TO) <8637>.

GO ABOUT – 1 ***šûṭ*** [verb: שׁוּט <7751>; a prim. root] ►

a. This word means to roam, to move to and fro, to wander. It has the sense of moving about here and there, to roam: hunting for something (Num. 11:8); to deliver a message throughout the land (2 Sam. 24:2, 8); or to find someone in city streets (Jer. 5:1). It is used of the scanning of an area with one's eyes, especially the Lord's eyes (2 Chr. 16:9; Zech. 4:10); of Satan's going about in the earth (Job 1:7; 2:2). It is used of sailors, mariners on a boat (Ezek. 27:8, 26); or of people going to and fro, searching out wisdom and knowledge (Dan. 12:4; Amos 8:12). Other ref.: Jer. 49:3. ¶

b. A verb meaning to row a boat. It is used in its participial form to indicate rowers (Ezek. 27:8, 26). ¶

– 2 Jer. 14:18 → MERCHANT <5503>.

GO DEEPER – Prov. 17:10 → BEND <5181>.

GO DOWN – 1 ***yāraḏ*** [verb: יָרַד <3381>; a prim. root] ► **This word means to descend. It is used of motion, either literally or figuratively, of someone or something coming down.** It is used figuratively of the Lord's coming down to observe something or to make an announcement, e.g., the Tower of Babel or the announcement of the Exodus (Gen. 11:5, 7; Ex. 3:8; 19:11, 18). It is used of people coming down from a mountain (Ex. 19:14); of birds descending from the air (Hos. 7:12), etc. It is used to describe valleys sinking (Ps. 104:8). A crown may "come down" as a sign of humility and falling from power (Jer. 13:17, 18). It is used figuratively of going down to Sheol (Gen. 37:35); or of breaking into, going down, apart, into tears (cf. Ps. 119:136; Is. 15:3). It depicts the falling or coming down of the pride of might (Ezek. 30:6). It describes fire from heaven or a pillar of fire coming down (Ex. 33:9; 2 Kgs. 1:10, 12, 14). It is used to depict the path of a boundary line descending down from one location to another (Josh. 16:3). *

– 2 Judg. 4:21 → GO THROUGH <6795> 3 Song 4:1; 6:5 → DESCEND <1570>.

GO ONE WAY OR THE OTHER – ***'āḥad*** [verb: אָחַד <258>; perhaps a prim. root] ▶ **This word, indicating to move in this direction or that, metaphorically describes the actions of the Lord's sword for destruction.** Ref.: Ezek. 21:16; also translated Swords at the ready!; Slash your sword; Show yourself sharp, go . . . ; Cut sharply. ¶

GO OUT – 1 ***yôṣē'ṯ, yāṣā'*** [יוֹצֵאת, יָצָא <3318>; a prim. root] ▶

a. A feminine noun meaning captivity. It is used of going forth from one's homeland into exile (Ps. 144:14). God's blessing on His people could prevent this from happening. ¶

b. A verb meaning basically to exit, to proceed, or to come in. It is used in many settings and contexts and is nuanced by those settings. It is used of the rising or coming forth of the sun or stars (Gen. 19:23; Neh. 4:21); of the birth and coming out of a child (Gen. 25:26); of the springing up of plants (1 Kgs. 4:33). It indicates general motion or movement, stepping forth for various purposes (1 Sam. 17:4; 2 Sam. 16:5); to set out (Ex. 17:9); to set out in a military sense (Deut. 20:1; 1 Sam. 8:20; 1 Chr. 5:18; Prov. 30:27). Of birds it is used with *šûḇ*, to return, to mean to fly back and forth or here and there (Gen. 8:7).

It has many figurative uses: "to come out from" (*yāṣā'* + *min*) means to be descended from (Gen. 10:14); to die is described as one's soul, life, going out, away (Gen. 35:18; Ezek. 26:18); to lack courage, to fail occurs when one's heart goes out (Gen. 42:28). The beginning of the year is described as the (old) year going out (Ex. 23:16); it is used of the effects of something wearing off (1 Sam. 25:37). It is used of manna "coming out of one's nose," meaning becoming sick over excessive eating of a food (Num. 11:20). It describes the removal of dross from a metal (Prov. 25:4), purifying it.

It has several nuanced meanings in different settings: to escape free (1 Sam. 14:41); to leave, to go away (Dan. 10:20). The removal of a scoffer causes a quarrel to cease, to go away (Prov. 22:10). It indicates the freeing of a slave (Lev. 25:25). The context in all its uses affects its meaning and translations. In its use as a causal stem verb, it takes on the idea of causing to go out, to go forth (Gen. 15:5; Josh. 2:3); to take away (Gen. 48:12); to lead an army (2 Sam. 5:2). Or it indicates bringing forth, producing plants from the ground (Gen. 1:12); a weapon by an iron worker or smith (Is. 54:16). Or it may, in the personal sphere, indicate bringing forth one's spirit or breath, indicating that a person makes his or her feelings known (Prov. 29:11), as is characteristic of a fool. It is used with the word justice to mean to bring forth or execute justice (Is. 42:1, 3). In its passive uses, it indicates that someone or something is led forth (Gen. 38:25; Ezek. 14:22; cf. Ezek. 38:22). *

– 2 Lev. 6:12, 13; 1 Sam. 3:3 ➔ QUENCH <3518> 3 Job 18:5, 6; Ps. 118:12; Prov. 13:9; 20:20 ➔ EXTINGUISH <1846> 4 Dan. 2:13, 14 ➔ TAKE OUT <5312>.

GO THROUGH – 1 ***ṣānaḥ*** [verb: צָנַח <6795>; a prim. root] ▶ **This word means to penetrate something and come out the other side.** Ref.: Judg. 4:21; also translated to go down, to fasten. The Hebrew word also means to get off, to dismount; see GET OFF <6795>. ¶

– 2 Ps. 48:13 ➔ CONSIDER <6448> 3 Is. 27:4 ➔ MARCH (verb) <6585>.

GO UP – 1 ***sālaq, s^e^lêq*** [verbs: סָלַק, סְלֵק <5559>; a prim. root] ▶

a. A verb meaning to climb up, used figuratively of going up to God's abode. Ref.: Ps. 139:8; also translated to ascend. ¶

b. An Aramaic verb meaning to travel up, to ascend; it is also translated to come up, to take up, to carry up. It is used of going up hill country, of ascending to Jerusalem from Persia, Babylon, etc. (Ezra 4:12); or to bring or carry something up (Dan. 3:22; 6:23). It describes what is coming up, growing, ascending (Dan. 7:3, 8, 20). It describes a person's thoughts ascending, i.e., focusing on something (Dan. 2:29). ¶

– 2 Ps. 139:8 ➔ ASCEND <5266>.

GO WITH, GO SOFTLY – ***dāḏāh*** [verb: דָּדָה <1718>; a doubtful root] ▶ **This word means to walk gently, to go along, to wander.** It describes the happy and joyous days of the psalmist as he led his group to the Temple to worship God (Ps. 42:4), using steps of delight and joy. On the other hand, it describes Hezekiah's anguished walk during his life in the bitterness of his soul (Is. 38:15). ¶

GOAD – [1] ***dorḇān, dorḇōn*** [masc. noun: דָּרְבָן, דָּרְבֹן <1861>; of uncertain deriv.] ▶ **It was an iron-tipped pole or a long stick used to drive cattle or oxen, an ox prod.** Ref.: 1 Sam. 13:21; NASB translates as hoes. It is also used figuratively of correctly chosen words used to stir up one's audience or students (Eccl. 12:11). ¶

[2] ***malmāḏ*** [masc. noun: מַלְמָד <4451>; from LEARN <3925> (in the sense of to teach)] ▶ **It was a farming tool, a prod, used to make an ox work more effectively.** Shamgar used it as a weapon (Judg. 3:31). ¶

GOAT – [1] ***'êz*** [Aramaic fem. noun: עֵז <5796>; corresponding to FEMALE GOAT <5795>] ▶ **A goat is a ruminant mammal related to the sheep. This word is used in the phrase he goats, male goats, *ṣ^e^p̱irê 'izzîn*. It refers to sacrificial goats at the Temple dedication ceremonies.** Ref.: Ezra 6:17. ¶

[2] ***'attûḏ*** [adv.: עַתּוּד <6260>; from READY (BE) <6257> (in the sense of something/someone prepared for a purpose)] ▶ **This word indicates a goat (a ruminant mammal related to the sheep), a male goat, a leader.** It refers to a strong animal of the flock, a ram, he goat (Gen. 31:10, 12). It is used figuratively, therefore, of a leader or people of strong character or position (Is. 14:9; Jer. 50:8; Ezek. 34:17; Zech. 10:3). It was used often in sacrifices (Num. 7:17, 23, 29; Ps. 66:15; Is. 34:6). *

[3] ***śā'iyr, śā'ir*** [masc. noun: שָׂעִיר, שָׂעִר <8163>; from SWEEP AWAY <8175> (in the sense of to storm; by implication, to shiver, i.e., to fear; by analogy, a goat could be a faun, a devil, a hairy creature)] ▶ **This word means a male goat (a ruminant mammal related to the sheep), a buck. Occasionally, the word can be used figuratively to mean a hairy one. Under the Israelite sacrificial system, a male goat was an acceptable sin offering.** This noun is used many times in conjunction with the sin offering, in which a male goat without any defects was offered by the priest to atone for the sins of himself and the people (Lev. 9:15; 2 Chr. 29:23; Ezek. 43:25). On the negative side, the Israelites worshiped the goat as an idol in times of rebellion against God; the same noun is used in these references (Lev. 17:7; 2 Chr. 11:15). *

[4] ***s^e^'iyrāh*** [fem. noun: שְׂעִירָה <8166>; fem. of <8163> above] ▶ **This word refers to a female goat (a ruminant mammal related to the sheep) of a flock designated as an offering to cover unintentional sins.** Refs.: Lev. 4:28; 5:6. ¶

[5] ***tayiš*** [masc. noun: תַּיִשׁ <8495>; from an unused root meaning to butt] ▶ **This word refers to a male goat (a ruminant mammal related to the sheep). It was a valuable member of a person's wealth and a part of a flock.** Refs.: Gen. 30:35; 32:14. It was considered a choice item for payment of a tribute (2 Chr. 17:11). It was among the four things impressive in their locomotion, their walk (Prov. 30:31). ¶

GOAT (WILD, MOUNTAIN) – ***yā'êl*** [masc. noun: יָעֵל <3277>; from PROFIT (verb) <3276> (in the sense of climbing)] ▶ **This word refers to the ibex or small mountain goat (a ruminant mammal related to the sheep).** Ref.: Ps. 104:18. The time and process of their calving was a wonder and mystery to people, noted by God Himself (Job 39:1). Other ref.: 1 Sam. 24:2. ¶

GOAT (YOUNG, LITTLE) – ***g^e^ḏiyyāh*** [fem. noun: גְּדִיָּה <1429>; fem. of KID <1423>] ▶ **This is a tender word referring to the young goats (a ruminant mammal related to the sheep) pastured by the young maiden that the lover is describing.** Ref.: Song 1:8; also translated kid. ¶

GOATH, GOAH – ***gō'āh*** [proper noun: גֹּעָה <1601>; fem. act. part. of LOW <1600>]: lowing, bellowing ▶ **A place near Jerusalem.** Ref.: Jer. 31:39. ¶

GOATSKIN – See BADGER <8476>.

GOB – ***gōḇ, gôḇ*** [proper noun: גּוֹב, גֹּב <1359>; from PLOWMAN <1461> (in the sense of one who digs)]: pit, cistern ▶ **A place where the Israelites fought twice against the Philistines.** Refs.: 2 Sam. 21:18, 19. ¶

GOBLET – [1] 1 Kgs. 10:21; 2 Chr. 9:20 → lit.: drinking vessel → DRINK (noun) <4945>, ARTICLE <3627> [2] Song 7:2 → BASIN <101> [3] Dan. 5:2, 3, 23 → VESSEL <3984>.

GOD – [1] ***'ēl*** [masc. noun: אֵל <410>; shortened from MIGHTY <352>] ▶ **This word means "The Mighty" when referring to the Supreme Being; it also means god, mighty one, hero. It is one of the most ancient terms for God, god, or deity. It appears most often in Genesis, Job, Psalms, and Isaiah and not at all in some books.** The root meaning of the word mighty can be seen in Job 41:25 and Micah 2:1. This word is used occasionally of other gods (Ex. 34:14; Deut. 3:24; Ps. 44:20; Mal. 2:11) but is most often used to mean the one true God (Ps. 5:4; Is. 40:18). It expresses various ideas of deity according to its context. The most common may be noted briefly: the holy God as contrasted to humans (Hos. 11:9); the High God El (Gen. 14:18; 16:13; Ezek. 28:2); the Lord (Yahweh) as a title of Israel according to the Lord's own claim (Gen. 33:20; Is. 40:18); God or god in general (Ex. 34:14; Deut. 32:21; Mic. 7:8); the God of Israel, the Lord (Num. 23:8; Ps. 118:27); God (Job 5:8).

This word is used with various descriptive adjectives or attributes: *'ēl* is God of gods (Ps. 50:1); God of Bethel (Gen. 35:7); a forgiving God (Ps. 99:8). He is the holy God (Is. 5:16). Especially significant are the assertions declaring that *'ēl* is with us, Immanuel (Is. 7:14); and He is the God of our salvation (Is. 12:2); a gracious God (Neh. 9:31); a jealous God (Ex. 20:5; 34:14). The closeness of this God is expressed in the hand of God (Job 27:11).

In the human realm, the word also designates men of power or high rank (Ezek. 31:11); mighty men (Job 41:25); or mighty warriors (Ezek. 32:21). The word is used to designate superior and mighty things in nature, such as mighty or high mountains (Ps. 36:6), lofty, high cedars, or stars (Ps. 80:10; Is. 14:13).

In conjunction with other descriptive words, it occurs as *'ēl šaday*, "God Almighty" <7706> (Gen. 17:1; 28:3; Ex. 6:3) or *'ēl 'elyôn*, "God Most High" <5945> (Gen. 14:18, 19; Ps. 78:35). Used with hand (*yāḏ*) in some settings, the word conveys power, strength (Gen. 31:29; Deut. 28:32; Prov. 3:27), or ability. *

[2] ***ᵉlāh*** [Aramaic masc. noun: אֱלָהּ <426>; corresponding to <433> below] ▶ **This noun means the Supreme, deity, divinity.** It can be used in a general sense to indicate a god (Dan. 3:15) or gods (Dan. 2:11; 3:12, 18, 25). In a specific sense, it signifies the God of Israel, namely, Yahweh (Ezra 5:1, 2, 8; 6:14; 7:15; Dan. 2:20, 28; 3:17). *

[3] ***ᵉlōhiym*** [masc. plur. noun: אֱלֹהִים <430>; plur. of <433> below] ▶ **This word means the true God, gods, judges, angels. Occurring more than 2,600 times in the Old Testament, it commonly designates the one true God (Gen. 1:1) and is often paired with God's unique name *yᵉhōwāh* <3068> (Gen. 2:4; Ps. 100:3).** When the word is used as the generic designation of God, it conveys in Scripture that God is the Creator (Gen. 5:1); the King (Ps. 47:7); the Judge (Ps. 50:6); the Lord (Ps. 86:12); and the Savior (Hos. 13:4). His character is compassionate (Deut. 4:31); gracious (Ps. 116:5); and faithful to His covenant (Deut. 7:9). In fewer instances, this word refers to foreign gods, such as Dagon (1 Sam. 5:7) or Baal (1 Kgs. 18:24). It also might refer to judges (Ex. 22:8, 9) or angels as gods (Ps. 97:7). Although the form of this word is plural, it is frequently used as if it were singular—i.e., with a singular verb (Gen. 1:1–31; Ex. 2:24). The plural form of this

word may be regarded (1) as intensive to indicate God's fullness of power; (2) as majestic to indicate God's kingly rule; or (3) as an allusion to the Trinity (Gen. 1:26). The singular form of this word *ᵉlôaḥ* <433> occurs only in poetry (Ps. 50:22; Is. 44:8). The shortened form of the word is *'ēl*: GOD <410>. *

[4] ***ᵉlôaḥ*** [masc. noun: אֱלוֹהַּ <433>; prob. prolonged (emphatically) from <410> above] ▶ **This word means god or God, the Supreme. It is thought by some to be the singular of the noun *ᵉlōhiym* <430>. This word is used of *yᵉhōwāh* <3068> (Ps. 18:31) and, with a negative, to describe what is not God (Deut. 32:17).** Most occurrences of this word are in the book of Job, where the speakers may not be Israelites and thus use other generic names for God (Job 3:4), of which this is one. It is used once in the name, "God of Jacob" (Ps. 114:7) and once in the phrase, "God of forgiveness" (Neh. 9:17). *

[5] ***yᵉhōwih*** [masc. proper noun: יֱהֹוִה <3069>; a variation of LORD <3068> used after LORD <136>] ▶ **Most translations render this word as GOD to distinguish it from *yᵉhōwāh*, LORD (see LORD <3068>; e.g., Gen. 15:2, 8; NASB, KJV, NKJV, ESV), but others chose to translate it as LORD (NIV, Gen. 15:2, 8; Deut. 3:24; 9:26; Josh. 7:7, etc.) based on recent studies of the word in various articles and grammars.** Its exact meaning is still being researched, but it is a form of the covenant name of Israel's God revealed to Moses at Sinai (Ex. 3:14, *hāyāh* [BE <1961>]). It means "He who is or is present," "He who will be who He will be" or "He who causes to be all that is" or an organic combination of the essence of all these renderings. *

GODLESS – ***ḥānēp̱*** [adj.: חָנֵף <2611>; from DEFILED (BE) <2610>] ▶ **This word means profane, filthy, impious; it is also translated hypocrite, ungodly. It is used as a substantive to refer to a person with such qualities. The root idea is to incline away (from God).** The word refers to a person whose moral uncleanness separates him or her from God (Job 13:16). It commonly describes someone without hope after this life (Job 8:13; 20:5; 27:8: godless, hypocrite), who can only expect anger from God (Job 36:13; Is. 33:14: godless, hypocrite). Such people come into conflict with the righteous (Job 17:8: godless, hypocrite, ungodly; Prov. 11:9: godless, hypocrite) and are known by their cruelty to others (Ps. 35:16: ungodly, godless, hypocritical, profane; Prov. 11:9). Other refs.: Job 15:34; 34:30; Is. 9:17; 10:6. ¶

GODLESS (BE) – Jer. 23:11 ➔ DEFILED (BE) <2610>.

GOG – ***gôg*** [proper noun: גּוֹג <1463>; of uncertain deriv.] ▶
a. The name of a descendant of Reuben, the son of Joel. Ref.: 1 Chr. 5:4. ¶
b. The name occurs often in Ezekiel 38 and 39. Ezekiel puts forth an inspired prophecy against him (Ezek. 38:2). He is pictured as a great enemy against God's people. He is from the land of Magog or possibly "from the land of Gog." The name appears in apocalyptic literature which often is highly symbolic and cryptic in meaning. The Lord, at any rate, sets Himself against Gog (Ezek. 38:2). Gog will lead a coalition of nations against God's people who are then dwelling securely in the land of Israel (Ezek. 38:14–16). But God, in fact, will bring Gog forth and will destroy him and his people. The Lord shows Himself holy in His actions against Gog (Ezek. 38:16; 39:1–8). The Lord spoke about this through other prophets (Ezek. 38:17, 18). The multitudes of Gog will be buried in the Valley of Hamon Gog, i.e., "multitudes of Gog" (Ezek. 39:15), while God's people will be liberated from the fear and threat of Gog (Ezek. 39:16–29). ¶

GOING – [1] 2 Sam. 5:24; 1 Chr. 14:15 ➔ MARCHING <6807> a. [2] Prov. 20:24 ➔ STEP (noun) <4703>.

GOING DOWN – [1] ***meʿāl*** [Aramaic masc. noun: מֶעָל <4606>; from ENTER <5954>] ▶ **This word means the setting (of the sun).** It is used once in Daniel to refer to sunset, "the going down of the sun" (Dan. 6:14), the official ending of the daylight hours. ¶

[2] ***nāḥēṯ*** [adj.: נָחֵת <5185>; from BEND <5181>] ▶ **This word is used of something in the process of descending, coming down in a geographical direction, e.g., an army.** Ref.: 2 Kgs. 6:9; also translated coming down. ¶

– [3] Josh. 7:5; 10:11; Jer. 48:5 ➔ DESCENT <4174>.

GOING FORTH – ***môṣā'āh*** [fem. noun: מוֹצָאָה <4163>; the same as GOING OUT, GOING FORTH <4161>] ▶ **This word means, in one nuance, the history of where one is issued out from and is also translated coming forth, origin.** It indicates the origin of the Messiah (Mic. 5:2) from Bethlehem Ephrathah. Other ref. in a second nuance: 2 Kgs. 10:27 (latrine, refuse dump, draught house). ¶

GOING OUT, GOING FORTH – ***môṣā'*** [masc. noun: מוֹצָא <4161>; from GO OUT <3318>] ▶ **This word indicates the action of going out in general, with many specific nuances.** Ref.: 2 Sam. 3:25. It designates an exit from the Temple in Ezekiel's vision (Ezek. 42:11); also the going forth of the Lord (Hos. 6:3); or a command (Dan. 9:25). It is used in a business sense of importing something, e.g., horses (1 Kgs. 10:28: brought out). It is used in an idiom for the rising, coming out, of the sun (Ps. 19:6); also indicating an easterly direction (Ps. 75:6). It has the sense of spring for an outlet of water (2 Kgs. 2:21; Ps. 107:33; Is. 58:11); in a more figurative sense, utterances that come forth from one's mouth (Num. 30:12). It is used in the idiom, the east and the west, literally, the goings forth of the morning and the evening (Ps. 65:8). And it indicates the sources(s) of something, e.g., silver (Job 28:1). *

GOINGS – [1] Ps. 17:5; Prov. 14:15 ➔ STEP (noun) <838> [2] Ps. 68:24 ➔ WAY <1979>.

GOLAN – ***gôlān*** [proper noun: גּוֹלָן <1474>; from CAPTIVITY <1473>]: exile, passage ▶ **A city of Bashan in the territory of Manasseh.** It was assigned to the Levites and became a city of refuge (Deut. 4:43; Josh. 20:8; 21:27; 1 Chr. 6:71). ¶

GOLD – [1] ***beṣer*** [masc. noun: בֶּצֶר <1220>; from GATHER <1219>] ▶ **This word refers to the very valuable yellow metallic element and then, using a play on the same word, depicts the Almighty as the true gold and silver of His people.** Refs.: Job 22:24, 25; KJV renders this noun as defense. ¶

[2] ***b***^{e}***ṣar*** [masc. noun: בְּצַר <1222>; another form for <1220> above] ▶ **This word is found in Job 36:19. It may be a term meaning in distress.** So, most translators understand the syntax of the verse differently and translate it as part of the phrase "not be in distress" (NIV) or similar renderings (NASB, NKJV). ¶

[3] ***d***^{e}***haḇ*** [Aramaic masc. noun: דְּהַב <1722>; corresponding to <2091> below] ▶ **Gold was the most precious metal in the ancient Near East and was considered the metal of the gods.** It was used in royal construction, clothing, furniture, and decorative items (Dan. 5:2–4, 7). A gold necklace was common dress for royalty and was presented as an award (Dan. 5:16, 29) for faithful or outstanding service. Nebuchadnezzar's dream involved a statue whose head was of gold (Dan. 2:32, 35, 38, 45), and he constructed a huge image of gold possibly depicting himself (Dan. 3:1, 5, 7, 10, 12, 14, 18). Many vessels in the Lord's Temple were of gold (Ezra 5:14; 6:5; 7:15, 16, 18; Dan. 5:23). ¶

[4] ***zāhāḇ*** [masc. noun: זָהָב <2091>; from an unused root meaning to shimmer] ▶ **This word is used to refer to gold in several ways.** In a raw or natural state (Gen. 2:11, 12; Jer. 10:9); as wealth in general (Gen. 13:2; 24:35); or as a precious metal (Job 28:17; Ps. 19:10; Prov. 22:1). It is referred to in its man-made form as bars (Josh. 7:21). Gold is referred to as booty or spoil from war (Josh. 6:19) and as merchandise (Ezek. 27:22). It was used to create money, shekels of gold (Gen. 24:22). Gold was used in jewelry (Gen. 24:22; Ex. 32:2; Judg. 8:24),

and some offerings of gold were given (Ex. 35:22; Num. 31:52). It was used in weight (Num. 7:14; Judg. 8:26). *

5 ***ḥārûṣ*** [adj.: חָרוּץ <2742>; pass. part. of MOVE <2782>] ▶ **This word refers to the golden wings of a dove in a simile.** Ref.: Ps. 68:13. Wisdom is always considered of greater value than gold (Prov. 3:14; 8:19; 16:16); as is knowledge (Prov. 8:10). The pagan city-state of Tyre piled up gold as her treasure (Zech. 9:3). The Hebrew word also means DECISION, DILIGENT, MOAT; see these entries. ¶

6 ***sᵉgôr*** [masc. noun: סְגוֹר <5458>; from CLOSE <5462>] ▶ **This word refers to high-quality, fine gold of great value.** Ref.: Job 28:15. The Hebrew word also means an enclosure; see CAUL <5458>. ¶

7 ***paz*** [fem. noun: פָּז <6337>; from REFINED (BE) <6338>] ▶ **This word designates pure gold, fine gold.** It refers to an especially valuable kind of gold (Job 28:17; Prov. 8:19). It is used figuratively to describe the beauty of the bridegroom (Song 5:11, 15). It was an extremely scarce commodity (Is. 13:12). Other refs.: Ps. 19:10; 21:3; 119:127; Lam. 4:2. ¶

GOLD (CHAINS OF) – Song 1:10 ➔ STRING OF JEWELS <2737>.

GOLD, FINE GOLD, PURE GOLD – ***keṯem*** [masc. noun: כֶּתֶם <3800>; from MARKED (BE) <3799>] ▶ **This word serves as a poetic synonym for *zāhāḇ* <2091>, gold.** Refs.: Job 31:24; Prov. 25:12. It is described in some places as gold of *'ôp̱îyr*, gold from the East (Job 28:16; Ps. 45:9; Is. 13:12); or pure gold (Job 28:19; Song 5:11; Lam. 4:1). Other ref.: Dan. 10:5. ¶

GOLDEN CITY – Is. 14:4 ➔ FURY <4062> b.

GOLDSMITH – 1 ***ṣōrpiy*** [masc. noun: צֹרְפִי <6885>; from REFINE <6884>] ▶ **This word refers to a person who is skilled in working with gold.** In context it may refer to a son of a goldsmith or to a goldsmith guild (*ben-ṣōrpᵉ pî*, Neh. 3:31). ¶
– 2 Neh. 3:8; Is. 41:7 ➔ REFINE <6884>.

GOLIATH – ***golyāṯ, golyaṯ*** [masc. proper noun: גָּלְיָת, גָּלְיַת <1555>; perhaps from REVEAL <1540>]: heap, great ▶ **A giant Philistine warrior around whom the Philistines rallied.** He came from the city of Gath and stood over nine feet tall (1 Sam. 17:4, 32). David slew him and later acquired his sword from Ahimelech at Nob (1 Sam. 21:8, 9; 22:10). Other refs.: 1 Sam. 17:23; 2 Sam. 21:19; 1 Chr. 20:5. ¶

GOMER – ***gōmer*** [masc. and fem. proper noun: גֹּמֶר <1586>; from END (COME TO AN) <1584>]: accomplished, ended ▶
a. A son of Japheth, Noah's son. Refs.: Gen. 10:2, 3; 1 Chr. 1:5, 6. ¶
b. The descendants, named as a people, who are among the hordes of Gog who will come against God's people. Ref.: Ezek. 38:6. ¶
c. The wife of Hosea the prophet, a daughter of Diblaim. Ref.: Hos. 1:3. ¶

GOMORRAH – ***ʿᵃmōrāh*** [proper noun: עֲמֹרָה <6017>; from SLAVE (TREAT AS A) <6014>]: submersion ▶ **This word designates the city located south, southwest of the Dead Sea that was destroyed, along with Sodom, for its heinous sins.** There were not enough righteous persons left in the city to rescue it from God's wrath (Gen. 18:20). It was on the border of the land occupied by Canaanites (Gen. 10:19). Its destruction resulted in a permanent change in the fertility and beauty of the land around Zoar (Gen. 13:10).

The city became a byword for wickedness and evil in the Prophets and Law (Deut. 29:23; Is. 1:9; Jer. 49:18; Amos 4:11; Zeph. 2:9). *

GONE – ***middaḏ*** [masc. noun: מִדַּד <4059>; from FLEE <5074>] ▶ **This word indicates flight.** It means gone, flown away, in flight (KJV, Job 7:4, lit.: when shall be the "flight" of night?), but see also MEASURE (verb) <4058>. ¶

GONE (BE) – Judg. 19:11 ➔ SUBDUE <7286>.

GONE (BE SOON) – Ps. 90:10 ➔ CUT OFF <1468>.

GONE ASIDE – 1 Kgs. 18:27 ➔ RELIEVE ONESELF <7873>.

GOOD – [1] ***ṭôḇ, ṭôḇāh, ṭōḇāh*** [adj.: טוֹב, טוֹבָה, טֹבָה <2896>; from HAPPY (BE) <2895>] ▶ **This word means well-pleasing, fruitful, morally correct, proper, convenient. It is frequently encountered in the Old Testament and is roughly equivalent to the English word *good* in terms of its function and scope of meaning.** It describes that which is appealing and pleasant to the senses (Num. 14:7; Esther 1:11; Ps. 52:9); is useful and profitable (Gen. 2:18; Zech. 11:12); is abundant and plentiful (Gen. 41:22; Judg. 8:32); is kind and benevolent (1 Sam. 24:18; 2 Chr. 5:13; Nah. 1:7); is good in a moral sense as opposed to evil (Gen. 2:17; Lev. 27:14; Ps. 37:27); is proper and becoming (Deut. 1:14; 1 Sam. 1:23; Ps. 92:1); bears a general state of well-being or happiness (Deut. 6:24; Eccl. 2:24); is the better of two alternatives (Gen. 29:19; Ex. 14:12; Jon. 4:3). The creation narrative of Genesis 1 best embodies all these various elements of meaning when the Lord declares each aspect of His handiwork to be "good." *
– [2] Ezra 5:17 ➔ FINE (adj.) <2869> [3] Eccl. 5:11 ➔ SKILL <3788>.

GOOD (BE, DO) – ***yāṭaḇ*** [verb: יָטַב <3190>; a prim. root] ▶ **This word means to be well, to be pleasing. In the causative stem, it means to do good, to do well, to please, to make pleasing.** It is often used in idiomatic expressions with heart (*lēḇ* [HEART <3820>]), meaning to be pleased or to be happy (Judg. 18:20; 19:6, 9; Ruth 3:7); and with eyes, to be pleasing to someone else (i.e., pleasing or good in their eyes [Gen. 34:18; 1 Sam. 18:5]). The term does not necessarily carry a moral weight but can be translated adverbially as "well." For instance, see Micah 7:3 where their hands do evil well (cf. 1 Sam. 16:17; Prov. 30:29; Is. 23:16). The word can also imply morality (Ps. 36:3; 119:68). *

GOOD (BE, SEEM, THINK) – ***šᵉp̱ar*** [Aramaic verb: שְׁפַר <8232>; corresponding to BEAUTIFUL (BE) <8231>] ▶ **This word means to be pleasing, to please, to be acceptable.** It indicates that something seems right, just, correct to a person (Dan. 4:2, 27; 6:1); especially to declare the greatness of God's mighty works or to appoint certain persons or things because of their character and performance. ¶

GOOD (SEEM) – ***yᵉṭaḇ*** [Aramaic verb: יְטַב <3191>; corresponding to GOOD (BE, DO) <3190>] ▶ **This word refers to what appears or is taken to be acceptable, good, helpful from various persons' perspectives.** Ref.: Ezra 7:18; also translated to seem best. ¶

GOOD, GOODLY – Ps. 16:6 ➔ BEAUTIFUL (BE) <8231>.

GOODLY – [1] Gen. 49:21 ➔ BEAUTIFUL <8233> [2] Job 39:13 ➔ ENJOY <5965> c. [3] Job 41:12 ➔ GRACEFUL <2433> [4] Ezek. 17:8 ➔ GARMENT <155> [5] Ezek. 17:23 ➔ MIGHTY <117> [6] Zech. 11:13 ➔ ROBE <145>.

GOODNESS – [1] ***ṭûḇ*** [masc. noun: טוּב <2898>; from HAPPY (BE) <2895>] ▶ **This word describes a quality or state, e.g., fairness, beauty. Concretely it refers to property, goods. The root concept of this noun is that of desirability for enjoyment.** It is used to identify the personal property of an individual (Gen. 24:10); the plentiful harvest of the land (Neh. 9:36; Jer. 2:7); items of superior quality and desirability (2 Kgs. 8:9); inward joy (Is. 65:14); the manifest goodness of the Lord (Ex. 33:19; Ps. 25:7). Notably, the psalmist employs the word to describe the state of spiritual blessing (Ps. 31:19; 65:4). *
– [2] See MERCY <2617>.

GOODS – [1] ***nᵉḵas*** [Aramaic noun: נְכַס <5232>; corresponding to WEALTH <5233>] ▶ **This word refers to resources or wealth.** It indicates the royal wealth or treasury (Ezra 6:8); or the property and goods of any person (Ezra 7:26). ¶

2 ***qinyān*** [masc. noun: קִנְיָן <7075>; from ACQUIRE <7069>] ▶ **This word means possessions, property.** It refers to all personal property acquired: sheep, goats (Gen. 31:18); capable of being moved, transferred (Gen. 34:23; 36:6; Josh. 14:4). It is used of the total work of God's creation as His possession (Ps. 104:24). It indicates a purchased slave (Zech. 13:5). *
– 3 Ex. 22:8 → PROPERTY (LOST) <9> 4 Judg. 18:21 → GLORIOUS <3520> b. 5 Neh. 10:31 → MERCHANDISE <4728> 6 Neh. 13:16 → MERCHANDISE <4377>.

GOPHER – ***gōp̱er*** [masc. noun: גֹּפֶר <1613>; from an unused root, prob. meaning to house in] ▶ **This word refers to a species of tree furnishing a light building material for the ark.** Ref.: Gen. 6:14 (NIV: cypress wood). The exact identity of this wood is unknown. ¶

GORE – ***nāgaḥ*** [verb: נָגַח <5055>; a prim. root] ▶ **The verb means to push; it is also translated to attack, to butt, to charge, to collide, to engage in battle; to thrust.** It is used of the goring of a horned animal (Ex. 21:28, 31, 32); the forceful expansion of a people or nation (Deut. 33:17; 1 Kgs. 22:11; 2 Chr. 18:10; Dan. 8:4; 11:40); or the defeat of enemies (Ps. 44:5). It is used of oppressing the poor, pushing them into subjection (Ezek. 34:21). ¶

GORGEOUSLY – Ezek. 23:12 → SPLENDIDLY <4358>.

GORING – ***naggāḥ*** [adj.: נַגָּח <5056>; from GORE <5055>] ▶ **The word describes an animal accustomed to behave violently by using its horns.** Refs.: Ex. 21:29, 36. ¶

GOSHEN – ***gōšen*** [proper noun: גֹּשֶׁן <1657>; prob. of Egyptian origin] ▶
a. This word refers to territory in Egypt where Israel was enslaved by the Egyptians. Refs.: Gen. 45–47; 50; Ex. 8, 9. It may have been called the "land of Rameses" in later history (Gen. 42:4–27). It was situated in the eastern part of the Nile Delta. *
b. It refers to a city in Judah in the southern mountainous area. Refs.: Josh. 10:41; 11:16; 15:51. It refers to a region in this area possibly. ¶

GOSSIP – Prov. 16:28; 18:8; 26:20, 22 → WHISPERER <5372>.

GOUGE – ***nāqar*** [verb: נָקַר <5365>; a prim. root] ▶ **This word means to dig something; to injure a person's eye.** It is used of putting out, gouging out the eyes of a person (Num. 16:14; 1 Sam. 11:2; Prov. 30:17); memorably of Samson's eyes blinded by the Philistines (Judg. 16:21). In a general sense, it means to dig something, e.g., a well (2 Kgs. 19:24); but in a figurative sense, it describes afflictions and pain that cut into a person (Job 30:17: to pierce, to rack). It is used in a figurative sense of God's digging wells as symbolic of His past acts of deliverance and help for His people (Is. 37:25); with Himself as the quarry or rock pile from which Israel was created or dug (Is. 51:1). ¶

GOURD – Jon. 4:6, 7, 9, 10 → PLANT (noun) <7021>.

GOURDS – 1 ***peqā'iym*** [masc. plur. noun: פְּקָעִים <6497>; from an unused root meaning to burst (since the gourds split open to shed their seeds)] ▶ **This word refers to gourds (hard-skinned fruits), knob shaped projections.** They were decorative ornamental gourds carved from cedar wood for the Temple. Refs.: 1 Kgs. 6:18; 7:24; also translated buds, knops. ¶
2 ***paqqu'ōṯ*** [masc. plur. noun: פַּקֻּעֹת <6498>; from the same as GOURDS <6497>] ▶ **In context this word refers to poisonous gourds (hard-skinned fruits) growing in the wild, capable of causing death to humans.** Ref.: 2 Kgs. 4:39. ¶

GOVERN – 1 Judg. 9:22 → RULE (verb) <7786> 2 Prov. 8:16 → RULE (verb) <8323>.

GOVERNMENT – ***miśrāh*** [fem. noun: מִשְׂרָה <4951>; from STRUGGLE <8280> (in the sense of to have power)] ▶ **This**

word indicates the extent of rulership; dominion that is under authority. Refs.: Is. 9:6, 7. ¶

GOVERNOR – [1] ***peḥāh*** [masc. noun: פֶּחָה <6346>; of foreign origin] ▶ ***The* primary meaning of this word is that of a lord over a given district or territory. It signified an office that is appointed and not received by virtue of birth or other right.** It was generally used of the leader of the Jewish nation after the exile (Neh. 12:26; Hag. 1:14; Mal. 1:8); but in other places it was used of a deputy bureaucrat in any given location (Esther 8:9; Jer. 51:23); or a military leader (1 Kgs. 20:24). *
[2] ***peḥāh*** [Aramaic masc. noun: פֶּחָה <6347>; corresponding to <6346> above] ▶ **This word means a ruler, magistrate, or other similarly appointed authority.** It was used particularly of a provincial governor in the Persian Empire (Ezra 5:6); the postexilic leader of the Jewish nation (Ezra 6:7); and various similar officers involved in the political structure (Dan. 6:7). *
[3] ***tiršāṯā'*** [תִּרְשָׁתָא <8660>; of foreign deriv.] ▶
a. A masculine noun meaning a ruler, magistrate. It refers to the political office of the person placed in charge of the small province of Judah on Israel's return from exile: governor (Ezra 2:63; Neh. 7:65, 70); possibly Zerubbabel or Sheshbazzar. Nehemiah is called the governor (Neh. 8:9).
b. A proper noun Tirshatha: title of the Persian ruler or magistrate of Judah. The KJV renders this a title (Ezra 2:63), the Tirshatha, but it is clear that it probably means governor (Neh. 7:65; 70). Nehemiah is called the Tirshatha in Nehemiah 8:9 (KJV). ¶
– [4] Gen. 42:6 ➔ POWER <7989> [5] 1 Kgs. 4:19 ➔ GARRISON <5333> [6] Dan. 2:48; 3:2, 3, 27; 6:7 ➔ PREFECT <5460> [7] Dan. 6:2–4, 6:6, 7 ➔ COMMISSIONER <5632>.

GOVERNORS – Ezra 4:9; 5:6; 6:6: lesser governors ➔ APHARSATHCHITES <671>.

GOZAN – ***gôzān*** [proper noun: גּוֹזָן <1470>; prob. from CUT OFF <1468>]: a cutting off ▶ **A city and its surrounding areas conquered by the Assyrians to which Israelites were exiled by the Assyrians.** Refs.: 1 Kgs. 17:6; 18:11; 19:12. It was located on a major route through upper Mesopotamia and situated due east of Haran and modern Aleppo. Other refs.: 1 Chr. 5:26; Is. 37:12. ¶

GRACE – ***ḥên*** [masc. noun: חֵן <2580>; from GRACIOUS (BE) <2603>] ▶ **This word means favor, acceptance. Genesis 6:8 stands as the fundamental application of this word, meaning an unmerited favor or regard in God's sight.** Beyond this, however, the word conveys a sense of acceptance or preference in a more general manner as well, such as the enticement of a woman (Prov. 31:30; Nah. 3:4); elegant speech (Eccl. 10:12); and some special standing or privilege with God or people (Num. 32:5; Esther 5:2; Zech. 12:10). *

GRACEFUL – [1] ***ḥiyn*** [masc. noun: חִין <2433>; another form for GRACE <2580>] ▶ **This word depicts beauty, elegance.** It indicates literally the grace (*ḥiyn*) or beauty of the form (*'ereḵ*) of Leviathan (Job 41:12); it is also translated orderly, goodly, comely. ¶
– [2] Song 7:1 ➔ CURVE <2542>.

GRACIOUS – [1] ***ḥannûn*** [adj.: חַנּוּן <2587>; from GRACIOUS (BE) <2603>] ▶ **This word refers to expressing favor, acceptance. It is used solely as a descriptive term of God.** The Lord used this word when He revealed Himself to Moses (Ex. 34:6), as One who is, above all else, merciful and abounding in compassion (Ps. 86:15; 103:8). Elsewhere, it expresses the Lord's response to the cry of the oppressed (Ex. 22:27); His treatment of those that reverence Him (Ps. 111:4; 112:4); His attitude toward those who repent (Joel 2:13); His mercy in the face of rebellion (Neh. 9:17, 31; Jon. 4:2); and His leniency toward His people in the midst of judgment (2 Chr. 30:9). Other refs.: Ps. 116:5; 145:8. ¶
– [2] Prov. 15:26; 16:24 ➔ BEAUTY <5278> [3] See FAITHFUL <2623>.

GRACIOUS (BE) – [1] ***ḥānan*** [verb: חָנַן <2603>; a prim. root (comp. ENCAMP <2583>)] ▶ **This word means to favor, to have mercy on.** In the wisdom literature, this verb is used primarily with human relations to denote gracious acts toward someone in need (Job 19:21; Prov. 19:17). Though the wicked may pretend to act graciously, they do not do so; neither should it be done so toward them (Ps. 37:21; Prov. 21:10; 26:25; Is. 26:10). Outside of the wisdom literature, the agent of graciousness is most frequently God, including the often repeated cry, "Have mercy on me!" (Ex. 33:19; Num. 6:25; Ps. 26:11; 27:7; 119:58). A mixture of divine and human agencies occurs when God, in judgment, sends nations that will show no mercy to punish other nations through warfare (Deut. 7:2; 28:50; Is. 27:11). *

[2] ***ḥannôṯ*** [verb: חַנּוֹת <2589>; from <2603> above (in the sense of prayer)] ▶ **This word refers to God's acts of mercy or graciousness in the past.** Ref.: Ps. 77:9; also translated to be merciful. The Hebrew word is also translated to entreat (see ENTREAT <2589>). ¶

GRAIN – [1] ***bar, bār*** [masc. noun: בַּר, בָּר <1250>; from PURIFY <1305> (in the sense of winnowing)] ▶ **This word means the small fruit of a cereal plant, the plant that produces grain; it is also translated corn, field.** This staple was one of the blessings the Lord gave to Israel from the land of Canaan (Ps. 65:13; Joel 2:24). It was abundant in Egypt during a time of drought in Israel (Gen. 41:35, 49; 42:3, 25). It was from a source of health and strength (Job 39:4; NASB, NIV, translate as referring to open fields or wilds; Prov. 11:26). It became a cause of judgment when Israel began to covet the wealth that flowed from selling it (Amos 8:5, 6). *

[2] ***mā'āh*** [fem. noun: מָעָה <4579>; fem. of BOWELS <4578> (in the sense of something internal)] ▶ **This word signifies a small particle of something.** It identifies granules of sand in context (Is. 48:19; KJV: gravel). ¶

[3] ***riyp̱āh, rip̱āh*** [fem. noun: רִיפָה, רִפָה <7383>; from TREMBLE <7322> (in the sense of triturate, e.g., in a mortar)] ▶ **This word refers to kernels of some kind of cereal crop; it is also translated ground grain, crushed grain, ground corn, wheat.** Ref.: 2 Sam. 17:19; some have suggested "beans." It has the same meaning in Proverbs 27:22 where it is used in a simile. ¶

[4] ***šeḇer*** [masc. noun: שֶׁבֶר <7668>; from BREAK <7665> (comp. DESTRUCTION <7667>)] ▶ **This word refers to that which is broken into kernels, corn, or food stuff. The word is used nine times in the Old Testament as a general term for grain, with seven being used in the Joseph narratives of Genesis.** This noun can connote grain that is for sale (Gen. 42:1, 2); especially that which is eaten during a famine (Gen. 42:19, 26; 43:2; 44:2; 47:14). This word is the food stuff eaten when people are less particular about what they eat. In Nehemiah, it describes the food brought in by neighboring countries to sell on the Sabbath. The remnant that had returned promised God they would not buy it (Neh. 10:31). The noun is also used in reference to Israel's greed and disobedience when they were waiting impatiently for the end of the Sabbath that they might once again sell grain (Amos 8:5). ¶

– [5] Lev. 11:37 ➔ SOWING <2221> [6] Job 15:29 ➔ PERFECTION <4512> [7] Amos 9:9 ➔ BAG <6872> b. [8] See CORN <1715>.

GRAIN (NEW) – Lev. 2:14; 23:14; 2 Kgs. 4:42 ➔ FIELD (FERTILE, FRUITFUL, PLENTIFUL) <3759> b.

GRAIN (HEAD OF, EAR OF) – ***šibbōleṯ*** [fem. noun: שִׁבֹּלֶת <7641>; from an unused root meaning to flow] ▶ **This word refers to the part of a cereal plant that contains the seeds, grains or kernels; the ears of grain that grow from a stalk.** Refs.: Gen. 41:5, 6, 7, 22–24, 26, 27. It contains the way the Ephraimites pronounced "Sibboleth" (Judg. 12:6). These heads or ears of grain were cut off in harvest (Job 24:24; Is. 17:5). It refers to branches or twigs in Zechariah 4:12, representing two anointed persons. Other ref.: Ruth 2:2. For another meaning of the Hebrew word, see STREAM <7641>. ¶

GRAIN (SHEAF OF, FALLEN) – *'āmiyr* [masc.: עָמִיר <5995>; from SLAVE (TREAT AS A) (this Hebrew root word also has the sense of to bind and tie up sheaves of grain) <6014>] ► **This word refers to a bound bundle of newly cut stalks of grain or to swath, i.e., a row of a cereal crop as it lies when reaped.** Ref.: Jer. 9:22. In English, the plural is sheaves. It is used figuratively in each context (Amos 2:13; Mic. 4:12; Zech. 12:6). ¶

GRANARY – 1 *ma'ᵃbûs* [masc. noun: מַאֲבוּס <3965>; from FATTENED <75>] ► **This word indicates a place for storing grain or other stores; it is also translated storehouse, barn.** It is used of Babylon (Jer. 50:26). ¶
2 *mammᵉgûrāh* [fem. noun: מַמְּגוּרָה <4460>; from DELIVER OVER <4048> (in the sense of depositing)] ► **This word refers to a storage building or area; a storage barn.** Ref.: Joel 1:17. Some suggest grain pit as a more accurate designation. ¶
– 3 Ex. 22:29 ➔ HARVEST <4395> 4 Ps. 144:13 ➔ BARN <4200>.

GRANT – Ezra 3:7 ➔ PERMISSION <7558>.

GRAPE – 1 *'ênāḇ* [masc. noun: עֵנָב <6025>; from an unused root prob. meaning to bear fruit] ► **This word refers to a small, smooth-skinned fruit that grows in clusters; the fruits of the grapevine.** Refs.: Gen. 40:10, 11; Amos 9:13. In Numbers 13:23, the phrase *'eškol ᵃnāḇîm* refers to a cluster of grapes. It is used figuratively of Israel in the parable of Isaiah (Is. 5:2, 4); and in a figurative sense with *dām*, blood, in Genesis 49:11. Grapes were used in the production of raisin cakes (Hos. 3:1), a food used in idolatrous worship as well as in a common meal. *
– 2 Is. 5:2, 4: wild grape ➔ WORTHLESS ONE <891>.

GRAPE (TENDER) – *sᵉmāḏar* [masc. noun: סְמָדַר <5563>; of uncertain deriv.] ► **This word refers to young fruits of the grapevine, grapes in blossom.** It refers to grapes as they are flowering, in blossom at various stages (Song 2:13, 15; 7:12), giving off a pleasant fragrance. ¶

GRAPE GATHERING, GRAPE HARVEST – Lev. 26:5; Judg. 8:2; Is. 24:13; 32:10; Jer. 48:32; Mic. 7:1 ➔ VINTAGE <1210>.

GRAPES – Hab. 3:17 ➔ INCREASE (noun) <2981>.

GRASP – 1 *tāmaḵ* [verb: תָּמַךְ <8551>; a prim. root] ► **This word means to seize something, to hold, to support.** It means to grasp, seize something, to take hold of a person's hand (Gen. 48:17); a person (Is. 41:10); a scepter or a pole (Amos 1:5, 8). It refers to grasping and supporting a person's hands and arms (Ex. 17:12). It is used figuratively of supporting someone, as God supports His people (Ps. 16:5; 41:12; 63:8); or of holding on firmly to God's ways (Ps. 17:5; Prov. 4:4). Those who hold to wisdom find her a tree of life (Prov. 3:18). Its passive sense refers to being held tightly, firmly, e.g., the evil person held fast by his sins (Prov. 5:22). *
– 2 Gen. 25:26 ➔ HOLD (TAKE) <270> 3 Judg. 16:29 ➔ HOLD OF (TAKE) <3943> 4 1 Kgs. 20:33 ➔ CATCH (verb) <2480> 5 Is. 22:17 ➔ WRAP AROUND <5844> b.

GRASPED – Ezek. 21:15 ➔ WRAPPED UP <4593>.

GRASPING – 1 Eccl. 1:14; 2:11, 17, 26; 4:4, 6; 6:9 ➔ STRIVING <7469> 2 Eccl. 1:17; 2:22; 4:16 ➔ STRIVING <7475>.

GRASS – 1 *deše', dāšā'* [masc. noun and verb: דֶּשֶׁא, דָּשָׁא <1877>; from PRODUCE (verb) <1876>] ►
a. This word refers to herbage; grass or tender green grass, which is a plant with narrow green leaves. It is the grass produced initially by the earth at God's command (Gen. 1:11), often after rain (2 Sam.

23:4). God causes it to spring forth (Job 38:27), and it is refreshed by rain (Deut. 32:2) but withers in drought (Is. 15:6). It is food for the wild donkey (Job 6:5) and the heifer (Jer. 50:11; ESV, KJV). Its frailty and transitory nature is a picture of the wicked (Ps. 37:2), but its ability also to flourish symbolizes God's people when the Lord blesses them (Is. 66:14). *

b. This word is rendered to thresh, threshing grain. Ref.: Jer. 50:11; NASB, NIV, NKJV, referring to Babylon's trampling of God's people. ¶

[2] ***deṯe'*** [Aramaic masc. noun: דְּתֵא <1883>; corresponding to <1877> above] ▶ **This word denotes also new grass (a plant with narrow green leaves), young herbage.** It refers to the grass in the field of Nebuchadnezzar's dream (Dan. 4:15, 23) that surrounds the tree stump. It possibly serves as a symbol of fertility and hope here. ¶

[3] ***ḥāṣiyr*** [masc. noun: חָצִיר <2682>; perhaps originally the same as ABODE <2681>, from the greenness of a courtyard] ▶

a. This word refers to grass (a plant with narrow, green leaves), hay, reed, herbage. It is food for animals (1 Kgs. 18:5; Job 40:15; Ps. 104:14). It is used in a simile to indicate abundant growth (Is. 44:4). Its brief life and fragile existence is used to symbolize something that easily or quickly dies (Job 8:12), especially grass that often grew on housetops in the Middle East (2 Kgs. 19:26; Ps. 129:6; Is. 37:27). Its frailty described the wicked (Ps. 37:2); or of human beings in general (Ps. 90:5; 103:15). Other refs.: Ps. 147:8; Prov. 27:25; Is. 15:6; 35:7; 40:6–8; 51:12. ¶

b. This word designates leeks. A large onion-like plant of the lily family (Num. 11:5), eaten by Israelites in Egypt. ¶

[4] ***yereq*** [masc. noun: יֶרֶק <3418>; from SPIT (verb) <3417> (in the sense of vacuity of color)] ▶ **This word also refers to herbs, green plants, trees; something green.** It refers to the greenery that sprouts from the earth and is edible by living creatures (Gen. 1:30). It defines grass as green (Ps. 37:2); or is used alone to mean grass (Num. 22:4). It was a desirable food for locusts (Ex. 10:15). Its withering was a sign of drought or scarcity (Is. 15:6); and it was easily killed by the heat (Is. 37:27 in some translations). Other refs.: Gen. 9:3; 2 Kgs. 19:26. ¶

[5] ***yārāq*** [masc. noun: יָרָק <3419>; from the same as <3418> above] ▶ **This word also indicates green herbs, garden vegetables.** It indicates a fresh growth of grass (Is. 37:27 in some translations) or herbs. It takes on the sense of green vegetables (Deut. 11:10; 1 Kgs. 21:2; 2 Kgs. 19:26; Is. 37:27). It describes a meal of vegetables (or herbs), considered a modest meal (Prov. 15:17). ¶

[6] ***'êśeḇ, ʿᵃśaḇ*** [masc. noun: עֵשֶׂב, עֲשַׂב <6212>, <6211>; from an unused root meaning to glisten (or be green)] ▶

a. This word indicates grass, herbage, plants, herbs. In a broad sense, it includes all green growth, including grass of the field (Gen. 3:18; Ex. 9:22). It is used of food for cattle (Deut. 11:15; Ps. 106:20); and, excluding grass, of food for people (Gen. 3:18). For grass, see *deše'*. The phrase *'ēśeḇ zôrēᵃʿ zeraʿ* indicates seed-bearing plants (Gen. 1:29). The frailty of grass depicts a fragile, failing heart (Ps. 102:4). The days of a person pass quickly like grass (Ps. 102:11). It is used in an inclusive sense of all the green plants of the earth (Ps. 72:16). *

b. An Aramaic masculine noun meaning grass (a plant with narrow green leaves), herbage. It is a collective noun referring to all green growth. It describes the earth (Dan. 4:15). Grass is not normally for human consumption but for animals (Dan. 4:25; 5:21). *

GRASS (DRY) – ***ḥᵃšaš*** [masc. noun: חֲשַׁשׁ <2842>; by variation for STUBBLE <7179>] ▶ **This word refers to the useless part of hay, straw, or grain; it is also translated chaff.** It is used in a figurative expression of chaff or dry grass bursting into flame to depict God's corrupted vineyard, Israel (Is. 5:24). It can refer to anything considered useless, worthless, and easily consumed (Is. 33:11). ¶

GRASSHOPPER – [1] Num. 13:33; Eccl. 12:5; Is. 40:22 ➔ LOCUST <2284>

2 1 Kgs. 8:37; 2 Chr. 6:28; Ps. 78:46 ➔ CATERPILLAR <2625> 3 Ps. 105:34; Jer. 51:14, 27 ➔ LOCUST (YOUNG, CRAWLING) <3218> 4 See LOCUST <697>.

GRATE – Ex. 27:4; 35:16; 38:4, 5, 30; 39:39 ➔ GRATING <4345>.

GRATING – ***miḵbār*** [masc. noun: מִכְבָּר <4345>; from MULTIPLY <3527> in the sense of covering (comp. SIEVE <3531>)] ▶ **This word refers to a structure of interlaced or intertwined metal pieces serving as a cover or grating on the bronze altar.** Refs.: Ex. 27:4; 35:16; 38:4, 5, 30; 39:39; KJV: grate. ¶

GRAVE (noun) – 1 ***qeḇer*** [masc. noun: קֶבֶר <6913>; from BURY <6912>] ▶ **This word means a burial place; it is also translated tomb, sepulcher.** The grave was a place of grief (2 Sam. 3:32; Ps. 88:11); the end of life in contrast to the womb (Job 10:19; Jer. 20:17). The dead were laid to rest, often with previously deceased relatives (2 Sam. 19:37). In the Old Testament, graves were associated with uncleanness: one who touched a grave (or a bone, cf. 2 Chr. 34:5) had to be ceremonially cleansed (Num. 19:16–19). Josiah sprinkled the dust of crushed idolatrous paraphernalia on graves of idol worshipers to defile the idols (2 Kgs. 23:6; 2 Chr. 34:4). In a figurative sense, Isaiah prophesied against his self-righteous countrymen as living among graves and eating the flesh of swine (Is. 65:4; cf. Matt. 23:27, 28). Ezekiel prophesied that God would revive the Israelites from their graves, i.e., from their exile and defilement among idolatrous nations (Ezek. 37:12, 13). *
– 2 Job 30:24 ➔ HEAP OF RUINS <1164> 3 Ps. 107:20 ➔ PIT <7825> 4 See SHEOL <7585>.

GRAVE (verb) – Ex. 32:16 ➔ ENGRAVE <2801>.

GRAVEL – 1 ***ḥāṣāṣ*** [masc. noun: חָצָץ <2687>; from DIVIDE <2686> a. (properly something cutting)] ▶ **This word is used figuratively of a mouthful of bread that tastes like gravel, i.e., small rock fragments.** Ref.: Prov. 20:17. Gravel, representing God's judgments, breaks one's teeth (Lam. 3:16). ¶
– 2 Is. 48:19 ➔ GRAIN <4579>.

GRAVEN – Hab. 2:18 ➔ CUT (verb) <6458>.

GRAVESTONE – 2 Kgs. 23:17 ➔ MONUMENT <6725>.

GRAVING – 1 Kgs. 7:31 ➔ CARVING <4734>.

GRAVING TOOL – ***ḥereṭ*** [masc. noun: חֶרֶט <2747>; from a prim. root meaning to engrave] ▶ **This word designates a carving implement, a chisel.** It is an instrument used by Aaron to "fashion" or "dress down" the golden calf (Ex. 32:4; also translated engraving tool, tool). Its use further implicated Aaron the guilt of the Israelites. The word is also used in Isaiah 8:1 (pen, stylus) as a writing utensil. ¶

GRAY, GRAY-HAIRED, GRAYHEADED (BE) – ***śiyḇ*** [verb: שִׂיב <7867>; a prim. root (properly, to become aged)] ▶ **This word means to be hoary, i.e., crowned with gray or grayish-white hair, an indication of becoming aged.** In Samuel's farewell speech, he stated that it was time for him to step down, for he was old and gray (1 Sam. 12:2). Eliphaz used the word in Job to designate those that have grown gray-haired and aged, in his somewhat skewed argument to Job. These people are denoted as having wisdom above anyone else of a younger age (Job 15:10). ¶

GRAY HAIR – See OLD AGE <7872>.

GRAY-SPOTTED – Gen. 31:10, 12 ➔ MOTTLED <1261>.

GRAZE – Ex. 22:5 ➔ BURN (verb) <1197> b.

GREAT – 1 ***gāḏôl, gāḏōl, haggᵉḏôliym*** [adj.: גָּדוֹל, גָּדֹל, הַגְּדוֹלִים <1419>; from GREAT

(BECOME) <1431>] ▶ **This word emphasizes the importance, size, and significance of something or someone.** It is used to attribute theological importance in various ways to things of great significance: God's great acts of redemption are emphasized, His great and awesome things (Deut. 10:21; Ps. 71:19; 106:21); His great acts in nature and in general are recognized (Job 5:9; 9:10; 37:5). It is used to describe the might and greatness of God's arm which brought Israel from Egypt (Ex. 15:16). God's presence and character in power, counsel, compassion, and mercy are described as great (Ps. 145:8; Is. 54:7; Jer. 32:19; Nah. 1:3). It designates persons as influential, masters, great (Gen. 39:9) or as leading persons (2 Kgs. 10:6). Elisha's miracles are great and influential (2 Kgs. 8:4). The word is used to describe an intensity or extent of fear (Deut. 4:34; Prov. 19:19); weeping (Is. 38:3); evil or sin (Gen. 4:13; 20:9; 39:9). It is used in general to describe whatever is large, numerous, or intent, such as a sea (Num. 34:6); river (Gen. 15:18); wilderness (Deut. 1:19); number (Gen. 12:2; 2 Kgs. 10:19; Jer. 31:8); sound (Gen. 39:14; Ex. 11:6); or one's age (Gen. 10:21; 27:1; 29:16). A few fixed expressions occur using this word: the great king, referring to the king of Assyria (2 Kgs. 18:19, 28); the great (high) priest (Lev. 21:10); the great sea, meaning the Mediterranean Sea (Num. 34:6); the great river meaning the Euphrates (Deut. 1:7). *

2 ***gārōl*** [adj.: גָּרֹל <1632>; from the same as LOT (noun) <1486>] ▶ **This word is used to describe excessive anger as great anger.** Ref.: Prov. 19:19, NASB, KJV, NKJV, ESV. Others prefer to translate it as indicating a "hot-tempered" person (NIV). ¶

3 ***raḇ*** [Aramaic adj.: רַב <7229>; corresponding to MANY <7227>] ▶ **This word means boastful, large.** Used to define words, it indicates words of insolence (Dan. 7:20). It indicates that a king is great (Dan. 2:10); a statue is huge (Dan. 2:31); a magician is the head, chief musician (Dan. 4:9); a nation is great (Dan. 4:30). *

4 ***śaggiy'*** [Aramaic adj.: שַׂגִּיא <7690>; corresponding to EXALTED <7689>] ▶ **This word means abundant, many, much.** It refers to the power, splendor, and influence of a king as being great (Ezra 5:11). It indicates an abundance, an extent or high degree of something, honor (Dan. 2:6); fury (Dan. 2:12); size (Dan. 2:31; 4:10); quality of gifts, great gifts (Dan. 2:48); fruit, meat (Dan. 4:12, 21; 7:5). It figuratively describes a person's emotions, e.g., great alarm, anxiety, dread (Dan. 5:9; 6:14, 23; 7:28). ¶

– 5 Ex. 11:8; 2 Chr. 25:10 ➔ FIERCE <2750> 6 Job 8:2; Is. 17:12 ➔ MIGHTY <3524> 7 Job 36:26; 37:23 ➔ EXALTED <7689> 8 Ezra 5:8; 6:4 ➔ HUGE <1560> 9 Is. 33:23 ➔ INCREASE (noun) 4766> 10 Ezek. 41:8 ➔ LONG (adj.) <679> 11 Hos. 5:13; 10:6 ➔ JAREB <3377> b.

GREAT (BECOME) – ***rᵉḇāh*** [Aramaic verb: רְבָה <7236>; corresponding to MANY (BE, BECOME) <7231>] ▶ **This word refers to raising a person's official rank or position.** Ref.: Dan. 2:48. It describes a process of growth (Dan. 4:11, 20, 33); and the process of the increase in a ruler's power and greatness (Dan. 4:22). ¶

GREAT (BECOME, MAKE) – ***gāḏal*** [verb: גָּדַל <1431>; a prim. root] ▶ **This word means to magnify, to grow up, to grow; to promote.** It refers to the natural process of a person's development, a child's growing up (Gen. 21:8, 20; 25:27; Ex. 2:10, 11). It indicates that something or someone becomes great or influential in wealth (Gen. 26:13; Jer. 5:27); value (1 Sam. 26:24); or importance (1 Kgs. 10:23; Eccl. 2:9; Dan. 8:9, 10). It indicates the greatness of the Messiah that extends throughout the earth (Mic. 5:4) or to the importance of Jerusalem (Ezek. 16:7).

The verb asserts the greatness of God (2 Sam. 7:22; Ps. 104:1) and His works (Ps. 92:5). In the sense of magnifying something, it refers to magnifying the Lord Himself (Ps. 35:27; 40:16; 70:4), along with His name (2 Sam. 7:26). In some forms, the word means to cause something to grow, become great: hair (Num. 6:5); plants (Is. 44:14; Jon. 4:10), but it refers to magnifying or making God great as well (Ps. 34:3). The Lord's acts of salvation are made great by Himself (Ps. 18:50). The Lord promised to make Abraham's name great (Gen. 12:2). It means to promote someone to a higher office or position (Esther 3:1). Used of children, it may mean to bring them up (Is. 1:2) or educate them (Dan. 1:5). Used in a reflexive sense, the word means to magnify oneself (Ezek. 38:23) or boast (Is. 10:15; Dan. 11:36, 37). *

GREAT (MAKE) – ***śāgā'*** [verb: שָׂגָא <7679>; a prim. root] ▶ **This word means to grow, to magnify, to exalt, to extol.** It refers to the growth and development of a nation (Job 12:23: KJV: to increase); and to the great acts and works of God in general (Job 36:24). ¶

GREAT NUMBER – Nah. 3:3 → HEAVINESS <3514>.

GREAT, GREAT THINGS – ***raḇraḇ*** [Aramaic adj.: רַבְרַב <7260>; from GREAT <7229>] ▶ **This word means abundant, huge (in size), domineering (in character); it refers to the value and significance of relatively important, large gifts, such as rulership, authority, etc.** Ref.: Dan. 2:48. It indicates the splendor and magnificence of God's signs and words as great (Dan. 4:3). It describes the awesome and powerful aspects of the four beasts of Daniel's vision (Dan. 7:3, 7, 8, 17). It may have the sense of boastful, arrogant words uttered (Dan. 7:11, 20). ¶

GREATEST PART – 1 Chr. 12:29 → INCREASE (noun) <4768>.

GREATLY – Is. 31:6 → DEEP, DEEP (BE) <6009>.

GREATNESS – [1] ***g^{e}ḏûllāh, g^{e}ḏullāh*** [fem. noun: גְּדוּלָּה, גְּדֻלָּה <1420>; fem. of GREAT (BECOME) <1419>] ▶ **This word depicts the surpassing deeds and acts of God.** Ref.: Ps. 145:6. It includes His great act in choosing David and making him king (2 Sam. 7:21, 23; 1 Chr. 17:19, 21). Greatness is ascribed to God Himself because of His actions (1 Chr. 29:11; Ps. 145:3). It is used in this way to refer to honorable persons, such as Mordecai (Esther 10:2; Ps. 71:21). It depicts the great majesty of kingship (Esther 1:4). It indicates dignity or recognition given as a reward (Esther 6:3). ¶

[2] ***gōḏel*** [masc. noun: גֹּדֶל <1433>; from GREAT (BECOME) <1431>] ▶ **This word means something large, important; it also indicates majesty.** It is used to describe anything large: a great tree (Ezek. 31:7); persons (Ezek. 31:2); in a figurative sense, God's grace (Num. 14:19) or greatness through His mighty acts (Deut. 3:24) and power (Ps. 79:11). The psalmist calls God's greatness excellent (NASB, KJV) or surpassing (NIV) (Ps. 150:2, lit., abundant). It takes on the meaning of arrogance or bravado (Is. 9:9) with respect to Israel's rebellions. It indicates the extreme arrogance of the heart of the great king of Assyria that the Lord would bring down (Is. 10:12). *

[3] ***r^{e}ḇû*** [Aramaic fem. noun: רְבוּ <7238>; from a root corresponding to MANY (BE, BECOME) <7235>] ▶ **This word indicates the magnitude and the importance of something; it is also translated majesty.** It is an abstract noun referring to the splendor, grandeur, and honor surrounding a great king or ruler (Dan. 4:22, 36); all the benefits bestowed by God (Dan. 5:18, 19). It indicates the majesty and greatness of all the kingdoms of the earth (Dan. 7:27). ¶

– [4] 2 Chr. 9:6 → INCREASE (noun) <4768> [5] Is. 9:7 → INCREASE (noun) <4766>.

GREAVES – ***miṣḥāh*** [fem. noun: מִצְחָה <4697>; from the same as FOREHEAD <4696>] ▶ **This word refers to leg armor, shin guards worn on a soldier's legs.** Ref.: 1 Sam. 17:6. ¶

GRECIAN – ***y^{e}wāniy*** [masc. proper noun: יְוָנִי <3125>; patron. from <3120>] ▶ **This word is a reference to the Greeks, i.e., a Javanite or descendant of Javan.** It is used only in Joel 3:6. ¶

GREEDY (BE) – Ps. 17:12 → LONG FOR <3700>.

GREEN, GREEN (BE) – 1 ***laḥ*** [adj.: לַח <3892>; from an unused root meaning to be new] ▶ **This word indicates that something is still green (grass-colored), fresh, moist, newly picked.** Jacob's rod (Gen. 30:37); grapes (Num. 6:3); bowstrings (Judg. 16:7, 8); wood (Ezek. 17:24; 20:47). ¶

2 ***ra'ᵃnān*** [adj.: רַעֲנָן <7488>; from an unused root meaning to be green] ▶ **This word means verdant, new, prosperous; it is also translated flourishing, luxuriant.** It refers to a luxuriant plant or tree, flourishing and full of vibrant life (Job 15:32); green and healthy looking, a place where fertility worship was often practiced (Deut. 12:2; 1 Kgs. 14:23; 2 Kgs. 16:4; Is. 57:5; Jer. 2:20; Ezek. 6:13). It is used in similes for comparisons (Ps. 37:35; 52:8). Used of oil, it means new, pure, fresh olive oil (Ps. 92:10); of a love seat, it means luxuriant, beautiful (Song 1:16). The Lord Himself is described as the true luxuriant cypress tree for His people (Hos. 14:8). *

3 ***rā'an, ra'ᵃnan*** [רְעַן, רַעֲנַן <7487>; corresponding to GREEN <7488>] ▶

a. This verb indicates to grow luxurious; to flourish. It indicates, with reference to a tree limb, a lively, fresh, tender green branch, flourishing and developing (Job 15:32).

b. This Aramaic adjective means flourishing; it is also translated prospering, prosperous. This adjective is used figuratively of the success of a person or a king, his prosperity (Dan. 4:4). ¶

– 4 2 Kgs. 19:26; Is. 37:27 ➔ GRASS <3419> 5 Esther 1:6 ➔ LINEN <3768> 6 Job 8:12 ➔ GREENNESS <3> 7 Job 8:16 ➔ LUSH <7373>.

GREEN (BE, BECOME, TURN) – Joel 2:22 ➔ PRODUCE (verb) <1876>.

GREEN THING – ***yārôq*** [masc. noun: יָרוֹק <3387>; from SPIT (verb) <3417>] ▶ **This word refers to that which is the color of grasses and herbs; a green plant, verdant plants.** It denotes edible green plants sought out by mountain goats as food (Job 39:8). ¶

GREEN, GREEN THING – Gen. 1:30; 9:3; Ex. 10:15; 2 Kgs. 19:26; Ps. 37:2; Is. 15:6; 37:27 ➔ GRASS <3418>.

GREENISH – ***yᵉraqraq*** [adj.: יְרַקְרַק <3422>; from the same as GRASS <3418>] ▶ **This word means having a grass-colored shade of yellow, a tawny shade of gold.** It indicates a sickening growth on leather or human skin, such as dry rot in a house (Lev. 13:49; 14:37). It has, however, a positive meaning in Psalm 68:13 (yellow, glistening, shimmering, shining) where a dove's wings are gilded with a glistening or yellow-gold color. ¶

GREENNESS – ***'ēḇ*** [masc. noun: אֵב <3>; from the same as EAR <24>] ▶ **The word means freshness, fresh green growth, new growth, verdure.** It refers to healthy papyrus and rush plants (Job 8:12); it is also translated green, growing, in flower. It refers as well to vigorous greenery or flourishing vegetation (Song 6:11) or perhaps blossoms of a valley; the word is translated blossom, fruit, growth, verdure. ¶

GREETING – Ezra 4:17; 5:7: greeting, greetings, cordial greetings ➔ PEACE <8001>.

GREETINGS – Ezra 7:12 ➔ PERFECT PEACE <1585>.

GREYHOUND – 1 Prov. 30:31 ➔ LOINS <4975> c. 2 Prov. 30:31 ➔ STRUTTING ROOSTER <2223>.

GRIDDLE – ***maḥᵃḇaṯ*** [fem. noun: מַחֲבַת <4227>; from the same as PANS <2281>] ▶ **This word indicates a flat pan.** It was a metal cooking utensil used for roasting or frying items prepared for sacrificial use (Lev. 2:5; 6:21; 7:9; Ezek. 4:3). In 1 Chronicles 23:29, it designates that which has been cooked in one of these pans or griddles. ¶

GRIEF – 1 ***mōrāh*** [fem. noun: מֹרָה <4786>; from BITTER (BE) <4843>] ▶ **This word means sorrow, bitterness.** It describes an emotional response of strong disappointment and sorrow of spirit over something (Gen. 26:35); a condition of one's soul known by one's heart (Prov. 14:10). ¶

2 *pûqāh* [fem. noun: פּוּקָה <6330>; from STUMBLE <6328> (in the sense of a stumbling-block)] ▶ **This word refers to a feeling of regret or guilt because of something that has occurred.** Ref.: 1 Sam. 25:31. ¶

– 3 Esther 6:12: in grief ➔ MOURNING <57> 4 Job 2:13; 16:6 ➔ PAIN (noun) <3511> 5 Ps. 119:28; Prov. 10:1; 14:13; 17:21 ➔ SORROW (noun) <8424> 6 Prov. 10:10 ➔ SORROW (noun) <6094> 7 Is. 17:11 ➔ SICK (BE) <2470> 8 Jer. 8:18; Ps. 31:10 ➔ SORROW (noun) <3015>.

GRIEF (BITTER) – Ezek. 21:6 ➔ BITTER GRIEF <4814>.

GRIEF (BRING, CAUSE) – Lam. 1:5; 3:32 ➔ AFFLICT <3013>.

GRIEVE – 1 *'āḏaḇ* [verb: אָדַב <109>; a prim. root] ▶ **This word means to sadden or cause to be sad.** It refers to the grief that Eli would experience at the death of his descendants (1 Sam. 2:33). ¶

– 2 1 Sam. 15:35; 16:1 ➔ MOURN <56> 3 1 Sam. 20:34 ➔ HURT <6087> 4 Lam. 1:4; Zeph. 3:18 ➔ AFFLICT <3013> 5 Ezek. 9:4 ➔ GROAN (verb) <584>.

GRIEVE, GRIEVED (BE) – Ps. 95:10; 119:158; 139:21 ➔ LOATHE <6962>.

GRIEVED – *'āḡêm* [adj.: אָגֵם <99>; prob. from the same as POND <98> (in the sense of stagnant water)] ▶

a. An adjective meaning sick or stagnant; hence stagnant pond. It refers to hired laborers of Egypt, describing them as those who make ponds, in Isaiah 19:10 (KJV). But see b. also. ¶

b. A collective masculine adjective meaning saddened, troubled, or sick. It describes the grieved spirit of laborers or wage earners in Isaiah 19:10 (NASB, NIV, NKJV, ESV). ¶

GRIEVED (BE) – 1 ***kā'āh*** [verb: כָּאָה <3512>; a prim. root] ▶ **This word means to be brokenhearted, to be disheartened; it is also translated to be afraid, to lose heart, to make sad, to dishearten. The word describes a feeling of depression or discouragement, a loss of hope.** It describes the discouraged or depressed reaction of a person toward a superior foe who cannot be defeated (Dan. 11:30). It refers to the act of discouraging or disheartening the righteous (Ezek. 13:22); as well as those already despondent (Ps. 109:16; also translated broken). ¶

2 ***k^erāh*** [Aramaic verb: כְּרָה <3735>; prob. corresponding to DIG <3738> in the sense of piercing (fig.)] ▶ **This word indicates an agitated, worried attitude and set of emotions; it is also translated to be troubled, to be anxious, to be distressed.** Ref.: Dan. 7:15. Daniel was put into this state by an overwhelming dream or vision (see Dan. 7:1). ¶

3 ***'āḡam*** [verb: עָגַם <5701>; a prim. root] ▶ **This word refers to a response of grief, sorrow, lamentation for something or someone, especially the poor.** Ref.: Job 30:25. ¶

– 4 Ps. 73:21 ➔ LEAVENED (BE) <2556>.

GRIEVOUS – 1 ***māraṣ*** [verb: מָרַץ <4834>; a prim. root] ▶ **This word indicates to be sick, painful.** It describes a curse as hurtful, pernicious (1 Kgs. 2:8; also translated malicious, violent, bitter); destruction or punishment as painful (Mic. 2:10; also translated sore); words as unsettling, irritating (Job 6:25; also translated forceful, forcible); an unknown motivation or cause as provoking an argument (Job 16:3: to embolden, to plague, to provoke, to ail). ¶

– 2 Prov. 15:1 ➔ PAIN (noun) <6089>.

GRIEVOUS (BE) – Is. 15:4 ➔ TREMBLE <3415>.

GRIEVOUS THINGS – Ps. 31:18 ➔ ARROGANCE <6277>.

GRIEVOUSNESS – Is. 21:15 ➔ HEAVINESS <3514>.

GRIND – 1 ***kāṯaš*** [verb: כָּתַשׁ <3806>; a prim. root] ▶ **This word refers to pounding, mashing or pulverizing something in a mortar with a pestle; it is also translated to pound, to crush, to bray.** It is used figuratively of grinding a fool in a mortar (Prov. 27:22), to no avail in removing his foolishness. ¶
– 2 Ex. 30:36 ➔ BEAT <7833> 3 Lam. 3:16 ➔ BREAK <1638> 4 Lam. 5:13 ➔ MILL <2911> 5 See BEAT <1854>.

GRIND, GRINDER (verb and fem. noun) – ***ṭaḥan, ṭōḥªnāh*** [טָחַן, טֹחֲנָה <2912>; a prim. root] ▶
a. A verb meaning to mill, to crush, to pulverize. It indicates the labor of grinding at a mill (Judg. 16:21), but it is used in special cases too: the golden calf was ground up (Ex. 32:20; Deut. 9:21); the grinding or gritting of one's teeth (Eccl. 12:3); the grinding of manna (Num. 11:8). It is used figuratively and literally of Babylon's punishment and destruction as her daughters grind with millstones (Is. 47:2); and of the "grinding" of the faces of the poor (Is. 3:15). In a different context, it indicates serving a person (Job 31:10). ¶
b. A feminine noun indicating a molar, a grinder. It is used to depict "grinders," i.e., the teeth of older people, their molars, that are deteriorating (Eccl. 12:3). Possibly it refers, instead, to female millers or grinders. ¶

GRINDING – ***ṭaḥªnāh*** [fem. noun: טַחֲנָה <2913>; from GRIND, GRINDER <2912>] ▶ **This word means a hand-mill, grinding mill, or a millstone.** Literally it refers to a mill, a grinding mill, but it may be used figuratively in this context for teeth or the chewing action of one's mouth (Eccl. 12:4). ¶

GRINDING MILL – Lam. 5:13 ➔ MILL <2911>.

GRIP – Ex. 15:14 ➔ HOLD (TAKE) <270>.

GRISLED – Gen. 31:10, 12; Zech. 6:3, 6 ➔ MOTTLED <1261>.

GRIT – Lev. 2:14, 16 ➔ CRUSHED <1643>.

GROAN (noun) – Ps. 79:11; 102:20 ➔ GROANING <603>.

GROAN (verb) – 1 ***'ānaḥ*** [verb: אָנַח <584>; a prim. root] ▶ **This word means and is also translated to moan, to sigh, to grieve, to mourn.** It indicates a universal response to grave oppression or despair as when Israel was in Egypt (Ex. 2:23). More generally, it is also the response of a people when they are ruled by a wicked government or of persons who are deprived of their pleasures or addictions (Is. 24:7). Groaning or moaning is the response of a people whom God judges, much as Lebanon (Jer. 22:23), or a desolated city (Lam. 1:4, 8, 11, 21), such as Jerusalem. Even animals moan because of destruction (Joel 1:18). The righteous groan because of injustice and corruption (Ezek. 9:4), and especially God's righteous prophets (Ezek. 21:6, 7) groan over the rebellion of God's people. Other ref.: Prov. 29:2. ¶
2 ***'ānaq*** [verb: אָנַק <602>; a prim. root] ▶ **This word means to cry out, to groan silently, to lament, to sigh.** It depicts the cries of the mortally wounded (Jer. 51:52), as well as those who cry out and groan because of the slaughter of war and judgment (Ezek. 26:15). It also describes the groans of those who are devastated and shocked by moral and spiritual atrocities, especially those committed in Jerusalem (Ezek. 9:4). Ezekiel groans, but silently and inwardly, as with strangled groans, over the death of his wife (Ezek. 24:17). ¶
3 ***nā'aq*** [verb: נָאַק <5008>; a prim. root] ▶ **This word means to moan, to make sounds of despair because of oppression; to seek help.** Refs.: Job 24:12; Ezek. 30:24. ¶
– 4 Ps. 38:8 ➔ ROARING <5100> 5 Prov. 5:11; Ezek. 24:23 ➔ ROAR (verb) <5098> 6 Is. 42:14 ➔ CRY (verb) <6463>.

GROANING – 1 ***ªnāḥāh*** [fem. noun: אֲנָחָה <585>; from GROAN (verb) <584>] ▶ **This word means and is also translated**

moaning, sighing. This response is brought on by physical (Job 3:24; 23:2), spiritual, or mental despair (Ps. 6:6). It involves both body and soul (Ps. 31:9, 10; 38:9; Lam. 1:22; Jer. 45:3). Babylon would be punished because of the groaning she caused to others (Is. 21:2). But sighing and groaning will be removed from the redeemed of the Lord (Is. 35:10). *
2 ***ᵃnāqāh*** [fem. noun: אֲנָקָה <603>; from GROAN (verb) <602>] ▶ **This word describes the cry and expression of those who are needy or are wrongfully imprisoned; it is also translated sighing, groan, crying.** Refs.: Ps. 12:5; 79:11; 102:20. Groaning may be misplaced because the one crying out is in the wrong (Mal. 2:13). ¶
3 ***nᵉ'āqāh*** [fem. noun: נְאָקָה <5009>; from GROAN (verb) <5008>] ▶ **This word means a sigh, the uttering of sounds of despair, especially because of oppression.** Refs.: Ex. 2:24; 6:5; Judg. 2:18; Ezek. 30:24. ¶
– 4 Ps. 5:1 ➔ MEDITATION <1901>.

GROPE – 1 ***gāšaš*** [verb: גָּשַׁשׁ <1659>; a prim. root] ▶ **This word means to feel about with the hand, to seek by feeling.** It is used in a figurative sense of people groping along a wall in blindness because of their wickedness (Is. 59:10). ¶
– 2 Deut. 28:29; Job 5:14; 12:25 ➔ FEEL <4959>.

GROUND – ***ᵃḏāmāh*** [fem. noun: אֲדָמָה <127>; from RUDDY (BE) <119>] ▶ **This word means dirt, earth, clay.** In its narrow sense, it signifies the earth or clay God used to form man (Gen. 2:7); dirt put on the head during mourning (2 Sam. 1:2; Neh. 9:1); the ground itself (Ex. 3:5); cultivated land (Gen. 4:2; Zech. 13:5). In a broader sense, it means the inhabited earth (Is. 24:21; Amos 3:2). The first man, Adam, both came from the ground and was assigned the task of tending the ground (see Gen. 2:7, 15). *

GROUND MEAL – Num. 15:20, 21; Neh. 10:37; Ezek. 44:30 ➔ DOUGH <6182>.

GROUP – 1 ***maḥlᵉqāh*** [Aramaic fem. noun: מַחְלְקָה <4255>; corresponding to ESCAPE (noun) <4256> b.] ▶ **This word indicates the sets of people into which the Levites were divided.** Ref.: Ezra 6:18; also translated division, course. ¶
– 2 1 Sam. 10:5, 10 ➔ ROPE <2256> 3 1 Sam. 19:20 ➔ COMPANY <3862> 4 2 Sam. 2:25 ➔ BUNCH <92> 5 2 Chr. 35:5 ➔ DIVISION <6391>.

GROUPING – 1 2 Chr. 35:5 ➔ DIVISION <6391> 2 2 Chr. 35:12 ➔ DIVISION <4651>.

GROVE – Gen. 21:33 ➔ TAMARISK TREE <815>.

GROVES – Deut. 12:3; 1 Kgs. 14:23; Jer. 17:2 ➔ ASHERAH <842>.

GROW – 1 ***gāḏêl*** [adj.: גָּדֵל <1432>; from GREAT (BECOME) <1431>] ▶ **This word indicates increasing, becoming great, great.** Used with certain verbs (*hālaḵ, hāloḵ*), it means to become greater and greater; i.e., to increase in wealth and influence (Gen. 26:13). It indicates growing up or getting older (1 Sam. 2:26), as well as increasing in power and greatness (2 Chr. 17:12). Its use in Ezekiel 16:26 is best translated figuratively as lustful neighbors (NASB, NIV; cf. KJV, lit., great of flesh). ¶
2 ***dāḡāh*** [verb: דָּגָה <1711>; a prim. root] ▶ **This verb means to multiply; it is also translated to increase. Its primary meaning is to cover.** It is used only in Genesis 48:16 where Jacob blessed Ephraim and Manasseh, the sons of Joseph. He desired that they multiply or grow into a multitude. Jacob prophesied that Ephraim, the younger brother, would be a multitude of nations, more populous than Manasseh (cf. Gen. 48:17–19) but that both would be a model of blessedness (cf. Gen. 48:20). ¶
3 ***ṣāmaḥ*** [verb: צָמַח <6779>; a prim. root] ▶ **This word means to spring forth, to sprout.** It refers to a plant as it breaks forth out of the ground (Gen. 2:5, 9); or to trees as they grow from the ground (Ex. 10:5). Both God and the ground cause plants, trees, etc. to sprout (Gen. 3:18). It describes human hair beginning to grow

(Judg. 16:22; 2 Sam. 10:5). It is used in figurative expressions: trouble or evil sprouting from the ground (Job 5:6); of the good man's offspring (Job 8:19); of truth growing up from the earth (Ps. 85:11); of the sprouting of the line of kings from David (Ps. 132:17; Jer. 33:15; Ezek. 29:21; Zech. 6:12); the springing forth of new things ordained by God (Is. 42:9; 43:19); of Israel growing up as a child (Ezek. 16:7). *

[4] ***śᵉgā'*** [Aramaic verb: שְׂגָא <7680>; corresponding to GREAT (MAKE) <7679>] ▶ **This word indicates that something increases, expands, whether good or bad; it is also translated to increase, to multiply, to abound.** This the case of royal finances (Ezra 4:22) or the well-being of a whole nation (Dan. 4:1; 6:25). ¶

[5] ***śāgāh*** [verb: שָׂגָה <7685>; from EMPTY <7324>] ▶ **This word means to increase, to develop; to thrive.** It refers to an increase or development of something: of life's benefits in general (Job 8:7); of wealth (Ps. 73:12). The righteous person thrives, grows like a cedar in Lebanon (Ps. 92:12). Other ref.: Job 8:11. ¶

[6] ***śûg*** [verb: שׂוּג <7735>; a prim. root] ▶ **This word means to develop, to raise.** It has the sense of to cause to grow (Is. 17:11) or to nurture a plant or seed that sprouts. Others prefer to render it as fence in in order to care for a plant, something sown (NASB). ¶

– [7] Job 8:11 ➔ RISE <1342> [8] Is. 17:11 ➔ ENCIRCLE <5473>.

GROW FAT – Jer. 50:11; Mal. 4:2 ➔ FROLIC <6335> b.

GROW UP – Ps. 129:6 ➔ DRAW OUT <8025>.

GROWER – Amos 7:14 ➔ DRESSER <1103>.

GROWING – Job 8:12 ➔ GREENNESS <3>.

GROWL – [1] ***nā'ar*** [verb: נָעַר <5286>; a prim. root] ▶ **This word describes the sound made by lion cubs in their desire to hurt prey; it is also translated to yell.** It is used figuratively of the Babylonians whom God would overthrow utterly (Jer. 51:38). ¶

– [2] Ex. 11:7 ➔ MOVE <2782>.

GROWLING – [1] Prov. 19:12; 20:2 ➔ ROAR (noun) <5099> [2] Is. 5:30 ➔ ROARING <5100>.

GROWN UP – ***'āpiyl*** [adj.: אָפִיל <648>; from the same as DARK <651> (in the sense of weakness)] ▶ **This word indicates a late ripening. It refers to wheat and spelt as grains which ripen late.** They were not destroyed, therefore, in the plague of hail (Ex. 9:32). ¶

GROWS OF ITSELF (WHAT) – ***sāpiyaḥ*** [masc. noun: סָפִיחַ <5599>; from JOIN <5596>] ▶ **This word referred to what develops in the fields of itself, generated by nature or from spilled seeds.** Refs.: Lev. 25:5, 11; 2 Kgs. 19:29. God used this growth as a sign for His people (2 Kgs. 19:29; Is. 37:30). The Hebrew word also means a torrent; see TORRENT <5599>. ¶

GROWTH – [1] Song 6:11 ➔ GREENNESS <3> [2] Amos 7:1 ➔ CROP <3954>.

GRUB – Is. 51:8 ➔ WORM <5580>.

GRUDGE – Lev. 19:18 ➔ KEEP <5201>.

GRUDGE (BEAR, HOLD) – Gen. 27:41; 50:15; Ps. 55:3 ➔ HATE <7852>.

GRUMBLE – [1] Ex. 15:24; etc. ➔ MURMUR <3885> [2] Deut. 1:27; Ps. 106:25 ➔ MURMUR <7279>.

GRUMBLING – ***tᵉlunāh*** [verb: תְּלֻנָּה <8519>; from MURMUR <3885>] ▶ **This word indicates rebellious expressions of complaint and dissatisfaction against the Lord in particular; it is also translated complaint, mumuring.** Refs.: Ex. 16:7–9, 12; Num. 14:27; 17:5, 10. ¶

GUARANTOR – Prov. 17:18 ➔ PLEDGE (noun) <6161>.

GUARD – [1] ***ṭabbāḥ*** [Aramaic masc. noun: טַבָּח <2877>; the same as GUARD, IMPERIAL GUARD <2876>] ▶ **This word refers to one who prevents the slaughter of a ruler, i.e., imperial guard, bodyguard; executioner (a guard whose duty was to inflict capital punishment).** It is used in the book of Daniel to refer to Arioch who is designated as the chief or captain (*raḇ*) of this bodyguard (Dan. 2:14). ¶

[2] ***maṭṭārāh, maṭṭārā'*** [fem. noun: מַטָּרָה, מַטְּרָא <4307>; from KEEP <5201>] ▶ **This word indicates a guardian, a ward, a prison.** It is used of the men on guard, security forces (Neh. 3:25; 12:39). Used with *ḥ^{a}ṣar*, it referred to the court of the guard; with *ša'ar* it denoted the gate of the guard (Jer. 32:2, 8, 12; 33:1; 37:21; 38:6, 13, 28; 39:14, 15). The Hebrew word also indicates a target, a mark: 1 Sam. 20:20; Job 16:12; Lam. 3:12. ¶

[3] ***mišma'aṯ*** [fem. noun: מִשְׁמַעַת <4928>; from HEARING <4926> (which comes form HEAR <8085>)] ▶ **This word means obedient subjects. It comes from the verb *šāma'*, meaning to hear and obey, and describes a group of people who are bound to obey.** In several instances of this word, it describes a king's personal guard (1 Sam. 22:14; 2 Sam. 23:23; 1 Chr. 11:25); it is also translated bodyguard. In the only other instance, it depicts a conquered people who are bound to obey (Is. 11:14: to obey, to be subject). ¶

[4] ***mišmereṯ*** [fem. noun: מִשְׁמֶרֶת <4931>; from CUSTODY <4929> (which comes from KEEP <8104>] ▶ **This word means charge, duty. This word comes from the verb *šāmar*, meaning to watch, to keep, to protect, or to guard, and has a multiplicity of usages.** In its most basic sense, it describes a guarded place (Num. 17:10; 1 Sam. 22:23); keeping for later use (Ex. 12:6; 16:32–34); or protection against enemies (2 Kgs. 11:5–7). In several instances, it is used of a guard post (Is. 21:8; Hab. 2:1). The idea of obedience (i.e., keeping the commandments) is often depicted, which leads to a translation of charge (Gen. 26:5; Deut. 11:1; Zech. 3:7) or duty (Num. 3:7; 9:23; 2 Chr. 8:14). *

[5] ***p^eqiḏuṯ*** [fem. noun: פְּקִדֻת <6488>] ▶ **This word means supervision, oversight.** It occurs only in Jeremiah 37:13, where it refers with the word *ba'al* (<1167>), meaning master, to an official or policeman as a master of supervision. In this passage, the officer was stationed at the Gate of Benjamin where financial transactions took place (cf. Deut. 21:19; Ruth 4:1 ff.); and where the king sometimes officiated (cf. Jer. 38:7). The office gave its bearer the legal power to arrest Jeremiah (Jer. 37:13). ¶

[6] ***šāmrāh*** [fem. noun: שָׁמְרָה <8108>; fem. of an unused root from KEEP <8104>] ▶ **This word refers to a state of careful observation and watchfulness over something, a protective and preventative measure.** Ref.: Ps. 141:3; KJV: watch. ¶

– [7] Dan. 1:11, 16 ➔ STEWARD <4453> [8] Nah. 3:17 ➔ CROWNED ONE <4502> b. [9] Zech. 9:8 ➔ GARRISON <4675>.

GUARD, IMPERIAL GUARD – ***ṭabbāḥ*** [masc. noun: טַבָּח <2876>; from SLAUGHTER (verb) <2873>] ▶ **In its plural form only, this word refers to bodyguard or special elite guard of the military.** Refs.: Gen. 37:36; 39:1; 40:3, 4; 41:10, 12. Potiphar was the head of a group of these men. Nebuzaradan was the captain of these forces for Nebuchadnezzar (2 Kgs. 25:8, 10–12, 15, 18, 20). The connection between these meanings and the following contextual meaning seems to be that these persons were the "royal executioners." In another context, this word takes on the meaning of butcher or cook (1 Sam. 9:23, 24). Other refs.: Jer. 39:9–11, 13; 40:1, 2, 5; 41:10; 43:6; 52:12, 14–16, 19, 24, 26, 30. ¶

GUARD, UNDER GUARD – Num. 15:34; 1 Chr. 26:16; Neh. 4:9, 22, 23; Jer. 51:12; etc. ➔ CUSTODY <4929>.

GUARD THE PALACE, GUARD THE TEMPLE – 2 Kgs. 11:6 ➔ DEFENSE <4535>.

GUARDROOM – 1 Kgs. 14:28; 2 Chr. 12:11; etc. ➔ ROOM <8372>.

GUARDSMAN – Nah. 3:17 ➔ CROWNED ONE <4502> b.

GUDGODAH – ***guḏgōḏah*** [proper noun: גֻּדְגֹּדָה <1412>; by reduplication from CUT (verb) <1413>]: incision ▶ **One of the Israelites' campsites in the desert.** Ref.: Deut. 10:7. ¶

GUEST – 2 Sam. 12:4 ➔ TRAVEL <732>.

GUIDANCE – Job 37:12; Prov. 1:5; 11:14; 24:6 ➔ COUNSEL (noun) <8458>.

GUIDE – [1] Ps. 112:5 ➔ CONTAIN <3557> [2] See LEAD <5144>.

GUIDEPOST – ***tamrûr*** [masc. noun: תַּמְרוּר <8564>; from an unused root meaning to be erect] ▶
a. This word refers to an object set up to direct someone to a location. It also designates a road mark. The Israelites were to set up markers, directions to the land of Israel so they could return to their homeland from exile (Jer. 31:21; NKJV: landmark).
b. A masculine noun meaning a high heap. It refers to piling up stone or dirt markers to lead Israel back to her homeland after being scattered (Jer. 31:21; KJV). ¶

GUILE – [1] Prov. 26:26 ➔ DECEPTION <4860> [2] Is. 30:12 ➔ PERVERSE <3868>.

GUILT – [1] ***'āšām*** [masc. noun: אָשָׁם <817>; from GUILTY (BE) <816>] ▶ **This word is used to express the concept of culpability or offense.** It can connote the deeds which bring about guilt (Ps. 68:21). It can also express the condition of being guilty, i.e., the results of the actions as shown in Genesis 26:10 (NIV), "You would have brought guilt upon us." This word can also refer to the restitution that the guilty party was to make to the victim in the case of property damage (Num. 5:7). The biblical writer also uses this term to designate the guilt offering, the offering which is presented to the Lord in order to absolve the person guilty of an offense against God or man, which can be estimated and compensated (Lev. 5:6). *
[2] ***'ašmāh*** [fem. noun: אַשְׁמָה <819>; fem. of GUILTY (adj.) <817>] ▶ **This word suggests the concept of sin or culpability; it is also translated trespass.** It is similar in meaning to *'āšām* above. It can represent wrong actions (2 Chr. 24:18); the status of guilt which comes on a person by virtue of his or her wrong actions (Ezra 10:10); the guilt offering itself (Lev. 6:5). *
– [3] Hos. 10:10 ➔ MARITAL RIGHTS <5772> b. [4] See INIQUITY <5771>.

GUILTY (adj.) – ***'āšêm*** [adj.: אָשֵׁם <818>; from GUILTY (BE) <816>] ▶ **This adjective describes one who is in a culpable state.** It describes Joseph's brothers, who declared, "Truly we are guilty concerning our brother" (Gen. 42:21, NASB); David in not bringing back Absalom (2 Sam. 14:13); and priests who had married foreign wives (Ezra 10:19). ¶

GUILTY (noun) – ***wāzār*** [masc. noun: וָזָר <2054>; presumed to be from an unused root meaning to bear guilt] ▶ **This word occurs only once in the Old Testament (Prov. 21:8), where the immoral path of the one who is culpable is contrasted to the pure behavior of the innocent.** The translators for the KJV understood the word to be a combination of the word *and* with the adjective meaning strange. Therefore, they translated this Hebrew word, "The way of man is froward (or perverse) and strange." But modern translators translate this word "guilty." ¶

GUILTY (BE) – [1] ***'āšam, āšêm*** [verb: אָשַׁם, אָשֵׁם <816>; a prim. root] ▶ **This word also means to do wrong. It is most often used to describe the product of sin—i.e., culpability before God.** It may be used of individuals (Lev. 5:2–5; Num. 5:6, 7); congregations (Lev. 4:13); or nations (Ezek. 25:12; Hos. 13:16). Because of the close connection between guilt and sin, this word may be used as a synonym for sin (Hos. 4:15; 13:1), while often the idea

of punishment for a wrong done is implied (Hos. 10:2; Zech. 11:5). See the related nouns, *'āšām* (GUILT <817>) and *'ašmāh* (GUILTINESS <819>). *
– [2] Job 9:20 ➔ CROOKED (MAKE, BE) <6140>.

GULL – Lev. 11:16; Deut. 14:15 ➔ SEA GULL <7828>.

GUM, AROMATIC GUM – Gen. 37:25; 43:11 ➔ SPICE <5219>.

GUM RESIN – Ex. 30:34 ➔ STACTE <5198>.

GUNI – ***gûniy*** [masc. proper noun: גּוּנִי <1476>; prob. from DEFEND <1598>]: protected ►
a. A son of Naphtali. Refs.: Gen. 46:24; Num. 26:48; 1 Chr. 7:13. ¶
b. An Israelite of the tribe of Gad. Ref.: 1 Chr. 5:15. ¶

GUNITE – ***gûniy*** [masc. proper noun: גּוּנִי <1477>; patron. from GUNI <1476>] ► **A member of the family of Guni.** Ref.: Num. 26:48. ¶

GUR – ***gûr*** [proper noun: גּוּר <1483>; the same as CUB <1482>]: young animal, lion's cub ► **A place where Ahaziah, the king of Judah, was mortally wounded.** Ref.: 2 Kgs. 9:27. ¶

GUR BAAL – ***gûr-ba'al*** [proper noun: גּוּר־בַּעַל <1485>; from SOJOURN <1481> and BAAL <1168>]: dwelling of Baal ► **A place in Arabia.** Ref.: 2 Chr. 26:7. ¶

GUSH – [1] ***giyaḥ, gûaḥ*** [verb: גִּיחַ, גּוּחַ <1518>; a prim. root] ► **This word is used literally to depict a river flowing out fast.** Ref.: Job 40:23. Figuratively it shows the sea bursting forth as if coming from a womb (Job 38:8). It is also translated to break forth, to rush, to surge. A child is cast forth from its mother's womb (Ps. 22:9: to bring out, to take out). It depicts Jerusalem going forth after travail into captivity (Mic. 4:10: to go). Egypt bursts forth from her rivers as a monster (Ezek. 32:2; also translated to break forth, to come forth, to thrash about). It describes an army breaking out of ambush (Judg. 20:33: to break out, to charge out, to come forth, to rush out). ¶
[2] ***zûb*** [verb: זוּב <2100>; a prim. root] ► **This word refers to water that pours from a rock.** Refs.: Ps. 78:20; 105:41. It refers to honey and milk that flow in the land of Canaan (Ex. 3:8, 17; Num. 13:27; Deut. 6:3). It describes an active flowing discharge from a person's body (Lev. 15:2) that renders a person unclean, man (2 Sam. 3:29) or woman (Lev. 15:19). Used figuratively, it describes valleys in Ammon that were flowing, eroding away (Jer. 49:4); or to a person pining away from hunger (Lam. 4:9). *
– [3] Prov. 15:2, 28 ➔ UTTER <5042>.

GUTTER – [1] Gen. 30:38, 41 ➔ TROUGH <7298> a. [2] 2 Sam. 5:8 ➔ WATER SHAFT <6794> [3] Ezek. 43:13, 14, 17 ➔ BOSOM <2436>.

H

HAAHASHTARI – ***ᵃḥaštāriy*** [masc. proper noun: אֲחַשְׁתָּרִי <326>; prob. of Persian deriv.]: courier ▶ **An Israelite of the tribe of Judah.** Ref.: 1 Chr. 4:6. ¶

HABAIAH – ***ḥᵃḇāyāh, ḥᵒḇāyyāh*** [masc. proper noun: חֲבָיָה, חֳבַיָּה <2252>; from HIDE <2247> and LORD <3050>]: the Lord has hidden ▶ **Father of some Jews who were excluded from the priesthood.** Refs.: Ezra 2:61; Neh. 7:63. ¶

HABAKKUK – ***ḥᵃḇaqqûq*** [masc. proper noun: חֲבַקּוּק <2265>; by reduplication from EMBRACE <2263>]: love, who embraces ▶ **This word designates Habakkuk (Hab. 1:1; 3:1), a prophet contemporary (ca. 620–609 B.C.) with Jeremiah who witnessed the terrible rise and power of the Babylonians against Israel.** He prophesied ca. 605 B.C. He was in constant debate/dialogue with the Lord in his prophecies. Hab. 2:4 is quoted as the chief principle of the gospel (Rom. 1:17; see also Heb. 10:38). ¶

HABAZZINIAH – ***ḥᵃḇaṣṣinyāh*** [masc. proper noun: חֲבַצִּנְיָה <2262>; of uncertain deriv.] ▶ **A Rechabite who lived before Jeremiah.** Ref.: Jer. 35:3. ¶

HABERGEON – Ex. 28:32; 39:23 ➔ COAT OF MAIL <8473> a.

HABIT (BE THE) – Num. 22:30 ➔ PROFITABLE (BE) <5532> a.

HABITATION – [1] ***gêrûṯ*** [fem. noun: גֵּרוּת <1628>; from SOJOURN <1481>] ▶
a. This word means an inn, a lodging place. It was a convenient place to stop on the way to Egypt (Jer. 41:17). Some translators prefer to render the word as part of the name of a location, Geruth Kimham (NIV, NASB, ESV). It was not far from Bethlehem. ¶
b. A feminine proper noun meaning Geruth. It indicated a location to stop and rest on the way to Egypt (Jer. 41:17). Some translators prefer to render it as habitation (KJV, NKJV). ¶

[2] ***zᵉḇûl, zᵉḇul*** [masc. noun: זְבוּל, זְבֻל <2073>; from DWELL <2082>] ▶ **This word indicates magnificence; lofty abode, exalted dwelling.** It designates the exalted habitation of God (Is. 63:15) or the lofty location of the sun and moon (Hab. 3:11; also translated place). In general, it may refer to any habitation (Ps. 49:14; also translated dwelling, mansion). Combined with house, it refers to the Temple of the Lord built by Solomon, the *bêyṯ* (HOUSE <1004>) *zᵉḇûl*, house of loftiness (1 Kgs. 8:13; 2 Chr. 6:2; Is. 63:15). ¶

[3] ***mā'ôn, mā'iyn*** [masc. noun: מָעוֹן, מָעִין <4583>; from the same as MARITAL RIGHTS <5772>] ▶ **This word refers to a dwelling, a refuge. It describes a dwelling place for various purposes.** It refers to God's heavenly abode (Deut. 26:15; 2 Chr. 30:27; Zech. 2:13); and the sanctuary where He dwells among His people (1 Sam. 2:29; 2 Chr. 36:15). It describes in a general sense the existence and dwelling of Jerusalem as God's chosen city (Zeph. 3:7). It refers to a dwelling in general (1 Chr. 4:41; but some translate as a people called Meunites [<4586>], NASB, NIV). It is used of the lairs of animals (Jer. 9:11; Nah. 2:11). *

[4] ***nāweh, nāwāh*** [noun: נָוֶה, נָוָה <5116>; from PRAISE (verb) <5115> b.] ▶
a. A masculine noun depicting a shepherd's abode, a camp; a flock. It refers to any dwelling place, natural or man-made. Its most famous reference is to the land of Canaan, Zion (Ex. 15:13; Ps. 79:7; Jer. 10:25). It refers to the pasturage used for sheep and the work of pasturing itself (2 Sam. 7:8). It refers to Jerusalem and the Temple as places of God's habitation (2 Sam. 15:25). It refers to any place of abode (Job 5:3, 24), figuratively or literally, (Prov. 3:33). It is used even of deserted areas (Is. 27:10; Ezek. 25:5). *
b. A feminine noun indicating a dwelling, a pasturage. It has many of the same uses as a. It refers to green pasturage in the beloved psalm (Ps. 23:2) and to other types of pasturage: wilderness pastures (Jer. 9:10; Joel 1:19); pasturage used by shepherds

(Amos 1:2). In an ironic passage, the sea-coast is termed "pastures" after God's judgments (Zeph. 2:6). It refers to the land of Jacob, Canaan (Lam. 2:2). *

c. An adjectival noun meaning a person dwelling, abiding. It refers to a person who remains in a location, e.g., in a home, a house, as opposed to fleeing (Ps. 68:12: to remain, to tarry). ¶

– [5] Gen. 49:5 → SWORD <4380> [6] Deut. 12:5 → DWELLING <7933> [7] Ezra 7:15 → DWELLING <4907> [8] Ps. 69:25 → CAMP <2918> [9] Ps. 89:14; 97:2 → DWELLING <4349> b. [10] Ps. 132:13 → SEAT <4186> [11] Jer. 21:13 → DWELLING PLACE <4585> [12] Ezek. 29:14 → ORIGIN <4351>.

HABITATION (HAVE ONE'S) – Dan. 4:21 → DWELL <7932>.

HABITATION (PREPARE A) – Ex. 15:2 → PRAISE (verb) <5115> a.

HABOR – ***ḥāḇôr*** [proper noun: חָבוֹר <2249>; from JOIN TOGETHER <2266>]: joined, united ▶ **A river of Assyria near where the Israelites were deported.** Refs.: 2 Kgs. 17:6; 18:11; 1 Chr. 5:26. ¶

HACALIAH, HACHALIAH – ***ḥᵃḵalyāh*** [masc. proper noun: חֲכַלְיָה <2446>; from the base of DARKER <2447> and LORD <3050>]: the Lord is hidden ▶ **The father of Nehemiah.** Refs.: Neh. 1:1; 10:1. ¶

HACHILAH, HAKILAH – ***ḥᵃḵiylāh*** [proper noun: חֲכִילָה <2444>; from the same as DARKER <2447>]: dark ▶ **A hill of the desert of Ziph where David hide.** Refs.: 1 Sam. 23:19; 26:1, 3. ¶

HACHMONI – ***ḥaḵmôniy*** [masc. proper noun: חַכְמוֹנִי <2453>; from WISE (MAKE) <2449>]: wise ▶

a. Father of Jehiel. Ref.: 1 Chr. 27:32. ¶

b. Hachmonite, the nationality of one of David's mighty men. Ref.: 1 Chr. 11:11. ¶

HACK IN/TO PIECES – [1] 1 Sam. 15:33 → HEW TO PIECES <8158> [2] Ezek. 16:40 → CUT TO PIECES <1333>.

HADAD – [1] ***ᵃḏaḏ*** [masc. proper noun: אֲדַד <111>; prob. an orthographical variation for <2301> below]: powerful, the highest ▶ **Name of an Edomite.** Ref.: 1 Kgs. 11:17, a variant form of the Hebrew name Hadad next; he was an adversary of Solomon. ¶

[2] ***hᵃḏaḏ*** [masc. proper noun: הֲדַד <1908>; prob. of foreign origin (comp. <111> above)] ▶

a. A descendant of Esau and a son of Bedad. He became king of Edom before any king reigned in Israel. His royal city was Avith, and he successfully defeated the Midianites in the territory of Moab (Gen. 36:35, 36; 1 Chr. 1:46, 47). Some translators prefer to find this name in Genesis 36:39 also, but most Masoretic manuscripts read Hadar here (NIV, Hadad; ESV, KJV, NASB, NKJV, Hadar; see b., c., below). ¶

b. A serious adversary of King Solomon. He was of the royal dynasty in Edom (1 Kgs. 11:14) and had fled to Egypt when a boy (1 Kgs. 11:17) from where he returned to Israel to harass Solomon (1 Kgs. 11:19, 21, 25). ¶

c. An Edomite king who reigned before any king reigned in Israel. Refs.: Gen. 36:39, NIV; ESV, KJV, NASB, NKJV read Hadar. His chief city was Pai (1 Chr. 1:50, 51). ¶

[3] ***ḥᵃḏaḏ*** [masc. proper noun: חֲדַד <2301>; from SHARPEN <2300>]: fierce ▶ **Son of Ishmael.** Refs.: Gen. 25:15; 1 Chr. 1:30: Hadar. ¶

HADAD RIMMON – ***hᵃḏaḏ-rimmôn*** [proper noun: הֲדַד־רִמּוֹן <1910>; from HADAD <1908> and RIMMON <7417>]: the names of two Syrian divinities ▶ **A place in the plain of Megiddo.** Ref.: Zech. 12:11. ¶

HADADEZER – ***hᵃḏaḏʿezer*** [masc. proper noun: הֲדַדְעֶזֶר <1909>; from HADAD <1908> and HELP (noun) <5828>]: Hadad *is his* help ▶ **This son of Rehob and king of Zobah was defeated by David.** Refs.: 2 Sam. 8:3, 5, 7–10, 12; 10:16, 19; 1 Kgs. 11:23; 1 Chr. 18:3, 5, 7–10; 19:16, 19. ¶

HADAR – [1] ***h^{a}ḏar*** [masc. proper noun: הֲדַר <1924>; the same as GLORY <1926>]: honor ▶ **Another spelling for *h^{a}ḏaḏ* (HADAD <1908> c.).** Ref.: Gen. 36:39. ¶
[2] ***ḥ^{a}ḏar*** [masc. proper noun: חֲדַר <2316>; another form for ROOM <2315>] ▶ **See HADAD <2301>.** Ref.: Gen. 25:15. ¶
– [3] 1 Chr. 1:30 ➔ HADAD <2301>.

HADAREZER – ***h^{a}ḏar'ezer*** [masc. proper noun: הֲדַרְעֶזֶר <1928>; from HADAR <1924> and HELP (noun) <5828>] ▶ **This name is another spelling of *h^{a}ḏaḏ'ezer* (see HADADEZER <1909>).** Refs.: 2 Sam. 10:16, 19; 1 Chr. 18:3, 5, 7–10; 19:16, 19. ¶

HADASHAH – ***ḥ^{a}ḏāšāh*** [proper noun: חֲדָשָׁה <2322>; fem. of NEW <2319>]: new ▶ **A village of the plain of Judah.** Ref.: Josh. 15:37. ¶

HADASSAH – ***h^{a}ḏassāh*** [fem. proper noun: הֲדַסָּה <1919>; fem. of MYRTLE TREE <1918>]: myrtle ▶ **Jewish name of queen Esther.** Ref.: Esther 2:7. ¶

HADID – ***ḥāḏiyḏ*** [proper noun: חָדִיד <2307>; from SHARPEN <2300>]: sharp, pointed ▶ **City of Benjamin in the mountains.** Refs.: Ezra 2:33; Neh. 7:37; 11:34. ¶

HADLAI – ***ḥaḏlay*** [masc. proper noun: חַדְלָי <2311>; from WORLD <2309> (in the sense of cessation, rest)]: resting, patient ▶ **An Israelite of the tribe of Ephraim.** Ref.: 2 Chr. 28:12. ¶

HADORAM – ***h^{a}ḏôrām*** [masc. proper noun: הֲדוֹרָם <1913>; prob. of foreign deriv.]: Hadad (a god) is exalted ▶
a. Son of Joktan. Refs.: Gen. 10:27; 1 Chr. 1:21. ¶
b. Son of Tou. Ref.: 1 Chr. 18:10. ¶
c. Another name for *^{a}ḏōrām* (ADORAM <151>). Ref.: 2 Chr. 10:18. ¶

HADRACH – ***ḥaḏrāḵ*** [proper noun: חַדְרָךְ <2317>; of uncertain deriv.] ▶ **This word refers to a city in northern Syria against which the Lord prophesied.** Ref.: Zech. 9:1. ¶

HAFT – Judg. 3:22 ➔ HILT <5325>.

HAGAB – ***ḥāgāḇ*** [masc. proper noun: חָגָב <2285>; the same as LOCUST <2284>]: locust ▶ **A founder of a Nethinim family.** Ref.: Ezra 2:46. ¶

HAGABAH – ***ḥ^{a}gāḇā', ḥ^{a}gaḇāh*** [masc. proper noun: חֲגָבָא, חֲגָבָה <2286>; fem. of HAGAB <2285>]: locust ▶ **A founder of a Nethinim family.** Refs.: Ezra 2:45; Neh. 7:48. ¶

HAGAR – ***hāgār*** [fem. proper noun: הָגָר <1904>; of uncertain (perhaps foreign) deriv.]: escape, stranger ▶ **She was Sarah's handmaid by whom Abraham fathered Ishmael whose descendants were numerous.** Refs.: Gen. 16:1–16; 25:12–18. She was driven from Abraham by Sarah (Gen. 21:9–17). ¶

HAGGAI – ***ḥaggay*** [masc. proper noun: חַגַּי <2292>; from FEAST <2282>]: feast ▶
a. A prophet who prophesied during the time of Ezra-Nehemiah (ca. 520 B.C.), encouraging the people and leaders to rebuild the Temple, the house of God. He warned the people to do the Lord's work and not put their own well-beings and economic prosperity ahead of that (Hag. 1:3, 4). Postexilic Israelites had become an unholy, defiled people (Hag. 2:10–14), but Haggai gave an encouraging message as well (Hag. 2:20–23). Refs.: Hag. 1:1, 3, 12, 13; 2:1, 10, 13, 14, 20. ¶
b. The Aramaic occurrence of the name Haggai. Refs.: Ezra 5:1; 6:14. ¶

HAGGERI – 1 Chr. 11:38 ➔ HAGRITE <1905>.

HAGGI, HAGGITE – ***ḥaggiy*** [masc. proper noun: חַגִּי <2291>; from FEAST (HOLD A) <2287>]: feast, happy ▶
a. Haggi, son of Gad. Refs.: Gen. 46:16; Num. 26:15. ¶
b. Haggite, descendant of Haggi. Ref.: Num. 26:15. ¶

HAGGIAH – ***ḥaggiyyāh*** [masc. proper noun: חַגִּיָּה <2293>; from FEAST <2282>

and LORD <3050>]: feast of the Lord ► **A Levite, descendant of Merari.** Ref.: 1 Chr. 6:30. ¶

HAGGITH – ***ḥaggiyṯ*** [fem. proper noun: חַגִּית <2294>; fem. of HAGGI <2291>]: festive ► **A wife of David, mother of Adonijah.** Refs.: 2 Sam. 3:4; 1 Kgs. 1:5, 11; 2:13; 1 Chr. 3:2. ¶

HAGRI – 2 Sam. 23:36; 1 Chr. 11:38 ➔ HAGRITE <1905>.

HAGRITE – ***hagriy, hagriy'iym*** [masc. proper noun: הַגְרִיאִים, הַגְרִי <1905>; perhaps patron. from HAGAR <1904>] ►
a. Jaziz the Hagrite was in charge of the flocks of King David. Ref.: 1 Chr. 27:31. ¶
b. Hagri, Haggeri, the father of Mibhar. Refs.: 2 Sam. 23:36; 1 Chr. 11:38. In 2 Samuel 23:36, some read "the son of Hagri," others read "Bani the Gadite." ¶
c. Hagrite, Arabian Bedouin tribes of the Transjordan region. Refs.: 1 Chr. 5:10, 19, 20; Ps. 83:6. ¶

HAIL (noun) – ***bārāḏ*** [masc. noun: בָּרָד <1259>; from HAIL (verb) <1258>] ► **This word denotes hail or hailstones, i.e., pellets of ice, of frozen rain, that fall from the clouds.** It is used to describe hail that came down as the seventh plague of Egypt (Ex. 9:18, 19, 22–26, 28, 29, 33, 34; Ps. 78:47, 48; 105:32), large enough to kill cattle, plants, and trees, nearly devastating the land (Ex. 10:5, 12, 15). Hailstones were a terrifying weapon of and accompaniment of the Lord's appearances (Josh. 10:11; Ps. 18:12, 13). The Lord stored up these hailstones (Job 38:22) and discharged them at His will (Is. 28:2, 17; Hag. 2:17) as His teaching and destructive agents. Other refs.: Ps. 148:8; Is. 30:30. ¶

HAIL (verb) – ***bāraḏ*** [verb: בָּרַד <1258>; a prim. root] ► **This word depicts a devastating storm.** It would lay a forest low (Is. 32:19) as part of God's reconstruction program. ¶

HAILSTONE – ***'elgāḇiyš*** [masc. noun: אֶלְגָּבִישׁ <417>; from GOD <410> and CRYSTAL <1378>] ► **This word means a stone of pellets of ice. It is a feature of God's judgment upon the inferior work of the false prophets.** Refs.: Ezek. 13:11, 13; 38:22. ¶

HAILSTONES – See HAIL (noun) <1259>.

HAIR – 1 ***miqšeh*** [masc. noun: מִקְשֶׁה <4748>; from HARD (BE) <7185 in the sense of knotting up round and hard] ► **This word refers to a coiffure, a well-groomed head of hair and scalp.** Ref.: Is. 3:24. ¶
2 ***ś*ᵉ*'ar*** [Aramaic masc. noun: שְׂעַר <8177>; corresponding to <8181> below] ► **This word refers to the natural covering of the human head.** Hair is easily singed by fire (Dan. 3:27). God's curse on Nebuchadnezzar caused his hair to grow wild like an eagle's feathers (Dan. 4:33). White hair represented antiquity, great age, and wisdom (Dan. 7:9). ¶
3 ***śê'ār*** [masc. noun: שֵׂעָר <8181>; from SWEEP AWAY <8175> in the sense of dishevelling] ► **This word refers to human and animal hair, e.g., the hair of animals used in certain materials.** Ref.: Gen. 25:25. It indicates human hair (Judg. 16:22). It can be used in an inclusive sense of the whole head (Lev. 14:8, 9); or of the hair in specific body areas (Is. 7:20). It refers to hairs involved in diagnosing leprosy (Lev. 13:3, 4, 10, etc.). *
4 ***śa*ᵃ*rāh*** [fem. noun: שַׂעֲרָה <8185>; fem. of HAIR <8181>] ► **This word is used to reference a single hair.** Refs.: Judg. 20:16; 1 Sam. 14:45; 2 Sam. 14:11; 1 Kgs. 1:52; Job 4:15; Ps. 40:12; 69:4. It is used often to illustrate God's care and protection of a person or to refer to the accuracy of a sling thrower who could sling a stone at a hair's breadth. It indicates the relative small value of losing a single hair. ¶
– 5 Num. 6:5; Ezek. 44:20 ➔ LOCK OF HAIR <6545> 6 Song 5:2, 11 ➔ LOCK, LOCK OF HAIR <6977> 7 Song 7:5 ➔ LOOM <1803>.

HAKKATAN – ***qāṭān, haqqāṭan*** [masc. proper noun: הַקָּטָן ,קָטָן <6997>; the same as SMALL <6996>]: small ► **Father of Johanan who returned from the Babylonian captivity.** Ref.: Ezra 8:12. ¶

HAKKEPHIRIM – Neh. 6:2 ➔ LION (YOUNG) <3715> b., c.

HAKKOZ – See KOZ <6976> b.

HAKUPHA – ***ḥ^{a}qûpā'*** [proper noun: חֲקוּפָא <2709>; from an unused root prob. meaning to bend]: bent, curved ▶ **A Nethinim who returned from the Babylonian captivity with Zerubbabel.** Refs.: Ezra 2:51; Neh. 7:53. ¶

HALAH – ***ḥ^{a}laḥ*** [proper noun: חֲלַח <2477>; prob. of foreign origin] ▶ **A region of Assyria where the Israelites were deported.** Refs.: 2 Kgs. 17:6; 18:11; 1 Chr. 5:26. ¶

HALAK – ***ḥālāq*** [proper noun: חָלָק <2510>; the same as SMOOTH <2509>]: bald, bare ▶ **A mountain in southern Judah.** Refs.: Josh. 11:17; 12:7. ¶

HALF – 1 ***beṯer*** [masc. noun: בֶּתֶר <1335>; from DIVIDE <1334>] ▶ **This word indicates a piece cut off, a half (one of two equal parts) cut off; it is also translated piece, part.** It describes the pieces of sacrificial meat produced when Abraham cut a three-year-old ram and a three-year-old goat in two during a covenantal ritual (Gen. 15:10). It also describes half of a calf cut in two for a pagan ritual (Jer. 34:18) and condemns to death those who took part in the ceremony (Jer. 34:19). ¶

2 ***ḥ^{a}ṣiy*** [masc. noun: חֲצִי <2677>; from DIVIDE <2673>] ▶ **This word means one of two equal parts; it also indicates middle.** It is used about 120 times to express half of something by placing it before the word: half of their beards (2 Sam. 10:4); with a pronoun suffix added to it, such as *nû*, us, it means half of us (2 Sam. 18:3). It is also used to indicate the middle measure of something: with *'aḏ* preceding, it means up to half of something (Ex. 27:5, height); with the preposition *b^e* followed by a time word, it means half of the days (Ps. 102:24; Jer. 17:11); or half of the night, midnight (Ex. 12:29). *

3 ***meḥ^{e}ṣāh*** [fem. noun: מֶחֱצָה <4275>; from DIVIDE <2673>] ▶ **This word indicates 50 percent of the whole of something: sheep, cattle, donkeys, soldiers.** Refs.: Num. 31:36, 31:43. ¶

4 ***maḥ^{a}ṣiyṯ*** [fem. noun: מַחֲצִית <4276>; from DIVIDE <2673>] ▶ **This word indicates the middle.** It indicates half of something: a shekel (Ex. 30:13, 15); chariotry (1 Kgs. 16:9); flour (Lev. 6:20). It is used before *hayyôm*, the day, to mean noon, midday (Neh. 8:3). *

5 ***p^{e}lag*** [Aramaic masc. noun: פְּלַג <6387>; from DIVIDE <6386>] ▶ **This term seems to assume a single division into two equal parts or halves.** It is used only once in the famous passage stating that the saints will be delivered for a time, times and a half time (Dan. 7:25; KJV: dividing). ¶

HALF-SHEKEL – See RANSOM (noun) <3724>.

HALHUL – ***ḥalḥûl*** [proper noun: חַלְחוּל <2478>; by reduplication from SHAKE <2342>]: trembling ▶ **A village in Judah.** Ref.: Josh. 15:58. ¶

HALI – ***ḥ^{a}liy*** [proper noun: חֲלִי <2482>; the same as ORNAMENT <2481>]: jewel, ornament ▶ **A village at the border of Judah.** Ref.: Josh. 19:25. ¶

HALLOHESH – ***hallôḥēš*** [masc. proper noun: הַלּוֹחֵשׁ <3873>; act. part. of WHISPER (verb) <3907>]: whisperer, charmer ▶ **His son Shallum repaired a section of the wall of Jerusalem.** Refs.: Neh. 3:12; 10:24. ¶

HALT – Gen. 32:31; Mic. 4:6, 7; Zeph. 3:19 ➔ LIMP <6760>.

HAM – 1 ***hām*** [proper noun: הָם <1990>; of uncertain deriv.]: hot ▶ **A place between Ashteroth-karnaim and the country of the Moabites.** Ref.: Gen. 14:5. ¶

2 ***ḥām*** [masc. proper noun: חָם <2526>; the same as WARM <2505>]: warm, hot ▶ **a. The second son of Noah.** Ref.: Gen. 6:10. He entered the ark along with his brothers and all their wives (Gen. 7:13). He became the father of Canaan (Gen.

9:18). Ham committed some grave sin with respect to his father after the flood, euphemistically described as "seeing his father's nakedness" (Gen. 9:24). God cursed Ham's son Canaan because of his father's behavior, illustrating God's cursing of a first through a fourth generation (Ex. 34:6, 7). Ham fathered many sons, including Canaan and Cush, who was the father of Nimrod (Gen. 10:8–10). Nimrod founded Babylon, Calneh, Assyria, and Nineveh (Gen. 10:11–20). One of his sons, Mizraim, is the name for Egypt (Gen. 10:6). *

b. Ham also is closely allied with the Egyptians. In poetic lines, the word Ham parallels the words Egypt or Egyptians (Ps. 78:51; 105:23, 27; 106:22). ¶

HAMAN – ***hāmān*** [masc. proper noun: הָמָן <2001>; of foreign deriv.]: magnificent ▶ **The name of the villain in Esther who sought to eradicate the Jews from the Persian Empire.** Refs.: Esther 3:7–15. Instead, his wicked plot was ironically turned upon his own head, and he was hanged on his own gallows (Esther 7:1–10) and his sons killed (Esther 9:5–10, 14, 9:24, 25). Haman was the son of Hammedatha, an Agagite, and may have been an Amalekite in ancestry. The destruction of Haman and his sons fulfilled the Lord's curse on the Amalekites (Ex. 17:8–15). *

HAMATH – ***ḥ^{a}māṯ, l^{e}ḇō ḥ^{a}māṯ*** [proper noun: חֲמָת, לְבֹא חֲמָת <2574>; from the same as WALL <2346>]: fortress ▶

a. A city explored by the ten spies of Joshua. Ref.: Num. 13:21. It is also listed as Lebo ("at the entrance" of) Hamath. It seems to refer to the larger territory of Hamath in some cases. It was located at the northern boundary of Canaan (Ezek. 47:16, 20; 48:1) and was the northernmost point of the land of Israel (Josh. 13:5; Judg. 3:3; 1 Chr. 13:5; Amos 6:14). As noted Hamath used alone may refer to a larger Hamath territory (Amos 6:2), evidently a land touched by northern Israel's territory during the monarchy (2 Sam. 8:9). The city was ca. 45 miles north of Damascus on the west side of the Orontes River. *

b. Much the same as a., but each context must be carefully checked to discern whether the larger territorial kingdom of Hamath is meant or the capital city itself. See a. above. Compare NIV, Lebo-Hamath; KJV, "to Hamath"; NLT, Lebo-Hamath (Num. 13:21). Compare Amos 6:2, 14. *

c. The name of an ancestor of the Rechabite clan, the father of the family itself. Ref.: 1 Chr. 2:55. ¶

HAMATH THE GREAT – ***ḥ^{a}maṯ rabbāh*** [proper noun: חֲמַת רַבָּה <2579>; from HAMATH <2574> and RABBAH <7237> (which means great)] ▶ **A place in Syria, possibly the same as HAMATH <2574> a., at the northern boundary of Canaan.** Ref.: Amos 6:2. ¶

HAMATH ZOBAH – ***ḥ^{a}maṯ ṣôḇāh*** [proper noun: חֲמַת צוֹבָה <2578>; from HAMATH <2574> and ZOBAH <6678>]: fortress of Zobah ▶ **Probably a place in Syria against which Solomon prevailed.** Ref.: 2 Chr. 8:3. ¶

HAMATHITE – ***ḥ^{a}māṯiy*** [proper noun: חֲמָתִי <2577>; patrial from HAMATH <2574>]: see HAMATH <2575> ▶ **An inhabitant of Hamath.** Refs.: Gen. 10:18; 1 Chr. 1:16. ¶

HAMMATH – ***ḥammaṯ*** [proper noun: חַמַּת <2575>; a variation for the first part of HAMMOTH DOR <2576>]: warm springs ▶

a. A city in Naphtali. Ref.: Josh. 19:35. ¶

b. Ancestral head of the Rechabite clan. Ref.: 1 Chr. 2:55. ¶

HAMMEDATHA – ***hamm^{e}ḏāṯā'*** [masc. proper noun: הַמְּדָתָא <4099>; of Persian origin] ▶ **Father of Haman.** Refs.: Esther 3:1, 10; 8:5; 9:10, 24. ¶

HAMMELECH – Jer. 36:26; 38:6 → MELECH, HAMMELECH <4429> b.

HAMMER (noun) – [1] ***halmûṯ*** [fem. noun: הַלְמוּת <1989>; from SMITE <1986>] ▶

This word means a pounding tool; it is also translated mallet. It refers to a hammer used by Jael, wife of Heber the Kenite, to drive a tent peg through Sisera's skull, killing him (Judg. 5:26). It could have been made of metal or wood. ¶
[2] ***kêylap̱*** [fem. noun: כֵּילָף <3597>; from an unused root meaning to clap or strike with noise] ▶ **This word refers to a tool or weapon used to smash the splendid work of the Temple; it is also translated hatchet.** It is paralleled in verse 5 by the ax (Ps. 74:6). ¶
[2] ***maqqeḇeṯ*** [fem. noun: מַקֶּבֶת <4717>; from PIERCE <5344>] ▶ **This word refers to an iron tool used to drive nails or pegs, or to break up and shape various materials.** Refs.: Judg. 4:21; 1 Kgs. 6:7; Is. 44:12; Jer. 10:4. ¶
[3] ***pattiyš*** [masc. noun: פַּטִּישׁ <6360>; intensively from an unused root meaning to pound] ▶ **This word depicts a tool used to hammer out or smooth out metal by pounding it or to break up rock.** Refs.: Is. 41:7; Jer. 23:29. It describes figuratively God's Word (Jer. 23:29). Babylon is described as God's hammer of the whole earth, pounding it down, devastating the nations (Jer. 50:23). ¶
– [4] Jer. 51:20 ➔ WAR CLUB <4661>.

HAMMER (verb) – [1] 1 Kgs. 6:32 ➔ SUBDUE <7286> [2] 1 Kgs. 10:16, 17; 2 Chr. 9:15, 16 ➔ BEAT <7820> [3] Is. 2:4; Mic. 4:3 ➔ CRUSH <3807>.

HAMMERED – [1] ***riqqûa'***, ***riqqua'*** [masc. noun: רִקֻּעַ, רִקּוּעַ <7555>; from BEAT <7554>] ▶ **This word means expansion (of metal plates), broad.** Signifying the stretching effect produced when metal is beaten, this word appears only in reference to the plates covering the altar of the Tabernacle (Num. 16:38). ¶
– [2] 1 Kgs. 7:29 ➔ DESCENT <4174>.

HAMMERED, HAMMERED WORK – ***miqšāh*** [fem. noun: מִקְשָׁה <4749>; from HAIR <4748> (in the sense of rounded work)] ▶ **This word describes metal work that has been smoothed out and often embossed in relief, featuring raised artwork.** Refs.: Ex. 25:18, 31, 36; 37:17, 22; Num. 8:4; 10:2. Other refs.: Ex. 37:7; Jer. 10:5 (KJV, NKJV: upright). ¶

HAMMOLECHETH, HAMMOLEKETH – ***hammōleḵeṯ*** [fem. noun: הַמֹּלֶכֶת <4447>; fem. act. part. of KING (BE) <4427>]: the queen ▶ **Daughter of Machir and sister of Gilead.** Ref.: 1 Chr. 7:18. ¶

HAMMON – ***ḥammôn*** [proper noun: חַמּוֹן <2540>; from WARM (BE) <2552>]: shining, hot; warm springs ▶
a. A town in Asher. Ref.: Josh. 19:28. ¶
b. A town in Naphtali. Ref.: 1 Chr. 6:76. ¶

HAMMOTH DOR – ***ḥammōṯ dō'r*** [proper noun: חַמֹּת דֹּאר <2576>; from the plur. of SUN <2535> (with the sense of warmth) and DOR <1756>]: hot springs of Dor ▶ **A Levitical city in Naphtali.** Ref.: Josh. 21:32. ¶

HAMMUEL – ***ḥammû'ēl*** [masc. proper noun: חַמּוּאֵל <2536>; from SUN <2535> and GOD <410>]: heat or wrath of God ▶ **An Israelite of the tribe of Simeon.** Ref.: 1 Chr. 4:26. ¶

HAMON GOG – ***hᵃmôn gôg*** [proper noun: הֲמוֹן גּוֹג <1996>; from MULTITUDE <1995> and GOG <1463>]: multitude of Gog ▶ **A valley on the east side of the Dead Sea.** Refs.: Ezek. 39:11, 15. ¶

HAMONAH – ***hᵃmônāh*** [proper noun: הֲמוֹנָה <1997>; fem. of MULTITUDE <1995>]: multitude ▶ **Symbolical name of the city where Gog must be destroyed.** Ref.: Ezek. 39:16. ¶

HAMOR – ***ḥᵃmôr*** [masc. proper noun: חֲמוֹר <2544>; the same as DONKEY <2543>]: donkey ▶ **The father of Shechem who was probably named after the city of Shechem.** Hamor was a Hivite (Gen. 33:19; 34:2). He negotiated with Jacob concerning his daughter Dinah whom his son Shechem had violated (Gen. 34:5–13). The sons of

Jacob dealt deceitfully with him and slew Shechem and the inhabitants of Shechem (Gen. 34:13–31). They also killed Hamor (Gen. 34:26). Other refs.: Josh. 24:32; Judg. 9:28. ¶

HAMPER – Prov. 4:12 → DISTRESSED (BE) <3334>.

HAMRAM – *ḥamrān* [masc. proper noun: חַמְרָן <2566>; from RED (BE) <2560>]: exalted people ▶ **He is designated as the son of Dishon and had three brothers.** Ref.: 1 Chr. 1:41; also written Amram. ESV and NIV have Hemdam; see Genesis 36:26. ¶

HAMSTRING – *'āqar* [verb: עָקַר <6131>; a prim. root] ▶
a. **A verb meaning to cut tendons, to cut the leg tendon.** It refers to cutting the large tendons at the back of the major joint of a four-legged animal's legs (Gen. 49:6, NASB: to lame; Josh. 11:6, 9; 2 Sam. 8:4; 1 Chr. 18:4; NASB: to lame). ¶
b. **A verb signifying to pluck up, to root out.** It is translated as to dig out, to tear down by some translators (KJV, Gen. 49:6). It is used of tearing out living plants and destroying, rooting out cities (Eccl. 3:2; Zeph. 2:4). ¶

HAMUEL – See HAMMUEL <2536>.

HAMUL – *ḥāmûl* [masc. proper noun: חָמוּל <2538>; from PITY (HAVE) <2550>]: pitied, spared ▶ **The youngest son of Perez who was one of the sons of Judah.** Refs.: Gen. 46:12; Num. 26:21; 1 Chr. 2:5. ¶

HAMULITE – *ḥāmûliy* [masc. proper noun: חָמוּלִי <2539>; patron. from HAMUL <2538>]: see HAMUL <2538> ▶ **A descendant of Hamul.** Ref.: Num. 26:21. ¶

HAMUTAL – *ḥamûṭal* [fem. proper noun: חֲמוּטַל <2537>; from FATHER-IN-LAW <2524> and DEW <2919>] ▶ **The daughter of Jeremiah of Libna; she was the wife of king Josiah and the mother**

of kings Jehoahaz and Zedekiah. Refs.: 2 Kgs. 23:31; 24:18; Jer. 52:1. ¶

HANAMEL, HANA-MEEL – *ḥªnam'ēl* [masc. proper noun: חֲנַמְאֵל <2601>; prob. by orthographical variation for HANA-NEEL <2606>]: God has mercy, gift of God ▶ **Cousin of the prophet Jeremiah.** Refs.: Jer. 32:7–9, 12. ¶

HANAN – *ḥānān* [masc. proper noun: חָנָן <2605>; from GRACIOUS (BE) <2603>]: merciful, compassion ▶
a. **One of David's mighty men.** Ref.: 1 Chr. 11:43. ¶
b. **A chief Benjamite.** Ref.: 1 Chr. 8:23. ¶
c. **Son of Azel.** Refs.: 1 Chr. 8:38; 9:44. ¶
d. **Head of the Nethinim.** Ref.: Ezra 2:46. ¶
e. **A Levite.** Refs.: Neh. 7:49; 8:7. ¶
f. **Son of Zaccur who signed the covenant of renewal with Nehemiah after the return from the Babylonian captivity.** Refs.: Neh. 10:10, 22; 13:13. ¶
g. **A Jewish leader who also signed the covenant of renewal with Nehemiah after the return from the Babylonian captivity.** Ref.: Neh. 10:26. ¶
h. **Son of Igdaliah.** Ref.: Jer. 35:4. ¶

HANANEEL, HANANEL – *ḥªnan'ēl* [masc. proper noun: חֲנַנְאֵל <2606>; from GRACIOUS (BE) <2603> and GOD <410>]: God has favored, God is compassionate ▶ **This word designates a tower of Jerusalem.** It probably refers to an Israelite (Neh. 3:1; 12:39; Jer. 31:38; Zech. 14:10). ¶

HANANI – *ḥªnāniy* [masc. proper noun: חֲנָנִי <2607>; from GRACIOUS (BE) <2603>]: gracious, compassionate ▶
a. **Son of Heman.** Refs.: 1 Chr. 25:4, 25. ¶
b. **A seer and the father of Jehu.** Refs.: 1 Kgs. 16:1, 7; 2 Chr. 16:7; 19:2; 20:34. ¶
c. **Brother of Nehemiah.** Refs.: Neh. 1:2; 7:2. ¶
d. **A priest.** Ref.: Ezra 10:20. ¶
e. **Another priest.** Ref.: Neh. 12:36. ¶

HANANIAH – *ḥªnanyāh, ḥªnanyāhû* [masc. proper noun: חֲנַנְיָה, חֲנַנְיָהוּ <2608>;

from GRACIOUS (BE) <2603> and LORD <3050>]: the Lord has given, the Lord is gracious ▶ **The name of fourteen persons in the Old Testament. Little is known about most of them.**
a. A son of Heman who served as a singer at the Temple. Heman was the king's prophet (seer) (1 Chr. 25:4, 23). ¶
b. A royal official who helped organize the army of Uzziah. Ref.: 2 Chr. 26:11. ¶
c. The father of Zedekiah who was a royal official under Jehoiakim. Ref.: Jer. 36:12. ¶
d. The son of Azur and a false prophet who opposed Jeremiah. He proclaimed that God would destroy Babylon and not permit it to destroy Jerusalem and God would bring back Jehoiachin as king in Judah. Jeremiah correctly predicted his death because of his false prophecies and rebellion (Jer. 28:1, 5, 10–13, 15, 17). ¶
e. His grandson Irijah accused Jeremiah of treason for leaving Jerusalem. Ref.: Jer. 37:13. ¶
f. A son of Shashak in the line of Benjamin through Saul. Refs.: 1 Chr. 8:24, 25. ¶
g. The Hebrew name of Shadrach, one of the three companions of Daniel in exile. Refs.: Dan. 1:6, 7, 11, 19; 2:17. ¶
h. A son of Zerubbabel. He had a brother and sister and returned with his father to Jerusalem after the exile. Refs.: 1 Chr. 3:19, 21. ¶
i. A descendant of Bebai who intermarried with the people of the land. Ref.: Ezra 10:28. ¶
j. A priest under Nehemiah and a perfumer who helped repair the wall and gates of Jerusalem. Ref.: Neh. 3:8. ¶
k. A priest, son of Shele, who helped repair the walls of Jerusalem. Ref.: Neh. 3:30. ¶
l. Nehemiah's brother whom he appointed to administer the city of Jerusalem. He feared God and was honest (Neh. 7:2). ¶
m. A leader of the Jews who affirmed the covenant of renewal set up by Nehemiah. Ref.: Neh. 10:23. ¶
n. A priest who was the head of a priestly family. Refs.: Neh. 12:12, 41. ¶

HAND – 1 ***ḥōp̱en*** [masc. noun: חֹפֶן <2651>; from an unused root of uncertain signification] ▶ **This word means fist and also means handful. It refers to a closed hand or a hand holding all that it can.** As such, it could serve as a means to measure ashes (Ex. 9:8); or ground incense (Lev. 16:12). In a metaphor, it describes the Lord's fists containing the wind (Prov. 30:4), or a fist or handful of "rest" (Eccl. 4:6). It is used of divine beings' hands filled with hot coals (Ezek. 10:2, 7). ¶
2 ***yāḏ, yaḏ 'aḇšālôm*** [fem. noun: יָד, יַד אַבְשָׁלוֹם <3027>; a prim. root] ▶ **This word literally refers to the part of the body that enables a human to perform many works; it also means strength. It frequently appears in the Old Testament with literal, figurative, and technical uses.** Literally, it implies the hand of a human being (Lev. 14:28; Jer. 36:14) and occasionally the wrist (Gen. 38:28). Metaphorically, it signifies strength or power (Deut. 32:36; Is. 37:27); authority or right of possession (Gen. 16:9; 2 Chr. 13:16); location or direction (Num. 24:24; Ps. 141:6); the side of an object (1 Sam. 4:18); a fractional portion of the whole (Gen. 47:24; Neh. 11:1). In a technical sense, the word is used to identify the upright supports for the bronze laver (1 Kgs. 7:35, 36); the tenons for the Tabernacle (Ex. 26:17); and an axle (1 Kgs. 7:32, 33). See also 2 Samuel 18:18 for the name of a pillar called Absalom's Monument (lit.: Absalom's Hand). *
3 ***yaḏ*** [Aramaic noun: יַד <3028>; corresponding to <3027> above] ▶ **This word also means power, control, possession.** It corresponds to the Hebrew noun of the same spelling (<3027> above) and refers to a literal hand (although not a human one) as writing (Dan. 5:5). From the ability of the hand to hold and manipulate objects, the word is used figuratively to describe control, power, or possession, such as Nebuchadnezzar's power over Israel (Ezra 5:12) and other people and animals (Dan. 2:38); God's power to do whatever He wishes (Dan. 4:35); the lions' power to hurt a person (Dan. 6:27; cf. 1 Sam. 17:37); the Jews' control over the rebuilding of the Temple

(Ezra 5:8). The stone cut out without hands (Dan. 2:34) refers to a kingdom set up by God independently of human power (Dan. 2:45). In Ezra 6:12, the word refers to an attempt to gain power to change the edict of Darius. *

[4] ***kap*** [fem. noun: כַּף <3709>; from BOW, BOW DOWN <3721> (in the sense of to bend)] ▶ **This word means the palm, and also means the flat of the hand, the flat of the foot, hollow, bent. The principal meaning is hollow, often used of the hollow of the physical hand or foot.** It also relates to cupped or bent objects such as spoons (Num. 7:80). In metaphysical overtones, Job declared his cleanness of hand (Job 9:30); and David linked clean hands with a pure heart (Ps. 24:4). The righteous correctly lift up their hands in God's name (Ps. 63:4; 141:2), but the wicked are snared by their own hands' work (Ps. 9:16). At wicked Jezebel's death, dogs devoured her but refused the palms of her hands (2 Kgs. 9:35). The Israelites inherited every place on which their soles treaded in the Promised Land (Deut. 11:24); the returning exiles were delivered from the hand of the enemy (Ezra 8:31). Ultimately, God is the skillful Shepherd, securely holding His own with a sovereign hand (Ps. 139:5). *

– [5] Job 33:7 ➔ PRESSURE <405>.

HAND (TURN TO THE RIGHT) – ***'āman*** [verb: אָמַן <541>; denom. from RIGHT HAND <3225>] ▶ **This word is always used with its opposite, *śāma'l*, meaning to go to the left or to use the left hand.** Lot could choose which direction he wanted to go (Gen. 13:9: *yāman* <3231>). God would guide Israel where they needed to go (Is. 30:21 <541>). God commanded Ezekiel to go the way God directed him (Ezek. 21:16: *yāman* <3231>). ¶

HAND OVER – [1] Is. 19:4 ➔ GIVE OVER <5534> [2] Jer. 18:21 ➔ SPILL <5064>.

HANDBAG – Is. 3:22 ➔ money purse ➔ BAG <2754>.

HANDBREATH – [1] ***ṭep̱aḥ, ṭap̱ḥāh*** [noun: טֶפַח, טְפָחָה <2947>; from SPREAD OUT <2946>] ▶

a. A masculine noun denoting a small lineal measurement, the breadth of a person's hand. It indicated the thickness of Solomon's great brass sea (1 Kgs. 7:26; 2 Chr. 4:5). ¶

b. A feminine noun indicating a small measurement of time. It was used by the psalmist to indicate the shortness and swiftness of the days of his life (Ps. 39:5). ¶

c. A feminine noun referring to a covering, coping, eave. Its meaning is not entirely certain, but it seems to refer to a coping or top layer of a wall or structure (1 Kgs. 7:9; NASB, KJV, ESV, coping; NKJV, NIV, eaves). ¶

[2] ***ṭōpaḥ*** [masc. noun: טֹפַח <2948>; from SPREAD OUT <2946> (the same as <2947> above)] ▶ **This was a small measurement about the width of a man's hand.** Several items bear this measurement in the Old Testament: the rim of the table of showbread (Ex. 25:25; 37:12); measuring instruments (Ezek. 40:5; 43:13); hooks for hanging (Ezek. 40:43). ¶

HANDFUL – [1] ***qōmeṣ*** [masc. noun: קֹמֶץ <7062>; from TAKE A HANDFUL <7061>] ▶ **This word indicates an abundance.** It refers to an amount of something equal to what a person's hand can hold (Lev. 2:2; 5:12; 6:15). It is used to mean a great amount of something; handfuls of grain, an abundant supply or crop (Gen. 41:47). ¶

[2] ***šō'al*** [masc. noun: שֹׁעַל <8168>; from an unused root meaning to hollow out] ▶ **This word also indicates the hollow of the hand.** In its context, it indicates figuratively a full handful of people, compared to the mere dust, the small population of Samaria (1 Kgs. 20:10; Is. 40:12; Ezek. 13:19). ¶

– [3] Ex. 9:8; Lev. 16:12; Eccl. 4:6 ➔ HAND <2651> [4] Ruth 2:16 ➔ BUNDLE <6653> [5] Ps. 72:16 ➔ ABUNDANCE <6451>.

HANDLE – [1] Judg. 3:22 ➔ HILT <5325> [2] Ps. 115:7 ➔ FEEL <4184> [3] Zeph. 1:11 ➔ WEIGH OUT <5187>.

HANDSOME – 1 Gen. 39:6 ➔ BEAUTIFUL <3303> 2 Ezek. 23:6, 12, 23 ➔ PLEASANT <2531> 3 Zech. 11:13 ➔ ROBE <145>.

HANDSOME (BE) – Ps. 45:2 ➔ BEAUTIFUL (BE, MAKE ONESELF) <3302>.

HANES – ***ḥānês*** [proper noun: חָנֵס <2609>; of Egyptian deriv.] ▶ **A place in Egypt.** Ref.: Is. 30:4. ¶

HANG – 1 ***ḥānaq*** [verb: חָנַק <2614>; a prim. root (comp. DEDICATE <2596>)] ▶ **This word means to strangle, to hang oneself, to kill.** It is used in its reflexive stem when the subject acts upon itself to mean to hang oneself (2 Sam. 17:23). It describes a lioness killing her prey which serves figuratively as a picture of the Assyrians destroying other peoples (Nah. 2:12: to kill, to strangle). ¶
2 ***sāraḥ*** [verb: סָרַח <5628>; a prim. root] ▶ **A verb also meaning to extend over, to spread, to sprawl.** It signifies something that is lapped over, folded over, doubled over (Ex. 26:12, 13). Used of a low-growing plant, it means to spread out over the ground (Ezek. 17:6: spreading). It is used of turbans that lap around one's head and shoulders (Ezek. 23:15). Used of a person lying on a couch, it means to sprawl out, stretch out over it (Amos 6:4: flowing). It means to act riotously, carefree at a banquet hall (Amos 6:7: to stretch, to recline, sprawler). The Hebrew word also means to decay, to degenerate; see VANISH <5628>. ¶
3 ***tālā'*** [verb: תָּלָא <8511>; a prim. root] ▶ **This word means to suspend and also means to be determined.** It refers to dangling in midair with the danger of falling or dropping (Deut. 28:66). It indicates hanging objects up, not touching the ground; of hanging people or their bones (2 Sam. 21:12). It refers to having a strong opinion, one that a person will not change (Hos. 11:7: to be bent, to be determined). ¶
4 ***tālāh*** [verb: תָּלָה <8518>; a prim. root] ▶ **This word means to suspend something or someone in the air.** The king's chief baker was hanged and executed (Gen. 40:19, 22). Hanging or execution on a tree was the penalty for a crime worthy of death (Deut. 21:22, 23; Esther 2:23). It was the fate of many in time of war (Josh. 8:29; 10:26). In the passive sense, it means to be hanged (Esther 2:23; Lam. 5:12). Objects are hung out as well (Ezek. 27:10). It is used figuratively of hanging an abstract quality or responsibility on a person (Is. 22:24). *
– 5 Num. 25:4; 2 Sam. 21:6, 9, 13 ➔ ALIENATED (BE) <3363> 6 Job 28:4 ➔ BRING LOW <1809> 7 Prov. 26:7: to hang down, useless, limp ➔ DRAW <1802>.

HANGED (BE) – Ezra 6:11 ➔ STRIKE <4223>.

HANGING – 1 Ex. 27:9, 11; etc. ➔ CURTAIN <7050> 2 Ex. 27:16; 35:17; etc. ➔ CURTAIN <4539> 3 1 Kgs. 7:29 ➔ DESCENT <4174>.

HANNAH – ***ḥannāh*** [fem. proper noun: חַנָּה <2584>; from GRACIOUS (BE) <2603>]: grace ▶ **The mother of Samuel, wife of Elkanah.** Ref.: 1 Sam. 1:2. Her name means "grace" (1 Sam. 2:21). She consecrated her child to the Lord as a Nazarite (1 Sam. 1:9–11, 21, 22) as she had promised before his birth. She named him Samuel, meaning "asked of God" (1 Sam. 1:20). Her song/prayer of praise and thanksgiving is also prophetic in both its tone and content (1 Sam. 2:1–11). Other refs.: 1 Sam. 1:5, 8, 13, 15, 19. ¶

HANNATHON – ***ḥannāṯōn*** [proper noun: חַנָּתֹן <2615>; prob. from GRACIOUS (BE) <2603>]: looked upon with grace ▶ **A place near the border of Zebulun.** Ref.: Josh. 19:14. ¶

HANNIEL – ***ḥanniy'êl*** [masc. proper noun: חַנִּיאֵל <2592>; from GRACIOUS (BE) <2603> and GOD <410>]: grace of God ▶ **a. Chief Manassite.** Ref.: Num. 34:23. ¶ **b. Chief Asherite.** Ref.: 1 Chr. 7:39. ¶

HANOCHITE – ***ḥ*ᵃ*nōḵiy*** [masc. proper noun: חֲנֹכִי <2599>; patron. from ENOCH

<2585>]: see ENOCH d. ▶ **A descendant of Hanoch (or Enoch), a son of Reuben.** Ref.: Num. 26:5. ¶

HANUN – ***ḥānûn*** [masc. proper noun: חָנוּן <2586>; from GRACIOUS (BE) <2603>]: favored, gracious ▶
a. The king of the Ammonites. Refs.: 2 Sam. 10:1–4; 1 Chr. 19:2–4, 6. He acted with hostility toward David's servants, shaming them. War resulted, and David defeated the Ammonites (see 2 Sam. 10:5–19). ¶
b. An Israelite leader who returned from the exile. He helped repair the walls of Jerusalem (Neh. 3:13, 30). ¶

HAP – Ruth 2:3 ➔ CHANCE <4745>.

HAPHARAIM – ***ḥ*ᵃ*p̄ārayim, ḥop̄ra'*** [proper noun: חֲפָרַיִם, חָפְרַע <2663>; dual of HEPHER <2660>]: double wells ▶
a. A city included in the inheritance of Issachar. Ref.: Josh. 19:19. ¶
b. This word designates Hophra, the pharaoh of Egypt. Ref.: Jer. 44:30. See also PHARAOH HOPHRA <6548>. ¶

HAPPEN – [1] ***qārāh*** [fen. noun: קָרָה <7136>; a prim. root] ▶
a. This word means to occur; to meet. It states that something happens, comes about, whether good or bad. Abraham's servant prayed that God would grant him success, to let it come about (Gen. 27:20); it refers to an entire episode of events (Gen. 42:29); or to a specific event (Gen. 44:29). It is used of an event in which God is involved or is behind the scenes working something out (Ex. 3:18; Ruth 2:3; Esther 4:7). It indicates what will happen in the future (Is. 41:22; Dan. 10:14).
b. A word meaning to lay beams of wood. It describes in a technical sense the putting of beams of wood into a structure, especially into the Temple (2 Chr. 34:11); into a new wall of Jerusalem (Neh. 2:8; 3:3, 6). It is used figuratively of God's laying beams in the structure of the heavens (Ps. 104:3). *
– [2] Ruth 2:3; 1 Sam. 6:9; Eccl. 2:15; 3:19; 9:2, 3 ➔ CHANCE <4745>.

HAPPIZZEZ – ***piṣṣêṣ*** [masc. proper noun: פִּצֵּץ <6483>; from an unused root meaning to dissever]: to break ▶ **A priest of Aaron's line who received an allotment when the lots were drawn to serve at the Temple.** Ref.: 1 Chr. 24:15. ¶

HAPPY – [1] ***'ōšer*** [masc. noun: אֹשֶׁר <837>; from BLESS <833>] ▶ **This word means gladness, contentment. The Hebrew word is found once in the Bible describing a feeling of joy.** Ref.: Gen. 30:13; lit.: with my happiness. ¶
– [2] Prov. 3:13; Deut. 33:29; etc. ➔ BLESSED <835>.

HAPPY (BE) – ***ṭôḇ*** [verb: טוֹב <2895>; a prim. root] ▶ **This word means to be cheerful and also means to please, to be loved, to be favored, to seem good, to be acceptable, to endure, to be valuable, to do well, to do right.** It means to be happy or glad, such as when Nabal, husband of Abigail, was joyous from drinking too much (1 Sam. 25:36; 2 Sam. 13:28; Esther 1:10). The word naturally expresses the idea of being loved or enjoying the favor of someone. Samuel grew up in favor before the Lord and people (1 Sam. 2:26). It is used with the idiom "in the eyes of" to express the idea of seeming good or advisable; Abner informed David of everything that was good in the eyes of Israel (2 Sam. 3:19; 15:26). The word is used to express the meaning of good, as when the Israelites asserted they were better off in Egypt than in the wilderness (Num. 11:18; cf. Deut. 5:29). The idea of being better or being valuable is expressed several times using this word: Jephthah asked the Ammonites whether they were better than Balak, son of Zippor (Judg. 11:25); while the psalmist asserted that it was good for him to have been afflicted, for thereby he learned the Lord's decrees (Ps. 119:71).

The verb is used four times in the causative stem to mean to deal rightly or to deal justly. The Lord informed David that he had done well to plan to build a Temple for God (2 Chr. 6:8) and informed Jehu that he had performed his assassination of Ahab's house well (2 Kgs. 10:30). *

HARA – ***hārā'*** [proper noun: הָרָא <2024>; perhaps from MOUNTAIN <2022>]: country of hills ▶ **A place to which were deported prisoners from among the 10 tribes.** Ref.: 1 Chr. 5:26. ¶

HARADAH – ***ḥ^arāḏāh*** [proper noun: חֲרָדָה <2732>; the same as TREMBLING <2731>]: trembling, fear ▶ **A place in the desert where the Israelites camped.** Refs.: Num. 33:24, 25. ¶

HARAN – 1 ***hārān*** [masc. proper noun: הָרָן <2039>; perhaps from HOR <2022>]: mountaineer, elevated ▶
a. Son of Terah and brother of Abraham. Refs.: Gen. 11:26–29, 31. ¶
b. A Levite, son of Shimei. Ref.: 1 Chr. 23:9. ¶
2 ***ḥārān*** [proper noun: חָרָן <2771>; from BURN (verb) <2787>]: parched ▶
a. The city in northern Mesopotamia to which Abraham migrated from Ur of the Chaldeans. It was about seven hundred miles from Ur of the Chaldeans. It was on the west side of the Balik River. Shepherding was an important agricultural pursuit there, including all kinds of livestock. Haran traded with many nations (Ezek. 27:23). It was a center for the worship of the moon god. Assyria, under Sennacherib, conquered it (2 Kgs. 19:12; Is. 37:12). Abraham left Haran with Lot when he was seventy-five years old (Gen. 12:4, 5). Laban lived there and, of course, Jacob lived there for a long period of time with Laban. Terah lived there briefly before he died. Rebekah, Isaac's wife, came from Haran. It was the birthplace of the twelve patriarchs, except Benjamin. Other refs.: Gen. 11:31, 32; 27:43; 28:10; 29:4. ¶
b. The son of Caleb through his concubine Ephah. Haran fathered Gazez (1 Chr. 2:46). ¶

HARARITE – ***hārāriy, h^arāriy*** [masc. proper noun: הָרָרִי, הֲרָרִי <2043>; apparently from MOUNTAIN <2042>] ▶ **Possibly an inhabitant of a village named Harar (mountain).** Refs.: 2 Sam. 23:11, 33; 1 Chr. 11:34, 35. ¶

HARASHIM – ***ḥ^arašiym*** [masc. plur. proper noun: חֲרָשִׁים <2798>; plur. of CRAFTSMAN <2796>]: craftsmen ▶ **The name of a valley according to some translators.** Ref.: 1 Chr. 4:14; KJV: the valley of Charashim. The word literally means craftsmen and should be translated as the valley of craftsmen (1 Chr. 4:14; see ESV, NASB, NKJV, NIV: Ge (Valley of) Harashim with a note). ¶

HARASS – 1 Gen. 49:23 ➔ HATE <7852> 2 Deut. 2:9, 19 ➔ BESIEGE <6696> b. 3 Judg. 2:18 ➔ AFFLICT <1766> 4 Judg. 10:8 ➔ SHATTER <7492>.

HARBONA – ***ḥarḇônā', ḥarḇônāh*** [masc. proper noun: חַרְבוֹנָא, חַרְבוֹנָה <2726>; of Persian origin] ▶ **One of the seven chamberlains of king Ahasuerus.** Refs.: Esther 1:10; 7:9. ¶

HARBOR – Is. 23:10 ➔ BELT <4206>.

HARD (BE) – 1 ***qāšāh*** [verb: קָשָׁה <7185>; a prim. root] ▶ **This word means to be hardened, cruel, stiff-necked.** It indicates that something is difficult, hard, cruel, severe, harsh, e.g., a difficult birth (Gen. 35:16, 17); harsh anger or wrath (Gen. 49:7). It is one of the words used to describe a hardened heart (Ex. 7:3; 13:15); a resentful heart or attitude (Deut. 15:18). It refers to a hardened spirit created by the Lord (Deut. 2:30). In its passive sense, it indicates a person oppressed, crushed (Is. 8:21). It is used figuratively of making circumstances difficult for persons, making heavy yokes for them (1 Kgs. 12:4). To harden or stiffen one's neck means to become stubborn (2 Kgs. 17:14; Jer. 7:26; 17:23; 19:15). *
2 ***qāšeh*** [adj.: קָשֶׁה <7186>; from <7185> above] ▶ **This word means harsh, cruel, severe, strong, violent, fierce. This term's basic function is to describe something as hard. The word modifies a variety of different subjects and encompasses a fairly broad range of meanings.** The labor the Egyptians imposed on the Hebrews was described as hard (i.e., harsh, Ex. 1:14; 6:9). Joseph spoke hard words to his brothers at

first (Gen. 42:7, 30; cf. 1 Sam. 20:10). A Calebite named Nabal was labeled as being hard, i.e., cruel and evil (1 Sam. 25:3). The Israelites were often characterized as being hard or stiff of neck, i.e., stubborn, rebellious, obstinate (Ex. 32:9, 33:3, 5; Deut. 9:6, 13; cf. Ezek. 3:7). An experience could be hard, i.e., painful (Ps. 60:3); as could a vision or revelation (Is. 21:2). Hannah was hard of spirit, i.e., deeply troubled (1 Sam. 1:15). Both battles and winds could be hard, i.e., fierce (2 Sam. 2:17; Is. 27:8). Moses chose capable men from all Israel to serve as judges; they judged minor cases while Moses himself judged the difficult ones (Ex. 18:26). *

HARD PRESSED (BE) – 1 Sam. 13:6 → OPPRESS <5065>.

HARD ROCK – Deut. 8:15; Ps. 114:8 → lit.: rock of flint → FLINT <2496>.

HARD THINGS – Ps. 31:18; 94:4 → ARROGANCE <6277>.

HARDEN – [1] ***qāšaḥ*** [verb: קָשַׁח <7188>; a prim. root] ► **This word means to make hard, to treat roughly. Used twice in the Old Testament, it implies a hardening similar to the formation of a callous.** It signifies the hardening of a mother's heart toward her offspring (Job 39:16: to treat harshly, to treat cruelly, to be hardened against, to deal cruelly); and is used by Isaiah to connote the spiritual dullness of the people toward God (Is. 63:17). ¶
– [2] Job 7:5 → MOMENT (BE FOR A) <7280> e. [3] Dan. 5:20 → STRONG (BE, BECOME, GROW) <8631>.

HARDEN ONESELF – Job 6:10 → REJOICE <5539> b.

HARDENED AGAINST (BE) – Job 39:16 → HARDEN <7188>.

HARDNESS – Lam. 3:65 → SORROW (noun) <4044>.

HARDSHIP – ***t^{e}lā'āh*** [fem. noun: תְּלָאָה <8513>; from WEARY (BE, BECOME) <3811>] ► **This word refers to unfavorable circumstances, oppressions, attacks, war, famine, etc., that Israel endured in Egypt as well as in their wilderness wanderings.** Refs.: Ex. 18:8; Num. 20:14; KJV: travail. In Nehemiah's prayer, it refers to the difficult circumstances Israel had to bear in exile after the fall of Jerusalem (Neh. 9:32; also translated trouble). It refers to personal oppression and discomfort (Lam. 3:5; also translated woe, travail, tribulation). It is used in a derisive, mocking manner by rebellious Israelites about their worship of the Lord that had become a burden and a hardship (Mal. 1:13; also translated weariness). ¶

HARE – Lev. 11:6; Deut. 14:7 → RABBIT <768>.

HAREPH – ***ḥārēp̱*** [masc. proper noun: חָרֵף <2780>; from REPROACH (verb) <2778>]: reproachful ► **One of the sons of Caleb.** Ref.: 1 Chr. 2:51. ¶

HARETH – 1 Sam. 22:5 → HERETH <2802>.

HARHAIAH – ***ḥarh^{a}yāh*** [masc. proper noun: חַרְהֲיָה <2736>; from ANGRY (GET) <2734> and LORD <3050>]: anger of the Lord, zeal of the Lord ► **Father of one of the goldsmiths who repaired the wall of Jerusalem.** Ref.: Neh. 3:8. ¶

HARHAS – ***ḥarḥas*** [masc. proper noun: חַרְחַס <2745>; from the same as SUN <2775>]: shining ► **Ancestor of Shallum, the husband of the prophetess Huldah.** Ref.: 2 Kgs. 22:14. ¶

HARHUR – ***ḥarḥûr*** [masc. proper noun: חַרְחוּר <2744>; a fuller form of HEAT (FIERY) <2746>]: great heat, fever ► **Members of his family came back from the Babylonian captivity.** Refs.: Ezra 2:51; Neh. 7:53. ¶

HARIM – ***ḥārim*** [masc. proper noun: חָרִם <2766>; from DESTROY <2763>]: flat-nosed ►

a. A priest. Ref.: 1 Chr. 24:8. ¶
b. An Israelite who signed the covenant of renewal with Nehemiah after the return from the Babylonian captivity. Ref.: Neh. 10:5). ¶
c. Head of a priestly course. Refs.: Ezra 2:39; 10:21; Neh. 7:42; 12:15. ¶
d. Head of a family. Refs.: Ezra 2:32; 10:31; Neh. 3:11; 7:35. ¶
e. A chief of the people who signed the covenant of renewal with Nehemiah after the return from the Babylonian captivity. Ref.: Neh. 10:27. ¶

HARIPH – ***ḥāriyp̱*** [masc. proper noun: חָרִיף <2756>; from WINTER (verb) <2778>]: autumnal rain ▶
a. Members of his family came back from the Babylonian captivity. Ref.: Neh. 7:24. ¶
b. A prince of this family who signed the covenant of renewal with Nehemiah after the return from the Babylonian captivity. Ref.: Neh. 10:19. ¶

HARLOTRY – See PROSTITUTION <8457>.

HARM (noun) – 1 ***'āsôn*** [masc. noun: אָסוֹן <611>; of uncertain deriv.] ▶ **This word means and is also translated calamity, mischief, injury.** It signifies potential danger during a journey (Gen. 42:4, 38; 44:29), bodily harm or personal loss (Ex. 21:22, 23). ¶
– 2 Dan. 3:25; 6:23 ➔ DAMAGE (noun) <2257> 3 Dan. 6:22 ➔ WRONG (noun) <2248>.

HARM (verb) – 1 Gen. 26:11 ➔ TOUCH <5060> 2 Prov. 8:36 ➔ VIOLENCE (DO) <2554>.

HARMFUL – 1 Ezra 4:15 ➔ DAMAGE (verb) <5142> 2 Ps. 52:4 ➔ DEVOURING <1105>.

HARMON – ***harmôn*** [proper noun: הַרְמוֹן <2038>; from the same as HORAM <2036>] ▶
a. This word indicates the destiny of Israelite refugees (when defeated by her enemies). Ref.: Amos 4:3; ESV, NASB, NIV, NKJV. ¶
b. A masculine noun denoting a palace. It refers to possibly a foreign palace, to which Israelite refugees will go (Amos 4:3, KJV). ¶

HARMONIOUS SOUND – Ps. 92:3 ➔ MEDITATION <1902>.

HARMONY (IN) – Dan. 3:5, 7, 10, 15 ➔ BAGPIPE <5481>.

HARNEPHER – ***ḥarnep̱er*** [masc. proper noun: חַרְנֶפֶר <2774>; of uncertain deriv.] ▶ **A descendant of Asher, son of Zophah.** Ref.: 1 Chr. 7:36. ¶

HARNESS – 1 ***rāṯam*** [verb: רָתַם <7573>; a prim. root] ▶ **This word means to hook up, to connect.** Used of hooking up horses to a chariot, it means to harness (Mic. 1:13: KJV: to bind). ¶
– 2 Ps. 32:9 ➔ CONTROL (verb) <1102>.

HAROD (WELL OF, SPRING OF) – ***'êyn ḥ***[a]***rōḏ*** [proper noun: עֵין חֲרֹד <5878>; from EYE (noun) <5869> (in the sense of fountain) and a deriv. of TREMBLE <2729>]: fountain of trembling ▶ **Gideon and all the people who were with him encamped beside this place.** Ref.: Judg. 7:1. ¶

HARODITE – ***ḥ***[a]***rōḏiy*** [proper noun: חֲרֹדִי <2733>; patrial from a deriv. of TREMBLE <2729>; comp. HAROD (WELL OF) <5878] ▶ **Designation of two of David's mighty men, i.e., Shammah and Elika.** Ref.: 2 Sam. 23:25. ¶

HAROEH – ***rō'eh, hārō'eh*** [masc. proper noun: רֹאֶה, הָרֹאֶה <7204>; from VISION <7203>]: seer, prophet ▶ **A man of the tribe of Judah.** Ref.: 1 Chr. 2:52. ¶

HARORITE – ***h***[a]***rôriy*** [masc. proper noun: הֲרוֹרִי <2033>; another form of HARARITE <2043>]: the mountaineer ▶ **Title given to Shammoth or designation of this man.** Ref.: 1 Chr. 11:27. ¶

HAROSHETH HAGGOYIM – ***ḥ**a**rōšeṯ haggôyim, ḥ**a**rōšeṯ*** [proper noun: חֲרֹשֶׁת הַגּוֹיִם, חֲרֹשֶׁת <2800>; the same as CUTTING <2799>]: Harosheth (workmanship) of the Gentiles ▶
a. Sisera, who was killed by Jael, dwelt there. Refs.: ESV, NASB, NIV, NKJV, Judg. 4:2, 13, 16.
b. Harosheth, used with the definite article and the plural of *gôy* (NATION <1471> a.). Refs.: KJV, Judg. 4:2, 13, 16. ¶

HARP – 1 ***nêḇel, neḇel*** [masc. noun: נֵבֶל, נֶבֶל <5035>; from WITHER <5034>] ▶ **The word indicates a lyre, a stringed instrument.** It refers to a stringed instrument (Amos 5:23; 6:5); a harp of ten strings (1 Sam. 10:5; 1 Kgs. 10:12; Ps. 33:2; 57:8; 92:3). It was used by prophets and at religious feasts, ceremonies, and in various common celebrations. The word also refers to a storage jar; see SKIN BOTTLE <5035>. *
– 2 Dan. 3:5, 7, 10, 15 ➔ LYRE <7030>, PSALTERY <6460> 3 See LYRE <3658>.

HARPOON – ***śukkāh*** [fem. noun: שֻׂכָּה <7905>; fem. of TABERNACLE <7900> in the sense of BARB <7899>] ▶ **This word refers to a weapon used to kill huge sea creatures.** In context Leviathan is in mind, the great monster God describes (Job 41:7; KJV: barbed iron). ¶

HARROW – 1 ***śāḏaḏ*** [verb: שָׂדַד <7702>; a prim. root] ▶ **This word refers to breaking up and leveling plowed ground, thus covering seeds and/or clearing the ground of weeds, small debris, etc.** Animals had to be trained to do this by pulling a harrowing tool over the ground (Job 39:10); as the farmer guided them (Is. 28:24). It is used figuratively of Jacob (Israel) harrowing the ground at God's command (Hos. 10:11). ¶
– 2 2 Sam. 12:31; 1 Chr. 20:3 ➔ PICK (noun) <2757>.

HARSH – Prov. 15:1 ➔ PAIN (noun) <6089>.

HARSH (BE) – Dan. 2:15 ➔ URGENT (BE) <2685>.

HARSH TREATMENT – Is. 66:4 ➔ CAPRICIOUS CHILDREN <8586>.

HARSHA – ***ḥaršā'*** [masc. proper noun: חַרְשָׁא <2797>; from HERESH <2792>]: mute, magician ▶ **His children came back from the Babylonian captivity.** Refs.: Ezra 2:52; Neh. 7:54. ¶

HARSHLY (TREAT) – Job 39:16 ➔ HARDEN <7188>.

HARSHNESS – Ezek. 34:4 ➔ SEVERITY <6530>.

HART – Deut. 12:15, 22; 1 Kgs. 4:23; Ps. 42:1 ➔ DEER <354>.

HARUM – ***hārûm*** [masc. proper noun: הָרוּם <2037>; pass. part. of the same as HORAM <2036>]: elevated, high ▶ **An Israelite of the tribe of Judah.** Ref.: 1 Chr. 4:8. ¶

HARUMAPH – ***ḥ**a**rûmap̱*** [masc. proper noun: חֲרוּמַף <2739>; from pass. part. of DESTROY <2763> and NOSE <639>]: with a snub or small nose ▶ **Father of Jedaiah who repaired the wall of Jerusalem.** Ref.: Neh. 3:10. ¶

HARUPHITE – ***ḥ**a**rûp̱iy*** [masc. proper noun: חֲרוּפִי <2741>; a patrial from (prob.) a collateral of HARIPH <2756>] ▶ **Designation of Shephatiah who came to David at Ziklag.** Ref.: 1 Chr. 12:5. ¶

HARUZ – ***ḥārûṣ*** [masc. proper noun: חָרוּץ <2743>; the same as DILIGENT <2742>]: diligent ▶ **Father of Meshullemeth who was the mother of Amon; he was king of Judah.** Ref.: 2 Kgs. 21:19. ¶

HARVEST – 1 ***m**e**lê'āh*** [fem. noun: מְלֵאָה <4395>; fem. of FULL (adj.) <4392>] ▶ **This word means an autumnal gathered crop, a produce of grain.** It is used to indicate the fullness or best quality of the harvest in the fall (Ex. 22:29; Deut. 22:9; also translated ripe fruits, ripe produce, granary, crop, yield) of grain or wine (Num. 18:27: fullness, full produce, juice). ¶

2 ***qāṣiyr*** [masc. noun: קָצִיר <7105>; from REAP <7114>] ▶
a. This word refers to the time of the year set by God when crops have ripened and are reaped (Gen. 8:22; 30:14, April-June); and to the activity of harvesting itself (2 Sam. 21:9). The failure of a harvest was devastating (Gen. 45:6). Certain feasts were centered around times of harvesting (Ex. 23:16).
b. A masculine noun meaning a bough, a branch. This word also refers to a fresh bough or sprig springing forth from a stump, an indication of life (Job 14:9). It is used figuratively of the wicked whose branch is dead, cut off (Job 18:16); and to the prosperity of Job in his earlier years (Job 29:19). It is used of Israel's prospering (Ps. 80:11), but also to her state of ruin as dry limbs (Is. 27:11). *
3 ***tᵉḇû'āh*** [fem. noun: תְּבוּאָה <8393>; from COME <935> (in the sense of to bring, to produce)] ▶ **This word also indicates a crop, an increase, a revenue.** It indicates the produce or yield from the ground (Ex. 23:10; Lev. 19:25; Josh. 5:12); and the fields (2 Kgs. 8:6; Ezek. 48:18). It indicates any increase or prosperity in general (Job 31:12; Prov. 10:16; 14:4). It describes the benefits or gains from wisdom (Prov. 3:14; 8:19). Even Israel's reaping of what she has sown is described as a harvest, an increase; but it is one she does not want to reap (Jer. 12:13). It means harvest in a general sense (Gen. 47:24), at the increase or at the harvest. The threshing floor and wine vats generated produce and products (Num. 18:30). It refers to increase or income (Eccl. 5:10). Every increase or income is from God. *
– 4 Lev. 26:10 ➔ SLEEP (verb) <3462> b. 5 Deut. 32:22; Ps. 67:6; 85:12 ➔ INCREASE (noun) <2981>.

HARVEST OF FRUIT – Is. 32:10 ➔ GATHERING <625>.

HARVEST TIME (SPEND) – Is. 18:6 ➔ WINTER (verb) <2778>.

HASADIAH – ***ḥᵃsaḏyāh*** [masc. proper noun: חֲסַדְיָה <2619>; from MERCY <2617> and LORD <3050>]: mercy of the Lord ▶ **A descendant of Solomon.** Ref.: 1 Chr. 3:20. ¶

HASHABIAH – ***ḥᵃšaḇyāh, ḥᵃšaḇyāhû*** [masc. proper noun: חֲשַׁבְיָה, חֲשַׁבְיָהוּ <2811>; from THINK <2803> and LORD <3050>]: considered by the Lord ▶
a. A Merarite Levite. Ref.: 1 Chr. 6:45. ¶
b. Son of Bunni. Refs.: 1 Chr. 9:14; Neh. 11:15. ¶
c. Son of Jeduthun. Refs.: 1 Chr. 25:3, 19. ¶
d. A Hebronite. Ref.: 1 Chr. 26:30. ¶
e. Son of Kemuel. Ref.: 1 Chr. 27:17. ¶
f. A Levite. Ref.: 2 Chr. 35:9. ¶
g. Another Levite. Refs.: Ezra 8:19, 24; Neh. 3:17; 10:11; 12:24. ¶
h. Son of Mattaniah. Ref.: Neh. 11:22. ¶
i. A priest. Ref.: Neh. 12:21. ¶

HASHABNAH – ***ḥᵃšaḇnāh*** [masc. proper noun: חֲשַׁבְנָה <2812>; fem. of SCHEME <2808>]: inventiveness ▶ **A chief of the people who signed the covenant of renewal with Nehemiah after the return from the Babylonian captivity.** Ref.: Neh. 10:25. ¶

HASHABNEIAH – ***ḥᵃšaḇnᵉyāh*** [masc. proper noun: חֲשַׁבְנְיָה <2813>; from SCHEME <2808> and LORD <3050>]: regarded by the Lord ▶
a. His son Hattush repaired the wall of Jerusalem. Ref.: Neh. 3:10. ¶
b. A Levite. Ref.: Neh. 9:5. ¶

HASHBADDANAH – ***ḥašbaddānāh*** [masc. proper noun: חַשְׁבַּדָּנָה <2806>; from THINK <2803> and JUDGE (verb) <1777>]: considerate in judging ▶ **One of those who stood beside Ezra when he addressed the people who had come back from captivity.** Ref.: Neh. 8:4. ¶

HASHEM – ***hāšêm*** [masc. proper noun: הָשֵׁם <2044>; perhaps from the same as HASHUM <2828>]: sleep ▶ **His sons were among David's mighty men.** Ref.: 1 Chr. 11:34. ¶

HASHMONAH – ***ḥašmōnāh*** [proper noun: חַשְׁמֹנָה <2832>; fem. of ENVOY

<2831>]: fertile ▶ **A place in the desert where the Israelites camped.** Refs.: Num. 33:29, 30. ¶

HASHUBAH – ***ḥ^{a}šuḇāh*** [masc. proper noun: חֲשֻׁבָה <2807>; from THINK <2803>]: consideration ▶ **One of the sons of Zerubbabel.** Ref.: 1 Chr. 3:20. ¶

HASHUM – ***ḥāšum*** [masc. proper noun: חָשֻׁם <2828>; from the same as ENVOY <2831>]: rich ▶ **Members of his family came back from the Babylonian deportation.** He stood beside Ezra when he addressed the people and later he sealed Nehemiah's covenant to follow the Law of God (Ezra 2:19; 10:33; Neh. 7:22; 8:4; 10:18). ¶

HASRAH – ***ḥasrāh*** [masc. proper noun: חַסְרָה <2641>; from LACKING (BE) <2637>]: poverty, wanting ▶ **Grandfather of Shallum who was the husband of the prophetess Huldah.** He had been the keeper of the wardrobe, i.e., the priestly clothes (2 Chr. 34:22). ¶

HASSENAAH – Neh. 3:3 ➔ SENAAH, HASSENAAH <5570>.

HASSENUAH – 1 Chr. 9:7 ➔ SENUAH, HASSENUAH <5574>.

HASSHUB – ***ḥaššûḇ*** [masc. proper noun: חַשּׁוּב <2815>; from THINK <2803>]: intelligent, considerate ▶
a. A chief Levite. Refs.: 1 Chr. 9:14; Neh. 11:15. ¶
b. A repairer of Jerusalem's wall. Refs.: Neh. 3:11; 10:23. ¶
c. Another repairer of Jerusalem's wall. Ref.: Neh. 3:23. ¶

HASSOPHERETH – Ezra 2:55 ➔ SOPHERETH, HASSOPHERETH <5618>.

HASTE (noun) – [1] ***b^{e}hiylû*** [Aramaic fem. noun: בְּהִילוּ <924>; from HASTE (BE IN) <927>] ▶ **This word describes quick travel and response to an urgent situation by the enemies of the Jews.** Ref.: Ezra 4:23. ¶
[2] ***ḥippāzôn*** [masc. noun: חִפָּזוֹן <2649>; from HURRY (verb) <2648>] ▶ **This word indicates readiness; also a hurried flight.** It indicates a state of watchfulness and readiness as necessary, as at the first Passover in Egypt (Ex. 12:11) when the Israelites ate their food in haste (Deut. 16:3). Or negated, the word means to do something without hurry; with the Lord as comforter and guardian (Is. 52:12). ¶
– [3] Ps. 71:12 ➔ HASTE (MAKE) <2439> [4] Prov. 20:21: to be in haste ➔ ABHOR <973>.

HASTE (BE IN) – ***b^{e}hal*** [Aramaic verb: בְּהַל <927>; corresponding to TERRIFIED (BE) <926>] ▶ **This word means to be in a hurry; it is also translated quickly, hurriedly, at once, to hurry; to terrify, to trouble, to alarm.** It occurs only in the book of Daniel, where it is used of someone in a hurry (Dan. 2:25; 3:24; 6:19) or someone who is terrified, frightened, or troubled (Dan. 4:5, 19; 5:6, 9, 10; 7:15, 28). In each of these cases, the people are terrified because of a dream or a vision from God. ¶

HASTE (MAKE) – ***ḥiyš*** [verb: חִישׁ <2439>; another form for HASTEN <2363>] ▶ **This verb means to act quickly, to hurry.** Its sense seems to be for God to hasten (or not remain distant) to the psalmist who is in need (Ps. 71:12); also translated to hasten, to come quickly. Some understand this as an adverb. ¶

HASTE (REQUIRE) – ***nāḥaṣ*** [verb: נָחַץ <5169>; a prim. root] ▶ **This word means to be urgent.** It describes a situation or a set of circumstances as pressing, demanding attention (1 Sam. 21:8). ¶

HASTE (verb) – [1] Job 9:26 ➔ SWOOP <2907> [2] Zeph. 1:14; Is. 8:1 ➔ QUICK, QUICKLY <4118> a.

HASTE (verb and noun) – 1 Sam. 23:26; 2 Sam. 4:4 ➔ haste, to make haste ➔ HURRY (verb) <2648>.

HASTEN – [1] ***ʾûṣ*** [verb: אוּץ <213>; a prim. root] ▶ **This word means to hurry, to urge, to insist, or to try.** It expresses urgency (Ex. 5:13; also translated to press, to force, to be urgent) directed towards workers by foremen. It is used to describe the failure of the sun to set in Joshua's famous battle in the Valley of Aijalon (Josh. 10:13; also translated to hurry). It is translated as narrow (confined), also (Josh. 17:15). It can carry the connotation of to insist upon in its causative usage (Gen. 19:15: to urge; Is. 22:4: to labour, to labor, to try). *
[2] ***ḥûš*** [verb: חוּשׁ <2363>; a prim. root] ▶ **a. The basic sense of this word is to hurry or do something quickly.** To carry out an ambush quickly (Judg. 20:37); to hurry to a place of safety (Ps. 55:8). It takes on the sense of disturbed, agitated, or unstable (1 Sam. 20:38; Job 20:2; 31:5; Is. 28:16; Hab. 1:8). * **b. A verb meaning to enjoy; to be anxious, to disturb, to dismay.** Some translators see this word indicating Job's disquiet in himself (Job 20:2) and in Isaiah 28:16. In a different context, it takes on the meaning to enjoy (Eccl. 2:25). ¶
[3] ***ʿûš*** [verb: עוּשׁ <5789>; a prim. root] ▶ **This word means to hurry.** It occurs once in the Hebrew Bible (Joel 3:11; KJV, NKJV: to assemble; NIV: to come quickly). Recent translations have abandoned the former translation, to lend aid, to come to help, for a different Arabic cognate, meaning to hurry. Joel used the word with the verb to come to summon all the nations to prepare for battle in the Valley of Jehoshaphat. At that location, God will judge them, trampling them like grapes in a winepress. ¶
– [4] 2 Chr. 26:20 ➔ TERRIFIED <926> [5] Esther 6:12 ➔ HURRY (verb) <1765> [6] Job 40:23; Ps. 104:7 ➔ HURRY (verb) <2648>.

HASTENING – Is. 16:5 ➔ SKILLED <4106>.

HASTILY – [1] Prov. 20:21: to get hastily, to gain hastily ➔ ABHOR <973> [2] Prov. 25:8 ➔ QUICK, QUICKLY <4118> b.

HASTING – Is. 16:5 ➔ SKILLED <4106>.

HASTY (BE) – [1] Eccl. 8:3 ➔ TERRIFIED <926> [2] Dan. 2:15 ➔ URGENT (BE) <2685>.

HASUPHA – ***ḥᵃśûpāʾ, ḥᵃśupāʾ*** [masc. proper noun: חֲשׂוּפָא, חֲשֻׂפָא <2817>; from STRIP <2834>]: uncovered ▶ **Members from his family came back from the Babylonian captivity.** Refs.: Ezra 2:43; Neh. 7:46. ¶

HAT – [1] ***karbᵉlāh*** [fem. Aramaic noun: כַּרְבְּלָה <3737>; from a verb corresponding to that of CLOTHED WITH <3736>] ▶ **This word indicates a cap, a turban.** It was an article of clothing worn on the heads of the three Hebrew young men thrown into a fiery furnace (Dan. 3:21). ¶
– [2] Ex. 28:40; 29:9; 39:28; Lev. 8:13 ➔ CAP <4021>.

HATACH, HATHACH – ***hᵃṯāḵ*** [masc. proper noun: הֲתָךְ <2047>; prob. of foreign origin]: verily ▶ **One of the king's eunuchs assigned to attend Esther.** Refs.: Esther 4:5, 6, 9, 10. ¶

HATCH – Jer. 17:11 ➔ GATHER <1716>.

HATCHET – [1] Ps. 74:6 ➔ AX <3781> [2] Ps. 74:6 ➔ HAMMER (noun) <3597>.

HATE – [1] ***śāṭam*** [verb: שָׂטַם <7852>; a prim. root] ▶ **This word means to dislike, to detest, to bear a grudge against, to harass, to assail.** It means to nurse hostility and bitterness toward someone (Gen. 27:41; 50:15; Ps. 55:3); or even to attack or harass a person physically (Gen. 49:23). It is rendered variously in Job 16:9 (KJV, "hateth"; NASB, "hunted"; NIV, "tears," all renderings indicating God's supposed attitude toward Job); likewise in Job 30:21. ¶
[2] ***śānêʾ*** [verb: שָׂנֵא <8130>; a prim. root] ▶ **This verb means to detest, to be unwilling, to be hated. It is the antonym of the Hebrew verb *ʾāhaḇ* (<157>), meaning to love.** The verb means to hate God or persons; God punishes children for the sins of their fathers to the third and fourth

generation of those who hate Him, but He shows kindness instead of punishment to those who love (*'āhab*) Him (Ex. 20:5). God hates as His enemies those who love cruelty and wickedness (Ps. 11:5); they do not keep His covenant and are not loyal to Him (Ex. 20:5). God's people were not to become allied to those who hated the Lord (2 Chr. 19:2; Ps. 139:21). God or persons can be the subject of the verb; God came to hate the palaces of Jacob (Amos 6:8; Hos. 9:15); and even the religious services of His own people because they were false (Amos 5:21). In fact, God hates all who do evil (Ps. 5:5); and wickedness (Ps. 45:7); thus, to fear God means to hate evil (Prov. 8:13).

God is different from all other so-called gods, so much so that He hates the corrupt things the heathen do when they worship these gods (Deut. 12:31). The word describes the haters or enemies of persons. David's enemies were those whom his soul hated (2 Sam. 5:8); the enemies of Rebekah would be those who might hate her descendants (Gen. 24:60). The lack of hatred toward a person cleared someone who accidentally killed another person without planning to do so and did not previously hate the person (Deut. 4:42). Absalom, on the other hand, hated his brother Ammon for humiliating his sister and planned his death because he hated him (2 Sam. 13:22). The negative rendition of love your neighbor as yourself asserted that you should not hate your brother in your heart (Lev. 19:17).

The word means to dislike, to be hostile to, or to loathe someone or something in some contexts: Isaac accused Abimelech of rejecting him or acting hostile toward him when he asked Isaac to move away from him (Gen. 26:27; Judg. 11:7); Joseph's brothers became bitter and hostile toward him and his dreams (Gen. 37:5); Malachi asserted that God hated Esau but loved Jacob to explain how God had dealt with their descendants (Mal. 1:3); God cared for Esau and gave him offspring. A similar use of this word is found concerning Jacob's love for Rachel and the hyperbolic statement that he hated Leah (Gen. 29:31, 33; Deut. 21:16, 17); Jethro instructed Moses to choose faithful men who despised increasing their wealth in dishonest ways (Ex. 18:21). In the passive stem of the verb, it is used once to refer to the poor who are despised by their friends or neighbors in contrast to the rich who have many friends (Prov. 14:20).

In the intensive stem, the word means one who radiates hatred (i.e., an enemy); Moses prayed for the Lord to strike the enemies of Levi (Deut. 33:11; 2 Sam. 22:41). The word described the enemies of the Lord (Num. 10:35; Deut. 32:41). The word also described the person who hates wisdom; such a person loves death (Prov. 8:36). *

3 ***śᵉnê'*** [Aramaic verb: שְׂנֵא <8131>; corresponding to <8130> above] ▶ **This word only occurs once in the Hebrew Bible and refers to those who detest a person.** In Daniel 4:19, this word is used when Daniel is speaking to King Nebuchadnezzar about the interpretation of his dream. The interpretation is so unfavorable that Daniel says he wishes it were for the king's enemies instead of being for the king himself. ¶

HATED – Deut. 21:15c → UNLOVED <8146>.

HATHATH – ***ḥᵃṯaṯ*** [masc. proper noun: חֲתַת <2867>; the same as TERROR <2866>]: dismay, terror ▶ **Son of Othniel.** Ref.: 1 Chr. 4:13. ¶

HATIPHA – ***ḥaṭiypā'*** [masc. proper noun: חֲטִיפָא <2412>; from CATCH (verb) <2414>]: captive ▶ **Members of his family came back from Babylon with Zerubbabel.** Refs.: Ezra 2:54; Neh. 7:56. ¶

HATITA – ***ḥᵃṭiyṭā'*** [masc. proper noun: חֲטִיטָא <2410>; from an unused root apparently meaning to dig out]: exploration ▶ **A Temple porter; members of his family came back from Babylon with Zerubbabel.** Refs.: Ezra 2:42; Neh. 7:45. ¶

HATRED – 1 ***śin'āh*** [fem. noun: שִׂנְאָה <8135>; from HATE <8130>] ▶ **This word means detestation, hating, abhorrence. It is most commonly used to describe hatred that one human feels towards**

another. This hate can be so strong that it leads to murder (Num. 35:20); or it can be a hate that causes unrest and dissension between people, yet not necessarily leading to violence (Prov. 10:12; 15:17). In one place, this noun is even used to describe sexual revulsion and is indicative of a strong hate (2 Sam. 13:15). This word can be used as a verb at times, such as in Deuteronomy 1:27 and 9:28. Here God is the subject, and the people were complaining that He hated them, although this was not true. The connotations the people had with this word showed through because they felt that God hated them so much that He would hand them over to be killed by their enemies. *
– [2] Ezek. 25:15; 35:5 ➔ ENMITY <342> [3] Hos. 9:7, 8 ➔ HOSTILITY <4895>.

HATRED (LOOK WITH) – Ps. 68:16 ➔ ENVY (LOOK WITH, GAZE IN, FUME WITH) <7520> a.

HATTIL – ***ḥaṭṭiyl*** [masc. proper noun: חַטִּיל <2411>; from an unused root apparently meaning to wave]: fluctuating ▶ **A servant of Solomon; members of his family came back from Babylon with Zerubbabel.** Refs.: Ezra 2:57; Neh. 7:59. ¶

HATTUSH – ***ḥaṭṭûš*** [masc. proper noun: חַטּוּשׁ <2407>; from an unused root of uncertain signification]: assembled ▶
a. An Israelite of the tribe of Judah, son of Shemiah. Ref.: 1 Chr. 3:22. ¶
b. A descendant of David who came back to Jerusalem with Ezra. Ref.: Ezra 8:2. ¶
c. Son of Hashabiah who made repairs to the wall of Jerusalem. Ref.: Neh. 3:10. ¶
d. A Jew who signed the covenant of renewal with Nehemiah after the return from the Babylonian captivity. Ref.: Neh. 10:4. ¶
e. A priest who came back from Babylon with Zerubbabel. Ref.: Neh. 12:2. ¶

HAUGHTILY – ***rômāh*** [adv.: רוֹמָה <7317>; fem. of HIGH, ON HIGH <7315>] ▶ **This word describes the way something is done or carried out, e.g., in a proud or arrogant manner.** Ref.: Mic. 2:3. ¶

HAUGHTINESS – [1] Job 20:6 ➔ LOFTINESS <7863> [2] Eccl. 7:8 ➔ PROUD <1362> [3] Is. 2:11, 17; Is. 10:12 ➔ HEIGHT <7312> [4] Is. 2:17 ➔ LOFTINESS <1365>.

HAUGHTY – [1] ***yāhiyr*** [adj.: יָהִיר <3093>; prob. from the same as MOUNTAIN <2022>] ▶ **This word describes what is proud, arrogant. It is used to define a person who is insolent, prideful, and narcissistically self-centered.** He or she acts in pride (Prov. 21:24). The use of wine by this person betrays and puts on display his or her supercilious, haughty character (Hab. 2:5), the opposite of the character of a person of faith. ¶
– [2] Ps. 75:5 ➔ ARROGANCE <6277> [3] Prov. 21:4; Is. 10:12 ➔ HEIGHT <7312> [4] Is. 2:11 ➔ LOFTINESS <1365> [5] Is. 13:11 ➔ PROUD <2086>.

HAURAN – ***ḥawrān*** [proper noun: חַוְרָן <2362>; apparently from PALE (GROW) <2357> (in the sense of HOLE <2352>)]: place of caverns ▶ **A region south of Damas.** Refs.: Ezek. 47:16, 18. ¶

HAVE (LET) – Gen. 25:30 ➔ FEED (verb) <3938>.

HAVE RESPECT – 2 Kgs. 1:13, 14 ➔ PRECIOUS (BE) <3365>.

HAVE YOU NOT – 1 Sam. 21:8 ➔ IS THERE NOT <371>.

HAVEN – [1] ***maḥôz*** [masc. noun: מָחוֹז <4231>; from an unused root meaning to enclose] ▶ **This word indicates an enclosure, a place of safety and peace to which God leads His people.** Ref.: Ps. 107:30. ¶
– [2] Gen. 49:13 ➔ COAST <2348>.

HAVILAH – ***ḥ^a^wiylāh*** [proper noun: חֲוִילָה <2341>; prob. from SHAKE <2342>]: circular ▶ **The name of two or three eastern regions.** Refs.: Gen. 2:11; 10:7, 29; 25:18; 1 Sam. 15:7; 1 Chr. 1:9, 23. ¶

HAVVOTH JAIR – ***ḥawwôṯ yā'iyr*** [proper noun: חַוֹּת יָאִיר <2334>; from the plur. of TOWN <2333> and a modification of JAIR <3265>]: villages of Jair ► **These villages were captured by Jair, son of Manasseh.** Refs.: Num. 32:41; Deut. 3:14; Judg. 10:4; 1 Chr. 2:23. ¶

HAWK – [1] ***nêṣ*** [masc. noun: נֵץ <5322>; from SPARKLE <5340> (in the sense of to flash, e.g., in relation to speed)] ► **This word refers to a bird of prey that classified as unclean in Israel, not edible.** Refs.: Lev. 11:16; Deut. 14:15. God's wisdom created the hawk and its ability to soar and fly (Job 39:26). The Hebrew word also means flower, blossom; see FLOWER <5322>. ¶ – [2] Is. 34:11 ➔ PELICAN <6893> [3] Is. 34:15 ➔ VULTURE <1772>.

HAZAEL – ***ḥ**ᵃ**zāh'ēl*** [masc. proper noun: חֲזָהאֵל <2371>; from SEE <2372> and GOD <410>]: God has seen ► **A king of Aram (Syria) (ca. 841–797? B.C.). He was a benefit to Israel in his early years.** Elijah anointed him, and he helped eradicate Baalism (worship of Baal) (1 Kgs. 19:15–18). He may have killed Ben-Hadad. He succeeded him as king at any rate. Elisha prophesied of the terror and devastation Hazael and Aram would bring on Israel (2 Kgs. 8:7–15). He fought against Israel (2 Kgs. 8:28, 29) successfully, but his victories were given because of the Lord's anger toward His corrupt people (2 Kgs. 10:32; 13:3). Joash of Judah bribed him to cease his attack on Jerusalem (2 Kgs. 12:17, 18). His son, Ben Hadad II, succeeded him (2 Kgs. 13:25). Amos announced God's judgment on Hazael and his house (Amos 1:4). *

HAZAIAH – ***ḥ**ᵃ**zāyāh*** [masc. proper noun: חֲזָיָה <2382>; from SEE <2372> and LORD <3050>]: the Lord has seen ► **An Israelite of the tribe of Judah.** Ref.: Neh. 11:5. ¶

HAZAR ADDAR – ***ḥ**ᵃ**ṣar 'addār*** [proper noun: חֲצַר אַדָּר <2692>; from VILLAGE <2691> and ADDAR <146>]: village of Addar ► **This word designates a city on the southern border of Canaan, possibly *'addar* (ADDAR <146>).** Ref.: Num. 34:4. ¶

HAZAR ENAN – [1] ***ḥ**ᵃ**ṣar 'êynôn*** [proper noun: חֲצַר עֵינוֹן <2703>; from VILLAGE <2691> and a deriv. of EYE <5869> (in the sense of spring, fountain)]: village of fountains ► **A city on the northeast border of Canaan.** Ref.: Ezek. 47:17. ¶
[2] ***ḥ**ᵃ**ṣar 'êynān*** [proper noun: חֲצַר עֵינָן <2704>; from VILLAGE <2691> and the same as ENAN <5881>]: village of fountains ► **The same as <2703> above.** Refs.: Num. 34:9, 10; Ezek. 48:1. ¶

HAZAR ENON – See HAZAR ENAN <2703>.

HAZAR GADDAH – ***ḥ**ᵃ**ṣar gaddāh*** [proper noun: חֲצַר גַּדָּה <2693>; from VILLAGE <2691> and a fem. of FORTUNE <1408>]: village of fortune ► **This word designates a city situated on the southern border of Judah.** Ref.: Josh. 15:27. ¶

HAZAR HATTICON – ***ḥ**ᵃ**ṣar hattiyḵôn*** [proper noun: חֲצַר הַתִּיכוֹן <2694>; from VILLAGE <2691> and MIDDLE <8484> with the art. interposed]: village of the middle ► **This word designates a city on the border of Hauran.** Ref.: Ezek. 47:16. ¶

HAZAR SHUAL – ***ḥ**ᵃ**ṣar šû'āl*** [proper noun: חֲצַר שׁוּעָל <2705>; from VILLAGE <2691> and FOX <7776>]: village of the jackal ► **A place assigned to the tribe of Simeon.** Refs.: Josh. 15:28; 19:3; 1 Chr. 4:28; Neh. 11:27. ¶

HAZAR SUSAH – ***ḥ**ᵃ**ṣar sûsāh*** [proper noun: חֲצַר סוּסָה <2701>; from VILLAGE <2691> and MARE <5484>]: village of the horse ► **A place belonging to the descendants of Simeon.** Ref.: Josh. 19:5; see also HAZAR SUSIM. ¶

HAZAR SUSIM – ***ḥ**ᵃ**ṣar sûsiym*** [proper noun: חֲצַר סוּסִים <2702>; from VILLAGE <2691> and the plur. of HORSE <5483> a.]: village of horses ► **A place belonging to the descendants of Simeon.** Ref.: 1 Chr. 4:31; the same as HAZAR SUSAH. ¶

HAZARMAVETH – ***ḥ**ᵃ**ṣarmāweṯ*** [masc. proper noun: חֲצַרְמָוֶת <2700>; from VILLAGE <2691> and DEATH <4194>]: court of death ▶ **One of the sons of Joktan.** Refs.: Gen. 10:26; 1 Chr. 1:20. ¶

HAZAZON-TAMAR – ***ḥaṣ**ᵉ**ṣôn tāmār*** [proper noun: חַצְצוֹן תָּמָר <2688>; from DIVIDE <2686> a. (in the sense of to cut off) and PALM TREE <8558>]: pruning of palm trees ▶ **A town inhabited by Amorites.** It was conquered in battle by Chedorlaomer, king of Elam and his allies (Gen. 14:7). It refers to the same town, evidently, in the reign of Jehoshaphat (2 Chr. 20:2), also named Engedi. ¶

HAZEL TREE – Gen. 30:37 ➔ ALMOND TREE <3869>.

HAZELELPONI – 1 Chr. 4:3 ➔ HAZZELELPONI <6753>.

HAZERIM – ***ḥ**ᵃ**ṣêriym*** [proper noun: חֲצֵרִים <2699>; masc. plur. of VILLAGE <2691>]: villages ▶ **The Avvim dwelt in Hazerim (or: in villages).** Ref.: Deut. 2:23. ¶

HAZEROTH – ***ḥ**ᵃ**ṣērôṯ*** [proper noun: חֲצֵרוֹת <2698>; fem. plur. of VILLAGE <2691>]: villages ▶ **A place in the desert where the Israelites remained.** Refs.: Num. 11:35; 12:16; 33:17, 18; Deut. 1:1. ¶

HAZEZON-TAMAR – Gen. 14:7; 2 Chr. 20:2 ➔ HAZAZON-TAMAR <2688>.

HAZIEL – ***ḥ**ᵃ**ziy'ēl*** [masc. proper noun: חֲזִיאֵל <2381>; from SEE <2372> and GOD <410>]: vision of God ▶ **A Levite, descendant of Guershon.** Ref.: 1 Chr. 23:9. ¶

HAZO – ***ḥ**ᵃ**zô*** [masc. proper noun: חֲזוֹ <2375>; from SEE <2372>]: seer, vision ▶ **A nephew of Abraham.** Ref.: Gen. 22:22. ¶

HAZOR – ***ḥāṣôr*** [proper noun: חָצוֹר <2674>; a coll. form of VILLAGE <2691>]: enclosure, courtyard ▶
a. A large royal town in northern Canaan. It was the capital city of several kingdoms in league in the area. Joshua captured it and gave it to the tribe of Naphtali (Josh. 11:1, 10; 12:19; 19:36). Barak and Deborah had to fight strong forces from this city (Jdg. 4:2, 17; 1 Sam. 12:9). Solomon strengthened it as a part of his kingdom (1 Sam. 9:15). It eventually fell into the hands of the Assyrians (2 Kgs. 15:29) and Babylon (Jer. 49:28). *
b. A town in southern Judah in the Negev. It was allotted to Judah (Josh. 15:23). ¶
c. Another southern city of Judah with the alternate name of Kerioth Hegron (city of Hegron). Ref.: Josh. 15:25. ¶
d. A town in which Benjamites settled after returning from exile. Ref.: Neh. 11:33. ¶

HAZOR-HADATTAH – ***ḥāṣôr ḥ**ᵃ**ḏattāh*** [proper noun: חָצוֹר חֲדַתָּה <2675>; from HAZOR <2674> and a Aramaic form of the fem. of NEW <2319> (comp. NEW <2323>)]: new village ▶ **A city in the south of Judah.** Ref.: Josh. 15:25. ¶

HAZZELELPONI – ***ṣ**ᵉ**lelpôniy, haṣṣ**ᵉ**lelpôniy*** [fem. proper noun: צְלֶלְפּוֹנִי, הַצְלֶלְפּוֹנִי <6753>; from SHADOW <6752> and the act. part. of TURN (verb) <6437>]: facing the shade ▶ **An Israelite woman from the tribe of Judah.** Ref.: 1 Chr. 4:3. ¶

HAZZOBEBAH – 1 Chr. 4:8 ➔ ZOBEBAH <6637> b.

HE GOAT – [1] See MALE GOAT <6841> and <6842> [2] See GOAT <8495>.

HE, SHE, IT – [1] ***hiy', hû'*** [masc., fem. pron.: הִיא, הוּא <1931>; a prim. word] ▶ **The major uses of these pronouns are as follows: as the third person independent pronoun meaning he, she, it, they (Gen. 3:15, 20; 13:1; 37:2; Judg. 11:1); as a demonstrative pronoun meaning i.e., there is (Gen. 2:11–13; Lev. 10:3; Deut. 30:20); as an emphatic word to emphasize a subject (Gen. 2:14).** Placed in front of a noun, it gives precision (Ex. 12:42); used with a pronoun, it indicates identity, *ᵃnî hû*, it is I (Is. 52:6). Used after a noun in agreement with the noun, it is a demonstrative adjective meaning that, e.g., that man (Job 1:1). It serves to tie two things together as the verb is, are (Lam. 1:18). It is combined with other words to form names, such as *ᵉlîyhû(')* (ELIHU <453>), He is my God. *

[2] ***hû', hiy'*** [Aramaic masc., fem. pron.: הוּא, הִיא <1932>; corresponding to <1931> above] ▶ **The major uses of these pronouns include an independent pronoun, he, she, it (Dan. 2:21, 22; 6:4; 7:7, 24); a demonstrative adjective meaning that (Dan. 2:32); a word indicating emphasis (Dan. 6:16); translated as himself, a semiverb meaning is, are (Dan. 2:28).** *

HEAD (noun) – [1] ***gulgōleṯ*** [fem. noun: גֻּלְגֹּלֶת <1538>; by reduplication from ROLL (verb) <1556>] ▶ **This word means the top part of the body; it is also translated skull, person, poll.** The author of Judges used it when he described Abimelech's skull being cracked when a woman dropped a millstone on it (Judg. 9:53). When Jezebel was killed, her skull was one of the few remnants of her body when people buried her (2 Kgs. 9:35). The Philistines hung up Saul's head in the temple of Dagon (1 Chr. 10:10). At other times, this word is used more generically to mean person, as when Moses instructed the Israelites to gather an omer of manna per person (Ex. 16:16); a beka of silver per person for the Tabernacle (Ex. 38:26); or to redeem the Levites (Num. 3:47). It is also used in passages concerning the taking of a census (Num. 1:2, 18, 20, 22; 1 Chr. 23:3, 24). This word means the same as the Aramaic word *Golgotha*—the name of the place where Jesus was crucified (Luke 23:33). ¶

[2] ***mᵉraᵃšôṯ*** [fem. noun: מְרַאֲשׁוֹת <4763>; formed like PRINCIPALITIES <4761>] ▶

a. This word refers to a place at or near a head. It refers to a location at or around a person's head (Gen. 28:11, 18; 1 Sam. 26:7, 11; 1 Kgs. 19:6; Jer. 13:18). Other refs.: 1 Sam. 19:16; 26:12. ¶

b. This word refers to a pillow, a bolster (for the head). It refers to a head support (Gen. 28:11) or something put in place to look like a person's head (1 Sam. 19:13; 26:7, 11, 12). An exact decipherment of the use of the word and hence its meaning is difficult. ¶

[3] ***rᵉ'ēš*** [Aramaic masc. noun: רֵאשׁ <7217>; corresponding to <7218> below] ▶ **The word is used to indicate the head of a man (Dan. 3:27); of an image constructed by Nebuchadnezzar (Dan. 2:32, 38); and a beast in Daniel's vision (Dan. 7:6, 20).** It is also used to denote a receptacle for dreams and visions (i.e., the head [Dan. 7:1]), and in the same verse it represents the sum total (i.e., essential matter). Ezra used this noun to indicate those people who served in the capacity of leaders (Ezra 5:10). *

[4] ***rō'š*** [masc. noun: רֹאשׁ <7218>; from an unused root apparently meaning to shake] ▶ **This word also means hair, a person, a point, the top, the beginning, the best, a chief, a leader. It is clear from the multitude of legitimate translations of this word that it has many metaphorical meanings.** In Scripture, the word is used to refer to a human head (Gen. 40:16); it also refers to animal heads as well, such as the serpent's head (Gen. 3:15); a dog; a donkey; a living being (2 Sam. 3:8; 2 Kgs. 6:25; Ezek. 1:22). It regularly indicates the heads of animals being sacrificed (Ex. 12:9; 29:15, 19).

This word is used in several Hebrew idioms: to bring something down on someone's head is to get vengeance (Ezek. 9:10); and to sprinkle dust on one's head is to mourn and show despair (Josh. 7:6; Ezek. 27:30).

The word can designate an individual person: It refers to Joseph's head as representative of his whole tribe (Gen. 49:26; Deut. 33:16). It refers to the top or peak of things and indicates the tops of mountains (Gen. 8:5); such as the top of Mount Olives in 2 Samuel 15:32 or even the top of a bed (Gen. 47:31).

This Hebrew word commonly designates the beginning of something: It refers to the head or beginning of the year (Ezek. 40:1); or month (Ex. 12:2). Its use extends to describing the best of something. The best spices or myrrh were depicted by this word (Ex. 30:23), as were the most influential persons: commanders (Deut. 20:9; Ezek. 10:11); the heads or leaders of families and chiefs (1 Kgs. 8:1; 1 Chr. 24:31); the chief priest of Israel (1 Chr. 27:5). It is used with a superlative connotation to describe the chief cornerstone (Ps. 118:22); or the most lofty stars (Job 22:12).

In some places, the word is best translated to indicate the entire or complete amount of something: the Lord made the chief part of the dust of the earth, i.e., all of it (Prov. 8:26). It also meant to take (or lift up) the total number of people, i.e., take a census (Ex. 30:12). The psalmist asserted that the sum total of God's words are righteous forever (Ps. 119:160).

It also indicates the source of a river or branch as its head (Gen. 2:10). When combined with the noun dog, it expresses a major insult. Abner used the term of himself, a dog's head, as a term of disgust (2 Sam. 3:8). *

5 ***raʾašōṯ*** [fem. noun: רַאֲשֹׁת <7226>; from <7218> above] ▶ **According to some, this word means a head place; for others it means a bolster.** Ref.: 1 Sam. 26:12. Some observe that it is not a known Hebrew form, and so assign this occurrence to the noun *meraʾašōṯ* (HEAD (noun) <4763> b.), a pillow or bolster. ¶

– 6 Ex. 9:31; Lev. 2:14 ➔ EAR <24> 7 Deut. 23:25 ➔ KERNEL <4425>.

HEAD (CROWN OF, TOP OF) – ***qoḏqōḏ*** [masc. noun: קָדְקֹד <6936>; from BOW DOWN <6915>] ▶ **This word refers to the pate, the top of the head.** The crown of the head represents the place where blessing would be most obvious and honoring (Gen. 49:26; Deut. 33:16). It means the entire person in the figurative expression, from the sole of one's foot to the top of one's head (Deut. 28:35; 2 Sam. 14:25; Job 2:7). It refers to a person's forehead in some contexts (Num. 24:17, NIV, NASB; corners, KJV). But in reference to a land, it may mean its corners, chief features, or cities. God destroys His adversaries by smiting (Ps. 68:21) them on the tops of their hairy heads (*qāḏqoḏ śêʿār*). It refers to the skin, scalp, or glorified hairdos of Judah's women (Is. 3:17). *

HEAD (verb) – Ex. 9:31: the barley had headed ➔ lit.: the barley was in the ear ➔ EAR <24>.

HEADBAND – 1 ***šaḇiys*** [masc. noun: שָׁבִיס <7636>; from an unused root meaning to interweave] ▶ **This word refers to a piece of luxurious clothing worn for beauty.** Ref.: Is. 3:18. ¶

– 2 1 Kgs. 20:38, 41 ➔ BANDAGE <666>.

HEADBANDS – Is. 3:20 ➔ ATTIRE <7196>.

HEADDRESS – Is. 3:20; 61:3, 10 ➔ TURBAN <6287>.

HEADLONG FLIGHT – 2 Kgs. 7:15 ➔ HURRY (verb) <2648>.

HEADS HELD HIGH (WITH) – Lev. 26:13 ➔ UPRIGHT <6968>.

HEADSTONE – Zech. 4:7 ➔ TOP <7222>.

HEAL – 1 ***rāpaʾ*** [verb: רָפָא <7495>; a prim. root] ▶ **This word describes the process of healing (i.e., mending health, curing), being restored to health, made healthy, usable, fertile. It also means to make fresh.** It is used in relation to Abimelech's household being restored to fertility (Gen. 20:17); of physical and spiritual healing (Is. 53:5); of wounds being restored (Lev. 13:18; Jer. 15:18); of water being restored to a healthy state, drinkable, wholesome (2 Kgs. 2:21, 22); of the repair, restoration of an altar (1 Kgs. 18:30); of many diseases being healed (Deut. 28:27, 35). In its participial forms, it refers to a person who acts as a physician, a healer: God, the Lord, as Israel's healer (Gen. 20:17; Ex. 15:26; Job 13:4). It describes the restoring of a person's soul, life (Ps. 41:4). In an emphatic construction, it indicates having a person healed, cared for (Ex. 21:19). It is used in its reflexive infinitive to note a purpose, in order to be (get) healed, from (*min*) wounds

inflicted in battle (2 Kgs. 8:29; 9:15). God alone was able to heal the wounds of His broken people (Hos. 5:13; 6:1; 7:1). A true leader in Israel was to heal, care for the people of Israel (Zech. 11:16). *
– [2] Hos. 5:13 ➔ CURE <1455>.

HEALING – [1] ***ᵃrûḵāh, ᵃruḵāh*** [fem. noun: אֲרוּכָה, אֲרֻכָה <724>; fem. pass. part. of PROLONG <748> (in the sense of restoring to soundness)] ▶ **This word means curing of a wound, restoration, repair; it is also translated health, recovery. The intuitive meaning is healing caused by the fleshly covering of a physical wound.** It signifies the restoration of Israel, both the need for it (Jer. 8:22) and the reality of it (Is. 58:8); and also the rebuilding of Jerusalem's walls that had been torn down (Jer. 33:6). Other refs.: 2 Chr. 24:13; Neh. 4:7; Jer. 30:17. ¶
[2] ***kêhāh*** [fem. noun: כֵּהָה <3545>; fem. of DARK <3544>] ▶ **This word has the sense of let up or partial cessation; it is also translated relief, easing.** There was no let up for the city of Nineveh from God's relentless judgment upon it (Nah. 3:19). ¶
[3] ***rip'ûṯ*** [fem. noun: רִפְאוּת <7500>; from HEAL <7495>] ▶ **This word refers to a process of restoration and refreshment to a person that brings healing; it is also translated health.** In context the fear of the Lord is the healing balm (Prov. 3:8). ¶
[4] ***tᵉ'ālāh*** [fem. noun: תְּעָלָה <8585>; from OFFER <5927> (in the sense of to raise, to recover, to restore)] ▶ **This word refers to an act, a medicine, or a process of healing (literally, as in new flesh and skin forming over a wound). It also means a remedy.** In its context, it refers to Judah's spiritual wounds and illnesses (Jer. 30:13). Gilead was famous for its restorative and healing medicines (Jer. 46:11). For another meaning of the Hebrew word, see TRENCH <8585>. ¶
[5] ***tᵉrûpāh*** [fem. noun: תְּרוּפָה <8644>; from TREMBLE <7322> in the sense of its congener HEAL <7495>] ▶ **This word means remedy; it is also translated medicine.** It refers in context to leaves on trees growing along the sides of Ezekiel's river of life (Ezek. 47:12). The ideas of healing, restoration, and renewal are figurative expressions for the total, wholistic healing and health of the people in God's new Temple world. ¶
– [6] Prov. 6:15; 29:1; Jer. 8:15; 14:19 ➔ REMEDY <4832> [7] Ezek. 30:21 ➔ MEDICINE <7499>.

HEALTH – [1] Prov. 3:8 ➔ HEALING <7500> [2] Prov. 4:22; 12:18; 13:17; 15:4; 16:24; Jer. 8:15 ➔ REMEDY <4832> [3] Ps. 38:3 ➔ SOUNDNESS <4974> [4] Jer. 8:22; 33:6; Is. 58:8 ➔ HEALING <724>.

HEALTH (RESTORE) – Is. 38:16 ➔ DREAM (verb) <2492> b.

HEALTHY – See FAT (adj.) <1277>.

HEAP (noun) – [1] ***gal*** [masc. noun: גַּל <1530>; from ROLL (verb) <1556>] ▶ **This word means heap (i.e., pile), large amount; it is also translated heap of stones, rock pile, stone heap, pile of rocks.** It indicates rocks piled over a person's grave to mark it (Josh. 7:26; 8:29) or a pile of rocks to which the roots of the wicked cling in vain (Job 8:17). A pile of rocks could indicate the ratification of a covenant or agreement (Gen. 31:46, 48, 51, 52). But in another context, it indicates a heap of uninhabitable ruins (2 Kgs. 19:25; Is. 25:2; Hos. 12:11). The word also refers to waves; see WAVE <1530>. *
[2] ***ḥômer*** [masc. noun: חֹמֶר <2563>; from RED (BE) <2560>] ▶ **This word means a pile; it is also translated surge, surging, churning.** Figuratively, it refers to a pile or heap of water (Hab. 3:15), a pile of dead frogs (Ex. 8:14), or even a heap of dead bodies (Judg. 15:16). The Hebrew word also means MIRE, CLAY (see MIRE <2563>) and indicates a dry measure (HOMER <2563>). ¶
[3] ***nêḏ*** [masc. noun: נֵד <5067>; from FLEE <5110> in the sense of piling up] ▶ **This word refers to something piled up on itself.** It refers to waters: the Red Sea (Ex. 15:8; Ps. 78:13; NIV: wall); the Jordan River (Josh. 3:13, 16); the sea (Ps. 33:7; NIV: jars). It refers to the remains of a failed harvest lying on the ground (Is. 17:11). ¶

4 ***ʿrēmāh*** [fem. noun: עֲרֵמָה <6194>; from PILED UP <6192>] ▶ **This word refers to a pile or heap of grain, wheat, fruit, rubble.** Refs.: Ruth 3:7; 2 Chr. 31:6–9; Neh. 4:2; Hag. 2:16. It describes the healthy, amorous appearance of the bride's belly (Song 7:2: NIV: mound). It is used figuratively again of overthrowing Babylon into heaps (Jer. 50:26). Other refs.: Neh. 13:15; Hag. 2:16. ¶

5 ***ṣibbur, ṣibbûr*** [masc. noun: צִבֻּר, צִבּוּר <6652>; from STORE UP <6651>] ▶ **This word refers to something gathered together and left in a certain spot, a number of things randomly stashed on top of each other; it is also translated pile.** Ref.: 2 Kgs. 10:8. ¶

6 ***šepek*** [masc. noun: שֶׁפֶךְ <8211>; from POUR OUT <8210>] ▶ **This word means a place of pouring, a place of emptying.** It is used in Leviticus to describe the place where the priest was to burn the remains of the bull sacrifice, i.e., next to the place where the ashes were poured out (Lev. 4:12). ¶

7 ***tēl*** [masc. noun: תֵּל <8510>; by contr. from LOFTY <8524>] ▶ **This word means a mound, ruins.** It refers to what signs may remain of a devastated and destroyed city, a ruin (Deut. 13:16; Josh. 8:28; 11:13; Jer. 49:2). The word also means mounds, small or large man-made hills on which cities were repeatedly destroyed and rebuilt. New cities could be erected on top of their ruins (Jer. 30:18). ¶

– 8 Ps. 79:1; Jer. 26:18; Mic. 1:6; 3:12 ➔ heap, heap of ruins, heap of rubble ➔ RUINS <5856> 9 Is. 17:1 ➔ RUIN (noun) <4596>.

HEAP (REFUSE) – Is. 25:10 ➔ DUNGHILL <4087>.

HEAP (REFUSE, ASH, RUBBISH) – Ezra 6:11; Dan. 2:5; 3:29 ➔ DUNGHILL <5122>.

HEAP OF RUINS – ***b^{e}ʿiy*** [masc. noun: בְּעִי <1164>; from BOIL (verb) <1158> (in the sense of being ransacked, plundered)] ▶ **This word means ruin (heap), against a ruin, or a mound of dirt over a grave; entreaty; figuratively, a grave.** In its only use in Job 30:24, it is probably best interpreted as an occurrence of the preposition *b^e* ("for" or "against") and *'iy* (RUINS <5856>), and should be translated as "against a ruin." However, some have interpreted this word as a derivative of *bāʿāh* [BOIL (verb) <1158>] and translated it as "entreaty" or "prayer," or in a derived meaning, "grave." Either translation would fit the context, for both communicate that the outstretched hand of God is present in the midst of destruction. This destroying hand has either brought a person (in this case, Job) to utter ruin or is the very thing against which there is no entreaty or prayer. Job is speaking from the shattered depths of utter personal ruin, where he perceives the hand of God as against him. ¶

HEAP OF STONES – Josh. 7:26; 8:29 ➔ HEAP (noun) <1530>.

HEAP (verb) – Prov. 25:22 ➔ TAKE <2846>.

HEAPS – 1 ***ḥ^{a}môrātayim*** [fem. dual noun: חֲמֹרָתַיִם <2565>; from RED (BE) <2560>; comp. HEAP (noun) <2563>] ▶ **This word means loads, piles. It is found in the dual form (in referring to heaps of dead Philistines) where it is preceded by *ḥ^{a}môr* (heap).** Ref.: Judges 15:16. ¶

– 2 Nah. 3:3 ➔ HEAVINESS <3514>.

HEAR – 1 ***šāmaʿ*** [verb: שָׁמַע <8085>; a prim. root] ▶ **This word means to perceive sounds. It also means to obey, to listen, to be heard of, to be regarded, to cause to hear, to proclaim, to sound aloud. The verb basically means to hear and in context expresses various connotations of this.** The most famous use of this word is to introduce the Shema, "Hear, O, Israel," followed by the content of what the Israelites are to understand about the Lord their God and how they are to respond to Him (Deut. 6:4). In a parallel usage, the heavens are commanded to "Hear, Oh heavens!" to the prophet's message about Israel (Is. 1:2). The word calls attention to hear various things: It means to hear another person speaking (Gen. 27:6); the Lord's voice (Gen. 3:10); or anything that can be perceived by the ear. Used with or without the preposition *'el* (TO <413>) following, the word means to listen to someone. The house of Israel was not willing to listen to Ezekiel (Ezek. 3:7); the Lord was not willing to listen to the beautiful worship services of God's people, for they were not following justice (Gen. 27:5; Amos 5:23).

The word takes on the connotation of obedience in certain contexts and with certain Hebrew constructions: It can mean to heed a request or command, such as Abraham's request concerning Ishmael (Gen. 17:20). The Lord listened to Hagar's prayer and gave her a son (Gen. 16:11; 30:6). It means to obey in certain contexts (Gen. 3:17; 22:18; Ex. 24:7; 2 Kgs. 14:11).

The word is used to connote the idea of understanding. God confused the speech of the people at the Tower of Babel so they could not understand each other (Gen. 11:7; Is. 33:19). Solomon wanted a heart of discernment and understanding (hearing) to govern his people (Deut. 1:16; 1 Kgs. 3:9); to be able to decide between good and evil (2 Sam. 14:17).

In the passive stem, the word means to be heard. Pharaoh heard the news that Joseph's brothers had arrived in Egypt (Gen. 45:16). No sound of a tool was heard as the Temple was being built (Deut. 4:32; 1 Kgs. 6:7). It also meant to be obedient to King David (2 Sam. 22:45); or to make hear, to call, or to summon as when Saul summoned his soldiers (1 Sam. 15:4; 23:8).

The word is used often in the causative stem to mean to cause to listen, to proclaim, to announce. When Israel assembled at Mount Horeb (Sinai), the Lord caused them to hear His words (Deut. 4:10; Josh. 6:10). It also means to proclaim, to summon; Isaiah spoke of those who proclaim peace (1 Kgs. 15:22; Is. 52:7); and the psalmist proclaimed the praise of the Lord (Ps. 26:7). *

2 ***šᵉma'*** [Aramaic verb: שְׁמַע <8086>; corresponding to <8085> above] ▶ **This verb, meaning to discern with the ear, to have the faculty of hearing, to show oneself obedient, is used only in the book of Daniel.** It is used when speaking of words that have been heard from another person (Dan. 5:14, 16); or when hearing sounds, such as the sounds of music from many instruments (Dan. 3:5, 7, 10). In a broader perspective, it can also mean to have a sense of hearing as opposed to being deaf (Dan. 5:23). This verb can also be used in the reflexive form and means that one shows one's obedience to what has been heard (Dan. 7:27). Other refs.: Dan. 3:15; 6:14. ¶

– 3 Deut. 32:1; Ps. 77:1; 80:1 ➔ EAR (GIVE) <238>.

HEAR (CAUSE TO) – Ezek. 24:26 ➔ REPORT <2045>.

HEARING – 1 ***mišmā'*** [masc. noun: מִשְׁמָע <4926>; from HEAR <8085>] ▶ **This word indicates that which is heard or reported, a rumor.** It indicates, in context, something heard but not properly confirmed or established at the time (Is. 11:3). ¶

2 ***šêma'*** [masc. noun: שֵׁמַע <8088>; from HEAR <8085>] ▶ **This word refers to something perceived by the ear and can mean hearing as opposed to, or in addition to, seeing.** Refs.: Job 42:5; Ps. 18:44. It can also be used to represent a rumor, a report, or an announcement, as these are things that have been announced and heard by others. These reports may be good news to be greeted joyously, such as a report of fame and good deeds (Gen. 29:13; 1 Kgs. 10:1); bad news to be concerned about (Is. 23:5); or even lies and malicious rumors causing others to suffer (Ex. 23:1). *

HEARS (WHAT HE) – Is. 11:3 ➔ HEARING <4926>.

HEART – 1 ***ḥōḇ*** [masc. noun: חֹב <2243>; by contr. from LOVE (verb) <2245>] ▶ **This word refers to Job's inner self, a place where he can hide his transgressions or guilt in his inner being or heart (i.e., properly, "a cherisher").** Ref.: Job 31:33; also translated bosom. ¶

[2] ***lêḇ*** [masc. noun: לֵב <3820>; a form of <3824> below] ▶ **This Hebrew word is usually rendered as heart but its range of meaning is extensive, e.g., inner man, mind, will, understanding.** It can denote the heart as a human physical organ (Ex. 28:29; 1 Sam. 25:37; 2 Kgs. 9:24); or an animal (Job 41:24). However, it usually refers to some aspect of the immaterial inner self or being since the heart is considered to be the seat of one's inner nature as well as one of its components. It can be used in a general sense (1 Kgs. 8:23; Ps. 84:2; Jer. 3:10); or it can be used of a specific aspect of personality: the mind (Gen. 6:5; Deut. 29:4; Neh. 6:8); the will (Ex. 35:5; 2 Chr. 12:14; Job. 11:13); the emotions (Gen. 6:6 [Note that God is the subject]; 1 Sam. 24:5; 25:31). In addition, the word can also allude to the inside or middle (Ex. 15:8; Deut. 4:11). *

[3] ***lêḇ*** [Aramaic masc. noun: לֵב <3821>; corresponding to <3820> above] ▶ **In this form, the only occurrence of this word in the Hebrew Bible is in Daniel 7:28.** See <3820> above. ¶

[4] ***lêḇāḇ*** [masc. noun: לֵבָב <3824>; from HEART (RAVISH THE) <3823>] ▶ **The primary usage of this word describes the entire disposition of the inner person.** God can discern it (1 Sam. 16:7); it can be devoted to the Lord (1 Kgs. 15:3); seek the Lord (2 Chr. 11:16); turn against people (Ex. 14:5); be uncircumcised (Lev. 26:41); be hardened (1 Sam. 6:6); be totally committed to the Lord (Deut. 6:5; 2 Chr. 15:15). It is also used to describe the place where the rational, thinking process occurs that allows a person to know God's blessings (Josh. 23:14); to plan for the future (1 Kgs. 8:18); to communicate (2 Chr. 9:1); and to understand God's message (Is. 6:10). Like our English usage, it often refers to the seat of emotions, whether it refers to joy (Deut. 28:47); discouragement (Josh. 2:11); comfort (Judg. 19:8); grief (1 Sam. 1:8); sorrow (Ps. 13:2); or gladness (Is. 30:29). *

[5] ***lêḇaḇ*** [Aramaic masc. noun: לְבַב <3825>; corresponding to <3824> above] ▶ **This word is used to describe the entire disposition of the inner person, which God can change.** Refs.: Dan. 4:16; 5:21; 7:4. This inner person can be lifted up in pride (Dan. 5:20) or made low in humility (Dan. 5:22). The rational, thinking process is demonstrated when Daniel described the thoughts of the king's mind (Dan. 2:30). ¶

[6] ***libbāh*** [fem. noun: לִבָּה <3826>; from <3820> above] ▶ **A variant of the word *lêḇ*, it suggests the seat of emotions or the will.** Ref.: Ezek. 16:30. Other refs.: Ps. 7:9; 125:4; Prov. 15:11; 17:3; 21:2; 24:12; Is. 44:18. ¶

– [7] 2 Sam. 22:46; Ps. 18:45 ➔ lose hearth ➔ WITHER <5034> [8] Job 38:36 ➔ MIND <7907> [9] Is. 16:11 ➔ BOWELS <4578> [10] Dan. 6:14 ➔ MIND <1079>.

HEART (LOSE) – [1] Is. 19:3 ➔ EMPTY (MAKE) <1238> [2] Dan. 11:30 ➔ GRIEVED (BE) <3512>.

HEART (RAVISH THE) – ***lāḇaḇ*** [verb: לָבַב <3823>; a prim. root] ▶ **This word is related to the common Hebrew nouns *lêḇ* (<3820>) and *lêḇāḇ* (<3824), which both mean heart, mind, or inner being. It means, among its many nuances, to transport (with love).** Solomon used this word twice in the same verse to express the stirring of his heart with affection for his lover (Song 4:9; also translated to captivate the heart, to steal the heart, to make the heart beat faster); Zophar used it to describe the mind of an idiot being made intelligent (Job 11:12: to be wise, to become wise, to get understanding, to become intelligent). In the only other instances of this word, it describes the making of bread or a cake that was kneaded and baked (2 Sam. 13:6, 8). ¶

HEART SET ON (HAVE ONE'S) – Gen. 34:8 ➔ DESIRE (verb) <2836>.

HEARTH – [1] ***môqêḏ*** [masc. noun: מוֹקֵד <4168>; from BURN <3344>] ▶ **This word refers to a burning, burning embers, a furnace.** It describes something scorched or burned, like charred bones (Ps. 102:3; also translated furnace, glowing embers). It is used to depict God's judgment as a burning fire or embers (Is. 33:14: burning, burnings). ¶

2 ***môqᵉḏāh*** [fem. noun: מוֹקְדָה <4169>; fem. of <4168> above] ▶ **This word indicates the top of an altar.** It is the same word as <4168> with the *āh* (Lev. 6:9; KJV: burning). It names the location where the burnt offering was to remain all night. ¶
– 3 Jer. 36:22, 23 ➔ BRAZIER <254>.

HEARTHS – ***mᵉḇaššᵉlôṯ*** [fem. plur. noun: מְבַשְּׁלוֹת <4018>; from COOK <1310>] ▶ **This word refers to cooking or boiling places.** It was constructed where the priests prepared sacrificial offerings in Ezekiel's vision of a new Temple (Ezek. 46:23). ¶

HEARTLESS – Lam. 4:3 ➔ CRUEL <393>.

HEAT (noun) – 1 ***ḥōreḇ*** [masc. noun: חֹרֶב <2721>; a collateral form of SWORD <2719>] ▶ **This word indicates hotness, drought, dryness. It basically refers to heat (i.e., high temperature) or dryness of some kind. In another nuance, it refers to desolation, a desolating, waste, a laying waste, ruin.** It refers to the heat of the day (Gen. 31:40; Is. 4:6; Jer. 36:30). In Gideon's test with the fleece of wool, it refers to the dryness of the ground or the fleece (Judg. 6:37, 39, 40). The dryness or feverishness of Job's skin is described with this word (Job 30:30). It indicates the destruction and devastation of cities that will be renewed (Is. 61:4: ruins, wastes); and a drought or dry spell that destroys the land (Hag. 1:11). Other refs.: Is. 25:4, 5; Jer. 49:13; 50:38; Ezek. 29:10; Zeph. 2:14. ¶
2 ***taᵃnāh*** [fem. noun: תַּאֲנָה <8385>; from BEFALL <579> (in the sense of to meet, to seek an occasion)] ▶ **This word refers to an occasion or a time of copulation. It refers to the time when a mare is ready to receive a male for procreation.** It is used mockingly of Israel as a wild female donkey (Jer. 2:24; also translated mating, occasion). For another meaning of the Hebrew word, see OCCASION <8385>. ¶
– 3 Deut. 29:24 ➔ FIERCE <2750> 4 Ps. 19:6 ➔ SUN <2535> 5 Ps. 32:4 ➔ heat, fever heat ➔ DROUGHT <2725> 6 Is. 21:15 ➔ HEAVINESS <3514> 7 Is. 49:10: heat, scorching heat, desert heat ➔ BURNING SAND <8273> 8 Jer. 2:24 ➔ DESIRE (noun) <185> 9 See WARMTH <2527>.

HEAT (BE IN) – Gen. 30:38, 39, 41; 31:10 ➔ CONCEIVE <3179>.

HEAT (FIERY, SCORCHING) – ***ḥarḥur*** [masc. proper noun: חַרְחֻר <2746>; from BURN (verb) <2787>] ▶ **This word indicates extreme hotness, feverish hotness.** It refers most likely to the feverish heat of a disease rather than to the sun's heat (Deut. 28:22; also translated extreme burning, severe burning). It was among possible curses the Lord could bring on a disobedient nation. ¶

HEAT (GET, HAVE) – 1 Kgs. 1:1; Eccl. 4:11 ➔ CONCEIVE <3179>.

HEAT (verb) – ***ᵃzā', ᵃzāh*** [Aramaic verb.: אֲזָא, אֲזָה <228>] ▶ **This word means to raise the temperature, of a furnace in context, to a very high degree; it is also translated to make hot, to overheat.** It is used by Nebuchadnezzar in its infinitive form to order the furnace to be heated seven times hotter than normal (Dan. 3:19, 22). ¶

HEATH – 1 Jer. 17:6 ➔ SHRUB <6199> 2 Jer. 17:6; 48:6 ➔ SHRUB <6176>.

HEAVEN – 1 ***šāmayim*** [masc. noun: שָׁמַיִם <8064>; from an unused root meaning to be lofty] ▶ **This word means sky, abode, firmament, air, stars. Although the word is plural or dual in form, it can be translated into English as singular or plural depending on the context. The word describes everything God made besides the earth. It also refers to the abode of God Himself.** God made the heavens of the universe (Gen. 1:1; 14:19); the firmament or expanse which He created around the earth was named sky or heaven as well (Gen. 1:8). He stretched out the heavens (Is. 40:22); creating them (Is. 42:5; 45:18).

The heavens that humans observe with their senses are indicated by this word. The stars are part of the heavens (Gen. 15:5) and are personified in some cases (Judg. 5:20); the sun and the moon, along with the stars, make up a major part of the hosts of heaven (Deut. 4:19). Unfortunately, these things were worshiped as gods by even the Israelites (Jer. 8:2). The heavens became a source of knowing the future and life in general, for scanners of the heavens and astrologers searched the heavens for signs (Is. 47:13). A favorite pagan deity was the Queen of Heaven whom the people worshiped (Jer. 7:18; 44:17). God created waters above and below the heavens (Gen. 1:8, 9). The clouds are a feature of the sky (Gen. 8:2; Judg. 5:4; 1 Kgs. 18:45; Job 26:13). The word indicates the total inhabited earth when it speaks of from under heaven, as when the Amalekites were to be destroyed from under heaven (Gen. 6:17; Ex. 17:14). The teacher of Ecclesiastes spoke of examining everything under heaven, i.e., everything done in the world in which humans live (Eccl. 1:13; 2:3; 3:1); birds and other fowl fly in the sky (Gen. 1:20). In God's new world, there will be a new heaven and a new earth (Is. 65:17; 66:22).

The invisible heavens are the abode of God. Heaven is the Lord's throne, the earth is the resting place of His feet—beautiful metaphor of God's sovereignty over the universe (Is. 66:1). He extends the heavens as the tent roof of the universe (Is. 40:22); He dwells in heaven (1 Kgs. 8:30, 32); yet He is not contained in even the heaven of heavens, the most exclusive part of the heavens (1 Kgs. 8:27). *

2 ***šemayin*** [Aramaic noun: שְׁמַיִן <8065>; corresponding to <8064> above] ▶ **This word has several different connotations, but the basic meaning is that of the sky (Dan. 4:11; 7:2).** Reaching beyond the simple meaning of sky, this word also referred to heaven, the dwelling place of God that is much higher than any other place (Dan. 2:28; 4:34). The heavens are great not because of what they are but because of who lives there. Not only does God dwell in heaven, but His messengers, the angels, also dwell there and are sent down to earth to do His work (Dan. 4:13). This word also signifies the whole universe where God showed His mighty signs and made His works known to all (Dan. 6:27). It is combined to form phrases such as the God of heaven (Ezra 5:11, 12; Dan. 2:18, 19, 28, 37, 44); birds of the sky (Dan. 2:38); winds of heaven (Dan. 7:2, 13). This noun corresponds to the Hebrew noun *šāmayim* (<8064>), that is very similar in meaning.

Heaven describes the place from which God operates: He calls to people from heaven (Gen. 21:17; 22:11). He sent down manna from heaven for His people in the desert (Ex. 16:4). The Ten Commandments were spoken from heaven (Ex. 20:22; Neh. 9:13). He is not merely a dweller in heaven, but He is the God of heaven (Gen. 24:3; 2 Chr. 36:23; Ezra 1:2). The heavens grow old and pass away, but God is eternal (Job 14:12; Is. 13:10; 65:17). Satan aspired to usurp God's reign in heaven and was cast out (Is. 14:12, 13). Elijah the prophet, because he faithfully followed the Lord, was taken up into heaven in a whirlwind (2 Kgs. 2:1, 11). *

– 3 Ps. 77:18 ➔ WHEEL <1534>.

HEAVENS – 1 Is. 5:30 ➔ CLOUD <6183> 2 Is. 47:13 ➔ those who divide the heavens ➔ ASTROLOGER <1895>.

HEAVILY – Ex. 14:25 ➔ DIFFICULTY <3514>.

HEAVINESS – 1 ***kōḇeḏ*** [masc. noun: כֹּבֶד <3514>; from HEAVY (BE) <3513>] ▶ **This word indicates weight, thickness. It basically means what is weighty, heavy, a burden.** It is used figuratively of the press or load weighing on a person in battle (Is. 21:15: press, grievousness, distress, heat). It has the sense of density or thickness, e.g., clouds (Is. 30:27: heavy, dense, tick); or a dense mass of corpses from battle (Nah. 3:3: mass, heaps, piles, great number). It refers to the actual weight of something, e.g., a stone (Prov. 27:3: heavy). ¶

– 2 Ezra 9:5 ➔ FASTING <8589> 3 Ps. 119:28; Prov. 10:1; 14:13 ➔ SORROW (noun) <8424> 4 Prov. 12: ➔ ANXIETY <1674> 5 Is. 29:2 ➔ MOURNING <8386> 6 Is. 61:3 ➔ DARK <3544>.

HEAVINESS (BE FULL OF) – Ps. 69:20 ➔ SICK (BE) <5136>.

HEAVY – 1 ***kāḇēḏ*** [adj.: כָּבֵד <3515>; from HEAVY (BE) <3513>] ▶ **This word describes something as heavy, e.g., weighty, great, grievous. It attributes the basic feature of heavy, weighty to things, but its sense is nuanced carefully by its context and usage.** Figuratively, a "yoke" of taxation can be heavy, burdensome (1 Kgs. 12:4); and heavy hands can be an expression of being tired, weary (Ex. 17:12). Various things are heavy in the sense of being oppressive or burdensome, such as famine (Gen. 12:10); hail (Ex. 9:18); an impressive or large group of officials (1 Kgs. 10:2). The word regularly means impressive, rich, noble (Gen. 13:2); large (Gen. 50:9–11). It takes on negative senses as well, for the heart can be hard, heavy (Ex. 7:14). Something can be clumsy, slow, dull. Ezekiel's tongue was *kāḇēḏ*, slow (Ezek. 3:5–6). The phrase *kāḇēḏ 'awôwn* has the meaning of heavy or loaded with guilt (Is. 1:4). Used after a noun, it may mean literally heavy, a heavy rock or perhaps a huge rock (Is. 32:2). *
– 2 1 Kgs. 20:43; 21:4 ➔ SULLEN <5620> 3 Ezra 5:8; 6:4 ➔ HUGE <1560> 4 Prov. 27:3; Is. 30:27 ➔ HEAVINESS <3514>.

HEAVY (BE) – 1 ***kāḇēḏ*** [verb: כָּבֵד <3513>; a prim. root] ▶ **This word means to weigh heavily, to be honored, to be made heavy, to get honor, to make dull, to let weigh down, to harden, to multiply. In the simple form, the verb means to be heavy, to weigh heavily, to be honored. The hands of both humans and God were described metaphorically as heavy, i.e., powerful.** The heavy hand of Joseph dispossessed the Amorites of their land, and the Lord's hand was heavy against the city of Ashdod (i.e., He brought devastation upon it [1 Sam. 5:6]). The Hebrew word refers to mere physical weight as well; the description of Absalom' hair is a celebrated example of this use (2 Sam. 14:26). The labor of the Israelites in Egypt became burdensome (Ex. 5:9). The word's metaphorical use extended to the description of failing senses, such as Jacob's eyes (Israel's) in old age (Gen. 48:10; Is. 59:1). This is one of three words describing the dulling or hardening of Pharaoh's heart in the plagues. Pharaoh's heart became dull, obstinate, heavy (Ex. 9:7) to the Lord's warnings. Yet the word also describes honor being bestowed on someone (Job 14:21; Is. 66:5).

In the passive form, the word expresses the idea of enjoying honor or glory. It describes the smug self-glorification of Amaziah (2 Sam. 6:22; 2 Kgs. 14:10); God's honoring Himself through the defeat of Pharaoh is also expressed by this stem (Ex. 14:4, 17, 18; Is. 26:15). In the factitive or intensive stem, the verb expresses the idea of causing or making something unfeeling (1 Sam. 6:6) but also the act of honoring people or God (Judg. 9:9; Ps. 22:23). God's people also honor some things: the Sabbath (Is. 58:13); Jerusalem; God's sanctuary (Is. 60:13); wisdom (Prov. 4:8). The causative form carries the ideas of making something heavy (1 Kgs. 12:10; Is. 47:6); or dull and heavy, especially Pharaoh's heart (Ex. 8:15, 32; Ex. 9:34). In two places, the word means to make into many or multiply (Jer. 30:19); as when God's people multiplied (cf. 2 Chr. 25:19). It is used once in the reflexive form meaning to act deceptively (i.e., to pretend something [Prov. 12:9]). *
2 ***rāzan*** [verb: רָזַן <7336>; a prim. root] ▶ **This word means to be weighty, to be honored, to be mighty. The term also occurs six times as a noun, meaning rulers, princes.** Five times the word is used in conjunction with the Hebrew word for king (*meleḵ* <4428>; Judg. 5:3; Ps. 2:2; Prov. 8:15; 31:4; Hab. 1:10); and once with judge (a participle of the verb *šāp̱aṭ* <8199>; Is. 40:23). Rulers were summoned to listen to Deborah's victory song (Judg. 5:3); warned to not conspire against the Lord and His anointed one (Ps. 2:2); enabled by wisdom to decree just laws (Prov. 8:15);

abstained from strong drink (Prov. 31:4); and were made as nothing by the Lord (Is. 40:23). The noun *rāzôn* (PRINCE <7333>) is derived from this verb; also see the verb *kāḇēḏ* (<3513> above). ¶

HEAVY, VERY HEAVY – ***ma‘ᵃmāsāh*** [fem. noun: מַעֲמָסָה <4614>; from LOAD (verb) <6006>] (in the sense of to carry a load) ▶ **This word indicates that something is weighty, almost immovable, dangerous to handle like a weight that is too great to lift; it is also translated immovable, burdensome.** It is used figuratively of Jerusalem becoming a heavy stone (Zech. 12:3). ¶

HEBER – ***ḥeḇer*** [masc. proper noun: חֶבֶר <2268>; the same as COMPANY <2267>]: companion, communion ▶
a. Son of Beriah, grandson of Asher. Refs.: Gen. 46:17; Num. 26:45; 1 Chr. 7:31, 32. ¶
b. Husband of Jael, the woman who killed Sisera. Refs.: Judg. 4:11, 17, 21; 5:24. ¶
c. Son of another Beriah, a descendant of Ezra. Ref.: 1 Chr. 4:18. ¶
d. Son of a third Beriah of the tribe of Benjamin. Ref.: 1 Chr. 8:17. ¶

HEBERITE – ***ḥeḇriy*** [masc. proper noun: חֶבְרִי <2277>; patron. from HEBER <2268>]: see HEBER ▶ **A descendant of Heber, grandson of Asher.** Ref.: Num. 26:45. ¶

HEBREW – ***‘iḇriy*** [proper noun: עִבְרִי <5680>; patron. from EBER <5677>] ▶ **The gentilic or ethnic form of the word means a Hebrew person, possibly a person from beyond the Euphrates River.** Abraham is called a Hebrew in Genesis 14:13, where the word was first used. This is usually traced back to Eber who was a Shemite. Abraham's lineage is traced back to Shem through Eber, Shem being the ancestor of all the sons of Eber (Gen. 10:21; 11:10). Eber features the root letters of "Hebrew" (*‘br*), without the gentilic or ethnic ending *iy* (י). The term Habiru found in documents throughout the Middle East is equal to the Old Testament *Hebrew* to some extent. It also had a strong social flavor to it as well and probably was used to describe a certain social or professional class of people. The word *Hebrew* seems to have had a negative sense to it at first. It was used of Joseph, "the Hebrew or the Hebrew slave" (Gen. 39:14, 17), by Potipher's wife. In Egypt the descendants of Abraham were referred to as Hebrews and God as the God of the Hebrews (Ex. 3:18; 5:3), i.e., slaves (cf. Ex. 21:2; Deut. 15:12; Jer. 34:9, 14). The Philistines referred to the Israelites at times as Hebrews (1 Sam. 4:6, 9). Jonah asserted that he was a Hebrew (Jon. 1:9). So in the Old Testament, the term is primarily an ethnic or gentilic term. *

HEBREW (IN) – ***yᵉhûḏiyṯ*** [fem. adj.: יְהוּדִית <3066>; fem. of JEW <3064>] ▶ **This adjective of nationality means: in Hebrew or in the Jewish language; it is also translated: in the Jews' language, in the language of Judah, in Judean.** It is used as an adverb indicating that someone is speaking Hebrew, in the Hebrew language, or literally in the language of Judah (2 Kgs. 18:26, 28; 2 Chr. 32:18; Neh. 13:24; Is. 36:11, 13). ¶

HEBRON – [1] ***ḥeḇrôn*** [proper noun: חֶבְרוֹן <2275>; from COMPANY <2267>]: association, companion ▶
a. A city in the hill country of Judah. In Genesis 23:2 it is called Kiriath Arba. Abraham build an altar (Gen. 13:18) by this ancient city (Num. 13:22). The cave of Machpelah was in this field, and the patriarchs and their wives were buried in the cave. It was given to Caleb and was designated as a city of refuge and a Levitical city (Josh. 20:7; 21:11). The spies visited the area (Num. 13:22–33). David was anointed king in Hebron and ruled from there for seven and a half years (2 Sam. 5:1–13). Absalom's rebellion and conspiracy began in Hebron (2 Sam. 15:1–6). *
b. A son of Kohath from the line of Moses, and a head of a family. Ref.: Ex. 6:18. It was a family/clan of Kohath (Num. 3:19). *

c. A descendant of Caleb, a brother of Jerahmeel. Refs.: 1 Chr. 2:42, 43. He fathered many sons (1 Chr. 15:9). ¶
– 2 Josh. 19:28 ➔ EBRON <5683>.

HEBRONITE – ***ḥeḇrôniy, ḥeḇrōniy*** [masc. proper noun: חֶבְרֹנִי, חֶבְרוֹנִי <2276>; patron. from HEBRON <2275>]: see HEBRON ▶ **A descendant of Hebron, the son of Kohath from the line of Moses.** Refs.: Num. 3:27; 26:58; 1 Chr. 26:23, 30, 31. ¶

HEDGE – ***meśûkāh, meśukāh*** [fem. noun: מְשׂוּכָה, מְשֻׂכָּה <4881>; from HEDGE (MAKE A) <7753>] ▶ **This word refers to a border of thorns. It refers to a stand of thorn-bearing shrubbery used to form a hedge.** The lazy person finds life as difficult as traveling through a hedge of thorns (Prov. 15:19). It is used in a more general sense of any hedge (Is. 5:5), e.g., one of grapevines. ¶

HEDGE (MAKE A, PUT A) – ***śûḵ*** [verb: שׂוּךְ <7753>; a prim. root] ▶ **This word refers to erecting a protective or restraining barrier of some kind.** Refs.: Job 1:10; Hos. 2:6: to hedge up, to block. It refers in a figurative sense to fencing a person about with sinews and bones (Job 10:11: to fence, to knit). ¶

HEDGE UP – Hos. 2:6 ➔ HEDGE (MAKE A, PUT A) <7753>.

HEED (GIVE) – Jer. 13:15 ➔ EAR (GIVE) <238>.

HEED (GIVE GOOD) – Eccl. 12:9 ➔ PONDER <239>.

HEED (TAKE) – 1 ***zehar*** [Aramaic verb: זְהַר <2095>; corresponding to WARN <2094>] ▶ **This word means to be admonished, to be cautious; it is also translated to beware, to take care, to be careful.** The word *zehar* is used only once in Scripture. King Artaxerxes told his secretaries and other men under his command to be careful to obey his order (Ezra 4:22). ¶
– 2 Deut. 27:9 ➔ SILENT (BE) <5535> b.

HEEL – 1 ***'āqēḇ*** [masc. sing. noun: עָקֵב <6119>; from SUPPLANT <6117>] ▶ **This word means the back of the foot, also footprints, a back, a rear.** The basic meaning of the word is heel and is seen in the passage where the serpent was told that he would strike at the heel of Eve's offspring (Gen. 3:15). Jacob grasped Esau's heel in the womb (Gen. 25:26). But the term can also be used to refer to the mark left by the heel (i.e., a footprint) (Ps. 56:6; 77:19; Song 1:8). It is also used in a military context to mean rear, i.e., at the heels (Gen. 49:19; Josh. 8:13). *
2 ***'āqēḇ*** [masc. noun: עָקֵב <6120>; from SUPPLANT <6117>] ▶
a. This word is taken to refer to the back of the feet of a person. In a figurative sense it refers to the way of life one's feet lead (Ps. 49:5). ¶
b. A masculine noun meaning a foe, a deceiver, one who cheats. It is used of one who attacks, withstands, accuses another person to bring him or her down (Ps. 49:5). ¶

HEEL (TAKE, GRASP BY THE) – Hos. 12:3 ➔ SUPPLANT <6117>.

HEELS (AT HIS) – Dan. 11:43 ➔ lit.: at his steps ➔ STEP (noun) <4703>.

HEGAI, HEGE – ***hêge', hêgay*** [masc. proper noun: הֵגֵא, הֵגַי <1896>; prob. of Persian origin]: eunuch ▶ **He was one of the eunuch of King Ahasuerus, in charge of the women, i.e., harem.** Refs.: Esther 2:3, 8, 15. ¶

HEIFER – 1 ***'eglāh, 'eglaṯ šelišiyyāh*** [fem. noun: עֶגְלָה, עֶגְלַת שְׁלִשִׁיָּה <5697>; fem. of CALF <5695>] ▶ **This word refers to a young cow.** These animals were used for milk, for certain sacrifices (Gen. 15:9); or symbolic rituals (Deut. 21:3, 4, 6). It is employed in a riddle to symbolize a woman, a wife (Judg. 14:18); and in a metaphor to refer to Egypt (Jer. 46:20); to Ephraim (Hos. 10:11). It refers to a calf, a heifer idol in Beth-aven, "house of iniquity" (Hos. 10:5). *
– 2 See COW <6510>.

HEIGHT – [1] ***gōḇah*** [masc. noun: גֹּבַהּ <1363>; from EXALTED (BE) <1361>] ▶ **This word means tallness, and refers also to grandeur, dignity.** Used literally, it refers to the tall aspects of something: buildings, trees, persons, heaven (1 Sam. 17:4; Job 11:8; Ezek. 1:18; 19:11; 31:10, 14; Amos 2:9). It is employed figuratively to depict grandeur or dignity (Job 40:10) and in a negative sense excessive pride or arrogance (Ps. 10:4; Prov. 16:18; Jer. 48:29). *
[2] ***mārôm*** [masc. noun: מָרוֹם <4791>; from RAISE UP <7311>] ▶ **This word means something or someone high, lifted up, literally or figuratively. It also means a high place, exaltedness.** It refers to something elevated, high (2 Kgs. 19:23; Job 5:11; Prov. 8:2; Is. 37:24); especially of Zion (Jer. 17:12; 31:12); figuratively, something worthy of praise or a place of authority or safety (Eccl. 10:6; Is. 26:5; Hab. 2:9). It has a more figurative meaning often: God sends from above, looks down from on high (2 Sam. 22:17; Ps. 18:16; 102:19); the high or exalted God (Mic. 6:6, literally God of the height); exaltedness as an attribute of the Lord (Ps. 92:8); as a direction with *l*ᵉ, to, toward, toward heaven (Is. 38:14; 40:26); as a description of a negative attitude of pride, arrogance (Ps. 56:2; 73:8). *
[3] ***qômāh*** [fem. noun: קוֹמָה <6967>; from STAND, STAND UP <6965>] ▶ **This word also means stature, length. It refers to the physical tallness of something.** E.g., height of the ark (Gen. 6:15; Ex. 25:10, 23; 2 Kgs. 25:17); a person (1 Sam. 16:7). The use of the word in 1 Samuel 28:20 refers to Saul's full stature lying on the ground. It has the sense of tall or high in 2 Kings 19:23, referring to the legendary tall cedars of Lebanon. It is used in a figurative sense of great and powerful people (Is. 10:33). Its use in Ezekiel 13:18 seems to refer to social stature more than physical size. *
[4] ***rûm, rum*** [masc. noun: רוּם, רֻם <7312>; from EXALT <7311>] ▶ **This word means physical tallness. It also indicates haughtiness, pride.** It refers to actual physical height (Prov. 25:3, the heavens). But it is used most often figuratively of the arrogance of persons, their haughtiness (Prov. 21:4: high, haughty; Is. 2:11, 17: haughtiness, loftiness, lofty pride, human pride), especially of the king of Assyria (Is. 10:12) and of Moab (Jer. 48:29). ¶
[5] ***rûm*** [Aramaic masc. noun: רוּם <7314>; from EXALT <7313>] ▶ **This word refers to the actual measured tallness of a structure or a natural object.** Refs.: Ezra 6:3; Dan. 3:1; 4:10, 11, 20. ¶
– [6] Josh. 11:2; 12:23; 1 Kgs. 4:11 → SIEVE <5299> b. [7] 1 Sam. 22:6 → HIGH PLACE <7413> [8] Job 20:6 → LOFTINESS <7863> [9] Ezek. 32:5 → CARCASS <7419> b.

HEIR – [1] ***ben*** [part of speech: alliteration <1121>] ***mešeq*** [masc. noun: מֶשֶׁק <4943>; from an unused root meaning to hold] ▶ **This expression is usually explained as meaning "the son of possession," i.e., the one who will possess a person's house after that person dies. Abram called Eliezer of Damascus by this term.** Ref.: Gen. 15:2; KJV: steward. ¶
– [2] Judg. 21:17 → POSSESSION <3425> [3] Prov. 29:21 → SON <4497>.

HEIR (BE) – ***yāraš*** [verb: יָרַשׁ <3423>; a prim. root] ▶ **This word means to take possession, to inherit, to dispossess, to drive out.** It is sometimes used in the generic sense of inheriting possessions (Gen. 15:3, 4). But the word is used usually in connection with the idea of conquering a land. This verb is a theme of Deuteronomy in particular where God's promise of covenantal relationship is directly related to Israelite possession (and thereby foreign dispossession) of the land of Israel. This theme continued throughout Israel's history and prophetic message. Possession of the land was directly connected to a person's relationship with the Lord; breaking the covenantal relationship led to dispossession. But even in exile, Israelites awaited the day when they would repossess the land (Jer. 30:3). *

HELAH – ***ḥel'āh*** [fem. proper noun: חֶלְאָה <2458>; the same as SCUM <2457>]: rust ▶ **One of the two wives of Ashhur.** Refs.: 1 Chr. 4:5, 7. ¶

HELAM – ***ḥêylām*** [proper noun: חֵילָם <2431>; from STRENGTH <2428>]: strength; army, fortress ▶ **A place east of the Jordan where David defeated Hadadezer, king of Syria.** Refs.: 2 Sam. 10:16, 17. ¶

HELBAH – ***ḥelbāh*** [proper noun: חֶלְבָּה <2462>; fem. of FAT (noun) <2459>]: fertility ▶ **A city of the territory of Asher; its inhabitants were not driven out by the Israelites.** Ref.: Judg. 1:31. ¶

HELBON – ***ḥelbôn*** [proper noun: חֶלְבּוֹן <2463>; from FAT (noun) <2459>]: fertile, fat ▶ **A city of Syria renowned for its wine.** Ref.: Ezek. 27:18. ¶

HELDAI – ***ḥelday*** [masc. proper noun: חֶלְדַּי <2469>; from HELED <2466>]: worldly ▶
a. One of David's mighty men. Ref.: 1 Chr. 27:15. ¶
b. A Jew who came back from the Babylonian captivity. Ref.: Zech. 6:10. Zechariah 6:14 has an alternate spelling; see HELEM <2494>. ¶

HELEB – ***ḥêleḇ*** [masc. proper noun: חֵלֶב <2460>; the same as FAT (noun) <2459>]: fat ▶ **One of David's mighty men.** Ref.: 2 Sam. 23:29. ¶

HELED – ***ḥeleḏ*** [masc. proper noun: חֵלֶד <2466>; the same as WORLD <2465>]: gliding, transient ▶ **One of David's mighty men.** Ref.: 1 Chr. 11:30; the same as HELEB <2460>. ¶

HELEK – ***ḥêleq*** [masc. proper noun: חֵלֶק <2507>; the same as PORTION <2506>]: portion ▶ **A son of Gilead of the tribe of Manasseh.** Refs.: Num. 26:30; Josh. 17:2. ¶

HELEKITE – ***ḥelqiy*** [proper noun: חֶלְקִי <2516>; patron. from HELEK <2507>] ▶ **A member of the clan of Helek, an Israelite of the tribe of Manasseh.** Ref.: Num. 26:30. ¶

HELEM – 1 ***ḥêlem*** [masc. proper noun: חֵלֶם <2494>; from DREAM (verb) <2492>]: dream or strength ▶ **This name refers to the same person as HELDAI <2469> b.** Ref.: Zech. 6:14. ¶
2 ***helem*** [masc. proper noun: הֶלֶם <1987>; from SMITE <1986>]: conqueror ▶ **An Israelite of the tribe of Asher.** Ref.: 1 Chr. 7:35. ¶

HELEPH – ***ḥêlep̱*** [proper noun: חֵלֶף <2501>; the same as RETURN FOR (IN) <2500>]: exchange ▶ **A city part of the boundary of Naphtali.** Ref.: Josh. 19:33. ¶

HELEZ – ***ḥêleṣ, ḥeleṣ*** [masc. proper noun: חֵלֶץ, חֶלֶץ <2503>; from DRAW OUT <2502>]: strength, deliverance ▶
a. One of David's mighty men. Refs.: 2 Sam. 23:26; 1 Chr. 11:27; 27:10. ¶
b. A man of the tribe of Judah. Ref.: 1 Chr. 2:39. ¶

HELIOPOLIS – Ezek. 30:17 → ON <204>.

HELKAI – ***ḥelqāy*** [masc. proper noun: חֶלְקָי <2517>; from SHARE (verb) <2505>]: portion of the Lord ▶ **A priest, head of the fathers' house of Meraioth.** Ref.: Neh. 12:15. ¶

HELKATH – ***ḥelqaṯ*** [proper noun: חֶלְקַת <2520>; a form of SMOOTH <2513>]: smoothness or portion of a land, field ▶ **A city of the border of Asher.** Refs.: Josh. 19:25; 21:31. ¶

HELKATH-HAZZURIM – ***ḥelqaṯ haṣṣuriym*** [proper noun: חֶלְקַת הַצֻּרִים <2521>; from HELKATH <2520> and the plur. of ROCK <6697>, with the art. inserted]: field of the sharp blades ▶ **A place near the pool of Gibeon where twelve young men killed each other.** Ref.: 2 Sam. 2:16. ¶

HELMET – 1 ***kôḇa'*** [masc. noun: כּוֹבַע <3553>; from an unused root meaning to be high or rounded] ▶ **A covering for a person's head for protection at work or in battle.** Goliath, the giant, wore a bronze helmet to go into battle (1 Sam. 17:5). Helmets were a key part of an army's military

dress (2 Chr. 26:14; Jer. 46:4; Ezek. 27:10; 38:5). Isaiah uses the word figuratively of the helmet of salvation (Is. 59:17). ¶
[2] ***qôḇa'*** [masc. noun: קוֹבַע <6959>; a form collateral to <3553> above] ▶ **This word refers to a warrior's protective headgear to guard against serious head injuries in battle.** Refs.: 1 Sam. 17:38; Ezek. 23:24. ¶

HELON – ***ḥêlōn*** [masc. proper noun: חֵלֹן <2497>; from STRENGTH <2428>]: strong, courageous ▶ **Father of Eliab, a chief of Zebulun.** Refs.: Num. 1:9; 2:7; 7:24, 29; 10:16. ¶

HELP (noun) – [1] ***'êzer*** [masc. noun: עֵזֶר <5828>; from HELP (verb) <5826>] ▶ **This word means succor, aid; one who aids, one who assists.** It refers to aid or assistance that is given, whether material or immaterial (Is. 30:5; Dan. 11:34). It is often help from the Lord who helps His people (Ps. 20:2; 121:1, 2; 124:8). He is called the shield or protection of Israel's help (Deut. 33:29). It indicates persons who give help: the woman created as Adam's complementary helper (Gen. 2:18, 20); the Lord as Israel's help (Hos. 13:9); the Lord as Israel's chief Helper (Ex. 18:4; Deut. 33:7; Ps. 33:20; 115:9–11). The name Eliezer means God (is) my helper (Ex. 18:4). *
[2] ***'ezrāh, 'ezrāth*** [fem. noun: עֶזְרָה, עֶזְרַת <5833>; fem. of <5828> above ▶ **This word indicates the assistance or aid given to a person.** It can be material or immaterial (Is. 10:3; 20:6; 31:1; Jer. 37:7; Lam. 4:17); especially help for the Lord (Judg. 5:23); and help from the Lord (Ps. 22:19; 38:22; 40:13, 17). It refers to the person who helps: persons (at the gate) who help (Job 31:21); of the Lord as Helper (Ps. 27:9; 40:17; 44:26; 46:1). *
– [3] 2 Sam. 22:36; Ps. 18:35 ➔ HUMILITY <6038> [4] Ps. 22:19 ➔ STRENGTH <360>.

HELP (CRY FOR) – Job 30:24; 36:19; Ps. 5:2 ➔ CRY (noun) <7769>.

HELP (LOOK FOR) – Is. 30:2 ➔ STRENGTHEN <5810>.

HELP (verb) – [1] ***'āzar*** [verb: עָזַר <5826>; a prim. root (in the sense of to surround)] ▶ **This word means to support, to give material or nonmaterial encouragement to a person.** God was the one who helped His people (Gen. 49:25). It is used mockingly of the inability of idols or pagan gods to aid their people (Deut. 32:38). It describes people helping each other to accomplish goals (Josh. 1:14; 10:4). The name Ebenezer means literally stone of help (1 Sam. 7:12). The participial form of the verb, *'ōzer*, may mean helper (Is. 31:3). In its passive use, it means to be helped, aided (Ps. 28:7). Zechariah 1:15 indicates that the nations helped and aided the evil, the devastation of God's people (Zech. 1:15). *
– [2] 1 Chr. 12:33 ➔ RANK (KEEP) <5737> [3] Ezra 5:2 ➔ SUPPORT (verb) <5583>.

HELPER – Gen. 2:18, 20 ➔ HELP (noun) <5828>.

HELPLESS – ***ḥêl^eḵāh*** [adj.: חֵלְכָה <2489>]; from an unused root prob. meaning to be dark or (fig.) unhappy ▶ **This word means defenseless, and also hapless, unfortunate; it is also translated poor, victims.** It indicates a person who is the object of a wicked person' hatred and evil plans (Ps. 10:8, 10). This same helpless or unfortunate person is the object of God's help (Ps. 10:14). ¶

HELPLESS (BE) – [1] Ps. 69:20 ➔ SICK (BE) <5136> [2] Ps. 88:15 ➔ DESPAIR (BE IN) <6323>.

HEM – ***šûl*** [masc. noun: שׁוּל <7757>; from an unused root meaning to hang down] ▶ **This word also means a skirt or the train of a robe. It refers to a border or edge on a garment or a piece of cloth.** It indicates the decorated hem of the high priest's robe (Ex. 28:33, 34; 39:24–26). It is used figuratively of the hem of the Lord's royal garment (Is. 6:1). It indicates more generally an entire skirt, a garment extending from a person's waist down (Jer. 13:22, 26). It figuratively indicates the skirts of Israel (Lam. 1:9; Nah. 3:5). ¶

HEMAM – ***hêymān*** [masc. proper noun: הֵימָן <1968>; prob. from NURSE (verb) <539> (in the sense of faithful, reliable)]: faithful ▶
a. A sage under Solomon. Refs.: 1 Kgs. 4:31; 1 Chr. 2:6. ¶
b. A chief singer. Refs.: 1 Chr. 6:33; 15:17, 19; 16:41, 42; 25:1, 4–6; 2 Chr. 5:12; 29:14; 35:15; Ps. 88:1. ¶

HEMAN – ***hêymām*** [masc. proper noun: הֵימָם <1967>; another form of HOMAM <1950>] ▶ **See HOMAM.** Ref.: Gen. 36:22, KJV, NASB. ¶

HEMDAM – 1 Chr. 1:41 ➔ HAMRAM <2566>.

HEMDAN – ***ḥemdān*** [masc. proper noun: חֶמְדָּן <2533>; from PLEASANT <2531>]: pleasant ▶ **A Horite, the older son of Dishon.** Refs.: Gen. 36:26; 1 Chr. 1:41. ¶

HEN – ***ḥên*** [masc. proper noun: חֵן <2581>; the same as GRACE <2580>]: grace ▶ **Son of Zephaniah.** Ref.: Zech. 6:14. ¶

HENA – ***hêna'*** [proper noun: הֵנַע <2012>; prob. of foreign deriv.] ▶ **A city taken by the Assyrians.** Refs.: 2 Kgs. 18:34; 19:13; Is. 37:13. ¶

HENADAD – ***ḥênāḏāḏ*** [masc. proper noun: חֵנָדָד <2582>; prob. from GRACE <2580> and HADAD <1908>]: favor of Hadad ▶ **Father of a family of Levites; his sons worked on the house of God.** Refs.: Ezra 3:9; Neh. 3:18, 24; 10:9. ¶

HEPHER – ***ḥêper*** [proper noun: חֵפֶר <2660>; from DIG <2658> or ASHAMED <2659>]: digger, well ▶
a. Son of Gilead. Refs.: Num. 26:32, 33; 27:1; Josh. 17:2, 3. ¶
b. Son of Naarah. Ref.: 1 Chr. 4:6. ¶
c. A Mecherathite, one of David's mighty men. Ref.: 1 Chr. 11:36. ¶
d. A city northwest of Jerusalem. Refs.: Josh. 12:17; 1 Kgs. 4:10. ¶

HEPHERITE – ***ḥepriy*** [masc. proper noun: חֶפְרִי <2662>; patron. from HEPHER <2660>] ▶ **Member of the family of Hepher.** Ref.: Num. 26:32. ¶

HEPHZIBAH – ***ḥepṣiy-ḇāh*** [fem. proper noun: חֶפְצִי־בָהּ <2657>; from DESIRE (noun) <2656> with suffixes]: my delight is in her ▶ **The wife of Hezekiah and the mother of king Manasseh.** Ref.: 2 Kgs. 21:1. It is also a symbolical name for Zion (Is. 62:4). ¶

HERALD – ***kārôz*** [Aramaic masc. noun: כָּרוֹז <3744>; from PROCLAMATION <3745>] ▶ **This word means one who cries out in proclamation; it is used of announcer at the dedication of Nebuchadnezzar's statue.** Ref.: Dan. 3:4. ¶

HERB – 2 Kgs. 4:39; Is. 26:19 ➔ LIGHT (noun) <219>.

HERBS – Deut. 11:10; 1 Kgs. 21:2; Prov. 15:17 ➔ GRASS <3419>.

HERD – [1] ***'elep*** [masc. noun: אֶלֶף <504>; from LEARN <502>] ▶ **This word means a large group of domestic animals; it is also translated cattle, oxen, kine.** Refs.: Deut. 7:13; 28:4, 18, 51; Ps. 8:7; Prov. 14:4; Is. 30:24. ¶
[2] ***bāqār*** [masc. noun: בָּקָר <1241>; from SEEK <1239>] ▶ **This noun refers to cattle, ox, oxen individually; collectively, it refers to the same animals as a large group.** It refers to female cattle, cows (Gen. 33:13), and is used to describe a herd of cattle or a single animal (Ex. 22:1). A *ben-bāqār*, a son of cattle, refers to a calf (Gen. 18:7). These animals were used as beasts of burden or for farming, plowing, etc. (2 Sam. 6:6; 1 Chr. 12:40). The possession of cattle was important and constituted wealth. *

HERDED TOGETHER (BE) – Is. 24:22 ➔ GATHERED TOGETHER (BE) <626>.

HERDMAN – [1] Amos 1:1 ➔ SHEEP BREEDER <5349> [2] Nah. 2:10 ➔ HERDSMAN <951>.

HERDS – Is. 60:6 ➔ ABUNDANCE <8229>.

HERDSMAN – ***bôqêr*** [masc. noun: בּוֹקֵר <951>; properly act. part. from SEEK <1239> as denom. from CATTLE <1241>] ▶ **This word means one who tends cattle; it is also translated shepherd, sheepbreeder.** It describes the work of Amos when he was called to be a prophet (Amos 7:14). He tended cattle and sheep and grew figs. ¶

HERE – 1 ***hênnāh*** [adv.: הֵנָּה <2008>; from THEY, THEM <2004>] ▶ **This word means in this place; it also indicates now. It is used most often of physical location or motion toward a location.** It means to go to a location (Gen. 15:16; 42:15; 45:5); it indicates a specific location reached (Gen. 45:8, 13; Josh. 2:2; 2 Kgs. 8:7). Repeated, it means hither . . . hither, to and fro, back and forth (2 Kgs. 4:35). It indicates a point reached in time and location (Num. 14:19; 2 Sam. 20:16). It indicates the end or extent of Jeremiah's words (Jer. 51:64). It is used to indicate an extent or process of time: It can indicate, with a negative, that a process has not been completed (Gen. 15:16). It refers to a period of past time that touches the present (Gen. 44:28; Judg. 16:13). It indicates a point to which something has been done, e.g., the declaration of God's wonders until now (Ps. 71:17). *

2 ***pō', pōh, pô*** [adv.: פֹּא, פֹּה, פּוֹ <6311>; prob. from a prim. inseparable particle "p" (of demonstrative force) and HE, SHE, IT <1931>] ▶ **This word means in this place, hither.** Its basic meaning is here (Gen. 19:12; 22:5). Combined with *min* (4480) in *mippōh,* it means on this or that side (Ezek. 40:10; 12, 21); with *'ad,* it means this far (1 Sam. 16:11; Ezra 4:2; Job 38:11). It is in the interrogative word *'êpōh.* *

HERE, HITHER – ***haᵃlōm*** [adv.: הֲלֹם <1988>; from the art. (see BEYOND <1973>)] ▶ **This word indicates a place which one approaches.** Refs.: Ex. 3:5; 1 Sam. 10:22. It indicates indefinite locations as well (1 Sam. 14:16). But it can also indicate the place where a person is currently located, i.e., here (Judg. 20:7; 1 Sam. 14:36, 38), even a spot where God has revealed Himself (Gen. 16:13). It is used figuratively or metaphorically to refer to the place in a person's life that the Lord has brought them (2 Sam. 7:18), as in the case of King David. It refers to the way of the wicked as a place to which people turn to follow (Ps. 73:10). Other refs.: Judg. 18:3; Ruth 2:14; 1 Chr. 17:16. ¶

HEREAFTER – Dan. 2:29, 45 ➔ lit.: after this ➔ AFTER <311>.

HERES – ***ḥeres*** [proper noun: חֶרֶס <2776>; the same as SUN <2775>]: shining ▶ **The Amorites dwelt in mount Heres.** Ref.: Judg. 1:35. For the word used in Judges 8:13, see SUN <2775>. ¶

HERESH – ***ḥereš*** [masc. proper noun: חֶרֶשׁ <2792>; the same as SECRETLY <2791>]: mute, silent ▶ **A Levite.** Ref.: 1 Chr. 9:15. ¶

HERETH – ***ḥereṯ*** [proper noun: חֶרֶת <2802>; from ENGRAVE <2801> (but equivalent to FOREST <2793>]: forest ▶ **A forest in the territory of the tribe of Judah where David took refuge when Saul was threatening his life.** Ref.: 1 Sam. 22:5; KJV, Hareth. ¶

HERITAGE – 1 Ex. 6:8; Deut. 33:4 ➔ POSSESSION <4181> 2 Ps. 61:5 ➔ POSSESSION <3425>.

HERMON – ***ḥermôn*** [proper noun: חֶרְמוֹן <2768>; from DESTROY <2763>]: destruction *or* devotion ▶ **This mountain became a landmark on the north-east boundary of Israel after the conquests under Moses and Joshua.** Refs.: Deut. 3:8, 9; 4:48; Josh. 11:3, 17; 12:1, 5; 13:5, 11; 1 Chr. 5:23; Ps. 89:12; 133:3; Song 4:8. ¶

HERMONITES – ***ḥermôniym*** [proper noun: חֶרְמוֹנִים <2769>; plur. of HERMON <2768>]: see HERMON ▶ **This word**

designates the peaks of Mount Hermon. Ref.: Ps. 42:6. ¶

HERO – Is. 33:7 ➔ VALIANT ONE <691>.

HERON – ***ᵃnāp̱āh*** [fem. noun: אֲנָפָה <601>; from ANGRY (BE) <599>] ▶ **This Hebrew word refers to an unclean bird; it could also be translated plover or cormorant.** This bird was forbidden as food (Lev. 11:19; Deut. 14:18) for God's holy people. ¶

HESED – ***ḥeseḏ*** [masc. proper noun: חֶסֶד <2618>; the same as MERCY <2617>]: mercy, kindness ▶ **One of the twelve governors of Solomon over Israel.** Ref.: 1 Kgs. 4:10. ¶

HESHBON – ***ḥešbôn*** [proper noun: חֶשְׁבּוֹן <2809>; the same as SCHEME (noun) <2803>]: intelligence, stronghold ▶ **This word designates the city where the king of the Amorites, Sihon, lived before it was captured by Israel.** Refs.: Num. 21:25–28, 30, 34; Judg. 11:19, 26. Reuben inherited the city, but it eventually was given to Gad. It also functioned as a Levitical city afterwards (Josh. 21:39). Interestingly, it was retaken by the Moabites (Is. 15:4; 16:8–9; Jer. 49:3). It was located east of the northern end of the Dead Sea. *

HESHMON – ***ḥešmôn*** [proper noun: חֶשְׁמוֹן <2829>; the same as ENVOY <2831>]: rich soil, fatness ▶ **A town in the extreme south of Judah.** Ref.: Josh. 15:27. ¶

HESITATE – 1 ***'āṣal*** [verb: עָצַל <6101>; a prim. root] ▶ **This word means not to act, to lay back; it is also translated to delay, to be slothful, to be slow.** In context it is used of Israel's hesitation to enter the Promised Land (Judg. 18:9). ¶
– 2 Gen. 19:16; 43:10 ➔ LINGER <4102>.

HETH – ***ḥēṯ*** [masc. proper noun: חֵת <2845>; from DISMAYED (BE) <2865>]: terror ▶ **Son of Canaan and grandson of Ham; he is the ancestor of the Hittites.** Refs.: Gen. 10:15; 23:3, 5, 7, 10, 16, 18, 20; 25:10; 27:46; 49:32; 1 Chr. 1:13. See HITTITE. ¶

HETHLON – ***ḥeṯlōn*** [proper noun: חֶתְלֹן <2855>; from SWADDLE <2853>]: enswathed, hideout ▶ **A place on the northern border of Israel's territory in Ezekiel's vision of the future.** Refs.: Ezek. 47:15; 48:1. ¶

HEW – 1 Ex. 34:1, 4; Deut. 10:1, 3; 1 Kgs. 5:18 ➔ CUT (verb) <6458> 2 Deut. 19:5 ➔ CUT (verb) <2404>.

HEW DOWN – Dan. 4:14, 23 ➔ CHOP DOWN <1414>.

HEW TO PIECES – ***šāsap̱*** [verb: שָׁסַף <8158>; a prim. root] ▶ **This word means to kill; it is also translated to hack in/to pieces, to put to death.** It refers to Samuel's violent destruction of Agag, a pagan king (1 Sam. 15:33). ¶

HEWER – 1 Deut. 29:11; Josh. 9:21, 23, 27; Jer. 46:22 ➔ lit.: one who hews ➔ CUT (verb) <2404> 2 See CUT (verb) <2672> b.

HEWN – ***maḥṣēḇ*** [masc. noun: מַחְצֵב <4274>; from CUT (verb) <2672>] ▶ **This word means something cut or carved. It is used of stone that has been quarried or cut out.** Refs.: 2 Kgs. 12:12; 22:6; 2 Chr. 34:11; also translated dressed. ¶

HEWN, HEWED – 1 Kgs. 5:17; 6:36; etc. ➔ DRESSED <1496>.

HEZEKI – 1 Chr. 8:17 ➔ HIZKI <2395>.

HEZEKIAH – 1 ***ḥizqiyyāh, ḥizqiyyāhû*** [masc. proper noun: חִזְקִיָּה, חִזְקִיָּהוּ <2396>; from STRONG (BE) <2388> and LORD <3050>]: the Lord is my strength ▶
a. The son of Ahaz who succeeded him as king in Judah (715–686 B.C.). He began to reign at twenty-five years of age and reigned twenty-nine years. He served the Lord faithfully and was considered possibly

the greatest king to rule over Judah alone (2 Kgs. 18:5); he wholly trusted the Lord. He carried reforms in his day and purified the Temple and the worship of Yahweh (2 Chr. 29:3–27), reestablishing the Passover (2 Chr. 30:26). With the help of the Lord and the prophet Isaiah, he stood against the king of Assyria (2 Kgs. 18:17–20:21). The Lord permitted him to live fifteen more years because of his trust in the Lord and total devotion to Him (2 Kgs. 20:23). At the end of his reign, he acted unwisely and arrogantly by allowing ambassadors from Babylon to examine the riches of the Temple and Jerusalem (2 Kgs. 20:12–21).

During his life, he was active in preserving Israel's written wisdom (Prov. 25:1). Micah prophesied during his reign (Jer. 26:18, 19; Hos. 1:1). *

b. The name of a son of Neariah who was of the royal line of David. Most read this as Hizkiah (e.g., ESV) (1 Chr. 3:23). ❡

c. The father of Amariah who was the son of Gedaliah. He was an ancestor of Zephaniah (Zeph. 1:1). ❡

d. The head or father of a clan that returned from the Babylonian exile (cf. Ezra 2:16). He, with others, sealed the covenant of Nehemiah (Neh. 10:17) to wholly follow the Lord. The name Ater is his Akkadian name (Neh. 7:21). ❡

2 ***yᵉḥizqiyyāh, yᵉḥizqiyyāhû*** [masc. proper noun: יְחִזְקִיָּה, יְחִזְקִיָּהוּ <3169>; from STRONG (BE) <2388> and LORD <3050>]: the Lord is my strength ►

a. A great king of Judah. See comments to HEZEKIAH <2396>.

b. A Jew who returned under Zerubbabel. Ref.: Ezra 2:16. ❡

c. A Jew, an Ephraimite, who disapproved of Israelites taking Judeans as prisoners of war. Ref.: 2 Chr. 28:12. ❡

HEZION – ***ḥezyôn*** [masc. proper noun: חֶזְיוֹן <2383>; from SEE <2372>]: vision ► **Grandfather of Ben-Hadad, king of Syria.** Ref.: 1 Kgs. 15:18. ❡

HEZIR – ***ḥêziyr*** [masc. proper noun: חֵזִיר <2387>; from the same as PIG <2386>]: enclosed, protected ►

a. A priest, descendant of Aaron. Ref.: 1 Chr. 24:15. ❡

b. A chief of the people, who signed the covenant of renewal with Nehemiah after the return from the Babylonian captivity. Ref.: Neh. 10:20. ❡

HEZRAI – 2 Sam. 23:35 → HEZRO <2695>.

HEZRO – ***ḥeṣrô*** [proper noun: חֶצְרוֹ <2695>; by an orthographical variation for HEZRON <2696>]: enclosure ► **One of David's mighty men.** Refs.: 2 Sam. 23:35: Hezro or Hezrai; 1 Chr. 11:37. ❡

HEZRON – ***ḥeṣrôn*** [proper noun: חֶצְרוֹן <2696>; from VILLAGE <2691>]: enclosed ►

a. Son of Pharez. Refs.: Gen. 46:12; Num. 26:21; Ruth 4:18, 19; 1 Chr. 2:5, 9, 18, 21, 24, 25; 4:1). ❡

b. Son of Reuben. Refs.: Gen. 46:9; Ex. 6:14; Num. 26:6; 1 Chr. 5:3. ❡

c. A city. Refs.: Josh. 15:2, 25. See also KERIOTH HEZRON b. ❡

HEZRONITE – ***ḥeṣrôniy*** [masc. proper noun: חֶצְרוֹנִי <2697>; patron. from HEZRON <2696>] ►

a. A descendant of Reuben through the line of his son Hezron. Ref.: Num. 26:6. ❡

b. A descendant of Pharez through the line of his son Hezron. Ref.: Num. 26:21. ❡

HID, HIDDEN – Ps. 17:14 → TREASURE, HIDDEN TREASURE <6840>.

HIDDAI – ***hidday*** [masc. proper noun: הִדַּי <1914>; of uncertain deriv.]: rejoicing of the Lord ► **One of David's mighty men.** Ref.: 2 Sam. 23:30. ❡

HIDDEKEL – ***ḥiddeqel*** [proper noun: חִדֶּקֶל <2313>; prob. of foreign origin]: rapid ► **This word designates the Tigris River, running on the eastern side of Mesopotamia and roughly parallel to a sister river, the Euphrates River.** It is one of the four rivers mentioned in

Genesis 2:14. Daniel was given an apocalyptic vision as he stood on its shore (Dan. 10:4). Its sources begin in the southeast of southern Turkey (ancient Hittite-Harrian territory) in the Armenian Mountains. It is ca. 1,500 miles long and empties into the Persian Gulf after it joins the Euphrates. The capital cities of Assyria, Assur, and Nineveh were on its banks. ¶

HIDDEN – Dan. 2:22 ➔ HIDE <5642>.

HIDDEN (BE) – 1 Is. 30:20 ➔ HIDE (verb) <3670> 2 Ezek. 28:3; 31:8 ➔ DIM (BECOME, GROW) <6004> 3 Hab. 3:4 ➔ HIDING <2253>.

HIDDEN THING – 1 Job 28:11 ➔ SECRET <8587> 2 Obad. 1:6 ➔ HIDDEN TREASURE <4710>.

HIDDEN TREASURE – ***maṣpôn*** [masc. noun: מַצְפּוֹן <4710>; from HIDE <6845>] ▶ **This word refers to the wealth and power of the kingdom of Edom (Esau) in its mountain strongholds.** Ref.: Obad. 1:6; KJV: hidden thing. ¶

HIDE – 1 ***ḥāḇā'*** [verb: חָבָא <2244>; a prim. root; comp. LOVE (verb) <2245>] ▶ **This word refers to drawing back, withdrawing oneself from any undesired person or situation, concealing oneself, as Adam did in the Garden of Eden.** Refs.: Gen. 3:8, 10. It indicates being in a safe, secure location metaphorically (Job 5:21) or literally to be hidden or hide (Job 29:10; Amos 9:3). It takes on the meaning of to hide something or someone (1 Kgs. 18:4, 13). It has the unusual meaning of water being ice or hard (Job 38:30) and the meaning to hush or be silent when referring to the voices of certain persons (Job 29:10). *
2 ***ḥāḇāh*** [verb: חָבָה <2247>; a prim. root; comp. LOVE (verb) <2245>] ▶ **This verb indicates to conceal, to withdraw.** It refers to persons secluding themselves for a time to escape a threat (Is. 26:20) or danger, either literally or figuratively. It literally means to hide oneself somewhere from something or someone (Josh. 2:16; 2 Kgs. 7:12), e.g., in the hills or fields. It indicates both a literal and figurative hiding from the Lord (Jer. 49:10). Other ref.: 1 Kgs. 22:25. ¶
3 ***ṭāman*** [verb: טָמַן <2934>; a prim. root] ▶ **This word means to bury, to conceal, to keep concealed.** Its basic sense is to hide something for various purposes, God or humans may be the subject: so that it would deteriorate (Jer. 13:4–7) in the crevice of a rock; so that it might ensnare others, e.g., a net (Ps. 9:15) or a trap (Ps. 64:5); so that it may be retrieved later, e.g., gold, silver, clothes (2 Kgs. 7:8). Moses hid an Egyptian's body in the sand (Ex. 2:12); and a miscarried child is placed in a grave (Job 3:16). It is used of person's being buried, hidden in the ground (Job 40:13) by God. Persons attempt to hide themselves "in the dust" from the Lord's judgments and majesty (Is. 2:10). It is used of hiding spies under stalks of grain (Josh. 7:21, 22). Proverbs describes the sluggard who "buries" his hand in a dish and is too lazy to draw it out (Prov. 19:24; 26:15). *
4 ***kānaḇ*** [verb: כָּנַף <3670>; a prim. root] ▶ **This word means to be concealed, to be put in a corner.** It is used only in a passive sense of being thrust aside, cornered, or hidden (Is. 30:20). ¶
5 ***mastêr*** [masc. noun: מַסְתֵּר <4564>; from <5641> below] ▶ **This word indicates an act of turning away.** In context it indicates desiring not to look at someone, because of his pathetic situation (Is. 53:3). ¶
6 ***sāṯar*** [verb: סָתַר <5641>; a prim. root] ▶ **This word means to conceal. It has the sense of preventing someone from knowing or seeing something, to keep something from public notice or from certain persons.** It has the sense of to guard and protect oneself from perceived danger (Prov. 22:3); and of trying to escape God's eyes, His presence (Gen. 4:14; Jer. 16:17). It is used of persons being hidden from each other, absent from each other's presence (Gen. 31:49). It is used in the sense of shielding and protecting a person or something from perceived danger (Ex. 3:6). It means to do something secretly, hidden, such as adultery (Num. 5:13); or to try to

hide oneself physically from danger and other persons (Deut. 7:20; 1 Sam. 20:5, 24; 1 Kgs. 17:3). It is used as a noun referring to secret things known only to God (Deut. 29:29). Persons are sometimes aware of hidden problems or errors in their own lives (Ps. 19:12). It is used of God's not hiding His face, i.e., removing His presence from a person (Ps. 22:24; Mic. 3:4). God will, however, hide His people from His wrath (Zeph. 2:3). *

7 ***s*ᵉ*ṯar*** [Aramaic verb: סְתַר <5642>; corresponding to <5641> above] ▶ **This word is derived from two separate roots. One of these means to conceal; the second means to destroy.** The first occurs as a passive participle in Daniel 2:22 where it refers to hidden things that God reveals to the wise. The second describes the actions of Nebuchadnezzar, the Chaldean, who destroyed God's Temple in Jerusalem (Ezra 5:12). It is possibly related to the Hebrew root *śāṯar* (BREAK OUT <8368>). ¶

8 ***'ālam*** [verb: עָלַם <5956>; a prim. root] ▶ **This word means to conceal, to ignore. It refers to something kept secret, not observed, not taken care of.** It is used by the psalmist to point out his hidden faults, unconscious errors (Ps. 90:8). It is used in various ways: to hide oneself, conceal oneself (Deut. 22:1, 3); to hide or conceal, to cover up something (1 Sam. 12:3). In its passive sense, it means things that are hidden (1 Kgs. 10:3). With *min* (FROM <4480>), it means to keep from, to hide from (2 Kgs. 4:27); to disregard, to hide eyes from (Is. 1:15). *

9 ***ṣāp̱an*** [verb: צָפַן <6845>; a prim. root] ▶ **This word means to conceal, to keep secret.** It is used of concealing something, often of great value, e.g., the baby Moses (Ex. 2:2, 3). Rahab concealed the Israelite spies (Josh. 2:4). It is used figuratively of keeping something hidden in a person's heart or mind (Job 10:13). It is used of God's protecting a person (Job 14:13). It is used of the storing up, the limiting of the days of the wicked and ruthless (Job 15:20). It refers to something hidden, stored up (Ps. 17:14). As a noun, it refers to God's treasured people (Ps. 83:3). It means to lie in wait for, to ambush someone (Prov. 1:11). It means to hide, to constrain a person (Prov. 27:16). It refers to holding something, saving it for another person (Song 7:13). The Temple or the Holy of Holies is referred to as God's hidden, secret habitation (Ezek. 7:22). It describes sin figuratively as being stored up (Hos. 13:12). *

– 10 Job 20:12; etc. ➔ CUT OFF <3582> 11 Job 23:9 ➔ TURN (verb) <5848> a. 12 Ps. 139:11 ➔ BRUISE (verb) <7779> c. 13 Ps. 139:12 ➔ DARKEN <2821>.

HIDING – ***ḥeḇyôn*** [masc. noun: חֶבְיוֹן <2253>; from HIDE <2247>] ▶ **This word refers to the covering or concealment of the Lord's power as He comes to deliver His people.** Ref.: Hab. 3:4: to be hidden, to be veiled. His power is hidden evidently by the rays shining from His hand or the splendor of His presence. ¶

HIDING PLACE – 1 ***maḥᵃḇê', maḥᵃḇō'*** [masc. noun: מַחֲבֵא, מַחֲבֹא <4224>; from HIDE <2244>] ▶

a. This word indicates a place of safety or refuge from the wind, especially a refuge under the protection of God's approved princes and rulers. Ref.: Is. 32:2. ¶

b. This word is used of any possible hideout that one could find in the desert areas of Judah. Ref.: 1 Sam. 23:23; also translated lurking place. ¶

2 ***mistār*** [masc. noun: מִסְתָּר <4565>; from HIDE <5641>] ▶ **This word defines a secret place, a place of ambush. It indicates a strategic secret or well-camouflaged location, literally or figuratively, from which to operate.** The wicked or oppressive person lurks there to catch the innocent (Ps. 10:8, 9; 17:12; 64:4; Hab. 3:14). It is used of hidden places where royal wealth was stored (Is. 45:3). It refers figuratively to a secret place where a sorrowful person can weep (Jer. 13:17). There is no hiding place that the Lord does not see clearly (Jer. 23:24; 49:10). Other ref.: Lam. 3:10. ¶

– 3 Deut. 32:38 ➔ COVERING <5643> b. 4 Judg. 9:35 ➔ AMBUSH <3993> 5 Ps. 32:7 ➔ COVERING <5643> a. 6 Is. 4:6 ➔ SHELTER <4563> 7 Jer. 25:38 ➔ ABODE <5520>.

HIEL – ***ḥiy'ēl*** [masc. proper noun: חִיאֵל <2419>; from ANIMAL <2416> (in the sense of a living thing) and GOD <410>]: God lives ▶ **An Israelite from Bethel who rebuilt Jericho.** Ref.: 1 Kgs. 16:34; cf. Josh. 6:26. ¶

HIGGAION – Ps. 9:16 ➔ MEDITATION <1902>.

HIGH – 1 ***gāḇôah, gāḇōah*** [adj.: גָּבֹהַּ, גָּבוֹהַּ <1364>; from EXALTED (BE) <1361>] ▶ **This word means elevated, and also exalted, proud.** It is used to denote items that are literally high: mountains (Gen. 7:19); trees (Is. 10:33); persons (1 Sam. 16:7); or any high or exalted thing (in a figurative sense, too) (Ezek. 21:26). It refers figuratively to haughty persons in the phrase the eyes of the proud (Is. 5:15) and also denotes a high position in rank or authority (Eccl. 5:8). *
– 2 Prov. 21:4 ➔ HEIGHT <7312> 3 Is. 13:2 ➔ STICK OUT <8192> 4 Ezek. 31:3 ➔ PROUD <1362>.

HIGH HEAP – Jer. 31:21 ➔ GUIDEPOST <8564> b.

HIGH OFFICIAL – Jer. 39:3, 13 ➔ RABMAG <7248>.

HIGH PLACE – 1 ***bāmāh*** [fem. noun: בָּמָה <1116>; from an unused root (meaning to be high)] ▶ **This word may refer to a physical elevated place, like a mountain (Ps. 18:33; Hab. 3:19); or a place of worship.** Although Samuel conducted sacrifices in these locations (1 Sam. 9:13), they were predominantly places of idol worship, which God hates (Ps. 78:58). These high places became symbolic of the idolatry of the Israelites (2 Kgs. 12:3; 14:4; 15:4; Jer. 19:5). *
2 ***rāmāh*** [fem. noun: רָמָה <7413>; fem. act. part. of EXALT <7311>] ▶ **This word indicates a height, a hill.** It refers to a hill or high ground in an area (1 Sam. 22:6; KJV, NKJV: Ramah). It indicates literally and figuratively an artificially constructed high place created for false worship in Israel or Judah (Ezek. 16:24, 25, 31, 39; also translated lofty place, lofty shrine). ¶
– 3 1 Sam. 13:6 ➔ STRONGHOLD <6877> b. 4 Ezek. 43:13 ➔ BACK <1354>.

HIGH, ON HIGH – ***rôm*** [adv.: רוֹם <7315>; from EXALT <7311>] ▶ **This adverb of direction means aloft, upwards.** It is used figuratively of the deep sea lifting high (*rôm*) its hands (Hab. 3:10). ¶

HIGHEST – ***gap̱*** [masc. noun: גַּף <1610>; from an unused root meaning to arch] ▶ **Coming from a root meaning to arch the back, this word refers to the back itself, and hence to a person's entire body or self. The signification of back in Hebrew is applied to any surface whatsoever, hence this word also means top, high elevated point.** It refers to the high points or tops of a city's structures or geographical features (Prov. 9:3). The Hebrew word also means a person alone; see ALONE <1610>. ¶

HIGHEST ONE – Dan. 7:18, 22, 25, 27 ➔ MOST HIGH <5946>.

HIGHEST PART – Judg. 9:37 ➔ CENTER <2872>.

HIGHWAY – 1 ***m^e^s̱illāh*** [fem. noun: מְסִלָּה <4546>; from EXALT <5549> (in the sense of to cast up a highway)] ▶ **This word means a public road.** It refers to key travel routes in antiquity (Num. 20:19; Judg. 20:31, 32, 45). Some were constructed of stone, gravel, or other materials; a few are named or located (2 Kgs. 18:17). The word is used in a figurative sense to describe the course of the stars (Judg. 5:20); the road of life lived by the righteous (Ps. 84:5); Prov. 16:17); or locusts' manner of marching (Joel 2:8). *
2 ***maslûl*** [masc. noun: מַסְלוּל <4547>; from EXALT <5549>] ▶ **This word describes a major roadway.** In context it is used figuratively of the Highway of Holiness that God's people will travel (Is. 35:8). ¶

HILEN – ***ḥiylên*** [proper noun: חִילֵן <2432>; from STRENGTH <2428>]: sandy ▶ **A city of Judah.** Ref.: 1 Chr. 6:58. It is the same place as Holon: Josh. 15:51; 21:15. ¶

HILKIAH – ***ḥilqiyyāh, ḥilqiyyāhû*** [masc. proper noun: חִלְקִיָּה, חִלְקִיָּהוּ <2518>; from PORTION <2506> and LORD <3050>]: the Lord is my portion ▶
a. This name refers to Hilkiah, the father of Eliakim, who was the administrator of Hezekiah's palace. Refs.: 2 Kgs. 18:18, 26, 37; Is. 22:20; 36:3, 22. ¶
b. The name of a high priest. He was in charge of the resources collected to repair the Temple (2 Chr. 35:8). He discovered the Book of the Law while renovating and cleaning out the Temple (2 Kgs. 22:8; 23:4–7) and delivered it to Shaphan the scribe or secretary. He, with others, went to Huldah the prophetess (2 Kgs. 22:14). He was an ancestor of Ezra (Ezra 7:1). All refs.: 2 Kgs. 22:4, 8, 10, 12, 14; 23:4, 24; 1 Chr. 6:3; 9:11; 2 Chr. 34:9, 14, 15, 18, 22; 35:8; Ezra 7:1. ¶
c. A descendant of Merari who helped to direct the worship and music of the Temple. Ref.: 1 Chr. 6:45. ¶
d. The son of Hosah, a Merarite, who served as a gatekeeper. Ref.: 1 Chr. 26:11. ¶
e. The son of Meshul, a priest who stood by Ezra as he read the Law to the people at the Water Gate. Ref.: Neh. 8:4. He became a new resident of Jerusalem to populate the city (Neh. 11:11; 12:7, 21). He returned from exile with Zerubbabel. ¶
f. The father of Gemariah. He with others took Jeremiah's letter to the exiles (Jer. 29:1–23). ¶

HILL – 1 ***giḇʿāh*** [fem. noun: גִּבְעָה <1389>; fem. from the same as GEBA <1387>] ▶ **This word often simply refers to a hill (i.e., an elevation of land, both high and low), not a mountain.** Refs.: Ex. 17:9, 10; 2 Sam. 2:25. Often it has negative implications that Israel used these natural locations as illicit places of worship of foreign gods (1 Kgs. 14:23; 2 Kgs. 17:10; Jer. 2:20). It often stands poetically in a parallel relationship with Hebrew *hār*, mountain, and means the same thing (Deut. 33:15; Ps. 72:3; 114:4, 6; Is. 2:2, 14; 30:17, 25; Joel 3:18). It is combined with a following word to designate a specific hill: teacher's hill; hill of Moreh (Judg. 7:1); hill of foreskins, Gibeath Haaraloth (Josh. 5:3); hill of God (1 Sam. 10:5; NIV, Gibeah of God). It designates in general the hills where Jerusalem is located (Zeph. 1:10). *
2 ***ʿōp̄el*** [masc. noun: עֹפֶל <6076>; from a verb meaning to be lifted up, see PRESUME <6075>] ▶ **This word means mound; it is also translated citadel, tower, fort, stronghold.** Refs.: 2 Kgs. 5:24; Is. 32:14; Mic. 4:8. The Hebrew word also means tumor; see TUMOR <6076>. ¶
– 3 Deut. 8:9 ➔ MOUNTAIN <2042> 4 1 Sam. 22:6 ➔ HIGH PLACE <7413> 5 2 Sam. 6:3, 4; etc. ➔ GIBEAH <1390> 6 See MOUNTAIN <2022>.

HILL (HIGH) – Ps. 68:15, 16 ➔ RUGGED <1386>.

HILL COUNTRY – Gen. 14:6 ➔ MOUNTAIN <2042>.

HILLEL – ***hillêl*** [masc. proper noun: הִלֵּל <1985>; from PRAISE (verb) <1984>]: praising ▶ **Father of Abdon, a judge in Israel.** Refs.: Judg. 12:13, 15. ¶

HILT – ***niṣṣāḇ*** [masc. noun: נִצָּב <5325>; pass. part. of STAND (verb) <5324>] ▶ **This word indicates the handle of something. It refers to the feature of something by which it is held, grasped.** In context it refers to the handle of a sword located on the end opposite the blade (Judg. 3:22; KJV: haft). ¶

HIMSELF, HERSELF (BY) – Ex. 21:3, 4 ➔ ALONE <1610>.

HIN – ***hiyn*** [masc. noun: הִין <1969>; prob. of Egyptian origin] ▶ **This word denotes a unit of liquid measure.** It indicates the amount of liquid used in a ritual (Ex. 29:40). It was used for measuring olive oil (Ex. 29:40; 30:24). The modern equivalent is about 3.8 liquid quarts or 3.3 dry quarts, although some would suggest a larger modern equivalent of over one quart liquid for a hin. *

HIND – 1 Gen. 49:21; Song 2:7; 3:5; 2 Sam. 22:34; Job 39:1; Ps. 18:33; 29:9;

Hab. 3:19 ➔ DOE <355> [2] Prov. 5:19; Jer. 14:5 ➔ DEER <365> a.

HINDER – [1] 1 Sam. 14:6 ➔ CUTTING TOOL <4621> [2] Ezra 6:8 ➔ CEASE <989> [3] Prov. 4:12 ➔ DISTRESSED (BE) <3334>.

HINDER PART – Joel 2:20 ➔ END <5490>.

HINGE – [1] ***pōṯ*** [masc. noun: פֹּת <6596>; from an unused root meaning to open] ▶ **This word refers to a device on which a door turned, probably a hole or socket in which rods, door-pivots turned, serving the same function as a modern hinge.** It identifies the hinges on which a door swings and is able to open and close (1 Kgs. 7:50; also translated socket). The Hebrew word also refers to the private parts of a woman and to a forehead; see SECRET PARTS <6596> and FOREHEAD <6596>. ¶
[2] ***ṣiyr*** [masc. noun: צִיר <6735>; from BESIEGE <6696> (in the sense of being pressed by turning in the case of a hinge)] ▶ **Based upon its usage in context, the word evidently refers to a device, probably a door pivot, on which the weight of the door rested and on which the door turns.** Ref.: Prov. 26:14. See also PAIN, LABOR PAINS <6735> and MESSENGER <6735> for other meanings of the Hebrew word. ¶

HINNOM – ***hinnōm*** [proper noun: הִנֹּם <2011>; prob. of foreign origin] ▶ **This word designates the valley that lies west and south of the hill of Jerusalem.** It became a place known for idolatrous practices located there (2 Kgs. 23:10; 2 Chr. 28:3; Jer. 7:31), especially the worship of the god Molech. It runs together with the Kidron Valley on the south end of the City of David. Other refs.: Josh. 15:8; 18:16; 2 Chr. 33:6; Neh. 11:30; Jer. 7:32; 19:2, 6; 32:35. ¶

HIP – [1] ***mip̱śā'āh*** [fem. noun: מִפְשָׂעָה <4667>; from MARCH <6585>] ▶ **This word refers to the upper thighs of a person which, in the Middle East, were to be covered.** Ref.: 1 Chr. 19:4; also translated buttocks. ¶
– [2] 2 Sam. 10:4 ➔ BUTTOCKS <8351> a. [3] 2 Sam. 10:4 ➔ BUTTOCKS <8357> [4] Dan. 5:6 ➔ LOINS <2783>.

HIP JOINT – ***qeṭar*** [Aramaic masc. noun: קְטַר <7001>; from a root corresponding to JOINED (BE) <7000>] ▶ **This word refers to the connecting articulation of a person's hips (the sides of the body below the waist). A very important articulation, it bears a person's body weight and allows him to stand upright.** Ref.: Dan. 5:6. For another meaning of the Hebrew word, see PROBLEM <7001>. ¶

HIRAH – ***ḥiyrāh*** [masc. proper noun: חִירָה <2437>; from PALE (GROW) <2357> in the sense of splendor]: nobility ▶ **An Adullamite, friend of Judah.** Refs.: Gen. 38:1, 12. ¶

HIRAM – [1] ***ḥûrām*** [masc. proper noun: חוּרָם <2361>; prob. from WHITE <2353>]: noble ▶
a. A king of Tyre (979–945 B.C.) with whom Solomon and also David had close ties and economic and political dealings. Hiram supplied logs and skilled workers to help build Solomon's Temple (2 Chr. 2:1–16). Hiram (Huram, a variant) also gave Solomon cities, ships, and crewmen (2 Chr. 8:18). He, with Solomon, imported gold from Ophir (2 Chr. 9:10, 21). *
b. The chief architect and skilled craftsman that Hiram sent to work for Solomon to help build the Temple. Refs.: 2 Chr. 2:13; 4:11, 16. ¶
c. The name of a Benjamite, a son of Bela and ancestor of Saul. Ref.: 1 Chr. 8:5. ¶
[2] ***ḥiyrôm, ḥiyrām*** [masc. noun: חִירוֹם, חִירָם <2438>; another form of <2361> above]: noble ▶
a. The king of Tyre who befriended David and recognized him as a national power. Ref.: 2 Sam. 5:11. He sent both supplies and skilled workers to help him prepare to build his palace. This helpful and peaceful relationship continued under Solomon (1 Kgs. 5:1, 2). The same person as discussed in entry <2361> a. above. *

b. The same as Huram in entry <2361> b. above. Refs.: 1 Kgs. 7:13, 40, 45; 2 Chr. 4:11. ¶

HIRE – [1] ***śāḵar, sāḵar*** [verb: שָׂכַר, סָכַר <7936>; a prim. root] ▶ **This word means to make an agreement with someone to do something for payment.** For procreation purposes (Gen. 30:16); for the purpose of prophesying (Deut. 23:4); for military use (Judg. 9:4; 2 Sam. 10:6; 2 Kgs. 7:6); for priestly services (Judg. 18:4); for political purposes (Ezra 4:5; Neh. 6:12, 13); for craftsmanship (Is. 46:6). In the passive or causative uses, it means to be hired or to hire oneself out (1 Sam. 2:5; Hag. 1:6). *

[2] ***tānāh*** [verb: תָּנָה <8566>; a prim. root] ▶ **This word means to sell oneself. It describes a harlot hiring out her body.** In context it refers to Israel's spiritual harlotry and attempts to make forbidden liaisons with the nations (Hos. 8:9, 10). ¶

– [3] Deut. 23:18; Ezek. 16:31, 41; Hos. 9:1 ➔ EARNINGS <868> [4] Ezek. 16:33 ➔ REWARD (GIVE A) <7809>.

HIRED – [1] ***śaḵiyr*** [masc. adj.: שָׂכִיר <7916>; from HIRE <7936>] ▶ **This word refers a person who is employed in exchange for a wage; it also refers to a rented animal.** Refs.: Ex. 12:45 (a person); 22:15 (an animal). Wages were to be paid promptly to hired workers (Lev. 19:13). Restrictions were laid on hired persons concerning Temple rituals and holy things (Lev. 22:10). Even a freeman's labor seems like the days of a hired man (Job 7:1). A hired soldier was a mercenary (Jer. 46:21). It is rendered as wage earner appropriately in Malachi 3:5 (NASB). *

[2] ***śᵉḵiyrāh*** [fem. adj.: שְׂכִירָה <7917>; fem. of <7916> above] ▶ **This word has the same meaning as <7916> above.** It is applied to an object, referring figuratively to Assyria as a rented, hired razor (Is. 7:20). ¶

HISS – ***šāraq*** [verb: שָׁרַק <8319>; a prim. root] ▶ **This word means to whistle, to scorn.** It describes a hissing or whistling of puzzled wonderment (1 Kgs. 9:8). It is a word of rejection and mockery in some cases (Job 27:23; Jer. 19:8; 49:17; 50:13; Lam. 2:15, 16). The great city of Tyre became an object of hissing at her fall (Ezek. 27:36); as did Ethiopia (Zeph. 2:15). It is used to call for, to whistle for someone or something to come (Is. 5:26; 7:18; Zech. 10:8). ¶

HISSING – [1] ***šᵉrēqāh*** [fem. noun: שְׁרֵקָה <8322>; from HISS <8319>] ▶ **This word indicates mocking as scorn or derision.** It refers to whistling or hissing at something: for instance, as an object of dread or horror (2 Chr. 29:8; Jer. 25:9); especially Jerusalem in her devastation (Jer. 19:8; 25:18). The people of Israel themselves because of their transgressions would become a hissing among the nations (Jer. 29:18; Mic. 6:16); but likewise so would Babylon (Jer. 51:37). ¶

– [2] Jer. 18:16 ➔ PIPING <8292>.

HIT – Ex. 21:22 ➔ SMITE <5062>.

HITHERTO – Dan. 7:28 ➔ POINT (AT THIS) <3537>.

HITTITE – ***ḥittiy*** [proper noun: חִתִּי <2850>; patron. from HETH <2845>] ▶ **a. The Hittites were descendants of Heth, some of whom lived in Canaan.** Ref.: Gen. 15:20. Abraham acquired Machpelah as a burial cave for the patriarchs (Gen. 23:10–20; 25:9) from the Hittites. Israelites were not to intermarry with them (Gen. 26:34–35). They were one of the peoples Israel took land from (Ex. 3:8, 17). The Hittites on the international scale made up a much larger group of people and occupied a larger area as a nation that encompassed the whole of Syria into modern day Turkey (see b.). The groups of Hittites in the Old Testament in Canaan lived mainly in the area of Hebron. Israel disinherited them and took Canaan. Uriah the Hittite served in David's army (2 Sam. 23:39). Esau married a Hittite woman (Gen. 27:46) and greatly grieved his parents. *

b. The greater Hittite population inhabited Anatolia (modern day areas of Turkey) and major parts of Syria. Solomon sold chariots to them and the Arameans. Refs.: 1 Kgs. 10:29; 2 Kgs. 7:6. Solomon even intermarried with them (1 Kgs. 11:1). Other ref.: 2 Chr. 1:17. ¶

HIVITE – ***ḥiwwiy*** [proper noun: חִוִּי <2340>; perhaps from TOWN <2333>] ▶ **The gentilic name of a group of people descended from Canaan.** Refs.: Gen. 10:17; 36:2. Hamor, father of Shechem, was a Hivite. A people that inhabited Canaan (Ex. 3:8; 23:28), along with various other peoples. They evidently lived mostly in Lebanon (Judg. 3:3, Judg. 3:5). They worked for Solomon as builders (1 Kgs. 9:20). They are sometimes confused with the Horites (cf. Gen. 36:2, 20–30). *

HIZKI – ***ḥizqiy*** [masc. proper noun: חִזְקִי <2395>; from STRONG (BE) <2388>]: strong ▶ **An Israelite of the tribe of Benjamin.** Ref.: 1 Chr. 8:17. ¶

HOAR FROST, HOARY FROST – Ex. 16:14; Job 38:29; Ps. 147:16 ➔ FROST <3713>.

HOARD – Amos 3:10 ➔ STORE (verb) <686>.

HOARDED (BE) – ***ḥāsan*** [verb: חָסַן <2630>; a prim. root] ▶ **This verb refers to storing up something for reserve or to piling up excess supplies irresponsibly; it is also translated to be laid up.** Ref.: Is. 23:18. ¶

HOBAB – ***ḥōḇāḇ*** [masc. proper noun: חֹבָב <2246>; from LOVE (verb) <2245>]: beloved ▶ **The son of Rehuel the Midianite; possibly the same as Jethro, the father-in-law of Moses.** Refs.: Num. 10:29; Judg. 4:11. ¶

HOBAH – ***ḥôḇāh*** [proper noun: חוֹבָה <2327>; fem. act. part. of HIDE <2247>]: hiding place ▶ **A city north of Damascus.** Ref.: Gen. 14:15. ¶

HOD – ***hôḏ*** [masc. proper noun: הוֹד <1936>; the same as VIGOR <1935>]: vigor, majesty ▶ **An Israelite of the tribe of Asher.** Ref.: 1 Chr. 7:37. ¶

HODAIAH – ***hôḏaywāhû*** [masc. proper noun: הוֹדַיְוָהוּ <1939>; a form of HODAVIAH <1938>]: praise of the Lord ▶ **He was a son of Elioenai and, therefore, was listed in the royal line of David's descendants.** Ref.: 1 Chr. 3:24, KJV. ¶

HODAVIAH – ***hôḏawyāh*** [masc. proper noun: הוֹדַוְיָה <1938>; from VIGOR <1935> and LORD <3050>]: praise of the Lord ▶
a. He was a son of Elioenai and, therefore, was listed in the royal line of David's descendants. Ref.: 1 Chr. 3:24. ¶
b. An Israelite of the tribe of Manasseh. Ref.: 1 Chr. 5:24. ¶
c. An Israelite of the tribe of Benjamin. Ref.: 1 Chr. 9:7. ¶
d. Members of his family came back from the Babylonian captivity. Ref.: Ezra 2:40. ¶

HODESH – ***ḥōḏeš*** [fem. proper noun: חֹדֶשׁ <2321>; the same as MONTH <2320>]: new moon ▶ **The wife of Shaharaim, an Israelite of the tribe of Benjamin.** Ref.: 1 Chr. 8:9. ¶

HODEVAH – ***hôdᵉwāh*** [masc. proper noun: הוֹדְוָה <1937>; a form of HODAVIAH <1938>]: praise of the Lord ▶ **Members of his family came back from the Babylonian captivity.** Ref.: Neh. 7:43. ¶

HODIAH – ***hôḏiyyāh*** [masc. proper noun: הוֹדִיָּה <1940>; a form for the fem. of JEW <3064>]: majesty of the Lord ▶ **An Israelite, most likely of the tribe of Judah.** Ref.: 1 Chr. 4:19, KJV. ¶

HODIJAH, HODIAH – ***hôḏiyyāh*** [masc. proper noun: הוֹדִיָּה <1941>; a form of HODIAH <1938>]: majesty, authority of the Lord ▶
a. An Israelite, most likely of the tribe of Judah. Ref.: 1 Chr. 4:19, NASB, NIV. ¶
b. A Levite who signed the covenant of renewal with Nehemiah after the return from the Babylonian captivity. Refs.: Neh. 8:7; 9:5; 10:10. ¶
c. Another Levite who sealed the same covenant. Ref.: Neh. 10:13. ¶

d. A Jewish chief who sealed the same covenant. Ref.: Neh. 10:18. ¶

HOE – [1] ***ma'dêr*** [masc. noun: מַעְדֵּר <4576>; from RANK (KEEP) <5737> (in the sense of to cultivate)] ▶ **This word depicts an agricultural tool for loosening the ground for cultivation.** Ref.: Is. 7:25; KJV: mattock. ¶
– [2] 1 Sam. 13:21 ➔ GOAD <1861> [3] Is. 5:6; 7:25 ➔ CULTIVATE <5737>.

HOGLAH – ***ḥoglāh*** [fem. proper noun: חָגְלָה <2295>; of uncertain deriv.]: partridge ▶ **One of the five daughters of Zelophehad.** Refs.: Num. 26:33; 27:1; 36:11; Josh. 17:3. ¶

HOHAM – ***hôhām*** [masc. proper noun: הוֹהָם <1944>; of uncertain deriv.]: the Lord impels ▶ **King of Hebron who was defeated by Joshua and executed.** Ref.: Josh. 10:3; read 1–27. ¶

HOLD (noun) – Judg. 9:46, 49 ➔ STRONGHOLD <6877> a.

HOLD (TAKE) – ***'aḥaz*** [verb: אָחַז <270>; a prim. root] ▶ **This word indicates to seize, to grasp, to grip, to hold firmly.** This meaning is employed quite uniformly. Someone or a thing can be seized (Gen. 25:26; Ex. 15:14). In its passive usage, it has the idea of caught or held fast (Gen. 22:13, the ram) or being settled in a land (Gen. 34:10: to acquire possessions, to get property), metaphorically. *

HOLD (verb) – [1] Gen. 25:26; Ex. 15:14 ➔ HOLD (TAKE) <270> [2] 1 Kgs. 7:26; Jer. 2:13; 6:11; 20:9; Ezek. 23:32 ➔ CONTAIN <3557> [3] 2 Kgs. 4:16 ➔ EMBRACE <2263> [4] Lam. 2:22 ➔ CARE FOR <2946>.

HOLD BACK – [1] Ex. 22:29 ➔ STAY (verb) <309> [2] Job 37:4 ➔ SUPPLANT <6117> [3] Is. 42:14; 63:15; 64:12 ➔ CONTROL (verb) <662> [4] Is. 48:9 ➔ RESTRAIN <2413> [5] Dan. 4:35 ➔ STRIKE <4223>.

HOLD FAST – [1] Deut. 4:4 ➔ JOINING <1695> [2] 2 Kgs. 6:32 ➔ OPPRESS <3905>.

HOLD IN, HOLD IN CHECK – Ps. 32:9 ➔ CONTROL (verb) <1102>.

HOLD OF (TAKE) – ***lāpaṯ*** [verb.: לָפַת <3943>; a prim. root] ▶ **This word means to grasp, to turn aside.** It is used of placing one's hand on something, grasping it (Judg. 16:29; also translated to grasp, to reach forward; Ruth 3:8: to turn). It describes the path of life as winding its way, winding along (Job 6:18: to turn aside, to wind along). ¶

HOLD OUT – ***yāšaṭ*** [verb: יָשַׁט <3447>; a prim. root] ▶ **This word refers to an act of granting something to a person in a formal royal setting by handing it to the one requesting it.** Refs.: Esther 4:11; 5:2; 8:4; also translated to extend. ¶

HOLD TOGETHER – Dan. 2:43 ➔ ADHERE <1693>.

HOLD, WITHHOLD – ***māna'*** [verb: מָנַע <4513>; a prim. root] ▶ **This word refers to keeping, keeping back, retaining, controlling something for some reason.** For instance: food or grain from the market (Prov. 11:26). In a figurative sense of holding back the rivers of a fallen nation, indicating its destruction (Ezek. 31:15); of holding back something from another person, as when God withheld pregnancy from Rachel (Gen. 30:2); to restrain someone from something (Num. 24:11; 1 Sam. 25:26). It is used of something being restrained (Job 38:15; Joel 1:13); or of persons permitting themselves to be controlled (Num. 22:16). In Israel the Lord often withheld rain to warn His people (Jer. 3:3; Amos 4:7). It is used figuratively of a person holding evil in his mouth (Job 20:13). Light, understanding is withheld from the wicked person (Job 38:15). Wisdom exhorts the wise to withhold their feet from walking with the wicked (Prov. 1:15). The wise person does not keep back a good deed from those who deserve it (Prov. 3:27).

Discipline is not to be withheld from a child (Prov. 23:13). *

HOLE – [1] ***ḥur*** [masc. noun: חֻר <2352>; from an unused root prob. meaning to bore] ▶ **This word is used of a cavity in the ground where a cobra or asp lives.** Ref.: Is. 11:8; also translated den. It takes on the meaning of a large hole or possibly a cave where Israelites hide in a time of oppression and judgment (Is. 42:22; also translated cave, pit). ¶
[2] ***ḥôr, ḥōr*** [masc. noun: חוֹר, חֹר <2356>; the same as HOLE <2352>] ▶ **This word designates a cavity, and also a cave.** It is used of a hole in a door, in a stone wall, or in the top of a chest (2 Kgs. 12:9; Song 5:4: hole, latch, opening, latch-opening; Ezek. 8:7), created by drilling or boring. It would designate holes or short caves, as hiding places for persons in danger (1 Sam. 14:11); or for the outcasts of society (Job 30:6: hole, cave). It describes the lodging places of lions, and it means lairs or dens (Nah. 2:12: hole, cave, lair). Other ref.: Zech. 14:12 (hole, socket). ¶
– [3] 1 Sam. 13:6 ➔ THORN <2336> [4] Is. 2:19 ➔ CAVE <4247> [5] Is. 7:19; Jer. 13:4; 16:16 ➔ CLEFT <5357>.

HOLES – 1 Sam. 13:6 ➔ THICKETS <2337>.

HOLIDAY – ***hᵃnāḥāh*** [fem. noun: הֲנָחָה <2010>; from REST (verb) <5117>] ▶ **This word denotes a day of rest; it is also translated remission of taxes, release.** It refers to a holiday declared by the Persian king Ahasueras (Xerxes) in honor of Esther's banquet (Esther 2:18). ¶

HOLINESS – See HOLY THING <6944>.

HOLLOW (noun) – [1] ***nāḇaḇ, nāḇûḇ*** [masc. noun: נָבַב, נָבוּב <5014>; a prim. root] ▶ **The word is considered as a set noun form meaning empty space, a place filled with air.** The meanings indicate a thing or person with the feature of hollowness, empty-headed (Ex. 27:8; 38:7; Job 11:12; Jer. 52:21). ¶
– [2] Zech. 1:8 ➔ RAVINE <4699>.

HOLLOW OF THE HAND – Is. 40:12 ➔ HANDFUL <8168>.

HOLLOW PLACE – ***maḵtēš*** [masc. noun: מַכְתֵּשׁ <4388>; from GRIND <3806>] ▶ **This word refers to a depression, an empty place in a jawbone or mortar bowl.** It is used of a hollow place in a jawbone where the molar tooth was (Judg. 15:19) and indicates by extension the depression in a mortar bowl (Prov. 27:22). In the case of Judges 15:19, it is probably used figuratively of a depression in the ground that resembled the molar cavity of a jawbone. ¶

HOLLOW (verb) – **to hollow, to make hollow, to be hollow: *nāḇaḇ, nāḇûḇ*** [masc. noun: נָבַב, נָבוּב <5014>; a prim. root] ▶ **The verb means to create an empty space inside something, a cavity.** The bronze altar was to be hollowed out inside (Ex. 27:8); the pillars of the Temple were hollow (Jer. 52:21). A person described as hollow is a fool, senseless (Job 11:12; also translated empty-headed, idiot, vain, stupid, witless).

HOLON – ***ḥōlôn*** [proper noun: חֹלוֹן <2473>; prob. from SAND <2344>]: sandy ▶
a. A city in Moab. Ref.: Jer. 48:21. ¶
b. A city in Judah. Refs.: Josh. 15:51; 21:15. ¶

HOLY – [1] ***qāḏôš*** [adj.: קָדוֹשׁ <6918>; from <6942> below] ▶ **This word is used to denote someone or something that is inherently sacred or has been designated as sacred by divine rite or cultic ceremony. It designates that which is the opposite of common or profane. It could be said the *qāḏôš* is a positive term regarding the character of its referent, where common is a neutral term and profane a very negative term.** This word is often used to refer to God as being inherently holy, sacred, and set apart (Ps. 22:3; Is. 6:3; 57:15); and as being free from the attributes of fallen humanity (Hos. 11:9). Therefore, in the Old Testament, God is accorded the title "The Holy One of Israel" (2 Kgs. 19:22; Ps. 78:41; Is. 17:7; Jer. 50:29). As such, God instructed that humanity should be holy because He is holy (Lev. 11:44, 45; 19:2). In addition to its divine references, this word can also modify places, like the court of the Tabernacle (Ex. 29:31); the camp of Israel (Deut. 23:14); Jerusalem (Eccl. 8:10); heaven (Is. 57:15); people, like the priests (Lev. 21:7, 8); a Nazirite (Num. 6:5, 8); the prophet Elisha (2 Kgs. 4:9); Levites (2 Chr. 35:3); saints [angels] (Job 5:1; 15:15; Dan. 8:13); water (Num. 5:17); time (Neh. 8:9–11; Is. 58:13). *

2 ***qaddîš*** [Aramaic masc. adj.: קַדִּישׁ <6922>; corresponding to <6918> above] ▶ **This term can modify the word *ᵉlāh* (<426>), meaning God or gods.** Refs.: Dan. 4:8, 9, 18; 5:11. As a substantive, it could stand for angel(s), the supernatural holy one(s) (Dan. 4:13, 17, 23). It could also refer to God's people, human holy ones, or saints (Dan. 7:18, 21, 22, 25, 27). ¶

– 3 See FAITHFUL <2623>.

HOLY (BE) – ***qāḏaš*** [verb: קָדַשׁ <6942>; a prim. root] ▶ **This word means to be set apart, in particular: to show oneself holy, to be treated as holy, to consecrate, to treat as holy, to dedicate, to be made holy, to declare holy or consecrated, to behave, to act holy, to dedicate oneself. The verb, in the simple stem, declares the act of setting apart, being holy (i.e., withdrawing someone or something from profane or ordinary use).** The Lord set aside Aaron and his sons, consecrated them, and made them holy for the priesthood (Ex. 29:21). The altar was made holy, and anything coming into contact with it became holy (Ex. 29:37). The Tabernacle, the ark, the table of showbread, the altar of burnt offering, and all the smaller accessories and utensils used in the cult of Israel were anointed with a special anointing oil so they became holy. Whatever came in contact with them became holy (Ex. 30:26–29). The men accompanying David as his military were declared holy (1 Sam. 21:5).

The word is used most often in the intensive stem, meaning to pronounce or to make holy, to consecrate. The Lord pronounced the Sabbath day holy (Gen. 2:3; Ex. 20:8). Places could be dedicated as holy, such as a part of the courtyard of the Temple (1 Kgs. 8:64); or Mount Sinai itself (Ex. 19:23). The Year of Jubilee, the fiftieth year, was declared holy (Lev. 25:10). Persons could be consecrated to holy duties: Aaron and his sons were consecrated to serve as priests of the Lord (Ex. 28:3, 41; 1 Sam. 7:1); the firstborn males of people or animals were consecrated to the Lord (Ex. 13:2). Holy times were designated using this word in the factitive stem: Jehu deceitfully proclaimed a holy assembly to Baal (2 Kgs. 10:20); a holy fast could be consecrated as Joel did (Joel 1:14). With the Lord as the subject, the word describes establishing something as holy. The Lord Himself consecrated or made holy His people (Ex. 31:13; Lev. 20:8; 21:8); through His judgments on Israel and the nations, God proved the holiness of His name (Ezek. 36:23). The priests' holy garments serving in Ezekiel's restored Temple will make those who touch them holy (Ezek. 44:19; 46:20).

In the causative stem, the meanings overlap with the meanings in the intensive stem. It indicates designating something as consecrated or holy; Jeremiah was declared holy (Jer. 1:5); as was the Temple (1 Kgs. 9:3). The word means to treat as holy or dedicated. Gifts, fields, or money could be treated as holy (Lev. 27:16; 2 Sam. 8:11; 2 Kgs. 12:18). God declared things holy to Himself (1 Kgs. 9:7); God Himself is to be treated as holy (Num. 20:12; 27:14; Is. 29:23).

In the passive stems, the word means to be consecrated, to be treated as holy, or to show oneself as holy. Ezekiel described the Zadokite priests as consecrated for service at a future Temple (Ezek. 48:11); Ezra 3:5 described the established holy feasts of the Lord in the return from exile. The entrance at the Tabernacle was to be treated as consecrated and holy through the Lord's glory (Ex. 29:43). The Lord showed Himself as holy (Lev. 10:3; 22:32; Ezek. 20:41).

In the reflexive stem, the verb means to show oneself holy or consecrated: the priests had to properly consecrate themselves before coming before the Lord (Ex. 19:22; Lev. 11:44); the Lord would prove Himself holy before the nations and Israel (Ezek. 38:23). The word indicates putting oneself or another into a state of holiness to the Lord (Num. 11:18; Josh. 3:5; 1 Sam. 16:5; 2 Chr. 31:18). *

HOLY PLACE – Josh. 24:26 ➔ SANCTUARY <4720>.

HOLY THING – ***qōḏeš*** [masc. noun: קֹדֶשׁ <6944>; from HOLY (BE) <6942>] ▶ **This word indicates something consecrated and set aside for sacred use only; it was not to be put into common use, for if it was, it became profaned and common (*ḥôl*), not holy. It also means holiness, sacredness.** This noun described holy offerings or things used in Israel's cult; it described the holy offerings which only the priest or his family could eat (Lev. 22:10). Some of the offerings of the Lord were described as Most Holy (Lev. 2:3, 10; Num. 18:9); various things could be consecrated as holy: warriors (1 Sam. 21:6); food (Ex. 29:33); and the places where the holy ark had been located (2 Chr. 8:11). Only holy priests could go into the Temple (2 Chr. 23:6). Many vessels and items used in the Tabernacle or Temple areas were holy (Ezra 8:28; Ex. 30:32, 35). The Sabbath was, of course, holy (Ex. 31:14).

This word also designates divine holiness: the Lord alone can swear by His own holiness (Ps. 89:35; Amos 4:2); and His ways are holy (Ps. 77:13). In fact, God is marvelous in holiness (Ex. 15:11).

Since the Lord is holy, He expected Israel to be holy. This word described the essence of the Israelites: They were His holy people (Ex. 22:31; 28:36).

The word describes holiness when it relates to various things: holiness adhered to the Lord's house and beautified it (Ps. 93:5). The Lord's name is holy (Lev. 20:3; 22:2; Ezek. 39:7, 25; Amos 2:7). The Lord will establish His holy mountain when all the earth will know Him (Is. 11:9; 56:7). Zion is God's holy hill (Dan. 9:20; Joel 3:17).

The word is also used when referring to holy places. God's presence is what makes any place, anything, or anyone holy (Ex. 3:5). The Holy Place in the Tabernacle (Ex. 26:33; 28:29) was separated from the Most Holy Place by a curtain (Ex. 26:33); it refers to the Most Holy Place in the Temple as well (1 Kgs. 6:16). This word with the definite article refers to the entire Tabernacle (Ex. 36:1, 3, 4; 38:27) and later the Temple Solomon built (1 Kgs. 8:8); literally, the Holy Place (Ps. 60:6; 63:2). *

HOMAM – ***hômām*** [masc. proper noun: הוֹמָם <1950>; from CONFUSE <2000>]: confusion, destruction ▶ **A king in the land of Edom.** Ref.: 1 Chr. 1:39. ¶

HOME – [1] Prov. 24:15 ➔ RESTING PLACE <7258> [2] Is. 34:13 ➔ ABODE <2681>.

HOME (BE AT) – Dan. 4:4 ➔ EASE (BE AT) <7954>.

HOME (HAVE ONE'S) – Dan. 4:21 ➔ DWELL <7932>.

HOME (KEEP AT, STAY AT) – Hab. 2:5 ➔ PRAISE (verb) <5115> a.

HOMEBORN – Ex. 12:49 ➔ NATIVE <249>.

HOMELESS – Is. 58:7 ➔ WANDERING <4788>.

HOMELESSNESS – Lam. 1:7 ➔ WANDERING <4788>.

HOMER – [1] ***ḥōmer*** [masc. noun: חֹמֶר <2563>; from RED (BE) <2560>] ▶ **This was a dry measure of barley or wheat.** Refs.: Lev. 27:16; Ezek. 45:13; Hos. 3:2. A dry homer equaled 354 dry quarts or 412 liquid quarts. Other refs.: Num. 11:32; Is. 5:10; Ezek. 45:11, 14. The Hebrew word also means MIRE, CLAY (see MIRE

<2563>), and a pile or heap [see HEAP (noun) <2563>]. ¶
– 2 Hos. 3:2 ➔ LETHECH <3963>.

HONEST – 1 Prov. 14:5 ➔ FAITHFUL <529> 2 Prov. 24:26 ➔ RIGHT <5228>.

HONESTY – Is. 59:14 ➔ RIGHT <5229>.

HONEY – ***d*^e*bas̆*** [masc. noun: דְּבַשׁ <1706>; from an unused root meaning to be gummy] ▶ **This word means the sweet substance produce by bees. It is combined often with milk (*ḥālāḇ*) to form the phrase milk and honey.** It is used literally but also stood for the richness and fertility of a land or country such as Canaan (Ex. 3:8, 17; 13:5; Lev. 20:24; Deut. 6:3; 11:9); for honey produced by bees (Judg. 14:8, 9, 18; 1 Sam. 14:25); sometimes in nests among rocks (Deut. 32:13; Ps. 81:16). It was a valuable trade article (Ezek. 27:17). It was not permitted as a burnt offering (Lev. 2:11). It is to the taste what wisdom is to life (Prov. 24:13). It is to be used only in moderation (Prov. 25:16, 27). The sweetness of God's law is like the sweetness of honey (Ps. 19:10); the sweetness of a lover's lips is like that of honey (Song 4:11). It is used figuratively as a metaphor for love (Song 5:1). *

HONEYCOMB – 1 ***ya*^a*rāh*** [fem. noun: יַעְרָה <3295>; fem. of FOREST <3293>] ▶ **a. This word refers to honey running from its comb as well as the honeycomb itself.** It is especially invigorating and gives a person quick energy (1 Sam. 14:27). ¶
b. The Hebrew word also refers to a forest. It is used in a metaphor in which the Lord's voice is so powerful that it lays low the trees and foliage of a forest (Ps. 29:9). ¶
2 ***nōpeṯ*** [fem. noun: נֹפֶת <5317>; from SPRINKLE <5130> in the sense of shaking to pieces] ▶ **This word means honey dripping from the comb.** It is used in parallel with honey and refers to the sweetest part of honey, the drippings (Ps. 19:10). It is used metaphorically, figuratively of the allurements of an adulteress' lips that drip honey (Prov. 5:3). Honey is symbolic of wisdom (Prov. 24:13). It is used in a good sense of the lips of one's wife that drip honey (Song 4:11). Other ref.: Prov. 27:7. ¶
3 ***ṣûp*** [masc. noun: צוּף <6688>; from FLOW OVER <6687>] ▶ **This word refers to a wax structure built by bees to house the honey they produce.** The honey from it is noted for its refreshing sweetness (Ps. 19:10; Prov. 16:24). ¶
– 4 Song 5:1 ➔ FOREST <3293>.

HONOR (noun) – 1 ***h*^a*ḏar*** [Aramaic masc. noun: הֲדַר <1923>; from HONOR (verb) <1922>] ▶ **This word means glory; it is also translated majesty.** In a meeting between Daniel and King Belshazzar, Daniel reminded Belshazzar that the Lord gave his father Nebuchadnezzar kingship, majesty, glory, and honor (Dan. 5:18). Other refs.: Dan. 4:30, 36. ¶
2 ***y*^e*qār*** [masc. noun: יְקָר <3366>; from PRECIOUS (BE) <3365>] ▶ **This word indicates splendor, value.** It indicates great value attached to something: lips that speak wisdom are more valuable than gold or jewels (Prov. 20:15: precious, rare). A monetary value can be called expensive or splendid (Zech. 11:13: price). The costly luxuries of a royal palace shows its splendor (Esther 1:4). In a figurative sense, the word refers to deference or respect, honor given to a person (Esther 1:20; 6:3, 6, 7, 11). An attitude of respect and appreciation can be shown to a people in general, i.e., the Jews (Esther 8:16). It refers to the valuables of a city in a collective sense, all of them together (Jer. 20:5: precious things, prized belongings, costly things, valuables; Ezek. 22:25: precious things). Other refs.: Esther 6:9; Job 28:10; Ps. 49:12, 20. ¶
3 ***y*^e*qār*** [Aramaic masc. noun: יְקָר <3367>; corresponding to <3366> above] ▶ **This word refers to glory, splendor.** It indicates an attitude of respect and great appreciation, sometimes recognized in an official way (Dan. 2:6). God is the ultimate giver of honor or glory (Dan. 2:37; 5:18, 20). A grave sin for humans is to attribute to themselves any honor or splendor from their labor and work (Dan. 4:30; 36). The Son of Man in Daniel 7 is granted great glory with a kingdom and special recognition from God Himself (Dan. 7:14). ¶

– [4] Job 30:15 ➔ DIGNITY <5082> [5] Prov. 14:28 ➔ GLORY <1927> [6] Mal. 1:6 ➔ FEAR (noun) <4172>.

HONOR (CLAIM) – Prov. 25:6 ➔ HONOR (verb) <1921>.

HONOR (TREAT WITH) – Gen. 30:20 ➔ DWELL <2082>.

HONOR (verb) – [1] ***h^{a}ḏûriym, hāḏar*** [verb: הֲדוּרִים, הָדַר <1921>; a prim. root] ▶ **This word means to respect, to venerate, to favor.** The Israelites were commanded not to show unjust bias toward the poor (Ex. 23:3: to show favoritism, to be partial, to countenance, to show partiality) and to honor older people (Lev. 19:32; also translated to fear). This did not always happen (Lam. 5:12; also translated to respect, to show respect), but Solomon said that a person should not honor himself (Prov. 25:6: to exalt, to claim honor). Isaiah used this word when he prophesied that the Lord would come dressed in glory (Is. 63:1: to be glorious, to be majestic). Other refs.: Lev. 19:15 (also translated to show favoritism); Is. 45:2. ¶

[2] ***h^{a}ḏar*** [Aramaic verb: הֲדַר <1922>; corresponding to <1921> above] ▶ **This verb means to glorify, to magnify.** Nebuchadnezzar built up Babylon to glorify himself until God took his power away and showed him who was sovereign. Then Nebuchadnezzar glorified God (Dan. 4:34, 37). Unfortunately, King Belshazzar did not learn from his ancestor's mistake and also decided to honor himself instead of God (Dan. 5:23). ¶

– [3] Gen. 30:20 ➔ DWELL <2082> [4] Esther 6:6, 7, 11 ➔ HONOR (noun) <3366>.

HONORABLE – [1] Ezra 4:10 ➔ NOBLE <3358> [2] Is. 32:5 ➔ RICH <7771> a.

HONORABLE, HONOURABLE – Is. 42:21 ➔ GLORIOUS <142>.

HOOF – [1] ***parsāh*** [fem. noun: פַּרְסָה <6541>; fem. of VULTURE <6538> (which is from DIVIDE <6536>)] ▶ **This word refers to the horny covering on the feet of ungulate animals.** It is sometimes used of the animal itself (Ex. 10:26; Lev. 11:3–7, 26; Deut. 14:6–8; Is. 5:28; Ezek. 32:13). Bronze hoofs are mentioned as weapons to pulverize the enemy (Mic. 4:13). The sound of horses' hoofs and people trampling the streets create dread and fear (Jer. 47:3; Ezek. 26:11). Tearing off, ripping off the hoofs of animals indicates violent ruthlessness (Zech. 11:16). ¶

– [2] Ps. 69:31 ➔ DIVIDE <6536>.

HOOK – [1] ***wāw*** [masc. noun: וָו <2053>; prob. a hook (the name of the sixth Hebrew letter)] ▶ **This word is used only in Exodus and indicates a nail, pin, or peg of some kind used to hang various hangings of the Tabernacle.** Some were of gold (Ex. 26:32, 37; 36:36); some of silver (Ex. 27:10, 11, 17; 38:10, 11). Other refs.: Ex. 36:38; 38:12, 17, 19, 28. ¶

[2] ***ḥāḥ*** [masc. noun: חָח <2397>; from the same as THORN <2336>] ▶ **This word normally indicates gold jewelry; it is also translated chain, bracelet, brooch.** It was used ironically as a hook to lead away prisoners of war (2 Kgs. 19:28; Ezek. 19:4, 9). It was among the sources of gold for the Tabernacle (Ex. 35:22). In a figurative sense, it refers to God's sovereign activity as He leads away the king of Assyria (Is. 37:29); Egypt (Ezek. 29:4); or Gog (Ezek. 38:4). ¶

[3] ***ḥakkāh*** [fem. noun: חַכָּה <2443>; prob. from WAIT <2442>] ▶ **This is a curved or bent piece of metal or wood used to catch and hold or to control something or someone.** Leviathan (Job 41:1); fish (Is. 19:8; NASB:, line; KJV: angle); prisoners of war (Hab. 1:15; KJV: angle). ¶

[4] ***ṣinnāh*** [fem. noun: צִנָּה <6793>; fem. of THORN <6791>] ▶

a. This word refers to a sharp instrument used to gouge and lead away prisoners. Ref.: Amos 4:2.

b. This word indicates a shield, a large shield, a buckler. It refers to a large, probably rectangular shield used in battle (1 Sam. 17:7, 41; 1 Kgs. 10:16; Jer. 46:3; Ezek. 23:24). Goliath's shield was carried

by someone for him. It is used figuratively often: God as a Shield (Ps. 5:12); of God as a Shield or a Warrior (Ps. 35:2); of God's faithfulness or truth as a shield (Ps. 91:4).
c. This word means cold, coolness. It refers to the impression given through the senses of something not hot, like ice or snow (Prov. 25:13). *
5 ***šᵉp̱attayim*** [masc. noun: שְׁפַתַּיִם <8240>; from ESTABLISH <8239>] ▶
a. A masculine noun indicating double-pronged pieces of metal. It refers to special meat forks used to handle sacrifices in Ezekiel's Temple (Ezek. 40:43).
b. A masculine dual noun referring to campfires. It refers to hot cooking stones (NASB, note) or campfires (KJV, pots) used in homes in Israel (Ps. 68:13).
c. A masculine dual noun meaning pots. This translation is given to the word by the KJV translators (Ps. 68:13).
d. A masculine dual noun indicating sheepfolds. This translation is given by many translators in Psalm 68:13. ¶
– 6 2 Chr. 33:11; Job 41:2 ➔ THORN <2336> 7 Job 41:2 ➔ ROPE <100> 8 Amos 4:2 ➔ THORN <5518> 9 Amos 4:2 ➔ THORN <6791>.

HOOPOE – ***dûḵiyp̱aṯ*** [fem. noun: דּוּכִיפַת <1744>; of uncertain deriv.] ▶ **This word refers to one of the birds that was unclean to Israel and therefore not to be eaten.** Refs.: Lev. 11:19; Deut. 14:18; also translated lapwing. ¶

HOP – Lev. 11:21 ➔ LEAP <5425>.

HOPE (noun) – 1 ***mabbāṭ*** [masc. noun: מַבָּט <4007>; from LOOK (verb) <5027>] ▶ **This word indicates expectation, an object of confidence.** It indicates the basis or goal of a person's hope. Israel put its hope in Cush and Egypt, not the Lord (Is. 20:5, 6). It indicates the object of hope even if it were a false hope (Zech. 9:5). ¶
2 ***miqwê', miqweh, qᵉwê', qᵉweh*** [masc. noun: מִקְוֵא, מִקְוֶה, קְוֵא, קְוֵה <4723>; from WAIT FOR <6960> (also in the sense of to hope for)] ▶ **This word means an object of expectation, confidence. It is used five times and is highly significant theologically. It is used twice as a designation for the Lord.** King David, shortly before he died, asserted that as for humans, their days were without any hope in this life (1 Chr. 29:15). But Jeremiah answered this challenge in the midst of drought, famine, and sword. Jeremiah cried out to the Lord, calling Him the Hope of Israel in parallel with Savior (Jer. 14:8). He also viewed the day of the Lord prophetically at a time when there was no positive outlook for Judah. Jeremiah asserted that the Lord was the only hope Judah had; to turn from Him would result in shame (Jer. 17:13).

Those who returned from exile and established the community found themselves near the brink of rejection, but one brave soul was moved to assert that there was still some hope for Israel to be spared (Ezra 10:2). The word has within its root meaning the thought of waiting for the Lord to act. Other ref.: Jer. 50:7. ¶
3 ***tôḥeleṯ*** [fem. noun: תּוֹחֶלֶת <8431>; from WAIT <3176>] ▶ **This word means and is also translated prospect, expectation.** It is found most often in the Wisdom Literature of Proverbs. Hope is associated with the prosperity of the righteous (Prov. 10:28; 11:7); and is seen as the spring from which the desire for life flows (Prov. 13:12). Jeremiah lamented that his soul was destitute because his hope in the Lord had perished (Lam. 3:18). Other refs.: Job 41:9; Ps. 39:7. ¶
4 ***tiqwāh*** [fem. noun: תִּקְוָה <8615>; from WAIT FOR <6960>] ▶ **This word refers to an attitude of anticipation with the expectation that something will happen, e.g., the hope of bearing a child.** Ref.: Ruth 1:12. A manner of life raises hope of certain consequences (Job 4:6). Because God cares for the oppressed and hopeless, even they have hope (Job 5:16; Ps. 9:18). Hope can be equivalent to a longing or a desire (Job 6:8). The righteous person's hope is ultimately and completely in God (Ps. 62:5); the same cannot be said of the wicked (Prov. 10:28). The fear of the Lord gives hope (Prov. 23:18). A self-conceited person or a person wise in his or her own thinking is more hopeless than a fool (Prov.

26:12). Even when they were in exile, God let His people know that He had a hope to give them, a positive future (Jer. 29:11). The hope for the success of Israel was lost in her captivity (Ezek. 19:5); but God gave Israel hope to return from there (Ezek. 37:11). Hosea speaks of Israel's recovery and hope of full restoration (Hos. 2:15; Zech. 9:12). For another meaning of the Hebrew word, see CORD <8615>. *
– [5] Eccl. 9:4 ➔ CONFIDENCE <986> [6] Job 8:14; 31:24; Ps. 78:7 ➔ LOINS <3689>.

HOPE (BE NO) – Is. 57:10; Jer. 2:25; 18:12 ➔ DESPAIR (verb) <2976>.

HOPE (verb) – [1] ***yāḥiyl*** [verb: יָחִיל <3175>; from WAIT <3176>] ▶ **This word occurs only in Lamentations 3:26 (KJV, NKJV), and its exact meaning is difficult to determine.** It could be derived from *yāḥal* (WAIT <3176>) and be an adjective meaning hopeful. Or it could also be a verb derived from *ḥûl* (SHAKE <2342>) and thus refer to waiting (cf. Ps. 37:7). In this case, the word might imply painful waiting as in childbirth, which would harmonize with the next verse. Whether hopefully or in pain (or both), the verse says it is good to wait in silence for the salvation of the Lord. ¶
[2] ***śēḇer*** [masc. noun: שֵׂבֶר <7664>; from WAIT <7663>] ▶ **This word indicates a feeling and a conviction that what one wants is going to come to pass.** In context it refers to a person's hope and expectation in God (Ps. 119:116; 146:5). ¶
– [3] Esther 9:1; Ps. 119:66; Is. 38:18 ➔ WAIT <7663> [4] Job 6:11; 13:15; Ps. 31:24; 33:18, 22; 38:15; 42:5, 11; etc. ➔ WAIT <3176>.

HOPELESS (BE) – Is. 57:10; Jer. 2:25; 18:12 ➔ DESPAIR (verb) <2976>.

HOPHNI – ***ḥopniy*** [masc. proper noun: חָפְנִי <2652>; from HAND <2651>]: strong, pugilist ▶ **A son of Eli; he served, with his brother Phinehas, as priest of the Lord at Shiloh.** They became wicked in their service at the Lord's altar and were slain as the Lord predicted (1 Sam. 2:34). They were in charge of the ark until it was captured and they were killed (1 Sam. 4:11). Other refs.: 1 Sam. 1:3; 4:4, 17. ¶

HOPHRA – Jer. 44:30 ➔ HAPHARAIM <2663> b.

HOR – ***hōr*** [proper noun: הֹר <2023>; another form for MOUNTAIN <2022>]: mountain ▶
a. A mountain near the border of Edom where Aaron was buried. Refs.: Num. 20:22–29. It was located in the area of Kadesh (Num. 33:37–39, 41). Other refs.: Num. 21:4; Deut. 32:50. ¶
b. A hill in northeastern Israel. Refs.: Num. 34:7, 8. It was a key marker for the northern border of Israel. It was probably in the northern part of the Lebanon Mountains. ¶

HOR HAGGIDGAD – ***ḥōr haggiḏgāḏ*** [proper noun: חֹר הַגִּדְגָּד <2735>; from HOLE <2356> and a collateral (masc.) form of GUDGODAH <1412>, with the art. interposed] ▶ **A place in the desert where the Israelites camped.** Refs.: Num. 33:32, 33. ¶

HORAM – ***hōrām*** [masc. proper noun: הֹרָם <2036>; from an unused root (meaning to tower up)]: elevated ▶ **King of Gezer in Canaan who was defeated and killed by Joshua.** Ref.: Josh. 10:33. ¶

HORDE – ***m^egammāh*** [fem. noun: מְגַמָּה <4041>; from the same as ALSO <1571> (properly, accumulation)] ▶ **The meaning of this word is uncertain, but it refers to the faces or advancement of the Babylonian army coming to attack Judah.** Ref.: Hab. 1:9. Totality or "all of" have been offered as meanings in context. ¶

HORDES – Ezek. 38:6, 9, 22; 39:4 ➔ TROOPS <102>.

HOREB – ***ḥōrēḇ*** [proper noun: חֹרֵב <2722>; from WASTE (LAY) <2717>]: dryness, desert ▶ **This word is another name for Mount**

Sinai where God gave the Law to the Israelites (SINAI <5514>). Refs.: Ex. 3:1; 17:6; 33:6; Deut. 1:2, 6, 19; 4:10, 15; 5:2; 9:8; 18:16; 29:1; 1 Kgs. 8:9; 19:8; 2 Chr. 5:10; Ps. 106:19; Mal. 4:4. ¶

HOREM – ***ḥ*°*rêm*** [proper noun: חֳרֵם <2765>; from DESTROY <2763> (in the sense of to devote)]: consecrated ▶ **A fortified city in the territory of Naphtali.** Ref.: Josh. 19:38. ¶

HORESH – 1 Sam. 23:15, 16, 18, 19 ➔ FOREST <2793>.

HORI – ***ḥôriy*** [masc. proper noun: חוֹרִי <2753>; the same as HORITE <2752>]: cave dweller ▶
a. Son of Lotan. Refs.: Gen. 36:22, 30 (KJV); 1 Chr. 1:39. ¶
b. A Simeonite. Ref.: Num. 13:5. ¶

HORITE – ***ḥōriy*** [masc. proper noun: חֹרִי <2752>; from HOLE <2356>]: cave dweller ▶ **Inhabitant of the hill country of Seir.** Refs.: Gen. 14:6; 36:20, 21, 29, 30 (ESV, NASB, NIV, NKJV); Deut. 2:12, 22. ¶

HORIZON – Job 26:10 ➔ to draw a circular horizon, to mark out the horizon ➔ CIRCLE (INSCRIBE A) <2328>.

HORMAH – ***ḥormāh*** [proper noun: חָרְמָה <2767>; from DESTROY <2763>]: destruction *or* devotion ▶ **The name of the city was originally Zephath. Judah and Simeon defeated its inhabitants, the Canaanites, and devoted it to destruction. So the name of the city was called Hormah.** See Judges 1:17. Other refs.: Num. 14:45; 21:3; Deut. 1:44; Josh. 12:14; 15:30; 19:4; 1 Sam. 30:30; 1 Chr. 4:30. ¶

HORN – [1] ***qeren, qarnayim*** [fem. noun: קֶרֶן, קַרְנַיִם <7161>; from HORNS (HAVE) <7160>] ▶
a. This word refers to the bony projections that grow out of the heads of various hoofed animals. Ref.: Gen. 22:13. But its meaning is expanded to refer to the horn-like protrusions on the corners or edges of altars, possibly representing strength, power (Ex. 27:2; Jer. 48:25); blood was applied to these horns during the use of the altar (Ex. 29:12). Iron horns were manufactured (1 Kgs. 22:11). Horns were used to make musical instruments, shophar, ram's horn, etc. (Josh. 6:5). The term describes strength, honor, rulership, dignity, fertility, descendants (1 Sam. 2:10); fertility, descendants (1 Sam. 2:1; Ps. 89:17); the power and source of salvation (2 Sam. 22:3). To raise up one's horn meant to act arrogantly, insolently (Ps. 75:4). The special anointing oil was sometimes kept in a horn, a container made of a hollowed-out horn (1 Kgs. 1:39). *
b. The Hebrew word also corresponds to Karnaim, a city located about twenty miles east of the Sea of Galilee. Ref.: Gen. 14:5. ¶
[2] ***qeren*** [Aramaic fem. noun: קְרַן <7162>; corresponding to <7161> above] ▶ **This word refers to a musical instrument made from a horn.** Refs.: Dan. 3:5, 7, 10, 15. A vision of a little horn will arise, representing a king (Dan. 7:7, 8, 11, 20, 21, 24). ¶
– [3] Ex. 21:29 ➔ to push with the horn, to thrust with the horn ➔ GORING <5056> [4] Num. 23:22; 24:8 ➔ STRENGTH <8443> b.

HORNED OWL – Lev. 11:16; Deut. 14:15; Job 30:29; Is. 13:21; 34:13; 43:20; Jer. 50:39; Mic. 1:8 ➔ OWL <3284>.

HORNED SNAKE – Gen. 49:17 ➔ VIPER <8207>.

HORNETS – ***ṣir'āh*** [coll. fem. noun: צִרְעָה <6880>; from LEPER (BE A) <6879>] ▶ **The term may be literal (a stinging wasp) or refer figuratively to the dread and fear that the Lord would put on the Canaanites.** Refs.: Ex. 23:28; Deut. 7:20; Josh. 24:12. ¶

HORNS (HAVE) – ***qāran*** [verb: קָרַן <7160>; a prim. root] ▶ **This word describes a young bull with horns (the permanent outgrowths on its head).** Such an animal was a choice sacrifice, but praise and thanksgiving is more pleasing to the

Lord (Ps. 69:31). For another meaning of the Hebrew word, see SHINE <7160>. ¶

HORONAIM – *ḥōrōnayim, ḥōrônayim* [proper noun: חֹרֹנַיִם, חוֹרוֹנַיִם <2773>; dual of a deriv. from HOLE <2356>]: two caverns ► **A city of Moab, possibly not far from Zoar.** Refs.: Is. 15:5; Jer. 48:3, 5, 34. ¶

HORONITE – *ḥōrōniy* [masc. proper noun: חֹרֹנִי <2772>; patrial from HORONAIM <2773>] ► **Designation of Sanballat who opposed Nehemiah in rebuilding the walls of Jerusalem.** Refs.: Neh. 2:10, 19; 13:28. ¶

HORRIBLE – Ps. 11:6 ➔ BURNING HEAT <2152>.

HORRIBLE THING – *ša^a^rûr, ša^a^rûrāh, ša^a^rûriy, ša^a^rûriyyāh* [fem. noun: שַׁעֲרוּר, שַׁעֲרוּרָה, שַׁעֲרוּרִי, שַׁעֲרוּרִיָּה <8186>; fem. from THINK <8176> in the sense of SWEEP AWAY <8175>] ► **This word is used to describe how bad the apostasy and apathy of the Israelites were; it is also translated shocking thing, appalling thing.** What they did in worshiping idols and prophesying falsely were truly horrible things in the eyes of God and the prophets who denounced them (Jer. 5:30; 23:14). There are two variant spellings of this word. One, *ša^a^rûriy-yāh*, is found in Hosea 6:10 and another, *ša^a^ruriṯ*, is found in Jeremiah 18:13. The uses of these variant spellings are exactly the same as the most common spelling. In every instance of the use of this word, it refers to the horror of the things that Israel was doing and the sins they were committing against the Lord. ¶

HORROR – [1] *za^a^wāh* [fem. noun: זַעֲוָה <2189>; by transposition from TERROR <2113>] ► **This word indicates a trembling, a terror.** It depicts Israel as an example of terror and horror before the nations because of the judgments the Lord will bring on her (Deut. 28:25; Jer. 15:4; 24:9; 29:18; 34:17). It refers to the acts of war and violence to which the Lord will deliver Israel (Ezek. 23:46). Other ref.: 2 Chr. 29:8. ¶

[2] *šimmāmôn* [masc. noun: שִׁמָּמוֹן <8078>; from DESTROYED (BE) <8074>] ► **This word refers to a state of shock and trepidation at what is happening; it is also translated dismay, dread, astonishment, despair.** In context it describes what was taking place in a besieged Jerusalem and land of Israel (Ezek. 4:16; 12:19). ¶

[3] *śa'ar* [masc. noun: שַׂעַר <8178>; from SWEEP AWAY <8175> (in the sense of to storm; by implication, to shiver), i.e., to fear)] ► **The horror described by the use of this noun is what people feel when witnessing the destruction that God allows to happen to evil people of this world.** In Job 18:20, it is said that people were seized with horror at the fate of an evil person. In Ezekiel 27:35 and 32:10, this word is used in the context of laments composed for the land of Tyre and Pharaoh of Egypt, who were both destroyed. When people see the destruction wrought on them, they are filled with horror at their fate. A less common use of this word holds the meaning of storm (Is. 28:2; NASB, ESV: tempest; NIV: wind). ¶

– [4] Gen. 15:12 ➔ TERROR <367> [5] Job 21:6; Ps. 55:5; Is. 21:4; Ezek. 7:18 ➔ TREMBLING <6427> [6] Ps. 119:53 ➔ BURNING HEAT <2152> [7] Jer. 15:4 ➔ TERROR <2113> [8] Jer. 48:39 ➔ RUIN (noun) <4288> [9] Jer. 49:16 ➔ TERROR <8606> [10] Ezek. 27:36; 28:19 ➔ TERROR <1091>.

HORROR, OBJECT OF HORROR – Ezek. 5:15 ➔ DESOLATION <4923>.

HORSE – [1] *sûs, sus* [masc. noun: סוּס, סֻס <5483>; from an unused root meaning to skip (properly, for joy)] ►

a. This Hebrew word is uniformly rendered as horse, the four-legged equine animal. It refers to any horse (Gen. 47:17; 49:17; Ex. 9:3). Horses were trained for special uses: chariotry and war (Ex. 14:9; 1 Kgs. 20:1; Is. 31:1; Ezek. 27:14). They were not to be multiplied by Israel's kings, but the kings were to trust the Lord for their might, not horses (Deut. 11:4; 17:16). *

b. A masculine noun referring to a swallow, a crane, a swift. This is the name of

a bird. It refers to a small, swift-flying type of bird, a swift or a swallow (Is. 38:14; Jer. 8:7). Understanding the word to refer to a crane is difficult. ¶
2 ***reḵeš*** [masc. noun: רֶכֶשׁ <7409>; from ACCUMULATE <7408> (in the sense of a relay of animals on a post-route; as stored up for that purpose)] ▶
a. This word means a horse, a steed. It refers to a pair or team of horses (1 Kgs. 4:28; Mic. 1:13); specially bred royal horses (Esther 8:10, 14).
b. This word is rendered as dromedaries, camels by some translators. They were camels trained for speed and efficiency in transport (1 Kgs. 4:28).
c. This word means a mule. It is rendered as mules, common royal possessions in the ancient Middle East (KJV, Esther 8:10, 14).
d. This word refers to a swift beast. It implies a chariot horse trained to pull a chariot with great speed (Mic. 1:13). ¶

HORSEFLY – Jer. 46:20 ➔ DESTRUCTION <7171>.

HORSELEACH – Prov. 30:15 ➔ LEECH <5936>.

HORSEMEN – 1 ***pārāš*** [masc. noun: פָּרָשׁ <6571>; from SCATTER <6567> (in the case of horses, as stretched out to a vehicle, not single nor for mounting)] ▶
This word also refers to cavalry. It is usually used to refer to a rider, a horseman, serving in a military capacity. Refs.: Gen. 50:9; Ex. 14:9, 17, 18, 23, 26, 28. It is often listed along with chariotry (Ex. 15:9; Josh. 24:6). It is employed in a powerful metaphor. When Elisha saw «a chariot of fire and horses of fire» with a whirlwind taking Elijah up, Elisha cried out «the chariots and horsemen of Israel,» their true army and defense (2 Kgs. 2:12); and of Elisha (2 Kgs. 13:14). It sometimes stands for horses (Is. 28:28; Ezek. 27:14; Joel 2:4). *
– 2 2 Kgs. 9:17 ➔ DRIVER OF A CHARIOT <7395>.

HORSES (COMPANY OF) – Song 1:9 ➔ MARE <5484>.

HOSAH – ***ḥōsāh*** [proper noun: חֹסָה <2621>; from REFUGE <2620>]: refuge ▶
a. A Levite, gatekeeper in the time of David. Refs.: 1 Chr. 16:38; 26:10, 11, 16. ¶
b. A location near the border in Asher. Ref.: Josh. 19:29. ¶

HOSE – Dan. 3:21 ➔ TROUSERS <6361>.

HOSHAMA – 1 ***hôšāmā'*** [masc. proper noun: הוֹשָׁמָע <1953>; from LORD <3068> and HEAR <8085>]: the Lord has heard ▶
A son of King Jeconiah. Ref.: 1 Chr. 3:18. ¶
2 ***hôša'yāh*** [masc. proper noun: הוֹשַׁעְיָה <1955>; from SAVE <3467> and LORD <3050>]: the Lord has saved, the Lord has heard ▶
a. A prince of Judah. Ref.: Neh. 12:32. ¶
b. The father of Jezaniah. Refs.: Jer. 42:1; 43:2. ¶

HOSHEA – ***hôšēa'*** [masc. proper noun: הוֹשֵׁעַ <1954>; from SAVE <3467>]: deliverance, salvation ▶
a. The name borne by Joshua before it was changed. Refs.: Num. 13:8; 16. His father was Nun. Other ref.: Deut. 32:44. ¶
b. The last king of Israel. He was considered evil, as were all the kings of northern Israel. Ref.: 2 Kgs. 15:30. He assassinated his predecessor Pekah, son of Remaliah. He was king when Israel went into exile in 722 B.C. He reigned nine years and was eventually put into prison by Shalmaneser, the Assyrian king (727–722 B.C.). Other refs.: 2 Kgs. 17:1, 3, 4, 6; 18:1, 9, 10. ¶
c. The prophet who prophesied in northern Israel in the central years of the eighth century B.C. He warned Israel of God's coming judgments by the Assyrians. Little is known about him. He was from northern Israel, the son of a man named Beeri (Hos. 1:1). He prophesied under several kings (Hos. 1:1, 2), but his message was primarily to the northern kingdom. He lived during the troublesome times of the last days of northern Israel, which was destroyed in 722 B.C. ¶
d. The name of a leader in Ephraim. He was the son of Azaziah (1 Chr. 27:20). ¶

e. The name of a leader of those who returned from exile. Ref.: Neh. 10:23. He supported Nehemiah's reforms. ¶

HOSTAGE – ***ta'ᵃrûḇāh*** [fem. noun: תַּעֲרוּבָה <8594>; from PLEDGE (BE A) <6148> (in the sense of to take as a guarantee)] ▶ **This word refers to a person taken in time of war in context and kept in the power of the conquering nation.** Refs.: 2 Kgs. 14:14; 2 Chr. 25:24. ¶

HOSTILE – Lev. 26:21, 23, 24, 27, 28, 40, 41 ➔ HOSTILITY <7147>.

HOSTILITY – [1] ***qeriy*** [masc. noun: קְרִי <7147>; from HAPPEN <7136> a.] ▶ **This word means opposition, contrariness; it is also translated contrary, hostile.** It is used with the verb *halaḵ* to mean to walk, to act with hostility (Lev. 26:21, 23, 24, 27, 40, 41). It is used with *ḥamāh* to mean with anger, hostility, extreme hostility (Lev. 26:28). ¶
[2] ***maśṭêmāh*** [fem. noun: מַשְׂטֵמָה <4895>; from the same as WHIP <7850>] ▶ **This word means strong opposition; it also describes hatred.** In context it indicates an attitude and state of animosity and rejection, especially toward God's prophets and spokesmen (Hos. 9:7, 8). ¶
– [3] Ps. 39:10 ➔ OPPOSITION <8409> [4] Ezek. 25:15; 35:5 ➔ ENMITY <342>.

HOSTS – See SERVICE <6635>.

HOT – [1] Ex. 11:8 ➔ FIERCE <2750> [2] Josh. 9:12; Job 37:17 ➔ WARM <2525> [3] Jer. 4:11 ➔ DAZZLING <6703> [4] Dan. 3:22: to be hot, to make hot ➔ HEAT (verb) <228>.

HOT (BE) – Lam. 5:10 ➔ YEARN <3648>.

HOT COAL – ***riṣpāh*** [fem. noun: רִצְפָּה <7531>; fem. of BAKED ON COALS <7529>] ▶ **This word refers to a coal (a black rock used as combustible) that is still actively burning, live, capable of being used for cooking, heating, etc.** It indicates a cooking fuel (1 Kgs. 19:6); and is used in a symbolic manner to remove uncleanness from a prophet's lips, purging Isaiah for his mission (Is. 6:6). For another meaning of the Hebrew word, see PAVEMENT <7531>. ¶

HOT SPRINGS – Gen. 36:24 ➔ MULE <3222> b.

HOT-TEMPERED – Prov. 19:19 ➔ GREAT <1632>.

HOTHAM – ***ḥôṯām*** [masc. proper noun: חוֹתָם <2369>; the same as SEAL (noun) <2368>]: seal, signet ring ▶
a. An inhabitant of Aroer, probably a town of Judah. Two of his sons were among the mighty men of David (1 Chr. 11:44). ¶
b. An Israelite of the tribe of Asher. Ref.: 1 Chr. 7:32. ¶

HOTHIR – ***hôṯiyr*** [masc. proper noun: הוֹתִיר <1956>; from REMAIN <3498> (in the sense of to have more than enough)]: fullness ▶ **A son of Heman. Hothir's father Heman was the king's seer and a supervisor of the music for the Temple of the Lord. Hothni was under his father's direction for music.** Refs.: 1 Chr. 25:4, 28. ¶

HOUR – Dan. 3:6, 15; 4:19, 33; 5:5 ➔ IMMEDIATELY <8160>.

HOUSE – [1] ***bayiṯ*** [masc. noun: בַּיִת <1004>; prob. from BUILD <1129> abbreviated] ▶ **This word means a building where people live. It also means dwelling, family, temple, palace.** It is used basically to denote a building in which a family lives (Deut. 20:5) but can also refer to the family or household itself (Gen. 15:2; Josh. 7:14; 24:15). It often is used of a clan such as "house of Aaron" (Ps. 115:10, 12; 118:3). Sometimes it means palace or dynasty when employed in the Hebrew phrase "house of the king" (Gen. 12:15; 1 Kgs. 4:6; Jer. 39:8). When the Old Testament speaks of the house of the Lord, it obviously refers to the Temple or Tabernacle (Ex. 23:19; Dan. 1:2). The word is also found in place names: Bethel, meaning "house of God" (Gen. 12:8); Beth Shemesh, meaning "house of the sun" (Josh. 15:10); and Bethlehem, meaning "house of bread" (Gen. 35:19). *

2 ***bayiṯ*** [Aramaic masc. noun: בַּיִת <1005>; corresponding to <1004> above] ▶ **This word refers to a temple, a royal residence.** It has in mind a palace (Dan. 4:4). In combination with other words, it takes on the meaning of royal treasury (Ezra 6:4); royal residence (Dan. 4:30); banquet hall (Dan. 5:10); treasure house (Ezra 5:17); archives (Ezra 6:1; KJV, house of rolls [scrolls]). It refers to the Temple often (Ezra 4:24; 7:23; Dan. 5:3, 23) as the house of God. *

HOUSEHOLD – Gen. 26:14; Job 1:3 ➔ SERVANTS <5657>.

HOUSEHOLD IDOL – ***tᵉrāp̱iym*** [masc. plur. noun: תְּרָפִים <8655>; plur. from HEAL <7495>] ▶ **This word means domestic gods, cultic objects, teraphim. This word refers to the kind of idols or objects of worship whose ownership was possibly tied to inheritance rights. They were employed in divination.** Rachel stole these objects from her father Laban for some reason not entirely clear to us now, but they were probably not tied to ancestor worship (Gen. 31:19, 34). These objects seemed to have had the shape of persons. But in one case, the word refers to something larger than the objects Rachel stole from Laban (1 Sam. 19:13, 16). Some have suggested that the teraphim used here were old pieces of cloth. The word refers to idols owned by Micah during the time of the judges (Judg. 17:5).

These objects are more strongly condemned in other passages: the wickedness of consulting teraphim is asserted in 1 Samuel 15:23 (see Ezek. 21:21; Zech. 10:2). Josiah cast them out when he got rid of the mediums and spiritists, literally, the ghosts and familiar spirits (2 Kgs. 23:24). *

HOVER – ***rāḥap̱*** [verb: רָחַף <7363>; a prim. root] ▶ **This word means to float in the air, to move, to tremble.** In a participial form, it describes God's Spirit hovering over the great waters at the beginning of God's creative acts (Gen. 1:2). It describes an eagle hovering over her young. It indicates the shaking or trembling of a person's bones because of fear and anxiety (Jer. 23:9). Other ref.: Deut. 32:11; also translated to flutter. ¶

HOW – ***hêyḵ*** [interr. adv.: הֵיךְ <1963>; another form for HOW?, HOW! <349>] ▶ **David used this word to ask how, in what way, he could move the ark of God to Jerusalem.** Ref.: 1 Chr. 13:12. It asks how it was possible for a divine being to communicate with Daniel (Dan. 10:17). ¶

HOW LONG – Ex. 10:3, 7; Num. 14:27; etc. ➔ WHEN <4970>.

HOW?, HOW! – ***'êyḵ, 'êyḵāh, 'êyḵāḵāh*** [interr. adv.: אֵיךְ, אֵיכָה, אֵיכָכָה <349>; prolonged from WHERE <335>] ▶

a. The Hebrew word is translated this way uniformly, but its connotation can be slightly different according to context. It can hint or connote doubt (Gen. 44:8); reproach (Judg. 16:15); mourning (2 Sam. 1:19); assertiveness (Jer. 3:19). *

b. The word connotes what? Ref.: 2 Kgs. 6:15. It functions rhetorically (Deut. 1:12). It further expresses mourning, reproach, where (Is. 1:21; Jer. 8:8). It functions in some cases as a technical literary word introducing a dirge (Is. 1:21). *

c. This word indicates a psychological impossibility. Refs.: Esther 8:6; Song 5:3. ¶

HOWEVER – See NEVERTHELESS <1297>.

HOWL – Is. 14:31; Mic. 1:8; etc. (KJV) ➔ WAIL (verb) <3213>.

HOWLING – 1 ***yᵉlêl*** [masc. noun: יְלֵל <3214>; from WAIL (verb) <3213>] ▶ **This word describes a crying or wailing of beasts.** It is used to depict the sounds and desolation of a wilderness or desert area (Deut. 2:10). ¶

– [2] Is. 15:8; Jer. 25:36; Zeph. 1:10; Zech. 11:3 ➔ WAIL (noun) <3215>.

HOZAI – ***ḥôzay*** [masc. proper noun: חוֹזָי <2335>; from SEER <2374>] ▶ **A professional title for a group of seers or prophets.** Ref.: 2 Chr. 33:19, NASB, NKJV. Some simply translate it as seers (ESV, KJV, NIV). ¶

HUB – ***ḥiššûr*** [masc. noun: חִשּׁוּר <2840>; from an unused root meaning to bind together] ▶ **This word refers to the center part of a wheel, the part normally fastened to the end of an axle.** These hubs were a part of the decorative great brass sea built by Solomon (1 Kgs. 7:33). ¶

HUBBAH – 1 Chr. 7:34 ➔ JEHUBBAH <3160>.

HUDDLE AROUND – Job 24:8 ➔ EMBRACE <2263>.

HUG – Job 24:8 ➔ EMBRACE <2263>.

HUGE – ***geᵉlāl*** [Aramaic adj.: גְּלָל <1560>; from a root corresponding to ROLL (verb) <1556>] ▶ **Properly, this word means rolling, hence (of) a considerable weight or size; it is also translated great, heavy, large.** It indicates literal stones that had to be rolled, i.e., larger stones or blocks of stones (Ezra 5:8; 6:4). ¶

HUKKOK – ***ḥuqōq*** [proper noun: חֻקֹק <2712>; from ENGRAVE <2710>] ▶
a. A location in Naphtali. Ref.: Josh. 19:34. ¶
b. Another name for *ḥelqāṯ* (HELKATH <2520>). Ref.: 1 Chr. 6:75. ¶

HUL – ***ḥûl*** [masc. proper noun: חוּל <2343>; from SHAKE <2342>]: circle ▶ **The second son of Aram.** Refs.: Gen. 10:23; 1 Chr. 1:17. ¶

HULDAH – ***ḥuldāh*** [fem. proper noun: חֻלְדָּה <2468>; fem. of WEASEL <2467>]: weasel ▶ **A prophetess, the wife of Shallum, who prophesied during the reign of Josiah.** She spoke a word of grace concerning the king of Judah, Josiah (2 Kgs. 22:18). Hilkiah and others sought her out and then reported her message to Josiah. She read the Book of the Law they brought to her and called forth the judgments written in it (2 Kgs. 22:14–20; 2 Chr. 34:22). ¶

HUMAN COMPANY, HUMAN SOCIETY – Job 30:5 ➔ COMMUNITY <1457>.

HUMBLE – [1] ***ʿānāw*** [adj.: עָנָו <6035>; from AFFLICTED (BE) <6031>] ▶ **This word means poor, oppressed, afflicted. It is used of persons who put themselves after others in importance; persons who are not proud, haughty, supercilious, self-assertive, persons low in rank or position.** Moses in the Old Testament is the prototype of the humble man before God and other human beings (Num. 12:3; also translated meek), but he was not poor or low in rank. The word also refers to persons who are poor, afflicted, low in societal standing, oppressed (Job 24:4; Ps. 10:12, 17; 22:26). God favors the humble or meek to inherit the land, to be blessed (Ps. 37:11); God gives help and grace to the afflicted (Prov. 3:34). A humble or contrite spirit is of great value (Prov. 16:19). God will finally give justice to the poor (Is. 11:4). The poor were oppressed by the rich and the immoral (Amos 2:7). *

[2] ***šaḥ*** [adj.: שַׁח <7807>; from BOW DOWN <7817>] ▶ **This word refers to a person who is not overly proud, overly self-assertive, possibly low in rank but not necessarily so.** It is a person who does not flaunt his or her abilities or achievements before others and, especially, is lowly and meek before God (Job 22:29; also translated lowly, downcast). ¶

[3] ***šāp̱āl*** [adj.: שָׁפָל <8217>; from HUMBLE, HUMBLE (MAKE) <8213>] ▶ **This word means low, lower, meek.** It refers to a tree being low (Ezek. 17:24) but often refers in a figurative way to low social positions (2 Sam. 6:22). It describes a short tree or a shrub in a parable (Ezek. 17:6). It has the sense of a humble, despondent, meek, or contrite spirit (Is. 57:15). *

– [4] Job 8:7 ➔ LITTLE ONE <4705>.

HUMBLE, HUMBLE (MAKE) – 1 ***šāp̱al*** [masc. noun: שָׁפֵל <8213>; a prim. root] ▶ **This word means to feel less important; also to humiliate, to bring down. It indicates that something is low, sinking down.** It is used literally/figuratively of bringing down trees representing the powerful, influential people of a society (Is. 10:33); of humbling persons (Is. 2:9; 5:15); even a city (Is. 32:19). It describes one's being humiliated, placed lower (Prov. 25:7; 29:23; Jer. 13:18). It describes a sound as being low (Eccl. 12:4). In its causative sense, it means to bring down (Ezek. 17:24); to lay something low (Is. 25:12); to put lower (Prov. 25:7); to humiliate (1 Sam. 2:7). God lowers or humbles Himself to observe the things of earth (Ps. 113:6). *
2 ***šᵉp̱al*** [Aramaic verb: שְׁפַל <8214>; corresponding to <8213> above] ▶ **This word means to bring down, to subdue.** It describes figuratively the bringing down or making humble the prideful person (Dan. 4:37); of humbling anyone whom God desires to humble (Dan. 5:19). Persons can humble themselves (Dan. 5:22). In a context of war, it may mean to overcome, to defeat, to subdue (Dan. 7:24). ¶

HUMBLE (BE) – 1 ***ṣānaʿ, ṣānûaʿ*** [צָנַע, צָנוּעַ <6800>; a prim. root] ▶
a. A verb used to describe those who are meek and act meekly. They are not arrogant, boastful (Prov. 11:2), especially before the Lord (Mic. 6:8).
b. A masculine noun indicating humility. Some translators take the forms of the word in the text as nouns, referring to a person in a state of humility, meekness (Prov. 11:2) and living accordingly (Mic. 6:8: humbly). ¶
– 2 See SUBDUE <3665>.

HUMBLE PLACE – Eccl. 10:6 ➔ LOW PLACE <8216>.

HUMBLE (verb) – 1 Ps. 68:30; Prov. 6:3 ➔ SUBMIT <7511> 2 See SUBDUE <3665>.

HUMBLED (BE) – Lam. 3:20 ➔ BOW DOWN <7743> a.

HUMBLY – Mic. 6:8 ➔ HUMBLE (BE) <6800> b.

HUMILIATED (BE) – Deut. 25:3 ➔ DESPISED (BE) <7034>.

HUMILIATING – Judg. 18:7 ➔ RESTRAINT <6114>.

HUMILIATION – 1 Is. 32:19 ➔ LOW PLACE <8218> 2 Jer. 23:40 ➔ SHAME <3640>.

HUMILITY – 1 ***ʿanwāh*** [fem. noun: עֲנָוָה <6037>; from HUMBLE <6035>] ▶ **This word refers to qualities of meekness, modesty, mildness, and patience.** It is appropriate for the king over God's people, along with truth and righteousness (Ps. 45:4). ¶
2 ***ʿnāwāh*** [fem. noun: עֲנָוָה <6038>; from HUMBLE <6035>] ▶ **This word indicates patience, mildness, tenderness; it is also translated gentleness, help, meekness.** These characteristics of God foster growth in His king, David (Ps. 18:35). It is found in Psalm 45:4, but see HUMILITY <6037> also. It indicates an attitude of humility that brings a person honor (Prov. 15:33; 18:12; 22:4); and possibly mercy in the day of judgment (Zeph. 2:3). Other ref.: 2 Sam. 22:36. ¶
– 3 Prov. 11:2 ➔ HUMBLE (BE) <6800> b.

HUMP – ***dabbešet*** [fem. noun: דַּבֶּשֶׁת <1707>; intens. from the same as HONEY <1706>] ▶ **This word denotes the bump on the back of a camel; it is also translated bunch, back.** It depicts the hump as a place where embassaries carried their treasures for tribute or for other reasons to various nations (Is. 30:6). ¶

HUMTAH – ***ḥumṭāh*** [proper noun: חֻמְטָה <2547>; fem. of SAND LIZARD <2546>]: low ▶ **A city in Judah.** Ref.: Josh 15:54. ¶

HUNCHBACK – ***gibbên*** [adj.: גִּבֵּן <1384>; from an unused root meaning to be arched or contracted] ▶ **This word**

describes a person with an abnormally curved or bent back. This condition disqualified a descendant of Aaron from serving at the Lord's altar (Lev. 21:20; KJV: crookbackt). ¶

HUNDRED – [1] ***mê'āh*** [fem. noun: מֵאָה <3967>; a prim. numeral] ▶ **This word means one hundred and may precede or follow a noun.** Refs.: Gen. 5:3; 17:17. In its dual form, it means two hundred, e.g., *mā'tayim 'îš*, two hundred men (1 Sam. 18:27). In its plural form *me'ôṯ*, it combines with other words to mean, e.g., three hundred, *šelōš me'ôṯ* (Judg. 15:4). Military units could be made up of hundreds (1 Sam. 29:2). *
[2] ***me'āh*** [Aramaic fem. noun: מְאָה <3969>; corresponding to <3967> above] ▶ **This word is used to indicate a hundred of something, often with other numbers to give exact figures.** Refs.: Ezra 6:17; 7:22; Dan. 6:1. In its dual form *mā'ṯayin*, it indicates two hundred (Ezra 6:17). ¶
– [3] Neh. 3:1; 12:39 ➔ MEAH <3968>.

HUNDREDFOLD – ***ša'ar*** [masc. noun: שַׁעַר <8180>; from THINK <8176> in its original sense of to split or open (thus indicating a measure as a section)] ▶ **This word indicates a huge increase in the yield of crops or produce from a field or land.** Ref.: Gen. 26:12. ¶

HUNGER – [1] ***rā'āḇ*** [masc. noun: רָעָב <7458>; from HUNGRY (BE) <7456>] ▶ **This word means starvation, famine. It refers to a general and acute failure of crops, a serious shortage of food, and/or water.** Canaan often experienced famines (Gen. 12:10; 26:1); but Egypt also suffered cycles of famine (Gen. 41:27, 30, 31). The word also refers to hunger itself, a strong need for certain kinds of food (Ex. 16:3; Deut. 28:48). God can and does preserve a person in time of famine (Job 5:20; Ps. 33:19). Famine or hunger can be the punishment or discipline of God on His people (Is. 5:13). It is one of the three judgments of God often mentioned together (Jer. 32:24), sword, famine, and pestilence. Amos mentions a famine of the Word of God, not food, that the Lord will send (Amos 8:11). *
– [2] Job 30:3 ➔ FAMINE <3720> [3] Mic. 6:14 ➔ CASTING DOWN <3445>.

HUNGRY – ***rā'êḇ*** [adj.: רָעֵב <7457>; from HUNGRY (BE) <7456>] ▶ **This word describes a state of craving, needing food. It also means famished.** It indicates the perpetual poor of the land who are in constant hunger, lacking enough food and care (1 Sam. 2:5); often lacking rest and water as well (2 Sam. 17:29). It was a common condition in the siege of a city (2 Kgs. 7:12). The wicked will suffer from hunger (Job 18:12). The Lord delivers from hunger (Ps. 107:5, 9, 36). The famous saying in Proverbs 25:21 urges people to feed hungry enemies. Hunger can cause a person to dream (Is. 29:8). A hungry person finds even bitter food to be enjoyable (Prov. 27:7). A righteous person helps feed the hungry (Ezek. 18:7, 16). *

HUNGRY (BE) – [1] ***rā'êḇ*** [verb: רָעֵב <7456>; a prim. root] ▶ **This word indicates that a person has a serious lack of food. It also means to be famished.** It describes an entire nation during a time of famine (Gen. 41:55). Israel suffered from hunger in the wilderness (Deut. 8:3). It indicates the hunger of lions (Ps. 34:10). God does not hunger as people do (Ps. 50:12). It is used of Israel, a people famished from hunger (Is. 8:21). God, however, cares for the hunger of His servants (Is. 65:13). *
– [2] Ps. 17:12 ➔ LONG FOR <3700>.

HUNT – [1] ***ṣûḏ, ṣiyḏ*** [verb: צוּד, צִיד <6679>; a prim. root (in the sense of to lie alongside, i.e., in wait)] ▶
a. This word means to chase animals, to ensnare. It describes hunting animals for food (Gen. 27:3, 5, 33; Job 10:16); including birds (Lev. 17:13; Lam. 3:52). It is used figuratively of hunting people, ensnaring them (Job 10:16; Mic. 7:2); of evil pursuing violent men (Ps. 140:11). An adulteress hunts down her prey (Prov. 6:26). It describes hunting down and catching, snaring souls (Ezek. 13:18, 20). ¶

b. This word means to take as provisions. It refers to taking along food provisions for a long journey, to prepare food provisions (Josh. 9:12, see c. below). It is used in the reflexive form in this verse. The verb is considered to be from the basic stem *ṣûḏ.* ¶
c. This word means to take as provisions. It means to pack and prepare food for taking on a long journey (Josh. 9:12, see b. above). Some consider the verb to be *ṣîḏ,* not *ṣûḏ,* its basic form. ¶
– [2] 1 Sam. 24:11 ➔ LIE IN WAIT <6658> [3] Job 18:2 ➔ SNARE (noun) <7078> a.

HUNT DOWN – Gen. 31:36; Ps. 10:2 ➔ BURN (verb) <1814>.

HUNTER – ***ṣayyāḏ*** [masc. noun: צַיָּד <6719>; from the same as FOOD <6718>] ▶ **This word refers to a person who tracks down and kills game.** It is used metaphorically of the hunters the Lord would send against His people to judge them (Jer. 16:16). ¶

HUPHAM – ***ḥûpām*** [masc. proper noun: חוּפָם <2349>; from the same as COAST <2348>]: protection ▶ **An Israelite of the tribe of Benjamin.** Ref.: Num. 26:39. ¶

HUPHAMITE – ***ḥûpamiy*** [masc. proper noun: חוּפָמִי <2350>; patron. from HUPHAM <2349>] ▶ **A descendant of Hupham.** Ref.: Num. 26:39. ¶

HUPPAH – ***ḥuppāh*** [masc. proper noun: חֻפָּה <2647>; the same as CHAMBER <2646>]: canopy, protection ▶ **Descendant of Aaron, head of the fourteenth sacerdotal course.** Ref.: 1 Chr. 24:13. ¶

HUPPIM – ***ḥuppiym, ḥuppim*** [masc. proper noun: חֻפִּים, חֻפִּם <2650>; plur. of CHAMBER <2646> (comp. HUPHAM <2349>)]: protection ▶ **One of the sons or descendants of Benjamin.** Refs.: Gen. 46:21; 1 Chr. 7:12, 15. ¶

HUR – ***ḥûr*** [masc. proper noun: חוּר <2354>; the same as WHITE <2353> or HOLE <2352>]: whiteness ▶
a. Companion of Aaron. Refs.: Ex. 17:10, 12; 24:14. ¶
b. A Judaite. Refs.: Ex. 31:2; 35:30; 38:22; 1 Chr. 2:19, 20, 50; 4:1, 4; 2 Chr. 1:5. ¶
c. A Midianite king. Refs.: Num. 31:8; Josh. 13:21. ¶
d. Officer of Solomon. Ref.: 1 Kgs. 4:8. ¶
e. The father of Rephaiah. Ref.: Neh. 3:9. ¶

HURAI – ***ḥûray*** [masc. proper noun: חוּרַי <2360>; prob. an orthographical variation for HURI <2359>]: linen-weaver ▶ **One of David's mighty men.** Ref.: 1 Chr. 11:32. ¶

HURAM – See HIRAM <2361>.

HURI – ***ḥûriy*** [masc. proper noun: חוּרִי <2359>; prob. from WHITE <2353>]: linen-weaver ▶ **An Israelite of the tribe of Gad.** Ref.: 1 Chr. 5:14. ¶

HURL – [1] Ex. 15:1, 21 ➔ THROW <7411> [2] Is. 22:17 ➔ CAPTIVITY <2925> [3] Jer. 10:18; 1 Sam. 25:29 ➔ SLING (verb) <7049>.

HURL AWAY – [1] Job 27:21 ➔ SWEEP AWAY <8175> [2] Is. 22:17 ➔ WRAP AROUND <5844> b.

HURRIEDLY – [1] Prov. 20:21: to gain hurriedly ➔ ABHOR <973> [2] Dan. 2:25 ➔ HASTE (BE IN) <927>.

HURRY (BE IN A) – 2 Chr. 26:20; Eccl. 8:3 ➔ TERRIFIED <926>.

HURRY (verb) – [1] ***dāḥap̱*** [verb: דָּחַף <1765>; a prim. root] ▶ **This word indicates doing something quickly, in haste; it is also translated to hasten, to rush.** Haman hurried to his house, mourning and with his head covered (Esther 6:12). Other refs.: 2 Chr. 26:20; Esther 3:15; 8:14. ¶
[2] ***ḥāpaz*** [verb: חָפַז <2648>; a prim. root] ▶ **This word indicates to hasten, also to fear, to flee.** It refers to hurrying away in haste or fear (2 Sam. 4:4: to make haste, to hurry, haste, hurry) or in military flight (1 Sam. 23:26: to hurry, to make haste; 2 Kgs. 7:15: haste, headlong flight).

Behemoth does not react in haste and fear to anything (Job 40:23: to be alarmed, to be disturbed, to be frightened, to hasten) nor become alarmed. It describes in figurative language how flood waters went down quickly at the Lord's command (Ps. 104:7: to hasten, to hurry, to take flight). Other refs.: Deut. 20:3; Ps. 31:32; 48:5; 116:11. ¶
3 ***māhar*** [verb: מָהַר <4116>; a prim. root] ▶ **This word means to do more quickly, to hasten.** It has the sense always of doing something quickly, in a hurry, hastily, or even rashly because of being in haste: to hasten to a location (Gen. 18:6); to modify any other verb adverbially in its performance (Gen. 19:22; 24:18; Ex. 2:18; 1 Sam. 23:27; 1 Kgs. 22:9); the infinitive *mahêr* is used various times as an adverb (Ex. 32:8); *lᵉmahêr* indicates haste (Ex. 12:33; 1 Chr. 12:8). Used of counsel, it means rash, headlong advice that is quickly and easily hindered (Job 5:13). In its participial form, it indicates persons who speak hastily, too quickly (Is. 32:4; Hab. 1:6). Used with *lêb*, heart, it refers to an agitated heart full of anxiety (Is. 35:4). *
– 4 Josh. 10:13 ➔ HASTEN <213> 5 Judg. 20:37; Ps. 55:8 ➔ HASTEN <2363> 6 Dan. 6:19 ➔ HASTE (BE IN) <927>.

HURT – 1 ***'āṣaḇ*** [verb: עָצַב <6087>; a prim. root] ▶ **This word means to pain, to grieve, to shape, to fashion.** This word has two separate meanings. The first meaning deals with physical pain (Eccl. 10:9); emotional pain (1 Sam. 20:34); or some combination of physical and emotional pain (1 Chr. 4:10). The word is also used of David's inaction when Adonijah attempted to usurp the throne (1 Kgs. 1:6). The second meaning generally refers to creative activity, such as the kind God exercised when He created human bodies (Job 10:8: to make, to fashion, to shape); or the creative activity of people (Jer. 44:19). In both these instances, the word occurs in parallel with the word *'āśāh* <6213>, which means to make or to do. *
– 2 Gen. 4:23 ➔ BRUISE (noun) <2250> 3 Ex. 21:22, 35 ➔ SMITE <5062> 4 Ezra 4:22 ➔ DAMAGE (verb) <5142> 5 Dan. 3:25; 6:23 ➔ DAMAGE (noun) <2257> 6 Dan. 6:22 ➔ WRONG (noun) <2248> 7 Zech. 12:3 ➔ CUT (verb) <8295>.

HURTFUL – Ezra 4:15 ➔ DAMAGE (verb) <5142>.

HURTING – Gen. 4:23 ➔ BRUISE (noun) <2250>.

HUSBAND – 1 Ex. 4:25, 26 ➔ SON-IN-LAW <2860> 2 See MAN <376>.

HUSBAND'S BROTHER – ***yāḇām*** [masc. noun: יָבָם <2993>; from MARRY <2992> (in the sense of a levirate marriage)] ▶ **This word indicates a brother-in-law.** It indicates the brother of a deceased husband, who was to marry the deceased brother's wife and raise up a son in his honor (Deut. 25:5, 25:7). ¶

HUSBANDMAN – 1 2 Kgs. 25:12 ➔ PLOWMAN <1461> 2 2 Chr. 26:10; Jer. 31:24; 51:23; Joel 1:11; Amos 5:16 ➔ FARMER <406>.

HUSBANDMAN (BE) – 2 Kgs. 25:12; Jer. 52:16 ➔ PLOWMAN (BE) <3009>.

HUSHAH – ***ḥûšāh*** [proper noun: חוּשָׁה <2364>; from HASTEN <2363>]: haste ▶ **A city of Judah.** Ref.: 1 Chr. 4:4. ¶

HUSHAI – ***ḥûšay*** [masc. proper noun: חוּשַׁי <2365>; from HASTEN <2363>]: hasty, quick ▶ **A faithful friend dedicated to helping and protecting King David.** Refs.: 2 Sam. 15:32–37; 17:5–16. He successfully confounded Ahithophel, David's deceitful earlier counselor. He was termed the "king's friend" (1 Chr. 27:33). His son was on Solomon's administrative staff (1 Kgs. 4:16); but possibly a different person who had a son who served under Solomon, Baanah (1 Kgs. 4:16). *

HUSHAM – ***ḥušām, ḥûšām*** [masc. proper noun: חֻשָׁם, חוּשָׁם <2367>; from HASTEN <2363>]: with haste ▶ **A man of the land**

of the Temani who reigned after Jobab on the throne of Edom. Refs.: Gen. 36:34, 35; 1 Chr. 1:45, 46. ¶

HUSHATHITE – ***ḥušāṯiy*** [masc. proper noun: חֻשָׁתִי <2843>; patron. from HUSHAH <2364>] ▶ **An inhabitant of Hushah, a town in Judah.** The word designates two of David's strong men: Sibbechai and Mebunnai (2 Sam. 21:18; 23:27; 1 Chr. 11:29; 20:4; 27:11). ¶

HUSHIM – ***ḥušiym, ḥûšiym*** [fem. and masc. proper noun: חֻשִׁים, חוּשִׁים <2366>; plur. from HASTEN <2363>]: in hasting ▶
a. The wife of Shaharaim. Refs.: 1 Chr. 8:8, 11. ¶
b. Son of Dan. Ref.: Gen. 46:23. ¶
c. Son of Aher. Ref.: 1 Chr. 7:12. ¶

HUSK – [1] Num. 6:4 ➔ SKIN <2085> [2] 2 Kgs. 4:42 ➔ SACK <6861> b.

HUT – ***mᵉlûnāh*** [fem. noun: מְלוּנָה <4412>; from LODGE <3885>] ▶ **It was a makeshift structure for those who guarded the fields at night; this word is also translated lodge, shack, cottage.** Refs.: Is. 1:8; 24:20. ¶

HYENA – ***'iy*** [masc. noun: אִי <338>; prob. identical with WOE! (interj.) <337> (through the idea of a doleful sound)] ▶ **A wild animal resembling a dog.** In the desolations left of a destroyed Babylon or other nation, jackals or hyenas prowl about and make their home (Is. 13:22; 34:14; Jer. 50:39). ¶

HYPOCRISY – [1] ***ḥōnep̱*** [masc. noun: חֹנֶף <2612>; from DEFILED (BE) <2610>] ▶ **This word means ungodliness, profaneness; it is also translated ungodliness. It is found only once in the Hebrew Bible.** Isaiah 32:6 uses the word in reference to the ungodly practices of vile or foolish persons. Such individuals have little nobility as their hearts are inclined to ruthlessness and their mouths speak nonsense and error. ¶
– [2] Dan. 11:34 ➔ FLATTERY <2519>.

HYPOCRITE – Job 8:13; 13:16; 20:5; 27:8; etc. ➔ GODLESS <2611>.

HYRAX – See BADGER <8227>.

HYSSOP – ***'ēzôḇ*** [masc. noun: אֵזוֹב <231>; prob. of foreign deriv.] ▶ **A woody plant with aromatic leaves and small flowers.** It was used as a brush to sprinkle items used in various purificatory (Lev. 14:4, 6) and other rites in Israel, especially the blood used in the Passover rites (Ex. 12:22). It was used in the ordinance concerning the red heifer (Num. 19:6, 18). It is used literally and figuratively of spiritual cleansing (Ps. 51:7). *

I

I – [1] *^{a}nā', ^{a}nāh* [Aramaic pron.: אֲנָא, אֲנָה <576>; corresponding to <589> below] ► **This word regularly means simply "I" but is used to reinforce other nouns, pronouns, or suffixes as well; it is also translated me.** Daniel 7:28 is a case in point: As for me, I, Daniel (cf. Ezra 6:12; 7:21). *
[2] *^{a}niy* [first person sing. pron.: אֲנִי <589>; contr. from <595> below] ► **This word may serve as subject or object.** It often serves as a subject of a participle, normally by following it (Gen. 18:17; Judg. 15:3; Jer. 1:12). Following a first person verb, it gives emphasis (Judg. 8:23; 2 Sam. 12:28). In answer to a question, it means I am, yes (Gen. 27:24; Judg. 13:11). With an interrogative Hebrew *ha* attached to it, it means do I? (Is. 66:9). Placed in front of the Lord's name, it serves as an introduction, I am the Lord; so also with Pharaoh, I am Pharaoh (Gen. 41:44; Ex. 6:6). It is synonymous with *'ānōḵiy* (see below). *
[3] *'ānōḵiy* [first person sing. pron.: אָנֹכִי <595>; a prim. pron.] ► **This common independent pronoun is used as a formula of introduction when placed before the Lord, I am the Lord (Ex. 20:2).** It is used in contrasts with other pronouns, you and I (Hos. 1:9). Placed before a first person verb form, it is emphatic, I myself gave (Hos. 2:8). It is used often as a predicate or verb meaning I am (Gen. 24:34; 1 Sam. 30:13; 2 Sam. 1:8). Sometimes biblical writers preferred to use *'ānōḵiy* and at other times *^{a}niy* (<589>), evidently for poetic or rhythmical reasons. *

I BEG YOU – *'ānnā', 'ānnāh* [interj.: אָנָּא, אָנָּה <577>; apparently contr. from LOVE (noun) <160> and PLEASE <4994>] ► **This interjection of entreaty also means ah now, alas, or oh. The primary use of the word is to intensify the urgency of request or the gravity of a given situation.** It is used to signify the pressing desire for forgiveness (Gen. 50:17); the great weight of sin (Ex. 32:31); earnestness in prayer of petition (2 Kgs. 20:3; Neh. 1:5, Jon. 1:14). *

I WILL BE – *^{e}hiy* [verb: אֱהִי <165>; apparently an orthographical variation for WHERE <346>] ►
a. This is a verb meaning, I will be, in the first person singular from *hāyah*, to be (KJV, NKJV, Hos. 13:10; see b.). However, some authorities consider this an interrogative pronoun.
b. This form is treated as an interr. pronoun by some (NIV, NASB Hos. 13:10; see a.) meaning where? (Also Hos. 13:14, KJV; see a.)

I WISH THAT! – 2 Kgs. 5:3 ➔ WOULD THAT <305>.

IBEX – *diyšôn* [masc. noun: דִּישׁוֹן <1788>; from THRESH <1758>] ► **This word refers to a gazelle, pygarg; it is also translated mountain goat.** It was an animal considered clean and suitable for eating (Deut. 14:5). ¶

IBHAR – *yiḇḥār* [masc. proper noun: יִבְחָר <2984>; from CHOOSE <977>]: choice ► **One of the sons of David.** Refs.: 2 Sam. 5:15; 1 Chr. 3:6; 14:5. ¶

IBLEAM – *yiḇl^{e}'ām* [proper noun: יִבְלְעָם <2991>; from SWALLOW <1104> and PEOPLE <5971>]: devouring the people ► **A city in Issachar assigned to Manasseh.** Its inhabitants, the Canaanites, were not driven out (Josh. 17:11; Judg. 1:27; 2 Kgs. 9:27). ¶

IBNEIAH – *yiḇn^{e}yāh* [masc. proper noun: יִבְנְיָה <2997>; from BUILD <1129> and LORD <3050>]: the Lord has built ► **Son of Jehoram, a Benjamite.** Ref.: 1 Chr. 9:8. ¶

IBNIJAH – *yiḇniyyāh* [masc. proper noun: יִבְנִיָּה <2998>; from BUILD <1129> and LORD <3050>]: the Lord builds ► **Father of Reuel, a Benjamite.** Ref.: 1 Chr. 9:8. ¶

IBRI – *'iḇriy* [masc. proper noun: עִבְרִי <5681>; the same as HEBREW <5680>]: Hebrew ► **A Levite of the family of Jaaziah.** Ref.: 1 Chr. 24:27. ¶

IBSAM – ***yiḇśām*** [masc. proper noun: יִבְשָׂם <3005>; from the same as SPICE <1314>]: of good odor, pleasant ▶ **Grandson of Issachar; also translated Jibsam.** Ref.: 1 Chr. 7:2. ¶

IBZAN – ***'iḇṣān*** [masc. proper noun: אִבְצָן <78>; from the same as BOIL (noun) <76>]: splendor ▶ **He judged Israel seven years.** Refs.: Judg. 12:8, 10. ¶

ICE – ***qeraḥ*** [masc. noun: קֶרַח <7140>; from SHAVE THE HEAD <7139> (as if bald, i.e., smooth, in the case of ice)] ▶ **This word refers to frozen water; it also indicates frost.** It indicates extreme cold in general (Gen. 31:40; Jer. 36:30). It refers to condensed frozen water that forms small ice crystals (Job 6:16). It is described as one of God's wonderful works (Job 37:10; 38:29; Ps. 147:17). It indicates a shiny, gleaming roof or ceiling (Ezek. 1:22); the word is translated crystal. ¶

ICHABOD – ***'iy-ḵāḇôḏ*** [masc. proper noun: אִי־כָבוֹד <350>; from NOT <336> and GLORY <3519>]: the glory has departed ▶ **The name of the son born of Phinehas, son of Eli, high priest in Israel.** Ref.: 1 Sam. 4:21. The meaning of the name refers to the capture of the ark of God by the Philistines. He was the uncle of Ahijah, the son of his brother Ahitub (1 Sam. 14:3). ¶

IDALAH – ***yiḏ*ᵉ*lāh*** [proper noun: יִדְאֲלָה <3030>; of uncertain deriv.] ▶ **A city of the tribe of Zebulun.** Ref.: Josh. 19:15. ¶

IDBASH – ***yiḏbāš*** [masc. proper noun: יִדְבָּשׁ <3031>; from the same as HONEY <1706>]: like honey ▶ **A man of the tribe of Judah.** Ref.: 1 Chr. 4:3. ¶

IDDO – 1 ***'iddô*** [masc. proper noun: אִדּוֹ <112>; of uncertain deriv.] ▶ **Name of an Israelite, a leader at the place Casiphia.** Ref.: Ezra 8:17. ¶
2 ***yiddô*** [masc. proper noun: יִדּוֹ <3035>; from THANKS (GIVE) <3034>]: praised ▶
a. A Manassite. Ref.: 1 Chr. 27:21. ¶
b. A Jew. Ref.: Ezra 10:43, an alternate reading for Jaddai. ¶
3 ***ye'dô*** [masc. proper noun: יֶעְדּוֹ <3260>; from APPOINT <3259>]: appointed, timely ▶ **A seer who wrote his visions concerning Jeroboam as well as events concerning Solomon.** Ref.: 2 Chr. 9:29. ¶
4 ***'iddō', 'iddô, 'iddô', 'iddo*** [masc. proper. noun: עִדֹּא, עִדּוֹ, עִדּוֹא, עִדּוֹ <5714>; from PASS OVER <5710>]: timely ▶
a. The father of Ahinadab. Ref.: 1 Kgs. 4:14. ¶
b. Grandfather of Zechariah the prophet. Refs.: Neh. 12:4, 16; Zech. 1:1, 7. ¶
c. Grandfather of Zechariah the prophet. Refs.: Ezra 5:1; 6:14. ¶
d. A Levite. Ref.: 1 Chr. 6:21. ¶
e. A seer. Refs.: 2 Chr. 12:15; 13:22. ¶

IDIOT – Job 11:12 → HOLLOW (verb) <5014>.

IDLE (STAND) – Eccl. 12:3 → CEASE <988>.

IDLE HANDS – Eccl. 10:18 → IDLENESS <8220>.

IDLENESS – 1 ***'aṣlûṯ*** [fem. noun: עַצְלוּת <6104>; from HESITATE <6101>] ▶ **This word refers to inactivity, slothfulness.** The description of a wise, worthy woman includes the assertion that she does not let idleness or laziness become a part of her life (Prov. 31:27). ¶
2 ***šiplûṯ*** [fem. noun: שִׁפְלוּת <8220>; from HUMBLE, HUMBLE (MAKE) <8213>] ▶ **This word indicates an attitude and state of laziness or inactivity that in context leads to the deterioration of the roof of a house; it is also translated slackness, indolence, idle hands.** It illustrated the result of sloth and laziness (Eccl. 10:18). ¶

IDOL – 1 ***sêmel, semel*** [masc. noun: סֵמֶל, סֶמֶל <5566>; from an unused root meaning to resemble] ▶ **This word means a forbidden object of worship such as a statue, an image, a figure.** Moses instructed the people to keep careful watch on themselves,

lest they make an idol and worship it (Deut. 4:16). Manasseh put a carved image in God's Temple but later humbled himself before God and removed it (2 Chr. 33:7, 15). In a vision, Ezekiel saw an idol of jealousy—an idol in the north gate that was standing near the glory of the God of Israel (Ezek. 8:3, 5). ¶
2 *'āṣāḇ* [masc. noun: עָצָב <6091>; from HURT <6087>] ► **This term always appears in the plural. It is derived from the second meaning of the verb *'āṣaḇ*, meaning to form or fashion, and thereby highlights the fact that these idols ("gods") were formed by human hands.** This term can allude to idols in general (Hos. 4:17); idols of silver (Hos. 13:2); or idols of gold and silver (Hos. 8:4). It appears in parallel with *massêḵāh* (COVERING <4541>), meaning a molten image (Hos. 13:2); and *gillûl* <1544>, meaning idols (Jer. 50:2). *
3 ***pāsiyl*** [masc. noun: פָּסִיל <6456>; from CUT (verb) <6458>] ► **This word comes from the verb *pāsal*, meaning to hew or to cut, which was done to create a carved image.** In the Law of the Old Testament, it was clear that such idols should be burned (Deut. 7:5, 25); and cut down (Deut. 12:3); for they provoked God to anger (Ps. 78:58; Jer. 8:19); and incited Him to judgment (Jer. 51:47, 52; Micah 1:7; 5:13). The presence of these idols were indicative of the sin and rebellion of the people (2 Chr. 33:19, 22; Hos. 11:2); while the removal of such idols was a sign of repentance (2 Chr. 34:3, 4, 7; Is. 30:22). *
4 ***pesel*** [masc. noun: פֶּסֶל <6459>; from CUT (verb) <6458>] ► **This word comes from the verb *pāsal*, meaning to hew or to cut, which was done to create an idol. It also means a graven image.** In the Law of the Old Testament, the Lord forbade Israel to create such images (Ex. 20:4; Lev. 26:1; Deut. 5:8); for they were an abomination to Him (Deut. 27:15). Those who served idols would be ashamed in the judgment (Ps. 97:7; Is. 42:17); and the Lord would cut them off from Him (Nah. 1:14). The presence of these idols were indicative of the sin and rebellion of the people (Deut. 4:16, 23, 25; 2 Chr. 33:7). The prophets often demonstrated the folly of these idols: they were profitable for nothing (Is. 44:10; Hab. 2:18); they could easily be burned (Is. 44:15); they had no breath (Jer. 10:14); and they could not save (Is. 45:20). Idols could be made of metal (Judg. 17:3, 4; Is. 40:19); wood (Is. 40:20; 44:15, 17); or possibly stone (Hab. 2:18; cf. Hab. 2:19). *
– 5 Lev. 19:4; Ps. 96.5; Is. 2:8; Hab. 2:18; etc. → WORTHLESSNESS <457> 6 1 Kgs. 15:13; 2 Chr. 15:16 → IMAGE <4656> 7 2 Chr. 34:7 → INCENSE ALTAR <2553> 8 Is. 45:16 → FORM (noun) <6736> 9 Is. 48:5 → PAIN (noun) <6090> 10 Jer. 22:28 → PAIN (noun) <6089> 11 Ezek. 8:12 → PICTURE <4906> 12 Zeph. 1:3 → RUIN, HEAP OF RUINS <4384>.

IDOLATROUS PRIEST – 2 Kgs. 23:5; Hos. 10:5; Zeph. 1:4 → PRIEST <3649>.

IDOLATRY – Jer. 14:14 → FUTILITY <434>.

IDOLS – ***gillûl*** [masc. noun: גִּלּוּל <1544>; from ROLL (verb) <1556>] ► **The Hebrew word is always found in the plural form. They are forbidden objects of worship. The term is used thirty-nine times in Ezekiel and nine times in the rest of the Old Testament. The people are told to destroy, abandon, and remove their idols.** Deuteronomy 29:17 implies idols can be made of wood, stone, silver, or gold. Ezekiel longs for a day when Israel will no longer worship idols (Ezek. 37:23). *

IEZER – ***'iy'ezer*** [masc. proper noun: אִיעֶזֶר <372>; from NOT <336> and HELP (noun) <5828>]: father of help ► **This noun designating Iezer is a form of Abiezer (see ABIEZER <44> a.).** Ref.: Num. 26:30. ¶

IEZERITE – ***'iy'ezriy*** [masc. proper noun: אִיעֶזְרִי <373>; patron. from IEZER <372>] ► **A descendant of Iezer.** Ref.: Num. 26:30. ¶

IF – 1 ***'illû*** [interj.: אִלּוּ <432>; prob. from NO <408>] ► **This word means but if, yea though.** It makes a sentence assert a

condition contrary to fact, "if . . ." (Esther 7:4, NKJV, Had we been . . . ; cf. NASB, Now if we had only . . . ; Eccl. 6:6). ¶
[2] ***hên*** [Aramaic particle: הֵן <2006>; corresponding to <2005> above] ▶ **This word means granting that, on condition that; it is also translated in case, whether.** It introduces conditional sentences meaning if (Ezra 4:13, 16; Dan. 2:6). When used in sequence with intervening words, it is translated as whether . . . or . . . or (Ezra 7:26). It is found in an indirect question meaning if or whether (Dan. 4:27; Ezra 5:17). *
– [3] See BEHOLD (interj.) <2005>, <2006> [4] See WHEN <518>.

IF NOT – ***lûlê', lûlêy*** [adv. particle: לוּלֵא, לוּלֵי <3884>; from OH THAT <3863> and NO <3808>] ▶ **This word introduces conditional sentences. It also means unless.** It may introduce a condition known to be contrary to fact (Gen. 31:42; 43:10; Deut. 32:27; Judg. 14:18; 2 Kgs. 3:14; Ps. 94:17). Sometimes the apodosis or concluding clause to the condition asserted in the *lûlê'* clause is understood but not written (Ps. 27:13). *Lûlê'* may be followed grammatically by the perfect form of a verb, the imperfect form, the participle form, or no verb at all. *

IF ONLY! – 2 Kgs. 5:3 ➔ WOULD THAT <305>.

IGAL – ***yig'āl*** [masc. proper noun: יִגְאָל <3008>; from REDEEM <1350>]: (God) redeems ▶
a. One of the twelve spies of the land of Canaan. Ref.: Num. 13:7. ¶
b. One of David's mighty men. Ref.: 2 Sam. 23:36. ¶
c. A descendant of Zerubbabel. Ref.: 1 Chr. 3:22. ¶

IGDALIAH – ***yigdalyāhû*** [masc. proper noun: יְגַדַּלְיָהוּ <3012>; from GREAT (BECOME) <1431> and LORD <3050>]: great is the Lord ▶ **Father of Hanan, a man of God.** Ref.: Jer. 35:4. ¶

IGNORED (BE) – Hab. 1:4 ➔ STUNNED (BECOME) <6313>.

IJE ABARIM – Num. 21:11; 33:44 ➔ IYE-ABARIM <5863>.

IJON – ***'iyyôn*** [proper noun: עִיּוֹן <5859>; from RUINS <5856>]: ruin ▶ **A town of Naphtali captured by Ben-hadad of Syria in agreement with King Asa.** Refs.: 1 Kgs. 15:20; 2 Kgs. 15:29; 2 Chr. 16:4. ¶

IKKESH – ***'iqqêš*** [masc. proper noun: עִקֵּשׁ <6142>; the same as PERVERSE <6141>] ▶ **Father of Ira, one of David's strong men.** Refs.: 2 Sam. 23:26; 1 Chr. 11:28; 27:9. ¶

ILAI – ***'iylay*** [masc. proper noun: עִילַי <5866>; from OFFER <5927> (in the sense of to go up)]: elevated ▶ **One of David's mighty men.** Ref.: 1 Chr. 11:29. ¶

ILL – [1] Lev. 15:33 ➔ FAINT (adj.) <1739> [2] Job 6:7 ➔ ILLNESS <1741>.

ILL (BECOME) – 2 Sam. 12:15 ➔ SICK (BE) <605>.

ILL SAVOUR – Joel 2:20 ➔ FOUL SMELL, FOUL ODOR <6709>.

ILLEGITIMATE BIRTH – Deut. 23:2 ➔ FORBIDDEN UNION (ONE BORN OF) <4464>.

ILLNESS – [1] ***d^eway*** [masc. noun: דְּוַי <1741>; from FAINT (adj.) <1739>] ▶ **This word describes the malady of a righteous man.** Ref.: Ps. 41:3; KJV: languishing. It is also translated by adjectives (loathsome, sorrowful, ill) in referring to odious or execrable food, intolerable for eating (Job 6:7). ¶
[2] ***ḥ^oliy*** [masc. noun: חֳלִי <2483>; from SICK (BE) <2470>] ▶ **This word indicates disease, sickness.** It denotes some kind of illness (1 Kgs. 17:17; 2 Kgs. 1:2, a serious illness). It is modified to indicate an illness that is strong or hangs on (Deut. 28:59). It is used of suffering brought on by the loss of one's wealth (Eccl. 6:2), "an evil disease." It is used figuratively of the ever-present evil of Jerusalem (Is. 1:5; Jer.

6:7) that could not be healed by seeking out foreign powers for healing (Hos. 5:13). Idolatry was an especially heinous sickness of Israel before the exile (Jer. 10:19). *

ILLUMINATION – Dan. 5:11, 14 ➔ LIGHT (noun) <5094>.

ILLUMINE – 1 2 Sam. 22:29; Ps. 18:28 ➔ LIGHTEN <5050> 2 Eccl. 8:1 ➔ LIGHT (GIVE) <215>.

ILLUSION – ***mahᵃṯallāh*** [fem. noun: מַהֲתַלָּה <4123>; from MOCK <2048>] ▶ **This word refers to what is not true or real, deception.** False prophecies or false visions the people wanted to hear were illusions (Is. 30:10; KJV, NKJV: deceit). ¶

IMAGE – 1 **obscene, horrid, abominable, repulsive, detestable image: *mipleṣeṯ*** [fem. noun: מִפְלֶצֶת <4656>; from SHAKE <6426>] ▶ **This word comes from the verb *pālaṣ* and describes something so horrible that one would shudder.** It was used only to describe an image (perhaps some sort of idol) that Maacah had made as an object of worship (1 Kgs. 15:13; 2 Chr. 15:16). ¶
2 ***ṣelem*** [masc. noun: צֶלֶם <6754>; from an unused root meaning to shade] ▶ **This word means a likeness, a statue, a model, a drawing, a shadow.** The word means image or likeness; its most celebrated theological and anthropological use was to depict human beings as made in God's own image (Gen. 1:26, 27; 5:3). People continue to be in His image even after the fall, although the image is marred (Gen. 9:6), and still serves as the basis of the prohibition not to kill human beings.

It is used metaphorically to depict persons as shadows, phantoms, or unknowing, senseless, fleeting beings carrying out the motions of life (Ps. 39:6); unless they have hope in God (see Ps. 39:7). In a similar vein, the wicked before the Lord are considered as mere dreams or fantasies (Ps. 73:20).

The word is also used in a concrete sense to depict images cut out of or molded from various materials. The word describes the images or idols of foreign or strange gods (2 Kgs. 11:18; Amos 5:26). The people of Israel produced images used as idols from their own jewelry (Ezek. 7:20; 16:17). Israel was, on its entrance into Canaan, to destroy all the molten images of the heathen (Num. 33:52). In Ezekiel 23:14, this word refers to pictures of Babylonians that enticed the people of Israel into apostasy when they saw them (Ezek. 23:14). *
3 ***ṣelem, ṣᵉlêm*** [Aramaic masc. noun: צְלֵם, צֶלֶם <6755>; corresponding to <6754> above] ▶ **This word is related to the Hebrew word *ṣelem*, meaning image, statue.** It was used to describe the statue in Nebuchadnezzar's dream (Dan. 2:31, 32, 34, 35); the image that Nebuchadnezzar built (Dan. 3:1–3, 5, 7); and the distortion of Nebuchadnezzar's face in anger when he heard the response of Shadrach, Meshach, and Abednego (Dan. 3:19). *
– 4 Lev. 26:1 ➔ PICTURE <4906> 5 2 Chr. 14:5; 34:4; Is. 17:8; 27:9; Ezek. 6:6 ➔ INCENSE ALTAR <2553> 6 Ezek. 8:3, 5 ➔ IDOL <5566> 7 Dan. 4:5 ➔ THOUGHT <2031>.

IMAGE (METAL, MOLDED, MOLTEN) – Is. 41:29; 48:5; Jer. 10:14 ➔ DRINK OFFERING <5262>.

IMAGERY – Ezek. 8:12 ➔ PICTURE <4906>.

IMAGINATION – 1 1 Chr. 29:18 ➔ FORMED <3336> 2 Ps. 73:7; Prov. 18:11 ➔ PICTURE <4906> 3 Jer. 16:12; 18:12; etc. ➔ STUBBORNNESS <8307>.

IMLAH – ***yimlā', yimlāh*** [masc. proper noun: יִמְלָא, יִמְלָה <3229>; from FULL (BE) <4390>]: fullness ▶ **Father of the prophet Micaiah.** Refs.: 1 Kgs. 22:8, 9; 2 Chr. 18:7, 8. ¶

IMMANUEL – ***'immānû'ēl*** [masc. proper noun: עִמָּנוּאֵל <6005>; from WITH <5973> and GOD <410>] ▶ **This word is the name of the child who would serve as a sign to King Ahaz in his day and, in the fuller meaning of the prophecy, as a sign**

to the Lord's people Israel in the future. The name means "God with us" (Is. 7:10–17). It was used as a cry to God Himself to be with Israel when the Assyrians threatened to destroy them (Is. 8:8). It is found in Isaiah 8:10 as well as in the Hebrew text ("God is with us"). ¶

IMMEDIATELY – [1] ***šā'āh*** [Aramaic fem. noun: שָׁעָה <8160>; from a root corresponding to LOOK WITH FAVOR OR IN DISMAY <8159>] ▶ **This word refers to a brief time span, almost instantly.** Refs.: Dan. 3:6, 15; 4:33; 5:5. It can refer to a slightly longer time span (Dan. 4:19: for a time, for a while, for *one* hour). ¶
– [2] Ezra 6:8 ➔ DILIGENTLY <629> [3] Esther 1:6 ➔ lit.: in haste ➔ HASTE (noun) <924>.

IMMER – ***'immēr*** [proper noun: אִמֵּר <564>; from SAY <559>]: he has said ▶
a. The name refers to a priest under the governor Zerubbabel who returned from Babylon. Refs.: Ezra 2:37; Neh. 7:40. Some of his descendants intermarried with the people of the land (Ezra 10:20). He had a son, Meshillemoth, among the new residents of Jerusalem (Neh. 11:13). Other refs.: 1 Chr. 9:12; Neh. 3:29; 7:61. ¶
b. It indicates a priest who is assigned during the time of David. Ref.: 1 Chr. 24:14. ¶
c. It indicates a Babylonian village from which Israelites returned from the Babylonian exile. Ref.: Ezra 2:59. They were supposedly descendants of Solomon's servants. ¶
d. It refers to the father of Pashhur, who attacked Jeremiah the prophet and had him constrained. Ref.: Jer. 20:1; see v. 2. ¶

IMMOVABLE – [1] Is. 33:20 ➔ FOLD (verb) <6813> [2] Zech. 12:3 ➔ HEAVY, VERY HEAVY <4614>.

IMNA – ***yimnā'*** [masc. proper noun: יִמְנָע <3234>; from HOLD, WITHHOLD <4513>]: holding back ▶ **A descendant of Asher, son of Helem.** Ref.: 1 Chr. 7:35. ¶

IMNAH – ***yimnāh*** [masc. proper noun: יִמְנָה <3232>; from RIGHT (GO TO THE) <3231>]: right hand, prosperity ▶ **Son of Asher.** Refs.: Gen. 46:17; Num. 26:44; 1 Chr. 7:30; 2 Chr. 31:14. ¶

IMPAIR – Ezra 4:13 ➔ DAMAGE (verb) <5142>.

IMPALE – ***zeqap̱*** [Aramaic verb: זְקַף <2211>; corresponding to RAISE UP <2210>] ▶ **This verb indicates to raise up, to lift up, to hang; if a man defied the edit of King Cyrus, the man was to be raised up, hung, on a erect timber pulled from his house; this verb is also translated to impale (i.e., to cause the point of an object to go through a human body).** It is used to indicate the impaling and raising up of a rebellious person on a piece of wood according to Persian law (Ezra 6:11; also translated to hang). ¶

IMPALED (BE) – Ezra 6:11 ➔ STRIKE <4223>.

IMPATIENT (BE) – Job 4:2, 5 ➔ WEARY (BE, BECOME) <3811>.

IMPATIENT (BECOME) – See SHORTEN <7114>.

IMPEDE – Prov. 4:12 ➔ DISTRESSED (BE) <3334>.

IMPENDING – Deut. 32:35 ➔ READY <6264> b.

IMPENETRABLE – Zech. 11:2 ➔ THICK <1208> or VINTAGE <1210>.

IMPERIOUS – Ezek. 16:30 ➔ BRAZEN <7986>.

IMPETUOUS (BE) – Job 6:3 ➔ SWALLOW (verb) <3886> b.

IMPLEMENT – [1] Gen. 4:22 ➔ CRAFTSMAN <2794> [2] Deut. 23:13 ➔ PEG <3489>.

IMPOSE – Ezra 7:24 ➔ THROW <7412>.

IMPOTENT – Is. 16:14 ➔ lit.: not mighty ➔ MIGHTY <3524>.

IMPOVERISH – Jer. 5:17; Mal. 1:4 ➔ DEMOLISH <7567>.

IMPOVERISHED – ***sāḵan*** [verb: סָכַן <5533>; prob. a denom. from KNIFE <7915> (properly, to cut, i.e., to damage)] ▶
a. This word refers to a person who is lacking in resources or the money to get them. Ref.: Is. 40:20. ¶
b. The Hebrew word refers to putting oneself in harm's way, getting into a dangerous situation; it is also translated to be endangered. Ref.: Eccl. 10:9. ¶

IMPOVERISHED (BE) – Judg. 6:6 ➔ BRING LOW <1809>.

IMPRESS – [1] Deut. 6:7 ➔ SHARPEN <8150> [2] Prov. 17:10 ➔ BEND <5181>.

IMPRISONMENT – ***ᵉsûr*** [Aramaic masc. noun: אֱסוּר <613>; corresponding to BOND <612>] ▶ **This word refers to the act of incarceration, confinement.** Ref.: Ezra 7:26. It indicates a strong band made of iron and bronze that could bind up a huge tree stump (Dan. 4:15, 23). ¶

IMPROVISE – ***pāraṭ*** [verb: פָּרַט <6527>; a prim. root] ▶
a. This word means to chant, to invent in singing, to sing idly. It refers to composing on the spot and possibly to performing at the same time in a rather vain, self-centered way according to context (Amos 6:5).
b. A verb meaning to strum. It means to strike the strings of a stringed instrument slowly and lightly (Amos 6:5). ¶

IMPUDENT – Prov. 7:13 ➔ STRENGTHEN <5810>.

IMPURE – [1] Lev. 7:18; 19:7; Ezek. 4:14 ➔ OFFENSIVE THING <6292> [2] Is. 30:22 ➔ FAINT (adj.) <1739>.

IMPURITIES – Is. 1:25 ➔ TIN <913>.

IMPURITY – ***niddāh*** [fem. noun: נִדָּה <5079>; from FLEE <5074> (in the sense of to reject)] ▶ **This word means a woman's menstrual cycle; it refers to a woman's flow of blood during her menstruation period. It also applies to anything unclean.** She was considered unclean and impure during this time, and the impurity had to be cleansed by water (Lev. 12:2; Num. 19:9; Ezek. 18:6; 22:10). Its meaning extended to refer to anything polluted, detestable, or unclean (Lev. 20:21; Ezra 9:11; Lam. 1:17). The phrase *hāyāh lᵉniddāh* means to become a detestable thing (Ezek. 7:19). *

IMRAH – ***yimrāh*** [masc. proper noun: יִמְרָה <3236>; prob. from <3231>]: rebel ▶ **A descendant of Asher, son of Zophah.** Ref.: 1 Chr. 7:36. ¶

IMRI – ***'imriy*** [masc. proper noun: אִמְרִי <566>; from IMMER <564>]: promised by the Lord ▶
a. A Judaite; son of Bani, a descendant of Pharez. Ref.: 1 Chr. 9:4. ¶
b. Father of Zaccur who rebuilt the wall of Jerusalem. Ref.: Neh. 3:2. ¶

IN – ***bᵉmô*** [prep.: בְּמוֹ <1119>; prolongation for prep. prefix] ▶ **This word means from, with, by. It serves as a poetic substitute for the common prose preposition *bᵉ* in Hebrew.** It is used to indicate the instrument by which or with which something is done (Job 9:30; 16:4, 5), such as snow, head, mouth. It indicates how something is done (Ps. 11:2; Is. 25:10; 43:2) or where it is done. *

INCANTATION – See COMPANY <2267>.

INCENSE – [1] ***lᵉḇônah, lᵉḇōnāh*** [fem. noun: לְבֹנָה, לְבוֹנָה <3828>; from WHITE <3836>] ▶ **Incense, or frankincense, is a white resin from a tree.** It was an ingredient of holy incense (Ex. 30:34; Jer. 6:20). It was put on certain offerings (Lev. 2:1, 2, 15, 16; 6:15; 24:7; Neh. 13:5, 9). It was used as a perfume by burning (Song 3:6; 4:6, 14); and it was considered a valuable tribute gift

(Is. 60:6; Jer. 41:5). Other refs.: Lev. 5:11; Num. 5:15; 1 Chr. 9:29; Is. 43:23; 66:3; Jer. 17:26. ¶
2 ***qᵉṭôrāh*** [masc. noun: קְטוֹרָה <6988>; from BURN (verb) <6999>] ► **This word refers to what goes up in a sweet-smelling, aromatic smoke to represent the prayers of God's people.** Ref.: Deut. 33:10. ¶
3 ***qiṭṭêr*** [fem. noun: קִטֵּר <7002>; from BURN <6999>] ► **This word refers to something that produces incense smoke; it is also translated smoking sacrifice, offering.** In context it indicates incense burned to pagan gods (Jer. 44:21). ¶
4 ***qᵉṭōreṯ*** [fem. noun: קְטֹרֶת <7004>; from BURN <6999>] ► **This word means smoke, the smell of a burning sacrifice.** Incense was one of the valid gifts Moses was to ask from the people (Ex. 25:6); and it played an important role in Aaron's atonement for the sin of the people (Lev. 16:13). David's plans for the Temple included an altar for incense (1 Chr. 28:18); and David prayed that his prayers would be like incense to the Lord (Ps. 141:2). God told Judah that the smell of worthless sacrifices was detestable (Is. 1:13). See the related Hebrew verb *qāṭar* [BURN (verb) <6999>]. *
– 5 Dan. 2:46 ➔ incense, fragrant incense ➔ PLEASING <5208>.

INCENSE ALTAR – ***ḥammān*** [masc. noun: חַמָּן <2553>; from SUN <2535>] ► **This word means sun pillar. It also means idol or pillar in general.** This is a pillar used in idolatrous worship of the solar deities, similar to the images Asa and Josiah tore down as part of their religious reforms (2 Chr. 14:5; 34:4). Isaiah also condemned the worship of these images (Is. 17:8; 27:9). Other refs.: Lev. 26:30; 2 Chr. 34:7; Ezek. 6:4, 6. ¶

INCEST – Lev. 20:12 ➔ PERVERSION <8397>.

INCITE – Is. 19:2 ➔ COVER (verb) <5526> b.

INCLINE – Prov. 2:18 ➔ BOW DOWN <7743> a.

INCLOSING – Ex. 39:13 ➔ SETTING <4396>.

INCLUDE – Job 3:6 ➔ REJOICE <2302>.

INCOME – 1 Kgs. 10:15 ➔ WARES <4536>.

INCREASE (noun) – 1 ***yᵉḇûl*** [masc. noun: יְבוּל <2981>; from BRING <2986>] ► **This word refers to a crop, produce; it is also translated harvest, yield, fruit, grapes.** It indicates the fruit or produce generated by well-watered land or soil (Lev. 26:4, 20; Ezek. 34:27; Zech. 8:12), a blessing from the Lord. It also refers to the produce brought forth by people's labor (Ps. 78:46). It refers to a person's acquired goods or possessions (Job 20:28). Other refs.: Deut. 11:17; 32:22; Judg. 6:4; Ps. 67:6; 85:12; Hab. 3:17; Hag. 1:10. ¶
2 ***marbeh*** [masc. noun: מַרְבֶּה <4766>; from MANY (BE) <7235>] ► **This word refers to an abundance. It indicates prosperity, success.** In context it refers to the prosperity and overflowing success to accrue to Israel's king (Is. 9:7; NIV: greatness). It is used of a huge, rich collection of booty or spoil taken from an enemy (Is. 33:23: abundance, abundant, great). ¶
3 ***marbiyṯ*** [fem. noun: מַרְבִּית <4768>; from MANY (BE) <7235>] ► **This word depicts greatness, a gain.** It indicates profit or gain from lending (Lev. 25:37); the increase of persons born to a family (house, *bayiṯ*) (1 Sam. 2:33; also translated descendants). It indicates the greatest part or majority (1 Chr. 12:29); the extent or breadth of something (2 Chr. 9:6). It has the sense of a large part (not necessarily a majority) of a group (2 Chr. 30:18: multitude, majority). ¶
– 4 Lev. 25:36; Ezek. 18:8, 13, 17; 22:12 ➔ PROFIT (noun) <8636> 5 Num. 32:14 ➔ BROOD <8635>.

INCREASE (verb) – 1 ***nûḇ*** [verb: נוּב <5107>; a prim. root] ► **This word means to flourish, to bear fruit, to bring forth.** It has the basic sense of causing something to increase, to succeed: wealth or riches to

multiply, to increase (Ps. 62:10). Figuratively, it speaks of the continued prosperity of a righteous person (Ps. 92:14; Prov. 10:31; also translated to flow). It indicates the prosperity and increase of the people of Judah and Ephraim when God blesses them (Zech. 9:17: to make flourish, to make cheerful, to make thrive). ¶
– 2 Gen. 48:16 ➔ GROW <1711> 3 Ezra 4:22 ➔ GROW <7680> 4 Job 8:7; Ps. 73:12 ➔ GROW <7685> 5 Job 10:16 ➔ RISE <1342> 6 Job 12:23 ➔ GREAT (MAKE) <7679> 7 Ps. 72:17 ➔ CONTINUE <5125>.

INCURABLE – 1 2 Chr. 21:18 ➔ REMEDY <4832> 2 Job 34:6; Is. 17:11; Jer. 15:18: incurable, to be incurable ➔ SICK (BE) <605>.

INDEED – 1 ***'omnāh*** [adv.: אָמְנָה <546>; fem. of TRUTH <544> (in its usual sense)] ▶ **This word indicates confirmation of something; it is also translated actually, truly, really.** Abraham used this word to express that he was being truthful when he said Sarah was his sister (Gen. 20:12)—although, in fact, he was lying. When Achan took loot from Jericho, he admitted his sin by saying he had indeed sinned against God (Josh. 7:20). ¶
– 2 Gen. 18:13 ➔ SURELY <552> 3 Gen. 47:23 ➔ BEHOLD (interj.) <1887> 4 Job 9:2; 19:4, 5 ➔ TRULY <551> 5 See TRULY <61>.

INDIA – ***hōddû*** [proper noun: הֹדּוּ <1912>; of foreign origin] ▶ **Ahasuerus reigned from India to Ethiopia.** Refs.: Esther 1:1; 8:9. ¶

INDIGNANT (BE) – ***zā'am*** [verb: זָעַם <2194>] ▶ **The root of this word means literally to foam at the mouth, to be enraged.** It is used to describe the fury of the king of the North against the holy covenant in Daniel's vision (Dan. 11:30). Because God is a righteous judge, He shows indignation against evil every day (Ps. 7:11). This theme is picked up again in Isaiah (Is. 66:14). God was angry with the towns of Judah (Zech. 1:12), and Edom was under the wrath of the Lord (Mal. 1:4). This anger can also show in one's face (Prov. 25:23). Other refs.: Num. 23:7, 8; Prov. 22:14; 24:24; Mic. 6:10. ¶

INDIGNATION – 1 ***za'am*** [masc. noun: זַעַם <2195>; from INDIGNANT (BE) <2194>] ▶ **This word means intense anger, denunciation, curse.** Although this noun can refer to a state of being or actions of a human being (Jer. 15:17; Hos. 7:16), it usually refers to those of the Lord (Is. 26:20; 30:27; Hab. 3:12). This word is also used in parallel with other words with the connotation of anger: *'ap̱* (NOSE <639>) (Ps. 69:24; Is. 10:5, 25; 30:27; Zeph. 3:8); *'eḇrāh* (WRATH <5678>) (Ps. 78:49; Ezek. 21:31; 22:31); and *qeṣep̱* (WRATH <7110>) (Ps. 102:10; Jer. 10:10). *
– 2 Ps. 119:53: indignation, burning indignation, hot indignation ➔ BURNING HEAT <2152>.

INDISPOSED – Lev. 15:33 ➔ FAINT (adj.) <1739>.

INDITE – Ps. 45:1 ➔ OVERFLOW (verb) <7370> b.

INDOLENCE – 1 Eccl. 10:18 ➔ IDLENESS <8220> 2 Eccl. 10:18 ➔ SLUGGARD <6103>.

INFAMY – Prov. 25:10; Ezek. 36:3 ➔ REPORT (BAD) <1681>.

INFANT – 1 ***yōnêq, yônêq*** [masc. noun: יֹנֵק, יוֹנֵק <3126>; act. part. of NURSE (verb and noun) <3243>] ▶ **This word indicates a tender shoot of a plant; a child, a suckling child.** It is used of the Suffering Servant of the Lord (Is. 53:2: tender plant, young plant, tender shoot), depicting Him as a fragile young plant. It is used of a nursing infant (1 Sam. 15:3; Song 8:1) and of nursing infants who suckle the breasts (Num. 11:12; Joel 2:16). When God brings judgment, even nursing infants are included (Deut. 32:25; Jer. 44:7). Other refs.: 1 Sam. 22:19; Ps. 8:2; Lam. 2:11; 4:4. ¶
– 2 Is. 65:20 ➔ NURSING CHILD <5764>.

INFANTS – Is. 3:4 ➔ CAPRICIOUS CHILDREN <8586>.

INFERIOR – Is. 3:5 ➔ DESPISED (BE) <7034>.

INFIRM – 2 Chr. 36:17 ➔ AGED <3486>.

INFIRMITY – Lev. 12:2 ➔ MENSTRUATION <1738>.

INFLAME – Is. 5:11 ➔ BURN (verb) <1814>.

INFLAMMATION – ***daleqet*** [fem. noun: דַּלֶּקֶת <1816>; from BURN (verb) <1814>] ▶ **This word designates an irritation, a swelling that God may bring on a disobedient people.** Ref.: Deut. 28:22. ¶

INFLICT – 1 Gen. 12:17 ➔ TOUCH <5060> 2 Lam. 1:12 ➔ AFFLICT <3013> 3 Zech. 14:18 ➔ SMITE <5062>.

INFLUENCES (SWEET) – Job 38:31 ➔ CHAINS <4575> b.

INGATHERING – ***'āsiyp, 'āsip*** [masc. noun: אָסִיף, אָסִף <614>; from GATHER <622>] ▶ **This word means a harvest, a crop.** It refers to an ingathering taken in before the rainy season from either the winepress or threshing floor (Ex. 23:16; 34:22). ¶

INHABITANT – 1 ***šākēn*** [adj.: שָׁכֵן <7934>; from SETTLE DOWN <7931>] ▶ **This word usually refers to a resident of a city.** Refs.: Is. 33:24; Hos. 10:5. It can also have the more specific meaning of neighbor. These neighbors can either be people who are friends or enemies (Ex. 3:22; Ruth 4:17); or nations (Deut. 1:7). Neighbors can also be extremely influential (Ezek. 16:26). Israel was said to have engaged in prostitution with her neighbor Egypt, meaning that she followed the gods and religions of Egypt rather than following the one true God. * – 2 Dan. 4:35 ➔ DWELL <1753>.

INHABITANT OF THE VILLAGE – Judg. 5:7, 11 ➔ VILLAGER <6520>.

INHERITANCE – 1 Deut. 33:4; Ezek. 33:24 ➔ POSSESSION <4181> 2 Josh. 12:7; Judg. 21:17; Ps. 61:5; Jer. 32:8 ➔ POSSESSION <3425>.

INIQUITY – 1 ***'ᵃwāyāh*** [Aramaic fem. noun: עֲוָיָה <5758>; from a root corresponding to INIQUITY (COMMIT) <5753>] ▶ **This word refers to perverseness, perversity, sin; it is related to a Hebrew word whose root meaning is iniquity or guilt (twist, twisted).** It is found only once in the Old Testament, in Daniel's interpretation of one of King Nebuchadnezzar's dreams (Dan. 4:27; NIV: wickedness). In his interpretation, Daniel warned the king that unless he repented of his sins and iniquities and began to act righteously and show mercy, judgment would fall on him. ¶ 2 ***'āwōn*** [masc. noun: עָוֹן <5771>; from INIQUITY (COMMIT) <5753>] ▶ **This word means evil, guilt, punishment; sin. This is one of the four main words indicating sin in the Old Testament. This word indicates sin that is particularly evil, since it strongly conveys the idea of twisting or perverting deliberately.** The noun carries along with it the idea of guilt from conscious wrongdoing (Gen. 44:16; Jer. 2:22). The punishment that goes with this deliberate act as a consequence is indicated by the word also (Gen. 4:13; Is. 53:11).

The Hebrew word means sin or transgression in a conscious sense, as when David kept (consciously) from transgression or sin (2 Sam. 22:24); Israel by choice returned to the sins their ancestors had committed (Jer. 11:10; 13:22).

This word for sin can also indicate the guilt that results from the act of sin: Moses prayed that the Lord would forgive the guilt and sin of rebellious Israel (Num. 14:19); the guilt of the Amorites was not yet full in the time of Abraham (Gen. 15:16); God would remove the guilt of His people when they returned from exile (Jer. 50:20); the guilt of the fathers was a recurring phrase in the Old Testament (Ex. 20:5; 34:7).

The word also indicates in some contexts the punishment that results from sin and guilt; Cain's punishment was unbearable for him (Gen. 4:13; Jer. 51:6). Edom was condemned for not helping Israel in the time of Israel's punishment (Ezek. 35:5); and the Levites had to bear their punishment because they strayed from following the Lord (Ps. 31:10; Ezek. 44:10, 12). *

[3] ***'alwāh*** [fem. noun: עַלְוָה <5932>; from INJUSTICE <5766>] ► **This word means injustice, unrighteousness.** Hosea 10:9 is the sole occurrence of this word in the Bible. It is used to denote the supreme wickedness and depravity of Israel. The prophet relates the current situation to an episode at Gibeah during the time of the judges (cf. Judg. 19:1–20:28). ¶

– [4] Ps. 10:7; Zech. 10:2 ➔ NOTHINGNESS <205> [5] Hos. 10:10 ➔ MARITAL RIGHTS <5772> b.

INIQUITY (COMMIT) – ***'āwāh*** [verb: עָוָה <5753>; a prim. root] ► **This word means to bend, to twist; it is also translated to do wrong.** In its various uses, the word means to do wrong, to commit iniquity (Esther 1:16; Dan. 9:5); or to be physically or emotionally distressed (Is. 21:3: to be distressed, to be bewildered, to be bowed down, to be staggered). It is used with reference to a person with a disturbed mind (Prov. 12:8: perverse, twisted, warped). In the intensive form, it can mean to distort something, such as the face of the earth (Is. 24:1: to distort, to twist, to ruin); or the path that one walks (Lam. 3:9). In its causative form, it refers to perverting right behavior (Job 33:27; Jer. 3:21); or simply doing that which is wrong (2 Sam. 7:14; 19:19; Jer. 9:5); referring to behavior acknowledged as wrong by the psalmist (Ps. 106:6); by David (2 Sam. 24:17); and by Solomon (1 Kgs. 8:47: to do perversely, to act perversely; 2 Chr. 6:37: to do amiss, to act perversely). Other refs.: 1 Sam. 20:30 (perverse); Ps. 38:6 (to be troubled, to be bent over, to be bowed down). ¶

INJUNCTION – Dan. 6:7–9, 12, 13, 15 ➔ DECREE (noun) <633>.

INJURE – [1] Ex. 21:35 ➔ SMITE <5062> [2] Lev. 24:19, 20 ➔ DEFECT <3971> [3] Prov. 8:36 ➔ VIOLENCE (DO) <2554> [4] Eccl. 10:9 ➔ HURT <6087> [5] Zech. 12:3 ➔ CUT (verb) <8295>.

INJURED – Is. 1:5 ➔ SICK <1742>.

INJURING – Gen. 4:23 ➔ BRUISE (noun) <2250>.

INJURY – [1] Ex. 21:22, 23 ➔ HARM (noun) <611> [2] Lev. 24:20; Prov. 9:7 ➔ DEFECT <3971> [3] Dan. 6:23 ➔ DAMAGE (noun) <2257>.

INJUSTICE – [1] ***muṭṭeh*** [masc. noun: מֻטֶּה <4297>; from STRETCH OUT <5186> (in the sense of acting in a hostile manner toward someone)] ► **This word means something perverted, twisted, warped; it is also translated perversity, perversion, perverseness.** Occurring only in Ezekiel 9:9, this word derives its meaning from a primitive root meaning to stretch, to incline, or to bend (see STRETCH OUT <5186>). It was used by the Lord to describe the perverseness of Judah in distorting His Law and justice. ¶

[2] ***'āwel, 'ewel, 'awlāh, 'ōlāṯāh*** [masc. sing. noun: עָוֶל, עֶוֶל, עַוְלָה, עֹלָתָה <5766>; from UNJUSTLY (DEAL) <5765>] ► **This word refers to anything that deviates from the right way of doing things; it is also translated unrighteousness.** It is often the direct object of *'āśāh* <6213>, meaning to do (Lev. 19:15; Deut. 25:16; Ps. 7:3; Ezek. 3:20; 33:13); and is in direct contrast to words like righteous (Prov. 29:27); upright (Ps. 107:42); and justice (Deut. 32:4). God has no part with injustice (Deut. 32:4; 2 Chr. 19:7; Job 34:10; Jer. 2:5). See the verb *'āwal* [UNJUSTLY (DEAL) <5765>]. *

– [3] Hos. 10:9 ➔ INIQUITY <5932>.

INK – ***deyô*** [masc. noun: דְּיוֹ <1773>; of uncertain deriv.] ► **It was the writing material Baruch used to write down Jeremiah's prophecies.** Ref.: Jer. 36:18. ¶

INKHORN – ***qeseṯ*** [fem. noun: קֶסֶת <7083>; from the same as CUP <3563>

(in the sense of a container)] ▶ **This word refers to a set of materials needed to write, to record something. The expression "writer's inkhorn" is also translated "writing kit," "writing case."** Refs.: Ezek. 9:2, 3, 11. ¶

INLAID – Song 5:14 ➔ COVER (verb) <5968>.

INLAY – ***rāṣap̱*** [verb: רָצַף <7528>; a denom. from BAKED ON COALS <7529>] ▶ **This word means to cover, to decorate; it is also translated to fit out, to pave.** It indicates the décor and decorative patterns worked into the inside of a royal sedan chair for the king's wedding day (Song 3:10). ¶

INLET – Judg. 5:17 ➔ LANDING <4664>.

INMOST BEING – Ps. 139:13 ➔ KIDNEY <3629>.

INN – Gen. 42:27; 43:21; Ex. 4:24 ➔ LODGING <4411>.

INNER – ***pᵉniymiy*** [adj.: פְּנִימִי <6442>; from FACE (noun) <6440>] ▶ **This word means interior and refers to something that is located inside, within another structure.** Refs.: 1 Kgs. 6:27, 36; 7:12, 50; Esther 4:11; 5:1. It is used often of the inner features of the Temple in Ezekiel (8:13; 46:1). *

INNER CHAMBER – Judg. 9:46, 49 ➔ STRONGHOLD <6877> a.

INNER PARTS – Is. 16:11 ➔ BOWELS <4578>.

INNERMOST BEING – Job 38:36; Ps. 51:6 ➔ INWARD PART <2910>.

INNOCENCE – 1 ***zāḵû*** [Aramaic fem. noun: זָכוּ <2136>; from a root corresponding to PURE (BE) <2135>] ▶ **This word indicates a state of guiltlessness, freedom from guile or blame; it indicates also purity.** This was the case of Daniel (Dan. 6:22) who was not guilty of the charges alleged against him; it is translated by an adjective: innocent, blameless. ¶

2 ***niqqāyôn, niqqāyōn*** [masc. noun: נִקָּיוֹן, נִקָּיֹן <5356>; from FREE (BE) <5352>] ▶ **The Hebrew word generally implies innocence or freedom from guilt; it also means cleanness, whiteness.** It is applied in the realm of sexual morality (Gen. 20:5); and ritual purification or personal conduct as it relates to worship (Ps. 26:6; 73:13; KJV: innocency). Choosing to embrace idolatry rather than innocence in their worship, Israel faced God's judgment (Hos. 8:5; NIV: purity). In Amos 4:6, this term appears in a phrase that literally means cleanness of teeth, which is an idiomatic expression implying empty stomachs or nothing to eat. ¶

INNOCENCY – Gen. 20:5; Ps. 26:6; 73:13; Hos. 8:5 ➔ INNOCENCE <5356>.

INNOCENT – 1 ***ḥap̱*** [adj.: חַף <2643>; from COVER (verb) <2653> (in the moral sense of covered from soil, thus clean, not dirty)] ▶ **This word describes a state of being pure, without iniquity (*'āwōn*: INIQUITY <5771>); it is also translated clean (ESV, NIV).** Ref.: Job 33:9. ¶

2 ***nāqiy, nāqiy'*** [adj.: נָקִי, נָקִיא <5355>; from FREE (BE) <5352>] ▶ **This word means clean, free from, exempt.** It frequently refers to innocent blood, i.e., the shed blood of an innocent individual (Deut. 19:10, 13; 21:8, 9; 1 Sam. 19:5; 2 Kgs. 21:16; 24:4; Ps. 94:21; 106:38; Prov. 6:17; Is. 59:7; Jer. 7:6; 22:3, 17). It also refers to a person who is innocent (Job 4:7; 17:8; 22:19, 30; 27:17; Ps. 10:8; 15:5; Prov. 1:11). According to Psalm 24:4, it is a necessary quality for those who will stand in the presence of the Lord. It also refers to those who are free from blame (Gen. 44:10); free from liability or punishment (Ex. 21:28; 2 Sam. 14:9); released from an oath (Gen. 24:41; Josh. 2:17, 19, 20); exempt from various obligations (Num. 32:22); or free from the obligation of military service (Deut. 24:5). *

– 3 Prov. 21:8 ➔ PURE <2134> 4 Dan. 6:22 ➔ INNOCENCE <2136>.

INORDINATE LOVE – Ezek. 23:11 → LUST (noun) <5691>.

INQUIRE – [1] Ezra 7:14 → SEARCH (MAKE) <1240> [2] Is. 21:12 → BOIL (verb) <1158> [3] See SEEK <1875>.

INQUIRIES (MAKE) – Ezra 7:14 → SEARCH (MAKE) <1240>.

INQUIRY (MAKE) – Prov. 20:25 → SEEK <1239>.

INSCRIBE – [1] ***rāšam*** [verb: רָשַׁם <7559>; a prim. root] ▶ **This word refers to the process of writing with an instrument or engraving a message on something.** In context it is used figuratively of writing or engraving in the book, writing of truth (Dan. 10:21; also translated to note, to write). ¶
[2] ***reśam*** [Aramaic verb: רְשַׁם <7560>; corresponding to <7559> above] ▶ **This word also means to write; to sign.** It refers to something written out (*reśîm*) in a language (Dan. 5:24, 25). It refers to the act of affixing signatures to a legal document (Dan. 6:8–10, 12, 13). ¶
– [3] Hab. 2:2 → EXPLAIN <874>.

INSCRIPTION – Dan. 5:7, 8, 15–17, 24, 25 → WRITING <3792>.

INSECT – Ps. 50:11; 80:13 → MOVING CREATURES <2123>.

INSIGHT – [1] Dan. 5:11, 14 → LIGHT (noun) <5094> [2] Dan. 5:11, 12, 14 → UNDERSTANDING <7924>.

INSIGNIFICANT – Job 8:7 → LITTLE ONE <4705>.

INSIGNIFICANT (BE) – 2 Sam. 7:19 → WORTHY (BE NOT) <6994>.

INSIGNIFICANT (BE, BECOME) – Job 14:21; Jer. 30:19 → BRING LOW <6819>.

INSOLENCE – [1] 1 Sam. 17:28; Prov. 13:10; 21:24 → PRIDE <2087> [2] 2 Kgs. 19:28; Is. 37:29 → EASE (AT) <7600> b.

INSOLENT – [1] Ps. 75:5 → ARROGANCE <6277> [2] Ps. 86:14; 119:21, 51, 69, 78, 85, 122; Jer. 43:2 → PROUD <2086> [3] Prov. 29:21 → SON <4497> [4] Is. 33:19 → FIERCE <3267>.

INSOLENT – Zeph. 3:4 → RECKLESS (BE) <6348>.

INSOLENT (BE) – Is. 3:5 → BOLD (BE, MAKE) <7292>.

INSOLENT THINGS – Ps. 31:18; 94:4 → ARROGANCE <6277>.

INSOLENTLY – Ps. 31:18 → ARROGANCE <6277>.

INSPECT – ***śāḇar*** [verb: שָׂבַר <7663>; a prim. root] ▶ **Nehemiah used this word to express an examination of the broken walls of Jerusalem before the returning exiles began rebuilding. This word is also translated to view, to examine.** Refs.: Neh. 2:13, 15. In this context, the verb did not only refer to Nehemiah's viewing of simply a broken wall but also a metaphorical viewing of Israel's brokenness and need for the return of the presence of God to Jerusalem. For another meaning of the Hebrew word, see WAIT <7663>. ¶

INSPECTION – ***mip̄qāḏ*** [proper noun: מִפְקָד <4663>; the same as APPOINTMENT <4662>] ▶ **This word (Neh. 3:31) is rendered in the transliterated form in the KJV (Miphkad).** But it is translated as the "Inspection Gate" in most modern translations; also translated "Muster Gate." ¶

INSTRUCTED (WHO) – 2 Chr. 35:3 → TAUGHT (WHO) <4000>.

INSTRUCTER – Gen. 4:22 → SHARPEN <3913>.

INSTRUCTION – [1] ***mûsār*** [masc. noun: מוּסָר <4148>; from ADMONISH <3256> (in the sense of to instruct)] ▶ **This word means teaching but also means discipline, correction. It occurs almost exclusively**

in the poetic and prophetic literature. In Proverbs, instruction and discipline come primarily through the father (or a father figure such as a teacher) and usually are conveyed orally but may come via the rod (Prov. 1:8; 13:1, 24). Those who are wise receive instruction, but fools reject it (Prov. 1:7; 8:33; 13:1; 15:5). The reception of instruction brings life, wisdom, and the favor of the Lord (Prov. 4:13; 8:33); however, rejection brings death, poverty, and shame (Prov. 5:23; 13:18). Apart from Proverbs, this noun is always associated with God—with two exceptions (Job 20:3; Jer. 10:8). When God's instruction is rejected, it results in punishments of various kinds (Job 36:10; Jer. 7:28; 17:23; 32:33; Zeph. 3:2). The discipline of the Lord is not to be despised, for it is a demonstration of His love for His children (Job 5:17; Prov. 3:11; cf. Heb. 12:5, 6). The supreme demonstration of God's love came when Jesus Christ bore the "chastisement of our peace" (Is. 53:5). *

2 ***mōsār*** [masc. noun: מֹסָר <4561>; from ADMONISH <3256>] ► **This word indicates some communication from God that imparts warnings or teachings to persons who are to deliver them.** Ref.: Job 33:16; also translated warnings. ¶

– 3 2 Sam. 7:19 ➔ TURN (noun) <8447> d. 4 Prov. 16:21, 23; Is. 29:24 ➔ LEARNING <3948>.

INSTRUCTOR – Gen. 4:22 ➔ SHARPEN <3913>.

INSTRUMENT – Gen. 4:22 ➔ CRAFTSMAN <2794>.

INSTRUMENT OF MUSIC – Dan. 6:18 ➔ ENTERTAINMENT <1761>.

INSTRUMENT OF TEN STRINGS – Ps. 33:2 ➔ HARP <5035>.

INSUBORDINATION – 1 Sam. 15:23 ➔ PRESS <6484>.

INSULT – Is. 51:7; Zeph. 2:8 ➔ SCORN (noun) <1421>.

INSULTS (HURL) – 1 Sam. 25:14 ➔ RUSH GREEDILY <5860> a.

INSURRECTION – Ps. 64:2 ➔ THRONG (noun) <7285>.

INSURRECTION (MAKE) – ***neśā'*** [Aramaic verb: נְשָׂא <5376>; corresponding to CARRY <5375>] ► **This word means to stand against, to resist authority or controls; it also means to take, to carry away.** It indicates a city rising up in rebellion against a foreign king ruling over it (Ezra 4:19; also translated to rise, to revolt). It refers to removing something, taking it elsewhere, e.g., vessels or chaff (Ezra 5:15: to take; Dan. 2:35: to carry). ¶

INTEGRITY – ***tummāh*** [fem. noun: תֻּמָּה <8538>; fem. of COMPLETENESS <8537>] ► **This word comes from the verb *tāmam*, meaning to be complete, and is the feminine equivalent of the word *tōm*, meaning completeness or integrity.** It is used only five times in the Old Testament and is only found in the Wisdom Literature of Job and the Psalms. In four of these instances, it is used by God, Job, and Job's wife to refer to Job's integrity (Job. 2:3, 9; 27:5; 31:6). In Proverbs 11:3, integrity guides the upright person. See the related adjective *tām* (PERFECT <8535>), meaning complete. ¶

INTELLIGENCE – 1 ***śeḵel, śêḵel*** [verb: שֶׂכֶל, שֵׂכֶל <7922>; from CONSIDER <7919>] ► **This word also means good sense. This intelligence is more than just mere book knowledge or learning about a particular subject. It has a greater significance and means insight or understanding.** This insight is a gift from God (1 Chr. 22:12); and God holds the freedom to give it or to take it away whenever He chooses (Job 17:4). The results from having this intelligence and insight is that it gives a person patience (Prov. 19:11); and wins praise from others (Prov. 12:8). Only fools despise this intelligence (Prov. 23:9). This noun is used once with a negative connotation in Daniel 8:25 where it stands for

cunning, requiring much intelligence; it is also translated shrewdness, policy. *
– 2 Dan. 5:11, 12, 14 ➔ UNDERSTANDING <7924>.

INTELLIGENT (BECOME) – Job 11:12 ➔ HEART (RAVISH THE) <3823>.

INTEND – Dan. 7:25 ➔ THINK <5452>.

INTENT – 1 Chr. 29:18 ➔ FORMED <3336>.

INTERCEDE – Ex. 8:9; etc. ➔ PRAY <6279>.

INTERCOURSE – ***šekōḇeṯ*** [fem. noun: שְׁכֹבֶת <7903>; from LIE DOWN <7901>] ▶ **This word refers to the act of sexual relations.** Refs.: Lev. 18:20; Num. 5:20. It also refers to intercourse or copulation with an animal which was considered perversion and punishable by death (Lev. 18:23; 20:15). ¶

INTEREST – 1 ***nešeḵ*** [masc. noun: נֶשֶׁךְ <5392>; from BITE <5391> (in the sense of to lend or borrow at interest)] ▶ **This word refers to the amount paid back to a creditor beyond the principal; it is also translated usury.** Refs.: Ex. 22:25; Lev. 25:36, 37. It was a practice forbidden in Israel with respect to other Israelites (Ps. 15:5; Prov. 28:8). A righteous man did not practice usury or charge an excessive amount of interest (Ezek. 18:8, 13, 17; 22:12). Other ref.: Deut. 23:19. ¶
– 2 Lev. 25:36 ➔ PROFIT (noun) <8636> 3 Neh. 5:7, 10 ➔ USURY <4855>.

INTERMARRY – Ezra 9:14 ➔ MARRIAGE <2859> a.

INTERMEDDLE – Prov. 18:1 ➔ BREAK OUT <1566>.

INTERMISSION – Lam. 3:49 ➔ INTERRUPTION <2014>.

INTERPRET – 1 ***ḥawāh*** [Aramaic verb: חֲוָה <2324>; corresponding to SHOW <2331>] ▶ **This word means to explain, to declare or to put forth the explanation of a dream or written message.** Refs.: Dan. 2:4, 6, 7, 9–11, 16; 5:7. It can mean also to publicize or make known something (Dan. 4:2). Dan. 5:12 indicates that the word was used to describe the declaration or interpretation of a variety of things. Other refs.: Dan. 2:24, 27; 5:15. ¶
2 ***pešar*** [Aramaic verb: פְּשַׁר <6590>; corresponding to <6622> below] ▶ **This word refers in a participial form (*mešappar*) to a person, Daniel in this case, who has the ability to explain dreams and visions.** Refs.: Dan. 5:12, 16. ¶
3 ***pāṯar*** [verb: פָּתַר <6622>; a prim. root (in the sense of to open up)] ▶ **This word describes Joseph's God-given ability to unravel the dreams of Pharaoh, a gift from God.** Refs.: Gen. 40:8, 16, 22; 41:8, 12, 13, 15. The term refers to this process in general since Pharaoh's magicians and wise men could not interpret his dreams. ¶
– 4 Ezra 4:7 ➔ TRANSLATE <8638>.

INTERPRETATION – 1 ***pešar*** [Aramaic masc. noun: פְּשַׁר <6591>; from INTERPRET <6590>] ▶ **This word refers to an explanation or explanations of dreams, visions.** It may mean to translate as well as to give the intent and meaning of something (Dan. 2:4–7; 5:7, 8, 12, 15–17, 26). It occurs in both singular and plural forms (Dan. 2:4, 7). It occurs with the definite article (Dan. 5:12); and with pronominal suffixes in the singular form (Dan. 4:18; 5:8). *
2 ***pêšer*** [masc. noun: פֵּשֶׁר <6592>; corresponding to <6591> above] ▶ **This word refers to the intention and meaning of something, how it should be understood and acted on; it is also translated explanation.** Ref.: Eccl. 8:1. ¶
3 ***piṯrôn*** [masc. noun: פִּתְרוֹן <6623>; from INTERPRET <6622>] ▶ **This word refers to explanation, meaning.** It refers to the answer, solution, the result of the interpretive process (Gen. 40:5, 8, 12, 18; 41:11). ¶
– 4 Prov. 1:6 ➔ SAYING <4426> 5 See INTERPRET <2324>.

INTERPRETING – Dan. 5:12 ➔ EXPLANATION <263>.

INTERRUPTION – ***hap̱ûgāh*** [fem. noun: הֲפוּגָה <2014>; from STUNNED <6313>] ▶ **This word means break, disruption; it is also translated intermission, stopping, respite, relief.** It is used with a preceding negative (*mē'ên*) to indicate weeping that is continuous, without relief (Lam. 3:49) over the fall of Jerusalem. ¶

INTERWOVEN – [1] 1 Kgs. 7:17 ➔ WREATH <1434> [2] Ps. 45:13 ➔ FILIGREE <4865>.

INTESTINES – [1] Ex. 29:14; Lev. 4:11; 8:17; 16:27; Num. 19:5 ➔ DUNG <6569> [2] 2 Sam. 20:10 ➔ BOWELS <4578>.

INTREAT – Gen. 25:21; etc. ➔ PRAY <6279>.

INTRIGUE – [1] Ps. 5:10 ➔ COUNSEL (noun) <4156> [2] Dan. 11:21, 34 ➔ FLATTERY <2519> [3] Hos. 7:6 ➔ AMBUSH <696>.

INVADE – Hab. 3:16 ➔ ATTACK (verb) <1464>.

INVENT – Neh. 6:8 ➔ DEVISE <908>.

INVENTION – Eccl. 7:29 ➔ DEVICE <2810>.

INWARD BEING – Ps. 51:6 ➔ INWARD PART <2910>.

INWARD PART – ***ṭuḥôṯ*** [fem. plur. noun: טֻחוֹת <2910>; from BOWSHOT <2909> (or OVERLAY <2902>) in the sense of overlaying] ▶ **This word indicates the inner being of a person.** It refers to a person's moral consciousness (Ps. 51:6; also translated inward being, innermost being, womb); the ability to perceive right and wrong or discern wisely (Job 38:36; also translated innermost being, mind). ¶

INWARD PARTS – [1] 2 Sam. 20:10 ➔ BOWELS <4578> [2] Ps. 139:13 ➔ KIDNEY <3629>.

IPHDEIAH – ***yip̱ḏᵉyāh*** [masc. proper noun: יִפְדְּיָה <3301>; from REDEEM <6299> and LORD <3050>]: the Lord will redeem ▶ **A Benjamite, son of Shashak.** Ref.: 1 Chr. 8:25. ¶

IPHEDEIAH – 1 Chr. 8:25 ➔ IPHDEIAH <3301>.

IPHTAH – Josh. 15:43 ➔ JEPHTHAH <3316> b.

IPHTAHEL – ***yip̱taḥ'ēl*** [proper noun: יִפְתַּח־אֵל <3317>; from OPEN <6605> and GOD <410>]: God opens ▶ **A valley at the border of Zebulon and Asher.** Refs.: Josh. 19:14, 27. ¶

IR – ***'iyr*** [masc. proper noun: עִיר <5893>; the same as CITY <5892>]: city ▶ **A descendant of Benjamin.** Ref.: 1 Chr. 7:12. ¶

IR-NAHASH – ***'iyr nāḥāš*** [masc. proper noun: עִיר נָחָשׁ <5904>; from CITY <5892> and SERPENT <5175>]: city of a serpent ▶ **An Israelite of the tribe of Judah (or a city of unspecified location).** Ref.: 1 Chr. 4:12. ¶

IR-SHEMESH – ***'iyr šemeš*** [proper noun: עִיר שֶׁמֶשׁ <5905>; from CITY <5892> and SUN <8121>]: city of the sun ▶ **A city given as inheritance to the tribe of Dan.** Ref.: Josh. 19:41. ¶

IRA – ***'iyrā'*** [masc. proper noun: עִירָא <5896>; from AWAKE <5782>]: wakeful ▶
a. A Jairite. Ref.: 2 Sam. 20:26. ¶
b. A son of Ikkesh. Refs.: 2 Sam. 23:26; 1 Chr. 11:28; 27:9. ¶
c. One of David's mighty men. Refs.: 2 Sam. 23:38; 1 Chr. 11:40. ¶

IRAD – ***'iyrāḏ*** [masc. proper noun: עִירָד <5897>; from the same as ARAD <6166>]: fugitive, wild donkey ▶ **An antediluvian descendant of Cain.** Ref.: Gen. 4:18. ¶

IRAM – ***'iyrām*** [masc. proper noun: עִירָם <5902>; from CITY <5892>]: belonging to a city ▶ **A leader among the Edomites.** Refs.: Gen. 36:43; 1 Chr. 1:54. ¶

IRI – ***'iyriy*** [masc. proper noun: עִירִי <5901>; from CITY <5892>]: belonging to a city ▶ **A Benjamite, son of Bela; he and his brothers were mighty warriors.** Ref.: 1 Chr. 7:7. ¶

IRIJAH – ***yir'iyyāyh*** [masc. proper noun: יִרְאִיָּיה <3376>; from FEARING <3373> and LORD <3050>]: fearful of the Lord ▶ **A captain of the guard who arrested Jeremiah the prophet.** Refs.: Jer. 37:13, 14. ¶

IRON (metal) – [1] ***barzel*** [masc. noun: בַּרְזֶל <1270>; perhaps from the root of BIRZAITH <1269>] ▶ **It is the most common and important of all metals. Its discovery and use was a major contribution to the development of civilization. It was also symbolic of power and strength. This word also means an iron ax head.** It is found in lists detailing various metals (Num. 31:22; Josh. 22:8; Dan. 2:35). It was found in the earth as ore and had to be smelted to purify it (Deut. 8:9; Job 28:2). Many ancient implements of all kinds were made of iron (Gen. 4:22), such as bedsteads (Deut. 3:11); tools (Gen. 4:22; Deut. 27:5; Josh. 8:31; 1 Kgs. 6:7); farming tools (Deut. 28:48; 2 Sam. 12:31). It was used in powerful chariots of war (Josh. 17:16, 18; Judg. 1:19; 4:3). The mention of iron stands out in importance several times: the iron ax head that Elisha caused to float (2 Kgs. 6:5, 6); tools made of iron (Job 19:24; Jer. 17:1); the iron scepter by which the Messiah will reign, indicating a rulership of power and authority (Ps. 2:9). It is used in a figurative sense many times: the sky is made like iron (Lev. 26:19); the limbs and sinews of Leviathan or Behemoth are like iron rods (Job 40:18); iron used to sharpen iron is like a mind sharpening another mind (Prov. 27:17); a horn strong like iron to thresh with (Mic. 4:13). *

[2] ***parzel*** [Aramaic masc. noun: פַּרְזֶל <6523>; corresponding to <1270> above] ▶ **See definition for *barzel* above.** It is used to symbolize strength, power, inhumaneness in the beast of Daniel 7, as well as strength and power in Daniel 2 (2:33–35, 40–43, 45; 7:7, 19). It was found in various kinds of tools and equipment (Dan. 4:15, 23); as well as in the production of idols (Dan. 5:4, 23). *

IRON (place) – ***yir'ôn*** [proper noun: יִרְאוֹן <3375>; from FEAR (VERB) <3372>]: fearing ▶ **A city of Nephtali.** Ref.: Josh. 19:38. ¶

IRON COLLAR – Jer. 29:26 ➔ NECK IRON <6729> a.

IRPEEL – ***yirp^{e}'ēl*** [proper noun: יִרְפְּאֵל <3416>; from HEAL <7495> and GOD <410>]: God will heal ▶ **One of the cities of the tribe of Benjamin.** Ref.: Josh. 18:27. ¶

IRREVERENCE – 2 Sam. 6:7 ➔ ERROR <7944>.

IRREVERENT ACT – 2 Sam. 6:7 ➔ ERROR <7944>.

IRRITANT – Num. 33:55 ➔ BARB <7899>.

IRRITATE – ***rā'am*** [verb: רָעַם <7481>; a prim. root] ▶ **This word means to be agitated, to be worried, to be anxious; it is also translated to make miserable, to keep provoking, to make fret.** It refers to agitating, picking on persons, possibly making fun of them or mocking them (1 Sam. 1:6). It refers to a worried or anxious countenance (face) because of a threatening situation (Ezek. 27:35: to be troubled, to be convulsed, to be distorted with fear). For another meaning of the Hebrew word, see THUNDER (verb) <7481>. ¶

IRU – ***'iyrû*** [masc. proper noun: עִירוּ <5900>; from CITY <5892>]: citizen ▶ **The oldest son of Caleb.** Ref.: 1 Chr. 4:15. ¶

IS THERE NOT – ***'iyn*** [neg. adv.: אִין <371>; apparently a shortened form of NO

<369>] ▶ **This word is found only in 1 Samuel 21:8.** It is also translated "Have you not." ❡

ISAAC – [1] ***yiṣḥāq*** [masc. proper noun: יִצְחָק <3327>; from LAUGH <6711>]: laughter (cf. Gen. 17:17) ▶ **The promised son and heir of Abraham and the Lord's promises to him.** Refs.: Gen. 15; 26:1–6. Abraham was one hundred years old when Isaac was born. Through him God would complete His goals for calling Abraham (Gen. 12:1–3). He was the son of Abraham through whom God would bless the nations and keep His covenant and promises to Abraham (Gen. 21:8–10; 25:1–6). His birth was a special act of God (Gen. 21:1–7). His preservation as the promised son was as much a miracle or more as his birth (Gen. 22). His wife Rebekah, a woman picked by God (Gen. 24), bore him Jacob, the father of the twelve patriarchs (Gen. 24; 25:21–26). He fell prey to Jacob and Rebekah's scheming and blessed Jacob instead of Esau with the birthright blessing (Gen. 27:1–33). *
[2] ***yiśḥāq*** [masc. proper noun: יִשְׂחָק <3446>; comp. <3327> above]: laughter ▶ **This word is a variant spelling of *yiṣḥāq* (<3327> above).** It is found in Psalm 105:9; Jeremiah 33:26; Amos 7:9, 16. ❡

ISAIAH – ***y^ešaʿyāh, y^ešaʿyāhû*** [masc. proper noun: יְשַׁעְיָה, יְשַׁעְיָהוּ <3470>; from SAVE <3467> and LORD <3050>]: the Lord has saved ▶
a. The prophet Isaiah who prophesied during the reigns of Uzziah, Jotham, Ahaz, and Hezekiah in Judah (ca. 792–686 B.C.). Refs.: Is. 1:1; see also 2 Kgs. 19:2, 5, 6, 20; 20:1, 4, 7–9, 11, 14, 16, 19; 2 Chr. 26:22; 32:20, 32. He was a prophet to the kingdom of Judah. His father was Amoz who lived in Jerusalem (Is. 37:2). He was an astute observer of the world of his day and moved easily and boldly among the rulers of Judah, both civil and religious. Many scholars conclude that he was of the line of David, of royal descent.

His call occurred dramatically in the year of Uzziah's death (Is. 6:1; 640 B.C.). His last historical appearance was probably in ca. 701 B.C. at the time of Sennacherib's threatened siege of Jerusalem (2 Kgs. 19–20; 37–38). He may have suffered a violent death (cf. Heb. 11:37). He was married (Is. 7:3) and had two sons whose names served as prophetic object lessons: Shear-Jashub, "a remnant will return" and Maher-Shalal-Hash-Baz, "hasten booty, speed the loot" (Is. 8:1–10). He warned kings, rebuked kings, and comforted kings as the Lord instructed him (Is. 7:1–16; 36–37; 38–39). He is the prophet most cited, alluded to, or echoed in the New Testament. Other refs.: Is. 2:1; 13:1; 20:2, 3; 37:5, 6, 21; 38:1, 4, 21; 39:3, 5, 8. ❡
b. A son of Jeduthun who took part in Temple worship, including prophecy and worship. Refs.: 1 Chr. 25:3, 15. ❡
c. A Levite, son of Rehabiah, who helped administer Temple treasuries. Ref.: 1 Chr. 26:25. ❡
d. A descendant of Hananiah of the royal line of Judah. Ref.: 1 Chr. 3:21. ❡
e. A descendant of Elam, a family head in Judah. Ref.: Ezra 8:7. ❡
f. A descendant of Merari of the tribe of Levi. He returned under Ezra as a Temple servant (Ezra 8:19). ❡
g. A new Benjamite resident of Jerusalem after the exile. His son was Ithiel (Neh. 11:7). ❡

ISCAH – ***yiskāh*** [fem. proper noun: יִסְכָּה <3252>; from an unused root meaning to watch]: one who looks forth ▶ **The daughter of Haran and sister of Milcah and Lot.** Ref.: Gen. 11:29. ❡

ISH-BOSHETH – ***'iyš bōšeṯ*** [masc. proper noun: אִישׁ בֹּשֶׁת <378>; from MAN <376> and SHAME <1322>]: man of shame ▶ **This name refers to one of Saul's sons whom Abner put forth as king against David after Saul's death.** Refs.: 2 Sam. 2:8, 10, 12, 15. He later offended Abner (2 Sam. 3:7, 8) and was killed (2 Sam. 4:5, 8, 12). David avenged his death by executing his assassins. Other refs.: 2 Sam. 3:11, 14, 15. ❡

ISH-TOB – ***'iyš-ṭôḇ, 'iyš ṭôḇ*** [proper noun: אִישׁ־טוֹב, אִישׁ טוֹב <382>; from MAN <376> and TOB <2897>]: man of Tob ▶

a. This word is translated by the KJV as the proper name Ish-tob. Refs.: 2 Sam. 10:6, 8.
b. In other versions, it is translated as the men of Tob, *'iyš* (MAN <376>) and *ṭôḇ* (TOB <2897>). Refs.: 2 Sam. 10:6, 8. ¶

ISHBAH – ***yišbāḥ*** [masc. proper noun: יִשְׁבָּח <3431>; from SOOTHE <7623> (in the sense of to praise)]: he gives thanks ▶ **A man of the tribe of Judah.** Ref.: 1 Chr. 4:17. ¶

ISHBAK – ***yišbāq*** [masc. proper noun: יִשְׁבָּק <3435>; from an unused root corresponding to LEAVE, LEAVE ALONE <7662>]: he will leave ▶ **A descendant of Abraham and Keturah.** Refs.: Gen. 25:2; 1 Chr. 1:32. ¶

ISHBI-BENOB – ***yišbiy b^{e}nōḇ*** [masc. proper noun: יִשְׁבִּי בְּנֹב <3430>; from DWELL <3427>, with a pron. suffix and a prep. interposed]: his dwelling is in Nob ▶ **A Philistine giant who thought to kill David, but was killed by Abishai.** Ref.: 2 Sam. 21:16. ¶

ISHDOD – ***'iyšhôḏ*** [masc. proper noun: אִישְׁהוֹד <379>; from MAN <376> and VIGOR <1935> (in the sense of authority, majesty)]: man of majesty ▶ **An Israelite of the tribe of Manasseh.** Ref.: 1 Chr. 7:18. ¶

ISHI – ***yiš'iy*** [masc. proper noun: יִשְׁעִי <3469>; from SAVE <3467>] ▶
a. A descendant of Jerahmeel. Ref.: 1 Chr. 2:31. ¶
b. A Manassite. Ref.: 1 Chr. 5:24. ¶
c. A Judaite. Ref.: 1 Chr. 4:20. ¶
d. A Simeonite. Ref.: 1 Chr. 4:42. ¶

ISHIAH – See ISSHIAH <3449>.

ISHIJAH – See ISSHIAH <3449>.

ISHMA – ***yišmā'*** [masc. proper noun: יִשְׁמָא <3457>; from DESOLATE (BE) <3456>]: desolate ▶ **A man of the tribe of Judah, descendant of Hur.** Ref.: 1 Chr. 4:3; see. v. 4. ¶

ISHMAEL – ***yišmā'ê'l*** [masc. proper noun: יִשְׁמָעֵאל <3458>; from HEAR <8085> and GOD <410>]: God will hear ▶
a. A son of Abraham by Hagar, his Egyptian concubine. He was not a city dweller but preferred the free range of the deserts (Gen. 16:11). He became an outdoors person, roamed freely in the desert wilderness, and produced a great progeny like him (Gen. 16:12). He was born when Abraham was eighty-six years old. He is considered to be the ancestor of many Arabs (Gen. 25:12–18). *
b. A Judahite who was the father of Zebadiah, the leader of Judah in Jehoshaphat's day. Refs.: 2 Chr. 19:8–11. ¶
c. A son of Azel, the head of a family in Jerusalem. Refs.: 1 Chr. 8:38; 9:44. ¶
d. The son of Jehohanan, a leader of a unit of one hundred. Ref.: 2 Chr. 23:1. ¶
e. A descendant of Pashur who intermarried with the people of the land. Ref.: Ezra 10:22. ¶
f. He was of the line of David and led an uprising that assassinated Gedeliah at Mizpah. He wanted to be king himself and believed that the Jews should not submit to the Babylonians (Jer. 41:1–3). *

ISHMAELITE – ***yišm^{e}'ê'liy*** [proper noun: יִשְׁמְעֵאלִי <3459>; patron. from ISHMAEL <3458>] ▶ **A descendant of Ishmael.** Refs.: Gen. 37:25, 27, 28; 39:1; Judg. 8:24; 1 Chr. 2:17; 27:30; Ps. 83:6. ¶

ISHMAIAH – ***yišma'yāh, yišma'yāhû*** [masc. proper noun: יִשְׁמַעְיָה, יִשְׁמַעְיָהוּ <3460>; from HEAR <8085> and GOD <410>]: the Lord will hear ▶
a. A Gibeonite. Ref.: 1 Chr. 12:4. ¶
b. A man of Zebulun. Ref.: 1 Chr. 27:19. ¶

ISHMERAI – ***yišm^{e}ray*** [masc. proper noun: יִשְׁמְרַי <3461>; from KEEP <8104>]: the Lord keeps ▶ **A man of the tribe of Benjamin, a son of Elpaal.** Ref.: 1 Chr. 8:18. ¶

ISHPAH – ***yišpāh*** [masc. proper noun: יִשְׁפָּה <3472>; perhaps from STICK OUT <8192>] ▶ **A Benjamite, son of Beriah.** Ref.: 1 Chr. 8:16. ¶

ISHPAN – ***yišpān*** [masc. proper noun: יִשְׁפָּן <3473>; prob. from the same as SHAPHAN <8227>]: he will hide ► **A Benjamite, son of Shashak.** Ref.: 1 Chr. 8:22. ¶

ISHUAH, ISHVAH – ***yišwāh*** [masc. proper noun: יִשְׁוָה <3438>; from LIKE (BE) <7737>]: he will be like, he will be equal ► **Second son of Asher.** Refs.: Gen. 46:17; 1 Chr. 7:30. ¶

ISHUAI – See ISHVI <3440> a.

ISHUI – See ISHVI <3440> b.

ISHVI – ***yišwiy*** [masc. proper noun: יִשְׁוִי <3440>; from LIKE (BE) <7737>]: he will be like, he will be equal ►
a. An Asherite. Refs.: Gen. 46:17; Num. 26:44; 1 Chr. 7:30. ¶
b. Son of Saul. Ref.: 1 Sam. 14:49. ¶

ISHVITE – ***yišwiy*** [masc. proper noun: יִשְׁוִי <3441>; patron. from ISHVI <3440>] ► **Member of the family of Ishvi.** Ref.: Num. 26:44. ¶

ISLAND – [1] Job 22:30 ➔ NOT <336> [2] Is. 13:22; 34:14; Jer. 50:39: wild beast of the islands ➔ HYENA <338> [3] Is. 20:6; 23:2, 6; etc. ➔ COASTLAND <339>.

ISMACHIAH – ***yismak̲yāhû*** [masc. proper noun: יִסְמַכְיָהוּ <3253>; from LAY ON <5564> (in the sense of to uphold, to sustain) and LORD <3050>]: the Lord sustains ► **A Gibeonite who joined David at Ziklag.** Ref.: 2 Chr. 31:13. ¶

ISMAKIAH – 2 Chr. 31:13 ➔ ISMACHIAH <3253>.

ISOLATED – [1] 2 Kgs. 15:5; 2 Chr. 26:21 ➔ SEPARATE (adj.) <2669> [2] Is. 27:10 ➔ ALONE <910>.

ISPAH – 1 Chr. 8:16 ➔ ISHPAH <3472>.

ISRAEL – [1] ***yiśrā'ēl*** [proper noun: יִשְׂרָאֵל <3478>; from STRUGGLE <8280> and GOD <410>]: he who struggles with God ►
a. The name given to Jacob after he wrestled with the messenger of God and prevailed. Ref.: Gen. 32:28. It was used of the descendants of Jacob who went to Egypt (70 in all) but was applied to the nation that developed from those descendants (Ex. 1:1, 7). This name is explained again in Genesis 35:10. The name Jacob had been interpreted in context as well (Gen. 25:26), "he deceives." *
b. The persons descended from Jacob who was renamed Israel (Gen. 35:10; see a. above). His descendants became known as Israel (Ex. 1:1, 7). They were known as the "twelve tribes of Israel [Jacob]" (Gen. 49:7, 16, 28). The Lord became "the Rock of Israel" (Gen. 49:24).

The land of Israel was ideally the territory first described to Abraham. It stretched from the river of Egypt (El-Arish) to the great Euphrates River and encompassed the territory of the Kenites, Kenizzites, Kadmonites, Hittites, Perizzites, Rephaites, Amorites, Canaanites, Girgashites, and Jebusites (Gen. 15:17–21; cf. also Gen. 10:15–18). The full expanse of this territory was occupied during the reign of David and Solomon and approached during the time of Israel-Judah under the respective contemporary reigns of Jeroboam II in Israel and Azariah (Uzziah) in Judah. Most often, however, the land of Israel in the Old Testament is designated as the territory from Dan (north) to Beersheba (south). After Israel divided into two kingdoms in 930 B.C., the name refers still to all of Israel but most often to northern Israel. After the return from exile in 538 B.C., the term is used of the whole restored community again regularly. *

[2] ***yiśra'ēl*** [Aramaic proper noun: יִשְׂרָאֵל <3479>; corresponding to <3478> above]: he who struggles with God ► **This word designates the Aramaic spelling of Israel. See ISRAEL <3478> b.** It occurs only in the Aramaic portions of Ezra (5:1, 11; 6:14, 16, 17; 7:13, 15). ¶

ISRAELITE – ***yiśrᵉ'ēliy*** [masc. proper noun: יִשְׂרְאֵלִי <3481>; patron. from ISRAEL <3478>] ► **A male descendant of Israel.** Refs.: Lev. 24:10; 2 Sam. 17:25. ¶

ISRAELITESS – ***yiśrᵉʾēliyṯ*** [fem. proper noun: יִשְׂרְאֵלִית <3482>; fem. of ISRAELITE <3481>] ▶ **A female descendant of Israel.** Refs.: Lev. 24:10, 11. ¶

ISRAELITISH – Lev. 24:10, 11 ➔ ISRAELITESS <3482>.

ISSACHAR – ***yiśśaśḵār*** [masc. proper noun: יִשָּׂשכָר <3485>; from CARRY <5375> and WAGES <7939> (in the sense of reward)]: he will bring a reward ▶
a. Jacob's fifth son by Leah. Refs.: Gen. 30:18; 35:23. Issachar is often paired with Zebulun (Gen. 49:14; Deut. 33:18, 19) and his wealth with maritime riches. He had four sons (1 Chr. 7:1). Other refs.: Gen. 46:13; Ex. 1:3; 1 Chr. 2:1. ¶
b. The descendants of Issachar (see a. above). The growth of the tribe is indicated in 1 Chronicles 7:1–5. During David's reign, the tribe provided many soldiers and leading commanders. Deborah was from Issachar's tribe (Judg. 5:1–15). Tola, a minor judge, was from Issachar (Judg. 10:1). King Baasha in Israel was from this tribe (1 Kgs. 15:27). The tribe was located among several other tribes: Zebulon and Manasseh, west; Naphtali, north; Manasseh, south; Gad, east. The men of Issachar were noted for their understanding and action by the time of David (1 Chr. 12:32). Issachar was allotted a place in Ezekiel's vision of a new Temple and a New Jerusalem (Ezek. 48:25–33). *
c. A son of Obed-Edom. He served as a gatekeeper at the Temple and city (1 Chr. 26:5). ¶

ISSHIAH – ***yiššiyyāhû, yiššiyyāh*** [masc. proper noun: יִשִּׁיָּהוּ, יִשִּׁיָּה <3449>; from LEND <5383> and LORD <3050>]: the Lord will lend ▶
a. One of David's mighty men. Ref.: 1 Chr. 12:6. ¶
b. A descendant of Issachar. Ref.: 1 Chr. 7:3. ¶
c. A Levite. Refs.: 1 Chr. 23:20; 24:25. ¶
d. A Levite. Ref.: 1 Chr. 24:21. ¶
e. A postexilic Jew. Ref.: Ezra 10:31. ¶

ISSHIJAH – See ISSHIAH <3449>.

ISSUE – [1] ***zirmāh*** [fem. noun: זִרְמָה <2231>; fem. of STORM (noun) <2230>] ▶ **This word denotes a flow or discharge of liquid; it is also translated emission.** It refers to a seminal discharge and is used figuratively of the excessive lustfulness of Israel's illicit lovers (Ezek. 23:20). ¶
[2] ***ṣᵉpiyʿāh*** [fem. noun: צְפִיעָה <6849>; from the same as VIPER <6848> (maybe in the sense of an outcast)] ▶ **This word means an offshoot.** It describes the descendants of a person, posterity; especially important will be the offspring of a messianic figure (Is. 22:24). ¶
– [3] Gen. 48:6 ➔ KINDRED <4138> [4] Lev. 12:7 ➔ FOUNTAIN <4726> [5] See DISCHARGE <2101>.

ISSUE FORTH – See FLOW (verb) <5047>.

ISUI – See ISHVI <3440> a.

IT MAY BE THAT – Gen. 16:2; Job 1:5 ➔ PERHAPS <194>.

ITCH – [1] ***ḥeres*** [masc. noun: חֶרֶס <2775>; from an unused root meaning to scrape] ▶ **The word indicates a skin disorder.** It is listed among the curses as one of the skin diseases the Lord will bring on Israel if they disobey the Sinai covenant (Deut. 28:27). The Hebrew word also refers to the sun; see SUN <2775>. ¶
– [2] Lev. 13:30–37; 14:54 ➔ SKIN DISEASE <5424>.

ITHAMAR – ***ʾiyṯāmār*** [masc. proper noun: אִיתָמָר <385>; from COASTLAND <339> and PALM TREE <8558>]: island of the palm tree ▶ **He was Aaron's youngest son who served in the newly established priesthood.** Refs.: Ex. 6:23; Num. 3:2 Ex. 28:1. He was involved in building the Tabernacle and keeping records about it (Ex. 38:21). He was present when Nadab and Abihu were killed (Lev. 10:6–16). He directed the work of the Merarites and Gershonites as they cared for the wagons transporting the Tabernacle (Num. 7:8). One of his descendants, Daniel, returned from the Babylonian Exile under Ezra (Ezra 8:2). *

ITHIEL – ***'iyṯiy'ēl*** [masc. proper noun: אִיתִיאֵל <384>; perhaps from HAPPY <837> and GOD <410>]: God is with me ▶
a. One of two persons instructed by Agur. Ref.: Prov. 30:1. ¶
b. An Israelite of the tribe of Benjamin; his descendants returned from Babylon. Ref.: Neh. 11:7. ¶

ITHLAH – ***yiṯlāh*** [proper noun: יִתְלָה <3494>; prob. from HANG <8518> (in the sense of suspending something in the air)]: height ▶ **A city of the tribe of Dan.** Ref.: Josh. 19:42. ¶

ITHMAH – ***yiṯmāh*** [masc. proper noun: יִתְמָה <3495>; from the same as ORPHAN <3490>]: orphan ▶ **A Moabite, one of David's strong men.** Ref.: 1 Chr. 11:46. ¶

ITHNAN – ***yiṯnān*** [proper noun: יִתְנָן <3497>; from the same as SERPENT <8577>]: extensive ▶ **A city at the extreme south of Judah.** Ref.: Josh. 15:23. ¶

ITHRA, JETHER – ***yiṯrā'*** [masc. proper noun: יִתְרָא <3501>; by variation for <3502>]: abundance ▶ **An Israelite who married Abigail the daughter of Nahash and became the father of Amasa.** Ref.: 2 Sam. 17:25. He is called Jether elsewhere; see JETHRO, JETHER <3500>. ¶

ITHRAN – ***yiṯrān*** [masc. proper noun: יִתְרָן <3506>; from REMAIN <3498> (in the sense of to excel; see REMAINDER <3499>)]: excellence ▶
a. An Edomite. Refs.: Gen. 36:26; 1 Chr. 1:41. ¶
b. An Asherite. Ref.: 1 Chr. 7:37. ¶

ITHREAM – ***yiṯreʿām*** [masc. proper noun: יִתְרְעָם <3507>; from REMAINDER <3499> (in the sense of excellence) and PEOPLE <5971>]: excellence of people ▶ **One of the sons of David born by his wife Eglah in Hebron.** Refs.: 2 Sam. 3:5; 1 Chr. 3:3. ¶

ITHRITE – ***yiṯriy*** [proper noun: יִתְרִי <3505>; patron. from JETHER <3500>] ▶ **This word designates two of David's mighty men.** Refs.: 2 Sam. 23:38; 1 Chr. 2:53; 11:40. ¶

ITTAH-KAZIN – ***'ittāh qāṣiyn*** [proper noun: עִתָּה קָצִין <6278>]: time of the judge ▶ **See ETH-KAZIN <6278>.** Ref.: Josh 19:13. ¶

ITTAI – ***'ittay*** [masc. proper noun: אִתַּי <863>; from WITH <854>]: with, near ▶
a. The name of one of David's faithful Philistine commanders, a Gittite. Refs.: 2 Sam. 18:2, 5, 12. He chose to stay with David rather than go away in safety while David fled from Absalom (2 Sam. 15:19–22). ¶
b. Also the name given to one of David's select warriors, one of his "thirty." Refs.: 2 Sam. 23:24–39. Other ref.: 1 Chr. 11:31. ¶

IVORY – ***šenhabbiym*** [masc. noun: שֶׁנְהַבִּים <8143>; from TOOTH <8127>] ▶ **This word refers to the white dentin of the tusks of elephants, walruses, etc.** It was highly prized in the ancient world and very scarce (1 Kgs. 10:22; 2 Chr. 9:21). Solomon imported ivory. ¶

IVVAH – See AVVA <5755>.

IYE-ABARIM – ***'iyyêy hāᵃ-ḇāriym*** [proper noun: עִיֵּי הָעֲבָרִים <5863>; from the plur. of RUINS <5856> and the plur. of the act. part. of PASS THROUGH, PASS OVER <5674>]: ruins of Abarim (i.e., the passers) ▶ **A place in the desert where the Israelites camped.** Refs.: Num. 21:11; 33:44. ¶

IYIM – ***'iyyiym*** [proper noun: עִיִּים <5864>; plur. of RUINS <5856>] ▶
a. Another name for IYE-ABARIM (<5863>). Ref.: Num. 33:45.
b. A city in Judah. Ref.: Josh. 15:29. ¶

IZHAR – [1] ***yiṣhār*** [masc. proper noun: יִצְהָר <3324>; the same as OIL <3323>]: oil ▶ **A Levite, son of Kohath.** Refs.: Ex.

6:18, 21; Num. 3:19; 1 Chr. 6:2, 18, 38; 23:12, 18. He was the father of Korah who revolted against Moses (Num. 16:1). ¶
2 ***yiṣḥar*** [masc. proper noun: יִצְחַר <3328>; from the same as WHITE <6713> b.] ▶ **A man of the tribe of Judah.** Ref.: 1 Chr. 4:7. ¶

IZHARITE – ***yiṣhāriy*** [proper noun: יִצְהָרִי <3325>; patron. from IZHAR <3324>] ▶ **A descendant of Izhar.** Refs.: Num. 3:27; 1 Chr. 24:22; 26:23, 29. ¶

IZLIAH – ***yizliy'āh*** [masc. proper noun: יִזְלִיאָה <3152>; perhaps from an unused root (meaning to draw out)]: the Lord will deliver ▶ **A man of the tribe of Benjamin.** Ref.: 1 Chr. 8:18. ¶

IZRAHIAH – ***yizraḥyāh*** [masc. proper noun: יִזְרַחְיָה <3156>; from RISE UP <2224> (also meaning to shine forth) and LORD <3050>]: the Lord will arise, the Lord will shine ▶ **a. A musical leader in the time of Nehemiah.** Ref.: Neh. 12:42. ¶
b. Grandson of Tola, from the tribe of Issachar. Ref.: 1 Chr. 7:3. ¶

IZRAHITE – ***yizrāḥ*** [masc. proper noun: יִזְרָח <3155>; a variation for EZRAHITE <250>] ▶ **A descendant of Zerah; the designation of Shamhuth.** Ref.: 1 Chr. 27:8. ¶

IZRI – ***yiṣriy*** [masc. proper noun: יִצְרִי <3339>; from FORM (verb) <3335>] ▶ **A Levite, son of Jeduthun; the leader of the fourth division of singers.** Ref.: 1 Chr. 25:11. His name is spelled Zeri in v. 3. ¶

IZZIAH – ***yizziyyāh*** [masc. proper noun: יִזִּיָּה <3150>; from the same as the first part of JEZIEL <3149> and LORD <3050>]: sprinkled of the Lord ▶ **He had married a foreign woman in Ezra's time.** Ref.: Ezra 10:25. ¶

J

JAAKAN – ***yaʿăqān*** [masc. proper noun: יַעֲקָן <3292>; from the same as AKAN <6130>]: one who twists ▶ **The people of Israel camped beside the descendants of Jaakan.** Ref.: Deut. 10:6. This man (spelled Akan) was the grandson of Seir (1 Chr. 1:42; see also Gen. 36:27). ¶

JAAKOBAH – ***yaʿăqōḇāh*** [masc. proper noun: יַעֲקֹבָה <3291>; from JACOB <3290>]: one taking advantage ▶ **A descendant of Simeon.** Ref.: 1 Chr. 4:36. ¶

JAALA – ***yaʿălaʾ, yaʿălāh*** [masc. proper noun: יַעֲלָא, יַעֲלָה <3279>; the same as DOE <3280> or direct from PROFIT (verb) <3276> (in the sense of climbing)]: little mountain goat ▶ **A Nethinim, i.e., a Temple servant, whose descendants returned from the Babylonian captivity.** Refs.: Ezra 2:56; Neh. 7:58. ¶

JAALAM – ***yaʿlām*** [masc. proper noun: יַעְלָם <3281>; from HIDE <5956>]: hidden ▶ **One of the sons of Esau and his wife Aholibamah.** He became one of the chiefs of Edom (Gen. 36:5, 14, 18; 1 Chr. 1:35). ¶

JAANAI – ***yaʿnay*** [masc. proper noun: יַעְנַי <3285>; from the same as OSTRICH <3283> (in the sense of paying attention; see BECAUSE <3282>)]: responsive ▶ **A chief in Israel from the tribe of Gad.** Ref.: 1 Chr. 5:12. ¶

JAAR – Ps. 132:6 ➔ FOREST <3293>.

JAARE-OREGIM – ***yaʿărêy ʾōrĕgiym*** [masc. proper noun: יַעֲרֵי אֹרְגִים <3296>; from the plur. of FOREST <3293> and the masc. plur. act. part. of WEAVE <707>]: forests of the weavers ▶ **A Bethlehemite; his son Elhanan slew the brother of Goliath the Gittite.** Ref.: 2 Sam. 21:19; see 1 Chr. 20:5. ¶

JAASAI – Ezra 10:37 ➔ JAASU <3299>.

JAASAU – Ezra 10:37 ➔ JAASU <3299>.

JAASIEL – ***yaʿăśiyʾēl*** [masc. proper noun: יַעֲשִׂיאֵל <3300>; from DO <6213> and GOD <410>]: God makes ▶
a. One of David's mighty men. Ref.: 1 Chr. 11:47. ¶
b. A Benjamite. Ref.: 1 Chr. 27:21. ¶

JAASU – ***yaʿăśāw*** [masc. proper noun: יַעֲשָׂו <3299>; from DO <6213>]: they will do ▶ **One of the sons of Bani; Ezra persuaded him to put away the foreign woman he had married.** Ref.: Ezra 10:37. ¶

JAAZANIAH – ***yaʾăzanyāhû, yaʾăzanyāh*** [masc. proper noun: יַאֲזַנְיָהוּ, יַאֲזַנְיָה <2970>; from EAR (GIVE) <238> and LORD <3050>]: heard by the Lord ▶
a. A Maachathite. Ref.: 2 Kgs. 25:23. ¶
b. A Rechabite. Ref.: Jer. 35:3. ¶
c. Son of Shaphan. Ref.: Ezek. 8:11. ¶
d. Son of Azur. Ref.: Ezek. 11:1. ¶

JAAZIAH – ***yaʿăziyyāhû*** [masc. proper noun: יַעֲזִיָּהוּ <3269>; from FIERCE <3267> and GOD <410>]: made strong by the Lord ▶ **A son or descendant of Merari the Levite.** Refs.: 1 Chr. 24:26, 27. ¶

JAAZIEL – ***yaʿăziyʾēl*** [masc. proper noun: יַעֲזִיאֵל <3268>; from FIERCE <3267> and GOD <410>]: made strong by God ▶ **A Levite appointed by David for the musical service related to the Tabernacle in Jerusalem.** Ref.: 1 Chr. 15:18. ¶

JABAL – ***yāḇāl, yabbeleṯ*** [masc. proper noun: יָבָל, יַבֶּלֶת <2989>; the same as STREAM (noun) <2988>]: stream ▶ **Son of Lamech, a descendant of Cain.** Ref.: Gen. 4:20. ¶

JABBOK – ***yabbōq*** [proper noun: יַבֹּק <2999>; prob. from EMPTY (MAKE) <1238>]: which flows, a pouring out ▶ **A proper noun designating the Jabbok, a Transjordanian river, swift flowing, from modern Amman, Jordan, north and west into the Jordan.** Jacob wrestled with the angel of the Lord (Gen. 32:22) along its shores. Because of his effort, his name was changed to Israel. The river bounded the Amorites on the north (Num. 21:24; Deut. 2:37). It also served as a boundary to the tribes of Manasseh and Reuben (Deut. 3:16; Josh. 12:2). Other refs.: Judg. 11:13, 22. ¶

JABESH – ***yāḇêš*** [proper noun and masc. proper noun: יָבֵשׁ <3003>; the same as DRIED, DRY <3002>]: dry ▶
a. A town in Gilead. It is located on the north side of the Jabbok, seven miles east of the Jordan River. The city kept aloof from the war against the Benjamites. As a result, the inhabitants were slaughtered, and the women served as wives to the Benjamites (Judg. 21:13, 14). Saul rescued the city in his day (1 Sam. 11:1, 9), and the inhabitants, in turn, later rescued his body from shameful exposure (1 Sam. 31:12, 13; 2 Sam. 2). It is located at Tell-el-Maglub by archaeologists today. *
b. He was the father of Shallum, a king of Israel who reigned only one month and was assassinated. Refs.: 2 Kgs. 15:8–14. ¶

JABEZ – ***ya'bêṣ*** [proper noun: יַעְבֵּץ <3258>; from an unused root prob. grieve]: sorrow, pain ▶
a. A descendant of the line of Judah, a family head. Refs.: 1 Chr. 4:9, 10. He is called an "honorable" man. His name means "he means or causes sorrow/pain," thus the expression of his mother. Jabez prays a prayer that, playing on the meaning of Jabez, asks that the Lord would grant him freedom from pain by blessing him. God did so! ¶
b. A city of Judah where the families of the scribes dwelt. Ref.: 1 Chr. 2:55. ¶

JABIN – ***yāḇiyn*** [masc. proper noun: יָבִין <2985>; from PERCEIVE <995>]: who understands ▶
a. King of Hazor. Ref.: Josh. 11:1. ¶
b. A different king of Hazor. Refs.: Judg. 4:2, 7, 17, 4:23, 24; Ps. 83:9. ¶

JABNEEL – ***yaḇnᵉ'êl*** [proper noun: יַבְנְאֵל <2995>; from BUILD <1129> and GOD <410>]: built by God ▶
a. A town in Judah. Ref.: Josh. 15:11. ¶
b. A town in Naphtali. Ref.: Josh. 19:33. ¶

JABNEH – ***yaḇneh*** [proper noun: יַבְנֶה <2996>; from BUILD <1129>]: building of God ▶ **Uzziah broke down the wall of this Philistine city.** Ref.: 2 Chr. 26:6. ¶

JACAN – ***ya'kān*** [masc. proper noun: יַעְכָּן <3275>; from the same as ACHAN <5912>]: troublesome ▶ **One of the chief men of the tribe of Gad.** Ref.: 1 Chr. 5:13. ¶

JACHAN – 1 Chr. 5:13 ➔ JACAN <3275>.

JACHIN – See JAKIN <3199>.

JACHINITE – ***yāḵiyniy*** [masc. proper noun: יָכִינִי <3200>; patron. from JAKIN <3199>]: God establishes ▶ **Member of a family descending from Jakin.** Ref.: Num. 26:12. ¶

JACINTH – ***lešem*** [masc. noun: לֶשֶׁם <3958>; from an unused root of uncertain meaning] ▶ **This word refers to a precious stone. Its exact nature is not clear.** In addition to jacinth, carnelian, and amber, several other identifications have been offered (Ex. 28:19; 39:12; KJV: ligure). It was placed in the high priest's breastplate. ¶

JACKAL – [1] ***tān*** [masc. noun: תַּן <8565>; from an unused root prob. meaning to elongate] ▶ **This word designates a wild scavenging animal or a dragon.** Jackal well is the name given to a well near the wall of Jerusalem (the NIV notes Serpent or Fig as translation possibilities as well) (Neh. 2:13). A jackal is a wild dog that gains much of its food as a scavenger, an outcast of the animals (Job 30:29); dwelling in the outskirts of the desert or wilderness (Ps. 44:19; Mal. 1:3). It tends to congregate in the ruins of cities (Is. 13:22; Jer. 9:11). It lets out a piercing, lonely howl like a lament (Mic. 1:8). It suckles its young on its breast, showing tenderness (Lam. 4:3). *
– [2] Ps. 63:10; Lam. 5:18; Ezek. 13:4 ➔ FOX <7776> [3] Is. 13:21 ➔ OWL <255>

4 Is. 34:14; Jer. 50:39 ➔ HYENA <338>
5 Mal. 1:3 ➔ DRAGON <8568>.

JACKAL WELL – Neh. 2:13 ➔ DRAGON'S SPRING <5886>.

JACKDAW – Lev. 11:18; Deut. 14:17 ➔ PELICAN <6893>.

JACOB – ***ya^{a}qōḇ*** [masc. proper noun: יַעֲקֹב <3290>; from SUPPLANT <6117>]: supplanter ▶
a. Son of Isaac. He had an older twin brother, Esau (Edom). Jacob became the father of the twelve patriarchs from whom the nation of Israel was formed. He moved with his sons to Egypt because of divine providence (Gen. 41; Ex. 1:1–7), probably sometime in the eighteenth century. He lived with his sons in Egypt until his death in Egypt (Gen. 49–50). He was embalmed in Egypt, carried out of Egypt many years before the Exodus, and buried in Canaan (Gen. 50:1–14) in the cave located in the area of Machpelah. Abraham had purchased this burial property from the Hittites living in the land (Gen. 50:12–14). Jacob produced seventy descendants (seventy-five according to the Septuagint) who went down to Egypt (Ex. 1:5).

Much of Genesis is occupied with tracing the birth, growth, and development of this father of the patriarchs. His name probably means something like "he seized or he seizes." Jacob took advantage of Esau and obtained the firstborn's birthright from him, thus supplanting him (Gen. 25:29–34). Later, he deceived Isaac into giving him the firstborn's blessing (Gen. 27:1–33).

The Lord confirmed the promises and covenants to Jacob previously made to Abraham (Gen. 28:1–22), and showed His special love for him and his progeny (Mal. 1:2). Jacob himself was deceived by Laban but eventually married Leah and Rachel through whom, with their handmaids, he fathered the ancestors of the twelve tribes (Gen. 29; 30; 35; 46). He was reconciled with Esau on his return to Canaan (Gen. 33:1–20). Israel's God, the Lord, became known as the God of Abraham, Isaac, and Jacob (Ex. 2:24; 3:15–16), and Canaan became the land sworn to Abraham, Isaac, and Jacob (Deut. 34:4).

Jacob purchased the land in Shechem. It later became the burial place for Joseph's bones (Gen. 33:19; Josh. 24:32). His name was used sometimes to refer to all of Israel (see b. below; 1 Sam. 12:8). His name was changed to Israel, "(he) has striven (wrestled) with God," after he encountered the angel of the Lord (Gen. 32:22–30) at the Jabbok River. *
b. The name Jacob often stands for all his descendants. Refs.: Lam. 1:17; Lam. 2:3; Ezek. 20:5. In fact, the name stands for all of Israel in some cases. In other contexts, it refers to northern Israel or Judah (Amos 3:13; 6:8; Mic. 1:5; Mal. 2:12; 3:6). His name, in fact, was changed to Israel (see a. above) and his descendants bore that designation and name. The seventy descendants from Jacob's "loins" became the Israelite nation in Egypt over a period of 400 years (Ex. 1:1–7). In poetry Jacob/Israel are used as parallel pairs (Ps. 14:7; 20:23). *

JADA – ***yāḏā‘*** [masc. proper noun: יָדָע <3047>; from KNOW <3045>]: knowing ▶ **Son of Onam; a descendant of Judah.** Refs.: 1 Chr. 2:28, 32. ¶

JADDUA – ***yaddûa‘*** [masc. proper noun: יַדּוּעַ <3037>; from KNOW <3045>]: known ▶
a. A chief of the people who signed the covenant of renewal with Nehemiah after the return from the Babylonian captivity. Ref.: Neh. 10:21. ¶
b. Son of Jonathan the high priest. Refs.: Neh. 12:11, 22. ¶

JADON – ***yāḏôn*** [masc. proper noun: יָדוֹן <3036>; from THANKS (GIVE) <3034>]: thankful ▶ **A Meronothite who participated in rebuilding the wall of Jerusalem.** Ref.: Neh. 3:7. ¶

JAEL – ***yā‘êl*** [fem. proper noun: יָעֵל <3278>; the same as GOAT (WILD, MOUNTAIN) <3277>]: mountain goat ▶ **This word designates the wife of Heber**

the Kenite. She killed Sisera, the commander of the army of Jabin, a great king of Canaan who reigned in Hazor (Judg. 4; 5). Specific refs.: Judg. 4:17, 18, 21, 22; 5:6, 24. ¶

JAGGED – Job 41:30 ➔ SHARP <2303>.

JAGGED POTSHERD – Job 41:30 ➔ EARTHENWARE <2789>.

JAGUR – ***yāḡûr*** [proper noun: יָגוּר <3017>; prob. from SOJOURN <1481>]: dwelling ▶ **A city on the extreme south of Judah.** Ref.: Josh. 15:21. ¶

JAHATH – ***yaḥaṯ*** [masc. proper noun: יַחַת <3189>; from UNITE <3161>]: unity ▶
a. Grandson of Judah. Ref.: 1 Chr. 4:2. ¶
b. A Levite, son of Gershom. Refs.: 1 Chr. 6:20, 43. ¶
c. A Levite, grandson of Gershom. Refs.: 1 Chr. 23:10, 11. ¶
d. A Levite of the family of Kohath. Ref.: 1 Chr. 24:22. ¶
e. A Levite of the family of Merari. Ref.: 2 Chr. 34:12. ¶

JAHAZ – ***yahaṣ, yahṣāh*** [proper noun: יַהַץ, יַהְצָה <3096>; from an unused root meaning to stamp]: trodden down ▶ **A place in the plain of Moab.** Refs.: Num. 21:23; Deut. 2:32; Josh. 13:18; 21:36; Judg. 11:20; 1 Chr. 6:78; Is. 15:4; Jer. 48:21, 34. ¶

JAHAZIAH – ***yaḥzᵉyāh*** [masc. proper noun: יַחְזְיָה <3167>; SEE <2372> and LORD <3050>]: the Lord will see ▶ **He was opposed to Ezra in the matter of separating from foreign woman married by men of Judah and Benjamin.** Ref.: Ezra 10:15. ¶

JAHAZIEL – ***yaḥᵃziy'ēl*** [masc. proper noun: יַחֲזִיאֵל <3166>; from SEE <2372> and GOD <410>]: seen by God ▶
a. A Benjamite who joined David at Ziklag. Ref.: 1 Chr. 12:4. ¶
b. A priest who participated in the removal of the ark by blowing the trumpet. Ref.: 1 Chr. 16:6. ¶
c. A Levite, the third son of Hebron. Refs.: 1 Chr. 23:19; 24:23. ¶
d. A Levite upon whom came the Spirit of the Lord; He encouraged king Jehoshaphat against the Moabites and Ammonites. Ref.: 2 Chr. 20:14. ¶
e. Father of Shechaniah who came back from the Babylonian captivity. Ref.: Ezra 8:5. ¶

JAHDAI – ***yāhday*** [masc. proper noun: יָהְדַי <3056>; perhaps from a form corresponding to JUDAH <3061>] ▶ **A man who appears among the descendants of Caleb.** Ref.: 1 Chr. 2:47. ¶

JAHDIEL – ***yaḥdiy'ēl*** [masc. proper noun: יַחְדִּיאֵל <3164>; from TOGETHER <3162> and GOD <410>]: unity of God ▶ **A descendant of Manasseh; he was a mighty warrior and famous man.** Ref.: 1 Chr. 5:24. ¶

JAHDO – ***yaḥdô*** [masc. proper noun: יַחְדּוֹ <3163>; from TOGETHER <3162> with pron. suffix]: unity ▶ **A descendant of Gad.** Ref.: 1 Chr. 5:14. ¶

JAHLEEL – ***yaḥlᵉ'ēl*** [masc. proper noun: יַחְלְאֵל <3177>; from WAIT <3176> and GOD <410>]: God waits ▶ **One of the sons of Zebulun.** Refs.: Gen. 46:14; Num. 26:26. ¶

JAHLEELITE – ***yaḥlᵉ'ēliy*** [masc. proper noun: יַחְלְאֵלִי <3178>; patron. from JAHLEEL <3177>] ▶ **Member of the family of Jahleel.** Ref.: Num. 26:26. ¶

JAHMAI – ***yaḥmay*** [masc. proper noun: יַחְמַי <3181>; prob. from CONCEIVE <3179> (in the sense of to be hot)]: hot ▶ **Member of the family of Issachar.** Ref.: 1 Chr. 7:2. ¶

JAHZEEL – ***yaḥṣᵉ'ēl*** [masc. proper noun: יַחְצְאֵל <3183>; from DIVIDE <2673> and GOD <410>]: God allots, God divides ▶ **First son of Naphtali.** Refs.: Gen. 46:24; Num. 26:48. ¶

JAHZEELITE – ***yaḥṣᵉ'ēliy*** [masc. proper noun: יַחְצְאֵלִי <3184>; patron. from JAHZEEL <3183>] ▶ **Member of the family of Jahzeel.** Ref.: Num. 26:48. ¶

JAHZERAH – ***yaḥzērāh*** [masc. proper noun: יַחְזֵרָה <3170>]: whom God leads back ▶ **A priest among the returned exiles.** Ref.: 1 Chr. 9:12. ¶

JAHZIEL – ***yaḥṣiy'ēl*** [masc. proper noun: יַחְצִיאֵל <3185>; from DIVIDE <2673> and GOD <410>]: God allots, God divides ▶ **One of the sons of Naphtali.** Ref.: 1 Chr. 7:13. ¶

JAIL – Gen. 39:20–23; 40:3, 5 ➔ PRISON <5470>.

JAÏR – [1] ***yā'iyr*** [masc. proper noun: יָאִיר <2971>; from LIGHT (GIVE) <215>]: he enlightens ▶
a. Son of Manasseh and patronym of *hawwôṯ yā'iyr* (HAVVOTH JAIR <2334>). Refs.: Num. 32:41; Deut. 3:14; Josh. 13:30; Judg. 10:4; 1 Kgs. 4:13; 1 Chr. 2:22, 23. ¶
b. A judge in Gilead. Refs.: Judg. 10:3, 5. ¶
c. Father of Mordecai. Ref.: Esther 2:5. ¶
[2] ***yā'ûr*** [masc. proper noun: יָעוּר <3265>; apparently the pass. part. of the same as FOREST <3293>]: he enlightens ▶ **Father of Elhanan who slew the brother of Goliath the Gittite.** Ref.: 1 Chr. 20:5. ¶

JAIRITE – ***yā'iriy*** [masc. proper noun: יָאִרִי <2972>; patron. from JAIR <2971>]: he enlightens ▶ **A descendant of Jair.** Ira the Jairite was David's priest (2 Sam. 20:26). ¶

JAKEH – ***yāqeh*** [masc. proper noun: יָקֶה <3348>; from an unused root prob. meaning to obey]: obedient ▶ **Father of Agur who wrote or compiled Proverbs 30.** Ref.: Prov. 30:1. ¶

JAKIM – ***yāqiym*** [masc. proper noun: יָקִים <3356>; from STAND, STAND UP <6965>]: he will raise ▶
a. A Benjamite. Ref.: 1 Chr. 8:19. ¶
b. A Levite. Ref.: 1 Chr. 24:12. ¶

JAKIN – ***yāḵiyn*** [proper noun: יָכִין <3199>; from SET UP <3559>]: He will establish ▶
a. The fourth son of Simeon. He fled to Egypt (Gen. 46:10; Ex. 6:15; Num. 26:12). ¶
b. The name of the southern pillar that Solomon erected in the portico of the Temple facing east; it is also written Jachin. Refs.: 1 Kgs. 7:21; 2 Chr. 3:17. ¶
c. A descendant of the priests who lived in Jerusalem and had resettled in Jerusalem. Refs.: 1 Chr. 9:10; 24:17. ¶
d. A priest living after the exile (538 B.C.) to whom the twenty-first lot fell. He was from Ithamar's descendants (Neh. 11:10). ¶

JAKINITE – See JACHINITE <3200>.

JALON – ***yālôn*** [masc. proper noun: יָלוֹן <3210>; from LODGE <3885>]: lodging ▶ **The youngest son of Ezra, of the tribe of Judah.** Ref.: 1 Chr. 4:17. ¶

JAMIN – ***yāmiyn*** [masc. proper noun: יָמִין <3226>; the same as RIGHT HAND <3225>]: right hand ▶
a. Second son of Simeon. Refs.: Gen. 46:10; Ex. 6:15; Num. 26:12; 1 Chr. 4:24. ¶
b. A man of the tribe of Judah. Ref.: 1 Chr. 2:27. ¶
c. A Levite who helped the people understand the law. Ref.: Neh. 8:7. ¶

JAMINITE – ***yāmiyniy, y****ᵉ****miy-niy*** [masc. proper noun: יָמִינִי, יְמִינִי <3228>; patron. from JAMIN <3226>]: right hand ▶
a. Member of the family of Jamin. Ref.: Num. 26:12. ¶
b. Benjamite, a shortened form of *ben-yᵉmiymiy* (BENJAMITE <1145>). Refs.: 1 Sam. 9:1, 4; 2 Sam. 20:1; Esther 2:5. ¶

JAMLECH – ***yamlēḵ*** [masc. proper noun: יַמְלֵךְ <3230>; from KING (BE) <4427>]: whom God makes king ▶ **A descendant of Simeon.** Ref.: 1 Chr. 4:34. ¶

JANAI – 1 Chr. 5:12 ➔ JAANAI <3285>.

JANIM – Josh. 15:53 ➔ JANUM <3241>.

JANOAH – ***yānôaḥ, yānôḥāh*** [proper noun: יָנוֹחַ, יָנוֹחָה <3239>; from REST (verb) <3240>]: rest ▶
a. A town in Naphtali. Ref.: 2 Kgs. 15:29. ¶
b. A town in Ephraim. Refs.: Josh. 16:6, 7. ¶

JANUM – ***yāniym*** [proper noun: יָנִים <3241>; from SLUMBER (verb) <5123>]: sleeping ▶ **A town in the mountains of Judah; also written Janim.** Ref.: Josh. 15:53. ¶

JAPHETH – ***yepet*** [masc. proper noun: יֶפֶת <3315>; from ENLARGE <6601>]: enlargement ▶ **The third son of Noah.** He was married and was on the ark during the great flood (Gen. 7:13). He and his descendants were blessed by Noah's prophetic words (Gen. 9:26, 27) and are listed first in the author's genealogical lists (Gen. 10:1–5). They were to share in Shem's blessing. Japheth fathered 14 nations, Ham 30, and Shem 26 for a total of seventy nations, a number indicating "all" nations (Gen. 10). Other refs.: Gen. 5:32; 6:10; 9:18, 23; 10:21; 1 Chr. 1:4, 5. ¶

JAPHIA – ***yāpiya'*** [proper noun: יָפִיעַ <3309>; SHINE, SHINE FORTH <3313>]: bright, shining ▶
a. King of Lachish. Ref.: Josh. 10:3. ¶
b. A border town of Zebulon. Ref.: Josh. 19:12. ¶
c. Son of David. Refs.: 2 Sam. 5:15; 1 Chr. 3:7; 14:6. ¶

JAPHLET – ***yaplêṭ*** [masc. proper noun: יַפְלֵט <3310>; from DELIVER <6403>]: he will deliver ▶ **A descendant of Asher, son of Heber.** Refs.: 1 Chr. 7:32, 33. ¶

JAPHLETITE – ***yaplêṭiy*** [masc. proper noun: יַפְלֵטִי <3311>; patron. from JAPHLET <3310>]: God will deliver ▶ **A descendant of a certain Japhlet, most likely not the same as JAPHLET <3310>.** The Japhletites were living near the border of Ephraim (Josh. 16:3). ¶

JAPHO – Josh. 19:46 → JOPPA <3305>.

JAR – 1 ***'āsûk*** [masc. noun: אָסוּךְ <610>; from ANOINT <5480>] ▶ **This word refers to a container; it is also translated pot.** It is used only once to refer to the jar of oil that belonged to a poor widow (2 Kgs. 4:2). It was made of clay. ¶

2 ***baqbuq*** [masc. noun: בַּקְבֻּק <1228>; from EMPTY (MAKE) <1238>] ▶ **This word refers to an earthenware vessel, a potter's creation; it is also translated a flask, a bottle.** Jeremiah's breaking of such a jar was an object lesson for Judah, whom the Lord would likewise break so it could not be restored (Jer. 19:1, 10). A similar jar was used to carry honey (1 Kgs. 14:3; KJV: cruse). ¶

3 ***kad*** [fem. noun: כַּד <3537>; from an unused root meaning to deepen] ▶ **This word indicates a large portable pottery vessel for domestic purposes; it is also translated pitcher.** It was used for water (Gen. 24:14; 1 Kgs. 18:33: also translated barrel, waterpot); or for flour (1 Kgs. 17:12; also translated barrel, bowl, bin). Such jars were used ingeniously by Gideon in war (Judg. 7:16, 19, 20); in Ecclesiastes 12:6, a pitcher was a symbol of life with its breaking indicating death. Other refs.: Gen. 24:15–18, 20, 43, 45, 46; 1 Kgs. 17:14, 16. ¶

4 ***qaśāh, qaśwāh*** [fem. noun: קְשָׂה, קַשְׂוָה <7184>; from an unused root meaning to be round] ▶
a. This word refers to some of the various utensils used in the Tabernacle and later the Temple. Refs.: Ex. 25:29; 37:16; Num. 4:71; 1 Chr. 28:17. They probably were used in pouring libation offerings and therefore were holy vessels.
b. In earlier translations, the word was rendered as cover or covers in certain passages. Refs.: KJV, NKJV, pitchers; Ex. 25:29; 37:16; Num. 4:7. ¶

5 ***ṣinṣenet*** [fem. noun: צִנְצֶנֶת <6803>; from the same as THORN <6791>] ▶ **This word refers to a container into which a sample of manna was placed for preservation and display; it is also translated pot.** Ref.: Ex. 16:33. It must have been a closed container with a lid. ¶

6 ***ṣappaḥat*** [fem. noun: צַפַּחַת <6835>; from an unused root meaning to expand] ▶ **This word refers to a container, a jug; it is also translated cruse.** It refers to a container to hold water for traveling or hunting (1 Sam. 26:11, 12, 16). It also describes a household storage jar or a jug for oil or water (1 Kgs. 17:12, 14, 16; 19:6). ¶

– [7] 2 Kgs. 2:20 ➔ BOWL <6746> [8] Job 38:37; Is. 22:24; Jer. 13:12; 48:12; Lam. 4:2 ➔ SKIN BOTTLE <5035> [9] Jer. 22:28 ➔ PAIN (noun) <6089> .

JARAH – ***ya‘rāh*** [masc. proper noun: יַעְרָה <3294>; a form of HONEYCOMB <3295>]: honeycomb, forest ▶ **A descendant of king Saul.** Ref.: 1 Chr. 9:42. ¶

JAREB – *yārēḇ* [masc. proper noun and masc. noun: יָרֵב <3377>; from STRIVE <7378>]: he will contend ▶
a. This word designates the Assyrian king Jareb. Refs.: KJV, NASB, NKJV, Hos. 5:13; 10:6. ¶
b. This word also means great. It is used in the NIV and the ESV in Hosea 5:13; 10:6. ¶

JARED – ***yereḏ*** [masc. proper noun: יֶרֶד <3382>; from GO DOWN <3381>]: descent ▶
a. Father of Enoch. Refs.: Gen. 5:15, 16, 18–20; 1 Chr. 1:2. ¶
b. Man of Judah, son of Mered. Ref.: 1 Chr. 4:18. ¶

JARESIAH – ***ya‘ᵃrešyāh*** [masc. proper noun: יַעֲרֶשְׁיָה <3298>; from an unused root of uncertain signification and LORD <3050>]: nourished by the Lord (?) ▶ **One of the sons of Jeroham of the tribe of Benjamin.** Ref.: 1 Chr. 8:27. ¶

JARHA – ***yarḥā‘*** [masc. proper noun: יַרְחָע <3398>; prob. of Egyptian origin] ▶ **Egyptian servant of a man of Judah, Sheshan, who gave him his daughter as a wife.** Refs.: 1 Chr. 2:34, 35. ¶

JARIB – ***yāriyḇ*** [masc. proper noun: יָרִיב <3402>; the same as CONTENDS (ONE WHO) <3401>]: contender, adversary ▶
a. Fourth son of Simeon. Refs.: 1 Chr. 4:24; Ezra 8:16; 10:18. ¶
b. One of the chief men who were with Ezra near the river that runs to Ahava. Refs.: Ezra 8:16; 10:18. ¶

JARMUTH – ***yarmûṯ*** [proper noun: יַרְמוּת <3412>; from RAISE UP <7311>]: height, elevation ▶
a. A Canaanite city in Judah. Refs.: Josh. 10:3, 5, 23; 12:11; 15:35; Neh. 11:29. ¶
b. A city in Issachar. Ref.: Josh. 21:29. ¶

JAROAH – ***yārôaḥ*** [masc. proper noun: יָרוֹחַ <3386>; perhaps denom. from MOON <3394>]: new moon ▶ **A man of the tribe of Gad.** Ref.: 1 Chr. 5:14. ¶

JARS – Ps. 33:7 ➔ HEAP (noun) <5067>.

JASHEN – ***yāšēn*** [masc. proper noun: יָשֵׁן <3464>; the same as SLEEPING <3463>]: sleeping ▶ **Many of his sons were among David's mighty men.** Ref.: 2 Sam. 23:32. ¶

JASHOBEAM – ***yāšoḇ‘ām*** [masc. proper noun: יָשָׁבְעָם <3434>; from TURN <7725> and PEOPLE <5971>]: the people will return ▶
a. A military leader under David. Ref.: 1 Chr. 11:11. ¶
b. A warrior under David, possibly the same person as in a. above. Ref.: 1 Chr. 12:6. ¶
c. Son of Zabdiel, in charge of a military division. Ref.: 1 Chr. 27:2. ¶

JASHUB – ***yāšûḇ*** [masc. proper noun: יָשׁוּב <3437>; from TURN <7725>]: he will return ▶
a. Son of Issachar. Refs.: Gen. 46:13; Num. 26:24; 1 Chr. 7:1. ¶
b. Son of Bani. Ref.: Ezra 10:29. ¶

JASHUBI LEHEM – ***yāšuḇiy lāḥem*** [proper noun: יָשֻׁבִי לָחֶם <3433>; from TURN <7725> and BREAD <3899>]: returner of bread ▶ **Probably a man, not a place; member of the tribe of Judah.** Ref.: 1 Chr. 4:22. ¶

JASHUBITE – ***yāšûḇiy*** [proper noun: יָשׁוּבִי <3432>; patron. from JASHUB <3437>] ▶ **A member of the family of Jashub.** Ref.: Num. 26:24. ¶

JASPER – [1] ***yāšᵉpēh*** [masc. noun: יָשְׁפֵה <3471>; from an unused root meaning to polish] ▶ **This word denotes a precious stone.** In context it was mounted on the

breastpiece of the high priest with other stones (Ex. 28:20; 39:13). It was part of the symbolic covering of the historical king of Tyre who served also as a symbol of Lucifer (Ezek. 28:13). ¶
– [2] Job 28:18 ➔ CRYSTAL <1378>.

JATHNIEL – ***yaṯniy'ēl*** [masc. proper noun: יַתְנִיאֵל <3496>; from an unused root meaning to endure and GOD <410>]: continued of God ▶ **A gatekeeper of the Korahites.** Ref.: 1 Chr. 26:2. ¶

JATTIR – ***yattiyr, yattir*** [proper noun: יַתִּר, יַתִּיר <3492>; from REMAIN <3498>]: plenty ▶ **A city in the mountain region of Judah.** Refs.: Josh. 15:48; 21:14; 1 Sam. 30:27; 1 Chr. 6:57. ¶

JAVAN – ***yāwān*** [masc. proper noun: יָוָן <3120>; prob. from the same as WINE <3196> (in the sense of effervescing, i.e., hot and active)]: effervescing ▶
a. Son of Japheth. Refs.: Gen. 10:2, 4; 1 Chr. 1:5, 7. ¶
b. The descendants of Javan or their territory. Refs.: Is. 66:19; Ezek. 27:13, 19; Dan. 8:21; 10:20; 11:2; Zech. 9:13. They settled in Greece. ¶

JAVELIN – [1] Num. 25:7 ➔ SPEAR <7420> [2] Josh. 8:18, 26; 1 Sam. 17:6, 45; Job 39:23; 41:29; Jer. 50:42 ➔ SPEAR <3591> [3] Job 41:26 ➔ ARMOR <8295> c.

JAW – [1] ***leḥiy*** [masc. noun: לְחִי <3895>; from an unused root meaning to be soft] ▶ **This word means the facial bone in which teeth are set; it is also means cheek.** It refers to the jawbone of an ass used by Samson (Judg. 15:15–17, 19); the jaw of any draft animal (Hos. 11:4). It is used metaphorically of the "jaws" of the nations/peoples (Is. 30:28). It seems to stand for cheek (1 Kgs. 22:24; Lam. 1:2; 3:30; Mic. 5:1) and in some cases refers to cheeks as an aspect of human beauty (Song 1:10; 5:13). To smite people on the cheek was to insult them (Job 16:10) and challenge them to battle (Ps. 3:7). It is used figuratively of the jaws of Egypt and Gog which the Lord will pierce with hooks (Ezek. 29:4; 38:4) and lead them about. It indicates also a part of a sacrifice belonging to the priest (Deut. 18:3; jowls, NIV; cheeks, NASB, KJV, NKJV). Other refs.: 2 Chr. 18:23; Job 41:2; Is. 50:6. ¶
[2] ***malqôaḥ*** [masc. noun: מַלְקוֹחַ <4455>; from TAKE <3947>] ▶ **This word refers to the inside of a person's mouth, the inner part of the cheek or palate.** Ref.: Ps. 22:15; NIV: roof of the mouth. The Hebrew word also refers to booty, prey; see PREY <4455>. ¶

JAWBONE – Judg. 15:15–17, 19 ➔ JAW <3895>.

JAWS – ***meṯalle'ôṯ*** [fem. plur. noun: מְתַלְּעוֹת <4973>; contr. from DEVOUR <3216>] ▶ **This word refers to a jawbone, jaw teeth, cheek teeth, fangs.** Breaking a person's jaw or jawbone means to incapacitate him or her thoroughly (Job 29:17). It is used of the fangs, the large teeth, of young lions in a figurative sense (Ps. 58:6). These jawbones were a weapon for attack (Prov. 30:14). It is used metaphorically of the teeth of the armies of Babylon (Joel 1:6). ¶

JAZER – ***ya'azêyr, ya'zêr*** [proper noun: יַעְזֵר, יַעֲזֵיר <3270>; from HELP (verb) <5826>]: helpful ▶ **A town east of the Jordan in Sihon's kingdom in southern Gilead. It was captured and allotted to the Gadites.** It served as a Levitical city (Josh. 21:39). It was later retaken by the Moabites (Is. 16:8, 9; Jer. 48:32). *

JAZIZ – ***yāziyz*** [masc. proper noun: יָזִיז <3151>; from the same as ABUNDANCE <2123> (in the sense of being conspicuous)]: He will make prominent ▶ **A Hagrite that David put over his personal flocks.** Ref.: 1 Chr. 27:31. ¶

JEALOUS – [1] ***qannā'*** [adj.: קַנָּא <7067>; from JEALOUS (BE) <7065>] ▶ **In every instance of this word, it is used to describe the character of the Lord. He demands loyalty, He does not share His glory with anyone else.** He is a jealous God who will not tolerate the worship of other gods (Ex. 20:5; Deut. 5:9). This word is always used to describe God's attitude toward the worship of false gods, which arouses His jealousy and anger in judgment against the idol worshipers (Deut. 4:24; 6:15). So closely is this characteristic associated with God that His name is Jealous (Ex. 34:14). ¶

[2] ***qannô'*** [adj.: קַנּוֹא <7072>; for <7067> above] ▶ **This word refers to Israel's God, a jealous God for His people; in judgment toward them or vengeance on their enemies.** Refs.: Josh. 24:19; Nah. 1:2. They were His own possession, His personal property. ¶

JEALOUS (BE) – ***qānā'*** [verb: קָנָא <7065>; a prim. root] ▶ **This word also means to be envious, to be zealous. This is a verb derived from a noun, and, as such, occurs in the extensive and causative forms only. The point of the verb is to express a strong emotion in which the subject is desirous of some aspect or possession pertaining to the object.** It can express jealousy, where persons are zealous for their own property or positions for fear they might lose them (Num. 5:14, 30; Is. 11:13); or envy, where persons are zealous for the property or positions of others, hoping they might gain them (Gen. 26:14; 30:1; 37:11). Furthermore, it can indicate someone being zealous on behalf of another (Num. 11:29; 2 Sam. 21:2); on behalf of God (Num. 25:13; 1 Kgs. 19:10, 14); as well as God being zealous (Ezek. 39:25; Joel 2:18; Zech. 1:14; 8:2). It is also used to denote the arousing of one's jealousy or zeal (Deut. 32:16, 21; 1 Kgs. 14:22; Ps. 78:58). *

JEALOUSY – ***qin'āh*** [fem. noun: קִנְאָה <7068>; from JEALOUS (BE) <7065>] ▶ **This word describes an intense fervor, passion, and emotion that is greater than a person's wrath and anger; it also means zeal.** Ref.: Prov. 27:4. It can be either good or bad: Phinehas was commended for taking up the Lord's jealousy (Num. 25:11); but such passion can also be rottenness to the bones (Prov. 14:30). It is used to describe a spirit of jealousy, which comes on a man for his wife (Num. 5:14, 15, 29). Most often, however, this word describes God's zeal, which will accomplish His purpose (2 Kgs. 19:31; Is. 9:7; 37:32); and will be the instrument of His wrath in judgment (Ps. 79:5; Ezek. 36:5, 6; Zeph. 3:8). *

JEARIM – ***yᵉ'āriym*** [proper noun: יְעָרִים <3297>; plur. of FOREST <3293>]: forests ▶ **A mountain on the border of Judah.** Ref.: Josh. 15:10. ¶

JEATERAI – ***yᵉ'āṯray*** [masc. proper noun: יְאָתְרַי <2979>; from the same as SPIES <871>]: stepping ▶ **A descendant of Gershom, the son of Levi.** Ref.: 1 Chr. 6:21. ¶

JEBERECHIAH – ***yᵉḇereḵyāhû*** [masc. proper noun: יְבֶרֶכְיָהוּ <3000>; from BLESS <1288> and LORD <3050>]: blessed by the Lord ▶ **Father of a man named Zechariah.** Ref.: Is. 8:2. ¶

JEBUS – ***yᵉḇûs*** [proper noun: יְבוּס <2982>; from TREAD DOWN <947>]: trodden under foot ▶ **An ancient name for Jerusalem.** It was formerly inhabited by Jebusites (Judg. 19:10, 11; 1 Chr. 11:4, 5). ¶

JEBUSITE – ***yᵉḇûsiy, yᵉḇusiy*** [proper noun: יְבוּסִי, יְבֻסִי <2983>; patrial from JEBUS <2982>]: see JEBUS ▶ **The word is gentilic, indicating an ethnic group or nationality.** The earliest inhabitants of Jerusalem (Gen. 10:16; Judg. 1:21; Josh. 15:63) were Jebusites. Jerusalem was also called Jebus in antiquity. The Jebusites were descended from Canaan, hence, were Canaanites whom Israel would displace in time (Gen. 15:17–21; Ex. 3:8, 17). They also lived in the mountain regions around Jerusalem (Num. 13:29). David gained control of the city of Jebus/Jerusalem (2 Sam. 5:6) and, hence, it was also called "the city of David." *

JECOLIAH – ***yᵉḵolyāh, yᵉḵolyāhû*** [fem. proper noun: יְכָלְיָה, יְכָלְיָהוּ <3203>; from ABLE (BE) <3201> and LORD <3050>]: the Lord is able, the Lord has prevailed ▶ **The wife of king Amaziah and mother of king Uzziah.** Refs.: 2 Kgs. 15:2; 2 Chr. 26:3. ¶

JECONIAH – ***yᵉḵônyāh, yᵉḵonyāh, yᵉḵonyāhû*** [masc. proper noun: יְכָנְיָה, יְכוֹנְיָה, יְכָנְיָהוּ <3204>; from SET UP <3559> (in the sense of to establish) and LORD <3050>]: the Lord establishes ▶ **This is another name for *yᵉhôyāḵiyn* (JEHOIACHIN <3078>); see also *konyāhû* (CONIAH <3659>).** Refs.: 1 Chr. 3:16, 17; Esther 2:6; Jer. 24:1; 27:20; 28:4; 29:2. ¶

JEDAIAH – 1 ***yᵉḏāyāh*** [masc. proper noun: יְדָיָה <3042>; from THANKS (GIVE) <3034> and LORD <3050>]: the Lord knows ▶
a. Son of Shimri; a descendant of Simeon. Ref.: 1 Chr. 4:37. ¶
b. Son of Harumaph; he participated in rebuilding the wall of Jerusalem. Ref.: Neh. 3:10. ¶
2 ***yᵉḏaʿyāh*** [masc. proper noun: יְדַעְיָה <3048>; from KNOW <3045> and LORD <3050>]: the Lord has known ▶
a. A priest under David. Ref.: 1 Chr. 24:7. ¶
b. A priest under Zerubbabel. Refs.: 1 Chr. 9:10; Ezra 2:36; Neh. 7:39; 11:10; 12:6, 19. ¶
c. A postexilic priest. Refs.: Neh. 12:7, 21. ¶
d. A Jew returning from the Babylonian captivity who brought gifts for the Temple. Refs.: Zech. 6:10, 14. ¶

JEDIAEL – ***yᵉḏiyᵃʿ'ēl*** [masc. proper noun: יְדִיעֲאֵל <3043>; from KNOW <3045> and GOD <410>]: known by God ▶
a. Son of Benjamin. Refs.: 1 Chr. 7:6, 10, 11. ¶
b. Son of Shimri; one of the mighty men of David. Ref.: 1 Chr. 11:45. ¶
c. A Manassehite who defected to David when he went to Ziklag. Ref.: 1 Chr. 12:20. ¶
d. A Korahite; one of the gatekeepers under the reign of David. Ref.: 1 Chr. 26:2. ¶

JEDIDAH – ***yᵉḏiyḏāh*** [fem. proper noun: יְדִידָה <3040>; fem. of BELOVED <3039>]: beloved ▶ **The mother of king Josiah.** Ref.: 2 Kgs. 22:1. ¶

JEDIDIAH – ***yᵉḏiyḏyāh*** [masc. proper noun: יְדִידְיָה <3041>; from BELOVED <3039> and LORD <3050>]: beloved of the Lord ▶ **The name given to Solomon by the Lord through Nathan the prophet.** Ref.: 2 Sam. 12:25. ¶

JEDUTHUN – ***yᵉḏûṯûn, yᵉḏûṯûn*** [masc. proper noun: יְדֻתוּן, יְדוּתוּן <3038>; prob. from THANKS (GIVE) <3034>]: praise, praising ▶ **A Levite, founder of a family filling the official functions of musicians under the reign of David.** Refs.: 1 Chr. 9:16; 16:38, 41, 42; 25:1, 3, 6; 2 Chr. 5:12; 29:14; 35:15; Neh. 11:17; Ps. 39:1; 62:1; 77:1. ¶

JEER – 2 Kgs. 2:23 ➔ MOCK <7046>.

JEGAR SAHADUTHA – ***yᵉgar śāhᵃḏûṯā'*** [proper noun: יְגַר שָׂהֲדוּתָא <3026>; from a word derived from an unused root (meaning to gather) and a deriv. of a root corresponding to ADVOCATE <7717>]: pile of testimony ▶ **Name given by Laban to the pile of stones where him and Jacob made a covenant; Jacob called it Galeed.** Ref.: Gen. 31:47. ¶

JEHALLELEL – ***yᵉhallel'ēl*** [masc. proper noun: יְהַלֶּלְאֵל <3094>; from PRAISE (verb) <1986> and GOD <410>]: who praises God ▶
a. A man of the tribe of Judah. Ref.: 1 Chr. 4:16; KJV: Jehaleleel. ¶
b. A Levite, descendant of Merari. Ref.: 2 Chr. 29:12; KJV: Jehalelel. ¶

JEHDEIAH – ***yeḥdᵉyāhû*** [masc. proper noun: יֶחְדְּיָהוּ <3165>; from TOGETHER <3162> and Lord <3050>]: unity of the Lord ▶
a. A Levite. Ref.: 1 Chr. 24:20. ¶
b. A royal officer. Ref.: 1 Chr. 27:30. ¶

JEHIAH – ***yᵉḥiyyāh*** [masc. proper noun: יְחִיָּה <3174>; from LIVE <2421> and LORD <3050>]: the Lord is alive ▶ **A doorkeeper for the ark of God.** Ref.: 1 Chr. 15:24. ¶

JEHIEL – ***y^{e}ḥiy'ēl, y^{e}ḥô'ēl*** [masc. proper noun: יְחִיאֵל, יְחוּאֵל <3171>; from LIVE <2421> and GOD <410>]: God is alive ▶
a. A Levite among those who played musical instruments before the ark of the Lord. Refs.: 1 Chr. 15:18, 20; 16:5. ¶
b. A Levite of the family of Gershon. Refs.: 1 Chr. 23:8; 29:8. ¶
c. A Jew, the son of Hachmoni; he was with king David's sons. Ref.: 1 Chr. 27:32. ¶
d. Son of Jehoshaphat who was killed by Jehoram, his older brother who was firstborn. Refs.: 2 Chr. 21:2–4. ¶
e. Son of Heman; he was among those who cleansed the house of the Lord under Hezekiah. Ref.: 2 Chr. 29:14; see verses 14 to 18. ¶
f. A Levite who, with others, prepared chambers in the house of the Lord. Ref.: 2 Chr. 31:13. ¶
g. A ruler in the Temple under king Josiah. Ref.: 2 Chr. 35:8. ¶
h. Father of Obadiah. Ref.: Ezra 8:9. ¶
i. Father of Shechaniah. Ref.: Ezra 10:2. ¶
j. A priest guilty of having married a foreign woman. Ref.: Ezra 10:21. ¶
k. A Jew guilty of having married a foreign woman. Ref.: Ezra 10:26. ¶

JEHIELI – ***y^{e}ḥiy'ēliy*** [masc. proper noun: יְחִיאֵלִי <3172>; patron. from JEHIEL <3171>]: the Lord is alive ▶ **A Gershonite of the family of Levi.** Refs.: 1 Chr. 26:21, 22. ¶

JEHOADAH – ***y^{e}hô'addāh*** [masc. proper noun: יְהוֹעַדָּה <3085>; from LORD <3068> and ADORN <5710>]: the Lord adorns ▶ **A descendant of Jonathan, the son of Saul.** Ref.: 1 Chr. 8:36. ¶

JEHOADDAN – ***y^{e}hô'addān*** [fem. proper noun: יְהוֹעַדָּן <3086>; from LORD <3068> and DELIGHT ONESELF <5727>]: in whom the Lord delights ▶ **The wife of king Joash, and mother of king Amaziah.** Refs.: 2 Kgs. 14:2; 2 Chr. 25:1. ¶

JEHOAHAZ – ***y^{e}hô'āḥāz*** [masc. proper noun: 3059> יְהוֹאָחָז] ▶
a. The sixth king of Judah who reigned one year (841 B.C.; 2 Chr. 21:17; 25:23). Jehoahaz is another name for Ahaziah (see AHAZIAH <274>). The name means "the Lord has seized." He was the son of Jehoram (848–841 B.C.). His mother was the infamous Athaliah, granddaughter of Omri (see 2 Kgs. 8:25–29). He was a relative of Ahab. Jehu assassinated Jehoahaz, also known as Ahaziah (see 2 Kgs. 9:27–29). ¶
b. The son of Jehu who reigned 814–798 B.C. (2 Kgs. 10:35). He was an evil king; therefore the Lord oppressed Israel by the Syrians during his reign (2 Kgs. 13:3). His army was devastated by the Arameans (2 Kgs. 13:7–9). His son Jehoash succeeded him. *
c. A king of Judah who reigned in Judah. Refs.: 2 Kgs. 23:31–34. He was crowned by the people. His father was Josiah, the great king. He reigned three months before the king of Egypt replaced him (2 Kgs. 23:30–34; 2 Chr. 36:1–4). Jeremiah called him Shallum (Jer. 22:11, 12). ¶

JEHOAHAZ, JOAHAZ – ***yô'āḥāz*** [masc. proper noun: יוֹאָחָז <3099>; a form of JEHOAHAZ <3059>]: whom the Lord sustains, whom the Lord holds ▶
a. A king of Judah who reigned three months (609 B.C.). The king of Egypt deposed him and installed Jehoiakim in his place. Pharaoh Neco exiled him to Egypt (2 Kgs. 23:31–34).
b. A king of Israel, son of Jehu. He reigned 814–798 B.C., seventeen years. He was an evil king who was stripped of his army and buffeted by Hazael, king of Aram, most of his reign (cf. 2 Kgs. 13:1–8).
c. The recorder or chronicler for King Josiah. His son helped repair the Temple under Jehoahaz (2 Chr. 34:8). ¶

JEHOASH – ***y^{e}hô'āš*** [masc. proper noun: יְהוֹאָשׁ <3060>; from LORD <3068> and (perhaps) FIRE <784>]: the Lord has given ▶
a. A king of Judah who was also known as Joash. He was son of Ahaziah and Zibiah. He reigned forty years (835–796 B.C.). He began to reign when he was seven years old, after being shielded for six years in the Temple by Jehoiada, the high priest

(2 Kgs. 11:1–21). He ironically sought to repair the Lord's house but was forced to decimate its wealth in order to buy off Hazael of Aram (2 Kgs. 12:17, 18). He was assassinated and buried in Jerusalem.
b. Another wicked king of northern Israel (798–782 B.C.), he reigned sixteen years (2 Kgs. 13:10–25; 14:1–17). His father was Jehoahaz. He continued to pursue the sins of previous kings in Israel. He fought against Amaziah, king of Judah. Jeroboam II followed him. Jehoash sought help from Elisha (2 Kgs. 13:14–19). He successfully recovered some cities and territory from Aram (2 Kgs. 13:24–25). He captured, destroyed, and looted parts of Jerusalem (2 Kgs. 14:11–14).

JEHOHANAN – *y*ᵉ*hôḥānān* [masc. proper noun: יְהוֹחָנָן <3076>; from LORD <3068> and GRACIOUS (BE) <2603>]: the Lord is gracious ▶
a. A Levite and descendant of Korah through Meshelemiah his father. One of his sons was a leader of Ephraim (1 Chr. 26:3; 2 Chr. 28:12). ¶
b. A commander of part of Jehoshaphat's military. He was from Judah (2 Chr. 17:15; 23:1). ¶
c. A priestly descendant of Bebai who had intermarried with people of the land. Ref.: Ezra 10:28. ¶
d. The head of a priestly family during the days of the high priest Joiakim. Ref.: Neh. 12:13.
e. A priest who took part in dedicating the newly restored wall of Jerusalem with Nehemiah. Ref.: Neh. 12:42. ¶
f. Son of Eliashib. Ezra stayed in his room at the Temple and mourned the condition and sins of the returned exiles (Ezra 10:6). ¶
g. A son of Tobiah, an Ammonite leader, who had married the daughter of a Jew Meshallam. Ref.: Neh. 6:18. This marriage was not approved in Israel. ¶

JEHOIACHIN – 1 *y*ᵉ*hôyāḵiyn* [masc. proper noun: יְהוֹיָכִין <3078>; from LORD <3068> and SET UP <3559> (in the sense of to establish)]: the Lord will establish ▶ **A king who reigned three months in Jerusalem (598–597 B.C.) but was forced to surrender to the Babylonians (2 Kgs. 24:8–20) under Nebuchadnezzar.** He was taken captive to Babylon along with the royal household. Nebuchadnezzar set up Mattaniah (Zedekiah) in his place as king in Judah. He was, after some years, treated with great respect by the Babylonian king Evil-Merodach (561 B.C.). This helped maintain hope among the exiles for a return to Jerusalem. His father was Jehoiachim. *
2 ***yôyaḵiyn*** [masc. proper noun: יוֹיָכִין <3112>; a form of <3078> above]: the Lord will establish ▶ **This is a variant spelling of *y*ᵉ*hôyāḵiyn* above.** Ref.: Ezek. 1:2. ¶

JEHOIADA – 1 *y*ᵉ*hôyāḏā'* [masc. proper noun: יְהוֹיָדָע <3077>; from LORD <3068> and KNOW <3045>]: the Lord knows ▶
a. The father of Benaiah who was in charge of the elite personal guard of David, the Kerethites and Pelethites. Refs.: 2 Sam. 8:18; 1 Chr. 11:22, 24. *
b. The son of Benaiah and grandson of Jehoiada, who counseled David and served as his wise man. Ref.: 1 Chr. 27:34. ¶
c. A high priest who notably kept Joash hidden from certain death at the hands of Athaliah. Refs.: 2 Kgs. 11:1–21. He led him forth and proclaimed him king (2 Kgs. 11:4–17). Jehoiada served as ruler de facto for Joash as he grew up and gave Joash important guidance (2 Kgs. 12:2–9; 2 Chr. 24:2–25). He was buried appropriately in a royal tomb. He was faithful to the Lord. *
d. A priest in the time of Jeremiah who was over the Temple. He was replaced by Zephaniah (Jer. 29:26). ¶
2 ***yôyāḏā'*** [masc. proper noun: יוֹיָדָע <3111>; a form of <3077> above]: the Lord knows ▶
a. A son of Paseah who helped repair the Jeshanah Gate under Nehemiah. Ref.: Neh. 3:6. ¶
b. A high priest, son of Eliashib and father of Jonathan, who returned from exile to Jerusalem. His son was driven out by Nehemiah for intermarrying with a foreigner (Neh. 12:10, 11, 22; 13:28). ¶

JEHOIAKIM – ***yᵉhôyāqiym*** [masc. proper noun: יְהוֹיָקִים <3079>; from LORD <3068> abbreviated and STAND, STAND UP <6965>]: the Lord will raise ▶ **A Judean king (609–598), son of Josiah. His mother's name was Zebidah. He was an evil king.** Pharaoh Neco made him king and changed his name from Eliakim to Jehoiakim. He servilely paid tribute thereafter to Egypt by overtaxing the people of Judah. In 605 B.C. the Babylonian king Nebuchadnezzar invaded the land and made Jehoiakim his vassal. He rebelled against Babylon (2 Kgs. 24:1), but the Lord brought judgment on Judah because of its previous sins (2 Kgs. 24:1–6). He was rejected by the Lord (Jer. 22:18, 19). Jeremiah prophesied during his reign (Jer. 1:3; 25:1; 35:1). In one of the most arrogant, ignominious acts recorded in Scripture, Jehoiakim cut up and burned the first draft of Jeremiah's prophecies (Jer. 36:1–32). During his reign, Daniel was taken captive to Babylon (Dan. 1:1, 2). Jehoiachin, his son, reigned after him. *

JEHOIARIB – ***yᵉhôyāriyḇ*** [masc. proper noun: יְהוֹיָרִיב <3080>; from LORD <3068> and STRIVE <7378> (in the sense of to oppose)]: the Lord defends ▶ **A priest living in Jerusalem, descendant of Aaron.** Refs.: 1 Chr. 9:10; 24:7. ¶

JEHONADAB – ***yᵉhônāḏāḇ*** [masc. proper noun: יְהוֹנָדָב <3082>; from LORD <3068> and GIVE WILLINGLY <5068>]: the Lord is generous ▶

a. The son of Rechab who opposed Baalism and the house of Ahab as adamantly as did Jehu. Refs.: 2 Kgs. 10:14–17, 23. He and the Rechabites also rejected the use of wine and various other culturally developed practices in Israel. They were so faithful to their original covenant that the prophet used them and their faithfulness to shame Israel's failure for keeping the Lord's covenant steadfastly (Jer. 35:8–18). ¶

b. A nephew of David through Shimeah. He set up Tamar for her fateful meeting with Amnon (2 Sam. 13:3–5), her half brother. ¶

JEHORAM – ***yᵉhôrām*** [masc. proper noun: יְהוֹרָם <3088>; from LORD <3068> and RAISE UP <7311> (in the sense of to be exalted)]: the Lord is exalted ▶

a. A king of Judah who ruled eight years (848–841 B.C.), son of Jehoshaphat. Ref.: 1 Kgs. 22:50. He became an evil king who led Judah into Baal worship and all the sins of Israel (2 Kgs. 8:16–19). He married a daughter of Ahab, king of Israel. During his reign, Edom revolted from Judah. He died unmourned by his people (1 Chr. 21:20). *

b. A king of Israel, son of Ahab, who ruled 852–841 B.C. He succeeded Ahaziah as his younger brother (2 Kgs. 1:17; 3:1, 6). He was an evil king but his rebellions did not equal those of his father. He even removed additional aspects of Baal worship (2 Kgs. 3:2), and the Lord granted him victory in defeating the Moabites (2 Kgs. 3:14–27). He was executed by Jehu who then reigned (2 Kgs. 9:21–26). *

c. The name of a priest who helped teach the Book of the Law to Judah in the days of Jehoshaphat. Refs.: 2 Chr. 17:7–9. ¶

JEHOSHABEATH – ***yᵉhôšaḇʿaṯ*** [fem. proper noun: יְהוֹשַׁבְעַת <3090>; a form of JEHOSHEBA <3089>]: the Lord is her oath ▶ **See JEHOSHEBA (2 Chr. 22:11).** ¶

JEHOSHAPHAT – ***yᵉhôšāpāṭ*** [proper noun: יְהוֹשָׁפָט <3092>; from LORD <3068> and JUDGE (verb) <8199>]: the Lord has judged ▶

a. A good king of Judah, son of Asa. He ruled twenty-five years (872–852 B.C.). He tried to keep Judah and Israel united as one people (1 Kgs. 22:4, 5). He kept peace (1 Kgs. 22:44) and followed the Lord in every way (1 Kgs. 22:41–43), consulting the true prophet of God for leadership (1 Kgs. 22:7; 2 Kgs. 3:11–25). He had the Law of God taught throughout Judah (2 Chr. 17:1–9). He led a great prayer gathering to deal with the approaching enemy armies and saw a great victory from the Lord (2 Chr. 20:1–30). He removed religious male prostitutes from the land (1 Kgs. 22:46). He built ships for commerce, but they were all wrecked at Ezion Geber (1 Kgs. 22:48).

His son Jehoram succeeded him. The Books of 1 and 2 Chronicles consider his reign a great success as well. *
b. The father of Jehu who was king in Israel. Refs.: 2 Kgs. 9:2, 14. His father was Nimshi. ¶
c. He was the recorder or secretary under David and son of Ahilud. Refs.: 2 Sam. 8:16; 20:24; 1 Kgs. 4:3; 1 Chr. 18:15. ¶
d. He was one of Solomon's twelve area governors. He was over Issachar and was son of Paruah (1 Kgs. 4:17). ¶
e. A valley into which the Lord will bring all nations for judgment. Refs.: Joel 3:2, 12. The name means "the Lord judges." The Lord will judge them with respect to how they treated His people Israel. It appears to be a symbolic use of the term or name or refers also to this valley near Jerusalem. ¶

JEHOSHEBA – ***yᵉhôšeḇaʿ*** [fem. proper noun: יְהוֹשֶׁבַע <3089>; from LORD <3068> and SWEAR <7650> (in the sense of to take an oath)]: the Lord is her oath ▶ **Daughter of king Joram. She stole Joash from among the king's sons and hid him, so that he would not be killed by wicked Athaliah.** Ref.: 2 Kgs. 11:2. She was the wife of the high priest Jehoiada (see 2 Chr. 22:11; her name is spelled Jehoshabeath). ¶

JEHOVAH – See LORD <3068>.

JEHOVAH JIREH – ***yᵉhōwāh yirʾeh*** [proper noun: יְהוָה יִרְאֶה <3070>; from LORD <3068> and SEE <7200>]: the Lord will see to it, the Lord will provide, or, possibly, the Lord will be seen ▶ **This is a proper name of the Lord. Abraham called Mount Moriah by this name in honor of the Lord and in appreciation for providing a sacrifice in place of Isaac.** Ref.: Gen. 22:14. ¶

JEHOVAH NISSI – ***yᵉhōwāh nissiy*** [proper noun: יְהוָה נִסִּי <3071>; from LORD <3068> and BANNER <5251> with pron. suffix]: the Lord is my banner *or* my standard ▶ **This name was given to the altar Moses built to the Lord after defeating the Amalekites.** Ref.: Ex. 17:15. ¶

JEHOVAH SHALOM – ***yᵉhōwāh šālôm*** [proper noun: יְהוָה שָׁלוֹם <3073>; from LORD <3068> and PEACE <7965>]: the Lord is peace ▶ **This name designates an altar built by Gideon.** Ref.: Judg. 6:24. This famous judge of Israel built it because the Lord confirmed that He was calling him to deliver Israel. It stood for many years. ¶

JEHOVAH SHAMMAH – ***yᵉhōwāh šāmmāh*** [proper noun: יְהוָה שָׁמָּה <3074>; from LORD <3068> and BEFORE <8033> with directive enclitic]: the Lord is there ▶ **This name is given to the New Jerusalem of Ezekiel's vision.** Ref.: Ezek. 48:35. ¶

JEHOVAH TSIDKENU – ***yᵉhōwāh ṣiḏqênû*** [proper noun: יְהוָה צִדְקֵנוּ <3072>; from LORD <3068> and RIGHTEOUSNESS <6664> with pron. suffix]: the Lord is our righteousness ▶ **This name occurs in a context referring to the messianic concept of "the Branch."** Ref.: Jer. 23:6; see verses 1 to 6. Other ref.: Jer. 33:16. ¶

JEHOZABAD – ***yᵉhôzāḇāḏ*** [masc. proper noun: יְהוֹזָבָד <3075>; from LORD <3068> and ENDOW <2064>]: the Lord gives ▶
a. Son of Shomer and of a Moabitess; a servant of king Joash and one of those who murdered him. Refs.: 2 Kgs. 12:21; 2 Chr. 24:26. ¶
b. Son of Obed-edom; he was a gatekeeper. Ref.: 1 Chr. 26:4. ¶
c. A Benjamite, commander of 180,000 men armed for war. Ref.: 2 Chr. 17:18. ¶

JEHOZADAK – ***yᵉhôṣāḏāq*** [masc. proper noun: יְהוֹצָדָק <3087>; from LORD <3068> and JUST (BE) <6663> (in the sense of to be righteous)]: the Lord is righteous ▶ **Father of the high priest; he was deported to Babylon.** Refs.: 1 Chr. 6:14, 15; Hag. 1:1, 12, 14; 2:2, 4; Zech. 6:11. He is also called Josedech in the KJV. ¶

JEHU – ***yêhûʾ*** [masc. proper noun: יֵהוּא <3058>; from LORD <3068> and HE, SHE, IT <1931>]: it is the Lord ▶
a. He was a king, Jehoshaphat's son, chosen by God to overthrow the dynasty

of Omri. He reigned 28 years (841–814 B.C.). Elijah anointed him to be king. His divinely appointed purpose was accomplished during his evil reign (2 Kgs. 9:10). He destroyed the house of Ahab and Jezebel (2 Kgs. 9:6–10). He was an army commander and was later anointed king by his men (2 Kgs. 9:13). He killed both King Joram (Israel) and King Ahaziah (Judah) (2 Kgs. 9:21–29). Jezebel's death soon followed (2 Kgs. 9:30–37), as well as the slaughter of Baal's prophets. *
b. A prophet, the son of Hanani, who prophesied the destruction of Baasha and his evil house. Refs.: 1 Kgs. 16:1–4, 11. *
c. The name of one of David's mighty skilled warriors, a relative of Saul and a Benjamite. Ref.: 1 Chr. 12:3. ¶
d. A Judahite traced to Judah's son Hezron through Jerahmeel, son of Hezron. Ref.: 1 Chr. 2:38. His father was Jesse. ¶
e. His father was Joshibiah, a Simeonite. He was the head of a clan (1 Chr. 4:35). ¶

JEHUBBAH – ***y^{e}ḥubbāh*** [masc. proper noun: יְחֻבָּה <3160>; from HIDE <2247>]: hidden ► **A descendant of Asher.** Ref.: 1 Chr. 7:34. ¶

JEHUCAL – ***y^{e}hûḵal*** [masc. proper noun: יְהוּכַל <3081>; from ABLE (BE) <3201>]: able ► **One of two men sent by king Zedekiah to the prophet Jeremy asking him to pray for himself and his people.** Ref.: Jer. 37:3. ¶

JEHUD – ***y^{e}huḏ*** [proper noun: יְהֻד <3055>; a briefer form of one corresponding to JUDAH <3061>]: praise ► **A city of the tribe of Dan.** Ref.: Josh. 19:45. ¶

JEHUDI – ***y^{e}hûḏiy*** [masc. proper noun: יְהוּדִי <3065>; the same as JEW <3064>]: Jew, man of Judah ► **A man sent to Baruch to tell him to come with the scroll containing the prophecies of Jeremiah.** He then had to read the scroll to the king and his officials, but the king burned the scroll (Jer. 36:14, 21, 23). ¶

JEHUDIJAH – ***y^{e}huḏiyyāh*** [fem. proper noun: יְהֻדִיָּה <3057>; fem. of JEW <3064>] ► **This word literally means the Jewess; it is also translated Jewish, Judahite, from the tribe of Judah.** Its only occurrence is in 1 Chronicles 4:18. See also *y^{e}hûḏiy* (JEW <3064>). ¶

JEIEL – [1] ***y^{e}'iy'êl, y^{e}'û'êl*** [masc. proper noun: יְעִיאֵל, יְעוּאֵל <3273>; from SWEEP AWAY <3261> and GOD <410>]: taken away by God ►
a. A Reubenite. Ref.: 1 Chr. 5:7. ¶
b. Father of Gibeon. Ref.: 1 Chr. 9:35. ¶
c. Son of Hotham. Ref.: 1 Chr. 11:44. ¶
d. A Musician. Refs.: 1 Chr. 15:18, 21; 16:5. ¶
e. Son of Mattaniah. Ref.: 2 Chr. 20:14. ¶
f. A scribe. Ref.: 2 Chr. 26:11. ¶
g. Son of Elizaphan. Ref.: 2 Chr. 29:13. ¶
h. A Levite. Ref.: 2 Chr. 35:9. ¶
i. Son of Adonikam. Ref.: Ezra 8:13. ¶
j. Son of Nebo. Ref.: Ezra 10:43. ¶
– [2] See JEHIEL <3171>.

JEISH – ***y^{e}'iyš*** [masc. proper noun: יְעִישׁ <3274>; from HASTEN <5789>]: hasty ► **This word designates Jeish, alternate spelling of *y^{e}'ûš*, Jeush:**
a. Son of Esau. Refs.: Gen. 36:5, 14. See also JEUSH <3266> a. ¶
b. A Benjamite. Ref.: 1 Chr. 7:10. See also JEUSH <3266> b. ¶

JEKABZEEL – ***y^{e}qaḇṣ^{e}'êl*** [proper noun: יְקַבְצְאֵל <3343>; from GATHER <6908> and GOD <410>]: God will gather ► **A city at the extreme south of Judah.** Ref.: Neh. 11:25. ¶

JEKAMEAM – ***y^{e}qam'ām*** [masc. proper noun: 3360> יְקַמְעָם; from STAND, STAND UP <6965> and PEOPLE <5971>]: the people will rise ► **A Levite, fourth son of Hebron and grandson of Kohath.** Refs.: 1 Chr. 23:19; 24:23. ¶

JEKAMIAH – ***y^{e}qamyāh*** [masc. proper noun: יְקַמְיָה <3359>; from STAND, STAND UP <6965> and LORD <3050>]: the Lord will raise ►
a. Fifth son of Jeconiah. Ref.: 1 Chr. 3:18. ¶
b. Son of Shallum. Ref.: 1 Chr. 2:41. ¶

JEKUTHIEL – ***y**^{e}**qûṯiy'êl*** [masc. proper noun: יְקוּתִיאֵל <3354>; from the same as JAKEH <3348> and GOD <410>]: obedience of God ▶ **A descendant of Caleb of the tribe of Judah.** Ref.: 1 Chr. 4:18. ¶

JEMIMA – Job 42:14 → JEMIMAH <3224>.

JEMIMAH – ***y**^{e}**miymāh*** [fem. proper noun: יְמִימָה <3224>; perhaps from the same as DAY <3117> (properly warm, i.e., affectionate, hence dove; comp. <3123>)]: dove ▶ **Oldest daughter of Job.** Ref.: Job 42:14. ¶

JEMUEL – ***y**^{e}**mû'êl*** [masc. proper noun: יְמוּאֵל <3223>; from DAY <3117> and GOD <410>]: day of God ▶ **Oldest son of Simeon.** Refs.: Gen. 46:10; Ex. 6:15. ¶

JEPHTHAH – ***yip̄tāḥ*** [proper noun: יִפְתָּח <3316>; from OPEN <6605>]: he will open, he will set free ▶ **This word designates Jephthah and Iphtah:**
a. Jephthah was a judge in Israel who had a Gileadite as a father and a prostitute as a mother, thus making him a rejected outcast in Israel. Refs.: Judg. 11:1–40. He was ostracized but subsequently recalled because he was a competent military leader (Judg. 11:8–11). He delivered Israel from the Ammonites. He made a foolish, rash vow concerning his only daughter that led to her death or to a life of celibacy (Judg. 11:29–40). He delivered and judged Israel six years then died (Judg. 12:7). Other refs.: Judg. 12:1, 2, 4; 1 Sam. 12:11. ¶
b. Iphtah was a town in Judah. Ref.: Josh. 15:43; also translated Jiphtah. ¶

JEPHUNNEH – ***y**^{e}**p̄unneh*** [masc. proper noun: יְפֻנֶּה <3312>; from TURN <6437>]: beholder, for whom a way is prepared ▶
a. Father of Caleb. Refs.: Num. 13:6; 14:6, 30, 38; 26:65; 32:12; 34:19; Deut. 1:36; Josh. 14:6, 13, 14; 15:13; 21:12; 1 Chr. 4:15; 6:56. ¶
b. An Asherite. Ref.: 1 Chr. 7:38. ¶

JERAH – ***yeraḥ*** [masc. proper noun: יֶרַח <3392>; the same as MONTH <3391>]: month ▶ **Fourth son of Joktan.** Refs.: Gen. 10:26; 1 Chr. 1:20. ¶

JERAHMEEL – ***y**^{e}**raḥm**^{e}**'êl*** [masc. proper noun: יְרַחְמְאֵל <3396>; from COMPASSION (HAVE) <7355> and GOD <410>]: God has compassion ▶
a. A Judaite. Refs.: 1 Chr. 2:9, 25–27, 33, 42. ¶
b. Son of Jehoiakim. Ref.: Jer. 36:26. ¶
c. A Levite. Ref.: 1 Chr. 24:29. ¶

JERAHMEELITE – ***y**^{e}**raḥm**^{e}**'êliy*** [masc. proper noun: יְרַחְמְאֵלִי <3397>; patron. from JERAHMEEL <3396>] ▶ **Descendant of Jerahmeel.** Refs.: 1 Sam. 27:10; 30:29. ¶

JEREMAI – ***y**^{e}**rêmay*** [masc. proper noun: יְרֵמַי <3413>; from RAISE UP <7311>]: elevated ▶ **An Israelite whom Ezra persuaded to put away his foreign wife.** Ref.: Ezra 10:33. ¶

JEREMIAH – ***yirm**^{e}**yāh, yirm**^{e}**yāhû*** [proper noun: יִרְמְיָה, יִרְמְיָהוּ <3414>; from RAISE UP <7311> and LORD <3050>]: the Lord will raise ▶
a. A great prophet of Judah who prophesied 626–586 B.C. The meaning of his name is difficult, but it seems to mean "the Lord raises up" or "the Lord loosens," which fits his task—to prophesy the rising and/or falling of nations. He was the son of Hilkiah, a priest (Jer. 1:1–6). He prophesied to Judah, warning them to submit to God's servant Nebuchadnezzar, the king of Babylon, or be taken into exile (Jer. 25:1–38). He prophesied the Lord's word under Josiah on through the debacle of Jehoiakim's reign and Zedekiah's reign, the last king of Judah. He continued to prophesy in a context in which he was harassed and threatened by both the people of Judah and their leaders and by false prophets, such as Hananiah (Jer. 26–28).

He counseled and prophesied submission to Babylon. He charged the people and nations with breaking the covenant (Jer. 11) but gave them a hope of a New Covenant (Jer. 31:31–34). He described the seventy-year exile they would undergo (Jer. 25) but also a glorious return (Jer. 25:12 ff.; Jer. 25:30–34).

He dictated a second version of his prophesies to Baruch his scribe after Jehoiakim burned an earlier draft (Jer. 36). He poured out oracles of judgment on the nations (Jer. 46–52), but he counseled Israel to circumcise their hearts (Jer. 4:4) to the Lord. His prophecies unheeded, he himself went into a forced exile in Egypt, where he uttered some concluding prophecies (Jer. 42–44). *

b. The father of Hamutal, mother of Zedekiah. Refs.: 2 Kgs. 23:31; 24:18. ¶

c. A Gadite who joined David while he was fleeing Saul. He was an army official or commander (1 Chr. 12:10). ¶

d. A family head of Manasseh who lived east of the Jordan River. Ref.: 1 Chr. 5:24. ¶

e. A leader of a group of Benjamites who defected to David while he was fleeing Saul; they were superb warriors. Ref.: 1 Chr. 12:4. ¶

f. A leader of a group of Gadites who followed David, not Saul; he was an army leader. Ref.: 1 Chr. 12:13. ¶

g. A priest who returned under Zerubbabel and Jeshua. The head of a priestly family (Neh. 12:1, 12). ¶

h. A leader of Levites who supported Nehemiah's covenant of renewal. He helped in the dedication of the wall (Neh. 10:2; 12:34). ¶

JEREMOTH – See JERIMOTH <3406>.

JERIAH – ***y^{e}riyyāh, y^{e}riyyāhû*** [masc. proper noun: יְרִיָּהוּ, יְרִיָּה <3404>; from SHOOT (verb) <3384> and LORD <3050>]: the Lord will throw ► **A Levite of the family of Kohath.** Refs.: 1 Chr. 23:19; 24:23; 26:31. ¶

JERIBAI – ***y^{e}riyḇay*** [masc. proper noun: יְרִיבַי <3403>; from CONTENDS (ONE WHO) <3401>]: contentious ► **Son of Elnaam, one of the mighty men of David.** Ref.: 1 Chr. 11:46. ¶

JERICHO – ***y^{e}rēḥô, y^{e}riyḥô*** [proper noun: יְרִיחוֹ, יְרֵחוֹ <3405>; perhaps from MOON <3394>]: its moon ► **An important city in the Old Testament for it was the first city taken by the Israelites as they entered Canaan ca. 1250 (or 1406) B.C.** Its defeat was to serve as a model of what God could and would do for His people if they were faithful to Him (Josh. 5–7). It was a great walled city that God delivered into the hands of His people by destroying its walls. Its destruction and capture stands in strong contrast to Israel's faithless failure at Ai (Josh. 8:1–29). The biblical story stresses the success of capturing this great barrier to the Promised Land by Israel's failure to keep the Law. After its destruction, Joshua placed a curse on it (Josh. 6:26, 27). It played a relatively subdued role in the history of Israel after Joshua's day.

The city is now reduced to an archaeological mound, Tell es-Sultan, covering about ten acres. It is located six miles west of the Jordan River, seven miles north of the Dead Sea. In antiquity it served as a major obstacle to invaders of Canaan and served as a sentinel to protect Canaan. It can be viewed from Mount Nebo (Deut. 34:1–4). It served as a well-armed, walled border city between Ephraim and Benjamin (Josh. 16:1, 7; 18:12, 21). Its fortress-like character and defenses would have been unassailable by Israel without the Lord's intervention. It is near a large spring that yields fresh water even today and in the past supported lush flora, including palm trees. *

JERIEL – ***y^{e}riy'ēl*** [masc. proper noun: יְרִיאֵל <3400>; from SHOOT (verb) <3384> (in the sense of to teach, to instruct) and GOD <410>]: taught by God ► **Son of Tola, of the tribe of Issachar.** Ref.: 1 Chr. 7:2. ¶

JERIMOTH – ***y^{e}rēmôṯ, y^{e}riymôṯ*** [masc. proper noun: יְרִימוֹת, יְרֵמוֹת <3406>; plur. from RAISE UP <7311>]: heights ►
a. Son of Bela. Ref.: 1 Chr. 7:7. ¶
b. Son of Becher. Ref.: 1 Chr. 7:8. ¶
c. Son of Beriah. Ref.: 1 Chr. 8:14. ¶
d. A Benjamite. Ref.: 1 Chr. 12:5. ¶
e. Son of Mushi. Refs.: 1 Chr. 23:23; 24:30. ¶

f. A Levite. Ref.: 1 Chr. 25:22. ¶
g. Son of Heman. Ref.: 1 Chr. 25:4. ¶
h. A Levite. Ref.: 2 Chr. 31:13. ¶
i. A Naphtalite. Ref.: 1 Chr. 27:19. ¶
h. Son of David. Ref.: 2 Chr. 11:18. ¶
k. Descendant of Elam. Ref.: Ezra 10:26. ¶
l. Descendant of Zattu. Ref.: Ezra 10:27. ¶
m. A Jew. Ref.: Ezra 10:29. ¶
n. A covenanter in Ezra's day. Ref.: also in Ezra 10:29. ¶

JERIOTH – ***yᵉriy'ôṯ*** [fem. proper noun: יְרִיעוֹת <3408>; plur. of CURTAIN <3407>]: curtains ▶ **One of Caleb's wives.** Ref.: 1 Chr. 2:18. ¶

JEROBOAM – ***yāroḇ'ām*** [masc. proper noun: יָרָבְעָם <3379>; from STRIVE <7378> and PEOPLE <5971>]: the people will contend ▶
a. Jeroboam I, son of Nebat, an Ephraimite, the first king of Israel. He unfortunately caused Israel to sin by building golden calves at Bethel and Dan, thus introducing idolatry in northern Israel and leading the people astray. His name possibly means "may he strive for the people (*'am* [PEOPLE <5971>])." He reigned 930–910 B.C., seventeen years. He pulled the Israelites away from God's chosen Temple worship at Jerusalem and started them on the way to spiritual harlotry and corruption. He thereby became the model of rebellion and sin for all the kings of northern Israel (1 Kgs. 16:2; 22:52; 2 Kgs. 3:3). Even after a stern rebuke by a prophet, he continued to establish false priests and corrupt worship in Israel (1 Kgs. 13:33, 34).

Although he had begun as one of Solomon's supporters and administrators he rebelled against the harsh policies of Solomon, but the Lord supported his move (1 Kgs. 11:29–33). Even before he was king, he had not followed the Lord in service and worship properly. The Lord gave Jeroboam the ten northern tribes to rule over, promising to prosper him if he served Him (1 Kgs. 11:34–39). Jeroboam was forced to seek asylum in Egypt with Pharaoh Shishak until Solomon died. When he returned, he tried to get Rehoboam to change Solomon's harsh policies toward Israel but to no avail (1 Kgs. 12:1–20). *
b. A king of Israel, son of Jehoash. He reigned, including his coregency with Jehoash, for forty-one years (793–753 B.C.). He was a powerful political king who enlarged the borders of Israel (2 Kgs. 14:23–25) and brought on prosperous economic times but continued to lead Israel in the way of Jeroboam I, who made Israel sin. He ruled in his capital, Samaria, and delivered Israel from her enemies. Amos predicted his death and judgment from God (Amos 1:1; 7:9–11). *

JEROHAM – ***yᵉrōḥām*** [masc. proper noun: יְרֹחָם <3395>; from COMPASSION (HAVE) <7355>]: compassionate ▶
a. Father of Elkanah. Refs.: 1 Sam. 1:1; 1 Chr. 6:27, 34. ¶
b. A Benjamite. Ref.: 1 Chr. 8:27. ¶
c. Another Benjamite. Ref.: 1 Chr. 9:8. ¶
d. A priest. Ref.: 1 Chr. 9:12. ¶
e. Another priest. Ref.: Neh. 11:12. ¶
f. Man from Gedor. Ref.: 1 Chr. 12:7. ¶
g. A Danite. Ref.: 1 Chr. 27:22. ¶
h. Father of Azariah. Ref.: 2 Chr. 23:1. ¶

JERUBBAAL – ***yᵉrubba'al*** [masc. proper noun: יְרֻבַּעַל <3378>; from STRIVE <7378> and BAAL <1168>]: Baal will contend ▶ **The surname of Gideon after he had destroyed the altar of Baal at Ophrah.** Refs.: Judg. 6:32; 7:1; 8:29, 35; 9:1, 2, 5, 16, 19, 24, 28, 57; 1 Sam. 12:11. ¶

JERUBBESHETH – ***yᵉrubbešeṯ*** [masc. proper noun: יְרֻבֶּשֶׁת <3380>; from STRIVE <7378> and SHAME <1322>]: shame will contend ▶ **A surname of Gideon.** Ref.: 2 Sam. 11:21. ¶

JERUEL – ***yᵉrû'ēl*** [proper noun: יְרוּאֵל <3385>; from SHOOT (verb) <3384> and GOD <410>]: foundation of God ▶ **A desert in the land of Judah.** Ref.: 2 Chr. 20:16. ¶

JERUSALEM – [1] ***yᵉrûšālam, yᵉrûšālayim*** [proper noun: יְרוּשָׁלַיִם ,יְרוּשָׁלֵם <3389>; prob. from the pass. part. of SHOOT (verb) <3384>

(in the sense of to lay) and COMPLETED (BE) <7999> (in the sense of to be at peace)]: founded peaceful ▶ **A proper noun designating Jerusalem, the city mentioned most often in the Old Testament and Israel's capital and most important city. It was formerly called Jebus when inhabited by the Jebusites, prior to David's conquest of the city.** After Israel was split into two parts, it was the capital of Judah, both before and after the exile (Ezra 1–2). Its name appears in written texts outside the Bible and in the Bible that recall a city predating Israel or the Hebrews in Egypt, throughout the nineteenth and eighteenth centuries B.C. An appropriate meaning for God's goal with and for His people is "shalom," "peace, well-being." The traditional meaning of the name is "city of peace." Jerusalem was the city of the Jebusites (Judg. 19:10) for many years. Even earlier, we hear of a Melchizedek, king of Salem (Jerusalem) functioning there (Gen. 14:14; Ps. 76:2). It was to be a city of righteousness but became a city of oppression. It was to be a city of peace but was torn apart. It was to be "the Holy City" (Is. 52:1), but it was corrupted (Ezek. 8). Its holiness was based on God's presence in its midst (1 Kgs. 6–8). God's presence over His ark (2 Sam. 6:1–15) sanctified the city, and His presence (Ex. 33:15–17) and made the people holy (Ezek. 48:35). Since David conquered the city, it could thereafter also be termed "the city of David" (2 Sam. 5:6–16). In 2 Samuel 5:7, it became associated with the designation "Zion," a powerful fortress or stronghold. It is called Ariel ("lion of God") several times (Is. 29). Ezekiel saw a new purified and cleansed city and Temple in his vision and appropriately named the new city "the Lord Is There" (Ezek. 48:35). The Arabic name for the city is "the Holy (City," el-Quds). Mohammed visited it (by tradition). It was and is the holiest city of Jews and Christians and the third holiest of Islam. See <3390> below. *

2 ***yᵉrûšᵉlem*** [Aramaic proper noun: יְרוּשְׁלֶם <3390>; corresponding to <3389> above] ▶ **See JERUSALEM <3389>. The city was rebuilt with a new Temple by Zerubbabel and later, walls by Nehemiah.** New residents inhabited the city, and Jerusalem again became the hoped-for "city of peace." Refs.: Ezra 4:8, 12; Dan. 5:2, 3, 6 (Daniel used the Aramaic name of Jerusalem in his historical account). See Neh. 2–7. *

JERUSHA – ***yᵉrûšāh, yᵉrûšā'*** [fem. proper noun: יְרוּשָׁה, יְרוּשָׁא <3388>; fem. pass. part. of HEIR (BE) <3423>]: possession ▶ **Wife of Uzziah, king of Judah, and mother of Jotham, his successor.** Refs.: 2 Kgs. 15:33; 2 Chr. 27:1. ¶

JESARELAH – 1 Chr. 25:14 ➔ JESHARELAH <3480>.

JESHANAH – ***yᵉšānāh*** [proper noun: יְשָׁנָה <3466>; fem. of OLD <3465>]: old ▶ **A city in Israel. It was taken, along with the smaller towns pertaining to it, from Jeroboam by Abijah.** Ref.: 2 Chr. 13:19. ¶

JESHARELAH – ***yᵉśar'ēlāh*** [masc. proper noun: יְשַׂרְאֵלָה <3480>; by variation from RIGHT <3477> and GOD <410>]: upright before God ▶ **Son of Asaph.** Ref.: 1 Chr. 25:14; same as Asharelah (or Asarelah) (v. 2). ¶

JESHEBEAB – ***yešeḇ'āḇ*** [masc. proper noun: יֶשֶׁבְאָב <3428>; from DWELL <3427> and FATHER <1>]: dwelling of the father ▶ **Head of the fourteenth division of priests.** Ref.: 1 Chr. 24:13. ¶

JESHER – ***yēšer*** [masc. proper noun: יֵשֶׁר <3475>; from STRAIGHT (BE) <3474>]: upright ▶ **One of the sons of Caleb.** Ref.: 1 Chr. 2:18. ¶

JESHIMON – ***yᵉšiymôn, yᵉšimôn*** [noun: יְשִׁימוֹן, יְשִׁמוֹן <3452>; from DESOLATE (BE) <3456>] ▶

a. A masculine proper noun denoting Jeshimon. It is used in two ways. First, it may refer to a desert or wilderness (see b. below), or it may refer to a location or territory called Jeshimon. Some translations render it Jeshimon (KJV, Num. 21:20; 23:28; 1 Sam. 23:19, 24; 26:1, 3). ¶

b. A masculine common noun referring to a desert, a wilderness, a wasteland.

See also a. above. It is taken as referring to a desert or wasteland by some translators (NKJV, ESV, NASB, NIV, Num. 21:20; 23:28). In some contexts, its use to refer to a desert or wilderness is accepted by all translators (Deut. 32:10; Ps. 68:7; 78:40; 106:14; 107:4; Is. 43:19, 20). ¶

JESHISHAI – ***yešiyšay*** [masc. proper noun: יְשִׁישַׁי <3454>; from AGED <3453>]: old, venerable ▶ **A man of the tribe of Gad.** Ref.: 1 Chr. 5:14. ¶

JESHOHAIAH – ***yešôḥāyāh*** [masc. proper noun: יְשׁוֹחָיָה <3439>; from CASTING DOWN <3445> and PEOPLE <3050>]: the Lord will cast down ▶ **A descendant of the tribe of Simeon.** Ref.: 1 Chr. 4:36. ¶

JESHUA – [1] ***yêšûaʿ*** [proper noun: יֵשׁוּעַ <3442>; from JOSHUAH <3091>]: he will save ▶
a. A priest. Refs.: 1 Chr. 24:11; Ezra 2:36; Neh. 7:39. ¶
b. A Levite. Refs.: 2 Chr. 31:15; Ezra 2:40; Neh. 7:43. ¶
c. A priest. Refs.: Ezra 2:2; 3:2, 8, 9; 4:3; 10:18; Neh. 7:7; 12:1, 7, 10, 26. See also ***yêšûaʿ*** (JESHUA <3443>). ¶
d. Father of Jozabad. Ref.: Ezra 8:33. ¶
e. Son of Pahath-Moab. Refs.: Ezra 2:6; Neh. 7:11. ¶
f. Father of Ezer. Ref.: Neh. 3:19. It may be the same as c. above. ¶
g. A Levite. Refs.: Neh. 8:7; 9:4, 5; 12:8, 24. ¶
h. Moses' successor. Ref.: Neh. 8:17. ¶
i. A Levite, son of Azaniah, who signed the covenant of renewal with Nehemiah after the return from the Babylonian captivity. Ref.: Neh. 10:9. ¶
j. A city in Benjamin. Ref.: Neh. 11:26. ¶
[2] ***yêšûaʿ*** [Aramaic masc. proper noun: יֵשׁוּעַ <3443>; corresponding to <3442> c. above]: he will save ▶ **The son of Jozadak who began building the house of God in Jerusalem with Zerubbabel.** Ref.: Ezra 5:2. It corresponds to the Hebrew JESHUA <3442> c. ¶

JESHURUN – ***yešurûn*** [masc. proper noun: יְשֻׁרוּן <3484>; from STRAIGHT (BE) <3474>]: the upright one ▶ **A word designating Israel.** It is found in poetry in the Song of Moses (Deut. 32:15), the blessings of Moses (Deut. 33:5, 26), and the prophecy of Isaiah (Is. 44:2). Hence, it is often termed the "poetic" name of Israel. It is clearly parallel with Jacob in Isaiah's prophecy. It seems to be used as an ideal designation of Israel. ¶

JESIAH – See ISSHIAH <3449>.

JESIMIEL – ***yeśiymiʾēl*** [masc. proper noun: יְשִׂימִאֵל <3450>; from PUT <7760> and GOD <410>]: God will place ▶ **A member of the tribe of Simeon, a prince in his clan.** Ref.: 1 Chr. 4:36. ¶

JESSE – ***yišay, ʾiyšay*** [masc. proper noun: יִשַׁי, אִישַׁי <3448>; from the same as BE <3426>]: extant ▶ **An Ephrathite from Bethlehem in Judah; the father of king David; his father was Obed.** Refs.: Ruth 4:21, 22. He helped Samuel find David so he could anoint him (1 Sam. 16). He was an old man during Saul's reign. *

JEST – Is. 57:4 ➔ DELIGHT (HAVE, FIND, TAKE) <6026>.

JESTER – Ps. 35:16 ➔ STAMMERING <3934>.

JESUI – See ISHVI <3440> a.

JESUITE – See ISHVITE <3441>.

JETHER – See JETHRO, JETHER <3500>.

JETHETH – ***yeṯēṯ*** [masc. proper noun: יְתֵת <3509>; of uncertain deriv.] ▶ **One of the chiefs of Edom.** Refs.: Gen. 36:40; 1 Chr. 1:51. ¶

JETHLAH – Josh. 19:42 ➔ ITHLAH <3494>.

JETHRO – ***yiṯrô*** [masc. proper noun: יִתְרוֹ <3503>; from REMAINDER <3499> with pron. suffix]: his excellence, his abundance ▶ **This word designates the**

father-in-law of Moses. He was a Midianite priest. He wisely advised Moses about how to structure his administration of justice to the people (Ex. 18). See JETHRO, JETHER <3500> a.

JETHRO, JETHER – ***yeṯer*** [masc. proper noun: יֶתֶר <3500>; the same as REMAINDER <3499>]: abundance, excellence ▶
a. Jethro, the father of Zipporah, Moses' wife taken in Midian. Ref.: Ex. 4:18. He is also called Reuel (Ex. 3:18) and functioned as a Midianite priest—but even more importantly as Moses' father-in-law (Ex. 3; 4; 18). See JETHRO <3503>. ¶
b. Jether, the oldest son of the great judge Gideon. He was only a young man in the biblical text and was afraid to kill the Midianite leaders, Zebah and Zalmunna (Judg. 8:18–21). ¶
c. Jether, the father of Amasa. Amasa served for a while as David's commander of his army. He was murdered by Joab (1 Kgs. 2:5, 32; 1 Chr. 2:17). ¶
d. Jether, son of Jada. He had no descendants and was in the line of Judah through Hegron (1 Chr. 2:32). ¶
e. Jether, from Judah and the son of a clan head, Ezrah. Ref.: 1 Chr. 4:17. ¶
f. Jether, an Asherite and a head of a clan family. Ref.: 1 Chr. 7:38. ¶

JETUR – ***yᵉṭûr*** [masc. proper noun: יְטוּר <3195>; prob. from the same as ROW <2905> (in the sense of forming an enclosure)]: enclosure ▶ **One of the sons of Ishmael.** Refs.: Gen. 25:15; 1 Chr. 1:31; 5:19. ¶

JEUEL – ***yᵉʿûʾēl*** [masc. proper noun: יְעוּאֵל <3262>; from SWEEP AWAY <3261> GOD <410>]: taken away by God ▶ **A man of the tribe of Judah, the son of Zerah.** Ref.: 1 Chr. 9:6. ¶

JEUSH – ***yᵉʿûš*** [masc. proper noun: יְעוּשׁ <3266>; from HASTEN <5789>]: hasty ▶
a. One of the sons of Esau and his wife Aholibamah. He became one of the chiefs of Edom (Gen. 36:5, 14, 18; 1 Chr. 1:35). ¶
b. A Benjamite, son of Bilhan. Ref.: 1 Chr. 7:10. ¶
c. A Benjamite, descendant of Jonathan. Ref.: 1 Chr. 8:39. ¶
d. A Levite of the family of Gershon. Refs.: 1 Chr. 23:10, 11. ¶
e. One of the sons of Rehoboam. Ref.: 2 Chr. 11:19. ¶

JEUZ – ***yᵉʿûṣ*** [masc. proper noun: יְעוּץ <3263>; from COUNSEL (TAKE) <3245>]: counselor ▶ **A man of the tribe of Benjamin, son of Shaharaim and Hodesh his wife.** Ref.: 1 Chr. 8:10. ¶

JEW – 1 ***yᵉhûḏay*** [Aramaic masc. proper noun: יְהוּדָי <3062>; patrial from JUDAH <3061>] ▶ **This word corresponds to the Hebrew word *yᵉhûḏiy* (<3064> below).** It is found in Ezra 4:12, 23; 5:1, 5; 6:7–8, 14; Daniel 3:8, 12. ¶
2 ***yᵉhûḏiy*** [proper noun: יְהוּדִי <3064>; patron. from JUDAH <3063>] ▶ **This word designates a Jew, a gentilic noun indicating nationality. An *iy* (י) ending indicated a male while *iyṯ* (ית) indicated a female. It referred originally to those Israelites living in Judah or of the tribe of Judah after the exile.** Refs.: 2 Kgs. 16:6; 25:25; Neh. 1:2; 2:16. The term was used by later writers to depict some inhabitants or persons of Judah who lived there earlier (1 Chr. 4:18). Foreign people used the term to describe the people of Judah in and after the eighth century B.C. (Zech. 8:23; Esther 2:5; 3:4; 8:11). The updating or final editing of Daniel used the designation (Dan. 3:8; 5:13). "Jew(s)" is a general term referring to males or females. "Jewess" refers to a female. *

JEWEL – 1 Prov. 31:10 ➔ MERCHANDISE <4377> 2 Song 4:9 ➔ CHAIN <6060> 3 Song 7:1 ➔ ORNAMENT <2481> 4 Dan. 11:20 ➔ GLORY <1925>.

JEWELRY – ***ḥelyāh*** [fem. noun: חֶלְיָה <2484>; fem. of ORNAMENT <2481>] ▶ **This word means ornaments for the body.** Israel's spiritual prostitution is pictured as a time when she adorned herself with jewelry or ornaments to pursue her religious and political lovers. Ref.: Hos. 2:13. She corrupted herself through harlotry. ¶

JEWELS – [1] ***pᵉniyniym*** [masc. plur. noun: פְּנִינִים <6443>; from the same as CORNER (noun) <6434> (in the sense of something being round)] ► **This word refers to ornaments worn for beautification; it is also translated rubies, pearls, costly stones, corrals.** Such ornaments are usually made of gold, silver, and precious stones (Prov. 3:15). Jewels are known for their great value as well. Other refs.: Job 28:18; Prov. 8:11; 20:15; 31:10; Lam. 4:7. ¶
– [2] Song 5:14 ➔ BERYL <8658> a. [3] Mal. 3:17 ➔ TREASURE POSSESSION <5459>.

JEWELS (STRING OF) – Song 1:10 ➔ STRING OF JEWELS <2737>.

JEWISH – 1 Chr. 4:18 ➔ JEHUDIJAH <3057>.

JEWISH LANGUAGE (IN THE) – 2 Kgs. 18:26, 28; 2 Chr. 32:18; Neh. 13:24; Is. 36:11, 13 ➔ HEBREW (IN) <3066>.

JEWS (BECOME, DECLARE THEMSELVES) – ***yāhaḏ*** [verb: יָהַד <3054>; denom. from a form corresponding to JUDAH <3061>] ► **This word is used of many of Israel's enemies who decide to cast their lot with the Jews and join them and their God because of the great deliverance God gave to the Jews.** Ref.: Esther 8:17. ¶

JEWS' LANGUAGE (IN THE) – 2 Kgs. 18:26, 28; 2 Chr. 32:18; Neh. 13:24; Is. 36:11, 13 ➔ HEBREW (IN) <3066>.

JEZANIAH – ***yᵉzanyāhû, yᵉzanyāh*** [masc. proper noun: יְזַנְיָהוּ, יְזַנְיָה <3153>; prob. from JAAZANIAH <2970>]: the Lord hears ►
a. A Judean. Ref.: Jer. 40:8. ¶
b. A Judean leader. Ref.: Jer. 42:1. ¶

JEZEBEL – ***'iyzeḇel*** [fem. proper noun: אִיזֶבֶל <348>; from NOT <336> and ZEBUL <2083> (habitation)]: no habitation ► **This woman was a Sidonian princess who married the Israelite King Ahab. Her father was Ethbaal, king of Tyre and a priest of Baal.** She introduced Tyrian Baal worship in Israel and promoted and fostered the priests of Baal (1 Kgs. 16:31). She killed the many prophets of the Lord (1 Kgs. 18:4). She attempted to kill Elijah ("the Lord is God") (1 Kgs. 19:1). She arranged to have Naboth killed (1 Kgs. 21:5–25). Elijah condemned her, and the Lord appointed Jehu to eradicate her and her family from Israel (2 Kgs. 9:6–10, 22–37). She was the queen mother for ten or more years after Ahab died. She died at Jehu's hand in ca. 842 B.C. She is mentioned as a negative symbol of a false prophet in the New Testament (Rev. 2:20). *

JEZER – ***yêṣer*** [masc. proper noun: יֵצֶר <3337>; the same as FORMED <3336>]: form, purpose ► **The third son of Naphtali.** Refs.: Gen. 46:24; Num. 26:49; 1 Chr. 7:13. ¶

JEZERITE – ***yiṣriy*** [proper noun: יִצְרִי <3340>; patron. from JEZER <3337>] ► **A member of the family of Jezer.** Ref.: Num. 26:49. ¶

JEZIAH – Ezra 10:25 ➔ IZZIAH <3150>.

JEZIEL – ***yᵉzû'êl*** [masc. proper noun: יְזוּאֵל <3149>; from an unused root (meaning to sprinkle) and GOD <410>]: sprinkled of God ► **A man of the tribe of Benjamin who joined David at Ziklag.** Ref.: 1 Chr. 12:3. ¶

JEZLIAH – 1 Chr. 8:18 ➔ IZLIAH <3152>.

JEZREEL – ***yizrᵉ'e'l*** [proper noun and masc. proper noun: יִזְרְעֶאל <3157>; from SOW <2232> and GOD <410>]: God sows ►
a. A town in Judah from which David's wife Ahinoam came. It was possibly located just south of Hebron to the west of the Dead Sea (1 Sam. 25:43). Other refs.: Josh. 15:56; 1 Sam. 29:1, 11. ¶
b. A city of Issachar. Ref.: Josh. 19:18. Saul used the city as did his son Ish-Bosheth later who was in charge of it (2 Sam. 2:9). One of Ahab's palaces was there (1 Kgs.

18:45). Naboth's vineyard, violently seized by Ahab, was in Jezreel and there Ahab's son, Joram, and Jezebel were executed by Jehu (2 Kgs. 8:29–10:11). *
c. The name of a fertile valley in northern Israel. Ref.: Hos. 2:22. Its name means "God sows." Many peoples battled for control of it (Josh. 17:16; Judg. 6:33). Hosea mentioned it as a place where God will judge Israel (Hos. 1:5). ¶
d. The son of Etam, a clan head in Judah. Ref.: 1 Chr. 12:3. ¶
e. A son of Hosea. He was so named as a symbol of the massacre and bloodshed that occurred there related to Jehu's house (Hos. 1:4). ¶
f. Another name for Israel (see e. also). The valley stands for all of Israel in the prophet's usage (Hos. 1:4, 11). ¶

JEZREELITE – ***yizr*ᵉ*'ê'liy*** [masc. proper noun: יִזְרְעֵאלִי <3158>; patron. from JEZREEL <3157>] ▶ **A male native of Jezreel.** Naboth was a Jezreelite (1 Kgs. 21:1, 4, 6, 7, 15, 16; 2 Kgs. 9:21, 25); see JEZREEL b. ¶

JEZREELITESS – ***yizr*ᵉ*'ê'liyṯ, yizr*ᵉ*'ê'liṯ*** [fem. proper noun: יִזְרְעֵאלִית, יִזְרְעֵאלִת <3159>; fem. of JEZREELITE <3158>] ▶ **A female native of Jezreel.** Ahinoam, one of David's wives, was a Jezreelitess; see JEZREEL a. Refs.: 1 Sam. 27:3; 30:5; 2 Sam. 2:2; 3:2; 1 Chr. 3:1. ¶

JIBSAM – 1 Chr. 7:2 ➔ IBSAM <3005>.

JIDLAPH – ***yiḏlāp̱*** [masc. proper noun: יִדְלָף <3044>; from LEAK <1811> (in the sense of to weep)]: weeping ▶ **One of the sons of Nahor and Milcah.** Ref.: Gen. 22:22. ¶

JINGLE – Is. 3:16 ➔ TINKLE <5913>.

JIPHTAH – Josh. 15:43 ➔ JEPHTHAH <3316> b.

JIPHTHAHEL – Josh. 19:14, 27 ➔ IPHTAHEL <3317>.

JISHUI – See ISHVI <3440> b.

JISSHIAH – See ISSHIAH <3449>.

JOAB – ***yô'āḇ*** [masc. proper noun: יוֹאָב <3097>; from LORD <3068> and FATHER <1>]: the Lord is father ▶
a. The name of David's nephew and the commander of his army. He was the son of Zeruiah, David's half-sister. With his brothers, Asahel and Abishai, he defeated Ish-Bosheth's attempt to be king (2 Sam. 8:8–17). David made him commander of all his forces (1 Chr. 11:6). He was a great commander but also took part in David's murder of Uriah the Hittite (2 Sam. 11:6–18). He showed no mercy or hesitation about executing a person he deemed dangerous to David or the kingdom (2 Sam. 3:6–39; 18:10–17). This aspect of his character caused David to replace him for a while by Amasa (2 Sam. 19:13) whom Joab slew and replaced before long (2 Sam. 20:4). He differed with David on some things and at the end of his life was executed before the altar at Gibeon because he had not supported Solomon as king but rather Adonijah (1 Kgs. 1:1–2:5). According to Solomon, Joab had shed innocent blood by killing Abner and Amasa. *
b. He was of the line of Judah. His father was Seraiah (1 Chr. 4:14). ¶
c. An exile who returned with Zerubbabel. He had a large posterity who returned after him (Ezra 2:6). Other refs.: Ezra 8:9; Neh. 7:11. ¶

JOAH – ***yô'āḥ*** [masc. proper noun: יוֹאָח <3098>; from LORD <3068> and BROTHER <251>]: the Lord is brother ▶
a. Son of Asaph. Refs.: 2 Kgs. 18:18, 26, 37; Is. 36:3, 11, 22. ¶
b. A Levite. Ref.: 1 Chr. 6:21. ¶
c. Another Levite. Ref.: 2 Chr. 29:12. ¶
d. Son of Joahaz. Ref.: 2 Chr. 34:8. ¶
e. Son of Obed-Edom. Ref.: 1 Chr. 26:4. ¶

JOASH – 1 ***yô'āš*** [masc. proper noun: יוֹאָשׁ <3101>; a form of JEHOASH <3060>]: the Lord has given ▶
a. A king of Judah who reigned (835–796 B.C.), forty years. He was a good king who repaired the Temple of the Lord. His

mother was Zibiah. He reigned during the time of the high priest Jehoiada who served as a counselor to him (2 Kgs. 12:1, 2). His reforms were not thorough (2 Kgs. 12:3), but he paid the workmen fair wages (2 Kgs. 12:14). Unfortunately, he was forced to pay tribute to Hazael, king of Aram (Syria). *

b. A king of Israel (798–782 B.C.) who reigned sixteen years. His reign was evil, for he followed in the footsteps of Jeroboam I, son of Nebat. He continued in the corrupt and false worship of his father. He fought with Amaziah of Judah (2 Kgs. 13:12, 13). He called upon and honored Elisha the prophet (2 Kgs. 13:14–19). *

c. The father of Gideon, a famous judge in Israel. He bravely defended Gideon and the Lord before the people of the city (Judg. 6:30–32). *

d. A son in the house of Ahab, one of Israel's most wicked kings. He was in charge of the prison (1 Kgs. 22:26, 27; 2 Chr. 18:25). ¶

e. One of David's mighty warriors and a Benjamite, very skilled in bow and arrow and in the use of slings. Refs.: 1 Chr. 12:1–3. ¶

f. A descendant of the tribe of Judah who in ancient times exercised some rulership in Moab and Lehem. Ref.: 1 Chr. 4:22. ¶

2 ***yô'āš*** [masc. proper noun: יוֹעָשׁ <3135>; from LORD <3068> and HASTEN <5789>]: the Lord hastens ▶

a. A Benjamite, son of Becher. Ref.: 1 Chr. 7:8. ¶

b. Officer under David; he was in charge of the stores of oil. Ref.: 1 Chr. 27:28. ¶

JOB – 1 ***'iyyôḇ*** [masc. proper noun: אִיּוֹב <347>; from ENEMY (BE AN) <340>]: hated, persecuted ▶ **This man is the central character of the Book of Job and is the object of testing. By the Lord's permission Satan ("adversary") was permitted to test Job to the limit twice.** (1) Job lost all his worldly possessions, riches, and family—yet remained faithful to God; (2) God permitted Satan to afflict Job sorely, almost unto death—yet again Job submitted to the mysterious will of God concerning his suffering (Job 40:1–5; 42:1–6). Even his friends forsook him in his suffering. Job was a non-Israelite of great value in God's eyes who said that Job was blameless, upright, God-fearing, and one who resisted evil (Job 1:1). He was considered a wise man as well. His wealth was legendary (Job 1:1–3). The location of the land of Uz is uncertain, but possibly it was east of Edom (Jer. 25:2; Lam. 4:21). Job is mentioned in the New Testament (Jas. 5:11) and in Ezekiel 14:14, 20 as a wise and righteous man. *

2 ***yôḇ*** [masc. proper noun: יוֹב <3102>; perhaps a form of JOBAB <3103>, but more prob. by erroneous transcription for JASHUB <3437>]: hated, persecuted ▶ **Fourth son of Issachar.** Ref.: Gen. 46:13. ¶

JOBAB – ***yôḇāḇ*** [masc. proper noun: יוֹבָב <3103>; from CRY, CRY OUT <2980>]: howler ▶

a. Son of Joktan. Refs.: Gen. 10:29; 1 Chr. 1:23. ¶

b. King of Edom. Refs.: Gen. 36:33, 34; 1 Chr. 1:44, 45. ¶

c. King of Madon. Ref.: Josh. 11:1. ¶

d. Son of Shaharaim. Ref.: 1 Chr. 8:9. ¶

e. A Benjamite. Ref.: 1 Chr. 8:18. ¶

JOCHEBED – ***yôḵeḇeḏ*** [fem. proper noun: יוֹכֶבֶד <3115>; from LORD <3068> contr. and HEAVY (BE) <3513> (in the sense of enjoying honor or glory)]: the Lord is glory ▶ **This is the name of Moses' mother, as well as mother of Miriam and Aaron.** She was from the line of Levi. Her husband was Amram (Hebrew, her nephew; Septuagint, her cousin) (Ex. 6:20; Num. 26:59). ¶

JOED – ***yô'ēḏ*** [masc. proper noun: יוֹעֵד <3133>; apparently the act. part. of APPOINT <3259>]: one who designates ▶ **A Benjamite, the son of Pedaiah.** Ref.: Neh. 11:7. ¶

JOEL – ***yô'ēl*** [masc. proper noun: יוֹאֵל <3100>; from LORD <3068> and GOD <410>]: the Lord is God ▶

a. A prophet of probably the ninth century B.C., although the date of this prophet is not certain. Ref.: Joel 1:1. Some locate him in the sixth century. His message was a warning to Judah of the coming Day of the Lord in which all nations, including a rebellious Israel, would be judged severely. His description of a plague of locusts, literal or figurative, was a powerful way to depict this perilous situation of the coming of God's judgment upon Israel. The nations of judgment would be real, whether the locusts were metaphorical or not. ¶

b. The elder son of Samuel who was a priest at Beersheba. Samuel's sons became corrupt and were part of the reason Israel asked for a king who could lead them in character and behavior, as well as serve as a military conqueror (1 Sam. 8:2; 1 Chr. 6:28). ¶

c. A prince or leader from the tribe of Simeon. Ref.: 1 Chr. 4:35. ¶

d. A leading descendant of the tribe of Reuben. Refs.: 1 Chr. 5:4, 8. ¶

e. One of the heads of the descendants of the tribe of Gad. He lived in Bashan (1 Chr. 5:12). ¶

f. A priest who served in the music and worship of the Temple. Ref.: 1 Chr. 6:36. ¶

g. A head or chief of the descendants of Issachar. Ref.: 1 Chr. 7:3. ¶

h. Listed among David's mighty warriors. Ref.: 1 Chr. 11:38. ¶

i. A chief or leader of the descendants of Manasseh. Ref.: 1 Chr. 27:20. ¶

j. A descendant of the Levites through Gershom. Refs.: 1 Chr. 15:7, 11, 17; 23:8; 26:22. ¶

k. A Levite through the Kohathites. His father was Azariah. Ref.: 1 Chr. 29:12. ¶

l. A descendant of Nebo who intermarried with the people of the land. Ref.: Ezra 10:43. ¶

m. The son of Zichri who served as a chief officer among the Benjamites. Ref.: Neh. 11:9. All were new residents of a resettled Jerusalem. ¶

JOELAH – ***yô'ē'lāh*** [masc. proper noun: יוֹעֵאלָה <3132>; perhaps fem. act. part. of PROFIT (verb) <3276>]: the Lord helps ▶ **A man of the tribe of Benjamin who joined David at Ziklag.** Ref.: 1 Chr. 12:7. ¶

JOEZER – ***yô'ezer*** [masc. proper noun: יוֹעֶזֶר <3134>; from LORD <3068> and HELP (noun) <5828>]: the Lord is help ▶ **A Korahite who joined David at Ziklag.** Ref.: 1 Chr. 12:6. ¶

JOGBEHA – ***yoḡbᵉhāh*** [proper noun: יָגְבְּהָה <3011>; fem. from EXALTED (BE) <1361>]: elevated, exalted ▶ **Gideon attacked a Midianite army who felt in security near that place in the territory of Gad.** Refs.: Num. 32:35; Judg. 8:11. ¶

JOGLI – ***yoḡliy*** [masc. proper noun: יָגְלִי <3020>; from REVEAL <1540> (in the sense of going into exile)]: exiled ▶ **Father of Bukki, of the tribe of Dan.** Ref.: Num. 34:22. ¶

JOHA – ***yôḥā'*** [masc. proper noun: יוֹחָא <3109>; prob. from LORD <3068> and a variation of LIVE <2421>]: the Lord is living ▶

a. A Benjamite. Ref.: 1 Chr. 8:16. ¶

b. One of David's mighty men. Ref.: 1 Chr. 11:45. ¶

JOHANAN – ***yôḥānān*** [masc. proper noun: יוֹחָנָן <3110>; a form of JEHOHANAN <3076>]: the Lord is gracious ▶

a. A priest who functioned during Ezra-Nehemiah's time. He was a son of the priest Eliashib (Neh. 12:22, 23). ¶

b. A Jewish officer, son of Kareah, who supported Gedaliah after the fall of Jerusalem. Ref.: 2 Kgs. 25:23. He tried to warn and protect the appointed governor to no avail (Jer. 40:13–16). He fled to Egypt. *

c. The oldest son of Josiah and of the descendants of Judah. Ref.: 1 Chr. 3:15. ¶

d. The son of Elioenai of the line of Judah. Ref.: 1 Chr. 3:24. ¶

e. The son of Azariah of the line of Levi. Refs.: 1 Chr. 6:9, 10. ¶

f. One of several persons from the tribe of Gad who joined David when he was fleeing from Saul. Ref.: 1 Chr. 12:4. ¶

g. A capable warrior from the Benjamites who defected to David when David was fleeing Saul. Ref.: 1 Chr. 12:12. ¶

h. A family head or leader who returned from exile to Jerusalem under Ezra. He was a descendant of Azgad (Ezra 8:12). ¶

JOIAKIM – ***yôyāqiym*** [masc. proper noun: יוֹיָקִים <3113>; a form of JEHOIACHIM <3079, cf. JOKIM <3137>]: the Lord sets up ► **A high priest, son and successor of Jeshua.** Refs.: Neh. 12:10, 12, 26. ¶

JOIARIB – ***yôyāriyḇ*** [masc. proper noun: יוֹיָרִיב <3114>; a form of JEHOIARIB <3080>]: whom the Lord defends ►
a. Name of a priestly family. Refs.: Neh. 11:10; 12:6, 19. ¶
b. Teacher of Ezra. Ref.: Ezra 8:16. ¶
c. A Judaite. Ref.: Neh. 11:5. ¶

JOIN – 1 ***dāḇaq*** [verb: דָּבַק <1692>; a prim. root] ► **This word means to cling to, to link with, to stay with.** It is used of something sticking to or clinging to something else (Ezek. 29:4); it describes Ezekiel's tongue clinging to the roof of his mouth (Ezek. 3:26). It is used figuratively or symbolically of a man cleaving or clinging to his wife (Gen. 2:24) or of evil deeds clinging to a person (Ps. 101:3). It depicts leprosy clinging to a person, not going away and persisting (2 Kgs. 5:27), as well as famine (Deut. 28:21; Jer. 13:11; 42:16). It depicts relationships created as an act of joining together, to follow (Josh. 23:12; 2 Sam. 20:2). In a spiritual sense, it describes Ruth joining and staying with Boaz's maids (Ruth 2:8, 21, 23) and Jehoram's following the sins of Jeroboam (2 Kgs. 3:3). To hold on to an inheritance or right is depicted using this verb (Num. 36:7). It depicts the scales of a crocodile tightly fastened together (Job 41:17) and clods of earth stuck to each other (Job 38:38). In certain uses, it has the idea of causing things to stick or be stuck (Ps. 22:15; Ezek. 29:4). *

2 ***lāwāh*** [verb: לָוָה <3867>; a prim. root] ► **This word has the meaning of attaching oneself to someone or something.** To one's wife through affection (Gen. 29:34); to a group of fellow tribesmen who have a common purpose of serving in the work of the priesthood (Num. 18:2, 4); to the Lord as one's God, even though the persons are foreigners, strangers or eunuchs (Is. 14:1; 56:3, 6), for the Lord will accept and prosper them. It is used of the Israelite's firm attachment to the Lord in devotion and worship (Jer. 50:5), along with many other nations in the Day of the Lord (Zech. 2:11). It is used of nations aligning themselves with the enemies of God's people taking on a common cause (Ps. 83:8); it is used of something that will remain with people and satisfy them during their lives, such as eating, drinking, and joy (Eccl. 8:15). Other refs.: Esther 9:27; Dan. 11:34. The word also means to borrow, to lend; see BORROW <3867>. ¶

3 ***sāp̱aḥ, śāp̱aḥ*** [verb: סָפַח, שָׂפַח <5596>; a prim. root] ► **This word means to be gathered together, to be united, to cleave, to unite oneself, to abide in.** The word refers to putting a priest into office, i.e., joining him to the office (1 Sam. 2:36). It refers to David remaining in Israel's inheritance in spite of death threats from Saul (1 Sam. 26:19); similarly, it refers to the Gentiles being joined to Israel (Is. 14:1). In Job 30:7, it refers to the gathering of foolish poor people for protection under a plant. It appears to refer to the joining of heat (i.e., poison) to a drink meant to make someone drunk; but the word here may be a copyist's error for *sap̱* (BASIN <5592>), meaning goblet (Hab. 2:15). In Isaiah 3:17, the word means to smite with a scab, but here it is spelled *śippaḥ* and may belong to another root of similar spelling. ¶

4 ***ṣāmaḏ*** [verb: צָמַד <6775>; a prim. root] ► **This word indicates to combine forces with someone, to attach oneself to someone or something, to become like each other; it also means to yoke, to harness.** Israel began to take part in worshiping Baal of Peor (Num. 25:3, 5; Ps. 106:28). In a physical sense, it refers to an object being tied to or fastened to another object (2 Sam. 20:8). It is used in a figurative sense to describe a person's tongue harnessing or latching on to deceit, producing it (Ps. 50:19). ¶

– 5 Gen. 49:6; Job 3:6; Is. 14:20 → UNITE <3161> 6 Ezra 4:12 → REPAIR <2338> 7 Job 3:6 → REJOICE <2302>.

JOIN TOGETHER – ***ḥāḇar*** [verb: חָבַר <2266>; a prim. root] ►

a. This word means to unite; to conjure, to charm; to heap up (words). It refers to simple physical proximity or touching of objects (Ex. 26:3, 6, 9, 11) or to the mental, emotional, and physical joining of forces or armies (Gen. 14:3; 2 Chr. 20:35, 36; Dan. 11:6). It is used figuratively of joining one's self in a deep religious sense to something, such as idols (Ps. 94:20; Hos. 4:17). Closely allied to this is its use to indicate the process of charming, conjuring, or casting a spell (Deut. 18:11; Ps. 58:5). It is used of composing or joining words to attack someone (Job 16:4). *
b. This word means to adorn, to make beautiful, to be brilliant; to heap up. It refers to the joining or composing of words, a speech (Job 16:4, NASB, NIV; KJV, heap up *words*). ¶

JOINED (BE) – [1] ***qāṭar*** [verb: קָטַר <7000>; a prim. root] ▶ **This word means to be connected; it is also translated to be enclosed.** It refers to the connection or the partitioned areas to serve as courts, used only of these areas in Ezekiel's Temple (Ezek. 46:22). ¶
– [2] 2 Chr. 3:12 ➔ JOINING <1695>.

JOINING – [1] ***dāḇêq*** [adj.: דָּבֵק <1695>; from JOIN <1692>] ▶ **This word indicates clinging to, holding to.** The wings of the cherubs in the Holy of Holies were touching and thus joining (2 Chr. 3:12); also translated to be attached, to be joined, to touch. In a spiritual sense, it depicts faithfulness to the Lord of Israel (Deut. 4:4: to cleave, to hold fast). It depicts the steadfast companionship of an intimate friend (Prov. 18:24: to stick close). ¶
– [2] 1 Chr. 22:3 ➔ FITTING <4226>.

JOINT – [1] ***deḇeq*** [masc. noun: דֶּבֶק <1694>; from JOIN <1692>] ▶ **This word designates a joining, a fastener, welding, a place of connecting.** It indicates the place where armor is joined and thus weak (1 Kgs. 22:34; 2 Chr. 18:33) or the spot where metal work in general is fastened in various ways (Is. 41:7: soldering, welding). ¶
– [2] 1 Chr. 22:3 ➔ FITTING <4226>
[3] Song 7:1 ➔ CURVE <2542>.

JOINT (PUT OUT OF) – Gen. 32:25 ➔ ALIENATED (BE) <3363>.

JOIST – 2 Chr. 34:11 ➔ FITTING <4226>.

JOKDEAM – ***yoqḏ**ᵉ**'ām*** [proper noun: יָקְדְעָם <3347>; from BURN (verb) <3344> and PEOPLE <5971>]: burning of the people ▶ **A city in the mountains of Judah.** Ref.: Josh. 15:56. ¶

JOKIM – ***yôqiym*** [masc. proper noun: יוֹקִים <3137>; a form of JOIAKIM <3113>]: the Lord sets up ▶ **A man of the tribe of Judah, son of Shelah.** Ref.: 1 Chr. 4:22. ¶

JOKMEAM – ***yoqm**ᵉ**'ām*** [proper noun: יָקְמְעָם <3361>; from STAND, STAND UP <6965> and PEOPLE <5971>]: the people will be raised ▶ **A Levitical city of Ephraim.** Refs.: 1 Kgs. 4:12; 1 Chr. 6:68. ¶

JOKNEAM – ***yoqn**ᵉ**'ām*** [proper noun: יָקְנְעָם <3362>; from LAMENT <6969> and PEOPLE <5971>]: the people will lament ▶ **A Levitical city of Zebulun.** Refs.: Josh. 12:22; 19:11; 21:34. ¶

JOKSHAN – ***yoqšān*** [masc. proper noun: יָקְשָׁן <3370>; from SNARE, BE SNARED <3369>]: insidious ▶ **Son of Abraham and Keturah.** Refs.: Gen. 25:2, 3; 1 Chr. 1:32. ¶

JOKTAN – ***yoqṭān*** [masc. proper noun: יָקְטָן <3355>; from NOT WORTHY (BE) <6994> (in the sense of to be small)]: small ▶ **The second son of Heber.** Refs.: Gen. 10:25, 26, 29; 1 Chr. 1:19, 20, 23. ¶

JOKTHEEL – ***yoqṯ**ᵉ**'ēl*** [proper noun: יָקְתְאֵל <3371>; prob. from the same as JAKEH <3348> and GOD <410>]: obedience to God ▶
a. A location in Judah. Ref.: Josh. 15:38. ¶
b. A location in Idumea. Ref.: 2 Kgs. 14:7. ¶

JOLTING – Nah. 3:2 ➔ DANCE (verb) <7540>.

JONADAB – ***yônāḏāḇ*** [masc. proper noun: יוֹנָדָב <3122>; a form of JEHONADAB <3082>]: the Lord is generous ▶
a. The son of Rechab and the father of the Rechabnites who were not to drink wine, build houses, raise grain, or plant vineyards. Refs.: Jer. 35:6, 10, 19. Instead Jonadab commanded them to live in tents (Jer. 35:6–10). ¶
b. David's nephew, the son of Shimeah, David's brother. He was cunning and helped arrange for Amnon to be alone with Tamar (2 Sam. 13:3–5). ¶

JONAH – ***yônāh*** [masc. proper noun: יוֹנָה <3124>; the same as DOVE <3123>]: dove ▶ **This word designates a prophet called to preach repentance to Nineveh. He came from Gath Hepher. His father's name was Amittai.** Jonah foretold the expansion of Israel under Jeroboam II (2 Kgs. 14:25). He was called by God to go to Nineveh and preach repentance to the capital of Assyria. Amazingly, it was his understanding and grasp of God's compassion and mercy toward the wicked that caused him to refuse, initially, to fulfill God's call (Jon. 4:1–3). *

JONATH ELEM REHOKIM – ***yônaṯ 'ēlem reḥōqiym*** [proper noun: יוֹנַת אֵלֶם רְחֹקִים <3128>; from DOVE <3123 and OAK TREES <482> and the plur. of FAR OFF <7350>] ▶ **This phrase occurs in the title of Psalm 56.** It is transliterated into English by some translators as Jonath elem rehokim (NASB, KJV), while others translate the words (Ps. 56:1): "The Silent Dove in Distant Lands" and note that this is a tune to which the psalm is set (NKJV); "A Dove on Distant Oaks" (NIV); "The Dove on Far-off Terebinths." ¶

JONATHAN – 1 ***yehônāṯān*** [masc. proper noun: יְהוֹנָתָן <3083>; from LORD <3068> and GIVE <5414>]: the Lord has given ▶
a. The son of Saul who befriended David despite the animosity of his father Saul toward David. He was a mighty warrior (1 Sam. 14:13, 14), but his father nearly executed him for a minor incident (1 Sam. 14:44, 45). He refused to kill David when Saul commanded him to do so but rather warned and shielded David (1 Sam. 19:1–7; 20:1–17). They became faithful friends and covenanted to keep faith between them (1 Sam. 20:42). David composed a powerful lament at Jonathan's death (2 Sam. 1:26, 27). *
b. The son of Abiathar, the high priest. He served as a liaison for David (2 Sam. 15:27, 36; 17:17–22). ¶
c. Son of Shimeah, David's brother. He slew a huge six fingered man at Gath who taunted Israel and her God (2 Sam. 21:21; 1 Chr. 20:7). ¶
d. Son of Shagee and one of David's top thirty mighty warriors. Ref.: 2 Sam. 23:32. Some translations read Shammah (1 Chr. 11:34), reflecting both Hebrew and Greek variants. ¶
e. He was a wise counselor to David, as well as a scribe. Ref.: 1 Chr. 27:32. ¶
f. A person in charge of the royal regional treasuries, a son of Uzziah. Ref.: 1 Chr. 27:25. ¶
g. A scribe who served in Jeremiah's day. His house was converted into a prison (Jer. 37:15, 20; 38:26). ¶
h. A Levite who helped teach the law to Israel under the king Jehoshaphat's directions. Refs.: 2 Chr. 17:7–9. ¶
i. The head of a priestly family in the time of Joiakim. Ref.: Neh. 12:18. ¶
j. The son of Gershom, son of Moses. He and his sons served idols among the Danites until northern Israel was taken into exile in 722 B.C. (Judg. 18:30). ¶
2 ***yônāṯān*** [masc. proper noun: יוֹנָתָן <3129>; a form of <3083> above]: the Lord has given ▶
a. The oldest son of Saul and became the close friend of David. He deferred to David as the Lord's anointed even though he himself was next in line for the kingship when his father died. He was a successful commander and warrior against the Philistines. He made a covenant with David to be loyal to him (see JONATHAN <3083> a.). *

b. A son of Abiathar, one of David's priests. However, Abiathar backed Adonijah, not Solomon for king against David's wishes (1 Kgs. 1:42, 43). ¶
c. One of David's mighty warriors, a son of Shagee who was a Hararite. Ref.: 1 Chr. 11:34. ¶
d. He took part in the musical aspect of worship at the second Temple. Ref.: Neh. 12:35. ¶
e. He supported Gedaliah, the governor in Judah after Jerusalem fell. He had a brother, Johanan, and his father was Kareah (Jer. 40:8). ¶
f. A Judahite who was son of Judah, Shammai's brother. He had sons as well (1 Chr. 2:32, 33). ¶
g. A descendant of Adin. His son was Ebed. They were from the family heads who returned under Ezra (Ezra 8:6). ¶
h. He was the son of Asahel and one of the few who did not support Ezra's reforms entirely. Ref.: Ezra 10:15. ¶
i. A priest who was head of the priestly family of Malluch. Ref.: Neh. 12:14. ¶
j. A son of Jehoida who was son of Eliashib, a high priest. Ref.: Neh. 12:11. ¶

JOPPA – ***yāpô', yāpô*** [proper noun: יָפוֹא, יָפוֹ <3305>; from BEAUTIFUL (BE) <3302>]: beautiful ▶ **A port city given to the Danites.** Ref.: Josh. 19:46. It was a convenient place to import building materials and other merchandise on the Mediterranean coast. Jonah tried to escape God's call by sailing from Joppa (Jon. 1:3). It was located just south of the north Yarkon River. It was still an important port in New Testament times (Act. 9:36–43, etc.). Other refs.: 2 Chr. 2:16; Ezra 3:7. ¶

JORAH – ***yôrāh*** [masc. proper noun: יוֹרָה <3139>; from SHOOT (verb) <3384> (in the sense of to pour)]: autumn rain ▶ **Members of his family came back from the Babylonian captivity.** Ref.: Ezra 2:18. ¶

JORAI – ***yôray*** [masc. proper noun: יוֹרַי <3140>; from SHOOT (verb) <3384> (in the sense of to pour)]: autumn rain ▶ **A descendant of Gad.** Ref.: 1 Chr. 5:13. ¶

JORAM – ***yôrām*** [masc. proper noun: יֹרָם <3141>; a form of JEHORAM <3088>]: the Lord is exalted ▶
a. A king of Judah, son of the righteous king Jehoshaphat. See comments to JEHORAM <3088> a.
b. A king of Israel, son of the wicked king Ahab. See comments to JEHORAM <3088> b.
c. A son of Tou who was king of Hamath and sought to make friends with David. Refs.: 2 Sam. 8:9, 10. ¶
d. A Levite who helped Shubael take care of the various treasuries or storehouses of the Temple. Refs.: 1 Chr. 26:24, 25. ¶

JORDAN – ***yardên*** [proper noun: יַרְדֵּן <3383>; from GO DOWN <3381>]: descender ▶ **This word designates the most famous river in Israel. It is named over 180 times in the Old Testament and numerous times in the New Testament. Its name is appropriate ("the one going down") for it becomes the lowest river on earth.** After starting at an altitude of 300 feet at the foot of Mount Hermon it drops to 1,200 feet below sea level at the Dead Sea. It runs through the Jordan Valley, a great archaeological fissure in the earth's surface averaging about ten miles in width. Its main riverbed runs 70 miles south from the Sea of Galilee to the northern part of the Dead Sea. It starts north of Hulah Lake north of the Sea of Galilee in the territory of ancient Dan and runs a meandering route to the Dead Sea. Four small tributaries join just north of Lake Hulah. Its meandering course makes it ca. 140 miles long between Galilee and the Dead Sea. *

JORKOAM – ***yorq^{o}'ām*** [masc. proper noun: יָרְקְעָם <3421>; from EMPTY <7324> and PEOPLE <5971>]: people will be poured forth ▶ **A descendant of Caleb.** Ref.: 1 Chr. 2:4. ¶

JOSEDECH – See JEHOZADAK <3087>.

JOSEPH – [1] ***y^{e}hôsēp*** [masc. proper noun: יְהוֹסֵף <3084>; a fuller form of <3130> below]: he (the Lord) will add ▶ **A spelling**

variant of Joseph. It is found only in Psalm 81:5; see JOSEPH <3130> b. ¶

2 ***yôsēp̱*** [masc. proper noun: יוֹסֵף <3130>; future of CONTINUE <3254> (in the sense of to increase)]: remover, increaser ► **a. Jacob's eleventh son, as well as his favorite son. He was also the first son Rachel bore. His brother was Benjamin, the twelfth patriarch.** The story of Joseph is a marvelous narrative of God's calling and leading in his life from the time he was young until the day he died (Gen. 34–50). God spoke to Joseph in dreams and revealed his future (Gen. 37) but also revealed, as he was dying, that his bones would be carried up from Egypt and buried in Canaan (Gen. 50:24, 25; Ex. 13:19; Josh. 24:32). The Lord used Joseph to provide for his father and family and endeared him to the Egyptians, even the Pharaoh, so that he became a powerful Egyptian vizier, second only to the Pharaoh (Gen. 41:41–45). The Lord carefully watched over his personal life and safety (Gen. 50:19–21). He demonstrated a magnanimous spirit of mercy and forgiveness toward his enemies, even his brothers. He bore two sons in Egypt who became patriarchs in Israel and provided two of the largest tribes of the nation, Ephraim and Manasseh (Gen. 41:51, 52). Through him the Lord fulfilled His promises and covenant to Abraham (Gen. 15:4–17). He may have been in Egypt sometime during the 1750–1550 B.C. era. Moses blessed him (Deut. 33:13, 16) as did Jacob (Gen. 49:22–26). *

b. A name used in this instance for the nation of Judah since Joseph's fruitfulness, in the form of his descendants, includes the entire nation in a figurative sense. Ref.: Ps. 80:1. ¶

c. The descendants of Joseph are referred to figuratively under the name of Joseph who represents all of his posterity. Refs.: Deut. 27:12; 33:13–16. ¶

d. Joseph is used to represent all of Israel or at least northern Israel. Refs.: Ps. 77:15; 78:67; Ezek. 37:16, 19; 47:13; 48:32; Amos 5:15; 6:6; Obad. 1:18. Sometimes the northern tribes are called Ephraim in honor of Joseph's son. ¶

e. A postexilic Jew who had married a foreign woman in Ezra's time. Ref.: Ezra 10:42. ¶

f. A man from Issachar with this name Joseph. He had a son Igal who was one of the twelve spies sent to Canaan (Num. 13:7). ¶

g. A son of Asaph who was a part of the musical worship at the Temple. Ref.: 1 Chr. 25:2. ¶

h. A priest who was head of the Levite family of Shecaniah. Ref.: Neh. 12:14. ¶

JOSHAH – ***yôšāh*** [masc. proper noun: יוֹשָׁה <3144>; prob. a form of JOSHAVIAH <3145>] ► **A member of the tribe of Simeon, of the family of Amaziah.** Ref.: 1 Chr. 4:34. ¶

JOSHAPHAT – ***yôšāp̱āṭ*** [masc. proper noun: יוֹשָׁפָט <3146>; a form of JEHOSHAPHAT <3092>]: the Lord has judged ►

a. One of David's mighty men. Ref.: 1 Chr. 11:43. ¶

b. One of the priests who blew the trumpets before the ark of God. Ref.: 1 Chr. 15:24. ¶

JOSHAVIAH – ***yôšawyāh*** [masc. proper noun: יוֹשַׁוְיָה <3145>; from LORD <3068> and LIKE (BE) <7737>] ► **One of David's mighty men.** Ref.: 1 Chr. 11:46. ¶

JOSHBEKASHAH – ***yošbᵉqāšāh*** [masc. proper noun: יָשְׁבְּקָשָׁה <3436>; from DWELL <3427> (in the sense of to sit) and HARD (BE) <7186>]: seated in a hard place ► **Son of Heman, head of a course of musicians.** Refs.: 1 Chr. 25:4, 24. ¶

JOSHEB-BASSHEBETH – See SEAT (WHO SAT IN THE) <3429>.

JOSHIBIAH – ***yôšiḇyāh*** [masc. proper noun: יוֹשִׁבְיָה <3143>; from DWELL <3427> and LORD <3050>]: who dwells with the Lord ► **A member of the tribe of Simeon, of the family of Asiel.** Ref.: 1 Chr. 4:35. ¶

JOSHUA – ***yᵉhôšûa'***, ***yᵉhôšua'*** [masc. proper noun: יְהוֹשֻׁעַ, יְהוֹשׁוּעַ <3091>; from LORD

<3068> and SAVE (verb) <3467> (in the sense of to deliver)]: the Lord delivers ▶
a. He was Moses' successor (Num. 27:12–23; Deut. 34:9–12), picked by the Lord to conquer the Promised Land (Josh. 1:1–5) that had been given to Israel. His name was previously Hoshea ("salvation"), son of Nun (Num. 13:16). He was from the tribe of Ephraim (Num. 13:8). In his first appearance, he showed himself an exceptionally capable military commander, defeating the Amalekites (Ex. 17:8–16). He became Moses' personal scribe, administrator, and intimate aide. He accompanied Moses often when others were not permitted to do so (Ex. 24:13; 32:17; 33:11). His respect and faithfulness to Moses as God's picked leader never wavered (Num. 11:28). He was one of the spies sent into Canaan and never doubted that Israel could conquer the land (Num. 14:5–9). He and Caleb lived to enter the Promised Land (Num. 26:65). He led Israel successfully, and the Lord fulfilled every promise He had made to Joshua and Israel (Josh. 21:43–45). He was buried in the land which he had conquered for God's people (Josh. 24:29–30). *
b. A person of Beth Shemesh in whose field the cart carrying the ark of God back to Jerusalem came to rest beside a large stone. The Philistines were sending it back to Israel. The stone remained a memorial of this event for many years (1 Sam. 6:13–18). ¶
c. A postexilic high priest in the time of Haggai and Zechariah. He was the son of Jehozadak. He returned from exile in Babylon (537 B.C.). The altar and Temple were rebuilt under his direction. Zechariah called him the Branch, a powerful messianic title (Zech. 6:11, 12). Under him the priesthood was to be cleansed and purified (Zech. 3:1–9), as well as the whole land. *
d. A governor of Jerusalem who had a gate named after him, the Gate of Joshua. Refs.: 2 Kgs. 23:8, 9. ¶

JOSIAH – ***yō'šiyyāhû, yô'šiyyāhû, yō'šiyyāh*** [masc. proper noun: יֹאשִׁיָּהוּ, יוֹאשִׁיָּהוּ, יֹאשִׁיָּה <2977>; from the same root as FOUNDATION <803> and LORD <3050>]: the Lord supports, the Lord heals ▶
a. A great reforming king in Judah. His coming was prophesied years earlier (1 Kgs. 13:2). He reigned 640–609 B.C.; he began to reign when he was eight years old after his father Amon died (2 Kgs. 21:24–26; 22:1, 2). He did what was right in the eyes of the Lord and walked in the Law as David had. He even removed the high places (2 Kgs. 23:15, 16). His extensive reforms resulted in the finding of the Book of the Law in ca. 622 B.C., which Josiah then followed rigorously in his reign (22:1–23:30). He held a renewal ceremony for the covenant in the Book of the Law (2 Kgs. 23:1–3). He died at an early age at Megiddo in a battle against Neco, king of Egypt (2 Chr. 35:20–24). He was so esteemed that Jeremiah wrote a lament about him (2 Chr. 35:24, 25). *
b. An exile who returned from Babylon. Ref.: Zech. 6:10. ¶

JOSIBIAH – 1 Chr. 4:35 ➔ JOSHIBIAH <3143>.

JOSIPHIAH – ***yôsip̱yāh*** [masc. proper noun: יוֹסִפְיָה <3131>; from act. part. of CONTINUE <3254> and LORD <3050>]: the Lord increases ▶ **He came back from the Babylonian captivity with Ezra.** Ref.: Ezra 8:10. ¶

JOSTLE – Joel 2:8 ➔ AFFLICT <1766>.

JOTBAH – ***yoṭḇāh*** [proper noun: יָטְבָה <3192>; from GOOD (SEEM) <3191>]: goodness ▶ **The native place of the grandfather of king Amon.** Ref.: 2 Kgs. 21:19. ¶

JOTBATHAH – ***yoṭḇāṯāh*** [proper noun: יָטְבָתָה <3193>; from JOTBAH <3192>]: goodness ▶ **A place in the desert where the Israelites camped.** Refs.: Num. 33:33, 34; Deut. 10:7. ¶

JOTHAM – ***yôṯām*** [masc. proper noun: יוֹתָם <3147>; from LORD <3068> and PERFECT <8535>]: the Lord is perfect, the Lord is upright ▶

a. A king of Judah, son of Azariah (Uzziah). He reigned 750–732 B.C., reigning with this father, who had leprosy, for ten years (2 Kgs. 15:5–7). His mother was Jerusha, Zadok's daughter (2 Kgs. 15:32–38). He was a good king and followed the Lord, except that the high places were not removed. He also helped restore the Temple. His son Ahaz reigned after he died. Isaiah, Hosea, and Micah prophesied during his reign. *
b. The youngest son of Gideon who escaped Abimelech's massacre of the seventy sons of Gideon. In a lengthy allegory, he urged the cities of Shechem and Beth Millo to rebel against Abimelech (Judg. 9:16–21), even placing a curse on them. *
c. A descendant of Caleb and the son of Jahdai. He was a Judahite (1 Chr. 2:47). ¶

JOURNEY (noun) – [1] ***mahᵃlāḵ*** [masc. noun: מַהֲלָךְ <4109>; from GO <1980>] ▶ **This word indicates a trip, a distance covered. It also indicates access of some kind: a passageway or walkway by the chambers of a temple.** Ref.: Ezek. 42:4: passage inward, inner passageway, walk, inner walk. It refers in general to any journey or trip (Neh. 2:6). It also takes on the sense of a "walk" as a trip or a distance covered (Jon. 3:3, 4; also translated walk). The plural form in Zechariah 3:7 is covered in ACCESS <4108>. ¶
– [2] See PATH <1870>.

JOURNEY (verb) – [1] ***massa'*** [verb: מַסַּע <4550>; from SET OUT <5265> (in the sense of to journey)] ▶ **This word means to travel about, to go from place to place with a purpose, especially with the Lord as leader.** Refs.: Gen. 13:3; Ex. 17:1; 40:36, 38. Trumpets gather Israel for setting out, journeying, breaking camp (Num. 10:2, 6). It is used in a summary sense of many travels (Num. 33:1). Other refs.: Num. 10:12, 28; 33:2; Deut. 10:11. ¶
[2] ***śûr*** [verb: שׁוּר <7788>; a prim. root] ▶ **This word means to depart, to go.** It describes the descent from a mountain height (Song 4:8; also translated to descend; to look); it indicates to travel, to go to a location or person (Is. 57:9). It indicates what is used to transport, to carry merchandise by ships, caravans, etc. (Ezek. 27:25; KJV: to sing). ¶

JOY – [1] ***giyl*** [masc. noun: גִּיל <1524>; from REJOICE <1523>] ▶
a. This word describes a happy state of affairs and actions compared to a previous state of suffering. Ref.: Job 3:22. The Lord Himself may cause one's rejoicing (Ps. 43:4). The hills rejoice at God's bountiful favors (Ps. 65:12; also translated gladness, rejoicing). Rejoicing is the result of having a righteous son (Prov. 23:24). Israel's right to rejoice depended on her faithfulness to God (Hos. 9:1; also translated exultation), and God could cut off her rejoicing with His judgments (Joel 1:16).
b. This word designates a circle, age, stage of life. It is used in a general sense of the age(s) of Daniel and other youths (Dan. 1:10; also translated sort). *
[2] ***giylāh*** [fem. noun: גִּילָה <1525>; fem. of <1524> above] ▶ **A word denoting happiness, rejoicing.** The dry land, the Arabah, is depicted as rejoicing (Is. 35:2) in a picture of the future restoration of Zion. Rejoicing is the goal for which God creates His people (Is. 65:18; also translated joy, delight). ¶
[3] ***ḥeḏwāh*** [fem. noun: חֶדְוָה <2304>; from REJOICE <2302>] ▶ **This word means rejoicing; it is also translated gladness.** The dwelling place of the Lord is the place of strength and joy (1 Chr. 16:27). It specifically indicates the joy of the Lord which serves as the strength of the Israelites (Neh. 8:10). ¶
[4] ***ḥeḏwāh*** [Aramaic fem. noun: חֶדְוָה <2305>; corresponding to <2304> above] ▶ **This word means rejoicing; it denotes the Israelites' attitude and response to the dedication of the new Temple in Ezra's day.** Ref.: Ezra 6:16. ¶
[5] ***māśôś*** [masc. noun: מָשׂוֹשׂ <4885>; from REJOICE <7797>] ▶
a. This word indicates a response of inner happiness in the way of the Lord; in anything a person chooses to rejoice in. Refs.: Job; 8:19; Is. 8:6. Jerusalem was considered to be the joy of the whole earth (Ps. 48:2);

especially of God's people (Is. 66:10; Lam. 2:15); music creates joy in those hearing it (Is. 24:8). It depicts the joy of a bridegroom (Is. 62:5). God's people are created for joy (Is. 65:18). It stands for the object of peoples' joy: wife, son, daughter, prophet (Ezek. 24:25). God, however, brings an end to the joy of a rebellious people and city (Hos. 2:11). *

b. Some translators read Job 8:19 as a negative assertion concerning decaying roots or other rotten objects. ¶

[6] ***śimḥāh*** [fem. noun: שִׂמְחָה <8057>; from JOYFUL <8056>] ▶ **This word means rejoicing, gladness, pleasure. It refers to the reality, the experience and manifestation of joy and gladness.** It refers to a celebration of something with joyful and cheerful activities (Gen. 31:27). It is practically equivalent to the Israelites' days of feasting and celebrating over their God and His blessings (Num. 10:10; Neh. 8:12; Zech. 8:19). The Israelites were expected to worship and serve their God with joy (Deut. 28:47). God's salvation consists of restoring or creating rejoicing in His people (Ps. 51:8). God even gives a person a glad heart in the toils of this earthly life (Eccl. 5:20). One's wedding day is a day of rejoicing (Song 3:11). It refers to great celebration and joy at conquering one's enemy (Judg. 16:23). The joy and gladness of the wicked does not last forever (Job 20:5). The Lord can remove rejoicing from His people (Is. 16:10; Joel 1:16). *

[7] ***śāśôn*** [masc. noun: שָׂשׂוֹן <8342>; from REJOICE <7797>] ▶ **This word means rejoicing; it is also translated gladness.** It refers to joy, exultation toward God's King (Ps. 45:7); given to God's people (Ps. 51:8, 12); in His own people at deliverance (Ps. 105:43); over the testimonies and laws of God (Ps. 119:111). God is the joy of His people (Is. 12:3). Joy will be removed from a rebellious people (Jer. 7:34; Joel 1:12). In God's restoration of His people, joy will be abundant (Zech. 8:19). *

– [8] Is. 65:18 ➔ to be a joy ➔ REJOICE <1523> [9] Ezek. 7:7 ➔ JOYFUL SHOUTING <1906>.

JOY (FIND) – Is. 58:14 ➔ DELIGHT (HAVE, FIND, TAKE) <6026>.

JOY (HAVE) – Job 10:20 ➔ SMILE (verb) <1082>.

JOY (verb) – Is. 9:3; 65:19 ➔ REJOICE <1523>.

JOYFUL – [1] ***śāmêaḥ*** [adj.: שָׂמֵחַ <8056>; from REJOICE <8055>] ▶ **This word means glad, happy, many. Its feminine form is *śemêḥāh*; its plural form is *śemêḥîm*. It means to be filled with joy, to be exceedingly glad.** The blessings of the Lord lead to great joy (Deut. 16:15, *'akśameaḥ*). Anointing Israel's king was cause for great joy (1 Kgs. 1:40, 45). Joy comes from having children (Ps. 113:9). God's people rejoice for what He does for them (Ps. 126:3). The wicked are perverted so that they are joyful at evil (Prov. 2:14; 17:5). A state and attitude of joy makes one's face appear healthy (Prov. 15:13). It may be rendered as pleased or happy in some contexts (Eccl. 2:10). *

– [2] Ps. 5:11 ➔ REJOICE <5970>.

JOYFUL (BE) – Ps. 9:14; 35:9; 89:16; 29:19; Is. 61:10; 66:10 ➔ REJOICE <1523>.

JOYFUL CRY – Job 3:7 ➔ JOYFUL SHOUT <7445>.

JOYFUL SHOUT – ***renānāh*** [fem. noun: רְנָנָה <7445>; from SHOUT (verb) <7442>] ▶ **This word means a ringing cry, a shout for joy; it also refers to singing.** It refers to a cry of delight over a marvelous event (Job 3:7). The joy of the godless is indicated to be brief, for a short time (Job 20:5: triumphing, exulting, mirth). It is used to indicate lips of joy, lips that offer praise to God (Ps. 63:5: joyful, singing). It refers to praise and worship before God in general (Ps. 100:2). ¶

JOYFUL SHOUTING – ***hêḏ*** [masc. noun: הֵד <1906>; from SHOUTING <1959>] ▶ **This word indicates a happy response of joy as opposed to tumult, confusion, or panic that God is bringing on His people.** Ref.: Ezek. 7:7; also translated rejoicing, joy, sounding again. ¶

JOYFUL VOICE – Job 3:7 ➔ JOYFUL SHOUT <7445>.

JOYFUL, JOYFUL SONGS – Ps. 63:5; 100:2 ➔ JOYFUL SHOUT <7445>.

JOZABAD – ***yôzāḇāḏ*** [masc. proper noun: יוֹזָבָד <3107>; a form of JEHOZABAD <3075>]: the Lord has bestowed ►
a. Soldier in David's army. Ref.: 1 Chr. 12:4. ¶
b. Manassite captain. Ref.: 1 Chr. 12:20. ¶
c. Another Manassite captain. Ref.: 1 Chr. 12:20. ¶
d. A Levite. Ref.: 2 Chr. 31:13. ¶
e. A chief Levite. Ref.: 2 Chr. 35:9. ¶
f. A priest. Ref.: Ezra 10:22. ¶
g. Another priest. Ref.: Ezra 10:23. ¶
h. A Levite. Ref.: Ezra 8:33. ¶
i. Another Levite. Ref.: Neh. 8:7. ¶
j. Another Levite. Ref.: Neh. 11:16. ¶

JOZACHAR – ***yôzāḵār*** [masc. proper noun: יוֹזָכָר <3108>; from LORD <3068> and REMEMBER <2142>]: the Lord remembers ► **Son of an Ammonite, he was one of the two murderers of Joash, king of Judah.** Ref.: 2 Kgs. 12:21. His name is Zabad in 2 Chronicles 24:26. ¶

JOZADAK – ***yôṣāḏāq*** [masc. proper noun: יוֹצָדָק <3136>; a form of JEHOZADAK <3087>]: the Lord is righteous ►
a. Father of the high priest Jeshua. Refs.: Ezra 3:2, 8; 10:18; Neh. 12:26. ¶
b. Aramaic proper noun for Jozadak. Ref.: Ezra 5:2, the same as in a. above. ¶

JUBAL – ***yûḇāl*** [masc. proper noun: יוּבָל <3106>; from BRING <2986>]: stream ► **Younger son of Lamech and Ada; he was the father of all those who play the lyre and pipe.** Ref.: Gen. 4:21. ¶

JUBILANT – ***'ālêz*** [adj.: עָלֵז <5938>; from REJOICE <5937>] ► **This word indicates that something is exalting, rejoicing.** It refers to the actions and state of people celebrating and exalting over something, a condition that Jerusalem lost (Is. 5:14). ¶

JUBILANT (BE) – 1 Chr. 16:32 ➔ REJOICE <5970>.

JUBILEE – Lev. 25:10–13, 15; etc. ➔ RAM <3104>.

JUCAL – ***yôḵeḇeḏ*** [fem. proper noun: יוֹכֶבֶד <3116>; a form of JEHUCAL <3081>]: able, powerful ► **One of two persons sent by Zedekiah to request Jeremiah to pray for the kingdom.** Ref.: Jer. 38:1; same as Jehucal: Jer. 37:3. ¶

JUDAH – [1] ***yᵉhûḏ*** [Aramaic proper noun: יְהוּד <3061>; contr. from a form corresponding to <3063> below]: praise ► **This word corresponds to the Hebrew entry JUDAH <3063>.** It is found in the Aramaic portions of Ezra and Daniel (Ezra 5:1, 8; 7:14; Dan. 2:25; 5:13; 6:13). ¶
[2] ***yᵉhûḏāh*** [masc. proper noun: יְהוּדָה <3063>; from THANKS (GIVE) <3034>]: praised, celebrated ►
a. The fourth son of Jacob through Leah (Gen. 29:35; 35:23). He married a Canaanite woman and bore two sons by her (Er, Onan). Er died and then Onan his brother died, leaving Tamar, Er's wife, without a child. Judah, heartlessly, refused to allow his third son to have a child by Tamar. Judah then committed an unwitting, but heinous sin with his daughter-in-law by hiring her as a prostitute and unwittingly fathered twins by her (Gen. 38). His lack of compassion is evident in the story. Judah himself bore many other sons (Gen. 46:12). Jacob prophesied of the high status Judah and his descendants would have among the patriarchs (Gen. 49:8–12). He and they would be above their enemies, their own kinsmen; he was compared to a lion. He would have royal prerogatives ("scepter," "rulership"); he would be prosperous and powerful in appearance (cf. also Deut. 33:7). From Judah would come the Star out of Jacob and Israel (Gen. 24:17). *
b. The territory of Judah ran north-south from north of Jerusalem and Aijalon and south to Kadesh Barnea. Its eastern border ran from Gath south to the El-Arish (River of Egypt). Its eastern border

was the Dead Sea and a boundary running from the Brook Zered southwest to Kadesh Barnea. Jerusalem, Hebron, and Bethlehem. All important cities in Israel and the Old Testament were within its boundaries.

The tribe took its territory in Canaan rather forcefully (Judg. 1:1–9) but could not totally capture Jerusalem. Judah seems gradually to have become isolated from the northern tribes (Judg. 4; 5).

Under David, Judah became powerful. David was crowned king in Judah at Hebron and then captured Jerusalem to consolidate Judah and to attract the other tribes to Jerusalem as the central capital and worship center of the nation (2 Sam. 5:1–16). Solomon attempted to consolidate the nation further, but through poor politics, poor economics, oppressive taxation, and megalomanical building projects, he forced those outside of Judah into a subordinate, almost slave-like position toward Judah and Jerusalem (2 Sam. 8–12). As a result, Israel split off from Judah after Solomon's death in 930 B.C. The nation of Israel went into exile in 722 B.C., while the nation of Judah, with the Davidic covenant and royal line intact, lingered on with a few good kings (Asa, Jehosaphat, Joash, Hezekiah, Josiah) until she too was destroyed because of her religious and moral corruption (2 Kgs. 25).

Within Judah, God had chosen a king and established an eternal covenant (2 Sam. 7). The tribe of Judah went into exile in 586 B.C., as predicted by Jeremiah, but likewise returned in 538 B.C. according to the prophet's word, still bearing the promised royal seed. The tribe was a mere shadow of itself from then until the end of the Old Testament. The high priest became dominant, for no kings were permitted in Judah, now a province of Persia, then Egypt, Syria, and Rome. *

c. A Levite who had intermarried with the foreign people of the land in Ezra's day. Ref.: Ezra 10:23. ¶

d. A district or sectional director in Jerusalem over its newly returned residents from exile or the surrounding region. Ref.: Neh. 11:9. ¶

e. A leading Levite who returned from exile from Babylon under Zerubbabel. Ref.: Neh. 12:8. ¶

f. A priest who took part in the procession celebrating the rebuilding of the wall of Jerusalem. Ref.: Neh. 12:34. ¶

JUDAH (FROM THE TRIBE OF) – 1 Chr. 4:18 ➔ JEHUDIJAH <3057>.

JUDAH (IN THE LANGUAGE OF) – 2 Kgs. 18:26, 28; 2 Chr. 32:18; Neh. 13:24; Is. 36:11, 13 ➔ HEBREW (IN) <3066>.

JUDAHITE – 1 Chr. 4:18 ➔ JEHUDIJAH <3057>.

JUDEAN (IN) – 2 Kgs. 18:26, 28; 2 Chr. 32:18; Neh. 13:24; Is. 36:11, 13 ➔ HEBREW (IN) <3066>.

JUDGE (noun) – [1] ***dayyān*** [masc. noun: דַּיָּן <1781>; from JUDGE (verb) <1777>] ▶ **David uses this word to refer to God as his judge, the one who makes a decision on a matter.** Ref.: 1 Sam. 24:15. The psalmist uses this term to describe God as the defender or judge of the widows (Ps. 68:5). ¶

[2] ***dayyān*** [Aramaic masc. noun: דַּיָּן <1782>; corresponding to <1781> above] ▶ **This word corresponds to the Hebrew word of the same spelling and meaning above.** It is used only in Ezra 7:25 where it refers to judges that Ezra was to appoint over those who knew God's laws. The judges were to judge diligently and had power to imprison, execute, and banish people in addition to confiscating property (cf. Ezra 7:26). ¶

[3] ***deṯāḇar*** [Aramaic masc. noun: דְּתָבַר <1884>; of Persian origin] ▶ **This word refers to a class of officials from the Babylonian provinces.** Refs.: Dan. 3:2, 3 (KJV, counselor; NASB, NKJV, NIV, judges; ESV: justices). ¶

[4] ***pāliyl*** [masc. noun: פָּלִיל <6414>; from PRAY <6419>] ▶ **This word refers to one making a decision; it is only used in the plural in the Hebrew Old Testament.** The song of Moses said that even the enemies

of Israel judged the Israelite God to be different from other gods (Deut. 32:31: also translated to judge, to concede). As Job listed all the sins he had not committed, he mentioned that it would be shameful to be judged by those sins (Job 31:11: also translated to be judged, judgment). See the related Hebrew root *pālal* (<6419>). Other ref.: Ex. 21:22 (also translated court). ¶
– 5 Dan. 3:2, 3 → COUNSELOR <148>.

JUDGE (verb) – 1 ***diyn*** [verb: דִּין <1777>; a prim. root (comp. LORD <113>)] ▶ **This word means to bring justice, to go to court, to pass sentence, to contend, to act as judge, to govern, to plead a cause, to be at strife, to quarrel.** The verb regularly involves bringing justice or acting as judge; the Lord Himself is the chief judge over the whole earth and especially over those who oppose Him (1 Sam. 2:10). The tribe of Dan, whose name means "He provides justice" and is followed by this verb, will indeed provide justice for His people (Gen. 30:6). The king of Israel was to deliver justice in righteousness (Ps. 72:2). Israel's many sins included failure to obtain justice in the case of the orphan (Jer. 5:28). The verb also signifies pleading a case: God's people often failed to plead the case of the orphan (Jer. 5:28); this was a heinous sin for the house of David, for Judah was to administer justice every day for all those who needed it (Jer. 21:12). Sometimes pleading a case resulted in vindication, as when God gave Rachel a son through her maidservant Bilhah, and Rachel in thanks named him Dan (Gen. 30:6). At other times, it resulted in redress for evils done, as when God judges the nations in the day of His anger (Ps. 110:6); Israel's plight because of their sin had become hopeless so they had no one to plead their cause (Jer. 30:13).

The verb also signifies governance, contention, or going to law or court. It is hopeless for individuals to contend with persons who are far more powerful and advantaged than they are (Eccl. 6:10). The high priest, Joshua, was given authority to govern, render justice, and judge the house of the Lord on the condition that he himself walked in the ways of the Lord (Zech. 3:7).

In the passive-reflexive stem, the verb signifies to be at strife or to quarrel (2 Sam. 19:10). *
2 ***diyn*** [Aramaic verb: דִּין <1778>; corresponding to <1777> above] ▶ **This word corresponds to the Hebrew word above that is spelled the same or spelled as *diyn* (<1777>).** It occurs only in Ezra 7:25, where Artaxerxes commanded Ezra to appoint people to judge those beyond the river who knew God's laws. ¶
3 ***yāḵaḥ*** [verb: יָכַח <3198>; a prim. root] ▶ **This word means to argue, to convince, to convict, to reprove.** The word usually refers to the clarification of people's moral standing, which may involve arguments being made for them (Job 13:15; Is. 11:4) or against them (Job 19:5; Ps. 50:21). The word may refer to the judgment of a case between people (Gen. 31:37, 42) or even (in the days before Christ) to someone desired to mediate between God and humankind (Job 9:33). The word may also refer to physical circumstances being used to reprove sin (2 Sam. 7:14; Hab. 1:12). Reproving sin, whether done by God (Prov. 3:12) or persons (Lev. 19:17), was pictured as a demonstration of love, but some people were too rebellious or scornful to be reproved (Prov. 9:7; 15:12; Ezek. 3:26). In Genesis 24:14, 44, the word referred to God's appointment (or judgment) of Rebekah as the one to be married to Isaac. *
4 ***šāp̱aṭ*** [verb: שָׁפַט <8199>; a prim. root] ▶ This word also means to govern. **This word, though often translated as judge, is much more inclusive than the modern concept of judging and encompasses all the facets and functions of government: executive, legislative, and judicial.** Consequently, this term can be understood in any one of the following ways. It could designate, in its broadest sense, to function as ruler or governor. This function could be fulfilled by individual judges (Judg. 16:31; 1 Sam. 7:16); the king (1 Kgs. 3:9); or even God Himself (Ps. 50:6; 75:7); since He is the source of authority (cf. Rom. 13:1) and will eventually conduct all judgments (Ps. 96:13). In a judicial sense, the word could also indicate, because of the exalted status

of the ruler, the arbitration of civil, domestic, and religious disputes (Deut. 25:1). As before, this function could be fulfilled by the congregation of Israel (Num. 35:24); individual judges (Ex. 18:16; Deut. 1:16); the king (1 Sam. 8:5, 6, 20); or even God Himself (Gen. 16:5; 1 Sam. 24:12, 15). In the executive sense, it could denote to execute judgment, to bring about what had been decided. This could be in the form of a vindication (Ps. 10:18; Is. 1:17, 23); or a condemnation and punishment (Ezek. 7:3, 8; 23:45). *

5 ***šepaṭ*** [Aramaic verb: שְׁפַט <8200>; corresponding to <8199> above] ▶ **This word means to govern. It is used only once in the Old Testament and is related to the Hebrew word *šāp̱aṭ* (<8199>), meaning to judge or to govern.** In Ezra 7:25, this word is used to describe one of the governing rulers that Ezra was to appoint. These rulers were to perform similar functions as the *dayyān* [JUDGE (noun) <1782>] or judges that Ezra was also to appoint. ¶

– 6 Deut. 32:31; Job 31:11 ➔ JUDGE (noun) <6414>.

JUDGED (BE) – Job 31:18 ➔ JUDGES (PUNISHABLE BY) <6416>.

JUDGES – Ezra 4:9 ➔ DINAITES <1784>.

JUDGES (PUNISHABLE BY) – ***peliyliy*** [fem. noun: פְּלִילִי <6416>; from JUDGE (noun) <6414>] ▶ **This word indicates liable for judgment.** It refers to an evil deed, adultery or idolatry, that would bring judgment, open to condemnation and punishment (Job 31:28; also translated deserving of judgment, to be judged). ¶

JUDGMENT – 1 ***diyn*** [masc. noun: דִּין <1779>; from JUDGE (verb) <1777>] ▶ **This word refers to a legal verdict; it also means condemnation, plea, cause. It carries a legal connotation and is found in poetic texts with most of its occurrences in the book of Job.** The idea of judgment is often followed by justice (Job 36:17). Judah is called a wicked nation, one that does not plead the cause of the less fortunate (Jer. 5:28). It also occurs in relation to strife in a legal case (Prov. 22:10). *

2 ***diyn*** [Aramaic masc. noun: דִּין <1780>; corresponding to <1779> above] ▶ **This word is used to signify punishment or the justice of God; it also means justice.** Refs.: Ezra 7:26; Dan. 4:37. It is related to the Aramaic word *dayyān* [JUDGE (noun) <1782>] and the Aramaic word *diyn* [JUDGE (verb) <1778>]. It is also similar to the Hebrew word *diyn* [JUDGE (verb) <1777>] and the Hebrew noun *diyn* (JUDGMENT <1779>). Other refs.: Dan. 7:10, 22, 26. ¶

3 ***peliylāh*** [fem. noun: פְּלִילָה <6415>; fem. of JUDGE (noun) <6414>] ▶ **This form of the word is used only once in the Hebrew Old Testament, i.e., in the book of Isaiah. It means a decision.** In the oracle against Moab, the women cried out for a judgment or settlement to be made for them (Is. 16:3; also translated decision, justice). See the masculine form of this word *pāliyl* [JUDGE (noun) <6414>] and the related Hebrew root *pālal* (PRAY <6419>). ¶

4 ***peliyliyyah*** [fem. noun: פְּלִילִיָּה <6417>; fem. of JUDGES (PUNISHABLE BY) <6416>] ▶ **This word is a feminine abstract noun referring to the process of rendering a verdict in a case.** Ref.: Is. 28:7; also translated decision. ¶

5 ***šepôṭ*** [masc. noun: שְׁפוֹט <8196>; from JUDGE (verb) <8199>] ▶ **This word means a decision, a punishment.** It is an abstract noun referring to both the declaration and enactment of judgment on someone (2 Chr. 20:9). It indicates, in context, the actual enactments of justice on God's people (Ezek. 23:10). ¶

6 ***šep̱eṭ*** [masc. noun: שֶׁפֶט <8201>; from JUDGE (verb) <8199>] ▶ **This word usually describes the active role of God in punishing.** In several instances, such judgment is described as the sword, famine, wild beasts, plagues, stoning, and burning (Ezek. 14:21; 16:41). The plagues that God inflicted on Egypt are described as judgments (Ex. 6:6; 7:4; 12:12; Num. 33:4). This word describes both the defeat of Israel (2 Chr. 24:24; Ezek. 5:10, 15); as well as the

defeat of other nations (Ezek. 25:11; 28:22, 26). In one instance, this word speaks more generally, not of specific nations, but of unruly scoffers who will receive physical chastisement (Prov. 19:29). *
– [7] Job 31:11 ➔ JUDGE (noun) <6414> [8] See JUSTICE <4941>.

JUDGMENT (DESERVING OF) – Job 31:18 ➔ JUDGES (PUNISHABLE BY) <6416>.

JUDGMENT (GOOD) – 1 Sam. 25:33; Ps. 119:66 ➔ TASTE (noun) <2940>.

JUDITH – ***yᵉhûḏiyṯ*** [fem. proper noun: יְהוּדִית <3067>; the same as HEBREW (IN) <3066>]: Jewess, praise ▶ **One of Esau's wives.** Ref.: Gen. 26:34. She was also named Oholibamah (Gen. 36:2). ¶

JUG – [1] 1 Sam. 1:24; 10:3; 25:18; 2 Sam. 16:1; Jer. 13:12 ➔ SKIN BOTTLE <5035> [2] 1 Sam. 16:20; Judg. 4:19 ➔ BOTTLE <4997> [3] 1 Sam. 26:11, 12, 16; 1 Kgs. 17:12, 14, 16 ➔ JAR <6835>.

JUICE – [1] ***miśrāh*** [fem. noun: מִשְׂרָה <4952>; from LOOSE (LET) <8281> in the sense of loosening] ▶ **This word refers to a flowing liquid and is used of the juice of grapes.** Ref.: Num. 6:3; KJV: liquor. A Nazarite could not drink this liquid. ¶
– [2] Ex. 22:29 ➔ VINTAGE <1831> [3] Num. 18:27 ➔ HARVEST <4395> [4] Song 8:2 ➔ WINE <6071>.

JUMP – Lev. 11:21 ➔ LEAP <5425>.

JUMPING – Nah. 3:2 ➔ DANCE (verb) <7540>.

JUNIPER – [1] Jer. 48:6 ➔ SHRUB <6176> [2] See CYPRESS <1265>.

JUNIPER, JUNIPER TREE – 1 Kgs. 19:4, 5; Job 30:4; Ps. 120:4 ➔ BROOM TREE, BROOM BUSH <7574>.

JUSHAB-HESED – ***yûšaḇ ḥeseḏ*** [masc. proper noun: יוּשַׁב חֶסֶד <3142>; from TURN <7725> and MERCY <2617> (also in the sense of goodness, love, kindness)]: goodness is rewarded ▶ **A descendant of David.** Ref.: 1 Chr. 3:20. ¶

JUST – ***ṣaddiyq*** [adj.: צַדִּיק <6662>; from JUST (BE) <6663>] ▶ **The term bears primarily a moral or ethical significance. Someone or something is considered to be just or righteous because of conformity to a given standard.** It could be used to describe people or actions in a legal context, indicating they were in accordance with the legal standards (2 Kgs. 10:9); or in a religious context, that they were in accordance with God's standards (Gen. 6:9). It is used of human beings, such as the Davidic king (2 Sam. 23:3); judges and rulers (Prov. 29:2; Ezek. 23:45); and individuals (Gen. 6:9). It is also often applied to God, who is the ultimate standard used to define justice and righteousness (Ex. 9:27; Ezra 9:15; Ps. 7:11). As a substantive, the righteous is used to convey the ideal concept of those who follow God's standards (Mal. 3:18). In this way, it is often in antithetic parallelism with the wicked, *rāšā'* (<7563>), the epitome of those who reject God and His standards (Prov. 29:7). *

JUST (BE) – ***ṣāḏaq*** [verb: צָדַק <6663>; a prim. root] ▶ **This word means to be right, to be righteous, to be innocent, to be put right, to justify, to declare right, to prove oneself innocent.** The word is used twenty out of forty times in the simple stem. In this stem, it basically means to be right or just. God challenged His own people to show they were right in their claims (Is. 43:26). The verb can also connote being innocent, for God's people, through the Lord, will be found innocent (Ps. 51:4; Is. 45:25). Job argued his case effectively, proving himself right and vindicated (Job 11:2; 40:8). The ordinances of God were declared right by the psalmist (Ps. 19:9).

In the passive stem, it means to be put right. The verb refers to the altar in the second Temple being put right after its defilement (Dan. 8:14). In the intensive stem, the verb means to make or to declare righteous.

Judah, because of her sin, made Samaria, her wicked sister, seem righteous (Ezek. 16:51, 52); the Lord asserted that northern Israel had been more just than Judah (Jer. 3:11; cf. Job 32:2).

In the causative stem, the verb takes on the meaning of bringing about justice: Absalom began his conspiracy against David by declaring that he would administer justice for everyone (2 Sam. 15:4). The Lord vindicates His servant (Is. 50:8); every person of God is to declare the rights of the poor or oppressed (Ps. 82:3). In Isaiah 53:11, it has the sense of the Servant helping other persons obtain their rights. Once in the reflexive stem, it means to justify oneself, as when Judah was at a loss as to how he and his brothers could possibly justify themselves before Pharaoh (Gen. 44:16). *

JUST AS – Dan. 3:25 ➔ BEHOLD (interj.) <1888>.

JUSTICE – [1] ***mišpāṭ*** [masc. noun: מִשְׁפָּט <4941>; from JUDGE (verb) <8199>] ▶ **This word means a judgment, a legal decision, a legal case, a claim, proper, rectitude. It connotes several variations in meanings depending on the context.** It is used to describe a legal decision or judgment rendered: it describes a legal decision given by God to be followed by the people (Is. 58:2; Zeph. 2:3; Mal. 2:17). These decisions could come through the use of the Urim and Thummim (Num. 27:21). The high priest wore a pouch called the breastpiece of justice, containing the Urim and Thummim by which decisions were obtained from the Lord (Ex. 28:30). Doing what was right and just in the Lord's eyes was far more important than presenting sacrifices to Him (Gen. 18:19; Prov. 21:3, 15). God was declared to be the Judge of the whole earth who rendered justice faithfully (Gen. 18:25; Is. 30:18). In the plural form, the word describes legal judgments, cases, examples, laws, and specifications.

The word describes the legal case or cause presented by someone. The Servant spoken of by Isaiah asked who brought his case of justice against him (Is. 50:8); Job brought his case to vindicate himself (Job 13:18; 23:4). The legal claim or control in a situation is also described by the word. Samuel warned the people of the civil and legal demands a king would place on them (1 Sam. 8:9); Moses gave legislation to protect the rightful claim of daughters (Ex. 21:9). The Hebrew word also described the legal right to property (Jer. 32:8). Not surprisingly, the place where judgments were rendered was also described by this word; disputes were to be taken to the place of judgment (Deut. 25:1). Solomon built a hall of justice where he served as judge (1 Kgs. 7:7).

The word also describes plans or instructions: it describes the building plans for the Tabernacle (Ex. 35–40); and the specifications for the Temple (1 Kgs. 6:38); the instructions the angelic messenger gave to Samson's parents about how he was to be brought up (Judg. 13:12). In a more abstract sense, it depicts the manner of life a people followed, such as the Sidonians (Judg. 18:7; 1 Sam. 2:13).

The word means simple justice in some contexts, often in parallel with synonymous words, such as *ḥōq* (<2706>) or *ṣeḏeq* (<6664>), meaning ordinance or righteousness. It describes justice as one thing Jerusalem was to be filled with along with righteousness (Is. 1:21). Justice and righteousness characterize the Lord's throne (Ps. 89:14); and these were coupled with love and faithfulness (cf. Ps. 101:1; 111:7). Executing or doing justice was the central goal that Yahweh had for His people (Jer. 7:5; Ezek. 18:8), for that equaled righteousness (Ezek. 18:9). *

– [2] Job 31:11 ➔ JUDGMENT <6415> [3] Dan. 3:2, 3 ➔ JUDGE (noun) <1884>.

JUTTAH – ***yûṭṭāh, yuṭṭāh*** [proper noun: יוּטָּה, יֻטָּה <3194>; from STRETCH OUT <5186>]: extended ▶ **A Levitical city in the mountain region of Judah.** Refs.: Josh. 15:55; 21:16. ¶

K

KAB – ***qab̲*** [masc. noun: קַב <6894>; from CURSE <6895> (which literally means to scoop out; thus a hollow)] ▶ **This word is a dry measure of about two quarts; it is also translated cab.** It is a small measure, but in a time of distress or siege, one-fourth of a kab sold for five shekels, a huge price (2 Kgs. 6:25). ¶

KABZEEL – ***qab̲ṣᵉ'êl*** [proper noun: קַבְצְאֵל <6909>; from GATHER <6908> and GOD <410>]: God has gathered ▶ **A city located in the southern part of Judah.** Refs.: Josh. 15:21; 2 Sam. 23:20; 1 Chr. 11:22. ¶

KADESH – ***qād̲êš*** [proper noun: קָדֵשׁ <6946>; from HOLY (BE) <6942>]: consecrated, holy ▶ **This word designates a city called Kadesh ten times and used by the Israelites for several years as a base of operations while still wandering in the desert.** It is also called Kadesh Barnea (10 times; see <6947>). It is fifty miles southwest of Beersheba and in the southern part of the Wilderness of Zin. It is called En Mishpat, "spring of Justice" (Kadesh) in Genesis 14:7. Hazar was not too far from it (Gen. 16:14). Abraham encamped between it and Shur (Gen. 20:1); it was located in the Desert of Paran (Num. 13:26). The twelve spies returned there to report. Miriam died there (Num. 20:1–22). Mount Hor, where Aaron died, was near it. *

KADESH BARNEA – ***qād̲êš barnêa'*** [proper noun: קָדֵשׁ בַּרְנֵעַ <6947>; from the same as KADESH <6946> and an otherwise unused root meaning desert of a fugitive]: holy place of the desert of a fugitive ▶ **The same as KADESH <6946> but here called Kadesh Barnea 14 times.** Refs.: Num. 32:8; Deut. 9:23; Josh. 10:41. It was allotted to Judah (Josh. 15:3). *

KADMIEL – ***qad̲miy'êl*** [masc. proper noun: קַדְמִיאֵל <6934>; from EAST <6924 (in the sense of earlier) and GOD <410>]: God is before ▶ **His descendants returned from the Babylonian captivity.** Refs.: Ezra 2:40; 3:9; Neh. 7:43; 9:4, 5; 10:9; 12:8, 24. ¶

KADMONITE – ***qad̲mōniy*** [proper noun: קַדְמֹנִי <6935>; the same as EASTERN <6931>]: easterner, former ▶ **A people who occupied the land of Canaan between Egypt and the Euphrates.** Ref.: Gen. 15:19. ¶

KAIN – See CAIN <7014>.

KALCOL – 1 Kgs. 4:31; 1 Chr. 2:6 ➔ CALCOL <3633>.

KALLAI – ***qāllāy*** [masc. proper noun: קַלָּי <7040>; from SLIGHT (BE) <7043>]: frivolous ▶ **Ancestor of Sallai, a priest who returned to Jerusalem.** Ref.: Neh. 12:20. ¶

KALNEH, KALNO – See **CALNEH, CALNO** <3641>.

KAMON – ***qāmôn*** [proper noun: קָמוֹן <7056>; from STAND, STAND UP <6965>]: raised ▶ **The place where Jair was buried.** Ref.: Judg. 10:5. ¶

KANAH – ***qānāh*** [proper noun: קָנָה <7071>; fem. of STALK <7070>]: place of reeds ▶
a. This seasonal stream (a *wadi* in Arabic, *nahal* in Hebrew) served as part of the boundary between west Ephraim and Manasseh. Refs.: Josh. 16:8; 17:9. The ravine ran east.
b. A city on the border of the tribe of Asher. Ref.: Josh. 19:28. It became the inheritance of Asher, located ca. eight miles southeast of Tyre. ¶

KANNEH – Ezek. 27:23 ➔ CANNEH <3656>.

KAREAH – ***qārêaḥ*** [masc. proper noun: קָרֵחַ <7143>; from SHAVE THE HEAD <7139>]: bald ▶ **Father of Johanan and Jonathan; these two supported Gedaliah, the governor of Judah.** Refs.: 2 Kgs. 25:23; Jer. 40:8, 13, 15, 16; 41:11, 13, 14, 16; 42:1, 8; 43:2, 4, 5. ¶

KARKA – ***qarqa'*** [proper noun: קַרְקַע <7173>; the same as FLOOR <7172>]: ground floor ▶ **A place on the southern border of Judah.** Ref.: Josh. 15:3. ¶

KARKAS – See CARCAS <3752>.

KARKOR – ***qarqōr*** [proper noun: קַרְקֹר <7174>; from DIG <6979> a.]: foundation ▶ **A place where two kings of Midian fought against Gideon.** Ref.: Judg. 8:10 (see 10 to 12). ¶

KARMI – See CARMI <3756>.

KARMITE – See CARMITE <3756>.

KARNAIM – Gen. 14:5 ➔ HORN <7160>.

KARSHENA – See CARSHENA <3771>.

KARTAH – ***qartāh*** [proper noun: קַרְתָּה <7177>; from CITY <7176>]: city ▶ **A city given to the Levites by the tribe of Zebulun.** Refs.: Josh. 21:34; 1 Chr. 6:77. ¶

KARTAN – ***qartān*** [proper noun: קַרְתָּן <7178>; from CITY <7176>]: two cities ▶ **A city given to the Levites by the tribe of Naphtali.** Ref.: Josh. 21:32. ¶

KASIPHIA – See CASIPHIA <3703>.

KATTAH – ***qaṭṭāṯ*** [proper noun: קַטָּת <7005>; from SMALL <6996>]: small ▶ **A town in Zebulun.** Ref.: Josh. 19:15. ¶

KATTATH – Josh. 19:15 ➔ KATTAH <7005>.

KEBAR – See CHEBAR <3529>.

KEDAR – ***qêḏār*** [proper noun: קֵדָר <6938>; from DARK (BE) <6937>]: dark ▶ **A son of Ishmael; also his descendants.** Refs.: Gen. 25:13; 1 Chr. 1:29; Ps. 120:5; Song 1:5; Is. 21:16, 17; 42:11; 60:7; Jer. 2:10; 49:28; Ezek. 27:21. *

KEDEMAH – ***qêḏ^{e}māh*** [masc. proper noun: קֵדְמָה <6929>; from MEET (verb) <6923> (in the sense of to come before)]: precedence ▶ **The youngest son of Ishmael.** Refs.: Gen. 25:15; 1 Chr. 1:31. ¶

KEDEMOTH – ***q^{e}ḏêmôṯ*** [proper noun: קְדֵמוֹת <6932>; from MEET (verb) <6923> (in the sense of to do something before the sun rises)]: beginning, eastern ▶ **One of the towns belonging to the tribe of Reuben.** Refs.: Deut. 2:26; Josh. 13:18; 21:37; 1 Chr. 6:79. ¶

KEDESH – ***qeḏeš*** [proper noun: קֶדֶשׁ <6943>; from HOLY (BE) <6942>]: holy place ▶
a. A town in upper Galilee northwest of Lake Hulah and due north of Hazor. It was conquered by Israel and allotted to Naphtali (Josh. 19:37). It was used as a Levitical city and a city of refuge (Josh. 20:7; 21:32; 1 Chr. 7:76). The Assyrians conquered it under their king Tiglath-Pileser III (2 Kgs. 15:29).
b. A town located in Judah in the southern Negev area. Current authorities do not equate the city with Kadesh Barnea.
c. A city assigned to the Levites. It was in Issachar, but its exact location is not certain (1 Chr. 6:72). *

KEDORLAOMER – See CHEDORLAOMER <3540>.

KEEP – [1] ***nāṭar*** [verb: נָטַר <5201>; a prim. root] ▶ **This word means to take care of, to be angry, to bear a grudge. It means to hold something against another person, to disdain him or her.** This attitude was forbidden in Israel (Lev. 19:18). God never maintains this disposition toward His people forever (Ps. 103:9; Jer. 3:5, 12); but He does display His wrath at times (Nah. 1:2; also translated to reserve). It is used to describe an attitude of anger toward someone (Song 1:6: keeper). It is used in its participial form to refer to those who care for vineyards (Song 8:11, 12). ¶
[2] ***n^{e}ṭar*** [Aramaic verb: נְטַר <5202>; corresponding to <5201> above] ▶ **This word means to hold on to, to bear in mind.** It is used of Daniel's keeping his dream and vision in his mind (Dan. 7:28). ¶

3 ***nāṣar*** [verb: נָצַר <5341>; a prim. root] ▶ **This word means to guard, to observe, to preserve, to hide.** The word refers to people's maintaining things entrusted to them, especially to keeping the truths of God in both actions and mind (Ps. 119:100, 115). God's Word is to be kept with our whole hearts (Ps. 119:69); our hearts, in turn, ought to be maintained in a right state (Prov. 4:23). The word also refers to keeping speech under control (Ps. 34:13; 141:3); the maintenance of a tree (Prov. 27:18); the work of God's character (Ps. 40:11); its reflection in humans as preserving them (Ps. 25:21; Prov. 2:11). Sometimes the word refers directly to God's preservation and maintenance of His people (Prov. 24:12; Is. 49:8). The passive participle form of the verb describes an adulteress' heart as guarded or kept secret (Prov. 7:10). It also describes a city as guarded or besieged (Is. 1:8). The active participle is used to signify a watchman (2 Kgs. 17:9; Jer. 31:6). *

4 ***šāmar*** [verb: שָׁמַר <8104>; a prim. root] ▶ **This word means to watch, to preserve, to guard, to be careful, to watch over, to watch carefully over, to be on one's guard.** The verb means to watch, to guard, to care for. Adam and Eve were to watch over and care for the Garden of Eden where the Lord had placed them (Gen. 2:15); cultic and holy things were to be taken care of dutifully by priests (2 Kgs. 22:14). The word can suggest the idea of protecting: David gave orders to keep Absalom safe (1 Sam. 26:15; 2 Sam. 18:12); the Lord keeps those who look to Him (Ps. 121:7). The word can mean to simply save or to preserve certain items; objects could be delivered to another person for safekeeping (Gen. 41:35; Ex. 22:7). The word also means to pay close attention to: Eli the priest continued to observe Hannah's lips closely as she prayed (1 Sam. 1:12; Is. 42:20). Closely related to this meaning is the connotation to continue to do something, as when Joab maintained his siege of the city of Rabbah (2 Sam. 11:16). The verb also indicates caring for sheep (1 Sam. 17:20).

The Hebrew word means to maintain or to observe something for a purpose and is followed by another verb indicating the purpose or manner, as in the following examples: Israel was to observe the laws of the Lord, so as to do them (Deut. 4:6; 5:1); Balaam had to observe accurately what he had been charged with (Num. 23:12); and Israel was responsible to keep the way of the Lord and walk in it (Gen. 17:9; 18:19).

The word naturally means to watch over some physical object, to keep an eye on it. In its participial form, the word means human guards, those who watch for people or over designated objects (Judg. 1:24; Neh. 12:25). The Lord, as the moral Governor of the world, watches over the moral and spiritual behavior of people (Job 10:14).

In the passive reflexive stem, it means to be taken care of. To take care in the passive aspect, the verb was used to assert that Israel was watched over (Hos. 12:13). Most often it means to take care, as when the Lord instructed Laban to take care not to harm Jacob (Gen. 31:29). Amasa did not guard himself carefully and was killed by Joab (2 Sam. 20:10). Pharaoh warned Moses to take care not to come into his presence again or he would die (Ex. 10:28; cf. Gen. 24:6; 2 Kgs. 6:10; Jer. 17:21).

The word in its intensive stem means to pay regard to or attach oneself to. In the participial form of this verb, it means those who give heed to useless vanities (Jon. 2:8). In the reflexive stem, it means to keep oneself. David declared he was blameless since he had kept himself from sin (2 Sam. 22:24; Ps. 18:23). *

– 5 Deut. 33:21 ➔ COVER (verb) <5603> b. 6 Eccl. 2:10 ➔ RESERVE (verb) <680> 7 Is. 33:15 ➔ SHAKE <5287>.

KEEP ALOOF – Prov. 20:3 ➔ LOSS OF TIME <7674>.

KEEP AWAY – Prov. 20:3 ➔ LOSS OF TIME <7674>.

KEEPER – Song 1:6; 8:11, 12 ➔ KEEP <5201>.

KEHELATHAH – ***q^ehêlāṯāh*** [proper noun: קְהֵלָתָה <6954>; from ASSEMBLE

<6950>]: place of gathering, convocation ▶ **A place where the Israelites camped in the wilderness.** Refs.: Num. 33:22, 23. ¶

KEILAH – ***qᵉʿiylāh*** [proper noun: קְעִילָה <7084>]: fortress ▶ **A town in the low-lying hills (Shephelah) of Judah that had been inherited by them.** Ref.: Josh. 15:44. David, not yet king, fought and delivered the city from attacking Philistines (1 Sam. 23:1–6) but later had to flee the city when Saul learned of his presence there (1 Sam. 23:7, 8–13). Postexilic Jews resettled the city (Neh. 3:17, 18). It was located ca. 20 miles southwest of Jerusalem and west of Hebron. *

KELAIAH – ***qêlāyāh*** [masc. proper noun: קֵלָיָה <7041>; from DESPISED (BE) <7034>]: insignificance ▶ **A Levite who had married a foreign wife.** Ref.: Ezra 10:23. ¶

KELAL – Ezra 10:30 ➔ CHELAL <3636>.

KELITA – ***qeliyṭā'*** [masc. proper noun: קְלִיטָא <7042>; from STUNTED (BE) <7038> (in the sense of to maim)]: maiming ▶ **A Levite who had married a foreign wife.** Refs.: Ezra 10:23; Neh. 8:7; 10:10. ¶

KEMUEL – ***qᵉmû'êl*** [masc. proper noun: קְמוּאֵל <7055>; from STAND, STAND UP <6965> AND GOD <410>]: raised of God ▶
a. A nephew of Abraham. Ref.: Gen. 22:21. ¶
b. An Ephraimite. Ref.: Num. 34:24. ¶
c. A Levite. Ref.: 1 Chr. 27:17. ¶

KENAANAH – See CHENAANAH <3668>.

KENAN – ***qêynān*** [masc. proper noun: קֵינָן <7018>; from the same as NEST <7064>]: fixed ▶ **Son of Enosh who lived 910 years.** Refs.: Gen. 5:9, 10, 12–14; 1 Chr. 1:2. ¶

KENANI – Neh. 9:4 ➔ CHENANI <3662>.

KENANIAH – 1 Chr. 15:22, 27; 26:29 ➔ CHENANIAH <3663>.

KENATH – ***qᵉnāṯ*** [proper noun: קְנָת <7079>; from ACQUIRE <7069>]: possession ▶ **A city in Gilead.** Refs.: Num. 32:42; 1 Chr. 2:23. ¶

KENAZ – ***qᵉnaz*** [masc. proper noun: קְנַז <7073>; from an unused root meaning to hunt]: hunter ▶
a. Grandson of Esau. Refs.: Gen. 36:11, 15, 42; 1 Chr. 1:36, 53. ¶
b. The father of Othniel. Refs.: Josh. 15:17; Judg. 1:13; 3:9, 11; 1 Chr. 4:13. ¶
c. Grandson of Caleb. Ref.: 1 Chr. 4:15. ¶

KENITE – ***qêyniy*** [proper noun: קֵינִי <7017>; patron. from CAIN <7014> b., c.] ▶ **Member of a people living in Canaan at the time of Abraham.** Refs.: Gen. 15:19; Num. 24:21, 22; Judg. 1:16; 4:11, 17; 5:24; 1 Sam. 15:6; 27:10; 30:29; 1 Chr. 2:55. ¶

KENIZZITE – ***qᵉnizziy*** [proper noun: קְנִזִּי <7074>; patron. from KENAZ <7073>] ▶ **A descendant of Kenaz.** Refs.: Gen. 15:19; Num. 32:12; Josh. 14:6, 14. ¶

KEPHAR AMMONI – See CHEPHAR-AMMONI <3726>.

KEPHIRAH – See CHEPHIRAH <3716>.

KEPHIRIM – Neh. 6:2 ➔ LION (YOUNG) <3715> b., c.

KERAN – See CHERAN <3762>.

KERCHIEF – Ezek. 13:18, 21 ➔ VEIL <4555>.

KEREN-HAPPUCH – ***qeren happûḵ*** [fem. noun: קֶרֶן הַפּוּךְ <7163>; from HORN <7161> and MAKEUP <6320>]: horn of cosmetic ▶ **The third of three daughters born to Job after his trial.** Ref.: Job 42:14. ¶

KERETHITES – ***kᵉrêṯiy*** [masc. proper coll. noun: כְּרֵתִי <3774>; prob. from CUT (verb) <3772> in the sense of executioner]: executioners ▶ **Nation or tribe inhabiting**

Philistia. Refs.: 1 Sam. 30:14; 2 Sam. 8:18; 15:18; 20:7, 23; 1 Kgs. 1:38, 44; 1 Chr. 18:17; Ezek. 25:16; Zeph. 2:5. ¶

KERIOTH, KERIOTH HEZBON – ***q^{e}riyyôṯ, q^{e}riyyôṯ ḥeṣrôn*** [proper noun: קְרִיּוֹת, קְרִיּוֹת חֶצְרוֹן <7152>; plur. of CITY <7151>]: cities ▶
a. A popular noun designating Kerioth, a Moabite city that would be judged. Refs.: Josh. 15:25 (KJV, NKJV); Jer. 48:24, 41; Amos 2:2.
b. A popular noun designating Kerioth Hezron, a city of Judah. Ref.: NASB, NIV, ESV, Josh. 15:25. ¶

KERNEL – [1] ***m^{e}liylāh*** [fem. noun: מְלִילָה <4425>; from SPEAK <4449> (in the sense of cropping) (comp. CIRCUMCISE <4135>, which also means to cut off, to cut short)] ▶ **This word designates an ear of grain, or a head of grain. It is mentioned as a head or heads of grain in a field of standing grain.** Ref.: Deut. 23:25, NASB. ¶
– [2] Num. 6:4 ➔ SEED <2785>.

KEROS – ***qêyrōs, qêrōs*** [masc. proper noun: קֵירֹס, קֵרֹס <7026>; from the same as FOOT <7166> (also translated ankle)]: ankled ▶ **Members of his family came back from the Babylonian captivity.** Refs.: Ezra 2:44; Neh. 7:47. ¶

KERUB – See CHERUB <3743>.

KESALON – Josh. 15:10 ➔ CHESALON <3693>.

KESED – See CHESED <3777>.

KESIL – See CHESIL <3686>.

KESULLOTH – Josh. 19:18 ➔ CHESULLOTH <3694>.

KETTLE – [1] 1 Sam. 2:14; 2 Chr. 35:13 ➔ BASKET <1731> [2] Mic. 3:3 ➔ CAULDRON <7037>.

KETURAH – ***q^{e}ṭûrāh*** [fem. proper noun: קְטוּרָה <6989>; fem. pass. part. of BURN (verb) <6999>]: perfumed, incense ▶ **Wife of Abraham after the death of Sarah.** Refs.: Gen. 25:1, 4; 1 Chr. 1:32, 33. ¶

KEY – ***mapṯêaḥ*** [masc. noun: מַפְתֵּחַ <4668>; from OPEN <6605>] ▶ **This word indicates a tool used to open a lock.** Ref.: Judg. 3:25. To be over (*'al*) the key means to be in charge of opening a door (1 Chr. 9:27: opening). It is used figuratively of the official right to be a part of the Davidic dynasty and its authority (Is. 22:22). ¶

KEZIA – ***q^{e}ṣiy'āh*** [fem. proper noun: קְצִיעָה <7103>; the same as CASSIA <7102>]: cassia ▶ **The second of three daughters born to Job after his trial.** Ref.: Job 42:14. ¶

KEZIB – Gen. 38:5 ➔ CHEZIB <3580>.

KEZIZ – ***q^{e}ṣiyṣ*** [proper noun: קְצִיץ <7104>; from CUT OFF <7112>]: cut off, abrupt ▶ **A place in Benjamin.** Ref.: Josh. 18:21. ¶

KIBROTH HATTAAVAH – ***qiḇrôṯ hatta^{a}wāh*** [proper noun: קִבְרוֹת הַתַּאֲוָה <6914>; from the fem. plur. of GRAVE (noun) <6913> and DESIRE <8378>]: grave of lust ▶ **A campsite of the Israelites in the wilderness on their way to the Promised Land.** Refs.: Num. 11:34, 35; 33:16, 17; Deut. 9:22. ¶

KIBZAIM – ***qiḇṣayim*** [proper noun: קִבְצַיִם <6911>; dual from GATHER <6908>]: two heaps, two gatherings ▶ **This is the name of a city given to the Levites and located between Geza and Beth Horon.** Ref.: Josh. 21:22. ¶

KICK – [1] ***bā'aṭ*** [verb: בָּעַט <1163>; a prim. root] ▶ **This word means to strike with the foot; to disdain, scorn.** It refers to the disrespectful attitude and unholy actions of the high priest's sons in the time of the birth and maturation of Samuel (1 Sam. 2:29). It refers to a rebellious disposition and action of Israel toward the Lord (Deut. 32:15). ¶
– [2] 2 Sam. 16:13 ➔ FLING <6080>.

KID – 1 ***gᵉḏiy*** [masc. noun: גְּדִי <1423>; from the same as BANK <1415>] ▶ **This word designates a young goat or the young of other animals.** Followed by the word for goats (*'izzîm*), it refers almost always to the young of goats (Gen. 27:9, 16; 38:17, 20; 1 Sam. 16:20). It was often used as food or a sacrificial animal (Judg. 6:19; 13:15, 19). It was never to be boiled in the milk of its mother (Ex. 23:19; 34:26; Deut. 14:21). *
– 2 Song 1:8 ➔ GOAT (YOUNG, LITTLE) <1429>.

KIDNEY – ***kilyāh*** [fem. noun: כִּלְיָה <3629>; from ARTICLE <3627> (only in the plur.)] ▶ **This word means the organ that removes the waste in the body; it also means the heart as the seat of emotions. It is always used in its plural form.** It is an animal's internal organ referred to often in sacrifices (Ex. 29:13; Lev. 4:9; 7:4; 9:10); it is the innermost and most private aspect of a person (Job 16:13; Ps. 139:13; Prov. 23:16; Jer. 11:20; Lam. 3:13). God created the kidneys (Ps. 139:13; translated inward parts, reins, inmost being). In a metaphor, it is used to refer to choice wheat, *kilyôṯ ḥittāh* (Deut. 32:14). *

KIDRON – ***qiḏrôn*** [proper noun: קִדְרוֹן <6939>; from DARK (BE) <6937>]: dark ▶ **This word designates the brook of Kidron. It is also called the Kidron Valley which is east of Jerusalem and separates it from the Mount of Olives.** It runs with water only during the rainy season. David crossed it to flee Jerusalem (2 Sam. 15:23). It seemed to mark the city limits in a sense for crossing it meant leaving Jerusalem (1 Kgs. 2:37). Many foreign idols and shrines were built in this valley. The good kings of Judah always attempted to destroy and remove them (1 Kgs. 15:13). Josiah cleared the Temple of these abominations and burned or trashed them in the Kidron Valley (2 Kgs. 23:4–12). God showed Jeremiah a time, however, when even the desecrated and polluted Kidron Valley will be made holy to the Lord (Jer. 31:38–40). *

KILL – 1 ***hārag*** [verb: הָרַג <2026>; a prim. root] ▶ **This verb means to murder, to slay. It carries a wide variety of usages.** Its first use in the Bible is in the fratricide of Abel by Cain (Gen. 4:8). The word is employed for war and slaughter (Josh. 8:24; 1 Kgs. 9:16; Esther 8:11); God's killing in judgment (Gen. 20:4; Ex. 13:15; Amos 2:3); humans killing animals (Lev. 20:15; Num. 22:29); animals killing humans (2 Kgs. 17:25; Job 20:16). *
2 ***rāṣaḥ*** [verb: רָצַח <7523>; a prim. root] ▶ **This word means to murder, to slay. The taking of a human life is the primary concept behind this word.** It is used to indicate a premeditated murder (Deut. 5:17; 1 Kgs. 21:19; Jer. 7:9); an accidental killing (Num. 35:11; Josh. 20:3); the ultimate act of revenge (Num. 35:27); and death by means of an animal attack (Prov. 22:13). Provocatively, Hosea refers to the lewdness of the priests that led people astray as being equal to murder (Hos. 6:9). *
3 ***šāḥaṭ*** [verb: שָׁחַט <7819>; a prim. root] ▶ **The primary meaning of the verb is to slaughter; it also means to offer, to shoot out, to slay.** In Leviticus, the word is used to indicate that the one who brings the sacrifice is the person who will slaughter the animal (Lev. 1:5). After the slaughtering, the priests brought the blood and other parts of the animal to the altar. In contrast to Leviticus, 2 Chronicles indicates that the worshipers could not slaughter their sacrifices because they did not consecrate themselves and were ceremonially unclean. In this case, the Levites (i.e., priests) had to slaughter the lambs for all who were ceremonially unclean (cf. 2 Chr. 30:17). This verb is also used to indicate an ineffective sacrifice where the offerers were only going through the motions of worship (Is. 66:3). Even though the object of their worship appears to be God, their hearts were still bent toward evil. This failure is the reason for their upcoming judgment. Another usage of the verb depicts Saul's army pouncing on the plunder, butchering sheep, cattle, and calves, and eating the meat together with the blood, which was forbidden in the Law (1 Sam. 14:32). This makes the actions of Saul's army in direct disobedience of God's Law.

The verb is also used to describe the process of a human sacrifice to Yahweh (i.e.,

the process used to test Abraham with his son Isaac [Gen. 22:10]). Since He does not desire human sacrifices, God stopped Abraham from sacrificing his son Isaac. When used in the context of a human sacrifice to false gods, the verb describes the actual process being carried out rather than the anticipated process such as that found with Abraham (Is. 57:5; Ezek. 16:21; 23:39). *
– [4] Num. 25:4; 2 Sam. 21:6, 9, 13 ➔ ALIENATED (BE) <3363> [5] Job 24:14 ➔ SLAY <6991> [6] Dan. 2:13, 14; etc. ➔ SLAY <6992> [7] Nah. 2:12 ➔ HANG <2614> [8] See OFFER <2076> [9] See SLAUGHTER (verb) <2873>.

KILN – Ex. 9:8, 10; 19:18 ➔ FURNACE <3536>.

KIN – Prov. 7:4 ➔ RELATIVE <4129>.

KINAH – ***qiynāh*** [proper noun: קִינָה <7016>; the same as LAMENTATION <7015>]: lamentation ▶ **A town on the southern boundary of Judah.** Ref.: Josh. 15:22. ¶

KIND (adj.) – [1] 2 Sam. 22:26b; Ps. 18:25b ➔ MERCIFUL <2616> [2] See FAITHFUL <2623>.

KIND (BE) – Dan. 4:27 ➔ MERCY (SHOW, ASK FOR) <2604>.

KIND (noun) – [1] ***zan*** [masc. noun: זַן <2177>; from WELL-FED <2109>] ▶ **This word means sort, various types.** It indicates a particular variety or group of something linked by similar traits (2 Chr. 16:14). Used in the phrase *mizzan 'el-zan*, it indicates of all sorts, of all kinds, of every kind (Ps. 144:13). ¶
[2] ***zan*** [Aramaic masc. noun: זַן <2178>; corresponding to <2177> above] ▶ **This word indicates a particular variety or group of things linked by similar traits.** Preceded by *kōl*, it indicates all kinds of (Dan. 3:5, 7, 10, 15). ¶
[3] ***miyn*** [masc. noun: מִין <4327>; from an unused root meaning to portion out] ▶ **This word indicates an animal or something that shares common characteristics.** Refs.: Gen. 1:11, 12, 21, 24, 25; 6:20; 7:14; Lev. 11:14–16, 19, 22, 29; Deut. 14:13–15, 18; Ezek. 47:10. It does not equal the modern scientific definition of and the use of species. ¶

KIND (DIFFERENT, DIVERSE, ANOTHER) – ***kil'ayim*** [masc. dual noun: כִּלְאַיִם <3610>; dual of PRISON <3608> in the original sense of separation] ▶ **This word indicates a mixing or mingling of two sorts.** It refers to mixing cattle, seeds, or vines as forbidden by the Law (Lev. 19:19; Deut. 22:9). ¶

KINDLE – [1] ***nāśaq*** [verb: נָשַׂק <5400>; a prim. root] ▶ **This word refers to starting a fire, creating a spark to get a blaze going.** It indicates God's anger being fired up against His people (Ps. 78:21; NIV: to break out). It refers to wooden idols being burned, kindled, to warm its former worshipers (Is. 44:15; NASB: to make a fire). It describes destroying weapons by burning them (Ezek. 39:9). ¶
[2] ***qāḏaḥ*** [verb: קָדַח <6919>; a prim. root] ▶ **This word means to set on fire.** It describes igniting a fire (Is. 64:2); but is used figuratively of the kindling of the Lord's anger (Deut. 32:22; Jer. 15:14; 17:4). It indicates those persons who wrongly, wickedly try to destroy the Lord's Servant or the righteous (Is. 50:11). ¶
– [3] Prov. 26:21 ➔ BURN (verb) <2787> [4] Ezek. 24:10; Obad. 1:18 ➔ BURN (verb) <1814>.

KINDLED (BE) – Hos. 11:8 ➔ YEARN <3648>.

KINDNESS – See MERCY <2617>.

KINDRED – [1] ***môleḏeṯ*** [fem. noun: מוֹלֶדֶת <4138>; from BIRTH (GIVE) <3205>] ▶ **This word indicates birth, family background. It has the basic sense of origin, common origin, relationship by birth.** It refers then to offspring, descendants (Gen. 48:6: children, offspring, issue); relations (Gen. 12:1; 24:4); birthed in the same

household or family (*bayit*) (Lev. 18:9). It is extended to refer to descent, parentage (Ezek. 16:3); in a figurative way of Israel, or even birth (Ezek. 16:4). Used in front of *'eres*, it indicates a land of birth, origin (Gen. 11:28; 24:7; Jer. 22:10). *
– 2 Ruth 3:2 ➔ RELATIVE <4130>.

KINDS (TWO) – Lev. 19:19; Deut. 22:9 ➔ KIND (DIFFERENT, DIVERSE, ANOTHER) <3610>.

KINE – Deut. 7:13; 28:4, 18, 51; Ps. 8:7 ➔ HERD <504>.

KING – 1 ***melek*** [masc. noun: מֶלֶךְ <4428>; from KING (BE) <4427>] ▶ **This word refers to one who rules or reigns over a kingdom. The feminine form of this word is *malkāh* (<4436>), meaning queen, though the concept is more of a king's consort than a monarchical ruler. The word *melek* appears over 2,500 times in the Old Testament. In many biblical contexts, this term is simply a general term, denoting an individual with power and authority.** It is parallel with and conceptually related to a number of other Hebrew words that are usually translated as lord, captain, prince, chief, or ruler. It is used in reference to men and often with a genitive of people or place (Gen. 14:1; Ex. 1:15; 2 Sam. 2:4); the Lord who demonstrates His power and authority over Israel (Is. 41:21; 44:6); and over each individual (Ps. 5:2; 44:4). In pagan worship, the worshipers of idols attribute this term with its connotations to their idols (Is. 8:21; Amos 5:26). *
2 ***melek*** [Aramaic masc. noun: מֶלֶךְ <4430>; corresponding to <4428> above] ▶ **This very common word is equivalent to the Hebrew word *melek* (<4428>) above, meaning king.** It is used to speak of the top government official. It is used to speak of the following kings: Artaxerxes (Ezra 4:8 ff.); Darius (Ezra 5:6 ff.; Dan. 6:2 ff.); Cyrus (Ezra 5:13 ff.); Nebuchadnezzar (Dan. 2:4 ff.); Belshazzar (Dan. 5:1 ff.); kings that will arise on the earth (Dan. 7:17, 24). *

KING (BE, MAKE) – ***mālak*** [verb: מָלַךְ <4427>; a prim. root] ▶ **This word is used approximately three hundred times in its simple form to mean to rule, to have sway, power, and dominion over people and nations.** God is King and will rule over the whole earth in the day when He judges the earth and establishes Mount Zion (Is. 24:23). Israel rejected God from ruling over them during the time of Samuel (1 Sam. 8:7; cf. Ezek. 20:33); the verb is used to proclaim the rulership of a king when he is installed, as when Adonijah prematurely attempted to usurp the throne of his father David (1 Kgs. 1:11). The Lord reigns as the Lord Almighty over both earthly and divine subjects (Is. 24:23; Mic. 4:7).

The verb also describes the rulership of human kings—the establishment of rulership and the process itself (Gen. 36:31; Judg. 9:8; Prov. 30:22). It describes the rule of Athaliah the queen over Judah for six years (2 Kgs. 11:3). In the causative form, it depicts the installation of a king. It describes God's establishment of Saul as the first king over Israel (1 Sam. 15:35). Hos. 8:4 indicates that the Israelites had set up kings without the Lord's approval. *

KINGDOM – 1 ***m^e^lûkāh*** [fem. noun: מְלוּכָה <4410>; fem. pass. part. of KING (BE) <4427>] ▶ **This word means royalty. It designates the position or authority of a king as well as kingship in general (1 Kgs. 2:15).** It is found in various expressions: with *'āśāh* plus *'al* to mean to rule over, to exercise kingship (1 Kgs. 21:7); with *qārā'* to announce or proclaim kingship (Is. 34:12); the justice or ruling principle of kingship is expressed by *mišpat hamm^e^lûkāh* (1 Sam. 10:25); *kissê' hamm^e^lûkāh* means the throne of the kingship or kingdom (1 Kgs. 1:46). The Lord bestowed rulership in Israel (2 Sam. 16:8). It is used figuratively of Jerusalem attaining rulership (Ezek. 16:13). A city of rulership is a royal city (2 Sam. 12:26). Isaiah 62:3 speaks of Zion's being a royal diadem. The expression seed of royalty refers to the royal family or dynasty (2 Kgs. 25:25; Jer. 41:1; Ezek. 17:13; Dan. 1:3). *
2 ***malkû*** [Aramaic fem. noun: מַלְכוּ <4437>; corresponding to <4438> below] ▶ **This**

word means royalty, reign, kingly authority. This word, corresponding to the word *malkût* (<4438>), distinguishes the propriety of royalty from all else (e.g., Dan. 5:20). It is used to denote the reign of a particular sovereign (Dan. 6:28); the extent of a king's authority (Ezra 7:13); the territorial or administrative dominion of a monarch (Dan. 6:3); the nation or kingdom in a general sense (Dan. 5:31). *

3 ***malkût*** [fem. noun: מַלְכוּת <4438>; from KING (BE) <4427>] ▶ **This word means royalty, reign, dominion. It chiefly describes that which pertains to royalty or the natural outflow of power from the royal station.** The book of Esther especially illustrates how this word is used to distinguish the royal from the ordinary, speaking of royal wine (1:7); a royal command (1:19); and royal clothing (5:1). It is specifically used to signify the reign of a monarch (2 Chr. 15:10; Dan. 1:1); and the kingdom or territorial realm under the authority of a particular sovereign (1 Chr. 12:23; 2 Chr. 11:17; Dan. 10:13). *

4 ***mamlākāh*** [fem. noun: מַמְלָכָה <4467>; from KING (BE) <4427>] ▶ **Often this term refers to the royal power an individual in sovereign authority possesses.** Because Solomon did not keep the Lord's covenant and commandments, his kingdom (i.e., his power to rule) was torn from his son (1 Kgs. 11:11; cf. 1 Sam. 28:17; 1 Kgs. 14:8). In many other places, however, the word is utilized concretely to denote a people under a king (i.e., a realm). The kingdom (or realm) of King Sihon of the Amorites and the kingdom (realm) of King Og of Bashan were given to the Gadites, Reubenites, and the half-tribe of Manasseh (Num. 32:33; cf. Ex. 19:6; Deut. 28:25; 1 Sam. 24:20). In some passages, the word functions as an adjective, meaning royal (e.g., city of the kingdom = royal city; Josh. 10:2; 1 Sam. 27:5; cf. 2 Kgs. 11:1; 2 Chr. 23:20; Amos 7:13). This noun derives from the verb *mālak* [KING (BE, MADE) <4427>], as does its synonym, *malkût* (<4438> above). *

5 ***mamlākût*** [fem. noun: מַמְלָכוּת <4468>; a form of <4467> above and equivalent to it] ▶ **This word means royal power.** Samuel told Saul that the Lord had torn the kingdom of Israel from him and given it to another better than he (1 Sam. 15:28). The Lord declared to Hosea that He was going to put an end to the kingdom of Israel (Hos. 1:4; cf. Josh. 13:12; 2 Sam. 16:3; Jer. 26:1). This noun is derived from the verb *mālak* [KING (BE) <4427>]. *

KINNERETH – See CHINNERETH <3672>.

KINSMAN – 1 Ruth 2:1 ➔ RELATIVE <4129> 2 Ruth 3:2 ➔ RELATIVE <4130>.

KINSWOMAN – 1 ***šarāh*** [fem. noun: שַׁאֲרָה <7608>; fem. of FLESH <7607>] ▶ **This word designates a woman as a close blood relative.** Intercourse was forbidden with this person (Lev. 18:17). ¶
– 2 Prov. 7:4 ➔ RELATIVE <4129>.

KIR – ***qiyr*** [proper noun: קִיר <7024>; the same as WALL <7023>]: wall ▶
a. A city in Mesopotamia. Refs.: 2 Kgs. 16:9; Is. 22:6; Amos 1:5; 9:7. ¶
b. A city in Moab, possibly the same as Kir Hareseth (<7024>). Ref.: Is. 15:1. ¶

KIR HARESETH, KIR HERES – ***qiyr ḥreśeṯ, qiyr ḥereś*** [proper noun: קִיר חֲרֶשֶׂת, קִיר חֶרֶשׂ <7025>; from WALL <7023> and EARTHENWARE <2789>]: wall of earthenware ▶ **A city in Moab.** Refs.: 2 Kgs. 3:25; Is. 16:7, 11; Jer. 48:31, 36. ¶

KIRIATH ARBA – ***qiryaṯ 'arba', qiryaṯ hā'arba'*** [proper noun: קִרְיַת אַרְבַּע, קִרְיַת הָאַרְבַּע <7153>; from CITY <7151> and ARBA <704> or FOUR <702>]: city of Arba ▶ **The name is an older name for Hebron.** Refs.: Gen. 23:2; 35:27. Sarah died there. Earlier, the city had been the home of the Anakites of whom Arba was the greatest (Josh. 14:15) and an ancestor of Anak (Josh. 15:13). It was used even after the return of the exiles to Judah (Neh. 11:25). Other refs.: Josh. 15:54; 20:7; 21:11; Judg. 1:10. ¶

KIRIATH BAAL – ***qiryaṯ ba‘al*** [proper noun: קִרְיַת בַּעַל <7154>; from CITY <7151> and BAAL <1168>]: city of Baal ▶ **A city that became part of the territory of Judah after the conquest of the Promised Land.** Refs.: Josh. 15:60; 18:14. ¶

KIRIATH HUZOTH – ***qiryaṯ ḥuṣôṯ*** [proper noun: קִרְיַת חֻצוֹת <7155>; from CITY <7151> and the fem. plur. of STREET <2351>]: city of streets ▶ **A city in Moab where Balaak brought Balaam to curse Israel.** Ref.: Num. 22:39. ¶

KIRIATH JEARIM – ***qiryaṯ yᵉ‘āriym, qiryaṯ ‘āriym, qiryaṯ*** [proper noun: קִרְיַת יְעָרִים, קִרְיַת עָרִים, קִרְיַת <7157>; from CITY <7151> and the plur. of FOREST <3293> or CITY <5892>]: city of forests (or) city of towns ▶
a. A city located about eight miles west of Jerusalem. It concluded a deceitful treaty with the Israelites (along with Gibeon and Beer) so that Israel was bound not to destroy its inhabitants. Ref.: Josh. 9:17. The men were reduced to woodcutters and water carriers (Josh. 9:18–21). It was identified with Kiriath Baal by the biblical writer (Josh. 18:14–15; see <7154>). It was located in Judah on its northern border touching Benjamin. The ark was temporarily stored there in David's time until he transferred it to Jerusalem (1 Sam. 6:21; 7:1, 2; 1 Chr. 13:5, 6). The city produced at least one prophet (Jer. 26:20). It was resettled by returned exiles (Neh. 7:29).
b. A city given to Benjamin, possibly the same as a. *

KIRIATH SEPHER, KIRIATH SANNAH – ***qiryaṯ sêp̱er, qiryath sannāh*** [proper noun: קִרְיַת סֵפֶר, קִרְיַת סַנָּה <7158>; from CITY <7151> and BOOK <5612>, or (for the latter name) a simpler fem. from the same as FRUIT <5577>]: city of the book ▶
a. A city of Judah captured by Othniel. Refs.: Josh. 15:15, 16; Judg. 1:11, 12. ¶
b. Same as a. Ref.: Josh. 15:49. ¶

KIRIATHAIM – ***qiryāṯayim*** [proper noun: קִרְיָתַיִם <7156>; dual of CITY <7151>]: two cities ▶
a. A city east of the Jordan River. Refs.: Num. 32:37; Josh. 13:19; Jer. 48:1, 23; Ezek. 25:9. ¶
b. A town in Naphtali. Ref.: 1 Chr. 6:76. ¶

KISH – ***qiyš*** [masc. proper noun: קִישׁ <7027>; from SNARE (LAY A) <6983> (in the original sense of bending)]: bent, bow ▶ **Name of five Israelites, including the father of King Saul.** Refs.: 1 Sam. 9:1, 3; 10:11, 21; 14:51; 2 Sam. 21:14; 1 Chr. 8:30, 33; 9:36, 39; 12:1; 23:21, 22; 24:29; 26:28; 2 Chr. 29:12; Esther 2:5. ¶

KISHI – ***qiyšiy*** [masc. proper noun: קִישִׁי <7029>; from SNARE (LAY A) <6983> (in the original sense of bending)]: bowed ▶ **A Merarite of the tribe of Levi, father of Ethan.** Ref.: 1 Chr. 6:44. ¶

KISHION – ***qišyôn*** [proper noun: קִשְׁיוֹן <7191>; from STUBBORNNESS <7185>, which is from HARD (BE) <7185>]: hard ground ▶ **A city given to the Levites by the tribe of Issachar.** Refs.: Josh. 19:20; 21:28. ¶

KISHON – ***qiyšôn*** [proper noun: קִישׁוֹן <7028>; from SNARE (LAY A) <6983> (in the original sense of bending)]: winding ▶ **The name of a river that played a part in the defeat of the Canaanites by the forces of Deborah and Barak.** It flowed out of the Jezreel Valley east to west to the Mediterranean. Elijah killed prophets of Baal here (1 Kgs. 18:40). It overflowed and helped bog down the iron chariots of Sisera's forces (Judg. 4:7, 13; 5:21). It was a great victory for Israel at Kishon and enshrined in the memory of Israel (Ps. 83:9). ¶

KISLEV – Neh. 1:1; Zech. 7:1 ➔ CHISLEV <3691>.

KISLON – Num. 34:21 ➔ CHISLON <3692>.

KISLOTH TABOR – Josh. 19:12 ➔ CHISLOTH TABOR <3694>.

KISS (noun) – ***nᵉšiyqāh*** [fem. noun: נְשִׁיקָה <5390>; from KISS (verb) <5401>] ▶

This word means a caress with the lips; it indicates an act showing an intimacy of a relationship. But in context it is used in a deceitful, false show of affection (Prov. 27:6). It describes an amorous show of love and affection (Song 1:2). ¶

KISS (verb) – ***nāšaq*** [verb: נָשַׁק <5401>; a prim. root (identical with KINDLE <5400>, through the idea of fastening up)] ▶ **The word means to caress with the lips; it rarely has romantic implications.** Refs.: Prov. 7:13; Song 1:2. Often, along with tears and embraces, kisses expressed the dearness of relationships between friends and family, especially at a farewell (Ruth 1:9, 14; 1 Sam. 20:41; 1 Kgs. 19:20); or a reunion (Gen. 45:15, cf. Rom. 16:16; 1 Pet. 5:14). Kisses also expressed acceptance of a person (Gen. 45:15; 2 Sam. 14:33); and even the mutual acceptance or harmony of moral qualities (Ps. 85:10). They also were associated with giving blessings (Gen. 27:27; 2 Sam. 19:39). Kisses sometimes expressed the worship of idols (1 Kgs. 19:18; Hos. 13:2); and the worship of the Messiah (Ps. 2:12; cf. Ps. 2:7; Heb. 1:5). Some kisses, however, were deceitful (2 Sam. 20:9). The meaning of lightly touching occurs in Ezekiel 3:13. *

KITE – ***dā'āh*** [fem. noun: דָּאָה <1676>; from FLY (verb) <1675>] ▶ **This word indicates an unclean bird of prey of which no varieties were to be eaten by the Israelites.** Refs.: Lev. 11:14; Deut. 14:13; KJV, vulture and glede. ¶

KITE, BLACK KITE – Lev. 11:14; Deut. 14:13 ➔ FALCON <344>.

KITHLISH – ***kiṯliyš*** [proper noun: כִּתְלִישׁ <3798>; from WALL <3786> and MAN <376>]: wall of a man ▶ **A town in the plain of Judah.** Ref.: Josh. 15:40. ¶

KITLISH – See KITHLISH <3798>.

KITRON – ***qiṭrôn*** [proper noun: קִטְרוֹן <7003>; from BURN <6999>]: incense ▶ **A town in Zebulun from which the Canaanites were not driven out.** Ref.: Judg. 1:30. ¶

KITTIM – ***kittiy*** [masc. proper noun: כִּתִּי <3794>; patrial from an unused name denoting Cyprus (only in the plur.)] ▶ **Son of Javan and grandson of Japheth; his descendants populated the island of Cyprus and other islands and coasts of the eastern part of the Mediterranean.** Refs.: Gen. 10:4; Num. 24:24; 1 Chr. 1:7; Is. 23:1, 12; Jer. 2:10; Ezek. 27:6; Dan. 11:30. ¶

KITTITE – See KITTIM <3794>.

KIYYUN – Amos 5:26 ➔ CHIUN <3594> a.

KNAPSACK – 2 Kgs. 4:42 ➔ SACK <6861> a.

KNEAD – ***lûš*** [verb: לוּשׁ <3888>; a prim. root] ▶ **This word is used of the preparation of dough for baking, working the dough, massaging it.** Refs.: Gen. 18:6; 1 Sam. 28:24; 2 Sam. 13:8. It is used of preparing bread to make cakes for the Queen of Heaven by apostate Israelites (Jer. 7:18). The kneading of the dough and the penetration of the leaven is a picture of the spread of corruption in Israel (Hos. 7:4). ¶

KNEADING BOWL, KNEADING TROUGH – ***miš'ereṯ*** [fem. noun: מִשְׁאֶרֶת <4863>; from REMAIN <7604> in the original sense of swelling] ▶ **This word denotes a vessel for preparing dough for baking or clay for some use.** Refs.: Ex. 8:3; 12:34; Deut. 28:5, 17); KJV translates store in Deuteronomy 28:5, 17. ¶

KNEE – 1 ***'arḵubbāh*** [Aramaic fem. noun: אַרְכֻבָּה <755>; from an unused root corresponding to RIDE <7392> (in the sense of bending the knee)] ▶ **This word means the middle joint of the human leg.** It refers to Belshazzar's knees knocking together because of his terror of the writing on the wall (Dan. 5:6). ¶

2 ***berêḵ*** [Aramaic fem. noun: בְּרֵךְ <1291>; corresponding to <1290> below] ▶ **This**

word is combined with the verb *b^{e}rak̲* to mean to kneel, literally, to kneel on his knees. Ref.: Dan. 6:10 ¶
3 ***berek̲*** [fem. noun: בֶּרֶךְ <1290>; from BLESS <1288>] ► **This word is used with the verb *kāra'*, to bend, meaning to bend the knee.** Isaiah declares that every knee will bow before the Lord (Is. 45:23) in the sense of worshiping and confessing the Lord. Solomon knelt before the Lord at the altar to worship his God (1 Kgs. 8:54; cf. 1 Kgs. 18:42). The phrase "on her knees" designates the lap of a mother (2 Kgs. 4:20 KJV). In Ezekiel's vision, water reached up to his knees (Ezek. 47:4). One of the curses the Lord would lay on a disobedient people was ailing knees (Deut. 28:35). Since the knees were a picture of strength, terror or fasting could weaken them (Job 4:4; Ps. 109:24; Is. 35:3; Nah. 2:10). *

KNEEL – Dan. 6:10 ➔ BLESS <1289>.

KNIFE – 1 ***ma^{a}k̲elet̲*** [fem. noun: מַאֲכֶלֶת <3979>; from EAT <398> (in the sense of something to eat with)] ► **This word refers to a large instrument for cutting used in sacrifices.** It was used by Abraham when he was about to slay Isaac and by the Levite to carve up his concubine (Gen. 22:6, 10; Judg. 19:29). It is parallel to a sword in Proverbs 30:14, giving an especially macabre aspect to the proverb. ¶
2 ***maḥ^{a}lāp̲*** [masc. noun: מַחֲלָף <4252>; from PASS ON <2496> b. (in the sense of to pierce, to strike through)] ► **This word refers to a cutting instrument for slaughter.** The meaning is not known for sure but several suggestions are (1) knives for slaughtering animals (KJV); (2) silver pans (NIV); duplicates (NASB); censers (ESV) (Ezra 1:9). ¶
3 ***śakkiyn*** [masc. noun: שַׂכִּין <7915>; intens. perhaps from the same as SECU <7906>] ► **This word refers to a sharp cutting or stabbing instrument, single or double-edged.** Ref.: Prov. 23:2. ¶
– 4 See SWORD <2719>.

KNIT – Job 10:11 ➔ HEDGE (MAKE A, PUT A) <7753>.

KNIT TOGETHER – Job 10:11; Ps. 139:13 ➔ COVER (verb) <5526> c.

KNIT TOGETHER (BE) – 1 ***śārag̲*** [verb: שָׂרַג <8276>; a prim. root] ► **This word means to be woven together.** It indicates the close, orderly entwinement of the sinews of someone's tendons (Job 40:17; also translated to be tightly knit, to be wrapped together, to be close-knit). It is used figuratively of sins being knit together (Lam. 1:14: to be wreathed, to be fastened together, to be woven together). ¶
– 2 Lam. 1:14 ➔ KNIT TOGETHER (BE) <8276>.

KNITTED – Lev. 13:48 ➔ MIXED <6154>.

KNOB – Ex. 25:31, 33–36; 37:17, 19–22 ➔ BULB <3730>.

KNOCK – 1 ***n^{e}qaš*** [Aramaic verb: נְקַשׁ <5368>; corresponding to ENSNARE <5367> (but use in the sense of CUT DOWN <5362> in the KJV, i.e., to smite)] ► **This word means to collide, to bang; it occurs only once in the Hebrew Bible.** Daniel 5:6 employed the idiomatic phase knocking (KJV: to smite) knees to express Belshazzar' fear when he saw a finger mysteriously writing on the wall. ¶
– 2 Song 5:2 ➔ DRIVE HARD <1849>.

KNOCKING – Nah. 2:10 ➔ SMITE TOGETHER <6375>.

KNOP – Ex. 25:31, 33–36; 37:17, 19–22 ➔ BULB <3730>.

KNOPS – 1 Kgs. 6:18; 7:24 ➔ GOURDS <6497>.

KNOW – 1 ***yād̲a'*** [verb: יָדַע <3045>; a prim. root] ► **This word means to learn, to perceive, to discern, to experience, to confess, to consider, to know people relationally, to know how, to be skillful, to be made known, to make oneself known, to make to know.** The simple meaning, to know, is its most common translation out of the eight hundred or more uses. One of the primary uses means to know relationally and experientially: it refers to knowing or not knowing persons (Gen. 29:5; Ex. 1:8) personally or by reputation (Job 19:13). The word also refers to knowing a person sexually (Gen. 4:1; 19:5; 1 Kgs. 1:4). It may even describe knowing or not knowing God or foreign gods (Ex. 5:2; Deut. 11:28; Hos. 2:20; 8:2), but it especially signifies knowing what to do or think in general, especially with respect to God (Is. 1:3; 56:10). One of its most important uses is depicting God's knowledge of people: The Lord knows their hearts entirely (Ex. 33:12; 2 Sam. 7:20; Ps. 139:4; Jer. 17:9; Hos. 5:3); God knows the suffering of His people (Ex. 2:25), and He cares.

The word also describes knowing various other things: when Adam and Eve sinned, knowing good and evil (Gen. 3:22); knowing nothing (1 Sam. 20:39); and knowing the way of wisdom (Job 28:23). One could know by observation (1 Sam. 23:22, 23), as when Israel and Pharaoh came to know God through the plagues He brought on Egypt (Ex. 10:2). People knew by experience (Josh. 23:14) that God kept His promises; this kind of experience could lead to knowing by confession (Jer. 3:13; 14:20). Persons could be charged to know what they were about to do (Judg. 18:14) or what the situation implied (1 Kgs. 20:7) so they would be able to discriminate between right and wrong, good and bad, what was not proper or advantageous (Deut. 1:39; 2 Sam. 19:35).

The word describes different aspects of knowing in its other forms. In the passive forms, it describes making something or someone known. The most famous illustration is Exodus 6:3 when God asserted to Moses that He did not make himself known to the fathers as Yahweh. *

2 ***yᵉḏaʻ*** [Aramaic verb: יְדַע <3046>; corresponding to <3045> above] ▶ **This word also means to communicate, to inform, to cause to know. The word primarily refers to knowledge sharing or awareness and occurs often in the books of Ezra and Daniel.** In Ezra, the men opposed to the rebuilding of Jerusalem wanted it to be known to Artaxerxes (Ezra 4:12, 13), and when opposing the Temple, they made it known to Darius (Ezra 5:8, 10). The book of Daniel presents a theological subtheme of true knowledge. In the desired and hidden meanings of life, only the God of Heaven truly knows the end from the beginning, and only He can ultimately reveal and wisely inform (Dan. 2:5, 21, 23, 28–30; 4:9; 5:8, 15, 16). Fearing Him is true knowing (Dan. 5:17, 21–23), a sovereign awareness that removes crippling human fear in circumstantial knowing (Dan. 3:18; 6:10). *Yᵉḏaʻ* compares with the Hebrew word *yāḏaʻ* (<3045> above), which is used with much broader variances of meaning in Scripture, ranging from cognitive to experiential to sexual relations. *

KNOW (LET), KNOWN (MAKE) – 1 Sam. 20:2, 12, 13 ➔ REVEAL <1540>.

KNOWLEDGE – 1 ***dêaʼ*** [noun: דֵּעַ <1843>; from KNOW <3045>] ▶ **This word means precise information, what one possesses intellectually, learning; it is possibly the masculine form of *dêʻāh* (<1844> below).** It is used only by Elihu in the book of Job, where it refers to Elihu's opinion that he was about to make known to Job and his three friends (Job 32:6, 10, 17); knowledge as brought in from a distance, perhaps from heaven, since Elihu has just claimed to speak for God (Job 36:3); and God's perfect knowledge demonstrated in the clouds and lightning (Job 37:16). The phrase "perfect in knowledge" occurs also in Job 36:4, apparently describing Elihu but using *dêʻāh* (<1844>). It might be thought that Elihu was using a more modest word in describing his own knowledge. The word *dêaʼ*, however, is also used to refer to God's knowledge (cf. 1 Sam. 2:3), and it is difficult to find any distinction of meaning between the two forms. ¶

2 ***dêʻāh*** [fem. noun: דֵּעָה <1844>; fem. of <1843> above] ▶ **This word comes from the verb *yāḏaʻ* <3045>, meaning to know, and is equivalent in meaning to the much more common form of this noun,**

da'at̲ **<1847>, also meaning knowledge.** This particular word refers to the knowledge within God (1 Sam. 2:3; Ps. 73:11). It also describes the knowledge of God that was known throughout the land (Is. 11:9) or taught either by God or by His faithful shepherds (Jer. 3:15). Other refs.: Job 36:4; Is. 28:9. ¶

3 ***da'at̲*** [fem. noun: דַּעַת <1847>; from KNOW <3045>] ▶ **This word means knowing, learning, discernment, insight, and notion.** It occurs forty of its ninety-one times in Proverbs as one of the many words associated with the biblical concept of wisdom. The root meaning of the term is knowledge or knowing. In Proverbs 24:3, 4, it is the third word in a chain of three words describing the building of a house by wisdom, the establishment of that house by understanding, and finally, the filling of the rooms of the house by knowledge. The word describes God's gift of technical or specific knowledge along with wisdom and understanding to Bezalel so he could construct the Tabernacle (Ex. 31:3; 35:31; cf. Ps. 94:10). It also describes the Israelites when they lacked the proper knowledge to please God (Is. 5:13; Hos. 4:6). God holds both pagan unbelievers and Israelites responsible to know Him. On the other hand, a lack of knowledge also describes the absence of premeditation or intentionality. That lack of knowledge clears a person who has accidentally killed someone (Deut. 4:42; Josh. 20:3, 5).

The word is also used in the sense of knowing by experience, relationship, or encounter. For example, Balaam received knowledge from the Most High who met him in a vision (Num. 24:16); the knowledge gained by the suffering Servant of Isaiah justified many people (Is. 53:11); and to truly know the Holy God leads to real understanding (Prov. 9:10). This moral, experiential knowledge of good and evil was forbidden to the human race in the Garden of Eden (Gen. 2:9, 17). But the Messiah will have the Spirit of understanding in full measure as the Spirit of the Lord accompanied Him (Is. 11:2).

The term is also used to indicate insight or discernment. God imparted discernment to the psalmist when he trusted in God's commands (Ps. 119:66). Job was guilty of speaking words without discernment (lit., words without knowledge, Job 34:35; 38:2).

God alone possesses all knowledge. No one can impart knowledge to God, for His knowledge, learning, and insight are perfect (Job 21:22); He alone has full knowledge about the guilt, innocence, or uprightness of a person (Job 10:7). God's knowledge of a human being is so profound and all-encompassing that the psalmist recognized that such knowledge is not attainable by people (Ps. 139:6).

Some knowledge is empty and useless (Job 15:2), but God's people and a wise person are marked by true knowledge of life and the divine (Prov. 2:5; 8:10; 10:14; 12:1). Knowledge affects behavior, for persons who control their speech have true knowledge (Prov. 17:27). While the preacher of Ecclesiastes admitted that knowledge may result in pain (Eccl. 1:18), he also asserted that having knowledge is, in the end, better, for it protects the life of the one who has it (Eccl. 7:12), and it is God's gift (Eccl. 2:26). *

4 ***maddā'*** [masc. noun: מַדָּע <4093>; from KNOW <3045>] ▶ **This word refers to the ability to gain knowledge by study and also to its resulting acquisition; it is also translated learning, thought.** Refs.: Dan. 1:4, 17. It is used of practical knowledge for administering a government (2 Chr. 1:10–12) and refers to something that has become known (Eccl. 10:20). ¶

5 ***manda'*** [Aramaic masc. noun: מַנְדַּע <4486>; corresponding to <4093> above] ▶ **This word means and is also translated reason, understanding, sanity. It is found only in Daniel.** When King Nebuchadnezzar was turned into an animal, he was said to have lost his reason and understanding. Upon his restoration to his human body, his mind was also restored (Dan. 4:36). Daniel himself was described as a man of understanding and knowledge with an excellent spirit (Dan. 5:12). Other refs.: Dan. 2:21; 4:34. ¶

KNOWN (BE WELL) – 1 Sam. 18:30 ➔ PRECIOUS (BE) <3365>.

KOA – ***qôaʻ*** [proper noun: קוֹעַ <6970>; prob. from SUMMER (verb) <6972> in the original sense of cutting off]: curtailment ▶ **A territory in Mesopotamia.** Ref.: Ezek. 23:23. ¶

KOHATH – ***qᵉhāṯ*** [masc. proper noun: קְהָת <6955>; from an unused root meaning to ally oneself]: allied ▶ **One of the three sons of Levi, along with Gershon and Merari.** Refs.: Gen. 46:11; Ex. 6:16. Among his descendants were Amram, Moses' father, and Jochebed, Moses' mother (Ex. 6:18; Num. 26:58–61). They took care of the sanctuary in the wilderness (Num. 3:28, 29; 4:1–20) and carried parts of it on their shoulders when traveling (Num. 7:9). Some of them rebelled against Moses (Num. 16:1) and were destroyed. They received Levitical cities to live in (Josh. 21:5, 20, 26). *

KOHATHITE – ***qᵉhāṯiy*** [proper noun: קְהָתִי <6956>; patron. from KOHATH <6955>] ▶ **The gentilic or ethnic form of the word Kohath <6955>.** This is indicated by the *iy* (י) on the end of the word, *iyṯ* (ית) that designates a woman. See KOHATH. *

KOL-HOZEH – See COL-HOZEH <3626>.

KOLAIAH – ***qôlāyāh*** [masc. proper noun: קוֹלָיָה <6964>; from VOICE <6963> and LORD <6950>]: voice of the Lord ▶
a. A Benjamite. Ref.: Neh. 11:7. ¶
b. The father of the false prophet Ahab. Ref.: Jer. 29:21. ¶

KOR – 1 Kgs. 4:22; 5:11; 2 Chr. 2:10; 27:5; Ezra 7:22; Ezek. 45:14 → COR <3734>.

KORAH – ***qōraḥ*** [masc. proper noun: קֹרַח <7141>; from SHAVE THE HEAD <7139>]: bald ▶
a. A son of Esau through his Canaanite wife Oholibamah, daughter of Anah and granddaughter of the Hivite, Zibeon. He was a chief or leader of Esau's descendants through Oholibamah (Gen. 36:5–18).
b. A chief or leader in Edom, the son of Eliphaz, Esau's oldest son—and grandson of Adah, his first Canaanite wife. Refs.: Gen. 36:15–16.
c. A Levite of the line of Kohath who rebelled against the leadership position of Moses in the wilderness wanderings. Refs.: Ex. 6:21, 24; Num. 16:1–49. He and his cohorts were "swallowed" up by an earthquake (Num. 16:28–35).
d. A descendent of Caleb through Hebron. Ref.: 1 Chr. 2:43. *

KORAHITE – ***qorḥiy*** [proper noun: קָרְחִי <7145>; patron. from KORAH <7141>] ▶ **A descendant of Korah, the son of Levi.** Refs.: Ex. 6:24; Num. 26:58; 1 Chr. 9:19, 31; 12:6; 26:1, 19; 2 Chr. 20:19. ¶

KORE – ***qôrê', qōrê'*** [masc. proper noun: קוֹרֵא, קֹרֵא <6981>; act. part. of CALL <7121>]: crier ▶
a. An ancestor of gatekeepers in David's day. Refs.: 1 Chr. 9:19; 26:1. ¶
b. A Levite under Hezekiah. Ref.: 2 Chr. 31:14. ¶

KOZ – ***qôṣ, haqqôṣ*** [masc. proper noun: קוֹץ, הַקּוֹץ <6976>; the same as THORN, THORNBUSH <6975>] ▶
a. A descendant of Caleb. Ref.: 1 Chr. 4:8. ¶
b. A proper noun designating Hakkoz, a priest returning from Babylonian exile. Refs.: 1 Chr. 24:10; Ezra 2:61; Neh. 3:4, 21; 7:63. ¶

KOZBI – Num. 25:15, 18 → COZBI <3579>.

KOZEBA – 1 Chr. 4:22 → COZEBA <3578>.

KUB – Ezek. 30:5 → CHUB <3552>.

KUN – 1 Chr. 18:8 → CHUN <3560>.

KUSHAIAH – ***qûšāyāhû*** [masc. proper noun: קוּשָׁיָהוּ <6984>; from the pass. part. of SNARE (LAY A) <6983> and LORD <3050>]: snare of the Lord ▶ **Father of Ethan, a Levite musician.** Ref.: 1 Chr. 15:17. ¶

L

LAADAH – ***la'dāh*** [masc. proper noun: לַעְדָּה <3935>; from an unused root of uncertain meaning] ▶ **Man of Judah, father of Mareshah.** Ref.: 1 Chr. 4:21. ¶

LABAN – ***lāḇān*** [proper noun: לָבָן <3837>; the same as WHITE <3836>]: white ▶
a. The brother of Rebekah, daughter of Bethuel, who was the son of Nahor, Abraham's brother. Refs.: Gen. 24:15, 16, 28–31. He and Bethuel permitted Rebekah to return with Abraham's servant to marry Isaac. He lived in northwest Mesopotamia (Aram Naha-raim) in the city of Nahor. Later, he arranged to his advantage Jacob's marriage with his daughters, first Leah and then Rachel, apparently requiring Jacob to labor fourteen years to get both wives (Gen. 29:14–30). He recognized Isaac and Jacob's God but maintained an idolatrous worship of other gods (Gen. 31:19–35) as well. He spoke at least some Aramaic (Gen. 31:47, Jegar Sahadutha, "witness pile"). Jacob and Laban were finally reconciled at Mizpah and made a covenant of respect and faith toward each other (Gen. 31:48–55). *
b. A location somewhere in the Sinai Desert or on the plains of Moab. Some believe it is the same place as Libnah (Num. 33:20, 21). ¶

LABOR (noun) – 1 ***y^e^giya'*** [masc. noun: יְגִיעַ <3018>; from WEARY (verb) <3021>] ▶ **This word indicates the performance of toil, physical or mental exertion toward a task; it denotes also the fruit of labor.** It refers to Jacob's toil for his father-in-law Laban (Gen. 31:42). It can refer to the products produced by the land and the labor expended on it (Deut. 28:33; Ps. 78:46; 109:11; 128:2; Hag. 1:11). In Nehemiah 5:13, it indicates the possessions (also translated property) obtained through one's labors (Ezek. 23:29). Human beings are the products of the labor of the Lord's hands (Job 10:3; also translated work). It may indicate all the tasks to be performed (Job 39:11; also translated heavy work). It is used of all the produce or production of a given nation (Is. 45:14; also translated products, wealth). It possibly indicates wages, as opposed to labor, which are spent unwisely in vain (Is. 55:2). It has the sense of efforts put forth in Hosea 12:8. Other refs.: Job 39:16; Jer. 3:24; 20:5. ¶
2 ***'āmāl*** [masc. sing. noun: עָמָל <5999>; from LABOR (verb) <5998>] ▶ **This word means trouble, toil. It can be used for the general difficulties and hardships of life.** This can be seen by its use in conjunction with sorrow (Jer. 20:18); affliction (Deut. 26:7; Ps. 25:18); and futility (Job 7:3). It can also refer to trouble or mischief directed at another person. The evil person talks of causing trouble (Prov. 24:2); and God cannot look at the trouble caused by sin (Hab. 1:3, 13). Its usage in Ecclesiastes and Psalms 105:44 and 107:12 is best rendered labor. The Teacher in Ecclesiastes repeatedly asked what benefit toil was (Eccl. 2:10, 11). *
– 3 Eccl. 1:8 ➔ full of labor ➔ WEARY (adj.) <3023> 4 Eccl. 8:16 ➔ TASK <6045> 5 Ps. 127:2; Prov. 5:10; 14:23 ➔ PAIN (noun) <6089> 6 Jer. 13:21 ➔ BIRTH (GIVE) <3205> b.

LABOR (HARD, FORCED) – Ex. 1:11; 2:11; 5:4, 5; 6:6, 7 ➔ BURDEN <5450>.

LABOR (verb) – 1 ***'āmal*** [verb: עָמַל <5998>; a prim. root] ▶ **This word means to toil. It refers to physical labor but is also used figuratively of God's building His house, His people.** Ref.: Ps. 127:1. It describes hunger working as a motivating force (Prov. 16:26). It is used of every possible kind of toil and labor in this life (Eccl. 1:3; 2:11; Jon. 4:10). *
2 ***š^e^ḏar*** [Aramaic verb: שְׁדַר <7712>; a prim. root] ▶ **This word means to exert oneself, to make every effort. It indicates strong efforts put forth to accomplish something.** Darius put forth every effort to rescue Daniel (Dan. 6:14). ¶
– 3 Josh. 7:3; Job 9:29; Prov. 23:4 ➔ WEARY (verb) <3021> 4 Job 20:18 ➔ that for which one labors ➔ FRUIT OF ONE'S TOIL <3022> 5 Eccl. 2:18, 22;

3:9; 4:8; 9:9 ➔ TOIL (noun and verb) <6001> 6 Is. 22:4 ➔ HASTEN <213>.

LABORER – 1 2 Chr. 34:13; Neh. 4:10 ➔ BURDEN-BEARER <5449> 2 Is. 58:3 ➔ WORKER <6092>.

LABOUR (noun) – Is. 58:3 ➔ WORKER <6092>.

LABOUR (verb) – Is. 22:4 ➔ HASTEN <213>.

LACE – Ex. 28:28, 37; 39:21, 31 ➔ CORD <6616>.

LACHISH – ***lāḵiyš*** [proper noun: לָכִישׁ <3923>; from an unused root of uncertain meaning] ▶ **Tell Lachish today witnesses to this large important city in the Shephelah or low hills of Judah. (Tell refers to a mound.) It is only about thirty miles west from Jerusalem and a few miles south.** It was first conquered by Joshua (Josh. 10:3–35; 12:11). Solomon fortified the city because it was a gateway and defense port for Jerusalem (2 Chr. 11:5–9). King Amaziah of Judah was killed in Lachish but buried in Jerusalem (2 Kgs. 14:17–20). Sennacherib, a great Assyrian king, besieged the city and conquered it (2 Kgs. 18:13–16). Nebuchadnezzar captured it again (Jer. 34:7; ca. 588 B.C.). The Jewish exiles resettled the city after 539 B.C. (Neh. 11:30). *

LACK – 1 Deut. 28:48, 57; Amos 4:6 ➔ WANT <2640> 2 Judg. 18:10; 19:19 ➔ NEED <4270>.

LACK, LACKING (BE) – ***'āḏar*** [verb: עָדַר <5737>; a prim. root] ▶ **This word means to be absent, to fall short; it is also translated to be missing, to be left, to remain, to fail.** It refers to something gone or missing, absent (1 Sam. 30:19); of people (2 Sam. 17:22); of food (1 Kgs. 4:27); of God's judgment (Is. 34:16); of the heavens God created (Is. 40:26); of truth (Is. 59:15). It is used of the fact that the Lord never falls short, never fails (Zeph. 3:5). The Hebrew word also means to keep rank, to help, to cultivate; see RANK (KEEP) <5737>, CULTIVATE <5737>. ¶

LACKING – 1 ***ḥāsêr*** [adj.: חָסֵר <2638>; from LACKING (BE) <2637>] ▶ **This word indicates in need of.** It can indicate a person who is lacking (1 Sam. 21:15). It can refer to some benefit or goodwill that is absent or lacking (1 Kgs. 11:22). One who "lacks heart" is deficient in understanding or character (Prov. 6:32; 7:7; 9:4; Eccl. 10:3). It refers to a person who lacks nothing he or she needs to enjoy life and security (Eccl. 6:2). * – 2 Deut. 28:48, 57 ➔ WANT <2640>.

LACKING (BE) – ***ḥāsêr*** [verb: חָסֵר <2637>; a prim. root] ▶ **This word indicates to be missing, to be absent; it also means to be needy, to decrease, to deprive.** In general, it refers to a failure of something to be fully complete, whole, sufficient (Ex. 16:18). It refers to a jar's being empty (of oil) (1 Kgs. 17:14). Psalm 23:1 indicates that the one whose shepherd is the Lord shall not lack. Used in a causative stem of the verb, it takes on the meaning of causing someone to lack something (Eccl. 4:8; Is. 32:6). The psalmist used the verb with *min* (FROM <4480>), thus, to indicate that a human being is less than (*min*), lower than (*min*) God (Ps. 8:5). It indicates a diminution of flood waters (Gen. 8:3, 5) or a diminution of numbers (Gen. 18:28). Other refs.: Deut. 2:7; 8:9; 15:8; 1 Kgs. 17:16; Neh. 9:21; Ps. 34:10; Prov. 13:25; 31:11; Eccl. 9:8; Song 7:2; Is. 51:14; Jer. 44:18; Ezek. 4:17. ¶

LACKING (WHAT IS) – ***ḥesrôn*** [masc. noun: חֶסְרוֹן <2642>; from LACKING (BE) <2637>] ▶ **This word indicates something that is absent; it is also translated that which is wanting (KJV).** It is used to refer to basic aspects of life and the world that are not present (Eccl. 1:15). ¶

LADAN – ***la'dān*** [masc. proper noun: לַעְדָּן <3936>; from the same as LAADAH <3935>] ▶
a. An Ephraimite. Ref.: 1 Chr. 7:26. ¶
b. A Gershonite. Refs.: 1 Chr. 23:7–9; 26:21. ¶

LADDER – ***sullām*** [masc. noun: סֻלָּם <5551>; from EXALT <5549> (in the sense of to build up, to lift up)] ▶ **This word refers in context to a series of steps, or treads, reaching from earth to heaven on which angels were ascending and descending. It was seen by Jacob in a dream and the Lord Himself stood at the top of this amazing avenue of communication.** Ref.: Gen. 28:12; NIV: stairway. ¶

LADE – Gen. 45:17 ➔ LOAD (verb) <2943>.

LADY – 1 Judg. 5:29; Esther 1:18 ➔ PRINCESS <8282> 2 Is. 47:5, 7 ➔ MISTRESS <1404>.

LAEL – ***lā'ēl*** [masc. proper noun: לָאֵל <3815>; from the prep. prefix and GOD <410>]: (belonging) to God ▶ **A Gershonite, father of Eliasaph.** Ref.: Num. 3:24. ¶

LAG – Deut. 25:18 ➔ FEEBLE (BE) <2826>.

LAHAD – ***lāhaḏ*** [masc. proper noun: לַהַד <3855>; from an unused root meaning to glow; comp. FLAME <3851> or STUDY (noun) <3854>]: glowing, earnest ▶ **Son of Jahath, a man of Judah.** Ref.: 1 Chr. 4:2. ¶

LAHMAM – Josh. 15:40 ➔ LAHMAS <3903>.

LAHMAS – ***laḥmās*** [proper noun: לַחְמָס <3903>; prob. by erroneous transcription for LACHMAM]: food ▶ **A city in Judah.** Ref.: Josh. 15:40. ¶

LAHMI – ***laḥmiy*** [masc. proper noun: לַחְמִי <3902>; from BREAD <3899>]: food ▶ **Brother of Goliath who was killed by Elhanan.** Ref.: 1 Chr. 20:5. ¶

LAID UP (BE) – Is. 23:18 ➔ HOARDED (BE) <2630>.

LAID WASTED – Is. 49:19 ➔ DESTRUCTION <2035>.

LAIR – 1 Ps. 10:9; Jer. 25:38 ➔ ABODE <5520> 2 Jer. 4:7 ➔ THICKET <5441> 3 Nah. 2:12 ➔ HOLE <2356> 4 Zeph. 2:15 ➔ RESTING PLACE <4769>.

LAISH – 1 ***lāwiš*** [masc. proper noun: לָוִשׁ <3889>; from KNEAD <3888> (comp. <3919> below: lion)]: kneading, lion ▶ **Father of Paltiel.** Ref.: 2 Sam. 3:15. ¶
2 ***layiš, layᵉšāh*** [proper noun: לַיִשׁ, לַיְשָׁה <3919>; the same as LION <3918>]: lion ▶ **a. A city in northern Israel.** Refs.: Judg. 18:6, 14, 27, 29. It was later renamed Dan (see DAN <1835>). ¶
b. Michal's father-in-law. Refs.: 1 Sam. 25:44; 2 Sam. 3:15. ¶
c. A village near Jerusalem. Ref.: Is. 10:30. ¶

LAKKUM – ***laqqûm*** [proper noun: לַקּוּם <3946>; from an unused root thought to mean to stop up by a barricade] ▶ **A place in Naphtali.** Ref.: Josh. 19:33. ¶

LAMB – 1 ***'immar*** [Aramaic masc. noun: אִמַּר <563>; perhaps from SAY <560> (in the sense of bringing forth)] ▶ **This word refers to the young sheep, along with other animals, supplied by the Persian kings, Darius and Artaxerxes, for the Temple being built in Jerusalem.** Refs.: Ezra 6:9; 7:17. Four hundred such lambs were offered at the dedication of the new Temple constructed in Jerusalem in 516 B.C. (Ezra 6:17). ¶
2 ***zeh*** [masc. noun: זֶה <2089>; by permutation for SHEEP <7716>] ▶ **This word indicates a young sheep taken from David's flock.** Ref.: 1 Sam. 17:34. ¶
3 ***ṭᵉlāh*** [masc. plur. noun: טְלָה <2922>; apparently from SPOTTED (BE) <2921> in the (original) sense of covering (for protection)] ▶ **This word refers to the Lord's people as young sheep for whom He is leader.** Ref.: Is. 40:11. ¶
4 ***ṭāleh*** [masc. noun: טָלֶה <2924>; by variation for <2922> above] ▶ **This word describes a suckling young sheep.** Ref.: 1 Sam. 7:9. Elsewhere, it denotes any lamb (Is. 40:11; 65:25) and describes God's people as lambs the Lord leads (Is. 40:11) or as lambs in the future new heavens and new earth which the Lord will create (Is. 65:25). ¶

5 ***kar*** [masc. noun: כַּר <3733>; from DANCE (verb) <3769> in the sense of plumpness] ▶ **This word means pasture, a young male sheep (a well-fed, frolicking lamb of the pasture), and a battering ram (an engine of war for assaulting the walls of besieged cities in the manner of a butting ram). When used to mean pasture, it describes a bountiful restoration for the Israelites.** Like sheep, they would have large pastures in which to graze (Is. 30:23); see also Psalm 37:20; 65:13. In reference to sheep, it means a male lamb as compared to ewes, lambs, or fatlings (1 Sam. 15:9). Tribute often came in the form of both ewes and rams, such as Mesha, king of Moab, paid to the king of Israel (2 Kgs. 3:4). This word also connotes a battering ram such as those used in siege warfare (Ezek. 4:2). It is also interpreted as a saddle (Gen. 31:34). *

6 ***kiśbāh*** [fem. noun: כִּשְׂבָּה <3776>; from SHEEP <3775>] ▶ **This word refers to a young female sheep.** Ref.: Lev. 5:6. It could be presented as a guilt offering. ¶

– 7 See SHEEP <3775>.

LAMB (EWE, FEMALE) – ***kibśāh, kabśāh*** [fem. noun: כִּבְשָׂה, כַּבְשָׂה <3535>; fem. of SHEEP <3532>] ▶ **This word refers to a young female sheep. This animal was valuable property and could be used as a gift to establish an oath.** Refs.: Gen. 21:28–30; 2 Sam. 12:3, 4, 6. It was used in certain sacrifices, such as cleansing a leper (Lev. 14:10); or in a Nazarite vow (Num. 6:14). ¶

LAMB (MALE) – See SHEEP <3532>.

LAME – 1 ***pisséaḥ*** [adj.: פִּסֵּחַ <6455>; from PASS OVER <6452>] ▶ **This word denotes a person who has a physical defect, an injured leg or foot, hindering a person's walking ability.** This disqualified a person for the priesthood (Lev. 21:18; 2 Sam. 9:13); or an animal for sacrifice (Deut. 15:21; Mal. 1:8, 13). Job had served as feet to the lame (Job 29:15). *

– 2 Gen. 49:6 ➔ HAMSTRING <6131> a. 3 2 Sam. 4:4; 9:3 ➔ CRIPPLED <5223> 4 Prov. 25:19 ➔ UNSTEADY <4154>.

LAME (BE) – Mic. 4:6, 7; Zeph. 3:19 ➔ LIMP <6760>.

LAME (BECOME) – 2 Sam. 4:4 ➔ PASS OVER <6452>.

LAMECH – ***lemek̲*** [masc. proper noun: לֶמֶךְ <3929>; from an unused root of uncertain meaning] ▶

a. A son of Methushael who married two women, the beginning of polygamy in the human race. Refs.: Gen. 4:18–24. He also displayed arrogance toward God and God's social restraints (Gen. 4:15, 16, 23, 24), as well as a lack of concern for harming another human being. ¶

b. The son of Methusalah, the oldest person recorded in the Bible. He was the father of Noah. He gave his son a name with prophetic significance, "rest," asserting that his son would give humankind rest from the labor and toil of God's curse on the ground (Gen. 5:25–31; 1 Chr. 1:3). ¶

LAMENT – 1 ***'ālāh*** [verb: אָלָה <421>; a prim. root, rather identical with CURSE (verb) <422> through the idea of invocation] ▶ **This word expresses sadness, regret; it is also translated to mourn, to wail.** It is used in Joel 1:8 to depict the mournful lament that needs to be made because of the coming devastation of the day of the Lord. ¶

2 ***'ānāh*** [verb: אָנָה <578>; a prim. root] ▶ **This word describes the despairing response of fishermen toward the loss of water in the Nile.** Ref.: Is. 19:8; also translated to mourn. Figuratively, it describes the hopeless reactions of the gates, the elders, of the cities of Judah at the judgment on them from the Lord (Is. 3:26). ¶

3 ***nāhāh*** [verb: נָהָה <5091>; a prim. root] ▶ **This word indicates weeping, showing deep sorrow and remorse for something or a situation; it is also translated to wail, to moan.** It is used in relation to the absence of the ark of the covenant from Jerusalem (1 Sam. 7:2); of the fall of a nation (Ezek. 32:18); especially God's chosen, Israel (Mic. 2:4). ¶

4 ***qûn, qiyn, qônên*** [verb: קוּן, קִין, קוֹנֵן <6969>; a prim. root] ▶ **This word means**

to present a dirge, a song, or a poem of lamentation and sorrow; it also means to chant, to mourn. It was presented over someone or an event (2 Sam. 1:17; 3:33). A lament (*qînāh*) was composed at Josiah's death by Jeremiah (2 Chr. 35:25). Ezekiel speaks of a lament sung for the fallen city of Tyre (Ezek. 27:32). Other refs.: Jer. 9:17; Ezek. 32:16. ¶
– 5 Judg. 5:28 ➔ CRY, CRY OUT <2980> 6 Ps. 5:1 ➔ MEDITATION <1901> 7 Is. 19:18; Lam. 2:8 ➔ MOURN <56> 8 Ezek. 9:4 ➔ GROAN (verb) <602> 9 Mic. 1:8 ➔ LAMENTATION <4553>.

LAMENTABLE – Dan. 6:20 ➔ TROUBLED <6088>.

LAMENTATION – 1 ***ᵃniyyāh*** [fem. noun: אֲנִיָּה <592>; from LAMENT <578>] ▶ **This word refers to an expression of sadness, of regret; it is also translated sorrow, mourning, moaning.** It functions with other words for mourning for emphasis (Is. 29:2; Lam. 2:5). In each usage, the Lord brings about the mourning over His city, Ariel, or Jerusalem. ¶
2 ***mispēḏ*** [masc. noun: מִסְפֵּד <4553>; from MOURN <5594>] ▶ **This word depicts wailing, mourning, lamenting.** It stands for deep, despairing emotional reactions by persons and animals at some calamity: the death of a patriarch (Gen. 50:10); the prospect of being slaughtered, annihilated (Esther 4:3); the opposite of dancing for joy (Ps. 30:11); at the approach of judgment from the Lord (Is. 22:12; Jer. 6:26; Amos 5:16, 17; Mic. 1:8); economic disaster (Ezek. 27:31). It is used of mourning for a person (Zech. 12:10, 11). Other refs.: Jer. 48:38; Joel 2:12; Mic. 1:11. ¶
3 ***qiynāh*** [fem. noun: קִינָה <7015>; from LAMENT <6969>] ▶ **This word refers to a lament, a funeral expression of sadness; a dirge.** It was a song or poem composed to recognize and to mourn the death of a person (2 Sam. 1:17; 2 Chr. 35:25); or of the people of a nation, especially Judah (Jer. 7:29). It lamented over even the cattle and lands of Israel (Jer. 9:10; Ezek. 2:10; Amos 5:1; 8:10). *
– 4 Jer. 31:15; Amos 5:16; Mic. 2:4 ➔ WAILING <5092> 5 Ezek. 31:15: to cause lamentation ➔ MOURN <56>.

LAMENTING – 1 Esther 4:3 ➔ LAMENTATION <4553> 2 Is. 29:2 ➔ MOURNING <8386> 3 Dan. 6:20 ➔ TROUBLED <6088>.

LAMP – 1 ***niyr, nêr, neyr*** [masc. noun: נִיר, נֵר, נֵיר <5216>; from a prim. root (see BREAK UP <5214>)] ▶ **This word referred to various sources of illumination.** The lamps of the Tabernacle (Ex. 27:20); the lamp in the Temple with Samuel (1 Sam. 3:3); the Word of God that lights the way (Ps. 119:105); and the noble wife that does not let her lamp go out at night (Prov. 31:18). The lamp can be used figuratively, as when God promised that David would always have a lamp before Him in Jerusalem (1 Kgs. 11:36; 2 Chr. 21:7). This word corresponds to the Aramaic noun *nûr* (<5135>), which can be masculine or feminine and means fire or flame. See the book of Daniel, where the fire does not harm the three Hebrews (see Dan. 3:27); and where fire describes the Ancient of Days (see Dan. 7:9, 10). *
– 2 Gen. 15:17; Judg. 7:16, 2; Job 12:5; Is. 62:1; Dan. 10:6; Ezek. 1:13 ➔ TORCH <3940> 3 Prov. 21:4 ➔ FALLOW GROUND <5215>.

LAMPSTAND – 1 ***mᵉnôrāh, mᵉnōrāh*** [fem. noun: מְנוֹרָה, מְנֹרָה <4501>; from BEAM <4500> (in the original sense of LAMP <5216>)] ▶ **This word refers to a stand, not the lamp itself. These were used to hold lamps or wicks and were in common use in a house.** Ref.: 2 Kgs. 4:10. Elaborate models were employed in the Tabernacle and the Temple (Ex. 25:31–35; 26:35; 30:27; 31:8; 1 Kgs. 7:49). It is used figuratively of Zerubbabel (Zech. 4:2, 11). *
2 ***neḇrᵉšāh*** [Aramaic fem. noun: נֶבְרְשָׁה <5043>; from an unused root meaning to shine] ▶ **This stand used oil and possibly wicks to produce its light; the word is also translated a candlestick in the KJV and certain other older translations, but**

actually refers to a lamp and lampstand. A royal lampstand was used in the palace at Babylon (Dan. 5:5). ¶

LANCE – [1] 1 Kgs. 18:28 ➔ SPEAR <7420> [2] Job 39:23; 41:29; Jer. 50:42 ➔ SPEAR <3591>.

LANCET – 1 Kgs. 18:28 ➔ SPEAR <7420>.

LAND – See EARTH <776>.

LAND (FERTILE, FRUITFUL) – 2 Chr. 26:10; Is. 10:18 ➔ FIELD (FERTILE, FRUITFUL, PLENTIFUL) <3759> a.

LAND APART, LAND INHABITED – Lev. 16:22 ➔ SOLITARY LAND <1509>.

LANDING – ***miprāṣ*** [masc. noun: מִפְרָץ <4664>; from BREAK OUT <6555> (in the sense of a break in the shore)] ▶ **This word describes a cove, a place for loading or unloading.** It depicts a place along a seashore where boats dock, load, and unload passengers and cargo (Judg. 5:17; also translated inlet, breach). ¶

LANDMARK – Jer. 31:21 ➔ GUIDEPOST <8564> a.

LANGUAGE – ***liššān*** [Aramaic common noun: לִשָּׁן <3961>; corresponding to TONGUE <3956>] ▶ **This word refers, literally, to the tongue of a person; it is found only in Daniel, where it is always used to mean verbal communication.** Refs.: Dan. 3:4, 7; 4:1; 5:19; 6:25; 7:14. There is perhaps one exception where it has the nuance of a "tongue that speaks anything offensive" (Dan. 3:29 NASB). ¶

LANGUAGE (OF STRANGE) – ***lā'az*** [verb: לָעַז <3937>; a prim. root] ▶ **This word means to speak in an incomprehensible foreign system of communication.** The term is used in a participial form to describe the Egyptians among whom the Hebrews lived for 430 years, a people who spoke a much different language (Ps. 114:1). See the verb *lā'ag* (MOCK <3932>) that appears to semantically overlap with this word. ¶

LANGUISH – [1] ***'āmal*** [verb: אָמַל <535>; a prim. root] ▶ **This word means to weaken, to deteriorate; it is also translated to become feeble, to wax feeble, to pine away, to wither, to fail.** It describes the languishing of a fertile woman with whom God has dealt harshly (1 Sam. 2:5). Metaphorically, it depicts the city gates of Judah languishing, i.e., her elders cry out at the cities' gates (Jer. 14:2). The crops of Moab languish in the fields under the Lord's judgment (Is. 16:8; Joel 1:10, 12). In a striking metaphor, the word depicts the hearts of His people pining away because they have committed spiritual prostitution (Ezek. 16:30). *

[2] ***lāhah, lāhāh*** [verb: לָהַהּ, לָהָה <3856>; a prim. root] ▶ **This word refers to the weakening and deterioration of a people because of hardship and oppression brought on by famine.** Ref.: Gen. 47:13; also translated to faint, to waste away. It has also the sense of to behave like a madman; see MADMAN <3856>. ¶

– [3] Is. 24:4 ➔ MOURN <56> [4] Jer. 31:12, 25 ➔ SORROW (verb) <1669>.

LANGUISHING – [1] Deut. 28:65 ➔ DESPAIR (noun) <1671> [2] Ps. 6:2 ➔ WEAK (adj.) <536> [3] Ps. 41:3 ➔ ILLNESS <1741>.

LAP (noun) – Neh. 5:13 ➔ BOSOM <2684>.

LAP (verb) – [1] ***lāqaq*** [verb: לָקַק <3952>; a prim. root] ▶ **This word indicates to drink something with quick movements of the tongue: to lap up, to lick. In its context in Judges, the text indicates lapping like a dog.** It refers to lapping up water like a dog (Judg. 7:5–7; 1 Kgs. 21:19; 22:38). In the 1 Kings references, dogs lick up Ahab's blood. ¶

– [2] Ezek. 17:6 ➔ HANG <5628>.

LAPIDATE – Ex. 8:26; 21:28; etc. ➔ STONE (verb) <5619>.

LAPIS LAZULI – Ex. 24:10; Ezek. 28:13; etc. ➔ SAPPHIRE <5601>.

LAPPIDOTH – ***lappiydôt*** [masc. proper noun: לַפִּידוֹת <3941>; fem. plur. of TORCH <3940>]: torches ▶ **Husband of the prophetess Deborah.** Ref.: Judg. 4:4. ¶

LAPSE – Ps. 40:4 ➔ TURN ASIDE <7750>.

LAPWING – Lev. 11:19; Deut. 14:18 ➔ HOOPOE <1744>.

LARGE – 1 2 Sam. 22:20; Ps. 18:19; 31:8; 118:5; Hos. 4:16 ➔ BREADTH <4800> 2 Ezra 5:8; 6:4 ➔ HUGE <1560> 3 Jer. 22:14 ➔ REFRESHED (BE) <7304>.

LASH – Job 5:21 ➔ WHIP <7752>.

LASHA – ***leša'*** [proper noun: לֶשַׁע <3962>; from an unused root thought to mean to break through]: fissure, boiling spring ▶ **A place east of the Dead Sea.** Ref.: Gen. 10:19. ¶

LAST – 1 ***'oḥ^orêyn*** [Aramaic adv.: אָחֳרֵין <318>; from ANOTHER <317>] ▶ **This word means in the end, finally, at length (literally: until afterwards).** Daniel came in before Nebuchadnezzar at the last, i.e., after a long series, all, of Babylon›s wise men had failed to interpret the dream (Dan. 4:8). ¶
– 2 Ex. 4:8; etc. ➔ NEXT <314>.

LAST HOUSE – ***bêyt hammerḥāq*** [phrase: בֵּית הַמֶּרְחָק <1023>; from HOUSE <1004> and FAR <4801> with the art. interposed]: house far away ▶ **Most translations treat this phrase as meaning last house (literally: house or remoteness), outskirts, a place that is far off, at the edge of the city.** It is listed by Strong as a proper noun (Beth-ham-Merchaq). David halted at this place on the edge of the city of Jerusalem, probably on the near side of the Kidron (cf. v. 23). Ref.: 2 Sam. 15:17. ¶

LAST TIME – See LATTER TIME <319>.

LATCH, LATCH-OPENING – Song 5:4 ➔ HOLE <2356>.

LATCHET – Gen. 14:23; Is. 5:27 ➔ STRAP <8288>.

LATER – Gen. 30:33 ➔ TOMORROW <4279>.

LATRINE – 1 ***maḥ^arā'āh*** [fem. noun: מַחֲרָאָה <4280>; from the same as DUNG <2716>] ▶ **This word means a place that serves as a toilet, a privy; it is also translated draught house, refuse dump.** Ref.: 2 Kgs. 10:27. ¶
– 2 2 Kgs. 10:27 ➔ GOING FORTH <4163>.

LATTER – Ex. 4:8; etc. ➔ NEXT <314>.

LATTER TIME – 1 ***'aḥ^ariyṯ*** [fem. noun: אַחֲרִית <319>; from BEHIND <310>] ▶ **This word means the end, last time.** Refs.: Gen. 49:1; Num. 23:10; 24:14, 20; Deut. 4:30; 8:16; 11:12; 31:29; 32:20, 29; Job 8:7; 42:12; Ps. 37:37, 38; 73:17; 109:13; 139:9; Prov. 5:4, 11; 14:12, 13; 16:25; 19:20; 20:21; 23:18, 32; 24:14, 20; 25:8; 29:21; Eccl. 7:8; 10:13; Is. 2:2; 41:22; 46:10; 47:7; Jer. 5:31; 12:4; 17:11; 23:20; 29:11; 30:24; 31:17; 48:47; 49:39; 50:12; Lam. 1:9; Ezek. 23:25; 38:8, 16; Dan. 8:19, 23; 10:14; 11:4; 12:8; Hos. 3:5; Amos 4:2; 8:10; 9:1; Mic. 4:1. ¶
2 ***'aḥ^ariyṯ*** [Aramaic fem. noun: אַחֲרִית <320>; from AFTER <311>, the same as BEHIND <310>] ▶ **This word is used to indicate the end time or last time(s).** It is rendered as latter days in Daniel (Dan. 2:28). ¶

LATTICE – 1 ***'ešnāḇ*** [masc. noun: אֶשְׁנָב <822>; apparently from an unused root (prob. meaning to leave interstices)] ▶ **This word describes the window with a crisscrossed frame through which Sisera's mother looked as she waited for her son.** Ref.: Judg. 5:28. It was more or less an empty hole in the wall. It was common in the walls of buildings located within villages (Prov. 7:6). ¶
2 ***ḥārāḵ*** [masc. noun: חָרָךְ <2762>; from ROAST <2760>] ▶ **This word refers to a**

structure of open crossed strips or bars of various materials such as wood or metal, perhaps a garden trellis. Ref.: Song 2:9. ¶ – 3 1 Kgs. 7:17 → NET <7638> 4 Is. 60:8 → WINDOW <699>.

LAUGH – 1 ***ṣāḥaq*** [verb: צָחַק <6711>; a prim. root] ► **This word is used as an expression of joy, merriment, humor, or scorn (properly: to laugh repeatedly); it also means to make jokes, to mock; to sport, to play.** It also can be used to mock or make light of something serious (Judg. 16:25); sometimes in jest (Gen. 19:14). It also expresses an attitude toward something that is claimed but seems impossible to realize, e.g., Abraham's and Sarah's laughing responses to God's promises (Gen. 17:17; 18:12, 13, 15). God can create laughter, joy, where otherwise there would be none (Gen. 21:6). It may refer to a display of playful marital affection (Gen. 26:8). It may have sexual, licentious overtones (Ex. 32:6). *
2 ***śāḥaq*** [verb: שָׂחַק <7832>; a prim. root] ► **This word refers to the expressing lively amusement (in merriment or derision); it means to celebrate; to rejoice; to mock.** It refers to a strong expression of joy: of celebration (Jer. 30:19); of making merry, rejoicing (2 Sam. 6:5, 21; Jer. 15:17); it means to play, to sport, to have fun (Ps. 104:26). But it is often used in a context where ridicule or mockery is directed at someone or something (Judg. 16:25). It is used in parallel with mocking (Prov. 1:26). Great kings mocked at lesser kings (Hab. 1:10). Samson was forced to serve as a tragic comedian for the Philistines (Judg. 16:27). It is used figuratively of wisdom personified, laughing, rejoicing at God's creation (Prov. 8:30, 31). The teacher taught that there is a time for genuine laughter (Eccl. 3:4). It has the sense of playing, enjoying life, in some contexts, especially in the prophet's vision of a restored people of God (Zech. 8:5). It means to sing and indicates singing women (1 Sam. 18:7). It means to play a sport, to hold a contest or a match (2 Sam. 2:14). In its causative stem, it means to cause laughter toward persons, to mock them (2 Chr. 30:10). *

LAUGHING MATTER – Hab. 1:10 → SCORN (noun) <4890>.

LAUGHINGSTOCK – 1 Gen. 38:23 → CONTEMPT <937> 2 Ex. 32:25 → DERISION <8103> 3 Ps. 44:1 → SHAKING OF THE HEAD <4493> 4 Ezek. 22:4 → MOCKERY <7048>.

LAUGHTER – 1 ***ṣeḥōq*** [masc. noun: צְחֹק <6712>; from LAUGH <6711>] ► **This word refers to the expression of happiness; it also refers to the expression of scorn.** It describes the act of laughing but also indicates the reason for the laughter (Gen. 21:6); or the object at which laughter is directed, e.g., Judah (Ezek. 23:32). ¶
2 ***śeḥôq, śeḥōq*** [verb: שְׂחוֹק, שְׂחֹק <7814>; from LAUGH <7832>] ► **This word refers to an expression of happiness; it also indicates ridicule, derision.** It refers to an expression of joy, humor, or relief usually (Job 8:21; Ps. 126:2); but laughter can be fabricated to deride and make fun of someone or something (Jer. 20:7; 48:26, 27, 39). The fool considers evil an object of laughter, humor, or even sport (Prov. 10:23; Eccl. 7:6; Lam. 3:14). Laughter can be only an outward façade with pain lying beneath it (Prov. 14:13). It does not really satisfy and may be deceptive (Eccl. 2:2); sorrow may be more beneficial (Eccl. 7:3). A meal often provides a setting for enjoyment, laughter (Eccl. 10:19). Other ref.: Job. 12:4. ¶

LAVER – 1 Ex. 30:18; 31:9; etc. → BASIN <3595> 2 1 Kgs. 7:37–39 → STAND (noun) <4350>.

LAVISH – ***zûl*** [verb: זוּל <2107>; a prim. root; comp. GLUTTON (BE) <2151>] ► **This verb means to give abundantly, to not spare; it is also translated to pour out.** It describes the act of providing gold to construct a useless idol (Is. 46:6). ¶

LAW – 1 ***dāṯ*** [fem. noun: דָּת <1881>; of uncertain (perhaps foreign) deriv.] ► **This word means edict, decree; an order enjoined publicly and nationally by an authority to direct the subjects of that**

authority. It is used to describe either a permanent rule that governed a nation or an edict sent out with the king's authority. The first meaning can be seen in Esther 1:13, 15, where the king counseled with those who knew the law (cf. Esther 3:8). The second meaning appears in the several occasions where King Ahasuerus (Xerxes) sent out a decree (Esther 2:8; 3:14, 15). At times, it is difficult to distinguish between these two meanings (Esther 1:8), for the edict of the king became a written law among the Persians (Esther 1:19). With several exceptions, this word occurs only in the book of Esther (Ezra 8:36; cf. debated Deut. 33:2). *

2 ***dāṯ*** [Aramaic fem. noun: דָּת <1882>; corresponding to <1881> above] ► **This word refers to a rule established by God or by a human authority. The decrees imposed by humans may agree more or less with God's Law, but God is always presented as controlling human rules.** The word describes God's changeless Law in Ezra 7:12 and Daniel 6:5. Elsewhere, it signifies a king's decree made in anger (Dan. 2:9, 13). In the case of the Medes and Persians, a king could make the law at his own will but could not change it even if it were wrong (Dan. 6:8, 12, 15). In Ezra 7:26, God's Law and the king's law coincide. In Daniel 7:25, a ruler was prophesied to speak against the Most High God and to set up laws in opposition to Him, but the ruler could only do so for a period of time set by God. *

3 ***tôrāh, tōrāh*** [fem. noun: תּוֹרָה, תֹּרָה <8451>; from SHOOT <3384> (in the sense of to teach, to instruct)] ► **This word means instruction, direction, rule, Torah, the whole Law. This noun comes from the verb *yārāh*, which has, as one of its major meanings, to teach, to instruct.** The noun means instruction in a general way from God; e.g., Eliphaz uttered truth when he encouraged Job and his readers to be willing to receive instruction from God, the Almighty (Job 22:22). In Israel, a father and mother were sources of instruction for life (Prov. 1:8; 6:20); along with wise persons (Prov. 13:14; 28:4). In contrast, rebellious people were not willing to accept God's instructions in any manner (Is. 30:8, 9); the scribes handled the instructions of the Lord deceitfully and falsely (Jer. 8:8). Various words are found in synonyms parallel with this term: It is paralleled by the sayings of the Holy One (Is. 5:24); the word of the Lord (Is. 1:10); and the testimony or witness (Is. 8:20). It is used regularly to depict priestly instructions in general or as a whole. The Lord rejected the priests of Israel for they had disregarded (lit., forgotten) the Law (Jer. 2:8; Hos. 4:6). They had been charged to carry out and teach all the instructions of the Lord (Deut. 17:11).

The term takes on the meaning of law in certain settings, although it is still currently debated about how to translate the various words that describe the laws, ordinances, commands, decrees, and requirements of the Lord. This word *tôrāh* is used as a summary term of various bodies of legal, cultic, or civil instructions. The word refers to the entire book of Deuteronomy and Moses' exposition of the Torah found in it (Deut. 1:5). By implication, the word here also refers to the laws given in Exodus, Leviticus, and Numbers. Numerous times this word refers to the whole Law of Moses, the Book of the Law of Moses, the Book of the Law of God, the Law of the Lord, and the Law of God given at Sinai (in order of titles listed, 1 Kgs. 2:3; Neh. 8:1; Josh. 24:26; Ps. 1:2; Neh. 10:28, 29). The kings of Israel were held to the standard of the Law of Moses (1 Kgs. 2:3; 2 Kgs. 10:31; 14:6; 23:25). The word can also refer to a single law, e.g., the law of the burnt offering (Lev. 6:9; 7:7; Neh. 12:44).

It is used of special laws for the Feast of Unleavened Bread (Ex. 13:9); the Passover (Ex. 12:49); of decisions by Moses (Ex. 18:16, 20); for the content of the Book of the Covenant (Ex. 24:12). The Law or Torah of God is pursued diligently by the psalmist; this word is found twenty-five times in Psalm 119 in parallel with various near synonyms. The word means the usual way, custom, or manner of God as David addressed his surprise to the Lord about the way He had dealt with him (2 Sam. 7:19). *

– 4 Is. 10:1 ➔ STATUTE <2711>.

LAWLESS – 2 Sam. 3:33 ➔ FOOLISH <5036>.

LAY, LAY CLAIM – 1 ***šāṯaṯ*** [verb: שָׁתַת <8371>; a prim. root] ▶
a. This word indicates that something is to be set or placed in a certain location. Ref.: Ps. 49:14. It is also translated in the phrase "to set one's mouth against," referring to an attitude of arrogance and harangue taken toward something (Ps. 73:9).
b. This word means to be appointed; to be destined. It indicates clearly that something is literally appointed or destined for something (Ps. 49:14).
c. This word means to lay claim (to assert one's right) to something. It indicates an arrogant claim of ownership or right with respect to something (Ps. 73:9). ¶
– 2 2 Sam. 19:32 (KJV) ➔ STAY (noun) <7871> 3 Ezra 6:3: to lay, to strongly lay, to firmly lay ➔ RETAIN <5446> 4 Esther 4:3 ➔ SPREAD (verb) <3331> 5 Job 38:6 ➔ SHOOT (verb) <3384> 6 Is. 38:21 ➔ APPLY <4799> 7 Lam. 3:28 ➔ OFFER <5190>.

LAY AWAY – Job 14:10 ➔ LAY LOW <2522>.

LAY BARE – Lev. 20:18, 19; Is. 3:17; Hab. 3:13; Zeph. 2:14 ➔ EMPTY (verb) <6168>.

LAY LOW – ***ḥālaš*** [verb: חָלַשׁ <2522>; a prim. root] ▶ **This word means to lie prostrate, to cause one to lie prostrate.** It means to weaken or overwhelm one's enemy in battle (Ex. 17:13: to overwhelm, to discomfit, to defeat, to overcome). It takes on the sense of to disappear, lying prostrate, dead, or totally weakened (Job 14:10; also translated to lay away, to lie prostrate, to waste away) when referring to an individual. The star of morning, the king of Babylon, was known as one who weakened, incapacitated the other nations of the world (Is. 14:12; also translated to weaken). ¶

LAY ON – ***sāmaḵ*** [verb: סָמַךְ <5564>; a prim. root] ▶ **This word indicates placing something on a person or animal, often in a ritualistic or legal setting; it means also to lean upon, to rest, to uphold, to support, to sustain.** A hand on a sacrificial animal (Ex. 29:10, 15, 19); hand(s) on a person to be punished (Lev. 24:14); or a hand on a person to be commissioned by the Lord (Num. 27:18, 23; Deut. 34:9); to lean against a wall with one's hand (Amos 5:19). It indicates figuratively God's wrath resting on someone (Ps. 88:7). It has the sense of supporting or sustaining someone (Gen. 27:37). The Lord upholds, supports, and sustains someone (Ps. 3:5; Is. 59:16; 63:5). In its passive participle, it describes a heart that is supported, sustained (Ps. 112:8). *

LAY OPEN – Hab. 3:13 ➔ EMPTY (verb) <6168>.

LAY UP – Ezra 6:1 ➔ BRING DOWN <5182>.

LAY, PUT – ***mišlôaḥ, mišlāḥ*** [masc. noun: מִשְׁלוֹחַ, מִשְׁלָח <4916>; from SEND FORTH <7971>] ▶
a. This word refers to sending, a stretching forth. It is used to refer to land and territory that covered and belonged to a nation (Is. 11:14; also translated to plunder). It has the meaning of sending out something, e.g., gifts (Esther 9:19, 22: to send, to give). ¶
b. The word also refers to an undertaking; putting forth. It refers to that which is covered or undertaken. In its context it is used with hand, the outstretching of a person's hand, what he or she is attempting to do (Deut. 12:7, 18; 15:10; 23:20; 28:8, 20). It has the sense of an area of land, a place, or a location that is covered or extended for some purpose, e.g., for pasturing (Is. 7:25; also translated sending fort, let loose, turned loose). ¶

LAYER, LYING – 1 ***niḏbāḵ*** [Aramaic masc. noun: נִדְבָּךְ <5073>; from a root meaning to stick] ▶ **This word refers to a single thickness of something, a stratum.** Ref.: Ezra 6:4 (also translated course). Layers of timber and stones were used in constructing the Temple. ¶
2 ***šᵉḵāḇāh*** [fem. noun: שְׁכָבָה <7902>; from LIE DOWN <7901>] ▶

a. This word refers to something forming a covering or a deposit over something else. E.g., a thin covering of dew over the ground (Ex. 16:13, 14).
b. This word also means the act of lying (in sexual relations); semen. It refers to semen, literally, a laying out of semen (Lev. 15:16–18, 32) which made a man unclean. It refers to sexual intercourse (Lev. 19:20; Num. 5:13). Other ref.: Lev. 22:4. ¶
– 3 Job 37:16: layers of tick clouds ➔ balancings of the clouds ➔ BALANCING <4657>.

LAYER OF FAT – Lev. 9:19; lit.: that which covers the entrails ➔ COVERING <4374>.

LAYING IN WAIT – Num. 35:20, 22 ➔ LYING IN WAIT <6660>.

LAZINESS – ***'aṣlāh*** [fem. noun: עַצְלָה <6103>; fem. of SLUGGARD <6102>] ▶ **This word means a state and attitude of sluggishness, of aversion or disinclination to work, activity, exertion; it is also translated slothfulness, indolence, sloth.** It destroys persons (Prov. 19:15); and their possessions (Eccl. 10:18). ¶

LAZY MAN – Prov. 13:4; 19:24; 20:4; 21:25; etc. ➔ SLUGGARD <6102>.

LEAD (noun) – ***'ôpereṯ, 'ōpereṯ*** [fem. noun: עוֹפֶרֶת, עֹפֶרֶת <5777>; fem. act. part. of FLING <6080> (in the sense of the dusty color of an object, e.g., lead)] ▶ **This word indicates a heavy metal.** It was a scarce but useful metal (Ezek. 27:12). It was used as a weight (Zech. 5:8). It is used figuratively of the way the Egyptians sank in the Red Sea, like lead (Ex. 15:10). It was used in some engraving processes (Job 19:24). It is used figuratively of the impurity of God's people (Jer. 6:29). It needed to be heated to remove its dross, as did God's people (Ezek. 22:18, 20). Other refs.: Num. 31:2; Zech. 5:7. ¶

LEAD (verb) – 1 ***nāhal*** [verb: נָהַל <5095>; a prim. root] ▶ **This word means to guide, to move along.** It means to move at a convenient speed and manner befitting travelers and their situations (Gen. 33:14; 47:17). It has the sense of guiding people, leading them in an orderly fashion and with great care (Ex. 15:13; 2 Chr. 28:15; Ps. 23:2; 31:3; Is. 40:11; 49:10; 51:18). Other ref.: 2 Chr. 32:22. ¶
2 ***nāḥāh*** [verb: נָחָה <5148>; a prim. root] ▶ **This word means to guide, usually in the right direction or on the proper path.** The verb sometimes occurs with a human subject (Ex. 32:34; Ps. 60:9; 108:10); however, it usually appears with the Lord as the subject (Gen. 24:27; Ex. 13:17; 15:13). This term is also used metaphorically to represent spiritual guidance in righteousness (Ps. 5:8; 27:11; 139:24). It also carries a connotation of treating kindly (Job 31:18); blessing (Ps. 23:3); deliverance (Ps. 31:3); protection (Ps. 61:2); or wisdom (Ps. 73:24). *
– 3 2 Sam. 6:3; 1 Chr. 20:1; etc. ➔ DRIVE <5090> a.

LEAD DOWN – Prov. 2:18 ➔ BOW DOWN <7743> a.

LEADER – 1 ***nāgiyḏ*** [masc. noun: נָגִיד <5057>; from TELL <5046>] ▶ **The word means a ruler, a prince; it is also translated captain, chief officer, commander, official in charge.** This term has a broad range of applications. At the top, it could allude to the king of Israel (1 Sam. 9:16; 13:14; 1 Kgs. 1:35); a ruler from a foreign land like Tyre (Ezek. 28:2); or Assyria (2 Chr. 32:21). It could also be used regarding cultic leaders and officials from the high priest down (1 Chr. 9:11, 20; 2 Chr. 31:12, 13; 35:8; Jer. 20:1). It could also be a label for various other lesser positions of leadership (1 Chr. 27:16; 2 Chr. 11:11, 22; 19:11; 29:10). The word is also used in an abstract sense to convey that which is princely, noble, and honorable (Prov. 8:6; also translated excellent, trustworthy). *
2 ***pera'*** [fem. noun: פֶּרַע <6546>; fem. of LOCK OF HAIR <6545> (in the sense of beginning)] ▶ **This specific singular form of the word is not used in the Hebrew Bible, but the related plural form is used;**

it means chiefs, commanders. In the song of Moses, the Lord proclaimed that He would overcome the enemy leaders (Deut. 32:42). See the Hebrew root *pāra'* [GO (LET) <6544>]. Other ref.: Judg. 5:2. ¶
– 3 Ex. 24:11 ➔ NOBLE <678> 4 Josh. 10:24; Judg. 11:6, 11; etc. ➔ CAPTAIN <7101> 5 1 Kgs. 21:8, 11 ➔ NOBLE <2715> 6 1 Chr. 26:6 ➔ DOMINION <4474> 7 Is. 14:9; etc. ➔ GOAT <6260> 8 Jer. 25:34–36 ➔ MIGHTY <117> 9 Ezek. 38:13 ➔ LION (YOUNG) <3715> b.

LEADING MAN – 2 Kgs. 24:15 ➔ BODY <193> b., MIGHTY <352>.

LEAF – 1 ***'āleh*** [masc. noun: עָלֶה <5929>; from OFFER <5927> (as coming up, e.g., a leaf on a tree] ► **This word refers to a flat structure on a stem produced by a tree; collectively: greenery, leaves, or foliage on trees or shrubs; it also signifies a branch.** Refs.: Gen. 3:7; 8:11; Neh. 8:15. Ezekiel speaks of leaves of healing (Ezek. 47:12); and Isaiah of fading leaves (Is. 1:30; 34:4). Proverbs employs a (flourishing, green) leaf as a symbol of a righteous person (Prov. 11:28). *
2 ***ᵓpiy*** [Aramaic masc. noun: עֳפִי <6074>; corresponding to BRANCHES <6073>] ► **This word is used of the foliage and branches put forth by the great symbolic tree of Nebuchadnezzar's dream.** Refs.: Dan. 4:12, 14, 21. The foliage is described as beautiful, splendid (*šappîr*). ¶

LEAFY – ***'āḇōṯ*** [adj.: עָבֹת <5687>; from WEAVE <5686>] ► **This word means thick with leaves, dense with leaves.** It refers to a tree loaded with leaves, that sends out a huge amount of foliage (Lev. 23:40; Neh. 8:15). These trees were used as places of apostate, pagan worship (Ezek. 6:13; 20:28). ¶

LEAH – ***lê'āh*** [fem. proper noun: לֵאָה <3812>; from WEARY (BE) <3811>]: weary ► **This word designates the first wife of Jacob, given to him by Laban in an act of deception.** She was Laban's daughter, an Aramean. She bore to Jacob Reuben, Simeon, Levi, Judah, Issachar, and Zebulun. Her maidservant Zilpah bore Gad and Asher (Gen. 35:23–26). Refs.: Gen. 29:16, 17, 23–25, 30–32; 30:9–14, 16:20; 31:4, 14, 33; 33:1, 2, 7; 34:1; 46:15, 18; 49:31; Ruth 4:11. ¶

LEAK – ***dālaḇ*** [verb: דָּלַף <1811>; a prim. root] ► **This word means to drop, to drip; e.g., a house drips, or leaks, because cracks in the roof are not mended; an eye weeps, or drops, tears.** Ref.: Eccl. 10:18; KJV: to drop through. It describes an eye weeping before God (Job 16:20: to pour out *tears*, to weep). Figuratively, it denotes a person weeping in grief (Ps. 119:28: to weep, to melt, to be weary). ¶

LEAN (adj.) – 1 ***rāzeh*** [adj.: רָזֶה <7330>; from LEAN (GROW) <7329>] ► **This word is an antonym of fat and means having little fat, skinny, thin, unproductive. It describes land as lean; i.e., without fertile soil to produce an abundance of crops, trees, shrubs.** Ref.: Num. 13:20; also translated poor. It refers figuratively to the strong in a society, the powerful, and those who oppress the weak (Ezek. 34:20). ¶
2 ***raq*** [adj.: רַק <7534>; from SPIT (verb) <7556> (in its original sense of diffusing)] ► **This word means skinny; it is also translated thin, gaunt.** It refers to emaciated, skinny cows from drought conditions seen in Pharaoh's dreams (Gen. 41:19, 20, 27). ¶

LEAN (GROW, BECOME, WAX) – 1 ***rāzāh*** [verb: רָזָה <7329>; a prim. root] ► **This word means to starve, to waste away.** It indicates the wasting away of healthy flesh, fatness as a result of God's judgments (Is. 17:4). It is used figuratively of God starving, destroying the gods of the nations (Zeph. 2:11; also translated to famish, to reduce to nothing). ¶
– 2 Is. 17:4 ➔ BRING LOW <1809>.

LEAN (verb) – 1 ***rāpāq*** [verb: רָפַק <7514>; a prim. root] ► **This word means to support oneself; to lean on, to rest on.** It means to find support from someone by leaning on him or her, especially a bridegroom or a beloved friend (Song 8:5). ¶

2 *šā'an* [verb: שָׁעַן <8172>; a prim. root] ► **This word means to rely, to support oneself. This verb is found only in the passive form, but it is active in meaning.** In its simplest meaning, it refers to leaning on things for support, such as trees (Gen. 18:4) and pillars (Judg. 16:26). The idea conveyed here is simply that of resting one's weight against something to give it support, but not all things leaned on will actually support (Job 8:15). This verb is also used in the sense of a king leaning or relying on his closest friends and advisors. This may mean literally leaning on someone's arm or trusting in his or her counsel (2 Kgs. 5:18; 7:2, 17). Leaning on can also mean trusting in persons, whether it be God (Mic. 3:11); other people (Ezek. 29:7); or oneself (Prov. 3:5). Ultimately, God should be trusted and leaned on, for He will never fail. *

LEANNESS – 1 *rāzôn* [masc. noun: רָזוֹן <7332>; from LEAN (GROW) <7329>] ► **This word refers to weakness, frailty, lack of strength; it is also translated wasting disease, wasting sickness.** It is used with respect to one's soul, life (Ps. 106:15; also translated a wasting disease); or to the deterioration of one's fatness, health (Is. 10:16). It indicates a reduced measure (ephah) used in business that is employed unfairly (Mic. 6:10: scant, short). ¶

2 *rāziy* [masc. noun: רָזִי <7334>; from LEAN (GROW) <7329>] ► **This word also indicates a wasting away.** It is used only in the expression *razî-lî, razî-lî.* Its meaning is not certain in Isaiah 24:16: "leanness to me" (KJV, NKJV); "woe to me, woe to me" (NASB); "I waste away" (NIV, ESV). ¶

– 3 Job 16:8 → LIE (noun) <3585>.

LEANNOTH – Psalm 88 (title) → ANSWER (verb) <6030> c.

LEAP – 1 *dālag* [verb: דָּלַג <1801>; a prim. root] ► **This word means to jump or jump over.** Ref.: Zeph. 1:9; in this instance, it was part of a pagan ritual act. It is an ability restored to the lame in the time of Zion's restoration (Is. 35:6). It is used figuratively in David's claim to leap over a wall with the Lord's help (2 Sam. 22:30; Ps. 18:29); also translated to scale. It is used of the joyous jumping and leaping of a groom coming to his bride (Song 2:8; also translated to climb). ¶

2 *zānaq* [verb: זָנַק <2187>; a prim. root] ► **This word means to spring, to jump forth.** It depicts Dan's action coming forth or leaping forth from Bashan, thus depicting a characteristic of Dan's nature (Deut. 33:22). ¶

3 *nāṯar* [verb: נָתַר <5425>; a prim. root] ► **This word indicates to jump, to startle, to make tremble.** It refers to the ability of certain insects to jump, leap; insects Israel could eat (Lev. 11:21; also translated to hop). It describes a rapid rush of the heartbeat at God's presence in nature (Job 37:1; also translated to move out); or His actions toward the nations that startle or shock them (Hab. 3:6: to startle, to drive asunder, to make tremble, to shake). The Hebrew word also means to loosen, to release; see LOOSE (LET) <5425>. ¶

– 4 2 Sam. 6:16 → AGILE (MAKE) <6338> b. 5 1 Chr. 15:29; Ps. 29:6; 114:4, 6; Is. 13:21; Joel 2:5 → DANCE (verb) <7540> 6 Job 41:22 → DANCE (verb) <1750> 7 Ps. 68:16 → ENVY (LOOK WITH, GAZE IN, FUME WITH) <7520> b. 8 Mal. 4:2 → FROLIC <6335> a.

LEAP DOWN – Song 4:1; 6:5 → DESCEND <1570>.

LEARN – 1 *'ālaḇ* [verb: אָלַף <502>; a prim. root, to associate with] ► **The meaning of this word apparently derives from a noun meaning association, familiarity, which leads to knowledge, learning. The verb also means, in a causative sense, to teach.** This root idea appears in Proverbs 22:25 where association with an angry man causes one to learn his ways. Other usages mean to teach without obvious reference to learning by association (Job 15:5; 33:33; 35:11). ¶

2 ***lāmad̲*** [verb: לָמַד <3925>; a prim. root] ▶ **This word means, to study, to teach, to be taught, to be learned.** The verb describes learning war, training for war, the lack of training (Is. 2:4; Mic. 4:3), or the acquisition of instruction (Is. 29:24). God's people were warned not to learn the ways of the nations, i.e., to acquire their corrupt and false practices and standards (Jer. 10:2) but to learn the ways of God instead (Jer. 12:16). The verb is sometimes used with an infinitive following it suggesting the meaning to learn to do something. Israel was not to learn to do the abominations of surrounding nations (Deut. 18:9); it describes metaphorically the actions of Jehoahaz against his countrymen as he tore them as a lion would tear its prey (Ezek. 19:3).

In the intensive or factitive form, the root takes on the meaning of imparting learning (i.e., teaching). The verb simply means to teach (2 Chr. 17:7, 9) or to teach people or things; the Lord taught His people (Jer. 31:34) His decrees and laws (Deut. 4:1). The participle of this form often means teacher (Ps. 119:99).

The passive forms of this verb mean to be teachable or to be knowledgeable or well-trained by the Lord (Jer. 31:18) or people (Is. 29:13). *

LEARNED – Is. 50:4 ➔ ACCUSTOMED <3928>.

LEARNING – **1** ***leqaḥ*** [masc. noun: לֶקַח <3948>; from TAKE <3947> (in the sense of something received)] ▶ **This word means something received, instruction; it is also translated teaching, doctrine, precepts, persuasiveness.** Having this basal sense, the word's usage can be divided further into three categories, each with its own distinctive variation of meaning. First, the word can signify the learning, insight, or understanding that a person receives, perceives, or learns through an instructor or some other means (Prov. 1:5; 9:9; Is. 29:24). The second variation is similar to the first, yet only slightly different in that it arises from the perspective of the one dispensing the knowledge (i.e., a teacher or instructor), rather than that of the learner. It describes that which is being communicated to others, therefore giving the sense of teaching, instruction, or discourse (Deut. 32:2; Prov. 4:2). Finally, the term seems to have the force of persuasive speech, whether for a positive or a deceitful intent (Prov. 7:21: enticing speech, fair speech, seductive speech, persuasions, persuasive words; 16:21). Other refs.: Job 11:4; Prov. 16:23. ¶

– **2** Dan. 1:4, 17 ➔ KNOWLEDGE <4093>.

LEAVE – **1** ***'āzab̲*** [verb: עָזַב <5800>; a prim. root] ▶ **This word can be used to designate going away to a new locale (2 Kgs. 8:6); or to separate oneself from another person (Gen. 44:22; Ruth 1:16).** When Zipporah's father found her without Moses, he asked, "Why did you leave him?" (Ex. 2:20). A man is to leave his parents to marry (Gen. 2:24). To leave in the hand of is an idiomatic expression meaning to entrust (Gen. 39:6). The word can also carry a much more negative connotation. Israelites abandoned their towns after the army fled (1 Sam. 31:7); the ultimate sign of defeat (and often God's judgment) were abandoned cities (Is. 17:9; Jer. 4:29; Zeph. 2:4). The Israelites often were warned and accused of forsaking God by sacrificing to other gods (Deut. 28:20; Judg. 10:10; Jer. 1:16). The prophets called on them to forsake idols and sin instead (Is. 55:7; Ezek. 20:8; 23:8). While the psalmist said that God would not abandon his soul (Ps. 16:10), God does on occasion abandon humans because of their sin (Deut. 31:17; Ezek. 8:12). But despite the psalmist's cry which Jesus quoted from the cross (Ps. 22:1), most Biblical writers took heart because God would not abandon them (Ezra 9:9; Is. 42:16). The word *'āzab̲* can also mean to restore or repair. It occurs only in Nehemiah 3:8 in reference to the walls of Jerusalem. *

– **2** 1 Sam. 17:20; Ps. 27:9 ➔ FORSAKE <5203> **3** Song 5:6 ➔ WITHDRAW <2559> **4** Zeph. 3:3 ➔ BREAK <1633> b.

LEAVE, LEAVE ALONE – ***šᵉbaq*** [Aramaic verb: שְׁבַק <7662>; corresponding to the root of SHOBEK <7733> (to leave)] ▶ **This word indicates to not interfere, to let alone.** It refers to not bothering or disturbing something (Dan. 4:15, 23, 26), to letting something remain as it is. It means to not become involved in or interfere with persons (Ezra 6:7). In its passive use, it means to leave something to another person or people, to change hands of rulership (Dan. 2:44). ¶

LEAVEN – 1 ***ḥāmêṣ, maḥmeṣeṯ*** [masc. noun: חָמֵץ, מַחְמֶצֶת <2557>; from LEAVENED (BE) <2556>] ▶ **This Hebrew word refers particularly to yeast that causes bread to rise. Bread was made without leaven when Israel went out of Egypt because there was not enough time to leaven it.** Thus, unleavened bread is known as "the bread of affliction" and is eaten the week after Passover as a celebration of the Exodus (Deut. 16:3). Leaven was later used in offerings (Lev. 7:13; 23:17) but was not allowed to be burned (Lev. 2:11). In Amos 4:5, leaven is associated with hypocrisy and insincerity, an association made more explicitly in the New Testament (Luke 12:1; 1 Cor. 5:6–8). *

2 ***śᵉ'ōr*** [masc. noun: שְׂאֹר <7603>; from REMAIN <7604>] ▶ **This word refers to a fungus that ferments sugars; it is also translated yeast. It is used to cause dough to rise and in other kinds of food productions.** It was not used in the unleavened bread of the Passover Feast (Ex. 12:15, 19; 13:7; Deut. 16:4); and it was forbidden in grain offerings (Lev. 2:11). ¶

LEAVENED (BE) – ***ḥāmêṣ*** [verb: חָמֵץ <2556>; a prim. root] ▶ **In connection with the Exodus from Egypt, the Israelites were told not to leaven the bread before their departure, i.e., not to mix yeast in the dough.** Refs.: Ex. 12:34, 39. In Hosea 7:4, the prophet used the image of a baker kneading dough until it was leavened. This verb was also used metaphorically to refer to the heart being soured or embittered (Ps. 73:21; also translated to be grieved). The word is translated cruel, ruthless in Psalm 71:4.

Another root, spelled exactly the same, is listed under this entry by Strong. It occurs in Isaiah 63:1 and means to be stained red; it is translated dyed, stained crimson, crimsoned. ¶

LEAVES – Ezek. 17:9 → PREY <2964>.

LEB-KAMAI – Jer. 51:1 → LIBNITE <3846> b.

LEBANAH – ***lᵉḇānāh*** [masc. proper noun: לְבָנָה <3838>; the same as MOON <3842>]: whiteness, moon ▶ **Some members of his family returned from the Babylonian captivity.** Refs.: Ezra 2:45; Neh. 7:48. ¶

LEBANON – ***lᵉḇānôn*** [proper noun: לְבָנוֹן <3844>; from WHITE (MAKE) <3835>]: white ▶ **A beautiful mountainous territory north of Israel. Its white, snow capped peaks and the white limestone of its mountains are associated with its name.** It paralleled the coast of the Mediterranean from roughly the Leontes River to the Eleutherus River. The range of mountains is about one hundred miles long. Its cedars were famous for their size, beauty, and use as building materials (Judg. 9:15; 1 Kgs. 5:6; Ps. 104:1, 16; Song 5:3, 15). The great strength of the cedar became legendary as well. *

LEBAOTH – ***lᵉḇā'ôṯ*** [proper noun: לְבָאוֹת <3822>; plur. of LION <3833>]: lionesses ▶ **A city at the extreme south of Judah.** Ref.: Josh. 15:32. ¶

LEBONAH – ***lᵉḇônāh*** [proper noun: לְבוֹנָה <3829>; the same as INCENSE <3828>]: frankincense ▶ **A town near Shiloh, north of Bethel.** Ref.: Judg. 21:19. ¶

LECAH – ***lêḵāh*** [proper noun: לֵכָה <3922>; from GO <3212>]: journey ▶ **According to the context, a village in Judah.** Ref.: 1 Chr. 4:21. ¶

LEDGE – 1 ***ᵃzārāh*** [fem. noun: עֲזָרָה <5835>; from HELP (verb) <5826> (in its original meaning of surrounding)] ▶ **This**

Hebrew word indicates an enclosure, a courtyard; it is also translated court. It indicates some kind of enclosure, a rail or edging around an object (Ezek. 43:14, 17, 20; 45:19; KJV: settle); or an enclosed area, a courtyard or court area (2 Chr. 4:9b; 6:13). ¶
2 ***karkōḇ*** [masc. noun: כַּרְכֹּב <3749>; expanded from the same as CABBON <3522>] ▶ **This word indicates a rim, an edge; KJV: compass.** It is used to describe a ledge or border around the edge of the bronze altar (Ex. 27:5; 38:4). The grating of the altar was located beneath the ledge. ¶
– 3 1 Kgs. 7:28, 29 ➔ FRAME <7948> 4 Ezek. 46:23 ➔ CAMP <2918>, ROW (noun) <2905>.

LEDGE (NARROW, NARROWED, OFFSET) – ***migrā'āh*** [fem. noun: מִגְרָעָה <4052>; from REDUCE <1639>] ▶ **This word means a recess.** It is a technical architectural term indicating a ledge, a rebatement of a wall, or offsets for timbers to rest on (1 Kgs. 6:6; also translated offset, narrowed rest). ¶

LEECH – ***ᵃlûqāh*** [fem. noun: עֲלוּקָה <5936>; fem. pass. part. of an unused root meaning to suck] ▶ **This is a blood-sucking worm-like creature.** According to Proverbs, it is never satisfied (Prov. 30:15; as spelled in the KJV: horseleach). ¶

LEES – Is. 25:6; Zeph. 1:12 ➔ DREGS <8105>.

LEFT – ***śᵉmō'wl, śᵉmō'l*** [masc. noun: שְׂמֹאול, שְׂמֹאל <8040>; a prim. word] ▶ **This word means left hand, left side (the sinistral side), north (i.e., when facing east).** It indicates directions to the left (Gen. 13:9; Ex. 14:22). It indicates northward in some contexts: with *'el* preceding (Josh. 19:27); by itself (Is. 54:3); with *'el* preceding and with a suffix, it means north of (suffix) (Ezek. 16:46). With *yaḏ* preceding the phrase, it means left hand (Judg. 3:21; 7:20; Jon. 4:11). The word takes suffixes, e.g., *ś 'mō'lô* means his left hand (Gen. 48:13, 14). Traditionally, the direction left meant wrong, bad, evil (Eccl. 10:2). To raise both the left and right hand toward heaven was part of a ritual for making a vow to God (Dan. 12:7). *

LEFT (BE) – 2 Sam. 17:22 ➔ LACK, LACKING (BE) <5737>.

LEFT (GO TO THE) – ***śim'ēl*** [verb: שְׂמְאֵל <8041>; a prim. root] ▶ **This word indicates movement to the left, toward the left hand (i.e., sinistral movement).** Refs.: Gen. 13:9; Ezek. 21:16. It is used of turning left or right, i.e., deviating from a given path or set of instructions (2 Sam. 14:19; Is. 30:21). It indicates the use of one's left hand (1 Chr. 12:2). ¶

LEFT, LEFT OVER – ***'āḏap*** [verb: עָדַף <5736>; a prim. root] ▶ **This word means to remain over, to be in excess.** It refers to whatever is left, the remains: quails (Ex. 16:23); part of a curtain (Ex. 26:12, 13); a balance or remainder of money paid (Lev. 25:27); persons, specifically firstborn Israelites (Num. 3:46, 48, 49). *

LEFT, ON THE LEFT – ***śᵉmā'liy*** [adj.: שְׂמָאלִי <8042>; from LEFT <8040>] ▶ **This word means situated on the left (i.e., sinistral) side as opposed to the right side; it also means the north. In Israel for a person facing east, the left was literally toward the north.** It defines the left palm or hand as opposed to the right (Lev. 14:15, 16, 26, 27). The left pillar, the north pillar of the Temple, was named Boaz, in it is power (1 Kgs. 7:21). A house may have a left side (2 Kgs. 11:11). The prophet was commanded to lie on his left side (Ezek. 4:4). Other refs.: 2 Chr. 3:17; 23:10. ¶

LEFT-HANDED – ***'iṭṭēr*** [adj.: אִטֵּר <334>; from CLOSE <332>] ▶ **This word literally describes a person bound or restricted as to the use of the right hand, hence one using mainly the left hand.** Ehud, a judge in Israel, was left-handed (Judg. 3:5). Seven hundred left-handed stone slingers, who were considered especially skilled, are mentioned as part of the tribe of Benjamin (Judg. 20:16). ¶

LEG – [1] ***kᵉraʻ*** [masc. noun: כְּרַע <3767>; from BOW (verb) <3766>] ▶ **This word refers to the lower limb.** The fibula bone of the Passover lamb (Ex. 12:9); a sacrificial ram (Ex. 29:17); and various sacrificial offerings (Lev. 1:9, 13; 4:11; 8:21; 9:14). It is used of a locust's legs (Lev. 11:21). Other ref.: Amos 3:12. ¶
[2] ***šôq*** [masc. noun: שׁוֹק <7785>; from OVERFLOW (verb) <7783>] ▶ **This word means a lower limb, a hip; a thigh (or shoulder) of a sacrificial animal.** It refers to the thigh or right leg portion of a sacrificial animal (Ex. 29:22, 27; Lev. 7:32–34; 8:25, 26; 9:21; Num. 6:20; 1 Sam. 9:24). It is used to refer to the entire leg or legs of a person (Deut. 28:35; Prov. 26:7; Is. 47:2). *
[3] ***šāq*** [Aramaic masc. noun: שָׁק <8243>; corresponding to <7785> above] ▶ **This word refers to the iron leg(s) of the great statue in the king's dream.** Ref.: Dan. 2:33. ¶
– [4] Is. 47:2 ➔ SKIRT <7640> [5] Dan. 5:6 ➔ his legs became weak ➔ the joints of his loins were loosed ➔ LOINS <2783>.

LEG ORNAMENT – Is. 3:20 ➔ MARCHING <6807> b.

LEHABITES – ***lᵉhāḇiym*** [masc. proper noun: לְהָבִים <3853>; plur. of FLAME <3851>]: flames ▶ **People of Egyptian origin or incorporated to the Egyptians.** Refs.: Gen. 10:13; 1 Chr. 1:11. ¶

LEHI – ***leḥiy*** [proper noun: לֶחִי <3896>; a form of JAW <3895>]: jawbone ▶ **A place in Judah where Samson killed 1,000 Philistines with a fresh jawbone.** Refs.: Judg. 15:9, 14, 19. ¶

LEISURE – Gen. 33:14: at my leisure ➔ SLOWLY <328>.

LEISURELY WALK – Deut. 33:25 ➔ STRENGTH <1679>.

LEMUEL – ***lᵉmû'ēl, lᵉmô'ēl*** [masc. proper noun: לְמוּאֵל, לְמוֹאֵל <3927>; from FOR <3926> and GOD <410>]: (dedicated) to God ▶ **A king who recalled the instructions taught by his mother.** Refs.: Prov. 31:1, 4. He is the author of Proverbs 31. ¶

LEND – [1] ***nāšāh, nāšā'*** [verb: נָשָׁה, נָשָׁא <5383>; a prim. root; it is rather identical with FORGET <5382>, in the sense of DEBT (BE IN) <5378>] ▶ **This word means to advance money; it also means to borrow. The word here is spelled with *he* (ה) instead of *aleph* (א). It means to let a person have a loan, to use the owner's money for a time.** Refs.: Ex. 22:25; Deut. 24:10, 11. Loans were canceled, released in the sabbatical years and in the Year of Jubilee (Deut. 15:2). In its participle form, it indicates a creditor, a person who had extended a loan (2 Kgs. 4:1; Ps. 109:11). Food and other items were loaned, as well as money (Neh. 5:7, 10, 11; also translated to exact). Other refs.: Is. 24:2: creditor, taker of usury; 50:1: creditor; Jer. 15:10: lend, lend on usury, lend for interest. ¶
[2] ***'āḇaṭ*** [verb: עָבַט <5670>; a prim. root] ▶ **This word means to advance money, to borrow, to take a pledge from.** It refers to extending credit to someone, to a people or nations (Deut. 15:6: to lend and to borrow, 8; 24:10: to collect, to fetch, to get, to take). A pledge was usually taken as collateral for the loan. The Hebrew word also means to swerve, to deviate; see SWERVE <5670>. ¶
– [3] Deut. 23:19, 20 ➔ BITE <5391> b.

LENGTH – ***'ōreḵ*** [masc. noun: אֹרֶךְ <753>; from PROLONG <748>] ▶ **This word is a measure of distance between two points; it also means long.** It is primarily used in describing physical measurements, e.g., Noah's ark (Gen. 6:15) and the land (Gen. 13:17). It is also used for the qualities of patience (forbearance) in Proverbs 25:15 and limitless presence (forever) in Psalm 23:6. In perhaps its most significant theological usage, it speaks of long life or "length of your days" (NASB), a desirable state of existence embodied in the Lord (Deut. 30:20), given to those who walk in obedience (Ps. 91:16; Prov. 3:2) and wisdom (Prov. 3:16). This kind of existence begins in the eternity of God and is granted to those He has chosen. *

LENGTHENING – ***'arkāh*** [Aramaic fem. noun: אַרְכָה <754>; from PROPER <749>] ▶ **This word means a continuation; it is also translated prolonging, extension.** It is used temporally (Dan. 4:27; 7:12). ¶

LENTILS – ***ʿᵃdāšiym*** [masc. plur. noun: עֲדָשִׁים <5742>; from an unused root of uncertain meaning] ▶ **A vegetable-like pea with small seeds that are edible.** Refs.: Gen. 25:34; 2 Sam. 17:28; Ezek. 4:9. It was cultivated in Canaan (2 Sam. 23:11). ¶

LEOPARD – 1 ***nᵉmar*** [Aramaic masc. noun: נְמַר <5245>; corresponding to <5246> below] ▶ **This word means a large, strong, spotted wild cat.** It is found in Daniel describing one of the beasts of his night visions (Dan. 7:6). ¶

2 ***nāmêr*** [masc. noun: נָמֵר <5246>; from an unused root meaning properly to filtrate, i.e., be limpid (comp. NIMRAH <5257> and NIMRIM <5249>), and thus to spot or stain as if by dripping] ▶ **This word refers to a panther, a large wild stalking animal of the cat family with spots.** Refs.: Hos. 13:7; Jer. 13:23. It was known for its speed (Hab. 1:8). It is used in a metaphor to represent the splendor and mysterious quality of a bridegroom (Song 4:8). In the messianic kingdom, even the leopard will be tame (Is. 11:6). It describes the Lord stalking His own rebellious people (Hos. 13:7). Other ref.: Jer. 5:6. ¶

LEPER (BE A) – ***ṣāraʿ*** [verb: צָרַע <6879>; a prim. root (to scourge; e.g., to be stricken with leprosy)] ▶ **This word means to have leprosy. It refers to having a skin disease in which the skin appears white.** Refs.: Ex. 4:6; Lev. 13:44, 45; 14:2, 3. It was possibly leprosy, but there were other similar diseases as well. Most translations still render the word as leprosy (2 Sam. 3:29; 2 Kgs. 5:1, 11, 27). Several people were struck with leprosy or a similar skin disease because of their rebellious attitudes (Num. 12:10; 2 Kgs. 15:5). *

LEPROSY – ***ṣarʿaṯ*** [fem. noun: צָרַעַת <6883>; from LEPER (BE A) <6879>] ▶ **This word refers to a skin disease on humans.** Refs.: Lev. 13:2, 3, 8; 2 Kgs. 5:3. It refers also to similarly appearing mold, mildew, or fungus in garments, walls of houses, etc. (Lev. 13:47, 49, 51, 52, 59). Most translations still render this as leprosy, but many scholars hold that it refers to leucodermia, etc. *

LEPROSY (HAVE) – See LEPER (BE A) <6879>.

LESHEM – ***lešem*** [proper noun: לֶשֶׁם <3959>; the same as JACINTH <3958>]: precious stone ▶ **A city of Dan.** Ref.: Josh. 19:47. ¶

LESSEN – Num. 17:5 ➔ SUBSIDE <7918>.

LET – Gen. 31:28 ➔ FORSAKE <5203>.

LET OUT – Prov. 17:14 ➔ OPEN <6362>.

LETHECH – ***leṯeḵ*** [masc. noun: לֶתֶךְ <3963>; from an unused root of uncertain meaning] ▶ **This word refers to a half homer, a dry measure.** This dry measure probably equaled about 110 liters or ca. 3.3 bushels. Its exact capacity is unknown (Hos. 3:2). ¶

LETHEK – Hos. 3:2 ➔ LETHECH <3963>.

LETTER – 1 ***'iggᵉrā'*** [Aramaic fem. noun: אִגְּרָא <104>; of Persian origin] ▶ **The word refers to a written communication or correspondence.** In Ezra it describes a letter sent to King Artaxerxes (Ezra 4:8, 11) and one sent to Darius (5:6). These were high-level letters of correspondence. ¶

2 ***'iggereṯ*** [fem. noun: אִגֶּרֶת <107>; fem. of <104> above] ▶ **The word indicates a written correspondence of some kind.** There are letters of invitation delivered by couriers of the king (2 Chr. 30:1, 6) and letters granting royal authority to Nehemiah (Neh. 2:7–9). The Feast of Purim is officially established in Esther 9:26, 29 by letters. *

3 ***ništᵉwān*** [verb: נִשְׁתְּוָן <5406>; prob. of Persian origin] ▶ **This word refers to a**

form of correspondence in writing on clay, parchment, etc. It refers to official letters sent by the government (Ezra 4:7; 7:11). Sometimes it is better understood as a document, a decree, or a report of some kind. ¶
[4] ***ništᵉwān*** [Aramaic masc. noun: נִשְׁתְּוָן <5407>; corresponding to <5406> above] ▶ **This word refers to a form of correspondence in writing on clay, parchment.** It is translated according to context as a letter, a decree, a document, etc. (Ezra 4:18, 23; 5:5). ¶
– [5] 2 Sam. 11:14, 15; etc. ➔ BOOK <5612> [6] 2 Chr. 21:12 ➔ WRITING <4385> [7] Ezra 5:7 ➔ ANSWER (noun) <6600>.

LETUSHITES – ***lᵉṭûšiym*** [masc. plur. proper noun: לְטוּשִׁם <3912>; masc. plur. of pass. part. of SHARPEN <3913>] ▶ **These people are mentioned as the sons or people descended from Abraham through Keturah.** Ref.: Gen. 25:3. She bore Jokshan, who bore Dedan, the father of the Letushites. ¶

LEUKODERMA – Lev. 13:39 ➔ SPOT (FRECKLED, WHITE) <933>.

LEUMMIM – ***lᵉ'ummiym*** [masc. proper noun: לְאֻמִּים <3817>; plur. of PEOPLE <3816>]: peoples, nations ▶ **Third son of Dedan, who was a grandson of Abraham and Keturah.** Ref.: Gen. 25:3. ¶

LEVEL (noun) – [1] ***mêyšār*** [masc. noun: מֵישָׁר <4339>; from STRAIGHT (BE) <3474>] ▶ **This word designates rightness, equity, smoothness. It is found only in the plural.** It is used figuratively: a level path of righteousness means a time free of difficulties and injustice (Is. 26:7). Used of wine, it indicates a smooth flow of wine (Prov. 23:31; Song 7:9). It is used as an adverb to mean justly, rightly (Ps. 17:2; Song 1:4). It is something that wisdom leads to and encourages: it indicates just, right things (Prov. 8:6); what is correct, fair (Prov. 1:3; 2:9); just governments (Ps. 9:8; 58:1; 75:2; 98:9); proper, fair speech or talk (Prov. 23:16; Is. 33:15). The Lord's promises are upright (Is. 45:19). Other refs.: 1 Chr. 29:17; Ps. 96:10; 99:4; Dan. 11:6. ¶
– [2] Is. 28:17 ➔ PLUMB LINE <4949>.

LEVEL (verb) – [1] Ps. 65:10 ➔ BEND <5181> [2] Jer. 51:58 ➔ STRIP <6209> a.

LEVEL, MAKE LEVEL – Ps. 78:50; Is. 26:7 ➔ WEIGH, WEIGH OUT <6424>.

LEVI – ***lêwiy*** [masc. proper noun: לֵוִי <3878>; from JOIN <3867>]: attached, joined ▶
a. The third son of Leah. His name means, in the biblical context, "joined" or "attached" based on the popular etymology Leah gave the word (cf. Num. 18:2, 4). Levi and Simeon avenged the rape of their sister Dinah (Gen. 34:25–30). This event influenced Jacob's blessing on Levi (Gen. 49:5–7). Moses mentioned Levi's testing of the Lord at Massah and Meribah (Deut. 33:8). Levi had three sons, Gershon (Gen. 46:11), Kohath, and Merari (Ex. 6:16–18). Moses' mother came from Levi descent (Ex. 2:1; 6:16). *
b. These were the descendants of Levi (see a. above) who were given the priesthood in Israel and were in charge of all of the holy things. Refs.: Num. 1:47–54; Num. 3:5–50. Within the tribe of Levi, only the sons of Aaron were to serve as high priests (Ex. 28–29). The descendants of Kohath, Gershon, and Merari were also special important family lines (Num. 2:1–31; 4:1–33; 10:11–33). In Exodus 32:26–28, the Levites showed their zeal for the Lord, not for senseless violence against other humans. Ezekiel had a place for the Levites in his New Temple Vision, although a reduced one (Ezek. 40:45–46); even a Gate of Levi is featured. Zadok and his sons were favored by Ezekiel's priestly scheme. Zadok was a Levite, a son of Eleazar, and hence high priest with Abiathar (2 Sam. 8:17). *

LEVIATHAN – ***liwyāṯān*** [masc. proper noun: לִוְיָתָן <3882>; from JOIN <3867>] ▶
a. This word describes a huge indomitable being that God created and whom

only He fully comprehends and controls. Refs.: Job 3:8; 41:1. Its exact meaning is complex and tied to ancient Near Eastern ideas of creatures. In Psalm 104:26, Leviathan frolics in the ocean, a harmless being made by God. In Psalm 74:14, Leviathan refers to the mighty waters of the Red Sea that the Lord subdued to rescue His people. In Isaiah 27:1, the word refers most likely to the rebellious nations whom God will slay as He slayed the monster of the sea. ¶
b. A masculine noun meaning mourning. Its traditional meaning has been rendered as mourning regarding Job's hated day of birth (Job 3:8). Most recent translators prefer to render this as Leviathan (NASB, NIV, NKJV, ESV). ¶

LEVITE – [1] ***lêwāy*** [Aramaic proper noun: לֵוָי <3879>; corresponding to GARLAND <3880>]: see LEVI <3878> (meaning attached, joined) ▶ **This word corresponds to the Hebrew name LEVITE <3881> below.** It is found in Ezra 6:16, 18; 7:13, 24. ¶
[2] ***lêwiy*** [proper noun: לֵוִי <3881>; patron. from LEVI <3878>] ▶ **This word designates a descendant of Levi, a member of the tribe of Levi (see LEVI <3878>).** Refs.: Ex. 4:14; 6:25; 38:21; Lev. 25:32, 33; Judg. 17:7, 9–13; Is. 66:21; Jer. 33:18, 21, 22. *

LEVY – [1] Num. 31:28, 37–41 ➔ TRIBUTE <4371> [2] 2 Kgs. 23:33 ➔ FINE (noun) <6066>.

LEWDNESS – [1] ***naḇlûṯ*** [fem. noun: נַבְלוּת <5040>; from FOOLISH <5036>] ▶ **The word refers to gross sexual behavior to excite sexual desire.** It is used of Israel's lewd actions to attract her forbidden lovers (Hos. 2:10). ¶
– [2] Ezek. 16:36 ➔ LUST (noun) <5178>.

LIAR – [1] Is. 44:25 ➔ TALK (EMPTY, IDLE) <907> [2] Jer. 15:18: as a liar ➔ DECEPTIVE <391>.

LIAR (BE A, DECLARE A, MAKE A) – ***kāzaḇ*** [verb: כָּזַב <3576>; a prim. root] ▶ **This word means to lie, i.e., to not tell the truth.** It occurs sixteen times and refers to false witnesses (Prov. 14:5); worshipers (Prov. 30:6); and figuratively of water (Is. 58:11). The book of Job, filled with courtroom rhetoric, debating the trustworthiness of the speakers' accounts, uses the verb four times (Job 6:28; 24:25; 34:6; 41:9). Other refs.: Num. 23:19; 2 Kgs. 4:16; Ps. 78:36; 89:35; 116:11; Is. 57:11; Ezek. 13:19; Mic. 2:11; Hab. 2:3. ¶

LIBERAL – Is. 32:8 ➔ DIGNITY <5082>.

LIBERALLY (FURNISH, SUPPLY) – ***ʿānaq*** [verb: עָנַק <6059>; a prim. root] ▶ **This word means to place around the neck; to give generously.** It indicates giving freely to persons to provide all their needs and more (Deut. 15:14). It refers to putting on or wearing a necklace (Ps. 73:6; the *mô* is a suffix, third masculine plural; KJV: to compass about as a necklace). ¶

LIBERTY – Lev. 25:10; Is. 61:1; Jer. 34:8, 15, 17; Ezek. 46:17 ➔ FREEDOM <1865> a.

LIBNAH – ***liḇnāh*** [proper noun: לִבְנָה <3841>; the same as POPLAR <3839> or PAVEMENT <3840>]: white or pavement ▶
a. A city in southwest Judah. Refs.: Josh. 10:29, 31, 32, 39; 12:15; 15:42; 21:13; 2 Kgs. 8:22; 19:8; 23:31; 24:18; 1 Chr. 6:57; 2 Chr. 21:10; Is. 37:8; Jer. 52:1. ¶
b. The site of an encampment in the Wilderness. Refs.: Num. 33:20, 21. ¶

LIBNI – ***liḇniy*** [proper noun: לִבְנִי <3845>; from WHITE (MAKE) <3835>]: white ▶ **The oldest son of Gershon and grandson of Levi.** Refs.: Ex. 6:17; Num. 3:18; 1 Chr. 6:17, 20, 29. ¶

LIBNITE – ***liḇniy, lêḇ qāmāy*** [masc. proper noun: לִבְנִי, לֵב קָמָי <3846>; patron. from LIBNI <3845>] ▶
a. A descendant of Libni. Refs.: Num. 3:21; 26:58. ¶
b. A cryptic name for Babylon. Ref.: Jer. 51:1; it is translated Leb-kamai. ¶

LIBYAN – See LUBIM <3864>.

LICE – Ex. 8:16–18; Ps. 105:31 ➔ GNAT <3654>.

LICK – 1 Kgs. 21:19; 22:38 ➔ LAP (verb) <3952>.

LICK, LICK UP – ***lāḥak*** [verb: לָחַךְ <3897>; a prim. root] ▶ **This word means to lap up or scoop up something.** Grass like an ox (Num. 22:4); water licked up by fire (1 Kgs. 18:38). It is used of licking up dust from the ground, from someone's feet (Ps. 72:9; Is. 49:23); or of a serpent as it seemingly licks up or eats the dust of the ground (Mic. 7:17). It is used figuratively of Israel's enemies in the last reference. ¶

LIE (noun) – [1] ***kāzāḇ*** [masc. noun: כָּזָב <3577>; from LIAR (BE A) <3576>] ▶ **This word means a deception, a falsehood. Indeed, the idea of nontruth is unequivocally presented as antithetical to God.** He destroys liars (Ps. 5:6; 62:4) and calls them an abomination (Prov. 6:19). Lies and deceptions place one against God and guarantee His punishment (Prov. 19:5, 9). Isaiah graphically depicted one taking shelter in lying and falsehood as equivalent to making a covenant with death and an agreement with hell-a contract that cannot save on Judgment Day (Is. 28:15, 17). Freedom from falsehood is both the character and heritage of God's children (Ps. 40:4; Zeph. 3:13). The verb *kāzaḇ* (to be a liar) also develops the anti-God theme of lying: God cannot lie (Num. 23:19); and His word will never deceive (Ps. 89:35), unlike false prophets and humans. *

[2] ***kaḥaš*** [masc. noun: כַּחַשׁ <3585>; from DENY <3584>] ▶ **This word means lying; it carries the meaning of deception and deceit.** Israel was lying to God (Hos. 10:13; 11:12). Nineveh, the capital of Assyria, was full of deceit and lies (Nah. 3:1). The wicked constantly utter lies (Ps. 59:12). In the context of Job 16:8, it means sickliness, leanness, or gauntness. Other ref.: Hos. 7:3. ¶

[3] ***šeqer*** [noun: שֶׁקֶר <8267>; from FALSELY (DEAL) <8266>] ▶ **This word means to not tell the truth; it also means vanity, without cause.** It is used of a lying witness (Deut. 19:18); of false prophets (Jer. 5:31; 20:6; 29:9); of telling lies (Lev. 19:12; Jer. 37:14); and of a liar (Prov. 17:4). In other cases, it describes something done in vain (1 Sam. 25:21; Ps. 33:17); or an action without cause (Ps. 38:19; 119:78, 86). *

– [4] Job 11:3; Is. 16:6; Jer. 48:30; 50:36 ➔ TALK (EMPTY, IDLE) <907> [5] Ezek. 24:12 ➔ TOIL (noun) <8383> b. [6] Mic. 1:14 ➔ DECEPTIVE <391>.

LIE (verb) – [1] Num. 23:19; 2 Kgs. 4:16; Job 6:28; 24:25; 34:6; 41:9; Ps. 78:36; 89:35; 116:11; Prov. 14:5; 30:6; Is. 57:11; 58:11; Ezek. 13:19; Mic. 2:11; Hab. 2:3. ➔ LIAR (BE A, DECLARE A, MAKE A) <3576> [2] 1 Sam. 15:29 ➔ FALSELY (DEAL) <8266>.

LIE CARNALLY, LIE SEXUALLY – Lev. 19:20; Num. 5:13 ➔ LAYER <7902> b.

LIE DOWN – [1] ***ṣā'āh*** [verb: צָעָה <6808>; a prim. root] ▶ **This word means to incline oneself; it is used with the word *zônāh*, prostitute, following, so it may mean to lie down, to bow oneself (for coitus).** In this context it would be for an act of prostitution (Jer. 2:20; also translated to bow down). Other refs (with very different nuances): Is. 51:14; 63:1; Jer. 48:12. ¶

[2] ***rāḇa'*** [verb: רָבַע <7250>; a prim. root] ▶ **This word means to rest; but it also indicates to mate with an animal.** It is used in its biblical context of lying with someone to mate, human or beast (Lev. 18:23; 19:19; 20:16). But it is used in a neutral context of the act merely of lying down to rest (Ps. 139:3). ¶

[3] ***rāḇaṣ*** [verb: רָבַץ <7257>; a prim. root] ▶ **This word means to rest; to lay something down.** It is used figuratively of sin lying, crouching at the door (Gen. 4:7); and it is used figuratively of a curse resting on a person (Deut. 29:20). It refers to animals lying down, domestic or wild (Gen. 49:9; Ex. 23:5). It describes birds sitting on their eggs (Deut. 22:6). It describes persons lying down in rest, reposing (Job 11:19; Is. 14:30); in security and safety (Ezek. 34:14).

It means in its causative stem to lay, to set stones (Is. 54:11); to cause one's flock to lie down to rest (Song 1:7). *

4 **šāḵaḇ** [verb: שָׁכַב <7901>; a prim. root] ► **This word means to put oneself in a reclining position when sleeping or resting.** Refs.: Gen. 19:4; Lev. 14:47; Deut. 6:7; Josh. 2:1; Ps. 3:5; Prov. 3:24. When ill, it means to recover (Lev. 15:4; 2 Kgs. 9:16). It is used of sexual intercourse, lying with a woman or man (Gen. 19:32–35; Num. 5:13, 19; Judg. 16:1; 2 Sam. 13:14); or an act of sex with an animal, bestiality (Ex. 22:19) that was punishable by death. It is used of Israel's spiritual harlotries, lying with her lovers (Ezek. 23:8). To lie with one's fathers means to die and be buried (Gen. 47:30). It refers to death in general (Job 3:13). It is used figuratively of lying, being covered by shame (Jer. 3:25). It takes the sense of making or letting persons lie down, causing them to lie down (1 Kgs. 3:20; 17:19; 2 Kgs. 4:21). Figuratively, it describes the Lord's betrothing Israel to Himself (Hos. 2:18). It is used of tipping or turning over a vessel, referring in a figurative sense to the clouds of the sky (Job 38:37). In a passive sense, it refers to someone or something being laid someplace (2 Kgs. 4:32; Ezek. 32:19, 32). Lying in one's bosom or lap indicates extreme intimacy (Mic. 3:5). *

LIE DOWN (PLACE TO) – Zeph. 2:15 ➔ RESTING PLACE <4769>.

LIE FALLOW, STILL, UNUSED – Ex. 23:11 ➔ FORSAKE <5203>.

LIE IN WAIT – **ṣāḏāh** [verb: צָדָה <6658>; a prim. root] ► **The word means to stay hidden, waiting for someone, possibly to attack that person. It occurs only twice in the Old Testament.** In Exodus 21:13, it signified deliberation and planning before a murder; those who were lying in wait were to be executed. Those, however, who committed a murder without lying in wait could flee to a city of refuge and be protected within its borders (cf. Num. 35:9–34). In 1 Samuel 24:11, the word signified Saul's attempt to hunt down David and kill him. ¶

LIE IN WAIT, LYING IN WAIT – Judg. 9:35; Ps. 10:8 ➔ AMBUSH <3993>.

LIE UPON – Is. 58:5 ➔ SPREAD (verb) <3331>.

LIE WITH – Deut. 28:30 ➔ RAPE <7693>.

LIEUTENANT – Ezra 8:36; Esther 3:12; 8:9; 9:3 ➔ SATRAP <323>.

LIFE – 1 Ezra 6:10; Dan. 7:12 ➔ LIVING (adj.) <2417> 2 Job 11:17; Ps. 89:47 ➔ WORLD <2465> 3 Dan. 3:28 ➔ BODY <1655> 4 Dan. 5:23 ➔ BREATH <5396>.

LIFE (ENJOY) – Ps. 39:13 ➔ SMILE (verb) <1082>.

LIFE-BREATH – Dan. 5:23 ➔ BREATH <5396>.

LIFEBLOOD – Is. 63:3, 6 ➔ BLOOD <5332>.

LIFELESS – Hab. 2:19 ➔ SILENCE (noun) <1748>.

LIFETIME – Ps. 39:5 ➔ WORLD <2465>.

LIFT – 1 Ps. 30:1 ➔ DRAW <1802> 2 Dan. 6:23 ➔ GO UP <5559> b.

LIFT, LIFT UP – 1 **n**ᵉ**ṭal** [Aramaic verb: נְטַל <5191>; corresponding to OFFER <5190> (in the sense of to take up, to lift up)] ► **This word is used figuratively of elevating one's eyes to heaven, recognizing God's authority.** Ref.: Dan. 4:34; also translated to raise. It also means to set something on its feet, to set it upright (Dan. 7:4). ¶
– 2 Is. 40:15; 63:9 ➔ OFFER <5190>.

LIFT ONESELF – **mārā'** [verb: מָרָא <4754>; a prim. root] ► **A verb meaning to fly, to propel with wings; it is also translated to rouse oneself. It refers to**

the ability to travel without touching the ground. It is used figuratively of the ostrich (Job 39:18), a wonder of God's creation. The Hebrew word also means filthy; see FILTHY (BE) <4754>. ¶

LIFT UP – [1] Job 10:16 ➔ RISE <1342> [2] Ps. 145:14; 146:8 ➔ RAISE UP <2210> [3] Is. 33:3 ➔ LIFTING UP <7427> [4] Jer. 13:26 ➔ STRIP <2834> [5] Ezek. 10:15, 17 ➔ EXALTED <7426> a. [6] Dan. 5:20, 23 ➔ EXALT <7313> [7] Dan. 6:23 ➔ TAKE UP <5267> [8] Zech. 14:10 ➔ RISE <7213>.

LIFTED UP (BE) – Hab. 2:4 ➔ PRESUME <6075>.

LIFTING UP – [1] ***mōʿal*** [masc. noun: מֹעַל <4607>; from OFFER <5927> (in the sense of to lift)] ▶ **This word means to raise something.** In context it is used of the lifting of peoples' hands to worship God (Neh. 8:6). ¶
[2] ***rōmêmuṯ, rômêmuṯ*** [masc. noun: רֹמֵמֻת, רוֹמֵמֻת <7427>; from the act. part. of EXALTED <7426>] ▶ **This word indicates a rising up.** It is used in a figurative sense to refer to the Lord's raising Himself up, of His beginning to act (Is. 33:3). ¶
– [3] Job 22:29 ➔ PRIDE <1466> [4] Ps. 141:2 ➔ GIFT <4864> [5] Is. 9:18 ➔ MAJESTY <1348>.

LIGHT (adj.) – [1] Num. 21:5 ➔ WORTHLESS <7052> [2] Judg. 9:4; Zeph. 3:4 ➔ RECKLESS (BE) <6348>.

LIGHT (noun) – [1] ***'ôr*** [masc. noun: אוֹר <216>; from LIGHT (GIVE) <215>] ▶ **In a literal sense, this word is used primarily to refer to light (illumination) from heavenly bodies (Jer. 31:35; Ezek. 32:7) but also for light itself (Gen. 1:3; Eccl. 12:2).** The pillar of fire was a light for the wandering Israelites (Ex. 13:21). One day God, who is clothed with light (a manifestation of His splendor), will replace the light of the heavens with His own light (Ps. 104:2; Is. 60:19, 20; cf. Rev. 21:23; 22:5). Light is always used as a positive symbol, such as for good fortune (Job 30:26); victory (Mic. 7:8, 9); justice and righteousness (Is. 59:9); guidance (Ps. 119:105); and a bearer of deliverance (Is. 49:6). Expressions involving light include the light of one's face, meaning someone's favor (Ps. 44:3); to see light, meaning to live (Ps. 49:19); and to walk in the light, meaning to live by God's known standards (Is. 2:5). *
[2] ***'ôrāh*** [fem. noun: אוֹרָה <219>; fem. of <216> above] ▶ **The primary stress of the word is on the life-giving properties. This word also means brightness, splendor, herbs.** It is used to signify light (Ps. 139:12); joyous well-being (Esther 8:16); vibrant green herbs (2 Kgs. 4:39). It also conveys the quality of living (the dew of herbs) (Is. 26:19); it is also translated morning, dawn. ¶
[3] ***mā'ôr, mā'ōr*** [masc. sing. noun: מָאוֹר, מָאֹר <3974>; from LIGHT (GIVE) <215>] ▶ **This word means luminary.** It is employed in connection with the lamp in the Tabernacle (Ex. 35:14; Lev. 24:2; Num. 4:16). It is also used to describe the heavenly lights in the creation story of Genesis 1:14–16. Other refs.: Ex. 25:6; 27:20; 35:8, 28; 39:37; Num. 4:9; Ps. 74:16; 90:8; Prov. 15:30; Ezek. 32:8. ¶
[4] ***nᵉhiyr, nahiyrû*** [Aramaic fem. noun: נְהִיר, נַהִירוּ <5094>; from the same as <5105> below] ▶ **This word means illumination, wisdom, or insight. It is found only in Daniel.** The story of the handwriting on the wall in Belshazzar's banquet hall established the fact that Daniel was able to discern things people found baffling. Belshazzar described Daniel's wisdom as light and understanding coming from the Spirit of God within him (Dan. 5:11, 14: light, illumination, insight). Other ref.: Dan. 2:22. ¶
[5] ***nᵉhārāh*** [fem. noun: נְהָרָה <5105>; from FLOW (verb) <5102> b. in its original sense of to shine, to glow] ▶ **This word refers to the light of dawn, the sunlight, which illumines something and makes it known or real.** Ref.: Job 3:4. ¶
– [6] 2 Sam. 22:29; Job 18:5; 22:28; Ps. 18:28 ➔ to turn into light, to give light ➔ LIGHTEN <5050> [7] Ps. 13:3; 18:28; 77:18; 97:4 ➔ LIGHT (GIVE) <215> [8] Is.

50:10; Ezek. 1:4, 27, 28 ➔ light, bright light, brilliant light ➔ BRIGHTNESS <5051>.

LIGHT (GIVE) – ***'ôr*** [verb: אוֹר <215>; a prim. root] ▶ **This word means to shine, to become light, day; it is also translated to lighten, to light, to light up, to enlighten, to brighten.** The heavenly bodies provide light (Gen. 1:15, 17), as does fire (Ex. 13:21). Lightning shines forth (Ps. 77:18; 97:4). The presence of the Lord can cause the earth to shine forth (Ezek. 43:2). A lamp or burning wood also gives off light (Ps. 18:28; Is. 27:11). Metaphorically, the Lord's face may shine on us (Num. 6:25), and His law enlightens our eyes (Ezra 9:8; Ps. 13:3; Prov. 29:13). In a beautiful idiom, it is asserted that wisdom lights up a person's face (Eccl. 8:1). *

LIGHT OFF – Josh. 15:18; Judg. 1:14 ➔ GET OFF <6795>.

LIGHT THING (BE A) – 1 Sam. 18:23 ➔ DESPISED (BE) <7034>.

LIGHTEN – 1 ***nāgah*** [verb: נָגַהּ <5050>; a prim. root] ▶ **This word means to shine, to illuminate. It always is used figuratively except once. It indicates the giving of light, illumination.** It is used figuratively of the Lord who shines into darkness in a moral sense (2 Sam. 22:29; Ps. 18:28); and of the life of the wicked which goes out (Job 18:5). It indicates God's approval (Job 22:28). It is used of God's breaking in to enlighten His people about Himself and His gospel (Is. 9:2). It is used of the light put forth by the heavenly luminaries (Is. 13:10). ¶
– 2 Ezra 9:8; Ps. 13:3; 77:18; 97:4; Prov. 29:13 ➔ LIGHT (GIVE) <215>.

LIGHTLY ESTEEMED (BE) – Prov. 12:9 ➔ DESPISED (BE) <7034>.

LIGHTNESS – Jer. 23:32 ➔ RECKLESSNESS <6350>.

LIGHTNING – 1 **flash of lightning, bolt of lightning: *bāzāq*** [masc. noun: בָּזָק <965>; from an unused root meaning to lighten] ▶ **This word refers to the flashes of light produced during an electrical storm; it is used in a figurative sense to describe the movement of the living beings in Ezekiel's chariot vision.** Ref.: Ezek. 1:14. ¶
2 ***bārāq*** [masc. noun: בָּרָק <1300>; from FLASH FORTH <1299>] ▶ **The most famous appearance of this word (see previous definition) is in the great theophany at Mount Sinai when God settles on the sacred mountain amid thundering and lightning.** Refs.: Ex. 19:16; Ps. 18:14. The Exodus was accompanied by lightning as well (Ps. 77:18), but this phenomenon witnesses to the presence of God in every storm (Ps. 97:4). The swiftness of lightning is used to describe war chariots (Nah. 2:4), while its blazing brightness describes the face of an angelic being (Dan. 10:6; cf. Ezek. 21:10, 21:15, Ezek. 21:28). *
– 3 Ex. 20:18 ➔ TORCH <3940> 4 Job 28:26; 38:25 ➔ THUNDERSTORM <2385> 5 Ps. 78:48 ➔ FLASH (noun) <7565> 6 Hab. 3:11 ➔ BRIGHTNESS <5051>.

LIGURE – Ex. 28:19; 39:12 ➔ JACINTH <3958>.

LIKE – 1 ***keᵉmô*** [particle: כְּמוֹ <3644>; a form of the prefix "k-", but used separately (comp. THEREFORE <3651>)] ▶ **A word used to assert that something is like something else or behaves in the same way that something else does; also meaning as.** The Egyptians sank like stones (Ex. 15:5). With a suffix as subject attached, it asserts a likeness of its suffix to something, e.g., *kāmōḵā kᵉp̱ar'ôh*, "you are like Pharaoh" (Gen. 44:18). There is no one like the Lord (Ex. 9:14). Something is asserted to be as (*kᵉ*) it used to be (Zech. 10:8). It has the sense of time, when, in some contexts (Gen. 19:15), lit., as it was. *
– 2 Job 41:33 ➔ AUTHORITY <4915>.

LIKE (BE) – 1 ***dāmāh*** [verb: דָּמָה <1819>; a prim. root] ▶ **This word can be used in the sense of to make oneself like someone or something; it also means to compare,**

to resemble; to use parables, to plan, to think. The king of Babylon aspired to make himself like the Most High God (Is. 14:14). It is used to compare things or persons: to compare oneself to something (Ps. 102:6); to compare God to something (Is. 40:18, 25; 46:5) and therefore indicates the use of parables in teaching, etc. (Hos. 12:10), especially in specific similes (Song 1:9; 2:9, 17; 7:7; 8:14). Its meaning extends to forming an idea or planning something (Num. 33:56; Judg. 20:5; 2 Sam. 21:5; Ps. 48:9; Ps. 50:21). *

[2] ***d*^e*māh*** [Aramaic verb: דְּמָה <1821>; corresponding to <1819> above] ▶ **This word indicates that something resembles something else.** The fourth man in the furnace was like a son of the gods (Dan. 3:25); the second beast of Daniel's vision resembled a bear (Dan. 7:5). ¶

LIKE (BE, BECOME) – ***šāwāh*** [verb: שָׁוָה <7737>; a prim. root] ▶

a. This word means to be or become equal, to match, to suffice. It means basically to be like or equivalent (Prov. 26:4; Is. 40:25). It also takes on the sense of being suitable or sufficient (Esther 3:8; 7:4). In its causative stem, it means to make like (2 Sam. 22:34); or to compare or equate (Is. 46:5; Lam. 2:13). It is used of leveling the ground (Is. 28:25). Wisdom is not to be compared even to jewels (Prov. 3:15; 8:11). It indicates that something is fitting, sufficient or not (Job 33:27). It takes on the meaning of to set, to place, to establish (Ps. 18:33. See b. below).

b. A verb meaning to set, to place, to put, to lay. It means to focus on someone (Ps. 16:8); or something (Ps. 119:30); it refers to God's granting something, such as deliverance to a person (Ps. 21:5; 89:19). It takes on the sense of producing something. In context it is used figuratively of God causing Israel to produce fruit (Hos. 10:1). *

LIKE AS – ***dimyôn*** [masc. noun: דִּמְיוֹן <1825>; from LIKE (BE) <1819>] ▶ **This word denotes similarity and means, literally, likeness, resemblance, image.** It depicts an oppressor of the psalmist who is likened to a lion awaiting its prey (Ps. 17:12, lit.: his likeness is as a lion), secretly and stealthily planning its attack. ¶

LIKENESS – [1] ***d*^e*mûṯ*** [fem. noun: דְּמוּת <1823>; from LIKE (BE) <1819>] ▶ **This word is often used to create a simile by comparing two unlike things.** For instance the wickedness of people and the venom of a snake (Ps. 58:4); the sound of God's gathering warriors and of many people (Is. 13:4); or the angelic messenger and a human being (Dan. 10:16). Additionally, it is used in describing humans being created in the image or likeness of God (Gen. 1:26; 5:1); the likeness of Seth to Adam (Gen. 5:3); the figures of oxen in the Temple (2 Chr. 4:3); the pattern of the altar (2 Kgs. 16:10). But most often, Ezekiel uses it as he describes his visions by comparing what he saw to something similar on earth (Ezek. 1:5, 16; 10:1). *

[2] ***t*^e*mûnāh*** [fem. noun: תְּמוּנָה <8544>; from KIND (noun) <4327>] ▶ **This word is related to the noun *miyn*, meaning kind or species. The main idea of this word is one of likeness or similarity; it is also translated form.** It is normally used to describe God's ban on creating images of anything that would attempt to resemble (or be like) Him (Ex. 20:4; Deut. 4:15, 16; 5:8). This word can also describe the form or likeness of a visible image (Job 4:16; Ps. 17:15). Synonyms for this word are *tabniyt* (<8403>) meaning plan, pattern, or form, and *demût* (<1823>), meaning likeness. Other refs.: Num. 12:8; Deut. 4:12, 23, 25. ¶

– [3] Deut. 4:16–18; etc. ➔ PLAN (noun) <8400>.

LIKHI – ***liqḥiy*** [masc. proper noun: לִקְחִי <3949>; from TAKE <3947> (see LEARNING <3948>)]: learned ▶ **A man of the tribe of Manasseh, son of Shemida.** Ref.: 1 Chr. 7:19. ¶

LILY – ***šûšan, šôšān, šôšannāh, šôšanniym***; [שׁוּשַׁן, שׁוֹשָׁן, שׁוֹשַׁנָּה, שׁוֹשַׁנִּים <7799>; from REJOICE <7797>] ▶

a. A masculine and feminine noun denoting a perennial plant that has large or

colorful flowers. It may indicate the flower of these plants, which was a major feature of their beauty (Hos. 14:5). It was often used in decorative designs, e.g., the lily design on the capitals or pillars (1 Kgs. 7:19, 22); or on other objects (1 Kgs. 7:26; 2 Chr. 4:5). It is found as the name of a song or tune in psalm titles (see refs. below). Its beauty was used in similes referring to one's bride (Song 2:1, 2; 7:2); or bridegroom (Song 5:13); and to the lilies of the Sharon valley area (Song 2:16). It describes part of an idyllic setting (Song 4:5; 6:2, 3).
b. A proper noun, a title of a song. It is used in several psalm titles and means literally lilies [Ps. 45 (title); 69 (title)], evidently indicting the title of a recognized song or tune at the time of the author or the time of the music director. ¶

LILY OF THE COVENANT, LILY OF THE TESTIMONY – Ps. 60 (title); Ps. 80 (title) ➔ SHUSHAN EDUTH <7802> a. and b.

LIMB – [1] Dan. 2:5; 3:29 ➔ PIECE <1917> [2] Dan. 5:6 ➔ his limbs gave way ➔ the joints of his loins were loosed ➔ LOINS <2783>.

LIMB TOO LONG – Lev. 21:18; 22:23 ➔ DEFORMED (BE) <8311>.

LIME – [1] Deut. 27:2, 4; Is. 33:12; Amos 2:1 ➔ PLASTER (noun) <7875> [2] Is. 27:9 ➔ CHALK <1615>.

LIMIT (noun) – [1] Job 11:7; 28:3 ➔ END <8503> [2] Ps. 71:15 ➔ NUMBER (noun) <5615>.

LIMIT (SET A) – Job 13:27 ➔ CARVE <2707>.

LIMIT (verb) – Ps. 78:41 ➔ VEX <8428> b.

LIMITS (PUT, SET) – Ex. 19:12, 23 ➔ BOUNDS (SET) <1379>.

LIMP – ***ṣāla‘*** [verb: צָלַע <6760>; a prim. root; prob. to curve] ▶ **To limp means to walk unevenly, vertically or horizontally, because of an injury. This word is also translated to be lame, to halt.** Ref.: Gen. 32:31. To be lame means to limp badly or to be crippled, disabled (Mic. 4:6, 7; Zeph. 3:19). ¶

LIMPNESS – ***ripyôn*** [masc. noun: רִפְיוֹן <7510>; from CEASE <7503>] ▶ **This word indicates a condition of weakness, slackness, a loss of strength, courage, firmness of resolve; it is also translated feebleness.** In context it refers to the inability to act, to be strong, to be brave in action (Jer. 47:3). ¶

LINE – [1] 1 Sam. 17:23 ➔ ARMY <4630> [2] 1 Kgs. 7:15; Jer. 52:2 ➔ THREAD <2339> [3] 2 Chr. 3:5, 7 ➔ COVER (verb) <2645> [4] Is. 19:8 ➔ HOOK <2443> [5] Is. 44:13 ➔ MARKER <8279> b.

LINE (DRAW A, RUN A) – Num. 34:10 ➔ MARK OUT <184>.

LINE, MEASURING LINE – [1] ***qaw, qāw*** [masc. noun: קַו, קָו <6957>; from WAIT FOR <6960> (in the sense of winding a strand of cord or rope)] ▶ **This word refers to an actual cord used in construction work as a line to evaluate a distance.** Ref.: 1 Kgs. 7:23. Figuratively, it indicates a measuring standard of justice to be applied to Jerusalem (2 Kgs. 21:13). It refers to the architectural plan, line, of the heavens that reflects God's work (Ps. 19:4). It refers to an instructive utterance of prophetic and legal speech from God (Is. 28:10, 13). It indicates God's judgments and His sovereign distribution of His power (Is. 34:11, 17). *
[2] ***qāweh*** [masc. noun: קָוֶה <6961>; from WAIT FOR <6960>] ▶ **See <6957> above.** Ref.: 1 Kgs. 7:23. ¶

LINEN – [1] ***'ēṭûn*** [masc. noun: אֵטוּן <330>; from an unused root (prob. meaning to bind)] ▶ **This word refers to a type of fabric; it is also translated fine linen and colored linen.** Ref.: Prov. 7:16. It was imported from Egypt. ¶
[2] ***baḏ*** [masc. noun: בַּד <906>; perhaps from ALONE (BE) <909> (in the sense of

divided fibers)] ▶ **This word describes a type of fabric used in the garments of the priests.** It is most likely linen (Ex. 28:42; 39:28; Lev. 16:23). It is used to describe the ephod of Samuel and other priests (1 Sam. 2:18; 22:18). It is a feature of the clothing of divine beings mentioned in Ezekiel and Daniel (Ezek. 9:2, 3, 11; 10:2, 6, 7; Dan. 10:5; 12:6, 7). *

[3] ***karpas*** [masc. noun: כַּרְפַּס <3768>; of foreign origin] ▶ **This word is used of white and violet fabric found in the palace of the Persian king, Ahasuerus.** Ref.: Esther 1:6; KJV: green. ¶

[4] ***pêšet̲*** [masc. noun: פֵּשֶׁת <6593>; from the same as TRANSGRESSION <6580> as in the sense of comminuting] ▶ **Linen was a highly valued material for certain kinds of clothing. It could be made of yarn, thread, or cloth made from flax, which consisted of threadlike fibers from various plants from the flax family. This word is also translated flax.** The flax was harvested (Josh. 2:6); and used in various garments (Lev. 13:47; Prov. 31:13; Jer. 13:1; Ezek. 44:17, 18). Wool and linen could not be mixed in a garment (Deut. 22:11). *

LINEN, FINE LINEN – ***šêš*** [masc. noun: שֵׁשׁ <8336>; for MARBLE <7893>] ▶
a. This word refers to a fine fabric from Egypt, exquisitely woven. It was used in garments (Gen. 41:42); sails, priestly clothing (Ex. 28:5, 39). It was spun by women (Ex. 35:25). *S:eš mašzar* refers to fine twisted linen (Ex. 28:6, 15; 36:8).
b. A masculine noun indicating marble. A fine-grained hard limestone of great beauty and ornamental value (Esther 1:6). It is rendered as alabaster as well, a fine-grained translucent variety of gypsum (Song 5:15). *

LINEN GARMENT – ***sād̲iyn*** [masc. noun: סָדִין <5466>; from an unused root meaning to envelop] ▶ **This word refers to a garment that was wrapped around a person. It is also translated linen wrap, fine garment, fine linen, sheet.** These garments were of great value (Judg. 14:12, 13; Prov. 31:24) and considered a luxury (Is. 3:23). ¶

LINEN WRAP – Judg. 14:12, 13 ➔ LINEN GARMENT <5466>.

LINGER – ***māhah*** [verb: מָהַהּ <4102>; apparently a denom. from WHAT? <4100>] ▶ **This word means to delay doing something. It also translated to hesitate, to delay, to tarry, to wait.** Lot halted, hesitated about leaving Sodom (Gen. 19:16; 43:10). Israel could not delay leaving Egypt (Ex. 12:39). It takes on the positive sense of wait in some contexts (2 Sam. 15:28). It refers to delaying religious action (Ps. 119:60). Prophetic visions may tarry or delay but do certainly reach fulfillment (Hab. 2:3; ESV: to seem slow). Other refs.: Judg. 3:26; 19:8; Is. 29:9. ¶

LINK – Song 4:9 ➔ CHAIN <6060>.

LINTEL – ***mašqôp̄*** [masc. noun: מַשְׁקוֹף <4947>; from LOOK DOWN <8259> in its original sense of overhanging] ▶ **This word refers to the upper part of a doorway. It indicates the crosspiece over a door (overhanging it). It is also translated upper door post, top of the doorframes.** It was to be smeared with blood at the Passover (Ex. 12:7, 22, 23). ¶

LINTEL OF THE DOOR, UPPER LINTEL – Amos 9:1; Zeph. 2:14 ➔ BULB <3730>.

LION – [1] ***ᵃriy, 'aryêh*** [masc. and fem. noun: אֲרִי, אַרְיֵה <738>; from PICK (verb) <717> (in the sense of violence)] ▶
a. As a masc. noun, this word refers to a big wild cat. Refs.: Judg. 14:5, 18; 1 Sam. 17:34, 36; 2 Sam. 23:20. Figuratively, it describes Israel's rise to a powerful nation (Num. 23:24; 24:9) and Israel's destroyers Assyria and Babylon (Jer. 50:17). Jerusalem's kings are depicted as destructive lions (Zeph. 3:3). The strength of lions was celebrated in songs and poetry (2 Sam. 1:23; Prov. 22:13). *
b. As a fem. noun, the word refers to an animal. It has the same basic function and meaning as a. In addition, it is used in the following ways: Judah and Dan in

particular are described as lions or a lion's whelps (Gen. 49:9; Deut. 33:22) using this word. One of the four living beings of Ezekiel's vision has the face of a lion (Ezek. 1:10; 10:14). The Lord roars as a lion (Hos. 11:10; Amos 3:4, Amos 3:8) as a protector of His people or, if necessary, as a judge of His people. *

c. As a masc. noun, the word describes the piercing of the psalmist's hands and feet, a prophetic assertion also applied to Christ. Ref.: Ps. 22:16. ¶

[2] ***'aryêh*** [Aramaic masc. noun: אַרְיֵה <744>; corresponding to <738> above] ▶ **This noun is used to describe the den of lions.** Refs.: Dan. 6:7, 12. It is employed figuratively to depict the first beast of Daniel's apocalyptic dream (Dan. 7:4), a lion representing Babylon and Nebuchadnezzar. *

[3] ***layiš*** [masc. noun: לַיִשׁ <3918>; from KNEAD <3888> (in the sense of crushing)] ▶ **This word clearly indicates a lion.** Ref.: Job 4:11. In context, it is representative of a strong being under God's control. The lion is reckoned as majestic among all beasts (Prov. 30:30). It was present in the Negev in early Israel (Is. 30:6). ¶

[4] ***šaḥal*** [masc. noun: שַׁחַל <7826>; from an unused root prob. meaning to roar] ▶ **This word refers to a lion, possibly a fierce (KJV, NASB) lion or a strong roaring lion (NIV).** Refs.: Job 4:10; 28:8. It is used to refer to God as a prowling lion (Job 10:16; Hos. 5:14; 13:7). The lion was a beast that brought great fear and dread (Prov. 26:13). Other ref.: Ps. 91:13. ¶

LION (YOUNG) – ***k^epiyr*** [masc. noun: כְּפִיר <3715>; from COVER (verb) <3722>] ▶

a. This word is used to indicate the animal, a young lion, one mature enough to hunt for its prey. Refs.: Ps. 17:12; Judg. 14:5. It is known for its ferocity (Job 4:10; Ps. 17:12). The nature and character of a lion is understood by God alone (Job 38:39). Its roar is compared to a king's anger (Prov. 19:12). It is used often figuratively of nations or persons. Pharaoh is a young lion among the nations, a terror to others (Ezek. 32:2) as were Dedan, Tarshish (Ezek. 38:13), and Assyria (Nah. 2:11, 13). The Lord is compared to an avenging lion (Hos. 5:14; Amos 3:4). *

b. A masculine noun indicating a village, a small town. It indicates an inhabited small town often situated in the shadow of larger cities (Neh. 6:2: village, Kephirim, Chephirim, Hakkephirim; Ezek. 38:13: village, leader, young lion). ¶

c. A masculine proper noun referring to the village, Kephirim. It indicates a small town in Benjaminite territory, possibly located near Joppa (Neh. 6:2; also translated Chephirim, Hakkephirim). ¶

LION, LIONESS – ***leḇe', liḇ'āh, l^eḇiyyā', lāḇiy'*** [masc. and fem. noun: לְבָא, לְבָאָה, לְבִיָּא, לָבִיא <3833>; from an unused root meaning to roar] ▶

a. A masculine noun indicating a lion, a lioness, a big wild cat. It is used figuratively of violent persons depicted as lions (Ps. 57:4). The prophet refers to allies of or parts of Assyria's empire as lionesses to be fed (Nah. 2:12) (see b.). ¶

b. A feminine noun referring to a lioness. See a. above. Its feminine form is used in Nahum 2:12. ¶

c. A feminine noun meaning lioness. It refers to a female lion, but in context it is used figuratively of Israel or Jerusalem (Ezek. 19:2). ¶

d. A masculine noun indicating a lion, a lioness. It refers to the animal itself but is used only figuratively in its contexts except once. In Job 38:39, the animal is referred to literally. Only God knows the way of the lion as it hunts its prey (Job 38:39); Judah behaves as a lion (Gen. 49:9); the people of Israel and Jacob behave as a strong lion (Num. 23:24; 24:9; 33:20). It refers to the nation God will call forth for vengeance on His people (Is. 5:29; 30:6; Joel 1:6); and of the Lord's fury against Israel (Hos. 13:8); and her enemies (Nah. 2:11). The word is used to describe the wicked in their ways and manner of life (Job 4:11). ¶

LIP – [1] ***śapāh*** [fem. noun: שָׂפָה <8193>; prob. from DESTROY <5595> or STICK OUT <8192> through the idea of termination] ▶ **This word means a soft part,**

the border, the edge of the mouth; it also means a language, an edge, a border. The most common use of this word is that of lip. It can be used merely to describe the organ of speech (Ex. 6:12, 30; Ps. 63:5); and the organ from where laughter comes (Job 8:21). Yet it can also be used as a feature of beauty in descriptions of a beautiful person (Song 4:3, 11). Finally, it can refer to the place from where divine speech comes, from the lips of God (Job 23:12; Ps. 17:4). A more general meaning is that of language that originates from the lips (Gen. 11:6, 7; Ps. 81:5; Is. 33:19). When an edge or a border is the meaning of this word, it can refer to a wide variety of things such as the shore of a sea (Gen. 22:17); the edge or brim of a variety of objects (1 Kgs. 7:23; Ezek. 43:13); or the boundary between geographical sites (Judg. 7:22). *
– [2] Lev. 13:45; Ezek. 24:17, 22; Mic. 3:7 ➔ BEARD <8222> [3] Zech. 4:2 ➔ PIPE <4166>.

LIQUID – Ex. 30:23 ➔ FREEDOM <1865> b.

LIQUOR – [1] Num. 6:3 ➔ JUICE <4952> [2] Song 7:2 ➔ WINE (MIXED, BLENDED) <4197> [3] Hos. 4:18 ➔ WINE <5433>.

LISTEN – [1] ***qāšaḇ*** [verb: קָשַׁב <7181>; a prim. root] ▶ **This word means to hear carefully, to pay attention, to give heed, to obey.** The basic significance of the term is to denote the activity of paying close attention to something, usually another person's words or sometimes to something that can be seen (e.g., Is. 21:7). Job pleaded for his three friends to listen to his words (Job 13:6; see also Is. 32:3; Jer. 23:18). Often the term functioned as an appeal to God to hear and respond to an urgent prayer (Ps. 17:1; 61:1; 66:19; cf. Ps. 5:2). At other times, it denoted the obedience that was expected after the hearing of the Lord's requirements (1 Sam. 15:22; Neh. 9:34; Is. 48:18). Israel's history, however, was characterized by a life of hard-heartedness and rebellion. Jeremiah declared that this was due to the fact that Israel's ears were uncircumcised; therefore, they could not listen so they were able to obey (Jer. 6:10). *
– [2] Deut. 32:1; Ps. 5:1 ➔ EAR (GIVE) <238>.

LIT – Ps. 77:18; 97:4 ➔ LIGHT (GIVE) <215>.

LITTER – Is. 66:20 ➔ COVERED <6632> b.

LITTLE (adj.) – [1] ***z^e'êyr*** [Aramaic adj.: זְעֵיר <2192>; corresponding to LITTLE (noun) <2191>] ▶ **This word describes the small horn that came up among the previous ten horns of Daniel's vision.** Ref.: Dan. 7:8. It surprisingly made arrogant claims for itself against God and His people. ¶
– [2] 2 Kgs. 19:26; Is. 37:27 ➔ SHORT <7116> [3] Dan. 8:9 ➔ SMALL <4704>.

LITTLE (noun) – [1] ***z^e'êyr*** [masc. noun: זְעֵיר <2191>; from an unused root (akin by permutation to BRING LOW <6819>), meaning to dwindle] ▶ **This word indicates a small quantity of something.** It refers to a small or insufficient amount of teaching or instruction from the prophet or wise men (Is. 28:10, 13). Elihu uses the word to appeal for a little time (Job 36:2). ¶
[2] ***m^e'aṭ*** [masc. noun: מְעַט <4592>; from DECREASE <4591>] ▶ **This word indicates a small amount, a few, a short time. It has the basic sense of littleness, smallness, not many.** It indicates a small amount of something (Gen. 18:4; 24:17; 43:11; Deut. 26:5). As a noun, it refers to a small thing, matter, issue (Gen. 30:15). It is used as an adjective to mean small, weak (Deut. 7:7; Eccl. 5:2). It also functions as an adverb indicating place, time, extent, etc. (2 Sam. 16:1; Job 10:20; 2 Kgs. 10:18; Zech. 1:15). Repeated, it means little by little (Ex. 23:30; Deut. 7:22). Prefaced with *h^a*, the interrogative particle, it means, (Was) it too little? (Gen. 30:15; Num. 16:9, 13). *'Ôḏ me'at* indicates a time phrase, Yet a little . . . (Jer. 51:33). It is often used with *k^e* (*kim'at*), almost, just about (Ps. 119:87; Prov. 5:14). At times placed before a verb

form, it is best rendered as just, only, hardly (2 Sam. 19:36; Ps. 2:12). Placed before *r^{e}gaʿ*, it indicates about a moment, for a little while (Ezra 9:8; Is. 26:20). *
– [3] Is. 54:8 ➔ SURGE <8241> b.

LITTLE BOY – ***ʿ^{a}wiyl*** [masc. noun: עֲוִיל <5759>; from NURSING CHILD <5764>] ▶ **This word means a young lad; it is also translated young child.** It describes little children hardly able to understand life but able to turn against someone without understanding (Job 19:18); or children in general (Job 21:11). In context it depicts the offspring of the wicked. ¶

LITTLE FINGER – ***qōṭen*** [masc. noun: קֹטֶן <6995>; from WORTHY (BE NOT) <6994>] ▶ **A word meaning smallness, pettiness. In context it refers to a person's small finger and is used in a figurative sense.** Refs.: 1 Kgs. 12:10; 2 Chr. 10:10. ¶

LITTLE ONE – ***miṣʿār*** [masc. noun: מִצְעָר <4705>; from BRING LOW <6819>] ▶ **This word depicts a small thing, a little while. It basically indicates a small amount or quantity or something of little importance.** A number in size (Gen. 19:20); an insignificant event (Job 8:7; NIV: humble); a small number (2 Chr. 24:24: small company, small number, few); a small period of time (Is. 63:18: a little while). ¶

LITTLE ONES – Zech. 13:7 ➔ BRING LOW <6819>.

LITTLE THING (SEEM A) – 1 Sam. 18:23 ➔ DESPISED (BE) <7034>.

LITTLE WHILE (A) – Is. 63:18 ➔ LITTLE ONE <4705>.

LIVE – [1] ***ḥ^{a}yāh, ḥ^{a}yā'*** [Aramaic verb: חֲיָה, חֲיָא <2418>; corresponding to <2421> below] ▶ **The main usage of this word is the polite address for the king to stay alive, keep living forever.** The astrologers used this verb to address Nebuchadnezzar when they asked him to tell them his dream (Dan. 2:4) and again when they informed him that certain Jews were not bowing down to his golden image (Dan. 3:9). The queen used the verb to advise Belshazzar that Daniel could interpret the handwriting on the wall (Dan. 5:10). The king's advisors also used these words when they tricked King Darius into making a decree to worship only the king (Dan. 6:6). Daniel also used this phrase when he explained to Darius that God saved him from the lions (Dan. 6:21). Other ref.: Dan. 5:19. ¶
[2] ***ḥāyāh*** [verb: חָיָה <2421>; a prim. root] ▶ **This word also means to be alive, to keep alive. It is found numerous times in Scripture.** It is used in the sense of flourishing (Deut. 8:1; 1 Sam. 10:24; Ps. 22:26); or to convey that an object is safe (Gen. 12:13; Num. 14:38; Josh. 6:17). It connotes reviving in Ezekiel 37:5 and 1 Kings 17:22 or healing in Joshua 5:8 and 2 Kings 8:8. Genesis often uses the word when people are kept alive in danger (Gen. 6:19, 20; 19:19; 47:25; 50:20). Also, the word is used in the genealogies of Genesis (Gen. 5:3–30; Gen. 11:11–26). Psalm 119 employs this word to say that God's Word preserves life (Ps. 119:25, 37, 40, 88). Many verses instruct hearers to obey a command (either God's or a king's) in order to live (Gen. 20:7; Prov. 4:4; Jer. 27:12). *
[3] ***ḥāyay*** [verb: חָיַי <2425>; a prim. root (comp. <2421> above)] ▶ **This word is often used in reference to the length of a person's life.** Refs.: Gen. 5:5; 11:12, 14; 25:7. Genesis 3:22 employs this word to describe eternal life represented by the tree of life. It is used in reference to life which is a result of seeing God (Ex. 33:20; Deut. 5:24) or looking at the bronze serpent (Num. 21:8, 9). It is also used to refer to living by the Law (Lev. 18:5; Ezek. 20:11, 13, 21). Cities of refuge were established to which people could flee and live (Deut. 4:42; 19:4, 5). This verb is identical in form and meaning to the verb *ḥāyāh* (LIVE <2421>). *
– [4] Ezra 4:17 ➔ SIT <3488> [5] Dan. 2:38; 4:1, 12 ➔ DWELL <1753> [6] Dan. 4:21 ➔ DWELL <7932>.

LIVE A LONG TIME – Deut. 4:25 ➔ SLEEP (verb) <3462> b.

LIVELY – Ex. 1:19 ➔ VIGOROUS <2422>.

LIVER – [1] ***kāḇēḏ*** [masc. noun.: כָּבֵד <3516>; the same as HEAVY <3515>] ▶ **A large glandular organ, the heaviest visceral organ.** In some animals it has lobes, appendages (Ex. 29:13, 22; Lev. 3:4, 10, etc.). A pierced liver was a deadly wound (Prov. 7:23). In pagan religions, the liver was a religious object and was carefully inspected in the process of divination (Ezek. 21:21). *
– [2] Job 20:25 ➔ GALL <4845>.

LIVES (WHO) – Dan. 4:34 ➔ LIVING (adj.) <2417>.

LIVESTOCK – [1] ***miqneh*** [masc. common noun: מִקְנֶה <4735>; from ACQUIRE <7069> (in the sense of to buy, to possess)] ▶ **This word refers to livestock (purchasable ruminants and other farm animals), a major source of wealth.** Most often: cattle, sheep, goats, horses, donkeys (Gen. 4:20; 26:14: possession; 47:6, 16–18; Ex. 9:3). It could also indicate collections of sheep, goats, and cows only (Gen. 13:2; 31:9; Num. 32:1). Men of cattle, *'anše miqneh*, were cattle herders or breeders (Gen. 46:32); there were herdsmen (*rō'îym*) of cattle (Gen. 13:7); foremen or guardians of cattle and livestock (Gen. 47:6). *
– [2] Ex. 22:5; Num. 20:4, 8, 11 ➔ ANIMAL <1165>.

LIVING (adj.) – ***ḥay*** [Aramaic adj.: חַי <2417>; from LIVE <2418>] ▶ **This word means alive, that lives. In the book of Daniel, the word is used of people.** Refs.: Dan. 2:30; 4:17. King Darius used this word in his description of God (Dan. 6:20, 26). Other refs.: Ezra 6:10 (life, well-being); Dan. 4:34 (who lives); 7:12 (life). ¶

LIVING (noun) – [1] ***ḥayyûṯ*** [fem. noun: חַיּוּת <2424>; from LIVE <2421>] ▶ **This word means lifetime.** It occurs only in 2 Samuel 20:3, where it states that David provided for the ten concubines who were left to watch the palace in Jerusalem (2 Sam. 15:16) and were later violated by David's son, Absalom (2 Sam. 16:21, 22). Although David kept them and provided for their needs, he did not lie with them; consequently, they were like widows during the lifetime of their husband. ¶
[2] **living thing, living creature, living substance: *yᵉqûm*** [masc. noun: יְקוּם <3351>; from STAND, STAND UP <6965>] ▶ **This word denotes something that subsists.** It is an all-inclusive generic term referring to all the living things God created whenever they existed (Gen. 7:4, 23). It is also inclusive of everything that was alive and tainted by the rebellion of Dathan and Abiram (Deut. 11:6; KJV, NKJV: substance). ¶

LIVING, LIVING THING – Judg. 6:4; 17:10 ➔ PRESERVATION OF LIFE <4241>.

LIZARD – [1] ***lᵉṭā'āh*** [fem. noun: לְטָאָה <3911>; from an unused root meaning to hide] ▶ **This word refers to an unclean reptile.** It was forbidden as food for the Israelites (Lev. 11:30) to set them apart from the surrounding nations. ¶
[2] ***śᵉmāmiyṯ*** [fem. noun: שְׂמָמִית <8079>; prob. from DESTROYED (BE) <8074> (in the sense of poisoning)] ▶
a. This word describes a reptile with a long, slender body and tail and four short legs, often with scaly skin. Ref.: Prov. 30:28. It probably refers to a gecko. It is able to inhabit unexpected places through stealth.
b. Early translators understood this word to refer to a spider. Ref.: Prov. 30:28. ¶
– [3] Lev. 11:30 ➔ SAND LIZARD <2546>.

LIZARD (GREAT, LARGE) – Lev. 11:29 ➔ COVERED <6632> c.

LIZARD (MONITOR) – ***kōaḥ, kôaḥ*** [masc. noun: כֹּחַ, כּוֹחַ <3581>] ▶ **This word refers to a long, slender reptile prescribed as unclean to Israel and therefore forbidden as food.** Ref.: Lev. 11:30; also translated chameleon, crocodile. The Hebrew word also means power or might; see STRENGTH <3581>. ¶

LO – Dan. 3:25 ➔ BEHOLD (interj.) <1888>.

LO-AMMI – *lō' 'ammiy* [proper noun: לֹא עַמִּי <3818>; from NO <3808> and PEOPLE <5971> with pron. suffix]: not my people ▶ **Symbolic name given by the prophet Hosea to his second son.** It signified the rejection of the kingdom of Israel by the Lord (Hos. 1:9; 2:23). ¶

LO DEBAR – *lō' ḏᵉḇār, lô ḏᵉḇār* [proper noun: לֹא דְבָר, לוֹ דְבָר <3810>; from NO <3808> and WORD <1699> (in the sense of pastureland)]: no pasture ▶ **A town in Gilead.** Refs.: 2 Sam. 9:4, 5; 17:27. ¶

LO-RUHAMAH – *lō' ruḥāmāh* [proper noun: לֹא רֻחָמָה <3819>; from NO <3808> and COMPASSION (HAVE) <7355>]: the one for whom one does not have compassion ▶ **Symbolic name of the daughter of the prophet Hosea and his wife Gomer.** It indicated the ruined condition of Israel (Hos. 1:6, 8; 2:23). ¶

LOAD (noun) – 1 *ṭōraḥ* [masc. noun: טֹרַח <2960>; from LOAD (verb) <2959>] ▶ **This word indicates a burden, especially a mental burden, as well as the responsibility of a task.** Moses' load was carrying and leading Israel (Deut. 1:12; also translated problems, weight, cumbrance). Or it indicates something that has become a burden or load that should have been otherwise, e.g., Israel's hypocritical worship of the Lord in her feasts and festivals (Is. 1:14: trouble, burden). ¶
– 2 Ex. 23:5; 2 Kgs. 5:17; etc. ➔ BURDEN (noun) <4853>.

LOAD (verb) – 1 *ṭā'an* [verb: טָעַן <2943>; a prim. root] ▶ **This word means to put into or on something to be carried or transported, such as provisions or necessities for a trip.** Ref.: Gen. 45:17; KJV, lade. ¶
2 *ṭāraḥ* [verb: טָרַח <2959>; a prim. root] ▶ **This word means to place in or on.** It refers to the Lord's activity of causing water to accumulate in clouds (Job 37:11; also translated to saturate, to weary), to absorb moisture, and eventually disperse as rain. ¶
3 *'āmas, 'āmaś* [verb: עָמַס, עָמַשׂ <6006>; a prim. root] ▶
a. This word means to carry a burden. It indicates putting a load or burden of some kind on persons or animals—wheat, taxes, labor demands. Refs.: Gen. 44:13; 1 Kgs. 12:11; 2 Chr. 10:11; Neh. 13:15. The Lord helps bear the burdens of His people (Ps. 68:19); as well as carry them Himself (Is. 46:3). It is used derisively of idols being loaded and carried in pack animals (Is. 46:1). It is used in a figurative way of Jerusalem being carried by the nations (Zech. 12:3). ¶
b. A verb meaning to transport, to carry a load. It is used here to distinguish a class of workmen (those who carried materials to the builders) from the class that removed rubble and the class that did the construction. It describes the task of carrying materials to reconstruct the wall of Jerusalem (Neh. 4:17). ¶

LOAF – 1 Judg. 7:13 ➔ CAKE <6742> 2 1 Sam. 2:36; 1 Sam. 10:3 ➔ ROUND (SOMETHING) <3603> 3 Hos. 7:8 ➔ CAKE <5692>.

LOAN – 1 *maššā'āh* [fem. noun: מַשָּׁאָה <4859>; from USURY <4855>] ▶ **This word means something lent; it also depicts a debt.** It indicates something given to a neighbor with the expectation that it will be paid back (Deut. 24:10; Prov. 22:26). ¶
2 *maššeh* [masc. noun: מַשֶּׁה <4874>; from LEND <5383>] ▶ **This word refers to something borrowed.** It is found in Deuteronomy 15:2 preceded by *ba'al*, lord, possessor. It refers to a loan or a debt. The phrase translates as creditor, literally, lord of debt. ¶
– 3 Hab. 2:6 ➔ PLEDGE (noun) <5671> a.

LOAN, LOAN (MAKE A) – Deut. 15:2; 24:10, 11 ➔ LEND <5383>.

LOATH – 1 Lev. 26:30; Jer. 14:19; Ezek. 16:45 ➔ ABHOR <1602> 2 Ezek. 16:5 ➔ LOATHING <1604>.

LOATHE – [1] ***qûṭ*** [verb: קוּט <6962>; a prim. root] ▶ **This word means to abhor; it is also translated to be weary, to grieve, to be grieved, to be angry, to be disgusted. It means to despise, to feel a revulsion toward something or someone.** Job loathed, despised his miserable condition (Job 10:1); God loathed, abhorred His rebellious people (Ps. 95:10). The righteous person loathes those who do not keep God's Word (Ps. 119:158; 139:21). It describes a people's feeling of disgust toward themselves (Ezek. 6:9; 20:43; 36:31). ¶
[2] ***qûṣ*** [verb: קוּץ <6973>; a prim. root (identical with SUMMER (verb) <6972>)] ▶ **This word means to be disgusted, to be sick of; it is also translated to abhor, to detest, to be weary, to be tired.** The word signifies God's revulsion toward pagan practices (Lev. 20:23); by Israel toward manna (ungratefully and wrongly) after eating it for years (Num. 21:5; cf. Ps. 78:22–25); by Rebekah toward her Hittite daughters-in-law (Gen. 27:46); and by Solomon's son toward the Lord's rebuke (Prov. 3:11). It also signified the loathing felt by enemies toward Israel's prosperity (Ex. 1:12; Num. 22:3). In Isaiah 7:6, the causative sense means to vex. By taking over, the enemies planned to cause Judah to abhor them. Other refs.: 1 Kgs. 11:25; Is. 7:16. ¶
– [3] Job 33:20 ➔ ABHOR <2092> [4] Prov. 27:7 ➔ TREAD DOWN <947> [5] Amos 6:8 ➔ ABHOR <8374>.

LOATHING – ***gōʿal*** [masc. noun: גֹּעַל <1604>; from ABHOR <1602>] ▶ **This word indicates a despising, an aversion, an abhorrence; it is translated by verbs: to loath, to abhor, to despise.** It depicts a attitude of rejection or neglect toward something, in this case, Israel when she was born (Ezek. 16:5). ¶

LOATHSOME – [1] ***zārāʾ*** [fem. noun: זָרָא <2214>; from STRANGER (BE) <2114> (in the sense of estrangement) (comp. SCRUTINIZE <2219>)] ▶ **This word indicates a disgusting thing or object.** It refers to the quail meat that was given in such abundance that it became detestable as food for the Israelites (Num. 11:20). ¶
– [2] Job 6:7 ➔ ILLNESS <1741> [3] Prov. 13:5: to be loathsome ➔ STINK <887> [4] Is. 66:24 ➔ ABHORRENCE <1860>.

LOATHSOME (BE) – [1] Ps. 38:7 ➔ ROAST <7033> c. [2] Ps. 77:9 ➔ ENTREAT <2589>.

LOBE – ***tᵉnûḵ*** [masc. noun: תְּנוּךְ <8571>; from PLUMB LINE <594> through the idea of protraction] ▶ **This word indicates the tip of the ear. It refers to the thick, soft, lower part of a person's ear.** It was anointed in a ritual to consecrate the priests to God and their sacred duties, indicating a demand for total commitment and obedience to the Lord's work (Ex. 29:20; Lev. 8:23, 24). The lobe of the ear was anointed with blood and oil taken from a guilt offering in a ritual that cleansed a leper (Lev. 14:14, 17, 25, 28). ¶

LOBE (LONG, FATTY) – ***yōṯereṯ*** [fem. noun: יֹתֶרֶת <3508>; fem. act. part. of REMAIN <3498>] ▶ **This word refers to an appendage, portions of the liver; also translated caul (KJV).** It designates the lobes of the liver in cattle, sheep, and goats (not humans) (Ex. 29:13, 22; Lev. 3:4, 10, 15; 4:9; 7:4; 8:16, 25; 9:10, 19). All references are related to sacrifices in Israel. ¶

LOCK (noun) – [1] ***maḥlāp̄āh*** [fem. noun: מַחְלָפָה <4253>; from PASS ON <2496> b. (maybe in the sense of to grow up)] ▶ **This word identifies a small piece of hair, braid of hair.** It is used of Samson's long hair as a Nazarite wherein lay his strength (Judg. 16:13, 19). ¶
[2] ***minʿāl*** [masc. noun: מִנְעָל <4515>; from LOCK (verb) <5274>] ▶
a. This word indicates a bar or bolt used to secure something. It is used figuratively of the locks of Asher to indicate the security of the tribe (Deut. 33:25, NASB, NIV, ESV). ¶
b. Some translators understand this to refer to a shoe or sandal, which is fitting for the context. Ref.: Deut. 33:25, KJV, NKJV. ¶

– [3] Neh. 3:3, 6, 13–15; Song 5:5 ➔ BOLT <4514> [4] Song 4:1, 3; 6:7; Is. 47:2 ➔ VEIL <6777> b. [5] Ezek. 8:3 ➔ TASSEL <6734>.

LOCK, LOCK OF HAIR – ***qᵉwuṣṣāh*** [fem. noun: קְוֻצָּה <6977>; fem. pass. part. of SUMMER (verb) <6972> in its original sense] ▶ **This word refers to tresses, curls, ringlets of hair hanging on a person's head.** It portrays the beauty of the bridegroom. Refs.: Song 5:2, 11. ¶

LOCK OF HAIR – ***pera'*** [masc. noun: פֶּרַע <6545>; from GO (LET) <6544>] ▶ **This word refers to the unbraided or natural free growth of loose hair on a person's head.** Ref.: Num. 6:5. It could be trimmed but not shaved according to Ezekiel's directions (Ezek. 44:20). ¶

LOCK (verb) – ***nā'al*** [verb: נָעַל <5274>; a prim. root] ▶ **This word indicates the securing of a door or doors; it is also translated to bolt.** Refs.: Judg. 3:23, 24; 2 Sam. 13:17, 18. It is used in a figurative sense of a virgin whose love and attentions are locked up in her for her future husband (Song 4:12; also translated to shut up, to enclose). The Hebrew word also means to furnish with footwear; see SHOD <5274>. ¶

LOCKS – Song 7:5 ➔ LOOM <1803>.

LOCUST – [1] ***'arbeh*** [masc. noun: אַרְבֶּה <697>; from MANY (BE, BECOME) <7235>] ▶ **This word refers to a species of migrating or desert grasshoppers, which are jumping and plant-eating insects; it is also translated grasshopper.** Infestations of locusts could destroy entire crops (Deut. 28:38). The eighth plague on Egypt was a locust plague of immense destructive proportions (Ex. 10:4, 12–14, 19). A locust plague, real or imagined, was used figuratively to describe the coming devastation of the day of the Lord (Joel 1:4; 2:25). It was, however, included in the Law of Moses among the insects that could be eaten (Lev. 11:22). The locust appeared suddenly and disappeared suddenly (Nah. 3:15, 3:17). Wise men noted that locusts were a well-organized group, even though they had no king (Prov. 30:27). They could thus be likened to an invading army (Judg. 6:5; 7:12). There were several kinds of locusts or perhaps several phases in the lives of locusts described in Joel 1:4. *

[2] ***gêḇ*** [masc. noun: גֵּב <1357>; prob. from PLOWMAN <1461> (comp. <1462> below)] ▶ **This word refers to a swarm of locusts, plant-eating insects, used figuratively to describe people engaged in plundering spoil.** Ref.: Is. 33:4. ¶

[3] ***gôḇ, gôḇay*** [masc. noun: גּוֹב, גּוֹבַי <1462>; from PLOWMAN <1461>] ▶ **This word depicts a swarm or multitude of locusts which are plant-eating insects.** They were indicative of the multitude of Assyria's military personnel (Nah. 3:17). Amos refers to a locust swarm being gathered to destroy crops (Amos 7:1). ¶

[4] ***gāzām*** [masc. noun: גָּזָם <1501>; from an unused root meaning to devour] ▶ **This word describes a certain kind of locust which normally does not totally devour a crop; it is also translated caterpillar, cutting locust, gnawing locust, locust swarm, palmerworm.** Refs.: Joel 1:4; 2:25. This locust was sent by God as judgment on His people (Amos 4:9). ¶

[5] ***ḥāgāḇ*** [masc. noun: חָגָב <2284>; of uncertain deriv.] ▶ **The context of this word influences its translation greatly. It refers most likely to grasshoppers as one of the clean insects the Israelites were permitted to eat.** Ref.: Lev. 11:22. It is used to indicate something very small (Num. 13:33; Is. 40:22) compared to the Nephilim giants in Canaan. It is translated as locusts based on the context in 2 Chronicles 7:13 but grasshoppers in Ecclesiastes 12:5. ¶

– [6] Deut. 28:42 ➔ WHIRRING <6767> c. [7] Ps. 78:46; Is. 33:4; Joel 1:4; 2:25 ➔ consuming locust, destroying locust, other locust, stripping locust, young locust ➔ CATERPILLAR <2625>.

LOCUST (BALD, DEVASTATING) – ***sol'ām*** [masc. noun: סָלְעָם <5556>; apparently from the same as ROCK <5553> in the sense of crushing as with a rock] ▶ **This word refers to a winged insect, a bald locust, a grasshopper that was permitted as food for the Israelites.** Ref.: Lev. 11:22. ¶

LOCUST (YOUNG, CRAWLING) – ***yeleq*** [masc. noun: יֶלֶק <3218>; from an unused root meaning to lick up] ▶ **This word refers to the creeping, early stage in the life of a grasshopper, an unwinged stage; it is also translated caterpiller, grasshopper, cankerworm (KJV).** Refs.: Joel 1:4; 2:25; Ps. 105:34; Jer. 51:14, 27; Nah. 3:15, 16. ¶

LOD – ***lōḏ*** [proper noun: לֹד <3850>; from an unused root of uncertain signification] ▶ **A town in the tribe of Benjamin.** Refs.: 1 Chr. 8:12; Ezra 2:33; Neh. 7:37; 11:35. ¶

LODGE (noun) – Is. 1:8; 24:20 ➔ HUT <4412>.

LODGE (verb) – ***liyn, lûn*** [verb: לִין, לוּן <3885>; a prim. root] ▶ **This word means to rest, to tarry, to stay, often overnight.** Persons may spend the night or lodge somewhere (Gen. 19:2; 24:23, 25, 54; 28:11). It is used figuratively of righteousness lodging permanently in Zion (Is. 1:21); and of evil thoughts taking residence in the city of Jerusalem (Jer. 4:14). It is used of weeping coming to "lodge" in the evening (Ps. 30:5). It describes the secure, peaceful rest of one living close to the Lord (Ps. 91:1). Used with *'ayin* (EYE <5869>) as subject, it has the sense of to set on, to look upon (Job 17:2). Job notes that his error originates and remains in him (Job 19:4). It indicates a wise person's proper existence, abiding among the wise (Prov. 15:31). It takes on the sense of resting or sleeping when one fears the Lord (Prov. 19:23). Something may remain through the night (Ex. 23:18; Lev. 19:13; Jer. 4:14); or stay the night (Job 39:28). It is used of a dead body remaining in a tree overnight (Deut. 21:23). The Hebrew word also means to grumble; see MURMUR <3885>. *

LODGING – ***mālôn*** [masc. noun: מָלוֹן <4411>; from LODGE <3885>] ▶ **This word is also translated inn, encampment, lodging place. It is used of a temporary place to stay, usually for a night.** Refs.: Gen. 42:27; 43:21; Ex. 4:24; 2 Kgs. 19:23; Is. 10:29; Jer. 9:2. It may mean simply a place in the open to sleep overnight (Josh. 4:3, 8). ¶

LOFTINESS – [1] ***gaḇhûṯ*** [fem. noun: גַּבְהוּת <1365>; from EXALTED (BE) <1361>] ▶ **This word indicates arrogance, pride, haughtiness.** It is used to refer to the arrogant or proud look of the eyes of persons (Is. 2:11) whose pride will be humbled by the Lord (Is. 2:17). ¶
[2] ***śiy'*** [masc. noun: שִׂיא <7863>; from the same as ARISE <7721>] ▶ **This word indicates an excessive degree of pride, superciliousness, arrogance, even to the point of persons thinking they are God; it is also translated haughtiness, excellency, height, pride.** Ref.: Job 20:6. ¶
– [3] Ps. 48:2 ➔ ELEVATION <5131> [4] Is. 2:11, 17 ➔ HEIGHT <7312>.

LOFTY – ***tālûl*** [adj.: תָּלוּל <8524>; a prim. root] ▶ **This word describes anything high like a high mountain.** Ref.: Ezek. 17:22; also translated prominent, eminent. ¶

LOFTY PLACE, LOFTY SHRINE – Ezek. 16:24, 25, 31, 39 ➔ HIGH PLACE <7413>.

LOG – [1] ***lōḡ*** [masc. noun: לֹג <3849>; from an unused root apparently meaning to deepen or hollow (like JAR <3537>)] ▶ **This word refers to a liquid measure of oil. It is used to designate an amount of liquid equal to about two-thirds of a pint (not quite one-third of a liter).** Refs.: Lev. 14:10, 12, 15, 21, 24. It was used in cleansing leprosy or a skin disease. ¶
– [2] 2 Kgs. 6:2, 5 ➔ BEAM <6982>.

LOINCLOTH – [1] Gen. 3:7 ➔ BELT <2290> [2] Job 12:18; Jer. 13:1, 2, 4, 6, 7, 10, 11 ➔ BELT <232>.

LOINS – [1] ***ḥᵃlāṣayim*** [fem. noun: חֲלָצַיִם <2504>; from DRAW OUT <2502> (in the sense of strength)] ▶ **This word is used only in the dual form. It refers to loins (the parts of the human body between the ribs and the hips) but often has a figurative sense.** In general, it is used figuratively to represent the source of strength or human virility (1 Kgs. 8:19; 2 Chr. 6:9). It represents the masculine virtue of acting like a man, being stable, strong, determined (Job 38:3); to face a rebuke (Job 40:7). To loosen or take off one's girded belt is to waver, weaken, or show fear (Is. 5:27). It can refer to one's waist where sackcloth was worn (Is. 32:11). It refers to a belt or sash of righteousness in a figurative sense (Is. 11:5). It refers to the lower stomach area that is full of pangs during childbirth (Jer. 30:6). Other refs.: Gen. 35:11; Job 31:20. ¶

[2] ***ḥᵃraṣ*** [Aramaic fem. noun: חֲרַץ <2783>; from a root corresponding to MOVE <2782> (in the sense of vigor)] ▶ **This word refers also to hip, hip joint. It is used of the hips or hip joints of the human body.** Belshazzar's loins or hips gave way at the appearance of a hand writing on the wall of his palace (Dan. 5:6). ¶

[3] ***kesel*** [masc. noun: כֶּסֶל <3689>; from FOOLISH (BE) <3688>] ▶ **This word means the waist area; it also means confidence, stupidity.** The first use can actually mean the waist area, the kidneys, etc. (Lev. 3:4, 10, 15; 4:9; 7:4; Job 15:27); also translated flanks. The second use is more ambiguous, meaning that in which one puts trust or confidence (Job 8:14; 31:24; Ps. 78:7; Prov. 3:26); also translated hope, trust, side. The final usage is a false self-trust or stupidity (Ps. 49:13; Eccl. 7:25). See the related Hebrew verb *kāsal* [FOOLISH (BE) <3688>] and Hebrew noun *kislāh* (FOLLY <3690>). Other ref.: Ps. 38:7 (loins, sides, back). ¶

[4] ***moṯnayim*** [masc. dual noun: מָתְנַיִם <4975>; from an unused root meaning to be slender] ▶

a. A masculine dual noun meaning loins, waist, body, side. It refers to the section of the human body which connects and supports the upper and lower parts of the body, including the buttocks lumbar region. The hips, loins, and lower back are included. In general use, it referred to the central area of the body (Ezek. 47:4). Sackcloth was placed on one's loins in times of mourning (Gen. 37:34). Clothing girded it during travel (Ex. 12:11); but a girdle was worn regularly (1 Kgs. 2:5). The righteous king is to be girded with righteousness in the messianic kingdom (Is. 11:5). The loins were regarded as full of strength (Deut. 13:11; 1 Kgs. 12:10). In this area, various things were attached and carried such as a sword (2 Sam. 20:8; Neh. 4:18). To gird up one's loins was to prepare for battle or action (1 Kgs. 18:46). *

b. A masculine dual noun referring to a strutting rooster. It depicts a rooster taking long steps, crowing and stretching its neck (Prov. 30:31, NASB, NIV, ESV). It is described as a splendid thing, a stately act. See c. ¶

c. A masculine dual noun describing a dog, a greyhound. Some translators prefer to translate this as the greyhound because of its impressive look and running style (Prov. 30:31, KJV). See b. ¶

LONELY – Ps. 25:16; 68:6 ➔ ONLY <3173>.

LONELY (BE) – Ps. 102:7 ➔ ALONE (BE) <909>.

LONG (adj.) – [1] ***'aṣṣiyl*** [fem. noun: אַצִּיל <679>; from RESERVE (verb) <680> (in its primary sense of uniting)] ▶ **This word is used to describe a cubit as long or great (KJV).** Ref.: Ezek. 41:8. The word also means wrist; see WRIST <679>. ¶

[2] ***'ārōḵ*** [adj.: אָרֹךְ <752>; from PROLONG <748>] ▶ **This word means extending for a great time or space; it occurs only in the feminine singular tense.** It is used to modify exile (Jer. 29:28); war (2 Sam. 3:1); and God's wisdom (Job 11:9, longer). See PROLONG <748>. ¶

– [3] Prov. 25:15; etc. ➔ LENGTH <753>.

LONG (verb) – [1] Gen. 34:8 ➔ DESIRE (verb) <2836> [2] Is. 21:4 ➔ DESIRE (noun) <2837> [3] Is. 26:9 ➔ DESIRE (verb) <183>.

LONG FOR – [1] ***yā'aḇ*** [verb: יָאַב <2968>; a prim. root] ▶ **This word means to desire, to crave.** It is used metaphorically of desiring, longing for the laws and commandments of God (Ps. 119:131). ¶

[2] ***kāsap̱*** [verb: כָּסַף <3700>; a prim. root] ▶ **This word refers to a strong, affectionate desire for someone or something, especially the presence of the Lord.** Refs.: Gen. 31:30; Ps. 84:2. It also indicates a lion's powerful hunger for food (Ps. 17:12: to be greedy, to be eager, to be hungry). It takes on the sense of shameless with regard to a nation so set on its rebellion and sin that it is not ashamed (Zeph. 2:1: shameless, without shame, undesirable, shameful, not desired). Other ref.: Job 14:15 (to desire, to long for). ¶

[3] ***šā'ap̱*** [verb: שָׁאַף <7602>; a prim. root] ▶ **a. A verb meaning to gasp, to pant; to wait eagerly for, to hurry for. It means to desire, to crave for, to seek for something.** It indicates a desire to obtain the wealth of others (Job 5:5); the desire of a laborer to rest in the shade (Job 7:2). It indicates a longing for the night (Job 36:20). It depicts a donkey in heat sniffing the wind (Jer. 2:24; 14:6). It describes the seeming hastening of the sun across the sky (Eccl. 1:5). It depicts the panting of a woman giving birth (Is. 42:14). It describes an evil eagerness, a panting after the needy to oppress them further (Amos 2:7). Other ref.: Ps. 119:131.

b. A verb meaning to pursue, to chase. It describes the psalmist's enemies pursuing him (Ps. 56:1, 2); threatening him (Ps. 57:3).

c. A verb meaning to swallow up. It is translated as to swallow up, to devour by some translators, but see a. Its use is figurative in Job 5:5. It refers to the evil enemies of the psalmist (Ps. 56:1, 2; 57:3). It describes the Lord's going forth to devour His enemies (Is. 42:14); and also the act of Israel's enemies devouring, destroying them (Ezek. 36:3). Other ref.: Amos 8:4.

d. A verb meaning to trample on; to crush. This is another alternative rendering of this word in some contexts: to trample on someone (Ps. 56:1, 2; 57:3). Israel's enemies are depicted as having crushed, trampled her (Ezek. 36:3). For Amos 2:7, see a. ¶

[4] ***tā'aḇ*** [verb: תָּאַב <8373>; a prim. root] ▶ **This word is used figuratively of a person's inherent desire for God's ethical and moral precepts.** Refs.: Ps. 119:40, 174. ¶

– [5] Ps. 63:1 ➔ FAINT <3642>.

LONG-SLEEVED – 2 Sam. 13:18, 19 ➔ COLORS (OF MANY) <6446> b.

LONGER (TAKE) – 2 Sam. 20:5 ➔ DELAY (verb) <3186>.

LONGING – [1] ***kāleh*** [adj.: כָּלֶה <3616>; from FINISH <3615>] ▶ **This word means yearning, desire; it is also translated to fail with longing, to yearn, to wear out.** It is used of parents' yearning for their absent children (Deut. 28:32). ¶

[2] ***ta'ᵃḇāh*** [fem. noun: תַּאֲבָה <8375>; from LONG FOR <8373>] ▶ **This word indicates a desire, an intense hunger to experience and follow God's laws and ordinances.** Ref.: Ps. 119:20. ¶

– [3] Ps. 107:9 ➔ RUSH (verb) <8264> b., c.

LONGING (WEARY WITH) – Deut. 28:65 ➔ FAILING <3631>.

LONGWINGED – Ezra 4:14 ➔ SLOW <750>.

LOOK (noun) – [1] ***hakkārāh*** [fem. noun: הַכָּרָה <1971>; from DETERMINE <5234>] ▶ **This word indicates appearance, expression.** The facial appearance or countenance that reveals a person's attitudes (Is. 3:9) and character; the word is also translated shew (KJV). ¶

– [2] Eccl. 5:11 ➔ BEHOLDING <7212>.

LOOK (verb) – [1] ***naḇaṭ*** [verb: נָבַט <5027>; a prim. root] ▶ **This verb means to gaze, and also to watch, to regard.** It has the sense of looking somewhat intensely in a focused way at something; to gaze: to gaze at the heavens (Gen. 15:5); at Sodom and Gomorrah (Gen. 19:17, 26); at the sea (1 Kgs. 18:43). It is used in a figurative sense of looking at, considering the commands of the Lord to follow them (Ps. 74:20; 119:6, 15, 18; also translated to have respect, to contemplate, to have regard, to have the eyes fixed, to see, to behold); to look on something for help, dependence (Is. 22:8, 11). It means to evaluate or consider by looking at something (1 Sam. 16:7; 17:42; Ps. 84:9; Amos 5:22). It is used of the keen observations of an eagle from a great distance (Job 39:29; also translated to observe, to detect); and of the Lord's gazing on the earth from His habitation (Ps. 102:19; also translated to behold, to view, to gaze). *

[2] **look out, look forth, look narrowly:** ***šāgāḥ*** [verb: שָׁגָה <7688>; a prim. root] ▶ **This word means to regard attentively; it also means to gaze, to watch, to stare.** It refers to a person's observing closely, looking intently at something, studying it but mainly appreciating something (Ps. 33:14; Song 2:9). It takes on a sense of looking at intently in surprise or wonder (Is. 14:16). ¶

[3] ***šûr*** [verb: שׁוּר <7789>; a prim. root, identical with JOURNEY (verb) <7788> through the idea of going round for inspection] ▶ **This word means to gaze on, to regard, to see, to observe.** It refers to simply looking at, observing something from the heights (Num. 23:9). It means to see a person (Job 7:8); or to regard something in one's thinking and emotions (Job 17:15). God can hide Himself so that He is not observable (Job 34:29). It means to gaze out over an area (Song 4:8, but see <7788> also). It is used of observing others to harm them (Jer. 5:26); lying in wait for them (Hos. 13:7). It describes in a prophetic figurative sense seeing something in the future (Num. 24:17); and to God's looking carefully over His people (Hos. 14:8). *

– [4] Job 10:15 ➔ CONSCIOUS <7202> [5] Ps. 104:27; 145:15 ➔ WAIT <7663> [6] Song 1:6 ➔ SEE <7805> a. [7] Song 2:9 ➔ BLOSSOM (verb) <6692> b. [8] Song 4:8 ➔ JOURNEY (verb) <7788> [9] See BEHOLD (interj.) <2009>.

LOOK! – [1] Ezek. 21:15 ➔ ALAS! <253> [2] Dan. 3:25 ➔ BEHOLD (interj.) <1888>.

LOOK AFTER – Ezek. 34:12 ➔ SEEK <1243>.

LOOK DOWN – ***šāqap*** [verb: שָׁקַף <8259>; a prim. root] ▶ **This word has the sense from context of a person, of God, looking down, observing from above; it also means to overlook.** It is used of people or angels (Gen. 18:16); Abraham (Gen. 19:28); God (Ex. 14:24; Ps. 14:2; 53:2; 102:19; Lam 3:50); evil (Jer. 6:1). It may mean simply to look over at something, to observe (Gen. 26:8; Prov. 7:6). It is used in the sense of to look forth, to shine forth (Song 6:10). *

LOOK FAVORABLY – Job 10:3 ➔ SHINE, SHINE FORTH <3313>.

LOOK WITH FAVOR OR IN DISMAY – ***šā'āh, šāta'*** [verb: שָׁעָה, שָׁתַע <8159>; a prim. root] ▶

a. This word means to consider something with approval, to accept it (Gen. 4:4, 5); or to consider some burdensome thing or situation in trepidation, discouragement (Ex. 5:9). It can mean simply to hope for, to desire, to look for (2 Sam. 22:42). It has the sense of looking at intently (Job 7:19; Ps. 39:13). It can have the sense of looking at with high regard and appreciation (Is. 17:7); or just the opposite according to context (Is. 17:8; 41:10). It has the sense of seeing with understanding (Is. 32:3).

b. This word indicates considering something with anxiety. This is a possible nuanced meaning given to this word by some translators (Is. 41:10, 23). *

LOOKING GLASS – Job 37:18 ➔ MIRROR <7209>.

LOOKOUT – 2 Chr. 20:24 ➔ WATCHTOWER <4707>.

LOOM – [1] ***'ereg*** [masc. noun: אֶרֶג <708>; from WEAVE <707>] ▶ **This word refers to a weaving apparatus or weaver's shuttle.** It describes a hairpiece or hair loom or web (Judg. 16:14). The speed of the motion of the weaver's shuttle is used metaphorically to refer to the days of Job's life passing by swiftly (Job 7:6). ¶

2 ***dallāh*** [fem. noun: דַּלָּה <1803>; from DRAW <1802>] ▶ **This word indicates a weaving apparatus on which thread or yarn was made into cloth by weaving or possibly the activity of the worker at the loom.** Ref.: Is. 38:12. It denotes the hair of the bridegroom (Song 7:5); also translated locks. The Hebrew word denotes also poverty; see POOR <1803>. ¶

LOOP – ***maḥberet̲*** [fem. noun: מַחְבֶּרֶת <4225>; from JOIN TOGETHER <2266>] ▶ **This word means a place of joining; that which is joined.** It is the juncture at which various parts of the priestly clothing were connected (Ex. 28:27; 39:20: seam, coupling); a tie or connecting loop on the curtains or hangings of the Tabernacle (Ex. 26:4, 5; 36:11, 12, 17). ¶

LOOPS – ***lulā'ôt̲*** [fem. plur. noun: לֻלָאוֹת <3924>; from the same as STAIRWAY <3883>] ▶ **This word indicates circular fasteners of cloth made to hold the curtains of the Tabernacle together with clasps through them.** Refs.: Ex. 26:4, 5, 10, 11; 36:11, 12, 17. ¶

LOOSE – 1 Lev. 13:40, 41 ➔ PULL, PULL OUT <4803> 2 Job 6:9; Ps. 105:20; 146:7 ➔ LOOSE (LET) <5425> 3 Job 31:39 ➔ BREATHE <5301> 4 Prov. 3:21 ➔ PERVERSE <3868> 5 Is. 33:9 ➔ SHAKE <5287>.

LOOSE (COME) – ***zāḥaḥ*** [verb: זָחַח <2118>; a prim. root] ▶ **This verb indicates to be removed; it is also translated to be loosed, to swing out.** It indicates the loosening or falling off of an object, such as the breastpiece of the priest's garments (Ex. 28:28; 39:21) that was tightly fastened to the ephod. ¶

LOOSE (LET) – 1 ***nāt̲ar*** [verb: נָתַר <5425>; a prim. root] ▶ **This word means to loosen, to undo, to set free, to release, to set, to make; it is also translated to loose.** It means to not regard or to remove oneself from the direction of something (2 Sam. 22:33: to make); to let something go (Job 6:9). It means to release, to set free a political prisoner or slave (Ps. 105:20); especially of the Lord freeing the oppressed (Ps. 146:7; Is. 58:6: to undo). The Hebrew word also means to jump; see LEAP <5425>. ¶
2 ***šārāh*** [verb: שָׁרָה <8281>; a prim. root] ▶ **This word means to let go. It occurs in the Old Testament only once.** In Job 37:3, it describes God's loosing of thunder and lightning; it is also translated to unleash, to let go, to direct, to send forth. ¶

LOOSE (LET, TURNED) – Is. 7:25 ➔ LAY, PUT <4916> b.

LOOSED (BE) – Ex. 28:28; 39:21 ➔ LOOSE (COME) <2118>.

LOOSEN – ***šᵉrê'*** [Aramaic verb: שְׁרֵא <8271>; a root corresponding to that of SET FREE <8293>] ▶ **This word means to make something untight, to free someone; it also means to dissolve; to solve (problems).** It carries a sense of support, to aid, to help (Ezra 5:2). It has the sense of dwelling with or being dispersed when used of light in relationship to God (Dan. 2:22). It refers to someone being loosed after being bound up (Dan. 3:25). It indicates loose joints or sockets (Dan. 5:6). With reference to problems, it means to solve them, to disentangle them (Dan. 5:12, 16). ¶

LOOT – 1 Is. 13:16 ➔ PLUNDER (verb) <8155> 2 Is. 42:24 ➔ SPOIL (noun) <4882> 3 See PLUNDER (verb) <962>.

LOP, LOP OFF – ***sā'ap̱*** [verb: סָעַף <5586>; a prim. root] ▶ **This word describes the cutting off, the pruning of tree branches.** Figuratively, it describes God's cutting off the Assyrian army (Is. 10:33). ¶

LOP OFF – 1 Is. 18:5 ➔ CUT DOWN <8456> 2 Dan. 4:14 ➔ CUT OFF <7113>.

LORD – 1 ***'ādôn*** [masc. noun: אָדוֹן <113>; from an unused root (meaning to rule)] ▶ **A word designating a master or a sovereign. The most frequent usage is of a**

human lord, but it is also used of divinity. Generally, it carries the nuances of authority rather than ownership. When used of humans, it refers to authority over slaves (Gen. 24:9; Judg. 19:11); people (1 Kgs. 22:17); a wife (Gen. 18:12; Amos 4:1); or a household (Gen. 45:8; Ps. 105:21). When used of divinity, it frequently occurs with *y*^{e}*hōwāh* (<3068> below), signifying His sovereignty (Ex. 34:23; Josh. 3:13; Is. 1:24). See the Hebrew noun ^{a}*ḏōnāy* below. *

2 ^{a}***ḏōnāy*** [masc. proper noun: אֲדֹנָי <136>; an emphatic form of <113> above] ► **This word is used exclusively of God. It means literally "my Lord" (Gen. 18:3). It is often used in place of the divine name *YHWH*: GOD (see <3068> below), which was held by later Jewish belief to be too holy to utter.** This designation points to the supreme authority or power of God (Ps. 2:4; Is. 6:1). The word was often combined with the divine name to reinforce the notion of God's matchlessness (e.g., Ezek. 20:3; Amos 7:6). *

3 ***ba'al*** [masc. noun: בַּעַל <1167>; from MARRY <1166>] ► **This word also means husband, owner, possessor, the title of a Canaanite deity (Baal).** It can also denote rulers and leaders (Is. 16:8). Commonly, it refers to legally owning something such as an ox or bull (Ex. 21:28); house (Ex. 22:8; or land (Job 31:38). It can also describe possessing a quality, attribute, or characteristic like anger (Prov. 22:24); wrath (Prov. 29:22); hair (2 Kgs. 1:8); appetite (Prov. 23:2); wisdom (Eccl. 7:12). When Joseph is called a dreamer, he is literally a possessor of dreams (Gen. 37:19). Further, the word can connote husband as used of Abraham (Gen. 20:3) and elsewhere (Ex. 21:3; Deut. 22:22). It often refers to the Canaanite deity, generally known as Baal in the Old Testament and other local manifestations (Num. 25:3). Worship of this deity seems to have been common in the Northern Kingdom which is attested in the preponderance of the Baal theophoric element in many proper nouns. The Lord may also have been referred to with this generic term for "lord." But in light of the worship of Baal in the north, Hosea longed for a time when this usage would cease (Hos. 2:16). *

4 ***g***^{e}***ḇiyr*** [masc. noun: גְּבִיר <1376>; from PREVAIL <1396>] ► **This word refers also to a ruler, master.** It occurs in Isaac's blessing of Jacob, describing Jacob as the future master and lord over his brother Esau and his descendants (Gen. 27:29, 37). ¶

5 ***yāh*** [neuter pronoun: יָהּ <3050>; contr. of <3068> below, and meaning the same] ► **This neuter pronoun of God, a shortened form of Yahweh, is often translated "LORD." This abbreviated noun for Yahweh is used in poetry, especially in the Psalms.** The word is found first in Exodus 15:2 and 17:16; in both cases, the LORD is exalted after He delivered His people from possible annihilation, first by Egypt and then by the Amalekites. These two poetic passages are then quoted later (Ps. 118:14; Is. 12:2). In a poetic prayer, Hezekiah used the endearing term also (Is. 38:11). All other uses of the shortened name are found in Psalms (Ps. 68:18; 77:11; 130:3). Many times it is found in the phrase, "Hallelujah, praise be to Yah!" (Ps. 104:35; 105:45; 106:1, 48). *

6 ***y***^{e}***hōwāh*** [proper noun: יְהוָה <3068>; from BE <1961>]: the existing One, the Eternal ► **This word means God. It refers to the proper name of the God of Israel, particularly the name by which He revealed Himself to Moses (Ex. 6:2, 3).** The divine name has traditionally not been pronounced, primarily out of respect for its sacredness (cf. Ex. 20:7; Deut. 28:58). Until the Renaissance, it was written without vowels in the Hebrew text of the Old Testament, being rendered as YHWH. However, since that time, the vowels of another word, ^{a}*ḏōnāy* (LORD <136>), have been supplied in hopes of reconstructing the pronunciation. Although the exact derivation of the name is uncertain, most scholars agree that its primary meaning should be understood in the context of God's existence, namely, that He is the "I AM THAT I AM" (Ex. 3:14), the One who was, who is, and who always will be (cf. Rev. 11:17). Older translations of the Bible and many newer ones employ the practice of rendering the divine name in capital letters, so as to distinguish it from other Hebrew words. It is

most often rendered as LORD (Gen. 4:1; Deut. 6:18; Ps. 18:31; Jer. 33:2; Jon. 1:9) but also as GOD (Gen. 6:5; 2 Sam. 12:22) or JEHOVAH (Ps. 83:18; Is. 26:4). The frequent appearance of this name in relation to God's redemptive work underscores its tremendous importance (Lev. 26:45; Ps. 19:14). Also, it is sometimes compounded with another word to describe the character of the Lord in greater detail (see Gen. 22:14; Ex. 17:15; Judg. 6:24). *

7 ***mārê'*** [Aramaic noun: 4756> מָרֵא; from a root corresponding to REBELLIOUS <4754> in the sense of domineering, a master>] ► **This word refers to one who is full of authority. It appears only four times, and all occurrences are found in the book of Daniel.** It is applied to King Nebuchadnezzar (Dan. 4:19, 24) and to God (Dan. 2:47; 5:23). This term appears in parallel with *meleḵ* (<4430>), meaning king (Dan. 2:47; 4:24) in two of the occurrences. It appears in reference to a human king (and in virtual parallelism with *meleḵ* [KING <4430>] in another occurrence (Dan. 4:19). In the final occurrence (Dan. 5:23), it appears in the phrase, *mārê' šᵉmayyā'* (HEAVEN <8065>), "the Lord of heaven," which is a reference to the divine monarch. Therefore, it is clear that this is a term that represents an individual with much power, authority, and respect. ¶

8 ***seren*** [masc. sing. noun: סֶרֶן <5633>; from an unused root of uncertain meaning] ► **This term is a Philistine loan word and was applied only to Philistine rulers.** Five rulers reigned in the five main cities of the Philistines: Ashdod, Gaza, Ashkelon, Gath, and Ekron (1 Sam. 6:16, 18). In one passage, the word is translated axle of brass, based on the Septuagint rendering (1 Kgs. 7:30), but the etymology is unknown. David and his men were sent away by the *seren* and not allowed to fight for the Philistines (1 Chr. 12:19). *

– 9 Jer. 25:34–36 ➔ MIGHTY <117> 10 Dan. 4:36; 5:1–3, 9, 10, 23; 6:17 ➔ NOBLE <7261>.

LORD IS MY BANNER (THE) – Ex. 17:15 ➔ JEHOVAH NISSI <3071>.

LORD IS OUR RIGHTEOUSNESS (THE) – Jer. 23:6; 33:16 ➔ JEHOVAH TSIDKENU <3072>.

LORD IS PEACE (THE) – Judg. 6:24 ➔ JEHOVAH SHALOM <3071>.

LORD IS THERE (THE) – Ezek. 48:35 ➔ JEHOVAH SHAMMAH <3074>.

LORD WILL PROVIDE (THE) – Gen. 22:14 ➔ JEHOVAH JIREH <3070>.

LORD (verb) – Num. 16:13 ➔ RULE (verb) <8323>.

LORD OVER – See RULE OVER <7980>, <7981>.

LORDLY – 1 Judg. 5:25 ➔ MIGHTY <117> 2 Zech. 11:13 ➔ ROBE <145>.

LOSE – Eccl. 3:6 ➔ PERISH <6>.

LOSS – 1 ***nêzeq*** [masc. noun: נֵזֶק <5143>; from an unused root meaning to injure] ► **This word indicates an annoying disturbance, a bother, or an agitation to someone; it is also translated damage, annoyance.** Ref.: Esther 7:4. ¶
– 2 Dan. 6:2 ➔ DAMAGE (verb) <5142>.

LOSS OF CHILDREN – ***šᵉḵôl*** [masc. noun: שְׁכוֹל <7908>; inf. of DEPRIVED OF CHILDREN <7921>] ► **This Hebrew word means bereavement. It primarily indicates a loss of children.** In Isaiah's oracle against Babylon, he stated that the woman who thought of herself as lasting forever would become a widow and suffer the loss of her children. The Virgin Daughter of Babylon, who once thought that there was none like her, would suffer the fate of a common person (Is. 47:8, 9). The word is also used to denote how the soul is left after a ruthless witness repays evil for good (Ps. 35:12; also translated spoiling, sorrow). ¶

LOSS OF LIFE – Job 11:20 ➔ lit.: breathing out life ➔ BREATHING OUT <4646>.

LOSS OF TIME – *šeḇeṯ* [masc. noun: שֶׁבֶת <7674>; from REST (verb) <7673>] ▶ **This word means a ceasing, a time of inactivity.** It indicates literally a sitting or a time of recovery, inactivity (Ex. 21:19); or a refusal to become involved in something, a holding back (Prov. 20:3: to stop, to keep away, to cease, to keep aloof, to avoid). It refers to a period of inactivity by a nation, an inability to act, referring to Egypt (Is. 30:7: to sit still, to do nothing). ¶

LOST (BE) – 1 Num. 17:12; Deut. 22:3 ➔ PERISH <6> 2 Lam. 3:54 ➔ CUT (verb) <1504>.

LOST PROPERTY, LOST THING – Lev. 6:3, 4; Deut. 22:3 ➔ PROPERTY (LOST) <9>.

LOT (noun) – *gôrāl* [masc. noun: גּוֹרָל <1486>; from an unused root meaning to be rough (as stone)] ▶ **This word indicates a portion, a share.** A lot was cast, probably a stone or stones, to decide questions or appoint persons for various reasons; for apportioning land (Num. 26:55; 33:54; Josh. 18:6, 11); for assignments of various kinds, such as goats on the Day of Atonement (Lev. 16:8–10); priests, singers, musicians, etc. to their duties (1 Chr. 24:5, 31; 25:8; 26:13); for living in Jerusalem (Neh. 11:1), etc. (Judg. 20:9; Neh. 10:34); for allotting slaves (Joel 3:3). Lots were cast to distribute garments (Ps. 22:18). The word also is used to refer to things allotted such as land (Josh. 15:1; 17:1; 21:40) or even the boundary itself of an allotment (Josh. 18:11). It refers figuratively to one's destiny or fortune (Prov. 1:14) but notes an allotted share or portion in the age to come (Dan. 12:13). Finally, it can designate a portion or allotment for someone in the sense of recompense or retribution (Is. 17:14; Jer. 13:25). *

LOT (proper noun) – *lôṭ* [masc. proper noun: לוֹט <3876>; from COVERING <3875>]: covering, veil ▶ **Nephew of Abraham.** Refs.: Gen. 11:27, 31; 12:4, 5; 13:1, 5, 7, 8, 10–12, 14; 14:12, 16; 19:1, 5, 6, 9, 10, 12, 14, 15, 18, 23, 29, 30, 36; Deut. 2:9, 19; Ps. 83:8. God preserved Lot at the destruction of Sodom (Luke 17:28, 29). His wife, who looked back, became a pillar of salt (Luke 17:32; see Gen. 19:26). God delivered Lot who was oppressed by the dissolute behavior of his fellow citizens; Lot is recognized a "righteous" man (2 Pet. 2:7). ¶

LOTAN – *lôṭān* [masc. proper noun: לוֹטָן <3877>; from COVERING <3875>]: covering, veil ▶ **One of the sons of Seir, the Horite.** Refs.: Gen. 36:20, 22, 29; 1 Chr. 1:38, 39. ¶

LOTH – Lev. 26:30; Jer. 14:19; Ezek. 16:45 ➔ ABHOR <1602>.

LOTHING – Ezek. 16:5 (KJV) ➔ LOATHING <1604>.

LOTUS PLANTS, LOTUS TREES – *ṣeʾliym* [masc. plur. noun: צֶאֱלִים <6628>; from an unused root meaning to be slender] ▶
a. This word refers to a species of thorny shrubs. It is one place where Behemoth lies down and makes his bed (Job 40:21, 22). Most consider it to be a reference to a lotus plant, a water lily.
b. Earlier translators took this to be a reference to shade trees under which Behemoth would lie. Refs.: Job 40:21, 22: shady trees. ¶

LOUDER – Ex. 19:19 ➔ STRONGER <2390>.

LOUDLY – Mic. 4:9 ➔ NOISE <7452>.

LOVE (noun) – 1 ***ʾahaḇ*** [masc. noun: אַהַב <158>; from LOVE (verb) <157>] ▶ **The Hebrew word means tender affection; it is translated loving and lover. Both occurrences of this Hebrew word are in the plural.** In Proverbs 5:19, it refers to marital love, while in Hosea 8:9, the word refers to Israel's trust in foreign alliances rather than in God. The foreign nations are Israel's hired lovers. ¶
2 ***ʾahᵃḇāh*** [fem. noun: אַהֲבָה <160>; fem. of <158> above and meaning the same] ▶

The word often signifies a powerful, intimate relationship between a man and a woman. Refs.: Gen. 29:20; Song 2:4, 5, 7. It signifies also love between friends (2 Sam. 1:26); God's love for His people (Is. 63:9; Hos. 3:1). Frequently, it is associated with forming a covenant, which enjoins loyalty (Deut. 7:8). When used in an abstract way, the word designates a desirable personal quality, which connotes affection and faithfulness (Prov. 15:17; 17:9). *

3 ***'ōhaḇ*** [masc. noun: אֹהַב <159>; from LOVE (verb) <157>, meaning the same as LOVE (noun) <158>] ▶ **The word means loved one, paramour.** It occurs twice in the Hebrew Bible, both times in the plural (Prov. 7:18; Hos. 9:10); it is also translated caresses in Proverbs 7:18. Both occurrences are associated with illicit sexual relations. ¶

4 ***'āḡāḇ*** [masc. plur. noun: עֲגָב <5690>; from LUST (verb) <5689>] ▶ **This word means lust.** It describes words of lustfulness, words or songs of love, words that have little meaning to the hearers (Ezek. 33:31, 32; also translated lustful, lovely, sensual). ¶

5 ***ra'yāh*** [fem. noun: רַעְיָה <7474>; fem. of PERSON (ANOTHER) <7453> (in the sense of associate, friend)] ▶ **This word indicates a female companion; it is also translated darling.** In Song of Solomon the beloved of the bridegroom is mentioned at least nine times (Song 1:9, 15; 2:2, 10, 13; 4:1, 7; 5:2; 6:4). ¶

– 6 Ps. 84:1 BELOVED <3039>.

LOVE (SET ONE'S) – Deut. 7:7 ➔ DESIRE (verb) <2836>.

LOVE (verb) – 1 ***'āhaḇ*** [verb: אָהַב <157>; a prim. root] ▶ **The semantic range of the verb includes various things.** Loving or liking objects and things such as bribes (Is. 1:23); wisdom (Prov. 4:6); wine (Prov. 21:17); peace, truth (Zech. 8:19); or tasty food (Gen. 27:4, 9, 14). The word also conveys love for other people (Gen. 29:32; Ruth 4:15; 1 Kgs. 11:1); love for God (Ex. 20:6; Ps. 116:1); and also God's love of people (Deut. 4:37; 1 Kgs. 10:9; Hos. 3:1). *

2 ***ḥāḇaḇ*** [verb: חָבַב <2245>; a prim. root (comp. HIDE <2244>, HIDE <2247>)] ▶ **This word occurs only once in the Old Testament, in which it describes God's love for the people of Israel.** Ref.: Deut. 33:3. This verse is in a poetical section of Scripture, which helps to explain why this word is used only once. It is related to *ḥōḇ* (HEART <2243>), which is used only in Job 31:33. Thus, the love expressed here probably signifies an embracing, motherly affection. ¶

LOVED ONE – See LOVER <1730>.

LOVELY – 1 2 Sam. 1:23; Ps. 135:3 ➔ PLEASANT <5273> a. 2 Ps. 84:1 BELOVED <3039> 3 Song 1:5; 2:14; 4:3; 6:4; Jer. 6:2 ➔ BEAUTIFUL <5000> 4 Ezek. 33:32 ➔ LOVE (noun) <5690> 5 Dan. 4:12, 21 ➔ BEAUTIFUL <8209>.

LOVELY (BE) – Song 1:10; Is. 52:7 ➔ BEAUTIFUL (BE) <4998>.

LOVER – 1 ***dôḏ*** [masc. noun: דּוֹד <1730>; from an unused root meaning properly to boil] ▶ **This word means beloved, loved one; uncle.** It is used most often in the Song of Solomon and has three clear meanings: (1) the most frequent is an address to a lover, beloved (Song 5:4; 6:3; 7:9); (2) love, used literally of an adulteress who seduced a naïve man (Prov. 7:18), and of Solomon and his lover (Song 1:2, 4; 4:10) (This meaning of love is also used symbolically of Jerusalem reaching the age of love [Ezek. 16:8] and Jerusalem's adultery [bed of love] with the Babylonians [Ezek. 23:17]); and finally, (3) uncle (Lev. 10:4; 1 Sam. 10:14–16; Esther 2:15). *

– 2 Hos. 8:9 ➔ LOVE (noun) <158>.

LOVERS – Jer. 4:30 ➔ LUST (verb) <5689>.

LOVING – Prov. 5:19 ➔ LOVE (noun) <158>.

LOVINGKINDNESS – See MERCY <2617>.

LOW – ***gā'āh*** [verb: גָּעָה <1600>; a prim. root] ▶ **This word imitates the sound cows made when taking the ark to Beth-shemesh.** Ref.: 1 Sam. 6:12. As well as the sound of an ox as it eats its fodder (Job 6:5; also translated to bellow). ¶

LOW ESTATE – Ps. 136:23 ➔ LOW PLACE <8216>.

LOW PLACE – [1] ***šēp̱el*** [masc. noun: שֵׁפֶל <8216>; from HUMBLE, HUMBLE (MAKE) <8213>] ► **This word means a humble estate.** It refers to a social position of relatively low power, influence, and esteem by the world's standards (Eccl. 10:6; also translated humble place, lowly place). It describes the people of Israel at a time when they were powerless and oppressed in the land of Canaan (Ps. 136:23: low estate). ¶
[2] ***šip̱lāh*** [fem. noun: שִׁפְלָה <8218>; fem. of <8216> above] ► **This word indicates lowliness, humiliation.** It refers to the bringing down or lowering of a city, literally, in lowliness the city will be laid low (Is. 32:19). ¶

LOWER, LOWEST – [1] ***taḥtôn*** [adj.: תַּחְתּוֹן <8481>; from UNDER <8478>] ► **This word refers to being below something.** A territory (Josh. 16:3; 18:13; 1 Kgs. 9:17); a story or room (1 Kgs. 6:6, 8); water pool (Is. 22:9); lower street or pavement (Ezek. 40:18); the lower of two ledges (Ezek. 43:14). *
[2] ***taḥtiy*** [adj.: תַּחְתִּי <8482>; from UNDER <8478>] ► **This word means below.** It refers to the lower as opposed to upper stories (Gen. 6:16), e.g., to lower millstones (Job 41:24). Used as a noun, it refers to what is in the lower parts, e.g., of the earth (Is. 44:23; Ezek. 26:20; 31:14). It indicates the lowest areas of Sheol (Deut. 32:22). The foot of Mount Sinai is indicated by *taḥtîṯ*, a feminine form of this word. *

LOWEST – Dan. 4:17 ➔ LOWLIEST <8215>.

LOWLAND – ***šᵉp̱ēlāh*** [שְׁפֵלָה <8219>; from HUMBLE, HUMBLE (MAKE) <8213>] ►
a. A feminine noun meaning a low country; a foothill; a valley. It refers to the lowland including not just a low-lying plain but also the low-lying foothills of western Judea looking out over the Mediterranean (Deut. 1:7; Josh. 9:1; Judg. 1:9; 1 Kgs. 10:27). It also describes the lowland near the seacoast north of Mount Carmel (Josh. 11:2).
b. A proper noun Shephelah. The name means lowlands (KJV, low plains), an area placed under the authority of Baal-Hanan the Gederite (1 Chr. 27:28; Obad. 1:19). *

LOWLIEST – ***šᵉp̱al*** [Aramaic adj.: שְׁפַל <8215>; corresponding to HUMBLE, HUMBLE (MAKE) <8214>] ► **This word means of least importance.** But it is placed before a masculine plural noun to indicate a superlative meaning; lowliest (Dan. 4:17; also translated lowest, basest). ¶

LOWLY – Job 22:29 ➔ HUMBLE <7807>.

LOWLY PLACE – Eccl. 10:6 ➔ LOW PLACE <8216>.

LUBIM – ***lûḇiy*** [masc. proper noun: לוּבִי <3864>; patrial from a name prob. derived from an unused root meaning to thirst] ► **People from Libya, a region situated between Egypt and Carthage.** Refs.: 2 Chr. 12:3; 16:8; Dan. 11:43; Nah. 3:9. ¶

LUCIFER – Is. 14:12 ➔ MORNING STAR <1966>.

LUD, LYDIA – ***lûḏ*** [masc. proper noun: לוּד <3865>; prob. of foreign deriv.] ► **One of the sons of Shem, ancestor of the Lydians.** Refs.: Gen. 10:22; 1 Chr. 1:17; Is. 66:19; Ezek. 27:10; 30:5. ¶

LUDITES, LYDIANS – ***lûḏiym*** [masc. proper noun: לוּדִים <3866>; patrial from LUD, LYDIA <3865>] ► **According to M. G. Easton, they are associated with African nations as mercenaries of the king of Egypt.** Refs.: Gen. 10:13; 1 Chr. 1:11; Jer. 46:9. ¶

LUHITH – ***lûḥiyṯ*** [proper noun: לוּחִית <3872>; from the same as BOARD <3871>]: boards ► **A place in Moab between Zoar and Horonaim.** Refs.: Is. 15:5; Jer. 48:5. ¶

LURK – See WAIT (LIE IN) <693>.

LURKING PLACE – 1 Sam. 23:23 ➔ HIDING PLACE <4224> b.

LURKING PLACES – Ps. 10:8 ➔ AMBUSH <3993>.

LUSH – ***rāṭōḇ*** [adj.: רָטֹב <7373>; from WET (BE) <7372>] ► **This word means well-watered, thriving.** It figuratively describes the prosperousness of the good person before God, his success (Job 8:16; also translated green). ¶

LUST (noun) – [1] ***neḥōšeṯ*** [common noun: נְחֹשֶׁת <5178>] ► **This word is used of female genitals or nakedness, shame, or some such obscene sense of the word; it is also translated lewdness, filthiness.** Ref.: Ezek. 16:36. The Hebrew word also means copper, bronze; see COPPER <5178>. ¶
[2] ***‛agāḇāh*** [fem. noun: עֲגָבָה <5691>; from LUST (verb) <5689>] ► **This word refers to inordinate love, sensual desire.** Figuratively, it indicates apostate desires and the unfaithfulness of the people of Judah (Ezek. 23:11). ¶

LUST (verb) – [1] ***‛āgaḇ*** [verb: עָגַב <5689>; a prim. root (it has the sense of to breathe after)] ► **This word means to sexually desire.** The word occurs in Ezekiel 23 six times (23:5, 7, 9, 12, 16, 20; KJV: to dote) where it refers to the desire of Jerusalem and Samaria for foreign ways under the figure of two sisters who lust after foreigners. Ezekiel warned that, just as Assyria, the object of Samaria's lust, had destroyed them, so sensual Babylon would destroy Jerusalem. The word also occurs as a participle in Jeremiah 4:30 and means lovers. Again, the word is used figuratively in a warning that Jerusalem's foreign lovers would despise and destroy them. ¶
[2] Deut. 12:15, 20, 21 ➔ DESIRE (noun) <185>.

LUSTER (LOSE) – Lam. 4:1 ➔ DIM (BECOME, GROW) <6004>.

LUSTFUL – Ezek. 33:31, 32 ➔ LOVE (noun) <5690>.

LUSTY – [1] ***śāḵāh*** [verb: שָׂכָה <7904>; a prim. root] ►
a. This word is used to describe a sexually aroused horse. It is used figuratively to condemn and illustrate the lustfulness of the people of Jerusalem (Jer. 5:8).
b. This word means to arise in the morning. It refers to well-nurtured horses rising early to neigh after their neighbors, again a figurative use (Jer. 5:8; KJV). ¶
– [2] Jer. 5:8 ➔ WELL-FED <2109>.

LUTE – Ps. 57:8; 92:3 ➔ HARP <5035>.

LUXURIANT (BE) – Hos. 10:1 ➔ EMPTY (MAKE) <1238>.

LUXURIOUS – Is. 13:22 ➔ DELIGHT (noun) <6027>.

LUXURIOUSLY – 2 Sam. 1:24 ➔ DELIGHT (noun) <5730> a.

LUXURY – Prov. 19:10 ➔ DELIGHT (noun) <8588>.

LUZ – ***lûz*** [proper noun: לוּז <3870>; prob. from ALMOND TREE <3869> (as growing there)]: almond tree ►
a. Another name for Bethel. Refs.: Gen. 28:19; 35:6; 48:3; Josh. 16:2; 18:13; Judg. 1:23. ¶
b. A Hittite city. Ref.: Judg. 1:26. ¶

LYE – Jer. 2:22 ➔ SODA <5427>.

LYING – [1] ***keḏaḇ*** [Aramaic adj.: כְּדַב <3538>; from a root corresponding to LIAR (BE) <3576>] ► **This word is used to refer to lying or deceitful words from Nebuchadnezzar's wise men; it is also translated misleading.** Ref.: Dan. 2:9. ¶
[2] ***keḥāš*** [adj.: כֶּחָשׁ <3586>; from DENY <3584>] ► **This word means deceitful; it is also translated false, deceitful.** It occurs only in Isaiah 30:9. The reference is to the deceitfulness of Israel. Their rebellious activities included urging prophets to prophesy falsely and to subvert the authority of the Lord (see Is. 30:10, 11). ¶

LYING DOWN – ***reḇa'*** [verb: רָבַע <7252>; from LIE DOWN <7250>] ► **This word means to lie down, to stretch out prostrate.** Ref.: Ps. 139:3. ¶

LYING IN WAIT – ***ṣᵉḏiyyāh*** [fem. noun: צְדִיָּה <6660>; from LIE IN WAIT <6658>] ► **This word indicates ambushing.** It refers to a person planning to harm someone, waiting to get a chance to do injury, to strike out in a premeditated attempt to harm someone (Num. 35:20, 22). This crime was punishable by death. ¶

LYRE – 1 ***kinnôr*** [masc. noun: כִּנּוֹר <3658>; from an unused root meaning to twang] ► **This word indicates a stringed instrument with a built-in acoustical chest or board; it is also translated harp.** Refs.: Gen. 4:21; 31:27. It was used for sacred (1 Sam. 10:5; 2 Sam. 6:5) or secular (Is. 24:8) music (1 Sam. 16:16; Is. 5:12). It was used in a figurative way of the Lord's heart lamenting like a harp for Moab (Is. 16:11). *

2 ***qiyṯārōs*** [Aramaic masc. noun: קִיתָרֹס <7030>; of Greek origin (*kithara*; from which *guitar* in English)] ► **This word is now generally taken to refer to a lyre or a lute, a stringed instrument of the harp family; it is also translated harp.** Refs.: Dan. 3:5, 7, 10, 15. ¶

– 3 Dan. 3:5, 7, 10, 15 ➔ TRIGON <5443>.

M

MAACAH – ***ma^{a}ḵāh*** [proper noun: מַעֲכָה <4601>; from CRUSH <4600>]: oppression ▶
a. A son of Nahor. Ref.: Gen. 22:24. ¶
b. A wife of Machir. Refs.: 1 Chr. 7:15, 16. ¶
c. A concubine. Ref.: 1 Chr. 2:48. ¶
d. The wife of Jeiel. Refs.: 1 Chr. 8:29; 9:35. ¶
e. A daughter of Talmai. Refs.: 2 Sam. 3:3; 1 Chr. 3:2. ¶
f. The father of Hanan. Ref.: 1 Chr. 11:43. ¶
g. The father of Shephatiah. Ref.: 1 Chr. 27:16. ¶
h. The father of Achish. Ref.: 1 Kgs. 2:39. ¶
i. The wife of Rehoboam. Refs.: 1 Kgs. 15:2, 10, 13; 2 Chr. 11:20–22; 15:16. ¶
j. A small Syrian kingdom near Mount Hermon. Refs.: 2 Sam. 10:6, 8; 1 Chr. 19:6, 7. ¶
k. A descendant of Maacah, a Maacathite. Ref.: Josh. 13:13. See also MAACATHITE <4602>. ¶

MAACATHITE – ***ma^{a}ḵāṯiy*** [proper noun: מַעֲכָתִי <4602>; patrial from MAACAH <4601>] ▶ **A proper noun designating an inhabitant of Maacah (see MAACAH <4601> k.).** Refs.: Deut. 3:14; Josh. 12:5; 13:11, 13; 2 Sam. 23:34; 2 Kgs. 25:23; 1 Chr. 4:19; Jer. 40:8. ¶

MAADAI – ***ma^{a}ḏay*** [masc. proper noun: מַעֲדַי <4572>; from ADORN <5710>]: ornament ▶ **An exile, son of Bani, who had married a foreign wife.** Ref.: Ezra 10:34. ¶

MAADIAH – ***ma'aḏyāh*** [masc. proper noun: מַעַדְיָה <4573>; from ADORN <5710> and LORD <3050>]: ornament of the Lord ▶ **A priest who returned from the Babylonian captivity.** Ref.: Neh. 12:5. ¶

MAAI – ***mā'ay*** [masc. proper noun: מָעַי <4597>; prob. from BOWELS <4578>]: compassionate ▶ **A priest who played a musical instrument at the dedication of the Temple.** Ref.: Neh. 12:36. ¶

MAARATH – ***ma^{a}rāṯ*** [proper noun: מַעֲרָת <4638>; a form of ARMY <4630>]: open place, bareness ▶ **A city of the tribe of Judah.** Ref.: Josh. 15:59. ¶

MAAREH-GEBA – Judg. 20:33 ➔ MEADOW (place) <4629> b.

MAASAI – ***ma'śay*** [masc. proper noun: מַעְשַׂי <4640>; from DO <6213>] ▶ **The name identifies a priest, a son of Adiel, who worked in Jerusalem in the Temple.** Ref.: 1 Chr. 9:12. ¶

MAASEIAH – ***ma^{a}śêyāh, ma^{a}śêyāhû*** [masc. proper noun: מַעֲשֵׂיָה, מַעֲשֵׂיָהוּ <4641>; from WORK <4639> and LORD <3050>]: work of the Lord ▶
a. A Levite. Refs.: 1 Chr. 15:18, 20. ¶
b. A son of Adaiah. Ref.: 2 Chr. 23:1. ¶
c. A ruler. Ref.: 2 Chr. 26:11. ¶
d. A son of Ahaz. Ref.: 2 Chr. 28:7. ¶
e. The father of Zephaniah. Refs.: Jer. 21:1; 29:25; 37:3. ¶
f. A governor of Jerusalem. Ref.: 2 Chr. 34:8. ¶
g. The father of Zedekiah, a false prophet. Ref.: Jer. 29:21. ¶
h. A son of Shallum. Ref.: Jer. 35:4. ¶
i. A son of Ithiel. Ref.: Neh. 11:7. ¶
j. The father of Azariah. Ref.: Neh. 3:23. ¶
k. A descendant of Jeshua. Ref.: Ezra 10:18. ¶
l. A descendant of Harim. Ref.: Ezra 10:21. ¶
m. A descendant of Pashhur. Ref.: Ezra 10:22. ¶
n. A son of Pahath-Moab. Ref.: Ezra 10:30. ¶
o. A priest. Refs.: Neh. 8:4, 7. ¶
p. A chief of the people who signed the covenant of renewal with Nehemiah after the return from the Babylonian captivity. Ref.: Neh. 10:25. ¶
q. A son of Baruch. Ref.: Neh. 11:5. ¶
r. A priest. Ref.: Neh. 12:41. ¶
s. A priest. Ref.: Neh. 12:42. ¶

MAAZ – ***ma'aṣ*** [masc. proper noun: מַעַץ <4619>; from WINK <6095> (in the sense of to close)]: closure ▶ **A man of the tribe of Judah, son of Ram.** Ref.: 1 Chr. 2:27. ¶

MAAZIAH – ***ma'azyāh, ma'azyāhû*** [masc. proper noun: מַעַזְיָה, מַעַזְיָהוּ <4590>; prob. from SAFETY (FLEE FOR) <5766> (in the sense of protection) and LORD <3050>]: the Lord is a refuge ▶
a. A priest under Nehemiah who signed the covenant of renewal with Nehemiah after the return from the Babylonian captivity. Ref.: Neh. 10:8. ¶
b. A priest under David. Ref.: 1 Chr. 24:18. ¶

MACHBANNAI – ***makbannay*** [masc. proper noun: מַכְבַּנַּי <4344>; patrial from MACHBENAH <4343>] ▶ **A mighty man who joined David in Ziklag.** Ref.: 1 Chr. 12:13. ¶

MACHBENAH – ***makbênāh*** [masc. proper noun: מַכְבֵּנָה <4343>; from the same as CABBON <3522>]: hilly ▶ **Grandson of Caleb.** Ref.: 1 Chr. 2:49. ¶

MACHI – ***mākiy*** [masc. proper noun: מָכִי <4352>; prob. from POOR (BECOME) <4134>]: decrease ▶ **A Gadite; his son Geuel was one of the twelve Israelites sent to spy out the land of Canaan.** Ref.: Num. 13:15. ¶

MACHINE – 2 Chr. 26:15 ➔ DEVICE <2810>.

MACHIR – ***makiyr*** [masc. proper noun: מָכִיר <4353>; from SELL <4376>]: salesman ▶
a. A son of Ammiel. Refs.: 2 Sam. 9:4, 5; 2 Sam. 17:27. ¶
b. A son of Manasseh. Refs.: Gen. 50:23; Num. 26:29; 27:1; 32:39, 40; 36:1; Deut. 3:15; Josh. 13:31; 17:1, 3; Judg. 5:14; 1 Chr. 2:21, 23; 7:14–17. ¶

MACHIRITE – ***mākiyriy*** [proper noun: מָכִירִי <4354>; patron. from MACHIR <4353>] ▶ **Member of the family descending from Machir.** Ref.: Num. 26:29. ¶

MACHNADEBAI – ***maknadbay*** [masc. proper noun: מַכְנַדְבַי <4367>; from WHAT? <4100> and GIVE WILLINGLY <5068> with a particle interposed]: what is like a liberal man ▶ **An Israelite who had married a foreign wife and pledged to put her away.** Ref.: Ezra 10:40. ¶

MACHPELAH – ***makpêlāh*** [proper noun: מַכְפֵּלָה <4375>; from DOUBLE (verb) <3717>]: double, fold ▶ **This word designates the cave in which the patriarchs were buried with their wives.** Abraham purchased it from the Hittites, from a man named Ephron in the land of Canaan. It was located in Hebron near Mamre (Gen. 23:9–19; 25:9; 49:30; 50:13). ¶

MAD (BE, DRIVE) – ***šaga'*** [verb: שָׁגַע <7696>; a prim. root] ▶ **This word means to be insane, to be demented.** Refs.: Deut. 28:34; 1 Sam. 21:14, 15; 21:15; 2 Kgs. 9:11; Jer. 29:26; Hos. 9:7. ¶

MADAI – ***māday*** [proper noun: מָדַי <4074>; of foreign deriv.]: middle land ▶
a. A descendant of Japheth. Refs.: Gen. 10:2; 1 Chr. 1:5. ¶
b. A people or land of Media. Refs.: 2 Kgs. 17:6; 18:11; Esther 1:3, 14, 18, 19; 10:2; Is. 13:17; 21:2; Jer. 25:25; 51:11, 28; Dan. 8:20; 9:1. ¶

MADMAN – ***lāhah, lāhāh*** [verb: לָהַהּ, לָהָה <3856>; a prim. root] ▶ **This word indicates to behave like a fool, a maniac.** It is used of irrational and senseless behavior and actions towards others (Prov. 26:18). It is also translated to languish; see LANGUISH <3856>. ¶

MADMANNAH – ***madmannāh*** [proper noun: מַדְמַנָּה <4089>; a variation for DUNGHILL <4087>]: dunghill ▶
a. A city in Judah. Ref.: Josh. 15:31. ¶
b. A descendant of Caleb. Ref.: 1 Chr. 2:49. ¶

MADMEN – ***madmên*** [proper noun: מַדְמֵן <4086>; from the same as DUNG <1828>]: dunghill ▶ **A town in Moab.** Ref.: Jer. 48:2. ¶

MADMENAH – ***madmênāh*** [proper noun: מַדְמֵנָה <4088>; the same as DUNGHILL <4087>]: dunghill ▶ **A town of the**

tribe of Benjamin, north of Jerusalem. Ref.: Is. 10:31. ¶

MADNESS – 1 ***hôlêlôṯ*** [fem. plur. noun: הוֹלֵלוֹת <1947>; fem. act. part. of PRAISE (verb) <1984> (in the sense of to act foolishly, to be mad)] ► **This word is found only in the book of Ecclesiastes and means the tendency to try anything to know its outcome. It refers also to delusion.** It is not a worthwhile experience to know madness but is rather vanity (Eccl. 1:17; 7:25), the opposite of wisdom. Wisdom excels madness and folly (Eccl. 2:12; see v. 13). The desire to know madness is, unfortunately, intrinsic in the human heart (Eccl. 9:3). ¶
2 ***hôlêlûṯ*** [fem. noun: הוֹלֵלוּת <1948>; from act. part. of PRAISE (verb) <1984>] ► **This word indicates the ultimate outcome and fruit of a fool's foolish talk.** Ref.: Eccl. 10:13. ¶
3 ***šiggā'ôn*** [masc. noun: שִׁגָּעוֹן <7697>; from MAD (BE) <7696>] ► **This word means insanity.** It is always used in a negative, accusatory way of persons who behave abnormally to a threatening and excessive extent (Deut. 28:28; Zech. 12:4); but it is used of especially agitated or excessive physical activity in general (2 Kgs. 9:20: furiously, like a maniac). ¶

MADON – ***māḏôn*** [proper noun: מָדוֹן <4068>; from STRIFE <4066>]: strife, quarrel ► **One of the main cities of Canaan before the conquest.** Refs.: Josh. 11:1; 12:19.

MAGBISH – ***magḇiyš*** [proper noun: מַגְבִּישׁ <4019>; from the same as CRYSTAL <1378>] ► **One of the exiles returning from captivity.** Ref.: Ezra 2:30. Some believe this is the name of a city. ¶

MAGDIEL – ***magdiy'êl*** [masc. proper noun: מַגְדִּיאֵל <4025>; from PRECIOUS THING <4022> and GOD <410>]: prince of God ► **One of the chiefs of Esau.** Refs.: Gen. 36:43; 1 Chr. 1:54. ¶

MAGGOT – 1 Ex. 16:20 → CRIMSON <8438> b. 2 Ex. 16:24; Is. 14:11; Job 25:6 → WORM <7415>.

MAGIC BAND – ***keseṯ*** [fem. noun: כֶּסֶת <3704>; from COVER (verb) <3680>] ► **This word describes a band, some kind of wristband for religious, supernatural purposes.** Refs.: Ezek. 13:18, 20; also translated magic charm, pillow. ¶

MAGIC CHARM – Ezek. 13:18, 20 → MAGIC BAND <3704>.

MAGIC SPELL – See COMPANY <2267>.

MAGICIAN – 1 ***ḥarṭōm*** [masc. noun: חַרְטֹם <2748>; from the same as GRAVING TOOL <2747>] ► **This word means engraver, a writer associated with the occult. These people seem to have had knowledge of astrology or divination and were commonly associated with the magicians of Egypt in Pharaoh's court.** Pharaoh could not find any magicians to interpret his dream, so he called Joseph (Gen. 41:24). Moses caused plagues to come upon Egypt which the magicians could not reverse (Ex. 9:11). Other refs.: Gen. 41:8; Ex. 7:11, 22; 8:7, 18, 19; Dan. 1:20; 2:2. ¶
2 ***ḥarṭōm*** [Aramaic masc. noun: חַרְטֹם <2749>; the same as <2748> above] ► **This word occurs only in the book of Daniel. See previous definition.** Refs.: Dan. 2:10, 27; 4:7, 9; 5:11. These people, who practiced sorcery and other occult practices, were advisors and counselors of kings. ¶

MAGISTRATE – 1 ***tiptāy*** [Aramaic masc. noun: תִּפְתָּי <8614>; perhaps from JUDGMENT <8199>] ► **This word refers to a group of civil officers with delegated power to administer the law and to perform other matters of state.** Refs.: Dan. 3:2, 3; KJV: sheriffs. ¶
– 2 Is. 60:17 → OPPRESS <5065>.

MAGNIFICENT – 1 Judg. 5:25 → MIGHTY <117> 2 Zech. 11:13 → ROBE <145>.

MAGNIFICENTLY – Ezek. 23:12 → SPLENDIDLY <4358>.

MAGNIFY – Job 36:24 ➔ GREAT (MAKE) <7679>.

MAGOG – ***māḡôg*** [proper noun: מָגוֹג <4031>; from GOG <1463>] ▶
a. Son of Japheth. Refs.: Gen. 10:2; 1 Chr. 1:5. ¶
b. A mountainous region north of Israel. Refs.: Ezek. 38:2; 39:6. ¶

MAGOR-MISSABIB – ***māḡôr mis-sāḇiyḇ*** [masc. proper noun: מָגוֹר מִסָּבִיב <4036>; from TERROR <4032> and ALL AROUND <5439> with the prep. inserted]: terror on every side ▶ **Name given by Jeremiah to Pashur, the priest.** He had beaten him and put him in the stocks (Jer. 20:3). ¶

MAGPIASH – ***magpiy'āš*** [masc. proper noun: מַגְפִּיעָשׁ <4047>; apparently from SHUT <1479> or SMITE <5062> and MOTH <6211>]: killer of the moth ▶ **A chief of the people who signed the covenant of renewal with Nehemiah after the return from the Babylonian captivity.** Ref.: Neh. 10:20. ¶

MAHALALEL – ***mah^alal'ēl*** [masc. proper noun: מַהֲלַלְאֵל <4111>; from PRAISE <4110> and GOD <410>]: praise of God ▶
a. Great-grandson of Seth. Refs.: Gen. 5:12, 13, 15–17; 1 Chr. 1:2. ¶
b. A Judaite. Ref.: Neh. 11:4. ¶

MAHALATH – 1 ***māḥ^alaṯ*** [fem. proper noun: מָחֲלַת <4257>; from SICK (BE) <2470> (maybe in the sense of asking for a favor; see c.)] ▶ **This word designates Mahalath, mahalath; part of a song title.** This is probably a musical term or a designation of some musical instrument (Ps. 53:1). It may mean "according to mahalath." Other ref.: Ps. 88:1. ¶
2 ***māḥ^alaṯ*** [fem. proper noun: מָחֲלַת <4258>; the same as <4257> above] ▶
a. A daughter of Ishmael. Ref.: Gen. 28:9. ¶
b. A granddaughter of David. Ref.: 2 Chr. 11:18. ¶

MAHANAIM – ***maḥ^anayim*** [proper noun: מַחֲנַיִם <4266>; dual of CAMP <4264>]: two camps ▶ **The word was used by Jacob to indicate that God had encamped in the midst of Jacob and his family.** Refs.: Gen. 32:1, 2. It is used as a boundary marker by Joshua (Josh. 13:26, 30). It became a city of the Levites (Josh. 21:38). It was located in Gilead, evidently (2 Sam. 8, 12, 29) in Gad. David escaped to Mahanaim when Absalom rebelled (2 Sam. 17:24, 27). Solomon established it as the center of one of his districts in Israel (1 Kgs. 4:14). *

MAHANEH DAN – ***maḥ^anēh-ḏān*** [proper noun: מַחֲנֵה־דָן <4265>; from CAMP <4264> and DAN <1835>]: camp of Dan ▶ **A campsite of the tribe of Dan.** Ref.: Judg. 18:12. ¶

MAHARAI – ***mah^aray*** [masc. proper noun: מַהֲרַי <4121>; from HURRY <4116>]: hasty, impetuous ▶ **One of David's mighty men.** Refs.: 2 Sam. 23:28; 1 Chr. 11:30; 27:13. ¶

MAHATH – ***maḥaṯ*** [masc. proper noun: מַחַת <4287>; prob. from WIPE, WIPE OUT <4229>]: grasping ▶
a. A son of Amasai. Ref.: 1 Chr. 6:35. ¶
b. A chief Levite. Refs.: 2 Chr. 29:12; 31:13. ¶

MAHAVITE – ***maḥ^awiym*** [proper noun: מַחֲוִים <4233>; apparently a patrial, but from an unknown place (in the plur. only for a sing.)] ▶ **The designation of Eliel, one of David's mighty men.** Ref.: 1 Chr. 11:46. ¶

MAHAZIOTH – ***maḥ^aziy'ôṯ*** [masc. proper noun: מַחֲזִיאוֹת <4238>; fem. plur. from SEE <2372>]: visions ▶ **Son of Heman.** Refs.: 1 Chr. 25:4, 30. ¶

MAHER-SHALEL-HASH-BAZ – ***mahêr šālāl ḥāš baz*** [proper noun: מַהֵר שָׁלָל חָשׁ בַּז <4122>] ▶ **A phrase meaning *The spoil speeds, the prey hastens*.** Refs.: Is. 8:1, 3. The phrase is made up of the words from *mahêr* (QUICK, QUICKLY <4118> a.), *šālāl* (SPOIL <7998>), *ḥûš* (HASTEN <2363> a.), and *baz* [PLUNDER (noun) <957>]. ¶

MAHLAH – ***maḥlāh*** [proper noun: מַחְלָה <4244>; from SICK (BE) <2470>]: disease ▶
a. One of the five daughters of Zelophehad. Refs.: Num. 26:33; 27:1; 36:11; Josh. 17:3. ¶
b. A Manassite. Ref.: 1 Chr. 7:18. ¶

MAHLI – ***maḥliy*** [masc. proper noun: מַחְלִי <4249>; from SICK (BE) <2470>]: sick, weak ▶
a. A Levite. Refs.: Ex. 6:19; Num. 3:20; 1 Chr. 6:19, 29; 23:21; 24:26, 28; Ezra 8:18. ¶
b. A son of Mushi. Refs.: 1 Chr. 6:47; 23:22, 23; 24:30. ¶

MAHLITE – ***maḥliy*** [proper noun: מַחְלִי <4250>; patron. from MAHLI <4249>] ▶ **Member of the family of Mahli.** Refs.: Num. 3:33; 26:58. ¶

MAHLON – ***maḥlôn*** [masc. proper noun: מַחְלוֹן <4248>; from SICK (BE) <2470>]: sickly (comp. CHILION <3630>) ▶ **The first husband of Ruth; son of Elimelech and Naomi.** Refs.: Ruth 1:2, 5; 4:9, 10. ¶

MAHOL – ***māḥôl*** [masc. proper noun: מָחוֹל <4235>; the same as DANCING <4234>]: dancing, dance ▶ **His four sons were very wise.** Ref.: 1 Kgs. 4:31. ¶

MAHSEIAH – ***maḥsêyāh*** [masc. proper noun: מַחְסֵיָה <4271>; from REFUGE <4268> and LORD <3050>]: the Lord is a refuge ▶ **Grandfather of Baruch.** Refs.: Jer. 32:12; 51:59. ¶

MAID – [1] ***'āmāh*** [fem. noun: אָמָה <519>; apparently a prim. word] ▶ **This word indicates a female servant or slave girl.** It depicts a simple maidservant (Gen. 30:3; 31:33; Ex. 2:5; 2 Sam. 6:20). It refers to a girl who is a servant in a legal sense (Ex. 20:10, 17; 21:20; Lev. 25:6; Job 31:13). It is applied to concubines (Gen. 20:17; 21:12; Ex. 23:12). In a figurative or metaphorical sense, it is used to express the humility of any person (Ruth 3:9; 1 Sam. 1:16; 25:24; 2 Sam. 20:17). It is used as a token of submission when addressing God (1 Sam. 1:11; Ps. 86:16; 116:16). *
– [2] Ex. 2:8 ➔ YOUNG WOMAN <5959> [3] 2 Kgs. 5:2; Job 41:5; etc. ➔ GIRL <5291>.

MAIDEN – Gen. 24:43; Ex. 2:8; Ps. 68:25; Prov. 30:19; Song 1:3; 6:8 ➔ YOUNG WOMAN <5959>.

MAIDSERVANT – ***šiphāh*** [fem. noun: שִׁפְחָה <8198>; from an unused root meaning to spread out (as a family; see CLAN <4940>)] ▶ **This word also means a female servant or slave.** People of wealth and power had female servants in the ancient world to carry out tasks for their masters, from great tasks to small ones (Gen. 12:16). Hagar was Sarah's handmaid and could be permitted to bear a child to her mistress's husband (Gen. 16:1–3, 5, 6, 8). A maidservant held a humble social position (Ruth 2:13; 1 Sam. 1:18; 25:27). She was evidently suitable for marriage (Lev. 19:20). *

MAIL – Job 41:13 ➔ BRIDLE <7448> b.

MAIMED – Lev. 22:22 ➔ MOVE <2782>.

MAINTAIN – Ps. 112:5 ➔ CONTAIN <3557>.

MAINTENANCE – [1] Judg. 17:10 ➔ PRESERVATION OF LIFE <4241> [2] Ezra 4:14 ➔ to have maintenance ➔ SALT (EAT THE) <4415>.

MAJESTIC – [1] Ex. 15:6, 11 ➔ GLORIOUS <142> [2] Ps. 8:1, 9; Is. 10:34; Ezek. 17:23 ➔ MIGHTY <117> [3] Song 6:4, 10 ➔ TERRIBLE <366> [4] Ezek. 17:8 ➔ GARMENT <155>.

MAJESTIC (BE) – [1] Is. 63:1 ➔ HONOR (verb) <1921> [2] Ezek. 31:7 ➔ BEAUTIFUL (BE, MAKE ONESELF) <3302>.

MAJESTY – [1] ***ga'ᵃwāh*** [fem. noun: גַּאֲוָה <1346>; from RISE <1342>] ▶ **This word means grandeur, dignity, splendor; it**

also refers to pride, arrogance, rage. In a good sense, it can refer to the exaltation or loftiness of God (Deut. 33:26; Ps. 68:34); it is also translated excellency, excellence. It refers figuratively to the pride of Israel, God, as her majesty (Deut. 33:29); it is also translated excellency, triumph. It describes the activity of the sea as a raging or swelling of its waters (Ps. 46:3). It describes the haughty, prideful attitude of the wicked (Ps. 10:2; 31:18, 23; Is. 9:9); a pride that destroys them (Prov. 29:23). The warriors of Babylon are termed God's instruments to judge His people and referred to as the Lord's proudly exulting ones (Is. 13:3; cf. Zeph. 3:11), a pride the Lord used to His purposes. *
2 ***gā'ôn*** [masc. noun: גָּאוֹן <1347>; from RISE <1342> (the same as <1346> above)] ▶ **This word means exaltation, excellence; it designates also pride, arrogance.** It refers to the exalted majesty or excellence of the Lord (Ex. 15:7; Is. 24:14; Mic. 5:4) and even to His redeemed people and their pride in Him (Is. 4:2). It is used in a neutral sense to describe the proud, high waves of the sea (Job 38:11) and the thick growth or thicket around some areas of the Jordan (Jer. 12:5). Jacob, Judah, and Israel are all depicted as possessing excessive pride (Jer. 13:9; Amos 6:8), or, in some cases, these references may have a positive thrust to them. *
3 ***gê'ûṯ*** [fem. abstract noun: גֵּאוּת <1348>; from RISE <1342> (the same as MAJESTY <1346>)] ▶ **This word refers to exaltation, excellence; it also refers to pride surging, swelling.** It praises the exaltation of God (Ps. 93:1; Is. 26:10) and His exalted or excellent works (Is. 12:5: excellent things, glorious things). It refers figuratively to the proud crown of Ephraim that will cause her to go into captivity (Is. 28:1, 3). In a negative sense, it mentions those who speak proudly (Ps. 17:10); it is also translated arrogantly, with arrogance. It describes the rising, swelling waves of the sea (Ps. 89:9) over which the Lord rules. Other ref.: Is. 9:18 (lifting up, rising, column). ¶
– 4 Dan. 4:22, 36; 5:18, 19 ➔ GREATNESS <7238> 5 Dan. 4:30, 36; 5:18 ➔ HONOR (noun) <1923> 6 See GLORY <1926> 7 See VIGOR <1935>.

MAJOR – 2 Kgs. 3:19 ➔ CHOICE, CHOICEST <4004>.

MAJORITY – 1 Chr. 12:29; 2 Chr. 30:18 ➔ INCREASE (noun) <4768>.

MAKAZ – ***māqaṣ*** [proper noun: מָקַץ <4739>; from CUT OFF <7112> b. (in the sense of to be at the end)]: end, limit ▶ **A place in the territory of the tribe of Judah Makaz.** Ref.: 1 Kgs. 4:9. ¶

MAKE – 1 ***ʿᵃḇaḏ*** [Aramaic verb: עֲבַד <5648>; corresponding to SERVE <5647>] ▶ **This word means to do, to carry out, to perform.** It takes on the particular meaning indicated by its specific context: to revolt, to rebel (Ezra 4:19); performing, doing, carrying out something (Ezra 4:22; 6:11; Dan. 6:10); it refers to the process of working, etc. (Ezra 5:8); it means to change something (Dan. 2:5); to perform signs and wonders (Dan. 6:22); to make, create the heavens and earth (Jer. 10:11). It describes God's performing of His will (Dan. 4:35); to make, wage, to engage in (Dan. 7:21). *
2 ***pā'al*** [verb: פָּעַל <6466>; a prim. root] ▶ **This word means to do, to practice.** It is used of constructing or making something (Ps. 7:13); or just to make (Is. 41:4). It takes the sense of doing or practicing something, e.g., deceit (Hos. 7:1); righteousness (Ps. 15:2). Hence, it means to accomplish, to do, to perform, to make: God made His mountain into His dwelling (Ex. 15:17); and performed His works for His people (Num. 23:23; cf. Deut. 32:27). Job refers to God, his Maker, Creator (Job 36:3), where the word has the sense of God's creative activity in it. It is used figuratively of persons acting against God (Job 7:20; 35:6). It refers to doing what God hates, evil, iniquity (Ps. 5:5; Prov. 10:29; Mic. 2:1); but also of doing the Lord's ordinances, His will (Zeph. 2:3). *
– 3 2 Sam. 22:33 ➔ LOOSE (LET) <5425> 4 Job 10:8 ➔ HURT <6087> 5 Job 17:13 ➔ SPREAD, SPREAD OUT <7502> 6 Ps. 78:50; Is. 26:7 ➔ WEIGH, WEIGH OUT <6424>.

MAKE, MAKE LIKE – ***šᵉwāh*** [Aramaic verb: שְׁוָה <7739>; corresponding to LIKE (BE, BECOME) <7737>] ► **This word means to become, to become like.** It is used in a reflexive verb stem indicating the making of something into something else, changing it (Dan. 3:29); and in a similar stem, it describes a human heart being made into the heart of a beast (Dan. 5:21). ¶

MAKE UP – Neh. 6:8 ➔ DEVISE <908>.

MAKE WAY – Gen. 41:43 ➔ BOW THE KNEE <86>.

MAKEUP – ***pûḵ*** [masc. noun: פּוּךְ <6320>; from an unused root meaning to paint] ► **This word indicates glistening pigment used to paint the eyes.** It describes Jezebel's adornment of her face shortly before her death (2 Kgs. 9:30: paint, makeup). It indicates figuratively of Judah's adornment of herself (Jer. 4:30). This word also refers to glistening stones; see ANTIMONY. ¶

MAKEUP (APPLY) – Ezek. 23:40 ➔ PAINT (verb) <3583>.

MAKHELOTH – ***maqhêlōṯ*** [proper noun: מַקְהֵלֹת <4722>; plur. of CONGREGATION <4721>]: assemblies ► **Encampment of Israel in the desert.** Refs.: Num. 33:25, 26. ¶

MAKKEDAH – ***maqqêḏah*** [proper noun: מַקֵּדָה <4719>; from the same as SPECKLED <5348> in the denom. sense of herding (comp. SHEEP BREEDER <5349>)]: place of shepherds ► **A city in Canaan conquered by Joshua.** Refs.: Josh. 10:10, 16, 17, 21, 28, 29; 12:16; 15:41. ¶

MAKTESH – ***maḵtêš*** [noun: מַכְתֵּשׁ <4389>; the same as HOLLOW PLACE <4388>]: hollow place, mortar ►
a. A proper noun designating a place inhabited by silver merchants. Ref.: KJV, Zeph. 1:11. ¶
b. A proper noun designating Mortar. Ref.: NASB, ESV, Zeph. 1:11. ¶
c. A masculine noun meaning market district. Ref.: NIV, Zeph. 1:11. ¶

MALACHI – ***mal'āḵiy*** [masc. proper noun: מַלְאָכִי <4401>; from the same as MESSENGER <4397>]: my messenger ► **The name traditionally given to the prophet of the book that bears his name.** Ref.: Mal. 1:1. Some scholars think that the word, which means "my messenger," was not a personal name but a title. ¶

MALCHAM – ***milkōm, malkām*** [masc. proper noun: מִלְכֹּם, מַלְכָּם <4445>; from KING <4428> and MOLECH <4432>]: Molech is king ►
a. A Benjaminite. He is listed as a descendant of Shaharaim in the land of Moab (1 Chr. 8:9). ¶
b. A proper noun designating Malcam, Molech, a false god. It designates Milcom as the idol of the Ammonites (1 Kgs. 11:5, 33; 2 Kgs. 23:13). It is rendered as Milcom in Zephaniah 1:5. In Jeremiah 49:1, 3, it is ambiguous. Some prefer to translate it as Molech (NIV), some as Malcam (NASB), and some as king (KJV). The preferred Hebrew text reads Malcam. ¶

MALCHI-SHUA – ***malkiyšûa', malkiy šûa'*** [masc. proper noun: מַלְכִּישׁוּעַ, מַלְכִּי שׁוּעַ <4444>; from KING <4428> and CRY (noun) <7769> b. (in the sense of riches, wealth]: king of wealth ► **One of the four sons of king Saul.** Refs.: 1 Sam. 14:49; 31:2; 1 Chr. 8:33; 9:39; 10:2. ¶

MALCHIEL – ***malkiy'êl*** [masc. proper noun: מַלְכִּיאֵל <4439>; from KING <4428> and GOD <410>]: God is king ► **Son of Beriah, grandson of Asher.** Refs.: Gen. 46:17; Num. 26:45; 1 Chr. 7:31. ¶

MALCHIELITES – ***malkiy'êliy*** [proper noun: מַלְכִּיאֵלִי <4440>; patron. from MALCHIEL <4439>] ► **Descendants of Malchiel.** Ref.: Num. 26:45. ¶

MALCHIJAH – ***malkiyyāh, malkiyyahû*** [masc. proper noun: מַלְכִּיָּה, מַלְכִּיָּהוּ <4441>;

from KING <4428> and LORD <3050>]: the Lord is king ►
a. Son of Ethni. Ref.: 1 Chr. 6:40. ¶
b. A priest. Ref.: 1 Chr. 24:9. ¶
c. Father of Pashhur. Refs.: 1 Chr. 9:12; Neh. 11:12; Jer. 21:1; 38:1. ¶
d. Son of Hammelech. Ref.: Jer. 38:6. ¶
e. A Jew, possibly two according to the Septuagint. Ref.: Ezra 10:25. ¶
f. Son of Harim. Refs.: Ezra 10:31; Neh. 3:11. ¶
g. Son of Rechab. Ref.: Neh. 3:14. ¶
h. Repairer of the wall of Jerusalem. Ref.: Neh. 3:31. ¶
i. A priest. Refs.: Neh. 8:4; 10:3; 12:42. ¶

MALCHIRAM – ***malkiyrām*** [masc. proper noun: מַלְכִּירָם <4443>; from KING <4428> and CRY (verb) <7311>]: king of exaltation ► **A member of the family of Jeconiah.** Ref.: 1 Chr. 3:18. ¶

MALE – 1 ***zᵉḵûr*** [masc. noun: זְכוּר <2138>; properly, pass. part. of REMEMBER <2142>, but used for MALE (BE), MALE <2145> b.] ► **This word denotes a man.** It refers to the males of Israel in a collective sense (Ex. 23:17; 34:23; Deut. 16:16) and once to the males of any foreign city (Deut. 20:13). ¶
– 2 1 Sam. 25:22, 34; 1 Kgs. 14:10; 16:11; 21:21; 2 Kgs. 9:8 → URINATE AGAINST THE WALL <8366> 3 See MAN <376>.

MALE (BE), MALE – ***zāḵar, zāḵār*** [verb and noun: זָכַר, זָכָר <2145>; from REMEMBER <2142>] ►
a. A verb meaning to be a male animal. It indicates firstborn male animals for sacrifice (Ex. 34:19). Its form in the verse, *tizzāḵār*, influences some translators to render this as a verb. Others take the oral tradition form and read the word as a noun rather than a verb and understand it to refer to sacrificial animals (see b.). ¶
b. A masculine noun indicating a man, male, human. It indicates a person as male as opposed to female (Gen. 1:27; Lev. 18:22). With *kol* preceding, it indicates every male that was to be circumcised at eight days of age (Gen. 17:12). With *bēn*, son, preceding, it denotes a male child or person (Lev. 12:2; Jer. 20:15). In its collective and plural forms, it denotes men (Ex. 13:12; Judg. 21:11; 1 Kgs. 11:15). Lying with a *zāḵār* indicates homosexuality (Lev. 18:22) while *miškab* (BED <4904>) *zāḵār* refers to heterosexual intercourse (Num. 31:17; Judg. 21:12). It refers to the Passover lamb (Ex. 12:5). *

MALE GENITALS – Deut. 25:11 → PRIVATE PARTS <4016>.

MALE GOAT – 1 ***ṣᵉp̱iyr*** [Aramaic masc. noun: צְפִיר <6841>; corresponding to <6842> below] ► **A small animal related to the sheep. This was a major sacrificial animal in Israel.** One goat was offered for each tribe of Israel as a mass sin offering for the nation at the dedication of the rebuilt Temple (516 B.C.) (Ezra 6:17). ¶
2 ***ṣāpiyr*** [masc. noun: צָפִיר <6842>; from DEPART <6852> (in the sense of to skip about)] ► **See previous definition.** One was offered for each tribe of Israel as a massive sin offering for the nation (Ezra 8:35) after Ezra›s journey from Babylon to Jerusalem (458 B.C.) (cf. 2 Chr. 29:21). It is used in apocalyptic literature to stand for Alexander the Great (Dan. 8:5, 8, 21). ¶
– 3 Gen. 37:31; Dan. 8:5, 8 → FEMALE GOAT <5795> 4 Ezra 6:17 → GOAT <5796> 5 See GOAT <8495>.

MALE ORGAN – ***šopḵāh*** [fem. noun: שָׁפְכָה <8212>; fem. of a deriv. from POUR OUT <8210>] ► **This word refers to a man's penis, literally a place of pouring out, a urinary organ.** Ref.: Deut. 23:1. ¶

MALICE – ***šᵉʼāṭ*** [masc. noun: שְׁאָט <7589>; from an unused root meaning to push aside] ► **This word indicates disrespect, hatred; it also means contempt and is translated scorn, disdain, despite.** It indicates strong disrespect at the misfortune of someone (Ezek. 25:6, 15); even hatred toward a person or people (Ezek. 36:5). ¶

MALICIOUS – 1 Kgs. 2:8 → GRIEVOUS <4834>.

MALICIOUS TALK – Ezek. 36:3 ➔ REPORT (BAD) <1681>.

MALIGN – Prov. 30:10 ➔ SLANDER <3960>.

MALIGNANT – Lev. 13:51, 52; 14:44 ➔ PAINFUL (BE) <3992>.

MALLET – Judg. 5:26 ➔ HAMMER (noun) <1989>.

MALLOTHI – ***mallôṯiy*** [masc. proper noun: מַלּוֹתִי <4413>; apparently from SPEAK <4448>]: I have spoken ▶ **A Kohathite Levite, one of the sons of Heman the singer.** Refs.: 1 Chr. 25:4, 26. ¶

MALLOW – ***mallûaḥ*** [masc. noun: מַלּוּחַ <4408>; from SEASON (verb) <4414>] ▶ **This word means herbs growing in salt marshes.** A food eaten by the poor and destitute, it was a salty plant (Job 30:4; also translated saltwort, salt herb). ¶

MALLUCH – ***mallûḵ, mallûḵiy*** [masc. proper noun: מַלּוּךְ, מַלּוּכִי <4409>; from KING (BE) <4427>]: who counsels, who reigns ▶
a. A son of Hashabiah. Ref.: 1 Chr. 6:44. ¶
b. A priest. Ref.: Neh. 12:2. ¶
c. A son of Bani. Ref.: Ezra 10:29. ¶
d. A son of Harim. Ref.: Ezra 10:32. ¶
e. An Israelite who signed the covenant of renewal with Nehemiah after the return from the Babylonian captivity. Ref.: Neh. 10:4. ¶
f. A chief of the people who signed the covenant of renewal with Nehemiah after the return from the Babylonian captivity. Ref.: Neh. 10:27. ¶
g. A priest. Ref.: Neh. 12:14. ¶

MAMRE – ***mamrê'*** [proper noun and masc. proper noun: מַמְרֵא <4471>; from LIFT ONESELF <4754> (in the sense of vigor)]: vigor ▶
a. A location north of Hebron. Refs.: Gen. 13:18; 18:1; 23:17, 19; 25:9; 35:27; 49:30; 50:13. ¶
b. A friend of Abram. Refs.: Gen. 14:13, 24. ¶

MAN – [1] ***'āḏām*** [masc. noun: אָדָם <120>; from RUDDY (BE) <119>]: ruddy ▶ **The word means a male, any human being, or generically the human race.** It is used to signify a man, as opposed to a woman (Gen. 2:18; Eccl. 7:28); a human (Num. 23:19; Prov. 17:18; Is. 17:7); the human race in general (Gen. 1:27; Num. 8:17; Ps. 144:3; Is. 2:17); and the representative embodiment of humanity, as the appellation "son of man" indicates (Ezek. 2:1, 3). This word was used as a proper noun for the first man, "Adam" (Gen. 2:20). *
[2] ***'iyš*** [masc. noun: אִישׁ <376>; contr. for <582> below (or perhaps rather from an unused root meaning to be extant)] ▶ **This word means an individual. It is also used to mean male or husband. It does not indicate humankind but the male gender in particular.** Its feminine counterpart is a woman or wife. In Hosea 2:16, this word describes God's special relationship to Israel. He will be their protective husband, not their master. Curiously, the word is also used of animals (Gen. 7:2), referring to a male and his mate. *
[3] ***'enôš*** [masc. noun: אֱנוֹשׁ <582>; from SICK (BE) <605> (in the sense of to be weak)] ▶ **This word means a male. In the singular, it occurs in poetry and prayers.** Ref.: 2 Chr. 14:11. It may derive from *'ānaš* <605>, meaning to be weak or sick. In comparison to *'îš* <376>, which also means man, *'nôš* often occurs in passages emphasizing man's frailty (Job 7:17; Ps. 8:4; 90:3). However, the plural of *'nôš* serves as the plural of *'îš* and occurs throughout the Old Testament. *
[4] ***'nāš*** [Aramaic masc. noun: אֱנָשׁ <606>; corresponding to <582> above] ▶ **This word is often used to differentiate man from deity. It can also be synonymous with human beings.** The most frequent usage occurs in the book of Daniel. It is used in a general, collective sense to mean everyone (Ezra 6:11; Dan. 3:10); and in the phrase "son of man" to mean a human being (Dan. 7:13). See the related Hebrew noun *'nôš* (<582> above). *
[5] ***geḇer*** [masc. noun: גֶּבֶר <1397>; from PREVAIL <1396>] ▶ **This word means**

a mighty (virile) man, a warrior. It is used of man but often contains more than just a reference to gender by referring to the nature of a man, usually with overtones of spiritual strength or masculinity, based on the verb *gāḇar* (see PREVAIL <1396>), meaning to be mighty. It is used to contrast men with women and children (Ex. 10:11) and to denote warrior ability (Jer. 41:16). The fifteen occurrences of the word in Job are significant, presenting a vast contrast between the essence of man (even a good one) and God (Job 4:17; 22:2). This contrast only adds more force to the passage in Zechariah 13:7 where God calls Himself *geḇer*. This passage points to the coming of Jesus—the One who as God would take on the sin debt for people with their sinful human nature. He is the Man (the Shepherd of the sheep). *

6 ***geḇar*** [masc. noun: גְּבַר <1399>; from PREVAIL <1396>] ▶ **This word is the construct of the Hebrew word *geḇer* (<1397> above) and has the same meaning. It is found in the Psalms to describe a male who is upright before the Lord.** He is described as a blameless man, literally, a man of no shame (Ps. 18:25). ¶

7 ***geḇar*** [Aramaic masc. noun: גְּבַר <1400>; corresponding to <1399> above] ▶ **See the word *geḇer* (<1397> above).** *

8 ***gibbar*** [Aramaic masc. noun: גִּבָּר <1401>; intens. of <1400> above] ▶ **This word means mighty one, warrior, hero; it is also translated soldier.** It is used only once in the Bible, where it is attached to another word meaning strength. It translates as "mighty one" or "strongest soldier" (Dan. 3:20). ¶

– 9 Ex. 23:17; 34:23; Deut. 16:16; 20:13 ➔ MALE <2138> 10 Deut. 2:34; 3:6; Is. 3:25 ➔ FEW IN NUMBER <4962>.

MANAHATH – ***mānaḥaṯ, mānaḥtiy*** [proper noun: מָנַחַת, מָנַחְתִּי <4506>; from REST (verb) <5117> a.]: rest ▶

a. A son of Shobal. Refs.: Gen. 36:23; 1 Chr. 1:40. ¶

b. A location in Judah. Ref.: 1 Chr. 8:6. ¶

c. A Manahathite. Refs.: 1 Chr. 2:52, 54. ¶

MANAHATHITES (HALF OF THE) –

1 ***ḥᵃṣiy hammᵉnuḥôṯ*** [חֲצִי הַמְּנֻחוֹת <2679>; from HALF <2677> and the plur. of RESTING PLACE <4496>, with the art. interposed] ▶ **This phrase refers to half of the Manahathites (also translated Manahethites, Manuhoth, Menuhoth), from *ḥᵃziy* (HALF <2677>) and *mānaḥtiy* (MANAHATH <4506> c.).** Ref.: 1 Chr. 2:52. See also <2680> below. ¶

2 ***ḥᵃṣiy hammᵉnaḥtiy*** [חֲצִי הַמְּנַחְתִּי <2680>; patron. from <2679> above] ▶ **This phrase refers to half of the Manahathites (also translated Manahethites, Manuhoth, Menuhoth), from *ḥᵃziy* (HALF <2677>) and *mānaḥtiy* (MANAHATH <4506> c.).** Ref.: 1 Chr. 2:54. See also <2679> above. ¶

MANAHETHITES – 1 Chr. 2:52 ➔ MANAHATHITES (HALF OF THE) <2679>.

MANASSEH – ***mᵉnaššeh*** [masc. proper noun: מְנַשֶּׁה <4519>; from FORGET <5382>]: cause to forget ▶

a. The firstborn son of Joseph in Egypt. His mother was Asenath, an Egyptian woman whose father was a priest in Heliopolis (On) (Gen. 41:50). The name means "cause to forget" and was given by Joseph because Manasseh's birth helped Joseph forget his family and hard times (Gen. 49:51). Jacob gave his firstborn blessing, however, to Ephraim whose descendants outstripped Manasseh's (Gen. 48:19, 20). Both became key tribes in northern Israel, and Jacob blessed both under Joseph's name (Gen. 49:22–26). Their fruitfulness and God's care for them are emphasized. Manasseh had a son named Machir (Gen. 50:23). Other refs.: Gen. 41:51; 46:20; 48:1, 5, 13, 14, 17. ¶

b. It refers to the descendants of Manasseh, a very fertile tribe. Refs.: Josh. 17:17, 18. One-half of the tribe settled east of the Jordan and as far north as Mount Hermon. Parts of the eastern half lived as far south as the Jabbok River (Josh. 16:1–17:18). The other half of the tribe lived west of the Jordan. Its western border was the Mediterranean coast. Dan, Ephraim, and Benjamin

touched its southern borders, and Asher, Zebulun, and Issachar touched its northern border. Key cities, such as Megiddo, Tirzah, Samaria, and Shechem were in its tribal territories. Both Mount Ebal and Gerazim were there. Gilgal and Jericho were just inside its southern tip (Josh. 13:8–13, 29–31). *
c. A king in Judah, an evil king, and a son of Hezekiah. He ruled 697–642 B.C., including a coregency with his father. He began to reign when he was twelve years old and reigned 55 years (2 Kgs. 21:1). He reversed all the good that his father had done, even rebuilding pagan high places for sacrifice and worship (2 Kgs. 21:1–18) and altars for Baal. He worshiped the heavenly bodies and sacrificed his own son in fire (2 Kgs. 21:6). He set up idolatrous Asherah poles in the Temple and led Israel astray (2 Kgs. 21:9). He sinned worse than the Amorites (2 Kgs. 21:11) of Canaan had. He shed innocent blood (2 Kgs. 21:16). As a result, the Lord declared He would wipe away Jerusalem and Judah as a person wipes a dish (2 Kgs. 21:13). According to the chronicler, Manasseh repented in his old age, and God had mercy on him, but God did not relent from His judgment on Judah. *
d. A man who had intermarried in the time of Ezra, son of Pahath-Moab. Ref.: Ezra 10:30. ¶
e. The son of Hashum who had intermarried during the time of Ezra or before. Ref.: Ezra 10:33. ¶
f. The father of Gershom (Judg. 18:30), according to some ancient Hebrew manuscripts. But the best reading indicates that he was the son of Moses (1 Chr. 23:15). *

MANASSITE – ***m*^{e}*naššiy*** [proper noun: מְנַשִּׁי <4520>; from MANASSEH <4519>] ► **A member of the tribe of Manasseh.** Refs.: Deut. 4:43; 29:8; 2 Kgs. 10:33; 1 Chr. 26:32. ¶

MANCHILD – Ex. 34:23 (KJV) ➔ MALE <2138>.

MANDRAKE – ***dûḏā'iym*** [masc. plur. noun: דּוּדָאִים <1736>; from BASKET <1731>] ► **A fragrant plant, the mandrake was considered a potent aphrodisiac.** Ref.: Song 7:13. This usage can be seen in Genesis 30:14–16, where the text describes Leah using these plants to attract Jacob. The Hebrew word also means a basket (Jer. 24:1). ¶

MANE – Job 39:19 ➔ THUNDER (noun) <7483>.

MANEH – Ezek. 45:12 ➔ MINA <4488>.

MANGER – Job 39:9; Prov. 14:4; Is. 1:3 ➔ CRIB <18>.

MANGLE – Lam. 3:11 ➔ PIECES (TEAR IN, TEAR TO, PULL IN) <6582>.

MANHOOD – Hos. 12:3 ➔ STRENGTH <202>.

MANIAC – Prov. 26:18 ➔ MADMAN <3856>.

MANIAC (LIKE A) – 2 Kgs. 9:20 ➔ MADNESS <7697>.

MANNA – ***mān*** [masc. noun: מָן <4478>; from WHAT? <4100>] ► **This word also means who, or what. This is the reaction that the Israelites had to the substance that the Lord gave them to eat.** Ref.: Ex. 16:15. They asked "What is it?" which translates into *mān*. This substance is described as tasting like wafers made with honey and like white coriander seeds in shape (Ex. 16:31). The manna could be ground into grain and cooked into cakes (see Num. 11:6–9). When the Israelites entered the Promised Land, God caused the manna to cease (Josh. 5:12). Other refs.: Ex. 16:33, 35; Deut. 8:3, 16; Neh. 9:20; Ps. 78:24. ¶

MANNER – [1] 2 Sam. 7:19 ➔ TURN (noun) <8447> d. [2] Ruth 4:7 ➔ TESTIMONY <8584>.

MANTLE – Judg. 4:18 ➔ BLANKET <8063>.

MANOAH – ***mānôaḥ*** [masc. proper noun: מָנוֹחַ <4495>; the same as RESTING PLACE <4494>]: rest ▶ **This word designates the father of Samson.** He and his wife carefully tried to bring up Samson as the messenger of the Lord had instructed them. They made Samson a Nazarite. Manoah conversed with the angel and was submissive to his message. He and his wife were broken and hurt when Samson married a Philistine woman (Judg. 14:3). Refs.: Judg. 13:2, 8, 9, 11–13, 15–17, 19–22; 16:31. ¶

MANSION – Ps. 49:14 ➔ HABITATION <2073>.

MANTLE – 1 ***maʿᵃṭepeṯ*** [fem. noun: מַעֲטֶפֶת <4595>; from TURN (verb) <5848> a. (in the sense of to wrap, to cover)] ▶ **This word refers to a part of the royal garments worn by officials of state or the rich; it is also translated outer tunic, cape.** Ref.: Is. 3:22. ¶
– 2 Josh. 7:21, 24; 1 Kgs. 19:13, 19; Zech. 13:4 ➔ GARMENT <155> 3 Is. 61:3 ➔ GARMENT <4594>.

MANUHOTH – 1 Chr. 2:52 ➔ MANAHATHITES (HALF OF THE) <2679>.

MANURE, MANURE PILE – Is. 25:10 ➔ DUNGHILL <4087>.

MANY – ***raḇ*** [adj.: רַב <7227>; from MANY (BE, BECOME) <7231>] ▶
a. This word also means much, great, long, mighty. The word indicates abundance, numerous. It indicates much in amount, e.g., gold (1 Kgs. 10:2); silver (2 Kgs. 12:10); wine (Esther 1:7); etc. It indicates a large number of people (Gen. 50:20; Ex. 5:5; Judg. 8:30); a long time, many days (Gen. 21:34; 37:34). It indicates an abundance of some things: blessings (Prov. 28:20); straw (Gen. 24:25). It is used with *min* (<4480>), from, than, following to indicate more . . . than (Ex. 1:9; Num. 22:15). Used as an adverb, it indicates much, exceedingly (Ps. 123:3); greatly, seriously (Ps. 62:2). It modifies and defines space at times, a long distance (1 Sam. 26:13); the depth of the sea or the deep itself (Gen. 7:11; Amos 7:4). It indicates something greater than something else (Deut. 7:1, 17; 9:14). The phrase *wayyêleḵ hālôḵ wārāḇ,* indicates in context, the sound became louder and louder, greater and greater (1 Sam. 14:19). Followed by *min* (<4480>), it may mean enough of . . . (Ex. 9:28). The phrase *raḇ lāḵem min-* means, too much for one to . . . (in context, to go up to Jerusalem; 1 Kgs. 12:28).
b. An adjective meaning chief, captain, high official. It indicates that someone or something is of great importance. It indicates the leader, the chief of a group (2 Kgs. 18:17; 25:8); the chief officer, head of the royal guard respectively (cf. Dan. 1:3). It indicates the captain of a ship (Jon. 1:6, *raḇ haḥoḇêl*). In the plural, it indicates the leading officers or officials (Jer. 39:13; 41:1). *

MANY (BE, BECOME) – 1 ***rāḇaḇ*** [verb: רָבַב <7231>; a prim. root] ▶ **This word means to be increased or multiplied.** It refers to the multiplication of the human race on earth (Gen. 6:1). It indicates the intensity, the multiplication of the cry against the cities of Sodom and Gomorrah (Gen. 18:20). In the intensive stem it may have the sense of a ten-thousand-fold increase (Ps. 144:13). With *min* (from, than) following, it means more than . . . (Jer. 46:23). *
2 ***rāḇāh, harbêh*** [verb: רָבָה, הַרְבֵּה <7235>; a prim. root] ▶
a. A verb meaning to become numerous or great; to be abundant. It expresses God's original mandate for humans to multiply on earth (Gen. 1:22, 28). It depicts the increase of Israelites in Egypt (Ex. 1:10, 12); it refers to an increase in volume, extent, power, or influence (Gen. 7:17, 18; Ps. 49:16; Daniel 12:4). It is used for both animals and inanimate things (Ex. 11:9; Deut. 7:22; 8:13; Ezek. 31:5). It refers to an increase or multiplication of time: days (Gen. 38:12); years (Prov. 4:10). It indicates in a comprehensive sense God's greatness over humans (Job 33:12). In the intensive or causative stems of the verb, it indicates the increasing or enlarging

of someone or something: (Judg. 9:29; Ps. 44:12; Lam. 2:22; Ezek. 19:2). God makes His followers great (2 Sam. 22:36; Ps. 18:35); the leaders of His people (1 Chr. 4:10). He increases in number persons, things (Deut. 17:16; Hos. 2:8). Adverbially (especially *harbêh*), it means to do something, to perform greatly (Amos 4:4). The phrase *harbāh 'arbeh* means I will increase, multiply greatly (Gen. 3:16; 16:10; 22:17).
b. An adjective indicating to be much, to be abundant. It refers to a great number of something (2 Sam. 1:4; Jon. 4:11). Used with a preposition and *m*ᵉ*'ōḏ*, it means very much (2 Chr. 11:12; 16:8; Neh. 5:18). As an adverb, it intensifies, usually used with *m*ᵉ*'ōḏ* following, much, very, very much . . . (Gen. 41:49; Josh. 13:1; Neh. 2:2), but it is found alone also (2 Kgs. 10:18; Eccl. 5:20). It may indicate a great amount of something, much brass (2 Sam. 8:8). *

MAOCH – ***mā'ôḵ*** [masc. proper noun: מָעוֹךְ <4582>; from CRUSH <4600>]: oppression ▶ **Father of Achish, king of Gath.** Ref.: 1 Sam. 27:2. ¶

MAON – ***mā'ôn*** [proper noun: מָעוֹן <4584>; the same as HABITATION <4583>]: habitation ▶
a. A son of Shammai. Ref.: 1 Chr. 2:45. ¶
b. A city in Judah. Refs.: Josh. 15:55; 1 Sam. 23:24, 25; 1 Sam. 25:2. ¶
c. An Arabian tribe. Ref.: Judg. 10:12. ¶

MARA – ***mārā'*** [proper noun: מָרָא <4755>; for BITTER <4751>]: bitter, bitterness ▶ **This word means bitter, bitterness.** Naomi called herself this name during the time of her bereavements. Ref.: Ruth 1:20. ¶

MARAH – ***mārāh*** [proper noun: מָרָה <4785>; the same as BITTER <4751>]: bitter, bitterness ▶ **The first encampment of the Israelites in the desert.** They murmured against Moses because the water was bitter (Ex. 15:23; Num. 33:8, 9). ¶

MARALAH – ***mar'ᵃlāh*** [proper noun: מַרְעֲלָה <4831>; from BRANDISH <7477> (in the sense of to shake)]: trembling. earthquake ▶ **A place on the boundary of Zebulun.** Ref.: Josh. 19:11. ¶

MARBLE – 1 ***šayiš*** [masc. noun: שַׁיִשׁ <7893>; from an unused root meaning to bleach] ▶ **This word indicates a beautiful, decorative, yet excellent grade of gypsum used in various ways in construction; it is also translated alabaster.** Ref.: 1 Chr. 29:2. ¶
– 2 Esther 1:6; Song 5:15 → LINEN, FINE LINEN <8336> b.

MARBLE (BLACK) – Esther 1:6 → PRECIOUS STONE <5508> b.

MARCH (noun) – Nah. 2:5 → WAY <1979>.

MARCH (verb) – 1 ***pāśa'*** [verb: פָּשַׂע <6585>; a prim. root] ▶ **This word means to tread on something, to press on it with one's foot; it is also translated to step.** In context it means to injure or destroy something (Is. 27:4). The sense may be to pass through or over something (KJV). ¶
2 ***ṣā'āh*** [verb: צָעָה <6808>; a prim. root] ▶ **This word means to travel, to wander.** It refers figuratively to the Lord traveling, going forth, (*ṣ'h*) in might and strength (Is. 63:1). It describes acting, behaving as a prostitute (Jer. 2:20). It refers to a person who travels without purpose and wanders about (Jer. 48:12). ¶

MARCHING – ***ṣᵉ'āḏāh*** [fem. noun: צְעָדָה <6807>; fem. of STEP (noun) <6806>] ▶
a. This word refers to the sound created by the Lord and His armies as they go forth in battle. Refs.: 2 Sam. 5:24; 1 Chr. 14:15. ¶
b. A feminine noun referring to an ankle bracelet, an ankle chain. These were items usually made of gold or silver, luxury items of jewelry for ornamentation (Is. 3:20: leg ornament, ankle chain, anklet, armlet). The Lord would remove them as an act of judgment on His part. ¶

MARDUK – Jer. 50:2 → MERODACH <4781>.

MARE – ***sûsāh*** [fem. noun: סוּסָה <5484>; fem. of HORSE <5483>] ▶ **This word indicates a female horse.** It refers to the bride in Song 1:9 (NKJV: filly; KJV: a company of horses) as an indication of her attractiveness. ¶

MARESHAH – ***mārēšāh, mārê'šāh*** [proper noun: מָרֵשָׁה, מָרֵאשָׁה <4762>; formed like PRINCIPALITIES <4761>]: principality ▶
a. A city in Judah. Refs.: Josh. 15:44; 2 Chr. 11:8; 14:9, 10; 20:37; Mic. 1:15. ¶
b. The father of Hebron. Ref.: 1 Chr. 2:42. ¶
c. A son of Laadah. Ref.: 1 Chr. 4:21. ¶

MARINER – ***mallāḥ*** [masc. noun: מַלָּח <4419>; from SEASON (verb) <4414>] ▶ **This word is used of the seamen of the merchant vessels of the city of Tyre; it is also translated sailor.** Refs.: Ezek. 27:9, 27, 29. They would all be judged with Tyre. Other ref.: Jon. 1:5. ¶

MARISH – Ezek. 47:11 ➔ CISTERN <1360>.

MARITAL RIGHTS – ***'ōnāh, 'ônāh*** [fem. noun: עֹנָה, עוֹנָה <5772>; from an unused root apparently meaning to dwell together] ▶
a. This word refers to conjugal rights, the duty of marriage. It refers to the right of a wife in a polygamous marriage to have intimacy with her husband (Ex. 21:10). ¶
b. The Hebrew word also means sin, guilt; it is also translated iniquity, transgression, furrow (KJV). It refers to the burden or responsible guilt someone bears (Hos. 10:10). ¶

MARK – 1 ***kṯōḇeṯ*** [fem. noun: כְּתֹבֶת <3793>; from WRITE <3789>] ▶ **This word indicates an inscription or imprint on a person's body, possibly tattooing of some kind; the word is also translated tattoo, tattoo mark.** The Israelites were not to make any tattoo marks on themselves (Lev. 19:28). ¶
2 ***tāw*** [masc. noun: תָּו <8420>; from SCRIBBLE <8427>] ▶ **This word is the name of the last letter of the Hebrew alphabet; it also means a signature.** It indicates a mark of some kind put on a person (Ezek. 9:4, 6); and also a person's identifying mark or signature (Job 31:35). In the case of Ezekiel, it was a sign of exemption from judgment. ¶
– 3 Lev. 13–14 ➔ SORE (noun) <5061> 4 1 Sam. 20:20; Job 16:12; Lam. 3:12 ➔ GUARD <4307> 5 Job 7:20 ➔ TARGET <4645> 6 Is. 44:13 ➔ OUTLINE (MAKE AN) <8388>.

MARK (BECOME A DISTINGUISHING) – Ezek. 27:7 ➔ SPREADING <4666>.

MARK (MAKE, PUT, SET A) – 1 Sam. 21:13; Ezek. 9:4 ➔ SCRIBBLE <8427>.

MARK, TATTOO MARK – Lev. 19:28 ➔ TATTOO <7085>.

MARK OUT – ***'āwāh*** [verb: אָוָה <184>; a prim. root] ▶ **This word means to draw.** In Numbers 34:10, it is used reflexively to indicate drawing out a line (for yourselves) to indicate the eastern border of the land of Israel's inheritance; it is also translated to run a line, to point out. ¶

MARKED (BE) – ***kāṯam*** [verb: כָּתַם <3799>; a prim. root] ▶ **This word means stained.** It is used in a figurative sense in context to refer to the "remaining stain" (participle form) of iniquity after Israel's ineffective attempt to remove it (Jer. 2:22). ¶

MARKER – 1 ***śereḏ*** [masc. noun: שֶׂרֶד <8279>; from REMAIN <8277>] ▶
a. This word refers to some kind of tool used by a craftsman to sketch out a design on newly dressed wood. Ref.: Is. 44:13; also translated pencil.
b. It could also refer to a line drawn on newly dressed wood or a string used to mark a line. Ref.: Is. 44:13.
c. It could also refer to a chalk marker used to make a pattern on newly dressed wood. Ref.: Is. 44:13. ¶
– 2 Ezek. 39:15 ➔ MONUMENT <6725>.

MARKET – 1 ***sḥōrāh*** [fem. noun: סְחֹרָה <5506>; from MERCHANT <5503>] ▶

This word depicts the various seabordering lands (isles?) as the marketplaces, the market of Tyre. It is also translated merchandise, customer. (Ref.: Ezek. 27:15). ¶
– [2] Is. 23:3 ➔ MERCHANDISE <5504> [3] Ezek. 27:13, 19, 25 ➔ MERCHANDISE <4627> [4] Ezek. 27:24 ➔ MERCHANDISE <4819>.

MARKET DISTRICT – Zeph. 1:11 ➔ MAKTESH <4389>.

MARKETPLACE – [1] Is. 23:3 ➔ MERCHANDISE <5504> [2] Ezek. 27:24 ➔ MERCHANDISE <4819>.

MARKS (PUT) – Job 13:27 ➔ CARVE <2707>.

MAROTH – ***mārôṯ*** [proper noun: מָרוֹת <4796>; fem. plur. of BITTER <4751>]: bitterness ▶ **A city of the tribe of Judah.** Ref.: Mic. 1:12. ¶

MARRED – ***mišḥaṯ, mošḥāṯ*** [masc. noun: מִשְׁחַת, מָשְׁחַת <4893>; from DESTROY <7843>] ▶
a. This word is used of the terrible disfigurement or distortion of a person's appearance. It describes the appearance of the Servant of the Lord (Is. 52:14; also translated disfigured). ¶
b. This word refers to a defect or blemish in an animal, making it unacceptable for sacrifice to the Lord. Ref.: Lev. 22:25: corruption, blemish. ¶

MARRIAGE – ***ḥāṯan, ḥōtên, ḥōṯeneṯ*** [verb, masc. noun, fem. noun: חָתַן, חֹתֵן, חֹתֶנֶת <2859>; a prim. root] ▶
a. A verb meaning to become related by marriage (the legal relationship between spouses); it is also translated to intermarry. It is used of the entire marriage process and ceremonial trappings (Ezra 9:14). It naturally takes on the idea of becoming a son-in-law (1 Sam. 18:21–23, 26, 27; 1 Kgs. 3:1). It could indicate a political liaison to ally oneself with powerful and beneficial persons (2 Chr. 18:1). ¶
b. A masculine noun indicating a father-in-law. It refers to the person who is the wife's father (Ex. 3:1; 4:18; 18:1, 2, 5–8, 12, 14, 15, 17, 24, 27; Num. 10:29; Judg. 1:16; 4:11). It usually refers to Moses' wife's father. ¶
c. A feminine noun indicating mother-in-law. It indicates the wife's mother and is used only once in Deuteronomy 27:23 where intercourse with one's mother-in-law is forbidden as a grave sin. ¶

MARRIAGE (DUTY OF) – Ex. 21:10 ➔ MARITAL RIGHTS <5772> a.

MARRIAGE RIGHTS – Ex. 21:10 ➔ MARITAL RIGHTS <5772> a.

MARROW – [1] ***mōaḥ*** [masc. noun: מֹחַ <4221>; from the same as FAT ANIMAL <4220>] ▶ **This word refers to bone marrow, the soft fatty tissue that fills a healthy person's bones.** It is a sign of strength and health (Job 21:24). ¶
– [2] Prov. 3:8 ➔ DRINK (noun) <8250>.

MARRY – [1] ***bāʿal*** [verb: בָּעַל <1166>; a prim. root] ▶ **This Hebrew word means for a man to espouse a woman (Deut. 24:1), and for a woman to espouse a man (Prov. 30:23). It also means to have dominion or to rule over (land or people).** Figuratively, it is used in connection with God's marriage to Israel (Jer. 3:14), as well as Judah and Israel's marriage to the daughter of a foreign god (Mal. 2:11). Other times, this verb means to have dominion over land (1 Chr. 4:22) or people (Is. 26:13). Used as a participle, it means to be married to (Gen. 20:3). *
[2] ***yābam*** [verb: יָבַם <2992>; a prim. root of doubtful meaning] ▶ **The word means to perform one's duty in a levirate marriage; to consummate a levirate marriage.** It indicates the duty of impregnating the wife of one's brother who has died so there will be offspring to him and so the family name will not die out (Gen. 38:8; also translated to perform the duty of a brother-in-law) in Israel (Deut. 25:5, 7: to perform the duty of the husband's brother). ¶

MARSENA – ***marsᵉnāʾ*** [masc. proper noun: מַרְסְנָא <4826>; of foreign deriv.] ▶ **One**

of the seven princes of Persia and Media counseling Ahasuerus. Ref.: Esther 1:14. ¶

MARSH – [1] ***biṣṣāh*** [fem. noun: בִּצָּה <1207>; intens. from MUD <1206>] ▶ **This word means a soft and wet ground; it is also translated mire, miry place, fens, swamp.** It refers to the place and type of water and soil conditions needed for the papyrus plant and reeds to grow (Job 8:11; 40:21). It refers to the places around the Salt Sea that will remain salty when the Lord transforms the land (Ezek. 47:11). ¶
– [2] Jer. 51:32 ➔ POND <98> [3] Ezek. 47:11 ➔ CISTERN <1360>.

MARSH GRASS – Gen. 41:2, 18 ➔ MEADOW (plant) <260>.

MARSHAL – ***ṭip̱sār*** [masc. noun: טִפְסָר <2951>; of foreign deriv.] ▶ **This word means a military commander.** In Jeremiah 51:27 (marshal, general, captain, commander), it appears to refer to the supreme commander of an army called to oppose Babylon. In the only other occurrence, Nahum 3:17 (marshals, captains, generals, scribes officials), it is plural and has a slightly different spelling. Here it refers to commanders in the army of Nineveh, the capital of Assyria. Interestingly, in both passages, comparison is made between military power and different kinds of locusts. ¶

MARSHAL (verb) – Mic. 5:1 ➔ GATHER <1413>.

MART – Is. 23:3 ➔ MERCHANDISE <5504>.

MARVELOUS – Ps. 17:7 ➔ DISTINCTION (MAKE) <6395>.

MASH – [1] ***maš*** [masc. proper noun: מַשׁ <4851>; of foreign deriv.] ▶ **One of the sons of Aram.** Ref.: Gen. 10:23. He is called Meshech in 1 Chronicles 1:17. ¶
– [2] Is. 30:24 ➔ SALTED <2548>.

MASHAL – ***māšāl*** [proper noun: מָשָׁל <4913>; from MISHAL <4861>] ▶ **An abbreviated form of *miš'āl* (see MISHAL <4861>).** Ref.: 1 Chr. 6:74. ¶

MASKIL – ***maśkiyl*** [masc. noun: מַשְׂכִּיל <4905>; from CONSIDER <7919> (in the sense of to understand, to contemplate)] ▶ **This word means a poem. It is an unknown musical or wisdom term applied as a title or descriptive phrase to several psalms.** Refs.: Ps. 32; 42; 44; 45; 52–55; 74; 78; 88; 89; 142, possibly wisdom psalms indicating insight. NKJV translates the word contemplation. ¶

MASON – 2 Kgs. 12:12 ➔ BUILD <1443>.

MASREKAH – ***maśrêqāh*** [proper noun: מַשְׂרֵקָה <4957>; a form of SOREK <7796> (vineyard) used as a denom.]: vineyard ▶ **A place in Edom.** Refs.: Gen. 36:36; 1 Chr. 1:47. ¶

MASS – [1] ***ḥaśrāh*** [fem. noun: חַשְׁרָה <2841>; from the same as HUB <2840>] ▶ **This word indicates a collection of water. It is used in one of David's poetic psalms to depict one feature of a theophany or appearance of God.** It pictures a mass of water collected around God (2 Sam. 22:12); NIV reads "dark rain clouds," following the Septuagint and Vulgate; ESV: a gathering of water; KJV, NKJV: dark waters. ¶
– [2] Nah. 3:3 ➔ HEAVINESS <3514>.

MASSA – ***maśśā'*** [masc. proper noun: מַשָּׂא <4854>; the same as BURDEN (noun) <4853>]: burden ▶ **A son of Ishmael.** Refs.: Gen. 25:14; 1 Chr. 1:30. ¶

MASSAH – ***massāh*** [proper noun: מַסָּה <4532>; the same as TRIAL <4531>]: testing ▶ **The name of a place where the Israelites arrogantly "tested" God.** The event was recorded to warn Israel not to act in such a way again (Ex. 17:7; Deut. 6:16; 9:22; Ps. 95:8). See TRIAL <4531>. ¶

MAST – [1] ***ḥibbêl*** [masc. noun: חִבֵּל <2260>; from PLEDGE (TAKE AS A) <2254> (in the sense of furnished with

ropes)] ► **This word indicates an upright support for sails; it also refers to a ship's rigging.** In context, the word points out in a simile that a drunken person is like someone lying on the top of a ship's mast or upper rigging (Prov. 23:34). ¶
– [2] Is. 33:23; Ezek. 27:5 ➔ FLAG <8650>.

MASTER – [1] Gen. 18:12; 24:9; Judg. 19:11; 1 Kgs. 22:17; Amos 4:1; etc. ➔ LORD <113> [2] Gen. 27:29, 37 ➔ LORD <1376> [3] Jer. 25:34–36 ➔ MIGHTY <117> [4] Song 7:1 ➔ ARTIST <542>.

MASTER OF (BE) – See RULE OVER <7980>, <7981>.

MASTER CRAFTSMAN – Prov. 8:30 ➔ MASTER WORKMAN <525>.

MASTER WORKMAN – ***'āmôn*** [masc. noun: אָמוֹן <525>; from NURSE (verb) <539>, prob. in the sense of training] ► **This word means an architect or a master craftsman.** It is used in Proverbs 8:30 as the personification of wisdom. Wisdom is portrayed as a craftsman at God's side, involved in designing the creation. ¶

MASTERY – ***šalliyṭ*** [Aramaic masc. adj.: שַׁלִּיט <7990>; corresponding to POWER <7989>] ► **This word is commonly used of God and His sovereignty that gives Him dominion, complete control over everything.** There is nothing that is not under His authority, including the kingdoms of people (Dan. 4:17; 5:21). God's mastery covers everything that exists. This adjective can also be used in describing the power that kings have (Ezra 4:20); and the authority they can exercise (Ezra 7:24). This word can also be used as a noun meaning captain or one who has authority and mastery over others (Dan. 2:15). *

MATCH – Ezek. 31:8 ➔ DIM (BECOME, GROW) <6004>.

MATCH (BE A) – Ezek. 28:3 ➔ DIM (BECOME, GROW) <6004>.

MATE (noun) – Is. 34:15, 16 ➔ NEIGHBOR <7468>.

MATE (verb) – Gen. 30:38, 39, 41; 31:10 ➔ CONCEIVE <3179>.

MATERIAL (TWO KINDS OF) – ***ša'aṭnêz*** [masc. noun: שַׁעַטְנֵז <8162>; prob. of foreign deriv.] ► **This word refers to mixed fabric; cloth of more than one kind.** It refers to something that combines differing materials together, thus creating something forbidden in Israel because of the inequity involved (Lev. 19:19; Deut. 22:11). Others suggest a reference to a material of wide mesh (spaces). ¶

MATERIALS – Neh. 4:17 ➔ BURDEN <5447>.

MATING – Jer. 2:24 ➔ HEAT (noun) <8385>.

MATRED – ***maṭrêḏ*** [fem. noun: מַטְרֵד <4308>; from CONTINUAL <2956>]: pushing forward ► **Mother-in-law of Hadad king of Edom.** Refs.: Gen. 36:39; 1 Chr. 1:50. ¶

MATRI – ***maṭriy*** [proper noun: מַטְרִי <4309>; from RAIN (verb) <4305>]: rainy ► **Family of Benjamin to which King Saul belonged.** Ref.: 1 Sam. 10:21. ¶

MATSOR – ***māṣôr*** [proper noun: מָצוֹר <4693>; the same as SIEGE <4692> in the sense of a limit] ► **This word is another name for Egypt as the border of Canaan. It is the singular form of the dual form commonly used for Egypt and seems to be used for Lower Egypt.** It indicates the land or territory of Egypt (2 Kgs. 19:24; Is. 19:6; 37:25; Mic. 7:12). ¶

MATTAN – ***mattān*** [masc. proper noun: מַתָּן <4977>; the same as GIFT <4976>]: gift ►
a. A priest of Baal. Refs.: 2 Kgs. 11:18; 2 Chr. 23:17. ¶
b. The father of Shephatiah. Ref.: Jer. 38:1. ¶

MATTANAH – ***mattānāh*** [proper noun: מַתָּנָה <4980>; the same as GIFT <4979>]: gift of the Lord ▶ **An encampment of the Israelites on the territory of Moab or near it.** Refs.: Num. 21:18, 19. ¶

MATTANIAH – ***mattanyāh, mattanyāhû*** [masc. proper noun: מַתַּנְיָה, מַתַּנְיָהוּ <4983>; from GIFT <4976> and LORD <3050>]: gift of the Lord ▶
a. A descendant of Asaph. Ref.: 2 Chr. 20:14. ¶
b. A Levite. Refs.: 1 Chr. 25:4, 16. ¶
c. A Levite, possibly the same as a. above. Ref.: 2 Chr. 29:13. ¶
d. A king of Judah. Ref.: 2 Kgs. 24:17. ¶
e. A son of Micah. Refs.: 1 Chr. 9:15; Neh. 11:17, 22; 12:8, 25, 35; 13:13. ¶
f. A son of Elam. Ref.: Ezra 10:26. ¶
g. A son of Zattu. Ref.: Ezra 10:27. ¶
h. A son of Pahath-Moab. Ref.: Ezra 10:30. ¶
i. A son of Bani. Ref.: Ezra 10:37. ¶

MATTATTAH – ***mattattāh*** [proper noun: מַתַּתָּה <4992>; for MATTITHIAH <4993>]: gift of the Lord ▶ **Ezra persuaded him to send back his foreign wife.** Ref.: Ezra 10:33. ¶

MATTENAI – ***matt^enay*** [masc. proper noun: מַתְּנַי <4982>; from GIFT <4976>]: gift ▶
a. A priest. Ref.: Neh. 12:19. ¶
b. A son of Hashum. Ref.: Ezra 10:33. ¶
c. A son of Bani. Ref.: Ezra 10:37. ¶

MATTER – [1] Ezra 5:5 ➔ COMMAND (noun) <2941> [2] Dan. 4:17 ➔ ANSWER (noun) <6600>.

MATTITHIAH – ***mattiṯyāh, mattiṯyāhû*** [masc. proper noun: מַתִּתְיָה, מַתִּתְיָהוּ <4993>; from GIFT <4991> and LORD <3050>]: gift of the Lord ▶
a. A Levite. Refs.: 1 Chr. 9:31; 15:18, 21; 16:5. ¶
b. A son of Jeduthun. Refs.: 1 Chr. 25:3, 21. ¶
c. A son of Nebo. Ref.: Ezra 10:43. ¶
d. A postexilic Jew. Ref.: Neh. 8:4. ¶

MATTOCK – [1] ***maḥ^arêšāh*** [fem. noun: מַחֲרֵשָׁה <4281>; from PLOW (verb) <2790>] ▶ **This word indicates a tool used in agriculture or farming; it may refer to a sickle, a hoe, a plowshare.** Refs.: 1 Sam. 13:20, 21 (NASB, NIV, NKJV, ESV; not in KJV). This tool was used for breaking up ground or plowing. ¶
– [2] Is. 7:25 ➔ HOE <4576>.

MATURITY – Hos. 12:3 ➔ STRENGTH <202>.

MAW – Deut. 18:3 ➔ STOMACH <6896>.

MAZZAROTH – ***mazzārôṯ*** [fem. plur. noun: מַזָּרוֹת <4216>; apparently from SEPARATE <5144> in the sense of distinction]: constellations, perhaps the zodiac ▶ **This word is known for a constellation of stars.** It refers to constellations, possibly Venus, an evening or morning star, or Hyades in the constellation Taurus (Job 38:32). Others suggest a reference to some southern constellation of the zodiac. The Bear is mentioned in the second half of the verse. ¶

ME – See I <576>.

ME JARKON – ***mêy hayyarqôn*** [proper noun: מֵי הַיַּרְקוֹן <4313>; from WATER <4325> and MILDEW <3420> (in the sense of paleness) with the art. interposed]: waters of a yellow color ▶ **A place in the territory of the tribe of Dan.** Ref.: Josh. 19:46. ¶

MEADOW (place) – [1] ***ma^areh, ma^arêh gāḇa‘*** [noun: מַעֲרֶה, מַעֲרֵה־גָבַע <4629>; from EMPTY (verb) <6168> (in the sense of to expose)] ▶
a. A masculine noun meaning a setting place. An alternative reading for WEST, WEST SIDE <4628>. The textual reading is not clear (Judg. 20:33, KJV). ¶
b. A proper noun meaning Maareh-geba. Another rendering (NASB, ESV) preferred by some scholars because of the uncertain reading of the Hebrew (Judg. 20:33). ¶
– [2] Ps. 37:20; 65:13; Is. 30:23 ➔ LAMB <3733> [3] Hos. 4:16 ➔ BREADTH <4800> [4] Zeph. 2:6 ➔ CAVE <3741>.

MEADOW (plant) – ***’āḥû*** [masc. noun: אָחוּ <260>; of uncertain (perhaps Egyptian) deriv.] ▶ **This word means reed, papyrus, marsh plant.** It is what grows in a marsh (Job 8:11), i.e., papyrus or marsh plant. Cows grazed among the marsh grass in Egypt according to Pharaoh's dream (Gen. 41:2, 18). ¶

MEAH – ***mê'āh*** [proper noun: מֵאָה <3968>; the same as HUNDRED <3967>]: a hundred ▶ **This is the name of the tower of the Hundred between the Sheep Gate and the Tower of Hananel of the wall of Jerusalem.** Refs.: Neh. 3:1; 12:39. ¶

MEAL – 1 Gen. 18:6; Num. 5:15; etc. ➔ FLOUR <7058> 2 Ezek. 27:17 ➔ CAKE <6436> b.

MEAN – Prov. 22:29 ➔ OBSCURE <2823>.

MEANING – Dan. 7:19 ➔ TRUTH <3321>.

MEANING, EXACT MEANING – Dan. 7:16 ➔ CERTAIN <3330>.

MEARAH, ARAH – ***me'ārāh, 'ārāh*** [proper noun: מְעָרָה, עָרָה <4632>; the same as CAVE <4631>]: cave ▶
a. A location east of Sidon. Ref.: KJV, NKJV, ESV, NASB, Josh. 13:4. ¶
b. Arah, a location east of Sidon. Ref.: NIV, Josh. 13:4. ¶

MEASURE (noun) – 1 ***middāh*** [fem. noun: מִדָּה <4060>; fem. of CLOTHES <4055>] ▶ **This word indicates the actual dimension or size of something.** Curtains for the Tabernacle (Ex. 26:2, 8); cherubim for the Temple (1 Kgs. 6:25); all kinds of measures (1 Chr. 23:29). It indicates both the process of measuring (Lev. 19:35) and the part measured or section (of a wall) (Neh. 3:11). It is used to indicate a large size, e.g., a person of great stature, literally, "a man of measure" (1 Chr. 11:23); a large house (Jer. 22:14). In certain contexts, it has an adverbial aspect translated usually as "by measure(ment)" (Ezek. 48:30). The Hebrew word also means tax, tribute; see TAX <4060>. *

2 ***me'śûrāh*** [fem. noun: מְשׂוּרָה <4884>; from an unused root meaning apparently to divide] ▶ **This word is used of a liquid amount of capacity or weight.** Ref.: Lev. 19:35. It is used for volume and size as well (1 Chr. 23:29; also translated volume, capacity, quantity). It is used in an adverbial expression with *be* attached, by measure or according to its measurement (Ezek. 4:11). It indicates the scarcity of something (Ezek. 4:16: by measure, rationed). ¶
– 3 Gen. 18:6; 1 Sam. 25:18; 1 Kgs. 18:32; 2 Kgs. 7:1, 16, 18 ➔ SEAH <5429> 4 1 Kgs. 4:22; 5:11; 2 Chr. 2:10; 27:5; Ezra 7:22; Ezek. 45:14 ➔ COR <3734> 5 Job 11:9; Jer. 13:25 ➔ CLOTHES <4055> 6 Job 38:5 ➔ MEASUREMENT <4461> 7 Is. 27:8 ➔ WARFARE <5432> 8 Ezek. 45:11 ➔ QUOTA <8506>.

MEASURE (verb) – 1 ***māḏaḏ*** [verb: מָדַד <4058>; a prim. root] ▶ **This word properly means to calculate the length of anything with a line stretched out; it is also translated to stretch. It serves as a general term for gauging the length, distance, quantity, size, etc. (of various things) by diverse methods and for varied purposes.** Distance or area (Num. 35:5; Deut. 21:2; Ezek. 40:5, 6, 8, Ezek. 40:20); an amount of grain of any kind, sand, the heavens, etc. (Ruth 3:15; Is. 40:12; Jer. 31:37; 33:22; Hos. 1:10); counting out payment for something (Is. 65:7). It is used to line up, measure off, and tally up prisoners of war for life or death (2 Sam. 8:2). It refers to God's actions of deliverance for His people as He measures them out for victory (Ps. 60:6; 108:7). It indicates Elijah's action as he "measured himself out," stretched himself over the widow's son to heal him (1 Kgs. 17:21). It is probably the preferred reading in Job 7:4, indicating the way the nights continued to drag on. *

2 ***môḏ*** [verb: מוֹד <4128>; a prim. root] ▶
a. This word refers to the Lord's surveying the earth as He prepares to demolish it. Ref.: Hab. 3:6, KJV, NKJV, NASB, ESV. ¶
b. The word means to shake. It refers to the convulsing or shaking of the earth

set in motion by the Lord as judgment. Ref.: Hab. 3:6, NIV. ¶

MEASUREMENT – [1] *mêmaḏ* [masc. noun: מֵמַד <4461>; from MEASURE (verb) <4058>] ▶ This word refers specifically to the extent or size of the earth, established by God at creation; it is also translated dimension, measure. Ref.: Job 38:5. ¶ – [2] Ex. 26:2, 8; Lev. 19:35; etc. → MEASURE (noun) <4060>.

MEAT – [1] Deut. 28:26; Ps. 79:2; etc. → FOOD <3978> [2] 1 Sam. 25:11 → SLAUGHTER (noun) <2878> [3] 1 Kgs. 19:8 → FOOD <396> [4] Ps. 111:5; Prov. 31:15 → PREY <2964> [5] Prov. 9:2 → SLAUGHTER (noun) <2874> [6] Dan. 1:5, 8, 13, 15, 16; 11:26 → FOOD, CHOICE FOOD <6598> [7] For this word used by the KJV, see FOOD.

MEAT (UNCLEAN, TAINTED, IMPURE) – Is. 65:4 → OFFENSIVE THING <6292>.

MEBUNNAI – *mᵉḇunnay* [masc. proper noun: מְבֻנַּי <4012>; from BUILD <1129>]: building, construction ▶ One of David's mighty men. Ref.: 2 Sam. 23:27. ¶

MECHERATHITE – *mᵉḵērātiy* [proper noun: מְכֵרָתִי <4382>; patrial from an unused name (the same as SWORD <4380) of a place elsewhere unknown] ▶ A native or a inhabitant of a place called Mecherah. Ref.: 1 Chr. 11:36. ¶

MECONAH – *mᵉḵōnāh* [proper noun: מְכֹנָה <4368>; the same as STAND <4350>] ▶ A village of the tribe of Judah probably near Ziklag. Ref.: Neh. 11:28. ¶

MEDAD – *mêyḏāḏ* [masc. proper noun: מֵידָד <4312>; from CAST LOTS <3032> in the sense of loving]: love, affectionate ▶ A man on whom the Spirit of the Lord rested and who prophesied in the camp of Israel. Refs.: Num. 11:26, 27. ¶

MEDAN – *mᵉḏan* [masc. proper noun: מְדָן <4091>; the same as STRIFES <4090>]:

strife ▶ A son of Abraham and Keturah. Refs.: Gen. 25:2; 1 Chr. 1:32. ¶

MEDDLE – Deut. 2:5, 19; 2 Kgs. 14:10; 2 Chr. 25:19 → STRIVE <1624>.

MEDDLE WITH – Prov. 17:14 → BREAK OUT <1566>.

MEDE – [1] *māḏiy* [proper noun: מָדִי <4075>; patrial from MADAI <4074>] ▶ The term Mede indicates that Darius (Dan. 11:1) was related to the kingdom of the Medes, a rival to the rising Persian Empire in its early stages and to the Assyrians. Darius the Mede may be a throne name for Cyrus II, who did have close connections with the Medes through a Medean father (Dan. 9:1). The country or territory was known as Media, those living there as Medes or Medians. It was rather powerful in the years ca. 600–500 B.C. but succumbed to the power of Persia under Cyrus II in ca. 550 B.C. ¶ [2] *māḏāy'ā* [proper noun: מָדָיָא <4077>; corresponding to <4075> above] ▶ This is the Aramaic equivalent to the Hebrew <4075> above. It occurs in only the Aramaic portions of Daniel. Ref.: Dan. 5:31. ¶

MEDEBA – *mêyḏᵉḇā'* [proper noun: מֵידְבָא <4311>; from WATER <4325> and STRENGTH <1679>]: water of strength, water of rest ▶ An ancient city of Moab assigned to the tribe of Reuben. Refs.: Num. 21:30; Josh. 13:9, 16; 1 Chr. 19:7; Is. 15:2. ¶

MEDES – *māḏay* [Aramaic proper noun: מָדַי <4076>; corresponding to MADAI <4074> b.] ▶ This name occurs in only the Aramaic portions of Ezra and Daniel. Refs.: Ezra 6:2; Dan. 5:28; 6:8, 12, 15. ¶

MEDICINE – [1] *gêhāh* [fem. noun: גֵּהָה <1456>; from CURE <1455>] ▶ This word means cure, remedy. A joyful heart is declared to be a good medicine, literally causes good "healing," as opposed to a broken spirit, which dries up the bones (Prov. 17:22). ¶

[2] ***rᵉp̲û'â*** [fem. noun: רְפוּאָה <7499>; fem. pass. part. of HEAL <7495>] ▶ **This word indicates a remedy, healing.** It refers to a process of restoration as well as the cure for a spiritual illness (Jer. 30:13); national corruption (Jer. 46:11); or a severely inflicted wound (Ezek. 30:21). ¶
– [3] Ezek. 47:12 ➔ HEALING <8644>.

MEDITATE – [1] ***hāg̲āh*** [verb: הָגָה <1897>; a prim. root (comp. MEDITATION <1901>)] ▶ **This verb means to growl, to groan, to sigh, to mutter, to speak; used figuratively: to contemplate, to ponder (properly, to speak to oneself in low tones, as often done by a person deep in thought).** The Lord told Joshua to meditate on the Law day and night (Josh. 1:8), and the Psalms proclaimed people blessed if they meditate on the Law (Ps. 1:2). Job promised not to speak wickedness (Job 27:4). The Hebrew verb can also refer to the mutterings of mediums and wizards (Is. 8:19); the moans of grief (Is. 16:7); the growl of a lion (Is. 31:4); the coos of a dove (Is. 38:14). *
[2] ***śûaḥ*** [verb: שׂוּחַ <7742>; a prim. root] ▶ **This Hebrew word is used of Isaac's walking in a field to observe or quietly think about matters.** Its translation is not certain but is traditionally given as to meditate (Gen. 24:63). ¶

MEDITATION – [1] ***hāg̲ûṯ*** [fem. noun: הָגוּת <1900>; from MEDITATE <1897>] ▶ **This word denotes reflection or musing.** The psalmist describes the pondering of his heart as meditation (Ps. 49:3). It is derived from the Hebrew word *hāg̲āh*, which means to moan or to growl. ¶
[2] ***hāg̲iyg*** [masc. noun: הָגִיג <1901>; from an unused root akin to MEDITATE <1897>] ▶ **This word refers to intense reflection, musing or sighing by the psalmist in prayer as he cries out to the Lord; it is also translated groaning, lament, musing.** Refs.: Ps. 5:1; 39:3. ¶
[3] ***higgāyôn*** [masc. noun: הִגָּיוֹן <1902>; intens. from MEDITATE <1897>] ▶ **This word denotes reflection or thinking in the heart as opposed to speech.** Ref.: Ps. 19:14: meditation. It refers to thoughts or musing (internal) or possibly mockery or whispering (external) of persons against someone (Lam. 3:62: thought, whispering, device). It is best rendered as music dedicated to the Lord in Psalm 92:3: solemn sound, harmonious sound, resounding music, melody. It refers to a musical instrument of some kind (Ps. 9:16, Higgaion) or possibly instructs the reader to meditate. ¶
[4] ***śiyḥāh*** [fem. noun: שִׂיחָה <7881>; fem. of COMPLAINT <7879>] ▶ **This word means reflection, matter of one's thoughts (especially pious thoughts, relating to divine matters), musing. It is primarily used to indicate meditation.** The psalmist indicated the proper procedure for an individual's response to God's Law. Because of his love for God's Law, the psalmist was prompted to meditate on it all day long. Due to his practice of meditation, the psalmist received more understanding than his elders (Ps. 119:97, 99). As Job expressed his feelings and frustrations, Eliphaz responded condemningly, stating that what Job was feeling and saying was hindering devotion (or prayer) to God (Job 15:4). Eliphaz's response was that of an ignorant man who did not realize the true nature of devotion to God. ¶

MEDIUM – [1] ***'ôḇ*** [masc. noun: אוֹב <178>; from the same as FATHER <1> (apparently through the idea of prattling a father›s name)] ▶ **This word means an individual who is a channel of communication between the earthly world and the one of the spirits; it also means a conjured spirit, a necromancer; or a leather bottle.**
a. The primary use of the word is connected to the occult practice of necromancy or consulting the dead. It is used to signify a conjurer who professes to call up the dead by means of magic, especially to give revelation about future uncertainties (1 Sam. 28:7; Is. 8:19); a man or woman who has a familiar spirit (Lev. 20:27; 1 Chr. 10:13; Is. 29:4); the conjured spirit itself, particularly when speaking through the medium (1 Sam. 28:9; 2 Kgs. 21:6; 2 Chr. 33:6). The Israelites were strictly forbidden

from engaging in such practices or consulting mediums (Lev. 19:31; Deut. 18:10–12). Other refs.: 2 Kgs. 23:24; Is. 19:3. ¶
b. Interestingly, the word is used once to signify a leather bottle that may burst under pressure. Ref.: Job 32:19: wineskin, bottle. There is no convincing evidence that this particular reference has any occult connotations. Rather, the connection between the two divergent meanings of this Hebrew word is probably that a medium was seen as a "container" for a conjured spirit. ¶
– 2 1 Sam. 28:7 ➔ MISTRESS <1172>.

MEEK – Num. 12:3 ➔ HUMBLE <6035>.

MEEKLY – 1 Kgs. 21:27 ➔ SLOWLY <328>.

MEEKNESS – 1 Ps. 45:4 ➔ HUMILITY <6037> 2 Zeph. 2:3 ➔ HUMILITY <6038>.

MEET (adj.) – Ezra 4:14 ➔ PROPER <749>.

MEET (verb) – 1 ***pāga'*** [verb: פָּגַע <6293>; a prim. root] ▶ **This word means to encounter, to reach.** It could simply mean to meet (Ex. 5:20; 1 Sam. 10:5). It could also signify to meet someone with hostility, where it is usually rendered to fall upon (Josh. 2:16; Judg. 8:21; Ruth 2:22). In addition, it could convey the concept of meeting with a request or entreaty and is usually rendered as intercession (Jer. 7:16). This verb is used to designate the establishment of a boundary, probably with the idea of extending the boundary to reach a certain point (Josh. 16:7; 19:11, 22, 26, 27, 34). *
2 ***pāgaš*** [verb: פָּגַשׁ <6298>; a prim. root] ▶ **This word means to encounter, to come in contact with, to come face to face.** Refs.: Gen. 32:17; 33:8; Ex. 4:27; 1 Sam. 25:20. It is used of God meeting Moses at a particular place for a particular purpose (Ex. 4:24). It describes figuratively the wicked encountering darkness or trouble in their lives daily (Job 5:14); or things meeting together in a positive, approving way (Ps. 85:10). It denotes opposites meeting (Prov. 29:13). *
3 ***qārā'*** [verb: קָרָא <7122>; a prim. root] ▶ **This word means to encounter, to come across, to happen.** It states that something has taken place, occurred, happened, good, bad, or neutral (Gen. 42:4, 38; Ex. 1:10). It refers to the entire sweep of events yet to happen to the sons of Jacob and their descendants (Gen. 49:1). It refers to divine encounters (Ex. 5:3). It indicates a chance happening (Deut. 22:6; 2 Sam. 1:6). It is used of divine judgments occurring (Is. 51:19; Jer. 13:22; 32:23; 44:23). *
4 ***qādam*** [verb: קָדַם <6923>; a prim. root] ▶ **This word means to come before, to confront.** It can mean to confront with hostility (2 Sam. 22:6, 10; Ps. 18:6, 19; Job 30:27); or as a friend (Deut. 23:4; Is. 21:14; Mic. 6:6). It means to proceed, to go before (Ps. 68:25). It carries the sense of getting in someone's face, confronting him or her (Ps. 17:13; Amos 9:10). It means to say or do something earlier, before (Jon. 4:2); something before the sun rises (Ps. 119:147); to think or meditate beforehand on something (Ps. 119:148). *

MEET FOR – Gen. 2:18, 20 ➔ BEFORE <5048>.

MEETING – 1 ***qir'āh*** [masc. noun: קְרָאָה <7125>; from MEET <7122>] ▶ **This word refers to an encounter. This is the *qal* infinitive construct of the verb *qārā'*, to meet, to encounter, etc. See MEET (verb) <7122>. It has the preposition *le* prefixed to it.** It is used most often with verbs indicating motion (Gen. 14:17; 19:1; 24:17; Judg. 4:18, 22; 7:24; 20:25, 31; 1 Sam. 4:1). It has the sense of to encounter, to experience (Josh. 11:20; Amos 4:12). It occurs several times following *hinneh*, behold, at once, thereupon (1 Sam. 10:10; 2 Sam. 15:32; 16:1). *
– 2 Neh. 5:7 ➔ ASSEMBLY <6952>.

MEGIDDO – ***m**e**giddô, m**e**giddôn*** [proper noun: מְגִדּוֹ, מְגִדּוֹן <4023>; from GATHER <1413>]: place of troops ▶ **This word designates a key Canaanite town located on the south side of the Jezreel Valley and situated at the meeting place of five or**

more major international routes. Joshua conquered it and allotted it to Manasseh who could not entirely subdue it (Josh. 12:21; 17:11; Judg. 1:27). It later became a central city of Solomon's twelve district capitals (1 Kgs. 4:12; 9:15). Several good kings of Judah were killed in it (2 Kgs. 9:27; 23:29, 30). It is depicted as a place of past mourning and a picture of future sorrow by Zechariah (Zech. 12:11). Other refs.: Judg. 5:19; 1 Chr. 7:29; 2 Chr. 35:22. ¶

MEHETABEL – ***m^ehêyṭaḇ'ēl*** [fem. and masc. proper noun: מְהֵיטַבְאֵל <4105>; from (GOOD (BE) <3190> (augmented) and GOD <410>]: goodness of God ▶
a. Edomite princess. Refs.: Gen. 36:39; 1 Chr. 1:50. ¶
b. An ancestor of Shemaiah. Ref.: Neh. 6:10. ¶

MEHIDA – ***m^eḥiyḏā'*** [masc. proper noun: מְחִידָא <4240>; from RIDDLE <2330> (in the sense of put forth)]: union, famous ▶ **His descendants returned from Babylon with Zerubbabel.** Refs.: Ezra 2:52; Neh. 7:54. ¶

MEHIR – ***m^eḥiyr*** [masc. proper noun: מְחִיר <4243>; the same as PRICE <4242>]: price, wages ▶ **A man of the tribe of Judah, son of Chelub.** Ref.: 1 Chr. 4:11. ¶

MEHOLATHITE – ***m^eḥōlāṯiy*** [proper noun: מְחֹלָתִי <4259>; patrial from ABEL MEHOLAH <65>] ▶ **An inhabitant of a city in the territory of Issachar.** Refs.: 1 Sam. 18:19; 2 Sam. 21:8. ¶

MEHUJAEL – ***m^eḥûyā'ēl, m^eḥiyyāy'ēl*** [masc. proper noun: מְחוּיָאֵל, מְחִיָּיאֵל <4232>; from WIPE, WIPE OUT <4229> and GOD <410>]: smitten by God ▶ **A descendant of Cain, grandson of Enoch.** Ref.: Gen. 4:18. ¶

MEHUMAN – ***m^ehûmān*** [masc. proper noun: מְהוּמָן <4104>; of Persian origin]: faithful ▶ **One of the seven eunuchs serving in the presence of King Ahasuerus.** Ref.: Esther 1:10. ¶

MELATIAH – ***m^elaṭyāh*** [masc. proper noun: מְלַטְיָה <4424>; from MORTAR <4423> (which is from ESCAPE (verb) <4422>) and LORD <3050>]: the Lord has delivered ▶ **A Gibeonite who helped rebuild the wall of Jerusalem.** Ref.: Neh. 3:7. ¶

MELCHIZEDEK – ***malkiy-ṣeḏeq*** [masc. proper noun: מַלְכִּי־צֶדֶק <4442>; from KING <4428> and RIGHTEOUSNESS <6664>]: king of righteousness, the king is righteous ▶ **This name designates the king and high priest of Salem (Jerusalem). Abraham paid a tithe of his spoils to this Canaanite priest of the Most High God. David speaks of his Lord, who is both a king and a priest forever after the order of Melchizedek, in powerful reference to Christ as "King-Priest."** Neither his birth or death, mother or father were recorded, although he was born, died, and had parents (Gen. 14:18; Ps. 110:4). ¶

MELECH, HAMMELECH – ***meleḵ, hammeleḵ*** [masc. proper noun: מֶלֶךְ, הַמֶּלֶךְ <4429>; the same as KING <4428>]: king, king's son ▶
a. A name designating Melech (son of Micah, a descendant of Saul and Jonathan). Refs.: 1 Chr. 8:35; 9:41.
b. A name designating Hammelech (father of Jerahmeel; father of Malchiah). The word is also translated "the king's son" (Jer. 36:26; 38:6). ¶

MELODIOUS – Ps. 81:2 ➔ PLEASANT <5273> b.

MELODY – [1] Ps. 92:3 ➔ MEDITATION <1902> [2] Ps. 98:5; Is. 51:3; Amos 5:23 ➔ SONG <2172>.

MELON – ***'aḇaṭṭiyaḥ*** [masc. noun: אֲבַטִּיחַ <20>; of uncertain deriv.] ▶ **This word means a watermelon, an Egyptian fruit that clings to the vine.** It is used only in the plural form (Num. 11:5) to refer to Egyptian melons of some kind, along with other Egyptian vegetables and fruits for which the Israelites longed after leaving Egypt. ¶

MELT – [1] ***māsāh*** [verb: מָסָה <4529>; a prim. root] ► **This word means to dissolve, to become liquefied.** It means to dissipate, to turn to liquid: to melt ice (Ps. 147:18). It is used figuratively most often: to lose heart, "a heart melted" (Josh. 14:8); to make something wet (Ps. 6:6: to drench, to dissolve, to water); to cause something to dissolve or dissipate (Ps. 39:11; NASB, ESV, consume). ¶
[2] ***māsas*** [verb: מָסַס <4549>; a prim. root] ► **This word means to dissolve. It indicates something is breaking up or turning into a liquid.** It is used figuratively: of persons wasting away in sickness (Is. 10:18); of mountains breaking down (Is. 34:3; Mic. 1:4); of persons' hearts "melting," losing courage (Deut. 1:28; Josh. 2:11; 2 Sam. 17:10; Ps. 22:14). The unrighteous eventually are broken down (Ps. 112:10). It also refers literally to objects dissolving or melting: manna evaporated (Ex. 16:21); hot wax melts (Ps. 68:2). It is used of the ropes binding Samson that came apart (Judg. 15:14). *
– [3] Job 6:17 ➔ WARM (BE, WAX) <2215> [4] Ps. 119:28 ➔ LEAK <1811>.

MELT AWAY – [1] ***mûg*** [verb: מוּג <4127>; a prim. root] ► **This word means to dissolve; to faint, to become weak, to become disheartened; it is also translated to be fainthearted, to disperse, to toss, to spoil, to totter, to quake.** It is used in a powerful metaphor to describe the weakening and fearful hearts of the people of Canaan before Israel (Ex. 15:15; Josh. 2:9, 24); the weakening and falling away of warriors in battle (1 Sam. 14:16; Is. 14:31; Jer. 49:23). It refers to the shattering and dissolution of a nation or person before God's actions (Job 30:22; Ps. 107:26; Amos 9:5). The people of the entire earth melt and cringe before the Lord (Ps. 46:6; 75:3). In a more literal sense, the word describes rain softening the earth (Ps. 65:10). Other refs.: Is. 64:7; Ezek. 21:15; Amos 9:13; Nah. 1:5; 2:6. ¶
[2] ***temes*** [masc. noun: תֶּמֶס <8557>; from MELT <4529>] ► **This word refers to a melting away (i.e., a dissolving, a liquification).** It describes a snail that seems to melt as it drags itself along in the sun (Ps. 58:8; ESV: to dissolve). ¶

MELTED (BE) – ***hittûḵ*** [masc. noun: הִתּוּךְ <2046>; from POUR OUT <5413>] ► **This word indicates a liquefaction (of a metal).** It is used as a simile or picture of the way Israel will be purified of her dross (Ezek. 22:22). ¶

MELZAR – Dan. 1:11, 16 ➔ STEWARD <4453>.

MEMBER – ***'êqer*** [masc. noun: עֵקֶר <6133>; from HAMSTRING <6131 b. (fig., in the sense of to transplant in the case of a person)] ► **This word indicates a descendant, a member of one's family (i.e., a person attached to the roots of one's family).** It refers to the offspring of a person or social group living among Israel (Lev. 25:47; KJV: stock). ¶

MEMBERS – ***yᵉṣuriym*** [masc. plur. noun: יְצֻרִים <3338>; pass. part. of FORM (verb) <3335>] ► **This word denotes thing formed.** In its context and with reference to Job's assertion, it refers to bodily parts, members, such as one's eye (Job 17:7; NIV: frame). ¶

MEMORANDUM – Ezra 6:2 ➔ RECORD <1799>.

MEMORIAL – [1] ***'azkārāh*** [fem. noun: אַזְכָּרָה <234>; from REMEMBER <2142>] ► **This word indicates a commemorative offering, referring to that part of the meal offering which was burned with frankincense on the altar.** It is the portion of the meal offering that was burned (Lev. 2:2, 9: Num. 5:26). Other refs.: Lev. 2:16; 5:12; 6:15; 24:7. ¶
[2] ***zikkārôn*** [masc. noun: זִכָּרוֹן <2146>; from REMEMBER <2142>] ► **This word means remembrance, record, reminder.** It conveys the essential quality of remembering something in the past that has a particular significance (Eccl. 1:11). It signifies stone monuments (Josh. 4:7); the shoulder ornamentation of the ephod (Ex. 28:12; 39:7); a sacrifice calling for explicit retrospection (Num. 5:15); the securing of a progeny (Is. 57:8); a written record (Ex.

17:14; Esther 6:1); a memorable adage or quote (Job 13:12); some proof of an historic claim (Neh. 2:20); a festival memorializing a pivotal event (Ex. 12:14; 13:9). *

MEMPHIS – [1] ***mōp̱*** [proper noun: מֹף <4644>; of Egyptian origin] ▶ **Moph, the capital of Lower Egypt; i.e., another Hebrew name for the Egyptian city of Memphis.** Ref.: Hos. 9:6. See *nōp̱* <5297> below. ¶
[2] ***nōp̱*** [proper noun: נֹף <5297>; a variation of <4644> above]: place of good abode ▶ **This word designates Noph, the name of an ancient capital of Egypt (Old Kingdom) but always a place of significance throughout Egypt's history.** It was an important religious center where certain great creator gods resided (e.g., Ptah). It was usually condemned roundly and judged harshly by the prophets (Is. 19:13; Jer. 2:16). Certain exiles from Judah settled in this area and received a prophetic word from Jeremiah (Jer. 44:1). Other refs.: Jer. 46:14, 19; Ezek. 30:13, 16. ¶

MEMUCAN – ***meᵉmûḵān*** [masc. proper noun: מְמוּכָן <4462>; of Persian deriv.] ▶ **This word designates one of the chief counselors to Ahasuerus.** Refs.: Esther 1:14, 16, 21. ¶

MENAHEM – ***mᵉnaḥêm*** [masc. proper noun: מְנַחֵם <4505>; from SORRY (BE) <5162> (in the sense of to comfort)]: comforter ▶ **This name designates a violent king of Israel (752–742 B.C.). He assassinated his predecessor Shallum in Samaria. He was the son of Gadi. He was evaluated as a wicked king by the biblical writer.** He was cruel and merciless in war (2 Kgs. 15:16). During his reign, the king of Assyria forced him to pay a heavy tribute (2 Kgs. 15:16–22). Other refs.: 2 Kgs. 15:14, 23. ¶

MEND – Eccl. 3:7 ➔ SEW <8609>.

MENE – ***mᵉnê'*** [Aramaic noun: מְנֵא <4484>; pass. part. of APPOINT <4483>] ▶ **This word indicates a unit of weight of gold and/or silver.** Refs.: Dan. 5:25, 26. ¶

MENSTRUAL – Is. 30:22 ➔ FAINT (adj.) <1739>.

MENSTRUAL PERIOD, MENSTRUAL IMPURITY – Ezek. 18:6; 22:10; etc. ➔ IMPURITY <5079>.

MENSTRUATION – ***dāwāh*** [verb: דָּוָה <1738>; a prim. root] ▶ **The Hebrew expression "the days of the separation for her infirmity" is also translated her monthly period, the time of her menstruation, the days of her menstruation, her customary impurity.** It indicates the time during a woman's menstrual period when she was considered unclean (Lev. 12:2). ¶

MENSTRUOUS – Lev. 20:18; Is. 30:22 ➔ FAINT (adj.) <1739>.

MENUHOTH – 1 Chr. 2:52 ➔ MANAHATHITES (HALF OF THE) <2679>.

MEONOTHAI – ***mᵉ'ônōṯay*** [proper noun: מְעוֹנֹתַי <4587>; plur. of DWELLING PLACE <4585>]: my dwelling places ▶ **Son of Othniel, the younger brother of Caleb.** Ref.: 1 Chr. 4:14. ¶

MEPHAATH – ***mêyp̱a'aṯ, môp̱a'aṯ*** [proper noun: מֵיפַעַת, מוֹפַעַת <4158>; from SHINE <3313>]: splendor, beauty ▶ **A Levitical city of the tribe of Reuben.** Refs.: Josh. 13:18; 21:37; 1 Chr. 6:79; Jer. 48:21. ¶

MEPHIBOSHETH – ***mᵉp̱iyḇōšeṯ*** [masc. proper noun: מְפִיבֹשֶׁת <4648>; prob. from PIECES (CUT TO) <6284> (in the sense of to scatter) and SHAME <1322>]: dispeller of shame ▶
a. The son of Saul by Rizpah. He and six others were executed and left unburied by the king of Gibeah to stop a famine in the land of Israel (2 Sam. 21:8). ¶
b. The son of Jonathan, Saul's son. He was spared from execution because of the oath between David and Jonathan (2 Sam. 21:7). He had been dropped as a baby and was lame in both feet (2 Sam. 4:4). David had spared him earlier because he was Jonathan's

son (2 Sam. 9:7). He had supported David faithfully (2 Sam. 19:24, 25, 30). *

MERAB – ***mêraḇ*** [fem. proper noun: מֵרַב <4764>; from MANY (BE) <7231>]: increase ▶ **Eldest daughter of king Saul.** She was promised to David but given instead to Adriel the Meholathite (1 Sam. 14:49; 18:17, 19). ¶

MERAIAH – ***mᵉrāyāh*** [masc. proper noun: מְרָיָה <4811>; from REBELLIOUS (BE) <4784>]: rebellion ▶ **A priest in the time of Joiakim.** Ref.: Neh. 12:12. ¶

MERAIOTH – ***mᵉrāyôṯ*** [masc. proper noun: מְרָיוֹת <4812>; from MERAIAH <4811>]: rebellious ▶
a. A priest. Refs.: 1 Chr. 6:6, 7, 52; Ezra 7:3. ¶
b. A son of Ahitub. Refs.: 1 Chr. 9:11; Neh. 11:11. ¶
c. The father of Helkai. Ref.: Neh. 12:15. ¶

MERARI – ***mᵉrāriy*** [masc. proper noun: מְרָרִי <4847>; from BITTER (BE) <4843>]: bitter ▶ **Third son of Levi.** Refs.: Gen. 46:11; Ex. 6:16, 19; Num. 10:17; 26:57; 2 Chr. 29:12; 34:12. *

MERARITE – ***mᵉrāriy*** [proper noun: מְרָרִי <4848>; from MERARI <4847>] ▶ **A member of the family of Merari.** Ref.: Num. 26:57. ¶

MERATHAIM – ***mᵉrāṯayim*** [proper noun: מְרָתַיִם <4850>; dual of BITTER <4751>]: double bitterness, double rebellion ▶ **This name is most likely a symbolical name given to Babylon.** Ref.: Jer. 50:21. ¶

MERCHANDISE – [1] ***meḵer*** [masc. noun: מֶכֶר <4377>; from SELL <4376>] ▶ **This word refers to something for sale and also a price, worth. It indicates purchase money or whatever the price for a purchase is.** Refs.: Num. 20:19: to pay; Prov. 31:10: jewel, ruby. Preceded by *kōl*, the phrase indicates merchandise of any kind (Neh. 13:16: merchandise, goods, ware). ¶

[2] ***maᵃrāḇ*** [masc. noun: מַעֲרָב <4627>; from PLEDGE (BE A) <6148>, in the sense of trading] ▶ **This word refers to products and materials ready to be sold by bartering, money, or exchange to a seller; items for sale; it is also translated wares, market.** Refs.: Ezek. 27:9, 13, 17, 19, 25, 27, 33, 34. ¶

[3] ***maqqāḥôṯ*** [fem. noun: מַקָּחוֹת <4728>; from TAKE <3947>] ▶ **This word refers to goods and products for sale.** Ref.: Neh. 10:31; also translated wares. ¶

[4] ***markōleṯ*** [fem. noun: מַרְכֹּלֶת <4819>; from MERCHANDISE (SELL) <7402>] ▶ **This word indicates the objects of trade and barter or the location where these items were offered for display and trade.** Ref.: Ezek. 27:24; also translated market, marketplace. ¶

[5] ***saḥar*** [masc. noun: סַחַר <5504>; from MERCHANT <5503>] ▶ **This word refers to profit, marketplace; it is also translated proceeds, gain, trading.** It figuratively indicates the benefits of wisdom (Prov. 3:14); and diligence through wisdom (Prov. 31:18). It is used in a metaphor for the merchant city of Tyre, the marketplace of the ancient world (Is. 23:3; also translated marketplace, market, mart); as well as her monetary gains (Is. 23:18). It describes the goods or merchandise of trade (Is. 45:14). ¶

[6] ***sāḥār*** [masc. noun: סָחָר <5505>; from MERCHANT <5503>] ▶ **This word refers to trafficked goods or gain from dealing in trafficked goods.** It refers to the goods or merchandise moved or traded or the gain and profit connected with it (Is. 23:3: revenue). It is rendered as merchandise (Is. 45:14). In Proverbs 3:14, it has the sense of profit or merchandise (cf. KJV, merchandise; other translations, profit or proceeds). ¶

[7] ***rᵉḵullāh*** [fem. noun: רְכֻלָּה <7404>; fem. pass. part. of MERCHANDISE (SELL) <7402>] ▶ **This word refers to the material wares traded or to the process of merchandising (trafficking in goods) and trading itself; it is also translated trade, trading, traffick.** Refs.: Ezek. 26:12; 28:5, 16, 18. ¶

– [8] Ezek. 27:12, 14, 16, 19, 22, 27, 33 → WARES <5801> [9] Ezek. 27:15 → MARKET <5506>.

MERCHANDISE (MAKE) – Deut. 21:14; 24:7 ➔ SLAVE (TREAT AS A) <6014>.

MERCHANDISE (SELL) – ***rāḵal*** [verb: רָכַל <7402>; a prim. root] ▶ **This word means to exchange for money goods and products; it also means to trade.** In its participial forms, it refers to a merchant, a tradesman, or a female merchant (1 Kgs. 10:15) who sells merchandise (Ezek. 17:4; 27:3, 13; Nah. 3:16). *

MERCHANT – [1] ***k^{e}na^{ca}niy*** [masc. noun: כְּנַעֲנִי <3669>; from CANAAN <3667>] ▶ **This word means a person selling goods or products for money; it also came to mean a tradesman as well, since the Canaanites were known as traders or merchants throughout the Mediterranean world.** Refs.: Prov. 31:24; Zech. 14:21. Other ref.: Job 41:6. See CANAANITE <3669>. ¶
[2] ***sāḥar*** [verb: סָחַר <5503>; a prim. root] ▶ **This Hebrew word means to travel as merchants, to trade.** It refers to a merchant, a commercial business man, a traveling trader (Gen. 23:16; 37:28; 1 Kgs. 10:28; Is. 23:2; Ezek. 27:12); the activity of carrying on trade, business (Gen. 34:10, 21). It has the sense of to go back and forth, to wander; to throb (of the heart) (Ps. 38:10: to pant, to throb, to pound; Jer. 14:18: to go about, to go roving, to ply one's trade). *
– [3] 1 Kgs. 10:15; Ezek. 17:4; 27:3, 13; Nah. 3:16 ➔ MERCHANDISE (SELL) <7402>.

MERCIFUL – [1] ***ḥāsaḏ*** [verb: חָסַד <2616>; a prim. root] ▶ **A verb which occurs three times in the Hebrew Bible with very different meanings.** It is used reflexively as David sang to the Lord, meaning to show oneself as loyal or faithful to a covenant (2 Sam. 22:26b; Ps. 18:25b); also translated faithful, kind. This verb is related to the common noun *ḥeseḏ* (MERCY <2617>). But in another context and in a different verbal stem, the same root carries the meaning to reproach or to bring shame upon (Prov. 25:10). ¶
– [2] Gen. 19:16 ➔ COMPASSION <2551> [3] Ex. 34:6; Deut. 4:31; etc. ➔ COMPASSIONATE <7349> [4] See FAITHFUL <2623>.

MERCIFUL (BE) – Ps. 77:9 ➔ GRACIOUS (BE) <2589>.

MERCILESS – Prov. 5:9 ➔ CRUEL <394>.

MERCY – [1] ***ḥeseḏ*** [masc. noun: חֶסֶד <2617>; from MERCIFUL <2616>] ▶ **This word indicates kindness, lovingkindness, goodness, faithfulness, love, acts of kindness.** This aspect of God is one of several important features of His character: truth; faithfulness; mercy; steadfastness; justice; righteousness; goodness. The classic text for understanding the significance of this word is Psalm 136 where it is used twenty-six times to proclaim that God's kindness and love are eternal. The psalmist made it clear that God's kindness and faithfulness serves as the foundation for His actions and His character: it underlies His goodness (Ps. 136:1); it supports His unchallenged position as God and Lord (Ps. 136:2, 3); it is the basis for His great and wondrous acts in creation (Ps. 136:4–9) and delivering and redeeming His people from Pharaoh and the Red Sea (Ps. 136:10–15); the reason for His guidance in the desert (Ps. 136:16); His gift of the land to Israel and defeat of their enemies (Ps. 136:17–22); His ancient as well as His continuing deliverance of His people (Ps. 136:23–25); His rulership in heaven (Ps. 136:26). The entire span of creation to God's redemption, preservation, and permanent establishment is touched upon in this psalm. It all happened, is happening, and will continue to happen because of the Lord's covenant faithfulness and kindness.

The other more specific uses of the term develop the ideas contained in Psalm 136 in greater detail. Because of His kindness, He meets the needs of His creation by delivering them from enemies and despair (Gen. 19:19; Ex. 15:13; Ps. 109:26; Jer. 31:3); He preserves their lives and redeems them from sin (Ps. 51:1; 86:13). As Psalm 136 demonstrates, God's kindness is abundant, exceedingly great, without end, and good (Ex. 34:6; Num. 4:19; Ps. 103:8; 109:21; Jer. 33:11). The plural of the noun indicates the many acts of God on behalf of His people (Gen. 32:10; Is. 63:7). He is the covenant-keeping God who maintains kindness and mercy (Deut. 7:9) to those who love Him.

People are to imitate God. They are to display kindness and faithfulness toward each other (1 Sam. 20:15; Ps. 141:5; Prov. 19:22), especially toward the poor, weak, and needy (Job 6:14; Prov. 20:28). Israel was to show kindness and faithfulness toward the Lord but often failed. In its youth, Israel showed faithfulness to God, but its devotion lagged later (Jer. 2:2). It was not constant (Hos. 6:4), appearing and leaving as the morning mist even though God desired this from His people more than sacrifices (Hos. 6:6; cf. 1 Sam. 15:22). He looked for pious people (Is. 57:1) who would perform deeds of piety, faithfulness, and kindness (2 Chr. 32:32; 35:26; Neh. 13:14); the Lord desired people who would maintain covenant loyalty and responsibility so that He could build His righteous community. *

– [2] Is. 63:9 ➔ COMPASSION <2551>
[3] Dan. 2:18 ➔ COMPASSION <7359>.

MERCY (HAVE) – See GRACIOUS (BE) <2603>.

MERCY (SHOW, ASK FOR) – ***ḥ^{a}nan*** [Aramaic verb: חֲנַן <2604>; corresponding to GRACIOUS (BE) <2603>] ▶ **This verb means to demonstrate compassion, to ask for compassion.** It refers to showing mercy to the poor, an action that would help Nebuchadnezzar break away from his iniquities (Dan. 4:27). Daniel was discovered asking God for mercy even though it was against the new law of the Medes and Persians to do so (Dan. 6:11). Here the word occurs alongside *b^{e}'ā'* (SEEK <1156>), meaning to request (it is translated to make supplication, to make plea, to ask). ¶

MERCY SEAT – ***kappōreṯ*** [noun: כַּפֹּרֶת <3727>; from COVER (verb) <3722>] ▶ **This word means a lid, propitiation. It refers to the lid that covered the ark of the testimony. It was made of gold and was decorated with two cherubim. The Shechinah glory, visible manifestation of God's presence, rested above this mercy seat. Here God met and communed with His people via the people's representative (Ex. 25:17–22).** Only at specific times could the high priest come before the mercy seat (Lev. 16:2). On the Day of Atonement, the high priest made atonement for himself, the Tabernacle, and the people by a sin offering, which included sprinkling blood on this lid (Lev. 16:13–15). Other refs.: Ex. 26:34; 30:6; 31:7; 35:12; 37:6–9; 39:35; 40:20; Num. 7:89; 1 Chr. 28:11. ¶

MERED – ***mereḏ*** [masc. proper noun: מֶרֶד <4778>; the same as REBELLION <4777>]: rebellion ▶ **One of the sons of Ezra from the tribe of Judah.** Refs.: 1 Chr. 4:17, 18. ¶

MEREMOTH – ***m^{e}rêmôṯ*** [masc. proper noun: מְרֵמוֹת <4822>; plur. from EXALT <7311>]: heights, elevations ▶
a. A priest under Zerubbabel. Ref.: Neh. 12:3. ¶
b. A priest under Ezra. Refs.: Ezra 8:33; Neh. 3:4, 21. ¶
c. A postexilic Jew. Ref.: Ezra 10:36. ¶
d. An Israelite who signed the covenant of renewal with Nehemiah after the return from the Babylonian captivity. Ref.: Neh. 10:5. ¶
e. The father of Helkai. Ref.: Neh. 12:15. ¶

MERES – ***meres*** [masc. proper noun: מֶרֶס <4825>; of foreign deriv.] ▶ **One of the seven princes of Persia and Media counseling Ahasuerus.** Ref.: Esther 1:14. ¶

MERI-BAAL – ***m^{e}riyḇ ba'al*** [masc. proper noun: מְרִיב בַּעַל <4807>; from STRIVE <7378> and BAAL <1168>]: contender with Baal ▶ **Another name for Mephibosheth, son of Jonathan and grandson of Saul.** Refs.: 1 Chr. 8:34; 9:40. ¶

MERIB-BAAL – ***m^{e}riy ḇa'al*** [masc. proper noun: מְרִי בַעַל <4810>; from REBELLIOUSNESS <4805> and BAAL <1168>]: contender with Baal ▶ **Another name for Mephibosheth, son of Jonathan and grandson of Saul.** Ref.: 1 Chr. 9:40. ¶

MERIBAH – [1] ***m^eriyḇāh, m^eriyḇaṯ qāḏêš*** [proper noun: מְרִיבָה, מְרִיבַה קָדֵשׁ <4809>; the same as STRIFE <4808>] ► **a. A word meaning "quarreling" or "contention" (from the Hebrew word *riyḇ*: to strive, quarrel). It was the location of a place near Rephidim where there was no drinking water for Israel.** The people verbally attacked Moses, and he struck a rock, at the Lord's command, to bring forth water (Ex. 17:7). The place is also called Massah, "testing." ¶
b. Evidently another occasion of "contention" forty years later (see a. above but c. below). Refs.: Num. 20:13, 24; 27:14; Deut. 33:8; Ps. 81:7; 95:8; 106:32. ¶
c. This location is placed at Kadesh Barnea, not near Rephidim according to most authorities. But it is a clear reference to the incident in the Desert of Zin (Num. 20:13, 24). See b. above.
– [2] Ps. 95:8; 106:32; Ezek. 47:19; 48:28 → STRIFE <4808>.

MERODACH – ***m^erōḏāḵ*** [masc. proper noun: מְרֹדָךְ <4781>; of foreign deriv.] ► **This is the name of the chief Babylonian god, Merodach.** In more recent translations, it is rendered as Marduk (Jer. 50:2). ¶

MERODACH-BALADAN – ***m^erō'ḏaḵ bal^aḏān*** [masc. proper noun: מְרֹאדַךְ בַּלְאֲדָן <4757>; of foreign deriv.]: Merodach (a god) has given a son ► **King of Babylon during the time of Hezekiah.** Ref.: Is. 39:1. ¶

MEROM – ***mêrôm*** [proper noun: מֵרוֹם <4792>; formed like HEIGHT <4791>]: high place ► **Joshua defeated a confederacy of Canaanites kings and their allies near the waters of Merom.** Refs.: Josh. 11:5, 7. ¶

MERONOTHITE – ***mêrōnōṯiy*** [masc. proper noun: מֵרֹנֹתִי <4824>; patrial from an unused noun] ► **This noun signifies the ethnicity or some other relational designation of a man named Jehdeiah, who was in charge of the donkeys as his administrative task.** Ref.: 1 Chr. 27:30. It is also descriptive of Jadon who helped restore government quarters in Jerusalem (Neh. 3:7). ¶

MEROZ – ***mêrôz*** [proper noun: מֵרוֹז <4789>; of uncertain deriv.]: place of refuge ► **The inhabitants of this city did not help the Israelites fight Sisera.** Ref.: Judg. 5:23. ¶

MERRY – Judg. 9:27 → OFFERING OF PRAISE <1974>.

MESHA – [1] ***mêyšā'*** [masc. proper noun: מֵישָׁא <4331>; from DEPART <4185>]: departure ► **A Benjamite, son of Shaharaim and Hodesh.** Ref.: 1 Chr. 8:9. ¶
[2] ***mêyšā'*** [masc. proper noun: מֵישָׁע <4337>; from SAVE <3467>]: safety, deliverance ► **The oldest son of Caleb.** Ref.: 1 Chr. 2:42. ¶
[3] ***mêyšaʻ*** [masc. proper noun: מֵישַׁע <4338>; a variation for <4337> above] ► **A king of Moab.** Ref.: 2 Kgs. 3:4. ¶
[4] ***mêšā'*** [proper noun: מֵשָׁא <4852>; of foreign deriv.] ► **A place in Arabia.** Ref.: Gen. 10:30. ¶

MESHACH – [1] ***mêyšaḵ*** [masc. proper noun: מֵישַׁךְ <4335>; borrowed from <4336> below] ► **This is the name of one of Daniel's royal Hebrew companions in Babylonian exile.** Refs.: Dan. 1:6, 7. The name is Babylonian and probably means "Who is like Aku?" or "Who is it that is Aku?" Others suggest "I am of little account" (cf. Is. 39:7). ¶
[2] ***mêyšaḵ*** [masc. proper noun: מֵישַׁךְ <4336>; of foreign origin and doubtful meaning] ► **This name is the Aramaic form of <4335> above.** The meaning is the same. Refs.: Dan. 2:49; 3:12–14, 16, 19, 20, 22, 23, 26, 28–30. ¶

MESHEC – ***mešeḵ*** [masc. proper noun: מֶשֶׁךְ <4902>; the same in form as BAG <4901>, but prob. of foreign deriv.]: drawing out ► **One of the sons of Japheth.** Refs.: Gen. 10:2, 23; 1 Chr. 1:5, 17; Ps. 120:5; Ezek. 27:13; 32:26; 38:2, 3; 39:1. ¶

MESHECH, MESHEK – 1 Chr. 1:17 → MASH <4851>.

MESHELEMIAH – ***m*^e*šelemyāh, m*^e*šelemyāhû*** [masc. proper noun: מְשֶׁלֶ־מְיָה, מְשֶׁלֶמְיָהוּ <4920>; from COMPLETED (BE) <7999> and LORD <3050>]: the Lord rewards ▶ **A gatekeeper at the entrance of the tent of meeting.** Refs.: 1 Chr. 9:21; 26:1, 2, 9. ¶

MESHEZABEL – ***m*^e*šêyzab̲'ēl*** [masc. proper noun: מְשֵׁיזַבְאֵל <4898>; from an equivalent to DELIVER <7804> and GOD <410>]: God delivers ▶
a. His grandson made repair to the wall of Jerusalem. Ref.: Neh. 3:4. ¶
b. A chief of the people who signed the covenant of renewal with Nehemiah after the return from the Babylonian captivity. Ref.: Neh. 10:21. ¶
c. A man of Judah, of the family of Zerah. Ref.: Neh. 11:24. ¶

MESHILLEMITH – ***m*^e*šillêmiyt̲*** [masc. proper noun: מְשִׁלֵּמִית <4921>; from COMPLETED (BE) <7999>]: reward ▶ **A priest, son of Immer.** Ref.: 1 Chr. 9:12. ¶

MESHILLEMOTH – ***m*^e*šillêmôt̲*** [masc. proper noun: מְשִׁלֵּמוֹת <4919>; plur. from COMPLETED (BE) <7999>]: reward ▶
a. The father of Berechiah. Ref.: 2 Chr. 28:12. ¶
b. A son of Immer. Ref.: Neh. 11:13. ¶

MESHOBAB – ***m*^e*šôb̲āb̲*** [masc. proper noun: מְשׁוֹבָב <4877>; from TURN <7725>]: returned, restored ▶ **A descendant of Simeon.** Ref.: 1 Chr. 4:34. ¶

MESHULLAM – ***m*^e*šullām*** [masc. proper noun: מְשֻׁלָּם <4918>; from COMPLETED (BE) <7999>]: friend ▶
a. A descendant of Benjamin. Ref.: 1 Chr. 8:17. ¶
b. A descendant of Gad. Ref.: 1 Chr. 5:13. ¶
c. Grandfather of Shaphan. Ref.: 2 Kgs. 22:3. ¶
d. An overseer in the repair of the Temple. Ref.: 2 Chr. 34:12. ¶
e. A son of Zerubbabel. Ref.: 1 Chr. 3:19. ¶
f. A son of Shephatiah. Ref.: 1 Chr. 9:8. ¶
g. A son of Zadok. Refs.: 1 Chr. 9:11; Neh. 11:11. ¶
h. A son of Joed. Refs.: 1 Chr. 9:7; Neh. 11:7. ¶
i. A son of Ezra. Refs.: Neh. 12:13, 33. ¶
j. A son of Meshillemith. Ref.: 1 Chr. 9:12. ¶
k. A Jewish leader. Refs.: Ezra 8:16; 10:15; Neh. 8:4; 10:20. ¶
l. A son of Bani. Ref.: Ezra 10:29. ¶
m. A son of Berechiah. Refs.: Neh. 3:4, 30; 6:18; 10:7. ¶
n. A son of Besodeiah. Ref.: Neh. 3:6. ¶
o. A descendant of Iddo. Ref.: Neh. 12:16. ¶
p. A Levite. Ref.: Neh. 12:25. ¶

MESHULLEMETH – ***m*^e*šullemet̲*** [fem. proper noun: מְשֻׁלֶּמֶת <4922>; fem. of MESHULLAM <4918>]: friend ▶ **The wife of King Manasseh and mother of King Amon.** Ref.: 2 Kgs. 21:19. ¶

MESOBAITE, MEZOBAITE – ***m*^e*ṣōb̲yāh*** [proper noun: מְצֹבָיָה <4677>; apparently from FIND <4672> and LORD <3050>]; found of the Lord ▶ **Designation of Jaasiel, one of David's mighty men.** Ref.: 1 Chr. 11:47. ¶

MESOPOTAMIA – See ARAM OF THE (TWO) RIVERS <763>.

MESSAGE – [1] ***mal'āk̲ût̲*** [fem. noun: מַלְאָכוּת <4400>; from the same as MESSENGER <4397>] ▶ **This word is used only once in the Old Testament, where it describes Haggai's communication from the Lord.** Ref.: Hag. 1:13. This word is related to the common noun *mal'āk̲* (<4397>), meaning messenger, which is also used in Haggai 1:13. ¶
[2] ***q*^e*riy'āh*** [masc. noun: קְרִיאָה <7150>; from CALL <7121>] ▶ **This word refers to public proclamation, a bold oral communication, literally, a crying.** Ref.: Jon. 3:2; literally, cry to it (Nineveh) the "crying"; the little word "to" (no longer "against") may hint at mercy, hence the translation "preaching." ¶

MESSENGER – [1] ***mal'āk̲*** [masc. noun: מַלְאָךְ <4397>; from an unused root meaning to be sent as a deputy] ▶ **The term often denotes one sent on business or for matters of diplomacy by another (human) personage. It also means an angel.** Jacob sent messengers on ahead to his brother Esau in the hope of finding favor in his eyes (Gen. 32:3, 6). The elders of Jabesh sent messengers throughout Israel in a desperate attempt to locate someone who could rescue their town from the dire threat of the Ammonites (1 Sam. 11:3, 4, 9; cf. 2 Sam. 11:19; 1 Kgs. 19:2; 2 Kgs. 5:10). Very often, the term referred to messengers sent from God. Sometimes these were human messengers, whether prophets (Is. 44:26; Hag. 1:13; Mal. 3:1); priests (Eccl. 5:6; Mal. 2:7); or the whole nation of Israel (Is. 42:19). More often, however, the term referred to heavenly beings who often assumed human form (Gen. 19:1; Judg. 13:6, 15, 16) and appeared to people as bearers of the Lord's commands and tidings (Judg. 6:11, 12; 13:3). They were often responsible for aiding, protecting, and fighting for those who trusted in the Lord (Gen. 24:7; Ex. 23:20; 33:2; 1 Kgs. 19:5; Ps. 34:7; 91:11). They also acted as instruments of divine judgment, meting out punishment on the rebellious and the guilty (2 Sam. 24:16, 17; Ps. 35:5, 6; 78:49; Is. 37:36). Sometimes the angel of the Lord and his message are so closely identified with the Lord Himself that the text simply refers to the angel as "the Lord" or "God" (Gen. 16:7; 22:11; 31:11; Ex. 3:2; Judg. 13:18; cf. Gen. 16:13; 22:12; 31:13, 16; Ex. 3:4; Judg. 6:22; 13:22). Many times this is considered a «Christophany,» an appearance of the pre-incarnate Christ (e.g., see Judges 6:11–24; 13:2–23). *

[2] ***ṣiyr*** [masc. noun: צִיר <6735>; from BESIEGE <6696> (in the sense of being constrained by someone)] ▶ **This word means an ambassador, an envoy.** It describes a person appointed to represent someone else or his nation faithfully (Prov. 13:17; 25:13; Is. 18:2; 57:9; Jer. 49:14; Obad. 1:1); a much sought after person. See also HINGE <6735> and PAIN, LABOR PAINS <6735> for other meanings of the Hebrew word. ¶

– [3] Dan. 4:13, 17, 23 ➔ WATCHER <5894>.

METAL – [1] Ezek. 1:4, 27; 8:2 ➔ glowing metal, gleaming metal ➔ AMBER <2830> [2] Nah. 2:3 ➔ STEEL <6393> a.

METAL IMAGE – ***nāsiyk̲*** [masc. noun: נָסִיךְ <5257>] ▶ **This term refers to metal (possibly gold or silver) idols or images brought home by the Egyptian ruler Ptolemy after defeating the Syrian army.** Ref.: Dan. 11:8. The Hebrew word also has other meanings; see DRINK OFFERING <5257> and PRINCE <5257>. ¶

METAL WORKER – 2 Kgs. 24:16; Jer. 24:1; 29:2 ➔ SMITH <4525>.

METE OUT – Ps. 58:2; Is. 18:2, 7 ➔ POWERFUL <6978> b.

METHEG AMMAH – ***meṯeg̲ hā'ammāh*** [מֶתֶג הָאַמָּה <4965>; from BRIDLE <4964> and AMMAH <522> b. with the art. interposed]: bridle of the metropolis ▶
a. The Philistine city Metheg Ammah. Ref.: 2 Sam. 8:1. ¶
b. A phrase meaning control of the chief city. Ref.: NASB, 2 Sam. 8:1. ¶

METHUSAEL – ***mᵉṯûšā'ēl*** [masc. proper noun: מְתוּשָׁאֵל <4967>; from FEW IN NUMBER <4962> (in the sense of man) and GOD <410>]: man of God ▶ **Father of Lamech, a descendant from Cain.** Ref.: Gen. 4:18. ¶

METHUSELAH – ***mᵉṯûšelaḥ*** [masc. proper noun: מְתוּשֶׁלַח <4968>; from FEW IN NUMBER <4962> (in the sense of man) and WEAPON <7973>]: man of the dart ▶ **The son of Enoch. He fathered Lamech, father of Noah.** He lived an astounding 969 years (Gen. 5:21, 22, 25–27; 1 Chr. 1:3). ¶

MEUNIM, MEUNITES – ***mᵉ'ûniym*** [proper noun: מְעוּנִים <4586>; prob. patrial from MAON <4584>] ▶
a. A people who lived south of Canaan. Refs.: 1 Chr. 4:41; 2 Chr. 20:1; 26:7.

b. A group of returning exiles (perhaps descendants of a.). Refs.: Ezra 2:50; Neh. 7:52. ¶

MEZAHAB – ***mêy zāhāḇ*** [fem. proper noun: מֵי זָהָב <4314>; from WATER <4325> and GOLD <2091>]: water of gold ► **Grandfather of Mehetabel, wife of Hadar, king of Edom.** Refs.: Gen. 36:39; 1 Chr. 1:50. ¶

MIBHAR – ***miḇḥār*** [masc. proper noun: מִבְחָר <4006>; the same as CHOICE <4005>]: choice, chosen ► **One of David's mighty men.** Ref.: 1 Chr. 11:38. ¶

MIBSAM – ***miḇśām*** [masc. proper noun: מִבְשָׂם <4017>; from the same as SPICE <1314>]: sweet fragrance ►
a. Son of Ishmael. Refs.: Gen. 25:13; 1 Chr. 1:29. ¶
b. A descendant of Simeon. Ref.: 1 Chr. 4:25. ¶

MIBZAR – ***miḇṣār*** [masc. proper noun: מִבְצָר <4014>; the same as FORTIFICATION <4013>]: fortress ► **One of the chiefs of Esau.** Refs.: Gen. 36:42; 1 Chr. 1:53. ¶

MICA – ***miyḵā'*** [masc. proper noun: מִיכָא <4316>; a variation from MICAH <4318>] ►
a. Son of Mephibosheth. Ref.: 2 Sam. 9:12. ¶
b. A Levite who signed the covenant of renewal with Nehemiah after the return from the Babylonian captivity. Refs.: 1 Chr. 9:15; Neh. 10:11. ¶
c. A Levite. Refs.: Neh. 11:17, 22. ¶

MICAH – 1 ***miyḵāh*** [masc. proper noun: מִיכָה <4318>; an abbreviation of MICAIAH <4320>] ►
a. A man from Ephraim who hired a young Levite to be his priest over his self-made shrine, ephod, and idols. His priest and religious objects were forcefully taken from him by the Danites (Judg. 17–18). ¶
b. A prophet mentioned by some Israelites in Jeremiah's day. He had correctly prophesied war in the time of Hezekiah of Judah and was not threatened for it by the establishment (Jer. 26:18). ¶
c. The head of a family from the tribe of Reuben, a son of Joel. Ref.: 1 Chr. 5:5. ¶
d. A son of Merib-Baal who was a son of Jonathan, the friend of David and son of Saul. Refs.: 1 Chr. 8:34, 35; 9:40, 41. ¶
e. A priest from the family of Kohath. Refs.: 1 Chr. 23:20; 24:24, 25. ¶
f. The son of Imlah who prophesied the defeat of Israel and death of Ahab. Refs.: 1 Kgs. 22:9; 2 Chr. 18:14. ¶
g. The father of Abdon who was an official under King Josiah. Ref.: 2 Chr. 34:20. ¶
2 ***miyḵāyᵉhû, miḵāyᵉhû*** [masc. proper noun: מִיכָיְהוּ, מִכָיְהוּ <4321>; abbreviation for MICAIAH <4322>] ►
a. Micah the Ephraimite, the same as <4318> a. above. Refs.: Judg. 17:1, 4. ¶
b. He always prophesied only what the Lord instructed him to say. Ref.: 1 Kgs. 22:14. It is the same as <4318> f. above. *
c. A son of Gemariah who reported the words of Jeremiah's first scroll to the leading officials of King Jehoiakim. Refs.: Jer. 36:11, 13. ¶

MICAIAH – 1 ***miyḵāhû*** [masc. proper noun: מִיכָהוּ <4319>; a contr. for MICAH <4321>] ► **This name is the same as the one in MICAH <4318> f.** Ref.: 2 Chr. 18:8. ¶
2 ***miyḵāyāh*** [masc. proper noun: מִיכָיָה <4320>; from WHO <4310> and (the prefix deriv. from) BECAUSE <3588> and LORD <3050>]: who is like the Lord ►
a. The prophet Micah, the same as MICAH <4318> b. Ref.: Jer. 26:18. ¶
b. An ancestor of Zechariah who took part in the dedication of the wall of Nehemiah. Ref.: Neh. 12:35. ¶
c. A priest who took part in celebrating the dedication of Nehemiah's wall. Ref.: Neh. 12:41. ¶
d. The father of Achbor who was an official under King Josiah. Ref.: 2 Kgs. 22:12. ¶
3 ***miyḵāyāhû*** [fem. and masc. proper noun: מִיכָיָהוּ <4322>; for <4320> above] ►
a. Mother of Abijah. Ref.: 2 Chr. 13:2. ¶
b. A prince under Jehoshaphat. Ref.: 2 Chr. 17:7. ¶

MICHAEL – ***miyḵā'ēl*** [masc. proper noun: מִיכָאֵל <4317>; from WHO <4310> and (the prefix deriv. from) BECAUSE <3588> and GOD <410>]: who is like God ▶
a. The angel who watches over Israel, Daniel's people, the holy people. Refs.: Dan. 10:31, 21; 12:1. ¶
b. The father of Sethur, a spy in Canaan. Ref.: Num. 13:13. ¶
c. A person from Gad, head of a family. Ref.: 1 Chr. 5:13. ¶
d. A Gadite, of the sons of Abihail or an ancestor. Ref.: 1 Chr. 5:14. ¶
e. A descendant of the Kohathites, Levites, who served in a musical capacity at the Temple. Ref.: 1 Chr. 6:40. ¶
f. A son of Izrahiah from Issachar. Ref.: 1 Chr. 7:3. ¶
g. From the line of Saul, from the sons of Elpaal. Ref.: 1 Chr. 8:16. ¶
h. A military captain who defected to David at Ziklag. Ref.: 1 Chr. 12:20. ¶
i. An officer from the tribe of Issachar. Ref.: 1 Chr. 27:18. ¶
j. A son of the good king Jehoshaphat. Ref.: 2 Chr. 21:2. ¶
k. A descendant of Shephatiah who returned from exile with Ezra. Ref.: Ezra 8:8. ¶

MICHAL – ***miyḵal*** [fem. proper noun: מִיכַל <4324>; apparently the same as BROOK <4323>]: small stream ▶ **Saul's younger daughter who married David.** She was severely disciplined by him when she sharply critiqued his supposed indecent behavior in front of the people (2 Sam. 6:16–23). She had fallen in love with David, and Saul used her to gain an advantage over David (1 Sam. 18:20–30). She, in fact, helped David escape from her father several times (1 Sam. 19:9–16). *

MICHMASH – ***miḵmās, miḵmāś*** [proper noun: מִכְמָס, מִכְמָשׂ <4363>; from STORE (LAY IN) <3647>]: hidden ▶ **This word designates a village in Benjamin's territory. It was the site of a significant battle with the Philistines.** Jonathan, Saul's son, proved himself a mighty warrior on this occasion (1 Sam. 13:2–14:31), but the Philistines made a successful counter assault. The town was resettled by Jews returning from exile in Babylon (Ezra 2:27; Neh. 7:31). ¶

MICHMETHAH – ***miḵmᵉṯāṯ*** [proper noun: מִכְמְתָת <4366>; apparently from an unused root meaning to hide]: concealed place ▶ **A city in the northern border of Ephraim and Manasseh.** Refs.: Josh. 16:6; 17:7. ¶

MICHRI – ***miḵriy*** [masc. proper noun: מִכְרִי <4381>; from SELL <4376>]: salesman ▶ **A Benjamite dwelling in Jerusalem.** Ref.: 1 Chr. 9:8. ¶

MICHTAM – ***miḵtām*** [masc. noun: מִכְתָּם <4387>; from MARKED (BE) <3799> (in the sense of engraving)] ▶ **This word is a technical musical term whose meaning is uncertain. It is found in the titles of psalms.** Words like inscription, epigrammatic (terse, witty, wisdom-like), wisdom psalm apply. Refs.: titles of Psalms 16; 56–60. ¶

MIDDIN – ***middiyn*** [proper noun: מִדִּין <4081>; a variation for MIDIAN <4080>]: quarrel ▶ **A city of Judah.** Ref.: Josh. 15:61. ¶

MIDDLE – [1] ***qereḇ*** [masc. noun: קֶרֶב <7130>; from COME NEAR <7126>] ▶ **This word means midst, interior, inner part, inner organs, bowels, inner being.** The term occurs 222 times in the Old Testament and denotes the center or inner part of anything, e.g., the middle of a battle (middle of the streets: Is. 5:25); but especially the inner organs of the body. In the ceremony to ordain Aaron and his sons as priests for ministry to the Lord, all the fat that covered the inner organs of the sacrifices was to be burned on the altar (Ex. 29:13, 22; see also Lev. 1:13, 9:14). On many other occasions, however, the word is utilized abstractly to describe the inner being of a person. This place was regarded as the home of the heart from which the emotions spring (Ps. 39:3; 55:4; Lam. 1:20). It was also viewed as the source of thoughts (Gen. 18:12; Ps. 62:4; Jer. 9:8), which are often deceitful, wicked, and full of cursing. Yet wisdom from God can reside there also (1 Kgs. 3:28). This inner being is also the seat of one's moral disposition and thus one's affections and desires. David, grieved over his sin with Bathsheba, pleaded with God to place a right or steadfast spirit within him (lit., in [his] inner being), so that he might always desire to stay close to God and obey His laws (Ps. 51:10). The Lord promised to place His Law in the inner beings of His people Israel (Jer. 31:33; see also Ezek. 11:19, 36:26, 27). *

2 ***tiyḵôn, tiyḵōn*** [adj.: תִּיכוֹן, תִּיכֹן <8484>; from MIDST (IN THE) <8432>] ▶
a. This word indicates the place halfway between certain points, times, or other limits; in the center. In context it refers to a central stabilizing bar in a part of the Tabernacle framework (Ex. 26:28; 36:33); to the time of a middle watch (Judg. 7:19). It indicates the middle story of a building (1 Kgs. 6:6, 8; Ezek. 41:7; 42:5, 6); and it designates a middle court area (2 Kgs. 20:4).
b. This word means lower, lowest. The word is translated as lower, lowest in some ancient versions. They are followed by the NASB (1 Kgs. 6:8). ¶
– 3 Judg. 9:37 ➔ CENTER <2872> 4 Dan. 2:32 ➔ BELLY <4577> 5 See HALF <2677>.

MIDIAN – ***miḏyān*** [proper noun: מִדְיָן <4080>; the same as CONTENTIONS <4079>]: disputes ▶
a. A son of Abraham by Keturah, his second wife. He had several sons himself (Gen. 25:2, 4; 1 Chr. 1:32, 33). ¶
b. The word refers to a people or tribe descended from Abraham's son Midian and called by his name. Ref.: Gen. 36:25. They had priests, one of which was Jethro, Moses' father-in-law (Ex. 2:16; 3:1; 18:1), and elders as rulers (Num. 22:4, 7). They helped Balak hire Balaam to curse Israel (Num. 22:7). They were instrumental in leading Israel astray (Num. 25:16–18). The Lord called for holy war against them (Num. 31:3–9; Josh. 13:21; Ps. 83:9]). They continued to harass Israel in Canaan (Josh. 6–9). The defeat of the Midianites, especially under Gideon, became a symbol of God's deliverance for His people (Is. 9:4; 10:26; Hab. 3:7), but its restoration was also envisioned (Is. 60:6). *
c. The territory of the tribe descended from Midian. The land of Midian is difficult to pinpoint. Midianites were often found in northwest Arabia to the east of the Gulf of Aqaba. They, however, ranged far and wide (Judg. 6; 7). They were often close to the Moabites (Num. 22:4–7; 1 Kgs. 11:18). They were sent east by Abraham (Gen. 25:1–6) and seem to have been a people on the move, although they were largely desert dwellers (cf. Gen. 37:28–36). Refs.: Ex. 2:15; 4:19; Num. 25:15; 1 Kgs. 11:18. ¶

MIDIANITE – 1 ***miḏyāniy*** [proper noun: מִדְיָנִי <4084>; patron. or patrial from MIDIAN <4080>] ▶ **A member of the people of Midian (see MIDIAN <4080> b.).** Refs.: Gen. 37:36; Num. 10:29; 25:6, 14, 15, 17; 31:2. ¶

2 ***mᵉḏāniy*** [proper noun: מְדָנִי <4092>; a variation of <4084> above] ▶ **A member of the people of Midian (see MIDIAN <4080> b.).** Ref.: Gen. 37:36. ¶

MIDNIGHT – 1 ***ḥᵃṣôṯ*** [fem. noun: חֲצוֹת <2676>; from DIVIDE <2673>] ▶ **This word means middle, mid-, half division; it refers to time, i.e., the middle of the night.** The Lord went forth about midnight to slay the firstborn of Egypt (Ex. 11:4); persons suddenly die in the middle of the night (Job 34:20). The psalmist asserted that he would praise the Lord in the middle of the night (Ps. 119:62). ¶
– 2 See NIGHT, MIDNIGHT <3915>.

MIDST – 1 ***gaw*** [Aramaic masc. noun: גַּו <1459>; corresponding to BACK <1460>] ▶ **This word denotes interior, middle.** It is always used with the preposition *bᵉ* meaning in (Ezra 5:7; Dan. 3:25; 4:10); the preposition *lᵉ* meaning into (Dan. 3:6, 11); or the preposition *min* meaning out from (Dan. 3:26). *
– 2 1 Kgs. 22:35 ➔ BOSOM <2436> 3 Ezek. 38:12 ➔ CENTER <2872>.

MIDST (IN THE) – ***tāweḵ*** [substantive: תָּוֶךְ <8432>; from an unused root meaning to sever] ▶ **This word means in the middle, at the heart.** The word can have the implication of something being surrounded on all sides, as when God made a firmament in the midst of the waters (Gen. 1:6). It can also refer to something in the middle of a line: Samson destroyed the Temple by pushing over two middle pillars that supported it (Judg. 16:29). In relation to people, it can mean dwelling among (1 Sam. 10:10); or taken from among a group (Num. 3:12). *

MIGDAL EDER – ***migdal-'êḏer*** [proper noun: מִגְדַּל־עֵדֶר <4029>; from TOWER <4026> and FLOCK <5739>]: tower of the flock ▶
a. Israel pitched his tents beyond Migdal Eder. Ref.: KJV, NASB, ESV, Gen. 35:21. ¶
b. Israel pitched his tents beyond the tower of Eder. Ref.: NIV, Gen. 35:21. ¶

MIGDAL EL – ***migdal 'ēl*** [proper noun: מִגְדַּל־אֵל <4027>; from TOWER <4026> and GOD <410>]: tower of God ▶ **A fortified city of Naphtali.** Ref.: Josh. 19:38. ¶

MIGDAL GAD – ***migdal gāḏ*** [proper noun: מִגְדַּל־גָּד <4028>; from TOWER <4026> and FORTUNE <1408>]: tower of Gad, of prosperity ▶ **A city of Judah.** Ref.: Josh. 15:37. ¶

MIGDOL – Ex. 14:2; Num. 33:7; Jer. 44:1; 46:14; Ezek. 29:10; 30:6 ➔ TOWER <4024> b.

MIGHT – [1] ***t^{e}qāp̱, t^{e}qōp̱*** [masc. noun: תְּקָף, תְּקֹף <8632>; corresponding to AUTHORITY <8633>] ▶
a. This word means strength, force. It refers to the actual effective force of some power, e.g., the royal power of Nebuchadnezzar (Dan. 4:30; also translated mighty).
b. This word refers to the strength of royal sovereignty, the strength God gives to kings when He sets them up to rule. Ref.: Dan. 2:37. ¶
– [2] Deut. 8:17; Job 30:21; Nah. 3:9 ➔ STRENGTH <6108> [3] Ps. 78:4; 145:6; Is. 42:25 ➔ STRENGTH <5807> [4] Dan. 2:20, 23 ➔ POWER <1370> [5] Dan. 11:17 ➔ AUTHORITY <8633> [6] See STRENGTH <1369>.

MIGHTY – [1] ***'āḇiyr*** [adj.: אָבִיר <46>; from FLY (verb) <82>] ▶ **This word means strong, powerful.** It functions as a noun for God in Genesis 49:24, meaning the Mighty One (of Jacob) (NASB) or Mighty God of Jacob (NKJV) and similarly in other places (Ps. 132:2, 5; Is. 1:24, the Mighty One of Israel; Is. 49:26; 60:16). ¶
[2] ***'abbiyr*** [adj.: אַבִּיר <47>; for <46> above] ▶ **This word means strong, powerful.** It is used frequently as a noun and it applies to God as the Mighty One (Ps. 132:2, 5; Is. 1:24). It also designates angels (Ps. 78:25); men (Ps. 76:5); bulls (Ps. 22:12); and horses (Jer. 8:16). When used to describe a person or a person's heart, it normally refers to a strength independent of or opposed to God (Job 34:20; Ps. 76:5; Is. 46:12). It is used once to mean chief of the shepherds (1 Sam. 21:7). *
[3] ***'addiyr*** [adj.: אַדִּיר <117>; from GLORIOUS <142>] ▶ **This word means excellent, majestic, lofty, or great.** When describing physical objects, it often denotes strength of the waters of the sea (Ex. 15:10; Ps. 93:4); the precious value of a bowl (Judg. 5:25: lordly, magnificent, fit for a noble, noble's); or both the strength and beauty of trees (also translated goodly, stately, noble, splendid, glorious) (Ezek. 17:23; Zech. 11:2). When describing humans, it refers to those who lead, either as rulers or royalty (Jer. 14:3: noble; 25:34–36: principal, master, leader, lord; 30:21; Nah. 3:18: noble). When describing God, this word describes His majestic power (1 Sam. 4:8; Ps. 8:1, 9; Is. 10:34) that is greater than the breakers of the sea (Ps. 93:4). *
[4] ***'ayil*** [masc. noun: אַיִל <352>; from the same as BODY <193>] ▶ **This word refers to a leader or a powerful man, i.e., a strong pillar or post for others to look to; see DOORPOST <352>. It has this meaning many times.** The leaders or mighty men in Moab are described figuratively with this word. It describes

the leading men of Israel (2 Kgs. 24:15) or of the nations (Ps. 58:1). For other meanings of the Hebrew word, see RAM <352>, OAK <352>. *

[5] ***ḥᵃsiyn*** [adj.: חָסִין <2626>; from HOARDED (BE) <2630>] ▶ **This word means powerful; it is also translated strong.** It describes God as mighty like no one else (Ps. 89:8), the leader of His hosts. ¶

[6] ***kabbiyr*** [adj.: כַּבִּיר <3524>; from MULTIPLY <3527>] ▶ **This word is found only in Job and Isaiah; it means great, powerful.** It is used of mighty or influential persons (Job 34:17; KJV and NKJV: most). It is used of God who is great and mighty but does not look down on anyone (Job 36:5). It can describe wealth as extensive and great or water as powerful (Is. 17:12); or a population as great or renowned (Is. 16:14: feeble, impotent, i.e., not mighty). It refers to an aged or honored person (Job 15:10: much, even). The means God uses with which to work are powerful, mighty (Is. 28:2). Other refs.: Job 8:2 (strong, mighty, great, blustering); 31:25 (much); 34:24; Is. 10:13 (NIV). ¶

[7] ***'āṣûm*** [adj.: עָצוּם <6099>; pass. part. of MIGHTY (BE) <6105>] ▶ **This word refers to the power and influence of a person, a people, a nation, or military forces.** It is used of the descendants of Abraham becoming a numerous, mighty, powerful nation (Gen. 18:18; Ex. 1:9); of a nation from Moses (Num. 14:12; Deut. 4:38). But it is used of all strong, powerful nations and peoples (Josh. 23:9; Zech. 8:22). It can stress the number in a group of people, many, a great many (Prov. 7:26). It can emphasize the influence and power of individuals (Prov. 18:18; Is. 53:12). It is used of cattle (Num. 32:1); or indicates a large amount of water in a great river (Is. 8:7). *

[8] ***taqqiyp̱*** [adj.: תַּקִּיף <8623>; from PREVAIL <8630>] ▶ **This word indicates power and ability.** This is especially the case in arguing, disputation, or in wisdom, e.g., such as God has (Eccl. 6:10; also translated strong). ¶

[9] ***taqqiyp̱*** [Aramaic adj.: תַּקִּיף <8624>; corresponding to <8623> above] ▶ **This word means and is also translated strong, powerful.** It describes the power and authority wielded by kings, especially the great kings over Jerusalem (Ezra 4:20); and to the massive power and influence exercised by mighty kingdoms (Dan. 2:40, 42). It describes the unsurpassing might and wonders of God among the nations (Dan. 4:3). It describes the terrifying power and strength of the fourth kingdom of Daniel, represented by a fourth indescribable beast (Dan. 7:7). ¶

– [10] 2 Kgs. 24:15 ➔ BODY <193> b. [11] Job 9:4, 19 ➔ BRAVE <533> [12] Ps. 74:15 ➔ STRENGTH <386> [13] Is. 11:15 ➔ SCORCHING <5868> b. [14] Is. 18:2, 7 ➔ POWERFUL <6978> a. [15] Dan. 4:30 ➔ MIGHT <8632> a. [16] See BRAVE <1368>.

MIGHTY (BE) – ***'āṣam*** [verb: עָצַם <6105>; a prim. root] ▶ **This word describes a person, people, or nation becoming or being powerful, strong; it also means to be numerous.** Israel and his family had become strong, numerous (Gen. 26:16); Israel multiplied to become a powerful people in Egypt (Ex. 1:7, 20; Ps. 105:24). It refers to the enemies of a righteous person (Ps. 38:19). God's wonders are declared to be too many to number or tell about (Ps. 40:5). The might and strength of horsemen is emphasized (Is. 31:1). It is used figuratively of the might of a male goat that represents Alexander the Great (Dan. 8:8, 24). The Hebrew word also means to shut, to close; see CLOSE <6105>. *

MIGHTY MAN – [1] Eccl. 7:19 ➔ POWER <7989> [2] Is. 1:31 ➔ STRONG <2634>.

MIGRON – ***migrôn*** [proper noun: מִגְרוֹן <4051>; from DELIVER OVER <4048> (in the sense of to throw)]: precipice ▶ **A town of Benjamin in the neighborhood of Gibeah.** Refs.: 1 Sam. 14:2; Is. 10:28. ¶

MIJAMIN – ***miyyāmin*** [masc. proper noun: מִיָּמִן <4326>; a form of MINIAMIN <4509>]: from the right hand ▶
a. A descendant of Aaron. Ref.: 1 Chr. 24:9. ¶

b. A postexilic Jew. Ref.: Ezra 10:25. ¶
c. A priest who signed the covenant of renewal with Nehemiah after the return from the Babylonian captivity. Ref.: Neh. 10:7. ¶
d. A priest who came up from the Babylonian captivity. Ref.: Neh. 12:5. ¶

MIKLOTH – ***miqlôṯ*** [proper noun: מִקְלוֹת <4732>; plur. of (fem.) STICK <4731>]: staves ▶
a. A Benjamite. Refs.: 1 Chr. 8:32; 9:37, 38. ¶
b. An officer under David. Ref.: 1 Chr. 27:4. ¶

MIKNEIAH – ***miqnêyāhû*** [masc. proper noun: מִקְנֵיָהוּ <4737>; from LIVESTOCK <4735> and LORD <3050>]: possession of the Lord ▶ **A gatekeeper of the ark; he played a musical instrument in the time of David.** Refs.: 1 Chr. 15:18, 21. ¶

MILALAI – ***milᵃlay*** [masc. proper noun: מִלֲלַי <4450>; from SPEAK <4448>]: talkative, eloquent ▶ **A Levite musician who played at the dedication of the walls of Jerusalem.** Ref.: Neh. 12:36). ¶

MILCAH – ***milkāh*** [fem. proper noun: מִלְכָּה <4435>; a form of QUEEN <4436>]: queen ▶
a. The wife of Nahor. Refs.: Gen. 11:29; 22:20, 23; 24:15, 24, 47. ¶
b. The daughter of Zelophehad. Refs.: Num. 26:33; 27:1; 36:11; Josh. 17:3. ¶

MILDEW – ***yêrāqôn*** [masc. noun: יֵרָקוֹן <3420>; from GRASS <3418>] ▶ **This word refers to a disease attacking grains and forming rust or mildew (a fungal disease) on the grain; it also refers to paleness.** It was often considered a curse or pestilence from the Lord because of Israel's sin (1 Kgs. 8:37; 2 Chr. 6:28; Amos 4:9; Hag. 2:17). It was used of people's faces turning "green," i.e., pale from fear of judgment (Jer. 30:6: paleness, pale, deathly pale). Other ref.: Deut. 28:22. ¶

MILK – ***ḥālāḇ*** [masc. noun: חָלָב <2461>; from the same as FAT (noun) <2459>] ▶ **This word denotes the rich, white liquid secreted by female mammals to nourish their young and also refers to cheese. It is best known from the phrase describing Canaan as a land "flowing with milk and honey."** Refs.: Ex. 3:8, 17; 13:5; Num. 13:27; Deut. 6:3; Josh. 5:6; Ezek. 20:6, 15. The hills will flow with milk in the time of God's blessings (Joel 3:18). Milk was a major part of the diet of Israel and her surrounding neighbors. It was served with wine as a special treat (Song 5:1; Is. 55:1) and pictured the Lord's other blessings as well. Its whiteness served as a ready comparison (Lam. 4:7). It is found three times in the command not to boil a kid in its mother's milk (Ex. 23:19; 34:26; Deut. 14:21). The phrase *ṭelê' ḥalāḇ* refers to a sucking lamb (1 Sam. 7:9). *

MILK OUT – Is. 66:11 ➔ DRINK DEEPLY <4711>.

MILK, MILCH – 1 Sam. 6:7, 10 ➔ NURSE (verb) <5763>.

MILL – ***ṭᵉḥôn*** [masc. noun: טְחוֹן <2911>; from GRIND, GRINDER <2912>] ▶ **This word means and is also translated a millstone, grinding mill, to grind.** It indicates a place of difficult and onerous labor at a mill or grinding mill (Lam. 5:13) experienced by Israel's young men when Jerusalem fell to the Babylonians. ¶

MILLET – [1] ***dōḥan*** [masc. noun: דֹּחַן <1764>; of uncertain deriv.] ▶ **This grain is depicted as part of a meager diet.** It was prescribed for Ezekiel to symbolize the food of a besieged city (Ezek. 4:9). ¶
– [2] Ezek. 27:17 ➔ CAKE <6436> b.

MILLO – ***millô'*** [noun: מִלּוֹא <4407>; from FULL (BE) <4390> (in the sense of to fill in)]: rampart ▶
a. A proper noun referring to the citadel in Jerusalem. It was a man-made construction built onto a terrace and was simply called a citadel or a fortress (2 Sam. 5:9). It was expanded in David and Solomon's reigns (1 Kgs. 9:15; 11:27; 2 Kgs. 12:20;

1 Chr. 11:8; 2 Chr. 32:5). Other ref.: 1 Kgs. 9:24. ¶
b. A masculine noun referring to supporting terraces. Some prefer to translate the word this way. See references listed above in a. ¶
c. A proper noun referring to the city of Millo, a small town near Shechem. It is preceded by the word *beyṯ*; hence, its full rendering is *beyṯ-millo*, house of Millo (Judg. 9:6, 20). ¶

MILLO (HOUSE OF) – Judg. 9:6, 20 ➔ BETH MILLO <1037>.

MILLSTONE – 1 ***rêḥeh, rêḥayim*** [masc. noun: רֵחֶה, רֵחַיִם <7347>; from an unused root meaning to pulverize] ▶ **In its dual form, this word indicates the two stones used at a hand mill where grain was ground.** Refs.: Ex. 11:5; Num. 11:8; Deut. 24:6. It was considered a difficult and arduous task to grind meal (Is. 47:2); but it was a sign of a thriving town or community (Jer. 25:10). ¶
– 2 Lam. 5:13 ➔ MILL <2911>.

MILLSTONE (UPPER) – ***reḵeḇ*** [masc. noun: רֶכֶב <7393>; from RIDE <7392>] ▶ **This word refers to a movable stone used to crush or squeeze grapes or olives, to grind grain, etc.** It was movable, usually circular in shape, with a hole in its center (Deut. 24:6; Judg. 9:53; 2 Sam. 11:21). See also CHARIOT <7393>, another meaning of the Hebrew word. ¶

MINA – ***māneh*** [masc. noun: מָנֶה <4488>; from COUNT <4487>] ▶ **This word means a weight of money; it is also translated in the KJV by pound and maneh. It was a unit of weight of gold or silver amounting to about one pound (1/2 kilogram).** Refs.: 1 Kgs. 10:17; Ezra 2:69; Neh. 7:71, 72; Ezek. 45:12. ¶

MINCE – ***ṭāp̱ap̱*** [verb: טָפַף <2952>; a prim. root] ▶ **This word indicates to trip along with quick little steps.** It refers to the proud, seductive "mincing" steps (NIV: swaying hips) of the corrupt daughters of Zion, often highlighted with tinkling jewelry on their feet (Is. 3:16). ¶

MIND – 1 ***bāl*** [Aramaic noun: בָּל <1079>; from WEAR OUT <1080>] ▶ **This word properly means anxiety, care, hence mind as the seat of agitated anxiety; it is also translated heart.** There is only one occurrence of it in Scripture (Dan. 6:14), where King Darius "set his heart on Daniel." The phrase expresses the concern the king had for Daniel. ¶
2 ***śeḵwiy*** [masc. noun: שֶׂכְוִי <7907>; from the same as SECU <7906>] ▶ **This word means a celestial appearance or phenomenon, the mind (the seat of understanding).** It is used in Job to denote the mind that has been given understanding (Job 38:36; KJV, NKJV: heart; NIV: rooster). In a rhetorical question, the Lord indicated His sovereignty over all, including the lives of His servants. The exact meaning of this word is unclear. ¶
– 3 Job 38:36 ➔ INWARD PART <2910> 4 Is. 46:8: to fix in mind ➔ SHOW YOURSELVES MEN <377>.

MIND (MAKE ONE'S MIND) – Dan. 1:8 ➔ PUT <7760>.

MINGLE – Ps. 102:9; Prov. 9:2, 5; Is. 5:22; 19:14 ➔ MIX <4537>.

MINIAMIN – ***minyāmiyn*** [masc. proper noun: מִנְיָמִין <4509>; from FROM <4480> and RIGHT HAND <3225>]: from the right hand ▶
a. A priest under Nehemiah. Refs.: Neh. 12:17, 12:41. ¶
b. A priest under Hezekiah. Ref.: 2 Chr. 31:15. ¶

MINISTER – 1 Ex. 28:35; 1 Kgs. 8:11 ➔ SERVE <8334> 2 Dan. 7:10 ➔ SERVE <8120>.

MINISTERING – Num. 4:12 ➔ SERVICE <8335>.

MINISTRY – Num. 4:12 ➔ SERVICE <8335>.

MINNI – ***minniy*** [proper noun: מִנִּי <4508>; of foreign deriv.] ▶ **A kingdom in Armenia which was part of a coalition to destroy Babylon.** Ref.: Jer. 51:27. ¶

MINNITH – ***minniyṯ*** [proper noun: מִנִּית <4511>; from the same as PORTION <4482>]: enumeration, distribution ▶ **A city of the Ammonites.** Refs.: Judg. 11:33; Ezek. 27:17. ¶

MIPHKAD – Neh. 3:31 ➔ INSPECTION <4663>.

MIRE – [1] ***ḥōmer*** [masc. noun: חֹמֶר <2563>; from RED (BE) <2560>] ▶ **This word denotes mortar, thick mud.** It refers to mud in the streets (Is. 10:6). It was a building material used with bricks (Ex. 1:14). Bitumen was used as mortar at the Tower of Babel (Gen. 11:3). Potters used clay, a form of mud, designated by this word (Is. 29:16; Jer. 18:4, 6). It is used metaphorically to describe people as opposed to God (Job 10:9; Is. 45:9; 64:8) who is the potter that forms the clay. Seals were pressed into this malleable substance (Job 38:14). It is symbolic of something weak, such as defenses (Job 13:12) or the frail human body (Job 4:19). Other refs.: Job 27:16; 30:19; 33:6; Is. 41:25; Nah. 3:15. The Hebrew word also means a pile or heap [see HEAP (noun) <2563>] and indicates a dry measure (HOMER <2563>). ¶
[2] ***repeś*** [masc. noun: רֶפֶשׁ <7516>; from FOUL <7515> (in the sense of to roil water)] ▶ **This word refers to what is not desirable, makes dirty, stinks; it is also translated refuse.** In context it refers to the moral, ethical, spiritual mire and refuse that wicked persons produce and throw out (Is. 57:20). ¶
– [3] 2 Sam. 22:43; Job 41:30; Ps. 18:42; 69:14; Jer. 38:6; Mic. 7:10; Zech. 9:3; 10:5 ➔ MUD <2916> [4] Job 8:11 ➔ MARSH <1207> [5] Ps. 40:2; 69:2 ➔ MIRY <3121> [6] Jer. 38:22 ➔ MUD <1206>.

MIRIAM – ***miryām*** [fem. proper noun: מִרְיָם <4813>; from REBELLIOUSNESS <4805>]: obstinacy, rebellion ▶
a. The daughter of Amram and Jochebed and sister to Aaron and Moses. Ref.: Num. 26:59. She was considered a leader sent by God (Mic. 6:4). She probably was the sister who watched over Moses when he was placed in the Nile River as a baby. She composed a song to celebrate the Lord's deliverance at the Red Sea (Ex. 15:20, 21) but later unwisely challenged Moses' authority and was soundly rebuked by the Lord with leprosy (Num. 12:1–15). She died and was buried at Kadesh (Num. 20:1). ¶
b. A Judahite, a daughter of Mered. Ref.: 1 Chr. 4:17. ¶

MIRMAH – ***mirmāh*** [masc. proper noun: מִרְמָה <4821>; the same as DECEIT <4820>]: deceit ▶ **One of the sons of Shaharaim, a Benjamite.** Ref.: 1 Chr. 8:10. ¶

MIRROR – [1] ***gillāyôn*** [masc. noun: גִּלָּיוֹן <1549>; from REVEAL <1540>] ▶ **This word means a reflective surface; it is found in a list of luxury items the Lord will take away from His rebellious people when He judges them.** Ref.: Is. 3:23. It also means a scroll or a tablet in Isaiah 8:1; see SCROLL <1549>. ¶
[2] ***r^{e}'iy*** [masc. noun: רְאִי <7209>; from SEE <7200>] ▶ **The primary meaning is that of a looking glass used to see one's own reflection.** Job uses the word metaphorically to refer to the sky (Job 37:18). ¶
– [3] Ex. 38:8 ➔ VISION <4759>.

MIRTH – Job 20:5 ➔ JOYFUL SHOUT <7445>.

MIRY – [1] ***ṭiyn*** [Aramaic masc. noun: טִין <2917>; perhaps by interchange for a word corresponding to MUD <2916>] ▶ **This word refers to common (ceramic, miry, soft) clay mixed with iron in Nebuchadnezzar's vision of the feet and toes of the great image.** Refs.: Dan. 2:41, 43. It actually represented diverse groups of people who could not become unified among themselves. ¶
[2] ***yāwên*** [masc. noun: יָוֵן <3121>; from the same as WINE <3196> (properly dreg, as effervescing)] ▶ **This word indicates something is mire (heavy, wet earth), mud. It denotes mud or mire that is both slippery and sticky, tending to endanger**

anyone's life who is bogged down in it. Refs.: Ps. 40:2; 69:2. It is found twice and is used metaphorically each time: it represents the dangerous conditions of life the psalmist had become caught in or the clutches of his enemies and circumstances that overwhelmed him. ¶

MIRY PLACE – Ezek. 47:11 ➔ MARSH <1207>.

MISCARRIAGE – Job 3:16; Ps. 58:8; Eccl. 6:3 ➔ STILLBORN <5309>.

MISCARRY – Ex. 23:26; Job 21:10 ➔ DEPRIVED OF CHILDREN <7921>.

MISCHIEF – [1] Gen. 42:4, 38; 44:29; Ex. 21:22, 23 ➔ HARM (noun) <611> [2] Is. 47:11; Ezek. 7:26 ➔ DISASTER <1943> [3] Dan. 11:27 ➔ EVIL <4827>.

MISER – Is. 32:5 ➔ SCOUNDREL <3596>.

MISERABLE – Num. 21:5 ➔ WORTHLESS <7052>.

MISERABLE (MAKE) – 1 Sam. 1:6 ➔ IRRITATE <7481>.

MISERY – [1] Gen. 16:11; 39:32 ➔ AFFLICTION <6040> [2] Job 9:18 ➔ BITTERNESS <4472> [3] Ps. 56:8 ➔ WANDERING <5112> [4] Lam. 1:7; 3:19 ➔ WANDERING <4788>.

MISFORTUNE – [1] 1 Kgs. 5:4 ➔ lit.: evil occurrence ➔ OCCURRENCE <6294> [2] Job 31:29 ➔ DISASTER <6365> [3] Eccl. 4:8, 5:14 ➔ TASK <6045> [4] Is. 65:23 ➔ TERROR <928> [5] Obad. 1:12 ➔ DISASTER <5235>.

MISGAB – Jer. 48:1 ➔ STRONGHOLD <4869> b.

MISHAEL – [1] ***miyšā'ēl*** [masc. proper noun: מִישָׁאֵל <4332>; from WHO <4310> and GOD <410>]: who is what God is? ▶
a. A cousin of Moses. Refs.: Ex. 6:22; Lev. 10:4. ¶
b. A companion of Daniel. Refs.: Dan. 1:6, 7, 11, 19. ¶
c. A postexilic Jew. Ref.: Neh. 8:4. ¶
[2] ***miyšā'ēl*** [Aramaic masc. proper noun: מִישָׁאֵל <4333>; corresponding to <4332> above] ▶ **This name corresponds to the Hebrew name in b.** Ref.: Dan. 2:17. ¶

MISHAL – ***miš'āl*** [proper noun: מִשְׁאָל <4861>; from ASK <7592>]: request ▶ **A city of the tribe of Asher.** Refs.: Josh. 19:26; 21:30. See also MASHAL <4913>. ¶

MISHAM – ***miš'ām*** [masc. proper noun: מִשְׁעָם <4936>; apparently from LOOK FOR FAVOR OR IN DISMAY <8159>]: inspection, cleansing ▶ **A Benjamite, son of Elpaal; him and his brothers built the cities of Ono and Lod.** Ref.: 1 Chr. 8:12. ¶

MISHMA – ***mišmā'*** [masc. proper noun: מִשְׁמָע <4927>; the same as HEARING <4926>]: hearing ▶
a. A son of Ishmael. Refs.: Gen. 25:14; 1 Chr. 1:30. ¶
b. A descendant of Simeon. Refs.: 1 Chr. 4:25, 26. ¶

MISHMANNAH – ***mišmannāh*** [masc. proper noun: מִשְׁמַנָּה <4925>; from FAT (BE) <8080>]: fatness ▶ **A Gadite warrior who joined David at Ziklag.** Ref.: 1 Chr. 12:10. ¶

MISHRAITE – ***mišrā'iy*** [proper noun: מִשְׁרָעִי <4954>; patrial from an unused root] ▶ **Member of a clan of Kiriath-jearim.** Ref.: 1 Chr. 2:53. ¶

MISLEAD – Ezek. 13:10 ➔ SEDUCE <2937>.

MISLEADING – [1] ***maddûaḥ*** [masc. noun: מַדּוּחַ <4065>; from DRIVE <5080> a. (in the sense of to banish, to drive away)] ▶ **This word refers to oracles from prophets, describing the oracles as misleading, i.e., deceptive, or false in some way.** Ref.: Lam. 2:14; also translated delusion, cause of banishment. It is used with *šāw'*, vain, worthless. ¶
– [2] Dan. 2:9 ➔ LYING <3538>.

MISPAR – ***misp̄ār*** [masc. proper noun: מִסְפָּר <4558>; the same as NUMBER (noun) <4457>]: number ► **One of those who returned from the Babylonian captivity with Zerubbabel.** Ref.: Ezra 2:2. ¶

MISPERETH – ***misperet̠*** [masc. proper noun: מִסְפֶּרֶת <4559>; fem. of NUMBER (noun) <4557>]: number ► **One of those who returned from the Babylonian captivity with Zerubbabel.** Ref.: Neh. 7:7; also called Mispar. ¶

MISREPHOTH MAIM – ***miśrᵉp̄ôt̠ mayim*** [proper noun: מִשְׂרְפוֹת מַיִם <4956>; from the plur. of BURNING (noun) <4955> and WATER <4325>]: hot waters ► **Joshua pursued his enemies as far as that place.** Refs.: Josh. 11:8; 13:6. ¶

MISSING (BE) – 1 Sam. 30:19 → LACK, LACKING (BE) <5737>.

MIST – 1 ***'ēd̠*** [masc. noun: אֵד <108>; from the same as FIREBRAND <181> (in the sense of enveloping)] ► **This word means condensed water vapor in the atmosphere; it is also translated spring, streams, vapor.** In the beginning, the mist watered the ground before it had rained (Gen. 2:6). In Job 36:27, it refers to the mist of the clouds from which rain distilled and fell to earth. ¶
– 2 Ps. 148:8 → SMOKE (noun) <7008>.

MISTAKE – ***mišgeh*** [masc. noun: מִשְׁגֶּה <4870>; from ERR <7686>] ► **This word refers to an error made or an incorrect action taken by someone; it also indicates an oversight.** This was the case in the placement of money in a bag in error (Gen. 43:12). ¶

MISTREAT – 1 Deut. 21:14; 24:7 → SLAVE (TREAT AS A) <6014> 2 Jer. 13:22 → VIOLENCE (DO) <2554>.

MISTRESS – 1 ***baᵃlāh*** [fem. noun: בַּעֲלָה <1172>; fem. of LORD <1167>] ► **This word means lady, owner, or possessor.** It occurs four times in the Bible, and three times it refers to possessing occult abilities: possessor of ghosts (1 Sam. 28:7: to be a medium, to possess a familiar spirit); and spells (Nah. 3:4: the mistress of sorceries). Other ref.: 1 Kgs. 17:17 (mistress, one who owns). ¶
2 ***gᵉḇiyrāh*** [fem. noun: גְּבִירָה <1377>; fem. of LORD <1376>] ► **This word depicts a queen, a lady.** In general, it denotes a woman or a mistress (Gen. 16:4, 8, 9; 2 Kgs. 5:3). As a more formal term, it means the title of the king's mother, the queen mother (1 Kgs. 15:13; 2 Kgs. 10:13). It is used as the title of Pharaoh's wife in Egypt (1 Kgs. 11:19). Sons of this female were considered full brothers of the king (2 Kgs. 10:13). *
3 ***gᵉḇeret̠*** [fem. noun: גְּבֶרֶת <1404>; fem. of LORD <1376>] ► **This word refers to a woman in authority over servants; it also means a woman at the head of a kingdom.** In many cases, it refers to either a woman who is a mistress or to the servant of a mistress (Gen. 16:4, 8, 9; 2 Kgs. 5:3; Prov. 30:23). Also, it refers to a lady of a kingdom, i.e., the queen (Is. 47:5, 7). Other refs.: Ps. 123:2; Is. 24:2. ¶

MISUSE – 2 Chr. 36:16 → DECEIVE <8591> a.

MITHCAH – ***mit̠qāh*** [proper noun: מִתְקָה <4989>; fem. of SWEETNESS <4987>]: sweetness ► **An encampment of the Israelites in the desert.** Refs.: Num. 33:28, 29. ¶

MITHNITE – ***mit̠niy*** [proper noun: מִתְנִי <4981>; prob. patrial from an unused noun meaning slenderness] ► **Designation of Joshaphat, one of the mighty men of David.** Ref.: 1 Chr. 11:43. ¶

MITHREDATH – ***mit̠rᵉd̠āt̠*** [masc. proper noun: מִתְרְדָת <4990>; of Persian origin]: gift of Mithra (a Persian god) ►
a. A treasurer of Cyrus. Ref.: Ezra 1:8. ¶
b. A Persian governor of Samaria. Ref.: Ezra 4:7. ¶

MITRE – 1 Ex. 28:4, 37, 39; 29:6; 39:28, 31; Lev. 8:9; 16:4 → TURBAN

<4701> 2 Ex. 39:28 ➔ TURBAN <6287> 3 Zech. 3:5 ➔ TURBAN <6797> c.

MIX – 1 ***bālal*** [verb: בָּלַל <1101>; a prim. root] ▶ **This word means to mingle, to tangle, to confuse, to bewilder, to perplex, to anoint.** It is often used in a technical sense to signify the mixing of oil with the fine flour used to bake cakes without yeast that were then presented as grain offerings (Lev. 2:4; 14:21). Similarly, oil was mixed with fine wheat flour to bake wafers without yeast in a sacrificial setting (Ex. 29:2). Sometimes oil was simply mingled with fine flour itself as part of a drink offering (Ex. 29:40). While these food items readily combined with positive results, the verb can also indicate confusion, bewilderment, or perplexity. The language of the whole earth was confused by the Lord at the tower of Babel so that people could not understand each other (Gen. 11:9).

Since the verb could mean to moisten or to dampen when used in the technical sacrificial examples noted above, it is a reasonable extension of that usage to the anointing of a person with oil. This usage is found (Ps. 92:10) where the psalmist rejoiced that he was anointed with fine oils.

The verb is used one time also to indicate the feeding of donkeys, (i.e., providing fodder for the animal to eat [Judg. 19:21]), but in this case, the verb is probably from a different original root. *

2 ***māhal*** [verb: מָהַל <4107>; a prim. root] ▶ **This word means to weaken, to dilute. It refers to something adulterated by water so that it loses its character and quality.** Ref.: Is. 1:22. ¶

3 ***māsaḵ*** [verb: מָסַךְ <4537>; a prim. root] ▶ **This word means to mingle together various things; it is also translated to mingle.** Honey or various spices with wine; wisdom mixes her wine to invite persons to drink with her (Prov. 9:2, 5); mixed strong drink was a favorite of valiant, if foolish, men (Is. 5:22). It is used twice in figurative poetry: the psalmist mixed his wine with tears (Ps. 102:9); and the Lord mixed into Egypt, as a part of His judgments on her, a spirit of confusion or distortion (Is. 19:14; also translated to pour). ¶

4 ***ʿarab̲*** [Aramaic verb: עֲרַב <6151>; corresponding to PLEDGE (BE A) <6148>] ▶ **This verb means to mingle, to join together.** Daniel used this word to describe the feet of the image Nebuchadnezzar saw in his dream (Dan. 2:41, 43). They were a curious mixture of clay and iron. Thus, the word implies an amalgamation of two uncomplementary materials, which is at best unstable. ¶

– 5 Ex. 30:33; etc. ➔ COMPOUND <7543>.

MIXED – 1 ***ʿêreb̲*** [masc. noun: עֵרֶב <6154>; from PLEDGE (BE A) <6148> (in the sense of to mingle)] ▶ **This word means a mixture, a mixed company, interwoven. The primary meaning is a grouping of people from various ethnic and cultural backgrounds.** It was used of any heterogeneous band associated with the nation of Israel as it departed Egypt (Ex. 12:38); the tribes not aligned with any specific culture (Jer. 25:24); and the mingled people resulting from the Babylonian captivity (Jer. 50:37). By extension, the word was also used of interwoven material of varying fibers (Lev. 13:48: woof, knitted). *

– 2 Ps. 75:8 ➔ MIXTURE <4538>.

MIXED (BE) – Dan. 4:22, 36; 5:18, 19 ➔ STIRRED <7246>.

MIXED RACE, MIXED PEOPLE – Zech. 9:6 ➔ FORBIDDEN UNION (ONE BORN OF) <4464>.

MIXED WINE – ***mimsāḵ*** [masc. noun: מִמְסָךְ <4469>; from MIX <4537>] ▶ **This word usually indicated wine mingled with water.** Refs.: Prov. 23:30; Is. 65:11; also translated drink offering, but other things were used such as milk or spices. ¶

MIXING – 1 Chr. 9:30 ➔ MIXTURE <4842>.

MIXTURE – 1 ***meseḵ*** [masc. noun: מֶסֶךְ <4538>; from MIX <4537>] ▶ **This word**

describes something fully mingled. It is used figuratively to describe a cup of wine, representing the judgments of the Lord, as well-mixed (Ps. 75:8). ¶

2 ***mirqaḥaṯ*** [fem. noun: מִרְקַחַת <4842>; from COMPOUND <7543>] ▶ **This word indicates a blend of ointment or perfume.** It indicates Israel's anointing oil, a combination of various items (Ex. 30:25; also translated compound, blend) prepared by priests (1 Chr. 9:30: mixing, ointment). It refers to the blending of spices etc., together (2 Chr. 16:14). ¶

MIZAR – ***miṣār*** [proper noun: מִצְעָר <4706>; the same as LITTLE ONE <4705>]: small ▶ **A hill or a mount.** It is found only in Psalm 42:6. ¶

MIZPAH – ***miṣpāh*** [proper noun: מִצְפָּה <4709>; fem. of MIZPEH <4708>]: lookout ▶ This word indicates a place where a panoramic view is possible. It refers to several places:

a. A city located in Judah where Hivites lived. Refs.: Josh. 11:3; Judg. 10:17; 11:11, 34. *

b. A city that was fortified by Asa, king of Judah. Refs.: 1 Kgs. 15:22; Neh. 3:7. ¶

c. A name given to the heap of stones "watchtower" Laban and Jacob set up as a witness between them. Ref.: Gen. 31:49. ¶

d. An administrative district administered by Shallun, son of Colhozeh after the return of the exiles. Ref.: Neh. 3:15. ¶

e. A town or area ruled by Jeshua. Ref.: Neh. 3:19. ¶

MIZPEH – ***miṣpeh*** [proper noun: מִצְפֶּה <4708>; from WATCHTOWER <4707>]: lookout ▶ **This word indicates a place where a panoramic view is possible. It refers to several places.**

a. A village given to the tribe of Judah. Probably near the city of Lachish (Josh. 15:38). Other refs.: Jer. 40:6, 8, 12, 13; 14:1. ¶

b. A city in Moab, where David sent his mother and father for safety. Ref.: 1 Sam. 22:3. It would be somewhere east of the Dead Sea in Moab. ¶

c. A city in Gad (Gilead) from which the infamous judge Jephthah came. It was located south of the Jabbok River and east of the Jordan (Judg. 10:17). Other ref.: Judg. 11:29. ¶

d. A city allotted to the tribe of Benjamin. All Israel gathered there to decide what to do about the rape and murder of the Levite's concubine (Judg. 20:1; 21:25). Later, it became a key worship center (1 Sam. 7:2–17; 1 Sam. 10:17). It was used briefly by Gedaliah after Jerusalem had been destroyed. It supplied workers to rebuild the wall of the city (Neh. 3:7). Other ref.: Josh. 18:26. ¶

e. A valley or region where Israelites defeated Canaanites, especially the Hivites. Refs.: Josh. 11:3, 8. ¶

MIZRAIM – ***miṣrayim*** [proper noun: מִצְרַיִם <4714>; dual of MATSOR <4693>] ▶

a. The son of Ham, Noah's son, and the ancestor of Egypt and its people. The name is the name of Egypt in Hebrew. Mizraim fathered several sons from whom other peoples came (1 Chr. 1:8). ¶

b. An ancient land and nation that has a history going back beyond 2000 B.C. The word Egypt comes from the Greek term *Aiguptos*. The Hebrew name in the Old Testament is *miṣrayim*. The meaning of this word is uncertain. It is in a dual form and may hint at the Upper and Lower geographical aspects of this ancient nation. It occupied the northeastern corner of the African continent. It has been called the "gift of the Nile," referring to its central river which is the lifeblood of the nation. The Nile (or river of Egypt; Gen. 15:18) flows from the south to the northern delta where it empties into the Mediterranean. The Nile's seasonal flooding provided the land and people yearly with rich soil and abundant crops for food. To the south, past the cataracts of the Nile, lay Nubia, Cush, and Ethiopia, as well as the White Nile and Blue Nile, the highland tributaries of the Nile itself. The nation Israel and her ancestors had both friendly and hostile encounters with Egypt (Gen. 12:40, 41; Ex. 1–15).

Egypt was famed for its reception and nurture of the patriarchs (Gen. 41, 42, 43–50) but was infamous for its enslavement and oppression of the Israelites until the Lord delivered His people at the Exodus (ca. 1446 B.C. or ca. 1220 B.C.). Throughout the Old Testament after the Exodus, Egypt was a thorn in the flesh of Israel.

The patriarchs encountered Egypt during the years ca. 2134–1786 B.C., the Middle Kingdom of Egypt. The Second Intermediate Period (1786–1540 B.C.) probably saw the appearance of Joseph and the Hebrews in the land of Goshen, a northeastern area of the Nile Delta region. During the New Kingdom Era (ca. 1552–1069 B.C.), Israel was enslaved and freed (Ex. 1–15).

It is not the purpose of this article to trace the contacts of Egypt and Israel throughout the Old Testament, but in general, Egyptian power and influence on Israel declined greatly after the Exodus event. The last king of northern Israel (Hoshea) hoped futilely that Egypt would help him against Assyria (2 Kgs. 17:1–4). Assyria became dominant in the affairs of Israel until ca. 612–605 B.C. Then Babylon became the dominant superpower of the Middle East (650–538 B.C.), then Persia (538–332 B.C.). All three of these secular powers exerted their influence in Egypt as well as Canaan. *

c. The designation of the inhabitants of Egypt (see a. and b. above) simply took on the name of the nation itself.

MIZZAH – ***mizzāh*** [masc. proper noun: מִזָּה <4199>; prob. from an unused root meaning to faint with fear]: fear ▶ **Son of Reuel and grandson of Esau.** Refs.: Gen. 36:13, 17; 1 Chr. 1:37. ¶

MOAB – ***mô'āḇ*** [proper noun: מוֹאָב <4124>; from a prolonged form of the prep. prefix m- and FATHER <1>]: from his father ▶

a. A son of Lot (Gen. 19:37) who was born through an incestuous relationship with his daughter. Refs.: Gen. 19:30–38. He became the father of the Moabites. ¶

b. The territory of Moab was east of the Dead Sea between the Zered River and the Arnon River. It stretched eastward to the eastern desert. It was largely mountainous terrain with some plateau land toward the Arnon River and at times beyond it.

The people were, according to the writer of Genesis, descendants of Lot and his older daughter (Gen. 19:36–38). The Moabites or Moab are mentioned over 190 times in the Bible. Moab usually had a hostile relationship with the Israelites (e.g., Judg. 3:12–30; 2 Sam. 8:2–12; 2 Kgs. 4:3–27). They refused Israel passage through their land (Judg. 11:17). They were excluded from Israel (Deut. 23:3–6) because of hostilities. Balak, king of Moab, so feared Israel that he hired Balaam, a Mesopotamian soothsayer to curse them; and Balaam and Moab seduced Israel at Baal-Peor (Num. 22–26; Deut. 23:3–6). Israel crossed into the Promised Land from Moab (Josh. 3:1). On the other hand, any Moabite who would confess and follow the Lord could do so (Ruth 1:1–22), and the ancestors of David includes Ruth, a Moabitess. The Moabites conspired with the Ammonites and Edomites more than once against Israel (2 Chr. 20:1–23). The people and country fell, as did Israel, under the power of the Assyrians, Babylonians, and Persians. They are included in many prophetic oracles of judgment (e.g., Jer. 40:11). After Israel was exiled (586 B.C.) and returned (538 B.C.), the Moabites as a nation had disappeared. *

MOABITE – ***mô'āḇiy*** [proper noun: מוֹאָבִי <4125>; patron. from MOAB <4124>] ▶ **A gentilic form of the word that indicates that a person was related to the inhabitants of Moab or a part of their descendants.** The ending *iy* or *iyṯ* in Hebrew indicates this clearly. (See MOAB <4124>.) Refs.: Deut. 2:11, 29; 23:3; Ruth 1:4, 22; 2:2, 6, 21; 4:5, 10; 1 Kgs. 11:1; 1 Chr. 11:46; 2 Chr. 24:26; Ezra 9:1; Neh. 13:1, 23. ¶

MOADIAH – ***mô'aḏyāh*** [masc. proper noun: מוֹעַדְיָה <4153>; from APPOINTED TIMES <4151> and LORD <3050>]: appointed time of the Lord ▶ **A priest who returned from exile with Zerubbabel.** Ref.: Neh. 12:17. ¶

MOAN – [1] Ps. 90:9 ➔ RUMBLING <1899> [2] Joel 1:18 ➔ GROAN (verb) <584> [3] Mic. 2:4 ➔ LAMENT <5091> [4] Nah. 2:7 ➔ DRIVE <5090> b.

MOANING – [1] Ps. 6:6 ➔ GROANING <585> [2] Is. 29:2 ➔ MOURNING <8386> [3] Lam. 2:5 ➔ LAMENTATION <592>.

MOAT – ***ḥārûṣ*** [adj.: חָרוּץ <2742>; pass. part. of MOVE <2782>] ▶ **This word refers to a channel of water around a city, especially Jerusalem; it is also translated trench, wall.** Ref.: Dan. 9:25. It was dug and filled in for defensive purposes. The Hebrew word also means DECISION, DILIGENT, GOLD; see these entries. ¶

MOCK – [1] ***hāṯal, tālal*** [verb: הָתַל, תָּלַל <2048>; a prim. root] ▶
a. This word means to deceive, to deride. It is a strong word of derision and attack used by Elijah to mock the prophets of Baal (1 Kgs. 18:27; also translated to taunt). ¶
b. A verb indicating to cheat, to deceive, to trifle with, to tease, to lead on falsely. It is used effectively to describe the deceitful ways Pharaoh dealt with Moses and Israel (Ex. 8:29: to deal deceitfully, to act deceitfully, to cheat) and the way Laban treated Jacob (Gen. 31:7: to deceive, to cheat). Samson led Delilah on falsely concerning his strength (Judg. 16:10, 13, 15); it is translated to mock, to deceive, to make a fool. It describes the deceived heart of an idolater (Is. 44:20: deceived, deluded) or the rampant social deception that was characteristic of Zion before she fell (Jer. 9:5: to deceive). Other ref.: Job 13:9. ¶
[2] ***lā'aḇ*** [verb: לָעַב <3931>; a prim. root] ▶ **This word means to not take seriously, to make fun of, to despise.** The Israelites mocked the prophets of God and did not listen to them (2 Chr. 36:16). ¶
[3] ***lûṣ, liyṣ, lêṣ*** [verb: לוּץ, לִיץ, לֵץ <3887>; a prim. root] ▶ **This word means to boast, to scorn, to deride, or to imitate.** This Hebrew verb is frequently found in the book of Proverbs (Prov. 9:7, 8; 13:1; 20:1), and means to deride or to boast so as to express utter contempt. The activity of the scornful is condemned as an abomination to people (Prov. 24:9) and contrary to the Law of the Lord (Ps. 1:1). Both Job (Job 16:20) and the psalmist (Ps. 119:51) expressed the pain inflicted by the scornful, but in the end, the scorner will reap what he has sown (Prov. 3:34). By extension the word is used to signify ambassadors (2 Chr. 32:31), interpreters (Gen. 42:23), and spokesmen (Is. 43:27). These meanings arise from the sense of speaking indirectly implied in the root word. Some grammarians view the participle of this verb as a separate noun. *
[4] ***lā'ag*** [verb: לָעַג <3932>; a prim. root] ▶ **This word means to deride, to ridicule.** It refers to disclaiming people, deriding them, despising them to their faces, ridiculing them as Jerusalem did to Assyria (2 Kgs. 19:21; 2 Chr. 30:10; Neh. 2:19; 4:1). It describes the sounds of a foreign language as stammering, unintelligible (Is. 33:19). It indicates strongly attacking and accusing people's positions and words (Job 21:3), ridiculing them. It includes sometimes the act of sneering, making faces at someone (Ps. 22:7). It is used of wisdom's deriding those who despise wisdom (Prov. 1:26). Anyone mocking the poor is said to do the same to his Creator (Prov. 17:5; cf. Prov. 30:17). Other refs.: Job 9:23; 11:3; 22:19; Ps. 2:4; 59:8; 80:6; Is. 37:22; Jer. 20:7. ¶
[5] ***qālas*** [verb: קָלַס <7046>; a prim. root] ▶ **This word means to deride, to scorn; it is also translated to jeer, to scoff, to disdain.** It means to make fun of persons, to insult them (2 Kgs. 2:23); or to mock or insult a whole nation (Ezek. 22:5). It means to hold someone or something in disrespect; not to fear or take something seriously (Hab. 1:10). It is used figuratively to describe Israel's money gained from harlotry (Ezek. 16:31). ¶
– [6] Ps. 73:8 ➔ SCOFF <4167> [7] Is. 37:22 ➔ DESPISE <936> [8] Is. 57:4 ➔ DELIGHT (HAVE, FIND, TAKE) <6026>.

MOCKER – [1] ***laṣôn*** [masc. noun: לָצוֹן <3944>; from MOCK <3887>] ▶ **This**

word refers to foolish, arrogant, bragging talk, as well as to the scoffers or babblers themselves, literally, "people of *laṣôn*." Refs.: Prov. 1:22; 29:8; Is. 28:14; also translated scoffer, scorner, scornful man. ¶
2 ***leṣaṣiym, lāṣaṣ*** [לְצָצִים, לָצַץ <3945>; a prim. root] ▶
a. A masculine noun meaning a scoffer, a scorner. It is used in a masculine plural participial form to indicate those who rebel or scorn. It has the sense of scoffing that is religiously and morally wrong in context (Hos. 7:5, KJV, NASB). See b. also. ¶
b. A verb meaning to treat somebody with scorn. It is understood to be from the word *lāṣaṣ*, not *liyṣ*, by some translators (NIV: Hos. 7:5). ¶
– 3 Ps. 35:16 ➔ STAMMERING <3934>.

MOCKERS – ***haṯuliym*** [masc. plur. noun: הֲתֻלִּים <2049>; from MOCK <2048> (only in plur. collectively)] ▶ **This word means to deride, to excoriate, to attack with derision.** Job uses the word to describe his "friends" and detractors who are crushing him with their words (Job 17:2). ¶

MOCKERY – 1 ***qallāsāh*** [fem. noun: קַלָּסָה <7048>; intens. from MOCK <7046>] ▶ **This word means to be the object of scorn and the brunt of jokes of humor and disrespect; it is also translated laughingstock, mocking.** Ref.: Ezek. 22:4. ¶
2 ***ta'tu'iym*** [masc. plur. noun: תַּעְתֻּעִים <8595>; from DECEIVE <8591>] ▶ **This word is a epithet of idols, termed a work of mockery (object of scorn or ridicule and bringing the same on those who trust in them); it is also translated mockings, errors.** Jeremiah used this word twice when he ridiculed the idols of the Israelites (Jer. 10:15; 51:18; ESV: delusion). These two verses are identical and are found in identical passages. Jeremiah assaulted the idols, saying how worthless they were and that they were works of mockery whose end will be judgment. ¶

MOCKING – 1 Gen. 27:12 ➔ DECEIVE <8591> a. 2 Jer. 20:10 ➔ REPORT (BAD) <1681> 3 Ezek. 22:4 ➔ MOCKERY <7048>.

MOCKING SONG – ***mangiynāh*** [fem. noun: מַנְגִּינָה <4485>; from PLAY (verb) <5059> (in the sense of playing a stringed instrument)] ▶ **This word refers to a song of insult and disrespect directed at someone; it is also translated song, music, taunt, taunting song.** Ref.: Lam. 3:63. ¶

MOIST – Num. 6:3 ➔ GREEN <3892>.

MOISTEN – ***rāsas*** [verb: רָסַס <7450>; a prim. root] ▶ **This word means to add water to something or to add a water substitute, such as oil, to help mix ingredients together.** Ref.: Ezek. 46:14; KJV: to temper. ¶

MOISTURE – 1 ***riy*** [masc. noun: רִי <7377>; from DRINK ONE'S FILL <7301>] ▶ **This word describes the water taken up into as well as formed within a cloud.** Ref.: Job 37:11 (also translated watering). ¶
– 2 Ps. 32:4 ➔ CAKE BAKED <3955>.

MOLADAH – ***môlāḏāh*** [proper noun: מוֹלָדָה <4137>; from BIRTH (GIVE) <3205>]: birth, place of birth ▶ **A city in the south of Judah.** Refs.: Josh. 15:26; 19:2; 1 Chr. 4:28; Neh. 11:26. ¶

MOLDEN – Ex. 34:17; Lev. 19:4; Deut. 27:15 ➔ COVERING <4541>.

MOLDING – ***zêr*** [masc. noun: זֵר <2213>; from SNEEZE <2237> (in the sense of scattering)] ▶ **This word means a decorative strip, an edging; it is also translated a crown, a border.** It refers to an edging or molding around the ark of the covenant (Ex. 25:11); the table of showbread (Ex. 25:24, 25); and the altar of incense (Ex. 30:3, 4). Other refs.: Ex. 37:2, 11, 12, 26, 27. ¶

MOLDY – ***niqqûḏiym*** [masc. plur. noun: נִקֻּדִים <5350>; from the same as SPECKLED <5348>] ▶ **This word is used to**

describe food, bread that is dry, stale from age, and crumbly. Refs.: Josh. 9:5, 12; also translated crumbled. But it refers also to good, edible baked cakes as well (1 Kgs. 14:3; KJV: cracknel). ¶

MOLE – 1 ***ḥ^aparpārāh, ḥ^apōr pêrāh*** [fem. noun: חֲפַרְפָּרָה, חֲפֹר פֵּרָה <2661>; from DIG <2658>] ▶
a. This word indicates a rodent. It is used in the plural form in Isaiah 2:20. Worthless idols, in the day of judgment, are cast to these vermin. ¶
b. This word indicates a digging rodent. It is possibly developed from the qal infinitive construct of *ḥāpar* and stands in a construct relationship to the noun *pêrāh* (Is. 2:20). ¶
2 ***pêrāh*** [fem. noun: פֵּרָה <6512>; from NOTHING (BRING TO) <6331>] ▶ **This word refers to digging rodents (*ḥ^epor pêrôṯ*).** It may refer to the diggings of moles in their holes and chambers underground or to the moles themselves (Is. 2:20). ¶
– 3 Lev. 11:29 ➔ WEASEL <2467> 4 Lev. 11:30 ➔ WHITE OWL <8580> d.

MOLECH – 1 ***mōleḵ*** [masc. proper noun: מֹלֶךְ <4432>; from KING (BE) <4427>]: king ▶ **A pagan god of the Ammorites to whom, among other abhorrent practices, children were sacrificed.** Refs.: Num. 18:21; Amos 5:26. The name means "king," and possibly the consonants were combined with the vowels of the Hebrew word *bōšeṯ* (<1322>) "shame" to produce Molech. Manasseh may have sacrificed his sons to this god to avert the horrors of warfare (2 Kgs. 23:10). Solomon was reduced to recognize this god (1 Kgs. 11:7). *
– 2 See MALCHAM <4445> b.

MOLEST – Esther 7:8 ➔ SUBDUE <3533>.

MOLID – ***môliyḏ*** [masc. proper noun: מוֹלִיד <4140>; from BIRTH (GIVE) <3205>]: begetter ▶ **A man of the tribe of Judah.** Ref.: 1 Chr. 2:29. ¶

MOLLIFY – Is. 1:6 ➔ FAINT (BE, MAKE) <7401>.

MOLTED – Ex. 34:17; Lev. 19:4; Deut. 27:15 ➔ COVERING <4541>.

MOLTEN – 1 Kgs. 7:16, 23; etc. ➔ CAST (noun) <4165>.

MOLTEN (BE) – Job 28:2 ➔ SMELT <6694>.

MOMENT – ***rega'*** [masc. noun: רֶגַע <7281>; from MOMENT (BE FOR A) <7280>] ▶ **This word means an instant.** It refers to a brief, definite moment in time (Ex. 33:5; Ezra 9:8; Is. 54:8); or to something done at once, instantly (Num. 16:21, 45); suddenly (Ps. 6:10). God's anger lasts only for a brief moment (Ps. 30:5). It is combined in the plural with *l^e* to mean every moment, moment by moment (Ezek. 32:10). At one time . . . at another time is found in Jeremiah 18:7, 9 (*rega'. . . w^erega'*). *

MOMENT (BE FOR A) – ***rāga'*** [verb: רָגַע <7280>; a prim. root] ▶
a. This word means to do something instantaneously, in an instant; to endure only for a short time. It indicates the fleeting life of something: falsity (Prov. 12:19); a passing condition (Jer. 49:19; 50:44).
b. This word means to stir up, to churn up. It is rendered by the NIV to indicate God's churning, agitating the sea (Job 26:12; Is. 51:15; Jer. 31:35). In b. and c., the context is largely responsible for the renderings chosen.
c. This word means to be at rest; to cease struggles; to bring rest. The NASB prefers to render this word much differently, as the opposite of stir up, churn. It renders it in certain places meaning to quiet, to cause to rest, to cease from activity, referring to people, animals, nations, and the seas (Deut. 28:65; Job 26:12; Is. 34:14; 51:4; Jer. 31:2; 47:6; 50:34). It has the sense of establishing in Isaiah 51:4.
d. This word means to break upon. The NIV renders this word to describe the breaking of a person's skin (Job 7:5).
e. A verb meaning to harden; to become crusty. The NASB translates this verb to indicate a hardening of Job's skin (Job 7:5). ¶

MONEY – 1 Ezek. 16:31, 34 ➔ EARNINGS <868> 2 See SILVER <3701>, SILVER <3702>.

MONGREL – Zech. 9:6 ➔ FORBIDDEN UNION (ONE BORN OF) <4464>.

MONITOR LIZARD – Lev. 11:30 ➔ LIZARD (MONITOR) <3581>.

MONKEY – 1 Kgs. 10:22; 2 Chr. 9:21 ➔ PEACOCK <8500> b.

MONTH – 1 ***ḥōḏeš*** [masc. noun: חֹדֶשׁ <2320>; from RENEW <2318>] ▶ **This word means a major division of the year; it also means new moon (first day of the lunar month).** Its use can be put into two categories: (1) the new moon; the day when the crescent moon is once again visible (2 Kgs. 4:23). It is used in various phrases in this sense to indicate the day after the new moon (1 Sam. 20:27); second day of the new moon (1 Sam. 20:34); (2) month; a time marked by thirty days normally. A full month is a *ḥōdeš yāmîm* (Gen. 29:14). Idioms are formed that mean month by (*bᵉ*) month, i.e., an entire month (Num. 28:14); the day of the month is indicated by the preposition *lᵉ*. A child who is *ben-ḥoḏes* is one month old (Lev. 27:6). It is used to indicate the time when a wild donkey is in heat, literally, in her month (heat) (Jer. 2:24). It is used with specific names of months, such as the month of Abib (Ex. 13:4; 23:15; 34:18; Neh. 2:1; Zech. 7:1). From month to month is indicated by *min* (FROM <4480>) + *ḥōḏes* + *lᵉ* + *ḥōḏes* (Esther 3:7). *

2 ***yeraḥ*** [masc. noun: יֶרַח <3391>; from an unused root of uncertain signification] ▶ **This word denotes a period of time, a month, and is probably a more recent word for month than *ḥōdes*.** It is a measure of time (Ex. 2:2; Job 39:2; Zech. 11:8). "A month of time (days)" is formed with *yāmîym* following *yerah* (Deut. 21:13; 2 Kgs. 15:13). *

3 ***yᵉraḥ*** [Aramaic masc. noun: יְרַח <3393>; corresponding to <3391> above] ▶ **This word depicts a period of time and may be used with a particular name attached to it.** Ref.: Ezra 6:15. There were twelve months in a normal year (Dan. 4:29). ¶

MONTHLY PERIOD – Lev. 12:2 ➔ MENSTRUATION <1738>.

MONUMENT – ***ṣiyyûn*** [masc. noun: צִיּוּן <6725>; from the same as DRYNESS <6723> in the sense of conspicuousness (comp. OVERSEE <5329>)] ▶ **This word indicates a roadmark, a guidepost, a sign.** It indicates a monument or a marker set up to recall and explain past significant persons and events (2 Kgs. 23:17; also translated gravestone, tombstone, title); or to serve as guideposts to earmark the way for travelers or to give other instructions (Jer. 31:21: waymark, signpost, roadmark, road marker, road sign; Ezek. 39:15: marker, sign). ¶

MOON – 1 ***yārêaḥ*** [masc. noun: יָרֵחַ <3394>; from the same as MONTH <3391>] ▶ **This word corresponds to the lesser light created by God.** Ref.: Gen. 1:16. It helped mark out the signs, seasons, festivals, days, and months of the year as well as giving light on the earth (Gen. 1:16; 37:9; Ps. 136:9; Is. 3:10; Joel 2:10, 31). It was often worshiped in error as a god (Job 31:26). *

2 ***lᵉḇānāh*** [fem. noun: לְבָנָה <3842>; from WHITE (MAKE) <3835>] ▶ **This word is used to refer to the moon in its full brightness.** It is found in a simile describing the beloved as beautiful and fair as the full moon (*kallᵉḇobāh*) (Song 6:10). Its brightness is, however, eclipsed by the Lord's reigning in Jerusalem in His glory (Is. 24:23). In that day of restoration, the moon will be as bright as the sun (Is. 30:26). ¶

– 3 Deut. 33:14 ➔ PRODUCE (noun) <1645>.

MOORINGS – Jon. 2:6 ➔ FORM (noun) <7095>.

MORASTHITE – ***môraštiy, mōraštiy*** [proper noun: מוֹרַשְׁתִּי, מֹרַשְׁתִּי <4183>; patrial from MORESHETH GATH <4182>] ▶

The prophet Micah was a Morasthite, i.e., an inhabitant of Moreshath Gath (<4182>). Refs.: Jer. 26:18; Mic. 1:1. ¶

MORDECAI – ***mordḵay*** [masc. proper noun: מָרְדֳּכַי <4782>; of foreign deriv.] ▶
a. One of the leaders of the exiles back to Judah from Babylonian exile. He was an aide to Zerubbabel (Ezra 2:2). Other ref.: Neh. 7:7. ¶
b. The cousin of Esther. His name indicates a recognition of or tie to the great Babylonian god Marduk. Like Daniel, he had been given or taken on a name that reflected the nation and culture where he lived. He was from the tribe of Benjamin (Esther 2:5, 6) and had gone into exile at the hands of Nebuchadnezzar.

Through divine providence, Mordecai was able to expose a plot to assassinate the Persian king Xerxes (Esther 2:7–23). And he successfully thwarted, again through a conjunction of events by divine providence, a plan by Haman (possibly an Amalekite) to destroy all the Jews in the empire (Esther 3–7). He encouraged Esther to use her position and power to deliver the Jews (Esther 4:12–17). He was honored highly by the king twice (Esther 6; 10). *

MORE, MORE THAN – ***yôṯêr, yōṯêr*** [masc. noun: יוֹתֵר, יֹתֵר <3148>; act. part. of REMAIN <3498>] ▶ **This word indicates profit, gain; advantage.** It is combined with the proposition *min* (FROM <4480>) after it to express more than . . . (Esther 6:6). The *min* can be separated from *yôṯêr* (Eccl. 6:8). It can take on the meaning of an adverb meaning extremely, excessively, or so very (Eccl. 2:15; 7:16). It can have the meaning of benefit, gain, or advantage (Eccl. 6:11: the better, advantage, profit; 7:11: profit). It has the sense in context sometimes of further, in addition (Eccl. 12:9: moreover, besides, in addition), or of in addition to this, to what has just been said (Eccl. 12:12: further, beyond, in addition). ¶

MORE AND MORE (HAVE) – Jer. 22:15 ➔ COMPETE <8474> b.

MOREH – ***môreh*** [proper noun: מוֹרֶה <4176>; the same as RAIN (noun) <4175> (this Hebrew word also means teacher or teaching)]: teacher ▶ **A plain near Shechem and Gilgal.** Refs.: Gen. 12:6; Deut. 11:30; Judg. 7:1. ¶

MOREOVER – Eccl. 12:9 ➔ MORE, MORE THAN <3148>.

MORESHETH GATH – ***môrešeṯ gaṯ*** [proper noun: מוֹרֶשֶׁת גַּת <4182>; from HEIR (BE) <3423> and GATH <1661>]: possession of Gath (winepress) ▶ **This was probably the birth place of the prophet Micah, a place most likely in the neighborhood of Gath.** Ref.: Mic. 1:14; see 1:1. ¶

MORIAH – ***môriyyāh, mōriyyāh*** [proper noun: מוֹרִיָּה, מֹרִיָּה <4179>; from SEE <7200> and LORD <3050>]: seen by the Lord ▶ **This was the mountain on which Isaac was nearly sacrificed. According to Scripture, it became the location of the Temple mount.** Today the Dome of the Rock stands on top of it, with a large rock under it, believed by some to be the rock on which Abraham had placed Isaac after binding him. Refs.: Gen. 22:2; 2 Chr. 3:1. ¶

MORNING – [1] ***bōqer*** [masc. noun: בֹּקֶר <1242>; from SEEK <1239>] ▶ **This word means daybreak and also next day. It indicates the time when this period of the day arrives and has various nuances.** Refs.: Gen. 29:25; Ex. 10:13; 14:27; Judg. 19:25; Ruth 3:13. It is the opposite of night (Gen. 29:25). It could refer to the time before people can recognize each other (Ruth 3:14). It denotes the coming of sunrise (Judg. 9:33).

To the psalmist, the morning was a time to praise God (Ps. 5:3). Genesis uses the formula: There was evening, and there was morning (Gen. 1:5, 8, 13). The phrase in Daniel 8:14 refers to 2,300 half-days, literally, until evening-morning. The phrase morning by morning (Ex. 16:21; 30:7; 36:3) is used with the verb *šāḵam*, to rise early, and means to rise early in the morning (Gen. 19:27; 20:8; 21:14). *

[2] ***mišḥār*** [masc. noun: מִשְׁחָר <4891>; from SEEK DILIGENTLY <7836. a. (in the sense of to seek early, e.g., at dawn)] ▶ **This word refers to the rising sun in the phrase, from the womb of the dawn** (***mišḥār***). Ref.: Ps. 110:3. ¶
[3] ***nōgah*** [Aramaic fem. noun: נֹגַהּ <5053>; corresponding to BRIGHTNESS <5051>] ▶ **The word refers to daylight.** It is used of sunrise, as soon as the dawn begins. Ref.: Dan. 6:19. ¶
– [4] 2 Sam. 2:29 ➔ BITHRON <1338> [5] Job 3:9; Is. 5:11 ➔ TWILIGHT <5399> [6] Prov. 4:18 ➔ morning sun ➔ shining light ➔ BRIGHTNESS <5051> [7] Is. 26:19 ➔ LIGHT (noun) <219> [8] Jer. 5:8 ➔ LUSTY <7904> b. [9] Ezek. 7:7, 10 ➔ CROWN (noun) <6843> c.

MORNING STAR – ***hêylêl*** [masc. noun: הֵילֵל <1966>; from PRAISE (verb) <1984> (in the sense of brightness)] ▶ **This word refers to the king of Babylon figuratively as the morning star (a planet seen at dawn).** Ref.: Is. 14:12. It is also translated Lucifer (which is from the Latin Vulgate's translation meaning shining one), day star. ¶

MORSEL – 1 Sam. 2:36 ➔ ROUND (SOMETHING) <3603>.

MORSEL (DAINTY, DELICIOUS, CHOICE) – ***lāham*** [verb: לָהַם <3859>; a prim. root] ▶ **This verb means to swallow greedily. As a passive noun, it means something gulped; KJV translates it wound.** It is used to describe gossip as something that most people will swallow whole (Prov. 18:8) and be permeated by it (Prov. 26:22). ¶

MORTAL AGONY – Ps. 42:10 ➔ BREAKING <7524>.

MORTAR – [1] ***m**ḏōḵāh*** [fem. noun: מְדֹכָה <4085>; from BEAT <1743>] ▶ **This was a stone bowl used to beat or grind manna.** Ref.: Num. 11:8. ¶
[2] ***meleṭ*** [masc. noun: מֶלֶט <4423>; from ESCAPE (verb) <4422> (in the sense of smoothness of a material)] ▶ **This word means a building material that could be dug up or into; hence, it refers to clay flooring or grout.** Ref.: Jer. 43:9; also translated clay. ¶
– [3] Ex. 1:14 ➔ MIRE <2563> [4] Prov. 27:22 ➔ HOLLOW PLACE <4388> [5] Ezek. 13:12 ➔ COATING <2915> [6] Zeph. 1:11 ➔ MAKTESH <4389>.

MOSERAH, MOSEROTH – ***môsêrāh, mōsêrôṯ*** [proper noun: מוֹסֵרָה, מֹסֵרוֹת <4149>; fem. of BOND <4147>]: bonds ▶ **A place in the desert where the Israelites camped.** Refs.: Num. 33:30, 31; Deut. 10:6. ¶

MOSES – [1] ***mōšeh*** [masc. proper noun: מֹשֶׁה <4872>; from DRAW <4871>] ▶ **This noun designates the chosen deliverer, prophet, man of God, servant of the Lord, and wise man of Israel in the Old Testament.** His name, based on the Hebrew word and its popular etymology, *māšāh* (<4871>), "to draw out," means the "one who draws out," i.e., delivers, draws out Israel from Egypt through the water of the Red Sea. He was named so by his Egyptian adoptive mother (but possibly by his own Hebrew mother) for she "drew him from the water" (Ex. 2:19).

God chose Moses to deliver His people (Ex. 3:10), to receive the "ten words" and the covenant and its accompanying laws at Sinai (Ex. 19–24), to lead Israel through the wilderness for forty years (Num. 14 to Deut. 34), to perform signs and wonders before Pharaoh and his people (Deut. 34:9–12), to oversee the construction of the Tabernacle and to bless it and Israel (Ex. 39:32–43), and to install his successor, Joshua (Deut. 33; 34:9). He was the covenant human figure in the Pentateuch, but his person and work is seen and felt throughout the Old Testament. Malachi, the last prophet of the Old Testament, cried out, "Remember the law of my servant Moses, the decrees and laws I gave him at Horeb for all Israel" (Mal. 4:4, NIV). Even in Egypt Moses became a great man (Ex. 11:3). *
[2] ***mōšeh*** [Aramaic masc. proper noun: מֹשֶׁה <4873>; corresponding to <4872> above] ▶ **The Aramaic name corresponding to the Hebrew word.** Ref.: Ezra 6:18. ¶

MOST – Job 34:17 ➔ MIGHTY <3524>.

MOST HIGH – 1 ***'illāy*** [Aramaic masc. adj.: עִלָּי <5943>; corresponding to UPPER <5942>] ▶ **This word means highest. It always refers to God and shows the supremacy of God over humanity and other gods.** It can occur as an adjective to modify *ᵉlāh* (<426>), meaning God. Nebuchadnezzar used this term of God to indicate His supremacy in general (Dan. 4:2). Daniel also used this term of God (Dan. 5:18, 21) to reveal the difference between God and Belshazzar, who had lifted up [himself] against the Lord of heaven (see Dan. 5:23). This term can also occur as a noun to represent God, especially in His role as the supreme Ruler of the kingdoms of humanity (Dan. 4:17, 24, 25, 32, 34). Other refs.: Dan. 3:26; 7:25. ¶

2 ***'elyôn*** [masc. noun: עֶלְיוֹן <5945>; from OFFER <5927> (in the sense of to elevate)] ▶ **This word means the Highest. The word serves as an epithet for God and is used thirty-one times in the Old Testament.** The most celebrated use of this word is in Genesis 14:18–20: Melchizedek was priest of God Most High (*'êl 'elyôn*), so the term in context defines the God whom he served. But in this same passage, Abraham equated the God Most High with the Lord his God, the Creator of heaven and earth (Gen. 14:20). In Numbers 24:16, this epithet stands in parallel to the epithet God and Shaddai; it depicts the God who gave Balaam his knowledge and visions. The term also stands in parallel with other names of God, such as the LORD (Deut. 32:8; 2 Sam. 22:14; Ps. 18:13); and God (Ps. 46:4; 50:14). *

3 ***'elyôn*** [Aramaic masc. noun: עֶלְיוֹן <5946>; corresponding to <5945> above] ▶ **This word means Most High God. This term always appears in the plural of majesty, comparable to the Hebrew word *ᵉlōhiym* (GOD <430>).** Furthermore, it always occurs in the construct with *qaddiyš* (HOLY <6922>), meaning the holy ones or saints of the Most High God, and in the context of Daniel's interpretation of Nebuchadnezzar's dream of the four beasts, where four kingdoms were represented (Dan. 7:18, 22, 25, 27). ¶

– 4 2 Sam. 23:1; Hos. 7:16; 11:7 ➔ ABOVE <5920> b.

MOST HOLY PLACE – ***dᵉḇiyr*** [masc. noun: דְּבִיר <1687>; from SPEAK <1696> (apparently in the sense of oracle)] ▶ **This word refers to the innermost part of Solomon's Temple, also called the Holy of Holies.** This cubical room, which took up one-third of the space of the Temple, housed the ark of the covenant (1 Kgs. 6:16, 19–23). The ark contained the original tablets of the Ten Commandments, was overarched by carved cherubim covered with gold, and was especially associated with God's presence. When it was first brought into the Holy of Holies, God's glory filled the Temple (1 Kgs. 8:6; cf. 1 Kgs. 8:10). In Psalm 28:2, David spoke of lifting his hands to the *dᵉḇiyr*. Since the Temple had not yet been built, this likely referred to the heavenly reality that was the model for the Temple and earlier Tabernacle (cf. Ps. 18:6; Heb. 8:5; 9:3–5) or perhaps to the room in the Tabernacle that housed the ark of the covenant. Other refs.: 1 Kgs. 6:5; 7:49; 8:8; 2 Chr. 3:16; 4:20; 5:7, 9. ¶

MOTH – ***'āš*** [masc. noun: עָשׁ <6211>; from WASTE AWAY <6244> (in the sense of to consume)] ▶ **This word refers to a rather fragile but destructive four-winged insect.** The fragility of human life is indicated by the fact that a moth can destroy houses of earth or clay, that is people made of clay (Job 4:19). These insects were known to be destructive (Job 13:28), eating human clothing and garments. It is used in a metaphor speaking of Job's body and in other similes (Ps. 39:11). Figuratively, it describes the consuming of the enemies of Isaiah (Is. 50:9; 51:8). The Lord pictures Himself as a moth consuming Ephraim in a time of judgment (Hos. 5:12). Other ref.: Job 27:18. ¶

MOTHER – ***'êm*** [fem. noun: אֵם <517>; a prim. word] ▶ **A woman with children.** Refs.: Ex. 20:12; Ps. 35:14. The word may also signify a female ancestor, animals, or humans in general (Gen. 3:20; 1 Kgs. 15:13). A nation or city is sometimes viewed as the mother of its people. So in that sense, this word is sometimes used to refer to a nation (Is. 50:1; Hos. 2:2, 5). *

MOTHER-IN-LAW – 1 ***ḥamôṯ*** [fem. noun: חָמוֹת <2545>; fem. of FATHER-IN-LAW <2524>] ▶ **This word is often used of Naomi, mother-in-law of the Moabitess, Ruth. Hence, it refers here to one's husband's mother.** Refs.: Ruth 1:14; 2:11, 18, 19, 23; 3:1, 6, 16, 17. Normally, there is unity and peace between mother-in-law and daughter-in-law reflecting God's will, but the presence of hostility is considered a failure among God's people (Mic. 7:6). ¶ – 2 Deut. 27:23 ➔ MARRIAGE <2859> c.

MOTHER-OF-PEARL – ***dar*** [masc. noun: דַּר <1858>; apparently from the same as FREEDOM <1865>] ▶ **This word refers to something white.** It is used once to describe one of the precious and luxurious materials in the flooring of Xerxes' or Ahasuerus' palace (Esther 1:6). ¶

MOTTLED – ***bārōḏ*** [adj.: בָּרֹד <1261>; from HAIL (verb) <1258>] ▶ **This word describes male goats and sheep marked with different colors.** Refs.: Gen. 31:10, 12: mottled, gray-spotted, grisled, spotted. It refers also to horses drawing one of the chariots in Zechariah's vision (Zech. 6:3, 6: grisled, dappled). It features either different shades or different colors or both. ¶

MOUND – 1 Josh. 11:13; Jer. 30:18; 49:2 ➔ HEAP (noun) <8510> 2 Song 7:2 ➔ HEAP (noun) <6194> 3 Is. 29:3 ➔ TOWER <4674> 4 Ezek. 43:13 ➔ BACK <1354>.

MOUNT – 1 Ex. 25:7 ➔ SETTING <4396> 2 Is. 29:3 ➔ TOWER <4674>.

MOUNT UP – 1 Ps. 89:9 ➔ ARISE <7721> 2 Is. 9:18 ➔ ROLL UPWARD <55>.

MOUNTAIN – 1 ***har*** [masc. noun: הַר <2022>; a shortened form of <2042> below] ▶ **This word indicates an important elevation of land; it means also a hill, a hill country, a mountain range**. With a following modifying word, it may mean a mountain range, such as the mountains or hill country of Gilead (Gen. 31:21; cf. Deut. 1:7; Josh. 17:15; Judg. 12:15) or denote individual mountains or Mount Ebal (Deut. 11:29). It indicates a particular mountain from the context without naming it (Gen. 22:2). Combined with the word for God, *ᵉlohiym*, preceding, it points out the mountain of God (Ex. 4:27; 18:5; 24:13; Ps. 68:15) or mountain of the Lord used with *yhwh* (GOD <3068>) (Num. 10:33). These mountains and hills were sacred places for the gods of the pagan peoples of Canaan (Deut. 12:2), also called gods of the mountains (1 Kgs. 20:23). It refers to the *har-mō'ēḏ* or the mountain of assembly, a dwelling place of the gods (Is. 14:13). The word is used in a figurative sense often: the Lord weighs the mountains in His hand (Is. 40:12) and can lay them waste as a sign of His judgments (Is. 42:15). God causes His people to thresh the mountains as a sign of their defeating their foes (Is. 41:15). God calls the mountains as His witnesses (Mic. 6:2) and speaks to them (Ezek. 36:1, 4, 8). They are expected to praise the Lord (Ps. 148:9), and they leap in praise (Ps. 114:4, 6). The mountains symbolize strength (Is. 2:14); great age, antiquity, and stability (Prov. 8:25), yet the Lord's love is even more enduring (Is. 54:10). *

2 ***hārār*** [masc. noun: הָרָר <2042>; from an unused root meaning to loom up] ▶ **This word refers to a region of hill country or mountainous terrain.** Of the Horites (Gen. 14:6); of the East (Num. 23:7); a place from which copper is obtained (Deut. 8:9); a region of ancient hill country or mountains (Deut. 33:15); a symbol for personal strength and stability (Ps. 30:7; cf. Hab. 3:6); of righteousness as permanent as the mountains of God (Ps. 36:6); a place where leopards dwell (Song 4:8); a symbol for Judah, God's mountain (Jer. 17:3). *

3 ***ṭûr*** [Aramaic masc. noun: טוּר <2906>; corresponding to ROCK <6697>] ▶ **This word refers to a large high point of land, representing God's kingdom.** It fills the

whole earth in Nebuchadnezzar's first great dream (Dan. 2:35, 45). ¶

MOUNTAIN GOAT – Deut. 14:5 ➔ IBEX <1788>.

MOUNTAIN SHEEP – ***zemer*** [masc. noun: זֶמֶר <2169>; apparently from SING <2167> or PRUNE <2168>] ▶ **This word denotes a gazelle; it is also translated a chamois.** It was one of the animals the Israelites could eat (Deut. 14:5), and, hence, was clean. ¶

MOUNTAINSIDE – Song 2:14 ➔ CLIFF <4095>.

MOUNTED (BE) – Ex. 25:7; 35:9, 27 ➔ SETTING <4394>.

MOUNTING – Ex. 39:13 ➔ SETTING <4396>.

MOURN – [1] ***'aḇal*** [verb: אָבַל <56>; a prim. root] ▶ **This word means to express sadness in its simple verb forms; it is also translated to grieve, to lament.** Those who mourn are persons who mourn for looking at God's coming judgments (Is. 19:8; Amos 8:8; 9:5). But figuratively, the gates of the city of Zion mourn because of her desolation (Is. 3:26) as does the earth itself (Is. 24:4) when God comes in judgment (Is. 33:9; cf. Amos 1:2). In the reflexive use of the verb, it indicates mourning for the dead (Gen. 37:34); for Jerusalem (Is. 66:10); over a particular person (1 Sam. 15:35; 16:1); or over sin or judgment (Ex. 33:4; Neh. 8:9). It is also used to indicate that God causes mourning (Lam. 2:8; Ezek. 31:15). In both cases, the word is used in a figurative sense. In the first instance, He causes the deep to mourn over Assyria, and in the second case, He causes the wall of Jerusalem to mourn over the fall of the city which it (the wall) was to surround and protect. *
[2] ***sāp̄aḏ*** [verb: סָפַד <5594>; a prim. root] ▶ **This word means to lament, to bewail.** It means to mourn for someone, to weep, to cry (Gen. 23:2; 50:10; Is. 32:12). In its passive sense, it means to be mourned over (Jer. 16:4–6; 25:33). In its participial forms, it refers to professional wailers or mourners (Eccl. 12:5; Zech. 12:12). *
– [3] Ps. 55:2 ➔ RESTLESS (BE, BECOME, GROW) <7300> [4] Ps. 88:9 ➔ SORROW (verb) <1669> [5] Prov. 5:11; Ezek. 24:23 ➔ ROAR (verb) <5098> [6] Prov. 29:2 ➔ GROAN (verb) <584> [7] Is. 19:8 ➔ LAMENT <578> [8] Is. 29:2 ➔ MOURNING <8386> [9] Joel 1:8 ➔ LAMENT <421> [10] Zeph. 3:18 ➔ AFFLICT <3013>.

MOURNER – [1] Job 29:25; Ps. 35:14; Is. 57:18; 61:2, 3 ➔ MOURNING <57> [2] Eccl. 12:5 ➔ MOURN <5594> [3] Hos. 9:4 ➔ NOTHINGNESS <205>.

MOURNERS (AS, LIKE) – Mal. 3:14 ➔ MOURNFULLY <6941>.

MOURNFUL – Mic. 2:4 ➔ BITTER, BITTERLY <5093>.

MOURNFULLY – ***qᵉḏōranniyṯ*** [adv.: קְדֹרַנִּית <6941>; from DARK (BE) <6937>] ▶ **This word describes the manner of those who acted as mourners (i.e., darkened, blackish, referring to those who were gloomy in their countenances or in the dark mourning attire of sackcloth).** It is used only once in the Old Testament (Mal. 3:14). ¶

MOURNING – [1] ***'āḇēl*** [adj.: אָבֵל <57>; from MOURN <56>] ▶ **This word means sorrowing, and, as a noun, mourner(s).** It describes Jacob's mourning for Joseph's supposed death (Gen. 37:35). It describes mourning for imminent calamity (Esther 6:12; also translated in grief). It functions as a noun in several passages (Job 29:25; Ps. 35:14; Is. 57:18; 61:2, 3). Other ref.: Lam. 1:4. ¶
[2] ***'ēḇel*** [masc. noun: אֵבֶל <60>; from MOURN <56>] ▶ **The word indicates manifestation of sorrow.** It may be for the dead (Gen. 27:41) or for calamity (Esther 4:3; 9:22; Job 30:31). In Isaiah 61:3 and 2 Samuel 14:2, it seems to indicate a garment for mourning, as well as mourning itself. A period of mourning is also depicted by the word (2 Sam. 11:27; Eccl. 7:2, 4). *

3 ***b^eḵiyṯ*** [fem. noun: בְּכִית <1068>; from WEEP <1058>] ▶ **This word means and is also translated weeping.** It depicts a period of mourning (Gen. 50:4). In the case of Jacob's death, the period may have been as long as 110 days. ¶
4 ***marzêaḥ*** [masc. noun: מַרְזֵחַ <4798>; formed like BANQUETING <4797> (i.e., from a root meaning to scream; e.g., a cry of grief)] ▶ **This word refers to a funeral meal.** It indicates a meal; in context a meal of mourning because of calamity and distress (Jer. 16:5; Amos 6:7). For Amos 6:7, see BANQUETING <4797> also. ¶
5 ***ta^aniyyāh*** [fem. noun: תַּאֲנִיָּה <8386>; from LAMENT <578>] ▶ **This word describes the emotional response of feeling sorry for someone or something, grieving for some reason.** Ref.: Is. 29:2: lamenting, heaviness, moaning, to mourn. It is a response toward great loss (Lam. 2:5). ¶
– 6 Deut. 26:14 ➔ NOTHINGNESS <205> 7 Ps. 30:11; Is. 22:12; Jer. 6:26; 48:38; Ezek. 27:31; Joel 2:12; Mic. 1:8; Zech. 12:10, 11 ➔ LAMENTATION <4553> 8 Is. 29:2 ➔ LAMENTATION <592> 9 Jer. 31:15 ➔ WAILING <5092> 10 Ezek. 2:10 ➔ RUMBLING <1899> 11 Ezek. 31:15: to cause mourning ➔ MOURN <56>.

MOURNING (IN) – Mal. 3:14 ➔ MOURNFULLY <6941>.

MOURNING APPAREL – 2 Sam. 14:2 ➔ MOURNING <60>.

MOURNING CLOTHES – 2 Sam. 14:2 ➔ MOURNING <60>.

MOURNING GARMENTS – 2 Sam. 14:2 ➔ MOURNING <60>.

MOURNS (AS ONE) – Zech. 12:10 ➔ LAMENTATION <4553>.

MOURNS (ONE WHO) – Job 29:25; Ps. 35:14; Is. 57:18; 61:2, 3 ➔ MOURNING <57>.

MOUSE – ***'aḵbār*** [masc. noun: עַכְבָּר <5909>; prob. from the same as SPIDER <5908> (in the secondary sense of attacking, e.g., nibbling)] ▶ **This word is used of a rodent, often infesting dwellings.** It was an unclean "swarming thing" to Israel and therefore not edible (Lev. 11:29). Other refs.: 1 Sam. 6:4, 5, 11, 18; Is. 66:17. ¶

MOUTH – 1 ***ḥêḵ*** [masc. noun: חֵךְ <2441>; prob. from DEDICATE <2596> in the sense of tasting] ▶ **This word refers to the roof or upper palate of one's oral cavity, which is used extensively to form sounds and words.** Ref.: Ps. 137:6. Its failure to function makes one mute (Ezek. 3:26). It indicates the sensation of the sweet taste of honey (Ps. 119:103: taste); or figuratively of the pleasant, sweet taste of love (Song 2:3; 5:16). The palate senses the taste of food (Job 12:11: mouth, palate, tongue). It is used figuratively of one's ability to discern calamities (Job 6:30: mouth, taste, palate). It is used to mean speech, the place where speech is formed (Prov. 5:3; 8:7). In a case of extreme thirst, one's tongue sticks to a person's palate (Lam. 4:4). *
2 ***miḏbār*** [masc. noun: מִדְבָּר <4057>; from SPEAK <1696>] ▶ **This word refers to the human organ of talking, the mouth.** But in context its beauty and pleasantness are stressed (Song 4:3; KJV: speech). It stands in parallel usage to lips which precedes it in the previous line. The Hebrew word also refers to a desert, a wilderness; see DESERT (noun) <4057>. ¶
3 ***peh*** [masc. sing. noun: פֶּה <6310>; from PIECES (CUT TO) <6284>] ▶ **Besides the literal meaning, this term is used as the instrument of speech and figuratively for speech itself.** When Moses claimed to be an ineffective speaker, he was heavy of mouth (Ex. 4:10); the psalmist also uses *peh* to mean speech (Ps. 49:13; Eccl. 10:13; Is. 29:13). The word is rendered edge in the expression the mouth of the sword (Judg. 4:16; Prov. 5:4); or in some measurements from edge to edge or end to end (2 Kgs. 10:21; 21:16; Ezra 9:11). It is also used for other openings like those in caves, gates, wells, or sacks. In land and inheritance references, it is translated as share or portion (Deut. 21:17; 2 Kgs. 2:9; Zech. 13:8). With

the preposition *lᵉ*, it means in proportion to or according to. *

4 ***pum*** [Aramaic masc. noun: פֻּם <6433>; prob. for <6310> above] ▶ **This is the human organ that produces words, whether righteous or evil.** Ref.: Dan. 4:31. It is used figuratively of the front opening of a cave or den (Dan. 6:17). Figuratively in literature, it personifies an object, makes it represent a person (Dan. 7:5, 8, 20). The word is also used in relation to lions (Dan. 6:22). ¶

– 5 Dan. 3:26 ➔ COURT <8651>.

MOVE – 1 ***ḥāraṣ*** [verb: חָרַץ <2782>; a prim. root] ▶ **This verb indicates to act promptly, sharply, to decide, to move against, to maim, to be eager for something.** It indicates a cutting or maiming that an animal has that makes it unacceptable for sacrifice (Lev. 22:22: maimed, mutilated). Of a dog it means to snarl or move against (Ex. 11:7: growl, bark, move *its tongue*); of persons it means to utter a word against, speak sharply against (Josh. 10:21: move *the tongue*, utter *a word*). It means to determine, to define, to decide something (2 Sam. 5:24: to advance quickly, to bestir oneself, to act promptly, to rise oneself, to move quickly; 1 Kgs. 20:40: to decide, to pronounce); in its passive usage, it means something fixed, determined (Job 14:5). It refers to something set or determined or decreed (Is. 10:23; 28:22; Dan. 9:27). The judgments of God are firmly and strictly determined (Dan. 11:36) and will come to pass. Other refs.: Is. 10:22; Dan. 9:26. ¶

2 ***nāsag*** [verb: נָסַג <5253>; a prim. root] ▶ **This word means to move away (turn back), to be turned.** It means to change something from what it was, possibly by moving it: a boundary, a boundary marker (Deut. 19:14; 27:17; Prov. 22:28; 23:10; also translated to remove); any object (Mic. 6:14). It is used figuratively of being turned away from God, justice (Is. 59:13, 14); changing God's standards (Hos. 5:10). It describes God's accusations and reproaches of the people being turned back (Mic. 2:6). ¶

3 ***'āṯaq*** [verb: עָתַק <6275>; a prim. root] ▶ **This word means to proceed, to grow old; it is also translated to remove, to proceed, to go.** It indicates going from one place to another (Gen. 12:8); leaving a location under pressure (Gen. 26:22). It describes figuratively God's moving of mountains (Job 9:5). It describes the weakening of the eyes as the person grows old (Ps. 6:7: to become old, to wax old, to grow weak, to fail). It is used of copying literary works from one location to another, transcribing them (Prov. 25:1: to copy, to transcribe, to compile). Other refs.: Job 14:18; 18:4; 21:7; 32:15 (to escape, to fail, to leave off). ¶

– 4 Gen. 1:2 ➔ HOVER <7363> 5 Deut. 19:14; Hos. 5:10 ➔ TURN BACK <5472> 6 Judg. 13:25 ➔ TROUBLED (BE) <6470> 7 Ps. 99:1 ➔ SHAKE <5120> 8 Is. 33:20 ➔ FOLD (verb) <6813> 9 Jer. 10:4 ➔ STUMBLE <6328>.

MOVE FOR – Esther 5:9 ➔ TREMBLE <2111>.

MOVE OUT – Job 37:1 ➔ LEAP <5425>.

MOVED (BE) – 1 Ps. 10:6; etc. ➔ REMOVED (BE) <4131> 2 Jer. 25:16; 46:7, 8 ➔ SHAKE <1607>.

MOVED (BE DEEPLY) – Gen. 43:30; 1 Kgs. 3:26 ➔ YEARN <3648>.

MOVES (ALL THAT, EVERYTHING THAT, WHATEVER) – Ps. 50:11; 80:13 ➔ MOVING CREATURES <2123>.

MOVING – Job 16:5 ➔ COMFORT (noun) <5205> b.

MOVING CREATURES – ***ziyz*** [masc. coll. noun: זִיז <2123>; from an unused root apparently meaning to be conspicuous] ▶ **This word indicates living creatures; it is also translated insect, wild beast.** These are small creatures that inhabit fields and belong to God's creation (Ps. 50:11). It is used figuratively of those who feed on Israel, contributing to its destruction (Ps. 80:13). The Hebrew word also means abundance; see ABUNDANCE <2123>. ¶

MOWING – Ps. 72:6; Amos 7:1 ➔ SHEARING <1488>.

MOWN GRASS, MOWN FIELD – Ps. 72:6 ➔ SHEARING <1488>.

MOZA – ***môṣā'*** [masc. proper noun: מוֹצָא <4162>; the same as GOING OUT, GOING FORTH <4161>]: exit, fountain ▶
a. A son of Caleb. Ref.: 1 Chr. 2:46. ¶
b. A descendant of Saul. Refs.: 1 Chr. 8:36, 37; 9:42, 43. ¶

MOZAH – ***mōṣāh*** [proper noun: מֹצָה <4681>; act. part. fem. of DRAIN <4680>]: drained ▶ **A city of the tribe of Benjamin.** Ref.: Josh. 18:26. ¶

MUCH – ***mirbāh*** [fem. noun: מִרְבָּה <4767>; from MANY (BE) <7235>] ▶ **This word signifies abundance. It indicates a large amount of something.** In context it refers to the impending judgments coming on Judah (Ezek. 23:32). ¶

MUD – 1 ***bōṣ*** [masc. noun: בֹּץ <1206>; prob. the same as FINE LINEN <948>] ▶ **This word describes wet, soggy, muddy ground; it also means salt, mire.** It is used figuratively in a metaphorical expression to depict the failure of Zedekiah to act and do what Jeremiah was telling him to do. The king thus would be sunk in the mud, unable to act (Jer. 38:22). ¶
2 ***ṭiyṭ*** [masc. noun: טִיט <2916>; from an unused root meaning apparently to be sticky (rather perhaps a demons. from SWEEP <2894>, through the idea of dirt to be swept away)] ▶ **This word denotes mire, clay.** It describes the foul clay mud at the bottom of a cistern (Jer. 38:6); the mud in which a crocodile lies (Job 41:30); the muck brought up by the sea (Is. 57:20; also translated dirt). It is used of the more valuable clay used by a potter (Is. 41:25); clay of bricks (Nah. 3:14) or walls. It is used in the figurative language of similes: an enemy is trampled like mire in the streets (Mic. 7:10; Zech. 10:5); enemies are poured out like mire into the streets (Ps. 18:42); gold is piled up like the mud or mire in the streets; it is everywhere (Zech. 9:3); the Lord delivers His faithful follower from the mire of the streets (Ps. 69:14). Other refs.: 2 Sam. 22:43; Ps. 40:2 (clay, bog). ¶
– 3 Is. 10:6 ➔ MIRE <2563>.

MUDDLED – Prov. 25:26 ➔ FOUL <7515>.

MUDDY – 1 ***mirpaś*** [masc. noun: מִרְפַּשׂ <4833>; from FOUL <7515> (in the sense of to make muddy by trampling)] ▶ **This word means that which is marked with mud, made to resemble mud.** It describes water made muddy, fouled by the trampling of the feet of animals (Ezek. 34:19; also translated to foul). ¶
– 2 Ezek. 32:2, 13 ➔ TROUBLE (verb) <1804> 3 Ezek. 32:2; 34:18 ➔ FOUL <7515>.

MUFFLER – Is. 3:19 ➔ VEIL <7479>.

MULBERRY TREE – See BALSAM TREE <1057>.

MULE – 1 ***yêm*** [masc. noun: יֵם <3222>; from the same as DAY <3117> (in the sense of hot)] ▶
a. A masculine noun referring to a pack animal and work animal. Some of which ran wild (Gen. 36:24, KJV) in the open fields. ¶
b. A masculine noun indicating hot springs. It is understood as referring to hot springs by recent translators (ESV, NIV, NASB; Gen. 36:24). Some have suggested vipers as a translation. ¶
2 ***pereḏ*** [masc. noun: פֶּרֶד <6505>; from DIVIDE <6504> (perhaps in the sense of being separated, not mixing with others)] ▶ **This word depicts the offspring of a donkey and a horse; this product of mixed species is nearly always sterile.** It indicates a beast of burden and transportation but also a valuable piece of property (2 Sam. 13:9). It and the horse were known for their need to be contained and guided; they were without understanding (Ps. 32:9). *
3 ***pirdāh*** [fem. noun: פִּרְדָּה <6506>; fem. of <6505> above] ▶ **This word indicates a female mule. It is a female cross between a donkey and horse. A mule was valuable**

property. In context it refers to a mule belonging to King David. Riding on it gave the rider some claim to royalty and supposedly the support of the king (1 Kgs. 1:33, 38, 44). ¶
– 4 Esther 8:10, 14 ➔ HORSE <7409> c.

MULTICOLORED – 1 ***beromiym*** [masc. plur. noun: בְּרֹמִים <1264>; prob. of foreign origin] ▶ **This word means of different colors; it also means of two colors.** It refers to multicolored rugs or carpets (Ezek. 27:24; also translated many colors, colored material), which were part of Tyre's rich export trade with the Mediterranean world; KJV and NKJV translate: chests of multicolored (rich) apparel. ¶
– 2 Ezek. 16:165 ➔ SPOTTED (BE) <2921>.

MULTIPLY – 1 ***kāḇar*** [verb: כָּבַר <3527>; a prim. root] ▶ **This word means to increase.** It is used of producing an overabundance of words (Job 35:16). Its use as a participle indicates the abundant production of something (Job 36:31: in abundance). ¶
2 ***'āthar*** [verb: עָתַר <6280>; a prim. root] ▶ **This word means to make larger, be more numerous, or to do often.** In context it refers to enemies of God, emphasizing and increasing their words against Him (Ezek. 35:13). It has the sense of being alluring or deceitful, false like the kisses of an enemy (Prov. 27:6; also translated to be profuse). ¶
3 ***šāraṣ*** [verb: שָׁרַץ <8317>; a prim. root] ▶
a. This word means to teem, to swarm in numbers and rate of birth and multiplication. It is used of the land and waters swarming with swarming creatures (Gen. 1:20, 21; Ex. 8:3; Ps. 105:30). It is used figuratively of Israel's birth rate in Egypt, her unusual multiplication (Ex. 1:7). Certain swarming things were unclean to Israel (Lev. 11:29, 41, 43, 46). But swarming creatures will be part of the new rejuvenated Israel (Ezek. 47:9).
b. A verb indicating to creep. The same verb (or its homonym) refers to creeping things, insects, lizards, etc., on the earth (Gen. 7:21; Lev. 11:29, 41, 42, 43, 46). These things were detestable to Israel. *
– 4 Dan. 4:1; 6:25 ➔ GROW <7680>.

MULTITUDE – 1 ***'ᵃsapsup*** [masc. noun: אֲסַפְסֻף <628>; by reduplication from STOREHOUSE <624>] ▶ **This word means a gathering or mixed crowd.** It is related to *'āsap̱* (GATHER <622>). It occurs only in Numbers 11:4; it is also translated rabble. ¶
2 ***hāmôn, hāman*** [masc. noun and verb: הָמוֹן, הָמַן <1995>; from MURMUR <1993>] ▶
a. A masculine noun denoting a crowd, noise, tumult. It often describes the sound or tumult of a crowd of people (2 Kgs. 7:13; Ps. 65:7; Is. 13:4; 33:3; Dan. 10:6) or of a city (Is. 5:14; 32:14; Ezek. 26:13) or of an army or troop (1 Sam. 14:19; 2 Sam. 18:29). But it also describes the roar of nature in the rain (1 Kgs. 18:41) or the rumbling of chariot wheels (Jer. 47:3). It especially is used of the tumult and roar of huge multitudes: great armies (Judg. 4:7; 1 Sam. 14:16; 1 Kgs. 20:13, 28); an entire nation (2 Sam. 6:19; Is. 5:13). In general usage, it also indicates wealth (Ps. 37:16) and a great supply or mass of things (1 Chr. 29:16; 2 Chr. 31:10; Jer. 49:32). *
b. A verb indicating to multiply. It indicates the multiplication of the people of Israel (Ezek. 5:7; KJV, NKJV) and Jerusalem. ¶
c. A verb meaning to be in turmoil. It depicts the turmoil and tumult of Israel (Ezek. 5:7; NASB, NIV, NKJV). ¶
– 3 2 Chr. 30:18 ➔ INCREASE (noun) <4768> 4 Ps. 42:4 (first mention) ➔ THRONG (noun) <5519> 5 Is. 60:6; Ezek. 26:10 ➔ ABUNDANCE <8229> 6 Jer. 52:15 ➔ CRAFTSMAN <527>.

MUNITION – Nah. 2:1 ➔ FORTIFIED PLACE <4694>.

MUPPIM – ***muppiym*** [masc. proper noun: מֻפִּים <4649>; apparently from SPRINKLE <5130>]: wavings ▶ **A son of Benjamin.** Ref.: Gen. 46:21. ¶

MURDER – 1 Ezek. 21:22 ➔ BREAKING <7524> 2 See KILL <2026>.

MURKY – Prov. 25:26 ➔ FOUL <7515>.

MURMUR – [1] ***hāmāh*** [verb: הָמָה <1993>; a prim. root; comp. STIR (verb) <1949>] ▶ **This Hebrew word means to say something quietly; it also means to growl, to roar, to howl. It takes its specific meaning from its context.** Its basic renderings are: (1) to indicate a strong emotional response by birds or animals (Ps. 59:6; Is. 59:11; Ezek. 7:16), often used in a simile or comparison; (2) to indicate the murmuring of one's soul in distress (Ps. 42:5; 11; Ps. 55:17; 77:3 but also of musical instruments (Is. 16:11; Jer. 48:36); (3) to describe the sound or roar of waves or great multitudes of people (Is. 51:15; Jer. 5:22; 31:35); to depict the noise or uproar of a city (1 Kgs. 1:41; Is. 22:2); (4) to describe the uproar or commotion of people in general (Ps. 39:6). It indicates the restlessness of the human heart (Jer. 4:19) or of humankind itself (Ps. 77:3). *

[2] ***liyn, lûn*** [verb: לִין, לוּן <3885>; a prim. root] ▶ **This word means and is also translated to complain, to grumble.** It refers to the Israelites' complaining during their escape from Egypt and their wandering in the desert (Ex. 15:24; 16:2, 7, 8; 17:3; Num. 14:2, 27, 29, 36; 16:11, 41; 17:5). It is also used of the people's justified grumbling against the leaders of Israel (Josh. 9:18); and of the violent attacks of enemies on righteous persons (Ps. 59:15). The Hebrew word also means to rest, to tarry; see LODGE <3885>. ¶

[3] ***rāgan*** [verb: רָגַן <7279>; a prim. root] ▶ **This word means to complain; it is also translated to grumble, to criticize.** It refers to Israel's complaining, murmuring in the wilderness against the Lord (Deut. 1:27; Ps. 106:25). It indicates excessive complaining in a way that evokes relational problems among persons (Prov. 16:28: see WHISPERER <5372>). It means a gossiper, a whisperer, a trouble causer (Prov. 18:8; 26:20, 22: see WHISPERER <5372>). It describes an act of criticism, complaining, faultfinding (Is. 29:24). ¶

MURMURING – Ex. 16:7–9, 12; Num. 14:27; 17:5, 10 ➔ GRUMBLING <8519>.

MUSCLE – ***šāriyr*** [masc. noun: שָׁרִיר <8306>; from ENEMY <8324> in the original sense as in NAVEL <8270>] ▶ **This word describes the powerful stomach muscles (body tissues that can produce movement) of Leviathan.** Ref.: Job 40:16; KJV: navel. ¶

MUSHI – ***mûšiy*** [masc. proper noun: מוּשִׁי <4187>; from FEEL <4184>]: sensitive ▶ **A Levite, son of Merari.** Refs.: Ex. 6:19; Num. 3:20; 1 Chr. 6:19, 47; 23:21, 23; 24:26, 30. ¶

MUSHITE – ***mûšiy*** [proper noun: מוּשִׁי <4188>; patron. from MUSHI <4187>] ▶ **Member of a family descending from Mushi.** Refs.: Num. 3:33; 26:58. ¶

MUSIC – [1] ***zᵉmār*** [Aramaic masc. noun: זְמָר <2170>; from a root corresponding to SING <2167>] ▶ **This word refers to musical sounds and instruments.** Refs.: Dan. 3:5, 7, 10, 15. They were heard at the dedication of Nebuchadnezzar's great image. ¶

– [2] Ps. 81:2; Amos 5:23 ➔ SONG <2172> [3] Is. 14:11 ➔ NOISE <1998> [4] Lam. 3:63 ➔ MOCKING SONG <4485> [5] Lam. 5:14 ➔ SONG <5058> a.

MUSICAL INSTRUMENT – Eccl. 2:8 ➔ CONCUBINE <7705>.

MUSICIAN – [1] Judg. 5:11 ➔ DIVIDE <2686> b. [2] Ezra 7:24 ➔ SINGER <2171> [3] Dan. 6:18 ➔ ENTERTAINMENT <1761>.

MUSING – Ps. 39:3 ➔ MEDITATION <1901>.

MUSTACHE – 2 Sam. 19:24; Ezek. 24:17, 22 ➔ BEARD <8222>.

MUSTER – [1] Neh. 3:31 ➔ INSPECTION <4663> [2] Mic. 5:1 ➔ GATHER <1413>.

MUTE – [1] ***'illêm*** [adj.: אִלֵּם <483>; from BIND <481>] ▶ **This word describes one**

who cannot speak; it is also translated speechless, dumb, who cannot speak, that cannot speak. God makes whom He will dumb or mute (Prov. 31:8). The mute will be able to speak when the Lord's full salvation is realized (Is. 35:6). The Lord's prophetic spokesmen are not to be mute but to proclaim His will. His Spirit loosens their tongues. One's enemies and fear can make a person like a mute or dumb person (Ps. 38:13). Pagan idols are mute, useless things (Hab. 2:18). Other refs.: Ex. 4:11; Is. 56:10. ¶
– [2] Hab. 2:19 ➔ SILENCE (noun) <1748>.

MUTE (BE, BECOME) – Ps. 31:18; 39:2, 9; Ezek. 3:26 ➔ BIND <481>.

MUTH-LABBEN – ***mûṯ labbên*** [phrase: מוּת לַבֵּן <4192>; from DIE <4191> and SON <1121> with the prep. and art. interposed]: death of the son ▶ **This phrase is found only in the superscription at the top of Psalm 9. It is part of the musical directions for the singing of this psalm, yet the meaning is ambiguous.** Various renderings have been offered by interpreters, the most likely options being that the phrase is either a title of a tune to which the psalm was to be sung or that the phrase means "death to the son" or "to die for the son." Also possible is the combination of these two options, namely, that the phrase is a title of a tune called "Death to the Son"/ "To die for the Son" to which Psalm 9 was to be sung. ¶

MUTILATED – Lev. 22:22 ➔ MOVE <2782>.

MUZZLE (noun) – ***maḥsôm*** [masc. noun: מַחְסוֹם <4269>; from MUZZLE (verb) <2629>] ▶ **This was something used to keep a person's mouth shut, possibly a piece of thin metal over one's mouth.** Ref.: Ps. 39:1; also translated bridle. ¶

MUZZLE (verb) – ***ḥāsam*** [verb: חָסַם <2629>; a prim. root] ▶ **This verb also means to block. It describes muzzling an ox as it is threshing (i.e., covering or fastening the animal's mouth to keep it shut).** Ref.: Deut. 25:4. It takes on the idea of hindering, obstructing travel (Ezek. 39:11: to block, to obstruct, to stop). ¶

MYRIAD – [1] ***rᵉḇāḇāh*** [fem. noun: רְבָבָה <7233>; from MANY (BE, BECOME) <7231>] ▶ **This word means ten thousand, countless.** It indicates great multitudes of people or things, thousands of ten thousands (Gen. 24:60); a number that cannot be counted (Num. 10:36). It indicates figuratively that Israel's hundred will chase ten thousands of the enemy (Lev. 26:8; Deut. 32:30; Ps. 91:7). It refers to multitudes of heavenly beings (Deut. 33:2); or to the multitudes of Israel (Deut. 33:17). It is used in proverbs and idioms to express a great multitude (Song 5:10; Mic. 6:7). *
[2] ***ribbô*** [fem. noun: רִבּוֹ <7239>; from MANY (BE, BECOME) <7231>] ▶ **This word also means ten thousand; a thousand.** It refers to a host that cannot be numbered, usually translated as ten thousand: persons (Ezra 2:64; Neh. 7:66; Jon. 4:11). The number intended is indefinite sometimes (Dan. 11:12); of things: of numerical values: 10,000 darics, 18,000 talents of brass (1 Chr. 29:7); 61,000 drachmas (Ezra 2:69), etc. It refers to twice ten thousand chariots (Ps. 68:17). *
[3] ***ribbô*** [Aramaic fem. noun: רִבּוֹ <7240>; corresponding to <7239> above] ▶ **This word means ten thousand. It refers to an innumerable host of persons.** Ten thousand is employed figuratively (Dan. 7:10). ¶

MYRRH – [1] ***lōṭ*** [masc. noun: לֹט <3910>; prob. from WRAP <3874>] ▶ **This word is traditionally understood to refer to the gum of a kind of cistus plant.** Refs.: Gen. 37:25; 43:11. Some suggest the resinous bark of the tree Pistacia mutica. ¶
[2] ***mōr, môr*** [masc. noun: מֹר, מוֹר <4753>; from BITTER (BE) <4843>] ▶ **This word refers to a fragrant resin exuded from several plants found mainly in Arabia or Africa.** It is bitter in taste. It was used in the anointing oil in Israel (Ex. 30:23); and as a beauty treatment and cosmetic (Esther 2:12; Ps. 45:8; Prov. 7:17; Song 3:6; 5:1, 5).

It is used figuratively of love (Song 1:13; 4:6, 14; 5:13). ¶

MYRTLE TREE – ***h^adas*** [masc. noun: הֲדַס <1918>; of uncertain deriv.] ▶ **God will place this tree in the desert as a part of His blessing on Israel.** Ref.: Is. 41:19. It is contrasted with the nettle tree or bush (Is. 55:13). Myrtle trees are pictured growing in a ravine (Zech. 1:8, 10, 11). Its branches were used to construct booths for the Feast of Booths or Tabernacles (Neh. 8:15). ¶

MYSTERIES – Job 12:22 ➔ DEEP (adj.) <6013>.

MYSTERY – ***raz*** [Aramaic masc. noun: רָז <7328>; from an unused root prob. meaning to attenuate, i.e., (fig.) hide] ▶ **This word refers to the meaning of a dream or a vision that is not clear; it is also translated secret.** Refs.: Dan. 2:18, 19, 27–30. God is recognized as the one who reveals and gives the meaning of mysteries (Dan. 2:47); but may impart that ability to His servants (Dan. 4:9). ¶

N

NAAM – ***naʿam*** [masc. proper noun: נַעַם <5277>; from PLEASANT <5276>]: softness, pleasantness ▶ **One of the sons of Caleb.** Ref.: 1 Chr. 4:15. ¶

NAAMAH – ***naʿᵃmāh*** [proper noun: נַעֲמָה <5279>; fem. of NAAM <5277>]: soft, beautiful ▶
a. A sister of Tubal-Cain. Ref.: Gen. 4:22. ¶
b. The mother of Rehoboam. Refs.: 1 Kgs. 14:21, 31; 2 Chr. 12:13. ¶
c. A city in Judah. Ref.: Josh. 15:41. ¶

NAAMAN – ***naʿᵃmān*** [masc. proper noun: נַעֲמָן <5283>; the same as PLEASANT <5282>]: pleasantness ▶
a. A descendant of Benjamin, son of Rachel. Refs.: Gen. 46:21; Num. 26:40; 1 Chr. 8:4, 7. ¶
b. A Syrian general blessed by the Lord who was willing to follow the instructions of Elisha the prophet. Refs.: 2 Kgs. 5:1–2. By dipping himself seven times in the Jordan River, he was cured of leprosy. Elisha noted that this event demonstrated that there was a God and a prophet in Israel (2 Kgs. 5:8, 15). Naaman took dirt from Israel to Aram and vowed to recognize only the Lord of Israel as the true and only God (2 Kgs. 5:7, 8). *

NAAMATHITE – ***naʿᵃmāṯiy*** [proper noun: נַעֲמָתִי <5284>; patrial from a place corresponding in name (but not identical) to NAAMAH <5279>] ▶ **An inhabitant of Naamah, an unknown site.** Refs.: Job 2:11; 11:1; 20:1; 42:9. ¶

NAAMITE – ***naʿᵃmiy*** [proper noun: נַעֲמִי <5280>; patron. from NAAMAN <5283> a.] ▶ **This word distinguishes a descendant of Naaman; see NAAMAN <5283> a.** Ref.: Num. 26:40.

NAARAH – ***naʿᵃrāh, naʿᵃrāṯāh*** [proper noun: נַעֲרָה, נַעֲרָתָה <5292>; the same as GIRL <5291>]: girl, maiden ▶
a. The wife of Ashur. Refs.: 1 Chr. 4:5, 6. ¶
b. A town located on the border of Ephraim. Ref.: Josh. 16:7. ¶

NAARAI – ***naʿᵃray*** [masc. noun: נַעֲרַי <5293>; from BOY <5288>]: youthful ▶ **One of David's mighty men.** Ref.: 1 Chr. 11:37. ¶

NAARAN – ***naʿᵃrān*** [proper noun: נַעֲרָן <5295>; from BOY <5288>]: youthful ▶ **A city in Ephraim, east of Bethel and not far from Jericho.** Ref.: 1 Chr. 7:28. ¶

NABAL – ***nāḇāl*** [masc. proper noun: נָבָל <5037>; the same as FOOLISH <5036>]: fool ▶ **The name of a rogue and boor who refused to give needed supplies to David and arrogantly insulted David and his men as they were fleeing Saul.** His name means a particularly boorish type of "fool" (1 Sam. 25:25). His wife revealed his own folly to him, and he died from the shock (1 Sam. 25:36–39). *

NABOTH – ***nāḇôṯ*** [masc. proper noun: נָבוֹת <5022>; from the same as NOB <5011>] ▶ **An Israelite from Jezreel. He owned a vineyard near Ahab's palace. He refused to sell his property to the king because it was his sacred inheritance.** Jezebel arranged to have him accused of treason and killed (1 Kgs. 21:7–10). Ahab then confiscated Naboth's vineyard. This was avenged by the Lord through Jehu (2 Kgs. 9:21–26). *

NACHON – ***nāḵôn*** [masc. proper noun: נָכוֹן <5225>; from SET UP <3559> (in the sense of to prepare)] ▶ **Uzzah was slain near the threshing floor of Nachon.** Ref.: 2 Sam. 6:6. ¶

NADAB – ***nāḏāḇ*** [masc. proper noun: נָדָב <5070>; from GIVE WILLINGLY <5068>]: generous ▶
a. The firstborn son of Aaron. He was slain by the Lord because of offering up incense offerings before the Lord using improper ("strange" or "profane") fire. Ref.: Lev. 10:1. He and Abihu served to

warn the nation about the danger of not properly worshiping the Lord. He died at Sinai and had no sons (Num. 3:1–4). Other refs.: Ex. 6:23; 24:1, 9; 28:1; Num. 26:60, 61; 1 Chr. 6:3; 24:1, 2. ¶
b. A son of Jeroboam. He succeeded his father as king and reigned 909–908 B.C., about two years. He sinned greatly by continuing the reprehensible religious practices of his father, son of Nebat. Baasha assassinated Nadab and ruled in his place (1 Kgs. 14:20; 15:25, 27, 31). ¶
c. A son of Shammai who was the son of Onam. They were Judahites through Caleb and Hezron (1 Chr. 2:28, 30). ¶
d. A Gibeonite who was son of Jeiel by his wife Maacah. Refs.: 1 Chr. 8:29–30; 9:36. ¶

NAHALAL, NAHALOL – ***nah**a**lōl, nah**a**lāl*** [proper noun: נַהֲלָל, נַהֲלֹל <5096>; the same as PASTURE <5097>]: pasture ▶ **One of the cities of Zebulun.** Refs.: Josh. 19:15; 21:35; Judg. 1:30. ¶

NAHALIEL – ***naḥ**a**liy'ēl*** [proper noun: נַחֲלִיאֵל <5160>; from WADI <5158> b. (in the sense of a stream, a torrent) and GOD <410>]: valley of God, torrent of God ▶ **An encampment of the Israelites in the desert.** Ref.: Num. 21:19. ¶

NAHAM – ***naḥam*** [masc. proper noun: נַחַם <5163>; from SORRY (BE) <5162> (in the sense of to comfort, to console, to have compassion)]: comfort, consolation ▶ **The brother or brother-in-law of Hodiah.** Ref.: 1 Chr. 4:19. ¶

NAHAMANI – ***naḥ**a**māniy*** [masc. proper noun: נַחֲמָנִי <5167>; from SORRY (BE) <5162> (in the sense of to comfort, to console, to have compassion)] ▶ **One of the exiles from Babylon who returned to Jerusalem with Zerubbabel.** Ref.: Neh. 7:7. ¶

NAHARAI – ***naḥ**a**ray, naḥray*** [proper noun: נַחְרַי, נַחֲרַי <5171>; from the same as SNORTING <5170>]: snorting ▶ **Armorbearer of Joab.** Refs.: 2 Sam. 23:37; 1 Chr. 11:39. ¶

NAHASH – ***nāḥāš*** [masc. noun: נָחָשׁ <5176>; the same as SERPENT <5175>]: serpent ▶
a. A king of the Ammonites who was going to put out the right eye of every person in the city of Jabesh Gilead. Refs.: 1 Sam. 11:1–5. But Saul and the Israelites defeated the Ammonites and rescued the men of Jabesh Gilead (1 Sam. 11:9–11). He was perceived as a threat to Israel, and so the Israelites sought a human king to protect them (1 Sam. 12:12). David was able to live in peace with Nahash (2 Sam. 10:1, 2). His son Hanun succeeded him. He had another son, Shobi (2 Sam. 17:27). Other refs.: 1 Chr. 19:1, 2. ¶
b. The father of Abigail who was married to Nabal. Abigail was the sister of Zeruiah, David's sister (2 Sam. 17:25). ¶

NAHATH – ***naḥaṯ*** [masc. proper noun: נַחַת <5184>; the same as REST (noun) <5183>]: rest ▶
a. Son of Reuel. Refs.: Gen. 36:13, 17; 1 Chr. 1:37. ¶
b. Grandson of Elkanah. Ref.: 1 Chr. 6:26. ¶
c. A Levite. Ref.: 2 Chr. 31:13. ¶

NAHBI – ***naḥbiy*** [masc. proper noun: נַחְבִּי <5147>; from HIDE <2247>]: hidden, secluded ▶ **The designated man of the tribe of Naphtali sent by Moses to explore Canaan.** Ref.: Num. 13:14. ¶

NAHOR – ***nāḥôr*** [masc. proper noun: נָחוֹר <5152>; from the same as SNORTING <5170>]: snorting ▶
a. The father of Terah, father of Abraham. Refs.: Gen. 11:22–26; 1 Chr. 1:26. ¶
b. The son of Terah and brother of Abraham. Lot was his nephew by Haran, his other brother (Gen. 11:27). He married Milcah who was Haran's daughter. He remained in Haran and did not move on to Canaan. He fathered twin sons, Uz and Buz (Gen. 22:20, 21). He supplied Isaac with a wife, Rebekah, through Bethuel his son (Gen. 24:10, 15, 24, 47). Laban was Nahor's grandson (Gen. 29:5). His God was evidently the same as Abraham's God who had called them to Haran (Gen. 31:53), but

he had earlier worshiped a god beyond the Euphrates River (Josh. 24:2). Other refs.: Gen. 11:26, 29; 22:23; 31:53. ¶

NAHSON – ***naḥšôn*** [masc. proper noun: נַחְשׁוֹן <5177>; from DIVINATION (PRACTICE) <5172>]: who foretells, enchanter ▶ **A prince of the tribe of Judah.** Boaz was a descendant of him (Ex. 6:23; Num. 1:7; 2:3; 7:12, 17; 10:14; Ruth 4:20; 1 Chr. 2:10, 11). ¶

NAHUM – ***naḥûm*** [masc. proper noun: נַחוּם <5151>; from SORRY (BE) <5162> (in the sense of to comfort, to console, to have compassion)]: comfort, consolation ▶ **This is the name of a prophet whose entire message announced and celebrated the Lord's destruction of the Assyrian capital, Nineveh.** He came after Jonah. God's long-suffering and patience finally came to an end for Nineveh (Nah. 1:3). ¶

NAIL – [1] ***ṭᵉpar*** [Aramaic masc. noun: טְפַר <2953>; from a root corresponding to DEPART <6852>, and meaning the same as <6856> below] ▶ **This word indicates a claw, a fingernail.** It refers to the bird-like claws which grew on Nebuchadnezzar's hands during his seven-year punishment from the Lord (Dan. 4:33); and to the terrible bronze claws of the fourth beast of Daniel's dream (Dan. 7:19). ¶

[2] ***masmêr, mismêr, maśmêr*** [masc. noun: מַסְמֵר, מִסְמֵר, מַשְׂמֵר <4548>; from STAND UP <5568>] ▶ **This word is used of fasteners for doors and other items in construction work of all kinds.** Refs.: 1 Chr. 22:3; 2 Chr. 3:9; Is. 41:7. It is used humorously of idols being fastened together with nails (Jer. 10:4). The wise preacher sought out ways to hammer home his wise teachings with nails (Eccl. 12:11). ¶

[3] ***maśmērāh*** [fem. noun: מַשְׂמֵרָה <4930>; for <4548> above fem.] ▶ **This word refers to metal fasteners.** But it is used figuratively of collected words and their authors and of the wise as firm nails which drive home instruction for life (Eccl. 12:11). ¶

[4] ***ṣippōren*** [masc. noun: צִפֹּרֶן <6856>; from DEPART <6852>; in the denom. sense (from BIRD <6833>) of scratching] ▶ **This word refers to a toenail or a fingernail; a pointed writing instrument. It refers to both human fingernails and toenails.** A female captive in Israel who was to be taken for a wife had to have all of her nails clipped (Deut. 21:12). It indicates the diamond point of a stylus, a writing instrument in context (Jer. 17:1). ¶

– [5] Judg. 4:21, 22; 5:26; Ezra 9:8; Is. 22:23; Zech. 10:4 ➔ PEG <3489>.

NAIOTH – ***nāyôṯ*** [proper noun: נָיוֹת <5121>; from PRAISE (verb) <5115> a. (in the sense of to dwell, to rest)]: habitations ▶ **A place near Ramah where gathered prophets to work under the direction of Samuel.** Refs.: 1 Sam. 19:18, 19, 22, 23; 20:1. ¶

NAKED – [1] ***ʿêyrōm, ʿêrōm*** [adj.: עֵירֹם, עֵרֹם <5903>; from CRAFTY (BE) <6191>] ▶ **It is equivalent to being without clothing.** Refs.: Gen. 3:7, 10, 11. It indicates a state of penury or scarcity (Deut. 28:48: nakedness; Ezek. 16:39; 23:29). It has the sense of being in a state of innocence (Ezek. 16:7); of infancy (Ezek. 16:22) when used figuratively of Israel. Other refs.: Ezek. 18:7, 16. ¶

[2] ***ʿārôm*** [adj.: עָרוֹם <6174>; from CRAFTY (BE) <6191>] ▶ **This word can allude to physical nudity.** Refs.: Gen. 2:25; 1 Sam. 19:24; Is. 20:2–4. It can also be used figuratively to relate to one who has no possessions (Job 1:21; Eccl. 5:15). Moreover, Sheol is described as being naked before God, a statement of its openness and vulnerability to God and His power (Job 26:6). *

– [3] Hab. 3:9 ➔ NAKEDNESS <6181>.

NAKED (MAKE) – [1] Lev. 20:18, 19; Lam. 4:21 ➔ EMPTY (verb) <6168> [2] Hab. 3:9 ➔ UNCOVER <5783>.

NAKED (ONE WHO IS) – ***maʿᵃrōm*** [masc. noun: מַעֲרֹם <4636>; from CRAFTY (BE) <6191>, in the sense of stripping] ▶ **This word is used in reference to a person without clothing, someone needing to be clothed and cared for.** Ref.: 2 Chr. 28:15. ¶

NAKED BODY – Hab. 2:15 ➔ NAKEDNESS <4589>.

NAKEDNESS – [1] ***māʿôr*** [masc. noun: מָעוֹר <4589>; from UNCOVER <5783>] ► **This word depicts a unclothed body.** It refers to the indecent exposure of parts of the human body, especially under the influence of strong drink (Hab. 2:15). ¶
[2] ***maʿar*** [masc. noun: מַעַר <4626>; from EMPTY (verb) <6168> (in the sense of to uncover)] ► **This word depicts the private aspects of the human body displayed in public in an inappropriate way.** It is used figuratively of opening up the city of Nineveh to destruction (Nah. 3:5). It is used of an open space or clear space on the surface of something (1 Kgs. 7:36; KJV: proportion). ¶
[3] ***ʿerwāh*** [fem. noun: עֶרְוָה <6172>; from EMPTY (verb) <6168>] ► **This word can pertain to physical nudity for either a man or a woman.** Refs.: Gen. 9:22, 23; Ex. 20:26. However, it is more often used in a figurative sense. When used with the verbs *gālāh* (<1540>), meaning to uncover or remove, and *rā'āh* (<7200>), meaning to see, one finds a common euphemism for sexual relations—to uncover one's nakedness (Lev. 18:6; 20:17). On the other hand, when combined with the verb *kāsāh* (<3680>), meaning to cover, one finds a common idiom for entering into a marriage contract (Ezek. 16:8). Nakedness is also a symbol of the shame and disgrace of Egypt (Is. 20:4); Babylonia (Is. 47:3); and Jerusalem (Ezek. 16:37). Furthermore, when in construct with *dāḇār* (<1697>), meaning a word, matter, or thing, this term forms an idiom for indecent or improper behavior (Deut. 23:14; 24:1). When in construct with the word *'ereṣ* (EARTH <776>), it can refer to exposed or undefended areas (Gen. 42:9, 12). *
[4] ***ʿeryāh*** [fem. noun: עֶרְיָה <6181>; for <6172> above] ► **This term is only used figuratively. It can function as a metaphor for shame and disgrace.** In the allegory of unfaithful Jerusalem, God stated that Jerusalem was naked and bare, *ʿêrōm* (NAKED <5903>) *wᵉʿeryāh* (Ezek. 16:7: bare). The inhabitants of Shaphir were considered to be in the nakedness of shame, *ʿeryāh bōšeṯ* (SHAME <1322>) (Mic. 1:11). It is also used to indicate the outpouring of God's wrath on the earth by the allusion to God's bow being naked or uncovered, meaning that it was taken from its storage place and put to use (Hab. 3:9: naked, bare, uncovered). Other refs.: Ezek. 16:22, 39; 23:29. ¶
– [5] Deut. 28:48 ➔ NAKED <5903>.

NAKEDNESS (EXPOSE ONE'S) – ***ʿārêl*** [verb: עָרֵל <6188>; a prim. root (properly, to strip)] ► **This word means to consider uncircumcised, forbidden; to be exposed.** It indicates setting something aside or apart as not available for regular use, in this case, unharvested fruit (Lev. 19:23; to regard, to count). In the context of Habakkuk, it has the sense of exposing one's nakedness, treating oneself in an uncircumcised, forbidden way (Hab. 2:16; also translated to be exposed as uncircumcised, to show one's uncircumcision). ¶

NAME (noun) – [1] ***šêm*** [masc. noun: שֵׁם <8034>; a prim. word] ► **It is what specifically identifies a person or anything: God's name, "I am who I am" (Ex. 3:15); or the name Yahweh, Lord, which is in small capital letters in English (Ps. 5:12); a person's name (Gen. 3:20); names of animals (Gen. 2:19). This word also means fame.** To make a name for oneself means to attain a renowned reputation (Gen. 11:4; 2 Sam. 8:13); as when God made Abraham's name great (Gen. 12:2). To become famous is to have one's name spread through the land (Ezek. 16:14). To have a good name is to have a good character, a good reputation (Eccl. 7:1). The expression the name (*haššem*) refers to the Lord, Yahweh. The Lord's name is to be blessed, praised (Job 1:21). A name may serve as a memorial or monument (Is. 55:13). The phrase *yaḏ wašem* means a remembrance, a memorial (Is. 56:5) and serves today in modern Israel as the name of a museum built to remember the victims of the Holocaust or Shoah. The names of other gods were forbidden in Israel, i.e., the recognition of them (Ex. 23:13; Josh. 23:7). Israel's God was to be called on to act according to His revealed name (Is. 48:9; Jer. 14:7, 21; Ezek. 20:9, 14). To continue the name of a man, a family line gave him a kind of ongoing life in his sons (Deut. 25:7; 2 Sam. 8:13). *

[2] ***šum*** [Aramaic masc. noun: שֻׁם <8036>; corresponding to <8034> above] ▶ **Names are important. They indicate the specific identity of a person, a (god) God, or a thing.** Prophets prophesied only in the name of the God of Israel (Ezra 5:1). The names of returning exiles were important because they helped indicate what tribe they belonged to in Israel (Ezra 5:4, 10, 14). God caused His name to dwell in Jerusalem, His holy name that stood for His presence (Ezra 6:12). The name of God is always to be blessed (Dan. 2:20). Daniel's name had been changed to Belteshazzar, a pagan name, to indicate his place in Babylonian society (Dan. 2:26; 4:8, 19; 5:12). ¶

NAME (verb) – Is. 44:5 ➔ FLATTER <3655>.

NAOMI – ***nā***ᵒ***miy*** [fem. proper noun: נָעֳמִי <5281>; from BEAUTY <5278>]: delight, pleasantness ▶ **She traveled to Moab with her two sons and her husband when a sever famine struck Israel.** While there only she and her two daughters-in-law were left alive. Ruth, a Moabitess, was so impressed with her mother-in-law that she decided to cling to her, live with her, and adopt her God, land, and people. In the providence of God, she married Boaz and bore a son named Obed. Obed was the father of Jesse, who was the father of the great king David. Naomi was made "delightful" again after much bitterness. Refs.: Ruth 1:2, 3, 8, 11, 19–22; 2:1, 2, 6, 20, 22; 3:1; 4:3, 5, 9, 14, 16, 17. ¶

NAPHISH – ***nāp̄iyš*** [masc. proper noun: נָפִישׁ <5305>; from REST (verb) <5314> (in the sense of to refresh oneself)]: refreshment ▶ **One of the sons of Ishmael.** Refs.: Gen. 5:15; 1 Chr. 1:31; 5:19. ¶

NAPHOTH – [1] ***nep̄eṯ, nāp̄ôṯ*** [fem. proper noun: נֶפֶת, נָפוֹת <5316>; for <SIEVE 5299> c. (see b. also)]: height ▶

a. A country or region. It refers to a tribal allotment to Manasseh, possibly referring to Dor, the third name in the list (Josh. 17:11). Also Naphoth Dor south of Carmel. ¶

b. It is taken as a city (NASB) in Asher. It was connected, however, to Manasseh (Josh. 17:11). ¶

c. This refers to a tribal allotment to Manasseh in Asher. Ref.: Josh. 17:11. See a., b. It is a short term for Naphoth Dor located on the coast south of Carmel. ¶

– [2] Josh. 11:2; 12:23; 1 Kgs. 4:11 ➔ SIEVE <5299> c.

NAPHTALI – ***nap̄tāliy*** [masc. proper noun: נַפְתָּלִי <5321>; from WRESTLE <6617>]: my struggle, my wrestling ▶

a. The sixth son of Jacob born by Bilhah, Rachel's servant. Ref.: Gen. 30:8. Jacob blessed him as "a doe set free that bears beautiful fawns" (Gen. 49:21, NIV; KJV, "a hind let loose: he giveth goodly words"). Moses' blessing urged him to take possession of his territory (Deut. 33:23). *

b. The descendants of Naphtali lived in the northern part of Israel. It was bounded on the east by the Sea of Galilee and eastern Manasseh; on the north by the Litani River and Mount Hermon; on the west by Asher and Zebulun; on the south by Issachar. Kedesh, a city of refuge, was in its northern half. The great city of Hazor was in its eastern border, below Lake Hulah.

Baruch, who helped Deborah subdue Sisera, came from Naphtali (Judg. 4:6–10). Its people were strong supporters of Gideon (Judg. 6:35; 7:23). Since it was so close to Syria, it often was battered in wars from Syrian kings and armies (1 Kgs. 15:20). The entire tribe/land was exiled by Tiglath-pileser, an Assyrian king (ca. 734 B.C.). *

NAPHTUHITES, NAPHTUHIM – ***nap̄tuḥiym*** [proper noun: נַפְתֻּחִים <5320>; of foreign origin] ▶ **An Egyptian tribe.** Refs.: Gen. 10:13; 1 Chr. 1:11. ¶

NARD – ***nêrd*** [masc. noun: נֵרְדְּ <5373>; of foreign origin] ▶ **This word refers to a pleasant, fragrant ointment used in amorous situations; it is also translated spikenard, perfume.** Ref.: Song 1:12. It refers to the spikenard or nard plant as well (Song 4:13, 14). ¶

NARROW – Josh. 17:15 ➔ HASTEN <213>.

NARROW (BE) – Is. 49:19 ➔ DISTRESSED (BE) <3334>.

NARROWNESS – ***ṣar*** [masc. noun: צַר <6862>; from TROUBLED (BE) <6887> a. (in the sense of to be cramped, to be hard-pressed)] ▶
a. This word indicates tightness, distress, application, misery. It refers to a narrow space or object, not wide, with a small distance across it (Num. 22:26). It is used figuratively of a person's pain and distress; oppression, a feeling of being hemmed in (Deut. 4:30; Job 7:11; 15:24). The Lord delivers His faithful follower from affliction and distress (Ps. 4:1). It describes oppressive political, economic, and military conditions suffered by a group, a people, or a nation (Judg. 11:7). It describes the threats and destruction that come on something, especially the Lord's house (1 Sam. 2:32). It indicates conditions during times of judgment on Israel (Is. 5:30). It refers to the time, trouble, and effort given to consider an issue (Esther 7:4). It is used figuratively to describe an adulterous woman as a narrow well with no escape (Prov. 23:27). It depicts a cry of destruction as one of great anguish (Jer. 48:5). Affliction or distress may cause a person to seek God (Hos. 5:15). It is sometimes difficult to decide whether to translate *ṣar* as a. or b., e.g., in Zechariah 8:10 (cf. NKJV, NASB).
b. This word indicates an enemy, a foe, an adversary, an oppressor. It refers to a personal enemy or foe rather than an impersonal situation of distress or affliction (Gen. 14:20; Num. 10:9). Nations as well as individuals may be one's adversaries (Num. 24:8; Deut. 32:27, 41, 43; 33:7; 2 Sam. 24:13; Amos 3:11). It refers to the enemies and adversaries of God's people in exile (Ezra 4:1; Neh. 4:11; 9:27; Esther 7:4). It indicates the adversary or oppressor of Job (6:23); and the psalmist (3:1; 13:4; 27:2). For Zechariah 8:10, see a.
c. This word indicates flint. It refers to a kind of chert stone that produces sparks when struck with certain metals. Used in a simile, it described the terrifying hoofs of warhorses (Is. 5:28). *

NATHAN – ***nāṯān*** [masc. proper noun: נָתָן <5416>; from GIVE <5414>]: he (God) has given ▶
a. A Judahite through the line of Jerahmeel, son of Hezron. His father was Attai (1 Chr. 2:36). ¶
b. The father of Igal, who was among David's mighty men. Refs.: 2 Sam. 23:36; 1 Chr. 11:38. ¶
c. The father of Azariah who administered a district. A chief official of Solomon (1 Kgs. 4:5). ¶
d. The prophet who charged David with adultery and murder (2 Sam. 12:1–31). His name means "(God) has given." He was also loyal to David as David followed the Lord. God revealed the covenant with David through Nathan (2 Sam. 7:4–16). He supported Solomon as king on David's death (1 Kgs. 1:1–53). Psalm 51 (title) notes his condemnation of David's adultery. *
e. One of David's many sons by various wives. Ref.: 2 Sam. 5:14. *
f. An Israelite leader summoned to help Ezra gather workers for the services of the Temple. Ref.: Ezra 8:16. ¶
g. An Israelite who had intermarried with the people of the land. Ref.: Ezra 10:39. ¶

NATHAN-MELECH – ***n^eṯan-meleḵ*** [masc. proper noun: נְתַן־מֶלֶךְ <5419>; from GIVE <5414> and KING <4428>]: gift of the king ▶ **The chamberlain in the court of King Josiah.** Ref.: 2 Kgs. 23:11. ¶

NATION – [1] ***'ummāh*** [Aramaic fem. noun: אֻמָּה <524>; corresponding to PEOPLE <523>] ▶ **This word corresponds to**

the Hebrew word *'êm* meaning mother (see MOTHER <517>), and when carried into the Aramaic, it shifts to mean mother in a collective sense (i.e., nation). Often a nation is found in the expression "peoples, nations, and languages" (Dan. 3:4, 7; 4:1; 5:19; 6:25; 7:14; cf. Ezra 4:10). For example, after Shadrach, Meshach, and Abednego came through the fiery furnace, Nebuchadnezzar issued a decree to every people, language, and nation concerning the God of the Hebrews (Dan. 3:29). ¶

2 ***gôy, gôyim, hăggôyim*** [proper noun: גּוֹי, גּוֹיִם, הַגּוֹיִם <1471>; apparently from the same root as BACK <1465> (see COMMUNITY <1460>)] ► **This word means people of the same ethnicity; it also means Gentiles, country.**

a. It is used to indicate a nation or nations in various contexts and settings. It especially indicates the offspring of Abraham that God made into a nation (Gen. 12:2) and thereby set the stage for Israel's appearance in history as a nation (Gen. 18:18; Ps. 106:5). Israel was to be a holy nation (Ex. 19:6). Even the descendants of Abraham that did not come from the seed of Isaac would develop into nations (Gen. 21:13). God can create a nation, even a holy nation like Israel, through the descendants of the person whom He chooses, as He nearly does in the case of Moses when Israel rebels (Ex. 32:10). Edom refers to Israel and Judah as two separate nations (Ezek. 35:10), but God planned for them to be united forever into one nation (Ezek. 37:22). Then they would become the head of the nations (Deut. 28:12). In this overall literary, theological, and historical context, it is clear that Israel would share common ancestors, and would have a sufficient increase in numbers to be considered a nation. It would have a common place of habitation and a common origin, not only in flesh and blood, but in their religious heritage. It would share a common history, culture, society, religious worship, and purposes for the present and the future.

b. This noun is used to mean nations other than Israel as well. Pagan, Gentile, or heathen nations (Ex. 9:24; 34:10; Ezek. 5:6–8), for all the earth and all the nations belong to God (cf. Ex. 19:5). Israel was to keep herself from the false religions, unclean practices, and views of these nations (Ezra 6:21). In the plural, the noun may indicate the generic humankind (Is. 42:6). In a few instances, the word refers to a group of people rather than to a nation (2 Kgs. 6:18; Ps. 43:1; Is. 26:2), although the exact translation is difficult in these cases.

c. The word is used in a figurative sense to refer to animals or insects. In Joel 1:6 it depicts locusts. *

– 3 Gen. 25:16 ➔ PEOPLE <523>.

NATIVE, NATIVE-BORN, BORN IN – ***'ezrāḥ*** [masc. noun: אֶזְרָח <249>; from RISE UP <2224>] ► **This word indicates a person of a land (Ezek. 47:22; it is also translated born in the country) as opposed to a stranger (*gêr*) or settler (*tôšaḇ*).** These persons had full rights to take part in Israel's rites and festivals (Ex. 12:19, 48, 49; Lev. 16:29; Josh. 8:33). Strangers could be treated as natives in some cases (Ex. 12:48) and were to have, in general, respect and humanitarian treatment just as the natives (Lev. 19:34). They were to be loved. It is used figuratively to describe native soil (Ps. 37:35). *

NATIVITY – Ezek. 21:30 ➔ ORIGIN <4351>.

NAVEL – 1 ***šōr*** [masc. noun: שֹׁר <8270>; from ENEMY <8324>] ► **This word indicates the hollow on the surface of the stomach; it also indicates a navel (umbilical) cord.** It refers to the bride's navel, which is praised as an ornament of beauty (Song 7:2). It is used figuratively of the navel cord of the infant Israel (Ezek. 16:4). It can be read as naval (*šōr*) or body, flesh (*baśar*) (Prov. 3:8). ¶

2 ***šōrer*** [masc. noun: שֹׁרֶר <8326>; from ENEMY <8324> in the sense of twisting] ► **This word refers to the navel of the bride as an ornament of beauty.** Ref.: Song 7:2. ¶

– 3 Job 40:16 ➔ MUSCLE <8306>.

NAVY – 1 Kgs. 9:26, 27; 10:11, 22: navy of ships ➔ FLEET OF SHIPS <590>.

NAZARITE – See NAZIRITE <5139>.

NAZIRITE – ***nāziyr*** [masc. noun: נָזִיר <5139>; from SEPARATE <5144> (also in the sense of to dedicate, to consecrate)] ▶ **This word means one consecrated, separated, devoted. The term Nazarite means one who is consecrated to God.** The Nazarite vow included abstinence from strong drink or the cutting of his hair, and no contact with dead bodies (Judg. 13:4–7). Samuel, as well as Samson, was dedicated before birth by his mother to be a Nazarite (cf. 1 Sam. 1:11). Less common is the meaning of a prince or ruler being consecrated, as was the case with Joseph, who was separated from his brothers (Gen. 49:26). A third meaning of this word depicts an untrimmed vine (Lev. 25:5; also translated undressed, untended). Other refs.: Num. 6:2, 13, 18–21; Deut. 33:16; Judg. 16:17; Lam. 4:7; Amos 2:11, 12. ¶

NEAH – ***nê'āh*** [proper noun: נֵעָה <5269>; from WANDER <5128>]: who wanders, motion ▶ **A place near the border of Zebulun.** Ref.: Josh. 19:13. ¶

NEAR – 1 ***qārôḇ, qārōḇ*** [adj.: קָרוֹב, קָרֹב <7138>; from COME NEAR <7126>] ▶ **This word means close by, closely related.** It indicates nearness in time or space: something is about to happen, is near at hand, e.g., judgment, calamity (Deut. 32:35); (not) near at hand, a prophetic fulfillment (Num. 24:17); a fool's destruction is not far off (Prov. 10:14). It refers to the imminent coming of God's day of judgment (Zeph. 1:7, 14); to a town that is close by (Gen. 19:20). Joseph lived near the area of Pharaoh's habitation (Gen. 45:10). It is used of a neighbor's house (Ex. 12:4); or indicates a road near by (Ex. 13:17). It is used in a figurative sense of a person's coming near to listen to words of wisdom (Eccl. 5:1). It indicates a relationship, a relative (Ex. 32:27; Num. 27:11; 2 Sam. 19:42; among humans, but also a relationship to God (Lev. 10:3; 1 Kgs. 8:46, 59; Ps. 119:151). It refers to a friend (Ps. 15:3). *
– 2 See WITH <854>.

NEAR (BE, COME, DRAW) – Ps. 73:28; Is. 58:2 ➔ NEARNESS <7132>.

NEAR OF KIN – Lev. 18:17 ➔ KINSWOMAN <7608>.

NEARIAH – ***n*ᵉ*'aryāh*** [masc. noun: נְעַרְיָה <5294>; from BOY <5288> and LORD <3050>]: servant of the Lord ▶
a. A descendant of David. Refs.: 1 Chr. 3:22, 23. ¶
b. A Simeonite. Ref.: 1 Chr. 4:42. ¶

NEARNESS – ***qirḇāh*** [adj.: קִרְבָה <7132>; from COME NEAR <7126>] ▶ **This word indicates an approach; a drawing close, being close.** It indicates a closeness, a proximity of someone to something; in its context, it refers to God's nearness (Ps. 73:28; Is. 58:2). ¶

NEBAI – ***nêḇāy*** [masc. proper noun: נֵיבָי <5109>; from FRUIT <5108>]: fruitful ▶ **A chief of the people who signed the covenant of renewal with Nehemiah after the return from the Babylonian captivity.** Ref.: Neh. 10:19. ¶

NEBAIOTH – ***n*ᵉ*ḇāyôṯ, n*ᵉ*ḇāyōṯ*** [masc. proper noun: נְבָיוֹת, נְבָיֹת <5032>; from INCREASE (verb) <5107>]: fruitfulness ▶
a. A son of Ishmael. Refs.: Gen. 25:13; 28:9; 36:3; 1 Chr. 1:29.
b. Another person. Ref.: Is. 60:7. ¶

NEBALLAT – ***n*ᵉ*ḇallaṭ*** [proper noun: נְבַלָּט <5041>; apparently from FOOLISH <5036> and ENCHANTMENT <3909> (in the sense of secrecy, mystery]: foolish secrecy ▶ **A town of Benjamin reoccupied after the captivity.** Ref.: Neh. 11:34. ¶

NEBAT – ***n*ᵉ*ḇāṭ*** [masc. proper noun: נְבָט <5028>; from LOOK <5027>]: regard, aspect ▶ **He was the father of Jeroboam I.** Refs.: 1 Kgs. 11:26; 12:2, 12:15; 15:1; 16:3, 26, 31; 2 Kgs. 3:3; 9:9; 10:29; 14:24; 23:15; 2 Chr. 9:29; 10:2, 15; 13:6. *

NEBO – ***n*ᵉ*ḇô, n*ᵉ*ḇû śar-s*ᵉ*kiym*** [proper noun: נְבוֹ, נְבוּ שַׂר־סְכִים <5015>; prob. of foreign deriv.] ▶

a. A specific mountain or range in Moab from which a person could view the Promised Land of Canaan. Refs.: Num. 33:47; Deut. 32:49; 34:1.
b. A specific town in Moab. Refs.: Num. 32:3, 38; 1 Chr. 5:8; Is. 15:2; Jer. 48:1, 22.
c. A city located northwest of Jerusalem. Some persons from here returned from exile to Jerusalem (Ezra 2:29; Neh. 7:33).
d. A Jewish ancestor. Some of Nebo's sons intermarried with the people of the land after returning from exile (Ezra 10:43).
e. A false Babylonian god, Nebo. It refers to a god of Babylon identified as an idolatrous god who would be destroyed by the Lord (Is. 46:1).
f. Nebo-Sarsekiym was the name of a Babylonian official who occupied Jerusalem when it fell. Ref.: Jer. 39:3. It is combined and rendered differently by translators: Samgar-nebo, NKJV, KJV; Nebo-Sarsekim, NIV; Samgar-nebu, NASB). ¶

NEBUCHADNEZZAR – 1 ***nᵉḇûḵaḏne'ṣṣar, nᵉḇûḵaḏre'ṣṣar*** [masc. proper noun: נְבוּכַדְנֶאצַּר, נְבוּכַדְרֶאצַּר <5019>; of foreign origin]: Nabu (a Babylonian god) has protected the accession right ► **A proper noun designating the great Chaldean king of the neo-Babylonian Empire. He ruled 605–562 B.C. and was the virtual embodiment of this empire.** He defeated Assyria in 605 B.C. and became the master of the Middle East. He invaded Judah and destroyed Jerusalem and Judah in 586 B.C. He destroyed the Temple and took its wealth to the stone house of his god Marduk in Babylon (2 Kings 24; 25; Daniel 1–3). The prophet Jeremiah called him the servant of the Lord to do his bidding (Jer. 25:9; 27:6). It was the Lord's judgment that submitted Judah to this pagan king (Jer. 28:14). He listened to and promoted Daniel and his God while Daniel served as a counselor, wise man, and administrator for the king. The Lord gave him dreams, interpreted by Daniel, a Jew, that were breathtaking in their sweeping portrayals of the march of history from his time down to the rise of the kingdom of God (Daniel 2). He suffered from megalomania in his last years, but God humbled him with a humiliating disease and emotional derangement (Dan. 4:1; 23:31) but later restored him to sanity. *
2 ***nᵉḇûḵaḏneṣṣar*** [Aramaic masc. proper noun: נְבוּכַדְנֶצַּר <5020>; corresponding to <5019> above] ► **A proper noun designating Nebuchadnezzar, the Aramaic form of the Hebrew name.** See <5019> above. The meaning of the name is the same. *

NEBUSHAZBAN – ***nᵉḇûšazbān*** [masc. proper noun: נְבוּשַׁזְבָּן <5021>; of foreign deriv.] ► **Chief officer of Nebuchadnezzar.** Ref.: Jer. 39:13. ¶

NEBUZARADAN – ***nᵉḇûzarᵃḏān*** [masc. proper noun: נְבוּזַרְאֲדָן <5018>; of foreign origin] ► **Captain of the royal guard of Nebuchadnezzar who took many of the Israelites into exile.** Refs.: 2 Kgs. 25:8, 11, 20; Jer. 39:9–11. *

NECHO – ***nᵉḵô*** [masc. proper noun: נְכוֹ <5224>; prob. of Egyptian origin] ► **An Egyptian Pharaoh who warned Josiah not to fight against him. Josiah did not listen and was killed. It would appear that the Lord used this Pharaoh to warn the Judean king.** Necho removed Jehoahaz as king in Judah and set up Jehoiakim (Eliakim) in his place (2 Chr. 36:2–4), taking Jehoahaz captive to Egypt. Other refs.: 2 Chr. 35:20, 22. ¶

NECK – 1 ***gargārôṯ*** [fem. plur. noun: גַּרְגְּרוֹת <1621>; fem. plur. from DRAG (verb) <1641>] ► **The neck (the part between the head and the body) is mentioned as the place where ornaments are hung.** Ref.: Prov. 1:9. In a figurative sense, wisdom, discretion, kindness, and truth are to be hung around the neck (Prov. 3:3, 22). As a place of importance and prominence, the neck was where the teaching and commandments of one's parents are to be displayed (Prov. 6:21). ¶
2 ***mapreqeṯ*** [fem. noun: מַפְרֶקֶת <4665>; from BREAK OFF <6561>] ► **It is the part of a human or animal that connects**

the head to the body and encloses portions of the backbone. Eli's neck was broken when he fell backward (1 Sam. 4:18). ¶

[3] ***ʿōrep̱*** [masc. noun: 6203> עֹרֶף; from NECK (BREAK THE) <6202>] ► **This word refers to the back of a person's neck (the part between the head and the body) or a neck in general.** Refs.: Gen. 49:8; Lev. 5:8. It is used in the statement to turn one's back to, to flee from (Ex. 23:27; Josh. 7:8, 12; 2 Sam. 22:41; Jer. 2:27). A stiff neck indicates an obstinate, stubborn attitude, a rebellious person or people (Ex. 32:9; 33:3; Deut. 9:6; 31:27). God's turning His back to His people indicates His displeasure (Jer. 18:17). Israel's turning their backs to God indicates their apostasy (Jer. 2:27; 32:33). To turn the back may demonstrate shame (Jer. 48:39). *

[4] ***ṣawwaʾr*** [Aramaic masc. noun: צַוַּאר <6676>; corresponding to <6677> below] ► **This word refers to the neck of a human being.** It was a great honor to have a gold chain placed around one's neck by the king, especially in Babylon, an empire enamored of gold (Dan. 5:7, 16, 29). ¶

[5] ***ṣawwāʾr, ṣawwārōniym*** [masc. noun: צַוָּאר, צַוְּרֹנִים <6677>; intens. from BESIEGE <6696> in the sense of binding] ►

a. A masculine noun referring to a person's neck, the part of a human or animal that fastens the head to the body, the backbone between the skull and shoulders included. It refers to a person's neck (Gen. 27:16). It is used figuratively in the expression to have a yoke on one's neck, to be enslaved (Gen. 27:40; Is. 10:27; Jer. 27:2; 28:10–12, 14; 30:8). In the Middle East, it was a show of affection to kiss another man's neck (Gen. 33:4); while putting one's foot on an enemy's neck indicated dominance over him (Josh. 10:24). To rush into someone with one's head was to use one's neck (Job 15:26). A neck held forward while talking indicates stubbornness or insolence (Ps. 75:5). A person's neck was a place for ornamentation (Song 1:10; 4:9); and a feature of beauty and strength (Song 4:4; 7:4). Swords on the neck of the wicked means to slay them (Ezek. 21:29). The idiom from neck to thigh means to destroy an enemy or person utterly (Hab. 3:13). *

b. A masculine plural noun indicating necklaces. It refers to a jewel, a gold chain, or other ornamentation worn around a person's neck. It was used to enhance the attraction of the wearer (Song 4:9). ¶

– [6] Is. 3:16 ➔ THROAT <1627>.

NECK (BREAK THE) – ***ʿārap̱*** [verb: עָרַף <6202>; a prim. root (identical with DROP, DROP DOWN <6201>] ► **This Hebrew word is used of breaking the neck of an animal, especially the firstborn of a donkey.** Refs.: Ex. 13:13; 34:20; Deut. 21:4, 6; Is. 66:3. It is used once of breaking down altars (Hos. 10:2; NIV: to demolish). ¶

NECK BAND – Judg. 8:26 ➔ CHAIN <6060>.

NECK IRON – ***ṣiynōq*** [masc. noun: צִינֹק <6729>; from an unused root meaning to confine] ►

a. This word indicates an instrument and form of punishment used to control madmen and make a public show of them; it is also translated iron collar. Ref.: Jer. 29:26.

b. Some translators rendered this word as stocks. The meaning of an iron collar is most likely correct (Jer. 29:26). ¶

NECKLACE – [1] ***kûmāz*** [masc. noun: כּוּמָז <3558>; from an unused root meaning to store away] ► **This word refers to an ornamental piece of jewelry for wearing around the neck or on the breast.** Refs.: Ex. 35:22; Num. 31:50; also translated bracelet, tablet, ornament, bead. These items were brought as gifts and offerings to the Lord. ¶

[2] ***rāḇiyḏ*** [masc. noun: רָבִיד <7242>; from SPREAD (verb) <7234>] ► **This word indicates an ornamental piece of jewelry worn around the neck to indicate authority and honor.** Ref.: Gen. 41:42. It indicates in general decorative ornamental chains (2 Chr. 3:16). Figuratively, it speaks of God's magnificent care for His people (Ezek. 16:11). ¶

– [3] Dan. 5:7, 16, 29 ➔ CHAIN <2002>.

NECKLACE (BE THE, SERVE AS THE) – Ps. 73:6 ➔ LIBERALLY (FURNISH, SUPPLY) <6059>.

NECROMANCER – Deut. 18:11; 1 Sam. 28:9; 2 Kgs. 21:6; Is. 8:19; etc. ➔ SPIRITIST <3049>.

NEDABIAH – ***n***^e^***ḏaḇyāh*** [masc. proper noun: נְדַבְיָה <5072>; from GIVE WILLINGLY <5068> and LORD <3050>]: the Lord is generous ► **One of the sons of Jeconiah, a descendant of David.** Ref.: 1 Chr. 3:18. ¶

NEED (noun) – [1] ***ḥašḥû*** [Aramaic fem. noun: חַשְׁחוּ <2819>; from a root corresponding to NEED (verb and noun) <2818>] ► **This word indicates what is required in order to carry on proper worship at the second Temple building in Ezra's day.** Ref.: Ezra 7:20; also translated required, needed, needful. ¶

[2] ***maḥsôr, maḥsōr*** [masc. noun: מַחְסוֹר, מַחְסֹר <4270>; from LACKING (BE) <2637>] ► **This word refers to a lack, poverty.** It indicates what is needed because of a lack (Deut. 15:8); or what is required to meet a need (Judg. 19:20). Its sense becomes focused on the want or lack. There can be no lack (Judg. 18:10; 19:19). To live in a constant state of need is equivalent to poverty (Prov. 6:11; 11:24; 14:23; 21:5; 28:27). *

[3] ***ṣōreḵ*** [masc. noun: צֹרֶךְ <6878>; from an unused root meaning to need] ► **This word refers to something that is required.** It refers to what is necessary with respect to a particular need of something (2 Chr. 2:16). ¶

– [4] Deut. 28:48, 57 ➔ WANT <2640>.

NEED (verb and noun) – ***ḥ***^a^***šaḥ, ḥašḥāh*** [Aramaic verb and fem. noun: חֲשַׁח, חַשְׁחָה <2818>; a collateral root to one corresponding to HASTEN <2363> in the sense of readiness] ►

a. This verb indicates some obligation or necessity to do or say something. Ref.: Dan. 3:16; KJV, to be careful. But the three Hebrew young men assert that they have no need or obligation to defend their God or themselves before Nebuchadnezzar. ¶

b. This noun refers to necessity, something required. In the context, it refers to what was needed for sacrifices (Ezra 6:9) and was to be supplied by the Persians or those living around the Israelites after their return from exile. ¶

NEED (BE) – Ps. 79:8; 116:6; 142:6 ➔ BRING LOW <1809>.

NEEDED – Ezra 7:20 ➔ NEED (noun) <2819>.

NEEDFUL – Ezra 7:20 ➔ NEED (noun) <2819>.

NEEDY – Ex. 23:6; Job 5:15; 24:4, 14; 29:16; 30:25; Ps. 9:18; 12:5; 40:17; Jer. 20:13; Amos 2:6; 4:1; 5:12; Is. 29:19 ➔ POOR <34>.

NEEDY (BE) – See LACKING (BE) <2637>.

NEESING – Job 41:18 ➔ SNEEZING <5846>.

NEGEB – See SOUTH <5045>.

NEGEV – See SOUTH <5045>.

NEGLECT (noun) – ***šālû*** [Aramaic fem. noun: שָׁלוּ <7960>; from the same as AMISS <7955>] ► **This word refers to an error, a failure to do something, an offense.** It refers to a failure to perform or to carry out one's responsibilities in a certain matter (Ezra 4:22; 6:9). It describes something hurtful or offensive in certain contexts (Dan. 3:29). It refers to neglect or failure to carry out one's responsibilities according to what is expected in a given political office (Dan. 6:4). ¶

NEGLECT (verb) – Deut. 32:18 ➔ UNMINDFUL (BE) <7876>.

NEGLIGENT (BE) – [1] ***šālāh*** [verb: שָׁלָה <7952>; a prim. root ► **This word means to be careless, to be thoughtless, to sin.** The sin described by this verb does not seem to be a deliberate sin but rather one that is committed by ignorance or inadvertence. The verb is used only in the passive and causative forms. In the passive form, it holds the meaning of being negligent or being careless of duties (2 Chr. 29:11). The causative form means to lead astray or to deceive. It is used in 2 Kings 4:28 when the Shunammite woman felt deceived that she had been promised a son who later died. Although the sins described by this verb were not intentional, they were still deserving of punishment in God's sight. ¶

– [2] 2 Chr. 29:11 → EASE (BE AT) <7951> b.

NEHELAMITE – ***neḥ***^{e}***lāmiy*** [proper noun: נֶחֱלָמִי <5161>; apparently a patron. from an unused name; apparently also pass. part. of DREAM (verb) <2492>]: dreamer ▶ **Designation of Shemaiah, a false prophet.** Refs.: Jer. 29:24, 31, 32. ¶

NEHEMIAH – ***n***^{e}***ḥemyāh*** [masc. proper noun: נְחֶמְיָה <5166>; from SORRY (BE) <5162> (in the sense of to comfort, to console, to have compassion) and LORD <3050>]: the Lord comforts ▶

a. The name is a fitting name for the man who was deeply distressed at the perilous and oppressive condition of his holy city Jerusalem and its Jewish inhabitants. He was cupbearer to the Persian king Artaxerxes I (465–424 B.C.), a highly prized position (Neh. 2:1–3). The king permitted Nehemiah to return to Judah and Jerusalem to aid them (Neh. 2:6–9). He led a large group of exiles back to Jerusalem and Judah (Neh. 7:4–73). When there (ca. 445 B.C.), he oversaw the rebuilding of the walls and the city in record time (Neh. 2:11–12:26). It was duly dedicated (Neh. 12:27–43). He helped repopulate the city (Neh. 11:1–36), led in a national day of prayer (Neh. 9), and helped Ezra establish the Mosaic Law again (Neh. 7:73–8:18). He returned to Persia in 433 B.C., then went back to Jerusalem again after an indefinite period. He dealt again with the problem of Jewish intermarriage (Neh. 13:23–28) with non-Israelites as Ezra had and restored and purified the priestly services in Israel (Neh. 13:1–13). He warned them severely about not keeping the Sabbath (Neh. 13:14–22). Specific references to the name: Neh. 1:1; 8:9; 10:1; 12:26, 47. ¶

b. A postexilic Jew who returned from exile. Refs.: Ezra 2:2; Neh. 7:7. ¶

c. The son of Azbuk who helped repair part of the wall of Jerusalem. Ref.: Neh. 3:16. ¶

NEHILOTH – ***n***^{e}***ḥiylāh*** [fem. proper noun: נְחִילָה <5155>; prob. denom. from FLUTE <2485>]: flute ▶

a. A proper name in a psalm title. Ref.: Ps. 5:1. It is a technical musical term not fully understood. ¶

b. A feminine proper noun. It is a technical musical term not fully understood. Some suggest that it refers to a flute or pipe. Ref.: Ps. 5:1. ¶

NEHUM – ***n***^{e}***ḥûm*** [masc. proper noun: נְחוּם <5149>; from SORRY (BE) <5162> (in the sense of to comfort, to console, to have compassion)]: comfort, consolation ▶ **One of those who came back from the Babylonian captivity with Zerubbabel.** Ref.: Neh. 7:7. ¶

NEHUSHTA – ***n***^{e}***ḥuštā'*** [fem. proper noun: נְחֻשְׁתָּא <5179>; from COPPER <5178>]: copper ▶ **The daughter of Elnathan of Jerusalem, and the wife of Jehoiakin, king of Judah.** Ref.: 2 Kgs. 24:8. ¶

NEHUSHTAN – ***n***^{e}***ḥuštān*** [proper noun: נְחֻשְׁתָּן <5180>; from COPPER <5178>]: a thing made of copper ▶ **This word is the name given to a bronze serpent Moses ordered to be made in the wilderness (see Num. 21:9).** This was probably a model of it created in the idolatrous times of Ahaz (2 Kgs. 18:4). ¶

NEIEL – ***n***^{e}***'iy'ēl*** [proper noun: נְעִיאֵל <5272>; from WANDER <5128> and GOD <410>]: moved by God ▶ **A place on the border of Asher.** Ref.: Josh. 19:27. ¶

NEIGHBOR – [1] ***'āmiyṯ*** [masc. noun: עָמִית <5997>; from a prim. root meaning to associate] ▶ **This word refers to one's fellow, a friend, a comrade, a companion (Lev. 6:2); a neighbor (Lev. 18:20); other persons in a community in general (Lev. 19:11, 15).** Every neighbor or friend was to be dealt with in truth (Lev. 25:14, 15, 17). But in times of God's judgments, things could be turned upside down against a neighbor (Zech. 13:7). Other refs.: Lev. 19:17; 24:19. ¶
[2] ***re'ûṯ*** [fem. noun: רְעוּת <7468>; from FEED (verb) <7462> b. (with the meaning to associate with)] ▶ **This word means a fellow woman, an associate.** In Jeremiah, the women were to teach one another (i.e., their associates or companions) a lament (Jer. 9:20). Isaiah used the word to denote the mates of falcons or birds of prey (Is. 34:15, 16). In a figurative use, Zechariah used the word to denote that the people who remained would be left to eat one another's flesh (Zech. 11:9). In Esther, King Xerxes was advised to make a decree stating that Vashti was never again to enter his presence and that her position was to be given to one of her associates that was better than she was (Esther 1:19). Other ref.: Ex. 11:2. ¶
– [3] Ex. 3:22; Ruth 4:17; etc. ➔ INHABITANT <7934>.

NEIGHING – ***miṣhālôṯ*** [fem. plur. noun: מִצְהָלוֹת <4684>; from CRY OUT <6670> (in the sense of to neigh)] ▶ **This word indicates the high-pitched cry of horses getting ready for battle.** Ref.: Jer. 8:16. It is used figuratively of Israel's rebellious neighing for her lewd suitors (Jer. 13:27). ¶

NEKEB – ***neqeḇ*** [נֶקֶב <5346>; the same as SETTING <5345>]; hollow, cavern ▶
a. A town in Naphtali. Ref.: KJV, Josh. 19:33. ¶
b. Part of the full name Adami Nekeb, see ADAMI <129> and NEKEB <5346> a. Other translations, Josh. 19:33. ¶

NEKODA – ***neqôḏā'*** [proper noun: נְקוֹדָא <5353>; from SPECKLED <5348> (in the figurative sense of marked)]: distinguished ▶
a. The head of a family of Temple slaves returning from the Babylonian exile. Refs.: Ezra 2:48; Neh. 7:50. ¶
b. The head of an exile family who could not prove their Israelite descent. Refs.: Ezra 2:60; Neh. 7:62. ¶

NEMUEL – ***nemû'ēl*** [proper noun: נְמוּאֵל <5241>; apparently for JEMUEL <3223>]: day of God ▶
a. One of Simeon's five sons. Refs.: Num. 26:12; 1 Chr. 4:24. ¶
b. A Reubenite, son of Eliab and brother of Dathan and Abiram. Ref.: Num. 26:9. ¶

NEMUELITE – ***nemû'ēliy*** [proper noun: נְמוּאֵלִי <5242>; from NEMUEL <5241>] ▶ **Member of the family of Nemuel.** Ref.: Num. 26:12. ¶

NEPHEG – ***nep̱eg*** [masc. proper noun: נֶפֶג <5298>; from an unused root probably meaning to spring forth] ▶
a. A Levite. Ref.: Ex. 6:21. ¶
b. A son of David. Refs.: 2 Sam. 5:15; 1 Chr. 3:7; 14:6. ¶

NEPHILIM – ***nepiyliym*** [masc. noun: נְפִילִים <5303>; from FALL (verb) <5307>] ▶ **This word is used only in the plural and means giants.** The celebrated, puzzling passage where this term is first used is Genesis 6:4 which merely transliterates the Hebrew word into English as Nephilim. These beings evidently appeared on the earth in the ancient past when possibly divine beings cohabited with women, and Nephilim, the mighty men or warriors of great fame, were the offspring. This huge race of Nephilim struck fear into the Israelite spies who had gone up to survey the land of Canaan (see Num. 13:31–33). The sons of Anak, a tall race of people, came from the Nephilim (Num. 13:33; cf. Deut. 2:10, 11; 9:2; Josh. 15:14). Ezekiel 2:21, 27 may have the Nephilim in mind, possibly equating them with the mighty men or mighty warriors in the passage. These beings were not divine but only at best great, powerful men. ¶

NEPHISHESIM, NEPHUSSIM – ***n^epiyś^esiym*** [proper noun: נְפִישְׁסִים <5304>; plur. from an unused root meaning to scatter] ▶ **The sons of Nephishesim were Temple servants.** Refs.: KJV, Ezra 2:50; Neh. 7:52. For the other versions, see NEPHUSHESIM, NEPHUSSIM <5300>. ¶

NEPHTOAH – ***neptôaḥ*** [proper noun: נֶפְתּוֹחַ <5318>; from OPEN <6605>]: opening ▶ **This word designates a fountain and a stream flowing from it between the territories of Judah and Benjamin.** Refs.: Josh. 15:9; 18:15. ¶

NEPHUSHESIM, NEPHUSSIM – ***n^epûś^esiym*** [proper noun: נְפוּשְׁסִים <5300>; from NEPHISHESIM, NEPHUSSIM <5304>] ▶ **The sons of Nephushesim were Temple servants.** Refs.: Ezr. 2:50; Neh. 7:52. For the KJV, see NEPHISHESIM, NEPHUSSIM <5304>. ¶

NER – ***nêr*** [masc. proper noun: נֵר <5369>; the same as LAMP <5216>]: lamp, light ▶
a. The father of Abner. Refs.: 1 Sam. 14:50, 51; 26:5, 26:14; 2 Sam. 2:8, 12; 3:23, 25, 28, 37; 1 Kgs. 2:5, 32; 1 Chr. 26:28. ¶
b. The father of Kish. Refs.: 1 Chr. 8:33; 9:39. ¶
c. The brother of Kish. Ref.: 1 Chr. 9:36. ¶

NERGAL – ***nêrgal*** [masc. proper noun: נֵרְגַל <5370>; of foreign origin] ▶ **This is the name of a god made by the people of Cuth, a city in southern Mesopotamia.** Ref.: 2 Kgs. 17:30. ¶

NERGAL-SHAREZER – ***nêrgal śar-'eṣer*** [masc. proper noun: נֵרְגַל שַׂר־אֶצֶר <5371>; from NERGAL <5370> and SHAREZER <8272>] ▶
a. A Babylonian official. Refs.: Jer. 39:3, 13. ¶
b. Another Babylonian official. Ref.: Jer. 39:3. ¶

NERIAH – ***nêriyyāh, nêriyyāhû*** [masc. proper noun: נֵרִיָּה, נֵרִיָּהוּ <5374>; from LAMP <5216> and LORD <3050>]: lamp of the Lord ▶ **This word designates the father of Baruch.** Refs.: Jer. 32:12, 16; 36:4, 8, 14, 32; 43:3, 6; 45:1; 51:59. ¶

NEST – [1] ***qên*** [masc. noun: קֵן <7064>; contr. from NEST (MAKE A) <7077>] ▶ **This word refers to the actual constructed homes of various animals or birds.** Refs.: Deut. 22:6; 32:11; Job 39:27. It is used in a figurative sense to describe a safe dwelling (Num. 24:21; Hab. 2:9). The Temple is described as a nest for God's people Israel (Ps. 84:3). It describes cells or units in Noah's ark (Gen. 6:14). *
– [2] Is. 60:8 ➔ WINDOW <699>.

NEST (MAKE, BUILD A) – ***qānan*** [verb: קָנַן <7077>; a prim. root (to erect), but used only as a denom. from NEST <7064>] ▶ **This word refers to the activity of a serpent or a bird constructing its home.** In context it notes God's wisdom and sovereignty being displayed (Ps. 104:17). It is used figuratively of the people living in Lebanon, a place of hills and tall trees in certain areas (Jer. 22:23); or in the hills of Moab (Jer. 48:28). It describes the nesting of birds within the Assyrian Empire (Ezek. 31:6). Other ref.: Is. 34:15. ¶

NESTING PLACES (HAVE) – Dan. 4:21 ➔ DWELL <7932>.

NET – [1] ***ḥêrem*** [masc. noun: חֵרֶם <2764>] ▶ **This word means a device for catching something, especially fish; it is also translated fishnet, trap.** Refs.: Eccl. 7:26; Ezek. 26:5, 14; 32:3; 47:10; Mic. 7:2; Hab. 1:15–17. For another meaning of the Hebrew word, see DEVOTED THINGS <2764>. ¶
[2] ***makmōr, mikmār*** [masc. noun: מַכְמֹר, מִכְמָר <4364>; from YEARN <3648> in the sense of blackening by heat] ▶ **This word means also ensnarement. It refers to a knotted or woven string or a rope fabric for catching birds, fish, or other animals.** It is used figuratively of the nets evil persons create (Ps. 141:10); and of God's people caught in the net of exile like animals (Is. 51:20). ¶
[3] ***mikmeret, mikmōret*** [masc. noun: מִכְמֶרֶת, מִכְמֹרֶת <4365>; from <4364> above] ▶ **This**

word indicates a fishnet, a dragnet. It refers to a net spread out in the waters to catch fish (Is. 19:8). It is used figuratively to describe the oppressive net that the Babylonians cast on Israel, a net of judgment from God on His people (Hab. 1:15, 16; also translated fishing net, drag). ❡

[4] ***māṣôḏ, mᵉṣôḏāh*** [masc. noun: מָצוֹד, מְצוֹדָה <4685>; from HUNT <6679>] ▶ **This word means a hunting implement, a siege tower.** Job claimed that God had surrounded him with a net (Job 19:6). Used figuratively, a wicked person delighted in catching other evil ones (Prov. 12:12; also translated catch, spoil, stronghold, booty); the seductress threw out nets to capture men (Eccl. 7:26; NIV: trap). Siegeworks or bulwarks described the method of attack against a city (Eccl. 9:14; NKJV: snare). ❡

[5] ***mᵉṣûḏāh*** [fem. noun: מְצוּדָה <4686>; for <4685> above] ▶ **This word identifies a net used for hunting prey, a fortress.** Refs.: Ps. 66:11; Ezek. 12:13; 17:20; also translated snare. It is used figuratively of the Lord's net for His own people and their leaders. It indicates a net in which fish are caught but is used as a picture of the snares of human life (Eccl. 9:12). The Hebrew word also means stronghold; see STRONGHOLD <4686>. ❡

[6] ***śāḇāḵ*** [masc. noun: שָׂבָךְ <7638>; from an unused root meaning to intwine] ▶ **This word means a netting; a grating. It refers to some type of artwork made of meshed fabric, wood, or metal.** It was featured in the Temple of Solomon in the form of a grating at the top of pillars (1 Kgs. 7:17; also translated lattice). ❡

[7] ***śᵉḇāḵāh*** [fem. noun: שְׂבָכָה <7639>; fem. of <7638> above] ▶ **This word indicates a lattice, a grating, a screen-material.** See entry <7638> above for 1 Kings 7:17. In 1 Kings 7:18, 20, 41, 42; 2 Kgs. 25:17, it refers to ornamental meshed grating, most likely used to decorate and to hold other items in place by covering them (Jer. 52:22, 23). It refers to a wooden lattice structure probably used as safety fencing in the upper chambers of a house (2 Kgs. 1:2). It refers figuratively to a kind of net serving as a trap or snare that catches the wicked (Job 18:8). *

[8] ***rešeṯ*** [fem. noun: רֶשֶׁת <7568>; from HEIR (BE) <3423> (maybe in the sense of to possess, to seize)] ▶ **This word indicates a metal network, a configuration of metal wires, strips of metal, etc., that crisscrosses at regular intervals.** The large bronze altar featured this kind of network or grating (Ex. 27:4, 5; 38:4). It refers to a network of small ropes, cords, or threads for trapping animals or birds (Prov. 1:17; Ezek. 12:13). It is used figuratively of wicked persons being cast into their own traps, their own nets (Job 18:8); as well as the nations of the world (Ps. 9:15). The wicked person also prepares a net to catch others in it (Ps. 10:9). Flattery or excessive praise is a net for the unwary (Prov. 29:5). In Israel corrupt priests became a net to the people to ensnare them (Hos. 5:1). The Lord can deliver a person ensnared in a net (Ps. 25:15); but He also may prepare Himself to ensnare His people (Hos. 7:12). *

NETAIM – ***nᵉṭāʿiym*** [proper noun: נְטָעִים <5196>; plur. of PLANT (noun) <5194>]: plants ▶ **This word refers to a small village in Moab.** Ref.: 1 Chr. 4:23. ❡

NETHANEL – ***nᵉṯan'ēl*** [masc. proper noun: נְתַנְאֵל <5417>; from GIVE <5414> and GOD <410>]: God has given ▶

a. The son of Zuar. Refs.: Num. 1:8; 2:5; 7:18, 23; 10:15. ❡

b. The father of Shemaiah. Ref.: 1 Chr. 24:6. ❡

c. The son of Jesse. Ref.: 1 Chr. 2:14. ❡

d. A priest. Ref.: 1 Chr. 15:24. ❡

e. The son of Obed-Edom. Ref.: 1 Chr. 26:4. ❡

f. A prince of Judah. Ref.: 2 Chr. 17:7. ❡

g. The brother of Cononiah. Ref.: 2 Chr. 35:9. ❡

h. The son of Jedaiah. Ref.: Neh. 12:21. ❡

i. The son of Pashur. Ref.: Ezra 10:22. ❡

j. A priest. Ref.: Neh. 12:36. ❡

NETHANIAH – ***nᵉṯanyāh, nᵉṯanyāhû*** [masc. proper noun: נְתַנְיָה, נְתַנְיָהוּ <5418>; from GIVE <5414> and LORD <3050>]: given of the Lord ▶

a. The son of Asaph. Refs.: 1 Chr. 25:2, 12. ¶
b. A Levite. Ref.: 2 Chr. 17:8. ¶
c. The father of Jehudi. Ref.: Jer. 36:14. ¶
d. The father of Ishmael. Refs.: 2 Kgs. 25:23, 25; Jer. 40:8, 14, 15; 41:1, 2, 6, 7, 9–12, 15, 16, 18. ¶

NETHINIM – 1 ***n*^e*ṯiyniym*** [plur. proper noun: נְתִינִים <5411>; from GIVE <5414>]: given ones ▶ **This word designates the servants in the Temple.** Refs.: 1 Chr. 9:2; Ezra 2:43, 58, 70; 7:7; 8:17, 20; 3:26, 31; 7:46, 60, 73; 10:28; 11:3, 21. ¶
2 ***n*^e*ṯiyniyn*** [Aramaic plur. proper noun: נְתִינִין <5412>; corresponding to <5411>, the same Hebrew word above]: given ones ▶ **This word designates the servants in the Temple.** Ref.: Ezr. 7:24. ¶

NETOPHAH – ***n*^e*ṭōpāh*** [proper noun: נְטֹפָה <5199>; from DROP (verb) <5197>]: distillation ▶ **A town in Judah.** Refs.: Ezra 2:22; Neh. 7:26. ¶

NETOPHATHITE – ***n*^e*ṭôpāṯiy*** [proper noun: נְטוֹפָתִי <5200>; patron. from NETOPHAH <5199>] ▶ **An inhabitant of Netophah.** Refs.: 2 Sam. 23:28, 29; 2 Kgs. 25:23; 1 Chr. 2:54; 9:16; 11:30; 27:13, 15; Neh. 12:28; Jer. 40:8. ¶

NETTLE – Is. 55:13 ➔ BRIER <5636>.

NETTLES – 1 ***ḥārûl*** [masc. noun: חָרוּל <2738>; apparently pass. part. of an unused root prob. meaning to be prickly] ▶ **This word refers to weeds, thistles.** It depicts weeds in an orchard, vineyard, or field (Prov. 24:31) belonging to a sluggard. They provided a temporary lodging place for the outcasts of society (Job 30:7: also translated undergrowth). It grew in deserted areas and fields like Gomorrah (Zeph. 2:9). ¶
2 ***qimmôś*** [masc. coll. noun: קִמּוֹשׂ <7057>; from an unused root meaning to sting] ▶ **This word refers to a large, hardy, prickly plant that grows wild and covers the face of ruins.** Ref.: Is. 34:13. Its presence is a sign of a lack of cultivation or care of the land (Prov. 24:31), especially after destruction (Hos. 9:6). ¶

NETWORKS – Is. 19:9 ➔ WHITE CLOTH <2355>.

NEVERTHELESS – ***b*^e*ram*** [Aramaic conjunctive adv.: בְּרַם <1297>; perhaps from EXALT <7313> (in the sense of to raise up) with a prep. prefix] ▶ **This word means but, however. It indicates that something is being done in spite of certain contrary circumstances or expectations.** Refs.: Ezra 5:13; Dan. 4:15, 23; 5:17. Daniel receives an answer from the Lord in spite of the impossible situation in which he found himself (Dan. 2:28). ¶

NEW – 1 ***b*^e*riy'āh*** [fem. noun: בְּרִיאָה <1278>; fem. from CREATE <1254>] ▶ **This word indicates something original, i.e., entirely new.** In its biblical context, it describes something as the result of divine activity (Num. 16:30) that can serve as a sign. ¶
2 ***ḥāḏāš*** [adj.: חָדָשׁ <2319>; from RENEW <2318>] ▶ **This word is used to describe many different items as renewed or fresh.** King over Egypt (Ex. 1:8); house (Deut. 20:5); covenant (Jer. 31:31); heaven and earth (Is. 65:17); wife (Deut. 24:5); harvest of grain (Lev. 23:16); garment (1 Kgs. 11:29, 30); vessel (2 Kgs. 2:20). It is used to indicate something new in an obsolete sense, never seen or done before (Eccl. 1:9, 10). It refers to a new song of praise God's people will sing to Him (Ps. 33:3; 40:3; 96:1; 98:1; 144:9; 149:1); and to a new spirit that God implants within them (Ezek. 11:19; 18:31; 36:26). *
3 ***ḥ*^a*ḏaṯ*** [Aramaic adj.: חֲדַת <2323>; corresponding to <2319> above] ▶ **In Ezra 6:4, this word refers to a new (fresh) timber (KJV, NKJV).** Other translators prefer to read *ḥaḏ* here and translate as one (course, layer) of timber (ESV, NASB, NIV). ¶
– 4 Judg. 15:15 ➔ FRESH <2961>.

NEW MOON – See MONTH <2320>.

NEW WINE – ***tiyrôš*** [masc. noun: תִּירוֹשׁ <8492>; from HEIR (BE) <3423> in the sense of expulsion (in the case of grapes, as just squeezed out)] ▶ **New (fresh, freshly**

pressed) wine was one of the blessings God promised to His people in Canaan. Refs.: Gen. 27:28, 37. The best of the new wine went to the priests (Num. 18:12). The NIV translates this word as follows: new wine (34), grapes (1), juice (1), new (1), wine (1). The NASB renders it: new wine (33), fresh wine (1), wine (3), grapes (1). It was intended to be a joyous blessing in Israel (Ps. 4:7; Hos. 2:8, 9); but abused, it became a curse (Hos. 4:11). God could and would therefore remove it (Hos. 9:2); but He will ultimately restore it in a renewed land (Hos. 2:22). *

NEWS – 1 ***bᵉśôrāh, bᵉśōrāh*** [fem. noun: בְּשׂוֹרָה, בְּשֹׂרָה <1309>; fem. from NEWS (BRING) <1319>] ► **This word indicates tidings, message.** It indicates a report delivered to someone about something: the report about the death of Saul was reported using this word (2 Sam. 4:10); news of the defeat of David's enemies (2 Sam. 18:20, 22, 25, 27). It is used for either bad news or good news (2 Kgs. 7:9). ¶
– 2 1 Sam. 17:18 → PLEDGE (noun) <6161>.

NEWS (BRING) – ***bāśar*** [verb: בָּשַׂר <1319>; a prim. root] ► **The general idea of this word is that of a messenger announcing a message.** It may either be bad news (1 Sam. 4:17, the death of Eli's sons) or good news (Jer. 20:15, the birth of Jeremiah). It is often used within the military setting: a messenger coming from battle lines to report the news (2 Sam. 18:19, 20, 26) or victory (1 Sam. 31:9; 2 Sam. 1:20). When used of God's message, this word conveys the victorious salvation which God provides to His people (Ps. 96:2; Is. 40:9; 52:7; 61:1). *

NEXT – ***'aḥᵃrôn, 'aḥᵃrōn*** [adj.: אַחֲרוֹן, אַחֲרֹן <314>; from STAY (verb) <309>] ► **The word means subsequent, last, afterwards.** Its use is quite consistent, but it is nuanced by its context to mean in second position (Gen. 33:2); or to the west, westward (Deut. 11:24). It is used in a temporal sense to mean latter (Ex. 4:8); future (Deut. 29:22); or present (Ruth 3:10). It also means last (2 Sam. 19:11, 12). God is called the first and the last (Is. 41:4). It takes on the meaning of finally in some contexts (2 Sam. 2:26; 1 Kgs. 17:13). *

NEXT DAY – ***moḥᵒrāṯ*** [fem. noun: מָחֳרָת <4283>; from the same as TOMORROW <4279>] ► **This word means the morrow.** It means the following day (Num. 11:32; 1 Chr. 29:21). In an adverbial sense, it means on the next day (Gen. 19:34; Ex. 18:13). With *min* (FROM <4480>) on the front, it indicates on (from) the day after the Sabbath, the new moon respectively (Lev. 23:11; 1 Sam. 20:27). *

NEXT TO – ***'ummāh*** [prep.: עֻמָּה <5980>; from DIM (BECOME) <6004> (in the sense of to associate)] ► **This word means close to, against, alongside. It indicates that something is touching, alongside of, opposite, or very near something else.** In the table of showbread, the rings were close up or up toward the rim (Ex. 25:27); it indicates a spot or location near a particular juncture or point (Ex. 28:27). It indicates that two people were opposite each other on opposing hillsides (2 Sam. 16:13); or in a choir (Neh. 12:24). The wings and wheels of cherubim were beside each other in Ezekiel's vision (Ezek. 11:22). *

NEZIAH – ***nᵉṣiyaḥ*** [masc. proper noun: נְצִיחַ <5335>; from OVERSEE <5329>]: leader ► **Members from his family came back with Zerubbabel from the Babylonian captivity.** Refs.: Ezra 2:54; Neh. 7:56. ¶

NEZIB – ***nᵉṣiyḇ*** [proper noun: נְצִיב <5334>; the same as GARRISON <5333>]: garrison ► **A town in the plain of Judah.** Ref.: Josh. 15:43. ¶

NIBHAZ – ***niḇḥaz*** [masc. proper noun: נִבְחַז <5026>; of foreign origin] ► **A false god.** It refers to one of the many gods of idolatry made by pagan nations, in this case made by the Avvites (2 Kgs. 17:31). ¶

NIBSHAN – ***niḇšān*** [proper noun: נִבְשָׁן <5044>; of uncertain deriv.] ► **One of the**

six cities of Judah that were in the wilderness. Ref.: Josh. 15:62. ¶

NIGHT – [1] **spend the night, pass the night:** ***biyṯ*** [Aramaic verb: בִּית <956>; apparently denom. from HOUSE <1005>] ▶ **This word means to spend, or pass, the time after the day closes.** Darius passed the night fasting and without sleep or diversions (Dan. 6:18). ¶

[2] ***lêylᵉyā'*** [Aramaic masc. noun: לֵילְיָא <3916>; corresponding to NIGHT, MIDNIGHT <3915>] ▶ **All the undisputed instances of this word occur in the book of Daniel. Most often, the term is utilized to declare the time in which several of Daniel's visions took place (i.e., after the close of day).** Refs.: Dan. 2:19; 7:2, 7, 13. However, it functions once to indicate when the assassination of the Babylonian king, Belshazzar, transpired (Dan. 5:30). The word closely corresponds with the Hebrew noun *layil* or *layᵉlāh* (NIGHT, MIDNIGHT <3915>). ¶

– [3] Gen. 19:34; 31:29, 42; Job 30:3: last night, at night, by night ➔ YESTERDAY <570>.

NIGHT BIRD, NIGHT CREATURE, NIGHT MONSTER – ***liyliyṯ*** [fem. noun: לִילִית <3917>; from NIGHT <3915>] ▶ **This word refers to a nocturnal creature that will settle among the ruins of the nations whom God judges.** Ref.: Is. 34:14. It is also translated screech owl in the KJV. ¶

NIGHT, MIDNIGHT – ***laylāh, lāyilā, layil*** [masc. noun: לַיְלָה, לָיִל, לֵיל <3915>; from the same as STAIRWAY <3883>] ▶ **This Hebrew word primarily describes the portion of day between sunset and sunrise.** Ref.: Gen. 1:5; cf. Ps. 136:9. Figuratively, it signifies the gloom or despair that sometimes engulfs the human heart from an absence of divine guidance (Mic. 3:6); calamity (Job 36:20); or affliction (Job 30:17). Nevertheless, even in the dark night of the soul, the Lord gives His people a song of joy (Job 35:10; Ps. 42:8). *

NIGHTHAWK – Lev. 11:16; Deut. 14:15 ➔ OWL <8464> b.

NIMRAH – ***nimrāh*** [proper noun: נִמְרָה <5247>]; from the same as LEOPARD <5246>]: limpid ▶ **A city of Gad on the east side of the Jordan.** Ref.: Num. 32:3. ¶

NIMRIM – ***nimriym*** [proper noun: נִמְרִים <5249>; plur. of a masc. corresponding to NIMRAH <5247>] ▶ **A place in Moab; its waters were to become desolate.** Refs.: Is. 15:6; Jer. 48:34. ¶

NIMROD – ***nimrōḏ*** [proper noun: נִמְרֹד <5248>; prob. of foreign origin]: rebel ▶
a. An ancient king of antiquity (possibly Sargon I of Akkad). He was celebrated both as a great warrior and as a kingdom builder in the area of ancient southern Mesopotamia and later in northern Mesopotamia near the Tigris River. Nineveh, Babylon, and Akkad are just three of the foundational cities he set up. Refs.: Gen. 10:8, 9; 1 Chr. 1:10. ¶
b. Another name for Assyria, the ancient founder of the nation. It stands in Hebrew poetry in parallelism with Assyria. Ref.: Mic. 5:6. ¶

NIMSHI – ***nimšiy*** [masc. proper noun: נִמְשִׁי <5250>; prob. from DRAW <4871>]: drawn, rescued ▶ **Father (or ancestor) of king Jehu.** Refs.: 1 Kgs. 19:16; 2 Kgs. 9:2, 14, 20; 2 Chr. 22:7. ¶

NINE – ***têša'*** [masc. number: תֵּשַׁע <8672>; perhaps from LOOK WITH FAVOR OR IN DISMAY <8159> through the idea of a turn to the next or full number ten] ▶ **This word is a cardinal counting number (nine). As an ordinal number it also indicates the ninth item in a series.** Refs.: Num. 29:26 (nine bulls); Josh. 15:44 (nine towns). It combines with other numbers to create larger numbers, e.g., nine hundred and thirty years (Gen. 5:5). *

NINETY – ***tiš'iym*** [masc. plur. number: תִּשְׁעִים <8673>; multiple from NINE <8672>] ▶ **This word is a cardinal counting number indicating the total number of something.** It refers to any item that needs to be counted: e.g., years (Gen. 5:9).

It combines with other numbers to form larger numbers (Gen. 5:17, 30), e.g., eight hundred and ninety-five years. *

NINEVEH – ***niyn*^e*wêh*** [proper noun: נִינְוֵה <5210>; of foreign origin] ▶ **This name designates the great capital city of the Assyrian Empire. It served as the last capital of the nation and was destroyed in 612 B.C. by the Babylonians.** It is the sole topic of two prophetic books. In the Book of Jonah, it received mercy from God and a period of reprieve (ca. 775–750 B.C.). But Nahum celebrated the destruction of the great city that had devastated and bloodied the cities and nations around it. Zephaniah indicated the complete collapse and enduring desolation of the city (Zeph. 2:13).

Its foundation is set in the time before the call of Abraham (Gen. 10:11, 12). Nimrod had a part in its founding. In ca. 701 B.C., Sennacherib fled there after his futile attempt to destroy Jerusalem (2 Kgs. 19:35, 36; Is. 37:37). Other refs.: Jon. 1:2; 3:2–7; 4:11; Nah. 1:1; 2:8; 3:7. ¶

NINTH – ***t*^e*šiy'iy*** [ordinal number: תְּשִׁיעִי <8671>; from NINE <8672>] ▶ **This word is used to indicate the ninth item in a series of nine or more.** Refs.: Lev. 25:22 (the ninth year), Num. 7:60 (the ninth day). *

NIP – Lev. 5:8 ➔ WRING OFF <4454>.

NISAN – ***niysān*** [proper noun: נִיסָן <5212>; prob. of foreign origin] ▶ **This word refers to the first month of the Old Testament year.** It was equal to our March/April period of time (Neh. 2:1; Esther 3:7), a period of thirty days. It was called Abib before the Babylonian exile. The Passover, The Feast of unleavened Bread, and the Feast of Firstfruits were festivals held during this month. ¶

NISROCK – ***nisrōḵ*** [masc. proper noun: נִסְרֹךְ <5268>; of foreign origin] ▶ **This word refers to a pagan god worshiped by Assyrians in a temple at Nineveh.** Refs.: 2 Kgs. 19:37; Is. 37:38. ¶

NITRE – Prov. 25:20 ➔ SODA <5427>.

NO (particle) – 1 ***'ayin*** [particle: אַיִן <369>; as if from a prim. root meaning to be nothing or not exist] ▶ **A particle or semi-verb of negation or nonexistence meaning no, none, nothing. It is used hundreds of times with various negative nuances.** It can simply negate something (Ex. 17:7; Ps. 135:17) or assert that something is as nothing in comparison (Is. 40:17). Used with the preposition *l*^e, it indicates non possession (Gen. 11:30; Prov. 13:7; Is. 27:4; Hos. 10:3). It refers to the lack of a successor (Dan. 9:26). It indicates those who lack strength or power (Is. 40:29, *ûl*^e*'êyn 'ōniym*). When used with an infinitive, it negates the thought of the infinitive (Ps. 32:9). When the preposition *l*^e is added to the negated infinitive (*'eyn* + *l*^e + infinitive), it gives the meaning not to permit + the meaning of the particular infinitive (Esther 4:2). The antonym of *'ayin* is *yeš*, there is, are. *

2 ***'al*** [adv.: אַל <408>; a neg. particle (akin to NO, NOT, NEVER <3808>)] ▶ **This word also means not, without; a basic adverb of negation.** It is used consistently with the imperfect form of the verb to render a negative imperative or prohibition (Gen. 15:1; 22:12; 37:27; Ps. 25:2; Jer. 18:18). With the regular imperative, it expresses purpose, such as, that we may not die (1 Sam. 12:19). In poetic sections, it may express the poet's strong emotions (Job 5:22; Ps. 41:2; Prov. 3:25; Is. 2:9). It is also used without a verb to express simple negation in an imperative mode, as in *'al-ṭal*, let there be no dew (2 Sam. 1:21). It can have the meaning of there is no (Prov. 12:28), i.e., there is no death. It can also function as a noun + *l*^e meaning something comes to naught, nothing (Job 24:25). Coupled with the particle *nā'*, it means please do not or therefore, do not (Gen. 18:3). *

NO (proper noun) – ***nō'*** [proper noun: נֹא <4996>; of Egyptian origin] ▶ **This word designates No, a Hebrew name for Thebes in southern Egypt, an ancient capital city of Egypt.** *No* represents the Egyptian *niw(t)* and means "the city." Jeremiah and Ezekiel both indicated that God was about to punish No (Thebes) and its gods, especially the god Amon. Nahum mentioned its fall in 663 B.C. to the Assyrians as a past event. Refs.: Jer. 46:25; Ezek. 30:14–16; Nah. 3:8. ¶

NO, NOT, NEVER – 1 ***lō', lô', lōh*** [adverb: לֹא, לוֹא, לֹה <3808>; a prim. particle] ▶ **This term is primarily utilized as an ordinary negation.** For example in Genesis 3:4: "You will not surely die" (NIV cf. Judg. 14:4; Ps. 16:10). Often it is used to express an unconditional prohibition, thus having the force of an imperative: "You shall not (= do not ever) steal"(Ex. 20:15 NIV; cf. Judg. 13:5). Frequently, it functions as an absolute in answer to a question (Job 23:6; Zech. 4:5). The word is also employed in questions to denote that an affirmative answer is expected (2 Kgs. 5:26; Jon. 4:11). When it is prefixed to a noun or adjective, it negates that word, making it have an opposite or contrary meaning (e.g., god becomes non-god; strong becomes weak; cf. Deut. 32:21; Prov. 30:25). When prefixed by the preposition *bᵉ*, meaning in or by, the combined term carries the temporal meaning of beyond or before (Lev. 15:25); the meaning without is also not uncommon for this combination (Job 8:11). A prefixed preposition *lᵉ*, meaning to or for, gives the term the meaning of without (2 Chr. 15:3) or as though not (Job 39:16). Occasionally, the word suggests the meaning not only, on account of the context (Deut. 5:3). *

2 ***lā'*** [Aramaic particle: לָא <3809>; corresponding to <3808> above] ▶ **This term is used to negate the assertions of clauses.** Refs.: Ezra 4:13; Jer. 10:11; Dan. 2:5. It is used with *'îytay* following to negate the existence of something (Ezra 4:16; Dan. 2:10). It negates particular words, e.g., with *bᵉ* attached to the noun, "not by means of any wisdom . . ." (Dan. 2:30). Used with *dîy* preceding, it means without (Ezra 6:8; Dan. 6:8). *

NOADIAH – ***nô'aḏyāh*** [proper noun: נוֹעַדְיָה <5129>; from APPOINT <3259> and LORD <3050>]: meeting with the Lord ▶
a. A Levite under Ezra. Ref.: Ezra 8:33. ¶
b. A prophetess. Ref.: Neh. 6:14. ¶

NOAH – 1 ***nôḥāh*** [masc. proper noun: נוֹחָה <5119>; from RESTING PLACE <5118>]: rest ▶ **The fourth son of Benjamin.** Ref.: 1 Chr. 8:2. ¶

2 ***nōaḥ*** [masc. proper noun: נֹחַ <5146>; the same as RESTING PLACE <5118>]: rest ▶ **He is the son of Lamech. Noah gave rest to humankind from the curse placed on the earth.** Refs.: Gen. 4:28–32. He was considered a righteous man in his generation who found favor with God (Gen. 6:8–10). He followed the Lord and constructed an ark to preserve humanity from destruction (Gen. 6:14–21). God preserved him and his family. God caused the flood waters to stop and recede when He remembered Noah (Gen. 8:1). Noah offered sacrifices to God after leaving the ark (Gen. 8:21). He was sinned against by his son Ham. Noah, inspired by God, placed a curse on Ham and his descendants, the Canaanites (Gen. 9:1–29). The earth was repopulated by the descendants of his three sons, Ham, Shem, and Japheth (Gen. 10). The prophets remembered the time of Noah as a moral-religious message to guide (Is. 54:9) and to warn them. *

3 ***nō'āh*** [fem. proper noun: נֹעָה <5270>; from WANDER <5128>]: who wanders, motion ▶ **One of the five daughters of Zelophehad.** Refs.: Num. 26:33; 27:1; 36:11; Josh. 17:3. ¶

NOB – ***nōḇ*** [proper noun: נֹב <5011>; the same as FRUIT <5108>]: fruit ▶ **A priestly city in Benjamin situated on a high place near Jerusalem.** Refs.: 1 Sam. 21:1; 22:9, 11, 19; Neh. 11:32; Is. 10:32. ¶

NOBAH – ***nōḇaḥ*** [masc. proper noun: נֹבַח <5025>; from BARK <5024>]: bark (made by a dog) ▶
a. A Manassite. Ref.: Num. 32:42.
b. A location in Gilead. Refs.: Num. 32:42; Judg. 8:11. ¶

NOBILITY – 1 Job 30:15 ➔ DIGNITY <5082> 2 Eccl. 10:17 ➔ NOBLE <2715>.

NOBILITY (WOMAN OF) – Esther 1:18 ➔ PRINCESS <8282>.

NOBLE – [1] ***'āṣiyl*** [masc. noun: אָצִיל <678>; from RESERVE (verb) <680> (in its secondary sense of separation)] ► **This term means and is also translated leader, chief man in Exodus 24:11.** See also FARTHEST CORNER <678>. ¶

[2] ***ḥōr*** [masc. noun: חֹר <2715>] ► **This word occurs only in the plural form and apparently comes from a root, unused in the Old Testament, which means free. The nobles were a social order having power over the lower classes of people.** Such power was sometimes misused, exacting usury (Neh. 5:7), even following a royal order to kill innocent Naboth (1 Kgs. 21:8, 11; also translated leader). In Nehemiah's time, they maintained strong family connections (Neh. 6:17). Ecclesiastes 10:17 indicates that nobility was inherited and could not be instantly attained by election or force; otherwise, all kings would be nobility by definition. Thus, nobles made the best kings (Eccl. 10:17), apparently because they came from a background of involvement in civic affairs and were not suddenly vaulted to such a high position. Other refs.: Neh. 2:16; 4:14, 19; 7:5; 13:17; Is. 34:12; Jer. 27:20; 39:6. ¶

[3] ***yaqqiyr*** [Aramaic adj.: יַקִּיר <3358>; corresponding to DEAR <3357>] ► **This word is used when referring to the king of Assyria to show great respect.** Ref.: Ezra 4:10; also translated honorable. In Daniel 2:11, the word takes on the sense of astonishing, outstanding, a difficult (KJV: rare) task that the king demanded of his wise men. ¶

[4] ***partᵉmiym*** [masc. noun: פַּרְתְּמִים <6579>; of Persian origin] ► **This word means and is also translated prince, nobility. It is only used in the plural form in the Hebrew Old Testament.** The most important people in the kingdom were invited to King Xerxes' banquet (Esther 1:3). Haman suggested to the king that the appropriate way to honor someone was to have a nobleman lead him around the kingdom in the king's robe and on the king's horse (Esther 6:9). When Babylon captured Jerusalem, the young Israelite nobility were taken into Nebuchadnezzar's service (Dan. 1:3). Shadrach, Meshach, Abednego, and Daniel were part of this group. ¶

[5] ***rabrᵉḇān*** [Aramaic masc. noun: רַבְרְבָן <7261>; from GREAT, GREAT THINGS <7260>] ► **This word means an important official; it is also translated lord. The term occurs only in the plural and is found only in the book of Daniel.** Nebuchadnezzar and Belshazzar, both kings of Babylon at one point, were served and sought by a great host of these important officials (Dan. 4:36; 5:1–3, 9, 10, 23; 6:17). ¶

– [6] Judg. 5:25; Jer. 14:3; Nah. 3:18 ➔ MIGHTY <117> [7] Ps. 68:31 ➔ ENVOY <2831> [8] Prov. 8:6 ➔ LEADER <5057> [9] Is. 32:8 ➔ DIGNITY <5082> [10] Ezek. 17:8 ➔ GARMENT <155> [11] Ezek. 17:23 ➔ MIGHTY <117>.

NOBLE WOMAN – Esther 1:18 ➔ PRINCESS <8282>.

NOBODY – Is. 3:5 ➔ DESPISED (BE) <7034>.

NOBODY (BE A) – Prov. 12:9 ➔ DESPISED (BE) <7034>.

NOCTURNAL EMISSION – ***qāreh*** [masc. noun: קָרֶה <7137>; from HAPPEN <7136>] ► **This word indicates a temporary pollution.** It refers to a man's nocturnal emission of semen during the night, which rendered him temporarily unclean (Deut. 23:10). ¶

NOD – ***nôḏ*** [proper noun: נוֹד <5113>; the same as WANDERING <5112>]: wandering ► **Cain went away from the Lord's presence and settled in the land of Nod.** Ref.: Gen. 4:16. ¶

NODAB – ***nôḏāḇ*** [proper noun: נוֹדָב <5114>; from GIVE WILLINGLY <5068>]: noble ► **The name of an Arab tribe.** Ref.: 1 Chr. 5:19. ¶

NOGAH – ***nōgah*** [masc. proper noun: נֹגַהּ <5052>; the same as BRIGHTNESS <5051>]: brightness ► **One of the sons of David.** Refs.: 1 Chr. 3:7; 14:6. ¶

NOISE – [1] ***hemyāh*** [fem. noun: הֶמְיָה <1998>; from MURMUR <1993>] ► **This word means and is also translated music, sound.** It depicts the noise or music of harps (Is. 14:11) standing for the pride and joy of Babylon. ¶
[2] ***h***^{a}***mullāh, h***^{a}***mûllāh*** [fem. noun: הֲמֻלָּה, הֲמוּלָּה <1999>; fem. pass. part. of an unused root] ► **This word means a rushing sound; it is also translated roar, tumult. The two occurrences of this word conjure up the sound of a great wind.** The first is in the prophecy of Jeremiah, where Israel was called a strong olive tree, but the Lord would set the tree on fire with a great rushing sound as a sign of judgment (Jer. 11:16). The word is also used in Ezekiel's vision, where the sound of the creatures' wings was like the roar of a rushing river (Ezek. 1:24). ¶
[3] ***rêa'*** [masc. noun: רֵעַ <7452>; from SHOUT (verb) <7321>] ► **This word refers to a loud shout, roar, thunder. It refers to the sound and the action of shouting.** It refers to the shouts of the idolatrous Israelites as they shouted (lit.: in its shouting) in rebellion and confusion to their gods (Ex. 32:17). It refers to the sound of thunder and lightning (Job 36:33; ESV: crashing). It refers to a cry of agony, reinforced by the use of its related verb (Mic. 4:9: aloud, loudly). ¶
– [4] Job 36:29; Is. 22:2 ➔ STORM (noun) <8663> [5] Job 37:2 ➔ TURMOIL <7267>.

NOISE (MAKE A) – Ps. 98:4 ➔ BREAK FORTH <6476> a.

NOMADS – Ps. 72:9 ➔ WILDERNESS <6728>.

NONE – See NO <369>.

NONSENSE – Zech. 10:2 ➔ NOTHINGNESS <205>.

NOON – ***ṣōhar*** [masc. noun: צֹהַר <6672>; from OIL <6671> (in the sense of to spend noon)] ► **This word means midday. It is used in a dual form *ṣoh***^{o}***rayim*.** At noon is *baṣṣoh*^{o}*rayim* (Gen. 43:16, 25); but also without *b*^{e} (1 Kgs. 18:29). It indicates noon as a time of prayer (Ps. 55:17). With *b*^{e}*tôḵ* preceding, it means at noonday, in broad daylight (Is. 16:3). An afternoon nap, lying down in the afternoon, is a time of rest, a siesta (2 Sam. 4:5). It is used figuratively as a time of blessing, joy, happiness (Is. 58:10). The Hebrew word also means window space, roof; see WINDOW <6672>. *

NOOSE – Prov. 7:22 ➔ FETTER <5914>.

NOPH – See MEMPHIS <5297>.

NOPHAH – ***nōp̱aḥ*** [proper noun: נֹפַח <5302>; from BREATHE <5301>] ► **A city in Moab.** Ref.: Num. 21:30. ¶

NORTH – [1] ***m***^{e}***zāreh*** [masc. noun: מְזָרֶה <4215>; apparently from SCATTER <2219>] ►
a. This word indicates the area of the north as opposed to the south. Ref.: Job 37:9; NASB, KJV. ¶
b. This word indicates a driving wind, a scattering wind. Some translations prefer this rendering of the word indicating winds that carry with them the cold of winter or a storm (Job 37:9; NKJV, ESV, NIV). ¶
[2] ***ṣāp̱ôn*** [common noun: צָפוֹן <6828>; from HIDE <6845> (i.e., dark; used only of the north as a quarter, gloomy and unknown)] ► **This word refers to the direction north; facing east, the left hand points north.** Refs.: Gen. 13:14; 28:14. It combines with other directions (Gen. 13:14). With *āh* on the end, it indicates a northward direction (Ex. 40:22; Jer. 23:8); followed by *'el,* it means toward the north (Eccl. 1:6; Ezek. 42:1); or with *l*^{e} on the front (Ezek. 40:23). From the north is expressed by *min* (<4480>) + *ṣāp̱on* (Is. 14:31). The north became a source of violence, evil (Jer. 1:14). It was used of the great Mount Hermon of the north (Ps. 48:2; 89:12; Ezek. 32:30). *

NORTHERN ARMY – ***ṣ***^{e}***p̱ôniy*** [adj.: צְפוֹנִי <6830>; from NORTH <6828>] ► **This word is an adjective form from *ṣāp̱on* meaning north.** It probably refers to an invading army (Joel 2:20); it is also translated northern horde, northerner. ¶

NORTHERN HORDE – Joel 2:20 ➔ NORTHERN ARMY <6830>.

NORTHERNER – Joel 2:20 ➔ NORTHERN ARMY <6830>.

NOSE – ***'ap̱*** [masc. noun: אַף <639>; from ANGRY (BE̱) <599>] ▶ **This word means the organ of smell; it also means nostril and anger.** These meanings are used together in an interesting wordplay in Proverbs 30:33. This word may, by extension, refer to the whole face, particularly in the expression, to bow one's face to the ground (Gen. 3:19; 19:1; 1 Sam. 24:8). To have length of nose is to be slow to wrath; to have shortness of nose is to be quick tempered (Prov. 14:17, 29; Jer. 15:14, 15). This Hebrew term is often intensified by being paired with another word for anger or by associating it with various words for burning (Num. 22:27; Deut. 9:19; Jer. 4:8; 7:20). Human anger is almost always viewed negatively with only a few possible exceptions (Ex. 32:19; 1 Sam. 11:6; Prov. 27:4). The anger of the Lord is a frequent topic in the Old Testament. The Old Testament describes how God is reluctant to exercise His anger and how fierce His anger is (Ex. 4:14; 34:6; Ps. 30:5; 78:38; Jer. 51:45). *

NOSTRIL – 1 ***nāḥiyr*** [masc. noun: נָחִיר <5156>; from the same as SNORTING <5170>] ▶ **This word is used of the breathing holes in the nose of Leviathan, a legendary monster or crocodile that God described.** Ref.: Job 41:20. ¶
– 2 See NOSE <639>.

NOT – 1 ***'iy*** [adv.: אִי <336>; prob. identical with WHERE <335> (through the idea of a query)] ▶ **This negative adverb is used to indicate one not innocent.** It is found in Job 22:30; KJV translates: island. ¶
2 ***bal*** [neg. particle: בַּל <1077>; from WEAR OUT <1086>] ▶ **This word means cannot; scarcely, hardly. This negative is used in poetry and is a synonym of Hebrew *lô'*.** It is often found repeated in certain contexts meaning no, not (Is. 26:10, 11, 14, 18; 33:20, 21, 23, 24; 44:8, 9). It is used often to negate the verb *môṭ*, to move, to choke, to stagger, to reel, e.g., Psalm 16:8, "I will not be shaken" (NASB) (Job 41:23; Ps. 10:6; 16:8; 21:7; 30:6; Prov. 10:30; 12:3). It means scarcely, hardly, no sooner in Isaiah 40:24, depicting the ephemeral nature of worldly rulers. *
3 ***b*^{e}*liy*** [neg. particle: בְּלִי <1097>; from WEAR OUT <1086>] ▶ **This word means without.** It is used as a noun with a negative implication often meaning destruction, failure (Ps. 72:7; Is. 38:17). More often it negates something by interjecting the idea of without, defective: without a name, nameless (Job 30:8); without a place, last place (Is. 28:8); and often with the meaning without: without water (Job 8:11); without clothing, naked (Job 24:10); without knowledge (Job 35:16; 42:3). It is used to negate an idea put forth in an adjective or participle of a verb (2 Sam. 1:21; Ps. 19:3).

A preposition may be prefixed to *beliy* to mean without (Job 35:16; 36:12, without knowledge; Is. 5:14; Jer. 2:15). With the preposition *min* (<4480>) prefixed, this combination expresses causation, because, since (Deut. 9:28; 28:55). Sometimes the same construction means for lack of or for want of (Is. 5:13; Ezek. 34:5; Hos. 5:6). The Lord's people are being destroyed for lack of knowledge (Hos. 4:6). This combination functions with a following ^{a}*šer* and as a conjunction meaning so that not . . . (Eccl. 3:11). Very rarely, it is used to negate a finite verb form (Gen. 31:20; Is. 32:10; Job 41:26). *
4 ***biltiy*** [neg. particle: בִּלְתִּי <1115>; constructive fem. of WEAR OUT <1086> (equivalent to <1097> above)] ▶ **This word is used often to negate an infinitive meaning: not to, plus infinitive, e.g., plus *'āḵal* <398>, not to eat.** Refs.: Gen. 3:11; cf. Gen. 4:15; 19:21; Deut. 4:21); in order that . . . not, negative purpose, is expressed by this construction (Gen. 4:15; 38:9; Ex. 8:22, Ex. 8:29; Deut. 17:12); so that . . . not, negative result, is expressed likewise (Is. 44:10; Jer. 7:8). It is used after verbs that assert a command or order (Gen. 3:11; 2 Kgs. 17:15; Jer. 35:8, 9, 14); verbs of

swearing (Josh. 5:6; Judg. 21:7); agreeing (2 Kgs. 12:8); interceding (Jer. 36:25).

It is used to negate a following noun, such as in the phrase *'âḏ-biltiy šāmayim*, until there be no heavens (Job 14:12; cf. Num. 21:35; Josh. 8:22; 2 Kgs. 10:11); to negate an adjective, he is not clean (Gen. 47:18; Judg. 7:14). In some cases when it is used alone, it means except (Gen. 43:3; Num. 11:6; Is. 10:4). *

NOTABLE – Dan. 8:5 ➔ VISION <2380>.

NOTE – Dan. 10:21 ➔ INSCRIBE <7559>.

NOTHING – 1 ***'epes, 'ōphes*** [masc. noun: אֶפֶס, אֹפֶס <657>; from FAIL <656>] ▶ **This word indicates ceasing, end, extremity, naught.** It is used essentially in three ways meaning ceasing, nonexistence, no effect. 1) to cease to exist or effect (Is. 34:12; 41:29); to act with no effect (Is. 52:4); 2) a cessation of something, such as until there is no place (Deut. 32:36; 2 Kgs. 14:26; Is. 45:6; Amos 6:10); 3) the idea of limiting, such as only (Num. 22:35; 23:13) or except that (Num. 13:28; Deut. 15:4; Judg. 4:9). The word is also used to mean ceasing in the sense of end or extremity: the ends of the earth (Deut. 33:17; 1 Sam. 2:10; Prov. 30:4; Jer. 16:19; Micah 5:4). This Hebrew word also means ankles or soles of the feet; see ANKLE <657>. *

2 ***'epa'*** [masc. noun: אֶפַע <659>; from an unused root prob. meaning to breathe] ▶ **This word means worthlessness; it is also translated of no account.** It refers to the absolute inability of pagan gods to act as gods (Is. 41:24). ¶

3 ***beliymāh*** [fem. noun: בְּלִימָה <1099>; from NOT <1097> and WHAT? <4100>] ▶ **This word means literally nothingness, what is nothing, not aught, not any thing.** In poetic language, it describes what God hangs the earth on—nothing (Job 26:7). ¶

– 4 Dan. 6:17 ➔ SITUATION <6640> 5 Is. 41:29; Amos 5:5 ➔ NOTHINGNESS <205> 6 See NO <369>.

NOTHING (BRING TO) – ***pûr*** [fem. noun: פּוּר <6331>; a prim. root] ▶ **This word means to make something to cease.** It refers to causing the plans or machinations of nations or peoples to come to nothing (Ps. 33:10; also translated to foil, to bring to nought, to nullify); or to cut off or stop something (Ps. 89:33: to take from, to remove, to break off; Ezek. 17:19: to break). ¶

NOTHINGNESS – ***'āwen*** [masc. noun: אָוֶן <205>; from an unused root perhaps meaning properly to pant (hence, to exert oneself, usually in vain] ▶ **The primary meaning of this word is that of emptiness and vanity. It also means trouble, sorrow, evil, or mischief.** It is used to signify empty or futile pursuits (Prov. 22:8: vanity, sorrow, calamity; Is. 41:29: nothing, worthless); nothingness, in the sense of utter destruction (Amos 5:5: nothing, nought, trouble); an empty word, implying falsehood or deceit (Ps. 10:7: iniquity, wickedness, vanity, evil; Prov. 17:4: false, wicked, deceitful; Zech. 10:2: vanity, iniquity, delusion, nonsense); wickedness or one who commits iniquity (Num. 23:21; Job 22:15; Ps. 14:4; 36:4; 101:8; Is. 58:9; Mic. 2:1); evil or calamity (Job 5:6; Prov. 12:21; Jer. 4:15); and great sorrow (Deut. 26:14: mourning; Ps. 90:10: sorrow, trouble; Hos. 9:4: mourner). In a metaphorical sense, the word is used once to signify an idol, strongly conveying the futility of worshiping an idol, which is, in fact, "nothing" (Is. 66:3). *

NOTICE (TAKE) – Jon. 1:6 ➔ CONCERNED (BE) <6245>.

NOUGHT – Amos 5:5 ➔ NOTHINGNESS <205>.

NOUGHT (BRING TO) – Ps. 33:10 ➔ NOTHING (BRING TO) <6329>.

NOURISH – Gen. 45:11 ➔ CONTAIN <3557>.

NOURISHER – Ruth 4:15 ➔ CONTAIN <3557>.

NOURISHMENT – Prov. 3:8 ➔ DRINK (noun) <8250>.

NOW – [1] ***kᵉʿan*** [Aramaic adv.: כְּעַן <3705>; prob. from THUS <3652>] ▶ **This word indicates at the present time, immediately; it also means now then, furthermore. It has both a time and logical sense in its use.** It occurs only at the beginning of its clause (Ezra 4:13, 14, 21; Dan. 2:23; 3:15). With *ʿaḏ-* preceding, the phrase means up to or until now (Ezra 5:16). *
[2] ***ʿattāh*** [adv.: עַתָּה <6258>; from TIME <6256>] ▶ **This word means already, then, therefore.** It refers to a certain point in time that has been reached (Gen. 3:22; 22:12) but also has a logical function at the same time: Since we are at this time and set of circumstances, therefore. So it is also a logical connector or indicator (Ex. 3:9, 10). It may stress the current time or situation (Gen. 12:19; Num. 24:17). With *ʿaḏ-ʿattāh,* it means up to now, until now (Gen. 32:4; Deut. 12:9). Combined with *min* (4480), *mêʿattāh,* it means from now on (Is. 48:6; Jer. 3:4). It can mean already, something has happened or is under way (Ex. 5:5). *
– [3] Gen. 47:23 ➔ BEHOLD (interj.) <1887> [4] Eccl. 2:16; 9:6, 7 ➔ ALREADY <3528> [5] See THEN <645>.

NOW, AND NOW – ***kᵉʿeneṯ, kᵉʿeṯ*** [Aramaic particle.: כְּעֶנֶת, כְּעֶת <3706>; fem. of NOW <3705>] ▶ **This Aramaic word is related to what follows and serves to introduce it.** Refs.: Ezra 4:10, 11, 17; 7:12. ¶

NULLIFY – Ps. 33:10 ➔ NOTHING (BRING TO) <6329>.

NUMB (BECOME, GROW) – Gen. 45:26; Ps. 77:2 ➔ STUNNED (BECOME) <6313>.

NUMBER (noun) – [1] ***miḵsāh*** [fem. noun: מִכְסָה <4373>; fem. of TRIBUTE <4371>] ▶ **This word means a figure, a counting; it also means an evaluation, an amount, worth.** It is used as a record of the number of persons in an Israelite family (Ex. 12:4); or the actual agreed upon evaluation or worth of a piece of land (Lev. 27:23). ¶
[2] ***mᵉniy*** [masc. noun: מְנִי <4507>; from COUNT <4487>] ▶
a. This word refers to the tally or reckoning of something by numbers. It refers to total persons in a group of troops (Is. 65:11, KJV). ¶
b. According to other translators, this word refers to a false god. It refers to the god of Fate, Meni (Is. 65:11; also translated Destiny) and stands parallel to Fortune. ¶
[3] ***minyān*** [Aramaic masc. noun: מִנְיָן <4510>; from APPOINT <4483> (in the sense of counted)] ▶ **This word refers to the tally or reckoning of something by numbers.** It refers to the count of the twelve tribes in Israel (Ezra 6:17). ¶
[4] ***mispār*** [masc. noun: מִסְפָּר <4557>; from NUMBER (verb) <5608>] ▶ **This word also means a count, an amount.** In general it indicates the quantity numerically of something: years (Dan. 9:2); persons (Num. 3:22); cities (Jer. 2:28), etc. It can take on the sense of recounting something that has happened, a story or narrative (Judg. 7:15). If something is numbered, it may mean that it is fixed or few (Deut. 33:6). Something that is *ʾêyn mispār* is without number, innumerable (Gen. 41:49); or unlimited (Ps. 40:12; 147:5). The verb *ʿāḇar,* to cross over, plus *bᵉmispār* means to be counted, enrolled (2 Sam. 2:15). *ʿĀlāh mispar* means to go into a record, into an account (1 Chr. 27:24). *
[5] ***sᵉp̄ōrāh*** [fem. noun: סְפֹרָה <5615>; from NUMBER (verb) <5608>] ▶ **This word indicates a sum, an amount; it is also translated limit.** It refers to the total count or full amount of something. It is used of the totality of God's righteousness, His salvation (Ps. 71:15). ¶
– [6] Ex. 5:8 ➔ PROPORTION <4971> [7] 2 Sam. 24:9 ➔ APPOINTMENT <4662>.

NUMBER (IN SUFFICIENT) – 2 Chr. 30:3 ➔ SUFFICIENTLY <4078>.

NUMBER (LARGE, GREAT) – ***rōḇ*** [masc. noun: רֹב <7230>; from MANY (BE, BECOME) <7231>] ▶ **This word indicates an abundance.** It is used to indicate that something is numerous, such as people (Gen. 16:10; 30:30); that there is an abundance of something (Gen. 27:28). Preceded by *mê* (*min*), it means because of the multitude (Gen. 32:12). It is used with various words to form phrases: *roḇ dereḵ*, a long distance, road (Josh. 9:13); *roḇ yāmîm*, many days, a long time, etc. (Is. 24:22). The idiom *lāroḇ* means in respect to a multitude, a number (Josh. 11:4). *

NUMBER (SAME) – Ex. 5:18 → QUOTA <8506>.

NUMBER (verb) – [1] ***sāpar, sōpêr, sôpêr*** [verb: סָפַר, סֹפֵר, סוֹפֵר <5608>; a prim. root] ▶
a. A verb meaning to count and also meaning to recount, to relate, to declare. It is used to signify the numbering or counting of objects (Gen. 15:5; Ps. 48:12); and people, as in a census (1 Chr. 21:2; 2 Chr. 2:17). It also refers to a quantity that is too great to number (Gen. 16:10; Jer. 33:22). God's numbering of one's steps is a sign of His care (Job 14:16; cf. Matt. 10:30). The word also means to relate or to recount and is used often to refer to the communication of important information and truths to those who have not heard them, especially to foreign nations (Ex. 9:16; 1 Chr. 16:24; Ps. 96:3); or to the children in Israel (Ps. 73:15; 78:4, 6; 79:13). The matter communicated included dreams (Gen. 40:9; 41:8, 12; Judg. 7:13); God's works (Ex. 18:8; Ps. 73:28; Jer. 51:10); and recounting one's own ways to God (Ps. 119:26). The word also signifies the silent witness of the creation to its Creator and His wisdom and glory (Job 12:8; 28:27; Ps. 19:1).
b. The participle form of the word *sōpêr*, means scribe and occurs about fifty times in the Old Testament. Scribes such as Ezra studied, practiced, and taught the Law (Ezra 7:11). Scribes also served kings, writing and sometimes carrying messages to and from court (2 Kgs. 18:18; 19:2; Esther 3:12; 8:9). In 2 Kings 22:10, a scribe read the recovered scroll of the Law to King Josiah, bringing about a personal revival. Scribes, as people who could read and count, also acted militarily, gathering the troops (2 Kgs. 25:19; Jer. 52:25). The occupation of scribe could belong to a family (1 Chr. 2:55). Also, some Levites occupied the position as part of their job (2 Chr. 34:13). *
– [2] Dan. 5:26 → APPOINT <4483> [3] See COUNT <4487>.

NUMBERING – [1] 2 Sam. 24:9; 1 Chr. 21:5 → APPOINTMENT <4662> [2] 2 Chr. 2:17 → CENSUS <5610>.

NUN, NON – ***nun, nôn*** [masc. proper noun: נוּן, נוֹן <5126>; from CONTINUE <5125>]: continuation ▶ **The father of Joshua.** Refs.: Ex. 33:11; Num. 11:28; Josh. 1:1; 2:1, 23; Judg. 2:8; 1 Kgs. 16:34; 1 Chr. 7:27; Neh. 8:17. *

NURSE (noun) – [1] 1 Kgs. 1:2, 4 → PROFITABLE (BE) <5532> b. [2] Ruth 4:16; 2 Sam. 4:4 → NURSE (verb) <539>.

NURSE (BECOME THE) – 1 Kgs. 1:2 → PROFITABLE (BE) <5532> a.

NURSE (verb) – [1] ***'āman*** [verb: אָמַן <539>; a prim. root] ▶ **This word means to be firm, to build up, to support, to nurture, or to establish. The primary meaning is that of providing stability and confidence, like a baby would find in the arms of a parent.** It is used to signify support of a pillar (2 Kgs. 18:16; see PILLAR <547>); nurture and nourishment (Num. 11:12; Ruth 4:16; thus, a nurse, 2 Sam. 4:4); cradling in one's arms (Is. 60:4); a house firmly founded (1 Sam. 2:35; 25:28); a secure nail that finds a solid (or firm, sure, secure) place to grip (Is. 22:23); a lasting permanence (Ps. 89:28: to stand firm, to stand fast; with negative particle, Jer. 15:18). Metaphorically, the word conveys the notion of faithfulness and trustworthiness, such that one could fully depend on (Deut. 7:9; Job 12:20; Ps. 19:7; Is. 55:3; Mic. 7:5). Therefore, the word can also signify certitude or assurance (Deut. 28:66; Job 24:22; Hos. 5:9) and belief, in the sense of receiving something as true and sure (Gen. 15:6; Ex. 4:5; 2 Chr. 20:20; Ps. 78:22; Is. 53:1; Jon. 3:5). *
[2] ***nûq*** [verb: נוּק <5134>; a prim. root] ▶ **This word means to feed a baby at its**

mother's breasts. Moses' mother was divinely chosen to nurse him (Ex. 2:9). ¶
3 ***'ûl*** [masc. noun: עוּל <5763>; a prim. root] ▶ **This word means to give suck.** It refers to the feeding process of young animals still nursing their mothers (Gen. 33:13); to the young calves still nursing (1 Sam. 6:7, 10: milk cows); or to suckling lambs (Ps. 78:71; Is. 40:11). ¶

NURSE (verb and noun) – ***yānaq*** [verb: יָנַק <3243>; a prim. root] ▶ **This word means to care for, to nurture, to suckle.** It is used to describe the nursing or feeding of children (Gen. 21:7; 1 Kgs. 3:21). It may indicate the person serving as a nurse (Gen. 24:59; Ex. 2:7) or the child nursing (Deut. 32:25; Job 3:12; Joel 2:16). It describes the nursing of young animals (Gen. 32:15). It is used figuratively in idioms, e.g., it describes the blessing the Lord bestows on Jacob, His people, making them "suck honey from a rock" (Deut. 32:13). And it is used of Zebulum describing how he will draw on the abundance of the seas and the wealth of the sand (Deut. 33:19). *

NURSING – Num. 11:12 ➔ NURSE (verb) <539>.

NURSING CHILD – ***'ûl*** [masc. noun: עוּל <5764>; from NURSE (verb) <5763>] ▶ **This word means and is also translated a sucking child, a baby at the breast, infant.** It describes a child still tenderly attached to its mother (Is. 49:15). In Isaiah 65:20, it is used of a nursing child or baby and in the immediate context indicates infant death. ¶

NUT – Gen. 43:11 ➔ PISTACHIO NUT <992>.

NUTS, NUT TREES – ***'gôz*** [masc. noun: אֱגוֹז <93>; prob. of Persian origin] ▶ **This word is found only in Song of Solomon in parallel with other beautiful features of nature. The precise meaning is elusive.** Ref.: Song 6:11. ¶

O

O THAT! – Ps. 119:5 ➔ WOULD THAT <305>.

OAK – [1] ***'ayil*** [masc. noun: אַיִל <352>; from the same as BODY <193>] ▶ **This word refers to an oak tree, terebinth tree, or other strong, robust tree. This sacred fertility tree was associated with pagan worship.** Refs.: Is. 1:29; 57:5. God's faithful people should rather be oaks of righteousness (NASB, Is. 61:3). It can refer to especially strong or huge trees (Ezek. 31:14). For other meanings of the Hebrew word, see RAM <352>, DOORPOST <352>, MIGHTY <352>. ¶

[2] ***'ēlāh*** [fem. noun: אֵלָה <424>; fem. of <352> above] ▶ **This word refers to an oak tree, terebinth tree, or some other thick, strong deciduous tree. This was a mighty tree often connected to a cultic setting or activity.** Refs.: Gen. 35:4; 1 Kgs. 13:14; Ezek. 6:13. The angel of the Lord came to it (Judg. 6:11), and Gideon served food under the tree. Absalom's hair caught in one of these trees (2 Sam. 18:9, 10, 14) and led to his death. Saul and his sons were buried under an oak (1 Chr. 10:12); the word is also translated tamarisk. Israel is likened to an oak with falling leaves (Is. 1:30; cf. Is. 6:13). Other refs.: Judg. 6:19; Hos. 4:13. ¶

[3] ***'allāh*** [fem. noun: אַלָּה <427>; variation of <424> above] ▶ **This word indicates an oak tree, a terebinth tree, or other strong tree. Cultic activity is recorded concerning this tree.** Joshua set up a sacred stone under this tree as a witness to the renewed covenant at Shechem (Josh. 24:26). ¶

[4] ***'ēlôn*** [masc. noun: אֵלוֹן <436>; prolonged from <352> above] ▶ **This word refers to a strong, hardy tree; it is also translated great tree, terebinth.** Refs.: Gen. 12:6; 13:18; 14:13; 18:1; Deut. 11:30; Judg. 4:11; 9:6, 37; 1 Sam. 10:3. ¶

[5] ***'allôn*** [masc. noun: אַלּוֹן <437>; a variation of <436> above] ▶ **This word refers to a strong deciduous tree. It was native to Bashan and its wood was crafted into oars; it is also translated allon, large tree, terebinth.** This tree marked the grave site of Deborah, Rebekah's nurse (Gen. 35:8), the oak of weeping (cf. Josh. 19:33; KJV: ALLON <438>, a proper noun). In the Prophets, it has several uses: it indicates illicit shrines (Hos. 4:13); materials for producing idols (Is. 44:14); a symbol, i.e., a stump as a devastated Israel (Is. 6:13). Elsewhere, it indicates strength (Is. 2:13; Amos 2:9) or it serves as a metaphor for mighty or prominent men (Zech. 11:2). Other ref.: Ezek. 27:6. ¶

OAK TREES – ***'ēlem*** [masc. noun: אֵלֶם <482>; from BIND <481>] ▶
a. This word is in the title of Psalm 56. It means oaks in a short phrase meaning according to the tune of the distant oaks (NKJV, distant lands; it is transliterated in the KJV and NASB); it is also translated terebinths. ¶
b. A masculine noun transliterated as part of *Jonath elem rehokim* in the NASB, KJV. Ref.: Ps. 56:1. See a. ¶
c. A noun meaning congregation, company. The translators vary in their rendering of this word. It has often been rendered as silence or silent one, but there are other possibilities. It means congregation (Ps. 58:1), but it is also translated gods, silent ones, rulers. ¶

OAR – [1] ***māšôṭ, miššôṭ*** [masc. noun: מָשׁוֹט, מִשּׁוֹט <4880>; from GO ABOUT <7751>] ▶ **This word identifies an instrument for rowing a boat, propelling it through water.** Refs.: Ezek. 27:6, 29. ¶

[2] ***šayiṭ*** [masc. noun: שַׁיִט <7885>; from GO ABOUT <7751>] ▶ **This word refers to a large paddle used, possibly, to row ships of war or large cargo ships.** Ref.: Is. 33:21. ¶

OATH – [1] ***'ālāh*** [fem. noun: אָלָה <423>; from CURSE (verb) <422>] ▶ **This word means a sworn covenant or a curse; it is also translated adjuration, swearing.** It signifies an oath to testify truthfully (Lev. 5:1; 1 Kgs. 8:31); a sworn covenant, bearing a curse if violated (Deut. 29:19; Neh. 10:29); a curse from God for covenant violations (Deut. 29:20; 2 Chr. 34:24; Dan. 9:11); God's judgment on sin (Deut. 30:7; Is. 24:6; Zech. 5:3); and that which is accursed because of unfaithfulness, such as an adulterous wife or the erring tribe of Judah (Num. 5:27; Jer. 29:18; 42:18; 44:12). *

2 ***šᵉḇûʿāh*** [fem. noun: שְׁבוּעָה <7621>; fem. pass. part. of SWEAR <7650>] ► **An oath is a sacred promise attesting to what one has done or will do.** God swore an oath to Abraham, Isaac, and Jacob that He would fulfill His covenant with them (Gen. 26:3; Deut. 7:8; 1 Chr. 16:16). An oath could also be sworn by a person to declare innocence (Ex. 22:11; Num. 5:21); to proclaim friendship (2 Sam. 21:7); to affirm a promise (Lev. 5:4; 1 Kgs. 2:43); to ratify a peace treaty (Josh. 9:20); to pledge loyalty to God (2 Chr. 15:15); or to another person (Neh. 6:18). An oath was considered to be an unbreakable contract; however, in two instances, the Bible presents well-defined possibilities in which an oath could be nullified and the obligated party could be acquitted. Abraham provided for his servant to be released from his obligation to find a bride for Isaac if the woman refused to follow (Gen. 24:8); and the spies provided for their own release from their oath to Rahab if she did not display the scarlet cord and stay in her house or if she revealed the intentions of the Israelites (Josh. 2:17, 20). *

– 3 1 Sam. 14:2; 1 Kgs. 8:31; 2 Chr. 6:22; Hos. 10:4: to take, to place under, to bind under, to swear an oath ➔ CURSE (verb) <422>.

OATH (TAKE AN) – See SWEAR <7650>.

OBADIAH – ***ʿōḇaḏyāh, ʿōḇaḏyāhû*** [masc. proper noun: עֹבַדְיָה, עֹבַדְיָהוּ <5662>; act. part. of SERVE <5647> and LORD <3050>]: servant of the Lord ►

a. Son of Izrahiah. One of four sons. All, including the father, were military chiefs (1 Chr. 7:3). ¶

b. A Gadite. The second in military command under the chief Ezar. He was a commander (1 Chr. 12:9). ¶

c. Father of Ishmaiah. Ishamiah, the son of Obadiah, was an officer of the twelve tribes of Israel (1 Chr. 27:19). ¶

d. Governor of Ahab's house. Obadiah was a faithful servant of the Lord. He helped Ahab, his master, find Elijah. Earlier, he had hidden one hundred prophets of the Lord from Jezebel who sought to kill all the Lord's prophets. Ahab respected him and his devout faith in the Lord (Yahweh). He found Elijah and took him to Ahab (see 1 Kgs. 18:3–7, 16). ¶

e. Prince of Judah. One of Jehoshaphat's officials (2 Chr. 17:7). ¶

f. Son of Azel. One of six sons. Listed in the genealogy of Saul (1 Chr. 8:38; 9:44). ¶

g. A Levite descended from Merari. The Levites were in charge of the workers under Josiah's reforms (2 Chr. 34:12). ¶

h. Descendant of David. Listed in the genealogy of David (1 Chr. 3:21). ¶

i. He was the son of Jehiel, and included in Ezra's list of people who returned to Jerusalem during the reign of Darius, king of Persia. Ref.: Ezra 8:9. ¶

j. Son of Shemiah. At the dedication of the wall, he was sought and brought to Jerusalem to join in the musical celebration. Ref.: 1 Chr. 9:16. ¶

k. A priest, a covenanter who signed an agreement and sealed it before the Lord to uphold Nehemiah's covenant of renewal. Ref.: Neh. 10:5. ¶

l. A Levite, possibly same as j. He was also a gatekeeper and guarded the gates where supplies were kept. Ref.: Neh. 12:25. ¶

m. The prophet. Neither his place of birth nor his parents are recorded. Ref.: Obad. 1:1. His prophecies proclaimed the Lord's judgment on Edom because they did not mourn or help Judah in the day when Babylon destroyed Jerusalem and Judah (605–686 B.C.). Edom will be destroyed, but Jerusalem and Mount Zion will be rescued and prosper (Obad. 1:18–21). The written report of his message is twenty-one verses, the shortest book in the Old Testament. ¶

OBAL – ***‘ôḇāl*** [masc. proper noun: עוֹבָל <5745>; of foreign deriv.]: stripped ▶ **One of the sons of Joktan.** Ref.: Gen. 10:28; his name is also spelled Ebal (1 Chr. 1:22). ¶

OBED – ***‘ôḇêḏ, ‘ōḇêḏ*** [masc. proper noun: עוֹבֵד, עֹבֵד <5744>; act. part. of SERVE <5647>]: serving ▶
a. A descendant of Sheshan. Refs.: 1 Chr. 2:37, 38. ¶
b. The son of Boaz. Refs.: Ruth 4:17, 21, 22; 1 Chr. 2:12. ¶
c. One of David's mighty men. Ref.: 1 Chr. 11:47. ¶
d. Son of Shemaiah. Ref.: 1 Chr. 26:7. ¶
e. A captain. Ref.: 2 Chr. 23:1. ¶

OBED-EDOM – ***‘ōḇêḏ *ḏôm*** [masc. proper noun: עֹבֵד אֱדוֹם <5654>; from the act. part. of SERVE <5647 and EDOM <123>]: servant of Edom ▶
a. He evidently was a Gittite from the city of Gath. The ark of the Lord remained in his house for three months, during which time he was blessed (2 Sam. 6:10–12). *
b. An ancestor of a group of doorkeepers at the Temple. Ref.: 1 Chr. 15:24. *

OBEDIENCE – ***y*qāhāh*** [fem. noun: יְקָהָה <3349>; from the same as JAKEH <3348>] ▶ **This means the act of obeying, submitting to someone.** In Jacob's prophecy to Judah, he said that the kingship would not depart from Judah's descendants until one came who would have the obedience of the nations (Gen. 49:10; KJV: gathering). This verse is considered by many to be prophetic of Jesus Christ. In the sayings of Agur, the disobedient child (one who scorns to obey; one who scorns obedience) should have his eyes pecked out by ravens and vultures (Prov. 30:17). ¶

OBESE (BE) – ***kāśāh*** [verb: כָּשָׂה <3780>; a prim. root] ▶ **This word is translated to be covered with fatness by KJV. It is difficult to translate, and its meaning is not certain.** The KJV and NKJV favor the idea of fatness, obesity, filled, or covered with fullness (Deut. 32:15). The NIV, NASB, and ESV render it as sleek. ¶

OBEY – [1] Prov. 30:17 ➔ OBEDIENCE <3349> [2] Is. 11:14 ➔ GUARD <4928>.

OBIL – ***’ôḇiyl*** [masc. proper noun: אוֹבִיל <179>; prob. from MOURN <56>]: mournful ▶ **An Ishmaelite in charge of David's camels.** Ref.: 1 Chr. 27:30. ¶

OBLATION – Ezek. 48:12 ➔ ALLOTMENT <8642>.

OBLIGATION – Ezra 4:14 ➔ to be under obligation ➔ SALT (EAT THE) <4415>.

OBLIVION – Ps. 88:12 ➔ FORGETFULNESS <5388>.

OBNOXIOUS – Gen. 34:30; Ex. 5:21: to make obnoxious ➔ STINK <887>.

OBOTH – ***’ōḇōṯ*** [proper noun: אֹבֹת <88>; plur. of MEDIUM <178>]: hollow, waterskin ▶ **A place in the wilderness where the Israelites camped.** Refs.: Num. 21:10, 11; 33:43, 44. ¶

OBSCENE IMAGE – 1 Kgs. 15:13; 2 Chr. 15:16 ➔ IMAGE <4656>.

OBSCURE – [1] ***ḥāšōḵ*** [adj.: חָשֹׁךְ <2823>; from DARKEN <2821>] ▶ **This word identifies something as insignificant.** It is a detrimental and belittling term used of certain persons who are nobodies (Prov. 22:29; also translated unknown, mean, of low rank) on the social scale or in political influence. ¶ – [2] Prov. 20:20 ➔ PUPIL <380> [3] Is. 33:19; Ezek. 3:5, 6 ➔ UNINTELLIGIBLE <6012>.

OBSCURE (BE) – Job 38:2 ➔ DARKEN <2821>.

OBSERVANCE – Ex. 12:42 ➔ WATCHING <8107>.

OBSERVE – Job 39:29 ➔ LOOK (verb) <5027>.

OBSESSED (BE) – 2 Sam. 13:2 ➔ DISTRESSED (BE) <3334>.

OBSTINATE – Is. 30:1; 65:2 ➔ REBELLIOUS <5637>.

OBSTRUCT – Ezek. 39:11 ➔ MUZZLE (verb) <2629>.

OBTAIN – ***pûq*** [verb: פּוּק <6329>; a prim. root (identical to STUMBLE <6328> through the idea of dropping out; comp. TAKE OUT <5312>)] ▶ **This word means to acquire, to bring out.** It has the sense of furthering or fostering something (Ps. 140:8: to further, to promote); or of the increase of flocks (Ps. 144:13: to afford, to provide, to furnish, to supply). It indicates the acquisition of something (Prov. 3:13: to get, to gain; 8:35: to obtain, to receive). It indicates in some contexts the bringing out or giving of oneself to others who are needy (Is. 58:10: to draw out, to pour out, to spend, to extend). Other refs.: Prov. 12:2; 18:22. ¶

OCCASION – [1] ***ta^{a}nāh*** [fem. noun: תַּאֲנָה <8385>; from BEFALL <579> (in the sense of to meet, to seek an occasion)] ▶ **This word means an opportunity. It refers to the right time or set of situations for accomplishing something.** Ref.: Judg. 14:4. For another meaning of the Hebrew word, see HEAT (noun) <8385>. ¶
– [2] Job 33:10 ➔ OPPOSITION <8569> [3] Jer. 2:24 ➔ HEAT (noun) <8385> [4] Dan. 6:4, 5 ➔ COMPLAINT (GROUND FOR) <5931>.

OCCURRENCE – ***pega'*** [masc. noun: פֶּגַע <6294>; from MEET (verb) <6293>] ▶ **This word points out a circumstantial event, a happening, something that takes place, an incident, an event.** In context it may mean a detrimental event or a chance happening (1 Kgs. 5:4); the literal expression evil occurrence in this verse is also translated misfortune, disaster. It refers to any chance occurrence in the lives of people (Eccl. 9:11). ¶

OCCURRENT – 1 Kgs. 5:4 ➔ OCCURRENCE <6294>.

OCRAN – ***'oḵrān*** [masc. proper noun: עָכְרָן <5918>; from TROUBLE (BRING) <5916>]: disturber ▶ **An Israelite of the tribe of Asher.** Refs.: Num. 1:13; 2:27; 7:72, 77; 10:26. ¶

ODED – ***'ōḏeḏ, ōḏeḏ*** [proper noun: עֹדֵד, עוֹדֵד <5752>; from WITNESS (BEAR) <5749> (in the sense of reiteration)]: restorer ▶
a. The father of the prophet Azariah. Refs.: 2 Chr. 15:1, 8. ¶
b. A prophet. Ref.: 2 Chr. 28:9. ¶

ODIOUS – Gen. 34:30; Ex. 5:21: to make odious ➔ STINK <887>.

ODOR – [1] ***rêyaḥ*** [masc. noun: רֵיחַ <7381>; from REFRESHED (BE) <7306>] ▶ **This word indicates an aroma, a fragrance.** It refers to the odor or scent produced by various things: clothes (Gen. 27:27); water (Job 14:9); aromatic oils (Song 1:3); sweet-smelling breath (Song 7:8). It is used figuratively, not literally, of God's sensing and approving of an odor of sacrifices (Gen. 8:21), especially as described in the various sacrifices depicted in Exodus (29:18, 25, 41), Leviticus (8:21, 28), and Numbers (18:17). In Exodus 5:21, it is combined with *b'š* to indicate making someone an offensive, stinking odor. It is found often in a romantic setting describing various pleasing fragrances (Song 1:3, 12; 2:13, etc.). It is used figuratively, e.g., the smell of Moab (Jer. 48:11); and the cedar-like fragrance of a restored Israel (Hos. 14:6). It is used to describe the aromas offered to pagan gods (Ezek. 6:13). *
– [2] Eccl. 10:1 ➔ to give a foul odor ➔ STINK <887>.

OFFAL – Ex. 29:14; Lev. 4:11; 8:17; 16:27; Num. 19:5 ➔ DUNG <6569>.

OFFENSE – Lev. 19:7 ➔ OFFENSIVE THING <6292>.

OFFENSIVE – Dan. 3:29 ➔ AMISS <7955>.

OFFENSIVE THING – [1] ***piggûl*** [masc. noun: פִּגּוּל <6292>; from an unused root

meaning to stink] ▶ **This word means a foul thing, refuse. It is a technical term for a part of a sacrifice that has become or been rendered unclean.** This was applied to the fellowship offering that was to be eaten the same day it was offered or the next day. If it remained until the third day, it was considered unclean (Lev. 7:18; 19:7); the word is also translated offense, abomination, tainted, impure. Isaiah recorded the prophecy of God where He defined the activities of people that rendered them unclean, including contact with the deceased and eating unclean food, namely pork (Is. 65:4: abominable things, unclean meat, tainted meat, impure meat). Ezekiel protested God's instruction to him because he had never eaten any unclean meat; however, he failed to define what unclean meat was (Ezek. 4:14; the word is translated abominable, unclean, tainted, impure). ¶
– 2 Job 23:13 ➔ WRONGDOING <8604>.

OFFER – 1 ***dᵉḇaḥ*** [Aramaic verb: דְּבַח <1684>; corresponding to <2076> below] ▶ **This word means to sacrifice, to offer sacrifices, to present sacrifices (literally, to sacrifice sacrifices).** When King Darius issued the decree permitting the rebuilding of the Temple, he specified that it would be a place to offer sacrifices (Ezra 6:3; also translated to present). This word is the equivalent of the Hebrew verb *zāḇaḥ* (<2076> below). ¶
2 ***zāḇaḥ*** [verb: זָבַח <2076>; a prim. root] ▶ **This word means to slaughter, to kill, to sacrifice. The word is used in its broadest sense to indicate the slaughtering of various animals.** It indicates the slaughter of animals for food (Deut. 12:21; 1 Sam. 28:24) or for sacrifice with strong political implications (1 Kgs. 1:9, 19); Elisha slaughtered his oxen to make his break with his past and establish his commitment to Elijah (1 Kgs. 19:21). The word describes a sacrifice made to create communion or to seal a covenant. Jacob made a sacrificial meal to celebrate the peace between him and Laban (Gen. 31:54); and the priests were to receive part of the bulls or sheep offered by the people (Deut. 18:3). These slaughtered sacrificial animals were presented to gods or the true God; Jacob's sacrifice was to God (Gen. 46:1) as were most of these sacrifices, but the nations sacrificed to other gods as well, such as Dagon (Judg. 16:23) or the gods of Damascus (2 Chr. 28:23).

Various kinds of sacrifices are given as the objects of this verb. For instance, sacrifices of the firstborn male that open the womb (or a substitute sacrifice to redeem that male) (Ex. 13:12–15); offerings of well-being, peace offerings, and burnt offerings (Ex. 20:24); and animals of the flock and herd (Num. 22:40). Certain slaughtered sacrifices were prohibited, such as a sacrifice with blood and yeast in it (Ex. 23:18; cf. Ex. 12:15). In an exceptional setting, however, a prophet proclaimed the slaughter and sacrifice of the defiled priests who served at the forbidden high places (1 Kgs. 13:2). God will exercise divine judgment on the enemies of His people, Gog and Magog, slaying and providing their carcasses as a great banquet for every kind of bird and animal (Ezek. 39:17, 19); Israel, in their rebellion, offered, although forbidden, their own sons as offerings (Ezek. 16:20). *
3 ***nāṭal*** [verb: נָטַל <5190>; a prim. root)] ▶ **This word means to lift up; by implication, to impose, to bear, to carry, to present, to take up.** It means to place before someone options from which to chose (2 Sam. 24:12; NIV: to give); or, in an unusual sense, of forcing or imposing something on someone (Lam. 3:28: to lay, to bear). It takes the sense of carrying something (Is. 40:15: to take up, to lift up, to weigh). It has the sense of removing afflictions or danger, of delivering from something (Is. 63:9: to lift up, to bear). ¶
4 ***nᵉsaḵ*** [Aramaic verb: נְסַךְ <5260>; corresponding to POUR OUT <5258>] ▶ **This word indicates to pour out, to present a libation.** It means literally in context to pour out a drink offering, i.e., to offer a sacrifice in honor of someone, in this case in honor of Daniel for reciting and interpreting the king's dream (Dan. 2:46; also translated to present). ¶
5 ***'ālāh*** [verb: עָלָה <5927>; a prim. root] ▶ This word also means to go up, to ascend, to

take away, to lift. **This Hebrew word carries with it the connotation of an upward motion, e.g., to bring up gifts.** It is used generically to denote an ascension to a higher place (Num. 13:17); a departure in a northerly direction (Gen. 45:25); the flight of a bird (Is. 40:31); the springing up of plants (Is. 34:13); the preference of one thing above another (Ps. 137:6); and the offering of a sacrifice (Judg. 6:28; 2 Kgs. 3:20). Theologically significant is the fact that this verb is used in relationship to a person's appearance before God. One must go up to stand before the Lord (Ex. 34:24; see also Gen. 35:1). *
– [6] Ruth 2:14 → SERVE <6642>.

OFFER FREELY – ***nᵉḏaḇ*** [Aramaic verb: נְדַב <5069>; corresponding to GIVE WILLINGLY <5068>] ▶ **This word means to present something willingly, to make a freewill offering.** This word is used exclusively in the book of Ezra and refers to those who could leave Babylon freely (Ezra 7:13). It also indicates the gifts given freely by a king (Ezra 7:15); and the Israelites (Ezra 7:16). See the related Hebrew verbs *nāḏaḇ* (GIVE WILLINGLY <5068>) and *nᵉḏāḇāh* (FREEWILL OFFERING <5070>). ¶

OFFERING – [1] ***'iššeh*** [fem. noun: אִשֶּׁה <801>; the same as FIRE <800>, but used in a liturgical sense] ▶ **This word means a presentation or sacrifice made by fire, fire offering. Its usage is highly religious and theological in a ritual context. The word describes how the various offerings were presented to the Lord; i.e., they were offerings made by means of fire.** This practice gave rise to referring to all the offerings the priests presented as fire offerings; hence, some consider this term a general term that applied to all the sacrifices of the Israelites (Deut. 18:1; 1 Sam. 2:28). The fire was actually not offered. Instead, it was the means by which the various offerings were presented to God. The fire caused the offering to go up in smoke, a fact indicated by the causative form of the Hebrew verb, and that created a pleasant aroma to the Lord. The fire also purified what was offered. In this sense, the offerings could be called fire offerings or offerings made by fire. The other words for sacrifice in the Old Testament are specific and describe a certain sacrifice, although *qorbān* (<7133> below) is used in a general sense a few times. The word *'iššeh* is slightly more specific.

The Levites were put in charge of all the offerings by fire to the Lord (Josh. 13:14). Both animal sacrifices and nonanimal sacrifices were presented to the Lord by fire (Lev. 1:9; 2:10), as well as such items as the sacred bread and frankincense placed in the Holy Place (Lev. 24:7). These offerings by fire cover at least the burnt offering (Lev. 1:3–17; 6:8–13); the grain offering (Lev. 2:1–16; 6:14–23; 7:9, 10); the fellowship or peace offering (Lev. 3:9; 7:11–21, 28–34); the sin offering (Lev. 4:1–35; 5:1–13; 6:24–30); the guilt offering (Lev. 5:14–19; 7:1–10). All of these offerings were the Lord's (Num. 28:2), but the phrase "to the Lord" is explicitly stated most of the time (Ex. 29:18; Lev. 2:11; Num. 28:13). As noted above, the offering by fire produced a pleasing or soothing aroma to the Lord as it ascended (cf. Lev. 1:9; Num. 15:13, 14; 29:13, 36), a phrase indicating that the Lord had accepted the sacrifice. *

[2] ***haḇhaḇ*** [masc. noun: הַבְהַב <1890>; by reduplication from GIVE <3051>] ▶ **This word means gift in the sense of sacrifice. This type of sacrifice is not made by one person but always occurs with a plural subject.** Israel (collectively) sacrificed animals to God as gift offerings—gifts God did not accept (Hos. 8:13). ¶

[3] ***minḥāh*** [Aramaic fem. noun: מִנְחָה <4504>; corresponding to GIFT <4503>] ▶ **This word means a gift, a sacrificial offering, an oblation, a grain offering.** When Daniel was promoted to chief administrator of Babylon, the celebration included the presentation of an offering signified by this Aramaic word (Dan. 2:46). King Artaxerxes also used this Aramaic word to command Ezra to offer sacrificial gifts on the altar of God when he arrived in Jerusalem (Ezra 7:17). This word corresponds directly to *minḥāh* (GIFT <4503>). ¶

[4] ***qorbān, qurbān*** [masc. noun: קָרְבָּן, קֻרְבָּן <7133>; from COME NEAR <7126>] ▶

This word means a gift. This is the most general term, used eighty times in the Old Testament, for offerings and gifts of all kinds. The word is found in Leviticus referring to animal offerings of all permissible types (Lev. 1:2, 3); grain offerings of fine flour (Lev. 2:1, 5); gifts or votive offerings of gold vessels. It is found in Numbers referring to silver vessels and rings (Num. 7:13; 31:50) and jewelry (Num. 31:50).

Ezekiel uses the word to designate an offering. Israel corrupted the land by presenting their offerings at every high hill, leafy tree, and high place (Ezek. 20:28). Happily, the second use in Ezekiel depicts the table where the flesh offering would be properly presented within the restored Temple (Ezek. 40:43). *

[5] ***t*ᵉ*rûmāh*** [fem. noun: תְּרוּמָה <8641>; from EXALT <7311>] ▶ **The basic idea of this Hebrew noun is something being lifted up, i.e., a heave offering.** It is normally used to describe a variety of offerings: a contribution of materials for building (Ex. 25:2; 35:5); an offering of an animal for sacrifice (Ex. 29:27; Num. 6:20); a financial offering for the priests (Num. 31:52); an allotment of land for the priests (Ezek. 45:6, 7); or even the materials for an idol (Is. 40:20). In one instance, this word is used to describe a ruler who received bribes (Prov. 29:4). *

– [6] Lev. 2:5; Num. 6:15 ➔ GIFT <4503> [7] Jer. 44:21 ➔ INCENSE <7002> [8] See SACRIFICE (noun) <2077>.

OFFERING BREAD – 1 Chr. 9:31 ➔ PANS <2281>.

OFFERING OF PRAISE – ***hillûl*** [masc. noun: הִלּוּל <1974>; from PRAISE (verb) <1984> (in the sense of rejoicing)] ▶ **This word means rejoicing, a joyous celebration.** It designates a praise offering with the fruit of the land (Lev. 19:24), holy unto the Lord. It can be translated as a joyous festival or a time of merriment (Judg. 9:27). ¶

OFFICE – [1] 1 Chr. 23:28 ➔ ATTENDANCE <4612> [2] Neh. 13:14 ➔ CUSTODY <4929>.

OFFICER – [1] Gen. 40:2, 7; 1 Sam. 8:15; etc. ➔ EUNUCH <5631> [2] 1 Kgs. 4:19 ➔ GARRISON <5333>.

OFFICIAL – [1] ***šilṭôn*** [Aramaic noun: שִׁלְטוֹן <7984>; corresponding to POWER <7983>] ▶ **This word means a lord, a magistrate; it is also translated ruler.** This noun is used only in Daniel 3:2, 3, where it is found at the end of a long list of officials whom King Nebuchadnezzar called together before him. This noun is the last word used and seems to be a catchall phrase to account for any official who was missed in the specific titles given before. Due to the lack of specificity, it would appear that this is a general noun used to name anyone who holds a position of authority. ¶

– [2] Num. 26:9 ➔ CHOSEN <7148> [3] Jer. 51:23, 28; etc. ➔ RULER <5461> [4] Nah. 3:17 ➔ MARSHAL <2951>.

OFFICIAL (HIGH) – [1] Dan. 3:24, 27; 4:36; 6:7 ➔ COUNSELOR <1907> [2] Dan. 6:2–4, 6:6, 7 ➔ COMMISSIONER <5632>.

OFFICIAL IN CHARGE – See LEADER <5057>.

OFFICIALS – [1] Ezra 4:9 ➔ TARPELITES <2967> [2] Ezra 4:9; 5:6; 6:6 ➔ APHARSATHCHITES <671>.

OFFSCOURING – Lam. 3:45 ➔ SCUM <5501>.

OFFSET – 1 Kgs. 6:6 ➔ LEDGE (NARROW, NARROWED, OFFSET) <4052>.

OFFSHOOT – Is. 22:24 ➔ ISSUE <6849>.

OFFSPRING – [1] ***niyn*** [masc. noun: נִין <5209>; from CONTINUE <5125>] ▶ **This word refers to the descendants of persons, their posterity; it is also translated son, child, descendant, posterity.** Ref.: Gen. 21:23. The wicked are said to have no offspring (Job 18:19). It indicates the survivors of a group of people, e.g., Babylon (Is. 14:22). ¶

2 ***ṣeʾṣāʾ*** [masc. noun: צֶאֱצָא <6631>; from GO OUT <3318> (in the sense of to produce)] ▶ **This word refers to those who come out of the womb of the mother or from the loins of the father.** It indicates offspring, descendants (Job 5:25; 21:8; 27:14; Is. 22:24; 34:1; 44:3). In the new heavens and new earth, the term refers to the offspring of the people blessed of the Lord (Is. 65:23). ¶
3 ***šeger*** [masc. noun: שֶׁגֶר <7698>; from an unused root prob. meaning to eject] ▶ **This word refers to the young of animals. It may be rendered in context as offspring, increase, calves.** It refers to animals born to their parents (Ex. 13:12; Deut. 28:4, 18, 51; NIV, calves). It is rendered as increase of flocks (Deut. 7:13) by the NASB (NIV, calves). ¶
– **4** Gen. 48:6 ➔ KINDRED <4138> **5** 2 Chr. 32:21 ➔ COMING FORTH <3329> **6** See SEED <2233>.

OG – ***ʿôg, ʿōg*** [masc. proper noun: עוֹג, עֹג <5747>; prob. from BAKE <5746>] ▶ **A powerful king who ruled the territory of Bashan on the east side of the Jordan River.** He was evidently from a race of giants (Num. 21:33; Josh. 13:12–31). His bed was an object of amazement and splendor (Deut. 3:11). He controlled a large kingdom for his time (Deut. 3:1–13), from the Jabbok River in the south to Mount Hermon in the north. Manasseh inherited Og's land (Deut. 3:1–13). It was located northeast of the Sea of Galilee (Num. 21:33). The Lord gave victory to Moses and Israel over Og (Num. 21:34, 35). He was killed along with his entire army and family. His defeat was celebrated in the worship and festivals of Israel (Neh. 9:22; Ps. 135:11; 136:20). ¶

OH, THAT – **1** ***ʾāḇeh*** [masc. sing. noun: אָבֶה <15>; from WILLING (BE) <14>] ▶ **This word indicates the desire of the speaker; it is also translated my desire is that, would that, ought to.** It is found in Job 34:36 as an interjection *ʾāḇiy*. It is well rendered as Oh, that! It may rather be a first person singular future verb (*bāyay*), indicating, similarly, the desire of the speaker Elihu. ¶

2 ***lu', lû, lûʾ*** [particle: לוּא, לוּ, לֻא <3863>; a conditional particle] ▶ **This word means if, oh, that.** It introduces conditional statements: "Oh, if only . . ." (Gen. 17:18; Num. 14:2; Deut. 32:29); "If . . ." (Gen. 23:13; Mic. 2:11). *

OH! – Ezek. 21:15 ➔ ALAS! <253>.

OHAD – ***ʾōhaḏ*** [masc. proper noun: אֹהַד <161>; from an unused root meaning to be united]: powerful, which brings together ▶ **The name of an Israelite, son of Simeon.** Refs.: Gen. 46:10; Ex. 6:15. ¶

OHEL – ***ʾōhel*** [masc. proper noun: אֹהֶל <169>; the same as TENT <168>]: tent, family ▶ **One of the sons of Zerubbabel.** Ref.: 1 Chr. 3:20. ¶

OHOLAH – ***ʾohᵒlah*** [fem. proper noun: אָהֳלָה <170>; from TENT <168>]: she has her tent ▶ **Symbolic name representing the unfaithfulness of Samaria and the kingdom of Israel.** Refs.: Ezek. 23:4, 5, 36, 44. ¶

OHOLIAB – ***ʾohᵒliyāḇ*** [masc. proper noun: אָהֳלִיאָב <171>; from TENT <168> and FATHER <1>]: tent of the father ▶ **Skillful Israelite worker of the tribe of Dan; he was appointed to execute artistic works for the Tabernacle.** Refs.: Ex. 31:6; 35:34; 36:1, 2; 38:23. ¶

OHOLIBAH – ***ʾohᵒliyḇāh*** [fem. proper noun: אָהֳלִיבָה <172>; from TENT <168>]: my tent is in her ▶ **Female personification of Jerusalem and the kingdom of Judah.** Refs.: Ezek. 23:4, 11, 22, 36, 44. ¶

OHOLIBAMAH – ***ʾohᵒliyḇāmāh*** [proper noun: אָהֳלִיבָמָה <173>; from TENT <168> and HIGH PLACE <1116>]: tent of the height ▶
a. Wife of Esau. Refs.: Gen. 36:2, 5, 14, 18, 25. ¶
b. An Edomite chief. Refs.: Gen. 36:41; 1 Chr. 1:52. ¶

OIL – **1** ***yiṣhār*** [masc. noun: יִצְהָר <3323>; from <6671> below] ▶ **This word means**

fresh oil, anointing oil. It most commonly refers to fresh oil produced from the land, most likely from olive trees. Refs.: 2 Kgs. 18:32. This oil could be in an unprocessed state (Deut. 7:13). Concerning religious uses, people gave this oil to the Levites and priests as a means of support (2 Chr. 31:5). The Hebrew word is also used once for the purpose of anointing (Zech. 4:14). *

[2] **to press out oil, to make oil, to produce oil:** ***ṣāhar*** [verb: צָהַר <6671>; used only as denom. from <3323> above] ▶ **This word means to crush olives, to produce olive oil. It refers to the production of olive oil that always involved squeezing or pressing olives to obtain oil from them.** Ref.: Job 24:11. Others have suggested that the usage here means to spend noon, to spend the noonday, understanding the root of the verb to be related to *ṣoh^{o}rayim,* noon, afternoon. ¶

[3] ***šemen*** [masc. noun: שֶׁמֶן <8081>; from FAT (BE, BECOME) <8080>] ▶ **This word has a wide range of figurative meanings relating to richness and plenty.** Most simply, it is used of food, relating to feasts of good, rich food (Is. 25:6). It is also used frequently of oil. This can be oil used for food and cooking (Deut. 8:8; 32:13); for oil which was used to anoint holy objects or kings (Ex. 30:25; 1 Sam. 10:1); or for oil used as an ointment to soothe and cleanse, leading to healing (Ps. 133:2; Is. 1:6). The figurative meanings are also important. This word can be used to signify strength, such as in Isaiah 10:27 where growing fat meant growing strong. It also frequently relates to fruitfulness and fertile places where good things grew (Is. 5:1; 28:1). The overall picture one gets from this word is that of richness, strength, and fertility. *

OIL, OLIVE OIL – ***m^{e}šaḥ*** [Aramaic noun: מְשַׁח <4887>; from a root corresponding to ANOINT <4886>] ▶ **See OIL <3323>.** This word appears only in two passages (Ezra 6:9; 7:22). These passages cite the provisions, including silver, livestock, wheat, salt, wine, and oil, that kings Darius and Artaxerxes supplied to the restoration priests at the Temple in Jerusalem. ¶

OINTMENT – [1] Ex. 30:25 ➔ PERFUME <7545> [2] 1 Chr. 9:30 ➔ MIXTURE <4842>.

OINTMENT (POT OF, JAR OF) – ***merqāḥāh*** [fem. noun: מֶרְקָחָה <4841>; fem. of SCENTED <4840>] ▶ **This word refers to a smooth oily preparation compounded to serve as an aromatic perfume or it may refer to a seasoning composed of spices that is added to condiments. It also refers to a vessel in which this blend is compounded.** Refs.: Job 41:31; Ezek. 24:10. ¶

OLD – [1] ***bāleh*** [adj.: בָּלֶה <1087>; from WEAR OUT <1086>] ▶ **This word means existing for some time; it is also translated worn out. It refers to old sacks, sandals, and clothing as a part of the deception of the Gibeonites.** Refs.: Josh. 9:4, 5. It describes the corrupt and lewd character of someone worn out by acts of prostitution (Ezek. 23:43). Ezekiel applies it to Israel and Judah. ¶

[2] ***b^{e}lôy*** [masc. noun: בְּלוֹי <1094>; from WEAR OUT <1086>] ▶ **This word indicates worn-out things.** It describes clothes and rags used to pull Jeremiah out of a pit (Jer. 38:11, 12). ¶

[3] ***yāšān*** [adj.: יָשָׁן <3465>; from SLEEP (verb) <3462>] ▶ **This word means inveterate, referring to leprosy, and also means dry, used of last year's harvest. It has the basic sense of that which is seasoned or has been around for a long time, aged.** It refers to crops from a previous year (Lev. 25:22; 26:10); or things that have been around a long time, e.g., an old gate or old pool (Neh. 3:6; 12:39; Is. 22:11); old as opposed to new. Fruit and vegetables can be old as opposed to new (Song 7:13). ¶

– [4] Lev. 13:11 ➔ SLEEP (verb) <3462> b. [5] Job 32:6; 12:12; 29:8 ➔ AGED <3453>.

OLD (BE, BECOME) – ***zāqên*** [verb: זָקֵן <2204>; a prim. root] ▶ **This word means to have lived a long time; it is related to the adjective *zāqên* <2205>, meaning old, and the noun *zāqān* <2206>, meaning beard.** In Psalm 37:25, David described himself as an aged person as opposed to a youth, *na'ar* (BOY <5288>), "I have been young, and now am old" (KJV). Solomon also used the same words to demonstrate the contrast between a person when young and when old (Prov. 22:6). This word is used of men (Gen. 24:1; Josh. 13:1; 1 Sam. 12:2); of women (Gen. 18:13; Prov. 23:22); or even a tree (Job 14:8). When used of older people, this word is often used to describe the last days of their lives (Gen. 27:1, 2; 1 Kgs. 1:1; 2 Chr. 24:15). *

OLD (BECOME, GROW, WAX) – Ps. 6:7; Job 21:7 ➔ MOVE <6275>.

OLD (GROW) – Deut. 4:25 ➔ SLEEP (verb) <3462> b.

OLD AGE – 1 ***zequniym*** [masc. plur. noun: זְקֻנִים <2208>; properly, pass. part. of OLD (BE) <2204> (used only in the plur. as a noun)] ▶ **This word is used only four times in the Old Testament, each time in the book of Genesis. It appears in reference to children born to parents late in life.** Particularly, it is used of Isaac as the son of Abraham's old age (Gen. 21:2, 7); and of Joseph (Gen. 37:3) and Benjamin (Gen. 44:20) as the sons of Jacob's old age. ¶
2 ***ziqnāh*** [fem. noun: זִקְנָה <2209>; fem. of OLD, OLD MAN <2205>] ▶ **This word is used most often to refer to people who are past their prime age.** For example, it describes Sarah who is past the normal childbearing age (Gen. 24:36). Psalm 71 uses the word to ask the Lord not to turn away from the psalmist in his old age (Ps. 71:9, 18). Isaiah 46:4 describes God's care for the aged, even though their bodies grow weak. Other refs.: 1 Kgs. 11:4; 15:23. ¶
3 ***śeyḇāh*** [fem. noun: שֵׂיבָה <7872>; fem. of AGE <7869>] ▶ **This word refers to advanced years and also means gray hair.** It is used to denote that Joseph's brothers would bring to the grave the gray head of their father (Gen. 44:31). Hosea uses the word figuratively to depict Ephraim being old before its natural time, i.e., its hair was sprinkled with gray (Hos. 7:9). In Proverbs, gray hair is a crown of splendor (Prov. 16:31); while 1 Kings denotes the gray head, not as wise, but simply old (1 Kgs. 2:6, 9). The psalmist uses the word to depict a point in life in which he could not perform the same deeds as before. On account of this, the psalmist asked God not to forsake him until he was able to declare God's glory to the coming generation (Ps. 71:18). Genesis uses the word to denote the time Abraham will be buried, i.e., a good old age (Gen. 15:15; 25:8). Naomi's friends predicted that her grandson Obed would renew her life and sustain her in her old age (Ruth 4:15). *

OLD AGE (REACH) – Job 21:7 ➔ MOVE <6275>.

OLD CORN – Josh. 5:11, 12 ➔ PRODUCE (noun) <5669>.

OLD, OLD MAN – ***zāqên*** [adj.: זָקֵן <2205>; from OLD (BE) <2204>] ▶ **This Hebrew word means elder, aged, old woman (as a noun), leader(s). The word's basic meaning is old or aged. But from this basic meaning, several different meanings arise. The word means aged persons, but the ideas of dignity, rank, and privilege also became attached to this concept.** The person referred to was usually an old man (Gen. 19:4; Judg. 19:16, 17). One of the most famous was the old man in a robe (Samuel) that the witch of Endor saw (1 Sam. 28:14). Abraham and Sarah were both described as old in Genesis 18:11; the oldest servant in the master's house evidently had some prerogatives of seniority (Gen. 24:2). Old men, women, and children were often spared in war and were given special care and protection (cf. Ezek. 9:6) but not in the corrupt city of Jerusalem at its fall.

The group of men called elders in Israel were a powerfully influential group. They represented the nation from the time of the wilderness period (Ex. 19:7) and earlier (Ex. 3:16; 4:29). Of the 180 times the phrase is found, it occurs thirty-four times in Exodus when Israel was being formed into a people. There were traditionally seventy elders, and they ate and drank before the Lord with

Moses and Joshua on Mount Sinai (Ex. 24:9, 11). The older priests held special respect among the priests (2 Kgs. 19:2). The elders were equal to the judges in influence and regularly took part in making decisions (Deut. 21:2, 19, 20). The elders of a city as a whole formed a major ruling group (Josh. 20:4; Ruth 4:2). For example, the elders of Jabesh tried to locate help and negotiated with the Ammonites who were besieging the city (1 Sam. 11:3). But the elders could lead in evil as well as good, for the picture Ezekiel painted of them was devastating and incriminating. The elders had become corrupt and helped lead the people astray. Their counsel would fail (Ezek. 7:26; 8:11, 12; Ezek. 9:6). *

OLIVE – Is. 17:6 ➔ BERRY <1620>.

OLIVE, OLIVE TREE – ***zayit*** [noun: זַיִת <2132>; prob. from an unused root (akin to ZIV <2099>)] ▶
a. A common noun indicating an olive (a green or black fruit), olive tree. Olive trees were a source and indication of property and wealth. Ref.: Ex. 23:11. The word depicts the olives themselves as well (Deut. 28:40). Used with *šemen*, oil, it indicates olive oil (Ex. 27:20; 30:24). It is used in the phrase, mount of the ascent of the olives; i.e., the Mount of Olives (Zech. 14:4). It refers to an olive tree (Judg. 9:8, 9; Job 15:33; Hos. 14:6). In all these cases, it also serves as a simile or other illustration of a person (cf. Zech. 4:3, 11); beauty, a wicked man respectively. It also is a symbol of prosperity (Ps. 52:8; Jer. 11:16). *
b. A masculine proper noun. It is used in a phrase to indicate the Mount of Olives (2 Sam. 15:30; cf. Zech. 14:4). ¶

OLIVES (CRUSH) – Job 24:11 ➔ OIL <6671>.

OMAR – ***'ômār*** [masc. proper noun: אוֹמָר <201>; from SAY <559>]: speaker, talkative ▶ **A descendant of Esau.** Refs.: Gen. 36:11, 15; 1 Chr. 1:36. ¶

OMEN – Num. 23:23; 24:1 ➔ ENCHANTMENT <5173>.

OMENS – Lev. 19:26; 2 Kgs. 17:17; 21:6; 2 Chr. 33:6 ➔ DIVINATION (PRACTICE) <5172>.

OMENS (INTERPRET) – Lev. 19:26; Deut. 18:10 ➔ DIVINATION (PRACTICE) <5172>.

OMER – ***'ōmer*** [masc. noun: עֹמֶר <6016>] ▶ **This word indicates a measure of grain. It is a dry measure of about two liters or two quarts.** Refs.: Ex. 16:16, 18, 22, 32, 33, 36. The Hebrew word also refers to a sheaf of grain; see SHEAF <6016>. ¶

OMRI – ***'omriy*** [masc. proper noun: עָמְרִי <6018>; from SLAVE (TREAT AS A) <6014>]: heaping ▶ **A powerful king in northern Israel who established the "house of Omri." His son Ahab was the most wicked king of Israel. He had been the army commander before he was made king.** He forced Zimri, the king in Tirzah, to commit suicide, and he reigned in his place (1 Kgs. 16:16–19). Omri reigned twelve years (885–874 B.C.), six in Tirzah. He then purchased a hill on which he built Samaria, the new capital of Samaria (1 Kgs. 16:21–24). He continued to follow the corrupt and rebellious ways of Jeroboam I, son of Nebat. He died and was buried in Samaria (1 Kgs. 16:25–28). He and his son became symbols of rebellion and evil (Mic. 6:16). *

ON – [1] ***'ôn*** [masc. proper noun: אוֹן <203>; the same as STRENGTH <202>]: strength ▶ **The son of Peleth of the tribe of Reuben who took part in the rebellion of Korah.** Ref.: Num. 16:1. ¶
[2] ***'ôn*** [proper noun: אוֹן <204>; of Egyptian deriv.] ▶ **A city in Egypt.** Asenath who was given as wife to Joseph was from On (Gen. 41:45, 50; 46:20). It is also translated Heliopolis (city of the sun) and Avan (see Ezek. 30:17). ¶

ONAM – ***'ônām*** [masc. proper noun: אוֹנָם <208>; a variation of ONAN <209>]: strong, wealthy ▶
a. An Edomite. Refs.: Gen. 36:23; 1 Chr. 1:40. ¶

b. A son of Jerahmeel, of the tribe of Judah. Refs.: 1 Chr. 2:26, 28. ¶

ONAN – ***'ônān*** [masc. proper noun: אוֹנָן <209>; a variation of ONO <207>]: strong, vigorous ▶ **A son of Judah who did not want to give offspring (raise up an heir) to his brother and whom the Lord killed.** Refs.: Gen. 38:4, 8, 9; 46:12; Num. 26:19; 1 Chr. 2:3. ¶

ONCE (AT) – Dan. 2:25 ➔ HASTE (BE IN) <927>.

ONE – 1 ***'eḥāḏ*** [numerical adj.: אֶחָד <259>; a numeral from GO ONE WAY OR THE OTHER <258>] ▶ **This word means first, once, the same.** It may mean simply one of various things: e.g., place (Gen. 1:9); soul, or person (Lev. 4:27); a person from among many (Gen. 3:22; 42:19; 1 Sam. 26:15). It has the idea of unity or integrity as when it designates one justice for all (Num. 15:16) or actual physical unity (Ex. 36:12). The Lord is one (Deut. 6:4). It expresses agreement or unity among persons (Ex. 24:3) or physical unity (Zeph. 3:9). It may serve as an indefinite article, one man (1 Sam. 1:1), or to indicate the first of something, e.g., the first day of the month (Gen. 8:5). The word is pluralized to mean several, few, or a while (Gen. 11:1; 27:44). *

2 ***ḥaḏ*** [numerical adj.: חַד <2297>; abridged from <259> above] ▶ **This word is used in the phrase *ḥaḏ 'eṯ-'aḥaḏ* meaning one to another or to one another.** Ref.: Ezek. 33:30. ¶

3 ***ḥaḏ*** [Aramaic numerical adj.: חַד <2298>; corresponding to <2297> above] ▶ **This word is employed several ways.** It follows *k^ešā'āh* as a short time, indicating a rather short period of time (Dan. 4:19); it was the sense of only one option (Dan. 2:9); or only one object involved (Ezra 4:8, a letter; Dan. 2:31), thus serving as an indefinite article; it indicates the first year in the phrase *bišnaṯ ḥaḏāh* (Ezra 5:13; Dan. 7:1); with a following number it means "x times," whatever that number is, e.g., seven times is *ḥaḏ-šiḇ'āh* (Dan. 3:19). With *k^e* attached to the front, *ḥaḏ* takes on the meaning of as one or together (Dan. 2:35). *

ONION – ***bāṣāl*** [masc. noun: בָּצָל <1211>; from an unused root apparently meaning to peel] ▶ **This word refers to one of the luxury foods that Israel ate in Egypt.** They longed again for it as they tracked about in the desert (Num. 11:5). ¶

ONLY – 1 ***'aḵ*** [particle: אַךְ <389>; akin to SURELY <403>] ▶ **This word means surely, but.** Its emphatic use is translated as indeed or surely (Gen. 26:9; 29:14; 1 Kgs. 22:32; Jer. 5:4). It takes on a restrictive meaning and is translated as only (Gen. 7:23; 9:4, NASB) or just as (Gen. 27:13; Judg. 10:15, NASB). Its contrastive sense, but, however, or nevertheless, is also found (Jer. 34:4, NASB). *

2 ***yāḥiyḏ*** [adj.: יָחִיד <3173>; from UNITE <3161>] ▶ **This word means sole, solitary. It is frequently used to refer to an only child.** Isaac was Abraham's only son by Sarah (Gen. 22:2, 12, 16). Jephthah's daughter was his only child, who came running out to greet him after his vow to sacrifice the first thing to come out of his door (Judg. 11:34). The father of an only child began teaching him wisdom when he was very young (Prov. 4:3). Mourning an only child was considered an especially grievous sorrow (Jer. 6:26; Amos 8:10; Zech. 12:10). The feminine form is used parallel to life or soul, portraying the precious (KJV: darling), only life we are given (Ps. 22:20; 35:17). It is also used to mean lonely or alone (Ps. 25:16: desolate, lonely; 68:6: solitary, lonely). See the related Hebrew root *yāḥaḏ* (UNITE <3161>). ¶

3 ***raq*** [adv.: רַק <7535>; the same as LEAN (adj.) <7534> as a noun (properly, leanness, i.e., fig., limitation)] ▶ **This word means nevertheless, but, except. Its exact meaning must be discovered from its context.** It has the sense of something being exclusive, the only thing being done, e.g., evil thoughts only (*raq*) all day long describes the fallen state of the human heart without grace (Gen. 6:5). It indicates a specific condition that must be fulfilled or maintained

and means only (Gen. 14:24; 24:8; 41:40; Ex. 8:28; Job 1:12). After a negative word, *raq* gives the sense of except, but for (1 Kgs. 8:9; 15:5; 22:16; 2 Kgs. 17:18). Used in front of a positive assertion, it means surely, indeed (Gen. 20:11; Deut. 4:6). With *bᵉ* following and attached to a following word, the phrase means only in, by, in the case of (Prov. 13:10). It is used to point out one from among many (Amos 3:2), e.g., Israel only (*raq*) as God's chosen instrument. *

ONO – ***'ônô*** [proper noun: אוֹנוֹ <207>; prolonged from STRENGTH <202>]: strong ▶ **City of Benjamin situated in a vast plain.** Refs.: 1 Chr. 8:12; Ezra 2:33; Neh. 6:2; 7:37; 11:35. ¶

ONYCHA – ***šᵉḥêleṯ*** [fem. noun: שְׁחֵלֶת <7827>; apparently from the same as LION <7826> through some obscure idea, perhaps that of peeling off by concussion of sound)] ▶ **This is an ingredient in the holy incense.** It is used only once, and its use indicates that it was a spice used in the preparation of holy incense (Ex. 30:34). The incense could not be used as a common perfume or cosmetic. ¶

ONYX – ***šōham*** [masc. noun: שֹׁהַם <7718>; from an unused root prob. meaning to blanch] ▶ **This word refers to a precious stone.** It has been translated as onyx, but carnelian or lapis lazuli have been suggested as well (Gen. 2:12). It was a stone featured in the ephod and breastpiece worn by the high priests of Israel (Ex. 25:7); even bearing the names of the twelve tribes of Israel (Ex. 28:9). Wisdom, however, far exceeds it in value (Job 28:16). It was a part of the splendor of the coverings of the "king of Tyre" in the Garden of Eden (Ezek. 28:13). *

OOZE OUT – 1 Sam. 14:26 ➔ DRIP (noun) <1982>.

OPEN – [1] ***pāṭûr*** [adj.: פָּטוּר <6358>; pass. part. of <6362> below] ▶ **This word refers to something that is in a state of access, that may be freely viewed.** Refs.: 1 Kgs. 6:18, 29, 32, 35. ¶

[2] ***pāṭar*** [verb: פָּטַר <6362>; a prim. root] ▶ **This word means to release, to separate, to expose.** It means to make one's getaway (1 Sam. 19:10). It describes flowers with open petals or buds (1 Kgs. 6:18, 29, 32, 35, *pᵉṭurê ṣiṣṣîm*). It indicates being free from certain duties (1 Chr. 9:33: to be free, to be exempt). It means to let off of a job, let off duty (2 Chr. 23:8: to go off duty). It is used of foolishly mocking someone with one's mouth, literally parting one's lips (Ps. 22:7: to shoot out). It refers to letting out water, emptying one's bladder for relief (Prov. 17:14: to let out, to release, to breach). ¶

[3] ***peṭer, piṭrāh*** [noun: פֶּטֶר, פִּטְרָה <6363>; from <6362> above] ▶

a. A masculine noun referring to the firstborn. It indicates the first animal to part or separate from the womb (Ex. 13:2, 12, 13, 15; 34:19, 20; Num. 3:12; 18:15; Ezek. 20:26). ¶

b. A feminine noun indicating the firstborn one. It indicates the first one to open, separate from a mother's womb (Num. 8:16). ¶

[4] ***pā'ar*** [verb: פָּעַר <6473>; a prim. root] ▶ **This word means to open wide one's mouth (to gape), to jeer.** It means to mock or jeer at someone with one's mouth opened wide (Job 16:10; also translated to gape); but in a different context, it means to open one's mouth to praise or accept someone respectfully or in positive wonderment (Job 29:23). It is used figuratively of an open mouth panting after God's commandments (Ps. 119:131). In a strong figurative illustration, Sheol, the place of the dead, is personified with a mouth open to receive its victims (Is. 5:14). ¶

[5] ***pāṣāh*** [verb: פָּצָה <6475>; a prim. root] ▶

a. This word means to open one's mouth, to utter. It is used in a strong figure of speech depicting the earth's opening its mouth to receive the innocent blood of Abel (Gen. 4:11); or to swallow the wicked in an earthquake (Num. 16:30; Deut. 11:6). It signifies the uttering of a word, speaking (Judg. 11:35, 36; Job 35:16); especially in an accusation (Ps. 22:13; Lam. 2:16; 3:46).

It is used of uttering or making a vow (Ps. 66:14). It refers to a bird opening its mouth (Is. 10:14); or the prophet Ezekiel opening his mouth to eat a scroll (Ezek. 2:8). ¶

b. This word means to rescue, to deliver. It is used in an imperative form when the psalmist implores the Lord to open up to him to rescue him from his enemies (Ps. 144:7, 10, 11). ¶

6 ***pāqaḥ*** [verb: פָּקַח <6491>; a prim. root] ▶ **This word refers figuratively to one's eyes being opened to wisdom, understanding, reality; or to some physical object not noticed before; or even of normally unseen spiritual forces.** Refs.: Gen. 3:5, 7; 21:19; 2 Kgs. 6:17, 20. Opening the eyes is a sign of life (2 Kgs. 4:35). To open one's eyes is an idiom meaning to pay attention, to be watchful, to notice what is going on (2 Kgs. 19:16; Dan. 9:18; Zech. 12:4); or to bring judgment on someone (Job 14:3). It also is used to mean to be diligent, industrious, not lazy (Prov. 20:13). It is used in a proverb to indicate the shortness of life or the possession of riches (Job 27:19). God is able to heal the blind, open their eyes (Ps. 146:8). *

7 ***pāṯaḥ*** [verb: פָּתַח <6605>; a prim. root] ▶ **This word also means to open wide, to loosen.** It is used to indicate the opening of many things: figuratively, the windows of heaven (Gen. 7:11, 8:6); storehouses opened to distribute grain (Gen. 41:56); a grave (Ezek. 37:12, 13); a cistern (Ex. 21:33); a mouth of a cave (Josh. 10:22); a letter (Neh. 6:5); one's hand (Ps. 104:28). Used of a river, it means to cause it to run, to flow with water (Is. 41:18); it means to move, to sell commodities (Amos 8:5). In Ezekiel 21:28, it refers to drawing out one's sword. It has a general sense in many contexts of loosing something: saddles (Gen. 24:32); armor (1 Kgs. 20:11). Of flowers, the petals bloom, open up (Song 7:12); of plowing, it means to open, loosen the ground (Is. 28:24). It indicates unopened wine, wine still under pressure (Job 32:19). *

8 ***peṯaḥ*** [Aramaic verb: פְּתַח <6606>; corresponding to <6605> above] ▶ **This word is used to describe open windows in an upper chamber and books (scrolls) rolled open before the Ancient of Days.** Refs.: Dan. 6:10; 7:10. ¶

9 ***piṯḥôn*** [masc. noun: פִּתְחוֹן <6610>; from <6605> above] ▶ **This word means opening.** In context it refers to speaking with one's mouth in a defensive or arrogant way (Ezek. 16:63); or in an expression of joy and thanksgiving for blessings (Ezek. 29:21). ¶

10 ***šemurāh*** [fem. noun: שְׁמֻרָה <8109>; fem. of pass. part. of KEEP <8104> (in the sense of to watch over)] ▶ **This Hebrew word indicates openness, watchfulness. It refers to an alertness or awareness when used of the eyes.** The Lord held and maintained the watchfulness of the psalmist's eyes (Ps. 77:4; KJV: waking). ¶

– 11 Num. 24:4 ➔ REVEAL <1540>.

OPEN, BE OPEN – ***šāṯam*** [verb: שָׁתַם <8365>; a prim. root] ▶ **This word indicates that something or someone is open with respect to his eye.** Refs.: Num. 24:3, 15: NIV: to see clearly. ¶

OPEN, OPEN WIDE – ***pāśaq*** [masc. noun: פָּשַׂק <6589>; a prim. root] ▶ **This word means to open one's mouth without control, without discipline.** Only evil comes from such an action (Prov. 13:3). It refers to a woman spreading her legs wide in a sensuous, seductive manner, but the action is applied figuratively to Israel who had played the prostitute (Ezek. 16:25). ¶

OPEN COUNTRY – Hos. 4:16 ➔ BREADTH <4800>.

OPENING – 1 ***miptaḥ*** [masc. noun: מִפְתָּח <4669>; from OPEN <6605>] ▶ **This word describes the act of opening. It refers to opening, expanding something.** It is used in an idiom for speaking or saying, e.g., "the opening of my lips" (Prov. 8:6). ¶

– 2 1 Chr. 9:27 ➔ KEY <4668> 3 Neh. 4:13 ➔ BARE <6706> 4 Song 5:4 ➔ HOLE <2356> 5 Dan. 3:26 ➔ COURT <8651> 6 See DOOR <6607>.

OPENING OF THE PRISON – ***peqaḥ-qôaḥ*** [masc. noun: פְּקַח־קוֹחַ <6495>; from OPEN <6491> redoubled] ▶ **This phrase**

indicates a release from captivity. It means literally, opening (of the eyes), referring to the blind who are granted vision. In context it indicates the freeing of those who had been bound (Is. 61:1; also translated release, freedom). ¶

OPHEL – ***'ōpel*** [proper noun: עֹפֶל <6077>; the same as <6076>]: hill ▶ **This word designates the name of a hill where Jotham did major repairs to the wall of Jerusalem.** Ref.: 2 Chr. 27:3. Manasseh enlarged the outer wall of the City of David that went around the hill of Ophel (2 Chr. 33:14). Postexilic repairs were made to the wall of Jerusalem by Levites who served in the Temple but lived on top of the hill of Ophel (Neh. 3:26, 27; 11:21). ¶

OPHIR – ***'ôpiyr*** [proper noun: אוֹפִיר <211>; of uncertain deriv.]: abundance, wealth ▶
a. A name describing the area from which Solomon imported great quantities of gold. Refs.: 1 Kgs. 9:28; 10:11; 1 Chr. 29:4. The place was renowned for its fine gold, its major product to the nations (Job 22:24; 28:16; Is. 13:12). Its exact location is still a puzzle but may have been in the south or southwest part of the Arabian Peninsula. *
b. A proper noun describing the son of Yoqtan (Joktan) in Shem's genealogical list. Refs.: Gen. 10:29; 1 Chr. 1:23. ¶

OPHNI – ***'opniy*** [proper noun: עָפְנִי <6078>; from an unused root of uncertain meaning]: mouldy ▶ **A city of Benjamin.** Ref.: Josh. 18:24. ¶

OPHRAH – [1] ***'oprāh*** [proper noun: עָפְרָה <6084>; from YOUNG <6082>]: female fawn ▶
a. A town in Benjamin. Refs.: Josh. 18:23; 1 Sam. 13:17. ¶
b. A town west of the Jordan River. Refs.: Judg. 6:11, 24; 8:27, 32; 9:5. Ophrah was Gideon's hometown. ¶
c. Son of Meonothai. Ref.: 1 Chr. 4:14. ¶
[2] ***'eprôn*** [proper noun: עֶפְרוֹן <6085>; from EPHER <6081>]: fawnlike ▶
a. A Hittite. Refs.: Gen. 23:8, 10, 13, 14, 16, 17; 25:9; 49:29, 30; 50:13. ¶
b. Mount Ephron. Ref.: Josh. 15:9. ¶
c. The city Ephron. Ref.: 2 Chr. 13:19. ¶

OPINION – [1] ***s^e'ippiym*** [noun: שְׂעִפִּים <5587>; from LOP, LOP OFF <5586> (in the sense of divided)] ▶ **In context, the word refers to belief, whether in the Lord or in Baal.** This word occurs in 1 Kings 18:21, where Elijah asked the Israelites how long they would halt between two opinions. The word is translated thought in Job 4:13; 20:2. ¶
– [2] Job 32:6, 10, 17 ➔ KNOWLEDGE <1843>.

OPPONENT – Jer. 18:19 ➔ CONTENDS (ONE WHO) <3401>.

OPPORTUNITY – Judg. 14:4 ➔ OCCASION <8385>.

OPPOSE – [1] Ex. 23:22 ➔ BESIEGE <6696> b [2] Num. 30:5, 8, 11 ➔ FORBID <5106> [3] Ps. 38:20; 71:13; 109:20; Zech. 3:1 ➔ ACCUSE <7853> [4] Jer. 50:24 ➔ STRIVE <1624>.

OPPOSITE (adv.) – [1] ***nêkaḥ*** [adv.: נֵכַח <5226>; from an unused root meaning to be straightforward] ▶ **This word means before, against, in front of. It refers to a physical location that lies opposite, in front of something.** It has the sense of opposite, in front of (Ex. 14:2). In Ezekiel 46:9, it means what is opposite, directly ahead of something. See <5227> below. This word is simply a form of that word. ¶
[2] ***nōkaḥ*** [adv.: נֹכַח <5227>; from the same as <5226> above] ▶ **This word means before, against, opposite of; see <5226> above also.** It has the meaning indicated there (Num. 19:4, with preposition *'el*, toward). It is used figuratively often. The phrase *nōkaḥ yhwh* means what reflects the Lord's will, what is acceptable to the Lord (Judg. 18:6). The preposition *l^e* on the following word strengthens the sense of opposite (Josh. 15:7). It has the sense of, on behalf of, with regard to, when used with the verb to pray (Gen. 25:21). It means directly or straight ahead with the verbs of

looking (Prov. 4:25). It is used metaphorically of something being before the eyes of the Lord (Prov. 5:21). The idiom "in front of your face" means in someone's presence (Jer. 17:16; Lam. 2:19; Ezek. 14:3), especially in the presence of the Lord. *

OPPOSITE (noun) – ***hêpek̲, hepek̲*** [masc. noun: הֵפֶךְ, הֶפֶךְ <2016>; from TURN (verb) <2015>] ▶ **This word indicates contrary, opposite, perversity.** It indicates a total reversal of what should be or what is normal (Is. 29:16: turning things upside down, around). Israel's spiritual prostitution was itself perverse for she received no pay from others (Ezek. 16:34; also translated different, contrary) for her deeds. ¶

OPPOSITION – 1 ***tigrāh*** [fem. noun: תִּגְרָה <8409>; from STRIVE <1624>] ▶ **This word designates a blow, strife, hostility.** It indicates in context God's oppression or attack on a person (Ps. 39:10; possibly stirring). The KJV renders it a blow in a figurative sense of God's hand and power. ¶

2 ***tᵉnû'āh*** [fem. noun: תְּנוּאָה <8569>; from FORBID <5106>] ▶ **This word means rejection, a pretext.** It refers to God's attitude of discipline that He took against Israel in the wilderness, His reasons for dealing with them as He did (Num. 14:34; also translated rejection, displeasure, breach of promise). It indicates causes, reasons for doing or acting in a certain way, e.g., God's actions against Job (Job 33:10: occasion, pretext, fault). ¶

OPPRESS – 1 ***yānāh*** [verb: יָנָה <3238>; a prim. root] ▶ **This word means to treat violently.** The term is used in Exodus 22:21, Leviticus 25:14, 17, and Deuteronomy 23:16 to refer to improper treatment of strangers and the poor. The participle functions as a noun meaning oppressor (Jer. 25:38; 46:16; 50:16). In the Prophets, the term is typically used of foreign oppressors (e.g., Ezek. 18:7, 12; Zeph. 3:1). *

2 ***lāḥaṣ*** [verb: לָחַץ <3905>; a prim. root] ▶ **This word means to dominate cruelly; it is also translated to press, to crush.** It has the sense of pressing, crowding, or even tormenting: Hebrews as slaves in Egypt (Ex. 3:9); a stranger (Ex. 22:21; 23:9); someone's foot (Num. 22:25; 2 Kgs. 6:32: to hold fast); to hem in and oppress in battle (2 Kgs. 13:4, 22); to confine or keep in a certain territory (Judg. 1:34: to force, to press, to confine). Other refs.: Judg. 2:18; 4:3; 6:9; 10:12; 1 Sam. 10:18; Ps. 56:1; 106:42; Is. 19:20; Jer. 30:20; Amos 6:14. ¶

3 ***nāgaś*** [verb: נָגַשׂ <5065>; a prim. root] ▶ **This verb refers to forcing someone or something to do something.** It is used of forcing persons to labor (also translated to exact, to exploit, to drive hard) (Is. 58:3); of forcing or exacting payment of money (2 Kgs. 23:35). It refers in its participial forms to taskmasters (also translated slave driver, oppressor) or workers of animals (Ex. 3:7; 5:6, 10, 13, 14; Job 3:18). It is used figuratively of righteousness being a good foreman or overseer (Is. 60:17: exactor, magistrate, overseer, taskmaster, ruler) in a restored Jerusalem. In its passive uses, it refers to those who are oppressed by others (1 Sam. 13:6: to be distressed, to be hard pressed). The Suffering Servant of Isaiah is a person oppressed, ill-treated by His enemies (Is. 53:7; cf. Is. 3:5). *

4 ***'āšaq*** [verb: עָשַׁק <6231>; a prim. root (comp. CONTEND <6229>)] ▶ **This word means to rob, to defraud.** It refers to extorting or exploiting someone (Lev. 6:2, 4), especially a servant. It has the sense of cheating or robbing in some contexts (Lev. 19:13); keeping what is rightfully someone else's. A righteous person does not oppress or exploit another person (1 Sam. 12:3, 4). Job thought that God was oppressing him (Job 10:3). God will curse the one who oppresses others (Ps. 72:4; 105:14). To oppress another person is to abuse, to revile one's Creator (Prov. 14:31). Even the poor may be oppressors (Prov. 28:3). It is used to designate the guilt of blood on a person (Prov. 28:17). In its passive usage, it refers to a person who is abused or defrauded in some way (Is. 23:12). The prophets spoke strongly against the oppressors of the poor (Amos 4:1; Mic. 2:2; Zech. 7:10; Mal. 3:5). *

5 ***ṣûq*** [verb: צוּק <6693>; a prim. root (in the sense of to compress)] ▶ **This word**

means to distress, to constrain. It indicates forcing someone to do something under duress, often by violent means (Deut. 28:53, 55, 57; Is. 29:7; Jer. 19:9). It refers to the Lord bringing distress on His people (Is. 29:2). It can refer to badgering persons, nagging them, constantly urging them to do something until they give in (Judg. 14:17; 16:16). In its causative participial form, it refers to an oppressor (Is. 51:13). Other ref.: Job 32:18 (to compel, to constrain). ¶

– 6 Dan. 7:25 ➔ WEAR OUT, WEAR DOWN <1080>.

OPPRESSED – 1 ***dak*** [adj.: דַּךְ <1790>; from an unused root (comp. CRUSH <1794>)] ► **This word means afflicted, crushed; it is also translated downtrodden.** It indicates persons who are pressed down, oppressed (Ps. 9:9; Ps. 10:18; 74:21), crushed down. The Lord cares for and is concerned for them. These persons may be the objects of verbal attacks (Prov. 26:28). ¶

2 ***ʿ^e^nāh*** [Aramaic verb: עֲנָה <6033>; corresponding to AFFLICTED (BE) <6031>] ► **This verb means to be afflicted, to be poor, to be needy.** It describes the poor and oppressed in a society; in context its reference is within the Babylonian Empire (Dan. 4:27). ¶

– 3 Amos 3:9 ➔ OPPRESSIONS <6217>.

OPPRESSED (BE) – distress, oppression: ***ʿošqāh*** [fem. noun: עָשְׁקָה <6234>; fem. of OPPRESSION <6233>] ► **This word has the same meanings discussed in OPPRESSION <6233>.** In context it is used of a person weighted down by sickness, illness (Is. 38:14; also translated to be threatened). ¶

OPPRESSED (ONE WHO IS) – Is. 1:17 ➔ OPPRESSOR <2541>.

OPPRESSION – 1 ***laḥaṣ*** [masc. noun: לַחַץ <3906>; from OPPRESS <3905>] ► **This word refers to the affliction or distress of Israel.** Refs.: Ex. 3:9; Deut. 26:7; 2 Kgs. 13:4. The term "bread of oppression (or affliction)" (*lāḥaṣ*) means, in context, a prisoner's ration, a small amount (1 Kgs. 22:27). It indicates the oppression the psalmist suffered at the hands of his enemies (Ps. 42:9; 43:2). It is used of a period of affliction or oppression given by the Lord (Is. 30:20). Other refs.: 2 Chr. 18:26; Job 36:15; Ps. 44:24. ¶

2 ***ʿōṣer*** [masc. noun: עֹצֶר <6115>; from RESTRAIN <6113>] ► **This word depicts affliction, barrenness.** It refers to any kind of pressure, maltreatment, or affliction that is put on someone or a people (Ps. 107:39). It takes on the meaning of barrenness for the ultimate oppression of the womb (Prov. 30:16: barren). It refers to military, religious, political, social rejection, and oppression in the case of the Suffering Servant (Is. 53:8; KJV, NKJV: prison). ¶

3 ***ʿāqāh*** [fem. noun: עָקָה <6125>; from WEIGHTED DOWN <5781>] ►

a. This word means tension; it is also translated pressure. It is used of tension and force exerted on someone to create distress (Ps. 55:3). ¶

b. A feminine noun referring to staring. It refers to hostile gazes directed at someone intended to create fear and distress (Ps. 55:3; NIV: threats). ¶

4 ***ʿōšeq*** [masc. noun: עֹשֶׁק <6233>; from OPPRESS <6231>] ► **This word means extortion. It refers to defrauding, robbing persons of what is theirs; denying justice to the poor, the laborer, the slave, the widow, the orphan.** Extortion or robbery, keeping what is another's is often in mind (Lev. 6:4). Oppression can be personal, political, military (Eccl. 5:8; Is. 54:14). Oppression is not to be a way of life for God's people (Ps. 62:10). Oppression or fraud is not the mark of a righteous person (Ezek. 18:18). *

5 ***tōḵ, tôḵ*** [masc. noun: תֹּךְ, תּוֹךְ <8496>; from the same base as MIDST (IN THE) <8432> (in the sense of cutting to pieces)] ► **This word refers to pressure; it is also translated fraud, threats, deceit.** It refers to pressure, anxiety, feeling weighed down, something that the mouth of the evil person delights in (Ps. 10:7); it stalks those in the city (Ps. 55:11). A righteous king will remove oppression (Ps. 72:14); and the Lord puts

hope into the life of the oppressed person (Prov. 29:13). ¶
– 6 Is. 1:17 ➔ OPPRESSOR <2541> 7 Is. 5:7 ➔ BLOODSHED <4939> 8 Lam. 3:59 ➔ WRONG (noun) <5792>.

OPPRESSIONS – 1 ***ma'ᵃšaqqôṯ*** [fem. plur. noun: מַעֲשַׁקּוֹת <4642>; from OPPRESS <6231>] ▶ **This word indicates a leader abusing his people by forcing them to pay money or contribute goods and services against their will.** Ref.: Prov. 28:16. Bribes or gain through extortion (*ḇᵉṣa' ma'ᵃšaqqôṯ*) is considered evil (Is. 33:15; NASB: unjust gain). ¶
2 ***'ᵃšûqiym*** [masc. plur. noun: עֲשׁוּקִים <6217>; pass. part. of OPPRESS <6231>] ▶ **Oppression, or domination, weighs down a person with physical or mental distress.** Ref.: Job 35:9. It causes the oppressed to weep and mourn (Eccl. 4:1). Samaria was filled with many oppressions, physical, political, military, or economic (Amos 3:9; also translated oppressed). ¶

OPPRESSIVE – Is. 18:2, 7 ➔ TREADING DOWN <4001>.

OPPRESSOR – 1 ***ḥāmôṣ*** [masc. noun: חָמוֹץ <2541>; from LEAVENED (BE) <2556> (in the sense of to oppress, to be ruthless)] ▶ **This word denotes also one who is oppressed; some versions translate it: ruthless, oppression.** It refers to a ruthless or oppressive person especially regarding orphans and widows (Is. 1:17). ¶
2 ***mêṣ*** [verb: מֵץ <4160>; a prim. root] ▶ **This Hebrew word means to extort, to oppress. It is used in a participial form with a definite article showing a person or group of persons devastating the land of Moab.** Ref.: Is. 16:4; also translated extortioner. Others read the word *ḥamûṣ* here, oppression. ¶
3 ***'āšôq*** [masc. noun: עָשׁוֹק <6216>; from OPPRESS <6231>] ▶ **This word refers to a person guilty of troubling or wearing out another person, crushing him or her.** Ref.: Jer. 22:3. ¶
4 ***tāḵaḵ*** [masc. noun: תָּכָךְ <8501>; from an unused root meaning to dissever, i.e., to crush] ▶ **This word refers to deceit. It refers to what is not straightforward, true, or faithful but rather is treacherous.** Ref.: Prov. 29:13; KJV: deceitful man. ¶
– 5 Job 3:18 ➔ OPPRESS <5065> 6 Ps. 27:111 ➔ ENEMY <8324> 7 Prov. 29:13 ➔ OPPRESSION <8496> 8 Is. 51:13 ➔ OPPRESS <6693>.

OR – ***'aw, 'ô*** [conj.: אַו, אוֹ <176>] ▶
a. This particle conjunction of choice usually means or, but also rather, except in some contexts but still in essence meaning or. It can be translated as either when used in conjunction with another *'ô* (Gen. 44:19) or whether (Lev. 5:1; cf. also Gen. 24:55; Ex. 21:31, or if; 1 Sam. 20:10; Is. 27:5). *
b. The Hebrew word is also a noun possibly meaning desire or craving. Ref.: Prov. 31:4; NASB, NIV. It is translated to desire, to take. ¶

ORATOR – Is. 3:3 ➔ CHARM <3908>.

ORCHARD – 1 Eccl. 2:5; Song 4:13 ➔ FOREST <6508> 2 Song 6:11 ➔ GARDEN <1594> 3 Is. 16:10 ➔ FIELD (FERTILE, FRUITFUL, PLENTIFUL) <3759> a.

ORDAIN – 1 Is. 26:12 ➔ ESTABLISH <8239> 2 Dan. 2:24 ➔ APPOINT <4483>.

ORDAINED (BE) – Ps. 139:16 ➔ FORM (verb) <3335>.

ORDER – 1 ***sêḏer*** [masc. noun: סֵדֶר <5468>; from an unused root meaning to arrange] ▶ **This word refers to orderliness. It describes a state or condition of things being in their places, not chaotic, not a state of confusion.** Ref.: Job 10:22. ¶
– 2 Ps. 110:4 ➔ CAUSE <1700> 3 Is. 28:10, 13 ➔ PRECEPT <6673> a.

ORDER (SET IN) – Ex. 26:17 ➔ PARALLEL (SET) <7947>.

ORDERLY – Job 41:12 ➔ GRACEFUL <2433>.

ORDINANCE – 1 Dan. 6:7, 15 ➔ STATUTE <7010> 2 See STATUTE <2706>, <2708>.

ORDINARY – 1 Sam. 21:4, 5 ➔ COMMON <2455>.

ORDINATION – Ex. 29:22; Lev. 7:37; 8:22 ➔ SETTING <4394>.

OREB – ***'ôrêḇ*** [proper noun: עֹרֵב <6159>; the same as RAVEN <6158>]: raven ▶ **One of the two princes of Midian killed at a place further called the rock of Oreb.** Refs.: Judg. 7:25; 8:3; Ps. 83:11; Is. 10:26. ¶

OREN – ***'ōren*** [masc. proper noun: אֹרֶן <767>; the same as ASH <766>]: strong, pine tree ▶ **An Israelite of the tribe of Judah.** Ref.: 1 Chr. 2:25. ¶

ORGAN – Gen. 4:21; Job 21:12; 30:31; Ps. 150:4 ➔ FLUTE <5748>.

ORIGIN – 1 ***mᵉḵûrāh, mᵉḵōrāh*** [fem. noun: מְכוּרָה, מְכֹרָה <4351>; from the same as FURNACE <3564> in the sense of digging] ▶ **This word means beginning, ancestry; it is also translated birth, habitation, ancestry, nativity.** It is used in the singular with *'ereṣ*, land, to indicate the land of a person's or nation's origin (Ezek. 29:14; cf. Ezek. 16:3; 21:30). ¶
– 2 Is. 23:7 ➔ FORMER TIME <6927> 3 Mic. 5:2 ➔ GOING FORTH <4163>.

ORNAMENT – 1 ***ḥᵃliy*** [masc. noun: חֲלִי <2481>; from SICK (BE) <2470> (in the sense of to be rubbed or worn)] ▶ **This word denotes a jewel, an object that decorates.** A piece of jewelry made of fine gold that was delightful to the eye (Prov. 25:12) and beautifully crafted (Song 7:1: jewel). ¶
2 ***'ᵃdiy*** [masc. noun: עֲדִי <5716>; from ADORN <5710>] ▶ **This word refers to jewelry.** It refers to articles of gold, silver, and precious stones worn by many in Israel (Ex. 33:4–6). They were, in good times, supplied by the Lord as blessings for His people (2 Sam. 1:24). It refers to the trappings and adornments put on horses to control them (Ps. 32:9). It indicates the blessings of God to come on His people (Is. 49:18). Its use in Psalm 103:5 is questionable. If used, its possible meanings are difficult: desires (NIV), years (NASB), mouth (KJV, NKJV). *
3 ***śahᵃrôn*** [masc. noun: שַׂהֲרוֹן <7720>; from the same as ROUNDED <5469>] ▶ **This word refers to decorative objects used to dress and emphasize the splendor of the camels of some Midianite kings.** Refs.: Judg. 8:21, 26; also translated crescent ornament. The word also refers to ornaments worn by persons as well, luxurious items (Is. 3:18). ¶
– 4 Ex. 35:22 ➔ NECKLACE <3558> 5 Prov. 1:9 ➔ CHAIN <6060> 6 Prov. 1:9; 4:9 ➔ GARLAND <3880> 7 Is. 30:22 ➔ EPHOD (garment) <642>.

ORNAMENT (TINKLING) – Is. 3:18 ➔ ANKLET <5914>.

ORNAMENTS – Song 1:10 ➔ TURN (noun) <8447> b.

ORNAN – ***'ornān*** or ***'ārnān*** [masc. proper noun: אָרְנָן <771>; prob. from ASH <766>]: strong, a great pine ▶ **This word is a variant reading of Araunah in 1 Chronicles 21:15, 18, 20–25, 28.** A Jebusite owned the "Ornan" threshing floor where the angel of the Lord stopped plaguing Israel. Other ref.: 2 Chr. 3:1. ¶

ORNATE – Gen. 37:3, 23, 32; 2 Sam. 13:18, 19 ➔ COLORS (OF MANY) <6446> a.

ORPAH – ***'orpāh*** [fem. proper noun: עָרְפָּה <6204>; fem. of NECK <6203>]: neck, i.e., obstinacy ▶ **Naomi's daughter-in-law, a Moabitess married to Chilion.** She did not follow her to Bethlehem (Ruth 1:4, 14). ¶

ORPHAN – ***yāṯôm*** [masc. noun: יָתוֹם <3490>; from an unused root meaning to be lonely] ▶ **This word refers to children who had no fathers or parental support group in Israel; it is also translated fatherless.** They, along with widows, the poor, and the oppressed, were of special concern to the Lord (Ex. 22:22, 24; Deut. 16:11, 14; 24:17; 26:12; Ps. 10:18; 68:5; 146:9; Hos. 14:3). God works on their behalf (Deut. 10:18); and those who oppress them are under judgment (Deut. 27:19; Mal. 3:5). Job was concerned to care for them (Job 29:12; 31:17, 21). Israel as a whole did not care for them sufficiently (Job 24:3, 9; Ps. 94:6; Is. 1:23; Jer. 5:28; Ezek. 22:7). *

OSNAPPAR – ***'osnappar*** [Aramaic masc. proper noun: אָסְנַפַּר <620>; of foreign deriv.] ▶ **An Assyrian king, probably a reference to Ashurbanipal; also spelled Osnapper, Asnapper.** Ref.: Ezra 4:10. ¶

OSNAPPER – Ezra 4:10 ➔ OSNAPPAR <620>.

OSPRAY – Lev. 11:13; Deut. 14:12 ➔ VULTURE (BLACK) <5822>.

OSPREY – Lev. 11:18; Deut. 14:17 ➔ CARRION VULTURE <7360>.

OSSIFRAGE – Lev. 11:13; Deut. 14:12 ➔ VULTURE.

OSTRICH – [1] ***yā'ên*** [masc. noun: יַעֵן <3283>; from the same as BECAUSE <3282>] ▶ **This word refers to the most powerful and swift of living birds.** But it is known to try to skirt difficulties by avoiding them. It is used in a simile for Israel (Lam. 4:3). ¶
[2] ***renen*** [masc. noun: רְנָן <7443>; from SHOUT (verb) <7442>] ▶
a. This word refers to the most powerful bird. It runs fast but does not fly; it has wings with which to gesture. Ref.: Job 39:13.
b. KJV translates the word peacock. It refers to a large bird with a crest of plumules and long, brightly colored tail coverts that can spread out like a circular fan. The bird often struts, seemingly showing off its feathers and colors (Job 39:13). ¶
– [3] Lev. 11:16; Deut. 14:15; Job 30:29; Is. 13:21; 34:13; 43:20; Jer. 50:39; Mic. 1:8 ➔ OWL <3284> [4] See STORK <2624>.

OTHER – ***'aḥêr*** [adj.: אַחֵר <312>; from STAY (verb) <309>] ▶ **The meaning of the word is nuanced according to its context.** It means other (Neh. 7:34) but in context also additional or further offspring (Gen. 4:25) and further or another in the flood story (Gen. 8:10, 12). It can take on a figurative meaning indicating that a person has become another person (1 Sam. 10:9, lit., with another heart). When used with a language, it means a foreign language (Is. 28:11) or tongue. Its most important theological use is to designate other gods whom Israel was not to worship or serve (Ex. 34:14; Deut. 5:7; in Deuteronomy 19 times and Jeremiah 18 times). *

OTHNI – ***'oṯniy*** [masc. proper noun: עָתְנִי <6273>; from an unused root meaning to force]: to force, forcible ▶ **A gatekeeper, son of Shemaiah, in the house of the Lord.** Ref.: 1 Chr. 26:7. ¶

OTHNIEL – ***'oṯniy'êl*** [masc. proper noun: עָתְנִיאֵל <6274>; from the same as OTHNI <6273> and GOD <410>]: force of God ▶ **Othniel was a nephew to Caleb and son to Kenaz, Caleb's younger brother.** He was married to Caleb's daughter Achsah (Judg. 1:13). The Lord raised him up to "judge" Israel and to deliver them from the king of Aram Naharaim, Cushan-Rishathaim. The Spirit of God led him, and the Lord gave Israel's enemies into his hands. The land enjoyed peace for forty years (Josh. 15:17; Judg. 1:13; 3:9, 11; 1 Chr. 4:13; 27:15). ¶

OUCH – Ex. 28:11; etc. ➔ FILIGREE <4865>.

OUGHT TO – Job 34:36: my desire is that ➔ OH, THAT <15>.

OUT OF JOINT – Prov. 25:19 ➔ UNSTEADY <4154>.

OUTBREAK – 1 Sam. 5:9 ➔ BREAK OUT <8368>.

OUTBURST – Is. 54:8 ➔ SURGE <8241> a.

OUTCAST – [1] Is. 56:8 ➔ DRIVE <1760> [2] Mic. 4:7 ➔ DRIVEN AWAY (BE) <1972>.

OUTCRY – Ps. 144:14; Is. 24:11 ➔ CRY (noun) <6682>.

OUTER – ***ḥiyṣôn*** [adj.: חִיצוֹן <2435>; from WALL <2434>] ▶ **This word describes an external entry of the Temple.** It was used by the king (2 Kgs. 16:18); to the outer court area of a palace (Esther 6:4); or of Ezekiel's Temple (Ezek. 10:5; 46:20). It refers to the external part of a wall or part of a house (Ezek. 41:17) or sanctuary (1 Kgs. 6:29, 30). It is used in general to refer to anything outside, such as work on the outside of the Temple in Ezra's and Nehemiah's day (Neh. 11:16). *

OUTER TUNIC – Is. 3:22 ➔ MANTLE <4595>.

OUTERMOST – ***qiyṣôn*** [adj.: קִיצוֹן <7020>; from SUMMER (verb) <6972> (in the sense of to clip off)] ▶ **This word means at the end.** It refers to a border or something that lies on the outer perimeter or edge of something (Ex. 26:4, 10; 36:11, 17). ¶

OUTLINE (MAKE AN) – ***tā'ar*** [verb: תָּאַר <8388>; a prim. root] ▶ **This word means to mark.** It describes the process of outlining, drawing a line, or determining a line using various tools (Is. 44:13). For another meaning of the Hebrew word, see TURN (verb) <8388>. ¶

OUTPOST – [1] 1 Sam. 10:5; 13:3, 4 ➔ GARRISON <5333> [2] 1 Sam. 14:1, 4, 6, 11, 15 ➔ GARRISON <4673> [3] 1 Sam. 14:12 ➔ GARRISON <4675>.

OUTRAGE – Judg. 19:23 ➔ FOLLY <5039>.

OUTRAGEOUS – Prov. 27:4 ➔ FLOOD <7858>.

OUTRAGEOUS THING – Gen. 34:7; Deut. 22:21; Josh. 7:15; Judg. 19:23, 24; Jer. 29:23 ➔ FOLLY <5039>.

OUTSKIRT – 2 Sam. 15:17 ➔ LAST HOUSE <1023>.

OUTSPREAD – Is. 8:8 ➔ SPREAD (noun) <4298>.

OUTSTANDING – Song 5:10 ➔ BANNERS (SET UP, LIFT UP) ➔ <1713>.

OUTWIT – Ps. 89:22 ➔ DEBT (IN) <5378>.

OVEN – Ps. 21:9 ➔ FURNACE <8574>.

OVER – ***'êllā'*** [Aramaic prep.: עֵלָּא <5924>; from UPON <5922>] ▶ **This word is used figuratively of a position of power over others, above them in rank.** Ref.: Dan. 6:2. ¶

OVER (BE) – [1] Judg. 19:11 ➔ SUBDUE <7286> [2] Is. 22:15 ➔ PROFITABLE (BE) <5532> a.

OVER AGAINST – Ezek. 46:9 ➔ OPPOSITE (adv.) <5226>.

OVERCOME – [1] Gen. 49:19 ➔ ATTACK (verb) <1464> [2] Ex. 17:13 ➔ LAY LOW <2522> [3] Ps. 78:65 ➔ SHOUT (verb) <7442> b. [4] Song 6:5 ➔ BOLD (BE, MAKE) <7292> [5] Zech. 9:15 ➔ SUBDUE <3533>.

OVERCOME (BE) – Ps. 88:15 ➔ DESPAIR (BE IN) <6323>.

OVERCOME (BEING) – Ex. 32:18 ➔ DEFEAT (noun) <2476>.

OVERDRIVE – Gen. 33:13 ➔ DRIVE HARD <1849>.

OVERFLOW (noun) – ***reۥwāyāh*** [fem. noun: רְוָיָה <7310>; from DRINK ONE'S FILL <7301>] ▶ **This word refers to abundance; a state of spreading over. It refers to an overabundance of something.** It is used figuratively of the cup of life and blessing from the Lord (Ps. 23:5; translated also by another verb: to run over). It refers to the richness, safety, and blessing of God's deliverance from enemies (Ps. 66:12: wealthy place, place of abundance, rich fulfillment). ¶

OVERFLOW (verb) – 1 ***rāḥaš*** [verb: רָחַשׁ <7370>; a prim. root] ▶
a. A verb meaning to be stirred, to spread over. It refers figuratively of a person's heart, emotions being moved by something in a good sense (Ps. 45:1).
b. A verb meaning to indite or compose, to put in words. It refers to putting something into prose or verse; in context it probably refers to writing it out (Ps. 45:1). ¶
2 ***šûq*** [verb: שׁוּק <7783>; a prim. root] ▶ **This word is used figuratively of God's creating abundance, an overflowing of crops in the earth.** Ref.: Ps. 65:9. It refers to the overflowing abundance of wine and oil both literally and figuratively (Joel 2:24; 3:13). ¶
– 3 Deut. 11:4 ➔ FLOW OVER <6687> 4 Ps. 65:11, 12 ➔ DRIP (verb) <7491>.

OVERFLOWING (noun) – 1 Is. 54:8 ➔ SURGE <8241> a. 2 Hab. 3:10 ➔ STORM (noun) <2230>.

OVERFLOWING OF WATER – Job 38:25 ➔ FLOOD <7858>.

OVERHANG – 1 Kgs. 7:6; Ezek. 41:25, 26 ➔ CANOPY <5646>.

OVERHANGING ROOF – 1 Kgs. 7:6; Ezek. 41:25, 26 ➔ CANOPY <5646>.

OVERHEAT – Dan. 3:22 ➔ HEAT (verb) <228>.

OVERJOYED (BE) – Dan. 6:23 ➔ lit.: to be exceedingly glad ➔ GLAD (BE) <2868>.

OVERLAID – Song 5:14 ➔ COVER (verb) <5968>.

OVERLAPPING PART – Ex. 26:12 ➔ REMNANT <5629>.

OVERLAY – 1 ***ṭûaḥ, ṭāḥaḥ*** [verb: טוּחַ, טָחַח <2902>; a prim. root] ▶
a. This word refers to daubing, plastering over. It indicates covering or overlaying various things with different materials: a house with clay (Lev. 14:42); walls with gold or silver (1 Chr. 29:4). It is used metaphorically of plastering over the walls of Jerusalem to hide its sin and corruption (Ezek. 13:10–12, 15). It is a figurative expression of the soothing messages from false prophets (Ezek. 22:28). Other refs.: Lev. 14:43, 48; Is. 44:18; Ezek. 13:14. ¶
b. This word means to smear, to spread over, to daub. Isaiah uses it in a powerful theological metaphor to describe the Lord's smearing over the eyes and hearts of the Israelites so they could not understand His message or His ways (Is. 44:18). ¶
2 ***ṣāp̱āh*** [verb: צָפָה <6823>; a prim. root, prob. identical to WATCH (verb) <6822> through the idea of expansion in outlook, transferring to action] ▶ **This word means to cover.** It is used to describe glazing, plating, or overlaying something (1 Kgs. 6:20; 2 Kgs. 18:16); especially of things for the Tabernacle (Ex. 25:11, 13, 24, 28; 26:29, 32, 37). In its passive tense, it points out what has been overlaid (Ex. 26:32; Prov. 26:23). *
– 3 2 Chr. 3:5, 7–9 ➔ COVER (verb) <2645>.

OVERLAYING – ***ṣippûy*** [masc. noun: צִפּוּי <6826>; from OVERLAY <6823>] ▶ **This word means a coating, a plating.** Overlaying refers to the thin coating of substances placed on various objects for beauty and decorative purposes (Ex. 38:17, 19). Plating was similar but may generally involve a thicker overlay of substances (Num. 16:38, 39; Is. 30:22). ¶

OVERLOOK – 2 Chr. 20:24: place overlooking, place that overlooks ➔ WATCHTOWER <4707>.

OVERPOWER – 1 Judg. 3:10; 6:2 ➔ STRENGTHEN <5810> 2 Job 14:20; 15:24; Eccl. 4:12 ➔ PREVAIL <8630>.

OVERRULE – Num. 30:5, 8, 11 ➔ FORBID <5106>.

OVERRUN – Zeph. 2:9 ➔ POSSESSED <4476>.

OVERSEE – ***nāṣaḥ*** [verb: נָצַח <5329>; a prim. root] ▶ **This word means to lead, to direct.** It is used of foremen or work supervisors (1 Chr. 23:4; 2 Chr. 2:2, 18; 34:12, 13; Ezra 3:8, 9). It is used in a participial form to refer to the act of continuing or being a ringleader in apostasy, rebellion (Jer. 8:5). It refers to a music leader or a choir director (1 Chr. 15:21; Hab. 3:19). It is used often in Psalms and is translated chief musician, choir director, choirmaster, director of music (Ps. 4–6, 8, 9, 11–14, 18–22, 31, 36, 39–42, 44–47, 49, 51–62, 64–70, 75–77, 80, 81, 84, 85, 88, 109, 139, 140). ¶

OVERSEER – 1 ***pāqiyḏ*** [masc. noun: פָּקִיד <6496>; from ATTEND <6485>] ▶ **This word means a commissioner, a deputy. Depending on the context, it has a broad range of possible meanings.** It could apply to government representatives whose positions are temporary, like the officers appointed by Pharaoh to collect grain during the seven plentiful years (Gen. 41:34). It could also represent a permanent position of leadership for a king (Judg. 9:28); a high priest (2 Chr. 24:11); or a Levite (2 Chr. 31:13). It could further signify a general leader of men, such as a military officer (2 Kgs. 25:19); a tribal leader (Neh. 11:9); or a priestly leader (Neh. 11:14). *
– 2 Is. 60:17 ➔ OPPRESS <5065>.

OVERSHADOW – Ezek. 31:3 ➔ DARK (BE, GROW) <6751>.

OVERSIGHT – Gen. 43:12 ➔ MISTAKE <4869>.

OVERSPREAD – Gen. 9:19 ➔ BREAK <5310> b.

OVERTAKE – 1 ***nāśag*** [verb: נָשַׂג <5381>; a prim. root] ▶ **This word means to reach, to get.** It often means to overtake, to catch up to someone (Gen. 31:25; 44:4, 6; Ex. 14:9; 15:9; Num. 6:21). It is used figuratively of age, of years attaining a certain level (Gen. 47:9); or of joy and rejoicing arriving, becoming a reality (Is. 35:10). It means to afford, to have at one's hand, the ability, to have sufficient (Lev. 5:11; 14:21); or to obtain, come into possession of property (Lev. 25:47). *
– 2 Job 20:22 ➔ DISTRESSED (BE) <3334> 3 Ps. 91:10; Prov. 12:21 ➔ BEFALL <579>.

OVERTHROW (noun) – 1 ***hᵃpêḵāh*** [fem. noun: הֲפֵכָה <2018>; fem. of OPPOSITE (noun) <2016>] ▶ **This word denotes an overthrowing, a destruction, a catastrophe.** It describes the overthrow of Sodom and Gomorrah (Gen. 19:29) brought about as both a natural and a divinely caused judgment. ¶
– 2 Ezek. 27:27 ➔ FALL (noun) <4658>.

OVERTHROW (noun and verb) – ***mahpêḵāh*** [fem. noun: מַהְפֵּכָה <4114>; from TURN <2015>] ▶ **This word is also translated destruction. It describes primarily the demolishing or wiping out of the city of Sodom.** It never was rebuilt or used again (Deut. 29:23). The word is used of various places decimated like Sodom and Gomorrah (Is. 13:19; Jer. 49:18; 50:40; Amos 4:11); and once, with reference to the cities, of the devastation of Judah (Is. 1:7). ¶

OVERTHROW (verb) – 1 ***mᵉgar*** [Aramaic verb: מְגַר <4049>; corresponding to DELIVER OVER <4048>] ▶ **This word means to cast down, to destroy.** In an edict decreed by King Darius, this verb describes what Darius hoped the God of heaven would do to any king or people who altered his edict or tried to destroy the Temple in Jerusalem (Ezra 6:12. ¶
2 ***maḏḥêp̄āh*** [fem. noun: מַדְחֵפָה <4073>; from HURRY (herb) <1765>] ▶ **This word refers to evil pursuing the violent man and giving him thrust upon thrust, blow upon blow until he experiences destruction.** Ref.: Ps. 140:11; also translated speedily. ¶
3 ***sālap̄*** [verb: סָלַף <5557>; a prim. root] ▶ **This word means to distort, subvert, or**

mislead from what is normal; it is also translated to pervert, to twist, to ruin, as well as to throw down, to frustrate. It is used of the effect of bribes on justice, hindering it (Ex. 23:8); and its process (Deut. 16:19); it is used of removing governmental powers as well (Job 12:19). It describes hindering or subverting the wicked and foolish in their ways (Prov. 13:6; 19:3; 21:12; 22:12). ¶
– 4 Ex. 14:27; Ps. 136:15 ➔ SHAKE <5287> 5 2 Sam. 18:7 ➔ SMITE <5062> 6 Job 19:6 ➔ BEND <5791> 7 Ps. 140:4 ➔ DRIVE <1760> 8 See PULL DOWN <2040>.

OVERTHROWN – Ezek. 21:27 ➔ RUIN (noun) <5754>.

OVERTURN – Ezek. 21:27 ➔ RUIN (noun) <5754>.

OVERWHELM – 1 Ex. 17:13 ➔ LAY LOW <2522> 2 Deut. 11:4 ➔ FLOW OVER <6687> 3 Job 15:24 ➔ PREVAIL <8630> 4 Ps. 139:11 ➔ BRUISE (verb) <7779> c. 5 Song 6:5 ➔ BOLD (BE, MAKE) <7292>.

OVERWHELMING – Prov. 27:4 ➔ FLOOD <7858>.

OVERWORK – Prov. 23:4 ➔ WEARY (verb) <3021>.

OWL – 1 ***'ōaḥ*** [masc. noun: אֹחַ <255>; prob. from ALAS! <253>] ▶ **This word refers to a bird that hunts during the night; it is also translated doleful creature, howling creature, jackal.** After Babylon was destroyed, it would become the haunt of owls and other scavengers (Is. 13:21). ¶
2 ***ya^anāh*** [fem. noun: יַעֲנָה <3284>; fem. of OSTRICH <3283>] ▶ **This word means an unclean bird; a horned owl or ostrich. It is probably referring to the horned or great owl.** In its context, it is considered unclean and detestable for Israelites, and they could not eat it (Lev. 11:16; Deut. 14:15). It was ranked on the animal social scale with jackals or wild dogs (Job 30:29; Is. 13:21; 34:13; 43:20; Jer. 50:39; Mic. 1:8). Its forlorn howling and barking indicated mourning. ¶
3 ***qippôz*** [masc. noun: קִפּוֹז <7091>; from an unused root meaning to contract, i.e., to spring forward] ▶
a. Translators are divided about whether this refers to an owl of some kind or a small tree snake. See b. also. In either case, it refers to a creature that makes its home among ruins, the wild, or in places of devastation (Is. 34:15).
b. This word could refer to a tree snake. Ref.: Is. 34:15. See a. ¶
4 ***taḥmās*** [masc. noun: תַּחְמָס <8464>; from VIOLENCE (DO) <2554>] ▶
a. This word refers to a bird that Israel was not permitted to eat. It was classified as unclean (NASB: Lev. 11:16; Deut. 14:15); it is also translated short-eared owl (NKJV), screech owl (NIV).
b. This word refers to the nighthawk. The KJV and the ESV favored this rendering of the verb (Lev. 11:16; Deut. 14:15). Its classification as inedible and unclean is the same. ¶
– 5 Is. 14:23; 34:11; Zeph. 2:14 ➔ PORCUPINE <7090> b.

OWL (GREAT, SCREECH, SHORT-EARED) – ***yanšûp̱, yanšôp̱*** [masc. noun: יַנְשׁוּף, יַנְשׁוֹף <3244>; apparently from BLOW (verb) <5398> (perhaps from the blowing cry)] ▶ **This word refers to an unclean bird of some kind, possibly a great horned owl.** Refs.: Lev. 11:17; Deut. 14:16; Is. 34:11. It was not to be eaten by the Israelites. ¶

OWL (SCREECH) – See NIGHT BIRD, NIGHT CREATURE, NIGHT MONSTER <3917>.

OWL (TAWNY, DESERT) – Lev. 11:18; Deut. 14:17; Ps. 102:6; Is. 34:11; Zeph. 2:14 ➔ PELICAN <6893>.

OWL, LITTLE OWL – ***kôs*** [fem. noun: כּוֹס <3563>] ▶ **This word denotes a bird that hunts during the night; a screech**

owl, a little owl. It is used to symbolize a forsaken, lonely, afflicted person, i.e., an owl in the wilderness (Ps. 102:6). The Israelites could not eat these birds (little owl) because they were unclean and forbidden (Lev. 11:17; Deut. 14:16). The Hebrew word is also translated cup; see CUP <3563>. ¶

OX – 1 ***šôr*** [masc. noun: שׁוֹר <7794>; from JOURNEY (verb) <7788>] ▶ **This word refers to a bull or a cow. It refers to a mature male bovine, a bull, an ox, a steer.** It is used as a collective noun referring to one or more of these animals. It may be used as a common noun for cattle (Gen. 32:5). They could constitute a major part of a person's wealth (Ex. 20:17). Special laws were laid out for the treatment of these animals (Ex. 21:28, 29, 32, 33, 35, 36; 22:1, 4). They were major sacrificial animals (Lev. 9:4, 18, 19; 17:3; 1 Kgs. 1:19, 25; Ps. 69:31). The strange creatures in Ezekiel's' vision each included a face like an ox (Ezek. 1:10). *
– 2 See BULL <8450>.

OX, OXEN – See CATTLE <1241>.

OXEN – Deut. 7:13; 28:4, 18, 51; Ps. 8:7; Prov. 14:4; Is. 30:24 ➔ HERD <504>.

OZEM – ***'ōṣem*** [masc. proper noun: אֹצֶם <684>; from an unused root prob. meaning to be strong]: strength ▶
a. A brother of David. Ref.: 1 Chr. 2:15. ¶
b. A descendant of Judah. Ref.: 1 Chr. 2:25. ¶

OZNI – ***'ozniy*** [masc. proper noun: אָזְנִי <244>; from EAR <241>]: who listens ▶ **Son of Gad, as well as the name of a clan, the Oznites.** Ref.: Num. 26:16. ¶

P

PAARAI – ***paʿᵃray*** [masc. proper noun: פַּעֲרַי <6474>; from OPEN <6473>]: yawning ▶ **One of David's mighty men.** Ref.: 2 Sam. 23:35. ¶

PACIFY – 1 ***kāpāh*** [verb: כָּפָה <3711>; a prim. root] ▶ **This word refers to the calming or reconciling of an attitude of anger toward someone.** Ref.: Prov. 21:14; also translated to soothe, to subdue, to advert. ¶
– 2 Gen. 32:20; Prov. 16:14 ➔ COVER (verb) <3722> 3 Esther 2:1; 7:10 ➔ SUBSIDE <7918>.

PACT – Is. 28:18 ➔ VISION <2380>.

PADDAN, PADDAN ARAM – ***paddān, paddan ᵃrām*** [fem. noun: פַּדַּן אֲרָם ,פַּדָּן <6307>; from the same as ARAM <758>]: the tableland of Aram ▶
a. Paddan, a shortened form of b. Ref.: Gen. 48:7. ¶
b. A plain of northern Mesopotamia. Refs.: Gen. 25:20; 28:2, 5–7; 31:18; 33:18; 35:9, 26; 46:15. ¶

PADDLE – Deut. 23:13 ➔ PEG <3489>.

PADON – ***pāḏôn*** [masc. proper noun: פָּדוֹן <6303>; from REDEEM <6299>]: ransom, redemption ▶ **Head of a family of Temple servants.** Refs.: Ezra 2:44; Neh. 7:47. ¶

PAGIEL – ***pagʿiyʾēl*** [masc. proper noun: פַּגְעִיאֵל <6295>; from OCCURRENCE <6294> and GOD <410>]: encounter with God ▶ **A chief of the tribe of Asher.** Refs.: Num. 1:13; 2:27; 7:72, 77; 10:26. ¶

PAHATH-MOAB – ***paḥaṯ môʾāḇ*** [masc. proper noun: פַּחַת מוֹאָב <6355>; from PIT <6354 and MOAB <4124>]: pit of Moab ▶
a. Some of the descendants of this man came back from the Babylonian captivity and married foreign women. Refs.: Ezra 2:6; 10:30; Neh. 3:11; 7:11. ¶
b. A descendant of this man returned from the Babylonian captivity. Ref.: Ezra 8:4. ¶
c. A Jewish leader who renewed the covenant with Nehemiah. Ref.: Neh. 10:14. ¶

PAI – 1 Chr. 1:50 ➔ PAU <6464>.

PAILS – Job 21:24 ➔ BODY <5845>.

PAIN (noun) – 1 ***ḥiyl, ḥiylāh*** [noun: חִיל, חִילָה <2427>; from SHAKE <2342> (in the sense of to grieve)] ▶
a. A masculine noun referring to fear, discomfort, anguish; it is also translated sorrow, pang, agony. It indicates an internal sense of fear among the nations stirred up by Israel's victory at the Red Sea (Ex. 15:14) or other great acts of God (Ps. 48:6). It indicates the fear the enemies of Israel created in them (Jer. 6:24; Mic. 4:9). Other refs.: Jer. 22:23; 50:43. ¶
b. A feminine noun indicating suffering, sorrow, anguish. It is used of Job's relentless agony as he wrestles with the physical and emotional torment of his plight (Job 6:10). ¶
2 ***ḥalḥālāh*** [fem. noun: חַלְחָלָה <2479>; fem. from the same as HALHUL <2478>] ▶ **This word means distress, anguish, trembling.** It indicates a response of great distress and shaking toward God's imminent destruction of Babylon (Is. 21:3); of Egypt (Ezek. 30:4, 9). It describes the anguish of the inhabitants of Nineveh which was about to fall (Nah. 2:10). ¶
3 ***kᵉʾēḇ*** [masc. noun: כְּאֵב <3511>; from PAIN (BE IN) <3510>] ▶ **This word means anguish, sorrow; it is also translated grief, suffering, distress.** It is used of Job's distress and pain from his calamities and disease (Job 2:13; 16:6). It has the sense of distress or perhaps despair for the psalmist (Ps. 39:2); and those under God's judgment (Is. 17:11; 65:14, "from a painful heart"; Jer. 15:18). ¶
4 ***ʿeṣeḇ*** [masc. noun: עֶצֶב <6089>; from HURT <6087>] ▶ **This word means hurt, toil, labor.** Since, like the noun *ʿōṣeḇ* (<6090>), it is derived from the verb *ʿāṣaḇ* (<6087>), this noun carries the same

variations of meaning. The word is used of physical pain, such as a woman's pain in childbirth (Gen. 3:16); or of emotional pain, such as that caused by inappropriate words (Prov. 15:1: grievous, harsh). The word can also express both meanings (cf. Prov. 10:22: sorrow, painful toil); and can also refer to hard work or toil (Ps. 127:2; Prov. 5:10; 14:23). It is also translated jar, pot, idol in Jeremiah 22:28. ¶

5 ***'iṣṣāḇôn*** [masc. noun: עִצָּבוֹן <6093>; from HURT <6087>] ▶ **This word means and is also translated sorrow, toil.** It occurs three times in Genesis, relating to the curse that God placed on fallen humanity. To the woman, God stated that she would have pain and toil during childbirth (Gen. 3:16a). To the man, God stated that he would have pain and toil in working the ground to produce food (Gen. 3:17; 5:29). ¶

6 ***'ōṣeḇ*** [masc. noun: עֹצֶב <6090>; a variation of <6089> above] ▶ **This word means toil, labor; it also means image, idol. Like the noun *'eṣeḇ* (PAIN (noun) <6089>), this word is derived from the verb *'āṣaḇ* (HURT <6087>), to make, to shape.** It can be used to depict the physical pain of childbirth (1 Chr. 4:9); a painful way, meaning a harmful habit like idolatry (Ps. 139:24; KJV: sorrow); and the sorrow and hardship of the Babylonian exile (Is. 14:3; NIV: suffering). In the final passage, this word is in parallel with *rōgez* (<7267>), meaning disquiet or turmoil. Other ref.: Is. 48:5 (idol). ¶

– 7 Job 9:28 ➔ SORROW (noun) <6094> 8 Job 33:19; Ps. 38:17; Eccl. 2:23; Jer. 30:15; 45:3; etc. ➔ SUFFERING <4341> 9 Ps. 73:4 ➔ BOND <2784> 10 Ps. 116:3 ➔ DISTRESS (noun) <4712>.

PAIN (BE IN) – *kā'aḇ* [verb: כָּאַב <3510>; a prim. root] ▶ **This word indicates to be sore, to grieve.** It asserts being in physical pain (Gen. 34:25; Job 14:22) but also is used of the distress of affliction as pain (Ps. 69:29). The heart suffers emotional pain (Prov. 14:13). In its causal stem, it can express acts of God or people causing pain or distress (Job 5:18; Ezek. 13:22; 28:24). In 2 Kings 3:19 in a context describing destructive acts, it describes ruining a field by scattering stones in it. ¶

PAIN, LABOR PAINS – *ṣiyr* [masc. noun: צִיר <6735>; from BESIEGE <6696> (in the sense of being harassed or oppressed)] ▶ **This word means a throe (a severe spasm of pain), pang, distress, sorrow, anguish.** It refers to labor pains in giving birth (1 Sam. 4:19; Is. 21:3); the dread and anxiety of a doomed nation (Is. 13:8). It refers to a feeling of distress and hopelessness in the face of a divine vision (Dan. 10:16). See also MESSENGER <6735> and HINGE <6735> for other meanings of the Hebrew word. ¶

PAIN (verb) – Ps. 78:41 ➔ VEX <8428> a.

PAINFUL – 1 Job 6:25; Mic. 2:10 ➔ GRIEVOUS <4834> 2 Ezek. 28:24 ➔ PAINFUL (BE) <3992>.

PAINFUL (BE) – *mā'ar* [verb: מָאַר <3992>; a prim. root] ▶ **This word means to prick, to be destructive.** It refers to a skin disease or an eruption that is destructive, hurtful (Lev. 13:51, 52); or to some growth or malignancy found in the structure or materials of a house (Lev. 14:44); it is translated fretting, active, malignant, persistent. It modifies the word *ṣāra'aṯ* each time. It is used to modify brier or thorn, a figure of speech for oppressive peoples around Israel who were painful or prickly briers or thorns (Ezek. 28:24: to prick, pricking, prickling, painful). ¶

PAINFUL TOIL – Prov. 10:22 ➔ PAIN (noun) <6089>.

PAINT (noun) – 2 Kgs. 9:30; Jer. 4:30 ➔ MAKEUP <6320>.

PAINT (verb) – 1 ***kāḥal*** [verb: כָּחַל <3583>; a prim. root] ▶ **This word means to color something, e.g., the eyes; it is also translated to apply makeup.** It means to put on luxurious, alluring, and enticing cosmetics to impress and attract someone (Ezek. 23:40). ¶

– 2 2 Kgs. 9:30 ➔ lit.: to put on paint, makeup ➔ MAKEUP <6320>.

PAINTING – Jer. 4:30 ➔ MAKEUP <6320>.

PAIR – ***ṣemeḏ*** [masc. noun: צֶמֶד <6776>] ▶ **a. This word refers to a couple, a yoke, a team of two.** It refers to two of something, a team or a pair (Judg. 19:3, 10; 2 Sam. 16:1; 1 Kgs. 19:19, 21; 2 Kgs. 5:17). A yoke of oxen refers to two oxen, a pair (1 Sam. 11:7). It is used in the idiom, yoke of land, about an acre, referring to the amount of land plowed in a day by one yoke of oxen (1 Sam. 14:14). Job possessed five hundred yoke of oxen (1:3). *
b. This word refers to about an acre of land; land plowed by a team of two oxen in a day. Isaiah 5:10 refers to "*ten ṣimdê-ḵerem,*" ca. ten acres. See also 1 Samuel 14:14 in a. above. ¶

PALACE – 1 ***'appeḏen*** [masc. noun: אַפֶּדֶן <643>; apparently of foreign deriv.] ▶ **This word refers to a royal tent (also translated royal pavilion, palatial tents) or structure.** The fierce king of the North will pitch such a tent before he is destroyed (Dan. 11:45). ¶
2 ***biyṯān*** [masc. noun: בִּיתָן <1055>; prob. from HOUSE <1004>] ▶ **This word refers to the king's residence in Susa.** Ref.: Esther 1:5. It is combined with garden (*ginnaṯ* <1594>) to indicate the palace garden (Esther 7:7, 8). ¶
– 3 Ps. 122:7; Amos 3:11; Is. 23:13; Lam. 2:5 ➔ STRONGHOLD <759> 4 Song 8:9; Ezek. 25:4 ➔ CAMP <2918> 5 Amos 4:3 ➔ HARMON <2038> b. 6 See CITADEL <1001>, <1002> 7 See TEMPLE <1964>, <1965>.

PALAL – ***pālāl*** [masc. proper noun: פָּלָל <6420>; from PRAY <6419>]: judge ▶ **He repaired the wall of Jerusalem in the time of Nehemiah.** Ref.: Neh. 3:25. ¶

PALANQUIN – Song 3:9 ➔ CARRIAGE <668>.

PALATE – Job 6:30; 12:11 ➔ MOUTH <2441>.

PALATIAL – Dan. 11:45: his palatial tents ➔ the tents of his palace ➔ PALACE <643>.

PALE (GROW, TURN) – Joel 2:6; Nah. 2:10 ➔ BLACKNESS <6289>.

PALE (GROW, TURN, WAX) – ***ḥāwar*** [verb: חָוַר <2357>; a prim. root] ▶ **This word refers to persons turning pallid or whitish because of shame or calamity.** Ref.: Is. 29:22. ¶

PALE, DEATHLY PALE – Jer. 30:6 ➔ MILDEW <3420>.

PALENESS – Jer. 30:6 ➔ MILDEW <3420>.

PALESTINA – Ex. 15:14 ➔ PHILISTIA <6429>.

PALLU – ***pallû'*** [masc. proper noun: פַּלּוּא <6396>; from DISTINCTION (MAKE) <6395>]: distinguished ▶ **The second son of Reuben.** Refs.: Gen. 46:9; Ex. 6:14; Num. 26:5, 8; 1 Chr. 5:3. ¶

PALLUITES – ***pallu'iy*** [proper noun: פַּלֻּאִי <6384>; patron. from PALLU <6396>] ▶ **Descendants of Pallu, the second son of Reuben.** Ref.: Num. 26:5. ¶

PALM – Dan. 5:5, 24 ➔ PART (noun) <6447>.

PALM BRANCH – Lev. 23:40; Job 15:32; Is. 9:14; 19:15 ➔ BRANCH <3712>.

PALM TREE – 1 ***tāmār*** [masc. noun: תָּמָר <8558>; from an unused root meaning to be erect] ▶ **This word refers to a water-loving date palm tree found around springs.** Refs.: Ex. 15:27; Num. 33:9. It also refers to a desert oasis where the date palm flourishes (Ps. 92:12). Its rich foliage, long leaves, and slim branches were used often in feasts and festivals to celebrate (Lev. 23:40). Jericho was known as the city of palm trees (Deut. 34:3). The righteous flourish as the date palm (Ps. 92:12). The bride is likened favorably to a date palm (Song 7:7, 8). In a time of severe judgment, Joel could envision even the date palm drying up (Joel 1:12). *

2 ***tōmer*** [masc. noun: תֹּמֶר <8560>; from the same root as <8558> above] ▶
a. This word refers to the place where Deborah sat to render judgment in Israel. Ref.: Judg. 4:5. The KJV renders the word as palm tree in Jeremiah 10:5.
b. A masculine noun meaning a scarecrow. The word is rendered as scarecrow by most translators now (NASB, NIV, ESV; Jer. 10:5). ¶
3 ***timōrāh*** [fem. noun: תִּמֹרָה <8561>; from the same root as <8558> above] ▶ **This word also means a palm tree ornament.** It refers to a carved palm tree ornament done by a skilled craftsman (1 Kgs. 6:29, 32, 35; 2 Chr. 3:5; Ezek. 40:16; 41:18–20). It was found in Solomon's Temple and in Ezekiel's visionary Temple. *

PALMERWORM – Joel 1:4; 2:25 ➔ LOCUST <1501>.

PALTI – ***palṭiy*** [masc. proper noun: פַּלְטִי <6406>; from DELIVER <6403>]: deliverance ▶
a. A man from the tribe of Benjamin among the twelve spies sent to check out the land of Canaan. Ref.: Num. 13:9. ¶
b. A man to whom Saul married his daughter Michal, David's wife. Ref.: 1 Sam. 25:44. ¶

PALTIEL – ***palṭiy'ēl*** [masc. proper noun: פַּלְטִיאֵל <6409>; from the same as PELET <6404> and GOD <410>]: deliverance by God ▶
a. A prince of the tribe of Issachar. Ref.: Num. 34:26. ¶
b. The same as PALTI <6406> b. Ref.: 2 Sam. 3:15. ¶

PALTITE – ***palṭiy*** [proper noun: פַּלְטִי <6407>; patron. from PALTI <6406>]: deliverance ▶ **A descendant of Palti or an inhabitant of Beth-Palet.** Ref.: 2 Sam. 23:26. ¶

PAMPER – ***pānaq*** [verb: פָּנַק <6445>; a prim. root] ▶ **This word means to treat someone with great care and concern, to help him or her along patiently.** Ref.: Prov. 29:21; KJV: to delicately bring up. ¶

PAN – 1 ***marḥešeṯ*** [fem. noun: מַרְחֶשֶׁת <4802>; from OVERFLOW <7370> a.] ▶ **This word refers to a cooking utensil for frying or possibly baking; it is translated by a frying pan, covered pan.** Refs.: Lev. 2:7; 7:9. ¶
2 ***maśrêṯ*** [fem. noun: מַשְׂרֵת <4958>; apparently from an unused root meaning to perforate, i.e., hollow out] ▶ **This word refers to a cooking dish used for baking or frying food.** Ref.: 2 Sam. 13:9. ¶
3 ***ṣêlāḥāh*** [fem. noun: צְלָחָה <6745>; from RUSH (verb) <6743> (something protracted or flattened out)] ▶ **This word describes a cooking utensil used for boiling food and sacrifices.** Ref.: 2 Chr. 35:13. ¶
– 4 Lev. 2:5; 6:21; 7:9; Ezek. 4:3 ➔ GRIDDLE <4227> 5 2 Chr. 35:13 ➔ DISH <6747> 6 Neh. 11:8 ➔ POT <6517>.

PANEL – 1 1 Kgs. 6:9; 7:3, 7; Jer. 22:14; Hag. 1:4 ➔ COVER (verb) <5603> a. 2 2 Chr. 3:5 ➔ COVER (verb) <2645>.

PANELED – ***śaḥiyp*** [verb: שָׂחִיף <7824>; from an unused root meaning to peel] ▶ **This word refers to a flat piece of wood or metal that forms a part of a surface of a wall, etc., usually square or rectangular in shape; it is also translated ceiled, covered.** This feature was found in Ezekiel's visionary Temple (Ezek. 41:16). ¶

PANG – 1 Ex. 15:14; Jer. 50:43; Mic. 4:9 ➔ PAIN (noun) <2427> 2 Ps. 73:4 ➔ BOND <2784> 3 Ps. 116:3 ➔ DISTRESS (noun) <4712> 4 Is. 13:8; Jer. 13:21; Hos. 13:13 ➔ ROPE <2256>.

PANIC – 1 ***reṭeṭ*** [masc. noun: רֶטֶט <7374>; from an unused root meaning to tremble] ▶ **This word denoted fear or hysteria in the face of impending attack; it also means fear, trembling.** It is found only in Jeremiah 49:24. ¶
– 2 Lev. 26:16 ➔ TERROR <928> 3 1 Sam. 5:9, 11; Is. 22:5; Ezek. 7:7; Zech. 14:13 ➔ CONFUSION <4103> 4 1 Sam. 14:15 ➔ TREMBLING <2731> 5 Zech. 12:4 ➔ CONFUSION <8541>.

PANNAG – Ezek. 27:17 ➔ CAKE <6436> b.

PANS – ***ḥ*^a*ḇittiym*** [masc. plur. noun: חֲבִתִּים <2281>; from an unused root prob. meaning to cook (comp. GRIDDLE <4227>)] ▶ **This word refers to something flat, a flat utensil for cooking, frying, or baking, flat bread (baked in a pan).** It refers to a category of food or bread that was baked in pans (1 Chr. 9:31: flat cakes, offering bread), an important part of Temple ritual. ¶

PANT – [1] ***'āraḡ*** [verb: עָרַג <6165>; a prim. root] ▶ **This word means to pant (to breathe with short, quick breaths) for, to long for. It is a passionate, emotional verb.** It is used in emblematic poetry to depict a deer's longing for flowing brooks of water (Ps. 42:1). It is used of languishing beasts of the field panting after God, their Creator (Joel 1:20; also translated to cry out). ¶
– [2] Ps. 38:10 ➔ MERCHANT <5503>.

PAPERREEDS – Is. 19:7 ➔ BULRUSHES <6169>.

PAPYRUS – [1] Ex. 2:3; Job 8:11; Is. 18:2; 35:7 ➔ BULRUSH <1573> [2] Job 9:26 ➔ REED <16> [3] Is. 19:7 ➔ BULRUSHES <6169>.

PARABLE – Prov. 1:6 ➔ SAYING <4426>.

PARAH – ***pārāh*** [proper noun: פָּרָה <6511>; the same as COW <6510>]: heifer ▶ **A town in Benjamin.** Ref.: Josh. 18:23. ¶

PARALLEL (SET) – ***šālaḇ*** [verb: שָׁלַב <7947>; a prim. root] ▶ **This word refers to setting two tenons or extensions parallel with each other at the end of a board or panel; it is also translated to fit, to set in order, to be equally distant, to bind.** Refs.: Ex. 26:17; 36:22. ¶

PARALYZED (BE) – Hab. 1:4 ➔ STUNNED (BECOME) <6313>.

PARAN – ***pā'rān*** [proper noun: פָּארָן <6290>; from GLORIFY <6286>]: ornamental; full of caverns ▶ **The desert where Ishmael settled. The Desert of Paran is hard to pinpoint. It refers to a rather large area in west central Sinai. Kadesh Barnea and lower southeast Judah are on its periphery. It lay below the Negev and touched southern Edom.** Paran is a shortened form of the expression but may designate a more confined area as well. The Israelites traversed it on their wanderings to Canaan (Num. 10:12; 13:3, 26; Deut. 1:1) as did others (1 Kgs. 11:18). The Lord "came forth" or "shone forth from Mount Paran" in this area (Deut. 33:2). *

PARAPET – ***ma*^a*qeh*** [masc. noun: מַעֲקֶה <4624>; from an unused root meaning to repress] ▶ **This word indicates a low wall or railing put to keep anyone from falling over the edge of a structure.** Ref.: Deut. 22:8; KJV: battlement. ¶

PARBAR – 1 Chr. 26:18 ➔ PRECINCTS <6503> b.

PARCEL – Gen. 33:19 ➔ SMOOTH <2513>.

PARCHED – ***ṣiḥeh*** [adj.: צִחֶה <6704>; from an unused root meaning to glow] ▶ **This word is also translated dried up. It refers to something or someone desiccated, dried out from a serious lack of refreshing water.** It is used figuratively of Israel as God's vineyard (Is. 5:13). ¶

PARCHED (BE) – Is. 41:17 ➔ DRY UP <5405>.

PARCHED GRAIN – ***qāliy, qāliy'*** [masc. non: קָלִי, קָלִיא <7039>; from ROAST <7033>] ▶ **This word designates something parched (dried) or roasted, particularly grain. It refers to grain that has been placed in the hot sun to parch it, to dry it out, or placed over fire to roast it. Lentils and beans were also parched.** Ref.: Lev. 23:14. It was a most desirable food (Ruth 2:14; 1 Sam. 17:17; 25:18; 2 Sam. 17:28). ¶

PARCHED GROUND – Is. 35:7 ➔ BURNING SAND <8273>.

PARCHED LAND – ***ṣᵉḥiyḥāh*** [fem. noun: צְחִיחָה <6707>; fem. of BARE (noun) <6706>] ▶ **This word indicates a sun-scorched land.** It indicates something dried up and shriveled, suffering from the need for water, thirsty (Ps. 68:6). ¶

PARCHED PLACE – ***ḥārêr*** [noun: חָרֵר <2788>; from BURN (verb) <2787>] ▶ **This word means a scorched place; it is also translated stony wastes.** It occurs only in Jeremiah 17:6 where it is plural and refers to places where lack of water keeps plants from prospering. This symbolizes the lives of those who trust in people rather than in God. In contrast, those who trust in God have enough water even in heat and drought (Jer. 17:7, 8). ¶

PARDON – Num. 14:20; Is. 55:7; etc. ➔ FORGIVE <5545>.

PARDON (READY TO) – Neh. 9:17 ➔ FORGIVENESS <5545>.

PARK – Neh. 2:8; Eccl. 2:5 ➔ FOREST <6508>.

PARLOR – Judg. 3:20, 24 ➔ ROOF CHAMBER <4747>.

PARMASHTA – ***parmaštā'*** [masc. proper noun: פַּרְמַשְׁתָּא <6534>; of Persian origin]: first, superior ▶ **One of the ten sons of Haman, the enemy of Mordecai and Esther.** Ref.: Esther 9:9. ¶

PARNACH – ***parnāḵ*** [masc. proper noun: פַּרְנָךְ <6535>; of uncertain deriv.] ▶ **Son of Elizaphan, of the tribe of Zebulun, who entered the Promise Land.** Ref.: Num. 34:25. ¶

PARNAK – Num. 34:25 ➔ PARNACH <6535>.

PAROSH – ***par'ōš*** [masc. proper noun: פַּרְעֹשׁ <6551>; the same as FLEA <6550>]: flea ▶ **Family members of this man came back from the Babylonian captivity.** Refs.: Ezra 2:3; 8:3; 10:25; Neh. 3:25; 7:8; 10:14. ¶

PARSHANDATHA – ***paršandāṯā'*** [masc. proper noun: פַּרְשַׁנְדָּתָא <6577>; of Persian origin] ▶ **One of the ten sons of Haman, the enemy of Mordecai and Esther.** Ref.: Esther 9:7. ¶

PARSIN – Dan. 5:25 ➔ DIVIDE <6537> d.

PART (noun) – [1] ***baḏ*** [masc. noun: בַּד <905>; from ALONE (BE) <909>] ▶ **This word indicates a portion or portions of something such as an amount of an ingredient used to make incense or anointing oil.** Ref.: Ex. 30:34. Or it indicates various parts of objects: persons, animals, trees, parts of a structure, etc. (Ex. 25:13–15; Job 18:13; 41:12; Ezek. 17:6; 19:14). It designates the poles used to carry the ark (Ex. 25:14, 15). The Hebrew word also means alone, apart from; see ALONE <905>. *
[2] ***gezer*** [masc. noun: גֶּזֶר <1506>; from CUT (verb) <1504>] ▶ **This word means portion, division. It is found only as a plural form.** It refers to the halves of animals that Abraham prepared in the covenant ceremony of Genesis 15:17 and the two halves of the Red Sea when God divided it (Ps. 136:13). ¶
[3] ***pas*** [Aramaic masc. noun: פַּס <6447>; from a root corresponding to COLORS (OF MANY) <6446> (properly, the palm of the hand)] ▶ **This word describes the palm or back of a person's hand.** In context it denotes the appearance of a strong human hand (Dan. 5:5, 24). ¶
– [4] Ex. 26:12 ➔ REMNANT <5629> [5] Neh. 3:9, 12, 14–18 ➔ DISTRICT <6418> [6] Jer. 34:18, 19 ➔ HALF <1335> [7] Amos 3:12 ➔ DAMASCUS <1833> b.

PART (verb) – [1] Lev. 2:6 ➔ BREAK <6626> [2] Lev. 11:3–7, 26; Deut. 14:6–8 ➔ DIVIDE <6536> [3] Lev. 11:3, 7, 26; Deut. 14:6, 7 ➔ SPLIT <8156>.

PART, PARTLY – Dan. 2:42 ➔ END <7118>.

PARTIAL (BE) – Ex. 23:3 ➔ HONOR (verb) <1921>.

PARTIALITY – ***maśśō'*** [masc. noun: מַשֹּׂא <4856>; from CARRY <5375> (as a lifting up)] ▶ **This word means to show favor to certain people in the phrase *maśśō' pānîym*, literally, "lifting up of faces," meaning special recognition.** Ref.: 2 Chr. 19:7; KJV: respect of persons. ¶

PARTIALITY (SHOW) – Ex. 23:3 ➔ HONOR (verb) <1921>.

PARTICULAR ONE – Dan. 8:13 ➔ CERTAIN ONE <6422>.

PARTING GIFT – ***šillûḥiym*** [masc. noun: שִׁלּוּחִים <7964>; from SEND FORTH, SEND AWAY <7971>] ▶ **This word means a present to someone when leaving; it also means a dowry.** It refers to something given as a gift in parting (Mic. 1:14; KJV: present); or as a dowry to one's daughter in a marriage (1 Kgs. 9:16). For Exodus 18:2, see SEND FORTH, SEND AWAY <7971>. ¶

PARTNER – Mal. 2:14 ➔ COMPANION <2278>.

PARTRIDGE – ***qōrê'*** [masc. noun: קֹרֵא <7124>; act. part. of CALL <7121>] ▶ **This word refers to a relatively small bird with an orange-brown head, grayish neck, and rust-colored tail.** It was difficult to spot and hunt (1 Sam. 26:20). It is used in a simile for comparison (Jer. 17:11). ¶

PARUAH – ***pārûaḥ*** [masc. proper noun: פָּרוּחַ <6515>; pass. part. of BREAK OUT <6524>]: flourishing ▶ **Father of Jehoshaphat.** Ref.: 1 Kgs. 4:17. ¶

PARVAIM – ***parwayim*** [proper noun: פַּרְוַיִם <6516>; of foreign origin]: oriental regions ▶ **King Solomon brought gold from this place to decorate the Temple.** Ref.: 2 Chr. 3:6. ¶

PARZITE – See PEREZITE <6558>.

PAS DAMMIM – ***pas dammiym*** [proper noun: פַּס דַּמִּים <6450>; from COLORS (OF MANY) <6446> (properly, the palm of the hand) and the plur. of BLOOD <1818>]: palm (i.e., dell) of bloodshed ▶ **A place in Judah where David and his men fought the Philistines.** Ref.: 1 Chr. 11:13. ¶

PASACH – ***pāsaḵ*** [masc. proper noun: פָּסַךְ <6457>; from an unused root meaning to divide]: one who limps ▶ **An Israelite of the tribe of Asher.** Ref.: 1 Chr. 7:33. ¶

PASEAH – ***pāsêaḥ*** [masc. proper noun: פָּסֵחַ <6454>; from PASS OVER <6452>]: one who limps ▶
a. A man of the tribe of Judah. Ref.: 1 Chr. 4:12. ¶
b. Ancestor of a family who returned from the Babylonian captivity. Refs.: Ezra 2:49; Neh. 7:51. ¶
c. Father of a man who helped repair the wall of Jerusalem. Ref.: Neh. 3:6. ¶

PASHUR – ***pašḥûr*** [masc. proper noun: פַּשְׁחוּר <6583>; prob. from PIECES (TEAR IN) <6582>]: freedom ▶
a. Son of Malchiah; he protested to King Zedekiah against Jeremiah's warning that Jerusalem would be given into the hand of Nebuchadnezzar's army. Therefore King Zedekiah sent him to take Jeremiah. Ref.: Jer. 21:1–3. He opposed Jeremiah and cast him into a cistern (Jer. 38:1–6). ¶
b. Son of Immer; he was chief officer in the Temple. Refs.: Jer. 20:1–6. ¶
c. Father of Gedaliah who was opposing Jeremiah. Ref.: Jer. 38:1. ¶
d. Members of his family came back from the Babylonian captivity. Refs.: 1 Chr. 9:12; Ezra 2:38; 10:22; Neh. 7:41; 11:12. ¶
e. He sealed the covenant during the time of Nehemiah. Ref.: Neh. 10:3. ¶

PASS (noun) – 1 Sam. 13:23; 14:4; Is. 10:29 ➔ FORD <4569>.

PASS (verb) – Ruth 2:14 ➔ SERVE <6642>.

PASS AWAY – Ps. 90:10 ➔ CUT OFF <1468>.

PASS ON – ***ḥālap*** [verb: חָלַף <2498>; a prim. root] ▶

a. This word means to go by, to change, to violate, to renew. It has the meaning of passing on, to go by something (Job 9:11; 11:10). It takes on the nuance of something passing away, being gone (Job 9:26; Ps. 102:26; Song 2:11). It describes the changing of garments or clothes (Gen. 35:2) or wages (Gen. 31:7, 41). *
b. This word indicates to pierce, to strike through. It describes the act of striking a person's head or temple (Judg. 5:26) or of an arrow piercing a person (Job 20:24). ¶

PASS OVER – 1 ***'āḏāh*** [verb: עָדָה <5710>; a prim. root] ▶ **This word means to pass on, to walk; to lay aside.** It refers to passing over, to walking over a place or an area of land (Job 28:8); or to removing a garment or clothing (Prov. 25:20: to take off, to take away). The Hebrew word also means to ornament, to deck; see ADORN <5710>. ¶
2 ***pasaḥ*** [verb: פָּסַח <6452>; a prim. root] ▶ **This word means to leap, to halt, to limp, to be lame.** The first occurrence of this verb is in Exodus, where God states that He will preserve the Israelites by passing over their homes when He goes through Egypt to kill the firstborn (Ex. 12:13, 23, 27). This sentiment is echoed by the prophet Isaiah (Is. 31:5). In 2 Samuel 4:4, the word is used of Saul's grandson who became lame. Before Elijah confronted the prophets of Baal, he confronted the Israelites for their syncretism. He asked them how long they would bounce back and forth between the Lord and Baal (1 Kgs. 18:21). Then during Elijah's confrontation, the prophets of Baal began to dance on the altar that they had constructed (1 Kgs. 18:26). This was probably some sort of cultic dance performed as part of the sacrifice ritual. ¶

PASS OVER, PASS BY – ***ḥᵃlap̱*** [Aramaic verb: חֲלַף <2499>; corresponding to PASS ON <2498>] ▶ **This word is used figuratively of a period or periods of time passing by.** In Daniel it refers to "seven times" or periods of time (probably seven years) passing by during which Nebuchadnezzar was judged by the Lord (Dan. 4:16, 23, 25, 32). ¶

PASS THROUGH, PASS OVER – ***'āḇar*** [verb: עָבַר <5674>; a prim. root] ▶ **This word means to cover, to go beyond, to go along, to be crossed over, to make to cross over, to go through, to go away. This verb indicates the physical act of crossing or passing over and takes on a figurative usage that exhibits many variations in meaning.** Two figurative meanings are of primary importance theologically; the verb means going beyond, overstepping a covenant or a command of God or man. Moses uses the word when charging the people with disobeying and overstepping the Lord's commands (Num. 14:41; Josh. 7:11, 15). Esther 3:3 depicts Mordecai's transgressing of the king's command. The word is used of God's passing over His people's rebellion (Mic. 7:18); but also of His decision not to pass over or spare them any longer (Amos 7:8; 8:2). The verb relates to the placement of a yoke of punishment on the neck of Ephraim, God's rebellious nation (Hos. 10:11; cf. Job 13:13).

The word indicates the literal movement of material subjects and objects in time and space in various contexts: a stream or river is passed over (Josh. 3:14); as are boundaries (Num. 20:17). An attacking army passes through its enemies' territories, conquering them like a flood (cf. Josh. 18:9; Is. 8:8; Dan. 11:10, 40); and as the literal flood waters of Noah's day covered the earth (Ps. 42:7; 88:16; Is. 54:9). In a figurative sense, the word describes the feeling of jealousy that can come over a suspecting or jealous husband (Num. 5:14, 30); or the movement of God's Spirit (1 Kgs. 22:24; 2 Chr. 18:23; Jer. 5:28). The location of an event could move or pass on, as when the Israelites routed the Philistines, and the battle, both in location and progress, passed by Beth Aven (1 Sam. 14:23; 2 Sam. 16:1; Jer. 5:22).

The word indicates passing away or leaving (emigrating) from a certain territory (Mic. 1:11). It indicates dying or perishing, as when the Lord described the perishing of Assyria's allies (Nah. 1:12); or the disappearance of Job's safety (Job 30:15; Job 33:18); it describes the passing of a law's validity or its passing out of use (Esther 1:19; 9:27).

The causative stem adds the aspect of making these things happen as described in the simple stem. Jacob caused his family to cross over the Jabbok River (Gen. 32:23). The word is used of the heinous act of devoting children to pagan gods (Jer. 32:35; Ezek. 23:37). A proclamation or the sound of the shofar can pass through the land (Ex. 36:6; Lev. 25:9).

The word means to cause something to pass away. Many things could be noted: God caused Saul's kingdom to pass over to David (2 Sam. 3:10); evil could be put away, as when Asa, king of Judah, put away male prostitutes from the religions of Israel (1 Kgs. 15:12); or holy persons turned away their eyes from vain things (Ps. 119:37).

The word is used one time in the passive stem to indicate a river that cannot be crossed (Ezek. 47:5); and in the factitive or intensive stem to describe Solomon's stringing gold chains across the front area inside the Holy Place in the Temple (1 Kgs. 6:21). *

PASSAGE – [1] Josh. 22:11; Jer. 22:20 ➔ SIDE <5676> b. [2] 1 Sam. 13:23; 14:4; Is. 10:29; Jer. 51:32 ➔ FORD <4569>.

PASSAGE INWARD – Ezek. 42:4 ➔ JOURNEY (noun) <4109>.

PASSAGE WAY (INNER) – Ezek. 42:4 ➔ JOURNEY (noun) <4109>.

PASSION – Jer. 2:24 ➔ DESIRE (noun) <185>.

PASSOVER – ***pesaḥ*** [masc. noun: פֶּסַח <6453>; from PASS OVER <6452>] ▶ **This word is first used to describe the Passover ritual while Israel was still in Egypt. It also means a Passover animal, a sacrifice. The word is used forty-nine times, usually referring to the Passover festival or celebration.** (Ex. 12:11, 27, 43, 48; 34:25). The first Passover ideally was constituted as follows: on the human level, the Israelites killed the Passover sacrifice on the evening of the fourteenth day of the first month, Abib or Nisan (March/April). They then took some of the blood of the slain Passover animal (Deut. 16:2, 5) and smeared it on the sides and tops of the doorframes of their houses (cf. Ex. 12:7). The Passover ritual and the Passover animal were directed to and belonged to the Lord (Ex. 12:11, 48; Deut. 16:1). They then roasted the animal (lamb, kid, young ram, goat—a one-year old without any defect) and ate it with their sandals on their feet and their staffs in their hands, ready to move out in haste at any time. The angel of death passed through Egypt and passed over the Israelites' houses with the blood of the lambs on the doorposts, but the angel struck the firstborn of all the Egyptian households (cf. Ex. 12:12, 13, 29). Later Passovers were held in commemoration of the historical event of Israel's deliverance from Egyptian bondage.

The animals eaten were also called the *pesaḥ*, the Passover sacrifice (Ex. 12:21; 2 Chr. 30:15; 35:1). The Passover was celebrated throughout Israel's history before and after the exile (Num. 9:4; Josh. 5:10; 2 Kgs. 23:22; Ezra 6:19, 20). *

PASTURE – [1] ***mir'eh*** [masc. noun: מִרְעֶה <4829>; from FEED <7462> a. in the sense of feeding] ▶ **This word refers to land suitable for grazing flocks of sheep or herds of other animals; it includes the habitats of wild animals.** Refs.: Gen. 47:4; 1 Chr. 4:39–41; Job 39:8; Lam. 1:6; Joel 1:18; Nahum 2:11. It is used as imagery for an overthrown, deserted city area (Is. 32:14). Restored pasturelands of rich quality are a part of a renewed Israel (Ezek. 34:14, 18). ¶

[2] ***mar'iyṯ*** [fem. noun: מַרְעִית <4830>; from FEED <7462> a. in the sense of feeding] ▶ **This word means a flock feeding in a pasture. It indicates a fertile field for feeding and raising flocks of sheep or other animals.** Figuratively, it is the pasture God provides for His people (Ps. 74:1; 79:13; 95:7; 100:3; Is. 49:9; Jer. 23:1; Ezek. 34:31). It refers to the people of Israel as the sheep of their rulers (Jer. 10:21). The Lord will destroy His pasture because of its rebellion (Jer. 25:36). Israel fed on their pasture

provided by the Lord and forgot their Shepherd (Hos. 13:6). ¶
3 ***nahᵃlōl*** [masc. noun: נַהֲלֹל <5097>; from LEAD <5095>] ▶ **This word is also translated bush, watering place, water hole. It refers to a place where water was available for people, flocks, and herds.** Such places were especially prized by people in the Middle East (Is. 7:19). ¶
4 ***rᵉʿiy*** [masc. noun: רְעִי <7471>; from FEED (verb) <7462> a.] ▶ **This word refers to animals that have been fed and raised on good pastureland, pasture-fed cattle, oxen, etc., not raised in a stall; it is also translated pasture-fed.** Ref.: 1 Kgs. 4:23. ¶
– 5 Ps. 37:20; 65:13; Is. 30:23 ➔ LAMB <3733> 6 Is. 5:17; Mic. 2:12 ➔ WORD <1699>.

PASTURE (RICH, FAT, WELL-WATERED) – Ezek. 45:15 ➔ DRINK (noun) <4945>.

PASTURE-FED – 1 Kgs. 4:23 ➔ PASTURE <7471>.

PASTURELAND – ***migrāš*** [masc. noun: מִגְרָשׁ <4054>; from CAST OUT <1644> (in the sense of flocks being driven for pasture)] ▶ **This word generally refers to a stretch of land lying outside a city and controlled by the city.** Refs.: Num. 35:2–5, 7; Josh. 14:4; 21:2); also translated common-land, suburb. It also indicates land around Ezekiel's holy city (Ezek. 48:15, 17) or Temple (Ezek. 45:2). *

PASTURING – Is. 7:25 ➔ LAY, PUT <4916> b.

PATCHED (BE) – Josh. 9:5 ➔ SPOTTED (BE) <2921>.

PATH – 1 ***'ōraḥ*** [masc. noun: אֹרַח <734>; from TRAVEL <732>] ▶ **This word means way, byway, or highway.** It describes the literal path one walks on (Judg. 5:6); the path or rank one walks in (Joel 2:7). Figuratively, this word describes the path of an individual or course of life (Job 6:18); the characteristics of a lifestyle, good or evil (Ps. 16:11); righteousness or judgment (Prov. 2:13). It is further used to mean traveler or wayfarer (Job 31:32). In the plural, it means caravans or troops (Job 6:19). *
2 ***ᵃraḥ'*** [Aramaic fem. noun: אֲרַח <735>; corresponding to <734> above] ▶ **This word means way, manner of life.** It describes the just ways of the King of heaven, His manner of dealing with things (Dan. 4:37) but also refers to the ways and manner of life of persons (Dan. 5:23). ¶
3 ***derek*** [masc. noun: דֶּרֶךְ <1870>; from TREAD <1869>] ▶ **This word means journey, way. It is derived from the Hebrew verb *dāraḵ*, meaning to walk or to tread, hence the basic idea of this word: the path that is traveled.** It may refer to a physical path or road (Gen. 3:24; Num. 22:23; 1 Kgs. 13:24) or to a journey along a road (Gen. 30:36; Ex. 5:3; 1 Sam. 15:18). However, this word is most often used metaphorically to refer to the pathways of one's life, suggesting the pattern of life (Prov. 3:6); the obedient life (Deut. 8:6); the righteous life (2 Sam. 22:22; Jer. 5:4); the wicked life (1 Kgs. 22:52). The ways are described as ways of darkness (Prov. 2:13); pleasant ways (Prov. 3:17); and wise ways (Prov. 6:6). *
4 ***miš'ôl*** [masc. noun: מִשְׁעוֹל <4934>; from the same as HANDFUL <8168> (i.e., an unused root meaning to hollow out)] ▶ **This word refers to a walkway, man-made or created by nature, large enough for donkeys to travel.** Ref.: Num. 22:24. ¶
5 ***naṯiyḇ, nᵉṯiyḇāh*** [noun: נָתִיב, נְתִיבָה <5410>; from an unused root meaning to tramp] ▶
a. A masculine noun indicating a path, a pathway, a wake. It refers to a trail or navigable pass made by humans or by nature. It indicates figuratively the path, the way of life, of the wicked (Job 18:10); and the path to wisdom (Job 28:7). It is used of a wake, the foam and waves left in the water (Job 41:32). God's tragic treatment of the Egyptians created a path for His people (Ps. 78:50); His commandments are a path of life (Ps. 119:35); as is the way (path) of righteousness (Prov. 12:28). ¶

b. A feminine noun indicating a path, a pathway, a wake. It indicates well-traveled paths or roads, highways (Judg. 5:6). Figuratively, it indicates the paths of life (Job 19:8); of ethical and moral guidance (Ps. 119:105; 142:3); as well as the way of the wicked (Prov. 1:15). It describes the paths of salvation and restoration which the Lord prepares for His people (Is. 42:16). The ancient way of obedience to the Lord, the ancient paths, are the sources of guidance for God's people (Jer. 6:16). The Lord is capable of hiding, blocking the true paths of His people (Hos. 2:6). *

[6] ***šāḇiyl, šāḇûl*** [masc. noun: שְׁבִיל, שָׁבוּל <7635>; from the same as SKIRT <7640> (as something flowing along, e.g., a path] ► **This word refers figuratively to the paths or ways of God in the many waters.** Ref.: Ps. 77:19. It also refers to the laws and ways of God given to Israel in ancient times (Jer. 18:15; also translated road). ¶

– [7] Job 23:11 ➔ STEP (noun) <838> [8] Job 29:6 ➔ STEP (noun) <1978> [9] Ps. 17:5; 23:3; 65:11; etc. ➔ ENCAMPMENT <4570> b.

PATHROS – ***paṯrôs*** [proper noun: פַּתְרוֹס <6624>; of Egyptian deriv.] ► **A part of Egypt, probably the southern part.** Refs.: Is. 11:11; Jer. 44:1, 15; Ezek. 29:14; 30:14. ¶

PATHRUSITE – ***paṯrusiym*** [proper noun: פַּתְרֻסִים <6625>; patrial from PATHROS <6624>] ► **An inhabitant of Pathros.** Refs.: Gen. 10:14; 1 Chr. 1:12. ¶

PATTERN – [1] Ex. 25:9, 40; etc. ➔ PLAN (noun) <8400> [2] Ezek. 43:11 ➔ PERFECTION <8508>.

PAU – ***pā'û, pā'iy*** [proper noun: פָּעוּ, פָּעִי <6464>; from CRY (verb) <6463>]: screaming, bleating ► **A city in Edom ruled by King Hadar.** Refs.: Gen. 36:39; 1 Chr. 1:50. ¶

PAVE – Song 3:10 ➔ INLAY <7528>.

PAVED WORK – Ex. 24:10 ➔ PAVEMENT <3840>.

PAVEMENT – [1] ***liḇnāh*** [fem. noun: לִבְנָה <3840>; from BRICK (MAKE) <3835>] ► **This word means flooring; it is also translated paved work.** It is used to describe the surface made of sapphire under the Lord's feet, when He appeared to Moses and the elders of Israel (Ex. 24:10). ¶

[2] ***marṣepeṯ*** [fem. noun: מַרְצֶפֶת <4837>; from INLAY <7528> (in the sense of to pave)] ► **This word refers to a stone pavement or a stone layer serving as a base on which to set something; it is also translated base, pedestal.** Ref.: 2 Kgs. 16:17. ¶

[3] ***riṣpāh*** [fem. noun: רִצְפָּה <7531>; fem. of BAKED ON COALS <7529>] ► **This word refers to the paved surface associated with the Temple.** Ref.: 2 Chr. 7:3. It refers to an elaborate mosaic pavement of various stones and other materials (Esther 1:6). It describes the pavement or covering of an outer courtyard in Ezekiel's Temple complex (Ezek. 40:17, 18; 42:3). For another meaning of the Hebrew word, see HOT COAL <7531>. ¶

PAVILION – [1] 2 Kgs. 16:18 ➔ COVERED WAY <4329> [2] Ps. 27:5 ➔ ABODE <5520> [3] Jer. 43:10 ➔ CANOPY <8237> [4] Dan. 11:45: royal pavilion ➔ PALACE <643>.

PAY – [1] ***'eṯnāh*** [fem. noun: אֶתְנָה <866>; from HIRE <8566>] ► **This word means hire paid to a prostitute; it is also translated wages, reward.** It is used figuratively to refer to Israel's vine and fig trees which she had received through her dealings of prostitution with the nations around her (Hos. 2:12). ¶

– [2] Num. 20:19 ➔ MERCHANDISE <4377> [3] Is. 19:10 ➔ REWARD (noun) <7938> a.

PAYMENT – [1] Ezek. 16:31, 34, 41 ➔ EARNINGS <868> [2] Ezek. 16:33 ➔ GIFT <5083> [3] Ezek. 27:15 ➔ GIFT <814>.

PEACE – [1] ***šālôm*** [masc. noun: שָׁלוֹם <7965>; from COMPLETED (BE) <7999> (in the primary sense of being safe or uninjured in mind and body)] ▶ **This word means tranquility. This Hebrew term is used 237 times in the Old Testament and is used to greet someone.** Refs.: Judg. 19:20; 1 Chr. 12:18; Dan. 10:19. It is common in Hebrew to ask how one's peace is (Gen. 43:27; Ex. 18:7; Judg. 18:15), which is equivalent to asking "How are you?" Moreover, this word was often used to describe someone's manner of coming or going; sometimes this took the form of a blessing: Go in peace (Judg. 8:9; 1 Sam. 1:17; Mal. 2:6). Another common expression involved dying or being buried in peace (Gen. 15:15; 2 Chr. 34:28; Jer. 34:5) Peace is present with the wise but absent from the wicked (Prov. 3:2, 17; Is. 57:21; 59:8). It is often pictured as coming from God; Gideon built an altar and called the altar *Yahweh-shalom* (the Lord Is Peace; Num. 6:26; Judg. 6:24; Is. 26:3). God instructed the Israelites in exile in Babylon to pray for the «peace» or «welfare» (multi-level well-being) of the city in which they lived (Jer. 29:7). *

[2] ***šᵉlām*** [masc. sing. noun: שְׁלָם <8001>; corresponding to <7965> above] ▶ **This word is most frequently used in the context of a greeting and may be used in both the singular and plural forms with the same meaning.** As a greeting, these words signified a wish for peace, prosperity, and general good welfare to those who were being greeted. This seems to have been a common way to begin letters in ancient biblical times. In Nebuchadnezzar's letter to his subjects, he started by wishing prosperity to all his subjects (Dan. 4:1); and in the letter which Tatnai sent to King Darius, he used this word as a greeting of well-wishing (Ezra 5:7). Other refs.: Ezra 4:17; Dan. 6:25. ¶

– [3] 2 Kgs. 7:9; Is. 62:1, 6; etc. ➔ to keep, to hold one's peace ➔ SILENT (BE, KEEP, REMAIN) <2814> [4] Ezra 7:12 ➔ PERFECT PEACE <1585> [5] Prov. 29:9 ➔ REST (noun) <5183>.

PEACE (AT) – Prov. 14:30 ➔ CALMNESS <4832>.

PEACE (BE AT, HAVE) – Job 3:26; 12:6 ➔ EASE (BE AT) <7951> a.

PEACE OFFERINGS – ***šelem*** [masc. noun: שֶׁלֶם <8002>; from COMPLETED (BE) <7999>] ▶ **This word is also called thanksgiving offerings. These offerings were voluntary, given to God in thanks or in praise to Him.** These offerings were first described in the book of Leviticus, and the word is used many times after that, especially in the remaining sections of the Law dealing with sacrifices (Lev. 3:1, 7:11; Num. 7:17). This noun is also used in the plural form, which has a wider significance (Amos 5:22). In this context, the thanksgiving offerings were offered in great distress, not out of thankful hearts. They were offered to try to gain God's favor, but God rejected them because they were not given out of love and thankfulness to Him. *

PEACOCK – [1] ***tukkiyyiym*** [masc. plur. noun: תֻּכִּיִּים <8500>; prob. of foreign deriv.] ▶ **a. This word refers to a highly sought-after male bird with a crest of plumules and long, brightly colored upper tail coverts that can spread out like a colorful fan.** They were imported by Solomon for displaying at court (1 Kgs. 10:22; 2 Chr. 9:21).
b. This word refers to baboons. The NIV translates this word as baboons, and the NKJV as monkeys. It is a type of monkey having a dog-like snout, long teeth, a large head with cheek pouches, and bare calluses on its rump (1 Kgs. 10:22; 2 Chr. 9:21). It was imported by Solomon for his court. ¶

– [2] Job 39:13 ➔ OSTRICH <7443> [3] See STORK <2624>.

PEAK – Ps. 95:4 ➔ STRENGTH <8443> c.

PEAKS (MANY) – Ps. 68:15, 16 ➔ RUGGED <1386>.

PEARL – Job 28:18 ➔ CRYSTAL <1378>.

PEARLS – Job 28:18 ➔ JEWELS <6443>.

PEASANTRY – Judg. 5:7, 11 ➔ VILLAGER <6520>.

PEBBLE – 2 Sam. 17:13 ➔ lit.: small stone ➔ BAG <6872> b.

PEDAHEL – ***p^{e}ḏah'ēl*** [masc. proper noun: פְּדַהְאֵל <6300>; from REDEEM <6299> and GOD <410>]: redeemed by God ▶ **A chief of the tribe of Naphtali.** Ref.: Num. 34:28. ¶

PEDAHZUR – ***p^{e}ḏāhṣûr*** [masc. proper noun: פְּדָהצוּר <6301>; from REDEEM <6299> and ROCK <6697>]: the rock (God) has redeemed ▶ **Father of a chief of a tribe of Benjamin.** Refs.: Num. 1:10; 2:20; 7:54, 59; 10:23. ¶

PEDAIAH – ***p^{e}ḏāyāh, p^{e}ḏāyāhû*** [masc. proper noun: פְּדָיָה, פְּדָיָהוּ <6305>; from REDEEM <6299> and LORD <3050>]: the Lord has redeemed ▶
a. Grandfather of Jehoiakim. Ref.: 2 Kgs. 23:36. ¶
b. Son of Jehoiakim. Refs.: 1 Chr. 3:17, 18. ¶
c. Son of Parosh. Ref.: Neh. 3:25. ¶
d. A helper of Ezra. Ref.: Neh. 8:4. ¶
e. A descendant of Benjamin. Ref.: Neh. 11:7. ¶
f. A Levite in Nehemiah's day. Ref.: Neh. 13:13. ¶
g. The father of Joel. Ref.: 1 Chr. 27:20. ¶

PEDESTAL – [1] 1 Kgs. 7:29, 31 ➔ STAND (noun) <3653> [2] 2 Kgs. 16:17 ➔ PAVEMENT <4837> [3] Song 5:15 ➔ BASE (noun) <134> [4] Amos 5:26 ➔ CHIUN <3594> b. [5] Zech. 5:11 ➔ BASE (noun) <4369> [6] Zech. 5:11 ➔ STAND (noun) <4350>.

PEEL – ***pāṣal*** [verb: פָּצַל <6478>; a prim. root] ▶ **This word means to strip bark off.** It indicates removing narrow, long pieces of bark from trees or wooden poles or rods (Gen. 30:37, 38; KJV: to pill). ¶

PEELED – Is. 18:2, 7 ➔ PULL, PULL OUT <4803>.

PEEP – Is. 8:19; 10:14 ➔ CHIRP <6850>.

PEER – Song 2:9 ➔ BLOSSOM (verb) <6692> b.

PEG – ***yaṯēḏ*** [fem. noun: יָתֵד <3489>; from an unused root meaning to pin through or fast] ▶ **This word denotes a pin, a stake.** It is used of a wooden peg or nail (Judg. 4:21, 22; 5:26). It could be driven into a wall for hanging something on it (Is. 22:23). It refers to a tool used for digging a hole in the ground (Deut. 23:13: implement, spade, paddle, trowel, something to dig); or a tool for working on a loom (Judg. 16:14: pin). Metal pegs for use in the Tabernacle are also a part of its range of meaning (Ex. 27:19). It is used metaphorically as a means of having a share in the Lord's plans (Ezra 9:8; also translated secure hold, firm place); or to symbolize a leader who will bring stability to God's people (Zech. 10:4). *

PEKAH – ***peqaḥ*** [masc. proper noun: פֶּקַח <6492>; from OPEN <6491>]: opened, vigilant ▶ **A king of Israel who ruled twenty years (752–732 B.C.). He was son of Remaliah and ruled from Samaria. He was a typical evil Israelite king who continued to follow the evil ways of Israel's first king, Jeroboam I.** Refs.: 2 Kgs. 15:27, 28. Assyria began to dismantle the northern kingdom in his reign (2 Kgs. 15:29). He was assassinated by Hoshea, the last king in Israel. *

PEKAHIAH – ***p^{e}qaḥyāh*** [masc. proper noun: פְּקַחְיָה <6494>; from OPEN <6491> and LORD <3050>]: the Lord has opened (the eyes) ▶ **A king of the northern kingdom of Israel who was murdered by his captain Pekah after two years.** Refs.: 2 Kgs. 15:22, 23, 26. ¶

PEKOD – ***p^{e}qôḏ*** [proper noun: פְּקוֹד <6489>; from ATTEND <6485>]: visitation, punishment ▶ **A people in the Babylonian army and a tribe in Babylonia.** Refs.: Jer. 50:21; Ezek. 23:23. ¶

PELAIAH – ***p^{e}lā'yāh, p^{e}lāyāh*** [masc. proper noun: פְּלָאיָה, פְּלָיָה <6411>; from WONDERFUL (DO SOMETHING) <6381> and LORD <3050>]: the Lord has done something wonderful ▶
a. A descendant of David. Refs.: Neh. 8:7; 10:10. ¶
b. A postexilic priest. Ref.: 1 Chr. 3:24. ¶

PELALIAH – ***pᵉlalyāh*** [masc. proper noun: פְּלַלְיָה <6421>; from PRAY <6419> (in the sense of to judge) and LORD <3050>]: the Lord judges ▶ **Ancestor of a priest who returned to Jerusalem after the Babylonian exile.** Ref.: Neh. 11:12. ¶

PELATIAH – ***pᵉlaṭyāh, pᵉlaṭyāhû*** [masc. proper noun: פְּלַטְיָה, פְּלַטְיָהוּ <6410>; from DELIVER <6403> and LORD <3050>]: the Lord delivers ▶
a. Son of Hananiah. Ref.: 1 Chr. 3:21. ¶
b. Son of Ishi. Ref.: 1 Chr. 4:42. ¶
c. A leader who signed Nehemiah's covenant. Ref.: Neh. 10:22. ¶
d. Son of Benaiah. Refs.: Ezek. 11:1, 13. ¶

PELEG – ***peleg*** [masc. proper noun: פֶּלֶג <6389>; from STREAM (noun) <6388> (which is from DIVIDE <6385>)]: division ▶ **A son of Eber. In his time the earth was divided into various languages and peoples.** Refs.: Gen. 11:1–9, 16–19. ¶

PELET – ***peleṯ*** [masc. proper noun: פֶּלֶט <6404>; from DELIVER <6403>]: deliverance, escape ▶
a. A descendant of Caleb. Ref.: 1 Chr. 2:47. ¶
b. One of David's mighty men. Ref.: 1 Chr. 12:3. ¶

PELETH – ***peleṯ*** [masc. proper noun: פֶּלֶת <6431>; from an unused root meaning to flee]: swiftness ▶ **A man of the tribe of Reuben, father of On who rebelled against Moses.** Refs.: Num. 16:1; 1 Chr. 2:33. ¶

PELETHITES – ***pᵉlêṯiy*** [proper noun: פְּלֵתִי <6432>; from the same form as PELETH <6431>] ▶ **They were members of David's royal guard and were faithful to him.** Refs.: 2 Sam. 8:18; 15:18; 20:7, 23; 1 Kgs. 1:38, 44; 1 Chr. 18:17. ¶

PELICAN – ***qā'aṯ*** [fem. noun: קָאַת <6893>; from VOMIT (verb) <6958>] ▶ **This word refers to a bird that was considered unclean to Israel as food; it is also translated tawny owl, desert owl, jackdaw, cormorant, hawk.** Refs.: Lev. 11:18; Deut. 14:17. Its exact identity is not known. Its character is used in a simile of the psalmist (Ps. 102:6). It inhabited desert places and the haunts of destroyed cities (Is. 34:11; Zeph. 2:14). ¶

PELONITE – ***pᵉlôniy*** [proper noun: פְּלוֹנִי <6397>; patron. from an unused name; from DISTINCTION (MAKE) <6395>, meaning separate] ▶ **An inhabitant of an unknown place.** Refs.: 1 Chr. 11:27, 36; 27:10. ¶

PELUSIUM – Ezek. 30:15, 16 ➔ SIN <5512> a.

PEN – [1] ***'êṭ*** [masc. noun: עֵט <5842>; from RUSH GREEDILY <5860> (contr.) in the sense of swooping, i.e., side-long stroke] ▶ **This word refers to an iron stylus, a tool to write.** It indicates a writing instrument (Job 19:24). It is used in a figurative way or referred to metaphorically several times (Ps. 45:1; Jer. 8:8). It is used figuratively of the recording of Judah's sins (Jer. 17:1). ¶
– [2] Ps. 50:9; 78:70; Hab. 3:17 ➔ FOLD (noun) <4356> [3] Is. 8:1 ➔ GRAVING TOOL <2747> [4] Mic. 2:12 ➔ FOLD (noun) <1223>.

PENALTY – Prov. 19:19 ➔ FINE (noun) <6066>.

PENCIL – Is. 44:13 ➔ MARKER <8279> a.

PENDANT – [1] ***nᵉṭiypāh, nᵉṭipāh*** [fem. noun: נְטִיפָה, נְטִפָה <5188>; from DROP (verb) <5197> (in the sense of to fall in drops)] ▶ **This word means a hanging ornament; it is also translated earrings, dangling earring, chains.** Ref.: Is. 3:19. The meaning is not certain in the context of Judges 8:26 (KJV: collars). ¶
– [2] Prov. 1:9 ➔ CHAIN <6060>.

PENIEL – See PENUEL <6439>.

PENINNAH – ***pᵉninnāh*** [fem. proper noun: פְּנִנָּה <6444>; prob. fem. for JEWELS <6443>]: jewel, corral ▶ **The other wife of Elkanah who had children; she provoked**

Hannah who was initially childless. Refs.: 1 Sam. 1:2, 4. ¶

PENITENT (BE) – 2 Kgs. 22:19 ➔ FAINT (BE, MAKE) <7401>.

PENUEL – ***p^enû'ēl, p^eniy'ēl*** [פְּנוּאֵל, פְּנִיאֵל <6439>; from TURN (verb) <6437>; comp. FACE (noun) <6440> and GOD <410>]: face of God ▶
a. A city on the Jabbok River. Refs.: Gen. 32:30, 31; Judg. 8:8, 9, 17; 1 Kgs. 12:25. ¶
b. A descendant of Judah. Ref.: 1 Chr. 4:4. ¶
c. A descendant of Benjamin. Ref.: 1 Chr. 8:25. ¶

PEOPLE – 1 ***'ummāh*** [fem. noun: אֻמָּה <523>; from the same as MOTHER <517>] ▶ **This word means a group of human beings; it is also translated tribe, nation.** It occurs three times in the Hebrew Bible (Gen. 25:16; Num. 25:15; Ps. 117:1) and is always plural. It is synonymous with *gôy* (NATION <1471>). ¶
2 ***l^e'ôm, l^e'ōm*** [masc. sing. noun: לְאוֹם, לְאֹם <3816>; from an unused root meaning to gather] ▶ **This poetic term is used often as a synonym for people (*'am* [<5971> below]) or nation (*gôy* [NATION <1471>]). It can refer to Israel or to humanity in general.** A well-known passage (Gen. 25:23) uses this term in regard to the two peoples in Rebekah's womb—Israel and Edom. *
3 ***'am, 'ām*** [masc. noun: עַם, עָם <5971>; from DIM (BECOME) <6004> (in the sense of to associate; by association, to overshadow by huddling together)] ▶ **This word also means peoples, people of the land, citizens. The word is used over eighteen hundred times to indicate groups of people that can be categorized in various ways.** The largest group of people is the one comprising the whole earth (see Gen. 11:1); it constituted one people (Gen. 11:6); who shared a common language (Gen. 11:6; Ezek. 3:5); a common location (see Gen. 11:2); and a common purpose and goal (see Gen. 11:4). However, the Lord scattered the group and brought about multiple languages, thereby producing many groups who would then develop into new peoples united around common languages, including common ancestors, religious beliefs, traditions, and ongoing blood relationships.

The word is used to describe various groups that developed. The people of the sons of Israel (Ex. 1:9; Ezra 9:1), was a term referring to all Israel. The people of Judah were a subgroup of Israel (2 Sam. 19:40), as was northern Israel (2 Kgs. 9:6). The people of Israel as a whole could be described in religious or moral terms as a holy, special people (Deut. 7:6; 14:2; Dan. 8:24); or the Lord's inheritance (Deut. 4:20). Above all, they were to be the Lord's people (Judg. 5:11; 1 Sam. 2:24); and the people of God (2 Sam. 14:13). They were the Lord's own people because He had rescued them from slavery to Pharaoh and his gods (Ex. 6:7). But the Lord Himself characterized His people as stiff-necked (Ex. 32:9; 33:3; 34:9; Deut. 9:13). To be a member of the Lord's people was to have the Lord as one's God (Ruth 1:16); if God's people rejected the Lord, they ceased to be His people. Therefore, it is clear that God's presence and ownership of His people gave them their identity (Ex. 33:13, 16; Hos. 1:9; cf. Deut. 32:21).

In the plural form, the word refers to many peoples or nations. Jerusalem, destroyed and lamenting, called for the people of the world to look on it and its guilt (Lam. 1:18). Israel was chosen from among all the peoples of the earth (Ex. 19:5, 7; Deut. 14:2). The Lord is in control of all the plans of the nations and peoples (Ps. 33:10). The word is used in parallel with *gôyim* (NATION <1471>). Isaac prayed for Jacob's offspring to become a community of peoples that would include the twelve tribes of Israel (Gen. 28:3).

The word described people in general—-i.e., nonethnic or national groups. It refers to all the people as individuals in the world (Is. 42:5). When persons died, they were gathered to their people (Gen. 25:8, 17). It also referred to people from a particular city (Ruth 4:9; 2 Chr. 32:18); or people from a specific land (e.g., Canaan [Zeph. 1:11]). Centuries earlier, Pharaoh referred to the Hebrews living in Egypt under slavery as the people of the land (Ex. 5:5). This phrase could refer to the population at large in Solomon's time and later (2 Kgs. 11:14, 18; 15:5); or to the population of Canaan in Abraham's time (Gen. 23:7).

The term also depicted foreign peoples and nations. The Moabites were the people of the god Chemosh (Num. 21:29). The word designated foreigners in general as strange or alien people (Ex. 21:8); the people of Egypt were considered the people of Pharaoh (Ex. 1:9, 22).

The word is even used to describe a gathering of ants (Prov. 30:25); or rock badgers (Prov. 30:26). *

4 ***'am*** [Aramaic masc. noun: עַם <5972>; corresponding to <5971> above] ▶ **This word was not used in reference to a disparate group of individuals or to a specific ethnic group.** This is seen especially in its parallel usage with *'ûmmāh* (<524>), meaning nation, and *liššān* (<3961>), meaning language (Dan. 3:4, 7, 29). The specific ethnic group being identified could be either the Israelites (Ezra 5:12; Dan. 7:27); or the Gentiles (Ezra 6:12; Dan. 2:44). *

PEOR – ***pᵉ'ôr*** [proper noun: פְּעוֹר <6465>; from OPEN <6473>]: opening, cleft ▶ **This word refers to a high point in Moab from which Balaam was to curse Israel.** Ref.: Num. 23:28. Israel later worshiped Baal of Peor (Num. 25:18; 31:16; Josh. 22:17). It was possibly located near Mount Nebo east of the northern end of the Dead Sea. ¶

PERADVENTURE – Gen. 18:24; Ex. 32:30; Num. 22:6; 1 Sam. 6:5; Jer. 20:10 ➔ PERHAPS <194>.

PERAZIM – ***pᵉrāṣiym*** [proper noun: פְּרָצִים <6559>; plur. of BREACH <6556>]: breaches ▶ **A mountain in Israel.** Ref.: Is. 28:21. Maybe the same as Baal Perazim (<1188>). ¶

PERCEIVE – 1 ***biyn*** [verb: בִּין <995>; a prim. root] ▶ **This word means to discern, to observe, to pay attention to, to be intelligent, to be discreet, to understand; in the causative sense, to give understanding, to teach; in the reflexive sense, to consider diligently.** People can perceive by means of their senses: eyes (Prov. 7:7); ears (Prov. 29:19); touch (Ps. 58:9); taste (Job 6:30). But actual discerning is not assured. Those who hear do not always understand (Dan. 12:8). In the final analysis, only God gives and conceals understanding (Is. 29:14). *

– 2 Prov. 31:18 ➔ TASTE (verb) <2938>.

PERES – Dan. 5:28 ➔ DIVIDE <6537> b.

PERESH – ***pereš*** [masc. proper noun: פֶּרֶשׁ <6570>; the same as DUNG <6569>]: dung ▶ **An Israelite of the tribe of Manasseh.** Ref.: 1 Chr. 7:16. ¶

PEREZ – ***pereṣ*** [proper noun: פֶּרֶץ <6557>; the same as BREACH <6556>]: breach ▶ **Twin son with Zerah, born of Tamar and Judah.** Refs.: Gen. 38:29; 46:12; Num. 26:20, 21; Ruth 4:12, 18; 1 Chr. 2:4, 5; 4:1; 9:4; 27:3; Neh. 11:4, 6. ¶

PEREZ UZZAH – ***pereṣ 'uzzā'*** [proper noun: פֶּרֶץ עֻזָּא <6560>; from BREACH <6556> and UZZAH, UZZA <5798>]: breach of Uzzah ▶ **The place where Uzzah was killed by the Lord.** Refs.: 2 Sam. 6:8; 1 Chr. 13:11. ¶

PEREZITE – ***parṣiy*** [proper noun: פַּרְצִי <6558>; patron. from PEREZ <6557>] ▶ **A descendant of Perez.** Ref.: Num. 26:20. ¶

PERFECT (adj.) – 1 ***tām*** [adj.: תָּם <8535>; from COMPLETE (BE) <8552>] ▶ **This word means having integrity, complete. This is a rare, almost exclusively poetic term often translated perfect but not carrying the sense of totally free from fault, for it was used of quite flawed people.** It describes the mild manner of Jacob in contrast to his brother Esau, who was characterized by shedding blood (Gen. 25:27; see also Prov. 29:10). The term often carries a rather strong moral component in certain

contexts (Job 1:1; 9:20–22; Ps. 37:37; 64:4). This word appears among a list of glowing terms describing the admirable qualities of the Shulamite lover (Song 5:2; 6:9). Other refs.: Job 1:8; 2:3; 8:20. ¶
– 2 2 Chr. 4:21 ➔ PUREST <4357> 3 Ps. 50:2 ➔ PERFECTION <4359> 4 Ps. 139:22 ➔ END <8503>.

PERFECT (MAKE) – ***kālal*** [verb: כָּלַל <3634>; a prim. root] ▶ **This word means to reach excellence, flawlessness; it is also translated to perfect, to bring to perfection.** Ezekiel lamented over Tyre's pride concerning her perfected beauty (Ezek. 27:4). Builders as well as war bounty came from all over the Near East to the port city of Tyre and added to the perfect beauty of the city (Ezek. 27:11). ¶

PERFECT (verb) – 1 Ps. 138:8 ➔ END (COME TO AN) <1584> 2 Ezek. 27:4, 11 ➔ PERFECT (MAKE) <3634>.

PERFECT PEACE – ***gᵉmar*** [Aramaic verb: גְּמַר <1585>; corresponding to END (COME TO AN) <1584>] ▶ **This word means to complete; it is also translated Peace, Greetings. It is used only once in the Old Testament.** It is found only in the introductory section of Artaxerxes' decree given to Ezra (Ezra 7:12). Although the exact meaning of this word is unclear, it is best to understand this word as an introductory comment similar to Ezra 5:7, where the Hebrew word *šᵉlām* <8001>, meaning peace, is used. ¶

PERFECT SEARCH – Ps. 64:6 ➔ PLAN (noun) <2665>.

PERFECTION – 1 ***miḵlāl*** [masc. noun: מִכְלָל <4359>; from PERFECT (MAKE) <3634>] ▶ **This word indicates a state or quality of the highest kind.** Used with *yop̱îy*, beauty, it means perfect (beauty), referring to Zion (Ps. 50:2). ¶
2 ***minleh*** [masc. noun: מִנְלֶה <4512>; from END (MAKE AN) <5239>] ▶ **Translators and scholars differ on the meaning of this word.** It indicates the success for a while of an evil person (Job 15:29; KJV) in context. According to other translators, the Hebrew word refers to grain or to possession. ¶
3 ***tiḵlāh*** [fem. noun: תִּכְלָה <8502>; from FINISH <3615>] ▶ **This word indicates what is without fault, complete, whole, not lacking in any way.** God's laws are the epitome of perfection (Ps. 119:96). ¶
4 ***toḵniyṯ*** [fem. noun: תָּכְנִית <8508>; from QUOTA <8506> (which refers to a goal to be reached)] ▶ **This word indicates completeness in every way, wisdom, beauty, environment, blessedness, anointed of God.** Ref.: Ezek. 28:12; KJV: sum. It also refers to a plan, a pattern. It refers appropriately to a blueprint, an arrangement laid out for the Temple, its plan (Ezek. 43:10). ¶
– 5 Job 28:3 ➔ END <8503>.

PERFECTION (BRING TO) – Ezek. 27:4, 11 ➔ PERFECT (MAKE) <3634>.

PERFORM – 1 Ps. 57:2 ➔ END (COME TO AN) <1584> 2 Is. 10:12 ➔ CUT OFF <1214>.

PERFUME – 1 ***rōqaḥ*** [masc. noun: רֹקַח <7545>; from COMPOUND <7543> (in the sense of to perfume)] ▶ **This word refers to an ointment, a fragrant substance. It refers to the product, substance produced by a perfumer as he mixes various ingredients.** Refs.: Ex. 30:25, 35. ¶
2 ***riquaḥ, riqûaḥ*** [masc. noun: רִקֻּחַ, רִקּוּחַ <7547>; from COMPOUND <7543>] ▶ **This word refers to the product, substance prepared by a professional perfumer or ointment preparer for various purposes, such as incense, anointing oil, aromatic cosmetics, etc.** Ref.: Is. 57:9. ¶
– 3 Song 1:12 ➔ NARD <5373>.

PERFUME-MAKER – Neh. 3:8 ➔ PERFUMER <7546>.

PERFUMER – 1 ***raqqāḥ*** [masc. noun: רַקָּח <7546>; from COMPOUND <7543>] ▶ **This word indicates a perfume maker. It refers to a person skilled in preparing ointments and perfumes.** It usually contained

olive oil to hold it together (Neh. 3:8; KJV: apothecary). ¶
[2] ***raqqāḥāh*** [fem. noun: רַקָּחָה <7548>; fem. of PERFUME <7547>] ▶ **This word refers to a female skilled in mixing and preparing various aromatic ointments and perfumes.** Ref.: 1 Sam. 8:13. ¶

PERHAPS – ***'ûlay, 'ulay*** [adv.: אוּלַי, אֻלַי <194>; from OR <176>] ▶ **This adverb or adverbial conjunction is also translated peradventure, it may be that; it asserts a note of contingency into a sentence that may express fear, hope, entreaty, or wish.** Refs.: Gen. 16:2; Ex. 32:30; Num. 22:6; 1 Sam. 6:5; Job 1:5; Jer. 20:10. It may be rendered as suppose, what if, in the structure of an expression (cf. Gen. 18:24). *

PERIOD – Lev. 20:18: during her menstrual period, monthly period ➔ FAINT (adj.) <1739>.

PERISH – [1] ***'āḇaḏ*** [verb: אָבַד <6>; a prim. root] ▶ **This word means to be lost, to wander, or, in a causative sense, to destroy, to reduce to some degree of disorder.** It is used to signify God's destruction of evil, both threatened (Lev. 26:38) and realized (Num. 17:12; also translated to be undone, to die); Israel's destruction of the Canaanites and their altars (Num. 33:52; Deut. 12:2, 3); the perishing of natural life (Ps. 49:10; Ps. 102:26; Eccl. 7:15); the perishing of abstract qualities such as wisdom and hope (Is. 29:14), (Lam. 3:18; also translated to be gone); and an item or animal being lost (Deut. 22:3), (Eccl. 3:6; also translated to give up, to lose). *
[2] ***ᵃḇaḏ*** [Aramaic verb: אֲבַד <7>; corresponding to <6> above] ▶ **This word means to be destroyed, or, in a causative sense, to destroy. It is closely connected to death.** It is used for the passing away of false gods (Jer. 10:11); the execution of the Babylonian wise men (Dan. 2:12, 18, 24); the bodily destruction of Daniel's apocalyptic "beast" (Dan. 7:11). See the Hebrew cognate *'āḇaḏ*: PERISH <6>. Other refs.: Dan. 7:26; Jer. 10:11. ¶
– [3] Num. 24:20, 24 ➔ RUIN (noun) <8> [4] Ps. 49:12 ➔ CEASE <1820> [5] Lam. 3:54 ➔ CUT (verb) <1504>.

PERIZZITE – ***pᵉrizziy*** [proper noun: פְּרִזִּי <6522>; from UNWALLED <6521>] ▶ **The name of one of the peoples who inhabited Canaan and were to be disinherited by Israel and destroyed.** Refs.: Gen. 13:7; 15:20. The name may mean "village dwellers." They seem to have been mixed in among the other peoples in various locations throughout the land (Gen. 34:30; Josh. 17:15; Judg. 1:4, 5; 3:5). *

PERMANENTLY – ***ṣᵉmiyṯuṯ*** [fem. noun: צְמִיתֻת <6783>; from END (PUT TO AN) <6789>] ▶ **This word means completion, finality; it is also translated in perpetuity, for ever.** It was used in the Levitical Law to describe the duration of property ownership (Lev. 25:23, 30). ¶

PERMISSION – ***rišyôn*** [masc. noun: רִשְׁיוֹן <7558>; from an unused root meaning to have leave] ▶ **This word means authority. It refers to official legal, royal approval given to someone to do something.** Ref.: Ezra 3:7; also translated grant, authorized. ¶

PERMIT – Gen. 31:28 ➔ FORSAKE <5203>.

PERPETUITY (IN) – Lev. 25:23, 30 ➔ PERMANENTLY <6783>.

PERPLEXED (BE) – [1] ***šᵉḇaš*** [Aramaic verb: שְׁבַשׁ <7672>; corresponding to WEAVE <7660> (in the sense of to entangle)] ▶ **This word indicates a state of astonishment accompanied by confusion and puzzlement about something, especially an unusual occurrence.** Ref.: Dan. 5:9; also translated to be astonished, to be baffled. ¶
– [2] Esther 3:15; Joel 1:18 ➔ WANDER <943>.

PERPLEXED (BE GREATLY) – Dan. 4:19 ➔ ASTONISHED <8075>.

PERPLEXITY – ***mᵉḇûḵāh*** [fem. noun: מְבוּכָה <3998>; from WANDER <943>] ▶ **This word refers to the conditions in a time, a day of the God of hosts, when He**

will create disorder and bewilderment among the peoples of the earth. Refs.: Is. 22:5; Mic. 7:4; also translated confusion, terror. ¶

PERSECUTE – 1 Is. 14:6 ➔ PERSECUTION <4783> 2 Dan. 7:25 ➔ WEAR OUT, WEAR DOWN <1080>.

PERSECUTION – ***murdāp*** [masc. noun: מֻרְדָּף <4783>; from PURSUE <7291> (in the sense of to chase, to persecute)] ▶ **This word is used of Babylon's political and military aggression, pressure, and violence against other nations.** Ref.: Is. 14:6; also translated aggression, to persecute. ¶

PERSIA – 1 ***pāras*** [proper noun: פָּרַס <6539>; of foreign origin] ▶ **This word designates the Persian Empire that ruled the Middle East from ca. 539–332 B.C. It is mentioned ca. 30 times in the Old Testament. It stretched from India to Cush in Egypt. It was finally conquered by Alexander the Great in 332 B.C. when Alexander pursued its last king (Darius III) until he killed him. In the Old Testament, its history impacts Israel late but in key ways.** The Jews were allowed to return from Exile under then great King Cyrus (538/39 B.C.) (2 Chr. 36:20–23; Ezra 1:1–8). Persia under several kings fostered the rebuilding of the city of Jerusalem and its Temple, which was completed in 516 B.C. (Ezra 3:4; 6; 7; 9; Is. 44; 45). Darius the Mede was kind to Daniel and honored him (5; 6; 9). Daniel lived into the third year of Cyrus (Dan. 10:1) but foresaw the demise of the empire (Dan. 2; 7; 8). Under King Xerxes (486–405 B.C.), a great deliverance occurred on behalf of the Jews (Dan. 1; 10). Persia is mentioned in Ezekiel's vision of a huge battle of the nations against Israel when they will be defeated (Ezek. 38:15). *
2 ***pāras*** [Aramaic proper noun: פָּרַס <6540>; corresponding to <6539> above] ▶ **See <6539> above. Aramaic was the lingua franca of the day when parts of Daniel and Ezra were composed.** See Dan. 2:4b-7:28; Ezra 4:8–6:18; 7:12–26. Specific refs.: Ezra 4:24; 6:14; Dan. 5:28; 6:8, 12, 15. ¶
– 3 Ezra 4:9: people of Persia ➔ APHARSITES <670> b.

PERSIAN – 1 ***parsiy*** [proper noun: פַּרְסִי <6542>; patrial from PERSIA <6539>] ▶ **This word designates someone who is from Persia.** In Nehemiah 12:22 it is used of Darius. Compare the following Aramaic entry <6543>. ¶
2 ***parsāyā'*** [Aramaic proper noun: פַּרְסָיָא <6543>; corresponding to <6542> above] ▶ **This word designates something or someone that came from Persia.** The word is used to describe Cyrus in Daniel 6:28. ¶

PERSIST – Josh. 17:12; Judg. 1:27, 35 ➔ CONTENT (BE) <2974>.

PERSISTENT – Lev. 13:51, 52; 14:44 ➔ PAINFUL (BE) <3992>.

PERSON – Ex. 16:16; 38:26 ➔ HEAD (noun) <1538>.

PERSON (ANOTHER) – ***rêa', rêya'*** [masc. noun: רֵעַ, רֵיעַ <7453>; from FEED (verb) <7462> b. (in the sense of to associate with, to be a companion)] ▶ **Most frequently, this term is used to refer to the second party in a personal interaction without indicating any particular relationship.** Refs.: Gen. 11:7; Judg. 7:13, 14; Ruth 3:14. It is extremely broad, covering everyone from a lover (Hos. 3:1); a close friend (Job 2:11); an acquaintance (Prov. 6:1); an adversary in court (Ex. 18:16); an enemy in combat (2 Sam. 2:16). Thus, this word is well-suited for its widely inclusive use in the Ten Commandments (see Ex. 20:16, 17; Deut. 5:20, 21; cf. Luke 10:29–37). *

PERSPIRE – Ezek. 44:18 ➔ that makes them perspire ➔ lit.: that causes sweat ➔ SWEAT <3154.

PERSUADE – 1 Sam. 24:7 ➔ SPLIT <8156>.

PERSUASIONS – Prov. 7:21 ➔ LEARNING <3948>.

PERSUASIVE WORDS – Prov. 7:21 ➔ LEARNING <3948>.

PERSUASIVENESS – Prov. 16:21, 23 ➔ LEARNING <3948>.

PERUDA, PERIDA – ***pᵉrûḏā', pᵉriyḏā'*** [masc. proper noun: פְּרוּדָא, פְּרִידָא <6514>; from DIVIDE <6504>]: separation ▶ **Members of his family came back from the Babylonian captivity.** Refs.: Ezra 2:55; Neh. 7:57. ¶

PERVERSE – 1 ***lûz*** [verb: לוּז <3868>; a prim. root] ▶ **This word indicates to be crooked, to be devious. It indicates what a person or nation trusts in.** In context it indicates guile, deviousness, etc. found in political alliances with Egypt rather than trust in God's word (Is. 30:12: perversity, guile, perverseness, deceit). The wicked and perverse follow a path of perversity, crookedness, deviousness (Prov. 2:15: devious, froward; 3:32: froward, devious, perverse), and the Lord abhors them. Their way of crookedness shows that they despise and reject the Lord (Prov. 14:2: devious, perverse). In two passages, it has the sense of losing sight of something or of something being lost sight of (Prov. 3:21: to depart, to vanish, to loose; 4:21: to depart, to escape). ¶

2 ***'iqqêš*** [adj.: עִקֵּשׁ <6141>; from CROOKED (MAKE, BE) <6140>] ▶ **This word is used to describe the moral, religious, and social perversion and crookedness of Israel, as well as of the perverse in general; it is also translated crooked, warped.** Refs.: Deut. 32:52; 2 Sam. 22:27; Ps. 18:26; Prov. 2:15; 17:20. It is used to describe a deceitful, perverse heart, the source of evil (Ps. 101:4; KJV: froward). The perversity of the rich destroys them (Prov. 28:6). Wisdom has no perverse or crooked way in her (Prov. 8:8); God hates the perverse (Prov. 11:20). A fool pours out perverse speech (Prov. 19:1). Other ref.: Prov. 22:5. ¶

3 ***tahpuḵāh*** [fem. noun: תַּהְפֻּכָה <8419>; from TURN <2015>; lit.: a perversity or fraud] ▶ **This word is used of a generation of Israelites who deviated and distorted the Lord's ways, turning from Him, for their true life is found in Him.** Ref.: Deut. 32:20. It describes deceptive and corrupt speech, things that are distorted (Prov. 2:12). Evil itself features perversity, a distortion of what is straight and right (Prov. 2:14). Evil persons create perversity in their hearts (Prov. 6:14). God hates a perverted mouth, perverted speech (Prov. 8:13). A slanderer is a perverted person (Prov. 16:28). *

– 4 1 Sam. 20:30; Prov. 12:8 ➔ INIQUITY (COMMIT) <5753> 5 Ps. 55:3 ➔ PERVERTED <6127> 6 Prov. 4:24 ➔ PERVERSITY <3891> 7 Prov. 6:12 ➔ CROOKED <6143> 8 Prov. 15:4: a perverse tongue ➔ lit.: perverseness ➔ CROOKEDNESS <5558> 9 Prov. 21:8 ➔ CROOKED <2019> 10 Is. 19:14 ➔ CONFUSION <5773>.

PERVERSE (BE) – Num. 22:32 ➔ TURN OVER <3399>.

PERVERSE, PERVERSE (BE) – Job 9:20; Prov. 28:18 ➔ CROOKED (MAKE, BE) <6140>.

PERVERSE AND STRANGE – Prov. 21:8 ➔ GUILTY (noun) <2054>.

PERVERSELY (ACT, DO) – 1 Kgs. 8:47; 2 Chr. 6:37 ➔ INIQUITY (COMMIT) <5753>.

PERVERSENESS – 1 Prov. 11:3; 15:4 ➔ CROOKEDNESS <5558> 2 Is. 30:12 ➔ PERVERSE <3868> 3 Ezek. 9:9 ➔ INJUSTICE <4297>.

PERVERSION – 1 ***teḇel*** [masc. noun: תֶּבֶל <8397>; from MIX <1101>] ▶ **This is a strong word used in condemning distorted sexual practices.** One such practice is human-animal copulation (Lev. 18:23; KJV: confusion). Intercourse between a man and his daughter-in-law was also considered perversion and incest (Lev. 20:12). ¶

– 2 Prov. 15:4 ➔ CROOKEDNESS <5558> 3 Ezek. 9:9 ➔ INJUSTICE <4297>.

PERVERSITY – 1 ***lāzûṯ*** [fem. noun: לָזוּת <3891>; from PERVERSE <3868>] ▶

This word means deceitfulness; it is translated perverse, devious. It is used in its construct form with lips (*śᵉp̱otayim*) following, which may be rendered as perverse or deceitful lips (Prov. 4:24). ¶
– 2 Prov. 4:24 → CROOKED <6143> 3 Prov. 11:3 → CROOKEDNESS <5558> 4 Is. 30:12 → PERVERSE <3868> 5 Ezek. 9:9 → INJUSTICE <4297>.

PERVERT – 1 Ex. 23:8; Deut. 16:19; Prov. 13:6; 19:3 → OVERTHROW (verb) <5557> 2 Job 8:3; 34:12 → BEND <5791> 3 Job 33:27; Jer. 3:21 → INIQUITY (COMMIT) <5753> 4 Prov. 10:9; Mic. 3:9 → CROOKED (MAKE, BE) <6140>.

PERVERTED – ***'āqal*** [verb: עָקַל <6127>; a prim. root] ► **This word means to be distorted, to be made wrong.** It refers to a twisted distortion of justice that results in injustice being done (Hab. 1:4; NKJV: perverse). ¶

PESTILENCE – 1 Hab. 3:5 → FLASH (noun) <7565> 2 See PLAGUE (noun) <1698>.

PESTLE – ***'ᵉliy*** [masc. noun: עֱלִי <5940>; from OFFER <5927> (in the sense of to lift)] ► **This word refers to a tool with a rounded end used to crush various substances in a mortar.** Ref.: Prov. 27:22. ¶

PETHAHIAH – ***pᵉṯaḥyāh*** [masc. proper noun: פְּתַחְיָה <6611>; from OPEN <6605> and LORD <3050>]: opened by the Lord ►
a. A priest in David's time. Ref.: 1 Chr. 24:16. ¶
b. A Levite who assisted Ezra, perhaps the same as c. below. Ref.: Neh. 9:5. ¶
c. A Jew returning from exile with a foreign wife, perhaps the same as b. above. Ref.: Ezra 10:23. ¶
d. A descendant of Judah and advisor to Zerubbabel. Ref.: Neh. 11:24. ¶

PETHOR – ***pᵉṯôr*** [proper noun: פְּתוֹר <6604>; of foreign origin] ► **Town in Mesopotamia, home of the pagan prophet Balaam.** Refs.: Num. 22:5; Deut. 23:4. ¶

PETHUEL – ***pᵉṯû'ēl*** [masc. proper noun: פְּתוּאֵל <6602>; from ENTICE <6601> and GOD <410>]: God enlarges ► **Father of the prophet Joel.** Ref.: Joel 1:1. ¶

PETITION – 1 ***ba'û*** [Aramaic fem. noun: בָּעוּ <1159>; from SEEK <1156>] ► **This word is related to *be'ā'*, meaning to ask, seek, or request. It occurs only twice in Scripture, both times in Daniel.** It conveys the idea of prayer (Dan. 6:7, 13). ¶
– 2 Ps. 20:5 → DESIRE (noun) <4862>.

PEULLETHAI – ***pᵉ'ullᵉṯay*** [masc. proper noun: פְּעֻלְּתַי <6469>; from WORK <6468>]: laborious ► **A Levite, one of the gate keepers in the Temple, son of Obed-Edom.** Ref.: 1 Chr. 26:5. ¶

PEULTHAI – 1 Chr. 26:5 → PEULLETHAI <6469>.

PHALLU – Gen. 46:9 → PALLU <6396>.

PHALTI – 1 Sam. 25:44 → PALTI <6406>.

PHARAOH – ***par'ōh*** [masc. proper noun: פַּרְעֹה <6547>; of Egyptian deriv.] ► **This word was a common title used of the kings of Egypt, especially in the Bible.** Refs.: Gen. 12:15; Ex. 1:11, 19, 22, etc. The word builds off of the Egyptian pr-'' meaning great house. At first it referred to the king's royal palace. Later (ca. 1500 B.C.), it began to refer to the king himself. Then in the Bible it is coupled with specific names of Pharaohs (2 Kgs. 23:29). The Pharaohs of the book of Exodus are symbolic of tyrants over God's people as well as historical individuals. *

PHARAOH HOPHRA – ***par'ōh ḥopra'*** [masc. proper noun: פַּרְעֹה חָפְרַע <6548>; of Egyptian deriv.] ► **This word designates the name of an Egyptian Pharaoh (589–570 B.C.).** The Lord, demonstrating His sovereignty over all nations, handed him over to his enemies to be executed (Jer. 44:30). The Greeks called him Pharaoh Apries (Jer. 37:5). ¶

PHARAOH NECO – ***par'ōh nᵉḵōh*** [masc. proper noun: פַּרְעֹה נְכֹה <6549>; of Egyptian deriv.] ▶ **This word designates an Egyptian Pharaoh (610–595 B.C.).** He attempted to aid the Assyrians against the Babylonians (2 Kgs. 23:29). Josiah, king of Judah, unwisely challenged him and was killed. Neco was wiped out by the Babylonians at the important Battle of Carchemish in 605 B.C. Jeremiah prophesied against him and Egypt (Jer. 46:1–28). Refs.: 2 Kgs. 23:29, 33–36; Jer. 48:2. ¶

PHAREZ – See PEREZ <6557>.

PHARPAR – ***parpar*** [proper noun: פַּרְפַּר <6554>; from BREAK <6565>]: swift ▶ **A river of Damascus.** Ref.: 2 Kgs. 5:12. ¶

PHARZITE – See PEREZITE <6558>.

PHICHOL – See PHICOL <6369>.

PHICOL – ***piyḵōl*** [proper noun: פִּיכֹל <6369>; from MOUTH <6310> and ALL <3605>]: mouth of all ▶ **The commander of the army of Abimelech, a Philistine king in the days of Abraham and Isaac.** Refs.: Gen. 21:22, 32; 26:26. ¶

PHILISTIA – ***pᵉlešeṯ*** [proper noun: פְּלֶשֶׁת <6429>; from ROLL IN <6428> (in the sense of migratory)]: country of sojourners ▶ **This word designates the land where the Philistines lived. It was also called "land of the Philistines," a section of the Mediterranean coastal plain. It stretched from the Nahal Besor (a small stream or wadi) in the south to the Yarkon River in the north. It contained key Philistine cities: Gaza, Ashkelon, Ashdon, Ekron, and Gath in its northern half.** It occurs only ca. seven times in the Old Testament. It is first mentioned in Moses' "song at the sea" in anticipation of Israel's march into Canaan (Ex. 15:14; KJV: Palestina). The Lord would rule over it (Ps. 60:8). Other refs.: Ps. 83:7; 87:4 (KJV: Philistines); 108:9; Is. 14:29, 31; Joel 3:4. ¶

PHILISTINE – ***pᵉlištiy*** [proper noun: פְּלִשְׁתִּי <6430>; patrial from PHILISTIA <6429>]: sojourner, emigrant ▶ **This Hebrew word designates the gentilic or ethnic form of *Philistine* indicating that a person belonged to the Philistines who had settled in Philistia.** Their biblical ancestors were Casluhites, sons of Mizraim (Gen. 10:14). The Philistines had been a part of the various migrations of the "sea peoples" (Amos 9:7). They were in the land in small numbers during the time of the patriarchs (Gen. 20:26). They were for many years Israel's chief enemy until David effectively disabled them (2 Sam. 15–22). Solomon ruled over them (1 Kgs. 4:20, 21). *

PHILISTINES – Ps. 83:7 ➔ PHILISTIA <6429>.

PHINEAS – ***piynᵉḥās*** [masc. proper noun: פִּינְחָס <6372>; apparently from MOUTH <6310> and a variation of SERPENT <5175>]: mouth of brass *or* mouth of serpent ▶

a. The son of Eleazar and Putiel. Ref.: Ex. 6:25. He showed his zeal for the Law of the Lord and his hatred of sexual immorality at Shittim. He executed an Israelite, Zimri, who arrogantly brought a Midianite woman, Cozbi, into Israel's camp in the presence of Moses and all Israel (Num. 25:6–9). Zimri had immoral relations with her and worshiped her pagan god (Num. 25:1–9). Phinehas's zeal for the Lord and his dedication to Him was remembered as a lasting memorial by the Lord (Num. 25:10–13; Ps. 106:30). This priest was also a leader who helped avert civil war in Israel (Josh. 22:10–25). Gibeah was allotted to him in Ephraim near Shiloh (Josh. 24:33). He served with his father Eleazar at the ark of the covenant (Judg. 20:28). ¶

b. A Phinehas was the younger son of the high priest Eli in the time of Samuel's birth. Refs.: 1 Sam. 1:3; 2:34. He and Hophni were killed for their wickedness (1 Sam. 4:4, 11, 17, 19). He had a son, Ahitub (1 Sam. 14:3). ¶

c. The son of a priest in the time of Ezra. Refs.: Ezra 7:5; 8:2, 33. ¶

PHYLACTERIES – Ex. 13:16 ➔ FRONTLETS <2903>.

PI-BESETH – *piy ḇeseṯ* [proper noun: פִּי בֶסֶת <6364>; of Egyptian origin] ▶ **An Egyptian city.** Its young men would fall by the sword and the women would go into captivity; also known as Bubastis (Ezek. 30:17). ¶

PI-HAHIROTH – *piy haḥiyrōṯ* [proper noun: פִּי הַחִירֹת <6367>; from MOUTH <6310> and the fem. plur. of a noun (from the same root as HOLE <2356>), with the art. interpolated] ▶ **A place where the Israelites camped after leaving Egypt and before crossing the Red Sea.** Refs.: Ex. 14:2, 9; Num. 33:7, 8. ¶

PICK (noun) – 1 *ḥāriyṣ* [masc. noun: חָרִיץ <2757>; from MOVE <2782> (in the sense of cutting)] ▶ **This word refers to a harrow, a wedge, a sharp instrument.** It was a tool of menial, hard labor and often used by prisoners of war set to hard labor (2 Sam. 12:31; 1 Chr. 20:3). The Hebrew word is also translated cheese; see CHEESE <2757>. ¶
– 2 Ezek. 17:21 → FUGITIVE <4015>.

PICK (verb) – *’ārāh* [verb: אָרָה <717>; a prim. root] ▶ **This word means and is also translated to pluck, to gather.** It is used figuratively to describe the way the nations had devastated Israel and taken away its strength (Ps. 80:12). It is used to describe the gathering of myrrh (Song 5:1). ¶

PICK UP – 1 Kgs. 20:33 → CATCH (verb) <2480>.

PICKED (FRESHLY) – Gen. 8:11 → freshly plucked → PLUCKED <2965>.

PICTURE – 1 *maśkiyṯ* [fem. noun: מַשְׂכִּית <4906>; from the same as SECU <7906>] ▶ **This word means an image, the imagination.** It is usually used of a carved image or sculpture, often idolatrous, whether of stone (Lev. 26:1: image, figured, carved, engraved); silver (Prov. 25:11; also translated setting); or of unspecified material (Num. 33:52: figured stone, carved image, engraved stone; Ezek. 8:12: idol,

imagery, carved image). It is also utilized as a metaphor for one's imagination or conceit (Ps. 73:7: imagination, folly; *maśkiyyōṯlēḇāḇ* [HEART <3824>], meaning images of the heart; cf. Prov. 18:11: imagination, conceit, esteem). ¶
– 2 Is. 2:16 → VESSEL <7914> b.

PIECE – 1 *ᵃgôrāh* [fem. noun: אֲגוֹרָה <95>; from the same as AGUR <94>] ▶ **This word refers to a piece or payment of silver.** Ref.: 1 Sam. 2:36. ¶
2 *’ešpār* [masc. noun: אֶשְׁפָּר <829>; of uncertain deriv.] ▶ **This word indicates a portion of something, such as meat, dates, etc.** It indicates a cake of dates as a special luxury gift to the Israelites on the arrival of the ark in Jerusalem (NKJV: piece of meat; KJV: piece of flesh; 2 Sam. 6:19; 1 Chr. 16:3). ¶
3 *bāḏāl* [masc. noun: בָּדָל <915>; from SEPARATE (verb) <914>] ▶ **This word is used figuratively to refer to Israel's enemies snatching a "piece of an ear" representing Israel during God's judgments on her.** Ref.: Amos 3:12. ¶
4 *haddām* [Aramaic masc. noun: הַדָּם <1917>; from a root corresponding to that of FOOTSTOOL <1916>] ▶ **This word indicates the various external limbs or parts of the body which can be torn limb from limb.** Ref.: Dan. 2:5. It is used figuratively of the limbs of people, a nation, or a tongue (Dan. 3:29) that can be torn apart as a form of punishment. ¶
5 *pelaḥ* [masc. noun: פֶּלַח <6400>; from CUT (verb) <6398>] ▶ **This word indicates a portion of something.** It refers to part of a millstone (Judg. 9:53; 2 Sam. 11:21; Job 41:24). It describes a slice of a cake of figs (1 Sam. 30:12); or of pomegranates (Song 4:3; 6:7). ¶
6 *paṯ, pᵉṯôṯ* [masc. noun: פַּת, פְּתוֹת <6595>; from BREAK <6626>] ▶
a. This word refers to a portion of bread large enough to serve to guests. Ref.: Gen. 18:5; *paṯ leḥem*. It refers to broken-off pieces of a grain or baked offering (Lev. 2:6). It represents pieces of ice or hail (Ps. 147:17). It indicates a small morsel of food or bread as symbolic of not having enough

or a modest amount (Prov. 17:1). It indicates how readily a person will sin for a morsel of food (Prov. 28:21). *
b. This word designates in context a portion or morsel of bread, emphasizing its insignificant and small value. Ref.: Ezek. 13:19. ¶
7 ***qera'*** [masc. noun: קֶרַע <7168>; from TEAR <7167>] ▶ **This word refers to a section of cloth or a garment that has been torn; rags, the clothing of the poor.** Refs.: 1 Kgs. 11:30, 31; 2 Kgs. 2:12; Prov. 23:21. ¶
8 ***raṣ*** [masc. noun: רַץ <7518>; contr. from BREAK <7533>] ▶ **This word refers to a bar (of silver).** It is used in context of tribute, bars or pieces (KJV) (of silver) to be presented to Israel and her God (Ps. 68:30) by foreign nations. ¶
– 9 Gen. 15:10; Jer. 34:18, 19 → HALF <1335> 10 Gen. 15:17 → PART (noun) <1506> 11 Neh. 3:11 → MEASURE (noun) <4060> 12 Is. 30:14 → FRAGMENT <4386> 13 Amos 6:11 → BREACH <1233> 14 Amos 6:11 → DEW <7447> b.

PIECE OF MONEY – ***q^e śiyṭāh*** [fem. noun: קְשִׂיטָה <7192>; from an unused root (prob. meaning to weigh out)] ▶ **This word refers to coins of silver money used by Jacob to purchase a piece of land.** Refs.: Gen. 33:19; Josh. 24:32. It refers to money given to Job to help restore his good health and fortune (Job 42:11). ¶

PIECE OF SILVER – Gen. 33:19; Josh. 24:32; Job 42:11 → PIECE OF MONEY <7192>.

PIECES – ***nêtaḥ*** [masc. noun: נֵתַח <5409>; from CUT (verb) <5408>] ▶ **This word indicates portions of meat.** It refers to the pieces of a sacrifice into which an animal has been cut (Ex. 29:17; Lev. 1:6, 8, 12; 8:20; 9:13); the parts into which a human body has been cut (Judg. 19:29). It is used figuratively to symbolize Judah, the city of Jerusalem, and the various classes of people in them who will be "pieces of meat" for cooking as in a pot of destruction and judgment (Ezek. 24:4, 6). ¶

PIECES (BREAK TO, IN) – ***dāqû*** [Aramaic verb: דְּקוּ <1751>; corresponding to BEAT <1854>] ▶ **This word means and is also translated to crush.** It is an emphatic word and describes the crushing of iron, clay, bronze, silver, and gold in the statue of Nebuchadnezzar's dream (Dan. 2:35). ¶

PIECES (CUT TO, DASH IN) – ***pā'āh*** [verb: פָּאָה <6284>; a prim. root] ▶ **This word means to divide into pieces or corners; it is also translated to scatter.** It is used in a violent manner and attitude of God's judging His people in a devastating way, visiting a covenant curse upon them (Deut. 32:26). ¶

PIECES (TEAR IN, TEAR TO, PULL IN) – ***pāšaḥ*** [verb: פָּשַׁח <6582>; a prim. root] ▶ **This word is also translated to mangle.** It is used in the figurative poetry of Lamentations 3:11 to describe God's actions against His people in devastating judgments. ¶

PIERCE – 1 ***dāqar*** [verb: דָּקַר <1856>; a prim. root] ▶ **This word is used of penetrating with a sharp instrument to kill another person.** In vengeance (Num. 25:8); according to law (Zech. 13:3); or in an act of mercy (Judg. 9:54; 1 Sam. 31:4). It describes the killing of enemies in war (Is. 13:15; Jer. 51:4). It is used to describe wounded men in battle, pierced (Jer. 37:10). Other refs.: 1 Chr. 10:4; Lam. 4:9; Zech. 12:10. ¶
2 ***ḥālal*** [verb: חָלַל <2490>; a prim. root; comp. SICK (BE) <2470>] ▶ **This word means to bore through and also to play the pipe, to profane. It has three distinct meanings.** The first meaning is to pierce or wound, either physically unto death (Is. 53:5; Ezek. 32:26) or figuratively unto despair (Ps. 109:22). The second meaning of this word is to play the pipe, which is used only twice in the Old Testament (1 Kgs. 1:40; Ps. 87:7). The third meaning is to profane or to defile, which is used primarily of the ceremonial objects of worship (Ex. 20:25; Ezek. 44:7; Dan. 11:31); of the Sabbath (Ex. 31:14; Neh. 13:17;

Ezek. 23:38); of God's name (Lev. 18:21; Jer. 34:16); of God's priests (Lev. 21:4, 6). However, it also refers to sexual defilement (Gen. 49:4; Lev. 21:9); the breaking of a covenant (Ps. 89:31, 34; Mal. 2:10); and making a vineyard common (Deut. 20:6; 28:30). In the causative form of this verb, it means to begin (Gen. 4:26; 2 Chr. 3:2). *

3 ***ṭā'an*** [verb: טָעַן <2944>; a prim. root] ▶ **This word means to stab; it is also translated to thrust through.** In context it refers to those persons who have been mortally stabbed, pierced with swords (Is. 14:19), an ignominious lot. ¶

4 ***kûr*** [verb: כּוּר <3564>; from an unused root meaning properly to dig through] ▶ **This word is used to describe stabbing or puncturing something.** The oppressed psalmist tells of his enemies piercing his hands and feet (Ps. 22:16), an adumbration or foreshadowing of what would happen to the Messiah. The Hebrew word is also translated furnace; see FURNACE <3564>. ¶

5 ***māḥaṣ*** [verb: מָחַץ <4272>; a prim. root] ▶ **This word means to wound severely, to pierce through, and to shatter.** It describes bodily destruction and is best illustrated in Judges 5:26, where Jael pierced through Sisera's head from temple to temple with a tent peg. David used this word to describe some of his victories in which those wounded were not able to rise again (2 Sam. 22:39; Ps. 18:38). In all other instances of this word, God is in complete control (Deut. 32:39; Job 5:18) and completely shatters His enemies (Ps. 68:21; 110:5, 6; Hab. 3:13). This word occurs only in the poetical passages of the Old Testament, which highlights its intensity. Other refs.: Num. 24:8, 17; Deut. 33:1; Job 26:12; Ps. 68:23. ¶

6 ***nāqab*** [verb: נָקַב <5344>; a prim. root] ▶ **This word means to penetrate with a sharp instrument; it also means to designate, to curse.** The word signifies the piercing of an animal's head, jaw, or nose with a spear (Job 40:24; 41:2; Hab. 3:14). It also signifies the piercing of a person's hand by a reed, symbolic of pain. Egypt was charged with bringing such pain on its allies (2 Kgs. 18:21; Is. 36:6). In Haggai 1:6, the passive participle described a bag as being pierced. This word can also refer to wages being paid (Gen. 30:28); and to men being singled out for some task or distinction (2 Chr. 28:15; Amos 6:1). The meaning to curse may also be derived from a different root, *qābab* [CURSE (verb) <6895>]. It signified the cursing or blaspheming of God's name (Lev. 24:11, 16); the speaking of a negative spiritual sentence on people (Num. 23:8; Prov. 11:26; 24:24); or things associated with people (Job 3:8; 5:3). *

7 ***rāṣā'*** [verb: רָצַע <7527>; a prim. root] ▶ **This word refers to the process of perforating a slave's ear to mark him as a permanent slave of his master.** It was an act done with the approval of the slave and at his request (Ex. 21:6; KJV, ESV: to bore). ¶

– 8 Judg. 5:26 ➔ CRUSH <4277> 9 Job 16:13; Prov. 7:23 ➔ CUT (verb) <6398> 10 Job 30:17 ➔ GOUGE <5365> 11 Ps. 38:2 ➔ BEND <5181>.

PIERCED – ***ḥālāl*** [masc. noun or adj.: חָלָל <2491>; from PIERCE <2490>] ▶ **This word means slain, mortally wounded, profaned.** This word denotes the carnage of battle; the dead, generally as a result of warfare (Gen. 34:27; Jer. 14:18; Ezek. 21:29); and those having sustained some fatal injury (Judg. 9:40; 1 Sam. 17:52). Also, by extension, the word is used twice to indicate a state of defilement or perversion. In the first instance, it denotes a woman whose virginity has been violated or, as it were, pierced (Lev. 21:7, 14). The other applies to a wicked regent of Israel destined for punishment, emphasizing that he is already, in a prophetic sense, mortally wounded (Ezek. 21:25). *

PIERCING – Prov. 12:18 ➔ THRUST (noun) <4094>.

PIG – ***ḥᵃziyr*** [masc. noun: חֲזִיר <2386>; from an unused root prob. meaning to enclose] ▶ **This word refers also to a hog, a wild boar; it is also translated swine, boar.** It is among the unclean animals Israel could not eat (Lev. 11:7; Deut. 14:8; cf. Is. 65:4; 66:17). Its blood was an abomination as an offering (Is. 66:3). It is used metaphorically to refer to Israel's enemy that devours her (Ps. 80:13). A ring in its snout is totally out of place (Prov. 11:22). ¶

PIGEON – Lev. 1:14; 5:7, 11; 12:6, 8; Num. 6:10; etc. ➔ DOVE <3123>.

PIGEON (YOUNG) – ***gôzzāl*** [fem. noun: גּוֹזָל <1469>; from ROB <1497> (as being comparatively nude of feathers)] ▶ **This was one of two birds Abraham used in a covenantal ritual.** Ref.: Gen. 15:9. In Deuteronomy 32:11, it refers specifically to the young of an eagle. ¶

PILDASH – ***pildāš*** [masc. proper noun: פִּלְדָּשׁ <6394>; of uncertain deriv.] ▶ **A relative of Abraham.** Ref.: Gen. 22:22. ¶

PILE – 1 ***m*ᵉ*ḏûrāh*** [fem. noun: מְדוּרָה <4071>; from DWELL <1752> in the sense of accumulation (the Hebrew word also means to heap up, to pile)] ▶ **This word refers to a mound of wood or anything else for burning.** Ref.: Is. 30:33; also translated pyre. In context it is used figuratively of the woodpile on which Jerusalem would be destroyed by Babylon (Ezek. 24:9; also translated pyre). ¶
– 2 Lev. 24:6, 7 ➔ ROW (noun) <4635> 3 2 Kgs. 10:8 ➔ HEAP (noun) <6652> 4 Ruth 3:7 ➔ HEAP (noun) <6194> 5 Ezek. 24:5 ➔ BALL <1754>.

PILE OF ROCKS – Josh. 7:26; 8:29; Job 8:17 ➔ HEAP (noun) <1530>.

PILE OF RUBBLE – Ezra 6:11; Dan. 2:5; 3:29 ➔ DUNGHILL <5122>.

PILED UP – ***'āram*** [verb: עָרַם <6192>; a prim. root] ▶ **This word means to be heaped up; it is also translated to be gathered together**. It occurs once in the Hebrew Bible in Exodus 15:8. In Moses' song at the sea, he describes God's miraculous act by singing about how the waters were piled up. ¶

PILEHA – Neh. 10:24 ➔ PILHA <6401>.

PILES – Nah. 3:3 ➔ HEAVINESS <3514>.

PILHA – ***pilḥā'*** [masc. proper noun: פִּלְחָא <6401>; from PIECE <6400>]: slicing ▶ **A chief of the people who signed the covenant of renewal with Nehemiah after the return from the Babylonian captivity.** Ref.: Neh. 10:24. ¶

PILL – Gen. 30:37, 38 ➔ PEEL <6478>.

PILLAGE – 1 Ezra 9:7 ➔ PLUNDER (noun) <961> 2 Nah. 3:1 ➔ PLUNDER (noun) <6563>.

PILLAGED – Nah. 2:10 ➔ EMPTY (adj.) <950>.

PILLAR – 1 ***maṣṣêḇāh*** [fem. noun: מַצֵּבָה <4676>; fem. (causatively) part. of STAND <5324>] ▶ **This word means something set upright. It most often refers to a standing, unhewn block of stone utilized for religious and memorial purposes.** After a powerful experience of the Lord in a dream, Jacob set up as a pillar the stone on which he had laid his head, in commemoration of the event (Gen. 28:18, 22; cf. Gen. 31:45; 35:20). Moses set up an altar and also twelve pillars at the base of Mount Sinai to represent the twelve tribes of Israel (Ex. 24:4). These pillars were erected as monuments to God (Hos. 3:4); or, more commonly, to pagan deities (1 Kgs. 14:23, Mic. 5:13). Many times in 2 Kings, the term refers to a sacred pillar that aided people in their worship of pagan gods, especially the Canaanite god Baal. In most of these passages, the sacred columns were used by Israelites, contrary to the Lord's prohibition concerning the worship of any other god (2 Kgs. 3:2; 10:26, 27; 18:4; 23:14; cf. Hos. 10:1, 2; Mic. 5:13). *
2 ***maṣṣeḇeṯ*** [fem. noun: מַצֶּבֶת <4678>; from STAND <5324>] ▶ **This word means a stump, a standing stone.** A monument could be set up to commemorate a divine appearance, such as the pillar of stone Jacob set up at Bethel (Gen. 35:14, 20). The word can also refer to a pillar or monument set up to honor oneself, such as the one Absalom set up for himself in order that his name would be remembered (2 Sam. 18:18). Other ref.: Is. 6:13 (stump, substance). ¶

[3] ***māṣûq*** [masc. noun: מָצוּק <4690>; from OPPRESS <6693> (in the sense of something narrow)] ► **This word signifies a foundation; standing like a pillar.** It is used metaphorically of the foundations or pillars of the earth (1 Sam. 2:8). It points out the rise or structure of a natural rocky hill or crag (1 Sam. 14:5: to rise, to face, to stand, to be situated). ¶
[4] ***'ammûḏ*** [masc. noun: עַמּוּד <5982>; from STAND (verb) <5975>] ► **This word refers to a column.** It is a general term referring to a column, a pole, a pillar of various kinds: tent post (Ex. 26:32); pillars in the Tabernacle (Ex. 27:10–12, 14–17); a column in a house or a small temple (Judg. 16:25); free-standing, large bronze columns before the Temple of Solomon (1 Kgs. 7:15–22) and Ezekiel (Ezek. 40:49). In the Song of Solomon, it refers to a small post featured in a royal chair (Song 3:10). It is used of the pillars of cloud and fire that led Israel (Ex. 13:21, 22). Figuratively, it depicts the foundation pillars of the earth (Job 26:11; Ps. 75:3). Pillars of strength are a feature of lady Wisdom's house (Prov. 9:1). *
– [5] Gen. 19:26 ➔ GARRISON <5333> [6] Judg. 9:6 ➔ TOWER <4674> [7] 1 Kgs. 10:12 ➔ SUPPORT (noun) <4552> [8] Ps. 144:12 ➔ CORNER (noun) <2106> [9] Song 3:6; Joel 2:30 ➔ COLUMN <8490> [10] Jer. 50:15 ➔ FOUNDATION <803>.

PILLOW – [1] ***kāḇiyr*** [masc. noun.: כָּבִיר <3523>; from MULTIPLY <3527> in the original sense of plaiting] ► **This word refers to a garment, a cover, a quilt.** It is used of a bedspread or quilt made of goat's hair (1 Sam. 19:13, 16). Possibly the word should be translated as a cushion or pillow of goat's hair. ¶
– [2] Gen. 28:11, 18 ➔ HEAD (noun) <4763> b. [3] Ezek. 13:18, 20 ➔ MAGIC BAND <3704>.

PILOT – Ezek. 27:8; 27–29 ➔ SAILOR <2259>.

PILTAI – ***pilṭāy*** [masc. proper noun: פִּלְטָי <6408>; for PALTITE <6407>]: the Lord delivers ► **A priest who returned from the Babylonian captivity with Zerubbabel.** Ref.: Neh. 12:17. ¶

PIN – Ex. 27:19; Judg. 16:14 ➔ PEG <3489>.

PINE – [1] ***tiḏhār*** [masc. noun: תִּדְהָר <8410>] ► **This Hebrew word indicates a beautiful, firm, enduring tree native to Lebanon; it is translated pine tree, but its exact identification is uncertain.** It is also translated box tree (NASB), plane (ESV), fir (NIV) in Isaiah 41:19; 60:13. ¶
– [2] Song 1:17 ➔ FIR <1266> [3] Is. 44:14 ➔ ASH <766>.

PINE AWAY – [1] Lev. 26:16 ➔ SORROW (CAUSE) <1727> [2] Lev. 26:39; 24:23; 33:10 ➔ WASTE AWAY <4743> [3] 1 Sam. 2:5 ➔ LANGUISH <535>.

PINING AWAY – Ps. 6:2 ➔ WEAK (adj.) <536>.

PINIONS – Ps. 91:4 ➔ WINGS <84>.

PINIONS (LONG) – Ezra 4:14 ➔ SLOW <750>.

PINON – ***piynōn*** [masc. proper noun: פִּינֹן <6373>; prob. the same as PUNON <6325>] ► **One of the chiefs of Edom.** Refs.: Gen. 36:41; 1 Chr. 1:52. ¶

PIPE – [1] ***mûṣāqāh*** [fem. noun: מוּצָקָה <4166>; from POUR, POUR OUT <3332>] ► **This word indicates metal castings (2 Chr. 4:3: when it was cast) for the Temple area.** It indicates casting as a means of bonding or joining items together (Zech. 4:2; also translated spout, lip, channel). ¶
– [2] Gen. 4:21; Job 21:12; 30:31; Ps. 150:4 ➔ FLUTE <5748> [3] 1 Sam. 10:5; 1 Kgs. 1:40; Is. 5:12; 30:29; Jer. 48:36 ➔ FLUTE <2485> [4] Ps. 5:1 ➔ NEHILOTH <5155> [5] Ezek. 28:13 ➔ SETTING <5345> b. [6] Dan. 3:5, 7, 10, 15 ➔ BAGPIPE <5481> [7] Dan. 3:5, 7, 10, 15 ➔ FLUTE <4953>.

PIPE (PLAY THE) – 1 Kgs. 1:40; Ps. 87:7 ➔ PIERCE <2490>.

PIPES – *ṣantārôṯ* [fem. plur. noun: צַנְתָּרוֹת <6804>; prob. from the same as WATER SHAFT <6794>] ▶ **This word refers to hollow tubes through which olive oil was carried to serve as fuel for lamps.** Ref.: Zech. 4:12. ¶

PIPING – ***šᵉriyqāh, šᵉriqāh*** [fem. noun: שְׁרוּקָה, שְׁרִקָה <8292>; fem. pass. part. of HISS <8319>] ▶ **This word refers to flute playing; it is also translated whistling, bleating.** It describes a shepherd's playing his flute for his flocks to keep them calm (Judg. 5:16). Its meaning in Jeremiah 18:16 must indicate scorn, possibly a mocking playing of the flute, piping in scorn, but most translators render it as a hissing or mocking. ¶

PIRAM – ***pir'ām*** [masc. proper noun: פִּרְאָם <6502>; from DONKEY (WILD) <6501>]: wild ▶ **A king in Canaan defeated by Joshua.** Ref.: Josh. 10:3. ¶

PIRATHON – ***pir'āṯôn*** [proper noun: פִּרְעָתוֹן <6552>; from LEADER <6546>]: princely ▶ **A place in Ephraim.** Ref.: Judg. 12:15. ¶

PIRATHONITE – ***pir'āṯôniy*** [proper noun: פִּרְעָתוֹנִי <6553>; patrial from PIRATHON <6552>] ▶ **An inhabitant of Pirathon.** Refs.: Judg. 12:13, 15; 2 Sam. 23:30; 1 Chr. 11:31; 27:14. ¶

PISGAH – ***pisgāh*** [proper noun: פִּסְגָּה <6449>; from CONSIDER <6448>]: cleft ▶ **This word designates a mountain top where Israel encamped on the way to Moab.** Ref.: Num. 21:20. From it Balaam tried to curse Israel (Num. 23:14). Moses viewed Canaan from its heights (Deut. 34:1). It was inherited by Reuben (Josh. 13:20). Sihon, king of the Amorites, had ruled it earlier. Other refs.: Deut. 3:17, 27; 4:49; Josh 12:3. ¶

PISHON – ***piyšôn*** [proper noun: פִּישׁוֹן <6376>; from FROLIC <6335> b. (in the sense of to scatter, to spread out)]: dispersive, flowing freely ▶ **One of the four rivers into which a main river coming out of Eden divided.** Ref.: Gen. 2:11. ¶

PISON – Gen. 2:11 ➔ PISHON <6376>.

PISPAH – ***pispāh*** [masc. proper noun: פִּסְפָּה <6462>; perhaps from VANISH <6461>]: dispersion ▶ **An Israelite of the tribe of Asher, one of the sons of Jether.** Ref.: 1 Chr. 7:38. ¶

PISS AGAINST THE WALL – 1 Sam. 25:22, 34 ➔ URINATE AGAINST THE WALL <8366>.

PISTACHIO NUT – ***boṭnāh*** [masc. noun: בָּטְנָה <992>; from WOMB <990> (i.e., what is inside)] ▶ **This word depicts an oval, belly-shaped nut that was considered a delicacy, one item among others carried into Egypt by Jacob's sons at his directions.** Ref.: Gen. 43:11; KJV, nuts. ¶

PIT – 1 ***gûmmāṣ*** [masc. noun: גּוּמָּץ 1475>] ▶ **Although this word is used only once in the Old Testament, its meaning is derived from a related Aramaic word, which means to dig. Thus, a pit is the result of digging.** The meaning is clear when it is used in Ecclesiastes 10:8, "He who digs a pit will fall into it" (ESV). Furthermore, this meaning is further verified in a similar passage found in Proverbs 26:27, in which a parallel word, *šaḥaṯ* <7845>, meaning pit, is used. ¶

2 ***miḵreh*** [masc. noun: מִכְרֶה <4379>; from DIG <3738>] ▶ **This word designates a pit of salt. It indicates a location where salt was mined or where it was located.** In context it was a metaphorical feature of the land of Moab following its destruction (Zeph. 2:9). ¶

3 ***paḥaṯ*** [masc. sing. noun: פַּחַת <6354>; prob. from an unused root apparently meaning to dig] ▶ **In the prophecies of Isaiah and Jeremiah, the term is used in judgment as a trap for the wicked enemies of the Lord and Israel.** Refs.: Is. 24:17, 18; Jer. 48:28, 43, 44. In Lamentations, it was a place for sinful Jerusalem (Lam. 3:47: snare, pitfall). The term is

used for the cave where David and his men were hiding (2 Sam. 17:9); and for the pit in which Absalom's body was thrown (2 Sam. 18:17). ¶

4 ***šûḥāh*** [fem. noun: שׁוּחָה <7745>; from BOW DOWN <7743>] ► **This word also means a ditch, a chasm. The primary meaning of the word is pit. It is used primarily to describe figuratively a trap that leads to ruin.** Proverbs uses this word in a figurative sense to describe a prostitute as a deep pit in comparison to a wayward wife as a narrow well (Prov. 23:27; KJV: ditch). This word could also be used to describe plots against someone, as where Jeremiah stated that his accusers had dug pits for him (Jer. 18:20, 22). The word also describes the mouth of an adulteress (i.e., a deep pit [Prov. 22:14]). Out of the five times that it is used in the Old Testament, only one is used in its literal sense, describing a rift through which God led His people (Jer. 2:6; NIV: ravine). ¶

5 ***šᵉḥûṯ*** [fem. noun: שְׁחוּת <7816>; from BOW DOWN <7812> (in the sense of to fall down)] ► **Metaphorically speaking, this is a trap that is created as one leads the upright along the path of evil.** Ref.: Prov. 28:10. This trap or pit will eventually ensnare its builder. As the wicked plot and scheme against the righteous, in the end, they will only succeed in being caught in their own traps. ¶

6 ***šᵉḥiyṯ*** [fem. noun: שְׁחִית <7825>; from BOW DOWN <7812> (in the sense of to fall down)] ► **This word means a trap, destruction, pitfall.** In Lamentations 4:20, the Lord's anointed, King Zedekiah, was caught in the trap of the Babylonians. In Psalms, the noun is used to indicate the crisis from which Yahweh saves those who cry out to Him in their troubles (Ps. 107:20; NIV: grave). By simply a mere utterance and sending forth His word, God heals and rescues from destruction those who cry out to Him. The proper response of those rescued is to give thank offerings and tell of His works through songs of joy. ¶

7 ***šaḥaṯ*** [fem. noun: שַׁחַת <7845>; from BOW DOWN <7743> (in the sense of to sink)] ► **This word denotes a large hole in the ground, a ditch, a grave, a hollow place. Its prominent usage is pit, i.e., a hole in the ground.** The word is used to describe the pit of destruction from which the Lord's love saves (Is. 38:17). The psalmist uses the word figuratively to designate a type of trap that those who are seeking his life have dug for him (Ps. 35:7). The occurrence of the word in Ezekiel metaphorically denotes a pit in which lions are caught (Ezek. 19:4). The term lion is used to represent Jehoahaz and is a metaphorical representation of his policies. He learned to tear prey and devour people. The noun is also used to denote Sheol (Job 33:24; Ezek. 28:8). Job uses the word in a rhetorical sense to describe a situation in which there is no hope (Job 17:14). He stated that if he allowed himself to call corruption his father and the worm his mother and sister, where would his hope lie? *

8 ***šiyḥāh*** [fem. noun: 7882> שִׁיחָה; from PIT <7745>] ► **Jeremiah used a metaphorical rendering of the word to describe his enemies' actions against him, they had dug a pit, i.e., a hole in the ground, to capture him.** Ref.: Jer. 18:22. The psalmist also used a similar rendering of the word to describe what his enemies had done. They had dug a pit for him but had fallen into it themselves (Ps. 57:6). In Psalm 119:85, the word was used to indicate attempts on the part of the arrogant to cause the psalmist to act contrary to God's Law. However, the psalmist's firm grounding in the laws and precepts of *Yahweh* kept him from falling into their traps. ¶

– 9 Gen. 14:10; Ps. 55:23; 69:15 ➔ WELL (noun) <875> 10 Is. 30:14 ➔ CISTERN <1360> 11 Is. 42:22 ➔ HOLE <2352> 12 Is. 51:1 ➔ QUARRY (noun) <4718> 13 Jer. 14:3 ➔ POOL (noun) <1356> 14 See CISTERN <953>.

PIT (MIRY, DEEP) – ***mahᵃmōr*** [fem. noun: מַהֲמֹר <4113>; from an unused root of uncertain meaning] ► **This word refers to a place of confinement from which a person could never rise; a deep miry hole in the ground of some kind.** Ref.: Ps. 140:10. ¶

PITCH – [1] ***zepeṯ*** [fem. noun: זֶפֶת <2203>; from an unused root (meaning to liquefy)] ▶ **A bitumen, black, sticky substance used for waterproofing.** The basket in which Moses was placed was waterproofed using this substance (Ex. 2:3). In figurative language, streams of Edom will be turned into pitch in a day of judgment (Is. 34:9), indicating a hot flowing tar or pitch. ¶
– [2] Prov. 20:20 ➔ PUPIL <380>.

PITCHER – [1] Gen. 24:14; Judg. 7:16, 19, 20; Eccl. 12:6; etc. ➔ JAR <3537> [2] Is. 22:24; Lam. 4:2 ➔ SKIN BOTTLE <5035>.

PITFALL – Lam. 3:47 ➔ PIT <6354>.

PITHOM – ***piṯōm*** [proper noun: פִּתֹם <6619>; of Egyptian deriv.] ▶ **A store city build by the Israelites in Egypt.** Ref.: Ex. 1:11. ¶

PITHON – ***piyṯôn*** [masc. proper noun: פִּיתוֹן <6377>; prob. from the same as HINGE <6596>]: expansive ▶ **A son of Micah, a descendant of Saul.** Refs.: 1 Chr. 8:35; 9:41. ¶

PITIES (THAT WHICH ONE) – Ezek. 24:21 ➔ DELIGHT (noun) <4263>.

PITIFUL – Lam. 4:10 ➔ COMPASSIONATE <7362>.

PITY – [1] ***ḥûs*** [verb: חוּס <2347>; a prim. root] ▶ **This verb means to show pity or mercy. Negated, it is used in the sense that the subject of the verb is not to be concerned or worried about himself or herself, i.e., do not pity yourself.** Ref.: Gen. 45:20. It is used of pitying an object or other person (Deut. 19:21; Ezek. 16:5; Jon. 4:10, 11). The righteous person was to have pity or compassion on the poor (Ps. 72:13). It extends to sparing a person's life, even an enemy if he were the anointed of the Lord (1 Sam. 24:10). The Lord is said to show no pity to His people (Jer. 13:14). *
[2] Is. 63:9 ➔ COMPASSION <2551> [3] Hos. 13:14 ➔ COMPASSION <5164>.

PITY (HAVE, SHOW) – ***ḥāmal*** [verb: חָמַל <2550>; a prim. root] ▶ **This verb also means to have compassion, to spare.** It expresses pity or compassion toward something or someone, a child or other persons (Ex. 2:6; 1 Sam. 15:9, 15; 23:21; 2 Sam. 12:6; Zech. 11:5, 6; Mal. 3:17). Without pity (*lō' ḥomal*) means to do something ruthlessly (Is. 30:14; Lam. 2:2) or without any restraint (Jer. 50:14). It can take on the nuance of holding on to something, desiring it, such as holding evil in one's mouth (Job 20:13) or being unwilling to do something right or that is costly to oneself (2 Sam. 12:4). *

PIVOTS (THAT TURNED ON) – 1 Kgs. 6:34 ➔ FOLDING <1550>.

PLACE (noun) – [1] ***ᵃṯar*** [Aramaic masc. noun: אֲתַר <870>; from a root corresponding to that of SPIES <871>] ▶ **This word indicates a location, site, in place of; after this.** It refers to the site of the Temple in Jerusalem in Zerubbabel's day (Ezra 5:15; 6:3, 5, 7). It seems to mean trace or evidence in Daniel 2:35 (NASB, NKJV, NIV; cf. KJV, place). With *bᵉ* on the front, it means in place of, i.e., after this (Dan. 7:6, 7). Other ref.: Dan. 2:39. ¶
[2] ***māqôm, māqōm*** [common noun: מָקוֹם, מָקֹם <4725>; from STAND <6965>] ▶ **This word indicates a spot, a space, a stand.** It basically indicates a location or space, in general of any place or location specified: figuratively of the place of the wicked (Ps. 37:10); a place at a table for eating (1 Sam. 20:25); a place to live (Deut. 1:33; 2 Kgs. 6:1); a spot where one is standing (Ex. 3:5; Josh. 5:15); unspecified: in any place (Gen. 1:9; 28:16, 17; Ex. 20:24; Judg. 2:5; Amos 4:6; 8:3). It is used often to indicate a city, the place of the city (Gen. 18:24; 20:11; 22:14; 26:7; Deut. 21:19; 2 Kgs. 18:25). It refers to spots on a person's body (Le. 13:19; 2 Kgs. 5:11). It indicates a place for a statue on a pedestal, a stand (1 Sam. 5:3). It refers often to special holy places: the place of the sanctuary (Lev. 10:13; 14:17); a holy place (*māqôm qāḏôš*) means a place around the Tabernacle area. Jerusalem is

called this holy place (1 Kgs. 8:30). It refers to places concerning the Temple or the Temple itself; the place which God chose, where His name is (1 Kgs. 8:29, 30, 1 Kgs. 8:35; 2 Chr. 6:20, 21, 26; Is. 18:7; 60:13). It is used of a holy place at any location or time (Eccl. 8:10). It has the sense of an open space or area (1 Sam. 26:13). It is found in the idiom "to yield ground" in battle (Judg. 20:36). It refers to pagan holy places (Deut. 12:2, 3; Ezek. 6:13). *
3 ***'ōmeḏ*** [masc. noun: עֹמֶד <5977>; from STAND (verb) <5975>] ► **This word refers to a position, also to a standing place.** It indicates an appointed position or function that a person is to fill (2 Chr. 30:16; 34:31; Neh. 8:7). It means simply where one stands (Dan. 8:18; 10:11), possibly in context meaning to stand upright in one's place. In Daniel 8:17, it functions as a participle with a suffix meaning (where) one was standing; in Daniel 11:1 it means I stood, I arose. Other refs.: 2 Chr. 35:10; Neh. 9:3; 13:11. ¶
– 4 Gen. 42:21; etc. ➔ COURTYARD <1508> 5 Josh. 4:3, 9 ➔ GARRISON <4673> 6 2 Chr. 35:15 ➔ ATTENDANCE <4612> 7 Ps. 69:25 ➔ CAMP <2918> 8 Hab. 3:11 ➔ HABITATION <2073>.

PLACE (CERTAIN, SUCH A) – 1 Sam. 21:2; 2 Kgs. 6:8 ➔ CERTAIN ONE <6423>.

PLACE (HIGHER, OPENED, EXPOSED) – ***ṣᵉḥiyḥiy*** [adj.: צְחִיחִי <6708>; from BARE (noun) <6706>] ► **This word indicates an exposed location. It refers to something lying open, vulnerable to the elements or to danger.** In context it refers to an exposed wall or an area where the wall is missing or broken down (Neh. 4:13). ¶

PLACE (SET IN, PUT IN) – Dan. 7:9 ➔ THROW <7412>.

PLACE (verb) – 1 Gen. 50:26 ➔ PUT <3455> 2 Ezra 6:5 ➔ BRING DOWN <5182> 3 Ps. 21:5 ➔ LIKE (BE, BECOME) <7737> b.

PLACED (BE) – Dan. 7:9 ➔ THROW <7412>.

PLACENTA – Deut. 28:57 ➔ AFTERBIRTH <7988> a.

PLACES FOR FIRE – Ezek. 46:23 ➔ HEARTHS <4018>.

PLAGUE (noun) – 1 ***deḇer*** [masc. noun: דֶּבֶר <1698>; from SPEAK <1696> (in the sense of destroying)] ► **This word means an epidemic disease; it is also translated pestilence. This plague is a dreaded disease similar to the bubonic plague in the Middle Ages.** It was likely carried by rat fleas and produced tumors on the infected person. First Samuel 5, 6 describes the plague on the Philistines as a punishment from God. The word is also used as the most dreaded threat of the Lord against His people (Lev. 26:25; Num. 14:12). The prophets use this word frequently to predict coming judgment and destruction as in the common phrase, sword, famine, and plague (Jer. 21:9; 38:2; Ezek. 6:11, NIV). *
2 ***maggēpāh*** [fem. noun: מַגֵּפָה <4046>; from SMITE <5062>] ► **This word is used of the plagues and blows God rained on Egypt.** It is used especially of the seventh to the tenth plagues (Ex. 9:14); as well as other plagues brought by God on His own people (Ps. 106:29, 30). It is also used of deadly pestilences (Num. 14:37; 1 Sam. 6:4; 2 Sam. 24:21); or slaughter in war (1 Sam. 4:17; 2 Sam. 17:9; 18:7). In the final days and judgments of God, it is used of horrible calamities coming on people (Zech. 14:12, 15, 18). *
3 ***negep̱*** [masc. noun: נֶגֶף <5063>; from SMITE <5062>] ► **This word comes from the verb *nāgap̱*, meaning to strike or to smite, and described the effect of being struck or smitten.** It usually described a plague that God sent on a disobedient people (Ex. 12:13; 30:12; Num. 8:19; 16:46, 47; Josh. 22:17). In one instance, it described the stone of stumbling (Is. 8:14). ¶
– 4 Gen. 12:17; Ex. 11:1; Leviticus 13–14; 1 Kgs. 8:37, 38 ➔ SORE (noun) <5061> 5 Deut. 32:24 ➔ FLASH (noun) <7565>.

PLAGUE (verb) – 1 Gen. 12:17; Ps. 73:5 ➔ TOUCH <5060> 2 Job 16:3 ➔ GRIEVOUS <4834>.

PLAIN (adj.) – Prov. 8:9 ➔ RIGHT <5228>.

PLAIN (noun) – 1 ***'āḇēl*** [fem. noun: אָבֵל <58>; from an unused root (meaning to be grassy)] ▶ **This word means a flat land or a meadow.** Ref.: Judg. 11:33. But it may be part of the name of a city (NASB, NKJV, ESV, NIV): Abel-keramim. ¶
2 ***biq'āh*** [Aramaic fem. noun: בִּקְעָה <1236>; corresponding to <1237> below] ▶ **This word is used to describe the location of the plain of Dura where Nebuchadnezzar set a huge obelisk gilded with gold.** Ref.: Dan. 3:1. ¶
3 ***biq'āh*** [fem. noun: בִּקְעָה <1237>; from DIVIDE <1234>] ▶ **This word describes a valley flat land, one of the most well known being the plain in the land of Shinar where the Tower of Babel was erected.** Ref.: Gen. 11:2. These areas were created by the will of God (Ps. 104:8). It is used literally and figuratively by the prophet Amos to describe the Valley of Aven, literally, the Valley of Wickedness (Amos 1:5). The plain or Valley of Megiddo, a huge sprawling plain, is the traditional place where the Battle of Armageddon (Har Megiddo) will take place (Rev. 16:12–16; 19:11–21). *
– 4 Gen. 13:10–12; 19:17, 25, 28, 29 ➔ ROUND (SOMETHING) <3603> 5 2 Sam. 15:28; 17:16 ➔ FORD <5679>.

PLAINLY – 1 Ezra 4:18 ➔ CLEAR (MAKE) <6568> 2 Is. 32:4 ➔ DAZZLING <6703>.

PLAITED – 1 Kgs. 7:29 ➔ DESCENT <4174>.

PLAN (noun) – 1 ***zimmāh*** [fem. noun: זִמָּה <2154>; from CONSIDER <2161>] ▶ **This word means purpose, counsel, wickedness, lewdness, sin. It refers to the thoughts and purposes of the mind which give rise to one's actions.** Yet the word rarely pertains to good intentions (Job 17:11). It is used in reference to the evil plotting of the wicked (Is. 32:7); the thoughts of foolish people (Prov. 24:9); and mischievous motivations (Ps. 119:150). Moreover, it relates to sexual sins that spring from lustful intentions, such as incest (Lev. 18:17); prostitution (Lev. 19:29); adultery (Job 31:11); and rape (Judg. 20:6). Figuratively, the word represents the wickedness of the people of Israel in their idolatry, calling to mind the connection with adultery (Jer. 13:27; Ezek. 16:27). *
2 ***ḥēpeś*** [masc. noun: חֵפֶשׂ <2665>; from SEARCH FOR <2664>] ▶ **In context, preceding a participle of the same basic meaning, this word means a plot or a plan that has been thought through thoroughly.** Ref.: Ps. 64:6. The two words together (search for, plan) are translated diligent search, perfect plan, shrewd scheme, well-conceived plot. ¶
3 ***m^ezimmāh*** [fem. noun: מְזִמָּה <4209>; from CONSIDER <2161>] ▶ **This word means a project, a thought. Most often the term denotes the evil plans, schemes, or plots humanity devises that are contrary to God's righteous decrees.** The Lord declared to Jeremiah that in carrying out their evil, idolatrous plans, His people forfeited their right to enter His house (i.e., the Temple, Jer. 11:15). The psalmist prayed that the wicked might be ensnared by the very schemes they had planned to unleash on the poor (Ps. 10:2). The cunning plans that God's enemies intend to execute against Him never succeed (Ps. 21:11; cf. Ps. 37:7). Moreover, those who plot evil are condemned and hated by Him (Prov. 12:2; 14:17). Often, the wicked are so blinded by pride that their only thought about God is that He doesn't exist (Ps. 10:4). Another significant use of this word occurs when it describes an intention of God and so conveys the idea of purpose or plan. After the Lord confronted Job in the whirlwind, Job was deeply humbled and acknowledged that no purpose of the Lord's can be thwarted (Job 42:2). The Lord's anger so burned on account of the false prophets of Jeremiah's day that it would not be turned back until He had executed and accomplished the purpose of His heart against them (Jer. 23:20; cf. Jer. 30:24). The Lord's purpose for Babylon was to utterly destroy it for all the evil they had committed against Jerusalem and the Temple (Jer. 51:11). In Proverbs, the

word often conveys the sense of prudence, discretion, and wisdom. In his prologue to the book of Proverbs, Solomon expressed that one reason he was writing the work was to impart discretion to young men (Prov. 1:4; cf. Prov. 5:2). Solomon urged them to hold on to wisdom and not let it out of their sight once they acquired it (Prov. 3:21). Wisdom and prudence go hand in hand (Prov. 8:12). This noun derives from the verb *zāmam* (CONSIDER <2161>). Other refs.: Job 21:27; Ps. 139:20; Prov. 2:11; 24:8. ¶
4 **'*êṣāh*** [fem. noun: עֵצָה <6098>; from COUNSEL (verb) <3289>] ▶ **This word also means advice.** It sometimes may suggest the idea of a plot (Neh. 4:15; Prov. 21:30); of a judgment or decision (Judg. 20:7; 2 Sam. 16:20; Ezra 10:3, 8). The term occurs in a positive sense in association with wisdom and understanding (Job 12:13; Prov. 8:14; 12:15). Thus, the meaning of advice came from the sages of Israel and the astrologers of Babylon who were viewed as wise in their communities (Is. 47:13; Jer. 18:18). Kings and would-be kings sought out advice but did not always have the discernment to choose the good (2 Sam. 17:7, 14, 23; 1 Kgs. 12:8, 13, 14). This term is used quite often as a possession of God and the promised Messiah (Prov. 19:21; Is. 5:19; 11:2; Jer. 32:19). *
5 ***tabniyṯ*** [fem. noun: תַּבְנִית <8403>; from BUILD <1129>] ▶ **This word means a pattern, a form. This noun comes from the verb *bānāh*, meaning to build, and refers to the plans of a building or an object.** For example such as the pattern of the Tabernacle and its contents (Ex. 25:9, 40); an altar (Josh. 22:28; 2 Kgs. 16:10); and the Temple and its contents (1 Chr. 28:11, 12, 18, 19). However, in other contexts, it refers to an image that was patterned after something else, such as a graven image of a god (Deut. 4:16–18: likeness); the calf at Horeb (Ps. 106:20); pillars (Ps. 144:12); or a person (Is. 44:13). In a few contexts, it refers to something in the form of an animal (Ezek. 8:10); or a hand (Ezek. 8:3; 10:8). Synonyms for this word are *temûnāh* (<8544>), meaning likeness or form, and *demûṯ* (<1823>), meaning likeness. ¶

– 6 Ps. 140:8 ➔ DEVICE <2162> 7 Ezek. 43:11 ➔ PERFECTION <8508> 8 Hos. 11:6 ➔ COUNSEL (noun) <4156>.

PLAN (DEVISE A) – Is. 8:10 ➔ COUNSEL (TAKE) <5779>.

PLAN (verb) – 1 ***ma'ᵃrāḵ*** [masc. noun: מַעֲרָךְ <4633>; from VALUE (verb) <6186> (in the sense of to set in order)] ▶ **This word refers to the aspirations and considerations that come from the heart of man according to biblical anthropology.** Ref.: Prov. 16:1; also translated preparation. ¶
2 ***'ᵃšiṯ, 'ᵃšiyṯ*** [Aramaic verb: עֲשִׁת, עֲשִׁית <6246>; corresponding to CONCERNED (BE) <6245>] ▶ **This word indicates consideration given to doing something, an intention to do something; it is also translated to think, to give thought.** Ref.: Dan. 6:3. ¶
– 3 2 Kgs. 19:25 ➔ FORM (verb) <3335>.

PLANE – 1 ***maqṣu'āh*** [fem. noun: מַקְצֻעָה <4741>; from SCRAPE <7106>] ▶ **This word means a chisel, a planing tool.** It was an instrument used to size and smooth wood, to shape it (Is. 44:13); a knife or chisel tool. ¶
– 2 Is. 41:19; 60:13 ➔ PINE <8410>.

PLANE TREE – ***'armôn*** [masc. noun: עַרְמוֹן <6196>; prob. from CRAFTY (BE) <6191> (in the sense of something smooth and that sheds, e.g., in the case of the bark of a tree)] ▶ **This word is generally considered to indicate the tree species platanus orientalis, a tree that is great and lofty, but less imposing than a cedar in Lebanon; it is also translated chestnut tree.** It refers to a tree from the plane tree family, a broad-leafed tree with maple-like leaves (Gen. 30:37) and large branches (Ezek. 31:8). ¶

PLANET – 2 Kgs. 23:5 ➔ CONSTELLATION <4208>.

PLANK – 1 Kgs. 6:9 ➔ RANK <7713> b.

PLANNING – Eccl. 9:10 ➔ SCHEME (noun) <2808>.

PLANT (noun) – 1 ***neṭa'*** [masc. noun: נֶטַע <5194>; from PLANT (verb) <5193>] ▶ **This word refers to a small tree, a shrub, or an herb.** It refers to a healthy well-watered plant that puts forth young shoots, green growth (Job 14:9; Is. 17:10, 11). It is used to describe the people of Judah as God's plants which He cares for as a gardener (Is. 5:7). The word is a proper noun in 1 Chronicles 4:23 (Netaim). ¶
2 ***nāṭiya'*** [masc. noun: נָטִיעַ <5195>; from PLANT (verb) <5193>] ▶ **This word refers to a small tree, a shrub, or an herb.** It is used figuratively to represent strong young plants (Ps. 144:12). ¶
3 ***qiyqāy>ôn*** [masc. noun: קִיקָיוֹן <7021>; perhaps from VOMIT <7006>] ▶ **This word refers to a shady, fast growing organism with leaves that was vulnerable to worms; it also means a vine, a gourd.** It refers to a fast-growing plant, a castor-oil plant capable of providing shade (Jon. 4:6, 7, 9, 10). It, like the fish and the worm, were all especially prepared by the Lord, according to the author. ¶
4 ***šᵉṯil, šāṯiyl*** [masc. noun: שְׁתִל, שָׁתִיל <8363>; from PLANT (verb) <8362>] ▶ **This word refers to a shoot. It figuratively describes children as plants in a house blessed by God.** Ref.: Ps. 128:3. ¶
– 5 Gen. 2:5 ➔ BUSH <7880>.

PLANT (CHOICE, PRINCIPAL) – ***śārōq*** [masc. noun: שָׂרֹק <8291>; pass. part. from the same as VINE (CHOICE) <8321>] ▶ **This word indicates a choice vine, a principal plant; it is also translated choice cluster, branch, choicest vine.** It refers to the best-producing sections of a vineyard, whether they have choice vines or the best plants (Is. 16:8). ¶

PLANT (TENDER, YOUNG) – Is. 53:2 ➔ INFANT <3126>.

PLANT (verb) – 1 ***nāṭa'*** [verb: נָטַע <5193>; a prim. root] ▶ **This word means to start, to establish, to found something.** A garden (Gen. 2:8); a vineyard (Gen. 9:20); a tree or vine (Num. 24:6); vineyards, orchards (Josh. 24:13). It is used of God's planting His people Israel (Ex. 15:17); and of Jeremiah's "planting" nations by his prophetic words (Jer. 1:10; 2:21; 12:2; cf. 2 Sam. 7:10). It has the sense of to create or to set in order, to establish the heavens by God (Is. 51:16); or of His placement of the ear in the human body (Ps. 94:9). It describes fasteners, nails being fixed, driven in (Eccl. 12:11). *
2 ***šāṯal*** [verb: שָׁתַל <8362>; a prim. root] ▶ **This word means to plant, to put a seed or seedling in the ground and cultivate it so it may grow; to transplant (e.g., a cropped tree branch).** Ref.: Ps. 1:3. It is used figuratively of a person planted in the Temple of the Lord (Jer. 17:8); and of nations or peoples (Ezek. 17:8, 10, 22, 23); especially Israel (Ezek. 19:10, 13; Hos. 9:13). Other ref.: Ps. 92:13. ¶

PLANTED (BE) – Ezek. 17:7; 31:4 ➔ PLANTING <4302>.

PLANTING – 1 ***maṭṭā'*** [masc. noun: מַטָּע <4302>; from PLANT (verb) <5193>] ▶ **This word means a place of establishing, an act of planting (setting in the ground for growth).** It indicates a place and act of planting something (Ezek. 17:7; 31:4; Mic. 1:6). It refers to a planting by the Lord in Zion of His people, His community (Is. 60:21; 61:3; Ezek. 34:29). ¶
– 2 Lev. 11:37 ➔ SOWING <2221>.

PLANTS – 1 ***šelaḥ*** [masc. noun: שֶׁלַח <7973>; from SEND FORTH, SEND AWAY <7971>] ▶ **This word refers to what is put forth, fresh green sprouts, shoots; it also means shoots, tendrils.** It is used in an amorous expression referring to the beloved as a fertile garden (Song 4:13). For another meaning of the Hebrew word, see WEAPON <7973>. ¶
– 2 Gen. 3:18; Ex. 9:22; etc. ➔ GRASS <6212> 3 Is. 19:7 ➔ BULRUSHES <6169> 4 Jer. 48:32 ➔ BRANCHES <5189>.

PLASTER (noun) – 1 ***giyr*** [Aramaic masc. noun: גִּיר <1528>; corresponding to CHALK <1615>] ▶ **This Aramaic word designates the external smooth covering of the wall**

on which the fingers of a man's hand wrote a puzzling riddle. Ref.: Dan. 5:5. ¶
[2] ***śiyḏ*** [masc. noun: שִׂיד <7875>; from PLASTER (verb) <7874>] ► **This word refers to a white substance obtained from heating limestone and grinding it; it is also translated lime.** It can then be used to make mortar and cement or to coat something (Deut. 27:2, 4). Bones could be burned to lime (Is. 33:12); completely consumed (Amos 2:1; NIV: ashes) and used to neutralize acidic soils. ¶
– [3] Ezek. 13:12 ➔ COATING <2915>.

PLASTER (verb) – [1] ***śiyḏ*** [verb: שִׂיד <7874>; a prim. root prob. meaning to boil up (comp. WASTE, LAY WASTE <7736>); used only as denom. from PLASTER (noun) <7875>] ► **This verb refers to whitewashing or putting a white coating of lime on something to serve as a writing surface; it is also translated to coat (with lime), to whitewash.** Refs.: Deut. 27:2, 4. ¶
– [2] Lev. 14:42; Ezek. 13:10–12, 15; 22:28 ➔ OVERLAY <2902> a.

PLATE – Ex. 28:36 ➔ FLOWER <6728> b.

PLATFORM – 2 Chr. 6:13 ➔ BASIN <3595>.

PLATTER – Ezra 1:9 ➔ BASIN <105>.

PLAY – [1] ***nāgan*** [verb: נָגַן <5059>; a prim. root] ► **This word refers to performing on stringed instruments of various kinds, often harps.** Refs.: 1 Sam. 16:16–18, 23; 18:10; Ps. 33:3; etc. It refers to the person playing the harp, the minstrel or musician (2 Kgs. 3:15; Ps. 68:25). The prophet Ezekiel was mockingly compared to a minstrel (Ezek. 33:32). *
– [2] Ex. 32:6 ➔ LAUGH <6711>.

PLEA (MAKE) – Dan. 6:11 ➔ MERCY (SHOW, ASK FOR) <2604>.

PLEAD – Gen. 25:21; etc. ➔ PRAY <6279>.

PLEAD, PLEAD URGENTLY – Prov. 6:3 ➔ BOLD (BE, MAKE) <7292>.

PLEASANT – [1] ***ḥemeḏ*** [masc. noun: חֶמֶד <2531>; from DESIRE (verb) <2530>] ► **This word means handsome, beautiful. It indicates what is desirable and appreciated, charming.** It is used to describe a pleasant or fruitful vineyard (Is. 27:2; 32:12; Amos 5:11) or handsome, desirable young men (Ezek. 23:6, 12, 23). ¶
[2] ***nā'iym*** [adj.: נָעִים <5273>; from <5276> below] ►
a. This word is used of persons who are pleasing, a joy to be around. They display attitudes that please others, such as David and Jonathan (2 Sam. 1:23; also translated lovely, admired). It refers to those who are delightful to enjoy (Job 36:11: pleasures, pleasantness, contentment; Ps. 16:11: pleasures); a life that has experienced good things and joy (Ps. 16:6). A famous proverb illustrates the meaning of the word: brothers living together in peace, getting along with each other (Ps. 133:1). The Lord's name is called pleasant (NASB: lovely) (Ps. 135:3). Wise words and wisdom generate pleasantness (Prov. 22:18; NIV: pleasing). It describes a bridegroom as delightful, pleasing (Song 1:16; also translated delightful, charming). Other refs.: Ps. 147:1; Prov. 23:8; 24:4. ¶
b. An adjective meaning sweet, sweet-sounding. It is used to describe David, the singer and writer of psalms, as the sweet, pleasant, pleasing psalmist of Israel (2 Sam. 23:1). It indicates pleasant-sounding music (Ps. 81:2: sweet, melodious), sweet to soul and mind. ¶
[3] ***nā'êm*** [verb: נָעֵם <5276>; a prim. root] ► **This word refers to what is pleasing, comfortable, delightful to enjoy.** It refers to the land of Canaan (Gen. 49:15); to a person (2 Sam. 1:26; NIV: dear); to spoken words (Ps. 141:6; also translated sweet, well spoken); to knowledge and wisdom (Prov. 2:10). It is used of an improper experience of pleasantness from doing what is not right (Prov. 9:17; also translated delicious). More properly, it refers to the pleasantness, delightfulness of a bride (Song 7:6). It depicts a nation, for even a nation has a national splendor and character (Ezek. 32:19: beauty). Other ref.: Prov. 24:25 (delight). ¶

[4] ***na***

[4] ***naʿᵃmān*** [masc. abstract noun: נַעֲמָן <5282>; from <5276> above] ▶ **This word describes pretty plants, grown for pleasure; it is also translated delightful, finest.** But it was in honor of a pagan god, exacerbating Israel's harlotry and idolatry (Is. 17:10). ¶
– [5] Prov. 3:17; 15:26; 16:24 ➔ BEAUTY <5278> [6] Is. 13:22 ➔ DELIGHT (noun) <6027> [7] Is. 30:10 ➔ SMOOTH <2513> [8] Jer. 31:20 ➔ DELIGHT (noun) <8191> [9] Hos. 9:6 ➔ PRECIOUS <4261> [10] Mic. 2:9 ➔ DELIGHT (noun) <8588>.

PLEASANT (BE) – Mal. 3:4 ➔ PLEASING (BE) <6149>.

PLEASANT THING – ***maḥᵃmōḏ*** [masc. noun: מַחְמֹד <4262>; from DESIRE (verb) <2530>] ▶ **This word designates a precious thing, a treasure.** It is used to designate things held in great esteem and considered valuable, not all of which are material (Lam. 1:7), although that is a major part of those things (Lam. 1:11). ¶

PLEASANTNESS – [1] Job 36:11 ➔ PLEASANT <5273> a. [2] Prov. 3:17 ➔ BEAUTY <5278> [3] Prov. 27:9 ➔ SWEETNESS <4986>.

PLEASE – [1] ***nā'*** [part.: נָא <4994>; a prim. particle of incitement and entreaty, which may usually be rendered: "I pray," "now," or "then"] ▶ **The most common use of this word is similar to the antiquated use of pray as in pray tell. Since it was frequently used as a polite form of asking for something, it was often left untranslated in many English versions of the Bible.** Abraham used this word when he asked Sarah to say she was his sister (Gen. 12:13); Moses used the word when he asked the people to listen to him (Num. 20:10). It was often used to ask permission (Num. 20:17). *
– [2] 1 Sam. 23:20; Hos. 10:10 ➔ DESIRE (noun) <185> [3] Ezra 5:17 ➔ it pleases the king ➔ lit.: *it seems* good ➔ FINE (adj.) <2869> [4] Dan. 6:1 ➔ GOOD (BE, SEEM, THINK) <8232> [5] Hos. 9:4 ➔ PLEASING (BE) <6149>.

PLEASED (BE) – [1] 1 Kgs. 9:1 ➔ DELIGHT (verb) <2654> [2] Ps. 5:4 ➔ PLEASURE IN (HAVE, TAKE) <2655> [3] Dan. 6:23 ➔ GLAD (BE) <2868>.

PLEASING – [1] ***niyḥôaḥ, niyḥōaḥ*** [masc. noun: נִיחוֹחַ, נִיחֹחַ <5207>; from REST (verb) <5117> (in the sense of indicating something restful, pleasant)] ▶ **This word is used of an odor that is acceptable to God, soothing.** Ref.: Gen. 8:21. It is used as an adjective often to describe a pleasing odor, aroma, a feature of an acceptable sacrifice to God (Ex. 29:18, 25, 41; NKJV: sweet). It is the pleasing aroma created in an offering by fire to the Lord (Lev. 1:9, 13, 17, etc.). It was offered by Israel even to idols (Ezek. 6:13; 16:19; 20:28). It describes Israel as a people approved of the Lord (Ezek. 20:41). *
[2] ***niyḥôaḥ, niyḥōaḥ*** [Aramaic masc. noun: נִיחוֹחַ, נִיחֹחַ <5208>; corresponding to <5207> above] ▶ **This word indicates something fragrant, soothing.** It is used to describe acceptable, pleasant-smelling sacrifices to the Lord (Ezra 6:10); and to a fragrant incense offered in honor of Daniel (Dan. 2:46; KJV: sweet odors). ¶
– [3] Prov. 22:18 ➔ PLEASANT <5273> a. [4] Song 7:6 ➔ PLEASANT <5276>.

PLEASING (BE) – [1] ***ʿāraḇ*** [verb: עָרַב <6149>; a prim. root, identical to PLEDGE (BE A) <6148> through the idea of close association] ▶ **This word asserts that something is acceptable, desired by someone, satisfying; it is also translated to be sweet.** It was the case for David's meditation or contemplation (Ps. 104:34); sleep that is satisfying (Prov. 3:24); attaining one's goals (Prov. 13:19). It means to fit one's desires or tastes (Jer. 6:20). It is used of the pleasure Israel derived from her prostitutions (Ezek. 16:37: to take pleasure). Pleasing offerings to God were given by those with pure hearts toward Him (Mal. 3:4; also translated to be pleasant, to be acceptable). Other refs.: Jer. 31:26; Hos. 9:4 (to please). ¶
– [2] Dan. 4:27 ➔ GOOD (BE, SEEM, THINK) <8232>.

PLEASURE – [1] ***rāṣôn, raṣōn*** [verb: רָצוֹן, רָצֹן <7522>; from PLEASURE (TAKE) <7521>] ► **This word means delight, desire, will, favor, acceptance. This term is ascribed both to human agents and to God.** For humans, the word often described what the heart was set on having or doing, whether for good or evil (Gen. 49:6; 2 Chr. 15:15; Neh. 9:24, 37; Esther 1:8; Ps. 145:16, 19; Dan. 8:4; 11:3). When attributed to God, the term expresses the divine goodwill which He extends to humanity as He sees fit (Deut. 33:16, 23; Ps. 5:12; 69:13; 106:4; Prov. 12:2; 18:22; Is. 49:8; 60:10; 61:2). In passages pertaining to the offering of sacrifices, offerings, or fasting in worship, the word designates the favorable reception of the worshipers (and thus their worship) by the Lord (Ex. 28:38; Lev. 1:3; 19:5; 22:19–21, 29; 23:11; Is. 56:7; 58:5; 60:7; Jer. 6:20). On a few occasions, the word denotes anything that is pleasing to God (i.e., His will [lit., His pleasure]; Ps. 40:8; 103:21; 143:10). This noun is derived from the verb *rāṣāh* (<7521>), to take pleasure. *
– [2] Gen. 18:12 ➔ DELIGHT (noun) <5730> b. [3] Ezra 5:17 ➔ DECISION <7470> [4] Ps. 36:8 ➔ DELIGHT (noun) <5730> a. [5] Eccl. 2:8 ➔ DELIGHT (noun) <8588> [6] Is. 21:4 ➔ DESIRE (noun) <2837>.

PLEASURE (BE THE) – Dan. 4:2 ➔ GOOD (BE, SEEM, THINK) <8232>.

PLEASURE (LOVER OF) – Is. 47:8 ➔ PLEASURES (GIVEN TO, LOVER OF) <5719>.

PLEASURE (TAKE) – [1] ***rāṣāh*** [verb: רָצָה <7521>; a prim. root] ► **This word means to delight, to treat favorably, to favor, to accept, to pay off, to pay for, to make up for.** Both humans (cf. Gen. 33:10; Deut. 33:24; 1 Chr. 29:3; Ps. 50:18; Prov. 3:12) and the Lord can be found as the subjects (1 Chr. 28:4; Ps. 51:16; 147:10; Mic. 6:7; Hag. 1:8). The Lord takes pleasure in uprightness (1 Chr. 29:17); in those who fear Him (Ps. 147:11); and in His Servant (Is. 42:1). The word is also utilized within texts concerning sacrifices, offerings, and worship, denoting that which was acceptable or unacceptable to the Lord (Lev. 1:4; 7:18; Ps. 119:108; Jer. 14:12; Hos. 8:13; Amos 5:22; Mal. 1:8). Less common is the employment of the term to communicate the satisfying of a debt (e.g., when the land must pay off or make up for the Sabbath years that it owes [Lev. 26:34; cf. Lev. 26:41, 43; 2 Chr. 36:21; Is. 40:2]). *
– [2] Ezek. 16:37 ➔ PLEASING (BE) <6149>.

PLEASURE IN (HAVE, TAKE) – ***ḥāpêṣ*** [adj.: חָפֵץ <2655>; from DELIGHT (verb) <2654>] ► **This word means to delight in, to be pleased with. It modifies both humans and God.** A good example is Psalm 35:27, which refers to people who delighted in the psalmist's vindication and the Lord who delighted in His servant's well-being. Psalm 5:4 notes that God does not take pleasure in wickedness. It can also mean simply to want or to desire, as in the men who wanted to be priests of the high places (1 Kgs. 13:33). See the related verb *ḥāpêṣ* [DELIGHT (verb) <2654>] and noun *ḥêpeṣ* [DESIRE (noun) <2656>]. Other refs.: 1 Kgs. 21:6; 1 Chr. 28:9; Neh. 1:11; Ps. 34:12; 40:14; 70:2; 111:2; Mal. 3:1. ¶

PLEASURES – Job 36:11; Ps. 16:11 ➔ PLEASANT <5273> a.

PLEASURES (GIVEN TO, LOVER OF) – ***'āḏiyn*** [adj.: עָדִין <5719>; from DELIGHT ONESELF <5727>] ► **This word means wanton, sensuous.** It refers figuratively to Babylon, a wanton, sensuous people, enamored with gold, silver, royal dominion, power, and banqueting (Is. 47:8; also translated sensual, lover of pleasure). ¶

PLEDGE (noun) – [1] ***ᵉsār, 'issār*** [masc. noun: אֱסָר, אִסָּר <632>; from BIND <631>] ► **This word is translated bond, binding obligation, agreement.** All references are in Numbers (Num. 30:2–5, 7, 10–14). It is used eleven times, most often with the verb *'āsar* (BIND <631>), to bind oneself with a vow of abstention or binding obligation (NKJV, agreement; NIV, pledge). ¶

2 ***ḥᵃḇōl, ḥᵃḇōlāh*** [masc. noun: חֲבֹל, חֲבֹלָה <2258>; from PLEDGE (TAKE AS A) <2254>] ▶ **This word is always used when speaking of those who do or do not return pledges, which were items taken to guarantee loans.** These items were usually people's cloaks, and the Law stated that they were to be returned to the owners before the sun set because they were the only covering they had (cf. Ex. 22:26, 27). Righteous persons returned the pledges (Ezek. 18:7) or did not even require them (Ezek. 18:16), whereas wicked persons kept the items used for the pledge (Ezek. 18:12). But if they repented and returned them, they would live instead of die for the evil they did (Ezek. 33:15). ¶

3 ***ᵃḇôṭ*** [masc. noun: עֲבוֹט <5667>; from LEND <5670>] ▶ **This word indicates something given, put forth to stand as collateral for something, especially for a loan.** Refs.: Deut. 24:10–13. ¶

4 ***'aḇṭiyṭ*** [masc. noun: עַבְטִיט <5671>; from LEND <5670> (in the sense of to take a pledge from)] ▶

a. This word refers to loans, i.e., to what is borrowed from a creditor, whether goods or money. Ref.: Hab. 2:6. It may have the sense of extortion (NIV) in context. ¶

b. A masculine noun meaning thick clay. Earlier translators rendered the word as thick clay, which does not fit the context as well (Hab. 2:6: KJV). ¶

5 ***ᵃrubbāh*** [fem. noun: עֲרֻבָּה <6161>; fem. pass. part. of PLEDGE (BE A) <6148> in the sense of a bargain or exchange] ▶ **Occurring only twice in the Hebrew Bible, this word implies a tangible sign of a current or soon-expected reality; it is also translated token, assurance.** It was used specifically in reference to an assurance of well-being brought from the battlefield (1 Sam. 17:18; also translated news); and a collateral exchanged at the making of a pledge (Prov. 17:18: surety, security, guarantor). ¶

6 ***'ērāḇôn*** [masc. noun: עֵרָבוֹן <6162>; from PLEDGE (BE A) <6148> (in the sense exchange)] ▶ **It is a deposit given as evidence and proof that something else will be done. When the act is accomplished, the pledge is returned.** Judah gave his seal and staff to Tamar, whom he believed was a temple prostitute, as a guarantee that he would return the next day so he might give her a young goat as payment for her services and then reacquire his seal and staff (Gen. 38:17, 18, 20). It is also probable that this word is what is meant in Job's reply to Eliphaz (see Job 17:3; KJV: surety). ¶

– 7 Lev. 6:2 ➔ SECURITY <8667>.

PLEDGE (BE A) – ***'āraḇ*** [verb: עָרַב <6148>; a prim. root] ▶ **This word means to exchange, to take as a guarantee, to give as a guarantee.** This word denotes the action of giving a pledge or a guarantee (Gen. 43:9); a pledge given in exchange for the delivery of material goods (2 Kgs. 18:23); the action of taking possession of exchanged material (Ezek. 27:9); and the mortgage of property (Neh. 5:3). By extension, it was used in reference to the scattering of the Jews among the nations (Ps. 106:35); and implied sharing or association at a meaningful level (Prov. 14:10; 20:19). In Jeremiah 30:21, it conveyed the idea of purposing or engaging to meet with the Lord. *

PLEDGE (TAKE AS A) – ***ḥāḇal, ḥōḇᵉliym*** [verb: חָבַל, חֹבְלִים <2254>; a prim. root] ▶ **This word means to take as guarantee; it also means to destroy. It is translated in a variety of ways.** Most commonly, it means taking a pledge for such things as a loan (Ex. 22:26; Deut. 24:6; Ezek. 18:16; Amos 2:8). The word is used in Job in reference to debts (Job 22:6; 24:3, 9). It also describes the destruction of the wicked (Prov. 13:13; Is. 32:7) or destruction of property (Is. 10:27; 13:5). This word can also mean to corrupt (Neh. 1:7; Job 17:1). Zechariah used it in a metaphor describing the union between Israel and Judah (Zech. 11:7, 14). *

PLEDGE (verb) – Ex. 22:16; Deut. 20:7; etc. ➔ BETROTH <781>.

PLEIADES – ***kiymāh*** [fem. proper noun: כִּימָה <3598>; from the same as NECKLACE

<3558>] ▶ **This word refers to a constellation of seven stars in the heavens.** It is referred to in three places: it is the creation of God (Job 9:9; Amos 5:8); it is beyond human power or ability to control the Pleiades (Job 38:31). ¶

PLENTEOUSNESS – Prov. 21:5 ➔ PROFIT (noun) <4195>.

PLENTY – [1] ***śāḇā'*** [masc. noun: שָׂבָע <7647>; from SATISFIED <7646>] ▶ **This word indicates an abundance, an overflow.** It refers to an exact amount of something, an overflowing, e.g., grain (Gen. 41:29–31, 34, 47, 53); wine (Prov. 3:10). It is used in context with a definite article to mean a full stomach (Eccl. 5:12). ¶
– [2] Job 20:22 ➔ SUFFICIENCY <5607> a. [3] Prov. 21:5 ➔ PROFIT (noun) <4195>.

PLIGHT – Job 9:23 ➔ TRIAL <4531>.

PLOT (noun) – [1] Ps. 31:20 ➔ CONSPIRACY <7407> a. [2] Ps. 64:2 ➔ THRONG (noun) <7285> [3] Ezek. 17:7, 10 ➔ BED <6170>.

PLOT (EVIL) – Ps. 140:8 ➔ DEVICE <2162>.

PLOT (WELL-CONCEIVED) – Ps. 64:6 ➔ PLAN (noun) <2665>.

PLOT (verb) – Gen. 37:18 ➔ DECEIVE <5230>.

PLOTTING – Hos. 7:6 ➔ AMBUSH <696>.

PLOW – [1] ***ḥāraš*** [verb: חָרַשׁ <2790>; a prim. root] ▶ **This word refers to cultivating, tilling the soil with animals; it also means to engrave.** Refs.: Deut. 22:10; 1 Kgs. 19:19. Hosea speaks metaphorically of Israel's "plowing wickedness" and receiving injustice as a reward (Hos. 10:13). It refers to devising or preparing evil against one's neighbor (1 Sam. 23:9; Prov. 3:29) or enemy. With the preposition ʿal, upon, it means to engrave (Jer. 17:1). Zion in judgment was plowed under as a field (Jer. 26:18; Mic. 3:12). The participial form of the verb indicates the person who does skilled work, a craftsman (*ḥōrêš*) (Gen. 4:22; 1 Kgs. 7:14). The Hebrew word also means to be deaf, silent; see SILENT (BE) <2790>. *
– [2] 1 Sam. 8:12 ➔ PLOWING <2758> [3] Job 39:10 ➔ HARROW <7702> [4] Ps. 141:7 ➔ CUT (verb) <6398>.

PLOWED – Hos. 10:4; 12:11: plowed field ➔ lit.: furrows of the field ➔ FURROW <8525>.

PLOWING – [1] ***ḥāriyš*** [masc. noun: חָרִישׁ <2758>; from PLOW <2790>] ▶ **This word means cultivating, tilling the soil with animals; tilling time; it is also translated to plow, to ear, earing, earing time, plowing season.** It refers to the tillage of the soil with a plow (1 Sam. 8:12) and the season or time of plowing the fields (Gen. 45:6; Ex. 34:21). ¶
– [2] Prov. 21:4 ➔ FALLOW GROUND <5215>.

PLOWMAN – [1] ***gûḇ*** [verb: גּוּב <1461>; a prim. root] ▶ **This word is used in a verb form indicating one who digs or plows the ground; it is also translated farmer, husbandman, one who works the field.** This job was filled by the poor of the land at the time Israel was sent to Babylon into exile (2 Kgs. 25:12). In general, it means one who works the ground. ¶
– [2] 2 Chr. 26:10; Is. 61:5; Jer. 14:4 ➔ FARMER <406>.

PLOWMAN (BE) – ***yāḡaḇ*** [verb: יָגַב <3009>; a prim. root] ▶ **This word is used in its participial form to refer to those who cared for the land and its produce in Israel; it is also translated to be husbandman, to work the fields, as farmer.** Ref.: 2 Kgs. 25:12. It was a low-class social position and included vinedressers (Jer. 52:16). ¶

PLOWSHARE – [1] ***'êṯ*** [masc. noun: אֵת <855>; of uncertain deriv.] ▶ **This word designates an iron farm implement.**

Refs.: 1 Sam. 13:20, 21. Plowshares would be beaten into swords in Joel's picture of the coming day of the Lord (Joel 3:10), but in the prophet Micah's vision, this process is reversed (Mic. 4:3). Other ref.: Is. 2:4. ¶

2 ***maḥ*ª*rešeṯ*** [fem. noun: מַחֲרֶשֶׁת <4282>; from PLOW (verb) <2790>] ► **This tool is used to break up tillable ground, to plow the ground.** Ref.: 1 Sam. 13:20; KJV, share. ¶

PLUCK – 1 ***qāṭap*** [verb: קָטַף <6998>; a prim. root] ► **This word means to break off, to pluck off, to cut off.** It indicates picking, removing ears of grain or small branches, etc. (Deut. 23:25; Job 30:4; Ezek. 17:4, 22). In the latter reference, it is used figuratively. In its passive sense, it means to be picked or cut off (Job 8:12). ¶
– 2 Deut. 28:63; Ps. 52:5 ➔ TEAR <5255> 3 Ezra 9:3; Neh. 13:25; Is. 50:6 ➔ PULL, PULL OUT <4803> 4 Ps. 80:12 ➔ PICK (verb) <717>.

PLUCK, PLUCK OFF – ***m*ᵉ*raṭ*** [Aramaic: מְרַט <4804>; corresponding to PULL, PULL OUT <4803>] ► **This word means to remove something, to tear off.** In context it is used of plucking off, pulling out wings (Dan. 7:4). ¶

PLUCK, PLUCK UP – Eccl. 3:2 ➔ HAMSTRING <6131> b.

PLUCKED – freshly plucked, plucked off: *ṭārāp* [adj.: טָרָף <2965>; from TEAR <2963>] ► **This word designates something as freshly picked, new.** It refers to a fresh olive leaf just plucked off (Gen. 8:11). And some prefer to read this word in Ezekiel 17:9 as a fresh sprouted leaf (see PREY <2964>). ¶

PLUMAGE – Job 39:13; Ezek. 17:3, 7 ➔ FEATHER <5133> a.

PLUMB – Zech. 4:10 ➔ TIN <913>.

PLUMB LINE – 1 ***ª*nāḵ** [masc. noun: אֲנָךְ <594>; prob. from an unused root meaning to be narrow] ► **This line is used to determine verticality or straightness; it was an absolute standard.** It was employed by the Lord through Amos to test His people (Amos 7:7, 8). ¶

2 ***mišqeleṯ, mišqōleṯ*** [fem. noun: מִשְׁקֶלֶת, מִשְׁקֹלֶת <4949>; from WEIGHT <4948> or LINTEL <4947>] ► **This word indicates a tool used to determine if something is level, horizontal; it is also translated plummet, level.** Righteousness was God's "level" to evaluate His people (Is. 28:17); the skewed plumb line of the house of Ahab was placed over a wicked Jerusalem to judge her (2 Kgs. 21:13). ¶

PLUMMET – Is. 28:17; 2 Kgs. 21:13 ➔ PLUMB LINE <4949>.

PLUNDER (noun) – 1 ***bag*** [masc. noun: בַּג <897>; a Persian word] ► **This word means spoil, booty.** It refers figuratively to Ammon being given to the nations as plunder or spoil (Ezek. 25:7). Most translators render *baz*, which is the suggested reading in the Hebrew text rather than *bag*, whose meaning is in doubt in this text. ¶

2 ***baz*** [masc. noun: בַּז <957>; from PLUNDER (verb) <962>] ► **This word means booty, prey, spoils; it describes the act of stealing or the objects taken in the process.** The Temple was despoiled, plundered (Ezek. 7:21; 23:46). Many things were taken as booty: various objects (Is. 10:6; 33:23; Ezek. 29:19) including human beings (Num. 14:3, 31; Jer. 2:14). Even the Lord's flock, Israel, became prey to evil shepherds as well as foreign enemies (Ezek. 34:8, 22). The word is part of a phrase in Isaiah 8:1 meaning, "Swift is the booty, speedy is the prey" (NASB; cf. NIV, "quick to the plunder, swift to the spoil"). *

3 ***bizzāh*** [fem. noun: בִּזָּה <961>; fem. of <957> above] ► **This word means to loot, to steal, to despoil. It is also translated spoil, plundering, pillage, prey. It refers to objects of plunder.** A city was looted for its objects worthy of plundering (2 Chr. 14:14; 25:13). It also refers to the activity of plunder itself (Ezra 9:7; Neh. 4:4; Dan. 11:33). It was significant that the Jews did not seize the spoil in the city of Susa (Esther

9:10, 15, 16). Other refs.: 2 Chr. 28:14; Dan. 11:24. ¶

4 ***pereq*** [masc. noun: פֶּרֶק <6563>; from BREAK OFF <6561>] ► **This word refers to the confiscation of goods by plundering people and to the property gained in this way; it is also translated robbery, pillage.** Ref.: Nah. 3:1. The Hebrew word also means a fork in the road; see CROSSROAD <6563>. ¶

5 ***šālāl*** [masc. noun: שָׁלָל <7998>; from PLUNDER (verb) <7997>] ► **This word refers to loot, spoils.** It refers to what is taken by force or violence usually in war (Gen. 49:27; Ex. 15:9; Num. 31:11; Ps. 68:12). Or it may be seized as an act of social and political aggression (Esther 3:13; 8:11). Taking plunder or spoil was an act of aggression by the wicked on the weak or righteous (Prov. 1:13). It has a positive sense of prosperity or gain in certain contexts (Prov. 31:11). The Lord will make the nations plunder for His people in Zion (Zech. 2:9; 14:1). *

– 6 Num. 31:11, 12, 26, 27, 32; Is. 49:24, 25 ➔ PREY <4455> 7 Is. 3:14 ➔ ROBBERY <1500>.

PLUNDER (verb) – 1 ***bāzaz*** [verb: בָּזַז <962>; a prim. root] ► **This word means to loot, to spoil, to rob.** It describes this destructive activity taken against cities or places (Gen. 34:27; 2 Kgs. 7:16), people and cattle (Num. 31:9; Is. 10:2; 11:14). Its passive uses are similar with the meaning of be plundered (Is. 24:3) or taken as spoil (Jer. 50:37). *

2 ***šā'as*** [verb: שָׁאַס <7601>; a prim. root] ► **This word means to plunder, to spoil.** It means to take the spoils or goods of oppression and war, to take violently, to seize the property or persons of another person or people, to abuse them for one's own enrichment (Jer. 30:16). ¶

3 ***šālāl*** [verb: שָׁלַל <7997>; a prim. root] ► **a. A verb meaning to despoil, to steal. It means to overcome someone or a group of persons and destroy their goods and take some of it for oneself.** It is used of God's robbing or despoiling the strong (Ps. 76:5). It was often an act of force and violence in war (Is. 10:6; Jer. 50:10; Ezek. 26:12; 29:19; 38:12; Hab. 2:8; Zech. 2:8). In its reflexive form, it means to turn oneself into prey, used of those who shun evil in a time when there is no justice (Is. 59:15). **b. This word means to pull or drain out.** It is used of extracting some grain from a larger bundle of grain (Ruth 2:16). *

4 ***šāsāh, šāśāh*** [verb: שָׁסָה, שָׂשָׂה <8154>; a prim. root] ► **This word means to loot, to rob; it is also translated to spoil. It is used only in the simple stem and in the participle form.** It can refer to the plundering of both land and objects (Judg. 2:14; 1 Sam. 14:48; Hos. 13:15). In almost every reference where this word is found, enemies were plundering the land and the people of Israel. God allowed this in judgment on the sins of the Israelites after they had been warned and refused to repent or as a warning to call them to repentance. The participle form of this verb refers to people who do the plundering (Is. 10:13; 42:22). Ultimately, God allowed any persons to be plunderers. But if they overstepped their boundaries, they too would be plundered as the punishment for their sins. *

5 ***šāsas*** [verb: שָׁסַס <8155>; a prim. root] ► **This word means to rob or to take possession of the property of others, usually in a time of war; it is also translated to spoil, to loot, to rifle, to ransack.** Refs.: Judg. 2:14; 1 Sam. 17:53; Ps. 89:41. In its passive sense, it refers to being plundered (Is. 13:16; Zech. 14:2). Israel was plundered because of her own sins (Ps. 89:41). ¶

– 6 Is. 11:14 ➔ LAY, PUT <4916> a.

PLUNDERED – 1 Job 12:17, 19 ➔ STRIPPED <7758> 2 Nah. 2:10 ➔ DESOLATE <4003>.

PLUNDERER – Judg. 2:14; etc. ➔ PLUNDER (verb) <8154>.

PLUNDERING – Ezra 9:7; Dan. 11:33; etc. ➔ PLUNDER (noun) <961>.

PLUNDERS (ONE WHO) – Ps. 137:3 ➔ TORMENTOR <8437>.

POINT – Jer. 17:1 ➔ NAIL <6856>.

POINT (AT THIS) – ***kāh*** [Aramaic adv.: כָּה <3542>; corresponding to THIS <3541>] ▶ **This word means thus, so, this point; it is also translated, hitherto.** But it is used one time only in the phrase *'aḏ-kāh*, which means "up to this point" or "at this point" (Dan. 7:28). ¶

POINT OUT – [1] Num. 34:7, 8 ➔ DRAW A LINE <8376> [2] Num. 34:10 ➔ MARK OUT <184>.

POINTED THINGS, MARKS – Job 41:30 ➔ DILIGENT <2742>.

POISED (HANG) – Job 37:16 ➔ BALANCING <4657>.

POISON (noun) – ***rō'š, rôš*** [masc. noun: רֹאשׁ, רוֹשׁ <7219>; apparently the same as HEAD (noun) <7218>] ▶ **This word refers to something that is a life-threatening substance; it also means bitterness, gall.** In context it refers to human hostility or bitterness (Deut. 29:18). It defines grapes as poisonous, grapes that represent pagan peoples (Deut. 32:32). It describes pagan wine as like the poison of cobras (Deut. 32:33). Job described the wicked person as one who partakes of the poison of cobras (Job 20:16). It refers to water that is poisoned (Jer. 8:14; 9:15; 23:15). In context it may have the sense of harshness, gall, bitterness (Lam. 3:5, 19). Justice and/or injustice is described as being poisonous, transformed into deadly corruption socially (Hos. 10:4; Amos 6:12). Other ref.: Psalm 69:21. ¶

POISON (verb) – Prov. 23:32 ➔ STING <6567>.

POISONOUS – Deut. 32:24 ➔ BITTER <4815>.

POKERETH-HAZZEBAIM – ***pōḵereṯ hașṣᵉḇāyiym*** [masc. proper noun: פֹּכֶרֶת הַצְּבָיִים <6380>; from the act. part. (of the same form as the first word) fem. of an unused root (meaning to entrap) and plur. of GLORY <6643> (in the sense of gazelle)]: trap of gazelles ▶ **Descendants of this servant of Solomon returned to Jerusalem with Zerubbabel.** Refs.: Ezra 2:57; Neh. 7:59. ¶

POLE – [1] ***môṭ*** [masc. noun: מוֹט <4132>; from REMOVED (BE) <4131>] ▶ **This word means a bar, that which shakes.** It refers to a pole or rod used for carrying things (Num. 13:23; also translated staff); or a carrying frame or structure (Num. 4:10, 12: bar, beam, frame). For Psalm 66:9 and Psalm 121:3 see REMOVED (BE) <4131>. It is used figuratively of a bar or yoke representing Assyria that confines Israel (Nah. 1:13). ¶ – [2] Ex. 25:14, 15 ➔ PART <905> [3] Num. 21:8, 9 ➔ BANNER <5251> [4] 2 Kgs. 6:2, 5 ➔ BEAM <6982> [5] 1 Chr. 15:15 ➔ YOKE <4133> [6] Is. 30:17 ➔ FLAG <8650>.

POLICY – Dan. 8:25 ➔ INTELLIGENCE <7922>.

POLISH – [1] ***māraq*** [verb: מָרַק <4838>; a prim. root] ▶ **This word describes a process of cleaning a bronze vessel.** Ref.: Lev. 6:28: to scour. It describes as well the process of beautifying it by polishing (buffing) (2 Chr. 4:16; also translated burnished, bright); any metal surface (Jer. 46:4; also translated to furbish). Figuratively, it refers to scouring or removing evil (Prov. 20:30). ¶ – [2] Ps. 144:12 ➔ CUT (verb) <2404> [3] Ezek. 21:9–11, 28 ➔ PULL, PULL OUT <4803>.

POLISHED – [1] ***'ešeṯ*** [masc. noun: עֶשֶׁת <6247>; from CONCERNED (BE) <6245>] ▶ **This word indicates a shining, a carving; it is also translated carved, bright.** It refers in context to the external appearance of the bridegroom's stomach as if it were made of carved ivory (Song 5:14). ¶ – [2] Ezra 8:27 ➔ SHINY <6668> [3] Dan. 10:6 ➔ BURNISHED (adj.) <7044>.

POLISHING – Lam. 4:7 ➔ COURTYARD <1508>.

POLL – Num. 1:2, 18, 20, 22; 3:47; 1 Chr. 23:3, 24 ➔ HEAD (noun) <1538>.

POLLUTE – [1] Num. 35:33; Ps. 106:38; Is. 24:5; Jer. 3:1, 2, 9; 23:11; Mic. 4:11 ➔ DEFILED (BE) <2610> [2] Ezra 2:62; Neh. 7:6; Mal. 1:7, 12; Lam. 4:14; Zeph. 3:14 ➔ DEFILE <1351>.

POLLUTED – Is. 64:6 ➔ FILTHY <5708>.

POLLUTION – Jer. 23:15 ➔ PROFANENESS <2613>.

POMEGRANATE – ***rimmôn, rimmōn*** [masc. noun: רִמּוֹן, רִמֹּן <7416>; from EXALTED <7426> a.] ▶ **This word refers to a round fruit, red in color, covered with a rind and containing many seeds. Its fleshy part is edible and juicy.** It was used often in Israel as a food but also as a decorative ornamental feature on priestly clothes, carved into wood, metal, etc. (Ex. 28:33, 34; 39:24–26; Num. 13:23; 1 Kgs. 7:18, 20, 42). It was a favorite food (Num. 20:5). It is used in an amorous description of a bride (Song 4:3, 13). Its abundance in the land of Israel depended on the Lord's blessing along with Israel's faithfulness (Hag. 2:19). *

POMMEL – 2 Chr. 4:12, 13 ➔ BOWL <1543>.

POND – ***ᵃgam*** [masc. noun: אֲגַם <98>; from an unused root (meaning to collect as water)] ▶ **This word refers to swampy or muddy water or to any type of small lake or pool of water.** Refs.: Ex. 7:19; 8:5; Ps. 107:35; Is. 14:23; 41:18. The pools in Exodus are an object of the plagues of blood and frogs. In Jeremiah 51:32, the abstract ending is added to the word, and it refers to a marsh or swamp; it is also translated reed. *

PONDER – [1] ***'āzan*** [verb: אָזַן <239>; a prim. root; rather identical with EAR (GIVE) <238> through the idea of scales as if two ears] ▶ **This word means to consider; it is also translated to give good heed, to weigh.** It describes the Preacher of Ecclesiastes thinking as he attempts to teach the people wisdom (Eccl. 12:9) and as he tries to find the best way to impart his instruction to the people. ¶
– [2] Prov. 4:26; 5:6, 21 ➔ WEIGH, WEIGH OUT <6424>.

POOL (noun) – [1] ***bᵉrêḵāh*** [fem. noun: בְּרֵכָה <1295>; from BLESS <1288>] ▶ **This word indicates a pond.** It refers to a small body of water in Jerusalem called the upper pool (2 Kgs. 18:17; Is. 36:2) and later a pool called the King's Pool (Neh. 2:14) and the famous Pool of Siloam (Neh. 3:15). It is used to describe Nineveh as a pool being drained of its resources in its destruction (Nah. 2:8). The cities of Hebron and Gibeon had small pools (2 Sam. 2:13; 4:12). The pools of Heshbon were known for their beauty and stillness (Song 7:4). *
[2] ***gêḇ*** [masc. noun: גֵּב <1356>; from PLOWMAN <1461> (in the sense of one who digs)] ▶ **This word means a ditch, a cistern; it is also translated pit, ditch, trench, cistern.** It refers figuratively to ditches (2 Kgs. 3:16) dug to receive a deluge of unexpected water predicted by Elisha. It also indicates cisterns (Jer. 14:3; KJV, pits). The Hebrew word also means a beam; see BEAM <1356>. Other ref.: 1 Kgs. 16:9. ¶
– [3] Ex. 7:19; 8:5; Ps. 107:35; Is. 41:18 ➔ POND <98>.

POOL (verb) – Ezek. 44:20 ➔ TRIM <3697>.

POOR – [1] ***'eḇyôn*** [adj.: אֶבְיוֹן <34>; from WILLING (BE) <14>, in the sense of want (especially in feeling)] ▶ **This word corresponds to the state of a person in want or need of material goods; it is also translated needy.** In Israel the poor were often subjected to oppression and abuse by the rich or those in power (Amos 2:6; 4:1; 5:12). Job, a righteous man, cared for these people as a father (Job 29:16; 30:25). However, the poor were not to be favored because they were poor in a case of justice (Ex. 23:6) nor were they to be taken advantage of. During the sabbatical seventh year, they were permitted to eat the produce of the fallow land. The Lord watched over these persons with special care (Job 5:15; Jer. 20:13). The Lord would deliver the poor in times of need (Ps. 9:18; 12:5; 40:17). They became—along with the widow, the orphan, and the oppressed—one of the disadvantaged groups in society for which God was especially concerned (Job 24:4, 14; Jer. 5:28). The oppressed or humble are sometimes equated with the poor (Is. 29:19). *

2 ***dal*** [adj.: דַּל <1800>; from BRING LOW <1809> a.] ▶ **This word is often used as a noun to designate needy and oppressed persons for whom the Lord has a special concern.** Ref.: Ex. 23:3. They are on the opposite social scale from the rich (Ex. 30:15; 1 Sam. 2:8; Prov. 10:15; 22:16) and their condition often separates them from even their friends (Prov. 19:4). The poor have no power and are weak, helpless (Job 34:28; Ps. 82:3; Prov. 22:22).

It is used to describe various things or persons that are poor, weak, thin, insignificant: cattle (Gen. 41:19); people (Lev. 14:21; 2 Sam. 13:4); a clan or family line (Judg. 6:15; 2 Sam. 3:1). It depicts poor, noninfluential persons who are the opposite of great, powerful, or influential ones (Jer. 5:4). *

3 ***dallāh*** [fem. noun: דַּלָּה <1803>; from DRAW <1802>] ▶ **This word refers to needy people in the land of Israel after the nation went into exile.** Refs.: 2 Kgs. 24:14; 25:12; Jer. 40:7; 52:15, 16. It indicates sickness which cuts a person's life (KJV, Is. 38:12). The Hebrew word denotes also hair, loom; see LOOM <1803>. ¶

4 ***miskên*** [adj.: מִסְכֵּן <4542>; possibly from FOOLISHNESS <5531>] ▶ **This word refers, in context, to a deprived young lad or a deprived man, both of whom were wise.** Refs.: Eccl. 4:13; 9:15, 16. ¶

5 ***'āniy*** [adj.: עָנִי <6041>; from AFFLICTED (BE) <6031>] ▶ **This word refers to those who are suffering, in a state of poverty, oppression, misery from various causes; it also means afflicted.** From being poor, needy (Ex. 22:25); unfortunate, in want (Deut. 24:15; 2 Sam. 22:28; Job 24:4). They cry out for help and for their needs (Ps. 9:12; 12:5; 37:14). Hope for deliverance is from the Lord (Ps. 69:29) who dispenses grace (Prov. 3:34; 14:21). They are constantly abused by rich and oppressive leaders (Is. 3:14; Amos 8:4; Hab. 3:14). God had commanded His people not to oppress the poor (Zech. 7:10); for their true King is humble Himself (Zech. 9:9). *

– 6 Num. 13:20 ➔ LEAN (adj.) <7330>
7 Ps. 10:8, 10, 14 ➔ HELPLESS <2489>
8 Dan. 4:27 ➔ OPPRESSED <6033>.

POOR (BE) – ***rûš*** [verb: רוּשׁ <7326>; a prim. root] ▶ **This word indicates a person who has few resources and little standing or influence in a society, such as David before he was king.** Ref.: 1 Sam. 18:23. Nathan used the concept of the poor man in a parable (2 Sam. 12:1, 3, 4). It describes a person in want (Ps. 34:10). This class of people was to be especially cared for (Ps. 82:3). A poor person in this world's goods may be, in reality, rich in God's eyes (Prov. 13:7). The subject of poverty and the poor person is stressed in wisdom proverbs (Prov. 13:8, 23; 14:20; 17:5; 18:23; Eccl. 4:14; 5:8). *

POOR (BECOME, BE) – ***mûḵ*** [verb: מוּךְ <4134>; a prim. root] ▶ **This word means to be, become impoverished; it describes the state of fellow Israelites who through various circumstances become needy, deprived.** Refs.: Lev. 25:25, 35, 39, 47; KJV: to wax poor. It has the sense of less valuable in certain contexts (Lev. 27:8). ¶

POPLAR – 1 ***liḇneh*** [masc. noun: לִבְנֶה <3839>; from WHITE (MAKE) <3835>] ▶ **This word refers to a tree which grows quickly (possibly whitish), or the wood from it.** It is used of rods or small poles of poplar used by Jacob for some obscure breeding process (Gen. 30:37); and to the poplar trees under which pagan sacrifices were carried out by Israel (Hos. 4:13). ¶

– 2 Is. 15:7; 44:4; Job 40:22; Ps. 137:2 ➔ WILLOW <6155>.

POPLAR TREE – See BALSAM TREE <1057>.

PORATHA – ***pôrāṯah*** [masc. proper noun: פּוֹרָתָה <6334>; of Persian origin] ▶ **One**

of the ten sons of Haman, the enemy of Mordecai and Esther. Ref.: Esther 9:8. ¶

PORCH – 1 ***misd^erôn*** [masc. noun: מִסְדְּרוֹן <4528>; from the same as ORDER <5468>] ▶ **This word could designate a vestibule; its meaning is uncertain.** In its context, it may refer to a latrine, a toilet, or, more generally, a vestibule where toilet facilities were located (Judg. 3:23). ¶
– 2 1 Kgs. 6:3; 1 Chr. 28:11; 2 Chr. 3:4; Ezek. 40:7–9; Joel 2:17; etc. ➔ VESTIBULE <197> 3 Ezek. 40:16, 21, 22; etc. ➔ VESTIBULE <361>.

PORCUPINE – ***qippôḏ, qippōḏ*** [masc. noun: קִפּוֹד, קִפֹּד <7090>; from ROLL UP <7088> a.] ▶
a. This word indicates a hedgehog, a small spiny animal that lives in the wild or among ruins. Refs.: Is. 14:23; 34:11; Zeph. 2:14. Here and in b., c. below, the exact meaning of these words is still being researched.
b. This word is taken by some translators as a reference to a short-eared owl. This translation fits the contextual references, as does the word hedgehog (Is. 14:23; 34:11; Zeph. 2:14).
c. This word refers to a bittern, a wading marsh bird. In some contexts, translators prefer this translation, referring to a long-legged, marsh loving wading bird (Is. 14:23; 34:11; Zeph. 2:14). ¶

PORPHYRY – ***bahaṭ*** [masc. noun: בַּהַט <923>; from an unused root (prob. meaning to glisten)] ▶ **This word refers to a precious or semiprecious stone; it is also translated alabaster, red (stone).** The garden floor of the king's palace in the citadel in Susa was made of porphyry (Esther 1:6). ¶

PORPOISE – See BADGER <8476>.

PORTER – 1 2 Kgs. 7:10, 11; etc. ➔ GATEKEEPER <7778> 2 Ezra 7:24 ➔ DOORKEEPER <8652>.

PORTICO – 1 1 Kgs. 6:3; 1 Chr. 28:11; 2 Chr. 3:4; Ezek. 40:7–9; Joel 2:17; etc. ➔ VESTIBULE <197> 2 Ezek. 40:16, 21, 22; etc. ➔ VESTIBULE <361>.

PORTION – 1 ***ḥêleq*** [masc. noun: חֵלֶק <2506>; from SHARE (verb) <2505>] ▶ **This word indicates a share, a piece, a part, a territory; it is used in many applications.** A part of booty or spoil (Gen. 14:24; Num. 31:36); of food (Lev. 6:17); a tract or portion of land (Josh. 19:9; Hos. 5:7; Mic. 2:4); of Israel as a possession of the Lord (Deut. 32:9). It is used metaphorically of a person's doing his or her part in something (Job 32:17); of one's association or part or sharing in another group or way of life (Ps. 50:18; Is. 57:6); or of the portion or share of fortune that the Lord gives to persons (Job 31:2). The portion or proper share for the wicked is punishment or calamity (Is. 17:14). *
2 ***ḥ^alāq*** [Aramaic masc. noun: חֲלָק <2508>; from a root corresponding to SHARE (verb) <2505>] ▶ **This word refers to one's share, possession.** It is used figuratively of ownership or political right or claim (Ezra 4:16). It takes on the meaning of sharing the nature and behavior of beasts of the field (Dan. 4:15, 23). ¶
3 ***mānāh*** [fem. noun: מָנָה <4490>; from COUNT <4487>] ▶ **This word indicates shares of something.** Sacrificial meat (1 Sam. 1:4, 5); of fine foods at festive times (Esther 9:19, 22); of officially appointed portions of food (Esther 2:9); of portions of food sent to others (Neh. 8:10, 12). It is used in a figurative sense of the Lord Himself as the portion of the psalmist's inheritance (Ps. 16:5). It also designates the judgment of the Lord on people as their portion (Jer. 13:25). *
4 ***mên*** [masc. noun: מֵן <4482>; from an unused root meaning to apportion] ▶ **This Hebrew word is understood by some to mean part; it is also translated share.** It is taken to mean a portion or lot by more recent translators in Psalm 68:23. In Psalm 45:8, it is taken to mean stringed instruments (see STRINGED INSTRUMENT <4482> and PORTION <4521>; KJV, "whereby"). ¶
5 ***m^enāṯ*** [fem. noun: מְנָת <4521>; from COUNT <4487>] ▶ **This word indicates a**

part or share of something. The king's share of something (2 Chr. 31:3); a share required by law (Neh. 12:44, 47). It can indicate a share of a drink (Ps. 11:6), but in this case, used figuratively, it indicates a portion of the "cup of the wicked." It can be equivalent to one's lot in life (Jer. 13:25). Other refs.: 2 Chr. 31:4; Neh. 13:10; Ps. 16:5; 63:10. ¶
– 6 2 Sam. 6:19; 1 Chr. 16:3 ➔ PIECE <829> 7 Neh. 11:23: certain portion ➔ COVENANT <548>.

PORTRAIT – Ezek. 8:10; 23:14 ➔ CARVE <2707>.

POSITION – Is. 22:19 ➔ ATTENDANCE <4612>.

POSSESS – ***ḥ**ᵃ**san*** [Aramaic verb: חֲסַן <2631>; corresponding to HOARDED (BE) <2630>] ▶ **This verb means to take possession of, to own.** It refers to the passing of the kingdom to the saints of the Most High, to their taking over its administration (Dan. 7:18; 22). ¶

POSSESSED – ***mimšāq*** [masc. noun: מִמְשָׁק <4476>; from the same as HEIR <4943>] ▶ **This word indicates characterized by.** It means to feature, to be permeated, or to be noted for something (Zeph. 2:9; also translated breeding, overrun). In context, it describes the destroyed, ruined locations of Moab and Ammon. ¶

POSSESSION – 1 ***ᵃḥuzzāh*** [fem. noun: אֲחֻזָּה <272>; fem. pass. part. from HOLD (TAKE) <270>] ▶ **This word literally means something seized.** It usually refers to the possession of land, especially of the Promised Land (Gen. 48:4; Deut. 32:49). Because the Promised Land is "an everlasting possession" (Gen. 17:8), this word often refers to land that is to pass down within families, never being permanently taken away (Lev. 25; Num. 27:4, 7, Ezek. 46:16–18). The Levites had God, instead of land, as their "possession" (Ezek. 44:28). *
2 ***yᵉrēšāh*** [fem. noun: יְרֵשָׁה <3424>; from HEIR (BE) <3423>] ▶ **This word means property. It refers to a nation and is used only once in the Hebrew Bible.** In Numbers 24:18, Edom and Seir would become the possession of someone else (i.e., they would be defeated). ¶
3 ***yᵉruššāh*** [fem. noun: יְרֻשָּׁה <3425>; from HEIR (BE) <3423>] ▶ **This word means inheritance. It refers to an inheritance given, to a possession taken by force, or both.** The word describes the land God gave to the Edomites, Moabites, and Ammonites (Deut. 2:5, 9, 19). The Edomites and Ammonites, however, seized land from other tribes (Deut. 2:12, 19). The Israelites, likewise, had to fight to gain their inheritance (Deut. 3:20; Josh. 12:6, 7). However, God later protected Israel's inheritance against the unjust claims of discontent Edomites, Moabites, and Ammonites (2 Chr. 20:11). The word is also used to refer to the possession of wives (Judg. 21:17) and land (Jer. 32:8), both of which still waited to be claimed (sinfully in the former passage). In Psalm 61:5, the word refers to God's presence as the inheritance (or heritage) of those who fear God. Other ref.: Josh. 1:15. ¶
4 ***môrāš*** [masc. noun: מוֹרָשׁ <4180>; from HEIR (BE) <3423>] ▶ **This word indicates an inheritance.** It indicates ownership of something as an inhabitant (Is. 14:23; Obad. 1:17) of the area. The Hebrew word also means desire, thought; see DESIRE (noun) <4180>. ¶
5 ***môrāšāh*** [fem. noun: מוֹרָשָׁה <4181>; fem. of <4180> above] ▶ **This word means and is also translated heritage, inheritance.** It is used to refer to God giving land to Israel as an inheritance (Ex. 6:8; Ezek. 11:15; 33:24), but it also refers to God giving the land to other nations to possess (Ezek. 25:10). In one instance, the Edomites took land as a possession for themselves (Ezek. 36:5). In its other instances, God gave the Law as a possession (Deut. 33:4); God delivered the people of Israel over to other nations for a possession (Ezek. 25:4; 36:3); and the people took the high places as possessions (Ezek. 36:2). ¶
6 ***naḥᵃlāh*** [fem. noun: נַחֲלָה <5159>; from POSSESSION (TAKE) <5157> (in its usual sense)] ▶ **This word means property,**

inheritance. It implied property that was given by means of a will or as a heritage. It denoted the land of Canaan given to Israel and distributed among the tribes (Num. 26:53–56; Ezek. 48:29); a portion or state of blessing assigned by God to His people (Is. 54:17), or any possession presented by a father (Num. 27:8, 9; Job 42:15). The Lord Himself was declared to be the portion and inheritance of the Levites who served Him (Num. 18:20). *
– [7] Gen. 23:18 ➔ PURCHASE (noun) <4736> [8] Gen. 34:10: to acquire, to get possessions ➔ HOLD (TAKE) <270> [9] Neh. 5:13 ➔ LABOR (noun) <3018> [10] Job 15:29 ➔ PERFECTION <4512> [11] Job 20:28 ➔ INCREASE (noun) <2981>.

POSSESSION (TAKE) – [1] ***nāḥal*** [verb: נָחַל <5157>; a prim. root] ► **This word means to receive, to take property as a permanent possession. The noun** *naḥ*^{a}*lāh* **(<5159>), which refers to a possession or inheritance, is derived from this verb.** It can refer to the actual taking of the Promised Land, whether it was the entire land of Canaan as a gift from God (Ex. 23:30; 32:13); a tribal allotment (Josh. 16:4); or a familial portion (Josh. 17:6). In addition to the taking of Canaan, God declared that Israel's remnant would possess the lands of Moab and Edom (Zeph. 2:9). It can also refer to the division and distribution of the land of Canaan to the tribal units (Josh. 14:1). This verb is further used of God acquiring possession of Israel (Ex. 34:9; Zech. 2:12); and the nations as His own private property (Ps. 82:8). In the causative form, the verb denotes the giving of a possession (Deut. 1:38; 3:28); or inheritance (Deut. 21:16). This term is used figuratively to indicate the acquiring of things other than real property, like testimonies (Ps. 119:111); glory (Prov. 3:35); good things (Prov. 28:10); lies (Jer. 16:19); wind (Prov. 11:29); simplicity (Prov. 14:18); blessings (Zech. 8:12). *
– [2] Dan. 7:22 ➔ POSSESS <2631> [3] See HEIR (BE) <3423>.

POSSESSIONS – [1] ***r***^{e}***ḵûš, r***^{e}***ḵuš*** [masc. noun: רְכוּשׁ, רְכֻשׁ <7399>; from pass. part. of ACCUMULATE <7408>] ► **This word describes property and goods obtained by labor, not by purchasing them with money.** Possessions one has accumulated (Gen. 12:5); cattle, flocks (Gen. 13:6; 31:18; 36:7). It refers to equipment of all kinds, utensils, stored items, military baggage (Gen. 46:6; Ezra 1:4, 6; Dan. 11:13). This type of property includes the spoils and booty of war (Gen. 14:11, 12, 16, 21; Dan. 11:24, 28). It indicates the king's own property (1 Chr. 27:31). *
– [2] Judg. 18:21 ➔ GLORIOUS <3520> b. [3] 2 Chr. 1:11, 12; Eccl. 5:19; 6:2 ➔ RICHES <5233>.

POSTERITY – [1] ***neḵeḏ*** [masc. noun: נֶכֶד <5220>; from an unused root meaning to propagate] ► **This word refers to the offspring and later progeny of a person or family.** Ref.: Gen. 21:23. The offspring of the wicked was often cut off, according to Bildad (Job 18:19). It is similar to survivors when used of a nation, e.g., Babylon (Is. 14:22). ¶
– [2] Job 18:19 ➔ OFFSPRING <5209> [3] Is. 22:24 ➔ ISSUE <6849> [4] See SEED <2233>.

POT – [1] ***siyr*** [common noun: סִיר <5518>; from a prim. root meaning to boil up, also a thorn (as springing up rapidly)] ► **This word refers to a cooking container for various food items.** Refs.: Ex. 16:3; 2 Kgs. 4:38–41; Mic. 3:3. Pots were used in the Temple area (2 Kgs. 25:14; Zech. 14:20, 21). The word is used in the sense of a bowl for washing one's feet (Ps. 60:8; Ps. 108:9). The Hebrew word also means thorn, hook; see THORN <5518>. *
[2] ***pārûr*** [masc. noun: פָּרוּר <6517>; pass. part. of BREAK <6565>] ► **This word refers to a hollow vessel used for cooking and boiling food; it is also translated pan.** Refs.: Num. 11:8; Judg. 6:19. It refers to a pot used by the priests to boil meat offerings (1 Sam. 2:14). ¶
– [3] Ex. 16:33 ➔ JAR <6803> [4] Lev. 11:35 ➔ ranges for pots, cooking pot ➔ STOVE, COOKING STOVE <3600> [5] 2 Kgs. 4:2 ➔ JAR <610> [6] Job 41:20; Ps. 81:6 ➔

BASKET <1731> [7] Ps. 68:13 ➔ HOOK <8240> c. [8] Jer. 22:28 ➔ PAIN (noun) <6089> [9] Lam. 4:2 ➔ SKIN BOTTLE <5035> [10] Zech. 12:6 ➔ BASIN <3595>.

POTENT – Is. 47:9 ➔ STRENGTH <6109>.

POTIPHAR – ***pôṭiyp̱ar*** [masc. proper noun: פּוֹטִיפַר <6318>; of Egyptian deriv.] ► **Officer of Pharaoh and chief of his guard.** Refs.: Gen. 37:36; 39:1. ¶

POTIPHERAH – ***pôṭiyp̱era'*** [masc. proper noun: פּוֹטִי פֶרַע <6319>; of Egyptian deriv.] ► **Priest of On (Heliopolis) and father of Asenath whom Pharaoh gave to Joseph for wife.** Refs.: Gen. 41:45, 50; 46:20. ¶

POTSHERD – ***ḥarsûṯ*** [fem. noun: חַרְסוּת <2777>; from ITCH <2763> (apparently in the sense of a red tile used for scraping)] ► **The word denotes a clay fragment.** It is used with *ša'ar*, gate, to indicate the potsherd gate as literally "the gate of the potsherd" (Jer. 19:2). It is not clear whether potsherds play a part in the construction of the gate or some other activity took place there regarding potsherds, e.g., a potsherd dump. ¶

POTSHERD, JAGGED POTSHERD, SHARP POTSHERD – Job 2:8; 41:30; Ps. 22:15 ➔ EARTHENWARE <2789>.

POTTAGE – Gen. 25:29, 34 ➔ STEW <5138>.

POTTER – [1] ***peḥār*** [Aramaic masc. noun: פְּחָר <6353>; from an unused root prob. meaning to fashion] ► **This word is used of a person who is skilled in and works with the craft of pottery.** Ref.: Dan. 2:41. ¶
– [2] 1 Chr. 4:23; Ps. 2:9; Is. 41:25; Zech. 11:13; etc. ➔ FORM (verb) <3335>.

POTTERY – Job 2:8 ➔ piece of broken pottery ➔ EARTHENWARE <2789>.

POUCH – ***yalqûṭ*** [masc. noun: יַלְקוּט <3219>; from GATHER <3950>] ► **This word indicates a bag; a shepherd's bag. It is used only once, referring to the pouch into which David placed five smooth stones for use in his sling.** This pouch was constructed within his shepherd's bag (*k*e*lî hārō'îym*) most likely (1 Sam. 17:40; KJV: scrip). ¶

POUNCE – 1 Sam. 14:32; 15:19 ➔ RUSH GREEDILY <5860> b.

POUND (noun) – 1 Kgs. 10:17; Ezra 2:69; Neh. 7:71, 72 ➔ MINA <4488>.

POUND (verb) – [1] Ps. 38:10 ➔ MERCHANT <5503> [2] Prov. 27:22 ➔ GRIND <3806> [3] Song 5:2 ➔ DRIVE HARD <1849>.

POUNDING WAVE – ***d*ᵒ*ḵiy*** [masc. noun: דֳּכִי <1796>; from CRUSH <1794>] ► **This word denotes a crushing or beating of waves. It is also translated roaring, wave.** It describes the mighty pounding and crashing of waves (Ps. 93:3), but the might of the Lord is far greater. ¶

POUR – [1] ***yāsaḵ*** [verb: יָסַךְ <3251>; a prim. root] ► **This word is used of dispensing a liquid, an anointing oil on the skin of a person as a perfume.** Ref.: Ex. 30:32. ¶
– [2] Job 36:28 ➔ DRIP (verb) <7491> [3] Ps. 75:8; Jer. 18:21; Lam. 3:49; Mic. 1:4, 6 ➔ to pour, to pour down, to pour out the *blood* ➔ SPILL <5064> [4] Is. 19:14 ➔ MINGLE <4537> [5] Jer. 48:12 ➔ TIP OVER <6808>.

POUR DOWN – Job 36:27 ➔ REFINE <2212>.

POUR OUT – [1] ***zāram*** [verb: זָרַם <2229>; a prim. root] ► **This word denotes to sweep away, to end; it is also translated to carry away.** It refers to one of the great acts of the Lord when He caused the clouds to pour out water like a flood (Ps. 77:17). It is used figuratively to indicate the death of persons, swept away by the Lord (Ps. 90:5). ¶

[2] ***nāsak*** [verb: נָסַךְ <5258>; a prim. root] ▶ **This term frequently refers to dispensing drink offerings or libations.** These offerings usually employed wine (Hos. 9:4); or another strong drink (Num. 28:7). But David offered water as a drink offering to the Lord (2 Sam. 23:16; 1 Chr. 11:18). In the books of Moses (Num. 28:7), God clearly outlined instructions for making proper sacrifices. For example, He prohibited pouring a drink offering on the altar of incense (Ex. 30:9). Scripture clearly condemned the practice of making drink offerings to false gods (Jer. 19:13; 44:17–19, 25); a practice that angered God and incurred His judgment (Jer. 7:18; 32:29; Ezek. 20:28). Infrequently, this Hebrew term referred to the casting of idols from metal (Is. 40:19; 44:10); and in one instance, to a deep sleep that the Lord poured over the inhabitants of Jerusalem (Is. 29:10). *

[3] ***nāṯak*** [verb: נָתַךְ <5413>; a prim. root] ▶ **This word means to dispense, to gush, to melt, to break out.** It describes many things under these concepts: water or rain pour out (Ex. 9:33; 2 Sam. 21:10); God's anger and curse flow out or rush out on persons (Jer. 7:20; 42:18; Dan. 9:11, 27; Nah. 1:6). It describes emptying out, pouring out money (2 Kgs. 22:9; 2 Chr. 34:17). It is used of melting so that something will flow, such as metals (Ezek. 22:20–22). It is used figuratively a few times, e.g., of Job's tears being poured out (Job 3:24). *

[4] ***šāpak*** [verb: שָׁפַךְ <8210>; a prim. root] ▶ **In its most basic sense, this word refers to the dispensing of something.** E.g., fluid on the ground (Ex. 4:9; Deut. 12:16; 1 Sam. 7:6); or blood on an altar (Ex. 29:12; Lev. 4:7; Deut. 12:27). In several instances, it describes the casting up of a mound against a city to form a siege ramp for attacking it (2 Sam. 20:15; Ezek. 4:2; Dan. 11:15). This word is also used idiomatically to refer to the shedding of blood (Gen. 9:6; 1 Kgs. 2:31); especially of innocent blood (2 Kgs. 21:16; Prov. 6:17). A dependent prayer is described as the pouring out of one's soul (1 Sam. 1:15; Ps. 42:4); one's heart (Ps. 62:8; Lam. 2:19); or one's inner parts before the Lord (Lam. 2:11). God poured out both His wrath (Ps. 69:24; Is. 42:25; Jer. 6:11; Hos. 5:10); and His grace (Joel 2:28, 29; Zech. 12:10) from heaven on people. *

– [5] Job 29:6; Is. 26:16 ➔ SMELT <6694> [6] Is. 46:6 ➔ LAVISH <2107> [7] Is. 58:10 ➔ OBTAIN <6329> [8] Jer. 6:7 ➔ DIG <6979> c.

POUR OUT TEARS – Job 16:20 ➔ LEAK <1811>.

POUR OUT, FORTH – Ps. 19:2; 94:4; Prov. 1:23; 15:2, 28 ➔ UTTER <5042>.

POUR, POUR OUT – [1] ***yāṣaq*** [verb: יָצַק <3332>; a prim. root] ▶ **The exact use of this word is determined, of course, by its context.** It is used of serving up food (2 Sam. 13:9; 2 Kgs. 4:40, 41); of dispensing liquids (Gen. 28:18; 1 Kgs. 18:33). It is used figuratively of pouring various things: something deceitful, evil (Ps. 41:8); grace (Ps. 45:2); the Lord's Spirit (Is. 44:3). It is used of pouring out molten metal to cast it (1 Kgs. 7:24); hence, it can be translated as to cast. The scales of Leviathan are firmly cast together (Job 41:23); and his heart is described as being as hard (set, *yāṣûq*) as stone (Job 41:24). *

– [2] Is. 32:15; 53:12 ➔ EMPTY (verb) <6168>.

POURED OUT – Lev. 4:12 ➔ HEAP (noun) <8211>.

POURTRAY – Ezek. 8:10; 23:14 ➔ CARVE <2707>.

POVERTY – [1] ***ḥeser*** [masc. noun: חֶסֶר <2639>; from LACKING (BE) <2637>] ▶ **This word means need, want. It indicates basically a lack of something.** It describes the state of the outcasts of society (Job 30:3) and a potential need that may arise because of an improper pursuit of wealth (Prov. 28:22). ¶

[2] ***rêyš, rê'š, riyš*** [masc. noun: רֵישׁ, רֵאשׁ, רִישׁ <7389>; from POOR (BE) <7326>] ▶ **This word describes a state of need, a lack of the necessary or common needs of life.**

In the Wisdom Literature, poverty is often a result of irresponsibility, laziness, or a lack of diligence (Prov. 6:11; 13:18); but is also looked on as a dangerous trap that ensnares some people (Prov. 10:15). Neither poverty nor riches is the ideal (Prov. 30:8). Other refs.: Prov. 24:34; 28:19; 31:7. ¶
– [3] Deut. 28:48 → WANT <2640>.

POWDER – ***^{a}ḇāqāh*** [fem. noun: אֲבָקָה <81>; fem. of DUST <80>] ► **This word means a dry substance composed of very fine particles; it is also translated fragrant powder, scented powder, spice.** It is found only in Song of Solomon 3:6. It clearly indicates some aromatic powder(s). ¶

POWER – [1] ***g^{e}ḇûrāh*** [fem. noun: גְּבוּרָה <1369>; fem. pass. part. from the same as BRAVE <1368>] ► **This word denotes strength, might. It depicts the nature of God's mighty deeds.** It describes the strength of the Lord's right hand that delivers His anointed (Ps. 20:6), meaning all of His powerful acts as well as His power and might in general (Deut. 3:24; 1 Chr. 29:11, 12; Job 26:14; Ps. 65:6; 66:7). It describes the strength of various things: animals (Job 41:12; Ps. 147:10); people (Judg. 8:21; Eccl. 9:16). It indicates the might or power by which the Lord's powerful king reigns (1 Chr. 29:30); or the bravery and valor of the king's warriors (Judg. 8:21; Prov. 8:14; Is. 3:25). It refers to the strength of persons that may prolong their lives (Ps. 90:10). Its usage is flexible and can refer to the power of the sun (Judg. 5:31); or the strength of an army or military plan (2 Kgs. 18:20). *
[2] ***g^{e}ḇûrāh*** [Aramaic fem. noun: גְּבוּרָה <1370>; corresponding to <1369> above] ► **See previous definition above; this word is also translated might. In context, it refers to God's revelation of His secrets to people.** In an important sequence of verses, it is asserted that God's power or strength to reveal His plans are His alone (Dan. 2:20), but He shares it to a limited extent with His servants (Dan. 2:23). ¶
[3] ***ḥ^{e}sēn*** [Aramaic masc. noun: חֲסֵן <2632>; from POSSESS <2631>] ► **This word means strength, authority.** It refers to the authority and influences given to a king in order to rule a kingdom (Dan. 2:37; 4:30), specifically a prerogative given by God. ¶
[4] ***šilṭôn*** [masc. noun: שִׁלְטוֹן <7983>; from RULE OVER <7980>] ► **This word means mastery.** It can be used to mean powerful, as in the words of a king that are described as being supreme, authoritative (Eccl. 8:4). It can also mean having power over. It is used in Ecclesiastes 8:8 to say that no one has power over the day of his or her death. This word carries the connotation of legitimate authority, not just power that persons claim they have or have taken from others. A king's words had legitimate authority, for he was the ruler of his people; and no one except God has legitimate authority over death. ¶
[5] ***šalliyṭ*** [adj.: שַׁלִּיט <7989>; from RULE OVER <7980>] ► **This word could be used to describe having authority over anything, but it is used in a limited context in the Old Testament.** With this meaning, it is only found in Ecclesiastes 8:8, where people are said to have no power over the wind. It can also be used as a noun meaning a ruler or one who has mastery (Gen. 42:6; also translated governor). Rulers can also be a cause of evil (Eccl. 10:5). Other ref.: Eccl. 7:19. ¶
[6] ***ta^{a}ṣumāh*** [fem. noun: תַּעֲצֻמָה <8592>; from MIGHTY (BE) <6105>] ► **This word refers to the moral, ethical, and spiritual vigor and health God furnishes to His people; it is also translated strength.** Ref.: Ps. 68:35. ¶
– [7] Gen. 49:3 → STRONG <5794> b. [8] Esther 10:2; Dan. 11:17 → AUTHORITY <8633> [9] Ps. 78:4; 145:6 → STRENGTH <5807> [10] Is. 40:29; 47:9 → STRENGTH <6109> [11] Is. 43:17 → STRONG <5808> [12] Dan. 11:3, 5 → DOMINION <4474> [13] Dan. 11:4 → AUTHORITY <4915> [14] See STRENGTH <3581>.

POWER (GREAT, TERRIFYING) – Is. 10:33 → TERROR <4637>.

POWER (HAVE) – [1] Gen. 32:28; Hos. 12:4 → STRUGGLE (verb) <8280> [2] See RULE OVER <7980>, <7981>.

POWERFUL – [1] ***qaw, qaw-qaw, qāw*** [masc. noun: קַו, קַו־קָו, קָו <6978>; from LINE, MEASURING LINE <6957>] ▶
a. A word referring to power, might. It means might, strength and was used to describe the armies of Ethiopia with their legendary fierce warriors (Is. 18:2, 7).
b. A word indicating a measure, a meting out. The words relate to the word for a measuring cord; hence, the meaning is understood as a meting out, measured and limited (Is. 18:2, 7).
c. A masculine noun meaning strange speech. It means speech that is gibberish, alien (Is. 18:2, 7). ¶
– [2] Ezra 4:20; Dan. 7:7 ➔ MIGHTY <8624> [3] Zech. 6:3, 7 ➔ STRONG <554>.

POWERFUL (MAKE MORE) – Eccl. 7:19 ➔ STRENGTHEN <5810>.

POWERLESS (BE) – Hab. 1:4 ➔ STUNNED (BECOME) <6313>.

PRAISE (noun) – [1] ***mah^alāl*** [masc. noun: מַהֲלָל <4110>; from PRAISE (verb) <1984>] ▶ **This word indicates strong appreciation and respect accorded to someone by others.** Ref.: Prov. 27:21. It serves as a way of testing for its recipient in context. ¶
[2] ***t^ehillāh*** [fem. noun: תְּהִלָּה <8416>; from PRAISE (verb) <1984>] ▶ **This word means adoration, thanksgiving; it also means a song of praise. It is a noun derived from the verb *hālal*, which connotes genuine appreciation for the great actions or the character of its object.** It is used especially of the adoration and thanksgiving that humanity renders to God (Ps. 34:1). By extension, it also represents the character of God that deserves praise (Ps. 111:10); and the specific divine acts that elicit human veneration (Ex. 15:11). It can also refer to the condition of fame and renown that comes with receiving this sort of praise and, as such, was applied to God (Deut. 10:21; Hab. 3:3); Israel (Deut. 26:19; Jer. 13:11); Jerusalem (Is. 62:7; Zeph. 3:19, 20); Damascus (Jer. 49:25); Moab (Jer. 48:2); Babylon (Jer. 51:41). In late Hebrew, this term became a technical term for a psalm of praise. In this capacity, it is used in the title of Psalm 145 to designate it as David's Psalm of Praise. It has also become the Hebrew title for the entire book of Psalms. *
– [3] Lev. 19:24: praise, offering of praise ➔ OFFERING OF PRAISE <1974> [4] Is. 57:19 ➔ FRUIT <5108> c.

PRAISE, HIGH PRAISE – [1] ***rômam*** [masc. noun: רוֹמָם <7318>; from EXALTED <7426> a.] ▶ **This word is used of lifting up, an exaltation of God by His holy people.** Refs.: Ps. 66:17; 149:6. ¶
[2] ***rôm^emāh*** [fem. noun: רוֹמְמָה <7319>; fem. act. part. of EXALTED <7426>] ▶ **This word is used of the lifting up, the exaltation of God by His holy people.** Ref.: Ps. 149:6. ¶

PRAISE (verb) – [1] ***hālal*** [Aramaic verb: הָלַל <1984>; a prim. root] ▶ **This verb means to adore, to commend, to boast, to shine. The root meaning may be to shine but could also be to shout.** The word most often means praise and is associated with the ministry of the Levites who praised God morning and evening (1 Chr. 23:30). All creation, however, is urged to join in (Ps. 148), and various instruments were used to increase the praise to God (Ps. 150). The word hallelujah is a command to praise *Yah* (the Lord), derived from the word *hālal* (Ps. 105:45; 146:1). The reflexive form of the verb is often used to signify boasting, whether in a good object (Ps. 34:2) or a bad object (Ps. 49:6). Other forms of the word mean to act foolishly or to be mad (1 Sam. 21:13; Eccl. 7:7; Is. 44:25). *
[2] ***nāwāh*** [verb: נָוָה <5115>; a prim. root] ▶ **a. A verb meaning to dwell, to abide, to rest. A word referring to the safety and security given to a person.** Early translators interpreted the word (Ex. 15:2: to prepare a habitation) as though it referred to Moses supposedly (and prematurely) proposing to prepare a dwelling place for the Lord. However contemporary scholars generally agree that the word means to glorify, to praise. See b. below. Other ref.: Hab.

2:5 (keep at home, stay at home, be at rest) Other ref.: Hab. 2:5 (keep at home, stay at home, be at rest). ¶

b. A verb meaning to beautify; to praise. It is an expression of thanks and honor. Moses and Israel sang to the Lord, saying "I will praise Him" (Ex. 15:2). ¶

3 ***šᵉḇaḥ*** [Aramaic verb: שְׁבַח <7624>; corresponding to SOOTHE <7623> (in the sense of to praise)] ▶ **This word means to adore. It occurs five times in the book of Daniel.** It denotes Daniel's praise of the Lord (Dan. 2:23); the praise of the Lord by a humbled Nebuchadnezzar (Dan. 4:34, 37); and the praise given to idols during Belshazzar's debaucherous feast (Dan. 5:4, 23). ¶

PRANSING – 1 Judg. 5:22 ➔ GALLOPING <1726> 2 Nah. 3:2 ➔ GALLOP <1725>.

PRAY – 1 ***'āṯar*** [verb: עָתַר <6279>; a prim. root (rather denom. from ETHER <6281>, which is from MULTIPLY <6280>)] ▶ **This word means to entreat, to supplicate; it is also translated to intreat, to plead, to intercede. The fundamental meaning of this word is that of a cry to the Lord for deliverance.** It was used in Isaac's prayer concerning his wife's barrenness (Gen. 25:21); and the prayers of Moses to stop the plagues in Egypt (Ex. 8:8, 9, 28–30; 9:28; 10:17, 18). Scripture says that the Lord is faithful to hear such prayers (Job 22:27; 33:26). Other refs.: Judg. 13:8; 2 Sam. 21:14; 24:25; 1 Chr. 5:20; 2 Chr. 33:13, 19; Ezra 8:23; Is. 19:22. ¶

2 ***pālal*** [verb: פָּלַל <6419>; a prim. root] ▶ **This word means to intercede. This is the most common Hebrew word used to describe the general act of prayer (Jer. 29:7).** It was often used to describe prayer offered in a time of distress, such as Hannah's prayer for a son (1 Sam. 1:10, 12); Elisha's prayer for the dead boy (2 Kgs. 4:33); Hezekiah's prayer for protection and health (2 Kgs. 19:15; 20:2); and Jonah's prayer from the fish (Jon. 2:1). In some contexts, this word described a specific intercession of one person praying to the Lord for another, such as Abraham for Abimelech (Gen. 20:7, 17); Moses and Samuel for Israel (Num. 11:2; 21:7; 1 Sam. 7:5); the man of God for the king (1 Kgs. 13:6); or Ezra and Daniel for Israel's sins (Ezra 10:1; Dan. 9:4, 20). This prayer of intercession could also be made to a false god (Is. 44:17; 45:14). *

3 ***ṣᵉlā'*** [Aramaic verb: צְלָא <6739>; prob. corresponding to LIMP <6760> in the sense of bowing] ▶ **Daniel was praying to God when the royal administrators found him after King Darius' edict legislating that petitions should only be made of the king (Dan. 6:10).** King Darius instructed his governors to give to the Israelites whatever they needed to rebuild the Temple so they could offer sacrifices to God and continue praying for him (Ezra 6:10). ¶

– 4 Dan. 6:7, 13 ➔ lit.: to make petition ➔ PETITION <1159>.

PRAYER – 1 ***tᵉpillāh*** [fem. noun: תְּפִלָּה <8605>; from PRAY <6419>] ▶ **The word is used to describe a prayer that was similar to a plea (1 Kgs. 8:38; 2 Chr. 6:29).** In Samuel, David is described as having the courage to offer his prayer to God (2 Sam. 7:27). King Hezekiah was instructed to pray for the remnant that still survived (2 Kgs. 19:4); and in Jeremiah, the word is used to denote what not to do, i.e., do not pray with any plea or petition (Jer. 7:16). The word is used by the psalmist as he cried to God to hear his prayer (Ps. 4:1). He asked God not to be deaf to his weeping but to take heed to the turmoil His servant was in. In a similar manner, the psalmist again uses the word in a plea to God to hear his prayer and to know that it did not come from deceitful lips (Ps. 17:1). The word is also used in Habakkuk as an introduction to the rest of the chapter, indicating that what followed was his prayer (Hab. 3:1). *

– 2 Job 15:4 ➔ MEDITATION <7881>.

PRAYER, WHISPERED PRAYER – Is. 26:16 ➔ CHARM <3908>.

PREACH – Ezek. 21:2; Amos 7:16 ➔ DROP (verb) <5197>.

PREACHER – ***qōheleṯ*** [noun: קֹהֶלֶת <6953>; fem. of act. part. from ASSEMBLE <6950>] ▶ **This word means a collector of wisdom; it is also translated teacher. The root meaning appears to indicate a person who gathered wisdom. The word has a feminine form because it referred to an office or position, but it was usually used with masculine verbs and always referred to a man.** *Qōheleṯ* only occurs in Ecclesiastes: three times at the beginning and end of the book and once in the middle (Eccl. 7:27). It is also the Hebrew name of the book. The word Ecclesiastes is a translation of this Hebrew word into Greek and referred to someone who addressed a public assembly. This is another meaning of the word based on the fact that the preacher had gathered knowledge to speak about life. Solomon used the word to describe himself as one who gathered wisdom (Eccl. 12:9, 10; cf. 1 Kgs. 4:32–34); and as one who spoke to people about wisdom (Eccl. 12:9; cf. 2 Chr. 9:23). Other refs.: Eccl. 1:2, 12; 12:8. ¶

PREACHING – [1] Ezra 6:14 ➔ PROPHESYING <5017> [2] Jon. 2:2 ➔ MESSAGE <7150>.

PRECEPT – [1] ***piqqûḏ, pᵉqûḏiym*** [masc. noun: פִּקּוּד ,פְּקוּדִים <6490>; from ATTEND <6485>] ▶ **This word means instruction; it is also translated statute, commandment. The root expresses the idea that God is paying attention to how He wants things ordered (see *pāqaḏ* [ATTEND <6485>]).** God's precepts strike those who love Him as right and delightful (Ps. 19:8). This word is always plural and is only found in the Psalms, mostly in Psalm 119 (twenty-one times). This psalm talked of seeking (Ps. 119:40, 45, 94); keeping (Ps. 119:63, 69, 134); and not forgetting God's instructions (Ps. 119:87, 93, 141); even when opposed by the proud (Ps. 119:69, 78). The psalmist's diligence in obeying God's precepts was rewarded with understanding and the hatred of evil (Ps. 119:100, 104); liberty (Ps. 119:45); confidence in asking God's help (Ps. 119:94, 173); and spiritual life (Ps. 119:93). *

[2] ***ṣaw, ṣāw*** [masc. noun: צַו, צָו <6673>; from COMMAND (verb) <6680>] ▶
a. This word means rule, command; a senseless word of mockery; unintelligible speech. In Isaiah 28:10, it refers to line on line of instruction (NASB: order). It describes the ineffective piling up of the Lord's words, line on line (Is. 28:13).
b. Some translators render this word as idol, filth. Ref.: Hos. 5:11. Its meaning is not certain (see a.). ¶

PRECEPTS – Prov. 4:2 ➔ LEARNING <3948>.

PRECINCTS – ***parbār*** [masc. noun: פַּרְבָּר <6503>; of foreign origin] ▶
a. A masculine noun designating a court area, a special area. It refers, according to context, to an area located within the Temple environs or very near the Temple area (2 Kgs. 23:11; also translated suburbs, court). Levites were stationed in the Parbar or certain court districts (1 Chr. 26:18: court, colonnade). ¶
b. A masculine noun Parbar; a court area in Solomon's Temple. It is given the status of a proper name for a courtly precinct area by some translators (1 Chr. 26:18). ¶

PRECIOUS – [1] ***yāqār*** [adj.: יָקָר <3368>; from HONOR (noun) <3365>] ▶ **This word means valuable, rare, worthy.** It carries the sense of being rare in some contexts (1 Sam. 3:1). It is used to describe precious and costly stones (2 Sam. 12:30; 1 Kgs. 10:2, 10, 11); the valuable foundation stones of buildings (1 Kgs. 5:17); any expensive building stones or materials (1 Kgs. 7:9–11). It is used of the Lord's lovingkindness (*ḥeseḏ* [MERCY <2617>]) to His people (Ps. 36:7; also translated excellent, priceless). Wisdom is asserted to be more valuable than jewels (Prov. 3:15). It is used as an abstract collective term for that which is valuable, noble, moral, ethical, or worthy compared to what is worthless (Jer. 15:19). In Job 31:26 (splendor, brightness), it is used in a negative sense of the alluring attraction of the moon's splendor as an invitation to idolatry or astrology. The

menacing figure in Daniel 11:38 (precious stones, costly stones) casts his religious affection on the god of violence, honoring it. It may be used in Zechariah 14:6 meaning luminaries or lights, but the reading is uncertain, for it could mean cold. *
2 ***maḥmāḏ*** [masc. noun: מַחְמָד <4261>; from DESIRE (verb) <2530>] ▶ **This word indicates a desire, a desirable thing, a valuable thing. It indicates whatever is desirable, something one wishes to have, to possess.** It is used of things (1 Kgs. 20:6; 2 Chr. 36:19; Hos. 9:6; Joel 3:5); of persons (Song 5:16). It is used especially of what is attractive to the eyes (1 Kgs. 20:6; Ezek. 24:16, 21, 25). Other refs.: Is. 64:11; Lam. 1:7, 10; 2:4; Hos. 9:16. ¶
– 3 Job 22:25 ➔ STRENGTH <8443> d. 4 Ps. 22:20; 35:17 ➔ ONLY <3173> 5 Ps. 126:6 ➔ BAG <4901> a.

PRECIOUS (BE) – ***yāqar*** [verb: יָקַר <3365>; a prim. root] ▶ **This word means to esteem, to be valuable, to be costly. It has the basic idea of being highly valuable, worthy.** It indicates a high evaluation put upon someone or something (1 Sam. 18:30: to be set; to be highly esteemed, to be well known; Zech. 11:13: to value, to price, to prise (KJV), to set). It indicates considering something worth preserving, such as human life (1 Sam. 26:21; 2 Kgs. 1:13, 14: to have respect; Ps. 72:14). It can take on the idea of making something rare in certain causative usages (Is. 13:12: to make more rare, more precious, scarcer). The process of redeeming a person is said to cost great effort (Ps. 49:8; also translated to be costly). It is used figuratively of making something scarce, rare, such as a visit to a neighbor's house (Prov. 25:17: to seldom set, to let seldom be, to let rarely be, to withdraw). Other refs.: Ps. 139:17; Is. 43:4. ¶

PRECIOUS (MAKE MORE) – Is. 13:12 ➔ PRECIOUS (BE) <3365>.

PRECIOUS, PRECIOUS THINGS – Prov. 20:15; Jer. 20:5; Ezek. 22:25 ➔ HONOR (noun) <3366>.

PRECIOUS STONE – ***sōḥereṯ*** [fem. noun: סֹחֶרֶת <5508>; similar to BUCKLER <5507>] ▶
a. This word indicates a costly stone used in making a mosaic pavement It describes a hard, shiny, stone of luxury used in the Persian state buildings (Esther 1:6: NASB, ESV, NIV). ¶
b. For other translators, this word refers to marble, black marble used in making a mosaic pavement. It is a stone used in royal palaces and houses of state in the Persian Empire (Esther 1:6). ¶

PRECIOUS THING – 1 ***meḡeḏ*** [masc. noun: מֶגֶד <4022>; from an unused root prob. meaning to be eminent] ▶ **This word indicates a choice thing, the best thing, valuable thing.** Fruit and all kinds of produce from the land and heaven (Deut. 33:13–16); in a figurative sense of the choice delights of a beloved bride (Song 4:13, 16); or of the finest fruits that decorate their celebrations of love (Song 7:13); it indicates precious valuables or gifts of all kinds (Gen. 24:53; 2 Chr. 21:3; 32:23; Ezra 1:6). ¶
2 ***migdānāh*** [fem. noun: מִגְדָּנָה <4030>; from the same as <4022> above] ▶ **This word refers to a costly gift.** The plural form is *migdānôṯ* and appears in Genesis 24:53; 2 Chronicles 21:3; 32:23; Ezra 1:6. It also has the expected *m*ᵉ*gāḏîym* plural. ¶
– 3 Lam. 1:7, 11 ➔ PLEASANT THING <4262>.

PRECIOUS THINGS – 2 Kgs. 20:13; Is. 39:2 ➔ TREASURE <5238>.

PREDATORY BIRD – Ezek. 39:4 ➔ BIRD OF PREY <5861>.

PREEMINENCE – 1 ***nōah*** [masc. noun: נֹהַּ <5089>; from an unused root meaning to lament] ▶
a. This word designates something of value, something eminent. It refers to something of significance, of a significant value. It is not further defined, and its exact meaning is difficult to determine (Ezek. 7:11). ¶
b. This word also refers to a wailing, a lament. It was a human cry mourning or

bewailing calamity and judgment (Ezek. 7:11: KJV, NKJV). ¶
– [2] Eccl. 3:19 ➔ PROFIT (noun) <4195>.

PREFECT – [1] ***s^egan*** [Aramaic masc. noun: סְגַן <5460>; corresponding to RULER <5461>] ▶ **This word means a ruler; it is also translated governor, administrator.** King Nebuchadnezzar positioned Daniel to be the head of all the governors of Babylon (Dan. 2:48). Daniel 3:2 lists the various officers of the neo-Babylonian Empire, one of which was the office signified by this term. Later, King Nebuchadnezzar summoned these and other officials to the dedication of the golden image he had erected. At this dedication, all the officials were expected to fall down and worship the image. Later, Darius the Mede issued a similar edict (Dan. 6:7). However, in both instances, some refused, including Daniel. Other refs.: Dan. 3:3, 27. ¶
– [2] Jer. 51:23, 28; etc. ➔ RULER <5461>.

PREGNANT – ***hāreh*** [fem. adj.: הָרֶה <2030>; from CONCEIVE <2029>] ▶ **This word describes the state of carrying a human being within the body, the result of conception.** Women of varied civic status and moral integrity were pregnant. E.g., a servant who was a secondary wife (Gen. 16:11). A legitimately married wife (1 Sam. 4:19). A woman taken in adultery by a powerful king (2 Sam. 11:5). A woman posing and behaving as a prostitute (Gen. 38:24). Uniquely and surpassingly, this sign was prophesied: the virgin shall conceive (be pregnant) and bear a Son (Is. 7:14). It takes on the meaning of a noun indicating pregnant women (2 Kgs. 8:12; 15:16; Jer. 31:8; Amos 1:13). The womb of Jeremiah's mother is described as pregnant, enlarged (Jer. 20:17). *

PREPARATION – [1] Prov. 16:1 ➔ PLAN (verb) <4633> [2] Esther 2:12 ➔ BEAUTIFICATION <4795>.

PREPARE – [1] 2 Kgs. 6:23 ➔ BUY <3739> [2] Ps. 78:50 ➔ WEIGH, WEIGH OUT <6424> [3] Jer. 1:17 ➔ GIRD <247> [4] Dan. 2:9 ➔ AGREE <2164> [5] Jon. 1:17; 4:6–8 ➔ COUNT <4487>.

PRESCRIBED (BE) – Ezra 7:23 ➔ COMMAND (noun) <2941>.

PRESCRIBING – Ezra 7:22 ➔ WRITING <3792>.

PRESENT (noun) – [1] ***t^ešûrāh*** [fem. noun: תְּשׁוּרָה <8670>; from JOURNEY <7788> in the sense of arrival] ▶ **This word indicates something given to a person to show respect, appreciation, and honor.** Ref.: 1 Sam. 9:7; also translated gift. ¶
– [2] 2 Sam. 11:8 ➔ GIFT <4864> [3] 1 Kgs. 9:16; Mic. 1:14 ➔ PARTING GIFT <7964> [4] Ezra 6:3 ➔ OFFER <1684> [5] Ps. 68:29; 76:11; Is. 18:7 ➔ GIFT <7862> [6] Ezek. 27:15 ➔ GIFT <814>.

PRESENT (verb) – [1] Gen. 30:20 ➔ ENDOW <2064> [2] Prov. 4:9 ➔ DELIVER <4042> [3] Dan. 2:46 ➔ OFFER <5260>.

PRESERVATION OF LIFE – ***miḥ^eyāh*** [fem. sing. noun: מִחְיָה <4241>; from LIVE <2421>] ▶ **This word means conservation, sustenance, raw flesh.** Joseph said he was sent to Egypt to preserve life (lit.: for the preservation of life) (Gen. 45:5). The term is also used to mean food or sustenance (Judg. 6:4: living thing; 17:10: maintenance, victual, living, food). The Levitical Law used the term to refer to raw flesh because of a skin disease (Lev. 13:10, 24; KJV: quick). Other refs.: 2 Chr. 14:13 (to recover); Ezra 9:8, 9 (reviving, revival). ¶

PRESERVE LIFE – Gen. 45:5 ➔ PRESERVATION OF LIFE <4241>.

PRESERVED – ***nāṣiyr*** [adj.: נָצִיר <5336>; from KEEP <5341>] ▶ **This word describes the Israelites whom God had kept in reserve for Himself and for restoration.** Ref.: Is. 49:6. ¶

PRESIDENT – Dan. 6:2–4, 6:6, 7 ➔ COMMISSIONER <5632>.

PRESS – [1] ***pāṣar*** [verb: פָּצַר <6484>; a prim. root] ▶ **This word means to peck at, to push.** It indicates a literal physical push against someone (Gen. 19:9); figuratively, it refers to urging someone (Gen. 33:11) to do something (Judg. 19:7). In a negative sense, it refers to rebellion against someone (1 Sam. 15:23: stubbornness, insubordination, presumption, arrogance). Other refs.: Gen. 19:3; 2 Kgs. 2:17; 5:16. ¶
[2] ***śāḥaṭ*** [verb: שָׂחַט <7818>; a prim. root] ▶ **This word refers to the process of preparing wine in Pharaoh's cup by squeezing juice out of grapes into it.** Ref.: Gen. 40:11. ¶
– [3] Ex. 5:13 ➔ HASTEN <213> [4] Ex. 22:29 ➔ VINTAGE <1831> [5] Num. 22:25 ➔ OPPRESS <3905> [6] Judg. 1:34 ➔ OPPRESS <3905> [7] Judg. 14:17; 16:16 ➔ OPPRESS <6693> [8] Judg. 16:16 ➔ URGE <509> [9] Is. 21:15 ➔ HEAVINESS <3514> [10] Ezek. 23:3, 21 ➔ CRUSH <4600> [11] Hab. 1:8 ➔ FROLIC <6335> a.

PRESS DOWN – Amos 2:13 ➔ WEIGHTED DOWN (BE) <5781>.

PRESS OUT – Is. 1:6 ➔ CRUSH <2115>.

PRESSED – Ex. 27:20; 29:40; Lev. 24:2; Num. 28:5; 1 Kgs. 5:11 ➔ BEATEN <3795>.

PRESSED (BE) – Amos 2:13 ➔ WEIGHTED DOWN (BE) <5781>.

PRESSED (BE HARD) – Ps. 118:5 ➔ DISTRESS (noun) <4712>.

PRESSING – Prov. 30:33 ➔ CHURNING <4330>.

PRESSURE – [1] ***'ekep*** [masc. noun: אֶכֶף <405>; from CRAVE <404>] ▶ **This word means burden, load, urgency.** The NASB and the ESV translate the Hebrew word as pressure in Job 33:7, while others render the word as hand (NKJV, KJV, NIV) using the Greek translation (Septuagint) as their source. ¶
– [2] Ps. 55:3 ➔ OPPRESSION <6125> a.

PRESUME – ***'āpal*** [verb: עָפַל <6075>; a prim. root] ▶ **This word describes carrying on an act of presumption, arrogance, against the best advice; it also means to be proud.** Ref.: Num. 14:44. It refers to a person who has become too audacious, proud (Hab. 2:4; also translated to be puffed up, to be lifted up). ¶

PRESUMPTION – [1] 1 Sam. 15:23 ➔ PRESS <6484> [2] 1 Sam. 17:28 ➔ PRIDE <2087>.

PRESUMPTUOUS – Ps. 19:13 ➔ PROUD <2086>.

PRESUMPTUOUSLY – Deut. 17:12; 18:22 ➔ lit.: presumption ➔ PRIDE <2087>.

PRETEXT – Job 33:10 ➔ OPPOSITION <8569>.

PREVAIL – [1] ***gāḇar*** [verb: גָּבַר <1396>; a prim. root] ▶ **This verb means to be or prove superior to opposing forces, in strength, power, might, greatness, or influence; it also means to be strong, to be mighty.** It may refer to human effort or physical strength (Eccl. 10:10). It is used to indicate superior strength or success over someone else or something, as when Israel prevailed over Amalek (Ex. 17:11). It indicates something is more abundant or superior to something else (Gen. 49:26); it swells and becomes dominant (Gen. 7:18–20; Jer. 9:3). In a temporal sense, it means to remain, to prevail (Gen. 7:24). It is used figuratively to describe the unity and strength of friendship (1 Sam. 1:23), such as David and Jonathan's. The godly prevail or are successful because the Lord strengthens them (1 Sam. 2:9; Zech. 10:6). In Daniel 9:27, it is used in a form of the verb that means to cause a covenant to be established or, possibly, to cause a covenant to prevail (NIV, confirm a covenant; NASB, make a firm covenant; KJV, confirm the covenant). *
[2] ***tāqēp*** [verb: תָּקֵף <8630>; a prim. root] ▶ **This word means to overwhelm, to overcome, to defeat; it is also translated**

to overpower. In context it refers to God's overpowering or overwhelming humankind with His sovereign acts in the world (Job 14:20). Eliphaz pictures the wicked as overcome with anxiety, despair, and anguish that crush and overwhelm them (Job 15:24). It means to gain mastery over, to defeat (Eccl. 4:12). ¶
– 3 Judg. 3:10; 6:2; Ps. 9:19; Dan. 11:12 ➔ STRENGTHEN <5810> 4 See ABLE (BE) <3201>, ABLE (BE) <3202>.

PREY – 1 ***ṭerep*** [masc. noun: טֶרֶף <2964>; from TEAR <2963>] ▶ **This word denotes the victim of a predator.** It indicates the prey of people or beasts: often the prey of a lion (Job 4:11; 38:39; Ps. 104:21; Amos 3:4). In a figurative way, it describes Judah conquering its prey (Gen. 49:9) or Israel (Num. 23:24) devouring its prey. The mighty empires of the ancient Near East attacked their prey: Assyrians (Is. 5:29; Nah. 2:12, 13). False prophets attacked their prey (Ezek. 22:25). It takes on the general meaning of food or nourishment for the poor and oppressed in Job 24:5 (prey, food, game). It is used surprisingly of human food (KJV, meat) in Psalm 111:5 provided by God and in Proverbs 31:15 by a good wife. In Ezekiel 17:9, it is used of the fruit or leaves of a tree representing Judah. Other refs.: Job 29:17; Ps. 76:4; 124:6; Is. 31:4; Ezek. 19:3, 6; 22:27; Nah. 3:1; Mal. 3:10. ¶
2 ***malqôaḥ*** [masc. noun: מַלְקוֹחַ <4455>; from TAKE <3947>] ▶ **This word is used in context of the spoils of war or political or military intrigue; it is also translated booty, plunder.** Refs.: Num. 31:11, 12, 26, 27, 32; Is. 49:24, 25. The Hebrew word refers also to a jaw, a palate; see JAW <4455>. ¶
3 ***'aḏ*** [masc. noun: עַד <5706>; the same as ETERNITY <5703> (in the sense of the aim of an attack)] ▶ **This word refers to the victim of a ravening wolf, the wolf representing Benjamin.** Ref.: Gen. 49:27. It is used in an inclusive sense of all spoil or booty taken in war (Is. 33:23; NIV: abundance). Zephaniah 3:8 is rendered as prey (KJV), but others translate it as witness.
– 4 Neh. 4:4 ➔ PLUNDER (noun) <961> 5 Prov. 23:28 ➔ ROBBER <2863> 6 Nah. 2:12 ➔ TORN (WHAT IS) <2966>.

PRICE – 1 ***mḥiyr*** [masc. noun: מְחִיר <4242>; from an unused root meaning to buy] ▶ **This word means wages, cost.** It refers to the value of a transaction, a market price, or the equivalent value in goods (2 Sam. 24:24; 1 Kgs. 10:28). It means money or price (Mic. 3:11). It is used figuratively of a recompense or cost for Israel's sins (Jer. 15:13); and of the Lord's selling His people without profit from their price (Ps. 44:12). It is used of the hire paid to a dog, that is a male prostitute (Deut. 23:18). Wisdom has no equivalent price (Job 28:15). *
– 2 Lev. 25:16, 51 ➔ PURCHASE (noun) <4736> 3 1 Sam. 13:21 ➔ CHARGE (noun) <6477> a. 4 Job 28:18 ➔ BAG <4901> a. 5 Zech. 11:1 ➔ HONOR (noun) <3366>.

PRICE (verb) – Zech. 11:13 ➔ PRECIOUS (BE) <3365>.

PRICELESS – Ps. 36:7 ➔ PRECIOUS <3368>.

PRICK (noun) – Num. 33:55 ➔ BARB <7899>.

PRICK (verb) – Ezek. 28:24 ➔ PAINFUL (BE) <3992>.

PRICKED (BE) – Ps. 73:21 ➔ SHARPEN <8150>.

PRICKING – Ezek. 28:24 ➔ PAINFUL (BE) <3992>.

PRICKLING – Ezek. 28:24 ➔ PAINFUL (BE) <3992>.

PRIDE – 1 ***gê'āh*** [fem. noun: גֵּאָה <1344>; fem. from RISE <1342>] ▶ **This word means exaltation, haughtiness.** This attitude and character trait is hated by true wisdom along with evil actions, perverted talk, and arrogance (Prov. 8:13). ¶

[2] ***gêwāh*** [fem. noun: גֵּוָה <1466>; the same as BACK <1465>] ▶ **In a good sense this word means lifting up, exaltation, an injection of confidence, referring to God's action to help a downhearted person. In a bad sense it means arrogance.** Ref.: NASB: Job 22:29; other translations: exaltation. Jeremiah uses it to describe pride that separates from God's benefits (Jer. 13:17). It designates something from which God tries to keep a person (Job 33:17). ¶

[3] ***gêwāh*** [Aramaic fem. noun: גֵּוָה <1467>; corresponding to <1466> above] ▶ **This word indicates an arrogant, self-centered evaluation of one's actions and character which God will humble.** Ref.: Dan. 4:37. ¶

[4] ***zāḏôn*** [masc. noun.: זָדוֹן <2087>; from PROUDLY (DEAL) <2102>] ▶ **A word meaning presumptuousness, arrogance, insolence.** David's brothers accused him of being presumptuous when he wanted to challenge Goliath (1 Sam. 17:28; also translated insolence, presumption). Obadiah 1:3 addresses the pride (or arrogance) of the Edomites who fatally presumed that they had a safe place in the cliffs. Proverbs also describes the negative aspects of pride (Prov. 11:2; 13:10; 21:24), while Ezekiel uses this word in his description of the day of judgment (Ezek. 7:10). Other refs.: Deut. 17:12; 18:22; Jer. 49:16; 50:31, 32. ¶

[5] ***zûḏ*** [Aramaic verb: זוּד <2103>; corresponding to PROUDLY (DEAL) <2102>] ▶ **This verb means to act proudly, arrogantly.** It describes the actions and attitude of Nebuchadnezzar which caused God to judge him harshly (Dan. 5:20).

[6] ***šaḥaṣ*** [masc. noun: שַׁחַץ <7830>; from an unused root apparently meaning to strut] ▶

a. This word indicates an inordinately high opinion of one's self and a demeaning attitude toward others. Ref.: Job 41:34. ¶

b. This word refers to a lion (as a proud beast). It stands in parallel to fierce lion (NASB) and, hence, the pride of the lion is emphasized in context (Job 28:8); both are, however, unable to find or discover where wisdom dwells. ¶

– [7] Job 20:6 ➔ LOFTINESS <7863> [8] Ps. 31:20 ➔ CONSPIRACY <7407> b. [9] Eccl. 7:8 ➔ PROUD <1362> [10] Is. 2:17 ➔ LOFTINESS <1365> [11] Is. 28:1 ➔ MAJESTY <1348>.

PRIDE (LOFTY, HUMAN) – Is. 2:11, 17 ➔ HEIGHT <7312>.

PRIEST – [1] ***kōhên*** [masc. noun: כֹּהֵן <3548>; act. part. of PRIEST (MINISTER AS) <3547>] ▶ **The word is used to designate the various classes of priests in Israel. These people offered sacrifices to God and performed the function of mediators between God and His people.** God called the nation of Israel to be a kingdom of priests (Ex. 19:6), but God also appointed a priesthood to function within the nation. All the priests were to come from the tribe of Levi (Deut. 17:9, 18). The Lord set up a high priest who was over all the priestly services. The high priest was literally the great priest or head priest: Jehoiada was described as a high or great priest (2 Kgs. 12:10). Joshua is called the high priest over the community that returned from the Babylonian exile (Hag. 1:12; 2:2). God appointed Aaron to serve as high priest and his sons as priests when the entire priestly order was established (Lev. 21:10; Num. 35:25). The high point of the religious year was the atonement ritual the high priest performed on the Day of Atonement (Lev. 16). Aaron's family line produced the Aaronic priests or priesthood. Zadok became the ancestor of the legitimate priests from the time of Solomon's reign (1 Kgs. 1:8, 38, 44); and the prophet Ezekiel approved of this line of priests from among the Levites (Ezek. 40:46; 43:19). The priests were in charge of all the holy things in Israel: they bore the ark (Josh. 3:13, 14) and trumpets (Num. 10:8). They even counseled kings (1 Sam. 22:21; 1 Kgs. 1:38, 44). However, there arose priests who were not appointed by the Lord and who functioned illegitimately, such as Micah's priests during the time of the judges (Judg. 17:5, 10, 12) or Jeroboam's priests who did not come from the sons of Levi (1 Kgs. 12:31).

Some priests who functioned in other religions or nations are mentioned in Scripture. The most famous was Melchizedek, who was also a king in Canaan (Gen. 14:18). His priesthood became the model for Christ's eternal priesthood (Heb. 6:20). Jethro, Moses' father-in-law, was a priest among the Midianites (Ex. 2:16; 3:1). Joseph married Asenath, the daughter of an Egyptian priest (Gen. 41:45). There were priests of the Philistines (1 Sam. 6:2); and priests who served the false gods, the Baals, and the Asherim (2 Chr. 34:5) of the heathen nations. *

[2] ***kāhên*** [Aramaic masc. noun: כָּהֵן <3549>; corresponding to <3548> above] ▶ **This word refers to people offering sacrifices to God and performing the function of mediators between God and His people. It applies specifically to those qualified by willingness, genealogy, purity, and freedom from physical deformity to act as priests when Israel returned from Babylonian exile.** Refs.: Ezra 6:9, 16, 18; 7:12, 13, 16, 21, 24. ¶

[3] ***kōmer*** [masc. noun: כֹּמֶר <3649>; from YEARN <3648>] ▶ **This word refers to a pagan priest offering sacrifices to please a god; it is also translated idolatrous priest. In the Old Testament, this word occurs three times.** In 2 Kings 23:5, Josiah's reformation got rid of priests who burned incense in the idolatrous high places. In Hosea 10:5, Hosea prophesied that priests would mourn over the calf statue they worshiped when it was carried off to Assyrian captivity. In Zephaniah 1:4 (chemarim; idolatrous priest), God promised to cut off the names of unfaithful priests, along with His own priests (cf. Zeph. 1:5, 6). ¶

PRIEST (MINISTER AS, SERVE AS) – ***kāhan*** [verb: כָּהַן <3547>; a prim. root, apparently meaning to mediate in religious services] ▶ **This word means to act as a priest, one who offers sacrifices to God and performs the function of mediator between God and His people. It is a denominative verb from the noun *kōhên* (PRIEST <3548>).** The verb occurs twenty-three times in the Hebrew Bible, and twelve of them occur in Exodus. The most unusual usage is Isaiah 61:10 (to clothe) where it seems to refer to dressing in a priestly (i.e., ornate) manner. Refs.: Ex. 28:1, 3, 4, 41; 29:1, 44; 30:30; 31:10; 35:19; 39:41; 40:13, 15; Lev. 7:35; 16:32; Num. 3:3, 4; Deut. 10:6; 1 Chr. 6:10; 24:2; 2 Chr. 11:14; Is. 61:10; Ezek. 44:13; Hos. 4:6. ¶

PRIESTHOOD – ***kᵉhunnāh*** [fem. noun: כְּהֻנָּה <3550>; from PRIEST (MINISTER AS) <3547>] ▶ **This word means the priest's office or function. See PRIEST <3548>.** The priest's office belonged to Aaron and his sons and involved making sacrifices and entering the Holy of Holies (Num. 18:7), work from which the other Levites were excluded (Num. 18:1, 7). Because of the holiness of the priesthood, those without right who presumed to act in it (Num. 16:10), as well as priests who misused the office, faced severe judgments. Levites outside of Aaron's descendants were permitted to do other service in the Tabernacle; and, thus, the priesthood was referred to as their inheritance in place of land (Josh. 18:7). The ordination of priests was described in Exodus 29 and included the use of anointing oil, special clothes, and sacrifices. Other refs.: Ex. 29:9; 40:15; Num. 3:10; 25:13; 1 Sam. 2:36; Ezra 2:62; Neh. 7:64; 13:29. ¶

PRIME OF LIFE – Eccl. 11:10 ➔ YOUTH <7839>.

PRINCE – [1] ***nāsiyḵ*** [masc. noun: נָסִיךְ <5257>; from POUR OUT <5258> (in the sense of to be anointed)] ▶ **This word refers to a prince (consecrated by anointing), duke, chief man, or leader.** Refs.: Josh. 13:21; Ps. 83:11; Ezek. 32:30; Dan. 11:8; Mic. 5:5. The Hebrew word also means drink offering or libation; see DRINK OFFERING <5257>]. ¶

[2] ***rāzôn*** [masc. noun: רָזוֹן <7333>; from HEAVY (BE) <7336> (in the sense of ruler, prince)] ▶ **This word means a dignitary, a ruler.** The term occurs once in the entire Old Testament in Proverbs 14:28 and is synonymous with the noun *meleḵ* (<4428>), meaning king. The proverb states that what

makes or breaks a prince is whether or not he has a multitude of subjects to rule over. The term is derived from the verb *rāzan* (<7336>), to be heavy. ¶

3 ***śar*** [masc. noun: שַׂר <8269>; from RULE <8323>] ▶ **This word means a chieftain, a chief, a ruler, an official, a captain, a prince. The primary usage is official in the sense that this individual has immediate authority as the leader.** While he was at Gath, David became the leader for those who were in distress, in debt, or were discontented (1 Sam. 22:2). The word describes the powers of a magistrate when a man posed a sarcastic question to Moses (Ex. 2:14). In Genesis, the noun refers to Phicol as the commander of Abimelech's forces (Gen. 21:22). In a similar usage of the word, Joshua was met by the commander of the Lord's army. This commander was so entrusted by God that Joshua had to take off his shoes due to the glory of God surrounding the man. Some see this as an appearance of the Angel of the Lord, the pre-incarnate Christ (Josh. 5:14). This word is used to describe the coming Messiah (*Sar Shalom*, «Prince of Peace») (Isaiah 9:6).

In terms of priesthood, *śar* designates a leading priest, i.e., a priest that is above the others (Ezra 8:24, 29). In this situation with Ezra, the leading priest was entrusted with the articles of the Temple and had to guard them with his life. The noun depicts Michael as one of the chief princes who came to Daniel's aid (Dan. 10:13). In Daniel 8:11, the word is used to denote the little horn setting itself up to be as great as the Prince of the host. This horn would set itself up, take away the daily sacrifice, and desecrate the Temple of God. *

– 4 Gen. 23:6 ➔ RULER <5387> 5 Judg. 5:3; Ps. 2:2; Prov. 8:15; 31:4; Hab. 1:10 ➔ HEAVY (BE) <7336> 6 Esther 1:3 (NIV); Dan. 1:3 (KJV) ➔ NOBLE <6579> 7 Ps. 68:31 ➔ ENVOY <2831> 8 Is. 41:25 ➔ RULER <5461> 9 Dan. 3:2, 3, 27; 6:1–4, 6, 7 ➔ SATRAP <324> 10 Nah. 3:17 ➔ CROWNED ONE <4502> a.

PRINCE (TO MAKE ONESELF A) – Num. 16:13 ➔ RULE (verb) <8323>.

PRINCELY – Zech. 11:13 ➔ ROBE <145>.

PRINCESS – ***śārāh*** [fem. noun: שָׂרָה <8282>; fem. of PRINCE <8269>] ▶ **This word always refers to women who had access to the royal court; it is also translated lady, noble woman, woman of nobility, queen.** It is used of the particular princesses who associated with Deborah, Solomon, and the nation of Persia (Judg. 5:29; 1 Kgs. 11:3; Esther 1:18). It is also used in a general sense to describe princesses who were humbled to become nurses and servants (Is. 49:23; Lam. 1:1). This word is also the root for SARAH. The Lord gave Abraham›s wife Sarai the new name «Sarah;» she would become «a mother of nations» and «kings» (Gen. 17:15–16). ¶

PRINCIPAL – 1 Is. 28:25 ➔ ROW (noun) <7795> b. 2 Jer. 25:34–36 ➔ MIGHTY <117>.

PRINCIPALITIES – ***mar'āšôṯ*** [fem. plur. noun: מַרְאָשׁוֹת <4761>; denom. from HEAD (noun) <7218>] ▶ **This word refers to the royal authority and splendor surrounding the office of kingship and held by the reigning king.** Ref.: Jer. 13:18, KJV; NKJV: rule. See HEAD (noun) <4763> also. ¶

PRINT (SET A) – Job 13:27 ➔ CARVE <2707>.

PRISE – Zech. 11:13 (KJV) ➔ PRECIOUS (BE) <3365>.

PRISON – 1 ***kele'*** [masc. noun: כֶּלֶא <3608>; from RESTRAIN <3607>] ▶ **This word refers to confinement, imprisonment.** A *bêyṯ kele'* is a house of confinement, a prison (1 Kgs. 22:27; Is. 42:22; Jer. 37:4; 52:33). Used in a genitive "of" form or phrase, it indicates something to do with imprisonment: *bigdêy kil'ô*, garments of imprisonment, a convict's clothing (2 Kgs. 25:29). *

2 ***keliy', kelû'*** [masc. noun: כְּלִיא, כְּלוּא <3628>; from RESTRAIN <3607> (comp. <3608> above)] ▶ **A place of confinement and incarceration.** Refs.: Jer. 37:4; 52:31.

Jeremiah spent time there. It was a good sign when Jehoiachin was freed from confinement in a Babylonian prison (Jer. 52:31). ¶
3 ***masgêr*** [masc. noun: מַסְגֵּר <4525>; from CLOSE <5462> (in the sense of to shut up, to give to someone in authority)] ▶ **This word designates a dungeon, a place of incarceration and detainment.** Used figuratively, it pictured a prison of the psalmist's soul (Ps. 142:7). It is used metaphorically of the place of imprisonment of the host of heaven and the dead kings of the earth, possibly Sheol (Is. 24:22), but it was a holding place, not a final abode. It is used both literally and figuratively in Isaiah 42:7. The Hebrew word also means a metal worker, an artisan; see SMITH <4525>. ¶
4 ***sōhar*** [masc. noun: סֹהַר <5470>; from the same as ROUNDED <5469> (in the sense of surrounded, e.g., by walls)] ▶ **This was a place for incarcerating prisoners, specifically those termed prisoners of the king. This word is also translated jail.** Refs.: Gen. 39:20–23. Those persons were formerly in the employment of the royal house in some way (Gen. 40:3, 5). ¶
– 5 Gen. 42:17, 19 ➔ CUSTODY <4929> 6 2 Chr. 16:10; Jer. 29:26 ➔ STOCKS <4115> 7 Neh. 3:25; 12:39; Jer. 32:2, 8, 12; 33:1; etc. ➔ GUARD <4307> 8 Ps. 66:11 ➔ NET <4686> 9 Is. 53:8 ➔ OPPRESSION <6115> 10 Jer. 37:15 ➔ BOND <612>.

PRISONER – ***'āsiyr*** [masc. noun: אָסִיר <615>; from BIND <631>] ▶ **This word refers to a variety of inmates or captives.** Prisoners of war (Is. 14:17); prisoners held in containment for various reasons (Gen. 39:20); or who had been under taskmasters (Job 3:18). These persons were also the object of God's special concern (Ps. 68:6; 69:33; 79:11). This word describes the freed captives, prisoners from the Babylonian exile, the exiles of Israel (Zech. 9:11). They were prisoners of hope (Zech. 9:12) awaiting their release from captivity in Babylon. Other refs.: Gen. 39:22; Judg. 16:21, 25; Ps. 102:20; 107:10; Lam. 3:34. ¶

PRISONERS – ***'assiyr*** [masc. coll. noun: אַסִּיר <616>; for PRISONER <615>] ▶ **This word is used to describe captives of war and plunder.** Ref.: Is. 10:4. In a highly theological usage, it refers to prisoners as those kings of earth and the host of heaven whom the Lord will gather into prison and eventually punish (Is. 24:22). Equally significant is the spiritual liberation and rescue given to prisoners suffering spiritual captivity. The Servant of the Lord will bring them out, liberating them (Is. 42:7). ¶

PRIVATE (IN) – 1 Sam. 18:22 ➔ ENCHANTMENT <3909>.

PRIVATE PARTS – ***m**ᵉ**bûšiym*** [masc. plur. noun: מְבוּשִׁים <4016>; from ASHAMED (BE) <954>] ▶ **This word refers to the external male reproductive organs, especially the scrotum and testicles.** Ref.: Deut. 25:11; also translated male genitals. ¶

PRIVATELY – 1 ***š**ᵉ**liy*** [masc. noun: שְׁלִי <7987>; from EASE (BE AT) <7951>] ▶ **This word indicates quietness, privacy.** Used in an adverbially sense, it means to do something in private, secretly, without witnesses, according to its context (2 Sam. 3:27; KJV: quietly). ¶
– 2 1 Sam. 18:22 ➔ ENCHANTMENT <3909>.

PRIVILY – 1 Sam. 24:4 ➔ ENCHANTMENT <3909>.

PRIVY MEMBER – Deut. 23:1 ➔ MALE ORGAN <8212>.

PRIZED BELONGINGS – Jer. 20:5 ➔ HONOR (noun) <3366>.

PROBLEM – ***q**ᵉ**ṭar*** [Aramaic masc. noun: קְטַר <7001>; from a root corresponding to JOINED (BE) <7000> (in the sense of a knot, as tied up)] ▶ **This word has the sense of a twisted connection (a knot).** In a figurative sense, it refers to a complicated problem to be solved, undone (Dan. 5:12, 16; also translated doubt, enigma, difficult problem). For another meaning of the Hebrew word, see HIP JOINT <7001>. ¶

PROBLEMS – Deut. 1:12 ➔ LOAD (noun) <2960>.

PROCEED – Gen. 12:8 ➔ MOVE <6275>.

PROCEEDING – ***tah^alukāh*** [fem. noun: תַּהֲלֻכָה <8418>; from GO <1980>] ▶ **This word refers to a festive procession, a formal march to some designated location.** Ref.: Neh. 12:31. ¶

PROCEEDS – Prov. 3:14 ➔ MERCHANDISE <5504>.

PROCEEDS (WHAT) – Num. 30:12 ➔ GOING OUT, GOING FORTH <4161>.

PROCESSION – 1 1 Sam. 10:5, 10 ➔ ROPE <2256> 2 Ps. 68:24 ➔ WAY <1979>.

PROCLAIM – Dan. 3:4; 4:14; etc. ➔ READ <7123>.

PROCLAIMED (BE) – Dan. 5:29 ➔ PROCLAMATION <3745>.

PROCLAMATION – 1 ***k^eraz*** [Aramaic noun: כְּרָז <3745>; prob. of Greek origin (to proclaim: *kērussō*)] ▶ **This word refers to a royal report issued by a king.** It refers in context to Belshazzar's official royal announcement concerning Daniel (Dan. 5:29). ¶
– 2 Jon. 2:2 ➔ MESSAGE <7150>.

PROD – Judg. 16:16 ➔ URGE <509>.

PRODUCE (noun) – 1 ***gereš*** [masc. noun: גֶּרֶשׁ <1645>; from CAST OUT <1644>] ▶ **This word has the sense of yield, something put forth.** It is used with respect to the months' yield, their produce (Deut. 33:14, ESV, NASB, NKJV). NIV and KJV understand the word for moon, not month, as the thing which produces the yield). ¶
2 ***^abûr*** [masc. noun: 5669> עֲבוּר; the same as BECAUSE <5670> (in the sense of to keep over)] ▶ **This word refers to food.** It is used of what fields produce or generate, especially the fields of Canaan (Josh. 5:11, 12; KJV: old corn). ¶
– 3 Lev. 26:4, 20; Deut. 11:17; Judg. 6:4; Ps. 67:6; 85:12; Ezek. 34:27; Hag. 1:10; Zech. 8:12 ➔ INCREASE (noun) <2981> 4 Deut. 22:9 ➔ HARVEST <4395> 5 Job 40:20 ➔ FOOD <944> 6 Ps. 78:46; etc. ➔ LABOR (noun) <3018>.

PRODUCE (verb) – ***dāšā'*** [verb: דָּשָׁא <1876>; a prim. root] ▶ **This word means and is also translated to bring forth, to sprout. It means to produce green plants or fresh green grass.** With the earth as its subject, it depicts the initial production of green vegetables or grass (Gen. 1:11). It depicts the pastures and the wilderness turning green from God's blessing and restoration after judgment (Joel 2:22; also translated to be green, to become green, to spring, to spring up). ¶

PRODUCT – 1 Gen. 43:11 ➔ FRUIT <2173> 2 Is. 45:14 ➔ LABOR (noun) <3018>.

PROFANE (adj.) – Lev. 10:10; Ezek. 22:26; 44:20, 23; 48:15 ➔ COMMON <2455>.

PROFANE (BE) – Jer. 23:11 ➔ DEFILED (BE) <2610>.

PROFANE (verb) – See PIERCE <2490>.

PROFANENESS – ***ḥ^anuppāh*** [fem. noun: חֲנֻפָּה <2613>; fem. from DEFILED (BE) <2610>] ▶ **This word means irreverence as well as filthiness, godlessness; it is also translated pollution, ungodliness.** It occurs only in Jeremiah 23:15 where it describes the wickedness, including Baal worship, promoted by false prophets. The prophets' profaneness included substituting their own words for God's words. This led the people to hope for peace when they should have expected God's wrath. ¶

PROFIT (noun) – 1 ***beṣa'*** [masc. noun: בֶּצַע <1215>; from CUT OFF <1214>] ▶ **This word denotes gain, dishonest gain, covetousness.** It refers to illegal or unjust gain or profit which God's people were to avoid (Gen. 37:26; Ex. 18:21; 1 Sam. 8:3; Ps. 119:36; Prov. 28:16). It is further qualified in some contexts as gain obtained by violent means (Judg. 5:19; Mic. 4:13) or profit gained with selfish goals in mind (Gen. 37:26; Mal. 3:14). *

2 ***yiṯrôn*** [fem. noun: יִתְרוֹן <3504>; from REMAIN <3498>] ► **This word means advantage, gain.** It is found only in Ecclesiastes. It is used of the benefit or gain that could be the result of one's labor or work (Eccl. 1:3; 5:16; 10:11); or knowledge (Eccl. 7:12; also translated excellence, excellency). Wisdom does prove to have some benefit or advantage for attaining success (Eccl. 10:10). Under the sun, i.e., in this life apart from God, there is no gain (Eccl. 2:11). All is vanity. Other refs.: Eccl. 2:13; 3:9; 5:9. ¶

3 ***môṯār*** [masc. noun: מוֹתָר <4195>; from REMAIN <3498>] ► **This word indicates abundance, advantage.** It indicates profit or benefit, material or otherwise. In context it is what comes as result of labor (Prov. 14:23) and faithful effort (Prov. 21:5; also translated plenty, plenteousness). It takes on the aspect of advantage or a more favorable position or superiority over something else (Eccl. 3:19; KJV: preeminence). ¶

4 ***tarbiyṯ*** [fem. noun: תַּרְבִּית <8636>; from MANY (BE, BECOME) <7235>] ► **This word means increase, excessive interest, usury, unjust gain.** It is used to indicate usurious interest; oppressive, unjust rates of interest (Lev. 25:36). It was a business practice condemned by the wisdom writers as well (Prov. 28:8; NKJV: extortion); and the prophets (Ezek. 22:12). The righteous person does not lend money to gain benefits, increase, or interest at the expense of others (Ezek. 18:8, 13, 17). ¶

– 5 Lev. 25:37 → INCREASE (noun) <4768> 6 Job 35:3 → PROFITABLE (BE) <5532> a. 7 Eccl. 5:11 → SKILL <3788> 8 Eccl. 6:11; 7:11 → MORE, MORE THAN <3148> 9 Is. 23:18 → MERCHANDISE <5504>.

PROFIT (verb) – 1 ***yāʿal*** [verb: יָעַל <3276>; a prim. root] ► **This word means to gain, to benefit. It indicates something that is done beneficially, resulting in success and betterment. It is used most often figuratively of spiritual benefits from the Lord.** Gods other than the Lord could not benefit His people (1 Sam. 12:21; Jer. 2:8, 11). It is possible to put forth effort to no gain or benefit (Jer. 12:13). Useless talk is of no profit (Job 15:3). Israel had come to believe that they would not gain anything (*yāʿal*) by serving the Lord (Job 21:15). Wealth gotten wrongly does not ultimately result in any gain (Prov. 10:2); righteousness delivers one before the Lord but not riches (Prov. 11:4). Wrong alliances with enemies of the Lord bring no gain (Is. 30:5, 6). *

– 2 Job 34:9 → PROFITABLE (BE) <5532> a.

PROFITABLE (BE) – ***sāḵan, sōḵên*** [סָכַן, סֹכֵן <5532>; a prim. root] ►

a. A verb indicating to be useful, gainful, to attend to, to be acquainted with. It means to be accustomed to acting in a certain way (Num. 22:30: to be the habit, to be accustomed, to be wont, to be disposed); to take care of things as needed (1 Kgs. 1:2: to care, to take care, to be in the service, to become the nurse, to cherish; Job 22:21: to acquaint, to yield, to agree, to submit). When negated, it means to do something in a useless manner, in a way that will not profit (Job 15:3: unprofitable, useless). In a different context, it means to be of value, to be useful (Job 22:2: to be profitable, to be of benefit, to be of use); to profit (Job 34:9: to profit; 35:3: advantage, profit). It has the sense of knowing someone intimately, closely (Ps. 139:3: to be acquainted, to be intimately acquainted, to be familiar). It may indicate being over or in charge of something (Is. 22:15: to be over, to be in charge). ¶

b. A feminine noun meaning a steward, a nurse. It means to care for people as needed, to be a nurse to them (1 Kgs. 1:2, 4). It is understood by some as a noun in Isaiah 22:15, meaning steward or administrator. ¶

PROFOUND – 1 ***ʿᵃmiyq*** [Aramaic adj.: עֲמִיק <5994>; corresponding to UNINTELLIGIBLE <6012> (in the sense of deep, unfathomable)] ► **This word means deep in a physical sense, as a deep valley.**

It is used in a figurative sense of the type of things God reveals, deep things that only He knows (Dan. 2:22). ¶
– [2] Ps. 92:5 ➔ DEEP, DEEP (BE) <6009> [3] Eccl. 7:24 ➔ DEEP (adj.) <6013>.

PROFUSE (BE) – Prov. 27:6 ➔ MULTIPLY <6280>.

PROLONG – ***'ārak*** [verb: אָרַךְ <748>; a prim. root] ▶ **This word means to be long, draw out, or postpone; it is also translated to defer, to delay. In most instances, it refers to the element of time.** Most commonly, it bears the causative sense: to prolong one's days (Deut. 5:16); to show continuance (Ex. 20:12); to tarry or to stay long (Num. 9:19); to survive after (Josh. 24:31); to postpone or defer anger (Is. 48:9); to draw out (1 Kgs. 8:8). Used literally, it describes the growth of branches (Ezek. 31:5); and as a command, to lengthen one's cords (Is. 54:2). *

PROLONGING – Dan. 4:27 ➔ LENGTHENING <754>.

PROMINENT – [1] Ezek. 17:22 ➔ LOFTY <8524> [2] Dan. 8:5 ➔ VISION <2380>.

PROMINENT MAN – 1 Kgs. 1:42 ➔ VALIANT MAN <381>.

PROMINENT PEOPLE – 2 Kgs. 24:15 ➔ BODY <193> b.

PROMISE – Lev. 19:20 ➔ BETROTH <2778>.

PROMOTE – Ps. 140:8 ➔ OBTAIN <6329>.

PROMPT – [1] Job 15:5 ➔ to teach ➔ LEARN <502> [2] Is. 16:5 ➔ SKILLED <4106>.

PRONOUNCE – 1 Kgs. 20:40 ➔ MOVE <2782>.

PROOFS – Is. 41:21 ➔ ARGUMENTS (STRONG) <6110>.

PROPER – ***^{a}riyḵ*** [Aramaic adj.: אֲרִיךְ <749>; properly corresponding to PROLONG <748>, but used only in the sense of reaching to a given point] ▶ **This word describes a political situation that is not appropriate to tolerate or condone; it is also translated fitting, meet.** Ref.: Ezra 4:14. ¶

PROPER (SEEM) – Esther 8:5 ➔ SUCCESS (BRING, GIVE) <3787>.

PROPER END – Prov. 16:4 ➔ ANSWER (noun) <4617> b.

PROPERTY – [1] Gen. 34:10: to acquire, to get property ➔ HOLD (TAKE) <270> [2] Neh. 5:13; Ezek. 23:29 ➔ LABOR (noun) <3018>.

PROPERTY (LOST) – ***^{a}ḇêḏāh*** [fem. noun: אֲבֵדָה <9>; from PERISH <6>] ▶ **This word means a lost object or possession.** The term is employed only in a legal context in the Hebrew Bible (Ex. 22:8; Lev. 6:4; Deut. 22:3). To keep a lost item in one's possession and lie about it to the rightful owner is listed among sins, such as deception concerning a deposit or pledge and robbery and fraud (Lev. 6:3). ¶

PROPHECY – ***n^{e}ḇû'āh*** [fem. noun: נְבוּאָה <5016>; from PROPHESY <5012>] ▶ **A word meaning prediction, foretelling; a prophetic word.** Shemaiah gave a false prophecy to Nehemiah in order to cause him to sin and to saddle him with a bad name (Neh. 6:12). The prophecy of Azariah, son of Oded, encouraged King Asa of Judah to implement religious reform in the country, bringing the people back to the Lord their God (2 Chr. 15:8). Once the word refers to a written prophecy by a prophet named Ahijah (2 Chr. 9:29). ¶

PROPHESY – [1] ***nāḇā'*** [verb: נָבָא <5012>; a prim. root] ▶ **This word means to speak by inspiration, to predict.** This most commonly refers to the way in which the word of the Lord came to the people (Jer. 19:14; Ezek. 11:13). There were various means in which people came to prophesy. Eldad and Medad became ecstatic when they prophesied (Num. 11:25–27); whereas the sons of Asaph used songs and instruments when they prophesied (1 Chr. 25:1). False prophets were also known to prophesy (Zech. 13:3). *

[2] ***n^{e}ḇā'*** [Aramaic verb: נְבָא <5013>; corresponding to <5012> above] ▶ **In context, this verb means to prophesy in the sense of addressing exhortations to the people of God in order to stir them up** Only found once in the Old Testament, it is used to describe the means by which Haggai and Zechariah prophesied to the people of Israel (Ezra 5:1). ¶

PROPHESYING – ***n^{e}ḇû'āh*** [Aramaic fem. noun: נְבוּאָה <5017>; corresponding to PROPHECY <5016>] ▶ **This word refers to the role and functions of a prophet; it is also translated preaching.** It appears only once in the Old Testament, where it is recorded that the elders prospered through the prophesying of Haggai the prophet and Zechariah the son of Iddo (Ezra 6:14). ¶

PROPHET – [1] ***n^{e}ḇiy'*** [Aramaic masc. noun: נְבִיא <5029>; corresponding to <5030> below] ▶ **The word refers to an individual in the role and fulfilling the functions of one who receives and communicates the will of God. He interprets the mind of God and speaks what God has given him to say.** Refs.: Ezra 5:1, 2; 6:14. It is probably closely related to the biblical Hebrew word (if not the same word), *nāḇiy'* <5030>; as such, it would share similar, if not the same, variations in meaning. ¶

[2] ***nāḇiy'*** [masc. noun: נָבִיא <5030>; from PROPHESY <5012>] ▶ **The meaning is consistently one of prophet and inspired spokesman; see previous definition.** Moses was the greatest prophet of the Old Testament (Deut. 34:10) and the example for all later prophets. He displayed every aspect of a true prophet, both in his call, his work, his faithfulness, and, at times, his doubts. Only Abraham is called a prophet before Moses (Gen. 20:7).

Moses received a call from God to speak His words and perform a specific task (see Ex. 3:4, 10; 4:17, 29; 5:1) with the promise that the Lord would be with him and help him accomplish it (see Ex. 3:12, 20; 4:12, 14–16). He responded, though reluctantly (see Ex. 3:11, 13; 4:1), and God did what He had said He would do (see Ex. 6:1; 14:30, 31; 40:34, 38). Moses' prophetic voice spoke to Israel of the past (see Deuteronomy 1–3), the present (see Deut. 4:1; 26:18), and the future (see Deut. 31:20–22), as would every major prophet after him. This pattern, or much of it, is found in the case of every true prophet (see Isaiah 6; Jeremiah 1; Ezekiel 1–3; Hos. 1:2; Amos 7:14, 15; Jon. 1:1). All the true prophets stood in the counsel of God to receive their messages (see 1 Kgs. 22:19; Jer. 23:22; Amos 3:7). This word describes one who was raised up by God and, as such, could only proclaim that which the Lord gave him to say. A prophet could not contradict the Law of the Lord or speak from his own mind or heart. To do so was to be a false prophet (Jer. 14:14; 23:16, 26, 30). What a prophet declared had to come true, or he was false (Deut. 18:22; Jer. 23:9).

The noun is found parallel to two other words meaning a seer, a prophet (*ḥōzeh* <2374>, *rō'eh* [1 Sam. 9:9; 2 Sam. 24:11]), which tends to stress the visionary or perceptive aspects of a prophet's experiences. There were "sons of the prophets," a phrase indicating bands or companies of prophets, "son" in this case meaning a member (1 Kgs. 20:35; 2 Kgs. 2:3, 5; 4:1). Kings sometimes had a group of prophets around them (1 Kgs. 22:22; 2 Chr. 18:21, 22). Prophets were designated from Israel (Ezek. 13:2, 4); Samaria (Jer. 23:13); and Jerusalem (Zeph. 3:4). In an unusual development, David set aside some of the sons of Asaph, Heman, and Jeduthun to serve as prophets. Their prophesying was accompanied with musical instruments and possibly was brought on and aided by these instruments. This phenomenon is described mainly in the book of 2 Chronicles (see 2 Chr. 20:14; 29:30). Evidently, Zechariah, the priest, also prophesied in that era. But

Moses himself desired that all God's people have the Spirit of God on them, as did the prophets (Num. 11:29). *

PROPHETESS – ***nᵉḇiy'āh*** [fem. noun: נְבִיאָה <5031>; fem. of PROPHET <5030>] ▶ **The word is the feminine form of the Hebrew *nāḇî'* <5030>, meaning a spokesman, a speaker, or a prophet.** The ancient concept of a prophetess was a woman who had the gift of song, like Miriam (Ex. 15:20) or Deborah (Judg. 4:4; cf. Judg. 5:1). The later concept of a prophetess, being more in line with the concept of a prophet, was one who was consulted in order to receive a word from the Lord, like Huldah (2 Kgs. 22:14; 2 Chr. 34:22). It also described a false prophetess, Noadiah (Neh. 6:14). A unique usage may be its reference to the wife of Isaiah as a prophetess (Is. 8:3). Is this because of her own position and work or because of her relationship with Isaiah, a prophet? It has been interpreted both ways. ¶

PROPORTION – [1] ***maṯkōneṯ*** [fem. noun: מַתְכֹּנֶת <4971>; from WEIGH <8505> in the transferred sense of measuring] ▶ **This word indicates a measure, a quota, specifications.** It indicates some kind of measurement: a quota of bricks (Ex. 5:8; also translated number, tale); a proper proportional mixing of quantities of ingredients (Ex. 30:32, 37; Ezek. 45:11; also translated composition, formula). It refers to architectural and construction specifications and proportions (2 Chr. 24:13; also translated original condition, original design, proper condition, state). ¶

– [2] 1 Kgs. 7:36 ➔ NAKEDNESS <4626>.

PROSPECT – Prov. 10:28 ➔ HOPE (noun) <8431>.

PROSPER – [1] ***ṣᵉlaḥ*** [Aramaic verb: צְלַח <6744>; corresponding to RUSH (verb) <6743> (in the sense of to advance)] ▶ **This word means to successfully complete a task or a building project.** Refs.: Ezra 5:8; 6:14. It describes God's prospering persons in their daily tasks and responsibilities (Dan. 3:30). It indicates the amazing success Daniel enjoyed under Persian kings (Dan. 6:28). ¶

– [2] Job 12:6; Ps. 122:6; Jer. 12:1; Lam. 1:5 ➔ EASE (BE AT) <7951> a. [3] Eccl. 11:6 ➔ SUCCESS (BRING, GIVE) <3787> [4] Is. 53:10; etc. ➔ RUSH <6743> [5] Dan. 4:1; 6:25: may you prosper greatly ➔ lit.: peace be multiplied to you ➔ PEACE <8001>.

PROSPERING – Dan. 4:4 ➔ GREEN (BE) <7487> b.

PROSPERITY – [1] ***kōshārāh*** [fem. noun: כּוֹשָׁרָה <3574>; from SUCCESS (BRING) <3787>] ▶

a. This word refers to spiritual liberty and freedom. The Lord restores them to the oppressed or lonely (Ps. 68:6), a place of abundance in figurative language. ¶

b. A feminine noun indicating singing. This is the preferred translation for this word by some. The lonely or oppressed are liberated by singing (Ps. 68:6). ¶

c. A feminine noun indicating chains. It is used of the Lord freeing those bound in chains. Again, some translators prefer this rendering, but see a. and b. above (Ps. 68:6). ¶

[2] ***šālû*** [masc. noun: שָׁלוּ <7959>; from EASE (BE AT) <7951>] ▶ **This word indicates a state of abundance including good health that gives a false sense of total security in one's present state.** Ref.: Ps. 30:6. ¶

[3] ***šalwāh*** [fem. noun: שַׁלְוָה <7962>; from EASE (BE AT) <7951>] ▶ **This word also means security, quietness. It indicates ease, a lack of anxiety.** It describes a state of prosperity for Jerusalem (Ps. 122:7); but also a state of prosperity that contributed to her downfall (Jer. 22:21); excessive ease, security (Ezek. 16:49). It has the sense of excessive complacency or unconcern (Prov. 1:32). It depicts a state and attitude of peacefulness and enjoyment between friends or family (Prov. 17:1); and in and among nations and peoples (Dan. 8:25; 11:21, 24). ¶

[4] ***šᵉlêwāh*** [Aramaic noun: שְׁלֵוָה <7963>; corresponding to <7962> above] ▶ **See definition for <7962> above; this word is also**

translated tranquillity. It refers to a peaceful condition and to national security, as well as prosperity in a city or nation (Dan. 4:27). ¶

PROSPEROUS – Dan. 4:4 ➔ GREEN (BE) <7487> b.

PROSTITUTE – 1 Kgs. 22:38 ➔ ARMOR <2185> b.

PROSTITUTE (FEMALE TEMPLE) – ***qᵉḏēšāh*** [fem. noun: קְדֵשָׁה <6948>; fem. of PROSTITUTE (MALE TEMPLE) <6945>] ► **Although the term refers to a person who was consecrated (set apart), it is important to know what they were consecrated to. When referring to a pagan temple cult, it connotes a woman set apart for pagan temple service, namely, female prostitution (having sexual relations outside marriage).** Refs.: Deut. 23:17; Hos. 4:14. It is also possible that this term was used as a general term for prostitution (Gen. 38:21, 22) because of its parallel usage with *zānāh* [PROSTITUTE (verb) <2181>] (see Gen. 38:15). However, it is at the same time possible that *zānāh* was merely the more general term for a prostitute, while *qᵉḏēšāh* was the exclusive term for a shrine prostitute. ¶

PROSTITUTE (MALE TEMPLE, CULT, SHRINE) – ***qāḏēs***]]] [masc. noun: קָדֵשׁ <6945>; from HOLY (BE) <6942>] ► The feminine form of this word is *qᵉḏēšāh* (<6948>). **Although the term denotes one who was consecrated (set apart), the question must be asked, "Consecrated to what?" In the context of a pagan temple cult, the proper context for this word, it connotes a man who was set apart for pagan temple service, namely, male prostitution (having sexual relations outside marriage).** Refs.: Deut. 23:17; 1 Kgs. 14:24; 15:12; 22:46. This term is sometimes translated as sodomite, which is an excellent expression of the likelihood that these were homosexual or at least bisexual prostitutes. Other refs.: 2 Kgs. 23:7; Job 36:14. ¶

PROSTITUTE (verb) – ***zānāh, zônāh, zōnāh*** [verb: זָנָה, זוֹנָה, זֹנָה <2181>; a prim. root (highly-fed and therefore wanton)] ► **This word means to fornicate, i.e., to have sexual relations outside marriage.** It is typically used for women and only twice in reference to men (Num. 25:1). It occurs in connection with prostitution (Lev. 21:7; Prov. 7:10); figuratively, Israel's improper relationships with other nations (Is. 23:17; Ezek. 23:30; Nah. 3:4); or other gods (Ex. 34:15, 16; Deut. 31:16; Ezek. 6:9; Hos. 9:1). As a metaphor, it describes Israel's breach of the Lord's covenant relationship (Ex. 34:16). *

PROSTITUTION – [1] ***zᵉnûniym*** [masc. noun: זְנוּנִים <2183>; from PROSTITUTE (verb) <2181>] ► **This word means having sexual relations outside marriage; it also means fornication, adultery, idolatry.** Judah's daughter-in-law Tamar was accused of prostitution (Gen. 38:24). This word can also be used to describe cities like Nineveh (Nah. 3:4). Most often, it is used in a religious sense to describe, for instance, the unfaithfulness of Israel. Jezebel practiced idolatry (2 Kgs. 9:22); and Jerusalem's idolatry was portrayed in a story where she was the prostitute Oholibah (Ezek. 23:11, 29). God commanded Hosea to take an unfaithful wife (Hos. 1:2), who was also a picture of Israel (Hos. 2:2, 4; 4:12; 5:4). ¶
[2] ***taznûṯ*** [noun: תַּזְנוּת <8457>; from PROSTITUTE (verb) <2181>] ► **See previous definition; this word is also translated whoredom, harlotry, whoring.** This word is found only in Ezekiel 16 and 23. Chapter sixteen is an allegorical story about Jerusalem's faithlessness to the Lord (Ezek. 16:26). In this chapter, the Lord indicts Jerusalem for acting like a prostitute, throwing herself to the gods of foreign nations (Ezek. 16:15, 20, 33, 36). Chapter twenty-three is a similar story about Judah and Israel portrayed as two sisters in whoredom with the foreign nations (Ezek. 23:7, 14, 18, 35). These passages expose the vileness of the Israelites' sin. *

PROSTRATE – Dan. 2:46 ➔ FALL, FALL DOWN <5457>.

PROSTRATE (LIE) – Job 14:10 ➔ LAY LOW <2522>.

PROTECT – Mic. 1:11 ➔ STANDING PLACE <5979>.

PROTECTION – [1] Deut. 32:38 ➔ COVERING <5643> b. [2] Is. 4:6 ➔ SHELTER <4563>.

PROUD – [1] ***gê'*** [adj.: גֵּא <1341>; from <1343> below] ▶ **This word means haughty, prideful, arrogant.** It describes the character and attitude of Moab toward Israel (Is. 16:6). It has the same meaning as *gē'eh* (<1343> below). ¶
[2] ***gê'eh*** [adj.: גֵּאֶה <1343>; from RISE <1342>] ▶ **This word describes arrogant persons; the Lord has reserved a time of judgment when they will be abased.** Refs.: Job 40:11, 12; Ps. 94:2; Prov. 15:25. The Lord will judge at the right time (Is. 2:12). A whole nation can be depicted as haughty (Jer. 48:29). These persons set traps and snares for the righteous (Ps. 140:5). The opposite attitude and character trait is humility which is preferred to an arrogant and proud demeanor (Prov. 16:19). ¶
[3] ***gaᵃyôn*** [adj.: גַּאֲיוֹן <1349>; from RISE <1342>] ▶ **This word means haughty, arrogant.** It refers to those persons who heap contempt and abuse on those who trusted in God (Ps. 123:4), acting arrogantly toward them. ¶
[4] ***gāḇōah*** [adj.: גָּבֹהַּ <1362>; from EXALTED (BE) <1361>] ▶ **This word denotes high, lofty; it is also translated arrogant.** It describes an attitude of haughtiness or arrogance (Ps. 101:5; Prov. 16:5), which the Lord hates. Patience is better than haughtiness (or: pride) (Eccl. 7:8). It refers to Assyria figuratively as a high tree (Ezek. 31:3: high). ¶
[5] ***zêḏ*** [adj.: זֵד <2086>; from PROUDLY (DEAL) <2102>] ▶ **This word means and is also translated presumptuous, willful; arrogant, insolent, haughty.** It most often occurs in the Psalms where it is used in connection with sin (Ps. 19:13) or to describe the ungodly (Ps. 86:14; 119:21, 85). Elsewhere in the Old Testament, *zēḏ* describes the proud who will be judged (Is. 13:11; Mal. 4:1) and the disobedience of the proud (Jer. 43:2). Other refs.: Ps. 119:51, 69, 78, 122; Prov. 21:24; Mal. 3:15. ¶
[6] ***rahaḇ*** [masc. noun: רַהַב <7293>; from BOLD (BE, MAKE) <7292>] ▶ **This word means pride, arrogance, strength.** It is treated as a common noun referring to someone arrogant, boastful, proud by some translators (Job 9:13; 26:12). It refers mockingly to the strength of Egypt, i.e., their sitting still, doing nothing (Is. 30:7). ¶
[7] ***rāhāḇ*** [adj.: 7295> רָהָב; from BOLD (BE, MAKE) <7292>] ▶ **This word is used to designate arrogant, haughty persons, having too high a view of themselves or their positions.** Ref.: Ps. 40:4. ¶
– [8] Job 28:8; 41:34 ➔ PRIDE <7830> [9] Ps. 124:5 ➔ RAGING <2121> [10] Is. 2:11 ➔ LOFTINESS <1365> [11] Hab. 2:4 ➔ PRESUME <6075> [12] Hab. 2:5 ➔ HAUGHTY <3093>.

PROUDLY – [1] Ps. 17:10 ➔ MAJESTY <1348> [2] Mic. 2:3 ➔ HAUGHTILY <7317>.

PROUDLY (ACT) – Is. 3:5 ➔ BOLD (BE, MAKE) <7292>.

PROUDLY (DEAL) – ***zûḏ, ziyḏ*** [verb: זוּד, זִיד <2102>; a prim. root] ▶
a. This verb means to treat insolently, presumptuously, arrogantly. It describes the Egyptians' arrogant and proud treatment of the Israelites in Egypt (Ex. 18:11; Neh. 9:10). It depicts the attitude of a person acting presumptuously toward his or her neighbor or with ill will to kill him (Ex. 21:14). Israel's disrespect and presumptuous actions toward God's commands are described using the word (Deut. 1:43; 17:13; Neh. 9:16). It means to speak presumptuously in God's name, having not received His command to do so (Deut. 18:20). It refers to the arrogant actions of Babylon against God and His people (Jer. 50:29). Other ref.: Neh. 9:29. ¶
b. A verb meaning to boil, to cook. It describes Jacob's action of boiling or preparing food (Gen. 25:29). ¶

PROVE – See TEST <974>.

PROVENDER – 1 Gen. 24:25, 32; 42:27; 43:24; Judg. 19:19 ➔ FODDER <4554> 2 Is. 30:24 ➔ FODDER <1098>.

PROVERB – 1 **speak in proverbs, make a proverb:** ***māšal*** [verb: מָשַׁל <4911>; denom. from <4912> below] ▶ **This word means to compare, to be like, to quote a proverb (a popular saying).** It is used to describe the delivery of a proverb or a comparison (Num. 21:27). It describes making something into or like something else, a proverb or byword (Job 17:6; 30:19; Ps. 28:1; 49:12, 20; 143:7; Is. 14:10). It compares one thing with another (Is. 46:5). Ezekiel uses the word often to mean to speak or to use a parable (Ezek. 12:23; 17:2; 18:2, 3). Its participial form indicates a person who produces parables and speaks in proverbs (Ezek. 20:49; 24:3). Other ref.: Ezek. 16:44. ¶

2 ***māšāl*** [masc. noun: מָשָׁל <4912>; apparently from RULE (verb) <4910> in some original sense of superiority in mental action] ▶ **This word means an oracle, a parable (proverbial saying, similitude, aphorism).** It is a literary genre, device, and style in the form of short, pithy sayings, prophetic utterances, or compositions of comparison (1 Sam. 10:12; 24:13; Ezek. 12:22, 23; 17:2; 20:49). It has the sense of a byword or object spoken of in contempt or derision (Deut. 28:37; 1 Kgs. 9:7; Ps. 44:14; 69:11). It describes a prophetic utterance (Num. 23:7, 18; 24:3, 15, 20, 21, 23; Is. 14:4; Mic. 2:4). Its meaning is extended to poetry, that often features comparisons, figurative language, etc. (1 Kgs. 4:32; Ps. 49:4; 78:2). This word describes short sayings or sentences of wisdom (Job 13:12; 27:1; 29:1; Prov. 10:1; 25:1, etc. in Proverbs). *

– 3 Hab. 2:6 ➔ ENIGMA <2420>.

PROVIDE – 1 ***māsar*** [verb: מָסַר <4560>; a prim. root] ▶ **This word means to commit, to deliver up.** It means to supply or deliver for use: to supply men for war (Num. 31:5; also translated to recruit, to furnish, to deliver, to supply). In Numbers 31:16, it has the meaning of committing or occasioning something, in this case, apostasy or unfaithfulness against the Lord. ¶

– 2 Gen. 45:11; Neh. 9:21 ➔ CONTAIN <3557> 3 Ps. 144:13 ➔ OBTAIN <6329> 4 Jon. 1:17; 4:6–8 ➔ COUNT <4487>.

PROVINCE – 1 ***m***^e^***ḏiynāh*** [fem. noun: מְדִינָה <4082>; from JUDGE (verb) <1777>] ▶ **This word means a district (as ruled by a judge), a realm allotted to the jurisdiction of responsibility of a judge or lord. It refers to a specific area established by the political process within national boundaries.** It is used in a general sense of all provinces (1 Kgs. 20:14, 15, 17, 19; Eccl. 2:8; 5:8; Ezek. 19:8); of Babylonian provinces or districts (Ezra 2:1; Neh. 7:6; Dan. 8:2); of Judah as a province (Neh. 1:3). It is used often of Persian provinces (Esther 1:1, 3, 16, 22; Dan. 11:24) that numbered one hundred and twenty-seven. Other refs.: Neh. 11:3; Esther 2:3, 18; 3:8, 12–14; 4:3, 11; 8:5, 9, 11–13, 17; 9:2–4, 12, 16, 20, 28, 30; Eccl. 5:8; Lam. 1:1. ¶

2 ***m***^e^***ḏiynāh*** [Aramaic fem. noun: מְדִינָה <4083>; corresponding to <4082> above] ▶ **This word means an administrative area politically designated; it is also translated district.** It refers to the satrapies, a Persian name for provinces of the Persian Empire (Ezra 4:15; 5:8; 6:2; Dan. 3:1–3). One province encompassed all of Babylon (Ezra 7:16; Dan. 2:48, 49; Dan. 3:1, 12, 30). ¶

PROVISION – Neh. 11:23: fixed provision ➔ COVENANT <548>.

PROVISION(S) – Gen. 45:23; 2 Chr. 11:23 ➔ FOOD <4202>.

PROVISIONED (BE) – 1 Kgs. 20:27 ➔ CONTAIN <3557>.

PROVISIONS – 2 Kgs. 25:30; Jer. 40:5; 52:34 ➔ ALLOWANCE <737>.

PROVISIONS (BE GIVEN) – 1 Kgs. 20:27 ➔ CONTAIN <3557>.

PROVISIONS (TAKE AS) – Josh. 9:12 ➔ HUNT b, c. <6675>.

PROVOCATION – [1] ***ka'as, ka'as*** [masc. sing. noun: כַּעַס, כַּעַשׂ <3708>; from ANGER (PROVOKE TO) <3707>] ► **This word means anger, vexation. The alternate spelling of the Hebrew word occurs only in Job.** The majority of occurrences are in poetic literature. Human sinfulness and idolatry (1 Kgs. 15:30; Ezek. 20:28) cause God's anger, while fools, sons, wives, and rival wives can also cause vexation (1 Sam. 1:6; Prov. 27:3; 17:25; 21:19, respectively). *
– [2] Neh. 9:18, 26 ➔ DISGRACE (noun) <5007>.

PROVOKE – [1] Deut. 2:5, 9, 19, 24; 2 Kgs. 14:10; 2 Chr. 25:19 ➔ STRIVE <1624> [2] Job 16:3 ➔ GRIEVOUS <4834> [3] Ps. 78:41 ➔ VEX <8428> a.

PROVOKING (KEEP) – 1 Sam. 1:6 ➔ IRRITATE <7481>.

PROWL – Job 28:8 ➔ PASS OVER <5710>.

PRUDENCE – [1] ***'êṭâh*** [Aramaic fem. noun: עֵטָה <5843>; from CONSULT TOGETHER <3272>] ► **This word means careful good judgment that allows a person to avoid danger, counsel (i.e., sound advice given in directing the conduct of another). It refers to the discerning manner in which someone replies or acts.** Ref.: Dan. 2:14 (ESV). It is also translated counsel (KJV, NKJV), discretion (NASB), wisdom (NIV). ¶
[2] ***'ormâh*** [fem. noun: עָרְמָה <6195>; fem. of CRAFTINESS <6193>] ► **This word means craftiness, but also practical wisdom, discernment.** Ex. 21:14 employs it adverbially (schemes craftily) as does Josh. 9:4, where the foreign kings tricked Joshua into making a treaty. In Proverbs, the word has a different connotation. Both in the instruction for a son (Prov. 1:4; KJV: subtilty) and in describing Lady Wisdom who has *'ormâh* with her (Prov. 8:5, 12), the term is best translated prudence. See the verb *'âram* [CRAFTY (BE) <6191>]. ¶
– [3] Prov. 15:5: to show prudence ➔ lit.: to be prudent ➔ CRAFTY (BE) <6191>.

PRUDENT – [1] ***'ârûm*** [adj.: עָרוּם <6175>; pass. part. of CRAFTY (BE) <6191>] ► **Positively, this word means wise, sensible. Negatively, it means crafty, shrewd.** In a positive connotation, it is understood as being prudent. As such, a prudent individual takes no offense at an insult (Prov. 12:16); does not flaunt his knowledge (Prov. 12:23); takes careful thought of his ways (Prov. 14:8); takes careful thought before action (Prov. 14:15); is crowned with knowledge (Prov. 14:18); and sees and avoids danger (Prov. 22:3; 27:12). When the word has a negative meaning, it means being crafty (Job 5:12; 15:5). This word is used when the Bible describes the serpent in the Garden of Eden. The serpent was more subtle [crafty] than any beast of the field (Gen. 3:1; also translated cunning). This description is presented in stark contrast to the situation of Adam and Eve. They sought to be crafty like the serpent, but they only realized that they were *'êyrôm* (<5903>), meaning naked. Other ref.: Prov. 13:16. ¶
– [2] Prov. 15:5 ➔ CRAFTY (BE) <6191>.

PRUNE – ***zâmar*** [verb: זָמַר <2168>; a prim. root (comp. SING <2167>, STAND UP <5568>, WOOL <6785>)] ► **This verb means to trim, to remove something not necessary.** It indicates the pruning of vines (Lev. 25:3, 4) or, in the case of Israel as the Lord's vine or vineyard, the lack of pruning; it will be left to perish (Is. 5:6) without the Lord's tender care. ¶

PRUNING HOOK – ***mazmêrâh*** [fem. noun: מַזְמֵרָה <4211>; from PRUNE <2168>] ► **It was a knife or short trimming tool often used to cut or prune vines, one of Israel's major agricultural products.** Refs.: Is. 2:4; 18:5; Joel 3:10; Mic. 4:3. It was mentioned in times of judgment or restoration in Israel. ¶

PRUNING KNIFE – Is. 18:5 ➔ PRUNING HOOK <4211>.

PSALM – [1] ***mizmôr*** [masc. noun: מִזְמוֹר <4210>; from SING <2167>] ► **This word is found in the titles of psalms (sacred**

songs accompanied by a musical instrument) designating them as a psalm or melody. These musical titles are still under investigation to pinpoint their exact meanings more clearly. Refs.: Ps. 3–6, 8, 9, 12, 13, 15, 19–24, 29–31, 38–41, 47–51, 62–68, 73, 75–77, 79, 80, 82–85, 87, 88, 92, 98, 100, 101, 108–110, 139–141, 143. ¶
– 2 Ps. 81:2; 98:5 ➔ SONG <2172> 3 Ps. 95:2 ➔ SONG <2158>.

PSALMIST – 2 Sam. 23:1 ➔ SONG <2158>.

PSALTERY – 1 ***pᵉsanṭêriyn, pᵉsantêriyn*** [Aramaic masc. plur. noun: פְּסַנְתֵּרִין, פְּסַנְטֵרִין <6460>; a transliteration of the Greek *psalterion*] ▶ **This word designates a stringed musical instrument; a harp (psaltery).** It refers to one of the many instruments present at the dedication of Nebuchadnezzar's golden statue (Dan. 3:5, 7, 10, 15). A harp and psaltery both had sounding boards to magnify the sound. ¶
– 2 1 Sam. 10:5; 1 Kgs. 10:12; Ps. 57:8; 92:3 ➔ HARP <5035>.

PUAH – 1 ***pû'āh, puwwāh*** [masc. proper noun: פּוּאָה, פֻּוָּה <6312>; from PIECES (CUT TO) <6284>]: a blast; splendor ▶
a. Son of Issachar. Refs.: Gen. 46:13; Num. 26:23; 1 Chr. 7:1. ¶
b. Son of Dodo. Ref.: Judg. 10:1. ¶
2 ***pû'āh*** [fem. proper noun: פּוּעָה <6326>; from an unused root meaning to glitter]: splendor ▶ **One of the two midwives ordered by Pharaoh to kill the Israelite male children during the time of Moses, but who did not obey.** Ref.: Ex. 1:15. ¶

PUFF – Ps. 10:5 ➔ BREATHE <6315>.

PUFFED UP (BE) – Hab. 2:4 ➔ PRESUME <6075>.

PUHITES – 1 Chr. 2:53 ➔ PUTHITES <6336>.

PUITE – Num. 26:23 ➔ PUNITES <6324>.

PUL – ***pûl*** [proper noun: פּוּל <6322>; of foreign origin] ▶
a. A shortened form of Tiglath-Pileser, an Assyrian king (<8407>). ¶
b. The nation of Pul, an Ethiopian tribe; probably Libya. Ref.: Is. 66:19. ¶

PULL – 1 ***māšak̲*** [verb: מָשַׁךְ <4900>; a prim. root] ▶ **This word means to draw off, to drag, to pull up, to prolong.** It is used of pulling someone out of a location (Gen. 37:28; Jer. 38:13); to pull an object (Deut. 21:3); to pick out and retrieve something (Ex. 12:21). It means to draw out something, such as a trumpet sound (Ex. 19:13; Josh. 6:5). Used with the word for hand, it means to extend the hand (Hos. 7:5); with reference to a bow, it means to pull the bowstring (1 Kgs. 22:34; 2 Chr. 18:33). It takes on a figurative sense when used of dragging along iniquity or evil (Ps. 10:9; Is. 5:18). It may refer to lovingly leading, drawing someone along (Jer. 31:3); of bearing with a person or being patient (Neh. 9:30); or, conversely, of maintaining, stretching out one's anger (Ps. 85:5). It has the sense of a formal procession following someone in a funeral (Job 21:33). It has an idiomatic sense of sowing seed, pulling it from a pouch and dispersing it (Amos 9:13); and of marching, proceeding somewhere (Judg. 4:6). It describes drawing out a period of time (Ps. 36:10; Prov. 13:12; Is. 13:22); or a delay of time (Ezek. 12:25, 28). It may carry the sense of titillating, drawing out the sensitivities of the flesh (Eccl. 2:3). *
2 ***nᵉsaḥ*** [Aramaic verb: נְסַח <5256>; corresponding to TEAR <5255>] ▶ **This word means to be pulled out, to draw.** Found only once in the Old Testament, it refers to the removal of a beam of wood from the house of any person who altered the decree of King Cyrus. As punishment for disregarding the decree, the offending party would be hung or impaled on the wooden beam (Ezra 6:11). ¶
– 3 2 Sam. 17:13 ➔ DRAG (verb) <5498>.

PULL, PULL OUT – 1 ***māraṭ*** [verb: מָרַט <4803>; a prim. root] ▶ **This word means to fall off, to pluck off, to polish.** It is used of pulling out a person's hair (Ezra 9:3; Neh. 13:25); as well as of a person's hair

falling out, becoming bald (Lev. 13:40, 41: to fall, to loose). It indicates the plucking of a person's beard, an act of humiliation (Is. 50:6: to pull out, to pluck). It is used in a passive sense of burnished, polished (KJV: furbished) bronze or swords (Ezek. 21:9–11, 28). Used of human skin, it means smooth, polished (Is. 18:2, 7; also translated peeled, smooth-skinned). Other refs.: 1 Kgs. 7:45; Ezek. 29:18. ¶
– 2 Ruth 2:16 ➔ PLUNDER (verb) <7997> b.

PULL DOWN – ***hāras*** [verb: הָרַס <2040>; a prim. root] ▶ **This verb means to break through, to overthrow, to destroy.** In Miriam and Moses' song, God threw down His enemies (Ex. 15:7). Elijah told God that the Israelites had pulled down God's altars (1 Kgs. 19:10, 14). The psalmist wanted God to break out the teeth of the wicked (Ps. 58:6) and also said that God would tear down the wicked and not build them up again (Ps. 28:5). The foolish woman tore down her own house (Prov. 14:1). On Mount Sinai, God cautioned Moses to warn the people not to force their way through to see God and then perish (Ex. 19:21). In Exodus, this word is used in an even stronger sense when God instructs the Israelites not to worship foreign gods but to utterly demolish them (Ex. 23:24). *

PULL UP – Jer. 13:26 ➔ STRIP <2834>.

PULSE – Dan. 1:12, 16 ➔ VEGETABLE <2235>.

PULVERIZE – See BEAT <1854>.

PUNISH – 1 Ex. 21:22; Prov. 17:26; 21:11 ➔ FINE (verb) <6064> 2 Job 34:26 ➔ STRIKE <5606>.

PUNISHMENT – 1 ***biqqōreṯ*** [fem. noun: בִּקֹּרֶת <1244>; from SEEK <1239>] ▶ **This word describes a reprimand or penalty in a case of improper sexual relationships.** Ref.: Lev. 19:20; it is also translated scourging, to be scourged. ¶
– 2 Deut. 17:8 ➔ SORE (noun) <5061> 3 Ps. 91:8 ➔ RECOMPENSE (noun) <8011> 4 Prov. 19:19 ➔ FINE (noun) <6066> 5 Is. 66:4 ➔ CAPRICIOUS CHILDREN <8586> 6 See INIQUITY <5771>.

PUNITES – ***pûniy*** [proper noun: פּוּנִי <6324>; patron. from an unused name meaning a turn] ▶ **This word designates the descendants of Puah (PUAH <6312> a.).** Ref.: Num. 26:23; NIV: Puite. ¶

PUNON – ***pûnōn*** [proper noun: פּוּנֹן <6325>; from DESPAIR (BE IN) <6323>]: distraction, perplexity ▶ **A campsite of the Israelites in the wilderness on their way to the Promised Land.** Refs.: Num. 33:42, 43. ¶

PUPIL – 1 ***'iyšôn, *šûn*** [masc. noun: אִישׁוֹן, אֱשׁוּן <380>; diminutive from MAN <376>] ▶ **The eye or pupil (the aperture in the iris) of the eye was considered a vital part of life (Prov. 20:20), the lamp or light of life; the word is translated obscure, deep, utter, pitch, and is used with the word darkness.** Israel is depicted lovingly and caringly as the pupil (or apple) of the Lord's eye (Deut. 32:10). The psalmist cries out for the Lord to consider him as the apple of His eye (Ps. 17:8). Wisdom is to be the apple of the eye of the wise person (Prov. 7:2). For another meaning of the Hebrew word, see TWILIGHT <380>. ¶
2 ***talmiyḏ*** [masc. noun: תַּלְמִיד <8527>; from LEARN <3925>] ▶ **This word refers to persons who are in the process of learning, of acquiring knowledge, applying themselves diligently to study; it is also translated student.** Ref.: 1 Chr. 25:8; KJV: scholar. ¶

PUR, PURIM – ***pûr*** [masc. noun: פּוּר <6332>; from NOTHING (BRING TO) <6331>] ▶ **This word refers to a lot cast to make decisions (as by means of a broken piece); in plural, Purim, a Jewish feast day in ironic celebration of the overturning of Haman's cruel plot, for which purpose he consulted the pur.** It refers to the Jewish feast day celebrating the great deliverance of the Jews under the Persian Empire (Esther 9:24, 26, 28, 29, 31, 32). The pur was an object used in deciding a matter seemingly by chance (Esther 3:7). ¶

PURAH – ***purāh*** [masc. proper noun: פֻּרָה <6513>; from BRANCH <6288>]: bough ▶ **The servant of Gideon.** Refs.: Judg. 7:10, 11. ¶

PURCHASE (noun) – [1] ***miqnāh*** [fem. noun: מִקְנָה <4736>; fem. of LIVESTOCK <4735>] ▶ **This word refers to the acquisition of something with money (*kesep*).** Refs.: Gen. 17:12, 13, 23, 27; Ex. 12:44; Lev. 27:22; the word is translated bought. It defines a document as a deed of purchase (Jer. 32:11, 12, 14, 16). It indicates the price itself of something (Lev. 25:16, 51); or a possession acquired by purchase (Gen. 23:18). ¶
– [2] Deut. 2:6 ➔ BUY <3739>.

PURE – [1] ***bar*** [adj.: בַּר <1249>; from PURIFY <1305> (in its various senses)] ▶ **This word means clean, radiant; clear, bright. It is extremely rare and occurs only in the poetic books.** It typically means purity or cleanness of heart (Ps. 24:4; 73:1; cf. Job 11:4). This term also describes a clean feeding trough (Prov. 14:4); it is also translated empty. Radiance is ascribed to both the commandments of the Lord and the Shulamite (Ps. 19:8; Song 6:10). The only other occurrence of this word also applies to the Shulamite and seems to indicate a select status, but this status is probably based on her purity (Song 6:9); it is also translated favorite, choice. ¶
[2] ***zak*** [adj.: זַךְ <2134>; from PURE (BE) <2141>] ▶ **This word is derived from the related verbs *zākāh*, meaning to be clear or pure, and *zākak*, meaning to be clean or pure.** It is used to describe objects used in the worship of God, such as pure oil (Ex. 27:20; Lev. 24:2) and pure frankincense (Ex. 30:34; Lev. 24:7). It also denotes the purity of the righteous, such as Job (Job 8:6; 33:9), in contrast with one living a crooked life (Prov. 21:8; also translated innocent). This word can also speak about all aspects of one's life: one's actions in general (Prov. 16:2; 20:11); one's teaching (Job 11:4; also translated flawless); or one's prayer (Job 16:17). ¶
[3] ***ṭāhôr, ṭāhōr*** [adj.: טָהוֹר, טָהֹר <2889>; from PURE (BE) <2891>] ▶ **This word means clean, genuine. It is used ninety times in the Old Testament, primarily to distinguish a broad range of entities (including persons, animals, places, utensils, and clothing) that were ceremonially pure, fit to be used in, or take part in the religious rituals of Israel.** The Lord decreed that Israel must mark off the clean from the unclean (Lev. 10:10; 11:47; Job 14:4). Persons could be ceremonially clean or unclean (Deut. 12:15). A human corpse was especially defiling, and contact with it made a person unclean for seven days (Num. 19:11). When persons were clean, they could eat clean meat, but an unclean person could not (Lev. 7:19). Certain animals were considered ceremonially clean (Gen. 7:2) and needed by Noah and his family for sacrifices after the flood (Gen. 8:20). Ceremonially clean birds were used in various rituals (Lev. 14:4).

Clean things were considered normal; unclean things were considered polluted, but they could be restored to their state of purity (Lev. 11–15). Some things, however, were permanently unclean, such as unclean animals (Lev. 11:7, 26, 29–31). Other things were temporarily unclean. A woman in her period (Lev. 12:2) and a person with an infectious disease (Lev. 13:8) could be cleansed and be clean again (Lev. 12:4; 14:7); spring water could be considered as clean; even seed could be clean or unclean depending on whether a dead carcass had fallen on it while it was dry or wet (Lev. 11:36–38). Leprosy made a person unclean (Lev. 13:45, 46).

God expected His people to be morally pure and to imitate Him (Hab. 1:13). This word served to express that state. Clean hands merited God's favor (Job 17:9), and pure words were pleasing to the Lord. God judged a sacrifice's value by the quality of the offerer's heart (Ps. 51:10); thus, David prayed for a pure heart.

The root meaning of the word shines through in its use to describe the quality of metals and other items. Pure gold was used in the construction of the ark of the covenant and many other items (Ex. 25:11, 17; 28:14; 30:3); pure frankincense was prepared for use on the altar of incense (Ex. 30:34, 35; 37:29). The fear of the Lord was proclaimed pure and therefore endured forever. It guided the psalmist to know God (Ps. 19:9). *

4 ***nᵉqê'*** [Aramaic adj.: נְקֵא <5343>; from a root corresponding to FREE (BE) <5352> (in the sense of to be clean, to be pure)] ▶ **This word refers to the color white, the quality of purity.** It points out the garments of the Ancient of Days and is symbolic of holiness and purity (Dan. 7:9; NIV: white). ¶

5 ***sāḡar*** [masc. noun: סָגַר <5462>; a prim. root] ▶ **This word means the finest gold, pure (unadulterated) gold.** It was used for overlaying (1 Kgs. 6:20); for Temple furniture (1 Kgs. 7:49, 50); Temple vessels (1 Kgs. 10:21). It was especially valuable and used in wise comparisons (Job 28:15). The Hebrew word also means to close, to shut up; see CLOSE <5462>. ¶

– 6 Ex. 30:23 ➔ FREEDOM <1865> b. 7 1 Kgs. 10:18 ➔ REFINED (BE) <6338> 8 Dan. 2:32 ➔ FINE (adj.) <2869>.

PURE (BE) – 1 ***zāḵāh*** [verb: זָכָה <2135>; a prim. root (comp. <2141> below)] ▶ **This word means to clean, to be clean, to cleanse.** Job's friends used this word twice, questioning how one born of a woman could be clean or righteous before God (Job 15:14; 25:4). It is also used to describe the state of the heart (Ps. 73:13; Prov. 20:9). In other uses, it carries the connotation of being pure or cleansed from sin (Ps. 119:9; Is. 1:16; Mic. 6:11). Other ref.: Ps. 51:4 (to be clear, to be blameless). ¶

2 ***zāḵaḵ*** [verb: זָכַךְ <2141>; a prim. root] ▶ **This word is used only four times in the Old Testament; it means to make clean.** Job uses it to describe washing his hands to make them clean (Job 9:30; also translated to cleanse). On two occasions, it speaks of the purity of the heavens (Job 15:15: to be pure, to be clean) and the stars (Job 25:5: to be pure). The final usage of the word describes certain people as being purer than snow (Lam. 4:7; also translated to be bright) in contrast with the blackness of soot (see Lam. 4:8). See the related verb, *zāḵāh* (<2135> above), and the related noun, *zaḵ* (PURE <2134>). ¶

PURE (BE, MAKE) – ***ṭāhêr*** [verb: טָהֵר <2891>; a prim. root] ▶ **This word means to be clean, to make clean.** The term occurs most frequently in Leviticus where it was used for ritual cleansing of either things or persons (Lev. 14:48; 16:19; 22:7). The Old Testament also speaks of ritual cleansing performed on persons within the sphere of false worship (Is. 66:17; Ezek. 22:24). Animals were not made clean (like people), for animals were either clean or unclean by nature; the concept did not apply to plants at all. Sometimes cleanness had a moral dimension that, of course, did not exclude the spiritual. One was not to think that persons made themselves clean nor that their cleanness exceeded that of their Maker (Job 17; Prov. 20:9). Exilic and postexilic prophets prophesied of a future purification for God's people like the purifying of silver (Jer. 33:8; Ezek. 36:25; Mal. 3:3). *

PURE (MAKE) – Dan. 11:35 ➔ WHITE (MAKE) <3835>.

PURENESS – ***ṭᵉhār, ṭᵒhār*** [masc. noun: טְהָר, טֳהָר <2890>; from PURE (BE) <2891>] ▶ **This word occurs only in Proverbs 22:11; it means the quality of something free from contamination and is also translated purity.** As it is written in Hebrew, it is unpronounceable and appears to be a misspelling of the adjective *ṭāhôr* (PURE <2889>). However, the noun "pureness," fits much better than the adjective "pure," both grammatically and contextually (cf. Prov. 23:7, 8) and is the choice of the KJV. Loving pureness of heart (rather than "loving [the] pure of heart") results in graceful speech. ¶

PUREST – ***miḵlāh*** [fem. noun: מִכְלָה <4357>; from FINISH <3615>] ▶ **This word indicates perfection, purity. It has a state of near perfection or purity.** It is used in combination with *zāhāḇ*, gold, to indicate purest gold (2 Chr. 4:21; also translated perfect, solid). ¶

PURGE – [1] Ezek. 20:38 ➔ PURIFY <1305> [2] Mal. 3:3 ➔ REFINE <2212>.

PURIFICATION – [1] Lev. 12:4, 6 ➔ CLEARNESS <2892> [2] Esther 2:3, 9, 12 ➔ COSMETICS <8562> [3] See CLEANSING <2893>.

PURIFIED (BE) – Dan. 12:10 ➔ WHITE (MAKE) <3835>.

PURIFY – [1] ***bārar, bārûr*** [verb: בָּרַר, בָּרוּר <1305>; a prim. root] ▶ **This word means to clean, to purge, to polish; it also means to select.** God declares that He will purge the rebels from Israel (Ezek. 20:38) and that He will give the people purified lips (Zeph. 3:9). The term can also mean to polish or make shine like polished arrows (Is. 49:2; Jer. 51:11). Primarily used in the books of Chronicles, it points out that which was choice or select: men (1 Chr. 7:40); gatekeepers (1 Chr. 9:22); musicians (1 Chr. 16:41); sheep (Neh. 5:18). It can also carry the connotation of testing or proving (Eccl. 3:18). *
– [2] Ps. 12:6 ➔ REFINE <2212>.

PURIFYING – Lev. 12:4, 6 ➔ CLEARNESS <2892>.

PURIM – See PUR, PURIM <6332>.

PURITY – [1] Prov. 22:11 ➔ PURENESS <2890> [2] Hos. 8:5 ➔ INNOCENCE <5356>.

PURPLE – [1] ***'argᵉwān*** [masc. noun: אַרְגְּוָן <710>; a variation from <713> below] ▶ **This word indicates a purple color (composed of red and blue hues) used to dye wool yarn and used in weaving.** Ref.: 2 Chr. 2:7. Some recent translators prefer to translate this as red purple. ¶
[2] ***'argᵉwān*** [Aramaic masc. noun: אַרְגְּוָן <711>; corresponding to <710> above] ▶ **This word refers to a color of blended red and blue hues; it is also translated scarlet.** It was the color of wool dyed purple and was a feature of royal garments (Dan. 5:7, 16, 29). ¶
[3] ***'argāmān*** [masc. noun: אַרְגָּמָן <713>; of foreign origin] ▶ **This wool dyed purple, a red and blue color, or red purple was featured in the high priest's clothing and its decorative features, such as pomegranates. The word is also used to refer to anything dyed purple, e.g., thread, wool, cloth.** Refs.: Ex. 28:5, 6, 8, 15, 33. It was the color of a purple cloth which covered the altar after the removal of ashes (Num. 4:13). This color was a feature of royal clothing (Judg. 8:26; Esther 8:15; Jer. 10:9); the hangings and decorations in royal palaces (Esther 1:6); and even royal couches (Song 3:10). *
– [4] See CRIMSON <8438> a. c.

PURPOSE (noun) – [1] ***diḇrāh*** [Aramaic fem. noun: דִּבְרָה <1701>; corresponding to CAUSE <1700>] ▶ **This word is similar to the Hebrew form of the same spelling (see CAUSE <1700>).** The Aramaic form occurs in Daniel 2:30 and Daniel 4:17. In both places, it is used with other words to create a purpose clause which is translated in order that, for the purpose of, or for the sake of. ¶
– [2] Prov. 16:4 ➔ ANSWER (noun) <4617> b. [3] 1 Chr. 29:18 ➔ FORMED <3336> [4] Is. 19:10 ➔ FOUNDATION <8356> b. [5] Dan. 6:17 ➔ SITUATION <6640>.

PURPOSE (verb) – Dan. 1:8 ➔ PUT <7760>.

PURSE – [1] Prov. 1:14; Is. 46:6 ➔ BAG <3599> [2] Is. 3:22 ➔ money purse ➔ BAG <2754>.

PURSUE – [1] ***rāḏap̱*** [verb: רָדַף <7291>; a prim. root] ▶ **This word means to chase, to persecute.** It means to chase after, to pursue someone in a hostile manner, as when Abraham pursued Lot's captors (Gen. 14:14, 15); or Pharaoh pursued Israel (Ex. 14:4, 8, 9, 23; 15:9). It refers to a pursuit of a less hostile nature, e.g., Laban's pursuit of Jacob (Gen. 31:23). It refers to the Lord's pursuit of persons or nations to punish and judge them (Jer. 29:18; Lam. 3:43). It refers

to hunting, chasing after animals (1 Sam. 26:20). It takes on the sense of persecuting persons, harassing them (Deut. 30:7); sometimes with words alone (Job 19:22). Figuratively, it describes chasing rewards (Is. 1:23); or strong drink (Is. 5:11). To pursue one's enemies to darkness means to utterly wipe them out (Nah. 1:8). In its passive sense, it means to be chased (Is. 17:13). In its passive stem in Ecclesiastes 3:15, it refers to what has vanished, passed away. *
– [2] Gen. 31:36; Ps. 10:2; Lam. 4:19: to pursue, to hotly pursue ➔ BURN (verb) <1814> [3] Ps. 56:1, 2; 57:3 ➔ LONG FOR <7602> b.

PURSUING – 1 Kgs. 18:27 ➔ RELIEVE ONESELF <7873>.

PUSH – [1] ***hāḏap*** [verb: הָדַף <1920>; a prim. root] ► **This word means to drive out, to shove away; it is also translated to cast out, to cast away, to thrust, to thrust away, to expel, to reject, to thwart, to depose.** It means to shove a person (sometimes violently (Num. 35:20, 22), to force out an enemy from Canaanite territory (Deut. 6:19). Israel sometimes does it, or God (Deut. 9:4; Josh. 23:5) does it for His people. It depicts the bullying, violent abuse of persons or groups of people by those in power (Ezek. 34:21). It is used of God's refusing the desires or cravings of the wicked (Prov. 10:3) and driving them into darkness (Job 18:18). It refers figuratively to deposing or humbling someone (Is. 22:19; Jer. 46:15). Other ref.: 2 Kgs. 4:27. ¶
– [2] Ex. 21:32; Deut. 33:17; 1 Kgs. 22:11; 2 Chr. 18:10; Ps. 44:5; Ezek. 34:21; Dan. 8:4; 11:40 ➔ GORE <5055> [3] Ex. 21:36 ➔ GORING <5056> [4] Ps. 118:13 ➔ DRIVE <1760> [5] Jer. 46:15 ➔ SWEEP <5502> [6] Joel 2:8 ➔ AFFLICT <1766>.

PUT (nation) – ***pûṭ*** [proper noun: פּוּט <6316>; of foreign origin] ► **This word designates a nation, probably Lydia.** Refs.: Gen. 10:6; 1 Chr. 1:8; Jer. 46:9; Ezek. 27:10; 30:5; 38:5; Nah. 3:9. ¶

PUT (verb) – [1] ***hāḏāh*** [verb: הָדָה <1911>; a prim. root (comp. THANKS (GIVE) <3034> (in the sense of to cast)] ► **This verb means to stretch out.** Used with the word *yāḏ* <3027>, hand in Hebrew, it describes the action of a child putting out his or her hand toward a viper's den (Is. 11:8). ¶
[2] ***yāśam*** [verb: יָשַׂם <3455>; a prim. root] ► **This word refers to the process of placing and arranging a person in a coffin.** Ref.: Gen. 50:26. Others prefer the reading from the verb with the same meaning, *siym* (PUT <7760>). Other ref.: Gen. 24:33. ¶
[3] ***śûm, śiym*** [verb: שׂוּם, שִׂים <7760>; a prim. root] ► **This Hebrew word means to appoint, to bring, to call, to change, to charge, to commit, to consider, to convey, to determine, to set one's mind (on something). The primary meaning of the verb is to put, to set, or to place.** The verb indicates that which God put on the earth, as noted in Genesis where God put the man and woman that He formed in the Garden of Eden (Gen. 2:8). The usage of the verb in this sense indicates God's sovereignty over all creation, especially that of humankind. The verb is also used to describe Samuel's action concerning the stone he named Ebenezer (1 Sam. 7:12). This stone was set up between Mizpah and Shen to remember God's deliverance of the Israelites from the Philistines. The verb is used to describe a committing of one's cause before God (Job 5:8). The word is used in Exodus in response to an interaction between Moses and God, in which God gave a new decree and law to the Israelites (Ex. 15:25). In this setting, the verb again emphasizes God's sovereignty, His ability to establish the order of things, and His ability to control the elements of nature and disease. In Deuteronomy, *śûm* is used to describe God's appointing of leaders over the different tribes of Israel, for their numbers were too great for Moses alone (Deut. 1:13). The word is also used to indicate a charging of someone, as where a man charged his wife with premarital sex (Deut. 22:14). *
[4] ***śûm, śiym*** [Aramaic verb: שׂוּם, שִׂים <7761>; corresponding to <7760> above] ► **This word means to issue (a decree), to appoint, to place.** It is used to describe

the putting forth or issuance of a formal decree (Ezra 4:19, 21; 5:3, 9, 13, 17; 6:1; Dan. 3:10); or a command (Dan. 4:6). It describes the placement or laying of wooden beams in a wall (Ezra 5:8). It is used in a formal sense of appointing a person to an official position (Ezra 5:14; Dan. 3:12). It is used in a reflexive passive stem to describe something being put into a state or turned into something (Dan. 2:5). It describes a decree being issued (passive) (Ezra 4:21). It is used of placing names on persons or changing their names (Dan. 5:12). It takes on the sense of paying attention to or giving respect to someone (Dan. 6:13); or focusing on something (Dan. 6:14). It describes setting or imprinting a seal on something (Dan. 6:17). ¶

5 ***šiyṯ***] [verb: שִׁית <7896>; a prim. root] ▶ **This word basically means to place something somewhere.** Hostility between the serpent and the seed of the woman (Gen. 3:15); to appoint or replace something (Gen. 4:25); to place or put sheep in a separate area (Gen. 30:40); to appoint or establish a person in an official position (Gen. 41:33; Ps. 21:6; 132:11; Is. 5:6; 26:1; Jer. 22:6). It is used of God's setting or establishing the earth on its foundations (1 Sam. 2:8). To set one's hand on a person's eyes at death means to close them (Gen. 46:4). It indicates merely placing one's hand on a person (Gen. 48:14, 17). To set one's heart on something means to pay attention to it (Ex. 7:23; 2 Sam. 13:20; Jer. 31:21). The phrase *šîṯ leḇaddô* means to set apart (Gen. 30:40). The phrases to set one's hand to means to help or to have a common goal (Ex. 23:1); to blame someone means to set sin upon them (Num. 12:11). It takes on the sense of to make, to constitute something as: to make someone turn the shoulder (Ps. 21:12); to make something like something else, e.g., Israel like a land of hunting, a wilderness (Jer. 2:15; Hos. 2:3); to make or appoint darkness (Ps. 104:20). It refers to appointing a feast (Jer. 51:39); or of setting, putting one's refuge in the Lord (Ps. 73:28). God sets, defines Israel's borders (Ex. 23:31). *

– 6 Ezra 5:15; 6:5 ➔ BRING DOWN <5182>.

PUT ASIDE, PUT OFF – Lam. 4:1 ➔ CHANGE (verb) <8132> a.

PUT AWAY, OFF, FAR OFF – Amos 6:3 ➔ DRIVE <5077>.

PUT ON – 1 Lev. 16:4 ➔ WEAR <6801> 2 2 Kgs. 4:38; Ezek. 24:3 ➔ ESTABLISH <8239> 3 Job 31:36 ➔ BIND <6029>.

PUT ON A BELT – See GIRD ONESELF <2296>.

PUT ONESELF FORWARD – 1 Kgs. 1:5 ➔ EXALT ONESELF <4984>.

PUT OUT – 1 Lev. 6:12; 2 Sam. 14:7 ➔ QUENCH <3518> 2 Job 18:5, 6; 21:17; Prov. 13:9; 20:20; 24:20 ➔ EXTINGUISH <1846>.

PUTHITES – ***pûṯiy*** [proper noun: פּוּתִי <6336>; patron. from an unused name meaning a hinge] ▶ **A family of Judah.** Ref.: 1 Chr. 2:53. ¶

PUTIEL – ***pûṭiy'ēl*** [masc. proper noun: פּוּטִיאֵל <6317>; from an unused root (prob. meaning to disparage) and GOD <410>]: afflicted by God ▶ **Father of the wife of Eleazar, the son of Aaron.** Ref.: Ex. 6:25.

PUTREFACTION – Is. 3:24 ➔ STENCH <4716>.

PUTREFYING, PUTRIFYING – Is. 1:6 ➔ FRESH <2961>.

PYGARG – Deut. 14:5 ➔ IBEX <1788>.

PYRE – Is. 30:33; Ezek. 24:9 ➔ PILE <4071>.

Q

QUAIL – ***śelāw*** [masc. noun: שְׂלָו <7958>; by orthographical variation from EASE (BE AT) <7951> through the idea of sluggishness] ▶ **This word refers to any of a number of small short-tailed birds (Phasianidae family).** God provided these birds as food for Israel in the desert in a miraculous way (Ex. 16:13; Num. 11:31, 32; Ps. 105:40). ¶

QUAKE – [1] Job 26:11 ➔ TREMBLE <7322> [2] Ps. 18:7 ➔ SHAKE <1607> [3] Ps. 75:3 ➔ MELT AWAY <4127> [4] Ps. 99:1 ➔ SHAKE <5120> [5] Is. 64:1, 3 ➔ GLUTTON (BE) <2151> b. [6] Ezek. 29:7 ➔ SHAKE <5976>.

QUAKING – Dan. 10:7 ➔ TREMBLING <2731>.

QUALITY (JUDGE THE) – Lev. 27:12, 14 ➔ VALUE (verb) <6183>.

QUANTITY – [1] 1 Chr. 23:29 ➔ MEASURE (noun) <4884> [2] Ezek. 45:11 ➔ QUOTA <8506>.

QUARREL (noun) – [1] 2 Kgs. 5:7: to seek a quarrel ➔ BEFALL <579> [2] Prov. 17:14 ➔ STRIFE <4066>.

QUARREL (verb) – [1] Num. 27:14 ➔ STRIFE <4808> [2] 2 Sam. 14:6 ➔ FIGHT <5327> [3] Prov. 20:3 ➔ BREAK OUT <1566> [4] Is. 41:12 ➔ CONTEND <4695>.

QUARREL AGAINST – Prov. 18:1 ➔ BREAK OUT <1566>.

QUARRELING – Gen. 13:8 ➔ STRIFE <4808>.

QUARRELLING – Prov. 18:19 ➔ STRIFE <4066>.

QUARRELS – Prov. 18:18; etc. ➔ CONTENTIONS <4079>.

QUARRELS AGAINST (START) – Prov. 18:1 ➔ BREAK OUT <1566>.

QUARRIED – 2 Kgs. 12:12; 22:6; 2 Chr. 34:11 ➔ HEWN <4274>.

QUARRY (noun) – [1] ***massā'*** [masc. noun: מַסָּע <4551>; from SET OUT <5265> (in the sense of moving something out)] ▶ **This word point out a stone quarry, a place where stone was located, measured, cut, dressed, and removed.** It was a source of stone for building and was usually a noisy place (1 Kgs. 6:7). The Hebrew word also means a projectile; see DART <4551>. ¶
[2] ***maqqeḇeṯ*** [fem. noun: מַקֶּבֶת <4718>; from PIERCE <5344>] ▶ **This word indicates also a hole, a pit.** It refers to a place where stones were dug out, measured, cut, and shaped (Is. 51:1). ¶

QUARRY (verb) – 1 Kgs. 5:18 ➔ CUT (verb) <6458>.

QUARTERS – Neh. 3:30 ➔ CHAMBER <5393>.

QUARTZ – Job 28:18 ➔ CRYSTAL <1378>.

QUEEN – [1] ***malkāh*** [Aramaic fem. noun: מַלְכָּה <4433>; corresponding to <4436> below] ▶ **This word designated the proper title of the wife of the king.** It is used twice in Daniel 5:10. Scholars disagree as to whether she was the wife or the mother of the last king of the neo-Babylonian Empire, Belshazzar. ¶
[2] ***malkāh*** [fem. noun: מַלְכָּה <4436>; fem. of KING <4428>] ▶ **This word means exclusively queen, but the queen stands in several possible social positions.** The queen is often merely the wife of the king; she was, e.g., subordinate to the king, and was expected to do his bidding (Esther 1:11, 12, 16, 17). She also had much court authority herself (Esther 1:9). The only time the word is used to apply to Israelite women is in the plural, and they were part of Solomon's harem (Song 6:8, 9).

The term means queen without stressing the spousal relationship to the king, but it is not used in this way of any Israelite woman in the time of the monarchy. The queen of Sheba, from southwest Arabia, was a powerful monarch in her own right, traveled extensively (1 Kgs. 10:1, 10), and was considered a wise woman and ruler (2 Chr. 9:1). Esther became queen in Persia because of her beauty but won over the king by gaining his approval and favor (see Esther 2:17, 18). *

3 ***m*ᵉ*leḵeṯ*** [fem. noun: מְלֶכֶת <4446>; from KING <4428> and GOD <410>] ▶ **Rather than being just another term for a female regent, this word's significance is found in the chronicle of Judah's idolatry.** It is used solely to designate a fertility goddess worshiped in Jeremiah's day, the queen of the heavens (*mᵉleḵeṯ haššāmayim*: HEAVEN <8064>). Although the references are cryptic, it is believed that this queen of the heavens was either the goddess Ashtoreth, symbolized by the moon, or Astarte, symbolized by the planet Venus. Women baked cakes to offer to this goddess (Jer. 7:18) and burned incense (Jer. 44:17–19) in hopes of securing the blessings of fertility. However, the judgment of the Lord on this practice made it counterproductive (cf. Jer. 44:25 ff.). ¶

4 ***šēgal*** [fem. noun: שֵׁגַל <7694>; a prim. root] ▶ **The primary meaning of this Hebrew word is queen. It also means a concubine, a harem favorite, a consort.** This noun was used by Nehemiah to describe the queen who sat beside the king (Neh. 2:6). In the book of Psalms, the psalmist used this noun to designate the queen who sat at the right hand of the king (Ps. 45:9; NIV: royal bride). Concubine, harem favorite, and consort are also possible definitions due to the close connection of this word with *šāgal* (<7693>), which can mean to sleep or to have sexual intercourse with. ¶

– 5 1 Kgs. 15:13; 2 Kgs. 10:13 ➔ MISTRESS <1377> 6 Is. 47:5, 7 ➔ MISTRESS <1404> 7 Is. 49:23; Lam. 1:1 ➔ PRINCESS <8282>.

QUENCH – 1 ***kāḇāh*** [verb.: כָּבָה <3518>; a prim. root] ▶ **This word means to put out, to extinguish; it is also translated to go out.** It is used of a fire being extinguished (Lev. 6:12, 13; 1 Sam. 3:3) as of cutting off the source of a line of descendants (2 Sam. 14:7); or of killing persons, extinguishing their lives (2 Sam. 21:17; Is. 43:17). It is used of extinguishing, putting out the hot wrath of the Lord (2 Kgs. 22:17). It is used also of quenching or putting out the flame of love toward a person (Song 8:7). In its strong participial form, it may mean persons who quench or put out (Is. 1:31). *

– 2 Ps. 118:12; Is. 43:17 ➔ EXTINGUISH <1846>.

QUESTION (HARD, DIFFICULT) – 1 Kgs. 10:1; 2 Chr. 9:1 ➔ ENIGMA <2420>.

QUICK – Lev. 13:10, 24 ➔ PRESERVATION OF LIFE <4241>.

QUICK, QUICKLY – ***mahêr*** [adj. and adv.: מַהֵר <4118>; from HURRY <4116>] ▶ **a. An adjective indicating swift.** It indicates the swiftness and, hence, nearness of something, e.g., the Day of the Lord (Zeph. 1:14: to haste, to come; Is. 8:1: to haste, speedy). ¶

b. An adverb meaning speedily, hastily. It occurs right after the verb it modifies and indicates the swiftness of its performance (Ex. 32:8; Deut. 4:26; Josh. 2:5; Judg. 2:17; Ps. 69:17; 79:8; Prov. 25:8). Other refs.: Deut. 7:4, 22; 9:3, 12, 16; 28:20; Ps. 102:2; 143:7. ¶

QUICKLY – 1 ***mᵉhêrāh*** [fem. noun: מְהֵרָה <4120>; fem. of QUICK, QUICKLY <4118>] ▶ **This word indicates at once, speedily.** It indicates adverbially how quickly, hurriedly something is done (Num. 16:46; 2 Kgs. 1:11; Is. 5:26; Jer. 27:16; Joel 3:4); or something occurs quickly (Ps. 147:15; Eccl. 4:12; 8:11 [negated]). God's judgments, if enacted, could cause His people to perish quickly from their land (Deut. 11:17). *

– 2 Ps. 90:10 ➔ SOON <2440> 3 Dan. 2:25 ➔ HASTE (BE IN) <927>.

QUICKLY (COME) – 1 Ps. 71:12 ➔ HASTE (MAKE) <2439> 2 Joel 3:11 ➔ HASTEN <5789>.

QUIET (adj.) – ***rāḡêa‘*** [adj.: רָגֵעַ <7282>; from MOMENT (BE FOR A) <7280>] ▶ **This word describes a state of rest and trust in which persons are at ease.** Ref.: Ps. 35:20. ¶

QUIET (BE) – ***šāṯaq*** [verb: שָׁתַק <8367>; a prim. root] ▶ **This word means to be calm.** It refers to a time of quietness and safety after a storm or great danger (Ps. 107:30; also translated to grow calm). It indicates the quieting down of quarreling and hostilities (Prov. 26:20; also translated to cease, to die down). It indicates that the waters of the sea are becoming calm, quieting down, a storm is subsiding (Jon. 1:11, 12). ¶

QUIET (noun) – [1] ***šeqeṭ*** [masc. noun: שֶׁקֶט <8253>; from STILL (BE) <8252>] ▶ **This word means quietness, tranquility.** The only occurrence is found in 1 Chronicles 22:9 and is parallel to the Hebrew word for peace (*šālôm*, <7965>). It is used to describe the state of tranquility during the reign of Solomon when all enemies were defeated and the united kingdom was at its height. ¶
– [2] Prov. 29:9; Eccl. 9:17 → REST (noun) <5183>.

QUIET (verb) – Num. 13:30; Neh. 8:11 → SILENCE!, KEEP SILENCE! <2013>.

QUIET DOWN – Prov. 26:20; Jon. 1:11, 12 → QUIET (BE) <8367>.

QUIETLY – [1] Judg. 4:21 → SOFTLY <3811> [2] 2 Sam. 3:27 → PRIVATELY <7987> [3] Ruth 3:7 → ENCHANTMENT <3909> [4] Lam. 3:26 → SILENCE (noun) <1748>.

QUIETNESS – [1] 1 Chr. 22:9 → QUIET (noun) <8253> [2] Eccl. 4:6; 9:17 → REST (noun) <5183>.

QUILT – 1 Sam. 19:13, 16 → PILLOW <3523>.

QUIVER – [1] ***'ašpāh*** [fem. noun: אַשְׁפָּה <827>; perhaps (fem.) from the same as ENCHANTER <825> (in the sense of covering)] ▶ **The quiver was a container for arrows; it rested against the sides of warhorses.** Ref.: Job 39:23. To take up the quiver was to prepare for battle (Is. 22:6). The prophet describes it as being like an open grave (Jer. 5:16) into which Israel would fall. Figuratively, it is pictured as a container for the arrows of the Lord (Lam. 3:13). Other refs.: Ps. 127:5; Is. 49:2. ¶
[2] ***tᵉliy*** [masc. noun: תְּלִי <8522>; from HANG <8518>] ▶ **This word refers to a container in which a hunter or soldier carried his arrows.** It was usually made of leather and wood (Gen. 27:3). ¶
– [3] Ezek. 29:7 → SHAKE <5976> [4] Hab. 3:16 → TINGLE <6750>.

QUIVERING – Ezek. 12:18 → TREMBLING <7269>.

QUOTA – ***tōḵen*** [masc. noun: תֹּכֶן <8506>; from WEIGH <8505>] ▶ **This word refers to quantity, a set amount, a goal to be reached.** Refs.: Ex. 5:18; Ezek. 45:11. It is also translated same number, tale, full quota; size, quantity, measure. ¶

R

RAAMAH – ***ra'māh, ra'mā'*** [proper noun: רַעְמָה, רַעְמָא <7484>; the same as THUNDER (noun) <7483> b.]: mane ▶
a. A son of Cush. Refs.: Gen. 10:7; 1 Chr. 1:9. ¶
b. A home of traders. Ref.: Ezek. 27:22. ¶

RAAMIAH – ***ra'amyāh*** [proper noun: רַעַמְיָה <7485>; from THUNDER (verb) <7481> and LORD <3050>]: thunder of the Lord ▶ **The same as *r^e'ēlāyāh* (REELAIAH <7480>).** Ref.: Neh. 7:7. ¶

RAAMSES, RAMESES – ***ra'amsēs, ra'meśēs*** [proper noun: רַעַמְסֵס, רַעְמְסֵס <7486>; of Egyptian origin] ▶ **A city built in Egypt by the Hebrews.** Refs.: Gen. 47:11; Ex. 1:11; 12:37; Num. 33:3, 5. ¶

RAB-MAG – ***rab̲-māg̲*** [רַב־מָג <7248>; from MANY <7227> and a foreign word for a Magian (a Babylonian official)] ▶
a. A proper noun designating Rab-mag, a position in Babylon. Refs.: KJV, NASB, ESV, NKJV, Jer. 39:3, 13.
b. A phrase meaning high official, from *rāb̲* (MANY <7227> b.) and *māg̲*, official. Refs.: NIV, Jer. 39:3, 13. ¶

RAB-SARIS – ***rab̲-sāriys*** [masc. noun: רַב־סָרִיס <7249>; from MANY <7227> and WATER (GIVE) <8248>) (in the sense of a chief butler)] ▶
a. This word refers to leading military officials. For the kings of Assyria (2 Kgs. 18:17); of Babylon (Jer. 39:3, 13). *Rab* in these titular names indicates a chief, a captain, a leader.
b. A military title for Babylon's chief officer. A person in charge of the eunuchs or chief officials of the Babylonian king (Jer. 39:3, 13). ¶

RABBAH – ***rabbāh*** [proper noun: רַבָּה <7237>; fem. of MANY <7227>]: great ▶ **This word designates a Transjordanian Ammonite city that housed the famous huge bed of Og, king of Bashan.** Ref.: Deut. 3:11. The iron bed was thirteen feet long and six feet wide. The city was in the eastern edge of Ammon toward the eastern desert, about twelve miles south of the Jabbok River. David captured the city (2 Sam. 11:1; 12:26–29). Later, its king acted kindly toward David and received him as a fugitive (2 Sam. 17:27). The prophets spoke of the city a few times in judgment, asserting that it would become a pile of ruins (Jer. 49:2, 3; Ezek. 21:20; 25:5; Amos 1:14). *

RABBIT – ***'arneb̲et̲*** [fem. noun: אַרְנֶבֶת <768>; of uncertain deriv.] ▶ **This word refers to some animal that chews the cud, but does not part the hoof. However, no known rabbit or hare (the common translations) chews the cud. The word could refer to an unidentified or extinct species of animal.** It indicates an unclean animal not to be eaten by Israelites (Lev. 11:6; Deut. 14:7). ¶

RABBITH – ***rabbiyt̲*** [proper noun: רַבִּית <7245>; from MANY (BE, BECOME) <7231>]: multitude ▶ **A town in Issachar.** Ref.: Josh. 19:20. ¶

RABBLE – [1] Num. 11:4 ➔ MULTITUDE <628> [2] Job 30:12 ➔ BROOD <6526>.

RABSHAKEH – ***rab̲-šāqēh*** [proper noun: רַב־שָׁקֵה <7262>; from MANY <7227> and WATER (GIVE) <8248>]: chief cup bearer ▶
a. Title of a military chief. Refs.: 2 Kgs. 18:17, 19, 26–28, 37; 19:4, 8; Is. 36:2, 4, 11–13, 22; 37:4, 8.
b. A phrase meaning a field commander in the Assyrian army. Refs.: NIV, 2 Kgs. 18:17, 19, 26–28, 37; 19:4, 8; Is. 36:2, 4, 11–13, 22; 37:4, 8. ¶

RACAL, RACHAL – ***rāk̲āl*** [proper noun: רָכָל <7403>; from MERCHANDISE (SELL) <7402>]: trade ▶ **A town in southern Judah to which David sent part of the spoil of his enemies.** Ref.: 1 Sam. 30:29. ¶

RACE – ***mērôṣ*** [masc. noun: מֵרוֹץ <4793>; from RUN <7323>] ▶ **This word indicates**

a physical contest of speed and endurance, a running race. It is used in context figuratively of life (Eccl. 9:11). ¶

RACE OVER – Job 39:24 ➔ DRINK (verb) <1572>.

RACHEL – ***rāḥêl*** [fem. proper noun: רָחֵל <7354>; the same as EWE <7353>]: ewe ▶ **This word designates the second wife of Jacob. She was a shepherdess, a daughter of Laban, Nahor's grandson.** Laban was Jacob's uncle. Rachel lived in Paddan Aram, Aramaic territory (Gen. 29:6–31). Through divine guidance, Jacob located and married Rachel. Jacob worked for fourteen years to acquire Rachel as a wife. Jacob favored her over Leah. She eventually bore two sons, Joseph and Benjamin (Gen. 30:22–24; 35:16–18). She died bearing Benjamin whom she had named Benoni ("son of my sorrow") but Jacob renamed him. She was buried at Bethlehem or in its vicinity (Gen. 35:19–21).

During her life, she had stolen her father's idols, household gods (Gen. 31:19–22, 33–37). She evidently continued to relate to these gods in some way. She and Leah had "built up" Israel (Ruth 4:11). She became the ancestor through Joseph of two tribes, Ephraim and Manasseh, plus a third tribe through her son Benjamin. *

RACK – Job 30:17 ➔ GOUGE <5365>.

RADDAI – ***radday*** [masc. proper noun: רַדַּי <7288>; intens. from RULE (verb) <7287>]: ruling ▶ **Fifth son of Jesse and older brother of David.** Ref.: 1 Chr. 2:14. ¶

RADIANCE – Ezek. 1:27, 28; 10:4; Hab. 3:4, 11 ➔ BRIGHTNESS <5051>.

RADIANT – [1] Ps. 19:8 ➔ PURE <1249> [2] Song 5:10 ➔ DAZZLING <6703>.

RADIANT (BE) – [1] Ex. 34:29, 30, 35 ➔ SHINE <7160> [2] Ps. 34:5; Is. 60:5; Jer. 31:12 ➔ FLOW (verb) <5102> b. [3] Ezek. 43:2 ➔ LIGHT (GIVE) <215>.

RAFT – ***rapsōḏāh*** [fem. noun: רַפְסֹודָה <7513>; from SUBMIT <7511> (in the sense of to trample)] ▶ **This word refers to a floating wooden platform used to transport merchandise from one location to another by sea.** Ref.: 2 Chr. 2:16; KJV: float. The merchandise itself may form the raft, e.g., logs. ¶

RAFTER – [1] ***mqāreh*** [masc. noun: מְקָרֶה <4746>; from HAPPEN <7136> (properly something meeting)] ▶ **This word indicates the supporting beams in a structure or the entire structure itself; most likely, it means roof beams. It is also translated roof, building.** Ref.: Eccl. 10:18. ¶
– [2] Hab. 2:11 ➔ BEAM <3714>.

RAFTERS – ***rāḥiyṭ, rāhiyṭ*** [masc. coll. noun: רָחִיט, רָהִיט <7351>; from the same as TROUGH <7298>] ▶ **This word refers to the main supporting and ornamental wooden supports in a structure.** Ref.: Song 1:17. ¶

RAFTS – ***doḇrôṯ*** [fem. plur. coll. noun: דֹּבְרוֹת <1702>; fem. act. part. of SPEAK <1696>] ▶ **This word refers to logs towed by a ship or floated to their destination.** Ref.: 1 Kgs. 5:9; KJV: floats. ¶

RAG – [1] ***sḥāḇāh*** [fem. noun: סְחָבָה <5499>; from DRAG (verb) <5498> (in the sense of dragging trash)] ▶ **This word refers to old, torn, worn-out cloths or clothing.** It refers to pieces of cloth good only as waste or for cleaning up (Jer. 38:11, 12; KJV: cast clout). ¶
– [2] Prov. 23:21 ➔ PIECE <7168>.

RAG (OLD, OLD ROTTEN) – Jer. 38:11, 12 ➔ WORN-OUT CLOTHES <4418>.

RAGE (noun) – [1] ***za'ap*** [masc. noun: זַעַף <2197>; from ANGRY (BE) <2196>] ▶ **This word means wrath, indignation.** It is used to refer to the rage of kings (2 Chr. 28:9) or the stormy raging of the sea (Jon. 1:15). Other refs.: 2 Chr. 16:10; Prov. 19:12; Is. 30:30; Mic. 7:9. ¶
[2] ***rgaz*** [Aramaic masc. noun: רְגַז <7266>; from ANGER (verb) <7265>] ▶ **This word**

means violent anger. The term occurs only once in the entire Old Testament. When King Nebuchadnezzar heard that three Jews—Shadrach, Meshach, and Abednego—refused to worship the image of gold that he had erected, he flew into a rage (Dan. 3:13). This term is derived from the Aramaic verb *r*e*gaz* (ANGER <7265>), to anger, and is related to the Hebrew noun *rōgez* (TURMOIL <7267>), commotion, raging. ¶
– 3 Job 39:24 ➔ TURMOIL <7267>.

RAGE (verb) – 1 ***rāgaš*** [verb: רָגַשׁ <7283>; a prim. root] ▶ **This word means to be in commotion, to rage against; it is also translated to be in an uproar, to conspire.** This word appears only in Psalm 2:1 where it denotes the uproar and plotting of the wicked against the righteous. The image of a gathering lynch mob conveys well the action suggested here. ¶
– 2 Jon. 1:15 ➔ ANGRY (BE, BECOME) <2196>.

RAGE AGAINST – Prov. 18:1 ➔ BREAK OUT <1566>.

RAGING – 1 ***zêḏôn*** [adj.: זֵידוֹן <2121>; from PROUDLY (DEAL) <2102>] ▶ **This word is used figuratively to describe the wicked sweeping over one's soul like churning or tumultuous water; it is also translated proud, swollen.** Ref.: Ps. 124:5. ¶
– 2 Job 3:17 ➔ TURMOIL <7267> 3 Ps. 89:9 ➔ MAJESTY <1348> 4 Jon. 1:15 ➔ RAGE (noun) <2197> 5 Hab. 3:10 ➔ STORM (noun) <2230>.

RAGUEL – Num. 10:29 ➔ REUEL <7467> b.

RAHAB – 1 ***rahaḇ*** [proper noun: רַהַב <7294>; the same as PROUD <7293>]: boaster (an epithet of Egypt) ▶
a. The word is used for Egypt, sometimes with connotations of Egypt as a rebellious sea monster. The word means "arrogance, hubris." Refs.: Ps. 87:4; Is. 30:7; 51:9.
b. A mythical sea monster but subject to the Lord God of Israel. Refs.: Job 9:13; Ps. 89:10. In other cultures, it was known as Tiamat (Babylon) or Leviathan (Ugarit). In Israel the "monster" became merely the forces of nature or historical evil against them, but totally subject to Israel's God, the Lord (Yahweh). ¶
2 ***rāḥaḇ*** [fem. proper noun: רָחָב <7343>; the same as BROAD <7342>]: wide, proud ▶ **This word designates a Canaanite woman of Jericho, a prostitute, who gave proof of fear and faith in the great acts of Israel's God and became a part of His people; she is even given special note in the New Testament genealogical record of the Messiah.** She sheltered two Israelite spies and received a blessing from God for doing so (Josh. 2:1–14). All refs.: Josh. 2:1, 3; 6:17, 23, 25. ¶

RAHAM – ***raḥam*** [masc. proper noun: רַחַם <7357>; the same as WOMB <7356>]: compassion ▶ **An Israelite of the tribe of Judah.** Ref.: 1 Chr. 2:44. ¶

RAID – Gen. 49:19 ➔ ATTACK (verb) <1464>.

RAIL – 1 Sam. 25:14 ➔ RUSH GREEDILY <5860> a.

RAIMENT – 1 Ex. 21:10; Deut. 22:12 ➔ COVERING <3682> 2 Judg. 3:16 ➔ CLOTHES <4055> 3 Job 27:16; Is. 63:3; Ezek. 16:13 ➔ CLOTHING <4403>.

RAIMENT (CHANGE OF) – Zech. 3:4 ➔ FESTAL APPAREL <4254>.

RAIN (noun) – 1 ***gešem*** [masc. noun: גֶּשֶׁם <1653>; from RAIN (CAUSE) <1652>] ▶ **This word is most often used literally, referring to falling water droplets or a rain shower.** Refs.: Gen. 7:12; 8:2. It is used figuratively of blessing, a shower of blessing on God's people (Ezek. 34:26) but also a shower of destruction as well (Ezek. 13:11, 13). It is combined with other words to form phrases: a (heavy) shower (Zech. 10:1); a roaring of rain (1 Kgs. 18:41), etc. *
2 ***môreh*** [masc. noun: מוֹרֶה <4175>; from SHOOT <3384> (in the sense of to rain, to

pour)] ▶ **This word means falling water droplets; it refers to and is translated early rains, autumn rains.** It refers to the early rains in the fall of the year (Ps. 84:6; Joel 2:23), as opposed to the latter rains in the spring. ❡

3 ***māṭār*** [masc. noun: מָטָר <4306>; from RAIN (verb) <4305>] ▶ **This word indicates the watering of the earth.** In season (Deut. 11:11); and as a blessing from God (Deut. 11:14, 17; 1 Kgs. 8:35, 36); as a time of replenishing the earth, a refreshing for God's people (Deut. 32:2; Job 29:23). It was used as a metaphor also for times of distress and hardship (Is. 4:6). It was not fitting during harvest (Prov. 26:1). It was part of God's judgment on Egypt (Ex. 9:33, 34). *

– 4 Job 24:8 ➔ STORM (noun) <2230>.

RAIN (AUTUMN, EARLY, FIRST, FORMER) – ***yôreh*** [masc. noun: יוֹרֶה <3138>; act. part. of SHOOT (verb) <3384> (in the sense of to pour)] ▶ **This word indicates the early rain (falling water droplets) that in Israel fell from the end of October to the beginning of December.** A regular period of early rain was considered a blessing from God (Deut. 11:14), for He was the one who gave it (Jer. 5:24). It is used in a simile to indicate the refreshing arrival of the Lord's presence (Hos. 6:3). ❡

RAIN (CAUSE, GIVE, BRING) – ***gāšam*** [verb: גָּשַׁם <1652>; a prim. root] ▶ **This word is used in its causative sense meaning to cause water droplets to fall with the implied argument that only Israel's God can do so, not false idols.** Ref.: Jer. 14:22. ❡

RAIN (GENTLE, SMALL) – Deut. 32:2 ➔ DROPLET <8164>.

RAIN (LATER, LATTER, SPRING) – ***malqôš*** [masc. noun: מַלְקוֹשׁ <4456>; from GLEAN <3953>] ▶ **This designates the water droplets that in Israel fell during the spring season, our months of March and April.** Refs.: Deut. 11:14; Zech. 10:1. It was a time of joy to see this refreshing rain on its way (Prov. 16:15). Other refs.: Job 29:23; Jer. 3:3; 5:24; Hos. 6:3; Joel 2:23. ❡

RAIN (verb) – ***māṭar*** [verb: מָטַר <4305>; a prim. root] ▶ **This word means to pour down rain; it indicates the falling of water droplets. It is applied to other things that God pours down abundantly from heaven, e.g., hail, lightning, fire with sulfur, manna.** Someone may be rained on (Amos 4:7). The Lord controlled the rain for His people (Is. 5:6; Amos 4:7). It is used as a metaphor describing anything falling like rain, e.g., brimstone (Gen. 19:24; Ex. 9:18, 23; Ps. 78:24, 27; Ezek. 38:22); in a figurative sense of the Lord's raining coals of fire and brimstone upon the wicked (Ps. 11:6). Other refs.: Gen. 2:5; 7:4; Ex. 16:4; Job 20:23; 38:26. ❡

RAIN DOWN – Is. 45:8 ➔ DRIP (verb) <7491>.

RAIN ON, UPON – ***gōšem*** [masc. noun, verb: גֹּשֶׁם <1656>; from RAIN (CAUSE) <1652>] ▶ **This noun designates water droplets, shower. It is used verbally in a figurative passive meaning of being rained on.** The Lord in His indignation had not rained on Israel (Ezek. 22:24) but had sent drought. ❡

RAINBOW – See BOW (noun) <7198>.

RAINDROP – Deut. 32:2 ➔ DROPLET <8164>.

RAISE – Dan. 4:34 ➔ LIFT, LIFT UP <5191>.

RAISE UP – 1 ***zāqap*** [verb: זָקַף <2210>; a prim. root] ▶ **This verb means to elevate; it is also translated to lift up.** It describes the Lord's raising up of people who are fallen or bowed down (Ps. 145:14), since He is their sustainer (Ps. 146:8) and helper. ❡

– 2 Is. 23:13 ➔ STRIP <6209> b. 3 Zech. 14:10 ➔ RISE <7213> 4 See EXALT <7311>.

RAISIN – Hos. 3:1 ➔ GRAPE <6025>.

RAISIN CAKES – ***ᵃšîyšāh*** [fem. noun: אֲשִׁישָׁה <809>; fem. of FOUNDATION <808>] ▶ **This was a special luxury gift to the people to celebrate the arrival of the ark in Jerusalem, where the ark was placed inside a tent.** Refs.: 2 Sam. 6:19; 1 Chr. 16:3. It was a food desired for its energizing qualities (Song 2:5). Raisin cakes were also tied to pagan worship in some cases (Hos. 3:1). ¶

RAISINS (CLUSTER OF, CAKE OF) – ***simmûq*** [masc. noun: צִמּוּק <6778>; from DRY (verb) <6784>] ▶ **This word refers to a cake of dried grapes.** It was an especially desirable food item in the Middle East (1 Sam. 25:18); a quick energy source and delightful gift (1 Sam. 30:12; 2 Sam. 16:1; 1 Chr. 12:40). ¶

RAKKATH – ***rāqqaṯ*** [proper noun: רַקַּת <7557>; from SPIT (verb) <7556> (in its original sense of diffusing)]: beach, shore ▶ **A fortified city in Naphtali.** Ref.: Ezra 3:7. ¶

RAKKON – ***raqqôn*** [proper noun: רַקּוֹן <7542>; from LEAN (adj.) <7534>]: thinness ▶ **A city that was part of the inheritance of Dan near Joppa.** Ref.: Josh. 19:46. ¶

RAM (animal) – [1] ***'ayil*** [masc. noun: אַיִל <352>; from the same as BODY <193>] ▶ **The word is generally used in reference to the male sheep as a sacrificial animal.** The most famous one was the ram God Himself provided in place of Isaac (Gen. 22:13). For other meanings of the Hebrew word, see DOORPOST, MIGHTY, OAK. *
[2] ***dᵉḵar*** [Aramaic masc. noun: דְּכַר <1798>; corresponding to MALE <2145> a.] ▶ **This word refers to male sheep used for sacrifice.** Refs.: Ezra 6:9, 17; 7:17. ¶
[3] ***yôḇēl*** [common noun: יוֹבֵל <3104>; apparently from BRING <2986>] ▶ **This word refers to a male sheep's horn, a trumpet, the jubilee.** It is used in the phrase *qeren yôḇēl*, "horn of a ram" (Josh. 6:5) or in the phrase *šôp̱ᵉrôṯ hayyôḇᵉlîym* "shophars (rams' horns) of rams" which is rendered as "trumpets of rams' horns" (e.g., NASB, Josh. 6:4). Its most famous use is in the phrase "year of the ram's horn," which means the Year of Jubilee that was announced by blowing a ram's horn (Lev. 25:13). The word is used alone with the definite article or without it to mean simply the Jubilee (Lev. 25:10–12, 15). Its most spectacular use was at Sinai to inaugurate God's appearance and the giving of the Law (Ex. 19:13). *

RAM (person) – ***rām*** [masc. proper noun: רָם <7410>; act. part. of EXALT <7311>]: high, exalted ▶
a. Son of Hezron. Refs.: Ruth 4:19; 1 Chr. 2:9, 10. ¶
b. Son of Jerahmeel. Refs.: 1 Chr. 2:25, 27. ¶
c. Relative of Elihu. Ref.: Job 32:2. ¶

RAM'S HORN – See TRUMPET <7782>.

RAMAH – [1] ***rāmāh*** [proper noun: רָמָה <7414>; the same as HIGH PLACE <7413>]: high place ▶
a. A town in Benjamin's territory. Ref.: Josh. 18:25. It was near where Deborah judged Israel (Judg. 4:5). It was located about five miles north of Jerusalem and north, northeast of Gibeah. It was also called Ramathaim. King Baasha of Israel strengthened its fortifications (1 Kgs. 15:17; 2 Chr. 16:1–6), while Asa king of Judah dismantled them (1 Kgs. 15:21, 22). Later invasions passed through it (Is. 10:29) and brought devastation (Jer. 31:15; 40:1; Hos. 5:8). Exiles from Babylon returned there to settle (Ezra 2:26; Neh. 7:30).
b. The town from which Israel's last great judge, Samuel, came. Refs.: 1 Sam. 1:19, 2:11. It was his administrative center at times (1 Sam. 7:17). Here Israel demanded a king to lead them (1 Sam. 8:4). Samuel came here after anointing David (1 Sam. 16:13). David later fled here to Samuel, and Saul pursued him (1 Sam. 19:18–22; 20:1). Samuel was buried here (1 Sam. 25:1; 28:3). It is best translated "hill, height" in 1 Samuel 22:6.

c. A town on Asher's border, near the Canaanite cities of Tyre and Sidon. Ref.: Josh. 19:29.
d. A town in Naphtali between upper and lower Galilee. Ref.: Josh. 19:36. It is located ca. twenty-five miles west of the north end of the Sea of Galilee.
e. A town located on the border of Simeon. Ref.: Josh. 19:8. It is probably ca. twenty miles east, southeast of Beersheba and about thirteen miles west of the southern end of the Dead Sea.
f. A town in Transjordan in the area of Gilead where Joram, king of Israel, fought with the Arameans. Ref.: 2 Kgs. 8:29. *
– [2] 1 Sam. 22:6 ➔ HIGH PLACE <7413>.

RAMATH LEHI – ***rāmaṯ lᵉḥiy*** [proper noun: רָמַת לְחִי <7437>; from HIGH PLACE <7413> and JAW <3895>]: height of a jawbone ► **A place named by Samson after he had killed 1,000 Philistines with the jawbone of a donkey.** Ref.: Judg. 15:17. ¶

RAMATH MITZPEH – ***rāmaṯ hammiṣpeh*** [proper noun: רָמַת הַמִּצְפֶּה <7434>; from HIGH PLACE <7413> and WATCHTOWER <4707>]: height of the watchtower ► **A place in Gilead that became part of the inheritance of Gad.** Ref.: Josh. 27:27. ¶

RAMATHAIM-ZOPHIM – ***rāmāṯayim ṣôp̱iym, rāmāṯayim*** [proper noun: רָמָתַיִם, רָמָתַיִם צוֹפִים <7436>; from the dual of HIGH PLACE <7413> and the plur. of the act. part. of WATCH (verb) <6822>]: double height of watchers ►
a. A place in Ephraim, hometown of Elkanah, the father of Samuel. The same as b. below and *rāmāh* (RAMAH <7414> f.) (1 Sam. 1:1).
b. A word designating Ramathaim, used with *ṣûp̱iy* (ZUPH <6689>). The same as a. above and *rāmāh* (RAMAH <7414> f.) (NIV, 1 Sam. 1:1). ¶

RAMATHITE – ***rāmāṯiy*** [proper noun: רָמָתִי <7435>; patron. of RAMAH <7414>] ► **An inhabitant of Ramah.** Ref.: Josh. 27:27. ¶

RAMIAH – ***ramyāh*** [masc. proper noun: רַמְיָה <7422>; from EXALT <7311> and LORD <3050>]: the Lord has raised ► **An Israelite who had married a foreign wife.** Ref.: Ezra 10:25. ¶

RAMOTH – ***rā'môṯ, rā'mōṯ*** [proper noun: רָאמוֹת, רָאמֹת <7216>; plur. of CORAL <7215> (which is from RISE <7213>)]: heights ►
a. A city in Gilead. Refs.: Deut. 4:43; Josh. 20:8; 21:38; 1 Chr. 6:80. See also Ramoth Gilead (<7433>). ¶
b. A city in Issachar. Ref.: 1 Chr. 6:73. ¶

RAMOTH, RAMOTH GILEAD – ***rāmôṯ, rāmôṯ gil'āḏ*** [proper noun: רָמוֹת, רָמוֹת גִּלְעָד <7433>; from the plur. of HIGH PLACE <7413> and GILEAD <1568> (which means hill of testimony)]: heights of Gilead ► **A city located in Transjordan Gilead.** It belonged to Gad and was also a city of refuge (Josh. 21:38) (See also RAMAH <7414> f.). It was an administrative center for Solomon (1 Kgs. 4:13). Israel and Judah engaged the Arameans in battle here (1 Kgs. 22:3–29). The Lord had Jehu anointed here to destroy Ahab and Jezebel (2 Kgs. 9:1–14). *

RAMOTH NEGEV – ***rāmôṯ negeḇ*** [proper noun: רָמוֹת נֶגֶב <7418>; from the plur. or construct form of HIGH PLACE <7413> and SOUTH <5045>]: high place of the south ► **This place mentioned in 1 Samuel 30:27 is the same as *rāmāh* (RAMAH <7414> e.).** ¶

RAMPART – [1] ***ḥêylāh*** [fem. noun: חֵילָה <2430>; fem. of STRENGTH <2428>] ► **This word indicates embankments of earth normally topped off with a defensive wall or steep banks; it is also translated bulwark.** The defenses of the city of Zion (Ps. 48:13) were pictured as exceptionally effective and impressive. ¶
– [2] Nah. 2:1 ➔ FORTIFIED PLACE <4694>.

RANGE (noun) – [1] ***yᵉṯûr*** [masc. noun: יְתוּר <3491>; pass. part. of REMAIN <3498>] ► **This word indicates roaming, an area of open land.** It is used of an area where the

wild donkey runs loose, searching for his pasture, as well as the act of roaming itself (Job 39:8). ¶
– [2] 2 Kgs. 11:8, 15; 2 Chr. 23:14 ➔ RANK <7713> a.

RANGE (verb) – Job 39:8 ➔ RANGE (noun) <3491>.

RANK – [1] ***śᵉḏērāh*** [fem. noun: שְׂדֵרָה <7713>; from an unused root meaning to regulate] ▶
a. This word refers to a row or array of soldiers. It describes a configuration of soldiers standing in orderly array (NASB, 2 Kgs. 11:8, 15; 2 Chr. 23:14; KJV, ranks, ranges of soldiers; see also c.), possibly to protect the king or an area.
b. A feminine noun indicating a board, a plank of wood. It refers to boards, long, flat pieces of wood sawed or cut and prepared for use in construction (1 Kgs. 6:9; see also c.).
c. A feminine noun used as an architectural term indicating rows or ranks; used as a technical building term of unknown meaning. Rows or ranks (2 Kgs. 11:8, 15; 2 Chr. 23:14; see also a.). Technical building term of unknown meaning (1 Kgs. 6:9 NASB footnote: lit. rows; see also b.). ¶
– [2] 1 Sam. 17:23 ➔ ARMY <4630> [3] 1 Chr. 17:17 ➔ TURN (noun) <8447> d. [4] Prov. 30:27 ➔ to advance in rank, to advance in ranks, to go out in ranks, to march in rank ➔ DIVIDE <2686> a. [5] Joel 2:7 ➔ PATH <734>.

RANK (KEEP) – ***ʿāḏar*** [verb: עָדַר <5737>; a prim. root] ▶ **This word means to set in order, to arrange (as an army for battle), to muster (verifying that no soldier is missing). It refers to organizing a group of soldiers, of their arranging themselves in order, in battle array.** Ref.: KJV, NKJV, 1 Chr. 12:33. It also means to help, to support, to come to the aid of (NASB, ESV, NIV, 1 Chr. 12:33). The Hebrew word also means to lack, to cultivate; see LACK, LACKING (BE) <5737>, CULTIVATE <5737>. ¶

RANK (OF LOW) – Prov. 22:29 ➔ OBSCURE <2823>.

RANKS – Is. 14:31 ➔ APPOINTED TIMES <4151>.

RANSACK – [1] Obad. 1:6 ➔ BOIL (verb) <1158> [2] Zech. 14:2 ➔ PLUNDER (verb) <8155>.

RANSOM (noun) – [1] ***kōp̄er*** [masc. noun: כֹּפֶר <3724>; from COVER (verb) <3722>] ▶ **This word means a monetary covering, e.g., a redemption price, a ransom, a price of life. It also means a bribe. The most common translation of the Hebrew word is ransom. In Exodus 30:12 it refers to the price (i.e., a half shekel, v. 13) demanded in order to redeem or rescue a person.** The irresponsible owner of a bull that killed someone and was known to have gored people previously could be redeemed by the ransom that would be placed on him (Ex. 21:30). When a census of people was taken in Israel, adult males had to pay a half-shekel ransom to keep the Lord's plague from striking them (Ex. 30:12). A murderer could not be redeemed by a ransom (Num. 35:31). Yet money, without God's explicit approval, could not serve as a ransom for a human being (Ps. 49:7). On the other hand, money could serve as a ransom to buy off a person's human enemies (Prov. 13:8). God sometimes used a wicked person as a ransom to redeem a righteous person (Prov. 21:18); God ransomed Israel from Babylonian captivity for the ransom price of three nations (Is. 43:3): Egypt, Seba, and Cush.

The meaning of the word becomes a bribe when used in certain circumstances. For example, Samuel declared that he had never taken a bribe (1 Sam. 12:3); and Amos castigated the leaders of Israel for taking bribes (Amos 5:12). Prov. 6:35 describes a jealous husband whose fury would not allow him to take a bribe to lessen his anger. *
– [2] Ex. 21:30; Num. 3:49, 51; Ps. 49:8 ➔ REDEMPTION <6306> [3] Num. 3:46, 48, 51 ➔ REDEMPTION <6302>.

RANSOM (verb) – See REDEEM <6299>.

RAPE – ***šāḡal*** [verb: שָׁגַל <7693>; a prim. root] ▶ **This word means to violate sexually; it is also translated to ravish, to**

lie with. It refers to violating a betrothed woman, a woman promised in marriage, as one of God's curses that He will bring on Israel (Deut. 28:30). It is used of raping or violating wives taken in war as prisoners (Is. 13:16; Zech. 14:2). It is used figuratively of spiritual and religious prostitution of all kinds (Jer. 3:2). ¶

RAPHA – ***rāp̱a', rāp̱āh*** [masc. proper noun: רָפָא, רָפָה <7498>; prob. the same as REPHAIM <7497>]: giant ►
a. The father of several giants among David's enemies. Refs.: 1 Sam. 21:16, 18, 20, 22; 1 Chr. 20:6, 8.
b. Son of Benjamin. Ref.: 1 Chr. 8:2.
c. Son of Binea, the same as Rephaiah (<7509> d.). Ref.: 1 Chr. 8:37. ¶

RAPHU – ***rāp̱û'*** [masc. proper noun: רָפוּא <7505>; pass. part. of HEAL <7495>]: healed ► **Father of Palti, the Benjamite spy of the Promised Land.** Ref.: Num. 13:9. ¶

RARE – [1] 1 Sam. 3:1 ➔ PRECIOUS <3368> [2] Prov. 20:15 ➔ HONOR (noun) <3366> [3] Dan. 2:11 ➔ NOBLE <3358>.

RARE (MAKE MORE) – Is. 13:12 ➔ PRECIOUS (BE) <3365>.

RARELY BE (LET) – Prov. 25:17 ➔ PRECIOUS (BE) <3365>.

RASH – [1] ***mispaḥaṯ*** [fem. noun: מִסְפַּחַת <4556>; from JOIN <5596> (with another Hebrew meaning of causing a scab upon)] ► **This word means a skin irritation or disease; it is also translated scab, eruption.** It was considered relatively harmless by the priests (Lev. 13:6–8). ¶
– [2] Lev. 13:2; 14:56 ➔ SCAB <5597>.

RASH (BE) – Job 6:3 ➔ SWALLOW (verb) <3886> b.

RASH (HARMLESS) – Lev. 13:39 ➔ SPOT (FRECKLED, WHITE) <933>.

RASH STATEMENT – ***miḇṭā'*** [masc. noun: מִבְטָא <4008>; from THOUGHTLESSLY (SPEAK) <981>] ► **This word means an impulsive, ill-considered utterance, a hasty vow. It refers to a promise, vow, or verbal commitment made without sufficient reflection** a foolish vow on the spur of the moment (Num. 30:6, 8; also translated thoughtless). ¶

RASHLY (SAY, DEVOTE, DEDICATE) – Prov. 20:25 ➔ DEVOUR <3216>, SWALLOW (verb) <3886> b.

RASHLY (SPEAK) – Ps. 106:33; Prov. 12:18 ➔ THOUGHTLESSLY (SPEAK) <981>.

RATION – 2 Kgs. 25:30; Jer. 40:5; 52:34 ➔ ALLOWANCE <737>.

RATIONED – Ezek. 4:16 ➔ lit.: by measure ➔ MEASURE (noun) <4884>.

RATTLE – ***rānāh*** [verb: רָנָה <7439>; a prim. root] ► **This word means to make a rapid succession of loud, short, knocking sounds.** It refers to the sound made by a container of arrows or darts banging against something, e.g., a war horse (Job 39:23). ¶

RAVAGE (noun) – ***šō'*** [masc. noun: שֹׁאָה <7722>; from an unused root meaning to rush over] ► **When used in the feminine form *šō'āh*, this word means devastation, ruin, desolation, or noise. The primary meaning of the word is devastation.** Often this word carries with it a sense of something sudden or unexpected like that of a devastating storm (Ezek. 38:9). In Isaiah, the word describes a coming disaster on the day of reckoning (Is. 10:3). The noun is used to depict a wasteland or a desert (Job 30:3; 38:27). Psalm 35:17 uses the masculine form of the word to indicate the ravages that held the psalmist down. *

RAVAGE (verb) – ***kirsēm*** [verb: כִּרְסֵם <3765>; from TRIM <3697>] ► **This word means to tear, to tear apart; it is also translated to uproot, to eat away, to waste.** It is used to describe the ravaging of God's people by a wild boar (Ps. 80:13), a symbol of their enemies. ¶

RAVEN – ***'ôrêḇ*** [masc. noun: עֹרֵב <6158>; from EVENING (BECOME) <6150> (in the case of the raven, in relation to its dusky hue)] ▶ **This word refers to several species of large crows, given this name because of their cry, a harsh sound. It has a voracious appetite.** It was considered unclean, not edible by Israelites (Lev. 11:15; Deut. 14:14). God feeds it (Job 38:41; Ps. 147:9); paradoxically, ravens fed Elijah, the man of God (1 Kgs. 17:4, 6), rather than eating the food themselves. It had both admirable (Song 5:11); and detestable characteristics (Prov. 30:17; Is. 34:11). Other ref.: Gen. 8:7. ¶

RAVENOUS – Is. 35:9 ➔ VIOLENT <6530>.

RAVENOUS BIRD – Is. 46:11; Ezek. 39:4 ➔ BIRD OF PREY <5861>.

RAVIN – Nah. 2:12 ➔ TORN (WHAT IS) <2966>.

RAVINE – [1] ***'āpiyq*** [masc. noun and adj.: אָפִיק <650>; from GATHER <622>] ▶
a. This word refers to a torrent, a stream channel; tube. It is found often in Ezekiel (Ezek. 6:3; 31:12; 32:6; 34:13; 35:8; 36:4, 36:6) indicating a stream channel. It refers to channels opened in the deep sea waters (2 Sam. 22:16) but also to the wadis or quickly appearing but swiftly vanishing streams in the desert (Job 6:15; Joel 1:20). It also, however, describes smooth flowing streams of peace (Song 5:12). It describes the tubes, sinews, of the Behemoth (NIV, ESV, NASB, Job 40:18; beam in NKJV).
b. In an adjectival form, this word also means strong, mighty, robust. It refers to strong persons of great wealth and influence (Ref.: Job 12:21). The strength of Behemoth is described by this word (KJV, Job 40:18). *
[2] ***m^e^ṣulāh*** [fem. noun: מְצֻלָה <4699>; from DARK (BE) <6751>] ▶ **This word is used of a long, deep depression in the land, forming a hollow.** Ref.: Zech. 1:8; also translated bottom, glen. ¶
– [3] Jer. 2:6 ➔ PIT <7745>.

RAVISH – Deut. 28:30; Is. 13:16; Jer. 3:2; Zech. 14:2 ➔ RAPE <7693>.

RAW – [1] ***nā'*** [adj.: נָא <4995>; apparently from FORBID <5106> in the sense of harshness from refusal] ▶ **This word describes meat as uncooked. It is used of meat prepared to be eaten.** Israel was not to eat raw meat with blood in it (Ex. 12:9). ¶
– [2] Lev. 13:10, 24 ➔ PRESERVATION OF LIFE <4241>.

RAWBONED – Gen. 49:14 ➔ BONE <1634>.

RAZE – Is. 3:17 ➔ EMPTY (verb) <6168>.

RAZED (COMPLETELY) – Jer. 51:58 ➔ STRIP <6209> a.

RAZOR – [1] ***môrāh*** [masc. noun: מוֹרָה <4177>; from EXCHANGE (verb) <4171> in the sense of shearing] ▶ **This word indicates a tool for shaving one's beard or hair.** Refs.: Judg. 13:5; 16:17; 1 Sam. 1:11. It was used regarding Samson and Samuel in their Nazarite vows. ¶
– [2] ***ta'ar*** [masc. noun: תַּעַר <8593>; from EMPTY (verb) <6168> (as making bare)] ▶ **See previous definition. This word also refers to a knife's sheath.** It refers to a sharp-edged cutting tool used to cut one's hair or beard (Num. 6:5); a Nazarite was not to cut his hair during the time of his Nazarite vow. Ezekiel used a razor to shave his hair and beard (Ezek. 5:1). It was used to shave the Levites' entire bodies to symbolically cleanse them for their sacred service (Num. 8:7). It also describes a knife (razor?) used to cut passages from a scroll (Jer. 36:23). It refers to the sheath for a sword (1 Sam. 17:51; 2 Sam. 20:8; Ezek. 21:3, 4, 5, 30). The tongue of an evil person is compared to a sharp razor that works deceit (Ps. 52:2). It is used figuratively of the Lord shaving Judah with His razor—Assyria's army (Is. 7:20). Other ref.: Jer. 47:6. ¶

REACH – [1] ***m^e^ṭā', m^e^ṭāh*** [Aramaic verb: מְטָא, מְטָה <4291>; apparently corresponding to FIND <4672> in the intransitive sense of

being found present] ▶ **This word means, to attain, to happen.** It is used to indicate that something physically or figuratively has touched or reached a certain location (Dan. 4:11, 20; 6:24; 7:13, 22); or something such as royal influence has reached a certain extent (Dan. 4:22). It is used of a decree or a sentence being fulfilled (Dan. 4:28: to come upon, to happen to). Other ref.: Dan. 4:24. ¶
– [2] Ruth 2:14 ➔ SERVE <6642> [3] Ezra 5:5 ➔ GO <1946> [4] Is. 16:8; Jer. 51:9; Jon. 3:6 ➔ TOUCH <5060>.

REACH FORWARD – Judg. 16:29 ➔ HOLD OF (TAKE) <3943>.

READ – ***qerā'*** [Aramaic verb: קְרָא <7123>; corresponding to CALL <7121>] ▶ **This word means to look at and understand words; it also means to call, to shout.** It refers to the act of reading a written document, silently or orally (Ezra 4:18, 23); or to calling out or proclaiming something aloud (Dan. 3:4; 4:14; 5:7, 8, 12, 15–17). ¶

READINESS (IN) – ***'ittiy*** [adj.: עִתִּי <6261>; from TIME <6256>] ▶ **This word means fit, prepared to stand.** It refers to someone prepared and waiting to perform a task, in this case, to send a goat into the wilderness on the Day of Atonement (Lev. 16:21; also translated suitable, appointed). ¶

READY – [1] ***'ăṯiyḏ*** [Aramaic adj.: עֲתִיד <6263>; corresponding to <6264> below] ▶ **This word means prompt; prepared to respond to a signal to do something.** In this case, it is spiritually and emotionally as well as physically (Dan. 3:15). ¶
[2] ***āṯiyḏ*** [adj.: עָתִיד <6264>; from READY (BE) <6257>] ▶
a. This word means prepared for something. It refers to being forewarned and set to respond to a situation that will arise soon (Esther 3:14; 8:13; Job 15:24). It means to be brave enough to do something (Job 3:8). ¶
b. This word means the things that are ready for anyone, i.e., impending; about to come. It is used of things about to occur, to happen, to come about, especially things to occur in Israel's future (Deut. 32:35). ¶
c. This word means the things that are prepared, acquired, stored up; i.e., wealth, treasures. It refers to the valued things of peoples and nations, what they consider of importance to them (Is. 10:13; also translated treasury). ¶
– [3] Ezra 7:6; Ps. 45:1 ➔ SKILLED <4106>.

READY (BE) – Deut. 1:41 ➔ EASY (THINK, REGARD AS) <1951>.

READY (BE, MAKE, GET) – ***'āṯaḏ*** [fem. plur. noun: עָתַד <6257>; a prim. root] ▶ **This word has the sense of something destined, prepared for a purpose or goal.** Ref.: Job 15:28. It is used of getting something ready beforehand to use later as needed (Prov. 24:27; also translated to make fit). ¶

READY (GET) – Jer. 1:17 ➔ GIRD <247>.

READY (MAKE) – Hab. 3:9 ➔ UNCOVER <5783>.

REAIA, REAIAH – ***re'āyāh*** [masc. proper noun: רְאָיָה <7211>; from SEE <7200> and LORD <3050>]: the Lord has seen ▶
a. An Israelite of the tribe of Reuben. Ref.: 1 Chr. 5:5. ¶
b. An Israelite of the tribe of Judah. Ref.: 1 Chr. 4:2. ¶
c. Ancestor of a family who returned from the Babylonian captivity. Refs.: Ezra 2:47; Neh. 7:50. ¶

REALLY – [1] Gen. 18:13 ➔ SURELY <552> [2] Gen. 20:12 ➔ INDEED <546>.

REAP – ***qāṣar*** [verb: קָצַר <7114>; a prim. root] ▶ **This word means to harvest, gather in a crop.** Refs.: Lev. 19:9; 23:10; 1 Sam. 6:13; 8:12. Its participial form *qôṣêr* refers to a reaper (Jer. 9:22; Amos 9:13). It is used in a figurative sense of reaping the fruits of righteousness (Hos. 10:12); of evil (Hos. 8:7). Psalm 126:5 records the famous phrase that they who sow in tears, reap in joy. For another meaning of the Hebrew word, see SHORTEN <7114>. *

REAR GUARD – Joel 2:20 ➔ END <5490>.

REASON – [1] Eccl. 7:25, 27 ➔ SCHEME (noun) <2808> [2] Dan. 4:34 ➔ KNOWLEDGE <4486>.

REASONS (STRONG) – Is. 41:21 ➔ ARGUMENTS (STRONG) <6110>.

REBA – ***reḇa'*** [masc. proper noun: רֶבַע <7254>; the same as FOURTH <7253>]: four ► **One of the five Midianite kings killed by the Israelites, as well as Balaam.** Refs.: Num. 31:8; Josh. 13:21. ¶

REBEKAH – ***riḇqāh*** [fem. proper noun: רִבְקָה <7259>; from an unused root prob. meaning to clog by tying up the fetlock]: ensnarer, fettering by beauty ► **She was the daughter of Bethuel and granddaughter of Nahor, Abraham's brother.** Refs.: Gen. 22:20–24. She became Isaac's wife and bore Esau and Jacob, twins (Gen. 25:21–26). She was an Aramean and also the sister of Laban (Gen. 25:20). Isaac gave her, deceitfully, to Abimelech for a while who quickly returned her when the Lord revealed the situation to him in a dream (Gen. 26:7–11). Esau grieved her and Isaac by marrying a Canaanite (Gen. 26:35). She helped Jacob surreptitiously get Esau's blessing (Gen. 27:1–28:9). She and Isaac happily sent Jacob to Paddan Aram to get a wife (Gen. 28:5). She died (an event not mentioned) and was buried in the burial cave in the field of Machpelah (Gen. 49:29–30). *

REBEL (noun) – Hos. 5:2 ➔ REVOLTER <7846> a.

REBEL (verb) – [1] ***māraḏ*** [verb: מָרַד <4775>; a prim. root] ► **This word usually means to resist authority.** It can be against the Lord (Num. 14:9; Dan. 9:9) or against human kings (Gen. 14:4; Neh. 2:19). In one instance, it is used to describe those who rebel against the light (i.e., God's truth [Job 24:13]). This word is also used to describe a general, rebellious character of a nation (Ezek. 2:3; 20:38); as well as a specific act of rebellion, such as Hezekiah's rebellion against Sennacherib (2 Kgs. 18:7, 20; Is. 36:5); or Zedekiah's rebellion against Nebuchadnezzar (2 Kgs. 24:20; Jer. 52:3; Ezek. 17:15). *

[2] ***pāša'*** [verb: פָּשַׁע <6586>; a prim. root; identical with MARCH (verb) <6585> through the idea of expansion] ► **This word means to transgress, to revolt, to sin. It is used about forty times in the simple stem of the verb. It means to sin, but the sin involved is one of revolt or rebellion in nearly every case.** It indicates rebellion against various parties; the people of Israel rebelled against their God (Is. 1:2; 66:24; Jer. 2:29; 3:13); especially their leaders (Jer. 2:8). Nations and peoples revolted or broke with one another: Israel broke from and rebelled against Judah (1 Kgs. 12:19); Moab rebelled against Israel (2 Kgs. 1:1; 3:5); and Edom revolted against Judah (2 Kgs. 8:20). Revolt and rebellion against the Lord, Isaiah said, was a part of the character of Israel from its birth and throughout its history (Is. 48:8; 59:13). Amos described Israel's insistence to worship at the unapproved sanctuaries at Bethel and Gilgal as revolt and rebellion (Amos 4:4). The postexilic community rebelled through intermarriages with pagans (Ezra 10:13). God asserted that He would restore His people, forgiving their sins of rebellion (Jer. 33:8). Unrestrained rebellion seems to be a mark of the end times as noted by Daniel 8:23. *

– [3] Num. 26:9 ➔ FIGHT <5327> [4] Num. 27:14 ➔ STRIFE <4808> [5] Deut. 9:23 ➔ REBELLIOUS (BE) <4784> [6] Is. 1:5 ➔ REBELLION <5627>.

REBELLION – [1] ***meraḏ*** [Aramaic masc. noun: מְרַד <4776>; from a root corresponding to REBEL (verb) <4775>] ► **This word is used to indicate defiance of authority.** In Ezra 4:19, this word described Jerusalem's past rebellion. ¶

[2] ***mereḏ*** [masc. noun: מֶרֶד <4777>; from REBEL (verb) <4775>] ► **This word is used to indicate defiance of authority.** In Joshua 22:22, it was used to describe the act of building another altar on the east of the Jordan River as rebellious. ¶

3 ***sārāh*** [fem. noun: סָרָה <5627>; from TURN ASIDE <5493>] ▶ **This word means a defection, a revolt, an apostasy; it is also translated to turn away, to revolt, to rebel, to defect.** Derived from a verb that means to turn aside, this term refers to God's people turning away from Him to follow false gods (Deut. 13:5). Frequently, it describes those who chose to rebel against God (Is. 1:5; 14:6; 31:6; 59:13; Jer. 28:16; 29:32). Although some translations of this term in Deuteronomy 19:16 suggest it simply means a general offense, its use elsewhere in Deuteronomy and the rest of the Old Testament indicates that this word refers to apostasy. ¶
– 4 Ps. 64:2 ➔ THRONG (noun) <7285>
5 Ps. 95:8 ➔ STRIFE <4808>.

REBELLION (ONE WHO IS IN) – Ps. 139:21 ➔ RISES UP (ONE WHO) <8618>.

REBELLIOUS – 1 ***mārāḏ*** [Aramaic adj.: מְרָד <4779>; from the same as REBELLION <4776>] ▶ **This word, meaning disobedient, insubordinate, is used only twice in the Old Testament and is related to the Hebrew word *mārad* (<4775>), meaning to rebel.** In Ezra 4:12, 15, it described the historically rebellious character of Jerusalem. ¶
2 ***mardûṯ*** [fem. noun: מַרְדּוּת <4780>; from REBEL (verb) <4775>] ▶ **This word means literally rebelliousness, i.e., opposition to, defiance of authority.** In 1 Samuel 20:30, Saul used it in his anger against Jonathan as a derogatory word to describe Jonathan's mother. ¶
3 ***sārar*** [verb: סָרַר <5637>; a prim. root (with the sense of to turn away)] ▶ **This word means to be stubborn, to be defiant, to be obstinate.** Israel was said to be stubborn for forming an alliance with Egypt against God's ordained plan (Is. 30:1); performing improper sacrifices, eating unclean things, and worshiping ancestors (Is. 65:2). They were even compared to a stubborn heifer (Hos. 4:16). They stubbornly turned their backs (lit., shoulders) on God and His words (Neh. 9:29; Zech. 7:11). The son who rebelled against his parents could be severely disciplined and was eventually stoned (Deut. 21:18, 21). The term is also used of an immoral woman (Prov. 7:11; also translated wayward, defiant). *

REBELLIOUS (BE) – ***mārāh*** [verb: מָרָה <4784>; a prim. root] ▶ **This word means to defy authority.** In one instance, it spoke of a son's rebellion against his parents (Deut. 21:18, 20). In all other instances, this word was used of rebellion against God, which provoked Him to action. This word is usually used as an indictment against a nation's rebellion, whether Israel's (Deut. 9:23, 24; Ps. 78:8; Jer. 5:23; Zeph. 3:1, KJV: filthy <4754>); Samaria's (Hos. 13:16); or David's enemies (Ps. 5:10). In a few instances, it is used to indict specific people, as Moses (Num. 20:24; 27:14), or a man of God who disobeyed (1 Kgs. 13:21, 26: to disobey, to defy). *

REBELLIOUSNESS – ***m*^e^*riy*** [masc. noun: מְרִי <4805>; from REBELLIOUS (BE) <4784>] ▶ **This word means obstinacy, stubbornness. The term consistently stays within this tight semantic range and most often describes the Israelites' determined refusal to obey the precepts laid down by the Lord in His Law or Torah.** This characteristic attitude was a visible manifestation of their hard hearts. Moses had the Book of the Law placed beside the ark of the covenant to remain there as a witness against the Israelites' rebelliousness after he died (Deut. 31:27; Num. 17:10). The Lord rejected Saul as king over Israel because of his rebellion against the command the Lord had earlier given him (1 Sam. 15:23). Continually in Ezekiel, the Lord refers to Israel as the "house of rebelliousness" (= rebellious people; Ezek. 2:5–8; 3:9, 26, 27; 12:2, 3, 9). This noun is derived from the verb *mārāh* [REBELLIOUS (BE) <4784>]. *

REBUKE (noun) – 1 ***g*^e^*'ārāh*** [fem. noun: גְּעָרָה <1606>; from REBUKE (verb) <1605>] ▶ **This word depicts one person's sharp criticism of another.** Both God and humans are the subject of such rebukes (2 Sam. 22:16; Is. 50:2). Other refs.: Job 26:11; Ps. 18:15; 76:6; 80:16; 104:7; Prov. 13:1, 8; 17:10; Eccl. 7:5; Is. 30:17; 51:20; 66:15. ¶

[2] ***miḡʿereṯ*** [fem. noun: מִגְעֶרֶת <4045>; from REBUKE (verb) <1605>] ▶ **This word means to blame, to scold sharply, to reprimand as God said He would do to His people.** Ref.: Deut. 28:20; ESV: frustration. ¶

[3] ***tôḵêḥāh, tôḵaḥaṯ*** [fem. noun: תּוֹכֵחָה, תּוֹכַחַת <8433>; from JUDGE (noun) <3198>] ▶ **This word means a correction, a reproof, an argument. The primary thrust of this word is that of correcting some wrong.** It is employed to express the concept of rebuking (Prov. 15:10); judgment (Hos. 5:9); reckoning (2 Kgs. 19:3); or the argument of a claim (Job 13:6; Hab. 2:1). *

REBUKE (verb) – [1] ***gāʿar*** [verb: גָּעַר <1605>; a prim. root] ▶ **This word means to reprove. It depicts one person's sharp criticism of another.** Jacob rebuked Joseph for telling his dream (Gen. 37:10), and Boaz commanded his servants not to rebuke Ruth's gleaning activity (Ruth 2:16). When depicting God's actions, this word is often used to describe the result of His righteous anger (Is. 54:9; Nah. 1:4) against those who rebel against Him, including wicked nations (Ps. 9:5; Is. 17:13); their offspring (Mal. 2:3); the proud (Ps. 119:21); and Satan (Zech. 3:2). So authoritative is the Lord's rebuke that even nature obeys His voice (Ps. 106:9; Nah. 1:4). Other refs.: Ps. 68:30; Jer. 29:27; Mal. 3:11. ¶

– [2] 1 Sam. 3:13 ➔ DIM (BE) <3543> b. [3] 1 Sam. 24:7 ➔ SPLIT <8156> [4] Prov. 9:7; 15:12; Ezek. 3:26 ➔ JUDGE (verb) <3198>.

RECAH, RECHAH, RECHABITE – ***rêḵāh, rêḵāḇiy*** [proper noun: רֵכָבִי, רֵכָה <7397>; fem. from FAINT (BE, MAKE) <7401>]: softness ▶

a. A name designating Recah, Rechah. Ref.: 1 Chr. 4:12. ¶

b. Living in the midst of the Israelites, the Rechabites had obeyed their chief Jonadab to live a simple nomadic life. Refs.: Jer. 35:1–19. ¶

RECEDE – Gen. 8:1 ➔ SUBSIDE <7918>.

RECEIVE – [1] ***qāḇal*** [Aramaic verb: קְבַל <6902>; corresponding to ACCEPT <6901>] ▶ **This word means to take over.** It means to get from persons, to receive from them (Dan. 2:6); especially in the sense of taking dominion (KINGDOM <4437>: *malkûtāʾ*) (Dan. 5:31; 7:18). ¶

– [2] Prov. 8:35 ➔ OBTAIN <6329>.

RECESS – Job 28:3 ➔ END <8503>.

RECESSES – Job 38:16 ➔ SEARCH (noun) <2714>.

RECHAB – ***rêḵāḇ*** [masc. proper noun: רֵכָב <7394>; from RIDE <7392>]: rider ▶

a. He, along with others, assassinated Saul's son, Ishbosheth ("man of shame"), who tried to become king after Saul. Refs.: 2 Sam. 4:2, 5, 6, 9. ¶

b. A person who was strongly opposed to Baal and Baalism. He and his descendants refused to drink wine, build houses, or sow crops. God honored his faithfulness to His principles (2 Kgs. 10:15, 23; 1 Chr. 2:55; Jer. 35:6, 8, 14, 16, 19) by making him and his followers an example of faithfulness to a covenant. He is apparently the ancestor of Malkijah who was a leader in postexilic Judah and repaired the Dung Gate (Neh. 3:14). ¶

RECITE – Judg. 5:11 ➔ RECOUNT <8567>.

RECKLESS (BE) – [1] ***pāḥaz*** [verb: פָּחַז <6348>; a prim. root] ▶ **This word means to be undisciplined, wild, insolent, to be arrogant; it is also translated light, fickle, unprincipled.** In its plural participial form, it refers to reckless persons (Judg. 9:4). It refers to prophets who are undisciplined and unrestrained in their false prophecies (Zeph. 3:4). ¶

– [2] Num. 22:32 ➔ TURN OVER <3399>.

RECKLESSNESS – 1 ***paḥaz*** [masc. noun: פַּחַז <6349>; from RECKLESS (BE) <6348>] ▶ **This word means wantonness, unbridled license. It also refers to uncontrollableness. In context, this abstract notion is used to convey the concrete picture of boiling or overflowing water. It is translated uncontrolled, unstable, turbulent.** It refers to persons who are without self-control or discipline, e.g., Reuben who defiled his father's bed (Gen. 49:4). ¶
2 ***paḥᵃzûṯ*** [fem. noun: פַּחֲזוּת <6350>; from RECKLESS (BE) <6348>] ▶ **This word indicates the undisciplined, unrestrained behavior and actions of false prophets.** Ref.: Jer. 23:32; KJV: lightness. ¶

RECKONING – Hos. 9:7 ➔ RECOMPENSE (noun) <7966>.

RECLINE – Amos 6:7 ➔ HANG <5628>.

RECOMPENSE (noun) – 1 ***gᵉmûlāh*** [fem. noun: גְּמוּלָה <1578>; fem. of DESERVES (WHAT ONE) <1576>] ▶ **This word indicates that which is done; it is also translated retribution, reward.** It is used to describe God as a God of recompense who pays back fully what is deserved (Jer. 51:56) to His enemies and the enemies of His people (Is. 59:18; Jer. 51:56). It indicates a free bestowal of benefits on someone (2 Sam. 19:36). ¶
2 ***šillûm, šillum*** [masc. noun: שִׁלּוּם, שִׁלֻּם <7966>; from COMPLETED (BE) <7999>] ▶ **This word means a requital, a retribution.** It is derived from the verb *šālam*, to be completed, to be at peace. In context, this noun is used as God's punishment of Israel for their repeated disobedience (Is. 34:8; Hos. 9:7). It is not something given on a whim but is deserved. This noun can also mean a reward, or more accurately, a bribe (Mic. 7:3). Only the corrupt accept these bribes, which are used to distort justice. Such people have no care for what is right or wrong but only in what they will receive. Ultimately, they will receive their retribution from God for their wrongdoings. ¶
3 ***šillêm*** [masc. noun: שִׁלֵּם <8005>; from COMPLETED (BE) <7999>] ▶ **This word is used when speaking of a deserved punishment, in the sense of a repayment for whatever wrong was done by a person; it is also translated retribution.** Ref.: Deut. 32:35. In addition, it can also signify rewards for good that has been done. The idea behind this word is that it is a reward or punishment that is deserved and is in conjunction with what was done beforehand. Ultimately, only God has the power of retribution. It is His right only to avenge wrongdoers and give those persons what they deserve or to reward those who have done right. ¶
4 ***šillumāh*** [fem. sing. noun: שִׁלֻּמָה <8011>; fem. of <7966> above] ▶ **This word means retribution, punishment, penalty; it is also translated reward. It has negative meanings when it is used in Scripture, e.g., persons were punished or repaid for whatever evil they did.** The word does not seem to have anything to do with repayment in the sense of receiving rewards for doing what is right, but this could be because of its limited use in the Old Testament. The righteous remained safe in God's protection, but the wicked received their punishment before the eyes of the righteous (Ps. 91:8). God Himself is the giver of this retribution. ¶

RECOMPENSE (verb) – See REWARD (verb) <1580>.

RECONSIDER – Prov. 20:25 ➔ SEEK <1239>.

RECORD – 1 ***diḵrôn, doḵrān*** [Aramaic masc. noun: דִּכְרוֹן, דָּכְרָן <1799>; corresponding to MEMORIAL <2146>] ▶ **This word refers to a decree, a writing; it is also translated memorandum, archives.** It refers to a written royal decree from King Cyrus (Ezra 6:2) allowing the returned exiles to rebuild the Temple in Jerusalem. It refers also to a written record of past events concerning Jerusalem located in the archives or records of Artaxerxes (Ezra 4:15). ¶
– 2 Job 16:19 ➔ ADVOCATE <7717>.

RECOUNT – ***tānāh*** [verb: תָּנָה <8567>; a prim. root (identical with HIRE <8566>

through the idea of attributing honor)] ► **This word means to retell; it is also translated to rehearse, to repeat, to recite.** It indicates the retelling, narrating, recounting of great events the Lord accomplished for His people (Judg. 5:11). The tragic story of Jephthah's daughter was rehearsed every year for four days in Israel (Judg. 11:40: to commemorate). ¶

RECOVER – [1] 2 Chr. 14:13 ➔ PRESERVATION OF LIFE <4241> [2] Ps. 39:13 ➔ SMILE (verb) <1082>.

RECOVERY – Is. 58:8 ➔ HEALING <724>.

RECRUIT – Num. 31:5 ➔ PROVIDE <4560>.

RED – [1] ***'āḏōm*** [masc. adj.: אָדֹם <122>; from RUDDY (BE) <119>] ► **The word means ruddy, the color of blood (red to reddish brown).** Its meaning is best demonstrated in 2 Kings 3:22, where the Moabites saw the sunrise reflecting off the water which the Lord had miraculously provided. The Moabites thought the water was "as red as blood." This word is also used to describe the color of lentil stew (Gen. 25:30); the health or attractiveness of a man (Song 5:10); the color of garments (Is. 63:2); the color of animals, like a red heifer (Num. 19:2) or chestnut or bay-colored horses (Zech. 1:8; 6:2). ¶
[2] ***'aḏmōniy, 'aḏmôniy*** [adj.: אַדְמוֹנִי, אַדְמֹנִי <132>; from RUDDY (BE) <119>] ► **See previous definition. This word is also translated ruddy, glowing with health.** Esau is the prime example of someone who was red (Gen. 25:25). The Edomites, or "red ones," descended from Esau. David is the other notable figure whose complexion was characterized as good-looking, bright-eyed, and ruddy (1 Sam. 16:12; 17:42). ¶
– [3] Gen. 49:12 ➔ DARKER <2447>.

RED, BRIGHT RED – Jer. 22:14; Ezek. 23:14 ➔ VERMILION <8350>.

RED (BE) – ***ḥāmar*** [verb: חָמַר <2560>; a prim. root] ► **This word means to ferment, burn, boil, foment, make red.** It describes a person's face made red from suffering and skin disease (Job 16:16; also translated to be flushed, to be foul) and the troubling of a person's mind or spirit because of calamity (Lam. 1:20; 2:11). It describes the fomenting and foaming of the waters of the earth (Ps. 46:3; also translated to be troubled) and the agitation of wine in a cup (Ps. 75:8). The word also means to cover with bitumen; see COAT (verb) <2560>. ¶

RED (BE, MAKE) – Prov. 23:31; Is. 1:18, Nah. 2:3 ➔ RUDDY (BE) <119>.

RED (STONE) – Esther 1:6 ➔ PORPHYRY <923>.

RED KITE – ***rā'āh*** [fem. noun: רָאָה <7201>; from SEE <7200>] ► **This word indicates a bird of prey; it is also translated glede.** It was among the unclean birds, forbidden food to the Israelites (Deut. 14:13). It is classed among accipitrine birds having long, pointed wings, possibly a forked tail. They feed on insects, reptiles, and small mammals. ¶

RED SEA – [1] Ex. 10:19; 13:18; Josh. 2:10; 1 Kgs. 9:26 ➔ lit.: Sea of Reeds ➔ REED <5488> [2] Num. 21:14 ➔ STORM (noun) <5492> c.

REDDISH – ***ᵃḏamdām*** [adj.: אֲדַמְדָּם <125>; reduplicated from RUDDY (BE) <119>] ► **This word refers to a color which is a shade of red; it is used only six times in the Old Testament.** It signifies the reddish appearance of leprosy on the skin (Lev. 13:19, 24, 42, 43); the mark of leprosy on a garment (Lev. 13:49); or the mark of leprosy within a house (Lev. 14:37). ¶

REDEEM – [1] ***gᵉ'ûliym, gā'al*** [verb: גְּאוּלִים, גָּאַל <1350>; a prim. root] ► **This word means to exchange something for money, as well as to act as a kinsman-redeemer.** It means to act as a redeemer for a deceased kinsman (Ruth 3:13); to redeem or buy back from bondage (Lev. 25:48); to redeem or buy back a kinsman's possessions

(Lev. 25:26); to avenge a kinsman's murder (Num. 35:19); to redeem an object through a payment (Lev. 27:13). Theologically, this word is used to convey God's redemption of individuals from spiritual death and His redemption of the nation of Israel from Egyptian bondage and also from exile (see Ex. 6:6). *

[2] ***pāḏāh*** [verb: פָּדָה <6299>; a prim. root] ▶ **This word means to ransom, to deliver. It is used to depict God's act of rescuing, buying back.** He redeemed His people with a mighty hand from Pharaoh and the slavery they were under in Egypt (Deut. 7:8; Mic. 6:4). Egypt was literally the house of slavery and became the symbol of slavery and oppression from which Israel was delivered (Deut. 9:26; 24:18). After Israel was in exile in Babylon, the Lord redeemed them from their strong enemies (Jer. 31:11). He had longed to redeem them from their apostasy before He gave them over to judgment, but they would not respond to His call (Hos. 7:13; 13:14).

The Lord also redeemed individuals in the sense of rescuing them. He delivered David (2 Sam. 4:9; 1 Kgs. 1:29); Abraham (Is. 29:22); Jeremiah (Jer. 15:21); and the psalmist (Ps. 26:11; 31:5).

The word often describes the process of ransoming persons in the cultic setting of ancient Israel. The firstborn was ransomed or redeemed (Ex. 13:13, 15; Num. 18:15); animals were redeemed by payment of a half-shekel of ransom money (Lev. 27:27; Num. 18:15). The firstborn of an ox, sheep, or goat could not be redeemed (Num. 18:17). The word described the action of both the community and friends to redeem individuals (1 Sam. 14:45; Job 6:23).

In the passive stem, the word means to be redeemed. The word is used to describe a female slave who has not been ransomed (Lev. 19:20). A person under the ban for destruction could not be ransomed either (Lev. 27:29). Zion would be redeemed through justice (Is. 1:27); one person could not be redeemed by the life of another (Ps. 49:7).

In the causative stem, it means to bring about deliverance or redemption; the master who did not accept his slave girl had to cause her to be redeemed (Ex. 21:8); the firstborn male of unclean animals and humans had to be redeemed as well (Num. 18:15, 16). *

– [3] Lev. 25:26, 31, 32, 48; etc. → REDEMPTION <1353> [4] Is. 50:2 → REDEMPTION <6304>.

REDEMPTION – [1] ***g^e'ullāh*** [fem. sing. noun: גְּאֻלָּה <1353>; fem. pass. part. of REDEEM <1350>] ▶ **This term means the repurchase of something that must be delivered or rescued (after having been lost or forfeited) by payment of a ransom. The concept is developed to encompass deliverance in a broad sense.** It is typically used in legal texts denoting who can redeem (Lev. 25:24, 31, 32, 48); what they can redeem (Lev. 25:26); when (Lev. 25:26, 51, 52); and for how much (Lev. 25:26, 51, 52). Redemption was a means by which property remained in families or clans. The best picture of this custom in the Bible is Ruth 4:6, 7. Other refs.: Lev. 25:29; Jer. 32:7, 8; Ezek. 11:15. ¶

[2] ***p^{e}ḏûyiym*** [masc. noun: פְּדוּיִים <6302>; pass. part. of REDEEM <6299>] ▶ **Like the word *piḏyôm* (<6306> below), it is a cognate of *pāḏāh*, a verb meaning to ransom. As such, it occurs three times in the context of Israel's ransoming their firstborn males.** In this context, this term is parallel with the silver that was used to redeem firstborn males and then given to Aaron and his sons (Num. 3:46, 48, 51). ¶

[3] ***p^{e}ḏûṯ*** [fem. noun: פְּדוּת <6304>; from REDEEM <6299>] ▶ **This word means ransom.** It is used four times in the Old Testament and could refer to redemption in general (Ps. 111:9); redemption from sins (Ps. 130:7); or redemption from exile (Is. 50:2: to redeem, to deliver). The meaning of the fourth occurrence of this word (Ex. 8:23) is difficult to ascertain. The Septuagint renders the Hebrew with *diastole* (<1293>, New Testament), meaning a division or distinction, and English translations follow suit. ¶

[4] ***piḏyôm, piḏyôn*** [masc. noun: פִּדְיוֹם, פִּדְיוֹן <6306>; from REDEEM <6299>] ▶ **These words mean ransom, ransom money.** The

word *pidyôm* refers to the ransoming of the Israelite firstborn males (Num. 3:49, 51).

Pidyôn is a masculine noun meaning ransom money. It refers to the money exchanged as a ransom, not simply to the concept of ransoming. In addition, this term always occurs in connection with the term *nepeš* (<5315>), meaning life (Ex. 21:30; Ps. 49:8). ¶

REDNESS – ***ḥakliylûṯ*** [fem. abstract noun: חַכְלִילוּת <2448>; from DARKER <2447>] ▶ **This word depicts the color of blood or darkness of the person's eyes who had drunk too much wine.** Ref.: Prov. 23:29; NIV: bloodshot. ¶

REDUCE – ***gāraʻ*** [verb: גָּרַע <1639>; a prim. root] ▶ **This verb means to diminish, to cut short, to trim; to withdraw, to remove.** It basically means to reduce or diminish something: a workload or quota (Ex. 5:8, 11, 19); marital rights (Ex. 21:10); length of a beard (Jer. 48:37); the Torah or law of God (Deut. 4:2); to remove or withdraw an inheritance (Num. 36:3, 4). It is used to indicate the taking away of worship or reverence (Job 15:4) or to ascribe wisdom only to one source (Job 15:8). With respect to God's eyes, used figuratively, it is asserted that He does not withdraw them in watchful care from the righteous (Job 36:7). In its passive use, it means to be reduced (Ex. 5:11). *

REDUCE TO NOTHING – Zeph. 2:11 → LEAN (GROW, BECOME, WAX) <7329>.

REED – [1] ***'ēḇeh*** [masc. sing. noun: אֵבֶה <16>; from WILLING (BE) <14>] ▶ **This word means a tall water plant; it is also translated papyrus.** Ref.: Job 9:26. The meaning in this context is probably swift, indicating swift ships (NKJV). This thought parallels the lightning fast flight of the eagle. But the meaning could be literal, indicating reed or papyrus boats (NIV, NASB, ESV). ¶

[2] ***sûp̱*** [masc. noun: סוּף <5488>; prob. of Egyptian origin] ▶ **This word uniformly means large water plants, rushes, reeds.** Refs.: Ex. 2:3, 5; Is. 19:6; KJV: flags. The phrase *yammāh sûp̱* means unto, toward the sea of reeds, the Red Sea (Ex. 10:19). The phrase *yam-sûp̱* refers to a sea of reeds, the traditional Red Sea (Ex. 13:18; Josh. 2:10). It is extended in usage to the Gulf of Suez, the Gulf of Aqaba (1 Kgs. 9:26, Red Sea). *

– [3] Gen. 41:2, 18; Job 8:11: reed, reed grass → MEADOW (plant) <260> [4] Job 41:2, 20; Is. 9:14; 19:15; 58:5 → ROPE <100> [5] Is. 18:2 → BULRUSH <1573> [6] Jer. 51:32 → POND <98>.

REEL – 2 Sam. 22:8; Ps. 18:7 → SHAKE <1607>.

REELAIAH – ***reʻēlāyāh*** [masc. proper noun: רְעֵלָיָה <7480>; from BRANDISH <7477> (which refers to shaking) and LORD <3050>]: fearful of the Lord ▶ **An Israelite who returned form the Babylonian captivity, the same as *raʻamyāh* (RAAMIAH <7485>).** Ref.: Ezra 2:2. ¶

REELING – [1] ***raʻal*** [masc. noun: רַעַל <7478>; from BRANDISH <7477>] ▶ **This word refers to a quaking, a shaking induced by fear in the face of some terrifying situation.** Ref.: Zech. 12:2. It is also translated trembling, staggering, drunkenness. It. ¶

– [2] Is. 51:17, 22 → STAGGER (THAT MAKES) <8653>.

REESTABLISHED (BE) – Dan. 4:36 → ESTABLISHED (BE) <8627>.

REFINE – [1] ***zāqaq*** [verb: זָקַק <2212>; a prim. root] ▶ **This word's literal meaning is to strain or extract; it is also translated to purify, to purge, to pour down, to distill.** It is used in reference to gold (1 Chr. 28:18; Job 28:1); silver (1 Chr. 29:4; Ps. 12:6); water (Job 36:27); wine (Is. 25:6; also translated finest). It is also used of the purification of the Levites, comparing it to refining gold and silver (Mal. 3:3). ¶

[2] ***ṣārap̱*** [verb: צָרַף <6884>; a prim. root (in the sense of to fuse, e.g., metal)] ▶ **This word means to smelt, refine, test. It describes the purifying process of a refiner, who heats metal, takes away the dross, and is left**

with a pure substance. Ref.: Prov. 25:4. As a participle, this word refers to a tradesman (i.e., a goldsmith or silversmith) who does the refining work (Judg. 17:4; Neh. 3:8; Is. 41:7). This word is also used to speak of the Word of God that is described as pure and refined (2 Sam. 22:31; Ps. 12:6; Prov. 30:5). When applied to people, this word refers to the purifying effects of external trials (Ps. 66:10; 105:19; Is. 48:10) that God often uses to purify His people from sin (Is. 1:25; Zech. 13:9); or to remove the wicked from His people (Jer. 6:29; Mal. 3:2, 3). *
– 3 Deut. 28:56 → DELIGHT (HAVE, FIND, TAKE) <6026>.

REFINED (BE) – 1 ***pāzaz*** [verb: פָּזַז <6338>; a prim. root] ▶ **This verb means to refine (remove impurities from a metal). It is used in a passive sense to describe gold that has had the impurities, the dross, removed from it.** Ref.: 1 Kgs. 10:18; also translated pure, best, finest, fine. ¶
– 2 Deut. 28:54, 56 → DELICATE <6028>.

REFINEMENT – ***rōḵ*** [masc. noun: רֹךְ <7391>; from FAINT (BE, MAKE) <7401> (in the sense of to be tender, to be soft)] ▶ **This word indicates gentleness, sensitivity.** It is used as an abstract noun indicating a cultured, sophisticated, overly sensitive way of life (Deut. 28:56; also translated tenderness, tender, gentle). ¶

REFINING POT – Prov. 17:3; 27:21 → CRUCIBLE <4715>.

REFLECT – Prov. 20:25 → SEEK <1239>.

REFRAIN – 1 ***'āgan*** [verb: עָגַן <5702>; a prim. root] ▶ **This word means to be shut up, to remain shut up. It is used with *bā'al* <1166> and means to remain unmarried.** It means to not take a spouse, to refrain from getting married (Ruth 1:13). ¶
– 2 Gen. 43:31; 45:1; Esther 5:10; Is. 42:14; 64:12 → CONTROL (verb) <662> 3 Is. 48:9 → RESTRAIN <2413>.

REFRAUB – Ps. 40:9 → RESTRAIN <3607> a.

REFRESH – 1 ***sā'aḏ*** [verb: סָעַד <5582>; a prim. root] ▶ **This word means to renew one's energy, to support, to sustain; it is also translated to comfort, to strengthen.** It is used of energizing people, of aiding them, refreshing them with nourishment (Gen. 18:5; Judg. 19:5); or with rest and food (1 Kgs. 13:7). It describes the strength and support of God's hand on a person (Ps. 18:35; 20:2); and of righteousness supporting a king's reign (Prov. 20:28); especially with respect to the government of the messianic king (Is. 9:7). *
2 ***rāp̄aḏ*** [verb: רָפַד <7502>; a prim. root] ▶ **This word means to reinvigorate, to comfort, and to restore a person who is weak and faint.** Ref.: Song 2:5; KJV: to comfort. For another meaning of the Hebrew word, see SPREAD, SPREAD OUT <7502>. ¶
– 3 Ex. 23:12; 31:17; 2 Sam. 16:14 → REST (verb) <5314>.

REFRESHED (BE) – 1 ***rāwaḥ*** [verb: רָוַח <7304>; a prim. root (identical with <7306> below)] ▶ **This word means to breathe freely, to be spacious, to smell. The primary meaning is to breathe freely because one has been set at large and revived.** This word is used to indicate a relief that comes to a troubled mind or spirit (1 Sam. 16:23; Job 32:20). Shallem, son of Josiah, stated that he would build a great palace with spacious upper rooms (Jer. 22:14). *Rāwah* was also used to dictate the smelling of aromas of both the burnt offering and incense (see Gen. 8:21; Ex. 30:38). In Genesis, the burnt offerings had a pleasing aroma to God, which in turn prompted Him to state His covenant. In Exodus, the people were warned against making the special mixture of incense (meant only for the use of an incense offering to God) simply to enjoy its aroma. The punishment for disobeying this command was to be cut off from one's own people. ¶
2 ***rûaḥ, riyaḥ*** [verb: רוּחַ, רִיחַ <7306>; a prim. root] ▶ **This word means to feel relief, to be spacious, to smell.** This verb is used rarely in the Hebrew Bible. In the simple stem, it occurs twice meaning to gain

or feel relief. When David played the harp, Saul found relief (1 Sam. 16:23); the verbose Elihu had to speak in order to get relief from his anxiety (Job 32:20). In its single use in the passive intensive stem, it means roomy or spacious. The vain King Shallum proposed to build himself a palace with spacious, roomy, upper chambers (Jer. 22:14).

The verb is used most often in the causative stem to mean to smell. Gods of wood cannot smell (Deut. 4:28); nor can idols of gold or silver (Ps. 115:6). Isaac smelled the clothes that Jacob wore to deceive him (Gen. 27:27). In 1 Samuel 26:19, however, the verb refers to God being pleased by the aroma of an offering (Gen. 8:21; Lev. 26:31). The verb evidently means to be burned with in Judges 16:9: Samson snapped the ropes, as a thread of flax snaps when it touches the fire. The Shoot of Jesse, the Branch, will respond (i.e., be sensitive) to the fear of the Lord (Is. 11:1, 2). ¶

REFRESHING – Is. 28:12 ➔ REPOSE <4774>.

REFRESHMENT – Prov. 3:8 ➔ DRINK (noun) <8250>.

REFUGE – **1 to take, to find, to seek refuge: *ḥāsāh*** [verb: חָסָה <2620>; a prim. root] ▶ **This word means to find a shelter, a safe place; it is also translated to trust, to take shelter.** It is used literally in reference to seeking a tree's shade (Judg. 9:15) and taking refuge in Zion (Is. 14:32). It is commonly used figuratively in relation to deities (Deut. 32:37), particularly of Yahweh. He is a shield providing refuge (2 Sam. 22:31). Refuge is sought under His wings (Ruth 2:12; Ps. 36:7; 57:1; 61:4; 91:4) and at the time of death (Prov. 14:32). *
2 *maḥseh* [masc. noun: מַחְסֶה <4268>; from <2620> above] ▶ **This word designates a shelter (literally or figuratively); the person to whom one flees.** It indicates a place of safety and protection, security. It is used figuratively most often of God as a refuge for His people (Ps. 14:6; 46:1; 61:3; 62:7; 71:7; 73:28; Prov. 14:26; Jer. 17:17; Joel 3:16). It is used of various types of sheltering: from storms (Is. 4:6; 25:4); from danger for people or animals (Ps. 104:18); a false retreat, a false haven of deceit or falsity (Is. 28:15, 17). *
3 *mānôs* [masc. noun: מָנוֹס <4498>; from FLEE <5127>] ▶ **This word indicates flight, a place of escape. It is used of a place of safety; a place to which to flee.** It is used metaphorically of the Lord as one's refuge (2 Sam. 22:3; Ps. 59:16; 142:4); flight itself in a time when one needs refuge, safety (Jer. 46:5). The refuge or escape of the wicked perishes (Job 11:20); and the escape of God's enemies fails (Jer. 25:35; Amos 2:14). Other ref.: Jer. 16:19. ¶
4 *miqlāṭ* [masc. noun: מִקְלָט <4733>; from STUNTED (BE) <7038> in the sense of taking in] ▶ **This word refers to a place of protection.** It is used to point out a city to which a person guilty of manslaughter could flee for protection (Num. 35:6, 11–15, 25–28, 32; Josh. 20:2, 3; 21:13, 21, 27, 32, 38; 1 Chr. 6:57, 67). ¶
– **5** Deut. 32:38 ➔ COVERING <5643> b. **6** Deut. 33:27; Jer. 21:13 ➔ DWELLING PLACE <4585> **7** Is. 32:2 ➔ HIDING PLACE <4224> a. **8** Is. 33:16 ➔ STRONGHOLD <4679>.

REFUGE (PLACE OF) – Ps. 55:8 ➔ SHELTER <4655>.

REFUGE (SEEK) – Ps. 52:7 ➔ STRENGTHEN <5810>.

REFUGE (SEEK, TAKE) – Is. 10:31; Jer. 4:6 ➔ SAFETY (FLEE FOR) <5756>.

REFUGE (TAKE) – Is. 30:2 ➔ STRENGTHEN <5810>.

REFUGEE – ***pāliyṭ, pālêṭ*** [verb: פָּלִיט, פָּלֵיט <6412>; from DELIVER <6403>] ▶
a. This word indicates persons or groups who have lived through a dangerous situation. They are survivors or those who have escaped what might have been sure death; fugitives (Gen. 14:13; Josh. 8:22; 2 Kgs. 9:15, etc.). *
b. This Hebrew word is the same as a. In context it refers to Moabite fugitives (Num.

21:29); and to a group of survivors in the time when God will restore His people and the nations (Is. 66:19). *

REFUSE (noun) – [1] ***mā'ôs*** [masc. noun: מָאוֹס <3973>; from REJECT <3988>] ▶ **This word means trash, garbage. It indicates what is rejected.** It refers to Israel in a figurative sense as God's rejected people (Lam. 3:45). ¶
[2] ***sûḥāh*** [fem. noun: 5478> סוּחָה; from the same as SUAH <5477>] ▶
a. This word means rubbish. It refers to decaying garbage or other trash left to decompose (Is. 5:25). ¶
b. This word means something torn. Some earlier translators rendered this word as something killed (Is. 5:25: KJV). ¶
– [3] Ex. 29:14; Lev. 4:11; 8:17; 16:27; Num. 19:5; Mal. 2:3 ➔ DUNG <6569> [4] Deut. 23:13 ➔ EXCREMENT <6627> [5] Judg. 3:22 ➔ DUNG <6574> [6] 1 Kgs. 14:10; Zeph. 1:17 ➔ DUNG <1557> [7] 2 Kgs. 9:37; Ps. 83:10; Jer. 8:2; 9:22; 16:4; 25:33 ➔ DUNG <1828> [8] Job 20:7; Zeph. 1:17 ➔ DUNG <1561> [9] Eccl. 2:10 ➔ RESERVE (verb) <680> [10] Is. 57:20 ➔ MIRE <7516> [11] Ezek. 32:5 ➔ CARCASS <7419> a. [12] Amos 8:6 ➔ CHAFF <4651>.

REFUSE (verb) – [1] ***mā'an*** [verb: מָאַן <3985>; a prim. root] ▶ **This word means to be unwilling. The basic idea of this word is a refusal or rejection of an offer or command.** It is used to describe the refusal to obey God (Ex. 16:28; Neh. 9:17; Is. 1:20; Jer. 9:6); His messengers, (1 Sam. 8:19); or other men (Esther 1:12). Jacob refused comfort when he thought Joseph had died (Gen. 37:35); Joseph refused Potiphar's wife's offer to sin (Gen. 39:8); Pharaoh refused to let Israel go (Ex. 4:23; 7:14); Balaam refused Balak's offer to curse Israel (Num. 22:13, 14); both Saul and Amnon refused to eat food offered to them (1 Sam. 28:23; 2 Sam. 13:9). *
[2] ***mā'ēn*** [adj.: מָאֵן <3986>; from <3985> above] ▶ **This word means refusing, disobeying; it is translated by the verb to refuse.** This word is found in the context of disobedience to a command. A prime example was that of the Israelites in bondage. God said that if Pharaoh refused to let His people go, He would bring various plagues on Egypt (Ex. 8:2; 9:2). King Zedekiah was warned that he would be captured by Babylon if he refused to surrender to the Lord (Jer. 38:21). Other ref.: Ex. 10:4. ¶
[3] ***mê'ên*** [adj.: מֵאֵן <3987>; from <3985> above] ▶ **This word means pertinaciously refusing, refractory; it is translated by the verb to refuse.** In Jeremiah 13:10, it described the people of Judah as those refusing to listen to God's words. ¶
– [4] Gen. 23:6 ➔ RESTRAIN <3607> a. [5] Judg. 11:17; Prov. 6:35 ➔ lit.: to not consent, to not be willing ➔ WILLING (BE) <14> [6] Ps. 141:5 ➔ FORBID <5106>.

REFUSE DUMP – 2 Kgs. 10:27 ➔ GOING FORTH <4163> or LATRINE <4280>.

REFUSE GATE – Neh. 2:13; 3:13, 14; 12:31 ➔ ASH HEAP <830>.

REFUSE HEAP – Is. 25:10 ➔ DUNGHILL <4087>.

REFUSES (WHO) – Ezek. 3:27 ➔ REJECTED <2310>.

REFUTE – Job 32:13 ➔ DRIVE AWAY <5086>.

REGARD (noun and verb) – Ps. 74:20; 119:15; Amos 5:22 ➔ to have regard; to regard ➔ LOOK (verb) <5027>.

REGARD (verb) – Lev. 19:23 ➔ NAKEDNESS (EXPOSE ONE'S) <6188>.

REGARD TO (IN, WITH) – Dan. 6:4 ➔ CONCERNING <6655>.

REGARDED – Dan. 4:35 ➔ ACCOUNTED (BE) <2804>.

REGEM – ***regem*** [masc. proper noun: רֶגֶם <7276>; from STONE (verb) <7275>]: stone heap ▶ **An Israelite of the tribe of Judah.** Ref.: 1 Chr. 2:47. ¶

REGEM-MELECH – ***regem melek*** [masc. proper noun: רֶגֶם מֶלֶךְ <7278>; from REGEM <7276> (meaning stone heap) and KING <4428>]: king's heap ▶ **A messenger sent to Zechariah to seek the favor of the Lord. The Lord replied through His representative, Zechariah, rebuking all the people of the land for the hypocrisy of their fasts.** Ref.: Zech. 7:2. ¶

REGION – 1 ***g*^e*liylāh*** [fem. noun: גְּלִילָה <1552>; fem. of GALILEE <1550>] ▶ **This word means a district, an area; it is also translated border, coast, country, district, territory.** It refers to a specific district or region around Ezekiel's Temple (Ezek. 47:8) and to the region of the Philistines (Josh. 13:2) and Philistia (Joel 3:4). *
– 2 1 Kgs. 4:11 ➔ SIEVE <5299> b.

REGISTER – Ezra 2:62 ➔ WRITING <3791>.

REGISTRATION – Ezra 2:62 ➔ WRITING <3791>.

REGULATION – Neh. 11:23: firm regulation ➔ COVENANT <548>.

REHABIAH – ***r*^e*ḥaḇyāh, r*^e*ḥaḇyāhû*** [masc. proper noun: רְחַבְיָה, רְחַבְיָהוּ <7345>; from ENLARGE <7337> and LORD <3050>]: the Lord has enlarged ▶ **The only son of Eliezer.** Refs.: 1 Chr. 23:17; 24:21; 26:25. ¶

REHEARSE – Judg. 5:11 ➔ RECOUNT <8567>.

REHOB – ***r*^e*ḥôḇ*** [proper noun: רְחוֹב <7340>; the same as STREET <7339>] ▶
a. A town near Hamath. Ref.: Num. 13:21. ¶
b. A town in Asher. Refs.: Josh. 19:28, 30; 21:31; Judg. 1:31; 1 Chr. 6:75. ¶
c. An Aramean town. Ref.: 2 Sam. 10:8. ¶
d. The father of Hadadezer. Refs.: 2 Sam. 8:3, 12. ¶
e. A covenanter in Nehemiah's day. Ref.: Neh. 10:11. ¶

REHOBOAM – ***r*^e*ḥaḇ'ām*** [masc. proper noun: רְחַבְעָם <7346>; from ENLARGE <7337> and PEOPLE <5971>]: enlarged people ▶ **This word designates the first king of the southern kingdom of Judah (930–813 B.C.).** He was Solomon's son and, unfortunately, continued the oppressive administrative policies of his father (1 Kgs. 12:12–15). His mother was an Ammonite, Naamah (1 Kgs. 14:21, 22). When he did so, the ten northern Israelite tribes withdrew from Judah and David (1 Kgs. 12:16). He led Israel into gross religious prostitution and immorality. King Shishak of Egypt humbled Judah (1 Kgs. 14:25–28). Rehoboam pursued hostilities of war with Jeroboam of Israel constantly (1 Kgs. 14:29–31). His son Abijah succeeded him. *

REHOBOTH – ***r*^e*ḥōḇôṯ, r*^e*ḥōḇôṯ 'iyr*** [proper noun: רְחֹבוֹת, רְחֹבוֹת עִיר <7344>; plur. of STREET <7339>]: wide place, streets ▶
a. A well dug by Isaac. Ref.: Gen. 26:22.
b. A city on the Euphrates River. Refs.: Gen. 36:37; 1 Chr. 1:48. See also c. and d. below.
c. The city of Shaul, king of Edom. Ref.: KJV, Gen. 10:11; possibly the same as b. above.
d. Rehoboth-Ir, from b. above and *'iyr* (CITY <5892>). Ref.: other versions, Gen. 10:11; possibly the same as b. ¶

REHUM – ***r*^e*ḥûm*** [masc. proper noun: רְחוּם <7348>; a form of COMPASSIONATE <7349>]: compassionate ▶
a. A leader returning with Zerubbabel. Refs.: Ezra 2:2; Neh. 12:3. ¶
b. A Jewish builder of Nehemiah's wall. Ref.: Neh. 3:17. ¶
c. A covenanter in Nehemiah's day, possibly the same as b. Ref.: Neh. 10:25. ¶
d. A commanding officer who opposed the rebuilding of Jerusalem. Refs.: Ezra 4:8, 9, 17, 23. ¶

REI – ***rê'iy*** [masc. proper noun: רֵעִי <7472>; from PERSON (ANOTHER) <7453> (in the sense of associate, friend)]: friend ▶ **A friend of King David who remained faithful to him during the rebellion of Adonijah.** Ref.: 1 Kgs. 1:8. ¶

REIGN – Judg. 9:22 ➔ RULE (verb) <7786>.

REINFORCEMENTS – Is. 43:17 ➔ STRONG <5808>.

REINS – Ps. 139:13 ➔ KIDNEY <3629>.

REJECT – 1 ***zānaḥ*** [verb: זָנַח <2186>; a prim. root meaning to push aside] ▶
a. This word means to cast off, to spurn. It is used to note the refusal to recognize or accept various things or persons. Israel rejects what is good (Hos. 8:3); ironically, the Lord rejects Samaria's paganized calf (Hos. 8:5); often it denotes the Lord's rejection of His people or supplicants (Ps. 43:2; 60:1; 77:7; 88:14; Zech. 10:6); individual kings rejected some holy persons and vessels (2 Chr. 11:14; 29:19). *
b. A verb meaning to stink, to smell foul. It refers to the stench emitted by Egyptian canals or streams because of drought (Is. 19:6; KJV, turn far away). ¶
2 ***mā'as*** [verb: מָאַס <3988>; a prim. root] ▶ **This word means to despise, to abhor, to refuse. The primary meaning of this word is to reject or treat as loathsome.** It designates people's actions in refusing to heed God or accept His authority (1 Sam. 10:19; Jer. 8:9); esteeming God's commands lightly (Lev. 26:15; Is. 30:12); and despising one's spiritual condition in an act of repentance (Job 42:6). Scripture also speaks of the Lord rejecting His people (Hos. 4:6) and their worship (Amos 5:21) because of their rejection of Him. A secondary and more rare meaning of the word is to run or flow. This use appears in Psalm 58:7 as David prayed for the wicked to melt away like a flowing river. *
3 ***sālāh*** [verb: סָלָה <5541>; a prim. root] ▶ **This word means to put out, to exclude, to refuse to accept, to treat as worthless; it is also translated to spurn, to tread down, to tread underfoot, to trample underfoot.** It describes God's refusal to accept those who do not walk in His ways (Ps. 119:118). It means to reject anyone for various reasons (Lam. 1:15). The Hebrew word also means to value, to pay for; see VALUE (verb) <5541>. ¶
– 4 Lev. 26:11 ➔ ABHOR <1602> 5 Deut. 32:15 ➔ FOOLISH (BE) <5034> 6 Ps. 27:9 ➔ FORSAKE <5203> 7 Prov. 10:3 ➔ PUSH <1920> 8 Lam. 2:7 ➔ RENOUNCE <5010>.

REJECTED – ***ḥāḏêl*** [adj.: חָדֵל <2310>; from CEASE <2308>] ▶ **This word means not accepted; it also means transient, fleeting.** It is the opposite of hearing, i.e., refusing to hear or respond positively (Ezek. 3:27). It describes the Servant of Isaiah as a person rejected by men (Is. 53:3). It takes on the idea of fleeting or transitory with respect to the impermanence of human life (Ps. 39:4: frail, fleeting, transient). ¶

REJECTION – 1 Num. 14:34 ➔ OPPOSITION <8569> 2 2 Kgs. 19:3; Is. 37:3 ➔ DISGRACE (noun) <5007>.

REJOICE – 1 ***giyl, gûl*** [verb: גִּיל, גּוּל <1523>; a prim. root] ▶ **This word means to be happy; it is also translated to be glad, to be joyful, to exult, to joy.** It is a response of persons both religiously, as when they divide the spoils of the Lord's victories (Is. 9:3); when they rejoice in His salvation (Is. 25:9; 65:18: to be a joy, to be a delight); or over idolatrous objects (Hos. 10:5). It describes the Lord's joyous response over His people and Jerusalem in the new heavens and earth (Is. 65:19). The dry land, the Arabah, will even rejoice (Is. 35:1, 2). Many things rejoice besides those just mentioned: the heart (Ps. 13:5; Prov. 24:17: be glad; Zech. 10:7); the soul (Ps. 35:9; Is. 61:10). Rejoicing in the Lord is accompanied with proper fear and trembling as well (Ps. 2:11; also translated to celebrate the rule). God's people rejoice in many things: Jerusalem (Is. 66:10); the Lord's salvation (Ps. 9:14); the Lord (Ps. 35:9; Is. 41:16); the Lord's name (Ps. 89:16); the Holy One of Israel (Is. 29:19). *
2 ***ḥāḏāh, yāḥaḏ*** [verb.: חָדָה, יָחַד <2302>; a prim. root] ▶
a. This word means to be glad, to make glad. It depicts a joyous response to something or someone; it is also translated to be delighted, to be glad. The goodness of

the Lord (Ex. 18:9); figuratively of a day of birth rejoicing (Job 3:6, ESV, NASB, NKJV); in certain verb forms to indicate the Lord's making someone happy (Ps. 21:6). ¶
b. This word is translated as meaning "to be joined" in Job's plea that the unwanted day of his birth might not be joined to the days of the year. Ref.: Job 3:6, KJV, NIV. ¶
3 ***sālad*** [verb: סָלַד <5539>; a prim. root] ▶ **a. This word means to take satisfaction in something, to feel good about it; it is also translated to exult.** It was used of Job's rejoicing in his faithfulness to God (Job 6:10). ¶
b. KJV understands the Hebrew word to mean to harden oneself. It means to stand firm, to take strength in upholding one's position or actions. God is determined to continue faithful in sorrow and oppression (Job 6:10). ¶
4 ***'ālaz*** [verb: עָלַז <5937>; a prim. root] ▶ **This word means to exult, to be jubilant.** It describes a state and act of celebration, approval, support for something (2 Sam. 1:20); especially in exalting over God (Ps. 28:7; Hab. 3:18; Zeph. 3:14). God Himself exalts and is jubilant about His possession, Israel (Ps. 60:6). The possession of wisdom causes a person to rejoice (Prov. 23:16). God can, however, remove the jubilation of His people (Is. 23:12). *
5 ***'ālaṣ*** [verb: עָלַץ <5970>; a prim. root] ▶ **This word means to be jubilant; it is also translated to exult, to be joyful, to triumph.** It is used of a person (*leḇ*, heart) rejoicing, especially the Lord (1 Sam. 2:1; Ps. 5:11; 9:2; 68:3); of nature exalting God (Prov. 11:10; 28:12). It is used of the rejoicing of one's enemies as well (Ps. 25:2). Other ref.: 1 Chr. 16:32. ¶
6 ***śûś, śiyś*** [verb: שׂוּשׂ, שִׂישׂ <7797>; a prim. root] ▶ **This word means to exult, to display joy. It indicates great rejoicing and jubilant celebration. It also means to be glad.** It refers to the Lord's taking delight or joy over (*'al*), blessing, punishing, or disciplining His people if they need it (Deut. 28:63; 30:9; Jer. 32:41; Zeph. 3:17). It indicates finding a cause to be happy, to rejoice even over death (Job 3:22). It describes a horse enjoying his strength (Job 39:21); the sun joyfully traveling across the sky (Ps. 19:5); but especially God's people rejoicing over Him (Ps. 35:9; 40:16; 68:3; Is. 61:10). It is used figuratively of the desert and the dry land rejoicing in its God-given fertility (Is. 35:1). *
7 ***śāmaḥ*** [verb: שָׂמַח <8055>; a prim. root] ▶ **This word means to be joyful, to be glad; to gloat.** It describes a state and agitation of rejoicing, of being happy: of people (1 Sam. 11:9); of tribes of Israel (Deut. 33:18); of God rejoicing in His works (Ps. 104:31); of people rejoicing in the Lord Himself (Deut. 12:12; Ps. 32:11). It takes on the sense of making others rejoice, to be glad in its intensive stem (Jer. 20:15); making people rejoice the heart of others (Ps. 19:8). Wine can gladden the hearts of persons (Eccl. 10:19). God gladdens His people with His presence (Is. 56:7); but also their enemies when He judges Israel (Ps. 89:42). Although the word is used of all rejoicing, it is found most often in Psalms and describes religious and spiritual rejoicing (Ps. 5:11; 9:2; 14:7; 16:9; 19:8; etc.; but also 1 Sam. 2:1; Deut. 12:7; Joel 2:23; etc.). *
– 8 Job 20:18 ➔ ENJOY <5965> a. 9 Is. 13:3 ➔ REJOICING <5947> 10 Jer. 31:12 ➔ FLOW (verb) <5102> b.

REJOICING – 1 ***'alliyz*** [adj.: עַלִּיז <5947>; from REJOICE <5937>] ▶ **This word means exultant, jubilant, joyous.** In context it is used of triumphant warriors who would destroy Babylon (Is. 13:3); and of persons rejoicing in general (Is. 22:2; 24:8; 32:13). It is used of Jerusalem itself (Is. 23:7; Zeph. 3:11); and of Nineveh (Zeph. 2:15). ¶
2 ***'aliyṣuṯ*** [fem. noun: עֲלִיצֻת <5951>; from REJOICE <5970>] ▶ **This word indicates gloating, exultation.** It refers to a celebration of victory over enemies, rejoicing or even gloating over their destruction (Hab. 3:14). ¶
– 3 Ps. 65:12 ➔ JOY <1524> 4 Is. 65:18 ➔ JOY <1525> 5 Ezek. 7:7 ➔ JOYFUL SHOUTING <1906>.

REKEM – ***reqem*** [proper noun: רֶקֶם <7552>; from WEAVER <7551>]: variegated color ▶ **a. A Midianite king.** Refs.: Num. 31:8; Josh. 13:21. ¶
b. A descendant of Caleb. Refs.: 1 Chr. 2:43, 44. ¶

c. A descendant of Manasseh. Ref.: 1 Chr. 7:16. ¶
d. City of Benjamin. Ref.: Josh. 18:27. ¶

RELATIONS – Gen. 12:1; 24:4 ➔ KINDRED <4138>.

RELATIVE – 1 ***mōḏā', môḏa'*** [masc. noun: מֹדָע, מוֹדַע <4129>; from KNOW <3045>] ▶ **This word indicates a person closely related to someone and having the right of the kinsman redeemer; it is also translated kinsman, relative.** Ref.: Ruth 2:1. It has the sense of a close, intimate friend or relative (Prov. 7:4; also translated kin, friend, kinswoman). ¶
2 ***môḏa'aṯ*** [fem. noun: מוֹדַעַת <4130>; from KNOW <3045>] ▶ **This word refers to kindred, kinship. It indicates a relative close enough to serve as a kinsman redeemer in Israel, e.g., Boaz to Naomi and Ruth.** Ref.: Ruth 3:2. ¶
– 3 Lev. 18:17: relative, blood relative, close relative ➔ KINSWOMAN <7608>.

RELEASE (noun) – 1 Lev. 25:10; Jer. 34:8, 15, 17 ➔ FREEDOM <1865> a. 2 Deut. 15:1, 2, 9; 31:10 ➔ REMISSION <8059> 3 Esther 2:18 ➔ HOLIDAY <2010> 4 Eccl. 8:8 ➔ DISCHARGE <4917> 5 Is. 61:1 ➔ OPENING OF THE PRISON <6495>.

RELEASE (verb) – 1 ***šāmaṭ*** [verb: שָׁמַט <8058>; a prim. root] ▶ **This word means to free; it also means to throw down, to cancel; to stumble; to let fall.** It indicates letting the land lie free, untilled (Ex. 23:11). It is used in its absolute participial form as a command, shall release, will release (a debt) (Deut. 15:2, 3). It means to knock something over, e.g., the ark (2 Sam. 6:6; 1 Chr. 13:9). It is used of tossing something down (2 Kgs. 9:33); in a figurative sense, it means removed from power (Ps. 141:6). It indicates letting go of something, losing it. In context Israel loses her inheritance from the Lord, gives it up under force (Jer. 17:4). ¶
– 2 Ps. 105:20 ➔ LOOSE (LET) <5425> 3 Prov. 17:14 ➔ OPEN <6362>.

RELIEF – 1 ***r'wāḥāh*** [fem. noun: רְוָחָה <7309>; fem. of SPACE <7305>] ▶ **This word means breathing space, respite. The term occurs only twice in the entire Old Testament and is derived from the verb** *rāwaḥ* **(<7304>), meaning to breathe, to have breathing room, or to feel relief.** In its first occurrence, the word denotes the alleviation that resulted from God's act of terminating the plague of frogs in Egypt (Ex. 8:15). The second use of the term involves a desperate cry to the Lord for deliverance and rest from merciless enemies (Lam. 3:56; also translated sighing, breathing). ¶
– 2 Esther 4:14 ➔ SPACE <7305> 3 Lam. 2:18 ➔ REST (noun) <6314> 4 Lam. 3:49 ➔ INTERRUPTION <2014> 5 Nah. 3:19 ➔ HEALING <3545>.

RELIEF (GET, FIND) – Job 32:20 ➔ REFRESHED (BE) <7304>.

RELIEVE ONESELF – 1 ***śiyg*** [masc. noun: שִׂיג <7873>; from TURN <7734>] ▶ **This Hebrew word means pursuit, a moving away.** It is used in a striking and mocking way of the pagan god, Baal, who evidently had gone aside to relieve himself (1 Kgs. 18:27; also translated busy, gone aside, pursuing). ¶
– 2 1 Kgs. 18:27 ➔ DROSS <5509>.

REMAIN – 1 ***yāṯar*** [verb: יָתַר <3498>; a prim. root] ▶ **This word means to be left over.** Jacob was left alone after he sent his family across the river (Gen. 32:24); nothing remained after the locusts came (Ex. 10:15); Absalom was thought to have killed all the king's sons with not one remaining (2 Sam. 13:30); Isaiah prophesied to Hezekiah that nothing would be left of his kingdom (2 Kgs. 20:17); God said that when He destroyed Judah, He would leave a remnant (Ezek. 6:8). *
2 ***šā'ar*** [verb: שָׁאַר <7604>; a prim. root] ▶ **This word means to be left over; to leave, to let remain, to spare. The term maintains a narrow semantic range throughout Old Testament literature.** The verb and the nouns that derive from

it (see LEAVEN <7603> and REMNANT <7611>) play a key role in the development of the remnant theme that unfolds and evolves over the course of Old Testament history. From the early beginnings of salvation history in Genesis and all the way through to the end of the Old Testament and beyond, God has sovereignly acted to preserve for Himself a remnant of people who will worship Him alone (cf. Gen. 7:23; 32:8; 1 Kgs. 19:18; Ezra 9:8; Is. 4:3; 11:11, 16; 37:31; Ezek. 9:8; Zeph. 3:12; see also Rom. 11:5). Nevertheless, though this usage became the most significant function of the term, the verb was also employed in a variety of other contexts. For instance, the Egyptians came to Joseph for help because they had no remaining money to buy food (Gen. 47:18). After the Israelites crossed the Red Sea, the waters caved in on Pharaoh's army. Not one person remained (Ex. 14:28). The blood that remained from the sin offering was to be drained out at the base of the altar (Lev. 5:9). *

3 ***śāraḏ*** [verb: שָׂרַד <8277>; a prim. root] ► **This word means to be left. It indicates that something remains of what was originally present.** In this case, some of the defeated enemy survived (Josh. 10:20). ¶

– 4 Gen. 32:4 ➔ STAY (verb) <309> 5 Ruth 1:13 ➔ REFRAIN <5702> 6 2 Sam. 17:22 ➔ LACK, LACKING (BE) <5737>.

REMAIN LONG – Deut. 4:25 ➔ SLEEP (verb) <3462> b.

REMAIN UNITED – Dan. 2:43 ➔ ADHERE <1693>.

REMAIN, REMAIN OVER – Ex. 16:12, 13, 23 ➔ LEFT, LEFT OVER <5736>.

REMAINDER – 1 ***yeṯer*** [masc. noun: יֶתֶר <3499>; from REMAIN <3498>] ► **This word means what is left, the rest, abundance, excellence, a cord.** It refers to that which is left over: the produce of a field not used by people (and left for beasts) (Ex. 23:11); the years of a life span not yet finished (Is. 38:10); Temple vessels besides the ones specifically mentioned (Jer. 27:19). The word also signifies abundance as what was left beyond the necessities of life (Job 22:20; Ps. 17:14). In Genesis 49:3, the word means excellence, referring to the extra honor and power accorded to the firstborn. The word may refer to the cord of a tent or to a bowstring (Job 30:11; Ps. 11:2), both apparently derived from the idea of a string hanging over something, being extra. The word may be used adverbially to mean abundantly or exceedingly (Dan. 8:9). *

2 ***šᵉʼār*** [Aramaic masc. noun: שְׁאָר <7606>; corresponding to REMNANT <7605>] ► **This word means the rest. It signifies that which was left over after the removal of everything else.** The fourth beast in Daniel's vision devoured, broke things in pieces, and stamped the remainder with its feet (Dan. 7:7, 19; cf. Dan. 2:18; 7:12). The people of Israel, the priests, the Levites, and the rest of the returned exiles joyfully celebrated the dedication of the newly rebuilt Temple (Ezra 6:16; cf. Ezra 4:9, 10, 17; 7:18, 20). ¶

– 3 Num. 3:46, 48, 49 ➔ LEFT, LEFT OVER <5736>.

REMAINS – Ezek. 32:5 ➔ CARCASS <7419> a.

REMALIAH – ***rᵉmalyāhû*** [masc. proper noun: רְמַלְיָהוּ <7425>; from an unused root and LORD <3050>]: the Lord has adorned ► **Father of Pekah, king of Israel.** Refs.: 2 Kgs. 15:25, 27, 30, 32, 37; 16:1, 5; 2 Chr. 28:6; Is. 7:1, 4, 5, 9; 8:6. ¶

REMEDY – 1 ***marpê'*** [masc. noun: מַרְפֵּא <4832>; from HEAL <7495>] ► **This word refers to the cure of an illness or sickness as well as the resulting restoration, renewal; it is also translated health, healing.** Jehoram had a sickness for which there was no remedy, cure (2 Chr. 21:18: incurable); Israel was spiritually sick so that there was no healing (2 Chr. 36:16; Jer. 14:19). It has the sense of health or healing with respect to the body (Prov. 4:22); a sluggard will not find a remedy for his problem

(Prov. 6:15); a wise word brings healing (Prov. 12:18; 13:17; 15:4; 16:24). Healing is the opposite of experiencing dread or terror, destruction (Jer. 8:15). God provides healing for His chosen, special possession (Mal. 4:2). Other ref.: Prov. 29:1. The Hebrew word also means composure, calmness; see CALMNESS <4832>. ¶

– [2] Mic. 2:10: beyond all remedy ➔ lit.: with a grievous destruction ➔ GRIEVOUS <4834>.

REMEMBER – ***zāḵar, mazkiyr*** [verb: זָכַר, מַזְכִּיר <2142>; a prim. root] ► **This word means to mention, to recall, to think about, to think on, to be remembered, to acknowledge, to make known. The basic meaning indicates a process of mentioning or recalling either silently, verbally, or by means of a memorial sign or symbol. The verb often means to mention, to think about.** The Lord warned the people and false prophets they would not remember the oracle of the Lord (Jer. 23:36); the Lord thought about Ephraim in a good sense (Jer. 31:20); and the psalmist thought or meditated on the Lord in his heart and mind without words (Ps. 63:6).

These meanings, of course, overlap with the primary translation of the verb, to remember. The psalmist remembered the Lord often, and 43 of the 165 uses of the simple stem are in the Book of Psalms. Remembering in ancient Israel was a major aspect of proper worship, as it is today.

Remembering involves many things, and various connotations are possible. God or people can be the subject that remembers. For example, because God had acted so often for His people, they were to remember Him and His acts on their behalf (Deut. 5:15; 15:15; 24:18). They were to remember His covenant and commandments without fail (Ex. 20:8; Mal. 4:4). Above all, they were to remember Him by His name. By remembering Him, they imitated the Lord, for He never forgot them (cf. Deut. 4:29–31). He faithfully remembered His people (Gen. 8:1), and they could beg Him to remember them, as Jeremiah did in his distress (Neh. 13:31; Jer. 15:15). The Lord especially remembered His covenant with the ancestors and fathers of Israel (Lev. 26:45; Deut. 9:27; Jer. 14:21) and with all humankind through Noah (Gen. 9:15, 16).

In the passive stem, the word expresses similar meanings. For example, the psalmist prayed that the sins of his accuser's parents would be remembered against his accuser (Ps. 109:14). Yet in an important passage on moral and religious responsibility before God, it was asserted that if righteous people abandoned their righteous ways and followed evil, their righteous deeds would not be remembered by the Lord. The opposite case is also true. None of the evil deeds people commit will be remembered against them if they turn to God (Ezek. 18:22), nor will the actions, good or evil, of their parents be held for or against them (Ezek. 18:22, 24). Righteous people will, in fact, be remembered throughout the ages (cf. Ps. 112:6).

The causative stem indicates the act of bringing to memory or bringing to attention. It means to recall, as when the Lord challenged His people in Isaiah to recall their past in order to state their argument for their case (Gen. 41:9; Is. 43:26). Eli, the high priest, recalled (i.e., mentioned) the ark and then died according to God's prophetic word (1 Sam. 4:18). The verb is used to indicate urging someone to remember something, such as sin (1 Kgs. 17:18; Ezek. 21:23; 29:16). It is also used to convey the idea of causing something to be acknowledged, as when the psalmist asserted that he would cause the Lord's righteousness to be acknowledged above all else (Ps. 71:16). In the infinitive form, this word sometimes means petition, as found in the superscriptions of some Psalms (Ps. 38:1, 70:1). It may also mean performing an act of worship (Is. 66:3). *

REMEMBRANCE – ***zêḵer*** [masc. noun: זֵכֶר <2143>; from REMEMBER <2142>] ► **God has given His people many memorials.** Himself (Ps. 102:12); His name (Ex. 3:15; Hos. 12:5); His works (Ps. 111:4); His goodness (Ps. 145:7); His holiness (Ps. 30:4; 97:12); His deliverance of the Jews (Esther 9:28). God also promises the remembrance of the righteous (Prov. 10:7) but often cuts off the remembrance of the wicked (Job 18:17; Ps. 34:16; 109:15; Prov. 10:7); wicked nations (Ex. 17:14; Deut. 25:19; 32:26); and the dead (Eccl. 9:5; Is. 26:14). In several instances of this word, it is used synonymously with *šêm* <8034>, meaning name, because one's name invokes the memory (Ex. 3:15; Prov. 10:7; Hos. 12:5). *

REMETH – ***remeṯ*** [proper noun: רֶמֶת <7432>; from THROW <7411>]: height ► **A city that was part of the inheritance of Issachar.** Ref.: Josh. 19:21. ¶

REMISSION – ***šᵉmiṭṭāh*** [fem. noun: שְׁמִטָּה <8059>; from RELEASE (verb) <8058>] ► **This word means a release, a suspension. It signifies the cancellation of a debt that was owed to another person. This was a debt which a person would, under ordinary circumstances, be obligated to pay back.** In Israel, at the end of every seven years, the people were to release and forgive their fellow people from debts owed to them. This word was used in this context of the seventh year to show that the debtor was released from any obligation to pay back what had been loaned to him before that time (Deut. 15:1, 2, 9; 31:10). In the Old Testament, this noun was used only in the context of forgiving debts at the end of every seven years. ¶

REMISSION OF TAXES – Esther 2:18 → HOLIDAY <2010>.

REMNANT – 1 ***seraḥ*** [masc. noun: סֶרַח <5629>; from VANISH <5628>] ► **This word means excess; it is also translated part, overlapping part. Derived from a verbal form that means to hang over or overrun, this noun form occurs only once in the Old Testament.** In Exodus 26:12, it refers to the remaining or excess material of the curtains in the Tabernacle. ¶

2 ***šᵉ'ār*** [masc. noun: שְׁאָר <7605>; from REMAIN <7604>] ► **This word means a remainder, the rest. The term plays an important role in the development of the remnant theme concerning God's people.** This theme is interwoven throughout Scripture, and a variety of words were employed to convey the idea (cf. Is. 10:20, 21, 22; 11:11, 16). However, this term is not limited to the designation of the remnant of God's people. For instance, it was also employed to denote the remnant of other nations: Assyria (Is. 10:19); Babylon (Is. 14:22); Moab (Is. 16:14); Aram (Is. 17:3); Kedar (Is. 21:17). Moreover, the word was always utilized as a collective, never referring to a single individual (cf. 1 Chr. 16:41; Ezra 3:8; 4:3, 7; Esther 9:16; Zeph. 1:4). See also the verb *šā'ar* (REMAIN <7604>), from which this noun is derived, and its corresponding feminine cognate *šᵉ'êriyṯ* (REMNANT <7611>). *

3 ***šᵉ'êriyṯ*** [fem. noun: שְׁאֵרִית <7611>; from REMAIN <7604>] ► **This word means a residue, the remainder. The primary meaning conveyed by this word is that which is left over or remains.** It was used with reference to scrap pieces of wood (Is. 44:17); undesignated territory (Is. 15:9); and any group of people that remained (Jer. 15:9; Amos 1:8). Most significant was the technical use of this word by the prophets to denote the few among Israel or Judah that remained faithful to God (Is. 37:32; Mic. 5:7, 8); or those who survived the calamity of the exile (Zech. 8:11). Joseph declared that the purpose of his captivity was to preserve a remnant of Jacob's lineage (Gen. 45:7). *

4 ***śāriyḏ*** [masc. noun: שָׂרִיד <8300>; from REMAIN <8277>] ► **This word means a survivor. It comes from the verb *śāraḏ*, meaning to escape.** In one instance of this word, it is used to describe physical things that had not been devoured (Job 20:21). In all other instances, it is used to describe people who had survived the onslaught of an enemy (Num. 24:19; Josh. 10:20; Jer. 31:2). It is often used with the negative to describe total desolation, i.e., there were no survivors (Num. 21:35; Josh. 10:28; Jer. 42:17). *

REMOTE AREA, REMOTE PLACE – Lev. 16:22 → SOLITARY LAND <1509>.

REMOTEST PART – Is. 41:9 → FARTHEST CORNER <678>.

REMOVE – [1] ***hāgāh*** [verb: הָגָה <1898>; a prim. root] ▶ **This verb means and is also translated to take away.** It is used of removing dross or impurities from silver (Prov. 25:4) and, in a parallel simile, of removing the wicked from a king's presence (Prov. 25:5). It refers to the Lord's driving away or taking away His rebellious people (Is. 27:8); also translated to expel, to drive out, to stay. ¶

[2] ***yāgāh*** [verb: יָגָה <3014>; a prim. root (prob. rather the same as AFFLICT <3013>) through the common idea of dissatisfaction] ▶ **This word means to take away; it also means to push away, to carry off, to take out.** It indicates the removal of something, e.g., the removal of a dead person from blocking the road (2 Sam. 20:13). ¶

[3] ***nāšal*** [verb: נָשַׁל <5394>; a prim. root] ▶ **This word means to drop off, to clear away, to drive out.** It means to take off or remove something: shoes (Ex. 3:5; Josh. 5:15); nations from a land (Deut. 7:1, 22; also translated to cast out); people (2 Kgs. 16:6); trees (Deut. 19:5: to slip); olives (Deut. 28:40). ¶

– [4] Gen. 12:8; 26:22; Job 9:5; 14:18; 18:4 ➔ MOVE <6275> [5] Deut. 19:14; 27:17; Prov. 22:28; Hos. 5:10 ➔ MOVE <5253> [6] Deut. 19:14; Hos. 5:10 ➔ TURN BACK <5472> [7] Ps. 89:33 ➔ NOTHING (BRING TO) <6329> [8] Ps. 119:22 ➔ ROLL (verb) <1556> [9] Zeph. 1:2, 3 ➔ CONSUME, BE CONSUMED <5486>.

REMOVED – Lam. 1:8 ➔ UNCLEAN <5206> b.

REMOVED (BE) – [1] ***môṭ*** [verb: מוֹט <4131>; a prim. root] ▶ **This word means to totter, to shake, to slip. It is used of a wavering, wobbling action, response, or condition in various situations. It also indicates to be moved, to fall.** It is used of the wavering or shaking of even mountains, an unheard of event (Is. 54:10); Mount Zion was considered unshakable or unmovable (Ps. 125:1); the earth under God's fierce judgments could move violently (Is. 24:19). It is used of the pressure or shaking of the wicked against the psalmist (Ps. 55:3, 22). It has the sense of fire flaming out (Ps. 140:10). It describes the instability of kingdoms (Ps. 46:6). It is used figuratively of a foot slipping; it indicates the failure of God's people (Deut. 32:35). It is found in the idiom, a hand wavers, i.e., the person becomes weak economically (Lev. 25:35). It is used figuratively of the person who is sound, safe, secure, and will not be moved (Ps. 10:6), a claim made by the wicked but realized in the righteous (Prov. 10:30; 12:3). *

– [2] Lam. 1:8 ➔ GLUTTON (BE) <2151> a.

REND – [1] Lev. 10:6; 13:45; 21:10 ➔ TEAR <6533> [2] Judg. 14:6 ➔ SPLIT <8156>.

RENEW – ***ḥāḏaš*** [verb: חָדַשׁ <2318>; a prim. root] ▶ **This word means to be new, to repair, to rebuild. It refers to the renovating or reconstructing of various items; it is also translated to repair, to restore.** The altar of the Lord, i.e., rebuilding it (2 Chr. 15:8); the Temple (2 Chr. 24:4, 12); the surface of the ground or earth (Ps. 104:30); the kingdom (1 Sam. 11:14). It is used figuratively in an intensive stem to indicate the restoring or revitalizing of one's spirit (Ps. 51:10). In a time of restoration, ruined cities will be rebuilt (Is. 61:4). It is used of the Lord's restoring the past blessed days of Jerusalem (Lam. 5:21). Other refs.: Job 10:17; Ps. 103:5. ¶

RENEWED (BE) – Job 33:25 ➔ FRESH (BE, BECOME) <7375>.

RENOUNCE – [1] ***nā'ar*** [verb: נָאַר <5010>; a prim. root] ▶ **This word means to abandon, to reject.** It means to reject something or someone in word and in deed: of God rejecting, spurning His covenant (Ps. 89:39; also translated to spurn, to make void); and leaving, abandoning His Temple and Jerusalem (Lam. 2:7; also translated to abandon, to abhor, to disown, to reject). ¶

– [2] Dan. 4:27 ➔ BREAK AWAY, BREAK OFF <6562>.

RENOWNED – Num. 1:16 ➔ CHOSEN <7148>.

RENT – [1] Is. 3:24 ➔ ROPE <5364> [2] Amos 5:11: to impose heavy rent ➔ TRAMPLE <1318>.

REPAIR – [1] ***bāḏaq*** [verb: בָּדַק <918>; a prim. root] ▶ **This word means to mend (a breach), to rebuild. It describes the workmen's cleaning and reparations made on the Temple during Josiah's reign.** Ref.: 2 Chr. 34:10. ¶
[2] ***ḥûṭ*** [Aramaic verb: חוּט <2338>; corresponding to the root of THREAD <2339>, perhaps as a denom.] ▶ **This word means to join, to fix, to mend. It refers to work done on the foundations of Jerusalem by the returned exiles.** Ref.: Ezra 4:12; KJV: to join. ¶
– [3] 2 Chr. 15:8; 24:4, 12; Is. 61:4 ➔ RENEW <2318> [4] Neh. 3:8 ➔ LEAVE <5800>.

REPEAT – Judg. 5:11 ➔ RECOUNT <8567>.

REPENTANCE – [1] Is. 30:15 ➔ RETURNING <7729> [2] Hos. 13:14 ➔ COMPASSION <5164>.

REPHAEL – ***r^{e}pā'ēl*** [masc. proper noun: רְפָאֵל <7501>; from HEAL <7495> and GOD <410>]: the Lord has healed ▶ **An Israelite who returned from the Babylonian captivity.** Ref.: 1 Chr. 26:7. ¶

REPHAH – ***repāḥ*** [masc. proper noun: רֶפַח <7506>; from an unused root apparently meaning to sustain]: support ▶ **Ancestor of Joshua.** Ref.: 1 Chr. 7:25. ¶

REPHAIAH – ***r^{e}pāyāh*** [masc. proper noun: רְפָיָה <7509>; from HEAL <7495> and LORD <3050>]: the Lord heals ▶
a. Son of Jeshaiah. Ref.: 1 Chr. 3:21. ¶
b. A Simeonite. Ref.: 1 Chr. 4:42. ¶
c. Grandson of Issachar. Ref.: 1 Chr. 7:2. ¶
d. A descendant of Saul, the same as Rapha (<7498> c.). Ref.: 1 Chr. 9:43. ¶
e. Son of Hur. Ref.: Neh. 3:9. ¶

REPHAIM – ***r^{e}pā'iym, rāpa', rāpah*** [masc. noun: רְפָאִים, רָפָא, רָפָה <7497>; from HEAL <7495> in the sense of invigorating]: strong, giant ▶ **This word means a giant, Rephaim (an ethnic people group), Valley of Rephaim. Frequently, the term (only with the plural form) designated a Canaanite tribe that inhabited the Promised Land prior to the Hebrew conquest. Members of this tribe were known for their unusually large size.** Refs.: Gen. 14:5; 15:20; Deut. 2:11, 20; 3:11, 13; Josh. 12:4; 13:12; 17:15. In two accounts, the singular form was utilized to refer to a particular giant, perhaps an ancestor of the tribe of the Rephaim (2 Sam. 21:16, 18, 20, 22; 1 Chr. 20:6, 8). In a different vein, the word (also only in the plural form) acted as the proper name of a valley located southwest of Jerusalem (Josh. 15:8; 18:16; 2 Sam. 5:18, 22; 23:13; 1 Chr. 11:15; 14:9; Is. 17:5). *

REPHIDIM – ***r^{e}piyḏiym*** [proper noun: רְפִידִים <7508>; plur. of the masc. of the same as SUPPORT (noun) <7507>]: supports, great spaces ▶ **A campsite of the Israelites in the desert on their way to Canaan.** Refs.: Ex. 17:1, 8; 19:2; Num. 33:14, 15. ¶

REPLY (noun) – [1] Ezra 4:17; 5:11 ➔ ANSWER (noun) <6600> [2] Prov. 15:23 ➔ ANSWER (noun) <4617> a.

REPLY (verb) – Dan. 3:16 ➔ RETURN (verb) <8421>.

REPORT – [1] ***hašmā'ûṯ*** [fem. noun: הַשְׁמָעוּת <2045>; from HEAR <8085>] ▶ **This word refers to an oral or written statement or telling of Jerusalem's destruction.** Ref.: Ezek. 24:26; also translated to cause to hear. ¶
[2] ***š^{e}mû'āh*** [fem. noun: שְׁמוּעָה <8052>; from HEAR <8085>]: something heard ▶ **This word refers to news; a rumor. Literally, it means what is heard, a passive participle from *šāma'*, to hear, to understand.** It refers to a report or announcement of news, a report of something, even a rumor (1 Sam. 2:24; 4:19; 2 Sam. 4:4; 13:30). Daniel uses the plural form of the word, rumors (Dan. 11:44). It indicates

what is heard by a prophet, the message, the prophecy (Is. 28:9, 19; 53:1); what is heard (Obad. 1:1). *
– 3 Josh. 9:9; Jer. 6:24 ➔ FAME <8089> 4 Ezra 5:5 ➔ COMMAND (noun) <2941> 5 Ezra 5:7 ➔ ANSWER (noun) <6600>.

REPORT (BAD) – ***dibbāh*** [fem. noun: דִּבָּה <1681>; from SPEAK <1680> (in the sense of furtive motion)] ▶ **This word means a description of a bad situation, as well as slander, calumny. It is also translated whispering, defaming, mocking.** It is used of the true but negative report of the ten spies to Canaan (Num. 13:32; 14:36, 37): bad report, but it also depicts an accurate report concerning evil things (Gen. 37:2). It describes a report given for an evil purpose, e.g., to defame someone (Prov. 10:18), i.e., slander, which will destroy the person who spreads the story as well. It includes whispering in the sense of spreading slander against someone (Ps. 31:13; Jer. 20:10) but also in the sense of repeating an unfortunate truth about people behind their backs (Ezek. 36:3: infamy, evil gossip, malicious talk, whispering). Other ref.: Prov. 25:10. ¶

REPOSE – ***margê'āh*** [fem. noun: מַרְגֵּעָה <4774>; from MOMENT (BE FOR A) <7280> c. (in the sense of to be at rest)] ▶ **This word refers to a place of rest.** It refers to a state of relaxation and a cessation from toil, fighting, and worry (Is. 28:12; also translated place of repose, refreshing). ¶

REPRESENTATIVE – Num. 16:2; 26:9 ➔ CHOSEN <7148>.

REPROACH (noun) – 1 ***ḥerpāh*** [fem. noun: חֶרְפָּה <2781>; from REPROACH (verb) <2778>] ▶ **This word means scorn, taunt.** The term can be used for a taunt hurled at an enemy such as barrenness (Gen. 30:23); uncircumcision (Gen. 34:14); and widowhood (Is. 54:4). *
– 2 Is. 43:28 ➔ SCORN (noun) <1421> 3 Jer. 20:8 ➔ DERISION <7047> 4 Ezek. 35:12 ➔ DISGRACE (noun) <5007>.

REPROACH (BRING) – Num. 15:30 ➔ BLASPHEME <1442>.

REPROACH (verb) – 1 ***ḥārap̱*** [verb: חָרַף <2778>; a prim. root] ▶ **The word means to taunt or agitate someone about something.** The psalmist was the object of taunting from his enemies. (Ps. 119:42). Nehemiah is the object of reproaches from his enemies (Neh. 6:13). Israel as a whole was taunted and reproached by the Philistine, Goliath. God is the object of His enemies' reproaches or revilings (2 Kgs. 19:4, 16, 22, 23; Ps. 79:12) and by the enemies of His people. To reproach one's own life (soul) is to stake one's faith or trust in something and support it (Judg. 5:18; 1 Sam. 17:10, 25, 26; Ps. 89:51). For other meanings of the Hebrew word, see WINTER (verb) <2778> and BETROTH <2778>. *
– 2 Num. 15:30 ➔ BLASPHEME <1442>.

REPROVE – Prov. 9:7; 15:12; Ezek. 3:26 ➔ JUDGE (verb) <3198>.

REPTILE – Mic. 7:17 ➔ CRAWL <2119>.

REPTILE (SAND) – Lev. 11:30 ➔ SAND LIZARD <2546>.

REPULSIVE (BE) – Ps. 77:9 ➔ ENTREAT <2589>.

REPULSIVE IMAGE – 1 Kgs. 15:13; 2 Chr. 15:16 ➔ IMAGE <4656>.

REPULSIVE THING – Job 23:13 ➔ WRONGDOING <8604>.

REPUTATION – Esther 9:4 ➔ FAME <8089>.

REPUTED – Dan. 4:35 ➔ ACCOUNTED (BE) <2804>.

REQUEST – 1 ***baqqāšāh*** [fem. noun: בַּקָּשָׁה <1246>; from SEEK <1245>] ▶ **This word means a demand, an invitation, as well as a desire, something sought.** It is used to describe a request in general (Ezra 7:6). In its biblical use, it especially refers to requests made to royalty (Esther 5:3, 6–8; 7:2, 3; 9:12). ¶

[2] ***mê'mar*** [Aramaic masc. noun: מֵאמַר <3983>; corresponding to COMMAND (noun) <3982>] ▶ **This noun means word, command. It is used only twice in the Old Testament.** It describes the words the priests spoke to request supplies for rebuilding the Temple (Ezra 6:9; also translated appointment, to require, requested); and it also refers to the words of the holy ones that issued the edict in Nebuchadnezzar's dream (Dan. 4:17: word, command). This noun comes from the common Aramaic verb, *ᵃmar* (<560>), meaning to say. ¶
[3] ***šᵉ'ēlāh, šēlāh*** [fem. noun: שְׁאֵלָה, שֵׁלָה <7596>; from ASK <7592>] ▶ **This term signifies demand, petition, thing asked for of another party by a person or group.** The request can be made of another human: Gideon, for gold earrings from the Ishmaelites (Judg. 8:24); Adonijah, for Abishag the Shunammite from Solomon with Bathsheba as intermediary (1 Kgs. 2:16, 20); Esther, for the king's presence at her banquet; also for the sparing of the Jews' and her own life (Esther 5:6–8; 7:2, 3; 9:12); or of God: Hannah, for a son (1 Sam. 1:17, 27; 2:20); Job, for death (Job 6:8); the Israelites, for delicious food (Ps. 106:15 [cf. Num. 11:4–6, 31–35]). ¶
– [4] Ps. 20:5 ➔ DESIRE (noun) <4862>.

REQUESTED – Ezra 6:9 ➔ REQUEST <3983>.

REQUIRE – [1] Ezra 6:9 ➔ REQUEST <3983> [2] Job 27:8 ➔ TAKE AWAY <7953>.

REQUIRED – Ezra 7:20 ➔ NEED (noun) <2819>.

RESCUE – [1] Ps. 144:7, 10, 11 ➔ OPEN <6475> b. [2] Dan. 3:15, 28; etc. ➔ DELIVER <7804>.

RESEMBLE – Dan. 7:5 ➔ LIKE (BE) <1821>.

RESEN – ***resen*** [proper noun: רֶסֶן <7449>; the same as BRIDLE <7448>]: bridle ▶ **A place in Assyria between Nineveh and Calah.** Ref.: Gen. 10:12. ¶

RESHEPH – ***rešep̱*** [masc. proper noun: רֶשֶׁף <7566>; the same as FLASH (noun) <7565>]: flash ▶ **A son of Ephraim.** Ref.: 1 Chr. 7:25. ¶

RESERVE (noun) – Gen. 41:36 ➔ DEPOSIT <6487>.

RESERVE (KEEP IN) – Deut. 32:34 ➔ STORE (LAY IN) <3647>.

RESERVE (verb) – [1] ***'āṣal*** [verb: אָצַל <680>; a prim. root] ▶ **This word means to remove, to hold back, to take part of.** It is used of taking away both a blessing and a birthright (Gen. 27:36). It describes removing some of the Spirit of God from Moses to place it on the seventy elders of Israel (Num. 11:17, 25). Its opposite means to give free reign to, to not refuse, to not keep (Eccl. 2:10), e.g., one's eyes. It can be used literally as an architectural term meaning to shorten, to be shortened, or to set back (Ezek. 42:6), such as Temple chambers. ¶
– [2] Lev. 19:18 ➔ KEEP <5201>.

RESERVED (BE) – Deut. 33:21 ➔ COVER (verb) <5603> b.

RESERVOIR – ***miqwāh*** [fem. noun: מִקְוָה <4724>; fem. of HOPE (noun) <4723> (in another sense of the Hebrew word meaning collection)] ▶ **This word refers to a large hole dug out of the ground for holding water for various purposes, e.g., to reserve water, to create defense, beauty, etc.** Ref.: Is. 22:11; KJV: ditch. ¶

RESIST – [1] Prov. 28:4 ➔ STRIVE <1624> [2] Zech. 3:1 ➔ ACCUSE <7853>.

RESOLVE – [1] Judg. 5:15 ➔ STATUTE <2711> [2] Dan. 1:8 ➔ PUT <7760>.

RESOUND – 1 Chr. 16:32; Ps. 96:11; 98:7 ➔ THUNDER (verb) <7481>.

RESOUNDING MUSIC – Ps. 92:3 ➔ MEDITATION <1902>.

RESPECT (noun) – Ps. 74:20; 119:6, 15 ➔ to have respect ➔ LOOK (verb) <5027>.

RESPECT (GIVE) – Esther 1:20 ➔ lit.: give respect, give honor ➔ HONOR (noun) <3366>.

RESPECT (SHOW) – Lam. 5:12 ➔ HONOR (verb) <1921>.

RESPECT (TREAT WITH) – Lev. 22:2 ➔ SEPARATE <5144>.

RESPECT (verb) – Lam. 5:12 ➔ HONOR (verb) <1921>.

RESPECT OF PERSONS – 2 Chr. 19:7 ➔ PARTIALITY <4856>.

RESPECTED – Is. 32:5 ➔ RICH <7771> a.

RESPITE – [1] Ex. 8:15 ➔ RELIEF <7309> [2] Lam. 3:49 ➔ INTERRUPTION <2014>.

RESPONSE – Prov. 29:19 ➔ ANSWER (noun) <4617> a.

RESPONSIVE (BE) – 2 Kgs. 22:19; 2 Chr. 34:27 ➔ FAINT (BE, MAKE) <7401>.

REST (noun) – [1] ***dᵉmiy, dᵒmiy*** [masc. noun: דֳּמִי, דְּמִי <1824>; from CEASE <1820>] ▶
a. This word refers to the act of watchmen reporting what they see and know. Ref.: Is. 62:6; KJV: silence. It refers also to the Lord's resting from establishing Zion, Jerusalem (Is. 62:7), or remaining silent towards one who prays to Him for help (Ps. 83:1). ¶
b. This word also denotes half, middle, the rest, the remainder. It is used of Hezekiah's concern that he die young, deprived of half or the rest of his life span (Is. 38:10). ¶
[2] ***margôaʻ*** [masc. noun: מַרְגּוֹעַ <4771>; from MOMENT (BE FOR A) <7280> c. (in the sense of to be at rest)] ▶ **This poetic word refers to the peace and safety promised to God's earthly people, which they will secure by adhering to His commandments.** Ref.: Jer. 6:16. ¶
[3] ***naḥaṯ*** [masc. noun: נַחַת <5183>; from BRING DOWN <5182>; also perhaps from REST (verb) <5117>] ▶ **This word refers to calmness, quietness; it is also translated peace, quiet, tranquility.** A word referring to respite, freedom from oppression, or strife (Job 17:16, KJV; Prov. 29:9; Eccl. 4:6; 6:5; 9:17; Is. 30:15). For Job 36:16, see BEND <5181> also and in general. The Hebrew word also means descending, descent; see DESCENT <5183>. ¶
[4] ***pûgāh*** [fem. noun: פּוּגָה <6314>; from STUNNED (BECOME) <6313>] ▶ **This word defines a respite from some activity or thought, from an oppressive or grievous situation; it is also translated relief.** Ref.: Lam. 2:18. ¶
[5] ***šabbāṯôn*** [masc. noun: שַׁבָּתוֹן <7677>; from SABBATH <7676>] ▶ **This word means a time to rest, a special holiday, a day of relaxation, a Sabbath feast.** The meaning most often denoted from this word is that of the day of rest (Ex. 31:15). In Leviticus, this noun is used to refer to the Day of Atonement (Lev. 16:31); the sabbatical year (Lev. 25:4); the Feast of Trumpets (Lev. 23:24); and the first and eighth days of the Feast of Tabernacles (Lev. 23:39).

During the sabbatical year, the land was not to be plowed but to be given a Sabbath rest, a time of refreshing to the Lord. This word was also used to describe the requirements of rest on the first and eighth days of the Feast of Tabernacles. In any context, however, the meaning of this noun is still one of a requirement for God's people to rest on the seventh day or any other holy day as directed. *

– [6] Gen. 49:15; Deut. 28:65; Lam. 1:3; etc. ➔ RESTING PLACE <4494>, <4496> [7] Ps. 22:2; 62:1 ➔ SILENCE (noun) <1747>.

REST (BE AT) – [1] Ex. 15:2 ➔ PRAISE (verb) <5115> a. [2] Dan. 4:4 ➔ EASE (BE AT) <7954>.

REST (BE AT, CAUSE TO) – Deut. 28:65; Job 26:12; etc. ➔ MOMENT (BE FOR A) <7280> c.

REST (GIVE NO) – Prov. 6:3 ➔ BOLD (BE, MAKE) <7292>.

REST (NARROWED) – 1 Kgs. 6:6 ➔ LEDGE (NARROW, NARROWED, OFFSET) <4052>.

REST (verb) – [1] ***yānaḥ*** [verb: יָנַח <3240>; a prim. root] ► **The word employed here is now considered to be from *nûaḥ*.** See <5117> a. below.

[2] ***nûaḥ, munnāḥ*** [verb: נוּחַ, מֻנָּח <5117>; a prim. root] ►

a. A verb indicating to relax, to pause. It has many uses. Its main uses are summarized here: (1) to rest, to settle, to settle down, e.g., of the ark (Gen. 8:4); of locusts on the crops (Ex. 10:14); of a spirit on a person (2 Kgs. 2:15); of the Lord's Spirit (Num. 11:25–26); of birds (2 Sam. 21:10); of the hand of the Lord on something (Is. 25:10); of wisdom which rests in one's heart (Prov. 14:33). (2) It means to repose, to pause for rest after laboring (Ex. 20:11; 23:12; Deut. 5:14); freedom, respite from one's enemies (Esther 9:16). (3) It means to leave something as it is, at rest: the nations (Num. 32:15; Judg. 2:23; 3:1; Jer. 27:11); to leave something behind (Gen. 42:33; 2 Sam. 16:21). (4) It can have the sense of departing from a position (Eccl. 10:4); or of God's abandoning a person (Ps. 119:121; Jer. 14:9). (5) It can mean to leave alone, to let be, to not bother (Ex. 32:10; Hos. 4:17). (6) It has the sense of permit, to let a person do something (Judg. 16:26). (7) It may mean, in its causative senses: (a) to cause to rest, to give rest to: to rest one's hands (Ex. 17:11); to give satisfaction to one's spirit, especially God's Spirit (Zech. 6:8); to calm someone (Prov. 29:17); it is used figuratively of letting a blessing rest, come down on a person, house, or family (Ezek. 44:30). (b) To lay something down, to deposit it somewhere, such as stones (Josh. 4:3, 8); the ark (1 Sam. 6:18); man, Adam (Gen. 2:15). In one passive usage, it is negated (*lō'*) and refers to those who are given no respite (Lam. 5:5).

b. The Hebrew word also means free space, an open area. See FREE SPACE <5117> *

[3] ***nāp̄aš*** [verb: נָפַשׁ <5314>; a prim. root] ► **This word means to refresh oneself.** It refers to a renewal of energy in mind and body and applies to persons and work animals (Ex. 23:12; 2 Sam. 16:14). It is used figuratively of the Lord resting after creation, ceasing from His labor (Ex. 31:17: to refresh). ¶

[4] ***šaḇaṯ*** [verb: שָׁבַת <7673>; a prim. root] ► **This word means to repose, to rid of, to still, to put away, to leave. Most often, it expresses the idea of resting (i.e., abstaining from labor), especially on the seventh day (see Ex. 20:8–11). It is from this root that the noun for *Sabbath* originates, a word designating the time to be set aside for rest.** The verb is used of God to describe His resting after the completion of creation (Gen. 2:2). This example of rest by God at creation set the requirement of rest that He desires for His people in order that they may live lives pleasing to Him, full of worship and adoration (Ex. 31:17). In Joshua, the verb expresses a cessation of the provision of manna by God to the Israelites (Josh. 5:12). The land was also depicted as enjoying a rest from the Israelite farmers while they were in exile (Lev. 26:34, 35).

Daniel uses this verb to indicate a ceasing of ritual sacrifice and offerings. In Daniel 9:24, Daniel was speaking of the Messiah's coming and the establishment of the New Covenant, when there would be no more need for ritual sacrifices. In another context, the verb can mean to exterminate or destroy a certain object, such as in Amos 8:4 in which Amos addresses those who trampled the needy and did away with the poor. The verb means to cause, to desist from, as in God's declaration of action against the shepherds (Ezek. 34:10). The word suggests a removing of people or other objects (Ex. 12:15; Ezek. 23:27, 48; Is. 30:11). In still other contexts, the causative stem means to fail or to leave lacking. In Ruth 4:14, God was praised because He did not leave Naomi without a kinsman-redeemer. *

– [5] Esther 9:16–18 ➔ RESTING PLACE <5118>.

RESTING PLACE – 1 ***mānôaḥ*** [masc. noun: מָנוֹחַ <4494>; from FREE SPACE <5117>] ▶ **This word refers to a location where someone or something settles down and remains or to the cessation of work in order to refresh oneself; it is also translated rest.** Israel, figuratively, could find no resting place for the soles of her feet (Deut. 28:65; Lam. 1:3). A resting place was or rest was a time or place of security (Ruth 3:1). It is used of rest for the soul because of the Lord's mercies and blessings (Ps. 116:7). The dove found no resting place for herself (Gen. 8:9). Other refs.: 1 Chr. 6:31; Is. 34:14. ¶

2 ***meNûḥāh, menuḥāh*** [fem. noun: מְנוּחָה, מְנֻחָה <4496>; fem. of MANOAH <4495>] ▶ **This word means rest, quiet. It is used in several ways to denote places where peace, quiet, and trust are found.** Refs.: Gen. 49:15; Ruth 1:9; Ps. 23:2; Is. 28:12. Canaan was intended to be a place where Israel could find rest (Judg. 20:43; 1 Kgs. 8:56). The rest of God is not possible when uncleanness and corruption abounds (Mic. 2:10). In Jeremiah 51:59, the word has the meaning of quartermaster, an army officer who provides soldiers with rest, fresh horses, and food. People cannot make a sufficient place of rest for the Lord (Is. 66:1), but the Lord will supply a marvelous resting for His restored people (Is. 11:10). *

3 ***marbêṣ*** [masc. noun: מַרְבֵּץ <4769>; from LIE DOWN <7257>] ▶ **This word describes a place of safety and rest for sheep, a sheepfold.** Ref.: Ezek. 25:5; also translated fold, couching place. It describes also a home for wild animals, a lair (Zeph. 2:15; also translated lair, place to lie down). ¶

4 ***nûaḥ, nôaḥ*** [masc. noun: נוּחַ, נֹחַ <5118>; from REST (verb) <5117>] ▶ **This later Hebrew word means quiet, rest (e.g., from troubles and calamities).** Refs.: Esther 9:16–18. It indicates the place where the Lord chose to let His name and glory dwell on earth, the Temple (2 Chr. 6:41). ¶

5 ***rêḇeṣ*** [masc. noun: 7258> רֵבֶץ; from LIE DOWN <7257>] ▶ **This word means a place of security; it is also translated home, dwelling place, fold.** Figuratively, it depicts a resting place, a place of security for the righteous person (Prov. 24:15). In a more literal sense, it indicates a safe resting place where danger is removed (Is. 35:7); a pleasant place to live, a home (Is. 65:10; Jer. 50:6). ¶

RESTLESS (BE, BECOME, GROW) – ***rûḏ*** [verb: רוּד <7300>; a prim. root] ▶ **This word means to wander agitatedly, to feel unhappy about one's circumstances, to roam.** Hosea uses the verb figuratively to refer to Judah's restlessness, i.e., their lack of obedience to God (Hos. 11:12: to rule, to walk, to be unruly). The Lord uses the verb in Jeremiah to ask why His people felt they were free to roam (Jer. 2:31). Esau, after Jacob deceived Isaac, was doomed to live by the sword and serve his brother. However, there would come a time when he would become restless and throw off his yoke (Gen. 27:40). Other ref.: Ps. 55:2 (to mourn). ¶

RESTORE – 1 2 Chr. 15:8; 24:4, 12 ➔ RENEW <2318> 2 Ezra 4:12, 13; etc. ➔ FINISH <3635>.

RESTORED (BE) – Dan. 4:36 ➔ ESTABLISHED (BE) <8627>.

RESTRAIN – 1 ***ḥāṭam*** [verb: חָטַם <2413>; a prim. root] ▶ **This means to keep something back, to keep it from happening.** In particular it refers to God's restraining His wrath from Israel (Is. 48:9); also translated to refrain, to hold back. Its usage in this verse parallels the word *'āraḵ* (PROLONG <748>). ¶

2 ***kālā'*** [verb: כָּלָא <3607>; a prim. root] ▶ **a. This word means to hold back, also to close, to hinder.** It refers to the cessation of rain (Gen. 8:2: to restrain, to stop falling). It means to hold back something (Gen. 23:6: to withhold, to refuse); or to restrain one's lips or speech (Ps. 40:9: to restrain, to refrain, to seal). It describes persons restraining themselves from something (Ex. 36:6); or being held back (Num. 11:28; 1 Sam. 25:33). It refers to penning up or keeping something in a location

(1 Sam. 6:10; Jer. 32:2). It is used figuratively of God's withholding His love and compassion (Ps. 40:11); and of restraining the wind (Eccl. 8:8). It describes the failure or refusal of the earth to bear its produce (Hag. 1:10). Other refs.: Ps. 88:8; 119:101; Is. 43:6; Jer. 32:3; Ezek. 31:15. ¶

b. A verb meaning to finish, to complete, to bring to an end. It describes the completion of God's plans for His people Israel (Dan. 9:24; also translated to make an end, to put an end). ¶

[3] ***'āṣar*** [verb: עָצַר <6113>; a prim. root] ▶ **This word means to shut in, to keep in slavery.** It means to keep from, prevent, as when the Lord kept Sarah from having children (Gen. 16:2); He closed the wombs of many women in the Old Testament (Gen. 20:18). It is used of stopping something, stopping a plague (Num. 16:48, 50; 25:8). The Lord could check or shut up the natural processes of nature, e.g., rain (Deut. 11:17). It is used in a technical sense to refer to a person who is in bondage, not free, held in slavery (Deut. 32:36). It is used of politely detaining persons according to their wills (Judg. 13:15, 16); or of imprisoning someone (2 Kgs. 17:4). It refers to retaining strength, being strong (Dan. 10:8, 16). It is used with the sense of controlling or restraining a people, ruling over them (1 Sam. 9:17); and of driving or controlling a horse (2 Kgs. 4:24). In its passive uses, it means to be detained, to be shut up (1 Sam. 21:7; 1 Kgs. 8:35). *

– [4] Gen. 43:31; 45:1; Esther 5:10; Is. 42:14; 63:15; 64:12 ➔ CONTROL (verb) <662> [5] 1 Sam. 3:13 ➔ DIM (BE) <3543> b. [6] 1 Sam. 14:6 ➔ CUTTING TOOL <4621> [7] 1 Sam. 24:7 ➔ SPLIT <8156> [8] Job 37:4 ➔ SUPPLANT <6117> [9] Dan. 4:35 ➔ STRIKE <4223>.

RESTRAINT – [1] ***ma'ṣôr*** [masc. noun: מַעְצוֹר <4622>; from RESTRAIN <6113>] ▶ **This word means a holding back, a hindrance.** It occurs only one time, where Jonathan tells his armor-bearer that "there is no restraint to the LORD to save by many or by few" (1 Sam. 14:6, KJV; also translated to restrain, to hinder). ¶

[2] ***'eṣer*** [masc. noun: עֶצֶר <6114>; from RESTRAIN <6113>] ▶

a. This word is used of a ruler ruling over, restricting the people of Laish. Ref.: Judg. 18:7. The NASB nuances the word to mean humility, humiliating (*yôrêš 'eṣer*). ¶

b. This word means prosperity. It is taken by some to refer to the prosperity of the land and people of Laish (Judg. 18:7), possessing prosperity (*yôrêš 'eṣer*). ¶

– [3] Job 30:11 ➔ BRIDLE <7448> a. [4] Job 36:16 ➔ CONSTRAINT <4164> [5] Is. 23:10 ➔ BELT <4206>.

RESTRICTION – Job 36:16 ➔ CONSTRAINT <4164>.

RETAIN – ***s^{e}ḇal*** [Aramaic verb: סְבַל <5446>; corresponding to BEAR (verb) <5445>] ▶ **This word means to bear a load.** In context it refers to older Temple foundations becoming load bearing, being restored or re-laid (Ezra 6:3; also translated to lay, to strongly lay, to firmly lay). ¶

RETRIBUTION – [1] Deut. 32:35 ➔ RECOMPENSE (noun) <8005> [2] Is. 34:8; Hos. 9:7 ➔ RECOMPENSE (noun) <7966> [3] Is. 59:18; Jer. 51:56 ➔ RECOMPENSE (noun) <1578>.

RETURN (noun) – ***t^{e}šûḇāh*** [fem. noun: תְּשׁוּבָה <8666>; from TURN <7725>] ▶

a. This word refers to a response or reply given in a conversation or debate. Refs.: Job 21:34; 34:36. It also indicates a literal return to a location or destination (1 Sam. 7:17).

b. A feminine noun indicating the coming back (of the year); spring. It indicates the beginning of an new yearly cycle in the spring (2 Sam. 11:1; 1 Kgs. 20:22, 26; 1 Chr. 20:1; 2 Chr. 36:10). This is the rendering of the NASB and the NIV.

c. A feminine noun indicating the turn of the year; the end of the year. Some translators take it to refer to the expiration of a yearly cycle, the close of a year, as does the KJV (2 Sam. 11:1; 1 Kgs. 20:22, 26; 1 Chr. 20:1; 2 Chr. 36:10). ¶

RETURN FOR (IN) – ***ḥêlep̱*** [masc. noun: חֵלֶף <2500>; from PASS ON <2498>] ▶ **This word means in exchange for.** It is used of giving something in return for services (Num. 18:21, 31), in particular the services of the sons of Levi. ¶

RETURN (verb) – ***tûḇ*** [verb: תּוּב <8421>; corresponding to TURN <7725>] ▶ **This word means to come back, to restore, to give back, to respond, to give a reply to someone orally.** Refs.: Ezra 5:5, 11. It means literally to take something back, to return it (Ezra 6:5); or of reason returning to a person, someone recovering his or her senses (Dan. 4:34, 36). It is used of an official reply (Dan. 2:14). The reply of the three Hebrew young men remains a classic response to a tyrant (Dan. 3:16). ¶

RETURNING – ***šûḇāh*** [fem. noun: שׁוּבָה <7729>; from TURN <7725>] ▶ **This word refers in a religious sense to an act of turning back to God, to committing oneself to Him, while turning from one's wayward ways; it is also translated repentance.** Ref.: Is. 30:15. ¶

REU – ***r^e'û*** [masc. proper noun: רְעוּ <7466>; for PASTURE <7471> in the sense of PERSON (ANOTHER) <7453> (which also means fellow, friend)]: friend ▶ **A descendant of Shem, the son of Noah.** Refs.: Gen. 11:18–21; 1 Chr. 1:25. In the New Testament, He appears in the genealogy of Jesus (Luke 3:35). ¶

REUBEN – ***r^e'ûḇên*** [masc. proper noun: רְאוּבֵן <7205>; from the imperative of SEE <7200> and SON <1121>]: behold (see) a son ▶ **The firstborn son of Jacob.** His mother was Leah (Gen. 29:32). He was more merciful toward Joseph than his other brothers (Gen. 37:21–29) and tried to save him (Gen. 42:22). During the famine, he told his father that he (Jacob) would kill his (Reuben's) sons if he did not bring Benjamin back from Egypt (Gen. 42:37). Unfortunately, Reuben slept with one of Jacob's concubines, a sin that impacted Jacob's blessing on him (Gen. 49:3, 4). He became indecisive and could no longer be a leader in Israel, he or his descendants. Jacob gave a double portion of blessing to Joseph, not Reuben as firstborn (Gen. 49:22–26). Reubenites took part in the rebellion against Moses in the wilderness (Num. 16:1). The tribe inherited territory east of the Dead Sea from the Arnon River (south) to the Jabbok River (north). Mount Nebo and Heshbon were in its territory. Ezekiel allotted a place for Reuben in his vision of the new Temple and New Jerusalem (Ezek. 48:6–31). *

REUBENITE – ***r^e'ûḇêniy*** [proper noun: רְאוּבֵנִי <7206>; patron. from REUBEN <7205>] ▶ **A descendant of Reuben.** Refs.: Num. 26:7; 34:14; Deut. 3:12, 16; 4:43; 29:8; Josh. 1:12; 12:6; 13:8; 22:1; 2 Kgs. 10:33; 1 Chr. 5:6, 26; 11:42; 12:37; 26:32; 27:16. ¶

REUEL – ***r^e'û'êl*** [masc. proper noun: רְעוּאֵל <7467>; from the same as REU <7466> and GOD <410>]: friend of God ▶
a. Son of Esau. Refs.: Gen. 36:4, 10, 13, 17; 1 Chr. 1:35, 37.
b. Moses' father-in-law. Refs.: Ex. 2:18; Num. 10:29.
c. The father of Eliasaph, the same as *d^e'û'êl* (DEUEL <1845>). Ref.: KJV, Num. 2:14.
d. The father of Shephatiah. Ref.: 1 Chr. 9:8. ¶

REUMAH – ***r^e'ûmāh*** [fem. proper noun: רְאוּמָה <7208>; fem. pass. part. of RISE <7213>]: elevated ▶ **The concubine of Nahor, the brother of Abraham.** Ref.: Gen. 22:24. ¶

REVEAL – [1] ***gālāh*** [verb: גָּלָה <1540>; a prim. root] ▶ **A verb meaning to let know, and also to make known, to uncover, to remove, to go into exile, to reveal oneself, to expose, to disclose, to show, to apprise.** It is used with the words ear (1 Sam. 9:15; 20:2, 12, 13) and eyes (Num. 24:4; translated open, uncovered), meaning to reveal. On occasion, it is used in the expression to uncover the nakedness of, which often implies sexual relations (Lev. 18:6). *

[2] ***g^{e}lāh, g^{e}lā'*** [Aramaic verb: גְּלָה, גְּלָא <1541>; corresponding to <1540> above] ▶ **The**

meaning of this word, as used In the book of Daniel, is to uncover. In the story of the dreams of Nebuchadnezzar, God is shown as the One who reveals hidden things, specifically the meanings of dreams (Dan. 2:22, 28–30, 47). The word has also the meaning of to carry away (Ezra 4:10; 5:12); see BRING OVER <1541>. ¶
– [3] Neh. 9:25 → DELIGHT ONESELF <5727> [4] Ps. 19:2 → SHOW <2331>.

REVELATION – 2 Sam. 7:17 → VISION <2384>.

REVELRY – Amos 6:7 → BANQUETING <4797>.

REVENGE – Judg. 16:28; Prov. 6:34; etc. → VENGEANCE <5357>.

REVENUE – [1] ***’appeṯōm*** [Aramaic masc. noun: אַפְּתֹם <674>; of Persian origin] ▶ **This word refers to the tribute, custom, and tolls that went to Persian kings; it is also translated treasury.** Ref.: Ezra 4:13. ¶
– [2] Is. 23:3 → MERCHANDISE <5505>.

REVENUES – 1 Kgs. 10:15 → WARES <4536>.

REVERENT (BE) – Mal. 2:5 → DISMAYED (BE) <2865>.

REVILE – [1] 1 Sam. 25:14 → RUSH GREEDILY <5860> a. [2] 2 Kgs. 19:6, 22; Ps. 44:16; Is. 37:6, 23 → BLASPHEME <1442>.

REVILEMENT – Is. 43:28 → SCORN (noun) <1421>.

REVILING – [1] 2 Kgs. 19:3; Is. 37:3; Ezek. 35:12 → DISGRACE (noun) <5007> [2] Is. 43:28; 51:7; Zeph. 2:8 → SCORN (noun) <1421> [3] Ezek. 5:15 → TAUNT (noun) <1422>.

REVIVAL – Ezra 9:8, 9 → PRESERVATION OF LIFE <4241>.

REVIVING – Ezra 9:8, 9 → PRESERVATION OF LIFE <4241>.

REVOLT (noun) – [1] Ezra 4:15, 19 → SEDITION <849> [2] Is. 59:13 → REBELLION <5627>.

REVOLT (verb) – [1] Ezra 4:19 → INSURRECTION (MAKE) <5376> [2] Is. 1:5; 31:6 → REBELLION <5627>.

REVOLTER – ***śêṭ, sêṭ*** [masc. noun: שֵׂט, סֵט <7846>; from TURN ASIDE <7750>] ▶
a. This word means a swerver, i.e., one who turns aside. It refers to God's people who are turning against Him and His laws, deviating from what is pleasing to Him (Hos. 5:2; NIV: rebel). ¶
b. A masculine noun meaning deeds that swerve, i.e., a departure from right, a defection, a deviation, a revolt. It has the same meaning as a. but is spelled differently. This time it refers to the object of the psalmist's hatred—those who turn away from God and defect from His ways (Ps. 101:3). ¶

REWARD (noun) – [1] ***nebizbāh*** [Aramaic fem. noun: נְבִזְבָּה <5023>; of uncertain deriv.] ▶ **This rare word refers to something offered to the Babylonian wise men and Daniel as a gesture of approval and appreciation for something said or done. The nature of the rewards offered is not specified but no doubt in keeping with the king's magnificence.** Refs.: Dan. 2:6; 5:17. ¶
[2] ***śeḵer*** [masc. noun: שֶׂכֶר <7938>; from HIRE <7936>] ▶
a. The term is used figuratively of the wages of truth literally, the reward of sowing righteousness. Ref.: Prov. 11:18. The phrase workers of wages means hired laborers (Is. 19:10; also translated pay). ¶
b. A masculine noun meaning sluice. It refers to an artificial channel or passage for water (Is. 19:10, KJV). It refers to workers in a highly prosperous, luxurious society. ¶
– [3] Gen. 15:1; etc. → WAGES <7939> [4] 2 Sam. 19:36 → RECOMPENSE (noun) <1578> [5] Ruth 2:12 → WAGES <4909> [6] Ps. 91:8 → RECOMPENSE (noun) <8011> [7] Is. 1:23 → GIFT <8021> [8] Ezek. 16:34; Hos. 9:1 → EARNINGS <868>

[9] Hos. 2:12 ➔ PAY <866> [10] Mic. 7:3 ➔ RECOMPENSE (noun) <7966>.

REWARD (GIVE A) – ***šāḥad*** [verb: שָׁחַד <7809>; a prim. root] ▶ **This word means to bribe.** It refers to the act of offering something unrighteously to persons to get them to act or think in a certain way (Job 6:22; also translated to make a gift); usually in a way they normally would not (Ezek. 16:33: to bribe, to hire). ¶

REWARD (verb) – ***gāmal*** [verb: גָּמַל <1580>; a prim. root] ▶ **This word means to recompense another, to bring to completion, to do good. It has a broad spectrum of meanings.** The predominant idea is to recompense either with a benevolent reward (1 Sam. 24:17; 2 Sam. 19:36) or an evil recompense (Deut. 32:6; 2 Chr. 20:11; Ps. 137:8). The idea of bringing to an end is demonstrated in verses that describe a child who is weaned (Gen. 21:8; 1 Sam. 1:22–24; Is. 11:8) or plants that have ripened (Num. 17:8; Is. 18:5). At times this word is best translated to do good or to deal bountifully (Ps. 119:17; Prov. 11:17; Is. 63:7). *

REZEPH – ***reṣep̱*** [proper noun: רֶצֶף <7530>; the same as BAKED ON COALS <7529>]: hot stone ▶ **A place that had been conquered by Assyria.** Refs.: 2 Kgs. 19:12; Is. 37:12. ¶

REZIA – ***riṣyā'*** [masc. proper noun: רִצְיָא <7525>; from PLEASURE (TAKE) <7521>]: delight ▶ **An Israelite of the tribe of Asher.** Ref.: 1 Chr. 7:39. ¶

REZIN – ***reṣiyn*** [masc. proper noun: רְצִין <7526>; prob. for PLEASURE <7522>]: pleasure ▶

a. A king of Aram (Syria) who, with Pekah, king of Israel, fought against Judah. Refs.: 2 Kgs. 15:37; 16:5–9. During his day, Isaiah uttered several famous prophecies (Is. 7:1–8; 8:6; 9:11) that called on King Ahaz of Judah to trust the Lord against these forces.

b. The head of a family who served in the second Temple after returning from exile. Refs.: Ezra 2:48; Neh. 7:50. ¶

REZON – ***rezôn*** [masc. proper noun: רְזוֹן <7331>; from HEAVY (BE) <7336> (in the sense of ruler, prince)]: prince ▶ **Son of Eliadah, a Syrian, who became the enemy of King Solomon.** Ref.: 1 Kgs. 11:23. ¶

RIB – ***'ala'*** [Aramaic fem. noun: עֲלַע <5967>; corresponding to SIDE <6763>] ▶ **This word refers to one of the protective chest bones encasing the chest cavity.** In context it represents a defeated nation or people (Dan. 7:5). ¶

RIB CAGE – Hos. 13:8 ➔ CAUL <5458>.

RIBAI – ***riyḇay*** [masc. proper noun: רִיבַי <7380>; from STRIVE <7378>]: judgment of the Lord ▶ **Father of Ittai, one of David's strong men.** Refs.: 2 Sam. 23:29; 1 Chr. 11:31. ¶

RIBBAND – Num. 15:38 ➔ CORD <6616>.

RIBBON – Song 4:3 ➔ THREAD <2339>.

RIBLAH – ***riḇlāh*** [proper noun: רִבְלָה <7247>; from an unused root meaning to be fruitful]: fertility ▶ **A city located on the Orontes River in Syria. It is ca. sixty miles north and east of Damascus, capital of Syria and ca. seven miles south of Hamath.** A number of destructive events for Israel occurred in this city: Pharaoh Neco of Egypt took Jehoahaz captive in chains (2 Kgs. 23:33); Zedekiah, the last king of Judah, was captured in Riblah and taken to Babylon (2 Kgs. 25:6–21; Jer. 39:5, 6; 52:9–27). Other ref.: Num. 34:11. ¶

RICH (adj.) – [1] Is. 30:23 ➔ FAT (adj.) <1879> [2] Job 34:19; Is. 32:5 ➔ RICH (noun) <7771> a.

RICH (BE, BECOME, GROW, MAKE) – ***'āšar*** [verb: עָשַׁר <6238>; a prim. root; properly, to accumulate] ▶ **This word means to be or to become wealthy in money, possessions, or influence.** Its simple meaning is to become rich; it describes an arrogant Ephraim, a self-seeking country

(Hos. 12:8). It also has the sense of making someone else rich (Gen. 14:23); especially regarding the Lord who makes a person poor or rich (1 Sam. 2:7). It is used of making oneself rich, obtaining riches (Ps. 49:16; Prov. 21:17; Dan. 11:2; Jer. 5:27). It is used figuratively of a city obtaining riches (Ezek. 27:33). It has the sense of persons enriching themselves (Prov. 13:7). *

RICH (noun) – 1 ***'āšiyr*** [masc. noun: עָשִׁיר <6223>; from RICH (BE) <6238>] ► **This word refers to wealthy, well-to-do persons with significant power and influence socially and politically.** It is the opposite of *dal,* poor, without means (2 Sam. 12:1, 2, 4). The rich were a significant social group in Israel (Ex. 30:15; Ruth 3:10). The strength of rich people lies in their wealth (Prov. 10:15; 18:11); it sustains them. The rich have many superficial friends (Prov. 14:20). The Suffering Servant of Isaiah would lie with the rich at his death (Is. 53:9). Rich people are not to brag about their wealth, for it is given by God (Jer. 9:23). *
2 ***šôa'*** [adj., masc. noun: שׁוֹעַ <7771>; from CRY (verb) <7768>] ►
a. This adjective indicates noble, distinguished, wealthy, generous; hence, a noble, a wealthy person. It refers to wealthy, rich, and influential persons as opposed to the poor and insignificant (*dal*) (Job 34:19). It indicates a highly respected and distinguished person of means and influence (Is. 32:5: bountiful, honorable, respected). ¶
b. This noun indicates a cry for help, an exclamatory plea. It describes a person's plea for help in a confusing and practically hopeless situation (Is. 22:5: crying). ¶
– 3 Dan. 11:24 ➔ FATNESS <4924> a.

RICH ROBE – ***p^etiygiyl*** [masc. noun: פְּתִי־גִיל <6614>; of uncertain deriv.] ►
a. This word indicates a fine robe, fine clothes. It refers to fine, expensive, sartorial clothing. It is contrasted to sackcloth (Is. 3:24).
b. Some take the word to refer to a girdle that holds in, forms, and shapes the body, especially the stomach area. Ref.: Is. 3:24; KJV: stomacher. ¶

RICH STORE – Is. 33:6 ➔ TREASURE <2633>.

RICHES – 1 ***'ōšer*** [noun: עֹשֶׁר <6239>; from RICH (BE) <6238>] ► **This word describes all kinds of wealth, e.g., land, possessions, cattle, and descendants.** Refs.: Gen. 31:16; 1 Kgs. 3:13; Esther 1:4; Prov. 14:24; Jer. 9:23. The expression *'āśāh 'ōšer* means to make money, riches (Jer. 17:11). *
– 2 Josh. 22:8 ➔ WEALTH <5233> 3 Job 36:18 ➔ SUFFICIENCY <5607> b. 4 Job 36:19 ➔ CRY (noun) <7769> 5 Prov. 15:6; 27:24 ➔ TREASURE <2633> 6 Is. 15:7; Jer. 48:36 ➔ ABUNDANCE <3502>.

RICHNESS – 1 Gen. 27:28 ➔ FAT, FATNESS <8082> b. 2 Gen. 27:28, 39 ➔ FATNESS <4924> a.

RID – Num. 17:5 ➔ SUBSIDE <7918>.

RIDDLE – 1 ***'^aḥiyḏāh*** [Aramaic fem. noun: אֲחִידָה <280>; corresponding to ENIGMA <2420>] ► **This word means a puzzle; it is also translated enigma, hard sentence.** Daniel was able to explain these riddles (Dan. 5:12). ¶
2 **to put forth, propound, propose a riddle: *ḥûḏ*** [verb: חוּד <2330>; a prim. root] ► **This Hebrew word means to express a problem or a puzzle in words, to present it, to set forth an allegory.** It is, however, used with the noun "riddle" (Judg. 14:12, 13, 16; Ezek. 17:2) each time as its object. ¶
– 3 Num. 12:8; Judg. 14:12–19; Ps. 49:4; Prov. 1:6; Ezek. 17:2; Hab. 2:6 ➔ ENIGMA <2420>.

RIDE – ***rāḵaḇ*** [verb: רָכַב <7392>; a prim. root] ► **This word means to travel on a horse, in a chariot.** It refers to the activity of mounting and riding an animal: a camel (Gen. 24:61); donkey (Ex. 4:20); horse (Gen. 49:17; Ex. 15:1, 21); mule (1 Kgs. 1:33). It refers to riding in general (Lev. 15:9). It includes riding in a chariot (2 Kgs. 9:16; Jer. 17:25). It is used figuratively of living, enjoying the best things on earth (Deut. 32:13). God Himself rides the heavens (Deut. 33:26) on a cherub (2 Sam. 22:11; Ps. 18:10). In its causative use, it can have the sense of making a person ride (Gen. 41:43; 2 Kgs. 9:28; Ps. 66:12). Used of handling a bow, it means to draw the bow (2 Kgs. 13:16). It describes harnessing, hooking up a heifer, in the context of Ephraim portrayed as a heifer (Hos. 10:11). *

RIDGE – [1] Ps. 65:10 ➔ FURROW <1417> [2] Ps. 65:10 ➔ FURROW <8525>.

RIDICULE – [1] Is. 57:4 ➔ DELIGHT (HAVE, FIND, TAKE) <6026> [2] See MOCK <3932>.

RIDICULE (OBJECT OF) – Deut. 28:37; 1 Kgs. 9:7; Jer. 24:9 ➔ BYWORD <8148>.

RIDING – Ezek. 27:20 ➔ SADDLE <7396> a.

RIE – Ex. 9:32; Is. 28:25 ➔ SPELT <3698>.

RIFLE – Zech. 14:2 ➔ PLUNDER (verb) <8155>.

RIGGING – Prov. 23:34 ➔ MAST <2260>.

RIGHT – [1] ***yāšār*** [adj.: יָשָׁר <3477>; from STRAIGHT (BE) <3474>] ▶ **This word means straight, just.** It can refer to something physical, such as a path (Ps. 107:7; Is. 26:7), but it more often means right in an ethical or an emotional sense, as agreeable or pleasing. Examples of this include what is right in God's eyes (Ex. 15:26; 1 Kgs. 11:33, 38; 2 Kgs. 10:30); or in the eyes of people (Prov. 12:15; Jer. 40:5). It also means upright, such as God (Ps. 25:8); and His ways (Hos. 14:9). Some people were considered upright, such as David (1 Sam. 29:6); and Job (Job 1:1). An ancient history book was called the book of Jashar or the book of the Upright (Josh. 10:13; 2 Sam. 1:18). See the Hebrew root *yāšar* [STRAIGHT (BE) <3474>]. *

[2] ***naḵōaḥ*** [adj.: נָכֹחַ <5228>; from the same as OPPOSITE (adv.) <5226>] ▶ **This word means straightforward, honest, plain.** In 2 Samuel 15:3, it is used to describe a legal case as straightforward, obviously deserving amends. In Proverb 8:9, it describes wisdom's words as straightforward, not perverted, to the one who has the right attitude to receive them. In Proverbs 24:26, the adjective describes words spoken honestly, without partiality (cf. Prov. 24:23–25); lips speaking this way kiss the hearer. The word occurs as a noun in Isaiah 57:2 (uprightness, upright way; also translated uprightly) and means straightforwardness or honesty. For the feminine form of the word, see *neḵōḥāh* (<5229> below). ¶

[3] ***neḵōḥāh*** [adj.: נְכֹחָה <5229>; fem. of <5228> above] ▶ **This word means upright; it is also translated uprightness, equity, honesty.** It is used to modify a land's social practices as upright, just (Is. 26:10). It indicates this is correct, straight, upright dealing (Is. 30:10; 59:14); correct practice in a situation (Amos 3:10). ¶

– [4] Ps. 17:2; Song 1:4; Is. 45:19 ➔ LEVEL (noun) <4339> [5] Eccl. 4:4 ➔ SKILL <3788> [6] Dan. 4:37 ➔ TRUTH <7187>.

RIGHT (GO TO THE, USE THE, TURN TO THE) – ***yāman*** [verb: יָמַן <3231>; a prim. root] ▶ **This word means to use the right (dextral) hand. It is used to indicate direction, in the direction of the right side or hand.** Refs.: Gen. 13:9; Ezek. 21:16. It is used in the phrase not to "turn to the right or to the left" to indicate steadfastness, a determination to keep on one's current path or maintain one's current attitude (Is. 30:21). It describes the use of one's right hand to shoot a bow (1 Chr. 12:2). Other ref.: 2 Sam. 14:19. ¶

RIGHT (SEEM) – Esther 8:5 ➔ SUCCESS (BRING, GIVE) <3787>.

RIGHT (TURN TO THE) – Is. 30:21 ➔ HAND (TURN TO THE RIGHT) <541>.

RIGHT CIRCUMSTANCE – Prov. 25:11 ➔ FITLY <655>.

RIGHT, RIGHT HAND – ***yᵉmāniy*** [adj.: יְמָנִי <3233>; from RIGHT (GO TO THE) <3231>] ▶ **This word indicates direction, the opposite of the left, i.e., dextral.** It refers to Aaron's right ear, the ear on the right side of his body. Refs.: Ex. 29:20; Lev. 8:23. It refers also to the right pillar on the porch of Solomon's Temple (1 Kgs. 7:21) or to anything on the right (2 Kgs. 11:11). When facing the east, it indicates the south or southern direction (1 Kgs. 7:39; Ezek. 47:1, 2). *

RIGHT HAND – [1] ***yāmiyn*** [fem. noun: יָמִין <3225>; from RIGHT (GO TO THE) <3231>] ▶ **This word indicates direction; it also refers to the south. It has several basic usages.** It is used to indicate something on the right side: hand (Gen. 48:13). Used as an adverb, it means a direction to the right (Gen. 13:9; Ps. 45:9). Something on the right is said to have special significance: God swears by His right hand (Is. 62:8); and delivers His people by His right hand (Ex. 15:6, 12); a right-handed oath is noted (Ps. 144:8, 11); a person of honor gets to sit at the right hand (1 Kgs. 2:19; Ps. 110:1). The right side also indicates a southerly direction (Josh. 17:7; 1 Kgs. 7:39). It is used figuratively of being morally upright (Deut. 17:11; 28:14; Josh. 1:7; 2 Kgs. 22:2). The right is indicative of being morally correct or just (Eccl. 10:2). *

[2] ***yᵉmiyniy*** [adj.: יְמִינִי <3227>; from <3225> above] ▶ **This word indicates the right side or right hand of anything, i.e., dextral.** In Ezekiel 4:6 it comes after and modifies the noun meaning side but is used in 2 Chronicles 3:17 with the definite article added to it to mean the right (pillar). ¶

RIGHTEOUS – See JUST <6662>.

RIGHTEOUS (BE) – See JUST (BE) <6663>.

RIGHTEOUSNESS – [1] ***ṣeḏeq*** [masc. noun: צֶדֶק <6664>; from JUST (BE) <6663>] ▶ **This word means a right relation to an ethical or legal standard. The Hebrew word occurs most often in the Psalms and Isaiah.** It is frequently connected with the term justice (Ps. 119:106; Is. 58:2). Kings, judges, and other leaders were to execute their duties based on righteous standards (Deut. 1:16; Prov. 8:15; Is. 32:1). God Himself acts in righteousness both in judgment and deliverance (Ps. 119:75, 160; Is. 51:5; 62:1). Furthermore, God can be credited for generating human righteousness (Ps. 4:1; Jer. 23:6). The concept of righteousness was so important in the Old Testament period that the community that housed the Dead Sea scrolls called their most prominent leader the "Teacher of Righteousness," a person whom many regard as the founder of the sect. *

[2] ***ṣiḏqāh*** [Aramaic fem. noun: צִדְקָה <6665>; corresponding to <6666> below] ▶ **This word occurs only in Daniel 4:27 where it signifies righteousness as positive action by which a person breaks off from sin.** The Hebrew word in that verse is parallel to a Hebrew word meaning to show mercy. Daniel warned Nebuchadnezzar that he would go insane because of his arrogance (see Dan. 4:25) but that righteousness might prolong his prosperous state. For the corresponding Hebrew noun, see *ṣᵉḏāqāh* below. ¶

[3] ***ṣᵉḏāqāh*** [fem. noun: צְדָקָה <6666>; from JUST (BE) <6663>] ▶ **This word describes justice, right actions, and right attitudes, as expected from both God and people when they judge; it also means blameless conduct, and integrity.** God came speaking justice and righteousness as the divine Judge (Is. 63:1; Jer. 9:24; Mic. 7:9); the Lord's holiness was made known by His righteousness in judgments (Is. 5:16; 10:22). Human judges were to imitate the divine Judge in righteousness and justice (Gen. 18:19; 2 Sam. 8:15; Ps. 72:3; Is. 56:1).

The word describes the attitude and actions God had and expected His people to maintain. He is unequivocally righteous; righteousness is entirely His prerogative. His people are to sow righteousness, and they will receive the same in return (Hos. 10:12). He dealt with His people according to their righteousness and blamelessness (2 Sam. 22:21; Ezek. 3:20). Faith in God was counted as righteousness to Abraham (Gen. 15:6); and obedience to the Lord's Law was further evidence of faith that God considered as righteousness (Deut. 6:25). Returning a poor man's cloak was an act of obedience that was considered righteous and just before the Lord (Deut. 24:13). Jacob declared that his integrity (honesty, righteousness) would speak for him in the future to Laban (Gen. 30:33). The lives of people are to reflect righteousness and integrity (Prov. 8:20; 15:9); even old age may be attained by living a life of righteousness (Prov. 16:31).

The noun describes the justice of God or His will: persons are to act according to God's righteousness toward other persons (Deut. 33:21; Is. 48:1). The word is also synonymous with truth or integrity. God declares His words are based on His own truthfulness (Is. 45:23). The word depicts God's salvation or deliverance, such as when Isaiah spoke of the Lord bringing near His righteousness as equal to bringing near His salvation (Is. 46:13; 51:6; 56:1).

The word may indicate a just claim before the king (2 Sam. 19:28); or the righteous claim for vindication God gives to His people (Neh. 2:20; Is. 54:17). A person who was denied justice but was righteous was, in fact, innocent (Is. 5:23). In the plural, the word referred to the righteous acts that God performed for His people (1 Sam. 12:7); or, in the plural used in an abstract sense, it depicted people living righteously (Is. 33:15). The word was used to mean legitimate and blameless, referring to the Lord's righteous Branch (Jer. 23:5; 33:15) who will act justly and righteously in the restored land. *

RIGHTEOUSNESS (THE LORD IS OUR) – Jer. 23:6; 33:16 ➔ JEHOVAH TSIDKENU <3072>.

RIGHTLY – Song 1:4 ➔ LEVEL (noun) <4339>.

RIGOR – Ex. 1:13, 14; etc. ➔ SEVERITY <6530>.

RIGOROUSLY – Ex. 1:13, 14 ➔ SEVERITY <6530>.

RIM – [1] ***misgeret*** [fem. noun: מִסְגֶּרֶת <4526>; from CLOSE <5462> (in the sense of to enclose)] ► **This word refers to a border, a fortress.** It is used most often to indicate a decorative and/or functional rim or edging of a table, stand, or base (Ex. 25:25, 27; 7:28, 29, 31; 2 Kgs. 16:17). It also has the sense of a fortress erected around persons for defense or protection (2 Sam. 22:46; Ps. 18:45; Mic. 7:17); also translated stronghold. Other refs.: Ex. 37:12, 14; 1 Kgs. 7:32, 35, 36. ¶
– [2] Ex. 27:5; 38:4 ➔ LEDGE <3749>
[3] 1 Kgs. 7:33; Ezek. 1:18 ➔ BACK <1354>.

RIMMON – ***rimmôn, rimmônô, rimmôn hammᵉtō'ār*** [proper noun: רִמּוֹן, רִמּוֹנוֹ, רִמּוֹן הַמְּתֹאָר <7417>; the same as POMEGRANATE <7416>]: pomegranate ►
a. A masculine proper noun referring to Rimmon: a Syrian god. It refers to the god Hadad, a storm god, under another name. He was revered in Damascus, the capital of Syria. Naaman worshiped him (2 Kgs. 5:18).
b. A masculine proper noun referring to Rimmon: a Benjaminite. He was from the city of Beeroth. He was the father of Baanah and Rechab (2 Sam. 4:2, 5, 9).
c. A proper noun, Rimmon: a rock in the wilderness of Benjamin. It refers to a cliff full of caves in the area of Gibeah (Judg. 20:45, 47; 21:13).
d. A proper noun, Rimmon: a town in an undisclosed place but in the south of Judah toward Edom. Refs.: Josh. 15:32; 19:7; 1 Chr. 4:32; Zech. 14:10.
e. A proper noun, Rimmon: a town in Zebulun. It may lie about ten kilometers north of Nazareth. It was a city of the Levites (Josh. 19:13; 1 Chr. 6:77).
f. A proper noun, Remmonmethoar: Rimmon. A town located on the northeast border of Zebulun, due west of the center of the Sea of Galilee. Ref.: Josh. 19:13. ¶

RIMMON PEREZ – ***rimmôn pereṣ*** [proper noun: רִמֹּן פֶּרֶץ <7428>; from POMEGRANATE <7416> and BREACH <6556>]: pomegranate of the breach ► **A campsite of the Israelites in the desert on their way to Canaan.** Refs.: Num. 33:19, 20. ¶

RING – [1] ***gāliyl*** [adj., masc. noun: גָּלִיל <1550>; from ROLL (verb) <1556>] ▶ **This word indicates circles or rods to which cords were attached.** Ref.: Esther 1:6. It is used by a bride to describe the groom's hands (Song 5:14), indicating their strength and beauty. It also means folding, pivot (1 Kgs. 6:34); see FOLDING <1550>. ¶
[2] ***ṭabba'aṯ*** [fem. noun: טַבַּעַת <2885>; from DROWN <2883> (properly as sunk into the wax in the case of a seal)] ▶ **This word designates a signet band with a seal on it.** Refs.: Gen. 41:42; Esther 3:10, 12. It designates also jewelry (Ex. 35:22; Is. 3:21). It is used to refer to large rings used to hang curtains on or to put the poles into to carry the ark (Ex. 25:12; 35:22; 36:29). *
[3] ***nezem*** [masc. noun: נֶזֶם <5141>; from an unused root of uncertain meaning] ▶ **This word designates an earring, a nose ring.** It is used to describe a circular piece of jewelry worn on the wrist, ear, or nose (Gen. 24:22, 30, 47; 35:4); sometimes associated with idolatry (Ex. 32:2, 3; Hos. 2:13). These items were considered ornaments of luxury (Is. 3:21); and beauty (Ezek. 16:12). Earrings were characteristic of Israelites (Judg. 8:24–26). These jewelry pieces are referred to in proverbs (Prov. 11:22) to make comparisons (Prov. 25:12). Other refs.: Ex. 35:22; Job 42:11. ¶

RINGSTRAKED – Gen. 30:35, 39, 40; 31:8, 10, 12 ➔ STRIPED <6124>.

RINNAH – ***rinnāh*** [masc. proper noun: רִנָּה <7441>; from SHOUT (verb) <7442>]: shout of joy ▶ **An Israelite of the tribe of Judah.** Ref.: 1 Chr. 4:20. ¶

RINSE – 2 Chr. 4:6; Jer. 51:34; Ezek. 40:38 ➔ WASH <1740>.

RIOTOUS – Prov. 28:7 ➔ GLUTTON (BE) <2151> a.

RIPE (BE) – Joel 3:13 ➔ COOK (verb) <1310>.

RIPE FRUITS, RIPE PRODUCE – Ex. 22:29 ➔ HARVEST <4395>.

RIPEN – ***ḥānaṭ, ḥ^{a}nuṭiym*** [verb: חָנַט, חֲנֻטִים <2590>; a prim. root] ▶ **This word is used poetically, meaning to spice, in the sense that the fig tree spices its fruit, filling it with fragrant juice as it matures. It means to form, to mature and redden.** It refers to the process of the ripening of the fig tree (Song 2:13) or its production of figs; also translated to put forth. The Hebrew word also means to embalm (EMBALM <2590>). ¶

RIPEN EARLY – Jer. 24:2 ➔ FIRST RIPE <1073>.

RIPENING GRAPE – Is. 18:5 ➔ UNRIPE GRAPE <1155>.

RIPHATH – ***riyp̱aṯ, diyp̱aṯ*** [proper noun: רִיפַת, דִּיפַת <7384>; of foreign origin] ▶
a. One of the sons of Gomer. Refs.: Gen. 10:3; 1 Chr. 1:6. ¶
b. Another spelling: Diphath. Refs.: Gen. 10:3; 1 Chr. 1:6. ¶

RISE – [1] ***gā'āh*** [verb: גָּאָה <1342>; a prim. root] ▶ **This verb means to grow up, to exalt, to lift up.** It is used physically of a stream in Ezekiel 47:5, "The waters were risen"; and of plants in Job 8:11, "Can the rush grow up without mire?" In a figurative sense, it speaks of a lifting up or exaltation (specifically of God). The verb emphatically describes God's matchless power in Miriam's song (Ex. 15:1, 21). This is the key usage of *gā'āh*: The Lord only is highly exalted (or: He has triumphed gloriously). The horse and rider He easily casts into the sea; He alone legitimately lifts up the head, as Job admits in Job 10:16. None can stand before Him. Some Hebrew words derived from this one express an important negative theme—that of lifting up of one's self in wrongful pride against the rightful place of God: *gê'eh* (PROUD <1343>); *ga^{a}wāh* (MAJESTY <1346>); and *gā'ôn* (MAJESTY <1347>). ¶
[2] ***rā'am*** [verb: רָאַם <7213>; a prim. root] ▶ **This word means to be lifted up. It refers to something being raised high above other things.** It refers to Jerusalem's

exalted place in the era of God's Great King (Zech. 14:10). ¶
– [3] 1 Sam. 14:5 → PILLAR <4690> [4] Ezra 4:19 → INSURRECTION (MAKE) <5376> [5] Ps. 89:9 → ARISE <7721>.

RISE AGAINST – Is. 3:5 → BOLD (BE, MAKE) <7292>.

RISE EARLY – ***šāḵam*** [verb: שָׁכַם <7925>; a prim. root] ▶ **This word uniformly indicates getting up early (at the very beginning of the day) to do something, often to pack and go on a journey.** This procedure is especially appropriate in Israel where the afternoons are extremely hot: even angels, messengers, rose early to travel (Gen. 19:2); as well as humans (Gen. 19:27; 20:8; 21:14; 22:3, etc.). Job rose early to sacrifice and pray for his family (Job 1:5). It can be used to indicate excessive labor on the part of a person trying to get ahead, to prosper (Ps. 127:2). Some things are not appropriate at such an early hour (Prov. 27:14). The Lord had risen early and had diligently, eagerly spoken to a rebellious people (Jer. 7:13, 25). It has the sense in several contexts of eagerness (Jer. 7:25; Zeph. 3:7). *

RISE UP – [1] ***zāraḥ*** [verb: זָרַח <2224>; a prim. root] ▶ **This verb means to lift up, also to dawn, to shine forth, to break out.** It refers to the rising or shining of the sun (Gen. 32:31). It refers figuratively to the rising reputation or approval of a person who does good to the hungry and poor (Is. 58:10) or to God dawning on Israel from Mount Seir (Deut. 33:2). Used of illnesses, it describes the breaking out of skin diseases (2 Chr. 26:19). *
– [2] Is. 33:3 → LIFTING UP <7427> [3] Ezek. 10:15 → EXALTED <7426> a.

RISES UP (ONE WHO) – ***teqômêm*** [masc. noun, part.: תְּקוֹמֵם <8618>; from STAND, STAND UP <6965>] ▶ **This word means in context to take a hostile stand against persons, to become their nemesis, to be hostile toward them.** Ref.: Ps. 139:21; NIV: one who is in rebellion. ¶

RISING – [1] ***zeraḥ*** [masc. noun: זֶרַח <2225>; from RISE UP <2224>] ▶ **This word indicates dawning of something.** It indicates sunrise or the shining forth of light (Is. 60:3), but it is used metaphorically of the Lord rising up over Zion. ¶
– [2] Ps. 19:6 → GOING OUT, GOING FORTH <4161> [3] Ps. 32:6 → FLOOD <7858> [4] Is. 9:18 → MAJESTY <1348>.

RISING, RISING UP – ***qiymāh*** [fem. noun: קִימָה <7012>; from STAND, STAND UP <6965>] ▶ **This word means literally an arising, a standing from a sitting position.** In context it refers to the actions and activities of persons, their sitting and rising, all they do all the time (Lam. 3:63). ¶

RISSAH – ***rissāh*** [proper noun: רִסָּה <7446>; from MOISTEN <7450> (as something dripping on pieces)]: ruin ▶ **A campsite of the Israelites in the desert on their way to Canaan.** Refs.: Num. 33:21, 22. ¶

RITMAH – ***riṯmāh*** [masc. proper noun: רִתְמָה <7575>; fem. of BROOM TREE <7574>]: broom tree ▶ **A campsite of the Israelites in the desert on their way to Canaan**. Refs.: Num. 33:18, 19. ¶

RIVAL (noun) – 1 Sam. 1:6 → TROUBLE (noun) <6869> b.

RIVAL (verb) – Ezek. 31:8 → DIM (BECOME, GROW) <6004>.

RIVER – [1] ***ye'ōr, ye'ôr*** [masc. noun: יְאֹר, יְאוֹר <2975>; of Egyptian origin] ▶ **This word means a watercourse in general. It refers to various streams of water, including, importantly, the Nile River.** It is used to designate the Nile River (Gen. 41:1–3; Ex. 1:22; 2 Kgs. 19:24; Amos 8:8; 9:5) often. It also refers to the branches and the canals of the Nile River (Ex. 7:19) and to various canals or streams (NASB, NIV) in general (Is. 33:21). The word designates the Tigris River (Dan. 12:5–7). It is used of hollow shafts dug out for mining (Job 28:10). The Egyptians and their military activities of invasion are compared to a rising Nile River (Jer. 46:7, 8). *

2 ***nᵉhar*** [Aramaic masc. noun: נְהַר <5103>; from a root corresponding to FLOW (verb) <5102>] ▶ **This word refers to a large, flowing body of water: the Euphrates River.** Refs.: Ezra 4:10, 11, 16; 5:3; 6:6; 7:21. It is used metaphorically of a flowing river of fire (Dan. 7:10). *

3 ***nāhār*** [masc. noun: נָהָר <5104>; from FLOW (verb) <5102>] ▶ **This word indicates a large, flowing body of water or a current within a sea.** Any river in general (Num. 24:6; Job 14:11); specific rivers (Gen. 2:10, 13, 14); Euphrates River (Gen. 15:18; 31:21; Num. 22:5); Tigris River (Dan. 10:4); Nile River or El Arish River (Gen. 15:18). It refers to a current of water within a sea (Jon. 2:3). It is used figuratively and literally of a river flowing around the city of God (Ps. 46:4); as well as to underground flows of water (Job 28:11). *

– 4 Job 20:17 ➔ DIVISION <6390> 5 Job 29:6; Ps. 1:3; 65:9; 119:36; Prov. 5:16; 21:1; Is. 30:25; 32:2; Lam. 3:48 ➔ STREAM (noun) <6388> 6 Jer. 17:8 ➔ STREAM (noun) <3105> 7 Dan. 8:2, 3, 6 ➔ CANAL <180>.

RIZPAH – ***riṣpāh*** [fem. proper noun: רִצְפָּה <7532>; the same as HOT COAL <7531>, PAVEMENT <7531>]: hot coal, pavement ▶ **A concubine of King Saul.** Refs.: 2 Sam. 3:7; 21:8, 10, 11. ¶

ROAD – 1 1 Sam. 4:13 ➔ WAYSIDE <3197> 2 Jer. 18:15 ➔ PATH <7635>.

ROAD MARKER – Jer. 31:21 ➔ MONUMENT <6725>.

ROAD SIGN – Jer. 31:21 ➔ MONUMENT <6725>.

ROADMARK – Jer. 31:21 ➔ MONUMENT <6725>.

ROAM – 1 Job 30:3 ➔ GNAW, GNAWING <6207> b. 2 Jer. 2:31 ➔ RESTLESS (BE, BECOME, GROW) <7300>.

ROAMING – Lam. 1:7; 3:19 ➔ WANDERING <4788>.

ROAR (noun) – 1 ***naham*** [masc. noun: נַהַם <5099>; from ROAR (verb) <5098>] ▶ **This word means a snarl, a growl. It is used of the threatening sound that a lion of prey makes when provoked.** In context it is used of the roaring of a king's wrath against those who agitate it (Prov. 19:12; 20:2; also translated growling). ¶

– 2 Job 37:2 ➔ TURMOIL <7267> 3 Ps. 96:11; 98:7 ➔ THUNDER (verb) <7481> 4 Jer. 11:16 ➔ NOISE <1999>.

ROAR (verb) – 1 ***nāham*** [verb: נָהַם <5098>; a prim. root] ▶ **This word means to groan, to growl loudly; to groan (in suffering).** It expresses the deep guttural, piercing growl of a lion, especially as it grasps its prey (Prov. 28:15; Is. 5:29, 30). It expresses the despairing groan of a person who is destroyed by immoral behavior (Prov. 5:11: to groan, to mourn). It is the groan of persons forced into captivity in exile (Ezek. 24:23). ¶

2 ***šā'ag*** [verb: שָׁאַג <7580>; a prim. root] ▶ **This Hebrew word means to shout loudly (in victory or distress).** It describes the sound of a lion as it is attacking (Judg. 14:5; Amos 3:4). It describes the Lord as He roars in unrelenting judgment against His people (Jer. 25:30; Hos. 11:10; Joel 3:16; Amos 1:2; 3:8). It describes the sound of thunder after lightning (Job 37:4). The enemies of the righteous roar as lions against them (Ps. 22:13; 74:4). It depicts the sound of aggressive, destroying rulers (Zeph. 3:3); or it indicates a person's crying out in distress (Ps. 38:8). *

3 ***šā'āh*** [verb: שָׁאָה <7582>; a prim. root] ▶ **This word means to make a loud noise, a din, crash or tumult. It indicates figuratively the commotion and confusion, the great noise of nations in their hostile actions.** Refs.: Is. 17:12, 13; also translated to rush, to rumble. For another meaning of the Hebrew word, see WASTE (LAY, LIE) <7582>. ¶

– 4 Ps. 38:8 ➔ ROARING <5100> 5 Is. 42:13 ➔ CRY (verb) <6873>.

ROARING – 1 ***nᵉhāmāh*** [fem. noun: נְהָמָה <5100>; from ROAR (noun) <5099>] ▶

This word refers to agitation. It indicates a loud, disturbing noise or emotion. It is used of a palpitating heart or a heart despairing of hope (Ps. 38:8). It indicates the sound made by the breakers of the sea on the seashore (Is. 5:30; also translated growling). ¶
[2] ***še'āgāh*** [fem. noun: שְׁאָגָה <7581>; from ROAR (verb) <7580>] ▶ **This word depicts the shouting of a lion; shouting in distress.** It describes the shouting and din of invading armies (Is. 5:29). It is used figuratively of the cry of destroying enemies (Zech. 11:3). It has the sense of a person moaning or groaning (Job 3:24; Ps. 22:1; 32:3). It refers literally to the roar of a lion (Job 4:10). It is used figuratively of the Lord's action against His corrupt leaders (Ezek. 19:7). ¶
– [3] Ps. 93:3 ➔ POUNDING WAVE <1796> [4] Prov. 19:12; 20:2 ➔ ROAR (noun) <5099>.

ROAST – [1] ***ḥāraḵ*** [verb: חָרַךְ <2760>; a prim. root] ▶ **This word means to cook game over the fire. Food prepared in this manner was more succulent than food prepared by boiling.** Ref.: Prov. 12:27. ¶
[2] ***ṣālāh*** [verb: צָלָה <6740>; a prim. root] ▶ **This word means to cook something over an open fire or in hot coals or embers.** Ref.: 1 Sam. 2:15. It describes roasting meat in a context that mocks idolatry (Is. 44:16, 19). ¶
[3] ***qālāh*** [verb: קָלָה <7033>; a prim. root] ▶
a. This word means to parch, to dry. It means to expose certain vegetables to heat, to dry them out, to parch them (Lev. 2:14; Josh. 5:11). It means to cook something or burn it in fire (Jer. 29:22).
b. This word means to be burning, searing. It is used figuratively of guilt causing great inner psychological terror and pain (Ps. 38:7).
c. This word means to be loathsome. It refers to a person feeling abhorrent, loathsome because of guilt and the need for penitence (Ps. 38:7). ¶

ROASTED – ***ṣāliy*** [adj.: צָלִי <6748>; pass. part. of ROAST <6740>] ▶ **This word refers to something cooked.** It indicates cooking meat over an open fire, coals, or embers (Ex. 12:8, 9; Is. 44:16). It describes satirically the roasting of part of an idol over a fire. ¶

ROASTED GRAIN – Lev. 23:14; Ruth 2:14; 1 Sam. 17:17; 25:18; 2 Sam. 17:28 ➔ PARCHED GRAIN <7039>.

ROB – [1] ***gāzal*** [verb: גָּזַל <1497>; a prim. root] ▶ **This word means to take away something illegally, by force.** It is used often figuratively, as evil leaders of Israel pulling off or tearing off the skin of God's people (Mic. 3:2). In another figurative usage, it means to take away or deprive persons of their rights (Is. 10:2) or for sleep to be taken away (Prov. 4:16). In a literal sense, it describes the seizing of the houses of the oppressed (Mic. 2:2). Other objects are seized or taken away: wells (Gen. 21:25) or women (Gen. 31:31). It means to rob persons of their personal property (Judg. 9:25; Job 24:2) or even children (Job 24:9). *
[2] ***qāḇa'*** [verb: קָבַע <6906>; a prim. root] ▶ **This word means to take something away, to plunder.** It refers to taking the life and property of the oppressed and afflicted in context (Prov. 22:23). It indicates keeping back what belongs properly to God (Mal. 3:8, 9). ¶

ROBBED OF HER CUBS – 2 Sam. 17:8; Prov. 17:12; Hos. 13:8 ➔ BEREAVED <7909>.

ROBBER – [1] ***ḥeṯep*** [masc. noun: חֶתֶף <2863>; from SNATCH AWAY <2862>] ▶ **This word literally means the violent seizure of someone's property. It is used in likening an adulterous woman's behavior to that of a "robber," one who takes what is not hers.** Ref.: Prov. 23:28; also translated bandit; KJV and NKJV: *for* a prey, *for* a victim. ¶
– [2] Job 5:5 ➔ SNARE (noun) <6782> [3] Jer. 7:11; Ezek. 7:22; 18:10; Dan. 11:14 ➔ VIOLENT <6530>.

ROBBERY – [1] ***gāzêl*** [masc. noun: גָּזֵל <1498>; from ROB <1497>] ▶ **This word**

indicates the violent seizure of property; concretely it refers to something taken away, stolen. It refers to the sin of robbery that can be atoned for by a guilt offering (Lev. 6:2; Ps. 62:10). The Lord hates this sin (Is. 61:8), but it was one of the oppressive sins of Israel (Ezek. 22:29), especially against the poor, the needy, and the sojourners. ¶

2 ***gêzel*** [masc. noun: גֵּזֶל <1499>; from ROB <1497>] ► **This word refers to stealing, denial.** It is a strong word indicating the denial or even violent perversion (KJV) of something such as the robbery of justice (Eccl. 5:8). It can indicate robbing one's relative, doing what is not good but evil (Ezek. 18:18), a characteristic of an unrighteous person. ¶

3 **what is taken by robbery: *gᵉzêlāh*** [fem. noun: גְּזֵלָה <1500>; fem. of <1498> above] ► **This word refers to something taken away, stolen.** It can be atoned for by a guilt offering (Lev. 6:4). Isaiah uses the word in the sense of plunder or spoil taken from the poor (Is. 3:14). The righteous person avoids this robbery or plunder (Ezek. 18:7), but the evil person engages in it (Ezek. 18:12; 33:15). Other ref.: Ezek. 18:16. ¶

– 4 Nah. 3:1 ➔ PLUNDER (noun) <6563>.

ROBE – 1 ***'eḏer*** [masc. noun: אֶדֶר <145>; from GLORIOUS <142>] ► **The word means a garment that is handsome, great, glorious; it also means something splendid.** In Micah 2:8, it refers to a rich robe or a splendid garment, while in Zechariah 11:13, it evidently means something magnificent (also translated goodly, princely, lordly, handsome) in relation to the price that would be paid for the potter's field. ¶

2 ***mᵉ'iyl*** [masc. noun: מְעִיל <4598>; from TRANSGRESS <4603> (which properly means to cover up)] ► **This garment was an important part of the clothing worn by key classes of persons in Israel and the ancient Middle East.** It is used of the robe of the high priest (Ex. 28:4, 31; 29:5; 39:22). It had fringes on the bottom (Ex. 28:34; 39:24). An opening, the *pîy* (mouth), was created for a person's head (Ex. 39:23). According to 2 Samuel 13:18, David's daughter wore this garment. It was worn by other persons of rank (1 Sam. 18:4; 24:4); Job (Job 1:20); Job's friends (Job 2:12); chief merchants (Ezek. 26:16); persons in training for high offices (1 Sam. 2:19). It is used also in a figurative sense of the character and attributes of the Lord: justice (Job 29:14); zeal for judgment (Is. 59:17); righteousness (Is. 61:10). It is used to describe the character of oppressors as one of shame, dishonor (Ps. 109:29). *

3 ***taḵriyḵ*** [masc. noun: תַּכְרִיךְ <8509>; apparently from an unused root meaning to encompass] ► **This word refers to a long, loose, regal garment without sleeves.** It was worn in the Persian palaces and awarded to Mordecai in its biblical context (Esther 8:15). ¶

– 4 Gen. 37:3; etc. ➔ COAT (noun) <3801> 5 Lev. 6:10; 1 Sam. 18:4 ➔ CLOTHES <4055> 6 Josh. 7:21, 24; Jon. 3:6; Zech. 13:4 ➔ GARMENT <155> 7 Is. 3:23 ➔ VEIL <7289> 8 Is. 47:2 ➔ SKIRT <7640> 9 Dan. 3:21, 27 ➔ COAT (noun) <5622>.

ROBE (FESTAL, FINE, RICH) – Is. 3:22; Zech. 3:4 ➔ FESTAL APPAREL <4254>.

ROBES – 1 Kgs. 10:5; 2 Kgs. 10:22b; 2 Chr. 9:4; Is. 63:3 ➔ CLOTHING <4403>.

ROCK – 1 ***kêp̱*** [masc. noun: כֵּף <3710>; from BOW, BOW DOWN <3721> (in the sense of to curve)] ► **This word refers to rocks (aggregates of minerals) in the hills or mountains.** Ref.: Jer. 4:29. It refers as well to rocks in the ground on the lowland (Job 30:6). ¶

2 ***ṣûr*** [masc. noun: צוּר <6697>; from BESIEGE <6696>] ► **This word refers properly to a cliff (or sharp rock, as compressed).** It relates to a large rock, a boulder (Judg. 6:21; 13:19; 2 Sam. 21:10); a cliff or wall of rock (Ex. 17:6). It is used in figurative expressions: honey from the rock, from rock clefts where some bees lived (Ps. 81:16); of Abraham as the ancestral rock of Israel (Is. 51:1); of a rock as a symbol

of stability (Job 14:18; Nah. 1:6); of God as the Rock to look to and depend on (Ps. 31:2; Is. 17:10); of a rock personified, e.g., as Israel (2 Sam. 23:3); of God as the Rock many times (Deut. 32:4, 18; Hab. 1:12). It is used of an insufficient rock, a god of the pagan nations (Deut. 32:31). *

3 ***sela'*** [masc. noun: סֶלַע <5553>; from an unused root meaning to be lofty] ▶ **This word means a high rock, a cliff, a towering rock, as a place of defense. Memorably, David used this word to describe God as his Rock.** Refs.: 2 Sam. 22:2; Ps. 18:2; 31:3; 42:9. It refers to single rocks (1 Sam. 23:25); a crag or cliff (Judg. 6:20; Is. 2:21); a hollowed-out place in a rock for a burial spot (Is. 22:16). It refers to the habitations of Edom in clefts of the rocks (Obad. 1:3). It is a symbol of total destruction for the city of Tyre (Ezek. 26:4, 14). It describes figuratively God's destruction of Babylon (Jer. 51:25). *

ROCK PILE – Job 8:17 ➔ HEAP (noun) <1530>.

ROD – 1 ***ḥōṭer*** [masc. noun: חֹטֶר <2415>; from an unused root of uncertain signification] ▶ **This word means a stick or a branch.** In Proverbs 14:3, this word describes a stick used for discipline. In Isaiah 11:1, it is nuanced by the context to mean a fresh shoot or fresh twig. It stands in parallelism with *nêṣer*, branch in this verse (Branch = Messiah, Anointed King). ¶

2 ***šêḇeṭ*** [masc. noun: שֵׁבֶט <7626>; from an unused root prob. meaning to branch off] ▶ **This word means a staff, and also a scepter, a tribe.** It is presented in parallel with the word *maṭṭeh* (STAFF <4294>) that designates a rod or a tribe (Is. 10:15). As a rod, it represents a common tool used as a shepherd's staff (Lev. 27:32; Ezek. 20:37); a crude weapon (2 Sam. 23:21); or for beating out cumin (Is. 28:27). It also refers to the shaft of a spear (2 Sam. 18:14). The rod was also used in meting out discipline, both literally for a slave (Ex. 21:20); a fool (Prov. 10:13; 26:3); and a son (Prov. 13:24; 22:15; 29:15); and figuratively of God against Solomon (2 Sam. 7:14); of God against Israel through Assyria (Is. 10:24); against Philistia (Is. 14:29); and of God against Assyria (Is. 30:31). Because of the association between smiting and ruling, the rod became a symbol of the authority of the one bearing it; thus, this word can also mean a scepter (Gen. 49:10; Judg. 5:14; Is. 14:5). Also, the connotation of tribe is based on the connection between this term and the concept of rulership. It can connote the tribes of Israel collectively (Gen. 49:16; Deut. 33:5); or individually (Josh. 7:16; Judg. 18:1). It can also represent a portion of one of the tribes (Num. 4:18; Judg. 20:12; 1 Sam. 9:21). Eventually, the term was used in the singular to denote Israel as a whole (Ps. 74:2; Jer. 10:16; 51:19). It is also interesting to note that this word was never used in reference to the tribes of other nations. *

– 3 Gen. 30:37–39, 41; Jer. 1:11; 48:17; Hos. 4:12 ➔ STICK <4731> 4 Lev. 27:32; Ezek. 20:37; etc. ➔ ROD <7626> 5 1 Sam. 17:7; 2 Sam. 21:19; 1 Chr. 11:23; 20:5 ➔ BEAM <4500> 6 Esther 1:6; Song 5:14 ➔ RING <1550> 7 Job 40:18 ➔ BAR <4300> 8 See STAFF <4294>.

RODANIM – Gen. 10:4; 1 Chr. 1:7 ➔ DODANIM <1721> b.

ROE – Prov. 5:19 ➔ DOE <3280>.

ROE DEER – Deut. 14:5 ➔ ROEBUCK <3180>.

ROEBUCK – ***yaḥmûr*** [masc. noun: יַחְמוּר <3180>; from RED (BE) <2560>] ▶ **This word refers to a roe, a deer, a member of a small species of deer; it is also translated roe deer, fallowdeer.** It refers to a roebuck (Deut. 14:5), an animal declared clean and edible for the Israelites by God. It was a choice sacrificial animal (1 Kgs. 4:23). ¶

ROGELIM – ***rōgliym*** [proper noun: רֹגְלִים <7274>; plur. of act. part. of WALK (TEACH TO) <7270> (in the sense of trampling something)]: place of fullers ▶ **Hometown of Barzillai the Gileadite, who was a faithful follower of King David; a place east of the Jordan.** Refs.: 2 Sam. 17:27; 19:31. ¶

ROGUE – Is. 32:5, 7 ➔ SCOUNDREL <3596>.

ROHGAH – ***rôhᵃgāh, rohgāh*** [masc. proper noun: רוֹהֲגָה, רָהְגָּה <7303>; from an unused root prob. meaning to cry out]: outcry ▶ **An Israelite of the tribe of Asher.** Ref.: 1 Chr. 7:34. ¶

ROLL (noun) – Ezra 6:1 ➔ BOOK <5609>.

ROLL (verb) – 1 ***gālal*** [verb: גָּלַל <1556>; a prim. root] ▶ **The root idea of the verb is to turn over and over. It means also to remove, to commit, to trust.** The Hebrew word often refers to rolling stones (Gen. 29:8; Josh. 10:18; Prov. 26:27) as well as other concrete objects. It can also describe abstract concepts, such as reproach being rolled off (removed, taken away) from someone (Ps. 119:22) or one's ways and works rolled onto (committed, entrusted) to someone (especially God) (Ps. 37:5; Prov. 16:3). This important root word is used to form many other names and words (cf. Gilgal in Josh. 5:9). *
2 ***gālam*** [verb: גָּלַם <1563>; a prim. root] ▶ **This word means to wrap up, to fold together. It describes the folding of the mantle of Elijah.** He used it to part the Jordan River and walk through on dry ground (2 Kgs. 2:8). ¶
– 3 Is. 22:18 ➔ WEAR <6801> 4 Jer. 5:22 ➔ SHAKE <1607>.

ROLL ABOUT – Jer. 6:26; 25:34; Ezek. 27:30 ➔ ROLL IN <6428>.

ROLL IN – ***pālaš*** [verb: פָּלַשׁ <6428>; a prim. root] ▶ **This word means to turn over and over or to turn from side to side; it is also translated to wallow in.** Rolling in ashes or dust depicted great distress and sorrow (Jer. 6:26; 25:34; Ezek. 27:30; Mic. 1:10). ¶

ROLL UP – ***qāpad̠*** [verb: קָפַד <7088>; a prim. root] ▶
a. This word indicates to fold something up into a tubular form. It is used figuratively of closing out, rolling up one's life (Is. 38:12).
b. This word could also mean to cut off. It describes a piece of cloth being cut off. In context it refers figuratively to Hezekiah's fear of the cutting off his life, like a weaver cuts off pieces of cloth (Is. 38:12). ¶

ROLL UPWARD – ***'āḇak̠*** [verb: אָבַךְ <55>; a prim. root] ▶ **This word is used in a reflexive sense in Isaiah 9:18 with the meaning to rise and roll upward; it is also translated to mount up.** In this context, it refers figuratively to the rolling, rising smoke of briars, thorns, and thickets that have been set on fire by Israel's wickedness. ¶

ROLLER – Ezek. 30:21 ➔ BANDAGE <2848>.

ROLLING THING – Is. 17:13 ➔ WHEEL <1534>.

ROMAMTI-EZER – ***rômamtiy 'ezer, rōmamtiy 'ezer*** [masc. proper noun: רוֹמַמְתִּי עֶזֶר, רֹמַמְתִּי עֶזֶר <7320>; from EXALT <7311> and HELP (noun) <5828>]: I have exalted a help ▶ **One of the sons of King David's musician Heman.** Refs.: 1 Chr. 25:4, 31. ¶

ROOF (noun) – 1 ***gāg̠*** [masc. noun: גָּג <1406>; prob. by reduplication from RISE <1342>] ▶ **This word indicates something that covers the top of a structure; it is also translated top.** It describes various roofs: a house roof (Deut. 22:8); a flat roof (1 Sam. 9:25, 26); a palace roof (2 Sam. 11:2); or roof of a tower (Judg. 9:51). Persons could walk about and gather on these roofs. Illicit altars were sometimes located on roofs (2 Kgs. 23:12; Jer. 19:13), as in the time of Ahaz, a wicked king. Lamentations and wailing took place on rooftops from where the destruction of a city or village was visible (Is. 15:3). The corner of a roof depicts a meager and inadequate place to live (Prov. 21:9). It refers to the top of the altar of incense (Ex. 30:3; 37:26). *
– 2 Gen. 6:16 ➔ WINDOW <6672> 3 Gen. 19:8 ➔ BEAM <6982> 4 Eccl. 10:18 ➔ RAFTER <4746>.

ROOF (verb) – Neh. 3:1 ➔ COVER (verb) <2926>.

ROOF CHAMBER – ***meqêrāh*** [fem. noun: מְקֵרָה <4747>; from the same as COLD (adj.) <7119>] ► **This word means and is also translated upper room, parlor.** It refers to a room or special patio-like chamber where the wind cools it during the day (Judg. 3:20, 24). ¶

ROOF OF THE MOUTH – 1 Ps. 22:15 ➔ JAW <4455> 2 Ps. 137:6; Lam. 4:4; Ezek. 3:26 ➔ MOUTH <2441>.

ROOM – 1 ***ḥeḏer*** [masc. noun: חֶדֶר <2315>; from SURROUND <2314>] ► **This word refers to a chamber, a parlor, an enclosure.** It combines with other words to indicate various rooms, spaces, or enclosures: a room of lying down, a sleeping room (Ex. 8:3; 2 Sam. 4:7; 2 Kgs. 6:12; Eccl. 10:20); a bedroom toilet or cool room (Judg. 3:24; 2 Kgs. 11:2); an inner chamber (1 Chr. 28:11). Repeated with *be* attached to the front of the second occurrence of the word, it means one room (in)to another (1 Kgs. 20:30). Preceded by *min* (FROM <4480>), it has the meaning of indoors (Deut. 32:25). It is combined figuratively before *beṭen*, belly, womb, to refer to internal parts of the body (Prov. 18:8); and before *māšeṯ*, death, to refer to the rooms or chambers of death or Sheol (Prov. 7:27). It is used in a technical sense of the southern constellations (Job 9:9; cf. Job 37:9). *

2 ***liškāh*** [fem. noun: לִשְׁכָּה <3957>; from an unused root of uncertain meaning] ► **This word refers to a chamber, a storeroom; a hall. It refers to an area in a building having three walls furnished with benches for worshipers.** The fourth wall was open facing the courtyard (1 Sam. 9:22; 2 Kgs. 23:11; Jer. 35:2, 4; 36:10, 12, 20, 21). It seems to refer to storerooms as well (1 Chr. 28:12; 2 Chr. 31:11). In Ezekiel's visionary Temple, it referred to cells for various temple personnel (Ezek. 40:17, 38, 44, 46; 42:1). In the Temple of Ezra and Nehemiah, the word is used of storerooms (Ezra 8:29; Neh. 10:38). *

3 ***tā'*** [masc. noun: תָּא <8372>; from (the base of) DRAW A LINE <8376> (in the sense of to circumscribe, e.g., a room)] ► **This word refers to a chamber, a guardroom.** It refers to a guardroom or a chamber of a palace or temple (1 Kgs. 14:28; 2 Chr. 12:11; Ezek. 40:7, 10, 12, 13, 16, 21, 29, 33, 36). ¶

– 4 Neh. 3:30; 12:4; 13:7 ➔ CHAMBER <5393> 5 Dan. 6:10: upper room, upstairs room ➔ CHAMBER <5952>.

ROOST – Is. 60:8 ➔ WINDOW <699>.

ROOSTER – Job 38:36 ➔ MIND <7907>.

ROOT (noun) – 1 ***kannāh*** [fem. noun: כַּנָּה <3657>; from SHOOT UP <3661>] ► **This word means and is also translated shoot, stock, vineyard.** It is used figuratively of Israel as the root God Himself planted, indicating His son or vine (Ps. 80:15). ¶

2 ***šereš*** [masc. noun: שֹׁרֶשׁ <8328>; from ROOT (TAKE) <8327>] ► **This word refers to the base of something; it also indicates depth. It is often used figuratively.** It refers to the life-generating tentacles that a plant puts out in the ground (2 Kgs. 19:30; Job 14:8; Jer. 17:8). In a figurative sense, it refers to the hostile attitudes found in persons that create strife and bitterness (Deut. 29:18). It refers to an origin, a beginning (Judg. 5:14). Figuratively, good persons put their roots around rocks (Job 8:17). It may be translated as soles (NASB) of one's feet, the foundation of one's life (Job 13:27; KJV: heels). The roots of the wicked are destined to destruction (Job 18:16); the roots of the righteous stand forever (Prov. 12:3). The base or foundation of a mountain is its roots (Job 28:9). It is used of Israel herself taking root and prospering (Ps. 80:9). The coming messianic king, the Branch, will spring from the roots of the Davidic line (Is. 11:1); the root of Jesse (Is. 11:10). The Suffering Servant's root source was fragile (Is. 53:2). The whole picture of Ezekiel 17:6, 7, 9 utilizes the figurative use of roots to describe nations and peoples. Roots imply descendants in Daniel 11:7.

Israel's roots in her future restoration will propel her to prosperity (Hos. 14:5). God's final acts of judgment will destroy the roots of evildoers with fire (Mal. 4:1). *
[3] ***šōreš*** [Aramaic masc. noun: שֹׁרֶשׁ <8330>; corresponding to <8328> above] ▶ **This word is employed figuratively and refers to the underground base of a huge tree in a dream which Nebuchadnezzar had.** Refs.: Dan. 4:15, 23, 26. ¶

ROOT (TAKE) – ***šāraš*** [verb: שָׁרַשׁ <8327>; prim. root] ▶ **This word means to grow roots; it also means to uproot. It is used often in a figurative sense.** It means to put out, to grow roots (Ps. 80:9; Is. 27:6; 40:24; Jer. 12:2). In its passive sense, it means to be uprooted (Job 31:8, 12). Even the foolish person may take root but will not be stable (Job 5:3). The wicked person will finally be uprooted from this life (Ps. 52:5). ¶

ROOT (verb) – Prov. 2:22 ➔ TEAR <5255>.

ROOT UP – Zeph. 2:4 ➔ HAMSTRING <6131> b.

ROOTED OUT – Ps. 52:5; Job 31:8 ➔ ROOT (TAKE) <8327>.

ROOTS – Jon. 2:6 ➔ FORM (noun) <7095>.

ROOTS (PLUCK UP, PLUCK OUT, PULL OUT BY THE) – ***ʿaqar*** [Aramaic verb: עֲקַר <6132>; corresponding to HAMSTRING <6131> b. (in the sense of to pluck out, to root out)] ▶ **This word means to tear something out, to destroy it, to remove it by the roots.** It is used figuratively of tearing out men or rulers (Dan. 7:8; NIV: to uproot). ¶

ROPE – [1] ***'agmôn*** [masc. noun: אַגְמוֹן <100>; from the same as POND <98>] ▶ **The word refers to a cord, reed, cord of reeds, or a rush.** Refs.: Job 41:2, 20; Is. 58:5. It is also translated as bulrush (Is. 9:14; 19:15; 58:5). In Isaiah 58:5, it is used figuratively to picture a humble person bowing his or her head as a reed. ¶

[2] ***ḥeḇel, ḥêḇel*** [masc. noun: חֶבֶל, חֵבֶל <2256>; from PLEDGE (TAKE AS A) <2254>] ▶ **This word has many meanings, depending on the context. The most basic meaning is a rope or a cord.** The spies used a rope to escape through Rahab's window (Josh. 2:15); cords were used to bind Jeremiah in the dungeon (Jer. 38:11–13). Although these cords may be decorative (Esther 1:6), they are usually used to bind and control objects, such as animals (Job 41:1) or buildings (Is. 33:20). This word is also used symbolically to speak of the cords of sin and death (2 Sam. 22:6; Ps. 18:4, 5; Prov. 5:22) or the pangs of childbirth (Is. 13:8; Jer. 13:21; Hos. 13:13). It can even be translated "destruction," "calamity" (Job 21:17). This word is also used to describe a dividing line (2 Sam. 8:2; Amos 7:17); a geographical region (Deut. 3:13, 14; 1 Kgs. 4:13; Zeph. 2:5, 6); or an allotment of an inheritance (Deut. 32:9; Josh. 17:5; Ps. 105:11). In a few instances, this word describes a company of prophets (1 Sam. 10:5, 10; also translated group, procession). *
[3] ***niqpāh*** [fem. noun: נִקְפָּה <5364>; from SURROUND <5362>] ▶
a. This word refers to a cord used to bind something or someone. It is found in a mocking sense of persons bound in ropes or cords, not belts of ornamentation (Is. 3:24). ¶
b. The KJV uses this word in opposition to a girdle. In place of a girdle, a tear will be evident (Is. 3:24: rent). ¶
[4] ***ʿaḇōṯ*** [common noun: עֲבוֹת <5688>; the same as LEAFY <5687> (something intertwined)] ▶ **This word means a cord, a line.** It refers to twisted, finely crafted cordage (Ex. 28:14, 22, 24, 25; 39:15); as well as ropes formed to be strong for binding prisoners (Judg. 15:13–14; 16:11, 12; Job 39:10; Ezek. 3:25). It is used figuratively of political or military bonds or ropes (Ps. 2:3); but also of relationships of love and tender care from the Lord (Hos. 11:4). The Hebrew word also means a branch, thick foliage, clouds; see BOUGH (THICK). *
– [5] Ex. 35:18; 39:40; Num. 3:26, 37; 4:26, 32; Jer. 10:20 ➔ STRING <4340> [6] Judg.

16:12 ➔ THREAD <2339> 7 Job 39:5 ➔ BOND <4147> b.

ROSE – ***ḥ**^a**ḇaṣṣeleṯ*** [fem. noun: חֲבַצֶּלֶת <2261>; of uncertain deriv.] ▶ **This word refers most likely to a plant or flower of the genus asphodel and of the lily family, lilylike flowers.** Ref.: Is. 35:1; also translated crocus. The word stands parallel with lily in Song of Solomon 2:1 and is translated as rose for poetic effect. ¶

ROSH – ***rō'š*** [masc. proper noun: רֹאשׁ <7220>; prob. the same as HEAD (noun) <7218>]: head ▶
a. Son or grandson of Benjamin. Ref.: Gen. 46:21. ¶
b. An unknown kingdom. Refs.: Is. 66:19; Ezek. 38:2, 3; 39:1. In the KJV and the NIV, these instances are interpreted as the noun meaning chief (HEAD <7218>). ¶

ROT (noun) – Is. 5:24 ➔ STENCH <4716>.

ROT (verb) – ***rāqaḇ*** [verb: רָקַב <7537>; a prim. root] ▶ **This word means to decay, to fall apart from decomposition, infection, etc.** It is used figuratively of the name of the wicked rotting (Prov. 10:7). Wood that would not decay or rot was chosen from which to make idols (Is. 40:20). See ROTTENNESS <7538>. ¶

ROT AWAY – 1 Lev. 26:39; Is. 34:4; Ezek. 4:17; 24:23; 33:10; Zech. 14:12 ➔ WASTE AWAY <4743> 2 Is. 19:6; 33:9 ➔ WITHER <7060>.

ROTTEN – 1 ***riqqāḇôn*** [masc. noun: רִקָּבוֹן <7539>; from ROTTENNESS <7538>] ▶ **This word refers to a process of decay and decomposition, as well as the results.** It is used in a comparison to describe wood as rotten, weak, falling apart. Leviathan treats bronze as if it were rotten wood (Job 41:27, lit. wood of rottenness). ¶
– 2 Jer. 29:17 ➔ VILE <8182>.

ROTTEN THING – Job 13:28 ➔ ROTTENNESS <7538>.

ROTTENNESS – 1 ***rāqāḇ*** [masc. noun: רָקָב <7538>; from ROT (verb) <7537>] ▶ **This word indicates the process or result of decay and decomposition.** Job likens himself to a rotten thing (Job 13:28). A shameful wife affects her husband as decay affects his bones and his strength (Prov. 12:4). Undue passion acts as rottenness to the heart and life (Prov. 14:30). God likens Himself to rottenness to Judah, for He will cause her to decay and fall apart because of her sin (Hos. 5:12). It describes the destructive feelings a person suffers when confronted by certain dangers and fears (Hab. 3:16). ¶
– 2 Is. 3:24; 5:24 ➔ STENCH <4716>.

ROUGH – 1 Is. 40:4 ➔ DECEITFUL <6121> 2 Jer. 51:27 ➔ BRISTLING <5569> a.

ROUGH PLACE – ***reḵes*** [masc. noun: רֶכֶס <7406>; from BIND <7405> (as of something tied, e.g., summits)] ▶ **This word indicates a roughness or unevenness of ground; bound up, impeded places that are difficult to pass, e.g., a mountain chain of tied summits.** God will turn it into a habitable plain or valley (Is. 40:4; also translated rugged terrain, rugged place). ¶

ROUGH PLACES – ***ma**^a**qaššiym*** [masc. plur. noun: מַעֲקַשִּׁים <4625>; from CROOKED (MAKE) <6140>] ▶ **This word means and is also translated crooked places, crooked things, rugged places.** It describes roads, trails, or terrain in general as bumpy, hilly, uneven, difficult to traverse (Is. 42:16). It is used figuratively in this context. ¶

ROUND – 1 1 Kgs. 7:23, 31, 35; 10:19; 2 Chr. 4:2 ➔ CIRCULAR <5696> 2 Song 7:2 ➔ ROUNDED <5469>.

ROUND (SOMETHING) – ***kikkār*** [fem. noun: כִּכָּר <3603>; from DANCE (verb) <3769> (in the sense of a circle)] ▶ **This word indicates something circular, such as a coin (a talent); a district; a loaf of bread.** It indicates something round, dish-shaped, circular: a loaf of bread (1 Sam. 2:36; 1 Sam.

10:3); a cover (Zech. 5:7; also translated disc, talent); a unit of weight, a talent (ca. 75 lbs.) (1 Kgs. 9:14; 10:10; 20:39). It is used to refer to a district in its circuit or environs, e.g., a southern area (Gen. 13:10–12: plain, valley); or a surrounding mountainous area (Gen. 19:17, 25, 28, 29: plain, valley). It is used of the district surrounding Jerusalem (Neh. 3:22; 12:28). *

ROUND THING – Is. 1:31 ➔ FLAKE-LIKE THING <2636>.

ROUNDABOUT WAY – Judg. 5:6 ➔ CROOKED <6128>.

ROUNDED – [1] ***sahar*** [masc. noun: סַהַר <5469>; from an unused root meaning to be round] ► **This word indicates roundness; it is also translated round. It refers to something shaped like a circle, a sphere, a cylinder.** It describes the rounded aspect of something, a person's navel like a goblet (Song 7:2, lit.: a bowl of roundness). ¶
– [2] 1 Kgs. 10:19 ➔ CIRCULAR <5696> [3] Song 7:1 ➔ CURVE <2542>.

ROUSE ONESELF – [1] 2 Sam. 5:24 ➔ MOVE <2782> [2] Job 39:18 ➔ LIFT ONESELF <4754>.

ROUT – 2 Sam. 18:7; 2 Kgs. 14:12 ➔ SMITE <5062>.

ROVING (GO) – Jer. 14:18 ➔ MERCHANT <5503>.

ROW (noun) – [1] ***ṭûr*** [masc. noun: טוּר <2905>; from an unused root meaning to range in a regular manner] ► **This word means an orderly alignment; it is also translated course.** It indicates a number of things arranged in a straight line, such as building stones in Solomon's Temple and palace (1 Kgs. 6:36; 7:12); or in a rectangle or square to form an enclosure (Ezek. 46:23; also translated ledge). It is used of beams or pillars as well (1 Kgs. 6:36; 7:12); or various designs (1 Kgs. 7:20, 24, 42). It is used to describe the arrangement of the jewels placed on the breastpiece of the high priest (Ex. 28:17–20; 39:10–13). Other refs.: 1 Kgs. 7:2–4, 18; 2 Chr. 4:3, 13. *
[2] ***maʿareḵeṯ*** [fem. noun: מַעֲרֶכֶת <4635>] ► **This word means an arrangement, an ordering, concretely an ordered display. It comes from the verb *ʿāraḵ*, meaning to arrange or to line up.** The first time this word appears is in Leviticus 24:6, 7 (also translated pile, stack), where it describes the arrangement of the showbread: two rows of bread with six pieces in a row. In the other seven instances of this word, it is best translated "showbread" (i.e., the bread that was lined up in a row) (1 Chr. 9:32; 23:29; 28:16; 2 Chr. 2:4; 13:11; 29:18; Neh. 10:33). ¶
[3] ***śôrah*** [fem. noun: שׂוֹרָה <7795>; from RULE (verb) <7786> in the primitive sense of TURN ASIDE <5493>] ►
a. This word is taken as a reference to the furrows or rows where wheat grains were sown. Ref.: Is. 28:25.
b. This word refers to grains of millet or wheat, principally wheat, that were sown in the ground. Ref.: Is. 28:25; KJV: principal. ¶
– [4] Song 1:10 ➔ TURN (noun) <8447> c. [5] Ezek. 46:23 ➔ CAMP <2918>.

ROW (verb) – Jon. 1:13 ➔ DIG <2864>.

ROWS OF STONES – ***talpiyyôṯ*** [fem. plur. noun: תַּלְפִּיּוֹת <8530>; fem. noun of an unused root meaning to tower] ►
a. This word is used figuratively to describe in Middle Eastern style the attractive neck of a beloved bride. Ref.: Song 4:4; NIV: courses of stones. The exact meaning of the word is uncertain.
b. This word indicates armories. It describes features of the neck of a beloved bride in Middle Eastern style (Song 4:4).
c. This word means elegance. It refers to the beloved bride's neck in Middle Eastern style (Song 4:4). ¶

ROYAL – [1] ***ʾaḥašterān*** [masc. noun: אֲחַשְׁתְּרָן <327>; of Persian origin] ► **This word relates to a king. It could also mean speedy or swift.** The term royal seems to be the better translation, but the idea of speed

is probably included in the designation of royal steeds or studs (Esther 8:10, 14). ¶
– [2] Dan. 11:45: his royal tents ➔ the tents of his palace ➔ PALACE <643>.

ROYAL BRIDE – Ps. 45:9 ➔ QUEEN <7694>.

ROYAL STUD – ***rammāḵ*** [fem. noun: רַמָּךְ <7424>; of foreign origin] ▶
a. This word refers to horses bred and cared for by the king and his workmen for government service. Ref.: Esther 8:10.
b. Some translators render a. as a camel or dromedary, a less likely translation of the word in our current understanding of it. Ref.: Esther 8:10, KJV, cf. NKJV. ¶

RUBBLE – [1] Ps. 79:1 ➔ RUINS <5856> [2] Zeph. 1:3 ➔ RUIN, HEAP OF RUINS <4384>.

RUBIES – Job 28:18; Prov. 3:15; 8:11; 20:15; 31:10; Lam. 4:7 ➔ JEWELS <6443>.

RUBY – [1] Ex. 28:17; 39:10 ➔ SARDIUS <124> [2] Prov. 31:10 ➔ MERCHANDISE <4377> [3] Is. 54:12; Ezek. 27:16 ➔ AGATE <3539>.

RUDDY – [1] 1 Sam. 16:12; 17:42 ➔ RED <132> [2] Song 5:10 ➔ RED <122>.

RUDDY (BE) – ***'āḏam*** [verb: אָדַם <119>] ▶
A word meaning to be red, to be dyed red, to make red. It is used to describe people: Esau (Gen. 25:25); David (1 Sam. 16:12; 17:42); and princes (Lam. 4:7). As for things, it describes ram skins that were dyed red (other translation: tanned) (Ex. 25:5; 26:14; 35:7), the shield of mighty men (Nah. 2:3), and red wine (Prov. 23:31). Metaphorically, this word describes sin as "red like crimson" (Is. 1:18). ¶

RUFFIANS – Job 16:11 ➔ UNGODLY <5760>.

RUG – [1] ***ṣāpiyṯ*** [fem. noun: צָפִית <6844>; from WATCH (verb) <6822>] ▶
a. This word refers figuratively to a cloth spread on a tabletop in anticipation of coming disaster in Babylon. Ref.: Is. 21:5.
b. This word also refers to a watchtower, a small elevated structure that could be fortified. Watchmen were stationed there to watch for the coming attack on Babylon (Is. 21:5). ¶
– [2] Judg. 4:18 ➔ BLANKET <8063> [3] Ezek. 27:24 ➔ TREASURE <1595>.

RUGGED – [1] ***gaḇnôn*** [adj. or masc. noun: גַּבְנֹון <1386>; from the same as HUNCHBACK <1384>] ▶ **As a noun this word means the hump or peak of hills, a rounded mountain summit. Taken as an adjective, this word means, many-peaked, high, arched high, having an irregular surface.** It describes the physical appearance of the mountain of Bashan (Ps. 68:15, 16). Some translate it as a high hill (KJV), many peaks (NASB), rugged (NIV), each trying to catch the impression conveyed by the psalmist of this sacred mountain. ¶
– [2] Song 2:17 ➔ BETHER <1336>.

RUGGED PLACES – Is. 42:16 ➔ ROUGH PLACES <4625>.

RUGGED TERRAIN, RUGGED PLACE – Is. 40:4 ➔ ROUGH PLACE <7406>.

RUIN (noun) – [1] ***'ōḇēḏ*** [masc. noun: אֹבֵד <8>; act. part. of PERISH <6>] ▶ **This word means destruction.** It is used this way only in Numbers 24:20, 24 where Balaam prophesies the destruction of three nations or areas, one of which is Eber; it is also translated by the verb "to perish." If Eber refers to the Hebrews, then the destruction is not to be understood as absolute. Other occurrences of this form, although spelled identically, are used differently and are included under *'āḇaḏ*: PERISH <6>. ¶
[2] ***hᵃriysāh*** [fem. noun: הֲרִיסָה <2034>; from PULL DOWN <2040>] ▶ **This word indicates something demolished, e.g., a destroyed building.** It is used figuratively of the line of David in ruins (Amos 9:11), which the Lord will raise up again. ¶
[3] ***ḥorbāh*** [fem. noun: חָרְבָּה <2723>; fem. of HEAT (noun) <2721>] ▶ **This word**

almost always refers to an area devastated by the judgment of God. The destroyed area is usually a country or city but may also be individual property (Ps. 109:10). Sometimes the ruins are referred to as being restored by God (Is. 51:3; 52:9; 58:12). The ruins of Job 3:14 may have been rebuilt by men; if so, the context makes clear that the rebuilding was unsuccessful. In Malachi 1:4, God would not allow Edom to rebuild his ruins successfully; similarly, Psalm 9:6 seems to refer to an eternal state of ruin. Ezekiel 26:20 and Isaiah 58:12 refer to ancient ruins, but it is difficult to identify them definitely. The ruins of the latter passage would be restored by those who seek God sincerely with fasting. *

[4] ***miḏḥeh*** [masc. noun: מִדְחֶה <4072>; from DRIVE <1760> (in the sense of harming persons)] ► **This word indicates the harm and destruction that a flattering mouth can bring about.** Ref.: Prov. 26:28. ¶

[5] ***mᵉḥittāh*** [fem. noun: מְחִתָּה <4288>; from TAKE <2846> (in the sense of to take away, to pile up] ► **This word properly means a destruction, a breaking; hence, it is also translated terror, undoing, downfall.** It is used most often in a figurative sense in Proverbs to describe the ruin of the foolish (Prov. 10:14; 13:3; 18:7); and the workers of iniquity (Prov. 10:29; 21:15). It also describes the result of poverty (Prov. 10:15); and the failure to support a prince (Prov. 14:28). Elsewhere, this word depicted the power of God bringing destruction (Ps. 89:40), which resulted in an object lesson to all around (Jer. 48:39: horror, dismay, dismaying, object of terror). It is the blessing of God that people live without this terror (Is. 54:14; Jer. 17:17). ¶

[6] ***mᵉʿiy*** [masc. noun: מְעִי <4596>; from INIQUITY (COMMIT) <5753> (in the sense of twisted, like a pile of rubbish)] ► **This word refers to the condition and status of a fallen, destroyed city; it is also translated heap.** Ref.: Is. 17:1. ¶

[7] ***mappālāh*** [fem. noun: מַפָּלָה <4654>; from FALL (verb) <5307>] ► **This word refers to a heap of devastated remains, rubble.** It is the opposite of an inhabited city or area; an uninhabitable place (Is. 23:13; 25:2). Damascus was reduced to a rubble, a ruin (Is. 17:1; KJV, NKJV: ruinous). ¶

[8] ***ʿawwāh*** [fem. noun: עַוָּה <5754>; intens. from INIQUITY (COMMIT) <5753> abbreviated] ► **This word indicates rubble, an overturning.** It indicates the overthrow of something, turning it into rubble so that it no longer exists or functions (Ezek. 21:27; also translated overthrown, overturn). ¶

[9] ***šᵉʾiyyāh*** [fem. noun: שְׁאִיָּה <7591>] ► **This word refers to a crash, what has come tumultuously crashing down. It is used only once in the Old Testament and comes from the verb *šāʾāh*, meaning to turn into devastated remains.** In Isaiah 24:12, it describes the destroyed gate of the city that had been battered into ruins. ¶

[10] ***šammāh*** [fem. sing. noun: שַׁמָּה <8047>; from DESTROYED (BE) <8074>] ► **This word means desolation, waste; hence it also means astonishment, consternation, horror, appalment. The primary meaning is that of ruin and wasting.** This noun can be used to refer to evil people and their households who deserved to be destroyed because of their sins (Ps. 73:19; Is. 5:9); also of land, towns, and buildings that were destroyed as a result of the evil people who lived there (Jer. 2:15). A second meaning of astonishment, dismay, and horror is not clearly related to the primary meaning, but it is used to describe feelings toward Israel and its cities in their times of disobedience. Israel is seen as a horror, an object of scorn to all who saw her (Deut. 28:37; Jer. 19:8). It is also used to describe the extreme dismay people can feel at seeing destruction, a horror that fills persons (Jer. 8:21). *

– [11] Deut. 13:16; Jer. 30:18 ➔ HEAP (noun) <8510> [12] Job 31:29; Prov. 24:22 ➔ DISASTER <6365> [13] Ps. 73:18 ➔ RUINS <4876> [14] Lam. 1:7 ➔ DOWNFALL <4868> [15] Lam. 3:47 ➔ DEVASTATION <7612> [16] Ezek. 27:27 ➔ FALL (noun) <4658> [17] Nah. 2:10 ➔ WASTE (MAKE, BE, LAY) <1110>.

RUIN, HEAP OF RUINS – ***maḵšēlāh*** [fem. noun: מַכְשֵׁלָה <4384>; from FALL (verb) <3782>] ► **This word means a pile**

of rubble. Isaiah prophesied to the people of Judah that because of their rebellion against the Lord, He was going to desolate their land so thoroughly that they would soon search for leaders to care for them and for the ruins of what remained, yet find none (Is. 3:6). Other ref.: Zeph. 1:3 (ruin, stumbling block, rubble, idol). ¶

RUIN (COME TO) – ***lāḇaṭ*** [verb: לָבַט <3832>; a prim. root] ▶ **This word means to be torn down, to be ruined; it is also translated to fall, to be trampled.** It means to become ruined from talking foolishly (Prov. 10:8, 10); or by acting wickedly and immorally from a lack of understanding (Hos. 4:14). ¶

RUIN (verb) – [1] Ex. 23:8; Deut. 16:19; Prov. 19:3 → OVERTHROW (verb) <5557> [2] Is. 24:1 → INIQUITY (COMMIT) <5753>.

RUINED (BE) – Prov. 10:8, 10; Hos. 4:14 → RUIN (COME TO) <3831>.

RUINED (LIE) – Is. 6:11 → WASTE (LAY, LIE) <7582>.

RUINOUS – [1] 2 Kgs. 19:25; Is. 37:26 → RUINS (BE, LIE IN) <5327> [2] Is. 17:1 → RUIN <4654>.

RUINS – [1] ***maššû'āh*** [plur. fem. noun: מַשּׁוּאָה <4876>; from WASTE (noun) <4875>] ▶ **This word means deceptions, destructions, and desolations.** The psalmist took solace in the fact that God would cause the destruction of the wicked (Ps. 73:18). He also called on God to remember the righteous who had been in the depths of desolation (Ps. 74:3). ¶

[2] ***'iy*** [masc. noun: עִי <5856>; from INIQUITY (COMMIT) <5753> (in the sense of to ruin)] ▶ **This word means and is also translated heap, heap of ruins, heap of rubble, rubble.** It refers to a pile of useless trash or garbage, a personal situation of helplessness and devastation (Job 30:24). It indicates a city that has been besieged and wiped out (Ps. 79:1; Jer. 26:18; Mic. 1:6; 3:12). ¶

– [3] Job 30:24 → HEAP OF RUINS <1164> [4] Is. 61:4 → HEAT (noun) <2721> [5] Dan. 2:5; 3:29 → DUNGHILL <5122>.

RUINS (BE, LIE IN) – ***nāṣāh*** [verb: נָצָה <5327>; a prim. root] ▶ **This word means to fall, to be devastated, to be ruined, to lay waste.** It is used of defeated and razed cities (2 Kgs. 19:25; Is. 37:26; Jer. 4:7). The Hebrew word also means to struggle, to strive; see FIGHT <5327>. ¶

RULE (noun) – [1] ***mišṭār*** [masc. noun: מִשְׁטָר <4896>; from SCRIBE <7860> (the Hebrew word also means an official, a magistrate)] ▶ **This word indicates authoritative governance and guidance of something or someone over the earth or in general.** Ref.: Job 38:33; also translated dominion. ¶

– [2] Prov. 25:28 → SELF-CONTROL <4623> [3] Jer. 13:18 → PRINCIPALITIES <4761> [4] Zech. 9:10 → AUTHORITY <4915>.

RULE (verb) – [1] ***māšal*** [verb: מָשַׁל <4910>; a prim. root] ▶ **This word denotes to reign or to have dominion over. Although its general tone communicates leadership and authority, its specific nuance and connotation are derived from the context in which it appears.** In the creation narratives on the fourth day, God created the great luminaries. The greater luminary was to rule the day, and the lesser was to rule the night (Gen. 1:18). It is also applied to people who rule: a servant over his master's household (Gen. 24:2); a king over his country (Josh. 12:5); or his people (Judg. 8:22, 23); a people over another people (Judg. 14:4). God is also said to rule over His people (Judg. 8:23); not over His adversaries (Is. 63:19); over the nations (2 Chr. 20:6; Ps. 22:28); over Jacob (Ps. 59:13); over all things (1 Chr. 29:12). *

[2] ***śûr*** [verb: שׂוּר <7786>; a prim. root] ▶ **This word also means to vanquish, to have power over, to prevail over. The primary meaning of this word is to be or act as a prince, to rule, to govern.** In Hosea, the

verb denotes what will happen to the parents of children (i.e., they will be vanquished and bereaved of their children) when God turns away from them (see Hos. 9:12).

The word is also used to describe Abimelech's ruling of Israel for three years (Judg. 9:22). God sent an evil spirit between Abimelech and the people of Shechem, and they acted treacherously against Abimelech. This was done so that the shedding of the blood of Jerub-Baal's seventy sons might be avenged on their brother Abimelech and the citizens of Shechem who helped him. The verb also denotes one of the reasons for Israel's upcoming punishment. Not only did they choose princes without Yahweh's approval, but Israel also made and worshiped idols in blatant disregard for the rulership and dominion of Yahweh over them (Hos. 8:4). ¶

[3] ***rāḏāh*** [verb: רָדָה <7287>; a prim. root] ▶ **This word means to have dominion, to subjugate. It conveys the notion of exercising domain, whether legitimate or not, over those who are powerless or otherwise under one's control.** It is related as the exercise of authority by the priesthood (Jer. 5:31); by slave owners over their slaves (Lev. 25:43); by supervisors over their workers (1 Kgs. 9:23); and by a king over his kingdom (1 Kgs. 4:24). Theologically significant is the use of this word to identify people's God-ordained relationship to the created world around them (Gen. 1:26, 28). *

[4] ***śārar*** [verb: שָׂרַר <8323>; a prim. root] ▶ **This word means to reign as a prince, to be a prince.** This Hebrew word means literally to rule or to govern as a prince, as is evident in Isaiah 32:1. This word also may imply an unwelcome exercise of authority over another, as the protest against Moses in Numbers 16:13 suggests. Other refs.: Esther 1:22; Prov. 8:16. ¶

– [5] 1 Chr. 4:22; Is. 26:13 ➔ MARRY <1166> [6] Hos. 11:12 ➔ RESTLESS (BE, BECOME, GROW) <7300>.

RULE OVER – [1] ***šālaṭ*** [verb: שָׁלַט <7980>; a prim. root] ▶ **This word denotes to have dominion over. It is also translated to be master of, to lord over.** In the simple form, it takes the connotation of ruling. This can be ruling over people (Neh. 5:15; Eccl. 8:9); or possessions which one has been given control of (Eccl. 2:19). It can also mean to obtain power or to get mastery over something. Examples of this would be how sin can have power over a person (Ps. 119:133); or people can have power over each other (Esther 9:1). This verb is also used in the causative form, meaning to give power (Eccl. 5:19; 6:2). In these contexts, God gives people power over their lives, possessions, honor, and wealth. God is the only legitimate source of power, and all power flows from Him. ¶

[2] ***šᵉlaṭ*** [Aramaic verb: שְׁלַט <7981>; corresponding to <7980> above] ▶ **This word means to have power. It is found in the intensive and causative forms only.** In the causative form, it means to make rule or to cause to rule, referring to someone in power who gives that power to another (Dan. 2:38, 39, 48). In the intensive form, it may mean merely to have power in the sense of controlling other people (Dan. 3:27, 6:24), or to rule or be a ruler. In this sense, it is used in the context of King Belshazzar, who promised that whoever could interpret his dream would become a ruler (Dan. 5:7, 16). ¶

RULER – [1] ***nāśiy'*** [masc. adj. or noun: נָשִׂיא <5387>; from CARRY <5375>] ▶ **This word means someone or something that is lifted up, a prince, a mist. The Hebrew word is formed from the verb *nāśā'*, meaning to carry, to lift.** It refers to a leader of the people (Gen. 23:6; Ex. 16:22; 22:28). Although rare, it can refer to the king (1 Kgs. 11:34); or to a non-Israelite leader (Gen. 34:2; Num. 25:18; Josh. 13:21). Some scholars have proposed that the term refers to elected officials, contending that these were common people who were elevated or lifted up. They often buttress their argument with Numbers 1:16, which talks of these leaders as the ones called, chosen, or appointed from the congregation. In a few instances, this word also indicates mist or vapors that rise from the earth to form clouds and herald the coming of rain (Ps. 135:7; Prov. 25:14; Jer. 10:13; 51:16). *

2 ***segen, sāgān*** [masc. noun: סֶגֶן, סָגָן <5461>; from an unused root meaning to superintend] ▶ **This word means and is also translated prince, prefect, commander, official, deputy.** Sometimes it refers to an official of the Assyrian or Babylonian Empire (Is. 41:25; Jer. 51:23, 28, 57; Ezek. 23:6, 12, 23). It can also refer to the head of a Jewish community (Ezra 9:2); as well as lesser officials of Judah (Neh. 2:16; 4:14, 19; 5:7, 17; 7:5; 12:40; 13:11). ¶
– 3 Gen. 42:6; Eccl. 7:19; 10:5 ➔ POWER <7989> 4 Judg. 5:3; Ps. 2:2; Prov. 8:15; 31:4; Hab. 1:10 ➔ HEAVY (BE) <7336> 5 1 Sam. 6:16, 18; 1 Chr. 12:19 ➔ LORD <5633> 6 1 Chr. 26:6 ➔ DOMINION <4474> 7 Is. 60:17 ➔ OPPRESS <5065> 8 Dan. 3:2, 3 ➔ OFFICIAL <7984> 9 See PRINCE <8269>.

RULERS – Ps. 58:1 ➔ OAK TREES <482>.

RULES (ONE WHO) – 1 Chr. 26:6 ➔ DOMINION <4474>.

RUMAH – ***rûmāh*** [proper noun: רוּמָה <7316>; from EXALT <7311>]: height ▶ **A place in Judah.** Ref.: 2 Kgs. 23:36. ¶

RUMBLE – Is. 17:12, 13 ➔ ROAR (verb) <7582>.

RUMBLING – ***hegeh*** [masc. noun: הֶגֶה <1899>; from MEDITATE <1897>] ▶ **This word means muttering, growling, moaning, or sighing sound. It generally describes a sound that comes from deep within the body.** The Lord's voice is also described as making a rumbling sound associated with thunder (Job 37:2; KJV: sound). The idea of moaning or sighing depicts the sound uttered in mourning, lamentation, woe (Ezek. 2:10), or in deep resignation (Ps. 90:9: sigh, tale, moan). ¶

RUMP – Ex. 29:22; Lev. 3:9; 7:3; 8:25; 9:19 ➔ FAT TAIL <451>.

RUN – 1 ***rûṣ*** [verb: רוּץ <7323>; a prim. root] ▶ **This word means to travel, to journey by moving one's legs more rapidly than in walking. It also means to guard.** Ref.: Gen. 18:2. It may carry with it a sense of urgency, a need to hurry (Gen. 18:7); or a sense of intense concern, care, excitement (Gen. 24:17, 20, 28, 29). It is used of horses (Amos 6:12). It describes, figuratively, the course of the sun across the sky (Ps. 19:5); or the road, way, or course of God's moral commandments (Ps. 119:32). In its intensive stem, it can indicate fright, running to and fro in battle (Nah. 2:4). In its causative stem, it has the sense of to cause someone to run, to bring them (Gen. 41:14, 1 Sam. 17:17; 2 Chr. 35:13); or to cause or make someone run away (Jer. 49:19; 50:44). Followed by *liqra'ṯ*, it means to meet (Gen. 24:17; 29:13). It is used in a figurative sense of a prophet's activity of prophesying (Jer. 23:21; Hab. 2:2); of the swift activity of God's Word (Ps. 147:15). In its participial form, it may refer to runners (2 Sam. 15:1; 1 Kgs. 1:5). *
2 ***rāṣā'*** [verb: רָצָא <7519>; a prim. root] ▶ **This word indicates to speed, to run quickly, to dart.** The infinitive absolute of the verb (*râsô'*) is combined with *šôḇ* to give the meaning of back and forth (Ezek. 1:14). ¶
– 3 Lev. 15:3 ➔ FLOW (verb) <7325> 4 Ps. 77:2 ➔ SPILL <5064> 5 Jer. 2:23 ➔ TRAVERSE <8308>.

RUN A LINE – Num. 34:7, 8 ➔ DRAW A LINE <8376>.

RUN AWAY – See FLEE <1272>.

RUN DRY – Jer. 18:14 ➔ DRY UP <5405>.

RUN OUT – Ezek. 47:2 ➔ TRICKLE <6379>.

RUN OVER – Ps. 23:5 ➔ OVERFLOW (noun) <7310>.

RUNNING – 1 ***meʻrûṣāh*** [fem. noun: מְרוּצָה <4794>; fem. of RACE <4793>] ▶ **This word denotes running (hastening on foot at a rapid pace), manner of running, and also a course (manner of life).**

It means the actual visible style and characteristics of a person in the process of running (2 Sam. 18:27); or the running itself (Jer. 8:6; 23:10). In the latter case, it is used figuratively of the course of life. ¶
– [2] Is. 33:4 → RUSHING <4943>.

RUNNING SORE – [1] Lev. 21:20; 22:22 → SCAB <3217> [2] Lev. 22:22 → DISCHARGE <2990>.

RUNNING WATER – Deut. 21:4 → STRENGTH <386>.

RURAL – Deut. 3:5; 1 Sam. 6:18; Esther 9:19 → UNWALLED <6521>.

RUSH (noun) – [1] Job 8:11 → MEADOW (plant) <260> [2] Job 8:11; Is. 35:7 → BULRUSH <1573> [3] Job 41:20; Is. 9:14; 19:15; 58:5 → ROPE <100> [4] Ps. 32:6 → FLOOD <7858>.

RUSH (verb) – [1] ***ṣālaḥ, ṣālêaḥ*** [verb: צָלַח, צָלֵחַ <6743>; a prim. root (in the sense of to push forward)] ▶
a. This word means to do something in a hurry, also to break forth, to come mightily. It describes the Holy Spirit's affect on persons, making them powerful (Judg. 14:6, 9; 15:14; 1 Sam. 16:13); or causing persons to prophesy (1 Sam. 10:6, 10; 11:6). It indicates the effect of an evil spirit as well (1 Sam. 18:10). It has the sense of persons breaking out, rushing forward in battle (2 Sam. 19:17); and of God breaking out in acts of judgment (Amos 5:6).
b. This word means to succeed, to be victorious. It is used of causing something to turn out successfully (Gen. 24:21, 40); of prospering a person (2 Chr. 26:5). It indicates a successful person (Gen. 39:2; Jer. 12:1). Some actions are not able to succeed, especially those breaking the commandments of the Lord (Num. 14:41; Deut. 28:29). It has the sense of succeeding in an endeavor (1 Kgs. 22:12, 15). It describes the success of a powerful weapon in warfare (Is. 54:17), its successful use. What the righteous person does will eventually prosper (Ps. 1:3); but the seeming prosperousness of the wicked will fail (Ps. 37:7). Concealed sins keep one from prospering (Prov. 28:13). The will of the Lord will prosper in the hand of His Suffering Servant (Is. 53:10). The judgment on Jerusalem renders her useless, without any hope of prospering (Ezek. 15:4). God allows the rebellious king of the end to prosper but only until a certain limit is reached (Dan. 11:36). *
[2] ***šāqaq, šôqêq*** [verb: שָׁקַק, שׁוֹקֵק <8264>; a prim. root] ▶
a. This word means to move about quickly and eagerly, to surge forward like a raging river; to charge. It describes a quick, powerful motion, a movement towards someone or something (Prov. 28:15); a confused activity here and there, like swarming locusts (Is. 33:4; Joel 2:9); or war chariots darting here and there in city streets (Nah. 2:4). ¶
b. This word also means to thirst; to long for. It means to experience a strong desire for liquids but is used figuratively of the desire, the longing of the soul (Ps. 107:9; Is. 29:8).
c. An adjective meaning thirsty. It describes a thirsty soul, desiring the spiritual food it needs (Ps. 107:9; Is. 29:8). ¶
– [3] 1 Sam. 14:32; 15:19 → RUSH GREEDILY <5860> b. [4] Esther 6:12 → HURRY (verb) <1765> [5] Is. 17:12, 13 → ROAR (verb) <7582>.

RUSH GREEDILY – ***'iyṭ*** [verb: עִיט <5860>; a prim. root] ▶
a. A verb meaning to scorn, to insult. It is used of the people's rushing upon the spoils of battle (1 Sam. 14:32), but most read *'āśāh* here, they acted, did. This meaning fits well in 1 Samuel 15:19 and has the sense of rushing upon carelessly, scornfully. See b. It has the sense of disrespect or scorn (1 Sam. 25:14; also translated to revile, to rail, to hurl insults). ¶
b. A verb meaning to pounce upon. It is conjectured that this is the meaning of the original reading in 1 Samuel 14:32 (also translated to rush, to fly, to pounce). The meaning fits well in 1 Samuel 15:19. ¶

RUSH, RUSH OUT – Judg. 20:33; Job 38:8 → GUSH <1518>.

RUSHING – [1] ***maššāq*** [masc. noun: מַשָּׁק <4944>; from RUSH <8264>] ▶ **This word signifies swarming.** It is used of an attack and onslaught by devouring locusts (Is. 33:4; also translated running, swarm). ¶
– [2] Prov. 18:4 ➔ to rush ➔ UTTER <5042>.

RUSHING DOWN – Mic. 1:4 ➔ literally: poured down ➔ SPILL <5064>.

RUST – Ezek. 24:6, 11, 12 ➔ SCUM <2457>.

RUTH – ***rûṯ*** [fem. proper noun: רוּת <7327>; from NEIGHBOR <7468> (in the sense of fellow woman)]: friendship ▶ **This word designates a Moabitess who converted to the God of Naomi and her people. She is honored with special mention in the New Testament genealogical record of the Messiah.** God cared for her providentially, and she became the grandmother of King David (Ruth 4:5, 10–13). She married Boaz, a kinsman "redeemer" in Israel, thus rescuing her from poverty and oblivion. All refs.: Ruth 1:4, 14, 16, 22; 2:2, 8, 21, 22; 3:9; 4:5, 10, 13. ¶

RUTHLESS – [1] ***'āriyṣ*** [adj.: עָרִיץ <6184>; from TREMBLE <6206> (in the sense of to cause to tremble)] ▶ **This word means without pity, and also strong, violent.** It refers to a ruler, a master, or anyone who behaves ruthlessly toward his subjects: tyrants (Job 6:23; 27:13; Is. 29:20; Ezek. 31:12; 32:12); a ruthless person (Job 15:20). It indicates a person of insolence, violence (Ps. 37:35; 54:3). A ruthless person is proud, haughty (Is. 13:11). The Lord is a mighty man of violence or ruthlessness, a dreaded master (Jer. 20:11). Nations and peoples may be termed ruthless, violent (Ezek. 28:7; 30:11). *
– [2] Ps. 71:4 ➔ LEAVENED (BE) <2556> [3] Is. 1:17 ➔ OPPRESSOR <2541>.

RUTHLESSLY – [1] Ex. 1:13, 14; etc. ➔ SEVERITY <6530> [2] Job 30:21 ➔ CRUEL <393>.

RYE – Ex. 9:32; Is. 28:25 ➔ SPELT <3698>.

S

SABBATH – [1] ***šabbāṯ*** [masc./fem. noun: שַׁבָּת <7676>; intens. from REST (verb) <7673>] ► **This word also means Day of Atonement, Sabbath week or year, weeks. It can be translated as Sabbath in practically every instance. The seventh day was set aside at creation, but the holy Sabbath was first given to Israel and first mentioned in the biblical text in Exodus 16:23 as a gift to God's people (Ex. 16:25, 26, 29).** The word describes the day as it was officially established in the Ten Commandments at Sinai. It was the seventh day, and it was to be kept holy, set apart to the Lord (Ex. 20:8, 10). That day was blessed by the Lord (Ex. 20:11); and was to be observed by Israel forever (Ex. 31:13–16; Ezek. 20:12). Not even a fire could be lit in any house on the Sabbath (Ex. 35:3; Lev. 23:32; Neh. 10:31; Is. 58:13; Jer. 17:22); nor could work, even on the Tabernacle, be performed (Ex. 35:2). Special offerings were presented on the Sabbath in addition to the regular daily burnt offerings, properly termed Sabbath offerings (Num. 28:9, 10). The purpose for the Sabbath was rest for all God's people; its basis was found in God's cessation from work at Creation (Ex. 20:11; cf. Ex. 31:17); and Israel's historic experience of forced labor in Egypt (Deut. 5:15). Unfortunately, God's people chose to utterly desecrate the Lord's Sabbaths (Ezek. 20:13, 16, 20).

The high point of the religious year for Israel was the Day of Atonement which the author described as a Sabbath of Sabbaths (Lev. 16:31; 23:32), a Sabbath of rest. Every seventh year was described as a Sabbath to the Lord or, using the same term employed for the Day of Atonement, a Sabbath of Sabbaths (Lev. 25:4). During this time, the land was to remain unplowed; thus, the land itself was to enjoy its Sabbaths (Lev. 25:6; 26:34). When Israel was in exile, God remembered the land, giving it rest, so that it was refreshed by lying fallow for seventy years (Lev. 26:34, 35, 43); enjoying its Sabbaths that Israel had not observed (2 Chr. 36:21). Seven Sabbaths or seven weeks of years were equal to forty-nine years (Lev. 25:8). The produce of the land that grew of itself during the Sabbath year is described as the Sabbath (produce) of the land (Lev. 25:6). *

– [2] Lam. 1:7 → DOWNFALL <4868>.

SABEAN – ***šᵉḇā'iy*** [proper noun: שְׁבָאִי <7615>; patron. from SHEBA <7614>] ► **A citizen of Sheba (<7614> d.).** Ref.: Joel 3:8. ¶

SABEANS – ***sᵉḇā'iym, sāḇā'iym*** [proper noun: סְבָאִים, סָבָאִים <5436>; patrial from SEBA <5434>] ► **These descendants of Seba were men of stature and from the wilderness.** Refs.: Is. 45:14; Ezek. 23:42. They were to bring gifts to God (see Ps. 72:10). ¶

SABTA, SABTAH – ***saḇtā', saḇtāh*** [masc. proper noun: סַבְתָּא, סַבְתָּה <5454>; prob. of foreign deriv.]: rest ► **The third son of Cush.** Refs.: Gen. 10:7; 1 Chr. 1:9. ¶

SABTECHA – ***saḇtᵉḵā'*** [masc. proper noun: סַבְתְּכָא <5455>; prob. of foreign deriv.] ► **The fifth son of Cush.** Refs.: Gen. 10:7; 1 Chr. 1:9. ¶

SACAR – ***śāḵār*** [masc. proper noun: שָׂכָר <7940>; from wages <7939>]: wages, reward ►

a. The father of Ahiam, the same as Sharar (<8325>). Ref.: 1 Chr. 11:35. ¶

b. A Korahite gatekeeper. Ref.: 1 Chr. 26:4. ¶

SACHIA, SACHIAH – ***šoḇyāh*** [fem. noun: שָׁבְיָה <7634>] ► **An alternate form for *śāḵyāh* (VESSEL <7914> c.), a descendant of Benjamin.** Ref.: 1 Chr. 8:10. ¶

SACHIA, SAKIA, SHACHIA – 1 Chr. 8:10 → VESSEL <7914> c.

SACK – [1] ***'amtaḥaṯ*** [fem. noun: אַמְתַּחַת <572>; from SPREAD, SPREAD OUT <4969>] ► **This word means bag, flexible container.** It is featured in the Joseph narrative as the container of grain, especially of the money hidden in them by order of Joseph. Refs.: Gen. 42:27, 28; 43:12, 18; 44:1. *

2 ***ṣiqlôn*** [masc. noun: צִקְלֹון <6861>; from an unused root meaning to wind] ▶
a. This word refers to a cloth container. It was large enough to hold twenty loaves of barley and a supply of ears of grain. Refs.: 2 Kgs. 4:42; also translated knapsack.
b. A masculine noun indicating a husk of an ear of corn. It refers to the husks, the dry or green outer coverings of various fruits or seeds (2 Kgs. 4:42). ¶

SACKBUT – Dan. 3:5, 7, 10, 15 ➔ TRIGON <5443>.

SACKCLOTH – ***śaq*** [masc. noun: שַׂק <8242>; from RUSH <8264>] ▶ **This word refers to a material of poor quality made of goat hair.** Ref.: 2 Sam. 21:10. It was worn traditionally to demonstrate mourning or despair; to convey the message dramatically. It might be placed only on one's loins (Gen. 37:34). Persons might tear their clothes as well, especially at the death of a son. The word is used of sacks used to transport various items of merchandise (Gen. 42:25, 27, 35). *

SACRED – See HOLY <6918>.

SACRIFICE (noun) – 1 ***dᵉḇaḥ*** [Aramaic masc. noun: דְּבַח <1685>; from OFFER <1684>] ▶ **It is the term used when King Cyrus ordered a decree for the rebuilding of the Temple, describing it as the place where the Israelites offered sacrifices, i.e., they would give up something valued.** Ref.: Ezra 6:3. ¶

2 ***zeḇaḥ*** [masc. noun: זֶבַח <2077>; from OFFER <2076>] ▶ **This word refers to an animal sacrifice in a general way as well as to a particular animal sacrifice, often termed the sacrifice of peace offerings, whereby a suitable slaughtered animal was offered to God. (Parts of the flesh of the latter sacrifice were reserved for God, parts were distributed to the priests, and parts were eaten by the offerer.)** The general practice was ancient and did not apply solely to sacrifices to the true God of Israel (Ex. 34:15; Num. 25:2). Other sacrifices of this type included the covenant between Jacob and Laban (Gen. 31:54); the Passover Feast (Ex. 34:25); the thank offering (Lev. 22:29); the annual sacrifice (1 Sam. 1:21); the sacrifice of a covenant with God (Ps. 50:5). See the related Hebrew verb *zāḇaḥ* (OFFER <2076>). *

SACRIFICE (verb) – See OFFER <2076>.

SAD – 1 Kgs. 21:5 ➔ SULLEN <5620>.

SAD (BE) – Gen. 40:6 ➔ ANGRY (BE, BECOME) <2196>.

SAD (MAKE) – Ezek. 13:22 ➔ GRIEVED (BE) <3512>.

SADDLE – 1 ***merkāḇ*** [masc. noun: מֶרְכָּב <4817>; from RIDE <7392>] ▶ **This word means properly a riding place. It is used of a riding seat for a mounted animal.** Ref.: Lev. 15:9. It was used to describe a two-wheeled vehicle used in battle, drawn by horses (1 Kgs. 4:26: chariot). In Song of Solomon 3:10, it is used of a seat (KJV: covering) for the king on his wedding day. ¶

2 ***riḵbāh*** [fem. noun: רִכְבָּה <7396>; fem. of CHARIOT <7393>] ▶
a. This word refers to a seat for a rider on a horse, a donkey, a camel. Ref.: Ezek. 27:20, NASB, NIV. Some suggest an abstract meaning, riding.
b. Some translators prefer to render this as chariot. Ref.: Ezek. 27:20, KJV. ¶
– 3 Gen. 31:34 ➔ LAMB <3733>.

SADDLECLOTH – ***ḥōp̄eš*** [masc. noun: חֹפֶשׁ <2667>; from FREE (BE) <2666> (in the sense of something spread loosely)] ▶ **This word refers to an expensive item of merchandise of trade between Dedan and Tyre used to make saddlecloths (cloths placed over the back of a mount) for riding.** Ref.: Ezek. 27:20. ¶

SAFE – ***šālêm*** [adj.: שָׁלֵם <8003>; from COMPLETED (BE) <7999> (in the sense of being safe or uninjured in mind or body)] ► **This word means full, complete, whole, peaceful. This adjective has several uses when it means complete, safe, unharmed, natural.** Moses instructed the Israelites to build the altar on Mount Ebal of natural, unhewn or whole stones (Deut. 27:6; Josh. 8:31). Stones that were whole, finished, and from a rock quarry could be used to build the Temple (1 Kgs. 6:7). The word describes the work on the Lord's Temple as finished, complete (2 Chr. 8:16). It describes weights that had to be solid, accurate, and fair for use in the marketplace (Deut. 25:15; Prov. 11:1); it described wages paid as full, complete, rich (Ruth 2:12). It described Jacob traveling safely to the city of Shechem (Gen. 33:18). When referring to groups of people, it means entire or whole, such as whole communities taken captive in Amos's day (Amos 1:6, 9). Something could be described as not yet complete or full; the sin of the Amorites was not yet complete (Gen. 15:16).

The word connotes the idea of whole or undivided; the hearts of the Israelites were to be wholly centered on the Lord and His decrees (1 Kgs. 8:61), but Solomon's heart was not so committed (1 Kgs. 11:4; 2 Kgs. 20:3; Is. 38:3).

The word means peaceful or peaceable when used of persons in certain relationships; the people of Shechem believed the Israelites intended to live in a peaceful relationship with them (Gen. 34:21). *

SAFE (BE) – See COMPLETED (BE) <7999>.

SAFETY (FLEE FOR) – ***'ûz*** [verb: עוּז <5756>; a prim. root] ► **This word means to seek refuge, to bring to safety, to take cover.** It refers to bringing something into shelter, safety, a place of protection from any kind of threat or danger (Ex. 9:19; Is. 10:31; Jer. 4:6; 6:1). ¶

SAFFRON – ***karkōm*** [masc. noun: כַּרְכֹּם <3750>; prob. of foreign origin] ► **This word means an orange powder made from the crocus flower. It is used in highly charged, romantic, figurative language of a bridegroom.** He regards the bride's garden of delights (Song 4:14). ¶

SAG – Eccl. 10:18 → BRING LOW <4355>.

SAHAR – Ezek. 27:18 → WHITE <6713> b.

SAILOR – 1 ***ḥōḇêl*** [masc. noun: חֹבֵל <2259>; act. part. from PLEDGE (TAKE AS A) <2254> (in the sense of handling ropes)] ► **This word refers to a seaman, a pilot.** It indicates a captain of a ship (Jon. 1:6; also translated shipmaster). It is used metaphorically of the skilled men of Tyre as her pilots in her maritime empire (Ezek. 27:8), but also literally it denotes pilots who transport wares in ships (Ezek. 27:27–29). ¶ – 2 Ezek. 27:9, 27, 29; Jon. 1:5 → MARINER <4419>.

SAKE (FOR THE) – Gen. 12:13; 30:27; 39:5; Deut. 1:37 → BECAUSE <1558>.

SAKIA – 1 Chr. 8:10 → SACHIA, SACHIAH <7634>.

SALE – 1 ***mimkār*** [masc. noun: מִמְכָּר <4465>; from SELL <4376>] ► **This word indicates the act of selling and that which is sold.** It is used in several ways: to indicate the act of selling (Lev. 25:27, 29, 33; Deut. 18:8); the things being sold, merchandise (Lev. 25:14; Neh. 13:20); something already sold (Lev. 25:25, 28; Ezek. 7:13); or the price of a sale (Lev. 25:50). ¶
2 ***mimkereṯ*** [fem. noun: מִמְכֶּרֶת <4466>; fem. of <4465> above] ► **This word indicates the process or transaction of selling.** Ref.: Lev. 25:42. In context God's people cannot be sold as slaves. ¶

SALECAH – ***salḵāh*** [proper noun: סַלְכָה <5548>; from an unused root meaning to walk]: walking ► **This word designates a city of Bashan.** Refs.: Deut. 3:10; Josh. 12:5; 13:11; 1 Chr. 5:11. ¶

SALEM – ***šālêm*** [proper noun: שָׁלֵם <8004>; the same as SAFE <8003>]: peaceful ► **This word designates a city where Melchizedek was high priest and king.**

The name means "peace" and is an early reference to Jerusalem. Abraham paid tithes to Melchizedek (Gen. 14:18; cf. Heb. 7:1, 2), and he blessed Abraham. He served as a pattern for the priesthood of Jesus. The God of Israel, the Lord, dwelt in the city after Israel took it over and the Temple was dedicated by Solomon (Ps. 76:2). ¶

SALIVA – [1] ***riyr*** [masc. noun: רִיר <7388>; from FLOW (verb) <7325>] ► **This word means the liquid secreted into the mouth. It is used when David feigned insanity and let saliva run down his beard.** Ref.: 1 Sam. 21:13; also translated spittle. The Hebrew word also refers to the white of an egg; see WHITE <7388>. ¶
– [2] Job 7:19 ➔ SPIT (noun and verb) <7536>.

SALLU, SALU – ***sallû, sallay, sālû', sallû', salu'*** [masc. proper noun: סַלּוּ, סַלַּי, סָלוּא, סַלּוּא, סַלָּא <5543>; from VALUE (verb) <5541>]: worthy, exalted ►
a. A priest. Refs.: Neh. 12:7, 20. ¶
b. A Simeonite. Ref.: Num. 25:14. ¶
c. A postexilic Jew. Refs.: 1 Chr. 9:7; Neh. 11:7. ¶
d. A Benjamite. Ref.: Neh. 11:8. ¶

SALMA – ***śalmā'*** [masc. proper noun: שַׂלְמָא <8007>; prob. for CLOTHING <8008>]: clothing ► **Father of Boaz who married Ruth.** Refs.: 1 Chr. 2:11, 51, 54. It is the same as Salmon (<8009>) and Salmon (<8012>). ¶

SALMON – [1] ***śalmāh*** [masc. proper noun: שַׂלְמָה <8009>; the same as SALMA <8008>]: clothing ► **Father of Boaz.** This name is the same as Salma (<8007>) and Salmon (<8012>). ¶
[2] ***śalmôn*** [masc. proper noun: שַׂלְמוֹן <8012>; from SALMA <8008>]: clothing ► **Father of Boaz.** This name is the same as Salma (<8007>) and Salmon (<8009>). ¶

SALT (noun) – [1] ***meᵉlaḥ*** [Aramaic masc. noun: מְלַח <4416>; from SALT (EAT THE) <4415>] ► **Salt was an important condiment and preservative in ancient times and of great value.** It was used in payment (barter) for trading or services rendered (Ezra 4:14). It was used in some sacrifices (Ezra 6:9; 7:22). ¶
[2] ***melaḥ*** [masc. noun: מֶלַח <4417>; from SEASON (verb) <4414>] ► **Salt was an important condiment (Job 6:6) and preservative in ancient times and of great value in itself and for trading and bartering.** It was used to purify water (2 Kgs. 2:20, 21) but also was scattered on the ground of a city to be destroyed (Judg. 9:45). The Dead Sea is literally, the Salt Sea, (Gen. 14:3). It occurred naturally in pits (Zeph. 2:9). Lot's wife became a pillar of salt (Gen. 19:26). It was used to season various offerings (Lev. 2:13; Ezek. 43:24). A covenant of salt was a permanent feature of some offerings (Num. 18:19; 2 Chr. 13:5). It will be a feature of a restored Temple and Zion (Ezek. 47:11). *
– [3] Jer. 17:6 ➔ BARRENNESS <4420> [4] Jer. 48:9 ➔ FLOWER <6731> d.

SALT (EAT THE) – ***meᵉlaḥ*** [Aramaic verb: מְלַח <4415>; corresponding to SEASON (verb) <4414>] ► **This word means to be in service. It means to pay with salt, to supply one's needs.** Both the noun and verb occur in Ezra 4:14, literally, "We are salted [paid] by the salt of the palace." Other translations: "we receive support from the palace," "we are in the service of the palace," "we have maintenance from the king's palace," "we are under obligation to the palace." ¶

SALT (RUB WITH) – Ezek. 16:4 ➔ SEASON (verb) <4414>.

SALT (verb) – Ex. 30:35; Ezek. 16:4 ➔ SEASON (verb) <4414>.

SALT HERB – Job 30:4 ➔ MALLOW <4408>.

SALT LAND, SALT FLATS – Job 39:6 ➔ BARRENNESS <4420>.

SALT WASTE, SALTY WASTE – Ps. 107:34 ➔ BARRENNESS <4420>.

SALTED – ***ḥāmiyṣ*** [adj.: חָמִיץ <2548>; from LEAVENED (BE) <2556>] ▶ **This word describes fodder that has been prepared with salt or seasoned by soaking, a delicacy for animals.** Ref.: Is. 30:24; also translated seasoned, cured, clean, mash. ¶

SALTWORT – Job 30:4 ➔ MALLOW <4408>.

SALVATION – 1 ***yᵉšû'āh*** [fem. noun: יְשׁוּעָה <3444>; pass. part. of SAVE <3467>] ▶ **This word means deliverance, help, victory, prosperity. The primary meaning is to rescue from distress or danger.** It is used to signify help given by other human beings (1 Sam. 14:45; 2 Sam. 10:11); help or security offered by fortified walls, delivering in the sense of preventing what would have happened if the walls were not there (Is. 26:1); one's welfare and safety (Job 30:15); salvation by God, with reference to being rescued by Him from physical harm (Ex. 14:13; 2 Chr. 20:17); being rescued from the punishment due for sin (Ps. 70:4; Is. 33:6; 49:6; 52:7). Used in the plural, it signifies works of help (Ps. 44:4; 74:12); and God's salvation (2 Sam. 22:51; Ps. 42:5; 116:13). *
2 ***yêša', yeša'*** [masc. noun: יֵשַׁע, יֶשַׁע <3468>; from SAVE <3467>] ▶ **This word means deliverance, rescue, liberty, welfare.** David used the word salvation to describe the hope and welfare he had in the midst of strife due to his covenant with God (2 Sam. 23:5). God saves communities, as when He promised relief to Jerusalem (Is. 62:11) as well as individuals (see Mic. 7:7). *
3 ***môšā'āh*** [fem. noun: מוֹשָׁעָה <4190>; from SAVE <3467>] ▶ **This word appears only once in the Bible, signifying the saving acts of the Lord; it is also translated deliverances, who saves.** Ref.: Ps. 68:20. ¶

SAMARIA – 1 ***šōmᵉrôn*** [proper noun: שֹׁמְרוֹן <8111>; from the act. part. of KEEP <8104> (in the sense of to watch over)]: watch mountain ▶ **The capital city of the Northern Kingdom of Israel.** Refs.: 1 Kgs. 16:24, 28, 29, 32; 2 Kgs. 17:1, 5, 6, 24, 26, 28. *
2 ***šāmᵉrayin*** [Aramaic proper noun: שָׁמְרַיִן <8115>; corresponding to <8111> above]: watch mountain ▶ **This word corresponds to the Hebrew entry <8111> above.** Ref.: Ezra 4:10. ¶

SAMARITAN – ***šōmᵉrōniy*** [proper noun: שֹׁמְרֹנִי <8118>; patrial from SAMARIA <8111>] ▶ **An inhabitant of Samaria (<8111>).** Ref.: 2 Kgs. 17:29. ¶

SAMGAR-NEBU, SAMGAR – ***samgar-nᵉḇô, samgar*** [סַמְגַּר נְבוֹ, סַמְגַּר <5562>; of foreign origin] ▶ **One of the princes who entered Jerusalem with Nebuchadnezzar to destroy it.** Ref.: Jer. 29:3. ¶

SAMLAH – ***śamlāh*** [masc. proper noun: שַׂמְלָה <8072>; prob. from the same as CLOTHING <8071>]: clothing ▶ **A king of Moab.** Refs.: Gen. 36:36, 37; 1 Chr. 1:47, 48. ¶

SAMSON – ***šimšôn*** [masc. proper noun: שִׁמְשׁוֹן <8123>; from SUN <8121>]: like the sun, sunlight ▶ **This word designates the last of the major judges or deliverers mentioned in Judges (13–16). He was called before his birth to be God's chosen vessel, a Nazarite.** The Lord's special messenger announced his birth and special calling to his parents before his birth (13:1–22). The author clearly gives God's purpose in His plan for Samson: to begin to deliver Israel from the Philistines's oppression (Judg. 13:5). God's Spirit "stirred him" to do His will as he reached manhood (Judg. 13:24). Even his parents, though they know he had been chosen by the Lord, failed to understand how the Lord was using Samson to accomplish His purposes (14:4). The Philistine men and women in his life were ultimately brought in and used by the Lord to enable Samson to begin the destruction of the Philistines. Samson's great strength was a result of the Spirit's action on him (14:6, 19; 15:15; 16:28), not a result of natural powers. Because he disobeyed the Lord by letting his hair be cut, the Spirit failed to energize him until he let his hair grow again. He killed more of Israel's enemy in his death than he had in his life (16:30). *

SAMUEL – ***šᵉmû'ēl*** [masc. proper noun: שְׁמוּאֵל <8050>; from the pass. part. of HEAR <8085> and GOD <410>]: God has heard ▶
a. A man of the tribe of Simeon. He was the son of Ammihud (Num. 34:20).
b. A man from the tribe of Issachar, a head of a family. Ref.: 1 Chr. 7:2.
c. The last judge of Israel. He anointed Saul and David as kings (1 Sam. 9:1–27; 16:1–13) in Israel. He was born to Hannah who dedicated him to the Lord (1 Sam. 1:21–28). He was a special child who grew up with the favor of God and people on him (1 Sam. 2:26). He served as a prophet, priest, and judge in Israel. He served all Israel (1 Sam. 4:1) for the Lord had called him (1 Sam. 3:10). He fearlessly spoke the Lord's word to priests or kings (1 Sam. 3:15–20; 15:17–33) or people (1 Sam. 8:10–22; 12). He was the key transition figure from the time of the judges to the kingship. He, however, warned the people about clamoring for a king and the oppressive nature of kingship. When he died, he was buried in Ramah ("height"). In an unusual appearance, he spoke once more from the grave to Saul, condemning Saul sternly and prophesying his imminent death at the hands of the Philistines (1 Sam. 28:1–20). *

SANBALLAT – ***sanḇallaṭ*** [masc. proper noun: סַנְבַלַּט <5571>; of foreign origin] ▶ **This word designates a Horonite who became an adamant enemy of the rebuilding of Jerusalem and its Temple and walls.** The name is a Babylonian name meaning "the moon god gives life" (Neh. 2:10, 19). He especially fumed against the rebuilding of the city walls and Nehemiah (Neh. 4:1, 2). He evidently was governor of Samaria. He threatened military intervention at Jerusalem (Neh. 4:7) and assassination of Nehemiah (Neh. 6:1–14). Other ref.: Neh. 13:28. ¶

SANCTUARY – ***miqdāš*** [masc. noun: מִקְדָּשׁ <4720>; from HOLY (BE) <6942>] ▶ **This word means a holy or sacred place. As a nominal form from the verb *qāḏaš* meaning to be set apart or to be consecrated, this noun designates that which has been sanctified or set apart as sacred and holy as opposed to the secular, common, or profane.** It is a general term for anything sacred and holy, such as the articles of the Tabernacle that were devoted for use during worship (Num. 10:21: holy objects, sanctuary); or the best portion of the offerings given to the Lord (Num. 18:29: consecrated part, sacred part, hallowed part, holiest part, best part). Most often, it connotes a sanctuary, the physical place of worship. In this sense, the word encompasses a variety of these concepts: the old Israelite sanctuaries (Josh. 24:26: sanctuary, holy place); the Tabernacle (Ex. 25:8; Lev. 12:4; 21:12: sanctuary); the Temple (1 Chr. 22:19; 2 Chr. 29:21; Dan. 11:31); the sanctuaries dedicated to false worship (Lev. 26:31; Is. 16:12; Amos 7:9). It can also denote a place of refuge or asylum because this status was accorded to sacred places among the Hebrews (Is. 8:14; Ezek. 11:16; cf. 1 Kgs. 1:50; 2:28). *

SAND – ***ḥôl*** [masc. noun: חוֹל <2344>; from SHAKE <2342>] ▶ **This word is used to refer to the tiny grains of disintegrated rock along the seashore as an example of the innumerable descendants that will belong to Abraham or as simply the major element of the seashore (Gen. 22:17; 32:12; Ex. 2:12).** In the time of Solomon, Israel and Judah were said to have numbered as many as the grains of sand along the seashore (1 Kgs. 4:20). It is used regularly in this figurative sense to indicate great quantities: corn or grain (Gen. 41:49); length of days (Job 29:18); of Solomon's wisdom (1 Kgs. 4:29). *

SAND LIZARD – ***ḥōmeṭ*** [masc. noun: חֹמֶט <2546>; from an unused root prob. meaning to lie low] ▶ **This word indicates a reptile, possibly a small lizard, skink.** It indicates some kind of unclean reptile, not edible by Israelites (Lev. 11:30), perhaps a skink. It is also translated sand reptile, snail. ¶

SAND REPTILE – Lev. 11:30 ➔ SAND LIZARD <2546>.

SANDAL – 1 ***na'al*** [fem. noun: נַעַל <5275>; from SHOD <5274>] ► **This word refers to footwear whose sole is bound to the foot by straps; it is also translated shoe. It was a basic form of footwear in the Middle East in ancient times.** It may indicate a sandal secured by leather straps (1 Kgs. 2:5; Is. 5:27). It is asserted in a figurative sense that the Israelites' sandals did not wear out during their forty years in the desert; God cared for all their needs (Deut. 29:5). It is used in several idioms: A sandal was used to strike a person who would not perform his levirate marriage duties (Deut. 25:9, 10). In his role as kinsman-redeemer, Boaz gave his sandal as part of the process of redeeming all that belonged to Elimelech, including receiving Ruth as his wife (Ruth 4:7–12); to throw one's shoe over meant to take possession of something (Ps. 60:8; 108:9); wearing sandals could be a mark of beauty (Song 7:1); removing one's sandals could be a sign of mourning (Is. 20:2; Ezek. 24:17, 23). A pair of sandals indicates an insignificant price for something (Amos 2:6; 8:6). *
– 2 Deut. 33:25 → LOCK (noun) <4515>
3 Is. 9:5 → BOOT <5430>.

SANDALS (GIVE, PUT) – 2 Chr. 28:15; Ezek. 16:10 → SHOD <5274>.

SANITY – Dan. 4:34 → KNOWLEDGE <4486>.

SANSANNAH – ***sansannāh*** [proper noun: סַנְסַנָּה <5578>; fem. of a form of FRUIT <5577> (in the sense of bough, branch)]: palm branch, bough ► **A town in the South of Judah.** Ref.: Josh. 15:31. ¶

SAP (FULL OF) – Ps. 92:14 → FAT (adj.) <1879>.

SAPH – ***sap̱*** [masc. proper noun: סַף <5593>; the same as THRESHOLD <5592>]: tall ► **A Philistine giant killed by Sibbecai at the battle of Gob.** Ref.: 2 Sam. 21:18. ¶

SAPHIR – ***šāp̱iyr*** [proper noun: שָׁפִיר <8208>; from BEAUTIFUL (BE) <8231>]: beautiful ► **A city of Judah whose behavior was shameful.** Ref.: Mic. 1:11. ¶

SAPPHIRE – ***sappiyr*** [masc. noun: סַפִּיר <5601>; from NUMBER (verb) <5608> (in the sense of to inscribe; perhaps the sapphire was used for scratching other substances)] ► **This word refers to a brilliant blue jewel; it is also translated lapis lazuli. It refers to precious stones.** In one case, it was placed in a pavement floor of God's throne room (Ex. 24:10); usually denoting separate stones for decoration, beauty, and ornamentation (Ex. 28:18; 39:11). It is used figuratively of the attractive abdomen of a bridegroom (Song 5:14). Jerusalem had been adorned by persons, figuratively, polished like sapphire or lapis lazuli stones (Lam. 4:7). These stones had been in the Garden of Eden (Ezek. 28:13). The future Zion is to have a foundation of sapphire stones (Is. 54:11). Other refs.: Job 28:6, 16; Ezek. 1:26; 10:1. ¶

SARAH – ***śārāh*** [fem. proper noun: שָׂרָה <8283>; the same as PRINCESS <8282>]: princess, woman of nobility ► **This word designates the wife of Abraham.** Her name was changed from Sarai to Sarah (Gen. 17:15, 17). The change in name indicated the multitude of persons who would come forth from her (but was also merely an updating of the form of the word). Kings, nations, and leaders came from her.

She bore the son of the promise, Isaac, by a special act of God (Gen. 17:19–22; 18:7–15; 21:1–6). Isaiah called her the mother who gave birth to Zion, Israel (51:2). She willingly took part in Abraham's deception of her relationship to him (Gen. 20:1; 18). She died at 127 years of age in Hebron and was buried in the cave in the field in Machpelah near Mamre which Abraham purchased as a burial plot (Gen. 23:12–20). *

SARAI – ***śāray*** [fem. proper noun: שָׂרַי <8297>; from PRINCE <8269>]: princess ► **This word designates the wife whom Abram (Abraham) married in Ur of the Chaldeans. She became the "princess" or "woman of nobility" of the covenant**

and promises to Abraham. This old name was changed to Sarah (Gen. 17:15). See SARAH <8283>. *

SARAPH – ***śārāp̱*** [masc. proper noun: שָׂרָף <8315>]: burning ► **An Israelite of the tribe of Judah who ruled in Moab.** Ref.: 1 Chr. 4:22. ¶

SARDIUS – ***'ōḏem*** [fem. noun: אֹדֶם <124>; from RUDDY (BE) <119>] ► **This word probably corresponds to the carnelian, a hard red precious stone; it is also translated ruby, carnelian.** Semiprecious stones are mentioned in Exodus (Ex. 28:17; 39:10) and Ezekiel (Ezek. 28:13). In Exodus they are mounted on the breastpiece of the high priest, and in Ezekiel they are part of the covering of the mysterious satanic being used to represent the king of Tyre. ¶

SARGON – ***sargôn*** [proper noun: סַרְגּוֹן <5623>; of foreign deriv.]: prince of the sun ► **An Assyrian king mentioned by Isaiah who sent his troops to attack Ashdod and capture it.** Ref.: Is. 20:1. He reigned 721–705 B.C. Isaiah responded with a prophetic perspective on the event. ¶

SARID – ***śāriyḏ*** [proper noun: שָׂרִיד <8301>; the same as REMNANT <8300>]: survivor ► **A city in the territory of Zebulun.** Refs.: Josh. 19:10, 12. ¶

SAR-SEKIM – ***śarsᵉḵiym*** [masc. proper noun: שַׂרְסְכִים <8310>; of foreign deriv.] ► **An official of the king of Babylon who took part in the destruction of Jerusalem.** Ref.: Jer. 39:3. ¶

SASH – 1 ***'aḇnêṭ*** [masc. noun: אַבְנֵט <73>; of uncertain deriv.] ► **This word designated a wide cloth worn across the chest.** It was made for the high priest (Ex. 28:4, 39; 39:29; Lev. 8:7; 16:4) and priests as well (Ex. 28:40; 29:9; Lev. 8:13). It refers to the Lord's placing of a sash or girdle upon His servant Eliakim, the son of Hilkiah (Is. 22:21; also translated belt). ¶

– 2 Prov. 31:24 ➔ GIRDED <2289> b. 3 Is. 3:24 ➔ BELT <2290> 4 Jer. 13:1, 2, 4, 6, 7, 10, 11 ➔ BELT <232>.

SASHES – Is. 3:20 ➔ ATTIRE <7196>.

SATAN – See ACCUSER <7854>.

SATISFIED (BE) – ***śāḇa', śāḇêa'*** [verb: שָׂבַע, שָׂבֵעַ <7646>; a prim. root] ► **This word means to be filled, to be full, to become full. It basically means to have had enough of something or even too much.** Israel had enough meat (quail) to eat in the desert, even more than enough (Ex. 16:8, 12); in Canaan Israel would be satisfied with all kinds of food and drink (Deut. 6:11). One of God's judgments was not to provide sufficient food to a disobedient people (Lev. 26:26; Hos. 4:10; Amos 4:8; Mic. 6:14). It is used figuratively of being filled with, satiated with anxiety, suffering (Job 7:4); weary of life (1 Chr. 23:1). It is used figuratively of God's having enough, being sated with burnt offerings (Is. 1:11). It describes a positive state of being satisfied with children, having ample offspring (Ps. 17:14); but also of, in place of offspring, being satisfied, full, with seeing God, enjoying His presence (Ps. 17:15). A sick person has enough troubles (Ps. 88:3); an evil person becomes satiated, sated, with their own evil deeds (Prov. 1:31). It depicts figuratively a sword in battle being satiated (Jer. 46:10). The prophet was filled with bitterness from the hand of the Lord (Lam. 3:15). Wine is depicted as causing an arrogant, proud, haughty person to become insatiable, like Sheol (Hab. 2:5). Persons who seek the Lord will become satisfied, even when they are afflicted (Ps. 22:26). *

SATISFIED (BE) – Prov. 6:35 ➔ WILLING (BE) <14>.

SATRAP – 1 ***'ᵃḥašdarpan*** [masc. noun: אֲחַשְׁדַּרְפַּן <323>; of Persian deriv.] ► **This word means a governor of a Persian province.** It occurs as a technical administrative term four times (Ezra 8:36; Esther 3:12; 8:9; 9:3); it is also translated lieutenant. ¶

[2] *ᵃḥašdarpan* [Aramaic masc. noun: אֲחַשְׁדַּרְפַּן <324>; corresponding to <323> above] ▶ **Satraps were officials who governed large provinces in Persia as representatives of the Persian sovereign. This word is also translated prince.** *Peḥāh* (GOVERNOR <6346>) denotes a smaller office within a satrapy. Daniel was one of three rulers over the satraps and became an object of their evil schemes (Dan. 6:1–4, 6, 7); the word also occurs in Daniel 3:2, 3, 27. All occurrences of this Chaldean word are in the book of Daniel, but the Hebrew equivalent (<323> above) is spelled the same and occurs in Ezra and Esther. ¶

SATURATE – Job 37:1 ➔ LOAD (verb) <2959>.

SAUL – ***šā'ûl*** [masc. proper noun: שָׁאוּל <7586>; pass. part. of ASK <7592>]: asked ▶
a. The first king of Israel. He was from the tribe of Benjamin and the son of Kish. He was impressive in physical appearance (1 Sam. 9:1, 2). He was anointed by the Lord through Samuel (1 Sam. 9:15–10:2) and was made king at Mizpah (1 Sam. 9:17–27). Saul made a good start but soon began to reject the word of the Lord through Samuel. As a result, the Lord rejected Saul as king (1 Sam. 15:1–31) over Israel and chose David as king (1 Sam. 16:11–13). Saul's kingship deteriorated as did his own personal condition. He lost a decisive battle to the Philistines and committed suicide in the field after being seriously wounded (1 Sam. 31:1–7). From being "head and shoulders" above his brethren, he was reduced to the most pitied of Israel's kings.
b. An ancient king of Edom who came from Rehoboth. Ref.: Gen. 36:37.
c. A son of Simeon. His mother was a Canaanite (Gen. 46:10).
d. A Levite who descended through Kohath, Levi's son. Ref.: 1 Chr. 6:24. *

SAVE – ***yāša'*** [verb: יָשַׁע <3467>; a prim. root] ▶ **This word means to help, to deliver, to defend. The underlying idea of this verb is bringing to a place of safety or broad pasture as opposed to a narrow strait, symbolic of distress and danger.** The word conveys the notion of deliverance from tribulation (Judg. 10:13, 14); deliverance from certain death (Ps. 22:21); rescue from one's enemies (Deut. 28:31; Judg. 6:14); victory in time of war (1 Sam. 14:6); the protective duty of a shepherd (Ezek. 34:22; cf. Judg. 10:1); avenging wrongs (1 Sam. 25:33); compassionate aid in a time of need (2 Kgs. 6:26, 27; Ps. 12:1); the salvation that only comes from God (Is. 33:22; Zeph. 3:17). *

SAVES (WHO) – Ps. 68:20 ➔ SALVATION <4190>.

SAVORY FOOD, SAVORY DISH – Gen. 27:4, 7, 9, 14, 17, 31 ➔ DELICIOUS FOOD <4303>.

SAVOURY MEAT – Gen. 27:4, 7, 9, 14, 17, 31 ➔ DELICIOUS FOOD <4303>.

SAW (noun) – [1] ***meg̱ērāh*** [fem. noun: מְגֵרָה <4050>; from DRAG <1641> (in the sense of sawing, as dragging a saw over wood)] ▶ **This word probably refers to a special cutting tool for stoneworking.** Refs.: 2 Sam. 12:31; 1 Kgs. 7:9; 1 Chr. 20:3. ¶
[2] ***maśśôr*** [masc. noun: מַשּׂוֹר <4883>; from an unused root meaning to rasp] ▶ **This word refers to a tool used for cutting wood or stones.** Ref.: Is. 10:15. ¶
– [3] 1 Chr. 20:3 ➔ SAW (verb) <7787>.

SAW (verb) – [1] ***śûr*** [verb: שׂוּר <7787>; a prim. root, identical with RULE (verb) <7786> through the idea of reducing to pieces] ▶ **This word means to cut persons with saws and other tools as an act of destruction.** Ref.: 1 Chr. 20:3. Another translation is to set people to labor, to work with saws. ¶
– [2] 1 Kgs. 7:9 ➔ DRAG (verb) <1641>.

SAY – [1] ***'āmar*** [verb: אָמַר <559>; a prim. root] ▶ **This word means to express something verbally; it is translated in various ways depending on the context.**

It is almost always followed by a quotation. In addition to vocal speech, the word refers to thought as internal speech (2 Sam. 13:32; Esther 6:6). Further, it also refers to what is being communicated by a person's actions along with his words (Ex. 2:14; 2 Chr. 28:13). *

2 ***ᵃmar*** [Aramaic verb: אֲמַר <560>; corresponding to <559> above] ▶ **This word means to tell, to command.** The root carries the same semantic range as its Hebrew cognate, *'āmar* (SAY <559>) (Ezra 5:3, 15; Dan. 2:4; 3:24–26; 4:7–9; 7:23). *

– 3 Gen. 22:16; Num. 14:28; 24:3, 4, 15, 16; 1 Sam. 2:30; Is. 14:22; 56:8; Ezek. 16:58; Hos. 2:13; Joel 2:12; Amos 2:11; Obad. 1:4; etc. ➔ DECLARE <5002> 4 Jer. 23:31a ➔ DECLARE <5001> 5 See SPEAK <1696>.

SAYING – 1 ***mᵉliyṣāh*** [fem. noun: מְלִיצָה <4426>; from MOCK <3887>] ▶ **This word refers to a literary style, literary device, or genre, a parable, a taunting song, a mocking expression, an aphorism.** It is rendered as proverb often (Prov. 1:6: enigma, figure, interpretation, saying, parable) and stands in a close relationship to the Hebrew *māšāl*, figure, parable; see PROVERB <4912>. Other ref.: Hab. 2:6 (taunting). ¶

– 2 Num. 12:8; Ps. 49:4; 78:2; Prov. 1:6 ➔ saying, dark saying ➔ ENIGMA <2420>.

SCAB – 1 ***gārāḇ*** [masc. noun: גָּרָב <1618>; from an unused root meaning to scratch] ▶ **This word designates skin disease of some kind; it is also translated a festering sore.** It prohibited a priest from offering sacrifices to the Lord (Lev. 21:20) and also disqualified an animal to be used for sacrifice (Lev. 22:22). This condition was one of the curses the Lord would place on His people for breaking His covenant (Deut. 28:27). ¶

2 ***yallepeṯ*** [fem. noun: יַלֶּפֶת <3217>; from an unused root apparently meaning to stick or scrape] ▶ **This word refers to a skin disease; it is also translated running sore, scabbed (KJV).** No persons of the line of Aaron were permitted to offer sacrifices if they had this skin disease (Lev. 21:20); likewise, a sacrificial animal with this type of skin disease was not to be offered to the Lord (Lev. 22:22). ¶

3 ***sappaḥaṯ*** [fem. noun: סַפַּחַת <5597>; from JOIN <5596> (in the other sense of to scrape out)] ▶ **This word refers to scaly skin, a dry rash; it is also translated eruption, rash.** Refs.: Lev. 13:2; 14:56. This condition had to be watched closely and tested for its seriousness by the priests. ¶

– 4 Lev. 13:6–8 ➔ RASH <4556>.

SCABBED – Lev. 21:20; 22:22 ➔ SCAB <3217>.

SCAFFOLD – 2 Chr. 6:13 ➔ BASIN <3595>.

SCALE (noun) – 1 ***qaśqeśeṯ*** [fem. noun: קַשְׂקֶשֶׂת <7193>; by reduplication from an unused root meaning to shale off as bark] ▶ **This word indicates scales; scale armor. It refers to thin, overlapping plates for protection, e.g., the scales of a fish.** Israel was permitted to eat these fish with fins and scales (Lev. 11:9, 10, 12; Deut. 14:9, 10). It refers to armor worn by a warrior made with overlapping protective materials (1 Sam. 17:5). It is used figuratively of the scales of Egypt (Ezek. 29:4). ¶

– 2 Lev. 13:30–37; 14:54 ➔ SKIN DISEASE <5424> 3 Prov. 16:11; Is. 40:12 ➔ BALANCE <6425>.

SCALE (verb) – 2 Sam. 22:30; Ps. 18:29 ➔ LEAP <1801>.

SCALE-ARMOR – Jer. 46:4; 51:3 ➔ ARMOR <5630>.

SCALES – 1 ***mō'zᵉnayim*** [dual noun: מֹאזְנַיִם <3976>; from PONDER <239>] ▶ **This word refers to a pair of scales, balances, balance scale, i.e., a device with two containers used to weigh something.** It is in a dual form and refers to scales for weighing various things: money (Jer. 32:10); hair (Ezek. 5:1); figuratively, the Lord has weighed the mountains in a balance (Is. 40:12); the nations are a speck of

dust on the scales to the Lord (Is. 40:15). Job wishes for his grief to be weighed in a balance (Job 6:2). Also, figuratively scales are used to weigh Job before the Lord as to his integrity (Job 31:6). Persons in general weigh nothing on the scales when it comes to righteousness before God (Ps. 62:9). Dishonest scales were a feature of Israel's ethical corruption in their business dealings (Hos. 12:7; Amos 8:5; Mic. 6:11). Such scales are an abomination to the Lord (Prov. 11:1; 20:23); He always uses just weights, as a righteous God (Prov. 16:11). Other refs.: Lev. 19:36; Ezek. 45:10. ¶
2 ***mō'zᵉnê'*** [Aramaic dual noun: מֹאזְנֵא <3977>; corresponding to <3976> above] ► **This word indicates a pair of scales, balances, balance scale, i.e., a device with two containers used to weigh something.** It is used in a figurative sense once in Daniel 5:27. Belshazzar, king of Babylon, was weighed in God's scales of justice and found unfit. ¶

SCALP – Is. 43:17 ➔ FOREHEAD <6596>.

SCANT – Mic. 6:10 ➔ LEANNESS <7332>.

SCAPEGOAT – ***ᵃzā'zêl*** [masc. noun: עֲזָאזֵל <5799>; from FEMALE GOAT <5795> and GO <235>] ► **This word is taken as a designation of the goat on which the sins of the nation were laid, hence, a scapegoat on the Day of Atonement.** Refs.: Lev. 16:8, 10, 26. Others suggest that this is the name (Azazel) of a desert demon. ¶

SCAR – Lev. 13:23, 28 ➔ BURNING (adj. and noun) <6867>.

SCARCENESS – Deut. 8:9 ➔ SCARCITY <4544>.

SCARCER (MAKE) – Is. 13:12 ➔ PRECIOUS (BE) <3365>.

SCARCITY – ***miskênuṯ*** [fem. noun: מִסְכֵּנֻת <4544>; from POOR <4542>] ► **This word indicates a lack or need for more of something, in this case food.** Ref.: Deut. 8:9; KJV: scarceness. ¶

SCARE – Job 7:14 ➔ DISMAYED (BE) <2865>.

SCARECROW – Jer. 10:5 ➔ PALM TREE <8560> b.

SCARF – Is. 3:19 ➔ VEIL <7479>.

SCARLET – 1 ***šāniy*** [masc. noun: שָׁנִי <8144>; of uncertain deriv.] ► **This word describes a bright red color with a tinge of orange in it. It was used to color ribbons, threads, etc., in the ancient world.** It was easily seen (Gen. 38:28, 30; Lev. 14:4). It was a featured color of various items in the Tabernacle (Ex. 25:4; 26:1; 27:16). *
2 **to be dress, cloth, clad in scarlet: *tāla'*** [verb: תָּלַע <8529>; a denom. from CRIMSON <8438> c.] ► **This word refers to the armies of Babylon being dressed in scarlet, a bright red with a tinge of orange, a dazzling sight in war.** Ref.: Nah. 2:3. ¶
– 3 Dan. 5:7, 16, 29 ➔ PURPLE <711>
4 See CRIMSON <8438> a., c., e.

SCATTER – 1 ***bᵉḏar*** [Aramaic verb: בְּדַר <921>; corresponding (by transposition) to DIVIDE <6504>] ► **This word means to disperse in various random directions. It describes the dispersion of the fruit, the people of the earth, from the tree in Nebuchadnezzar's dream.** Ref.: Dan. 4:14. ¶
2 ***bāzar*** [verb: בָּזַר <967>; a prim. root] ► **This word means to disperse, to dissipate, to put to flight.** It refers to the dispersal and confusion of peoples who were engaged in warfare (Ps. 68:30). It depicts the dispersal or distribution of booty and plunder to allies in war (Dan. 11:24). ¶
3 ***zārāh*** [verb: זָרָה <2219>; a prim. root; comp. STRANGER (BE) <2114>] ► **This word means to winnow, to disperse; to smear, to spread.** It is used of the scattering or spreading out of people (Lev. 26:33; 1 Kgs. 14:15; Jer. 49:32, 36; 51:2); of objects, such as bones (Ezek. 6:5). It is used figuratively of scattering or winnowing the wicked (Prov. 20:26) as well as the Lord's dispersing His own people among

the nations (Ps. 44:11; 106:27). The wicked are scattered with no place to live (Job 18:15). It is used to describe the preparation or spreading of a net for the wicked (Prov. 1:17). It describes God smearing the refuse or dung of Israel's corrupt feasts on their faces (Mal. 2:3). The word is used as an active noun to refer to winds that disperse the cold (Job 37:9). The Hebrew word also means to scrutinize, to discern; see SCRUTINIZE <2219>. *

4 ***pûṣ*** [verb: פּוּץ <6327>; a prim. root] ► **a. This word means to spread something out, to disperse something.** Of humanity on the earth (Gen. 10:18; 11:4); enemies (Num. 10:35; 1 Sam. 11:11); especially of Israel dispersed among the nations in fulfillment of God's curse (Ezek. 34:5); pictured as a scattered flock (Zech. 13:7). In its passive sense, it means to be scattered, dispersed: of an army (2 Kgs. 25:5; Jer. 52:8); peoples in general (Gen. 10:18). It has the sense of causing something to be dispersed, scattered: peoples (Gen. 11:8, 9); especially among the peoples, nations (Deut. 4:27; 28:64; Jer. 9:16; Ezek. 11:16). It is used figuratively of lightning being sent forth, scattering an enemy (2 Sam. 22:15; Ps. 18:14). * **b. A verb meaning to shatter, to crush, to break in pieces.** It points out figuratively the Lord's apparent attack on Job in sickness (Job 16:12). It describes God's word, crushing rock like a sledgehammer (Jer. 23:29); and of His look breaking, shattering mountains (Hab. 3:6). *

5 ***pāraš*** [verb: פָּרַשׁ <6567>; a prim. root] ► **This word means to separate in a disorderly way, to disperse, creating confusion.** It is used of people scattered as sheep (Ezek. 34:12). The Hebrew word also means to make clear, to sting; see CLEAR (BE, MAKE) <6567> and STING <6567>. ¶

– 6 Gen. 9:19; 1 Sam. 13:11 ➔ BREAK <5310> b. 7 Deut. 32:26 ➔ PIECES (CUT TO, DASH IN) <6284> 8 Zech. 7:14 ➔ to scatter with a whirlwind, to scatter with a storm wind ➔ TEMPESTUOUS (BE, GROW) <5590> 9 See SPRINKLE <2236>.

SCATTER, SCATTERED (BE) – ***pāzar*** [verb: פָּזַר <6340>; a prim. root] ► **This word means to disperse or distribute something or someone.** Of the Jews among the Persian Empire (Esther 3:8; Joel 3:2); of the bones of the dead lying about wherever they fell (Ps. 53:5); of one's enemies (Ps. 89:10). It signifies in a good sense the sharing of things, scattering them (Prov. 11:24); but it is used of apostasy and prostitutions as well (Jer. 3:13). Other refs.: Ps. 112:9; 141:7; 147:16; Jer. 50:17. ¶

SCATTERED – 1 Is. 11:12 ➔ DRIVE <1760> 2 Zech. 11:16 ➔ YOUNG, YOUNG ONE <5289>.

SCATTERED (BE) – Nah. 3:8 ➔ FROLIC <6335> b.

SCATTERING – Is. 30:30 ➔ CLOUDBURST <5311>.

SCENTED, SWEET-SCENTED – ***merqāḥ*** [masc. noun: מֶרְקָח <4840>; from COMPOUND <7543> (in the sense of to mix perfume)] ► **This word refers to perfume, a sweet smelling scent.** It indicates sweet-smelling, aromatic herbs that create a pleasant aroma (Song 5:13). ¶

SCEPTER – ***šarḇiyṭ*** [masc. noun: שַׁרְבִיט <8275>; for ROD <7626>] ► **This word denotes a staff used as emblem of royal authority.** It is only found in the book of Esther. In Esther's response to Mordecai, she stated that anyone who went to see the king without being summoned would die unless the king extended the gold scepter in a symbolic act that saved the life of the individual (Esther 4:11). In Esther 5:2, Esther went before the king, touched the scepter that was extended to her, then stated her request that Haman come to a feast that she had provided for him and the king. Finally, Esther went again before the king and fell at his feet weeping and begging that he would stop Haman's evil plan. King Xerxes again extended the scepter to Esther, who in turn stood and restated her request (Esther 8:4). ¶

SCHEME (noun) – 1 ***ḥešbôn*** [masc. noun: חֶשְׁבּוֹן <2808>; from THINK <2803>] ►

This word means planning, a reason for things. It is also translated explanation, account. It indicates an understanding, a grasping, or a knowledge of the scheme of things (Eccl. 7:25); the result of searching out (Eccl. 7:27). It is an activity carried out by a living person; the dead (Eccl. 9:10: device, activity, thought, planning) do not understand nor can they plan anything. ¶
– [2] Num. 25:18 ➔ TRICK <5231> [3] Eccl. 7:29 ➔ DEVICE <2810>.

SCHEME (SHREWD) – Ps. 64:6 ➔ PLAN (noun) <2665>.

SCHEME (WICKED) – Ps. 140:8 ➔ DEVICE <2162>.

SCHEME (verb) – Mic. 7:3 ➔ WEAVE <5686>.

SCHEMER – [1] Job 5:5 ➔ SNARE (noun) <6782> [2] Is. 32:7 ➔ SCOUNDREL <3596>.

SCHOLAR – [1] 1 Chr. 25:8 ➔ PUPIL <8527> [2] Eccl. 12:11: words of scholars, council of scholars ➔ ASSEMBLY <627>.

SCOFF – [1] ***mûq*** [verb: מוּק <4167>; a prim. root] ► **This word means to mock, to deride; it is also translated to be corrupt (KJV).** It is used only once in the Old Testament. In Psalm 73:8, it describes the proud, mocking speech of the wicked. ¶
– [2] Deut. 32:15 ➔ to scoff at ➔ FOOLISH (BE) <5034> [3] 2 Chr. 36:16 ➔ DECEIVE <8591> a. [4] Hab. 1:10 ➔ MOCK <7046>.

SCOFFER – [1] Prov. 1:22; 29:8; Is. 28:14 ➔ MOCKER <3944> [2] Hos. 7:5 ➔ MOCKER <3945>.

SCOFFING – [1] Job 36:18 ➔ SUFFICIENCY <5607> c. [2] See SCORN (noun) <3933>.

SCOOP – Is. 30:14:9 ➔ STRIP <2834>.

SCORCH – [1] ***'āṯam*** [verb: עָתַם <6272>; a prim. root (prob. to glow)] ► **This word refers figuratively to Israel being ignited and consumed by fire because of the Lord's anger. It is difficult to pinpoint the exact nuance of this rare word.** Ref.: Is. 9:19; also translated to burn, to darken. ¶
– [2] Prov. 6:28; Is. 43:2 ➔ BURN (verb) <3554> [3] Ezek. 20:47 ➔ BURN (verb) <6866>.

SCORCHED – [1] ***šᵉḏêmāh*** [fem. noun: שְׁדֵמָה <7709>] ► **This Hebrew word apparently refers to blasting, e.g., the withering and drying up of grass by the hot sun or the blighting of corn/grain by disease.** It is used to depict the inhabitants of Egypt destroyed by the Lord's judgments (Is. 37:27; also translated blighted, blasted). For another meaning of the Hebrew word, see FIELD <7709>. ¶
[2] ***šāḏap*** [verb: שָׁדַף <7710>; a prim. root] ► **This verb means to blast. It refers to the effect of the wind on grain; it is also translated blighted.** Ears of corn were dried up, dehydrated, and withered by a hot east wind (Gen. 41:6, 23, 27). ¶
[3] ***šᵉḏêpāh, šiddāpôn*** [שְׁדֵפָה, שִׁדָּפוֹן <7711>; from <7710> above] ►
a. A feminine noun indicating something withered. It has the same meaning as <7709> above (Is. 37:27) and is used in the same way to depict, this time in general, the withering of the people of Egypt.
b. A masculine noun indicating a blight, withering, blasting (KJV). It is one of the curses that God may send on His disobedient people (Deut. 28:22), a disease or drying up of crops, grain, etc. It could be removed by prayer to the Lord and the repentance of His people (1 Kgs. 8:37; 2 Chr. 6:28; Amos 4:9; Hag. 2:17). ¶

SCORCHED LAND – [1] Is. 35:7 ➔ BURNING SAND <8273> [2] Is. 58:11 ➔ SCORCHED PLACE <6710>.

SCORCHED PLACE – ***ṣaḥṣāḥāh*** [fem. noun: צַחְצָחָה <6710>; from WHITER <6705>] ► **This word refers to an area desiccated, dried up, shriveled by a burning hot sun.** It is used of habitations where the conditions of life are like a parched area (Is. 58:11; also translated drought). ¶

SCORCHING – [1] ***ḥ*ᵃ*riyšiy*** [adj.: חֲרִישִׁי <2759>; from SILENT (BE) <2790>] ▶ **This word describes the hot desert east wind that helped kill Jonah's shade plant.** Ref.: Jon. 4:8; also translated vehement. ¶
[2] ***ᵃyām*** [masc. noun: עֲיָם <5868>; of doubtful origin and authenticity (prob. meaning strength)] ▶
a. This word refers most likely to the wind that dried up the Red Sea. Ref.: Is. 11:15: NASB, ESV, NIV. It could also possibly refer to a khamsin, a hot dry wind. ¶
b. This word refers to a mighty wind. It refers most likely to the wind that dried up the Red Sea, a mighty east wind (Is. 11:15: KJV, NKJV) or possibly a strong khamsin wind. ¶
– [3] Deut. 28:22; Amos 4:9 → SCORCHED <7711> b. [4] Ps. 11:6 → BURNING HEAT <2152> [5] Is. 49:10 → BURNING SAND <8273>.

SCORN (noun) – [1] ***giddûp̱*** [masc. noun: גִּדּוּף <1421>; from TAUNT (noun) <1422>] ▶ **This word means and is also translated reproach, revilement, reviling, insult, taunt.** It describes God's rejection and scorn of Israel because of their rebellion and scorn toward Him (Is. 43:28). It describes the scorn Israel's enemies heap on them (Zeph. 2:8). On the other hand, God's people are to endure and not fear the scorn, rejection, and revilings of others (Is. 51:7). ¶
[2] ***la'ag̱*** [masc. noun: לַעַג <3933>; from MOCK <3932>] ▶ **This word indicates derision, mocking. Used with *śāp̱āh*, lips, tongue, following, it indicates stammering lips.** It generally means derision, scorn in a negative sense (Ezek. 23:32: to hold in derision). Job was able to endure the scorn poured upon him (Job 34:7: scorn, scoffing, derision). It is used of the Lord's treatment of His rebellious people, making them an object of scorn before Himself and others (Ps. 44:13; 79:4; Hos. 7:16). The wicked mock the righteous (Ps. 123:4). Other ref.: Ezek. 36:4. ¶
[3] ***miśḥāq*** [masc. noun: מִשְׂחָק <4890>; from SHAHAZUMAH <7831> (which means proudly)] ▶ **This word indicates an object of laughter or of little concern or respect.** In context other rulers or dignitaries were scorned by the mighty Babylonians (Hab. 1:10; also translated laughing matter). ¶
– [4] Jer. 18:16 → PIPING <8292> [5] Ezek. 25:6, 15; 36:5 → MALICE <7589>.

SCORN (verb) – [1] 1 Sam. 2:29 → KICK <1163> [2] 1 Sam. 25:14 → RUSH GREEDILY <5860> a. [3] Ps. 22:24 → DETEST <8262> [4] Prov. 13:13; 23:9; 30:17; Song 8:7; Is. 37:22 → DESPISE <936> [5] Ezek. 16:31 → MOCK <7046> [6] Ezek. 16:57; 28:24, 26 → DESPISE <7590>.

SCORNER – [1] Prov. 1:22; 29:8; Is. 28:14 → MOCKER <3944> [2] Hos. 7:5 → MOCKER <3945>.

SCORNFUL MAN – Prov. 29:8; Is. 28:14 → MOCKER <3944>.

SCORPION – ***'aqrāḇ, 'aqraḇḇiym*** [masc. noun and proper noun: עַקְרָב, עַקְרַבִּים <6137>; of uncertain deriv.] ▶
a. This word denotes an order of arachnids (spiderlike) with front pinchers, a slim body, and a poisonous stinger at the end of its body. Ref.: Deut. 8:15. It is used figuratively of some kind of scourge or pestilence (1 Kgs. 12:11, 14); and of evil leaders among God's people (Ezek. 2:6). Other refs.: 2 Chr. 10:11, 14. ¶
b. A proper noun, Akrabbim. It is used of a hilly ascent at the south end of the Dead Sea. It has the contours of a scorpion's body (Num. 34:4; Josh. 15:3; Judg. 1:36). ¶

SCORPION PASS – ***ma*ᵃ*lêh 'aqrab-biym*** [proper noun: מַעֲלֵה עַקְרַבִּים <4610>; from ASCENT <4608> and (the plur. of) SCORPION <6137> b.] ▶
a. A location on the southeastern section of the boundary of Canaan and Judah, so named because the mountainous region resembled the back of a scorpion. The name is in its plural form. Refs.: Num. 34:4; Josh. 15:3; Judg. 1:36. ¶
b. The transliteration of the Hebrew for «Scorpion Pass.» The same as a. above. Ref.: Josh. 15:3. ¶
c. This is a literal translation of the Hebrew for Scorpion Pass: literally, "the

ascent of Akrabbim," "the ascent of scorpions." Refs.: Num. 34:4; Josh. 15:3; Judg. 1:36. ¶

SCOUNDREL – ***kiylay, kêlay*** [masc. noun: כִּילַי, כֵּלַי <3596>; from CONTAIN <3557> in the sense of withholding] ► **This word indicates a person of low, scandalous reputation, akin to a fool; it is also translated rogue, miser, churl, schemer.** Ref.: Is. 32:5. Israel's sin so blinded her that this person was held in esteem. Other ref.: Is. 32:7. ¶

SCOUR – Lev. 6:28 ➔ POLISH <4838>.

SCOUR AWAY – Prov. 20:30 ➔ COSMETICS <8562>.

SCOURGE – 1 Josh. 23:13 ➔ WHIP <7850> 2 Job 5:21; 9:23; Is. 10:26; 28:15, 18 ➔ WHIP <7752>.

SCOURGED (BE) – 1 Lev. 19:20 ➔ PUNISHMENT <1244> 2 Job 30:8 ➔ DRIVE OUT <5217>.

SCOURGING – 1 Lev. 19:20 ➔ PUNISHMENT <1244> 2 Is. 53:5 ➔ BRUISE (noun) <2250>.

SCRABBLE – 1 Sam. 21:13 ➔ SCRIBBLE <8427>.

SCRAPE – 1 ***gāraḏ*** [verb: גָּרַד <1623>; a prim. root] ► **The word indicates to scratch to relieve irritations.** A piece of broken pottery served Job as a tool to scrape himself because of skin irritations (Job 2:8). ¶
2 ***sāḥāh*** [verb: סָחָה <5500>; a prim. root] ► **This word means to sweep up, to clean up something by rubbing or pulling an abrasive tool over it; clearing an area of debris or filth.** Ref.: Ezek. 26:4. ¶
3 ***qāṣa'*** [verb: קָצַע <7106>; a prim. root] ► **This word means to rub or to move a sharp-edged tool or a rough tool over a surface, such as a plastered wall, to remove unwanted features or materials.** Ref.: Lev. 14:41. For another meaning of the Hebrew word, see CORNER (verb) <7106>. ¶
– 4 Lev. 14:41, 43 ➔ CUT OFF <7096>.

SCRATCH – 1 Sam. 21:13 ➔ SCRIBBLE <8427>.

SCREECH OWL – See NIGHT BIRD, NIGHT CREATURE, NIGHT MONSTER <3917>.

SCRIBBLE – ***tāwāh*** [verb: תָּוָה <8427>; a prim. root] ► **This word means to make a mark. It means, according to context, to write incoherently, in a confusing manner, illegibly.** Ref.: 1 Sam. 21:13; also translated to scratch, to scrabble. In a different context, it may have the sense of making an identifying mark, in this case, marking the righteous among God's people (Ezek. 9:4). ¶

SCRIBE – 1 ***sāp̱ar*** [Aramaic masc. noun: סָפַר <5613>; from the same as BOOK <5609>] ► **This word can refer to someone who had the ability to read and write documents, but it can also refer to someone who held a special government office; it is also translated a secretary.** A Persian official named Shimshai was identified as a scribe, whose duties probably included copying documents as well as translating documents from and into Aramaic (Ezra 4:8, 9, 17, 23). As a scribe of the law of the God of heaven, Ezra was especially qualified to interpret and teach the Law of God (Ezra 7:12, 21; NIV: teacher). ¶
2 ***šōṭêr*** [masc. noun: שֹׁטֵר <7860>; act. part. of an otherwise unused root prob. meaning to write] ► **This word means an official, a magistrate, a record keeper, and an officer. The word is used primarily to denote an officer or overseer.** While the ant has no overseer or ruler, it stores up in the summer and gathers at harvest in contrast to the sluggard who does not (Prov. 6:7). The word is also used to denote an officer in the military (2 Chr. 26:11). In Joshua, the word denoted the person that was responsible for organizing the camp for departure (Josh. 1:10; 3:2). In addition,

šōṭêr denoted those that organized the army and appointed its officers (Deut. 20:5, 8, 9). In Exodus, the slave drivers appointed Israelite foremen over the other workers (Ex. 5:14). The word is used to denote the officials appointed over Israel (Num. 11:16); and the designation of the Levites as officials (2 Chr. 19:11). *
– 3 Ezra 7:11; 2 Kgs. 18:18; 19:2; Esther 3:12; etc. ➔ NUMBER (verb) <5608> b.
4 Nah. 3:17 ➔ MARSHAL <2951>.

SCRIP – 1 Sam. 17:40 ➔ POUCH <3219>.

SCRIPT – Esther 1:22 ➔ WRITING <3791>.

SCROLL – 1 ***gillāyôn*** [masc. noun: גִּלָּיוֹן <1549>; from REVEAL <1540>] ▶ **In Isaiah 8:1, this word points to a tablet or parchment used for writing.** This Hebrew word also means a mirror in Isaiah 3:23; see MIRROR <1549>. ¶
2 ***m^egillāh*** [fem. noun: מְגִלָּה <4039>; from ROLL (verb) <1556>] ▶ **This word means roll, volume, writing, book. This Hebrew word is approximately equivalent to the English word "book." In ancient Israel, instead of pages bound into a cover, "books" were written on scrolls of leather or other durable material and rolled together.** The importance of this word is found in its reference to the sacred volume recording God's own words (cf. Jer. 36:2). Other refs.: Ps. 40:7; Jer. 36:2, 4, 6, 14, 20, 21, 23, 25, 27–29, 32; Ezek. 2:9; 3:1–3, Zech. 5:1, 2. ¶
3 ***m^egillāh*** [Aramaic noun: מְגִלָּה <4040>; corresponding to <4039> above] ▶ **This word means roll.** The term is used to describe the object upon which was written an official record of King Cyrus' decree concerning the rebuilding of the Temple at Jerusalem (Ezra 6:2). ¶

SCRUB AWAY – Prov. 20:30 ➔ COSMETICS <8562>.

SCRUTINIZE – ***zārāh*** [verb: זָרָה <2219>] ▶ **This word indicates keeping a careful watch on people, watching their paths closely; it is also translated to compass, to comprehend, to search out, to discern.** Ref.: Ps. 139:3. The Hebrew word also means to scatter, to disperse; see SCATTER <2219>. ¶

SCULPTED – ***ṣa^{ʿa}ṣuʿiym*** [masc. plur. noun: צַעֲצֻעִים <6816>; from an unused root meaning to bestrew with carvings] ▶ **This word refers to the skill of carving wood, chiseling stone; casting, cutting, or molding metal or clay into three dimensional artifacts.** The cherubim in the Most Holy Place of the Temple were sculpted, probably of wood and then overlaid with gold (2 Chr. 3:10; also translated sculptured, image). ¶

SCULPTURE – Ps. 144:12 ➔ CUT (verb) <2404>.

SCULPTURED – 2 Chr. 3:10 ➔ SCULPTED <6816>.

SCUM – 1 ***ḥel'āh*** [fem. noun: חֶלְאָה <2457>; from DISEASED (BE) <2456>] ▶ **This word is used figuratively to refer to the moral and religious corruption and rebellion of Jerusalem.** The Lord would consume it by fire and heat (Ezek. 24:6, 11, 12; also translated rust, corrosion, deposit). ¶
2 ***s^eḥiy*** [masc. noun: סְחִי <5501>; from SCRAPE <5500>] ▶ **This word refers to trash or what is rejected, left over, thrown away, unwanted.** Ref.: Lam. 3:45; also translated offscouring. ¶

SEA – 1 ***yām*** [masc. noun: יָם <3220>; from an unused root meaning to roar] ▶ **This points out significant bodies of water in general as created by God and nature at the time of God's bringing order on the earth. It denotes also the west.** Ref.: Gen. 1:26. It refers to all bodies of water collectively (Ex. 20:11); all the water collected into bodies of water (Dan. 11:45). The word refers often to specific bodies of water, designating them seas: the Great Sea, the Mediterranean (Josh. 1:4); the sea of the Philistines, also the Mediterranean (Ex. 23:31); the Dead Sea, literally, the Salt Sea (Gen. 14:3); the sea of the Arabah, again the Dead Sea (2 Kgs. 14:25); the sea of reeds or Red Sea (Ex. 10:19); the sea of Egypt (Is. 11:15); the Sea of Galilee (Num. 34:11; Josh. 13:27). It was used to refer to large rivers: the Nile (Is. 18:2); the Euphrates (Jer. 51:36).

It is used in the geographical phrase "from sea to sea" (Amos 8:12). Since it often referred to the Mediterranean Sea, the Great Sea, *yām* came to mean west (Gen. 13:14); from the west meant on the west side of (*miyyām*; Josh. 8:9). With *āh* added to the end of *yam*, the word means westward (Num. 3:23). It is used of the model bronze sea built by Solomon and used in Temple worship (1 Kgs. 7:23–25). Finally, it combines in word combinations to give the shore of the sea (Josh. 11:4); sand of the sea (*ḥōl hayyām*) (Gen. 32:12; 41:49). *

2 ***yam*** [Aramaic masc. noun: יַם <3221>; corresponding to <3220> above] ► **This word is used of the Great Sea, the Mediterranean Sea, from which Daniel sees four kingdoms arise.** Refs.: Dan. 7:2, 3. ¶

SEA GULL – ***šaḥap̱*** [masc. noun: שַׁחַף <7828>; from an unused root meaning to peel, i.e., emaciate] ► **This refers to a bird that was declared unclean in Israel.** It was forbidden as an edible food to them (Lev. 11:16; Deut. 14:15; also translated cuckow, gull). ¶

SEAH – ***sᵉʾāh*** [fem. noun: סְאָה <5429>; from an unused root meaning to define] ► **This word indicates a measure of flour or grain. An ancient dry measure of flour or grain that was equal to 6.6 dry quarts, 7.7 liquid quarts. It was probably used as a liquid as well as a dry measure. It equaled one-third of an ephah/bath.** It was used in the Old Testament to measure fine meal (Gen. 18:6); fine grain (1 Sam. 25:18); seed (1 Kgs. 18:32); fine flour (2 Kgs. 7:1, 16, 18). ¶

SEAL (noun) – 1 ***ḥôṯām, ḥōṯām*** [masc. noun: חוֹתָם, חֹתָם <2368>; from SEAL (verb) <2856>] ► **A seal was usually made of baked clay, metal, or stones and was used to identify someone. This word is also translated signet, signet ring.** It served much like an ancient identity card (Gen. 38:18) by bearing a person's distinctive mark. It also refers to a metal or other type of mold containing a person's seal that was then impressed on clay (Job 38:14) or another substance. A jeweler engraved the markings of a seal or signet ring (Ex. 28:11). It indicated a ring bearing a seal to be imposed on clay. It was a precious and intimate possession of its owner (Jer. 22:24); hence, a signet ring could be used figuratively of a person closely connected to someone (Hag. 2:23). Other refs.: Ex. 28:21, 36; 39:6, 14, 30; 1 Kgs. 21:8; Job. 41:15; Song 8:6. ¶

2 ***ḥōṯemeṯ*** [fem. noun: חֹתֶמֶת <2858>; fem. act. part. of SEAL (verb) <2856>] ► **See previous definition.** A seal that was unique to a person, imprinted on a signet ring in this case, was Judah's personal property (Gen. 38:25). It could be used to help identify a person. ¶

SEAL (verb) – 1 ***ḥāṯam*** [verb: חָתַם <2856>; a prim. root] ► **This word means to set a seal (a person's distinctive mark) on, to seal up. It indicates the act of affixing an impression to serve as a seal on something, then sealing it up as well.** It could be done to any clay object: a letter (1 Kgs. 21:8); a bill of sale, such as the one used by Jeremiah (Jer. 32:10, 11, 14, 44); a house could be sealed up (Job 24:16); something could be sealed up or stopped up (Lev. 15:3). It is used often figuratively: Daniel's vision of seventy weeks when fulfilled will seal up the prophetic vision (Dan. 9:24); Israel's testimony or law is "sealed" among his followers for future reference (Is. 8:16). It is used in Song of Solomon 4:12 to describe the bride of the bridegroom as a spring sealed up with promise of delights in marriage. It indicates sealing something so it can be opened only by the one who has the key that will open the seal (Is. 29:11). *

2 ***ḥᵃṯam*** [Aramaic verb: חֲתַם <2857>; a root corresponding to <2856> above] ► **This word refers to sealing something, to seal (i.e., affixing a person's distinctive**

mark on an object). Darius' lion's den was tamped, imprinted with the king's seal, his own signet ring imprint. Only he would release the royal seal (Dan. 6:17). ¶
– [3] Ps. 40:9 ➔ RESTRAIN <3607> a. [4] Is. 33:15 ➔ CLOSE <6105>.

SEAM – [1] Ex. 28:27; 39:20 ➔ LOOP <4225> [2] Ezek. 27:9, 27 ➔ DAMAGE (noun) <919>.

SEAR – Prov. 6:28 ➔ BURN (verb) <3554>.

SEARCH (noun) – ***ḥêqer*** [masc. noun: חֵקֶר <2714>; from SEARCH (verb) <2713>] ▶ **This word refers also to an inquiry, something to be examined.** It refers to the self-examination of one's heart (Judg. 5:16: searching); or to a general listing of things that have been examined by others (Job 8:8). The Lord's understanding is declared to be unsearchable (that cannot be fathomed, past finding, unfathomable, beyond searching out, inscrutable), among other things (*'ên ḥêqer*; Job 5:9; 9:10; Ps. 145:3; Is. 40:28). In Job the word refers to the foundations, bases or recesses of the deep or abyss (Job 38:16). Used figuratively, it denotes the deep things or depths of God to be examined (Job 11:7). Other refs.: Job 34:24; 36:26; Prov. 25:3, 27. ¶

SEARCH (MAKE) – **b^e*qar*** [Aramaic verb: בְּקַר <1240>; corresponding to SEEK <1239>] ▶ **This verb means to seek, to search for, to investigate, to find out.** It refers to a formal search made for official documents (Ezra 4:15, 19; 5:17; 6:1) and to a formal oral investigation to be made by Ezra at the command of King Artaxerxes (Ezra 7:14: to enquire, to inquire, to make inquiries). ¶

SEARCH (verb) – [1] ***ḥāqar*** [verb: חָקַר <2713>; a prim. root] ▶ **This word means to examine, to explore, to seek out.** It means to scout or explore various things: a city (2 Sam. 10:3); land (Judg. 18:2). The foundations of the earth are said to be unsearchable (Jer. 31:37; cf. 46:23). Something can be, in general, unsearchable, unmeasured (1 Kgs. 7:47; 2 Chr. 4:18). It is used of the preacher's process of searching out or even inventing proverbs or parables to communicate with his listeners (Eccl. 12:9). *
– [2] Gen. 31:34, 37 ➔ FEEL <4959>.

SEARCH FOR – ***ḥāp̱aś*** [verb: חָפַשׂ <2664>; a prim. root] ▶ **This word means to look for, to examine; to disguise oneself.** It refers to searching out, looking for something with one's mind and imagination (Ps. 64:6); or it denotes something sought out, such as valuable booty or spoil in war (Obad. 1:6). It means to search for spoil or booty (1 Kgs. 20:6). The Lord Himself tracks down His enemies (Amos 9:3). A person's conscience examines the inner aspects of his or her being (Prov. 20:27), as appointed by God; a person's spirit tries to understand the Lord's dealings with His people (Ps. 77:6). In a reflexive of the verb, it means to disguise oneself (1 Kgs. 20:38), literally, to let oneself be searched out. *

SEARCH OUT – Ps. 139:3 ➔ SCRUTINIZE <2219>.

SEARCHING – [1] Judg. 5:15 ➔ STATUTE <2711> [2] Judg. 5:16 ➔ SEARCH (noun) <2714>.

SEARING – Ps. 38:7 ➔ ROAST <7033> b.

SEASON (noun) – Eccl. 3:1 ➔ appointed time ➔ TIME <2165>.

SEASON (IN THE DRY) – Job 6:17 ➔ WARM (BE, WAX) <2215>.

SEASON (verb) – ***mālaḥ*** [verb: מָלַח <4414>; a prim. root] ▶
a. This word means to apply salt, giving flavor to various things. On a cereal or tribute offering (Lev. 2:13); on a newborn child (Ezek. 16:4: to rub with salt, to salt). In a passive sense, it is used of something being salted, such as incense (Ex. 30:35: to be salted, to be seasoned with salt). The Hebrew word also means to dissipate, to vanish: see VANISH <4414>. ¶

b. It indicates the dissipation or drifting away of the sky or heavens like smoke disappearing. Ref.: Is. 51:6. ¶

SEASONED – Is. 30:24 ➔ SALTED <2548>.

SEAT – [1] ***môšāḇ*** [masc. noun: מוֹשָׁב <4186>; from DWELL <3427>] ▶ **This word means a habitation, a dwelling place, inhabitants. The primary notion giving rise to this word is that of remaining or abiding in a given location.** It signifies a place to be seated (1 Sam. 20:18; Job 29:7); the sitting of an assembly (Ps. 107:32); the location or situation of a city (2 Kgs. 2:19); a place of habitation (Gen. 27:39: dwelling; Num. 24:21: dwelling place); the inhabitants of a particular residence (2 Sam. 9:12). The psalmist stated that the Lord Himself chose Zion as His dwelling place (Ps. 132:13; also translated habitation). *

[2] ***šeḇeṯ*** [fem. noun: שֶׁבֶת <7675>; inf. of DWELL <3427>] ▶ **This word means a dwelling place, a site; a place to sit. It comes from the verb *yāšaḇ,* to sit, to dwell, to inhabit.** It can indicate the site or location of a city (Num. 21:15); or the place of habitation, figuratively or literally, of the wicked (2 Sam. 23:7). It indicates the physical place where a people lives (Obad. 1:3). It is understood as part of a name by the NASB and NIV (2 Sam. 23:8); but as a common noun by the KJV (2 Sam. 23:8). It refers to a place to sit, a seat (1 Kgs. 10:19; 2 Chr. 9:18). It refers figuratively to a seat or a location of violence (Amos 6:3). ¶

[3] ***tᵉkhûnāh*** [fem. noun: תְּכוּנָה <8499>; from SET UP <3559> or prob. identical with ARRANGEMENT <8498>] ▶ **This word means a place of dwelling. It refers to the place or location established where someone is.** In its current context, it indicates God's dwelling or location (Job 23:3). See also ARRANGEMENT <8498> b. ¶

– [4] Song 3:10 ➔ SADDLE <4817>.

SEAT (TAKE ONE'S) – Dan. 7:9 ➔ SIT <3488>.

SEAT (WHO SAT IN THE) – ***yōšēḇ baššeḇeṯ*** [יֹשֵׁב בַּשֶּׁבֶת <3429>; from the act. part. of DWELL <3427> and LOSS OF TIME <7674> (in the sense of a time of inactivity), with a prep. and the art. interposed] ▶

a. A phrase consisting of qal active participle of *yāšaḇ* [DWELL <3427>] and *šeḇeṯ* [SEAT <7675>] with prefix preposition *bᵉ* and the definite article. It is translated in the KJV who sat in the seat (KJV, 2 Sam. 23:8). ¶

b. Josheb-Basshebeth: a chief among the captains of David. Ref.: 2 Sam. 23:8. ¶

SEATED (BE) – [1] Deut. 33:21 ➔ COVER (verb) <5603> b. [2] Dan. 26 (NKJV) ➔ SIT <3488>.

SEBA – ***sᵉḇā'*** [proper noun: סְבָא <5434>; of foreign origin] ▶

a. The firstborn son of Cush. Refs.: Gen. 10:7; 1 Chr. 1:9. ¶

b. The land or nation of Seba. Refs.: Ps. 72:10; Is. 43:3. ¶

SEBAM, SIBMAH – ***śᵉḇām, śiḇmāh*** [proper noun: שְׂבָם, שִׂבְמָה <7643>; prob. from SPICE <1313>]: fragrance, freshness ▶ **A town allotted to the tribe of Reuben in Moab.** Refs.: Num. 32:3, 38; Josh. 13:19; Is. 16:8, 9; Jer. 48:32. ¶

SECACAH – ***sᵉḵāḵāh*** [proper noun: סְכָכָה <5527>; from COVER (verb) <5526>]: enclosure ▶ **A place in the desert of Judah.** Ref.: Josh. 15:61. ¶

SECLUDED – Deut. 33:28 ➔ ALONE <910>.

SECOND – [1] ***šēniy*** [adj.: שֵׁנִי <8145>; from CHANGE (verb) <8138>] ▶ **This word refers to the second item in a series.** Refs.: Gen. 1:8; 2:13. It indicates something done for a second time (Gen. 22:15). In a conversation, it means secondly, and second, or besides (2 Sam. 16:19; Ezek. 4:6; Mal. 2:13). The plural is *šᵉniyyim* (Gen. 6:16). *

[2] ***tinyān*** [Aramaic ordinal number: תִּנְיָן <8578>; corresponding to TWO <8147>] ▶ **This word points out the second item in a series, a narrative, or a list.** Daniel's vision featured a second beast (Dan. 7:5). ¶

– [3] Gen. 41:43; 2 Kgs. 23:4 ➔ DOUBLE <4932> [4] Ezra 4:24 ➔ TWO <8648>.

SECOND TIME – ***tinyānûṯ*** [Aramaic adv.: תִּנְיָנוּת <8579>; from SECOND <8578>] ▶ **This word means again, e.g., to repeat a response, to respond again, as the king's wise men did.** Ref.: Dan. 2:7. ¶

SECRET – [1] ***taᵃlumāh*** [fem. noun: תַּעֲלֻמָה <8587>; from HIDE <5956>] ▶ **This word refers to that which is not evident, not public, concealed; it also means a hidden thing.** It refers to the concealed aspects of wisdom (Job 11:6). God is able to reveal the hidden things of wisdom (Job 28:11). More importantly, God understands and knows the secrets of the heart, what a person is truly like (Ps. 44:21). ¶
– [2] Judg. 13:18 ➔ WONDERFUL <6383> [3] Prov. 11:13; 20:19 ➔ COUNSEL (noun) <5475> [4] Dan. 2:18, 19, 27–30, 47; 4:9 ➔ MYSTERY <7328> [5] Dan. 2:22 ➔ HIDE <5642>.

SECRET ARTS – [1] Ex. 7:11 ➔ FLAMING <3858> [2] Ex. 7:22; 8:7, 18 ➔ ENCHANTMENT <3909>.

SECRET PARTS – ***pōṯ*** [masc. noun: פֹּת <6596>; from an unused root meaning to open] ▶ **This word refers to the private parts of a woman.** It may designate such private parts of women exposed in the judgments God visited on His people because of their prostitutions (Is. 3:17). The Hebrew word also refers to a door hinge and to a forehead; see HINGE <6596> and FOREHEAD <6596>. ¶

SECRET PLACE – Ps. 10:8; etc. ➔ HIDING PLACE <4565>.

SECRET SEARCH – Jer. 2:34 ➔ BREAKING IN <4290>.

SECRETARIES – Ezra 4:9 ➔ APHARSITES <670> c.

SECRETARY – Ezra 4:8, 9, 17, 23 ➔ SCRIBE <5613>.

SECRETLY – [1] ***ḥereš*** [adv.: חֶרֶשׁ <2791>; from SILENT (BE) <2790>] ▶ **This word describes doing something without giving it public exposure and keeping it from certain persons.** Joshua sent out spies into Canaan secretly (Josh. 2:1). ¶
– [2] Judg. 4:21 ➔ SOFTLY <3811> [3] Ruth 3:7; 1 Sam. 18:22; 24:4 ➔ ENCHANTMENT <3909> [4] Ps. 10:9 ➔ HIDING PLACE <4565>.

SECRETLY (DO) – ***ḥāpā'*** [verb: חָפָא <2644>; an orthographical variation of COVER (verb) <2645>] ▶ **This verb indicates to cover; to attribute something to someone.** In the stem in which it is used, it attributes Israel's doing of things, possibly secretively (2 Kgs. 17:9). It attributes to Israel certain things not approved by God. ¶

SECTION – [1] 2 Chr. 35:5 ➔ DIVISION <6391> [2] 2 Chr. 35:12 ➔ DIVISION <4651> [3] Neh. 3:11 ➔ MEASURE (noun) <4060>.

SECU, SECHU – ***śēḵû*** [proper noun: שֶׂכוּ <7906>; from an unused root apparently meaning to surmount]: observatory, watchtower ▶ **A place near Ramah with a large well.** Ref.: 1 Sam. 19:22. ¶

SECURE – [1] ***baṭṭuḥôṯ*** [fem. plur. noun: בַּטֻּחוֹת <987>; fem. plur. from TRUST (verb) <982>] ▶ **This Hebrew noun means security, safety.** Its only occurrence is Job 12:6. ¶
– [2] Deut. 33:28 ➔ ALONE <910> [3] Ps. 30:6: when I felt secure ➔ lit.: in my prosperity ➔ PROSPERITY <7959> [4] Is. 22:23 ➔ NURSE (verb) <539>.

SECURE (BE) – Jer. 12:1 ➔ EASE (BE AT) <7951> a.

SECURE HOLD – Ezra 9:8 ➔ PEG <3489>.

SECURITY – [1] ***beṭaḥ*** [masc. noun or adj.: בֶּטַח <983>; from TRUST (verb) <982>] ▶ **As a noun, this word primarily means safety or calm assurance.** Refs.: Gen. 34:25; Is. 32:17. As an adjective, it

means assurance or confidence. It is primarily a positive term: to dwell in safety because of God's protection (Lev. 25:18); to lie down safely or in security (Hos. 2:18); to walk securely or assuredly (Prov. 10:9). In other instances, it is a negative term meaning to be too self-assured or careless (Ezek. 30:9; 39:6). *
2 ***tᵉśûmeṯ*** [fem. noun: תְּשׂוּמֶת <8667>; from PUT <7760>] ▶ **This word refers to something left in safety as a pledge.** It refers to what is delivered to a person to keep in security; the person receiving it is responsible for it (Lev. 6:2). ¶
– 3 Ps. 122:7 ➔ PROSPERITY <7962> 4 Prov. 17:18 ➔ PLEDGE (noun) <6161>.

SEDAN CHAIR – Song 3:9 ➔ CARRIAGE <668>.

SEDITION – ***'eštaddûr*** [Aramaic masc. noun: אֶשְׁתַּדּוּר <849>; from LABOR (verb) <7712> (in a bad sense)] ▶ **This word means revolt, rebellion.** Refs.: Ezra 4:15, 19. ¶

SEDUCE – 1 ***ṭā'āh*** [verb: טָעָה <2937>; a prim. root] ▶ **This word refers to giving false information, saying the opposite of what is the case, whitewashing something.** Ref.: Ezek. 13:10; also translated to lead astray, to mislead. Deception is a part of the meaning of the Hebrew word. ¶
– 2 Num. 25:18 ➔ DECEIVE <5230> 3 Dan. 11:32 ➔ DEFILED (BE) <2610>.

SEDUCTIVE – Is. 3:16 ➔ WANTONLY (GLANCE) <8265>.

SEE – 1 ***ḥᵃzāh, ḥᵃzā'*** [Aramaic verb: חֲזָה, חֲזָא <2370>; corresponding to <2372> below] ▶ **This verb means to behold, to witness, to observe. It appears only in the books of Ezra and Daniel.** It signifies the literal sense of sight (Dan. 5:23); the observation of something with the eye (Dan. 3:25; 5:5); the witnessing of a king's dishonor (Ezra 4:14); beholding something in a dream (Dan. 2:41; 4:20); and having a dream (Dan. 7:1). On one occasion, the verb is used to imply the usual condition or customary state of the furnace set to receive Shadrach, Meshach, and Abednego (Dan. 3:19). This use probably stresses the difference in the appearance of the furnace, which would be obvious to the observer. *
2 ***ḥāzāh*** [verb: חָזָה <2372>; a prim. root] ▶ **This term means to behold, to observe, to perceive. It is more poetic than the common *rā'āh* (<7200> below).** It refers to seeing God (Ex. 24:11; Job 19:26, 27; Ps. 11:7; 17:15); astrological observations (Is. 47:13); prophetic vision and insight (Is. 1:1; Lam. 2:14; Ezek. 12:27; Hab. 1:1; Zech. 10:2). *
3 ***rā'āh, rō'eh*** [verb: רָאָה, רֹאֶה <7200>; a prim. root] ▶ **The basic denotation of this word is to see with the eyes (Gen. 27:1).** It can also have the following derived meanings, all of which require the individual to see physically outside of himself or herself: to see so that one can learn to know, whether it be another person (Deut. 33:9) or God (Deut. 1:31; 11:2); to experience (Jer. 5:12; 14:13; 20:18; 42:14); to perceive (Gen. 1:4, 10, 12, 18, 21, 25, 31; Ex. 3:4); to see by volition (Gen. 9:22, 23; 42:9, 12); to look after or to visit (Gen. 37:14; 1 Sam. 20:29); to watch (1 Sam. 6:9); to find (1 Sam. 16:17); to select (2 Kgs. 10:3); to be concerned with (Gen. 39:23). It is also possible for this verb to require the individual to make a mental observation. As an imperative, it can function as an exclamation similar to *hinnêh* (<2009>), which means to behold (Gen. 27:27; 31:50). Further, it can denote to give attention to (Jer. 2:31); to look into or inquire (1 Sam. 24:15); to take heed (Ex. 10:10); to discern (Eccl. 1:16; 3:13); to distinguish (Mal. 3:18); to consider or reflect on (Eccl. 7:14). It can also connote a spiritual observation and comprehension by means of seeing visions (Gen. 41:22; Is. 30:10). *
4 ***šāzap̱*** [verb: שָׁזַף <7805>; a prim. root] ▶ **a. In its context this word refers to observing, regarding a person while still alive.** Ref.: Job 20:9. It describes the observation or sighting of a falcon's eye (Job 28:7). It has the sense of looking intently in some contexts (Song 1:6).
b. This word means to burn, to darken (the result of the sun looking on one). It

refers to the effect of the sun's rays shining (looking) on persons, making them dark and swarthy (Song 1:6). ¶
– 5 Job 10:15 ➔ CONSCIOUS <7202> 6 Job 39:29; Ps. 119:18 ➔ LOOK (verb) <5027> 7 Prov. 31:18 ➔ TASTE (verb) <2938> 8 Eccl. 5:11 ➔ BEHOLD (verb) <7207> 9 Eccl. 5:11 ➔ BEHOLDING <7212>.

SEE CLEARLY – Num. 24:3, 15 ➔ OPEN, BE OPEN <8365>.

SEED – 1 ***zera'*** [masc. noun: זֶרַע <2233>; from SOW <2232>] ▶ **This word means the part of a plant from which a new plant can grow. It also means sowing, descendants, offspring, children, and posterity. The literal use of the word indicates seed of the field (i.e., seed planted in the field).** When Israel entered Egypt, Joseph instructed the Israelites to keep four-fifths of the crop as seed to plant in their fields and to serve as food for them (Gen. 47:24); the season for planting seed was guaranteed by God to continue without fail (Gen. 8:22); and successful, abundant harvests were promised right up until the sowing season if Israel followed the Lord's laws and commands (Lev. 26:5). God had created the seed of the field by decreeing that plants and trees would be self-perpetuating, producing their own seed (Gen. 1:11) and that the seed-producing plants would be edible (Gen. 1:29). Manna, the heavenly food, resembled coriander seed (Ex. 16:31). Any seed could be rendered unclean and not usable if a dead body fell on it after the seed had been moistened (Lev. 11:38).

The noun is used to describe the seed (i.e., the offspring) of both people and animals. The seed of Judah and Israel would be united and planted peacefully in the land together with animals in a pleasant setting (Jer. 31:27). Seed can be translated as son (i.e., seed as when God gives Hannah a promise of a son [1 Sam. 1:11]). The seed of a woman mentioned in Genesis 3:15 is her offspring, ultimately pointing to the Messiah, the seed of Abraham and of David (see Gen. 22:17, 18; Matt. 1:1; Gal. 3:16, 29).

The offspring of humans is described many times by this word. Hannah was given additional children to replace Samuel, whom she gave to the Lord's service (1 Sam. 2:20). The most important seed that the author of Genesis describes is the seed of Abraham, the promised seed, referring to Isaac, Jacob, and his twelve sons (Gen. 12:7; 15:3). The author of Genesis uses the word twenty-one times in this setting (Ex. 32:13; Deut. 1:8). The seed of the royal line of David was crucial to Israel's existence, and the term is used nine times to refer to David's offspring or descendants (2 Sam. 7:12). In a figurative sense, seed refers to King Zedekiah and perhaps to Israelites of royal lineage, whom Nebuchadnezzar established in Jerusalem (Ezek. 17:5). Royal lines or seed were found outside Israel, such as in Edom, where Hadad belonged to the royal line (1 Kgs. 11:14), and in Judah, where the wicked Athaliah attempted to destroy the royal seed (2 Kgs. 11:1; 25:25; Jer. 41:1).

The seed or offspring of a particular nation can be characterized in moral and religious terms as well. Three verses stand out: The seed of Israel was called a holy seed (Ezra 9:2; Is. 6:13); and, in the case of Ezra 9:2, the seed corrupted itself by mixing with the peoples around them. The seed of Israel is a seed of God or a divine seed (Mal. 2:15) through its union with God (cf. 2 Pet. 1:4). An offspring could be described as deceitful and wicked (Ps. 37:28; Is. 57:4). It was important in Israel to prove that one's origin or seed stemmed from an Israelite ancestor, for some Israelites and Israelite priests who returned from exile could not show their origin (Ezra 2:59). The word also refers to the seed or posterity of the Messiah (Is. 53:10). *

2 ***zᵉra'*** [Aramaic masc. noun: זְרַע <2234>; corresponding to <2233> above] ▶ **This word is used only once in Daniel 2:43 in the idiomatic phrase "with the seed of men" (KJV).** In this passage, Daniel interpreted King Nebuchadnezzar's dream about the gold, silver, bronze, iron, and clay statue. This mixing of people with the seed of men is a reference to other people groups

joining a community or nation. Those who come afterward lack the national spirit to adhere to one another, just as iron does not mix with clay. ¶

3 ***ḥarṣān*** [masc. noun: חַרְצָן <2785>; from MOVE <2782> (in the sense of something sharp, e.g., in taste] ▶ **This word refers to the kernels of the grape.** Ref.: Num. 6:4. Some have suggested that its reference is to unripe grapes. ¶

4 ***pᵉruḏōṯ*** [fem. noun: פְּרֻדֹת <6507>; fem. pass. part. of DIVIDE <6504>] ▶ **This word refers to separated grain that has been planted in the ground after plowing.** Ref.: Joel 1:17. ¶

– 5 Is. 61:11 ➔ SOWING <2221>.

SEED (BEAR) – See SOW <2232>.

SEED PODS – 1 2 Kgs. 6:2 ➔ DOVE'S DUNG <2755> 2 2 Kgs. 6:25 ➔ DOVE'S DUNG <1686>.

SEEDLING – Is. 17:10 ➔ BRANCH <2156>.

SEEING – ***piqqêaḥ*** [masc. adj.: פִּקֵּחַ <6493>; from OPEN <6491>] ▶ **This word is derived from the verb *pāqaḥ* (<6491>), meaning to open the eyes and ears; it describes those with the faculty of sight (as opposed to the blind).** In a literal sense, it occurs in Exodus 4:11 when God answered Moses' objections for leading the people out of Egypt. In a metaphorical sense, this term represented those who could see clearly but could be blinded by a gift (Ex. 23:8: clear-sighted, discerning, wise). ¶

SEEK – 1 ***bᵉʿā'*** [Aramaic verb: בְּעָא <1156>; corresponding to BOIL (verb) <1158> (in the sense of to ask, to request)] ▶ **This word means to ask, to request, to desire.** It is found only in Daniel, it connotes the idea to ask, request, or petition (2:18). It also conveys the idea of praying to God or seeking out a person (2:13); asking a person for something (6:7); making other inquiries (7:16); or seeking out a fault (6:4). *

2 ***bāqar*** [verb: בָּקַר <1239>; a prim. root] ▶ **This verb means to look for, to consider, to investigate.** It describes the process the priest goes through to see whether someone is unclean (Lev. 13:36) or religious inquiring in general at the bronze altar (2 Kgs. 16:15). It describes concern in general about an issue (Lev. 27:33). The psalmist's greatest desire was the object sought by this verb: to dwell in the house of the Lord (Ps. 27:4). On the other hand, the object the Lord seeks and cares for is His sheep, His people (Ezek. 34:11, 12). Other ref.: Prov. 20:25 (to make inquiry, to reconsider, to consider, to reflect). ¶

3 ***baqqārāh*** [fem. noun: בַּקָּרָה <1243>; intens. from <1239> above] ▶ **This word indicates the searching and caring of a shepherd for his flock when they are scattered.** Ref.: Ezek. 34:12; also translated to look after. In context, it depicts the Lord's care for His flock at a crucial time. ¶

4 ***bāqaš*** [verb: בָּקַשׁ <1245>; a prim. root] ▶ **This verb means to require, to try to obtain.** It is used to describe subjects seeking or requiring various things for various reasons: a stolen object (Gen. 31:39); persons (Gen. 37:15, 16); someone's life (Ex. 4:19; 24); evil against someone (1 Sam. 25:26) or good (Neh. 2:10; Ps. 122:9).

It denotes seeking someone's presence, especially the Lord's (1 Kgs. 10:24; Hos. 5:15) or His word (Amos 8:12). Prayer was a means of seeking the Lord's will (Dan. 9:3). In the passive use of the verb, something is sought for (Jer. 50:20; Ezek. 26:21) or is examined (Esther 2:23). *

5 ***dāraš*** [verb: דָּרַשׁ <1875>; a prim. root] ▶ **This word means to inquire of, to examine, to require.** Figuratively, it may refer to seeking out or inquiring about lovers (Jer. 30:14) or to care for Zion (Jer. 30:17). It denotes inquiring about persons (2 Sam. 11:3) or their welfare (souls) (Ps. 142:4). It indicates the Lord's care for His land (Deut. 11:12). It carries the general sense of seeking out property, such as a lost ox or cattle (Deut. 22:2), or examining a matter (Deut. 13:14; Judg. 6:29; 1 Kgs. 22:7) or event. It takes on the meaning of requiring or demanding someone's blood in a moral or legal sense (Gen. 9:5; 2 Chr. 24:22; Ps. 10:13) but also of seeking good itself (Amos 5:14).

Its most important theological meaning involves studying or inquiring into the Law of the Lord (Ezra 7:10) or inquiring of God (Gen. 25:22; Ex. 18:15; Deut. 12:5; 1 Kgs. 22:5; 2 Kgs. 3:11). God's people seek after their God (Deut. 4:29; Hos. 10:12; Amos 5:4). Seeking the Lord will be greatly rewarded (Ps. 34:10). Seeking heathen gods or persons who deal with the dead is to be avoided (1 Sam. 28:7; Is. 8:19; Ezek. 14:10). The works of God, however, are to be examined and studied (Ps. 111:2). *

SEEK DILIGENTLY – ***šāḥar*** [verb: שָׁחַר <7836>; a prim. root; properly, to dawn, i.e., (fig.) be up early at any task (with the implication of earnestness)] ▶
a. A verb meaning to look for persistently; to search for. It means to inquire after something or someone carefully. A person (Job 7:21); God (Job 8:5; Ps. 63:1; 78:34; Is. 26:9; Hos. 5:15); wisdom (Prov. 1:28; 8:17). It describes a harlot seeking a man (Prov. 7:15). Other ref.: Job 24:5. ¶
b. A verb meaning to conjure away; to charm away. It describes a process or ritual of pagan religion employed to get rid of unwanted conditions or evil (Is. 47:11). But it can be used in a proper context of Israel's properly seeking her God. For Hosea 5:15, see a. above and DAWN (noun) <7837>. ¶

SEEK OUT – ***tûr*** [verb: תּוּר <8446>; a prim. root] ▶ **This word means to explore, to spy out.** It refers to going into a land or country to search it out, e.g., Canaan (Num. 10:33; 13:2, 16, 17, 21, 25, 32; 14:6, 7, 34, 36, 38). It depicts persons following their own hearts or desires, seeking them out to pursue them rather than the Lord's will (Num. 15:39). It refers to merchants, those who seek out wares (1 Kgs. 10:15; 2 Chr. 9:14). It is used of the instincts and inclinations of an animal to search out its habitat (Job 39:8). It refers to a person serving as a guide who explores the way for others (Prov. 12:26). It is used figuratively of exploring and investigating wisdom and its ways (Eccl. 1:13; 2:3; 7:25). It refers to the Lord's previous exploration (NASB: selection) of the land of Canaan before giving it to His people (Ezek. 20:6). Other refs.: Num. 15:39; Judg. 1:23. ¶

SEEMLY – Prov. 19:10; 26:1 → BEAUTIFUL <5000>.

SEER – 1 ***ḥōzeh, chōzeh*** [masc. noun: חֹזֶה, חֹזֶה <2374>; act. part. of SEE <2372>] ▶ **This word is used only seventeen times in the Old Testament, always in the present active participle. The word means one who sees or perceives; it is used in parallel with the participle of the verb that means literally to see, to perceive.** In Isaiah a rebellious people sought to curb the functions of these seers (Is. 30:10). In 1 Samuel 9:9, the author parenthetically states that the word for prophet in his day, *nāḇiy'* (PROPHET <5030>), was formerly called a seer. However, for seer, he did not use *ḥôzeh* but a present participle of the verb *rā'āh* (SEE <7200>), meaning to see, to perceive. It appears that the participles of *ḥôzeh* and of *rā'āh* function synonymously. But, terminology aside, a seer functioned the same as a prophet, who was moved by God and had divinely given insight. This Hebrew word is also used in parallel with the word prophet (2 Kgs. 17:13; Amos 7:12, 14); hence, its meaning overlaps with that term as well (cf. 2 Chr. 33:18; Is. 29:10). Seers sometimes served a specific person: Gad served as King David's seer and did not hesitate to declare the words the Lord gave him for the king (2 Sam. 24:11). David had more than one seer (cf. 1 Chr. 25:5; 2 Chr. 29:25).

The functions of a seer as indicated by this term included, besides receiving and reporting the word of the Lord, writing about David's reign (1 Chr. 29:29); receiving and writing down visions (2 Chr. 9:29); writing genealogical records under Rehoboam's reign (2 Chr. 12:15). In general, the Lord forewarned His people through His prophets and seers (2 Kgs. 17:13; 2 Chr. 33:18). In many cases, these warnings were recorded in writing (2 Chr. 33:19). Other refs.: 1 Chr. 21:9; 2 Chr. 19:2; 29:30; 35:15; Ezek. 22:28; Mic. 3:8. ¶
– 2 2 Chr. 33:19 → HOZAI <2335>.

SEETHE – Job 30:27 ➔ BOIL (verb) <7570>.

SEETHING – Job 41:20; Jer. 1:13 ➔ BREATHE <5301>.

SEGUB – ***śᵉgûḇ*** [masc. proper noun: שְׂגוּב <7687>; from EXALTED (BE) <7682>]: exalted ▶
a. Son of Hiel. Ref.: 1 Kgs. 16:34. ¶
b. Son of Hezron. Refs.: 1 Chr. 2:21, 22. ¶

SEIR – ***śê'iyr*** [proper noun: שֵׂעִיר <8165>; formed like GOAT <8163>]: rough ▶
a. A mountain and also a mountain range in Edom usually taken to mean territory east of the Arabah Valley rift in Judah (sometimes it seemed to reach west [Deut. 1:2, 44] of the Arabah Valley). It ran from the brook Zered on the south of the Dead Sea to the Gulf of Aqaba. Genesis 32:3 identifies it with the country of Edom. Esau and his descendants settled in these areas. It is connected with Sinai and the Desert of Paran in the west of the Arabah (Deut. 33:2). The name designates a particular mountain in some texts (Gen. 14:6; Ezek. 35:15). Before the Edomites, the Horites lived in the territory (Gen. 36:8–30; Deut. 2:12). Some Amalekites settled in the area (1 Chr. 4:42). Ezekiel refers to the people of Seir who came to despise Israel (25:8), and he directed the Lord's judgment against it (35:1–30).
b. An ancient ancestor of the Horites who settled Edom before Esau. Refs.: Gen. 36:20, 21; 1 Chr. 1:38.
c. A boundary marker on the north of Judah. Ref.: Josh. 15:10. It was about ten miles west of Jerusalem. *

SEIRAH – ***śᵉ'iyrāh*** [proper noun: שְׂעִירָה <8167>; formed as GOAT <8166>]: roughness ▶ **A place in Ephraim where Ehud escaped after having killed Eglon, the king of Moab.** Ref.: Judg. 3:26. ¶

SEIZE – [1] Ex. 15:14 ➔ HOLD (TAKE) <270> [2] Judg. 21:21; Ps. 10:9 ➔ CATCH (verb) <2414> [3] Is. 22:17 ➔ WRAP AROUND <5844> b.

SELA – ***sela'*** [proper noun: סֶלַע <5554>; the same as ROCK <5553>]: rock ▶ **The capital of Edom.** Refs.: Judg. 1:36; 2 Kgs. 14:7; Is. 16:1; 42:11. ¶

SELA-HAMMAHLEKOTH – ***sela' hammaḥlᵉqôṯ*** [proper noun: סֶלַע הַמַּחְלְקוֹת <5555>; from ROCK <5553> and the plur. of ESCAPE <4256> b. with the art. interposed]: rock of division ▶ **The name of a gorge between Hachilah and Maon.** Ref.: 1 Sam. 23:28. ¶

SELAH! – ***selāh*** [verb: סֶלָה <5542>; from REJECT <5541> (possibly in the sense of to put out, to suspend)] ▶ **This word is possibly a fixed imperative form. Its exact meaning is uncertain. Perhaps it marks places for pauses in singing.** It is used over seventy times in Psalms (Ps. 3:2, 4, 8; 4:2, 4; 7:5; etc.). It may give musical instructions or indicate a pause for various reasons (Hab. 3:3, 9, 13). *

SELDOM SET, SELDOM BE – Prov. 25:17 ➔ PRECIOUS (BE) <3365>.

SELED – ***seleḏ*** [masc. proper noun: סֶלֶד <5540>; from REJOICE <5539>]: exultation ▶ **A man of the tribe of Judah.** Ref.: 1 Chr. 2:30. ¶

SELF-ABASEMENT – Ezra 9:5 ➔ FASTING <8589>.

SELF-CONTROL – ***ma'ṣār*** [masc. noun: מַעְצָר <4623>; from RESTRAIN <6113>] ▶ **This word is negated in its only occurrence. It characterizes a person as one who has no restraint; it is also translated rule, control.** This person is also compared to a ruined city without walls (Prov. 25:28). ¶

SELL – [1] ***māḵar*** [verb: מָכַר <4376>; a prim. root] ▶ **This word is a basic verb of exchange; it also means to give up something.** The selling of the right of the firstborn by Esau (Gen. 25:31); land (Gen. 47:20); cattle (Ex. 21:35); oil (2 Kgs. 4:7); even persons were sold (Gen. 31:15); sometimes persons or slaves were sold (Gen. 37:27, 28; Ex. 21:8); often persons captured in battle (Deut. 21:14). It is used in a figurative sense of selling an abstract quality like wisdom or truth (Prov. 23:23). It has the nuanced sense of handing over, surrendering something: God may give up His people (1 Sam. 12:9); or a person (Judg. 4:9). It is used of persons selling themselves (Lev. 25:47, 48); or letting oneself be sold (Deut. 28:68). Used with *lᵉ* plus *'ebeḏ*, it indicates being sold as a slave (Ps. 105:17); with *laᵃśôṯ*, it may mean, in its reflexive use, to sell oneself to do evil (1 Kgs. 21:20, 25; 2 Kgs. 17:17). * – 2 Gen. 41:57; Deut. 2:6; etc. ➔ BUY <7666> 3 Hos. 8:9, 10 ➔ HIRE <8566>.

SEM – See SHEM <8035>.

SENAAH, HASSENAAH – ***sᵉnā'āh, hassᵉnā'āh*** [masc. proper noun: סְנָאָה, הַסְּנָאָה <5570>; from an unused root meaning to prick]: thorny ▶ **The sons of Senaah rebuit the Fish Gate.** Ref.: Neh. 3:3. Descendants of Senaah came back from the Babylonian captivity with Zerubbabel (Ezra 2:35; Neh. 7:38). ¶

SEND – Esther 9:19, 22 ➔ LAY, PUT <4916> a.

SEND, BE SENT – ***šᵉlaḥ*** [Aramaic verb: שְׁלַח <7972>; corresponding to SEND FORTH, SEND AWAY <7971>] ▶ **This word describes God or a person putting forth, causing someone or something to go.** God sending a messenger (Dan. 3:28; 6:22); a person sending a letter or report (Ezra 4:11, 18); sending to inform someone (Ezra 4:14); or sending an answer, a reply (Ezra 4:17). It describes a person being sent (Ezra 7:14); one who is sent or a word from God that is sent (Dan. 5:24). The phrase who sends forth his hand to change (it), indicates an attempt to change Darius' decree (Ezra 6:12). It is used as a technical term to indicate the sending or issuing of a royal decree (Ezra 6:13); or command (Dan. 3:2). *

SEND FORTH – 1 Job 37:3 ➔ LOOSE (LET) <8281> 2 Ps. 144:6 ➔ FLASH FORTH <1299> 3 Eccl. 10:1 ➔ UTTER <5042>.

SEND FORTH, SEND AWAY – ***šālaḥ*** [verb: שָׁלַח <7971>; a prim. root] ▶ **This word means to let go, causing someone or something to go; to put.** The word is used to describe God's sending forth or away in a providential manner or purpose (Gen. 45:5; 1 Sam. 15:18); even an angel or divine messenger can be sent by God (Gen. 24:7); or of commissioning someone by sending him or her, e.g., Moses (Ex. 3:12; Judg. 6:14); or Gideon to do a task (cf. Num. 21:6; Deut. 7:20; 2 Kgs. 17:13, 26). The Lord sends forth His prophets (Jer. 7:25); and His plagues on Egypt (Ex. 9:14). It is used figuratively of the Lord's sending forth arrows (2 Sam. 22:15; Ps. 18:14); or is used literally of a person shooting arrows (1 Sam. 20:20, in an intensive stem). God sends forth His Word (Is. 9:8; 55:11; Zech. 7:12). It can have a strong sense of casting out someone (Lev. 18:24; 20:23; Jer. 28:16). In its intensive stem, it means to set free (Ex. 4:23; 5:2). Referring to an animal, it can mean let loose (Ex. 22:5).

It can have the sense of putting forth or reaching out one's hand (Gen. 37:22; 1 Sam. 24:10). It is used in a figurative sense of God's stretching out His hand, His power, against the leaders of Israel (Ex. 24:11). It may take on the idea of sending away, of letting loose (Gen. 28:5; Judg. 11:38; Ps. 50:19). In its passive sense, it refers to something being sent out (Gen. 44:3; Esther 3:13).

It is found in contexts in which it means to put forth (branches) (Ps. 80:11; Jer. 17:8; Ezek. 31:5). To put down, to let down, e.g., Jeremiah into a cistern (Jer. 38:6). The phrase to set the city on fire is literally to cast against the city with fire (Judg. 1:8; 20:48).

In its intensive passive stem, the word is used to describe a woman sent forth or divorced (Is. 50:1), but it is used in a figurative sense. It has the sense of unrestrained, let loose, in reference to a spoiled child (Prov. 29:15). In its causative stem use, it means to send forth, to cause to go out: famine (Ezek. 14:13; Amos 8:11); wild beasts (Lev. 26:22); flies of a plague (Ex. 8:21); an enemy (2 Kgs. 15:37). *

SEND OUT – Ezek. 17:7 ➔ BEND <3719>.

SENDING – Ps. 78:49 ➔ DISCHARGE <4917>.

SENDING FORTH – Is. 7:25 ➔ LAY, PUT <4916> b.

SENEH – ***senneh*** [proper noun: סֶנֶּה <5573>; the same as BUSH <5572>]: thorn ▶ **The name of a rocky crag on the side of the pass that Jonathan intended to cross to go over to the Philistine.** Ref.: 1 Sam. 14:4. ¶

SENIR, SHENIR – ***ś^eniyr, š^eniyr*** [proper noun: שְׂנִיר, שְׁנִיר <8149>; from an unused root meaning to be pointed]: peak, snow mountain ▶ **The name given by the Amorites to Mount Hermon.** Refs.: Deut. 3:9; 1 Chr. 5:23; Song 4:8; Ezek. 27:5. ¶

SENNACHERIB – ***sanḥēriyḇ*** [masc. proper noun: סַנְחֵרִיב <5576>; of foreign origin] ▶ **An Assyrian king (705–681 B.C.) who steam rolled through Israel and Judah, devastating the land, its cities, and inhabitants. His name means "(the) moon god has prospered his kinsmen."** He destroyed Lachish, a Judean city, after a long and horrifying siege (2 Kgs. 18:14–17; 19:8). He attempted to besiege Jerusalem and raze it in 701 B.C. when Hezekiah was king and Isaiah was prophesying (2 Kgs. 18; 19; Is. 36; 37). The Lord destroyed his army by an act of divine providence. Sennacherib was assassinated thereafter by his sons. *

SENSE – Prov. 31:18 ➔ TASTE (verb) <2938>.

SENSE (HAVE NO) – Jer. 5:4 ➔ FOOLISHLY (BE, DO, ACT) <2973>.

SENSELESS – ***ba‘ar*** [adj.: בַּעַר <1198>; from BURN (verb) <1197>] ▶ **This word means without intelligence; it is also translated foolish, brutish, stupid.** Asaph uses it concerning himself in one of his psalms (Ps. 73:22). It refers to a person who is senseless about riches (Ps. 49:10) or a person who will not learn discipline (Prov. 12:1). As a general term, it depicts any person who stands before the unsearchable wisdom of God as stupid (Prov. 30:2, 3). Other ref.: Ps. 92:6. ¶

SENSIBLE – [1] Prov. 14:15, 18 ➔ PRUDENT <6175> [2] Prov. 15:5 ➔ CRAFTY (BE) <6191>.

SENSITIVE – [1] Deut. 28:54, 56 ➔ DELICATE <6028> [2] Deut. 28:56 ➔ DELIGHT (HAVE, FIND, TAKE) <6026>.

SENSITIVITY – Deut. 28:56 ➔ REFINEMENT <7391>.

SENSUAL – [1] Is. 47:8 ➔ PLEASURES (GIVEN TO, LOVER OF) <5719> [2] Ezek. 33:32 ➔ LOVE (noun) <5690>.

SENTENCE – [1] Eccl. 8:11 ➔ EDICT <6599> [2] Dan. 4:17 ➔ ANSWER (noun) <6600> [3] Dan. 4:17 ➔ DECISION <7595> [4] Dan. 5:12: hard sentence ➔ RIDDLE <280>.

SENTRY – Jer. 37:13 ➔ lit.: captain of the guard ➔ GUARD <6488>.

SENUAH, HASSENUAH – ***ś^enû'āh, hass^eu'āh*** [masc. proper noun: סְנוּאָה, הַסְּנֻאָה <5574>; from the same as SENAAH, HASSENAAH <5570>]: pointed, thorny ▶
a. Father of a certain Judah. Ref.: Neh. 11:9: Senuah. ¶
b. A Benjamite. Ref.: 1 Chr. 9:7: Hassenuah. ¶

SEORIM – ***ś^e‘ōriym*** [masc. proper noun: שְׂעֹרִים <8188>; masc. plur. of BARLEY <8184>]: barley ▶ **A priest in the time of David chosen to serve in the Tabernacle.** Ref.: 1 Chr. 24:8. ¶

SEPARATE (adj.) – [1] ***ḥop̄šiyṯ*** [fem. noun: חָפְשִׁית <2669>; from FREE (BE) <2666>] ▶ **This Hebrew noun denotes freedom, separateness; it is also translated isolated,**

separate, several. It refers to a special house for King Azariah because he was leprous; it was separate from other state buildings (2 Kgs. 15:5; 2 Chr. 26:21). ¶

2 ***miḇdālāh*** [fem. noun: מִבְדָּלָה <3995>; from SEPARATE (verb)] ▶ **This Hebrew noun indicates a place set apart; singled out.** It refers to something selected, set apart, for a specific purpose, i.e., cities and villages for the sons of Ephraim (Josh. 16:9; also translated that is set apart, that is set aside). ¶

SEPARATE (verb) – 1 ***bāḏal*** [verb: בָּדַל <914>; a prim. root] ▶ **This word means to divide, to detach. It is used most often of the various words that indicate these ideas.** It is used both literally and figuratively in two different stems. The first stem is reflexive or passive in its function, and the second is causative. The reflexive sense of the word is used to express Israel's separation of themselves from intermarriage and the abominations and pollution of the nations around them (Ezra 6:21; 10:11) in order to dedicate themselves to the Lord and His Law (Neh. 10:28). Its passive usage indicates those being set apart for something (1 Chr. 23:13) or, in a negative sense, being excluded from something (e.g., from the community of Israel [Ezra 10:8]).

The verb is used most often in its active causative meanings that are the active counterparts to its passive reflexive meanings. Perhaps the most famous example of this is found in the creation story as God produces a separation between light and darkness (Gen. 1:4). Just as significant is the distinction He makes between His people Israel and the peoples and nations surrounding them (Lev. 20:24). The fact that Moses set aside the Levites to administer and to carry out their holy duties is described by this word (Num. 8:14), as is the exclusion of a person from the Israelite community (Deut. 29:21). In the religious and ritualistic sphere, this word indicates a sharp division between the holy and unholy (profane) and the clean and unclean (Lev. 20:25). It also describes priests dividing sacrificial animals into pieces (Lev. 1:17).

The use of this word by the writer indicates that God desires to make discriminations between this people and the nations, among groups within His own people and within His larger creation, both animate and inanimate. These differences are important to God and are to be observed carefully, especially by His chosen nation. *

2 ***nāzar*** [verb: נָזַר <5144>; a prim. root] ▶ **This word means to dedicate, to consecrate, to abstain.** In the passive or reflexive form, it can signify a dedication to (Hos. 9:10; also translated to consecrate, to devote) or a separation from a deity (Ezek. 14:7). It can also indicate considering something as sacred and consecrated (Lev. 22:2; also translated to treat with respect, to be careful). This verb also expresses the idea of consecrating oneself by fasting (Zech. 7:3; also translated to fast). In the causative form, it can denote to separate or to refrain from something (Lev. 15:31; also translated to keep separated); or to take on the obligations of a Nazirite, a *nāziyr* (NAZIRITE <5139>) (Num. 6:2, 5, 12). Other refs.: Num. 6:3, 6. ¶

– 3 1 Kgs. 5:9 ➔ BREAK <5310> b.

SEPARATE AREA – Gen. 42:21; etc. ➔ COURTYARD <1508>.

SEPARATED – Gen. 49:26 ➔ NAZIRITE <5139>.

SEPARATED (BE) – Ex. 33:16 ➔ DISTINCTION (MAKE) <6395>.

SEPARATED (KEEP) – Lev. 15:31 ➔ SEPARATE <5144>.

SEPHAR – ***sᵉpār*** [proper noun: סְפָר <5611>; the same as CENSUS <5610>]: numbering ▶ **A mountain in Arabia.** Ref.: Gen. 10:30. ¶

SEPHARAD – ***sᵉp̄āraḏ*** [proper noun: סְפָרַד <5614>; of foreign deriv.] ▶ **Exiles from Jerusalem lived there.** Ref.: Obad. 1:20. ¶

SEPHARVAIM – ***sᵉp̄arwayim*** [proper noun: סְפַרְוַיִם <5617>; of foreign deriv.] ▶

A city and/or region possibly in the territory of Aram (Syria). People were settled from Aram into northern Israel by the Assyrians (2 Kgs. 17:24–31). *

SEPHARVITE – ***separwiy*** [proper noun: סְפַרְוִי <5616>; patrial from SEPHARVAIM <5617>] ▶ **An inhabitant of Sepharvaim (<5617>).** Ref.: 2 Kgs. 17:31. ¶

SEPULCHRE – See GRAVE (noun) <6913>.

SERAH – ***śeraḥ*** [fem. proper noun: שֶׂרַח <8294>; by permutation from REMNANT <5629>]: abundance ▶ **The sister of the sons of Asher.** Refs.: Gen. 46:17; Num. 26:46; 1 Chr. 7:30. ¶

SERAIAH – ***śerāyāh, śerāyāhû*** [masc. proper noun: שְׂרָיָה, שְׂרָיָהוּ <8304>; from STRUGGLE <8280> and LORD <3050>]: the Lord has prevailed ▶

a. Secretary to David. Ref.: 2 Sam. 8:17. ¶
b. A Judaite, father of Joab. Refs.: 1 Chr. 4:13, 14. ¶
c. A Simeonite. Ref.: 1 Chr. 4:35. ¶
d. An officer of King Jehoiakim. Ref.: Jer. 36:26. ¶
e. A friend and associate of Jeremiah. Refs.: Jer. 51:59, 61. ¶
f. Associate of Gedaliah. Refs.: 2 Kgs. 25:23; Jer. 40:8. ¶
g. Chief priest when Jerusalem fell. Refs.: 2 Kgs. 25:18; 1 Chr. 6:14; Jer. 52:24, possibly the same as h. ¶
h. The father or ancestor of Ezra. Ref.: Ezra 7:1, possibly the same as g. ¶
i. One who returned from exile with Zerubabbel. Ref.: Ezra 2:2.
j. One who signed a covenant with Nehemiah. Ref.: Neh. 10:2, possibly the same as k. ¶
k. A priest in the restored Temple. Refs.: Neh. 11:11; 12:1, 12, possibly the same as j. ¶

SERAPHIM – Is. 6:2, 6 ➔ SERPENT <8314>.

SERED – ***sered*** [masc. proper noun: סֶרֶד <5624>; from a prim. root meaning to tremble]: fear ▶ **One of the sons of Zebulun.** Refs.: Gen. 46:14; Num. 26:26. ¶

SEREDITE – ***sardiy*** [proper noun: סַרְדִּי <5625>; patron. from SERED <5624>] ▶ **A descendant of Sered (<5624>).** Ref.: Num. 26:26. ¶

SERPENT – [1] ***nāḥāš*** [masc. noun: נָחָשׁ <5175>; from DIVINATION (PRACTICE) <5172>] ▶ **This word is used to refer to an actual serpent or snake.** Refs.: Ex. 4:3; Num. 21:6; Deut. 8:15; Eccl. 10:8; Amos 5:19. It refers also to an image of one (Num. 21:9). It is also used figuratively. Some of these symbolic uses include the tempter (Gen. 3:1, 2, 4, 13, 14); the tribe of Dan (Gen. 49:17); wicked rulers (Ps. 58:4); and enemies (Is. 14:29; Jer. 8:17; 46:22). *

[2] ***śārāp*** [masc. noun: שָׂרָף <8314>; from BURN (verb) <8313>] ▶ **This word generally refers to a poisonous snake, deriving its origin from the burning sensation of the serpent's bite (see Deut. 8:15).** It is used specifically of the fiery serpents that were sent as judgment. The likeness of a serpent was made of brass at the Lord›s command (Num. 21:8). The word is used twice by Isaiah to apparently denote a dragon (Is. 14:29; 30:6). Other ref.: Num. 21:6. The Hebrew word is also translated seraphim in Isaiah 6:2, 6 and refers to an angelic being. ¶

[3] ***tanniyn*** [masc. noun: תַּנִּין <8577>; intens. from the same as JACKAL <8565>] ▶ **This word means a snake; it also means a dragon and a sea monster.** It can connote a creature living in the water (Gen. 1:21; Job 7:12; Ps. 148:7). When the word is used this way, it is also used figuratively to represent the crocodile, which was the symbol of Pharaoh and Egypt (Ps. 74:13; Is. 27:1; 51:9; Ezek. 29:3). This imagery may help us better understand the confrontation between Moses and Pharaoh, when Aaron's staff became a serpent and then swallowed the staff-serpents of Pharaoh's magicians (Ex. 7:9, 10, 12). God was providing a graphic sign of what was to come. It can also connote a creature that lives on the land (Deut. 32:33; Ps. 91:13; Jer. 51:34). There is one other occurrence of this term in the Old Testament where it is used as a descriptor or part of a proper name for a

well or a spring (Neh. 2:13). In all its occurrences, this term has either a neutral (Gen. 1:21; Ps. 148:7); or a negative meaning (Is. 27:1; 51:9; Jer. 51:34). In a few instances, the negative meaning is somewhat lessened, as when God provides a serpent to save His people (Ex. 7:9, 10, 12); or when a serpent was divinely restrained (Ps. 91:13). *
– [4] Deut. 32:24 ➔ CRAWL <2119>
[5] See ASP <6620>.

SERPENT WELL – Neh. 2:13 ➔ DRAGON'S SPRING <5886>.

SERUG – ***śᵉrûg*** [masc. proper noun: שְׂרוּג <8286>; fem. of KNIT TOGETHER (BE) <8276> (in the sense of to be entwined)]: branch ▶ **Great grandfather of Abraham.** Refs.: Gen. 11:20–23; 1 Chr. 1:26. ¶

SERVANT – [1] ***ʿᵃḇaḏ*** [Aramaic masc. sing. noun: עֲבַד <5649>; from MAKE <5648>] ▶ **This word means a person serving another; it could also mean a slave. It is used for servants of God or of human beings.** King Nebuchadnezzar refers to Shadrach, Meshach, and Abednego as servants of the Most High God (Dan. 3:26). Darius calls Daniel the servant of the living God (Dan. 6:20). One could also be known as a servant of the king (Dan. 2:7). This noun is derived from the verb *ʿᵃḇaḏ* (<5648>), meaning to do or make. See the Hebrew cognate *ʿeḇeḏ* (<5650> below). Other refs.: Ezra 4:11; 5:11; Dan. 2:4; 3:28. ¶
[2] ***ʿeḇeḏ*** [masc. noun: עֶבֶד <5650>; from SERVE <5647>] ▶ **This word refers to a person rendering service to another. It could also mean a slave. Although the most basic concept of this term is that of a slave, slavery in the Bible was not the same as the slavery of modern times.** The period of slavery was limited to six years (Ex. 21:2). Slaves had rights and protection under the Law (Ex. 21:20). It was also possible for slaves to attain positions of power and honor (Gen. 24:2; 41:12). In addition, the people under the king were called his servants (Gen. 21:25); as well as his officers (1 Sam. 19:1); officials (2 Kgs. 22:12); ambassadors (Num. 22:18); vassal kings (2 Sam. 10:19); tributary nations (1 Chr. 18:2, 6, 13). This word is also a humble way of referring to one's self when speaking with another of equal or superior rank (Gen. 33:5). The term is also applied to those who worship God (Neh. 1:10); and to those who minister or serve Him (Is. 49:5, 6). The phrase, the servant of the Lord, is the most outstanding reference to the Messiah in the Old Testament, and its teachings are concentrated at the end of Isaiah (Is. 42:1, 19; 43:10; 49:3, 5–7; 52:13; 53:11). *
– [3] Gen. 18:7; 22:3 ➔ BOY <5288>.

SERVANT (FEMALE) – See MAID <519>.

SERVANTS – ***ʿᵃḇuddāh*** [fem. noun: עֲבֻדָּה <5657>; pass. part. of SERVE <5647>] ▶ **This word usually refers to an entire household of servants, individuals performing work for others.** The Philistines were jealous of Isaac because of his wealth, including his livestock and servants (Gen. 26:14). Job was considered the wealthiest man of the East because of all his possessions, including his multitude of servants (Job 1:3). See the related Hebrew root *ʿāḇaḏ* (SERVE <5647>), Aramaic root *ʿᵃḇaḏ* (MAKE <5648>), Aramaic noun *ʿᵃḇēḏ* (SERVANT <5649>), and Hebrew noun *ʿeḇeḏ* (SERVANT <5650>). ¶

SERVE – [1] ***ʿāḇaḏ*** [verb: עָבַד <5647>; a prim. root] ▶ **This word means to work, to be used for something. This labor may be focused on things, other people, or God.** When it is used in reference to things, that item is usually expressed: to till the ground (Gen. 2:5; 3:23; 4:2); to work in a garden (Gen. 2:15); or to dress a vineyard (Deut. 28:39). Similarly, this term is also applied to artisans and craftsmen, like workers in fine flax (Is. 19:9); and laborers of the city (Ezek. 48:19). When the focus of the labor is another person, that person is usually expressed: Jacob's service to Laban (Gen. 29:15); the Israelites' service for the Egyptians (Ex. 1:14); and a people's service to the king (Judg. 9:28; 1 Sam. 11:1).

When the focus of the labor is the Lord, it is a religious service to worship Him. Moreover, in these cases, the word does not have connotations of toilsome labor but instead of a joyful experience of liberation (Ex. 3:12; 4:23; 7:16; Josh. 24:15, 18). Unfortunately, this worship service was often given to false gods (Deut. 7:16; 2 Kgs. 10:18, 19, 21–23). *

2 ***pᵉlaḥ*** [Aramaic verb: פְּלַח <6399>; corresponding to CUT (verb) <6398> (maybe in the sense of to bring forth)] ▶ **This word means to revere, to worship.** King Nebuchadnezzar was amazed when Daniel's three friends were not harmed in the furnace; he recognized their God for rescuing them because they would not serve any other (Dan. 3:28). King Darius referred to God as the One Daniel served continually (Dan. 6:16, 20). Later, Daniel wrote of his vision of the Ancient of Days and how all nations worshiped Him (Dan. 7:14). This thought is echoed later in the same passage (Dan. 7:27). This word was also used to denote servants of the Temple (Ezra 7:24). Other refs.: Dan. 3:12, 14, 17, 18. ¶

3 ***ṣāḇā'*** [verb: צָבָא <6633>; a prim. root] ▶ **This word means to serve (e.g., to perform service at the sacred tent of meeting), to wage war. It is primarily used to describe a gathering of people waging war against another city or country.** Refs.: Num. 31:7, 42; Is. 29:7, 8; Zech. 14:12. In one instance, it was used to depict the Lord waging war (Is. 31:4). In several contexts, this word referred to the mustering of people into service (2 Kgs. 25:19; Jer. 52:25). Finally, this word described the religious service in the Tabernacle (Ex. 38:8; Num. 4:23; 8:24; 1 Sam. 2:22). ¶

4 ***ṣāḇaṭ*** [verb: צָבַט <6642>; a prim. root] ▶ **This word means to reach out, to hand something over.** It means to serve food to a guest, to serve generously (Ruth 2:14; also translated to pass, to offer); thereby Boaz showed his respect and love toward Ruth. ¶

5 ***šᵉmaš*** [Aramaic verb: שְׁמַשׁ <8120>; corresponding to the root of SUN <8121> through the idea of activity implied in daylight] ▶ **This word means to minister to, to attend to. It is used only in Daniel 7:10 in a stunning vision of God, the Ancient of Days, on His throne.** Thousands attend God, serving Him only. In this limited context, we get the idea that this verb is one that signifies much more than just serving or attending someone as a paid servant or a slave would do out of necessity. The connotation here seems to be that of having absolute devotion to the person, just as all who serve God must be wholeheartedly devoted to Him. This serving is voluntary for those who love God. ¶

6 ***šāraṯ*** [verb: שָׁרַת <8334>; a prim. root] ▶ **This Hebrew word means to wait upon, to minister unto. It was utilized in a generic sense to describe various activities; it is also translated to minister.** Such activities included that of a domestic servant serving a ranking official (Gen. 39:4; 2 Sam. 13:17, 18); a chief assistant to an authority figure, such as Joshua was to Moses (Ex. 24:13); the angelic host to God (Ps. 103:21); and assistants to kings (Is. 60:10). More particularly, the word is used in the context of religious service before the Lord, such as that required of the priests (Ex. 28:35; 1 Kgs. 8:11); or Levites (Num. 3:6). *

SERVICE – 1 ***polḥan*** [Aramaic masc. abstract noun: פָּלְחָן <6402>; from SERVE <6399>] ▶ **This word describes the entire process involved in worshiping God; it is also translated worship.** Ref.: Ezra 7:19. ¶

2 ***ṣāḇā'*** [masc. noun: צָבָא <6635>; from SERVE <6633>] ▶ **This word means work done for another person; it also means servants.** It may apply to military service (Num. 1:3; 1 Sam. 17:55); hard, difficult service (Job 7:1; Is. 40:2); or divine service (Num. 4:3; 8:24, 25; Ps. 68:11). The angels and the heavens alike are in divine service and therefore come under this term (Gen. 2:1; 1 Kgs. 22:19; Jer. 33:22; cf. Luke 2:13). Over half of its nearly five hundred uses come in the phrase, the Lord [or God] of hosts. The phrase is absent from the first five book of the Bible. But frequently in the Prophets, the phrase introduces a divine declaration. At least once the hosts (always plural) in this expression are identified as

human armies, but elsewhere they most likely refer to angelic forces (Josh. 5:13–15; 1 Sam. 17:55; Ps. 103:21; Is. 1:9). The title the Lord of hosts was often translated in the Septuagint as the Lord of powers or the Lord Almighty (Ps. 24:10; Zech. 4:6). On other occasions, the Hebrew word for hosts was transliterated into Greek (1 Sam. 1:3, 11). This Greek form of the Hebrew word shows up twice in the New Testament as the "Lord of Sabaoth," once in a quotation from Isaiah (cf. Rom. 9:29; Jas 5:4). *
3 ***šārêṯ*** [masc. noun: שָׁרֵת <8335>; inf. of SERVE <8334>] ▶ **This word means religious ministry. Service in the place of worship underlies the primary meaning of this word.** It is used twice in reference to the instruments used by those ministering in the Tabernacle (Num. 4:12); and the vessels used for ritual in the Temple (2 Chr. 24:14). The stress was upon the connection to the functions of the priestly office. ¶
– 4 Ex. 1:14; Num. 4:26; etc. ➔ WORK <5656> 5 Ex. 31:10; 35:19; 39:1, 41 ➔ WOVEN <8278> b. 6 Ezra 4:14 ➔ to be in the service ➔ SALT (EAT THE) <4415> 7 Ezra 6:18 ➔ WORK <5673> 8 Neh. 13:14 ➔ CUSTODY <4929>.

SERVICE (BE IN THE) – 1 Kgs. 1:2 ➔ PROFITABLE (BE) <5532> a.

SET – 1 ***yāṣag*** [verb: יָצַג <3322>; a prim. root] ▶ **This word means to place, to present. It is a synonym of the Hebrew** ***śim*****, to place, to put.** It is used of placing objects or persons in a certain location or a certain way (Gen. 30:38; Judg. 8:27; 1 Sam. 5:2; 2 Sam. 6:17). It has the sense of giving persons to someone as helpers (Gen. 33:15) in certain contexts. It means to set forth someone for a purpose or with a certain result (Job 17:6), e.g., Job was set forth, made a byword, a joke of scorn. To set justice in the land means to establish justice, what is right, in the land (Amos 5:15). In Judges 7:5, it has the sense of to set out, to separate out. *
– 2 Ex. 25:7 ➔ SETTING <4396> 3 Ex. 28:20 ➔ WEAVE <7660> 4 Ezra 4:10 (KJV); Dan. 7:10 (KJV) ➔ SIT <3488> 5 Ezra 10:14; Neh. 10:34 ➔ APPOINTED <2163> 6 Ps. 73:9 ➔ LAY, LAY CLAIM <8371> a. 7 Is. 19:2 ➔ COVER (verb) <5526> b. 8 Jer. 5:26 ➔ SUBSIDE <7918>.

SET, BE SET – 1 Sam. 18:30; Zech. 11:13 ➔ PRECIOUS (BE) <3365>.

SET, SET OVER – Ezra 7:25; Dan. 2:49; 3:12 ➔ APPOINT <4483>.

SET ABOUT – Song 7:2 ➔ ENCIRCLE <5473>.

SET APART – Ex. 8:22; Ps. 4:3 ➔ DISTINCTION (MAKE) <6395>.

SET BACK – Ezek. 42:6 ➔ RESERVE (verb) <680>.

SET FREE – ***šᵉrûṯ*** [fem. noun: שְׁרוּת <8293>; from LOOSE (LET) <8281>] ▶ **This word may mean a beginning, freedom; to let something go.** In Jeremiah 15:11, this word refers to God setting Jeremiah free. ¶

SET IN ORDER – Eccl. 12:9 ➔ STRAIGHT (MAKE) <8626>.

SET LIGHT – Deut. 25:3 ➔ DESPISED (BE) <7034>.

SET OUT – ***nāsa'*** [verb: נָסַע <5265>; a prim. root] ▶ **This word has the basic meaning of moving something out, pulling it out, taking it away; causing something to move out. It also indicates to travel, to journey.** Samson pulled out the gates (foundations included) and carried them away (Judg. 16:3); to set out on a journey (Gen. 33:12, 17; Ex. 12:37); to make or cause to set out (Ex. 15:22; Ps. 78:26, 52); of being stirred up by God (Num. 11:31). It describes pulling up a tent in order to move on (Is. 38:12). It is used figuratively of a person's death, his or her "tent-rope" is pulled up (Job 4:21). It describes the quarrying, cutting, and carrying away of stones (1 Kgs. 5:17; Eccl. 10:9). With *min* (FROM <4480>) following, it means to journey or to depart from (Gen. 37:17). *

SET UP – [1] ***kûn*** [verb: כּוּן <3559>; a prim. root] ▶ **The primary meaning of this verb is to cause to stand in an upright position, and thus the word also means fixed or steadfast. This word also means to make firm, to establish, to prepare.** It signifies the action of setting in place or erecting an object (Is. 40:20; Mic. 4:1); establishing a royal dynasty (2 Sam. 7:13; 1 Chr. 17:12); founding a city (Hab. 2:12); creating the natural order (Deut. 32:6; Ps. 8:3; Prov. 8:27); fashioning a people for oneself (2 Sam. 7:24); adjusting weapons for targets (Ps. 7:12; 11:2); appointing to an office (Josh. 4:4); confirming a position (1 Kgs. 2:12); making ready or preparing for use (2 Chr. 31:11; Ps. 103:19; Zeph. 1:7); attaining certainty (Deut. 13:14; 1 Sam. 23:23). *
– [2] Dan. 5:19, 23 ➔ EXALT <7313> [3] Dan. 7:9 ➔ THROW <7412>.

SETH – ***šēṯ*** [masc. proper noun: שֵׁת <8352>; from PUT <7896>, i.e., substituted] ▶ **He was the third son of Adam and Eve. He was named Seth, which means "substitute, compensation" in place of Abel.** Seth fathered Enosh, a name meaning "mortal, weak." He had more sons and daughters and lived to be 912 years old (Gen. 5:6–8). Refs.: Gen. 4:25, 26; 5:3, 4, 6–8; Num. 24:17; 1 Chr. 1:1. ¶

SETHUR – ***s***^***e***^***ṯûr*** [masc. proper noun: סְתוּר <5639>; from HIDE <5641>]: hidden ▶ **A spy from the tribe of Asher sent to explore Canaan.** Ref.: Num. 13:13. ¶

SETTING – [1] ***millu', millû'*** [masc. noun: מִלֻּא, מִלּוּא <4394>; from FULL (BE) <4390>] ▶ **This word designates a mounting of a jewel; an ordination of a priest.** It refers to the surrounding and enclosing metal environment in which jewels were set (Ex. 25:7; 35:9, 27). But it also extends its meaning to placing a priest in office; his ordination, consecration, installation by a special ordination, filling, offering (Ex. 29:22; Lev. 7:37; 8:22, etc.). *
[2] ***millu'āh*** [fem. noun: מִלֻּאָה <4396>; fem. of <4394> above] ▶ **This word refers to a filling, a setting (of gem stones); it is also translated enclosing, filigree, mounting.** It describes a prepared location by a jeweler for precious stones (Ex. 28:17, 20; 39:13), but see also <4394> above. ¶
[3] ***neqeḇ*** [masc. noun: נֶקֶב <5345>; no information on root] ▶
a. This word is a technical term relating to the work of a jeweler. It refers to a socket, hole, or cavity (e.g., a bezel) for securing a precious stone. In context it speaks of mountings created by God, the master craftsman. Ref.: Ezek. 28:13. ¶
b. This word indicates a conduit, a cylinder for conducting something. Ref.: Ezek. 28:13; KJV, NKJV: pipe. ¶
– [4] Prov. 25:11 ➔ PICTURE <4906> [5] Song 5:12 ➔ FITLY <4402> [6] Ezek. 28:13 ➔ TAMBOURINE <8596>.

SETTLE – [1] Ezra 4:10 ➔ SIT <3488> [2] Ps. 65:10 ➔ BEND <5181> [3] Ezek. 43:14, 17, 20; 45:19 ➔ LEDGE <5835>.

SETTLE DOWN – ***šāḵan*** [verb: שָׁכַן <7931>; a prim. root (apparently akin to LIE DOWN <7901> through the idea of lodging)] ▶ **In its most simple form, three slight variations of meaning are found for this verb: to settle down, to rest, to abide.** First, it simply means to settle down (Ex. 24:16; Num. 24:2; Ps. 102:28); used of the Lord settling down in the Tabernacle (Ex. 25:8; 40:35). Second, it can mean to lie down or rest. When used this way, it can refer to objects (Num. 9:17; Job 3:5); animals (Is. 13:21); and people (Jer. 23:6; 33:16). When people are the object of the verb, it means that they are resting in peace and security. Third, it may mean to dwell or abide. Again, this can have several referents such as people (Ps. 37:27; Prov. 2:21); the dead (Job 26:5); God (1 Kgs. 8:12; Is. 8:18); or objects such as the Tabernacle (Josh. 22:19). In the intensive form, it means to establish. The word is used in this way in Deuteronomy 12:11 and Psalm 78:60 to describe how God set up a dwelling place for His name, establishing Himself in Israel. Finally, the causative form means to lay, to place, to set (Gen. 3:24; Josh. 18:1); or to cause to dwell (Job 11:14; Ps. 78:55). *

SETTLED (BE) – Prov. 8:25 ➔ DROWN <2883>.

SETTLEMENT – [1] Gen. 25:16; 1 Chr. 6:54 ➔ CAMP <2918> [2] Num. 32:41; Josh. 13:30; 1 Kgs. 4:13; 1 Chr. 2:23 ➔ TOWN <2333>.

SEVEN – [1] ***šāḇûa'*** [masc. noun: שָׁבוּעַ <7620>; pass. part. of SWEAR <7650> as a denom. of <7651> below] ► **This word means a heptad; a week, a group of seven days or years.** It indicates a unit of seven: a week, seven days (Lev. 12:5; Deut. 16:9); of a marriage feast (Gen. 29:27, 28); a week of days (Dan. 10:2, 3). It is used in a technical sense to name a festival, the Feast of Weeks (Ex. 34:22; Deut. 16:10). It refers to seven years, a *heptad* of years (Dan. 9:24–27). * [2] ***šeḇa', šiḇ'āh*** [masc. or fem. noun: שֶׁבַע, שִׁבְעָה <7651>; from SWEAR <7650> (properly to be complete; the number seven is as the sacred full one)] ► **This word is a counting number that indicates a total number of something, such as years (e.g., Gen. 5:7, 25).** It combines with other numbers, e.g., *šᵉḇa' 'ęsreh,* 17, (lit., seven and ten) (Gen. 37:2). Repeated, it means groups of seven (seven by seven) by sevens (Gen. 7:2). Its plural form in – *îm* means seventy (Gen. 50:10). The term *bᵉšiḇ'a laḥōḏeš* indicates the seventh day of the month (Ezek. 30:20). * [3] ***šiḇ'āh, šᵉba'*** [Aramaic masc. or fem. noun: שִׁבְעָה, שְׁבַע <7655>; corresponding to <7651> above] ► **This word is used in its masculine form (*šiḇ'āh*) with masculine nouns and in its feminine form (*šᵉba'*) with feminine nouns.** It indicates seven periods of time (Dan. 4:16, 23, 25, 32); the seven advisors of the Persian king (Ezra 7:14). The phrase *ḥaḏ-šiḇ'āh* means seven (Dan. 3:19). ¶ [4] ***šiḇ'ānāh*** [masc. noun: שִׁבְעָנָה <7658>; prolonged for the masc. of <7651> above] ► **This word is used once as a counting number.** It indicates Job's seven restored sons (Job 42:13). ¶

SEVEN TIMES – See SEVENFOLD <7659>.

SEVENFOLD – ***šiḇ'āṯayim*** [masc. dual noun: שִׁבְעָתַיִם <7659>; dual (adv.) of SEVEN <7651>] ► **This word indicates that something is increased seven times, consists of seven parts.** Refs.: Gen. 4:15, 24. It is employed in an expression, seven times, to indicate the purity of the Lord's words (Ps. 12:6); or, in a different context, the sevenfold judgment of the Lord (Ps. 79:12). Sevenfold repayment of a theft is noted (Prov. 6:31). In a restored world, a sun shining sevenfold brighter is mentioned, indicating the joyous nature of that environment (Is. 30:26). ¶

SEVENTH – ***šᵉḇiy'iy, šᵉḇiy'iṯ*** [adj.: שְׁבִיעִי, שְׁבִיעִית <7637>; ordinal from SEVENTY <7657>] ► **This word is an ordinal number indicating the seventh in a series; it is normally used in relation to time.** The seventh day (Lev. 13:5, 6; Josh. 6:4; Esther 1:10); the seventh week (Lev. 23:16); the seventh month (Lev. 23:27; Jer. 28:17; Hag. 2:1); and the seventh year (Lev. 25:4; 2 Kgs. 11:4; 2 Chr. 23:1). When this word refers to the seventh day, it can refer to the Sabbath (Gen. 2:2; Ex. 20:10, 11; Deut. 16:8). In other usages, this word describes the seventh of a series of events (Josh. 6:16; 1 Kgs. 18:44); the seventh lot (Josh. 19:40; 1 Chr. 24:10); the seventh son (1 Chr. 2:15; 26:3); the seventh mighty man (1 Chr. 12:11); and the seventh commander (1 Chr. 27:10). *

SEVENTY – ***šiḇ'iym*** [common noun: שִׁבְעִים <7657>; multiple of SEVEN <7651>] ► **This word is the plural form of *šeḇa'*. It combines with other numbers to form larger numbers, e.g., seventy-seven (Gen. 4:24).** It is used as a counting number to indicate seventy of something: seventy years (Gen. 5:12; 11:26); seventy persons (Ex. 1:5); seventy trees, seventy years (figurative?) of exile (Jer. 25:11, 12; 29:10; Zech. 1:12; 7:5); seventy weeks (or sevens) (Dan. 9:2, 24). *

SEVERAL – 2 Kgs. 15:5; 2 Chr. 26:21 ➔ SEPARATE (adj.) <2669>.

SEVERE – Eccl. 12:6 ➔ BIND <7576>.

SEVERED (BE) – Job 8:14 ➔ CUT OFF (BE) <6990> a.

SEVERITY – ***perek̲*** [masc. noun: פֶּרֶךְ <6531>; from an unused root meaning to break apart] ▶ **This word refers to ruthlessness, cruelty; it is also translated, harshness, rigor, rigorously, ruthlessly, as slaves.** It refers to a manner in which something is carried out. Israel was made to labor without mercy, cruelly by Egypt (Ex. 1:13, 14). God warned Israel not to force slaves to labor in this manner (Lev. 25:43, 46, 53; Ezek. 34:4). ¶

SEW – 1 ***tāp̲ar*** [verb: תָּפַר <8609>; a prim. root] ▶ **This word indicates to join or fasten (something) by means of stitches made with a needle and thread. It describes the skill of making clothes or other items by stitching materials together**. Refs.: Gen. 3:7; Ezek. 13:18. It is used figuratively of sewing sackcloth, a garment for mourning, over one's skin (Job 16:15); or perhaps of simply attaching sackcloth to one's body. It is used in a figurative sense of a time to sew, a time to be productive and enjoy stability (Eccl. 3:7; also translated to mend). ¶
– 2 Job 14:17 ➔ SMEAR <2950>.

SHAALBIM, SHAALABBIN – ***šaʿalb̲iym, šaʿᵃlabbiyn*** [proper noun: שַׁעַלְבִים, שַׁעֲלַבִּין <8169>; plur. from FOX <7776>]: foxholes ▶ **A town in Dan taken by the Amorites.** Refs.: Josh. 19:42; Judg. 1:35; 1 Kgs. 4:9. ¶

SHAALBONITE – ***šaʿalb̲ōniy*** [proper noun: שַׁעַלְבֹנִי <8170>; patrial from SHAALBIM <8169>] ▶ **An inhabitant of Shaalbim (<8169>).** Refs.: 2 Sam. 23:32; 1 Chr. 11:33. ¶

SHAAPH – ***šāʿap̲*** [proper noun: שַׁעַף <8174>; from LOP, LOP OFF <5586>]: division, fluctuation ▶
a. Son of Caleb, the brother of Jerahmeel. Ref.: 1 Chr. 2:49. ¶
b. Another descendant of Caleb, the brother of Jerahmeel. Ref.: 1 Chr. 2:47. ¶

SHAARAIM – ***šaʿᵃrayim*** [proper noun: שַׁעֲרַיִם <8189>; dual of GATE <8179>]: two gates ▶
a. A town in Judah. Refs.: Josh. 15:36; 1 Sam. 17:52. ¶
b. A town in Simeon. Ref.: 1 Chr. 4:31. ¶

SHAASHGAZ – ***šaʿašgaz*** [masc. proper noun: שַׁעַשְׁגַז <8190>; of Persian deriv.]: servant of what is beautiful ▶ **A eunuch in the palace of the Assyrian king Ahasuerus who was in charge of his concubines.** Ref.: Esther 2:14. ¶

SHABBETHAI – ***šabbᵉt̲ay*** [masc. proper noun: שַׁבְּתַי <7678>; from SABBATH <7676>]: restful ▶ **A Levite in the time of Ezra and Nehemiah.** Refs.: Ezra 10:15; Neh. 8:7; 11:10. ¶

SHACHIA – 1 Chr. 8:10 ➔ SACHIA, SACHIAH <7634>.

SHACK – Is. 24:20 ➔ HUT <4412>.

SHACKLES – Ps. 105:18; 149:8 ➔ FETTERS <3525>.

SHADDAI – See ALMIGHTY <7706>.

SHADE (noun) – 1 Job 40:22 ➔ SHADOW <6752> 2 Is. 14:9; 26:14 ➔ DEAD <7496> 3 See SHADOW <6738>.

SHADE (FIND) – ***ṭᵉlal*** [Aramaic verb: טְלַל <2927>; corresponding to COVER (verb) <2926>] ▶ **This word means to find a place which is not in the direct sunlight; it is also translated to find shelter, to have shadow.** It describes the beasts of the field as they procure rest, shade, and shelter under the huge tree of Nebuchadnezzar's dream (Dan. 4:12). ¶

SHADE (verb) – Ezek. 31:3 ➔ DARK (BE, GROW) <6751>.

SHADOW – 1 ***ṣêl*** [masc. noun: צֵל <6738>; from DARK (BE, GROW) <6751>] ▶ **This word means literally a dark shape cast by a body that comes between rays of light and a surface; it is frequently used as a symbol for protection or refuge.** This can be seen in the allegory of the trees (Judg.

9:15); and of the vine (Ps. 80:10). God protects in the shadow of His wings (Ps. 17:8; 36:7; 57:1). The Lord is portrayed as the shade (Ps. 121:5); and hid His servant in the shadow of His hand (Is. 49:2). The writer of Ecclesiastes taught that money and wisdom are both forms of protection, but wisdom could save one's life (Eccl. 7:12). *

2 ***ṣêlel*** [masc. noun: צֵלֶל <6752>; from DARK (BE, GROW) <6751>] ► **See previous definition. This word occurs only four times in the Old Testament.** In Job it described the shade of trees (Job 40:22). In the other instances, it depicted the time of day when the shadows fled (Song 2:17; 4:6) or lengthened (Jer. 6:4). ¶

– 3 Ezek. 31:3 ➔ DARK (BE, GROW) <6751>.

SHADOW (HAVE) – Dan. 4:12 ➔ SHADE (FIND) <2927>.

SHADOW OF DEATH – ***ṣalmāweṯ*** [masc. noun: צַלְמָוֶת <6757>; from SHADOW <6738> and DEATH <4194>] ► **This Hebrew word is used to describe various types of darkness; it also means a deep shadow.** In some contexts, this word was used to describe death (Job 38:17); or those close to death (Ps. 107:10, 14). In other contexts, it was used to describe a physical darkness (Job 24:17; Amos 5:8); a spiritual darkness (Is. 9:2); a darkness of understanding (Job 12:22); a gloomy countenance (Job 16:16); or a dangerous land (Jer. 2:6). Occasionally, both elements of death and darkness are present in the context (Job 3:5; 10:21, 22). *

SHADRACH – 1 ***šaḏraḵ*** [masc. proper noun: שַׁדְרַךְ <7714>; prob. of foreign origin] ► **This word designates the Babylonian name of the Jewish royal youth named Hananiah.** The change of name was subsequent to forced deportation and immersion in a heathen culture (Dan. 1:6, 7). ¶

2 ***šaḏraḵ*** [Aramaic masc. proper noun: שַׁדְרַךְ <7715>; the same as <7714> above] ► **The meaning of this word is the same as the previous one.** Refs.: Dan. 2:49; 3:12–14, 16, 19, 20, 22, 23, 26, 28–30. ¶

SHADY TREES – Job 40:21, 22 ➔ LOTUS PLANTS, LOTUS TREES <6628>.

SHAGEE – ***šāḡêh*** [masc. proper noun: שָׁגֵה <7681>; prob. from ERR <7686>]: erring ► **Father of one of David's mighty man.** Ref.: 1 Chr. 11:34. ¶

SHAHARAIM – ***šaḥ^a^rayim*** [masc. proper noun: שַׁחֲרַיִם <7842>; dual of DAWN (noun) <7837>]: double dawn ► **An Israelite of the tribe of Benjamin.** Ref.: 1 Chr. 8:8. ¶

SHAHAZIMAH – Josh. 19:22 ➔ SHAHAZUMAH <7831>.

SHAHAZUMAH – ***šahaḥ^a^ṣûm, šaḥ^a^ṣiym*** [proper noun: שַׁחֲצוּם, שַׁחֲצִים <7831>; from the same as PRIDE <7830>]: proudly ► **A town in Issachar with directional *hê*.** Ref.: NASB, NIV, ESV, Josh. 19:22. The word is also spelled Shahazimah (KJV, NKJV, Josh. 19:22). ¶

SHAKE – 1 ***ga'aš*** [verb: גָּעַשׁ <1607>; a prim. root] ► **This word means to quake, to move, to surge. It indicates a violent rising and falling.** It is attended sometimes with loud noises of the earth and its foundations (Ps. 18:7; also translated to reel, to quake); of waves or the sea itself (Jer. 5:22: to toss, to roll). It is used figuratively to describe drunken nations (Jer. 25:16) as they stagger and Egypt in particular as it surges about in its pride (Jer. 46:7, 8; also translated to be moved). Other refs.: 2 Sam. 22:8 (also translated to reel, to tremble); Job 34:20 (also translated to be troubled). ¶

2 ***ḥûl, ḥiyl*** [verb: חוּל, חִיל <2342>; a prim. root] ► **This word means to whirl, to fear, to dance, to writhe, to grieve. It has many different meanings, most of which derive from two basic ideas: to whirl in motion and to writhe in pain.** The first of these ideas may be seen in the shaking of the earth (Ps. 29:8); the stirring of the waters (Ps. 77:16); or the trembling of the mountains (Hab. 3:10). At times, this word is used in a context of shaking with fear (Deut. 2:25; Jer. 5:22); worshiping in trembling awe (1 Chr. 16:30; Ps. 96:9); or

anxiously waiting (Gen. 8:10; Ps. 37:7). It is also used to describe dancing women (Judg. 21:21, 23). The second idea of writhing in pain can be either physical, as when Saul was wounded in battle (1 Sam. 31:3), or emotional, as when Jeremiah grieved in anguish over Jerusalem's refusal to grieve (Jer. 4:19). This word is often used to describe the labor pains of giving birth (Ps. 29:9; Is. 26:17, 18; 51:2) but can also imply God's creating work (Deut. 32:18; Job 15:7; Ps. 90:2; Prov. 8:24, 25). *

3 ***nûṭ*** [verb: נוּט <5120>; no information on root] ▶ **This word means to quake, to be moved. It describes the quivering, quick, violent movements of the earth as a response to the enthronement of the Lord.** Ref.: Ps. 99:1; it is also translated to move, to quake. ¶

4 ***nā'ar*** [verb: נָעַר <5287>; a prim. root (prob. identical with GROWL <5286>), through the idea of the rustling of mane, which usually accompanies the lion's roar] ▶ **This Hebrew word means to shake off, to shake out; it is also translated to shake free, to throw, to overthrow, to sweep.** It means to shake off, to defeat by casting off: the Egyptians in the midst of the Red Sea by an overwhelming power of surging waters (Ex. 14:27; Ps. 136:15); one's enemies by exercising force (Judg. 16:20). It has the idiomatic sense of disciplining, separating persons from their wealth and families, getting rid of (Neh. 5:13). It indicates shaking one's hands to show innocence (Is. 33:15; also translated to gesture, to keep). It describes the shaking down, the judging of a nation (Is. 33:9; also translated to loose, to drop). It is used figuratively of Jerusalem shaking off the dust of captivity (Is. 52:2). Its figurative use describes a person shaken off like a locust by affliction from God (Ps. 109:23; KJV: to toss up and down); or the wicked shaken out of the earth, swept away, removed (Job 38:13). ¶

5 ***'āmaḏ*** [verb: עָמַד <5976>; for SLIP <4571> (in the sense of to shake, to wobble)] ▶ **This word means either to quake (the generally preferred translation) or to stand, to be at a stand. The former signification refers to something that is trembling or violently shaken by some force, physical or spiritual.** It is used of the trembling, quaking that came on those who trusted in vain in Egypt (Ezek. 29:7; also translated to be wrenched, to quiver). ¶

6 ***pālaṣ*** [verb: פָּלַץ <6426>; a prim. root] ▶ **This word means to quake, to quiver, to move back and forth.** It describes the shaking or trembling of the pillars or foundations of the earth (Job 9:6). ¶

7 ***rāgaz*** [verb: רָגַז <7264>; a prim. root] ▶ **This word means to tremble, to agitate, to disturb, to rouse up, to rage, to provoke. This term occurs forty-one times in the Old Testament and is utilized most often to express the idea of the physical moving or shaking of someone or something.** Lands (1 Sam. 14:15; Amos 8:8); mountains (Ps. 18:7; Is. 5:25); the heavens (2 Sam. 22:8); kingdoms (Is. 23:11); and even the whole earth (Joel 2:10) are described as being shaken in this way, with the Lord's anger often given as the basis for the quaking. Often people, whether groups or individuals, would shake, i.e., were moved or stirred by deep emotions in response to specific circumstances. They trembled in fear (Ex. 15:14; Deut. 2:25; Is. 64:2; Joel 2:1; Mic. 7:17); or shook in agitation or anger (Prov. 29:9; Ezek. 16:43); and even grief (2 Sam. 18:33). Sometimes the word signifies the disturbing or rousing up of someone (1 Sam. 28:15; 2 Sam. 7:10; 1 Chr. 17:9). Occasionally, it conveys the act of rebelling or raging against another, literally, to shake oneself against someone (cf. 2 Kgs. 19:27, 28; Is. 37:28, 29). This verb is related to the verbs *rāga'* and *rāgaš* (<7283>), meaning to rage, to be in an uproar. The noun *rōgez* (TURMOIL <7267>), meaning commotion, raging, is directly derived from it. *

8 ***rā'aš*** [verb: רָעַשׁ <7493>; a prim. root] ▶ **This word means to quake, to tremble, to leap, to be abundant. The word occurs thirty times in the Old Testament and most often refers to the physical, forceful (often violent), quick, back-and-forth movement of a physical body by an outside force.** Frequently, the trembling or shaking takes place as nature's response to God's presence or to His activity of

rendering divine judgment. Things shaken included the walls of a city (Ezek. 26:10); the thresholds of doors (Amos 9:1); the heavens (Joel 2:10, 3:16; Hag. 2:6); the mountains (Jer. 4:24; Nah. 1:5); coastlands or islands (Ezek. 26:15); kingdoms (Is. 14:16); the earth or lands (Judg. 5:4; 2 Sam. 22:8; Ps. 60:2; 68:8; 77:18; Is. 13:13; Jer. 8:16; 10:10; 49:21); Gentile nations (Ezek. 31:16; Hag. 2:7); and every living creature of creation (Ezek. 38:20). Twice the term conveys a much different action than the one related above. In the first rare usage, the verb portrays the leaping ability of a warhorse (Job 39:20). The second unique use expresses the psalmist's desire that there be an abundance of grain in the land (Ps. 72:16). *

– [9] 1 Kgs. 14:15; Jer. 18:16 ➔ FLEE <5110> [10] Is. 64:1, 3 ➔ GLUTTON (BE) <2151> b. [11] Jer. 23:9 ➔ HOVER <7363> [12] Hab. 3:6 ➔ LEAP <5425> [13] Nah. 2:3 ➔ BRANDISH <7477> [14] Hab. 3:6 ➔ MEASURE (verb) <4128>.

SHAKE OFF – [1] Job 15:33 ➔ VIOLENCE (DO) <2554> [2] Dan. 4:14 ➔ STRIP OFF <5426>.

SHAKE TOGETHER – Nah. 2:10 ➔ SMITE TOGETHER <6375>.

SHAKEN – Lev. 26:36 ➔ DRIVE AWAY <5086>.

SHAKEN (BE) – 1 Sam. 28:21 ➔ TERRIFIED <926>.

SHAKING – [1] ***nōqep*** [masc. noun: נֹקֶף <5363>; from SURROUND <5362>] ▶ **This word denotes a beating. In general, it means to strike, to whip, to jerk back and forth.** It describes the beating of olives off olive trees in an agricultural setting (Is. 17:6; 24:13). ¶

[2] ***ra'aš*** [masc. noun: רַעַשׁ <7494>; from SHAKE <7493>] ▶ **This word refers to an earthquake, a rumbling, a commotion.** It indicates a quaking of the surface of the earth (1 Kgs. 19:11, 12); the quivering and shaking of a warhorse as it engages a battle (Job 39:24); or the brandishing, shaking of a javelin (Job 41:29). It refers to the roar and commotion, the clatter of a battle itself (Is. 9:5); or the preparations for war (Jer. 10:22). It depicts the noise of a rolling chariot wheel, hastening into battle (Nah. 3:2). It is used of the sounds made by the Lord's chariot appearance and movement (Ezek. 3:12). It stands for an earthquake itself, a great shaking, trembling (Amos 1:1; Zech. 14:5). *

SHAKING OF THE HEAD – ***mānôḏ*** [masc. noun: מָנוֹד <4493>; from FLEE <5110> (in the sense of moving or shaking)] ▶ **This word refers to a negative gesture of turning the head from side to side, indicating a pitiful but accusatory attitude toward someone.** Ref.: Ps. 44:14; NASB, ESV: laughingstock. ¶

SHALIM, SHAALIM – ***ša'aliym*** [proper noun: שַׁעֲלִים <8171>; plur. of FOX <7776>]: foxes ▶ **A land where Saul passed as he searched for missing donkeys.** Ref.: 1 Sam. 9:4. ¶

SHALISHAH – ***šālišāh*** [proper noun: שָׁלִשָׁה <8031>; fem. of DIVIDE INTO THREE PARTS <8027>]: third ▶ **This word indicates a land or small area.** Saul passed through it looking for donkeys (1 Sam. 9:4). This place is about sixteen miles northeast of Jerusalem. ¶

SHALLECHETH – ***šalleḵeṯ*** [proper noun: שַׁלֶּכֶת <7996>; the same as FELLING <7995>]: overthrow, felling of trees ▶ **This word refers to a gate on the west of the Temple.** Ref.: 1 Chr. 26:16. ¶

SHALLUM – [1] ***šallûm, šallum*** [masc. proper noun: שַׁלּוּם, <7967> שַׁלֻּם; the same as RECOMPENSE <7966>]: retribution ▶

a. King of Israel. Refs.: 2 Kgs. 15:10, 13–15. ¶

b. The husband of Huldah the prophetess. Refs.: 2 Kgs. 22:14; 2 Chr. 34:22. ¶

c. The father of Jekamiah. Refs.: 1 Chr. 2:40, 41. ¶

d. King of Judah, fourth son of Josiah. Refs.: 1 Chr. 3:15; Jer. 22:11. ¶

e. A descendant of Jacob. Ref.: 1 Chr. 4:25. ¶
f. A priest. Refs.: 1 Chr. 6:12, 13; Ezra 7:2. ¶
g. Son of Naphtali, also called Shillem (<8006>). Ref.: 1 Chr. 7:13. ¶
h. A Levite. Refs.: 1 Chr. 9:17, 19, 31; Ezra 2:42; Neh. 7:45. ¶
i. An Ephraimite chief. Ref.: 2 Chr. 28:12. ¶
j. A Levite. Ref.: Ezra 10:24. ¶
k. Son of Bani. Ref.: Ezra 10:42. ¶
l. A repairer of Jerusalem's wall, son of Halohesh. Ref.: Neh. 3:12. ¶
m. Uncle of Jeremiah the prophet. Ref.: Jer. 32:7. ¶
n. The father of Maaseiah. Ref.: Jer. 35:4. ¶
– [2] 1 Chr. 7:13 → SHILLEM <8006>.

SHALLUM, SHALLUN – ***šallûn*** [masc. proper noun: שַׁלּוּן <7968>; prob. for SHALLUM <7967>]: retribution ▶ **He repaired the gate of the fountain.** Ref.: Neh. 3:15. ¶

SHALMAI – ***šalmay, šalmay*** [masc. proper noun: שַׁלְמַי, שַׂלְמַי <8014>; from CLOTHING <8008>]: clothed ▶ **His descendants returned from the Babylonian captivity with Zerubbabel.** Refs.: Ezra 2:46; Neh. 7:48. ¶

SHALMAN – ***šalman*** [masc. proper noun: שַׁלְמַן <8020>; of foreign deriv.]: worshipper of fire ▶ **A contraction for Shalmaneser (<8022>), king of Assyria.** Ref.: Hos. 10:14. ¶

SHALMANESER – ***šalman'eser*** [masc. proper noun: שַׁלְמַנְאֶסֶר <8022>; of foreign deriv.]: Shalmana (a god) is chief ▶ **This word designates the Assyrian king (727–722 B.C.) usually identified as the one who destroyed northern Israel (722 B.C.) and took them into exile among various nations and cities of the Middle East.** Ref.: 2 Kgs. 17:6. Hoshea, northern Israel's last king, had stopped paying tribute to Shalmaneser. He then transported foreigners into Israel to live and till the land. He besieged Samaria for three years (2 Kgs. 18:9). Shalmaneser I's son Sargon II reigned in his place. ¶

SHAMA – ***šāmā'*** [masc. proper noun: שָׁמָע <8091>; from HEAR <8085>]: who listens ▶ **One of David's mighty men.** Ref.: 1 Chr. 11:44. ¶

SHAME – [1] ***bûšāh*** [fem. noun: בּוּשָׁה <955>; fem. part. pass. of ASHAMED (BE) <954>] ▶ **Although this word is used only four times in the Old Testament, its meaning is clear from an understanding of the verb *bôš* <954> meaning to be ashamed, to act shamefully, or to put to shame. It means embarrassment, humiliation.** This word refers to the shame that came on David during his distress (Ps. 89:45), as well as the shame associated with the destruction of an enemy (Mic. 7:10); of Edom (Obad. 1:10); and of the people in the land of Israel (Ezek. 7:18). ¶
[2] ***bošnāh*** [fem. noun: בָּשְׁנָה <1317>; fem. of ASHAMED (BE) <954>] ▶ **This word indicates the painful emotion and feeling Israel will experience, along with a sense of guilt, disgrace, and embarrassment, because of her worship of idols.** Ref.: Hos. 10:6. Its calf idol will be packed off to Assyria. ¶
[3] ***bōšeṯ*** [fem. noun: בֹּשֶׁת <1322>; from ASHAMED (BE) <954>] ▶ **This word denotes humiliation, disgrace.** It depicts the feelings of guilt, disgrace, and embarrassment persons experience because of unfortunate acts or words committed (1 Sam. 20:30; 2 Chr. 32:21). Humiliation and disgrace was brought on God's people through the exile at the hands of Babylon (Ezra 9:7), but He could also bring shame on one's enemies (Job 8:22). Used with its related verb *bôš*, it could express deep shame (Is. 42:17); with the word face following, it could express a face of shame (2 Chr. 32:21; Ezra 9:7; Jer. 7:19; Dan. 9:7, 8) meaning their "own shame." To be clothed with shame is a figurative expression of the psalmist (Ps. 35:26; 132:18). The phrase "shame of your youth" (Is. 54:4) refers to Israel's early indiscretions. The biblical authors would sometimes substitute this word for the word *ba'al* in a person's name, emphasizing the shame of ever recognizing such a pagan god (2 Sam. 2:8; Judg. 6:32). In other places and

ways, it replaces the word *ba'al* that became so closely attached to the gods of Canaan (Jer. 3:24; cf. Jer. 11:13; Hos. 9:10). *

4 ***kᵉlimmāh*** [fem. noun: כְּלִמָּה <3639>; from ASHAMED (BE) <3637>] ▶ **This word refers to disgrace, humiliation.** It has the meaning of embarrassment, i.e., Israel would eventually be ashamed because of its attempt to gain protection from Egypt (Is. 30:3; cf. Is. 45:16; 61:7). It has the sense of shame or humiliation through judgment (Mic. 2:6). It is referred to figuratively as a covering, clothing (Ps. 35:26; 109:29). It is often found in Ezekiel with the verb *nāśa'*, rendering the phrase to bear, to carry, to endure ignoring or shame (Ezek. 16:52). A word or rebuke can humiliate a person (Job 20:3). *

5 ***kᵉlimmûṯ*** [fem. noun: כְּלִמּוּת <3640>; from <3639> above] ▶ **This word means disgrace; it is also translated humiliation.** It is used of disgrace to be brought upon false prophets because of their false claims in God's name (Jer. 23:40). ¶

6 ***qālôn*** [masc. noun: קָלוֹן <7036>; from DESPISED (BE) <7034>] ▶ **This word refers to disgrace.** It refers to a feeling and condition of shame, of being put on display in mockery (Job 10:15); or of being dishonored (Ps. 83:16). The characters of fools make a show of dishonor; it clings to them (Prov. 3:35). It refers to losing a high social position and being ruined, shamed (Is. 22:18). God will change the glory of His rebellious people to shame and dishonor (Hos. 4:7; Nah. 3:5). *

– 7 Ex. 32:25 ➔ DERISION <8103> 8 Hab. 2:16 ➔ DISGRACE (noun) <7022>.

SHAME (WITHOUT) – Zeph. 2:1 ➔ LONG FOR <3700>.

SHAMED – 1 Chr. 8:12 ➔ SHEMER, SHAMER <8106>.

SHAMEFUL – Zeph. 2:1 ➔ LONG FOR <3700>.

SHAMEFUL SPEWING – Hab. 2:16 ➔ DISGRACE (noun) <7022>.

SHAMELESS – Zeph. 2:1 ➔ LONG FOR <3700>.

SHAMER – 1 Chr. 7:34 ➔ SHEMER, SHAMER <8106>.

SHAMGAR – ***šamgar*** [masc. proper noun: שַׁמְגַּר <8044>; of uncertain deriv.] ▶ **A minor judge in Israel. He was the son of Anath.** He killed six hundred Philistines with an oxgoad, a mighty deliverance for Israel (Judg. 3:31; 5:6). ¶

SHAMHUTH – ***šamhûṯ*** [masc. proper noun: שַׁמְהוּת <8049>]: ruin, astonishment ▶ **A commander in King David's army.** Ref.: 1 Chr. 27:8. ¶

SHAMIR – ***šāmiyr*** [proper noun: שָׁמִיר <8069>; the same as BRIER <8068>]: point, thorn ▶
a. A town in Judah. Ref.: Josh. 15:48. ¶
b. A town in Ephraim. Refs.: Judg. 10:1, 2. ¶
c. A Levite in David's day. Ref.: 1 Chr. 24:24. ¶

SHAMLAI – ***šamlay*** [proper noun: שַׁמְלַי <8073>; for SHALMAI <8014>] ▶ **This name stands in the place of Shalmai (<8014>).** Ref.: Ezra 2:46. ¶

SHAMMA – ***šammā'*** [masc. proper noun: שַׁמָּא <8037>; from DESTROYED (BE) <8074>]: desolation ▶ **An Israelite of the tribe of Asher.** Ref.: 1 Chr. 7:37. ¶

SHAMMAH – ***šammāh*** [masc. proper noun: שַׁמָּה <8048>; from RUIN (noun) <8047>]: ruin, astonishment ▶
a. An Edomite chief, son of Reuel. Refs.: Gen. 36:13, 17; 1 Chr. 1:37. ¶
b. The third son of Jesse. Refs.: 1 Sam. 16:9; 17:13. ¶
c. Son of Agee the Hararite. Refs.: 2 Sam. 23:11, 33. ¶
d. One of David's mighty men. Ref.: 2 Sam. 23:25. ¶

SHAMMAI – ***šammay*** [masc. proper noun: שַׁמַּי <8060>]: desolate ▶
a. Son of Onam. Refs.: 1 Chr. 2:28, 32. ¶
b. Son of Rekem. Refs.: 1 Chr. 2:44, 45. ¶
c. Son of Mered. Ref.: 1 Chr. 4:17. ¶

SHAMMOTH – ***šammôṯ*** [masc. proper noun: שַׁמּוֹת <8054>; plur. of RUIN (noun) <8047>]: ruins, desolation ▶ **One of David's mighty men.** Ref.: 1 Chr. 11:27. ¶

SHAMMUA – ***šammûaʿ*** [masc. proper noun: שַׁמּוּעַ <8051>; from HEAR <8085>]: renowned ▶
a. Son of David. Refs.: 2 Sam. 5:14; 1 Chr. 14:4. ¶
b. A Reubenite. Ref.: Num. 13:4. ¶
c. A Levite. Ref.: Neh. 11:17. ¶
d. Head of a Levite family. Ref.: Neh. 12:18. ¶

SHAMSHERAI – ***šamšᵉray*** [masc. proper noun: שַׁמְשְׁרַי <8125>; apparently from SUN <8121>]: like the sun ▶ **An Israelite of the tribe of Benjamin.** Ref.: 1 Chr. 8:26. ¶

SHAMUR – ***šāmûr*** [masc. proper noun: שָׁמוּר <8053>] ▶ **This name stands in place of Shamir (<8069> c.).** Ref.: 1 Chr. 24:24. ¶

SHAPE (noun) – 1 Kgs. 6:25; 7:37 ➔ FORM (noun) <7095>.

SHAPE (verb) – 1 Job 10:8 ➔ HURT <6087> 2 Hab. 2:18 ➔ CUT (verb) 6458>.

SHAPED (BE) – Prov. 8:25 ➔ DROWN <2883>.

SHAPHAM – ***šāp̄ām*** [masc. proper noun: שָׁפָם <8223>; formed like SHEPHAM <8221>]: naked, bald ▶ **An Israelite of the tribe of Gad.** Ref.: 1 Chr. 5:12. ¶

SHAPHAN – ***šāp̄ān*** [masc. proper noun: שָׁפָן <8227>; from TREASURE <8226> (in the sense of something hidden)]: badger ▶
a. This word refers to Josiah's secretary who helped carry out Josiah's great reforms. Refs.: 2 Kgs. 22:3, 8–10, 12, 14. He even helped to make public the Book of the Law found in the Temple.
b. Perhaps the same as a., the father of Ahikam. He was closely involved in all the issues surrounding the discovery of the Book of the Law. Refs.: 2 Kgs. 25:22; 2 Chr. 34:20; Jer. 26:24; 39:14. He was the grandfather of Gedeliah, governor of Judah (Jer. 40:5; 41:2; 43:6).
c. The father of Elasah; perhaps the same as a. His son delivered Jeremiah's letter to the exiles (Jer. 29:3).
d. The father of Gemariah; perhaps the same as a. His son Gemariah had his own room or chamber in the Temple near the New Gate (Jer. 36:10–12).
e. The father of Jaazeniah; perhaps the same as a. His son Jaazeniah was a participant in heinous abominations in the Lord's Temple (Ezek. 8:11).
f. For another meaning of the Hebrew word, see BADGER <8227>. *

SHAPHAT – 1 ***šāp̄āṭ*** [masc. proper noun: שָׁפָט <8202>; from JUDGE (verb) <8199>]: judge ▶
a. A Simeonite. Ref.: Num. 13:5. ¶
b. The father of the prophet Elisha. Refs.: 1 Kgs. 19:16, 19; 2 Kgs. 3:11; 6:31. ¶
c. A descendant of David. Ref.: 1 Chr. 3:22. ¶
d. A Gadite. Ref.: 1 Chr. 5:12. ¶
e. Son of Adlai. Ref.: 1 Chr. 27:29. ¶
2 ***šᵉp̄aṭyāhû, šᵉp̄aṭyāh*** [masc. proper noun: שְׁפַטְיָהוּ, שְׁפַטְיָה <8203>; from JUDGE (verb) <8199> and LORD <3050>]: the Lord is judge ▶
a. A Benjamite warrior. Ref.: 1 Chr. 12:5. ¶
b. A Simeonite official. Ref.: 1 Chr. 27:16. ¶
c. A son of David. Refs.: 2 Sam. 3:4; 1 Chr. 3:3. ¶
d. Son of Jehoshaphat. Ref.: 2 Chr. 21:2. ¶
e. A prince who opposed Jeremiah. Ref.: Jer. 38:1. ¶
f. The head of a family returning from exile with Zerubbabel. Refs.: Ezra 2:4; 8:8; Neh. 7:9. ¶
g. Descendant of one of Solomon's servants. Refs.: Ezra 2:57; Neh. 7:59. ¶
h. Ancestor of Meshullam. Ref.: 1 Chr. 9:8. ¶
i. A descendant of Perez. Ref.: Neh. 11:4. ¶

SHAPHER – Num. 33:23, 24 ➔ SHEPHER <8234>.

SHARAI – ***šāray*** [masc. proper noun: שָׁרַי <8298>; prob. from ENEMY <8324>]: hostile ▶ **An Israelite who had married a foreign woman.** Ref.: Ezra 10:40. ¶

SHARAR – ***šārār*** [masc. proper noun: שָׁרָר <8325>; from ENEMY <8324>]: enemy ▶ **Father of one of David's mighty men.** Ref.: 2 Sam. 23:33, the same as Sacar (<7940> a.). ¶

SHARD – Is. 30:14 ➔ EARTHENWARE <2789>.

SHARE (noun) – 1 Sam. 13:20 ➔ PLOWSHARE <4282>.

SHARE (verb) – 1 ***ḥālaq*** [verb: חָלַק <2505>; a prim. root] ▶ **This word indicates to divide, to split among two or more persons.** It indicates receiving or obtaining one's share of something (1 Sam. 30:24; Jer. 37:12). It means to allot something (Deut. 4:19; 29:26), to give a share to someone. Of persons it means to divide up into sections or groups or even to scatter them (Gen. 49:7; 1 Chr. 23:6; 24:3); of objects it means to divide them up (Ezek. 5:1); or distribute them (2 Chr. 23:18). It takes on the nuance of to be a sharer or partner with (Prov. 29:24). *
– 2 Is. 58:7 ➔ DIVIDE <6536>.

SHARED – Prov. 21:9; 25:24 ➔ COMPANY <2267>.

SHAREZER – ***šar'eṣer, śar'eṣer*** [masc. proper noun: שַׁרְאֶצֶר, שַׂרְאֶצֶר <8272>; of foreign deriv.]: prince of fire ▶
a. Son of Sennacherib. Refs.: 2 Kgs. 19:37; Is. 37:38. ¶
b. An Israelite in Zechariah's day. Ref.: Zech. 7:2. ¶

SHARON, LASHARON – ***šārôn, laššārôn*** [proper noun: שָׁרוֹן, לַשָּׁרוֹן <8289>; prob. abridged from STRAIGHT (BE) <3474>]: plain ▶
a. Lasharon is the name of a Canaanite king conquered by Joshua, evidently on the west of the Jordan. The location is not known. It may be a separate town. Ref.: Josh. 12:18.
b. Sharon is the name given to a stretch of the coastal plain on the Mediterranean shore. It was between the Yarkon River and Mount Carmel. Cattle pastured here. It was fertile, but God judged even this territory and its inhabitants (Is. 33:9; 35:2). God would, however, restore its fertility (Is. 65:10). The Philistine plain lay to its south.
c. A plain east of the Jordan in Gilead. Ref.: 1 Chr. 5:16.
d. A king in Lasharon. The location is not certain. (See a. above.) It may have been a town. The Septuagint indicates a "king of Aphek" named Lasharon (Josh. 12:18).
e. Other refs.: 1 Chr. 27:29; Song 2:1. ¶

SHARONITE – ***šārôniy*** [proper noun: שָׁרוֹנִי <8290>; patrial from SHARON <8289>] ▶ **Inhabitant of Sharon.** Ref.: 1 Chr. 27:29. ¶

SHARP – 1 ***ḥaḏ*** [adj.: חַד <2299>; from SHARPEN <2300>] ▶ **This word describes metaphorically the harsh tongues of those attacking the psalmist. It also means able to cut, pointed.** Ref.: Ps. 57:4. It describes the deadly seduction of an adulteress as sharp as a two-edged sword (Prov. 5:4). The Servant's mouth is like a sharp sword (Is. 49:2; also translated sharpened). Other ref.: Ezek. 5:1. ¶
2 ***ḥaddûḏ*** [masc. noun: חַדּוּד <2303>; from SHARPEN <2300>] ▶ **This word means pointed, sharpened.** It defines some features of Leviathan described in Job (Job 41:30). His undersides or parts are like jagged or sharp potsherds or stones. ¶
– 3 Josh. 5:2, 3 ➔ FLINT <6864> 4 Ps. 120:4; Prov. 25:18 ➔ SHARPEN <8150> 5 Ezek. 21:16: Show yourself sharp ➔ GO ONE WAY OR THE OTHER <258>.

SHARP (BE, MAKE) – Ps. 45:5; 140:3; Is. 5:28 ➔ SHARPEN <8150>.

SHARP INSTRUMENT – 2 Sam. 12:31; 1 Chr. 20:3 ➔ PICK (noun) <2757>.

SHARP POTSHERD – Job 41:30 ➔ EARTHENWARE <2789>.

SHARP STONE – Ex. 4:25 ➔ FLINT <6864>.

SHARPEN – 1 ***ḥāḏaḏ, ḥāḏāh*** [verb.: חָדַד, חָדָה <2300>; a prim. root] ► **a. A verb meaning to be keen; to slash, be quick, be fierce.** It describes the horses of the Babylonian cavalry in the evening as more quick, keen, or fierce than wolves (Hab. 1:8). It depicts a sharpened sword as both literal and symbolic of the Lord's "sword" of imminent judgment on Israel (Ezek. 21:9–11, 16). ¶
b. A verb used of iron sharpening iron from which comes the simile of one person sharpening the face of another, i.e., contributing to the improvement of another. Ref.: Prov. 27:17. ¶
2 ***lāṭaš*** [verb: לָטַשׁ <3913>; a prim. root] ► **This word means to make sharper, to hammer, to instruct.** It indicates the process of sharpening a tool (1 Sam. 13:20). It is used figuratively of God's sharpening a weapon, a sword (Ps. 7:12); the tongue of an evil person is described as a sharpened razor (Ps. 52:2). It is used of God's squinting or whetting His eyes against Job (Job 16:9). It is used in its active participial form to indicate a smith or forger of metal tools or instruments (Gen. 4:22: forger, instructor, instructer, to forge). ¶
3 ***šānan*** [verb: שָׁנַן <8150>; a prim. root] ► **This word is used in three of the basic stems.** In its simple meaning of sharpen, it can be used to refer to the sharpening of a sword. In context it refers to God sharpening His sword of judgment (Deut. 32:41; also translated to whet). Also, it can be used in reference to sharp arrows (Ps. 45:5; Is. 5:28: to be sharp). Figuratively, this verb can be used to signify sharp words that a person says in order to hurt someone else (Ps. 64:3; 140:3). In the intensive form of the verb, it means to teach incisively (Deut. 6:7: to teach diligently, to impress). The idea here is that just as words are cut into a stone tablet with a sharp object, so the Law should be impressed on the hearts of the children of every generation. Finally, in the reflexive stem, this verb means to be pierced by grief or envy or to be wounded (Ps. 73:21: to be pricked, to be vexed, to be embittered). Other refs. (sharp): Ps. 120:4; Prov. 25:18. ¶

SHARPENED – Is. 49:2 → SHARP <2299>.

SHARPLY – Ezek. 21:16: cut sharply → GO ONE WAY OR THE OTHER <258>.

SHARUHEN – ***šārûḥen*** [proper noun: שָׁרוּחֶן <8287>; prob. from LOOSE (LET) <8281> (in the sense of dwelling) and GRACE <2580>]: pleasant dwelling ► **A city that became part of the inheritance of Simeon.** Ref.: Josh. 19:6. ¶

SHASHAI – ***šāšay*** [masc. proper noun: שָׁשַׁי <8343>; perhaps from LINEN, FINE LINEN <8336>]: whitish ► **A man who took a foreign wife and then divorced her during Ezra's day.** Ref.: Ezra 10:40. ¶

SHASHAK – ***šāšāq*** [masc. proper noun: שָׁשָׁק <8349>; prob. from the base of LEG <7785>]: pedestrian ► **An Israelite of the tribe of Benjamin.** Refs.: 1 Chr. 8:14, 25. ¶

SHATTER – 1 ***ḥᵃšal*** [Aramaic verb: חֲשַׁל <2827>; a root corresponding to FEEBLE (BE) <2826>] ► **This word refers to iron as the metal which smashes into pieces everything it is used against, a symbol of the fourth kingdom.** Ref.: Dan. 2:40; also translated to smash, to subdue. ¶
2 ***rāʿaṣ*** [verb: רָעַץ <7492>; a prim. root] ► **This word means to destroy; it also means to afflict.** It refers to a violent breaking of the power of an enemy, disarming them (Ex. 15:6; also translated to dash in pieces). It refers also to a constant oppression placed on a people or nation by force, a constant harassment of them (Judg. 10:8; also translated to harass, to crush, to vex). ¶
– 3 Job 16:12; Jer. 23:29; Hab. 3:6 → SCATTER <6483> 4 Mal. 1:4 → DEMOLISH <7567>.

SHATTERED – 1 Sam. 2:4 → DREAD (noun and adj.) <2844> b.

SHATTERING – 1 Jer. 25:34 → DISPERSING <8600> b. 2 Ezek. 9:2 → SLAUGHTER (noun) <4660>.

SHAULITE – ***šā'ûliy*** [proper noun: שָׁאוּלִי <7587>; patron. from SAUL <7586>] ► **A descendant of Simeon (SAUL <7586> c.).** Ref.: Num. 26:13.

SHAVE, SHAVE OFF – ***gālaḥ*** [verb: גָּלַח <1548>; a prim. root] ► **The verb indicates cutting or removing hair with a razor.** Refs.: Lev. 13:33; 14:9; Num. 6:19; Judg. 16:17, 22; 2 Sam. 10:4; 14:26; Is. 7:20. In a figurative sense, it speaks of Assyria as God's razor that He will use to shave and shame His people Judah (Is. 7:20). *

SHAVE THE HEAD – ***qāraḥ*** [verb: קָרַח <7139>; a prim. root] ► **This word refers to cutting off one's hair; it also means to make bald.** It was done as a sign of mourning (Lev. 21:5; Ezek. 27:31; Mic. 1:16); the practice was forbidden to Israelite priests for various reasons. It is a sign of great effort and of labor expended, of wearing down a person (Ezek. 29:18). Other ref.: Jer. 16:6. ¶

SHAVED HEAD – See BALDNESS <7144>.

SHAVEH – ***šāwêh*** [proper noun: שָׁוֵה <7740>; from LIKE (BE, BECOME) <7737> (properly, to level)]: plain ► **A valley where the king of Sodom met Abraham after a battle.** Ref.: Gen. 14:17. ¶

SHAVEH-KIRIATHAIM – ***šāwêh qiryāṯayim*** [proper noun: שָׁוֵה קִרְיָתַיִם <7741>; from the same as SHAVEH <7740> and the dual of CITY <7151>]: plain of double city ► **A place where Chedorlaomer and the kings that were with him defeated the Emim.** Ref.: Gen. 14:5. ¶

SHAVSHA – ***šawšā'*** [masc. proper noun: שַׁוְשָׁא <7798>; from REJOICE <7797>]: joyful ► **The secretary of King David.** Ref.: 1 Chr. 18:16. ¶

SHAWL – [1] Ruth 3:15 ➔ CLOAK <4304> [2] Song 5:7; Is. 3:23 ➔ VEIL <7289>.

SHEAF – ***'ōmer*** [masc. noun: עֹמֶר <6016>; from a verb meaning to bind sheaves, see SLAVE (TREAT AS A) <6014>] ► **This word refers to a bundle of grain. It indicates ears of grain recently cut off the stalks.** Refs.: Lev. 23:10–12, 15; Deut. 24:19; Ruth 2:7, 15. Sheaves were to be left for the poor and hungry (Job 24:10). The Hebrew word also indicates a measure of grain; see OMER <6016>. ¶

SHEAF, SHEAF OF GRAIN – Job 21:32 ➔ STACKED GRAIN <1430>.

SHEAL – ***šᵉ'āl*** [masc. proper noun: שְׁאָל <7594>]: request ► **An Israelite who had married a foreign wife.** Ref.: Ezra 10:29. ¶

SHEALTIEL – [1] ***šᵉ'altiy'êl, šaltiy'êl*** [masc. proper noun: שְׁאַלְתִּיאֵל, שַׁלְתִּיאֵל <7597>; from ASK <7592> and GOD <410>]: I have asked God ►
a. Father of Zerubbabel, the governor of Judah after the Babylonian captivity. Refs.: 1 Chr. 3:17; Ezra 3:2, 8; Neh. 12:1; Hag. 1:1; 2:23. See the Aramaic entry <7598> below.
b. A slightly different name in Hebrew than a. above. Refs.: Hag. 1:12, 14; 2:2. ¶
[2] ***šᵉ'altiy'êl*** [masc. proper noun: שְׁאַלְתִּיאֵל <7598>; corresponding to <7597> above]: I have asked God ► **This name corresponds to the entry <7597> a. above and refers to the same individual.** Ref.: Ezra 5:2. ¶

SHEAR – [1] Gen. 31:19 ➔ CUT (verb) <1494> [2] Song 4:2 ➔ CUT, CUT OFF, CUT DOWN <7094>.

SHEAR-JASHUB – ***šᵉ'ār yāšûḇ*** [masc. proper noun: שְׁאָר יָשׁוּב <7610>; from REMNANT <7605> and TURN <7725>]: a remnant will return ► **A symbolical name given to the son of Isaiah the prophet.** Ref.: Is. 7:3. ¶

SHEARIAH – ***šᵉ'aryāh*** [masc. proper noun: שְׁעַרְיָה <8187>; from THINK <8176> (in the sense of to calculate, to estimate) and LORD <3050>]: the Lord weighs the value ► **A Benjamite of the family of Saul and his son Jonathan.** Refs.: 1 Chr. 8:38; 9:44. ¶

SHEARING – ***gêz*** [masc. noun: גֵּז <1488>; from CUT (verb) <1494>] ▶ **This word is also translated fleece, mown field.** It refers to wool sheared from sheep (Deut. 18:4) and to clothing made from it (Job 31:20). It designates the object cut or mown, such as a mown field (Ps. 72:6) as well as the act or process of mowing (Amos 7:1). ¶

SHEATH – 1 ***nāḏān*** [masc. noun: נָדָן <5084>; of uncertain deriv.] ▶ **This word indicates a case for holding a sword in place.** It is used to hold, in context, the sword blade of a divine being (1 Chr. 21:27). ¶
– 2 1 Sam. 17:51; 2 Sam. 20:8 ➔ RAZOR <8593> 3 Dan. 7:15 ➔ BODY <5085>.

SHEATHED – Ps. 68:13 ➔ COVER (verb) <2645>.

SHEAVE – ***ᵃlummah*** [fem. noun: אֲלֻמָּה <485>; pass. part. of BIND <481>] ▶ **The word refers to a bundle of cut stalks of grain or similar growth bound with twine or straw.** Ref.: Ps. 126:6. It is used to describe some aspects of Joseph's dreams (Gen. 37:7). ¶

SHEAVES – See GRAIN (SHEAF OF, FALLEN) <5995>.

SHEBA – 1 ***šᵉḇā'*** [masc. proper noun: שְׁבָא <7614>; of foreign origin]: fulness, oath ▶
a. A descendant of Shem. Refs.: Gen. 10:28; 1 Chr. 1:22.
b. A descendant of Ham. Refs.: Gen. 10:7; 1 Chr. 1:9.
c. A descendant of Abraham through Keturah. His father was Jokshan (Gen. 25:3; 1 Chr. 1:32).
d. A nation in Arabia. Refs.: 1 Kgs. 10:1, 4; etc. *
2 ***šeḇa'*** [proper noun: שֶׁבַע <7652>; the same as SEVEN <7651>]: seven, oath ▶
a. A Benjamite. Refs.: 2 Sam. 20:1, 2, 6, 7, 10, 13, 21, 22. ¶
b. A Gadite. Ref.: 1 Chr. 5:13. ¶
c. A town in Simeon. Ref.: Josh. 19:2. ¶

SHEBAH – Gen. 26:33 ➔ SHIBAH <7656>.

SHEBANIAH – ***šᵉḇanyāhû, šᵉḇanyāh*** [masc. proper noun: שְׁבַנְיָהוּ, שְׁבַנְיָה <7645>; for the same as SHEBNA <7644> and LORD <3050>]: increased by the Lord ▶
a. A priest in David's day. Ref.: 1 Chr. 15:24.
b. A Levite who led worship in Nehemiah's day, possibly the same as d. or e. Refs.: Neh. 9:4, 5; 10:10.
c. A priest in Ezra's day. Refs.: Neh. 10:4; 12:14, NIV, see SHECANIAH <7935> c.
d. A Levite who signed Nehemiah's covenant, possibly the same as b. Ref.: Neh. 10:10.
e. Another Levite who signed Nehemiah's covenant, possibly the same as b. Ref.: Neh. 10:12. ¶

SHEBARIM – ***šᵉḇāriym*** [שְׁבָרִים <7671>; plur. of DESTRUCTION <7667>]: ruins ▶
a. A masculine proper noun designating a place near Ai. Ref.: Josh. 7:5.
b. A masculine plural noun meaning stone quarries. Ref.: NIV, Josh. 7:5. ¶

SHEBAT – ***šᵉḇāṭ*** [proper noun: שְׁבָט <7627>; of foreign origin] ▶ **This word refers to the eleventh month of postexilic Israel, equal to a modern date of February-March.** In context the exact date given refers to February 15, 519 B.C. Only ref.: Zech. 1:7. ¶

SHEBER – ***šeḇer*** [masc. proper noun: שֶׁבֶר <7669>; from BREAK <7665> (comp. DESTRUCTION <7667>)]: breaking ▶ **A son of Caleb, from the tribe of Judah.** Ref.: 1 Chr. 2:48. ¶

SHEBNA, SHEBNAH – ***šeḇnā', šeḇnāh*** [masc. proper noun: שֶׁבְנָא, שֶׁבְנָה <7644>; from an unused root meaning to grow]: vigor, youth ▶ **The scribe of King Hezekiah of Judah.** He spoke to the representative of the Assyrians when they were attacking Jerusalem (2 Kgs. 18:18, 26, 37; 19:2; Is. 22:15; 36:3, 11, 22; 37:2). ¶

SHEBUEL, SHUBAEL – ***šᵉḇû'ēl, šûḇā'ēl*** [masc. proper noun: שְׁבוּאֵל, שׁוּבָאֵל <7619>; from CAPTIVE (TAKE) <7617>

(abbreviated) or TURN <7725> and GOD <410>]: captive of God ▶
a. A Levitical official descended from Gershom. Refs.: 1 Chr. 23:16; 24:20; 26:24. ¶
b. A Levitical musician, son of Heman. Refs.: 1 Chr. 25:4, 20. ¶

SHECHANIAH – ***š[e]ḵanyāhû, š[e]ḵanyāh*** [masc. proper noun: שְׁכַנְיָהוּ, שְׁכַנְיָה <7935>; from SETTLE DOWN <7931> and LORD <3050>]: dwelling of the Lord ▶
a. A priest. Ref.: 1 Chr. 24:11. ¶
b. A Levite. Ref.: 2 Chr. 31:15.
c. A priest. Refs.: Neh. 12:3, 14 (see also <7645> c.). ¶
d. A descendant of Zerubbabel. Refs.: 1 Chr. 3:21, 22; Ezra 8:3; Neh. 3:29. ¶
e. Son of Jahaziel. Ref.: Ezra 8:5. ¶
f. Son of Jehiel. Ref.: Ezra 10:2. ¶
g. Son of Arah. Ref.: Neh. 6:18. ¶

SHECHEM – [1] ***šeḵem*** [proper noun: שְׁכֶם <7927>; the same as SHOULDER <7926>]: shoulder, ridge ▶ **This word designates an important biblical and middle-eastern city located on the border of Ephraim and Manasseh.** Refs.: Josh. 17:2, 7. It lay between Mount Ebal on the northwest and Mount Gerazim on the southeast. It also served in Israel as a Levitical city as well as a city of refuge (Josh. 20:7; 21:21). It was the first capital city of the Northern Kingdom briefly (Tirzah and then Samaria took its place). It lies ca. thirty miles north of Jerusalem. Abraham had a vision and received promises from God in Shechem at the tree of Moreh (Gen. 12:6). Jacob purchased land in it from Hamor, father of Shechem (Gen. 33:18) and committed himself and his family to the Lord there (Gen. 35:4), as Israel and Joshua did many years later (Josh. 24:1–32). Here Dinah was raped and savagely avenged by Simon and Levi (Gen. 37). Shechem continued to be a city intertwined with Israel at various times during its history (Judg. 8:31; 9:1–57). Jeroboam I was made king at Shechem (1 Kgs. 12:1, 25).

It was God's intent to give Shechem to *His* people, for He owned it (Ps. 60:6; 108:7). Inhabitants of the city supported Gedaliah as governor, God's chosen vessel, after the fall of Jerusalem (Jer. 41:5). *

[2] ***šeḵem*** [masc. proper noun: שְׁכֶם <7928>; for SHOULDER <7926>]: shoulder, neck ▶
a. A man of Manasseh and descendant of Gilead. Through him the family/clan of Shechem was built up (Num. 26:31; Josh. 17:2). ¶
b. The son of Hamor, a Hivite. His son Shechem raped Dinah, daughter of Jacob. Simeon and Levi took vengeance, killing Hamor, Shechem, and everyone in their city (Gen. 33:19; 34:2, 4, 6, 8, 11, 13, 18, 20, 24, 26). ¶
c. A son of Shemediah (Shemida, NIV) from the tribe of Manasseh. Ref.: 1 Chr. 7:19. ¶
– [3] Hos. 6:9 → SHOULDER <7926>.

SHECHEMITE – ***šiḵmiy*** [proper noun: שִׁכְמִי <7930>; patron. from SHECHEM <7928>] ▶ **A descendant of Shechem.** Ref.: Num. 26:31; see SHECHEM <7928> a. ¶

SHED – Ezek. 35:5 → to shed the *blood* → SPILL <5064>.

SHEDEUR – ***š[e]ḏêy'ûr*** [masc. proper noun: שְׁדֵיאוּר <7707>; from the same as FIELD <7704> (to spread out) and LIGHT <216>]: spreader of light ▶ **Father of Elizur, a chief of the tribe of Reuben.** Refs.: Num. 1:5; 2:10; 7:30, 35; 10:18. ¶

SHEEP – [1] ***keḇeś*** [masc. noun: כֶּבֶשׂ <3532>; from an unused root meaning to dominate] ▶ **This word refers to a male lamb.** These animals were usually mentioned as sacrificial animals (Ex. 12:5; 29:38–41; Lev. 4:32; 9:3; Num. 6:12, 14; 7:15; 28:3; Ezra 8:35; Is. 1:11; Ezek. 46:4–7). They are mentioned as a source of raw material for clothing (Job 31:20; Prov. 27:26). Their nature was renowned for gentleness, and the word is used to refer to Jeremiah in a simile (Jer. 11:19). *

[2] ***keśeḇ*** [masc. noun: כֶּשֶׂב <3775>; apparently by transposition for <3532> above ▶ **This word indicates lambs or young sheep used for sacrifices.** Refs.: Lev. 1:10;

3:7; 4:35; 22:19, 27; Num. 18:17. These animals could also be used in food preparation (Lev. 7:23; 17:3; Deut. 14:4). They constituted wealth and property (Gen. 30:32, 33, 35, 40). ¶

3 ***ṣō'n*** [coll. fem. noun: צֹאן <6629>; from an unused root meaning to migrate] ▶ **This word refers also to a flock. It is used literally most often to refer to small cattle, i.e., goats and/or sheep.** Refs.: Gen. 4:2, 4; 30:31, 32; 1 Sam. 25:2. The phrase *bᵉnê ṣō'n* refers to individual sheep or goats (Ps. 114:4). The flock was important for food (Amos 6:4); clothing materials (Gen. 31:19); drink, milk (Deut. 32:14); especially sacrificial victims (Gen. 4:4; Lev. 1:2, 10); and as a major part of a person's wealth (Gen. 12:16; 13:5). It is used figuratively often of children, of persons, multitudes of people, of Israel as sheep especially (Num. 27:17; 1 Kgs. 22:17; Job 21:11); of Israel wandering as sheep in sin (2 Sam. 24:17; Is. 53:6; Ezek. 24:5; 34:2, 3, etc.; Zech. 9:16; 10:2; 11:4; 13:7); of Israel as sheep led by the Lord (Ps. 77:20; 78:52); of a scattered, destroyed Babylon as confused sheep (Is. 13:14; Jer. 50:45). Edom is pictured as a flock (Jer. 49:20). *

4 ***ṣōnê', ṣōneh*** [common noun צֹנֶא, צֹנֶה <6792>; for <6629> above] ▶ **This word is another word referring to a flock, sheep, goats.** Ref.: Num. 32:24. God has made humankind ruler over all flocks of sheep (Ps. 8:7). ¶

5 ***śeh*** [common noun: שֶׂה <7716>; prob. from ROAR <7582> (in the sense of to rush, through the idea of pushing out to graze)] ▶ **This word refers to a young lamb of sheep or a young kid of goats, a part of a larger unit of animals, a flock (*ṣō'n*).** Ref.: Gen. 22:7. The animals were of great value for wealth in general, food, sacrifices, milk. They were a favorite subject in figures of speech indicating lost or straying persons, as well as sheep themselves (Ps. 119:176). They were used figuratively of Israel (Ezek. 34:17). The Suffering Servant was slaughtered like a sheep (Is. 53:7). The lamb was used in the Passover ritual (Ex. 12:3–5). *

– 6 Gen. 31:38; Song 6:6; Is. 53:7 ➔ EWE <7353 7 1 Sam. 17:34 ➔ LAMB <2089>.

SHEEP BREEDER – ***nōqēḏ*** [masc. noun: נֹקֵד <5349>; act. part. from the same as SPECKLED <5348>] ▶ **This word refers to a shepherd; it is also translated sheepmaster, herdman.** It refers literally to a person who grazes sheep but extends to include the total care involved in raising them. Even a king or a prophet could be a sheep breeder or grazer (2 Kgs. 3:4; Amos 1:1). ¶

SHEEP PEN – Gen. 49:14; Judg. 5:16 ➔ BURDEN a. and b.<4942>.

SHEEPBREEDER – Nah. 2:10 ➔ HERDSMAN <951>.

SHEEPFOLD – 1 Gen. 49:14 ➔ BURDEN a., b.<4942> 2 Ps. 68:13 ➔ HOOK <8240> d.

SHEEPMASTER – 2 Kgs. 3:4 ➔ SHEEP BREEDER <5349>.

SHEERAH – ***šeʾᵉrāh*** [fem. proper noun: שֶׁאֱרָה <7609>; the same as KINSWOMAN <7608>]: kinswoman ▶ **Daughter of Ephraim.** She built Beth-horon and Uzzen-sheerah (1 Chr. 7:24). ¶

SHEET – Judg. 14:12, 13 ➔ LINEN GARMENT <5466>.

SHEHARIAH – ***šᵉḥaryāh*** [masc. proper noun: שְׁחַרְיָה <7841>; from SEEK DILIGENTLY <7836> and LORD <3050>]: sought by the Lord ▶ **An Israelite of the tribe of Benjamin.** Ref.: 1 Chr. 8:26. ¶

SHEJA – ***šᵉyā'*** [masc. proper noun: שְׁיָא <7864>; for SHEVA <7724>] ▶ **This name stands in place of the name Sheva (<7724> a.) in Hebrew manuscripts.** Ref.: 2 Sam. 20:25. ¶

SHEKEL – ***šeqel*** [masc. noun: שֶׁקֶל <8255>; from WEIGH <8254>] ▶ **This word indicates a unit of weight for metals that was probably around twelve grams or one-half ounce.** A silver shekel is expressed as *šeqel kesep̱* (Gen. 23:15); *šeqel* *haqqōdeṣ* refers to a shekel of the sanctuary (Ex. 30:13). There was also a king's shekel (2 Sam. 14:26). A half shekel was *maḥᵃṣîṯ haššeqel* (Ex. 38:24–26); *reḇaʿ* indicated one-fourth shekel (1 Sam. 9:8). *

SHELAH – 1 ***šêlāh*** [masc. proper noun: שֵׁלָה <7956>; the same as REQUEST <7596>]: request ▶ **The youngest son of Judah.** Refs.: Gen. 38:5, 11, 14, 26; 46:12; Num. 26:20; 1 Chr. 2:3; 4:21. ¶
2 ***šelaḥ*** [masc. proper noun: שֶׁלַח <7974>; the same as PLANTS <7973> or WEAPON <7973>]: weapon, plants ▶ **Father of Eber.** Refs.: Gen. 10:24; 11:12–15; 1 Chr. 1:18, 24. ¶
– 3 Neh. 3:15 ➔ SHILOAH <7975> b.

SHELANITE – ***šêlāniy*** [proper noun: שֵׁלָנִי <8024>; from SHELAH <7956>] ▶ **A descendant of Shelah (<7956>).** Refs.: Num. 26:20; Neh. 11:5. ¶

SHELEMIAH – ***šelemyāh, šelemyāhû*** [masc. proper noun: שֶׁלֶמְיָה, שֶׁלֶמְיָהוּ <8018>; from PEACE OFFERINGS <8002> and LORD <3050>]: peace offerings of the Lord ▶
a. A gatekeeper. Ref.: 1 Chr. 26:14. ¶
b. A son of Cushi. Ref.: Jer. 36:14. ¶
c. Son of Abdeel. Ref.: Jer. 36:26. ¶
d. The father of Jehucal. Refs.: Jer. 37:3; 38:1. ¶
e. The father of Irijah. Ref.: Jer. 37:13. ¶
f. Son of Bani. Ref.: Ezra 10:39. ¶
g. Another son of Bani. Ref.: Ezra 10:41. ¶
h. The father of Hananiah. Ref.: Neh. 3:30. ¶
i. A priest in Nehemiah's day. Ref.: Neh. 13:13. ¶

SHELEPH – ***šelep̱*** [masc. proper noun: שֶׁלֶף <8026>; from DRAW OUT <8025>]: drawing out ▶ **Second son of Joktan.** Refs.: Gen. 10:26; 1 Chr. 1:20. ¶

SHELESH – ***šêleš*** [masc. proper noun: שֵׁלֶשׁ <8028>; from DIVIDE INTO THREE PARTS <8027>]: third, might ▶ **An Israelite of the tribe of Asher.** Ref.: 1 Chr. 7:35. ¶

SHELOMI – ***šᵉlōmiy*** [masc. proper noun: שְׁלֹמִי <8015>; from PEACE <7965>]: peaceful ▶ **An Israelite from the tribe of Asher, father of a leader Ahihud.** Ref.: Num. 34:27. ¶

SHELOMITH – ***šᵉlōmiyṯ*** [proper noun: שְׁלוֹמִית <8019>; from PEACE <7965>]: peaceful, peacefulness ▶
a. A Danite woman. Ref.: Lev. 24:11. ¶
b. Daughter of Zerubbabel. Ref.: 1 Chr. 3:19. ¶
c. A Gershonite Levite. Ref.: 1 Chr. 23:9. It is the same as Shelomith (<8013> b.). ¶
d. A Levite, son of Izhar. Ref.: 1 Chr. 23:18. It is the same as Shelomith (<8013> a.). ¶
e. A Levite descended from Eliezer. Refs.: 1 Chr. 26:25; 26, 28. It is the same as Shelomith (<8013> c.). ¶
f. Son of Rehoboam. Ref.: 2 Chr. 11:20. ¶
g. The head of a family. Ref.: Ezra 8:10. ¶

SHELOMOTH, SHELOMITH – ***šᵉlōmôṯ*** [masc. proper noun: שְׁלֹמוֹת <8013>; fem. plur. of PEACE <7965>]: peacefulness ▶
a. A Levite, son of Izhar. Ref.: 1 Chr. 24:22. It is the same as Shelomith (<8019> d.).
b. A Gershonite Levite. Ref.: 1 Chr. 23:9. It is the same as Shelomith (<8019> c.).
c. A Levite descended from Eliezer. Refs.: 1 Chr. 26:25, 26, 28. It is the same as Shelomith (<8019> e.). ¶

SHELTER – 1 ***ḥāsûṯ*** [fem. noun: חָסוּת <2622>; from REFUGE <2620>] ▶ **This word means refuge, trust.** Isaiah uses it to describe the false hope or trust that Israel put in Egypt (Is. 30:3). ¶
2 ***mistôr*** [masc. noun: מִסְתּוֹר <4563>; from HIDE <5641>] ▶ **This word depicts a hiding place, place of protection.** It refers to a shelter or place of protection from a storm, used figuratively and literally (Is. 4:6; also translated covert). ¶
3 ***mip̱lāṭ*** [masc. noun: מִפְלָט <4655>; from DELIVER <6403>] ▶ **This word depicts a location or place of safety and security; it is also translated a place of shelter, place of refuge, escape.** Ref.: Ps. 55:8. Used figuratively, it describes the psalmist's escape from the storm and tempest of suffering brought on by his enemies. ¶

– [4] Deut. 32:38 ➔ COVERING <5643> b. [5] Judg. 6:2 ➔ DEN <4492> [6] Ps. 27:5 ➔ ABODE <5520> [7] Ps. 61:4 ➔ COVERING <5643> a. [8] Is. 4:6; 25:4; etc. ➔ REFUGE <4268> [9] Is. 32:2 ➔ HIDING PLACE <4224> a. [10] Zeph. 2:6 ➔ CAVE <3741>.

SHELTER (FIND) – Dan. 4:12 ➔ SHADE (FIND) <2927>.

SHELTER (TAKE) – Judg. 9:15 ➔ REFUGE <2620>.

SHELTER (verb) – Deut. 33:12 ➔ COVER (verb) <2653>.

SHELUMIEL – ***š^{e}lumiy'ēl*** [masc. proper noun: שְׁלֻמִיאֵל <8017>; from PEACE <7965> and GOD <410>]: peace of God, friend of God ▶ **An Israelite leader of the tribe of Simeon.** Refs.: Num. 1:6; 2:12; 7:36, 41; 10:19. ¶

SHEM – ***šēm*** [masc. proper noun: שֵׁם <8035>; the same as NAME <8034>]: name, fame ▶ **This word designates the first son of Noah.** God established His rainbow covenant with Noah and his sons and their families (Gen. 6:18). They survived the flood (Gen. 7:13). The human race multiplied from these persons after the flood (Gen. 9:18, 19). Shem was blessed above his other brothers who were to be subordinate to him and his descendants. Shem fathered many peoples and was the ancestor of Abraham and Eber (Gen. 10:21–31; 11:10–32). The blessings of Shem were worked out most fully, in a special way in the descendants of Abraham. *

SHEMA – [1] ***šema'*** [masc. proper noun: 8087> שֶׁמַע; for the same as HEARING <8088>]: heard, renown ▶
a. Son of Hebron. Refs.: 1 Chr. 2:43, 44. ¶
b. A Benjamite. Ref.: 1 Chr. 8:13. ¶
c. A postexilic Jew. Ref.: Neh. 8:4. ¶
d. A Reubenite. Ref.: 1 Chr. 5:8. ¶
[2] ***š^{e}ma'*** [proper noun: שְׁמַע <8090>; for <8087> above]: renowned ▶ **A city in the south of the territory of Judah.** Ref.: Josh. 15:26. ¶

SHEMAAH – ***š^{e}mā'āh*** [masc. proper noun: שְׁמָעָה <8094>; for SHIMEA <8093>]: renowned ▶ **One of David's mighty men.** Ref.: 1 Chr. 12:3. ¶

SHEMAIAH – [1] ***š^{e}ma'yāh, š^{e}māyāhû*** [masc. proper noun: שְׁמַעְיָה, שְׁמַעְיָהוּ <8098>; from HEAR <8085> and LORD <3050>]: the Lord has heard ▶
a. A man from the line of Reuben. Ref.: 1 Chr. 5:4. Reuben was the firstborn of the sons of Jacob.
b. A chief from the line of Simeon. Ref.: 1 Chr. 4:37.
c. He was a Levite and a leader during David's reign. Refs.: 1 Chr. 15:8, 11.
d. This Shemaiah was a Levite scribe during David's day and son of Nethanel. Ref.: 1 Chr. 24:6.
e. He held the position of gatekeeper. His sons also had positions of responsibility and were leaders in their families (1 Chr. 26:4).
f. The brother of Zerubbabel and son of Pedaiah. Refs.: 1 Kgs. 12:22; 2 Chr. 11:2; 12:5, 7, 15.
g. A teacher who taught the Book of the Law throughout Judah. Ref.: 2 Chr. 17:8 (see v. 9).
h. May be the same as i. He was a Levite during Hezekiah's day (2 Chr. 31:15).
i. Possibly the same as h. in Hezekiah's day. Kore was the keeper of the East Gate and was in charge of the freewill offering, and Shemaiah was one of his assistants (2 Chr. 31:15).
j. A chief Levite under Josiah who helped provide Passover offerings. Ref.: 2 Chr. 35:9.
k. Father of Uriah the prophet. May be same as l. or m. (Jer. 26:20).
l. Father of Delaiah during time of Jeremiah the prophet. May be same as k. or m. (Jer. 36:12).
m. A descendant of Gershon; hence, a Gershonite. In Hezekiah's day he helped cleanse, purify, and restore the Temple (2 Chr. 29:14).
n. A priest. May be the same as o. Refs.: Neh. 10:8; 12:6, 18.
o. A Levite who returned to Jerusalem from exile in Babylon. Ref.: Ezra 8:13.

p. Another Levite who was also among those who returned from Exile in Babylon. Ref.: Neh. 12:35.
q. A layman who returned from Babylonian exile. Ref.: Neh. 10:8.
r. A priest who was guilty of intermarriage; he married a foreign woman. Ref.: Ezra 10:21.
s. A priest who married a foreign woman in Ezra's day. Ref.: Ezra 10:31.
t. Descended from Zerubbabel, the royal line after the Exile. Refs.: 1 Chr. 3:22; Neh. 3:29.
u. He was a false prophet during the time of Nehemiah. Ref.: Neh. 6:10.
v. During Nehemiah's day, an official. May be same as w. (Neh. 12:36).
w. Possibly the same as v. or x. Grandfather of the priest Zechariah (Neh. 12:35, 42).
x. Possibly the same as w. He was a Levite and a musician during the time of Nehemiah (Neh. 12:42). *
2 ***sᵉmaḵyāhû*** [proper noun: סְמַכְיָהוּ <5565>; from LAY ON <5564> and LORD <3050>]: the Lord has sustained ▶ **A gatekeeper in the house of the Lord.** Refs.: 1 Chr. 26:4–7. ¶

SHEMARIAH – ***šᵉmaryāhû, šᵉmaryāh*** [masc. proper noun: שְׁמַרְיָהוּ, שְׁמַרְיָה <8114>; from KEEP <8104> and LORD <3050>]: kept by the Lord ▶
a. A Benjamite warrior. Ref.: 1 Chr. 12:5. ¶
b. Son of King Rehoboam. Ref.: 2 Chr. 11:19. ¶
c. A man who divorced a foreign wife in the time of Ezra. Ref.: Ezra 10:32. ¶
d. Another man who divorced a foreign wife in the time of Ezra. Ref.: Ezra 10:41. ¶

SHEMEBER – ***šem'ēḇer*** [masc. proper noun: שֶׁמְאֵבֶר <8038>; apparently from NAME <8034> and <83>]: illustrious ▶ **The king of Zeboim, an ally of the king of Sodom in the days of Abraham.** Ref.: Gen. 14:2. ¶

SHEMER, SHAMER – ***šemer, šāmed*** [masc. proper noun: שֶׁמֶר, שָׁמֶד <8106>; from the same as DREGS <8105>]: kept, preserved ▶
a. Owner of the hill where Samaria was built. Ref.: 1 Kgs. 16:24. ¶
b. A Levite. Ref.: 1 Kgs. 16:24. ¶
c. An Asherite. Refs.: Shamer, 1 Chr. 7:34. It is the same person as Shomer (<7763> b.). ¶
d. A Benjamite. Ref.: Shamed, 1 Chr. 8:12. ¶

SHEMIDA – ***šᵉmiyḏā'*** [masc. proper noun: שְׁמִידָע <8061>; apparently from NAME <8034> and KNOW <3045>]: name of knowing ▶ **Grandson of Manasseh.** Refs.: Num. 26:32; Josh. 17:2; 1 Chr. 7:19. ¶

SHEMIDAITE – ***šᵉmiyḏā'iy*** [proper noun: שְׁמִידָעִי <8062>; patron. from SHEMIDA <8061>] ▶ **A descendant of Shemida (<8061>).** Ref.: Num. 26:32. ¶

SHEMINITH – ***šᵉmiyniyṯ*** [fem. noun: שְׁמִינִית <8067>; fem. of EIGHTH <8066>] ▶ **This word is used as a musical term; it may signify an instrument or an octave. Its meaning is not clear.** The NASB has "lyres tuned to the sheminith" (1 Chr. 15:21); ESV, "lyres according to the Sheminith"; KJV, harps on the Sheminith. It occurs in Psalm 6 (title); 12 (title). Perhaps it refers to an eight-stringed lyre (NASB) or tune (KJV); for NIV it is probably a musical term. ¶

SHEMIRAMOTH – ***šᵉmiyrāmôṯ*** [masc. proper noun: שְׁמִירָמוֹת <8070>; prob. from NAME <8034> and plur. of HIGH PLACE <7413>]: name of heights, name highly exalted ▶
a. A Levite harpist in David's day. Refs.: 1 Chr. 15:18, 20; 16:5. ¶
b. A Levite teacher in Jehoshaphat's day. Ref.: 2 Chr. 17:8. ¶

SHEN – ***šēn*** [proper noun: שֵׁן <8129>; the same as TOOTH <8127>]: crag ▶ **Samuel took a stone and set it between Mizpah and Shen, and named it Ebenezer (thus far the Lord has helped us).** Ref.: 1 Sam. 7:12. ¶

SHENAZZAR – ***šen'aṣṣar*** [masc. proper noun: שֶׁנְאַצַּר <8137>; apparently of Babylonian origin]: light of the splendor ▶ **An Israelite of the tribe of Judah.** Ref.: 1 Chr. 3:18. ¶

SHEOL – ***še'ôl, še'ōl*** [noun: שְׁאוֹל, שְׁאֹל <7585>; from ASK <7592>] ► **This word means the world of the dead, the grave, death, the depths. It describes the underworld but usually in the sense of the grave and is most often translated as grave.** Jacob described himself as going to the grave upon Joseph's supposed death (Gen. 37:35; 42:38); Korah, Dathan, and Abiram went down into the ground, which becomes their grave, when God judges them (Num. 16:30, 33; 1 Sam. 2:6). David described his brush with death at the hands of Saul as feeling the ropes or bands of the grave clutching him (2 Sam. 22:6). The Lord declares that He will ransom His people from the grave or Sheol (Hos. 13:14). Habakkuk declared that the grave's desire for more victims is never satiated (Hab. 2:5).

The word means depths or Sheol. Job called the ways of the Almighty higher than heaven and lower than Sheol or the depths of the earth (Job 11:8). The psalmist could not escape the Lord even in the lowest depths of the earth, in contrast to the high heavens (Ps. 139:8; Amos 9:2). It means the deepest valley or depths of the earth in Isaiah 7:11.

In a few cases, Sheol seems to mean death or a similar concept; that Abaddon (destruction) lies uncovered seems to be matched with Sheol's meaning of death (Job 26:6). It means death or the grave, for neither is ever satisfied (Prov. 7:27; cf. Is. 38:10) The word is best translated as death or the depths in Deuteronomy 32:22.

Sheol or the grave is the place of the wicked (Ps. 9:17; 31:17); Ezekiel pictured it as the place of the uncircumcised (Ezek. 31:15; 32:21, 27). Israel's search for more wickedness and apostasy took them to the depths of Sheol (Is. 57:9). On the other hand, the righteous were not made for the grave or Sheol; it was not their proper abode. They were not left in the grave or Sheol (Ps. 16:10) but were rescued from that place (Ps. 49:15). Adulterers and fornicators were, metaphorically, described as in the lower parts of Sheol or the grave (Prov. 9:18). Sheol and Abaddon (Destruction) are as open to the eyes of God as are the hearts and thoughts of humankind; there is nothing mysterious about them to Him (Prov. 15:11). *

SHEPHAM – ***šepām*** [proper noun: שְׁפָם <8221>; prob. from STICK OUT <8192>]: naked, bald ► **A place identifying the border of Israel.** Refs.: Num. 34:10, 11. ¶

SHEPHELAH – 1 Chr. 27:28; Obad. 1:19 ➔ LOWLAND <8219>.

SHEPHER – ***šeper*** [proper noun: שֶׁפֶר <8234>; the same as BEAUTIFUL <8233>]: beauty ► **A mount where the Israelites camped on their way to Canaan.** Refs.: Num. 33:23, 24. ¶

SHEPHERD – 1 ***rō'iy*** [masc. noun: רֹעִי <7473>; from act. part. of FEED (verb) <7462> a.] ► **This word refers to one who pastures, cares for, and shepherds flocks.** It may function in poetry as a simile, like the tent of a shepherd (Is. 38:12). A useless or worthless shepherd is used to describe a corrupt leader in Israel (Zech. 11:17). ¶
– 2 Amos 1:1 ➔ SHEEP BREEDER <5349> 3 Nah. 2:10 ➔ HERDSMAN <951>.

SHEPHERD (BE A) – See FEED (verb) <7462> a.

SHEPHO, SHEPHI – ***šepô, šepiy*** [masc. proper noun: שְׁפוֹ, שְׁפִי <8195>; from STICK OUT <8192>; comp. BARE (noun) <8205>] ► **An Edomite, son of Shobal.** Refs.: Gen. 36:23; 1 Chr. 1:40. ¶

SHEPHUPHAM, SHEPHUPHAN – ***šepûpam, šepûpān*** [masc. proper noun: שְׁפוּפָם, שְׁפוּפָן <8197>; from the same as VIPER <8207>]: serpent ►
a. A descendant of Benjamin. Ref.: Num. 26:39. ¶
b. Son of Bela. Ref.: 1 Chr. 8:5. It is perhaps the same as a. ¶

SHERAH – See SHEERAH <7609>.

SHERD – Is. 30:14 ➔ EARTHENWARE <2789>.

SHEREBIAH – ***šêrêḇyāh*** [masc. prooper noun: שֵׁרֵבְיָה <8274>; from BURNING SAND <8273> and LORD <3050>]: the Lord has scorched ▶
a. A Levite returning from exile with Ezra. Refs.: Ezra 8:18, 24. Perhaps the same as b. below.
b. A Levite who assisted Ezra. Refs.: Neh. 8:7; 9:4, 5; 10:12. Perhaps the same as a. or c.
c. A Levite who returned with Zerubbabel. Refs.: Neh. 12:8, 24. ¶

SHERESH – ***šereš*** [masc. proper noun: שֶׁרֶשׁ <8329>; the same as ROOT (noun) <8328>]: root ▶ **Grandson of Manasseh.** Ref.: 1 Chr. 7:16. ¶

SHERIFF – Dan. 3:2, 3 ➔ MAGISTRATE <8612>.

SHESHACH – ***šêšaḵ*** [masc. proper noun: שֵׁשַׁךְ <8347>; of foreign deriv.] ▶ **A symbolic name for Babylon (of uncertain signification).** Refs.: Jer. 25:26; 51:41. ¶

SHESHAI – ***šêšai*** [masc. proper noun: שֵׁשַׁי <8344>; for SHASHAI <8343>]: whitish ▶ **Son of Anak, one of the giants in Canaan.** Refs.: Num. 13:22; Josh. 15:14; Judg. 1:10. ¶

SHESHAN – ***šêšān*** [masc. proper noun: שֵׁשָׁן <8348>; perhaps for LILY <7799>]: lily ▶ **An Israelite of the tribe of Judah.** Refs.: 1 Chr. 2:31, 34, 35. ¶

SHESHBAZZAR – [1] ***šešbaṣṣar***] [masc. proper noun: שֵׁשְׁבַּצַּר <8339>; of foreign deriv.] ▶ **A prince of Judah in Babylon who was in charge of the Temple vessels returned to Babylon.** Refs.: Ezra 1:8, 11. The name is Babylonian. It may mean "Shamash (sun god) protect the father." He served as governor in Judah and helped rebuild the Temple. Many feel that he is none other than Zerubbabel (cf. Ezra 3:2–8; 5:14). Babylonian names were regularly given to ranking officials in Babylon (Dan. 1:7, etc.). But, Sheshbazzar could have been a non-Jew, a governor of Samaria (cf. Ezra 5:14). ¶

[2] ***šêšbaṣṣār*** [Aramaic masc. proper noun: שֵׁשְׁבַּצַּר <8340>; corresponding to <8339 above] ▶ **A word designating the Aramaic name for Sheshbazzar.** Refs.: Ezra 5:14, 16. The facts and meaning are the same. ¶

SHETHAR – ***šêṯar*** [fem. proper noun: שֵׁתָר <8369>; of foreign deriv.]: star ▶ **One of the seven princes of Persia and Media next to King Ahasuerus.** Ref.: Esther 1:14. ¶

SHETHAR-BOZENAI – ***š^{e}ṯar bôz^{e}nay*** [masc. proper noun: שְׁתַר בּוֹזְנַי <8370>; of foreign deriv.]: star of splendor ▶ **An associate of Tattenai, governor of the Trans-Euphrates area (west of Jordan), who opposed the building of the Temple by the Jews.** He and his associates sent letters to Darius in Persepolis, Persia (Ezra 5:3–6). Darius refused their request to stop the building activity (Ezra 6:6–13). ¶

SHEVA – ***š^{e}wā'*** [masc. proper noun: שְׁוָא <7724>; from the same as EMPTINESS <7723>] ▶
a. A scribe. Ref.: 2 Sam. 20:25. ¶
b. A descendant of Caleb. Ref.: 1 Chr. 2:49. ¶

SHEW – Is. 3:9 ➔ LOOK (noun) <1971>.

SHIBAH – ***šiḇ'āh*** [proper noun: שִׁבְעָה <7656>; masc. of SEVEN <7651>]: seven, oath ▶ **Name of a well dug by Isaac's servants near Beersheba.** Ref.: Gen. 26:33. ¶

SHIBBOLETH, SIBBOLETH – Judg. 12:6 ➔ GRAIN (HEAD OF, EAR OF) <7641>.

SHIELD (noun) – [1] ***māḡên*** [masc. noun: מָגֵן <4043>; from DEFEND <1598>] ▶ **This word indicates some kind of protection, literal or figurative.** A shield as a weapon (Judg. 5:8; 2 Sam. 1:21; 1 Kgs. 14:27; Job 15:26); a shield as an ornament or decorative display (1 Kgs. 10:17; 14:26); as the protective scales of a crocodile (Job 41:15). Metaphorically, it refers to persons

or God as sources of protection or escape, a refuge: a king (Ps. 84:9; 89:18). God is often referred to as a shield of refuge (Gen. 15:1; Ps. 3:3; 7:10; 18:2; Prov. 2:7); also the rulers of the earth are referred to as shields (Ps. 47:9). *
2 ***šeleṭ*** [masc. noun: שֶׁלֶט <7982>; from RULE OVER <7980>] ▶ **Most commonly, this word is used to refer to defensive pieces of armor used for protection in battle.** In Ezekiel 27:11, they were hung on walls; in Jeremiah 51:11, they were to be taken up as warriors prepared to defend themselves. Another context in which this word is used is in describing the gold shields that King David took from people he defeated (2 Sam. 8:7). They were then kept in the Temple and used when Jehoida presented Joash as king (2 Kgs. 11:10). Other refs.: 1 Chr. 18:7; 2 Chr. 23:9; Song 4:4. ¶
– 3 1 Sam. 17:7, 41; 1 Kgs. 10:16; Ps. 35:2; etc. ➔ HOOK <6793> b. 4 Job 39:23; 1 Sam. 17:45 (KJV) ➔ SPEAR <3591>.

SHIELD (verb) – Deut. 33:12 ➔ COVER (verb) <2653>.

SHIGGAION – ***šiggāyôn, šiggāyōnāh*** [proper noun: שִׁגָּיוֹן, שִׁגְיֹנָה <7692>; from ERR <7686>] ▶ **This word is probably a musical or liturgical term; its meaning is not certain.** The NASB suggests that it is a song of passionate feeling, a dithyramb. But this term and definition is Greek in origin. The NIV notes only that it is a musical or literary term and the ESV that it is a musical or liturgical term. Refs.: Ps. 7 (title); Hab. 3:1: Shigionoth. ¶

SHIGIONOTH – Hab. 3:1 ➔ SHIGGAION <7692>.

SHIHOR – ***šiyḥôr*** [proper noun: שִׁיחוֹר <7883>; prob. from BLACK (BE) <7835>]: dark ▶ **This word designates a river that was a branch of the Nile.** Refs.: Josh. 13:3; 1 Chr. 13:5; Is. 23:3; Jer. 2:18. ¶

SHIHOR LIBNATH – ***šiyḥôr libnaṯ*** [proper noun: שִׁיחוֹר לִבְנָת <7884>; from the same as SHIHOR <7883> (which means dark) and WHITE (MAKE) <3835>]: darkness of whiteness ▶ **A stream on the border of the territory of Asher.** Ref.: Josh. 19:26. ¶

SHIKKERON, SHICRON – ***šikkᵉrôn*** [proper noun: שִׁכְּרוֹן <7942>; from DRUNKENNESS <7943>]: drunkenness ▶ **A city on the border of the territory of Judah.** Ref.: Josh. 15:11. ¶

SHILHI – ***šilḥiy*** [masc. proper noun: שִׁלְחִי 7977>; from WEAPON <7973>]: armed ▶ **Grandfather of King Jehoshaphat.** Refs.: 1 Kgs. 22:42; 2 Chr. 20:31. ¶

SHILHIM – ***šilḥiym*** [proper noun: שִׁלְחִים <7978>; plur. of WEAPON <7973>]: armed ▶ **A city in the south of the territory of Judah.** Ref.: Josh. 15:32. ¶

SHILLEM – ***šillêm*** [masc. proper noun: שִׁלֵּם <8006>; the same as RECOMPENSE (noun) <8005>]: recompense ▶ **Son of Naphtali.** Refs.: Gen. 46:24; Num. 26:49; 1 Chr. 7:13. ¶

SHILLEMITE – ***šillêmiy*** [masc. proper noun: שִׁלֵּמִי <8016>; patron. from SHILLEM <8006>] ▶ **A descendant of Shillem.** Ref.: Num. 26:49. ¶

SHILOAH – ***šilōaḥ, šelaḥ*** [proper noun: שִׁלֹחַ, שֶׁלַח <7975>; in imitation of SHELAH <7974>]: sent ▶
a. A pool in southeast Jerusalem. Ref.: Is. 8:6.
b. A word designating Shelah, another name for a. Ref.: Neh. 3:15. ¶

SHILOH – 1 ***šiylōh*** [masc. proper noun: שִׁילֹה <7886>; from EASE (BE AT) <7951>] ▶ **This word means whose it is or he whose it is (a name alluding to the Messiah).** Ref.: Gen. 49:10. The NIV renders it to whom it belongs; the NASB uses Shiloh with a note. The KJV translates it as Shiloh. ¶
2 ***šiylōh, šilōh, šiylô, šilô*** [proper noun: שִׁילֹה, שִׁלֹה, שִׁילוֹ, שִׁלוֹ <7887>; from the same as <7886> above]: who makes peace, place

of rest ▶ **This word designates the location of the ark of God and presumably the Tabernacle tent during the time of the judges in Israel.** Refs.: Josh. 18:1–22:12; Judg. 18:31–21:21. It was Israel's religious center located in the hills of Ephraim between Shechem and Bethel (Judg. 21:12–21). Eli and Samuel both served at Shiloh (1 Sam. 2:14; 14:3). Prophets gathered to the location (1 Kgs. 14:1–4). At some point, the Lord deserted the Tabernacle site at Shiloh, perhaps when the Philistines captured the ark of God (1 Sam. 4:3–12). This event became a religious and moral lesson for Israel (Jer. 7:12–14). The Temple of Jeremiah's day would be destroyed as the Tabernacle site at Shiloh was deserted (Jer. 26:6, 9), although the town continued to be inhabited (Jer. 41:5). *

SHILONI – ***šilōniy*** [proper noun: שִׁלֹנִי <8023>; the same as SHILONITE <7888>] ▶ **An inhabitant of Shiloh.** Ref.: Neh. 11:5. ¶

SHILONITE – ***šiylōniy, šiylôniy, šilōniy*** [proper noun: שִׁילֹנִי, שִׁילוֹנִי, שִׁלֹנִי <7888>; from SHILOH <7887>] ▶ **An inhabitant of Shiloh.** Refs.: 1 Kgs. 11:29; 12:15; 15:29; 1 Chr. 9:5; 2 Chr. 9:29; 10:15; Neh. 11:5 (KJV, see *šilōniy* [SHILONI <8023>]; NIV, see *šêlāniy* [SHELANITE <8024>]. ¶

SHILSHAH – ***šilšāh*** [masc. proper noun: שִׁלְשָׁה <8030>; from DIVIDE INTO THREE PARTS <8027>]: third, powerful ▶ **An Israelite of the tribe of Asher.** Ref.: 1 Chr. 7:37. ¶

SHIMEA – ***šim'ā'*** [masc. proper noun: שִׁמְעָא <8092>; for SHIMEA <8093>]: fame ▶
a. A brother of David, the third born, David being the seventh. Refs.: 1 Chr. 2:13; 20:7. ¶
b. A son of David, his seventh (NIV, **Shammua).** Ref.: 1 Chr. 3:5. ¶
c. A descendant of Levi through the family of Merari, his third born. Ref.: 1 Chr. 6:30. ¶
d. A descendant of Levi through the family of Kohath. Ref.: 1 Chr. 6:39. ¶

SHIMEAH – [1] ***šim'āh*** [masc. proper noun: שִׁמְאָה <8039>; perhaps for <8093> below]: report ▶ **An Israelite of the tribe of Benjamin, the same as Shimeam (<8043>).** Ref.: 1 Chr. 8:32. ¶
[2] ***šim'āh*** [masc. proper noun: שִׁמְעָה <8093>; fem. of HEARING <8088>]: fame ▶ **The brother of David.** Refs.: 2 Sam. 13:3, 32; 21:21. It is the same as Shimea (<8092> a.). ¶

SHIMEAM – ***šim'ām*** [masc. proper noun: שִׁמְאָם <8043>; for SHIMEAH <8039>]: report ▶ **The same as Shimeah (<8039>).** Ref.: 1 Chr. 9:38. ¶

SHIMEATH – ***šim'aṯ*** [fem. proper noun: שִׁמְעָת <8100>; fem. of HEARING <8088>]: report ▶ **The mother of Zabad who conspired to kill King Joash of Judah.** Refs.: 2 Kgs. 12:21; 2 Chr. 24:26. ¶

SHIMEATHITES – ***šim'āṯiym*** [proper noun: שִׁמְעָתִים <8101>; patron. from SHIMEAH <8093>]: report ▶ **A family of scribes.** Ref.: 1 Chr. 2:55. ¶

SHIMEI – ***šim'iy*** [masc. proper noun: שִׁמְעִי <8096>; from HEARING <8088>]: renowned ▶
a. A grandson of Levi and son of Gershon. The Gershonites were responsible to transport part of the Tabernacle when Israel journeyed in the wilderness (Num. 3:18; 4:24–28). And Shimei worked with the Temple servants in his day (1 Chr. 6:42).
b. Closely related to Saul, he treated King David arrogantly and cursed him. He favored Absalom as king over David and called David a murderer of Saul and his family (2 Sam. 16:5–13). David believed that perhaps Shimei's actions and words were from the Lord. Shimei repented of these things later (2 Sam. 19:18–23). Solomon, however, confined Shimei to Jerusalem and eventually was forced to execute him (1 Kgs. 2:44–46).
c. This Shimei was the brother of David and the father of Jonathan. Ref.: 2 Sam. 21:21.
d. Supporter of Solomon; possibly the same as Shimei in e. Ref.: 1 Kgs. 1:8. He

may have been the son of Ela or Elah but not the same Shimei in c. above.

e. An officer for Solomon. Maybe the same Shimei as above in d. He is specifically called the son of Ela (1 Kgs. 4:18).

f. This Shimei was the brother of Zerubbabel. He was a descendant of the royal line after the exile (1 Chr. 3:19).

g. He is listed in the genealogy of Simeon. This clan settled in part of the territory of Judah. Shimei had sixteen sons and five daughters (1 Chr. 4:26–27).

h. A Reubenite. This family was descended from Reuben, the firstborn of Jacob (1 Chr. 5:4).

i. Descended from the tribe of Levi, Shimei was descended from Merari. Ref.: 1 Chr. 6:30.

j. Head of a family of Benjamin from whom Saul is descended. Ref.: 1 Chr. 8:32.

k. David set apart sons of Asaph to be ministers of prophecy, a group to which this Shimei belonged. They used musical instruments to accompany their singing and prophesying (1 Chr. 25:17).

l. This Shimei was a minister of David's property and was in charge of the grape vineyards. Ref.: 1 Chr. 27:27.

m. A descendant of Heman, he was a Levite official during Hezekiah's reign. Maybe the same Shimei as in n. below (2 Chr. 29:14).

n. Probably the same as above in m. With Conaniah, his brother, they were in charge of the storerooms of Hezekiah (2 Chr. 31:12, 13).

o. He married a pagan woman and then divorced her after Ezra's condemnation. A Levite (Ezra 10:23).

p. He was not a priest; he was a layman who divorced his pagan wife in Ezra's day. Ref.: Ezra 10:33.

q. Another man who took a foreign wife and then divorced her during Ezra's day. Ref.: Ezra 10:38.

r. An ancestor of Mordecai from the tribe of Benjamin. May be the same as b. above (Esther 2:5). *

SHIMEITES – ***šim'iy*** [proper noun: שִׁמְעִי <8097>; patron. from SHIMEI <8096>] ▶ **Descendants of Shimei (<8096> a.).** Refs.: Num. 3:21; Zech. 12:13. ¶

SHIMMERING – [1] Ps. 68:13 ➔ GREENISH <3422> [2] Is. 18:4 ➔ DAZZLING <6703>.

SHIMON – ***šiymôn*** [masc. proper noun: שִׁימוֹן <7889>; apparently for JESHIMON <3452>]: desolation, desert ▶ **An Israelite of the tribe of Judah.** Ref.: 1 Chr. 4:20. ¶

SHIMRATH – ***šimrāṯ*** [masc. proper noun: שִׁמְרָת <8119>; from KEEP <8104>]: guard ▶ **An Israelite of the tribe of Benjamin, son of Shimei.** Ref.: 1 Chr. 8:21. ¶

SHIMRI – ***šimriy*** [masc. proper noun: שִׁמְרִי <8113>; from KEEP <8104> (in the sense of to watch over)]: watchful ▶

a. A Simeonite. Ref.: 1 Chr. 4:37. ¶

b. The father of Jediael and Joha. Ref.: 1 Chr. 11:45. ¶

c. A Levite gatekeeper in David's day. Ref.: 1 Chr. 26:10. ¶

d. A Levite in Hezekiah's day. Ref.: 2 Chr. 29:13. ¶

SHIMRITH – ***šimriyṯ*** [fem. proper noun: שִׁמְרִית <8116>; fem. of SHIMRI <8113>]: watchful ▶ **The same as Shomer (<7763> a.).** Ref.: 2 Chr. 24:26. ¶

SHIMRON – ***šimrôn*** [masc. proper noun: שִׁמְרוֹן <8110>; from KEEP <8104> (in the sense of to watch over)]: watch station, watch mountain ▶

a. Son of Issachar. Refs.: Gen. 46:13; Num. 26:24; 1 Chr. 7:1. ¶

b. A Canaanite city. Refs.: Josh. 11:1; 19:15. ¶

SHIMRON MERON – ***šimrôn me***

SHIMRON MERON – ***šimrôn mᵉrôn*** [proper noun: שִׁמְרוֹן מְרוֹן <8112>; from SHIMRON <8110> and a deriv. of LIFT ONESELF <4754>]: guard of the high place ▶ **A Canaanite city alloted to Zebulun; possibly the same as Shimron <8110> b.** Ref.: Josh. 12:20. ¶

SHIMRONITE – ***šimrōniy*** [proper noun: שִׁמְרֹנִי <8117>; patron. from SHIMRON

<8110>] ► **A descendant of Shimron (<8110> a.).** Ref.: Num. 26:24. ¶

SHIMSHAI – ***šimšay*** [masc. proper noun: שִׁמְשַׁי <8124>; from SUN <8122>]: sunny ► **A scribe who wrote to King Artaxerxes to stop the rebuilding of Jerusalem.** Refs.: Ezra 4:8, 9, 17, 23. ¶

SHINAB – ***šin'āb*** [masc. proper noun: שִׁנְאָב <8134>; prob. from CHANGE <8132> and FATHER <1>]: tooth of the father ► **This word designates the king of Admah in the days of Abraham.** Ref.: Gen. 14:2. ¶

SHINAR – ***šin'ār*** [proper noun: שִׁנְעָר <8152>; prob. of foreign deriv.] ► **This word designates the name of the plain where the Tower of Babel was built and the city and nation of Babylon were begun by Nimrod.** Refs.: Gen. 10:8–10; 11:2–4. Shinar lay in the area between the Tigris and Euphrates Rivers near the Persian Gulf. Amraphel is listed as an early king (Gen. 14:1, 9). It is rendered "Babylonia" by some translations (e.g., NIV, Babylonia for Shinar, Josh. 7:21; Is. 11:11; Dan. 9:1; Zech. 5:11). Many great ancient cities were in the area: Akkad, Babylon, Calneh, Erech, Lagash, Nippur. ¶

SHINE – 1 ***'āhal*** [verb: אָהַל <166>; a prim. root] ► **This word means and is also translated to be bright, to have brightness.** It is used only in Job 25:5. ¶
2 ***ṣāhal*** [verb: צָהַל <6670>; a prim. root] ► **This word means to make gleaming. It describes the healthy effect of oil on a person's skin to make it appear shiny, strong, and healthy; it is also translated to glisten.** Ref.: Ps. 104:15. The Hebrew word also means cry out, to shout; see CRY OUT <6670>. ¶
3 ***qāran*** [verb: קָרַן <7160>; a prim. root] ► **This word describes the skin of Moses' face as luminous, sending out light from its surface.** Refs.: Ex. 34:29, 30, 35; also translated to be radiant. For another meaning of the Hebrew word, see HORNS (HAVE) <7160>. ¶
– 4 Num. 6:25; Eccl. 8:1; Ezek. 43:2 ➔ LIGHT (GIVE) <215> 5 Job 18:5; 22:28; Is. 9:2; 13:10 ➔ LIGHTEN <5050> 6 Jer. 5:28 ➔ SLEEK (BE) <6245> 7 Dan. 12:3 ➔ WARN <2094> 8 Zech. 9:16 ➔ SPARKLE <5264> a.

SHINE, SHINE FORTH – ***yāpa'*** [verb: יָפַע <3313>; a prim. root] ► **This word means to send out beams, to be bright, to show self; it is often used in regard to God Himself. It is used to indicate a bright streak of lightning.** Ref.: Job 37:15; also translated to flash. It is used of the Lord's coming as if He shone forth from Mount Paran (Deut. 33:2) as well as out of Zion (Ps. 50:2). It is used of light lighting up something (Job 3:4). In an ironical statement, it depicts the deep shadow or utter gloom shining forth as darkness (Job 10:22). It is used in certain contexts to mean to look at with approval (Job 10:3; also translated to smile, to look favorably). It describes God's action for His people as shining forth on their behalf (Ps. 80:1; 94:1). ¶

SHINE FORTH – Job 11:17 ➔ DECEIVE <8591> b.

SHINING – 1 2 Sam. 23:4; Prov. 4:18; Is. 4:5; Hab. 3:11 ➔ BRIGHTNESS <5051> 2 Ps. 68:13 ➔ GREENISH <3422>.

SHINY – ***ṣāhab*** [verb: צָהַב <6668>; a prim. root] ► **This verb means to gleam with a golden color; as a participle it also means fine, polished.** It refers to bronze of a high quality with a shiny surface (Ezra 8:27). ¶

SHION – ***šiy'ōn*** [proper noun: שִׁיאֹן <7866>; from the same as RAVAGE <7722>]: destruction, ruin ► **A city of Issachar.** Ref.: Josh. 19:19. ¶

SHIP – 1 ***ᵉniyyāh*** [fem. noun: אֳנִיָּה <591>; fem. of FLEET OF SHIPS <590>] ► **This word designates a floating vessel, a boat.** Refs.: Gen. 49:13; Deut. 28:68; Prov. 30:19. These ships are further designated as a ship sailing to Tarshish (2 Chr. 9:21; Jonah 1:3); merchant ships (Prov. 31:14); swift ships (Job 9:26). Combined with the word for

men in the construct form, it designates seamen (1 Kgs. 9:27). *
2 *sᵉpiynāh* [fem. noun: סְפִינָה <5600>; from COVER (verb) <5603>] ▶ **This word refers to a floating vessel, a boat.** In context it refers to a large vessel with a deck capable of carrying many persons, plus cargo (Jon. 1:5). ¶
3 *ṣiy* [masc. noun: צִי <6716>; from COMMAND (verb) <6680>] ▶ **From its usage, this word seems to refer to warships.** Refs.: Num. 24:24; Is. 33:21; Ezek. 30:9; Dan. 11:30. ¶
– 4 1 Kgs. 9:26, 27; 10:11, 22: ships, navy of ships ➔ FLEET OF SHIPS <590>.

SHIPMASTER – Jon. 1:6 ➔ SAILOR <2259>.

SHIPHI – *šip̱ʿiy* [masc. proper noun: שִׁפְעִי <8230>; from ABUNDANCE <8228>]: abundant ▶ **An Israelite of the tribe of Simeon.** Ref.: 1 Chr. 4:37. ¶

SHIPHRAH – *šiprāh* [fem. proper noun: שִׁפְרָה <8236>; the same as FAIR <8235>]: fair, brightness ▶ **One of the Hebrew midwives who refused to kill the male Israelite babies as ordered by the king of Egypt.** Ref.: Ex. 1:15. ¶

SHIPHTAN – *šip̱ṭān* [masc. proper noun: שִׁפְטָן <8204>; from JUDGE (verb) <8199>]: like a judge ▶ **The father of Kemuel.** Ref.: Num. 34:24. ¶

SHISHA – *šiyšāʾ* [masc. proper noun: שִׁישָׁא <7894>; from an unused root meaning to bleach]: whiteness ▶ **Father of two secretaries under the reign of Solomon.** Ref.: 1 Kgs. 4:3. ¶

SHISHAK – *šiyšaq* [masc. proper noun: שִׁישַׁק <7895>; of Egyptian deriv.] ▶ **This word designates an Egyptian king (945–924 B.C.) who fought against Rehoboam of Judah, humiliated him, and took away much wealth from Jerusalem and the Temple.** He had earlier harbored Jeroboam I before he became king of Israel. Refs.: 1 Kgs. 11:40; 14:25; 2 Chr. 12:2, 5, 7, 9. ¶

SHITRAI – *šiṭray* [proper noun: שִׁטְרַי <7861>; from the same as SCRIBE <7860>]: scribe, magistrate ▶ **An official of King David who was in charge of his cattle in Sharon.** Ref.: 1 Chr. 27:29. ¶

SHITTIM – 1 *šiṭṭiym* [proper noun: שִׁטִּים <7851>; the same as the plur. of ACACIA <7848>]: acacia trees ▶
a. A location in the plains of Moab. Refs.: Num. 25:1; Josh. 2:1; 3:1; Mic. 6:5. This is a shortened form of Abel Shittim (<63>). ¶
b. A valley northwest of the Dead Sea. Ref.: Joel 3:18. ¶
– 2 See ACACIA <7848>.

SHIZA – *šiyzāʾ* [masc. proper noun: שִׁיזָא <7877>; of unknown deriv.] ▶ **An Israelite of the tribe of Reuben and father of Adina, one of David's might men.** Ref.: 1 Chr. 11:42. ¶

SHOA – *šôaʿ* [proper noun: שׁוֹעַ <7772>; the same as RICH (noun) <7771>]: noble, rich ▶ **A nomadic tribe living in Mesopotamia.** Ref.: Ezek. 23:23. ¶

SHOBAB – *šôḇāḇ* [masc. proper noun: שׁוֹבָב <7727>; the same as BACKSLIDING <7726>]: backslider ▶
a. Son of David. Refs.: 2 Sam. 5:14; 1 Chr. 3:5; 14:4. ¶
b. Son of Caleb. Ref.: 1 Chr. 2:18. ¶

SHOBACH – *šôḇāḵ* [masc. proper noun: שׁוֹבָךְ <7731>; perhaps for THICK BRANCH <7730>]: thicket ▶ **A commander in the Syrian army defeated by the Israelites and King David; the same as *šôp̄āḵ* (SHOPHACH <7780>).** Refs.: 2 Sam. 10:16, 18. ¶

SHOBAI – *šōḇāy* [masc. proper noun: שֹׁבָי <7630>; for SHOBI <7629>]: captor ▶ **Ancestor of a family who returned from the Babylonian captivity.** Refs.: Ezra 2:42; Neh. 7:45. ¶

SHOBAL – *šôḇal* [masc. proper noun: שׁוֹבָל <7732>; from the same as SKIRT <7640>]: flowing ▶

a. An Edomite leader. Refs.: Gen. 36:20, 23, 29; 1 Chr. 1:38, 40. ¶
b. Son of Caleb. Refs.: 1 Chr. 2:50, 52. ¶
c. Son of Judah. Refs.: 1 Chr. 4:1, 2. ¶

SHOBEK – ***šôḇêq*** [masc. proper noun: שׁוֹבֵק <7733>; act. part. from a prim. root meaning to leave (comp. LEAVE, LEAVE ALONE <7662>)]: free ▶ **An Israelite leader who sealed the covenant with Nehemiah.** Ref.: Neh. 10:24. ¶

SHOBI – ***šōḇiy*** [masc. proper noun: שֹׁבִי <7629>; from CAPTIVE (TAKE) <7617>]: captor ▶ **An Israelite who supported David during the rebellion of Absalom.** Ref.: 2 Sam. 17:27. ¶

SHOCK – Ezek. 26:9 ➔ BLOW (noun) <4239>.

SHOCK, SHOCK OF CORN – Judg. 15:5; Job 21:32 ➔ STACKED GRAIN <1430>.

SHOCKING THING – Jer. 5:30 ➔ HORRIBLE THING <8186>.

SHOD – ***nā'al*** [verb: נָעַל <5274>; a prim. root] ▶ **This word means to furnish with footwear; it is also translated to give sandals, to put sandals.** It indicates furnishing sandals or some kind of footwear to persons in a general sense (2 Chr. 28:15). It is used of God's putting shoes of the highest quality on His peoples' feet (Ezek. 16:10). The Hebrew word also means to shut up; see LOCK (verb) <5274>. ¶

SHOE – [1] Deut. 33:25 ➔ LOCK (noun) <4515> [2] See SANDAL <5275>.

SHOHAM – ***šōham*** [masc. proper noun: שֹׁהַם <7719>; the same as ONYX <7718>]: onyx ▶ **An Israelite from the tribe of Levi.** Ref.: 1 Chr. 24:27. ¶

SHOMER – ***šômêr, šōmêr*** [proper noun: שׁוֹמֵר, שֹׁמֵר <7763>; act. part. of KEEP <8104>]: keeper ▶
a. Mother of Jehozabad, the same as Shimrith (<7762> c.). Ref.: 2 Kgs. 12:21. ¶
b. An Asherite, the same person as Shamer (<8106> c.). Refs.: 1 Chr. 7:32, 34. ¶

SHOOT (noun) – [1] **shoot, new shoot, tender shoot, young shoot: *yôneqeṯ*** [fem. noun: יוֹנֶקֶת <3127>; fem. of INFANT <3126>] ▶ **This word means a new plant growth; it is also translated branch, tender branch.** It is used of tender twigs from the top of a tree (Ezek. 17:22: young twig, tender sprig), so it indicates the fresh young growth on a tree limb or other shrubbery. It is used of the Israelites sprouting as God brings forth His renewed people (Hos. 14:6). It indicates the fresh young sprouts of a garden (Job 8:16) and the green sprouts coming from the stump of a tree (Job 14:7). The growth and spread of the people of Israel in Canaan is described as shoots stretching toward water as they multiplied in the land (Ps. 80:11: shoot, branch). Other ref.: Job 15:30. ¶
[2] ***šilluḥāh*** [fem. noun: שְׁלֻחָה <7976>; fem. of PARTING GIFT <7964>] ▶ **This word means and is also translated branch, tendril.** It refers figuratively to the lively growth of Moab, represented by the vibrant clinging tendrils it puts forth (Is. 16:8). ¶
– [3] Ps. 80:15 ➔ ROOT (noun) <3657> [4] Ps. 128:3 ➔ PLANT (noun) <8363> [5] Is. 11:1 ➔ ROD <2415> [6] Is. 18:5 ➔ SPRIG <2150> [7] Ezek. 17:4 ➔ TWIG <3242> [8] Ezek. 17:6 ➔ BRANCH <6288> a.

SHOOT (TENDER) – Is. 53:2 ➔ INFANT <3126>.

SHOOT (verb) – ***yārāh, yôreh, môreh, yārah*** [verb: יָרָה, יוֹרֶה, מוֹרֶה, יָרַה <3384>; a prim. root] ▶ **This word means to throw, to pour, to cast.** God hurled Pharaoh's army into the sea (Ex. 15:4); Joshua cast lots (Josh. 18:6); and God asked Job who laid the cornerstone of the earth (Job 38:6). This word is used often in reference to shooting with arrows, as Jonathan (1 Sam. 20:36); and those who killed some of David's men (2 Sam. 11:24). King Uzziah made machines that shot arrows (2 Chr. 26:15); and the wicked shot arrows at the upright of heart (Ps. 11:2; 64:4). In the sense of throwing, people were overthrown (Num. 21:30); and Job said that God had thrown him in the mud (Job 30:19). *

SHOOT, SHOOT OUT – ***rāḇaḇ*** [verb: רָבַב <7232>; a prim. root] ▶ **This word means to project (arrows, possibly implying to shower with many arrows). It describes archers shooting arrows.** Ref.: Gen. 49:23. Figuratively, it describes God's sending forth His protective arrows (Ps. 18:14; also translated to flash, to flash forth). ¶

SHOOT OUT – Ps. 22:7 ➔ OPEN <6362>.

SHOOT UP – ***kānan*** [verb: כָּנַן <3661>; a prim. root] ▶ **This word is probably the root for *kānāh*. *See* ROOT <3657>.** ¶

SHOOTS – Song 4:13 ➔ PLANTS <7973>.

SHOPHACH – ***šôp̱āḵ*** [masc. proper noun: שׁוֹפָךְ <7780>; from POUR OUT <8210>]: poured, expansion ▶ **This is another name for Shobach (<7731>).** Refs.: 1 Chr. 19:16, 18. ¶

SHORE – Gen. 49:13; Judg. 5:17; Jer. 47:7 ➔ COAST <2348>.

SHORN – 2 Kgs. 19:26; Is. 37:27 ➔ SHORT <7116>.

SHORT – ***qāṣār*** [adj.: קָצָר <7116>; from SHORTEN <7114>] ▶ **This word means weak, few, hasty.** It means literally lacking of something: of might, strength (2 Kgs. 19:26; Is. 37:27; also translated: small, little, shorn, drained); of days, short-lived (Job 14:1); of nostrils, an idiom for short-tempered, irascible (Prov. 14:17); of a short spirit, impatience (Prov. 14:29). ¶

SHORTEN – [1] ***qāṣar*** [verb: קָצַר <7114>; a prim. root] ▶ **This word means to abridge; it also means to become impatient.** It describes something not being too short, e.g., the Lord's power to deliver (Num. 11:23). It refers to a shortening of time because of wickedness (Prov. 10:27). It refers figuratively to impatience or anxiety, annoyance (Num. 21:4; Judg. 10:16; 16:16; Job 21:4; Mic. 2:7); used with *min* (<4480>), it expresses a comparison of too short for something (Is. 28:20). It has the sense of the Lord's shortening Himself, of holding back (Ps. 89:45). *

– [2] Ezek. 42:6 ➔ RESERVE (verb) <680>.

SHORTENED (BE) – Job 18:7 ➔ DISTRESSED (BE) <3334>.

SHOSHANNIM – Ps. 45 (title); 69 (title) ➔ LILY <7799>.

SHOSHANNIM EDUTH – Ps. 80 (title) ➔ SHUSHAN EDUTH <7802> b.

SHOULDER – [1] ***kāṯêp̱*** [fem. noun: כָּתֵף <3802>; from an unused root meaning to clothe] ▶ **This word indicates literally the upper arm and/or the shoulder (the place of the body where the arm is attached) of a living being: a person or animal (Ex. 28:12; Judg. 16:3); choice meat (Ezek. 24:4); it also means a side.** It is used often in figures of speech: to turn or give a stubborn shoulder is to be hostile, difficult, or rebellious (Zech. 7:11); to dwell between the shoulders of the Lord is to live in safety (Deut. 33:12). The meaning is extended to inanimate objects: the high priest's ephod had shoulder pieces (Ex. 28:7); the laver had side supports (1 Kgs. 7:30); a mountain slope is termed a shoulder, a slope (Num. 34:11; Josh. 15:8; Ezek. 25:9). As a construction term, it means a side of something, e.g., a door (Ex. 27:14, 15; 1 Kgs. 6:8; 7:39). *

[2] ***šeḵem*** [masc. noun: שְׁכֶם <7926>; from RISE EARLY <7925>] ▶

a. This word refers to the place of the body where the arm is attached; it also refers to the upper back and neck area. Refs.: Gen. 9:23; 21:14. Often things were carried on one's shoulder (Gen. 24:15, 45; Ex. 12:34; Josh. 4:5; Judg. 9:48). To turn one's shoulder to (*le*) someone or something means to turn to leave (1 Sam. 10:9). To set one's shoulder, back is to turn away (Ps.

21:12). To carry the government on one's shoulder is to bear the burden of rulership (Is. 9:4, 6; 22:22). A yoke is worn on the shoulders, literally or figuratively (Is. 10:27; 14:25). In Genesis 48:22, the word refers to a geographical feature, a ridge.

b. A masculine noun used to indicate consent, shoulder to shoulder. The phrase shoulder to shoulder indicates sharing in a common effort or open consent to something, whether bad (Hos. 6:9; KJV; other translations, Shechem) or good (Zeph. 3:9). *

2 ***šiḵmāh*** [fem. noun: שִׁכְמָה <7929>; fem. of <7926> above] ▶ **This word refers to the upper part of a person's bicep, tricep, and deltoid muscle area, supported by a structural skeleton and featuring a socket where several bones come together. It is also translated shoulder blade, socket.** This is normally considered a strong feature of the human body (Job 31:22). ¶

SHOULDER BLADE – Job 31:22 ➔ SHOULDER <7929>.

SHOUT (noun) – 1 ***t^erû'āh*** [fem. noun: תְּרוּעָה <8643>; from SHOUT (verb) <7321>] ▶ **This word indicates a loud cry of joy; a loud cry of alarm, a battle cry.** It refers to a loud, sharp shout or cry in general, but it often indicates a shout of joy or victory (1 Sam. 4:5, 6); a great shout anticipating a coming event (Josh. 6:5, 20). It can refer to the noise or signal put out by an instrument (Lev. 23:24; 25:9). Amos used the word to refer to war cries (Amos 1:14; 2:2; cf. Job 39:25; Zeph. 1:16). The Lord puts shouts of joy into His people (Job 8:21; 33:26). *

– 2 Job 39:7; Zech. 4:7 ➔ STORM (noun) <8663> 3 Job 39:25 ➔ THUNDER (noun) <7482> 4 Psalm 32:7 ➔ SONG <7438> 5 Is. 16:9; Jer. 25:30; 48:33; 51:14 ➔ SHOUTING <1959>.

SHOUT (verb) – 1 ***ṣāwaḥ*** [verb: צָוַח <6681>; a prim. root] ▶ **This word is used of crying out, crying aloud in joy because of what God is doing for His people.** Ref.: Is. 42:11. ¶

2 ***rûa'*** [verb: רוּעַ <7321>; a prim. root] ▶ **This word means to sound a blast. The term occurs thirty-three times in the Old Testament and was utilized fundamentally to convey the action of shouting or the making of a loud noise.** Shouting often took place just before a people or army rushed into battle against opposition; sometimes the war cry became the very signal used to commence engagement with the enemy (Josh. 6:10, 16, 20; Judg. 15:14; 1 Sam. 4:5; 17:20; 2 Chr. 13:15). Many times the shout was a cry of joy, often in response to the Lord's creating or delivering activity on behalf of His people (Job 38:7; Ps. 47:1; 95:1, 2; Is. 44:23; Zeph. 3:14; Zech. 9:9). In several other instances, the shout expressed triumph and victory over a foe (Ps. 41:11; 60:8; 108:9); and occasionally mourning (Is. 15:4; Mic. 4:9). A few times, the term denotes the shout of a trumpet (i.e., the blast), usually as a signal calling on the Lord and to begin battle (Num. 10:9; 2 Chr. 13:12–14; cf. Hos. 5:8; Joel 2:1). *

3 ***rānan, rûn*** [verb: רָנַן, רוּן <7442>; a prim. root] ▶

a. This word means to shout for joy; to sing joyfully. It indicates the utterance or crying out of a person or persons. The character of the cry must be discerned by the context or actual intended use of the verb. Often it indicates crying out in joy, exaltation (Is. 12:6; 24:14; Jer. 31:7). It is used most often of exalting or praising the Lord (Is. 26:19; 35:2; 52:8; Jer. 31:12; 51:48); especially in Psalms (Ps. 5:11; 67:4; 81:1; 90:14; 92:4; 149:5). The absence of a cry like this is sometimes an indication of God's judgment (Is. 16:10). God makes even a widow's heart sing for joy (Job 29:13). God causes even nature to shout for delight (Ps. 65:8); and commands His just, righteous people to shout for joy (Ps. 32:11). Its opposite is a cry of distress (Is. 65:14; Lam. 2:19). It is used in general of putting forth a cry of encouragement, exhortation, instruction (Prov. 1:20; 8:3).

b. This word means to be overcome. It indicates a person who is under the influence of wine, who is making sounds, responses as a staggering person or one barely awake (Ps. 78:65).

c. This word means to awake out of stupor. It refers to a person coming from under the influence of wine, still not fully alert (Ps. 78:65). *
– [4] Dan. 3:4; 4:14; etc. ➔ READ <7123>.

SHOUT ALOUD – Is. 42:13 ➔ CRY (verb) <6873>.

SHOUT JOYFULLY – Ps. 98:4 ➔ BREAK FORTH <6476> a.

SHOUTED (AS THEY) – Ex. 32:17 ➔ NOISE <7452>.

SHOUTING – [1] ***hêyḏāḏ*** [masc. noun: הֵידָד <1959>; from an unused root (meaning to shout)] ▶ **This word indicates a cheer or shout.** It refers to jubilant shouting heard at harvest time (Is. 16:9, 10; Jer. 48:33). It refers also to Moab's shouts of mourning or the shouts of their enemies (Jer. 48:33; cf. Jer. 51:14). It indicates the Lord's shout over the nations as He treads them in judgment (Jer. 25:30). ¶
– [2] Job 39:7; Is. 22:2; Zech. 4:7 ➔ STORM (noun) <8663>.

SHOVE – Ezek. 34:21 ➔ PUSH <1920>.

SHOVEL – [1] ***yāʿ*** [masc. noun: יָע <3257>; from SWEEP AWAY <3261>] ▶ **A tool with a broad flat blade adapted for scooping, or similar utensil, used for cleaning the ashes and other material remains from an altar after sacrifices have been offered.** Refs.: Ex. 27:3; 38:3; Num. 4:14; 1 Kgs. 7:40, 45; 2 Kgs. 25:14; 2 Chr. 4:11, 16; Jer. 52:18. ¶
[2] ***raḥaṯ*** [fem. noun: רַחַת <7371>; from REFRESHED (BE) <7306> (in the sense of to blow; e.g., as blowing the chaff away)] ▶ **This word refers to a winnowing shovel or fork used to separate the chaff from grain.** Ref.: Is. 30:24. ¶

SHOW – [1] ***ḥāwāh*** [verb: חָוָה <2331>; a prim. root (comp. INTERPRET <2324>, LIVE <2421>)] ▶ **This word means to announce, to tell, to explain; to reveal, to display. It is also translated to declare.** It indicates the knowledge the heavens put forth in their movements and appearance (Ps. 19:2). But also the wisdom and knowledge a person puts forth in speech (Job 15:17; 32:6, 10, 17; 36:2), whether old or young. ¶
– [2] Lev. 24:12 ➔ CLEAR (BE, MAKE) <6567> [3] 1 Sam. 20:2, 12, 13 ➔ REVEAL <1540>.

SHOW FEAR – Esther 5:9 ➔ TREMBLE <2111>.

SHOW YOURSELVES MEN – ***ʾiyš, ʾāšaš*** [verb: אִישׁ, אָשַׁשׁ <377>; denom. from MAN <376>] ▶
a. A verbal root meaning to show oneself a man, to be strong, firm. It is employed in a reflexive form in the text. It is used in Isaiah 46:8 to mean show yourselves men (NKJV, KJV). It is nuanced to mean fix it in mind (NIV) or be assured (NASB).
b. A verb stem meaning to fix in mind (NIV) or to be assured (NASB). It is debatable whether two separate verbal roots are spelled *ʾiyš* or whether one root has a semantic range covering a larger range of meaning than was earlier thought. It is translated as to fix in mind (NIV) or be assured (NASB) in Isaiah 46:8. The KJV and NKJV render it as to show oneself a man, to be brave and courageous; ESV: to stand firm. ¶

SHOWBREAD – 1 Chr. 9:32; 23:29; etc. ➔ ROW (noun) <4635>.

SHOWER – [1] ***rāḇiyḇ*** [masc. noun: רְבִיב <7241>; from MANY (BE, BECOME) <7231> (as an accumulation of drops in the case of a shower)] ▶ **This word indicates a precipitation of rain.** It refers to a refreshing, mild rain (Deut. 32:2); showers (Ps. 65:10) that invigorate the grass (Ps. 72:6; Jer. 3:3). God is the giver of the rain (Jer. 14:22). It is used in similes (Mic. 5:7). ¶
– [2] Deut. 32:2 ➔ DROPLET <8164> [3] Job 24:8 ➔ STORM (noun) <2230> [4] Is. 45:8 ➔ DRIP (verb) <7491> [5] See RAIN (verb) <1653>.

SHOWER WITH – 2 Sam. 16:13 ➔ FLING <6080>.

SHOWING – Dan. 5:12 ➔ EXPLANATION <263>.

SHRANK (WHICH, THAT) – ***nāšeh*** [masc. noun: נָשֶׁה <5384>; from FORGET <5382>, in the sense of failure] ▶
a. This word refers to a portion of the sinew or tendon that was reduced in size upon Jacob's extraordinary encounter with a divine being. Ref.: Gen. 32:32: KJV, NKJV. ¶
b. A masculine noun referring to a sinew, a tendon. It is described as the tendon or sinew of the hip or thigh (Gen. 32:32: NASB, ESV, NIV). ¶

SHRED – 2 Kgs. 4:39 ➔ CUT (verb) <6398>.

SHREWD – [1] 1 Sam. 23:22; Ps. 83:3 ➔ CRAFTY (BE) <6191> [2] Job 5:12 ➔ PRUDENT <6175>.

SHREWD (BE) – 2 Sam. 22:27; Ps. 18:26 ➔ WRESTLE <6617>.

SHREWD SCHEME – Ps. 64:6 ➔ PLAN (noun) <2665>.

SHREWDNESS – [1] Job 5:13 ➔ CRAFTINESS <6193> [2] Dan. 8:25 ➔ INTELLIGENCE <7922>.

SHRINE – Amos 5:26 ➔ SIKKUTH <5522>.

SHRIVEL – [1] ***'āḇaš*** [verb: עָבַשׁ <5685>; a prim. root] ▶ **This word means to wrinkle and contract, especially due to lack of moisture. It indicates a process of decay or death.** In context it describes seeds dying, shriveling instead of germinating, beginning to grow (Joel 1:17; KJV: to rot). ¶
[2] ***qāmaṭ*** [verb: קָמַט <7059>; a prim. root] ▶
a. This word means to cause to shrink; to fill with wrinkles. It describes Job's pathetic, weakened condition with his devastating skin disease. It was used both literally (skin) and figuratively (Job's life, influence) (Job 16:8).
b. This word means to bind. It is used in a figurative sense of Job's being hemmed in, pressed on by his friends and illness, almost to utter despair (Job 16:8).
c. A verb indicating to snatch away; to cut down. It is used as an euphemism for the death of the wicked, taking them away (Job 22:16). ¶

SHRIVELED UP (BE) – ***ṣāp̱aḏ*** [verb: צָפַד <6821>; a prim. root] ▶ **This word means to dry up and shrink, become wrinkled.** It describes the skin of those suffering under a long siege from an attacking enemy (Lam. 4:8; also translated to cleave, to cling). ¶

SHROUD – [1] Is. 25:7 ➔ COVERING <3875> [2] Ezek. 31:3 ➔ FOREST <2793>.

SHRUB – [1] ***'ᵃrô'ēr*** [masc. noun: עֲרוֹעֵר <6176>; from STRIP <6209> a. reduplicated] ▶ **This word refers to a tree, a bush; juniper. It refers to some kind of desert bush or plant; KJV: heath.** Its isolation in the desert is used to make a point in a simile (Jer. 17:6). It possibly refers to a juniper bush in both references (Jer. 48:6). ¶
[2] ***'ar'ār*** [adj.: עַרְעָר <6199>; from STRIP <6209>] ▶ **This word refers to a bush or a shrub living in the desert or dry wilderness.** It is used to compare a person who trusts only in people to this hopeless, isolated shrub (Jer. 17:6; KJV: heath). The Hebrew word also means a person who is poor in Psalm 102:17; see DESTITUTE <6199>. ¶
– [3] Gen. 2:5; 21:15 ➔ BUSH <7880>.

SHUA – [1] ***šûa'*** [masc. proper noun: שׁוּעַ <7770>; the same as CRY (noun) <7769> b. (in the sense of riches, possessions)]: wealth ▶ **Father-in-law of Judah, the son of Jacob.** Refs.: Gen. 38:2, 12; 1 Chr. 2:3, for NASB, see *baṯ šûa'* [BATHSHUA <1340> a.]. ¶
[2] ***šû'ā'*** [fem. proper noun: שׁוּעָא <7774>; from CRY (verb) <7768> (in the sense of to be free)]: wealth ▶ **Daughter of Heber.** Ref.: 1 Chr. 7:32. ¶

SHUAH – [1] ***šûaḥ*** [masc. proper noun: שׁוּחַ <7744>; from BOW DOWN <7743>]:

wealth ▶ **A son of Abraham and Keturah.** Refs.: Gen. 25:2; 1 Chr. 1:32. ¶
– [2] 1 Chr. 4:11 ➔ SHUHAH <7746>.

SHUAL – ***šû'āl*** [proper noun: שׁוּעָל <7777>; the same as FOX <7776>]: fox, jackal ▶
a. An Asherite. Ref.: 1 Chr. 7:36. ¶
b. A district in Benjamin. Ref.: 1 Sam. 13:17. ¶

SHUDDERING – Job 21:6; Ezek. 7:18 ➔ TREMBLING <6427>.

SHUHAH – ***šûḥāh*** [masc. proper noun: שׁוּחָה <7746>; the same as PIT <7745>] ▶ **An Israelite of the tribe of Judah.** Ref.: 1 Chr. 4:11. ¶

SHUHAM – ***šûḥām*** [masc. proper noun: שׁוּחָם <7748>; from BOW DOWN <7743>]: humble ▶ **A son of Dan.** Ref.: Num. 26:42. ¶

SHUHAMITE – ***šûḥāmiy*** [proper noun: שׁוּחָמִי <7749>; patron. from SHUHAM <7748>] ▶ **A descendant of Shuham.** Refs.: Num. 26:42, 43. ¶

SHUHITE – ***šûḥiy*** [masc. proper noun: שׁוּחִי <7747>; patron. from SHUAH <7744>] ▶ **This word designates Bildad, one of Job's supposed comforters.** Refs.: Job 2:11; 8:1; 18:1; 25:1; 42:9. ¶

SHUMATHITE – ***šumāṯiy*** [proper noun: שֻׁמָתִי <8126>; patron. from an unused name from GARLIC <7762> prob. meaning garlic-smell] ▶ **A member of a family of Kiriath-jearim.** Ref.: 1 Chr. 2:53. ¶

SHUNAMMITE – [1] ***šûlammiyṯ*** [proper noun: שׁוּלַמִּית <7759>; from COMPLETED (BE) <7999> (in the sense of to be at peace)]: peaceful ▶ **The name of the beloved woman in the Song of Solomon.** It refers to her most likely as a Shulamite/Shunnamite woman (1 Kgs. 2:21, 22). ¶
[2] ***šûnammiyṯ*** [proper noun: שׁוּנַמִּית <7767>; patrial from SHUNEM <7766>] ▶ **An inhabitant of Shunem.** Refs.: 1 Kgs. 1:3, 15; 2:17, 21, 22; 2 Kgs. 4:12, 25, 36. ¶

SHUNEM – ***šûnêm*** [proper noun: שׁוּנֵם <7766>; prob. from the same as SHUNI <7764>]: double resting place ▶ **It was a town inherited by Issachar.** Ref.: Josh. 19:18. It is mentioned as a city near which the Philistines encamped (1 Sam. 28:4). Abishag, a wise person, came from here, and Elisha received help from a lady of Shunem (2 Kgs. 4:8). ¶

SHUNI – ***šûniy*** [masc. proper noun: שׁוּנִי <7764>; from an unused root meaning to rest]: fortunate, rest ▶ **Third son of Gad.** Refs.: Gen. 46:16; Num. 26:15. ¶

SHUNITE – ***šûniy*** [proper noun: שׁוּנִי <7765>; patron. from SHUNI <7764>] ▶ **Descendant of Shuni.** Ref.: Num. 26:15. ¶

SHUPHAM – Num. 26:39 ➔ SHEPHUPHAM <8197>.

SHUPHAMITE – ***šûp̱āmiy*** [proper noun: שׁוּפָמִי <7781>; patron. from SHEPHUPHAM <8197>] ▶ **A descendant of Shephupham (<8197> a.).** Ref.: Num. 26:39. ¶

SHUPPIM – ***šuppiym*** [masc. proper noun: שֻׁפִּים <8206>; plur. of a unused noun from the same as VIPER <8207> and meaning the same]: serpents ▶
a. A Benjamite. Refs.: 1 Chr. 7:12, 15. ¶
b. A Levite gatekeeper. Ref.: 1 Chr. 26:16. ¶

SHUR – ***šûr*** [proper noun: שׁוּר <7793>; the same as WALL <7791>]: wall ▶ **The Israelites passed through the desert of Shur after leaving Egypt.** Refs.: Gen. 16:7; 20:1; 25:18; Ex. 15:22; 1 Sam. 15:7; 27:8. ¶

SHUSHAN – ***šûšan*** [proper noun: שׁוּשַׁן <7800>; the same as LILY <7799>]: lily ▶ **One of several capitals of the Persian Empire. It was located on the upper reaches of the Karun River in southwest Persia.** Esther's story begins here (Esther 1:5, etc.). In Nehemiah 1:1, Artaxerxes is king in this city. Daniel had a vision in which he was transported to this city (Dan. 8:2). *

SHUSHAN EDUTH – ***šûšan 'ēḏûṯ, šôšanniym 'ēḏûṯ*** [proper noun: שׁוֹשַׁן עֵדוּת, שׁוֹשַׁנִּים עֵדוּת <7802>; from LILY <7799> and TESTIMONY <5715>] ▶ **a. This word indicates a song title, Shushan Eduth, Lily of the Covenant.** It is a titular phrase; covenant refers to the covenant of the ten words or to the stone tablets where they were written [Ps. 60 (title)]. Covenant may also be rendered as Testimony.
b. A proper noun Shoshannim Eduth, a song title meaning literally Lilies of the Covenant. See a. also. It is found in Psalm 80 (title); it may be rendered as the Lilies of the Testimony also. ¶

SHUT – 1 ***gûp̱*** [verb: גּוּף <1479>; a prim. root] ▶ **This word indicates closing a city gate.** Ref.: Neh. 7:3. In this case, the gates of Jerusalem during its reconstruction under Nehemiah. ¶
2 ***sᵉgar*** [Aramaic verb: סְגַר <5463>; corresponding to CLOSE <5462>] ▶ **This word means to close something.** In context it refers to the Lord's closing the lions' mouths (Dan. 6:22); an act of deliverance by the Lord on Daniel's behalf. ¶
3 ***qapaṣ*** [verb: קָפַץ <7092>; a prim. root] ▶ **This word indicates the closing off one's feelings (hand) toward a person, ceasing to give regard to.** Ref.: Deut. 15:7. It is used figuratively of unrighteousness, injustice shutting its mouth (Job 5:16; Ps. 107:42). It depicts God's withholding His compassion (Ps. 77:9). Other refs.: Job 24:24; Song 2:8; Is. 52:15. ¶
– 4 Is. 29:10 ➔ CLOSE <6105> 5 Prov. 16:30 ➔ WINK <6095> 6 Prov. 17:28 ➔ STOP <331> 7 Ps. 69:15 ➔ CLOSE <332>.

SHUT UP – Song 4:12 ➔ LOCK (verb) <5274>.

SHUTHELAH – ***šûṯelaḥ*** [masc. proper noun: שׁוּתֶלַח <7803>; from WASTE (LAY, LIE) <7582> and the same as TELAH <8520>]: breakage ▶ **Son of Ephraim.** Refs.: Num. 26:35, 36; 1 Chr. 7:20, 21. ¶

SHUTHELAHITE – ***šuṯalḥiy*** [proper noun: שֻׁתַלְחִי <8364>; a prim. root] ▶ **A descendant of Shuthelah, son of Ephraim.** Ref.: Num. 26:35. ¶

SIAHA – ***siy'ā', siyᵉhā'*** [proper noun: סִיעָא, סִיעֲהָא <5517>; from an unused root meaning to converse]: congregation, assembly ▶ **Members of this family of Nethinim returned from the Babylonian captivity with Zerubbabel.** Refs.: Ezra 2:44; Neh. 7:47. ¶

SIBBECAI – ***sibbᵉḵai*** [masc. proper noun: סִבְּכַי <5444>; from ENTWINE <5440>] ▶ **One of the strong men of David.** Refs.: 2 Sam. 21:18; 1 Chr. 11:29; 20:4; 27:11. ¶

SIBBOLETH – ***sibbōleṯ*** [fem. noun: סִבֹּלֶת <5451>; from GRAIN (HEAD OF, HEAR OF) <7641>] ▶ **This word describes an ear of grain, wheat. The word was used to ascertain tribal identity.** It was the way an Ephraimite pronounced *šibbōleṯ*, "s" instead of "sh", as in the dialect of the Gileadites (Judg. 12:6). ¶

SIBRAIM – ***siḇrayim*** [proper noun: סִבְרַיִם <5453>; dual from a root corresponding to THINK <5452>]: double hope ▶ **A place named by Ezekiel between the border of Damascus and the border of Hamath.** Ref.: Ezek. 47:16. ¶

SICK – 1 ***dawwāy*** [adj.: דַּוָּי <1742>; from FAINT (adj.) <1739>] ▶ **This word means faint (of heart), figuratively, troubled; it is also translated injured.** Used figuratively, it describes the spiritual sickness of Israel's head (Is. 1:5). It describes the heart sorely afflicted because of the treachery of Judah (Jer. 8:18; Lam. 1:22). ¶
– 2 Lev. 15:33; Lam. 5:17 ➔ FAINT (adj.) <1739> 3 2 Chr. 24:25 ➔ DISEASE <4251> 4 Is. 19:10 ➔ GRIEVED <99>.

SICK (BE) – 1 ***'ānaš*** [verb: אָנַשׁ <605>; a prim. root] ▶ **This word means to have a weak condition of health; it is also translated to become ill, to be incurable, to be in poor health.** It describes a weakened condition that can lead to death (2 Sam. 12:15; Job 34:6; Is. 17:11:

desperate, incurable) or an incurable pain or ill health (Jer. 15:18). In its most potent theological usage, it describes the incurably wicked, desperately sick condition of the human heart (Jer. 17:9) that only God knows. Other refs.: Jer. 17:16; 30:12, 15; Mic. 1:9. ¶

[2] ***ḥālāh, naḥ^{a}lāh*** [חָלָה, נַחֲלָה <2470>; a prim. root (comp. SHAKE <2342>, PIERCE <2490>)] ►

a. A verb indicating to be weak, to be in poor health, to be a patient. It is used to mean becoming weak or sick (Gen. 48:1; 1 Kgs. 14:1, 5; 2 Kgs. 1:2). It indicates becoming diseased in some body part (1 Kgs. 15:23). Used with *lāmûwt*, it means "sick unto death (dying)" (2 Kgs. 20:1). It takes on some nuanced meanings according to its context: to be lovesick (Song 2:5); *rā'āh ḥōlāh* meaning a great evil, a sickening evil (Eccl. 5:13); to feel pain, regret, to feel sorry for (*ḥōleh . . . 'al*, 1 Sam. 22:8). *

b. A feminine noun denoting disease; also translated grief, sickliness. It describes a sickness or disease brought upon Damascus when God judged her (Is. 17:11). ¶

c. A verb meaning to appease, to entreat, to appeal to. It refers to a specific attempt to get the Lord to relent from judgment (Ex. 32:11; Dan. 9:13). It is used to ask for the favor of the Lord in general (Jer. 26:19; Zech. 8:21, 22) or for a specific purpose or policy (1 Sam. 13:12). It describes the nations' entreaty to the Lord for His favor (Ps. 45:12). It is used to entreat the favor of persons also (Job 11:19; Prov. 19:6). *

[3] ***nûš*** [verb: נוּשׁ <5136>; a prim. root] ► **This word means and is also translated to be helpless, to be full of heaviness, to be in despair.** It refers to a debilitated, weak person, depressed from the oppression of his enemies (Ps. 69:20). ¶

SICK MAN – ***nāsas*** [verb: נָסַס <5263>; a prim. root] ►

a. A verb meaning to be sick. It is used in its participial form to refer to a sick person, one who is sick (Is. 10:18). ¶

b. A verb meaning to raise as a beacon. The verb is understood to be from a root meaning to raise up a sign. In its participial form, it, therefore, refers to a standard-bearer (*nês nōsês*) (Is. 10:18). ¶

SICKLE – [1] ***ḥermêš*** [masc. noun: חֶרְמֵשׁ <2770>; from DESTROY <2763>] ► **A farming or agricultural implement used to cut or harvest grain, to cut weeds and overgrowth of bushes, etc.** Ref.: Deut. 23:25. "To put the sickle" to standing grain means to begin harvesting it (Deut. 16:9). It is found in the Septuagint of 1 Samuel 13:20 as the last item mentioned, but the Hebrew text reads plowshare (NASB, hoe; ESV, NIV, NKJV, sickle; KJV, mattock). ¶

[2] ***maggāl*** [fem. noun: מַגָּל <4038>; from an unused root meaning to reap] ► **This word refers to an instrument for harvesting grain or clearing land.** Refs.: Jer. 50:16; Joel 3:13. It is used metaphorically of God's reaping with a sickle among the nations. ¶

SICKLINESS – Is. 17:11 ➔ SICK (BE) <2470>.

SICKNESS – [1] ***taḥ^{a}lû', taḥ^{a}lu'*** [masc. noun: תַּחֲלוּא, תַּחֲלֻא <8463>; from DISEASED (BE, BECOME) <2456>] ► **This word refers to various diseases or illnesses which God may bring on His people to curse them in the case of disobedience.** Refs.: Deut. 29:22; Jer. 14:18; 16:4. It refers to suffering and pain from a mortal illness (2 Chr. 21:19). God, however, heals all diseases (Ps. 103:3). ¶

– [2] Lev. 20:18: during sickness, having her ➔ FAINT (adj.) <1739> [3] 2 Chr. 21:15; etc. ➔ DISEASE <4245> [4] Is. 38:12 ➔ POOR <1803>.

SIDDIM – ***śiddiym*** [proper noun: שִׂדִּים <7708>; plur. from the same as FIELD <7704> (to spread out)]: flats, plain ► **A valley near the Red Sea where the king of Elam and his allies fought the kings of Sodom and Gomorrah and their allies.** Refs.: Gen. 14:3, 8, 10. ¶

SIDE – [1] ***^{e}ḇar*** [Aramaic masc. noun: עֲבַר <5675>; corresponding to <5676> below] ► **This word indicates a region,**

an area beyond, across from. It is used of the area west of the Euphrates River, on the other side from Persia proper (Ezra 4:10, 11, 16, 17, 20; 7:21, 25), which was administered by the government of Persia. *

2 ***'ēḇer*** [masc. noun: עֵבֶר <5676>; from PASS THROUGH, PASS OVER <5674>] ▶

a. This word means a region beyond, a region across from. It refers to an area across from another, one of two sides situated opposite each other (1 Sam. 14:1; 26:13); an area opposite, beyond a marker, a river, etc. (Gen. 50:10, 11; Num. 21:13). It indicates what is over against, in the front of (Ex. 25:37; Ezek. 1:9). Several phrases are found: from one side and the other (1 Sam. 14:4; 40); from every side (1 Kgs. 4:24; Jer. 49:32). It indicates the edge or side of something (Ex. 28:26); the shore of a river or sea (Deut. 30:13; Is. 18:1). The phrase, beyond, over the Jordan means east or west depending on where the speaker is locating himself (Gen. 50:10; Deut. 3:20, 25; Josh. 12:7; 17:5). It indicates the two sides of the tablets containing the Ten Commandments, the ten words of God (Ex. 32:15). When God restores His people, they will come from beyond (*'ēḇer*) the river of Ethiopia to serve Him (Zeph. 3:10). *

b. A masculine noun indicating a passage, a place of crossing over. It refers to an area located near or beside a place where a river was crossed (Josh. 22:11); as well as a passage itself (Jer. 22:20). ¶

3 ***ṣaḏ*** [masc. noun: צַד <6654>; from an unused root meaning to sidle off] ▶ **This word refers to the left or right half of a person, an animal, or a boundary area of something in any direction, north, south, east, west.** It refers to the side of any object, e.g., a window (Gen. 6:16); a lampstand (Ex. 25:32); a person (Num. 33:55; 2 Sam. 2:16). At the side of or beside something may be expressed with *min* (FROM <4480>) plus *ṣaḏ, miṣṣaḏ* (1 Sam. 6:8; 20:20). It is used of Ezekiel lying on his side, side to side (Ezek. 4:4, 6, 9). On this side . . . from that side (1 Sam. 23:26). *

4 ***ṣēlā'*** [fem. noun: צֵלָע <6763>; from LIMP <6760> (in the sense of something curved)] ▶ **This word means the left or right of something; it also means a side room (chamber), a hillside, a wall.** It refers to a side or rib from a side of a human body (Gen. 2:21, 22); or the side of an object (Ex. 25:12, 14; 26:20). It may in context be translated as hillside, the side of a hill (2 Sam. 16:13). It may have the sense of side (rooms) or side (chambers) (1 Kgs. 6:5; 7:3); or the wing or extension of a building (Ezek. 41:5). It is taken by some to mean side in Job 18:12 (cf. STUMBLING <6761>). It refers to planks or boards, building materials (1 Kgs. 6:15, 16); or to sections or leaves of doors (1 Kgs. 6:34). *

5 ***s*ᵉ*ṭar*** [Aramaic masc. noun: שְׂטַר <7859>; of uncertain deriv.] ▶ **This word refers to the flank of a bear on which the bear was lying.** Ref.: Dan. 7:5. Its side as opposed to its front or back. ¶

– 6 Ex. 27:14, 15; 1 Kgs. 6:8; 7:39; etc. → SHOULDER <3802> 7 Lev. 1:11; Num. 3:29, 35 → THIGH <3409> 8 Ps. 38:7; Prov. 3:26 → LOINS <3689>.

SIDE PILLAR – Ezek. 40:9, 10, 16 → DOORPOST <352>.

SIDES – Job 21:24 → BODY <5845>.

SIDON – ***ṣiyḏôn, ṣiyḏōn*** [proper noun: צִידֹן, צִידוֹן <6721>; from HUNT <6679> in the sense of catching fish]: fishery ▶ **One of Phoenicia's principal walled port cities. It was on the coast of the Mediterranean north of Tyre and Carmel. It was situated on a major commercial route.** Sidon was also the first son of Canaan (Gen. 10:15, 19). Sidon the city and its surrounding areas were a part of Canaan. Zebulun was to expand toward Sidon (Gen. 49:17). Asher, closest to Sidon, did not drive out its inhabitants (Judg. 1:31). Israel was enticed often to worship the Sidonian gods (Judg. 10:6). Elijah visited the widow of Zarephath in Sidonian territory (1 Kgs. 17:9). The city, like Tyre, was renowned for its trade with merchants (Is. 23:2; Ezek. 27:8). Jeremiah and other prophets announce God's wrath to come on it (Jer. 25:22; Joel 3:4; Zech. 9:2). *

SIDONIAN – ***ṣiyḏōniy*** [proper noun: צִידֹנִי <6722>; patrial from SIDON <6721>] ► **An inhabitant of Sidon.** Refs.: Deut. 3:9; Josh. 13:4, 6; Judg. 3:3; 10:12; 18:7; 1 Kgs. 5:6; 11:1, 5, 33; 16:31; 2 Kgs. 23:13; 1 Chr. 22:4; Ezra 3:7; Ezek. 32:30. ¶

SIEGE – ***māṣôr*** [masc. noun: מָצוֹר <4692>; from BESIEGE <6696>] ► **This word indicates a military operation, such as surrounding a city to try to overcome it; it also indicates a besieged, fortified area.** It indicates a methodical attack on people, city, or country in order to overcome and conquer it or to the period of time when this occurs (Ezek. 4:8; 5:2); siege (Mic. 5:1; Zech. 12:2); with *bô'* it expressed the idea of coming into a state of siege (Deut. 20:19; 2 Kgs, 24:10; 25:2; Jer. 52:5); the distressful time of the siege (Deut. 28:53, 55, 57; Jer. 19:9). It indicates also the entrenchment or features of the siege itself: engines of siege (Deut. 20:20); a rampart or defense structure (Eccl. 9:14; Zech. 9:3); a besieged city (Ps. 31:21; 60:9). *

SIEGE MOUND – Ezek. 26:8 ➔ SIEGE WORK <1785>.

SIEGE MOUND, SIEGE RAMP – ***sōlelāh, sôlelāh*** [fem. noun: סֹלְלָה, סוֹלְלָה <5550>; act. part. fem. of EXALT <5549> (in the sense of to build up, to lift up)] ► **This word describes a huge amount of dirt and earthen debris, rocks, etc., piled up by an attacking army in order to put a city under siege.** Ref.: 2 Sam. 20:15. The Lord prevented Israel from being besieged in the year 701 B.C. by the Assyrians (2 Kgs. 19:32). The related verb *šāpaḵ*, to cast, to throw, is always used to describe the process of setting up, casting up a siege ramp or mound. *

SIEGE TOWER – ***baḥûn, baḥiyn*** [masc. noun: בַּחוּן, בַּחִין <971>; another form of WATCHTOWER <975>] ► **This word depicts an ancient, often-used tool of ancient warfare.** It was effective in scaling and battering high walls and gates of enemy cities during a time of war (Is. 23:13). ¶

SIEGE WALL – 2 Kgs. 25:1; Jer. 52:4; Ezek. 4:2; 17:17; 21:22; 26:8 ➔ SIEGE WORK <1785>.

SIEGE WORK – [1] ***dāyêq*** [masc. noun: דָּיֵק <1785>; from a root corresponding to PIECES (BREAK IN) <1751>] ► **This word means siege mound, siege walls, bulwarks; it is also translated forts. It describes the engines and weapons of ancient warfare.** These works were built at the site of an attack and enabled Nebuchadnezzar to capture Jerusalem (2 Kgs. 25:1; Jer. 52:4; Ezek. 4:2; 17:17; 21:22). Siege works were erected against the coastal city of Tyre (Ezek. 26:8) by Babylon, including a causeway out to the island city itself. ¶
– [2] Is. 29:3 ➔ FORTIFIED PLACE <4694>.

SIEGEWORK – [1] Eccl. 9:14 ➔ NET <4685> [2] Is. 29:3: I will set siegeworks ➔ lit.: I will besiege with towers ➔ TOWER <4674>.

SIEVE – [1] ***keḇārāh*** [fem. noun: כְּבָרָה <3531>; from MULTIPLY <3527>] ► **This word refers to tools or utensils with small openings or perforations through which chaff and other small particles could be shaken loose from various kinds of grains.** Ref.: Amos 9:9. It is used in a simile of the Lord shaking Israel/Jerusalem in a sieve in order to cleanse her. ¶
[2] ***nāphāh, nāpôṯ*** [נָפָה, נָפוֹת <5299>; from SPRINKLE <5130> in the sense of lifting] ►
a. A feminine noun referring to a farm instrument used to separate chaff and other impurities from certain foods, grain, etc., by letting the grain pass through a sieve or a winnow but holding back the undesirable parts. Ref.: Is. 30:28. ¶
b. A feminine noun indicating height, elevation, a region, a border. It refers to the highlands, the tops of low-lying hills. Refs.: Josh. 11:2; 12:23; 1 Kgs. 4:11. ¶
c. A proper noun. Naphoth refers to an area just south of Mount Carmel on the Mediterranean coast. Refs.: Josh. 11:2; 12:23; 17:11; 1 Kgs. 4:11. ¶

SIGH (noun) – Ps. 90:9 ➔ RUMBLING <1899>.

SIGH (verb) – 1 Ex. 2:23; Is. 24:7; Lam. 1:4, 8, 11, 21; Ezek. 9:4; 21:6, 7 ➔ GROAN (verb) <584> 2 Ezek. 24:17 ➔ GROAN (verb) <602>.

SIGHING – 1 Job 3:24; Ps. 6:6; 31:10; 38:9; Is. 21:2; 35:10 ➔ GROANING <585> 2 Ps. 12:5; 79:11 ➔ GROANING <603> 3 Lam. 3:56 ➔ RELIEF <7309>.

SIGHT – 1 ***ḥ**ᵃ**zôṯ*** [Aramaic fem. noun: חָזוֹת <2379>; from SEE <2370>] ▶ **This word refers to something that can be seen and is visible.** In Nebuchadnezzar's dream, he saw a tree visible from anywhere on earth (Dan. 4:11, 20). ¶
2 ***mar'eh*** [masc. noun: מַרְאֶה <4758>; from SEE <7200>] ▶ **This word means an appearance, a vision. Derived from the verb *rā'āh*, meaning to see, this noun bears many of the same shades of meaning as the verb.** It can represent the act of seeing (Gen. 2:9; Lev. 13:12); the appearance of the object (Lev. 13:3; Dan. 1:13); the object which is seen (Ex. 3:3); the face, being that part of the person which is visible (Song 2:14; 5:15); a supernatural vision (Ezek. 8:4; 11:24; Dan. 8:16, 27); the ability to see (Eccl. 6:9); the shining light of a fire (Num. 9:15) or of lightning (Dan. 10:6). *
3 ***r**ᵒ**'iy*** [masc. noun: רְאִי <7210>; from SEE <7200>] ▶ **This word means an appearance, a spectacle. The basic force of this word is that of a visible appearance.** It is used in reference to God's ability to see (Gen. 16:13); the outward look of an individual (1 Sam. 16:12); and a visual spectacle that drew attention to itself (Nah. 3:6). Other refs.: Job 7:8; 33:21. ¶
– 4 Prov. 29:13: to give sight ➔ LIGHT (GIVE) <215>.

SIGN (noun) – 1 ***'ôṯ*** [masc. noun: אוֹת <226>; prob. from CONSENT <225> (in the sense of appearing)] ▶ **This word means a signal, a mark, a miracle.** It is used most often to describe awe-inspiring events: God's work to bring the Hebrew people out of Egypt (Ex. 4:8, 9; Num. 14:22; Deut. 7:19; Ps. 78:43; Jer. 32:20, 21); miracles verifying God's message (1 Sam. 2:34; 10:7, 9; Is. 7:11, 14). Moreover, this word may also denote signs from false prophets (Deut. 13:1, 2; Is. 44:25); circumstances demonstrating God's control (Deut. 28:46; Ps. 86:17). Associate meanings of the word denote physical emblems (Num. 2:2); a promise to remember (Gen. 17:11; Deut. 6:8; Josh. 2:12; 4:6); an event to occur in the future (Is. 20:3; Ezek. 4:3). *
2 ***'āṯ*** [Aramaic masc. noun: אָת <852>; corresponding to <226> above ▶ **This word means miraculous sign.** It refers to the dreams and the personal humbling that Nebuchadnezzar had gone through as part of God's righteous judgment on him (Dan. 4:2, 3; 6:27). These signs were communications and messages in various ways that communicated effectively to the king concerning his own life and the history of the world. ¶
– 3 Num. 26:10 ➔ BANNER <5251> 4 Ezek. 39:15 ➔ MONUMENT <6725>.

SIGN (verb) – Dan. 6:8–10, 12, 13 ➔ INSCRIBE <7560>.

SIGNAL – Is. 11:10; 18:3; Jer. 4:6 ➔ BANNER <5251>.

SIGNATURE – Job 31:35 ➔ MARK (noun) <8420>.

SIGNET, SIGNET RING – 1 ***'izqāh*** [Aramaic fem. noun: עִזְקָה <5824>; from a root corresponding to DIG <5823> (in the sense of to be engraved)] ▶ **This word refers to a band bearing the seal of someone and used to seal various items for authorization purposes.** Ref.: Dan. 6:17. ¶
– 2 Gen. 38:18; Ex. 28:11; Jer. 22:24; Hag. 2:23; etc. ➔ SEAL (noun) <2368> 3 Gen. 38:25 ➔ SEAL (noun) <2858>.

SIGNPOST – Jer. 31:21 ➔ MONUMENT <6725>.

SIHON – ***siyḥôn*** [masc. proper noun: סִיחוֹן <5511>; from the same as SUAH <5477>] ▶

This word designates a king of the Amorites (ca. 1200 B.C.). Joshua conquered his kingdom. His capital was at Heshbon. He at one time ruled over Moab (Num. 21:21–36). His territory stretched from the Arnon in the south to the Jabbok River in the north. The Jordan was its western border. He refused to let Israel pass through his territory on their way to Canaan (Numbers 21). For this he was conquered and slain. Reuben and Gad received much of his conquered territory (Num. 32:33). His defeat was a great victory of Israel's God, the Lord (Deut. 34:1; Josh. 9:10; Ps. 135:11; Ps. 136:19). *

SIKKUTH – ***sikkûṯ*** [masc. sing. noun: סִכּוּת <5522>; fem. of THRONG (noun) <5519> (which is from COVER (verb) <5526> a.)] ▶ **This obscure word occurs only in Amos 5:26 and may mean Tabernacle.** This passage clearly describes the Israelites' false and improper worship. The question is how detailed the prophet's charge was. Some have translated the phrase as booth or shrine, while the Septuagint (Greek Old Testament) reads "shrine of Molech." Some have suggested that both terms represent Akkadian astral deities, Sakkut and Kaiwan. ¶

SILENCE (noun) – 1 ***dûmāh*** [fem. noun: דּוּמָה <1745>; from an unused root meaning to be dumb (comp. CEASE <1820>] ▶ **This word is used figuratively to refer to death, literally the land of silence (i.e., absence of sound) where the Lord is not praised.** Refs.: Ps. 94:17; 115:17. ¶
2 ***dûmiyyāh, dumiyyāh*** [fem. noun: דּוּמִיָּה, דֻּמִיָּה <1747>; from CEASE <1820>] ▶ **This word denotes a quiet wait; it is also translated rest, silent, silently.** It indicates a time of silence in the sense of rest (Ps. 22:2) or a self-imposed period of silence in the presence of evil persons (Ps. 39:2). It may, on the other hand, indicate a time of reverential silence and patience as one waits for God (Ps. 62:1) or a period of awesome silence in anticipation of praise to the Lord (Ps. 65:1). ¶
3 ***dûmām*** [masc. noun: דּוּמָם <1748>; from STAND STILL <1826>] ▶ **This word indicates a quiet wait, in muteness.** It refers to a stone of silence or mute stone that is addressed by a deluded idolater (Hab. 2:19: mute, dumb, silent, lifeless). It is used adverbially to refer to a person's patient, silent waiting on the LORD (Lam. 3:26: quietly, silently). It describes the silent, subdued state of a defeated Babylonian facing destruction (Is. 47:5: in silence, silent, silently). ¶
– 4 Job 4:16 ➔ STILL <1827> 5 Ps. 83:1; Is. 62:6 ➔ REST (noun) <1824>.

SILENCE (KEEP) – Deut. 27:9 ➔ SILENT (BE) <5535> a.

SILENCE (PUT TO) – Ps. 31:18 ➔ BIND <481>.

SILENCE (verb) – 1 Num. 13:30 ➔ SILENCE!, KEEP SILENCE! <2013> 2 Ps. 31:18; 39:9 ➔ BIND <481> 3 Ps. 63:11 ➔ CLOSE <5532>.

SILENCE!, KEEP SILENCE! – ***hās, hāsāh*** [interj. and verb: הַס, הָסָה <2013>; a prim. root] ▶
a. An interjection meaning Hush! Quiet! It is a serious request or an order to keep quiet. As the order of a king to his attendants (Judg. 3:19); as a command to not mention the name of the Lord (Amos 6:10); as a command for silence in a time of pestilence and destruction (Amos 8:3); as the proper response before the Lord in His holy Temple (Hab. 2:20); as the day of the Lord approaches (Zeph. 1:7) when He will act on behalf of Jerusalem (Zech. 2:13). It is used to indicate the proper response to a holy day of the Lord (Neh. 8:11, but is pointed as a verb form here). ¶
b. A verb indicating to hush, to quiet, to silence, to still. It is employed in the causal form of the verb meaning caused to be silent or stilled (Num. 13:30). ¶

SILENCED (WHO IS) – Ezek. 27:32 ➔ DESTROYED <1822>.

SILENT – 1 Ps. 22:2; 39:2 ➔ SILENCE (noun) <1747> 2 Is. 47:5; Hab. 2:19 ➔ SILENCE (noun) <1748>.

SILENT (BE) – 1 ***ḥāraš*** [verb: חָרַשׁ <2790>; a prim. root] ▶ **This word means to not utter words; it also means to be deaf, to be mute.** It indicates a person's keeping still or being silent (Gen. 24:21; 2 Kgs. 18:36). It refers to keeping silent as indicating approval or consent (Num. 30:4) or as indicating a lack of conviction to act about something that needs to be done (2 Sam. 19:10). Keeping silent can be a way to fake being dumb (1 Sam. 10:27). To become silent is to cease speaking, to stop communicating with a person (Jer. 38:27). It can refer to a person silenced by shock, fear, or the inability to answer someone (Job 11:3). It describes God as being silent about evil (Ps. 50:21; Is. 42:14; Hab. 1:13). The Hebrew word also means to plow, to engrave; see PLOW (verb) <2790>. *
2 ***sāḵaṯ*** [verb: סָכַת <5535>; a prim. root] ▶ **a. This word means to pay attention, to listen, to stop talking in order to focus and hear an important statement.** Ref.: Deut. 27:9; ESV: to keep silence. ¶
b. The Hebrew word is also translated to take heed. It means to take care, to listen, and take seriously something that is being said. Ref.: Deut. 27:9. ¶

SILENT (BE, KEEP, REMAIN) – ***ḥāšāh*** [verb: חָשָׁה <2814>; a prim. root] ▶ **This word describes refraining from telling some news or information.** Refs.: 2 Kgs. 7:9; Is. 62:1, 6. It describes also simply to refrain from speech or even mourning (2 Kgs. 2:3, 5; Neh. 8:11). It also means to be inactive; to do nothing, to sit still and do nothing (Judg. 18:9; 1 Kgs. 22:3). It can refer to the stilling of nature (Ps. 107:29). It is used of God's not addressing or acting about iniquity (Is. 57:11; 65:6). Other refs.: Ps. 28:1; 39:2; Eccl. 3:7; Is. 42:14; 64:12. ¶

SILENT (BE, REMAIN) – Ps. 39:2; Is. 53:7; Ezek. 3:26 ➔ BIND <481>.

SILENT (WHO IS) – Ezek. 27:32 ➔ DESTROYED <1822>.

SILENT ONES – Ps. 58:1 ➔ OAK TREES <482>.

SILENTLY – 1 Ps. 62:1 ➔ SILENCE (noun) <1747> 2 Is. 47:5; Lam. 3:26 ➔ SILENCE (noun) <1748>.

SILK – ***mešiy*** [masc. noun: מֶשִׁי <4897>; from DRAW <4871> (in the case of silk, as drawn from the cocoon)] ▶ **This word refers to expensive and luxurious material made into clothing, possibly woven of very fine threads; silk as we know it is not specifically identified.** Refs.: Ezek. 16:10, 13; NIV: costly garments, costly fabric. ¶

SILLA – ***sillā'*** [proper noun: סִלָּא <5538>; from EXALT <5549> (in the sense of to build up)] ▶ **An unidentified place near Millo.** Ref.: 2 Kgs. 12:20. ¶

SILVER – 1 ***kesep̱*** [masc. noun: כֶּסֶף <3701>; from LONG FOR <3700>] ▶ **This word refers to a gleaming grayish and very valuable metal and also to money.** It refers to silver used as a metal (Job 28:1; Prov. 2:4; Zech. 13:9; Mal. 3:3); silver used in making various vessels (Gen. 24:53; Ezek. 27:12); silver as a medium of exchange (Gen. 23:9; 44:1, 2, 8). It was a sign of wealth (Gen. 13:2). Some silver was more choice, more pure (Prov. 8:19; 10:20). It was used in a system of weights and measures, especially shekels (Ex. 21:32; Le. 5:15; Num. 18:16); and talents (ca. 75 lbs. in weight) of silver (Ex. 38:27; 1 Kgs. 20:39). It was used as a means of atonement and ransom for the lives of individual Israelites (Ex. 30:16; Num. 3:49). It was used in idioms and figurative senses: a figure of a dove's wings (Ps. 68:13); standing for a slave (Ex. 21:21); the tongue of a righteous person (Prov. 10:20). It is often found with verbs indicating refining and buying silver: to refine (Is. 48:10; Zech. 13:9); to weigh out silver (Gen. 23:16; Ezra 8:25; Jer. 32:9); to buy something with silver (Jer. 32:25, 44; Amos 8:6. In Numbers 18:16 only, it is used with the verb to redeem. The phrase *miqnaṯ kesep̱* indicates a person purchased for money (Gen. 17:12, 13, 23, 27; Ex. 12:44; or *kesep̱ miqnaṯ* in Lev. 25:51). *
2 ***keₑsap̱*** [Aramaic masc. noun: כְּסַף <3702>; corresponding to <3701> above] ▶ **This**

word denotes both the metal and money. It is used in biblical Aramaic to indicate both a metal (Ezra 5:14; Dan. 2:32, 35), second only in value to gold, or a medium of exchange, money (Ezra 7:17; 22). *

SILVER PAN – Ezra 1:9 ➔ KNIFE <4252>.

SILVERSMITH – Judg. 17:4 ➔ REFINE <6884>.

SIMEON – ***šim'ôn*** [masc. proper noun: שִׁמְעוֹן <8095>; from HEAR <8085>]: heard, hearing ▶
a. The second of Leah's sons from Jacob. His name means "hearing" (Gen. 29:33; 35:23). He and Levi savagely avenged the rape of their sister Dinah by Shechem, son of Hamor the Hivite (Gen. 34:1–4). He had many sons, one by a Canaanite woman (Gen. 46:10). Jacob noted his violent nature in his prophetic utterance (Gen. 49:5). Simeon's tribal inheritance lay within Judah. It included some strategic cities, such as Beersheba, Hormah and Ziklag in the Negev area. Ezekiel alloted Simeon's descendant a place in his vision of a new Temple and New Jerusalem (Ezek. 48:24–33).
b. The name of an Israelite who intermarried with the people of the land during or after the exile. Ref.: Ezra 10:31. *

SIMEONITES – ***šim'ōniy*** [proper noun: שִׁמְעֹנִי <8099>; patron. from SIMEON <8095>] ▶ **Descendants of Simeon (<8095> a.).** Refs.: Num. 25:14; 26:14; Josh. 21:4; 1 Chr. 27:16. ¶

SIMPLE – [1] ***peṯiy*** [adj.: פְּתִי <6612>; from ENTICE <6601> (in the sense of to be deceived, to be gullible] ▶ **This word means foolish, simpleminded.** It refers to a person who is naive concerning the complexities and challenges of life, inexperienced, lacking insight but made wise by God's words and laws (Ps. 19:7; 119:130); but also sometimes rescued by the Lord (Ps. 116:6). The book of Proverbs is written to give insight, perception, and prudence to the simple (Prov. 1:4); wisdom can make the simple wise (Prov. 1:22); for their indecision can destroy them (Prov. 1:32). It refers to being deficient in observing or understanding the Law of God (Ezek. 45:20). *
[2] ***p^{e}ṯayyûṯ*** [fem. noun: פְּתַיּוּת <6615>; from <6612> above] ▶ **This word refers to simplicity; the state of being naïve.** It refers to persons who are not aware of the impact their actions have nor of the complexities and disciplines of life (Prov. 9:13). ¶

SIN (common noun) – [1] ***ḥēṭ^{e}'*** [masc. noun: חֵטְא <2399>; from SIN (verb) <2398>] ▶ **This word means an offense, a fault.** The word suggests the accumulated shortcomings that lead to punishment (Gen. 41:9); errors or offenses that cause the wrath of a supervisor (Eccl. 10:4); and the charge against an individual for his or her actions contrary to the Law (Lev. 24:15; Num. 9:13; Deut. 15:9; 23:21). Isaiah uses the word to reinforce the tremendous sinfulness of Judah in contrast to the Messiah's redemptive suffering (Is. 53:12). *
[2] ***ḥ^{a}ṭā'āh*** [fem. noun: חֲטָאָה <2401>; fem. of <2399> above] ▶ **The word generally stands as a synonym for transgression.** Ref.: Ps. 32:1. It is used to convey the evil committed by Abimelech in taking Sarah into his harem (Gen. 20:9); the wickedness of idolatry committed by the Israelites at Sinai (Ex. 32:21, 30, 31); and the perversion foisted on the Northern Kingdom by Jeroboam (2 Kgs. 17:21). Conversely, the psalmist uses the Hebrew word once to mean a sin offering (Ps. 40:6). Other ref.: Ps. 109:7. ¶
[3] ***ḥaṭṭā'āh*** [fem. noun: חַטָּאָה <2402>] ▶ **This word is used only twice in the Old Testament and is equivalent to the Hebrew word *ḥaṭṭā'ṯ* (<2403> below).** It is used in Exodus 34:7 to speak of what God, in the greatness of His lovingkindness, will forgive. It is also used in Isaiah 5:18 to describe God's woe against those who sin greatly. ¶
[4] ***ḥaṭṭā'ṯ*** [fem. noun: חַטָּאת <2403>; from SIN (verb) <2398>] ▶ **This word means evil, transgression, sin offering, punishment.** The word denotes youthful indiscretions (Ps. 25:7); evil committed against

another (Gen. 50:17); trespasses against God (2 Chr. 33:19; Ps. 51:2; Amos 5:12); a general state of sinfulness (Is. 6:7); and the specific occasion of sin, particularly in reference to idolatry (Deut. 9:21; Hos. 10:8). It also implies an antidote to sin, including purification from ceremonial impurity (Num. 19:9, 17); the sacrificial offering for sin (Ex. 29:14; Lev. 4:3); and the punishment for sin (Lam. 4:6; Zech. 14:19). In the story of Cain and Abel, sin appears as a creature, ready to pounce, lurking "at the door" of Cain's heart (Gen. 4:7). *

[5] ***ḥ^{a}ṭāy*** [Aramaic masc. noun: חֲטָי <2408>; from a root corresponding to SIN (verb) <2398>] ▶ **This word is used only once in the Old Testament and is equivalent to the Hebrew word *ḥaṭṭā'ṯ* (<2403> above).** Daniel advised King Nebuchadnezzar to turn from his sins (Dan. 4:27). ¶

– [6] Hos. 10:10 ➔ MARITAL RIGHTS <5772> b.

SIN (proper noun) – ***siyn*** [proper noun: סִין <5512>; of uncertain deriv.] ▶

a. An Egyptian border town fortress (Pelusium, ESV, NIV; Sin, KJV) mentioned by Ezekiel as an object of God's wrath. Refs.: Ezek. 30:15, 16. It has been located thirteen miles east of the Suez Canal and about two miles from the Mediterranean coast on a major route to Memphis. It is placed just east of Migdol. ¶

b. A desert located west of Sinai between Elim and Rephidim. Its exact location depends on where Sinai is located. Refs.: Ex. 16:1; 17:1; Num. 33:11, 12. ¶

SIN (verb) – ***ḥeṭ'āh, ḥāṭā'*** [verb: חֵטְאָה, חָטָא <2398>; a prim. root] ▶ **This word means to miss the mark, to wrong, to lead into sin, to purify from sin, to free from sin. Four main Hebrew words express the idea of sin in the Hebrew Bible, with this word used most often. Its central meaning is to miss the mark or fail. It is used in a non-moral or nonreligious sense to indicate the simple idea of missing or failing in any task or endeavor.** In Judges 20:16, it indicated the idea of a slinger missing his target. The verb also indicated the situation that arose when something was missing (Job 5:24); or it described a failure to reach a certain goal or age (Prov. 19:2; Is. 65:20). These are minor uses of the verb. The word is used the most to describe human failure and sin. It indicates failure to do what is expected; the one who fails to find God in this life destroys himself (Prov. 8:36). Many times the word indicates being at fault (Gen. 20:9; Ex. 10:16; 2 Kgs. 18:14; Neh. 6:13) as Pharaoh was toward Moses or to be guilty or responsible (Gen. 43:9; 44:32). It regularly means to sin; Pharaoh sinned against God (Ex. 10:16). People can also sin against other human beings (Gen. 42:22; 1 Sam. 19:4, 5) or against their own souls (Prov. 20:2). The verb is used to indicate sin with no object given, as when Pharaoh admitted flatly that he had sinned (Ex. 9:27; Judg. 10:15) or when Israel was described as a "sinful nation" (Is. 1:4). Sometimes the writer used the noun from this same verbal root as the object of the verb for emphasis, such as in Exodus 32:30, 31, where Moses asserted that Israel had sinned a great sin (Lev. 4:3; Num. 12:11). Sinning, unfortunately, is a universal experience, for there is no one who does not sin (Eccl. 7:20). Persons may sin with various parts of their bodies or in certain ways or attitudes. They may sin with their tongues or lips (Job 2:10; Ps. 39:1). Persons may sin innocently or in such a way as to bring guilt on others (Lev. 4:2, 3; Num. 15:27).

Three other stems of this verb are used less often. The intensive stem is used to indicate people bearing their own material losses or failures (Gen. 31:39); one freeing oneself from sin or purifying an object or person (Lev. 8:15; Ps. 51:7); and one bringing a sin offering (Lev. 6:26; 2 Chr. 29:24). The causative stem, besides indicating failure to miss a literal target, means to lead into sin, to lead astray. Jeroboam was an infamous king who caused all Israel to walk in sin (1 Kgs. 14:16; 15:26). The reflexive stem communicates the idea of freeing oneself from sin. The Levites purified themselves (i.e., set themselves apart from sin) so they could work at the sanctuary (Num. 8:21). *

SIN OFFERING – ***ḥaṭṭāyā'*** [Aramaic fem. noun: חַטָּיָא <2409>; from the same as SIN (noun) <2408>] ▶ **This Aramaic word appears only in Ezra 6:17, where it indicates the particular sacrifice made at the dedication of the rebuilt Temple, following the return from exile.** The text states that the "sin offering" consisted of twelve rams for the sins of the twelve tribes of Israel. ¶

SINAI – ***siynay*** [proper noun: סִינַי <5514>; of uncertain deriv.] ▶ **This word designates the "mountain of God."** Refs.: Ex. 3:1; 4:27; 18:5; 24:13. Moses received there the laws of God and concluded the "Sinai Covenant" (Ex. 19:1–24:18). It is the place where God met with the Israelites after their exodus from Egypt (Ex. 16:1; 19:1, 2, 11, 18, 20, 23; 24:16; 31:18; 34:2, 4, 29, 32; Lev. 7:38; 25:1; 26:46; 27:34). Many places have been suggested for its location. It has traditionally been placed at Jebel Musa ("Mountain of Moses," Arabic) in the central southern region of southern Sinai. In every instance of its use, it is tied to Moses and the giving of the Law (Ex. 19–34; Num. 1; 3; 4; 9; Deut. 33:2). The mountain was called Horeb one time (Ex. 33:6), Horeb elsewhere referring to a mountain range (Ex. 3:1; 17:6; Deut. 1:2, 6; 4:10; Deut. 29:1). Israel encamped at Sinai for ca. eleven months (Num. 10:11, 12). God's giving of the Law at Sinai was celebrated in Israel's worship (Ps. 68:8, 17), the One of Sinai (NIV), the God of Israel (Judg. 5:5). *

SINEW – 1 ***giyḏ*** [masc. noun: גִּיד <1517>; prob. from ATTACK (verb) <1464>] ▶ **This word refers to the tendon of a person's body, e.g., of the neck, hip, or thigh.** Refs.: Gen. 32:32; Job 10:11; 40:17. Israel's obstinacy is likened to an iron sinew of the neck (Is. 48:4). It is used to describe the "iron" sinew of the thighs of Behemoth, possibly a hippopotamus (Job 40:17). The Lord restores sinews and flesh to Israel represented by the bones in the valley of dry bones (Ezek. 37:6, 8). ¶
– 2 Gen. 32:32 ➔ SHRANK (WHICH, THAT) <5384> b.

SINEWS – Job 30:17 ➔ GNAW, GNAWING <6207> c.

SING – 1 ***zāmar*** [verb: זָמַר <2167>; a prim. root (perhaps identified with PRUNE <2168> through the idea of striking with the fingers)] ▶ **This word means to play an instrument, to perform songs with musical accompaniment; it is also translated to make melody, to make music.** Stringed instruments are commonly specified in connection with this word, and the tambourine is also mentioned once (Ps. 33:2; 71:22, 23; 149:3). The term occurs frequently in a call to praise—usually a summons to oneself (2 Sam. 22:50; 1 Chr. 16:9; Ps. 66:4; Is. 12:5). In the Bible, the object of this praise is always the Lord, who is lauded for both His attributes and His actions (Judg. 5:3; Ps. 101:1; 105:2). Besides the above references, this verb appears exclusively in the Book of Psalms, contributing to a note of praise in psalms of various types: hymns (Ps. 104:33); psalms of thanksgiving (Ps. 138:1); and even psalms of lament (Ps. 144:9). *
2 ***šiyr*** [verb: שִׁיר <7891>; a prim. root (identical with JOURNEY <7788> through the idea of strolling minstrels)] ▶ **See previous definition. This word occurs often in a call to praise the Lord.** The call may be directed toward oneself or others (Ps. 27:6; 96:1, 2; 101:1; Jer. 20:13). This term is frequently associated with the Levitical worship established by David and emphasized by postexilic writers (1 Chr. 15:16; Ezra 2:41; Neh. 7:1). Although the Levitical singers were all men, women also were singers in ancient Israel both in religious and secular settings (Ex. 15:21; Judg. 5:1–3; Eccl. 2:8). Secular occasions for singing included celebration of victory in battle (1 Sam. 18:6); mourning over death (2 Chr. 35:25); entertainment (2 Sam. 19:35); and an expression of love (Is. 5:1). The Bible once mentions the singing of birds (Zeph. 2:14). *
– 3 Ex. 15:21; 1 Sam. 18:7; etc. ➔ ANSWER (verb) <6030> b. 4 Ezek. 27:25 ➔ JOURNEY (verb) <7788>.

SING IDLY – Amos 6:5 ➔ IMPROVISE <6527> a.

SINGED (BE) – ***ḥ^{a}raḵ*** [Aramaic verb: חֲרַךְ <2761>; a root prob. allied to the equivalent of BURN (verb) <2787>] ▶ **This word means to be burned slightly or superficially, but enough to see and smell.** Ref.: Dan. 3:27. It was miraculous that the clothing of the three Israelites was not singed at all from the high heat of the furnace. ¶

SINGER – [1] ***zammār*** [Aramaic masc. noun: זַמָּר <2171>; from the same as MUSIC <2170>] ▶ **This word refers to vocalists among the Temple personnel; they were free from any tax, tribute, or toll.** Ref.: Ezra 7:24; also translated musician. ¶
– [2] Judg. 5:11 ➔ DIVIDE <2686> b.

SINGING – [1] ***rannên*** [intens. verb: רַנֵּן <7444>; intens. from SHOUT (verb) <7442>] ▶ **This word refers to shouting, performing songs. It describes singing, a joyful cry.** It usually describes a cry of jubilation or praise to the Lord (Is. 35:2). ¶
– [2] Ps. 68:6 ➔ PROSPERITY <3574> [3] Ps. 98:5; Is. 51:3 ➔ SONG <2172> [4] Song 2:12; Is. 24:16 ➔ SONG <2158>.

SINGING, JOYFUL SINGING – Ps. 63:5; 100:2 ➔ JOYFUL SHOUT <7445>.

SINIM – ***siyniym*** [proper noun: סִינִים <5515>; plur. of otherwise unknown name] ▶
a. A masculine proper noun designating the Sinim people, perhaps from southern China. Ref.: KJV, NKJV, NASB, Is. 49:12. ¶
b. The people of Aswan. Ref.: NIV, Is. 49:12; ESV translates Syene. ¶

SINITE – ***siyniy*** [proper noun: סִינִי <5513>; from an otherwise unknown name of a man] ▶ **The name of a people mentioned twice.** Refs.: Gen. 10:17; 1 Chr. 1:5. ¶

SINK – [1] ***ṣālal*** [verb: צָלַל <6749>; a prim. root (properly, to tumble down)] ▶ **This word means to descend rapidly into the dark, shadowy depths of the sea.** Ref.: Ex. 15:10. ¶
– [2] Ex. 15:4; 1 Sam. 17:49; Ps. 69:2; Jer. 38:6, 22; Lam. 2:9 ➔ DROWN <2883> [3] Ps. 38:2 ➔ BEND <5181>.

SINK DOWN – [1] Ps. 44:25; Prov. 2:18; Lam. 3:20 ➔ BOW DOWN <7743> a. [2] Ezek. 21:30 ➔ BRING LOW <4355>.

SINK IN – Eccl. 10:18 ➔ BRING LOW <4355>.

SINNER – ***ḥaṭṭā'*** [masc. noun and adj.: חַטָּא <2400>] ▶ **This word comes from the common verb *ḥāṭā'* <2398> and is related to the common noun *ḥaṭṭā'ṯ* <2403>. As a noun, it is used to describe those who, by their actions, are under the wrath and judgment of God.** Ref.: Ps. 1:5. They face ultimate destruction (Gen. 13:13; Ps. 104:35; Is. 1:28). The influence of these people is to be avoided (Ps. 1:1; 26:9; Prov. 1:10), but they are to be instructed in the way of righteousness (Ps. 25:8; 51:13). As an adjective, the word describes the sinful people the tribes of Reuben and Gad were raising (Num. 32:14). *

SION – ***śiy'ōn*** [proper noun: שִׂיאֹן <7865>; from LOFTINESS <7863>]: elevated ▶ **Another name for Mount Hermon.** Ref.: Deut. 4:48.

SIPHMITE – ***šip̄miy*** [proper noun: שִׁפְמִי <8225>; patrial from SHEPHAM <8221>] ▶ **An inhabitant of Shepham.** Ref.: 1 Chr. 27:27. ¶

SIPHMOTH – ***śip̄môṯ*** [proper noun: שִׂפְמוֹת <8224>; fem. plur. of SHEPHAM <8221>]: fruitful, bald ▶ **A city of Judah.** Ref.: 1 Sam. 30:28. ¶

SIPPAI – ***sippay*** [masc. proper noun: סִפַּי <5598>; the same as THRESHOLD <5592>]: threshold ▶ **One of the descendants of the giants killed by Sibbecai at Gezer.** Ref.: 1 Chr. 20:4. ¶

SIRAH – ***sirāh*** [proper noun: סִרָה <5626>; from TURN ASIDE <5493> (in the sense of to depart)]: retiring, departure ▶ **A well, or cistern, from which Abner was brought back at the command of Joab.** Ref.: 2 Sam. 3:26. ¶

SIRION – ***śiryōn*** [proper noun: שִׂרְיֹן <8303>; the same as SERAIAH <8304>]: armor ▶ **The name given by the Sidonians to Mount Hermon.** Refs.: Deut. 3:9; Ps. 29:6. ¶

SISERA – ***siysᵉrā'*** [masc. proper noun: סִיסְרָא <5516>; of uncertain deriv.] ▶
a. The commander in charge of the Canaanite troops of Jabin, king of Hazor. He was slain by Jael, wife of Heber the Kenite (Judg. 5:24–27). *
b. The father of a postexilic family. Refs.: Ezra 2:53; Neh. 7:55. ¶

SISMAI – ***sismāy*** [masc. proper noun: סִסְמַי <5581>; of uncertain deriv.] ▶ **A man of the tribe of Judah.** Ref.: 1 Chr. 2:40. ¶

SISTER – ***'āḥôṯ*** [fem. noun: אָחוֹת <269>; irregular fem. of BROTHER <251>] ▶ **Besides a biological sister (female sibling), it also refers to more intimate female relatives.** Song of Solomon uses the word to refer to a bride (Song 4:9, 10, 12; 5:1, 2). In Numbers 25:18, it is used as a generic term for female relatives. Poetically, it sometimes refers to a geographical location (Jer. 3:7, 8, 10; Ezek. 16:45, 52). For inanimate objects, it can often be translated as the English word *another* (Ex. 26:3, 5, 6, 17; Ezek. 1:9; 3:13). *

SISTER-IN-LAW – Ruth 1:15 ➔ BROTHER'S WIFE <2994>.

SIT – 1 ***yᵉṯiḇ*** [Aramaic verb: יְתִב <3488>; corresponding to DWELL <3427>] ▶ **This word means to take a seat; it also means to dwell, to cause to dwell.** It is used of taking a seat, sitting down (Dan. 7:9, 10, 26). It also has the sense of dwelling or causing to dwell or settle somewhere (Ezra 4:10). It can be translated to live in an area (Ezra 4:17). ¶
– 2 See DWELL <3427>.

SIT DOWN – ***tāḵāh*** [verb: תָּכָה <8497>; a prim. root] ▶
a. This word indicates sitting or paying homage (to bow down) to God. This was the case as He delivered His Law at Sinai (Deut. 33:3).
b. This word means to follow. It refers to God's people walking after, accepting the laws of the Lord (Deut. 33:3). ¶

SIT ON – Jer. 17:11 ➔ GATHER <1716>.

SIT STILL – Is. 30:7 ➔ LOSS OF TIME <7674>.

SITE – See PLACE (noun) <870>.

SITHRI – ***siṯriy*** [masc. proper noun: סִתְרִי <5644>; from COVERING <5643>]: protected ▶ **A Levite, son of Uzziel.** Ref.: Ex. 6:22. ¶

SITNAH – ***śiṭnāh*** [proper noun: שִׂטְנָה <7856>; the same as ACCUSATION <7855>]: accusation, opposition, hostility ▶ **This word designates the second well dug by Isaac.** Ref.: Gen. 26:21. ¶

SITUATED (BE) – 1 Sam. 14:5 ➔ PILLAR <4690>.

SITUATION – 1 ***ṣᵉḇû*** [Aramaic fem. noun: צְבוּ <6640>; from WISH <6634>] ▶ **This word refers to the circumstances or conditions under which people find themselves.** Other translations render it so that nothing would be changed (Dan. 6:17); the KJV translates it as purpose. ¶
– 2 2 Kgs. 2:19 ➔ SEAT <4186> 3 Ps. 48:2 ➔ ELEVATION <5131>.

SIVAN – ***siywān*** [proper noun: סִיוָן <5510>; prob. of Persian origin] ▶ **This word refers to the third month of the year, equaling our May-June, the time of the Feast of Weeks.** It is used in Esther 8:9. ¶

SIX, SIXTH – 1 ***šēš, šiššāh*** [verb: שֵׁשׁ, שִׁשָּׁה <8337>; a prim. number] ▶ **This word indicates a cardinal number identifying the sixth item in counting.** It combines with other numbers (Gen. 7:6, 11; 8:13; 16:16). *
2 ***šēṯ, šiṯ*** [Aramaic numerical adj.: שֵׁת, שִׁת <8353>; corresponding to <8337> above] ▶

This word is used as an ordinal, e.g., the sixth year. Ref.: Ezra 6:15, year of six, the sixth year. It is also used as a cardinal counting number, six cubits (Dan. 3:1). ¶

SIXTH – ***šiššiy*** [numerical ordinal adj.: שִׁשִּׁי <8345>; from SIX, SIXTH <8337>] ▶ **This word points out the sixth item in a series.** Refs.: Gen. 1:31; 30:19; Ex. 16:5, 22, 29; Hag. 1:1, 15. *

SIXTH PART (GIVE A) – ***šāšāh*** [verb: שָׁשָׁה <8341>; a denom. from SIX, SIXTH <8337>] ▶ **This word refers to contributing one-sixth of an ephah from a homer of wheat or barley.** It was an offering to the Prince in Ezekiel's new Temple (Ezek. 45:13). ¶

SIXTH PART (LEAVE A) – Ezek. 39:2 ➔ DRIVE <8338> b.

SIXTY – [1] ***šiššiym*** [numerical plur. adj.: שִׁשִּׁים <8346>; multiple of SIX, SIXTH <8337>] ▶ **This word is the plural of** *šêš (six).* **It indicates the sixtieth item in a counting series of items.** Ref.: Gen. 46:26. It combines with other numbers, e.g., sixty-five (Gen. 5:15, 18, 20). *

[2] ***šittiyn*** [Aramaic numerical plur. adj.: שִׁתִּין <8361>; from <8346> above] ▶ **This word indicates the cardinal number sixty, indicating sixty items.** Refs.: Ezra 6:3; Dan. 3:1. It combines with other numbers, e.g., sixty-two (Dan. 5:31). ¶

SIXTY-TWO – Dan. 5:31 ➔ TWO <8648>.

SIZE – [1] Ex. 26:2, 8; 1 Kgs. 6:25 ➔ MEASURE (noun) <4060> [2] 1 Kgs. 6:25; 7:37 ➔ FORM (noun) <7095> [3] Ezek. 45:11 ➔ QUOTA <8506>.

SKILL – [1] ***kišrôn*** [noun: כִּשְׁרוֹן <3788>; from SUCCESS (BRING) <3787>] ▶ **This word means skill (of work, i.e., skillful work), profit, productivity. It occurs three times and refers to increase which brings no lasting satisfaction.** In Ecclesiastes 2:21 (KJV: equity), it refers to the profit from labor which, at an owner's death, is given to one who did not labor for it. In Ecclesiastes 4:4 (NKJV, KJV: skillful, right), the word refers to the profit produced by hard work which is caused by or results in competition with and is the envy of one's neighbors. In Ecclesiastes 5:11 (advantage, profit, benefit, good), the word refers to the (lack of) profit in producing more than one can use. ¶

– [2] Is. 25:11 ➔ TRICKERY <698>.

SKILLED – ***māhiyr*** [adj.: מָהִיר <4106>; from HURRY <4116>] ▶ **This word means quick; hence prompt, ready, apt. It describes an expertise in a domain; it is also translated well-versed, skillful, ready.** It refers to extraordinary expertise in some area, such as the Law of Moses (Ezra 7:6; Is. 16:5: prompt, hasting, hastening, swift, to speed); or a fluent ability to speak glowingly of Israel's king (Ps. 45:1). It extends to a person's work of any kind (Prov. 22:29: diligent, who excels). ¶

SKILLFUL – [1] Ps. 45:1; Prov. 22:29 ➔ SKILLED <4106> [2] Eccl. 4:4 ➔ SKILL <3788>.

SKIN – [1] ***gêleḏ*** [masc. noun: גֶּלֶד <1539>; from an unused root prob. meaning to polish] ▶ **This word means the natural layer covering the human body. It is an archaic Hebrew word, since it is found only one time in the book of Job.** It is used when the text describes Job expressing his grief by sewing sackcloth over his skin (Job. 16:15)—a common custom of mourning in ancient Israel. ¶

[2] ***zāḡ*** [masc. noun: זָג <2085>; from an unused root prob. meaning to enclose] ▶ **This word refers to a grape skin.** It was one of the least desirable parts of the grape vintage (Num. 6:4; also translated husk). ¶

[3] ***'ôr*** [masc. sing. noun: עוֹר <5785>; from UNCOVER <5783>] ▶ **This word is used literally of human skin, the natural layer covering the body.** It is used of Moses' shining face (Ex. 34:29); also in connection with regulations regarding leprosy or skin diseases (Lev. 13:2). It is employed

figuratively in the expression, skin of my teeth (Job 19:20). It can also denote skins of animals, typically already skinned (with the exception of Job 41:7). Skins were used for the garments that God made for Adam and Eve (Gen. 3:21); and for coverings of items like the Tabernacle (Ex. 25:5); and the ark (Num. 4:6). *
– [4] Gen. 21:14, 15, 19 ➔ WATERSKIN <2573> [5] 1 Sam. 16:20; Judg. 4:19 ➔ BOTTLE <4997>.

SKIN BOTTLE – ***nêḇel, neḇel*** [masc. noun: נֵבֶל, נֶבֶל <5035>; from WITHER <5034>] ▶ **The word indicates a storage jar, a skin container.** A jug or other container for wine (1 Sam. 1:24; 10:3; 25:18; 2 Sam. 16:1); water (Job 38:37); figuratively for all kinds of purposes (Is. 22:24; Jer. 13:12; 48:12). It is used figuratively of persons (Lam. 4:2). Some vessels were made of clay (cf. Is. 30:14). The word also refers to a stringed instrument; see HARP <5035>. ¶

SKIN DISEASE – ***neṯeq*** [masc. noun: נֶתֶק <5424>; from BREAK <5423>] ▶ **This word refers to a scab, a type of leprosy; it is also translated scale, dry scall, itch. It refers to a skin disease of some kind.** It has been suggested that it was leprosy, but others prefer ringworm or eczema. It probably referred to various skin eruptions under the same name (Lev. 13:30–37; 14:54). ¶

SKINK – Lev. 11:30 ➔ SAND LIZARD <2546>.

SKIP – [1] Job 21:11; Ps. 29:6; 114:4, 6 ➔ DANCE (verb) <7540> [2] Jer. 50:11; Mal. 4:2 ➔ FROLIC <6335> a.

SKIRT – [1] ***šōḇel*** [masc. noun: שֹׁבֶל <7640>; from an unused root meaning to flow] ▶ **This word refers in context to a woven or latticed garment, a flowing train of a woman's skirt, or hem of a dress or skirt.** Ref.: Is. 47:2; KJV: leg; ESV: robe. ¶
– [2] Is. 3:24 ➔ GIRDING <4228> [3] Jer. 13:22, 26; Lam. 1:9; Nah. 3:5 ➔ HEM <7757>.

SKULL – Judg. 9:53; 2 Kgs. 9:35 ➔ HEAD (noun) <1538>.

SLACK – Prov. 10:4; 12:24 ➔ DECEIT <7423> b.

SLACKED (BE) – Hab. 1:4 ➔ STUNNED (BECOME) <6313>.

SLACKNESS – Eccl. 10:18 ➔ IDLENESS <8220>.

SLANDER – [1] ***dᵉp̱iy*** [masc. noun: דֳּפִי <1848>; from an unused root (meaning to push over)] ▶ **This Hebrew word means blemish, fault; it refers to alleging a fault, harming one's own brother by verbal statements that injure his reputation.** Ref.: Ps. 50:20. ¶
[2] ***lāšan*** [verb: לָשַׁן <3960>; a prim. root] ▶ **This word refers to uttering false, damaging statements against a third party.** Ref.: Ps. 101:5. God avenges this with destruction. Even a slave was not to be slandered to his owner (Prov. 30:10; also translated to accuse, to malign). ¶
[3] ***rāḡal*** [verb: רָגַל <7270>; a prim. root] ▶ **This word means verbally abusing someone in spoken language.** Ref.: 2 Sam. 19:27. God's people should not slander (Ps. 15:3). For other meanings of the Hebrew word, see SPY OUT <7270> and WALK (TEACH TO) <7270>. *
– [4] Num. 14:36; Ps. 31:13; Prov. 10:18 ➔ REPORT (BAD) <1681>.

SLANDER, SLANDERER – [1] ***rāḵiyl*** [masc. noun: רָכִיל <7400>; from MERCHANDISE (SELL) <7402> (in the sense of to travel about, e.g., to carry tales)] ▶ **This word refers to gossip; it also means and is translated talebearer. It refers to one who goes about spreading rumors or falsities about someone.** It is always used in a negative manner. Such a practice was prohibited by the Mosaic Law (Lev. 19:16). Wisdom Literature condemns it. It entails revealing things that should not be made public (Prov. 11:13; 20:19). God condemns the whole people of being talebearers, especially certain leaders (Jer. 6:28; 9:4; Ezek. 22:9). ¶

– [2] Prov. 16:28; 18:8; 26:20, 22 ➔ WHISPERER <5372>.

SLASH – Jer. 48:37 ➔ GASH (noun) <1418>.

SLASH OPEN – Job 16:13 ➔ CUT (verb) <6398>.

SLAUGHTER (noun) – [1] ***'iḇḥāh*** [fem. noun: אִבְחָה <19>; from an unused root (apparently meaning to turn)] ▶ **In Ezekiel, it is the killing resulting from the avenging sword of the Lord as it strikes His rebellious and corrupt people.** Ref.: Ezek. 21:15. ¶

[2] ***hereg*** [masc. noun: הֶרֶג <2027>; from KILL <2026>] ▶ **This word means killing, destruction.** The Jews had a great victory and struck down all their enemies (Esther 9:5), while the book of Proverbs advises that one should rescue those unwise people heading for the slaughter (Prov. 24:11). Isaiah uses the "day of the great slaughter" to refer to the time of Israel's deliverance (Is. 30:25). In the prophecy against Tyre, Ezekiel warns of the day when a slaughter will take place there (Ezek. 26:15). Other ref.: Is. 27:7. ¶

[3] ***hᵃrêḡāh*** [fem. noun: הֲרֵגָה <2028>; fem. of <2027> above] ▶ **This word means killing, destruction. It is used only five times in the Old Testament. Two of these instances are found in the phrase "valley of slaughter" (Jer. 7:32; 19:6).** In both of these occurrences, the Lord renames the Hinnom Valley because of the slaughter He will bring on the Israelites who have done horrifying deeds by sacrificing their children to other gods. Jeremiah also uses the word when he pleads with the Lord for the wicked to be taken away for the "day of slaughter" (Jer. 12:3, NIV). Zechariah uses this word twice in a metaphor describing Israel as the "flock marked for slaughter" (Zech. 11:4, 7 NIV). ¶

[4] ***ṭeḇaḥ*** [masc. noun: טֶבַח <2874>; from SLAUGHTER (verb) <2873>] ▶ **Originally, the term referred to the actual killing of animals for food (lit.: to slaughter a slaughter).** Refs.: Gen. 43:16: animal; Prov. 9:2: meat, beast. However, this term has also been used metaphorically. It describes the condition of a man seduced by an adulteress (Prov. 7:22), as well as the slaughter of the Suffering Servant (Is. 53:7). Furthermore, it characterizes the destinies of Edom (Is. 34:6); Moab (Jer. 48:15); Babylon (Jer. 50:27); and all those who forsake God (Is. 34:2; 65:12). A parallel term is *zeḇaḥ* (SACRIFICE <2077>), meaning slaughtering for a sacrifice. Other refs.: Ezek. 21:10, 15, 28. ¶

[5] ***ṭiḇḥāh*** [fem. noun: טִבְחָה <2878>; fem. of <2874> above and meaning the same] ▶ **This word means killing; it also means slaughtered meat.** In 1 Samuel, Nabal questioned why he should give his food to David and his men (1 Sam. 25:11; KJV, flesh). But in Psalm 44:22 and Jeremiah 12:3, it is a generic term for slaughter. In both passages, it compared the punishment of people to the slaughtering of sheep. See the cognate verb *ṭāḇaḥ* (SLAUGHTER (verb) <2873>). ¶

[6] ***mappāṣ*** [masc. noun: מַפָּץ <4660>; from BREAK <5310> a.] ▶ **This word means a smashing, a shattering.** It is used in this form only once and refers to a dangerous weapon for smashing (Ezek. 9:2; also translated deadly). See the related Hebrew root *nāp̄aṣ* (BREAK <5310>), as well as the Hebrew words *nep̄eṣ* (CLOUDBURST <5311>) and *mappêṣ* (WAR CLUB <4661>). ¶

[7] ***qeṭel*** [masc. noun: קֶטֶל <6993>; from SLAY <6991>] ▶ **This word refers to a mass killing of people in battle and in pillage in Edom as part of the Lord's judgment on this rebellious nation.** Ref.: Obad. 1:9. ¶

[8] ***šᵉḥiyṭāh, šaḥᵃṭāh*** [fem. noun: שְׁחִיטָה, שַׁחֲטָה <7821>; from KILL <7819>] ▶
a. This technical word refers to the sacrificial killing and preparation of lambs for the Passover, carried out by certain Levites. Ref.: 2 Chr. 30:17. ¶
b. In context this word refers to the willful rejection of God's ways and the concomitant descent into rebellious and depraved behavior as measured by God's will and laws. Ref.: Hos. 5:2; also translated depravity in the NASB. ¶

– [9] Ezek. 21:22 ➔ BREAKING <7524>.

SLAUGHTER (verb) – 1 ***ṭāḇaḥ*** [verb: טָבַח <2873>; a prim. root] ▶ **This word signifies killing livestock to prepare it for food; it is also translated to kill, to slay.** Refs.: Gen. 43:16; Ex. 22:1; 1 Sam. 25:11. The Hebrew word *zāḇaḥ* (OFFER <2076>), in contrast, signifies slaughtering livestock for sacrifice. Slaughter was used as a picture of destruction, whether attempted against righteous people (Ps. 37:14; Jer. 11:19) or brought on those being judged by God (Lam. 2:21; Ezek. 21:10). The slaughter of lambs, which do not comprehend or expect slaughter, symbolized an unexpected destruction (Jer. 11:19). In Proverbs 9:2, the slaughtering of livestock symbolizes a feast prepared by wisdom. Other refs.: Jer. 25:34; 51:40. ¶
– 2 See KILL <7819> 3 See OFFER <2076>.

SLAUGHTER, PLACE OF SLAUGHTER – ***maṭbêaḥ*** [masc. noun: מַטְבֵּחַ <4293>; from SLAUGHTER (verb) <2873>] ▶ **This word defines a place where sacrificial killing or killing in general takes place.** It is used figuratively of a slaughtering place where God will judge the Babylonians (Is. 14:21). ¶

SLAVE (TREAT AS A) – ***'āmar*** [verb: עָמַר <6014>; a prim. root] ▶ **This word means to treat someone without humane compassion; it is also translated to make merchandise, to treat brutally, to deal violently, to mistreat.** It means to treat a person harshly, without humane consideration, without compassion (Deut. 21:14); or to be brutal physically to a person (Deut. 24:7). This word also refers to a person who binds and ties up sheaves of grain (Ps. 129:7: binder). Some translators find a different word, therefore, in Psalm 129:7 (NIV: one who gathers). ¶

SLAVE DRIVER – Ex. 3:7; 5:6, 10, 13, 14; Job 3:18 ➔ OPPRESS <5065>.

SLAVERY – Ezra 9:8, 9; Neh. 9:17 ➔ BONDAGE <5659>.

SLAVERY (BRING INTO) – Neh. 5:5 ➔ SUBDUE <3533>.

SLAVES (AS) – Ex. 1:13, 14 ➔ SEVERITY <6530>.

SLAY – 1 ***qāṭal*** [verb: קָטַל <6991>; a prim. root] ▶ **This word properly means to cut off; it is also translated to kill. It means to destroy persons by illness, cause them to die, to perish.** It is used by Job about himself (Job 13:15). It describes the activity of a murderer (Job 24:14). It indicates God's possible slaying of the wicked. Other ref.: Ps. 139:19. ¶
2 ***qᵉṭal*** [Aramaic verb: קְטַל <6992>; corresponding to <6991> above] ▶ **This word means to destroy persons, to cut off their lives.** It is used in an official royal decree to kill the wise men of Babylon (Dan. 2:13, 14; cf. 5:19, 30; 7:11). It describes the death of a person by burning (Dan. 3:22). ¶
– 3 Lev. 26:17; 2 Sam. 18:7 ➔ SMITE <5062> 4 See KILL <2026> 5 See SLAUGHTER (verb) <2873>.

SLEEK (BE) – 1 ***'āšaṯ*** [verb: עָשַׁת <6245>; a prim. root] ▶ **This word means to shine, to excel.** It means to become slick in actions, in excelling at something (Jer. 5:28; KJV: to shine). The Hebrew word also means to consider, to think upon; see [CONCERNED (BE) <6245>]. ¶
– 2 Deut. 32:15 ➔ OBESE (BE) <3780>.

SLEEP (noun) – 1 ***šᵉnāh*** [Aramaic fem. noun: שְׁנָה <8139>; corresponding to <8142> below] ▶ **See next definition.** Darius was not able to sleep; his sleep went from him; he would not fall asleep (Dan. 6:18). ¶
2 ***šênā', šênāh*** [fem. noun: שֵׁנָא, שֵׁנָה <8142>; from SLEEP (verb) <3462>] ▶ **This word refers to a state of rest that occurs naturally and regularly during which there is little or no conscious thought. A person dreams intermittently.** In the Old Testament, God often used the time of sleep as a time to display Himself and His will to His servants and people (Gen. 28:16; Judg. 16:14, 20). God spoke in dreams to pagans during their sleep (Dan. 2:1). The loss of sleep is serious and must be regained (Gen. 31:40). It is

used as a euphemism for death (Job 14:12; Ps. 76:5). Sleep can be put off for a time (Ps. 132:4). Excessive sleep leads to poverty (Prov. 20:13); but the sleep of a laboring worker is sweet (Eccl. 5:12). *

3 ***šᵉnaṯ*** [fem. noun: שְׁנַת <8153>; from SLEEP (verb) <3462> a.] ► **This word is used figuratively of closing one's eyelids for sleep in context.** Ref.: Ps. 132:4. In this case, it was for a worthy cause. ¶

– 4 Ps. 78:65 ➔ SLEEPING <3463>.

SLEEP (verb) – 1 ***hāzāh*** [verb: הָזָה <1957>; a prim. root (comp. SEE <2372>)] ► **This verb is used in a derisive way of useless, lazy persons who love to slumber and lounge about, mere dreamers among God's people; it is also translated to dream.** Ref.: Is. 56:10. ¶

2 ***yāšên*** [verb: יָשֵׁן <3462>; a prim. root] ► **a. A verb meaning to fall asleep, to sleep; it also means to be dead.** It indicates the process of going into a sleeping state (Gen. 2:21). It indicates the state of being asleep without fear or danger (Ezek. 34:25). It is used as a euphemism for one who is dead (Job 3:13). It is used of God's failure to act or inactivity on behalf of His people (Ps. 44:23). But, in fact, the psalmist asserts that God, who watches over His people, does not sleep (Ps. 121:4). In its intensive form, it means to make someone go to sleep (Judg. 16:19), as when Delilah caused Samson to fall asleep. *

b. A verb meaning to become old, to be chronic, to linger. It presents the concept of a long duration of time in general (Deut. 4:25: to grow old, to remain long, to live a long time); or for a specific situation (Lev. 26:10: store, supply, harvest); or disease (Lev. 13:11: old, chronic). ¶

– 3 1 Kgs. 3:20; 18:27; Dan. 12:2; Hos. 7:6 ➔ SLEEPING <3463>.

SLEEPING – ***yāšên*** [adj.: יָשֵׁן <3463>; from SLEEP (verb) <3462>] ► **This word designates someone in a state of rest during which there is little or no conscious thought.** It refers to persons in a sleeping state or condition (1 Sam. 26:7, 12; 1 Kgs. 3:20); of God seemingly sleeping, being inactive (Ps. 78:65). It is used mockingly to describe the god Baal sleeping on the job (1 Kgs. 18:27). It describes those dead in the ground (Dan. 12:2). It has the sense of smoldering or active human passion that has been inordinately aroused (Hos. 7:6); others prefer to read the verb; see SLEEP (verb) <3462> a. here. Other refs.: Song 5:2; 7:9. ¶

SLEET – Ps. 78:47 ➔ FROST <2602>.

SLEEVE – Jer. 38:12 ➔ WRIST <679>.

SLICE – 2 Kgs. 4:39 ➔ CUT (verb) <6398>.

SLIGHT (BE) – ***qālal*** [verb: קָלַל <7043>; a prim. root] ► **This word means to be trivial, to be swift. It is used in many different ways, but most uses trace back to the basic idea of this word, which is lightness.** In its most simple meaning, it referred to the easing of a burden (Ex. 18:22); lightening judgment (1 Sam. 6:5); lessening labor (1 Kgs. 12:9, 10; 2 Chr. 10:9, 10); or the lightening of a ship (Jon. 1:5). This idea leads to its usage to describe people who were swifter than eagles (2 Sam. 1:23); swift animals (Hab. 1:8); or days that pass quickly (Job 7:6; 9:25). When describing an event or a circumstance, it means trivial (1 Sam. 18:23; 1 Kgs. 16:31; Is. 49:6). In many instances, it is used to describe speaking lightly of another or cursing another: a person cursing another person (Ex. 21:17; 2 Sam. 16:9–11; Neh. 13:2); people cursing God (Lev. 24:11); or God cursing people (Gen. 12:3; 1 Sam. 2:30; Ps. 37:22). *

SLIGHTED (BE) – Prov. 12:9 ➔ DESPISED (BE) <7034>.

SLIME – Gen. 11:3; 14:10; Ex. 2:3 ➔ TAR <2564>.

SLING (noun) – 1 ***margêmāh*** [fem. noun: מַרְגֵּמָה <4773>; from STONE (verb) <7275>] ► **This word is a weapon made of cords or ropes fastened by one end to a piece of leather broad enough to enwrap**

a small stone. Ref.: Prov. 26:8. The cords are whirled, and the stone is released to strike its target. ¶
2 ***qela'*** [masc. noun: קֶלַע <7050>; from SLING (verb) <7049>] ▶ **This word refers to a weapon used to throw stones with great speed and accuracy.** It was made of a piece of leather to hold the stone and then fastened to two cords (1 Sam. 17:40, 50; 25:29; 2 Chr. 26:14). The term *'aḇnê-qᵉla'* refers to slingstones (Job 41:28; Zech. 9:15). For another meaning of the Hebrew word, see CURTAIN <7050>. ¶

SLING (verb) – ***qāla'*** [verb: קָלַע <7049>; a prim. root] ▶ **This word means to throw with force or hurl something.** It indicates the casting or throwing stones by using a weapon devised for this purpose (1 Sam. 17:49). It is used figuratively of destroying Israel's enemies (1 Sam. 25:29); or casting, slinging Israel out of the land of promise (Jer. 10:18). Other ref.: Judg. 20:16. For another meaning of the Hebrew word, see CARVE <7049>. ¶

SLINGER – ***qallā'*** [masc. noun: קַלָּע <7051>; intens. from SLING (verb) <7049>] ▶ **This word refers to a man armed with a sling (a weapon designed to throw stones).** It refers to men armed with slings who, in context, went about slinging stones in a destructive manner as an act of war, ruining the land (2 Kgs. 3:25). ¶

SLINGSTONE – Job 41:28; Zech. 9:15 ➔ SLING (noun) <7050>.

SLIP – 1 ***mā'aḏ*** [verb: מָעַד <4571>; a prim. root] ▶ **This word means to slide, to waver, to give way.** It indicates an action of something or someone that shakes, wobbles, slips; to have one's feet (figuratively) slip, to fail (2 Sam. 22:37; Job 12:5; Ps. 18:36).

In a strong figurative sense, it means to be indecisive, to be tempted to turn away, to waver (Ps. 26:1). A fool that slips is like a faithless person or nation, unstable, untrustworthy (Prov. 25:19; Ezek. 29:7). Other refs.: Ps. 37:1; 69:23. ¶
– 2 Deut. 19:5 ➔ REMOVE <5394>.

SLIPPERY – Ps. 35:6 ➔ FLATTERY <2519>.

SLIPPERY WAYS, SLIPPERY PATHS – Jer. 23:12 ➔ FLATTERY <2519>.

SLIPS (THAT) – Prov. 25:19 ➔ UNSTEADY <4154>.

SLOOP – Is. 2:16 ➔ VESSEL <7914> a.

SLOPE – 1 ***'āšēḏ*** [masc. noun: אֶשֶׁד <793>; from an unused root meaning to pour] ▶ **This word refers to the slanted banks and surrounding area of the temporary streams or wadis in the territory that separated the Moabites and the Amorites from each other.** Ref.: Num. 21:15; also translated stream. The word is found in the poetry of the book of the wars of Yahweh. ¶
2 ***'ᵃšēḏāh*** [fem. noun: אֲשֵׁדָה <794>; from <793> above] ▶ **This word refers to slanted ground; it is found three times.** Twice it refers to the mountain slopes of Mount Pisgah (Deut. 3:17; 4:49). It is rendered as slopes of the south from which the Lord comes to His people in the remaining usage (NIV, Deut. 33:2). Others prefer to translate this difficult word differently (NASB, flashing lightning; NKJV, KJV, fiery law). ¶
3 ***'ēšdāṯ*** [fem. noun: אֵשְׁדָּת <799>; from FIRE <784> and LAW <1881>] ▶ **The NIV prefers to render the word as slopes (slanting grounds) in Deuteronomy 33:2 since it refers to the Lord as coming from the south (*yomin*) down from the mountains.** The Hebrew word is also translated FIERY LAW and FLASHING LIGHTNING; see these entries. ¶

SLOTH – Eccl. 10:18 ➔ SLUGGARD <6103>.

SLOTHFUL – Prov. 19:24; 21:25; etc. ➔ SLUGGARD <6102>.

SLOTHFUL (BE) – Judg. 18:9 ➔ HESITATE <6101>.

SLOTHFULNESS – Prov. 19:15; Eccl. 10:18 ➔ SLUGGARD <6103>.

SLOW – ***'ārēk*** [adj.: אָרֵךְ <750>; from PROLONG <748>] ► **This word primarily describes feelings pertaining to a person: either being slow of temper or patient. It also means long, drawn out.** In wisdom literature, the person who is patient and does not anger quickly is extolled as a person of understanding (Prov. 14:29; Eccl. 7:8). When used to describe God, the Hebrew word means slow to anger and is immediately contrasted with God's great love, faithfulness, and power, demonstrating His true nature and His long-suffering (Ex. 34:6). Also, this Hebrew word is used of an eagle's long pinions or feathers (Ezek. 17:3). *

SLOW (BE) – Judg. 18:9 ➔ HESITATE <6101>.

SLOW (SEEM) – Hab. 2:3 ➔ LINGER <4102>.

SLOWLY – ***'aṭ, 'iṭṭiym*** [adv.: אַט, אִטִּים <328>; from an unused root (perhaps meaning to move softly)] ► **This word means gently, with gentleness; it is also translated softly, dejectedly, despondently, meekly.** It occurs five times (Gen. 33:14; 2 Sam. 18:5; 1 Kgs. 21:27; Job 15:11; Is. 8:6). ¶

SLUG – Ps. 58:8 ➔ SNAIL <7642>.

SLUGGARD – ***'āṣēl*** [adj.: עָצֵל <6102>; from HESITATE <6101>] ► **This word means sluggish, lazy; it is also translated lazy man, slothful.** It is best known for its translation as sluggards, useless, lazy persons who always fail because of laziness that becomes moral failure (Prov. 6:6, 9); their souls want nothing, and they get nothing (Prov. 13:4). These persons take no initiative (Prov. 19:24); don't do their tasks on time (Prov. 20:4); will not work (Prov. 21:25). They create imaginary excuses (Prov. 22:13). Their wealth and health deteriorate (Prov. 24:30); but they consider themselves wise (Prov. 26:13–16). Other refs.: Prov. 10:26; 15:19. ¶

SLUICE – Is. 19:10 ➔ REWARD (noun) <7938> b.

SLUMBER (noun) – [1] ***tenûmāh*** [fem. noun: תְּנוּמָה <8572>; from SLUMBER (verb) <5123>] ► **This word indicates a state of sleep, rest, when persons most often dream.** Ref.: Job 33:15. Sleep and slumber are parallel in Psalm 132:4 and Prov. 6:4, 10. Too much sleep and slumber leads to the downfall of the fool and the sluggard (Prov. 24:33). ¶
– [2] Prov. 23:21 ➔ DROWSINESS <5124>.

SLUMBER (verb) – ***nûm*** [verb: נוּם <5123>; a prim. root] ► **This word indicates to sleep, to rest.** It is found in Isaiah 5:27; 56:10; Nah. 3:18. It is used figuratively of God's sending a spirit of slumber (or somnolence, drowsiness) on His enemies (Ps. 76:5; lit.: they slumbered their sleep). God Himself never sleeps or slumbers (Ps. 121:3, 4). ¶

SMALL – [1] ***miṣ'iyrāh*** [adj.: מִצְעִירָה <4704>; fem. of LITTLE ONE <4705>] ► **This word indicates that something is little in size, especially compared to other things of the same kind.** Ref.: Dan. 8:9. In this context, a horn stands for a person. ¶
[2] ***qāṭān, qāṭōn*** [adj.: קָטָן, קָטֹן <6996>; from LOATHE <6962> (which properly means to cut off)] ►
a. This word also means little, insignificant, unimportant. It describes what is not large but diminutive in size. It describes what is small in respect to something else: animals and fish, both small and great (Ps. 104:25); vessels (2 Chr. 36:18); weights (Deut. 25:13, 14). It is used to indicate small children (Gen. 44:20; 2 Sam. 9:12); the small or smallest child, which can also mean the younger or youngest child (Gen. 9:24; 27:15; Judg. 15:2; 1 Sam. 16:11; 17:14). It can have the sense of weak or insignificant (1 Sam. 9:21; 2 Kgs. 18:24). It is used of uttering a minor prophecy (Num. 22:18). It refers to what may appear as insignificant times and events in general (Zech. 4:10).
b. This word also means little, insignificant. Its meanings are basically the same as a. It refers to: persons who are young (1 Sam. 20:35); persons young compared

to others (Gen. 48:19); with the definite article, it may indicate the youngest (Gen. 42:13, 15, 20). Used in the phrase young (*Qāṭān, gāḏôl*) and old, it means everyone (Gen. 19:11; cf. Deut. 1:17; 1 Kgs. 22:31). It describes things as small: a little robe (1 Sam. 2:19); the idea of too small employs *qāṭôn + min* (<4480>) (1 Kgs. 8:64). It is used in a figurative sense to indicate trifling, unimportant things (Ex. 18:22, 26; 1 Sam. 20:2; Jer. 49:15; Obad. 1:2); weak things (Amos 7:2, 5). *
– [3] Gen. 19:20; Job 8:7 ➔ LITTLE ONE <4705> [4] 2 Kgs. 19:26; Is. 37:27 ➔ SHORT <7116> [5] Is. 16:14 ➔ VERY <4213>.

SMALL (BE) – [1] Is. 49:19 ➔ DISTRESSED (BE) <3334> [2] Jer. 30:19 ➔ BRING LOW <6819>.

SMALL (MAKE) – Amos 8:5 ➔ WORTHY (BE NOT) <6994>.

SMALL COMPANY – 2 Chr. 24:24 ➔ LITTLE ONE <4705>.

SMALL MATTER (BE A) – 1 Sam. 18:23 ➔ DESPISED (BE) <7034>.

SMALL NUMBER – 2 Chr. 24:24 ➔ LITTLE ONE <4705>.

SMALL SERVING – Prov. 15:17 ➔ ALLOWANCE <737>.

SMALL THING (BE A) – 2 Sam. 7:19; 1 Chr. 17:17 ➔ WORTHY (BE NOT) <6994>.

SMASH – [1] Judg. 5:26 ➔ CRUSH <4277> [2] Dan. 2:40 ➔ SHATTER <2827>.

SMEAR – ***ṭāpal*** [verb: טָפַל <2950>; a prim. root] ► **This word means to cover or to plaster.** It is used figuratively of persons covering over or smearing (Job 13:4: to smear, to be a forger, to whitewash; Ps. 119:69: to smear, to forge) over the truth or to the Lord's plastering over or sealing over one's iniquity (Job 14:17: to sew, to cover, to wrap). ¶

SMELL (noun) – [1] ***rêyaḥ*** [Aramaic fem. noun: רֵיחַ <7382>; corresponding to ODOR <7381>] ► **This word indicates the odor produced by fire when it singes or burns clothing.** Ref.: Dan. 3:27. ¶
– [2] Eccl. 10:1: to give a bad smell ➔ STINK <887>.

SMELL (verb) – Ex. 7:21; 16:20 ➔ STINK <887>.

SMELT – ***ṣûq*** [verb: צוּק <6694>; a prim. root (identical with OPPRESS <6693> through the idea of narrowness, e.g., of orifice)] ► **This word means to pour out, to refine.** It refers to a process of removing impurities, dross, from ores containing metals (Job 28:2). It describes God's disciplining of a people (Is. 26:16: to pour out). It is used of pure oil pouring forth like refined metal from a rock (Job 29:6). ¶

SMILE (verb) – [1] ***bālag*** [verb: בָּלַג <1082>; a prim. root] ► **This word means to exhibit a pleasant expression, to rejoice, to flash up, to gain strength. It is also translated to take comfort, to have a cheer, to find a cheer, to have joy; to recover, to regain strength, to enjoy life; to wear a smile, to be cheerful, to be of good cheer, to comfort oneself; to flash forth, to strengthen.** It indicates a recovery of fortune because God turns His anger away (Job 10:20; Ps. 39:13). The word in this context means a recovery of strength and good spirits. It is the opposite of a depressed state of mind (Job 9:27). On the other hand, it depicts God's swift action in judgment against the strong (Amos 5:9). ¶
– [2] Job 10:3 ➔ SHINE, SHINE FORTH <3313>.

SMILE (WEAR A) – Job 9:27 ➔ SMILE (verb) <1082>.

SMITE – [1] ***hālam*** [verb: הָלַם <1986>; a prim. root] ► **This word means to hammer, to strike down. It carries the**

implication of conquering and disbanding. The author of Judges used this word to describe Jael hammering the tent peg through Sisera's head (Judg. 5:26). Isaiah employed this word figuratively to describe nations breaking down grapevines (Is. 16:8) and people overcome by wine (Is. 28:1). Other refs.: Judg. 5:22; 1 Sam. 14:16; Ps. 74:6; 141:5; Prov. 23:35; Is. 41:7. ¶

2 ***nāgap*** [verb: נָגַף <5062>; a prim. root] ▶ **The verb means to strike; it is also translated to defeat, to strike down, to slay, to overthrow, to rout.** It is most often used within the context of warring nations when one nation struck another (Lev. 26:17; Num. 14:42; Deut. 28:7, 25). At times, this was followed by the death of many (Judg. 20:35; 1 Sam. 4:10; 2 Sam. 18:7; at others, it merely signified defeat in war, with no mention of death (1 Kgs. 8:33; 2 Kgs. 14:12). God is often the One who smote, which led to incurable illness (2 Chr. 21:18; Zech. 14:12, 18); or even death (1 Sam. 25:38; 2 Sam. 12:15). This word is also used to describe the stumbling of the foot (Prov. 3:23; Jer. 13:16); the causing of injury to another person (to hurt, to hit, to strike) (Ex. 21:22); or to an animal (to hurt, to butt, to injure) (Ex. 21:35). *

– 3 Num. 24:10; Jer. 31:19; Ezek. 21:12 ➔ STRIKE <5606> 4 2 Kgs. 15:5; Job 1:19 ➔ TOUCH <5060> 5 Dan. 2:34, 35 ➔ STRIKE <4223> 6 Dan. 5:6 ➔ KNOCK <5368>.

SMITE TOGETHER – ***piyq*** [masc. noun: פִּיק <6375>; from OBTAIN <6329> (which is from a root identical with STUMBLE <6328>)] ▶ **This word means tottering. It only occurs in one passage, where the devastation of Nineveh is portrayed.** "She is empty, and void, and waste: and the heart melteth, and the knees smite together, and much pain is in all loins, and the faces of them all gather blackness" (Nah. 2:10: KJV); it is also translated: to shake together, knocking, to tremble, to give way. ¶

SMITER – Ps. 35:15 ➔ ATTACKER <5222>.

SMITH – ***masgêr*** [masc. noun: מַסְגֵּר <4525>; from CLOSE <5462> (in the sense of to fit things together)] ▶ **This word indicates someone skilled to work with various metals and perform many tasks; it is also translated metal worker, artisan.** Refs.: 2 Kgs. 24:14, 16; Jer. 24:1; 29:2. He was highly prized by any captor. The Hebrew word also means a prison, a place of incarceration; see PRISON <4525>. ¶

SMOKE (noun) – 1 ***'āšān*** [masc. noun: עָשָׁן <6227>; from SMOKE (noun and verb) <6225>] ▶ **Smoke is a vaporous matter with suspended particles of carbon in it, arising from something burning.** It is a feature of a mysterious smoking oven at the time God made a covenant with Abraham (Gen. 15:17); and was a part of the theophany at Mount Sinai, created because of God's presence (Ex. 19:18). It is also used in figurative depictions of the Lord going forth in battle or in anger (2 Sam. 22:9); as well as in God's depiction of Leviathan's nostrils (Job 41:20). Its quick dissipation is used in similes and metaphors (Ps. 37:20; 68:2; Prov. 10:26; Hos. 13:3). Smoke is a feature of the Day of the Lord (Joel 2:30). *

2 ***maśśā'āh*** [fem. noun: מַשָּׂאָה <4858>; from CARRY <5375> (in the sense of a conflagration, e.g., from the rising of smoke)] ▶

a. This word refers also to a cloud of smoke. It is used of the visible vaporous matter arising from something burning. It also will accompany the coming of the Lord (Is. 30:27). ¶

b. Some translators prefer this rendering of the noun as something lifted up, carried, a burden or message or a lifting up of heavy clouds. Ref.: Is. 30:27. ¶

3 ***qiyṭôr, qiyṭōr*** [fem. noun: קִיטוֹר, קִיטֹר <7008>; from BURN <6999>] ▶ **This word indicates thick, dense smoke; vapor, figuratively cloud.** It refers to the cloud of fine particles that arise from burning something (Gen. 19:28); the smoke arising from the land and cities of Sodom and Gomorrah (Gen. 19:28). It is difficult to discern something through smoke (Ps. 119:83). It indicates rising smoke, but in

context it could be translated figuratively as clouds (Ps. 148:8; also translated vapours, mist). ¶
– [4] Ezek. 8:11 ➔ the smoke of the cloud ➔ lit.: the fragrance (or the thickness) of the cloud ➔ WORSHIPPER <6282> b., c.

SMOKE (IN) – Ex. 20:18 ➔ SMOKING <6226>.

SMOKE (noun and verb) – ***'āšan*** [verb: עָשַׁן <6225>; a prim. root] ▶ **The literal meaning of this Hebrew word is literally or figuratively to smolder or smoke, (to be) a smoke; it also means to be angry, to be furious.** Refs.: Ex. 19:18; Ps. 144:5. Metaphorically, it was used by the psalmist to convey the idea of fuming anger (Ps. 74:1; 80:4). Other refs.: Deut. 29:20; 104:32. ¶

SMOKING – [1] ***'āšēn*** [adj.: עָשֵׁן <6226>; from SMOKE (noun and verb) <6225>] ▶ **This word indicates that something is smoking, has smoke coming off of it or out of it; it also means smoldering.** It is used of Mount Sinai when God descended on it (Ex. 20:18); and to logs that are burnt up, used up but still smoking. In the latter case, it is used figuratively of political leaders (Is. 7:4). ¶
– [2] Is. 42:3 ➔ DARK <3544>.

SMOKING SACRIFICE – Jer. 44:21 ➔ INCENSE <7002>.

SMOLDER – Deut. 29:20; 104:32; Ps. 74:1; 80:4 ➔ SMOKE (noun and verb) <6225>.

SMOLDERING – [1] Is. 7:4 ➔ SMOKING <6226> [2] Is. 42:3 ➔ DARK <3544>.

SMOOTH – [1] ***ḥālāq*** [adj.: חָלָק <2509>; from SHARE (verb) <2505>] ▶ **This word indicates soft, not rough; it also indicates flattering.** It refers to smooth stones in a riverbed or ravine (Is. 57:6) that possibly represent idolatrous objects. Used figuratively, the word depicts slippery or dangerous conditions of life (Ps. 73:18); or a mouth that spins things deceitfully (Prov. 26:28; Ezek. 12:24; Dan. 11:32) and falsely (Ps. 12:2, 3). An adulteress uses smooth and sweet-tasting speech (Prov. 5:3). ¶
[2] **smoothness: *ḥallāq*** [masc. noun: חַלָּק <2511>; from SHARE (verb) <2505>] ▶ **Some translate this word as *ḥālāq* (<2509> above) in Isaiah 57:6.** But it has essentially the same meaning and refers to smooth stones in a ravine or dry riverbed. ¶
[3] ***ḥalluq*** [adj.: חַלֻּק <2512>; from SHARE (verb) <2505>] ▶ **This word means, polished, not rough.** It describes the five stones that David picked up from a streambed to use against Goliath and put in his sling (1 Sam. 17:40). ¶
[4] ***ḥelqāh*** [fem. noun: חֶלְקָה <2513>; fem. of PORTION <2506>] ▶
a. This word denotes flattery, sleekness, a smooth part. It indicates an area of skin without hair (Gen. 27:16). It indicates the smooth or flattering lips of the treacherous (Ps. 12:2, 3); of the adulterous (Prov. 6:24); or unstable circumstances (Ps. 73:18). False prophets spoke with deceitful and slippery words (Is. 30:10; also translated pleasant). ¶
b. This word denotes ground, portion. It is used to indicate a plot of ground (Gen. 33:19; Josh. 24:32; Ruth 4:3; Amos 4:7); of good, productive ground (2 Kgs. 3:19). It is used of an assigned portion of a field or plot (Deut. 33:21). It designates a particular location in the phrase *ḥelqaṯ haṣṣûrîy*, the field of swords (2 Sam. 2:16). *
[5] ***môrāṭ*** [adj.: מוֹרָט <4178>; from TURN OVER <3399>] ▶ **This word describes the people of Ethiopia who were a smooth-skinned people.** Ref.: Is. 18:2, 7. ¶

SMOOTH (MAKE) – Is. 26:7 ➔ WEIGH, WEIGH OUT <6424>.

SMOOTH WORD – Dan. 11:32 ➔ FLATTERY <2514>.

SMOOTH, SMOOTH-SKINNED – Is. 18:2, 7 ➔ PULL, PULL OUT <4803>.

SNAIL – [1] ***šablûl*** [masc. noun: שַׁבְּלוּל <7642>; from an unused root meaning to flow] ▶ **This word is used in a figure of**

speech to indicate the melting away of persecutors and the wicked, like a snail, a slow-moving gastropod that leaves a slimy trail behind it that soon disappears; it is also translated slug. Ref.: Ps. 58:8. ¶
– [2] Lev. 11:30 ➔ SAND LIZARD <2546>.

SNAKE – [1] Ex. 4:3; Num. 21:6; Deut. 8:15; etc. ➔ SERPENT <5175> [2] Is. 30:6; 59:5 ➔ VIPER <660> [3] Mic. 7:17 ➔ CRAWL <2119>.

SNAP – Eccl. 12:6 ➔ BIND <7576>.

SNARE (noun) – [1] ***môqêš*** [masc. noun: מוֹקֵשׁ <4170>; from SNARE, BE SNARE <3369>] ▶ **This word means a trap, bait. The proper understanding of this Hebrew word is the lure or bait placed in a hunter's trap. From this sense comes the primary use of the term to mean the snare itself.** It is used to signify a trap by which birds or beasts are captured (Amos 3:5); a moral pitfall (Prov. 18:7; 20:25); and anything that lures one to ruin and disaster (Judg. 2:3; Prov. 29:6). *
[2] ***paḥ*** [masc. sing. noun: פַּח <6341>; from TRAPPED (BE) <6351>] ▶ **This word means a trap, a device to catch a prey; it is translated bird trap.** It is used in its literal sense in Amos 3:5, Proverbs 7:23, and Ecclesiastes 9:12. But more often it is used figuratively for a human ensnarement. Jeremiah prophesied that a snare awaited Moab (Jer. 48:43); while Proverbs said that snares were set for the wicked (Prov. 22:5). Eliphaz told Job that snares surrounded him (Job 22:10). The psalmist's path was filled with the snares of his enemies (Ps. 140:5; 142:3). But retribution was envisioned as the enemies' tables turned into a snare (Ps. 69:22). *
[3] ***qeneṣ*** [masc. noun: קֶנֶץ <7078>; from an unused root prob. meaning to wrench] ▶
a. This word signifies a trap for hunting. It is used figuratively of catching, laying a snare for right words, seeking for right words to express one's position (to hunt for words) (Job 18:2).
b. This word is taken by some to refer to an ending, a conclusion to the speaking of many words by Job. Ref.: Job 18:2: end. ¶
[4] ***ṣammiym*** [masc. noun: צַמִּים <6782>; from the same as VEIL <6777>] ▶ **This word refers to a trap, a robber.** It seems to refer to a robber or someone out to take a person's riches (Job 5:5: schemer, robber; thirsty); but in Job 18:9 it has the sense of a snare, a hindrance that traps the wicked. ¶
– [5] Job 18:9 ➔ SNARE (noun) <6782> [6] Eccl. 9:14 ➔ NET <4685> [7] Lam. 3:47 ➔ PIT <6354>.

SNARE (LAY A) – ***qôš*** [verb: קוֹשׁ <6983>; used only as denom. for SNARE, BE SNARED <3369>] ▶ **This word means to set a trap; it is also translated to ensnare. The root idea may be that of bending, as the energy stored in bent wood powers a snare.** *Qôš* occurs only in Isaiah 29:21 where it figuratively refers to the laying of a snare to cause trouble and to silence the person who judges justly and thwarts the wicked. ¶

SNARE (noun and verb) – Jer. 5:26 ➔ FOWLER <3353>.

SNARE (verb) – Deut. 12:3; 1 Sam. 28:9; Ps. 9:16 ➔ ENSNARE <5367>.

SNARE, BE SNARED – ***yāqōš*** [verb: יָקֹשׁ <3369>; a prim. root] ▶ **The word refers primarily to catching animals, especially birds.** Refs.: Ps. 124:7; Eccl. 9:12. However, this word always refers figuratively to the catching of a person or people in an undesirable situation. The bait of these snares is people's desire for other gods (Deut. 7:25; Ps. 141:9, cf. Ps. 141:4). Pride makes persons susceptible to snares (Jer. 50:24 [cf. Jer. 50:31, 32]) while humility (Prov. 6:2) and the help of God may deliver them. In two similar passages in Isaiah, Israel is snared by their rejection of God's word (Is. 8:15; 28:13). ¶

SNARED (BE) – Is. 42:22 ➔ TRAPPED (BE) <6351>.

SNARED (FROM BEING) – Prov. 3:26 ➔ CAPTURE (noun) <3921>.

SNARES (LAY) – Ps. 38:12 ➔ ENSNARE <5367>.

SNATCH – [1] Judg. 21:21 ➔ CATCH (verb) <2414> [2] Ps. 52:5 ➔ TAKE <2846>.

SNATCH AWAY – [1] ***ḥāṯap*** [verb: חָתַף <2862>; a prim. root] ▶ **This word refers to taking away.** It refers to a person's sudden death brought about by the Lord (Job 9:12) who alone knows our day of birth and day of death. ¶
– [2] Job 22:6 ➔ SHRIVEL <7059> c. [3] Jer. 8:13 ➔ CONSUME, BE CONSUMED <5486>.

SNEER – [1] Ps. 10:5 ➔ BREATHE <6315> [2] Mal. 1:13 ➔ BREATHE <5301>.

SNEEZE – ***zārar*** [verb: זָרַר <2237>; a prim. root; comp. STRANGER (BE) <2114>] ▶ **This word properly means to scatter, to spread out over a large area; hence, to sneeze (in doing which particles of mucus are scattered from the nostrils).** It describes the reaction of the Shunammite's son as he was being restored to life by Elisha (2 Kgs. 4:35), evidently breathing in air once again. ¶

SNEEZING – ***ᵃṭiyšāh*** [fem. noun: עֲטִישָׁה <5846>; from an unused root meaning to sneeze] ▶ **The word is also translated snorting (NIV), neesing (KJV, obsolete for sneezing).** It is used to describe the sneezing, the sudden sharp coughing of Leviathan, a magnificent animal created by God (Job 41:18). ¶

SNIFF – Mal. 1:13 ➔ BREATHE <5301>.

SNOOP – Prov. 6:27 ➔ TAKE <2846>.

SNORT – [1] Ps. 10:5 ➔ BREATHE <6315> [2] Mal. 1:13 ➔ BREATHE <5301>.

SNORTING – [1] ***naḥar, naḥᵃrāh*** [נַחַר, נַחֲרָה <5170>; from an unused root meaning to snort or snore] ▶
a. A masculine noun used of the neighing or forcing air through the nostrils of a horse. Ref.: Job 39:20. ¶
b. A feminine noun used of the snorting or neighing of horses. Ref.: Jer. 8:16. ¶
– [2] Job 41:18 ➔ SNEEZING <5846>.

SNOW – [1] ***bōr*** [masc. noun: בֹּר <1253>; the same as CLEANNESS <1252>] ▶ **This word refers to lye, washing, soda, potash; a substance formed from wood and plant ashes. It was used as a cleansing agent.** It parallels the word for soap or snow (Job 9:30) and is described as something with which Job would wash his hands. It was used to remove dross, according to Isaiah (Is. 1:25). ¶
[2] ***šeleg*** [masc. noun: שֶׁלֶג <7950>; from SNOW (BE AS WHITE AS) <7949>] ▶
a. This word refers to frozen white crystals of water that fall from the sky. Its white color was considered the example of choice for whiteness (Ex. 4:6; Num. 12:10; 2 Kgs. 5:27); leprosy was as white as snow. The coldness of snow is noted (Prov. 25:13). Snowy days were rare and memorable in Israel (2 Sam. 23:20). The Lord would make one's sins as white as snow and cleanse them away (Is. 1:18). David prayed for the Lord›s cleansing from his sin, making him «whiter than snow» (Ps. 51:7).
b. The Hebrew word also means soap, soapwort. The NIV renders this word as soap in the text (Job 9:30). Soapwort is a genus of plants whose sap forms a lather with water for washing. *
[3] ***tᵉlag*** [Aramaic masc. noun: תְּלַג <8517>; corresponding to <7950> above] ▶ **This word refers to frozen crystals of water having a white color.** The white color of snow is used to describe the appearance of the Ancient of Days (Dan. 7:9). ¶

SNOW (BE AS) – Ps. 68:14 ➔ SNOW (BE AS WHITE AS) <7949>.

SNOW (BE AS WHITE AS) – ***šālag*** [verb: שָׁלַג <7949>; a prim. root (properly, meaning to be white)] ▶ **This word properly means to be white, to be as snow. It refers to the falling of snow at the time of the Lord's giving Israel a great victory in the wintertime (or perhaps an allusion to the numerous slain enemies fallen to the ground in battle).** Ref.: Ps. 68:14. Zalmon is probably located in the area of Bashan, 60 miles southeast of Damascus. ¶

SNUFF – Mal. 1:13 ➔ BREATHE <5301>.

SNUFF OUT – Job 18:5; 21:17; Prov. 13:9; 20:20; 24:20 ➔ EXTINGUISH <1846>.

SNUFFERS – 1 ***mᵉzammereṯ*** [fem. plur. noun: מְזַמֶּרֶת <4212>; from PRUNE <2168>] ▶ **This word designates wick trimmers. It is used in the plural form only.** It was used as its name indicates to put out lamps and to trim wicks (1 Kgs. 7:50; 2 Kgs. 12:13; 25:14; 2 Chr. 4:22; Jer. 52:18). ¶
– 2 Ex. 25:38; 37:23; Num. 4:9; 1 Kgs. 7:49; 2 Chr. 4:21 ➔ WICK TRIMMER <4457>.

SO – ***sô'*** [masc. proper noun: סוֹא <5471>; of foreign deriv.] ▶ **A king of Egypt.** Ref.: 2 Kgs. 17:4. ¶

SO THAT – 1 ***ma'an*** [particle: מַעַן <4616>; from ANSWER (verb) <6030> a.] ▶ **This word is used with the preposition *lᵉ* prefixed also meaning because of, for the sake of, with respect to, in order that.** Its use as a preposition is found often (Deut. 30:6; 1 Kgs. 8:41; 11:39; 2 Kgs. 19:34; Ps. 23:3; 25:11; 31:3; Ezek. 20:9); with an infinitive following to express purpose, in order to, in order that (Gen. 37:22; Ex. 1:11; 9:16; 10:1; 11:9; 2 Kgs. 10:19). Followed by the imperfect form of the verb with or without *ᵃšer*, it expresses either purpose or result in order that, so that (Gen. 12:1318:19; Deut. 27:3; Josh. 3:4; Jer. 27:15; 42:6; Hos. 8:4). *
2 ***pen*** [conj.: פֶּן <6435>; from TURN (verb) <6437>] ▶ **This word indicates the prevention of a possible event or of an event that will occur unless it is stopped.** Refs.: Gen. 3:22; 11:4; 19:19; 26:7, 9; 2 Sam. 20:6. It indicates a negative purpose or result (Gen. 3:3). It is found at the beginning of a sentence meaning in order that not, lest (Is. 36:18). Used with the perfect form of the verb, the condition may have already been fulfilled (2 Kgs. 2:16 and above in 2 Sam. 20:6). *

SOAP – 1 ***bōriyṯ*** [fem. noun: בֹּרִית <1287>; fem. of SNOW <1253> (in the sense of washing)] ▶ **This Hebrew word refers to soap, alkali. Its cleaning agent is derived from a soap-bearing plant.** It removes external dirt but could not remove the stain from Israel's guilt before God (Jer. 2:22). It is designated as the soap of a person who washes cloth or a fuller (Mal. 3:2) and so would be of high quality. ¶
– 2 Job 9:30 ➔ SNOW <1253> 3 Job 9:30 ➔ SNOW <7950>.

SOAR – Job 39:26 ➔ FLY (verb) <82>.

SOCKET – 1 Ex. 26:19, 21, 25; 35:11; Num. 3:36, 37 ➔ BASE (noun) <134> 2 Job 31:22 ➔ SHOULDER <7929> 3 Zech. 14:12 ➔ HOLE <2356>.

SOCKINGS (THAT TURNED IN) – 1 Kgs. 6:34 ➔ FOLDING <1550>.

SOCO, SOCOH – ***śôḵô, śôḵōh, śôkōh, śôḵô*** [proper noun: שׂוֹכוֹ, שׂוֹכֹה, שֹׂכֹה, שׂוֹכוֹ <7755>; from HEDGE (MAKE A) <7753>]: edge, fence ▶
a. Son of Heber. Ref.: 1 Chr. 4:18. ¶
b. A city in Judah. Ref.: Josh. 15:48. ¶
c. A city in Judah-Shephelah. Refs.: Josh. 15:35; 1 Sam. 17:1; 1 Kgs. 4:10; 2 Chr. 11:7; 28:18. ¶

SOD – Gen. 25:29 (past tense of to seethe) ➔ to boil ➔ PROUDLY (DEAL) <2102>.

SODA – ***neṯer*** [masc. noun: נֶתֶר <5427>; from LOOSE (LET) <5425>] ▶ **This word indicates natron, a substance used in detergents, native soda (potassium nitrate, sodium nitrate); it is also translated nitre, lye.** Refs.: Prov. 25:20; Jer. 2:22. ¶

SODDEN – Ex. 12:9; Num. 6:19 ➔ BOILED <1311>.

SODI – ***sôḏiy*** [masc. proper noun: סוֹדִי <5476>; from COUNSEL (noun) <5475>]: a confidant ▶ **Father of Gaddiel, the spy representing Zebulun.** Ref.: Num. 13:10. ¶

SODOM – ***sᵉḏōm*** [proper noun: סְדֹם <5467>; from an unused root meaning to scorch]: burning ▶ **A city destroyed by the Lord for its egregious sins, especially "sodomy."** Lot lived in it for a short while (Gen. 13) but was rescued from its destruction. It was located in the southern area of Canaan (Gen. 10:19), southeast of the Dead Sea. It engaged in war with several northern kings (Gen. 14:2–22). The story of its destruction illustrates its wickedness, for there were not enough righteous persons in it to deliver it (Gen. 18:16–26; 19:1–28). It became a symbol of wickedness (Ezek. 16:46–56). *

SODOMITE – See PROSTITUTE (MALE TEMPLE, CULT, SHRINE) <6945>.

SOFT – Dan. 2:41, 43 ➔ MIRY <2917>.

SOFT (MAKE) – Ps. 65:10 ➔ MELT AWAY <4127>.

SOFT (MAKE, BE) – Job 23:16: Ps. 55:21 ➔ FAINT (BE, MAKE) <7401>.

SOFTEN – [1] Ps. 65:10 ➔ MELT AWAY <4127> [2] Is. 1:6 ➔ FAINT (BE, MAKE) <7401>.

SOFTLY – [1] ***lā'ṭ*** [masc. noun: לָאט <3814>; from COVER (verb) <3813> (or perhaps for the act. part. of WRAP <3874>)] ▶ **This word indicates silence, softness, or secrecy. It means quietness, stealth, care.** Used once with *b*ᵉ on the front, it functions as an adverb meaning secretly, carefully, quietly (Judg. 4:21; also translated: quietly, secretly). ¶
– [2] Gen. 33:14; 1 Kgs. 21:27; Is. 8:6 ➔ SLOWLY <328> [3] Ruth 3:7 ➔ ENCHANTMENT <3909>.

SOIL – ***ṭānap̱*** [verb: טָנַף <2936>; a prim. root] ▶ **This word means to defile, to make dirty.** In context it refers to making feet that have just been washed dirty again, soiled (Song 5:3). ¶

SOJOURN – ***gûr*** [verb: גּוּר <1481>; a prim. root] ▶ **This word means to stay, to dwell as a foreigner; in the reflexive sense, to seek hospitality with.** The term is commonly used of the patriarchs who sojourned in Canaan (Gen. 26:3; 35:27); places outside Canaan (Gen. 12:10; 20:1; 21:23; 32:4; 47:4); Naomi and her family in Moab (Ruth 1:1); the exiles in Babylonia (Jer. 42:15). Metaphorically, the term is used of one who worships in God's Temple (Ps. 15:1; 61:4). It is used reflexively with the meaning to seek hospitality within 1 Kings 17:20. *

SOJOURNER – [1] ***tôšāḇ, tōšāḇ, tišbêy*** [masc. noun: תּוֹשָׁב, תֹּשָׁב, תִּשְׁבֵּי <8453>; from DWELL <3427>] ▶ **This word implies temporary visitors who were dependent in some way on the nation in which they were residing; it also means a foreigner.** It denotes a sojourner who received shelter from a priest (Lev. 22:10); foreigners who were closely linked to the economy of the people (Lev. 25:40, 47); and a wanderer with close ties to the land occupied by another people (Gen. 23:4). David proclaimed himself to be such a sojourner with the Lord (Ps. 39:12). *
– [2] See STRANGER <1616>.

SOJOURNING – ***māḡûr, maḡôr*** [masc. noun: מָגוּר, מָגֻר <4033>; from SOJOURN <1481> in the sense of lodging] ▶ **This word means a stay for a certain time; it also means a dwelling place.** Most often, this word is used to describe Israel as a sojourning people, who will inherit the land of Canaan, where they sojourned (Gen. 17:8; 37:1; Ex. 6:4). The psalmist described the preciousness of God's statutes in his sojourning (Ps. 119:54). The wicked are described as having evil in their dwelling places (Ps. 55:15), which will result with God removing them from their dwelling places (Ezek. 20:38). As a result, the wicked will have no offspring in their dwelling places (Job 18:19). Other refs.: Gen. 28:4; 36:7; 47:9. ¶

SOLACE (noun) – Job 16:5 ➔ COMFORT (noun) <5205> a.

SOLACE (verb) – Prov. 7:18 ➔ ENJOY <5965> a.

SOLDERING – Is. 41:7 ➔ JOINT <1694>.

SOLDIER – Dan. 3:20 ➔ MAN <1401>.

SOLEMN ASSEMBLY – See ASSEMBLY <6116>.

SOLEMN SOUND – Ps. 92:3 ➔ MEDITATION <1902>.

SOLID – 2 Chr. 4:21 ➔ PUREST <4357>.

SOLITARY – [1] ***galmûḏ*** [adj.: גַּלְמוּד <1565>; prob. by prolongation from ROLL (verb) <1563>] ▶ **This word means and is also translated barren, desolate.** It can depict a barren night, one in which a child was not born, as Job wished (Job 3:7). It describes Zion as a barren woman without children (Is. 49:21) or the failure of the godless company to bear offspring (Job 15:34). It indicates a picture of solitary waste or desolation for the outcasts of society (Job 30:3) and the utterly despised and disdained of the community. ¶
– [2] Ps. 68:6 ➔ ONLY <3173> [3] Is. 27:10 ➔ ALONE <910>.

SOLITARY LAND – ***gᵉzērāh*** [fem. noun: גְּזֵרָה <1509>; from CUT (verb) <1504>] ▶ **This word denotes a secluded place; it is also translated land apart, land not inhabited, remote area, remote place.** It refers to an isolated, infertile place or land to which the scapegoat was sent on the Day of Atonement (Lev. 16:22). It includes the idea of an uninhabitable land, possibly the desert. ¶

SOLOMON – ***šᵉlōmōh*** [masc. proper noun: שְׁלֹמֹה <8010>; from PEACE <7965>]: peaceful ▶ **He was the second most renowned king of all Israel during the monarchy. He was David's son through Bathsheba. In contrast to his father David, a man of war, Solomon was noted for the peace given by the Lord to Israel during his days, thus typifying the Messiah during His coming reign of peace.** He was born in Jerusalem (2 Sam. 5:14). The Lord instructed Nathan the prophet that the child was to be named Jedidiah, meaning "beloved by the Lord" (2 Sam. 12:24, 25). David named him Solomon. The Lord's special name indicated His continued love for David's descendants (2 Sam. 7). Solomon became king in 970 B.C. and ruled forty years. He was known for his wisdom, but in his old age, he was led away from serving the Lord (1 Kgs. 3:1–28). He organized Israel effectively, completed many building projects, including his own palace and the Lord's Temple (1 Kgs. 6, 7). He dedicated the Temple, and the Lord appeared to him (1 Kgs. 8, 9) for a second time (cf. 1 Kgs. 3:4–15). His first and most important request from the Lord was for wisdom to rule his people (1 Kgs. 3:4–15). His wisdom was the greatest the world had ever seen (1 Kgs. 4:29–34; 10). He built many other projects, and his wisdom attracted visitors from the ends of the earth (1 Kgs. 10) as his greatness and wealth increased (1 Kgs. 10:14–29).

After Solomon's apostasy due to his pagan wives, the Lord raised up many adversaries to harass and bring him down (1 Kgs. 11:14–40). Solomon's oppressive use of taxation, state-forced work teams, and heavy tribute, especially in northern Israel, resulted in a state of rebellion by the time he died. Solomon's name is etched on the Wisdom Literature of the Old Testament (Proverbs, Ecclesiastes, Song of Solomon). *

SON – [1] ***bên*** [masc. noun: בֵּן <1121>; from BUILD <1129>] ▶ **This word occurs almost five thousand times in the Old Testament. Although the most basic meaning and general translation is son, the direct male offspring of human parents (Gen. 4:25; 27:32; Is. 49:15), it is more generally a relational term because of its variety of applications.** This word can express an adopted child (Ex. 2:10); children in general, male and female (Gen. 3:16; 21:7; Ex. 21:5); descendants, such as grandsons (Josh. 22:24, 25, 27; 2 Kgs. 10:30); relative age (Gen. 5:32; 17:12; Prov. 7:7; Song 2:3); the male offspring of animals (Lev. 22:28; Deut. 22:6, 7; 1 Sam. 6:7, 10); a member of a guild, order, or class (1 Kgs.

20:35; 1 Chr. 9:30; Ezra 4:1); a person with a certain quality or characteristic (1 Sam. 14:52; 2 Sam. 3:34; 2 Kgs. 14:14). It may also have a gentilic sense and designate a person from a certain place (Gen. 17:12; Ps. 149:2; Ezek. 23:15, 17). *

2 ***bᵉnêy*** [Aramaic masc. noun: בְּנֵי <1123>; corresponding to <1121> above] ▶ **This word is the Aramaic equivalent of the Hebrew word *bên* <1121>, meaning son.** Thus, it is only used in the Aramaic sections of the Old Testament (Ezra 4:8–6:18; 7:12–26; Dan. 2:4–7:28; Jer. 10:11). Although it may refer to the offspring of animals (Ezra 6:9), it is used mostly of the sons of particular groups of people: of Israel (Ezra 6:16); of captives (Dan. 2:25; 5:13; 6:13); of kings (Ezra 6:10; 7:23); of those who accused Daniel (Dan. 6:24); of people in general (Dan. 2:38; 5:21). ¶

3 ***bar*** [Aramaic masc. noun: בַּר <1247>; corresponding to <1121> above] ▶ **This word refers to sons in general or to specific sons.** Refs.: Ezra 5:1, 2; 6:10; Dan. 5:22; 6:24. In its plural form, it refers to Israelites (Ezra 6:16) or captives, exiles (Ezra 6:16; Dan. 2:25; 5:13). In its singular and plural forms, it is combined with the word for mankind, humankind (*'ᵉnāš*) to denote a human being (Dan. 7:13) in general or people in general (Dan. 2:38; 5:21). In Daniel 7:13 with the preposition *bᵉ* added to *bar*, it denotes a being "like" a son of man. Combined with the word for god(s), it refers to a divine or angelic creature (Dan. 3:25). *

4 ***bar*** [masc. noun: בַּר <1248>; borrowed (as a name) from <1247> above] ▶ **This word refers to the specially anointed Son of the Lord to whom the nations will pay homage.** Refs.: Ps. 2:12. But it may also depicts any son in general who needs to learn wisdom (Prov. 31:2). ¶

5 ***mānôn*** [masc. noun: מָנוֹן <4497>; from CONTINUE <5125>] ▶ **This word refers to a slave who has become a son through his master's careful nurture and care.** Ref.: Prov. 29:21; ESV: heir. Some translators and scholars, because of the word *pampers* earlier in the proverb, prefer to render this verb as grief, sorrow, pain (Prov. 29:21; NIV: insolent). ¶

– 6 Gen. 21:23; Job 18:19; Is. 14:22 → OFFSPRING <5209> 7 2 Sam. 21:16, 18 → DESCENDANT <3211> 8 2 Chr. 32:21 → COMING FORTH <3329>.

SON-IN-LAW – 1 ***ḥāṯān*** [masc. noun: חָתָן <2860>; from MARRIAGE <2859>] ▶ **This word refers to a daughter's husband, a bridegroom.** It is used to indicate a daughter's husband (Gen. 19:12, 14; Judg. 15:6; 19:5; 1 Sam. 18:18; Neh. 6:18). It is used of Ahaziah as the son-in-law of Ahab's family because his mother, Athaliah, was Ahab's daughter (2 Kgs. 8:27). In Exodus 4:25, Moses' wife addressed him with this word as her bridegroom (KJV, NKJV: husband). It is used figuratively of the Lord's gracious treatment of His oppressed people as His bridegroom (Is. 61:10; 62:5). Other refs.: Ex. 4:26; 1 Sam. 22:14; Neh. 13:28; Ps. 19:5; Jer. 7:34; 16:9; 25:10; 33:11; Joel 2:16. ¶

– 2 1 Sam. 18:21–23, 26, 27; 1 Kgs. 3:1 → MARRIAGE <2859> a.

SONG – 1 ***zāmiyr*** [masc. noun: זָמִיר <2158>; from SING <2167>] ▶ **This word means a melody with words; it also indicates a singer, a psalmist.** It indicates songs (2 Sam. 23:1), and in this verse, David is called the pleasant (sweet) singer of songs of Israel. It refers to other types of songs: a hostile song of the ruthless (Is. 25:5; KJV: branch); a praise song to the Lord (Ps. 95:2; also translated psalm, song of praise); songs of joy even in the night given by God (Job 35:10); the statutes of the Lord as songs to God (Ps. 119:54). Preceded by *'ēṯ*, time, it defines the time as the time of songs, singing (Song 2:12), a festive time. Other ref.: Is. 24:16 (song, song of praise, singing). ¶

2 ***zimrāh*** [fem. noun: זִמְרָה <2172>; from SING <2167>] ▶ **This word means a melody with words; it is also translated melody, singing, sound, music, psalm.** It is used of the sound or playing of a musical instrument or of singing (Is. 51:3; Amos 5:23) as one feature of a revived Zion. It is used as a metaphor for God as Israel's song (Ex. 15:2; Ps. 118:14; Is. 12:2); NIV translates the word defense. Other refs.: Ps. 81:2; 98:5. ¶

3 ***zimrāṯ*** [fem. noun: זִמְרָת <2176>; from SING <2167>] ▶ **This word is used as a metaphor to indicate the Lord as Israel's song (a melody with words).** Refs.: Ex. 15:2; Ps. 118:14; Is. 12:2, but see also <2172> above. ¶

4 ***neḡiynāh, neḡiynaṯ*** [fem. noun: נְגִינָה, נְגִינַת <5058>; from PLAY <5059>] ▶

a. The word is used of a taunting song (a melody with words) in some contexts, a song of mocking or ridicule. Refs.: Job 30:9; Ps. 69:12; 77:6; Lam. 3:14. It is used also of stringed instruments or music (Is. 38:20; Lam. 5:14).

b. It denotes a stringed instrument. It describes certain psalms in their titles (4, 6, 54, 55, 61, 67, 76) and is found at the end of Hab. 3:19 as a technical musical term, "stringed instruments."

c. A feminine proper noun indicating Neginah (singular), Neginoth (plural); proper names for stringed instruments. It is used only in the psalm titles listed previously. ¶

5 ***rōn*** [masc. noun: רֹן <7438>; from SHOUT (verb) <7442>] ▶ **This word in Psalm 32:7 refers to songs (or shouts) of deliverance.** See SHOUT (verb) <7442> a. ¶

6 ***šiyrāh, šiyr*** [masc. noun: שִׁירָה, שִׁיר <7892>; from SING <7891>] ▶ **This word is used to indicate a type of lyrical song (a melody with words), a religious song, or a specific song of Levitical choirs.** In Amos, God uses the word to indicate that He will turn their joyful singing into mourning because of their unfaithfulness to Him (Amos 8:10). This time of mourning will be like that of mourning for an only son, and it will end in a bitter day. In a similar usage, Laban asks Jacob why he ran off secretly without telling Laban. If Jacob would have stated he wanted to leave, Laban would have sent him off with joy and singing (Gen. 31:27). Isaiah uses the word to indicate the type of songs that will no longer be sung when the Lord lays waste the earth (Is. 24:9). The type of drunken revels associated with drinking wine and beer will no longer be heard.

This word is also used in Nehemiah to denote songs of praise (Neh. 12:46). In this particular context, Nehemiah indicates that the music directors in the days of David and Asaph led songs of praise. The noun is also used to indicate specific songs of Levitical choirs accompanied by musical instruments. When David and the Israelites brought the ark of the Lord from Baalah of Judah (Kiriath Jearim), they celebrated with songs (1 Chr. 13:8). Amos uses the word to denote complacency and apathy. Many Israelites lay on ivory couches and strummed their musical instruments while dining on fattened calves and choice lambs. These people were so caught up in themselves that they did not even give thought to the threat of destruction by the Lord. *

– 7 Lam. 3:63 ➔ MOCKING SONG <4485>.

SOON – 1 ***ḥiyš*** [adv.: חִישׁ <2440>; from HASTE (MAKE) <2439>] ▶ **This word means quickly; it indicates the haste with which fleeting days are gone.** Ref.: Ps. 90:10; also translated quickly. ¶

– 2 Deut. 4:26 ➔ QUICK, QUICKLY <4118> b.

SOOT – ***šeḥôr*** [masc. noun: שְׁחוֹר <7815>; from BLACK (BE) <7835>] ▶ **This word means dinginess, blackness.** It is used to describe a punishment of Israel, i.e., they were blacker than soot, and their skin had shriveled on their bones (Lam. 4:8; KJV: coal). The people of different nations told the Israelites that they must leave for they were seen as unclean. This is similar to the descriptions of the results of the Day of the Lord, which will be a day of blackness (see Joel 2:2). This blackness figuratively represents an army of locusts with which Yahweh will punish those who live in the land for their sin. For this reason, the prophet declared that all who live in the land should and will tremble in fear. ¶

SOOTH – Is. 1:6 ➔ FAINT (BE, MAKE) <7401>.

SOOTHE – ***šāḇaḥ*** [verb: שָׁבַח <7623>; a prim. root] ▶ **The primary meaning of this word is to calm or still; it also means**

to stroke, to praise. It was used particularly in reference to the calming of the sea (Ps. 65:7). A secondary current of meaning associated with this word is that of praise. In this sense, it was employed to denote either the exaltation of God (Ps. 63:3); or the holding of something in higher esteem (Eccl. 4:2). The connection between the two may stem from the soothing effect of praise on the ego. *

SOOTHING – Gen. 8:21; Ex. 29:18, 25, 41; Lev. 1:9, 13, 17; Ezek. 6:13; 16:19; 20:28, 41; etc. ➔ PLEASING <5207>.

SOOTHING (BE) – Job 23:16: Ps. 55:21 ➔ FAINT (BE, MAKE) <7401>.

SOOTHSAYER – [1] Dan. 2:27; 4:7; 5:7, 11 ➔ CUT (verb) <1505> [2] Deut. 18:10, 14 ➔ WITCHCRAFT (PRACTICE) <6049>.

SOPHERETH, HASSOPHERETH – ***sōp̱eret̲, hassōp̱eret̲*** [proper noun: סֹפֶרֶת, הַסֹּפֶרֶת <5618>; fem. act. part. of NUMBER <5608> b.]: scribe ▶
a. **The sons of Sophereth returned with Zerubbabel from the Babylonian captivity.** Refs.: Ezra 2:55 (KJV, NKJV); Neh. 7:57. ¶
b. **Hassophereth.** The same as a. Ref.: Ezra 2:55 (NASB, ESV, NIV). ¶

SORCERER – [1] ***kaššāp̱*** [masc. sing. noun: כַּשָּׁף <3786>; from WITCHCRAFT (USE) <3784>] ▶ **This word refers to a magician.** It occurs once in the Hebrew Bible, i.e., in Jeremiah 27:9. ¶
– [2] Dan. 2:2; Mal. 3:5 ➔ WITCHCRAFT (USE, PRACTICE) <3784>.

SORCERESS – Is. 57:3 ➔ WITCHCRAFT (PRACTICE) <6049>.

SORCERY – [1] ***kešep̱*** [masc. noun: כֶּשֶׁף <3785>; from WITCHCRAFT (USE) <3784>] ▶ **This word means occult magic, witchcraft.** While specific practices included under this term cannot be established, the word occurs along with other similar terms such as enchantments and soothsaying, thus providing clues through association (Is. 47:9, 12; Mic. 5:12). This word always appears in a plural form, and half the time, it is modified by the word "numerous" (2 Kgs. 9:22; Is. 47:9, 12). The plurals may indicate different manifestations, or they may represent plurals of intensification. Twice this term is linked with metaphorical harlotry (2 Kgs. 9:22; Nah. 3:4). In the Old Testament, magic was connected with several nations: Babylon, Nineveh, the Northern Kingdom and the Southern Kingdom (2 Kgs. 9:22; Is. 47:9–12; Mic. 5:12; Nah. 3:4). ¶
– [2] Num. 23:23; 24:1 ➔ ENCHANTMENT <5173>.

SORCERY (PRACTICE) – Deut. 18:10, 14 ➔ WITCHCRAFT (PRACTICE) <6049>.

SORCERY (USE, PRACTICE) – 2 Chr. 33:6; etc. ➔ WITCHCRAFT (USE, PRACTICE) <3784>.

SORE (adj.) – Mic. 2:10 ➔ GRIEVOUS <4834>.

SORE (LAY) – Judg. 14:17 ➔ OPPRESS <6693>.

SORE (noun) – [1] ***nega‘*** [masc. noun: נֶגַע <5061>; from TOUCH <5060>] ▶ **This word means a blemish, a mark, a stroke, a plague.** It comes from the verb *nāga‘*, meaning to touch or to strike, and is best understood as a blemish that has been created by touching or striking. In the majority of instances, it described a blemish inflicted by leprosy or a skin disease that the priest was to discern (used over sixty times in Lev. 13–14). It also referred to a physical injury (stroke, assault, punishment) inflicted by another person (Deut. 17:8; 21:5; Is. 53:8); or by God Himself (stripes, flogging) (Ps. 89:32). When describing land or property, it is best translated plague (Gen. 12:17; Ex. 11:1; 1 Kgs. 8:37). At times, this word described a nonphysical blemish (also translated affliction, blow, burden, plague, wound) (1 Kgs. 8:38; 2 Chr. 6:29; Prov. 6:33). *
– [2] Jer. 30:13; Hos. 5:13 ➔ WOUND (noun) <4205>.

SORE (RUNNING) – Lev. 21:20; 22:22 ➔ SCAB <3217>.

SOREK – ***śôrêq, śōrêq*** [proper noun: שׂוֹרֵק, שֹׂרֵק <7796>; the same as VINE (CHOICE) <8321>]: vineyard ▶ **The valley where Delilah lived.** Ref.: Judg. 16:4. ¶

SORREL – ***śārōq*** [masc. noun: שָׂרֹק <8320>; from HISS <8319> in the sense of redness] ▶
a. This word refers to a reddish brown color; it is also translated brown. It is the color of certain horses that Zechariah sees in a vision. Sorrel is a light reddish-brown color (Zech. 1:8).
b. This word is also translated speckled in the KJV. It is another color of certain horses seen in Zechariah's vision (Zech. 1:8). It is any color with various small specks of a different color scattered in it. ¶

SORROW (noun) – 1 ***ᵃḇôy*** [interj.: אֲבוֹי <17>; from WILLING (BE) <14>] ▶ **An exclamation of anxiety or pain found in Proverbs 23:29.** It translates well as woe. It parallels four other words that refer to sorrow, complaints, undeserved wounds, and red eyes. ¶
2 ***dᵉʾāḇāh*** [fem. noun: דְּאָבָה <1670>; from SORROW (verb) <1669>] ▶ **This word means and is also translated dismay, terror.** It depicts the hopelessness and dismay that Leviathan produces in those lying before him (Job 41:22) or the fact that sorrow or dismay themselves go before his advance (cf. KJV, sorrow is turned to joy; NKJV, sorrow dances before him). ¶
3 ***yāḡôn*** [masc. noun: יָגוֹן <3015>; from AFFLICT <3013>] ▶ **This word indicates grief, torment, trouble.** It indicates a state or condition of utter loss and despair (Gen. 42:38; 44:31) that seems beyond cure (Jer. 8:18). It is an emotion that is the opposite of gladness or joy (Esther 9:22) and equal to a state of mourning. It is brought on by the oppression of an enemy and the absence of the Lord in one's life (Ps. 13:2) but also by one's sin (Ps. 31:10; also translated anguish). It is related to being overcome by drunkenness (Ezek. 23:33). This condition is the bedfellow of misery and oppression (Ps. 107:39). The redeemed of the Lord experience a liberty from sorrow (Is. 35:10). Other refs.: Ps. 116:3; Is. 51:11; Jer. 20:18; 31:13; 45:3. ¶
4 ***mᵉginnāh*** [fem. noun: מְגִנָּה <4044>; from DELIVER <4042> (in the bad sense of a covering)] ▶ **This word may mean sorrow, hardness, but insolence fits the context also.** It is used only once in a difficult context. Ref.: Lam. 3:65; also translated hardness, dullness). ¶
5 ***ʿaṣṣeḇeṯ*** [fem. noun: עַצֶּבֶת <6094>; from HURT <6087>] ▶ **This noun means hurt, injury, pain, suffering.** It is used only in Hebrew poetry and refers to the grief or sorrow that causes fear of discipline (Job 9:28); the grief caused by idolatry (Ps. 16:4); the grief that comes with being brokenhearted (Ps. 147:3: wound); the grief caused by one who winks with the eye (Prov. 10:10: trouble, grief); or grief that causes the spirit to be broken (Prov. 15:13). Although sometimes portrayed in physical terms (Ps. 147:3), this term clearly refers to emotional suffering and not physical pain or injury. ¶
6 ***tûgāh*** [fem. noun: תּוּגָה <8424>; from AFFLICT <3013>] ▶ **This word means and is also translated grief, heaviness.** It refers to the emotion and process of feeling a great loss and loneliness (Ps. 119:28). A son who is a fool creates grief in his parents (Prov. 10:1; 17:21). For the wicked, even the end of joy is grief (Prov. 14:13). ¶
– 7 Gen. 3:16a, 17 ➔ PAIN (noun) <6093> 8 Ex. 3:7; Ps. 38:17; Eccl. 2:23; Is. 53:3, 4; Jer. 30:15; 45:3; etc. ➔ SUFFERING <4341> 9 Ex. 15:14; Job 6:10 ➔ PAIN (noun) <2427> 10 Deut. 28:65 ➔ DESPAIR (noun) <1671> 11 Ps. 35:12 ➔ LOSS OF CHILDREN <7908> 12 Ps. 39:2; Is. 17:11; 65:14 ➔ PAIN (noun) <3511> 13 Ps. 139:24; Is. 14:3 ➔ PAIN (noun) <6090> 14 Prov. 10:22 ➔ PAIN (noun) <6089> 15 Prov. 22:8; Ps. 90:10 ➔ NOTHINGNESS <205> 16 Is. 29:2 ➔ LAMENTATION <592> 17 Is. 50:11 ➔ TORMENT (noun) <4620>.

SORROW (CAUSE) – ***dûḇ*** [verb: דּוּב <1727>; a prim. root] ▶ **This verb means**

to waste away, to pine away, to consume. It describes a pining away or wasting away of the souls (*nepheš*) of God's people because they rejected the statutes of the Lord (Lev. 26:16; KJV, cause sorrow of heart). ¶

SORROW (verb) – 1 ***dā'aḇ*** [verb: דָּאַב <1669>; a prim. root] ► **This word means to become faint, sad. It indicates to fail or waste away.** Negated, it indicates a spiritual and physical renewal, for a redeemed Israel will never faint away or languish again (Jer. 31:12: to sorrow, to languish). The Lord will restore those who languish (Jer. 31:25). It refers to eyesight wasting away (Ps. 88:9); also translated to mourn, to be dim, to grow dim. ¶
– 2 Zeph. 3:18 → AFFLICT <3013>.

SORROWFUL – Job 6:7 → ILLNESS <1741>.

SORROWFUL (BE) – Zeph. 3:18 → AFFLICT <3013>.

SORRY (BE) – 1 ***nāḥam*** [verb: נָחַם <5162>; a prim. root] ► **This word means to feel sadness, disappointment; it also means to pity, to comfort, to avenge. The verb often means to be sorry or to regret.** The Lord was sorry that He had made people (Gen. 6:6); He led Israel in a direction to avoid war when they left Egypt, lest they became so sorry and grieved that they would turn back (Ex. 13:17). The Lord had compassion on His people (i.e., He became sorry for them because of the oppression their enemies placed on them [Judg. 2:18]). While the Lord could be grieved, He did not grieve or become sorry so that He changed His mind as a human does (1 Sam. 15:29). The word also means to comfort or console oneself. Isaac was comforted after Sarah, his mother, died (Gen. 24:67).

The verb always means to console or comfort. Jacob refused to be comforted when he believed that Joseph had been killed (Gen. 37:35). To console is synonymous with showing kindness to someone, as when David consoled Hanun, king of the Ammonites, over the death of his father (2 Sam. 10:2). God refused to be consoled over the destruction of His people (Is. 22:4; 40:1); yet He comforts those who need it (Ps. 119:82; Is. 12:1). The passive form of the word means to be comforted: the afflicted city of Zion would be comforted by the Lord (Is. 54:11; 66:13). In the reflexive stem, it can mean to get revenge for oneself (Gen. 27:42; Ezek. 5:13); to let oneself be sorry or have compassion (Num. 23:19; Deut. 32:36); and to let oneself be comforted (Gen. 37:35; Ps. 119:52). *
– 2 Ps. 38:18 → ANXIOUS (BE, BECOME) <1672>.

SORT – Dan. 1:10 → JOY <1524>.

SOTAI – ***sôṭay*** [masc. proper noun: סוֹטַי <5479>; from TURN ASIDE <7750>]: roving, unfaithful ► **Members of his family came back from the Babylonian captivity with Zerubbabel.** Refs.: Ezra 2:55; Neh. 7:57. ¶

SOUL – Job 30:15 → DIGNITY <5082>.

SOUND – 1 ***qāl*** [Aramaic masc. noun: קָל <7032>; corresponding to VOICE <6963>] ► **This word means something audible, a voice.** It refers often to the sound of musical instruments (Dan. 3:5, 7, 10, 15); to a voice uttering words from heaven (Dan. 4:31); to a human voice crying out (Dan. 6:20); to the sound of words uttered by the little horn (Dan. 7:11). ¶
2 ***têqa'*** [masc. noun: תֵּקַע <8629>; from BLOW (verb) <8628>] ► **This word refers to the sound of a trumpet.** It refers to the sound put forth by a shophar, a ram's horn (*b'têqa' šôp̱ār*) (Ps. 150:3; NIV: sounding), although it is normally translated as the sound of a trumpet. ¶
– 3 Job 37:2 → RUMBLING <1899> 4 Prov. 14:308 → CALMNESS <4832> 5 Is. 14:11 → NOISE <1998> 6 Amos 5:23 → SONG <2172>.

SOUND SLEEP – See DEEP SLEEP <8639>.

SOUNDING – Ps. 150:3 → SOUND <8629>.

SOUNDING AGAIN – Ezek. 7:7 → JOYFUL SHOUTING <1906>.

SOUNDNESS – ***m^etōm*** [masc. noun: מְתֹם <4974>; from COMPLETE (BE) <8552> (in the sense of to be whole)] ▶
a. This word indicates wholeness, entirety, entire; it is also translated health. It refers to a healthy, sound spot, a sign of wholeness, health (Ps. 38:3; Is. 1:6). In Judges 20:48 some translators render the word as "entire" (NASB) or "all" (NIV). Others take the Hebrew word in that verse as <4962> and render it as "men." See b., below. Other ref.: Ps. 38:7. ¶
b. Some translators translate the phrase in Judges 20:48 like this: "men" and beasts. The men of Israel struck down the tribe of Benjamin, from men down to beasts (Judg. 20:48, KJV, NKJV, ESV). It could refer to all the men but it is more probably comprehensive, including all women and children. See a. above for an alternate translation. ¶

SOUR GRAPE – Is. 18:5; Jer. 31:29, 30; Ezek. 18:2 → UNRIPE GRAPE <1155>.

SOUTH – 1 ***negeḇ*** [נֶגֶב <5045>; from an unused root meaning to be parched] ▶
a. A masculine noun meaning the South, south (see definition for <8486> below). It refers to the area around Beersheva and south of it (Gen. 12:9; 13:1; 20:1), but see b. below. It refers in general to the dry desert area in the south (Gen. 13:14; 24:62). It takes the definite article to mean the South, the southland. With *āh* added to it, the directive gives the sense of southward, to the south (Gen. 13:14). It is nuanced by the use of prepositions: *l^e*, from (Josh. 17:9, 10); *min-*, from or on the *negev*, south (1 Sam. 14:5). It is used to give directions, southward (Dan. 8:4, 9). Compound directions are expressed using several words: *qêḏ^emāh mimmûl negeḇ*, eastward toward the south, southeast (1 Kgs. 7:39); *p^e'aṯ-negeḇ* refers to a southern area or boundary of land in a geographical context (Num. 34:3). It is used of an Egyptian king of the South often in Daniel (Dan. 11:5, 6, 9, 11, etc.).
b. A proper noun, Negev, the southern district of Judah. It is used more specifically in contexts to indicate the area south of Judah (Jer. 13:19; 17:26). These areas are not always defined exactly. It may indicate land south of Babylon or southern Israel (Is. 21:1). *
2 ***têymān*** [fem. noun: תֵּימָן <8486>; denom. from RIGHT HAND <3225>] ▶ **This word refers to the direction lying to the right of a person facing east.** Refs.: Ex. 26:18, 35; 27:9; 36:23; 38:9. It can refer to a southern area of land (Josh. 15:1). With *āh* on the end, it means toward the south, southward (Ex. 26:18). It is used with reference to the entire south country (Zech. 6:6). It stands for a south wind controlled by God (Ps; 78:26; Song 4:16). It is used figuratively of the south personified (Is. 43:6; Ezek. 20:46). *
– 3 See RIGHT HAND <3225>.

SOUTH, SOUTHWARD – ***dārôm*** [masc. noun: דָּרוֹם <1864>; of uncertain deriv.] ▶ **This word indicates the south (Ezek. 42:18) or toward the south, southward (Job 37:17; Ezek. 40:24, 27). See definition in SOUTH <8486>.** It can give definition to something, e.g., a south gate (lit., the gate of the south, Ezek. 40:28). It indicates the opposite of the north (Eccl. 1:6; 11:3; Ezek. 41:11; 42:13). Other refs.: Deut. 33:23; Ezek. 20:46; 40:44, 45. ¶

SOW – ***zāra'*** [verb: זָרַע <2232>; a prim. root] ▶ **This word indicates the act of planting seed in the ground or field; it also means to bear seed.** Refs.: Gen. 47:23; Ex. 23:16; Deut. 22:9; Jer. 12:13. The verb can take two objects and mean to sow a city with salt (Judg. 9:45). It is used figuratively of sowing the wind (Hos. 8:7). It is the product of a plant or tree that produces its own seed in itself (Gen. 1:11, 29). *

SOWING – 1 ***zêrûa'*** [masc. noun: זֵרוּעַ <2221>; from SOW <2232>] ▶ **This word is a passive noun that indicates seed used for planting or that has already been planted in the ground.** Ref.: Lev. 11:37 (also translated planting, grain); Is. 61:11: the thing sown, what is sown, seed. It serves as a symbol that God will make righteousness and praise to spring up in the future. ¶ – [2] Ps. 126:6 ➔ BAG <4901> c. [3] See SEED <2233>.

SOWN – ***mizrā'*** [masc. noun: מִזְרָע <4218>; from SOW <2232>] ► **This word indicates that which is planted, a planted field.** It depicts a fertile land sown with gracious seeds, specifically land sown in Egypt along the Nile River (Is. 19:7). ¶

SOWN (THE THING, WHAT IS) – Is. 61:11 ➔ SOWING <2221>.

SPACE – ***rewaḥ*** [masc. noun: רֶוַח <7305>; from REFRESHED (BE) <7304> (in the sense of to be spacious)] ► **This word means distance, an interval, a respite, a relief, a liberation.** In Genesis, the word is used in Jacob's command to keep a space between the herds that were given as gifts to his brother Esau (Gen. 32:16). This space gave Jacob more time to prepare, looked more impressive to the receiver (i.e., controlled herds), and gave a better impression of the size or amount of the gift. In Esther, Mordecai indicated that if Esther kept silent, then relief for the Jews would arise from another place, and she and her father's family would die (Esther 4:14; KJV: enlargement). ¶

SPACE, CLEAR SPACE – 1 Kgs. 7:36 ➔ NAKEDNESS <4626>.

SPACIOUS – [1] 2 Sam. 22:20; Ps. 18:19; 31:8; 118:5 ➔ BREADTH <4800> [2] Jer. 22:14 ➔ REFRESHED (BE) <7304>.

SPACIOUS PLACE – Job 36:16 ➔ BROAD PLACE <7338>.

SPADE – Deut. 23:13 ➔ PEG <3489>.

SPAN – [1] ***zereṯ*** [fem. noun: זֶרֶת <2239>; from SCATTER <2219>] ► **This word indicates the width of a man's hand as a convenient means of measurement, about 25 centimeters.** Ref.: Ex. 28:16. It was the width of the breastpiece the high priest wore (Ex. 39:9), as well as the width of the border on the sacrificial altar of Ezekiel's vision (Ezek. 43:13). Goliath stood six cubits (about 9 feet) and a span (about four inches) (1 Sam. 17:4). The Lord, in great accuracy, measured the heavens to the span (Is. 40:12). ¶ – [2] Is. 48:13 ➔ SPREAD OUT <2946>.

SPAN LONG (OF A) – Lam. 2:20 ➔ CARED FOR (ONES) <2949>.

SPAN OF THE YEARS, OF LIFE – Ps. 39:5; 89:47 ➔ WORLD <2465>.

SPARE – [1] Job 33:24 ➔ DELIVER <6308> [2] See PITY (HAVE, SHOW) <2550>.

SPARK – [1] ***kiyḏôḏ*** [masc. noun: כִּידוֹד <3590>; from the same as DESTRUCTION <3589> (comp. AGATE <3539>)] ► **This word refers to a glowing or flashing bit of something.** In context it refers to a flash or sparkle of fire from Leviathan's mouth (Job 41:19) and stands in parallel with torches, lamps, or firebrands in the preceding line. ¶
[2] ***niyṣôṣ*** [masc. noun: נִיצוֹץ <5213>; from SPARKLE <5340>] ► **This word refers to a flash of light indicating a fire or that something has been consumed.** Ref.: Is. 1:31. ¶ – [3] Job 5:7 ➔ FLASH (noun) <7565> [4] Job 18:5 ➔ FLAME <7632> [5] Is. 50:11 ➔ FIREBRAND <2131> a.

SPARKLE – [1] ***nāṣaṣ*** [verb: נָצַץ <5340>; a prim. root] ► **This word is used of putting forth buds, blossoms, blooms, to gleam forth in beauty.** Refs.: Eccl. 12:5; Song 6:11; 7:12. It depicts the sparkle or shining of four strange living beings like the gleam of burnished bronze (Ezek. 1:7). ¶
[2] ***nāsas*** [verb: נָסַס <5264>; a prim. root] ►
a. This word is taken by some translators to be from a verb meaning to gleam, to display, to shine. It indicates the features of the stones of a crown, i.e., sparkling, shining. The sparkling stones symbolize God's people (Zech. 9:16). ¶
b. A verb meaning to raise as a beacon. It is used to indicate the raising up of a

symbol or a sign for something. It is used in a reflexive stem to indicate the raising of God's people as an ensign for the land of Israel (Zech. 9:16: to lift like a banner, an ensign). ¶

SPARKLING JEWEL – Is. 54:12 ➔ CRYSTAL <688>.

SPEAK – 1 ***dāḇaḇ*** [verb: דָּבַב <1680>; a prim. root (comp. STRENGTH <1679>)] ▶ **This word means to move slowly, to glide over. It is used in late Hebrew to mean to flow slowly or to drop. In the Old Testament, it suggests something that causes one to talk.** In the discourse of the Shulamite and the beloved, this word identifies the way wine gently or slowly moves over the taster's lips and teeth (Song 7:9). ¶

2 ***dāḇar*** [verb: דָּבַר <1696>; a prim. root] ▶ **This word means to say; it can also mean to promise, to sing, to think, etc.** God told Moses to tell Pharaoh what He said (Ex. 6:29). It can mean to promise (Deut. 1:11). When used with the word song, it can mean to sing or chant (Judg. 5:12). The word *dāḇar* can also mean to think, as when Solomon spoke in his heart (Eccl. 2:15). In Jeremiah, it means to pronounce judgment (Jer. 1:16). This verb also refers to speaking about or against someone (Mal. 3:13) or someone speaking to someone else (Mal. 3:16). It is closely related to the Hebrew noun *dāḇār* (WORD <1697>). *

3 ***mālal*** [verb: מָלַל <4448>; a prim. root] ▶ **This word means to say, to declare, to utter.** Except for an occurrence found in Proverbs 6:13 (a wicked man "speaks" [i.e., gives a sign] with his feet), the verb is utilized mostly with the intensive stem. Sarah said, "Who would have said to Abraham that Sarah would nurse children?" (Gen. 21:7). Elihu stated that his lips would utter upright knowledge to Job (Job 33:3; cf. Job 8:2). The psalmist exclaimed that no one can declare the mighty acts of God (Ps. 106:2). The term compares closely in meaning with the Hebrew verb *dāḇar* (<1696> above). ¶

4 ***mᵉlal*** [Aramaic verb: מְלַל <4449>; corresponding to <4448> above] ▶ **This word means to say, to talk. All undisputed instances of this term occur in the Aramaic sections of the book of Daniel.** In Daniel's vision of the four beasts, the fourth beast had a little horn upon which was a mouth speaking arrogantly (Dan. 7:8, 11, 20). This horn (symbolic of a king) spoke words against the Most High (Dan. 7:25). This term is closely related to the Hebrew verb *mālal* (<4448> above). Other ref.: Dan. 6:21. ¶

– 5 Is. 50:4 ➔ SUSTAIN <5790>.

SPEAK (WHO CANNOT, THAT CANNOT) – Prov. 31:8; Hab. 2:18 ➔ MUTE <483>.

SPEAR – 1 ***ḥᵃniyṯ*** [fem. noun: חֲנִית <2595>; from ENCAMP <2583>] ▶ **This word means a weapon with a long handle and a sharp point. It refers to the spear itself (1 Sam. 13:19); the wooden spear shaft when preceded by *'ēṣ* (1 Sam. 17:7); or even the head of the spear when used with *lahebeṯ* preceding it (1 Sam. 17:7).** The end or butt of the spear is indicated by the phrase *'aḥᵉrêy hahᵃniyṯ* (2 Sam. 2:23). It is used in a negative sense to refer to people's teeth as spears (Ps. 57:4). In the phrase *hêyrîq hᵃniyt*, it means to employ one's sheath of a spear or javelin (Ps. 35:3). *

2 ***kiyḏôn*** [masc. noun: כִּידוֹן <3591>; from the same as SPARK <3589>] ▶ **This word refers to a weapon of some kind, traditionally a spear (see previous definition) or javelin; it is also translated javelin.** It could possibly refer to a short sword for close fighting (Josh. 8:18, 26; 1 Sam. 17:6, 45). It is rendered as spear (Jer. 6:23, NIV, NASB); lance (Jer. 50:42, KJV); or javelin (Jer. 50:42, NASB). Other refs.: Job 39:23; 41:29. ¶

3 ***rōmaḥ*** [masc. noun: רֹמַח <7420>; from an unused root meaning to hurl] ▶ **This word refers to a weapon of war or a hunting tool with a long shaft and a pointed sharp end; it is also translated javelin.** Refs.: Num. 25:7; Judg. 5:8. It was capable of cutting one's flesh like a knife or sword (1 Kgs. 18:28). It was a major emblem of war (Ezek. 39:9; Joel 3:10). *

– 4 Job 41:7 ➔ WHIRRING <6767> b.

SPEAR, SPEARHEAD – ***qayin*** [masc. noun: קַיִן <7013>; from ACQUIRE <7069> in the original sense of fixity] ► **This word refers to the weapon wielded by Ishbi-Benob, a descendant of giants.** Its reference is probably to the entire weapon, including its shaft and metal end (2 Sam. 21:16). ¶

SPECIFICATION – 2 Chr. 24:13 ➔ PROPORTION <4971>.

SPECKLED – [1] ***nāqōḏ*** [adj.: נָקֹד <5348>; from an unused root meaning to mark (by puncturing or branding)] ► **This word indicates that something has marks of contrasting colors. It refers to a certain color scheme.** In context it refers to speckled cattle, sheep, or goats (Gen. 30:32, 33, 35, 39; 31:8, 10, 12). ¶
[2] ***ṣāḇûa'*** [adj.: צָבוּעַ <6641>; pass. part. of the same as DYED WORK, DYED MATERIALS <6648>] ► **This word is used to describe a bird of prey as having small, contrasting dots or marks of color, specks.** Ref.: Jer. 12:9. It was a detestable bird in Israel, unclean and therefore not to be eaten. ¶
– [3] Gen. 30:35, 39, 40; 31:8, 10, 12 ➔ STRIPED <6124> [4] Zech. 1:8 ➔ SORREL <8320> b.

SPEECH – [1] Prov. 5:3 ➔ MOUTH <2441> [2] Song 4:3 ➔ MOUTH <4057> [3] See WORD <1697>.

SPEECH (ENTICING, FAIR, SEDUCTIVE) – Prov. 7:21 ➔ LEARNING <3948>.

SPEECHLESS – Prov. 31:8; Hab. 2:18 ➔ MUTE <483>.

SPEECHLESS (BE, BECOME) – Dan. 10:15 ➔ BIND <481>.

SPEED (noun) – Ezra 6:12: with speed ➔ DILIGENTLY <629>.

SPEED (verb) – Is. 16:5 ➔ SKILLED <4106>.

SPEEDILY – [1] Ezra 6:13; 7:17, 21, 26 ➔ DILIGENTLY <629> [2] Ps. 140:11 ➔ OVERTHROW (verb) <4073> [3] Eccl. 8:11 ➔ QUICKLY <4120>.

SPEEDY – Is. 8:1 ➔ QUICK, QUICKLY <4118> a.

SPELT – ***kussemeṯ*** [fem. noun: כֻּסֶּמֶת <3698>; from TRIM <3697>] ► **This word refers to a species of wheat; it is also translated rie, rye, emmer, fitches.** It refers to a grain with split kernels which ripened later than flax and barley (Ex. 9:32; Is. 28:25; Ezek. 4:9). ¶

SPEND – Is. 58:10 ➔ OBTAIN <6329>.

SPENT (BE) – [1] Judg. 19:11 ➔ SUBDUE <7286> [2] 1 Sam. 9:7 ➔ GO <235>.

SPEW – Ps. 59:7 ➔ UTTER <5042>.

SPEW OUT – Jer. 51:34 ➔ WASH <1740>.

SPICE – [1] ***bāśām*** [masc. noun: בָּשָׂם <1313>; from an unused root meaning to be fragrant] ► **This word means an aromatic substance used to add flavor to food; it is also translated balsam. It is used figuratively in Song of Solomon 5:1 to refer to spices, some of the delights of the lover's beloved.** The beloved is pictured as the lover's garden of delight. ¶
[2] ***beśem, bōśem*** [masc. noun: בֶּשֶׂם, בֹּשֶׂם <1314>; from the same as <1313> above] ► **See previous definition. This word designates also balsam; fragrance, perfume. This item was highly prized.** It is mentioned several times in Song of Solomon to describe a fragrance and pleasant aroma (Song 4:10, 14; 5:1, 13; 6:2; 8:14). It is best translated as fragrance in Song of Solomon 4:16 (KJV, NKJV, spices). It was featured in beauty treatments (Esther 2:12). It was an ingredient in the anointing oil and fragrant incense used in the Tabernacle rituals (Ex. 25:6; 30:23; 35:8, 28). It was one of the gifts to Solomon from the Queen of Sheba and was a feature in the king's storehouses (2 Kgs. 20:13; Is. 39:2; Ezek. 27:22). *

[3] ***neḵō'ṯ*** [fem. noun: נְכֹאת <5219>; from CRUSHED <5218>] ▶ **This word means and is also translated gum, aromatic gum, spicery.** It refers to a highly desired spice from Gilead (Gen. 37:25) and transported by the Israelites to Egypt; but it was found in Canaan also (Gen. 43:11). ¶
– [4] Song 3:6 ➔ POWDER <81>.

SPICED – ***reqaḥ*** [masc. noun: רֶקַח <7544>; from COMPOUND <7543> (properly, perfumery)] ▶ **This word refers to something seasoned with spice; what is spiced.** It refers to something that has powdered spice added to it, e.g., spiced wine, to improve its taste and aroma (Song 8:2). ¶

SPICERY – Gen. 37:25 ➔ SPICE <5219>.

SPICES – Ezek. 24:10 ➔ OINTMENT (POT OF, JAR OF) <4841>.

SPIDER – [1] ***'akkāḇiyš*** [masc. noun: עַכָּבִישׁ <5908>; prob. from an unused root in the literal sense of entangling] ▶ **A group of arachnids that spin out silk threads made into webs.** Webs are weak and flimsy, very fragile and frail (Job 8:14). The unjust weave spider webs to catch people in evil plans (Is. 59:5). ¶
– [2] Prov. 30:28 ➔ LIZARD <8079> b.

SPIES – ***aṯāriym*** [masc. plur. noun and masc. proper noun: אֲתָרִים <871>; plur. from an unused root (prob. meaning to step)] ▶ **a. This word refers to secrets observers, individuals seeking secret information.** It is found in Numbers 21:1 (KJV). ¶
b. The name Atharim is found in other versions. ESV, NKJV, NASB, NIV, Num. 21:1. ¶

SPIKENARD – Song 1:12; 4:13, 14 ➔ NARD <5373>.

SPILL – ***nāgar*** [verb: נָגַר <5064>; a prim. root] ▶ **This verb indicates to pour, to pour out, to flow, to flow away. It has the sense of something gushing out, pouring forth.** It is used of water poured out on the ground (2 Sam. 14:14); of wine poured out as a symbol of judgment (Ps. 75:8); of a hand put forth (Ps. 77:2: to stretch, to run); of tears flowing from weeping eyes (Lam. 3:49; translated to flow, to pour down, to trickle down). It is used of the loss of possessions by the wicked (Job 20:28); and the giving over of persons to the sword (also translated to fall, to deliver, to pour out the *blood*, to hand over, to shed the *blood*) (Ps. 63:10; Jer. 18:21; Ezek. 35:5). It is used of the stones of cities cast down during God's judgments (Mic. 1:6); also Mic. 1:4. ¶

SPIN – ***ṭāwāh*** [verb: טָוָה <2901>; a prim. root] ▶ **This word means to make yarn from various materials.** It describes the tasks of the women of Israel as they skillfully spun goats' hair and blue, purple, and scarlet material, as well as linen for the Tabernacle or its accessories (Ex. 35:25, 26). ¶

SPINDLE – [1] ***peleḵ*** [masc. noun: פֶּלֶךְ <6418>; from an unused root meaning to be round] ▶ **This word also refers to a walking stick, a crutch; it also refers to a spool used for spinning.** It is a support device used by persons crippled or feeble, too weak to walk alone (2 Sam. 3:29: also translated staff, distaff). It refers to a spool or spindle holding thread or to cords for spinning (Prov. 31:19). For another meaning of the Hebrew word, see DISTRICT <6418>. ¶
– [2] Prov. 31:19 (KJV) ➔ DISTAFF <3601>.

SPIRIT – [1] ***rûaḥ*** [fem. noun: רוּחַ <7307>; from REFRESHED (BE) <7306> (in the sense of to blow)] ▶ **This word is used to refer to the Spirit of God or the Lord; it also means wind, breath.** The Spirit of the Lord inspired prophets to utter their prophecies (Num. 11:17, 25; 1 Sam. 10:6; 19:20); the Spirit of the Lord moved the prophets in time and space, as in the case of Elijah (1 Kgs. 18:12; Ezek. 2:2). The word could be modified by an adjective to refer to an evil spirit from the Lord (1 Sam. 16:15, 16; 1 Kgs. 22:22, 23). The Spirit of God is properly referred to as the Holy Spirit (Ps. 51:11; 106:33; Is. 63:10, 11). The Spirit produced and controlled the message of the prophets, even of a Mesopotamian prophet like Balaam (Num. 24:2). David was inspired to speak as a prophet by the Spirit (2 Sam. 23:2). The Spirit was present among the returned exiles in Jerusalem (Hag. 2:5; Zech. 4:6); and will be poured out in the latter days on all flesh, imparting prophecy, dreams, and visions (Joel 2:28). The Spirit of God was grieved by the rebellion of God's people (Is. 63:10).

The Lord's Spirit imparted other gifts: giving Bezalel skill and ability in all kinds of work (Ex. 31:3; 35:31); including the skill to teach others (see Ex. 35:34); the Spirit gave understanding as well (Job 32:8). The Spirit of the Lord had a part in creating the universe; the Spirit hovered over the deep and imparted life to persons (Gen. 1:2; Job 33:4); and even revived the dead (Ezek. 37:5, 10; 39:29).

The human spirit and the Spirit of God are closely linked with moral character and moral attributes. God will give His people a new spirit so they will follow His decrees and laws (Ezek. 11:19; 36:26). God's Spirit will rest on His people, transforming them (Is. 59:21). The Lord preserves those who have heavy spirits and broken hearts (Ps. 34:18; Is. 65:14).

The human spirit is sometimes depicted as the seat of emotion, the mind, and the will. In a song of praise, Isaiah asserted that the spirit desires the Lord (Is. 26:9; Job 7:11). The spirit imparts wisdom for understanding (Ex. 28:3; Deut. 34:9); and carrying out one's responsibilities. David prayed for a willing spirit to aid him (Ex. 35:21; Ps. 51:10).

The spirit made flesh alive and is the life force of living humans and animals. The Lord makes the spirits of people that give them life (Zech. 12:1). This spirit is from God and leaves at death (Gen. 6:3; Ps. 78:39; Eccl. 3:21). The spirit is pictured as giving animation, agitation, or liveliness; the Queen of Sheba was overcome in her spirit when she saw the splendors of Solomon's world (1 Kgs. 10:5). Not to have any spirit is to lose all courage; the Amorite kings had no spirit in them when they learned how Israel had crossed the Jordan. To be short of spirit is to be despondent or impatient (Eccl. 6:9).

The word also describes the breath of a human being or the natural wind that blows. The idols of the goldsmith have no breath in them; they are inanimate (Jer. 10:14; 51:17). Human speech is sometimes only words of wind that mean nothing (Job 16:3). By the gust of his nostrils, the Lord piled up the waters of the Red Sea (Ex. 15:8). Often, the word refers to wind or a synonym of wind. The Lord sent a wind over the earth to dry up the floodwaters (Gen. 8:1; Ex. 15:10; Num. 11:31). Jeremiah spoke of the four winds, referring to the entire earth (Jer. 49:36; Ezek. 37:9). The word is also used to mean wind in the sense of nothing (Eccl. 1:14; 2:11; Is. 26:18). The wind, like the Spirit, cannot be caught, tamed, or found (Eccl. 2:11). *

[2] ***rûaḥ*** [Aramaic noun: רוּחַ <7308>; corresponding to <7307> above] ▶ **This word means wind; spirit of a person, mind; spirit divine. All occurrences of the word are located in the book of Daniel.** For the Hebrew mind, the term at its heart encapsulated the experience of any mysterious, invisible, awesome, living power. This included such forces as the wind (Dan. 2:35; 7:2); the active inner being of a person where attitudes, feelings, and intellect resided (Dan. 5:12, 20; 6:3; 7:15); the divine Spirit that could come down from God and indwell individuals, often giving them supernatural abilities, such as Daniel's ability to interpret dreams (Dan. 4:8, 9, 18; 5:11, 14). This term is identical in form and meaning to the Hebrew noun *rûaḥ* (<7307> above). ¶

SPIRIT (POSSESS A FAMILIAR) – 1 Sam. 28:7 → MISTRESS <1172>.

SPIRIT, DEPARTED SPIRIT – Job 26:5; Ps. 88:10; Is. 14:9; 26:14, 19 → DEAD <7496>.

SPIRITIST – ***yidd^e'ōniy*** [masc. noun: יִדְּעֹנִי <3049>; from KNOW <3045>] ▶ **This word describes a medium contacting spirits; it is also translated wizard,**

necromancer. In Levitical Law, this type of person was considered an abomination to the Lord (Deut. 18:11). King Saul consulted such a medium when he desired to know the outcome of his war against the Philistines (1 Sam. 28:9). King Manasseh's evil deeds included the practice of consulting mediums and wizards (2 Kgs. 21:6). Isaiah condemned the people of Israel for turning to the way of the Canaanites, who sought out mediums and wizards in order to hear from their dead (Is. 8:19). Other refs.: Lev. 19:31; 20:6, 27; 1 Sam. 28:3; 2 Kgs. 23:24; 2 Chr. 33:6; Is. 19:3. ¶

SPIT (noun) – ***tōpeṯ*** [fem. noun: תֹּפֶת <8611>; from the base of TAMBOURINES (PLAYING) <8608>] ▶
a. This word indicates an object of spitting, something expulsed from the mouth. It indicates an object of disgust and rejection, of no value (Job 17:6).
b. This word refers to a tabret (a drum). Job used it metaphorically to refer to himself as once in good standing with people, a drum that drew attention, was listened to, and was respected (KJV, Job 17:6). ¶

SPIT (noun and verb) – ***rōq*** [masc. noun: רֹק <7536>; from SPIT (verb) <7556>] ▶ **This word refers to the moisture or liquid present in a person's mouth; it is also translated spittle, spitting, saliva.** Job's condition was such that he did not have time to swallow his spittle before new calamities hit him (Job 7:19). To spit at persons was to utterly demean and detest them (Job 30:10). Even the Lord's Suffering Servant suffered this ultimate expression of rejection and disdain (Is. 50:6). ¶

SPIT (verb) – [1] ***yāraq*** [verb: יָרַק <3417>; a prim. root] ▶ **This word refers to ejecting saliva.** In context it refers to spitting in someone's face as a sign of disapprobation or cursing (Num. 12:14; Deut. 25:9). ¶
[2] ***rāqaq*** [verb: רָקַק <7556>; a prim. root (it has the original sense of diffusing)] ▶ **This word refers to a person's ejecting saliva from his or her mouth.** In context, such an act is capable of making another person unclean if the saliva is ejected on them (Lev. 15:8). ¶

SPIT OUT – Jer. 51:34 ➔ WASH <1740>.

SPITTING – Is. 50:6 ➔ SPIT (noun and verb) <7536>.

SPITTLE – [1] 1 Sam. 21:13 ➔ SALIVA <7388> [2] Job 7:19 ➔ SPIT (noun and verb) <7536>.

SPLENDID – [1] Ezek. 17:8 ➔ GARMENT <155> [2] Ezek. 17:23 ➔ MIGHTY <117> [3] Ezek. 23:41 ➔ GLORIOUS <3520> a.

SPLENDIDLY – ***miḵlôl*** [masc. noun: מִכְלוֹל <4358>; from PERFECT (MAKE) <3634>] ▶ **This word indicates magnificence, completeness with respect to something.** In context it is used in reference to splendid or magnificent clothing (Ezek. 23:12: gorgeously, magnificently, in full dress, in full armor). It is used also of the splendid uniforms of an army (Ezek. 38:4; also translated in full armor, fully armed, with all sorts of armour). ¶

SPLENDOR – [1] ***yip'āh*** [fem. noun: יִפְעָה <3314>; from SHINE, SHINE FORTH <3313>] ▶ **This word denotes brightness.** It is used of the glamour and glitter of a city or nation, its splendor or reputation (Ezek. 28:7). This splendor often led to pride and corruption (Ezek. 28:17). ¶
– [2] 1 Chr. 16:29; 2 Chr. 20:21; Ps. 29:2; 96:9 ➔ GLORY <1927> [3] Esther 1:4 ➔ HONOR (noun) <3366> [4] Job 31:26 ➔ PRECIOUS <3368> [5] Dan. 2:31; 4:36 ➔ BRIGHTNESS <2122> [6] Dan. 11:20 ➔ GLORY <1925> [7] Hab. 3:4 ➔ BRIGHTNESS <5051>.

SPLINT – Ezek. 30:21 ➔ BANDAGE <2848>.

SPLINTER – ***qᵉṣāpāh*** [fem. noun: קְצָפָה <7111>; from ANGRY (BE) <7107> (in the original sense of to crack off)] ▶ **This word refers to a splintering, a peeling of bark. It refers to wood that is cracking,**

breaking up into many small pieces. In Joel it is caused by a vicious attack of locusts (Joel 1:7). ¶

SPLIT – [1] ***šāsa‘*** [verb: שָׁסַע <8156>; a prim. root] ► **This word means and is also translated to divide, to tear, to cleave, to part, to rend.** It means to pull something apart, to separate it wholly or partly (Lev. 1:17). The animal that had a divided, separated hoof was edible for Israel (Lev. 11:3, 7, 26; Deut. 14:6, 7). In Samson's great might, he tore and mangled a lion (Judg. 14:6). It probably has the sense of to disperse, to separate, or to persuade (1 Sam. 24:7; also translated to stay, to rebuke). ¶
– [2] See CLEFT <8157> [3] See DIVIDE <1234>.

SPLIT OPEN – [1] Job 16:13 ➔ CUT (verb) <6398> [2] Ps. 60:2 ➔ TEAR OPEN <6480>.

SPLIT-OPEN – Jer. 29:17 ➔ VILE <8182>.

SPOIL (noun) – [1] ***ḥ*ᵃ*liyṣāh*** [fem. noun: חֲלִיצָה <2488>; from DRAW OUT <2502>] ► **This word refers to the clothing and/or personal effects stripped off a person who has been overcome.** Ref.: Judg. 14:19; also translated apparel. In a militant setting, it is used to describe the weapons taken from or stripped off a soldier or armed man (2 Sam. 2:21; also translated armor, armour, weapons). ¶
[2] ***m*ᵉ*šûsāh*** [fem. noun: מְשׁוּסָה <4882>; from an unused root meaning to plunder] ► **This word means plunder, loot.** It refers to the defeat and plunder of Israel by her enemies, in particular the spoil itself that was taken but also the devastation of the people themselves (Is. 42:24). ¶
[3] ***m*ᵉ*šissāh*** [fem. noun: מְשִׁסָּה <4933>; from PLUNDER <8155>] ► **This word refers to the material gains, both persons and goods, acquired through war.** It indicates Israel (2 Kgs. 21:14; Is. 42:22, 24; Hab. 2:7); and those who plunder Israel, God's people (Jer. 30:16; Zeph. 1:13). ¶
– [4] Gen. 49:27; Ex. 15:9; etc. ➔ PLUNDER (noun) <7998> [5] 2 Chr. 14:14; 25:13; Ezra 9:7; Dan. 11:33; etc. ➔ PLUNDER (noun) <961> [6] Prov. 12:12 ➔ NET <4685> [7] Is. 3:14; Ezek. 18:7, 12; 33:15 ➔ ROBBERY <1500> [8] Ezek. 25:7 ➔ PLUNDER (noun) <897> [9] See PLUNDER (noun) <957>.

SPOIL (verb) – [1] Judg. 2:14; 1 Sam. 14:48; etc. ➔ PLUNDER (verb) <8154> [2] Judg. 2:14; 1 Sam. 17:53; Ps. 89:41; Is. 13:16; Zech. 14:2 ➔ PLUNDER (verb) <8155> [3] Job 30:22 ➔ MELT AWAY <4127> [4] Is. 18:2, 7 ➔ DIVIDE <958> [5] Jer. 30:16 ➔ PLUNDER (verb) <7601> [6] See PLUNDER (verb) <962>.

SPOILED – Job 12:17, 19 ➔ STRIPPED <7758>.

SPOILING – Ps. 35:12 ➔ LOSS OF CHILDREN <7908>.

SPOILS – Is. 25:11 ➔ TRICKERY <698>.

SPOKE – ***ḥiššuq*** [masc. noun: חִשֻּׁק <2839>; from DESIRE (verb) <2836> (in the sense of being conjoined)] ► **This word is used to refer to the braces or bars that gave support between the hub and rim of a wheel.** They hold up Solomon's great brass sea (1 Kgs. 7:33). ¶

SPORT – Is. 57:4 ➔ DELIGHT (HAVE, FIND, TAKE) <6026>.

SPOT – [1] ***ḥ*ᵃ*ḇarburāh*** [fem. noun: חֲבַרְבֻּרָה <2272>; by reduplication from JOIN TOGETHER <2266>] ► **This word refers in context to markings on the fur coat of a wild animal; the marks could be small roundish shapes, or more probably stripes.** It is traditionally taken to refer to the spots of a leopard or panther (Jer. 13:23) that the animal cannot change. In a similar way, evil Israelites cannot change their characters to do good. ¶
– [2] Deut. 32:5; Job 11:15; Song 4:7 ➔ DEFECT <3971>.

SPOT (BRIGHT, SHINY) – ***baheret*** [fem. noun: בַּהֶרֶת <934>; fem. act. part. of the same as BRIGHT <925>] ▶ **These small round marks were potentially dangerous or pathogenic and had to be watched until their natures could be identified more accurately.** Refs.: Lev. 13:2, 4, 19, 23–26, 28, 38, 39; 14:56. ¶

SPOT (FRECKLED, WHITE) – ***bōhaq*** [masc. noun: בֹּהַק <933>; from an unused root meaning to be pale] ▶ **This word describes a harmless skin rash; it is also translated harmless rash, leukoderma, eczema.** It did not render a person unclean (Lev. 13:39). ¶

SPOTLESS (MAKE) – Dan. 12:10 ➔ WHITE (MAKE) <3835>.

SPOTTED – Gen. 31:10, 12 ➔ MOTTLED <1261>.

SPOTTED (BE) – ***ṭālā'*** [verb: טָלָא <2921>; a prim. root (properly to cover with pieces)] ▶ **This word is used to depict pied cattle, goats, and sheep (i.e., having patches of two or more colors).** Refs.: Gen. 30:32, 33, 35, 39. It also indicates clothing: sandals (Josh. 9:5: to be patched, to be clouted; Ezek. 16:16: multicolored, various colors, divers colors, colorful, gaudy). ¶

SPOUT – [1] Prov. 15:2 ➔ UTTER <5042> [2] Zech. 4:2 ➔ PIPE <4166>.

SPOUTING – Ps. 27:12 ➔ BREATH OUT <3307>.

SPRAWLER – Amos 6:7 ➔ HANG <5628>.

SPREAD (noun) – ***muṭṭāh*** [fem. noun: מֻטָּה <4298>; from STRETCH OUT <5186>] ▶ **This word refers to extending, stretching out. It describes the stretching out of a bird's wings as the picture of the flood waters of the Euphrates.** This, in turn, was a picture of God's judgment on Samaria (Is. 8:8; ESV, NIV: outspread wings), a mixed metaphor literary device. ¶

SPREAD (verb) – [1] ***yāṣa'*** [verb: יָצַע <3331>; a prim. root] ▶ **This verb means to extend widely; it indicates making a bed, laying.** It means to lie down for various reasons: for mourning and fasting on ashes and sackcloth (Esther 4:3). It indicates the act of spreading out or preparing sackcloth and ashes to lie upon (Is. 58:5). It is used figuratively of making one's bed or couch in Sheol (Ps. 139:8); God is also there. It figuratively describes maggots spread out as a bed in Sheol (Is. 14:11). ¶
[2] ***nāsak*** [verb: נָסַךְ <5259>; a prim. root (prob. identical with POUR OUT <5288> through the idea of fusion)] ▶ **This word means to stretch out, to cover. It means to intertwine, to spread out something like a net or a veil.** It is used figuratively of a covering that surrounds, hinders, or enshrouds the sight of the nations in a spiritual or religious sense (Is. 25:7). It indicates pouring out a drink offering (*massêkāh*), concluding a treaty or alliance (Is. 30:1; KJV: to cover with a covering). ¶
[3] ***paršêz*** [verb: פַּרְשֵׁז <6576>; a root apparently formed by compounding CLEAR (BE, MAKE) <6567> and that of WARRIOR <6518> (to separate) (comp. DUNG <6574>)] ▶ **This word means to cover something by putting an opaque substance over it or in front of it.** Ref.: Job 26:9. ¶
[4] ***pāśāh*** [verb: פָּשָׂה <6581>; a prim. root] ▶ **This word means to be extensive, to be propagated; it describes the growth or permeation of an infection or various skin diseases, their spread.** The condition was closely watched and diagnosed by the priests (Lev. 13:5–8, 34–36; 14:39, 44, 48). *
[5] ***rābad*** [verb: רָבַד <7234>; a prim. root] ▶ **This word means to lay out a covering over something.** It is used of laying a blanket, a covering of some kind, over a couch; it was probably a decorative covering (Prov. 7:16; also translated to cover, to deck). ¶
– [6] 1 Kgs. 6:32 ➔ SUBDUE <7286> [7] Job 36:29; Ezek. 27:7 ➔ SPREADING <4666> [8] Ps. 37:35 ➔ EMPTY (verb) <6168> [9] Ezek. 16:25 ➔ OPEN WIDE <6589> [10] Hab. 1:8 ➔ FROLIC <6335> b.

SPREAD, SPREAD OUT – [1] ***māṭah*** [verb: מָתַח <4969>; a prim. root] ▶ **This**

word refers to stretching out. It is used of God's act of expanding the sky like spreading out a curtain (Is. 40:22). ¶

2 ***pāraś*** [verb: פָּרַשׂ <6566>; a prim. root] ▶ **This word means to stretch, stretch out; to break in pieces; to scatter, to be scattered.** A garment (Judg. 8:25); a fishing net or snare (Is. 19:8; Hos. 5:1); wings (1 Kgs. 6:27); spreading a tent out (Ex. 40:19); hands in praise and prayer (1 Kgs. 8:38); or helping someone (Prov. 31:20). It indicates covering something over (1 Sam. 17:19). Micah 3:3 used the verb figuratively to depict the violent ways of Israel's rulers over her, breaking (pulling apart, spreading out) her bones. It describes the breaking or distribution of bread, food (Lam. 4:4). In its passive use, it refers to Israel's being scattered, spread out because of God's judgment (Ezek. 17:20). *

3 ***rāpad̲*** [verb: רָפַד <7502>; a prim. root] ▶ **A word meaning to extend; to spread a blanket.** It describes figuratively persons making themselves at home, at rest as permanent inhabitants of Sheol (Job 17:13). In another figurative expression, it describes the lying down, the spreading out of Leviathan (Job 41:30). For another meaning of the Hebrew word, see REFRESH <7502>. ¶

– 4 Is. 14:11 ➔ SPREAD (verb) <3331>.

SPREAD OUT – 1 ***ṭāpaḥ*** [verb: טָפַח <2946>; a prim. root] ▶ **This word is used in a magnificent metaphor to describe the unfolding of the heavens by the Lord's right hand, as a person might spread out a scroll.** Ref.: Is. 48:13; also translated to span, to stretch. In Lamentation 2:22, the word has the meaning of to swaddle, to bear, to hold, to care; see CARE FOR <2946>. ¶

2 ***šāṭaḥ*** [verb: שָׁטַח <7849>; a prim. root] ▶ **This word means to stretch out; to enlarge.** It means to place something out, to spread it out over a large area rather than putting it into piles, as Israel did with an abundance of quails (Num. 11:32; Jer. 8:2). It indicates spreading out one's hands to God in prayer or worship (Ps. 88:9). It refers to spreading out a blanket or some kind of covering (2 Sam. 17:19). It describes God's dispersing, leading away the nations as He pleases, demonstrating His sovereignty (Job 12:23). ¶

SPREADING – 1 ***mip̄rāś*** [masc. noun: מִפְרָשׂ <4666>; from SPREAD <6566>] ▶ **This word means an expansion, e.g., the spreading of clouds across the sky.** Ref.: Job 36:29. It indicates the chief merchandising item of Tyre, fine embroidered linen. It was Tyre's "spreading out" her sail to attract merchants to her (Ezek. 27:7; also translated to serve as a banner, to become a distinguishing mark). ¶

2 ***mišṭôaḥ*** [masc. noun: מִשְׁטוֹחַ <4894>; from SPREAD OUT <7849>] ▶ **This word refers to a place for spreading.** It points out a location where fishing nets can be stretched out for commercial fishing (Ezek. 26:5, 14; 47:10). ¶

– 3 Ex. 26:12, 13 ➔ HANG <5628>
4 Hos. 10:1 ➔ EMPTY (MAKE) <1238>.

SPREADING BRANCHES – Is. 18:5 ➔ BRANCHES <5189>.

SPRIG – 1 ***zalzal*** [masc. noun: זַלְזַל <2150>; by reduplication from GLUTTON (BE) <2151> a.] ▶ **This word denotes a twig, tender shoot.** It refers to a fresh shoot of a vine just before it bears fruit (Is. 18:5). ¶

– 2 Ezek. 17:6 ➔ BRANCH <6288> a.

SPRIG (TENDER) – Ezek. 17:22 ➔ SHOOT (noun) <3127>.

SPRING – 1 ***gullāh*** [fem. noun: גֻּלָּה <1543>; fem. from ROLL (verb) <1556>] ▶ **This word indicates water outflowing from underground.** Refs.: Josh. 15:19; Judg. 1:15. It also means a bowl (1 Kgs. 7:41, 42; 2 Chr. 4:12, 13; Eccl. 12:6; Zech. 4:2); see BOWL <1543>. ¶

2 ***mabbûa'*** [masc. noun: מַבּוּעַ <4002>; from UTTER <5042>] ▶ **This word indicates a spring (source) of water.** It indicates a source, a well from which water is drawn by a pitcher (Eccl. 12:6; also translated fountain). Its abundant presence in a restored Zion is evidence of its powerful

symbolism of life (Is. 35:7) and the Lord's salvation (Is. 49:10). ¶

3 ***nêḇeḵ*** [masc. noun: נֵבֶךְ <5033>; from an unused root meaning to burst forth] ▶ **The word refers to water that flows of its own pressure from the ground or the floor of a sea or a lake.** Ref.: Job 38:16. ¶

– 4 Gen. 2:6 ➔ MIST <108> 5 Gen. 7:11; 8:2; Lev. 11:36; etc. ➔ FOUNTAIN <4599> 6 2 Kgs. 2:21; Ps. 107:33; Is. 58:11 ➔ GOING OUT, GOING FORTH <4161> 7 Prov. 25:26; Hos. 13:15; Jer. 2:13; 17:13; 51:36 ➔ FOUNTAIN <4726> 8 Song 4:12 ➔ WAVE <1530>.

SPRING OUT – Deut. 33:22 ➔ LEAP <2187>.

SPRING, SPRING UP – Joel 2:22 ➔ PRODUCE (verb) <1876>.

SPRINGS FROM THE SAME (WHAT) – ***šāḥiys, sāḥiyš*** [masc. noun: שָׁחִיס, סָחִישׁ <7823>; from an unused root prob. meaning to sprout] ▶

a. This Hebrew word refers to edible crops that spring up by themselves without human cultivation. Ref.: Is. 37:30.

b. A masculine noun referring to aftergrowth, that which grows by itself. It has the same meaning as a. It refers to what springs up by itself from last year's crops (2 Kgs. 19:29). ¶

SPRINKLE – 1 ***zāraq*** [verb: זָרַק <2236>; a prim. root] ▶ **This word means to scatter a liquid over something; it is most often used to describe the actions of the priests performing the sacrificial rituals.** They sprinkled the blood of the sacrifices (Lev. 1:5; 2 Kgs. 16:13; 2 Chr. 29:22). It is also used of water (Num. 19:13; Ezek. 36:25). In a time of grief, Job's friends sprinkled dust on their heads (Job 2:12). King Josiah destroyed the false gods and scattered their pieces (powder, NASB) over the graves of those who had worshiped them (2 Chr. 34:4). *

2 ***nûp̄*** [verb: נוּף <5130>; a prim. root] ▶ **This verb only occurs in the basic verbal form once, where it refers to scattering a bed over with myrrh.** Ref.: Prov. 7:17. Most often, it occurs in the causative form, where it can carry a similar semantic idea, namely making rain fall (Ps. 68:9). However, it usually carries the idea of moving back and forth or waving. It could be used to represent the reciprocating motion of a tool, like a sword (Ex. 20:25); a sickle (Deut. 23:25); a tool for dressing stone (Deut. 27:5); or a saw (Is. 10:15). It could also be used of the motion of one's hand as a healing ritual (2 Kgs. 5:11); as retribution (Is. 11:15; 19:16); or as a signal (Is. 13:2). In a cultic context, this verb is a technical term that referenced the actions of the priest as he offered a sacrifice to God by waving it before the altar (Ex. 29:24; Lev. 23:11; Num. 5:25). *

3 ***nāzāh*** [verb: נָזָה <5137>; a prim. root] ▶ **This verb means to spurt, to spatter, to spring, to leap.** It appears only a few times in the basic verbal form and carries the connotation of blood spurting or spattering (Lev. 6:27; 2 Kgs. 9:33; Is. 63:3). In the causative form, the verb connotes the sprinkling of a liquid as part of a ritual cleansing. The sprinkled liquid could be blood (Lev. 5:9; 14:7); oil (Lev. 8:11); water (Num. 19:18, 19); blood and oil (Ex. 29:21); or blood and water (Lev. 14:51). Also in the causative form, this verb could signify to leap or to spring, especially with the connotation of surprise or joy (Is. 52:15). *

SPROUT – Gen. 1:11 ➔ PRODUCE (verb) <1876>.

SPUN – Ex. 35:25, 26 ➔ SPIN <2901>.

SPUN (THAT WHICH IS) – ***maṭweh*** [masc. noun: מַטְוֶה <4299>; from SPIN <2901>] ▶ **This word described the things spun, clothing, cords, curtains, etc., by the skilled women of Israel for use in the Tabernacle.** Ref.: Ex. 35:25. ¶

SPUR – Is. 9:11 ➔ COVER (verb) <5526> b.

SPURN – 1 ***nā'aṣ*** [verb: נָאַץ <5006>; a prim. root] ▶ **This verb means to revile, to scorn, to reject; it is also translated to despise, to contemn.** It is related to *nāṣaṣ*

<5340>, meaning to scorn or to blaspheme. This word often refers to rejecting the counsel of a wise person. This scornful attitude results in an unhappy life: people live in affliction because they reject God's counsel (Ps. 107:11). Another example of a passage that uses this word is Proverbs 1:30, where wisdom laments that people scorn her reproof. In another instance of this word, the Israelites were chastised because they had despised the word of the Holy One of Israel (Is. 5:24). *
– [2] Ps. 89:39 ➔ RENOUNCE <5010> [3] Ps. 119:118 ➔ REJECT <5541>.

SPY OUT – [1] ***rāgal*** [verb: רָגַל <7270>; a prim. root] ▶ **This word refers to roaming, going through a land to observe it secretly.** Refs.: Num. 21:32; Deut. 1:24; Judg. 18:2, 14, 17; 2 Sam. 10:3. Its participial form in its intensive stem indicates spies, a person who secretly scouts out a land (Gen. 42:9, 11). For other meanings of the Hebrew word, see SLANDER <7270> and WALK (TEACH TO) <7270>. *
– [2] Num. 14:6, 7; etc. ➔ SEEK OUT <8446>.

SQUARE (BE) – ***rāḇaʻ*** [verb: רָבַע <7251>; a prim. root] ▶ **This word defines something as being square, having four equal sides, ends, tops, bottoms; it is used of various items.** In the Tabernacle complex (Ex. 27:1; 28:16); Solomon's palace (1 Kgs. 7:5, 31); Ezekiel's court for his Temple (Ezek. 40:47); and various other items (Ezek. 41:21; 43:16; 45:2). *

SQUEEZE – [1] Gen. 40:11 ➔ PRESS <7818> [2] Judg. 6:38 ➔ CRUSH <2115>.

STACK – Lev. 24:6, 7 ➔ ROW (noun) <4635>.

STACK OF CORN – Ex. 22:6 ➔ STACKED GRAIN <1430>.

STACKED GRAIN – ***gāḏiyš*** [masc. noun: גָּדִישׁ <1430>; from an unused root (meaning to heap up)] ▶ **These heaped piles were found in the harvest fields and were easily ignited by fire.** Ref.: Ex. 22:6; also translated stack of corn. Samson destroyed a whole harvest of the Philistines by burning these stacks (Judg. 15:5; also translated shock). They stood in the field and were used when it was well cured (Job 5:26; translated sheaf, sheaf of grain, stacking of grain, shock of corn). The Hebrew word also means a grave mound (Job 21:32); see TOMB <1430>. ¶

STACING OF GRAIN – Job 21:32 ➔ STACKED GRAIN <1430>.

STACTE – ***nāṭāp̱, neṭep*** [masc. noun: נָטָף, נֶטֶף <5198>; from DROP (verb) <5197> (in the sense of to drip)] ▶
a. This word refers to drops of a sweet spice, resin of some trees. It was one of the spices used by the priests to prepare the sacred incense (Ex. 30:34; NIV: gum resin). ¶
b. This word refers to a drop of water. It is used of the evaporation of water into the upper atmosphere that returns as drops of rain. Ref.: Job 36:27. ¶

STAFF – [1] ***maṭṭeh, maṭṭāh*** [masc. noun: מַטֶּה, מַטָּה <4294>; from STRETCH OUT <5186> (in the sense of extending something such as a staff)] ▶ **This word means a rod, a branch, a tribe.** It signifies, variously, a walking stick (Ex. 4:2); a branch of a tree (Ezek. 19:11 ff.); a spear used in battle (Hab. 3:14); an instrument of chastisement (Is. 10:24); an instrument used in the threshing process (Is. 28:27). Metaphorically, the image of a staff symbolizes the supply of food (Lev. 26:26); strength (Is. 14:5); and authority (Ps. 110:2). Uniquely, the word also signifies a tribe, such as one of the twelve tribes of Israel (Num. 36:3, 4; Josh. 13:29). The origin of this use derives from the image of the leader of the tribe going before the company with his staff in hand (cf. Num. 17:2). *
– [2] Gen. 32:10; Ex. 12:11; Num. 22:27; 1 Sam. 17:40, 43; Jer. 48:17; Hos. 4:12; Zech. 11:7, 10, 14 ➔ STICK <4731> [3] Ex. 21:19; Num. 21:18; Zech. 8:4 ➔ SUPPORT (noun) <4938> a. [4] Num. 13:23 ➔ POLE <4132> [5] Judg. 6:21; 2 Kgs. 4:29,

31; 18:21; Ps. 23:4; Is. 3:1; 36:6; Ezek. 29:6 ➔ SUPPORT (noun) <4938> a. [6] 2 Sam. 3:29 ➔ SPINDLE <6418>.

STAG – Song 2:9, 17; etc. ➔ DEER <354>.

STAGGER – Jer. 25:16; 46:7, 8 ➔ SHAKE <1607>.

STAGGER (THAT MAKES) – ***tar'ēlāh*** [fem. noun: תַּרְעֵלָה <8653>; from BRANDISH <7477>] ► **This word indicates an unsteady walk or a swagger of body and mind brought on by wine.** In context, it was brought on by God's actions against His people (Ps. 60:3; also translated confusion, astonishment). In Isaiah it again refers to the dizziness and confusion brought on God's people by His cup of staggering and reeling (Is. 51:17, 22; also translated trembling). ¶

STAGGERED (BE) – Is. 21:3 ➔ INIQUITY (COMMIT) <5753>.

STAGGERING – [1] Is. 51:17, 22 ➔ STAGGER (THAT MAKES) <8653> [2] Zech. 12:2 ➔ REELING <7478>.

STAGNANT (BE) – Zeph. 1:12 ➔ CONGEAL <7087>.

STAIN – [1] Is. 59:3; 63:3 ➔ DEFILE <1351> [2] Jer. 2:22 ➔ MARKED (BE) <3799>.

STAIRS – Song 2:14 ➔ CLIFF <4095>.

STAIRS, WINDING STAIRS – 1 Kgs. 6:8 ➔ STAIRWAY <3883>.

STAIRWAY – [1] ***lûl*** [masc. noun: לוּל <3883>; from an unused root meaning to fold back] ► **This word means and is also translated stairs, winding stairs.** It is a technical architectural term referring traditionally to a set of spiral stairs (1 Kgs. 6:8) in Solomon's Temple. Some have suggested that it indicates a trapdoor. ¶
– [2] Gen. 28:12 ➔ LADDER <5551>.

STALK – ***qāneh*** [masc. noun: קָנֶה <7070>; from ACQUIRE <7069>] ► **This word means a rod, a reed, a calamus reed; beam of scales. It is a general term that can be used of any object in the form of a long stalk or tubular shape.** It refers to stalks of grain (Gen. 41:5, 22); certain tall, slim water plants, reeds (1 Kgs. 14:15; Is. 19:6); weak supports in a figurative sense, e.g., Egypt (2 Kgs. 18:21; Is. 36:6); aromatic, fragrant cane (Ex. 30:23; Jer. 6:20). The word was used in various ways of other items or concepts, objects: a measuring rod, a reed of about nine feet (Ezek. 40:3, 5); as a part of a scale, it is used to indicate a whole scale (Is. 46:6). It is used often in descriptions of lamps, lampstands, and their branches extending from them (Ex. 25:31–33, 35, 36; 37:17, 18). It refers to the upper part of a person's arm (Job 31:22). *

STALL – [1] ***ᵃwērôṯ*** [fem. plur. noun: אֻוֵרוֹת <220>; by transposition for <723> below] ► **This word indicates pens for cattle.** Ref.: 2 Chr. 32:28. ¶
[2] ***'urwāh*** [fem. noun: אֻרְוָה <723>; from PICK (verb) <717> (in the sense of feeding)] ► **This term is used to describe the huge complex of quarters constructed for Solomon's horses.** These horses pulled his chariots and provided steeds for his horsemen (1 Kgs. 4:26; 2 Chr. 9:25; 32:28). ¶
[3] ***repeṯ*** [masc. noun: רֶפֶת <7517>; prob. from CEASE <7503> (in the sense of a place to rest)] ► **This word indicates an enclosure, a pen of a stable.** It refers to an area prepared to house and protect cattle, horses, etc., a place where the offspring of these animals can be safely confined and cared for (Hab. 3:17). ¶
– [4] Amos 6:4; Mal. 4:2 ➔ FAT, FATTED, FATTENED <4770>.

STALLION – Jer. 8:16 ➔ lit.: strong one ➔ MIGHTY <47>.

STAMMERER – Is. 32:4: the tongue of the stammerers ➔ lit.: the stammering tongue ➔ STAMMERING <5926>.

STAMMERING – [1] ***lā'ēg*** [adj.: לָעֵג <3934>; from MOCK <3932>] ► **This word is used to describe the language**

spoken by foreign lip(s) as (*b^e*) stammering (speaking with hesitation and repetitions). Ref.: Is. 28:11. It is also used of certain persons as jesters, mockers (Ps. 35:16, NIV, "maliciously mocked"). ¶
2 ***'illêg*** [adj.: עִלֵּג <5926>; from an unused root meaning to stutter] ► **This word refers to the inability to speak clearly and smoothly without hesitation.** Ref.: Is. 32:4. ¶
– 3 Is. 33:19 ➔ MOCK <3932>.

STAMP – Dan. 7:7, 19 ➔ TRAMPLE <7512>.

STAMPING – ***ša^{ca}ṭāh*** [fem. noun: שַׁעֲטָה <8161>; fem. from an unused root meaning to stamp] ► **This word means bringing the hoofs down heavily; it is also translated galloping.** In context it refers to the noisy, powerful galloping of warhorses (Jer. 47:3). ¶

STAND (noun) – 1 ***kên*** [masc. noun: כֵּן <3653>; the same as THEREFORE <3651>, used as a noun] ► **This word means a structure designed to support; it is also translated base, foot, pedestal.** It is used to indicate a foundational stand for a water basin (Ex. 30:18, 28; 31:9; Lev. 8:11; 1 Kgs. 7:29, 31). It refers to the housing for a ship's mast (Is. 33:23; NASB: base). *
2 ***m^eḵônāh, m^eḵōnāh*** [fem. noun: מְכוֹנָה, מְכֹנָה <4350>; from DWELLING <4349>] ► **This word indicates a movable base, a supporting structure.** It is used of equipment used in the Temple functions; stands (1 Kgs. 7:27, 28, 30, 32, 34, 35, 37; Jer. 27:19; 52:17, 20); or basins (1 Kgs. 7:37–39). It is used to denote the foundations of a structure (Ezra 3:3). It indicates a stand or pedestal (Zech. 5:11). *
– 3 1 Sam. 14:5 ➔ PILLAR <4690>.

STAND (BE AT) – Ezek. 29:7 ➔ SHAKE <5976>.

STAND (TAKE A, MAKE A) – ***yāṣaḇ*** [verb: יָצַב <3320>; a prim. root] ► **This word indicates to confront, to take a position on a matter.** It is used in a reflexive stem and means to station oneself, to take a firm stand (1 Sam. 3:10). It has the sense of to present oneself at a location (Deut. 31:14) or to take a firm position on something (2 Sam. 18:13). It is used of putting oneself in a place of honor (Prov. 22:29); of a soldier taking his place in the armed forces (Jer. 46:4); or a person placing himself among the people of Israel in assembly (Judg. 20:2). To not allow someone to stand before you means to disapprove of him or her (Ps. 5:5). To direct one's life in a certain way is to set oneself on a certain path of life (Ps. 36:4). It is used of resisting people by taking a stand against them (Josh. 1:5; Ps. 2:2). *

STAND (verb) – 1 ***nāṣaḇ*** [verb: נָצַב <5324>; a prim. root] ► **This word means to station, to appoint, to erect, to take a stand.** Abraham's servant stationed himself beside the well to find a wife for Isaac (Gen. 24:13); Jacob set up a stone pillar (Gen. 35:14, 20); the people stood up when Moses went out to the tent to meet God (Ex. 33:8); God established the boundaries for Israel (Deut. 32:8); Boaz asked the work supervisor (the one who stands over) about Ruth (Ruth 2:5, 6). See the related Hebrew noun *niṣṣāḇ* (HILT <5325>) and the Aramaic noun *niṣbāh* (STRENGTH <5326>). *
2 ***'āmaḏ*** [verb: עָמַד <5975>; a prim. root] ► **This word, opposing to sit, means to rise up; to take one's stand.** The basic uses of the word can be noted here: to stand on one's feet, not sit (Gen. 18:22; 24:30; 41:1, 3); to remain motionless or stay behind (Gen. 19:17; 24:31). It has the sense of ceasing, to stop doing something, e.g., to stop bearing children (Gen. 29:35; 30:9). It has the sense of serving before someone, as Joseph served, stood before Pharaoh (Gen. 41:46). It can mean to delay, to hold back from doing something (Gen. 45:9). It has the sense of presenting, introducing someone to someone else (Gen. 47:7). It indicates living somewhere, standing, remaining there (Ex. 8:22). It is used of taking a position (physically, spatially) somewhere (Ex. 14:19). It is used of something enduring, lasting, being preserved (Jer. 32:14). Used with *'al* following, it means to stand over, upon, to exercise authority over (Num. 7:2); with *lip̄nê*, it

indicates standing before (1 Kgs. 1:28). To stand over one's life (*nep̱eš*) is to defend, protect one's life (Esther 8:11). In its causative uses, it means to set up, station, appoint, restore, etc. It is used of causing persons to do something or putting them somewhere (Judg. 16:25); of setting up, standing up someone (2 Sam. 22:34; Ps. 18:33); to cause someone to endure, to continue (Ex. 9:16); to set up, to erect a structure, a temple (Ezra 2:68); to appoint, set up guards on duty (Neh. 7:3). It is used in a figurative sense of Moab standing, remaining undisturbed or unchanged (Jer. 48:11); and of a prophet standing in the presence of God, i.e., receiving a message from God (Jer. 23:18, 22). In its few passive forms, it means to be presented (of a sacrifice) before the Lord (Lev. 16:10); to be set straight again or propped up (2 Chr. 18:34). *

3 ***tᵉqûmāh*** [fem. noun: תְּקוּמָה <8617>; from STAND, STAND UP <6965>] ► **This word indicates the ability to rise up. It means to be strong, to stand in an erect position, to maintain one's position.** In context Israel loses this ability to withstand her enemies because of breaking the covenant (Lev. 26:37). ¶

STAND (PLACE TO) – Mic. 1:11 ➔ STANDING PLACE <5979>.

STAND, STAND FAST – Dan. 6:12 ➔ CERTAIN <3330>.

STAND, STAND UP – 1 ***qûm*** [verb: קוּם <6965>; a prim. root] ► **This word means to arise; there are also various other meanings.** Its basic meaning is the physical action of rising up (Gen. 19:33, 35; Ruth 3:14); or the resultant end of that action, standing (Josh. 7:12, 13). However, a myriad of derived and figurative meanings for this term have developed. It can designate the following attributes: to show honor and respect (Gen. 27:19; Ex. 33:10; Num. 23:18); to move (Ex. 10:23); to recover (Ex. 21:19); to belong (Lev. 25:30); to cost (Lev. 27:14, 17); to be valid (Num. 30:5); to appear (Deut. 13:1); to follow (Deut. 29:22); to be hostile (Judg. 9:18); to endure (1 Sam. 13:14); to replace (1 Kgs. 8:20). The word can also mean to ratify (Ruth 4:7); to obligate (Esther 9:21, 27, 31); to establish or strengthen (Ps. 119:28); to fulfill (Ezek. 13:6). In the causative form, it means to provide (Gen. 38:8; 2 Sam. 12:11); to rouse (Gen. 49:9); to perform (Deut. 9:5); to revive (Ruth 4:5, 10); to keep one's word (1 Sam. 3:12); to erect (1 Kgs. 7:21); to appoint (1 Kgs. 11:14); to be victorious (Ps. 89:43); to bring to silence (Ps. 107:29). *

2 ***qûm*** [verb: קוּם <6966>; corresponding to <6965> above] ► **This word means to arise, to set up, to establish.** It means to get up from a sitting or lying position, to stand erect (Dan. 3:24); to arise, get up from sleeping (Dan. 6:19). It describes the beginning and development of nations (Dan. 7:17); or the beginning of a process, the preparation to build (Ezra 5:2). It carries the sense of something being in a standing position (Dan. 2:31; 3:3). It indicates durability of something, its continuance (Dan. 2:44). In legal language, it means to set up, to put through a legal ruling, a law (Dan. 6:8). In its passive usage, it means to be set up (Dan. 7:4, 5). In its causative stem, it is used often of setting something up: a statue (Dan. 3:1, 3, 5; 6:8); a kingdom (Dan. 2:44); various persons to their offices (Ezra 6:18; Dan. 5:11). *

STAND STILL – ***dāmam*** [verb: דָּמַם <1826>; a prim. root; comp. ASTONISHED (BE) <1724> and CEASE <1820>] ► **This verb means to be silent, to be still.** It depicts the state of being motionless (1 Sam. 14:9; Jer. 47:6). It can be used to command something to be motionless, to stand still (Josh. 10:12, 13), such as the sun. It means to refrain from speech (Lev. 10:3) at an appropriate time (Amos 5:13). It refers to persons being traumatized, rigid, or frozen from fear and fright (Ex. 15:16) like a stone or the silencing of persons through war or other means (Jer. 8:14; 48:2; 49:26; 50:30). It indicates, on the other hand, the absence of emotional distress and churning and the ability to be quiet and relax (Job 30:27; Ps. 4:4; 30:12; 131:2), which Job could not accomplish. *

STAND UP – ***sāmar*** [verb: סָמַר <5568>; a prim. root] ▶ **This word means to bristle up; to tremble. It is used of something caused to straighten up, to bristle, to become erect.** In context it is used of human hair (Job 4:15). It takes on the sense of quiver, shake, tremble before God's Word (Ps. 119:120). ¶

STANDARD – [1] Num. 1:52; 2:2; etc. ➔ BANNER <1714> [2] Num. 21:8, 9; Is. 18:3; 31:9 ➔ BANNER <5251> [3] 1 Chr. 17:17 ➔ TURN (noun) <8447> d.

STANDARD-BEARER – Is. 10:18 ➔ SICK MAN <5263> b.

STANDING – [1] Ps. 69:2 ➔ FOOTHOLD <4613> [2] Lam. 3:63 ➔ RISING, RISING UP <7012> [3] Mic. 1:11 ➔ STANDING PLACE <5979>.

STANDING GRAIN, STANDING CORN – ***qāmāh*** [masc. noun: קָמָה <7054>; fem. of act. part. of STAND, STAND UP <6965>] ▶ **This word means a stalk.** It indicates grain still growing in the field, not yet cut, easily ignited and burned by fire (Ex. 22:6; Deut. 16:9; Judg. 15:5; 2 Kgs. 19:26). Reapers gathered it by cutting it down with sickles (Is. 17:5). See also STAND, STAND UP <6965>. *

STANDING PLACE – ***'emdāh*** [fem. noun.: עֶמְדָּה <5979>; from STAND (verb) <5975>] ▶ **This word indicates support, protection.** It refers to that which gives security, stability, safety and protection to someone (Mic. 1:11; also translated place to stand, standing, to protect). ¶

STAR – ***kôḵāḇ*** [masc. noun: כּוֹכָב <3556>; prob. from the same as CABBON <3522> (in the sense of rolling) or BURN (noun) <3554> (in the sense of blazing)] ▶ **The primary referents of this word are a star (the luminous celestial objects) and/or the stars of heaven which God created.** Ref.: Gen. 1:16. These shining heavenly bodies have several functions: to rule over the night (Gen. 1:16; Ps. 136:9); to give light; to praise God (Ps. 148:3). They were used in idioms and metaphors often: to symbolize rulership and a coming ruler (Num. 24:17). Pagans and apostate Israelites worshiped them as gods (Deut. 4:19); they were used in pagan astrology or augury seeking to know the future (Is. 47:13); yet the Lord of Israel communicates with them and commands them (Job 9:7); they were used to represent Joseph's brothers (Gen. 37:9): their number is used figuratively to represent the many descendants of Abraham and the patriarchs (Gen. 15:5; 22:17; 26:4; Ex. 32:13); prideful and haughty nations are represented as stars (Obad. 1:4), especially the king of Babylon (Is. 14:13); the Lord can use stars in battle to fight for His people (Judg. 5:20); they shout for joy in personification (Job 38:7). The Lord has numbered them (Ps. 147:4); but even these shining bodies are not pure or clean in His sight (Job 25:5). *

STARE – Is. 14:16 ➔ LOOK (verb) <7688>.

START – Prov. 17:14; 20:3 ➔ BREAK OUT <1566>.

START OFF – Prov. 22:6 ➔ DEDICATE <2596>.

STARTLE – Hab. 3:6 ➔ LEAP <5425>.

STARVE – Zeph. 2:11 ➔ LEAN (GROW, BECOME, WAX) <7329>.

STARVING – Gen. 42:19, 33 ➔ FAMINE <7459>.

STATE – [1] 2 Chr. 24:13 ➔ PROPORTION <4971> [2] Is. 22:19 ➔ ATTENDANCE <4612>.

STATELY – [1] Ezek. 17:23; Zech. 11:2 ➔ MIGHTY <117> [2] Ezek. 23:41 ➔ GLORIOUS <3520> a.

STATION – 2 Chr. 35:15; Is. 22:19 ➔ ATTENDANCE <4612>.

STATURE – [1] ***māḏôn*** [masc. noun: מָדוֹן <4067>; from the same as GARMENT

<4063>] ► **This word is used once and indicates a man of great height or size, the son of a giant.** Ref.: 2 Sam. 21:20. ¶
– 2 1 Chr. 11:23 ➔ MEASURE (noun) <4060>.

STATUTE – 1 ***ḥōq*** [masc. noun: חֹק <2706>; from ENGRAVE <2710>] ► **This word means regulation, law, ordinance, decree, custom. Primarily, this word represents an expectation or mandate prescribed by decree or custom.** It is used to speak of the general decrees of God (Jer. 5:22; Amos 2:4); the statutes of God given to Moses (Ex. 15:26; Num. 30:16; Mal. 4:4); the lawful share deserved by virtue of status (Gen. 47:22; Lev. 10:13, 14); the declared boundaries or limits of something (Job 14:5; 26:10); the prevailing cultural norm (Judg. 11:39); the binding legislation made by a ruler (Gen. 47:26); and that which must be observed by strict ritual (Ex. 12:24). *

2 ***ḥuqqāh*** [fem. noun: חֻקָּה <2708>; fem. of <2706> above] ► **This word mean an ordinance, anything prescribed. It serves as the feminine of *ḥōq*. Since its basic meaning is not specific, the word takes on different connotations in each context. Its most common meaning is decrees, statutes, or a synonym of these words. The decrees of the Lord could be oral or written; they made God's will known and gave divine directions to His people.** Abraham kept them, evidently, before they were written down (Gen. 26:5). Moses and his assistants were to teach the statutes of the Lord to Israel (Ex. 18:20; Lev. 10:11) so that the Israelites could discern between the clean and the unclean. The decrees of the Lord, along with His laws, regulations, and commandments, covered all areas of life. The Israelites were to follow His decrees so they would separate themselves from the practices of the pagan nations around them (Lev. 18:3, 4). Moses admonished the Israelites to keep God's decrees and statutes (Lev. 19:37; 20:22; 25:18). Blessing was the reward for keeping them (Lev. 26:3), but curses were promised for those who didn't obey them (Lev. 26:15, 43).

Throughout the passing of Israel's history, new decrees were added (Josh. 24:25), and the people and leaders were judged with respect to their faithfulness in observing God's decrees, laws, statutes, and commandments. David was renowned for having observed them (2 Sam. 22:23). The Davidic covenant would be realized if later kings followed the Lord's decrees as David had (1 Kgs. 6:12). However, most of the kings failed, including Solomon (1 Kgs. 11:11; 2 Kgs. 17:15, 34). Josiah renewed the covenant and exerted himself to follow the Lord's decrees (2 Kgs. 23:3), but it was too late to save Judah from exile (see 2 Kgs. 23:25–27).

The psalmist found great joy in the decrees, laws, commandments, precepts, ordinances, and instructions of the Lord; they were not burdensome (Ps. 18:22; 119:5). However, some leaders of Israel distorted God's decrees and established their own oppressive decrees on the people (see Is. 10:1).

God's issuance of a decree was effective and permanent: by His decree, He established the order of creation forever, the functions of the sun and the moon (Job 28:26; Jer. 31:35). The prophets without fail condemned Israel and its leaders for not keeping the decrees of the Lord (Ezek. 11:12; 20:13; Amos 2:4) but saw a future time when a redeemed people would follow them (Ezek. 36:27; 37:24). *

3 ***ḥêqeq*** [masc. noun: חֵקֶק <2711>; from ENGRAVE <2710>] ► **This word means something prescribed, a decree, a thought. This word is the construct of *ḥōq* (<2706> above) and is only found twice in the Old Testament.** When Deborah and Barak sang a song to commemorate the victory over the Canaanites, they sang of the "great thoughts of the heart" (KJV), referring to the thoughts and statues within a person (Judg. 5:15: resolve, searching, thought). In the other occurrence, Isaiah declared that the judgment of God was on those who enacted wicked statutes (Is. 10:1: decree, statute, law). ¶

4 ***qᵉyām*** [Aramaic masc. noun: קְיָם <7010>; from STAND, STAND UP <6966> (in the sense of arising in law in the case of a

statute)] ▶ **This word means something prescribed, a decree; it is also translated ordinance, edict. A form of this word is only used twice in the Hebrew Old Testament, both times in the book of Daniel.** When King Darius' advisors wanted to get rid of Daniel, they persuaded Darius to make a law that forbade worship of anyone but himself (Dan. 6:7). When Daniel broke this law, the advisors compelled Darius to enforce the punishment because the edict he issued could not be revoked (Dan. 6:15). ¶
– [5] See PRECEPT <6490>.

STAVE – [1] Num. 21:18 ➔ SUPPORT (noun) <4938> b. [2] 1 Chr. 15:15 ➔ YOKE <4133>.

STAY (noun) – [1] ***šiyḇāh*** [fem. noun: שִׁיבָה <7871>; from DWELL <3427>] ▶ **This word indicates a sojourn.** It refers to a period of time, a sojourn, of King David at Mahanaim (2 Sam. 19:32) during which Barzillai took care of him. ¶
– [2] 2 Sam. 22:19; Ps. 18:18; Is. 3:1 ➔ SUPPORT (noun) <4937> a.

STAY (verb) – [1] ***'āḥar*** [verb: אָחַר <309>; a prim. root] ▶ **This word means to delay or hold back.** It means to delay or remain (Gen. 32:4; 2 Sam. 20:5, [written tradition]). In its intensive usage, it can mean to hesitate (Ex. 22:29; Judg. 5:28). In its causal stem, it means to come too late (2 Sam. 20:5, [oral tradition]). *
– [2] Gen. 26:3; 35:27; 1 Kgs. 17:20; etc. ➔ SOJOURN <1481> [3] 1 Sam. 24:7 ➔ SPLIT <8156> [4] Ruth 1:13 ➔ REFRAIN <5702> [5] Job 37:4 ➔ SUPPLANT <6117> [6] Is. 27:8 ➔ REMOVE <1898> [7] Dan. 4:35 ➔ STRIKE <4223> [8] See JOIN <1692>.

STEADFAST – Dan. 6:26 ➔ ENDURING <7011>.

STEAL – ***gānaḇ*** [verb: גָּנַב <1589>; a prim. root] ▶ **This word denotes to take away by theft, to carry away secretly, to sweep away.** It indicates wrongfully taking objects or persons (Gen. 31:19, 32; Ex. 21:16), sometimes for a good reason (2 Kgs. 11:2). It has the sense of deceiving when used with the word for heart, as when Jacob literally stole Laban's heart (Gen. 31:20, 26). With storm as its subject, the word means to carry away quickly and violently (Job 21:18), especially the wicked (Job 27:20). In its passive uses, it means to be stolen away (Gen. 40:15; Ex. 22:12). Used in the reflexive sense, it means to steal away, to go by stealth (2 Sam. 19:3). *

STEALTHILY – 1 Sam. 24:4 ➔ ENCHANTMENT <3909>.

STEEL – ***p^{e}lāḏāh*** [fem. noun: פְּלָדָה <6393>; from an unused root meaning to divide] ▶
a. This word refers to metal of some kind; some translators prefer steel. It is used then of steel chariot frames or coverings (Nah. 2:3: NASB, ESV, NIV).
b. Some translators earlier rendered the word as torch. Ref.: Nah. 2:3: KJV, NKJV.

STEEP – Is. 7:19 ➔ DESOLATE <1327>.

STEEP PATHWAY – Song 2:14; Ezek. 38:20 ➔ CLIFF <4095>.

STEEP PLACE – Ezek. 38:20 ➔ CLIFF <4095>.

STEM – Is. 40:24 ➔ STUMP <1503>.

STENCH – [1] ***b^{e}'ōš*** [masc. noun: בְּאֹשׁ <889>; from STINK <887>] ▶ **This word indicates a foul odor; it is translated stink in KJV.** It is used literally to describe the smell of rotting corpses (Is. 34:3; Joel 2:20; Amos 4:10) of both Israel's enemies and her own armies. ¶
[2] ***maq*** [masc. noun: מַק <4716>; from WASTE AWAY <4743>] ▶ **This word indicates a putrid, unpleasant smell or a state of decay, the opposite of sweet-smelling, healthy.** Refs.: Is. 3:24; 5:24. It is also translated rottenness, stink, putrefaction, rot, to decay. ¶
– [3] Prov. 13:5; Eccl. 10:1: to make a stench, to give a stench ➔ STINK <887>.

STENCH (BE A) – Ps. 77:9 ➔ ENTREAT <2589>.

STENCH (EMIT A) – Is. 19:6 ➔ REJECT <2186> b.

STEP (noun) – 1 ***'oššur, 'aššur*** [fem. noun: אֻשֻּׁר, אַשֻּׁר <838>; from BLESS <833> in the sense of going] ► **This word means pace; it is also translated path, goings. It is often used figuratively to describe a person's walk or manner of life.** It describes the path that is pleasing to God (Job 23:11; 31:7; Ps. 17:5) and the steps of a wise or sensible person (Prov. 14:15). *
2 ***hāliyḵ*** [masc. noun: הָלִיךְ <1978>; from GO <1980>] ► **This word is used figuratively to refer to Job's successful life, steps, before calamity struck him.** Ref.: Job 29:6; also translated path. ¶
3 ***miṣ'āḏ*** [masc. noun: מִצְעָד <4703>; from WALK <6805>] ► **This word means a footstep. It is used picturesquely of the way a person's life unfolds, i.e., as one walks along a path by moving his or her feet.** Ref.: Ps. 37:23. The Lord orders peoples' steps (Prov. 20:24; KJV: goings) as they go through life. To follow a person's steps (translated: at his heels, in his train, in submission) is to imitate and adopt their actions and goals (Dan. 11:43). ¶
4 ***peśa'*** [masc. noun: פֶּשַׂע <6587>; from MARCH (verb) <6585>] ► **This word refers to the time needed to take one step or the small amount of space represented by a step.** Ref.: 1 Sam. 20:3. ¶
5 ***ṣa'aḏ*** [masc. noun: צַעַד <6806>; from WALK (verb) <6805>] ► **This word refers to a step taken, a stride.** It refers to actual steps taken or the distance covered by a step (2 Sam. 6:13). It bears a figurative sense of success in life, prosperity (2 Sam. 22:37). The Lord numbers the steps of persons, determining their extent and their path (Job 14:16; Prov. 16:9; Jer. 10:23). Wisdom helps make life's steps successful and easier (Prov. 4:12). *
– 6 1 Kgs. 10:12 ➔ SUPPORT (noun) <4552>.

STEP (verb) – Is. 27:4 ➔ MARCH (verb) <6585>.

STEW – ***nāziyḏ*** [masc. noun: נָזִיד <5138>; from PROUDLY (DEAL) <2102> b. (in the sense of to boil, to cook)] ► **This word is used to refer to the boiled or simmered dish Jacob prepared.** Refs.: Gen. 25:29, 34; KJV: pottage. The exact contents of the food are not known. Other refs.: 2 Kgs. 4:38–40; Hag. 2:12. ¶

STEWARD – 1 ***melṣar*** [masc. noun: מֶלְצַר <4453>; of Persian deriv.] ► **This word identifies a person as an overseer, someone in authority over designated areas or persons.** Refs.: Dan. 1:11, 16; also translated guard, Melzar. ¶
– 2 Gen. 15:2 ➔ HEIR <4943> 3 Is. 22:15 ➔ PROFITABLE (BE) <5532> b.

STICK – ***maqqēl*** [masc. noun: מַקֵּל <4731>; from an unused root meaning apparently to germinate] ► **This word refers to a rod, a thin branch, a staff of wood for various uses; it is also translated staff, rod branch.** Jacob cut rods from poplar and peeled white stripes in them for use in a mysterious breeding process (Gen. 30:37–39, 41); a walking stick or shepherd's stick (Gen. 32:10; Ex. 12:11; 1 Sam. 17:40); a prodding or riding rod (Num. 22:27); a weapon (Ezek. 39:9: club). It is used figuratively of covenants with Israel and Judah (Zech. 11:7, 10, 14). Hosea describes it as a kind of staff or wand used by a sorcerer or diviner (Hos. 4:12). It is used symbolically several more times (Jer. 1:11; 48:17 [of Moab]). Other ref.: 1 Sam. 17:43. ¶

STICK CLOSE – Prov. 18:24 ➔ JOINING <1695>.

STICK FAST – Ps. 38:2 ➔ BEND <5181>.

STICK OUT – ***šāp̱āh*** [verb: שָׁפָה <8192>; a prim. root] ► **This word refers to something protruding out or becoming visible: the bones of a chastened person before God.** Ref.: Job 33:21. It is used of hoisting up a flag or a banner on a hill for all to see (Is. 13:2: high, bare). ¶

STIFF – Ps. 75:5 ➔ ARROGANCE <6277>.

STILL (adj.) – ***d^{e}māmāh*** [fem. noun: דְּמָמָה <1827>; fem. from STAND STILL <1826>] ▶ **This word indicates a soft gentle blowing or whisper; it is also translated calm, whisper, silence.** It in contrast to the roar of an earthquake, fire, or a storm at sea (1 Kgs. 19:12: still; Ps. 107:29: calm, still, whisper). It indicates the absence of any sound or voice (Job 4:16: silence). ¶

STILL (adv.) – Eccl. 4:2 ➔ YET <5728>.

STILL (BE) – [1] ***šāqaṭ*** [verb: שָׁקַט <8252>; a prim. root] ▶ **This word means to be quiet, to be undisturbed. The primary meaning of this verb is the state or condition of tranquility (cf. Job 37:17).** It signifies the condition during the absence of war (Judg. 3:30; 2 Chr. 20:30); a sense of safety and security (Ezek. 38:11); inactivity or passivity (Ps. 83:1; Is. 18:4); keeping silent (Ruth 3:18; Is. 62:1); and an inner confidence or peace (Is. 7:4). Scripture declares that righteousness brings true security and tranquility (Is. 32:17); but also warns of the false security that comes to the unrighteous (Ezek. 16:49). *
– [2] 2 Kgs. 2:3, 5; Neh. 8:11; etc. ➔ SILENT (BE, KEEP, REMAIN) <2814>.

STILLBORN – ***nêp̱el, nep̱el*** [masc. noun: נֵפֶל, נֶפֶל <5309>; from FALL (verb) <5307>] ▶ **This word means and is also translated untimely birth, miscarriage.** Job thought it might have been better to have been stillborn than to be born and live with his trouble (Job 3:16). The psalmist hoped the wicked would be put away like a miscarried infant (Ps. 58:8). The teacher in Ecclesiastes thought it would have been better for people to never be born than not to be able to enjoy their riches and have proper burials (Eccl. 6:3). ¶

STING – ***pāraš*** [verb: פָּרַשׁ <6567>; a prim. root] ▶ **This word refers to a sharp, smarting pain, such as a pinprick or a bee sting, sometimes accompanied with the injection of poison into the penetrated area.** Ref.: Prov. 23:32. The Hebrew word also means to make clear, to scatter; see CLEAR (BE, MAKE) <6567> and SCATTER <6567>. ¶

STINK – [1] ***bā'aṣh*** [verb: בָּאַשׁ <887>; a prim. root] ▶ **This word means to be offensive, to be repulsive; it is also translated to smell, to become foul, to make obnoxious, to make odious, to make abhorrent, to make a stench, to be loathsome, etc.** It denotes a bad physical smell, like the reeking odor of blood in the Nile River (Ex. 7:21) or the odor of spoiled manna (Ex. 16:20). In a figurative sense, it speaks of a person who becomes strongly revolting to another, a metaphorical "stench in the nostrils." Jacob worried that his sons' retributive murder of the Shechemites caused him to stink before the people of the land (Gen. 34:30. The Israelites fretted that Moses' preaching caused them to be offensive to Pharaoh (Ex. 5:21), thus risking their lives. The verb also negatively expresses the actions of the wicked (Prov. 13:5); folly (Eccl. 10:1); and the stinking of wounds resulting from God's reproof of sin (Ps. 38:5). *
– [2] Is. 3:24 ➔ STENCH <4716> [3] Is. 19:6 ➔ REJECT <2186> b.

STINK (noun) – Is. 34:3; Joel 2:20; Amos 4:10 ➔ STENCH <889>.

STINKWEED – ***bo'šāh*** [fem. noun: בָּאְשָׁה <890>; fem. of STENCH <889>] ▶ **This word indicates a useless category of weeds; it is also translated weed, foul weed, cockle.** It is some kind of Eurasian grass which some translators render a darnel (Job 31:40). ¶

STIR (noun) – Is. 22:2 ➔ STORM (noun) <8663>.

STIR (verb) – [1] ***hûm*** [verb.: הוּם <1949>; a prim. root (comp. CONFUSE <2000>)] ▶ **This verb means to be in a stir, to be in commotion. It describes an emotional reaction or rousing, such as occurred in Bethlehem when Ruth and Naomi returned from Moab.** Ref.: Ruth 1:19: to be excited, to be stirred, to be moved. Such a stir would occur

in the nations when God would confuse them before their destruction (Deut. 7:23). On several occasions, the audible effects of the rousing was emphasized, such as when Solomon was anointed king, the roar of the city could be heard (1 Kgs. 1:45; cf. 1 Sam. 4:5; Mic. 2:12). In the only other occurrence of this verb, David described himself as restless and roused (Ps. 55:2). ¶
– [2] Judg. 13:25 ➔ TROUBLED (BE) <6470> [3] Ps. 147:18 ➔ DRIVE <5380> [4] Ezek. 32:13 ➔ TROUBLE (verb) <1804> [5] Dan. 11:10, 25 ➔ STRIVE <1624>.

STIR UP – [1] ***giyaḥ, gûaḥ*** [Aramaic verb: גִּיחַ, גּוּחַ <1519>; corresponding to GUSH <1518>] ▶ **This word indicates rushing forth, churning up; it is also translated to break forth, to strive upon.** It is used of the four winds of heaven churning the sea, from which four beasts arise (Dan. 7:2). ¶
– [2] Job 26:12; Is. 51:15; Jer. 31:35 ➔ MOMENT (BE FOR A) <7280> b. [3] Is. 9:11; 19:2 ➔ COVER (verb) <5526> b.

STIRRED – ***rāḇaḵ*** [verb: רָבַךְ <7246>; a prim. root] ▶
a. This word is used only in a passive form of the verb meaning something mixed, stirred. Usually olive oil is mixed with dough, cakes, etc. (Lev. 6:21; 7:12; 1 Chr. 23:29).
b. This word means to bake, to fry. It describes the baking, frying, preparations for dough or cakes (Lev. 6:21; 7:12; 1 Chr. 23:29). ¶

STIRRED (BE) – [1] Gen. 43:30; 1 Kgs. 3:26; Hos. 11:8 ➔ YEARN <3648> [2] Ps. 45:1 ➔ OVERFLOW (verb) <7370> a.

STIRRING – Prov. 30:33 ➔ CHURNING <4330>.

STOCK – [1] Lev. 25:47 ➔ MEMBER <6133> [2] Job 14:8; Is. 11:1; 40:24 ➔ STUMP <1503> [3] Ps. 80:15 ➔ ROOT (noun) <3657> [4] Is. 3:1 ➔ SUPPORT (noun) <4937> a. [5] Is. 44:19 ➔ FOOD <944>.

STOCKS – [1] ***mahpeḵeṯ*** [fem. noun: מַהְפֶּכֶת <4115>; from TURN <2015>] ▶ **This word is used of implements, a punishment device, used to confine prisoners in a stooped posture.** Refs.: Jer. 20:2, 3; 29:26. Once combined with *bêyt*, it is used of a prison or a house of confinement (2 Chr. 16:10). ¶
[2] ***saḏ*** [masc. noun: סַד <5465>; from an unused root meaning to stop or impede] ▶ **This word refers to a device for confining a prisoner's feet so he or she could not walk or wander away, a form of punishment or discipline.** Refs.: Job 13:27; 33:11; NIV: shackles. It is used figuratively in both passages. ¶
– [3] Prov. 7:22 ➔ FETTER <5914> [4] Jer. 29:26 ➔ NECK IRON <6729> b.

STOLEN (WHAT IS) – Ex. 22:4 ➔ THEFT <1591>.

STOMACH – [1] ***ḥōmeš*** [masc. noun: חֹמֶשׁ <2570>; from an unused root prob. meaning to be stout] ▶ **This word refers to the digestive organ; it is also translated belly; it means a fifth rib.** It refers to a person's stomach (2 Sam. 2:23; 3:27; 20:10), a vulnerable and accessible part of the body for an enemy to strike at. Other ref.: 2 Sam. 4:6. ¶
[2] ***kārêś*** [masc. noun: כָּרֵשׂ <3770>; by variation from STOOP <7164> (in the sense of the belly swelling out)] ▶ **This word is used in a figure of speech referring to Nebuchadnezzar's digestive organ.** "He has filled his stomach from my best foods" (Jer. 51:34). ¶
[3] ***qêḇāh*** [fem. noun: קֵבָה <6896>; from CURSE (verb) <6895> (which is from a root meaning to scoop out; thus a cavity)] ▶ **This word is used as a general term for the stomach (the digestive organ) or belly.** It is translated body (NASB) by some but is more specific than that (Num. 25:8). It refers to the internal organ itself. In a ruminate animal, its stomach was given to the priest as food in a sacrifice (Deut. 18:3). ¶
– [4] Num. 5:22 ➔ BOWELS <4578>.

STOMACHER – Is. 3:24 ➔ RICH ROBE <6614> b.

STONE (noun) – 1 ***'eben*** [fem. noun: אֶבֶן <68>; from the root of BUILD <1129>] ▶ **The word means a fragment of a rock; it is used often and has both literal and figurative meanings depending upon its context.** It is also used as a major source of raw material for all kinds of projects produced by various skilled craftsmen or merchants. Both precious and nonprecious stones are mentioned in Scripture.

In its natural or adapted states, stone was used as a pillow (Gen. 28:11, 18); a cover of a well (Gen. 29:2, 3, 8); a weapon of opportunity (Ex. 21:18); a weapon of official executions (Lev. 20:2, 27; 24:23; Num. 14:10); sling stones (1 Sam. 17:40, 49); memorial stones (Josh. 4:3, 5–9); sacred pillars (Gen. 28:18). In Joshua 24:26, 27, they are used as witnesses by Joshua.

Various items were made of stone: the tablets of the Ten Commandments (Ex. 31:18; 34:1; Deut. 5:22); vessels (Ex. 7:19); and pavement (2 Kgs. 16:17). Washed stones are mentioned (Lev. 14:40, 42, 43, 45), and they were used in walls, tombs, and buildings (2 Kgs. 22:6; Neh. 4:2; Is. 14:19). Stones were especially important for use as foundation stones or cornerstones (Job 38:6; Is. 28:16; Jer. 51:26); and capstones (Zech. 3:9; 4:7).

Many precious stones are noted in various passages (Gen. 2:12; Ex. 28:9–12, 17–21), especially those featured in the breastplate of Israel's high priest. They are also featured in the Garden of Eden as mentioned in Ezekiel 28:13–16.

The word indicates some tools or equipment used by merchants and builders such as weights (Prov. 20:10, 23; 27:3). They were described as plummets or a plumb line (Is. 34:11) in a literal and figurative sense as well by the biblical writer. *

2 ***'eben*** [Aramaic fem. noun: אֶבֶן <69>; corresponding to <68> above] ▶ **The word means a fragment of a rock; it is found only in the Aramaic portions of Daniel and Ezra in the Old Testament.** The stones referred to in Ezra (Ezra 5:8; 6:4) are heavy or huge stones used to build the second Temple. The word is used as powerful imagery in Daniel (Dan. 2:34, 35, 45) to refer to the kingdom of God. In Daniel 5:4, 23, stone gods/idols are referred to. In Daniel 6:17, a special stone is used to seal the lion's den. ¶

– 3 Lev. 21:20 ➔ TESTICLE <810> 4 2 Sam. 17:13 ➔ BAG <6872> b. 5 Job 40:17 ➔ THIGH <6344> b.

STONE HEAP – Job 8:17; Hos. 12:11 ➔ HEAP (noun) <1530>.

STONE QUARRIES – Josh. 7:5 ➔ SHEBARIM <7671> b.

STONE (verb) – 1 ***sāqal*** [verb: סָקַל <5619>; a prim. root (properly to be weighty)] ▶ **This word means to throw stones at, to kill by stoning.** It describes a fairly common way of killing or executing persons in the Middle East (Ex. 8:26; 17:4; 19:13; Josh. 7:25); or animals (Ex. 21:28). A false prophet was stoned to death (Deut. 13:10). It is used in a causative way meaning to clear or remove stones (Is. 5:2; 62:10). *

2 ***rāgam*** [verb: רָגַם <7275>; a prim. root] ▶ **This word means to kill persons by stoning them.** Refs.: Lev. 20:2, 27; Num. 14:10; Deut. 21:21. The preposition *b^e^* is usually used in the construction indicating the stone (*'eben*) or the person stoned (1 Kgs. 12:18). Sometimes *b^e^* is not used at all (Josh. 7:25; Ezek. 23:47). *

STONECUTTER – See CUT (verb) <2672> b.

STONES (CLEAR, REMOVE, TAKE OUT) – Is. 5:2; 62:10 ➔ STONE (verb) <5619>.

STONY WASTES – Jer. 17:6 ➔ PARCHED PLACE <2788>.

STOOL – Ex. 1:16: stool, delivery stool ➔ WHEEL <70>.

STOOP – 1 ***qāras*** [verb: קָרַס <7164>; a prim. root] ▶ **This word means to bend low.** It is used mockingly of Bel, a Babylonian idol, that stoops over, wavers, for Babylon is destroyed (Is. 46:1, 2). ¶

– 2 Eccl. 12:3 ➔ BEND <5791>.

STOOPED FOR AGE – 2 Chr. 36:17 ➔ AGED <3486>.

STOP – [1] ***'āṭam*** [verb: אָטַם <331>; a prim. root] ▶ **This word means to shut up, to be narrow, to frame.** It refers to stopping one's ears (Is. 33:15) or closing one's mouth (Prov. 17:28). It also indicates a framed, shuttered, or latticed window (1 Kgs. 6:4; Ezek. 40:16). *
– [2] Gen. 8:2; Ps. 63:11 ➔ CLOSE <5532> [3] 1 Sam. 10:2 ➔ FORSAKE <5203> [4] Ezra 4:21, 23, 24; 5:5; 6:8 ➔ CEASE <989> [5] Prov. 20:3 ➔ LOSS OF TIME <7674> [6] Is. 33:1 ➔ END (MAKE AN) <5239> [7] Ezek. 39:11 ➔ MUZZLE <2629> [8] See CEASE <2308>.

STOP, STOP UP – ***sāṯam, śāṯam*** [verb: סָתַם, שָׂתַם <5640>; a prim. root] ▶ **This word means to plug up, to halt the function of a well by filling the well cylinder with dirt and debris.** Refs.: Gen. 26:15, 18. It describes the filling in of springs as well (2 Kgs. 3:19, 25); or gaps in a broken wall (Neh. 4:7). It is used, with *bᵉ* on the front, as an adverb to mean secretly, in secret (Ps. 51:6). It means to hide or to keep something hidden, secret (Dan. 8:26; 12:4). *

STOPPING – Lam. 3:49 ➔ INTERRUPTION <2014>.

STORAGE – ***miskᵉnôṯ*** [fem. plur. noun: מִסְכְּנוֹת <4543>; by transposition from GATHER <3664>] ▶ **This word refers to storehouses, storage areas, i.e., places to put things away.** It indicates a structure or even a city used for storage or supplies of various kinds, chiefly military supplies (Ex. 1:11; 1 Kgs. 9:19; 2 Chr. 8:4, 6; 17:12); grain (2 Chr. 16:4); or wine and oil (2 Chr. 32:28). ¶

STORE (noun) – [1] Gen. 41:36 ➔ DEPOSIT <6487> [2] Ex. 1:11; 1 Kgs. 9:19; 2 Chr. 8:4, 6; 16:4; 17:12 ➔ STORAGE <4543> [3] Lev. 26:10 ➔ SLEEP (verb) <3462> b. [4] Deut. 28:5, 17 ➔ KNEADING BOWL, KNEADING TROUGH <4863> [5] 2 Kgs. 20:17; Is. 39:6: to lay up in store ➔ STORE (verb) <686> [6] Neh. 12:44 ➔ STOREHOUSE <214> [7] Is. 3:1 ➔ SUPPORT (noun) <4938> a. [8] Jer. 41:8 ➔ TREASURE <4301>.

STORE (LAY IN) – ***kāmas*** [verb: כָּמַס <3647>; a prim. root] ▶ **This word indicates to store up, i.e., to put things away, to save. It is used of preserving or saving up something.** In context it is used of God saving up judgment for His people (Deut. 32:34; NIV: to keep in reserve). ¶

STORE (verb) – [1] ***'āṣar*** [verb: אָצַר <686>; a prim. root] ▶ **This word means to store up (i.e., to put things away), or put in charge of stored items.** It refers to everything stored in Hezekiah's palace and the Temple (2 Kgs. 20:17; Is. 39:6). It indicates Nehemiah's (Neh. 13:13) placing certain persons in charge of the tithes kept in the storehouses. It is used figuratively of the wealth, wages, and gains of Tyre, a city of prostitution, which would be destroyed by the Lord. Her wealth would be decimated, not stored up (Is. 23:18); also translated to be treasured. Amos uses the word to refer to hoarding up evil or violence (Amos 3:10). ¶
– [2] Ezra 6:1 ➔ BRING DOWN <5182>.

STORE UP – ***ṣāḇar*** [verb: צָבַר <6651>; a prim. root] ▶ **This word means to heap up, to gather together.** It means to pile up, to reserve an abundance of grain (Gen. 41:35, 49). It refers to piling up, heaping up anything (Ex. 8:14); to hoard money, wealth (Job 27:16; Ps. 39:6; Zech. 9:3); to pile up rubble to besiege a city (Hab. 1:10). ¶

STOREHOUSE – [1] ***'ôṣār*** [masc. noun: אוֹצָר <214>; from STORE (verb) <686>] ▶ **This word means a place where things are put away; it is also translated treasure, treasury, storeroom, store.** Various items were stored up, such as supplies (Neh. 12:44) or treasures of a palace or temple (1 Kgs. 7:51; Jer. 15:13). The Lord also has treasures in the heavens (Deut. 28:12) and in the winds (Jer. 10:13). The word refers to storehouses themselves (Neh. 13:12, 13). *

[2] ***'āsōp̱, ᵃsuppiym*** [masc. noun: אֲסֻפִּים ,אָסֹף <624>; pass. part. of GATHER <622>] ▶ **This word means a collection, a treasury; it is also translated gatehouse, storeroom.** The primary meaning of the root is that which is gathered. It is used three times in the Old Testament to signify the storehouses near the gates of a temple (1 Chr. 26:15, 17; Neh. 12:25). ¶
– [3] Deut. 28:8 ➔ BARN <618> [4] 1 Chr. 28:11 ➔ TREASURY <1597> [5] 2 Chr. 32:28 ➔ STORAGE <4543> [6] Jer. 50:26 ➔ GRANARY <3965>.

STOREROOM – [1] 1 Chr. 28:11 ➔ TREASURY <1597> [2] Neh. 12:25 ➔ STOREHOUSE <624> [3] Neh. 12:44 (lit.: rooms of the storehouse); 13:12, 13 ➔ STOREHOUSE <214>.

STORK – ***ḥᵃsiyḏāh*** [fem. noun: חֲסִידָה <2624>; fem. from FAITHFUL <2623>] ▶ **a. This word identifies a bird declared unclean to Israel, not to be eaten.** Refs.: Lev. 11:19; Deut. 14:18. Its behavior is a witness to God's work in nature (Job 39:13; others read ostrich here: ESV, NIV, NKJV, NASB; KJV, peacock; Ps. 104:17; Jer. 8:7). Its wings are described in a simile by Zechariah as the wings of two women (Zech. 5:9). ¶
b. This word also means an ostrich. It is a picture of a bird displaying its beauty as God's handiwork (Job 39:13; KJV, peacock). ¶

STORM (noun) – [1] ***zerem*** [masc. noun: זֶרֶם <2230>; from POUR OUT <2229>] ▶ **This word indicates a violent rain, a rain shower, cloudburst; it is also translated tempest, shower, rain.** God's remnant will be protected from the storm of their enemies seeking to destroy them (Is. 4:6). God Himself becomes a refuge from the storm (Is. 25:4), and His king and princes in a restored Israel will bring shelter from the storms of life (Is. 32:2). But God also brings a storm of judgment on His enemies (Is. 28:2; 30:30; Hab. 3:10: overflowing, downpour, torrent, raging). Other ref.: Job 24:8. ¶
[2] ***sûp̱āh*** [סוּפָה <5492>; from CONSUME, BE CONSUMED <5486>] ▶ **a. A feminine noun indicating a wind, a stormy wind.** It indicates a storm with strong winds that blow away chaff like nothing (Job 21:18; NIV: gale). In general, it refers to a storm with destructive powers, a tempest, a hurricane-type storm (Job 27:20: tempest, whirlwind). It is used in a figurative sense of God's pursuit of the wicked (Ps. 83:15; Is. 66:15; Amos 1:14; Nah. 1:3); or of any calamity on humankind (Prov. 1:27). God's chariots are like a tempest or a whirlwind (Jer. 4:13). *
b. A proper noun, Suphah. It refers to a region in Moab near the Arnon River. Ref.: Num. 21:14. ¶
c. A proper noun referring to the Red Sea, Sea of Reeds. It is taken by some translators as a reference to the Red Sea (KJV, Num. 21:14). ¶
[3] ***šaᵃwāh*** [fem. noun: שַׁאֲוָה <7584>; from ROAR (verb) <7582>] ▶ **This type of storm is used to describe the aftermath of rejecting Wisdom's advice on how to live wisely.** Ref.: Prov. 1:27. ¶
[4] ***tᵉshu'āh, tᵉshûwāh*** [fem. noun: תְּשֻׁאָה, תְּשֻׁוָה <8663>; from RAVAGE <7722>] ▶ **This word means a violent weather condition, a crashing, a noise; a substance.** God breaks Job in the storm, noise, crashing (Job 30:22; KJV: substance). It refers to the thundering of the storms from God's dwelling (KJV, Tabernacle); to His displays in nature (Job 36:29). It refers to the shouting or crying out of the drivers in the center of great cities (Job 39:7); and to the noise and bustling activity of Babylon in her prosperity (Is. 22:2; also translated stir, commotion). It refers to formal shouting accompanying a religious ritual in Jerusalem (Zech. 4:7). ¶
– [5] Job 9:17; Nah. 1:3 ➔ TEMPEST <8183> [6] Job 30:22 ➔ SUBSTANCE <7738> [7] Ps. 55:8 ➔ WIND <5584> [8] Is. 28:2 ➔ HORROR <8178> [9] Nah. 2:9 ➔ ARRANGEMENT <8498> a.

STORM (verb) – Dan. 11:40 ➔ SWEEP AWAY <8175>.

STORM AGAINST – Is. 3:5 ➔ BOLD (BE, MAKE) <7292>.

STORY – [1] ***midrāš*** [masc. noun: מִדְרָשׁ <4097>; from SEEK <1875>] ▶ **This word designates a record, a treatise; it is also translated annals, annotations.** It is used of an official writing or composition recording the official acts of a king and other events surrounding him (2 Chr. 13:22; 24:27). ¶
– [2] 1 Kgs. 6:5, 6, 10 ➔ BED <3326> b.

STOUT OF HEART – Amos 2:16 ➔ BRAVE <533>.

STOUT WARRIORS – Is. 10:16 ➔ FATNESS <4924> a.

STOUTHEARTED – Ps. 76:5; Is. 46:12 ➔ lit.: mighty of heart ➔ MIGHTY <47>.

STOVE, COOKING STOVE – ***kiyr*** [masc. noun: כִּיר <3600>; a form of FURNACE <3564> (only in the dual)] ▶ **This word means an oven, a range, a cooking pot.** It probably refers to a small stove for two pots (Lev. 11:35); it is also translated ranges for pots, cooking pot. ¶

STRAGGLE – Deut. 25:18 ➔ FEEBLE (BE) <2826>.

STRAGGLER (BE) – Is. 14:31 ➔ ALONE (BE) <909>.

STRAIGHT – [1] ***miyšôr*** [masc. noun: מִישׁוֹר <4334>; from STRAIGHT (BE) <3474>] ▶ **This word means plain, evenness, straightness, righteousness, equity.** Evenness is the fundamental sense of this word. It denotes straight, as opposed to crooked (Is. 40:4; 42:16); level land, such as a plain (Deut. 3:10; 1 Kgs. 20:23); and a safe, unobstructed path (Ps. 27:11). By analogy, it is likewise used to imply a righteous lifestyle (Ps. 143:10); and equitable leadership (Ps. 45:6; Is. 11:4). *
– [2] Ezek. 46:9 ➔ OPPOSITE (adv.) <5226>.

STRAIGHT (BE) – ***yāšar*** [verb: יָשַׁר <3474>; a prim. root] ▶ **This word means to be upright, to be smooth, to be pleasing. When it means straight, it applies in a physical and an ethical sense, i.e., as in straightforward.** Therefore, this word can be used to refer to a path (1 Sam. 6:12); water (2 Chr. 32:30); the commands of God (Ps. 119:128); or of a person (Hab. 2:4). This word is also used to mean pleasing, as Samson found a Philistine woman pleasing to him (Judg. 14:7); but the cities that Solomon gave to Hiram were not pleasing (1 Kgs. 9:12). It can also mean to make (or be) smooth or even, as with gold (1 Kgs. 6:35); or a level road (Is. 40:3). *

STRAIGHT (MAKE) – ***tāqan*** [verb: תָּקַן <8626>; a prim. root] ▶ **This word means to make right; to straighten out, to straighten what is crooked.** It is used figuratively of straightening the moral, ethical, and religious ills of the world (Eccl. 1:15), the things God Himself has allowed humankind to make crooked or bent (Eccl. 7:13). It indicates putting a writing composition into proper order, especially a series of sayings or proverbs (Eccl. 12:9: to set in order, to arrange). ¶

STRAIGHTEN – Eccl. 1:15; 7:13 ➔ STRAIGHT (MAKE) <8626>.

STRAIGHTFORWARD – Prov. 8:9 ➔ RIGHT <5228>.

STRAITEN – [1] Prov. 4:12 ➔ DISTRESSED (BE) <3334> [2] Ezek. 42:6 ➔ RESERVE (verb) <680>.

STRAITENED (BE) – [1] Job 18:7 ➔ DISTRESSED (BE) <3334> [2] Job 37:10 ➔ CONSTRAINT <4164>.

STRAITNESS – [1] Deut. 28:53, 55, 57; Jer. 19:9 ➔ DISTRESS (noun) <4689> [2] Job 36:16 ➔ CONSTRAINT <4164>.

STRAITS – Lam. 1:3 ➔ DISTRESS (noun) <4712>.

STRAITS (BE IN) – Job 20:22 ➔ DISTRESSED (BE) <3334>.

STRAKE – Gen. 30:37 ➔ STRIPE <6479>.

STRAND – [1] Ex. 39:3 ➔ CORD <6616> [2] Song 4:3 ➔ THREAD <2339> [3] Song 4:9 ➔ CHAIN <6060>.

STRANGE – [1] ***nokriy*** [adj.: נָכְרִי <5237>; from SET UP <5235> (in the sense of strange)] ▶ **This word means foreign; stranger, foreigner.** It refers to someone who was not part of the family (Gen. 31:15; cf. Gen. 31:14; Ps. 69:8), especially the extended family of Israel (Deut. 17:15). Under the Law, strangers were not allowed to rule in Israel (Deut. 17:15); they were not released from their debts every seven years as Hebrews were (Deut. 15:3); and could be sold certain ceremonially unclean food (Deut. 14:21). Strangers were regarded as unholy (Deut. 14:21); and were often looked down on (Ruth 2:10; Job 19:15). Some hope for the conversion of foreigners was offered (Ruth 2:10; 1 Kgs. 8:41, 43); but with this word, more emphasis was placed on avoiding the defilement of foreign women (1 Kgs. 11:1; Ezra 10:2, 10, 11, 14, 17, 18, 44; Prov. 6:24); and foreign ways (Is. 2:6; Jer. 2:21; Zeph. 1:8). The word *gêr* (STRANGER <1616>), meaning sojourner, alien, focuses more sympathetically on foreigners in Israel. *
– [2] Is. 28:11 ➔ STAMMERING <3934> [3] Ezek. 3:5, 6 ➔ UNINTELLIGIBLE <6012>.

STRANGE (TO MAKE ONESELF) – Job 19:3 ➔ WRONG (verb) <1970> b.

STRANGE PUNISHMENT – Job 31:3 ➔ DISASTER <5235>.

STRANGE SPEECH – Is. 18:2, 7 ➔ POWERFUL <6978> c.

STRANGER – [1] ***gêyr, gêr*** [masc. noun: גֵּיר, גֵּר <1616>; from SOJOURN <1481>] ▶ **This word means a sojourner, an alien.** It indicates in general anyone who is not native to a given land or among a given people (Ex. 12:19). It is used most often to describe strangers or sojourners in Israel who were not native-born Israelites and were temporary dwellers or newcomers. A person, family, or group might leave their homeland and people to go elsewhere because of war or immediate danger as Moses had done (Ex. 2:22; cf. 2 Sam. 4:3); Naomi and her family were forced to travel to Moab to sojourn because of a famine in Israel (Ruth 1:1). God's call to Abraham to leave his own land of Ur of the Chaldeans made him a sojourner and an alien in the land of Canaan (Gen. 12:1). Israel's divinely orchestrated descent into Egypt resulted in their becoming an alien people in a foreign land for four hundred years (Gen. 15:13). Abraham considered himself an alien, although he was in the land of Canaan, the land of promise, because he was living among the Hittites at Hebron (Gen. 23:4).

This evidence indicates that strangers or aliens were those living in a strange land among strange people. Their stay was temporary or they did not identify with the group among whom they were living, no matter how long they stayed. The transitory nature of aliens' status is indicated in passages that describe them as seeking overnight lodging or accommodations (Job 31:32; Jer. 14:8).

Sojourners or strangers in Israel were not to be oppressed but were to receive special consideration for several reasons: Israel knew about being aliens, for they had been aliens in Egypt (Ex. 23:9); aliens had a right to rest and cessation from labor just as the native Israelites did (Ex. 20:10); aliens were to be loved, for God loved them (Deut. 10:18) just as He loved widows and orphans; aliens had a right to food to satisfy their needs just as orphans and widows did (Deut. 14:29). In Ezekiel's vision of a new Temple and Temple area, the children of aliens and sojourners were given an allotment of land (Ezek. 47:22), for they were to be considered as native children of Israel. However, this shows that sojourners had to receive special concessions because they did not have all the rights of native Israelites. Aliens could eat the Lord's Passover only if they and their entire household submitted to circumcision (Ex. 12:48, 49). They were then not allowed to eat anything with yeast in it during the celebration of the Passover, just like native Israelites (Ex. 12:19, 20). However, major distinctions did exist between sojourners or aliens and native Israelites. Unclean food could be given to aliens to eat, but the Israelites were prohibited from eating the same food. To have done so would violate their holiness and consecration to the Lord God. Unfortunately, David himself laid forced labor on the shoulders of aliens in Israel to prepare to build the Temple (1 Chr. 22:2; cf. 2 Chr. 8:7–9). *

– [2] Obad. 1:12: the day that he became a stranger ➔ the day of his misfortune ➔ DISASTER <5235>.

STRANGER (BE) – ***zûr*** [verb: זוּר <2114>; a prim. root] ▶ **The basic meaning of this word is to turn aside (particularly for lodging); therefore, it refers to being alien or foreign.** It can mean to go astray, to be wayward (Ps. 58:3). The participle is used frequently as an adjective, signifying something outside the law of God (Ex. 30:9; Lev. 10:1); a person outside the family (Deut. 25:5); the estranged way Job's guests and servants viewed him (Job 19:15); hallucinations from drunkenness (Prov. 23:33). This word is used several times in Proverbs of the adulterous woman (Prov. 2:16; 5:3, 20; 7:5; 22:14). *

STRANGLE – 2 Sam. 17:23; Nah. 2:12 ➔ HANG <2614>.

STRANGLING – ***maḥ***[a]***naq*** [masc. noun: מַחֲנָק <4267>; from HANG <2614>] ▶ **This word means suffocation, as a mode of death.** It refers figuratively to a means of death, a way of Job's soul (life) being snuffed out (Job 7:15). ¶

STRAP – ***ś***[e]***rûḵ*** [masc. noun: שְׂרוֹךְ <8288>; from TRAVERSE <8308>] ▶ **This word refers in context to binding strips used to keep sandals on a person's feet.** Refs.: Gen. 14:23; Is. 5:27; also translated latchet, thong. If the straps break, it slows a person's progress. ¶

STRATA – Amos 9:6 ➔ BUNCH <92>.

STRATEGY (DEVISE A) – Is. 8:10 ➔ COUNSEL (TAKE) <5779>.

STRAW – [1] ***maṯbên*** [masc. noun: מַתְבֵּן <4963>; denom. from STRAW <8401>] ▶ **This word refers to hollow stalks or stems of grain after being threshed.** It was used for fodder, for beds, or for making huts, pillows, etc. (Is. 25:10). ¶

[2] ***teḇen*** [masc. noun: תֶּבֶן <8401>; prob. from BUILD <1129>] ▶ **It was chopped stalks or stems of grain used for feed, fodder, and bedding for animals.** Refs.: Gen. 24:25; Judg. 19:19. It was mixed with clay to make strong bricks (Ex. 5:7). In poetry it describes the wicked blown in the wind (Job 21:18). In the reign of the Messiah, the lion will eat straw (Is. 11:7). It is used in a negative comparison by Jeremiah 23:28. *

STREAK – Gen. 30:37 ➔ STRIPE <6479>.

STREAK (INGRAINED, HOLLOW) – Lev. 14:37 ➔ DEPRESSION <8258>.

STREAKED – Gen. 30:35, 39, 40; 31:8, 10, 12 ➔ STRIPED <6124>.

STREAM (noun) – [1] ***yāḇāl*** [masc. noun: יָבָל <2988>; from BRING <2986>] ▶ **This word describes water currents or rivulets located on the tops of mountains and high hills.** In a time of God's judgments (Is. 30:25), they will be judged. But also it describes streams of water that will feed trees in a time of God's great blessings (Is. 44:4). ¶

[2] ***yûḇal*** [masc. noun: יוּבַל <3105>; from BRING <2986>] ▶ **This word refers to water, a canal; it is also translated river.** It indicates a source of water from which a tree can draw its sustenance and thrive (Jer. 17:8). ¶

[3] ***peleg*** [masc. noun: פֶּלֶג <6388>; from DIVIDE <6385>] ▶ **This word means a large channel of water; it is also translated river, channel.** It indicates any abundant flow of oil or water (Job 29:6); small or relatively large (Ps. 1:3). It refers to a channel or tributaries of a river, used figuratively

of the streams of the city of God (Ps. 46:4). God is the creator of the many streams (Ps. 65:9) that so abundantly water the earth. It is used figuratively of a man's fertility or vigor, as well as his offspring (Prov. 5:16). It signifies the heart of the king whose streams are in God's control (Prov. 21:1). It designates man-made water channels (Is. 30:25). Other refs.: Ps. 119:136; Is. 32:2; Lam. 3:48. ¶

4 ***šibbōleṯ*** [fem. noun: שִׁבֹּלֶת <7641>; from an unused root meaning to flow] ► **This word means a torrent, a flood.** This root has the sense of a flood or a mass of water (Ps. 69:2); a flood of water (Ps. 69:15). It refers to the powerful waters flowing in a river (Is. 27:12). For another meaning of the Hebrew word, see GRAIN (HEAD OF, EAR OF) <7641>. ¶

– 5 Num. 21:15 ➔ SLOPE <793>.

STREAM (verb) – Is. 2:2; 60:5; Jer. 31:12; 51:44; Mic. 4:1 ➔ FLOW (verb) <5102> a.

STREAMS – Gen. 2:6; Job 36:27 ➔ MIST <108>.

STREET – 1 ***ḥûṣ*** [masc. noun: חוּץ <2351>; from an unused root meaning to sever] ► **This word means an urban road; it also means the outside.** It indicates a location or direction: to the outside (Judg. 19:25); in a phrase, it can modify a noun, e.g., outer gate (Ezek. 47:2). It takes on the meaning of street, lane. Used with a following word in a construct phrase, it identifies a particular street, e.g., bakers' street (*ḥûṣ hā'ōp̱îym*; Jer. 37:21). It indicates direction to the outside: from the wall outward (Num. 35:4); outside, in the street (1 Kgs. 6:6). Prepositions are added to indicate direction (*bᵉ, lᵉ, 'el, min* (FROM <4480>) (Gen. 9:22; 2 Kgs. 4:3; Ezek. 41:9; 42:7). The phrase *ḥûṣ min*, which literally means outside from me, is rendered as more than I (Eccl. 2:25). *

2 ***rᵉḥōḇ, rᵉḥôḇ*** [fem. noun: רְחֹב, רְחוֹב <7339>; from ENLARGE <7337>] ► **This word means an urban road; it refers also to a public square, an open place.** It uniformly indicates an open area, a plaza, a public square of a town or village where most people met (Gen. 19:2). Nearly all cities had such an area (Deut. 13:16; Judg. 19:15, 17, 20). Wisdom cries out to people in the town square, a public place (Prov. 1:20). It refers to the entire network of open areas and streets in some cases (Ps. 55:11; 144:14; Prov. 5:16; Zech. 8:45). It would be a feature included in a rebuilt Jerusalem (Dan. 9:25). *

3 ***šûq*** [masc. noun: שׁוּק <7784>; from OVERFLOW (verb) <7783>] ► **This word refers to a public city road that is bounded by houses.** Refs.: Prov. 7:8; 12:4, 5. It is used to indicate all the streets of a city (Song 3:2). ¶

STRENGTH – 1 ***'on*** [masc. noun: אוֹן <202>; prob. from the same as NOTHINGNESS <205> (in the sense of effort, but successful)] ► **This word means manhood, maturity, generative power.** Reuben was the firstfruits of Jacob's generative power and strength (Gen. 49:3) as is any firstborn (Deut. 21:17). It refers to the fleeting strength of the wicked (Job 18:12); physical strength (Hos. 12:3); and riches as strength (Hos. 12:8: wealth, substance, wealthy). *

2 ***ᵉyāl*** [masc. noun: אֱיָל <353>; a variation of MIGHTY <352>] ► **This word refers to energy.** Ref.: Ps. 88:4. ¶

3 ***ᵉyālûṯ*** [fem. noun: אֱיָלוּת <360>; fem. of <353> above] ► **This word means a source of support.** The psalmist pleas that the Lord would be his strength (Ps. 22:19; also translated help). ¶

4 ***'êyṯān*** [masc. noun: אֵיתָן <386>; from an unused root (meaning to continue)] ► **The word means strong; it also indicates permanence, endurance.** Figuratively, it describes the usual, constant position of a stream or sea (Ex. 14:27; also translated normal course, normal state). It indicates the ancient, enduring feature of a nation, such as Babylon (Jer. 5:15). Literally, it depicts the perennial (constant) watering of a pasture (Jer. 49:19: strong) or the flooding or overflow of a dry river bed (wadi, Deut. 21:4). Used as a noun, it envisions constant overflowing streams (Ps. 74:15). *

5 ***'amṣāh*** [fem. noun: אַמְצָה <556>; from STRONG (BE) <553>] ▶ **This word refers to strong support against threats of danger as supplied by those who are living in Jerusalem.** Ref.: Zech. 12:5. ¶

6 ***dōḇe'*** [masc. noun: דֹּבֶא <1679>; from an unused root (comp. SPEAK <1680>)] ▶ **This word depicts the strength (NASB, leisurely walk) of Asher in Moses' blessing on the twelve tribes.** Ref.: Deut. 33:25. ¶

7 ***ḥêzeq*** [masc. noun: חֵזֶק <2391>; from STRONG (BE) <2388>] ▶ **This particular word is used only once in the Old Testament; it means strength, help.** God is the strength of the psalmist (Ps. 18:1). See the related Hebrew root *ḥāzaq* [STRONG (BE) <2388>] and the feminine form of this noun, *ḥezqāh* (<2393> below). ¶

8 ***ḥōzeq*** [masc. noun: חֹזֶק <2392>; from STRONG (BE) <2388>] ▶ **This word is used to describe the Lord's power in delivering Israel out of Egyptian bondage.** Refs.: Ex. 13:3, 14, 16. It is also used to describe the military strength of Israel (Amos 6:13) and of other kingdoms (Hag. 2:22). Although this particular word is used only five times in the Old Testament, its related verb *ḥāzaq* [STRONG (BE) <2388>] and its related adjective *ḥāzāq* (STRONG <2389>) are used many times. ¶

9 ***ḥezqāh*** [fem. noun: חֶזְקָה <2393>; fem. of <2391> above] ▶ **This word refers to the hand of the Lord on Isaiah as the Lord spoke to him.** Ref.: Is. 8:11. It is also used to describe the power of kings. When Rehoboam became strong and established his kingdom, he and his people abandoned the Law of the Lord (2 Chr. 12:1). When King Uzziah became strong, he became proud and went into the Temple to burn incense, even though that was the job of the priests (2 Chr. 26:16). In Daniel's vision, the fourth king gained power through his great wealth (Dan. 11:2). See the related Hebrew root *ḥāzaq* [STRONG (BE) <2388>] and the masculine form of this noun *ḥêzeq* (<2391> above). ¶

10 ***ḥozqāh*** [fem. noun: חָזְקָה <2394>; fem. of <2392> above] ▶ **This word means power; it always occurs with the preposition *b^e* (with or by).** It can be used to modify oppression (Judg. 4:3); rebuke (Judg. 8:1); capture (1 Sam. 2:16); ruling (Ezek. 34:4); crying to God (Jon. 3:8). Only the last of these references has a positive connotation. All the others connote a harsh, cruel, and self-serving connotation of the use of one's strength and power. ¶

11 ***ḥayil*** [masc. noun: חַיִל <2428>; from SHAKE <2342>] ▶ **This word has the basic idea of strength and influence; it also means wealth, army.** It can be used to speak of the strength of people (1 Sam. 2:4; 9:1; 2 Sam. 22:40); of horses (Ps. 33:17); or of nations (Esther 1:3). God is often seen as the supplier of this strength (2 Sam. 22:33; Hab. 3:19). When describing men, it can speak of those who are strong for war (Deut. 3:18; 2 Kgs. 24:16; Jer. 48:14); able to judge (Ex. 18:21, 25); or are righteous in behavior (1 Kgs. 1:52). When describing women, it speaks of virtuous character (Ruth 3:11; Prov. 12:4; 31:10). This idea of strength often is used to imply a financial influence (i.e., wealth) (Job 31:25; Ps. 49:6; Zech. 14:14); a military influence (i.e., an army) (Ex. 14:9; 2 Chr. 14:8, 9; Is. 43:17); or a numerical influence (i.e., a great company) (1 Kgs. 10:2; 2 Chr. 9:1). *

12 ***ḥayil*** [Aramaic masc. noun: חַיִל <2429>; corresponding to <2428> above] ▶ **This word means power, army.** In the book of Ezra, Rehum and Shimshai forced the Jews to stop rebuilding the city (Ezra 4:23). It can mean a loud or powerful voice, such as Nebuchadnezzar's herald (Dan. 3:4); a messenger from heaven (Dan. 4:14); and King Belshazzar to his enchanters (Dan. 5:7). Nebuchadnezzar had the most powerful soldiers bind up Shadrach, Meshach, and Abednego (Dan. 3:20). See the related Hebrew noun *ḥayil* (<2428> above). Other ref.: Dan. 4:35. ¶

13 ***kōaḥ, kôaḥ*** [masc. noun: כֹּחַ, כּוֹחַ <3581>; from an unused root meaning to be firm] ▶ **This is a general term referring to power or might in many different settings.** The strength of people (Judg. 16:5; Josh. 17:17); the prophet filled with the power and Spirit of the Lord (Mic. 3:8). It is used of animals (Prov. 14:4); or even of the fertility of a field

or the ground (Gen. 4:12). A son born to a father is his strength or vigor (Gen. 49:3). It is used of human labor in the fields to procure food (Lev. 26:20). Good food provides energy and strength for travel (1 Kgs. 19:8). It refers to all kinds of social, political, and economic forces (Eccl. 4:1); or general physical and intellectual capacity and determination (Eccl. 9:10). It indicates all the benefits and gains a person has accumulated (Prov. 5:10). The Hebrew word also means a lizard; see LIZARD MONITOR <3581>. *

14 ***niṣbāh*** [Aramaic fem. noun: נִצְבָּה <5326>; from a root corresponding to STAND (verb) <5324> (in the sense of brilliancy)] ► **This word refers to the ability of something to hold together or to perform difficult tasks; it is also translated toughness, firmness.** It refers to the iron in the feet of Daniel's vision (Dan. 2:41). ¶

15 ***ᵉzûz*** [masc. noun: עֱזוּז <5807>; from STRENGTHEN <5810>] ► **This word means might, power, violence.** It is used of God's power and strength displayed in His mighty work of salvation for His people (Ps. 78:4; 145:6). It describes the rage and violence of battle or war (Is. 42:25; NASB: fierceness). ¶

16 ***'ōṣem*** [masc. noun: עֹצֶם <6108>; from MIGHT (BE) <6105>] ► **This word indicates might, endurance as opposed to being weak, tired.** It refers to the supposed power and effectiveness of magical spells or enchantments. It refers to the power and influence of a political ally (Nah. 3:9). Other refs.: Deut. 8:17; Job 30:21. The Hebrew word also means frame, substance (lit.: bones) (Ps. 139:15). ¶

17 ***'oṣmāh*** [fem. noun: עָצְמָה <6109>; fem. of <6108> above] ► **This word indicates might.** It refers to the strength of persons, usually their social and political power as well as their physical or emotional strength (Is. 40:29). Other ref.: Is. 47:9 (abundance, power, potent). ¶

18 ***rōhaḇ*** [masc. noun: רֹהַב <7296>; from BOLD (BE, MAKE) <7292>] ► **This word refers in context to health, vigor of life, the ability to continue in life's pursuits.** Ref.: Ps. 90:10. ¶

19 ***tô'āp̱āh*** [fem. noun: תּוֹעָפָה <8443>; from FAINT <3286> (indicating exhaustion to obtain something)] ►

a. This word describes the power and might figuratively of the mythical unicorn as well as the might of the hills. Refs.: Num. 23:22; 24:8; Ps. 95:4. They are all demonstrations of God's power to deliver His people.

b. This word refers figuratively to the strength or horns of a wild ox as illustrative of God's power in delivering Israel. Refs.: Num. 23:22; 24:8.

c. This word refers to the peak of a mountain. Ref.: Ps. 95:4. It is rendered as peaks by the NIV and the NASB, but is still illustrative of God's power and strength.

d. This word means choice; abundance. It denotes a high-quality, pure silver, which is used to describe the value of the Lord (Job 22:25).

– 20 Deut. 34:7 ➔ VIGOR <3893> 21 Judg. 5:21; Ps. 8:2 ➔ STRONG <5797> 22 1 Sam. 2:33: sap your strength ➔ grieve your hearth ➔ GRIEVE <109> 23 Job 17:9 ➔ STRONGER <555> 24 Ps. 32:4 ➔ CAKE BAKED <3955> 25 Ps. 68:35 ➔ POWER <8592> 26 Ps. 73:4 ➔ BODY <193> a. 27 Prov. 3:8 ➔ DRINK (noun) <8250> 28 Is. 23:10 ➔ BELT <4206> 29 Is. 30:7 ➔ PROUD <7293> 30 Is. 40:26: the strength of his power, gained strength ➔ he is strong (or brave) in power, grew strong ➔ BRAVE <533> 31 Jer. 20:5; Is. 33:6 ➔ TREASURE <2633> 32 Dan. 2:37 ➔ MIGHT <8632> b. 33 Dan. 11:17 ➔ AUTHORITY <8633> 34 See HAND <3027> 35 See STRENGTH <1369>.

STRENGTH (REGAIN) – Ps. 39:13 ➔ SMILE (verb) <1082>.

STRENGTHEN – 1 ***'āzaz*** [verb: עָזַז <5810>; a prim. root] ► **This word means to make firm, to be strong, to prevail, to overpower; it is also translated to triumph, to remain triumphant.** It depicts being victorious, prevailing, being victorious in battle (Judg. 3:10; 6:2; Dan. 11:12) or in various settings. It describes people triumphing instead of God (Ps. 9:19). It has the sense

of being fixed, determined in a course of action (Ps. 52:7: to be strong, to grow strong, to seek refuge). It indicates a prostitute's face in her arrogance, an insolent or shameless countenance (Prov. 7:13: impudent, brazen, bold). It is used of the Lord's fixing or establishing the springs of the great deep at creation (Prov. 8:28; also translated to establish, to fix securely). It describes the affect of wisdom in establishing a person (Eccl. 7:19: also translated to make more powerful). It has the sense of to be or to find strength when in its infinitive form (Is. 30:2; also translated to take refuge, to look for help). Other refs.: Ps. 68:28; 89:13; Prov. 21:29. ¶
– 2 Judg. 19:5; Ps. 20:2 ➔ REFRESH <5582> 3 Ps. 138:3 ➔ BOLD (BE, MAKE) <7292> 4 Is. 45:5 ➔ GIRD <247> 5 Amos 5:9 ➔ SMILE (verb) <1082>.

STRETCH – 1 ***śāra'*** [verb: שָׂרַע <8311>; a prim. root] ▶ **This word means to stretch out. It refers to extending one's body fully and comfortably on a bed.** The whole context refers to Israel figuratively (Is. 28:20). For another meaning of the Hebrew word, see DEFORMED <8311>. ¶
– 2 Ps. 77:2 ➔ SPILL <5064> 3 Is. 25:7 ➔ SPREAD (verb) <5259> 4 Is. 48:13 ➔ SPREAD OUT <2946> 5 Amos 6:7 ➔ HANG <5628>.

STRETCH ONESELF – ***gāhar*** [verb: גָּהַר <1457>; a prim. root] ▶ **This word means to crouch down, to bend.** It is used to describe Elijah's posture in prayer on Mount Carmel as he beseeches the Lord for rain (1 Kgs. 18:42: to bow down, to cast oneself down, to bend down). It describes Elisha's crouching over or stretching himself out on the Shunammite's dead son in order to restore him to life (2 Kgs. 4:34, 35). ¶

STRETCH OUT – ***nāṭāh*** [verb: נָטָה <5186>; a prim. root] ▶ **This word is used often of simply extending or reaching out something: a hand, an arm is extended or a staff or javelin is pointed.** Refs.: Ex. 6:6; 7:5, 19; 9:22, 23; 10:12, 13, 21, 22; Josh. 8:18. It indicates spreading sackcloth for mourning (2 Sam. 21:10). The Lord extends His arm or hand to deliver His people (Ex. 6:6; Deut. 4:34; Jer. 32:21); or to bring judgments on them and the nations (Is. 5:25; 23:11; Ezek. 6:14). The idiom, to stretch out one's hand against someone, means to act in a hostile manner toward that person (Job 15:25). It is used of setting up a tent or tabernacle, stretching it out (Gen. 12:8; 26:25; Ex. 33:7; 2 Sam. 6:17; 16:22). The Lord has stretched out the sky, the firmament of the heavens (Jer. 10:12). It is used of God stretching out a plumb line in judgment (2 Kgs. 21:13). It describes in its passive forms something stretched out, e.g., wings (Is. 8:8), used figuratively. It is used figuratively of establishing a people, stretching out a tent (Jer. 10:12). It has the sense of turning something, inclining to: Balaam's ass turned aside (Num. 22:23); it is used of a person turning aside (2 Sam. 2:19). It has the figurative sense of inclining one's heart and mind a certain way, of giving attention: of turning from being loyal (1 Kgs. 2:28); turning from righteousness or justice (Ex. 23:2; 1 Sam. 8:3); or preventing it (Prov. 18:5). It is used of turning one's heart (mind) in a certain direction (1 Sam. 14:7); of being loyal (Josh. 24:23); it means to turn, to show love (*ḥeseḏ*) to someone (Ezra 7:28). It describes the apostasy of Solomon's heart turning after other gods and foreign women in his old age (1 Kgs. 11:2, 4). It is used of iniquities and sin thrusting away, turning away the good benefits of God from His people (Jer. 5:25). Finally, there are those who turn aside, away, in context to twisted, crooked ways (Ps. 125:5). *

STRETCHING OUT – Is. 8:8 ➔ SPREAD (noun) <4298>.

STRICKEN – 1 Is. 16:7 ➔ CRUSHED <5218> b. 2 Is. 53:8 ➔ he was stricken ➔ literally: to whom the stroke ➔ SORE (noun) <5061>.

STRICTLY – Ezra 7:26 ➔ DILIGENTLY <629>.

STRIDE – ***ṣā'āh*** [verb: צָעָה <6808>; a prim. root] ▶ **This word indicates walking forth**

with purpose, marching; in context it means to bring judgment. Ref.: Is. 63:1. ¶

STRIFE – [1] ***māḏôn*** [masc. noun: מָדוֹן <4066>; from JUDGE (verb) <1777> (in the sense of to be at strife, to quarrel)] ▶ **This word refers to dissension; it is also translated quarrel, contention, quarrelling, dispute.** Its plural is *m^eḏāniym, miḏyāniym*. It refers to a quarrel or dispute that cannot be stopped once it starts (Prov. 17:14); or to arguments and contentions that create barriers between persons (Prov. 18:19). It is preceded by *'iyš* to indicate Jeremiah as a man of strife or contention (Jer. 15:10). God can make His people an object of strife and contention (Ps. 80:6). An evil heart spreads dissension and strife (Prov. 6:14, 19); as does hatred (Prov. 10:12). A person with a temper creates strife (Prov. 15:18). A contentious, quarreling wife is a curse (Prov. 25:24). *

[2] ***maṣṣāh*** [fem. noun: מַצָּה <4683>; from FIGHT (verb) <5327>] ▶ **This word relates to contention.** It refers to wrangling, quarreling, and contention (Prov. 13:10; 17:19), especially brought on by arrogant or insolent attitudes, transgressions, and trespasses. It refers to the results of false fasts that brought on fighting, quarreling, and violence (Is. 58:4; KJV, NKJV: debate). ¶

[3] ***m^eriyḇāh*** [fem. noun: מְרִיבָה <4808>; from STRIVE <7378>] ▶ **This word indicates contention. It is used of a state of quarreling or wrangling over something, a condition of hostility.** Refs.: Gen. 13:8; Num. 27:14. The name Meribah means striving, strife (Num. 27:14; Ps. 95:8; 106:32; Ezek. 47:19; 48:28). ¶

[4] ***riyḇ, riḇ, riyḇāh*** [masc. noun: רִב, רִיב, רִיבָה <7379>; from STRIVE <7378>] ▶ **This word means a controversy, a contention. The primary idea of this noun is that of a quarrel or dispute.** It appears in reference to an argument over land-use rights (Gen. 13:7); the logical dispute the Lord has with sinners (Jer. 25:31); any general state of contention between individuals (Prov. 20:3); the clamoring of people for station or possessions (2 Sam. 22:44); and open hostilities with an enemy (Judg. 12:2). Israel is commanded not to pervert justice in a lawsuit (Ex. 23:2). Similarly, the word is used in a legal sense to refer to an argument or case made in one's defense (Deut. 21:5; Prov. 18:17; Mic. 7:9). *

STRIFES – ***m^eḏāniym*** [masc. plur. noun: מְדָנִים <4090>; a form of STRIFE <4066>] ▶ **This word designates discords. It is the plural of *māḏôn* and has the same meaning and usage.** Refs.: Prov. 6:14, 19; 10:12. See STRIFE <4066>. ¶

STRIKE – [1] ***m^eḥā'*** [Aramaic verb: מְחָא <4223>; corresponding to CLAP <4222>] ▶ **This term corresponds closely to the Hebrew verbs *māḵāh* (WIPE, WIPE OUT <4229>) and *nāḵāh* (STRIKE <5221>).** When combined with the prepositional phrase *b^eyaḏ* (HAND <3027>) meaning on the hand, the term attains the idiomatic sense to restrain, to hinder, to prevent, or to stay (Dan. 4:35: to restrain, to stay, hold back, ward off). On one occasion, the word vividly described the penalty of impalement (on a beam) which awaited any individual who dared to alter King Darius' edict concerning the rebuilding of the Temple in Jerusalem (Ezra 6:11: to be impaled, to be hanged). Other refs.: Dan. 2:34, 35 (to smite, to strike). ¶

[2] ***nāḵāh*** [verb: נָכָה <5221>; a prim. root] ▶ **This word means to beat, to wound.** There are many instances of striking physically (Ex. 21:15, 19; Job 16:10; Ps. 3:7; Song 5:7). This word is also used in a different sense, as when the men of Sodom and Gomorrah were stricken blind by the two angels (Gen. 19:11); when a priest stuck a fork into the kettle (1 Sam. 2:14); when people clapped their hands (2 Kgs. 11:12); or when people verbally abused Jeremiah (Jer. 18:18). God struck the Egyptians with plagues (Ex. 3:20); and struck people down in judgment (Is. 5:25). *

[3] ***sāp̄aq, śāp̄aq*** [verb: סָפַק, שָׂפַק <5606>; a prim. root] ▶ **This word means to clap, to smite.** It signifies the clapping of hands in derision or disrespect, sometimes accompanied by hissing (Job 27:23; 34:37; Lam. 2:15); the clapping of the hand on the thigh

as a sign of grief or shame (Jer. 31:19; Ezek. 21:12: to beat); or the clapping of the hands in anger (Num. 24:10). The word is used to refer to God's striking of people in public rebuke for backsliding (Job 34:26; NIV: to punish); and the wallowing or splashing of Moab in its vomit (Jer. 48:26: to wallow). In Isaiah 2:6, the word referred to the striking of hands, i.e., making deals with foreigners. The meaning, "suffice," found in 1 Kings 20:10, appears to belong under another root, and this may also be true of Isaiah 2:6 (both passages spell the word with *ś* instead of *s*). ¶

STRIKE, STRIKE DOWN – 1 Gen. 12:17; Ps. 73:5; 2 Kgs. 15:5; Job 1:19; Is. 53:4; Ezek. 17:10 ➔ TOUCH <5060> 2 Ex. 21:22 Lev. 26:17; Num. 14:42; Judg. 20:35; 1 Sam. 25:38; 2 Sam. 12:15; 2 Chr. 21:18; Zech. 14:12, 18 ➔ SMITE <5062>.

STRIKING – Gen. 4:23 ➔ BRUISE (noun) <2250>.

STRING – 1 ***mêyṯār*** [masc. noun: מֵיתָר <4340>; from REMAIN <3498>] ▶ **This word refers to a strong cord or rope-like string.** A bowstring, used in a figurative sense (Ps. 21:12); or, especially, tent cords (Ex. 35:18; 39:40; Jer. 10:20). It is used of decorative cords in the Tabernacle (Num. 3:26, 37; 4:26, 32). Other ref.: Is. 54:2. ¶
– 2 Judg. 16:9 ➔ TOW <5296> 3 Ps. 45:8; 150:4 ➔ STRINGED INSTRUMENT <4482>.

STRING OF BEADS – Song 1:10 ➔ STRING OF JEWELS <2737>.

STRING OF JEWELS – ***ḥārûz*** [masc. noun: חָרוּז <2737>; from an unused root meaning to perforate] ▶ **This word indicates a string of beads or jewels, a necklace of shells; it is also translated string of jewels, chain of gold.** It was an ornament, a beautifying piece of jewelry which the writer of Song of Solomon 1:10 places on the beloved's neck. ¶

STRINGED INSTRUMENT – 1 ***mên*** [masc. noun: מֵן <4482>] ▶ **This word refers to musical instruments with stretched cords; it also refers to music of strings.** Refs.: Ps. 45:8; 150:4. The Hebrew word also means portion share; see PORTION <4482>. ¶
– 2 1 Sam. 10:5; 1 Kgs. 10:12; Amos 5:23; 6:5 ➔ HARP <5035> 3 Psalm 4, 6, 54, 55, 61, 67, 76; Hab. 3:19 ➔ SONG <5058> b.

STRIP – 1 ***ḥāśap*** [verb: חָשַׂף <2834>; a prim. root] ▶ **This word indicates to make bare, to take off.** It is used in contexts giving the effect of locusts stripping bark off of vines and trees (Joel 1:7); figuratively, of the Lord baring His arm (Is. 52:10); or stripping the forests bare by His voice (Ps. 29:9; KJV, to discover); of water (Is. 30:14: to dip, to scoop, to take); or wine (Hag. 2:16: to draw). It indicates Babylon stripping off a garment in a figurative sense (Is. 47:2: to strip off, to make bare, to bare, to take off; Jer. 13:26: to uncover, to strip, to discover, to lift up, to pull up). Other refs.: Is. 20:4; Jer. 49:10; Ezek. 4:7. ¶
2 ***'ārar*** [verb: עָרַר <6209>; a prim. root] ▶ **a. A verb meaning to remove clothes, to undress oneself; to raze.** It indicates the complete destruction, stripping, and demolishing of a city or nation, especially its most splendid features, its palaces and walls (Is. 23:13; Jer. 51:58). Prisoners of war were stripped of their luxurious garments (Is. 32:11). ¶
b. A verb meaning to raise up. It is translated as raised up since the translators understand a different contextual milieu (Is. 23:13). ¶
– 3 Gen. 30:37 ➔ STRIPE <6479> 4 Ezek. 17:9 ➔ CUT OFF <7082> 5 Hab. 3:9 ➔ UNCOVER <5783>.

STRIP OFF – 1 ***n^eṯar*** [Aramaic verb: נְתַר <5426>; corresponding to LOOSE (LET) <5425>] ▶ **This word is used of pulling off, plucking off the fruit and greenery of a tree or large shrub.** Ref.: Dan. 4:14; KJV: to shake off. ¶
2 ***pāšaṭ*** [verb: פָּשַׁט <6584>; a prim. root] ▶ **This word means to undress; it also means to raid, to invade.** It is used of forcefully removing clothing from a

person (Gen. 37:23); and of removing the skin from a sacrificial animal (Lev. 1:6). But it also refers to persons' removal of their inner clothing, as a matter of course (Lev. 6:11; 1 Sam. 18:4); or under duress (Is. 32:11). It indicates plundering or stripping a defeated enemy (1 Sam. 31:8; 2 Sam. 23:10). It means to break forth in a raid, to rush against an enemy (Judg. 9:33; 20:37). Figuratively, it describes the ruthless way the rulers of Israel treated the people (Mic. 3:3); and of how God would strip His people because of their rebellion (Hos. 2:3). *

STRIP, STRIP BARE, STRIP NAKED – Lam. 4:21; Hab. 3:13 ➔ EMPTY (verb) <6168>.

STRIPE – 1 ***peṣālāh*** [fem. noun: פְּצָלָה <6479>; from PEEL <6478>] ▶ **This word indicates a peeled spot, stripe, or place; it is also translated strip, strake, streak.** It refers to an exposed area on fresh wooden poles or rods where the bark has been removed (Gen. 30:37). ¶
– 2 Ex. 21:25; Prov. 20:30; Is. 53:5 ➔ BRUISE (noun) <2250> 3 Ps. 89:32; Is. 53:8 ➔ SORE (noun) <5061>.

STRIPED – ***'āqōḏ*** [adj. עָקֹד <6124>; from BIND <6123>] ▶ **This word refers to male goats that were striped (NASB, ESV), speckled (NKJV), streaked (NIV), ringstraked (KJV).** The various ways that the word is translated shows how difficult it is to give it an exact rendering (Gen. 30:35, 39, 40; 31:8, 10, 12). ¶

STRIPES – Prov. 19:29 ➔ BEATINGS <4112>.

STRIPLING – 1 Sam. 17:56 ➔ YOUNG MAN <5958>.

STRIPPED – 1 ***šôlāl*** [adj.: שׁוֹלָל <7758>; from PLUNDER (verb) <7997> a.] ▶ **This word means barefoot, without shoes, a shameful condition for some.** Refs.: Job 12:17, 19; also translated plundered, spoiled. Micah, the prophet, went barefoot as he lamented the coming destruction of Israel (Mic. 1:8). The KJV and other versions render this word as stripped (Mic. 1:8). ¶
– 2 Nah. 2:10 ➔ WASTE (MAKE, BE, LAY) <1110>.

STRIPPED (BE) – Ezek. 12:19 ➔ DESOLATE (BE, BECOME) <3456>.

STRIVE – 1 ***gārāh*** [verb: גָּרָה <1624>; a prim. root] ▶ **This verb means and is also translated to resist, to contend, to meddle, to provoke, to stir.** It is used in Proverbs always with the object being strife (Prov. 15:18; 28:25; 29:22) or those who forsake God's law (Prov. 28:4). Used reflexively, it basically means to stir up one's self against someone or something: peoples (Deut. 2:5, 19); a king (2 Kgs. 14:10; 2 Chr. 25:19); a people or nation to provoke war (Deut. 2:9, 24; Dan. 11:10, 25). Other ref.: Jer. 50:24. ¶
2 ***riyḇ, rûḇ*** [verb: רִיב, רוּב <7378>; a prim. root] ▶ **This word means to contend, to dispute, and to conduct a lawsuit or legal case, with all that it involves.** The Lord conducts His case against the leaders of His people (Is. 3:13). He relents in His case from accusing humankind, knowing how weak they are (Is. 57:16). David pleaded with the Lord to give him vindication in his case (1 Sam. 24:15); as did Israel when God contended for them (Mic. 7:9).

The word means to contend or to strive for some reason in a non-legal setting as well. The servants of Isaac and Abimelech contended over wells they had dug or claimed to own (Gen. 26:21). Two men could quarrel and come to blows (Ex. 21:18; Judg. 11:25). Jacob and Laban disputed with one another (Gen. 31:36). The people of Israel complained bitterly against the Lord at Meribah (Num. 20:13).

The word means to raise complaints or accusations against others. The tribes of Israel complained because some of their women were taken and given as wives to the Benjamites (Judg. 21:22). An arrogant Israel would dare to bring charges against the Lord (Is. 45:9; Jer. 2:29; 12:1). The tribe of Levi contended with the Lord at Meribah as well (Deut. 33:8; cf. Num. 20:13).

The causative stem of this verb means to bring a case against (i.e., to oppose). The Lord will judge those who oppose Him (1 Sam. 2:10). *
– [3] Gen. 32:28; Hos. 12:4 ➔ STRUGGLE (verb) <8280> [4] Ex. 2:13; 21:22; Num. 26:9; Deut. 25:11; Lev. 24:10; 2 Sam. 14:6 ➔ FIGHT <5327> [5] Ps. 35:1 ➔ CONTENDS (ONE WHO) <3401>.

STRIVE UPON – Dan. 7:2 ➔ STIR UP <1519>.

STRIVING – [1] ***rᵉʿûṯ*** [masc. noun: רְעוּת <7469>; prob. from FEED (verb) <7462> a.] ▶ **This word refers to a person's efforts to attain something, to achieve or master something, to find out all about the world and its purposes. It is also translated grasping, chasing, vexation.** In Ecclesiastes, these efforts are considered vain (Eccl. 1:14; 2:11, 17, 26; 4:4, 6; 6:9). All striving ends up being a striving after nothing, the wind. ¶
[2] ***raʿyôn*** [masc. noun: רַעְיוֹן <7475>; from FEED (verb) <7462> in the sense of <7469> above] ▶ **This word indicates an effort to attain something or to gain some knowledge or wisdom about life under the sun. It is also translated grasping, chasing, vexation.** It is considered useless striving after the wind, nothing (Eccl. 1:17; 4:16); or simply without benefit or merit (Eccl. 2:22). ¶

STROKE – [1] ***maḥaṣ*** [masc. sing. noun: מַחַץ <4273>; from PIERCE <4272>] ▶ **This word means a severe wound.** It occurs only once in the Hebrew Bible (Is. 30:26; also translated blow), referring to God healing His wounded people. ¶
– [2] Deut. 17:8; 21:5; Is. 53:8 ➔ SORE (noun) <5061> [3] Job 36:18 ➔ SUFFICIENCY <5607> c. [4] Is. 30:32 ➔ FORD <4569>.

STROKES – Prov. 18:6 ➔ BEATINGS <4112>.

STRONG – [1] ***'āmōṣ*** [adj.: אָמֹץ <554>; prob. from STRONG (BE) <553>] ▶ **The basic meaning of this word is endowed with strength, power; active, nimble.** Some versions render this term as strong steeds (horses) (NKJV, Zech. 6:3), while others prefer powerful (NIV, Zech. 6:3, 7; cf. KJV, bay horses). ¶
[2] ***ḥāzāq*** [masc. adj.: חָזָק <2389>; from STRONG (BE) <2388>] ▶ **This word means firm, mighty. The feminine form of this word is *ḥᵃzāqāh*.** It can refer to human strength or power (Num. 13:18; Josh. 14:11); to human persistence or stubbornness (Ezek. 2:4; 3:8, 9); or to divine strength or power (Ex. 3:19; Is. 40:10). In addition, it can refer to the strength of things, but it must be translated to fit the context: a *loud* trumpet blast (Ex. 19:16); a *sore* war (1 Sam. 14:52); the *hottest* battle (2 Sam. 11:15); a *sore* sickness (1 Kgs. 17:17); a *severe* famine (1 Kgs. 18:2); a *strong* wind (Ex. 10:19). This adjective can also be used as a substantive for a strong or mighty person (Job 5:15; Is. 40:10; Ezek. 34:16). *
[3] ***ḥasōn*** [adj.: חָסֹן <2634>; from HOARDED (BE) <2630>] ▶ **This word indicates mighty; it is also translated strong man, mighty man.** It describes a powerful person (Is. 1:31) in Jerusalem. The Amorites were designated as strong as oaks (Amos 2:9), yet the Lord gave them over to Israel. ¶
[4] ***ʿaz*** [עַז <5794>; from the verb STRENGTHEN <5810>] ▶
a. An adjective meaning powerful; insolent. When referring to a person's attitude of anger or wrath, it means insolent, excessive, fierce (Gen. 49:7); used of physical strength or power, it means strong, forceful (Ex. 14:21; Judg. 14:14). The phrase *ʿaz pānîm*, strong of faces means determined, defiant (Deut. 28:50; Dan. 8:23); in context *ʿaz nep̱eš* indicates that persons are greedy, covetous, insatiable (Is. 56:11). Describing bold or arrogant speech, it means arrogantly, insolently (Prov. 18:23). Ants are not considered strong but are wise (Prov. 30:25). Used as a noun, it means a strong person (Amos 5:9). *
b. A masculine noun meaning power, strength. It is used as an abstract noun to refer to procreative power and the power of offspring (Gen. 49:3). ¶

5 **'ōz, 'ôz** [masc. noun: עֹז, עוֹז <5797>; from STRENGTHEN <5810>] ▶ **This word refers to strength, power.** It depicts the Lord as one's strength (Ps. 61:3; Prov. 18:10; Is. 12:2); and the power by which God led His people (Ex. 15:13). It is used of the power or strength of a people, a nation (Lev. 26:19); or the internal fortitude and strength of an individual (Judg. 5:21). It indicates the defense, the strength of a fortified tower (Judg. 9:51). It indicates the ability and might of God's anointed king, given by God (1 Sam. 2:10). The phrase, strength, might of the Lord, is found often as well as other combinations with *'ōz* (Job 12:16; Is. 49:5; Hab. 3:4; Mic. 5:4). The phrase *qôl 'ōz* means a strong voice (Ps. 68:35). The Lord delivered by the arm of His might, His strong arm (Is. 62:8). Political and national strength is recognized (Jer. 48:17). In Ecclesiastes 8:1, it is used in a phrase to indicate a sternness or impudence of a person. In a figurative sense, it refers to the strength or witness for God from the mouths of infants (Ps. 8:2). *

6 **'izzûz** [adj.: עִזּוּז <5808>; from STRENGTHEN <5810>] ▶ **This word describes the Lord as one who is mighty, powerful, and able to defend or fight for His people.** Ref.: Ps. 24:8. It refers to a mighty man or to strength, might for battle (Is. 43:17; also translated power, warrior, reinforcements). ¶

– 7 Gen. 49:14 ➔ BONE <1634> 8 2 Sam. 15:12; Job 9:19; Is. 28:2; 40:26 ➔ BRAVE <533> 9 Job 8:2 ➔ MIGHTY <3524> 10 Ps. 22:12; Jer. 8:16 ➔ MIGHTY <47> 11 Ps. 89:8 ➔ MIGHTY <2626> 12 Eccl. 6:10 ➔ MIGHTY <8623> 13 Jer. 49:19 ➔ STRENGTH <386> 14 Dan. 2:40, 42; Dan. 7:7 ➔ MIGHTY <8624> 15 See BRAVE <1368>.

STRONG, STRONG SUPPORT – Zech. 12:5 ➔ STRENGTH <556>.

STRONG (BE) – 1 **'āmaṣ** [verb: אָמַץ <553>; a prim. root] ▶ **This word means to be determined, bold, courageous; to conquer.** This idea is translated by the NKJV as prevailed when referring to men of Judah in war (2 Chr. 13:18; NASB: conquered). A people or nation can be considered strong (Gen. 25:23). The emphatic stem of the verb means to make strong or cause to grow strong (Prov. 8:28; 31:17; Is. 44:14) of inanimate objects. It is used of human activity in repairing or strengthening a house or building (2 Chr. 24:13). Metaphorically, it means to strengthen or harden one's attitude or heart (Deut. 2:30; 15:7; 2 Chr. 36:13). It is also used in some contexts to mean to show courage or to show or prove oneself strong (Ps. 27:14; 31:24); to persist in an activity (Ruth 1:18); or make haste (1 Kgs. 12:18). With a slight change, it means to be better or superior (2 Chr. 13:7). *

2 **ḥāzaq** [verb: חָזַק <2388>; a prim. root] ▶ **This verb means to strengthen, to be courageous, to overpower.** It is widely used to express the strength of various phenomena, such as the severity of famine (2 Kgs. 25:3; Jer. 52:6); the strength of humans to overpower each other: the condition of Pharaoh's heart (Ex. 7:13); David and Goliath (1 Sam. 17:50); Amnon and Tamar (2 Sam. 13:14); a battle situation (2 Chr. 8:3); Samson's strength for his last superhuman performance (Judg. 16:28). This word occurs in the commonly known charge, "Be strong and of good courage!" (Josh. 1:9). Moses urges Joshua (Deut. 31:6, 7) to be strong. The Lord also bids Joshua to be strong in taking the Promised Land (Deut. 31:23; Josh. 1:6, 7, 9), after which Joshua encourages the people in the same way (Josh. 10:25). *

STRONG (BE, BECOME, GROW) – **tqēp̱** [Aramaic verb: תְּקֵף <8631>; corresponding to PREVAIL <8630>] ▶ **This word is related to the Hebrew verb *tāqaēp̱* (<8630>), meaning to prevail over.** It describes the growing strength of the tree in Nebuchadnezzar's dream (Dan. 4:11, 20) that referred to the growing strength of the king (Dan. 4:22). It was also used to describe the growing arrogance of Belshazzar (Dan. 5:20: to harden). In its only other instance, it describes a strong enforcement of an edict (Dan. 6:7: to make firm, to enforce). ¶

STRONG (BE, GROW) – Ps. 52:7 ➔ STRENGTHEN <5810>.

STRONG (BECOME) – Job 39:4 ➔ DREAM (verb) <2492> b.

STRONG (MAKE) – Gen. 49:24 ➔ AGILE (MAKE) <6338> a.

STRONG (ONE WHO IS) – Is. 59:10 ➔ VIGOROUS PEOPLE <820>.

STRONG DRINK – ***šêḵār*** [masc. noun: שֵׁכָר <7941>; from DRUNK, DRUNKEN <7937>] ▶ **This word refers to an intoxicating drink and is usually understood as some kind of beer.** Priests were not to drink it when serving at the Tabernacle or Temple (Lev. 10:9). The Nazarite was not to touch it (Num. 6:3; Judg. 13:4, 7, 14). The drinkers of strong drink (*šôṯê šêḵār*) were none other than drunkards (Ps. 69:12; Is. 5:11, 22; 28:7; 29:9; 56:12). Such drinking causes violent behavior (Prov. 20:1); kings should stay away from it (Prov. 31:4); though it may be a sedative for the dying and bitter (Prov. 31:6; Is. 24:9). It is used in a context of mockery by Micah (2:11). *

STRONGER – 1 ***'ōmeṣ*** [masc. noun: אֹמֶץ <555>; from STRONG (BE) <553>] ▶ **This word means strength. It refers to a basic strength of character generated by a righteous and clean life.** Ref.: Job 17:9. ¶
2 ***ḥāzêq*** [adj.: חָזֵק <2390>; from STRONG (BE) <2388>] ▶ **This word means having more strength. It is used only twice in Scripture.** In Exodus 19:19, it described the trumpet blast on Mount Sinai as the Lord's presence descended around Moses; it is translated louder. In 2 Samuel 3:1, it described the strength of David's house over the house of Saul. ¶

STRONGHOLD – 1 ***'armôn*** [masc. noun: אַרְמוֹן <759>; from an unused root (meaning to be elevated)] ▶ **This word means fortress, citadel, palace.** Amos frequently equated God's judgment with the destruction of a fortress (Amos 3:11). The word is used in parallel construction with strength (Amos 3:11); siege tower (Is. 23:13); rampart (Ps. 122:7: citadel, palace); fortification (Lam. 2:5: palace). *
2 ***biṣṣārôn*** [masc. noun: בִּצָּרוֹן <1225>; masc. intens. from GATHER <1219>] ▶ **This word refers to a place of strength and fortification.** The exiles of Judah will return to such a place, probably the rebuilt city of Jerusalem as Zion (Zech. 9:12; also translated fortress). ¶
3 ***mā'ôz, mā'ôzen*** [masc. noun: מָעוֹז, מָעוֹזֶן <4581>; from STRENGTHEN <5810>] ▶ **a. A masculine noun meaning a refuge, a fortress, a shelter.** It signifies a stronghold or fortress (Ezek. 24:25; 30:15; Dan. 11:7, 10, 19, 39); or a protected location or place of safety (Judg. 6:26). It is used to modify sanctuary as a stronghold, indicating a temple possibly (Dan. 11:31). It also is used in the expression "god of fortresses," indicating a god of war (Dan. 11:38). It is used figuratively of God as a fortress (2 Sam. 22:33; Nah. 3:11); the joy of God as a shelter or strength (Neh. 8:10); of God as one's strength or defense (Ps. 27:1); the way of God as a stronghold or refuge (Prov. 10:29). *
b. A masculine noun meaning a stronghold, a fortified place. It refers to all kinds of fortified locations and structures in Canaan (Is. 23:11). ¶
4 ***m*ᵉ*ṣāḏ, m*ᵉ*ṣaḏ*** [masc. noun: מְצָד, מְצַד <4679>] ▶ **This word refers to a fort, a mountain-fastness and also defines a fortress. It refers to a place with powerful natural or man-made defenses, difficult of access, and a place for refugees, etc.** Also, it refers to a place for further fortification by military engines and soldiers; strongholds (Judg. 6:2; 1 Sam. 23:14, 19, 29; 1 Chr. 12:8, 16; Jer. 48:41; 51:30; Ezek. 33:27). Jerusalem became David's major stronghold (1 Chr. 11:7), sometimes rendered as a refuge (of the righteous) (Is. 33:16: refuge, place of defense). ¶
5 ***m*ᵉ*ṣûḏāh*** [fem. noun: מְצוּדָה <4686>; for NET <4685> (in the sense of stronghold)] ▶ **This word refers to a wilderness or mountainous places for hiding, defense, and gathering supplies for battle.** Refs.: 1 Sam. 22:4, 5; 24:22; especially

David's Zion (2 Sam. 5:7, 9). In nature, eagles have their safe havens, inaccessible nests, or strongholds (Job 39:28). The Lord Himself is the greatest stronghold (2 Sam. 22:2; Ps. 18:2; 31:2, 3; 71:3; 91:2; 144:2). The Hebrew word also means a net used for hunting prey; see NET <4686>. *

[6] ***miśgāḇ*** [מִשְׂגָּב <4869>; from EXALTED (BE) <7682> (in the sense of to be high, to defend)] ▶

a. A masculine noun indicating a place naturally fortified or fortified by man. A high hill or cliff, a rock (Is. 33:16; Jer. 48:1); walls built by men (Is. 25:12). It is used often of God as a safe haven, a place of refuge (2 Sam. 22:3; Ps. 9:9; 18:2; 46:7, 11; 48:3, etc.). *

b. A proper noun, Misgab, in Moab. It is taken by some translators as a name for a city (Jer. 48:1, KJV). See a. above also. ¶

[7] ***ṣᵉriyaḥ*** [masc. noun: צְרִיחַ <6877>; from CRY (verb) <6873> (which is from a root meaning to be clear; here in the sense of clearness of vision)] ▶

a. This word means and is also translated inner chamber, hold. It refers to a room located in the innermost part of a religious temple or fortress (Judg. 9:46, 49). From context it is clear that it may refer to an underground hiding place or cellar as well (1 Sam. 13:6).

b. This word refers to a high place. Some translators rendered this word as high place, a place for sacrifices to be offered (1 Sam. 13:6). In context this is understandable. ¶

– [8] 2 Sam. 22:46; Ps. 18:45; Mic. 7:17 ➔ RIM <4526> [9] Prov. 12:12 ➔ NET <4685> [10] Mic. 4:8 ➔ HILL <6076>.

STRUCTURE – [1] ***miḇneh*** [masc. noun: מִבְנֶה <4011>; from BUILD <1129>] ▶ **This word refers to a vision of buildings resembling a city; it is also translated buildings, frame.** Hence, the prophet saw an entire complex not just a mere building (Ezek. 40:2). ¶

[2] ***mûsaḇ*** [masc. noun: מוּסַב <4141>; from AROUND (GO) <5437>] ▶ **This word refers to a surrounding circuitous structure as a part of the inner Temple.** Ref.: Ezek. 41:7; KJV: winding about. ¶

– [3] 1 Kgs. 6:5, 6, 10 ➔ BED <3326> b. [4] Ezra 5:3, 9 ➔ WALL <846>.

STRUGGLE (noun) – [1] Gen. 30:8 ➔ WRESTLINGS <5319> [2] Ps. 73:4 ➔ BOND <2784>.

STRUGGLE (verb) – [1] ***śārāh*** [verb: שָׂרָה <8280>; a prim. root] ▶ **This word means to persist, to exert oneself, to persevere; it is also translated to strive, to have power, to wrestle. The primary meaning is to exert oneself.** In Genesis, the word depicts Jacob, who had struggled with God and persons and prevailed. This achievement resulted in a name change to Israel (Gen. 32:28; also translated to strive, to have power). The word is used figuratively in Hosea, recollecting on the memory of Jacob's struggle with God at Peniel to describe a reason for Ephraim's punishment (Hos. 12:4). This comparison relates Ephraim back to Jacob, the father of their tribe, as a call to repentance. ¶

– [2] Ex. 2:13; 21:22; Deut. 25:11; Lev. 24:10; 2 Sam. 14:6 ➔ FIGHT <5327> [3] Job 9:29 ➔ WEARY (verb) <3021>.

STRUM – Amos 6:5 ➔ IMPROVISE <6527> b.

STRUTTING ROOSTER – [1] ***zarziyr*** [masc. noun: זַרְזִיר <2223>; by reduplication from CRUSH <2115>] ▶ **This word indicates some animal, perhaps a rooster showing off, cock, or greyhound.** It is specifically stated to be one of four animals which is impressive or stately in its walk (Prov. 30:31), a feature of created beings that causes the wise person to marvel at God's works. ¶

– [2] Prov. 30:31 ➔ LOINS <4975> b.

STUB OF FIREWOOD – Is. 7:4 ➔ FIREBRAND <181>.

STUBBLE – ***qaš*** [masc. noun: קַשׁ <7179>; from GATHER <7197>] ▶ **This word refers to the short dry stumps of grain, corn, wheat, etc., left in a field after harvesting; it is also translated chaff.** It burned quickly once it was ignited (Mal. 4:1). It was of little value and not highly prized. It was a poor substitute for straw in brick making (Ex. 5:12; 15:7). Job refers to himself as dried-out chaff or stubble in a metaphor (Job 13:25). God turns His enemies into stubble or chaff (Ps. 83:13). God scattered His people like stubble in the wind (Jer. 13:24). ¶

STUBBORN – [1] Prov. 7:11; Is. 30:1; Hos. 4:16 ➔ REBELLIOUS <5637> [2] Is. 46:12: stubborn of heart, stubborn-hearted, stubborn-minded ➔ MIGHTY <47>.

STUBBORNNESS – [1] ***qᵉšiy*** [masc. noun: קְשִׁי <7190>; from HARD (BE) <7185>] ► **This word indicates a current condition of attitude as well as a past history of demonstrated refusal to obey the Lord's covenantal words.** Ref.: Deut. 9:27. ¶
[2] ***šᵉriyrûṯ, šᵉrirûṯ*** [fem. noun: שְׁרִירוּת, שְׁרִרוּת <8307>; from ENEMY <8324>] ► **This word has the basic idea of firmness or hardness, but in its ten usages in the Old Testament, it is always used in conjunction with the word *lêḇ* (<3820>), meaning heart, to describe disobedient Israel.** Thus, it is best to translate this word stubbornness; it is also translated imagination, dictates. It is used to describe those who did evil (Jer. 16:12); who walked after their own plans (Jer. 18:12); who refused to listen to God's words (Jer. 13:10); who did not obey God's counsel (Jer. 7:24; 9:14; 11:8); and who were deluded to think they were at peace (Deut. 29:19; Jer. 23:17). God gave such people over to their own devices (Ps. 81:12). Other ref.: Jer. 3:17. ¶
– [3] 1 Sam. 15:23 ➔ PRESS <6484>.

STUD – ***nᵉquddāh*** [fem. noun: נְקֻדָּה <5351>; fem. of SPECKLED <5348>] ► **This word refers to small spheres of silver placed on a necklace or bracelet ornament.** Ref.: Song 1:11; also translated bead, studded. ¶

STUDDED – Song 1:11 ➔ STUD <5351>.

STUDENT – 1 Chr. 25:8 ➔ PUPIL <8527>.

STUDY (noun) – ***lahag*** [masc. noun: לַהַג <3854>; from an unused root meaning to be eager] ► **This word refers to learning, a devotion to learning.** In its context, it means study or examination (Eccl. 12:12; NASB: devotion to books). The context speaks of excessive (*harbêh*) study or searching. ¶

STUDY (verb) – See LEARN <3925>.

STUMBLE – [1] ***pûq*** [verb: פּוּק <6328>; a prim. root] ► **This word means to reel, to totter. It is used in regard to persons who are incapacitated, unable to render judgments with integrity.** Ref.: Is. 28:7. It is used derisively of idols who must be shored up so they are stable and will not totter (Jer. 10:4; also translated to move, to topple). ¶
– [2] Prov. 3:23; Jer. 13:16 ➔ SMITE <5062>.

STUMBLING – [1] ***dᵉḥiy*** [masc. noun: דְּחִי <1762>; from DRIVE <1760>] ► **This word denotes falling, a thrusting down, an overthrowing (from which the feet need to be rescued).** The Lord delivered the psalmist from this, probably tripping over or falling (Ps. 56:13; 116:8). ¶
[2] ***ṣela'*** [masc. noun: צֶלַע <6761>; from LIMP <6760>] ► **This word means a fall, a slip.** It is taken by many translators to mean a fall or stumbling, used figuratively of a person falling, being overtaken (Job 18:12; Ps. 35:15; 38:17; Jer. 20:10). Some prefer to translate it as side (<6763>) in Job 18:12. ¶
– [3] Prov. 16:18 ➔ FALL (noun) <3783> [4] Is. 8:14 ➔ PLAGUE (noun) <5063>.

STUMBLING BLOCK – [1] ***mikšôl*** [masc. noun: מִכְשׁוֹל <4383>; from FALL (verb) <3782>] ► **This word means an obstacle. Sometimes the term refers to something an individual can literally trip over.** For instance, the Lord commanded the people of Israel not to put a stumbling block before the blind (Lev. 19:14). More often, however, it is used in a figurative sense. The Lord Himself will become the obstacle over which both houses of Israel will stumble (Is. 8:14). Much later in Isaiah,

it is written that the Lord will demand that the obstacle be removed from His people's way (Is. 57:14). In other places, the word refers to that which causes people to stumble morally, i.e., to sin: gold and silver (Ezek. 7:19); idols (Ezek. 14:3); the Levites (Ezek. 44:12). In other places, the term describes something that causes people to fall to their ruin. Because of Israel's persistent rejection of God's Law, He laid a stumbling block before them so they would trip and perish (Jer. 6:21; cf. Ps. 119:165; Ezek. 3:20; 18:30). This term is derived from the verb *kāšal* [FALL (verb) <3782>]. Other refs.: 1 Sam. 25:31; Ezek. 14:4, 7; 21:15. ¶
– [2] Zeph. 1:3 ➔ RUIN, HEAP OF RUINS <4384>.

STUMP – [1] ***geza'*** [masc. noun: גֶּזַע <1503>; from an unused root meaning to cut down (trees)] ► **This word refers to a stem, a trunk; it is also translated stock.** It indicates a tree stump left in the ground (Job 14:8) which can still revive if watered. Isaiah pictures a righteous branch springing from this kind of stump (Is. 11:1). It is used figuratively of the brief establishment of the "roots" of earthly rulers before they wither away (Is. 40:24). ¶
[2] ***'iqqar*** [Aramaic masc. noun: עִקַּר <6136>; a prim. root] ► **This word means the base of a tree primarily but seems to include the taproot or rootstock attached to it as well.** Refs.: Dan. 4:15, 23, 26. ¶
– [3] Is. 6:13 ➔ PILLAR <4678>.

STUNNED (BECOME) – ***pûg*** [verb: פּוּג <6313>; a prim. root] ► **This word means to be greatly astonished; it also means to be paralyzed, to be feeble.** It indicates a response of great surprise or astonishment about something (Gen. 45:26; also translated to become numb, to faint); or a condition brought on by severe illness (Ps. 38:8; also translated to be benumbed). It indicates weakness, frailty in an emotional or physical way (Ps. 77:2: to grow numb, to cease, to weary). It has the sense of something being paralyzed in usage, not used, ignored (Hab. 1:4; also translated to be slacked, to be powerless). ¶

STUNTED (BE) – ***qālaṭ*** [verb: קָלַט <7038>; a prim. root (to maim)] ► **This word indicates to lack body parts, to be deformed, to be maimed. It refers to an animal that has a deformed or injured member, not fully or properly developed.** The animal could be used in a freewill offering but not a vow offering (Lev. 22:23). ¶

STUPID – [1] ***ṭāmāh*** [verb: טָמָה <2933>; a collateral form of UNCLEAN (BE) <2930>] ► **A verb which occurs once in the Hebrew Bible (Job 18:3; KJV, to be reputed).** It is translated "stopped up," "stupid," or possibly "unclean." ¶
– [2] Job 11:12 ➔ HOLLOW (verb) <5014> [3] Ps. 49:10; 92:6; Prov. 12:1; 30:2 ➔ FOOLISH <1198>.

STUPID (BE) – Jer. 10:8, 14 ➔ BURN (verb) <1197> c.

STURDY WARRIORS – Is. 10:16 ➔ FATNESS <4924> a.

STYLUS – [1] Job 19:24; Jer. 17:1 ➔ PEN <5842> [2] Is. 8:1 ➔ GRAVING TOOL <2747>.

SUAH – ***sûaḥ*** [masc. proper noun: סוּחַ <5477>; from an unused root meaning to wipe away]: sweeping ► **Son of Zophah, a descendant of Asher.** Ref.: 1 Chr. 7:36. ¶

SUBDIVISION – 2 Chr. 35:12 ➔ DIVISION <4651>.

SUBDUE – [1] ***kāḇaš*** [verb: כָּבַשׁ <3533>; a prim. root] ► **This word means to bring into subjection, to enslave. It means basically to overcome, to subjugate someone.** It is used to describe God's mandate to humans to subdue the created order (Gen. 1:28). It describes Israel's taking of the Promised Land, Canaan (Num. 32:22, 29; Josh. 18:1: also translated to bring under control). King David subjugated the land (2 Sam. 8:11). It means to put into bondage or to degrade in general (Neh. 5:5: to bring under bondage, to enslave, to bring into slavery). It is used once of Haman's supposed assault

on Queen Esther (Esther 7:8: to assault, to molest, to force). It is used in its causative stem to indicate subduing or subjugating peoples (Jer. 34:11, 16). It is used figuratively of the Lord's subduing, removing, crushing the iniquities of His people (Mic. 7:19: also translated to tread underfoot). It is used of the Lord's people overcoming their enemies with His help (Zech. 9:15; also translated to tread down, to overcome, to trample). ¶
2 ***kāna'*** [verb: כָּנַע <3665>; a prim. root] ▶ **This word indicates to humble, to be humble. It has the basic sense of being lowly, meek.** It is used of the Lord's humbling an uncircumcised, prideful heart (Lev. 26:41); or defeating Israel's enemies (Deut. 9:3; Judg. 3:30; 4:23; 8:28; 1 Chr. 17:10; 18:1; 20:4). It is used of humbling oneself as well (1 Kgs. 21:29), especially before the Lord. The key to the Israelites' success after failure was to repent and humble themselves before the Lord (2 Chr. 7:14). The Lord challenges Job that only He can humble and crush the wicked in due time (Job 40:12). *
3 ***rāḏaḏ*** [verb: רָדַד <7286>; a prim. root] ▶ **This word means to beat down; to be almost gone.** It indicates that something is about to pass away, is almost gone (Judg. 19:11: to be spent, to be over, to be gone). It is used of overlaying gold on a surface by beating it into thin sheets (1 Kgs. 6:32: to spread, to hammer). It has the sense of subduing persons, a people (Ps. 144:2; Is. 45:1). ¶
– 4 Dan. 2:40 → SHATTER <2827>.

SUBJECT (BE) – Is. 11:14 → GUARD <4928>.

SUBJECTION (BRING INTO) – Jer. 34:11, 16 → SUBDUE <3533>.

SUBJUGATION – Is. 22:5 → TREADING DOWN <4001>.

SUBMISSION (IN) – Dan. 11:43 → lit.: at his steps → STEP (noun) <4703>.

SUBMIT – Job 22:21 → PROFITABLE (BE) <5532> a.

SUBSTANCE – 1 Gen. 7:4, 23; Deut. 11:6 → LIVING (noun) <3351> 2 Job 22:20 → ADVERSARY <7009> b. 3 Is. 6:13 → PILLAR <4678> 4 Hos. 12:8 → STRENGTH <202>.

SUBMIT – ***rāpas*** [verb: רָפַס <7511>; a prim. root] ▶ **This word means to humble oneself. It is translated as submit by some translators to indicate surrender or submission, in context the submission of warring peoples.** But others render this as a further picture of the enemy nations of Israel trampling down the wealth of nations (Ps. 68:30). The thought of submission or humility is prominent in Proverbs 6:3. ¶

SUBSIDE – ***šāḵaḵ*** [verb: שָׁכַךְ <7918>; a prim. root] ▶ **This word means to go down, to get lower.** It refers to a lowering of the great flood waters (Gen. 8:1; also translated to assuage, to recede); to an abatement of anger (Esther 2:1; 7:10; also translated to appease, to abate, to pacify). In its causative use, it means to lower something: personal attacks or accusations (Num. 17:5: to make to cease, to rid, to lessen). It is rendered to set a snare (KJV, Jer. 5:26); to set a trap (NASB); to set up a snare (NIV). ¶

SUBSTANCE – 1 ***šāwāh*** [fem. noun: שָׁוָה <7738>; a prim. root] ▶ **In context this word refers to a person's physical and/or spiritual essence or being.** Ref.: Job 30:22, KJV. Other versions translate success, storm. ¶
– 2 Job 30:22 → STORM (noun) <8663> 3 Ps. 139:15 → STRENGTH <6108> 4 Ps. 139:16: unformed substance → UNFORMED SUBSTANCE <1564>.

SUBTIL – Gen. 3:1 → PRUDENT <6175>.

SUBTILLY – 1 Sam. 23:22 → CRAFTY (BE) <6191>.

SUBTILLY (DEAL) – Ps. 105:25 → DECEIVE <5230>.

SUBTILTY – 1 2 Kgs. 10:19 → CUNNING <6122> 2 Prov. 1:4 → PRUDENCE <6195>.

SUBURB – Num. 35:2–5, 7; Josh. 14:4; etc. ➔ PASTURELAND <4054>.

SUBURBS – 2 Kgs. 23:11 ➔ PRECINCTS <6503> a.

SUBVERT – Ex. 23:8; Deut. 16:19; Prov. 13:6 ➔ OVERTHROW (verb) <5557>.

SUCATHITES – ***śûḵāṯiym*** [proper noun: שׂוּכָתִים <7756>; prob. patron. from a name corresponding to BRANCH <7754> (fem.)]: who dwell in tents ▶ **A family of scribes who lived at Jabez from the tribe of Judah.** Ref.: 1 Chr. 2:55. ¶

SUCCEED – Eccl. 10:10; 11:6 ➔ SUCCESS (BRING, GIVE) <3787>.

SUCCESS – Job 30:22 ➔ SUBSTANCE <7738>.

SUCCESS (BRING, GIVE) – ***kāšêr*** [verb: כָּשֵׁר <3787>; a prim. root] ▶ **This word means to achieve something significant, to prosper.** In Ecclesiastes 10:10 (KJV: to direct), the word refers to success as the result of wisdom that enables one to go through difficult situations like a sharp ax through wood. In Ecclesiastes 11:6 (also translated to prosper), the word refers to the success of seeds in growing, a matter beyond complete human control. Like other human ventures, successful farming calls for diligence and diversification. In Esther 8:5 (to seem right, to seem proper), the word is used to confirm the king's opinion of Esther's proposal, whether in his view it would work smoothly. ¶

SUCCOTH – ***sukkôṯ*** [proper noun: סֻכּוֹת <5523>; plur. of BOOTH <5521>]: booths, tents ▶
a. A city in Canaan. Refs.: Gen. 33:17; Josh. 13:27; Judg. 8:5, 6, 8, 14–16; 1 Kgs. 7:46; 2 Chr. 4:17; Ps. 60:6; 108:7. ¶
b. A campsite in Egypt. Refs.: Ex. 12:37; 13:20; Num. 33:5, 6. ¶

SUCCOTH BENOTH – ***sukkôṯ bᵉnôṯ*** [proper noun: סֻכּוֹת בְּנוֹת <5524>; from SUCCOTH <5523> and the (irregular) plur. of DAUGHTER <1323>]: tents of daughters ▶ **An idol made by Babylonian settlers in Samaria.** Ref.: 2 Kgs. 17:30. ¶

SUCH – 1 Sam. 21:2; 2 Kgs. 6:8 ➔ A ONE <492>.

SUCK – Is. 66:11 ➔ DRINK DEEPLY <4711>.

SUCK UP – ***'āla'*** [verb: עָלַע <5966>; a prim. root] ▶ **This word means to take something in, i.e., a liquid, by drawing it out with the mouth.** The young of the hawk eat blood (Job 39:30; NIV: to feast on). ¶

SUCKING CHILD – Is. 49:15 ➔ NURSING CHILD <5764>.

SUDDENLY – [1] ***piṯ'ôm*** [adv.: פִּתְאוֹם <6597>; from <6621> below] ▶ **This word means instantly, in a moment, surprisingly, unexpectedly.** It refers to things occurring all at once, surprisingly, all of a sudden: death (Num. 6:9; Job 9:23); an action or word by God (Num. 12:4); at once, immediately (Job 5:3; Ps. 64:4); fear that comes on unexpectedly (Prov. 3:25; Mal. 3:1); a catastrophe, calamity (Eccl. 9:12). Hezekiah›s revival «came about suddenly» (2 Chr. 29:36). *
[2] ***peṯa'*** [masc. noun: פֶּתַע <6621>; from an unused root meaning to open (the eyes)] ▶ **This word refers to the quickness or an unexpected aspect of an event.** Refs.: Num. 6:9; 35:22; Hab. 2:7. A foolish and stubborn person is broken by calamity all of a sudden (Prov. 6:15; 29:1). Jerusalem's enemies would be instantly destroyed (Is. 29:5); her own destruction would be sudden (Is. 30:13). ¶

SUET – ***peḏer*** [masc. noun: פֶּדֶר <6309>; from an unused root meaning to be greasy] ▶ **This word refers to hard fat that collects around the kidneys and loins of cattle and sheep.** Refs.: Lev. 1:8, 12; 8:20. ¶

SUFFER – [1] Gen. 31:28 ➔ FORSAKE <5203> [2] Ezra 4:13 ➔ DAMAGE (verb) <5142>.

SUFFERING – 1 ***mak'ôḇ*** [masc. noun: מַכְאוֹב <4341>; from PAIN (BE IN) <3510>] ▶ **This word refers to pain, physical or emotional; it is also translated sorrow.** It depicts pain and suffering born by the Servant of the Lord (Is. 53:4), who was literally a "man of pain" (Is. 53:3); of pain inflicted on him. It indicates the pain placed on the Hebrews by the Egyptians and noted by God (Ex. 3:7). Israel brought great pain on herself through her sin (Jer. 30:15; 45:3). Pain and suffering is the lot of humankind (Job 33:19; Ps. 38:17; Eccl. 2:23), but the wicked are especially prone to pain and suffering (Ps. 32:10; Jer. 51:8). Even great knowledge may lead to pain in this age (Eccl. 1:18). Other refs.: 2 Chr. 6:29; Ps. 69:26; Lam. 1:12, 18. ¶
– 2 Job 2:13; 16:6 ➔ PAIN (noun) <3511> 3 Job 9:28 ➔ SORROW (noun) <6094> 4 Ps. 22:24 ➔ AFFLICTION <6039> 5 Is. 14:3 ➔ PAIN (noun) <6090>.

SUFFICE – 1 Kgs. 20:10 ➔ STRIKE <5606>.

SUFFICIENCY – ***sêpeq, śep̄eq, sep̄eq*** [masc. noun: סֵפֶק, שֶׂפֶק, שֶׂפֶק <5607>; from STRIKE <5606>] ▶
a. This word refers to plenty, an abundance. It indicates an overabundance of goods and wealth beyond what is needed (Job 20:22). ¶
b. A masculine noun understood as riches by some translators. Its exact meaning in context is difficult (NIV, Job 36:18). Its meaning depends on the interpretation of other difficult words in the text, as well as the difficulty of the word itself. ¶
c. A masculine noun referring to a stroke, scoffing, chastisement. It is understood as scoffing by some (NASB, ESV, Job 36:18); as a blow or stroke by others (KJV, NKJV, Job 36:18). See b. ¶

SUFFICIENTLY – ***madday*** [adv.: מַדַּי <4078>; from WHAT? <4100> and ENOUGH <1767>] ▶ **This word means and is also translated enough, in sufficient number.** It indicates adequacy for a purpose or goal (2 Chr. 30:3), e.g., adequate numbers. ¶

SUFFOCATION – Job 7:15 ➔ STRANGLING <4267>.

SUITABLE – Lev. 16:21 ➔ READINESS (IN) <6261>.

SUITABLE FOR – Gen. 2:18, 20 ➔ BEFORE <5048>.

SUKKITES – ***sukkiyyiym*** [proper noun: סֻכִּיִּים <5525>; patrial from an unknown name (perhaps ABODE <5520>)] ▶ **They came with Shishak, king of Egypt, against Jerusalem.** Ref.: 2 Chr. 12:3. ¶

SULFUR – Gen. 19:24; Deut. 29:23; Job 18:15; Ps. 11:6; Is. 30:33; 34:9; Ezek. 38:22 ➔ BRIMSTONE <1614>.

SULLEN – ***sar*** [adj.: סַר <5620>; contr. from REBELLIOUS <5637>] ▶ **This word means and is also translated vexed (ESV), heavy (KJV), sad (KJV).** It refers to a state of depression, without hope, of vexation (1 Kgs. 20:43); over even a minor issue (1 Kgs. 21:4, 5). ¶

SUM – 1 Ps. 71:15 ➔ NUMBER (noun) <5615> 2 Ezek. 28:12 ➔ PERFECTION <8508>.

SUM, EXACT SUM – ***pārāšāh*** [fem. noun: פָּרָשָׁה <6575>; from CLEAR (BE, MAKE) <6567>] ▶ **This word indicates an accurate assessment of something in exact detail; the total sum of something; or a complete, detailed account of an incident or story.** Refs.: Esther 4:7; 10:2; also translated exact amount, account, full account, declaration. ¶

SUMMER (noun) – ***qayiṭ*** [fem. noun: קַיִט <7007>; corresponding to SUMMER, SUMMER FRUIT <7019>] ▶ **This word indicates the driest and hottest time of the year when chaff would be easily wafted away by the wind.** Ref.: Dan. 2:35. ¶

SUMMER (SPEND THE) – Is. 18:6 ➔ SUMMER (verb) <6972>.

SUMMER, SUMMER FRUIT – ***qayiṣ*** [masc. noun: קַיִץ <7019>; from SUMMER (verb) <6972>] ▶ **This word refers to the summer season, the hottest and driest time of the year (ca. May-October) as it was established by the Lord.** Refs.: Gen. 8:22; Amos 3:15. It also refers to summer fruits (2 Sam. 16:1, 2; Amos 8:1, 2). It refers figuratively to a time of drought, a lack of rain (Ps. 32:4), when the heat is scorching (Zech. 14:8). *

SUMMER (verb) – ***qûṣ, qiyṣ*** [verb: קוּץ, קִיץ <6972>; a prim. root] ▶ **This word means to spend the summer (see the related entry for a noun). It refers to using up one's time during the summer months, to be active then.** Ref.: Is. 18:6. In context it is the chronological setting for birds of prey to spend their time in the ruins remaining after God's judgment had created devastation. ¶

SUN – [1] ***ḥammāh*** [fem. noun: חַמָּה <2535>; from WARM <2525>] ▶ **This word refers to the glow and heat of the sun or to the heavenly body itself.** Ref.: Ps. 19:6: heat, warmth. With God's restoration and healing of Israel, the light of the sun (*ḥammāh*) will be seven times brighter (Is. 30:26). It takes on the sense of comfort in Job 30:28, i.e., without heat or comfort (NASB; but, ESV, KJV, NIV, NKJV, sun). Other refs.: Song 6:10; Is. 24:23. ¶
[2] ***ḥeres*** [masc. noun: חֶרֶס <2775>; from an unused root meaning to scrape] ▶ **This word also refers to the sun.** Refs.: KJV, Judg. 8:13; 14:18; Job 9:7. But others read a proper name in Judges 8:13 (ESV, NKJV, NASB, NIV) referring to the ascent or pass of Heres. The Hebrew word also means a skin disorder; see ITCH <2775>. ¶
[3] ***šemeš*** [common noun: שֶׁמֶשׁ <8121>; from an unused root meaning to be brilliant] ▶ **This word refers to the heavenly body, the sun; it also means daylight.** It sets, *bô'* (Gen. 15:12, 17; 28:11); rises, *yāṣa'* (Gen. 19:23). The sun becomes hot (*ḥam*) during the day (Ex. 16:21). The place of the going down or setting of the sun, sunset, indicates direction or west (Deut. 11:30); the place of its rising or shining forth indicates east (Judg. 11:18). The phrase before (*neged*) the sun means in public, in the open (2 Sam. 12:12). In a glorified Zion, the sun will not set (Is. 60:20). Isaiah 38:8 refers to a sundial made up of steps. The Israelites time and again fell into sun worship (2 Kgs. 23:5; Jer. 8:2; Ezek. 8:16), believing the sun to be a god. The phrase under the sun (Eccl. 1:3, etc.) means on the earth in this present secular life. It refers to some shining ornamental pinnacle (Is. 54:12). It is used metaphorically of the Lord being our Sun and Shield (Ps. 84:11). *
[4] ***šemeš*** [Aramaic common noun: שְׁמַשׁ <8122>; corresponding to <8121> above] ▶ **This word is used in the phrase *me'ālê šimšā'*, from the coming up of the sun, i.e., until sunset.** Ref.: Dan. 6:14. ¶
– [5] Prov. 4:18 ➔ morning sun ➔ shining light ➔ BRIGHTNESS <5051> [6] Is. 19:18 ➔ DESTRUCTION <2041>.

SUN (SETTING, GOING DOWN OF) – Deut. 11:30; Mal. 1:11 ➔ ENTRANCE <3996>.

SUN-SCORCHED LAND – Ps. 68:6 ➔ PARCHED LAND <6707>.

SUNRISE – See EAST <4217>.

SUNSHINE – 2 Sam. 23:4 ➔ BRIGHTNESS <5051>.

SUPERFLUOUS – Lev. 21:18; 22:23 ➔ DEFORMED (BE) <8311>.

SUPH – ***sûp̱*** [proper noun: סוּף <5489>; for REED <5488> (by ellipsis of SEA <3220>)]: reed (the Red Sea) ▶
a. A proper noun designating the place Suph, near Mount Horeb. Ref.: Deut. 1:1. ¶
b. Red [reed] from *sûp̱* (REED <5488>), a designation for the Red Sea. Ref.: KJV, Deut. 1:1. ¶

SUPHAH – Num. 21:14 ➔ STORM (noun) <5492> b.

SUPPLANT – ***'āqaḇ*** [verb: עָקַב <6117>] ▶ **This word means to grasp by the heel, to**

deceive, to cheat, to take advantage. This verb is derived from the noun meaning heel *'āqēḇ* (HEEL <6119>) and is connected etymologically to the name Jacob (*ya'ᵃqōḇ*). The first occurrence sets the backdrop for the other uses. After Jacob tricked his brother Esau out of Isaac's blessing, Esau says, "He is rightly called 'Jacob'—for he has tricked (*Jacobed*) me twice" (Gen. 27:36). In Jeremiah 9:4, reflecting on the Jacob story, the prophet said every brother deceives. Hosea used the term in its more literal meaning when he recalled that Jacob grasped the heel of his brother in the womb (Hos. 12:3). Other ref.: Job 37:4 (to restrain, to hold back, to stay). ¶

SUPPLE – Ezek. 16:4 ➔ CLEANSING <4935>.

SUPPLIANT – Zeph. 3:10 ➔ WORSHIPPER <6282> a.

SUPPLICATION – [1] ***tᵉḥinnāh*** [fem. noun: תְּחִנָּה <8467>; from GRACIOUS (BE) <2603>] ▶ **This word means a request for favor.** Such a request is always directed toward God—with two exceptions when the request is made to the king (Jer. 37:20; 38:26). This seldom-used term occurred predominately in connection with the dedication of the Temple by Salomon (1 Kgs. 8:28, 30, 38, 45, 49, 52, 54; 2 Chr. 6:14–42). In these passages, the request was often connected with prayer and associated with a distinct relationship to God. On two occasions, the word was used to refer to favor itself (Josh. 11:20; Ezra 9:8). *

[2] ***taḥᵃnûn*** [masc. noun: תַּחֲנוּן <8469>; from GRACIOUS (BE) <2603>] ▶ **This word refers to an entreaty for favor and is used in a comparison of a rich man with a poor man.** The rich man answers harshly, while the poor man pleads for mercy (Prov. 18:23). Daniel used the word to indicate how he turned to the Lord in a prayer of petition, i.e., he pleaded with Him in prayers of petition with fasting and in sackcloth and ashes (Dan. 9:3). He also called to God to hear the prayers and petitions of His servant (Dan. 9:17). The noun was also used by the psalmist, who made a plea to God to hear his cry for mercy (Ps. 28:2; 31:22; 86:6). In Jeremiah, a cry was heard on the barren heights, along with weeping and pleading by the people of Israel (Jer. 3:21). The word was also used to inform Daniel that as soon as he began his prayer or petition, an answer would be given to him (Dan. 9:23). *

SUPPLICATION (MAKE) – Dan. 6:11 ➔ MERCY (SHOW, ASK FOR) <2604>.

SUPPLY (noun) – [1] Lev. 26:10 ➔ SLEEP (verb) <3462> b. [2] Is. 3:1 ➔ SUPPORT (noun) <4937> b. [3] Is. 3:1 ➔ SUPPORT (noun) <4938> a.

SUPPLY (verb) – [1] Num. 31:5 ➔ PROVIDE <4560> [2] Ps. 144:13 ➔ OBTAIN <6329>.

SUPPORT (noun) – [1] ***miš'ān, maš'ēn*** [masc. noun: מִשְׁעָן, מַשְׁעֵן <4937>; from LEAN <8172> (in the sense of to rely, to support oneself)] ▶

a. This word designates a staff, a supply; it is also translated stay, stock. It indicates something serving to make one firm, to keep one stable. It is used figuratively of the Lord who encourages His people and supplies their needs (2 Sam. 22:19; Ps. 18:18). He can remove that protective support (Is. 3:1). ¶

b. This word means support, supply. It is used of the entire spectrum of the Lord's caring for His people (Is. 3:1). See a. ¶

[2] ***maš'ēnāh, miš'eneṯ*** [fem. noun: מַשְׁעֵנָה, מִשְׁעֶנֶת <4938>; fem. of <4937> above] ▶

a. This word is used of what firms up, keeps stable, furnishes needed supplies; it is also translated supply, store, staff. It is a synonym to SUPPORT (noun) <4937>, a. The Lord is able to remove the support and supply needed by Jerusalem and Judah (Is. 3:1). ¶

b. A feminine noun also indicates a pole, a staff. It refers to a physical support, such as a cane or crutch (Ex. 21:19), especially for the elderly (Zech. 8:4). It serves as a symbol of authority along with a scepter (Num. 21:18;

also translated stave). It indicates a rod used by a divine being (Judg. 6:21); and the staff of a prophet or a man of God that represents his authority (2 Kgs. 4:29, 31). In context it can refer to nations as feeble, frail staffs, not to be trusted (2 Kgs. 18:21; Is. 36:6; Ezek. 29:6). The staff of the Lord, His presence and protection, comforts His people (Ps. 23:4). ¶

3 ***misʿāḏ*** [masc. noun: מִסְעָד <4552>; from REFRESH <5582> (this word also means to support, to sustain)] ▶ **This word designates a pillar.** It refers to wooden supporting or stabilizing structures and used in various ways and for different objects (1 Kgs. 10:12; NKJV: step). ¶

4 ***r^{e}piyḏāh*** [fem. noun: רְפִידָה <7507>; from REFRESH <7502>] ▶ **This word refers to the bottom or back of something (a sedan chair). It refers to a part of a splendid chair for a king to sit/ride in while being carried.** In context it is made of gilded gold or golden cloth (Song 3:10; also translated base). Sedan comes from a Latin word meaning to sit, to recline. ¶

– 5 Ezra 4:14 ➔ to receive support ➔ SALT (EAT THE) <4415>.

SUPPORT (verb) – 1 ***s^{e}ʿaḏ*** [Aramaic verb: סְעַד <5583>; corresponding to REFRESH <5582> (in the sense of to support, to sustain)] ▶ **This word refers to assisting, lending support or giving encouragement to someone; it is also translated to help.** It describes the prophetic support given to those building the second Temple (Ezra 5:2). ¶

– 2 Ps. 20:2 ➔ REFRESH <5582>.

SUPPOSE – Gen. 18:24 ➔ PERHAPS <194>.

SUPREME – Eccl. 8:4 ➔ POWER <7983>.

SUPREME COMMANDER – 2 Kgs. 18:17; Is. 20:1 ➔ TARTAN <8661> b.

SUR – ***sûr*** [proper noun: סוּר <5495>; the same as DEGENERATE <5494>]: deteriorated ▶ **This word designates a Temple gate.** Ref.: 2 Kgs. 11:6. ¶

SURE – 1 Is. 22:23 ➔ NURSE (verb) <539> 2 Dan. 2:45 ➔ TRUST (verb) <540> 3 Dan. 4:26 ➔ ENDURING <7011>.

SURE (MAKE) – Prov. 6:3 ➔ BOLD (BE, MAKE) <7292>.

SURELY – 1 ***ʾāḵên*** [adv.: אָכֵן <403>; from SET UP <3559> (comp. THEREFORE <3651>)] ▶ **This word means truly or yet. It basically gives expression to something or some situation that was unexpected.** Jacob was surprised to find the Lord's presence where he had slept (Gen. 28:16), and Moses was amazed to find that Pharaoh knew of his killing an Egyptian (Ex. 2:14; cf. 1 Sam. 15:32). It is used to show contrast with what was expected. Against all odds, the servant of the Lord would receive from the Lord (Is. 49:4). This use is found several times after the verb to say, *ʾāmartiy* (Is. 49:4; 53:4; Jer. 3:20; Zeph. 3:7). *

2 ***ʾumnām*** [interr. particle: אֻמְנָם <552>; an orthographical variation of TRULY <551>] ▶ **This word means verily, truly, indeed; it is also translated really, of a surety. It occurs only in questions.** An example is Genesis 18:13, where Sarah doubted that she would have a child, "Shall I of a surety bear a child . . . ?" Other refs.: Num. 22:37; 1 Kgs. 8:27; 2 Chr. 6:18; Ps. 58:1. ¶

– 3 Gen. 47:23 ➔ BEHOLD (interj.) <1887> 4 Ezra 7:26 ➔ DILIGENTLY <629> 5 Job 36:4 ➔ TRULY <551> 6 Dan. 2:47 ➔ TRUTH <7187> 7 See ONLY <389> 8 See TRULY <61>.

SURETY – 1 Job 17:3 ➔ PLEDGE (noun) <6162> 2 Prov. 17:18 ➔ PLEDGE (noun) <6161>.

SURETY (OF A) – Gen. 18:13 ➔ SURELY <552>.

SURGE – 1 ***šeṣep*** [masc. noun: שֶׁצֶף <8241>; from WASH <7857> (in the sense of to gush, to overflow)] ▶

a. This word refers to the Lord's burst of angry emotion toward a disobedient

nation. Ref.: Is. 54:8; also translated overflowing, outburst.
b. This word means a little. It is used to describe the extent of God's anger rather than its nature, a little wrath. Ref.: Is. 54:8. ¶
– [2] Job 38:8 ➔ GUSH <1518> [3] Hab. 3:15 ➔ HEAP (noun) <2563>.

SURGING – Hab. 3:15 ➔ HEAP (noun) <2563>.

SURNAME (verb) – Is. 44:5; 45:4 ➔ FLATTER <3655>.

SURPRISE (BE TAKEN BY) – Jer. 14:9 ➔ ASTONISHED (BE) <1724>.

SURROUND – [1] ***'āpap*** [verb: אָפַף <661>; a prim. root] ▶ **This word means to entangle, to engulf, to encompass. It is also translated to compass, to close in, to swirl about.** Literally, it depicts waves of water enshrouding Jonah (Jon. 2:5). It refers figuratively to waves of death or evil surrounding and wrapping up the psalmist (Ps. 40:12; 116:3). Other refs.: 2 Sam. 22:5; Ps. 18:4. ¶
[2] ***ḥāḏar*** [verb: חָדַר <2314>; a prim. root] ▶ **This word means to enclose, to enter deeply.** It is used of the penetration or the enclosing of the Lord's sword of judgment on His people (Ezek. 21:14). ¶
[3] ***kāṯar*** [verb: כָּתַר <3803>; a prim. root] ▶ **This word means to enclose; to crown. It has the basic meaning of encircling something.** It is used figuratively of being surrounded by political or religious foes (Ps. 22:12: to surround, to compass, to encompass; Hab. 1:4: to surround, to compass, to hem in); and literally of being pressed by an army and encircled (Judg. 20:43: to surround, to enclose). To be surrounded by the righteous is to have God's blessing and protection (Ps. 142:7: to surround, to compass, to gather about). To surround, to enclose in the sense of to gather around and wait, seems to be the sense of the word in Job 36:2 (to suffer, to wait, to bear). Others would see a different root word here. Other ref.: Prov. 14:18: the prudent are crowned with knowledge. ¶
[4] ***nāqap*** [verb: נָקַף <5362>; a prim. root] ▶ **This word means to go around, to compass.** Refs.: Lev. 19:27; Josh. 6:3, 11; 1 Kgs. 7:24; 2 Kgs. 6:14; 11:8; Lam. 3:5; etc. *
– [5] Deut. 33:12 ➔ COVER (verb) <2653> [6] 1 Sam. 23:26; Ps. 5:12 ➔ CROWN (noun and verb) <5849> b. [7] Ps. 140:9 ➔ AROUND <4524>.

SURVIVORS – Gen. 45:7; Judg. 21:17 ➔ DELIVERANCE <6413>.

SUSA – See SHUSHAN <7800>.

SUSANCHITES – ***šûšanḵiy*** [proper noun: שׁוּשַׁנְכִי <7801>; of foreign origin] ▶ **This word designates the inhabitants of Susa or Shushan <7800>.** Ref.: Ezra 4:9. ¶

SUSI – ***sûsiy*** [masc. proper noun: סוּסִי <5485>; from HORSE <5483>]: horseman ▶ **Father of Gaddi, the spy representing Manasseh.** Ref.: Num. 13:11. ¶

SUSPICION (LOOK WITH) – 1 Sam. 18:9 ➔ EYE (verb) <5770>.

SUSTAIN – [1] ***'ûṯ*** [verb: עוּת <5790>; from HASTEN <5789> (in the sense of to lend aid, to come to help)] ▶ **This word occurs once in the Hebrew Bible (Is. 50:4). It is traditionally translated to help but the meaning is uncertain.** In this context, Isaiah proclaimed that the Lord gave him a tongue to help (KJV, NKJV: to speak to) the weary. ¶
– [2] Ruth 4:15; Neh. 9:21 ➔ CONTAIN <3557> [3] Prov. 18:14 ➔ CONTAIN <3557>.

SUSTAINER – Ruth 4:15 ➔ CONTAIN <3557>.

SUSTENANCE – [1] Gen. 45:23 ➔ FOOD <4202> [2] Judg. 6:4; 17:10 ➔ PRESERVATION OF LIFE <4241>.

SWADDLE – [1] ***ḥāṯal*** [verb: חָתַל <2853>; a prim. root] ▶ **This word describes wrapping a newborn infant in cloths at**

birth. It is used figuratively of Israel at her birth (Ezek. 16:4). ¶
– [2] Lam. 2:22 ➔ CARE FOR <2946>.

SWADDLING BAND – ***ḥ**a**ṯullāh*** [fem. noun: חֲתֻלָּה <2854>; from SWADDLE <2853>] ▶ **This word is used in a metaphor that describes God's placement of darkness over the earth as a narrow, long piece of cloth wrapped around an infant at birth.** Ref.: Job 38:9. Its context stresses God's sovereignty and wisdom in creation. ¶

SWALLOW (noun) – [1] ***d**e**rôr*** [masc. noun דְּרוֹר <1866>; the same as FREEDOM <1865>] ▶ **This word indicates one of the birds that found a nesting place in the house of the Lord.** Ref.: Ps. 84:3. The darting and erratic flight of this bird serves as a simile for the flight patterns of a curse (Prov. 26:2). ¶
– [2] Is. 38:14; Jer. 8:7 ➔ CRANE <5693> [3] Is. 38:14; Jer. 8:7 ➔ HORSE <5483> b.

SWALLOW (verb) – [1] ***bāla'*** [verb: בָּלַע <1104>; a prim. root] ▶ **The word means to gulp; it also means to engulf.** The literal meaning of this word is to swallow, as a person swallows a fig (Is. 28:4) or as the great fish swallowed Jonah (Jon. 1:17). It further describes how the earth consumed Pharaoh's army (Ex. 15:12) and the rebellious Israelites (Num. 16:32); and a consuming destruction that comes on people (2 Sam. 17:16; Job 2:3; Ps. 21:9); cities (2 Sam. 20:19); or nations (Lam. 2:5). *
[2] ***lā'a'*** [verb: לָעַע <3886>; a prim. root] ▶ **a. This word indicates to devour, to gulp, to drink.** It means in context to lick up, to devour words (Job 6:3, KJV). It has the sense of the nations slurping down God's judgments (Obad. 1:16). It is used of the improper treatment of holy things (Prov. 20:25, KJV). ¶
b. A verb meaning to act impetuously, to act rashly. Most translators render the word to indicate that Job's words were spoken rashly (Job 6:3, NIV, NKJV, NASB, ESV). It indicates ill-timed and irrational speech (Prov. 20:25, NASB, NIV, NKJV, ESV). ¶
– [3] Jer. 51:44 ➔ DEVOURING <1105>.

SWALLOW UP – Ps. 56:1, 2; 57:3 ➔ LONG FOR <7602> c.

SWAMP – Ezek. 47:11 ➔ MARSH <1207>.

SWAN – Lev. 11:18; Deut. 14:16 ➔ WHITE OWL <8580> c.

SWARM – [1] Lev. 11:29, 41; etc. ➔ MULTIPLY <8317> a. [2] Is. 33:4 ➔ RUSHING <4943> [3] Jer. 51:27 ➔ BRISTLING <5569> b.

SWARM OF FLIES – ***'ārōḇ*** [masc. noun: עָרֹב <6157>; from PLEDGE (BE A) <6148> (in the sense of to mingle, to swarm)] ▶ **This word means a group of insects.** It is found in Psalm 78:45; 105:31. It is used exclusively of the insects involved in the fourth plague against Egypt (Ex. 8:29, 31), a swarm of harmful and noxious insects (Ex. 8:21, 22, 24). ¶

SWARTHY – Song 1:6 ➔ DARK <7840>.

SWAY – [1] 1 Kgs. 14:15; Is. 24:20 ➔ FLEE <5110> [2] Is. 3:16 ➔ MINCE <2952>.

SWEAR – [1] ***šaḇa'*** [verb: שָׁבַע <7650>; a prim. root] ▶ **This word means to take an oath, to make to swear an oath. In the passive reflexive stem, the verb means to swear, to take an oath.** Abimelech and Phicol asked Abraham to swear his kindness and integrity to them and their descendants (Gen. 21:23; Judg. 21:1; 2 Sam. 21:2). The Lord swears by Himself, since there is nothing greater to swear by. God swore to multiply and bless Abraham's descendants (Gen. 22:16; Jer. 22:5). God also swore an oath to Abraham personally (Gen. 24:7; Ex. 13:11). God swore by His holiness to lead Israel into captivity (Amos 4:2).

In the causative stem, the verb means to make, to cause someone to take an oath: Abraham made his servant swear an oath to get Isaac a wife from Abraham's own people (Gen. 24:37). A wife suspected of adultery was forced to take an oath affirming the proposed curse on her if she were found

guilty (Num. 5:21). Saul had ordered the people to take an oath not to eat honey or food while they were engaged in battle with the Philistines (1 Sam. 14:27; 1 Kgs. 18:10). In this stem, the word can mean to charge someone or to adjure that person. David's men adjured him not to go into battle with them again (2 Sam. 21:17; 1 Kgs. 22:16). The land of Canaan became the Promised Land the Lord gave to His people based on His oath. He brought them into the land as He had promised by oath to their fathers (Ex. 13:5; Deut. 1:8, 35; 6:10; Josh. 1:6; Judg. 2:1; Jer. 11:5). *
– 2 Hos. 4:2; 10:4 ➔ CURSE (verb) <422>.

SWEARING – Lev. 5:1 ➔ OATH <423>.

SWEAT – 1 ***zê'āh*** [fem. noun: זֵעָה <2188>; from TREMBLE <2111> (in the sense of SWEAT <3154>)] ▶ **This word means perspiration; it indicates a curse; it is the physical result of man's hard labor on the ground after God had cursed it.** Ref.: Gen. 3:19. ¶
2 ***yeza'*** [masc. noun: יֶזַע <3154>; from an unused root meaning to ooze] ▶ **This word refers to perspiration, the sweat secreted by certain glands of the skin because of clothing or overheating from work.** Ref.: Ezek. 44:18. ¶

SWEEP – 1 ***ṭê'ṭê'*** [verb: טֵאטֵא <2894>; a prim. root] ▶ **This word means to clean with a broom. It is used in a metaphor describing how the Lord will "sweep" Babylon with His broom to destroy it, removing it from the world scene forever.** Ref.: Is. 14:23. ¶
2 ***sāḥap̱*** [verb: סָחַף <5502>; a prim. root] ▶ **This word means to brush away, to cast down to the ground, to throw someone off their feet; it is also translated to drive, to beat, to thrust, to push.** It indicates rain water washing away crops in a field; it depicts those who have political or military power being swept away (Prov. 28:3; Jer. 46:15). ¶
– 3 Ex. 14:27; Ps. 136:15 ➔ SHAKE <5287>.

SWEEP AWAY – 1 ***gārap̱*** [verb: גָּרַף <1640>; a prim. root] ▶ **This word is used in poetry of a strong current of water washing away the armies of Israel's enemy.** Ref.: Judg. 5:21. ¶
2 ***yā'āh*** [verb: יָעָה <3261>; a prim. root] ▶ **This word indicates to brush aside. It refers figuratively to a tool used to remove something, from context possibly with a sweeping motion.** Ref.: Is. 28:17. It is used figuratively of hail "sweeping away" Jerusalem since it is a place of deceit and lies. ¶
3 ***śā'ar*** [verb: שָׂעַר <8175>; a prim. root] ▶ **The image brought to mind when this verb is used is that of a stormy wind sweeping things away that cannot stand against its power. The word is also translated to whirl away, to hurl away, to take away.** It appears in the simple, passive, intensive, and reflexive stems of the verb, but the meanings in each stem are all comparable. This verb is often used to describe the fate of evil persons (Job 27:21; Ps. 58:9). Their punishment from God is that they will be swept away suddenly, just as a stormy wind arises suddenly to sweep things away. Another use of this word is to describe God in all His power and glory, the Ruler of the universe (Ps. 50:3: to be tempestuous); and it can also be used to describe a battle where one ruler storms out against another (Dan. 11:40: to come like a whirlwind, to storm, to rush like a whirlwind). ¶
– 4 Ps. 90:5 ➔ POUR OUT <2229> 5 Prov. 21:7 ➔ DRAG (verb) <1641> 6 Zeph. 1:2, 3 ➔ CONSUME, BE CONSUMED <5486>.

SWEEPING – 1 Jer. 30:23 ➔ DRAG (verb) <1641> 2 Amos 8:6 ➔ CHAFF <4651>.

SWEET – 1 ***mālaṣ*** [verb: מָלַץ <4452>; a prim. root] ▶ **This word means to be smooth, slippery. It means to be delightful, agreeable.** In context God's words of Torah are satisfying (Ps. 119:103). ¶
2 ***māṯôq*** [adj.: מָתוֹק <4966>; from SWEETNESS <4985>] ▶ **This word refers to something that has a taste similar to sugar**

or honey. Ref.: Prov. 24:13. It is the opposite of bitter or sour (Is. 5:20). It is used to convey the idea of pleasantness, agreeableness (Judg. 14:14, 18). God's laws are sweeter than honey (Ps. 19:10); pleasant words are as sweet as honey (Prov. 16:24). It is used figuratively in amorous expressions (Song 2:3). Other refs.: Prov. 27:7; Eccl. 5:12; 11:7; Ezek. 3:3. ¶

[3] ***sam*** [masc. noun: סַם <5561>; from an unused root meaning to smell sweet] ► **This word means an aroma, fragrant; fragrant spice.** It is used of spices from which fragrant perfumes were made (Ex. 25:6; 30:7, 34, etc.). The phrase *qᵉṭoreṯ* (*ha*)*ssammîm* indicates an incense of spices. *

[4] ***ʿārēḇ*** [adj.: עָרֵב <6156>; from PLEASING (BE) <6149> (in the sense of to mingle)] ► **This word describes something tasting like sugar or honey, sweet and invigorating.** But is used figuratively of things obtained and enjoyed falsely (Prov. 20:17). In Song of Solomon 2:14, it is used of the pleasant sound of the beloved's voice. ¶

– [5] Ex. 29:18, 25, 4141; Lev. 1:9, 13, 17; Ezek. 6:13; 16:19; 20:28, 41; etc. → PLEASING <5207> [6] 2 Sam. 23:1; Ps. 81:2 → PLEASANT <5273> b. [7] Ezra 6:10 → PLEASING <5208> [8] Neh. 8:10; Song 5:16 → SWEETNESS <4477> [9] Ps. 141:6 → PLEASANT <5276>.

SWEET (BE) – [1] Ps. 104:34; Prov. 3:24; 13:19; Jer. 6:20; 31:26; Hos. 9:4 → PLEASING (BE) <6149> [2] See SWEETNESS <4985>.

SWEET INFLUENCES – Job 38:31 → CHAINS <4575> b.

SWEET ODORS – Dan. 2:46 → PLEASING <5208>.

SWEET, SWEET-SMELLING – Song 5:13 → SCENTED, SWEET-SCENTED <4840>.

SWEETLY (FEED) – ***māṯāq*** [verb: מָתַק <4988>; from SWEETNESS <4985>] ► **This word indicates to eat with pleasure, as feeding on a sweet morsel.** It refers to someone or something that feeds on something, in context a worm (*rimmāh*, Job 24:20) feeding on the wicked in their graves. See SWEETNESS <4985>. ¶

SWEETNESS – [1] ***mamtaqqiym*** [masc. plur. noun: מַמְתַּקִּים <4477>; from <4985> below] ► **This word is used of a drink with a taste like sugar or with an agreeable taste and smell.** Ref.: Neh. 8:10: sweet. In Song of Solomon 5:16 (also translated sweet), it is used figuratively of the mouth of the beloved groom. ¶

[2] ***māṯaq*** [verb: מָתַק <4985>; a prim. root] ► **This word means to be sweet, to be pleasant. It indicates something having a taste like sugar or honey.** It is used figuratively of evil as tasting deceptively sweet (Job 20:12; Prov. 9:17). It describes a worm enjoying its food (Job 24:20); it describes, ironically, clods of earth sweetly, gently covering a person in burial (Job 21:33). It indicates the pleasantness of a friendship in the Lord (Ps. 55:14). Other ref.: Ex. 15:25. ¶

[3] ***māṯēq*** [masc. noun: מֶתֶק <4986>; from <4985> above] ► **This word describes a taste of something like sugar or honey.** Refs.: Prov. 16:21; 27:9. Manner of speech and good counsel give the effects of pleasantness. ¶

[4] ***mōṯeq*** [masc. noun: מֹתֶק <4987>; from <4985> above] ► **This word refers to the sweet taste of ripe figs, a taste similar to honey.** Ref.: Judg. 9:11. ¶

SWELL – [1] ***bāṣaq*** [verb: בָּצֵק <1216>; a prim. root] ► **This verb means to become swollen, to increase in size.** It was used of the failure of the Israelites' feet to swell in their desert marches in Sinai (Deut. 8:4). God's providential kindness and care for His people was recorded and remembered by the exiles returned from Babylon (Neh. 9:21). ¶

[2] ***ṣāḇāh*** [verb: צָבָה <6638>; a prim. root] ► **This word means to increase in size, to puff up from disease or from stomach and intestinal gases in this context.** Refs.: Num. 5:22, 27. ¶

3 *ṣāḇeh* [adj.: צָבֶה <6639>; from <6638> above] ► **This word means swollen. It describes something puffed up, extended because of a curse and trial by ordeal.** Ref.: Num. 5:21. ¶
– 4 Is. 30:13 ➔ BOIL (verb) <1158>.

SWELLING – 1 Lev. 13:2, 10; etc. ➔ DIGNITY <7613> b. 2 Ps. 89:9 ➔ MAJESTY <1348>.

SWELLING, SWELLING PRIDE – Ps. 46:3 ➔ MAJESTY <1346>.

SWERVE – *'āḇaṭ* [verb: עָבַט <5670>; a prim. root] ► **This word means to turn aside, to get out of line, to deviate from one's course; it is also translated to deviate, to break.** Ref.: Joel 2:7. The Hebrew word also means to borrow, to lend; see LEND <5670>. ¶

SWIFT – 1 *qal* [adj.: קַל <7031>; from SLIGHT (BE) <7043>] ► **This word means rapid, speedy. It describes something as agile, quick.** It refers to a swift warrior (Amos 2:14); a fast horse (Is. 30:16); a swift messenger from Ethiopia (Is. 18:2); a swift-footed runner such as Asahel (2 Sam. 2:18); a fast-moving army (Is. 5:26). The Lord is pictured as traveling on a swift-flying cloud (Is. 19:1). *
– 2 Esther 8:10, 14 ➔ ROYAL <327> 3 Job 9:26 ➔ REED <16> 4 Is. 16:5 ➔ SKILLED <4106> 5 Is. 38:14; Jer. 8:7 ➔ HORSE <5483> b.

SWIFT BEAST – 1 Is. 66:20 ➔ CAMEL <3753> 2 Mic. 1:13 ➔ HORSE <7409> d.

SWIFT FLIGHT – Dan. 9:21 ➔ WEARINESS <3288> b.

SWIFT STEED – 1 Kgs. 4:28; Mic. 1:13 ➔ HORSE <7409> d.

SWIFTLY (FLY) – Dan. 9:21 ➔ WEARINESS <3288> b.

SWIM – 1 *śāḥāh* [verb: שָׂחָה <7811>; a prim. root] ► **This word refers to using one's hands to move through the water in a breast-stroke fashion; it also means to cause to swim, to flood.** Refs.: Ps. 6:6; Is. 25:11.
– 2 2 Kgs. 6:6 ➔ FLOW OVER <6687> 3 Ezek. 32:6 ➔ DISCHARGE <6824> b. 4 Ezek. 47:5 ➔ SWIMMING <7813>.

SWIMMING – *śāḥû* [masculine noun: שָׂחוּ <7813>; from SWIM <7811>] ► **This is used of the action of swimming. The phrase *mê śāḥû* means literally, water of swimming, i.e., water deep enough to swim in.** Ref.: Ezek. 47:5. ¶

SWINDLER – Mal. 1:14 ➔ DECEIVE <5230>.

SWINE – Deut. 14:8; Prov. 11:22; Is. 65:4; 66:3, 17; Lev. 11:7 ➔ PIG <2386>.

SWING – Deut. 19:5; 20:19 ➔ DRIVE <5080> b.

SWING OUT – Ex. 28:28; 39:21 ➔ LOOSE (COME) <2118>.

SWINGING – Ezek. 41:24 ➔ ENCLOSED <4142>.

SWIRL ABOUT – 2 Sam. 22:5 ➔ SURROUND <661>.

SWOLLEN – Ps. 124:5 ➔ RAGING <2121>.

SWOOP – 1 *ṭûś* [verb: טוּשׂ <2907>; a prim. root] ► **This word means to dart.** It describes the quick flight of an eagle attacking its prey (Job 9:26; KJV, to haste). It demonstrates how quickly Job's days are flying by and the frailty of life for even a righteous man. ¶
– 2 Deut. 28:49; Jer. 48:40; 49:22 ➔ FLY (verb) <1675>.

SWORD – 1 *ḥereḇ* [fem. noun: חֶרֶב <2719>; from WASTE (LAY) <2717>] ► **This word means an offensive weapon with a long blade; it also means a knife, a cutting tool. The word frequently pictures the sword, along with the bow and**

shield, as the standard fighting equipment of the times. Refs.: Gen. 48:22; Ps. 76:3; Hos. 1:7. Warriors are referred to as those drawing the sword (Judg. 20; 1 Chr. 21:5). The sword may also stand for a larger unit of military power, sometimes pictured as coming on a people or land (Lev. 26:25; Lam. 1:20; Ezek. 14:17). The cutting action of a sword is likened to eating, and its edges are literally referred to as mouths. Similarly, the mouths of people are likened to swords (Ps. 59:7; Prov. 30:14; Is. 49:2). The sword is also a symbol of judgment executed by God (Gen. 3:24; Deut. 32:41; Jer. 47:6); or His people (Ps. 149:6). The word can refer to a knife (Josh. 5:2, 3); or a tool for cutting stones (Ex. 20:25). *

[2] ***mᵉḵērāh*** [masc. noun: מְכֵרָה <4380>; prob. from the same as PIERCE <3564> in the sense of stabbing] ► **In context the meaning of this word is difficult, but it may be rendered as swords (see previous definition).** Refs.: Gen. 49:5. It is rendered by some translations as a dwelling, a habitation; perhaps houses, i.e., biological groups is meant (Gen. 49:5). ¶

– [3] 1 Kgs. 18:28 ➔ SPEAR <7420> [4] Ps. 42:10 ➔ BREAKING <7524> [5] Ezek. 21:16: Swords at the ready!; Slash your sword ➔ GO ONE WAY OR THE OTHER <258>.

SWORD (DRAWN) – ***pᵉṯiyḥāh*** [fem. noun: פְּתִיחָה <6609>; from OPEN <6605>] ► **This word is used to indicate a sword (see entry for this word) ready for engagement, taken out of its sheath.** Ref.: Ps. 55:21. ¶

SWORN COVENANT – Deut. 29:19 ➔ OATH <423>.

SYCAMORE – ***šiqmāh*** [fem. noun: שִׁקְמָה <8256>; of uncertain deriv.] ► **This word designates a tall fig tree having a thick trunk and leaves which are downy on the underside. The fig tree, with its edible fruit, is native to Asia Minor and Egypt.** It was abundant in Israel's territory (1 Kgs. 10:27); these trees were destroyed by the Lord in times of judgment (Ps. 78:47). It made an inferior construction material (Is. 9:10). Amos grew and cultivated these trees (Amos 7:14). Other refs.: 1 Chr. 27:28; 2 Chr. 1:15; 9:27. ¶

SYENE – [1] ***sᵉwênêh*** [proper noun: סְוֵנֵה <5482>; of Egyptian deriv.] ► **A city in Egypt on the border of Ethiopia.** Refs.: Ezek. 29:10; 30:6. ¶

– [2] Is. 49:12 ➔ SINIM <5515> b.

SYMBOL – Ex. 13:16; Deut. 6:8; 11:18 ➔ FRONTLETS <2903>.

SYRIAC – See ARAMAIC <762>.

SYRIAN – [1] ***rammiy*** [proper noun: רַמִּי <7421>; for ARAMEAN <761>] ► **This word designates an inhabitant from Syria.** Ref.: 2 Chr. 22:5; NASB, NIV: Aramean. ¶

– [2] 2 Kgs. 16:6 ➔ ARAMEAN <726> [3] See ARAMEAN <761>.

SYSTRUM – 2 Sam. 6:5 ➔ CASTANETS <4517> a.

T

TAANACH – ***ta'nāḵ, ta'naḵ*** [proper noun: תַּעְנָךְ, תַּעֲנָךְ <8590>; of uncertain deriv.] ▶ **This word designates a city southeast of Megiddo.** Joshua captured it (Josh. 12:21; 17:11). Manasseh inherited it and it was a Levitical city as well (Josh. 21:25). It was near the western border of Issachar. Manasseh failed to drive out the Canaanites from it (Judg. 1:27). The battle of Deborah and Barak took place partly at Taanach and Megiddo (Judg. 5:19). It lay within Solomon's fifth administrative district of Israel (1 Kgs. 4:12; 1 Chr. 7:29). ¶

TAANATH-SHILOH – ***ta'ᵃnaṯ šilōh*** [proper noun: תַּאֲנַת שִׁלֹה <8387>; from OCCASION <8385> and SHILOH <7887>]: approach of Shiloh ▶ **A place on the border of Ephraim's territory.** Ref.: Josh. 16:6. ¶

TABBAOTH – ***ṭabbā'ôṯ*** [masc. proper noun: טַבָּעוֹת <2884>; plur. of RING <2885>]: rings ▶ **His children came back from the Babylonian captivity.** Refs.: Ezra 2:43; Neh. 7:46. ¶

TABBATH – ***ṭabbāṯ*** [proper noun: טַבָּת <2888>; of uncertain deriv.]: famous, celebrated ▶ **A town in Ephraim mentioned in relation to the flight of the army of Midian.** Ref.: Judg. 7:22. ¶

TABEEL, TABEAL – ***ṭāḇᵉ'ēl, ṭāḇᵉ'al*** [masc. proper noun: טָבְאֵל, טָבְאַל <2870>; from HAPPY (BE) <2895> (in the sense of to please) and GOD <410>]: pleasing to God ▶

a. Tabeel, a Persian official. Ref.: Ezra 4:7. ¶

b. A Syrian. Ref.: Is. 7:6. ¶

TABERAH – ***taḇ'ērāh*** [proper noun: תַּבְעֵרָה <8404>; from BURN <1197>]: burning ▶ **A place in the desert of Paran where the Israelites provoked the Lord to wrath.** Refs.: Num. 11:3; Deut. 9:22. ¶

TABERNACLE – **1** ***miškān*** [masc. noun: מִשְׁכָּן <4908>; from SETTLE DOWN <7931> (in the sense of to dwell or abide)] ▶ **This word means dwelling, tabernacle, or sanctuary. The most significant meaning of the word indicates the dwelling place of the Lord, the Tabernacle.** The word is often used in Exodus to indicate the temporary lodging of God and His glory among His people, the Tabernacle (Lev. 26:11; Ps. 26:8). It is used parallel to the word meaning sanctuary or holy place in the preceding verse (Ex. 25:9, cf. v. 8). The noun is formed from the verbal root *šāḵan* (DWELL <7931>), which indicates temporary lodging (Ex. 25:9; 26:1, 6; 2 Sam. 7:6). This noun is also often found in parallel with or described by the Hebrew word for tent (Ex. 26:35; Jer. 30:18).

The Tabernacle was often called the Tent of Meeting (1 Chr. 6:32; see Ex. 28:43; 30:20; 40:32), for there the Lord met with His people. Exodus 33:7–11 refers to a «tent of meeting» outside the camp to which Moses went prior to the Tabernacle being set up. The Tabernacle was also called the Tent of Testimony (Ex. 38:21; Num. 9:15; cf. Num. 17:22, 23; 18:2), since the covenantal documents, the Ten Commandments, were lodged in the Holy of Holies. The Hebrew noun is used with the definite article in 74 of 130 times, indicating that the author expected the reader to know what Tabernacle he meant. God gave Moses the pattern of the structure for the Tabernacle (Ex. 25:9; 26:30). The Lord had His Tabernacle set up at Shiloh in Canaan, but it was later abandoned (Ps. 78:60). The word is hardly ever used regarding the later Temple of Solomon, of Ezekiel's visionary Temple (2 Chr. 29:6; Ps. 26:8; 46:4; Ezek. 37:27); or the Lord's dwelling place in Zion (Ps. 132:5, 7). The word used most often to describe Solomon's Temple and the postexilic Temple is *bayiṯ* (<1004>), meaning house.

The word also indicates the dwelling places of the Israelites and other peoples; it describes Korah's dwelling place (Num. 16:24, 27); Israel's dwelling place (Num. 24:5; Is. 32:18; Jer. 30:18). Twice the word indicates

the dwelling of the dead, i.e., the grave Jerusalem made for herself, and the abode of all classes of men (Ps. 49:11; Is. 22:16). *
2 ***śōḵ*** [masc. noun: שׂךְ <7900>; from COVER (verb) <5526> in the sense of HEDGE (MAKE A) <7753>] ► **This word is used figuratively of Israel as the tabernacle or holy place where God would dwell; it is also translated booth, dwelling.** Ref.: Lam. 2:6. ¶
– 3 Ps. 76:2 ➔ ABODE <5520> 4 Amos 5:26 ➔ SIKKUTH <5522> 5 See TENT <168>.

TABLE – 1 ***šulḥān*** [masc. noun: שֻׁלְחָן <7979>; from SEND FORTH, SEND AWAY <7971> (in the sense of to spread out, e.g., a table)] ► **The most significant referent of this word (a piece of furniture with a flat top) is the table of showbread.** It was featured in the Tabernacle (Ex. 25:23); and then in the Temple (1 Kgs. 7:48), including Ezekiel's Temple (Ezek. 40:39–43). The idiom to eat at one's table indicated a special honor given to a person (1 Kgs. 2:7). The word refers to a table where the king dined (1 Kgs. 4:27). *
– 2 Song 1:12 ➔ AROUND <4524>.

TABLET – 1 Ex. 31:18; Hab. 2:2; etc. ➔ BOARD <3871> 2 Ex. 35:22; Num. 31:50 ➔ NECKLACE <3558> 3 Is. 8:1 ➔ SCROLL <1549>.

TABOR – ***tāḇôr*** [proper noun: תָּבוֹר <8396>; from a root corresponding to BRITTLE (BE) <8406>]: broken region ►
a. It was a high mountain on the northwest boundary of Issachar. Refs.: Josh. 19:22; Jer. 46:18. It is noted in the Deborah-Barak cycle of stories (Judg. 4:6, 12, 14; 8:18). God created it along with Mount Hermon (Ps. 89:12). It is used in a figure of speech (Hos. 5:1). Two hostile princes were slain near it (Judg. 8:18).
b. It was a Levitical city in Zebulun. Ref.: 1 Chr. 6:77. Its location is not yet known.
c. This is the name of a small area or city in which the oak of Tabor was located. It was not far from Bethel (1 Sam. 10:3). The KJV has the plain of Tabor. ¶

TABRET – Job 17:6 ➔ SPIT (noun) <8611> b.

TABRETS – Ezek. 28:13 ➔ TAMBOURINE <8596>.

TABRIMMON – ***ṭaḇrimmōn*** [masc. proper noun: טַבְרִמֹּן <2886>; from HAPPY (BE) <2895> (in the sense of to be good) and RIMMON <7417>]: goodness of Rimmon ► **Father of Ben-Hadad I, king of Syria.** Ref.: 1 Kgs. 15:18. ¶

TACHE – Ex. 26:6, 11, 33; etc. ➔ CLASP <7165>.

TADMOR – ***taḏmōr*** [proper noun: תַּדְמֹר <8412>; apparently from PALM TREE <8558>]: palm tree ► **A city that King Solomon built in the desert.** Refs.: 1 Kgs. 9:18; 2 Chr. 8:4. ¶

TAHAN – ***taḥan*** [masc. proper noun: תַּחַן <8465>; from ENCAMP <2583>]: camp, station ► **An Israelite of the tribe of Ephraim.** Refs.: Num. 26:35; 1 Chr. 7:25. ¶

TAHANITE – ***taḥ***[a]***niy*** [proper noun: תַּחֲנִי <8470>; patron. from TAHAN <8465>] ► **Descendant of Tahan.** Ref.: Num. 26:35. ¶

TAHASH, THAHASH – ***taḥaš*** [masc. proper noun: תַּחַשׁ <8477>; the same as BADGER <8476>]: badger ► **Son of Nahor and nephew of Abraham.** Ref.: Gen. 22:24. ¶

TAHATH – ***taḥaṯ*** [proper noun: תַּחַת <8480>; from an unused root meaning to depress]: hollow ►
a. A Kohathite. Refs.: 1 Chr. 6:24, 37.
b. Son of Ephraim. Ref.: 1 Chr. 7:20.
c. Grandson of b. above. Ref.: 1 Chr. 7:20.
d. A wilderness location. Refs.: Num. 33:26, 27. ¶

TAHKEMONITE – ***taḥk***[e]***mōniy*** [masc. proper noun: תַּחְכְּמֹנִי <8461>; prob. from HACHMONI <2453>] ► **This word is found in 2 Samuel 23:8.** It is the same as Hachmonite (see HACHMONI <2453> b.). ¶

TAHPANHES – ***taḥpanḥês, tᵉḥapnᵉḥês*** [proper noun: תַּחְפַּנְחֵס, תְּחַפְנְחֵס <8471>; of Egyptian deriv.] ► **An Egyptian city in the eastern delta. It was located south of Lake Manzaleh on the Pelusaic branch of the Nile River. It took part in the devastation of Israel. Jeremiah was taken into exile here and many Jewish refugees fleeing Nebuchadnezzar passed through it.** Jeremiah prophesied here (Jer. 2:16; 43:8–13). Pharaoh's palace was in the city at that time. The Babylonians conquered Egypt, passing through Tahpanhes (Jer. 46:14; Ezek. 30:18) (568–567 B.C.). ¶

TAHPENES – ***taḥpᵉnêys*** [fem. proper noun: תַּחְפְּנֵיס <8472>; of Egyptian deriv.] ► **The name of a Pharaoh's queen (prior to ca. 945 B.C.).** The Pharaoh gave Hadad a sister of the queen for a wife (1 Kgs. 11:19, 20). ¶

TAHREA – ***taḥrêaʻ*** [masc. proper noun: תַּחְרֵעַ <8475>; for TAREA <8390>] ► **An Israelite of the tribe of Benjamin.** Ref.: 1 Chr. 9:41. ¶

TAHTIM-HODSHI – ***taḥtiym ḥoḏšiy*** [proper noun: תַּחְתִּים חָדְשִׁי <8483>; apparently from the masc. plur. of LOWER, LOWEST <8482> and MONTH <2320>]: lowest moon ► **A land near Gilead.** Ref.: 2 Sam. 24:6. ¶

TAIL – ***zānāḇ*** [masc. noun: זָנָב <2180>; from ATTACK (verb) <2179> (in the original sense of flapping)] ► **This word refers to the posterior appendage part of an animal or reptile.** Of a snake or fox (Ex. 4:4; Judg. 15:4); figuratively of the lowest place of influence among nations (Deut. 28:13, 44); of the tail of Behemoth (Job 40:17); metaphorically, of the end of a burning stump (Is. 7:4); or of a false prophet (Is. 9:15). Coupled with head, it indicates the totality of something (Is. 9:14, 15). ¶

TAINTED – Lev. 7:18; 19:7; Ezek. 4:14 ➔ OFFENSIVE THING <6292>.

TAKE – 1 ***ḥāṯāh*** [verb: חָתָה <2846>; a prim. root] ► **This word indicates to take away, to snatch away; to get and place something. It means to take away when used with the preposition "from" (*min* <4480>).** In context, it indicates taking fire or coals from a hearth (Is. 30:14) or people from a location (Ps. 52:5). Without *min*, the word can mean to get and bring into, take into, such as fire into one's bosom (Prov. 6:27; also translated to carry, to snoop). In Proverbs 25:22 (to heap), burning coals stand for an act of kindness or warming one's enemy (cf. Rom. 12:20). ¶

2 ***lāqaḥ*** [verb: לָקַח <3947>; a prim. root] ► **This word means to get. Its exact meaning must be discerned from its context.** It is used of grasping or seizing a person or an animal (Gen. 12:5; Ex. 17:5; Ezek. 8:3; Hos. 14:2). The ark was captured (1 Sam. 4:11, 17, 19). It has the sense of keeping what one has (Gen. 14:21). It may mean in context to receive or acquire, to buy (2 Kgs. 5:20; Prov. 31:16). It is used of a bird carrying or loading its young onto its wings (Deut. 32:11). It is used figuratively of obeying, "taking on" commands, instructions (Prov. 10:8). It is used of taking a wife (Gen. 25:1). With *nāqām* as its object, it means to take vengeance (Is. 47:3). One's ear can "receive," hearken to God's Word (Jer. 9:20). It is used of one's heart sweeping away, carrying away oneself (Job 15:12). In its passive usage, it means to be brought in (Gen. 12:15; Esther 2:8, 16). It takes on the nuance of flashing, bolting here and there like fire or lightning (Ex. 9:24; Ezek. 1:4). *

– 3 Num. 11:17, 25 ➔ RESERVE (verb) <680> 4 Deut. 24:10 ➔ LEND <5670> 5 Ezra 5:15 ➔ INSURRECTION (MAKE) <5376> 6 Prov. 31:4 ➔ OR <176> b. 7 Is. 30:14:9 ➔ STRIP <2834>.

TAKE A HANDFUL – ***qāmaṣ*** [verb: קָמַץ <7061>; a prim. root] ► **This word refers to gathering up an amount of something equal to what a person's hand can hold of flour or grain.** Refs.: Lev. 2:2; 5:12; Num. 5:26. ¶

TAKE AWAY – 1 ***šālāh*** [verb: שָׁלָה <7953>; a prim. root] ► **This word means literally to draw out or off, i.e., to remove**

(the soul by death). Ref.: Job 27:8; also translated to require. ¶
– 2 Job 9:12 ➔ SNATCH AWAY <2862> 3 Ps. 58:9 ➔ SWEEP AWAY <8175> 4 Ps. 119:22 ➔ ROLL (verb) <1556> 5 Prov. 25:4, 5 ➔ REMOVE <1898> 6 Jer. 8:13 ➔ CONSUME, BE CONSUMED <5486>.

TAKE BACK – Ezra 6:5 ➔ GO <1946>.

TAKE DOWN – Is. 33:20 ➔ FOLD (verb) <6813>.

TAKE FROM – Ps. 89:33 ➔ NOTHING (BRING TO) <6329>.

TAKE OFF – Ex. 3:5; Josh. 5:15 ➔ REMOVE <5394>.

TAKE OFF, TAKE AWAY – Prov. 25:20 ➔ PASS OVER <5710>.

TAKE, TAKE OUT – ***gāzāh*** [verb: גָּזָה <1491>; a prim. root (akin to CUT OFF <1468>)] ▶ **This word means to cut; it is also translated to bring forth.** It refers to the cutting of the umbilical cord (Ps. 71:6). Figuratively, it describes God as taking a child from its mother's womb. ¶

TAKE OUT – 1 ***n^{e}p̱aq*** [Aramaic verb: נְפַק <5312>; a prim. root] ▶ **This word indicates to go or come out, to bring or come forth.** The vessels of the Solomonic Temple were removed (Ezra 5:14; 6:5; Dan. 5:2, 3); Shadrach, Meshach, and Abednego came out from the fiery furnace (Dan. 3:26). It also means to go out, to issue a decree, an order, to send forth fire (Dan. 2:13, 14; 7:10); and the appearance of a hand (Dan. 5:5: to appear, to come forth, to emerge). ¶
– 2 2 Sam. 20:13 ➔ REMOVE <3014> 3 Ps. 22:9 ➔ GUSH <1518>.

TAKE UP – 1 ***n^{e}saq*** [Aramaic verb: נְסַק <5267>; corresponding to ASCEND <5266>] ▶ **This word means to bring up an object, to carry it higher; it is also translated to carry up, to lift.** It is used of carrying up persons (Dan. 3:22; 6:23). ¶
– 2 1 Kgs. 20:33 ➔ CATCH (verb) <2480> 3 Is. 40:15 ➔ OFFER <5190> 4 Dan. 3:22; 6:23 ➔ GO UP <5559> b.

TAKEN (FROM BEING) – Prov. 3:26 ➔ CAPTURE (noun) <3921>.

TAKEN FROM – Is. 28:9 ➔ ANCIENT <6267> b.

TAKEN UP – Ezek. 21:15 ➔ WRAPPED UP <4593>.

TAKING – ***miqqaḥ*** [masc. noun: מִקָּח <4727>; from TAKE <3947>] ▶ **This word means the act of taking, receiving. It means to accept something.** In context it is used of the wrongful acceptance of bribes (2 Chr. 19:7). ¶

TALE – 1 Ex. 5:18 ➔ QUOTA <8506> 2 Ps. 90:9 ➔ RUMBLING <1899>.

TALEBEARER – 1 Lev. 19:16; Prov. 11:13; 20:19; Jer. 6:28 ➔ SLANDER, SLANDERER <7400> 2 Prov. 18:8; 26:20, 22 ➔ WHISPERER <5372>.

TALENT – 1 ***kakkar*** [fem. Aramaic noun: כַּכַּר <3604>; corresponding to ROUND (SOMETHING) <3603>] ▶ **This word refers to a coin or a measure of weight, a talent.** It is used to refer to the talents (about 75 lbs.) of silver given to the Jews by King Artaxerxes (Ezra 7:22). ¶
– 2 1 Kgs. 9:14; 10:10; 20:39; Zech. 5:7 ➔ ROUND (SOMETHING) <3603>.

TALK (EMPTY, IDLE) – ***baḏ*** [masc. noun: בַּד <907>; from DEVISE <908>] ▶ **This word is also translated babble, boast, lie, boasting; liar, boaster, babbler, false prophet.** It describes boasting or vain talk, such as Zophar claimed Job was uttering (Job 11:3). An arrogant nation utters false boasts (Is. 16:6; Jer. 48:30; 50:36) as do false prophets (Is. 44:25). ¶

TALMAI – ***talmay*** [masc. proper noun: תַּלְמַי <8526>; from FURROW <8525>] ▶

a. A descendant of the Anakim from Anak. He lived in Hebron (Num. 13:22). Joshua drove the Anakim from the area (Josh. 15:14; Judg. 1:10). ¶
b. The grandfather of Absalom, David's son. He was the son (king?) of the king of Geshur, Ammihud (2 Sam. 3:3; 13:37; 1 Chr. 3:2). ¶

TALMON – ***ṭalmôn, ṭalmōn*** [masc. proper noun: טַלְמֹן, טַלְמוֹן <2929>; from the same as TELEM <2728>]: oppression ▶ **A Levite porter; his descendants returned from the Babylonian captivity.** Refs.: 1 Chr. 9:17; Ezra 2:42; Neh. 7:45; 11:19; 12:25. ¶

TAMAR – ***tāmār*** [proper noun: תָּמָר <8559>; from the same as plam tree]: palm tree ▶
a. The daughter-in-law of Judah. She married Judah's son Er who died childless (Gen. 38:1–24). Onan, his second son, died at the hand of the Lord because he would not raise up seed for Israel through Tamar according to the Levirate law of marriage (Gen. 38:9–10). She then disguised herself as a prostitute, solicited Judah, and lay with him to conceive a son. She bore twins, Perez and Zerah, by Judah (Gen. 38:28–30). Perez, her son, and his fruitfulness became a model for the hoped-for offspring of Ruth and Boaz (Ruth 4:12).
b. A beautiful daughter of David, with whom his son Amnon, son by his wife Ahinoam, fell in love. The name means "palm." He raped her and then rejected and hated her after the attack (2 Sam. 13:1–32). She was Absalom's full sister by Maacah their mother. Absalom avenged Tamar and slew Amnon. Thus began the destruction of David's family because of his adultery and murder concerning Bathsheba.
c. The daughter of Absalom (not his sister) who also became a beautiful woman. Ref.: 2 Sam. 14:27.
d. A city on the border of the tribe of Gad. It was built by Solomon (1 Kgs. 9:18). Some translations give Tadmor (NIV). Ezekiel envisioned the city as part of a rebuilt Israel and located on the southeast border (Ezek. 47:18; 48:28). ¶

TAMARISK – 1 Chr. 10:12 ➔ OAK <424>.

TAMARISK TREE – ***'êšel*** [masc. noun: אֵשֶׁל <815>; from a root of uncertain signification] ▶ **This tree has small leaves and survives well in the dry, hot climate of Israel.** The word appears only three times in the Old Testament: when Abraham planted a tamarisk tree near the well in Beersheba (Gen. 21:33; also translated grove); the place where Saul and his men gathered (1 Sam. 22:6); and where Saul's bones were buried at Jabesh (1 Sam. 31:13). ¶

TAMBOURINE – ***tōp̱*** [masc. noun: תֹּף <8596>; from TAMBOURINES (PLAYING) <8608>] ▶
a. This word refers to a small, shallow, single-headed hand drum, also called a timbrel. It may have jingles around the rim, played by shaking it and/or striking it with the knuckles (Gen. 31:27). Miriam used this instrument to lead the women in a song of praise to the Lord for deliverance at the Red Sea. The KJV renders this word as tabrets in Ezekiel 28:13.
b. A masculine noun referring to the setting for a jewel. It refers to the tiny sockets, their arrangements, and the precious jewels placed into them by a jeweler (Ezek. 28:13; KJV: tabrets). *

TAMBOURINES (PLAYING, BEATING) – ***tāp̱ap̱*** [verb: תָּפַף <8608>; a prim. root] ▶ **This word means to beat one's knuckles on a tambourine and shake it slightly.** Ref.: Ps. 68:25; also translated playing timbrels. But in Nahum 2:7, the objects being struck were the breasts (lit., hearts) of the mourners. ¶

TAMMUZ – ***tāmmûz*** [masc. proper noun: תַּמּוּז <8542>; of uncertain deriv.] ▶ **This word refers to a popular and widely known fertility god in the ancient Middle East.** Ref.: Ezek. 8:14. It had other names in different nations, Astarte, Ishtar, etc. ¶

TAN – Song 1:6 ➔ SEE <7805> b.

TANGLED – Nah. 1:10 ➔ ENTWINE <5440>.

TANHUMETH – ***tanḥumeṯ*** [masc. proper noun: תַּנְחֻמֶת <8576>; for CONSOLATION <8575>]: consolation ▶ **Father of Seraiah, an associate of Gedaliah.** Refs.: 2 Kgs. 25:23; Jer. 40:8. ¶

TANNED (BE) – Ex. 25:5; 26:14; 35:7 ➔ RUDDY (BE) <119>.

TAPESTRY, COVERING OF TAPESTRY – Prov. 7:16; 31:22 ➔ COVERING <4765>.

TAPHATH – ***ṭāp̱aṯ*** [fem. proper noun: טָפַת <2955>; prob. from DROP (verb) <5197>]: drop (of ointment) ▶ **Daughter of Solomon and wife of the son of Abinadab.** Ref.: 1 Kgs. 4:11. ¶

TAPPUAH – ***tappûaḥ*** [proper noun: תַּפּוּחַ <8599>; the same as APPLE, APPLE TREE <8598>]: apple ▶
a. Descendant of Caleb. Ref.: 1 Chr. 2:43. ¶
b. A city in Judah. Ref.: Josh. 15:34. ¶
c. A city on the border of Ephraim. Refs.: Josh. 12:17; 16:8; 17:8. ¶

TAR – ***ḥêmār*** [masc. noun: חֵמָר <2564>; from COAT (verb) <2560>] ▶ **This word refers to slime, pitch, bitumen, asphalt.** Ref.: Gen. 14:10. It was used as cement in construction work (Gen. 11:3) and used in coating the basket in which Moses was placed (Ex. 2:3; parallel to *zep̱eṯ*: see PITCH <2203>). ¶

TARALAH – ***tarᵃlāh*** [verb: תַּרְאֲלָה <8634>; for STAGGER (THAT MAKES) <8653>]: reeling ▶ **A city in the territory of Benjamin.** Ref.: Josh. 18:27. ¶

TAREA – ***taᵃrêaʿ*** [masc. proper noun: תַּאֲרֵעַ <8390>; perhaps from EARTH <772>] ▶ **An Israelite of the tribe of Benjamin.** Ref.: 1 Chr. 8:35. ¶

TARGET – 1 ***mip̱gāʿ*** [masc. noun: מִפְגָּע <4645>; from MEET (verb) <6293> (in the sense of to reach)] ▶ **This word refers to the object at which a marksman aims; it is also translated mark.** It is used figuratively of Job being the target of God's attacks (Job 7:20). ¶
– 2 1 Sam. 17:6 (KJV) ➔ SPEAR <3591> 3 1 Sam. 20:20; Job 16:12; Lam. 3:12 ➔ GUARD <4307>.

TARPELITES – ***ṭarpᵉlāy*** [proper noun: טַרְפְּלָי <2967>; from a name of foreign deriv.] ▶ **They were conquered by the Assyrians.** Ref.: Ezra 4:9: KJV and NKJV. Other translators believe it was the titles of some Persian officials in Samaria (see NASB, ESV, and NIV). ¶

TARRY – 1 Ex. 12:39; Judg. 3:26; 19:8; 19:8; 2 Sam. 15:28; Hab. 2:3 ➔ LINGER <4102> 2 Judg. 5:28; 2 Sam. 20:5 ➔ STAY (verb) <309> 3 1 Sam. 10:8; 13:8 ➔ WAIT <3176> 4 2 Sam. 20:5 ➔ DELAY (verb) <3186>.

TARSHISH (common noun) – See BERYL <8658> b.

TARSHISH (proper noun) – ***taršiyš*** [proper noun: תַּרְשִׁישׁ <8659>; prob. the same as BERYL <8658>]: beryl or another gemstone ▶
a. The name of a son of Javan, his second son. Refs.: Gen. 10:4; 1 Chr. 1:7.
b. A descendant of Benjamin, a son of Bilhan. He was the head of a family (1 Chr. 7:10).
c. The name of a Persian advisor. He was a wise man who could interpret current events and the world situation. He had access to the Persian king and was one of the highest officials in the nation (Esther 1:14). ¶

TARTAK – ***tartāq*** [masc. proper noun: תַּרְתָּק <8662>; of foreign deriv.] ▶ **An Avvite deity. This name of the god of the Avvites is not described fully anywhere.** The Avvites made an idol of this god evidently (2 Kgs. 17:31). ¶

TARTAN – ***tartān*** [תַּרְתָּן <8661>; of foreign deriv.] ▶

a. A proper noun designating Tartan, an Assyrian general. Refs.: 2 Kgs. 18:17; Is. 20:1. **b. A masculine noun meaning supreme commander.** Refs.: NIV, 2 Kgs. 18:17; Is. 20:1. ¶

TASK – ***'inyān*** [masc. noun: עִנְיָן <6045>; from AFFLICTED (BE) <6031>] ▶ **This word refers to a job to be performed, a responsibility to be met, a need to be satisfied; it is also translated travail, business, burden, work, labor.** To examine all of life, to understand it (Eccl. 1:13; 2:23); both by good and evil persons (Eccl. 2:26; 3:10); concerning what is past, present, and future (Eccl. 8:16). It indicates the effort put forth as well as the task itself (Eccl. 5:3: effort, activity, cares). Other refs.: Eccl. 4:8, 5:14 (misfortune, venture). ¶

TASKMASTER – Ex. 3:7; 5:6, 10, 13, 14; Job 3:18; Is. 60:17 ➔ OPPRESS <5065>.

TASSEL – 1 ***gāḏil*** [masc. noun: גְּדִל <1434>; from GREAT (BECOME) <1431> (in the sense of twisting)] ▶ **This word indicates an edging on a garment.** Ref.: Deut. 22:12; also translated fringe. The Hebrew word also means a twisted thread (1 Kgs. 7:17); see WREATH <1434>. ¶
2 ***ṣiyṣiṯ*** [fem. noun: צִיצִת <6734>; fem. of FLOWER <6731>] ▶ **This was an ornamental tuft of threads, cords, short strings, etc. of the same length and thickness made to hang from the edge or fringe of a garment, a knob, or some other object.** Refs.: Num. 15:38, 39. These tassels served as reminders. It is used of a tassel or bunch of hair (Ezek. 8:3: lock). ¶

TASTE (noun) – 1 ***ṭa'am*** [masc. noun: טַעַם <2940>; from TASTE (verb) <2938>] ▶ **This word means flavor (e.g., of food); it also means judgment, discernment, discretion. The word is used only thirteen times in the Old Testament but is a key word when considering the concept of taste, perception, or decree.** It is used to describe the experience of taste: it describes the physical taste of manna as something like wafers or cakes made with honey (Ex. 16:31); or as something made with olive oil (Num. 11:8); it also refers to tasteless food needing salt in order to be eaten (Job 6:6; also translated flavor). The word has several abstract meanings. It can mean mental or spiritual perception, discretion, or discernment. David thanked Abigail for her good discretion that kept him from killing Nabal and his men (1 Sam. 25:33: advice, discretion, good judgment). This Hebrew word is ranked along with knowledge as something the psalmist wanted from the Lord (i.e., good discernment or judgment [Ps. 119:66: good judgment, discernment]); and in a famous proverb, the beautiful woman without discretion is unfavorably compared to a gold ring in a pig's snout (Prov. 11:22). The word can also mean an oral or written proclamation (i.e., a decree). It depicts the proclamation of the king of Nineveh (Jon. 3:7). Finally, its Aramaic equivalent *ṭa'am* (<2941>) means decree or command. Other refs.: 1 Sam. 21:13: behavior; Job 12:20: discernment, understanding; Ps. 34 title: behavior; Prov. 26:16; Jer. 48:11. ¶
– 2 Job 6:30; Ps. 119:103; Song 2:3 ➔ MOUTH <2441>.

TASTE (verb) – 1 ***ṭā'am*** [verb: טָעַם <2938>; a prim. root] ▶ **This word refers to eating, discerning the flavor, experiencing.** It refers to the sense of taste, of discerning the taste of food or beverages (2 Sam. 19:35). It means to eat food (parallel to *'ākal*, to eat) (1 Sam. 14:24, 29, 43) even if it were a small amount. To refrain from eating food was akin to mourning (Jon. 3:7). It is used in a figurative sense of tasting to see that the Lord is indeed good (Ps. 34:8). The good wife senses ("tastes") that her merchandise is excellent (Prov. 31:18: to perceive, to sense, to see). Other refs.: 2 Sam. 3:35; Job 12:11; 34:3. ¶
– 2 Dan. 5:2 ➔ DECREE (noun) <2942>.

TASTY FOOD – Gen. 27:4, 7, 9, 14, 17, 31 ➔ DELICIOUS FOOD <4303>.

TATNAI, TATTENAI – ***tatt'nay*** [masc. proper noun: תַּתְּנַי <8674>; of foreign deriv.]: gift ▶ **A Persian governor who was against**

the rebuilding of Jerusalem's Temple. Refs.: Ezra 5:3, 6; 6:6, 13. ¶

TATTOO – ***qa'qa'*** [masc. noun: קַעֲקַע <7085>; from the same as KOA <6970> in the original sense of cutting off] ▶ **The word indicates incised marks or patterns on a person's body.** The practice was forbidden in Israel (Lev. 19:28). ¶

TATTOO, TATTOO MARK – Lev. 19:28 ➔ MARK <3793>.

TAUGHT (WHO) – ***mᵉbûniym*** [masc. noun: מְבוּנִים <4000>; from PERCEIVE <995>] ▶ **This word occurs only once in 2 Chronicles 35:3 where it refers to those who instruct or teach others.** This is a variant form of the participle from *biyn* (PERCEIVE <995>). ¶

TAUNT (noun) – 1 ***gᵉdûpāh*** [fem. noun: גְּדוּפָה <1422>; fem. pass. part. from BLASPHEME <1442>] ▶ **This word designates an address or speech placing scorn and reproach on someone or something before others.** Jerusalem would become the object of taunts or revilings (NASB) because of her abominations (Ezek. 5:15). ¶
– 2 Deut. 28:37; 1 Kgs. 9:7; 2 Chr. 7:20; Jer. 24:9 ➔ BYWORD <8148> 3 Lam. 3:63 ➔ MOCKING SONG <4485> 4 Zeph. 2:8 ➔ SCORN (noun) <1421>.

TAUNT (verb) – 1 Kgs. 18:27 ➔ MOCK <2048>.

TAUNTING – Hab. 2:6 ➔ SAYING <4426>.

TAUNTING SONG – Lam. 3:63 ➔ MOCKING SONG <4485>.

TAX (noun) – 1 ***middāh*** [fem. noun: מִדָּה <4060>; fem. of CLOTHES <4055>, which is from MEASURE (verb) <4058>, as counting payment for something] ▶ **In context this word describes a royal due or tribute.** Ref.: Neh. 5:4. The Hebrew word also indicates measurement, size; see MEASURE (noun) <4060. ¶
– 2 Amos 5:11: to impose a tax, to exact taxes ➔ TRAMPLE <1318>.

TAX (verb) – 2 Kgs. 23:35 ➔ VALUE (verb) <6183>.

TEACH – 1 Ex. 18:20 ➔ WARN <2094> 2 Job 15:5; 33:33; 35:11 ➔ LEARN <502> 3 See LEARN <3925>.

TEACH DILIGENTLY – Deut. 6:7 ➔ SHARPEN <8150>.

TEACHER – 1 Ezra 7:12, 21 ➔ SCRIBE <5613> 2 Eccl. 1:2, 12; 7:27; etc. ➔ PREACHER <6953>.

TEACHING – Deut. 32:2; Job 11:4; Prov. 4:2 ➔ LEARNING <3948>.

TEAR – 1 **to tear, to tear in pieces, to tear to pieces: *ṭārap*** [verb: טָרַף <2963>; a prim. root] ▶ **This word means to rend, to pull to pieces. It is used especially of things pulled in pieces by wild animals.** Refs.: Gen. 37:33; Ex. 22:13; Jer. 5:6. In Proverbs 30:8 (to feed with), it takes a much milder sense of God's providing persons with their food. It is used figuratively often: to describe Benjamin and Gad as animals that tear their prey (Gen. 49:27; Deut. 33:20); and of Jacob's remnant in Judah (Mic. 5:8). It is used of the king of Nineveh (Nah. 2:12) who is depicted as a lion tearing his prey. Evil oppressors are often described as animals that tear their intended victims (Ps. 17:12). It is used of God's supposed wrath attacking and tearing Job (Job 16:9); and of the Lord's judgment on the wicked (Hos. 5:14). *
2 ***nāsaḥ*** [verb: נָסַח <5255>; a prim. root] ▶ **This word means to tear down, to tear out, i.e., to pull apart; it is also translated to pluck, to root, to uproot, to destroy. In the Hebrew Old Testament, this verb almost always occurs in poetical literature and always occurs in contexts of judgment.** For example, as the result of disobedience to God's covenant, He promised to remove Israel from the land. According to the psalmist, God would snatch the unrighteous from the comforts of their homes for putting

trust in material wealth rather than in Him (Ps. 52:5). Similarly, Proverbs 2:22 indicates that the righteous would remain in the land while the unrighteous would be removed from it. The Lord promised to tear down or destroy the house of the proud person (Prov. 15:25). Other ref.: Deut. 28:63. ¶

3 ***pāram*** [verb: פָּרַם <6533>; a prim. root] ▶ **This word indicates ripping something apart, especially clothing or garments as a sign of mourning; it is also translated to rend.** Refs.: Lev. 10:6; 21:10. Torn clothes were also worn to indicate that a person was a leper (Lev. 13:45). ¶

4 ***qāra'*** [verb: קָרַע <7167>; a prim. root] ▶ **This word means to rend. It refers to ripping apart a piece of clothing, parchment, or cloth.** Refs.: Gen. 37:29, 34; Ex. 28:32; Jer. 36:23, 24). Sometimes it was a sign of mourning or fear (Gen. 44:13; 1 Sam. 4:12). It is used figuratively of tearing away, removing a king's authority (1 Kgs. 11:11–13); of God's tearing the heavens (Is. 64:1); of Israel's tearing her heart instead of her garments (Joel 2:13). It describes the process of cutting out a window in a house (Jer. 22:14). It refers figuratively to tearing apart one's eyes with cosmetics, i.e., expanding them, enlarging them (Jer. 4:30). In its passive form, it means to be torn apart, torn up (Ex. 39:23; 1 Kgs. 13:3, 5). It is used of the tearing, ripping of wild beasts (Ps. 35:15; Hos. 13:8). In the latter reference, it refers to the Lord's activity. *

– 5 Lev. 1:17; Judg. 14:6 ➔ SPLIT <8156> 6 Judg. 8:7 ➔ THRESH <1758>.

TEAR OFF – Dan. 7:4 ➔ PLUCK, PLUCK OFF <4803>.

TEAR OPEN – ***pāṣam*** [verb: פָּצַם <6480>; a prim. root] ▶ **This word means to split open, to break. It refers to making a tear, crevasse, or deep crack in something.** In context it describes the effects of an earthquake on the surface of the earth (Ps. 60:2). ¶

TEARS – ***dim'āh*** [fem. noun: דִּמְעָה <1832>; from VINTAGE <1831> (in the sense of juice)] ▶ **This word means tears (drops shed by the eyes), weeping. It is used in various settings to refer to the shedding of tears whether for good or deceptive reasons.** In times of distress (Ps. 6:6; 39:12; 42:3; 80:5), especially in the case of Jeremiah (Jer. 9:18; 13:17; 14:17); on behalf of someone or something (Is. 16:9); to gain God's compassion and help in time of danger or illness (2 Kgs. 20:5; Is. 38:5); useless weeping because of one's own hypocrisy before God (Mal. 2:13). In many of these references, tears are described figuratively or metaphorically as food or drink (Ps. 42:3; 80:5). *

TEATS – Ezek. 23:3, 21 ➔ BREAST <1717>.

TEBAH – 1 ***ṭeḇaḥ*** [masc. proper noun: טֶבַח <2875>; the same as SLAUGHTER (noun) <2874>]: slaughter ▶ **Son of Nachor, Abraham's brother, and his concubine Reumah.** Ref.: Gen. 22:24. ¶

– 2 1 Chr. 18:8 ➔ TIBHATH <2880>.

TEBALIAH – ***ṭᵉḇalyāhû*** [masc. proper noun: טְבַלְיָהוּ <2882>; from DIP <2881> (in view of purification) and LORD <3050>]: the Lord has purified ▶ **The third son of Hosah.** Ref.: 1 Chr. 26:11. ¶

TEBETH – ***ṭêḇêṯ*** [proper noun: טֵבֵת <2887>; prob. of foreign deriv.] ▶ **This word refers to the tenth month of the seventh year of the reign of King Ahasuerus of Persia.** Esther was queen (Esther 2:16), a feature of storytelling that argues for the book's historicity. ¶

TEETH – Is. 41:15 ➔ TWO-EDGED <6374>.

TEETH (GREAT) – Ps. 58:6 ➔ FANGS <4458>.

TEETH (JAW, CHEEK) – Ps. 58:6; Joel 1:6 ➔ JAWS <4973>.

TEHINNAH – ***tᵉḥinnāh*** [masc. proper noun: תְּחִנָּה <8468>; the same as SUPPLICATION <8467>]: grace, supplication ▶ **An Israelite of the tribe of Judah.** Ref.: 1 Chr. 4:12. ¶

TEKEL – Dan. 5:25, 27 → WEIGH <8625>.

TEKOA – ***t*****e*****qôa'*** [proper noun: תְּקוֹעַ <8620>; a form of TRUMPET <8619>]: trumpet ▶ **This word designates the city from which the prophet Amos came.** Ref.: Amos 1:1. It was in the hill country of Judah. It was a city known for its wise women, for a wise woman came from here to argue a case for David's son Absalom (2 Sam. 14:2–24). She was successful. The word is used to establish an effective wordplay on "signal" in Hebrew, a favorite literary tool of the prophets (Jer. 6:1). *

TEKOITE – ***t*****e*****qô'iy, t*****e*****qō'iy*** [proper noun: תְּקוֹעִי, תְּקֹעִי <8621>; patron. from TEKOA <8620>] ▶ **This word designates an inhabitant of Tekoa (<8620>).** Refs.: 2 Sam. 14:4, 9; 23:26; 1 Chr. 11:28; 27:9; Neh. 3:5, 27. ¶

TEL-ABIB – ***têl 'āḇiyḇ*** [proper noun: תֵּל אָבִיב <8512>; from HEAP (noun) <8510> and EAR <24>]: hill of ear (of barley) ▶ **A city in Babylon where the prophet Ezekiel visited exiles of Judah.** Ref.: Ezek. 3:15. ¶

TEL ASSAR – ***t*****e*****la'ššār*** [proper noun: תְּלַאשָּׂר <8515>; of foreign deriv.] ▶ **A city conquered by the Assyrians.** Refs.: 2 Kgs. 19:12; Is. 37:12. ¶

TEL HARSHA – ***tel ḥarša'*** [proper noun: תֵּל חַרְשָׁא <8521>; from HEAP (noun) <8510> and the fem. of HARASHIM <2798>]: mound of workmanship ▶ **A town in Judah to which the returned captives came after the exile in Babylon.** They could not demonstrate they were Israelites (Ezra 2:59; Neh. 7:61). ¶

TEL MELAH – ***têl m*****e*****laḥ*** [proper noun: תֵּל מֶלַח <8528>; from HEAP <8510> and SALT <4417>]: mound of salt ▶ **A town in Judah to which returned captives came after the exile in Babylon.** They could not demonstrate they were Israelites (Ezra 2:59; Neh. 7:61). ¶

TELAH – ***telaḥ*** [masc. proper noun: תֶּלַח <8520>; prob. from an unused root meaning to dissever]: breach ▶ **A son of Ephraim.** Ref.: 1 Chr. 7:25. ¶

TELAIM – ***ṭ*****e*****lā'iym*** [proper noun: טְלָאִים <2923>; from the plur. of LAMB <2922>]: young lambs ▶ **A place where Saul gathered his army to attack the Amalekites.** Ref.: 1 Sam. 15:4. ¶

TELEM – ***ṭelem*** [proper noun: טֶלֶם <2928>; from an unused root meaning to break up or treat violently]: oppression ▶ **a. A town in Judah.** Ref.: Josh. 15:24. ¶ **b. A gatekeeper who pledged to put away the foreign woman he had married.** Ref.: Ezra 10:24. ¶

TELL – [1] ***nāḡaḏ*** [verb: נָגַד <5046>; a prim. root] ▶ **This verb means to report, to make known, to explain, to be reported. The root idea of the word and the causative form in which it is used is to declare something. The manner and context in which this is done creates the various shades of meaning of the verb.** Its simplest use is to announce, to report, to share. Samuel, when a child, was afraid to report the vision he had to Eli (1 Sam. 3:15, 18; 1 Kgs. 1:23). In some cases, it means to solve or explain, to make known. God asked Adam who had made him know he was naked (Gen. 3:11; 12:18); it indicated the resolution of a riddle (Judg. 14:12, 15); or dream (Job 11:6; Dan. 2:2). Close to this is its meaning to share with or to inform someone of something, to speak out. People were responsible to speak out when they knew something relevant to a case (Lev. 5:1; Josh. 2:14; Prov. 29:24). It is used to proclaim or announce something, often proclaiming the character and attributes of the Lord. The psalmist proclaimed the great deeds of the Lord (Ps. 9:11); the posterity of the righteous psalmist would declare God's righteousness (Ps. 22:31); the Lord's love was regularly proclaimed (Ps. 92:2). The participle of the verb may indicate a messenger (Jer. 51:31). The passive use of the verb means to be told, to be announced. If an Israelite turned and followed false gods, this act of rebellion was to be brought to the attention of the leaders (Deut. 17:4); anything that needed to be reported could be covered by this verb (Judg. 9:25; 2 Sam. 10:17). The Queen of Sheba used this verb when she declared that not even half the splendor of Solomon's wisdom and wealth had been told her (1 Kgs. 10:7; Is. 21:2). *

2 ***śiyaḥ*** [verb: שִׂיחַ <7878>; a prim. root] ▶ **This word means to ponder, to converse, to utter, to complain, to meditate, to pray, to speak. Its primary use is to complain.** In Job, the word denotes the action that Job took against the bitterness in his soul, i.e., his complaints (Job 7:11). God's people were instructed to sing praises to Him and to tell of all His wondrous works (1 Chr. 16:9; Ps. 105:2). This singing tells of all His wondrous acts. The word is used in Job to denote speaking to the earth (Job 12:8); while Isaiah used it to depict Christ's dying without children, i.e., descendants (Is. 53:8; but note v. 10). Isaiah's rhetorical question denoted that an absence of descendants was normally a shameful thing in the culture. *

– 3 1 Sam. 9:15; 20:2, 12 ➔ REVEAL <1540> 4 Job 15:17; 32:6, 10, 17 ➔ SHOW <2331>.

TEMA – ***têymā'*** [masc. proper noun: תֵּימָא <8485>; prob. of foreign deriv.] ▶ **One of the sons of Ishmael.** Refs.: Gen. 25:15; 1 Chr. 1:30; Job 6:19; Is. 21:14; Jer. 25:23. ¶

TEMAH – ***temaḥ*** [masc. proper noun: תֶּמַח <8547>; of uncertain deriv.] ▶ **Forefather of a family who returned from the Babylonian captivity.** Refs.: Ezra 2:53; Neh. 7:55. ¶

TEMAN – ***têymān*** [proper noun: תֵּימָן <8487>; the same as SOUTH <8486>]: south ▶

a. The grandson of Esau. Refs.: Gen. 36:11, 15, 42; 1 Chr. 1:36, 53.

b. The area in Edom occupied by the descendants of a. above. Refs.: Jer. 49:7, 20; Ezek. 20:46; 25:13; Amos 1:12; Obad. 1:9; Hab. 3:3. ¶

TEMANI – Gen. 36:34 ➔ TEMANITE <8489>.

TEMANITE – ***têymāniy*** [proper noun: תֵּימָנִי <8489>; patron. from TEMAN <8487>] ▶ **A descendant of Teman or an inhabitant of the same name area in Edom.** Refs.: Gen. 36:34 (KJV: Temani); 1 Chr. 1:45; Job 2:11; 4:1; 15:1; 22:1; 42:7, 9. ¶

TEMENI – ***têymᵉniy*** [masc. proper noun: תֵּימְנִי <8488>; prob. for TEMANITE <8489>]: southern ▶ **An Israelite of the tribe of Judah.** Ref.: 1 Chr. 4:6. ¶

TEMPER – Ezek. 46:14 ➔ MOISTEN <7450>.

TEMPEST – 1 ***sa'ar, sᵉ'ārāh*** [סַעַר, סְעָרָה <5591>; from TEMPESTUOUS (BE, GROW) <5590>] ▶

a. A masculine noun meaning a stormy wind, a storm, a whirlwind. It refers to a strong gale, a windstorm. It is used figuratively of one's enemies (Ps. 55:8); of God's pursuit of them (Ps. 83:15); and God's wrath in judgment (Jer. 23:19; Amos 1:14). It refers to a storm at sea (Jon. 1:4, 12). *

b. A feminine noun indicating a strong wind, a storm, a whirlwind. It is similar to a. It indicates a powerful gale, high winds, a windstorm. It was such a whirlwind that took Elijah up to heaven (2 Kgs. 2:1, 11). The Lord speaks from such a windstorm (Job 38:1; 40:6); and uses it to shield His presence (Ezek. 1:4; Zech. 9:14). It was God's tool at the Exodus (Ps. 107:25, 29); and His tool in judgment (Is. 29:6; 40:24; Jer. 30:23). *

2 ***śᵉ'ārāh*** [fem. noun: שְׂעָרָה <8183>; fem. of HORROR <8178>] ▶ **This word refers figuratively and literally to the calamitous storms or illnesses suffered by Job.** Ref.: Job 9:17. The Lord clothes Himself in storms and displays aspects of His character in them (Nah. 1:3). ¶

– 3 Job 27:20; etc. ➔ STORM (noun) <5492> a. 4 Ps. 50:3 ➔ SWEEP AWAY <8175> 5 Is. 28:2 ➔ HORROR <8178> 6 Is. 28:2; 30:30; 32:2 ➔ STORM (noun) <2230>.

TEMPESTUOUS – Ps. 50:3 ➔ SWEEP AWAY <8175>.

TEMPESTUOUS (BE, GROW) – ***sā‘ar*** [verb: סָעַר <5590>; a prim. root] ▶ **This word means to storm, to blow strongly; to be enraged.** It is used of the violent raging and movement of a stormy sea (Jon. 1:11, 13; also translated to become stormier, to grow wild). It indicates a stormy wind that drove Israel into exile among the nations (Zech. 7:14: to scatter with a whirlwind, to scatter with a storm wind; cf. Hos. 13:3; Hab. 3:14), a figurative usage. In its passive forms, it means to be blown away, driven off (Is. 54:11). It means to be agitated and angry when applied to the human heart (2 Kgs. 6:11). ¶

TEMPLE (building) – [1] ***hêyḵāl*** [masc. noun: הֵיכָל <1964>; prob. from ABLE (BE) <3201> (in the sense of capacity)] ▶ **This word means a building for worship; it also means a palace.** It refers to a king's palace or other royal buildings (1 Kgs. 21:1; Is. 13:22) and, likely by extension, to the dwelling of God, whether on earth (Ps. 79:1) or in heaven (Is. 6:1). The word is used of Solomon's Temple, the second Temple (Ezra 3:6; Neh. 6:10) and also of the Tabernacle. In reference to foreign buildings, it is sometimes difficult to say whether a palace or the temple of a false god is meant (2 Chr. 36:7; Joel 3:5). A special usage of the word designates the holy place of the Temple as opposed to the Holy of Holies (1 Kgs. 6:17; Ezek. 41:4, 15). *
[2] ***hêyḵal*** [Aramaic masc. noun: הֵיכַל <1965>; corresponding to <1964> above] ▶ **This word means a building for worship; it also means a palace. It is the Aramaic form of the Hebrew word *hêyḵāl* (<1964> above).** It is used most often in relation to a king's palace (Ezra 4:14). When Belshazzar sees the handwriting on the wall of the palace, this is the word used (Dan. 5:5). It is also used in reference to the Temple of God in Jerusalem (Ezra 5:14, 15), as well as the temple in Babylon (Ezra 5:14). *
– [3] Is. 15:2 ➔ BAJITH <1006>.

TEMPLE (of the head) – ***raqqāh*** [fem. noun: רַקָּה <7541>; fem. of LEAN (adj.) <7534> (in the sense of thin in relation, for instance, to the side of the head)] ▶ **This word refers to either of the flat areas alongside the forehead just in front of each ear.** Jael, Heber's wife, drove a tent peg through the temple of Sisera, general of the army of Jabin, king of Canaan (Judg. 4:21, 22; 5:26). It is likened to a piece or slice of pomegranate, considered a compliment in Middle Eastern imagery (Song 4:3; 6:7; ESV: cheek). ¶

TEMPTATION – Deut. 4:34; 7:19; 29:3 ➔ TRIAL <4531>.

TEN – [1] ***‘āśôr*** [masc. noun: עָשׂוֹר <6218>; from <6235> below] ▶ **This word also means tenth, ten-stringed instruments.** It refers to a collection of ten things: days (Gen. 24:55); ten strings arranged to produce music (Ps. 33:2; 92:3; 144:9). It is used as an ordinal number to designate a tenth day, a tenth month, etc. in what is called a date formula (Josh. 4:19; 2 Kgs. 25:1; Jer. 52:4, 12). *
[2] ***‘eśer, ᵃśārāh*** [fem., masc. numerical adj. and counting number: עֶשֶׂר, עֲשָׂרָה <6235>; from TITHE (GIVE) <6237>] ▶ **This word indicates a number of items equaling ten: animals, donkeys, cities, cubits, days, etc.** Refs.: Gen. 5:14; 45:23. Its masculine form is *ᵃśārāh*. Exodus 18:21, 25 refers to captains/heads (over) tens. It may be used with other numbers either preceding or following them (Gen. 5:14; Ezra 8:12; Jer. 32:9; Ezek. 45:12). A period of time equaling ten days is possibly an idiom (Dan. 1:12, 14, 15). The phrase *‘eśer yāḏôṯ* meaning ten times, is a hyperbolic expression indicating greatly (Dan. 1:20). *
[3] ***ᵃśar, ‘aśrāh*** [fem., masc. Aramaic numerical adj.: עֲשַׂר, עַשְׂרָה <6236>; corresponding to <6235> above] ▶ **This word indicates a collection of items numbering ten.** Refs.: Dan. 7:7, 20, 24. The phrase *ṯᵉrê-ᵃśar* means twelve (Ezra 6:17; Dan. 4:29). ¶
[4] ***‘āśār*** [numerical noun, adj.: עָשָׂר <6240>; for <6235> above] ▶ **This word is used in combination with other numerals from eleven to nineteen.** Used with masculine nouns, *’aḥaḏ ‘āśār,* eleven (Gen. 32:22). With feminine nouns, it has a companion

form *'eśrêh,* e.g., *ḥ^a^mêš 'eśrêh,* fifteen (years) (Gen. 5:10). It is used both as a cardinal (counting) number and an ordinal number. Hence, *'aḥaṯ 'eśrêh,* eleven (feminine) *'aḥaḏ 'āśār* (masculine); *'aštê 'āśar,* eleven (masculine) (Num. 29:20), *'aštê 'eśrêh,* eleven (feminine) (Ex. 26:7). The numbers are followed by the nouns being numbered in the singular but also in the plural. If they follow the noun, the noun is in the plural form (Josh. 15:36; Ezra 8:35). *

5 ***'iśśārôn*** [masc. noun: עִשָּׂרוֹן <6241>; from <6235> above] ► **This word refers to a tenth part of something.** One-tenth of an ephah (Ex. 29:40); three-tenths of an ephah (Lev. 14:10). *

TEN-STRINGED LYRE – Ps. 33:2 ➔ HARP <5035>.

TEN STRINGS (INSTRUMENT OF) – See TEN <6218>.

TENDER – 1 Deut. 28:56 ➔ REFINEMENT <7391> 2 Amos 7:14 ➔ DRESSER <1103>.

TENDER (BE) – 2 Kgs. 22:19; 2 Chr. 34:27 ➔ FAINT (BE, MAKE) <7401>.

TENDER CARE – Lam. 2:20 ➔ CARED FOR (ONES) <2949>.

TENDERNESS – Deut. 28:56 ➔ REFINEMENT <7391>.

TENDON – 1 Gen. 32:32 ➔ SHRANK (WHICH, THAT) <5384> b. 2 Gen. 32:32; Job 10:11; Is. 48:4; Ezek. 37:6, 8 ➔ SINEW <1517>.

TENDRIL – Is. 16:8 ➔ SHOOT (noun) <7976>.

TENDRILS – Jer. 48:32 ➔ BRANCHES <5189>.

TENT – 1 ***'ōhel*** [masc. noun: אֹהֶל <168>; from SHINE <166>] ► **The word is used literally to indicate a habitation of nomadic peoples and patriarchs.** Refs.: Gen. 9:21; 25:27. It can be used figuratively for a dwelling (Ps. 91:10; 132:3); or a people group (Gen. 9:27; Jer. 35:7; 49:29). As a generic collective, it describes cattle (Gen. 4:20) or wickedness (Job 15:34; Ps. 84:10). The word is also employed in reference to the Tabernacle, the "tent" (Num. 12:5, 10; Ezek. 41:1). *

2 ***qubbāh*** [fem. noun: קֻבָּה <6898>; from CURSE (verb) <6895> (which is from a root meaning to scoop out; thus a domed cavity)] ► **This word means a large tent, a domed cavity, a pavilion. It is not found often in the Old Testament, but where it does appear, it refers to some sort of habitation.** Phinehas chased a man and woman who were idolaters into one of these large tents and thrust them through with a javelin, thus ending a plague on Israel (Num. 25:8; ESV: chamber). ¶

– 3 Ps. 76:2 ➔ ABODE <5520>.

TENT (MOVE, REMOVE, PITCH A) – ***'āhal*** [verb: אָהַל <167>; a denom. from TENT <168>] ► **This word means to move one's tent from place to place: pitching it in one place and removing it to another, in the manner of nomads.** In particular, it describes Lot pitching his tent in Sodom while Abraham placed his tent by the oaks of Mamre in Hebron (Gen. 13:12, 18). God's judgment on Babylon would keep the Arab from pitching his tent there again (Is. 13:20). ¶

TENT (PITCH ONE'S) – See ENCAMP <2583>.

TENTH – 1 ***ma^a^śêr*** [masc. noun: מַעֲשֵׂר <4643>; from TEN <6240>] ► **This word is related to *'eśer* (TEN <6235>), meaning ten, and often means tenth (Gen. 14:20; Ezek. 45:11, 14).** In the Levitical system of the Old Testament, this word refers to the tenth part, which came to be known as the tithe. Israelites were to tithe from their land, herds, flocks, and other sources (Lev. 27:30–32). Such tithes were intended to support the Levites in their priestly duties (Num. 18:21, 24, 26, 28); as well as strangers, orphans, and widows (Deut. 26:12). When Israel failed to give the tithe, it was a

demonstration of their disobedience (Mal. 3:8, 10); when they reinstituted the tithe, it was a sign of reform, as in Hezekiah's (2 Chr. 31:5, 6, 12) and Nehemiah's times (Neh. 10:37, 38; Neh. 12:44). *
[2] ***ʿaśiyriy*** [numerical adj.: עֲשִׂירִי <6224>; from TEN <6235>] ▶ **This word indicates a tenth, one-tenth.** It is an ordinal number used to indicate the tenth of a series (Gen. 8:5; 1 Chr. 12:13; Zech. 8:19); or a fractional number indicating a tenth part of something (Ex. 16:36); a tenth generation (Deut. 23:3). *
– [3] Josh. 4:19; 2 Kgs. 25:1; etc. ➔ TEN <6218>.

TENTH (GIVE, RECEIVE, TAKE A) – Gen. 28:22; etc. ➔ TITHE (GIVE, RECEIVE) <6237>.

TERAH – ***teraḥ*** [proper noun: תֶּרַח <8646>; of uncertain deriv.] ▶
a. The father of Abraham. He lived beyond the Euphrates and served pagan gods (Josh. 24:1–13) but migrated to Haran (Gen. 11:24–28, 31, 32). He fathered also Nahor and Haran and died in Haran. Other ref.: 1 Chr. 1:26. ¶
b. A place in the wilderness where Israel camped on the way to Canaan. It lay between Tahath and Mithcah (Num. 33:27, 28). ¶

TERAPHIM – Ps. 60:3 ➔ STAGGER (THAT MAKES) <8653>.

TEREBINTH – [1] Gen. 12:6; 13:18; 14:13; 18:1; Deut. 11:30; Judg. 4:11; 9:6, 37; 1 Sam. 10:3 ➔ OAK <436> [2] Gen. 35:4; Judg. 6:11, 19; 2 Sam. 18:9, 10, 14; Is. 1:30; 6:13 ➔ OAK <424> [3] Gen. 35:8; Josh. 19:33 ➔ OAK <437> [4] Josh. 24:26 ➔ OAK <427>.

TEREBINTHS – title of Psalm 56 ➔ OAK TREES <482>.

TERESH – ***tereš*** [masc. proper noun: תֶּרֶשׁ <8657>; of foreign deriv.]: strictness, authority ▶ **One of the two enunuchs who planned to killed King Ahasuerus.** Refs.: Esther 2:21; 6:2. ¶

TERRACE – [1] Job 24:11 ➔ WALL <7790> b. [2] Jer. 31:40 ➔ FIELD <8309>.

TERRACES – 2 Sam. 5:9; 1 Kgs. 9:15; 11:27; etc. ➔ MILLO <4407>.

TERRIBLE – [1] ***ʾāyōm*** [adj.: אָיֹם <366>; from an unused root (meaning to frighten)] ▶ **This word means horrible, dreadful, awesome.** It means awesome in an amorous setting in Song of Solomon 6:4, 10; it is also translated majestic, terrible. It depicts a dreadful or terrible people in Habakkuk 1:7; it is also translated dreaded. ¶
[2] ***ʾêmṯān*** [Aramaic adj.: אֵימְתָן <574>; from a root corresponding to that of LOINS <4975>] ▶ **This word means terrifying, frightful.** It is one of the words describing the fourth beast of Daniel's dream (Dan. 7:7). ¶
– [3] Lam. 5:10 ➔ BURNING HEAT <2152> [4] Dan. 2:31 ➔ FEAR (verb) <1763>.

TERRIBLENESS – Jer. 49:16 ➔ TERROR <8606>.

TERRIFIED – Jer. 46:5 ➔ DREAD (noun and adj.) <2844> b.

TERRIFIED (BE) – ***bāhal*** [verb: בָּהַל <926>; a prim. root] ▶ **This word means and is also translated to be dismayed, to be amazed, to be troubled, to be shaken.** It is sometimes used when a sudden threat conveys great fear (Ex. 15:15; 1 Sam. 28:21). This word can also mean hasten or to be in a hurry (2 Chr. 26:20; Eccl. 8:3). *

TERRIFY – [1] Esther 7:6; Job 3:5; 7:14; 9:34; Ps. 18:4 ➔ TROUBLE (verb) <1204> [2] Dan. 4:5, 19; 5:6, 9, 10; 7:15, 28 ➔ HASTE (BE IN) <927>.

TERRIFYING – [1] Dan. 7:7 ➔ TERRIBLE <574> [2] Dan. 7:7, 19 ➔ FEAR (verb) <1763>.

TERRITORY – [1] Josh. 13:2 ➔ REGION <1552> [2] See PORTION <2506>.

TERROR – [1] ***'ēymāh*** [fem. noun: אֵימָה <367>; from the same as TERRIBLE <366>] ▶ **This word means fear, dread, or horror. The basic meaning is that of fear.** It is used to signify the dread of the darkness that fell on Abraham (Gen. 15:12); a fear of hostile opponents (Josh. 2:9; Ezra 3:3); the terror of the Lord's judgment (Ex. 15:16; 23:27; Job 9:34); dread of the wrath of an earthly king (Prov. 20:2); something fierce or fearsome (Job 39:20). In a metaphorical sense, it refers once to pagan idols (Jer. 50:38). *

[2] ***behālāh*** [fem. noun: בֶּהָלָה <928>; from TERRIFIED (BE) <926>] ▶ **This word means and is also translated panic, calamity, trouble, misfortune, dismay, fear.** One of the curses for not obeying the commands of the Lord is sudden terror (Lev. 26:16). When God makes the new heaven and earth, children will not be doomed to this terror (Is. 65:23). But the people in Jerusalem will be the object of such terror for not remaining faithful to God (Jer. 15:8). Other ref.: Ps. 78:33. ¶

[3] ***ballāhāh*** [fem. noun: בַּלָּהָה <1091>; from AFRAID (MAKE) <1089>] ▶ **This word indicates calamity; it is also translated dreadful end, horrible end, horror, trouble.** It describes fearful, threatening events or circumstances that beset a wicked person (Job 18:11, 14). God may bring on these calamities (Ezek. 26:21) so that the object is terrified (Ezek. 27:36; 28:19). Various terrors are depicted: the king of terrors (Job 18:14); terrors of deep darkness (Job 24:17); terrors that pursue a person relentlessly (Job 27:20; 30:15); instantaneous, unexpected terrors (Ps. 73:19; Is. 17:14). ¶

[4] ***beʻāṯāh*** [fem. noun: בְּעָתָה <1205>; from TROUBLE (verb) <1204>] ▶ **This word means and is also translated trouble.** It describes a state of illness and destruction brought on by the Lord (Jer. 8:15; 14:19); a time devoid of peace, the opposite of what Judah had hoped for (Jer. 14:19). ¶

[5] ***zewāʻāh*** [fem. noun: זְוָעָה <2113>; from TREMBLE <2111>] ▶ **This word indicates an object of terror, horror, trembling.** It refers to a scourge or pestilence that becomes an object of horror to those who experience it (Is. 28:19; also translated sheer terror, vexation). Judah becomes an object of horror because of her sins under Manasseh (Jer. 15:4: horror, trouble, abhorrent). Both Judah and Jerusalem become objects of terror, horror, and derision before the Lord and the nations because of their sins (2 Chr. 29:8: trouble). Other refs.: Jer. 24:9; 29:18; 34:17. ¶

[6] ***ḥāggā'*** [fem. noun: חָגָּא <2283>; from an unused root meaning to revolve; comp. FEAST (HOLD A) <2287>] ▶ **This word speaks of the reeling terror that Judah would cause in Egypt.** It occurs only once in the Old Testament in Isaiah 19:17. ¶

[7] ***ḥittāh*** [fem. noun: חִתָּה <2847>; from DISMAYED (BE) <2865>] ▶ **This word means great fear.** The Lord sent terror before Jacob into the land of Canaan as he returned from Mesopotamia so he and his family could pass through without being attacked by the native population (Gen. 35:5). ¶

[8] ***ḥaṯḥaṯ*** [noun: חַתְחַת <2849>; from DREAD (noun and adj.) <2844>] ▶ **This word occurs in the plural in Ecclesiastes 12:5, referring to terrors on the road; it is also translated fears, dangers.** It is part of a list of coming negative situations. The word is derived from the verbal root *ḥāṯaṯ* (<2865>), meaning to be dismayed or to be shattered. ¶

[9] ***ḥittiyṯ*** [fem. noun: חִתִּית <2851>; from DISMAYED (BE) <2865>] ▶ **This word is found exclusively in Ezekiel's writings where he described the reign of terror that powerful nations and cities brought on the Promised Land.** For example, in Ezekiel's oracles to the nations, he described the terror that would come on Tyre when it was destroyed (Ezek. 26:17). When Assyria's slain army fell to the sword, they could no longer cause terror in the land (Ezek. 32:23–27, 30, 32). ¶

[10] ***ḥaṯaṯ*** [masc. noun: חֲתַת <2866>; from DISMAYED (BE) <2865>] ▶ **This word means and is also translated calamity, casting down, something dreadful.** It is something that inspires fear in Job's "friends," evidently his condition or other frightening things in the world (Job 6:21). ¶

[11] ***māgôr*** [masc. noun: מָגוֹר <4032>; from SOJOURN <1481> in the sense of fearing] ► **The fundamental concept underlying this word is a sense of impending doom; it is also translated fear.** It is used to signify the fear that surrounds one whose life is being plotted against (Ps. 31:13); the fear that causes a soldier to retreat in the face of an invincible foe (Is. 31:9; Jer. 6:25); and the horrors that befall those facing God's judgment (Lam. 2:22). Of interest is the prophecy of Jeremiah concerning Pashur after he had Jeremiah placed in the stocks for prophesying against the idolatry of Jerusalem (cf. Jer. 20:1–6). The Lord would no longer call Pashur by his name. He gave him a new one, Magormissabib or Magor-Missabib ("fear on every side"), because the Lord would make him, as it were, afraid of his own shadow (Jer. 20:4). Other refs.: Jer. 20:10; 46:5; 49:29. ¶

[12] ***maʿᵃrāṣāh*** [fem. noun: מַעֲרָצָה <4637>; from TREMBLE <6206>] ► **This word is used of the forcefulness and decisiveness with which the boughs of a tree are cut off; it is also translated great power, terrible crash, terrifying power.** It is used figuratively of the Lord's activity against Assyria, Israel's foe (Is. 10:33). ¶

[13] ***qᵉp̱āḏāh*** [fem. noun: קְפָדָה <7089>; from ROLL UP <7088> b. (in the sense of to cut off)] ► **Early Jewish interpreters translated the word as destruction; however, terror follows better from the root, which means to roll up, to contract (*qāp̱aḏ* <7088>).** The word occurs only in Ezekiel 7:25 (NASB, ESV: anguish) where it refers to the fear that would come on Israel, causing them to seek peace they would not find. Ezekiel was prophesying of the coming Babylonian invasion, which led to the fall of Jerusalem in 586 B.C. ¶

[14] ***tip̱leṣeṯ*** [fem. noun: תִּפְלֶצֶת <8606>; from SHAKE <6426>] ► **This word refers to dread, horror, fear.** In context it refers to the dread that Bozrah, a city in Moab, with great arrogance, had put upon others (Jer. 49:16; also translated fierceness, terribleness). ¶

– [15] Gen. 9:2 ➔ DREAD (noun and adj.) <2844> a. [16] Deut. 4:34; 34:12; Jer. 32:21 ➔ FEAR (noun) <4172> [17] Job 41:22 ➔ SORROW (noun) <1670> [18] Ps. 116:3 ➔ DISTRESS (noun) <4712> [19] Prov. 21:15; Is. 54:14; Jer. 17:17; 48:39 (object of terror) ➔ RUIN (noun) <4288> [20] Is. 22:5 ➔ PERPLEXITY <3998> [21] Ezek. 7:18 ➔ TREMBLING <6427> [22] Dan. 10:7 ➔ TREMBLING <2731> [23] See DREAD (noun) <6343> [24] See HORROR <2189>.

TERRORIZE – 1 Sam. 16:14, 15 ➔ TROUBLE (verb) <1204>.

TERRORS – ***biʿûṯiym*** [masc. plur. noun: בִּעוּתִים <1161>; masc. plur. from TROUBLE (verb) <1204>] ► **This word denotes horror.** It describes terrifying experiences and impressions from God (Job 6:4) which are devastating and destructive (Ps. 88:16; also translated dreadful assaults). ¶

TEST – [1] ***nāsāh*** [verb: נָסָה <5254>; a prim. root] ► **This word means to try, to prove. Appearing nearly forty times in the Old Testament, this term often refers to God testing the faith and faithfulness of human beings.** This includes Abraham (Gen. 22:1); the nation of Israel (Ex. 15:25; 16:4; 20:20; Deut. 8:2, 16; 13:3; Judg. 2:22; 3:1, 4); Hezekiah (2 Chr. 32:31); David (Ps. 26:2). Although people were forbidden from putting God to the test, they often did so (Ex. 17:2, 7; Num. 14:22; Deut. 6:16; 33:8; Ps. 78:18, 41, 56; 95:9; 106:14; Is. 7:12). Testing, however, does not always suggest tempting or enticing someone to sin, as when the Queen of Sheba tested Solomon's wisdom (1 Kgs. 10:1; 2 Chr. 9:1); and Daniel's physical appearance was tested after a ten-day vegetarian diet (Dan. 1:12, 14). Finally, this term can refer to the testing of equipment, such as swords or armor (1 Sam. 17:39). Other refs.: Deut. 4:34; 28:56; Judg. 6:39; Job 4:2; Eccl. 2:1; 7:23. ¶

[2] ***bāḥan*** [verb: בָּחַן <974>; a prim. root] ► **This word means to examine, to try, to prove.** It can refer to any type of test. Joseph tested his brothers (Gen. 42:15, 16); while Job and Elihu indicated that the ear tests words as the palate tastes food (Job 12:11; 34:3), thereby indicating that the

hearer should be able to vindicate his or her assertions. However, it generally refers to God's testing of humanity. The psalmist acknowledges this fact (Ps. 11:4, 5) and even requests it (Ps. 139:23). The biblical writers sometimes compare God's testing to the refining of precious metals, like gold and silver (Job 23:10; Zech. 13:9). There are also a few passages in which people test God, but these clearly state that this is not normal (Ps. 95:9; Mal. 3:10, 15). *
– 3 Eccl. 3:18 ➔ PURIFY <1305> 4 Is. 48:10 ➔ CHOOSE <977> 5 Jer. 6:27 ➔ GATHER <1219>.

TESTED – ***bōḥan*** [masc. noun also used as adj.: בֹּחַן <976>; from TEST <974>] ▶ **This word means testing. It is derived from the verb *bāḥan*, meaning to examine, to try, or to prove. The idea is that the testing verifies or authenticates.** In Ezekiel 21:13, the strength of the sword is verified in its testing. In Isaiah 28:16, the stone is verified in that it has been tested (or tried) and proved. ¶

TESTER – 1 Jer. 6:27 ➔ ASSAYER <969> 2 Jer. 6:27 ➔ FORTIFICATION <4013> b, c.

TESTICLE – ***'ešeḵ*** [masc. noun: אֶשֶׁךְ <810>; from an unused root (prob. meaning to bunch together)] ▶ **Crushed testicles (the male sex glands) were a defect that disqualified a descendant of Aaron from the priesthood.** Ref.: Lev. 21:20; KJV: stones. ¶

TESTIFIES (HE WHO) – Job 16:19 ➔ ADVOCATE <7717>.

TESTIMONY – 1 ***'ēḏûṯ*** [fem. noun: עֵדוּת <5715>; fem. of WITNESS <5707>] ▶ **This word means witness; it also means precept, warning sign. It is always used in connection with the testimony of God and most frequently in association with the Tabernacle (Ex. 38:21; Num. 1:50, 53).** The stone tablets containing the Ten Commandments are identified as God's testimony (Ex. 25:16; 31:18; 32:15). Because the Ten Commandments represent the covenant that God made with Israel (see Ex. 34:27, 28), they are also called the "tables of the covenant"(see Deut. 9:9; 11:15); and they were preeminent in the Tabernacle. As a result, the Tabernacle is sometimes called the Tabernacle of the testimony (Ex. 38:21; Num. 1:50, 53); and the ark is sometimes called the ark of the testimony (Ex. 25:22; 26:33–34; 30:6, 26). This term is also used alone to represent the ark (Ex. 16:34; 27:21; 30:36; Lev. 16:13). In time, this term came to stand for the laws or precepts that God had delivered to humanity (Ps. 19:7; 119:88; 122:4). *
2 ***te'ûḏāh*** [noun: תְּעוּדָה <8584>; from WITNESS (BEAR) <5749>] ▶ **This word means witness and also a custom. It is used in Isaiah 8:16, 20 in combination with the word law.** In these verses, the testimony was the law of God's people that instructed them on how to live. In Ruth 4:7, this word refers to the common custom of sealing a legal agreement. ¶

TESTING – Deut. 4:34 ➔ TRIAL <4531>.

TEXT – Ezra 4:7; Esther 3:14 ➔ WRITING <3791>.

THANK – Dan. 2:23 ➔ THANKS (GIVE) <3029>.

THANKS (GIVE) – 1 ***yāḏāh*** [verb: יָדָה <3034>; a prim. root] ▶ **This word means to express appreciation; it also means to praise, to confess, to cast.** The essential meaning is an act of acknowledging what is right about God in praise and thanksgiving (1 Chr. 16:34). It can also mean a right acknowledgment of self before God in confessing sin (Lev. 26:40) or of others in their God-given positions (Gen. 49:8). It is often linked with the word *hālal* [PRAISE (verb) <1984>] in a hymnic liturgy of "thanking and praising" (1 Chr. 16:4; 23:30; Ezra 3:11; Neh. 12:24, 46). This rightful, heavenward acknowledgment is structured in corporate worship (Ps. 100:4; 107:1, 8, Ps. 107:15, 21, 31), yet is also part of personal lament and deliverance (Ps. 88:11). Several uses of *yāḏāh* evidence an essence of motion or action (as something given), intensively referring twice to cast or to throw down (Lam. 3:53; Zech. 1:21), and once it means to shoot (as an arrow; Jer. 50:14). *

2 ***yᵉḏā'*** [Aramaic verb: יְדָא <3029>; corresponding to <3034> above] ▶ **This word means to express appreciation, to offer praise. Twice this word appears in the Old Testament, both times in Daniel.** It is solely directed to the Lord, signifying the thanks given to God for answered prayer (Dan. 2:23) and in reference to Daniel's daily devotional practice (Dan. 6:10). ¶

THANKSGIVING – 1 ***huyyᵉḏôṯ*** [fem. plur. noun: הֻיְּדוֹת <1960>; from the same as SHOUTING <1959>] ▶ **This word refers to the songs of praise and gratitude which the Levites directed in the time of Nehemiah.** Ref.: Neh. 12:8. ¶

2 ***tôḏāh*** [fem. noun: תּוֹדָה <8426>; from THANKS (GIVE) <3034>] ▶ **This word describes an offering of thanks or a sacrifice of thanksgiving; it also means praise.** It is a subcategory of the fellowship offering or the offering of well-being; the fellowship offering could be presented as a thank offering (Lev. 7:12, 13, 15; 22:29; 2 Chr. 29:31; Amos 4:5). The word depicts worship by the presentation of songs of thanksgiving and praise that extolled the mighty wonders of the Lord (Neh. 12:27; Ps. 26:7; Is. 51:3). It refers to shouts of jubilation and thanksgiving (Ps. 42:4; Jon. 2:9). It describes the purpose of the choirs used by Nehemiah, i.e., they were choirs of praise (Neh. 12:31, 38). The goodness and praise of God were to be on the lips of even an enemy of the Lord, such as Achan, in the sense of proclaiming the glory of God while confessing and abandoning sin (Josh. 7:19). *

THANKSGIVING OFFERINGS – See PEACE OFFERINGS <8002>.

THAT – See WHICH <834>.

THEBES – Jer. 46:25; Ezek. 30:14–16; Nah. 3:8 ➔ NO (city) <4996>.

THEBEZ – ***têḇêṣ*** [proper noun: תֵּבֵץ <8405>; from the same as FINE LINEN <948>]: seen from far away ▶ **A city captured by Abimelech, the son of Gideon; but he was killed there.** Refs.: Judg. 9:50; 2 Sam. 11:21. ¶

THEFT – ***gᵉnêḇāh*** [fem. noun: גְּנֵבָה <1591>; from STEAL <1589>] ▶ **This word designates the act of stealing something or robbery itself, as well as the object stolen (e.g., an animal).** Refs.: Ex. 22:3, 4. ¶

THEN – 1 ***'ᵉḏayin*** [Aramaic adv.: אֱדַיִן <116>; of uncertain deriv.] ▶ **This word is found in the Aramaic portions of Ezra and Daniel. It is rendered quite uniformly as then, thereupon in most translations.** Refs.: Ezra 4:9, 23, 24; 5:2, 4; Dan. 2:14, 15; 3:3, 13; 4:7, 4:19; 5:3, 6; 6:3–6; 7:1, 11, 19. *

2 ***'āz, mê'āz*** [adv.: אָז, מֵאָז <227>; a demons. adv.] ▶ **This word means at that time, since.** It may introduce something that used to be so (Gen. 12:6); what happened next in a narrative (Ex. 15:1); or what will happen in the future (Is. 35:5, 6). On occasion, it is also used as a preposition, such as in Ruth 2:7, "Even from the morning" (KJV). *

3 ***'ᵃzay*** [adv.: אֲזַי <233>; prob. from <227> above] ▶ **This word means in that case, or possibly if not . . . then.** It is the first word in each line of Psalm 124:3–5 and is closely related in meaning to *'āz* (THEN <227>). ¶

4 ***'êpô, 'êpô'*** [particle: אֵפוֹ, אֵפוֹא <645>; from HERE <6311>] ▶ **This word means now.** It is sometimes used after an interrogative word (Gen. 27:33; Ex. 33:16) but also before an interrogative word (Gen. 27:37). It is found in wishes meaning would that (Job 19:23) or oh that! It is employed in conditional sentences with *'im* (WHEN <518>) or *'im lô'* meaning if then or if then . . . not (Job 9:24; 24:25). It expresses a logical result, such as know then, know now (2 Kgs. 10:10). *

THERE – ***tām, tammāh*** [Aramaic adv.: תָּם, תַּמָּה <8536>; corresponding to BEFORE

<8033>] ▶ **This word indicates a place where, a specific location.** Refs.: Ezra 5:17; 6:1, 6, 12. In context a city or temple area are in mind. ¶

THERE IS, THERE ARE – ***'iṯay*** [Aramaic particle: אִיתַי <383>; corresponding to BE <3426>] ▶ **This word makes an assertion of existence.** Refs.: Dan. 2:28, 30. It is used with *hên* preceding it to mean whether it is, thus forming a conditional sentence (Ezra 5:17). It can serve as a verb meaning be when placed before a participle or adjective (Dan. 3:17). Compare to Hebrew *yêš* (BE <3426>). *

THERE IS ONE – ***'iš*** [adv.: אִשׁ <786>; identical (in origin and formation) with FIRE <784>] ▶ **This word also means "Is there one?"** It is used in combination with *'im* <518> meaning if in 2 Samuel 14:19, and the same phrase means if there is, in the sense of either, is there one, or no one (NASB, NIV, NKJV; KJV none). It is coupled with the question word *h*[a] in Micah 6:10 and means is there (NASB) or are there (NKJV, KJV). The phrase is impersonal so that it may be translated as am I (NIV, Mic. 6:10) as well. ¶

THEREFORE – [1] ***kên*** [adv. or adj.: כֵּן <3651>; from SET UP <3559>] ▶ **This word is used either as an adverb or adjective, depending on the context of the sentence. It is derived from the verb meaning to stand upright or to establish.** As an adjective, it means correct, according to an established standard (Num. 27:7); upright and honest (Gen. 42:11); it is used as a statement of general agreement (Gen. 44:10; Josh. 2:21). As an adverb, it is usually translated as "thus" or "so" but conveys quality (Esther 4:16; Job 9:35; Nah. 1:12); quantity (Judg. 21:14); cause and effect (Judg. 10:13; Is. 5:24); or time (Neh. 2:16). *

[2] ***lāhên*** [adv. particle: לָהֵן <3860>; from the prep. prefix meaning to or for and BEHOLD <2005>] ▶ **This word means on this account.** It points out the motivation or conclusion for a previous statement or event, e.g., Naomi's encouragement for Ruth and Orpah to return to their own country (Ruth 1:13), since her sons are dead, and she will have no more. ¶

[3] ***lāhên*** [Aramaic particle: לָהֵן <3861>; corresponding to <3860> above] ▶ **This word means on this account.** It introduces the reason or cause of something (Ezra 5:12; Dan. 2:6, 9). *

THESE – ***'êl*** [Aramaic plur. noun: אֵל <412>; corresponding to THESE, THOSE <411>] ▶ **This word is found in Ezra 5:15 referring to articles of the Temple.** ¶

THESE, THOSE – [1] ***'êl*** [demons. plur. pron.: אֵל <411>; a demons. particle (only in a plur. sense)] ▶ **This Hebrew word occurs only in the Pentateuch and 1 Chronicles.** Refs.: Gen. 19:8, 25; 26:3, 4; Lev. 18:27; Deut. 4:42; 7:22; 19:11; 1 Chr. 20:8. ¶

[2] ***'êlleh*** [demons. pron. or adj.: אֵלֶּה <428>; prolonged from <411> above] ▶ **This word usually refers to preceding items and functions as a demonstrative adjective.** Refs.: Gen. 6:9; 15:1; 2 Sam. 23:22. Referring to following items, it functions as a demonstrative pronoun meaning these are (Gen. 6:9; Deut. 27:12, 13; 1 Sam. 4:8). *

[3] ***'êlleh*** [Aramaic plur. demons. adj. or pron.: אֵלֶּה <429>; corresponding to <428> above] ▶ **This word refers to items for the Temple.** Ref.: Ezra 5:15. It is used in a wordplay of irony concerning the heavens in Jeremiah 10:11. ¶

[4] ***'illêyn*** [Aramaic plur. demons. pron. or adj.: אִלֵּין <459>; prolonged from THESE <412>] ▶ **The term is used only in Daniel.** Refs.: Dan. 2:40, 44; 6:2, 6; 7:17. ¶

[5] ***'illêḵ*** [Aramaic plur. demons. pron.: אִלֵּךְ <479>; prolonged from THESE <412>] ▶ **The term refers to both persons and walls.** Refs.: Ezra 4:21; 5:9. In Daniel the word points out various groups of persons (Dan. 3:12, 13; 6:5, 11). *

THEY – ***'innûn, 'inniyn*** [Aramaic demons. pron.: אִנּוּן, אִנִּין <581>; corresponding to THEY, THESE <1992>] ▶ **This word regularly means they or those.** Ref.: Dan. 2:44. It also functions as a linking verb meaning were, are (Ezra 5:4). It serves as the object, them, of the verb in Daniel 6:24. Other ref.: Dan. 7:17. ¶

THEY, THEM – [1] ***hên*** [fem. pron.: הֵן <2004>; fem. plur. from HE, SHE, IT <1931>] ► **This word is used only with prefixes *b^e*, in, among; *k^e*, like, as; *l^e*, to, for; *min*, from.** It refers to either persons or things: in them (cities) (Gen. 19:29); for them (sons) (Ruth 1:13); like them, likewise (sins) (Ezek. 18:14); (more) than they (Israelites) (Ezek. 16:47). *

[2] ***hênnāh*** [fem. plur. pron.: הֵנָּה <2007>; prolongation for <2004> above] ► **This word is the long form of *hēn* and is used the same way with the same meanings (see THEY, THEM <2004>).** But note its use with (*māh*) *hênnāh* meaning these things (Gen. 21:29). *

THEY, THESE – ***hêm, hêmmāh*** [masc. plur. pron.: הֵם, הֵמָּה <1992>; masc. plur. from GO <1981>] ► **Both forms are used alike.** Its basic uses are: (1) with a verb form to serve as its subject or to emphasize its subject, meaning they or they themselves respectively (Gen. 6:4; Ex. 5:7; 18:22); (2) as a linking verb meaning is, are (Gen. 3:7; 48:5; Ex. 5:8; Job 6:7; Prov. 30:24); (3) as a demonstrative adjective coming after a noun and bearing the definite article (Gen. 6:4; Ex. 2:11) meaning those (Num. 14:38); (4) as an object of prepositions (Ex. 30:4; 36:1) meaning them, whom (Jer. 36:32) and translated as the particular preposition demands. *

THEY, THESE, THEM – ***himmô, himmōn*** [Aramaic pron.: הִמּוֹ, הִמּוֹן <1994>; corresponding to THEY, THESE <1992>] ► **This word is used as a linking verb meaning is or are.** Ref.: Ezra 5:11. It is used mostly as the accusative object of a verb meaning them (Ezra 4:23; 5:5; Dan. 2:34, 35). *

THICK – ***bāṣûr, bāṣiyr*** [adj.: בָּצוּר, בָּצִיר <1208>; from GATHER <1219>] ► **This word depicts something as inaccessible, impenetrable, dense.** It refers to the farmer's thick cedar forests of Lebanon (Zech. 11:2; NKJV, NASB, ESV, NIV). The Lord would destroy this forest in judgment. It also depicts vintage or time of grape harvest. It is an idiom used to describe the "vintage" forest of the magnificent cedars of Lebanon (Zech. 11:2; KJV). ¶

– [2] Lev. 23:40; Neh. 8:15; Ezek. 6:13; 20:28 ➔ LEAFY <5687> [3] 1 Kgs. 7:26; 2 Chr. 4:5; Job 15:26; Jer. 52:21 ➔ THICKNESS <5672> [4] Ps. 74:5 ➔ THICKET <5441>.

THICK (BE, GROW) – ***'āḇāh*** [verb: עָבָה <5666>; a prim. root] ► **This word means to be large in diameter or to grow large, to be great (greater).** Ref.: Deut. 32:15; also translated to grow fat. It refers to something being thick, heavy, e.g., a person's thigh (1 Kgs. 12:10; 2 Chr. 10:10); it is used as a symbol of oppression. ¶

THICK BOUGH – 2 Sam. 18:9 ➔ THICK BRANCH <7730>.

THICK BRANCH – ***śôḇeḵ*** [masc. noun: שׂוֹבֶךְ <7730>; for THICKET <5441>] ► **This word refers to the heavy, dense limb of a tree, in context of a great oak tree.** Ref.: 2 Sam. 18:9; also translated thick bough. Absalom, David's son, was caught by his head and neck in such a branch. ¶

THICK CLAY – Hab. 2:6 ➔ PLEDGE (noun) <5671> b.

THICK CLOUD – ***'āḇ*** [common noun: עָב <5645>; from CLOUD (COVER WITH A) <5743>] ► **This word refers to a dense, impenetrable covering or mass of clouds.** God came to Israel at Sinai in this setting (Ex. 19:9; 1 Kgs. 18:44, 45). It is used of a mist formed from dew (Is. 18:4). It has plurals in both *-îm, ôṯ*. The Hebrew word has two other meanings; see THICKET <5645> and CLAY <5645>. *

THICK PLANKS – 1 Kgs. 7:6; Ezek. 41:25, 26 ➔ CANOPY <5646>.

THICKET – [1] ***s^eḇōḵ*** [masc. noun: סְבֹךְ <5441>; from ENTWINE <5440>] ► **This**

word refers to a dense growth of a forest, a brush. Ref.: Ps. 74:5; also translated thick. It is used figuratively of the lair or home of a lion representing an attacking nation (Jer. 4:7). ¶

2 ***sᵉḇaḵ*** [masc. noun: סְבַךְ <5442>; from ENTWINE <5440>] ▶ **This word refers to a dense growth of heavy shrubs, small trees, or underbrush.** Refs.: Gen. 22:13; Is. 9:18; 10:34. ¶

3 ***'āḇ*** [common noun: עָב <5645>] ▶ **This word indicates a thick growth of underbrush in a forest or a growth of thick shrubs.** Ref.: Jer. 4:29. The Hebrew word has two other meanings; see THICK CLOUD <5645> and CLAY <5645>. ¶

– 4 1 Sam. 13:6 ➔ THORN <2336> 5 Ps. 10:9 ➔ ABODE <5520>.

THICKETS – ***ḥᵃwāḥiym*** [masc. plur. noun: חֲוָחִים <2337>; perhaps the same as THORN <2336>] ▶ **This word refers to an area heavily covered by thornbushes or similar shrubs and small trees.** It could serve as a place of hiding from one's enemies (1 Sam. 13:6; also translated holes). ¶

THICKLY – Job 15:26 ➔ THICKNESS <5672>.

THICKNESS – ***ᵃḇiy, ᵒḇiy*** [masc. noun: עֲבִי, עֳבִי <5672>; from THICK (BE, GROW) <5666>] ▶ **This word refers to the size of different things.** The bronze sea constructed by Solomon (1 Kgs. 7:26; 2 Chr. 4:5). The two pillars of the Solomonic Temple (Jer. 52:21). A military armor (Job 15:26). ¶

THIEF – 1 ***gannāḇ*** [masc. noun: גַּנָּב <1590>; from STEAL <1589>] ▶ **This word denotes a person who breaks in, who steals; a stealer.** Refs.: Ex. 22:2, 7, 8. It can happen in various ways (Jer. 49:9; Joel 2:9). One who commits the act of stealing (Ps. 50:18; Prov. 6:30; Is. 1:23). A slave dealer (Deut. 24:7) or one who steals people. *

– 2 Jer. 7:11 ➔ VIOLENT <6530>.

THIGH – 1 ***yārēḵ*** [fem. sing. noun: יָרֵךְ <3409>; from an unused root meaning to be soft] ▶ **This word means the top part of the leg; it also means a side, a base.** It is used of Jacob's thigh in the story of his wrestling with God (Gen. 32:25, 32) and is most likely used euphemistically of genitals (Gen. 46:26; Ex. 1:5; Judg. 8:30). It is best translated side in the cultic language of Leviticus 1:11 and Num. 3:29, 35. The Pentateuch also employs it with the meaning of a base (Ex. 25:31). *

2 ***yarḵāh*** [Aramaic fem. noun: יַרְכָה <3410>; corresponding to BORDER <3411>] ▶ **This word refers to the upper thigh, the area between the knee and the hip in humans, made of bronze in the statue envisioned by Nebuchadnezzar in his dream.** Ref.: Dan. 2:32. ¶

3 ***paḥaḏ*** [noun: פַּחַד <6344>; the same as DREAD (noun) <6343>] ▶

a. This word refers to the upper front part of a person's legs; it is used in the plural. It is used to describe Leviathan, God's masterful creation (Job 40:17). ¶

b. This word is rendered in the KJV as stones, meaning testicles. It describes a feature of Leviathan's body (Job 40:17). ¶

THIN – 1 ***daq*** [adj.: דַּק <1851>; from BEAT <1854>] ▶ **This word means skinny, slim. It also means gaunt, fine; dwarfish; low.** It indicates that something is weak, undernourished, fine, small: lean cows (Gen. 41:3, 4); lean ears of corn/grain (Gen. 41:6, 7); thin people or dwarfs (Lev. 21:20); fine manna (Ex. 16:14); or hair, incense, or dust (Lev. 13:30; 16:12; Is. 29:5). Once it is used to describe a soft whisper (1 Kgs. 19:12). Used in a simile, the islands are described as fine dust (Is. 40:15). Other refs.: Gen. 41:23, 24. ¶

– 2 Gen. 41:19, 20, 27 ➔ LEAN (adj.) <7534> 3 1 Kgs. 7:29 ➔ DESCENT <4174>.

THIN LOAF – Ex. 29:2, 23; Lev. 2:4; 7:12; 8:26; etc. ➔ WAFER <7550>.

THING OF NOUGHT – Jer. 14:14 ➔ FUTILITY <434>.

THINK – 1 ***ḥāšaḇ, ḥōšēḇ*** [verb: חָשַׁב, חֹשֵׁב <2803>; a prim. root] ▶ **This word means**

to devise, to reckon, to regard, to invent, to consider, to be accounted, to consider, to reckon oneself. When the subject of this verb is God, the verb means to consider, to devise, to plan, to reckon. Job cried out to God and asked why God considered him His enemy (Job 13:24; 33:10); however, Job was falsely accusing his Creator. Through the evil actions of Joseph's brothers, God had intended good for all of them (Gen. 50:20; Ps. 40:17). Against a wicked people, the Lord planned destruction (Jer. 18:11; Micah 2:3). God also "reckoned" Abraham's faith as righteousness (Gen. 15:6).

When humans are the subjects of this verb, the word has similar meanings: the king of Assyria thought he would destroy many nations (Is. 10:7); people devised or planned evil (Gen. 50:20; Ps. 35:4; Ezek. 38:10); Shimei begged David not to reckon his behavior as sin against him (2 Sam. 19:19; Ps. 32:2). In addition, the word is used to mean to regard or to invent: the Medes did not esteem gold or silver as the Persians did (Is. 13:17); and the Servant of Isaiah's passage was not highly esteemed by men (Is. 53:3). God endowed people with the ability to invent new things, such as artistic and practical devices (Ex. 31:4; 35:32, 35; 2 Chr. 2:14); and instruments for music (Amos 6:5).

When the verb is passive, the word expresses being valuable or being considered. Silver was not considered valuable in Solomon's reign (1 Kgs. 10:21). In the time of Israel's wandering, the Anakim were regarded as Rephaim, but the Moabites called them Emim (or Emites) and the Ammonites called the Rephaim Zamzummim (Deut. 2:11, 20).

This verb can also mean to plot, to think upon, to think out something. A person could think out his or her course of life (Prov. 16:9; Hos. 7:15); the evil person in Daniel 11:24 plotted the overthrow of all resistance to him; the boat that Jonah shipped out in came to the point of destruction in the storm (Jon. 1:4, lit., "it was thinking to be destroyed"). *

2 ***sᵉḇar*** [Aramaic verb: סְבַר <5452>; a prim. root] ▶ **This word means to do, to try.** It has the sense of attempting or intending to do something, to change something from what it was (Dan. 7:25). ¶

3 ***śā'ar*** [verb: שָׂעַר <8176>; a prim. root] ▶ **This word means to cleave, to divide, but it took on the meaning of to calculate, to estimate, to set a price on. The meaning was transferred to the sense of judging something, thereby setting a price to it.** There are no references to the verb meaning to cleave in the Old Testament, but in Proverbs 23:7, this verb is used to mean to calculate or to set a price on. The context here is that of misers who count the cost of everything that their guests eat or drink. They find no enjoyment in their guests but only worry about the cost of it all. ¶

– 4 Dan. 6:3 ➔ PLAN (verb) <6246>.

THINK ABOUT – Dan. 7:8 ➔ CONSIDER <7920>.

THINK UPON – Jon. 1:6 ➔ CONCERNED (BE) <6245>.

THIRD – 1 ***šāliyš*** [masc. noun: שָׁלִישׁ <7991>; from THREE <7969>] ▶ **This word carries many different meanings associated with the number three.** First of all, it can be used to signify a measure, perhaps originally a third or an ephah. From the contexts in which it is used, it is clear the word stands for a large measure (Ps. 80:5; Is. 40:12). It is also used once as a noun for a type of musical instrument—perhaps a three-cornered one with strings, such as a lute. This instrument was played with songs of celebration (1 Sam. 18:6). Finally, this word can signify a particular type of high-ranking officer or the third man in a chariot during battle (Ex. 14:7; 2 Sam. 23:8; 2 Kgs. 9:25). *

2 ***šᵉliyšiy, šališiy*** [שְׁלִישִׁי, שָׁלִשִׁי <7992>; ordinal from THREE <7969>] ▶

a. A masculine adjective meaning third in a series of three or more or a third part of something. It refers to any third in a series. Its feminine form is *šᵉliyšîṯ* and *šᵉlîšiyyah.* It indicates the third in any series of things (Gen. 1:13; 2:14). Its plural form means third also (1 Sam. 19:21), a third

group of messengers (*mal'āḵîm š^{e}lišîm*). The third day means the day after tomorrow (1 Sam. 20:5). With the definite article, it can mean a fraction or one-third of the whole (2 Sam. 18:2).
b. An adjective meaning third in a series or a third part of something. With the definite article added, according to context, it refers to David's three greatest men, the three (2 Sam. 23:8, 18; NASB, captains). Its use in Ezekiel 42:3 indicates three stories or levels in the chambers of the Temple.
c. An adjective in the plural meaning thirty. The NASB reads thirty (men), a leading part of David's personal army. Not all ancient manuscripts read thirty here (2 Sam. 23:18).
d. An adjective meaning three years old. This is combined with the word preceding it to form a proper noun of a city, Eglath-shelishiyah (Is. 15:5; Jer. 48:34, NASB). But it is rendered as an adjective defining a heifer in other translations, a heifer three years old (Is. 15:5; Jer. 48:34). *
[3] ***šillêš*** [adj.: שִׁלֵּשׁ <8029>; from DIVIDE INTO THREE PARTS <8027>] ▶ **In context this word refers to a third generation in a family.** Refs.: Gen. 50:23; Ex. 20:5; 34:7; Num. 14:18; Deut. 5:9. ¶
[4] ***t^{e}liyṯāy, taltay*** [Aramaic ordinal number: תְּלִיתָי, תַּלְתַּי <8523>; ordinal from THREE, THIRD <8532>] ▶ **In Daniel it refers to the third kingdom to arise in a series of four.** It probably represents Greece (Dan. 2:39) or the third ruler in the kingdom (Dan. 5:7). ¶
[5] ***t^{e}laṯ, taltā'*** [Aramaic ordinal number: תְּלַת, תַּלְתָּא <8531>; from THREE, THIRD <8532>] ▶ **This word indicates third highest.** It is used in a context indicating the third ranking political position in Babylon after the king and his son (Dan. 5:7).

THIRST – [1] ***ṣāmā'*** [masc. noun: צָמָא <6772>; from THIRSTY (BE) <6770>] ▶ **This word describes a desire for water to drink or some other liquid, e.g., milk or wine. It also refers to something parched.** It indicates a literal thirsting for water (Ex. 17:3). It describes the throat of a righteous man before his enemies (Ps. 69:21). The Lord meets the thirsty needs of His creatures (Ps. 104:11). It is used of spiritual and emotional needs, the thirsts of God's rebellious people (Is. 5:13); and the physical needs of the poor (Is. 41:17). Thirst may be a feature of God's judgments (Is. 50:2). It stands for parched places and land (Jer. 48:18). It refers to thirsting, desiring the Word of God (Amos 8:11). *
[2] ***ṣim'āh*** [fem. noun: צִמְאָה <6773>; fem. of <6772> above] ▶ **This word refers to dryness. It refers to a desire and a need for water.** In context it indicates a condition that Israelites can keep from if they follow the Lord, not their own desires (Jer. 2:25). ¶

THIRSTY – [1] ***ṣāmê'*** [adj.: צָמֵא <6771>; from THIRSTY (BE) <6770>] ▶ **This word indicates being in need of water, being dried out.** It is used to describe a thirsty land, a dried-out land needing water (Deut. 29:19; Is. 44:3); a people suffering from lack of water in desert heat (2 Sam. 17:29). Hunger and thirst are often mentioned together (Ps. 107:5). A thirsty enemy should be given water (Prov. 25:21); but a fool withholds help from a thirsty person (Is. 32:6). God will meet the needs of His people in a thirsty land (Is. 44:3). In its most famous use, the word is used figuratively of those who thirst after God, for free wine and milk will be given to meet their needs (Is. 55:1). Other refs.: Is. 21:14; 29:8. ¶
– [2] Job 5:5 ➔ SNARE (noun) <6782> [3] Ps. 107:9; Is. 29:8 ➔ RUSH (verb) <8264> b., c.

THIRSTY (BE) – ***ṣāmê'*** [verb: צָמֵא <6770>; a prim. root] ▶ **This word indicates a strong desire and need for water to drink.** Israel thirsted in the desert and grumbled against Moses (Ex. 17:3); Samson nearly died of thirst (Judg. 15:18); and Jael used Sisera's great thirst to trick him (Judg. 4:19). It is used in beautiful metaphors of the soul thirsting for God (Ps. 42:2; 63:1). God met the need for water for His people (Is. 48:21); and in the future will remove their thirst (Is. 49:10). But rebellious people will continue to thirst (Is. 65:13). ¶

THIRSTY GROUND – ***ṣimmā'ôn*** [fem. noun: צִמָּאוֹן <6774>; from THIRSTY <6771>] ► **This word means a parched ground or land; it also means drought.** It may stand for thirsty or parched ground, earth (Deut. 8:15; Is. 35:7); which God can transform at His will (Ps. 107:33). ¶

THIRSTY LAND – Deut. 8:15; Is. 35:7 ➔ THIRSTY GROUND <6774>.

THIRTY – 1 ***šᵉlôšiym, šᵉlōšiym*** [masc. plur. noun: שְׁלוֹשִׁים, שְׁלֹשִׁים <7970>; multiple of THREE <7969>] ► **This word is the plural of *šālôš*, <7969>, meaning thirty of something.** Refs.: Judg. 14:11–13, 19; Prov. 22:20, NIV; Zech. 11:12, 13. It combines with other numbers, e.g., one hundred and thirty (Gen. 5:3); thirty-five (Gen. 11:12). *

2 ***tᵉlāṯiyn*** [Aramaic plur. noun: תְּלָתִין <8533>; multiple of THREE, THIRD <8532>] ► **This word is *tᵉlaṯ* (third) pluralized. It refers to thirty days.** It was a special time during which Daniel was watched carefully to catch him in some error (Dan. 6:7, 12). ¶

THIS – 1 ***gêh*** [demons. pron.: גֵּה <1454>; prob. a clerical error for THIS, THESE <2088>] ► **This word stands undoubtedly for *zeh* <2088>, this, the normal demonstrative pronoun.** This list begins a description of the boundaries of Ezekiel's land (Ezek. 47:13). ¶

2 ***dā'*** [Aramaic demons. pron.: דָּא <1668>; corresponding to THIS, THESE <2088>] ► **This word is used to point out and designate something, such as a city (Dan. 4:30) or horn (Dan. 7:8).** With *min* <4480>, than, in between, it distinguishes one thing from another, this from that, from each other (Dan. 7:3). With the letter lamedh (ל), to, between, two appearances of the word means this to (against) that (Dan. 5:6). ¶

3 ***dêḵ, dāḵ*** [Aramaic demons. pron.: דֵּךְ, דָּךְ <1791>; prolonged from <1668> above] ► **This word is used to point out something and always comes after the noun with which it is used.** Refs.: Ezra 4:13, 15, 16, 19, 21; 5:8, 16, 17; 6:7, 8, 12. ¶

4 ***zōh*** [fem. pron.: זֹה <2090>; for THIS, THESE <2088>] ► **This word is used as the feminine form of *zeh* (THIS, THESE <2088>) in a few places.** Refs.: 2 Sam. 11:25; 2 Kgs. 6:19; Eccl. 2:24; 5:16; 9:13; Ezek. 40:45. *

THIS, IN THIS WAY, THIS IS WHAT – ***kōh*** [particle: כֹּה <3541>; from the prefix k and HE, SHE, IT <1931>] ► **This word is used as a function word in various ways.** Its three main uses are as follows: a. to indicate location or direction (Ex. 2:12; Num. 23:15); or direction to a certain place (Gen. 22:5); b. to indicate a temporal issue, such as up to now, *'aḏ-kōh*, (Ex. 7:16; Josh. 17:14); or meanwhile in the phrase *'aḏ-kōh wᵉ'aḏ-kōh* (1 Kgs. 18:45); c. in an adverbial expression meaning so, thus, in this way, as follows (Gen. 15:5; 24:30); to introduce a message from people (Gen. 32:4); especially from God or the Lord (over 400 times; e.g., Ex. 4:22; Jer. 9:22). It is found several times in idiomatic expressions: "thus may he do and thus may he do again" (*kōh yaʿᵃśeh wᵉkōh yôsîyp*, 1 Sam. 3:17); "one (said or did) this, and another person (said, did) another" (*zeh* THIS, THESE <2088> *bᵉḵōh wᵉzeh beḵōh*, 1 Kgs. 22:20). It is present in the idiomatic phrase, "if he says," *'im koh yo'mar* (Gen. 31:8; 1 Sam. 14:9, 10; 20:7; 2 Sam. 15:26). *

THIS, THAT – 1 ***dikkên*** [Aramaic demons. pron.: דִּכֵּן <1797>; prolonged from THIS <1791>] ► **This word points out something.** An image (Dan. 2:31); a horn (Dan. 7:20, 21). ¶

2 ***hallāz*** [demons. pron.: הַלָּז <1975>; from <1976> below] ► **This word points out specific objects.** That (other) side (1 Sam. 14:1); this Philistine (1 Sam. 17:26); this Shunamite (woman) (2 Kgs. 4:25). It is used regarding men, this one (Dan. 8:16, with *lᵉ*, to, prefixed). Other refs.: Judg. 6:20; 2 Kgs. 23:17; Zech. 2:4. ¶

3 ***hallāzeh*** [masc. demons. pron.: הַלָּזֶה <1976>; from the art. (see BEYOND <1973>) and THIS, THESE <2088>] ► **This word points out a person.** That man, Isaac (Gen. 24:65); this dreamer (Joseph) (Gen. 37:19) in a disrespectful slur. ¶

4 ***hallêzû*** [fem. demons. pron.: הַלֵּזוּ <1977>; another form of <1976> above] ► **This word is used once and points out the land of Israel, this desolate land.** Ref.: Ezek. 36:35. ¶
5 ***zô*** [demons. pron.: זוֹ <2097>; for THIS, THESE <2088>] ► **This word has the meaning which.** It refers to a whole preceding sentence or thought (Hos. 7:16). It is a relative pronoun referring to the Lord's testimony (Ps. 132:12). ¶

THIS, THEREFORE – ***dᵉnāh*** [Aramaic demons. pron. and adj.: דְּנָה <1836>; an orthographical variation of THIS <1791>] ► **This word points out something and may come before or after the noun.** Refs.: Ezra 5:4; Dan. 6:3. Used as a pronoun, it is translated as this is (Dan. 2:28). It is combined with *kᵉ* several times meaning like this or this (Ezra 5:7; Jer. 10:11; Dan. 3:29). *

THIS, THESE – ***zeh*** [masc. demons. pron.: זֶה <2088>; a prim. word] ► **Used alone, the word may mean this one (man).** Refs.: Gen. 5:29; Ex. 10:7; 1 Sam. 10:27. It may mean also an event, concept, action (Ex. 13:8; Job 15:17; Prov. 24:12; Eccl. 1:17). When repeated *zeh . . . zeh,* it means this . . . that or the one . . . the other, etc. (Ex. 14:20; 1 Kgs. 3:23; 22:20; Is. 6:3). It points out a noun that it precedes or follows (Ex. 32:1, 23; Deut. 21:20; Josh. 2:14, 20; 9:12; Judg. 5:5). Used as a semiverb, it means this is, these are (Gen. 5:1; 20:13; 2 Kgs. 3:23). It is coupled with certain words to make idioms, etc.: *'êy-zeh mîy zeh* meaning why, who is this, respectively (1 Sam. 17:55, 56; Job 28:12; Jer. 49:19); further one finds *mah-zeh*, how, what is this? (Gen. 27:20). With *hennêh* it means, behold, right here! (1 Kgs. 19:5; Song 2:8, 9; Is. 21:9). It functions as the relative pronoun *'ašer*, who, which, what, etc. in poetry: which (Ps. 74:2; Ps. 78:54; 104:8). It is used often with prefixes added to it: *bāzeh*, in this place (Gen. 38:21, 22; 1 Sam. 1:26); *mizzeh*, from here (Gen. 42:15); *mizzeh . . . mizzeh* means one side . . . on the other side (Ex. 17:12; 25:19). After the preposition *'al*, it means for this reason, on this account (Esther 6:3; Lam. 5:17). *

THIS, WHICH – ***zû*** [demons. pron.: זוּ <2098>; for THIS, THESE <2088>] ► **This word is used to point something out.** This strength or whose strength (Hab. 1:11); this generation (Ps. 12:7); there (are) (Ps. 62:11). As a relative pronoun, it refers to or is connected to something: (the people) which (Ex. 15:13; Ps. 9:15); (against) whom (Is. 42:24; 43:21). *

THIS ONE – ***zō'ṯ*** [fem. pron.: זֹאת <2063>; irregular fem. of LAMB <2089>] ► **This word also means this woman, this. It is the feminine form of *zeh* (THIS, THESE <2088>).** It functions in various ways of which the most important are: alone it means this one, standing for a feminine noun (Gen. 2:23; 2 Sam. 13:17); it refers to any act or event itself standing alone (Gen. 3:14; 20:5, 6; 45:19); it stands next to a noun to clarify it, in apposition to it (Gen. 24:8); it can act as the verb is, are, was, were (Is. 23:7; Ezek. 5:5); it is attached closely to other words as an adverb meaning this (Song 3:6; 6:10; 8:5), e.g., *mah-zō'ṯ*, means what is this? (Gen. 3:13; 12:18). It is used with prefixes attached: *bᵉzōṯ*, with this (Gen. 34:15, 22; 1 Sam. 11:2; Mal. 3:10); *kᵉzō'ṯ*, as follows, like this (Gen. 45:23; Judg. 13:23). It is used with a separate preposition, e.g., *'alzō'ṯ*, on this account (Amos 8:8; Mic. 1:8). *

THISTLE – 1 ***darda'*** [masc. noun: דַּרְדַּע <1863>; of uncertain deriv.] ► **This word depicts weedy, prickly plants that were part of God's curse on the ground.** Ref.: Gen. 3:18. It was a plant that grew of itself in places abandoned by humans (Hos. 10:8). ¶
– 2 2 Kgs. 14:9; 2 Chr. 25:18; Job 31:40 → THORN <2336> 3 Ezek. 2:6 → BRIER <5621>.

THONG – Gen. 14:23 → STRAP <8288>.

THORN – 1 ***ḥôaḥ*** [masc. noun: חוֹחַ <2336>; from an unused root apparently meaning to pierce] ► **This word means a sharp point on a plant; it is also translated thornbush, bramble, thistle, thicket, brier, hook.** It refers to a thorn (Prov. 26:9; Is. 34:13) which was despised compared to a lily (Song 2:2). It indicates a thornbush in the parable of King Jehoash (2 Kgs. 14:9; 2 Chr. 25:18). It depicts thickets where persons could hide (1 Sam. 13:6; also translated hole). Most likely, it is best rendered as briars in some contexts (Job 31:40). It depicts a hook (thorn?) that could not penetrate Leviathan's jaw (Job 41:2). Other refs.: 2 Chr. 33:11; Hos. 9:6. ¶

2 ***siyr*** [common noun: סִיר <5518>; from a prim. root meaning to boil up, also a thorn (as springing up rapidly)] ► **This word refers to a prickly shrub; it also means a hook.** It refers to thornbushes commonly used to fire a pot (Eccl. 7:6). They were a sign of an uncultivated area (Is. 34:13); or a barrier (Hos. 2:6). It clearly means a hook to hang something on or to use to catch something (Amos 4:2). Other ref.: Nah. 1:10. The Hebrew word also refers to a cooking pot; see POT <5518>. ¶

3 ***sallôn*** [masc. noun: סַלּוֹן <5544>; from REJECT <5541>] ► **This word is used in a figurative sense both times of persons who will prove to be troublesome "thorns" to Ezekiel and to the problems and threats of neighboring nations, such as Sidon.** Refs.: Ezek. 2:6; 28:24. ¶

4 ***ṣên*** [masc. noun: צֵן <6791>; from an unused root meaning to be prickly] ► **This word refers to a sharp, prickly plant or to individual spines sticking out from its branches.** It is often used figuratively of undesirable places or locations (Job 5:5; Prov. 22:5). The word is also used of sharp hooks used to lead prisoners (Amos 4:2). ¶

5 ***ṣāniyn*** [masc. noun: צָנִין <6796>; from the same as <6791> above] ► **It is a prickly, spiny, short growth from a branch that can stick and penetrate human skin.** It is used figuratively to represent the danger and trouble that the people whom Israel did not drive out of Canaan would be to Israel (Num. 33:55; Josh. 23:13). ¶

6 ***šayiṯ*** [masc. noun: שַׁיִת <7898>; from PUT <7896>] ► **This word indicates a small tree or shrub bearing hard, leafless, prickly stems.** Refs.: Is. 5:6; 7:23–25. Evil and wickedness consumes even thorns, it is so destructive (Is. 9:18). It is easily consumed by fire (Is. 27:4). Other ref.: Is. 10:17. ¶

– 7 Ps. 58:9 → BRAMBLE <329> a. 8 Prov. 15:19 → BRIER <2312> 9 Is. 7:19; 55:13 → THORN BUSH <5285>.

THORN BUSH – ***naʿᵃṣûṣ*** [masc. noun: נַעֲצוּץ <5285>; from an unused root meaning to prick] ► **This word refers to a small shrub featuring sharp-pointed needles sticking out from it; it is also translated thorn.** In context a figurative use of the word showed how extensive the attack of Judah's enemies will be (Is. 7:19). Since it was not considered a desirable plant, in the time of God's blessings, it will, figuratively and literally, be replaced (Is. 55:13). ¶

THORN EDGE – ***mᵉsûḵāh*** [fem. noun: מְסוּכָה <4534>; for HEDGE <4881>] ► **This was a prickly shrub bearing sharp, pointed stems; or a detested, undesirable plant as well.** Ref.: Mic. 7:4. ¶

THORN, THORNBUSH – ***qôṣ*** [masc. noun: קוֹץ <6975>; from SUMMER (verb) <6972> (in the sense of pricking)] ► **This word refers to an undesirable, inedible shrub that became part of God's curse on the ground.** Ref.: Gen. 3:18. Such shrubs were a fire hazard, easily ignited (Ex. 22:6). This word is used in similes to designate an undesirable thing (2 Sam. 23:6); and to represent enemies of the psalmist in some passages (Ps. 118:12). *

THORNBUSH – 1 Judg. 9:14, 15 → BRAMBLE <329> a. 2 2 Kgs. 14:9; 2 Chr. 25:18; Prov. 26:9 → THORN <2336>.

THORNS – ***qimmaśôn*** [masc. coll. noun: קִמָּשׁוֹן <7063>; from the same as NETTLES <7057>] ► **This word refers to a prickly shrub bearing sharp prickles on its stems.** Its presence in an area indicated a lack of care and cultivation; thorns, thorn bushes growing wild (Prov. 24:31). ¶

THOUGHT – 1 ***harhōr*** [Aramaic masc. noun: הַרְהֹר <2031>; from a root corresponding to CONCEIVE <2029>] ▶ **This word means ideas; it is also translated image, fantasy, fancy.** It denotes the thoughts (KJV, NKJV) or images (NIV) which King Nebuchadnezzar had while lying on his bed (Dan. 4:5). ¶

2 ***maḥ^a^šāḇāh, maḥ^a^šeḇeṯ*** [fem. noun: מַחֲשָׁבָה, מַחֲשֶׁבֶת <4284>; from THINK <2803>] ▶ **This word means a purpose, a device, an intention. Largely poetic in its use, this Hebrew word means thought or the inventions that spring from such thoughts.** It denotes the thoughts of the mind, either belonging to people (1 Chr. 28:9; Ps. 94:11); or God (Jer. 29:11; Mic. 4:12); the plans or intentions that arise from these thoughts (Prov. 15:22; 19:21); the schemes of a wicked heart (Lam. 3:60); skillful inventions coming from the mind of an artist (Ex. 31:4; 2 Chr. 26:15). *

3 ***'aštôṯ*** [fem. plur. noun: עַשְׁתּוֹת <6248>; from CONCERNED (BE) <6245>] ▶ **This word refers to plans, ideas. Its use seems to require the meaning of thought or attitude.** It refers to the attitude of those at ease, people who were not disturbed (Job 12:5). ¶

4 ***'eštōnāh*** [fem. plur. noun: עֶשְׁתֹּנָה <6250>; from CONCERNED (BE) <6245>] ▶ **This word refers to the ideas, imaginations, desires produced by a person during his lifetime; it is also translated plan.** Ref.: Ps. 146:4. ¶

5 ***rêa'*** [masc. noun: רֵעַ <7454>; from FEED (verb) <7462> b. (in the sense of association, e.g., of ideas)] ▶ **This word indicates what persons have in mind, what their intents or purposes are.** Ref.: Ps. 139:2. It is used also of the thoughts of God Himself (Ps. 139:17). ¶

6 ***ra'yôn*** [Aramaic masc. noun: רַעְיוֹן <7476>; corresponding to STRIVING <7475> (in the sense of a grasp, i.e., fig., mental conception)] ▶ **This word refers to what a person is thinking about or to the process itself, what is going through a person's mind.** It refers to the visionary thoughts of Babylonian kings (Dan. 2:29, 30; 4:19; 5:6, 10), as well as to the thoughts of Daniel's visions that passed through his head (Dan. 7:28). ¶

7 ***śêaḥ*** [masc. noun: שֵׂחַ <7808>; from COMPLAINT <7879> (in the sense of contemplation, meditation)] ▶ **This word refers to the ideas and imaginations formed in a person's mind, consciously or unconsciously.** They are all known to God (Amos 4:13). ¶

– 8 Judg. 5:15 ➔ STATUTE <2711> 9 Job 4:13; 20:2 ➔ OPINION <5587> 10 Ps. 94:19; 139:23 ➔ ANXIETY <8312> 11 Eccl. 9:10 ➔ SCHEME (noun) <2808> 12 Eccl. 10:20 ➔ KNOWLEDGE <4093> 13 Lam. 3:62 ➔ MEDITATION <1902>.

THOUGHT (GIVE) – 1 Dan. 6:3 ➔ PLAN (verb) <6246> 2 Jon. 1:6 ➔ CONCERNED (BE) <6245>.

THOUGHT (GIVE, GIVE CAREFUL) – Prov. 4:26; 5:6 ➔ WEIGH OUT <6424>.

THOUGHTLESS – Num. 30:6, 8 ➔ RASH <4008>.

THOUGHTLESSLY (SPEAK) – ***bāṭāh, bāṭā'*** [verb: בָּטָה, בָּטָא <981>; a prim. root] ▶ **This word means to speak rashly, to babble.** It connotes a foolish utterance with an oath spoken thoughtlessly or flippantly (Lev. 5:4). Other refs.: Ps. 106:33; Prov. 12:18. ¶

THOUSAND – 1 ***'elep*** [masc. noun: אֶלֶף <505>; properly the same as HERD <504>] ▶ **This word was commonly used for people, weights (including money), measures, and livestock.** Ref.: Judg. 8:26. Though it is usually literal, sometimes it is used poetically to suggest a large number (Gen. 24:60; Job 9:3). In a few cases, it carries the sense of an extended family or clan (Judg. 6:15). *

2 ***^a^lap*** [Aramaic masc. noun: אֲלַף <506>; corresponding to <505> above] ▶ **This word is found only in the book of Daniel.** For example, Belshazzar held a magnificent feast and invited the lords of the land, whose total number was one thousand (Dan. 5:1). Daniel had a dream of people

ministering to the Ancient of Days; Daniel called these people the thousand thousands (Dan. 7:10). ¶

THOUSANDS (BRING FORTH) – ***'ālap̱*** [verb: אָלַף <503>; denom. from THOUSAND <505>] ► **A masculine verb presenting the idea of bringing forth thousands or making a thousandfold.** It is found only once in the Old Testament. The psalmist asked God for his granaries to be filled and his sheep to bring forth thousands (Ps. 144:13). ¶

THOUSANDS (UPON, OF) – ***šin'ān*** [masc. noun: שִׁנְאָן <8136>; from CHANGE (verb) <8132>] ► **This Hebrew word means repeating, repetition.** This word is used only once in the Old Testament, in Psalm 68:17, where it is preceded by the word that means a thousand. Therefore, it means a thousand in repetition or thousands of thousands; KJV translated thousands of angels. Here it is in reference to the chariots of God, which shows how mighty and powerful God is because He is the ruler over so much. Chariots were also a sign of wealth; and since God had so many chariots, it showed that all the wealth in the world belongs to Him alone. ¶

THRASH – Judg. 8:7 ➔ THRESH <1758>.

THRASH ABOUT – Ezek. 32:2 ➔ GUSH <1518>.

THREAD – **1** ***ḥûṭ*** [masc. noun: חוּט <2339>; from an unused root prob. meaning to sew] ► **This word refers to a cord, ribbon, strand, rope. It was a light, fine, string-like fabrication.** It can mean an insignificant piece of material of little worth (Gen. 14:23). It was used of larger and broader pieces of material of various colors (Josh. 2:18; Song 4:3) or strong cords or ropes (Judg. 16:12; Eccl. 4:12). It was used in a proper size and form as a measuring line (1 Kgs. 7:15; Jer. 52:21: KJV, fillet). ¶
– **2** Ex. 39:3; Num. 15:38 ➔ CORD <6616>.

THREAT – Ezra 4:22 ➔ DAMAGE (noun) <2257>.

THREATS – **1** Ps. 10:7; 55:11 ➔ OPPRESSION <8496> **2** Ps. 55:3 ➔ OPPRESSION <6125> b.

THREE – ***šālôš, šālōš, šᵉlōšāh*** [masc./fem. noun: שָׁלוֹשׁ, שָׁלֹשׁ, שְׁלֹשָׁה <7969>; a prim. number] ► **This word is a cardinal counting number indicating three of something.** Ref.: 2 Sam. 24:12. It combines with other numbers, e.g., three hundred (Gen. 5:22, 23); three hundred fifty-six; *šᵉlōš 'eśreh,* thirteen (1 Kgs. 7:1). The phrase *šᵉlōšeṯ hayyāmîm* indicates within three days (Ezra 10:8, 9), literally three of days. *

THREE, THIRD – ***tᵉlāṯ, tᵉlāṯāh*** [Aramaic numerical noun: תְּלָת, תְּלָתָה <8532>; corresponding to THREE <7969>] ► **This word indicates an ordinal counting number referring to the third item being counted, the third layer, the third day.** Refs.: Ezra 6:4, 15. It also functions as a cardinal counting number (Dan. 3:23, 24), three men. Daniel prayed three times a day (Dan. 6:10, 13). Other refs.: Dan. 6:2; 7:5, 8, 20, 24. ¶

THREESCORE – See SIXTY <8346>.

THRESH – **1** ***'āḏôš*** [verb: אָדוֹשׁ <156>; a prim. root] ► **This word is possibly the infinitive of *dûš* (<1758> below).** In Isaiah 28:28, this word refers to the threshing of grain for bread; to thresh is to separate the seeds from the plant. ¶
2 ***dûš, diyš*** [verb: דּוּשׁ, דִּישׁ <1758>; a prim. root] ► **This word means and is also translated to tread out, to trample, to break.** It means to trample grain (Deut. 25:4; Hos. 10:11) or other objects (Job 39:15). It is used figuratively of Israel's threshing the mountains (her enemies) (Is. 41:15); of the Arameans' devastation of Israel's army and chariots under Jehoahaz, as if they were the dust left over after threshing grain (2 Kgs. 13:7); of the Lord's devastation and trampling of Moab like straw in a manure pile (Is. 25:10; cf. Amos

1:3; Hab. 3:12). Other refs.: Judg. 8:7 (to tear, to thrash, to flail); 1 Chr. 21:20; Is. 28:27; Jer. 50:11; Mic. 4:13. ¶

3 ***ḥabaṯ*** [verb: חָבַט <2251>; a prim. root] ► **This verb refers to the threshing or beating out of various things.** Grain (Judg. 6:11); olive trees (Deut. 24:20); or cumin (Is. 28:27). Figuratively, it indicates the Lord's gathering His people by threshing them from among the nations (Is. 27:12). Other ref.: Ruth 2:17. ¶

– 4 Jer. 50:11 ➔ GRASS <1877>.

THRESHED – Is. 21:10 ➔ THRESHING <4098>.

THRESHING (adj.) – threshing sledge, threshing instrument, threshing implement: *môrag* [masc. noun: מוֹרַג <4173>; from an unused root meaning to triturate] ► **This word indicates an agricultural tool made of a heavy slab of wood with flint or iron points on the bottom for threshing grain, i.e., separating the seeds from the plant.** Refs.: 2 Sam. 24:22; 1 Chr. 21:23. It is used figuratively to illustrate Israel's power and might to subdue her enemies (Is. 41:15). ¶

THRESHING (noun) – 1 ***dayiš*** [masc. noun: דַּיִשׁ <1786>; from THRESH <1758>] ► **This word refers to the process and period of time given to grape gathering and sowing.** Ref.: Lev. 26:5. This would be an extended time if Israel would walk in obedience to her God. ¶

2 ***meḏušāh*** [fem. noun: מְדֻשָׁה <4098>; from THRESH <1758>] ► **This word means that which is threshed.** It refers to something threshed or, figuratively, to someone threshed, e.g., it refers to persons God has "threshed" in judgment (Is. 21:10). ¶

THRESHING FLOOR – 1 ***'iddar*** [Aramaic fem. noun: אִדַּר <147>; intens. from a root corresponding to GLORIOUS <142>] ► **The word refers to summer threshing floors. See definition below (<1637>).** Ref.: Dan. 2:35. ¶

2 ***gōren*** [masc. noun: גֹּרֶן <1637>; from an unused root meaning to smooth] ► **This word indicates the place where various grains were beaten to remove the chaff (1 Kgs. 22:10) and where they were stored (1 Sam. 23:1; 2 Kgs. 6:27; Joel 2:24).** It is used to describe Israel as a threshed people because the Lord had, so to speak, put them on the threshing floor of judgment (Is. 21:10; cf. Jer. 51:33; Hos. 13:3). The word is combined with other words to indicate names for various locations: the threshing floor of Atad (Gen. 50:10, 11); the threshing floor of Nacon (2 Sam. 6:6); the threshing floor of Chidon (1 Chr. 13:9). *

THRESHING SLEDGE, INSTRUMENT – Is. 28:27; 41:15; Job 41:30 ➔ DILIGENT <2742>.

THRESHOLD – 1 ***miptān*** [masc. noun: מִפְתָּן <4670>; from the same as ASP <6620>] ► **This word indicates the beginning or entrance of something.** A doorsill (1 Sam. 5:4, 5), a temple, or other building (Ezek. 9:3; 10:4, 18; 46:2; 47:1; Zeph. 1:9). ¶

2 ***sap*** [masc. noun: סַף <5592>; from DOORKEEPER (BE A) <5605> (in the sense of to wait at the threshold)] ► **This word means the opening, sill, or entrance into a house, a building, a temple, a palace.** Refs.: Judg. 19:27; 1 Kgs. 14:17. The doorkeeper, the keeper of the door was an important person (2 Kgs. 25:18; Esther 2:21; Jer. 35:4). The Hebrew word also means a basin, a bowl; see BASIN <5592>. *

– 3 1 Kgs. 7:6; Ezek. 41:25, 26 ➔ CANOPY <5646>.

THRESHOLD (STAND AT THE) – Ps. 84:10 ➔ DOORKEEPER (BE A) <5605>.

THRIVE – Hos. 13:15 ➔ FRUITFUL (BE) <6500>.

THRIVE (MAKE) – Zech. 9:17 ➔ INCREASE (verb) <5107>.

THROAT – 1 ***gārôn*** [masc. noun: גָּרוֹן <1627>; from DRAG (verb) <1641>] ► **This word means the front of the neck; it is also translated neck.** It indicates the

throat as a location of thirst (Jer. 2:25) or figuratively as one's voice raised like a trumpet (Is. 58:1). The throat could be an organ of praise to God (Ps. 149:6) or an organ of pleading with Him (Ps. 69:3). The throat of the wicked is a conduit of death (Ps. 5:9). It was a favorite place for ornamentation (Ezek. 16:11). An outstretched neck was a sign of pride and haughtiness (Is. 3:16). Other ref.: Ps. 115:7. ¶
[2] ***lōa'*** [masc. noun: לֹעַ <3930>; from SWALLOW (verb) <3886>] ▶ **This word refers to a person's throat, that part of the body used for swallowing.** In context it is used figuratively to indicate controlling one's appetite (Prov. 23:2). ¶

THROB – Ps. 38:10 ➔ MERCHANT <5503>.

THROES OF DEATH – 2 Sam. 1:9 ➔ ANGUISH <7661>.

THRONE – [1] ***kēs*** [masc. noun: כֵּס <3676>; apparently a contr. for <3678> below, but prob. by erroneous transcription for BANNER <5251>] ▶ **This word is used once to designate the seat, or chair of the Lord.** Ref.: Ex. 17:16: ESV, NIV. ¶
[2] ***kissê', kissêh*** [masc. noun: כִּסֵּא, כִּסֵּה <3678>; from COVER (verb) <3680>] ▶ **This word means a place of honor.** Pharaoh put Joseph over everything in his kingdom except his throne (Gen. 41:40). Other references to leaders on the throne include Pharaoh (Ex. 11:5; 12:29); Solomon and Bathsheba (1 Kgs. 2:19); King Ahasuerus (Esther 5:1); departed kings (Is. 14:9); the princes of the coast (Ezek. 26:16); the prophetic one who will build the Temple of the Lord (Zech. 6:13). Scripture also depicts God as sitting on a throne (Is. 6:1; Ezek. 1:26). The throne can also be a symbol of a kingdom or power (2 Sam. 7:16; 14:9; Is. 16:5). *
[3] ***korsê'*** [Aramaic masc. noun: כָּרְסֵא <3764>; corresponding to <3678> above] ▶ **This word means a place of honor.** Daniel reminded Belshazzer that Nebuchadnezzar had been deposed from his kingly throne because of pride (Dan. 5:20). Daniel had a dream about thrones and a throne in particular that belonged to the Ancient of Days (Dan. 7:9). See the related Hebrew nouns *kissê'* and *kissêh* (<3678> above). ¶

THRONG (noun) – [1] ***sāḵ*** [masc. noun: סָךְ <5519>; from COVER (verb) <5526> c. (in the sense of to join together)] ▶ **This word refers to a group or gathering of people worshiping the Lord.** Ref.: Ps. 42:4; KJV, NKJV: multitude. ¶
[2] ***rigmāh*** [fem. noun: רִגְמָה <7277>; fem. of the same as REGEM <7276> (in the sense of a pile of stones)] ▶
a. This word refers to a large number of persons. In context it indicates a great number of rulers from Judah (Ps. 68:27; also translated company).
b. This word means a council. It refers to a group of people serving as advisors and counselors for someone. In its context it indicates the leaders of Judah (Ps. 68:27). ¶
[3] ***regeš*** [noun: רֶגֶשׁ <7285>; from RAGE (verb) <7283>] ▶ **This word means a crowd, a company, an insurrection. The basic meaning of this word is that of a cramming mass of people.** The word refers to worshipers going to the Temple in a large group (Ps. 55:14); and the riotous scheming that could result from a large gathering of people whose minds were not directed toward God (Ps. 64:2; also translated rebellion, tumult, insurrection, plot). ¶
– [4] Hab. 3:14 ➔ WARRIOR <6518>.

THRONG (verb) – [1] Jer. 5:7 ➔ GATHER <1413> [2] Dan. 6:6, 11, 15 ➔ ASSEMBLE TOGETHER <7284>.

THROW – [1] ***rāmāh*** [verb: רָמָה <7411>; a prim. root] ▶ **This word means to push someone off; it also means to shoot (an arrow).** It is used of the Lord's throwing the Egyptian horsemen into the Red Sea (Ex. 15:1, 21; also translated to hurl). It indicates the shooters of bows, archers (Ps. 78:9; Jer. 4:29). For another meaning of the Hebrew word see DECEIVE <7411>. ¶
[2] ***reᵉmāh*** [Aramaic verb: רְמָה <7412>; corresponding to <7411> above] ▶ **This word means to cast down; to impose (tribute,**

custom, etc.). It is used once in a context to indicate imposing a tax upon (*'al*). It is negated since a tribute or a tax could not be imposed on certain classes of Temple workers (Ezra 7:24). It refers to the throwing down of someone or something (Dan. 3:20, 21, 24; 6:16, 24). It is used in the sense of establishing, setting a throne in place (Dan. 7:9). In its passive reflexive use, it means to be thrown down (Dan. 3:6, 11, 15; 6:7, 12). ¶
[3] ***šālak̲*** [verb: שָׁלַךְ <7993>; a prim. root] ► **In the causative form, several different variations of meaning are associated with this verb. The basic meaning to cast or throw is found in Genesis 21:15 and Numbers 35:20.** It can also mean to cast away in the sense of getting rid of something that hinders, such as sin (Ezek. 18:31); or fetters (Ps. 2:3). This verb is also used to describe God's rejection of someone (2 Kgs. 17:20; 24:20). In a good sense, God will sustain those who cast their cares on Him (Ps. 55:22). In the passive causative form, this verb means to be cast, to be thrown or to be cast out. Usually, this is used in a negative sense, as when someone was cast out of his or her burial site (Is. 14:19; Jer. 36:30); or when people were cast away because of their disobedience to God (Jer. 14:16). Yet it can also be used in a good sense. In Psalm 22:10, the writer says that from birth he had been cast on God. So this verb can have either positive or negative connotations. *
– [4] Ex. 14:27 ➔ SHAKE <5287> [5] 2 Sam. 16:13 ➔ FLING <6080> [6] Job 16:11 ➔ TURN OVER <3399> [7] Is. 22:18 ➔ TOSS (noun) <6802> [8] Ezek. 21:12 ➔ DELIVER OVER <4048>.

THROW DOWN – [1] Ps. 36:12 ➔ DRIVE <1760> [2] Prov. 21:12 ➔ OVERTHROW (verb) <5557>.

THRUSH – Is. 38:14; Jer. 8:7 ➔ CRANE <5693>.

THRUST (noun) – ***mad̲qērāh*** [fem. noun: מַדְקֵרָה <4094>; from PIERCE <1856>] ► **This word means stabbing; it is also translated piercing.** It describes harmful and merciless words that are like sword thrusts to those receiving them (Prov. 12:18). ¶

THRUST (verb) – [1] Ex. 21:36 ➔ GORING <5056> [2] Num. 35:20, 22; Deut. 6:19; 9:4; Josh. 23:5; 2 Kgs. 4:27; Job 18:18; Is. 22:19; Jer. 46:15; Ezek. 34:21: to thrust of, to thrust out ➔ PUSH <1920> [3] Jer. 46:15 ➔ SWEEP <5502> [4] Ezek. 34:21 ➔ GORE <5055> [5] Joel 2:8 ➔ AFFLICT <1766>.

THRUST DOWN – [1] Job 32:13 ➔ DRIVE AWAY <5086> [2] Ps. 36:12; Prov. 14:32 ➔ DRIVE <1760>.

THRUST THROUGH – [1] Is. 14:19 ➔ PIERCE <2944> [2] Ezek. 16:40 ➔ CUT TO PIECES <1333>.

THRUST TOGETHER – Judg. 6:38 ➔ CRUSH <2115>.

THUMB – ***bōhen*** [masc. noun: בֹּהֶן <931>; from an unused root apparently meaning to be thick] ► **This word indicates the opposable thumb on a hand and also a big toe. It refers to the right thumb and right big toe of the high priest that were smeared with blood as part of his consecration ceremony.** Refs.: Ex. 29:20; Lev. 8:23, 24. This process was also part of the cleansing ritual of a leper (Lev. 14:14, 17, 25, 28). It refers to big toes and right thumbs in general (Judg. 1:6, 7). ¶

THUMMIN – ***tummiym*** [proper noun: תֻּמִּים <8550>; plur. of COMPLETENESS <8537>]: perfections ► **The meaning of this word is not certain. It may mean perfection(s), truth, integrity.** It refers to one of two small sacred lots used by the high priest to discern God's will (Ex. 28:30; Lev. 8:8; Deut. 33:8). It disappeared after the exile (Ezra 2:63; Neh. 7:65). The word begins with the last letter of the alphabet; the word urim begins with the first letter. See URIM <224>. ¶

THUNDER (noun) – [1] ***ra'am*** [masc. noun: רַעַם <7482>; from THUNDER (verb)

<7481>] ▶ **This word refers literally to a peal of thunder; it indicates the mighty works and power of God as displayed in His actions in nature, but goes infinitely beyond that.** Refs.: Job 26:14; Ps. 77:18. It refers to the din and thunderous noise of warfare (Job 39:25; also translated shout). It describes a *sêṯer,* a thundercloud (Ps. 81:7, literally, a hiding place of thunder). His voice, thunder, awes the entire creation (Ps. 104:7). It was one feature of the Lord's great acts of punishment (Is. 29:6). ¶

2 ***ra'māh*** [fem. noun: רַעְמָה <7483>; fem. of <7482> above] ▶

a. This word is taken by the KJV and the NKJV to refer to the mane growing on the top of a horse's neck, paralleling its strength. Ref.: Job 39:19.

b. This word is translated thunder, paralleling the strengths, the might of the horse on the previous poetic line. Ref.: Job 39:19. ¶

– 3 Job 36:29 ➔ STORM (noun) <8663> 4 Job 36:33 ➔ NOISE <7452> 5 Job 37:2 ➔ TURMOIL <7267>.

THUNDER (verb) – ***rā'am*** [verb: רָעַם <7481>; a prim. root] ▶ **This word means to be stirred up, agitated, noisy; confused.** It describes the Lord's thundering action in judgment (1 Sam. 2:10); especially in meting out military confusion against His and Israel's enemies (1 Sam. 7:10; 2 Sam. 22:14). God's voice is heard in the thunder of a storm (Job 37:4, 5; 40:9; Ps. 18:13; 29:3). It describes the roaring power of the seas (Ps. 96:11; 98:7: to roar, to resound). Other ref.: 1 Chr. 16:32. For another meaning of the Hebrew word, see IRRITATE <7481>. ¶

THUNDERBOLT – 1 Job 28:26; 38:25 ➔ lit.: lightning of the thunder ➔ THUNDERSTORM <2385> 2 Ps. 78:48 ➔ FLASH (noun) <7565>.

THUNDERCLOUD – Ps. 81:7 ➔ THUNDER (noun) <7482>.

THUNDERING – Job 36:29 ➔ STORM (noun) <8663>.

THUNDERSTORM – ***ḥ^{a}ziyz*** [masc. noun: חֲזִיז <2385>; from an unused root meaning to glare] ▶ **This word indicates lightning, a thunderbolt; a strong, sudden wind.** The Lord makes the *ḥ^{a}ziyz,* the storm clouds, thunderbolt, or strong wind of a storm (Zech. 10:1: flashing cloud, storm cloud, bright cloud, thunderstorm), so it indicates a major feature of storms or heavy rain. It seems to refer to the lightning or thunder of a storm (Job 28:26; 38:25): lightning (<2385>) of the thunder (VOICE <6963>), thunderbolt, thunderstorm. ¶

THUS – 1 ***kāḵāh*** [adv. particle: כָּכָה <3602>; from THIS <3541>] ▶ **This word also means so, in this way, as follows.** It indicates how something is to be done, in this manner, thus (Ex. 12:11; Deut. 25:9); or how a person is to be treated, thus (you shall do) (Ex. 29:35; Num. 8:26). It is used to indicate the condition of something or someone (2 Sam. 13:4; Ps. 144:15). It is used in the phrase *ka^{a}šer . . . kākāh,* just as . . . so . . . (Eccl. 11:5); or to indicate that one (said) this, another that, *zeh* (THIS, THESE <2088>) . . . *kākāh w^{e}zeh . . . kākāh* (2 Chr. 18:19). With *'al* preceding, it means upon this basis, for this reason (Esther 9:26). *

2 ***kên*** [Aramaic particle: כֵּן <3652>; corresponding to THEREFORE <3651>] ▶ **This word also means so.** It is used with reference to only what follows in context, such as something written or said (Ezra 5:3; 6:2; Dan. 2:24, 25; 4:14; 6:6; 7:5, 23). ¶

3 ***k^{e}nêmā'*** [Aramaic adv.: כְּנֵמָא <3660>; corresponding to LIKE <3644>] ▶ **This word also means so, as follows.** It refers to what follows, e.g., as something said (Ezra 4:8; 5:4, 9, 11); or to what precedes (Ezra 6:13 refers to Darius' previous decree) and may be translated as "then" if appropriate. ¶

THWART – 1 Ps. 33:10 ➔ FORBID <5106> 2 Prov. 10:3 ➔ PUSH <1920>.

TIBHATH – ***ṭiḇḥaṯ*** [proper noun: טִבְחַת <2880>; from SLAUGHTER (noun) <2878>]: slaughter ▶ **A Syrian town.** Ref.: 1 Chr. 18:8. ¶

TIBNI – ***tiḇniy*** [masc. proper noun: תִּבְנִי <8402>; from STRAW <8401>]: strawy ▶ **A contender for the throne of Israel's northern kingdom.** He died and his rival Omni became king (1 Kgs. 16:21, 22). ¶

TICK – [1] Is. 30:27 ➔ HEAVINESS <3514> [2] Ezek. 8:11 ➔ WORSHIPPER <6282> c.

TIDAL – ***tiḏʻāl*** [masc. proper noun: תִּדְעָל <8413>; perhaps from FEAR (verb) <1763>]: fear, reverence ▶ **The king of Goiim (nations) and an ally of Chedorlaomer.** Refs.: Gen. 14:1, 9. ¶

TIDINGS – 2 Sam. 4:10; 18:20, 22, 25, 27; 2 Kgs. 7:9 ➔ NEWS <1309>.

TIE – [1] Ex. 28:28; 39:21 ➔ BIND <7405> [2] Lev. 8:7 ➔ GIRD <640>.

TIE UP – Dan. 3:20, 21, 23, 24 ➔ BIND <3729>.

TIGHTLY KNIT (BE) – Job 40:17 ➔ KNIT TOGETHER (BE) <8276>.

TIGLATH-PILESER – ***tiglaṯ pil'eser, tilgaṯ pilneser, tilgaṯ piln*^{e}*'eser*** [masc. proper noun: תִּגְלַת פִּלְאֶסֶר, תִּלְגַת פִּלְנֶסֶר, תִּלְגַת פִּלְנְאֶסֶר <8407>; of foreign deriv.] ▶
a. A great Assyrian king, Tiglath-pileser III (745–727 B.C.). He had another name, Pul (2 Kgs. 15:29; 16:7, 10; 1 Chr. 5:26). He captured many cities in Aram, including Damascus (732 B.C.). He overran Gilead, Galilee, including Naphtali in upper Galilee. He deported the Israelites into various places in Assyria. He also took tribute from Ahaz of Judah (2 Chr. 28:20, 21). The name is also found rendered as Tiglath-pilneser (see b. below).
b. See a. above. Tiglath-pilneser is a variant of the name and may be unique to Hebrew. ¶

TIGLATH-PILNESER – See TIGLATH-PILESER <8407> b.

TIKVAH – ***tiqwāh*** [masc. proper noun: תִּקְוָה <8616>; the same as HOPE (noun) <8615>]: cord, hope ▶
a. The father-in-law of the prophetess Huldah. Refs.: 2 Kgs. 22:14; 2 Chr. 34:22; the same as Tokhath (<8445>).
b. The father of Jahaziah. Ref.: Ezra 10:15. ¶

TILL – Job 39:10 ➔ HARROW <7702>.

TILLAGE – Prov. 13:23 ➔ FALLOW GROUND <5215>.

TILON – ***tiylôn*** [masc. proper noun: תִּילוֹן <8436>; from LOFTY <8524>]: elevated, eminent ▶ **An Israelite of the tribe of Judah.** Ref.: 1 Chr. 4:20. ¶

TIMBER – ***'āʻ*** [Aramaic masc. noun: אָע <636>; corresponding to TREE <6086>] ▶ **This word means and is also translated beam, wood.** It refers to the beams used to construct the new Temple in the time of Zerubbabel (Ezra 5:8) and approved by Cyrus and Darius, kings of Persia (Ezra 6:4, 11). It refers to idols made of wood as well (Dan. 5:4, 23). ¶

TIMBREL – See TAMBOURINE <8596>.

TIMBRELS (PLAYING) – Ps. 68:25 ➔ TAMBOURINES (PLAYING, BEATING) <8608>.

TIME – [1] ***z*^{e}*man*** [masc. noun: זְמַן <2165>; from APPOINTED <2163>] ▶ **This word means an appointed time, a season. It occurs only four times in the Old Testament.** Two of these are in the book of Esther, referring to the time set for the Feast of Purim (Esther 9:27, 31); it is translated appointed time, prescribed time, designated time. In the book of Nehemiah, it refers to an appointed time to return from a journey (Neh. 2:6). In Ecclesiastes, it occurs in an often-quoted verse, "To every thing there is a season" (Eccl. 3:1) to say that everything has a predestined time. The word translated time throughout Ecclesiastes 3 is *ʻēṯ* (<6256> below). Thus, *z*^{e}*man* bears a different sense, emphasizing the specificity in time. ¶
[2] ***z*^{e}*mān*** [Aramaic masc. noun: זְמָן <2166>; from <2165> above] ▶ **This word means a**

specific time, a time period. It is used in Daniel indicating a duration of time or a period of time (Dan. 2:16; 7:12) and also in reference to the feast times (Dan. 7:25). See the Hebrew cognate (<2165> above). Other refs.: Ezra 5:3; Dan. 2:21; 3:7, 8; 4:36; 6:10, 13; 7:22. ¶

3 ***mōneh*** [masc. noun: מֹנֶה <4489>; from COUNT <4487>] ► **This word designates a counted number of instances.** It refers to the act of performing something, an occurrence of something (Gen. 31:7, 41). ¶

4 ***'iddān*** [Aramaic masc. noun: עִדָּן <5732>; from a root corresponding to that of FILTHY <5708>] ► **This word indicates a period of time, a moment of time.** It indicates a prolongation of time or some time (Dan. 2:8); a period or length of time (Dan. 7:12). It has the sense of a time, a period when things change, changing circumstances (Dan. 2:9, 21). It refers to a proper time, a time when something should occur (Dan. 3:5, 15). From context it may refer to a year as a duration of time (Dan. 4:16, 23, 4:25, 32; 7:25). ¶

5 ***'ēṯ*** [masc. and fem. noun: עֵת <6256>; from ETERNITY <5703>] ► **This Hebrew word basically means time. But in context, it expresses many aspects of time and kinds of time. It is used most often to express the time of the occurrence of some event.** The word means at that time in a general sense, as when Abimelech and Phicol spoke to Abraham during the days when Ishmael was growing up (Gen. 21:22; 38:1). The time described can be more specific, such as when Moses refers to the time of crisis in the wilderness when the people wanted meat to eat (Deut. 1:9). It may refer to a specific date (Ex. 9:18; 1 Sam. 9:16); or a part of a day, as when the dove returned to Noah in the evening (Gen. 8:11; 24:11). The word can refer to a duration of time, as for all time (Ex. 18:22; Prov. 8:30); or for any time in general (Lev. 16:2). The time referred to may be past, present, or future (Num. 23:23; Judg. 13:23; Is. 9:1). The word can describe times of the Lord's anger (Ps. 21:9); or times of trouble (Ps. 9:9). In fact, this word can be made to refer to about any kind of time or duration of time by its modifying words and context.

It is used to describe the time when certain appropriate things took place in general. For example, kings customarily went forth to war in the spring (2 Sam. 11:1; 1 Chr. 20:1). It can depict times that are fitting or suitable for certain reasons, such as rain falling on the land in its season (Deut. 11:14; Jer. 5:24); and fruit trees bearing fruit at the proper time (Ps. 1:3). The author of Proverbs 15:23 spoke of a proper time for fitting words. Ecclesiastes 3 described all of life as a grand mosaic of times and seasons; there is a time to do everything—to be born, to die, to plant, to uproot, to kill, to heal, to love, to hate (Eccl. 3:1–3, 8). This word occurs nineteen times in these verses (Eccl. 3:1–8), along with a synonym of this word, *zᵉmān* (<2165> above), to make twenty references to time.

The Hebrew word can be used to designate a time even more accurately. When the exiles returned, it was time for the house of the Lord to be rebuilt (Hag. 1:2). The word designated the set time of marriage (1 Sam. 18:19). It pinpointed the time of God's judgments (Is. 13:22; Ezek. 7:7, 12); but also the many times in the past when He delivered them (Neh. 9:28). The Lord stands in readiness to judge every nation when its time comes (Jer. 27:7). There will be a time of the end for all the nations as well (Dan. 8:17; 11:35; 12:4, 9). In contrast, the word in context can be combined with chance to indicate uncertain time (Eccl. 9:11); and, appropriately, it describes life in general and its content, whether good or bad (Ps. 31:15; Is. 33:6). *

6 ***pa'am*** [common noun: פַּעַם <6471>; from TROUBLED (BE) <6470> (in the sense of to beat regularly)] ► **This word indicates a specific period; it also indicates occurrence, foot.** It refers to a specific time when an occurrence takes place (Gen. 2:23; 46:30). In its dual form, it means twice (*paᵃmayim*). The phrase *kᵉpa'am-bᵉpa'am* means formerly or as is usually the case (Num. 24:1). Repeated but separated, it means at one time . . . at another time (Prov. 7:12). The phrase *kap̱ pᵉ'āmay* means sole of one's foot (2 Kgs. 19:24). *

– 7 Ps. 89:47 ➔ WORLD <2465> 8 Dan. 4:19 ➔ IMMEDIATELY <8160>.

TIME APPOINTED – Ps. 81:3 ➔ FULL MOON <3677>.

TIMID (BE) – Job 32:6 ➔ CRAWL <2119>.

TIMNA – ***timnā'*** [proper noun: תִּמְנָע <8555>; from HOLD, WITHHOLD <4513>]: restraint ▶
a. Concubine of Eliphaz. Refs.: Gen. 36:12, 22; 1 Chr. 1:39. ¶
b. A chief of Edom. Refs.: Gen. 36:40; 1 Chr. 1:51.
c. Son of Eliphaz. Ref.: 1 Chr. 1:36. ¶

TIMNAH – ***timnāh*** [proper noun: תִּמְנָה <8553>; from COUNT <4487>]: portion ▶
a. A city in northern Judah. Judah visited the city (Gen. 38:12–14). It was allotted to the tribe of Dan (Josh. 15:10). Samson loved and married a Philistine woman in Timnah (Judg. 14:1–5), so it went back into Philistine control at some point. In Ahaz's day, Edomites raided it (2 Chr. 28:18). It was likely south of Hebron. ¶
b. A city in the southern hill country of Judah. Ref.: Josh. 15:57. ¶

TIMNATH HERES, TIMNATH SERAH – ***timnaṯ ḥeres, timnaṯ seraḥ*** [תִּמְנַת חֶרֶס, תִּמְנַת סֶרַח <8556>; from TIMNA <8553> and SUN <2775>]: portion of the sun ▶ **A place in the hill coutry of Ephraim where Joshua was buried.** Ref.: Judg. 2:9. It was part of the inheritance of Joshua (Timnath Serah: Josh. 19:50; 24:30). ¶

TIMNITE – ***timniy*** [proper noun: תִּמְנִי <8554>; patrial from TIMNAH <8553>] ▶ **An inhabitant of Timnah.** Ref.: Judg. 15:6. ¶

TIN – ***bᵉḏiyl*** [masc. noun: בְּדִיל <913>; from SEPARATE <914>] ▶ **This word means a metallic element; it describes booty taken from the Midianites that had to be purified by fire.** Ref.: Num. 31:22. Israel is described as tin that needs to be purified in the furnace of God's judgments (Ezek. 22:18, 20). It is also translated as alloy and impurities (Is. 1:25) in a difficult passage to decipher. Other refs.: Ezek. 27:12; Zech. 4:10 (plumb). ¶

TINDER – Is. 1:31 ➔ TOW <5296>.

TINGLE – ***ṣālal*** [verb: צָלַל <6750>; a prim. root (identical with SINK <6749> through the idea of vibration)] ▶ **This word indicates a sensitive feeling in a person's ears or lips with a corresponding quivering reaction; it also means to quiver.** In context it was a result of hearing about a horrifying deed the Lord would do (1 Sam. 3:11; 2 Kgs. 21:12; Jer. 19:3). Other ref.: Hab. 3:16 (to quiver). ¶

TINKLE – ***'āḵas*** [verb: עָכַס <5913>; a prim. root] ▶ **This word is also translated to jingle, to make a tinkling sound. It means to jingle an ornament or bracelet.** It is used of the seductive, sophisticated women of Zion who tinkled or jingled foot jewelry (Is. 3:16). ¶

TINKLING (MAKE A) – Is. 3:16 ➔ TINKLE <5913>.

TINKLING ORNAMENT – Is. 3:18 ➔ ANKLET <5914>.

TIP OVER – ***ṣā'āh*** [verb: צָעָה <6808>; a prim. root] ▶ **This word literally means to incline a vessel which is to be emptied, figuratively to depopulate (implying to imprison or conquer). It refers to an act of destruction, in which vessels are emptied of their contents; it is also translated to pour.** God will bring these events to pass on Moab (Jer. 48:12). ¶

TIPHSAH – ***tipsaḥ*** [proper noun: תִּפְסַח <8607>; from PASS OVER <6452>]: ford ▶
a. A city in northern Syria. Ref.: 1 Kgs. 4:24. ¶
b. A city in northern Israel. Ref.: 2 Kgs. 15:16. ¶

TIRAHITES – ***tir'āṯiym*** [proper noun: תִּרְעָתִים <8654>; patrial from an unused name meaning gate]: gate ▶ **A family of scribes.** Ref.: 1 Chr. 2:55. ¶

TIRAS – ***tiyrās*** [masc. proper noun: תִּירָס <8494>; prob. of foreign deriv.] ▶ **Son of Japheth and grandson of Noah.** Refs.: Gen. 10:2; 1 Chr. 1:5. ¶

TIRE – Ezek.: 24:17, 23 ➔ TURBAN <6287>.

TIRED (BE) – Gen. 27:46 ➔ LOATHE <6973>.

TIRED (GROW) – 2 Sam. 23:10 ➔ WEARY (verb) <3021>.

TIRESOME – Mal. 1:13 ➔ WEARINESS <4972>.

TIRHAKAH – ***tirhāqāh*** [masc. proper noun: תִּרְהָקָה <8640>; of foreign deriv.] ▶ **King of Ethiopia in the time of King Hezekiah.** Refs.: 2 Kgs. 19:9; Is. 37:9. ¶

TIRHANAH – ***tirḥ^{a}nāh*** [masc. proper noun: תִּרְחֲנָה <8647>; of uncertain deriv.] ▶ **This word refers to one of Caleb's descendants, born to him by his concubine Maacah and, hence, a part of the genealogy of David.** Ref.: 1 Chr. 2:48. ¶

TIRIA – ***tiyryā'*** [masc. proper noun: תִּירְיָא <8493>; prob. from FEAR (verb) <3372>]: fear ▶ **An Israelite of the tribe of Judah.** Ref.: 1 Chr. 4:16. ¶

TIRSHATHA – See GOVERNOR <8660> b.

TIRZAH – ***tirṣāh*** [proper noun: תִּרְצָה <8656>; from PLEASURE (TAKE) <7521>]: agreeable ▶
a. A daughter of Zelophehad, evidently the youngest. Ref.: Num. 26:33. She and her sisters successfully raised the issue of the inheritance laws in Israel when a man bore no sons, only daughters. ¶
b. A city conquered by Joshua. It was the second capital of northern Israel after Shechem (1 Kgs. 14:17). Menahem, an Israelite king, was governor here (2 Kgs. 15:14–33). The Song of Solomon refers to its beauty and location (Song 6:4). It lay north, northeast from Shechem and east, northeast of Samaria. Baasha was buried there, a king of Israel (1 Kgs. 16:6). The reigns of short-lived kings in the city (Elah, Zimri, Tibni, Omri [6 years]) hastened its demise as a capital. Omri moved the capital to Samaria. ¶

TISHBITE – ***tišbey*** [proper noun: תִּשְׁבִּי <8664>; patrial from an unused name meaning recourse] ▶ **A designation of Elijah.** Refs.: 1 Kgs. 17:1; 21:17, 28; 2 Kgs. 1:3, 8; 9:36. ¶

TITHE – Gen. 14:20; etc. ➔ TENTH <4643>.

TITHE (GIVE, RECEIVE) – ***'āśar*** [verb: עָשַׂר <6237>; a prim. root (identical with RICH (BE) <6238>, in the sense of to accumulate)] ▶ **This word means to give a tenth part, to take a tenth part, to give the tithe, to receive the tithe.** This pivotal Hebrew word first appears in reference to a vow made by Jacob (Gen. 28:22). He promised to return one-tenth of his possessions to the Lord if the Lord would go with him. Under the Law given by Moses, this tithe was made mandatory on all increase (Deut. 14:22; see also Deut. 26:12). It was the duty of the priest to receive these tithes (Neh. 10:37, 38). Samuel also used this word to describe the taxes imposed by a king (1 Sam. 8:15, 17). Genesis 14:20 records that Abraham gave king/priest Melchizedek "a tenth of all," the word "tenth" being rooted in the same Hebrew word as "tithe." See TENTH (<4643> from <6235>). ¶

TITLE – 2 Kgs. 23:17 ➔ MONUMENT <6725>.

TIZITE – ***tiyṣiy*** [proper noun: תִּיצִי <8491>; patrial from an unused noun of uncertain meaning] ▶ **An inhabitant of a place (Tiz?).** Ref.: 1 Chr. 11:45. ¶

TO – ***'ēl, 'el*** [prep.: אֵל, אֶל <413>; a prim. particle] ▶ **This word means toward, into, concerning. It has the basic meaning of toward.** It is used in all kinds of situations indicating direction (Gen. 2:19; 16:11;

18:7; Lev. 1:16). It is used metaphorically to refer to speaking to someone (Gen. 8:15) or sexual intercourse (Gen. 16:2; Num. 25:1). It indicates direction when things face each other (Num. 12:8). Its use in the idiom *hinᵉni 'êl* indicates motion toward (Gen. 4:8). Other meanings according to context are: as far as (Jer. 51:9); into (Jon. 1:5); to sit at (Gen. 24:11; 1 Kgs. 13:20). Used figuratively, it can mean with regard to something (2 Sam. 1:24). When used with other prepositions, it indicates direction or location according to the preposition it is being combined with (Josh. 15:13; 1 Kgs. 8:6; 2 Kgs. 9:18).

It is used in place of or interchangeably for the preposition *'al* and takes on the meaning of upon, on (Josh. 5:14; Judg. 6:37). *

TOAH – ***tôaḥ*** [masc. proper noun: תּוֹחַ <8430>; from an unused root meaning to depress]: lowly, humble ▶ **An ancestor of the prophet Samuel, the same as Tohu (<8459>).** Ref.: 1 Chr. 6:34. ¶

TOB – ***ṭôḇ*** [proper noun: טוֹב <2897>; the same as GOOD <2896>]: good ▶ **A place where Jephthah took refuge when he fled from his brothers.** Refs.: Judg. 11:3, 5; 2 Sam. 10:6, 8. See also *'iyš ṭôḇ* (ISH-TOB <382>). ¶

TOB-ADONIJAH – ***ṭôḇ ᵃḏôniyyāh*** [masc. proper noun: טוֹב אֲדוֹנִיָּה <2899>; from GOOD <2896> and ADONIJAH <138>]: the Lord is good ▶ **One of the Levites sent by Jehoshaphat to teach the Law in the cities of Judah.** Ref.: 2 Chr. 17:8. ¶

TOBIJAH – ***ṭôḇiyyāh, ṭôḇiyyāhû*** [masc. proper noun: טוֹבִיָּה, טוֹבִיָּהוּ <2900>; from GOOD <2896> and LORD <3050>]: the Lord is good ▶ **a. He assisted other officials in teaching the Book of the Law throughout Judah.** Ref.: 2 Chr. 17:8. ¶
b. A few descendants who returned from exile in Babylon but could not demonstrate from records that they were Jews. Refs.: Ezra 2:60; Neh. 7:62.
c. An Ammonite leader who opposed the Jews who returned to Jerusalem from exile. Ref.: Neh. 2:10. He actively tried to stop the rebuilding of walls, etc. (Neh. 2:19; 4:3), and verbally attacked Nehemiah personally (Neh. 6:19). Nehemiah expelled him from the Temple area (Neh. 13:4, 7, 8). Other refs.: Neh. 4:7; 6:1, 12, 14, 17. ¶
d. A returned exile who possessed gold and was a leader in Israel. Refs.: Zech. 6:10, 14. ¶

TOE – See FINGER <676>, FINGER <677>.

TOE (BIG, GREAT) – See THUMB <931>.

TOGARMAH – ***tôḡarmāh, tōḡarmāh, bêyṯ tôḡarmāh*** [proper noun: תּוֹגַרְמָה, תֹּגַרְמָה, בֵּית תּוֹגַרְמָה <8425>; prob. of foreign deriv.] ▶
a. Son of Gomer, grandson of Japheth and great grandson of Noah. Refs.: Gen. 10:3; 1 Chr. 1:6; Ezek. 27:14 (KJV); 38:6 (KJV).
b. This word also designates Beth Togarmah, a territory settled by the descendants of Togarmah. Refs.: NASB, NIV, Ezek. 27:14; 38:6. ¶

TOGETHER – ***yaḥaḏ, yaḥdāw, yaḥdāyw*** [יַחַד, יַחְדָּו, יַחְדָּיו <3162>; from UNITE <3161>] ▶
a. A masculine noun denoting unitedness, community, association. It indicates persons being put into proximity with each other. When *yaḥaḏ* is placed last, it has the meaning of together (1 Sam. 11:11); all together (Is. 27:4); completely. It is used of encountering an enemy and fighting against each other, together (1 Sam. 17:10). It is used with verbs of gathering, as when the Arameans gathered themselves together for battle (2 Sam. 10:15). It is used of time, as when things are done at the same time, together (Is. 42:14). It has an inclusive sense of gathering up many things at once, leaving none out (Ps. 33:15).
b. An adverb meaning to do things all at once, jointly. It is used of action performed or plans and counsels made by a group together. Persons may exalt God's name together (Is. 52:9) or gather together for counsel (Neh. 6:7; Ps. 71:10;

83:5); persons may be forced to do something together, at the same time, e.g., go into exile (Amos 1:15). It is used figuratively of persons agreeing enough to be in harmony (Amos 3:3). It is used to emphasize doing something at the same time as well as together (Ex. 19:8). It may indicate something is like something else, for it is said that both the clean and the unclean "together" may eat it (Deut. 12:22; 15:22; 1 Sam. 30:24). In other words, they may share in it alike, "together." *

TOHU – ***tōḥû*** [masc. proper noun: תֹּחוּ <8459>; from an unused root meaning to depress]: lowly ► **The same as Toah (<8430>).** ¶

TOI – 2 Sam. 8:9, 10 ➔ TOU <8583> b.

TOIL (noun) – [1] ***tᵉ'un*** [masc. noun: תְּאֻן <8383>; from NOTHINGNESS <205>] ►
a. This word indicates an effort. It refers figuratively to work, energy, and attention. God has gone through toil for His people and Jerusalem, yet they rebel still more (Ezek. 24:12).
b. This word indicates a lie. It refers to self-deception, the employment of untruth and irreality with respect to Jerusalem, in this case (Ezek. 24:12). ¶
– [2] Gen. 3:17; 5:29 ➔ PAIN (noun) <6093> [3] Gen. 31:42; etc. ➔ LABOR (noun) <3018> [4] Job 20:18 ➔ FRUIT OF ONE'S TOIL <3022>.

TOIL (noun and verb) – ***'āmêl*** [verbal adj.: עָמֵל <6001>; from LABOR (verb) <5998>] ► **The overall use of the word is to stress the meaninglessness of human efforts; it is also translated to labor.** This form is used exclusively in Ecclesiastes (Eccl. 2:18, 22; 3:9; 4:8; 9:9) and always as a predicate adjective. Toiling under the sun appears to the writer to have no lasting value. One must leave the rewards to those who come afterward (Eccl. 2:18). This working results in nothing more than pain and grief (Eccl. 2:22). See the word *'āmāl*: LABOR (noun) <5999>. Other refs.: Judg. 5:26; Job 3:20; 20:22; Prov. 16:26. ¶

TOIL (verb) – [1] Josh. 7:3; Prov. 23:4; Job 9:29 ➔ WEARY (verb) <3021> [2] Job 20:18 ➔ what one toils for ➔ FRUIT OF ONE'S TOIL <3022>.

TOKEN – [1] ***tōḵen*** [proper noun: תֹּכֶן <8507>; the same as QUOTA <8506> (which is from WEIGH <8505>)]: measure, fixed quantity ► **A town in the territory of Simeon.** Ref.: 1 Chr. 4:32. ¶
– [2] 1 Sam. 17:18 ➔ PLEDGE (noun) <6161>.

TOKHATH – ***towqᵉhaṯ***, ***toqhaṯ*** [masc. proper noun: תּוֹקְהַת, תָּקְהַת <8445>; from the same as OBEDIENCE <3349>]: obedience ► **Father of Shallum who was married with the prophetess Huldah, the same as Tikvah (<8616> a.).** Ref.: 2 Chr. 34:22. ¶

TOLA – ***tôlā'*** [masc. proper noun: תּוֹלָע <8439>; from DEVOUR <3216>]: worm ►
a. The first son of Issachar and head of his clan. Refs.: Gen. 46:13; Num. 26:23; 1 Chr. 7:1, 2.
b. The name of a judge in Israel. He was son of Puah. He was from the city of Shamir in the hill country of Ephraim. He delivered Israel twenty-three years (Judg. 10:1). ¶

TOLAD – ***tôlāḏ*** [proper noun: תּוֹלָד <8434>; from BIRTH (GIVE) <3205>]: posterity, generation ► **A town in the territory of Simeon.** Ref.: 1 Chr. 4:29. ¶

TOLAITE – ***tôlā'iy*** [proper noun: תּוֹלָעִי <8440>; patron. from TOLA <8439>] ► **A descendant of Tola.** Ref.: Num. 26:23. ¶

TOMB – ***gāḏiyš*** [masc. noun: גָּדִישׁ <1430>; from an unused root (meaning to heap up)] ► **This word refers to the tomb or burial mound of an influential but wicked person.** His tomb is guarded after his burial (Job 21:32). The Hebrew word also means stacked grain; see STACKED GRAIN <1430>. ¶

TOMBSTONE – 2 Kgs. 23:17 ➔ MONUMENT <6725>.

TOMORROW – ***māḥār*** [masc. noun: מָחָר <4279>; prob. from STAY <309> (in the sense of to delay)] ▶ **This word refers to the immediate next day; it also means later, in the future.** Refs.: Gen. 30:33; Ex. 8:10, 29; Josh. 11:6; 1 Sam. 20:5; 1 Kgs. 19:2. It expands to have the broader sense of in time to come, the future (Ex. 13:14; Deut. 6:20; Josh. 4:6, 21). *

TONGS – [1] Ex. 25:38; 37:23; Num. 4:9; 1 Kgs. 7:49; 2 Chr. 4:21; Is. 6:6 ➔ WICK TRIMMER <4457> [2] Is. 44:12 ➔ CUTTING TOOL <4621>.

TONGUE – [1] ***lāšôn, lāšōn*** [common noun: לָשׁוֹן, לָשֹׁן <3956>; from SLANDER <3960>] ▶ **This word means the small, flexible organ in the mouth that is used to speak; it also means language. It is used literally as a part of a person or animal.** Of a person (Ex. 4:10; Lam. 4:4); of a dog (Ex. 11:7); metaphorically of the tongue of the Lord as a consuming fire (Is. 30:27). The tongue is the instrument of speech (2 Sam. 23:2). Being heavy of tongue meant to speak poorly (Ex. 4:10). A slanderer is a man of a tongue (Ps. 140:11). The phrase *ba'al hallāšôn* referred to a charmer (Eccl. 10:11) of snakes. The same word means language (Gen. 10:5; Neh. 13:24). The tongue is a source of flattery, smooth talk (Ps. 5:9); falsehood (Ps. 78:36); a lying tongue (Ps. 109:2; Prov. 6:17; 12:19; 21:6; 26:28). But the righteous use their tongues to praise the Lord (Ps. 51:14). In figurative language, the tongue is pictured in various ways: a bar of gold (Josh. 7:21); a tongue of fire (Is. 5:24); a bay along the seashore (Josh. 15:5; Is. 11:15). *
– [2] Job 12:11 ➔ MOUTH <2441> [3] Dan. 3:29 ➔ LANGUAGE <3961>.

TOOL – [1] Gen. 4:22 ➔ CRAFTSMAN <2794> [2] Ex. 32:4 ➔ tool, engraving tool, graving tool ➔ GRAVING TOOL <2747> [3] Deut. 23:13 ➔ EQUIPMENT <240> [4] Job 19:24; Jer. 17:1 ➔ PEN <5842>.

TOOL (CUTTING) – See SWORD <2719>.

TOOTH – [1] ***šēn***] [common noun: שֵׁן <8127>; from SHARPEN <8150>] ▶ **This word means one of the hard white structures in the mouth which is used to bite and chew; it also means ivory, a fang, a sharp projecting rock.** It refers to a person's teeth (Gen. 49:12; Ex. 21:24; Lev. 24:20); animal teeth (Deut. 32:24; Job 41:14; Joel 1:6); ivory tusks (1 Kgs. 10:18; Ezek. 27:15); the prong of a metal fork (1 Sam. 2:13). It is used figuratively of a jagged cliff or rock (1 Sam. 14:4). The famous *lex talionis* law, eye for eye, tooth for tooth is found in Exodus 21:24. This law limits the penalty in a case at law. *
[2] ***šēn***] [Aramaic masc. noun: שֵׁן <8128>; corresponding to <8127> above] ▶ **See previous definition (<8127>).** This word describes the teeth mentioned in Daniel's vision of four great beasts, especially the great iron teeth of the fourth beast (Dan. 7:5, 7, 19). ¶

TOP – [1] ***ṣammereṯ*** [fem. noun: צַמֶּרֶת <6788>; from the same as WOOL <6785>] ▶ **This word refers to the highest branch, the treetop.** It is used in a long parable from Ezekiel to refer to various nations, e.g., Judah (Ezek. 17:3, 22) or a part of the Davidic line. It indicates the topmost branches of a tree, its top, in referring to Assyria (Ezek. 31:3, 10, 14). ¶
[2] ***rō'šāh*** [fem. noun: רֹאשָׁה <7222>; fem. of HEAD (noun) <7218>] ▶ **This word means head, chief, and it is used in word or expression such as top stone, capstone, headstone.** It occurs only in Zechariah 4:7 where it describes a stone. The adjective sometimes indicates that the stone is the cornerstone, the first stone laid (see *rō'š* [HEAD <7218>]). However, it often refers to the top stone as being at a prominent place on the Temple structure (cf. Matt. 4:5), like the head is atop the body. The latter makes better sense in context because the foundation was already laid at the time of the prophecies that use this word (cf. Ezra 5; Zech. 1:1; 4:9). The stone may be the same stone mentioned in Zechariah 3:9 and 4:10, which is clearly a symbol of Christ (cf. Zech. 4:10; Rev. 5:6). It would make sense

for Jesus, the Alpha and the Omega (Rev. 1:8), to be both the first stone (cf. Is. 28:16; 1 Pet. 2:4–8) and the last stone laid in the Temple. ¶
– [3] Judg. 15:8, 11; Is. 2:21 ➔ CLEFT <5585> [4] 2 Kgs. 9:13 ➔ BONE <1634> [5] Prov. 9:3 ➔ HIGHEST <1610> [6] Ezek. 24:7, 8; 26:4, 14 ➔ BARE <6706> [7] See ROOF (noun) <1406>.

TOP OF THE PILLAR – Amos 9:1; Zeph. 2:14 ➔ BULB <3730>.

TOPAZ – [1] ***piṭdāh*** [fem. noun: פִּטְדָה <6357>; of foreign deriv.] ▶ **This word depicts a precious stone. The stone indicated is a light-colored or colorless stone used for beauty and splendor.** Refs.: Ex. 28:17; 39:10; Job 28:19; Ezek. 28:13. Ethiopia was famous for its topaz stones. They were found in the Garden of Eden (Ezek. 28:13). ¶
– [2] Ex. 28:20; 39:13; Song 5:14; Ezek. 1:16; 10:9; 28:13; Dan. 10:6 ➔ BERYL <8658> a.

TOPHEL – ***tōp̱el*** [proper noun: תֹּפֶל <8603>; from the same as FOOLISH <8602> a.]: tasteless, dry ▶ **A place in the desert through which the Israelites traveled on their way to Canaan.** Ref.: Deut. 1:1. ¶

TOPHET – ***top̱teh*** [proper noun: תָּפְתֶּה <8613>; prob. a form of <8612>]: a place to burn ▶ **Same place as Topheth <8612>.** Ref.: Is. 30:33. ¶

TOPHETH – ***tōp̱eṯ*** [proper noun: תֹּפֶת <8612>; the same as SPIT (noun) <8611>] (in the sense of a smiting): a place to burn ▶ **A place in the valley of Hinnom where children were sacrificed to the Ammonite god Molech.** Refs.: 2 Kgs. 23:10; Jer. 7:31, 32; 19:6, 11–14. ¶

TOPMOST BRANCHES – Is. 17:6, 9 ➔ BOUGH <534>.

TOPPLE – Jer. 10:4 ➔ STUMBLE <6328>.

TORCH – [1] ***lappiyḏ*** [masc. noun: לַפִּיד <3940>; from an unused root prob. meaning to shine] ▶ **This word means a burning stick, a source of light; it is also translated lamp (KJV).** It is used mainly of a fiery light (Gen. 15:17; Judg. 7:16, 20; 15:4, 5) but also depicts bright flashes of lightning (Ex. 20:18; Nah. 2:4). It is used figuratively of Judah's conquering clans (Zech. 12:6); and the eyes of a divine being (Dan. 10:6). Flames of fire may be called torches (Ezek. 1:13). Jerusalem's salvation will be seen like a flaming torch (Is. 62:1). Leviathan's mouth shoots forth burning torches (Job 41:19; also translated burning lamps, burning lights, flames, flaming torches). Other ref.: Job 12:5. ¶
– [2] Is. 50:11 ➔ FIREBRAND <2131> a. [3] Nah. 2:3 ➔ STEEL <6393> b.

TORMENT (noun) – ***maʿᵃṣēḇāh*** [fem. noun: מַעֲצֵבָה <4620>; from HURT <6087> (in the sense of to pain, to grieve)] ▶ **This word indicates a place of punishment, in context for those who attack God's servants; it is also translated sorrow.** Ref.: Is. 50:11. ¶

TORMENT (verb) – [1] 1 Sam. 16:14, 15 ➔ TROUBLE (verb) <1204> [2] Job 19:2 ➔ AFFLICT <3013>.

TORMENTATOR – Is. 51:23 ➔ AFFLICT <3013>.

TORMENTED (BE) – 2 Sam. 13:2 ➔ DISTRESSED (BE) <3334>.

TORMENTOR – ***tôlāl*** [masc. proper noun: תּוֹלָל <8437>; from WAIL <3213> (also translated to howl)] ▶ **This word refers to a person who willfully brings about pain, dread, fear in another person, psychological or physical.** Ref.: Ps. 137:3; also translated one who plunders, one who wastes. ¶

TORN (BE) – Is. 5:25 ➔ REFUSE <5478>.

TORN (WHAT IS) – ***ṭᵉrēp̱āh*** [fem. noun: טְרֵפָה <2966>; fem. (collectively) of PREY <2964>] ▶ **This word is often used of animal flesh pulled apart by wild beasts.** Refs.: Gen. 31:39; Ex. 22:13, 31. Torn flesh was not to be eaten by Israel; it was unclean and forbidden (Lev. 7:24; 17:15; 22:8; Ezek. 4:14; 44:31). It is used to describe the nations that served as prey to the lion, the king of Nineveh (Nah. 2:12: ravin, flesh, torn flesh, prey). ¶

TORN FLESH – Nah. 2:12 → TORN (WHAT IS) <2966>.

TORRENT – [1] ***sāpiyaḥ*** [masc. noun: סָפִיחַ <5599>; from JOIN <5596>] ▶ **This word refers to a powerful, fast stream of water.** It is used of God's power to remove the aspirations of people (Job 14:19) if He so desires. The Hebrew word also means an aftergrowth; see GROWS OF ITSELF (WHAT) <5599>. ¶
– [2] Prov. 27:4 → FLOOD <7858> [3] Hab. 3:10 → STORM (noun) <2230>.

TORRENTS OF RAIN – Job 38:25 → FLOOD <7858>.

TORTOISE – Lev. 11:29 → COVERED <6632> d.

TORTUOUS (BE) – 2 Sam. 22:27; Ps. 18:26 → WRESTLE <6617>.

TOSS (noun) – ***ṣᵉnēpāh*** [verb: צְנֵפָה <6802>; from WEAR <6801>] ▶
a. This word indicates to throw. It refers to the action of rolling a ball or throwing it. Used figuratively, it indicates the exiling of a person in a distant land (Is. 22:18). ¶
b. This word indicates to roll tightly. It is used figuratively to express even more emphatically the way the Lord will indeed roll Shebna into a ball tightly and cast him out (Is. 22:18: to cast, to throw). ¶

TOSS (verb) – [1] Job 16:11 → TURN OVER <3399> [2] Job 30:22 → MELT AWAY <4127> [3] Jer. 5:22 → SHAKE <1607>.

TOSS UP AND DOWN – Ps. 109:23 → SHAKE <5287>.

TOSSED TO AND FRO – Prov. 21:6 → DRIVE AWAY <5086>.

TOSSING – [1] ***nᵉḏuḏiym*** [masc. plur. noun: נְדֻדִים <5076>; pass. part. of FLEE <5074>] ▶ **This word refers to turning back and forth in bed, turning this way and that.** Ref.: Job 7:4; also translated tossing to and fro, to toss and turn. ¶
– [2] Ps. 56:8 → WANDERING <5112>.

TOTTER – [1] Ps. 75:3 → MELT AWAY <4127> [2] Is. 24:20 → FLEE <5110> [3] Is. 28:7; Jer. 10:4 → STUMBLE <6328>.

TOTTERING – Ps. 62:3 → DRIVE <1760>.

TOU – ***tō'û, tō'iy*** [masc. proper noun: תֹּעוּ, תֹּעִי <8583>; from WANDER <8582>]: error ▶
a. King of Hamath during David's time, the same as b. Refs.: 1 Chr. 18:9, 10.
b. A noun designating Toi, the same as a. Refs.: 2 Sam. 8:9, 10. ¶

TOUCH – [1] ***nāga'*** [verb: נָגַע <5060>; a prim. root] ▶ **The verb means to reach, to strike. The basic import of this verb is physical contact of one person with another. Since interpersonal contact can come in one (or more) of many varieties, this verb carries a range of semantic possibilities.** Its use could represent mere physical contact (Gen. 3:3; 1 Kgs. 6:27; Esther 5:2). On a deeper level, it could designate striking (Job 1:19; Is. 53:4; Ezek. 17:10). Along these lines is the figurative use to identify God's judgment (1 Sam. 6:9; Job 1:11; 19:21). On an even deeper level, it indicates doing actual harm (Gen. 26:11; Josh. 9:19; 2 Sam. 14:10). In a metaphorical sense, this verb can also portray the concept to reach or extend (Is. 16:8; Jer. 51:9; Jon. 3:6). In the passive form, it denotes the idea to allow oneself to be beaten in a military context (Josh. 8:15). In the intensive form, this verb means to afflict or to be afflicted (Gen. 12:17; 2 Kgs. 15:5; Ps. 73:5). *
– [2] Gen. 27:12, 22 → FEEL <4959> [3] Gen. 27:21 → FEEL <4184> [4] 2 Chr. 3:12 → JOINING <1695>.

TOUGHNESS – Dan. 2:41 → STRENGTH <5326>.

TOW – [1] ***nᵉʿōreṯ*** [fem. noun: נְעֹרֶת <5296>; from SHAKE <5287> (in the sense of something shaken out)] ▶ **Tow is a weak "rope" of coarse and broken fibers from flax, hemp, or similar material. This word is also translated string, yarn, flax; tinder.** String is a weak fastener compared to a regular rope or cord and is easily snapped (Judg. 16:9: tow, yard, flax, string). Tow or string could be used to start a fire (Judg. 16:9; Is. 1:31).
– [2] Is. 43:17 ➔ FLAX <6594>.

TOWARD – ***neḡeḏ*** [Aramaic prep.: נֶגֶד <5049>; corresponding to BEFORE <5048>] ▶ **This preposition indicates a direction, e.g., westward, toward Jerusalem, from Babylon.** Ref.: Dan. 6:10. ¶

TOWER – [1] ***migdôl, migdōl*** [מִגְדּוֹל, מִגְדֹּל <4024>; prob. of Egyptian origin] ▶
a. A masculine noun meaning a tall structure attached, or not, to a building. Refs.: 2 Sam. 22:51; Ezek. 29:10; 30:6. ¶
b. A proper noun designating Migdol, a city on the northeast border of Egypt. Refs.: Ex. 14:2; Num. 33:7; Jer. 44:1; 46:14; Ezek. 29:10; 30:6. ¶
[2] ***migdāl*** [masc. noun: מִגְדָּל <4026>; from GREAT (BECOME) <1431>] ▶ **This word refers to various kinds of tall structures.** The Tower of Babel (Gen. 11:4); a watchtower in a vineyard (Is. 5:2); a tower built into a wall (2 Chr. 14:7); storage structures (1 Chr. 27:25); central defense towers in the centers of cities (Judg. 9:51, 52). In Nehemiah 8:4, the word refers to a structure for someone to stand on in order to address a crowd. It is used figuratively of God as a tower of refuge (Ps. 61:3; Prov. 18:10); and of the breasts of the beloved in Song of Solomon 8:10. An ivory tower is mentioned (Song 7:4); as are several towers in specific locations (Judg. 8:17; 9:46, 47, 49; Neh. 3:1, 11; Song 4:4; 7:4; Jer. 31:38; Zech. 14:10). *
[3] ***muṣṣāḇ*** [masc. noun: מֻצָּב <4674>; from STAND <5324>] ▶ **This word means siege work.** It is used of a military engine used against cities (Is. 29:3; also translated mound, mount) but also of a specific structural location, possibly a column, pillar, or military structure (Judg. 9:6). ¶
– [4] 2 Kgs. 5:24 ➔ HILL <6076> [5] Song 8:9 ➔ CAMP <2918> [6] Is. 21:5 ➔ RUG <6844> b. [7] Is. 23:13 ➔ SIEGE TOWER <971> [8] Is. 32:14 ➔ WATCHTOWER <975> [9] Jer. 6:27 ➔ ASSAYER <969> [10] Jer. 50:15 ➔ FOUNDATION <803> [11] Lam. 4:17 ➔ WATCHING <6836>.

TOWN – [1] ***ḥawwāh*** [fem. noun: חַוָּה <2333>; properly, the same as EVE <2332> (life-giving, i.e., living-place) ▶ **This word refers to an urban area; it is also translated village, settlement.** It refers to various villages that were taken by Jair, son of Manasseh (Num. 32:41; Josh. 13:30; 1 Kgs. 4:13; 1 Chr. 2:23) in Gilead. ¶
– [2] Prov. 8:3; 9:3, 14 ➔ CITY <7176> [3] See VILLAGE <2691>.

TOWN (UNWALLED, RURAL) – ***pᵉrāzāh*** [fem. noun: פְּרָזָה <6519>; from the same as WARRIOR <6518>] ▶ **This word refers to rural country and the unwalled open villages in its confines.** Refs.: Esther 9:19; Ezek. 38:11; Zech. 2:4. ¶

TRADE – Ezek. 28:5, 16, 18 ➔ MERCHANDISE <7404>.

TRADE (PLY ONE'S) – Jer. 14:18 ➔ MERCHANT <5503>.

TRADE WITH – Zeph. 1:11 ➔ WEIGH OUT <5187>.

TRADER – [1] Gen. 37:28 ➔ MERCHANT <5503> [2] Job 41:6 ➔ COMPANION <2271> [3] Zech. 14:21 ➔ MERCHANT <3669>.

TRADESMAN – Prov. 31:24 ➔ MERCHANT <3669>.

TRADING – [1] Prov. 31:18 ➔ MERCHANDISE <5504> [2] Ezek. 28:5, 16, 18 ➔ MERCHANDISE <7404>.

TRAFFIC – 1 Kgs. 10:15 ➔ WARES <4536>.

TRAFFICK – Ezek. 28:5, 18 ➔ MERCHANDISE <7404>.

TRAIN – Prov. 22:6 ➔ DEDICATE <2596>.

TRAIN, TRAIN OF A ROBE – Is. 6:1 ➔ HEM <7757>.

TRAIN (IN HIS) – Dan. 11:43 ➔ lit.: at his steps ➔ STEP (noun) <4703>.

TRAINED – ***ḥāniyk̲*** [adj.: חָנִיךְ <2593>; from DEDICATE <2596>] ▶ **This word means instructed, skilled.** It designates the men of Abraham's house whom he takes with him to rescue Lot (Gen. 14:14), hence, men trained by him. ¶

TRAITOR – Mic. 2:4 ➔ BACKSLIDING <7728>.

TRAMP – Gen. 49:19 ➔ ATTACK (verb) <1464>.

TRAMPLE – [1] ***bāšas*** [verb: בָּשַׁס <1318>; a prim. root] ▶ **This word means to tread down. It indicates the oppression that the rich and powerful exercised on Israel's poor by treading them down; it is also translated to tread.** Ref.: Amos 5:11. It may mean to effect this abuse literally by levying heavy rent on the poor (NASB). ¶
[2] ***dûš*** [Aramaic verb: דּוּשׁ <1759>; corresponding to THRESH <1758>] ▶ **This word indicates crushing or smashing something by walking on it; it is also translated to tread down.** Daniel's fourth beast will tread down the whole earth (Dan. 7:23). ¶
[3] ***rāmas*** [verb: רָמַס <7429>; a prim. root] ▶ **This word means to trample underfoot, to tread down.** It indicates the trampling of clay by a potter (Is. 41:25), of grapes. It is used figuratively of God's trampling in judgment (Is. 63:3); of trampling God's courts in justice (Is. 1:12); of trampling a person in time of famine (2 Kgs. 7:17, 20); of Jezebel's being trampled by horses (2 Kgs. 9:33). It is used figuratively of trampling a person's soul or life (Ps. 7:5); of God's people stepping on, treading down dangerous serpents (Ps. 91:13). *
[4] ***rāp̄as*** [Aramaic verb: רְפַס <7512>; corresponding to SUBMIT <7511>] ▶ **This word means to stomp on something, to tread on it, to destroy it.** In context it refers to political and military action (Dan. 7:7, 19; KJV: to stamp). ¶
– [5] Job 39:15; Is. 25:10; Hab. 3:12 ➔ THRESH <1758> [6] Ps. 44:5; 60:12; Is. 14:25; 63:18; 63:6; Zech. 10:5 ➔ TREAD DOWN <947> [7] Lam. 3:16 ➔ COWER (MAKE) <3728> [8] Zech. 9:15 ➔ SUBDUE <3533> [9] Mal. 4:3 ➔ TREAD DOWN <6072>.

TRAMPLE ON – Ps. 56:1, 2; 57:3 ➔ LONG FOR <7602> d.

TRAMPLE UNDER FOOT – Lam. 1:15 ➔ REJECT <5541>.

TRAMPLED – Prov. 25:26 ➔ FOUL <7515>.

TRAMPLED, TRAMPLED DOWN – ***mirmās*** [masc. noun: מִרְמָס <4823>; from TRAMPLE <7429>] ▶ **This word refers to a location or something that has been stepped on, destroyed.** A vineyard (Is. 5:5); a field (Is. 7:25; Ezek. 34:19, used figuratively); God's people with acts of judgments on them (Is. 10:6; 28:18; Mic. 7:10). It is used of the holy people of God and His holy place being "trodden down," trampled by pagans (Dan. 8:13). ¶

TRAMPLED (BE) – Hos. 4:14 ➔ RUIN (COME TO) <3831>.

TRAMPLING – Is. 22:5 ➔ TREADING DOWN <4001>.

TRANQUIL – Prov. 14:30 ➔ CALMNESS <4832>.

TRANQUILLITY – [1] Eccl. 4:6 ➔ REST (noun) <5183> [2] Dan. 4:27 ➔ PROSPERITY <7963>.

TRANSCRIBE – Prov. 25:1 ➔ MOVE <6275>.

TRANSGRESS – ***mā'al*** [verb: מָעַל <4603>; a prim. root (prob. to cover up)] ▶ **This word means to violate one's duty. The term is used often as a synonym for sin; however, this word almost always denotes a willful act.** Refs.: Num. 5:6; Ezek. 14:13. It occurs principally in the later books of the Old Testament and is almost exclusively a religious term. There are only two secular uses: one for a wife's unfaithfulness to her husband and the other for a king's unfaithfulness in judgment (Num. 5:12, 27; Prov. 16:10). Although the offense is usually against God Himself, three times the unfaithfulness is directed against something under divine ban and not directly against God (Josh. 22:20; 1 Chr. 10:13; Ezek. 18:24). The writer of 1 and 2 Chronicles often connected national unfaithfulness with God's sending of punitive wars; ultimately, the outcome meant deportation for the Northern Kingdom and destruction and exile for the Southern Kingdom (1 Chr. 5:25; 2 Chr. 12:2; 28:19, 22; 36:14). *

TRANSGRESSION – 1 ***ma'al*** [masc. noun: מַעַל <4604>; from TRANSGRESS <4603>] ▶ **This word means an unfaithful act, a treacherous act. Of its twenty-nine occurrences, it appears twenty times as a cognate accusative to the verb *mā'al* (TRANSGRESS <4603>), meaning to act unfaithfully or treacherously.** It can apply to actions against another person, such as a wife against her husband (Num. 5:12, 27); Job by his "comforters" (Job 21:34). However, it usually applies to actions against God, whether those actions be committed by an individual (Lev. 5:15; 6:2; Josh. 7:1; 22:20); or by the nation of Israel collectively (Josh. 22:22; 1 Chr. 9:1; Ezra 9:2, 4; 10:6; Ezek. 39:26). *

2 ***paš*** [masc. noun: פַּשׁ <6580>; from an unused root meaning to disintegrate] ▶ **This word conveys a strong sense of rebellion. It refers to sin or rebellion against God. It is also translated folly, wickedness.** Many consider the word to be a misspelled form of *peša'*, rebellion, revolt, which is, of course, in a broader sense, transgression (Job 35:15). ¶

3 ***peša'*** [masc. noun: פֶּשַׁע <6588>; from REBEL (verb) <6586>] ▶ **This word means rebellion, revolt.** Though it can be a transgression of one individual against another (Gen. 31:36; 50:17; Ex. 22:9); or of one nation against another (Amos 1:3, 6, 9, 11, 13; 2:1); this word primarily expresses a rebellion against God and His laws (Is. 58:1; 59:12; Amos 5:12). Since it is possible for humanity to recognize this transgression (Ps. 32:5; 51:3), God's first step in dealing with it is to reveal it and call His people to accountability (Job 36:9; Mic. 3:8). He then punishes the guilty (Is. 53:5, 8; Amos 2:4, 6) in the hope of restoring the relationship and forgiving the transgressors who repent (Ezek. 18:30, 31). In addition to the act of transgression itself, this term can also be used to convey the guilt that comes from the transgression (Job 33:9; 34:6; Ps. 59:3); the punishment for the transgression (Dan. 8:12, 13; 9:24); or the offering that is presented to atone for the transgression (Mic. 6:7). *

– 4 Hos. 10:10 ➔ MARITAL RIGHTS <5772> b.

TRANSIENT – Ps. 39:4 ➔ REJECTED <2310>.

TRANSLATE – ***tirgam*** [verb: תִּרְגַּם <8638>; a denom. from STONE (verb) <7275> in the sense of throwing over] ▶ **This word describes rendering one language into another or giving the sense of a written or oral communication.** Ref.: Ezra 4:7; KJV: to interpret. ¶

TRANSPORTER – 1 Kgs. 5:15 ➔ BURDEN-BEARER <5449>.

TRAP – 1 ***māzôr*** [masc. noun: מָזוֹר <4204>; from STRANGER (BE) <2114> in the sense of turning aside from truth] ▶ **This word indicates some kind of ambush or ruse prepared to take someone unawares.** Ref.: Obad. 1:7; KJV: wound. Some suggest a net in a figurative sense. ¶

2 ***malkōdeṯ*** [fem. noun: מַלְכֹּדֶת <4434>; from CAPTURE <3920>] ▶ **This word means a snare, a noose.** It is found only in

Job 18:10. In his disputation with Job, Bildad the Shuhite used the word to describe the pitfalls that lay before the wicked. ¶
– 3 Prov. 20:25 ➔ SNARE (noun) <4170> 4 Prov. 28:10 ➔ PIT <7816> 5 Eccl. 7:26 ➔ NET <2764> 6 Eccl. 7:26 ➔ NET <4685> 7 Jer. 9:8 ➔ AMBUSH <696> 8 Lam. 4:20 ➔ PIT <7825>.

TRAPPED (BE) – ***pāḥaḥ*** [verb: פָּחַח <6351>; a prim. root] ▶ **This word refers to being confined, to be held captive by circumstances; it is also translated to be snared.** In its immediate context, Israel became ensnared as a result of her own blindness (Is. 42:22). *

TRAPPER – Ps. 91:3 ➔ FOWLER <3353>.

TRAPS (SET) – Ps. 38:12 ➔ ENSNARE <5367>.

TRAVAIL (noun) – 1 Ex. 18:8; Num. 20:14; Lam. 3:5 ➔ HARDSHIP <8513> 2 Eccl. 1:13; 2:23, 26; 3:10; 4:8; 5:14 ➔ TASK <6045>.

TRAVAIL (verb) – Jer. 13:21 ➔ BIRTH (GIVE) <3205> b.

TRAVEL – 1 ***'āraḥ*** [verb: אָרַח <732>; a prim. root] ▶ **This word means to go from place to place.** Figuratively, it refers to sharing or agreeing with another person, good or bad (Job 34:8). The participle of the verb refers to a traveler or wanderer (Judg. 19:17; 2 Sam. 12:4); it is also translated wayfaring man, wayfarer, guest. A wanderer or wayfarer in the desert was a common sight (Jer. 9:2). It refers to the seemingly temporary stay of the Lord with Israel during a time of judgment (Jer. 14:8). ¶
– 2 Is. 63:1 ➔ MARCH (verb) <6808> 3 Ezek. 27:25 ➔ JOURNEY (verb) <7788>.

TRAVELER – 1 Judg. 19:17; 2 Sam. 12:4; Jer. 9:2; 14:8 ➔ TRAVEL <732> 2 2 Sam. 12:4 ➔ DRIP (noun) <1982>.

TRAVERSE – ***śāraḵ*** [verb: שָׂרַךְ <8308>; a prim. root] ▶ **This word means to crisscross; it is also translated to entangle, to break loose, to run.** It refers to Israel, using the figure of a camel, entangling herself with the nations (Jer. 2:23). ¶

TREACHEROUS – 1 ***bōg^eḏôṯ*** [fem. plur. noun: בֹּגְדוֹת <900>; fem. plur. act. part. of TREACHEROUSNESS <899>] ▶ **This word depicts deceitfulness, faithlessness.** It describes prophets of Israel who deal treacherously (Zeph. 3:4). ¶
2 ***bāḡôḏ*** [adj.: בָּגוֹד <901>; from DECEITFULLY (DEAL) <898>] ▶ **This word means perfidious; it is also translated unfaithful.** It describes Judah's attitude and actions, even after she sees Israel's rebellious actions (Jer. 3:7, 10). It contains the idea of false pretense. ¶

TREACHEROUSLY – Jer. 3:20; Mal. 2:14; etc.: to depart, to deal, to act treacherously ➔ DECEITFULLY (DEAL) <898>.

TREACHEROUSNESS – ***beḡeḏ*** [masc. noun: בֶּגֶד <899>; from DECEITFULLY (DEAL) <898>] ▶ **This word means deceit, fraud. It is accompanied by the verb *bāḡaḏ*, to deal falsely, deceitfully for emphasis.** Refs.: Is. 24:16; Jer. 12:1. It describes the way of the wicked who deal in deceit or treachery. The Hebrew word also describes clothing or garment; see GARMENT <899>. ¶

TREAD – 1 ***dāraḵ*** [verb: דָּרַךְ <1869>; a prim. root] ▶ **This verb refers to walking on, over, or along or to pressing something with one's feet, trampling. It also takes on the sense of subduing something or someone or simply going forth.** Its main usages can be: a star or person may go forth, march forth (Num. 24:17; Judg. 5:21); to tread on land or one's enemy (Deut. 1:36; 11:25; Judg. 20:43; Job 28:8); a path, meaning life itself (Is. 59:8); to defeat enemies by treading on them (Deut. 33:29); the march or assault of an enemy (1 Sam. 5:5; Ps. 11:2; 37:14; 91:13; Mic. 1:3). It is used to indicate treading wine or oil presses (Neh. 13:15; Job 24:11; Mic. 6:15) and figuratively to depict the

Lord treading the winepress of judgment (Is. 63:3). In its extended meaning, it indicates directing or bending a bow (Jer. 51:3; Zech. 9:13). It refers to the spiritual walk in high places made possible by the Lord (Hab. 3:19). *
– [2] Deut. 25:4; Is. 25:10; Hos. 10:11 ➔ THRESH <1758> [3] Dan. 7:23 ➔ TRAMPLE <1759> [4] Amos 5:11 ➔ TRAMPLE <1318>.

TREAD DOWN – [1] ***bûs*** [verb: בּוּס <947>; a prim. root] ▶ **This word signifies to trample underfoot.** This term generally has a negative connotation, implying a destructive action (Zech. 10:5). God is often the subject of this verb, when He states that He will trample His enemies (Ps. 60:12; Is. 14:25; 63:6). It can also be used with people as the subject but with the understanding that they are only God's instruments (Ps. 44:5). This expression can also have a figurative meaning: to reject (Prov. 27:7: to loathe) and to desecrate (Is. 63:18). *
[2] ***hāḏaḵ*** [verb: הָדַךְ <1915>; a prim. root (comp. BEAT <1854>)] ▶ **This word means to crush, to trample.** It describes the crushing or subduing of the wicked, rendering them justice (Job 40:12). ¶
[3] ***ʿāsas*** [verb: עָסַס <6072>; a prim. root] ▶ **This word means to step on over and over, to flatten out, to mash into the ground; it is also translated to trample.** In context it is used figuratively of treading down the wicked (Mal. 4:3). ¶
– [4] Zech. 9:15 ➔ SUBDUE <3533>.

TREAD DOWN, TREAD UNDER FOOT – Ps. 119:118; Lam. 1:15 ➔ REJECT <5541>.

TREADING DOWN – ***m^{e}ḇûsāh*** [fem. noun: מְבוּסָה <4001>; from TREAD DOWN <947>] ▶ **This word indicates subjugation, downtreading; it is also translated trodden under foot, oppressive, conquering, aggressive, trampling.** It is applied to the people of Ethiopia (Is. 18:2, 7). It describes oppressive trampling activities creating violence and confusion on the Day of the Lord (Is. 22:5), according to Isaiah's vision about the Valley of Vision. ¶

TREASURE – [1] ***g^{e}nāziym*** [masc. plur. noun: גְּנָזִים <1595>; from an unused root meaning to store] ▶ **This word refers to the royal treasury or coffers of King Artaxerxes.** Refs.: Esther 3:9; 4:7. Its meaning in Ezekiel 27:24 is not certain, since it could mean rugs or carpets (NASB, NIV, ESV) or possibly chests (NKJV, KJV). ¶
[2] ***g^{e}naz*** [Aramaic masc. noun: גְּנַז <1596>; corresponding to <1595> above] ▶ **This word indicates treasury, archives.** Used in the plural, it refers to treasure house (Ezra 5:17; 7:20). It refers to the objects or treasures themselves (Ezra 6:1; also translated documents). ¶
[3] ***ḥōsen*** [masc. noun: חֹסֶן <2633>; from HOARDED (BE) <2630>] ▶ **This word indicates riches, strength, wealth.** It refers to individual wealth (Prov. 15:6: treasure, wealth; 27:24: riches) taken honestly or by violence (Ezek. 22:25: treasure). Collectively, it indicates the wealth of an entire city (Jer. 20:5: strength, wealth). The Lord is called the wealth of salvation (Is. 33:6: abundance, rich store, strength, wealth). ¶
[4] ***maṭmôn, maṭmun*** [masc. noun: מַטְמוֹן, מַטְמֻן <4301>; from HIDE <2934>] ▶ **This word indicates hidden treasure, riches.** It refers to valuables, such as silver coins kept in a sack (Gen. 43:23); or hidden in a field (Jer. 41:8; also translated store). It is used in a metaphor for death (Job 3:21). Wisdom is to be sought out even more than hidden treasure (Prov. 2:4). Cyrus was awarded hidden riches and wealth to show him that the Lord had called him (Is. 45:3). ¶
[5] ***miḵmān*** [masc. noun: מִכְמָן <4362>; from the same as CUMIN <3646> in the sense of hiding (the root means to store up or preserve)] ▶ **This word refers to something stored for safekeeping and hidden from common knowledge; it is also translated hidden treasure.** In context it denoted a treasure of gold and silver in Egypt (Dan. 11:43). ¶
[6] ***n^{e}ḵōṯ*** [masc. noun: נְכֹת <5238>; prob. for SPICE <5219> (in the sense of valuables,

precious things)] ▶ **This word refers to precious possessions, goods; KJV translates precious things.** It is used of any material wealth that a person possesses, especially a king (2 Kgs. 20:13; Is. 39:2); a king's treasure house. ¶

7 *'āṯûḏ* [adj.: עָתוּד <6259>; pass. part. of READY (BE) <6257> (in the sense of something prepared for a purpose)] ▶ **The Hebrew word means treasured.** It is used as a noun to refer to the treasures, supplies, and goods of nations and peoples (Is. 10:13; NKJV: treasury). ¶

8 *śāp̄an* [verb: שָׂפַן <8226>; a prim. root] ▶ **This word means to cover as a treasure.** It is used to describe valuable wealth, minerals, metals, etc., in the land of Israel dug from the sand in the territory of Zebulun (Deut. 33:19). ¶

– 9 Ex. 1:11 ➔ STORAGE <4543> 10 Deut. 28:12; Neh. 12:44; 1 Kgs. 7:51; Jer. 10:13; 15:13 ➔ STOREHOUSE <214> 11 Is. 10:13 ➔ READY <6264> c. 12 Lam. 1:7, 11 ➔ PLEASANT THING <4262> 13 Nah. 2:9 ➔ ARRANGEMENT <8498> a.

TREASURE (PECULIAR, SPECIAL) – Ex. 19:5; Deut. 7:6; 14:2; 26:18; Ps. 135:4; Mal. 3:17 ➔ TREASURED POSSESSION <5459>.

TREASURE, HIDDEN TREASURE – *ṣāp̄iyn* [adj.: צָפִין <6840>; from HIDE <6845>] ▶ **This word refers to something hidden.** In context something of significant worth is in mind, satisfying those who live for this life (Ps. 17:14). ¶

TREASURED (BE) – Is. 23:18 ➔ STORE (verb) <686>.

TREASURED POSSESSION – *s^eg̱ullāh* [fem. noun: סְגֻלָּה <5459>; fem. pass. part. of an unused root meaning to shut up (in the sense of something being closely shut up)] ▶ **This word means something owned personally, a special possession, property; it is also translated peculiar treasure, special treasure.** This noun is used only eight times, but it gives one of the most memorable depictions of the Lord's relationship to His people and the place established for them.

The primary meaning of the word theologically is its designation "unique possession." God has made Israel His own unique possession (Ex. 19:5). Israel holds a special position among the nations of the world, although all nations belong to the Lord. Israel's position, function, character, responsibility, and calling create its uniqueness (Deut. 7:6; 14:2; 26:18; Ps. 135:4). Israel is to be a priestly community that honors and fears the Lord, to be His alone (Mal. 3:17). In the New Testament, 1 Peter 2:9 quotes Exodus 19:5, applying it to the church.

The word is used in a secular sense to indicate personal possessions, such as when David gave his own gold and silver to the Lord (1 Chr. 29:3; Eccl. 2:8). ¶

TREASURER – 1 *g^eḏāḇar* [Aramaic masc. noun: גְּדָבַר <1411>; corresponding to <1489> below] ▶ **This is one of the many bureaucratic officials of the royal administrators of Babylon. He was in charge of the monies of the king and the kingdom.** Refs.: Dan. 3:2, 3. ¶

2 *gizbār* [masc. noun: גִּזְבָּר <1489>; of foreign deriv.] ▶ **This word designates a person in charge of the monetary resources and treasures of a king or nation.** Ref.: Ezra 1:8. He was responsible for the numbering, evaluation, safekeeping, and disbursement of these things. ¶

3 *gizbar* [Aramaic masc. noun: גִּזְבַּר <1490>; corresponding to <1489> above] ▶ **This word indicates a person in charge of the monetary resources and treasures of a king or a nation.** Ref.: Ezra 7:21. He was responsible for the safekeeping and dispensing of these things. ¶

– 4 2 Kgs. 12:5, 7 ➔ ACQUAINTANCE <4378>.

TREASURY – 1 *ganzaḵ* [masc. noun: גַּנְזַךְ <1597>; prolonged from TREASURE <1595>] ▶ **This word refers in the plural form to the storehouses of Solomon's Temple as prescribed in the building plans.** Ref.: 1 Chr. 28:11; also translated storeroom, storehouse. ¶

– 2 Deut. 28:12; 1 Kgs. 7:51; Neh. 13:12, 13; Jer. 10:13 ➔ STOREHOUSE <214> 3 Ezra 4:13 ➔ REVENUE <674> 4 Ezra 6:1; 7:20 ➔ TREASURE <1596> 5 Ezra 6:8 ➔ GOODS <5232> 6 Is. 10:13 ➔ READY <6264> c. 7 Is. 10:13 ➔ TREASURE <6259>.

TREAT BRUTALLY – Deut. 21:14 ➔ SLAVE (TREAT AS A) <6014>.

TREE – 1 ***'iylān*** [Aramaic masc. noun: אִילָן <363>; corresponding to MIGHTY, OAK <352>] ▶ **This word refers to the huge, powerful tree depicted in Daniel.** Refs.: Dan. 4:10, 11, 14, 20, 23, 26. It symbolizes the kingdom of Babylon and its king and God's provision for the whole earth. ¶
2 ***'ēṣ*** [masc. noun: עֵץ <6086>; from a verb meaning to make firm, see WINK <6095>] ▶ **This Hebrew word refers to a tree itself and also to wood, timber, a stick, a plank.** It refers to trees of all kinds (Gen. 1:11; Ps. 104:16); garden trees (Gen. 2:9, 16); special trees used figuratively (Gen. 2:17; 3:22, 24; Prov. 3:18; 11:30; 13:12; 15:4); a specific kind of tree, olive tree (1 Kgs. 6:23, 31, 33; Hab. 2:19). The word refers to wood, pieces of wood for various purposes (2 Kgs. 12:12); concerning specific kinds of wood, gopher wood (Gen. 6:14; Ex. 25:5, 10); articles made of wood (Ex. 7:19); timbers in a building or house (1 Kgs. 15:22; Hab. 2:11; Zech. 5:4). It refers to a tree or pole on which a slain person was hanged (Gen. 40:19; Deut. 21:22, 23; Josh. 8:29; 10:26); also to a wooden gallows (Esther 2:23). It is used of firewood (Gen. 22:3). *

TREE (GREAT) – Gen. 12:6; 13:18; 14:13; 18:1; Deut. 11:30; Judg. 4:11; 9:6, 37; 1 Sam. 10:3 ➔ OAK <436>.

TREE (LARGE) – Josh. 19:33 ➔ OAK <437>.

TREES – ***'ēṣāh*** [fem. coll. noun: עֵצָה <6097>; from TREE <6086>] ▶ **This word refers to trees surrounding Jerusalem that were to be destroyed by a siege.** Ref.: Jer. 6:6. ¶

TREMBLE – 1 ***zûa'*** [verb: זוּעַ <2111>; a prim. root] ▶ **This word means to quiver, to be nervous.** Haman was angry when Mordecai did not tremble at his sight (Esther 5:9; also translated to show fear, to move for). This word is also used to describe an old man (Eccl. 12:3). In Habakkuk, it occurs in a causative sense, meaning to cause to tremble. This verse refers to the debtors of Israel (used figuratively for Babylon) who would make Israel tremble with fear (Hab. 2:7). See the related Aramaic verb *zû'a* (<2112> below). ¶
2 ***zûa'*** [Aramaic verb: זוּעַ <2112>; corresponding to <2111> above] ▶ **This word is used to describe the quivering fear of the people before the mighty Nebuchadnezzar.** Ref.: Dan. 5:19. In Daniel 6:26, it describes the same trembling fear that people ought to have before the God of Daniel. In both instances, it is used synonymously with another Aramaic word meaning to fear, *deḥal* [FEAR (verb) <1763>]. ¶
3 ***ḥārad*** [verb: חָרַד <2729>; a prim. root] ▶ **This word means to quake, to be terrified.** The term is used in reference to mountains (Ex. 19:18); islands (Is. 41:5); birds and beasts (Jer. 7:33); and people (Ezek. 32:10). It can mark a disturbance, such as being startled from sleep (Ruth 3:8); or terror brought on by a trumpet's sound (Amos 3:6); or an act of God (1 Sam. 14:15). It is often connected with terrifying an enemy in battle. It is also used in the causative, meaning to terrify (Judg. 8:12; 2 Sam. 17:2; Zech. 1:21). See the word *ḥarādāh* (TREMBLING <2731>). *
4 ***'āraṣ*** [verb: עָרַץ <6206>; a prim. root] ▶ **This word means to cause to tremble, to strike with awe, to strike with dread.** The Lord's splendor can make the earth tremble (Is. 2:19, 21). Job wondered why God must overwhelm humans who are nothing more than driven leaves (Job 13:25). God and His leaders continually reminded the Israelites before battle not to be terrified by the enemy because God would fight for them (Deut. 1:29; 7:2120:3; 31:6; Josh. 1:9). If God is with us, we have no need to dread humans and their conspiracies and plots (Is. 8:12: to be afraid, to dread, to be in dread, to be troubled). *

5 ***yāraʻ*** [verb: יָרַע <3415>; a prim. root] ▶ **This word occurs only in Isaiah 15:4; it is also translated to be burdensome, to be grievous, to be faint.** As the result of the sudden devastation of Moab, his (i.e., Moab's or possibly an individual soldier's) life (or soul) trembles. The sentence could refer to inner turmoil: his soul trembles within him; or it could refer to an objective sense that his prospects of surviving are shaky; his life trembles before him (cf. Deut. 28:66). Of course, both meanings could be true; both could even be implied. ¶

6 ***rûp̱, rāp̱ap̱*** [verb: רוּף, רָפַף <7322>; a prim. root] ▶

a. This word describes the shaking, vibrating of the pillars of heaven, a figurative expression. Ref.: Job 26:11; also translated to quake. The root is *rûp̱*.

b. Some translators understand this verbal root to be *rāp̱ap̱* (Job 26:11). It has the same meaning as a. ¶

7 ***rāʻaḏ*** [verb: רָעַד <7460>; a prim. root] ▶ **This word means to quake.** The psalmist uses it in a description of the holiness, majesty, and power of God, where the earth is depicted as trembling at the mere gaze of the Lord. Ref.: Ps. 104:32. Daniel trembled in fear and reverence at the sight and presence of the vision before he heard the words that the messenger had been sent to deliver (Dan. 10:11). Other ref.: Ezra 10:9 (NIV: to be greatly distressed). ¶

– 8 Ex. 20:18 ➔ WANDER <5128> 9 2 Sam. 22:8 ➔ SHAKE <1607> 10 Ps. 119:120 ➔ STAND UP <5568> 11 Is. 64:1, 3 ➔ GLUTTON (BE) <2151> b. 12 Jer. 23:9 ➔ HOVER <7363> 13 Nah. 2:10 ➔ SMITE TOGETHER <6375>.

TREMBLE (MAKE) – Hab. 3:6 ➔ LEAP <5425>.

TREMBLES (WHO) – Ezra 9:4; Is. 66:2 ➔ TREMBLING <2730>.

TREMBLING – 1 ***ḥārēḏ, ḥᵃrōḏ*** [adj.: חָרֵד, חָרֹד <2730>; from TREMBLE <2729>] ▶ **This word means shaking slightly; it also means reverential.** God told Gideon to limit the number of warriors by telling those who were afraid or trembling to return to their camp at Gilead (Judg. 7:3). God honors and looks upon those who are contrite in spirit and tremble at His word (Is. 66:2). Those who tremble at God's words are also accounted as obedient (Ezra 9:4). Other refs.: 1 Sam. 4:13; Ezra 10:3; Is. 62:5. ¶

2 ***ḥᵃrāḏāh*** [fem. noun: חֲרָדָה <2731>; fem. of <2730> above] ▶ **This word means trembling, anxiety, extreme anxiety, anxious care and also quaking, fear. This trembling is often brought on by acts of God.** It is the terror of God that overcame the enemy (1 Sam. 14:15; also translated panic); and startled Daniel's friends (Dan. 10:7; also translated dread, terror, quaking). Humans can also inspire fear (Prov. 29:25). See the cognate verb *ḥāraḏ* (TREMBLE <2729>). Other refs.: Gen. 27:33; 2 Kgs. 4:13; Is. 21:4; Jer. 30:5; Ezek. 26:16. ¶

3 ***pallāṣûṯ*** [fem. noun: פַּלָּצוּת <6427>; from SHAKE <6426>] ▶ **This word describes the physical reaction of the body in response to fear. It is also translated shuddering, horror, fearfulness, fear, terror.** Job shuddered at the fate of the wicked (Job 21:6); David shuddered in fear of his enemy (Ps. 55:5); Isaiah shuddered because of God's judgment (Is. 21:4); and those about to be judged by God will shudder (Ezek. 7:18). See the word *mip̱leṣeṯ* (IMAGE <4656>). ¶

4 ***raggāz*** [adj.: רַגָּז <7268>; intens. from SHAKE <7264>] ▶ **This word means shaking. It describes a fainting heart that is full of uneasiness.** Deuteronomy 28:65 records the sole occurrence of this word. ¶

5 ***rogzāh*** [fem. noun: רָגְזָה <7269>; fem. of TURMOIL <7267>] ▶ **In Ezekiel 12:18, this word is used to imply a shaking or quivering hand.** The suggestion is that of tremendous worry or unsteadiness even during routine activities. ¶

6 ***raʻaḏ, rᵉʻāḏāh*** [masc. noun: רַעַד, רְעָדָה <7461>; from TREMBLE <7460>] ▶ **In the song of Moses and Miriam, the leaders of Moab were described as being seized with trembling before the power of the Lord.** Ref.: Ex. 15:15. In a cry to God, the psalmist uses the word to state that fear and trembling had bent him (Ps.

55:5). He cried out for God to come to his rescue and deliver him from his enemies. Other refs.: Ps. 2:1; 48:6; Is. 33:14. ¶

7 ***r^eṯēṯ*** [masc. noun: רְתֵת <7578>; from PANIC <7374>] ► **This word refers to an emotional response of fear or dread before a powerful person or group.** Ref.: Hos. 13:1. ¶

– 8 Is. 51:17, 22 ➔ STAGGER (THAT MAKES) <8653> 9 Zech. 12:2 ➔ REELING <7478>.

TREMBLING (COME) – ***ḥārag*** [verb: חָרַג <2727>; a prim. root] ► **This verb means to be afraid, to quake, to come quaking. It is also translated to come frightened.** The word occurs only in Psalm 18:45 where foreigners came quaking from their strongholds. The idea of foreigners coming out derives from the word *min* (<4480>), meaning from. However, a similar passage in Micah 7:17 (using a different verb but dependent on *min* for the idea of coming out) justifies the translation "to come quaking." The passage thus pictures foreigners surrendering their strongholds to David and coming out. ¶

TRENCH – 1 ***t^e'ālāh*** [fem. noun: תְּעָלָה <8585>; from OFFER <5927> (in the sense of to raise, to take away)] ► **This word refers to a channel, an aqueduct. It indicates a conduit constructed to convey water or to hold it.** Refs.: 1 Kgs. 18:32, 35, 38. It could deliver water into a pool (2 Kgs. 18:17; Is. 7:3; 36:2). Hezekiah's conduit is the most famous and was hewn out of solid rock (2 Kgs. 20:20). It refers to naturally occurring channels that carry away floodwaters (Job 38:25); or channels connected to rivers (Ezek. 31:4). For another meaning of the Hebrew word, see HEALING <8585>. ¶

– 2 1 Sam. 17:20; 26:5, 7 ➔ ENCAMPMENT <4570> a. 3 2 Kgs. 3:16 ➔ POOL (noun) <1356>.

TRESPASS – 1 Lev. 6:5; 2 Chr. 24:18; Ezra 10:10 ➔ GUILT <819> 2 See TRANSGRESSION <4604>.

TRESS – Song 7:5 ➔ TROUGH <7298> b.

TRIAL – ***massāh*** [fem. noun: מַסָּה <4531>; from TEST <5254>] ► **This word means despair, test, proving.** The Hebrew word is actually two homographs-words that are spelled the same yet have distinct origins and meanings. The first homograph is derived from the verb *māsas* (MELT <4549>), meaning to dissolve or melt, and it means despair. This word occurs only in Job 9:23; also translated calamity, plight, despair. The second homograph is derived from the verb *nāsāh* (TEST <5254>), meaning to test or try, and denotes a test, a trial, or proving. It is used in reference to the manifestations of God's power and handiwork before the Egyptians at the Exodus (Deut. 4:34; 7:19; 29:3; KJV: temptation). Furthermore, this term has become a proper noun, *massāh* (MASSAH <4532>), to designate the place where the Israelites tested God (Ex. 17:7; Deut. 6:16; 9:22; Ps. 95:8); and where Levi was tested (Deut. 33:8). ¶

TRIBAL – Gen. 25:16; Num. 25:15 ➔ PEOPLE <523>.

TRIBE – 1 ***š^eḇaṭ*** [Aramaic masc. noun: שְׁבַט <7625>; corresponding to ROD <7626> (this word also means a tribe)] ► **This noun is used in reference to the family divisions of Israel.** It occurs only in Ezra 6:17 (cf. Gen. 49:28). ¶

– 2 Gen. 25:16 ➔ PEOPLE <523> 3 Judg. 13:2; etc. ➔ CLAN <4940> 4 Job 30:12 ➔ BROOD <6526>.

TRIBULATION – Lam. 3:5 ➔ HARDSHIP <8513>.

TRIBUTE – 1 ***b^elô*** [Aramaic masc. noun: בְּלוֹ <1093>; from a root corresponding to WEAR OUT <1086>] ► **This word describes a tax or custom paid in kind.** Refs.: Ezra 4:13, 20; 7:24. ¶

2 ***middāh, mindāh*** [Aramaic fem. noun: מִדָּה, מִנְדָּה <4061>; corresponding to TAX (noun) <4060>] ► **This word refers to revenues collected to run a nation.** In context it refers to royal revenues of the kings of Persia (Ezra 4:13; 6:8) and of the

kings of Israel (Ezra 4:20). The personnel of the second Temple were exempt from this imposition of taxes (Ezra 7:24). ¶
[3] ***meḵes*** [masc. noun: מֶכֶס <4371>; prob. from an unused root meaning to enumerate] ▶ **This word means tax.** It indicates a portion or levy of booty or spoil taken in war to go to the priests (Num. 31:28, 37–41). ¶
[4] ***missāh*** [fem. noun: מִסָּה <4530>; from MELT <4549> (in the sense of flowing)] ▶ **This word designates something given as a free offering during the presentation of a freewill offering to the Lord.** Ref.: Deut. 16:10. ¶
– [5] 2 Kgs. 23:33 ➔ FINE (noun) <6066> [6] Is. 18:7 ➔ GIFT <7862> [7] Neh. 5:4 ➔ TAX (noun) <4060>.

TRICK – ***nêḵel*** [masc. noun: נֵכֶל <5231>; from DECEIVE <5230>] ▶ **This word refers to deceitfulness. A noun from the root meaning of *nāḵal* describing an act of deception, trickery used to deceive a person or a people.** Ref.: Num. 25:18; also translated wile, scheme, to deceive. ¶

TRICKERY – ***'orbāh*** [fem. noun: אָרְבָּה <698>; fem. of AMBUSH <696> (only in the plur.)] ▶ **This word depicts deceit, artifice; it is also translated spoils, skill, cleverness.** It refers literally to the tricks of one's hands; in context, it describes the deceit or trickery of Moab's actions (Is. 25:11). ¶

TRICKING – Gen. 27:12 ➔ DECEIVE <8591> a.

TRICKLE – ***pāḵāh*** [verb: פָּכָה <6379>; a prim. root] ▶ **This word indicates to flow, to run out.** It refers to a small running stream or flow of water (Ezek. 47:2). ¶

TRICKLE DOWN – Lam. 3:49 ➔ SPILL <5064>.

TRIED – Is. 28:16 ➔ TESTED <976>.

TRIGON – ***sabbᵉḵā', śabbᵉḵā'*** [Aramaic fem. noun: שַׂבְּכָא, סַבְּכָא <5443>; from a root corresponding to ENTWINE <5440>] ▶ **This word indicates a musical instrument; it is also translated sackbut, lyre.** It refers to one of the instruments from the huge ensemble of musical instruments celebrating the dedication of Nebuchadnezzar's golden statute (Dan. 3:5, 7, 10, 15). ¶

TRIM – ***kāsam*** [verb: כָּסַם <3697>; a prim. root] ▶ **This word indicates cutting one's hair.** It refers to clipping one's hair, the requirement for priests in Ezekiel's new Temple (Ezek. 44:20; KJV: to poll). Long hair may have indicated a Nazarite vow (see Num. 6) during Ezekiel's day as well. ¶

TRIM OFF – Dan. 4:14 ➔ CUT OFF <7113>.

TRIMMERS – 1 Kgs. 7:50; 2 Kgs. 12:13; 25:14; 2 Chr. 4:22; Jer. 52:18 ➔ SNUFFERS <4212>.

TRIP – Ps. 140:4 ➔ DRIVE <1760>.

TRIUMPH (noun) – Deut. 33:29 ➔ MAJESTY <1346>.

TRIUMPH (verb) – [1] Ps. 25:2; Prov. 28:12 ➔ REJOICE <5970> [2] Dan. 11:12 ➔ STRENGTHEN <5810>.

TRIUMPHANT (REMAIN) – Dan. 11:12 ➔ STRENGTHEN <5810>.

TRIUMPHED GLORIOUSLY (HAVE) – Ex. 15:1, 21 ➔ RISE <1342>.

TRIUMPHING – Job 20:5 ➔ JOYFUL SHOUT <7445>.

TRIVIAL (BE) – 1 Sam. 18:23 ➔ DESPISED (BE) <7034>.

TRODDEN UNDER FOOT – [1] Is. 18:2, 7 ➔ TREADING DOWN <4001> [2] Dan. 8:13 ➔ TRAMPED, TRAMPLED DOWN <4823>.

TROOP – [1] 2 Sam. 2:25; Amos 9:6 ➔ BUNCH <92> [2] Job 6:19 ➔ WAY <1979> [3] Is. 65:11 ➔ FORTUNE <1408>

or <1409> [4] Jer. 5:7 ➔ GATHER <1413> [5] See BAND (noun) <1416>.

TROOPS – [1] ***ʾᵃgap̱*** [masc. noun: אֲגַף <102>; prob. from SMITE <5062> (through the idea of impending)] ▶ **This word means and is also translated bands, hordes.** It refers to troops of Israel whom the Lord will scatter (Ezek. 12:14; 17:21) and to the multitude of troops gathered around Gog whom the Lord will destroy in a great eschatological battle (Ezek. 38:6, 9, 22; 39:4). ¶
– [2] 2 Kgs. 9:17 ➔ ABUNDANCE <8229> [3] Job 6:19 ➔ PATH <734> [4] Prov. 30:31 ➔ ARMY <510> a.

TROUBLE (noun) – [1] ***ṣārāh*** [fem. noun: צָרָה <6869>; fem. of NARROWNESS <6862>] ▶
a. This word means distress, anguish. It refers to a situation or a time of extreme discomfort, an affliction for many different reasons. God delivers His people from this condition (Gen. 35:3; Job 5:19; Ps. 9:9). The pursuit of wisdom is also a refuge in a time of distress (Prov. 1:27). God is the author of destruction and distress in judgment on the earth (Is. 8:22; Jer. 4:31). Daniel speaks of a final time of distress that will never be superseded (Dan. 12:1). *
b. This word refers to a person who is threatening or a source of despair for various reasons. Ref.: 1 Sam. 1:6: rival, adversary. ¶
– [2] 1 Sam. 5:9, 11; Prov. 15:16; Is. 22:5; Ezek. 7:7 ➔ CONFUSION <4103> [3] 2 Chr. 29:8; Jer. 15:4 ➔ TERROR <2113> [4] Neh. 4:8 ➔ ERROR <8442> [5] Neh. 9:32 ➔ HARDSHIP <8513> [6] Job 3:26; 14:1 ➔ TURMOIL <7267> [7] Ps. 78:33; Is. 65:23 ➔ TERROR <928> [8] Ps. 90:10; Amos 5:5 ➔ NOTHINGNESS <205> [9] Prov. 1:27 ➔ DISTRESS (noun) <6695> b. [10] Prov. 10:10 ➔ SORROW (noun) <6094> [11] Is. 1:14 ➔ LOAD (noun) <2960> [12] Is. 17:14 ➔ TERROR <1091> [13] Is. 47:11 ➔ DISASTER <1943> [14] Jer. 8:15; 14:19 ➔ TERROR <1205> [15] Dan. 4:5, 19; 5:6, 9, 10; 7:15, 28 ➔ HASTE (BE IN) <927> [16] See HORROR <2189>.

TROUBLE (BRING) – ***ʿāḵar*** [verb: עָכַר <5916>; a prim. root] ▶ **This word indicates stirring up resentment, to bring about hatred or danger.** Ref.: Gen. 34:30. It is used of bringing a curse on Israel (Judg. 11:35). It depicts a harsh law or order placed on people, troubling them, agitating them (1 Sam. 14:29). Elijah was called by the Lord to constantly harass the evil leaders and kings of Israel. He was called "the troubler of Israel" (1 Kgs. 18:17, 18). It is used of something growing worse, increasing (Ps. 39:2). Persons who are cruel and violent, harm and trouble themselves (Prov. 11:17). The wicked are made for and live with trouble (Prov. 15:6, 27). Other refs.: Josh. 6:18; 7:25; 1 Chr. 2:7; Prov. 11:29. ¶

TROUBLE (verb) – [1] ***bāʿaṯ*** [verb: בָּעַת <1204>; a prim. root] ▶ **This word means to fear, to be or to make afraid, to startle. It is also translated to torment, to terrorize, to terrify. The basic ideas of it can be summarized as an individual's realization that he or she is less powerful than someone or something else and can be overcome.** An evil spirit tormented Saul (1 Sam. 16:14, 15), but God is also accused of making people afraid (Job 7:14; 9:34). It is used of humans, as when Haman was terrified (Esther 7:6). This word can also mean to fall upon or to overwhelm (Job 3:5; Ps. 18:4). *
[2] ***dālaḥ*** [verb: דָּלַח <1804>; a prim. root] ▶ **This verb means and is also translated to churn, to muddy, to stir.** It is used figuratively of troubling or stirring up the rivers of Egypt like a monster (Ezek. 32:2) or of a person's foot polluting water (Ezek. 32:13). ¶
– [3] Ezra 4:4 ➔ AFRAID (MAKE) <1089> [4] Dan. 4:9 ➔ BAFFLE <598>.

TROUBLE, TROUBLESOME, TROUBLOUS – Dan. 9:25 ➔ DISTRESS (noun) <6695> a.

TROUBLED – [1] ***ʿᵃṣiyḇ*** [Aramaic verb: עֲצִיב <6088>; corresponding to HURT <6087>] ▶ **This word means to pain, to grieve. It appears only one time in the form of a passive participle and is used as an adjective to modify *qôl* (<6963>),**

meaning voice. In this instance, King Darius called into the lion's den for Daniel with a pained voice to see if God had preserved Daniel and kept him safe from harm (Dan. 6:20; also translated lamenting, lamentable, anguished, anguish). ¶
– [2] Prov. 25:26 ➔ FOUL <7515> [3] Is. 19:10 ➔ GRIEVED <99>.

TROUBLED (BE) – [1] ***pā'am*** [verb: פָּעַם <6470>; a prim. root] ▶ **This word means to stir, to be stirred, to be agitated.** It indicates a troubling or agitation bothering persons, making them act (Gen. 41:8); especially God's Spirit stirring up persons to motivate them (Judg. 13:25). Sometimes this anxiety keeps people from being able to act (Ps. 77:4); or to rest (Dan. 2:1, 3). ¶
[2] ***ṣārar*** [verb: צָרַר <6887>] ▶
a. This word means to bind up, to tie up, to be distressed, to be oppressed, to be cramped. It refers to something being bound up, tied up physically (Ex. 12:34). It means to be hard-pressed, anxious, worried, distressed about what to do (Gen. 32:7). It is used to describe the action of an enemy, a famine, or an army pressing upon a city, besieging it (Deut. 28:52). It is used figuratively of one's life (soul, *nep̱eš*) being bound in a bag (1 Sam. 25:29; cf. Hos. 4:19; 13:12); and of the law being bound for safekeeping (Is. 8:16). It means to keep out, shut out a person (2 Sam. 20:3). It indicates something being cramped, shortened, cut back (Job 18:7).
b. A verb indicating to be an enemy, an adversary, an oppressor, a rival. It means to oppose persons, to fight against, to be hostile toward them. The Lord promised to be an adversary, an enemy to His people's enemies, if His people obeyed Him (Ex. 23:22). It is used of taking a second wife who would compete with the first wife (Lev. 18:18). The adversary of the psalmist is mentioned often (Ps. 6:7; 7:4; 74:4). It has the sense of those who harass someone (Is. 11:13). *
– [3] Gen. 40:6 ➔ ANGRY (BE, BECOME) <2196> [4] 1 Sam. 28:21 ➔ TERRIFIED <926> [5] Job 34:20 ➔ SHAKE <1607> [6] Ps. 38:18 ➔ ANXIOUS (BE, BECOME) <1672> [7] Ps. 46:3; Lam. 1:20; 2:11 ➔ RED (BE) <2560> [8] Ezek. 27:35 ➔ IRRITATE <7481> [9] Dan. 7:15 ➔ GRIEVED (BE) <3735>.

TROUBLESOME – Ezra 4:15 ➔ DAMAGE (verb) <5142>.

TROUBLING – Job 3:17 ➔ TURMOIL <7267>.

TROUGH – [1] ***rahaṭ*** [masc. noun: רַהַט <7298>; from an unused root apparently meaning to hollow out] ▶
a. This word refers to a hollowed, narrow open container made of wood or stone to hold water or food for animals. Refs.: Gen. 30:38, 41; Ex. 2:16; also translated gutter.
b. This word refers to a tress, a lock of hair. It describes a braid or plait of human hair, a long, thick piece of hair hanging and falling loosely (Song 7:5).
c. This word refers to a gallery. It usually indicates a covered walk, a long, narrow balcony, or an area for seating. But it may have a theatric intention in the KJV meaning to act in a way so as to please someone (Song 7:5). ¶
[2] ***šōqeṯ*** [fem. noun: שֹׁקֶת <8268>; from WATER (GIVE) <8248>] ▶ **This word indicates a water trough, a hollow structure for holding drinking water for animals.** It was a standard piece of farming and agriculture in the ancient Near East (Gen. 24:20; 30:38). ¶
– [3] Prov. 14:4 ➔ CRIB <18>.

TROUSERS – [1] ***pattiyš*** [Aramaic noun: פַּטִּישׁ <6361>; from a root corresponding to that of HAMMER (noun) <6360>] ▶ **This Hebrew word refers to a wide garment (as if spread out), probably a coat or trousers, that was part of the elaborate Persian outfits worn by the Hebrew men when they were thrown into the fiery furnace.** Ref.: Dan. 3:21; also translated hose. Other translations, such as, tunics, robes, shirts, have been suggested.
– [2] Ex. 28:42; 39:28; Lev. 6:10; 16:4; Ezek. 44:18 ➔ UNDERGARMENT <4370> [3] Dan. 3:21, 27 ➔ COAT (noun) <5622>.

TROWEL – Deut. 23:13 ➔ PEG <3489>.

TRUE – [1] ***ṣᵉḏā'*** [Aramaic adj. and masc. noun: צְדָא <6656>; from an unused root corresponding to LIE IN WAIT <6658> in the sense of intentness] ▶ **This word means purpose, (sinister) design and it refers to doing something with malicious intent. The word is found once in the Old Testament, where it appears in the form of a question: "Is it (done) of design?".** Nebuchadnezzar approached Shadrach, Meshach, and Abednego, asking them if their intent was to defy him by not serving his gods or the golden image (Dan. 3:14). ¶
– [2] Dan. 2:45; 3:24 ➔ CERTAIN <3330>.

TRULY – [1] ***'ᵃḇāl*** [adv.: אֲבָל <61>; apparently from MOURN <56> through the idea of negation] ▶ **The word means indeed, surely, verily in several passages.** Refs.: Gen. 42:21; 2 Sam. 14:5; 1 Kgs. 1:43; 2 Kgs. 4:14. It is more adversative in other verses, being translated by however, but (Gen. 17:19; 2 Chr. 1:4; 19:3; Ezra 10:13). *
[2] ***'omnām*** [adv.: אָמְנָם <551>; adv. from TRUTH <544>] ▶ **This word means admittedly or surely; it is also translated indeed, no doubt, doubtless. It is used to acknowledge that something is true but not the whole truth.** Hezekiah admitted that Assyria destroyed other nations and their gods but claimed that it was because they were false gods (2 Kgs. 19:17; Is. 37:18). Job admitted the truth of his friends' sayings but claimed that they did not see the whole truth (Job 9:2; 12:2, 19:4, 5). Eliphaz used the word to deny negative statements about God and himself (Job 34:12; 36:4). Other ref.: Ruth 3:12 (it is true). ¶
– [3] Gen. 20:12; Josh. 7:20 ➔ INDEED <546> [4] Dan. 2:47 ➔ TRUTH <7187>.

TRUMPET – [1] ***ḥᵃṣōṣᵉrāh*** [fem. noun: חֲצֹצְרָה <2689>; by reduplication from TRUMPET (BLOW A) <2690>] ▶ **This word refers to a long metal instrument used for signaling.** It was used both in sacred (Num. 10:2, 8–10; 2 Kgs. 12:13; Ps. 98:6) and secular spheres (2 Kgs. 11:14; 2 Chr. 23:13; Hos. 5:8). *
[2] ***šôp̄ār, šōp̄ār*** [masc. noun: שׁוֹפָר, שֹׁפָר <7782>; from BEAUTIFUL (BE) <8231> in the original sense of incising] ▶ **This word refers to a trumpet or horn made out of a curved ram's horn.** It was used to signal a time of meeting together or a significant event, especially at Sinai (Ex. 19:16, 19; Lev. 25:9; Josh. 6:4–6, 8, 9, 13:16, 20). It was used at the time of proclaiming a new king in Israel (1 Kgs. 1:34, 39, 41; 2 Kgs. 9:13). It was sounded at the celebration of God as King over all the earth (Ps. 47:5). It also warned of approaching danger (Hos. 5:8; 8:1); especially the Day of the Lord (Joel 2:1, 15). *
[3] ***tāqôa'*** [masc. noun: תָּקוֹעַ <8619>; from BLOW (verb) <8628>] ▶ **This word describes an instrument with a bright, sometimes shrill, tone; it consists of a looped tube and a flared bell at the end.** It was used to sound the call to battle (Ezek. 7:14). ¶
– [4] Ex. 19:13 ➔ RAM <3104>.

TRUMPET (BLOW A) – ***ḥaṣṣar*** [verb: חִצֵּר <2690>; a prim. root] ▶ **This word is also translated to sound the trumpet (*ḥᵃṣōṣᵉrāh*) in order to announce a major event or to bring people together.** Refs.: 1 Chr. 15:24; 2 Chr. 5:12, 13; 7:6; 13:14; 29:28. ¶

TRUST (noun) – [1] ***biṭḥāh*** [fem. noun: בִּטְחָה <985>; fem. of BETAH <984> (i.e., security, assurance)] ▶ **This word means and is also translated confidence. It is used only in Isaiah 30:15 where this trust was to characterize the people of God.** Used as such, it explicates a key theme of Isaiah's theology: true belief in God should be exhibited by implicit trust (confidence) in Him (cf. Is. 26:3, 4). The people of God, even in their sinful failure, should glorify Him by quiet trust instead of reliance on self-stratagems and other powers (cf. Is. 7:4). This confident trust would bring divine strength and salvation. The failure to trust could only provoke judgment (cf. Is. 31:1). Such trust or confidence as indicative of belief is echoed throughout the Old Testament, particularly in the Psalms. ¶

[2] ***miḇṭāḥ*** [masc. noun: מִבְטָח <4009>; from TRUST (verb) <982>] ▶ **This word refers to persons or things in which one trusts or an attitude of confidence itself.** People who do not trust in God have a trust like a spider's web, fragile in the extreme (Job 8:14); the wicked are torn from whatever trust or security they may have (Job 18:14). Confidence in God results in a person being blessed by Him (Ps. 40:4; Jer. 17:7). Israel often trusted in Egypt or other foreign powers to help her (Jer. 2:37). The fear of God is a source of great trust for His people (Prov. 14:26). God is the ultimate trust of the entire earth, the confidence of all nations (Ps. 65:5), as well as the secure dwelling of His people (Is. 32:18). *
– [3] 2 Kgs. 18:19; Is. 36:4 ➔ CONFIDENCE <986> [4] Job 8:14; 31:24; Ps. 78:7 ➔ LOINS <3689> [5] Is. 30:3 ➔ SHELTER <2622>.

TRUST (verb) – [1] ***ʾᵉman*** [Aramaic verb: אֲמַן <540>; corresponding to NURSE (verb) <539>] ▶ **This word means to believe in, to put one's faith in someone or something. It occurs only three times in the Hebrew Bible.** In Daniel 6:23, it states that Daniel trusted in his God. In the other occurrences, the verb is in the form of a passive participle and functions as an adjective meaning trustworthy or faithful: the interpretation of the king's dream is trustworthy or sure (Dan. 2:45); and Daniel is described as a faithful man without negligence or corruption (Dan. 6:4). ¶
[2] ***bāṭaḥ*** [verb: בָּטַח <982>; a prim. root] ▶ **This word indicates to be confident, to rely on; it is also translated to put confidence, to put trust, to depend.** It expresses the feeling of safety and security that is felt when one can rely on someone or something else. It is used to show trust in God (2 Kgs. 18:5; Ps. 4:5; Jer. 49:11); in other people (Judg. 9:26; 20:36; Is. 36:5, 6, 9); or in things (Ps. 44:6; Jer. 7:4; Hab. 2:18). In addition, this expression can also relate to the state of being confident, secure, without fear (Judg. 18:7, 10, 27; Job 11:18; Prov. 28:1). *
[3] ***rᵉḥaṣ*** [Aramaic verb: רְחַץ <7365>; corresponding to WASH AWAY <7364>] ▶ **This word indicates a person's attitude of trust in the Lord, confidence in Him, commitment to Him.** Ref.: Dan. 3:28. ¶
– [4] Deut. 32:37; Judg. 9:15; 2 Sam. 22:31; Is. 14:32; etc. ➔ REFUGE <2620>.

TRUSTED – Job 12:20 ➔ NURSE (verb) <539>.

TRUSTWORTHY – [1] Prov. 8:6 ➔ LEADER <5057> [2] Prov. 13:17; 14:5; 20:6 ➔ FAITHFUL <529> [3] Dan. 2:45; 6:4 ➔ TRUST (verb) <540>.

TRUTH – [1] ***ʾᵉmûnāh*** [fem. noun: אֱמוּנָה <530>; fem. of FAITHFUL <529>] ▶ **This word means and is also translated faithfulness. It is used to describe God's character and His actions in Deuteronomy 32:4.** The psalmists often use this word in their praise of the Lord and His faithfulness (Ps. 33:4; 100:5; 119:90). When people are faithful, good comes their way (2 Chr. 19:9; Prov. 12:22; 28:20). The word *ʾᵉmûnāh* is also used with righteousness to describe the character (Prov. 12:17; Is. 59:4; Jer. 5:1). *
[2] ***ʾōmen*** [masc. noun: אֹמֶן <544>; from NURSE (verb) <539> (in the sense of being sure, secure)] ▶ **This word means faithfulness, full reliability. It stresses both the truthfulness of something and, therefore, its reliability simultaneously.** God's wonders and plans are planned and executed in faithfulness and truth (or: with perfect faithfulness) (Is. 25:1). ¶
[3] ***ʾᵉmeṯ*** [fem. noun: אֱמֶת <571>; contr. from NURSE (verb) <539> (in the sense of to support, to establish)] ▶ **This word means faithfulness.** It is frequently connected with lovingkindness (Prov. 3:3; Hos. 4:1) and occasionally with other terms such as peace (2 Kgs. 20:19); righteousness (Is. 48:1); and justice (Ps. 111:7). To walk in truth is to conduct oneself according to God's holy standards (1 Kgs. 2:4; 3:6; Ps. 86:11; Is. 38:3). Truth was the barometer for measuring both one's word (1 Kgs. 22:16; Dan. 11:2) and actions (Gen. 24:49; Josh. 2:14). Accordingly, God's words (Ps. 119:160; Dan. 10:21) and actions (Neh. 9:33) are characterized by this Hebrew term

also. Indeed, God is the only God of truth (Ex. 34:6; 2 Chr. 15:3; Ps. 31:5). *

4 ***yᵉṣaḇ*** [Aramaic verb: יְצַב <3321>; corresponding to STAND (TAKE A) <3320> (in the sense of to be firm; hence to speak surely)] ▶ **This word means to take, to make a stand, to gain certainty, to know the truth.** It is used only once in the entire Old Testament, in Daniel 7:19, where Daniel desired to know the truth (also translated meaning) of the fourth beast's identity. This corresponds with the Hebrew word *yāṣaḇ* [STAND (TAKE, MAKE A) <3320>], meaning to make one's stand, to take one's stand, or to present oneself. ¶

5 ***qāšôṭ, qᵉšōṭ*** [Aramaic masc. noun: קְשׁוֹט, קְשֹׁט <7187>; corresponding to <7189> below] ▶ **This word is equivalent to the Hebrew term *qōšeṭ* (<7189> below). It is utilized twice, with both occurrences embedded within the book of Daniel.** After being deeply humbled by the Lord, Nebuchadnezzar praised God and acknowledged that all His works were truth (Dan. 4:37; also translated right). Prior to this humbling, King Nebuchadnezzar had declared Daniel's God in truth to be the God of gods, i.e., truly (Dan. 2:47). Nevertheless, this knowledge failed to penetrate his proud heart, because in the very next section of text, Nebuchadnezzar built a monumental golden idol. ¶

6 ***qōšeṭ, qōšᵉṭ*** [masc. noun: קֹשֶׁט, קֹשְׁטְ <7189>] ▶ **This word means certainty. It comes from an unused root meaning to balance, as in a scale.** It appears twice in the Wisdom Literature, meaning the vindication of a true assessment by reality (Ps. 60:4); and the realization of a person's truthfulness by an intimate knowledge of the individual (Prov. 22:21). ¶

– 7 Is. 26:2 ➔ FAITHFUL <529> 8 Dan. 7:16 ➔ CERTAIN <3330>.

TRY – 1 Is. 22:4 ➔ HASTEN <213> 2 Dan. 7:25 ➔ THINK <5452> 3 See TEST <974>.

TUBAL – ***tûḇal, tuḇal*** [masc. proper noun: תּוּבַל, תֻּבַל <8422>; prob. of foreign deriv.] ▶ **Son of Japheth and grandson of Noah.** Refs.: Gen. 10:2; 1 Chr. 1:5; Is. 66:19; Ezek. 27:13; 32:26; 38:2, 3; 39:1. ¶

TUBAL-CAIN – ***tûḇal qayin*** [masc. proper noun: תּוּבַל קַיִן <8423>; apparently from BRING <2986> and CAIN <7014>]; offspring of Cain ▶ **Son of Lamech; he is the first recorded metal worker.** Ref.: Gen. 4:22. ¶

TUBE – Job 40:18 ➔ RAVINE <650> b.

TUCK – 1 Kgs. 18:46: tucking his cloak into his belt ➔ lit.: girding up his loins ➔ GIRD UP <8151>.

TUMBLEWEED – Is. 17:13 ➔ WHEEL <1534>.

TUMOR – ***'ōpel*** [masc. noun: עֹפֶל <6076>; from a verb meaning to be puffed up, see PRESUME <6075>] ▶ **This word means a growth, a lump; it is also translated emerod (KJV).** Refs.: Deut. 28:27; 1 Sam. 5:6, 9, 12; 6:4, 5. The Hebrew word also means citadel, hill; see HILL <6076>. ¶

TUMORS – ***ṭᵉḥôr*** [masc. noun: טְחוֹר <2914>; from an unused root meaning to burn] ▶ **This word is used in the plural only of some pestilence or diseased growth, evidently anal hemorrhoids (KJV, emerods) inflicted on the Philistines.** Refs.: 1 Sam. 6:11, 17. Models of these tumors were presented to Israel as guilt offerings by the Philistines. Other refs.: Deut. 28:27; 1 Sam. 5:6, 9, 12; 6:4, 5. ¶

TUMULT – 1 ***šā'ôn*** [masc. noun: שָׁאוֹן <7588>; from ROAR (verb) <7582>] ▶ **This word means a roar, a din, a crash.** It is found mostly in the prophets and generally refers to the din of battle (Hos. 10:14; Amos 2:2); or the crash of waves (Is. 17:12). A less frequent use of the word describes the merriment or uproar of revelers (Is. 24:8). *

– 2 2 Kgs. 19:28; Is. 37:29 ➔ EASE (AT) <7600> b. 3 Ps. 64:2 ➔ THRONG (noun) <7285> 4 Is. 22:5; Ezek. 7:7; 22:5; Amos 3:9; Zech. 14:13 ➔ CONFUSION <4103> 5 Ezek. 1:24 ➔ NOISE <1999>.

TUNIC – [1] Gen. 37:3; etc. ➔ COAT (noun) <3801> [2] 1 Sam. 17:38, 39; 2 Sam. 20:8 ➔ CLOTHES <4055> [3] Dan. 3:21 ➔ TROUSERS <6361>.

TURBAN – [1] ***miṣnepet̲*** [fem. noun: מִצְנֶפֶת <4701>; from WEAR <6801>] ▶ **This word depicts a headband.** It was worn by either the king (Ezek. 21:26; KJV: diadem) or the high priest (Ex. 28:4, 37, 39; 29:6; 39:28, 31; Lev. 8:9; 16:4; KJV: mitre). ¶

[2] ***pᵉ'ēr*** [masc. noun: פְּאֵר <6287>; from GLORIFY <6286>] ▶ **This word indicates a headband; it is also translated mitre, bonnet. It refers to a style of headdress worn by men in the Middle East or South Asia.** It is made up of lengths of cloth wound in folds around the head (Ex. 39:28). There were many styles of these, sometimes called headdresses (Is. 3:20). The word has the sense of a garland in some contexts, a wreath or woven chain of flowers, even leaves worn on one's head (Is. 61:3, 10). Other refs.: Ezek.: 24:17, 23; 44:18. ¶

[3] ***ṣāniyp̲*** [masc. noun: צָנִיף <6797>; from WEAR <6801>] ▶

a. This word indicates a headpiece often worn by persons in authority in the ancient Near East. It was fashioned by folding long pieces of cloth around a person's head. It was worn by the high priest of Israel (Zech. 3:5). It is used figuratively of righteousness (Job 29:14). People considered it a valued luxury in some cases (Is. 3:23). Zion is described as the royal turban or diadem of the Lord (Is. 62:3). ¶

b. A masculine noun referring to a diadem. It is translated as diadem in some cases, indicating a golden crown but used figuratively of righteousness. Ref.: Job 29:14. ¶

c. A masculine noun meaning mitre. It is translated as mitre or miter by some translators, indicating a turban, a headband of the high priest of Israel (Zech. 3:5). ¶

– [4] Ezek. 23:15 ➔ FLOWING TURBAN <2871> [5] Dan. 3:21 ➔ HAT <3737>.

TURBULENT – Gen. 49:4 ➔ RECKLESSNESS <6349>.

TURMOIL – [1] ***rōgez*** [masc. noun: רֹגֶז <7267>; from SHAKE <7264>] ▶ **This word means commotion, raging, excitement; it is also translated fear, wrath, trouble, raging, troubling, rage; noise, thunder, roar. The primary meaning of this word is a state of agitation or uproar.** It denotes the tumult that comes from fear (Is. 14:3); the fury of the Lord's judgment (Hab. 3:2); a general state of upheaval (Job 3:26); and the chaos of ordinary life in this world (Job 14:1). Other refs.: Job 3:17; 37:2; 39:24. ¶

– [2] 2 Chr. 15:5; Prov. 15:16; Is. 22:5; Ezek. 22:5 ➔ CONFUSION <4103>.

TURN (noun) – [1] ***tôr, tōr*** [masc. noun: תּוֹר, תֹּר <8447>; from SEEK OUT <8446>] ▶

a. This word indicates an opportunity. It refers to a person's allotted time and place in a predetermined series (Esther 2:12, 15).

b. This word refers to ornaments, earrings. It describes jewelry and decorative items of all kinds worn by a bride for beauty (Song 1:10).

c. This word indicates a row, a border. It describes an orderly set of something. In context it refers to rows of jewelry (KJV, Song 1:10).

d. This word means a standard, a manner; it is also translated custom, instruction, decree. It refers in context back to the previous manner or way in which God had dealt with David and his family (2 Sam. 7:19). In 1 Chronicles 17:17, it has a slightly different nuance, referring to the high estate or the high manner in which God regarded David in dealing with him. ¶

[2] ***tᵉqûp̄āh*** [fem. noun: תְּקוּפָה <8622>; from SURROUND <5362>] ▶ **This word indicates a turning around, a circuit.** It indicates the completion of a yearly cycle (Ex. 34:22; 2 Chr. 24:23); the gestation period of a child (1 Sam. 1:20). It is used to describe the circuit or passage of the sun across the sky (Ps. 19:6). ¶

TURN (verb) – [1] ***hāp̄ak̲*** [verb: הָפַךְ <2015>; a prim. root] ▶ **This verb means to move in a different direction, to change, to**

throw down, to overturn, to pervert, to destroy, to be turned against, to turn here and there, to wander. The verb is used to describe the simple act of turning something over (2 Kgs. 21:13; Hos. 7:8) but also to indicate turning back from something (Ps. 78:9). These turnings indicate that Jerusalem would lose all its inhabitants by being turned over as a dish is turned over after wiping it; "Ephraim has become a cake not turned," i.e., overdone on one side, uncooked on the other, and not edible (Hos. 7:8, NASB).

The verb becomes more figurative when it describes the act of overthrowing or destroying. Second Kings 21:13 is relevant here also, but Haggai speaks of God overthrowing the thrones of kingdoms (Persia) as well as chariots and riders (Hag. 2:22). Even more violently, the verb describes the overthrow of the enemies of God and His people; Sodom and Gomorrah were especially singled out (Gen. 19:21, 25; Deut. 29:23; cf. 2 Sam. 10:3). The word also indicates a change or is used to indicate defeat in battle when an army turned in flight (Josh. 7:8) or simply the change in direction of something (1 Kgs. 22:34). Metaphorically, the word comes to mean to change (by turning). For example, the Lord changed the curse of Balaam into a blessing (Deut. 23:5); He will change the mourning of His people into joy and gladness (Jer. 31:13). The simple stem is also found in a reflexive sense; the men of Israel turned themselves about in battle against the Benjamites (Judg. 20:39, 41; cf. 2 Kgs. 5:26; 2 Chr. 9:12).

The verb is used a few times in the reflexive stems to indicate turning oneself about: The Israelites are pictured as having turned themselves back against their enemies (Josh. 8:20); and Pharaoh changed his heart in himself (Ex. 14:5; Hos. 11:8), thus changing his mind. The word is used in the sense of being overwhelmed or overcome by pain (1 Sam. 4:19); the clouds rolled about (Job 37:12); the sword placed by the Lord to guard the Garden of Eden turned itself about (Gen. 3:24); and the earth's surface was shaped and moved like clay being impressed under a seal (Job 38:14). *

2 ***'āṭap̱*** [verb: עָטַף <5848>; a prim. root] ▶ **a. A word meaning to move in a different direction, to wrap, to cover.** It is used figuratively of God's mysterious, overwhelming actions with Job, turning them to the left (Job 23:9; KJV: to hide). The wicked are covered with violence (Ps. 73:6; NIV: to clothe, to cover). ¶

b. A word meaning to be feeble, to be faint, to be weak. It refers to animals of a flock that are born unhealthy, feeble, in a weakened state (Gen. 30:42). It is used of persons becoming weary, worn out in spirit from God's dealings with them (Is. 57:16: to faint, to grow faint); or from other causes so that they call on God (Ps. 61:2; 77:3; 142:3; Jon. 2:7). For Ps. 65:13, see a. Faint, weak persons pour out their prayers to God (Ps. 102:1). *

3 ***pānāh*** [verb: פָּנָה <6437>; a prim. root] ▶ **This word is used in various contexts.** It has the following basic meanings: to turn toward (plus *'el*) (Judg. 6:14; Is. 13:14; Jer. 50:16); to turn in a direction (plus *'al*) (Gen. 24:10); to turn from, away (plus *min* [FROM <4480>]) (Gen. 18:22); to turn with the goal, intention of doing something (Num. 21:33; Deut. 1:7; 1 Kgs. 10:13; Eccl. 2:12); to take a specific direction, north, south, etc. (Ex. 16:10; Num. 16:42; Josh. 15:7). In its intensive and causative stems, it may mean to turn, remove, or put something out of the way (Judg. 15:4; Jer. 48:39; Zeph. 3:15). In its passive use, it refers to being turned (Jer. 49:8). It is found in many figurative or idiomatic expressions: to turn to God in worship and time of need (Is. 45:22); to turn and follow one's own desires (Is. 53:6); to turn toward evening, for evening to come (Gen. 24:63); likewise for morning to come (Ex. 14:27). To turn to persons can mean to regard them compassionately, to give consideration to them (2 Sam. 9:8); it is used of inanimate things as well (Eccl. 2:11). *

4 ***šûḇ*** [verb: שׁוּב <7725>; a prim. root] ▶ **This word means to move in a different direction, to return, to go back, to do again, to change, to withdraw, to bring back, to reestablish, to be returned, to bring back, to take, to restore, to recompense, to answer, to hinder.** The verb

is used over one thousand times and has various shades of meaning in its four stems. In the simple stem, it is used to describe divine and human reactions, attitudes, and feelings. The verb describes the possibility that Israel might change (turn) their minds and return to Egypt (Ex. 13:17). Josiah the king turned back to the Lord with all his heart, soul, and strength (2 Kgs. 23:25; Jer. 34:15). Nevertheless, the Lord did not turn from the anger He held toward Judah (2 Kgs. 23:26; Jer. 4:28). Job pleaded with his miserable comforters to relent (i.e., turn away) from him (Job 6:29). God's people will return (repent) and seek Him in the last days (Deut. 30:2; Is. 59:20; Hos. 3:5) instead of turning away from Him as they are now; to return to Egypt (Is. 6:10; Hos. 11:5). God's call was persistently for His people to return to Him (1 Kgs. 8:33; Jer. 4:1). Any nation can repent and turn to God for forgiveness (Jer. 18:8).

The word is used metaphorically to describe things returning: God's Word will not be revoked (returned) once it has been uttered (Is. 45:23; 55:11); Jacob stayed with Laban until Esau's anger cooled off (turned back) (Gen. 27:44, 45); blood guilt could return on one's own head (1 Kgs. 2:33; Ps. 7:16). This word also describes the sword of Saul that did not return without success from the battlefield (2 Sam. 1:22).

The verb also indicates to return to or to change into. For example, human beings return to the dust of the earth (Gen. 3:19; Eccl. 12:7); but a person cannot naturally return to life (2 Sam. 12:23); unless God's Spirit brings it about (1 Kgs. 13:6). A land of great natural fertility can be reduced (turned into) to a farmer's cropland (Is. 29:17).

In its simplest sense, the word means to return, to restore, to go back. Abraham's descendants in their fourth generation would return to Canaan (Gen. 15:16); God returned to visit His people (Gen. 8:9; 18:10). It is also used to describe turning chariots about when needed (1 Kgs. 22:33; Mic. 2:8).

This verb is used with other verbs of motion, all in their infinitive or participial forms, to describe a back and forth motion; the ravens Noah sent out went back and forth (Gen. 8:7). Used with another verb in general, *šûḇ* is either not translated or means to do again whatever action is indicated by the other verb, such as when Isaac dug again the wells his father had previously dug (Gen. 26:18). A similar meaning is to take back or recapture when this verb is used with the Hebrew verb *lāqaḥ* (<7725>), meaning to take or to receive (2 Kgs. 13:25; Mic. 7:19). Finally, if this verb is used with a following infinitive of another verb, it means to do over and over or more and more; Israel angered the Lord more and more than they had already angered Him by performing pagan rituals (Ezek. 8:17). *

5 ***śûg*** [verb: שׂוּג <7734>; a prim. root] ▶ **This word refers to someone or something refraining from an act of some kind.** Jonathan's bow did not turn back from slaying Israel's enemies (2 Sam. 1:22). ¶

6 ***tā'ar*** [verb: תָּאַר <8388>; a prim. root] ▶ **This word indicates to incline; to stretch out.** It describes the direction and shape of something, e.g., a borderline that curves, bends (Josh. 15:9, 11); turns, inclines in one way (Josh. 18:14, 17). It also indicates a line or a direction that continues to a certain point (Josh. 19:13). For another meaning of the Hebrew word, see OUTLINE (MAKE AN) <8388>. ¶

– 7 2 Kgs. 19:25; Is. 6:11; 37:26 → WASTE (LAY, LIE) <7582> 8 Is. 22:18 → WEAR <6801> 9 Is. 59:13, 14; Mic. 2:6 → turn back, turn away → MOVE <5253> 10 Dan. 11:32 → DEFILED (BE) <2610>.

TURN, TURN AWAY – Prov. 4:15 → ASIDE (GO, TURN) <7847>.

TURN ASIDE – 1 ***sûr, sār*** [verb: סוּר, סָר <5493>; a prim. root] ▶ **This word means to turn away, to go away, to desert, to quit, to keep far away, to stop, to take away, to remove, to be removed, to make depart. It is used equally in the simple and causative stems. The basic meaning of the root, to turn away, takes on various connotations in the simple stem according to context.** In the simple stem, the verb means to turn aside, as Moses turned aside to see why the bush was not being consumed by the fire (Ex. 3:3, 4); it is used metaphorically to describe turning away from the Lord because of a rebellious heart (Jer. 5:23); or taking time to turn aside and seek someone's welfare (Jer. 15:5). The word describes leaving or going away literally (Ex. 8:31); or figuratively, the scepter would not leave Judah (Gen. 49:10); but Samson's strength left him (Judg. 16:19). Its meaning extends further to indicate falling away, as when one is enticed to fall away from following the Lord to pursue other gods (Deut. 11:16; 1 Sam. 12:20; Ps. 14:3). It means to stop something; e.g., the banqueting and carousing of Israel would cease at the time of exile (Hos. 4:18; Amos 6:7). It also indicates the act of keeping away from something, such as evil (Is. 59:15); or when the Lord kept Himself from His people (Hos. 9:12). Wise teaching helps keep a person far from the dangers of death (Prov. 13:14, 19).

The causative stem adds the idea of making something move, go away, turn away, or simply to put aside. The priests would set aside burnt offerings to be offered up (2 Chr. 35:12); and clothing was put aside as Tamar removed her widow's clothes to deceive Judah (Gen. 38:14; 1 Sam. 17:39; 1 Kgs. 20:41). God removed Israel from His presence because He was angry with them (2 Kgs. 17:18, 23; 23:27); Jacob charged his entire clan to get rid of their strange gods (Gen. 35:2; Josh. 24:14, 23).

When the verb is passive, it means to be removed, such as when the fat of offerings was removed by the priests (Lev. 4:31, 35). In Daniel 12:11, the word expresses the idea that the daily sacrifice was removed. *

2 ***śûṭ, sûṭ*** [verb: שׂוּט, סוּט <7750>; a prim. root] ▶ **This word indicates going away from the Lord to someone else.** An act of unfaithfulness (Ps. 40:4; also translated to go astray, to lapse); to fall away or to apostatize (Ps. 101:3). ¶

TURN AWAY – Deut. 13:5 ➔ REBELLION <5627>.

TURN AWAY (THOSE WHO) – ***yāsûr*** [masc. noun: יָסוּר <3249>; from TURN ASIDE <5493>] ▶ **This word indicates persons who go away. In this case, they turn away from following the Lord, "they that depart from me" (KJV, NKJV, Jer. 17:13).** Some translators edit the word to read *w^e ṣore(y)ḵa* (NIV, ESV, NASB), with the translation then becoming "those who turn away" (NASB) or "those who turn away from you" (NIV, ESV). ¶

TURN AWAY, TURN IN DISGUST – Jer. 6:8; Ezek. 23:17, 18 ➔ ALIENATED (BE) <3363>.

TURN BACK – ***sûg*** [verb: סוּג <5472>; a prim. root] ▶ **This word means to turn away, to backslide. It has the sense of deviating from or turning from an accepted or expected path or commitment.** To move something, e.g., a boundary line (Deut. 19:14; Hos. 5:10; KJV: to remove); to lose heart, to fail to perform (2 Sam. 1:22); to be thwarted from evil plans (Ps. 35:4; 40:14); to become disloyal, to be disloyal, to apostate (Ps. 53:3; 78:57); to change one's heart, to backslide (Prov. 14:14). Those who follow wrong paths will be turned back (Is. 42:17). *

TURN OF AFFAIRS – 1 Kgs. 12:15 ➔ TURN OF EVENTS <5438>.

TURN OF EVENTS – ***sibbāh*** [fem. noun: סִבָּה <5438>; from AROUND (GO, TURN) <5437>] ▶ **This word indicates a cause; it is also translated a turn of affairs.** It refers to a sudden change in the way things are going, a result coming about that was not expected (1 Kgs. 12:15). ¶

TURN OUT – Ruth 2:3 ➔ CHANCE <4745>.

TURN OVER – ***yāraṭ*** [verb: יָרַט <3399>; a prim. root] ▶ **This word means to be reckless, to be contrary, to throw recklessly; steep, difficult.** It carries the idea of tossing something or someone without care or concern into danger (Job 16:11: to toss, to cast, to throw). It refers to a difficult or steep road or path (Num. 22:32: to be perverse, to be contrary, to be reckless). ¶

TURN, TURN ASIDE – Ruth 3:8; Job 6:18 ➔ HOLD OF (TAKE) <3943>.

TURN, TURN AWAY – Song 5:6 ➔ WITHDRAW <2559>.

TURNCOAT – Mic. 2:4 ➔ BACKSLIDING <7728>.

TURNING – 1 Neh. 3:19, 20, 24, 25 ➔ CORNER (noun) <4740> 2 Ezek. 41:24 ➔ ENCLOSED <4142>.

TURNING AWAY – 1 ***mᵉšûḇāh*** [fem. noun: מְשׁוּבָה <4878>; from TURN <7725>] ► **This word refers to an apostasy, a backsliding.** It indicates figuratively a way of life that is fluctuating, vacillating, insecure (Prov. 1:32; also translated waywardness). In a religious sense, it indicates apostasy, turning from truth (Jer. 2:19; also translated backsliding); a lack of constancy, a defection (Jer. 3:6, 8, 11, 12, 22; 5:6; 8:5; 14:7; Hos. 14:4); or an act of turning away, a transgression (Ezek. 37:23; Hos. 11:7). *
– 2 Is. 57:17 ➔ BACKSLIDING <7726> 3 Mic. 2:4 ➔ BACKSLIDING <7728>.

TURNING THINGS AROUND, UPSIDE DOWN – ***hōpeḵ*** [masc. noun: הֶפֶךְ <2017>; from TURN (verb) <2015>] ► **This word is the same in meaning as OPPOSITE <2016>.** The KJV translates Isaiah 29:16 as, "Your turning of things upside down." ¶

TURQUOISE – 1 ***nōpeḵ*** [masc. noun: נֹפֶךְ <5306>; from an unused root meaning to glisten] ► **This word refers to a precious stone worn on the breastpiece of the high priest in the second row of stones; it is also translated emerald.** It represented one of the tribes of Israel (Ex. 28:18; 39:11). It was used to trade and barter for goods (Ezek. 27:16; 28:13). ¶
– 2 1 Chr. 29:2; Is. 54:11 ➔ ANTIMONY <6320>.

TURTLEDOVE – ***tôr, tōr*** [masc. noun: תּוֹר, תֹּר <8449>; prob. the same as TURN (noun) <8447>] ► **This word refers to wild doves known for their cooing and their affectionate ways of behaving toward each other.** It was a sacrificial animal in Israel, especially for the poor (Lev. 1:14; 5:7, 11; 12:6, 8; 14:22, 30; 15:14, 29). It is used charmingly of the psalmist or of Israel being the Lord's turtledove (Ps. 74:19). It was a harbinger of spring (Song 2:12); and had its built-in homing instincts (Jer. 8:7). Other refs.: Gen. 15:9; Num. 6:10. ¶

TWELVE – Ezra 6:17; Dan. 4:29 ➔ TWO <8648>.

TWENTY – 1 ***'eśriym*** [plur. number, adj., noun: עֶשְׂרִים <6242>; from TEN <6235>] ► **This word designates twenty items of a group or one twentieth of something: twenty years (Gen. 6:3).** It is used with other numbers to form larger numbers (Gen. 11:24). It is used as an ordinal number to represent the twentieth of something, in the twentieth year (1 Kgs. 15:9), with its noun before it in the construct form and state. *
2 ***'eśriyn*** [Aramaic plur. number, noun; adj.: עֶשְׂרִין <6243>; corresponding to <6242> above] ► **This word is used once in the larger number one hundred and twenty.** Ref.: Dan. 6:1. It is connected to one hundred (*mᵉ'āh*) with a waw, *wᵉ*. ¶

TWIG – 1 ***yᵉniyqāh*** [fem. noun: יְנִיקָה 3242>; from NURSE (verb and noun) <3243>] ► **This word denotes a young shoot. It refers to fresh young growth found on trees and shrubs, often in their top branches.** It is used figuratively in Ezekiel 17:4. ¶
– 2 Ezek. 8:17 ➔ BRANCH <2156>.

TWIG (YOUNG) – Ezek. 17:22 ➔ SHOOT (noun) <3127>.

TWIGS – Is. 64:2 ➔ BRUSHWOOD <2003>.

TWILIGHT – 1 ***'iyšôn, *šûn*** [masc. noun: אִישׁוֹן, אֱשׁוּן <380>; diminutive from MAN <376>] ► **A masculine noun indicating the approach of darkness or time of nightfall.** It describes twilight as the

time when prostitutes go forth to ply their trades (Prov. 7:9). The Hebrew word also means pupil of the eye; see PUPIL <380>. ¶
2 ***nešep̱*** [masc. noun: נֶשֶׁף <5399>; from BLOW (verb) <5398> (properly a breeze, i.e., by implication, dusk, when the evening breeze prevails)] ► **This word means and is also translated morning, dawn, dawning, dusk.** It refers to the period after the sun has set but before darkness has settled down (Job 3:9); when the adulterer made his way out (Job 24:15). It describes the early part of the day just before the sun rises or at the time of the rising of the sun (Job 7:4; Ps. 119:147; Is. 5:11). *
– 3 Ezek. 12:6, 7, 12 ➔ DARKNESS <5939>.

TWIN – ***tā'ôm, tô'ām*** [masc. noun: תָּאוֹם, תּוֹאָם <8380>; from DOUBLE (BE) <8382>] ► **This word refers to two children or animals born at the same birth.** Two boys (Gen. 25:24; 38:27); two animals (Song 4:5; 7:3). See DOUBLE (BE) <8382>. ¶

TWINS (BEAR, HAVE) – Song 4:2; 6:6 ➔ DOUBLE (BE) <8382>.

TWIST – 1 ***šāzar*** [verb: שָׁזַר <7806>; a prim. root] ► **This word means to twist, be twisted, to be finely twined.** It refers to finely worked threads, features of linen cloth (Ex. 26:1, 31, 36; 27:9, 16). *
– 2 Ex. 23:8; Deut. 16:19; Prov. 19:3 ➔ OVERTHROW (verb) <5557> 3 Is. 24:1 ➔ INIQUITY (COMMIT) <5753> 4 Mic. 3:9 ➔ CROOKED (MAKE, BE) <6140>.

TWISTED – 1 Ex. 28:14 ➔ BRAIDED <4020> 2 Deut. 32:5 ➔ CROOKED <6618> 3 Prov. 12:8 ➔ INIQUITY (COMMIT) <5753> 4 Is. 27:1 ➔ TWISTING <6129>.

TWISTED THREAD – 1 Kgs. 7:17 ➔ WREATH <1434>.

TWISTING – ***ʿaqallāṯôn*** [adj.: עֲקַלָּתוֹן <6129>; from PERVERTED <6127>] ► **This word means twined; it is also translated crooked, twisted.** It refers to a coiling, wiry, motion made by a serpent creature, Leviathan (Is. 27:1). ¶

TWITTER – Is. 38:14 ➔ CHIRP <6850>.

TWO – 1 ***šenayim, šettayim*** [adj., dual adj.: שְׁנַיִם, שְׁתַּיִם <8147>; dual of SECOND <8145>] ► **This word also means both, a pair.** It refers to two of anything, e.g., two of us (Gen. 21:27; 31:37); two brothers (Gen. 9:22); two slices of bread (1 Sam. 10:4). The phrase *šenayim šenayim* means two by two (Gen. 7:9). Its forms may precede *ʿāśa]r* to mean twelve (Gen. 14:4; 17:20). It combines to form larger numbers, e.g., two hundred thirty-two (1 Kgs. 20:15). *
2 ***terêyn*** [Aramaic number: תְּרֵין <8648>; corresponding to <8147> above] ► **This word also means second. Its feminine form is** *tartên.* It serves as a counting number (Ezra 4:24). It combines to form larger numbers: *terê-ʿaśar,* twelve (Ezra 6:17; Dan. 4:29); sixty-two (Dan. 5:31), *šittîn wetartên.* ¶

TWO-EDGED – ***piyp̱iyyôṯ*** [fem. plur. noun: פִּיפִיּוֹת <6374>; from EDGE <6366>] ► **This word is used to describe a sword or any blade that has been sharpened on both edges, an especially effective weapon.** Ref.: Ps. 149:6; also translated double-edged. Even both edges on a threshing sledge could be sharpened (Is. 41:15: teeth, double edges). ¶

TYRE – ***ṣōr, ṣôr*** [proper noun: צֹר, צוֹר <6865>; the same as FLINT <6864>]: a rock ► **This word designates a town located on the northern boundary of Asher. The city was renowned as a trading and shipping center for the world's merchants. Its main center was originally on an island. It is mentioned ca. 50 times in the Old Testament. Israel never did control the city but worked closely with several of its kings.** Refs.: Josh. 19:29; 2 Sam. 24:7. It was called to severe judgment by the prophets, especially Ezekiel (Ezek. 28). The psalmist pictured the king of Tyre bringing gifts (tribute?) to the king of Israel (45:12). It is listed among the enemies of Israel's God in Psalm 83:7, but Psalm 87:4 speaks of Tyre's recognition of the Lord in worship. Ezekiel could find no better ancient symbol to represent the hubris and arrogance of the king(s) of Tyre than the first Adam or Satan before his rebellion (Ezek. 28:1–10; 11–15). The city supplied David with materials for his own palace (2 Sam. 5:11). Hiram of Tyre helped Solomon with his many building projects, especially the Temple and palace (1 Kgs. 5:1), even supplying chief craftsmen for him (1 Kgs. 7:13). Solomon ceded cities to Hiram as partial payment (1 Kgs. 9:11–12). *

TYRIAN – ***ṣōriy*** [proper noun: צֹרִי <6876>; patrial from TYRE <6865>] ► **An inhabitant of Tyre.** Refs.: 1 Kgs. 7:14; 1 Chr. 22:4; 2 Chr. 2:14; Ezra 3:7; Neh. 13:16. ¶

TYRUS – See TYRE <6865>.

U

UCAL – ***'ukkāl*** [masc. proper noun: אֻכָּל <401>; apparently from EAT <398>]: I will prevail ▶ **One of two persons instructed by Agur.** Ref.: Prov. 30:1. ¶

UEL – ***'ûêl*** [masc. proper noun: אוּאֵל <177>; from OR <176> b. (in the sense of wish, desire), and GOD <410>]: desire of God ▶ **An Israelite who had married a foreign woman.** Ref.: Ezra 10:34. ¶

ULAI – ***'ûlay*** [proper noun: אוּלַי <195>; of Persian deriv.]: muddy water ▶ **A river (or canal) of Persia beside which Daniel had a vision.** Refs.: Dan. 8:2, 16. ¶

ULAM – ***'ûlām*** [masc. proper noun: אוּלָם <198>; apparently from BIND <481> (in the sense of dumbness)]: solitary ▶

a. A descendant of Manasseh. Refs.: 1 Chr. 7:16, 17. ¶

b. A descendant of Benjamin. Refs.: 1 Chr. 8:39, 40. ¶

ULCER – Lev. 22:22 ➔ DISCHARGE <2990>.

ULLA – ***'ullā'*** [proper masc. noun: עֻלָּא <5925>; fem. of YOKE <5923>]: yoke, burden ▶ **An Israelite of the tribe of Asher.** Ref.: 1 Chr. 7:39. ¶

UMMAH – ***'ummāh*** [proper noun: עֻמָּה <5981>; the same as NEXT TO <5980> (in the sense of association)]: next to, union ▶ **A city give to Asher as part of their inheritance.** Ref.: Josh. 19:30. ¶

UNCIRCUMCISED – ***'ārêl*** [masc. adj.: עָרֵל <6189>; from NAKEDNESS (EXPOSE ONE'S) <6188>] ▶ **In the literal sense, this word was used to designate a specific individual (Gen. 17:14; Ex. 12:48); a group (Josh. 5:7); or a nation, especially the Philistines (1 Sam. 14:6; Is. 52:1).** In addition to the simple statement of physical condition, the term could also convey an attitude of derision since the object was considered unclean and impure (Judg. 14:3; 15:18). Furthermore, the term could be used metaphorically to describe the corrupted nature of certain body parts: uncircumcised lips denoted an inability to speak effectively (Ex. 6:12, 30; cf. Is. 6:5); uncircumcised in heart represented a flawed character and precluded entrance to the Temple (Ezek. 44:7, 9); and uncircumcised in the ear signified an inability to hear (Jer. 6:10). Also, the fruit of newly planted trees was considered uncircumcised (unclean) for the first three years (Lev. 19:23). *

UNCIRCUMCISED (BE EXPOSED AS) – Hab. 2:16 ➔ NAKEDNESS (EXPOSE ONE'S) <6188>.

UNCIRCUMCISION (SHOW ONE'S) – Hab. 2:16 ➔ NAKEDNESS (EXPOSE ONE'S) <6188>.

UNCLE – Lev. 10:4; 1 Sam. 10:14–16; Esther 2:15 ➔ <1730>.

UNCLE'S WIFE – Lev. 20:20 ➔ FATHER'S SISTER <1733>.

UNCLEAN – 1 ***ṭāmê'*** [adj.: טָמֵא <2931>; from UNCLEAN (BE) <2930>] ▶ **This word denotes impure or defiled.** Refs.: Is. 6:5; Ezek. 22:5. It can also refer to ritually unclean items such as people, things, foods, and places. The land east of the Jordan (Josh. 22:19) and foreign lands (Amos 7:17) were unclean in contrast to the land of Israel. *

2 ***niyḏāh*** [fem. noun: נִידָה <5206>; fem. of COMFORT (noun) <5205> (in the sense of to move)] ▶

a. This word refers to something polluted, detestable. It is used of Jerusalem, a city that had become detestable because of her sins and harlotries (Lam. 1:8; also translated filthy, vile). ¶

b. This word indicates something that has been removed. It describes Jerusalem as removed by God in His judgments on her (Lam. 1:8, KJV). ¶

– 3 Ezra 2:62; Neh. 7:64 ➔ DEFILE <1351> 4 Is. 30:22 ➔ FAINT (adj.)

<1739> [5] Ezek. 4:14 → OFFENSIVE THING <6292>.

UNCLEAN (BE) – ***ṭāmê', ṭām'āh*** [verb: טָמֵא, טָמְאָה <2930>; a prim. root] ▶ **This word means to be impure, to become impure and also to desecrate, to defile, to make impure. The main idea of this action was that of contaminating or corrupting, especially in the sight of God.** The Levitical Law often spoke in terms of sexual, religious, or ceremonial uncleanness. Any object or individual who was not clean could not be acceptable to the Holy God of Israel. Examples of actions that caused a state of impurity would include eating forbidden food (Hos. 9:4); worshiping idols (Ps. 106:39; Hos. 5:3); committing adultery or engaging in sexual relations outside of marriage (Gen. 34:5; Num. 5:13; Ezek. 18:6); touching unclean objects or individuals (Lev. 5:3; 18:24; 19:31); and any action that violated the sacredness of the Lord (Jer. 32:34). It was the duty of the priesthood to discern matters of impurity (Lev. 13:3; Hag. 2:13) and to see that the strict rituals of purification were followed. *

UNCLEAN (BECOME) – Lam. 1:8 → GLUTTON (BE) <2151> a.

UNCLEANNESS – ***ṭum'āh*** [fem. noun: טֻמְאָה <2932>; from UNCLEAN (BE) <2930>] ▶ **This word means impurity; it is also translated filthiness.** It refers to the sexual impurity of a woman during the menstrual cycle (Num. 5:19; Lam. 1:9). It can also denote any unclean thing from which the Temple needed to be purified (2 Chr. 29:16). Finally, both ethical and religious uncleanness were dealt with: in the laws referring to proper behavior (Lev. 16:16); and in the heart, referring to an unclean spirit that causes one to lie (Ezek. 24:13). *

UNCONTROLLED – Gen. 49:4 → RECKLESSNESS <6349>.

UNCOVER – [1] ***'ûr*** [verb: עוּר <5783>; a primitive root] ▶ **This word means to be exposed; it is also translated to make ready, to make bare, to make naked, to strip.** It is used of God's bow, His weapon, being readied for battle (Hab. 3:9). ¶
– [2] Lev. 18:6 → REVEAL <1540> [3] Is. 22:6; Zeph. 2:14 → EMPTY (verb) <6168> [4] Jer. 13:26 → STRIP <2834>.

UNDER – [1] ***teḥôṯ*** [Aramaic prep.: תְּחוֹת <8460>; corresponding to <8478> below] ▶ **This word locates something below something else.** It is used figuratively and literally (Jer. 10:11). In the king's dream, the beasts of the field found shade under a great tree (Dan. 4:12, 14, 21). God has all dominion under the heavens, and He has all rulership under Him (Dan. 7:27). ¶
[2] ***taḥaṯ***] [prep.: תַּחַת <8478>; from an unused root meaning to depress] ▶ **This word means beneath; in place of. It indicates a position below or underneath some other reference point (Gen. 1:7, 9; 2:21; with suffix *taḥten-nāh*; Gen. 18:4).** It can mean in place of, instead of (Gen. 4:25; Ex. 21:26). *Taḥaṯ meh* means under what? why? (Jer. 5:19). Under something may be indicated by *le*, to, following this word (Ezek. 10:2). Out from under has *min*, from, attached to the front of *taḥaṯ* (Ex. 6:7), out from under the oppression of the Egyptians. It may be used as a noun (see Gen. 2:21 above) to indicate the place under someone or something, on the spot (NASB) (2 Sam. 2:23). *
[3] ***taḥaṯ*** [Aramaic prep.: תַּחַת <8479>; corresponding to <8478> above] ▶ **This word refers to a place or a time below or before something else.** Ref.: Dan. 4:14. ¶

UNDERFOOT (TREAD) – Mic. 7:19 → SUBDUE <3533>.

UNDERGARMENT – ***miḵnās*** [masc. noun: מִכְנָס <4370>; from STORE (LAY IN) <3647> in the sense of hiding] ▶ **This word designates breeches, underwear.** These were trousers or breeches for the priests, a garment for the hips and thighs (Ex. 28:42; 39:28; Lev. 6:10; 16:4; Ezek. 44:18). ¶

UNDERGROWTH – Job 30:7 → NETTLES <2738>.

UNDERSTAND – See PERCEIVE <995>.

UNDERSTANDING – [1] ***biynāh*** [fem. noun: בִּינָה <998>; from PERCEIVE <995>] ▶ **This word means comprehension, discernment, righteous action. It is found mainly in wisdom literature, the Psalms, in several of the major prophets, and 1 and 2 Chronicles. In nearly all the literary contexts in the Bible where it occurs with these basic meanings, it carries strong moral and religious connotations.** In Job 28:28, the act of turning away from evil was said to be understanding and was based on a prior proper discernment of what was evil. A lack of this kind of understanding was morally culpable and resulted in sin and even drove away God's compassion for persons who did not have it (Is. 27:11). Happily, understanding as a moral or religious entity can be acquired (Prov. 4:5, 7) and even increased (Is. 29:24) by seeking after it diligently. The understanding that God desires has a cognitive dimension, therefore, as further illustrated when the author of Proverbs spoke of words of "understanding" (Prov. 1:2). The understanding and discernment that is the object of all knowing is the knowledge of the Holy One (Prov. 9:10). Understanding is to mark God's people. It is not surprising, therefore, to learn that by means of understanding, God made all His created order (cf. Ps. 136:5).

God has graciously endowed human beings with the ability of understanding and comprehension, but this faculty is not infallible, and, therefore, we are to ask God for guidance at all times (Prov. 3:5). Our own ability of understanding should, however, function to give us discernment, for instance, in showing a proper attitude toward seeking the riches of this world (Prov. 23:4). Our understanding is also the ability that enables us to understand languages (Is. 33:19), literature, visions, and dreams (Dan. 1:20). It is the ability that decodes the symbols of communication for us. The writer of Proverbs personifies understanding along with wisdom in the famous wisdom chapter of Proverbs (Prov. 2:3; Prov. 8:14). *

[2] ***biynāh*** [Aramaic fem. noun: בִּינָה <999>; corresponding to <998> above] ▶ **The Hebrew root for this word means to distinguish, to separate, to perceive. This word is also translated discerning.** Therefore, this word carries the idea of discernment, as one separates the truth from lies (Dan. 2:21). ¶

[3] ***śoḵlᵉṯānû*** [Aramaic fem. noun: שָׂכְלְתָנוּ <7924>; from CONSIDER <7920>] ▶ **This word means and is also translated insight, intelligence.** It is used in Daniel 5:11, 12, and 14. In this context, it described Daniel's wisdom and insight into the interpretation of dreams. It was obvious to the people around Daniel that his wisdom was not merely human wisdom, for they said he had the spirit of the gods living in him and that he was like the gods. Thus, this wisdom cannot be gained by mere human training. It comes as a gift from God. The pagan culture did not attribute it to the one true God but to their gods. ¶

[4] ***tᵉḇûnāh*** [fem. noun: תְּבוּנָה <8394>; from PERCEIVE <995>] ▶ **This word occurs primarily in the Wisdom Literature and is associated with both wisdom and knowledge; it also means insight.** Refs.: Ex. 35:31; Prov. 8:1; 21:30). It is contrasted with foolishness (Prov. 15:21; 18:2). A person of understanding is slow to wrath and walks uprightly (Prov. 14:29; 15:21). God has understanding and gives it (Job 12:13; Ps. 147:5; Prov. 2:6; Is. 40:28). On the other hand, idolaters, who fashion idols by their own understanding, have no understanding at all (Is. 44:19; Hos. 13:2). *

– [5] Job 12:20 ➔ TASTE (noun) <2940> [6] Dan. 4:34 ➔ KNOWLEDGE <4486>.

UNDERSTANDING (BEYOND) – Judg. 13:18 ➔ WONDERFUL <6383>.

UNDERSTANDING (GET) – Job 11:12 ➔ HEART (RAVISH THE) <3823>.

UNDERTAKE – [1] Gen. 18:27; Deut. 1:5 ➔ CONTENT (BE) <2974> [2] Deut. 12:7, 18; 15:10; 23:20; 28:8, 20 ➔ LAY, PUT <4916> b.

UNDERTAKER – Amos 6:10 ➔ BURN (verb) <5635>.

UNDESIRABLE – Zeph. 2:1 ➔ LONG FOR <3700>.

UNDIMMED (BE) – Deut. 34:7 ➔ lit.: to no be dim ➔ DIM (BE) <3543> a.

UNDIVIDED – Ps. 86:11 ➔ give me an undivided heart (NIV) ➔ lit.: unite my heart ➔ UNITE <3161>.

UNDO – Is. 58:6 ➔ LOOSE (LET) <5425>.

UNDOING – Prov. 18:7 ➔ RUIN (noun) <4288>.

UNDONE (BE) – [1] Num. 17:12 ➔ PERISH <6> [2] Is. 6:5 ➔ CEASE <1820>.

UNDRESSED – Lev. 25:5 ➔ NAZIRITE <5139>.

UNEVEN – Is. 40:4 ➔ DECEITFUL <6121>.

UNFAITHFUL – [1] Deut. 32:20 ➔ lit.: not faithful ➔ FAITHFUL <529> [2] Jer. 31:22; 49:4 ➔ BACKSLIDING <7728>.

UNFAITHFULLY (ACT) – See TRANSGRESS <4603>.

UNFAMILIAR – Ezek. 3:5, 6 ➔ UNINTELLIGIBLE <6012>.

UNFATHOMABLE – See SEARCH (noun) <2714>.

UNFOLDING – ***pêṯaḥ*** [masc. noun: פֵּתַח <6608>; from OPEN <6605>] ▶ **This word indicates a place of access into something; it is also translated entrance.** Used of God's words, it refers to the understanding and wisdom they give to a person (Ps. 119:130). ¶

UNFORMED BODY – Ps. 139:16 ➔ UNFORMED SUBSTANCE <1564>.

UNFORMED SUBSTANCE – ***gōlem*** [masc. noun: גֹּלֶם <1564>; from ROLL (verb) <1563>] ▶ **This word designates a fetus or embryo; it is also translated unperfect substance, unformed body.** It refers to the unformed child or embryo in the womb, something that God's eyes saw before its birth (Ps. 139:16). ¶

UNFORTUNATE – [1] Ps. 10:8, 10, 14 ➔ HELPLESS <2489> [2] Prov. 31:8 ➔ DESTRUCTION <2475>.

UNGODLINESS – [1] Is. 32:6 ➔ HYPOCRISY <2612> [2] Jer. 23:15 ➔ PROFANENESS <2613>.

UNGODLY – [1] ***ʿᵃwiyl*** [masc. noun: עֲוִיל <5760>; from UNJUSTLY (DEAL) <5765>] ▶ **This word means an unjust one, an evil one. Derived from a verb meaning to act wrongfully, this term appears once in the Old Testament, where it has the sense of ungodly or evil people.** Ref.: Job 16:11; NASB: ruffians. Job used the term to describe Bildad, Zophar, and Eliphaz, his accusers, whom he sarcastically referred to as his friends (cf. Job 16:20). ¶
– [2] See GODLESS <2611>.

UNGODLY (BE) – Jer. 23:11 ➔ DEFILED (BE) <2610>.

UNHOLY – Lev. 10:10; Ezek. 22:26; 44:23 ➔ COMMON <2455>.

UNICORN – Num. 23:22; 24:8; Ps. 22:21; etc. ➔ WILD OX <7214>.

UNINTELLIGIBLE – ***ʿāmêq*** [adj.: עָמֵק <6012>; from DEEP, DEEP (BE) <6009>] ▶ **This word means deep, unfathomable; it is also translated obscure, unfamiliar, strange, foreign. Both times it is used to describe the speech of foreign peoples as unintelligible.** Isaiah spoke of the return from Babylon, telling the people that they would no longer hear the unintelligible speech of foreigners (Is. 33:19). When God called Ezekiel, He told him that he was to speak to the house of Israel, not to people of unintelligible speech (Ezek. 3:5, 6). ¶

UNIT – 2 Sam. 2:25 ➔ BUNCH <92>.

UNITE – ***yāḥad*** [verb: יָחַד <3161>; a prim. root] ► **This word means to join, to be united.** It refers to entering into the plan or thinking of a group, uniting with them (Gen. 49:6), letting one's honor be united to their cause. Job asks that the night of his birth not be joined or united to the days of the year (Job 3:6). It is used figuratively of the psalmist's desire for the Lord to unite his heart to walk in God's ways and to fear him (Ps. 86:11). It refers to persons going to the grave or Sheol upon death to "unite" with those they have known (Is. 14:20). ¶

UNJUST – Job 31:3 ➔ WICKED <5767>.

UNJUST GAIN – 1 Prov. 28:8 ➔ PROFIT (noun) <8636> 2 Prov. 28:16 ➔ OPPRESSIONS <4642>.

UNJUSTLY (DEAL) – ***'āwal*** [verb: עָוַל <5765>; a prim. root] ► **This word means to act wrongfully, to act unjustly, to deviate from the moral standard; it is also translated to deal corruptly, to go on doing evil.** The word is derived from the noun meaning injustice or iniquity. It occurs in Isaiah 26:10, where the prophet bemoaned the fact that despite God's showing grace to the wicked, they continued to act wrongfully. The verb occurs as a substantive participle where the psalmist prayed for deliverance from the clutches of the unrighteous (Ps. 71:4; also translated wrongdoer, unjust, one who is evil). See the noun *'āwel* (INJUSTICE <5766>]). ¶

UNKNOWN – Prov. 22:29 ➔ OBSCURE <2823>.

UNLEASH – Job 37:3 ➔ LOOSE (LET) <8281>.

UNLEAVENED BREAD – ***maṣṣāh*** [fem. noun: מַצָּה <4682>; from DRINK DEEPLY <4711> in the sense of greedily devouring for sweetness] ► **This food was a staple in Israelite diets and could be prepared in a hurry for a meal.** Refs.: Gen. 19:3, 1 Sam. 28:24. Each week priests placed fresh unleavened bread on the table of showbread in the Tabernacle and ate the past week's bread (Ex. 25:30; Lev. 24:5–9). One of the seven Israelite feasts was the Feast of Unleavened Bread where the people ate flat bread for seven days to commemorate their deliverance from Egypt (Ex. 23:15). Unleavened bread or cakes could also be anointed with oil and presented to the priests as a sacrifice (Ex. 29:2). *

UNLOVED – ***śāniy'*** [fem. adj.: שְׂנִיא <8146>; from HATE <8130>] ► **This word means one who is hated or held in aversion. It is used in Deuteronomy 21:15 contrasting a wife who is loved with a wife who is hated.** There does not seem to be a connotation of extreme hate here but rather of dislike, preferring one wife to the other. The terms are used as opposites, but the strength of opposition cannot be determined accurately. In this limited context, it is difficult to tell how strong of a connotation the word really holds, but here it seems to connote more dislike or neglect than strong hate that would lead to overtly hateful actions toward that person. ¶

UNMINDFUL (BE) – ***šāyāh*** [verb: שָׁיָה <7876>; a prim. root] ► **This word means to not pay attention to something, to disregard it, in this case Israel's Rock, God.** Ref.: Deut. 32:18; also translated to neglect, to desert. ¶

UNNI – ***'unniy*** [masc. proper noun: עֻנִּי <6042>; from AFFLICTED (BE) <6031>]: poor, afflicted ►
a. A Levite who took part at the celebration when the ark of the covenant was brought to Jerusalem. Refs.: 1 Chr. 15:18, 20. ¶
b. A Levite who returned to Jerusalem from the Babylonian captivity. Ref.: Neh. 12:9. ¶

UNNOTICED – 1 Sam. 24:4 ➔ ENCHANTMENT <3909>.

UNPERFECT SUBSTANCE – Ps. 139:16 ➔ UNFORMED SUBSTANCE <1564>.

UNPLOWED FIELD – Prov. 13:23; 21:4 ➔ FALLOW GROUND <5215>.

UNPLOWED GROUND – Jer. 4:3; Hos. 10:12 ➔ FALLOW GROUND <5215>.

UNPRINCIPLED – Zeph. 3:4 ➔ RECKLESS (BE) <6348>.

UNPROFITABLE – Job 15:3 ➔ PROFITABLE (BE) <5532> a.

UNRELIABLE – Jer. 15:18 ➔ DECEPTIVE <391>.

UNREST – Amos 3:9 ➔ CONFUSION <4103>.

UNRIGHTEOUS – Job 18:21; 29:17; 31:3; Zeph. 3:5 ➔ WICKED <5767>.

UNRIPE GRAPE – 1 ***beser*** [masc. noun: בֶּסֶר <1154>; from an unused root meaning to be sour] ▶ **This word is used to depict the distasteful character of the success of the wicked man.** His renown and good fortune drop off like a sour or unripe grape at the peak of his success (Job 15:33). ¶
2 ***bōser*** [masc. noun: בֹּסֶר <1155>; from the same as <1154> above] ▶ **This word depicts a sour grape or unripe grape.** It describes the infamous fortune of a wicked man that is quickly gone like a vine casts off unripe or sour grapes (Job 15:33). It is also used of ripening grapes (Is. 18:5, NASB; KJV, sour grape). It was used figuratively with the meaning sour grapes to describe something that had a destructive impact upon the descendants of the fathers who ate the sour grapes (Jer. 31:29, 30; Ezek. 18:2). ¶

UNRULY (BE) – Hos. 11:12 ➔ RESTLESS (BE, BECOME, GROW) <7300>.

UNSAVORY THING – Job 23:13 ➔ WRONGDOING <8604>.

UNSAVOURY – Job 6:6 ➔ FOOLISH <8602> a.

UNSEARCHABLE – See SEARCH (noun) <2714>.

UNSHOD – Jer. 2:25 ➔ BAREFOOT <3182>.

UNSTABLE – Gen. 49:4 ➔ RECKLESSNESS <6349>.

UNSTEADY – ***mû'edet*** [fem. noun: מוּעֶדֶת <4154>; fem. pass. part. of SLIP <4571>] ▶ **This word is used of a weak foot that cannot be counted on; it is also translated out of joint, lame, that slips.** Ref.: Prov. 25:19. ¶

UNSUITED – Prov. 17:7 ➔ not beautiful ➔ BEAUTIFUL <5000>.

UNTEMPERED MORTAR – Ezek. 13:10, 11, 14, 15; 22:28 ➔ FOOLISH <8602> c.

UNTENDED – Lev. 25:5 ➔ NAZIRITE <5139>.

UNTIL – 1 ***'ad*** [prep. and adv.: עַד <5704>; the same as ETERNITY <5703>] ▶ **This word means as far as, up to, unto, while.** It is used of time meaning until (Gen. 3:19; 8:5; 33:3; Judg. 6:31; 1 Sam. 1:14); of space indicating distance (Gen. 11:31; 12:6; 13:3); of the inclusiveness of a category of things (Gen. 6:7; 7:23). It is used adverbially to express degree: *'ad m^e'ōd*, greatly, quickly (Ps. 147:15); up to half of something (Esther 5:6); the extent of something (Deut. 2:5). It may function as a conjunction as well, meaning basically until: of a past time (Ex. 32:20); of a future time (Gen. 27:44). It may indicate the time while something is being done (1 Sam. 14:9). It is found in various phases and idioms: *'ad merāḥôq*, unto a distant (place) (Is. 57:9); *min* (<4480> . . . (*w^e*) *'ad*, from . . . as far as, to (Gen. 10:19); *min . . . w^e'ad*, from . . . to (Gen. 19:4), from a boy to an old person, both. *
2 ***'ad*** [Aramaic particle: עַד <5705>; corresponding to <5704> above] ▶ **This particle**

functions as a preposition or a conjunction meaning until, unto. It is used of spatial ideas: right up to, as far as (Dan. 7:13); up to this point (Dan. 7:28); and of temporal ideas: until evening (Dan. 6:14); until right now (Ezra 5:16); until the end, finally (Dan. 4:5). As a conjunction in the phrase *'aḏ dî* (Dan. 2:9, 34; 4:23, 25, 32, 33; 5:21), it means until. It is also used to indicate a limit in quantity (Ezra 7:22; Dan. 7:22, 25, 26, 28). Used alone, it means until (Ezra 4:21; 5:5). *

UNTIMELY BIRTH – Job 3:16 ➔ STILLBORN <5309>.

UNTRIMMED – Lev. 25:5 ➔ NAZIRITE <5139>.

UNWALLED – ***pᵉrāziy*** [masc. noun: פְּרָזִי <6521>; from TOWN (UNWALLED, RURAL) <6519>] ► **This word designates a village, a town not surrounded by walls.** It refers to rural areas and open villages as well as the peasantry living there (Deut. 3:5; 1 Sam. 6:18; Esther 9:19). ¶

UNWELL – Lev. 15:33 ➔ FAINT (adj.) <1739>.

UNWILLING – Is. 30:15 ➔ lit.: not willing ➔ WILLING (BE) <14>.

UNWORTHY (BE) – Gen. 32:10 ➔ WORTHY (BE NOT) <6994>.

UPHAZ – ***'ûpāz*** [proper noun: אוּפָז <210>; perhaps a corruption of OPHIR <211>]: island of gold ► **A country producing gold.** Refs.: Jer. 10:9; Dan. 10:5. ¶

UPON – 1 ***'al*** [prep.: עַל <5921>; the same as ABOVE <5920>] ► **This Hebrew word means on, over, against, by, to, for. The various nuances of this preposition are wide-ranging, and the context determines its exact meaning and usage.** Here are some basics: on, upon (Gen. 1:11, 26; Ex. 20:12; 2 Sam. 4:7); in front of (Gen. 18:8; Ex. 27:21); to, unto plus *mî*, "to whom" (Jer. 6:10); with *zô'ṯ* or *kên* following, it means because of, therefore with respect to, concerning (Gen. 20:3; Ruth 4:7); as or according to (Ps. 110:4); besides or over against (Ex. 20:3); to come on (one's) heart, means to come to mind, to think of (Jer. 3:16); to add to, in addition to (*yāsaḇ 'al*) (Gen. 28:9; 31:50; Deut. 19:9); it has the sense of with, met with (Ex. 3:18). Other phrases include: *kᵉ'al-ḵōl*, according to all (Is. 63:7); from upon, upon, e.g., a camel (Gen. 2:5; 19:24; 24:64); *'al-bᵉlî*, that . . . not (Gen. 31:20); *'al-ᵃšer*, because (Ex. 32:35). It is used to indicate God's provincial care, His hand on (*'al*) someone (Neh. 2:8); and to indicate a burden on someone (Ex. 5:8; 21:22; Job 7:20; Ps. 42:6; Is. 1:14). It indicates the thing one speaks about or is concerned with when used with verbs of speaking, hearing (Judg. 9:3; Jer. 16:3). It has the sense of eminence or exaltation, above (Deut. 26:19; Ps. 57:5, 11). It indicates what one exercises authority over (Is. 22:15). It is used in the idiom, to fall asleep, sleep falls on someone (Gen. 2:21; 15:12); and of the activity of the mind setting on (*'al*) something (2 Sam. 14:1; Jer. 22:17; Mal. 3:13). It is used of an army attacking against (*'al*) a foe (Gen. 34:25; Deut. 19:11; Amos 7:9). *

2 ***'al*** [Aramaic prep.: עַל <5922>; corresponding to <5921> above] ► **This Aramaic word means on, to, against, for.** Its basic meanings are evident in context: upon something (Dan. 2:10, 28, 46; 5:5, 7; 6:10). It indicates with respect to whom emotion or appearance changes (Dan. 5:9; 7:28). Other senses of the word: on account of, because (Dan. 3:16); concerning (Dan. 2:18). With verbs of authority or rulership, it indicates what is ruled over (Dan. 2:48, 49; 3:12; 4:17). It may express direction toward (Ezra 4:11, 17, 18; 5:6; Dan. 2:24; 4:34, 36). *

UPPER – ***'illiy*** [adj.: עִלִּי <5942>; from OFFER <5927> (in the sense of high)] ► **This word describes what is located physically higher, more elevated than something else.** E.g., upper springs as opposed to lower springs (Josh. 15:19; Judg. 1:15). ¶

UPPER ROOM – 1 ***ᶜᵃliyyāh*** [fem. noun: עֲלִיָּה <5944>; fem. from OFFER <5927> (in the sense of something lofty)] ► **This**

word indicates a chamber, a parlor. It is used of a rooftop chamber or room (Judg. 3:20, 23–25; Jer. 22:13, 14); an upper room over a gate (2 Sam. 18:33). Figuratively, it depicts God's structuring upper chambers at the time of creation (Ps. 104:3, 13). *
– [2] Judg. 3:20, 24 → ROOF CHAMBER <4747>.

UPRIGHT – [1] ***qôm^e^miyyûṯ*** [fem. noun: קוֹמְמִיּוּת <6968>; from STAND, STAND UP <6965>] ▶ **This word indicates uprightness, erectness. It is used of something standing straight and tall.** In a figurative sense, it refers to Israel's self-worth, reasonable pride (Lev. 26:13). ¶
– [2] 1 Kgs. 3:6 (NIV) → UPRIGHTNESS <3483> [3] 1 Kgs. 7:28, 29 → FRAME <7948> [4] Jer. 10:5 → HAMMERED, HAMMERED WORK <4749>.

UPRIGHT WAY – Is. 57:2 → RIGHT <5228>.

UPRIGHTLY – Is. 57:2 → RIGHT <5228>.

UPRIGHTNESS – [1] ***yišrāh*** [fem. noun: יִשְׁרָה <3483>; fem. of RIGHT <3477>] ▶ **This word means straightness, equity; it is derived from *yāšar* [STRAIGHT (BE) <3474>].** It occurs only in 1 Kings 3:6 where Solomon's prayer referred to the uprightness of David's heart. It was rewarded with lovingkindness, especially the lovingkindness of having his son reign after him. David's life ruled out any meaning of sinlessness and pointed to repentance, faith, and knowledge of God as central to his uprightness (cf. Rom. 4:6–8). ¶
[2] ***yōšer*** [verb: יֹשֶׁר <3476>; from STRAIGHT (BE) <3474>] ▶ **This word means straightness, equity.** The Old Testament often talks of two paths in life and warns people to stay on the straight path and not to stray onto the crooked path (Prov. 2:13). David was praised for walking in an upright manner before the Lord (1 Kgs. 9:4). Uprightness was also praised as a good quality to possess (Prov. 17:26). The word can also designate virtuous words that one speaks (Job 6:25). Another meaning less common is related to equity: one should give to another what is due to him or her (Prov. 11:24). *
– [3] Is. 26:10; 59:14 → RIGHT <5229> [4] Is. 57:2 → RIGHT <5228>.

UPROAR (BE IN AN) – Ps. 2:1 → RAGE (verb) <7283>.

UPROOT – [1] ***nāṯaš*** [verb: נָתַשׁ <5428>; a prim. root] ▶ **This word means to pluck up by the roots, to root out. It means to tear something out, to pull out by its roots.** God pulled out pagan gods or worship symbols, Asherim (Mic. 5:14); He uprooted His people from His land (Deut. 29:28; 1 Kgs. 14:15; Jer. 12:14, 15, Jer. 12:17); Jeremiah as a prophet uprooted, plucked up nations (Jer. 1:10). In its passive sense, it means to be uprooted, to be plucked out (Ezek. 19:12; Dan. 11:4). *
– [2] Deut. 28:63; Prov. 2:22 → TEAR) <5255> [3] Ps. 80:13 → RAVAGE (verb) <3765> [4] Eccl. 3:2; Zeph. 2:4 → HAMSTRING <6131> b. [5] Dan. 7:8 → ROOTS (PLUCK UP . . .) <6132>.

UPROOTED (BE) – Ps. 52:5; Job 31:8 → ROOT (TAKE) <8327>.

UPSIDE DOWN, AROUND (TURNING THINGS) – Is. 29:16 → OPPOSITE (noun) <2016>.

UR – ***'ûr*** [proper noun: אוּר <218>; the same as FIRE <217>]: brilliance, fire, i.e., the East, the region of light ▶
a. The name of the city that Terah and Abraham left to go to Haran. Refs.: Gen. 11:28, 31; 15:7; Neh. 9:7. It is called "Ur of the Chaldeans." It was most likely in southeast Iraq on the Euphrates River. It is probably ancient Tell el-Muqayyar. A few scholars have argued that it is somewhere in northern Mesopotamia or even southeast Turkey. Many ancient tablets have been uncovered there, and the "Law Code" of Ur-Nammu has been found and deciphered. It became the location of the much later neo-Babylonian kings (626–538 B.C.). ¶
b. The father of one of David's mighty men. Ref.: 1 Chr. 11:35. ¶

URGE – 1 ***'ālaṣ*** [verb: אָלַץ <509>; a prim. root] ▶ **This word means to press, to press upon someone.** Delilah urged Samson in her efforts to wring information out of him. Ref.: Judg. 16:16; also translated to press, to prod. ¶
– 2 Gen. 19:15 ➔ HASTEN <213> 3 Gen. 33:11; Judg. 19:7 ➔ PRESS <6484> 4 Prov. 16:26 ➔ CRAVE <404>.

URGENT (BE) – 1 ***ḥ*****ª*****ṣap*** [Aramaic verb: חֲצַף <2685>; a prim. root] ▶ **This word means to be pressing, harsh, severe.** It indicates something that is either urgent or severe, such as Nebuchadnezzar's command to kill the wise men of Babylon (Dan. 2:15; also translated to be harsh, to be hasty); or his order to heat the furnace seven times hotter than normal to kill the three Jewish young men (Dan. 3:22) when they were thrown into it. ¶
– 2 Ex. 5:13 ➔ HASTEN <213> 3 1 Sam. 21:8 ➔ HASTE (REQUIRE) <5169>.

URI – ***'ûriy*** [masc. proper noun: אוּרִי <221>; from FIRE <217>]: the Lord is light ▶
a. The name of the father of Bezaleel of the tribe of Judah. Refs.: Ex. 31:2; 35:30; 38:22; 1 Chr. 2:20; 2 Chr. 1:5. ¶
b. The father of an official of Solomon. Ref.: 1 Kgs. 4:19. ¶
c. A gatekeeper. Ref.: Ezra 10:24. ¶

URIAH – ***'ûriyyah*** [masc. proper noun: אוּרִיָּה <223>; from FIRE <217> and LORD <3050>]: the Lord is light ▶
a. A Hittite who served in David's army. Ref.: 2 Sam. 11. David eventually had him killed in battle. Bathsheba was his wife. He was a member of David's elite forces (2 Sam. 23:39; 1 Chr. 11:41). He proved himself to be an honorable man before David had him killed (Deut. 23:10, 11; 2 Sam. 11:11). *
b. The name of a priest who served as a witness for Isaiah the prophet at God's directions. Refs.: Is. 8:1–4. He would witness a legal action to which he could later bear witness. He served as a priest under King Ahaz (735–715 B.C.) (2 Kgs. 16:10, 11). He took part in the construction of an idolatrous altar in Judah (2 Kgs. 16:12–16). *
c. The name of a prophet in Judah. He is famous for his prophecies against Jerusalem that were in complete agreement with Jeremiah's prophecies. Refs.: Jer. 26:20–23. He fled from Jehoiakim but was eventually captured and put to death in Jerusalem (Jer. 26:23; cf. Luke 11:47). ¶
d. The name of a returned exile. His name is recorded in Nehemiah 3:4, 21. He was a priest and the father of Meremoth (cf. Ezra 8:33). ¶
e. The name of a returned exile from Babylon. He stood by and supported Ezra's reading of the Law at the Watergate (Neh. 8:4). He may be the Uriah listed in d. above. ¶

URIEL – ***'ûriyêl*** [masc. proper noun: אוּרִיאֵל <222>; from FIRE <217> and GOD <410>]: God is light ▶
a. The name of a Levite, a descendant of Kohath. Ref.: 1 Chr. 6:24. ¶
b. A Levite under David. Refs.: 1 Chr. 15:5, 11. ¶
c. The grandfather of Abijah, king of Judah. Ref.: 2 Chr. 13:2. ¶

URIM – ***'ûriym*** [masc. plur. noun: אוּרִים <224>; plur. of FIRE <217>]: lights ▶ **This word occurs seven times in the Old Testament, usually with "the Thummim." Our knowledge of the Urim and Thummim (lights and perfections) is limited.** They were kept in the breastplate which the high priest wore over his heart (Ex. 28:30; Lev. 8:8) and were given to the Levites as part of Moses' blessing (Deut. 33:8). Some believe they were flat objects which were cast to determine the will of God, one providing a negative answer and the other a positive, much like casting lots. However, that is somewhat conjectural. Joshua received God's revelation by Eleazer's use of the Urim (Num. 27:21). God didn't answer Saul when he consulted the Lord with the use of the Urim (1 Sam. 28:6). The Urim and Thummim were also used to approve priestly qualifications (Ezra 2:63; Neh. 7:65). ¶

URINATE AGAINST THE WALL – ***šaṯan*** [verb: שָׁתַן <8366>; a prim. root] ▶

This Hebrew word describes a male. It is a derogatory phrase making light of enemies, threatening to destroy them down to the last man (KJV, 1 Sam. 25:22, 34). It is translated politely as all who belong to him (NASB, NIV) by some translators. Likewise, compare the remaining references to see how it is translated euphemistically, except by the KJV translators. Its idiomatic sense is that every male will be cut off. Other refs.: 1 Kgs. 14:10; 16:11; 21:21; 2 Kgs. 9:8. ¶

URINE – ***šayin*** [masc. noun: שַׁיִן <7890>; from an unused root meaning to urinate] ▶ **This word refers to the waste product in liquid form secreted by the kidneys.** The context refers to a desperate time of siege when persons will be reduced to drinking their own urine (2 Kgs. 18:27; Is. 36:12). ¶

USE (BE NO) – Is. 57:10; Jer. 2:25; 18:12 ➔ DESPAIR (verb) <2976>.

USE (BE OF) – Job 22:2 ➔ PROFITABLE (BE) <5532> a.

USELESS – Job 15:3 ➔ PROFITABLE (BE) <5532> a.

USURY – 1 ***maššā'*** [masc. noun: מַשָּׁא <4855>; from LEND <5383>] ▶ **This word indicates an excessive profit, often in high interest charges.** Refs.: Neh. 5:7, 10. It has the meaning of debt (Neh. 10:31; Prov. 22:26). ¶
– 2 Ex. 22:25; Lev. 25:36, 37; etc. ➔ INTEREST <5392>.

USURY (GIVER OF) – Is. 24:2 ➔ DEBT (IN) <5378>.

USURY (TAKER OF) – Is. 24:2 ➔ LEND <5383>.

UTENSIL – Ezra 5:14, 15; 6:5; 7:19 ➔ VESSEL <3984>.

UTHAI – ***'ûṯay*** [proper noun: עוּתַי <5793>; from SUSTAIN <5790>]: succoring ▶
a. A son of Ammihud. Ref.: 1 Chr. 9:4. ¶
b. A son of Bigvai. Ref.: Ezra 8:14. ¶

UTMOST – 1 Ps. 139:22 ➔ END <8503> 2 Jer. 9:26; 25:23; 49:32 ➔ CUT OFF <7112> b.

UTMOST BOUND – ***ta'ᵃwāh*** [fem. noun: תַּאֲוָה <8379>; from DRAW A LINE <8376>] ▶ **This word indicates an outer limit.** It refers to the geographical extent of an area, the farthest boundary or distance (Gen. 49:26). ¶

UTTER – 1 ***nāḇa'*** [verb: נָבַע <5042>; a prim. root] ▶ **A verb meaning to spew out, to say something. It refers to something pouring forth, bubbling out.** The language and speech of the heavens (Ps. 19:2); evil persons, foolish talk (Ps. 59:7; 94:4); wise speech (Ps. 78:2). It is used of the spirit of wisdom being poured out profusely on persons (Prov. 1:23; 18:4). When fools speak, they are spouting out (also translated gushing out) foolishness, folly that creates dissension (Prov. 15:2, 28). It may have the sense of to cause to exude (Eccl. 10:1; also translated to send forth, to give, to cause to give, to give off). Other refs.: Ps. 119:171; 145:7. ¶
– 2 Prov. 20:20 ➔ PUPIL <380>.

UTTERLY – Ps. 73:19 ➔ CONSUME, BE CONSUMED <5486>.

UTTERMOST – Ex. 26:4, 10; 36:11, 17 ➔ OUTERMOST <7020>.

UZ – ***'ûṣ*** [proper noun: עוּץ <5780>; apparently from COUNSEL (TAKE) <5779>]: consultation ▶
a. One of the twins born to Nahor, the other was Buz. Refs.: Gen. 22:20, 21. ¶
b. A grandson of Seir, the Horite, and son of Dishan. Refs.: Gen. 36:28; 1 Chr. 1:17, 42. ¶
c. Son of Aram. Ref.: Gen. 10:23. ¶
d. A land east of Israel. Refs.: Job 1:1; Jer. 25:20; Lam. 4:21. ¶

UZAI – ***'ûzay*** [masc. proper noun: אוּזַי <186>; perhaps by permutation for UZZI <5813>]: speed of the Lord ▶ **Father of an Israelite whose son helped Nehemiah rebuild the wall.** Ref.: Neh. 3:25. ¶

UZAL – ***'ûzāl*** [masc. proper noun: אוּזָל <187>; of uncertain deriv.] ▶ **Son of Joktan.** Refs.: Gen. 10:27; 1 Chr. 1:21. ¶

UZZAH, UZZA – ***'uzzā', 'uzzāh*** [masc. proper noun: עֻזָּא, עֻזָּה <5798>; fem. of STRONG <5797>]: strength ▶
a. A son of Abinadab in whose house the ark was housed briefly. He helped his brother Ahio direct the cart carrying the ark. Uzzah touched the ark to steady it and was struck dead by the Lord (2 Sam. 6:3–8). David was angry because of the event and named the place where it happened Perez Uzzah, "breaking out (against) Uzzah." Other refs.: 1 Chr. 13:7, 9–11. ¶
b. The son of Gera who deported certain Jews. Ref.: 1 Chr. 8:7. ¶
c. A Levite descended through the line of Merari. Ref.: 1 Chr. 6:29. ¶
d. A Jew in whose garden Manasseh, king of Judah, was buried. Refs.: 2 Kgs. 21:18, 26. ¶
e. He was a Levite and served at the Temple. Refs.: Ezra 2:49; Neh. 7:51. ¶

UZZEN SHEERAH – ***'uzzên šeᵉrāh*** [proper noun: אֻזֵּן שֶׁאֱרָה <242>; from EAR (GIVE) <238> and SHERAH <7609>]: ear of Sheerah ▶ **A village in Israel built by Sheerah, the daughter of Ephraim.** Ref.: 1 Chr. 7:24. ¶

UZZI – ***'uzziy*** [masc. proper noun: עֻזִּי <5813>; from STRENGTHEN <5810>]: strong ▶
a. An Israelite of the tribe of Issachar. Refs.: 1 Chr. 7:2, 3. ¶
b. A Levite, ancestor of Ezra. Refs.: 1 Chr. 6:5, 6, 51; Ezra 7:4. ¶
c. A member of the tribe of Benjamin. Ref.: 1 Chr. 7:7. ¶
d. Another member of the tribe of Benjamin. Ref.: 1 Chr. 9:8. ¶
e. The overseer of the Levites in Jerusalem. Ref.: Neh. 11:22. ¶
f. A priest in the days of Joiakim. Ref.: Neh. 12:19. ¶
g. One of the priests who attended the dedication of the wall of Jerusalem. Ref.: Neh. 12:42. ¶

UZZIA – ***'uziyyā'*** [masc. proper noun: עֻזִּיָּא <5814>; perhaps for UZZIAH <5818>]: the Lord is my strength ▶ **One of King David's strong men.** Ref.: 1 Chr. 11:44. ¶

UZZIAH – ***'uzziyyāhû, 'uzziyyāh*** [masc. proper noun: עֻזִּיָּהוּ, עֻזִּיָּה <5818>; from STRONG <5797> and LORD <3050>]: the Lord is my strength ▶
a. The father of Jehonathan. He was overseer of the various treasuries and storehouses of the districts set up by David (1 Chr. 27:25). ¶
b. The son of Uriel and a priestly descendant of the family of Kohath. Ref.: 1 Chr. 6:24. ¶
c. A king of Judah and son of Amaziah. He reigned the same time as Azariah (see AZARIAH <5838> m.). He reigned 792–767 B.C. including a coregency, a total of fifty-two years (see esp. 2 Kgs. 15:1–7; 2 Chr. 26:1–23). A great earthquake took place during his reign (Zech. 14:5). *
d. A son of Zechariah who resettled in Jerusalem in the time of Nehemiah. Ref.: Neh. 11:4. ¶
e. A son of Harim who had married a foreigner during the exile. Ref.: Ezra 10:21. ¶

UZZIEL – ***'uzziy'êl*** [masc. proper noun: עֻזִּיאֵל <5816>; from STRONG <5797> and GOD <410>]: strength of God, power of God ▶
a. A son of Bela. Ref.: 1 Chr. 7:7. ¶
b. A son of Kohath. Refs.: Ex. 6:18, 22; Lev. 10:4; Num. 3:19, 30; 1 Chr. 6:2, 18; 15:10; 23:12, 20; 24:24. ¶
c. A son of Heman. Refs.: 1 Chr. 25:4; 2 Chr. 29:14. ¶
d. A Simeonite. Ref.: 1 Chr. 4:42. ¶
e. A son of Harhaiah. Ref.: Neh. 3:8. ¶

UZZIELITE – ***'ozziy'êliy*** [proper noun: עָזִּיאֵלִי <5817>; patron. from UZZIEL <5816>] ▶ **A descendant of Uzziel, son of Kohath.** Refs.: Num. 3:27; 1 Chr. 26:23. ¶

V

VAGABOND – Gen. 4:12, 14 ➔ FLEE <5110>.

VAIL – [1] Ruth 3:15 ➔ CLOAK <4304> [2] Is. 3:23 ➔ VEIL <7289> [3] See VEIL <6532>.

VAIN – [1] Job 11:12 ➔ HOLLOW (verb) <5014> [2] Ps. 119:113 ➔ DOUBLE-MINDED <5588>.

VAIN (BECOME) – ***hāḇal*** [verb: הָבַל <1891>; a prim. root] ▶ **This word indicates to fill with false hopes, to become empty, void. It is also translated to become worthless, to become false.** It notes that those who reject God's covenants and statues become vain (2 Kgs. 17:15) in their pursuits as well (Ps. 62:10; Jer. 2:5). It refers to foolish and vain talk and action (Job 27:12) and especially to futile prophecies of false prophets (Jer. 23:16). ¶

VAIZATHA, VAJEZATHA – ***wayzāṯa'*** [masc. proper noun: וַיְזָתָא <2055>; of foreign origin] ▶ **A son of Haman.** Ref.: Esther 9:9. ¶

VALIANT FIGHTER – 2 Sam. 23:20 ➔ VALIANT MAN <381>.

VALIANT MAN – ***'iyš-ḥayil*** [masc. noun: אִישׁ־חַיִל <381>; from MAN <376> and STRENGTH <2428>] ▶ **This word means brave man, courageous man, mighty man.** It is found in 1 Samuel 31:12; 2 Samuel 23:20; 24:9; 1 Kings 1:42. It is also translated valiant fighter, able-bodied man, worthy man, prominent man. ¶

VALIANT ONE – ***'er'ēl*** [masc. noun: אֶרְאֵל <691>; prob. for ARIEL <739>] ▶ **This word means and is also translated brave man, hero. It depicts the brave men of Jerusalem who weep in her streets because of the devastation the city has suffered.** Ref.: Is. 33:7. These men may be priests, inhabitants of Jerusalem, or heroes. ¶

VALLEY – [1] ***gay', gay*** [common noun: גַּיְא, גֵּי <1516>; prob. from the same root as PRIDE <1466> (abbreviated) (in the sense of a lifting up)] ▶ **This word refers to low-lying land in general.** Ref.: 2 Kgs. 2:16. But often it specifies valleys, such as a valley in Moab (Num. 21:20); a valley near Beth-peor (Deut. 3:29; 4:46); or near Gedor (1 Chr. 4:39). It is used to form names of valleys, such as the Valley of Hinnom, the most often cited valley (Josh. 15:8; 18:16; Neh. 11:30) or the Valley of Ben Hinnom (2 Kgs. 23:10; 2 Chr. 28:3). Names are formed to indicate events or activities that have or will take place in a valley, e.g., the Valley of Slaughter (Jer. 7:32); Valley of Vision (Is. 22:1); Valley of Hamon Gog (Ezek. 39:11). *
[2] ***'ēmeq*** [masc. noun: עֵמֶק <6010>; from DEEP, DEEP (BE) <6009>] ▶
a. This word refers to a vale, a lowland, the opposite of hilly or mountainous land. It is used of this kind of land in general (Is. 22:7; Jer. 31:40). It is used of the Jordan Valley area (Josh. 13:19, 27). It was a place where chariotry would be used in battle (Josh. 17:16). Many specific places have names featuring *'ēmeq*, valley, e.g., the Valley of Siddim, the Valley of the King, etc. (Gen. 14:17). *
b. The phrase *'ēmeq qᵉṣiys* occurs in Joshua 18:21 as the proper name Emek-Keziz. It was a valley that was given in inheritance to Benjamin. Keziz means abrupt. ¶
– [3] Gen. 13:10–12; 19:17, 25, 28, 29 ➔ ROUND (SOMETHING) <3603>.

VALUABLE – Lam. 4:2 ➔ WORTH THEIR WEIGHT <5537>.

VALUABLES – [1] Judg. 18:21 ➔ GLORIOUS <3520> b. [2] Jer. 20:5 ➔ HONOR (noun) <3366>.

VALUE (SET A) – Lev. 27:8 ➔ VALUE (verb) <6183>.

VALUE (SOMETHING OF) – Ezek. 7:11 ➔ PREEMINENCE <5089> a.

VALUE (verb) – ① *sālāh* [verb: סָלָה <5541>; a prim. root] ▶ **This word means to weigh against (as in a balance), to estimate in (e.g., gold), to buy with (e.g., gold).** Wisdom cannot be valued even in the finest gold (Job 28:16, 19; NIV: to buy). The Hebrew word also means to reject, to tread down; see REJECT <5541>. ¶
② *'āraḵ* [verb: עָרַךְ <6186>; a prim. root] ▶ **This word means to set a value, to judge the quality; to levy a tax.** It describes the process of a priest setting a value on someone or something (Lev. 27:8, 12, 14); as well as the process of leveling a tax evaluation and collection on a people (2 Kgs. 23:35: to tax). The Hebrew word also means to arrange, to set in order; see ARRANGE <6186>. ¶

VANIAH – *wanyāh* [masc. proper noun: וַנְיָה <2057>; perhaps for ANAIAH <6043>]: the Lord is praise ▶ **An Israelite who had married a foreign woman.** Ref.: Ezra 10:36. ¶

VANISH – ① *mālaḥ* [verb: מָלַח <4414>; a prim. root] ▶ **This word means to tear away, to dissipate.** It indicates the dissipation or drifting away of the sky or heavens like smoke disappearing (Is. 51:6). The Hebrew word also means to salt, to season: see SEASON (verb) <4414>. ¶
② *sāraḥ* [verb: סָרַח <5628>; a prim. root] ▶ **This word means to dissipate; it is also translated to decay, i.e., to degenerate.** It means to thin out, to become weak (Jer. 49:7); it is used of the loss of wisdom from among people (those who understand). The Hebrew word also means to spread, to sprawl; see HANG <5628>. ¶
③ *pāsas* [verb: פָּסַס <6461>; a prim. root] ▶ **This word means to disappear, to cease to be present.** It depicts what happens to the righteous when the wicked are in control (Ps. 12:1; KJV: to fail). ¶
– ④ Job 6:17 ➔ EXTINGUISH <1846>
⑤ Ps. 77:8; Is. 29:20 ➔ FAIL <656>
⑥ Prov. 3:21 ➔ PERVERSE <3868>.

VANITY – ① *heḇel* [common noun: הֶבֶל <1892>; from VAIN (BECOME) <1891>] ▶

This word refers to emptiness, meaninglessness; idols. It is used seventy times, thirty-five of which are in Ecclesiastes. It refers to breath because of its transitory fleeting character (Is. 57:13) and is used as a symbol for life (Job 7:16). It refers to the vanity and ultimate emptiness and meaninglessness of all things in this life, whether they seem good or bad (Eccl. 1:2, 14; 2:11, 15, 3:19; 4:4, 7, 8; 5:7; 6:2, 4, 9; 7:6, 15; 8:10; 9:9; 11:8). Combined with itself in the plural, it means absolute meaninglessness (Eccl. 1:2). Idols and the vain religious customs associated with them are all delusions (Jer. 10:3, 15). It denotes an empty, vain life (Eccl. 6:12). Used with the verb *hāḇal* (<1891>), it means to carry out vain talk or action or what is empty (Job 27:12). As an adverb, it means to talk in vain, emptily (Job 35:16). To walk after *heḇel* means to go after or follow vanity (2 Kgs. 17:15; Jer. 2:5). Anything obtained through evil is vain, such as wealth (Prov. 13:11). *
– ② Ps. 10:7; Prov. 22:8; Zech. 10:2 ➔ NOTHINGNESS <205>.

VANQUISH – Job 32:13 ➔ DRIVE AWAY <5086>.

VAPOR – Job 36:27 ➔ MIST <108>.

VAPOURS – Ps. 148:8 ➔ SMOKE (noun) <7008>.

VARICOLORED – Gen. 37:3, 23, 32 ➔ COLORS (OF MANY) <6446> a.

VARIOUS KINDS – 2 Chr. 16:14 ➔ KIND (noun) <2177>.

VASHNI – *wašniy* [masc. proper noun: וַשְׁנִי <2059>; prob. from ISHMERAI <3461>] ▶ **An Israelite of the tribe of Levi; the firstborn of the prophet Samuel.** Ref.: 1 Chr. 6:28, KJV. He is named Joel in other manuscripts. ¶

VASHTI – *waštiy* [fem. proper noun: וַשְׁתִּי <2060>; of Persian origin]: beautiful ▶ **She was debarred from the king's presence and her royal position was given to another** (Esther 1:9–2:4; 484–83 B.C.)

on account of her disobedience to the king's command. Esther, the Jewess, was made queen in her place (Esther 2:17). After Esther's brief reign as queen or at her death, Vashti was reinstalled as queen. Other refs.: Esther 1:9, 11, 12, 15–17, 19; 2:1, 4. ¶

VAT – Ex. 22:29 ➔ VINTAGE <1831>.

VAULT – 1 Job 22:14; Is. 40:22 ➔ CIRCLE <2329> 2 Amos 9:6 ➔ BUNCH <92>.

VAULTED CELL – Jer. 37:16 ➔ CELL <2588>.

VAULTED DOME – Amos 9:6 ➔ BUNCH <92>.

VEDAN – ***wᵉḏān*** [proper noun: וְדָן <2051>; perhaps for DELIGHT <5730>] ▶ **A place with whom Tyre was trading.** Ref.: Ezek. 27:19, NASB. ¶

VEGETABLE – ***zêrōa', zêr'ōn*** [masc. noun: זֵרֹעַ, זֵרְעֹן <2235>; from SOW <2232>] ▶ **This word describes the food, probably edible plants, Daniel and his friends ate in place of the king's rich foods and wine.** Refs.: Dan. 1:12, 16; KJV, pulse. ¶

VEGETABLES – Deut. 11:10; 1 Kgs. 21:2; Prov. 15:17 ➔ GRASS <3419>.

VEHEMENT – Jon. 4:8 ➔ SCORCHING <2759>.

VEIL – 1 ***masweh*** [masc. noun: מַסְוֶה <4533>; apparently from an unused root meaning to cover] ▶ **This word is used of the covering which Moses placed over his face to keep its glow from frightening the people.** Refs.: Ex. 34:33–35. ¶
2 ***mispāḥāh*** [fem. noun: מִסְפָּחָה <4555>; from JOIN <5596>] ▶ **This word denotes a covering. It indicates an identifying covering placed on persons marked for some specific purpose.** Refs.: Ezek. 13:18, 21; KJV: kerchief. It was probably a head covering. ¶
3 ***pārōḵeṯ*** [fem. noun: פָּרֹכֶת <6532>; fem. act. part. of the same as SEVERITY <6531> (in the sense of to separate)] ▶ **This word means and is also translated curtain.** It refers to the veil hung in front of the most holy place in the Tabernacle (Ex. 26:31, 33, 35; Lev. 4:6, 17; 16:2; Num. 4:5; 18:7; 2 Chr. 3:14). *
4 ***ṣammāh*** [fem. noun: צַמָּה <6777>; from an unused root meaning to fasten on] ▶
a. This word refers to a covering of cloth placed over a person's eyes. Refs.: Song 4:1, 3; 6:7. It is used figuratively of the uncovering and destruction of Babylon (Is. 47:2, see also b.).
b. This word indicates a lock of hair in the KJV. It refers to the beautiful, thick curls of hair on the bride (Song 4:1, 3; 6:7). Uncovering the locks refers to stripping bare the city and kingdom of Babylon (Is. 47:2, see also a.). ¶
5 ***ṣa'iyp̱*** [masc. noun: צָעִיף <6809>; from an unused root meaning to wrap over] ▶ **This word refers to a piece of cloth used to cover a bride's face, a wrap.** Ref.: Gen. 24:65. Some prefer to understand a shawl in this context, a covering for a woman's head and shoulders (Gen. 38:14, 19). ¶
6 ***rᵉḏiyḏ*** [masc. noun: רְדִיד <7289>; from SUBDUE <7286> in the sense of spreading] ▶ **This word refers to a cloak, a shawl.** It refers to a garment worn to cover someone (Song 5:7). It is a piece of fine clothing worn by the well-dressed women of Israel (Is. 3:23). ¶
7 ***rᵉ'ālāh*** [fem. noun: רְעָלָה <7479>; fem. of REELING <7478> (in the sense of fluttering in the case of a veil)] ▶ **This word refers to a light cloth covering worn over a woman's face or head or draped over the head and shoulders to conceal, protect, and beautify, a woman's face.** Ref.: Is. 3:19; also translated scarf, muffler. It was worn much less often by men and for different reasons. ¶

VEILED (BE) – Hab. 3:4 ➔ HIDING <2253>.

VENGEANCE – 1 ***nāqām*** [masc. noun: נָקָם <5359>; from VENGEANCE (TAKE) <5358>] ▶ **This word means revenge, retribution; it is also translated revenge or**

by the verb to be avenged. This term is employed to signify human vengeance. For example, Samson sought revenge against the Philistines for gouging out his eyes (Judg. 16:28). According to Proverbs, a jealous husband will show no mercy when he exacts vengeance on his wife's adulterous lover (Prov. 6:34). More often, however, this Hebrew term refers to divine repayment (Lev. 26:25; Deut. 32:35, 41, 43; Ezek. 24:8; Mic. 5:15). For example, the psalmist encouraged the righteous with the hope that someday they will be avenged, and God will redress the wrongs committed against them (Ps. 58:10). In fact, He will judge those who have acted with vengeance toward His people (Ezek. 25:12, 15). Ultimately, the judgment of God's enemies will mean redemption for His people (Is. 34:8; 35:4; 47:3; 59:17; 61:2; 63:4). ¶

[2] ***n*^{e}*qāmāh*** [fem. sing. noun: נְקָמָה <5360>; from <5359> above] ▶ **Jeremiah employed this word most frequently, referring to the revenge, retribution of God.** Refs.: Jer. 11:20; 46:10; 50:15, 28; 51:6, 11, 36. The worship of false gods, improper sacrifices, and a plot against Jeremiah himself all stirred up the vengeance of God. But it is also used with Israel as the subject (Num. 31:2; Ps. 149:7); and object (Lam. 3:60; Ezek. 25:15). Even when Israel took vengeance on an enemy, it was God's vengeance that they delivered (Num. 31:2, 3). *

VENGEANCE (TAKE) – ***nāqam*** [verb: נָקַם <5358>; a prim. root] ▶ **This word means to avenge, to take revenge, to be avenged, to suffer vengeance, to take one's revenge. In actual usage, the following ideas come out: in the simple, intensive, and reflexive stems, the word can mean to take vengeance, to avenge.** The Lord instructed His people not to seek revenge against each other, for to do so was unworthy of them (Lev. 19:18); the Lord took vengeance on His enemies and the enemies of His people (Nah. 1:2); but He would also take vengeance on His own people if necessary (Lev. 26:25); and He would avenge the death of His servants, the prophets (2 Kgs. 9:7); and His city, Jerusalem (Jer. 51:36). The reflexive idea of taking one's vengeance is found in the Lord's avenging Himself on Judah (Jer. 5:9). *

VENISON – See FOOD <6718> a.

VENOM – [1] Job 20:14 ➔ GALL <4846> [2] Hab. 2:15 ➔ WATERSKIN <2573>.

VENTURE – Eccl. 5:14 ➔ TASK <6045>.

VERDICT – Dan. 4:17 ➔ DECISION <7595>.

VERDURE – Song 6:11 ➔ GREENNESS <3>.

VERILY – See TRULY <61>.

VERMILION – ***šāšêr*** [masc. noun: שָׁשֵׁר <8350>; perhaps from the base of ENEMY <8324> in the sense of that of SORREL <8320>] ▶ **This is a pigment used to color paint.** It was the color of red ocher or even bright red, a bright ostentatious color (Jer. 22:14; Ezek. 23:14). ¶

VERY – [1] ***m*^{e}*'ōḏ*** [substantive, adv., or adj.: מְאֹד <3966>; from the same as FIREBRAND <181>] ▶ **This word means greatly, great, abundance; might, power.** It is used as a noun indicating might, power, will (Deut. 6:3; 2 Kgs. 23:25). As an adverb, it usually means very, i.e., all that God created was very good (Gen. 1:31). It takes on the sense of exceedingly as an extension of very and may come at the end of a phrase (Gen. 13:13). It can precede the word it is emphasizing as in greatly exalted (Ps. 47:9). Repeated, it emphasizes something greatly (Gen. 7:19); exceedingly (Gen. 17:2; Ex. 1:7). The phrase *'aḏ-m*^{e}*'ōḏ* adds an exceptional emphasis to a preceding assertion (Gen. 27:33; 1 Sam. 11:15; 2 Sam. 2:17; Is. 64:9). *

[2] ***miz'ār*** [masc. noun: מִזְעָר <4213>; from the same as LITTLE <2191>] ▶ **This word indicates a short time, a little while, a few. It indicates that something is small, not large in size, duration, or number.**

It is used of the short duration in time of God's anger (Is. 10:25); a short time before something will come to pass (Is. 29:17); the small number of persons who will remain after God's judgments (Is. 16:14: small; 24:6: few). ¶

3 *qāṭ* [adj.: קָט <6985>; from CUT OFF (BE) <6990> in the sense of abbreviation (a little)] ▶ **This word means little, very little, soon. It indicates something of relatively small significance.** It was used specifically to state that it was an insignificant thing that Israel had not committed the abominations of Samaria and Sodom, considering the sins and rebellions they had committed (Ezek. 16:47). ¶

VESSEL – 1 ***mā'n*** [Aramaic masc. noun: מָאן <3984>; prob. from a root corresponding to <579> in the sense of an enclosure by sides] ▶ **This word refers to a gold or silver vessel or receptacle used in the Temple; it is also translated utensil, article, goblet.** Refs.: Ezra 5:14, 15; 6:5; 7:19; Dan. 5:2, 3, 23. They were taken from the Temple and many were later returned under Persia. ¶

2 ***śᵉḵiyyāh, śāḵᵉyāh*** [שְׂכִיָּה, שָׂכְיָה <7914>; fem. from the same as SECU <7906>] ▶

a. A feminine noun indicating a ship, a sloop. It refers to seagoing vessels, further qualified in Isaiah 2:16 as pleasing, pleasant.

b. A feminine noun referring to a picture. The KJV rendered this word as pictures (Is. 2:16; ESV: craft), now known to be an improbable rendering. See also a.

c. A masculine proper noun Sachia. A descendant of Benjamin. Shaharaim had children in Moab by his wife Hodesh, one of which was Sachia (1 Chr. 8:10). ¶

VESTIBULE – 1 ***'ûlām*** [masc. noun: אוּלָם <197>; from BIND <481> (in the sense of tying)] ▶ **This word means a porch, a portico.** The most famous porch was located in front of the nave of Solomon's Temple, measuring 20 x 10 cubits (30 x 15 feet) (1 Kgs. 6:3; 1 Chr. 28:11; 2 Chr. 3:4; Joel 2:17). Ezekiel's visionary Temple had a porch in the gates (Ezek. 40:7–9, 15, 39, 40) and elsewhere (Ezek. 41:15, 25). *

2 ***'êylām*** [masc. noun: אֵילָם <361>; prob. from DOORPOST <352>] ▶ **This word means and is also translated arch, porch, portico, archway.** It is used fifteen times in Ezekiel to refer to the portico of the gates of the new Temple complex (Ezek. 40:16, 21, 22, 24–26). *

– 3 Judg. 3:23 ➔ PORCH <4528>.

VESTMENT – 2 Kgs. 10:22b ➔ CLOTHING <4403>.

VESTMENT (PURE) – Zech. 3:4 ➔ FESTAL APPAREL <4254>.

VESTRY – 2 Kgs. 10:22 ➔ WARDROBE <4458>.

VESTURE – Dan. 7:9 ➔ CLOTHING <3831>.

VEX – 1 ***tāwāh*** [verb: תָּוָה <8428>; a prim. root (or perhaps identical with SCRIBBLE <8427> through a similar idea of scraping to pieces)] ▶

a. This word refers to causing another person discomfort or annoyance because of one's behavior or attitude. Ref.: Ps. 78:41; also translated to pain, to provoke. In this case, Israel caused God to experience wounding from her unfaithfulness. See also b.

b. This word means to limit. It has the sense of restraining persons from what they can do because of one's own attitudes or actions. Ref.: Ps. 78:41, see also a. ¶

– 2 Judg. 2:18 ➔ AFFLICT <1766> 3 Judg. 10:8 ➔ SHATTER <7492> 4 Job 19:2 ➔ AFFLICT <3013>.

VEXATION – 1 Deut. 28:20; 2 Chr. 15:5 ➔ CONFUSION <4103> 2 Eccl. 1:14; 2:11, 17, 26; 4:4, 6; 6:9 ➔ STRIVING <7469> 3 Eccl. 1:17; 2:22; 4:16 ➔ STRIVING <7475> 4 Is. 9:1 ➔ CONSTRAINT <4164> 5 Is. 28:19 ➔ TERROR <2113>.

VEXED – 1 1 Kgs. 20:43; 21:4 ➔ DISPLEASED <2198> 2 1 Kgs. 20:43; 21:4,

5 (ESV) ➔ SULLEN <5620> [3] Is. 22:5; Ezek. 22:5 ➔ CONFUSION <4103>.

VEXED (BE) – [1] 2 Sam. 13:2 ➔ DISTRESSED (BE) <3334> [2] Ps. 73:21 ➔ SHARPEN <8150>.

VIAL – 1 Sam. 10:1 ➔ FLASK <6378>.

VICIOUS – Is. 35:9 ➔ VIOLENT <6530>.

VICTIM – Prov. 23:28 ➔ ROBBER <2863>.

VICTIMS – Ps. 10:8, 10, 14 ➔ HELPLESS <2489>.

VICTORY – Prov. 11:14; 21:31; 24:6; etc. ➔ DELIVERANCE <8668>.

VICTUAL – [1] Judg. 17:10 ➔ PRESERVATION OF LIFE <4241> [2] 2 Chr. 11:23 ➔ FOOD <4202>.

VICTUALS – Jer. 40:5 ➔ ALLOWANCE <737>.

VIEW – [1] Neh. 2:13, 15 ➔ INSPECT <7663> [2] Ps. 48:13 ➔ CONSIDER <6448> [3] Ps. 102:19 ➔ LOOK (verb) <5027>.

VIGIL – Ex. 12:42 ➔ WATCHING <8107>.

VIGOR – [1] ***hôḏ*** [masc. noun: הוֹד <1935>; from an unused root] ▶ **This word means vitality; it also means authority, majesty.** It refers to human physical vigor (Prov. 5:9; Dan. 10:8); the fighting vigor of a horse in battle (Zech. 10:3); and the growing vigor of an olive plant (Hos. 14:6). The word also implies authority, such as what Moses bestowed on Joshua (Num. 27:20); and royal majesty (1 Chr. 29:25; Jer. 22:18). Thus, it is used to describe God's majesty (Job 37:22; Ps. 145:5; Zech. 6:13). The word often describes God's glory as displayed above the heavens (Ps. 8:1; 148:13; Hab. 3:3; cf. Ps. 96:6; 104:1, where the word is related to God's creation of the heavens). *

[2] ***kelaḥ*** [masc. noun: כֶּלַח <3624>; from an unused root meaning to be complete] ▶ **This word indicates full strength.** It indicates maturity of vigor when one is in the bloom of health (Job 5:26; also translated full vigor, full age, ripe old age). If it has gone from persons, they are weak and often inactive, not good for much labor (Job 30:2; KJV: old age). ¶

[3] ***lêaḥ*** [masc. noun: לֵחַ <3893>; from the same as GREEN <3892>] ▶ **This word means and is also translated strength, natural force, natural vigor.** It refers to a drive or spark of the energy of life, such as Moses still possessed at 120 years of age (Deut. 34:7). ¶

– [4] Eccl. 11:10 ➔ YOUTH <7839>.

VIGOR (ONE WHO IS FULL OF) – Is. 59:10 ➔ VIGOROUS PEOPLE <820>.

VIGOROUS – ***ḥāyeh*** [adj.: חָיֶה <2422>; from LIVE <2421>] ▶ **This word means strong; it is also translated lively.** It is found only in Exodus 1:19, where the Egyptian midwives explained to Pharaoh that the Hebrew women were so vigorous in childbirth that they delivered before the midwives arrived. ¶

VIGOROUS PEOPLE – ***'ašmān*** [masc. noun: אַשְׁמָן <820>; prob. from OIL <8081> (i.e., strength)] ▶ **This word is taken by some translators as a description of vigorous or strong people among whom God's weakened people stumble about.** Ref.: ESV, NIV, NASB, Is. 59:10. See also DESOLATE PLACES <820>. ¶

VILE – [1] ***šōʻār*** [adj.: שֹׂעָר <8182>; from THINK <8176> in the sense of to cleave, to divide] ▶ **This word means horrid, bad, disagreeable; it is also translated rotten, split-open.** This word is used only once in the Old Testament in Jeremiah 29:17 when describing figs that are so bad they cannot be eaten. There is absolutely no use for them but to be thrown away. This is used to explain what would become of the Israelites who remained in their land instead of going into exile. God would

send the sword, famine, and plague against them so that in the end they too would be as worthless as bad figs. They would not be slightly disagreeable but would be so ruined and so horrid that they would simply be destroyed. ¶
– [2] 1 Sam. 15:9 ➔ DESPISED <5240> [3] Lam. 1:8 ➔ UNCLEAN <5206> a. [4] Dan. 11:21 ➔ DESPISE <959> [5] Nah. 3:6 ➔ to make vile ➔ FOOLISH (BE) <5034>.

VILE (BE, BECOME) – [1] Job 30:8 ➔ DRIVE OUT <5217> [2] Jer. 15:19; Lam. 1:8 ➔ GLUTTON (BE) <2151> a.

VILE (REPUTE) – Job 18:3 ➔ STUPID <2933>.

VILE THING – Judg. 19:23, 24 ➔ FOLLY <5039>.

VILENESS – [1] ***zullûṯ*** [fem. noun: זֻלּוּת <2149>; from GLUTTON (BE) <2151> a. (in the sense of being vile)] ▶ **This word denotes worthlessness.** It indicates a wicked and vile situation existing among human beings that fosters the wicked (Ps. 12:8). ¶
– [2] Mic. 6:14 ➔ CASTING DOWN <3445>.

VILLAGE – [1] ***ḥāṣêr*** [masc. noun: חָצֵר <2691>; from TRUMPET (BLOW A) <2690> in its original sense (a yard as enclosed by a fence)] ▶ **This word denotes a town, a courtyard.** It indicates a settlement without walls (Gen. 25:16; Josh. 15:46; Ps. 10:8; Is. 42:11); or an enclosed area, a courtyard (2 Sam. 17:18); a palace area or court (1 Kgs. 7:8; Jer. 36:20). Temples often featured these "Temple courts" (2 Kgs. 21:5; Ezek. 40:14). Solomon's Temple featured an inner court with cut stone and cedar beams (1 Kgs. 6:36; 7:12). It is combined with many words to indicate specific courts or aspects of courts (Jer. 32:2; 39:14, 15); the court of the Tabernacle (Ex. 27:9); the gate of the court (Ex. 35:17). It is used poetically of the courts of the Lord (Is. 1:12; 62:9). *

[2] ***kāp̄ār*** [masc. noun: כָּפָר <3723>; from COVER (verb) <3722> (as protected by walls)] ▶ **This word refers to a small town, usually unwalled.** Ref.: 1 Chr. 27:25. It was a pleasant place to spend time with one's beloved (Song 7:11). ¶
– [3] Num. 32:41; 1 Kgs. 4:13; 1 Chr. 2:23 ➔ TOWN <2333> [4] Neh. 6:2; Ezek. 38:13 ➔ LION (YOUNG) <3715> b. [5] Hab. 3:14 ➔ WARRIOR <6518>.

VILLAGER – ***pᵉrāzôn*** [masc. noun: פְּרָזוֹן <6520>; from the same as WARRIOR <6518>] ▶ **This word refers to a village population, people who dwell in a town without walls, rural people.** It refers to the inhabitants of rural areas, the peasants, small farmers, and sheepherders (Judg. 5:7, 11). ¶

VILLANY – Jer. 29:23 ➔ FOLLY <5039>.

VINDICATION – Is. 62:1 ➔ BRIGHTNESS <5051>.

VINE – [1] ***gep̱en*** [masc. noun: גֶּפֶן <1612>; from an unused root meaning to bend] ▶ **This word refers to any type of climbing plant.** But all except once, it refers to a grape-bearing vine: a poisonous wild vine bearing gourds (2 Kgs. 4:39); grapevine (Gen. 40:9, 10). It is often mentioned along with other fruits or the fig tree (1 Kgs. 4:25). It often is used symbolically to refer to Israel (Ps. 80:8; Ezek. 15:2, 6; 17:6, 8; Hos. 10:1) and has other figurative uses: the wicked drop off like unripe grapes from a vine (Job 15:33); a fertile wife (Ps. 128:3); enemies stem from the evil vine of Sodom (Deut. 32:32); a withering vine represents the collapsing prosperity of Moab (Is. 16:8, 9). *
– [2] Is. 17:10; Nah. 2:2 ➔ BRANCH <2156>.

VINE (CHOICE, CHOICEST, NOBLE) – [1] ***śōrêq, śōrêqāh*** [masc./fem. noun: שֹׂרֵק, שֹׂרֵקָה <8321>; from HISS <8319> in the sense of redness] ▶ **This word refers to choice species of vine, select grapes, evidently featuring a certain color.** Refs.: Is. 5:2; Jer. 2:21. It seems to refer to a choice vine in Genesis 49:11, the best growth in the land. ¶

– [2] Is. 16:8 ➔ PLANT (CHOICE, PRINCIPAL) <8291>.

VINE BRANCH – Is. 17:10; Nah. 2:2 ➔ BRANCH <2156>.

VINE GROWER – Joel 1:11 ➔ VINEDRESSER <3755>.

VINE ROW – Jer. 5:10 ➔ VINEYARD <8284> a.

VINEDRESSER – ***kōrêm*** [masc. noun: כֹּרֵם <3755>; act. part. of an imaginary denom. from VINEYARD <3754>] ▶ **This word refers to those people who cared for and husbanded vineyards in Israel.** It is a plural participial form of the verb *kāram* (2 Kgs. 25:12; 2 Chr. 26:10; Is. 61:5; Jer. 52:16; Joel 1:11). ¶

VINEGAR – ***ḥōmeṣ*** [masc. noun: חֹמֶץ <2558>; from LEAVENED (BE) <2556>] ▶ **This word refers to a fermented sour-tasting liquid from which a Nazarite had to abstain.** Ref.: Num. 6:3. Diners dipped bread in this drink (Ruth 2:14). It was administered as a drink to those who were under oppression and attack (Ps. 69:21). It was injurious and bitter to the teeth (Prov. 10:26) and caused an agitated reaction when poured on soda (Prov. 25:20). ¶

VINEYARD – [1] ***kerem*** [common noun: כֶּרֶם <3754>; from an unused root of uncertain meaning] ▶ **An area where grapevines and their fruits are grown and cultivated intensely. On occasion the word is also translated vines, vintage. Wine, as well as grapes, are produced from vineyards.** It is referred to many times in the Old Testament (Gen. 9:20; Judg. 15:5; 1 Kgs. 21:1, 2, 6, 7, 15–16, 18; Song 2:15). It is used as a figure of Israel with the Lord as the owner of the vineyard (Is. 5:1, 3–5, 7, 10; Jer. 12:10). It is used of the appearance of the beloved's skin (Song 1:6) and of her in general (Song 8:12). Various verbs used with the noun indicate that a vineyard is planted (*nṭ'*) (Gen. 9:20; Amos 5:11); seeded (*zr'*) (Deut. 20:6; 22:9); pruned (*zmr*), harvested (*bṣr*), gleaned (Lev. 19:10). Locusts may, as a warning from the Lord, consume a vineyard (Amos 4:9). *

[2] ***śārāh, śûrāh*** [fem. noun: שָׂרָה, שׂוּרָה <8284>; prob. fem. of WALL <7791>] ▶ **a. This word refers to rows of grapevines in the fields around Israel, but in context it is applied figuratively to the destruction of the city of Jerusalem.** Ref.: Jer. 5:10; also translated vine row. See also b. **b. This word also designates a wall.** It is understood to refer to the high protective walls surrounding Jerusalem (Jer. 5:10, see also a.). ¶

– [3] 2 Kgs. 25:12; 2 Chr. 26:10; Is. 61:5; Jer. 52:16 ➔ one working the vineyard ➔ VINEDRESSER <3755> [4] Ps. 80:15 ➔ ROOT (noun) <3657>.

VINTAGE – [1] ***bāṣiyr*** [masc. noun: בָּצִיר <1210>; from GATHER <1219>] ▶ **This word means and is also translated grape gathering, grape harvest.** It refers to the time of grape harvesting (Lev. 26:5; Is. 32:10) or the actual yield of wine or grapes from an area (Judg. 8:2; Jer. 48:32; Mic. 7:1). It implies the thoroughness of a grape harvest (Is. 24:13) as a metaphor for the extent of God's judgments on the earth. It is used idiomatically to describe the excellence of the cedar forests of Lebanon (Zech. 11:2, KJV; cf. NASB, NKJV, NIV: tick, impenetrable, dense). ¶

[2] ***dema'*** [masc. noun: דֶּמַע <1831>; from WEEP <1830>] ▶ **This word means overflowing; it is also translated juice, press, vat.** It indicates the abundance of oil and/or wine the Lord gives to Israel in her harvests (Ex. 22:29). ¶

VIOL – Amos 5:23; 6:5 ➔ HARP <5035>.

VIOLATE – [1] Deut. 28:30; Jer. 3:2 ➔ RAPE <7693> [2] Ezek. 22:26 ➔ VIOLENCE (DO) <2554>.

VIOLENCE – [1] ***ḥāmās*** [masc. noun: חָמָס <2555>; from VIOLENCE (DO) <2554>]

► **This word means violent (dealing), oppression, wrong. It implies cruelty, damage, and injustice.** Abraham's cohabiting with Hagar is described as a wrong done to Sarah (Gen. 16:5). In relation to physical violence, cruelty is implied (Judg. 9:24). When coupled with the term instrument or weapon, it becomes an attributive noun describing weapons or instruments of violence (Ps. 58:2). When it describes a person, it can mean an oppressor or a violent man (Prov. 3:31). *
[2] ***m^{e}rûṣāh*** [fem. noun: מְרוּצָה <4835>; from BREAK <7533> (in the sense of to oppress)] ► **This word is used of evil and hurtful activities of oppression and distress directed against others.** Ref.: Jer. 22:17; also translated extortion. ¶
– [3] Is. 42:25 ➔ STRENGTH <5807>.

VIOLENCE (DO) – ***ḥāmas*** [verb: חָמַס <2554>; a prim. root] ► **This word means to be violent, to act violently, to act wrongly. The term can be used to describe one who treats people badly.** The prophet Jeremiah condemned the wrong treatment of widows and orphans (Jer. 22:3). The word can also denote unethical behavior in a construction that takes *tôrāh* (see LAW <8451>) as an object (Ezek. 22:26; Zeph. 3:4) (lit., "do violence to the law"); the word is also translated "violate" in Ezekiel 22:26. God did violence to His dwelling when Jerusalem was sacked (Lam. 2:6; also translated to treat violently, to lay waste). Job thought his accusers treated him wrongly (Job 21:27: to wrong). Other refs.: Job 15:33 (to shake off, to drop off); Prov. 8:36 (to wrong, to injure, to harm); Jer. 13:22 (to make bare, to suffer violence, to mistreat, to expose). ¶

VIOLENCE (SUFFER) – Jer. 13:22 ➔ VIOLENCE (DO) <2554>.

VIOLENT – [1] ***pariyṣ*** [masc. noun: פָּרִיץ <6530>; from BREAK OUT, BREAK DOWN <6555>] ► **This word means a violent individual; the word is also translated destroyer, thief, robber. The term was usually applied to a person or people.** David claimed to have refrained from the ways of the violent (Ps. 17:4). God asked if the Temple had become the dwelling place of the violent (Jer. 7:11). God proclaimed through the prophet Ezekiel that the end would come when the violent desecrate God's treasured place (Ezek. 7:22); they would be punished (Ezek. 18:10). The prophet Isaiah also applied this term to wild animals like the lion (Is. 35:9: ravenous, vicious). Other ref.: Dan. 11:14. ¶
– [2] 1 Kgs. 2:8 ➔ GRIEVOUS <4834>.

VIOLENTLY (TREAT) – Lam. 2:6 ➔ VIOLENCE (DO) <2554>.

VIOLET – See BLUE <8504>.

VIPER – [1] ***'ep'eh*** [masc. noun: אֶפְעֶה <660>; from NOTHING <659> (in the sense of hissing)] ► **This word means a poisonous snake; it is also translated adder, snake.** This creature is found in the desert (Is. 30:6). The tongue or (metaphorically) the venom of this snake slays a wicked person (Job 20:16). It refers figuratively to the evil that the rebellious Israelites encounter when they seek help from the wrong source (Is. 59:5). ¶
[2] ***'aḵšûḇ*** [masc. noun: עַכְשׁוּב <5919>; prob. from an unused root meaning to coil] ► **This word is also translated asp, adder. It refers to a snake from a family of venomous snakes, including adders.** The tongue of this reptile is long and sharp (Ps. 140:3). ¶
[3] ***ṣepa', ṣip̱'ôniy*** [masc. noun: צֶפַע, צִפְעוֹנִי <6848>; from an unused root meaning to extrude (as thrusting the tongue, i.e., hissing, in the case of a viper)] ►
a. This word refers to a poisonous serpent; it is also translated adder, cockatrice. It indicates a venomous serpent or snake but is used figuratively to refer to a dangerous, destructive people that will destroy Philistia (Is. 14:29).
b. This word also refers to a poisonous serpent; it is also translated adder, cockatrice. It indicates a venomous serpent or snake. It illustrates the danger of drinking wine to excess (Prov. 23:32). The nature of the viper or serpent will be changed in

the messianic kingdom (Is. 11:8). It is used to represent the vile, evil character of who God's people have become in their rebellions (Is. 59:5). Figuratively, it describes the enemies God will bring against His rebellious people (Jer. 8:17). ¶

4 ***šᵉpiypōn*** [masc. noun: שְׁפִיפֹן <8207>; from an unused root meaning the same as BRUISE <7779> (which is used in reference to the attack of the serpent)] ▶ **This word means and is also translated horned snake, adder.** It is said of Dan that he shall be a viper by the path (Gen. 49:17). ¶

– 5 Deut. 32:24 ➔ CRAWL <2119>.

VIRGIN – 1 ***bᵉṯûlāh*** [fem. noun: בְּתוּלָה <1330>; fem. pass. part. of an unused root meaning to separate] ▶ **This word is traditionally understood to refer to a virgin, so called from being chaste, i.e., separated and secluded from intercourse with a man. Some scholars prefer to translate the term loosely as maiden or young woman. Yet in Genesis 24:16, Rebekah is described as a beautiful woman and a *bᵉṯûlāh*. The text states that no man had known Rebekah—i.e., had sexual relations with her.** Also, Judges 21:12 states that there were "four hundred young *bᵉṯûlāh*, that had known no man by lying with any male." In these verses, this Hebrew word certainly connotes virginity. But in Joel 1:8, the Lord describes the *bᵉṯûlāh* mourning for the husband of her youth. In this case, the word means young woman. Moreover, it also refers to cities or countries that are personified as females (Is. 37:22; 47:1; Jer. 18:13; 31:4, 21; Amos 5:2). For further occurrences of this Hebrew word, see Deuteronomy 22:23, 28; Judg. 19:24; 2 Sam. 13:2, 18; 1 Kgs. 1:2; Esther 2:2; Zech. 9:17. *

2 ***bᵉṯûliym*** [fem. noun: בְּתוּלִים <1331>; masc. plur. of the same as <1330> above] ▶ **This word also means virginity or maiden. It is primarily used to describe the sexual purity or chastity of a young woman.** Variations on this theme show it is used in contrast to a defiled or impure woman (Deut. 22:14); to signify the virginal state of a woman to be married (Lev. 21:13); or to signify the virginal state of young women in general (Judg. 11:37). Other refs.: Deut. 22:15, 17, 20; Judg. 11:38; Ezek. 23:3, 8. ¶

– 3 Gen. 24:43; Ps. 68:25; Prov. 30:19; Song 1:3; 6:8; Is. 7:14 ➔ YOUNG WOMAN <5959>.

VISAGE – Dan. 3:19 ➔ FACE (noun) <600>.

VISIBLE (BE) – Dan. 4:11, 20 ➔ VISIBLE <2379>.

VISION – 1 ***ḥêzû*** [Aramaic masc. noun: חֵזוּ <2376>; from SEE <2370>] ▶ **This word means a supernatural appearance, something seen in dream; it is found exclusively in the book of Daniel and draws attention to the nature of revelation.** It denotes the nighttime dreams of Nebuchadnezzar (Dan. 2:19, 28; 4:5, 13) and Daniel (Dan. 7:2, 7, 13) that have prophetic significance. There appears to be some connection with the ominous or troubling nature of these revelations (Dan. 7:15; cf. Dan. 2:1). Once the word pertains to the outward appearance of an object in the vision of the fourth beast (Dan. 7:20: look, appearance). Other refs.: Dan. 4:9, 10; 7:1. ¶

2 ***ḥāzôn*** [masc. noun: חָזוֹן <2377>; from SEE <2372>] ▶ **This word means a revelation by means of a vision, an oracle, a divine communication. The primary essence of this word is not so much the vision or dream itself as the message conveyed.** It signifies the direct, specific communication between God and people through the prophetic office (1 Sam. 3:1; 1 Chr. 17:15; Ps. 89:19) or the collection of such messages (2 Chr. 32:32; Is. 1:1; Obad. 1:1; Nah. 1:1; Hab. 2:2, 3). Also, the word is used of the messages of false prophets (Jer. 14:14; 23:16); a guiding communication from the Lord, often restricted when a people are under judgment (Lam. 2:9; Ezek. 7:26; Mic. 3:6); and the revelation of future events on a grand scale (Dan. 9:24; 10:14). People who disregard this divine communication face certain doom (Prov. 29:18). Other refs.: Is. 29:7; Ezek. 7:13; 12:22–24,

27; 13:16; Dan. 1:17; 8:1, 2, 13, 15, 17, 26; 9:21; 11:14; Hos. 12:10. ¶

3 ***ḥăzôṯ*** [fem. noun: חָזוֹת <2378>; from SEE <2372>] ► **This word means a revelation.** This particular word is used only once in the description of a book of prophetic writings called the visions of Iddo (2 Chr. 9:29). See the related Hebrew verb *ḥāzāh* (SEE <2372>). ¶

4 ***ḥāzûṯ*** [fem. noun: חָזוּת <2380>; from SEE <2372>] ► **This word means a striking supernatural appearance.** A difficult vision appeared to Isaiah (Is. 21:2); and another vision seemed to the Israelites to be words on a scroll (Is. 29:11). Daniel saw in his vision a goat with a visible (large) horn (Dan. 8:5, 8; notable, conspicuous, prominent). This word can also mean commitment or agreement, as in Isaiah's oracle against Ephraim (Is. 28:18: agreement, pact). See the related Hebrew root *ḥāzāh* (SEE <2372>). ¶

5 ***ḥizzāyôn*** [masc. noun: חִזָּיוֹן <2384>; from SEE <2372>] ► **This word means a dream, a revelation. The primary stress of this word lies on the means and manner of divine revelation.** It is used in reference to revelations that come in the night (2 Sam. 7:17; Job 4:13; 33:15); visions imparted (Zech. 13:4); and dreams in a general sense (Job 7:14; 20:8). Metaphorically, Jerusalem is called the "valley of vision," alluding to the city as the center of prophetic activity (Is. 22:1, 5; cf. Luke 13:33). Other ref.: Joel 2:28. ¶

6 ***maḥᵃzeh*** [masc. noun: מַחֲזֶה <4236>; from SEE <2372>] ► **This word means a supernatural appearance; it is used only four times in the Old Testament.** God came to Abram in a vision (Gen. 15:1); Balaam could rightly prophesy because he saw a vision of the Almighty (Num. 24:4, 16). However, false prophets saw a false vision and thus prophesied falsely (Ezek. 13:7). ¶

7 ***mar'āh*** [fem. noun: מַרְאָה <4759>] ► **This word means a supernatural appearance, a mirror. This noun is derived from the verb *rā'āh* (<7200>), meaning to see.** As a supernatural vision, it is a means of divine revelation (Num. 12:6). This term can stand by itself (1 Sam. 3:15); or it can function as a cognate accusative (Dan. 10:7, 8). The word is sometimes used in the expression *mar'ōṯ halaylāh* (<3915>), meaning visions of the night (Gen. 46:2); and *mar'ōṯ ᵉlōhiym* (<430>), meaning visions of God (Ezek. 1:1; 8:3; 40:2). The word is only used once in the Hebrew Bible to signify a mirror or a polished metal plate (Ex. 38:8). Other refs.: Num. 12:6; 1 Sam. 43:3; Dan. 10:16. ¶

8 ***rō'eh*** [masc. noun: רֹאֶה <7203>; act. part. of SEE <7200>] ► **This word is habitually used to mean a seer, a prophet; on occasion to mean a prophetic supernatural appearance.** The word is the active participle of *rā'āh* (<7200>), which signifies a prophet (see 1 Chr. 9:22, Is. 30:10). It refers to the vision or insight that the prophet receives (Is. 28:7). ¶

– 9 Ezek. 8:4; 11:24; etc. → SIGHT <4758>.

VITALITY – Ps. 32:4 → CAKE BAKED <3955>.

VOICE – 1 ***qôl*** [masc. noun: קוֹל <6963>; from an unused root meaning to call aloud] ► **This word means a sound, a noise, a cry. This is an all-encompassing word that is used of any kind of sound.** It describes God's voice in the Garden of Eden (Gen. 3:8, 10); human voices, speech (Gen. 27:22; Josh. 6:10; 2 Kgs. 7:10); singing (Ex. 32:18); laughter (Jer. 30:19); horses hoofs (Jer. 47:3); animal sounds (1 Sam. 15:14; Jer. 8:16). It is used of noises and sounds from inanimate objects: musical instruments, e.g., a shophar (Ex. 19:16; 20:18); a clap of thunder (Is. 30:30; Amos 1:2); feet marching (1 Kgs. 14:6); chariots (Nah. 3:2), etc. It refers to the content of speech, what is actually conveyed (Gen. 3:17; Ex. 3:18); also the contents of a written message (2 Kgs. 10:6). In a special use, it refers to the sound meaning of a divine sign (Ex. 4:8). The speech and utterances of the Lord as *qôl* are found often (Gen. 22:18; 26:5; Ex. 5:2; Zech. 6:15). The phrase *qôl gāḏôl* means a loud (great) voice (Gen. 39:14). The idiom to lift up one's voice means to cry out, to plead (Gen. 21:16); to raise up one's voice

means to prepare to cry out (Gen. 39:15). The phrase *qôl qōre'* means a voice calls (Is. 40:3, 6). It may bear the meaning of news, a report, hearsay (Gen. 45:16). The word is used as a personification of a person's blood crying out (Gen. 4:10). *
– [2] Dan. 4:31; 6:20; 7:11 ➔ SOUND <7032>.

VOID – [1] ***bōhû*** [masc. noun: בֹּהוּ <922>; from an unused root (meaning to be empty)] ▶ **This word indicates emptiness, desolation.** It depicts the state of matter after God had created it but before He had fashioned it for habitation (Gen. 1:2); it is also translated empty. It, therefore, describes the state of the land or earth after God judges it (Is. 34:11; Jer. 4:23). It is used in combination with *tōhû*, without form, each time. ¶
– [2] Nah. 2:10 ➔ DESOLATE <4003>.

VOID (MAKE) – [1] Ps. 89:39 ➔ RENOUNCE <5010> [2] Jer. 19:7 ➔ EMPTY (MAKE) <1238>.

VOLUME – 1 Chr. 23:29 ➔ MEASURE (noun) <4884>.

VOMIT (noun) – ***qê', qêy'*** [masc. noun: קֵא, 6892> קֵיא; from VOMIT (verb) <6958>] ▶
a. This word refers to the material, food, etc., ejected from an animal's or a person's stomach through the mouth. It is used in a proverb to parallel folly (Prov. 26:11).
b. This word is used in a simile to represent confusion, disarray. Ref.: Is. 19:14. It is used to describe the corrupt character of everything in Ephraim (Israel) (Is. 28:8). It is used figuratively of Moab wallowing in the confusion and destruction it has brought upon itself (Jer. 48:26). ¶

VOMIT (verb and noun) – ***qiy'*** [קִיא <7006>; a prim. root] ▶
a. A verb meaning to spew out the contents of one's stomach. It is used several times in a figurative sense of Canaan vomiting out its inhabitants (Lev. 18:25, 28; 20:22). It refers to a rich man spewing out his riches (Job 20:15). It represents the possible self-pollution of eating with a self-centered man (Prov. 23:8). Eating to excess, especially rich food, will result in vomiting (Prov. 25:16). It describes the action of a great fish spewing Jonah out of his mouth (Jon. 2:10). ¶
b. A masculine noun referring to what is vomited out, spewed out, filth. Refs.: Is. 19:14; 28:8. It figuratively indicates a nation wallowing in its corruption, vomit (Jer. 48:26). Other ref.: Jer. 25:27. ¶

VOMIT (verb) – ***qôh, qāyāh*** [verb: קוֹה, קָיָה <6958>; a prim. root] ▶
a. This word refers to the emptying of the contents of a person's stomach. It is used figuratively of the land of Canaan spewing the Israelites out of it because of their uncleanness. Refs.: Lev. 18:25, 28; 20:22. It is also used of a rich man vomiting out his riches (Job 20:15). Eating in excess may result in vomiting (Prov. 25:16). Jonah was vomited by a great fish (Jon. 2:10), a scene that served to humiliate the prophet for not obeying God's call. Other ref.: Prov. 23:8.
b. This word is used literally and figuratively of the nations becoming drunk only to vomit, to spew out their consumed corruptions. Ref.: Jer. 25:27. ¶

VOPHSI – ***wop̱siy*** [masc. proper noun: וָפְסִי <2058>; prob. from CONTINUE <3254>]: additional ▶ **An Israelite of the tribe of Naphtali.** He was the father of Nahbi, one of the spies of the land of Canaan (Num. 13:14). ¶

VOW (noun) – ***nêḏer, neḏer*** [masc. noun: נֵדֶר, נֶדֶר <5088>; from VOW, MAKE A VOW <5087>] ▶ **The word basically means a solemn promise to God or the thing promised. Several times, the word refers to the specific words given in a vow.** Jacob vowed that the Lord would be his God and he would give Him a tenth of everything the Lord gave him (Gen. 28:20; 31:13; Num. 21:2; Judg. 11:30). The word is used to describe the object or intent of vows: a Nazirite vow (Num. 6:2, 5, 21); a vow made by a wife (Num. 30:9); or by people in a difficult situation who made a promise before the Lord (Jon. 1:16). The object of the vow can be a sacrifice (Lev. 7:16; 22:21); or a person dedicated to the Lord (Lev. 27:2). Neither money earned by prostitution nor deformed animals could be used as part of a vow (Lev. 22:23; Deut. 23:18). Once made, a vow had to be paid by the one who made it, for if he or she did not pay, it was considered a sin (Deut. 23:21; 2 Sam. 15:7; Ps. 56:12). Prov. 20:25 warned against making a vow before carefully considering the wisdom of doing so. Jephthah made a rash vow without considering its implications and suffered greatly for it (Judg. 11:30, 39). The word also describes the vow of some of the Israelites and their wives to burn incense and give libation offerings to the Queen of Heaven in the time of Jeremiah (Jer. 44:25). *

VOW, MAKE A VOW (verb) – ***nāḏar*** [verb: נָדַר <5087>; a prim. root] ► **The verbal concept denotes the making of an oral, voluntary promise to give or do something as an expression of consecration or devotion to the service of God.** Jacob vowed to return a tenth of all that God bestowed on him if God would protect and preserve him on his journey (Gen. 28:20). Leviticus 27:8 discusses the special vow offerings to the Lord and the cost of redeeming someone or something which had been dedicated to the Lord. King David also made a vow that he would deny himself the pleasures of his house and his bed until the time came when he had established a resting place and a habitation for the Lord (Ps. 132:2). The sailors, unable to save themselves and having cast Jonah into the sea with the resulting calm, greatly feared the Lord, offered sacrifices, and made vows to Him (Jon. 1:16). *

VULTURE – [1] ***dayyāh*** [fem. noun: דַּיָּה <1772>; intens. from FLY (verb) <1675>] ► **This word means a bird of prey; it is also translated falcon, hawk.** It indicates an unclean bird of prey not edible for Israel (Deut. 14:13). It is a sinister and threatening presence predicted for the ruin of the nations that God judges (Is. 34:15). ¶

[2] ***peres*** [masc. noun: פֶּרֶס <6538>; from DIVIDE <6536>] ► **This word refers to a bird of prey that chiefly eats raw meats, carrion; it is also translated ossifrage, bearded vulture.** It was forbidden as food for Israel (Lev. 11:13; Deut. 14:12). ¶

– [3] Gen. 15:11; Job 28:7; Is. 18:6 ➔ BIRD OF PREY <5861> [4] Lev. 11:14 ➔ KITE <1676> [5] Job 28:7 ➔ FALCON <344>.

VULTURE (BLACK) – ***'ozniyyāh*** [fem. noun: עָזְנִיָּה <5822>; prob. fem. of STRONG <5797> (referring to strength, power)] ► **This word refers to an unclean bird: a buzzard, a black vulture.** It was forbidden to Israel as food; it was unclean (Lev. 11:13; Deut. 14:12; also translated buzzard, ospray). ¶

W

WADI – ***naḥªlāh, naḥal*** [נַחַל, נַחֲלָה <5158>; from POSSESSION (TAKE) <5157> in its original sense (i.e., to inherit, as a figurative mode of descent)]
a. A feminine noun referring to a seasonal or semi-permanent small river, often termed the River of Egypt (El-Arish?). It served as a boundary of the land of Israel in Ezekiel's vision (Ezek. 47:19; 48:28: wadi, brook, river). ¶
b. A masculine noun indicating a stream, a torrent. A stream bed or wadi with water in it permanently (a spring) or only during the rainy season (Gen. 26:19; Deut. 8:7; 1 Sam. 17:40). When it is full, it flows violently (Deut. 9:21; Judg. 5:21). It usually describes specific small streams, rivers, and brooks such as the Jabbok or Arnon (Gen. 32:23; Lev. 11:9, 10; Num. 21:14; Josh. 12:2). It is used of hollows or pits dug for graves, ravines, mining, etc. (Neh. 2:15; Job 28:4). It is used figuratively of streams, veins of oil (Mic. 6:7); wadis of death (2 Sam. 22:5; Ps. 18:4); a torrent of asphalt (*gop̱rîṯ*) describing Topheth, a stream of tears (Lam. 2:18); or a brook of wisdom (Prov. 18:4). Water breaking out from a rock is described by this term (Ps. 78:20). *

WAFER – [1] ***ṣapiyḥiṯ*** [fem. noun: צַפִּיחִת <6838>; from the same as JAR <6835> (i.e., an unused root meaning to expand)] ▶ **This Hebrew word describes a thin baked cake, like a small wafer.** Its appearance was used to describe manna (Ex. 16:31). ¶
[2] ***rāqiyq*** [masc. noun: רָקִיק <7550>; from SPIT (verb) <7556> (in its original sense of diffusing)] ▶ **This word refers to a thin cake; it is also translated thin loaf. It denotes a thin, flat, crisp cookie or cracker like cake or bread.** It is used in several situations: to consecrate priests (Ex. 29:2, 23; Lev. 8:26); in grain offerings (Lev. 2:4); peace offerings or offerings of well-being (Lev. 7:12); Nazarite offerings (Num. 6:15, 19). It was prepared by priests (1 Chr. 23:29). ¶

WAG – Jer. 18:16 ➔ FLEE <5110>.

WAGES – [1] ***maśkōreṯ*** [fem. noun: מַשְׂכֹּרֶת <4909>; from HIRE <7936>] ▶ **This word refers to various kinds of payment for services rendered to a person; it was fixed and not to be changed arbitrarily.** Refs.: Gen. 29:15; 31:7, 41. Wages were considered to be determined by God in Israel (Ruth 2:12; also translated reward). ¶
[2] ***śāḵār*** [masc. noun: שָׂכָר <7939>; from HIRE <7936>] ▶ **This word indicates a reward, pay.** It refers to monetary pay or pay consisting of material goods (Gen. 30:28, 32, 33; Ex. 2:9; Num. 18:31). It refers to a reward given by God to Abraham for faithfulness (Gen. 15:1). It can be rendered as hire, the amount paid to rent or hire a person or object (Ex. 22:15). It is used in the sense of ordinary expenses or the costs of maintenance or travel (Jon. 1:3; Zech. 8:10). The Lord's gift of children is considered a reward to His people (Ps. 127:3). When God comes to comfort His people, His reward is with Him, just payment for what each person deserves (Is. 40:10). *
– [3] Deut. 23:18; Is. 23:17, 18; Hos. 9:1; Mic. 1:7 ➔ EARNINGS <868> [4] Is. 19:10 ➔ REWARD (noun) <7938> a. [5] Is. 55:2 ➔ LABOR (noun) <3018> [6] Hos. 2:12 ➔ PAY <866>.

WAGON – ***ʿᵃgālāh*** [fem. noun: עֲגָלָה <5699>; from the same as CIRCULAR <5696>] ▶ **This word refers to a royal carriage or cart used for transporting people and their property.** Refs.: Gen. 45:19, 21, 27; 46:5; also translated cart. Carts or wagons in general were considered valuable gifts and offerings (Num. 7:3, 6–8); and used to carry produce (Amos 2:13). It indicates wagons or chariots used in warfare (Ps. 46:9). Some carts were pulled by ropes (Is. 5:18). The phrase *'ôpan ʿᵃgolāh* indicates a cartwheel (Is. 28:27). *

WAHEB – ***wāhêḇ, eṯwᵉhaḇ*** [proper noun and masc. noun: וָהֵב, אֶתְוָהֵב <2052>; of uncertain deriv.]: which is done ▶
a. A location in Moab. Ref.: Num. 21:14, ESV, NASB, NKJV; NIV: Zahab. ¶

b. A masculine noun meaning that which is done, that which is accomplished. Ref.: Num. 21:14, KJV. ¶

WAIL (noun) – ***yᵉlālāh*** [fem. noun: יְלָלָה <3215>; fem. of HOWLING <3214>] ▶ **This word describes a deep mourning of despair or distress; it is also translated wailing, howling.** Because of God's judgment on Moab, a cry of distress sounds throughout the land; Babylon wails because of God's judgment on her (Jer. 25:36); as does Judah (Zeph. 1:10); and Lebanon (Zech. 11:3). Other ref.: Is. 15:8. ¶

WAIL (verb) – 1 ***yālal*** [verb: יָלַל <3213>; a prim. root] ▶ **This is an onomatopoetic word that means to make a howling, to cry out in lamentation. It refers to deep mourning or distress; KJV translates to howl.** It is used to express dismay at the coming of the day of the Lord (Is. 13:6). All the nations will wail at that time (Is. 14:31; Mic. 1:8; Zeph. 1:11; Zech. 11:2), often in temples and high places (Is. 15:2, 3; 16:7; 23:1, 6). Even palace and temple songs will turn into wailing (Amos 8:3). *
– 2 Judg. 5:28 ➔ CRY, CRY OUT <2980> 3 Ezek. 32:18 ➔ LAMENT <5091> 4 Joel 1:8 ➔ LAMENT <421>.

WAILING – 1 ***nᵉhiy*** [masc. noun: נְהִי <5092>; from LAMENT <5091>] ▶ **This word describes lamentation, a song of mourning. On occasion it refers to the wailing of professional mourners. Generally, it depicts an expression of sorrow and distress, with a display of emotion, over a calamity of some kind.** Judgment on the hills and mountains of Israel (Jer. 9:10, 18–20); the loss of the people in Israel (Jer. 31:15: lamentation, mourning); the judgment of the Lord on His people (Amos 5:16; Mic. 2:4). ¶
2 ***niy*** [masc. noun: נִי <5204>; a doubtful word] ▶ **This word describes a mournful expression of despair and lament. In context it gives rise to a composed verbal expression of grief.** It describes formal wailing expressed by uttering a lament (Ezek. 27:32). ¶
– 3 Esther 4:3; Ps. 30:11; Is. 22:12; Jer. 6:26; Ezek. 27:31; Amos 5:16, 17; Mic. 1:8 ➔ LAMENTATION <4553> 4 Is. 15:8; Jer. 25:36; Zeph. 1:10; Zech. 11:3 ➔ WAIL (noun) <3215> 5 Ezek. 7:11 ➔ PREEMINENCE <5089> b.

WAIST – Ezek. 47:4 ➔ LOINS <4975> a.

WAISTBAND – 1 Ex. 28:27, 28; etc. ➔ BAND (noun) <2805> 2 Job 12:18; Is. 5:27; Jer. 13:1, 2, 4, 6, 7, 10, 11 ➔ BELT <232>.

WAISTCLOTH – Job 12:18 ➔ BELT <232>.

WAIT – 1 ***ḥāḵāh*** [verb: חָכָה <2442>; a prim. root (apparently akin to CARVE <2707> through the idea of piercing)] ▶ **This verb indicates to delay, to tarry.** It indicates also delaying an action (2 Kgs. 7:9; 9:3; Job 32:4). It refers to longing or hoping for something to happen (Job 3:21), such as death or, in a good sense, for the Lord to act (Ps. 33:20; Is. 8:17; Hab. 2:3; Zeph. 3:8); or to resurrect (Dan. 12:12). But it means to wait in order to accomplish one's purpose, good or bad (Hos. 6:9). Other refs.: Ps. 106:13; Is. 30:18; 64:4. ¶
2 ***yāḥal*** [verb: יָחַל <3176>; a prim. root] ▶ **This word means to hope, to tarry.** It is used of Noah (Gen. 8:12); Saul (1 Sam. 10:8; 13:8); Joab (2 Sam. 18:14); the king of Aram (2 Kgs. 6:33); Job (Job 6:11; 13:15; 14:14); Elihu (Job 32:11, 16). In the Psalms, it frequently means to wait with hope (Ps. 31:24; 33:18, 22; 38:15; 42:5, 11). This meaning also occurs in Isaiah (Is. 42:4; 51:5); Lamentations (Lam. 3:21, 24); Ezekiel (Ezek. 19:5); and Micah (Mic. 7:7). *
3 ***śāḇar*** [verb: שָׂבַר <7663>; a prim. root] ▶ **This word means to expect with hope and patience, to hope, to tarry, to look.** Refs.: Ruth 1:13; Esther 9:1; Ps. 104:27; 119:166; 145:15; Is. 38:18. The Hebrew word also means to view, to examine; see INSPECT <7663>. ¶
– 4 Ex. 12:39; Judg. 3:26; 19:8; 2 Sam. 15:28 ➔ LINGER <4102>.

WAIT (LIE IN) – ***'ārab*** [verb: אָרַב <693>; a prim. root] ► **This word means to ambush, to lurk. It describes the activity of the wicked man as he lurks, seeking to oppress or destroy the afflicted.** Refs.: Deut. 19:11; Ps. 10:9. It describes lying in ambush as a military tactic with intent to kill (Josh. 8:2, 4, 7). It can mean to put or set up an ambush (Judg. 9:25; 1 Sam. 15:5). *

WAIT (LIE IN, LAY HIS) – Jer. 9:8; Hos. 7:6 → AMBUSH <696>.

WAIT FOR – ***qāwāh*** [verb: קָוָה <6960>; a prim. root] ► **This word means to look for, to hope for. The root meaning is that of twisting or winding a strand of cord or rope, but it is uncertain how that root meaning relates to the idea of hope. Possibilities include: to wait, as being held back by being bound with a cord; to wait, as an allusion to the tension (as of a twisted cord) of waiting; to wait with endurance (an allusion to the strength of a cord).** The word is used to signify depending on and ordering activities around a future event (Job 7:2; Mic. 5:7). The hopes of someone can remain unfulfilled, especially when a person or a nation is sinning (Job 3:9; Ps. 69:20; Is. 5:2, 4, 7). Hoping, however, for what God has promised will not ultimately be disappointed, although it may not appear to succeed in the short run (Job 30:26; Is. 59:11; cf. Is. 59:15–21). The Lord will give strength to those who hope in Him (Ps. 27:14 [2 times]; Is. 40:31). Because He is all-powerful (Jer. 14:22), He will eventually bring His promises to pass (Lam. 3:25). These promises include the establishing of His kingdom on earth (Ps. 37:9, 34; Is. 25:9 [2 times]). The word also means to be gathered and refers to the gathering of waters (Gen. 1:9) and of people (Jer. 3:17). *

WAKE – Ps. 78:65 → SHOUT (verb) <7442> c.

WAKE UP – Gen. 41:4, 7; Hab. 2:7; etc. → AWAKEN <3364>.

WAKING – Ps. 77:4 → OPEN <8109>.

WALK (noun) – Nah. 2:5 → WAY <1979>.

WALK, INNER WALK – Ezek. 42:4; Jon. 3:3, 4 → JOURNEY (noun) <4109>.

WALK (verb) – 1 ***ṣā'aḏ*** [verb: צָעַד <6805>; a prim. root] ► **This word means to move on foot, to march, to run.** It describes the process of locomotion: walking, stepping, moving forward (2 Sam. 6:13); of the growth of limbs, stems, and branches over a wall (Gen. 49:22). It depicts God figuratively marching, moving from the land of Edom (Judg. 5:4; cf. Hab. 3:12); it is used derisively of the inability of pagan gods to walk (Jer. 10:5). It depicts God's leading His people in the wilderness, walking before them (Ps. 68:7). It indicates the arrogant stride of an adulterer (Prov. 7:8). Other ref.: Job 18:14. ¶
– 2 Hos. 11:12 → RESTLESS (BE, BECOME, GROW) <7300> 3 See GO <1980>, <1981>.

WALK (PLACES TO) – Zech. 3:7 → ACCESS <4108>.

WALK (TEACH TO) – 1 ***rāgal*** [verb: רָגַל <7270>; a prim. root] ► **This word is used in its causative stem to describe instructing someone to walk, causing him or her to walk.** Ref.: Hos. 11:3. For other meanings of the Hebrew word, see SPY OUT <7270> and SLANDER <7270>. *
2 ***tirgal*** [verb: תִּרְגַּל <8637>; from <7270> above] ► **This word is used to describe how a person instructs or trains, with care, a child to begin walking.** It was God who, in a spiritual and parental sense, taught His people, Israel, to walk (Hos. 11:3; KJV: to teach to go). ¶

WALK SLOWLY, CAREFULLY, HUMBLY – Is. 38:15 → GO WITH, GO SOFTLY <1718>.

WALL – 1 ***'uššarnā'*** [Aramaic masc. noun: אֻשַּׁרְנָא <846>; from a root corresponding to BLESS <833>] ► **This word most likely**

indicates a structure (ESV, NASB, NIV, Ezra 5:3, 9) rather than a wall. It occurs in the context of rebuilding the Temple. ¶

2 ***geḏer*** [masc. noun: גֶּדֶר <1444>; from BUILD <1443>] ▶ **This word refers to a partition, a fence.** It depicts a stone wall, broken down by a sluggard's neglect (Prov. 24:31). The eastern wall of Ezekiel's visionary Temple is indicated with this word (Ezek. 42:10). ¶

3 ***gāḏêr*** [masc. noun: גָּדֵר <1447>; from BUILD <1443>] ▶ **This word means a fence, a hedge, a defensive structure.** It depicts a stone wall of loose stones (Num. 22:24) but also a city wall (Mic. 7:11) or a wall in general (Eccl. 10:8). It denotes a wall of Ezekiel's Temple (Ezek. 42:7). Used in a figurative sense, it refers to the hedge or wall of the Lord's vineyard (Ps. 80:12; Is. 5:5), which no one could build up and make firm (Ezek. 22:30). An unstable wall is used to depict threatening persons (Ps. 62:3). *

4 ***geḏêrāh*** [fem. noun: גְּדֵרָה <1448>; fem. of WALL <1447>] ▶ **This word designates a hedge, a sheepfold, a defensive structure.** It refers to a stone pen or sheepfold (Num. 32:16, 36; 1 Sam. 24:3) but also a city wall (Ps. 89:40) or a Temple wall (Ezek. 42:12). The wall served as a major defense or stronghold (Ps. 89:40). *

5 ***ḥômāh*** [fem. noun: חוֹמָה <2346>; fem. act. part. of an unused root apparently meaning to join] ▶ **This word is used of the wall of a city.** Refs.: Lev. 25:29; 2 Kgs. 3:27. It indicates walls placed around parts of a city or temple (Deut. 28:52; Ezek. 40:5; 42:20). Nehemiah rebuilt the walls of Jerusalem (Neh. 4:1). It is found in figurative uses where a bronze wall (Jer. 1:18) or a wall of water (Ex. 14:22, 29) is indicated. It is used as a metaphor for a beloved woman (Song 8:9) and as a symbol for Israel (Amos 7:7) as a slanted wall because of her unrighteousness. High walls around cities were signs of strong defenses (Deut. 3:5). The famous wall of Babylon became a symbol of her power (Jer. 51:58). The Lord Himself says He will be a wall of fire around Jerusalem for its protection (Zech. 2:5). The wealth of a rich man is said to be his (high) wall in his mind (Prov. 18:11). To be without a wall is a sign of vulnerability (Prov. 25:28). *

6 ***ḥêyl, ḥêl*** [masc. noun: חֵיל, חֵל <2426>; a collateral form of STRENGTH <2428>] ▶ **This word means entrenchment, fortress, army, defense, fortified wall.** The wall of Jezreel was the location where the dogs would gnaw on Jezebel's dead body (1 Kgs. 21:23). The psalmist prayed for peace within the walls of Jerusalem (Ps. 122:7). The Lord decided to tear down the wall around Israel (Lam. 2:8). A surrounding river was the defense of Thebes (Nah. 3:8). See the related noun *ḥayil* (STRENGTH <2428>). Other refs.: 2 Sam. 20:15; 2 Kgs. 18:17; Ps. 10:10; 48:13; Is. 26:1; Obad. 1:20. ¶

7 ***ḥayiṣ*** [masc. noun: חַיִץ <2434>; another form for STREET <2351>] ▶ **This word indicates a thin, flimsy wall.** It is used in a context that indicates an unstable or weak wall that will easily fall under stress (Ezek. 13:10). ¶

8 ***kōṯel*** [masc. noun: כֹּתֶל <3796>; from an unused root meaning to compact] ▶ **This word indicates a barrier surrounding an area or living space for protection or landscaping beauty.** Ref.: Song 2:9. ¶

9 ***keṯal*** [Aramaic masc. noun: כְּתַל <3797>; corresponding to <3796> above ▶ **This word indicates a barrier surrounding an area or living space for protection or beauty.** It refers to the Temple walls being rebuilt in the time of Zerubbabel (Ezra 5:8); and it describes the interior wall of a banqueting room (Dan. 5:5). ¶

10 ***qiyr, qir, qiyrāh*** [masc. noun: קִיר, קִר, קִירָה <7023>; from DIG <6979> a. (as building something in a trench)] ▶ **This word refers to a wall in numerous aspects, e.g., generally: a wall as a solid vertical building component; the interior, exterior, thickness of a wall; the wall of a house (including the house of the Lord), of a room, of a city; a decorated wall; a wall as a barrier, etc.** Balaam's donkey, afraid of the angel, pressed against a wall and crushed Balaam's foot (Num. 22:25). Saul wanted to pin David to a wall with his spear (1 Sam. 18:11). This word also was used to describe a place one thought was safe (Amos

5:19). Solomon lined the interior walls of the Temple with cedar (1 Kgs. 6:15); and Jezebel's blood splattered on a wall (2 Kgs. 9:33). The Hebrew phrase, walls of one's heart, means something like the depths of one's soul in Jeremiah 4:19. The KJV translates that Hebrew phrase as, my very heart. In Ezekiel's vision of the new Temple, the walls were six cubits thick (Ezek. 41:5). *
11 ***šûr, šûrāh*** [שׁוּר, שׁוּרָה <7791>; from JOURNEY (verb) <7788> (as going about, e.g., a wall)] ►
a. A masculine noun meaning a wall. It refers to a wall around a well (Gen. 49:6; but note OX <7794>); a boundary-marking wall (2 Sam. 22:30; Ps. 18:29). It indicates a wall around a field or a vineyard (Gen. 49:22).
b. A feminine noun indicating a terrace, a supporting wall. It refers to the walls of an olive vineyard, within which the poor labor oppressively to produce oil that does not benefit them (Job 24:11). ¶
12 ***šûr*** [Aramaic masc. noun: שׁוּר <7792>; corresponding to <7791> above] ► **This word refers to the stone walls of Jerusalem needed for the protection of the city and for encouraging persons to settle in it again.** Refs.: Ezra 4:12, 13, 16. ¶
– 13 Ex. 15:8; Ps. 78:13 ➔ HEAP (noun) <5067> 14 Jer. 5:10 ➔ VINEYARD <8284> b.

WALLOW – Jer. 48:26 ➔ STRIKE <5606>.

WALLOW IN – Jer. 6:26; 25:34; Ezek. 27:30 ➔ ROLL IN <6428>.

WANDER – 1 ***bûḵ*** [verb: בּוּךְ <943>; a prim. root] ► **This word means to be confused, complexed; to mill around, to wander aimlessly; it is also translated to be bewildered, to be entangled, to be perplexed.** It indicates a confused state of mind and activity (Ex. 14:3; Esther 3:15) because of not knowing what to do. The word describes the endless wandering of animals during the Lord's judgments on His people (Joel 1:18). ¶
2 ***nûaʻ*** [verb: נוּעַ <5128>; a prim. root] ► **This word means to shake, to stagger.** It refers to a displaced person, a wanderer, a vagrant (Gen. 4:12; 14: fugitive). It describes a person physically shaking or trembling from fear (Ex. 20:18); and of a person's lips quivering or mumbling (1 Sam. 1:13). It depicts the wandering of Israel in the wilderness for forty years (Num. 32:13; cf. Amos 4:8). Figuratively, it describes a tree reigning, "swaying" over the other trees (Judg. 9:9, 11, 13). It is used of inanimate things moving, shaking, being shaken, tottering, etc. (2 Kgs. 23:18; Job 28:4; Is. 6:4; 7:2; Amos 9:9; Nah. 3:12). It is used of shaking one's head or hand (2 Kgs. 19:21; Ps. 22:7; Zeph. 2:15). It indicates the Lord's judgments that make the whole house of Israel shake in dread (Amos 9:9). *
3 ***tāʻāh*** [verb: תָּעָה <8582>; a prim. root] ► **This Hebrew word means to err, to go astray.** Its meaning primarily rests in the notion of wandering about (Ex. 23:4; Job 38:41). Figuratively, it is used in reference to one who is intoxicated (Is. 28:7). Most often, however, it refers to erring or being misled in a moral or religious sense (Is. 53:6; Ezek. 44:10 [2 times]; Hos. 4:12). *
– 4 Jer. 2:20 ➔ MARCH (verb) <6808> 5 Jer. 31:22 ➔ WITHDRAW <2559>.

WANDER ALONE – Hos. 8:9 ➔ ALONE (BE) <909>.

WANDERER – 1 Gen. 4:12, 14 ➔ FLEE <5110> 2 Is. 58:7 ➔ WANDERING <4788>.

WANDERING – 1 ***mārûḏ*** [masc. noun: מָרוּד <4788>; from RESTLESS (BE) <7300> in the sense of maltreatment] ► **This word means and is also translated roaming, misery, homelessness.** It indicates a condition of being without a permanent place to live, homeless (Is. 58:7; also translated wanderer, one cast out). It refers to Jerusalem destitute of all her past inhabitants as well as to persons exiled from their native city and land (Lam. 1:7). It has the sense of aimless wandering from one place to the next (Lam. 3:19). ¶
2 ***nôḏ*** [masc. noun: נוֹד <5112>; from FLEE <5110>] ► **This word refers to**

walking about, traveling about with no home to return to and no goal in mind. It is used of David's flight from his enemies in the wilderness (Ps. 56:8; also translated tossing, misery). ¶

WANT – 1 ***ḥôser*** [masc. noun: חֹסֶר <2640>; from LACKING (BE) <2637>] ▶ **This word indicates need, lack; it is also translated lacking, poverty.** It describes a basic shortage or privation of the necessities of life (Deut. 28:48, 57). A lack of bread was a sign from the Lord of His displeasure with Israel (Amos 4:6). ¶
– 2 Deut. 12:15, 20, 21 ➔ DESIRE (noun) <185> 3 Job 30:3; Prov. 28:22 ➔ POVERTY <2639>.

WANTING – ***ḥassiyr*** [Aramaic adj.: חַסִּיר <2627>; from a root corresponding to LACKING (BE) <2637>] ▶ **This word means deficient, of poor quality.** It refers to some deficiency in a person, such as Belshazzar (Dan. 5:27). ¶

WANTING (THAT WHICH IS) – Eccl. 1:15 ➔ LACKING (WHAT IS) <2642>.

WANTON – Is. 3:16 ➔ WANTONLY (GLANCE) <8265>.

WANTONLY (GLANCE) – ***śāqar*** [verb: שָׂקַר <8265>; a prim. root] ▶ **This word means to flirt.** It describes the seductive eyes of the proud women of Judah, eyes painted for the purpose of flirting, looking enticing (Is. 3:16). ¶

WAR – 1 ***lāḥem*** [masc. noun: לָחֶם <3901>; from FIGHT <3898>] ▶ **This word is used in the song of Deborah, a poetic section, to represent conflict or battle.** Ref.: Judg. 5:8. ¶
2 ***milḥāmāh*** [fem. noun: מִלְחָמָה <4421>; from FIGHT <3898>] ▶ **This word indicates a formal military combat declared and engaged in by peoples and nations.** The Lord was a "man of war" on behalf of His people (Ex. 15:3); a mighty one of battle (Ps. 24:8); the one in charge of the battle (1 Sam. 17:47; Ps. 76:3); for they were His battles (1 Sam. 18:17). It was a general term for battle, war, fighting (Gen. 14:8; Ex. 1:10; 1 Sam. 17:1; 31:3; 1 Kgs. 20:14). It refers to the place of war, a battlefield (1 Sam. 14:20). A soldier would be a man of war, a warrior (1 Sam. 16:18; Is. 3:2). The host of the armies is indicated by the phrase *ṣᵉḇā' milḥāmāh* (Num. 31:14; Is. 13:4). Various verbs are used with the noun: *'ārak̲*, get ready for battle (Judg. 20:22); *qāraḇ*, to join into battle (1 Kgs. 20:29); *'āśāh*, to make war (Prov. 20:18; 24:6). *
3 ***qᵉrāḇ*** [Aramaic masc. noun: קְרָב <7129>; corresponding to BATTLE <7128>] ▶ **This word refers to formal acts of hostility against someone, constituting a military attack, a war, a battle.** Ref.: Dan. 7:21. It is used figuratively of a battle carried out against someone on a personal or a spiritual level (see Ps. 55:18). It describes an attitude or a state of the heart (see Ps. 55:21). The Lord will fight as on a day of battle for His people to establish and defend them (see Zech. 14:3). ¶
– 4 Job 38:23; Ps. 55:21; etc. ➔ BATTLE <7128>.

WAR (MAKE, WAGE) – Num. 31:7, 42; etc. ➔ SERVE <6633>.

WAR (PREPARE FOR) – See DRAW OUT <2502>.

WAR (WAGE) – Is. 41:12 ➔ CONTEND <4695>.

WAR CLUB – ***mappêṣ*** [masc. noun: מַפֵּץ <4661>; from BREAK <5310> a.] ▶ **It was a weapon with a heavy blade, used in war. This word is also translated hammer, battle-ax.** It is used figuratively of Babylon as God's battle-ax against His own people (Jer. 51:20). ¶

WARD – 1 Gen. 40:3, 4, 7; 42:17, 19; Lev. 24:12; Num. 15:34; 1 Chr. 26:16 ➔ CUSTODY <4929> 2 Jer. 37:13 ➔ GUARD <6488>.

WARD OFF – Dan. 4:35 ➔ STRIKE <4223>.

WARDROBE – ***meltāḥāh*** [fem. noun: מֶלְתָּחָה <4458>; from an unused root meaning to spread out] ▶ **This word depicts a storeroom with its contents of garments or clothing.** Ref.: 2 Kgs. 10:22; KJV: vestry. In this case, it refers to an inventory of pagan priestly garments worn by the priests of Baal. ¶

WARE – Neh. 13:16 ➔ MERCHANDISE <4377>.

WARES – [1] ***misḥār*** [masc. noun: מִסְחָר <4536>; from MERCHANT <5503>] ▶ **This word depicts merchandise, the sale of merchandise.** It refers to materials and goods being offered for purchase or trade (1 Kgs. 10:15; also translated business, revenues, income, traffic). ¶
[2] ***'izzāḇôn*** [masc. noun: עִזָּבוֹן <5801>; from LEAVE <5800> in the sense of letting go (for a price, i.e., selling)] ▶ **This word refers to goods or merchandise available for trade and barter.** Refs.: Ezek. 27:12, 14, 16, 19, 22, 27, 33; KJV: fairs. ¶
– [3] Neh. 10:31 ➔ MERCHANDISE <4728> [4] Jer. 10:17 ➔ BUNDLE <3666> [5] Ezek. 27:9, 13, 17, 19, 25, 33, 34 ➔ MERCHANDISE <4627>.

WARFARE – ***sa'ss^e'āh*** [fem. noun: סַאסְּאָה <5432>; from SEAH <5429> (a measure of flour or grain)] ▶
a. A word indicating a driving away, conflict. It refers to banishing someone, especially one's enemy or advisory expelling them (Is. 27:8). ¶
b. A word referring to moderation, a measured response. It was formerly taken to indicate something done in a controlled, measured way (Is. 27:8; KJV, cf. NKJV; see also a.). ¶

WARM – ***ḥām*** [adj.: חָם <2525>; from WARM (BE) <2552>] ▶ **This word describes something as giving off a moderate amount of heat; it is also translated hot.** Bread that is still warm from being baked (Josh. 9:12); something that is warm because it has been heated, e.g., clothes from the hot sun and south wind (Job 37:17). ¶

WARM (BE) – ***ḥāmam*** [verb: חָמַם <2552>; a prim. root] ▶ **This word means to be hot, to become warm, to enflame oneself with, to warm, to warm oneself. It refers to bodily heat.** Refs.: 1 Kgs. 1:1, 2; 2 Kgs. 4:34. It refers also to the use of fire to warm oneself (Is. 44:15, 16). It indicates the act of becoming warm. It is used figuratively of anger and wrath arising within a person (Deut. 19:6); to the weather as it warms (Job 6:17); or to the sun's rays warming the day (1 Sam. 11:9). It depicts the Babylonians as lions becoming heated in riotous banqueting or debauchery (Jer. 51:39). *

WARM (BE, WAX) – ***zāraḇ*** [fem. noun: זָרַב <2215>; a prim. root] ▶ **This word means and is also translated to melt, to become waterless, in the dry season.** It describes the drying up of streams, especially wadis, streams that flow only at certain times (Job 6:17). ¶

WARM (GET, KEEP) – 1 Kgs. 1:1; Eccl. 4:11 ➔ CONCEIVE <3179>.

WARM (GROW) – Gen. 43:30; Hos. 11:8 ➔ YEARN <3648>.

WARMTH – [1] ***ḥôm*** [masc. noun: חֹם <2527>; from WARM (BE) <2552>] ▶ **This word functions as a predicate adjective to indicate warm bread, fresh bread; it is also translated heat.** Ref.: 1 Sam. 21:6. It refers to the heat of the day, the hottest period of the day (Gen. 18:1) or specifically to the heat of the sun (1 Sam. 11:9). In a general sense, it indicates the heat of summer as opposed to the cold of winter (Gen. 8:22). It creates certain effects: it melts snow (Job 24:19) and can threaten plants (Jer. 17:8) or trees. *
– [2] Ps. 19:6 ➔ SUN <2535>.

WARN – ***zāhar*** [verb: זָהַר <2094>; a prim. root] ▶ **This word means to caution, to advise against; it also means to teach, to shine. Ezekiel uses this verb more than any other Old Testament writer.** In chapter 3, he uses *zāhar* seven times consecutively when God commands him to warn the wicked and righteous about their sin (Ezek. 3:17–21). Similarly, Ezekiel 33 uses this word eight times to describe coming judgment for sin (Ezek. 33:3–9). Other books also use *zāhar* to mean warn (2 Kgs. 6:10; 2 Chr. 19:10) or admonish (Eccl. 4:13; 12:12). Exodus uses this word to mean teach (Ex. 18:20). Daniel is the only book which uses the future tense of the word (Dan. 12:3: to shine). Other ref.: Ps. 19:11. ¶

WARNING – Num. 26:10 ➔ BANNER <5251>.

WARNING SIGN – Num. 26:10 ➔ BANNER <5251>.

WARNINGS – Job 33:16 ➔ INSTRUCTION <4561>.

WARP – ***šᵉṯiy*** [masc. noun: שְׁתִי <8359>; from PUT <7896>] ▶ **This word indicates the lengthwise threads on a loom.** It refers to a set of threads running lengthwise in the loom and crossed by the woof or weft, the intertwining of cloth material (Lev. 13:48, 49, 51–53, 56–59). ¶

WARPED – [1] Deut. 32:5 ➔ PERVERSE <6141> [2] Prov. 12:8 ➔ INIQUITY (COMMIT) <5753>.

WARRIOR – [1] ***sā'an*** [verb: סָאַן <5431>; a prim. root] ▶ **This word means to be shod, to have boots; to be a soldier.** It refers to a person (*sō'ên*) wearing boots as he marched along in military gear and in military array (Is. 9:5; ESV: tramping warrior). ¶
[2] ***pārāz*** [masc. noun: פְּרָז <6518>; from an unused root meaning to separate, i.e., to decide] ▶ **This word means a crowd; it is also translated throng, village.** It refers to a throng of attacking warriors (Hab. 3:14). The Majority Text is difficult to decipher. ¶
– [3] Is. 43:17 ➔ STRONG <5808> [4] Dan. 3:20 ➔ MAN <1401>.

WARTS – Lev. 22:22 ➔ DISCHARGE <2990>.

WASH – [1] ***dûaḥ*** [verb: דּוּחַ <1740>; a prim. root] ▶ **This word means to cleanse; it is also translated to rinse. It is used only four times in the Old Testament.** On two occasions, it is used within the sacrificial context to describe offerings that needed to be washed (2 Chr. 4:6; Ezek. 40:38). In other contexts, it describes the washing away of the sins of those in Jerusalem (Is. 4:4) and Nebuchadnezzar's carrying away (or washing away) of Judah in the Babylonian exile (Jer. 51:34); also translated to cast out, to spew out, to spit out. ¶
[2] ***kāḇas*** [verb: כָּבַס <3526>; a prim. root] ▶ **The root meaning of the verb is to trample, which was the means of washing clothes.** The word most often refers to washing clothes (Gen. 49:11; 2 Sam. 19:24), especially ceremonially (Ex. 19:10; Lev. 15; Num. 19). As a participle, the word means fuller, one who left clothes to dry in the fuller's field (2 Kgs. 18:17; Is. 7:3; 36:2). An intensive form of the verb is used of the fuller in Malachi 3:2, whose soap is a symbol of Christ's demand for purity. In Jeremiah 2:22, the word may refer literally to ceremonial washings but also implies mere human effort used in an external attempt to overcome sin. In Psalm 51:2, 7, the word refers to God's internal cleansing of the heart, making it whiter than snow. Jer. 4:14, however, showed that God's people must work to cleanse their hearts and avoid temporal destruction. *
[3] ***šāṭap*** [verb: שָׁטַף <7857>; a prim. root] ▶ **This word means to gush, to cleanse, to conquer, to drown, to overflow, to overwhelm, to rinse, to run, to rush, to wash away. In its prominent meaning, the word means to wash away.** It is used to depict what the Lord will do to a hiding place, i.e., He will overflow it (Is. 28:17). This word is used to describe God's power as a flooding downpour (Is. 28:2). It also describes a medium through which God delivers punishment (Jer. 47:2). The Lord declared that the time had come to destroy the Philistines, and He would do so, metaphorically speaking, by raising up the waters into an overflowing torrent. If a man with a discharge touched another without rinsing his hands,

the person touched had to wash the infected clothing and take a bath with water; he or she would be unclean until evening (Lev. 15:11). Ezekiel used *šāṭap̱* metaphorically to describe the Lord cleansing His bride (Ezek. 16:9). The Song of Songs uses this word to depict what cannot be done to love, i.e., waters cannot flood or quench it. True love withstands all tests (Song 8:7). The psalmist made use of *šāṭap̱* to indicate a weariness of life and its trials, speaking metaphorically of sinking into the miry depths in which there is no foothold (Ps. 69:2). In Psalm 124:4, the psalmist used the word to indicate a physical or material tragedy that is avoided with God on his side. Isaiah used the verb to indicate divine judgment against Judah (Is. 8:8); and Ephraim (Is. 28:2, 15, 17, 18). The usage of this word can also indicate a flooding over or utter destruction at the hands of another nation, sometimes dictated by God and at other times simply by the nature of people (Jer. 47:2; Dan. 11:10, 22, 40). *

WASH AWAY, WASH OFF – ***rāḥaṣ*** [verb: רָחַץ <7364>; a prim. root] ▶ **This word means to lave, to wash; it also means to bathe. Usually, it refers to washing a body, whether a part or the whole, of a person or an animal. Once it is used of washing armor and occasionally it is used figuratively. This Hebrew word carries the connotation of washing with water in order to make clean.** It describes the action involved in washing the hands or feet (Ex. 30:19); the face (Gen. 43:31); the body (2 Sam. 11:2); clothes (Lev. 14:9); or the parts of a sacrificial offering (Lev. 1:9). Symbolically, such a washing was declarative of innocence (Deut. 21:6); and was figurative of cleansing from sin (Prov. 30:12; Is. 4:4). *

WASHBASIN – ***raḥaṣ*** [masc. noun: רַחַץ <7366>; from WASH AWAY <7364>] ▶ **This word appears twice where it refers to a washing pot.** Refs.: Ps. 60:8; 108:9; also translated washpot, washbowl. In both instances, it was a term of derision and was meant to convey a sense of utter contempt. ¶

WASHBOWL – Ps. 60:8; 108:9 ➔ WASHBASIN <7366>.

WASHING – ***raḥṣāh*** [fem. noun: רַחְצָה <7367>; fem. of WASHBASIN <7366>] ▶ **The primary meaning of this word is found in its two uses in the Song of Solomon.** Both times it referred to the bathing of sheep in water that caused them to be clean and white (Song 4:2; 6:6). ¶

WASHPOT – Ps. 60:8; 108:9 ➔ WASHBASIN <7366>.

WASTE (noun) – [1] ***mešô'āh, mešō'āh*** [fem. noun: מְשׁוֹאָה, מְשֹׁאָה <4875>; from the same as RAVAGE <7722>] ▶ **This word indicates desolation, barrenness.** It is descriptive of land devoid of life, barren, almost useless (Job 30:3; 38:27). It is used to depict a day of judgment on Nineveh (Zeph. 1:15). ¶

– [2] 2 Kgs. 18:27; Is. 36:12 ➔ DUNG <2716> [3] Ezek. 4:12 ➔ EXCREMENT <6627> [4] Ezek. 4:12, 15 ➔ DUNG <1561> [5] Is. 5:6 ➔ WASTELAND <1326>.

WASTE (LAY) – [1] ***ḥārêḇ, ḥāraḇ*** [verb: חָרֵב, חָרַב <2717>; a prim. root] ▶ **This verb means to be desolate, to be destroyed, to be dry, to dry up. Two related themes constitute the cardinal meaning of this word, devastation and drying up.** Although each aspect is distinct from the other, both convey the notion of wasting away. The word is used to describe the drying of the earth after the flood (Gen. 8:13); the drying of green vines (Judg. 16:7); the utter destruction of a physical structure (Ezek. 6:6); the devastation of war (Is. 37:18); the removal of human inhabitants (Ezek. 26:19); the slaughter of animals (Jer. 50:27). *

– [2] Ezra 4:15 ➔ DESTROYED (BE) <2718> [3] Is. 24:1, 3; Nah. 2:2 ➔ EMPTY (MAKE) <1238> [4] Jer. 4:7 ➔ RUINS (BE, LIE IN) <5327> [5] Lam. 2:6 ➔ VIOLENCE (DO) <2554>.

WASTE (LAY, LIE) – ***šā'āh*** [verb: שָׁאָה <7582>; a prim. root] ▶ **This word means to crush, to turn into ruins, to devastate,**

to be wasted, to lie ruined. It means to demolish, to ruin, to devastate. In context it describes making strong cities into trash heaps (2 Kgs. 19:25). It means to make cities desolate, without inhabitants (Is. 6:11; 37:26). For another meaning of the Hebrew word, see ROAR <7582>. ¶

WASTE (MAKE, BE, LAY) – ***bālaq*** [verb: בָּלַק <1110>; a prim. root] ► **This verb means to destroy; it is also translated to be stripped, ruin, to make desolate.** It describes the devastated state of a city (Nah. 2:10) or the earth itself (Is. 24:1) brought about by the Lord's acts of judgment. ¶

WASTE, LAY WASTE – ***šûḏ*** [verb: שׁוּד <7736>; a prim. root] ► **This word refers to rendering something useless, devastating or destroying it.** It is used in a general sense of any calamity or act of destruction (Ps. 91:6). ¶

WASTE (verb) – Ps. 80:13 ➔ RAVAGE (verb) <3765>.

WASTE AWAY – 1 ***māqaq*** [verb: מָקַק <4743>; a prim. root] ► **This word means to dissipate, to decompose, to putrefy; it is also translated to rot away, to pine away, consume away, wear away.** It is used of Israel as a people in exile (Lev. 26:39; Ezek. 4:17; 24:23; 33:10); of parts of the body (Zech. 14:12: NKJV: to dissolve); of injuries (Ps. 38:5: to be corrupt, to fester). It is used of anything, even in the heavens, wearing down, falling apart (Is. 34:4). ¶
2 ***'āšēš*** [verb: עָשֵׁשׁ <6244>; a prim. root, prob. to shrink] ► **This word means to deteriorate, to destroy; it is also translated to consume, to grow weak. It is from the same root as moth, *'āš*.** It refers to the deterioration or destruction of something: people's eyes, their sight (Ps. 6:7; 31:9); their bodies (Ps. 31:10). ¶
– 3 Gen. 47:13 ➔ LANGUISH <3856> 4 Job 14:10 ➔ LAY LOW <2522> 5 Is. 10:18 ➔ MELT <4549> 6 Is. 17:4 ➔ BRING LOW <1809> 7 Is. 17:4 ➔ LEAN (GROW, BECOME, WAX) <7329> 8 Ezek. 21:30 ➔ BRING LOW <4355>.

WASTE AWAY (I) – Is. 24:16 ➔ LEANNESS <7334>.

WASTED – 1 ***māzeh*** [adj.: מָזֶה <4198>; from an unused root meaning to suck out] ► **This word describes persons who are exhausted, debilitated, in this case, from famine.** Ref.: Deut. 32:24; also translated burnt, wasting. ¶
– 2 See DRY (adj.) <2720>.

WASTED (BE) – Is. 6:11 ➔ WASTE (LAY, LIE) <7582>.

WASTELAND – ***bāṯāh*** [fem. noun: בָּתָה <1326>; prob. an orthographical variation for DESOLATE <1327>] ► **This word indicates devastation, desert, waste.** Isaiah prophesied that the Lord would turn Jerusalem into a wasteland because of its failure to produce good fruit (Is. 5:6). ¶

WASTES – Is. 61:4 ➔ HEAT (noun) <2721>.

WASTES (ONE WHO) – Ps. 137:3 ➔ TORMENTOR <8437>.

WASTES (STONY) – Jer. 17:6 ➔ PARCHED PLACE <2788>.

WASTING – Deut. 32:24 ➔ WASTED <4198>.

WASTING DISEASE – Lev. 26:16; Deut. 28:22 ➔ CONSUMPTION <7829>.

WASTING DISEASE, WASTING SICKNESS – Ps. 106:15; Is. 10:16 ➔ LEANNESS <7332>.

WATCH (noun) – 1 ***'ašmûrāh, 'ašmōreṯ*** [fem. noun: אַשְׁמוּרָה, אַשְׁמֹרֶת <821>; from KEEP <8104>] ► **This word refers to a night guard's duty in general (Judg. 7:19, the middle watch which lasted from 10 p.m. to 2 p.m.; Ps. 90:4).** It may point to the last watch (period) of the night (Ex. 14:24; 1 Sam. 11:11), literally, the watch (period) of the morning. Other refs.: Ps. 63:6; 119:148; Lam. 2:19. ¶

– [2] Ex. 12:42 ➔ GUARD <8108> [3] 1 Chr. 26:16; Neh. 4:9; Jer. 51:12 ➔ CUSTODY <4929>.

WATCH (verb) – [1] ***ṣāp̱āh*** [verb: צָפָה <6822>; a prim. root] ► **This word means to keep an eye on something or someone, to guard someone, to monitor someone.** It refers to God's watching over persons while they are apart (Gen. 31:49); over the nations (Ps. 66:7). A person who watches is a watchman (1 Sam. 14:16; 2 Sam. 13:34; Is. 21:6; Mic. 7:4). The prophets were called watchmen for God (Jer. 6:17; Ezek. 3:17; 33:7; Hos. 9:8). It is used figuratively of waiting to see something, what God will do (Ps. 5:3; Nah. 2:1; Hab. 2:1). The wicked watch the righteous to do them harm (Ps. 37:32). *

[2] ***šāqaḏ*** [verb: שָׁקַד <8245>; a prim. root] ► **This word also means to guard. It means to keep a close observation on something or someone.** E.g., the Temple utensils (Ezra 8:29); a tomb (Job 21:32); a city (Ps. 127:1). It describes figuratively a person's diligent pursuit of wisdom (Prov. 8:34). It indicates an intent or attitude of a person set on doing something (Is. 29:20). It indicates a state of being vigilant, lying awake, watching (Ps. 102:7); especially of God's watching over His word to do it (Jer. 1:12; 31:28; 44:27). He brings devastations and calamities to pass, carefully watching over them (Dan. 9:14). Other ref.: Jer. 5:6. ¶

– [3] Gen. 24:21 ➔ GAZE <7583> [4] Ps. 33:14 ➔ LOOK (verb) <7688> [5] Prov. 4:26; 5:21 ➔ WEIGH, WEIGH OUT <6424>.

WATCHER – ***'iyr*** [Aramaic masc. noun: עִיר <5894>; from a root corresponding to AWAKE <5782>] ► **This word indicates a divinely commissioned being, portrayed as a watchful one, who communicated God's decrees and was responsible to God**. Refs.: Dan. 4:13, 17, 23; NIV: messenger. ¶

WATCHING – [1] ***ṣᵉp̱iyyāh*** [fem. noun: צְפִיָּה <6836>; from WATCH (verb) <6822>] ► **This word indicates a lookout tower.** It refers to a lookout structure from which to spy out approaching enemies or to keep aware of what is going on in the vicinity. KJV translates the word abstractly: watching (Lam. 4:17). ¶

[2] ***šimmur*** [masc. noun: שִׁמֻּר <8107>; from KEEP <8104> (in the sense of to watch over)] ► **This word means a vigil, an observance.** It refers to an act and a time of keen observation, vigilant watchfulness, especially on the night of the Passover (Ex. 12:42). ¶

WATCHMAN – 1 Chr. 26:16 ➔ CUSTODY <4929>.

WATCHTOWER – [1] ***baḥan*** [masc. noun: בַּחַן <975>; from TEST <974> (in the sense of keeping a look-out)] ► **This word indicates a garrisoned tower from which Israel's watchmen could guard their fields, cities, and nation.** Ref.: Is. 32:14. ¶

[2] ***miṣpeh*** [masc. noun: מִצְפֶּה <4707>; from WATCH (verb) <6822>] ► **This word describes a lookout in the wilderness, a lookout tower.** Ref.: 2 Chr. 20:24; also translated a place overlooking, that overlooks. It describes also a sentry post for spotting an enemy (Is. 21:8). ¶

– [3] Is. 21:5 ➔ RUG <6844> b.

WATER (noun) – ***mayim*** [masc. dual or plural noun: מַיִם <4325>; dual of a prim. noun (but used in a sing. sense)] ► **This word indicates the clear element in its various functions.** As a basic element of the earth (Gen. 1:2); as water descending as rain (2 Sam. 21:10); gathered water, as seas, wells, springs, etc. (Num. 20:17; Amos 5:8; Is. 22:9). Urine is designated as *mêymêy raglayim* (2 Kgs. 18:27). Water is used in various metaphors: as a picture of justice running down like abundant waters (Amos 5:24); powers of the underworld (Ps. 18:16); frailty or weakness (Josh. 7:5); distress (Is. 43:2); sudden violence (Job 27:20; Is. 28:2, 17; Hos. 2:5); the ephemeral character of things or persons (Job 11:16); God's wrath (Hos. 5:10). Numbers 5:17 speaks of holy water. Running water is "living water" (Lev. 14:5, 6, 50–52; Num. 19:17). *

WATER (GIVE) – ***šāqāh*** [verb: שָׁקָה <8248>; a prim. root] ► **This word means to cause one to drink.** It is used often of watering camels and other animals and of giving water or other liquids to persons to drink (Gen. 19:32–35; 21:19; 24:14, 18, 19; Ex. 2:16, 17, 19). This was done sometimes as a polite social gesture, sometimes forcefully (Ex. 32:20). It is used in an impersonal sense of watering the land (Gen. 2:6, 10; Joel 3:18). In reference to humans bones, it means to be damp, moist, wet (Job 21:24), meaning to be healthy. *

WATER (PLACE OF DRAWING) – Judg. 5:11 ➔ WATERING PLACE <4857>.

WATER HOLE – Is. 7:19 ➔ PASTURE <5097>.

WATER SHAFT – ***ṣinnôr*** [masc. noun צִנּוֹר <6794>; from an unused root perhaps meaning to be hollow] ► **This word refers to a water shaft hollowed out of stone, a water tunnel.** Ref.: 2 Sam. 5:8; KJV: gutter. It also describes water that drops suddenly and quickly, creating a rushing sound of turbulent water (Ps. 42:7: waterfall, waterspout), thus conveying a certain impression and response in the hearer. ¶

WATER TUNNEL – 2 Sam. 5:8 ➔ WATER SHAFT <6794>.

WATER (noun and verb) – ***zarziyp̱, zārap̱*** [זַרְזִיף <2222>; by reduplication from an unused root meaning to flow] ►
a. A masculine noun indicating a downpour, a hard rain. It is used as a simile indicating heavy rain descending on the earth (Ps. 72:6; KJV). ¶
b. A verb meaning to water, drip, pour down. It is considered a verb form with the subject being showers that water or pour down on the earth (Ps. 72:6; ESV, NASB, NIV, NKJV). ¶

WATER (verb) – 1 Ps. 6:6 ➔ MELT <4529> 2 Ps. 65:9 ➔ OVERFLOW (verb) <7783>.

WATERED – ***rāweh*** [adj.: רָוֶה <7302>; from DRINK ONE'S FILL <7301>] ► **This word describes a garden that has been watered; it also means well-watered. In another context it means satiated (as with intoxicating drink).** It refers to a condition of saturation or of having sufficient water or rain (Deut. 29:19); especially a garden, a figure of a renewed people of God (Is. 58:11; Jer. 31:12). It is used figuratively, e.g., of being satiated with dishonor, shame (Job 10:15: to be full). ¶

WATERFALL – Ps. 42:7 ➔ WATER SHAFT <6794>.

WATERING – Job 37:11 ➔ MOISTURE <7377>.

WATERING PLACE – 1 ***maš'āḇ*** [masc. noun: מַשְׁאָב <4857>; from DRAW <7579>] ► **This word refers to a place for drawing up water.** It indicates a well or spring from which water was drawn, a watering place where social conversation occurred as well (Judg. 5:11). ¶
– 2 Is. 7:19 ➔ PASTURE <5097> 3 Ezek. 45:15 ➔ DRINK (noun) <4945>.

WATERLESS (BECOME) – Job 6:17 ➔ WARM (BE, WAX) <2215>.

WATERPOT – 1 Kgs. 18:33 ➔ JAR <3537>.

WATERSKIN – ***ḥêmeṯ*** [masc. noun: חֵמֶת <2573>; from the same as WALL <2346>] ► **This word refers to a container for holding something to drink; it was made of hide and is also translated bottle, skin. It is most often taken to mean a bottle or wineskin.** Ref.: Hab. 2:15; but NASB, venom. It was probably tied and stopped with pitch at both ends to hold wine, water, or oil (Gen. 21:14, 15, 19). ¶

WATERSPOUT – Ps. 42:7 ➔ WATER SHAFT <6794>.

WATERY DEEP – Is. 44:27 ➔ DEEP (noun) <6683>.

WAVE – 1 ***gal*** [masc. noun: גַּל <1530>; from ROLL (verb) <1556>] ► **This word**

refers to waves of the sea, i.e., a long body of water curling into a rolling arched form. Refs.: Job 38:11; Is. 51:15; Jer. 5:22; 31:35. In a figurative sense, it denotes chastisement from the Lord (Ps. 42:7; Jon. 2:3) or the armies of an enemy approaching (Jer. 51:42, 55). In a different context, it indicates the bride of the lover as a barred spring (Song 4:12), a spring sealed up (KJV, a spring shut up), to assert her chastity. The word also refers to a heap of stones; see HEAP (noun) <1530>. *

2 ***mišbār*** [masc. noun: מִשְׁבָּר <4867>; from BREAK <7665>] ▶ **This word is used of breakers, incoming waves on a seashore.** It is used figuratively of the waves of death (2 Sam. 22:5); or the waves of despair (Ps. 42:7; 88:7; Jon. 2:3). They are used to compare the Lord's might with the sea's breakers (Ps. 93:4). ¶

– 3 Ps. 93:3 ➔ POUNDING WAVE <1796>.

WAVE OFFERING, WAVING, OFFERING – ***tᵉnûp̱āh*** [fem. noun: תְּנוּפָה <8573>; from SPRINKLE <5130>] ▶ **This word basically means swinging, waving (as of the hand). In a general sense, this word implies the side to side motion involved in waving. In its most important and frequent use it is translated wave offering. It is translated simply offering in other contexts.** It is used specifically as a technical term for the wave offering, e.g., involving a sacrificial animal and other accompanying offerings (Ex. 29:24; Lev. 8:27). This could be accompanied with oil in the case of a particular type of wave offering: the tresspass offering (Lev. 14:24). Leviticus 23:15S speaks of the sheaf of the wave offering and following verses speak of wave loaves. Levites themselves (a living sacrifce to execute the service of the Lord) are termed an offering (Num. 8:11) Three times this exact word is taken to mean an offering in general, i.e., of gold (Ex. 35:22 38:24), of brass (Ex. 38:29. It is used in its basic sense in Isaiah (Is. 19:16; 30:32. *

WAVE PROUDLY – Job 39:13 ➔ ENJOY <5965> b.

WAVER – 1 Ps. 26:1 ➔ SLIP <4571> 2 Jer. 31:22 ➔ WITHDRAW <2559>.

WAVY – ***taltal*** [תַּלְתַּל <8534>; by reduplication, from LOFTY <8524> through the idea of vibration] ▶

a. An adjective meaning curly, bushy. It describes the bridegroom's black, bushy locks lying in bunches. Ref.: Song 5:11. Its exact nuance is not entirely clear.

b. A feminine noun meaning a cluster of dates. It refers to the hair of the bridegroom, bundled into clusters that look like bunches of dates (Song 5:11), a cluster of flowers or dates of the date palm tree. ¶

WAX – ***dônag*** [masc. noun: דּוֹנַג <1749>; of uncertain deriv.] ▶ **This word is always used figuratively to form similes symbolizing something melting or soft.** Mountains melt before the Lord (Ps. 97:5; Mic. 1:4); the heart is like wax in times of distress (Ps. 22:14); the wicked melt away before the Lord (Ps. 68:2). ¶

WAY – 1 ***hᵃliyḵah*** [fem. noun: הֲלִיכָה <1979>; fem. of STEP (noun) <1978>] ▶ **This word indicates a going, a march, a procession, a traveling group.** It describes the confused march or scurrying about of the people of Nineveh under attack (Nah. 2:5: march, walk). It is used to describe those proceeding or traveling; caravans (Job 6:19: caravan, troop). It indicates the activity and lifestyle of a family (Prov. 31:27: way, affair). The psalmist uses it of God's procession or proceeding into the sanctuary (Ps. 68:24: procession, goings), and it denotes God's ways in general (Hab. 3:6). ¶

– 2 Ps. 77:19 ➔ PATH <7635> 3 See PATH <1870>.

WAY (LITTLE) – Gen. 35:16; 48:7; 2 Kgs. 5:19 ➔ DISTANCE (SOME, LITTLE) <3529>.

WAYFARER – 2 Sam. 12:4; Jer. 9:2 ➔ TRAVEL <732>.

WAYFARING MAN – Judg. 19:17; 2 Sam. 12:4; Jer. 9:2; 14:8 ➔ TRAVEL <732>.

WAYMARK – Jer. 31:21 ➔ MONUMENT <6725>.

WAYSIDE – ***yak̲*** [masc. noun: יָךְ <3197>; by erroneous transcription from HAND <3027>] ▶ **This word is placed in front of the word *derek̲*, road, way, indicating where Eli the priest was sitting.** It means side (of the road) or a more specific location along the road. Some prefer to read *yad̲* here, and they translate it as along the side of (the road) (1 Sam. 4:13). ¶

WAYWARD – Prov. 7:11 ➔ REBELLIOUS <5637>.

WAYWARDNESS – Prov. 1:32 ➔ TURNING AWAY <4878>.

WE – [1] ***ᵃnû*** [pron.: אֲנוּ <580>; contr. from <587> below] ▶ **This word serves as the subject of a participle.** Ref.: Jer. 42:6. ¶
[2] ***ᵃnaḥnā', ᵃnaḥnāh*** [Aramaic plur. pron.: אֲנַחְנָא, אֲנַחְנָה <586>; corresponding to <587> below] ▶ **This word is the standard first common plural independent pronoun in biblical Aramaic.** In Scripture it is used with a participle (Ezra 4:16; Dan. 3:16, 17) and with the infinitive (Ezra 5:11). ¶
[3] ***ᵃnaḥnû*** [pron.: אֲנַחְנוּ <587>; apparently from I <595>] ▶ **This word is a first common plural independent pronoun.** Its use is quite uniform in meaning we (Gen. 13:8; 29:4; 37:7; Num. 9:7; Deut. 1:28). It may precede or follow (Gen. 19:13; Num. 10:29; Judg. 19:18) a participle. It can follow a verb for emphasis (Judg. 9:28; 2 Kgs. 10:4). It also can be used in a reflexive construction following a preposition to mean with ourselves (Gen. 13:8, lit., with us, we). *
[4] ***naḥnû*** [pron.: נַחְנוּ <5168>; for <587> above] ▶ **This word serves as a shortened first person plural pronoun used for both men or women.** Refs.: Gen. 42:11; Ex. 16:7, 8; Num. 32:32; 2 Sam. 17:12; Lam. 3:42. ¶

WEAK (adj.) – [1] ***'umlal*** [adj.: אֻמְלַל <536>; from LANGUISH <535>] ▶ **This word means and is also translated faint, pining away, languishing.** It is used to describe the despair seizing the psalmist in a time of grave trouble (Ps. 6:2). ¶
[2] ***ᵃmêlāl*** [adj.: אֲמֵלָל <537>; from LANGUISH <535>] ▶ **This word means feeble; it describes the supposed feebleness of the Jewish people who had returned from exile in Babylon.** It was at least through the eyes of Sanballat (Neh. 4:2), as they tried to rebuild the city wall. ¶
[3] ***rāp̄eh*** [adj.: רָפֶה <7504>; from CEASE <7503>] ▶ **This word means slack (in body or mind). It refers to the lack of vigor, strength, or power of a people, an ethnic group, especially politically and militarily; it also means and is translated feeble.** Ref.: Num. 13:18. It is used with hands (*yād̲ayim*) following or preceding to mean weak of strength, worn out, frail (2 Sam. 17:2; Job 4:3; Is. 35:3). ¶
– [4] 2 Chr. 36:17 ➔ AGED <3486>.

WEAK (BE, GROW) – [1] Gen. 30:42; Ps. 102:1 ➔ TURN (verb) <5848> b. [2] Ps. 6:7 ➔ MOVE <6275> [3] Ps. 6:7; 31:9, 10 ➔ WASTE AWAY <6244>.

WEAK (NOT TO BE) – Deut. 34:7 ➔ lit.: to not be dim ➔ DIM (BE) <3543> a.

WEAK (noun) – ***ḥallāš*** [masc. noun: חַלָּשׁ <2523>; from LAY LOW <2522>] ▶ **This word refers to one who is sick.** It designates a person who is powerless, weak as opposed to a mighty (*gibbôr*) person (Joel 3:10; also translated weakling). ¶

WEAKEN – Is. 14:12 ➔ LAY LOW <2522>.

WEAKENED (BE) – Job 18:7 ➔ DISTRESSED (BE) <3334>.

WEAKLING – Joel 3:10 ➔ WEAK (noun) <2523>.

WEAKNESS – Lev. 26:36 ➔ FAINTNESS <4816>.

WEALTH – [1] ***hôn*** [masc. noun: הוֹן <1952>; from the same as EASY (THINK) <1951>

in the sense of STRENGTH <202>] ▶ **This word refers to abundance, benefit, substance, enough. It is used mainly in the Wisdom Books.** It is used to refer to goods or wealth that is sufficient or enough (Prov. 30:15); to fire that consumes and wants more (Prov. 30:16). God sold His people but not for a sufficient benefit or profit (Ps. 44:12) in their eyes. It regularly refers simply to wealth: wealth is a feature of the Lord's house (Ps. 112:3); it is present with true wisdom (Prov. 8:18); it is to be used to honor God (Prov. 3:9); it is the security of the rich person (Prov. 10:15); sinners pursue it (Prov. 1:13; 28:22); wealth cannot, however, purchase love (Song 8:7); wealth made a nation or city important in world trade markets (Ezek. 27:12, 18, 27, 33). Wealth will be useless in a time of God's judgment and wrath (Prov. 11:4). Virtues are of great value, however, such as diligence (Prov. 12:27). Sometimes true wealth is not visible but is a personal possession of an abundant life (Prov. 13:7). Ill-gotten wealth eventually is gone (Prov. 13:11), but wealth obtained through godly wisdom is true riches (Prov. 24:4). *

2 ***hām*** [masc. noun: הָם <1991>; from MURMUR <1993>] ▶ **This word denotes the abundance accumulated by the wicked in the land of Israel.** Ref.: Ezek. 7:11. But it was part of their idolatry. ¶

3 ***neḵes*** [masc. noun: נֶכֶס <5233>; from an unused root meaning to accumulate] ▶ **This word refers to all kinds of property and abundance in general; it is also translated riches, possessions.** In context it refers to the riches gained as spoils of war (Josh. 22:8). It refers to wealth and material prosperity in general (2 Chr. 1:11, 12). These things are considered as gifts from God (Eccl. 5:19; 6:2). ¶

– 4 Gen. 31:16; 1 Kgs. 3:13; etc. ➔ RICHES <6239> 5 Prov. 15:6; Jer. 20:5; Is. 33:6 ➔ TREASURE <2633> 6 Is. 15:7; Jer. 48:36 ➔ ABUNDANCE <3502> 7 Is. 45:14 ➔ LABOR (noun) <3018> 8 Hos. 12:8 ➔ STRENGTH <202>.

WEALTHY – Hos. 12:8 ➔ STRENGTH <202>.

WEALTHY (BE, BECOME) – Gen. 28:22; etc. ➔ RICH (BE, BECOME, GROW, MAKE) <6238>.

WEALTHY PLACE – Ps. 66:12 ➔ OVERFLOW (noun) <7310>.

WEAPON – 1 ***šelaḥ*** [masc. noun: שֶׁלַח <7973>; from SEND FORTH, SEND AWAY <7971>] ▶ **This word refers to a missile of attack generally and specifically it indicates a sword, a dart.** It refers to some kind of military weapon, perhaps a short sword (2 Chr. 23:10; Neh. 4:17, 23); and further, to all kinds of weapons of war (2 Chr. 32:5). God rescues from the sword (Job 33:18; 36:12). It describes the sword as a weapon of war in Joel's vision (Joel. 2:8; but NASB, defenses). The Hebrew word also means shoots, plants; see PLANTS <7973>. ¶

– 2 Deut. 23:13 ➔ EQUIPMENT <240> 3 Ezek. 23:24 ➔ CHARIOT <2021>.

WEAPONS – 1 ***nêšeq, nešeq*** [noun: נֵשֶׁק, נֶשֶׁק <5402>; from KISS (verb) <5401> (this Hebrew word also means, as a mode of attachment, to equip with weapons)] ▶ **The word refers to a variety of weapons, both offensive (bows, arrows, spears, and clubs) and defensive (shields).** Weapons were sometimes given as gifts (1 Kgs. 10:25; 2 Chr. 9:24); and were kept in the palace Solomon built (Is. 22:8); thus, they probably involved a high level of craftsmanship and were sometimes made of precious metals (cf. 1 Kgs. 10:16, 17, shields of gold); as well as iron and bronze (Job 20:24). In Nehemiah 3:19, the word means armory, a place where weapons were kept. The word also referred to a battle (Job 39:21; Ps. 140:7) as a place where horses charged, weapons flew, and one's head needed God's protection. Other refs.: 2 Kgs. 10:2; Ezek. 39:9, 10. ¶

– 2 2 Sam. 2:21 ➔ SPOIL (noun) <2488>.

WEAR – 1 ***ṣānap̱*** [verb: צָנַף <6801>; a prim. root] ▶ **This word means to wrap around, to roll up tightly.** It describes the wrapping, folding, and fastening of a turban

on a person's head (Lev. 16:4: to be attired, to wear, to put on). It is used figuratively of God's rolling up, judging, and destroying a rebellious person (Is. 22:18: to roll, to turn, to whirl). In the latter reference, the verb used is in an emphatic construction. ¶
– [2] 2 Kgs. 1:8 ➔ GIRD <247>.

WEAR AWAY – Is. 34:4 ➔ WASTE AWAY <4743>.

WEAR ONESELF OUT – Gen. 19:11 ➔ WEARY (BE, BECOME) <3811>.

WEAR OUT – [1] ***bālāh*** [verb: בָּלָה <1086>; a prim. root] ▶ **This word means to grow old, to be exhausted; to waste away; to enjoy.** Various things wear out or become used up: clothing (Deut. 8:4; 29:5) is often the subject; figuratively, the heavens and the earth wear out (Ps. 102:26; Is. 51:6); the bones of a guilty person (Ps. 32:3); persons in general (Gen. 18:12; Job 13:28). In some forms of the verb, it means to cause something to wear out or be wiped out (1 Chr. 17:9; Ps. 49:14; Lam. 3:4). This usage takes on the idea of using something to the full, hence, to enjoy something (Job 21:13; Is. 65:22). *
– [2] Ex. 18:18 ➔ WITHER <5034> [3] Deut. 28:32 ➔ LONGING <3616> [4] Ps. 6:6; 69:3; Prov. 23:4; Jer. 45:3 ➔ WEARY (verb) <3021>.

WEAR OUT, WEAR DOWN – ***b***^{e}***lā'*** [Aramaic verb: בְּלָא <1080>; corresponding to WEAR OUT <1086> (used only in a mental sense)] ▶ **This verb means and is also translated to persecute, to oppress.** It indicates a partially successful attempt to defeat or weary the saints of the Most High (Dan. 7:25). ¶

WEARINESS – [1] ***y***^{e}***giy'āh*** [fem. noun: יְגִיעָה <3024>; fem. of WEARY (adj.) <3019>] ▶ **This word indicates a condition of being worn out or exhausted, especially from excessive study or devotion to books.** Ref.: Eccl. 12:12; also translated wearisome, wearying, to weary. ¶
[2] ***y***^{e}***'āp*** [masc. noun: יְעָף <3288>; from FAINT (verb) <3286>] ▶
a. This word has traditionally been translated as weariness and interpreted in regard to Daniel. Ref.: Dan. 9:21. It has the preposition *b*^{e} in the front, indicating that it is being used adverbially (*bîy'āp*). See also b. ¶
b. This word indicates swift flight, swiftness. "In (swift) flight" is another way to translate this word with *b*^{e}on the front of it (Dan. 9:21), thus referring to the flight of Gabriel. ¶
[3] ***matt***^{e}***lā'āh*** [fem. noun: מַתְּלָאָה <4972>; from WHAT? <4100> and HARDSHIP <8513>] ▶ **The state of being bored with something or despising it, thinking it a nuisance, troublesome. This word is an exclamation translated "What a weariness it is!"** Ref.: Mal. 1:13; also translated burden, tiresome. ¶
– [4] Eccl. 1:8 ➔ full of weariness ➔ WEARY (adj.) <3023> [5] Mal. 1:13 ➔ HARDSHIP <8513>.

WEARING – Ezek. 23:15 ➔ GIRDED <2289> a.

WEARISOME – [1] Eccl. 1:8 ➔ WEARY (adj.) <3023> [2] Eccl. 12:12 ➔ WEARINESS <3024>.

WEARY (adj.) – [1] ***yāgiya'*** [adj.: יָגִיעַ <3019>; from WEARY (verb) <3021>] ▶ **This word means tired, exhausted.** It indicates a weariness, exhaustion, and turmoil experienced by persons, from which only the grave gives a respite (Job 3:17) or rest. ¶
[2] ***yāgêa'*** [adj.: יָגֵעַ <3023>; from WEARY (verb) <3021>] ▶ **This word means tired, tiresome. It refers to a state of weakness or exhaustion from physical exertion and oppression.** Refs.: Deut. 25:18; 2 Sam. 17:2. It refers in general to the weariness, exhaustion, and monotony of the endless cycle of repetitiveness in the world (Eccl. 1:8: full of labor, wearisome, full of weariness). ¶
[3] ***yā'êp*** [adj.: יָעֵף <3287>; from FAINT (verb) <3286>] ▶ **This word depicts someone as exhausted.** It describes the state of those coming in from desert travel

(2 Sam. 16:2), of an enemy (Judg. 8:15). It also describes emotional or spiritual weariness which the Lord can heal (Is. 40:29; also translated faint). The Servant of the Lord spoke a word of encouragement to the weary person (Is. 50:4). ¶

[4] ***'āyêp̱*** [adj.: עָיֵף <5889>; from WEARY (BE) <5888>] ► **This word means weak, tired; it is also translated faint, exhausted, famished.** It describes a person becoming weak from hard work and needing nourishment (Gen. 25:29, 30); or from exhausting travels, escapees (Deut. 25:18). It is used of a weary soul, life, needing good news (Prov. 25:25). It is used figuratively of the nations who fought against Israel being weary like a man faint from thirst (Is. 29:8). When used of a land suffering from drought, it means parched, dried-out land (Is. 32:2). It describes an exhausted beast or animal that must carry heavy loads (Is. 46:1). God refreshes the weary, both physically and spiritually (Jer. 31:25). *

WEARY (BE) – [1] ***nāqaṭ*** [verb: נָקַט <5354>; a prim. root] ► **This word means to be tired, worn out, with the desire to be done with something.** It is used of being weary of one's life (KJV, Job 10:1). Others take the word from *qûṭ*, to feel a loathing for. See LOATHE <6962>. ¶

[2] ***'iyp̱*** [verb: עִיף <5888>; a prim. root] ► **This word indicates physical weariness, exhaustion; it is also translated to be exhausted, to be faint.** Refs.: Judg. 4:21; 1 Sam. 14:28, 31; 2 Sam. 21:15. In a figurative sense, it describes the exhaustion of Zion because of her oppressors (Jer. 4:31). ¶

– [3] Gen. 27:46; Prov. 3:11 ➔ LOATHE <6973> [4] 1 Sam. 30:10, 21 ➔ EXHAUSTED (BE) <6296> [5] Job 10:1 ➔ LOATHE <6962> [6] Ps. 119:28 ➔ LEAK <1811>.

WEARY (BE, BECOME) – ***lā'āh*** [verb: לָאָה <3811>; a prim. root] ► **This word refers to becoming exhausted, impatient at doing something.** Refs.: Gen. 19:11; Job 4:2, 5. It refers to physical exhaustion (Jer. 12:5); but it also indicates wearing oneself out even in religious efforts (Is. 16:12; Jer. 6:11); or in seeking a multitude of advice (Is. 47:13). The wicked frustrate themselves in their evil activities (Jer. 9:5). The sluggard is weary; he is lazy (Prov. 26:15). It has the idea of worn out, impoverished (Ps. 68:9). The Egyptians wearied themselves finding drinking water; i.e., they were hardly able to do so (Ex. 7:18). In its causative stem, it takes on the sense of making someone tired, weary, trying their patience (Job 16:7; Is. 7:13; Mic. 6:3), as Israel tried the Lord's endurance with them. Other refs.: Is. 1:14; Jer. 15:6; 20:9; Ezek. 24:12. ¶

WEARY (BE, GROW) – Zech. 11:8 ➔ ABHOR <973>.

WEARY WITH LONGING – Deut. 28:65 ➔ FAILING <3631>.

WEARY, WEARY (BE, GROW) – Jer. 2:24; 51:58, 64; Hab. 2:13 ➔ FAINT (verb) <3286>.

WEARY (verb) – [1] ***yāg̱a'*** [verb: 3021 יָגַע>; a prim. root] ► **This word indicates to work, to become tired with work.** It indicates putting forth great effort and exertion to accomplish something (Josh. 7:3; also translated to labor, to toil), especially in battle (2 Sam. 23:10; also translated to grow tired), so that one becomes enervated or exhausted. It takes on the idea of putting forth effort to continue to function in the face of great obstacles (Job 9:29: to labor, to toil, to struggle). It indicates the loss of energy or spirit from one's hopeless responses to illness (Ps. 6:6; 69:3; also translated to wear out) or adversity (Jer. 45:3; also translated to wear out, to faint). Wise persons are told not to use up their energy just to acquire wealth (Prov. 23:4; also translated: to labor, to overwork, to toil, to wear out). A foolish person's labor is so poorly structured that it weakens him or her excessively (Eccl. 10:15). Israel, in her rebellion, became weary of following the Lord (Is. 43:22) and in turn "wearied" Him (Is. 43:24; Mal. 2:17). The nations in their rebellions weary themselves against the Lord (Hab. 2:13). *

– [2] Job 37:1 ➔ LOAD (verb) <2959> [3] Ps. 77:2 ➔ STUNNED (BECOME) <6313> [4] Eccl. 12:12 ➔ WEARINESS <3024>.

WEARYING – Eccl. 12:12 ➔ WEARINESS <3024>.

WEASEL – ***ḥōleḏ*** [masc. noun: חֹלֶד <2467>; from the same as WORLD <2465>] ▶ **This word refers to a small animal, a weasel or a mole.** These animals were declared unclean for Israel (Lev. 11:29). ¶

WEAVE – [1] ***'āraḡ*** [verb: אָרַג <707>; a prim. root] ▶ **This word means to make cloth by interlacing fibrous strands; it also means to braid. It describes the work of a skilled craftsman, an expert at fashioning interwoven or braided textiles.** Egyptians were known for their fine woven white cloth (Is. 19:9). The fringe or binding around the neck of the high priest's robe was the work of a weaver (Ex. 28:32; 35:35; 39:22, 27), as well as other priestly garments. The participle of the verb indicates a weaver (1 Sam. 17:7). It describes the intertwining of human hair (Judg. 16:13) or the production of pagan cult hangings (2 Kgs. 23:7). It is used figuratively to indicate the rolling up of one's life like a weaver (Is. 38:12) rolls up his equipment. *
[2] ***'āḇaṯ*** [verb: עָבַת <5686>; a prim. root] ▶ **This word means to weave together, to conspire, to wrap up. It means to intertwine something.** In context it is used figuratively of forming a plan or a conspiracy to do evil (Mic. 7:3; also translated to scheme, to wrap). ¶
[3] ***šāḇaṣ*** [verb: שָׁבַץ <7660>; a prim. root] ▶ **This word means to weave in; to set (a gem).** It describes the skillful work and placement of a precious stone or stones into a gold filigree or milieu (Ex. 28:20). Other ref.: Ex. 28:39. ¶

WEAVER – [1] ***rāqam*** [verb: רָקַם <7551>; a prim. root (in the sense of to variegate color)] ▶ **This word means to work in variegated colors, i.e., to embroider, to do needlework.** It is used in its simple participial form to designate the person skilled in doing all kinds of embroidery work, an embroiderer (Ex. 26:36). The phrase *ma'ᵃśêh rōqêm* occurs often (Ex. 26:36; 27:16; 28:39; 36:37; 38:18; 39:29). It is used in a figurative sense of a human embryo's being woven into existence (Ps. 139:15). Other refs.: Ex. 35:35; 38:23. ¶
– [2] 1 Sam. 17:7 ➔ WEAVE <707>.

WEAVER'S SHUTTLE – Judg. 16:14; Job 7:6 ➔ LOOM <708>.

WEB – [1] ***masseḵeṯ*** [fem. noun: מַסֶּכֶת <4545>; from SPREAD <4537> in the sense of spreading out] ▶ **This word depicts a web of fabric. It consisted of the unfinished set of long warp threads stretched out on a loom, ready to receive the horizontal filler threads.** In context it is used of weaving Samson's hair into this web-like pattern (Judg. 16:13, 14). ¶
[2] ***qûr*** [masc. noun: קוּר <6980>; from DIG <6979> a.] ▶ **This word designates a spider's web. It depicts the construction spun out by an arachnid.** In context the web stands for a sinister trap or snare devised by God's corrupted people (Is. 59:5, 6). ¶

WEDDING – [1] ***ḥᵃṯunnāh*** [fem. noun: חֲתֻנָּה <2861>; from MARRIAGE <2859>] ▶ **This word refers to a person's marriage, an especially festive time.** Ref.: Song 3:11; KJV, espousals. In context Solomon's wedding day is literally or possibly symbolically referred to. ¶
– [2] Ps. 84:1 BELOVED <3039>.

WEED – Job 31:40: weed, foul weed ➔ STINKWEED <890>.

WEEDS – Prov. 24:31; Zeph. 2:9 ➔ NETTLES <2738>.

WEEK – Dan. 10:2, 3; etc. ➔ SEVEN <7620>.

WEEP – [1] ***bāḵāh*** [verb: בָּכָה <1058>; a prim. root] ▶ **The word means to shed tears; it also means to wail. The weeping may be because of grief, pain, humiliation, or joy.** Refs.: Gen. 42:24; 43:30; Ex. 2:6; Num. 11:4, 10; Ps. 78:64; Joel 1:5. It is the opposite of laughing (Eccl. 3:4). It depicts weeping in general, or used with

modifiers, it indicates bitter, intense weeping (1 Sam. 1:10; Is. 30:19; Jer. 22:10; Mic. 1:10). It is used to describe a penitent's weeping before the Lord (Deut. 1:45; Judg. 20:23; 2 Kgs. 22:19). Weeping and fasting are mentioned together as an act of mourning (Judg. 20:26; 2 Sam. 12:21, 22). *
[2] ***dāma'*** [verb: דָּמַע <1830>; a prim. root] ► **This verb means to shed tears.** It indicates one's intense weeping (Jer. 13:17) and the shedding of tears over the threats of captivity facing Judah. It is found twice in this verse for emphasis. ¶
– [3] Job 16:20; Ps. 119:28 ➔ LEAK <1811>.

WEEPING – [1] ***beḵeh*** [masc. noun: בֶּכֶה <1059>; from WEEP <1058>] ► **Weeping, i.e., shedding tears, is described as an act of deep penitence before the Lord, along with confession; praying and prostration.** Ref.: Ezra 10:1. ¶
[2] ***bᵉḵiy*** [masc. noun: בְּכִי <1065>; from WEEP <1058>] ► **This word also means tears. It describes weeping that expresses various accompanying emotions.** It affects one's facial appearance (Job 16:16); it is paralleled only by deep mourning (Esther 4:3; Jer. 31:9, 15); it expresses humiliation (Is. 22:12; Joel 2:12); and it is profoundly bitter (Is. 22:4). It indicates the flow of dribbling streams in mines (Job 28:11). *
– [3] Gen. 50:4 ➔ MOURNING <1068>.

WEIGH – [1] ***šāqal*** [verb: שָׁקַל <8254>; a prim. root] ► **This word means to weigh out money, to pay. It indicates the process of calculating the actual weight of money (silver) or food items usually with the purpose of making payment for something.** Refs.: Gen. 23:16; Ex. 22:17; 2 Sam. 18:12; Job 28:15. Absalom's hair was weighed and registered 200 shekels in weight (2 Sam. 14:26). The gold and silver vessels of the Temple were weighed out (Ezra 8:33). It is used figuratively of weighing sorrow and suffering (Job 6:2); or of weighing a person in a moral, ethical sense (Job 31:6). *
[2] ***tāḵan*** [verb: תָּכַן <8505>; a prim. root] ► **This word means to determine the weight of something; it also means to be equal.** It describes God's weighing actions as a process of moral evaluation (1 Sam. 2:3; Prov. 16:2; 21:2; 24:12); but it is used of weighing money as well (2 Kgs. 12:11). It indicates parceling out water (Job 28:25). It indicates the weighing of the pillars of the earth in the sense of establishing them (Ps. 75:3). It is used figuratively of God's weighing even the mountains (Is. 40:12). It is used in the sense of testing or perhaps informing the Spirit of God (Is. 40:13). It means measured or weighed in the sense of being correct (Ezek. 18:25, 29; 33:17, 20; KJV: not equal). *
[3] ***tᵉqal, tᵉqêl*** [תְּקַל, תְּקֵל <8625>; corresponding to <8254> above] ►
a. A verb meaning literally to determine the weight of something. But in context, it is used figuratively of the failure of the moral, ethical, and humanness of Belshazzar's reign to meet God's expectations (Dan. 5:27). It is used in the *peil* passive form, "You have been weighed."
b. A proper passive noun *ṯekᵉl*: a unit of weight, a shekel. The significance of the word is given in Daniel 5:27 (see a.). In verse 25, it was a unit of measure and weight but is understood as a passive participle meaning having been weighed, referring to Belshazzar and his kingdom. ¶
– [4] Eccl. 12:9 ➔ PONDER <239> [5] Is. 40:15 ➔ OFFER <5190>.

WEIGH, WEIGH OUT – ***pālas*** [verb: פָּלַס <6424>; a prim. root] ► **This word means to calculate the weight of something; it also means to make level, to ponder.** It is used figuratively of weighing out, pondering evil (Ps. 58:2; also translated to deal out, to mete out); and of the Lord's leveling or cleansing a path for His anger to pass over in judgment (Ps. 78:50: to level, to make, to prepare). It means to guard, to watch carefully one's way of life (Prov. 4:26: to watch, to ponder, to give careful thought). It describes making one's way of life just, fair, level (Is. 26:7). Other refs.: Prov. 5:6, 21. ¶

WEIGH OUT – ***naṭiyl*** [adj.: נָטִיל <5187>; from OFFER <5190> (also in the sense of to carry)] ► **This word indicates to trade**

in something. It is used to describe persons who weigh out silver for trading and merchandising (Zeph. 1:11; also translated to trade with, to handle, to bear). ¶

WEIGHT – [1] ***mišqôl*** [masc. noun: מִשְׁקוֹל <4946>; from WEIGH <8254>] ▶ **This word signifies how much something weighs, its heaviness.** Used with the preposition *b*^{e}, by, it is rendered by weight, as to weight (Ezek. 4:10). ¶
[2] ***mišqāl*** [masc. noun: מִשְׁקָל <4948>; from WEIGH <8254>] ▶ **This word refers to how much something weighs, its heaviness.** Weight was expressed in various ways: shekels or part of a shekel (Gen. 24:22; Num. 7:13, 19, 25); money was valued according to its weight (Gen. 43:21, money according to its weight). To misrepresent the weight of money, food, or goods was wrong (Lev. 19:35). To serve something by weight was to use it sparingly (Lev. 26:26; Ezek. 4:16). The weight of something was determined by using scales (Ezek. 5:1). The phrase *'ên mišqāl* means something so great that it is not able to be weighed (1 Chr. 22:3; cf. 2 Kgs. 25:16; Jer. 52:20). *
– [3] Deut. 1:12 ➔ LOAD (noun) <2960> [4] Prov. 16:11 ➔ BALANCE <6425>.

WEIGHTED – Lam. 4:2 ➔ WORTH THEIR WEIGHT <5537>.

WEIGHTED DOWN (BE) – ***'ûq*** [verb: עוּק <5781>; a prim. root] ▶ **This word means to be burdened, to be crushed.** It is used of a heavy weight pressing down on something. In context it is used figuratively of the weight of Israel's rebelliousness pressing down on God (Amos 2:13). ¶

WEIGHTY – Prov. 27:3 ➔ BURDEN <5192>.

WELDING – Is. 41:7 ➔ JOINT <1694>.

WELL (noun) – [1] ***b*^{e}*'ēr*** [fem. noun: בְּאֵר <875>; from EXPLAIN <874> (maybe with the sense of making clear)] ▶ **This word defines a source of water whether natural (Gen. 16:14; Ex. 2:15) or dug out by workers (Gen. 21:25, 30; 26:15, 18; Num. 21:16–18).** It defines a pit which is a source of bitumen (Gen. 14:10). It is used metaphorically to refer to a pit of destruction (Ps. 55:23; NIV, pit of corruption) or in a positive sense to the well of water represented by one's own wife rather than a strange woman (Prov. 5:15). It refers to underground water sources or even the underworld (Ps. 69:15). It refers to a specific desert location (Num. 21:16). *
[2] ***bō'r*** [masc. noun: בֹּאר <877>; from EXPLAIN <874> (maybe with the sense of making clear)] ▶ **This word refers to a common well for drawing and drinking water.** A famous one was located by Bethlehem (2 Sam. 23:15, 16, 20). It is used figuratively to describe broken cisterns (Jer. 2:13). See also WELL <953>. ¶
– [3] Prov. 10:11; 25:26 ➔ FOUNTAIN <4726> [4] Eccl. 12:6 ➔ SPRING <4002> [5] Zeph. 2:6 ➔ CAVE <3741> [6] See CISTERN <953>.

WELL-BEING – Ezra 6:10 ➔ LIVING (adj.) <2417>.

WELL-CONCEIVED PLOT – Ps. 64:6 ➔ PLAN (noun) <2665>.

WELL-FED – ***zûn, yāzan*** [verb: זוּן, יָזַן <2109>; a prim. root] ▶
a. This verb is used figuratively of lusty horses that, in turn, stand for the Israelites who rushed after spiritual prostitution. Ref.: Jer. 5:8. See also b. ¶
b. A verb meaning to be rutting, in a state of rut; to be sexually excited. Used figuratively to symbolize the Israelites, it denotes horses well fed in the morning who eagerly displayed their sexuality (Jer. 5:8). See also a. ¶

WELL SPOKEN – Ps. 141:6 ➔ PLEASANT <5276>.

WELL-VERSED – Ezra 7:6 ➔ SKILLED <4106>.

WELL WATERED – Gen. 13:10 ➔ DRINK (noun) <4945>.

WELL-WATERED – Job 8:16 ➔ LUSH <7373>.

WELLSPRING – Prov. 16:22; 18:4 ➔ FOUNTAIN <4726>.

WEN – Lev. 22:22 ➔ DISCHARGE <2990>.

WEST – Gen. 13:14; etc. ➔ SEA <3220>.

WEST, WEST SIDE – ***maʿarāḇ*** [masc. noun: מַעֲרָב <4628>; from EVENING (BECOME) <6150>, in the sense of shading] ▶ **This word is used of the area and direction west.** Refs.: 1 Chr. 7:28; 12:15; Ps. 75:6; Is. 43:5; Dan. 8:5. It indicates a westward direction sometimes with *min* (FROM <4480>) prefixed, it means from the . . . (Judg. 20:33). Used with *le*, to, it means to the west of something or the west side of it (2 Chr. 32:30; 33:14). *

WESTERN RANKS – Joel 2:20 ➔ END <5490>.

WESTERN SEA – Deut. 11:24 ➔ lit.: the uttermost sea, i.e., the Mediterranean ➔ NEXT <314>.

WET (BE) – 1 ***ṣeḇaʿ*** [Aramaic verb: צְבַע <6647>; a root corresponding to that of DYED WORK, DYED MATERIALS <6648>] ▶ **This word describes a state of being covered with water; water running in droplets on something by a heavy dew from the sky; it is also translated to be drenched.** It depicts the state of a tree stump and later Nebuchadnezzar himself according to his dream (Dan. 4:15, 23, 25, 33; 5:21). ¶

2 ***rāṭaḇ*** [verb: רָטַב <7372>; a prim. root] ▶ **This word refers to falling water, rain; it is also translated to be drenched.** In context it refers to mountain rains that are especially threatening to those caught in them, especially in the Middle East (Job 24:8). ¶

WHAT – ***māʾ*** [Aramaic particle: מָא <3964>; corresponding to WHAT? <4100>] ▶ **This word is an indefinite interr. pronoun referring to what is to be done for the elders of Israel.** Ref.: Ezra 6:8. ¶

WHAT? – 1 ***māh, meh*** [indefinite interrogative pron.: מָה, מֶה <4100>; a prim. particle] ▶ **This word is used hundreds of times and its exact function must be determined from its contextual usage.** The main categories of usage are noted here: (1) as an interrogative meaning what? It is used in a direct question before verbs or nouns (Gen. 4:10; 15:2; 37:26; Ex. 3:13); with *zeh* (THIS, THESE <2088>) following, it means what, now? (1 Sam. 10:11); following a word in the construct, of, state, it means of what (Num. 23:3). It is used in indirect questions after such words as see, *rāʾāh* (Gen. 2:19; 37:20); it is used to indicate something of little or no value (Gen. 23:15); it is used in the idiom, "What to me and to you" (Judg. 11:12; 2 Sam. 16:10). (2) It is used as an adverb meaning how? (Gen. 44:16; Num. 23:8; Job 31:1); why? (Ex. 14:15, How! in the sense of an exclamation (Gen. 38:29). It is used as an indefinite pronoun meaning anything, whatever (Num. 23:3; 1 Sam. 19:3). (3) It combines with prepositions to express various nuances of its basic meanings: wherein, whereby, wherewith, by what means, for what reason (Gen. 15:8; Ex. 22:27; 33:16; Judg. 16:5; 2 Sam. 21:3; Is. 1:5; Mic. 6:6). *Kammeh* means how many, how much (Gen. 47:8; 2 Sam. 19:34); *ʿad-mah* (Ps. 4:2) means until when? *

2 ***māh*** [Aramaic interr. pron.: מָה <4101>; corresponding to <4100> above] ▶ **This word also means why?** It serves as a question marker, what (Dan. 4:35); a relative pronoun (Ezra 6:9; Dan. 2:22); with *diy* following, it means whatever (Dan. 2:28). Like its Hebrew counterpart, it combines with prepositions: *kemāh*, how . . . (Dan. 4:3); *lemāh*, for what purpose, *diy lemāh*, for what purpose (Ezra 4:22; 7:23) or lest. In context *ʾal-māh* for what reason, why? (Dan. 2:15). Other refs.: Ezra 7:18; Dan. 2:29; 45. ¶

WHAT IF – Gen. 18:24 ➔ PERHAPS <194>.

WHEAT – [1] ***ḥiṭṭāh*** [fem. noun: חִטָּה <2406>; of uncertain deriv.] ► **A major food product of the land of Canaan, a staple product and staff in Israel.** Ref.: Joel 1:11. It refers to grain in several stages: the wheat plant (Ex. 9:32); wheat grain and plant (Deut. 8:8); the ears or stalks beaten out (Judg. 6:11); the grain threshed, beaten out (1 Kgs. 5:11). It is used in the plural following *qᵉṣîyr*, harvest, to refer to a wheat harvest (lit., harvest of wheat) (Gen. 30:14; Ex. 34:22; Judg. 15:1). Following *sōleṯ*, the phrase means fine wheat flour (Ex. 29:2). *

[2] ***ḥinṭāh*** [Aramaic masc. noun: חִנְטָה <2591>; corresponding to <2406> above] ► **This word refers to wheat provided by the Persian authorities to the returning exiles.** Refs.: Ezra 6:9; 7:22. It was a staple needed in religious worship and in a healthy diet. ¶

– [3] Prov. 27:22 ➔ GRAIN <7383>.

WHEEL – [1] ***'ōḇen*** [fem. dual noun: אֹבֶן <70>; from the same as STONE (noun) <68>]: lit., pair of stone discs ► **The word describes a low, flat cylinder of various sorts and functions, e.g., a potter's wheel (Jer. 18:3).** It describes also the two stones on which a pregnant woman placed herself in order to deliver her child (Ex. 1:16). The NASB translates the literal Hebrew word "the two stones" as the birthstool while the NKJV renders it as birthstools. ¶

[2] ***'ôpān*** [masc. noun: אוֹפָן <212>; from an unused root meaning to revolve] ► **This word indicates one of the revolving disks fixed under a chariot. God caused the chariot wheels of the Egyptians to come off while they were chasing the Israelites through the Red Sea.** Ref.: Ex. 14:25. This word is also used to describe the movable stands in Solomon's Temple (1 Kgs. 7:30, 32, 33); the wheels of threshing carts (Prov. 20:26; Is. 28:27); and the wheels of Ezekiel's chariot that supported the four living creatures (Ezek. 1:15, 16, 19–21). *

[3] ***galgal*** [masc. noun: גַּלְגַּל <1534>; by reduplication from ROLL (verb) <1556>] ► **This word primarily describes an object circling or rotating around and around.** This can be seen in the related verb *gālal* <1556>. This word is often used to describe wheels (also translated chariots), like those on a chariot (Ezek. 23:24; 26:10); an instrument used to draw water from a cistern (Eccl. 12:6); or the objects in Ezekiel's vision (also translated whirling wheels) (Ezek. 10:2, 6, 13), which are similar to *'ôp̱ān* <212>, meaning wheels. In most passages, a sense of a whirling movement is found in swift wheels (Is. 5:28); rumbling, noisy wheels (Jer. 47:3); swirling chaff (also translated rolling thing, tumbleweed, whirling dust) (Is. 17:13); thunder in the swirling storm (also translated whirlwind, heaven) (Ps. 77:18). *

[4] ***galgal*** [Aramaic masc. noun: גַּלְגַּל <1535>; corresponding to <1534> above] ► **This word occurs only in Daniel 7:9, where it describes fiery wheels on the blazing throne of the Ancient of Days.** It is thought that the throne is seen as connected to a chariot. The wheeled cherubim (cf. Ezek. 10:15, 20) may be related to the wheels of this throne (cf. 1 Chr. 28:18; Ps. 99:1). ¶

[5] ***gilgāl*** [masc. noun: גִּלְגָּל <1536>; a variation of <1534> above] ► **It is the cart wheel used in the process of threshing or crushing grain (Is. 28:28).** This word is a variation of the Hebrew word *galgal* <1534> above. ¶

WHELP – [1] Gen. 49:9; Deut. 33:22; Ezek. 19:2, 3, 5; Nah. 2:11 ➔ CUB <1482> [2] Jer. 51:38; Nah. 2:12 ➔ CUB <1484>.

WHEN – [1] ***'im*** [particle: אִם <518>; a prim. part.] ► **This word means once, if, whenever.** It introduces conditional sentences capable of being fulfilled regularly, both in legal and everyday settings (Gen. 18:3; 43:4; Ex. 22:2; 1 Sam. 14:9, 10). Some conditions introduced cannot be fulfilled (Gen. 13:16; Num. 22:18). It introduces wishes meaning if only (Ps. 81:8; 95:7; Ps. 139:19). It is found in oaths (Num. 14:8; 1 Sam. 3:17); in some cases, it means not, or used with *lô'*, it means indeed, surely (Ps. 89:35; Is. 5:9). In a few cases, *'im* <518> introduces questions (Gen. 17:17; Josh. 5:13; Judg. 5:8, KJV; 1 Kgs. 1:27) which are direct or indirect (Gen. 18:21; Ex. 22:7). It introduces concessive clauses meaning although or even if (Jer. 15:1). Finally, it combines with other particles or conjunctions: *kî 'im* means unless, rather; *'im lô'* means if not but rather (Gen. 24:38); *biltiy 'im* means except, except if; *raq 'im* means only if. When *'im* is followed with another *'im* in close proximity, it means whether . . . or (Ex. 19:13; Deut. 18:3). It can serve as a prohibition used with the future or imperfect form of the verb (Song 2:7). *

2 ***māṯay*** [interr. adv.: מָתַי <4970>; from an unused root meaning to extend] ▶ **This adverb of time also means how long.** Used alone or with *lᵉ* on the front, it means when (Gen. 30:30; Ex. 8:9). With *'aḏ-* on the front, it has the sense of how long, until when (Ex. 10:3, 7; Num. 14:27; 1 Sam. 1:14; 1 Kgs. 18:21; Hos. 8:5). *

WHENEVER – See WHEN <518>.

WHERE – 1 ***'ēy*** [adv.: אֵי <335>; perhaps from <370> below] ▶ **This word also means whence. Its use is quite uniform.** It takes suffixes and can mean where are you? (Gen. 3:9). It takes on the meaning of which, e.g., *'ēy zeh* (THIS, THESE <2088>) *hadderek*: which way then? (2 Chr. 18:23). With *min* (FROM <4480>) on the front, it indicates from where (Gen. 16:8). And it can mean why? (Jer. 5:7). *

2 ***'ayyêh*** [adv.: אַיֵּה <346>; prolonged from <335> above] ▶ **The rendering of this Hebrew word is uniformly, "Where?".** Refs.: Gen. 18:9; Ex. 2:20; Job 14:10. Combined with *'êpô'*, it means, "Where then?" (Judg. 9:38). It is used to posit a theological question about God (2 Kgs. 2:14) or His word (Jer. 17:15). *

3 ***'êykōh*** [adv.: אֵיכֹה <351>; prob. a variation for HOW?, HOW! <349>, but not as an interr.] ▶ **This word functions as an interrogative (2 Kgs. 6:13) for the whereabouts of Elisha.** ¶

4 ***'ayin*** [adv.: אַיִן <370>; prob. identical with NO <369> in the sense of query (comp. NOT <336>)] ▶ **This word is always connected to *min* <4480>, from, and it means from where.** Refs.: Gen. 29:4; 42:7; Num. 11:13. It is used in an indirect question, as in Joshua 2:4 on the lips of Rahab. *

5 ***'eyp̄ōh*** [adv.: אֵיפֹה <375>; from WHERE <335> and HERE <6311>] ▶ **This word is employed in direct questions (1 Sam. 19:22) and indirect questions (Gen. 37:16).** In Judges it means what kind (Judg. 8:18), "What kind of men?" *

6 ***'ān*** [adv.: אָן <575>; contr. from <370> above] ▶ **This word also means whither. It is sometimes spelled with the letter ה, *h* on the end to show direction toward, whither. The *h* is not accented.** The word can be rendered quite uniformly: with reference to time, it means to what point or how long? (Ex. 16:28; Job 8:2). With the ה of direction added to indicate place, it means to which, whither? (Gen. 16:8; 32:17; 2 Kgs. 6:6; Is. 10:3). Preceded by *'āneh* it means to any place, whither (1 Kgs. 2:36, 42; 5:25). *

WHEREBY – Ps. 45:8 (KJV) ➔ PORTION <4482>.

WHEREFORE – ***maddûa', maddûa'*** [adv.: מַדּוּעַ, מַדֻּעַ <4069>; from WHAT? <4100> and the pass. part. of KNOW <3045>] ▶ **This word regularly means why, for what reason.** Refs.: Gen. 26:27; Ex. 1:18; 2:18; Ezek. 18:19. It is used in an indirect question (Ex. 3:3). Jeremiah used the word sixteen times and sometimes to ask a rhetorical question (Jer. 2:31; 8:5, 19, 22; 14:19; 22:28; 49:1). It is found after a compound or double question introduced by *hᵃ. . .'im* (WHEN <518>) . . . *maddûa'* (Jer. 2:14). It introduces a question expressing grief and pain and not expecting an answer (Job 3:12). *

WHET – Deut. 32:41; Ps. 64:3 ➔ SHARPEN <8150>.

WHICH – ***'ᵃšer*** [relative pron.: אֲשֶׁר <834>; a prim. relative pronoun (of every gender and number)] ▶ **This word functions as (a) a relative pronoun meaning which, who, that or (b) a conjunction meaning that, because, so that, as, so that.** The use of the word is determined by its function in the sentence in which it is used. Its basic usage: a relative pronoun (Gen. 21:2; Deut. 1:22; Is. 5:28; Hos. 3:1); a relative pronoun with a preposition prefixed (Gen. 21:17; Ex. 5:11; 33:12); or with nouns placed before *ᵃšer* in the construct or "of" state, e.g., Gen. 39:20, "The place where the king's prisoners were confined." *

WHILE – 1 *'ôḏ* [Aramaic adv.: עוֹד <5751>; corresponding to AGAIN <5750>] ▶ **This word indicates that something is still going on.** Ref.: Dan. 4:31; NIV: even as;, e.g., Nebuchadnezzar's words were still in his mouth. ¶
– 2 Dan. 4:19 ➔ IMMEDIATELY <8160>.

WHIP – 1 *šôṭ* [masc. noun: שׁוֹט <7752>; from GO ABOUT <7751>] ▶ **This word means a flagellating instrument to inflict pain, a lash (literally or figuratively); it is also translated scourge.** It refers to a lash or a whip of leather often used to make horses gallop (Nah. 3:2); or to control them (Prov. 26:3). It is used in a figurative sense of abusive political and economic oppression (1 Kgs. 12:11, 14; 2 Chr. 10:11, 14); of being scourged by an accusatory tongue (Job 5:21); or by a great calamity (Job 9:23; ESV: disaster); of a scourge of punishment brought by the Lord (Is. 10:26; 28:15, 18). ¶
2 *šōṭêṭ* [masc. noun: שֹׁטֵט <7850>; act. part. of an otherwise unused root meaning to flog] ▶ **This word means a whipping or lashing instrument used to punish; it is also translated scourge.** It indicates figuratively the effect the nations that Israel did not drive out of Canaan would have on them, as they acted as a punishing whip against Israel (Josh. 23:13). ¶

WHIPPED OUT (BE) – Job 30:8 ➔ DRIVE OUT <5217>.

WHIRL – 1 2 Sam. 6:16 ➔ DANCE (verb) <3769> 2 1 Chr. 15:29 ➔ DANCE (verb) <7540> 3 Is. 22:18 ➔ WEAR <6801>.

WHIRL AWAY – Job 27:21; Ps. 58:9 ➔ SWEEP AWAY <8175>.

WHIRLING – Jer. 30:23 ➔ DRAG (verb) <1641>.

WHIRLING DUST – Is. 17:13 ➔ WHEEL <1534>.

WHIRLWIND – 1 Job 27:20; etc. ➔ STORM (noun) <5492> a. 2 Ps. 77:18 ➔ WHEEL <1534>.

WHIRLWIND (COME LIKE, RUSH LIKE) – Dan. 11:40 ➔ SWEEP AWAY <8175>.

WHIRRING – *ṣilṣāl, ṣᵉlāṣal, ṣelṣᵉliym* [masc. noun: צִלְצָל, צְלָצַל, צֶלְצְלִים <6767>; from TINGLE <6750> reduplicated] ▶
a. This word describes the insects (locusts) of ancient Ethiopia (Nubia) or their armies. It is a word meant to imitate the sound or object it describes (Is. 18:1), technically an onomatopoeic word. ¶
b. This word means a spear (as rattling, whizzing). A long, sharp weapon or hunting gear used to bring down wild game (Job 41:7). ¶
c. This word refers to destroying insects (as making a strident noise), crickets or locusts that ravage crops, trees, all kinds of produce. Ref.: Deut. 28:42. ¶
d. This masc. plur. noun refers to cymbals (as making a tinkling, clinking sound), one or two circular, concave brass plates that create musical sound by being struck or by being struck together. Refs.: 2 Sam. 6:5; Ps. 150:5. ¶

WHISPER (noun) – 1 *šêmeṣ* [masc. noun: שֶׁמֶץ <8102>; from an unused root meaning to emit a sound] ▶ **This word refers to a faint sound.** It depicts a low, almost indiscernible speech or indicates hearing a snippet or a part of an oral statement (Job 4:12). Even God's mighty deeds are said to be a mere whisper of what a full display of His wisdom and power would be (Job 26:14). ¶
– 2 Ps. 107:29 ➔ STILL <1827>.

WHISPER (verb) – 1 *lāḥaš* [masc. noun: לָחַשׁ <3907>; a prim. root] ▶ **This word**

means to talk in a soft and quiet way; it is used only three times in the Old Testament. In two of these cases, this word is best translated as whisper to describe the quiet talk of David's servants at the death of his child (2 Sam. 12:19); and the secretive talk of David's enemies (Ps. 41:7). The other instance of this word described the snake charmers (Ps. 58:5; lit.: whispers). See also the related noun, *laḥaš* (CHARM <3908>), meaning whispering or charming. ¶

– [2] Is. 8:19; 29:4 ➔ CHIRP <6850>.

WHISPERER – ***nirgān*** [masc. noun: נִרְגָּן <5372>; from an unused root meaning to roll to pieces] ▶ **This word indicates a gossiper, a slanderer; it is also translated talebearer, gossip.** It depicts a person who harms others by attacking them verbally falsely (Prov. 16:28). It indicates a person who whispers things that will harm others, things that should be kept secret (Prov. 16:28; 18:8; 26:22), creating tension and strife (Prov. 26:20). ¶

WHISPERING – [1] Ps. 31:13; Jer. 20:10; Ezek. 36:3 ➔ REPORT (BAD) <1681> [2] Lam. 3:62 ➔ MEDITATION <1902>.

WHISTLING – Judg. 5:16 ➔ PIPING <8292>.

WHITE – [1] ***ḥûr*** [masc. noun: חוּר <2353>; from PALE (GROW) <2357>] ▶ **This word is used of linen hangings in the Persian king's garden and of the royal robes of honor in blue and white placed on Mordecai.** Refs.: Esther 1:6; 8:15. ¶

[2] ***ḥiwwār*** [Aramaic adj.: חִוָּר <2358>; from a root corresponding to PALE (GROW) <2357>] ▶ **This word indicates a color white like (*kᵉ*) snow as the garments of the Ancient of Days.** Ref.: Dan. 7:9. ¶

[3] ***lāḇān*** [adj.: לָבָן <3836>; from WHITE (MAKE) <3835>] ▶ **This word is used of various things.** Teeth (Gen. 49:12); sheep (Gen. 30:35); hair in the process of detecting a possible case of leprosy or a skin disease (Lev. 13:3, 4); skin of reddish-white, again indicating possible leprosy (Lev. 13:42, 43); or skin of a dull or faint white (Lev. 13:39); wood (Gen. 30:37); manna (Ex. 16:31); clothing (Eccl. 9:8); horses in a vision (Zech. 1:8; 6:3, 6). Other refs.: Lev. 13:10, 13, 16, 17, 19–21, 24–26, 38. ¶

[4] ***ṣaḥar*** [צַחַר <6713>; from an unused root meaning to dazzle] ▶

a. A masculine noun meaning white; light-colored. It is used to define wool as white, white wool, one of the luxury items of trade processed by Tyre (Ezek. 27:18). ¶

b. A proper noun, Zahar (or Sahar). Some translators prefer to render this word as a proper noun referring to a land, Zahar. If so, it may be the same as Sahra, northwest of Damascus (Ezek. 27:18). ¶

[5] ***ṣāḥōr*** [adj.: צָחֹר <6715>; from the same as <6713> above] ▶ **This word means light-colored.** It describes a white donkey ridden by the wealthy, an especially sought after animal (Judg. 5:10). ¶

[6] ***riyr*** [masc. noun: רִיר <7388>; from FLOW (verb) <7325>] ▶ **This word refers to the white of an egg.** It refers, evidently, to the tasteless nature of an egg white (Job 6:6). Some translators have suggested a slimy, tasteless excretion from a bugloss plant. The Hebrew word also means saliva; see SALIVA <7388>. ¶

– [7] Esther 1:6 ➔ MOTHER-OF-PEARL <1858> [8] Song 5:10 ➔ DAZZLING <6703> [9] Dan. 7:9 ➔ PURE <5343>.

WHITE (MAKE) – ***lāḇên*** [verb: לָבֵן <3835>; a prim. root] ▶ **This word indicates to make spotless, pure.** Its most important use is to describe the Lord's washing of persons from their sin and corruption, making them clean, white (Ps. 51:7; Is. 1:18). Persecution is a means of the Lord's purification of His people (Dan. 11:35; 12:10; also translated to make pure, to be purified, to make spotless). It has a negative sense when used of the whitening of a vine from an attack of locusts (Joel 1:7). The Hebrew word also means to make brick; see BRICK (MAKE) <3835>. ¶

WHITE CLOTH – ***ḥôrāy*** [masc. noun: חוֹרָי <2355>; the same as white <2353>] ▶ **This word is used of the white woven cloth produced in Egypt.** It was a luxurious item of international trade (Is. 19:9; also translated white cotton, fine linen, fine fabric, networks). ¶

WHITE COTTON – Is. 19:9 ➔ WHITE CLOTH <2355>.

WHITE OWL – ***tinšemeṯ*** [fem. noun: תִּנְשֶׁמֶת <8580>; from GASP <5395>] ▶
a. A word referring to a white owl, barn owl. It is classified in the Mosaic Law as a bird that was unclean, inedible for Israel (Lev. 11:18). ¶
b. A word meaning a chameleon. The NASB renders this as a chameleon, a kind of lizard with the ability to change color to fit its surroundings (Lev. 11:30). It was classified as a swarming thing, unclean and inedible to Israel. ¶
c. A word meaning swan. It is rendered as a swan, a fowl unclean and inedible to Israel (KJV; Lev. 11:18; Deut. 14:16). ¶
d. A word meaning a mole. It is rendered as mole (KJV; Lev. 11:30), a small burrowing animal that feeds on insects and lives underground. ¶

WHITE, WHITE BREAD – ***ḥōriy*** [masc. noun: חֹרִי <2751>; from the same as WHITE <2353>] ▶ **This word is used of a cake or bun of bread made of fine, white flour, the best cooking flour available.** Ref.: Gen. 40:16. ¶

WHITER – ***ṣāḥaḥ*** [verb: צָחַח <6705>; a prim. root] ▶ **This word is used of something exceedingly pure, white, whiter than fresh milk, indicating purity and cleanness, as well as holiness.** Ref.: Lam. 4:7. ¶

WHITEWASH – [1] Deut. 27:2, 4 ➔ PLASTER (verb) <7874> [2] Job 13:4 ➔ SMEAR <2950> [3] Ezek. 13:10, 11, 14, 15; 22:28 ➔ FOOLISH <8602> b. [4] Ezek. 13:12 ➔ COATING <2915>.

WHITHER – See WHERE <575>.

WHO – [1] ***diy*** [Aramaic particle: דִּי <1768>; apparently for THIS <1668>] ▶ **This word also means which, of which. A demonstrative and relative particle.** It often means "of" after a noun (Dan. 2:15; 7:10), and sometimes indicates the material of which something is made (Dan. 2:33). It introduces a relative clause meaning who, which, what (Dan. 2:26; 4:16; Dan. 5:2). Combined with *kōl,* it means everything that (Ezra 7:23). Its other uses are readily discernible if the context and words it is combined with are carefully noted: interrogative (Dan. 3:6); conjunction (Dan. 2:8; Ezra 5:14); introducing direct speech (Dan. 2:25); purpose (Dan. 4:6); result (Ezra 5:10); the reason or cause for something (Dan. 2:20). *
– [2] See WHICH <834>.

WHO, WHICH WHAT – ***ša, še,*** $\check{s}^e$ [relative pron.: שַׁ, שֶׁ, שְׁ <7945>; for the relative pron. WHICH <834>] ▶ **Each usage must be noted in its context carefully.** It has these basic uses: (1) as a pronoun, who, which, what, whom, whomever, him who, he who, that which, etc. (Judg. 7:12; Ps. 122:3; 124:6; Eccl. 1:11; Song 1:7; 3:1); (2) as an adverbial pronoun, where, e.g., place where (Eccl. 1:7; 11:3); (3) as a conjunction meaning that (Eccl. 2:13; 3:18); or introducing a cause, a causal clause (Song 1:6; 5:2). It is used in many compounds, such as b^e + we, *b^eše,* meaning in that, since (Eccl. 2:16); *k^eše,* according as (Eccl. 5:18; 12:7); *miššе,* from whom, from these (Eccl. 5:5). The phrase in Genesis 6:3, *bešaggam,* means, in the (fact) that they also . . . For Genesis 49:10, see SHILOH <7886>. It has the sense of when or until (Judg. 5:7, *šaqqamti*). *

WHO, WHOEVER, WHAT – ***man*** [Aramaic interr. pron.: מַן <4479>; from WHAT? <4101>] ▶ **This word refers to persons, things, gods.** To persons, who (Ezra 5:3, 9; Dan. 3:6, 11); to things, e.g., whose names or what names (Ezra 5:4); or to gods (Dan. 3:15). It is used in an indefinite sense, who(m)ever (Dan. 4:17, 25, 32; 5:21). ¶

WHO, WHOSE, WHOM – ***miy*** [pron.: מִי <4310>; an interr. pron. of persons, as WHAT? <4100> is of things, who?

(occasionally, by a peculiar idiom, of things)] ▶ **This word is usually used interrogatively meaning who. Nearly always it is used of persons, not things.** Refs.: Gen. 24:23, 65; 2 Kgs. 10:13. Used with prepositions or as an object, it means whom (1 Sam. 12:3; 17:28). It means what in some cases (Mic. 1:5). The expression *miyyittên* means literally who would grant and only if (Job 23:3). Repeated as in *miy wāmiy*, it means who each, who individually (Ex. 10:8). *

WHOLE – ***kāliyl*** [adj.: כָּלִיל <3632>; from PERFECT (MAKE) <3634>] ▶ **This word means entire, perfect, complete.** This word can refer to an offering that was entirely consumed (Deut. 33:10; 1 Sam. 7:9); figuratively, it refers to burning a whole town that worshiped other gods (Deut. 13:16). The ephod had to be all purple (Ex. 28:31; 39:22); Isaiah prophesied of a day when idols would completely disappear (Is. 2:18). This word also referred to Jerusalem's complete beauty (Lam. 2:15; Ezek. 16:14); or Tyre's (Ezek. 27:3; 28:12). See the Hebrew root *kālal*: see PERFECT (MAKE) <3634>. Other refs.: Lev. 6:22, 23; Num. 4:6; Judg. 20:40; Ps. 51:19. ¶

WHOREDOM – See PROSTITUTION <8457>.

WHORING – See PROSTITUTION <8457>.

WICK – Is. 42:3; 43:17 ➔ FLAX <6594>.

WICK TRIMMERS – ***melqāḥayim, malqāḥayim*** [masc. dual noun: מֶלְקָחַיִם, מַלְ־קָחַיִם <4457>; from TAKE <3947>] ▶ **This word describes an instrument used to put out the flames of lamps and lamp wicks; it is also translated snuffers, tongs.** Usually there was a pair of snuffers (Ex. 25:38; 37:23; Num. 4:9; 1 Kgs. 7:49; 2 Chr. 4:21). These tongs were used to remove coals from the altar as well (Is. 6:6). ¶

WICKED – [1] ***bi'ysh*** [Aramaic adj.: בְּאִישׁ <873>; from DISPLEASED (BE) <888>] ▶ **This word means and is also translated evil, bad.** Israel's enemies use the word to describe their perception of Jerusalem as a rebellious city and dangerous to the Persian kings (Ezra 4:12). ¶

[2] ***'awwāl*** [masc. sing. noun: עַוָּל <5767>; intens. from UNJUSTLY (DEAL) <5765>] ▶ **This word means and is also translated unjust, unrighteous, evil man. This word occurs five times in the Hebrew Bible with four of them occurring in the Book of Job.** Job said that an *'awwāl* deserved God's punishment (Job 31:3). But he countered the implications of his friends by stating adamantly that he was not such a person (Job 29:17). Likewise, Zephaniah argued that God is righteous and not an *'awwāl*, contrary to the corrupted leaders of Jerusalem (Zeph. 3:5). Other refs.: Job 18:21; 27:7. ¶

[3] ***rāšā'*** [adj.: רָשָׁע <7563>; from WICKEDLY (ACT) <7561>] ▶ **This word means guilty, in the wrong, criminal, transgressor. This adjective is used 264 times, many more times than the verb formed from it. It means essentially someone guilty or in the wrong and is an antonym to the Hebrew word *ṣaddiyq* (<6662>), meaning righteous, in the right.** Moses accused the Hebrew man who was in the wrong and was fighting with another Hebrew (Ex. 2:13); no one was to aid wicked persons in their wickedness (Ex. 23:1). A murderer worthy of death could not be ransomed (Num. 35:31); guilty, wicked persons accept bribes (Prov. 17:23; 18:5). The word may describe wicked people as murderers (2 Sam. 4:11).

The word indicates people who are enemies of God and His people: the psalmist prayed to be rescued from the wicked (Ps. 17:13). Those described by this word are evil and do not learn righteousness. Instead, they pursue their wicked ways among the righteous (Is. 26:10); but the Lord will eventually slay the wicked (Is. 11:4). Pharaoh admitted he was in the wrong in his attitude and actions against Moses, the Lord, and His people (Ex. 9:27; Is. 14:5).

The word indicates the guilt engendered by sinning against others, including God. The Lord moved to destroy the leaders and the wicked people who revolted against Him in the desert (Num. 16:26); the wicked are those who do not serve God and are as a result wicked and guilty before Him (Mal. 3:18). If wicked people continue in their ways toward God or others, they will die in their sins (Ezek. 3:18); but the righteous do not die with the wicked (Gen. 18:23, 25). The counsel of the wicked is avoided by the persons blessed by God (Job 10:3; 21:16; Ps. 1:1). Several phrases became idiomatic when talking about the wicked described by this word: the counsel of the wicked (Ps. 1:1); the way of the wicked (Prov. 15:9); the path of the wicked (Mic. 6:10); the tent of the wicked (Job 8:22); the life (literally, candle) of the wicked (Job 21:7). All these terms describe things, people, and locations that God's people are to avoid so He will not destroy them in the end. *

– [4] Prov. 17:4 ➔ NOTHINGNESS <205> [5] See WORTHLESS <1100>.

WICKED WOMAN – ***miršaʿat̲*** [fem. noun: מִרְשַׁעַת <4849>; from WICKEDLY (ACT) <7561>] ► **This word describes a person with evil intent.** In this case, Queen Athaliah apostatized from the Lord and served the Baals (2 Chr. 24:7). ¶

WICKEDLY (ACT) – ***rāšaʿ*** [verb: רָשַׁע <7561>; a prim. root] ► **This word means to be in the wrong, to be guilty, to be wicked, to do wickedly, to condemn.** In the simple stem, this verb means to be or to become guilty, to act wickedly. When God's people confessed that they acted wickedly, then the Lord forgave them (1 Kgs. 8:47; Eccl. 7:17; Dan. 9:15); to depart from the Lord is an act of wickedness (2 Sam. 22:22; Ps. 18:21).

In the causative stem, the word carries the idea of condemning others or doing wickedness; the people confessed that they had done wickedness (Neh. 9:33; Ps. 106:6; Dan. 12:10). The verb also means to condemn. God declares who is guilty in cases of illegal possession (Ex. 22:9; Deut. 25:1); when a moral or ethical offense has occurred, the Lord will judge in order to declare the guilty (1 Kgs. 8:32; Job 9:20). *

WICKEDNESS – [1] ***rešaʿ*** [masc. noun: רֶשַׁע <7562>; from WICKEDLY (ACT) <7561>] ► **This word means injustice and unrighteousness. It embodies that character which is opposite the character of God.** Refs.: Job 34:10; Ps. 5:4; 84:10. It is also placed in opposition to justice and righteousness, *ṣed̲eq* (<6664>), which is often used to describe God's character (Ps. 45:7). This word is presented as the bad and evil actions that are done by humanity (Job 34:8); and, as such, these actions became the object of God's judgment (see Job 34:26). It describes those actions that are violent. In Proverbs 4:17, this word is a parallel to *ḥāmās* (<2555>), meaning violence. In addition, the Hebrew word means violations of civil law, especially fraud and deceit (Prov. 8:7; note the word's opposition to *'emet̲* (<571>), which means truth; cf. Mic. 6:10, 11). It can also denote the actions of enemy nations (Ps. 125:3; note its opposition to *ṣad̲d̲iyq* (<6662>), which means just or righteous; cf. Ezek. 31:11). In a general sense, it may represent wrongful deeds (Deut. 9:27; note the parallel with *ḥaṭṭā't̲* (<2403>), which means sin). *

[2] ***rišʿāh*** [fem. noun: רִשְׁעָה <7564>; fem. of <7562> above] ► **This word means guilt. It refers to immorality in a wide range of evil.** It indicates a crime worthy of punishment (Deut. 25:2); the unrestrained evil that lurks in the human heart (Is. 9:18); the vileness of surrounding enemies (Mal. 1:4); the breach of a religious expectation (Mal. 4:1); or an unlawful act in general (Ezek. 33:19). *

– [3] Job 35:15 ➔ TRANSGRESSION <6580> [4] Ps. 10:7 ➔ NOTHINGNESS <205> [5] Dan. 4:27 ➔ INIQUITY <5758>.

WICKER – Ex. 2:3 ➔ BULRUSH <1573>.

WIDOW – ***'almānāh*** [fem. noun: אַלְמָנָה <490>; fem. of FORSAKEN <488>] ► **This word means a woman whose husband is dead. The word occurs many times in the Law and the Prophets, where the well-being and care of the widow are the subject.** Refs.: Deut. 14:29; Is. 1:17;

Jer. 7:6; Zech. 7:10. Israel's concern for the widow was founded in the Lord's own concern (Ps. 68:5; 146:9; Prov. 15:25; Jer. 49:11). Figuratively, the term occurs twice in reference to a devastated city: Jerusalem (Lam. 1:1) and Babylon (Is. 47:8). *

WIDOW'S, AS WIDOWS – 2 Sam. 20:3; Ps. 38:14, 19 ➔ WIDOWHOOD <491>.

WIDOWHOOD – [1] ***'almōn*** [masc. noun: אַלְמֹן <489>; from BIND <481> and FORSAKEN <488>] ► **It was one of the disasters that could befall a city under judgment by the Lord.** Ref.: Isaiah 47:9. The husbands of many women would be killed or captured, leaving the wives without husbands. ¶
[2] ***'almānûṯ*** [fem. noun: אַלְמָנוּת <491>; fem. of FORSAKEN <488>] ► **The word is used adjectively to describe a widow's garment.** Refs.: Gen. 38:14, 19. It indicates the state of a woman after the death of her husband. Other refs.: 2 Sam. 20:3; Is. 54:4. ¶

WIDTH – [1] ***peṯāy*** [Aramaic masc. noun: פְּתָי <6613>; from a root corresponding to ENLARGE <6601>] ► **This word is used as an architectural term to indicate the width, or breadth, of a structure or statue (obelisk).** Refs.: Ezra 6:3; Dan. 3:1. ¶
– [2] Gen. 6:15; Ex. 25:10; etc. ➔ BREADTH <7341>.

WIELD – Deut. 19:5; 20:19 ➔ DRIVE <5080> b.

WIFE – [1] ***šēgal*** [Aramaic fem. noun: שֵׁגַל <7695>; corresponding to QUEEN <7694>] ► **This is a word referring to royal spouses of the king.** It may refer to the more favored wives of the royal harem (Dan. 5:2, 3, 23). ¶
– [2] See WOMAN <802>.

WILD ASS – [1] Job 39:5 ➔ WILD DONKEY <6171> [2] Dan. 5:21 ➔ WILD DONKEY <6167>.

WILD BEAST – Ps. 50:11; 80:13 ➔ MOVING CREATURES <2123>.

WILD DONKEY – [1] ***ʿarāḏ*** [Aramaic masc. noun: עֲרָד <6167>; corresponding to <6171> below] ► **This word refers to the wild donkey, a horse-like animal, that ran free in the wilderness.** It is used in a passage to depict the extreme change that took place in Nebuchadnezzar's character. He then lived with the wild animals of the field (Dan. 5:21). ¶
[2] ***ʿārôḏ*** [masc. noun: עָרוֹד <6171>; from the same as ARAD <6166>] ► **This word refers to a horse-like animal that roamed wild in the wilderness under God's supervision alone.** Ref.: Job 39:5. ¶

WILD GOAT – ***'aqqô*** [masc. noun: אַקּוֹ <689>; prob. from GROAN (verb) <602>] ► **An animal that the Israelites could eat and still be holy.** Ref.: Deut. 14:5. ¶

WILD OX – [1] ***re'ēm, re'ēym, rêym, rêm*** [masc. noun: רְאֵם, רְאֵים, רֵים, רֵם <7214>; from RISE <7213>] ► **This word refers to a large animal with horns, which are powerful offensive as well as defensive weapons.** Refs.: Num. 23:22; 24:8; Ps. 22:21. God is its creator and provider (Job 39:9, 10). It is used figuratively of Joseph's strength and fecundity (Deut. 33:17); and of the strength God gives His people, their exalted horn indicating their success (Ps. 92:10). It stands for powerful persons, influential people (Is. 34:7). Other ref.: Ps. 29:6. ¶
– [2] Deut. 14:5; Is. 51:20 ➔ ANTELOPE <8377> b.

WILDERNESS – [1] **they that dwell in the wilderness, creatures of the wilderness: *ṣiyyiym*** [masc. plur. noun: צִיִּים <6728>; the same as DRYNESS <6723>] ► **This word refers to desert creatures, desert people.** It refers to nomadic people of the desert, possibly Bedouins included, a wild bunch that could not be tamed or controlled (Ps. 72:9). It describes animals of the desert; figuratively, of God's defeating Leviathan and giving it to desert creatures to devour (Ps. 74:14). The desert animals and creatures are often mentioned as those

beings that inhabit the remains of destroyed cities and the habitations of defeated peoples (Is. 13:21; 23:13; 34:14; Jer. 50:39), especially the ruins of Babylon. ¶
– [2] Gen. 37:22; Job 38:26; etc. ➔ DESERT (noun) <4057> [3] Num. 21:20; 23:28; Deut. 32:10; Ps. 68:7; 78:40; 106:14; 107:4; Is. 43:19, 20 ➔ JESHIMON <3452>.

WILE – Num. 25:18 ➔ TRICK <5231>.

WILL – Ezra 5:17 ➔ DECISION <7470>.

WILLFUL – Ps. 19:13 ➔ PROUD <2086>.

WILLING – [1] ***nāḏiyḇ*** [adj.: נָדִיב <5081>; from GIVE WILLINGLY <5068>] ▶ **This word means generous, noble; as a noun, those of noble birth. The word often denotes an attitude of heart which consents or agrees (often readily and cheerfully) to a course of action.** The Hebrews who were of willing hearts gave as offerings to the Lord jewelry and gold for the construction of the Tabernacle and its accessories (Ex. 35:5, 22; cf. 2 Chr. 29:31; Ps. 51:12). In many other places, the term describes an individual as one of excellent moral character. Proverbs states that to punish the noble for their integrity is wrong (Prov. 17:26; cf. Prov. 17:7; Is. 32:5, 8). At other times, the word signifies those born into lineages of nobility. The Lord lifts the needy from the ash heap and causes them to sit with princes (1 Sam. 2:8; cf. Num. 21:18; Job 12:21; 34:18; Ps. 47:9; Ps. 107:40; 113:8; 118:9; Prov. 25:7; Is. 13:2). This term is closely related to the verb *nāḏaḇ* (GIVE WILLINGLY <5068>). *
– [2] Ps. 51:12 ➔ DIGNITY <5082>.

WILLING (BE) – [1] ***'āḇāh*** [verb: אָבָה <14>; a prim. root] ▶ **This word means to consent, to be acquiescent, to yield, to desire. Its primary meaning is to be positively inclined to respond to some authority or petition.** The word is used to signify willingness or desire (Gen. 24:5, 8; Judg. 19:25; 2 Chr. 21:7; Is. 30:15); agreement in principle (Judg. 11:17; 1 Kgs. 20:8); consent to authority (Job 39:9; Is. 1:19); yielding, as to sin (Deut. 13:8; Prov. 1:10); and, by extension, to be content (Prov. 6:35; Eccl. 7:8). *
– [2] Ex. 2:21; Josh. 7:7; Judg. 19:6 ➔ CONTENT (BE) <2974>.

WILLOW – [1] ***'ereḇ*** [masc. noun: עֲרָב <6155>; from PLEDGE (BE A) <6148> (in the sense of to mingle, e.g., osiers used as wattles)] ▶ **This word refers to a willow tree, a poplar tree.** It is used to refer to particular trees: poplars (Is. 44:4); willows (Lev. 23:40; Job 40:22; Ps. 137:2). It is given as a proper noun, brook of Arabim, by some translators (NASB); other translations: the Brook of the willows (KJV, NKJV, ESV), the Ravine of the Poplars (NIV) (Is. 15:7). ¶
[2] **willow, willow tree, willow twig: *ṣapṣāpāh*** [fem. noun: צַפְצָפָה <6851>; from TROUBLED (BE) <6887> a. (in the sense of being hard-pressed, as something growing in overflowed places)] ▶ **This word refers to a large tree that flourishes where it has an ample supply of water.** Ref.: Ezek. 17:5. ¶

WILTED – Ezek. 31:15 ➔ FAINTED <5969>.

WIMPLE – Is. 3:22 ➔ CLOAK <4304>.

WIND – [1] ***sā'āh*** [verb: סָעָה <5584>; a prim. root] ▶ **This word indicates to blow strongly.** It is used to describe a fierce wind from a gale-like storm, from which one needs to seek refuge (Ps. 55:8; KJV, NKJV: storm). ¶
– [2] Is. 28:2 ➔ HORROR <8178> [3] See SPIRIT <7307>, <7308>.

WIND (DRIVING, SCATTERING) – Job 37:9 ➔ NORTH <4215> b.

WIND ALONG – Job 6:18 ➔ HOLD OF (TAKE) <3943>.

WINDBLOWN – Lev. 26:36; Is. 13:25; 41:2 ➔ DRIVE AWAY <5086>.

WINDING ABOUT – Ezek. 41:7 ➔ STRUCTURE <4141>.

WINDING PATH – Judg. 5:6 ➔ CROOKED <6128>.

WINDOW – [1] ***ᵃrubbāh*** [fem. noun: אֲרֻבָּה <699>; fem. part. pass. of WAIT (LIE IN) <693> (as if for lurking)] ▶ **This word refers to an opening in a wall; it is also translated floodgate.** It refers generally to windows in a house (Eccl. 12:3), but here possibly to eye sockets. Figuratively, it refers to windows or floodgates of the sky (Gen. 7:11; 8:2) which God controls. In general, it refers to God's ability to provide an abundance of anything (2 Kgs. 7:2, 19) but also to the windows through which God pours judgments from on high (Is. 24:18). The word refers symbolically to lattices, nests (NASB, NIV), or roosts (NKJV) for safety (Is. 60:8). It depicts as well a window in a wall through which smoke escapes (Hos. 13:3); it is also translated chimney. Other ref.: Mal. 3:10. ¶

[2] ***ḥallôn*** [common noun: חַלּוֹן <2474>] ▶ **It was usually an opening in the wall created for light and air.** Refs.: Gen. 8:6; 1 Kgs. 6:4. The window of the ark could be opened (Gen. 8:6). There were latticed windows (1 Kgs. 6:4; Ezek. 40:16); palace windows (Jer. 22:14); gate windows (Ezek. 40:16, 22, 25); Temple windows (Ezek. 41:16) which were evidently covered. *

[3] ***kawwāh*** [Aramaic masc. noun: כַּוָּה <3551>; from a root corresponding to STUDY (noun) <3854> in the sense of piercing] ▶ **This word refers to an opening through a wall or roof to look through and to let in light and air.** It was through such an opening located on his roof chamber that Daniel prayed three times a day toward Jerusalem (Dan. 6:10) when he was still in exile under Persia. ¶

[4] ***meḥᵉzāh*** [fem. noun: מֶחֱזָה <4237>; from SEE <2372>] ▶ **This word designates an opening made to let in light.** Refs.: 1 Kgs. 7:4, 5. The phrase *mᵉḥezāh 'el-mᵉḥezāh* is rendered "window toward (opposite) window." ¶

[5] ***ṣōhar*** [masc. noun: צֹהַר <6672>; from OIL <6671> (in the sense of to spend noon)] ▶ **This word refers to the window Noah made for the ark.** Ref.: Gen. 6:16; also translated roof. For another meaning of the Hebrew word, see NOON <6672>. ¶
– [6] 1 Kgs. 7:5 ➔ FRAME <8260>.

WINE – [1] ***ḥemer*** [masc. noun: חֶמֶר <2561>; from RED (BE) <2560>] ▶ **This word indicates fermenting wine.** Figuratively, in context, Israel drank of this wine as the Lord nurtured the nation (Deut. 32:14); KJV translates pure. In the future, Israel will drink of it again (Is. 27:2); also translated red wine, fruitful (*ḥemeḏ*). ¶

[2] ***ḥᵃmar*** [masc. Aramaic noun: חֲמַר <2562>; corresponding to <2561> above] ▶ **This word refers to wine furnished by Persian kings to the returned exiles.** Refs.: Ezra 6:9; 7:22. It was used to excess by the Babylonians under Belshazzar (Dan. 5:1, 2, 4, 23). ¶

[3] ***yayin*** [masc. noun: יַיִן <3196>; from an unused root meaning to effervesce] ▶ **This word indicates the juice of the grapevine and its fruits, a common drink for refreshment in the Old Testament.** Refs.: Gen. 14:18; 27:25; Judg. 19:19. It, along with grain and oil, were three great blessings to Israel in the Promised Land. It was used as a tonic (Prov. 31:6); a valuable commercial item (Neh. 13:15; Ezek. 27:18). Used properly, it made people's hearts glad (2 Sam. 13:28; Zech. 9:15) and was used figuratively to describe the fertility of the land of Israel (Is. 40:12). In moderation, it was used in the worship of the Lord (Deut. 14:26). It was forbidden to Nazarites (Num. 6:3). Wise persons, especially kings, had no need of it for it might distort their powers of judgment (Prov. 31:4). It could intoxicate a person (Gen. 9:21, 24; 1 Sam. 1:14; Prov. 21:17). The Rechabites abstained from it (Jer. 35:2, 5). God did not approve of heavy drinkers (Prov. 23:20). Priests were not to use it while serving at the sanctuary (Lev. 10:9), but it was employed as a drink offering (Ex. 29:40; Lev. 23:13; Num. 15:5, 7, 10). In the Old Testament, different qualities of wine are noted: good wine (Song 7:9); royal wine (Esther 1:7); spiced wine (Song 8:2). Wine is used in the figurative language of metaphors: wisdom's drink (Prov. 9:2, 5); the wine of the Lord's wrath

(Jer. 25:15); the wine that creates confusion, wandering (Ps. 60:3). Babylon is likened to a cup of wine, causing the nations to go mad (Jer. 51:7). True love is said to surpass the intoxication of wine (Song 1:2; 4:10). *

4 ***sōḇe'*** [masc. noun: סֹבֶא <5435>; from DRUNKARD <5433>] ▶ **This word is also translated choice wine, best wine.** It refers to a drink (Is. 1:22, NASB). Some suggest a form of beer or liquor, but it may refer to a form of wine (Hos. 4:18: drink, liquor; Nah. 1:10: drink, wine). ¶

5 ***'āsiys*** [masc. noun: עָסִיס <6071>; from TREAD DOWN <6072>] ▶ **This word is also translated sweet wine, new wine, juice.** It refers to grape juice (Is. 49:26; Amos 9:13); or to the nectar or juice from pomegranates (Song 8:2). It is used of sweet wine (Joel 1:5; 3:18). Sweet wine is probably grape juice, fresh and unfermented. ¶

WINE (MIXED, BLENDED) – ***mezeg*** [masc. noun: מֶזֶג <4197>; from an unused root meaning to mingle (water with wine)] ▶ **This word means spiced wine, sweetened and flavored; it is also translated liquor, blended beverage.** It was considered desirable and a delightful treat (Song 7:2). ¶

WINE (NEW) – See NEW WINE <8492>.

WINEPRESS – 1 ***gaṯ*** [fem. noun: גַּת <1660>; prob. from PLAY (verb) <5059> (in the sense of treading out grapes)] ▶ **This word refers to the upper trough or basin where grapes are pressed out, usually by treading on them.** Ref.: Neh. 13:15. God's harsh judgments against Jerusalem were like the city's being trodden in a winepress (Lam. 1:15) because Israel had filled the winepress with her evil deeds (Joel 3:13). The Lord is pictured as the treader of grapes pressing out His people in judgment (Is. 63:2). Wheat and other grains were also beaten out in this press (Judg. 6:11). ¶

2 ***pûrāh*** [fem. noun: פּוּרָה <6333>; from NOTHING (BRING TO) <6331> (in the sense of crushing)] ▶ **This word refers to a vat constructed to hold grapes so they could be pressed to give their juice.** Ref.: Is. 63:3. To tend the winepress became a reference to executing judgment or justice (Hag. 2:16). ¶

WINEPRESS, WINE VAT – ***yeqeḇ*** [verb: יֶקֶב <3342>; from an unused root meaning to excavate] ▶ **This word refers to an arrangement of two or more rocks, one to press the grapes, one to collect the juice.** In Isaiah 5:2, it is referred to as part of the vineyard, the wine vat, representing Israel. It was a place of refreshment and energy during famine or war (2 Kgs. 6:27). A person often treads out the wine at the presses (Is. 16:10). Wine from the press or wine vat was acceptable in sacrifices (Num. 18:27). The king often had his own wine vats (Zech. 14:10). *

WINESKIN – 1 Josh. 9:4, 13: lit.: wine bottle; Ps. 119:83 ➔ BOTTLE <4997> 2 Job 32:19 ➔ MEDIUM <178> b.

WING – 1 ***'êḇer*** [masc. noun: אֵבֶר <83>; from FLY (verb) <82>] ▶ **This noun indicates a bird's limb for flying or pinion.** It is used of the wings of a dove in Psalm 55:6 and of an eagle in Isaiah 40:31. The word is used figuratively to describe the wings of the king of Babylon (Nebuchadnezzar), depicted as a huge eagle (Ezek. 17:3). ¶

2 ***gap*** [Aramaic masc. noun: גַּף <1611>; from HIGHEST <1610>] ▶ **This word is used to describe the wings of an eagle and in general the wings of a bird.** Refs.: Dan. 7:4, 6. ¶

3 ***kānāp*** [common noun: כָּנָף <3671>; from HIDE (verb) <3670>] ▶ **This word means also the skirt or corner of a garment. It has the basic sense of to cover; an attached extremity.** It indicates the wings of various birds or winged creatures in general (Gen, 1:21; 7:14; Ex. 19:4; Is. 8:8). It is used of wings of other beings as well: cherubim (1 Kgs. 6:24); seraphs (Is. 6:2); visionary beings like women (Zech. 5:9); insects (Is. 18:1). It took on the sense of the outer edges, corners, or extremities of something, living or inanimate, i.e., the end(s) of the world (Is. 11:12; 24:16; Ezek.

7:2). God carried Israel to Himself on the wings of an eagle (Ex. 19:4). It indicates the edge of a garment (1 Sam. 15:27). The idiom to spread (one's) wings over means to take to wife (Ezek. 16:8). It is used in other idioms to mean an attacking king (Is. 18:1; Jer. 48:40; 49:22; Ezek. 17:3, 7); the healing wings of God's sun of righteousness (Mal. 4:2). God is often noted as providing a shadow of protection for His people under His wings (Ruth 2:12; Ps. 17:8; 36:7; 57:1; 61:4; 63:7; 91:4). *

– [4] Jer. 48:9 ➔ FLOWER <6728> c.

WINGS – ***'eḇrāh*** [fem. noun: אֶבְרָה <84>; fem. of WING <83>] ▶ **This noun indicates feathers or wings.** It describes the wings of an ostrich (Job 39:13); of an eagle spreading its wings to carry its young (Deut. 32:11); as Yahweh carried His people (cf. Ex. 19:4). It is used metaphorically of the wings of protection which the Lord gives those who rest under them (Ps. 91:4: feathers, pinions). The wings of a dove gilded with gold and silver are descriptive of Israel's prosperity in Psalm 68:13. ¶

WINK – [1] ***'āṣāh*** [verb: עָצָה <6095>]: a prim. root ▶ **This word refers to closing one eye, usually to indicate deception.** Ref.: Prov. 16:30; KJV: to shut. ¶

[2] ***qāraṣ*** [verb: קָרַץ <7169>; a prim. root] ▶ **a. This word means to blink the eyes, to compress the lips.** It refers to persons' blinking or winking their eyes with mocking, malicious, or deceitful intent (Ps. 35:19). Such actions indicate worthless, useless persons (Prov. 6:13; 10:10; 16:30). ¶ **b. This word also means to make, to form out; a man is formed from clay (Job 33:6).** It would mean to compress from clay and therefore is the same word as a. ¶

– [3] Job 15:12 ➔ FLASH (verb) <7335>.

WINTER (noun) – [1] ***ḥōrep̱*** [masc. noun: חֹרֶף <2779>; from WINTER (verb) <2778>] ▶ **The word refers to the season of winter or harvest time.** Ref.: Zech. 14:8. It indicates one of the four seasons; in the Middle East, it was also a time of sowing and the beginning of the land's new produce (Gen. 8:22). In the phrase "days of winter (autumn)" (*yᵉmêy ḥōrep̱*), it means the prime of one's life (Job 29:4). The rich were able to afford autumn/winter houses or palaces (Jer. 36:22; Amos 3:15). It was the time of harvesting, not plowing (Prov. 20:4). God has made summer and winter (Ps. 74:17). ¶

[2] ***sᵉṯāw*** [masc. noun: סְתָו <5638>; from an unused root meaning to hide] ▶ **This word indicates the cold, rainy season, winter.** Snow falls in some areas during this time (Song 2:11). ¶

WINTER (verb) – ***ḥārap̱*** [verb: חָרַף <2778>; a prim. root] ▶ **The word means to remain to winter or to remain in harvest time.** It is used in a context that refers to spending the winter at something, e.g., the wild animals spending the winter eating the remains of the Cushites (Is. 18:6) after the Lord's judgments. The Hebrew word also has the meaning of to reproach, to betroth; see REPROACH (verb) <2778> and BETROTH <2778>. ¶

WIPE, WIPE OUT – ***māḥāh*** [verb: מָחָה <4229>; a prim. root] ▶ **This term is often connected with divine judgment.** It is used of God wiping out all life in the flood (Gen. 7:23); destroying Jerusalem (2 Kgs. 21:13); and threatening to wipe out Israel's name (Deut. 9:14). God also wipes out sin (Ps. 51:1; Is. 43:25); and wipes away tears (Is. 25:8). Humans also act as the subject of this verb; the Israelites nearly wiped out the Benjamites (Judg. 21:17); and a prostitute wipes her mouth after eating (Prov. 30:20). *

WIRE – Ex. 39:3 ➔ CORD <6616>.

WISDOM – [1] ***ḥoḵmāh*** [fem. noun: חָכְמָה <2451>; from WISE (MAKE) <2449>] ▶ **This Hebrew word means understanding; it also means skill, experience, shrewdness. This is one of the wisdom words that cluster in Proverbs, Ecclesiastes, Job, and other wisdom literature scattered throughout the Old Testament.** The high point of this word and its concept is reached in Proverbs 8:1, 11, 12. In Proverbs 8:22–31, wisdom is personified. It is God's gracious creation and is thus inherent in the created order. God alone knows where wisdom dwells and where it originates (Job 28:12, 20); no other living being possesses this knowledge about wisdom (see Job 28:21). For humans, the beginning of wisdom and the supreme wisdom is to properly fear and reverence God (Job 28:28; Prov. 1:7; cf. Prov. 8:13); God is the master, creator, and giver of wisdom (see Job 28:27; Prov. 8:22, 23). He employed wisdom as His master craftsman to create all things (Ps. 104:24; Jer. 10:12). Rulers govern wisely by means of wisdom provided by God (1 Kgs. 3:28; cf. Prov. 8:15, 16). Wisdom keeps company with all the other virtues: prudence, knowledge, and discretion (Prov. 8:12). The portrayal of wisdom in Proverbs 8:22–24 lies behind Paul's magnificent picture of Christ in Colossians 1:15, 16, for all the treasures of wisdom are lodged in Christ (cf. Col. 2:3).

Wisdom, ordained and created by God, manifests itself in many ways in the created universe. It is expressed as a technical capability (Ex. 28:3; 31:3, 6; 1 Kgs. 7:14). It becomes evident in experience and prudence as evidenced in a wise woman (2 Sam. 20:22) who fears the Lord (see Prov. 31:30) or in a wise king (1 Kgs. 2:6). Wisdom in general, and worldly wisdom in particular, was universal to humankind created in the image of God; Babylonians, men of the East, Egyptians, and Edomites could obtain it or be found with it (Is. 47:10; Jer. 49:7). Wrongly used, however, for self-adulation or self-aggrandizement, this wisdom could be deadly. For unbelievers, wisdom led to piety, holiness, and devotion to the Lord and His will. The psalmist asked God to give him a wise heart (Ps. 90:12). God imparted wisdom to His people by His Spirit (Ex. 31:3), but His Anointed One, the Messiah, the Branch, would have His Spirit rest upon Him, the Spirit of wisdom (Is. 11:2), in abundance. Wisdom is also personified as a woman who seeks whoever will come and listen to her, thus receiving a blessing (Prov. 1:20; 2:2; 3:13, Prov. 3:19). Wisdom ends its presentation in Proverbs 8 with the striking assertion that all who hate wisdom love death. *

[2] ***ḥoḵmāh*** [Aramaic fem. noun: חָכְמָה <2452>] ► **This word is used only eight times in the Old Testament and is equivalent to the Hebrew word *ḥoḵmāh* <2451> above.** In these few instances, this word is used to speak of God's wisdom (Ezra 7:25; Dan. 2:20). It is God who gives this wisdom (Dan. 2:21, 23, 30) that was recognized by Belshazzar and the queen mother (Dan. 5:11, 14). ¶

[3] ***ḥoḵmôṯ*** [fem. noun: חָכְמוֹת <2454>] ► **Found exclusively in the wisdom literature of the Old Testament, this word is a form of the Hebrew word *ḥoḵmāh* <2451> above.** It denotes a wise woman (Prov. 14:1); the feminine personification of wisdom (Prov. 1:20; 9:1); and the wisdom that exceeds a fool's understanding (Prov. 24:7); or wisdom that reveals deep understanding (Ps. 49:3). ¶

[4] ***tûšiyyāh*** [fem. noun: תּוּשִׁיָּה <8454>; from an unused root prob. meaning to substantiate] ► **This word means sound wisdom, continuing success. The primary meaning of this Hebrew word is wisdom or ability that brings continued advancement.** Used in the Wisdom Literature of the Old Testament, it describes the wisdom of the Lord that keeps a person on the right path (Prov. 3:21; Is. 28:29); the wisdom that recognizes the things of God (Mic. 6:9); and the success that comes from heeding wise counsel (Job 5:12; 6:13). Other refs.: Job 11:6; 12:16; 26:3; 30:22; Prov. 2:7; 8:14; 18:1. ¶

– [5] Prov. 8:5 (KJV) → PRUDENCE <6195>
[6] Dan. 2:14 → DECREE (noun) <2942>
[7] Dan. 2:14 → PRUDENCE <5843>.

WISE – [1] ***ḥakkiym*** [Aramaic adj.: חַכִּים <2445>; from a root corresponding to WISE (MAKE) <2449>] ► **See next definition for <2450>.** This word is used in the singular with a definite article to denote a wise man (Dan. 2:21); in the plural to refer to a group of Babylonian wise men (Dan. 2:12–14; 4:6, 18; 5:7, 8, 15). Other refs.: Dan. 2:18, 24, 27, 48. ¶

[2] ***ḥāḵām*** [adj.: חָכָם <2450>; from WISE (MAKE) <2449>] ▶ **This word is used to describe one who is skilled or experienced.** It was used in the physical arena to describe those men who were skilled as builders (Ex. 31:6; 36:1, 2); as craftsmen of all sorts (1 Chr. 22:15); as precious metal workers (2 Chr. 2:7); those women who could spin fabrics (Ex. 35:25). This word was used in the social arena to express those who were the leaders of the day (Jer. 51:57); who could interpret dreams (Gen. 41:8; Ex. 7:11); who were able to rule (Deut. 1:13, 15); who knew the law (Esther 1:13); who were counselors (Esther 6:13; Jer. 18:18). In the personal arena, this word denoted skill in living, which was embodied in Solomon like no other before or since (1 Kgs. 3:12). The wise person is the one who learns (Prov. 1:5; 9:9; 13:1); who heeds a rebuke (Prov. 9:8; 15:31); and who speaks properly (Prov. 14:3; 15:2; 16:23). See the verb *ḥāḵam* [WISE (MAKE) <2449>], meaning to be wise, and the noun *ḥoḵmāh* (WISDOM <2451>). *
– [3] Ex. 23:8 ➔ SEEING <6493>.

WISE (BE, BECOME) – Job 11:12 ➔ HEART (RAVISH THE) <3823>.

WISE (MAKE) – ***ḥāḵam*** [verb: חָכַם <2449>; a prim. root] ▶ **This verb means to be wise, to act according to wisdom, to make wise decisions, to manifest wisdom.** This word is used to convey the act of instructing which if received brings wisdom (Job 35:11; Ps. 105:22); the wise activity that derives from such instruction (Prov. 6:6; 8:33); the way of conduct contrary to that of the wicked (Prov. 23:19); the wisdom manifested in the animal kingdom (Prov. 30:24). In the reflexive sense, the verb implies the tangible manifestation of wisdom (Eccl. 2:19); the exaggerated perception of one's own wisdom (Eccl. 7:16); and the cunning activities of the deceiver (Ex. 1:10). The psalmist declares that the Lord delights in dispensing wisdom to the simpleminded (Ps. 19:7). *

WISH – ***ṣᵉḇā'*** [Aramaic verb: צְבָא <6634>; corresponding to INTERPRETATION <6623> in the figurative sense of summoning one's wishes] ▶ **This word means to desire, to choose.** Refs.: Dan. 4:17, 25, 32, 35; 5:19, 21; 7:19. ¶

WITCHCRAFT – 2 Kgs. 9:22; Mic. 5:12; Nah. 3:4 ➔ SORCERY <3785>.

WITCHCRAFT (PRACTICE) – ***'ānan*** [verb: עָנַן <6049>; a prim. root] ▶ **This word means to practice soothsaying, fortune-telling, divining, magic. While it is clear from the contexts and the versions that this term is used for some type of magic or witchcraft, its etymology is unclear.** Therefore, the specifics of the practice it connotes are equally unclear. However, it is clear that it was strictly forbidden, and the one who practiced this act was detestable to God (Deut. 18:10, 14; also translated fortune-teller, to practice sorcery, to practice witchcraft, soothsayers). Isaiah appears to use the term figuratively to demean the idolatrous Israelites (Is. 57:3: sorceress). The Hebrew word also means "to bring" in the expression "to bring (<6049>) a cloud (<6050>)" in Genesis 9:14. Other refs.: Lev. 19:28; Judg. 9:37; 2 Kgs. 21:6; 2 Chr. 33:6; Is. 2:6; 57:3; Jer. 27:9; Mic. 5:12. ¶

WITCHCRAFT (USE, PRACTICE) – ***kāšap*** [verb: כָּשַׁף <3784>; a prim. root] ▶ **This word means to practice magic, to practice sorcery.** It occurs with words of similar meaning in Deuteronomy 18:10 and 2 Chronicles 33:6. While the exact meaning of the word is obscure, it involved the use of supernatural powers that hardened hearts against the truth (Ex. 7:11). Those in Israel who used such powers were to be executed (Ex. 22:18). King Manasseh's involvement in sorcery to the point of making his children pass through fire, helped lead Judah to the breaking point of God's patience (2 Chr. 33:6; cf. 2 Kgs. 24:3, 4). Judgment is promised against sorcerers when the Messiah returns (Mal. 3:5). However, in a pagan country, where sorcery was practiced with greater ignorance, Daniel acted to save magicians from death while demonstrating that God's power exceeded that of the sorcerers (Dan. 2:2). ¶

WITH – [1] *'ēṯ* [prep.: אֵת <854>; prob. from BEFALL <579>] ▶ **This word also means against, near, among. It indicates closer proximity than the Hebrew *'im* (WITH <5973>).** It may indicate together with, such as to walk with (2 Sam. 16:17) or simply bunched together, included with (Gen. 6:13; Judg. 1:3; 14:11). It is found often in the phrase "the people who were with him" (*hā'ām ᵃšer 'ittô*, Judg. 4:13; 7:1; 1 Sam. 14:20). It indicates one can walk with God as a friend (Gen. 5:22, 24). Verbs of fighting, striving, and similar verbs are followed often by *'ēṯ*, with (Num. 20:13; Prov. 23:11; Is. 45:9; 50:8). It is used to indicate location, e.g., near or at a place (Judg. 3:19; 4:11; 1 Kgs. 9:26). It also means near one's person, care, or space, i.e., with me (Gen. 27:15; 30:29; Lev. 6:4; 19:13). Coupled with *min* <4480>, from, it is used often to indicate from or away from proximity with (Gen. 25:10; 42:24; Ex. 25:2; Num. 17:2). It can be used figuratively in this area to indicate rights, obligation, or special benefits from various persons (Gen. 47:22; Ex. 27:21; Num. 3:9; Deut. 18:3). *

[2] *'im* [prep.: עִם <5973>; from DIM (BECOME) <6004> (in the sense of to associate)] ▶ **This word also means for, against, toward.** It is used to indicate something done together or in common with (Gen. 3:6, 12; 13:1; 18:16); to eat with, to talk with, to travel with, to have companionship with. It ties separate things together, such as blood and flesh (Deut. 12:23); the wicked and the righteous (Gen. 18:23). It is used with the verbs *yāraš, ḥalaq*, to possess (with), to inherit along (with) (Gen. 21:10; 26:28); and words that indicate a competition or contest (with), to fight, to argue, to wrestle (with), to dispute (with), etc. (Gen. 26:20; 30:8; 32:24). It indicates an attitude taken when dealing with someone: kindness (Gen. 24:12); to be hostile toward (Ps. 94:16); be pleased with (Job 34:9; Ps. 50:18). It indicates the person or persons with whom one contends (Gen. 26:20; 30:8; 32:24). It is used sometimes to indicate the person spoken to (with) (Ex. 19:9), by God or man. It refers to the object to whom or for whom something is done, e.g., to do (show) kindness to someone (Gen. 24:12). It is used to show proximity in a physical sense, to be close by (Gen. 23:4; 25:11; Josh. 19:46); or of closeness in spirit, as God said He would be with His people, a chief defining characteristic of Israel's God (Ex. 3:12). It indicates time: how long (Ps. 72:5); time when (2 Chr. 21:19). The phrase *min* (FROM <4480>) + *'im* (WHEN <518>), *mê'im* means, from (being) with someone (Gen. 26:16; 1 Sam. 16:14; 2 Sam. 3:26; 2 Kgs. 2:9); the verb *nāqāh*, to be innocent, guiltless, plus *mê'im*, means to be innocent from something, from before (2 Sam. 3:28; 1 Kgs. 2:33). It may be used to indicate possession, meaning something is with someone, belongs to them, is beside them (Deut. 17:19; Job 28:4). It has the sense of in addition to or besides in some contexts (2 Chr. 14:11); or against, as to stand against, defend against (2 Chr. 20:6). It is used often with the word heart, meaning mind, to indicate a purpose or thought someone has, e.g., you will know in your heart (mind) (Deut. 8:5; 15:9; Josh. 14:7; 1 Kgs. 8:17). A person can commune with his or her own heart (Ps. 77:6; Eccl. 1:16). It is used to indicate the origin of something, e.g., God, etc. (1 Sam. 20:7); especially of God as originator (Gen. 41:32; 1 Kgs. 2:33; Job 34:33; Is. 8:18). The phrase *wᵉ'im zeh* (THIS, THESE <2088>) means yet, in spite of (Neh. 5:18). Careful attention to the usage and context will normally reveal the nuanced usage of this word. *

[3] *'im* [Aramaic prep.: עִם <5974>; corresponding to <5973> above] ▶ **This word also means for. It is used to indicate connection to, action with.** It indicates things that accompany something or each other (Ezra 5:2; 6:8; 7:13, 16; 2:18, 43; 7:13). It indicates relationship to, dwelling, living with (Dan. 2:11, 22; 4:15; 5:21); speaking with (Dan. 6:21); making war with (Dan. 7:21). It is used to indicate time during which (Dan. 7:2); or a duration of time, with (unto) all generations (Dan. 4:3, 34). *

[4] *'immāḏ* [prep.: עִמָּד <5978>; prolonged for <5973> above] ▶ **This word also means**

to. It indicates the company or presence of someone and is always used with a suffix attached, *'immāḏî* or *'immî*. See also WITH <5973>. Its meanings are the same as *'im* with suffixes. It means with respect to someone (Gen. 21:23; 31:7). It indicates the person one strives (with) (Ex. 17:2). It means in company with, beside someone (Deut. 5:31). It describes God's special presence with a person (Ps. 23:4; 101:6). *

WITHDRAW – 1 *ḥāmaq* [verb: חָמַק <2559>; a prim. root] ▶ **This verb means to turn around, to turn away. It describes the retreat or departure of one person from another.** Ref.: Song 5:6; also translated to turn, to turn away, to leave. In another reflexive verb form, it means to wander here and there (Jer. 31:22; also translated to waver, to go about, to go here and there, to gad about). ¶
– 2 Prov. 25:17 ➔ PRECIOUS (BE) <3365>.

WITHER – 1 *nāḇêl* [verb: נָבֵל <5034>; a prim. root] ▶ **The verb means to languish, to fade.** It refers to something wearing out, drying up, dying, falling off: grass (Ps. 37:2); leaves (Is. 1:30; Jer. 8:13; Ezek. 47:12); flowers (Is. 28:1). It is used figuratively of humans (Ex. 18:18; 2 Sam. 22:46; Ps. 18:45); the land and earth (Is. 24:4). It also means to be foolish, to act disdainfully; see FOOLISH (BE) <5034>. *
2 *qāmal* [verb: קָמַל <7060>; a prim. root] ▶ **a. This word means to decay, to rot away.** It refers to the decaying and destruction of the reeds and rushes of the Nile River as a result of God's judgment on Egypt (Is. 19:6). A similar fate was suffered by the cedars and forests of Lebanon that dried up, withered (Is. 33:9a).
b. This word describes, as does a., the withering of the forests and cedars of Lebanon. Ref.: Is. 33:9. ¶
– 3 Is. 16:8; Joel 1:12 ➔ LANGUISH <535> 4 Job 14:2; Ps. 37:2 ➔ CUT DOWN <5243>.

WITHERED – 1 *ṣānam* [verb: צָנַם <6798>; a prim. root] ▶ **This word means to be**

dried up. It refers to withered ears of corn/grain seen in Pharaoh's dream and representing years of drought (Gen. 41:23). ¶
– 2 Ezek. 31:15 ➔ FAINTED <5969>.

WITHHOLD – 1 *ḥāśaḵ* [verb: חָשַׂךְ <2820>; a prim. root] ▶ **This word indicates to hold back, to spare; to keep from doing something. It means to hold something back, to retain.** It is used of Abraham's not withholding Isaac from possible sacrifice (Gen. 22:12); of a parent sparing the rod in discipline (Prov. 3:24); to keep a person from something, such as God keeping Abimelech from sinning (Gen. 20:6); of the Lord's keeping David from killing Nabal (1 Sam. 25:39); of Joab holding back the people in battle pursuit (2 Sam. 18:16); of restraining one's speech and keeping one's mouth shut (Job 7:11; Prov. 10:19; 17:27); of refraining from something (Is. 54:2; 58:1); or of sparing or holding back one's hand from a person such as Naaman (2 Kgs. 5:20). It takes on the idea of treasuring up or holding something in reserve (Job 38:23). In its passive use, it refers to something being spared (Job 16:6; 21:30). It is used in a figurative sense of not wandering into error both physically and spiritually by keeping one's feet in check (Jer. 14:10). *
– 2 Gen. 23:6 ➔ RESTRAIN <3607> a.
3 Is. 63:15 ➔ CONTROL (verb) <662>.

WITHIN – *pᵉniymāh* [adv.: פְּנִימָה <6441>; from FACE (noun) <6440>] ▶ **This word means inside, inner. It refers to the inner recesses of a structure, what lies within, what is internal.** It can mean to the inside, inward (Lev. 10:18; Ezek. 41:3); or located inside, within (1 Kgs. 6:18, 19; Ezek. 40:16). It can refer to something shared within a family or household (2 Kgs. 7:11). *

WITHOUT – See NOT <1097>.

WITLESS – Job 11:12 ➔ HOLLOW (verb) <5014>.

WITNESS – 1 *'êḏ* [masc. noun: עֵד <5707>; contr. from WITNESS (BEAR) <5749>] ▶ **This word refers to someone who will be**

accepted to bear a true testimony in various situations for various reasons. It also refers to the testimony given, written or oral, such as a covenant (Gen. 31:44; Deut. 31:19, 21); or a symbol established to confirm a covenant (Gen. 31:48). The evidence itself may be called a witness (Ex. 22:13). God Himself serves as a witness (Gen. 31:50, 52; Josh. 22:27, 28, 34; Job 16:19). *
[2] ***'êḏāh*** [fem. noun: עֵדָה <5713>; fem. of <5707> above] ▶ **Derived from a word that denotes permanence, this term refers to the act of testifying to a fact or an event.** For example, by accepting Abraham's gift of ewe lambs, Abimelech acknowledged the truth of Abraham's statement about the ownership of the well at Beersheba (Gen. 21:30). Likewise, a heap of stones became a witness to the boundary agreement reached between Jacob and Laban (Gen. 31:52). Within the context of a covenant renewal ceremony, Joshua placed a single large stone to function as a witness of the covenant established between the Lord and His people (Josh. 24:27). Other ref.: Jer. 6:18 (NIV; others: congregation). ¶

WITNESS (BEAR) – ***'ûḏ*** [verb: עוּד <5749>; a prim. root] ▶ **Specifically, this word can signify either to serve as a witness or to testify against someone, albeit falsely (1 Kgs. 21:10, 13); or in favor of someone (Job 29:11).** It can also mean either to admonish someone (Gen. 43:3; Neh. 9:26, 30); or to warn solemnly (Gen. 43:3; Ex. 19:21; Deut. 32:46; 1 Sam. 8:9; 1 Kgs. 2:42; 2 Chr. 24:19; Neh. 9:29; 13:15, 21; Jer. 42:19; Amos 3:13). Such warnings frequently came from the Lord (2 Kgs. 17:13, 15; Jer. 11:7); but they were also mediated through His prophets (2 Chr. 24:19; Jer. 42:19). In the causative form, it can mean to call to witness, to take as a witness (Deut. 4:26; Is. 8:2); or to obtain witnesses, i.e., authentication (Jer. 32:10, 25, 44). *

WIVES – ***n^ešiyn*** [fem. plur. noun: נְשִׁין <5389>; irregular fem. plur. of MAN <606>] ▶ **In context the word refers to the spouses of those royal officials and conspirators who tried to have Daniel killed.** Ref.: Dan. 6:24. ¶

WIZARD – Deut. 18:11; 1 Sam. 28:9; 2 Kgs. 21:6; Is. 8:19; etc. ➔ SPIRITIST <3049>.

WOE (interj.) – [1] ***'ôy*** [interj.: אוֹי <188>; prob. from DESIRE (verb) <183> (in the sense of crying out after)] ▶ **This word indicates distress, unhappiness; it also means alas!** In general its meaning is woe (Num. 21:29). This woe can be directed to oneself (Jer. 4:13; 10:19). It functions as a noun in Proverbs 23:29 indicating woe! *
[2] ***'ôyāh*** [interj.: אוֹיָה <190>; fem. of <188> above] ▶ **This word is the poetic form of *'ôy* above, meaning woe! alas!** It is found in Psalm 120:5, depicting the distress of one who has lived too long among a violent people. ¶
[3] ***'iy*** [interj.: אִי <337>; shortened from <188> above] ▶ **This word indicates a cry of warning for both persons and metaphorically a land that has a child for a king.** Refs.: Eccl. 4:10; 10:16. ¶
[4] ***'allay*** [interj.: אַלְלַי <480>; by reduplication from LAMENT <421>] ▶ **This word depicts the hopeless emotional outlook of Job before God. It expresses the anxiety and distress of the prophet Micah.** Refs.: Job 10:15; Mic. 7:1. ¶
– [5] Ezek. 30:2 ➔ ALAS! <1929>.

WOE (noun) – [1] ***hiy*** [masc. noun: הִי <1958>; for WAILING <5092>] ▶ **This word refers to distress and destruction found written in Ezekiel's scroll, along with laments and mournings.** Ref.: Ezek. 2:10. ¶
– [2] Is. 24:16 ➔ LEANNESS <7334> [3] Lam. 3:5 ➔ HARDSHIP <8513>.

WOLF – [1] ***z^e'ēḇ*** [masc. noun: זְאֵב <2061>; from an unused root meaning to be yellow] ▶ **A wild animal mentioned several ways by biblical writers.** It will be tame in the time of the Messianic Age (Is. 11:6), with even the wolf eating grass (Is. 65:25). It was a symbol of the violent, ravenous, and fierce nature of Benjamin (Gen. 49:27)

who devoured his prey. Its guile and effective actions were used to describe the cavalry of the Babylonian army (Hab. 1:8). Various classes of persons were personified as bloodthirsty wolves destroying persons: Judah's princes (Ezek. 22:27); her enemies in general (Jer. 5:6); judges who were unjust, oppressive (Zeph. 3:3). ¶
– [2] Is. 34:14 ➔ HYENA <338>.

WOMAN – [1] ***'iššāh*** [fem. noun: אִשָּׁה <802>; fem. of MAN <376> or MAN <582>] ▶ **This word also means wife, female. Its origin has been recorded in Genesis 2:23, where Adam said, "She shall be called Woman (*'iššāh* <802>), because she was taken out of Man (*'iyš* <376>) (NASB)."** While this word predominantly means woman or wife, it is further used in various ways: those able to bear children (Gen. 18:11); a widow (Ruth 4:5; 1 Sam. 27:3); an adulteress (Prov. 6:26; 7:5); female children (Num. 31:18); or female animals (Gen. 7:2). *
– [2] Judg. 5:30 ➔ WOMB <7361>.

WOMB – [1] ***beṭen*** [fem. noun: בֶּטֶן <990>; from an unused root prob. meaning to be hollow] ▶ **This word means belly, inner body, rounded projection. With perhaps the general meaning of inside, *beṭen* often refers to the physical belly.** It also frequently refers to the womb, where it is at times significantly linked with God's sovereign care, comfort, and the calling of His elect (Ps. 22:9; 139:13; Is. 44:2; 49:1; Jer. 1:5). Defined as womb, the Hebrew word is sometimes used with the word *reḥem,* also meaning womb <7358>. First Kings 7:20 uses the word to refer to a rounded projection of a temple pillar. In a figurative sense, *beṭen* means the inner being of a person. Ancient wisdom literature pictured the belly, or inmost part, as the place where thoughts were treasured and the spiritual being expressed itself and was satisfied (Job 32:18; Prov. 20:27). *
[2] ***raḥam*** [verb: רַחַם <7356>; from COMPASSION (HAVE) <7355>] ▶ **This word means the physical womb; it also means compassion, mercy, affection, maiden.** The singular form of this word always signified the physical womb of a woman and was commonly used in this way (Gen. 49:25). Yet when the plural form was used, the author had in mind the idea of compassion, tenderness, or mercy. The Old Testament authors thought of the womb or bowels as the seat of warm and tender emotions. For example, when Joseph saw his brother Benjamin, he became overwhelmed with tender affection (lit., wombs [Gen. 43:30]). Through the prophet Zechariah, the Lord commanded His people to show compassion to one another (Zech. 7:9; cf. Deut. 13:17; Ps. 25:6; 103:4; Is. 47:6). *
[3] ***reḥem*** [verb: רֶחֶם <7358>; from COMPASSION (HAVE) <7355>] ▶ **This word refers to the belly or womb of an animal or woman.** It is the place where a fetus is developed and from which it exits at birth (Gen. 20:18; 29:31). The phrase *mêreḥem* means from birth (Job 3:11; Ps. 22:10; 58:3; Jer. 20:17). The first births of Israel were the Lord's special possession (Ex. 13:12, 15; 34:19). The phrase *raḥam raḥ^{a}māṯayim* indicates a woman, two women (Judg. 5:30). A delay, a stoppage of a womb, indicates a barren womb (Prov. 30:16). A womb that miscarried could be a curse from God but not necessarily (Hos. 9:14). *
[4] ***raḥ^{a}māh*** [fem. noun: רַחֲמָה <7361>; fem. of <7356> above] ▶ **This word refers literally to a womb but stands for a wife taken in war, someone to carry on descendants.** Ref.: Judg. 5:30. It also means a maiden, a girl, a woman. ¶
– [5] Ps. 51:6 ➔ INWARD PART <2910>.

WONDER (noun) – [1] ***môpēṯ*** [masc. noun: מוֹפֵת <4159>; from BEAUTIFUL (BE) <3302> in the sense of conspicuousness] ▶ **This word means a sign, a portent, a token.** It is often a phenomenon displaying God's power, used to describe some of the plagues God placed on Egypt (Ex. 7:3; 11:9) directly or through Moses and Aaron (Ex. 4:21; 11:10); the psalmists sang of these wonders (Ps. 105:5); false prophets could work counterfeit wonders (Deut. 13:1, 2); God worked these signs in the heavens sometimes (Joel 2:30). Even people can become signs and tokens. Both Isaiah and his children served as signs to Israel (Is. 8:18), as did Ezekiel (Ezek. 12:6, 11; Zech. 3:8). The curses that God described in the Law would be signs and wonders to cause His people to see His activity in judging them if they broke His covenant (Deut. 28:46). *

[2] ***pele'*** [masc. noun: פֶּלֶא <6382>; from WONDERFUL (DO SOMETHING) <6381>] ▶ **This word means a miracle, a marvel. It is used to represent something unusual or extraordinary.** Except for Lamentations 1:9, this term always appears in the context of God's words or deeds. The Lord asked Abraham, «Is anything too difficult (<6381>, *pālā'*) for the Lord?» pointing to His full abilities (Gen. 18:14). It is used of God's actions among His people (Is. 29:14); the Law of God (Psalm 119:129); God's acts of judgment and deliverance (Ex. 15:11; Ps. 78:12; Is. 25:1); and the child to be born as the Messiah (Is. 9:6: Wonderful). These things then become the focus of people's worship of God (Ps. 77:11, 14). This word is also used as an adverb to reveal how astounding, significant, and extreme was the fall of the city of Jerusalem (Lam. 1:9). Other refs.: Ps. 88:10, 12; 89:5; Dan. 12:6. ¶

[3] ***t^emah*** [Aramaic masc. noun: תְּמַהּ <8540>; from a root corresponding to ASTONISHED (BE) <8539>] ▶ **This word is related to the Hebrew verb *tāmah* (<8539>), meaning to be astonished. In its only three instances, this word speaks of the wondrous and perhaps miraculous deeds of God.** Refs.: Dan. 4:2, 3; 6:27. In every instance, it is used in close connection with *'āṯ* (<852>), meaning signs. ¶

– [4] Job 37:16 ➔ WONDROUS WORK <4652>.

WONDER (verb) – Gen. 24:21 ➔ GAZE <7583>.

WONDERFUL – [1] ***pil'iy, peliy'*** [masc. adj.: פִּלְאִי, פֶּלִיא <6383>; from WONDERFUL (DO SOMETHING) <6381>] ▶ **This word also means incomprehensible.** The feminine form of this adjective is *p^eli'āyh* or *pil'iyyāh*. It was used as a description of the name of the angel of the Lord (Judg. 13:18; also translated secret, beyond understanding); and as a description of the knowledge of the Lord (Ps. 139:6). ¶

– [2] Is. 9:6 ➔ WONDER (noun) <6382>.

WONDERFUL (DO SOMETHING) – ***pālā'*** [verb: פָּלָא <6381>; a prim. root; properly, perhaps to separate (i.e., distinguish)] ▶ **This word means to do something extraordinary, or difficult. It frequently signifies the wondrous works of God, especially His deliverance and judgments.** Refs.: Ex. 3:20; Ps. 106:22; 136:4; Mic. 7:15. Because God's extraordinary deeds inspire thanksgiving and praise, this Hebrew word occurs often in the hymnic literature of the Bible and of the Dead Sea Scrolls (Ps. 9:1; 107:8; 145:5). While nothing is too extraordinary for God, various things are said to be beyond the abilities of some individuals to do or comprehend (Deut. 17:8; Prov. 30:18; Jer. 32:17); however, obeying God's commandments is not too difficult a task (Deut. 30:11). A rare use of this Hebrew word expresses the performance of a special vow beyond the ordinary commitment (Lev. 27:2; Num. 6:2; 15:3, 8). *

WONDERFULLY MADE (BE) – Ps. 139:14 ➔ DISTINCTION (MAKE) <6395>.

WONDROUS – Ps. 17:7 ➔ DISTINCTION (MAKE) <6395>.

WONDROUS WORK – ***miplā'āh*** [fem. noun: מִפְלָאָה <4652>; from WONDERFUL (DO SOMETHING) <6381>] ▶ **This word is a description of the marvelous and awe-inspiring works of God in the atmosphere.** Ref.: Job 37:16; also translated wonder. ¶

WONT (BE) – Num. 22:30 ➔ PROFITABLE (BE) <5532> a.

WOOD – [1] 1 Sam. 23:15, 16, 18, 19 ➔ FOREST <2793> [2] Dan. 5:4, 23 ➔ TIMBER <636>.

WOODED HILLS, WOODED AREAS – 2 Chr. 27:4 ➔ FOREST <2793>.

WOODS – ***yᵉʿôriym*** [masc. plur. noun: יְעוֹרִים <3264>; a variation of FOREST <3293>] ▶ **This word refers to a forest. It can indicate a thick growth of trees and accompanying shrubs and flora. It is considered a dangerous place.** God's will makes even the woods a safe place for His people to sleep (Ezek. 34:25; NIV: forests). ¶

WOOF – Lev. 13:48 ➔ MIXED <6154>.

WOOL – 1 ***ʿᵃmar*** [Aramaic masc. noun: עֲמַר <6015>; corresponding to <6785> below] ▶ **This word indicates white wool, the color of the hair of the Ancient of Days as well as His antiquity.** Ref.: Dan. 7:9. ¶

2 ***ṣemer*** [masc. noun: צֶמֶר <6785>; from an unused root prob. meaning to be shaggy] ▶ **This word refers to the soft, curly hair of sheep or of other animals with hair of the same or similar texture.** It was used in the production of clothing (Lev. 13:47, 48, 52, 59; Deut. 22:11; Prov. 31:13). Its whiteness was used in figures of speech (Ps. 147:16; Is. 1:18). It constituted a valuable merchandise of trade (Ezek. 27:18). Levites wore wool and linen garments (Ezek. 44:17). It is used in figurative expressions concerning Israel's prostitution (Hos. 2:5, 9). *

WORD – 1 ***'êmer*** [masc. noun: אֵמֶר <561>; from SAY <559>] ▶ **This term also means speech, saying. The primary meaning is something said.** The term is used like *dāḇār* below; however, it occurs (with the exception of Josh. 24:27) only in poetry, usually in the plural, often in the phrase "the words of my mouth" (Deut. 32:1; Ps. 19:14). Words are seen as taking from their context qualities such as truth (Prov. 22:21); beauty (Gen. 49:21); deception (Is. 32:7); knowledge (Prov. 23:12). This term may refer to God's words (Job 6:10; Ps. 138:4) as well as people's words. *

2 ***'ōmer*** [masc. noun: אֹמֶר <562>; the same as <561> above] ▶ **This term also means utterance, speech.** It is used only in poetry in parallel constructions with *dāḇār* below (Ps. 19:3; Prov. 2:16; 4:10, 20); *millāh* (<4405>), meaning words (Job 32:12, 14; 33:3; 34:37); *miṣwāh* (<4687>), meaning commandment (Job 23:12; Prov. 2:1; 7:1). Refs.: Job 22:28; Ps. 19:2, 3; 68:11; 77:8; Hab. 3:9. ¶

3 ***'emrāh, 'imrāh*** [fem. noun: אִמְרָה ,אֶמְרָה <565>; fem. of <561> above and meaning the same] ▶ **This rare poetic term occurs more in Psalm 119 than everywhere else combined.** It is used in parallel with teaching, covenant, commandment, and voice (Deut. 32:2; 33:9; Ps. 119:172; Is. 28:23). This noun most often designates God's Word, which is the psalmist's guide for life and his basis for requesting God's kindness, graciousness, and deliverance (Ps. 119:11, 41, 58, 76, 116, 133, 154, 170). The keeping of God's Word is a frequent topic in Scripture (Deut. 33:9; Ps. 119:67, 158; cf. Is. 5:24). God's Word is pure, sweeter than honey, and has been magnified with His name (Ps. 119:103; 138:2; Prov. 30:5). *

4 *dāḇār* [masc. noun: דָּבָר <1697>; from SPEAK <1696>] ▶ **This frequently used term has a wide range of meanings associated with it.** It signified spoken words or speech (Gen. 11:1; Is. 36:5; Jer. 51:64); a command or royal decree (Esther 1:12, 19); a report or tidings (Ex. 33:4); advice (Judg. 20:7); poetic writings of David (2 Chr. 29:30); business affairs (1 Chr. 26:32); a legal cause (Ex. 18:16); the custom or manner of activity (Esther 1:13); and something indefinite (thing, Gen. 22:16). Most important was the use of this word to convey divine communication. Often the word of the Lord signified the revelation given to prophets (2 Sam. 7:4; Jer. 25:3; Hos. 1:1). Similarly, the Ten Commandments were literally called the ten words of the Lord (Ex. 34:28; Deut. 4:13). *

5 ***dōḇer, dibbêr*** [masc. noun: דִּבֵּר ,דֹּבֶר <1699>; from SPEAK <1696> (in its original sense)] ▶ **This term describes the word that a prophet communicates (Jer. 5:13).** In a different context it refers to an ideal pastureland; on the one hand, where God will collect and pasture His people

(Mic. 2:12) but, on the other hand, where sheep will graze in the pasture of His devastated land (Is. 5:17). ¶

[6] ***dabbereṯ*** [fem. noun: דַּבֶּרֶת <1703>; intens. from SPEAK <1696>] ► **This term is found only once in the Old Testament (Deut. 33:3), where it is best translated words.** In this context, it poetically describes the words God gave Moses to deliver to the people. It comes from the verb *dāḇar* (SPEAK <1696>) and is related to the much-used Hebrew noun *dāḇār* (<1697> above). ¶

[7] ***millāh*** [fem. sing. noun: מִלָּה <4405>; from SPEAK <4448>] ► **This Hebrew term means a word; collectively, a discourse.** It is the poetic equivalent of *dāḇār* (<1697> above); it carries the same range of meaning (2 Sam. 23:2; Ps. 19:4; Ps. 139:4; Prov. 23:9). Of its thirty-eight uses in the Hebrew portion of the Old Testament, Job contains thirty-four (Job 4:2, 4; 6:26; 8:10; etc.). *

[8] ***millāh*** [Aramaic fem. sing. noun: מִלָּה <4406>; corresponding to <4405> above] ► **This term means an utterance. It also means command, matter.** Used only in Daniel, it is equivalent to the Hebrew term *millāh*: WORD <4405>; it means word or speech, and comes from the Hebrew verb *mālal* (<4448>), meaning to speak or say. This word is used to describe words that were spoken (Dan. 4:31; 7:11, 25), which, depending on the context, can be translated as command (Dan. 2:5; 3:22; 5:10). Often this word described an entire series of circumstances or matters (Dan. 2:9–11; 4:33; 7:1). *

– [9] Dan. 4:17 ➔ REQUEST <3983>.

WORK – [1] ***mᵉlā'ḵāh*** [fem. sing. noun: מְלָאכָה <4399>; from the same as MESSENGER <4397>] ► **This word means occupation, business, something made, property, workmanship.** It is used for God's creative work (Gen. 2:2, 3); as well as for human labor (Ex. 20:9, 10); skilled craftsmanship (Lev. 13:48); and agricultural tasks (1 Chr. 27:26). It is used for livestock (Gen. 33:14); property (Ex. 22:8); public and religious business. For instance, Ezra 10:13 employs the term in reference to the divorce of foreign wives. *

[2] ***maᵃḇāḏ*** [masc. noun: מַעֲבָד <4566>; from SERVE <5647> (in the sense of to work)] ► **This word indicates something done, performed: the deeds of people, the conduct of their lives.** Ref.: Job 34:25. ¶

[3] ***maᵃḇāḏ*** [Aramaic masc. noun: מַעֲבָד <4567>; corresponding to <4566> above] ► **In context this word refers to God's actions and deeds among the nations, executed in His sovereignty.** Ref.: Dan. 4:37. ¶

[4] ***maᵃśeh*** [masc. noun: מַעֲשֶׂה <4639>; from DO <6213>] ► **This word also means a deed, workmanship. It has an extremely broad range of meanings, but they can be deciphered by carefully examining the context of each use.** Here are some main categories: the works and deeds of God, whatever they may be, especially His work of salvation and judgment (Judg. 2:7, 10; Josh. 24:31; Ps. 8:6; 33:4; Eccl. 7:13; 8:17; Eccl. 11:5; Is. 26:12). The expression "the work(s) of His hands" occurs (Ps. 28:5; 92:4; Is. 5:12). God created, made Israel (Is. 60:21); Assyria (Is. 19:25; 64:8); various things (Job 14:15; Ps. 8:6; 19:1; Hab. 3:17).

The word refers to various deeds or works accomplished by people: it refers to any type of deed or act performed, good or bad (Num. 16:28; Ezra 9:13; Is. 59:6); including the worship of idols (Deut. 31:29; Jer. 25:6, 7; 32:30). People's labor such as husbandry (Gen. 5:29; Ex. 23:16; Judg. 19:16); especially Israel's enforced labor in Egypt (Ex. 5:4, 13). It refers to things produced by humans (Gen. 40:17; Ex. 26:1, 31, 36; Is. 3:24); especially things made for the Temple (1 Kgs. 7:17); or of detestable idols (Deut. 4:28; 2 Kgs. 19:18). For things God makes, see the first paragraph above. *

[5] ***mip̱'āl, mip̱'ālāh*** [מִפְעָל, מִפְעָלָה <4659>; from MAKE <6466>] ►

a. A masculine noun describing an act, a deed. It refers to acts, works, deeds, and the results as well; the things produced (Prov. 8:22). ¶

b. A feminine noun meaning a work, a deed. It is used of the destructive acts of God and their results by wars and battles in the earth (Ps. 46:8); but also in context to His magnificent deeds and accomplishments of deliverance for His people (Ps. 66:5). ¶

[6] ***ʿᵃbôḏāh, ʿᵃbōḏāh*** [fem. noun: עֲבוֹדָה, עֲבֹדָה <5656>; from SERVE <5647> (also in the sense of to work)] ► **This word also means service. It encompasses the wide variations of meaning of the English word "work"—from delicate artistry to forced labor.** The Egyptians made the Israelites do slave labor (Ex. 1:14); for certain feast days, the Israelites were not allowed to do any work (Lev. 23:7 ff.); different parts of the Tabernacle were considered to be in its service (Num. 4:26, 32); the descendants of Judah included workers of linen (1 Chr. 4:21). God handed the Israelites into the hand of Shishak so they would learn the difference between serving Him and serving other kings (2 Chr. 12:8). See the related Hebrew root *ʿāḇaḏ* (SERVE <5647>). *

[7] ***ʿᵃbiyḏāh*** [Aramaic fem. noun: עֲבִידָה <5673>; from MAKE <5648> (in the sense of to work)] ► **This word also means service, administration.** It refers to the process of construction (Ezra 4:24; 5:8; 6:7); and the ministry of serving at the holy places (Ezra 6:18: service). It also is used to describe the process of administering a city or area, a portion of a governing system (Dan. 2:49; 3:12: administration, affairs). ¶

[8] ***pōʿal*** [masc. noun: פֹּעַל <6467>; from MAKE <6466>] ► **This word also indicates a deed, an act. It indicates what is performed, completed, done.** God's work in all of His dealings with people (Deut. 32:4; Ps. 44:1; 64:9); the work and toil of people in every way (Ruth 2:12; Job 24:5; Ps. 104:23). It is used of deeds that express character (Prov. 20:11; 24:12, 29). It depicts evil acts, deeds indicated from context (Jer. 25:14; 50:29); and good actions (Prov. 21:8). It refers to the product of God's work and toil (Is. 45:9, 11). It may have the sense of the work to acquire something (Prov. 21:6). It stands for the wages or what is due to a worker (Jer. 22:13); or it refers to one's accomplishments in life (Is. 1:31). *

[9] ***pᵉʿullāh*** [fem. noun: פְּעֻלָּה <6468>; fem. pass. part. of MAKE <6466>] ► **This word also refers to wages, rewards.** It indicates the deeds of people or God (Ps. 17:4; 28:5); whether good or bad (2 Chr. 15:7; Prov. 11:18; Is. 65:7). It refers to rewards or wages earned (Lev. 19:13; Prov. 10:16); a reward from the Lord for doing what is right (Is. 49:4; 61:8). It is used once of punishment earned (Ps. 109:20). It describes the divinely guided deeds and actions of a pagan king (Ezek. 29:20). *

– [10] Ex. 31:10; 35:19; 39:1, 41 ➔ WOVEN <8278> b. [11] Job 10:3 (work); 39:11 (heavy work) ➔ LABOR (noun) <3018> [12] Eccl. 2:23 ➔ TASK <6045> [13] Eccl. 9:1 ➔ DEED <5652> [14] Jer. 32:19 ➔ DEED <5950>.

WORKER – ***ʿāṣêḇ*** [masc. noun: עָצֵב <6092>; from HURT <6087>] ► **This noun is derived from the verb *ʿāṣaḇ* (HURT <6087>), which conveys the idea of physical or emotional pain and suffering.** God condemned the people of Israel for not properly fasting because they sacrificed nothing personally while exploiting their laborers or workers (Is. 58:3; NKJV: laborer; KJV: labour). ¶

WORKMAN – Song 7:1: skillful workman, cunning workman ➔ ARTIST <542>.

WORLD – [1] ***ḥeḏel*** [masc. noun: חֶדֶל <2309>; from CEASE <2308>] ► **This word means cessation, rest. It occurs only in Isaiah 38:11 in the lamentation of Hezekiah.** Despite the fact it is translated "world" (KJV), it conveys the idea of a place of termination or repose (NIV: death). By considering the context in the Old Testament, one comes to understand that the word refers to the grave, or more exactly, Sheol (ESV, NASB, NKJV) (cf. Is. 38:10). ¶

[2] ***ḥeleḏ*** [masc. noun: חֶלֶד <2465>; from an unused root apparently meaning to glide swiftly] ► **This word also means age, duration of life, lifetime, span of the years. The primary sense of the word is a duration or span of time.** It signifies the world, i.e., this present existence (Ps. 17:14;

49:1); life itself (Job 11:17); and the span of a person's life (Ps. 39:5). Other refs.: Ps. 89:47: time, life, span of life; Is. 38:11. ¶

[3] ***têḇêl*** [fem. noun: תֵּבֵל <8398>; from BRING <2986>] ► **This word means the earth and also the globe.** It is used in a description of the clouds responding to the command of God, i.e., they swirled over the face of the whole earth (Job 37:12). In Proverbs, the created world was a reason for rejoicing (Prov. 8:31). This word is also used to indicate the foundations of the earth, as in 2 Samuel where the foundations of the earth were laid bare at the rebuke of the Lord (2 Sam. 22:16). *Têḇêl* is also used to denote what was firmly established, i.e., the world (Ps. 93:1; 96:10); something that would be punished for its evil (Is. 13:11); and what will be filled by Israel upon their blossoming (Is. 27:6). In Nahum, the world and all who live in it will tremble at the presence of the Lord (Nah. 1:5). *

WORM – [1] ***sās*** [masc. noun: סָס <5580>; from the same as HORSE <5483>] ► **This word refers to a grub worm (the root of the verb relates to the agility of the fly). It indicates an insect or worm that eats clothing.** In context it is used symbolically of what will devour Israel's enemies (Is. 51:8). ¶

[2] ***rimmāh*** [fem. noun: רִמָּה <7415>; from EXALTED <7426> b. (in the sense of breading, i.e., rapidly breeding in the case of worms)] ► **This word refers to worm-like insect larva; it is also translated maggot.** It often appears in any decaying matter (Ex. 16:24); such as decaying manna or a decomposing corpse (Job 7:5; 21:26; 24:20). It is used in various literary ways by Job: as my mother (Job 17:14); a feature of Sheol (Is. 14:11). Humankind is figuratively compared to a maggot in its lowliness (Job 25:6). ¶

– [3] Mic. 7:17 → CRAWL <2119> [4] See CRIMSON <8438> b. and d.

WORMWOOD – ***laʿănāh*** [fem. noun: לַעֲנָה <3939>; from an unused root supposed to mean to curse] ► **This word indicates bitterness; it is also translated bitter fruit, bitter poison, bitter food, gall. It is always used in a figurative, metaphorical sense.** It describes the character of an adulteress as bitter (of wormwood) (Prov. 5:4). It is used of a rebellious or bitter root or spirit in persons (Deut. 29:18) that, appropriately, results in judgments of bitterness (of wormwood), i.e., the judgments of God (Jer. 9:15; 23:15; Lam. 3:15, 19). It is used to describe the opposite of justice and righteousness which should be sweet experiences (Amos 5:7; 6:12). ¶

WORN OUT – [1] Josh. 9:4, 5; Ezek. 23:43 → OLD <1087> [2] Jer. 38:11, 12 → OLD <1094>.

WORN-OUT CLOTHES – ***melaḥ*** [masc. noun: מֶלַח <4418>; from VANISH <4414>] ► **This expression means rag.** It indicates a torn cloth or even scraps of clothing (Jer. 38:11, 12; also translated old rags, old rotten rags). In context rags were made into a rope and used to rescue Jeremiah. ¶

WORRY – 1 Sam. 9:5; 10:2; Is. 57:1 → ANXIOUS (BE, BECOME) <1672>.

WORSE – 2 Kgs. 14:12 → to put to the worse → SMITE <5062>.

WORSE (BE) – Dan. 1:10 → ANGRY (BE, BECOME) <2196>.

WORSHIP – See BOW DOWN <7812>.

WORSHIPPER – ***ʿāṯār*** [masc. noun: עָתָר <6282>; from MULTIPLY <6280>] ►

a. This word is used of persons who seek, entreat, and, hence, offer worship to God; they are mentioned in a projection of God's restored earth. Ref.: Zeph. 3:10; also translated suppliant. ¶

b. This word is translated fragrant, fragrance. It refers to the aroma, the smell that arose from burning incense (Ezek. 8:11). In this case, it took place in a forbidden pagan worship ritual. ¶

c. This word means thickness; it is translated thick. It refers to the heavy density of a cloud of incense sent up to God (Ezek. 8:11). ¶

WORTH THEIR WEIGHT – [1] ***sālā'*** [verb: סָלָא <5537>; a prim. root] ▶ **This word means to weigh, to compare.** In a figurative sense, it compares Israel's lack of moral and religious value against that of the purity of fine gold (Lam. 4:2; also translated weighed against, comparable to, valuable as. ¶
– [2] Lev. 27:23 ➔ NUMBER (noun) <4373>.

WORTHLESS – [1] ***b^{e}liyya'al*** [masc. noun: בְּלִיַּעַל <1100>; from NOT <1097> and PROFIT (verb) <3276>] ▶ **This word means unimportance, worthlessness; it is also translated wicked.** Often a strong moral component in the context suggests the state of being good for nothing and therefore expresses the concept of wickedness (Job 34:18; Prov. 6:12; Nah. 1:11). It is always used in reference to persons with only two exceptions, once for a disease and once for a nonspecific thing (Ps. 41:8; 101:3). The term is applied to the hard-hearted (Deut. 15:9; 1 Sam. 30:22); perjurers (1 Kgs. 21:13; Prov. 19:28); and those promoting rebellion against a king's authority (2 Sam. 20:1; 2 Chr. 13:7) or God's authority (Deut. 13:13). This word was not treated as a proper name by the Septuagint translators of the Old Testament, but it does appear in its Greek form as a name for the devil in the Dead Sea scrolls and in the New Testament (cf. 2 Cor. 6:15). *
[2] ***q^{e}lōqêl*** [adj.: קְלֹקֵל <7052>; from SLIGHT (BE) <7043>] ▶ **This word is also translated miserable, light.** It describes food that is unappetizing, unattractive, barely edible (Num. 21:5). ¶
– [3] Job 13:4; Zech. 11:17 ➔ WORTHLESSNESS <457> [4] Is. 41:29 ➔ NOTHINGNESS <205> [5] Lam. 2:14 ➔ FOOLISH <8602> a.

WORTHLESS (BE) – Jer. 15:19 ➔ GLUTTON (BE) <2151> a.

WORTHLESS (BECOME) – 2 Kgs. 17:15; Jer. 2:5; 23:16 ➔ VAIN (BECOME) <1891>.

WORTHLESS ONE – ***bā'uš*** [masc. noun: בְּאֻשׁ <891>; plur. of STENCH <889>] ▶ **This word indicates a useless, valueless thing. The word is used in parallel with (good) grapes but means the opposite of good grapes.** So it is bad grapes or bad fruit (NIV, Is. 5:2, 4). It is rendered worthless ones (grapes) by the NASB. ¶

WORTHLESS THING – Jer. 14:14 ➔ FUTILITY <434>.

WORTHLESSNESS – ***^{e}liyl*** [masc. noun: אֱלִיל <457>; apparently from NO <408>] ▶ **The term means having no value; it is frequently used to describe false gods and idols.** Refs.: Lev. 19:4; Ps. 96.5; Is. 2:8; Hab. 2:18. Sometimes, this noun is used in a prepositional phrase, such as in Zechariah 11:17, where the Hebrew literally says "shepherd of worthlessness," and in Job 13:4, "physicians of worthlessness." In those verses, *^{e}liyl* functions as an adjective. *

WORTHY – Jer. 15:19 ➔ PRECIOUS <3368>.

WORTHY (BE NOT) – ***qāṭan*** [verb: קָטֹן <6994>; a prim. root (rather a denom. from SMALL <6996>)] ▶ **This word means to be a small matter, insignificant; to be small, to make small.** It is used to refer to oneself as being trifling, insignificant, not worthy (Gen. 32:10); of something being considered as unimportant by God (2 Sam. 7:19; 1 Chr. 17:17). It is used in its causative sense to indicate making something smaller, but in context it describes an act of cheating (Amos 8:5). ¶

WORTHY MAN – 1 Kgs. 1:42 ➔ VALIANT MAN <381>.

WOULD THAT – Job 34:36: my desire is that ➔ OH, THAT <15>.

WOULD THAT! – ***aḥ^{a}lêy, 'aḥ^{a}lay*** [interj.: אַחֲלֵי, אַחֲלַי <305>; prob. from ALAS! <253> and a variant of OH THAT <3863>] ▶ **This word is also translated if only!, I wish that!, O that!** It represents a polite wish or desire (2 Kgs. 5:3) or a mere cry of the soul for integrity and stability (Ps. 119:5). ¶

WOUND (noun) – [1] ***māzôr*** [masc. noun: מָזוֹר <4205>; from CRUSH <2115> in the sense of binding] ► **This word indicates some kind of injury or a wound from disease; corruption in context. It is also translated sore.** It is used figuratively of Israel and Judah's moral and religious corruption before God (Jer. 30:13; Hos. 5:13). ¶
[2] ***peṣa'*** [common noun: פֶּצַע <6482>; from WOUND (verb) <6481>] ► **This word refers to an injury or bruise that has been inflicted, usually by striking.** Refs.: Gen. 4:23; Ex. 21:25. Job speaks of the wounds or injuries he has sustained from his illness (Job 9:17). Wounds, on the other hand, physical or emotional, may serve a good purpose (Prov. 20:30; 27:6). The word refers to all kinds of possible wounds (Prov. 23:29). The presence of wounds is used in a figurative sense to indicate Israel's spiritual sickness (Is. 1:6). ¶
– [3] Ps. 147:3 ➔ SORROW (noun) <6094> [4] Prov. 6:33 ➔ SORE (noun) <5061> [5] Prov. 18:8; 26:22 ➔ MORSEL (DAINTY, DELICIOUS, CHOICE) <3859> [6] Is. 53:5 ➔ BRUISE (noun) <2250> [7] Dan. 6:23 ➔ DAMAGE (noun) <2257> [8] Obad. 1:7 ➔ TRAP <4204>.

WOUND (verb) – ***pāṣa'*** [verb: פָּצַע <6481>; a prim. root] ► **This word means to destroy or ruin something by violently inflicting blows on it.** It describes the emasculating of a man's testicles by crushing (Deut. 23:1). It has the sense of injuring or bruising someone (1 Kgs. 20:37; Song 5:7). ¶

WOUNDED – [1] 2 Chr. 24:25 ➔ DISEASE <4251> [2] Prov. 18:14 ➔ CRUSHED <5218> a.

WOUNDED (BE) – Deut. 23:1 ➔ CRUSHING <1795>.

WOUNDING – Gen. 4:23 ➔ WOUND (noun) <6482>.

WOVEN – [1] ***śᵉrāḏ*** [masc. noun: שְׂרָד <8278>; from REMAIN <8277> (properly, to puncture)] ►
a. This word indicates woven work; it is also translated finely worked. It refers to skillfully integrated and entwined materials in certain garments (Ex. 31:10); and the garment itself (Ex. 35:19; 39:1, 41).
b. A masculine noun meaning service, work; it is also translated ministry. It is used of the work done by the priests and Levites in Israel (Ex. 31:10; 35:19; 39:1, 41). ¶
[2] ***tašbêṣ*** [masc. noun: תַּשְׁבֵּץ <8665>; from WEAVE <7660>] ► **This word indicates woven work fabricated like network. It is also translated checkered work, broidered.** It refers to the design of material used to make garments for the priests: breastpiece, ephod, robe, tunic, turban, and belt or sash (Ex. 28:4). Such beauty was worked into the clothes of the priest for splendor and dignity. ¶
– [3] Ps. 45:13 ➔ FILIGREE <4865> [4] Ps. 139:15 ➔ WEAVER <7551>.

WOVEN TOGETHER (BE) – Lam. 1:14 ➔ KNIT TOGETHER (BE) <8276>.

WRAP – [1] ***lûṭ*** [verb: לוּט <3874>; a prim. root] ► **This word indicates enveloping or folding a cover over or around something.** Goliath's sword was wrapped in a cloth (1 Sam. 21:9). Elijah covered his face with his mantle (1 Kgs. 19:13). It is used figuratively of the inability of persons to perceive something clearly (Is. 25:7, for a fuller discussion, see the noun form *ôṭ* [COVERING <3873>]). ¶
– [2] Job 14:17 ➔ SMEAR <2950> [3] Job 38:9 ➔ and wrapped it in thick darkness ➔ lit.: and thick darkness its swaddling band ➔ SWADDLING BAND <2854> [4] Ps. 77:18 ➔ ROLL (verb) <1563> [5] Is. 61:10 ➔ COVER (verb) <3271> [6] Mic. 7:3 ➔ WEAVE <5686>.

WRAP AROUND – ***'āṭāh*** [verb: עָטָה <5844>; a prim. root] ►
a. This word indicates to cover. It refers to shielding something, keeping it out of sight (Lev. 13:45); to put on a garment or a robe (1 Sam. 28:14). It is used to describe rain as it falls over an area (Ps. 84:6). Figuratively,

it describes being wrapped with or clothed in shame (Ps. 71:13). It may mean to wrap someone in or with something (Ps. 89:45; cf. Is. 61:10). To cover one's mouth is to show astonishment (Jer. 43:12). *
b. A verb meaning to take hold, to grasp. It is used of seizing someone, grasping him or her (Is. 22:17). In its immediate context, it is used figuratively. It may mean to wrap up something for use (KJV, NASB, Ezek. 21:15, see a.) or to grasp something (NIV: to hurl away) for immediate deployment. ¶

WRAP AROUND, WRAP ABOUT – Job 8:17 ➔ ENTWINE <5440>.

WRAP IN CLOTHS – Ezek. 16:4 ➔ SWADDLE <2853>.

WRAP ONESELF – Is. 28:20 ➔ GATHER <3664>.

WRAPPED TOGETHER (BE) – Job 40:17 ➔ KNIT TOGETHER (BE) <8276>.

WRAPPED UP – ***meʿuṭṭāh*** [adj.: מְעֻטָּה <4593>; pass. adj. of DECREASE <4591>] ► **This word means grasped, drawn, taken up.** It indicates something held in readiness for action, especially in battle (Ezek. 21:15). See also WRAP AROUND <5844>. ¶

WRATH – 1 ***ʿeḇrāh*** [fem. noun: עֶבְרָה <5678>; fem. of SIDE <5676>] ► **This word also means fury. It is derived from the word *ʿāḇar* (PASS THROUGH, PASS OVER <5674>) and thus implies an overflowing anger.** When the word is used of people, it usually describes a fault of character, a cruel anger (Gen. 49:7; Amos 1:11); associated with pride (Prov. 21:24; Is. 16:6). The wrath of a king toward shameful servants, however, is justifiable, representing God's anger (Prov. 14:35, cf. Prov. 14:34; Rom. 13:4). The word most often signifies God's wrath, an attribute people generally fail to properly appreciate (Ps. 90:11). God's wrath disregards a person's wealth (Prov. 11:4); and brings fiery judgment, purging the sin of His people (Ezek. 22:21, cf. Ezek. 22:22); and ultimately bringing wickedness and wicked people to an end on earth (Zeph. 1:15, 18). The instrument of wrath is sometimes pictured as a rod (Prov. 22:8; Lam. 3:1). *
2 ***qeṣap*** [Aramaic masc. noun: קְצַף <7109>; from ANGRY (BE) <7108>] ► **Like the word *qeṣap* [ANGRY (BE) <7108>], this word refers to anger aroused by someone's failure to fulfill a duty properly.** The word occurs only in Ezra 7:23 where Artaxerxes commanded that work necessary for the second Temple was to be done diligently, lest God's wrath fall on Persia. Artaxerxes understood that his responsibility was to see that his subjects did their duties. ¶
3 ***qeṣep*** [masc. noun: קֶצֶף <7110>; from ANGRY (BE) <7107>] ► **The word refers to anger aroused by someone's failure to do a duty.** For example, a wife in Persia who showed contempt for her husband by not doing her duties would arouse his wrath (Esther 1:18). This word usually refers to God's wrath aroused by people failing to do their duties (Deut. 29:28; Ps. 38:1; Is. 34:2). In some cases, this wrath was directed against sinful Gentile nations (Is. 34:2; Zech. 1:15; cf. Rom. 1:18). In Israel's case, this duty was expressed in the Law of Moses (2 Chr. 19:10; Zech. 7:12; cf. Rom. 4:15). Atonement performed by priests turned away God's wrath when laws were broken (Num. 16:46; 2 Chr. 29:8; 27:24; 2 Chr. 29:8). *
– 4 Dan. 3:19 ➔ FURY <2528> 5 Hab. 3:2 ➔ TURMOIL <7267>.

WRATH (PROVOKE TO) – Ezra 5:12 ➔ ANGER (verb) <7265>.

WREATH – 1 ***gāḏil*** [masc. noun: גְּדִל <1434>; from GREAT (BECOME) <1431> (in the sense of twisting)] ► **This word is an architectural term, it denotes chain-like decorations on the capitals of pillars.** Ref.: 1 Kgs. 7:17; also translated twisted thread, interwoven. The Hebrew word also means a tassel on a garment (Deut. 22:12), see TASSEL <1434>. ¶
2 ***lōyāh*** [fem. noun: לֹיָה <3914>; a form of GARLAND <3880>] ► **This word is a technical architectural term indicating**

some kind of ornamental work featured on the stands for the great molten sea that Solomon built. Refs.: 1 Kgs. 7:29, 30, 36; KJV: addition. ¶
– [3] Prov. 1:9 ➔ GARLAND <3880>.

WREATHED (BE) – Lam. 1:14 ➔ KNIT TOGETHER (BE) <8276>.

WREATHEN – Ex. 28:14 ➔ BRAIDED <4020>.

WRENCHED (BE) – [1] Gen. 32:25 ➔ ALIENATED (BE) <3363> [2] Ezek. 29:7 ➔ SHAKE <5976>.

WRESTLE – [1] ***'āḇaq*** [verb: אָבַק <79>; a prim. root, prob. to float away (as vapor), but used only as denom. from DUST <80>] ▶ **This word is found only in the story of Jacob's contest or wrestling/striving with a mysterious Man by the Jabbok River.** Refs.: Gen. 32:24, 25. Jacob's name was subsequently changed to Israel. ¶
[2] ***pāṯal*** [verb: פָּתַל <6617>; a prim. root] ▶ **This word means to be shrewd, to be cunning, to be devious.** It is used to describe spiritual and relational tensions that arise, difficult situations, wrestlings (Gen. 30:8). It refers to being insightful and understanding about things (2 Sam. 22:27; Ps. 18:26); but this can become a vice (Job 5:13; Prov. 8:8). ¶
– [3] Hos. 12:4 ➔ STRUGGLE (verb) <8280>.

WRESTLINGS – ***nap̱tûliym*** [masc. plur. noun: נַפְתּוּלִים <5319>; from WRESTLE <6617>] ▶ **This word describes contention and violent fighting between opponents.** It refers in context to strife, competition, and jealousy between two wives competing for the affection and recognition of their husband (Gen. 30:8; NIV: struggle). ¶

WRETCH – Ps. 35:15 ➔ ATTACKER <5222>.

WRING – Lev. 1:15; 5:9; Judg. 6:38; Ps. 73:10; 75:8; Is. 51:17; Ezek. 23:34 ➔ DRAIN <4680>.

WRING OFF – ***mālaq*** [verb: מָלַק <4454>; a prim. root] ▶ **This word describes pinching off, removing of the head of a bird.** The birds in context then serve as a burnt offering (Lev. 1:15) or guilt offering (Lev. 5:8). In the latter case, its head was not entirely severed. Rather, its head was nipped. ¶

WRIST – ***'aṣṣiyl*** [fem. noun: אַצִּיל <679>; from RESERVE (verb) <680> (in its primary sense of uniting)] ▶ **This word also means joint, armpit.** It refers to the joint of a person's hand or wrist (Ezek. 13:18); it is also translated sleeve. It indicates the arm joints or armpits (Jer. 38:12) by which Jeremiah was rescued. See also LONG (adj.) <679>. ¶

WRITE – [1] ***kāṯaḇ*** [verb: כָּתַב <3789>; a prim. root] ▶ **This word refers to communicating through a system of visible signs written down.** It is used to indicate the process of recording information in many ways and settings: writing in or on a stone or book (Ex. 17:14; Deut. 27:3; 2 Kgs. 23:3). The Ten Commandments or ten words were written by the finger of God on stone tablets (Ex. 31:18; 32:15; 34:1, 27, 28); covenants were written down (Ex. 24:4, 12). Descriptions of the land of Canaan were written down (Josh. 18:4). The second recording of Jeremiah's words were dictated as Baruch wrote them down again (Jer. 36:2, 4). It refers to inscribing or engraving on a crown of pure gold for the high priest to wear (Ex. 39:30). Job wished that his words would be written down (Job 19:23, 24). The Lord had a written book of remembrance that contained the names of those who feared Him (Mal. 3:16). The preacher tried to write down words of truth to teach and make the people wise (Eccl. 12:10). *
[2] ***keṯaḇ*** [Aramaic verb: כְּתַב <3790>; corresponding to <3789> above] ▶ **This word refers to recording information of any kind through a system of visible signs. It is used of the process in many ways and settings.** In Ezra it is used to describe writing letters, reports, name lists, and archives (Ezra 4:8; 5:7, 10; 6:2). In Daniel it is used

of writing on a wall by a mysterious hand (Dan. 5:5); in an official decree from a king (Dan. 6:25); in recording the summary of a vision (Dan. 7:1). ¶
– 3 Deut. 27:8; Hab. 2:2 ➔ EXPLAIN <874> 4 Dan. 5:24, 25 ➔ INSCRIBE <7560> 5 Dan. 10:21 ➔ INSCRIBE <7559>.

WRITING – 1 ***kᵉṯāḇ*** [masc. noun: כְּתָב <3791>; from WRITE <3789>] ► **This word indicates the process of writing or the symbols used to write; it is also translated script, document, edit, text, register, registration.** It is used of the particular writing form or system of an area (Esther 1:22); a written document (Esther 3:14); an official written list (Ezra 2:62); the actual language or text in a document (Ezra 4:7). With *bᵉ*, with, in, it describes a means to gain understanding by putting something in writing (*biḵṯāḇ*) (1 Chr. 28:19; 2 Chr. 35:4). It is modified to refer to a special source of truth, the writing of truth (Dan. 10:21). *
2 ***kᵉṯāḇ*** [Aramaic masc. noun: כְּתָב <3792>; corresponding to <3791> above] ► **See previous definition. This word is also translated inscription, document.** It refers to something that has been written down (Dan. 5:7, 8, 15–17, 24, 25). It indicates an official document and its contents (Dan. 6:8–10). It refers to specific instructions and commands written in the Law of Moses (Ezra 6:18). The phrase *dîy-lā' ḵᵉṯāḇ* means with no limit or with no written prescription (NASB, as needed) (Ezra 7:22). ¶
3 ***miḵṯāḇ*** [masc. noun: מִכְתָּב <4385>; from WRITE <3789>] ► **This word designates something written.** It is used of God's actual writing on the two stone tablets (Ex. 32:16); the engraving on the high priest's golden plate or crown that he wore (Ex. 39:30). With the preposition *bᵉ*, it means in writing (Deut. 10:4). It designates an entire written letter or document (2 Chr. 21:12; Is. 38:9); a set of instructions or directives (2 Chr. 35:4); or a royal decree or proclamation (2 Chr. 36:22). Other ref.: Ezra 1:1. ¶

WRITING KIT, WRITING CASE – Ezek. 9:2, 3, 11 ➔ INKHORN <7083>.

WRITTEN – Ezra 6:18 ➔ WRITING <3792>.

WRONG (noun) – 1 ***ḥᵃḇûlāh*** [Aramaic fem. noun: חֲבוּלָה <2248>; from DESTROY <2255>] ► **This word indicates a hurtful deed; it is also translated crime, hurt, harm.** Daniel was cleared of being guilty of this kind of evil action against Darius (Dan. 6:22) in any way. ¶
2 ***'awwāṯāh*** [fem. sing. noun: עַוָּתָה <5792>; from BEND <5791>] ► **This word is used only in Lamentations 3:59 (NASB: oppression) where the poet declared that God had seen the perversion of justice done to Jerusalem (i.e., its destruction).** This passage is interesting because the writer saw God's judgment as severe. See the verb *'āwaṯ* (BEND <5791>). ¶
– 3 Job 1:22; 24:12 ➔ WRONGDOING <8604>.

WRONG (DO) – 2 Sam. 7:14; 19:19; Esther 1:16; Dan. 9:5; etc. ➔ INIQUITY (COMMIT) <5753>.

WRONG (MAKE) – Ps. 55:3 ➔ PERVERTED <6127>.

WRONG (PUT IN THE) – Job 19:6 ➔ BEND <5791>.

WRONG (verb) – 1 ***hāḵar, ḥāḵar*** [verb: הָכַר, חָכַר <1970>; a prim. root] ►
a. A verb meaning to injure, to attack. It indicates unduly aggressive or injurious actions toward someone (Job 19:3; NKJV, NASB, NIV). ¶
b. A verb meaning to act as a stranger toward. It describes actions, words, and attitudes that indicate alienation towards another person (Job 19:3, KJV). ¶
– 2 Job 19:6 ➔ BEND <5791> 3 Prov. 8:36 ➔ VIOLENCE (DO) <2554>.

WRONGDOING – ***tiḇlāh*** [fem. noun: תִּפְלָה <8604>; from the same as FOOLISH <8602> a.] ► **This word indicates improper action, injustice, wrong. It also means folly.** It was something Job refused to attribute to God (Job 1:22). According to

Job, it is something God fails to pay attention to in some situations (Job 24:12). Prophecy by Israel's prophets through Baal is designated as *tiplāh,* a wrong thing, not right, disgusting (Jer. 23:13; also translated offensive thing, unsavory thing, repulsive thing). ¶

WROTH (BE) – 2 Chr. 26:19 ➔ ANGRY (BE, BECOME) <2196>.

WROUGHT – 1 ***'āšôṯ*** [adj.: עָשׁוֹת <6219>; from SLEEK (BE) <6245> (in the sense of to shine)] ▶ **This word means fabricated. Most recent translators prefer to render this word as wrought, rather than bright, when coupled with iron.** Ref.: Ezek. 27:19. It was a valuable trade commodity between Tyre and Javan (Greece). ¶
– 2 Ps. 45:13 ➔ FILIGREE <4865>.

Y

YARD – Gen. 42:21; etc. ➔ COURTYARD <1508>.

YARN – Judg. 16:9 ➔ TOW <5296>.

YEAR – 1 ***šᵉnāh*** [Aramaic fem. noun: שְׁנָה <8140>; corresponding to <8141> below] ▶ **This word refers to a cycle of the lunar year, the major division of time used in the ancient world (Ezra 4:24).** In Ezra's time, Solomon's Temple had been built many years earlier (Ezra 5:11). The first year of a king was always important (Ezra 5:13; 6:3; Dan. 7:1). The second Temple was completed in the sixth year of Darius, king of Persia (Ezra 6:15). It is used in calculating ages of persons (Dan. 5:31). ¶

2 ***šānāh*** [fem. noun: שָׁנָה <8141>; from CHANGE (verb) <8138>] ▶ **This word is used quite uniformly in its application, but its context must be noted carefully.** It means simply a division of time, a year (Gen. 1:14). Something done yearly or year upon year is *baššānāh, šānāh bᵉšānāh* respectively (Ex. 23:14; Deut. 14:22; 15:20). It expresses a person's age, *ben šānāh,* a son of a year, means one year old (Ex. 12:5). The accession year of a king is *šᵉnaṯ malkô,* year of his reigning (2 Kgs. 25:27). With a dual ending, *-ayim,* it means two full years (Gen. 41:1). The phrase *kᵉšānîm qaḏmōniyyôṯ* means according to (in) former (earlier) years (Mal. 3:4). *

YEARN – 1 ***kāmar*** [verb: כָּמַר <3648>; a prim. root] ▶ **This word indicates to be deeply affected with passion (e.g., love pity), to be aroused, to be deeply moved.** It indicates something being agitated or moved with respect to something else, i.e., Joseph was moved at seeing his brother Benjamin (Gen. 43:30; also translated to be stirred, to be deeply moved, to grow warm). A mother is gripped by feeling and emotion for her baby (1 Kgs. 3:26; also translated to be deeply moved, to be deeply stirred). It is used of skin tingling, sweating, or being feverish from lack of nourishment (Lam. 5:10: to be hot, to be black). God's own being is aroused in love for His rebellious people (Hos. 11:8: to be kindled, to grow warm, to be stirred, to be aroused). ¶

– 2 Deut. 28:32 ➔ LONGING <3616>
3 Is. 26:9 ➔ DESIRE (verb) <183>.

YEARN FOR – Ps. 63:1 ➔ FAINT <3642>.

YEARNING – Ezek. 24:21 ➔ DELIGHT (noun) <4263>.

YEAST – See LEAVEN <7603>.

YEAST (BREAD WITHOUT) – Gen. 19:3, 1 Sam. 28:24 ➔ STRONGHOLD <4679>.

YELL – Jer. 51:38 ➔ GROWL <5286>.

YELLOW – Ps. 68:13 ➔ GREENISH <3422>.

YELLOW, YELLOWISH – ***ṣāhoḇ*** [adj.: צָהֹב <6669>; from SHINY <6668>] ▶ **Hair of this color in an area of infected skin was dangerous** It indicated leprosy or some serious skin disease making a person unclean (Lev. 13:30, 32, 36). ¶

YESTERDAY – 1 ***'emeš*** [adv. of time: אֶמֶשׁ <570>] ▶ **This word refers to the evening of the previous day; it also means last night.** Refs.: Gen. 19:34; 31:29, 42. But it also has the sense of yesterday (2 Kgs. 9:26) or recently. It seems to have the meaning by night in Job (Job 30:3). ¶

2 ***'eṯmôl, 'eṯmûl*** [proper noun: אֶתְמוֹל, אֶתְמוּל <865>; prob. from the untranslated particle <853> or WITH <854> and AGAINST <4136>] ▶ **This word indicates yesterday and also formerly, recently.** It often means yesterday (Ps. 90:4). Used before *šilšôm* <8032>, it literally means yesterday and the third day, i.e., formerly, as formerly (1 Sam. 4:7; 14:21; 2 Sam. 5:2). Used with the preposition *min* <4480>, from, it means already (Is. 30:33; Mic. 2:8). Other refs.: 1 Sam. 10:11; 19:7. ¶

YET – ***ʿ^{e}ḏen, ʿ^{e}ḏenāh*** [adv.: עֲדֶן, עֲדֶנָה <5728>; from UNTIL <5704> and THEY, THEM <2004>] ▶
a. This word indicates an imagined thing, a state, or a condition that has not yet occurred; it also means still. Ref.: Eccl. 4:3. ¶
b. This word refers to something that is currently happening, the current situation or status; it also means still. Ref.: Eccl. 4:2. ¶

YIELD – [1] Deut. 13:8 ➔ WILLING (BE) <14> [2] Deut. 22:9 ➔ HARVEST <4395> [3] Deut. 32:22 ➔ INCREASE (noun) <2981> [4] Job 22:21 ➔ PROFITABLE (BE) <5532> a.

YIELDING – Eccl. 10:4 ➔ CALMNESS <4832>.

YOKE – [1] ***môṭāh*** [fem. noun: מוֹטָה <4133>; fem. of POLE <4132>] ▶ **This word means a bar. It is used of a harness collar but is employed figuratively of forces that oppress God's people (Is. 58:6, 9), especially in Egypt (Lev. 26:13).** This yoke was used in prophetic messages as well (Jer. 27:2; 28:10, 12, 13), representing political subjection (Ezek. 30:18; 34:27). It describes carrying poles for the ark of God (1 Chr. 15:15; KJV: staves). ¶
[2] ***ʿōl*** [masc. noun.: עֹל <5923>; from DO <5953> (in the sense of to treat severely)] ▶ **This word describes a wooden frame or a bar placed on the neck of work animals to harness them for labor.** Its usage includes a yoke for cattle (Deut. 21:3; 1 Sam. 6:7). It was a favorite figurative word to express servitude (1 Kgs. 12:4, 10, 11, 14). It is used of a yoke of transgressions (Lam. 1:14); or hardship (Lam. 3:27). *

YOKE, YOKE BAR – Nah. 1:13 ➔ POLE <4132>.

YOU – [1] ***ʾantah, ʾan^{e}t*** [Aramaic independent personal pron.: אַנְתָּה, אַנְתְּ <607>; corresponding to <859> below] ▶ **This word is used to mean simply you (Dan. 6:16) but is also employed to point out and emphasize, as in, you Ezra (Ezra 7:25).** It precedes the expression, O king (Dan. 2:29, 31), regularly as an expression of respect and court demeanor. *
[2] ***ʾantûn*** [Aramaic independent plur. pron.: אַנְתּוּן <608>; plur. of <607> above] ▶ **This word is found only in Daniel 2:8.** It refers to the Chaldeans of Babylon. ¶
[3] ***ʾattāh*** [personal pron.: אַתָּה <859>; a prim. pron. of the second person] ▶ **This word is also written *ʾattā* in a few places (1 Sam. 24:18; Ps. 6:3). Its basic use is as the independent personal pronoun meaning you.** Refs.: Num. 11:15; Deut. 5:27; 2 Chr. 14:11; Ezek. 28:14. It is used for emphasis before finite verb forms and then may mean you, yourself. It may also be used after (appended) a verb for emphasis (Ex. 18:19; 1 Sam. 17:56; 20:8). Used after a previous suffix referring to you, it is again emphatic (2 Chr. 35:21). *

YOUNG – [1] ***ʿōp̱er*** [masc. noun: עֹפֶר <6082>; from FLING <6080>] ▶ **This word refers to a not very old deer, a fawn.** It is used in a simile to compare one's bridegroom to a young stag, a young deer (Song 2:9, 17; 8:14); and of the breasts of the bride (Song 4:5; 7:3). ¶
[2] ***ṣāʿiyr*** [adj.: צָעִיר <6810>; from BRING LOW <6819> (in the sense of to be small)] ▶ **This word means young in the sense of having lived or existed for only a short time. It refers to the age of a person, someone young in years. It also means younger, little, small.** Used with the definite article, it can be the younger or the young one of two (Gen. 19:31, 34); or even the youngest (Ps. 68:27). It may indicate merely the one born first (Gen. 25:23). It indicates what is little, small, smaller, or smallest in size or number (1 Sam. 9:21; Ps. 119:141; Is. 60:22). It refers to servants, young ones (Jer. 14:3). It has the sense of so small! or too small followed by the prepositions *l^{e}* plus the infinitive of *hāyāh,* to be (Mic. 5:2). *
– [3] Deut. 32:11 ➔ PIGEON (YOUNG) <1469>.

YOUNG CHILD – Job 19:18; 21:11 ➔ INIQUITY <5758>.

YOUNG, YOUNG ONE – 1 ***na'ar*** [masc. noun: נַעַר <5289>; from SHAKE <5287> in its deriv. sense of tossing about] ▶
a. This word means a person not very old. It is the translation given to the word in Zechariah 11:16 (KJV, NKJV, ESV, NIV) to indicate persons who need to be cared for, instructed, prohibited. ¶
b. A masculine noun meaning scattered. It is understood as related to SHAKE <5287> and refers, therefore, to those shaken off, scattered (Zech. 11:16, NASB). ¶
– 2 Lam. 4:3 ➔ CUB <1482>.

YOUNG GIRL, YOUNG WOMAN – Gen. 34:4 ➔ GIRL <3207>.

YOUNG MAN – 1 ***baḥûr*** [masc. noun: בָּחוּר <970>; part. pass. of CHOOSE <977>] ▶ **This word is usually in its plural form. It refers to an unmarried adult male in his prime.** Refs.: 1 Sam. 9:2; Eccl. 11:9; Is. 62:5. It is used as a collective noun meaning young men (Jer. 15:8). It is used with the word for virgin, *beṯûlāh*, to indicate young men and virgins (Deut. 32:25; 2 Chr. 36:17; Jer. 51:22) and with *zeqêniym* to indicate young and old men (Jer. 31:13). *
2 ***'elem*** [masc. noun: עֶלֶם <5958>; from HIDE <5956> (properly, something kept out of sight; comp. YOUNG WOMAN <5959>)] ▶ **This word is also translated youth, stripling, boy. The feminine counterpart of this word is found in the word *'almāh* (YOUNG WOMAN <5959>). The focus of this term is probably sexual maturity.** It connotes an individual who has gone through puberty and is therefore sexually mature. Thus, *'elem* is the picture of an individual who has crossed (or is crossing) the threshold from boyhood or girlhood to manhood or womanhood, and, as such, is of marriageable age. Saul applied this term to David after he killed Goliath (1 Sam. 17:56); and Jonathan used it to refer to his armorbearer (1 Sam. 20:22). ¶
– 3 Gen. 18:7; 22:3 ➔ BOY <5288>.

YOUNG MAN, YOUNG ONE – 1 Kgs. 12:8, 10; Job 38:41; 39:3; etc. ➔ CHILD <3206>.

YOUNG ONE – 1 ***'eprōaḥ*** [masc. noun: אֶפְרֹחַ <667>; from BREAK OUT <6524> (in the sense of bursting the shell)] ▶ **This word describes young birds still in the nest with their mother.** The young birds could be taken, but the mother had to be left (Deut. 22:6). It refers to baby hawks (Job 39:30) and swallows (Ps. 84:3). ¶
– 2 Deut. 28:57 ➔ AFTERBIRTH <7988> b.

YOUNG WOMAN – ***'almāh*** [fem. noun: עַלְמָה <5959>; fem. of YOUNG MAN <5958> (a lass, as veiled or private)] ▶ **The word describes young women in different categories. It also means a maiden, a girl, and a virgin; it is also translated maid, damsel.** Rebekah was understood to be a marriageable young woman by Abraham's servant (Gen. 24:43); as was the maiden described in Proverbs 30:19, for in this case, the man was wooing her as a possible wife. Moses' sister was probably in this category (Exodus 2:8). Sometimes it is unclear how old or mature these young maidens were (Psalm 68:25). The most famous passage where this term is used is Isaiah 7:14, where it asserts an *'almāh* will give birth to a son. The author of Matthew 1:23 understood this woman to be a virgin. Other refs.: Song 1:3; 6:8. ¶

YOUTH – 1 ***beḥûrôṯ, beḥûriym*** [masc. plur. abstract noun: בְּחוּרִים ,בְּחוּרוֹת <979>; from YOUNG MAN <970>] ▶ **This word means age or time when a person is not very old.** The early years of life were considered times of joy, opportunity, and enjoyment—but above all, a vital time to remember one's Creator (Eccl. 11:9; 12:1). The word refers to one's early years as the time of youth (Num. 11:28). ¶
2 ***yalḏûṯ*** [fem. noun: יַלְדוּת <3208>; abstractly from CHILD <3206>] ▶ **This word refers to childhood, a period of youth.** It designates an early period in a person's life, childhood or youth, when it is especially important to serve the Creator (Eccl. 11:9, 10). In Psalm 110:3, it refers to the period of youth of the Israelite king or to the young people of his nation (NASB)

who are especially refreshing and invigorating to him. ¶

3 ***nᵉʿûriym, nᵉʿûrôṯ*** [נְעוּרִים, נְעוּרוֹת <5271>; properly, pass. part. from BOY <5288> as denom.] ▶

a. A masculine plural abstract noun. It refers to the early stages and years of a person's life and the experiences and characteristics of that time. Every person, all humankind experiences this time of life (Gen. 8:21). It is a time when skills are best learned (Gen. 46:34); a time of dependence on parents (Lev. 22:13; Num. 30:3, 16). Even a nation has a time of youth (Hos. 2:15). A husband is to be satisfied with the wife of his youth (Prov. 5:18; Mal. 2:14, 15). *

b. A feminine plural abstract noun. It is used to refer to the early period or stage of a person's life, the early years and its experiences and characteristics. It is used of a nation's youth, its early formative years (Jer. 32:30). ¶

4 ***nōʿar*** [masc. noun: נֹעַר <5290>; from SHAKE <5287> (comp. BOY <5288>)] ▶ **This word refers to childhood; it is also translated by the adjective youthful.** It is considered a time when life is exciting, and a person is energetic and healthy (Job 33:25); and it is not a time to die (Job 36:14; Ps. 88:15). It is a time when intimate and healthy relationships can begin to be formed (Prov. 29:21). ¶

5 ***ᵃlûmiym*** [masc. plur. noun: עֲלוּמִים <5934>; pass. part. of HIDE <5956> in the denom. sense of YOUNG MAN <5958>] ▶ **This word refers to the early years of a person's life, unencumbered by old age and illnesses.** It is used in a positive way of youth as a time of health and vigor (Job 20:11; 33:25; Ps. 89:45). But it also depicts youth as a time of indiscretions, of doing shameful things, as Israel did as a people (Is. 54:4). ¶

6 ***ṣᵉʿiyrāh*** [fem. noun: צְעִירָה <6812>; fem. of YOUNG <6810>] ▶ **This word has the meaning of chronological age; in context it is used to rank persons.** Ref.: Gen. 43:33. ¶

7 ***šaḥᵃrûṯ*** [fem. noun: שַׁחֲרוּת <7839>; from SEEK DILIGENTLY <7833> (in the sense of to dawn)] ▶ **This word refers to the most healthy and vigorous period of a person's life; it is also translated prime of life, dawn of life, vigor.** However, this time is fleeting (Eccl. 11:10). ¶

– 8 1 Sam. 17:56; 20:22 ➔ YOUNG MAN <5958> 9 Job 30:12 ➔ BROOD <6526>.

YOUTHFUL – 1 Job 20:11; 33:25 ➔ lit.: of the youth ➔ YOUTH <5934> 2 Job 33:25 ➔ YOUTH <5290>.

Z

ZAANAN – ***ṣa'ănan*** [proper noun: צַאֲנָן <6630>; from the same as SHEEP <6629> used denominatively]: sheep pasture ▶ **A town in Judah.** Ref.: Mic. 1:11. ¶

ZAANANNIM – ***ṣa^{a}nanniym*** [proper noun: צַעֲנַנִּים <6815>; plur. of FOLD (verb) <6813>]: removals, great migrations ▶ **A town in Naphtali near Kedesh.** Refs.: Josh. 19:33; Judg. 4:11. ¶

ZAAVAN – ***za^{a}wān*** [masc. proper noun: זַעֲוָן <2190>; from TREMBLE <2111>]: agitated ▶ **A son of Ezer the Horite.** Refs.: Gen. 36:27; 1 Chr. 1:42. ¶

ZABAD – ***zāḇāḏ*** [masc. proper noun: זָבָד <2066>; from ENDOW <2064>]: gift ▶
a. Son of Nathan, of the tribe of Judah. Refs.: 1 Chr. 2:36, 37. ¶
b. Son of Tahath, of the tribe of Ephraim. Ref.: 1 Chr. 7:21. ¶
c. Son of Ahlai, of the tribe of Judah. Ref.: 1 Chr. 11:41. ¶
d. Son of Shimeath (2 Chr. 24:26); the same as Jozachar. Ref.: 2 Kgs. 12:21. ¶
e. Son of Zattu, who had married a foreign woman. Ref.: Ezra 10:27. ¶
f. Son of Hashum, who had married a foreign woman. Ref.: Ezra 10:33. ¶
g. Son of Nebo, who had married a foreign woman. Ref.: Ezra 10:43. ¶

ZABBAI – ***zabbay*** [masc. proper noun: זַבַּי <2079>; prob. by orthographical error for ZACCAI <2140>]: pure ▶ **An Israelite who had married a foreign woman.** Ref.: Ezra 10:28. His son Baruch worked at rebuilding the wall (Neh. 3:20). ¶

ZABBUD – ***zabbûḏ*** [masc. proper noun: זַבּוּד <2072>; a form of ZABUD <2071>]: gift, given ▶ **An Israelite who came back from Babylon with Ezra.** Ref.: Ezra 8:14. ¶

ZABDI – ***zaḇdiy*** [masc. proper noun: זַבְדִּי <2067>; from GIFT <2065>]: gift, giving ▶
a. Grandfather of Achan, of the tribe of Judah. Refs.: Josh. 7:1, 17, 18; he is called Zimri in 1 Chr. 2:6. ¶
b. Son of Shimhi, of the tribe of Benjamin. Ref.: 1 Chr. 8:19. ¶
c. A Shiphmite who was in charge of the produce of the vineyards under David. Ref.: 1 Chr. 27:27. ¶
d. A Levite, son of Asaph. Ref.: Neh. 11:17. ¶

ZABDIEL – ***zaḇdiy'ēl*** [masc. proper noun: זַבְדִּיאֵל <2068>; from ZABDI <2065> and GOD <410>]: gift of God ▶
a. An Israelite, father of Jashobeam. Ref.: 1 Chr. 27:2. ¶
b. A priestly official. Ref.: Neh. 11:14. ¶

ZABUD – ***zāḇûḏ*** [masc. proper noun: זָבוּד <2071>; from ENDOW <2064>]: gift, given ▶ **Son of Nathan; he was a priest and King Solomon's friend.** Ref.: 1 Kgs. 4:5. ¶

ZACCAI – ***zakkay*** [masc. proper noun: זַכַּי <2140>; from PURE (BE) <2141>]: pure, innocent ▶ **Members of his family came back from Babylon with Zerubbabel.** Refs.: Ezra 2:9; Neh. 7:14. Compare ZABBAI <2079>. ¶

ZACCUR – ***zakkûr*** [masc. proper noun: זַכּוּר <2139>; from REMEMBER <2142>]: who remembers, mindful ▶
a. The father of Shammuah. Ref.: Num. 13:4. ¶
b. Son of Hamuel. Ref.: 1 Chr. 4:26. ¶
c. A Merarite. Ref.: 1 Chr. 24:27. ¶
d. Son of Asaph. Refs.: 1 Chr. 25:2, 10; Neh. 12:35. ¶
e. Son of Imri. Ref.: Neh. 3:2. ¶
f. A Levite who signed the covenant of renewal with Nehemiah after the return from the Babylonian captivity. Ref.: Neh. 10:12. ¶
g. Ancestor of Hanan. Ref.: Neh. 13:13. ¶
h. A Simeonite. Ref.: Ezra 8:14. ¶

ZACHER – 1 Chr. 8:31 ➔ ZECHER, ZEKER <2144>.

ZADOK – *ṣāḏôq* [masc. proper noun: צָדוֹק <6659>; from JUST (BE) <6663>]: righteous ▶
a. He was one of the priests in David's day who served along with Abiathar. Ref.: 2 Sam. 8:17. He was the son of Ahitub (1 Chr. 6:8, 53). He helped care for the ark. He, instead of Abiathar, supported Solomon, David's choice as king before David's death (1 Kgs. 1:7 45; 2:35). His descendants, therefore, were favored to serve in the Temple until its destruction (1 Kgs. 4:2; 586 B.C.) and even after (Ezra 7:2). His line replaced the rejected priestly line of Eli (1 Sam. 2:25–36). Ezekiel placed him and his descendants in charge of the Temple in his vision (Ezek. 40:46, etc.).
b. A Levite who supported David at Hebron when David became king. Ref.: 1 Chr. 12:28. (See a. also)
c. A descendant of Zadok (see a. above). He had a son Shallum (1 Chr. 6:12).
d. The son of Meraioth and father of Meshullam. His grandfather Ahitub had been in charge of the Temple (1 Chr. 9:11).
e. The grandfather of King Jotham. His mother's name was Jerusha (2 Chr. 27:1).
f. He served as a scribe under Nehemiah and was over the treasuries in the second Temple. Ref.: Neh. 13:13.
g. He supported Nehemiah and his covenant of renewal for the returned exiles. Ref.: Neh. 10:21.
h. The son of Baana. He helped repair a section of the wall of Jerusalem. Ref.: Neh. 3:4.
i. The son of Immer. He repaired the wall in front of his own house. Ref.: Neh. 3:29. *

ZAHAB – Num. 21:14 ➔ WAHEB <2052>.

ZAHAM – *zaham* [masc. proper noun: זַהַם <2093>; from ABHOR <2092>]: loathing ▶ **One of the sons of Rehoboam.** Ref.: 2 Chr. 11:19. ¶

ZAHAR – Ezek. 27:18 ➔ WHITE <6713> b.

ZAIR – *ṣā'iyrāh* [proper noun: צָעִירָה <6811>; the same as YOUNG <6810>]: young, little ▶ **A place in Edom.** Ref.: 2 Kgs. 8:21. ¶

ZALAPH – *ṣālāp̱* [proper noun: צָלָף <6764>; from an unused root of unknown meaning] ▶ **Father of Hanun who participated in the rebuilding of the wall of Jerusalem.** Ref.: Neh. 3:30. ¶

ZALMMUNNA – *ṣalmunnā'* [masc. proper noun: צַלְמֻנָּע <6759>; from SHADOW <6738> and HOLD, WITHHOLD <4513>]: deprived of shade ▶ **A Midianite king killed by Gideon.** Refs.: Judg. 8:5–7, 10, 12, 15, 18, 21; Ps. 83:11. ¶

ZALMON – *ṣalmôn* [proper noun: צַלְמוֹן <6756>; from IMAGE <6754>]: shady ▶
a. A wooded place near Shechem. Refs.: Judg. 9:48; Ps. 68:14. ¶
b. One of David's warriors. Ref.: 2 Sam. 23:28. ¶

ZALMONAH – *ṣalmōnāh* [proper noun: צַלְמֹנָה <6758>; fem. of SHADOW OF DEATH <6757>]: shadiness ▶ **A campsite of the Israelites in the wilderness on their way to the Promised Land.** Refs.: Num. 33:41, 42. ¶

ZAMSUMMITE, ZAMZUMMIM – *zamzummiym* [proper noun: זַמְזֻמִּים <2157>; from CONSIDER <2161>] ▶ **Name given by the Ammonites to a tribe of the land of Rephaim.** Ref.: Deut. 2:20. ¶

ZANOAH – *zānôaḥ* [proper noun: זָנוֹחַ <2182>; from REJECT <2186>]: rejected ▶
a. A city in Judah near En-gannim. Refs.: Josh. 15:34; 1 Chr. 4:18; Neh. 3:13; 11:30. ¶
b. A city in Judah near Juttah. Ref.: Josh. 15:56. ¶

ZAPHENATH-PANEAH – *ṣāp̱naṯ pa'nêaḥ* [masc. proper noun: צָפְנַת פַּעְנֵחַ <6847>; of Egyptian deriv.]: this living is the provision for the country ▶ **A name (rich in meaning but still enigmatic to us) given to Joseph by the Egyptian Pharaoh. Numerous suggestions have**

been put forth as to the meaning of this name. Ref.: Gen. 41:45. ¶

ZAPHON – ***ṣāp̱ôn*** [proper noun: צָפוֹן <6829>; the same as NORTH <6828>]; boreal, hidden ▶ **A city in Gad on the east bank of the Jordan River.** Refs.: Josh. 13:27; Judg. 12:1; Ps. 48:2. The occurrences in Judges 12:1 and Psalm 48:2 are interpreted in some versions as the noun meaning north, northward (<6828>), which is spelled the same in Hebrew. ¶

ZAREAH – See ZORAH <6881>.

ZARED – See ZERED <2218>.

ZAREPHATH – ***ṣārᵉpaṯ*** [proper noun: צָרְפַת <6886>; from REFINE <6884>]: refinement ▶ **God sent Elijah to that place, a Phoenician city south of Sidon.** Refs.: 1 Kgs. 17:9, 10; Obad. 1:20. ¶

ZARETHAN, ZARETAN – ***ṣārᵉṯān*** [proper noun: צָרְתָן <6891>; perhaps rom ZEREDA <6868>] ▶ **A place in the Jordan valley.** Refs.: Josh. 3:16; 1 Kgs. 4:12; 7:46; 2 Chr. 4:17. ¶

ZARHITE – ***zarḥiy*** [masc. proper noun: זַרְחִי <2227>; patron. from ZERAH <2226>]: see ZERAH ▶
a. Descendant of Zerah, son of Judah (ZERAH <2226> c.). Refs.: Num. 26:20; Josh. 7:17; 1 Chr. 27:11, 13. ¶
b. Descendant of Zerah, son of Simeon (ZERAH <2226> d.). Ref.: Num. 26:13. ¶

ZATTU – ***zattû'*** [masc. proper noun: זַתּוּא <2240>; of uncertain deriv.] ▶ **Members of his family came back from the Babylonian captivity.** Refs.: Ezra 2:8; 10:27; Neh. 7:13; 10:14. ¶

ZAZA – ***zāzā'*** [masc. proper noun: זָזָא <2117>; prob. from the root of ABUNDANCE <2123>]: fullness ▶ **An Israelite of the tribe of Judah.** Ref.: 1 Chr. 2:33. ¶

ZEAL – 2 Kgs. 19:31; Is. 9:7; 37:32; etc. → JEALOUSY <7068>.

ZEAL (WITH) – Ezra 7:23 → DILIGENTLY <149>.

ZEBADIAH – ***zᵉḇaḏyāh, zᵉbaḏyāhû*** [masc. proper noun: זְבַדְיָה, זְבַדְיָהוּ <2069>; from ENDOW <2064> and LORD <3050>]: the Lord has given ▶
a. Grandson of Elpaal, of the tribe of Benjamin. Ref.: 1 Chr. 8:15. ¶
b. Son of Elpaal, of the tribe of Benjamin. Ref.: 1 Chr. 8:17. ¶
c. Son of Jeroham; he came to David at Ziklag. Ref.: 1 Chr. 12:7. ¶
d. A Korahite. Ref.: 1 Chr. 26:2. ¶
e. Son of Asahel, the brother of Joab. Ref.: 1 Chr. 27:7. ¶
f. A Levite sent by Jehoshaphat to teach the Law. Ref.: 2 Chr. 17:8. ¶
g. A ruler of the tribe of Judah; he was established by Jehoshaphat to deal with judicial matters. Ref.: 2 Chr. 19:11. ¶
h. Son of Shephatiah; he came back with Ezra from Babylon. Ref.: Ezra 8:8. ¶
i. A priest who had married a foreign woman. Ref.: Ezra 10:20. ¶

ZEBAH – ***zeḇaḥ*** [masc. proper noun: זֶבַח <2078>; the same as SACRIFICE (noun) <2077>]: sacrifice ▶ **One of two princes of Midian pursued and killed by Gideon.** Refs.: Judg. 8:5–7, 10, 12, 15, 18, 21; Ps. 83:11. ¶

ZEBIDAH – ***zᵉḇiyḏāh*** [fem. proper noun: זְבִידָה <2080>; fem. from ENDOW <2064>]: given ▶ **The mother of King Jehoiakim.** Ref.: 2 Kgs. 23:36; also spelled Zebudah. ¶

ZEBINA – ***zᵉḇiyna'*** [masc. proper noun: זְבִינָא <2081>; from an unused root (meaning to purchase)]: acquired ▶ **An Israelite who had married a foreign woman.** Ref.: Ezra 10:43. ¶

ZEBOIIM – ***ṣᵉḇō'iym, ṣᵉḇōyiym*** [proper noun: צְבֹאִים, צְבֹיִים <6636>; plur. of GLORY <6643> (which also means gazelle)]: gazelles ▶ **This word designates a city on the southeast edge of Canaan.** Ref.: Gen. 10:19. It is mentioned among the five cities of the plain (Gen. 14:2, 8; Deut. 29:23). Based on Hosea 11:8, it perished with Sodom and Gomorrah. ¶

ZEBOIM – ***ṣᵉḇōʻiym*** [proper noun: צְבֹעִים <6650>; plur. of SPECKLED <6641>]: multicolored, gazelles ▶ **A valley in Benjamin and a city occupied by the Benjamites after their return from the Babylonian captivity.** Refs.: 1 Sam. 13:18; Neh. 11:34. ¶

ZEBOYIM – See ZEBOIIM <6636>.

ZEBUDAH – 2 Kgs. 23:36 ➔ ZEBIDAH <2080>.

ZEBUL – ***zᵉḇul*** [masc. proper noun: זְבֻל <2083>; the same as HABITATION <2073>]: dwelling ▶ **An officer of Shechem at the time of Abimelech.** Refs.: Judg. 9:28, 30, 36, 38, 41. ¶

ZEBULUN – ***zᵉḇûlûn, zᵉḇûlun, zᵉḇulûn*** [masc. proper noun: זְבֻלוּן, זְבוּלֻן, זְבוּלוּן <2074>; from DWELL <2082>]: dwelling ▶
a. The sixth son of Jacob. His mother was Leah (Gen. 35:23). He and his sons went to Egypt (Gen. 46:14). He lived near the shore of the Mediterranean and had some access to the sea (Gen. 49:13), evidently Galilee. Other refs.: Gen. 30:20; Ex. 1:3; 1 Chr. 2:1. ¶
b. The name of the tribe and territory of Zebulun. The territory, in lower Galilee, was bounded on the east by Asher, on the north and south by Issachar and Naphtali, on the southeast by Issachar, and on the southwest by Manasseh. It was located near major trade routes through the Jezreel Valley to the south (Josh. 19:10–16; Judg. 1:30). The tribe failed to drive out some Canaanites from a few cities. This tribe showed itself valiant for the Lord in various battles (Judg. 4:6, 10; 5:14, 18; 6:35; 1 Chr. 12:33, 40). Its population was conquered and deported by the Assyrians (722 B.C.). Ezekiel's new Temple vision reserves a place for this tribe (Ezek. 48:26, 27, 33). *

ZEBULUNITE – ***zᵉḇûlōniy*** [masc. proper noun: זְבוּלֹנִי <2075>; patron. from ZEBULUN <2074>] ▶ **A person belonging to the tribe of Zebulun or living on its territory.** Refs.: Num. 26:27; Judg. 12:11, 12. ¶

ZECHARIAH – ***zᵉḵaryāh, zᵉḵaryāhû*** [masc. proper noun: זְכַרְיָה, זְכַרְיָהוּ <2148>; from REMEMBER <2142> and LORD <3050>]: the Lord remembers ▶ **About thirty men in the Old Testament are named Zechariah. Little more than their name is known about some of them.**
a. The best known is Zechariah who prophesied during the time of Zerubbabel, the postexilic period. His message encouraged the Israelites to rebuild the Temple and to dedicate themselves wholly to the Lord. Then the days of "small things" would blossom by the power of God's Spirit. His father was Berekiah, son of Iddo (Zech. 1:1, 7). He came from Babylon with the exiles to Jerusalem (538 B.C.) under Zerubbabel. His contemporary was Haggai (Ezra 5:1).
b. It refers to a descendant of Reuben. Ref.: 1 Chr. 5:6, 7.
c. He was son of Meshelemiah and served as the gatekeeper at the Tent of Meeting. He was a wise counselor (1 Chr. 9:21).
d. He came from the line of Saul. Jeiel was his father who came from Gibeon (1 Chr. 9:35–37).
e. The name of Levite who served in the worship at the Temple, even before the ark. Ref.: 1 Chr. 16:5.
f. He served as a trumpet blower before the ark of God. Ref.: 1 Chr. 15:24.
g. The son of Isshiah and grandson of Micah. Ref.: 1 Chr. 24:25.
h. A son of Horah a Merarite and a gatekeeper. Refs.: 1 Chr. 26:10, 11.
i. The father of Iddo, an officer over the half-tribe of Manasseh. Ref.: 1 Chr. 27:21.
j. An official responsible to teach the Law of the Lord in Judah. Ref.: 2 Chr. 17:7.
k. He was the father of a prophet, Jahaziel, who prophesied to Jehoshaphat. Ref.: 2 Chr. 20:14.
l. The son of Jehoshaphat and the brother of Jehoram who became king in Judah. Ref.: 2 Chr. 21:2.
m. A prophet, son of Jehoiada the priest who prophesied to Joash and a wicked people. Ref.: 2 Chr. 24:20.

n. A prophet who counseled and taught King Uzziah. Ref.: 2 Chr. 26:5.
o. A son of Jeroboam II who succeeded to the kingship. He reigned six months (753 B.C.). He was assassinated by Shallum who took his place (752 B.C.) (2 Kgs. 15:8–10).
p. The father of Abi (Abijah) the mother of Hezekiah. Ref.: 2 Chr. 29:1.
q. A Levite, a descendant of Asaph, who helped restore the Temple under Hezekiah. Ref.: 2 Chr. 29:13.
r. A man asked by Isaiah to serve as one of two witnesses for him. Ref.: Is. 8:2.
s. A descendant of Kohath who directed repairs on the Temple. Ref.: 2 Chr. 34:12.
t. An administrator of worship at the Temple. Ref.: 2 Chr. 35:8.
u. One of the returnees from exile under Zerubbabel and a family head; same as a. Ref.: Ezra 5:1.
v. A descendant of Bebai and a family head. Ref.: Ezra 8:11.
w. A leader who helped Ezra gather persons to serve at the Temple; same as a. Ref.: Ezra 6:14.
x. A descendant of Elam who intermarried with people of the land. Ref.: Ezra 10:26.
y. A Levite present when Ezra read the Law at the Water Gate. Ref.: Neh. 8:4.
z. A new resident in Jerusalem after returning from exile and from the tribe of Judah. He was the father of Uzziah, son of Amariah, a descendant of Perez (Neh. 11:4).
aa. The father of Joiarib. He was descended from Shelah, a descendant of Perez (Neh. 11:5).
bb. A new priestly resident in Jerusalem from the returned exiles, father of Amzi and son of Phashhur. Ref.: Neh. 11:12.
cc. A head of a priestly family from Iddo's family. Ref.: Neh. 12:16.
dd. A priest who took part in the dedication of the wall of Jerusalem in Nehemiah's day. Ref.: Neh. 12:35.
ee. Another priest who took part in the dedication of the wall of Jerusalem in Nehemiah's day. Ref.: Neh. 12:41.

ZECHER, ZEKER – ***zeḵer*** [masc. proper noun: זֶכֶר <2144>; the same as REMEMBRANCE <2143>]: remembrance, memorial ► **An Israelite of the tribe of Benjamin.** Ref.: 1 Chr. 8:31; also spelled Zacher. ¶

ZEDAD – ***ṣᵉḏāḏ*** [proper noun: צְדָד <6657>; from the same as SIDE <6654>]: siding ► **One of the landmarks of Israel's northern border.** Refs.: Num. 34:8; Ezek. 47:15. ¶

ZEDEKIAH – ***ṣiḏqiyyāh, ṣiḏqiyyāhû*** [masc. proper noun: צִדְקִיָּה, צִדְקִיָּהוּ <6667>; from RIGHTEOUSNESS <6664> and LORD <3050>]: the Lord is righteous or the Lord is my righteousness ►
a. One of the many false prophets under Ahab who always said what the king wanted to hear, a "state" prophet. Ref.: 1 Kgs. 22:11.
b. The last king of Judah. He reigned 597–586 B.C., eleven years. His original name was Mattaniah; Nebuchadnezzar changed it to Zedekiah. Refs.: 2 Kgs. 24:15–20. His nephew was the deported king, Jehoiachin. His mother's name was Hamutal, a daughter of Jeremiah. Since he followed the evil ways of Jehoiakim, the Lord destroyed him and his sons as they fled from the Babylonians at Riblah. The enemy put his eyes out and took him to Babylon in chains where he died (Jer. 52:1–11). He would not listen to the prophetic warning of Jeremiah to submit to Babylon, so he was taken into exile and executed (Jer. 34; 37:1, 2). He had shown some mercy toward Jeremiah (37:21; 38:7–16; 14–26) but wavered even in that.
c. A son of Maaseiah. He was a false prophet in Jeremiah's time. Refs.: Jer. 29:21, 22. Jeremiah condemned him and his message as well as predicting his death.
d. A son of Hananiah. Ref.: Jer. 36:12. A leader or prince in Judah who listened to the reading of Jeremiah's scroll (Jer. 36:12–21).
e. He supported and confirmed Nehemiah's covenant of renewal among the returned exiles. Ref.: Neh. 10:1. *

ZEEB – ***zᵉ'ēḇ*** [masc. proper noun: זְאֵב <2062>; the same as WOLF <2061>]: wolf ► **A prince of the Midianites.** Refs.: Judg. 7:25; 8:3; Ps. 83:11. ¶

ZELAH – ***ṣêla'*** [proper noun: צֵלַע <6762>; the same as STUMBLING <6761>]: limping

► **A city in Benjamin.** Refs.: Josh. 18:28; 2 Sam. 21:14. ¶

ZELEK – ***ṣeleq*** [masc. proper noun: צֶלֶק <6768>; from an unused root meaning to split]: fissure ► **An Ammonite, one of David's mighty men.** Refs.: 2 Sam. 23:37; 1 Chr. 11:39. ¶

ZELOPHEHAD – ***ṣ*^e*lāp*^e*ḥāḏ*** [masc. proper noun: צְלָפְחָד <6765>; from the same as ZALAPH <6764> and ONE <259>]: first-born ► **A descendant of Manasseh, son of Hepher. He had only daughters.** Refs.: Num. 26:33; 27:1, 7. His daughters argued convincingly that they should receive their father's inheritance (Num. 27:3–11), but to keep the inheritance within their father's clan, they had to marry within that clan (Num. 36:2–11). Each tribe was to keep its tribal inheritances permanently (Num. 36:7–9). The daughter married cousins on their father's side. This interesting case illustrates the "living nature" of the laws God gave to Israel. They were to be interpreted in such a way to (1) preserve their original intent and (2) to treat the persons involved fairly. Other refs.: Josh. 17:3; 1 Chr. 7:15. ¶

ZELZAH – ***ṣelṣaḥ*** [proper noun: צֶלְצַח <6766>; from SHADOW <6738> and DAZZLING <6703>]: clear shade ► **A place on the boundary of the tribe of Benjamin.** Ref.: 1 Sam. 10:2. ¶

ZEMARAIM – ***ṣ*^e*mārayim*** [proper noun: צְמָרַיִם <6787>; dual of WOOL <6785>]: double fleece ►

a. A city in Benjamin near Bethel. Ref.: Josh. 18:22. ¶

b. A hill in Ephraim. Ref.: 2 Chr. 13:4. ¶

ZEMARITE – ***ṣ*^e*māriy*** [proper noun: צְמָרִי <6786>; patrial from an unused name of a city in Canaan] ► **A Hamite tribe descended from Canaan.** Refs.: Gen. 10:18; 1 Chr. 1:16. ¶

ZENAN – ***ṣ*^e*nān*** [proper noun: צְנָן <6799>; prob. from ZAANAN <6630>]: places of flocks ► **A town belonging to the tribe of Judah.** Ref.: Josh. 15:37. ¶

ZEPHANIAH – ***ṣ*^e*p̱anyāh, ṣ*^e*p̱anyāhû*** [masc. proper noun: צְפַנְיָה, צְפַנְיָהוּ <6846>; from HIDE <6845> and LORD <3050>]: hidden by the Lord ►

a. The prophet who zealously proclaimed the Day of the Lord. He was the son of Cushi (Zeph. 1:1). He prophesied in ca. 630 B.C. and was contemporary with Jeremiah, Nahum, and Habakkuk, other prophets who were equally zealous and emotional at this critical time in Israel's history. He proclaimed judgment on Judah and the nations, but he also declared that God would preserve a remnant and Israel would rise again (Zeph. 3:14–20). ¶

b. The second-ranking priest in Jeremiah's day. He was taken captive at the fall of Jerusalem, moved to Riblah, and was put to death there (2 Kgs. 25:18). Jeremiah had warned him of this danger (Jer. 21:1; 29:24–32). Other refs.: Jer. 37:3; 52:24. ¶

c. An ancestor of Heman. Heman was a Kohathite who served as a musician in the Temple (1 Chr. 6:33–36). ¶

d. The father of Josiah. He carried out key instructions with others as directed by the prophet Zechariah concerning the crowning of Joshua son of Jehozadak (Zech. 6:9–15). ¶

ZEPHATH – ***ṣ*^e*p̱aṯ*** [proper noun: צְפַת <6857>; from WATCH (verb) <6822>]: watchtower ► **A city in Canaan taken by Judah and Simeon; it was destroyed and renamed Hormah.** Ref.: Judg. 1:17. ¶

ZEPHATHAH – ***ṣ*^e*p̱āṯāh*** [proper noun: צְפָתָה <6859>; the same as ZEPHATH <6857>]: watchtower ► **A valley in western Judah.** Ref.: 2 Chr. 14:10. ¶

ZEPHI – 1 Chr. 1:36 → ZEPHO <6825>.

ZEPHO – *ṣ*^e*p̱ô, ṣ*^e*p̱iy* [masc. proper noun: צְפוֹ, צְפִי <6825>; from WATCH (verb) <6822>]: watch ► **Grandson of Esau and an Edomite chief.** Refs.: Gen. 36:11, 15; 1 Chr. 1:36. ¶

ZEPHON – ***ṣᵉpôn*** [masc. proper noun: צְפוֹן <6827>; prob. from ZIPHON <6837>] ▶ **A son of Gad; the same as Ziphion (<6837>).** Ref.: Num. 26:15. ¶

ZEPHONITE – ***ṣᵉpôniy*** [proper noun: צְפוֹנִי <6831>; patron. from ZEPHON <6827>] ▶ **A descendant of Zephon.** Ref.: Num. 26:15. ¶

ZER – ***ṣêr*** [proper noun: צֵר <6863>]: flint, rock ▶ **A fortified town in Naphtali.** Ref.: Josh. 19:35. ¶

ZERAH – ***zeraḥ*** [masc. proper noun: זֶרַח <2226>; the same as RISING <2225>]: rising, sunrise ▶
a. Son of Reuel. Refs.: Gen. 36:13, 17; 1 Chr. 1:37. ¶
b. The father of Joab. Refs.: Gen. 36:33; 1 Chr. 1:44. ¶
c. Son of Judah. Refs.: Gen. 38:30; 46:12; Num. 26:20; Josh. 7:1, 18, 24; 22:20; 1 Chr. 2:4, 6; 9:6; Neh. 11:24. ¶
d. Son of Simeon, the same as *ṣōhar* (ZOHAR <6714> b.). Refs.: Num. 26:13; 1 Chr. 4:24. ¶
e. A Gershonite. Ref.: 1 Chr. 6:21. ¶
f. The father of Ethni. Ref.: 1 Chr. 6:41. ¶
g. King of Ethiopia. Ref.: 2 Chr. 14:9. ¶

ZERAHIAH – ***zᵉraḥyāh*** [masc. proper noun: זְרַחְיָה <2228>; from RISING <2225> and LORD <3050>]: the Lord has risen ▶
a. A priest. Refs.: 1 Chr. 6:6, 51; Ezra 7:4. ¶
b. Head of a family. Ref.: Ezra 8:4. ¶

ZERED – ***zereḏ*** [proper noun: זֶרֶד <2218>; from an unused root meaning to be exuberant in growth]: exuberant ▶ **A brook east of the Dead Sea crossed by the Israelites at the end of their 38 years spent in the wilderness.** Refs.: Num. 21:12; Deut. 2:13, 14. ¶

ZEREDA – ***ṣᵉrêḏāh, ṣᵉrêḏaṯah*** [proper noun: צְרֵדָה, צְרֵדָתָה <6868>; apparently from an unused root meaning to pierce]: puncture ▶
a. The place where Jeroboam was born. Ref.: 1 Kgs. 11:26. ¶
b. A place in the plain of Jordan. Ref.: 2 Chr. 4:17. ¶

ZERERAH – ***ṣᵉrêrāh*** [proper noun: צְרֵרָה <6888>; apparently by erroneous transcription for ZEREDA <6868>] ▶ **A place in Manasseh.** Ref.: Judg. 7:22. ¶

ZERESH – ***zereš*** [fem. proper noun: זֶרֶשׁ <2238>; of Persian origin]: gold, star of worship ▶ **The wife of Haman.** Refs.: Esther 5:10, 14; 6:13. ¶

ZERETH – ***ṣereṯ*** [masc. proper noun: צֶרֶת <6889>; perhaps from OIL <6671> (in the sense of to glisten)]: splendor ▶ **An Israelite of the tribe of Judah.** Ref.: 1 Chr. 4:7. ¶

ZERETH SHAHAR – ***ṣereṯ haššaḥar*** [proper noun: צֶרֶת הַשַּׁחַר <6890>; from the same as ZERETH <6889> and DAWN <7837>]: splendor of the dawn ▶ **A town in Reuben.** Ref.: Josh. 13:19. ¶

ZERI – 1 ***ṣᵉriy*** [masc. proper noun: צְרִי <6874>; the same as BALM <6875>]: distillation ▶ **Son of Jeduthun who gave thanks and praised the Lord with his brothers.** Ref.: 1 Chr. 25:3. ¶
– 2 1 Chr. 25:3 ➔ IZRI <3339>.

ZEROR – 1 Sam. 9:1 ➔ BAG <6872> c.

ZERUAH – ***ṣᵉrû'āh*** [fem. proper noun: צְרוּעָה <6871>; fem. pass. part. of LEPER (BE A) <6879>]: leprous ▶ **The mother of Jeroboam, the first king of the northern kingdom of Israel.** Ref.: 1 Kgs. 11:26. ¶

ZERUBBABEL – 1 ***zᵉrubbāḇel*** [masc. proper noun: זְרֻבָּבֶל <2216>; from WARM (BE) <2215> and BABEL <894>]: born in Babylon ▶ **One of the leaders who led the exiles back from Babylonian captivity.** Refs.: Ezra 2:2; Neh. 7:7; 12:1. He was the son of Shealtiel (Ezra 3:2). He helped organize the returned group as their civil leader, as well as helping rebuild the altar (Ezra 3:8; 4:2, 3). He received prophetic messages from Haggai the prophet (Hag. 1:1, 12) and from Zechariah (Zech. 4:6–10). He was of the line of David and evidently could have become king if Israel had obeyed the Lord's instructions (Hag. 2:21–23). *

2 ***zᵉrubbāḇel*** [Aramaic masc. proper noun: זְרֻבָּבֶל <2217>; corresponding to <2216> above]: born in Babylon ▶ **This name is found in Ezra 5:2 and corresponds to entry <2216> above.** ¶

ZERUIAH – ***ṣᵉrûyāh*** [fem. proper noun: צְרוּיָה <6870>; fem. pass. part. from the same as BALM <6875>]: balsam ▶ **Sister of David and mother of three of his strong men.** Refs.: 1 Sam. 26:6; 2 Sam. 2:13, 18; 3:39; 8:16; 14:1; 16:9, 10; 17:25; 18:2; 19:21, 22; 21:17; 23:18, 37; 1 Kgs. 1:7; 2:5, 22; 1 Chr. 2:16; 11:6, 39; 18:12, 15; 26:28; 27:24. ¶

ZETHAM – ***zêṯām*** [masc. proper noun: זֵתָם <2241>; apparently a variation for ZETHAN <2133>]: olive tree ▶ **An Israelite of the tribe of Levi.** Refs.: 1 Chr. 23:8; 26:22. ¶

ZETHAN – ***zêyṯān*** [masc. proper noun: זֵיתָן <2133>; from OLIVE, OLIVE TREE <2132>]: olive tree ▶ **An Israelite of the tribe of Benjamin.** Ref.: 1 Chr. 7:10. ¶

ZETHAR – ***zêṯar*** [masc. proper noun: זֵתַר <2242>; of Persian origin] ▶ **One of the seven eunuchs who served in the presence of King Ahasuerus.** Ref.: Esther 1:10. ¶

ZIA – ***ziya‘*** [masc. proper noun: זִיעַ <2127>; from TREMBLE <2111>]: fear, agitation ▶ **An Israelite of the tribe of Gad.** Ref.: 1 Chr. 5:13. ¶

ZIBA – ***ṣiyḇā’*** [masc. proper noun: צִיבָא <6717>; from the same as ZOBAH <6678>]: station ▶ **He was a servant in Saul's house.** He informed David about Saul's remaining family members (2 Sam. 9:2–4). He was cared for by David and Ziba and his servants cared for Saul's grandson Mephibosheth (2 Sam. 9:9–13). He had been faithful to David, but when Ziba claimed that Mephibosheth wavered in his loyalty to David, David gave Ziba all of Mephibosheth's wealth (2 Sam. 19:15–18). Later, David discovered that Ziba had slandered Mephibosheth. David then divided the wealth between the two men (2 Sam. 19:24–30). Other refs.: 2 Sam. 16:1–4. ¶

ZIBEON – ***ṣiḇ‘ôn*** [masc. proper noun: צִבְעוֹן <6649>; from the same as DYED WORK, DYED MATERIALS <6648>]: multicolored ▶ **Grandfather of Aholibamah, a wife of Esau.** Refs.: Gen. 36:2, 14, 20, 24, 29; 1 Chr. 1:38, 40. He was possibly the son of Seir the Horite. ¶

ZIBIA – ***ṣiḇyā’*** [masc. proper noun: צִבְיָא <6644>; from ZIBIAH <6645>]: gazelle ▶ **An Israelite of the tribe of Benjamin.** Ref.: 1 Chr. 8:9. ¶

ZIBIAH – ***ṣiḇyāh*** [fem. proper noun: צִבְיָה <6645>; from GAZELLE <6646>]: gazelle ▶ **Mother of King Joash of Judah.** Refs.: 2 Kgs. 12:1; 2 Chr. 24:1. ¶

ZICHRI, ZICRI – ***ziḵriy*** [masc. proper noun: זִכְרִי <2147>; from REMEMBER <2142>]: memorable, remembered ▶
a. A Levite, son of Izhar. Ref.: Ex. 6:21. ¶
b. A Benjamite, son of Shimei. Ref.: 1 Chr. 8:19. ¶
c. A Benjamite, son of Shashak. Ref.: 1 Chr. 8:23. ¶
d. A Benjamite, son of Jeroham. Ref.: 1 Chr. 8:27. ¶
e. A Levite, son of Asaph. Ref.: 1 Chr. 9:15. ¶
f. A Levite, descendant of Eliezer, the son of Moses. Ref.: 1 Chr. 26:25. ¶
g. A Reubenite, father of Eliezer. Ref.: 1 Chr. 27:16. ¶
h. A man of Judah, the father of Amasiah. Ref.: 2 Chr. 17:16. ¶
i. The father of Elishaphat. Ref.: 2 Chr. 23:1. ¶
j. An Ephramite. Ref.: 2 Chr. 28:7. ¶
k. An Israelite of the tribe of Benjamin. Ref.: Neh. 11:9. ¶
l. A priest. Ref.: Neh. 12:17. ¶

ZIDDIM – ***ṣiddiym*** [proper noun: צִדִּים <6661>; plur. of SIDE <6654>]: sides ▶ **A fortified town in Naphtali.** Ref.: Josh. 19:35. ¶

ZIHA – ***ṣiyḥā'*** [masc. proper noun: צִיחָא <6727>; as if fem. of PARCHED <6704>]: drought ▶
a. An ancestor of a family of Temple slaves. Refs.: Ezra 2:43; Neh. 7:46. ¶
b. An overseer of Temple slaves, possibly the same as a. above. Ref.: Neh. 11:21. ¶

ZIKLAG – ***ṣiyqlag*** [proper noun: צִיקְלַג <6860>; of uncertain deriv.] ▶ **A southern town in the Negev given to Judah and to Simeon.** Refs.: Josh. 15:20–31; 19:5. David, as a fugitive from Saul, stayed in this town for some time (1 Sam. 27:6; 30:1–26). Some Jews returning from exile settled here (Neh. 11:28). *

ZILLAH – ***ṣillāh*** [fem. proper noun: צִלָּה <6741>; fem. of SHADOW <6738>]: shade ▶ **Second wife of Lamech and mother of Tubal-cain.** Refs.: Gen. 4:19, 22, 23. ¶

ZILLETHAI – ***ṣillᵉṯay*** [masc. proper noun: צִלְּתַי <6769>; from the fem. of SHADOW <6738>]: shady ▶
a. An Israelite of the tribe of Benjamin. Ref.: 1 Chr. 8:20. ¶
b. One of David's mighty men. Ref.: 1 Chr. 12:20. ¶

ZILPAH – ***zilpāh*** [fem. proper noun: זִלְפָּה <2153>; from an unused root apparently meaning to trickle, as myrrh]: distillation, drooping ▶ **She was the servant of Laban whom he gave to Leah to be her handmaid or maidservant.** Ref.: Gen. 29:24. She bore Jacob Gad and Asher (Gen. 35:26) who were in turn fruitful vines in Israel (Gen. 46:18). Other refs.: Gen. 30:9, 10, 12; 37:2. ¶

ZILTHAI – 1 Chr. 8:20; 12:20 ➔ ZILLETHAI <6769>.

ZIMIRAH, ZEMIRA – ***zᵉmiyrah*** [masc. proper noun: זְמִירָה <2160>; fem. of SONG <2158>]: song ▶ **An Israelite of the tribe of Benjamin.** Ref.: 1 Chr. 7:8. ¶

ZIMMAH – ***zimmāh*** [masc. proper noun: זִמָּה <2155>; the same as PLAN (noun) <2154>]: plan, thought ▶
a. Son of Janath. Ref.: 1 Chr. 6:20. ¶
b. A Gershomite. Ref.: 1 Chr. 6:42. ¶
c. The father of Joah. Ref.: 2 Chr. 29:12. ¶

ZIMRAN – ***zimrān*** [masc. proper noun: זִמְרָן <2175>; from SING <2167>]: musical, musician ▶ **A son of Abraham by Keturah.** Refs.: Gen. 25:2; 1 Chr. 1:32. ¶

ZIMRI – ***zimriy*** [proper noun: זִמְרִי <2174>; from SING <2167>]: music, song ▶
a. A man from the tribe of Simeon who arrogantly brought a Midianite woman into his tent. His father was Salu, a Simeonite leader. Phinehas put him to death (Num. 25:14). ¶
b. A grandson of Judah, a descendant of Hezron, son of Zerah. Ref.: 1 Chr. 2:6. ¶
c. A king of Israel (1 Kgs. 16:9–20) who reigned 876 B.C. for only one week in Tirzah. He assassinated Elah, the king of Israel, and eradicated the family of Baasha (1 Kgs. 16:11, 12). He later burned himself and his palace. His name is used to indicate an "assassin" by Jezebel (2 Kgs. 9:31). ¶
d. One of Saul's descendants whose father was Jehoaddah. Ref.: 1 Chr. 8:36. He was the father of Moza (1 Chr. 9:42). ¶
e. The name of a land or nation with rulers, kings. Its location is not known (Jer. 25:25). ¶

ZIN – ***ṣin*** [proper noun: צִן <6790>; from an unused root meaning to prick] ▶ **This word designates the Desert or Wilderness of Zin. It was the territory just north of Kadesh Barnea and south of the Negev, about one-half of the way between the coastal plains and the Arabale (the Rift Valley).** Its northern boundary was part of the southern boundary of Canaan (Num. 34:3, 4) and Judah (Josh. 15:1–3). The twelve spies went out from here (Num. 13:21), and they traveled all the way to Rehob north of Israel, just beyond Dan. *

ZINA – ***ziynā'*** [masc. proper noun: זִינָא <2126>; from WELL-FED <2109>]: well-fed ▶ **Same person as ZIZAH <2125>.** Ref.: 1 Chr. 23:10. ¶

ZION – ***ṣiyyôn*** [proper noun: צִיּוֹן <6726>; the same (regularly) as MONUMENT <6725>] ▶ **The meaning of the word is most likely "fortress," and the word refers to (1) the city of Jerusalem, the City of David (2 Sam. 5:7); (2) the Temple Mount or Temple (Ps. 9:11); or (3) to the area or cities of larger Judah (Ps. 69:35).** It was God's chosen location for His people. It was recognized ideally to be none other than a reference on earth to "the city of our God, His holy mountain" (Ps. 48:2, NASB), the city and country that God would show to Abraham and his descendants (Gen. 12:1). The word occurs most often in poetic/prophetic literature, only ca. seven times in historical prose. It occurs most often in Psalms, Isaiah, Jeremiah, Lamentations (a small book, but the word occurs 15 times in this poetic material lamenting the fall of Jerusalem in 586 B.C.), Micah, and Zechariah. *

ZIOR – ***ṣiy'ōr*** [proper noun: צִיעֹר <6730>; from BRING LOW <6819>]: smallness ▶ **A town in the mountains of Judah.** Ref.: Josh. 15:54. ¶

ZIPH – ***ziyp*** [proper noun: זִיף <2128>; from the same as PITCH <2203>]: flowing ▶
a. A city located in southern Judah near the border of Edom. Ref.: Josh. 15:24. The area around it was desert (1 Sam. 23:14). David fled there (1 Sam. 26:2). Other refs.: 1 Sam. 23:15, 24; 2 Chr. 11:8. ¶
b. A city in the hill country of Judah, possibly south of Jerusalem. Ref.: Josh. 15:55. ¶
c. A son of Jehallelel (Jehaleleel). He had three brothers and was a descendant of Judah (1 Chr. 4:16). ¶
d. A descendant of Caleb. His father was Mesha. His son was Mareshah (1 Chr. 3:42). ¶

ZIPHAH – ***ziypāh*** [masc. proper noun: זִיפָה <2129>; fem. of ZIPH <2128>] ▶ **An Israelite of the tribe of Judah.** Ref.: 1 Chr. 4:16. ¶

ZIPHITE – ***ziypiy*** [masc. proper noun: זִיפִי <2130>; patrial from ZIPH <2128>] ▶ **An inhabitant of Ziph or someone who is a native of this city.** Refs.: 1 Sam. 23:19; 26:1; Ps. 54:1. ¶

ZIPHON – ***ṣipyôn*** [masc. proper noun: צִפְיוֹן <6837>; from WATCH (verb) <6822>] ▶ **A son of Gad; the same as Zephon (<6827>).** Ref.: Gen. 46:16. ¶

ZIPHRON – ***ziprōn*** [proper noun: זִפְרֹן <2202>; from an unused root (meaning to be fragrant)]: perfume, sweet odor ▶ **A place of the northern border of the Promised Land.** Ref.: Num. 34:9. ¶

ZIPPOR – ***ṣippôr*** [masc. proper noun: צִפּוֹר <6834>; the same as BIRD <6833>]: small bird ▶ **Father of Balak the Moabite king.** Refs.: Num. 22:2, 4, 10, 16; 23:18; Josh. 24:9; Judg. 11:25. ¶

ZIPPORAH – ***ṣippōrāh*** [fem. proper noun: צִפֹּרָה <6855>; fem. of BIRD <6833>]: bird ▶ **The Midianite priest Jethro (Reuel) gave his daughter Zipporah to Moses as a wife.** Ref.: Ex. 2:21. She bore Moses' two sons, Gershom and Eliezer (Ex. 18:2–4). Other ref.: Ex. 4:25). ¶

ZITHRI – See SITHRI <5644>.

ZIV, ZIT – ***ziw*** [masc. proper noun: זִו <2099>; prob. from an unused root meaning to be prominent] ▶ **This word designates the second month in Israel's calendar year in Canaan.** Equal to our April-May (1 Kgs. 6:1, 37), it was the time of barley harvest when the dry season began. ¶

ZIZ – ***ṣiyṣ*** [proper noun: צִיץ <6732>; the same as FLOWER <6731>]: flower ▶ **A pass between the Dead Sea and the wilderness of Judah.** Ref.: 2 Chr. 20:16. ¶

ZIZA – ***ziyzā'*** [masc. proper noun: זִיזָא <2124>; apparently from the same as ABUNDANCE <2123>]: abundance, shining ▶
a. An Israelite of the tribe of Simeon. Ref.: 1 Chr. 4:37. ¶
b. A son of Rehoboam and Maacah. Ref.: 2 Chr. 11:20. ¶

ZIZAH – ***ziyzāh*** [masc. proper noun: זִיזָה <2125>; another form for ZIZA <2124>] ▶ **An Israelite of the tribe of Levi, same person as ZINA <2126>.** Ref.: 1 Chr. 23:11. ¶

ZOAN – ***ṣōʿan*** [proper noun: צֹעַן <6814>; of Egyptian deriv.] ▶ **This word designates a city in Egypt built seven years after Hebron in Judah.** Ref.: Num. 13:22. Some of the ten plagues hit this area (Ps. 78:12, 43). It was probably in the northeastern delta area of Egypt and west of the Nile. It was supposed to house Egypt's wise counselors (Is. 19:11, 13; 30:4), but Isaiah called them fools. Ezekiel predicted its destruction by fire (Ezek. 30:14). ¶

ZOAR – 1 ***ṣōḥar*** [masc. proper noun: צֹחַר <6714>; from the same as WHITE <6713>]: whiteness ▶

a. The father of Ephron the Hittite. Refs.: Gen. 23:8; 25:9. ¶

b. Son of Simeon, the same as Zerah (<2226> d.). Refs.: Gen. 46:10; Ex. 6:15. ¶

c. Son of Ashur. Ref.: 1 Chr. 4:7. See also 3328 (KJV, NASB). ¶

2 ***ṣôʿar*** [proper noun: צוֹעַר <6820>; from BRING LOW <6819>]: insignificant ▶ **Before the destruction of Sodom and Gomorrah it was located in a beautiful fertile plain of the Jordan.** Ref.: Gen. 13:10. It was also called Bela (Gen. 14:2, 8). The name Zoar also means "little, small" (Gen. 19:22, 23, 30). Lot fled there for safety. Its territory could be seen from Mount Pisgah (Deut. 34:3). Other refs.: Is. 15:5; Jer. 48:34. ¶

ZOBAH – ***ṣôḇāʾ, ṣôḇāh*** [proper noun: צוֹבָא, צוֹבָה <6678>; from an unused root meaning to station]: station ▶ **This word designates a small city-state power with a king that Saul successfully defeated along with many others.** Ref.: 1 Sam. 14:47. It was located north of Dan in the area of Lebanon and was evidently inhabited by Arameans. One of its later kings was named Hadedezer. David had to capture it again (2 Sam. 8:3–12; 10:6–8). *

ZOBEBAH – ***ṣōḇêḇāh, haṣṣōḇêḇāh*** [masc. proper noun: הַצֹּבֵבָה, צֹבֵבָה <6637>; fem. act. part. of the same as COVERED <6632>]: canopy ▶

a. This word designates Zobebah of the tribe of Judah, the son of Coz, used with the definite article. Ref.: 1 Chr. 4:8.

b. A proper noun designating Hazzobebah, the son of Coz. Ref.: 1 Chr. 4:8. This is the same individual as a. above, but the NIV interprets the prefix as part of the name rather than as the definite article. ¶

ZOHELETH – ***zōḥeleṯ*** [proper noun: זֹחֶלֶת <2120>; fem. act. part. of CRAWL <2119>]: crawling, serpent ▶ **A boundary stone near Jerusalem, which is beside En-rogel.** Ref.: 1 Kgs. 1:9. ¶

ZOHETH – ***zôḥêṯ*** [masc. proper noun: זוֹחֵת <2105>; of uncertain origin] ▶ **An Israelite of the tribe of Judah.** Ref.: 1 Chr. 4:20. ¶

ZOPHAH – ***ṣôp̄aḥ*** [masc. proper noun: צוֹפַח <6690>; from an unused root meaning to expand, breadth] ▶ **An Israelite of the tribe of Asher.** Refs.: 1 Chr. 7:35, 36. ¶

ZOPHAR – ***ṣôp̄ar*** [masc. proper noun: צוֹפַר <6691>; from DEPART <6852>]: departing ▶ **Zophar is called a Naamathite (<5284>).** Except for its appearance in Job (Job 2:11; 11:1; 20:1; 42:9), the word Naamathite is not found elsewhere. There is no connection with Naaman. He was one of Job's antagonists more than he was a true friend. He held that Job had sinned and was suffering for it. God did not approve of what he said (Job 42:9). ¶

ZOPHIM – ***ṣōp̄iym*** [proper noun: צֹפִים <6839>; plur. of act. part. of WATCH (verb) <6822>]: watchers ▶ **A place near the top of Mount Pisgah where Balak wanted Balaam to curse the Israelites.** Ref.: Num. 23:14. ¶

ZORAH – ***ṣorʿāh*** [proper noun: צָרְעָה <6881>; apparently another form of HORNETS

<6880>]: hornet ▶ **A town in Dan, where Manoah and Samson lived.** Refs.: Josh. 15:33; 19:41; Judg. 13:2, 25; 16:31; 18:2, 8, 11; 2 Chr. 11:10; Neh. 11:29. ¶

ZOREAH – See ZORAH <6881>.

ZORITE, ZORATHITE – ***ṣor'iy, ṣor'āṯiy*** [proper noun: צָרְעָתִי, צָרְעִי <6882>; patrial from ZORAH <6881>] ▶ **An inhabitant of Zorah.** Refs.: 1 Chr. 2:53, 54; 4:2. ¶

ZUAR – ***ṣû'ār*** [proper noun: צוּעָר <6686>; from BRING LOW <6819>]: small ▶ **Father of Nethanel, a chief of the tribe of Issachar.** Refs.: Num. 1:8; 2:5; 7:18, 23; 10:15. ¶

ZUPH – ***ṣûp̱, ṣôp̱ay*** [proper noun: צוּף, צוֹפַי <6689>; from HONEYCOMB <6688>]: honeycomb ▶
a. An ancestor of Samuel. Refs.: 1 Sam. 1:1; 1 Chr. 6:26, 35. ¶
b. A district in Judah. Ref.: 1 Sam. 9:5. ¶

ZUR – ***ṣûr*** [masc. proper noun: צוּר <6698>; from the same as ROCK <6697>]: rock ▶
a. A Midianite prince. Refs.: Num. 25:15; 31:8; Josh. 13:21. ¶
b. Saul's uncle. Refs.: 1 Chr. 8:30; 9:36. ¶

ZURIEL – ***ṣûriy'ēl*** [masc. proper noun: צוּרִיאֵל <6700>; from ROCK <6697> and GOD <410>]: rock of God ▶ **A chief of the Levites.** Ref.: Num. 3:35. ¶

ZURISHADDAI – ***ṣûriyšadday*** [masc. proper noun: צוּרִישַׁדָּי <6701>; from ROCK <6697> and ALMIGHTY <7706>]: rock of the Almighty ▶ **Father of chief of the Simeonites.** Refs.: Num. 1:6; 2:12; 7:36, 41; 10:19. ¶

ZUZIMS, ZUZITES – ***zûziym*** [plur. proper noun: זוּזִים <2104>; plur. prob. from the same as MOVING CREATURE <2123>] ▶ **A people living in a territory named Ham, to the east of the Jordan; they were defeated by Chedorlaomer.** Ref.: Gen. 14:5. ¶

Untranslated Particles

____ – ***'ēṯ*** [particle: אֵת <853>; apparently contracted from SIGN (noun) <226> in the demons. sense of entity] ▶ **This particle points out the definite direct object in a biblical Hebrew sentence. It is usually not translatable. It is normally employed in Hebrew prose but may often be missing in Hebrew poetry.** It occurs as *'eṯ, 'eṯ-, or 'ēṯ-*. It may take pronominal suffixes, *'ôtiy*, me; *'ôtka*, you, etc. (1 Sam. 8:7). Used before *miy, 'eṯ miy,* it indicates whom. In fact, it is able to point out any kind of accusative in a sentence (cf. 1 Kgs. 15:23). It is used thousands of times in the Old Testament. *

____ – ***yāṭ*** [Aramaic particle: יָת <3487>; corresponding to the untranslated particle <853> above] ▶ **This particle serves as the indicator of the accusative direct object in a sentence. It is not translated into English but helps to locate and define the direct object.** Ref.: Dan. 3:12. In its only use, it refers to the three Hebrews appointed by Nebuchadnezzar. ¶

Part II

Hebrew-English Lexicon

Hebrew-English Lexicon

א Aleph

<1> אָב ***'āḇ*** [FATHER] 1,215x
<2> אַב ***'aḇ*** [FATHER] 9x
<3> אֵב ***'êḇ*** [GREENNESS] 2x
<4> אֵב ***'êḇ*** [FRUIT] 3x
<5> אֲבַגְתָא ***ᵃḇagṯā'*** [ABAGTHA] 1x
<6> אָבַד ***'aḇaḏ*** [PERISH] 184x
<7> אֲבַד ***ᵃḇaḏ*** [PERISH] 7x
<8> אֹבֵד ***'ōḇêḏ*** [RUIN (noun)] 2x
<9> אֲבֵדָה ***ᵃḇêḏāh*** [PROPERTY (LOST)] 4x
<10> אֲבַדֹּה ***ᵃḇaddōh*** [DESTRUCTION] 1x
<11> אֲבַדּוֹן ***ᵃḇaddôn*** [DESTRUCTION] 6x
<12> אַבְדָן ***'aḇḏān*** [DESTRUCTION] 1x
<13> אָבְדָן ***'oḇḏān*** [DESTRUCTION] 1x
<14> אָבָה ***'āḇāh*** [WILLING (BE)] 54x
<15> אָבֶה ***'āḇeh*** [OH, THAT] 1x
<16> אֵבֶה ***'êḇeh*** [REED] 1x
<17> אֲבוֹי ***ᵃḇôy*** [SORROW (interj.)] 1x
<18> אֵבוּס ***'êḇûs*** [CRIB] 3x
<19> אִבְחָה ***'iḇḥāh*** [SLAUGHTER (noun)] 1x
<20> אֲבַטִּיחַ ***ᵃḇaṭṭiyaḥ*** [MELON] 1x
<21> אֲבִי ***ᵃḇiy*** [ABI] 1x
<22> אֲבִיאֵל ***ᵃḇiy'êl*** [ABIEL] 3x
<23> אֲבִיאָסָף ***ᵃḇiy'āsāp̄*** [ABIASAPH] 1x
<24> אָבִיב ***'āḇiyḇ*** [ABIB] 6x, [EAR (noun)] 2x
<25> אֲבִי גִּבְעוֹן ***ᵃḇiy giḇ'ôn*** [ABI GIBEON] 2x
<26> אֲבִיגַיִל ***ᵃḇiyḡayil*** [ABIGAIL] 17x
<27> אֲבִידָן ***'aḇiyḏān*** [ABIDAN] 5x
<28> אֲבִידָע ***ᵃḇiyḏā'*** [ABIDA] 2x
<29> אֲבִיָּה ***ᵃḇiyyāh,*** אֲבִיָּהוּ ***ᵃḇiyāhû*** [ABIJAH] 25x
<30> אֲבִיהוּא ***ᵃḇiyhû'*** [ABIHU] 12x
<31> אֲבִיהוּד ***ᵃḇiyhûḏ*** [ABIHUD] 1x
<32> אֲבִיחַיִל ***ᵃḇiyhayil*** [ABIHAIL] 6x
<33> אֲבִי הָעֶזְרִי ***ᵃḇiy hā'ezriy*** [ABIEZRITE] 3x
<34> אֶבְיוֹן ***'eḇyôn*** [POOR] 61x
<35> אֲבִיּוֹנָה ***ᵃḇiyyônāh*** [DESIRE (noun)] 1x
<36> אֲבִיטוּב ***ᵃḇiyṭûḇ*** [ABITUB] 1x
<37> אֲבִיטַל ***ᵃḇiyṭal*** [ABITAL] 2x
<38> אֲבִיָּם ***ᵃḇiyyām*** [ABIJAM] 4x
<39> אֲבִימָאֵל ***ᵃḇiymā'êl*** [ABIMAEL] 2x
<40> אֲבִימֶלֶךְ ***ᵃḇiymeleḵ*** [ABIMELECH] 67x
<41> אֲבִינָדָב ***ᵃḇiynāḏāḇ*** [ABINADAB] 12x
<42> אֲבִינֹעַם ***ᵃbiynō'ām*** [ABINOAM] 4x
<43> אֶבְיָסָף ***'eḇyāsāp̄*** [EBIASAPH] 3x
<44> אֲבִיעֶזֶר ***ᵃḇiy'ezer*** [ABIEZER] 7x
<45> אֲבִי עַלְבוֹן ***ᵃḇiy 'alḇôn*** [ABI-ALBON] 1x

<46> אָבִיר ***'āḇiyr*** [MIGHTY] 6x
<47> אַבִּיר ***'abbiyr*** [MIGHTY] 17x
<48> אֲבִירָם ***ᵃḇiyrām*** [ABIRAM] 11x
<49> אֲבִישַׁג ***ᵃḇiyšag*** [ABISHAG] 5x
<50> אֲבִישׁוּעַ ***ᵃḇiyšûa'*** [ABISHUA] 5x
<51> אֲבִישׁוּר ***ᵃḇiyšûr*** [ABISHUR] 2x
<52> אֲבִישַׁי ***ᵃḇiyšay*** [ABISHAI] 52x
<53> אֲבִישָׁלוֹם ***ᵃbiysālôm,*** אַבְשָׁלוֹם ***'aḇšālôm*** [ABSALOM] 111x
<54> אֶבְיָתָר ***'eḇyāṯār*** [ABIATHAR] 30x
<55> אָבַךְ ***'āḇaḵ*** [ROLL UPWARD] 1x
<56> אָבַל ***'aḇal*** [MOURN] 39x
<57> אָבֵל ***'āḇêl*** [MOURNING] 8x
<58> אָבֵל ***'āḇêl*** [PLAIN (noun)] 1x
<59> אָבֵל ***'āḇêl*** [ABEL] 4x
<60> אֵבֶל ***'êḇel*** [MOURNING] 24x
<61> אֲבָל ***ᵃḇāl*** [TRULY] 11x
<62> אָבֵל בֵּית־מַעֲכָה ***'āḇêl bêyṯ-mᵃ'aḵāh*** [ABEL BETH MAACAH] 2x
<63> אָבֵל הַשִּׁטִּים ***'āḇêl haššiṭṭiym*** [ABEL SHITTIM] 1x
<64> אָבֵל כְּרָמִים ***'āḇêl kᵉrāmiym*** [ABEL KERAMIM] 1x
<65> אָבֵל מְחוֹלָה ***'āḇêl mᵉḥôlāh*** [ABEL MEHOLAH] 3x
<66> אָבֵל מַיִם ***'āḇêl mayim*** [ABEL MAIM] 1x
<67> אָבֵל מִצְרַיִם ***'āḇêl miṣrayim*** [ABEL MIZRAIM] 1x
<68> אֶבֶן ***'eḇen*** [STONE (noun)] 269x
<69> אֶבֶן ***'eḇen*** [STONE (noun)] 8x
<70> אֹבֶן ***'ōḇen*** [WHEEL] 2x
<71> אֲבָנָה ***ᵃḇānāh*** [ABANA] 1x
<72> אֶבֶן הָעֵזֶר ***'eḇen hā'êzer*** [EBENEZER] 3x
<73> אַבְנֵט ***'aḇnêṭ*** [SASH] 9x
<74> אַבְנֵר, ***ᵃḇnêr,*** אֲבִינֵר ***ᵃḇiynêr*** [ABNER] 63x
<75> אָבַס ***'āḇas*** [FATTENED] 2x
<76> אֲבַעְבֻּעֹת ***ᵃḇa'bu'ōt*** [BOIL (noun)] 2x
<77> אֶבֶץ ***'eḇeṣ*** [EBEZ] 1x
<78> אִבְצָן ***'iḇṣān*** [IBZAN] 2x
<79> אָבַק ***'āḇaq*** [WRESTLE] 2x
<80> אָבָק ***'āḇāq*** [DUST] 6x
<81> אֲבָקָה ***ᵃḇāqāh*** [POWDER] 1x
<82> אָבַר ***'āḇar*** [FLY (verb)] 1x
<83> אֵבֶר ***'êḇer*** [WING] 3x
<84> אֶבְרָה ***'eḇrāh*** [WINGS] 4x
<85> אַבְרָהָם ***'aḇrāhām*** [ABRAHAM] 175x
<86> אַבְרֵךְ ***'aḇrêḵ*** [BOW THE KNEE] 1x
<87> אַבְרָם ***'aḇrām*** [ABRAM] 61x
<88> אֹבֹת ***'ōḇōṯ*** [OBOTH] 4x
<89> אָגֵא ***'āḡê'*** [AGEE] 1x
<90> אֲגַג ***ᵃḡaḡ*** [AGAG] 8x
<91> אֲגָגִי ***ᵃḡāḡiy*** [AGAGITE] 5x
<92> אֲגֻדָּה ***ᵃḡuddāh*** [BUNCH] 4x
<93> אֱגוֹז ***ᵉḡôz*** [NUTS, NUT TREES] 1x
<94> אָגוּר ***'āḡûr*** [AGUR] 1x
<95> אֲגוֹרָה ***ᵃḡôrāh*** [PIECE] 1x
<96> אֶגֶל ***'eḡel*** [DROP (noun)] 1x

<97> אֶגְלַיִם ***'eg̱layim*** [EGLAIM] 1x
<98> אֲגַם ***^{a}g̱am*** [POND] 9x
<99> אָגֵם ***'āg̱êm*** [GRIEVED] 1x
<100> אַגְמוֹן ***'ag̱môn*** [ROPE] 5x
<101> אַגָּן ***'aggān*** [BASIN] 3x
<102> אֲגַף ***^{a}g̱ap̱*** [TROOPS] 6x
<103> אָגַר ***'āg̱ar*** [GATHER] 3x
<104> אִגְּרָא ***'igg^{e}rā'*** [LETTER] 3x
<105> אֲגַרְטָל ***^{a}g̱arṭāl*** [BASIN] 2x
<106> אֶגְרֹף ***'eg̱rōp̱*** [FIST] 2x
<107> אִגֶּרֶת ***'iggereṯ*** [LETTER] 10x
<108> אֵד ***'êḏ*** [MIST] 2x
<109> אָדַב ***'āḏaḇ*** [GRIEVE] 1x
<110> אַדְבְּאֵל ***'aḏb^{e}'ēl*** [ADBEEL] 2x
<111> אֲדַד ***^{a}ḏaḏ*** [HADAD] 1x
<112> אִדּוֹ ***'iddô*** [IDDO] 2x
<113> אָדוֹן ***'āḏôn*** [LORD] 335x
<114> אַדּוֹן ***'addôn*** [ADDON] 1x
<115> אֲדוֹרַיִם ***^{a}ḏôrayim*** [ADORAIM] 1x
<116> אֱדַיִן ***^{e}ḏayin*** [THEN] 57x
<117> אַדִּיר ***'addiyr*** [MIGHTY] 27x
<118> אֲדַלְיָא ***'Aḏalyā'*** [ADALIA] 1x
<119> אָדַם ***'āḏam*** [RUDDY (BE)] 10x
<120> אָדָם ***'āḏām*** [MAN] 552x
<121> אָדָם ***'āḏām*** [ADAM] 15x
<122> אָדֹם ***'āḏōm*** [RED] 9x
<123> אֱדוֹם ***^{e}ḏôm,*** אֱדֹם ***^{e}ḏōm*** [EDOM] 100x
<124> אֹדֶם ***'ōḏem*** [SARDIUS] 3x
<125> אֲדַמְדָּם ***^{a}ḏamdām*** [REDDISH] 6x
<126> אַדְמָה ***'aḏmāh*** [ADMAH] 5x
<127> אֲדָמָה ***^{a}ḏāmāh*** [GROUND] 225x
<128> אֲדָמָה ***^{a}ḏāmāh*** [ADAMAH] 1x
<129> אֲדָמִי ***^{a}ḏāmiy*** [ADAMI] 1x
<130> אֱדֹמִי ***^{e}ḏōmiy*** [EDOMITE] 12x
<131> אֲדֻמִּים ***^{a}ḏummiym*** [ADUMMIM] 2x
<132> אַדְמֹנִי ***'aḏmōniy,*** אַדְמוֹנִי ***'aḏmôniy*** [RED] 3x
<133> אַדְמָתָא ***'aḏmāṯā'*** [ADMATHA] 1x
<134> אֶדֶן ***'eḏen*** [BASE (noun)] 57x
<135> אַדָּן ***'addān*** [ADDAN] 1x
<136> אֲדֹנָי ***^{a}ḏōnāy*** [LORD] 434x
<137> אֲדֹנִי בֶזֶק ***^{a}ḏōniy ḇezeq*** [ADONI-BEZEK] 3x
<138> אֲדֹנִיָּה ***^{a}ḏōniyyah,*** אֲדֹנִיָּהוּ ***^{a}ḏōniyyāhû*** [ADONIJAH] 26x
<139> אֲדֹנִי צֶדֶק ***^{a}ḏōniy ṣeḏeq*** [ADONI-ZEDEK] 2x
<140> אֲדֹנִיקָם ***^{a}ḏōniyqām*** [ADONIKAM] 3x
<141> אֲדֹנִירָם ***^{a}ḏōniyrām*** [ADONIRAM] 2x
<142> אָדַר ***'āḏar*** [GLORIOUS] 3x
<143> אֲדָר ***^{a}ḏār*** [ADAR] 8x
<144> אֲדָר ***^{a}ḏār*** [ADAR] 1x
<145> אֶדֶר ***'eḏer*** [ROBE] 2x
<146> אַדָּר ***'addār*** [ADDAR] 2x
<147> אִדַּר ***'iddar*** [THRESHING FLOOR] 1x

<148> אֲדַרְגָּזֵר ***ʼᵃḏargāzêr*** [COUNSELOR] 2x

<149> אַדְרַזְדָּא ***ʼaḏrazdāʼ*** [DILIGENTLY] 1x

<150> אֲדַרְכֹּן ***ʼᵃḏarkōn*** [DARIC] 2x

<151> אֲדֹרָם ***ʼᵃḏōrām*** [ADORAM] 2x

<152> אַדְרַמֶּלֶךְ ***ʼaḏrammeleḵ*** [ADRAMMELECH] 3x

<153> אֶדְרָע ***ʼeḏrāʻ*** [FORCE (noun)] 1x

<154> אֶדְרֶעִי ***ʼeḏreʻiy*** [EDREI] 8x

<155> אַדֶּרֶת ***ʼaddereṯ*** [GARMENT] 12x

<156> אָדוֹשׁ ***ʼāḏôš*** [THRESH] 1x

<157> אָהַב ***ʼāhaḇ*** [LOVE (verb)] 208x

<158> אַהַב ***ʼahaḇ*** [LOVE (noun)] 2x

<159> אֹהַב ***ʼōhaḇ*** [LOVE (noun)] 2x

<160> אַהֲבָה ***ʼahᵃḇāh*** [LOVE (noun)] 40x

<161> אֹהַד ***ʼōhaḏ*** [OHAD] 2x

<162> אֲהָהּ ***ʼᵃhāh*** [ALAS!] 30x

<163> אַהֲוָא ***ʼahᵃwāʼ*** [AHAVA] 3x

<164> אֵהוּד ***ʼêhûḏ*** [EHUD] 9x

<165> אֱהִי ***ʼᵉhiy*** [I WILL BE] 3x

<166> אָהַל ***ʼāhal*** [SHINE] 1x

<167> אָהַל ***ʼāhal*** [TENT (MOVE, REMOVE, PITCH A)] 3x

<168> אֹהֶל ***ʼōhel*** [TENT] 345x

<169> אֹהֶל ***ʼōhel*** [OHEL] 1x

<170> אָהֳלָה ***ʼohᵒlah*** [OHOLAH] 5x

<171> אָהֳלִיאָב ***ʼohᵒliyāḇ*** [OHOLIAB] 5x

<172> אָהֳלִיבָה ***ʼohᵒliyḇāh*** [OHOLIBAH] 6x

<173> אָהֳלִיבָמָה ***ʼohᵒliyḇāmāh*** [OHOLIBAMAH] 8x

<174> אֲהָל ***ʼahāl*** [ALOES] 4x

<175> אַהֲרוֹן ***ʼahᵃrôn*** [AARON] 347x

<176> אַו ***ʼaw,*** אוֹ ***ʼô*** [OR] 21x

<177> אוּאֵל ***ʼûêl*** [UEL] 1x

<178> אוֹב ***ʼôḇ*** [MEDIUM] 17x

<179> אוֹבִיל ***ʼôḇiyl*** [OBIL] 1x

<180> אוּבָל ***ʼûḇāl,*** אֻבָל ***ʼuḇāl*** [CANAL] 3x

<181> אוּד ***ʼûḏ*** [FIREBRAND] 3x

<182> אוֹדוֹת ***ʼôḏôṯ,*** אֹדוֹת ***ʼōḏôṯ*** [BECAUSE] 11x

<183> אָוָה ***ʼāwāh*** [DESIRE (verb)] 26x

<184> אָוָה ***ʼāwāh*** [MARK OUT] 1x

<185> אַוָּה ***ʼawwāh*** [DESIRE (noun)] 7x

<186> אוּזַי ***ʼûzay*** [UZAI] 1x

<187> אוּזָל ***ʼûzāl*** [UZAL] 2x

<188> אוֹי ***ʼôy*** [WOE (interj.)] 24x

<189> אֱוִי ***ʼᵉwiy*** [EVI] 2x

<190> אוֹיָה ***ʼôyāh*** [WOE (interj.)] 1x

<191> אֱוִיל ***ʼᵉwiyl*** [FOOLISH] 26x

<192> אֱוִיל מְרֹדַךְ ***ʼᵉwiyl mᵉrōḏaḵ*** [EVIL-MERODACH] 2x

<193> אוּל ***ʼûl*** [BODY] 2x

<194> אוּלַי ***ʼûlay,*** אֻלַי ***ʼulay*** [PERHAPS] 11x

<195> אוּלַי ***ʼûlay*** [ULAI] 2x

<196> אֱוִלִי ***ʼᵉwiliy*** [FOOLISH] 1x

<197> אוּלָם ***ʼûlām*** [VESTIBULE] 34x

<198> אוּלָם ***ʼûlām*** [ULAM] 4x

<199> אוּלָם ***'ûlām*** [BUT] 19x

<200> אִוֶּלֶת ***'iwweleṯ*** [FOLLY] 25x

<201> אוֹמָר ***'ômār*** [OMAR] 3x

<202> אוֹן ***'ôn*** [STRENGTH] 12x

<203> אוֹן ***'ôn*** [ON] 1x

<204> אוֹן ***'ôn*** [ON] 3x

<205> אָוֶן ***'āwen*** [NOTHINGNESS] 78x

<206> אָוֶן ***'āwen*** [AVEN] 3x

<207> אוֹנוֹ ***'ônô*** [ONO] 5x

<208> אוֹנָם ***'ônām*** [ONAM] 4x

<209> אוֹנָן ***'ônān*** [ONAN] 8x

<210> אוּפָז ***'ûp̱āz*** [UPHAZ] 2x

<211> אוֹפִיר ***'ôp̱iyr*** [OPHIR] 13x

<212> אוֹפָן ***'ôp̱ān*** [WHEEL] 36x

<213> אוּץ ***'ûṣ*** [HASTEN] 10x

<214> אוֹצָר ***'ôṣār*** [STOREHOUSE] 79x

<215> אוֹר ***'ôr*** [LIGHT (GIVE)] 43x

<216> אוֹר ***'ôr*** [LIGHT (noun)] 123x

<217> אוּר ***'ûr*** [FIRE] 6x

<218> אוּר ***'ûr*** [UR] 5x

<219> אוֹרָה ***'ôrāh*** [LIGHT (noun)] 4x

<220> אֲוֵרוֹת ***ᵃwêrôṯ*** [STALL] 1x

<221> אוּרִי ***'ûriy*** [URI] 8x

<222> אוּרִיאֵל ***'ûriyêl*** [URIEL] 4x

<223> אוּרִיָּה ***'ûriyyah*** [URIAH] 39x

<224> אוּרִים ***'ûriym*** [URIM] 7x

<225> אוּת ***'ûṯ*** [CONSENT] 4x

<226> אוֹת ***'ôṯ*** [SIGN (noun)] 79x

<227> אָז ***'āz,*** מֵאָז ***mê'āz*** [THEN] 22x

<228> אֲזָא ***ᵃzā',*** אֲזָה ***ᵃzāh*** [HEAT (verb)] 3x

<229> אֶזְבַּי ***'ezbay*** [EZBAI] 1x

<230> אַזָּד ***'azāḏ*** [FIRM] 2x

<231> אֵזוֹב ***'êzôḇ*** [HYSSOP] 10x

<232> אֵזוֹר ***'êzôr*** [BELT] 14x

<233> אֱזַי ***ᵉzay*** [THEN] 3x

<234> אַזְכָּרָה ***'azkārāh*** [MEMORIAL] 7x

<235> אָזַל ***'āzal*** [GO] 6x

<236> אֲזַל ***ᵃzal*** [GO] 7x

<237> אֶזֶל ***'ezel*** [EZEL] 1x

<238> אָזַן ***'āzan*** [EAR (GIVE)] 41x

<239> אָזַן ***'āzan*** [PONDER] 1x

<240> אָזֵן ***'āzên*** [EQUIPMENT] 1x

<241> אֹזֶן ***'ōzen*** [EAR] 187x

<242> אֻזֵּן שֶׁאֱרָה ***'uzzên šeᵉrāh*** [UZZEN SHEERAH] 1x

<243> אַזְנוֹת תָּבוֹר ***'aznôṯ tāḇôr*** [AZNOTH TABOR] 1x

<244> אָזְנִי ***'ozniy*** [OZNI] 1x

<245> אֲזַנְיָה ***ᵃzanyāh*** [AZANIAH] 1x

<246> אֲזֵק ***ᵃzêq*** [CHAIN] 2x

<247> אָזַר ***'āzar*** [GIRD] 16x

<248> אֶזְרוֹעַ ***'ezrôa'*** [ARM] 2x

<249> אֶזְרָח ***'ezrāḥ*** [NATIVE, NATIVE-BORN, BORN IN] 17x

<250> אֶזְרָחִי ***’ezrāḥiy*** [EZRAHITE] 3x
<251> אָח ***’āḥ*** [BROTHER] 606x
<252> אַח ***’aḥ*** [BROTHER] 1x
<253> אָח ***’āḥ*** [ALAS!] 2x
<254> אָח ***’aḥ*** [BRAZIER] 3x
<255> אֹחַ ***’ōaḥ*** [OWL] 1x
<256> אַחְאָב ***’aḥ’āḇ*** [AHAB] 94x
<257> אַחְבָּן ***’aḥbān*** [AHBAN] 1x
<258> אָחַד ***’āḥaḏ*** [GO ONE WAY OR THE OTHER] 1x
<259> אֶחָד ***’eḥāḏ*** [ONE] 951x
<260> אָחוּ ***’āḥû*** [MEADOW (plant)] 3x
<261> אֵחוּד ***’êḥûḏ*** [EHUD] 1x
<262> אַחְוָה ***’aḥwāh*** [DECLARATION] 1x
<263> אַחֲוָיַת ***’aḥ^{a}wāyah*** [EXPLANATION] 1x
<264> אַחֲוָה ***’aḥ^{a}wāh*** [BROTHERHOOD] 1x
<265> אֲחוֹחַ ***^{a}ḥôaḥ*** [AHOAH] 1x
<266> אֲחוֹחִי ***’aḥôḥiy*** [AHOHITE] 5x
<267> אֲחוּמַי ***^{a}ḥûmay*** [AHUMAI] 1x
<268> אָחוֹר ***’āḥôr*** [BACK] 41x
<269> אָחוֹת ***’āḥôṯ*** [SISTER] 114x
<270> אָחַז ***’aḥaz*** [HOLD (TAKE)] 67x
<271> אָחָז ***’āḥāz*** [AHAZ] 41x
<272> אֲחֻזָּה ***^{a}ḥuzzāh*** [POSSESSION] 66x
<273> אַחְזַי ***’aḥzay*** [AHZAI] 1x
<274> אֲחַזְיָהוּ ***^{a}ḥazyāhû,*** אֲחַזְיָה ***^{a}ḥazyāh*** [AHAZIAH] 37x
<275> אֲחֻזָּם ***^{a}ḥuzzām*** [AHUZZAM] 1x
<276> אֲחֻזַּת ***^{a}ḥuzzaṯ*** [AHUZZATH] 1x
<277> אֲחִי ***^{a}ḥiy*** [AHI] 2x
<278> אֵחִי ***’êḥiy*** [EHI] 1x
<279> אֲחִיאָם ***^{a}ḥiy’ām*** [AHIAM] 2x
<280> אֲחִידָה ***^{a}ḥiyḏāh*** [RIDDLE] 1x
<281> אֲחִיָּה ***^{a}ḥiyyāh*** [AHIJAH] 24x
<282> אֲחִיהוּד ***^{a}ḥiyhûḏ*** [AHIHUD] 1x
<283> אַחְיוֹ ***’aḥyô*** [AHIO] 6x
<284> אֲחִיחֻד ***^{a}ḥiyḥuḏ*** [AHIHUD] 1x
<285> אֲחִיטוּב ***^{a}ḥiyṭûḇ*** [AHITUB] 15x
<286> אֲחִילוּד ***^{a}ḥiylûḏ*** [AHILUD] 5x
<287> אֲחִימוֹת ***^{a}ḥiymôṯ*** [AHIMOTH] 1x
<288> אֲחִימֶלֶךְ ***^{a}ḥiymeleḵ*** [AHIMELECH] 17x
<289> אֲחִימַן ***^{a}ḥiyman,*** אֲחִימָן ***^{a}ḥiymān*** [AHIMAN] 4x
<290> אֲחִימַעַץ ***^{a}ḥiyma‘aṣ*** [AHIMAAZ] 15x
<291> אַחְיָן ***’aḥyān*** [AHIAN] 1x
<292> אֲחִינָדָב ***^{a}ḥiynāḏāḇ*** [AHINADAB] 1x
<293> אֲחִינֹעַם ***^{a}ḥiynō‘am*** [AHINOAM] 7x
<294> אֲחִיסָמָךְ ***^{a}ḥiysāmāḵ*** [AHISAMACH] 3x
<295> אֲחִיעֶזֶר ***^{a}ḥiy‘ezer*** [AHIEZER] 6x
<296> אֲחִיקָם ***^{a}ḥiyqām*** [AHIKAM] 20x
<297> אֲחִירָם ***^{a}ḥiyrām*** [AHIRAM] 1x
<298> אֲחִירָמִי ***^{a}ḥirāmiy*** [AHIRAMITE] 1x
<299> אֲחִירַע ***^{a}ḥiyra‘*** [AHIRA] 5x
<300> אֲחִישַׁחַר ***^{a}ḥiyšaḥar*** [AHISHAHAR] 1x

<301> אֲחִישָׁר ***ᵃḥiyšār*** [AHISHAR] 1x
<302> אֲחִיתֹפֶל ***ᵃḥiytōpel*** [AHITOPHEL] 20x
<303> אַחְלָב ***ᵃḥlāb*** [AHLAB] 1x
<304> אַחְלַי ***ᵃḥlay*** [AHLAI] 2x
<305> אַחֲלֵי ***aḥalêy,*** אַחֲלַי ***ʼaḥalay*** [WOULD THAT!] 2x
<306> אַחְלָמָה ***ʼaḥlāmāh*** [AMETHYST] 2x
<307> אַחְמְתָא ***ʼaḥmᵉṯaʼ*** [ACHMETHA] 1x
<308> אֲחַסְבַּי ***ᵃḥasbay*** [AHASBAI] 1x
<309> אָחַר ***ʼāḥar*** [STAY (verb)] 17x
<310> אַחַר ***ʼaḥar*** [BEHIND] 709x
<311> אַחֲרֵי ***ʼaḥᵃrêy*** [AFTER] 3x
<312> אַחֵר ***ʼaḥêr*** [OTHER] 166x
<313> אַחֵר ***ʼaḥêr*** [AHER] 1x
<314> אַחֲרוֹן ***ʼaḥᵃrôn,*** אַחֲרֹן ***ʼaḥᵃrōn*** [NEXT] 51x
<315> אַחְרַח ***ʼaḥraḥ*** [AHARAH] 1x
<316> אֲחַרְחֵל ***ᵃḥarḥêl*** [AHARHEL] 1x
<317> אָחֳרִי ***ʼoḥᵒriy*** [ANOTHER] 6x
<318> אָחֳרֵין ***ʼoḥᵒrêyn*** [LAST] 1x
<319> אַחֲרִית ***ʼaḥᵃriyṯ*** [LATTER TIME] 61x
<320> אַחֲרִית ***ʼaḥᵃriyṯ*** [LATTER TIME] 1x
<321> אָחֳרָן ***ʼoḥᵒrān*** [ANOTHER] 5x
<322> אֲחֹרַנִּית ***ᵃḥōranniyṯ*** [BACKWARD] 7x
<323> אֲחַשְׁדַּרְפַּן ***ᵃḥašdarpan*** [SATRAP] 4x
<324> אֲחַשְׁדַּרְפַּן ***ᵃḥašdarpan*** [SATRAP] 9x
<325> אֲחַשְׁוֵרוֹשׁ ***ᵃḥašwêrôš*** [AHASUERUS] 31x
<326> אֲחַשְׁתָּרִי ***ᵃḥaštāriy*** [HAAHASHTARI] 1x
<327> אֲחַשְׁתְּרָן ***ᵃḥaštᵉrān*** [ROYAL] 2x
<328> אַט ***ʼaṭ,*** אִטִּים ***ʼiṭṭiym*** [SLOWLY] 5x
<329> אָטָד ***ʼāṭāḏ*** [BRAMBLE] 6x
<330> אֵטוּן ***ʼêṭûn*** [LINEN] 1x
<331> אָטַם ***ʼāṭam*** [STOP] 8x
<332> אָטַר ***ʼāṭar*** [CLOSE] 1x
<333> אָטֵר ***ʼāṭêr*** [ATER] 5x
<334> אִטֵּר ***ʼiṭṭêr*** [LEFT-HANDED] 2x
<335> אֵי ***ʼêy*** [WHERE] 16x
<336> אִי ***ʼiy*** [NOT] 1x
<337> אִי ***ʼiy*** [WOE! (interj.)] 2x
<338> אִי ***ʼiy*** [HYENA] 3x
<339> אִי ***ʼiy*** [COASTLAND] 36x
<340> אָיַב ***ʼāyaḇ*** [ENEMY (BE AN)] 1x
<341> אֹיֵב ***ʼōyêḇ*** [ENEMY] 282x
<342> אֵיבָה ***ʼêyḇāh*** [ENMITY] 5x
<343> אֵיד ***ʼêyḏ*** [CALAMITY] 24x
<344> אַיָּה ***ʼayyāh*** [FALCON] 3x
<345> אַיָּה ***ʼayyāh*** [AIAH] 6x
<346> אַיֵּה ***ʼayyêh*** [WHERE] 44x
<347> אִיּוֹב ***ʼiyyôḇ*** [JOB] 58x
<348> אִיזֶבֶל ***ʼiyzeḇel*** [JEZEBEL] 22x
<349> אֵיךְ ***ʼêyḵ,*** אֵיכָה ***ʼêyḵāh,*** אֵיכָכָה ***ʼêyḵāḵāh*** [HOW?, HOW!] 75x
<350> אִי־כָבוֹד ***ʼiy-ḵāḇôḏ*** [ICHABOD] 2x
<351> אֵיכֹה ***ʼêyḵōh*** [WHERE] 1x

<352> אַיִל ***’ayil*** [DOORPOST], [MIGHTY], [OAK], [RAM] 185x
<353> אֱיָל ****yāl*** [STRENGTH] 1x
<354> אַיָּל ***’ayyāl*** [DEER] 11x
<355> אַיָּלָה ***’ayyālāh*** [DOE] 8x
<356> אֵלוֹן ***’êlôn,*** אֵילוֹן ***’êylôn*** [ELON] 7x
<357> אַיָּלוֹן ***’ayyālôn,*** אַיָלוֹן ***’ayālôn*** [AIJALON] 10x
<358> אֵילוֹן בֵּית חָנָן ***’êylôn bêyt ḥānān*** [ELON BETHHANAN] 1x
<359> אֵילַת ***’êylaṯ,*** אֵילוֹת ***’êylôṯ*** [ELATH] 8x
<360> אֱיָלוּת ****yālûṯ*** [STRENGTH] 1x
<361> אֵילָם ***’êylām*** [VESTIBULE] 15x
<362> אֵילִם ***’êylim*** [ELIM] 6x
<363> אִילָן ***’iylān*** [TREE] 6x
<364> אֵיל פָּארָן ***’êyl pā’rān*** [EL PARAN] 1x
<365> אַיֶּלֶת ***’ayyeleṯ*** [DEER] 3x
<366> אָיֹם ***’āyōm*** [TERRIBLE] 3x
<367> אֵימָה ***’êymāh*** [TERROR] 17x
<368> אֵימִים ***’êymiym*** [EMIM, EMITES] 3x
<369> אַיִן ***’ayin*** [NO] 29x
<370> אַיִן ***’ayin*** [WHERE] 17x
<371> אִין ***’iyn*** [IS THERE NOT] 1x
<372> אִיעֶזֶר ***’iy‘ezer*** [IEZER] 1x
<373> אִיעֶזְרִי ***’iy‘ezriy*** [IEZERITE] 1x
<374> אֵיפָה ***’êyp̱āh,*** אֵפָה ***’êp̱āh*** [EPHAH] 40x
<375> אֵיפֹה ***’eyp̱ōh*** [WHERE] 10x
<376> אִישׁ ***’iyš*** [MAN] 1,639x
<377> אִישׁ ***’iyš,*** אָשַׁשׁ ***’āšaš*** [SHOW YOURSELVES MEN] 1x
<378> אִישׁ בֹּשֶׁת ***’iyš bōšeṯ*** [ISH-BOSHETH] 11x
<379> אִישְׁהוֹד ***’iyšhôḏ*** [ISHDOD] 1x
<380> אִישׁוֹן ***’iyšôn,*** אֱשׁוּן ****šûn*** [PUPIL] 3x, [TWILIGHT] 1x
<381> אִישׁ־חַיִל ***’iyš-ḥayil*** [VALIANT MAN] 4x
<382> אִישׁ־טוֹב ***’iyš-ṭôḇ,*** אִישׁ טוֹב ***’iyš ṭôḇ*** [ISH-TOB] 2x
<383> אִיתַי ***’iṯay*** [THERE IS, THERE ARE] 17x
<384> אִיתִיאֵל ***’iyṯiy’êl*** [ITHIEL] 3x
<385> אִיתָמָר ***’iyṯāmār*** [ITHAMAR] 21x
<386> אֵיתָן ***’êytān*** [STRENGTH] 13x
<387> אֵיתָן ***’êyṯān*** [ETHAN] 8x
<388> אֵיתָנִים ***’eṯāniym*** [ETHANIM] 1x
<389> אַךְ ***’aḵ*** [ONLY] 22x
<390> אַכַּד ***’akkaḏ*** [ACCAD] 1x
<391> אַכְזָב ***’aḵzāḇ*** [DECEPTIVE] 2x
<392> אַכְזִיב ***’aḵziyḇ*** [ACHZIB] 4x
<393> אַכְזָר ***’aḵzār*** [CRUEL] 4x
<394> אַכְזָרִי ***’aḵzāriy*** [CRUEL] 8x
<395> אַכְזְרִיּוּת ***’aḵzᵉriyyûṯ*** [CRUEL] 1x
<396> אֲכִילָה ****ḵiylāh*** [FOOD] 1x
<397> אָכִישׁ ***’āḵiyš*** [ACHISH] 21x
<398> אָכַל ***’āḵal*** [EAT] 802x
<399> אֲכַל ****ḵal*** [EAT] 7x
<400> אֹכֶל ***’ōḵel*** [FOOD] 44x
<401> אֻכָּל ***’ukkāl*** [UCAL] 1x
<402> אָכְלָה ***’oḵlāh*** [FOOD] 18x

<403> אָכֵן ***'āḵên*** [SURELY] 18x
<404> אָכַף ***'āḵap̄*** [CRAVE] 1x
<405> אֶכֶף ***'eḵep̄*** [PRESSURE] 1x
<406> אִכָּר ***'ikār*** [FARMER] 7x
<407> אַכְשָׁף ***'aḵšāp̄*** [ACHSHAPH] 3x
<408> אַל ***'al*** [NO] 675x
<409> אַל ***'al*** [DO NOT] 3x
<410> אֵל ***'êl*** [GOD] 245x
<411> אֵל ***'êl*** [THESE, THOSE] 9x
<412> אֵל ***'êl*** [THESE] 1x
<413> אֵל ***'êl,*** אֶל ***'el*** [TO]
<414> אֵלָא ***'êlā'*** [ELA] 1x
<415> אֵל אֱלֹהֵי יִשְׂרָאֵל ***'êl ᵉlōhey yisrā'êl*** [EL ELOHE ISRAEL] 1x
<416> אֵל בֵּית אֵל ***'êl bêyṯ 'êl*** [EL BETHEL] 1x
<417> אֶלְגָּבִישׁ ***'elgāḇiyš*** [HAILSTONE] 3x
<418> אַלְגּוּמִּים ***'algûmmiym*** [ALGUM TREES] 3x
<419> אֶלְדָּד ***'eldāḏ*** [ELDAD] 2x
<420> אֶלְדָּעָה ***'eldā'āh*** [ELDAAH] 2x
<421> אָלָה ***'ālāh*** [LAMENT] 1x
<422> אָלָה ***'ālāh*** [CURSE (verb)] 6x
<423> אָלָה ***'ālāh*** [OATH] 36x
<424> אֵלָה ***'êlāh*** [OAK] 13x
<425> אֵלָה ***'êlāh*** [ELAH] 19x
<426> אֱלָהּ ***ᵉlāh*** [GOD] 95x
<427> אַלָּה ***'allāh*** [OAK] 1x
<428> אֵלֶּה ***'êlleh*** [THESE, THOSE] 20x
<429> אֵלֶּה ***'êlleh*** [THESE, THOSE] 2x
<430> אֱלֹהִים ***ᵉlōhiym*** [GOD] 2,606x
<431> אֱלוּ ***ᵉlû*** [BEHOLD (interj.)] 5x
<432> אִלּוּ ***'illû*** [IF] 2x
<433> אֱלוֹהַּ ***ᵉlôah̩*** [GOD] 57x
<434> אֱלוּל ***ᵉlûl*** [FUTILITY] 1x
<435> אֱלוּל ***ᵉlûl*** [ELUL] 1x
<436> אֵלוֹן ***'êlôn*** [OAK] 9x
<437> אַלּוֹן ***'allôn*** [OAK] 8x
<438> אַלּוֹן ***'allôn*** [ALLON] 2x
<439> אַלּוֹן בָּכוּת ***'allôn bāḵûṯ*** [ALLON BACUTH] 1x
<440> אֵלוֹנִי ***'êlôniy*** [ELEONITE] 1x
<441> אַלּוּף ***'allûp̄,*** אַלֻּף ***'allup̄*** [GENTLE] 69x
<442> אָלוּשׁ ***'ālûš*** [ALUSH] 2x
<443> אֶלְזָבָד ***'elzāḇāḏ*** [ELZABAD] 2x
<444> אָלַח ***'ālaḥ*** [CORRUPT (BECOME)] 3x
<445> אֶלְחָנָן ***'elḥānān*** [ELHANAN] 4x
<446> אֱלִיאָב ***ᵉliy'āḇ*** [ELIAB] 21x
<447> אֱלִיאֵל ***ᵉliy'êl*** [ELIEL] 12x
<448> אֱלִיָּתָה ***ᵉliyyāṯah,*** אֱלִיאָתָה ***ᵉliy'āṯah*** [ELIATAH] 2x
<449> אֱלִדָּד ***ᵉliḏāḏ*** [ELIDAD] 1x
<450> אֶלְיָדָע ***'elyāḏā'*** [ELIADA] 4x
<451> אַלְיָה ***'alyāh*** [FAT TAIL] 5x
<452> אֵלִיָּה ***'êliyyāh,*** אֵלִיָּהוּ ***'êliyyāhû*** [ELIJAH] 71x
<453> אֱלִיהוּ ***ᵉliyhû,*** אֱלִיהוּא ***ᵉliyhû'*** [ELIHU] 11x

<454> אֶלְיְהוֹעֵינַי ***’ely^{e}hô‘êynay,*** אֶלְיוֹעֵינַי ***’elyô‘êynay*** [ELIOENEAI] 9x
<455> אֶלְיַחְבָּא ***’elyaḥbā’*** [ELIAHBA] 2x
<456> אֱלִיחֹרֶף ****liyḥōrep̱*** [ELIHOREPH] 1x
<457> אֱלִיל ****liyl*** [WORTHLESSNESS] 20x
<458> אֱלִימֶלֶךְ ****liymeleḵ*** [ELIMELECH] 6x
<459> אִלֵּין ***’illêyn*** [THESE, THOSE] 5x
<460> אֶלְיָסָף ***’elyāsāp̱*** [ELIASAPH] 6x
<461> אֱלִיעֶזֶר ****liy‘ezer*** [ELIEZER] 15x
<462> אֱלִיעֵינַי ****liy‘êynay*** [ELIENAI] 1x
<463> אֱלִיעָם ****liy‘ām*** [ELIAM] 2x
<464> אֱלִיפַז ****liyp̱az*** [ELIPHAZ] 15x
<465> אֱלִיפָל ****liyp̱āl*** [ELIPHAL] 1x
<466> אֱלִיפְלֵהוּ ****liyp̱^{e}lêhû*** [ELIPHELEHU] 2x
<467> אֱלִיפֶלֶט ****liyp̱eleṭ*** אֶלְפֶּלֶט ***’elpeleṭ*** [ELIPHELET] 9x
<468> אֱלִיצוּר ****liyṣûr*** [ELIZUR] 5x
<469> אֱלִיצָפָן ****liyṣāp̱ān,*** אֶלְצָפָן ***’elṣāp̱ān*** [ELIZAPHAN] 6x
<470> אֱלִיקָא ****liyqā’*** [ELIKA] 1x
<471> אֶלְיָקִים ***’elyāqiym*** [ELIAKIM] 12x
<472> אֱלִישֶׁבַע ****liyšeḇa‘*** [ELISHEBA] 1x
<473> אֱלִישָׁה ****liyšāh*** [ELISHAH] 3x
<474> אֱלִישׁוּעַ ****liyšûa‘*** [ELISHUA] 2x
<475> אֶלְיָשִׁיב ***’elyāšiyḇ*** [ELIASHIB] 12x
<476> אֱלִישָׁמָע ****liyšāmā‘*** [ELIASHAMA] 17x
<477> אֱלִישָׁע ****liyšā‘*** [ELISHA] 58x
<478> אֱלִישָׁפָט ****liyšāp̱āṭ*** [ELISHAPHAT] 1x
<479> אִלֵּךְ ***’illêḵ*** [THESE, THOSE] 14x
<480> אַלְלַי ***’allay*** [WOE (interj.)] 2x
<481> אָלַם ***’ālam*** [BIND] 9x
<482> אֵלֶם ***’êlem*** [OAK TREES] 2x
<483> אִלֵּם ***’illêm*** [MUTE] 6x
<484> אַלְמֻגִּים ***’almuggiym*** [ALMUG] 2x
<485> אֲלֻמָּה ****lummah*** [SHEAVE] 5x
<486> אַלְמוֹדָד ***’almôḏāḏ*** [ALMODAD] 2x
<487> אַלַּמֶּלֶךְ ***’allammeleḵ*** [ALAMMELECH] 1x
<488> אַלְמָן ***’almān*** [FORSAKEN] 1x
<489> אַלְמֹן ***’almōn*** [WIDOWHOOD] 1x
<490> אַלְמָנָה ***’almānāh*** [WIDOW] 55x
<491> אַלְמָנוּת ***’almānûṯ*** [WIDOWHOOD] 4x
<492> אַלְמֹנִי ***’almōniy*** [A ONE] 3x
<493> אֶלְנַעַם ***’elna‘am*** [ELNAAM] 1x
<494> אֶלְנָתָן ***’elnāṯān*** [ELNATHAN] 7x
<495> אֶלָּסָר ***’ellāsār*** [ELLASAR] 2x
<496> אֶלְעָד ***’el‘āḏ*** [ELEAD] 1x
<497> אֶלְעָדָה ***’el‘āḏāh*** [ELADAH] 1x
<498> אֶלְעוּזַי ***’el‘ûzay*** [ELUZAI] 1x
<499> אֶלְעָזָר ***’el‘āzār*** [ELEAZAR] 72x
<500> אֶלְעָלֵא ***’el‘ālê’*** [ELEALEH] 5x
<501> אֶלְעָשָׂה ***’el‘āśāh*** [ELEASAH] 6x
<502> אָלַף ***’ālap̱*** [LEARN] 4x
<503> אָלַף ***’ālap̱*** [THOUSANDS (BRING FORTH)] 1x
<504> אֶלֶף ***’elep̱*** [HERD] 7x

<505> אֶלֶף ***'elep̱*** [THOUSAND] 505x
<506> אֲלַף ***'^{a}lap̱*** [THOUSAND] 4x
<507> אֶלֶף ***'elep̱*** [ELEPH] 1x
<508> אֶלְפַּעַל ***'elpa'al*** [ELPAAL] 3x
<509> אָלַץ ***'ālaṣ*** [URGE] 1x
<510> אַלְקוּם ***'alqûm*** [ARMY] 1x
<511> אֶלְקָנָה ***'elqānāh*** [ELKANAH] 21x
<512> אֶלְקֹשִׁי ***'elqōšiy*** [ELKOSHITE] 1x
<513> אֶלְתּוֹלַד ***'eltôlaḏ*** [ELTOLAD] 2x
<514> אֶלְתְּקֵא ***'elt^{e}qê'*** [ELTEKEH] 2x
<515> אֶלְתְּקֹן ***'elt^{e}qōn*** [ELTEKON] 1x
<516> אַל תַּשְׁחֵת ***'al tašḥêṯ*** [AL-TASHHETH] 4x
<517> אֵם ***'êm*** [MOTHER] 220x
<518> אִם ***'im*** [WHEN] 43x
<519> אָמָה ***'āmāh*** [MAID] 55x
<520> אַמָּה ***'ammāh*** [CUBIT] 245x
<521> אַמָּה ***'ammāh*** [CUBIT] 4x
<522> אַמָּה ***'ammāh*** [AMMAH] 2x
<523> אֻמָּה ***'ummāh*** [PEOPLE] 3x
<524> אֻמָּה ***'ummāh*** [NATION] 8x
<525> אָמוֹן ***'āmôn*** [MASTER WORKMAN] 1x
<526> אָמוֹן ***'āmôn*** [AMON] 17x
<527> אָמוֹן ***'āmôn*** [CRAFTSMAN] 3x
<528> אָמוֹן ***'āmôn,*** נֹא אָמוֹן ***nō' 'āmôn*** [AMON] 2x
<529> אֵמוּן ***'êmûn*** [FAITHFUL] 5x
<530> אֱמוּנָה ***'^{e}mûnāh*** [TRUTH] 49x
<531> אָמוֹץ ***'āmôṣ*** [AMOZ] 13x
<532> אָמִי ***'āmiy*** [AMI] 1x
<533> אַמִּיץ ***'ammiyṣ,*** אַמִּץ ***'ammiṣ*** [BRAVE] 6x
<534> אָמִיר ***'āmiyr*** [BOUGH] 2x
<535> אָמַל ***'āmal*** [LANGUISH] 16x
<536> אֻמְלַל ***'umlal*** [WEAK (adj.)] 1x
<537> אֲמֵלָל ***'^{a}mêlāl*** [WEAK (adj.)] 1x
<538> אֲמָם ***'^{a}mām*** [AMAM] 1x
<539> אָמַן ***'āman*** [NURSE (verb)] 108x
<540> אֲמַן ***'^{a}man*** [TRUST (verb)] 3x
<541> אָמַן ***'āman*** [HAND (TURN TO THE RIGHT)] 1x
<542> אָמָּן ***'ommān*** [ARTIST] 1x
<543> אָמֵן ***'āmên*** [AMEN] 27x
<544> אֹמֶן ***'ōmen*** [TRUTH] 1x
<545> אָמְנָה ***'omnāh*** [CARE (UNDER THE)] 1x
<546> אָמְנָה ***'omnāh*** [INDEED] 2x
<547> אֹמְנָה ***'ōm^{e}nāh*** [DOORPOST] 1x
<548> אֲמָנָה ***'^{a}mānāh*** [COVENANT] 2x
<549> אֲמָנָה ***'^{a}mānāh*** [AMANA] 1x
<550> אַמְנוֹן ***'amnôn,*** אֲמִינוֹן ***'amiynôn*** [AMNON] 28x
<551> אָמְנָם ***'omnām*** [TRULY] 9x
<552> אֻמְנָם ***'umnām*** [SURELY] 5x
<553> אָמַץ ***'āmaṣ*** [STRONG (BE)] 41x
<554> אָמֹץ ***'āmōṣ*** [STRONG] 2x
<555> אֹמֶץ ***'ōmeṣ*** [STRONGER] 1x

<556> אַמְצָה ***ʼamṣāh*** [STRENGTH] 1x
<557> אַמְצִי ***ʼamṣiy*** [AMZI] 2x
<558> אֲמַצְיָה ***ʼ^{a}maṣyāh,*** אֲמַצְיָהוּ ***ʼ^{a}maṣyāhû*** [AMAZIAH] 40x
<559> אָמַר ***ʼāmar*** [SAY] 5,308x
<560> אֲמַר ***ʼ^{a}mar*** [SAY] 71x
<561> אֵמֶר ***ʼêmer*** [WORD] 49x
<562> אֹמֶר ***ʼōmer*** [WORD] 6x
<563> אִמַּר ***ʼimmar*** [LAMB] 3x
<564> אִמֵּר ***ʼimmêr*** [IMMER] 10x
<565> אֶמְרָה ***ʼemrāh,*** אִמְרָה, ***ʼimrāh*** [WORD] 37x
<566> אִמְרִי ***ʼimriy*** [IMRI] 2x
<567> אֱמֹרִי ***ʼ^{e}mōriy*** [AMORITE] 87x
<568> אֲמַרְיָה ***ʼ^{a}maryāh,*** אמַרְיָהוּ ***ʼ^{a}maryāhû*** [AMARIAH] 16x
<569> אַמְרָפֶל ***ʼamrāpel*** [AMRAPHEL] 2x
<570> אֶמֶשׁ ***ʼemeš*** [YESTERDAY] 5x
<571> אֱמֶת ***ʼ^{e}meṯ*** [TRUTH] TRUTH
<572> אַמְתַּחַת ***ʼamtaḥaṯ*** [SACK] 15x
<573> אֲמִתַּי ***ʼ^{a}mittay*** [AMITTAI] 2x
<574> אֵימְתָן ***ʼêmṯān*** [TERRIBLE] 1x
<575> אָן ***ʼān*** [WHERE] 40x
<576> אֲנָא ***ʼ^{a}nāʼ,*** אֲנָה ***ʼ^{a}nāh*** [I] 16x
<577> אָנָּא ***ʼānnāʼ,*** אָנָּה ***ʼānnāh*** [I BEG YOU] 13x
<578> אָנָה ***ʼānāh*** [LAMENT] 2x
<579> אָנָה ***ʼānāh*** [BEFALL] 4x
<580> אֲנוּ ***ʼ^{a}nû*** [WE] 1x
<581> אִנּוּן ***ʼinnûni,*** אִנִּין ***ʼinniyn*** [THEY] 4x
<582> אֱנוֹשׁ ***ʼenôš*** [MAN] 564x
<583> אֱנוֹשׁ ***ʼ^{e}nôš*** [ENOSH] 7x
<584> אָנַח ***ʼānaḥ*** [GROAN (verb)] 12x
<585> אֲנָחָה ***ʼ^{a}nāḥāh*** [GROANING] 11x
<586> אֲנַחְנָא ***ʼ^{a}naḥnāʼ,*** אֲנַחְנָה ***ʼ^{a}naḥnāh*** [WE] 4x
<587> אֲנַחְנוּ ***ʼ^{a}naḥnû*** [WE] 6x
<588> אֲנָחֲרָת ***ʼ^{a}nāḥ^{a}rāṯ*** [ANAHARATH] 1x
<589> אֲנִי ***ʼ^{a}niy*** [I] 18x (NAS)
<590> אֳנִי ***ʼ^{o}niy*** [FLEET OF SHIPS] 7x
<591> אֳנִיָּה ***ʼ^{o}niyyāh*** [SHIP] 64x
<592> אֲנִיָּה ***ʼ^{a}niyyāh*** [LAMENTATION] 2x
<593> אֲנִיעָם ***ʼ^{a}niyʻām*** [ANIAM] 1x
<594> אֲנָךְ ***ʼ^{a}nāḵ*** [PLUMB LINE] 2x
<595> אָנֹכִי ***ʼānōḵiy*** [I] 6x (NAS)
<596> אָנַן ***ʼānan*** [COMPLAIN] 2x
<597> אָנַס ***ʼānas*** [COMPEL] 1x
<598> אֲנַס ***ʼ^{a}nas*** [BAFFLE] 1x
<599> אָנַף ***ʼānap̱*** [ANGRY (BE)] 14x
<600> אֲנַף ***ʼ^{a}nap̱*** [FACE (noun)] 2x
<601> אֲנָפָה ***ʼ^{a}nāpāh*** [HERON] 2x
<602> אָנַק ***ʼānaq*** [GROAN (verb)] 4x
<603> אֲנָקָה ***ʼ^{a}nāqāh*** [GROANING] 4x
<604> אֲנָקָה ***ʼ^{a}nāqāh*** [FERRET] 1x
<605> אָנַשׁ ***ʼānaš*** [SICK (BE)] 9x
<606> אֱנָשׁ ***ʼ^{e}nāš*** [MAN] 25x

<607> אַנְתָּה ***'antah,*** אַנְתְּ ***'an^{e}t*** [YOU] 14x
<608> אַנְתּוּן ***'antûn*** [YOU] 1x
<609> אָסָא ***'āsā'*** [ASA] 58x
<610> אָסוּךְ ***'āsûk*** [JAR] 1x
<611> אָסוֹן ***'āsôn*** [HARM (noun)] 5x
<612> אֵסוּר ***'êsûr*** [BOND] 3x
<613> אֱסוּר ***'^{e}sûr*** [IMPRISONMENT] 3x
<614> אָסִיף ***'āsiyp,*** אָסִף ***'āsip*** [INGATHERING] 2x
<615> אָסִיר ***'āsiyr*** [PRISONER] 14x
<616> אַסִּיר ***'assiyr*** [PRISONERS] 3x
<617> אַסִּיר ***'assiyr*** [ASSIR] 5x
<618> אָסָם ***'āsām*** [BARN] 2x
<619> אַסְנָה ***'asnāh*** [ASNAH] 1x
<620> אָסְנַפַּר ***'osnappar*** [OSNAPPAR] 1x
<621> אָסְנַת ***'ās^{e}nat*** [ASENATH] 3x
<622> אָסַף ***'āsap*** [GATHER] 208x
<623> אָסָף ***'āsāp*** [ASAPH] 46x
<624> אָסֹף ***'āsōp,*** אֲסֻפִּים ***'^{a}suppiym*** [STOREHOUSE] 3x
<625> אֹסֶף ***'ōsep*** [GATHERING] 3x
<626> אֲסֵפָה ***'^{a}sêpāh*** [GATHERED TOGETHER (BE)] 1x
<627> אֲסֻפָּה ***'^{a}suppah*** [ASSEMBLY] 1x
<628> אֲסַפְסֻף ***'^{a}sapsup*** [MULTITUDE] 1x
<629> אָסְפַּרְנָא ***'osparnā'*** [DILIGENTLY] 7x
<630> אַסְפָּתָא ***'aspātā'*** [ASPATHA] 1x
<631> אָסַר ***'āsar*** [BIND] 72x
<632> אֱסָר ***'^{e}sār,*** אִסָּר ***'issār*** [PLEDGE (noun)] 11x
<633> אֱסָר ***'^{e}sār*** [DECREE (noun)] 7x
<634> אֵסַרְחַדּוֹן ***'êsarhaddôn*** [ESARHADDON] 3x
<635> אֶסְתֵּר ***'estêr*** [ESTHER] 55x
<636> אָע ***'ā'*** [TIMBER] 5x
<637> אַף ***'ap*** [ALSO] 17x
<638> אַף ***'ap*** [ALSO] 4x
<639> אַף ***'ap*** [NOSE] 276x
<640> אָפַד ***'āpad*** [GIRD] 2x
<641> אֵפֹד ***'êpōd*** [EPHOD (person)] 1x
<642> אֲפֻדָּה ***'^{a}puddāh*** [EPHOD (garment)] 3x
<643> אַפֶּדֶן ***'appeden*** [PALACE] 1x
<644> אָפָה ***'āpāh*** [BAKE] 25x
<645> אֵפוֹ ***'êpô,*** אֵפוֹא ***'êpô'*** [THEN] 15x
<646> אֵפוֹד ***'êpôd,*** אֵפֹד ***'êpōd*** [EPHOD (garment)] 49x
<647> אֲפִיחַ ***'^{a}piyah*** [APHIAH] 1x
<648> אָפִיל ***'āpiyl*** [GROWN UP] 1x
<649> אַפַּיִם ***'appayim*** [APPAIM] 2x
<650> אָפִיק ***'āpiyq*** [RAVINE] 19x
<651> אָפֵל ***'āpêl*** [DARK] 1x
<652> אֹפֶל ***'ōpel*** [DARKNESS] 9x
<653> אֲפֵלָה ***'^{a}pêlāh*** [DARKNESS] 10x
<654> אֶפְלָל ***'eplāl*** [EPHLAL] 2x
<655> אֹפֶן ***'ōpen*** [FITLY] 1x
<656> אָפֵס ***'āpês*** [FAIL] 5x
<657> אֶפֶס ***'epes,*** אֹפֶס ***'ōphes*** [ANKLE] 1x, [NOTHING] 42x

<658> אֶפֶס דַּמִּים ***’epes dammiym*** [EPHES-DAMMIM] 1x

<659> אֶפַע ***’ep̱a‘*** [NOTHING] 1x

<660> אֶפְעֶה ***’ep̱‘eh*** [VIPER] 3x

<661> אָפַף ***’āp̱ap̱*** [SURROUND] 5x

<662> אָפַק ***’āp̱aq*** [CONTROL (verb)] 7x

<663> אֲפִיק ***’ªp̱iyq,*** אֲפֵק ***’ªp̱êq*** [APHEK] 9x

<664> אֲפֵקָה ***’ªp̱êqāh*** [APHEKAH] 1x

<665> אֵפֶר ***’êp̱er*** [ASHES] 22x

<666> אֲפֵר ***’ªp̱êr*** [BANDAGE] 2x

<667> אֶפְרֹחַ ***’ep̱rōaḥ*** [YOUNG ONE] 4x

<668> אַפִּרְיוֹן ***’appiryôn*** [CARRIAGE] 1x

<669> אֶפְרַיִם ***’ep̱rayim*** [EPHRAIM] 180x

<670> אֲפָרְסָי ***’ªp̱ārᵉsāy*** [APHARSITES] 1x

<671> אֲפַרְסְכָי ***’ªp̱arsᵉḵāy,*** אֲפַרְסַתְכַי ***’ªp̱arsaṯḵāy*** [APHARSATHCHITES] 3x

<672> אֶפְרָת ***’ep̱rāṯ,*** אֶפְרָתָה ***’ep̱rāṯāh*** [EPHRATH] 10x

<673> אֶפְרָתִי ***’ep̱rāṯiy*** [EPHRAIMITE] 3x, [EPHRATHITE] 2x

<674> אַפְּתֹם ***’appᵉṯōm*** [REVENUE] 1x

<675> אֶצְבּוֹן ***’eṣbôn*** [EZBON] 2x

<676> אֶצְבַּע ***’eṣba‘*** [FINGER] 32x

<677> אֶצְבַּע ***’eṣba‘*** [FINGER] 3x

<678> אָצִיל ***’āṣiyl*** [FARTHEST CORNER] 1x, [NOBLE] 1x

<679> אַצִּיל ***’aṣṣiyl*** [LONG (adj.)] 1x, [WRIST] 2x

<680> אָצַל ***’āṣal*** [RESERVE (verb)] 5x

<681> אֵצֶל ***’êṣel*** [BESIDE] 59x

<682> אָצֵל ***’āṣêl,*** אָצַל ***’āṣal*** [AZEL] 7x

<683> אֲצַלְיָהוּ ***’ªṣalyāhû*** [AZALIAH] 2x

<684> אֹצֶם ***’ōṣem*** [OZEM] 2x

<685> אֶצְעָדָה ***’eṣ‘āḏāh*** [ARMLET] 2x

<686> אָצַר ***’āṣar*** [STORE (verb)] 5x

<687> אֵצֶר ***’êṣer*** [EZER] 5x

<688> אֶקְדָּח ***’eqḏāḥ*** [CRYSTAL] 1x

<689> אַקּוֹ ***’aqqô*** [WILD GOAT] 1x

<690> אֲרָא ***’ªrā’*** [ARA] 1x

<691> אֶרְאֵל ***’er’êl*** [VALIANT ONE] 1x

<692> אַרְאֵלִי ***’ar’êliy*** [ARELI] 3x

<693> אָרַב ***’āraḇ*** [WAIT (LIE IN)] 42x

<694> אֲרָב ***’ªrāḇ*** [ARAB] 1x

<695> אֶרֶב ***’ereḇ*** [DEN] 2x

<696> אֹרֶב ***’ōreḇ*** [AMBUSH] 1x

<697> אַרְבֶּה ***’arbeh*** [LOCUST] 24x

<698> אָרְבָּה ***’orbāh*** [TRICKERY] 1x

<699> אֲרֻבָּה ***’ªrubbāh*** [WINDOW] 9x

<700> אֲרֻבּוֹת ***’ªrubbôṯ*** [ARUBBOTH] 1x

<701> אַרְבִּי ***’arbiy*** [ARBITE] 1x

<702> אַרְבַּע ***’arba‘,*** אַרְבָּעָה ***’arbā‘āh*** [FOUR] 316x

<703> אַרְבַּע ***’arba‘*** [FOUR] 8x

<704> אַרְבַּע ***’arba‘*** [ARBA] 2x

<705> אַרְבָּעִים ***’arbā‘iym*** [FORTY, FORTIETH] 136x

<706> אַרְבַּעְתַּיִם ***’arba‘tayim*** [FOURFOLD] 1x

<707> אָרַג ***’ārag*** [WEAVE] 13x

<708> אֶרֶג ***’ereg̱*** [LOOM] 2x

<709> אַרְגֹּב **'argōḇ** [ARGOB] 5x
<710> אַרְגְּוָן **'arg^{e}wān** [PURPLE] 1x
<711> אַרְגְּוָן **'arg^{e}wān** [PURPLE] 3x
<712> אַרְגָּז **'argāz** [CHEST] 3x
<713> אַרְגָּמָן **'argāmān** [PURPLE] 38x
<714> אַרְדְּ **'ard** [ARD] 2x
<715> אַרְדּוֹן **'ardôn** [ARDON] 1x
<716> אַרְדִּי **'ardiy** [ARDITE] 1x
<717> אָרָה **'ārāh** [PICK (verb)] 2x
<718> אֲרוּ **^{a}rû** [BEHOLD (interj.)] 5x
<719> אַרְוַד **'arwaḏ** [ARVAD] 2x
<720> אֲרוֹד **^{a}rôḏ** [AROD] 1x
<721> אַרְוָדִי **'arwāḏiy** [ARVADITE] 2x
<722> אֲרוֹדִי **^{a}rôḏiy** [ARODI] 2x
<723> אֻרְוָה **'urwāh** [STALL] 3x
<724> אֲרוּכָה **^{a}rûḵāh,** אֲרֻכָה **^{a}ruḵāh** [HEALING] 6x
<725> אֲרוּמָה **^{a}rûmāh** [ARUMAH] 1x
<726> אֲרוֹמִים **^{a}rômiym** [ARAMEAN] 1x
<727> אָרוֹן **'ārôn,** אָרֹן **'ārōn** [ARK] 202x
<728> אֲרַוְנָה **^{a}rawnāh** [ARAUNAH] 9x
<729> אָרוּז **'ārûz** [CORD] 1x
<730> אֶרֶז **'erez** [CEDAR, CEDAR TREE] 73x
<731> אַרְזָה **'arzāh** [CEDAR WORK, BEAM OF CEDAR] 1x
<732> אָרַח **'āraḥ** [TRAVEL] 5x
<733> אָרַח **'āraḥ** [ARAH] 4x
<734> אֹרַח **'ōraḥ** [PATH] 58x
<735> אֲרַח **^{a}raḥ'** [PATH] 2x
<736> אֹרְחָה **'ōr^{e}ḥāh** [CARAVAN] 2x
<737> אֲרֻחָה **^{a}ruḥāh** [ALLOWANCE] 6x
<738> אֲרִי **^{a}riy,** אַרְיֵה **'aryêh** [LION] 80x
<739> אֲרִיאֵל **^{a}riy'êl** [ARIEL] 2x
<740> אֲרִיאֵל **^{a}riy'êl** [ARIEL] 4x
<741> אֲרִיאֵל **^{a}riy'êl,** אֲרִאֵל **^{a}ri'êl** [ALTAR HEARTH] 2x
<742> אֲרִידַי **^{a}riyḏay** [ARIDAI] 1x
<743> אֲרִידָתָא **^{a}riyḏāṯā'** [ARIDATHA] 1x
<744> אַרְיֵה **'aryêh** [LION] 10x
<745> אַרְיֵה **'aryêh** [ARIEH] 1x
<746> אַרְיוֹךְ **'aryôḵ** [ARIOCH] 7x
<747> אֲרִיסַי **^{a}riysay** [ARISAI] 1x
<748> אָרַךְ **'āraḵ** [PROLONG] 34x
<749> אֲרִיךְ **^{a}riyḵ** [PROPER] 1x
<750> אָרֵךְ **'ārêḵ** [SLOW] 15x
<751> אֶרֶךְ **'ereḵ** [ERECH] 1x
<752> אָרֹךְ **'ārōḵ** [LONG (adj.)] 3x
<753> אֹרֶךְ **'ōreḵ** [LENGTH] 95x
<754> אַרְכָה **'arḵāh** [LENGTHENING] 2x
<755> אַרְכֻבָּה **'arḵubbāh** [KNEE] 1x
<756> אַרְכְּוָי **'ark^{e}wāy** [ARCHEVITE] 1x
<757> אַרְכִּי **'arkiy** [ARCHITE, ARKITE] 6x
<758> אֲרָם **^{a}rām** [ARAM] 132x
<759> אַרְמוֹן **'armôn** [STRONGHOLD] 32x

<760> אֲרַם צוֹבָה ***ªram ṣôḇāh*** [ARAM-ZOBAH] 1x

<761> אֲרַמִּי ***ªrammiy*** [ARAMEAN] 11x

<762> אֲרָמִית ***ªrāmiyṯ*** [ARAMAIC] 5x

<763> אֲרַם נַהֲרַיִם ***ªram nahª-rayim*** [ARAM OF THE (TWO) RIVERS] 6x

<764> אַרְמֹנִי ***'armōniy*** [ARMONI] 1x

<765> אֲרָן ***ªrān*** [ARAN] 2x

<766> אֹרֶן ***'ōren*** [ASH] 1x

<767> אֹרֶן ***'ōren*** [OREN] 1x

<768> אַרְנֶבֶת ***'arneḇeṯ*** [RABBIT] 2x

<769> אַרְנוֹן ***'arnôn*** [ARNON] 25x

<770> אַרְנָן ***'arnān*** [ARNAN] 1x

<771> אָרְנָן ***'ornān or 'ārnān*** [ORNAN] 12x

<772> אֲרַע ***ªra'*** [EARTH] 21x

<773> אַרְעִי ***'ar'iy*** [BOTTOM] 1x

<774> אַרְפָּד ***'arpāḏ*** [ARPAD] 6x

<775> אַרְפַּכְשַׁד ***'arpaḵšaḏ*** [ARPHAXAD] 9x

<776> אֶרֶץ ***'ereṣ*** [EARTH] 2,495x

<777> אַרְצָא ***'arṣā'*** [ARZA] 1x

<778> אֲרַק ***ªraq*** [EARTH] 1x

<779> אָרַר ***'ārar*** [CURSE (verb)] 63x

<780> אֲרָרַט ***ªrāraṭ*** [ARARAT] 4x

<781> אָרַשׂ ***'āraś*** [BETROTH] 11x

<782> אֲרֶשֶׁת ***ªrešeṯ*** [DESIRE (noun)] 1x

<783> אַרְתַּחְשַׁשְׂתָּא ***'artaḥšaśtā'*** [ARTAXERXES] 15x

<784> אֵשׁ ***'ēš*** [FIRE] 379x

<785> אֶשָּׁא ***'eššā'*** [FIRE] 1x

<786> אִשׁ ***'iš*** [THERE IS ONE] 2x

<787> אֹשׁ ***'ōš*** [FOUNDATION] 3x

<788> אַשְׁבֵּל ***'ašbêl*** [ASHBEL] 3x

<789> אַשְׁבֵּלִי ***'ašbêliy*** [ASHBELITE] 1x

<790> אֶשְׁבָּן ***'ešbān*** [ESHBAN] 2x

<791> אַשְׁבֵּעַ ***'ašbêa'*** [ASHBEA] 1x

<792> אֶשְׁבַּעַל ***'ešba'al*** [ESH-BAAL] 2x

<793> אָשֵׁד ***'āšêḏ*** [SLOPE] 1x

<794> אֲשֵׁדָה ***ªšêḏāh*** [SLOPE] 3x

<795> אַשְׁדּוֹד ***'ašdôḏ*** [ASHDOD] 17x

<796> אַשְׁדּוֹדִי ***'ašdôḏiy*** [ASHDODITE] 5x

<797> אַשְׁדּוֹדִית ***'ašdôḏiyṯ*** [ASHDOD (LANGUAGE OF)] 1x

<798> אַשְׁדּוֹת הַפִּסְגָּה ***'ašdôṯ happisgāh*** [ASHDOTHPISGAH] 3x

<799> אֵשְׁדָּת ***'êšdāṯ*** [FIERY LAW] 1x, [FLASHING LIGHTNING] 1x, [SLOPE] 1x

<800> אֶשָּׁה ***'eššāh*** [FIRE] 1x

<801> אִשֶּׁה ***'iššeh*** [OFFERING] 65x

<802> אִשָּׁה ***'iššāh*** [WOMAN] 780x

<803> אָשְׁיָה ***'āšyāh*** [FOUNDATION] 1x

<804> אַשּׁוּר ***'aššûr*** [ASSHUR] 151x

<805> אַשּׁוּרִי ***'aššûriy*** [ASSHURITE] 2x

<806> אַשְׁחוּר ***'ašḥûr*** [ASHHUR] 2x

<807> אֲשִׁימָא ***ªšiymā'*** [ASHIMA] 1x

<808> אָשִׁישׁ ***'āšiyš*** [FOUNDATION] 1x

<809> אֲשִׁישָׁה ***ªšiyšāh*** [RAISIN CAKES] 4x

<810> אֶשֶׁךְ ***'ešeḵ*** [TESTICLE] 1x

<811> אֶשְׁכּוֹל ***'eškôl,*** אֶשְׁכֹּל ***'eškōl*** [CLUSTER] 9x

<812> אֶשְׁכֹּל ***'eškōl,*** אֶשְׁכּוֹל ***'eškôl*** [ESHCOL] 6x

<813> אַשְׁכְּנַז ***'ašk^{e}naz*** [ASHKENAZ] 3x

<814> אֶשְׁכָּר ***'eškār*** [GIFT] 2x

<815> אֵשֶׁל ***'ēšel*** [TAMARISK TREE] 3x

<816> אָשַׁם ***'āšam,*** אָשֵׁם ***āšêm*** [GUILTY (BE)] 35x

<817> אָשָׁם ***'āšām*** [GUILT] 46x

<818> אָשֵׁם ***'āšêm*** [GUILTY (adj.)] 3x

<819> אַשְׁמָה ***'ašmāh*** [GUILT] 19x

<820> אַשְׁמָן ***'ašmān*** [DESOLATE PLACES] 1x, [VIGOROUS PEOPLE] 1x

<821> אַשְׁמוּרָה ***'ašmûrāh,*** אַשְׁמֹרֶת ***'ašmōreṯ*** [WATCH (noun)] 7x

<822> אֶשְׁנָב ***'ešnāḇ*** [LATTICE] 2x

<823> אַשְׁנָה ***'ašnāh*** [ASHNAH] 2x

<824> אֶשְׁעָן ***'eš'ān*** [ESHAN] 1x

<825> אַשָּׁף ***'aššāp̱*** [ENCHANTER] 2x

<826> אָשַׁף ***'āšap̱*** [ENCHANTER] 6x

<827> אַשְׁפָּה ***'ašpāh*** [QUIVER] 6x

<828> אַשְׁפְּנַז ***'ašp^{e}naz*** [ASHPENAZ] 1x

<829> אֶשְׁפָּר ***'ešpār*** [PIECE] 2x

<830> אַשְׁפֹּת ***'ašpōṯ,*** אַשְׁפּוֹת ***'ašpôṯ*** [ASH HEAP] 7x

<831> אַשְׁקְלוֹן ***'ašq^{e}lôn*** [ASHKELON] 12x

<832> אֶשְׁקְלוֹנִי ***'ešq^{e}lôniy*** [ASHKELONITE] 1x

<833> אָשַׁר ***'āšar*** [BLESS] 16x

<834> אֲשֶׁר ***^{a}šer*** [WHICH] 111x

<835> אֶשֶׁר ***'ešer*** [BLESSED] 45x

<836> אָשֵׁר ***'āšêr*** [ASHER] 43x

<837> אֹשֶׁר ***'ōšer*** [HAPPY] 1x

<838> אָשֻּׁר ***'oššur,*** אַשֻּׁר ***'aššur*** [STEP (noun)] 9x

<839> אֲשֻׁרִים ***^{a}šuriym*** [ASHURITES] 1x

<840> אֲשַׂרְאֵל ***^{a}śar'êl*** [ASAREL] 1x

<841> אֲשַׂרְאֵלָה ***^{a}śar'êlāh*** [ASARELAH] 1x

<842> אֲשֵׁרָה ***^{a}šêrāh,*** אֲשֵׁירָה ***^{a}šêyrāh*** [ASHERAH] 40x

<843> אָשֵׁרִי ***'āšêriy*** [ASHERITE] 1x

<844> אַשְׂרִיאֵל ***'aśriy'êl*** [ASRIEL] 3x

<845> אַשְׂרִאֵלִי ***'aśri'êliy*** [ASRIELITE] 1x

<846> אֻשַּׁרְנָא ***'uššarnā'*** [WALL] 2x

<847> אֶשְׁתָּאוֹל ***'eštā'ōl*** [ESHTAOL] 7x

<848> אֶשְׁתָּאֻלִי ***'eštā'uliy*** [ESHTAOLITE] 1x

<849> אֶשְׁתַּדּוּר ***'eštaddûr*** [SEDITION] 2x

<850> אֶשְׁתּוֹן ***'eštôn*** [ESHTON] 2x

<851> אֶשְׁתְּמוֹעַ ***'ešt^{e}môa',*** אֶשְׁתְּמֹה ***'ešt^{e}mōh*** [ESHTEMOA] 6x

<852> אָת ***'āṯ*** [SIGN (noun)] 3x

<853> אֵת ***'êṯ*** [____] 1x (NAS)

<854> אֵת ***'êṯ*** [WITH] 24x

<855> אֵת ***'êṯ*** [PLOWSHARE] 5x

<856> אֶתְבַּעַל ***'eṯba'al*** [ETHBAAL] 1x

<857> אָתָה ***'āṯāh,*** אָתָא ***'āṯā'*** [COME] 21x

<858> אֲתָה ***^{a}ṯāh,*** אֲתָא ***^{a}ṯā'*** [COME] 16x

<859> אַתָּה ***'attāh*** [YOU] 23x (NAS)

<860> אָתוֹן ***'āṯôn*** [DONKEY] 34x

<861> אַתּוּן ***'attûn*** [FURNACE] 10x

<862> אַתּוּק ***'attûq,*** אַתִּיק ***'attiyq*** [GALLERY] 5x
<863> אִתַּי ***'ittay*** [ITTAI] 9x
<864> אֵתָם ***'ēṯām*** [ETHAM] 4x
<865> אֶתְמוֹל ***'eṯmôl,*** אֶתְמוּל ***'eṯmûl*** [YESTERDAY] 8x
<866> אֶתְנָה ***'eṯnāh*** [PAY] 1x
<867> אֶתְנִי ***'eṯniy*** [ETHNI] 1x
<868> אֶתְנַן ***'eṯnan*** [EARNINGS] 11x
<869> אֶתְנָן ***'eṯnān*** [ETHNAN] 1x
<870> אֲתַר ***^{a}ṯar*** [PLACE (noun)] 8x
<871> אֲתָרִים ***^{a}ṯāriym*** [SPIES] 1x

ב Beth

<872> בִּאָה ***bi'āh*** [ENTRANCE] 1x
<873> בִּאִישׁ ***bi'ysh*** [WICKED] 1x
<874> בָּאַר ***bā'ar*** [EXPLAIN] 3x
<875> בְּאֵר ***b^{e}'ēr*** [WELL (noun)] 37x
<876> בְּאֵר ***b^{e}'ēr*** [BEER (proper noun)] 2x
<877> בֹּאר ***bō'r*** [WELL (noun)] 4x
<878> בְּאֵרָא ***b^{e}'ērā'*** [BEERA] 1x
<879> בְּאֵר אֵלִים ***b^{e}'ēr 'ēliym*** [BEER-ELIM] 1x
<880> בְּאֵרָה ***b^{e}'ērāh*** [BEERAH] 1x
<881> בְּאֵרוֹת ***'b^{e}'ērôṯ*** [BEEROTH] 6x
<882> בְּאֵרִי ***b^{e}'ēriy*** [BEERI] 2x
<883> בְּאֵר לַחַי רֹאִי ***b^{e}'ēr laḥay rō'iy*** [BEER-LAHAI-ROI] 3x
<884> בְּאֵר שֶׁבַע ***b^{e}'ēr šeḇa'*** [BEERSHEBA] 34x
<885> בְּאֵרֹת בְּנֵי־יַעֲקָן ***b^{e}'ērōṯ b^{e}nêy ya^{a}qān*** [BEEROTH BENE-JAAKAN] 1x
<886> בְּאֵרֹתִי ***b^{e}'ērōṯiy*** [BEEROTHITE] 5x
<887> בָּאַשׁ ***bā'ash*** [STINK] 17x
<888> בְּאֵשׁ ***b^{e}'ēš*** [DISPLEASED (BE)] 1x
<889> בְּאֹשׁ ***b^{e}'ōš*** [STENCH] 3x
<890> בָּאְשָׁה ***bo'šāh*** [STINKWEED] 1x
<891> בָּאֻשׁ ***bā'uš*** [WORTHLESS ONE] 2x
<892> בָּבָה ***bāḇāh*** [APPLE] 1x
<893> בֵּבַי ***bêḇay*** [BEBAI] 5x
<894> בָּבֶל ***bāḇel*** [BABEL] 262x
<895> בָּבֶל ***bāḇel*** [BABEL] 25x
<896> בָּבְלָי ***bāḇelāy*** [BABYLONIAN] 1x
<897> בַּג ***bag̱*** [PLUNDER (noun)] 1x
<898> בָּגַד ***bāg̱aḏ*** [DECEITFULLY (DEAL)] 49x
<899> בֶּגֶד ***beg̱eḏ*** [GARMENT] 215x, [TREACHEROUSNESS] 2x
<900> בֹּגְדוֹת ***bōg̱^{e}ḏôṯ*** [TREACHEROUS] 1x
<901> בָּגוֹד ***bāg̱ôḏ*** [TREACHEROUS] 2x
<902> בִּגְוַי ***bigway*** [BIGVAI] 6x
<903> בִּגְתָא ***bigṯā'*** [BIGTHA] 1x
<904> בִּגְתָן ***bigṯān,*** בִּגְתָנָא ***bigṯānā'*** [BIGTHAN or BIGTHANA] 2x
<905> בַּד ***baḏ*** [ALONE], [PART (noun)] 56x
<906> בַּד ***baḏ*** [LINEN] 23x
<907> בַּד ***baḏ*** [TALK (EMPTY, IDLE)] 5x

<908> בָּדָא ***bāḏā'*** [DEVISE] 2x
<909> בָּדַד ***bāḏaḏ*** [ALONE (BE)] 3x
<910> בָּדָד ***bāḏāḏ*** [ALONE] 11x
<911> בְּדַד ***b^{e}ḏaḏ*** [BEDAD] 2x
<912> בֵּדְיָה ***bêḏ^{e}yāh*** [BEDEIAH] 1x
<913> בְּדִיל ***b^{e}ḏiyl*** [TIN] 6x
<914> בָּדַל ***bāḏal*** [SEPARATE (verb)] 44x
<915> בָּדָל ***bāḏāl*** [PIECE] 1x
<916> בְּדֹלַח ***b^{e}ḏōlaḥ*** [BDELLIUM] 2x
<917> בְּדָן ***b^{e}ḏān*** [BEDAN] 2x
<918> בָּדַק ***bāḏaq*** [REPAIR] 1x
<919> בֶּדֶק ***beḏeq*** [DAMAGE (noun)] 10x
<920> בִּדְקַר ***biḏqar*** [BIDKAR] 1x
<921> בְּדַר ***b^{e}ḏar*** [SCATTER] 1x
<922> בֹּהוּ ***bōhû*** [VOID] 3x
<923> בַּהַט ***bahaṭ*** [PORPHYRY] 1x
<924> בְּהִילוּ ***b^{e}hiylû*** [HASTE (noun)] 1x
<925> בָּהִיר ***bāhiyr*** [BRIGHT] 1x
<926> בָּהַל ***bāhal*** [TERRIFIED (BE)] 39x
<927> בְּהַל ***b^{e}hal*** [HASTE (BE IN)] 11x
<928> בֶּהָלָה ***behālāh*** [TERROR] 4x
<929> בְּהֵמָה ***b^{e}hêmāh*** [ANIMAL] 189x
<930> בְּהֵמוֹת ***b^{e}hêmôṯ*** [BEHEMOTH] 1x
<931> בֹּהֶן ***bōhen*** [THUMB] 16x
<932> בֹּהַן ***bōhan*** [BOHAN] 2x
<933> בֹּהַק ***bōhaq*** [SPOT (FRECKLED, WHITE)] 1x
<934> בַּהֶרֶת ***baheret*** [SPOT (BRIGHT, SHINY)] 13x
<935> בּוֹא ***bô'*** [COME] 2,577x
<936> בּוּז ***bûz*** [DESPISE] 12x
<937> בּוּז ***bûz*** [CONTEMPT] 11x
<938> בּוּז ***bûz*** [BUZ] 3x
<939> בּוּזָה ***bûzāh*** [DESPISED] 1x
<940> בּוּזִי ***bûziy*** [BUZITE] 2x
<941> בּוּזִי ***bûziy*** [BUZI] 1x
<942> בַּוַּי ***bawway*** [BAVVAI] 1x
<943> בּוּךְ ***bûḵ*** [WANDER] 3x
<944> בּוּל ***bûl*** [FOOD] 2x
<945> בּוּל ***bûl*** [BUL] 1x
<946> בּוּנָה ***bûnāh*** [BUNAH] 1x
<947> בּוּס ***bûs*** [TREAD DOWN] 12x
<948> בּוּץ ***bûṣ*** [FINE LINEN] 8x
<949> בּוֹצֵץ ***bôṣêṣ*** [BOZEZ] 1x
<950> בּוּקָה ***bûqāh*** [EMPTY (adj.)] 1x
<951> בּוֹקֵר ***bôqêr*** [HERDSMAN] 1x
<952> בּוּר ***bûr*** [DECLARE] 1x
<953> בּוֹר ***bôr*** [CISTERN] 69x
<954> בּוֹשׁ ***bôš*** [ASHAMED (BE)] 109x
<955> בּוּשָׁה ***bûšāh*** [SHAME] 4x
<956> בִּית ***biyṯ*** [NIGHT] 1x
<957> בַּז ***baz*** [PLUNDER (noun)] 25x
<958> בָּזָא ***bāzā'*** [DIVIDE] 2x

<959> בָּזָה ***bāzāh*** [DESPISE] 43x
<960> בָּזֹה ***bāzōh*** [DESPISED] 1x
<961> בִּזָּה ***bizzāh*** [PLUNDER (noun)] 10x
<962> בָּזַז ***bāzaz*** [PLUNDER (verb)] 43x
<963> בִּזָּיוֹן ***bizzāyôn*** [DISRESPECT] 1x
<964> בִּזְיוֹתְיָה ***bizyôṯyāh*** [BIZIOTHIAH] 1x
<965> בָּזָק ***bāzāq*** [LIGHTNING] 1x
<966> בֶּזֶק ***bezeq*** [BEZEK] 3x
<967> בָּזַר ***bāzar*** [SCATTER] 2x
<968> בִּזְּתָא ***bizz^{e}ṯā’*** [BIZTHA] 1x
<969> בָּחוֹן ***bāḥôn*** [ASSAYER] 1x
<970> בָּחוּר ***baḥûr*** [YOUNG MAN] 45x
<971> בַּחוּן ***baḥûn,*** בַּחִין ***baḥiyn*** [SIEGE TOWER] 1x
<972> בָּחִיר ***bāḥiyr*** [CHOSEN] 13x
<973> בָּחַל ***bāḥal*** [ABHOR] 2x
<974> בָּחַן ***bāḥan*** [TEST (verb)] 29x
<975> בַּחַן ***baḥan*** [WATCHTOWER] 1x
<976> בֹּחַן ***bōḥan*** [TESTED] 2x
<977> בָּחַר ***bāḥar*** [CHOOSE] 172x
<978> בַּחֲרוּמִי ***baḥ^{a}rûmiy*** [BAHARUMITE] 1x
<979> בְּחוּרוֹת ***b^{e}ḥûrôṯ,*** בְּחוּרִים ***b^{e}ḥûriym*** [YOUTH] 3x
<980> בַּחוּרִים ***baḥûriym,*** בַּחֻרִים ***baḥuriym*** [BAHURIM] 5x
<981> בָּטָה ***bāṭāh,*** בָּטָא ***bāṭā’*** [THOUGHTLESSLY (SPEAK)] 4x
<982> בָּטַח ***bāṭaḥ*** [TRUST (verb)] 120x
<983> בֶּטַח ***beṭaḥ*** [SECURITY] 42x
<984> בֶּטַח ***beṭaḥ*** [BETAH] 1x
<985> בִּטְחָה ***biṭḥāh*** [TRUST (noun)] 1x
<986> בִּטָּחוֹן ***biṭṭāḥôn*** [CONFIDENCE] 3x
<987> בַּטֻּחוֹת ***baṭṭuḥôṯ*** [SECURE] 1x
<988> בָּטַל ***bāṭal*** [CEASE] 1x
<989> בְּטֵל ***b^{e}ṭêl*** [CEASE] 6x
<990> בֶּטֶן ***beṭen*** [WOMB] 72x
<991> בֶּטֶן ***beṭen*** [BETEN] 1x
<992> בָּטְנָה ***boṭnāh*** [PISTACHIO NUT] 1x
<993> בְּטֹנִים ***b^{e}ṭōniym*** [BETONIM] 1x
<994> בִּי ***biy*** [EXCUSE ME] 12x
<995> בִּין ***biyn*** [PERCEIVE] 170x
<996> בַּיִן ***bayin*** [BETWEEN] 32x
<997> בֵּין ***bêyn*** [BETWEEN] 2x
<998> בִּינָה ***biynāh*** [UNDERSTANDING] 38x
<999> בִּינָה ***biynāh*** [UNDERSTANDING] 1x
<1000> בֵּיצָה ***bêyṣāh*** [EGG] 6x
<1001> בִּירָה ***biyrāh*** [CITADEL] 1x
<1002> בִּירָה ***biyrāh*** [CITADEL] 16x
<1003> בִּירָנִיּוֹת ***biyrāniyyôṯ*** [FORTRESS] 2x
<1004> בַּיִת ***bayiṯ*** [HOUSE] 2,055x
<1005> בַּיִת ***bayiṯ*** [HOUSE] 44x
<1006> בַּיִת ***bayiṯ*** [BAJITH] 1x
<1007> בֵּית אָוֶן ***bêyṯ ’āwen*** [BETH AVEN] 8x
<1008> בֵּית־אֵל ***bêyṯ–‘êl*** [BETHEL] 70x
<1009> בֵּית אַרְבֵּאל ***bêyṯ ’arbê’l*** [BETH ARBEL] 1x

<1010> בֵּית בַּעַל מְעוֹן ***bêyṯ ba‘al m^{e}‘ôn,*** בֵּית מְעוֹן ***bêyṯ m^{e}‘ôn*** [BETH BAAL MEON, BETH MEON] 2x
<1011> בֵּית בִּרְאִי ***bêyṯ bir’iy*** [BETH BIRI] 1x
<1012> בֵּית בָּרָה ***bêyṯ bārāh*** [BETH BARAH] 1x
<1013> בֵּית־גָּדֵר ***bêyṯ-gāḏêr*** [BETH GADER] 1x
<1014> בֵּית גָּמוּל ***bêyṯ gāmûl*** [BETH GAMUL] 1x
<1015> בֵּית דִּבְלָתַיִם ***bêyṯ diḇlāṯayim*** [BETH DIBLATHAIM] 1x
<1016> בֵּית־דָּגוֹן ***bêyṯ-dāḡôn*** [BETH DAGON] 2x
<1017> בֵּית הָאֱלִי ***bêyṯ hā*liy*** [BETHELITE] 1x
<1018> בֵּית הָאֵצֶל ***bêyṯ hā’êṣel*** [BETH EZEL] 1x
<1019> בֵּית הַגִּלְגָּל ***bêyṯ haggilgāl*** [BETH GILGAL] 1x
<1020> בֵּית הַיְשִׁימוֹת ***bêyṯ hay^{e}šiymôṯ*** [BETH JESHIMOTH] 4x
<1021> בֵּית הַכֶּרֶם ***bêyṯ hakkerem*** [BETH HAKKEREM] 2x
<1022> בֵּית הַלַּחְמִי ***bêyṯ hallaḥmiy*** [BETHLEHEMITE] 4x
<1023> בֵּית הַמֶּרְחָק ***bêyṯ hammerḥāq*** [LAST HOUSE] 1x
<1024> בֵּית הַמַּרְכָּבוֹת ***beyṯ hammarkāḇôṯ*** [BETH MARCABOTH] 2x
<1025> בֵּית הָעֵמֶק ***bêyṯ hā‘êmeq*** [BETH EMEK] 1x
<1026> בֵּית הָעֲרָבָה ***bêyṯ hā‘^{a}rāḇāh*** [BETH ARABAH] 4x
<1027> בֵּית הָרָם ***bêyṯ hārām*** [BETH HARAM] 1x
<1028> בֵּית הָרָן ***bêyṯ hārān*** [BETH HARAN] 1x
<1029> בֵּית הַשִּׁטָּה ***bêyṯ haššiṭṭah*** [BETH SHITTAH] 1x
<1030> בֵּית הַשִּׁמְשִׁי ***bêyṯ haššimšiy*** [BETHSHEMITE] 2x
<1031> בֵּית חָגְלָה ***bêyṯ ḥoḡlāh*** [BETH HOGLAH] 3x
<1032> בֵּית חוֹרוֹן ***bêyṯ ḥôrôn*** [BETH HORON] 14x
<1033> בֵּית כָּר ***bêyṯ kār*** [BETH CAR] 1x
<1034> בֵּית לְבָאוֹת ***bêyṯ l^{e}ḇā’ôṯ*** [BETH LEBAOTH] 1x
<1035> בֵּית לֶחֶם ***beyṯ leḥem*** [BETHLEHEM] 41x
<1036> בֵּית לְעַפְרָה ***beyṯ l^{e}‘ap̄rāh*** [BETH OPHRAH] 1x
<1037> בֵּית מִלּוֹא ***bêyṯ millô’*** [BETH MILLO] 3x
<1038> בֵּית מַעֲכָה ***bêyṯ ma‘^{a}ḵāh*** [BETH MAACAH] 2x
<1039> בֵּית נִמְרָה ***bêyṯ nimrāh*** [BETH NIMRAH] 2x
<1040> בֵּית עֶדֶן ***bêyṯ ‘eḏen*** [BETH EDEN] 1x
<1041> בֵּית עַזְמָוֶת ***bêyṯ ‘azmāweṯ*** [BETH AZMAVETH] 1x
<1042> בֵּית עֲנוֹת ***bêyṯ ‘^{a}nôṯ*** [BETH ANOTH] 1x
<1043> בֵּית עֲנָת ***bêyṯ ‘^{a}nāṯ*** [BETH ANATH] 3x
<1044> בֵּית עֵקֶד ***bêyṯ ‘êqeḏ*** [BETH EKED] 2x
<1045> בֵּית עַשְׁתָּרוֹת ***bêyṯ ‘aštarôṯ*** [BETH ASHTAROTH] 1x
<1046> בֵּית פֶּלֶט ***bêyṯ peleṭ*** [BETH PELET] 2x
<1047> בֵּית פְּעוֹר ***bêyṯ p^{e}‘ôr*** [BETH PEOR] 4x
<1048> בֵּית פַּצֵּץ ***bêyṯ paṣṣêṣ*** [BETH PAZZEZ] 1x
<1049> בֵּית צוּר ***bêyṯ ṣûr*** [BETH ZUR] 4x
<1050> בֵּית רְחוֹב ***bêyṯ r^{e}ḥôḇ*** [BETH REHOB] 2x
<1051> בֵּית רָפָא ***bêyṯ rāp̄ā’*** [BETH RAPHA] 1x
<1052> בֵּית שְׁאָן ***bêyṯ š^{e}’ān,*** בֵּית שָׁן ***bêyṯ šān*** [BETH SHEAN] 9x
<1053> בֵּית שֶׁמֶשׁ ***bêyṯ šemeš*** [BETH SHEMESH] 21x
<1054> בֵּית תַּפּוּחַ ***bêyṯ tappûaḥ*** [BETH TAPPUAH] 1x
<1055> בִּיתָן ***biyṯān*** [PALACE] 3x
<1056> בָּכָא ***bāḵā’*** [BACA] 1x
<1057> בָּכָא ***bāḵā’*** [BALSAM TREE] 4x
<1058> בָּכָה ***bāḵāh*** [WEEP] 114x

<1059> בֶּכֶה ***beḵeh*** [WEEPING] 1x
<1060> בְּכוֹר ***bᵉḵôr,*** בְּכֹר ***bᵉḵōr*** [FIRSTBORN] 117x
<1061> בִּכּוּרִים ***bikkûriym*** [FIRSTFRUITS] 18x
<1062> בְּכוֹרָה ***bᵉḵôrāh,*** בְּכֹרָה ***bᵉḵōrāh*** [BIRTHRIGHT] 15x
<1063> בִּכּוּרָה ***biḵkûrāh*** [FIRST RIPE FRUIT, FIRST RIPE FIG] 4x
<1064> בְּכוֹרַת ***bᵉḵôraṯ*** [BECORATH] 1x
<1065> בְּכִי ***bᵉḵiy*** [WEEPING] 30x
<1066> בֹּכִים ***bōḵiym*** [BOCHIM] 2x
<1067> בְּכִירָה ***bᵉḵiyrāh*** [FIRSTBORN] 6x
<1068> בְּכִית ***bᵉḵiyṯ*** [MOURNING] 1x
<1069> בָּכַר ***bāḵar*** [BORN FIRST (BE)] 4x
<1070> בֵּכֶר ***bêḵer*** [CAMEL (YOUNG)] 1x
<1071> בֶּכֶר ***beḵer*** [BECHER] 5x
<1072> בִּכְרָה ***biḵrāh*** [CAMEL (YOUNG)] 1x
<1073> בַּכֻּרוֹת ***bakkûrôṯ*** [FIRST RIPE] 1x
<1074> בֹּכְרוּ ***bōḵᵉrû*** [BOCHERU] 2x
<1075> בִּכְרִי ***biḵriy*** [BICHRI] 8x
<1076> בַּכְרִי ***baḵriy*** [BECHERITE] 1x
<1077> בַּל ***bal*** [NOT] 71x
<1078> בֵּל ***bêl*** [BEL] 3x
<1079> בָּל ***bāl*** [MIND] 1x
<1080> בְּלָא ***bᵉlā'*** [WEAR OUT, WEAR DOWN] 1x
<1081> בַּלְאֲדָן ***balᵃḏān*** [BALADAN] 2x
<1082> בָּלַג ***bālag̲*** [SMILE (verb)] 4x
<1083> בִּלְגָּה ***bilgāh*** [BILGAH] 3x
<1084> בִּלְגַּי ***bilgay*** [BILGAI] 1x
<1085> בִּלְדַּד ***bildaḏ*** [BILDAD] 5x
<1086> בָּלָה ***bālāh*** [WEAR OUT] 16x
<1087> בָּלֶה ***bāleh*** [OLD] 5x
<1088> בָּלָה ***bālāh*** [BALAH] 1x
<1089> בָּלַהּ ***bālah*** [AFRAID (MAKE)] 1x
<1090> בִּלְהָה ***bilhāh*** [BILHAH] 11x
<1091> בַּלָּהָה ***ballāhāh*** [TERROR] 10x
<1092> בִּלְהָן ***bilhān*** [BILHAN] 4x
<1093> בְּלוֹ ***bᵉlô*** [TRIBUTE] 3x
<1094> בְּלוֹי ***bᵉlôy*** [OLD] 3x
<1095> בֵּלְטְשַׁאצַּר ***bêlṭᵉša'ṣṣar*** [BELTESHAZZAR] 2x
<1096> בֵּלְטְשַׁאצַּר ***bêlṭᵉša'ṣṣar*** [BELTESHAZZAR] 8x
<1097> בְּלִי ***bᵉliy*** [NOT] 58x
<1098> בְּלִיל ***bᵉliyl*** [FODDER] 3x
<1099> בְּלִימָה ***bᵉliymāh*** [NOTHING] 1x
<1100> בְּלִיַּעַל ***bᵉliyyaʻal*** [WORTHLESS] 26x
<1101> בָּלַל ***bālal*** [MIX] 44x
<1102> בָּלַם ***bālam*** [CONTROL (verb)] 1x
<1103> בָּלַס ***bālas*** [DRESSER] 1x
<1104> בָּלַע ***bālaʻ*** [SWALLOW (verb)] 48x
<1105> בֶּלַע ***belaʻ*** [DEVOURING] 2x
<1106> בֶּלַע ***belaʻ*** [BELA] 14x
<1107> בַּלְעֲדֵי ***balʻᵃḏêy,*** בִּלְעֲדֵי ***bilʻᵃḏêy*** [APART FROM] 17x
<1108> בַּלְעִי ***balʻiy*** [BELAITE] 1x
<1109> בִּלְעָם ***bilʻām*** [BILEAM] 61x

<1110> בָּלַק ***bālaq*** [WASTE (MAKE, BE, LAY)] 2x
<1111> בָּלָק ***bālāq*** [BALAK] 43x
<1112> בֵּלְשַׁאצַּר ***bêlša'ṣṣar*** [BELSHAZZAR] 1x
<1113> בֵּלְשַׁאצַּר ***bêlša'ṣṣar*** [BELSHAZZAR] 7x
<1114> בִּלְשָׁן ***bilšān*** [BILSHAN] 2x
<1115> בִּלְתִּי ***biltiy*** [NOT] 30x
<1116> בָּמָה ***bāmāh*** [HIGH PLACE] 102x
<1117> בָּמָה ***bāmāh*** [BAMAH] 1x
<1118> בִּמְהָל ***bimhāl*** [BIMHAL] 1x
<1119> בְּמוֹ ***b^{e}mô*** [IN] 10x
<1120> בָּמוֹת ***bāmôṯ,*** בָּמוֹת בַּעַל ***bāmôṯ baʻal*** [BAMOTH] 4x
<1121> בֵּן ***bên*** [SON] 4,904x
<1122> בֵּן ***bên*** [BEN] 1x
<1123> בְּנֵי ***b^{e}nêy*** [SON] 11x
<1124> בְּנָה ***b^{e}nāh,*** בְּנָא ***b^{e}nā'*** [BUILD] 22x
<1125> בֶּן־אֲבִינָדָב ***ben ^{a}ḇiynāḏāḇ*** [BEN-ABINADAB] 1x
<1126> בֶּן־אוֹנִי ***ben 'ôniy*** [BEN-ONI] 1x
<1127> בֶּן־גֶּבֶר ***ben-geḇer*** [BEN-GEBER] 1x
<1128> בֶּן־דֶּקֶר ***ben-deqer*** [BEN-DEKER] 1x
<1129> בָּנָה ***bānāh*** [BUILD] 376x
<1130> בֶּן־הֲדַד ***ben h^{a}ḏaḏ*** [BEN-HADAD] 25x
<1131> בִּנּוּי ***binnûy*** [BINNUI] 7x
<1132> בֶּן־זוֹחֵת ***ben zôḥêṯ*** [BEN-ZOHETH] 1x
<1133> בֶּן־חוּר ***ben ḥûr*** [BEN-HUR] 1x
<1134> בֶּן חַיִל ***ben ḥayil*** [BEN-HAIL] 1x
<1135> בֶּן־חָנָן ***ben-ḥānān*** [BEN-HANAN] 1x
<1136> בֶּן־חֶסֶד ***ben-ḥeseḏ*** [BEN-HESED] 1x
<1137> בָּנִי ***bāniy*** [BANI] 15x
<1138> בּוּנִּי ***bûnniy*** [BUNNI] 3x
<1139> בְּנֵי־בְרַק ***b^{e}nêy ḇ^{e}raq*** [BENE-BERAK] 1x
<1140> בִּנְיָה ***binyāh*** [BUILDING] 1x
<1141> בְּנָיָה ***b^{e}nāyāh,*** בְּנָיָהוּ ***b^{e}nāyāhû*** [BENAIAH] 42x
<1142> בְּנֵי יַעֲקָן ***b^{e}nêy ya^{a}qān*** [BENE-JAAKAN] 2x
<1143> בֵּנַיִם ***bênayim*** [CHAMPION] 2x
<1144> בִּנְיָמִין ***binyāmiyn*** [BENJAMIN] 161x
<1145> בֶּן־יְמִינִי ***ben-y^{e}miyniy*** [BENJAMITE] 18x
<1146> בִּנְיָן ***binyān*** [BUILDING] 7x
<1147> בִּנְיָן ***binyān*** [BUILDING] 1x
<1148> בְּנִינוּ ***b^{e}niynû*** [BENINU] 1x
<1149> בְּנַס ***b^{e}nas*** [ANGRY (BE)] 1x
<1150> בִּנְעָא ***binʻā'*** [BINEA] 2x
<1151> בֶּן־עַמִּי ***ben-ʻammiy*** [BEN-AMMI] 1x
<1152> בְּסוֹדְיָה ***b^{e}sôḏ^{e}yāh*** [BESODEIAH] 1x
<1153> בֵּסַי ***bêsay*** [BESAI] 2x
<1154> בֶּסֶר ***beser*** [UNRIPE GRAPE] 1x
<1155> בֹּסֶר ***bōser*** [UNRIPE GRAPE] 5x
<1156> בְּעָא ***b^{e}ʻā'*** [SEEK] 16x
<1157> בַּעַד ***baʻaḏ*** [FOR] 19x
<1158> בָּעָה ***bāʻāh*** [BOIL (verb)] 5x
<1159> בָּעוּ ***baʻû*** [PETITION] 2x
<1160> בְּעוֹר ***b^{e}ʻôr*** [BEOR] 10x

<1161> בִּעוּתִים ***biʿûṯiym*** [TERRORS] 2x
<1162> בֹּעַז ***bōʿaz*** [BOAZ] 24x
<1163> בָּעַט ***bāʿaṭ*** [KICK] 2x
<1164> בְּעִי ***b^{e}ʿiy*** [HEAP OF RUINS] 1x
<1165> בְּעִיר ***b^{e}ʿiyr*** [ANIMAL] 6x
<1166> בָּעַל ***bāʿal*** [MARRY] 16x
<1167> בַּעַל ***baʿal*** [LORD] 82x
<1168> בַּעַל ***baʿal*** [BAAL] 80x
<1169> בְּעֵל ***b^{e}ʿêl*** [COMMANDER] 3x
<1170> בַּעַל בְּרִית ***baʿal b^{e}riyṯ*** [BAAL-BERITH] 2x
<1171> בַּעַל גָּד ***baʿal gāḏ*** [BAAL-GAD] 3x
<1172> בַּעֲלָה ***baʿ^{a}lāh*** [MISTRESS] 4x
<1173> בַּעֲלָה ***baʿ^{a}lāh*** [BAALAH] 6x
<1174> בַּעַל הָמוֹן ***baʿal hāmôn*** [BAAL-HAMON] 1x
<1175> בְּעָלוֹת ***b^{e}ʿālôṯ*** [BEALOTH] 3x
<1176> בַּעַל זְבוּב ***baʿal z^{e}ḇûḇ*** [BAAL-ZEBUB] 4x
<1177> בַּעַל חָנָן ***baʿal ḥānān*** [BAAL-HANAN] 5x
<1178> בַּעַל חָצוֹר ***baʿal ḥāṣôr*** [BAAL HAZOR] 1x
<1179> בַּעַל חֶרְמוֹן ***baʿal ḥermôn*** [BAAL HERMON] 2x
<1180> בַּעֲלִי ***baʿ^{a}liy*** [BAALI] 1x
<1181> בַּעֲלֵי בָמוֹת ***baʿ^{a}lêy bāmôṯ*** [BAALE-BAMOTH] 1x
<1182> בְּעֶלְיָדָע ***b^{e}ʿelyāḏāʿ*** [BEELIADA] 1x
<1183> בְּעַלְיָה ***b^{e}ʿalyāh*** [BEALIAH] 1x
<1184> בַּעֲלֵי יְהוּדָה ***baʿ^{a}lêy y^{e}hûḏāh*** [BAALE JUDAH] 1x
<1185> בַּעֲלִיס ***baʿ^{a}liys*** [BAALIS] 1x
<1186> בַּעַל מְעוֹן ***baʿal m^{e}ʿôn*** [BAAL MEON] 3x
<1187> בַּעַל פְּעוֹר ***baʿal p^{e}ʿôr*** [BAAL PEOR] 6x
<1188> בַּעַל פְּרָצִים ***baʿal p^{e}rāṣiym*** [BAAL PERAZIM] 2x
<1189> בַּעַל צְפוֹן ***baʿal ṣ^{e}p̱ôn,*** בַּעַל צְפֹן ***baʿal ṣ^{e}p̱ōn*** [BAAL ZEPHON] 3x
<1190> בַּעַל שָׁלִשָׁה ***baʿal šālišāh*** [BAAL SHALISHAH] 1x
<1191> בַּעֲלָת ***baʿ^{a}lāṯ*** [BAALATH] 3x
<1192> בַּעֲלַת בְּאֵר ***baʿ^{a}laṯ b^{e}ʾêr*** [BAALATH BEER] 1x
<1193> בַּעַל תָּמָר ***baʿal tāmār*** [BAAL TAMAR] 1x
<1194> בְּעֹן ***b^{e}ʿōn*** [BEON] 1x
<1195> בַּעֲנָא ***baʿ^{a}nāʾ*** [BAANA] 3x
<1196> בַּעֲנָה ***baʿ^{a}nāh*** [BAANAH] 9x
<1197> בָּעַר ***bāʿar*** [BURN (verb)] 94x
<1198> בַּעַר ***baʿar*** [SENSELESS] 5x
<1199> בַּעֲרָא ***baʿ^{a}rāʾ*** [BAARA] 1x
<1200> בְּעֵרָה ***b^{e}ʿêrāh*** [FIRE] 1x
<1201> בַּעְשָׁא ***baʿšāʾ*** [BAASHA] 28x
<1202> בַּעֲשֵׂיָה ***baʿ^{a}śêyāh*** [BAASEIAH] 1x
<1203> בְּעֶשְׁתְּרָה ***b^{e}ʿešt^{e}rāh*** [BEESHTERAH] 1x
<1204> בָּעַת ***bāʿaṯ*** [TROUBLE (verb)] 16x
<1205> בְּעָתָה ***b^{e}ʿāṯāh*** [TERROR] 2x
<1206> בֹּץ ***bōṣ*** [MUD] 1x
<1207> בִּצָּה ***biṣṣāh*** [MARSH] 3x
<1208> בָּצוּר ***bāṣûr,*** בָּצִיר ***bāṣiyr*** [THICK] 1x
<1209> בֵּצָי ***bêṣāy*** [BEZAI] 3x
<1210> בָּצִיר ***bāṣiyr*** [VINTAGE] 7x
<1211> בָּצָל ***bāṣāl*** [ONION] 1x

<1212> בְּצַלְאֵל ***bᵉṣal’ēl*** [BEZALEL] 9x
<1213> בַּצְלוּת ***baṣlûṯ*** [BAZLUTH] 2x
<1214> בָּצַע ***bāṣaʿ*** [CUT OFF] 16x
<1215> בֶּצַע ***beṣaʿ*** [PROFIT (noun)] 23x
<1216> בָּצַק ***bāṣaq*** [SWELL] 2x
<1217> בָּצֵק ***bāṣēq*** [DOUGH] 5x
<1218> בָּצְקַת ***boṣqaṯ*** [BOZKATH] 2x
<1219> בָּצַר ***bāṣar*** [GATHER] 38x
<1220> בֶּצֶר ***beṣer*** [GOLD] 2x
<1221> בֶּצֶר ***beṣer*** [BEZER] 5x
<1222> בְּצַר ***bᵉṣar*** [GOLD] 1x
<1223> בָּצְרָה ***boṣrāh*** [FOLD (noun)] 1x
<1224> בָּצְרָה ***boṣrāh*** [BOZRAH] 9x
<1225> בִּצָּרוֹן ***biṣṣārôn*** [STRONGHOLD] 1x
<1226> בַּצֹּרֶת ***baṣṣōreṯ*** [DROUGHT] 2x
<1227> בַּקְבּוּק ***baqbûq*** [BAKBUK] 2x
<1228> בַּקְבֻּק ***baqbuq*** [JAR] 3x
<1229> בַּקְבֻּקְיָה ***baqbuqyāh*** [BAKBUKIA] 3x
<1230> בַּקְבַּקַּר ***baqbaqqar*** [BAKBAKKAR] 1x
<1231> בֻּקִּי ***buqqiy*** [BUKKI] 5x
<1232> בֻּקִּיָּהוּ ***buqqiyyāhû*** [BUKKIAH] 2x
<1233> בָּקִיעַ ***bāqiyaʿ*** [BREACH] 2x
<1234> בָּקַע ***bāqaʿ*** [DIVIDE] 51x
<1235> בֶּקַע ***beqaʿ*** [BEKA] 2x
<1236> בִּקְעָה ***biqʿāh*** [PLAIN (noun)] 1x
<1237> בִּקְעָה ***biqʿāh*** [PLAIN (noun)] 20x
<1238> בָּקַק ***bāqaq*** [EMPTY (MAKE), EMPTY (verb)] 9x
<1239> בָּקַר ***bāqar*** [SEEK] 7x
<1240> בְּקַר ***bᵉqar*** [SEARCH (MAKE)] 5x
<1241> בָּקָר ***bāqār*** [HERD] 182x
<1242> בֹּקֶר ***bōqer*** [MORNING] 205x
<1243> בַּקָּרָה ***baqqārāh*** [SEEK] 1x
<1244> בִּקֹּרֶת ***biqqōreṯ*** [PUNISHMENT] 1x
<1245> בָּקַשׁ ***bāqaš*** [SEEK] 276x
<1246> בַּקָּשָׁה ***baqqāšāh*** [REQUEST] 8x
<1247> בַּר ***bar*** [SON] 8x
<1248> בַּר ***bar*** [SON] 4x
<1249> בַּר ***bar*** [PURE] 7x
<1250> בַּר ***bar,*** בָּר ***bār*** [GRAIN] 14x
<1251> בַּר ***bar*** [FIELD] 8x
<1252> בֹּר ***bōr*** [CLEANNESS] 6x
<1253> בֹּר ***bōr*** [SNOW)] 2x
<1254> בָּרָא ***bārā’*** [CREATE] 54x
<1255> בְּרֹאדַךְ בַּלְאֲדָן ***bᵉrō’ḏaḵ bal’ᵃḏān*** [BERODACH-BALADAN] 1x
<1256> בְּרָאיָה ***bᵉrā’yāh*** [BERAIAH] 1x
<1257> בַּרְבֻּר ***barbur*** [FOWL] 1x
<1258> בָּרַד ***bāraḏ*** [HAIL (verb)] 1x
<1259> בָּרָד ***bārāḏ*** [HAIL (noun)] 29x
<1260> בֶּרֶד ***bereḏ*** [BERED] 2x
<1261> בָּרֹד ***bārōḏ*** [MOTTLED] 4x
<1262> בָּרָה ***bārāh*** [EAT] 7x

<1263> בָּרוּךְ ***bārûḵ*** [BARUCH] 26x
<1264> בְּרֹמִים ***b***^{e}***rōmiym*** [MULTICOLORED] 1x
<1265> בְּרוֹשׁ ***b***^{e}***rôš*** [CYPRESS] 20x
<1266> בְּרוֹת ***b***^{e}***rôṯ*** [FIR] 1x
<1267> בָּרוּת ***bārûṯ*** [FOOD] 1x
<1268> בֵּרוֹתָה ***bêrôṯāh,*** בֵּרֹתַי ***bêrōṯay*** [BEROTHAH, BEROTHAI] 2x
<1269> בִּרְזָוִת ***birzāwiṯ*** [BIRZAITH] 1x
<1270> בַּרְזֶל ***barzel*** [IRON] 76x
<1271> בַּרְזִלַּי ***barzillay*** [BARZILLAI] 12x
<1272> בָּרַח ***bāraḥ*** [FLEE] 65x
<1273> בַּרְחֻמִי ***barḥumiy*** [BARHUMITE] 1x
<1274> בְּרִי ***b***^{e}***riy*** [FAT (adj.)] 1x
<1275> בֵּרִי ***bêriy*** [BERI] 1x
<1276> בֵּרִי ***bêriy*** [BERITE] 1x
<1277> בָּרִיא ***bāriy'*** [FAT (adj.)] 13x
<1278> בְּרִיאָה ***b***^{e}***riy'āh*** [NEW] 1x
<1279> בִּרְיָה ***biryāh*** [FOOD] 3x
<1280> בְּרִיחַ ***b***^{e}***riyaḥ*** [BAR] 41x
<1281> בָּרִחַ ***bāriaḥ,*** בָּרִיחַ ***bāriyaḥ*** [FLEEING] 4x
<1282> בָּרִיחַ ***bāriyaḥ*** [BARIAH] 1x
<1283> בְּרִיעָה ***b***^{e}***riy‘āh,*** בְּרִעָה ***b***^{e}***ri‘āh*** [BERIAH] 12x
<1284> בְּרִיעִי ***b***^{e}***riy‘iy*** [BERIITE] 1x
<1285> בְּרִית ***b***^{e}***riyṯ*** [COVENANT] 284x
<1286> בְּרִית ***b***^{e}***riyṯ*** [BERITH] 1x
<1287> בֹּרִית ***bōriyṯ*** [SOAP] 2x
<1288> בָּרַךְ ***bāraḵ*** [BLESS] 330x
<1289> בְּרַךְ ***b***^{e}***raḵ*** [BLESS] 5x
<1290> בֶּרֶךְ ***bereḵ*** [KNEE] 25x
<1291> בְּרֵךְ ***b***^{e}***rêḵ*** [KNEE] 1x
<1292> בַּרַכְאֵל ***baraḵ'êl*** [BARACHEL] 2x
<1293> בְּרָכָה ***b***^{e}***rāḵāh*** [BLESSING] 69x
<1294> בְּרָכָה ***b***^{e}***rāḵāh*** [BERACAH] 3x
<1295> בְּרֵכָה ***b***^{e}***rêḵāh*** [POOL (noun)] 17x
<1296> בֶּרֶכְיָה ***bereḵyah,*** בֶּרֶכְיָהוּ ***bereḵyāhû*** [BERECHIAH, BERKIAH] 11x
<1297> בְּרַם ***b***^{e}***ram*** [NEVERTHELESS] 5x
<1298> בֶּרַע ***bera'*** [BERA] 1x
<1299> בָּרַק ***bāraq*** [FLASH FORTH] 1x
<1300> בָּרָק ***bārāq*** [LIGHTNING] 21x
<1301> בָּרָק ***bārāq*** [BARAK] 13x
<1302> בַּרְקוֹס ***barqôs*** [BARKOS] 2x
<1303> בַּרְקָנִים ***barq***^{o}***niym*** [BRIERS] 2x
<1304> בָּרֶקֶת ***bāreqeṯ,*** בָּרְקַת ***bār***^{e}***qath*** [EMERALD] 3x
<1305> בָּרַר ***bārar,*** בָּרוּר ***bārûr*** [PURIFY] 18x
<1306> בִּרְשַׁע ***birša‘*** [BIRSHA] 1x
<1307> בֵּרֹתִי ***bêrōṯiy*** [BEROTHITE] 1x
<1308> בְּשׂוֹר ***b***^{e}***sôr*** [BESOR] 3x
<1309> בְּשׂוֹרָה ***b***^{e}***śôrāh,*** בְּשֹׂרָה ***b***^{e}***śōrāh*** [NEWS] 6x
<1310> בָּשַׁל ***bāšal*** [COOK (verb)] 28x
<1311> בָּשֵׁל ***bāšêl*** [BOILED] 2x
<1312> בִּשְׁלָם ***bišlām*** [BISHLAM] 1x
<1313> בָּשָׂם ***bāśām*** [SPICE] 1x

<1314> בֶּשֶׂם ***beśem,*** בֹּשֶׂם ***bōśem*** [SPICE] 29x
<1315> בָּשְׂמַת ***bāś^{e}maṯ*** [BASHEMATH, BASEMATH] 7x
<1316> בָּשָׁן ***bāšān*** [BASHAN] 60x
<1317> בָּשְׁנָה ***bošnāh*** [SHAME] 1x
<1318> בָּשַׁס ***bāšas*** [TRAMPLE] 1x
<1319> בָּשַׂר ***bāśar*** [NEWS (BRING)] 24x
<1320> בָּשָׂר ***bāśār*** [FLESH] 269x
<1321> בְּשַׂר ***b^{e}śar*** [FLESH] 3x
<1322> בֹּשֶׁת ***bōšeṯ*** [SHAME] 30x
<1323> בַּת ***baṯ*** [DAUGHTER] 588x
<1324> בַּת ***baṯ*** [BATH] 13x
<1325> בַּת ***baṯ*** [BATH] 2x
<1326> בָּתָה ***bāṯāh*** [WASTELAND] 1x
<1327> בַּתָּה ***battāh*** [DESOLATE] 1x
<1328> בְּתוּאֵל ***b^{e}ṯû’ēl*** [BETHUEL] 10x
<1329> בְּתוּל ***b^{e}ṯûl*** [BETHUL] 1x
<1330> בְּתוּלָה ***b^{e}ṯûlāh*** [VIRGIN] 50x
<1331> בְּתוּלִים ***b^{e}ṯûliym*** [VIRGIN] 10x
<1332> בִּתְיָה ***biṯyāh*** [BITHIAH] 1x
<1333> בָּתַק ***bāṯaq*** [CUT TO PIECES] 1x
<1334> בָּתַר ***bāṯar*** [DIVIDE] 2x
<1335> בֶּתֶר ***beṯer*** [HALF] 3x
<1336> בֶּתֶר ***beṯer*** [BETHER] 1x
<1337> בַּת רַבִּים ***baṯ rabbiym*** [BATH RABBIM] 1x
<1338> בִּתְרוֹן ***biṯrôn*** [BITHRON] 1x
<1339> בַּת־שֶׁבַע ***baṯ-šeḇa‘*** [BATHSHEBA] 11x
<1340> בַּת שׁוּעַ ***baṯ šûa‘*** [BATHSHUA] 2x

ג Gimel

<1341> גֵּא ***gê’*** [PROUD] 1x
<1342> גָּאָה ***gā’āh*** [RISE] 7x
<1343> גֵּאֶה ***gê’eh*** [PROUD] 8x
<1344> גֵּאָה ***gê’āh*** [PRIDE] 1x
<1345> גְּאוּאֵל ***g^{e}’û’ēl*** [GEUEL] 1x
<1346> גַּאֲוָה ***ga’^{a}wāh*** [MAJESTY] 19x
<1347> גָּאוֹן ***gā’ôn*** [MAJESTY] 49x
<1348> גֵּאוּת ***gê’ûṯ*** [MAJESTY] 8x
<1349> גַּאֲיוֹן ***ga’^{a}yôn*** [PROUD] 1x
<1350> גְּאוּלִים ***g^{e}’ûliym,*** גָּאַל ***gā’al*** [REDEEM] 104x
<1351> גָּאַל ***gā’al*** [DEFILE] 11x
<1352> גֹּאַל ***gō’al*** [DEFILEMENT] 1x
<1353> גְּאֻלָּה ***g^{e}’ullāh*** [REDEMPTION] 14x
<1354> גַּב ***gaḇ*** [BACK] 13x
<1355> גַּב ***gaḇ*** [BACK] 1x
<1356> גֵּב ***gêḇ*** [BEAM] 2x, [POOL (noun)] 3x
<1357> גֵּב ***gêḇ*** [LOCUST] 1x
<1358> גֹּב ***gōḇ*** [DEN] 10x
<1359> גֹּב ***gōḇ,*** גּוֹב ***gôḇ*** [GOB] 2x

<1360> גֶּבֶא ***geḇe'*** [CISTERN] 2x
<1361> גָּבַהּ ***gāḇah*** [EXALTED (BE)] 34x
<1362> גָּבֹהַּ ***gāḇōah*** [PROUD] 4x
<1363> גֹּבַהּ ***gōḇah*** [HEIGHT] 17x
<1364> גָּבוֹהַּ ***gāḇôah,*** גָּבֹהַּ ***gāḇōah*** [HIGH] 37x
<1365> גַּבְהוּת ***gaḇhûṯ*** [LOFTINESS] 2x
<1366> גְּבוּל ***gᵉḇûl*** [BORDER] 241x
<1367> גְּבוּלָה ***gᵉḇûlāh*** [BORDER] 10x
<1368> גִּבּוֹר ***gibbôr,*** גִּבֹּר ***gibbōr*** [BRAVE] 157x
<1369> גְּבוּרָה ***gᵉḇûrāh*** [POWER] 61x
<1370> גְּבוּרָה ***gᵉḇûrāh*** [POWER] 2x
<1371> גִּבֵּחַ ***gibbêaḥ*** [BALD] 1x
<1372> גַּבַּחַת ***gabbaḥaṯ*** [BALD] 4x
<1373> גַּבַּי ***gabbay*** [GABBAI] 1x
<1374> גֵּבִים ***gêḇiym*** [GEBIM] 1x
<1375> גָּבִיעַ ***gāḇiya'*** [CUP] 11x
<1376> גְּבִיר ***gᵉḇiyr*** [LORD] 2x
<1377> גְּבִירָה ***gᵉḇiyrāh*** [MISTRESS] 6x
<1378> גָּבִישׁ ***gāḇiyš*** [CRYSTAL] 1x
<1379> גָּבַל ***gāḇal*** [BOUNDS (SET)] 5x
<1380> גְּבַל ***gᵉḇal*** [GEBAL] 1x
<1381> גְּבָל ***gᵉḇāl*** [GEBAL] 1x
<1382> גִּבְלִי ***giḇliy*** [GEBALITES] 2x
<1383> גַּבְלֻת ***gaḇluṯ*** [END] 2x
<1384> גִּבֵּן ***gibbên*** [HUNCHBACK] 1x
<1385> גְּבִינָה ***gᵉḇiynāh*** [CHEESE] 1x
<1386> גַּבְנֹן ***gaḇnôn*** [RUGGED] 2x
<1387> גֶּבַע ***geḇa'*** [GEBA] 19x
<1388> גִּבְעָא ***giḇ'ā'*** [GIBEA] 1x
<1389> גִּבְעָה ***giḇ'āh*** [HILL] 69x
<1390> גִּבְעָה ***giḇ'āh*** [GIBEAH] 44x
<1391> גִּבְעוֹן ***giḇ'ôn*** [GIBEON] 37x
<1392> גִּבְעֹל ***giḇ'ōl*** [BUD (IN)] 1x
<1393> גִּבְעוֹנִי ***giḇ'ôniy*** [GIBEONITE] 8x
<1394> גִּבְעַת ***giḇ'aṯ*** [GIBEATH] 1x
<1395> גִּבְעָתִי ***giḇ'āṯiy*** [GIBEATHITE] 1x
<1396> גָּבַר ***gāḇar*** [PREVAIL] 25x
<1397> גֶּבֶר ***geḇer*** [MAN] 68x
<1398> גֶּבֶר ***geḇer*** [GEBER] 1x
<1399> גְּבַר ***gᵉḇar*** [MAN] 1x
<1400> גְּבַר ***gᵉḇar*** [MAN] 21x
<1401> גִּבָּר ***gibbar*** [MAN] 1x
<1402> גִּבָּר ***gibbār*** [GIBBAR] 1x
<1403> גַּבְרִיאֵל ***gaḇriy'êl*** [GABRIEL] 2x
<1404> גְּבֶרֶת ***gᵉḇereṯ*** [MISTRESS] 9x
<1405> גִּבְּתוֹן ***gibbᵉṯôn*** [GIBBETHON] 6x
<1406> גָּג ***gāg*** [ROOF (noun)] 30x
<1407> גַּד ***gaḏ*** [CORIANDER] 2x
<1408> גַּד ***gaḏ*** [FORTUNE] 1x
<1409> גַּד ***gaḏ*** [FORTUNE] 2x
<1410> גָּד ***gāḏ*** [GAD] 70x

<1411> גְּדָבָר ***gᵉḏāḇar*** [TREASURER] 2x
<1412> גֻּדְגֹּדָה ***guḏgōḏah*** [GUDGODAH] 1x
<1413> גָּדַד ***gāḏaḏ*** [CUT (verb)] 5x, [GATHER] 3x
<1414> גְּדַד ***gᵉḏaḏ*** [CHOP DOWN] 2x
<1415> גָּדָה ***gāḏāh*** [BANK] 4x
<1416> גְּדוּד ***gᵉḏûḏ*** [BAND (noun)] 34x
<1417> גְּדוּד ***gᵉḏûḏ*** [FURROW] 1x
<1418> גְּדוּדָה ***gᵉḏûḏāh*** [GASH (noun)] 1x
<1419> גָּדוֹל ***gāḏôl,*** גָּדֹל ***gāḏōl,*** הַגְּדוֹלִים ***haggᵉḏôliym*** [GREAT] 529x
<1420> גְּדוּלָּה ***gᵉḏûllāh,*** גְּדֻלָּה ***gᵉḏullāh*** [GREATNESS] 12x
<1421> גִּדּוּף ***giddûp̱*** [SCORN (noun)] 3x
<1422> גְּדוּפָה ***gᵉḏûp̱āh*** [TAUNT (noun)] 1x
<1423> גְּדִי ***gᵉḏiy*** [KID] 16x
<1424> גָּדִי ***gāḏiy*** [GADI] 2x
<1425> גָּדִי ***gāḏiy*** [GADITE] 16x
<1426> גַּדִּי ***gaddiy*** [GADDI] 1x
<1427> גַּדִּיאֵל ***gaddiy'êl*** [GADDIEL] 1x
<1428> גִּדְיָה ***giḏyāh*** [BANK] 2x
<1429> גְּדִיָּה ***gᵉḏiyyāh*** [GOAT (YOUNG, LITTLE)] 1x
<1430> גָּדִישׁ ***gāḏiyš*** [STACKED GRAIN] 3x, [TOMB] 1x
<1431> גָּדַל ***gāḏal*** [GREAT (BECOME, MAKE)] 115x
<1432> גָּדֵל ***gāḏêl*** [GROW] 4x
<1433> גֹּדֶל ***gōḏel*** [GREATNESS] 13x
<1434> גָּדִל ***gāḏil*** [TASSEL]. [WREATH] 2x
<1435> גִּדֵּל ***giddêl*** [GIDDEL] 4x
<1436> גְּדַלְיָה ***gᵉḏalyāh,*** גְּדַלְיָהוּ ***gᵉḏalyāhû*** [GEDALIAH] 32x
<1437> גִּדַּלְתִּי ***giddaltiy*** [GIDDALTI] 2x
<1438> גָּדַע ***gāḏa'*** [CUT DOWN, OFF, IN PIECES] 23x
<1439> גִּדְעוֹן ***giḏ'ôn*** [GIDEON] 39x
<1440> גִּדְעֹם ***giḏ'ōm*** [GIDOM] 1x
<1441> גִּדְעֹנִי ***giḏ'ōniy*** [GIDEONI] 5x
<1442> גָּדַף ***gāḏap̱*** [BLASPHEME] 7x
<1443> גָּדַר ***gāḏar*** [BUILD] 10x
<1444> גֶּדֶר ***geḏer*** [WALL] 2x
<1445> גֶּדֶר ***geḏer*** [GEDER] 1x
<1446> גְּדוֹר ***gᵉḏôr*** [GEDOR] 7x
<1447> גָּדֵר ***gāḏêr*** [WALL] 12x
<1448> גְּדֵרָה ***gᵉḏêrāh*** [WALL] 10x
<1449> גְּדֵרָה ***gᵉḏêrāh*** [GEDERAH] 1x
<1450> גְּדֵרוֹת ***gᵉḏêrôṯ*** [GEDEROTH] 2x
<1451> גְּדֵרִי ***gᵉḏêriy*** [GEDERITE] 1x
<1452> גְּדֵרָתִי ***gᵉḏêrāṯiy*** [GEDERATHITE] 1x
<1453> גְּדֵרֹתַיִם ***gᵉḏêrōṯayim*** [GEDEROTHAIM] 1x
<1454> גֵּה ***gêh*** [THIS] 1x
<1455> גָּהָה ***gāhāh*** [CURE] 1x
<1456> גֵּהָה ***gêhāh*** [MEDICINE] 1x
<1457> גָּהַר ***gāhar*** [STRETCH ONESELF] 3x
<1458> גַּו ***gaw*** [BACK] 3x
<1459> גַּו ***gaw*** [MIDST] 13x
<1460> גֵּו ***gêw*** [BACK] 6x, [COMMUNITY] 1x
<1461> גּוּב ***gûḇ*** [PLOWMAN] 1x

<1462> גּוֹב ***gôḇ,*** גּוֹבַי ***gôḇay*** [LOCUST] 2x

<1463> גּוֹג ***gôg*** [GOG] 10x

<1464> גּוּד ***gûḏ*** [ATTACK (verb)] 3x

<1465> גֵּוָה ***gêwāh*** [BACK] 1x

<1466> גֵּוָה ***gêwāh*** [PRIDE] 3x

<1467> גֵּוָה ***gêwāh*** [PRIDE] 1x

<1468> גּוּז ***gûz*** [BRING] 1x, [CUT OFF] 1x

<1469> גּוֹזָל ***gôzzāl*** [PIGEON (YOUNG)] 2x

<1470> גּוֹזָן ***gôzān*** [GOZAN] 5x

<1471> גּוֹי ***gôy,*** גּוֹיִם ***gôyim,*** הַגּוֹיִם ***hāggôyim*** [NATION] 558x

<1472> גְּוִיָּה ***g^{e}wiyyāh*** [BODY] 13x

<1473> גּוֹלָה ***gôlāh,*** גֹּלָה ***gōlāh*** [CAPTIVITY] 42x

<1474> גּוֹלָן ***gôlān*** [GOLAN] 4x

<1475> גּוּמָּץ ***gûmmāṣ*** [PIT] 1x

<1476> גּוּנִי ***gûniy*** [GUNI] 4x

<1477> גּוּנִי ***gûniy*** [GUNITE] 1x

<1478> גָּוַע ***gāwaʿ*** [DIE] 24x

<1479> גּוּף ***gûp̱*** [SHUT] 1x

<1480> גּוּפָה ***gûp̱āh*** [BODY] 2x

<1481> גּוּר ***gûr*** [SOJOURN] 98x

<1482> גּוּר ***gûr*** [CUB] 7x

<1483> גּוּר ***gûr*** [GUR] 1x

<1484> גּוֹר ***gôr*** [CUB] 2x

<1485> גּוּר־בַּעַל ***gûr-baʿal*** [GUR BAAL] 1x

<1486> גּוֹרָל ***gôrāl*** [LOT (noun)] 77x

<1487> גּוּשׁ ***gûš*** [CRUST] 1x

<1488> גֵּז ***gêz*** [SHEARING] 4x

<1489> גִּזְבָּר ***gizbār*** [TREASURER] 1x

<1490> גִּזְבַּר ***gizbar*** [TREASURER] 1x

<1491> גָּזָה ***gāzāh*** [TAKE, TAKE OUT] 1x

<1492> גִּזָּה ***gizzāh*** [FLEECE] 7x

<1493> גִּזוֹנִי ***gizôniy*** [GIZONITE] 1x

<1494> גָּזַז ***gāzaz*** [CUT (verb)] 15x

<1495> גָּזֵז ***gāzêz*** [GAZEZ] 2x

<1496> גָּזִית ***gāziyṯ*** [DRESSED] 11x

<1497> גָּזַל ***gāzal*** [ROB] 30x

<1498> גָּזֵל ***gāzêl*** [ROBBERY] 4x

<1499> גֵּזֶל ***gêzel*** [ROBBERY] 2x

<1500> גְּזֵלָה ***g^{e}zêlāh*** [ROBBERY] 6x

<1501> גָּזָם ***gāzām*** [LOCUST] 3x

<1502> גַּזָּם ***gazzām*** [GAZZAM] 2x

<1503> גֶּזַע ***gezaʿ*** [STUMP] 3x

<1504> גָּזַר ***gāzar*** [CUT (verb)] 13x

<1505> גְּזַר ***g^{e}zar*** [CUT (verb)] 6x

<1506> גֶּזֶר ***gezer*** [PART (noun)] 2x

<1507> גֶּזֶר ***gezer*** [GEZER] 15x

<1508> גִּזְרָה ***gizrāh*** [COURTYARD] 8x

<1509> גְּזֵרָה ***g^{e}zêrāh*** [SOLITARY LAND] 1x

<1510> גְּזֵרָה ***g^{e}zêrāh*** [DECREE (noun)] 2x

<1511> גִּזְרִי ***gizriy*** [GIRZITES] 1x

<1512> גָּחוֹן ***gāḥôn*** [BELLY] 2x

<1513> גַּחֶלֶת ***gaḥeleṯ*** [COAL] 18x
<1514> גַּחַם ***gaḥam*** [GAHAM] 1x
<1515> גַּחַר ***gaḥar*** [GAHAR] 2x
<1516> גַּיְא ***gay',*** גַּיְ ***gay*** [VALLEY] 60x
<1517> גִּיד ***giyḏ*** [SINEW] 7x
<1518> גִּיחַ ***giyaḥ,*** גּוּחַ ***gûaḥ*** [GUSH] 6x
<1519> גִּיחַ ***giyaḥ,*** גּוּחַ ***gûaḥ*** [STIR UP] 1x
<1520> גִּיחַ ***giyaḥ*** [GIAH] 1x
<1521> גִּיחוֹן ***giyḥôn*** [GIHON] 6x
<1522> גֵּיחֲזִי ***gêyḥ[a]ziy,*** גֵּחֲזִי ***gêḥ[a]ziy*** [GEHAZI] 12x
<1523> גִּיל ***giyl,*** גּוּל ***gûl*** [REJOICE] 44x
<1524> גִּיל ***giyl*** [JOY (noun)] 10x
<1525> גִּילָה ***giylāh*** [JOY (noun)] 2x
<1526> גִּילֹנִי ***giylōniy*** [GILONITE] 2x
<1527> גִּינַת ***giynaṯ*** [GINATH] 2x
<1528> גִּיר ***giyr*** [PLASTER] 1x
<1529> גֵּישָׁן ***gêyšān*** [GESHAN] 1x
<1530> גַּל ***gal*** [HEAP (noun)], [WAVE] 35x
<1531> גֹּל ***gōl*** [BOWL] 1x
<1532> גַּלָּב ***gallāḇ*** [BARBER] 1x
<1533> גִּלְבֹּעַ ***gilbōa'*** [GILBOA] 8x
<1534> גַּלְגַּל ***galgal*** [WHEEL] 11x
<1535> גַּלְגַּל ***galgal*** [WHEEL] 1x
<1536> גִּלְגָּל ***gilgāl*** [WHEEL] 1x
<1537> גִּלְגָּל ***gilgāl*** [GILGAL] 41x
<1538> גֻּלְגֹּלֶת ***gulgōleṯ*** [HEAD (noun)] 12x
<1539> גֶּלֶד ***gêleḏ*** [SKIN] 1x
<1540> גָּלָה ***gālāh*** [REVEAL] 188x
<1541> גְּלָה ***g[e]lāh,*** גְּלָא ***g[e]lā'*** [BRING OVER] 2x, [REVEAL] 7x
<1542> גִּלֹה ***gilōh*** [GILOH] 2x
<1543> גֻּלָּה ***gullāh*** [BOWL] 6x, [SPRING] 2x
<1544> גִּלּוּל ***gillûl*** [IDOLS] 48x
<1545> גְּלוֹם ***g[e]lôm*** [CLOTHES] 1x
<1546> גָּלוּת ***gālûṯ*** [CAPTIVITY] 15x
<1547> גָּלוּ ***gālû*** [CAPTIVITY] 4x
<1548> גָּלַח ***gālaḥ*** [SHAVE, SHAVE OFF] 23x
<1549> גִּלָּיוֹן ***gillāyôn*** [MIRROR] 1x, [SCROLL] 1x
<1550> גָּלִיל ***gāliyl*** [FOLDING] 2, [RING] 2x
<1551> גָּלִיל ***gāliyl,*** גָּלִילָה ***gāliylāh*** [GALILEE] 6x
<1552> גְּלִילָה ***g[e]liylāh*** [REGION] 5x
<1553> גְּלִילוֹת ***g[e]liylôt*** [GELILOT] 3x
<1554> גַּלִּים ***galliym*** [GALLIM] 2x
<1555> גָּלְיָת ***golyāṯ,*** גָּלְיַת ***golyaṯ*** [GOLIATH] 6x
<1556> גָּלַל ***gālal*** [ROLL (verb)] 18x
<1557> גָּלָל ***gālāl*** [DUNG] 2x
<1558> גָּלָל ***gālāl*** [BECAUSE] 10x
<1559> גָּלָל ***gālāl*** [GALAL] 3x
<1560> גְּלָל ***g[e]lāl*** [HUGE] 2x
<1561> גֵּלֶל ***gêlel*** [DUNG] 4x
<1562> גִּלֲלַי ***gil[a]lay*** [GILALAI] 1x
<1563> גָּלַם ***gālam*** [ROLL (verb)] 1x

<1564> גֹּלֶם ***gōlem*** [UNFORMED SUBSTANCE] 1x

<1565> גַּלְמוּד ***galmûḏ*** [SOLITARY] 4x

<1566> גָּלַע ***gāla‘*** [BREAK OUT] 3x

<1567> גַּלְעֵד ***gal‘êḏ*** [GALEED] 2x

<1568> גִּלְעָד ***gil‘āḏ*** [GILEAD] 133x

<1569> גִּלְעָדִי ***gil‘āḏiy*** [GILEADITES] 11x

<1570> גָּלַשׁ ***gālaš*** [DESCEND] 2x

<1571> גַּם ***gam*** [ALSO] 34x

<1572> גָּמָא ***gāmā’*** [DRINK (verb)] 2x

<1573> גֹּמֶא ***gōme’*** [BULRUSH] 4x

<1574> גֹּמֶד ***gōmeḏ*** [CUBIT] 1x

<1575> גַּמָּדִים ***gammāḏiym*** [GAMMADIM] 1x

<1576> גְּמוּל ***g^{e}mûl*** [DESERVES (WHAT ONE)] 18x

<1577> גָּמוּל ***gāmûl*** [GAMUL] 1x

<1578> גְּמוּלָה ***g^{e}mûlāh*** [RECOMPENSE (noun)] 3x

<1579> גִּמְזוֹ ***gimzô*** [GIMZO] 1x

<1580> גָּמַל ***gāmal*** [REWARD (verb)] 37x

<1581> גָּמָל ***gāmāl*** [CAMEL] 54x

<1582> גְּמַלִּי ***g^{e}malliy*** [GEMALLI] 1x

<1583> גַּמְלִיאֵל ***gamliy’ēl*** [GAMALIEL] 5x

<1584> גָּמַר ***gāmar*** [END (COME TO AN)] 5x

<1585> גְּמַר ***g^{e}mar*** [PERFECT PEACE] 1x

<1586> גֹּמֶר ***gōmer*** [GOMER] 6x

<1587> גְּמַרְיָה ***g^{e}maryāh,*** גְּמַרְיָהוּ ***g^{e}maryāhû*** [GEMARIAH] 5x

<1588> גַּן ***gan*** [GARDEN] 42x

<1589> גָּנַב ***gānaḇ*** [STEAL] 39x

<1590> גַּנָּב ***gannāḇ*** [THIEF] 17x

<1591> גְּנֵבָה ***g^{e}nêḇāh*** [THEFT] 2x

<1592> גְּנֻבַת ***g^{e}nuḇaṯ*** [GENUBATH] 2x

<1593> גַּנָּה ***gannāh*** [GARDEN] 12x

<1594> גִּנַּת ***ginnāṯ*** [GARDEN] 4x

<1595> גְּנָזִים ***g^{e}nāziym*** [TREASURE] 3x

<1596> גְּנַז ***g^{e}naz*** [TREASURE] 3x

<1597> גַּנְזַךְ ***ganzaḵ*** [TREASURY] 1x

<1598> גָּנַן ***gānan*** [DEFEND] 8x

<1599> גִּנְּתוֹי ***ginn^{e}ṯôy,*** גִּנְּתוֹן ***ginn^{e}ṯôn*** [GINNETHON] 3x

<1600> גָּעָה ***gā‘āh*** [LOW] 2x

<1601> גֹּעָה ***gō‘āh*** [GOATH, GOAH] 1x

<1602> גָּעַל ***gā‘al*** [ABHOR] 10x

<1603> גַּעַל ***ga‘al*** [GAAL] 10x

<1604> גֹּעַל ***gō‘al*** [LOATHING] 1x

<1605> גָּעַר ***gā‘ar*** [REBUKE (verb)] 14x

<1606> גְּעָרָה ***g^{e}‘ārāh*** [REBUKE (noun)] 15x

<1607> גָּעַשׁ ***ga‘aš*** [SHAKE] 9x

<1608> גַּעַשׁ ***ga‘aš*** [GAASH] 4x

<1609> גַּעְתָּם ***ga‘tām*** [GATAM] 3x

<1610> גַּף ***gap̱*** [ALONE] 2x, [HIGHEST] 1x

<1611> גַּף ***gap̱*** [WING] 3x

<1612> גֶּפֶן ***gep̱en*** [VINE] 55x

<1613> גֹּפֶר ***gōp̱er*** [GOPHER] 1x

<1614> גָּפְרִית ***gop̱riyṯ*** [BRIMSTONE] 7x

<1615> גִּר ***gir*** [CHALK] 1x
<1616> גֵּיר ***gêyr,*** גֵּר ***gêr*** [STRANGER] 92x
<1617> גֵּרָא ***gêrā'*** [GERA] 9x
<1618> גָּרָב ***gārāḇ*** [SCAB] 3x
<1619> גָּרֵב ***gārêḇ*** [GAREB] 3x
<1620> גַּרְגֵּר ***gargêr*** [BERRY] 1x
<1621> גַּרְגָּרוֹת ***gargārôṯ*** [NECK] 4x
<1622> גִּרְגָּשִׁי ***girgāšiy*** [GIRGASHITE, GIRGASITE] 7x
<1623> גָּרַד ***gāraḏ*** [SCRAPE] 1x
<1624> גָּרָה ***gārāh*** [STRIVE] 14x
<1625> גֵּרָה ***gêrāh*** [CUD] 11x
<1626> גֵּרָה ***gêrāh*** [GERAH] 5x
<1627> גָּרוֹן ***gārôn*** [THROAT] 8x
<1628> גֵּרוּת ***gêrûṯ*** [HABITATION] 1x
<1629> גָּרַז ***gāraz*** [CUT OFF (BE)] 1x
<1630> גְּרִזִים ***gᵉriziym*** [GERIZIM] 4x
<1631> גַּרְזֶן ***garzen*** [AX, AXE] 4x
<1632> גָּרֹל ***gārōl*** [GREAT] 1x
<1633> גָּרַם ***gāram*** [BREAK] 3x
<1634> גֶּרֶם ***gerem*** [BONE] 5x
<1635> גְּרַם ***gᵉram*** [BONE] 1x
<1636> גַּרְמִי ***garmiy*** [GARMITE] 1x
<1637> גֹּרֶן ***gōren*** [THRESHING FLOOR] 36x
<1638> גָּרַס ***gāras*** [BREAK] 2x
<1639> גָּרַע ***gāra'*** [REDUCE] 21x
<1640> גָּרַף ***gārap̱*** [SWEEP AWAY] 1x
<1641> גָּרַר ***gārar*** [DRAG (verb)] 5x
<1642> גְּרָר ***gᵉrār*** [GERAR] 10x
<1643> גֶּרֶשׂ ***gereś*** [CRUSHED] 2x
<1644> גָּרַשׁ ***gāraš*** [CAST OUT] 47x
<1645> גֶּרֶשׁ ***gereš*** [PRODUCE (noun)] 1x
<1646> גְּרֻשָׁה ***gᵉrušāh*** [EVICTION] 1x
<1647> גֵּרְשׁוֹם ***gêršôm,*** גֵּרְשֹׁם ***gêršōm*** [GERSHOM] 14x
<1648> גֵּרְשׁוֹן ***gêršôn*** [GERSHON] 17x
<1649> גֵּרְשֻׁנִּי ***gêršunniy*** [GERSHONITE] 13x
<1650> גְּשׁוּר ***gᵉšûr*** [GESHUR] 9x
<1651> גְּשׁוּרִי ***gᵉšûriy*** [GESHURITE] 6x
<1652> גָּשַׁם ***gāšam*** [RAIN (CAUSE, GIVE, BRING)] 1x
<1653> גֶּשֶׁם ***gešem*** [RAIN (verb)] 35x
<1654> גֶּשֶׁם ***gešem,*** גַּשְׁמוּ ***gašmû*** [GESHEM] 4x
<1655> גְּשֵׁם ***gᵉšêm*** [BODY] 5x
<1656> גֹּשֶׁם ***gōšem*** [RAIN ON, UPON] 1x
<1657> גֹּשֶׁן ***gōšen*** [GOSHEN] 15x
<1658> גִּשְׁפָּא ***gišpā'*** [GISHPA, GISPA] 1x
<1659> גָּשַׁשׁ ***gāšaš*** [GROPE] 2x
<1660> גַּת ***gaṯ*** [WINEPRESS] 5x
<1661> גַּת ***gaṯ*** [GATH] 33x
<1662> גַּת־הַחֵפֶר ***gaṯ-haḥêp̱er,*** גִּתָּה־חֵפֶר ***gittāh-ḥêp̱er*** [GATH-HEPHER] 2x
<1663> גִּתִּי ***gittiy*** [GITTITE] 10x
<1664> גִּתַּיִם ***gittayim*** [GITTAIM] 2x
<1665> גִּתִּית ***gittiyṯ*** [GITTITH] 3x

<1666> גֶּתֶר ***geṯer*** [GETHER] 2x
<1667> גַּת־רִמּוֹן ***gaṯ-rimmôn*** [GATH-RIMMON] 4x

ד Daleth

<1668> דָּא ***dā'*** [THIS] 6x
<1669> דָּאַב ***dā'aḇ*** [SORROW (verb)] 3x
<1670> דְּאָבָה ***d^e'āḇāh*** [SORROW (noun)] 1x
<1671> דְּאָבוֹן ***d^e'āḇôn*** [DESPAIR] 1x
<1672> דָּאַג ***dā'ag*** [ANXIOUS (BE, BECOME)] 7x
<1673> דֹּאֵג ***dō'ēg̱,*** דּוֹאֵג ***dô'ēg̱*** [DOEG] 6x
<1674> דְּאָגָה ***d^e'āg̱āh*** [ANXIETY] 6x
<1675> דָּאָה ***dā'āh*** [FLY (verb)] 4x
<1676> דָּאָה ***dā'āh*** [KITE] 3x
<1677> דֹּב ***dōḇ,*** דּוֹב ***dôḇ*** [BEAR (noun)] 12x
<1678> דֹּב ***dōḇ*** [BEAR (noun)] 1x
<1679> דֹּבֶא ***dōḇe'*** [STRENGTH] 1x
<1680> דָּבַב ***dāḇaḇ*** [SPEAK] 1x
<1681> דִּבָּה ***dibbāh*** [REPORT (BAD)] 9x
<1682> דְּבוֹרָה ***d^{e}ḇôrāh*** [BEE] 4x
<1683> דְּבוֹרָה ***d^{e}ḇôrāh*** [DEBORAH] 10x
<1684> דְּבַח ***d^{e}ḇaḥ*** [OFFER] 1x
<1685> דְּבַח ***d^{e}ḇaḥ*** [SACRIFICE (noun)] 1x
<1686> דִּבְיוֹנִים ***diḇyôniym*** [DOVE'S DUNG] 1x
<1687> דְּבִיר ***d^{e}ḇiyr*** [MOST HOLY PLACE] 16x
<1688> דְּבִיר ***d^{e}ḇiyr*** [DEBIR] 13x
<1689> דִּבְלָה ***diḇlāh*** [DIBLAH] 1x
<1690> דְּבֵלָה ***d^{e}ḇêlāh*** [FIGS (CAKE, LUMP, POULTICE OF)] 5x
<1691> דִּבְלַיִם ***diḇlayim*** [DIBLAIM] 1x
<1692> דָּבַק ***dāḇaq*** [JOIN] 52x
<1693> דְּבַק ***d^{e}ḇaq*** [ADHERE] 1x
<1694> דֶּבֶק ***deḇeq*** [JOINT] 3x
<1695> דָּבֵק ***dāḇêq*** [JOINING] 3x
<1696> דָּבַר ***dāḇar*** [SPEAK] 1,139x
<1697> דָּבָר ***dāḇār*** [WORD] 1,439x
<1698> דֶּבֶר ***deḇer*** [PLAGUE (noun)] 49x
<1699> דֹּבֶר ***dōḇer,*** דִּבֵּר ***dibbêr*** [WORD] 3x
<1700> דִּבְרָה ***diḇrāh*** [CAUSE] 5x
<1701> דִּבְרָה ***diḇrāh*** [PURPOSE (noun)] 2x
<1702> דֹּבְרוֹת ***doḇ^{e}rôṯ*** [RAFTS] 1x
<1703> דַּבֶּרֶת ***dabbereṯ*** [WORD] 1x
<1704> דִּבְרִי ***diḇriy*** [DIBRI] 1x
<1705> דָּבְרַת ***dāḇ^{e}raṯ*** [DABERATH] 3x
<1706> דְּבַשׁ ***d^{e}ḇaš*** [HONEY] 54x
<1707> דַּבֶּשֶׁת ***dabbešeṯ*** [HUMP] 1x
<1708> דַּבֶּשֶׁת ***dabbešeṯ*** [DABBESHETH] 1x
<1709> דָּג ***dāg̱*** [FISH (noun)] 20x
<1710> דָּגָה ***dāg̱āh*** [FISH (noun)] 15x
<1711> דָּגָה ***dāg̱āh*** [GROW] 1x

<1712> דָּגוֹן ***dāg̱ôn*** [DAGON] 13x
<1713> דָּגַל ***dāg̱al*** [BANNERS (SET UP, LIFT UP)] 4x
<1714> דֶּגֶל ***deg̱el*** [BANNER] 14x
<1715> דָּגָן ***dāg̱ān*** [CORN] 40x
<1716> דָּגַר ***dāg̱ar*** [GATHER] 2x
<1717> דַּד ***daḏ*** [BREAST] 4x
<1718> דָּדָה ***dāḏāh*** [GO WITH, GO SOFTLY] 2x
<1719> דְּדָן ***dᵉḏān,*** דְּדָנֶה ***dᵉḏāneh,*** רֹדָן ***rōḏān*** [DEDAN] 11x
<1720> דְּדָנִי ***dᵉḏāniy*** [DEDANITE, DEDANIM] 1x
<1721> דֹּדָנִים ***dōḏāniym,*** רֹדָנִים ***rōḏāniym*** [DODANIM] 2x
<1722> דְּהַב ***dᵉhaḇ*** [GOLD] 23x
<1723> דֶּהָוֵא ***dehāwê'*** [DEHAVITES] 1x
<1724> דָּהַם ***dāham*** [ASTONISHED (BE)] 1x
<1725> דָּהַר ***dāhar*** [GALLOP] 1x
<1726> דַּהֲרָה ***dahᵃrāh*** [GALLOPING] 2x
<1727> דּוּב ***dûḇ*** [SORROW (CAUSE)] 1x
<1728> דַּוָּג ***dawwāg̱*** [FISHERMAN] 2x
<1729> דּוּגָה ***dûg̱āh*** [FISHHOOK] 1x
<1730> דּוֹד ***dôḏ*** [LOVER] 61x
<1731> דּוּד ***dûḏ*** [BASKET] 7x
<1732> דָּוִד ***dāwiḏ,*** דָּוִיד ***dāwiyḏ*** [DAVID] 1,076x
<1733> דּוֹדָה ***dôḏāh*** [FATHER'S SISTER] 3x
<1734> דּוֹדוֹ ***dôḏô*** [DODO] 5x
<1735> דֹּדָוָהוּ ***dōḏāwāhû*** [DODAVAHU, DODAVAH] 1x
<1736> דּוּדָאִים ***dûḏā'iym*** [MANDRAKE] 7x
<1737> דּוֹדַי ***dôḏay*** [DODAI] 1x
<1738> דָּוָה ***dāwāh*** [MENSTRUATION] 1x
<1739> דָּוֶה ***dāweh*** [FAINT (adj.)] 5x
<1740> דּוּחַ ***dûaḥ*** [WASH] 4x
<1741> דְּוַי ***dᵉway*** [ILLNESS] 2x
<1742> דַּוָּי ***dawwāy*** [SICK] 3x
<1743> דּוּךְ ***dûḵ*** [BEAT] 1x
<1744> דּוּכִיפַת ***dûḵiypaṯ*** [HOOPOE] 2x
<1745> דּוּמָה ***dûmāh*** [SILENCE (noun)] 2x
<1746> דּוּמָה ***dûmāh*** [DUMAH] 4x
<1747> דּוּמִיָּה ***dûmiyyāh,*** דֻּמִיָּה ***dumiyyāh*** [SILENCE (noun)] 4x
<1748> דּוּמָם ***dûmām*** [SILENCE (noun)] 3x
<1749> דּוֹנַג ***dônag̱*** [WAX] 4x
<1750> דּוּץ ***dûṣ*** [DANCE (verb)] 1x
<1751> דָּקוּ ***dāqû*** [PIECES (BREAK TO, IN)] 1x
<1752> דּוּר ***dûr*** [DWELL] 1x
<1753> דּוּר ***dûr*** [DWELL] 7x
<1754> דּוּר ***dûr*** [BALL] 3x
<1755> דּוֹר ***dôr*** [GENERATION] 167x
<1756> דֹּאר ***dō'r,*** דּוֹר ***dôr*** [DOR] 6x
<1757> דּוּרָא ***dûrā'*** [DURA] 1x
<1758> דּוּשׁ ***dûš,*** דִּישׁ ***diyš*** [THRESH] 14x
<1759> דּוּשׁ ***dûš*** [TRAMPLE] 1x
<1760> דָּחָה ***dāḥāh*** [DRIVE] 10x
<1761> דַּחֲוָה ***daḥᵃwāh*** [ENTERTAINMENT] 1x
<1762> דְּחִי ***dᵉḥiy*** [STUMBLING] 2x

<1763> דְּחַל ***d^{e}ḥal*** [FEAR (verb)] 6x
<1764> דֹּחַן ***dōḥan*** [MILLET] 1x
<1765> דָּחַף ***dāḥap̱*** [HURRY (verb)] 4x
<1766> דָּחַק ***dāḥaq*** [AFFLICT] 2x
<1767> דַּי ***day*** [ENOUGH] 38x
<1768> דִּי ***diy*** [WHO] 19x
<1769> דִּיבֹן ***diyḇôn*** [DIBON] 11x
<1770> דִּיג ***diyg̱*** [FISH (verb)] 1x
<1771> דַּיָּג ***dayyāg̱*** [FISHERMAN] 2x
<1772> דַּיָּה ***dayyāh*** [VULTURE] 2x
<1773> דְּיוֹ ***d^{e}yô*** [INK] 1x
<1774> דִּי זָהָב ***diy zāhāḇ*** [DIZAHAB] 1x
<1775> דִּימוֹן ***diymôn*** [DIMON] 2x
<1776> דִּימוֹנָה ***diymônāh*** [DIMONAH] 1x
<1777> דִּין ***diyn*** [JUDGE (verb)] 24x
<1778> דִּין ***diyn*** [JUDGE (verb)] 1x
<1779> דִּין ***diyn*** [JUDGMENT] 20x
<1780> דִּין ***diyn*** [JUDGMENT] 5x
<1781> דַּיָּן ***dayyān*** [JUDGE (noun)] 2x
<1782> דַּיָּן ***dayyān*** [JUDGE (noun)] 1x
<1783> דִּינָה ***diynāh*** [DINAH] 8x
<1784> דִּינָיֵא ***diynāyê’,*** דַּיָּנַיֵּא ***dayyānayyā’*** [DINAITES] 1x
<1785> דָּיֵק ***dāyêq*** [SIEGE WORK] 6x
<1786> דַּיִשׁ ***dayiš*** [THRESHING (noun)] 1x
<1787> דִּישֹׁן ***diyšōn,*** דִּשׁוֹן ***dišôn,*** דִּשֹׁן ***dišōn*** [DISHON] 7x
<1788> דִּישׁוֹן ***diyšôn*** [IBEX] 1x
<1789> דִּישָׁן ***diyšān*** [DISHAN] 5x
<1790> דַּךְ ***daḵ*** [OPPRESSED] 4x
<1791> דֵּךְ ***dêḵ,*** דָּךְ ***dāḵ*** [THIS] 13x
<1792> דָּכָא ***dāḵā’*** [CRUSH] 18x
<1793> דַּכָּא ***dakkā’*** [CRUSHED] 3x
<1794> דָּכָה ***dāḵāh*** [CRUSH] 5x
<1795> דַּכָּה ***dakkāh*** [CRUSHING] 1x
<1796> דֳּכִי ***d^{o}ḵiy*** [POUNDING WAVE] 1x
<1797> דִּכֵּן ***dikkên*** [THIS, THAT] 3x
<1798> דְּכַר ***d^{e}ḵar*** [RAM] 3x
<1799> דִּכְרוֹן ***diḵrôn,*** דָּכְרָן ***doḵrān*** [RECORD] 3x
<1800> דַּל ***dal*** [POOR] 48x
<1801> דָּלַג ***dālag̱*** [LEAP] 5x
<1802> דָּלָה ***dālāh*** [DRAW] 5x
<1803> דַּלָּה ***dallāh*** [LOOM] 2x, [POOR] 6x
<1804> דָּלַח ***dālaḥ*** [TROUBLE (verb)] 3x
<1805> דְּלִי ***d^{e}liy*** [BUCKET] 2x
<1806> דְּלָיָה ***d^{e}lāyāh,*** דְּלָיָהוּ ***d^{e}lāyāhû*** [DELAIAH] 7x
<1807> דְּלִילָה ***d^{e}liylāh*** [DELILAH] 6x
<1808> דָּלִית ***dāliyṯ*** [BRANCH] 8x
<1809> דָּלַל ***dālal*** [BRING LOW] 9x
<1810> דִּלְעָן ***dil‘ān*** [DILEAN] 1x
<1811> דָּלַף ***dālap̱*** [LEAK] 3x
<1812> דֶּלֶף ***delep̱*** [DRIPPING] 2x
<1813> דַּלְפוֹן ***dalp̱ôn*** [DALPHON] 1x

<1814> דָּלַק ***dālaq*** [BURN (verb)] 9x
<1815> דְּלַק ***d***^{e}***laq*** [BURNING (verb)] 1x
<1816> דַּלֶּקֶת ***daleqeṯ*** [INFLAMMATION] 1x
<1817> דָּל ***dāl,*** דֶּלֶת ***deleṯ*** [DOOR] 88x
<1818> דָּם ***dām*** [BLOOD] 362x
<1819> דָּמָה ***dāmāh*** [LIKE (BE)] 29x
<1820> דָּמָה ***dāmāh*** [CEASE] 16x
<1821> דְּמָה ***d***^{e}***māh*** [LIKE (BE)] 2x
<1822> דֻּמָה ***dumāh*** [DESTROYED] 1x
<1823> דְּמוּת ***d***^{e}***mûṯ*** [LIKENESS] 25x
<1824> דֳּמִי ***d***^{o}***miy,*** דְּמִי ***d***^{e}***miy*** [REST (noun)] 4x
<1825> דִּמְיוֹן ***dimyôn*** [LIKE] 1x
<1826> דָּמַם ***dāmam*** [STAND STILL] 30x
<1827> דְּמָמָה ***d***^{e}***māmāh*** [STILL (adj.)] 3x
<1828> דֹּמֶן ***dōmen*** [DUNG] 6x
<1829> דִּמְנָה ***dimnāh*** [DIMNAH] 1x
<1830> דָּמַע ***dāma'*** [WEEP] 2x
<1831> דֶּמַע ***dema'*** [VINTAGE] 1x
<1832> דִּמְעָה ***dim'āh*** [TEARS] 23x
<1833> דְּמֶשֶׂק ***d***^{e}***mešeq*** [DAMASCUS] 1x
<1834> דּוּמֶּשֶׂק ***dûmmeśeq,*** דַּמֶּשֶׂק ***dammeśeq,*** דַּרְמֶשֶׂק ***darmeśeq***
[DAMASCUS] 43x
<1835> דָּן ***dān*** [DAN] 71x
<1836> דְּנָה ***d***^{e}***nāh*** [THIS, THEREFORE] 57x
<1837> דַּנָּה ***dannāh*** [DANNAH] 1x
<1838> דִּנְהָבָה ***dinhāḇāh*** [DINHABAH] 2x
<1839> דָּנִי ***dāniy*** [DANITES] 5x
<1840> דָּנִאֵל ***dāni'êl,*** דָּנִיֵּאל ***dāniyyê'l*** [DANIEL] 29x
<1841> דָּנִיֵּאל ***dāniyyê'l*** [DANIEL] 43x
<1842> דָּן יַעַן ***dān ya'an*** [DAN JAAN] 1x
<1843> דֵּעַ ***dêa'*** [KNOWLEDGE] 5x
<1844> דֵּעָה ***dê'āh*** [KNOWLEDGE] 6x
<1845> דְּעוּאֵל ***d***^{e}***'û'êl*** [DEUEL] 5x
<1846> דָּעַךְ ***dā'aḵ*** [EXTINGUISH] 9x
<1847> דַּעַת ***da'aṯ*** [KNOWLEDGE] 91x
<1848> דֳּפִי ***d***^{o}***piy*** [SLANDER] 1x
<1849> דָּפַק ***dāp̱aq*** [DRIVE HARD] 3x
<1850> דָּפְקָה ***dop̱qāh*** [DOPHKAH] 2x
<1851> דַּק ***daq*** [THIN] 14x
<1852> דֹּק ***dōq*** [CURTAIN] 1x
<1853> דִּקְלָה ***diqlāh*** [DIKLAH] 2x
<1854> דָּקַק ***dāqaq*** [BEAT] 13x
<1855> דְּקַק ***d***^{e}***qaq*** [CRUSH] 9x
<1856> דָּקַר ***dāqar*** [PIERCE] 11x
<1857> דֶּקֶר ***deqer*** [DEKER] 1x
<1858> דַּר ***dar*** [MOTHER-OF-PEARL] 1x
<1859> דָּר ***dār*** [GENERATION] 4x
<1860> דְּרָאוֹן ***d***^{e}***rā'ôn,*** דֵּרָאוֹן ***dêrā'ôn*** [ABHORRENCE] 2x
<1861> דָּרְבָן ***dorḇān,*** דָּרְבֹן ***dorḇōn*** [GOAD] 2x
<1862> דַּרְדַּע ***darda'*** [DARDA] 1x
<1863> דַּרְדַּע ***darda'*** [THISTLE] 2x

<1864> דָּרוֹם ***dārôm*** [SOUTH, SOUTHWARD] 17x
<1865> דְּרוֹר ***dᵉrôr*** [FREEDOM] 8x
<1866> דְּרוֹר ***dᵉrôr*** [SWALLOW (noun)] 2x
<1867> דָּרְיָוֶשׁ ***dārᵉyāweš*** [DARIUS] 10x
<1868> דּרְיָוֶשׁ ***dārᵉyāweš*** [DARIUS] 15x
<1869> דָּרַךְ ***dāraḵ*** [TREAD] 62x
<1870> דֶּרֶךְ ***derek*** [PATH] 705x
<1871> דַּרְכְּמָה ***darkᵉmāh*** [DRACHMA] 4x
<1872> דְּרָע ***dᵉrā‘*** [ARM (noun)] 1x
<1873> דָּרַע ***dāra‘*** [DARA] 1x
<1874> דַּרְקוֹן ***darqôn*** [DARKON] 2x
<1875> דָּרַשׁ ***dāraš*** [SEEK] 164x
<1876> דָּשָׁא ***dāšā'*** [PRODUCE (verb)] 2x
<1877> דֶּשֶׁא ***deše',*** דָּשָׁא ***dāšā'*** [GRASS] 15x
<1878> דָּשֵׁן ***dāšên*** [FAT (MAKE, GROW)] 11x
<1879> דָּשֵׁן ***dāšên*** [FAT (adj.)] 3x
<1880> דֶּשֶׁן ***dešen*** [FATNESS] 15x
<1881> דָּת ***dāṯ*** [LAW] 22x
<1882> דָּת ***dāṯ*** [LAW] 14x
<1883> דֶּתֶא ***deṯe'*** [GRASS] 2x
<1884> דְּתָבַר ***dᵉṯāḇar*** [JUDGE (noun)] 2x
<1885> דָּתָן ***dāṯān*** [DATHAN] 10x
<1886> דֹּתָן ***dōṯān*** [DOTHAN] 3x

ה Hê

<1887> הֵא ***hê'*** [BEHOLD (interj.)] 2x
<1888> הָא ***hā',*** הֵא ***hê'*** [BEHOLD (interj.)] 2x
<1889> הֶאָח ***he'āḥ*** [AHA] 13x
<1890> הַבְהַב ***haḇhaḇ*** [OFFERING] 1x
<1891> הָבַל ***hāḇal*** [VAIN (BECOME)] 5x
<1892> הֶבֶל ***heḇel*** [VANITY] 70x
<1893> הֶבֶל ***heḇel*** [ABEL] 8x
<1894> הָבְנִים ***hoḇniym*** [EBONY] 1x
<1895> הָבַר ***hāḇar*** [ASTROLOGER] 1x
<1896> הֵגֶא ***hêge',*** הֵגַי ***hêgay*** [HEGAI, HEGE] 4x
<1897> הָגָה ***hāḡāh*** [MEDITATE] 25x
<1898> הָגָה ***hāḡāh*** [REMOVE] 3x
<1899> הֶגֶה ***hegeh*** [RUMBLING] 3x
<1900> הָגוּת ***hāḡûṯ*** [MEDITATION] 1x
<1901> הָגִיג ***hāḡiyg*** [MEDITATION] 2x
<1902> הִגָּיוֹן ***higgāyôn*** [MEDITATION] 4x
<1903> הָגִין ***hāḡiyn*** [DIRECTLY] 1x
<1904> הָגָר ***hāḡār*** [HAGAR] 12x
<1905> הַגְרִי ***haḡriy,*** הַגְרִיאִים ***haḡriy'iym*** [HAGRITE] 7x
<1906> הֵד ***hêḏ*** [JOYFUL SHOUTING] 1x
<1907> הַדָּבַר ***haddāḇar*** [COUNSELOR] 4x
<1908> הֲדַד ***hᵃḏaḏ*** [HADAD] 12x
<1909> הֲדַדְעֶזֶר ***hᵃḏaḏ‘ezer*** [HADADEZER] 21x

<1910> הֲדַד רִמּוֹן ***hᵃḏaḏ-rimmôn*** [HADAD RIMMON] 1x

<1911> הָדָה ***hāḏāh*** [PUT (verb)] 1x

<1912> הֹדּוּ ***hōddû*** [INDIA] 2x

<1913> הֲדוֹרָם ***hᵃḏôrām*** [HADORAM] 4x

<1914> הִדַּי ***hidday*** [HIDDAI] 1x

<1915> הָדַךְ ***hāḏaḵ*** [TREAD DOWN] 1x

<1916> הֲדֹם ***hᵃḏôm*** [FOOTSTOOL] 6x

<1917> הַדָּם ***haddām*** [PIECE] 2x

<1918> הֲדַס ***hᵃdas*** [MYRTLE TREE] 6x

<1919> הֲדַסָּה ***hᵃḏassāh*** [HADASSAH] 1x

<1920> הָדַף ***hāḏap̱*** [PUSH] 11x

<1921> הֲדוּרִים ***hᵃḏûriym,*** הָדַר ***hāḏar*** [HONOR (verb)] 7x

<1922> הֲדַר ***hᵃḏar*** [HONOR (verb)] 3x

<1923> הֲדַר ***hᵃḏar*** [HONOR (noun)] 3x

<1924> הֲדַר ***hᵃḏar*** [HADAR] 1x

<1925> הֶדֶר ***heḏer*** [GLORY] 1x

<1926> הָדָר ***hāḏār*** [GLORY] 30x

<1927> הֲדָרָה ***hᵃḏārāh*** [GLORY] 5x

<1928> הֲדַרְעֶזֶר ***hᵃḏarʿezer*** [HADAREZER] 12x

<1929> הָהּ ***hāh*** [ALAS!] 1x

<1930> הוֹ ***hô*** [ALAS!] 2x

<1931> הִיא ***hiy',*** הוּא ***hû'*** [HE, SHE, IT] 38x

<1932> הוּא ***hû',*** הִיא ***hiy'*** [HE, SHE, IT] 8x

<1933> הָוָה ***hāwāh*** [FALL (verb)] 6x

<1934> הֲוָה ***hᵃwāh*** [BE] 69x

<1935> הוֹד ***hôḏ*** [VIGOR] 24x

<1936> הוֹד ***hôḏ*** [HOD] 1x

<1937> הוֹדְוָה ***hôḏᵉwāh*** [HODEVAH] 1x

<1938> הוֹדַוְיָה ***hôḏawyāh*** [HODAVIAH] 4x

<1939> הוֹדַיְוָהוּ ***hôḏaywāhû*** [HODAIAH] 1x

<1940> הוֹדִיָּה ***hôḏiyyāh*** [HODIAH] 1x

<1941> הוֹדִיָּה ***hôḏiyyāh*** [HODIJAH, HODIAH] 6x

<1942> הַוָּה ***hawwāh*** [DESTRUCTION] 15x

<1943> הֹוָה ***hōwāh*** [DISASTER] 3x

<1944> הוֹהָם ***hôhām*** [HOHAM] 1x

<1945> הוֹי ***hôy*** [ALAS] 52x

<1946> הוּךְ ***hûḵ*** [GO] 4x

<1947> הוֹלֵלוֹת ***hôlēlôṯ*** [MADNESS] 4x

<1948> הוֹלֵלוּת ***hôlēlûṯ*** [MADNESS] 1x

<1949> הוּם ***hûm*** [STIR (verb)] 6x

<1950> הוֹמָם ***hômām*** [HOMAM] 1x

<1951> הוּן ***hûn*** [EASY (THINK, REGARD AS)] 1x

<1952> הוֹן ***hôn*** [WEALTH] 26x

<1953> הוֹשָׁמָע ***hôšāmāʿ*** [HOSHAMA] 1x

<1954> הוֹשֵׁעַ ***hôšēaʿ*** [HOSHEA] 17x

<1955> הוֹשַׁעְיָה ***hôšaʿyāh*** [HOSHAMA] 3x

<1956> הוֹתִיר ***hôṯiyr*** [HOTHIR] 2x

<1957> הָזָה ***hāzāh*** [SLEEP (verb)] 1x

<1958> הִי ***hiy*** [WOE (noun)] 1x

<1959> הֵידָד ***hêyḏāḏ*** [SHOUTING] 7x

<1960> הֻיְּדוֹת ***huyyᵉḏôṯ*** [THANKSGIVING] 1x

<1961> הָיָה ***hāyāh*** [BE] 1,249x (NAS)
<1962> הַיָּה ***hayyāh*** [DESTRUCTION] 1x
<1963> הֵיךְ ***hêyk̲*** [HOW] 2x
<1964> הֵיכָל ***hêyk̲āl*** [TEMPLE] 80x
<1965> הֵיכַל ***hêyk̲al*** [TEMPLE] 13x
<1966> הֵילֵל ***hêylêl*** [MORNING STAR] 1x
<1967> הֵימָם ***hêymām*** [HEMAN] 1x
<1968> הֵימָן ***hêymān*** [HEMAM] 17x
<1969> הִין ***hiyn*** [HIN] 22x
<1970> הָכַר ***hāk̲ar,*** חָכַר ***ḥāk̲ar*** [WRONG (verb)] 1x
<1971> הַכָּרָה ***hakkārāh*** [LOOK (noun)] 1x
<1972> הָלָא ***hālā'*** [DRIVEN AWAY (BE)] 1x
<1973> הָלְאָה ***hāl^{e}'āh*** [BEYOND] 14x
<1974> הִלּוּל ***hillûl*** [OFFERING OF PRAISE] 2x
<1975> הַלָּז ***hallāz*** [THIS, THAT] 7x
<1976> הַלָּזֶה ***hallāzeh*** [THIS, THAT] 2x
<1977> הַלֵּזוּ ***hallêzû*** [THIS, THAT] 1x
<1978> הָלִיךְ ***hāliyk̲*** [STEP (noun)] 1x
<1979> הֲלִיכָה ***h^{a}liyk̲ah*** [WAY] 6x
<1980> הָלַךְ ***hālak̲*** [GO] 771x (NAS)
<1981> הֲלַךְ ***h^{a}lak̲*** [GO] 6x
<1982> הֵלֶךְ ***hêlek̲*** [DRIP (noun)] 2x
<1983> הֲלָךְ ***h^{a}lāk̲*** [CUSTOM] 3x
<1984> הָלַל ***hālal*** [PRAISE (verb)] 165x
<1985> הִלֵּל ***hillêl*** [HILLEL] 2x
<1986> הָלַם ***hālam*** [SMITE] 9x
<1987> הֶלֶם ***helem*** [HELEM] 1x
<1988> הֲלֹם ***h^{a}lōm*** [HERE, HITHER] 12x
<1989> הַלְמוּת ***halmût̲*** [HAMMER (noun)] 1x
<1990> הָם ***hām*** [HAM] 1x
<1991> הָם ***hām*** [WEALTH] 1x
<1992> הֵם ***hêm,*** הֵמָּה ***hêmmāh*** [THEY, THESE] 44x
<1993> הָמָה ***hāmāh*** [MURMUR] 34x
<1994> הִמּוֹ ***himmô,*** הִמֹּן ***himmōn*** [THEY, THESE, THEM] 11x
<1995> הָמוֹן ***hāmôn,*** הָמֹן ***hāman*** [MULTITUDE] 83x
<1996> הֲמוֹן גּוֹג ***h^{a}môn gôg*** [HAMON GOG] 2x
<1997> הֲמוֹנָה ***h^{a}mônāh*** [HAMONAH] 1x
<1998> הֶמְיָה ***hemyāh*** [NOISE] 1x
<1999> הֲמֻלָּה ***h^{a}mullāh,*** הֲמוּלָּה ***h^{a}mûllāh*** [NOISE] 2x
<2000> הָמַם ***hāmam*** [CONFUSE] 12x
<2001> הָמָן ***hāmān*** [HAMAN] 54x
<2002> הַמְנִיךְ ***hamniyk̲*** [CHAIN] 3x
<2003> הֲמָסִים ***h^{a}māsiym*** [BRUSHWOOD] 1x
<2004> הֵן ***hên*** [THEY, THEM] 16x
<2005> הֵן ***hên*** [BEHOLD (interj.)] 99x (NAS)
<2006> הֵן ***hên*** [BEHOLD (interj.)] 15x (NAS)
<2007> הֵנָּה ***hênnāh*** [THEY, THEM] 26x
<2008> הֵנָּה ***hênnāh*** [HERE] 24x (NAS)
<2009> הִנֵּה ***hinnêh*** [BEHOLD (interj.)] 1,046x (NAS)
<2010> הֲנָחָה ***h^{a}nāḥāh*** [HOLIDAY] 1x
<2011> הִנֹּם ***hinnōm*** [HINNOM] 11x

<2012> הֵנַע **hênaʻ** [HENA] 3x
<2013> הָס **hās,** הָסָה **hāsāh** [SILENCE!, KEEP SILENCE!] 8x
<2014> הֲפוּגָה **hap̱ûḡāh** [INTERRUPTION] 1x
<2015> הָפַךְ **hāp̱aḵ** [TURN (verb)] 93x
<2016> הֵפֶךְ **hêp̱eḵ,** הֶפֶךְ **hep̱eḵ** [OPPOSITE (noun)] 2x
<2017> הֹפֶךְ **hōp̱eḵ** [TURNING THINGS AROUND, UPSIDE DOWN] 1x
<2018> הֲפֵכָה **h^{a}p̱êḵāh** [OVERTHROW (noun)] 1x
<2019> הֲפַכְפַּךְ **h^{a}p̱aḵpaḵ** [CROOKED] 1x
<2020> הַצָּלָה **haṣṣālāh** [DELIVERANCE] 1x
<2021> הֹצֶן **hōṣen** [CHARIOT] 1x
<2022> הַר **har** [MOUNTAIN] 546x
<2023> הֹר **hōr** [HOR] 12x
<2024> הָרָא **hārā'** [HARA] 1x
<2025> הַרְאֵל **har'êl** [ALTAR HEARTH] 1x
<2026> הָרַג **hāraḡ** [KILL] 167x
<2027> הֶרֶג **hereḡ** [SLAUGHTER (noun)] 5x
<2028> הֲרֵגָה **h^{a}rêḡāh** [SLAUGHTER (noun)] 5x
<2029> הָרָה **hārāh** [CONCEIVE] 45x
<2030> הָרֶה **hāreh** [PREGNANT] 16x
<2031> הַרְהֹר **harhōr** [THOUGHT] 1x
<2032> הֵרוֹן **hêrôn,** הֵרָיוֹן **hêrāyôn** [CONCEPTION] 2x
<2033> הֲרוֹרִי **h^{a}rôriy** [HARORITE] 1x
<2034> הֲרִיסָה **h^{a}riysāh** [RUIN (noun)] 1x
<2035> הֲרִיסוּת **h^{a}riysûṯ** [DESTRUCTION] 1x
<2036> הֹרָם **hōrām** [HORAM] 1x
<2037> הָרוּם **hārûm** [HARUM] 1x
<2038> הַרְמוֹן **harmôn** [HARMON] 1x
<2039> הָרָן **hārān** [HARAN] 6x
<2040> הָרַס **hāras** [PULL DOWN] 43x
<2041> הֶרֶס **heres** [DESTRUCTION] 1x
<2042> הָרָר **hārār** [MOUNTAIN] 13x
<2043> הָרָרִי **hārāriy,** הֲרָרִי **h^{a}rāriy** [HARARITE] 4x
<2044> הָשֵׁם **hāšêm** [HASHEM] 1x
<2045> הַשְׁמָעוּת **hašmāʻûṯ** [REPORT] 1x
<2046> הִתּוּךְ **hittûḵ** [MELTED (BE)] 1x
<2047> הֲתָךְ **h^{a}ṯāḵ** [HATACH, HATHACH] 4x
<2048> הָתַל **hāṯal,** תָּלַל **tālal** [MOCK] 10x
<2049> הֲתֻלִים **h^{a}ṯuliym** [MOCKERS] 1x
<2050> הָתַת **haṯaṯ,** הוּת **hûṯ** [ATTACK (verb)] 1x

ו Waw

<2051> וְדָן **w^{e}ḏān** [VEDAN] 1x
<2052> וָהֵב **wāhêḇ,** אֶתְוְהַב **eṯw^{e}haḇ** [WAHEB] 1x
<2053> וָו **wāw** [HOOK] 13x
<2054> וָזָר **wāzār** [GUILTY (noun)] 1x
<2055> וַיְזָתָא **wayzāṯa'** [VAIZATHA, VAJEZATHA] 1x
<2056> וָלָד **wālāḏ** [CHILD] 1x
<2057> וַנְיָה **wanyāh** [VANIAH] 1x

<2058> וָפְסִי ***wop̱siy*** [VOPHSI] 1x
<2059> וַשְׁנִי ***wašniy*** [VASHNI] 1x
<2060> וַשְׁתִּי ***waštiy*** [VASHTI] 10x

ז Zayin

<2061> זְאֵב ***z***^{e}***'êḇ*** [WOLF] 7x
<2062> זְאֵב ***z***^{e}***'êḇ*** [ZEEB] 6x
<2063> זֹאת ***zō'ṯ*** [THIS ONE] 41x
<2064> זָבַד ***zāḇaḏ*** [ENDOW] 1x
<2065> זֶבֶד ***zeḇeḏ,*** זֵבֶד ***zêḇeḏ*** [GIFT] 1x
<2066> זָבָד ***zāḇāḏ*** [ZABAD] 8x
<2067> זַבְדִּי ***zaḇdiy*** [ZABDI] 6x
<2068> זַבְדִּיאֵל ***zaḇdiy'êl*** [ZABDIEL] 2x
<2069> זְבַדְיָה ***z***^{e}***ḇaḏyāh,*** זְבַדְיָהוּ ***z***^{e}***baḏyāhû*** [ZEBADIAH] 9x
<2070> זְבוּב ***z***^{e}***ḇûḇ*** [FLY (noun)] 2x
<2071> זָבוּד ***zāḇûḏ*** [ZABUD] 1x
<2072> זַבּוּד ***zabbûḏ*** [ZABBUD] 1x
<2073> זְבוּל ***z***^{e}***ḇûl,*** זְבֻל ***z***^{e}***ḇul*** [HABITATION] 5x
<2074> זְבוּלוּן ***z***^{e}***ḇûlûn,*** זְבוּלֻן ***z***^{e}***ḇûlun,*** זְבֻלוּן ***z***^{e}***ḇulûn*** [ZEBULUN] 45x
<2075> זְבוּלֹנִי ***z***^{e}***ḇûlōniy*** [ZEBULUNITE] 3x
<2076> זָבַח ***zāḇaḥ*** [OFFER] 134x
<2077> זֶבַח ***zeḇaḥ*** [SACRIFICE (noun)] 162x
<2078> זֶבַח ***zeḇaḥ*** [ZEBAH] 12x
<2079> זַבַּי ***zabbay*** [ZABBAI] 2x
<2080> זְבִידָה ***z***^{e}***ḇiyḏāh*** [ZEBIDAH] 1x
<2081> זְבִינָא ***z***^{e}***ḇiyna'*** [ZEBINA] 1x
<2082> זָבַל ***zāḇal*** [DWELL] 1x
<2083> זְבֻל ***z***^{e}***ḇul*** [ZEBUL] 5x
<2084> זְבַן ***z***^{e}***ḇan*** [GAIN (verb)] 1x
<2085> זָג ***zāg̱*** [SKIN] 1x
<2086> זֵד ***zêḏ*** [PROUD] 13x
<2087> זָדוֹן ***zāḏôn*** [PRIDE] 11x
<2088> זֶה ***zeh*** [THIS, THESE] 1,469x (NAS)
<2089> זֶה ***zeh*** [LAMB] 1x
<2090> זֹה ***zōh*** [THIS] 9x (NAS)
<2091> זָהָב ***zāhāḇ*** [GOLD] 389x
<2092> זָהַם ***zāham*** [ABHOR] 1x
<2093> זַהַם ***zaham*** [ZAHAM] 1x
<2094> זָהַר ***zāhar*** [WARN] 22x
<2095> זְהַר ***z***^{e}***har*** [HEED (TAKE)] 1x
<2096> זֹהַר ***zōhar*** [BRIGHTNESS] 2x
<2097> זוֹ ***zô*** [THIS, THAT] 2x
<2098> זוּ ***zû*** [THIS, WHICH] 14x (NAS)
<2099> זִו ***ziw*** [ZIV, ZIT] 2x
<2100> זוּב ***zûb*** [GUSH] 42x
<2101> זוֹב ***zôḇ*** [DISCHARGE] 10x
<2102> זוּד ***zûḏ,*** זִיד ***ziyḏ*** [PROUDLY (DEAL)] 10x
<2103> זוּד ***zûḏ*** [PRIDE] 1x

<2104> זוּזִים ***zûziym*** [ZUZIMS, ZUZITES] 1x

<2105> זוֹחֵת ***zôḥêṯ*** [ZOHETH] 1x

<2106> זָוִית ***zāwiyṯ*** [CORNER (noun)] 2x

<2107> זוּל ***zûl*** [LAVISH] 1x

<2108> זוּלָה ***zûlāh*** [EXCEPT] 16x

<2109> זוּן ***zûn,*** יָזַן ***yāzan*** [WELL-FED] 1x

<2110> זוּן ***zûn*** [FEED (verb)] 1x

<2111> זוּעַ ***zûaʿ*** [TREMBLE] 3x

<2112> זוּעַ ***zûaʿ*** [TREMBLE] 2x

<2113> זְוָעָה ***zᵉwāʿāh*** [TERROR] 6x

<2114> זוּר ***zûr*** [STRANGER (BE)] 77x

<2115> זוּר ***zûr*** [CRUSH] 4x

<2116> זוּרֶה ***zûreh*** [CRUSHED] 1x

<2117> זָזָא ***zāzā'*** [ZAZA] 1x

<2118> זָחַח ***zāḥaḥ*** [LOOSE (COME)] 2x

<2119> זָחַל ***zāḥal*** [CRAWL] 3x

<2120> זֹחֶלֶת ***zōḥeleṯ*** [ZOHELETH] 1x

<2121> זֵידוֹן ***zêḏôn*** [RAGING] 1x

<2122> זִיו ***ziyw*** [BRIGHTNESS] 6x

<2123> זִיז ***ziyz*** [ABUNDANCE] 1x, [MOVING CREATURES] 2x

<2124> זִיזָא ***ziyzā'*** [ZIZA] 2x

<2125> זִיזָה ***ziyzāh*** [ZIZAH] 1x

<2126> זִינָא ***ziynā'*** [ZINA] 1x

<2127> זִיעַ ***ziyaʿ*** [ZIA] 1x

<2128> זִיף ***ziyp̱*** [ZIPH] 10x

<2129> זִיפָה ***ziyp̱āh*** [ZIPHAH] 1x

<2130> זִיפִי ***ziyp̱iy*** [ZIPHITE] 3x

<2131> זֵק ***zêq,*** זִיקָה ***ziyqāh*** [FIREBRAND] 7x

<2132> זַיִת ***zayiṯ*** [OLIVE, OLIVE TREE] 38x

<2133> זֵיתָן ***zêyṯān*** [ZETHAN] 1x

<2134> זַךְ ***zaḵ*** [PURE] 11x

<2135> זָכָה ***zāḵāh*** [PURE (BE)] 8x

<2136> זָכוּ ***zāḵû*** [INNOCENCE] 1x

<2137> זְכוֹכִית ***zᵉḵôḵiyṯ*** [CRYSTAL] 1x

<2138> זְכוּר ***zᵉḵûr*** [MALE] 4x

<2139> זַכּוּר ***zakkûr*** [ZACCUR] 10x

<2140> זַכַּי ***zakkay*** [ZACCAI] 2x

<2141> זָכַךְ ***zāḵaḵ*** [PURE (BE)] 4x

<2142> זָכַר ***zāḵar,*** מַזְכִּיר ***mazkiyr*** [REMEMBER] 233x

<2143> זֵכֶר ***zêḵer*** [REMEMBRANCE] 23x

<2144> זֶכֶר ***zeḵer*** [ZECHER, ZEKER] 1x

<2145> זָכַר ***zāḵar,*** זָכָר ***zāḵār*** [MALE (BE), MALE] 81x

<2146> זִכָּרוֹן ***zikkārôn*** [MEMORIAL] 24x

<2147> זִכְרִי ***ziḵriy*** [ZICHRI, ZICRI] 12x

<2148> זְכַרְיָה ***zᵉḵaryāh,*** זְכַרְיָהוּ ***zᵉḵaryāhû*** [ZECHARIAH] 43x

<2149> זֻלּוּת ***zullûṯ*** [VILENESS] 1x

<2150> זַלְזַל ***zalzal*** [SPRIG] 1x

<2151> זָלַל ***zālal*** [GLUTTON (BE)] 8x

<2152> זַלְעָפָה ***zalʿāp̱āh*** [BURNING HEAT] 3x

<2153> זִלְפָּה ***zilpāh*** [ZILPAH] 7x

<2154> זִמָּה ***zimmāh*** [PLAN (noun)] 29x

<2155> זִמָּה ***zimmāh*** [ZIMMAH] 3x

<2156> זְמוֹרָה ***z^{e}môrāh*** [BRANCH] 5x

<2157> זַמְזֻמִּים ***zamzummiym*** [ZAMSUMMITE, ZAMZUMMIM] 1x

<2158> זָמִיר ***zāmiyr*** [SONG] 7x

<2159> זָמִיר ***zāmiyr*** [BRANCH] 1x

<2160> זְמִירָה ***z^{e}miyrah*** [ZIMIRAH, ZEMIRA] 1x

<2161> זָמַם ***zāmam*** [CONSIDER] 12x

<2162> זָמָם ***zāmām*** [DEVICE] 1x

<2163> זָמַן ***zāman*** [APPOINTED] 3x

<2164> זְמַן ***z^{e}man*** [AGREE] 1x

<2165> זְמַן ***z^{e}man*** [TIME] 4x

<2166> זְמָן ***z^{e}mān*** [TIME] 11x

<2167> זָמַר ***zāmar*** [SING] 45x

<2168> זָמַר ***zāmar*** [PRUNE] 3x

<2169> זֶמֶר ***zemer*** [MOUNTAIN SHEEP] 1x

<2170> זְמָר ***z^{e}mār*** [MUSIC] 4x

<2171> זַמָּר ***zammār*** [SINGER] 1x

<2172> זִמְרָה ***zimrāh*** [SONG] 7x

<2173> זִמְרָה ***zimrāh*** [FRUIT] 1x

<2174> זִמְרִי ***zimriy*** [ZIMRI] 15x

<2175> זִמְרָן ***zimrān*** [ZIMRAN] 2x

<2176> זִמְרָת ***zimrāṯ*** [SONG] 3x

<2177> זַן ***zan*** [KIND] 2x

<2178> זַן ***zan*** [KIND] 4x

<2179> זָנַב ***zānaḇ*** [ATTACK (verb)] 2x

<2180> זָנָב ***zānāḇ*** [TAIL] 11x

<2181> זָנָה ***zānāh,*** זוֹנָה ***zônāh,*** זֹנָה ***zōnāh*** [PROSTITUTE (verb)] 93x

<2182> זָנוֹחַ ***zānôaḥ*** [ZANOAH] 5x

<2183> זְנוּנִים ***z^{e}nûniym*** [PROSTITUTION] 12x

<2184> זְנוּת ***z^{e}nûṯ*** [FORNICATION] 9x

<2185> זֹנוֹת ***zōnôṯ*** [ARMOR] 1x

<2186> זָנַח ***zānaḥ*** [REJECT] 20x

<2187> זָנַק ***zānaq*** [LEAP] 1x

<2188> זֵעָה ***zêʿāh*** [SWEAT] 1x

<2189> זַעֲוָה ***za^{a}wāh*** [HORROR] 7x

<2190> זַעֲוָן ***za^{a}wān*** [ZAAVAN] 2x

<2191> זְעֵיר ***z^{e}ʿêyr*** [LITTLE (noun)] 5x

<2192> זְעֵיר ***z^{e}ʿêyr*** [LITTLE (adj.)] 1x

<2193> זָעַךְ ***zāʿaḵ*** [EXTINCT (BE)] 1x

<2194> זָעַם ***zāʿam*** [INDIGNANT (BE)] 12x

<2195> זַעַם ***zaʿam*** [INDIGNATION] 22x

<2196> זָעַף ***zāʿap̱*** [ANGRY (BE, BECOME)] 5x

<2197> זַעַף ***zaʿap̱*** [RAGE (noun)] 6x

<2198> זָעֵף ***zāʿêp̱*** [DISPLEASED] 2x

<2199> זָעַק ***zāʿaq*** [CRY OUT] 73x

<2200> זְעַק ***z^{e}ʿaq*** [CRY OUT] 1x

<2201> זְעָקָה ***z^{e}ʿāqāh*** [CRY (noun)] 18x

<2202> זִפְרֹן ***zip̱rōn*** [ZIPHRON] 1x

<2203> זֶפֶת ***zep̱eṯ*** [PITCH] 3x

<2204> זָקֵן ***zāqên*** [OLD (BE, BECOME)] 27x

<2205> זָקֵן ***zāqên*** [OLD, OLD MAN] 180x

<2206> זָקָן ***zāqān*** [BEARD] 19x
<2207> זֹקֶן ***zōqen*** [AGE, OLD AGE] 1x
<2208> זְקֻנִים ***z^{e}quniym*** [OLD AGE] 4x
<2209> זִקְנָה ***ziqnāh*** [OLD AGE] 6x
<2210> זָקַף ***zāqap̱*** [RAISE UP] 2x
<2211> זְקַף ***z^{e}qap̱*** [IMPALE] 1x
<2212> זָקַק ***zāqaq*** [REFINE] 7x
<2213> זֵר ***zêr*** [MOLDING] 10x
<2214> זָרָא ***zārā'*** [LOATHSOME] 1x
<2215> זָרַב ***zāraḇ*** [WARM (BE, WAX)] 1x
<2216> זְרֻבָּבֶל ***z^{e}rubbāḇel*** [ZERUBBABEL] 21x
<2217> זְרֻבָּבֶל ***z^{e}rubbāḇel*** [ZERUBBABEL] 1x
<2218> זֶרֶד ***zereḏ*** [ZERED] 4x
<2219> זָרָה ***zārāh*** [SCATTER] 38x, [SCRUTINIZE] 1x
<2220> זְרוֹעַ ***z^{e}rôa',*** זְרֹעַ ***z^{e}rōa'*** [ARM (noun)] 91x
<2221> זֵרוּעַ ***zêrûa'*** [SOWING] 2x
<2222> זַרְזִיף ***zarziyp̱, zārap̱*** [WATER (noun and verb)] 1x
<2223> זַרְזִיר ***zarziyr*** [STRUTTING ROOSTER] 1x
<2224> זָרַח ***zāraḥ*** [RISE UP] 18x
<2225> זֶרַח ***zeraḥ*** [RISING] 1x
<2226> זֶרַח ***zeraḥ*** [ZERAH] 21x
<2227> זַרְחִי ***zarḥiy*** [ZARHITE] 6x
<2228> זְרַחְיָה ***z^{e}raḥyāh*** [ZERAHIAH] 5x
<2229> זָרַם ***zāram*** [POUR OUT] 2x
<2230> זֶרֶם ***zerem*** [STORM (noun)] 9x
<2231> זִרְמָה ***zirmāh*** [ISSUE] 2x
<2232> זָרַע ***zāra'*** [SOW] 56x
<2233> זֶרַע ***zera'*** [SEED] 229x
<2234> זְרַע ***z^{e}ra'*** [SEED] 1x
<2235> זֵרֹעַ ***zêrōa',*** זֵרְעֹן ***zêr'ōn*** [VEGETABLE] 2x
<2236> זָרַק ***zāraq*** [SPRINKLE] 35x
<2237> זָרַר ***zārar*** [SNEEZE] 1x
<2238> זֶרֶשׁ ***zereš*** [ZERESH] 4x
<2239> זֶרֶת ***zereṯ*** [SPAN] 7x
<2240> זַתּוּא ***zattû'*** [ZATTU] 4x
<2241> זֵתָם ***zêṯām*** [ZETHAM] 2x
<2242> זֵתַר ***zêṯar*** [ZETHAR] 1x

ח Heth

<2243> חֹב ***ḥōḇ*** [HEART] 1x
<2244> חָבָא ***ḥāḇā'*** [HIDE] 33x
<2245> חָבַב ***ḥāḇaḇ*** [LOVE (verb)] 1x
<2246> חֹבָב ***ḥōḇāḇ*** [HOBAB] 2x
<2247> חָבָה ***ḥāḇāh*** [HIDE] 5x
<2248> חֲבוּלָה ***ḥ^{a}ḇûlāh*** [WRONG (noun)] 1x
<2249> חָבוֹר ***ḥāḇôr*** [HABOR] 3x
<2250> חַבּוּרָה ***ḥabbûrāh,*** חַבֻּרָה ***ḥabburāh,*** חֲבֻרָה ***ḥ^{a}ḇurāh*** [BRUISE (noun)] 7x
<2251> חָבַט ***ḥaḇaṭ*** [THRESH] 5x

<2252> חֲבָיָה ***ḥ^{a}ḇāyāh,*** חֳבַיָּה ***ḥ^{o}ḇāyyāh*** [HABAIAH] 2x

<2253> חֶבְיוֹן ***ḥeḇyôn*** [HIDING] 1x

<2254> חבל ***ḥāḇal,*** חֹבְלִים ***ḥōḇ^{e}liym*** [PLEDGE (TAKE AS A)] 29x

<2255> חֲבַל ***ḥ^{a}ḇal*** [DESTROY] 6x

<2256> חֶבֶל ***ḥeḇel,*** חֵבֶל ***ḥêḇel*** [ROPE] 60x

<2257> חֲבָל ***ḥ^{a}ḇāl*** [DAMAGE (noun)] 3x

<2258> חֲבֹל ***ḥ^{a}ḇōl,*** חֲבֹלָה ***ḥ^{a}ḇōlāh*** [PLEDGE (noun)] 4x

<2259> חֹבֵל ***ḥōḇêl*** [SAILOR] 5x

<2260> חִבֵּל ***ḥibbêl*** [MAST] 1x

<2261> חֲבַצֶּלֶת ***ḥ^{a}ḇaṣṣeleṯ*** [ROSE] 2x

<2262> חֲבַצִּנְיָה ***ḥ^{a}ḇaṣṣinyāh*** [HABAZZINIAH] 1x

<2263> חָבַק ***ḥāḇaq*** [EMBRACE] 13x

<2264> חִבֻּק ***ḥibbuq*** [FOLDING] 2x

<2265> חֲבַקּוּק ***ḥ^{a}ḇaqqûq*** [HABAKKUK] 2x

<2266> חָבַר ***ḥāḇar*** [JOIN TOGETHER] 29x

<2267> חֶבֶר ***ḥeḇer*** [COMPANY] 7x

<2268> חֶבֶר ***ḥeḇer*** [HEBER] 11x

<2269> חֲבַר ***ḥaḇar*** [COMPANION] 3x

<2270> חָבֵר ***ḥāḇêr*** [COMPANION] 12x

<2271> חַבָּר ***ḥabbār*** [COMPANION] 1x

<2272> חֲבַרְבֻּרָה ***ḥ^{a}ḇarburāh*** [SPOT] 1x

<2273> חַבְרָה ***ḥaḇrāh*** [FELLOW] 1x

<2274> חֶבְרָה ***ḥeḇrāh*** [COMPANY] 1x

<2275> חֶבְרוֹן ***ḥeḇrôn*** [HEBRON] 71x

<2276> חֶבְרוֹנִי ***ḥeḇrôniy,*** חֶבְרֹנִי ***ḥeḇrōniy*** [HEBRONITE] 5x

<2277> חֶבְרִי ***ḥeḇriy*** [HEBERITE] 1x

<2278> חֲבֶרֶת ***ḥ^{a}ḇereṯ*** [COMPANION] 1x

<2279> חֹבֶרֶת ***ḥōḇereṯ*** [COUPLING] 3x

<2280> חָבַשׁ ***ḥāḇaš*** [BIND] 33x

<2281> חֲבִתִּים ***ḥ^{a}ḇittiym*** [PANS] 1x

<2282> חָג ***ḥāg̱,*** חַג ***ḥag̱*** [FEAST] 62x

<2283> חָגָּא ***ḥāggā'*** [TERROR] 1x

<2284> חָגָב ***ḥāg̱āḇ*** [LOCUST] 5x

<2285> חָגָב ***hāg̱āḇ*** [HAGAB] 1x

<2286> חֲגָבָא ***ḥ^{a}g̱āḇā',*** חֲגָבָה ***ḥ^{a}g̱aḇāh*** [HAGABAH] 2x

<2287> חָגַג ***ḥāg̱ag̱*** [FEAST (HOLD A)] 16x

<2288> חָגָו ***ḥāg̱āw,*** חָגוּ ***ḥāg̱û*** [CLEFT] 3x

<2289> חָגוֹר ***ḥāg̱ôr,*** חֲגוֹר ***ḥ^{a}g̱ôr*** [GIRDED] 4x

<2290> חֲגוֹרָה ***ḥ^{a}g̱ôrāh,*** חֲגֹרָה ***h^{a}g̱ōrāh*** [BELT] 5x

<2291> חַגִּי ***ḥaggiy*** [HAGGI, HAGGITE] 2x

<2292> חַגַּי ***ḥaggay*** [HAGGAI] 11x

<2293> חַגִּיָּה ***ḥaggiyyāh*** [HAGGIAH] 1x

<2294> חַגִּית ***ḥaggiyṯ*** [HAGGITH] 5x

<2295> חָגְלָה ***ḥog̱lāh*** [HOGLAH] 4x

<2296> חָגַר ***ḥāg̱ar*** [GIRD ONESELF] 43x

<2297> חַד ***ḥaḏ*** [ONE] 1x

<2298> חַד ***ḥaḏ*** [ONE] 14x

<2299> חַד ***ḥaḏ*** [SHARP] 4x

<2300> חָדַד ***ḥāḏaḏ,*** חָדָה ***ḥāḏāh*** [SHARPEN] 6x

<2301> חֲדַד ***ḥ^{a}ḏaḏ*** [HADAD] 1x

<2302> חָדָה ***ḥāḏāh,*** יָחַד ***yāḥaḏ*** [REJOICE] 3x

<2303> חַדּוּד ***ḥaddûḏ*** [SHARP] 1x
<2304> חֶדְוָה ***ḥeḏwāh*** [JOY] 2x
<2305> חֶדְוָה ***ḥeḏwāh*** [JOY] 1x
<2306> חֲדֵה ***ḥ^{a}ḏêh*** [CHEST] 1x
<2307> חָדִיד ***ḥāḏiyḏ*** [HADID] 3x
<2308> חָדַל ***ḥāḏal*** [CEASE] 57x
<2309> חֶדֶל ***ḥeḏel*** [WORLD] 1x
<2310> חָדֵל ***ḥāḏêl*** [REJECTED] 3x
<2311> חַדְלַי ***ḥaḏlay*** [HADLAI] 1x
<2312> חֵדֶק ***ḥêḏeq*** [BRIER] 2x
<2313> חִדֶּקֶל ***ḥiddeqel*** [HIDDEKEL] 2x
<2314> חָדַר ***ḥāḏar*** [SURROUND] 1x
<2315> חֶדֶר ***ḥeḏer*** [ROOM] 38x
<2316> חֲדַר ***ḥ^{a}ḏar*** [HADAR] 1x
<2317> חַדְרָךְ ***ḥaḏrāḵ*** [HADRACH] 1x
<2318> חָדַשׁ ***ḥāḏaš*** [RENEW] 10x
<2319> חָדָשׁ ***ḥāḏāš*** [NEW] 53x
<2320> חֹדֶשׁ ***ḥōḏeš*** [MONTH] 276x
<2321> חֹדֶשׁ ***ḥōḏeš*** [HODESH] 1x
<2322> חֲדָשָׁה ***ḥ^{a}ḏāšāh*** [HADASHAH] 1x
<2323> חֲדַת ***ḥ^{a}ḏaṯ*** [NEW] 1x
<2324> חֲוָה ***ḥ^{a}wāh*** [INTERPRET] 14x
<2325> חוּב ***ḥûḇ*** [ENDANGER] 1x
<2326> חוֹב ***ḥôḇ*** [DEBTOR] 1x
<2327> חוֹבָה ***ḥôḇāh*** [HOBAH] 1x
<2328> חוּג ***ḥûg*** [CIRCLE (INSCRIBE A)] 1x
<2329> חוּג ***ḥûg*** [CIRCLE] 3x
<2330> חוּד ***ḥûḏ*** [RIDDLE] 4x
<2331> חָוָה ***ḥāwāh*** [SHOW] 6x
<2332> חַוָּה ***ḥawwāh*** [EVE] 2x
<2333> חַוָּה ***ḥawwāh*** [TOWN] 4x
<2334> חַוֹּת יָאִיר ***ḥawwôṯ yā'iyr*** [HAVVOTH JAIR] 4x
<2335> חוֹזַי ***ḥôzay*** [HOZAI] 1x
<2336> חוֹחַ ***ḥôaḥ*** [THORN] 11x
<2337> חֲוָחִים ***ḥ^{a}wāḥiym*** [THICKETS] 1x
<2338> חוּט ***ḥûṭ*** [REPAIR] 1x
<2339> חוּט ***ḥûṭ*** [THREAD] 7x
<2340> חִוִּי ***ḥiwwiy*** [HIVITE] 25x
<2341> חֲוִילָה ***ḥ^{a}wiylāh*** [HAVILAH] 7x
<2342> חוּל ***ḥûl,*** חִיל ***ḥiyl*** [SHAKE] 62x
<2343> חוּל ***ḥûl*** [HUL] 2x
<2344> חוֹל ***ḥôl*** [SAND] 23x
<2345> חוּם ***ḥûm*** [DARK-COLORED] 4x
<2346> חוֹמָה ***ḥômāh*** [WALL] 133x
<2347> חוּס ***ḥûs*** [PITY] 24x
<2348> חוֹף ***ḥôp̱*** [COAST] 7x
<2349> חוּפָם ***ḥûp̱ām*** [HUPHAM] 1x
<2350> חוּפָמִי ***ḥûp̱amiy*** [HUPHAMITE] 1x
<2351> חוּץ ***ḥûṣ*** [STREET] 164x
<2352> חֻר ***ḥur*** [HOLE] 2x
<2353> חוּר ***ḥûr*** [WHITE] 2x

<2354> חוּר ***ḥûr*** [HUR] 16x
<2355> חוֹרָי ***ḥôrāy*** [WHITE CLOTH] 1x
<2356> חוֹר ***ḥôr,*** חֹר ***ḥōr*** [HOLE] 7x
<2357> חָוַר ***ḥāwar*** [PALE (GROW, TURN, WAX)] 1x
<2358> חִוָּר ***ḥiwwār*** [WHITE] 1x
<2359> חוּרִי ***ḥûriy*** [HURI] 1x
<2360> חוּרַי ***ḥûray*** [HURAI] 1x
<2361> חוּרָם ***ḥûrām*** [HIRAM] 12x
<2362> חַוְרָן ***ḥawrān*** [HAURAN] 2x
<2363> חוּשׁ ***ḥûš*** [HASTEN] 20x
<2364> חוּשָׁה ***ḥûšāh*** [HUSHAH] 1x
<2365> חוּשַׁי ***ḥûšay*** [HUSHAI] 14x
<2366> חֻשִׁים ***ḥušiym,*** חוּשִׁים ***ḥûšiym*** [HUSHIM] 4x
<2367> חֻשָׁם ***ḥušām,*** חוּשָׁם ***ḥûšām*** [HUSHAM] 4x
<2368> חוֹתָם ***ḥôṯām,*** חֹתָם ***ḥōṯām*** [SEAL (noun)] 14x
<2369> חוֹתָם ***ḥôṯām*** [HOTHAM] 2x
<2370> חֲזָה ***ḥ^{a}zāh,*** חֲזָא ***ḥ^{a}zā'*** [SEE] 31x
<2371> חֲזָהאֵל ***ḥ^{a}zāh'êl*** [HAZAEL] 23x
<2372> חָזָה ***ḥāzāh*** [SEE] 51x
<2373> חָזֶה ***ḥāzeh*** [BREAST] 13x
<2374> חֹזֶה ***ḥōzeh,*** חוֹזֶה ***chōzeh*** [SEER] 17x
<2375> חֲזוֹ ***ḥ^{a}zô*** [HAZO] 1x
<2376> חֵזוּ ***ḥêzû*** [VISION] 12x
<2377> חָזוֹן ***ḥāzôn*** [VISION] 35x
<2378> חָזוֹת ***ḥāzôṯ*** [VISION] 1x
<2379> חֲזוֹת ***ḥ^{a}zôṯ*** [SIGHT] 2x
<2380> חָזוּת ***ḥāzûṯ*** [VISION] 5x
<2381> חֲזִיאֵל ***ḥ^{a}ziy'êl*** [HAZIEL] 1x
<2382> חֲזָיָה ***ḥ^{a}zāyāh*** [HAZAIAH] 1x
<2383> חֶזְיוֹן ***ḥezyôn*** [HEZION] 1x
<2384> חִזָּיוֹן ***ḥizzāyôn*** [VISION] 9x
<2385> חֲזִיז ***ḥ^{a}ziyz*** [THUNDERSTORM] 3x
<2386> חֲזִיר ***ḥ^{a}ziyr*** [PIG] 7x
<2387> חֵזִיר ***ḥêziyr*** [HEZIR] 2x
<2388> חָזַק ***ḥāzaq*** [STRONG (BE)] 253x
<2389> חָזָק ***ḥāzāq*** [STRONG] 56x
<2390> חָזֵק ***ḥāzêq*** [STRONGER] 2x
<2391> חֵזֶק ***ḥêzeq*** [STRENGTH] 1x
<2392> חֹזֶק ***ḥōzeq*** [STRENGTH] 5x
<2393> חֶזְקָה ***ḥezqāh*** [STRENGTH] 4x
<2394> חָזְקָה ***ḥozqāh*** [STRENGTH] 5x
<2395> חִזְקִי ***ḥizqiy*** [HIZKI] 1x
<2396> חִזְקִיָּה ***ḥizqiyyāh,*** חִזְקִיָּהוּ ***ḥizqiyyāhû*** [HEZEKIAH] 87x
<2397> חָח ***ḥāḥ*** [HOOK] 8x
<2398> חֶטְאָה ***ḥeṭ'āh,*** חָטָא ***ḥāṭā'*** [SIN (verb)] 238x
<2399> חֵטְא ***ḥêṭ^{e}'*** [SIN (common noun)] 33x
<2400> חַטָּא ***ḥaṭṭā'*** [SINNER] 18x
<2401> חֲטָאָה ***ḥ^{a}ṭā'āh*** [SIN (common noun)] 8x
<2402> חַטָּאָה ***ḥaṭṭā'āh*** [SIN (common noun)] 2x
<2403> חַטָּאת ***ḥaṭṭā'ṯ*** [SIN (common noun)] 306x
<2404> חָטַב ***ḥāṭaḇ*** [CUT (verb)] 9x

<2405> חֲטֻבוֹת ***ḥaṭuḇôṯ*** [COLORED] 1x

<2406> חִטָּה ***ḥiṭṭāh*** [WHEAT] 30x

<2407> חַטּוּשׁ ***ḥaṭṭûš*** [HATTUSH] 5x

<2408> חֲטָי ***ḥaṭāy*** [SIN (common noun)] 1x

<2409> חַטָּיָא ***ḥaṭṭāyā'*** [SIN OFFERING] 1x

<2410> חֲטִיטָא ***ḥaṭiyṭā'*** [HATITA] 2x

<2411> חַטִּיל ***ḥaṭṭiyl*** [HATTIL] 2x

<2412> חֲטִיפָא ***ḥaṭiyp̱ā'*** [HATIPHA] 2x

<2413> חָטַם ***ḥāṭam*** [RESTRAIN] 1x

<2414> חָטַף ***ḥāṭap̱*** [CATCH (verb)] 2x

<2415> חֹטֶר ***ḥōṭer*** [ROD] 2x

<2416> חַי ***ḥay,*** חַיָּה ***ḥayyāh*** [ANIMAL] 501x

<2417> חַי ***ḥay*** [LIVING (adj.)] 7x

<2418> חֲיָה ***ḥayāh,*** חֲיָא ***ḥayā'*** [LIVE] 6x

<2419> חִיאֵל ***ḥiy'ēl*** [HIEL] 1x

<2420> חִידָה ***ḥiyḏāh*** [ENIGMA] 17x

<2421> חָיָה ***ḥāyāh*** [LIVE] 262x

<2422> חָיֶה ***ḥāyeh*** [VIGOROUS] 1x

<2423> חֵיוָה ***ḥêywāh*** [BEAST] 20x

<2424> חַיּוּת ***ḥayyûṯ*** [LIVING (noun)] 1x

<2425> חָיַי ***ḥāyay*** [LIVE] 23x

<2426> חֵיל ***ḥêyl,*** חֵל ***ḥêl*** [WALL] 10x

<2427> חִיל ***ḥiyl,*** חִילָה ***ḥiylāh*** [PAIN (noun)] 7x

<2428> חַיִל ***ḥayil*** [STRENGTH] 243x

<2429> חַיִל ***ḥayil*** [STRENGTH] 7x

<2430> חֵילָה ***ḥêylāh*** [RAMPART] 1x

<2431> חֵילָם ***ḥêylām*** [HELAM] 2x

<2432> חִילֵן ***ḥiylên*** [HILEN] 1x

<2433> חִין ***ḥiyn*** [GRACEFUL] 1x

<2434> חַיִץ ***ḥayiṣ*** [WALL] 1x

<2435> חִיצוֹן ***ḥiyṣôn*** [OUTER] 25x

<2436> חֵיק ***ḥêyq,*** חֵק ***ḥêq*** [BOSOM] 39x

<2437> חִירָה ***ḥiyrāh*** [HIRAH] 2x

<2438> חִירוֹם ***ḥiyrôm,*** חִירָם ***ḥiyrām*** [HIRAM] 24x

<2439> חִישׁ ***ḥiyš*** [HASTE (MAKE)] 1x

<2440> חִישׁ ***ḥiyš*** [SOON] 1x

<2441> חֵךְ ***ḥêḵ*** [MOUTH] 18x

<2442> חָכָה ***ḥāḵāh*** [WAIT] 14x

<2443> חַכָּה ***ḥakkāh*** [HOOK] 3x

<2444> חֲכִילָה ***ḥaḵiylāh*** [HACHILAH, HAKILAH] 3x

<2445> חַכִּים ***ḥakkiym*** [WISE] 14x

<2446> חֲכַלְיָה ***ḥaḵalyāh*** [HACALIAH, HACHALIAH] 2x

<2447> חַכְלִילִי ***ḥaḵliyliy*** [DARKER] 1x

<2448> חַכְלִילוּת ***ḥaḵliylûṯ*** [REDNESS] 1x

<2449> חָכַם ***ḥāḵam*** [WISE (MAKE)] 27x

<2450> חָכָם ***ḥāḵām*** [WISE] 137x

<2451> חָכְמָה ***ḥoḵmāh*** [WISDOM] 149x

<2452> חָכְמָה ***ḥoḵmāh*** [WISDOM] 8x

<2453> חַכְמוֹנִי ***ḥaḵmôniy*** [HACHMONI] 2x

<2454> חָכְמוֹת ***ḥoḵmôṯ*** [WISDOM] 5x

<2455> חֹל ***ḥōl*** [COMMON] 7x

<2456> חָלָא ***ḥālā'*** [DISEASED (BE, BECOME)] 1x
<2457> חֶלְאָה ***ḥel'āh*** [SCUM] 3x
<2458> חֶלְאָה ***ḥel'āh*** [HELAH] 2x
<2459> חֵלֶב ***ḥêleḇ*** [FAT (noun)] 92x
<2460> חֵלֶב ***ḥêleḇ*** [HELEB] 1x
<2461> חָלָב ***ḥālāḇ*** [MILK] 44x
<2462> חֶלְבָּה ***ḥelbāh*** [HELBAH] 1x
<2463> חֶלְבּוֹן ***ḥelbôn*** [HELBON] 1x
<2464> חֶלְבְּנָה ***ḥelbināh*** [GALBANUM] 1x
<2465> חֶלֶד ***ḥeleḏ*** [WORLD] 6x
<2466> חֵלֶד ***ḥeleḏ*** [HELED] 1x
<2467> חֹלֶד ***ḥōleḏ*** [WEASEL] 1x
<2468> חֻלְדָּה ***ḥuldāh*** [HULDAH] 2x
<2469> חֶלְדַּי ***ḥelday*** [HELDAI] 2x
<2470> חָלָה ***ḥālāh,*** נַחֲלָה ***naḥ^{a}lāh*** [SICK (BE)] 665x
<2471> חַלָּה ***ḥallāh*** [CAKE] 14x
<2472> חֲלוֹם ***ḥ^{a}lôm*** [DREAM (noun)] 65x
<2473> חֹלוֹן ***ḥōlôn*** [HOLON] 3x
<2474> חַלּוֹן ***ḥallôn*** [WINDOW] 31x
<2475> חֲלוֹף ***ḥ^{a}lôp̱*** [DESTRUCTION] 1x
<2476> חֲלוּשָׁה ***ḥ^{a}lûšāh*** [DEFEAT (noun)] 1x
<2477> חֲלַח ***ḥ^{a}laḥ*** [HALAH] 3x
<2478> חַלְחוּל ***ḥalḥûl*** [HALHUL] 1x
<2479> חַלְחָלָה ***ḥalḥālāh*** [PAIN (noun)] 4x
<2480> חָלַט ***ḥālaṭ*** [CATCH (verb)] 1x
<2481> חֲלִי ***ḥ^{a}liy*** [ORNAMENT] 2x
<2482> חֲלִי ***ḥ^{a}liy*** [HALI] 1x
<2483> חֳלִי ***ḥ^{o}liy*** [ILLNESS] 24x
<2484> חֶלְיָה ***ḥelyāh*** [JEWELRY] 1x
<2485> חָלִיל ***ḥāliyl*** [FLUTE] 6x
<2486> חָלִילָה ***ḥāliylāh*** [FAR BE IT] 21x
<2487> חֲלִיפָה ***ḥ^{a}liyp̱āh*** [CHANGE (noun)] 12x
<2488> חֲלִיצָה ***ḥ^{a}liyṣāh*** [SPOIL (noun)] 2x
<2489> חֵלְכָה ***ḥêl^{e}ḵāh*** [HELPLESS] 3x
<2490> חָלַל ***ḥālal*** [PIERCE] 141x
<2491> חָלָל ***ḥālāl*** [PIERCED] 94x
<2492> חָלַם ***ḥālam*** [DREAM (verb)] 29x
<2493> חֵלֶם ***ḥêlem*** [DREAM (noun)] 22x
<2494> חֵלֶם ***ḥêlem*** [HELEM] 1x
<2495> חַלָּמוּת ***ḥallāmûṯ*** [EGG] 1x
<2496> חַלָּמִישׁ ***ḥallāmiyš*** [FLINT] 5x
<2497> חֵלֹן ***ḥêlōn*** [HELON] 5x
<2498> חָלַף ***ḥālap̱*** [PASS ON] 28x
<2499> חֲלַף ***ḥ^{a}lap̱*** [PASS OVER, PASS BY] 4x
<2500> חֵלֶף ***ḥêlep̱*** [RETURN FOR (IN)] 2x
<2501> חֵלֶף ***ḥêlep̱*** [HELEPH] 1x
<2502> חָלַץ ***ḥālaṣ*** [DRAW OUT] 44x
<2503> חֵלֶץ ***ḥêleṣ,*** חֶלֶץ ***ḥeleṣ*** [HELEZ] 5x
<2504> חֲלָצַיִם ***ḥ^{a}lāṣayim*** [LOINS] 10x
<2505> חָלַק ***ḥālaq*** [SHARE (verb)] 65x
<2506> חֵלֶק ***ḥêleq*** [PORTION] 60x

<2507> חֵלֶק **ḥêleq** [HELEK] 2x
<2508> חֲלָק **ḥ^{a}lāq** [PORTION] 3x
<2509> חָלָק **ḥālāq** [SMOOTH] 8x
<2510> חָלָק **ḥālāq** [HALAK] 2x
<2511> חַלָּק **ḥallāq** [SMOOTH] 1x
<2512> חַלֻּק **ḥalluq** [SMOOTH] 1x
<2513> חֶלְקָה **ḥelqāh** [SMOOTH] 29x
<2514> חֲלַקָּה **ḥ^{a}laqqāh** [FLATTERY] 1x
<2515> חֲלֻקָּה **ḥ^{a}luqqāh** [DIVISION] 1x
<2516> חֶלְקִי **ḥelqiy** [HELEKITE] 1x
<2517> חֶלְקָי **ḥelqāy** [HELKAI] 1x
<2518> חִלְקִיָּה **ḥilqiyyāh,** חִלְקִיָּהוּ **ḥilqiyyāhû** [HILKIAH] 34x
<2519> חֲלַקְלַקּוֹת **ḥ^{a}laqlaqqôṯ** [FLATTERY] 4x
<2520> חֶלְקַת **ḥelqaṯ** [HELKATH] 2x
<2521> חֶלְקַת הַצֻּרִים **ḥelqaṯ haṣṣuriym** [HELKATH-HAZZURIM] 1x
<2522> חָלַשׁ **ḥālaš** [LAY LOW] 3x
<2523> חַלָּשׁ **ḥallāš** [WEAK (noun)] 1x
<2524> חָם **ḥām** [FATHER-IN-LAW] 4x
<2525> חָם **ḥām** [WARM] 2x
<2526> חָם **ḥām** [HAM] 16x
<2527> חֹם **ḥōm** [WARMTH] 14x
<2528> חֱמָא **ḥ^{e}mā'** [FURY] 2x
<2529> חֶמְאָה **ḥem'āh,** חֵמָה **ḥêmāh** [BUTTER] 10x
<2530> חָמַד **ḥāmaḏ,** חֲמוּדָה **ḥ^{a}mûḏāh,** חֲמֻדָה **ḥ^{a}muḏāh** [DESIRE (verb)] 21x
<2531> חֶמֶד **ḥemeḏ** [PLEASANT] 6x
<2532> חֶמְדָּה **ḥemdāh** [DESIRE (noun)] 25x
<2533> חֶמְדָּן **ḥemdān** [HEMDAN] 2x
<2534> חֵמָה **ḥêmāh,** חֵמָא **ḥêmā'** [ANGER (noun)] 124x
<2535> חַמָּה **ḥammāh** [SUN] 6x
<2536> חַמּוּאֵל **ḥammû'êl** [HAMMUEL] 1x
<2537> חֲמוּטַל **ḥamûṭal** [HAMUTAL] 3x
<2538> חָמוּל **ḥāmûl** [HAMUL] 3x
<2539> חָמוּלִי **ḥāmûliy** [HAMULITE] 1x
<2540> חַמּוֹן **ḥammôn** [HAMMON] 2x
<2541> חָמוֹץ **ḥāmôṣ** [OPPRESSOR] 1x
<2542> חַמּוּק **ḥammûq** [CURVE] 1x
<2543> חֲמוֹר **ḥ^{a}môr,** חֲמוֹרָה **ḥ^{a}môrah** [DONKEY] 97x
<2544> חֲמוֹר **ḥ^{a}môr** [HAMOR] 13x
<2545> חֲמוֹת **ḥamôṯ** [MOTHER-IN-LAW] 10x
<2546> חֹמֶט **ḥōmeṭ** [SAND LIZARD] 1x
<2547> חֻמְטָה **ḥumṭāh** [HUMTAH] 1x
<2548> חָמִיץ **ḥāmiyṣ** [SALTED] 1x
<2549> חֲמִישִׁי **ḥ^{a}miyšiy,** חֲמִשִּׁי **ḥamiššiy** [FIFTH] 45x
<2550> חָמַל **ḥāmal** [PITY (HAVE, SHOW)] 41x
<2551> חֶמְלָה **ḥemlāh** [COMPASSION] 2x
<2552> חָמַם **ḥāmam** [WARM (BE)] 11x
<2553> חַמָּן **ḥammān** [INCENSE ALTAR] 8x
<2554> חָמַס **ḥāmas** [VIOLENCE (DO)] 8x
<2555> חָמָס **ḥāmās** [VIOLENCE] 60x
<2556> חָמֵץ **ḥāmêṣ** [LEAVENED (BE)] 6x
<2557> חָמֵץ **ḥāmêṣ,** מַחְמֶצֶת **maḥmeṣeṯ** [LEAVEN] 13x

<2558> חֹמֶץ ***ḥōmeṣ*** [VINEGAR] 6x
<2559> חָמַק ***ḥāmaq*** [WITHDRAW] 2x
<2560> חָמַר ***ḥāmar*** [COAT (verb)] 1x, [RED (BE)] 5x
<2561> חֶמֶר ***ḥemer*** [WINE] 2x
<2562> חֲמַר ***ḥ^{a}mar*** [WINE] 6x
<2563> חֹמֶר ***ḥōmer*** [HEAP (noun)] 3x, [HOMER] 7x, [MIRE] 21x
<2564> חֵמָר ***ḥêmār*** [TAR] 3x
<2565> חֲמוֹרָתַיִם ***ḥ^{a}môrāṯayim*** [HEAPS] 1x
<2566> חַמְרָן ***ḥamrān*** [HAMRAM] 1x
<2567> חָמַשׁ ***ḥāmaš*** [FIFTH (TAKE A)] 1x
<2568> חָמֵשׁ ***ḥāmêš,*** חֲמִשָּׁה ***ḥ^{a}mis-šāh*** [FIVE] 341x
<2569> חֹמֶשׁ ***ḥōmeš*** [FIFTH] 1x
<2570> חֹמֶשׁ ***ḥōmeš*** [STOMACH] 4x
<2571> חֲמֻשִׁים ***ḥ^{a}mušiym*** [BATTLE (EQUIPPED FOR, ARRAYED FOR)] 4x
<2572> חֲמִשִּׁים ***ḥ^{a}miššiym*** [FIFTY] 162x
<2573> חֵמֶת ***ḥêmeṯ*** [WATERSKIN] 4x
<2574> חֲמָת ***ḥ^{a}māṯ,*** לְבֹא חֲמָת ***l^{e}ḇō ḥ^{a}māṯ*** [HAMATH] 30x
<2575> חַמַּת ***ḥammaṯ*** [HAMMATH] 2x
<2576> חַמֹּת דֹּאר ***ḥammōṯ dō'r*** [HAMMOTH DOR] 1x
<2577> חֲמָתִי ***ḥ^{a}māṯiy*** [HAMATHITE] 2x
<2578> חֲמַת צוֹבָה ***ḥ^{a}maṯ ṣôḇāh*** [HAMATH ZOBAH] 1x
<2579> חֲמַת רַבָּה ***ḥ^{a}maṯ rabbāh*** [HAMATH THE GREAT] 1x
<2580> חֵן ***ḥên*** [GRACE] 69x
<2581> חֵן ***ḥên*** [HEN] 1x
<2582> חֵנָדָד ***ḥênāḏāḏ*** [HENADAD] 4x
<2583> חָנָה ***ḥānāh*** [ENCAMP] 143x
<2584> חַנָּה ***ḥannāh*** [HANNAH] 11x
<2585> חֲנוֹךְ ***ḥ^{a}nôḵ*** [ENOCH] 18x
<2586> חָנוּן ***ḥānûn*** [HANUN] 10x
<2587> חַנּוּן ***ḥannûn*** [GRACIOUS] 13x
<2588> חָנוּת ***ḥānûṯ*** [CELL] 1x
<2589> חַנּוֹת ***ḥannôṯ*** [ENTREAT] 1x, [GRACIOUS] 1x
<2590> חָנַט ***ḥānaṭ,*** חֲנֻטִים ***ḥ^{a}nuṭiym*** [EMBALM] 4x, [RIPEN] 1x
<2591> חִנְטָה ***ḥinṭāh*** [WHEAT] 2x
<2592> חַנִּיאֵל ***ḥanniy'êl*** [HANNIEL] 2x
<2593> חָנִיךְ ***ḥāniyḵ*** [TRAINED] 1x
<2594> חֲנִינָה ***ḥ^{a}niynāh*** [FAVOR (noun)] 1x
<2595> חֲנִית ***ḥ^{a}niyṯ*** [SPEAR] 47x
<2596> חָנַךְ ***ḥānaḵ*** [DEDICATE] 5x
<2597> חֲנֻכָּה ***ḥ^{a}nukkāh*** [DEDICATION] 4x
<2598> חֲנֻכָּה ***ḥ^{a}nukkāh*** [DEDICATION] 8x
<2599> חֲנֹכִי ***ḥ^{a}nōḵiy*** [HANOCHITE] 1x
<2600> חִנָּם ***ḥinnām*** [FREELY] 32x
<2601> חֲנַמְאֵל ***ḥ^{a}nam'êl*** [HANAMEL, HANA-MEEL] 4x
<2602> חֲנָמָל ***ḥ^{a}nāmāl*** [FROST] 1x
<2603> חָנַן ***ḥānan*** [GRACIOUS (BE)] 78x
<2604> חֲנַן ***ḥ^{a}nan*** [MERCY (SHOW, ASK FOR)] 2x
<2605> חָנָן ***ḥānān*** [HANAN] 12x
<2606> חֲנַנְאֵל ***ḥ^{a}nan'êl*** [HananeEl, Hananel] 4x
<2607> חֲנָנִי ***ḥ^{a}nāniy*** [HANANI] 11x
<2608> חֲנַנְיָה ***ḥ^{a}nanyāh,*** חֲנַנְיָהוּ ***ḥ^{a}nanyāhû*** [HANANIAH] 29x

<2609> חָנֵס ***ḥānês*** [HANES] 1x

<2610> חָנֵף ***ḥānêp̱*** [DEFILED (BE)] 11x

<2611> חָנֵף ***ḥānêp̱*** [GODLESS] 13x

<2612> חֹנֶף ***ḥōnep̱*** [HYPOCRISY] 1x

<2613> חֲנֻפָּה ***ḥᵃnuppāh*** [PROFANENESS] 1x

<2614> חָנַק ***ḥānaq*** [HANG] 2x

<2615> חַנָּתֹן ***ḥannāṯōn*** [HANNATHON] 1x

<2616> חָסַד ***ḥāsaḏ*** [MERCIFUL] 3x

<2617> חֶסֶד ***ḥeseḏ*** [MERCY] 248x

<2618> חֶסֶד ***ḥeseḏ*** [HESED] 1x

<2619> חֲסַדְיָה ***ḥᵃsaḏyāh*** [HASADIAH] 1x

<2620> חָסָה ***ḥāsāh*** [REFUGE] 37x

<2621> חֹסָה ***ḥōsāh*** [HOSAH] 5x

<2622> חָסוּת ***ḥāsûṯ*** [SHELTER] 1x

<2623> חָסִיד ***ḥāsiyḏ*** [FAITHFUL] 32x

<2624> חֲסִידָה ***ḥᵃsiyḏāh*** [STORK] 6x

<2625> חָסִיל ***ḥāsiyl*** [CATERPILLAR] 6x

<2626> חֲסִין ***ḥᵃsiyn*** [MIGHTY] 1x

<2627> חַסִּיר ***ḥassiyr*** [WANTING] 1x

<2628> חָסַל ***ḥāsal*** [CONSUME] 1x

<2629> חָסַם ***ḥāsam*** [MUZZLE (verb)] 2x

<2630> חָסַן ***ḥāsan*** [HOARDED (BE)] 1x

<2631> חֲסַן ***ḥᵃsan*** [POSSESS] 2x

<2632> חֱסֵן ***ḥᵉsên*** [POWER] 2x

<2633> חֹסֶן ***ḥōsen*** [TREASURE] 5x

<2634> חָסֹן ***ḥasōn*** [STRONG] 2x

<2635> חֲסַף ***ḥᵃsap̱*** [CLAY] 9x

<2636> חַסְפַּס ***ḥaspas*** [FLAKE-LIKE THING] 1x

<2637> חָסֵר ***ḥāsêr*** [LACKING (BE)] 21x

<2638> חָסֵר ***ḥāsêr*** [LACKING] 19x

<2639> חֶסֶר ***ḥeser*** [POVERTY] 2x

<2640> חֹסֶר ***ḥōser*** [WANT] 3x

<2641> חַסְרָה ***ḥasrāh*** [HASRAH] 1x

<2642> חֶסְרוֹן ***ḥesrôn*** [LACKING (WHAT IS)] 1x

<2643> חַף ***ḥap̱*** [INNOCENT] 1x

<2644> חָפָא ***ḥāp̱ā'*** [SECRETLY (DO)] 1x

<2645> חָפָה ***ḥāp̱āh*** [COVER (verb)] 12x

<2646> חֻפָּה ***ḥuppāh*** [CHAMBER] 3x

<2647> חֻפָּה ***ḥuppāh*** [HUPPAH] 1x

<2648> חָפַז ***ḥāp̱az*** [HURRY (verb)] 9x

<2649> חִפָּזוֹן ***ḥippāzôn*** [HASTE (noun)] 3x

<2650> חֻפִּים ***ḥuppiym,*** חֻפִּם ***ḥuppim*** [HUPPIM] 3x

<2651> חֹפֶן ***ḥōp̱en*** [HAND] 6x

<2652> חָפְנִי ***ḥop̱niy*** [HOPHNI] 5x

<2653> חָפַף ***ḥāp̱ap̱*** [COVER (verb)] 1x

<2654> חָפֵץ ***ḥāp̱êṣ,*** חָפַץ ***ḥāp̱aṣ*** [DELIGHT (verb)] 75x

<2655> חָפֵץ ***ḥāp̱êṣ*** [PLEASURE IN (HAVE, TAKE)] 11x

<2656> חֵפֶץ ***ḥêp̱eṣ*** [DESIRE (noun)] 39x

<2657> חֶפְצִי־בָהּ ***ḥep̱ṣiy-ḇāh*** [HEPHZIBAH] 2x

<2658> חָפַר ***ḥāp̱ar*** [DIG] 22x

<2659> חָפֵר ***ḥāp̱êr*** [ASHAMED (BE)] 17x

<2660> חֵפֶר ***ḥêp̱er*** [HEPHER] 9x
<2661> חֲפַרְפָּרָה ***ḥᵃparpārāh,*** חֲפֹר פֵּרָה ***ḥᵃp̱ōr pêrāh*** [MOLE] 1x
<2662> חֶפְרִי ***ḥep̱riy*** [HEPHERITE] 1x
<2663> חֲפָרַיִם ***ḥᵃp̱ārayim,*** חָפְרַע ***ḥopraʻ*** [HAPHARAIM] 2x
<2664> חָפַשׂ ***ḥāp̱aś*** [SEARCH FOR] 23x
<2665> חֵפֶשׂ ***ḥêp̱eś*** [PLAN (noun)] 1x
<2666> חָפַשׁ ***ḥapaš*** [FREE (BE)] 1x
<2667> חֹפֶשׁ ***ḥōp̱eš*** [SADDLECLOTH] 1x
<2668> חֻפְשָׁה ***ḥup̱šāh*** [FREEDOM] 1x
<2669> חָפְשִׁית ***ḥop̱šiyṯ*** [SEPARATE (adj.)] 2x
<2670> חָפְשִׁי ***ḥop̱šiy*** [FREE] 17x
<2671> חֵץ ***ḥêṣ*** [ARROW] 53x
<2672> חָצַב ***ḥāṣaḇ,*** חָצֵב ***ḥāṣêḇ,*** חֹצֵב ***ḥōṣêḇ*** [CUT (verb)] 25x
<2673> חָצָה ***ḥāṣāh*** [DIVIDE] 15x
<2674> חָצוֹר ***ḥāṣôr*** [HAZOR] 19x
<2675> חָצוֹר חֲדַתָּה ***ḥāṣôr ḥᵃḏattāh*** [HAZOR-HADATTAH] 1x
<2676> חֲצוֹת ***ḥᵃṣôṯ*** [MIDNIGHT] 3x
<2677> חֲצִי ***ḥᵃṣiy*** [HALF] 125x
<2678> חֵצִי ***ḥêṣiy*** [ARROW] 5x
<2679> חֲצִי הַמְּנֻחוֹת ***ḥᵃṣiy hammᵉnuḥôṯ*** [MANAHATHITES (HALF OF THE)] 1x
<2680> חֲצִי הַמְּנַחְתִּי ***ḥᵃṣiy hammᵉnaḥtiy*** [MANAHATHITES (HALF OF THE)] 1x
<2681> חָצִיר ***ḥāṣiyr*** [ABODE] 1x
<2682> חָצִיר ***ḥāṣiyr*** [GRASS] 21x
<2683> חֵצֶן ***ḥêṣen*** [BOSOM] 1x
<2684> חֹצֶן ***ḥōṣen*** [BOSOM] 3x
<2685> חֲצַף ***ḥᵃṣap̱*** [URGENT (BE)] 2x
<2686> חָצַץ ***ḥāṣaṣ*** [DIVIDE] 3x
<2687> חָצָץ ***ḥāṣāṣ*** [GRAVEL] 2x
<2688> חַצְצוֹן תָּמָר ***ḥaṣᵉṣôn tāmār*** [HAZAZON-TAMAR] 2x
<2689> חֲצֹצְרָה ***ḥᵃṣōṣᵉrāh*** [TRUMPET] 29x
<2690> חַצְצַר ***ḥaṣṣar*** [TRUMPET (BLOW A)] 6x
<2691> חָצֵר ***ḥāṣêr*** [VILLAGE] 189x
<2692> חֲצַר אַדָּר ***ḥᵃṣar ʼaddār*** [HAZAR ADDAR] 1x
<2693> חֲצַר גַּדָּה ***ḥᵃṣar gaddāh*** [HAZAR GADDAH] 1x
<2694> חֲצַר הַתִּיכוֹן ***ḥᵃṣar hattiyḵôn*** [HAZAR HATTICON] 1x
<2695> חֶצְרוֹ ***ḥeṣrô*** [HEZRO] 2x
<2696> חֶצְרוֹן ***ḥeṣrôn*** [HEZRON] 18x
<2697> חֶצְרוֹנִי ***ḥeṣrôniy*** [HEZRONITE] 2x
<2698> חֲצֵרוֹת ***ḥᵃṣêrôṯ*** [HAZEROTH] 6x
<2699> חֲצֵרִים ***ḥᵃṣêriym*** [HAZERIM] 1x
<2700> חֲצַרְמָוֶת ***ḥᵃṣarmāweṯ*** [HAZARMAVETH] 2x
<2701> חֲצַר סוּסָה ***ḥᵃṣar sûsāh*** [HAZAR SUSAH] 1x
<2702> חֲצַר סוּסִים ***ḥᵃṣar sûsiym*** [HAZAR SUSIM] 1x
<2703> חֲצַר עֵינוֹן ***ḥᵃṣar ʻêynôn*** [HAZAR ENAN] 1x
<2704> חֲצַר עֵינָן ***ḥᵃṣar ʻêynān*** [HAZAR ENAN] 3x
<2705> חֲצַר שׁוּעָל ***ḥᵃṣar šûʻāl*** [HAZAR SHUAL] 4x
<2706> חֹק ***ḥōq*** [STATUTE] 127x
<2707> חָקָה ***ḥāqāh*** [CARVE] 4x
<2708> חֻקָּה ***ḥuqqāh*** [STATUTE] 104x
<2709> חֲקוּפָא ***ḥᵃqûp̱āʼ*** [HAKUPHA] 2x
<2710> חָקַק ***ḥāqaq*** [ENGRAVE] 19x

<2711> חֵקֶק **ḥêqeq** [STATUTE] 2x
<2712> חֻקֹּק **ḥuqōq** [HUKKOK] 2x
<2713> חָקַר **ḥāqar** [SEARCH (verb)] 27x
<2714> חֵקֶר **ḥêqer** [SEARCH (noun)] 12x
<2715> חֹר **ḥōr** [NOBLE] 13x
<2716> חֶרֶא **ḥere'** [DUNG] 3x
<2717> חָרֵב **ḥārêḇ,** חָרַב **ḥāraḇ** [WASTE (LAY)] 40x
<2718> חֲרַב **ḥ^{a}raḇ** [DESTROYED (BE)] 1x
<2719> חֶרֶב **ḥereḇ** [SWORD] 413x
<2720> חָרֵב **ḥārêḇ** [DRY (adj.)] 10x
<2721> חֹרֶב **ḥōreḇ** [HEAT (noun)] 16x
<2722> חֹרֵב **ḥōrêḇ** [HOREB] 17x
<2723> חָרְבָּה **ḥorbāh** [RUIN (noun)] 42x
<2724> חָרָבָה **ḥārāḇāh** [DRY LAND, DRY GROUND] 8x
<2725> חֲרָבוֹן **ḥ^{a}rāḇôn** [DROUGHT] 1x
<2726> חַרְבוֹנָא **ḥarḇônā',** חַרְבוֹנָה **ḥarḇônāh** [HARBONA] 2x
<2727> חָרַג **ḥārag̱** [TREMBLING (COME)] 1x
<2728> חַרְגֹּל **ḥargōl** [CRICKET] 1x
<2729> חָרַד **ḥāraḏ** [TREMBLE] 39x
<2730> חָרֵד **ḥārêḏ,** חֲרֹד **ḥ^{a}rōḏ** [TREMBLING] 6x
<2731> חֲרָדָה **ḥ^{a}rāḏāh** [TREMBLING] 9x
<2732> חֲרָדָה **ḥ^{a}rāḏāh** [HARADAH] 2x
<2733> חֲרֹדִי **ḥ^{a}rōḏiy** [HARODITE] 1x
<2734> חָרָה **ḥārāh,** נָחַר **nāḥār** [ANGRY (GET)] 90x
<2735> חֹר הַגִּדְגָּד **ḥōr haggiḏgāḏ** [HOR HAGGIDGAD] 2x
<2736> חַרְהֲיָה **ḥarh^{a}yāh** [HARHAIAH] 1x
<2737> חָרוּז **ḥārûz** [STRING OF JEWELS] 1x
<2738> חָרוּל **ḥārûl** [NETTLES] 3x
<2739> חֲרוּמַף **ḥ^{a}rûmap̱** [HARUMAPH] 1x
<2740> חָרוֹן **ḥārôn** [ANGER (noun)] 41x
<2741> חֲרוּפִי **ḥ^{a}rûp̱iy** [HARUPHITE] 1x
<2742> חָרוּץ **ḥārûṣ** [DECISION] 1x, [DILIGENT] 9x, [GOLD] 6x, [MOAT] 1x
<2743> חָרוּץ **ḥārûṣ** [HARUZ] 1x
<2744> חַרְחוּר **ḥarḥûr** [HARHUR] 2x
<2745> חַרְחַס **ḥarḥas** [HARHAS] 1x
<2746> חַרְחֻר **ḥarḥur** [HEAT (FIERY, SCORCHING)] 1x
<2747> חֶרֶט **ḥereṭ** [GRAVING TOOL] 2x
<2748> חַרְטֹם **ḥarṭōm** [MAGICIAN] 11x
<2749> חַרְטֹם **ḥarṭōm** [MAGICIAN] 5x
<2750> חֳרִי **ḥ^{o}riy** [FIERCE] 6x
<2751> חֹרִי **ḥōriy** [WHITE, WHITE BREAD] 1x
<2752> חֹרִי **ḥōriy** [HORITE] 7x
<2753> חוֹרִי **ḥôriy** [HORI] 4x
<2754> חָרִיט **ḥāriyṭ** [BAG] 2x
<2755> חֲרֵי יוֹנִים **ḥ^{a}rêy yôniym** [DOVE'S DUNG] 1x
<2756> חָרִיף **ḥāriyp̱** [HARIPH] 2x
<2757> חָרִיץ **ḥāriyṣ** [CHEESE] 1x, [PICK (noun)] 2x
<2758> חָרִישׁ **ḥāriyš** [PLOWING] 3x
<2759> חֲרִישִׁי **ḥ^{a}riyšiy** [SCORCHING] 1x
<2760> חָרַךְ **ḥāraḵ** [ROAST] 1x
<2761> חֲרַךְ **ḥ^{a}raḵ** [SINGED (BE)] 1x

<2762> חָרַךְ ***ḥārāḵ*** [LATTICE] 1x
<2763> חָרַם ***ḥāram*** [DESTROY] 52x
<2764> חֵרֶם ***ḥêrem*** [DEVOTED THINGS] 29x, [NET] 9x
<2765> חֳרֵם ***ḥ^orêm*** [HOREM] 1x
<2766> חָרִם ***ḥārim*** [HARIM] 11x
<2767> חָרְמָה ***ḥormāh*** [HORMAH] 9x
<2768> חֶרְמוֹן ***ḥermôn*** [HERMON] 13x
<2769> חֶרְמוֹנִים ***ḥermôniym*** [HERMONITES] 1x
<2770> חֶרְמֵשׁ ***ḥermêš*** [SICKLE] 2x
<2771> חָרָן ***ḥārān*** [HARAN] 12x
<2772> חֹרֹנִי ***ḥōrōniy*** [HORONITE] 3x
<2773> חֹרֹנַיִם ***ḥōrōnayim,*** חוֹרוֹנַיִם ***ḥōrônayim*** [HORONAIM] 4x
<2774> חַרְנֶפֶר ***ḥarnep̱er*** [HARNEPHER] 1x
<2775> חֶרֶס ***ḥeres*** [ITCH] 1x, [SUN] 3x
<2776> חֶרֶס ***ḥeres*** [HERES] 1x
<2777> חַרְסוּת ***ḥarsûṯ*** [POTSHERD] 1x
<2778> חָרַף ***ḥārap̱*** [BETROTH] 1x, [REPROACH (verb)] 39x, [WINTER (verb)] 1x
<2779> חֹרֶף ***ḥōrep̱*** [WINTER (noun)] 7x
<2780> חָרֵף ***ḥārêp̱*** [HAREPH] 1x
<2781> חֶרְפָּה ***ḥerpāh*** [REPROACH (noun)] 73x
<2782> חָרַץ ***ḥāraṣ*** [MOVE] 12x
<2783> חֲרַץ ***ḥ^araṣ*** [LOINS] 1x
<2784> חַרְצֻבָּה ***ḥarṣubbāh*** [BOND] 2x
<2785> חַרְצָן ***ḥarṣān*** [SEED] 1x
<2786> חָרַק ***ḥāraq*** [GNASH] 5x
<2787> חָרַר ***ḥārar*** [BURN (verb)] 10x
<2788> חָרֵר ***ḥārêr*** [PARCHED PLACE] 1x
<2789> חֶרֶשׂ ***ḥereś*** [EARTHENWARE] 17x
<2790> חָרַשׁ ***ḥāraš*** [PLOW] 25x, [SILENT (BE)] 48x
<2791> חֶרֶשׁ ***ḥereš*** [SECRETLY] 1x
<2792> חֶרֶשׁ ***ḥereš*** [HERESH] 1x
<2793> חֹרֶשׁ ***ḥōreš,*** חֹרֶשׁ ***ḥōres*** [FOREST] 7x
<2794> חֹרֵשׁ ***ḥōrêš*** [CRAFTSMAN] 1x
<2795> חֵרֵשׁ ***ḥêrêš*** [DEAF] 9x
<2796> חָרָשׁ ***ḥārāš*** [CRAFTSMAN] 33x
<2797> חַרְשָׁא ***ḥaršā'*** [HARSHA] 2x
<2798> חֲרָשִׁים ***ḥ^arašiym*** [HARASHIM] 1x
<2799> חֲרֹשֶׁת ***ḥ^arōšeṯ*** [CUTTING] 4x
<2800> חֲרֹשֶׁת הַגּוֹיִם ***ḥ^arōšeṯ haggôyim,*** חֲרֹשֶׁת ***ḥ^arōšeṯ*** [HAROSHETH HAGGOYIM] 3x
<2801> חָרַת ***ḥāraṯ*** [ENGRAVE] 1x
<2802> חֶרֶת ***ḥereṯ*** [HERETH] 1x
<2803> חָשַׁב ***ḥāšaḇ,*** חֹשֵׁב ***ḥōšêḇ*** [THINK] 124x
<2804> חֲשַׁב ***ḥ^ašaḇ*** [ACCOUNTED (BE)] 1x
<2805> חֵשֶׁב ***ḥêšeḇ*** [BAND (noun)] 8x
<2806> חַשְׁבַּדָּנָה ***ḥašbaddānāh*** [HASHBADDANAH] 1x
<2807> חֲשֻׁבָה ***ḥ^ašuḇāh*** [HASHUBAH] 1x
<2808> חֶשְׁבּוֹן ***ḥešbôn*** [SCHEME (noun)] 3x
<2809> חֶשְׁבּוֹן ***ḥešbôn*** [HESHBON] 38x
<2810> חִשָּׁבוֹן ***ḥiššāḇôn*** [DEVICE] 2x
<2811> חֲשַׁבְיָה ***ḥ^ašaḇyāh,*** חֲשַׁבְיָהוּ ***ḥ^ašaḇyāhû*** [HASHABIAH] 15x
<2812> חֲשַׁבְנָה ***ḥ^ašaḇnāh*** [HASHABNAH] 1x

<2813> חֲשַׁבְנְיָה ***ḥᵃšaḇnᵉyāh*** [HASHABNEIAH] 2x

<2814> חָשָׁה ***ḥāšāh*** [SILENT (BE, KEEP, REMAIN)] 16x

<2815> חַשּׁוּב ***ḥaššûḇ*** [HASSHUB] 5x

<2816> חֲשׁוֹךְ ***ḥᵃšôḵ*** [DARKNESS] 1x

<2817> חֲשׂוּפָא ***ḥᵃśûp̱āʼ,*** חֲשֻׂפָא ***ḥᵃśup̱āʼ*** [HASUPHA] 2x

<2818> חֲשַׁח ***ḥᵃšaḥ,*** חַשְׁחָה ***ḥašḥāh*** [NEED (verb and noun)] 2x

<2819> חַשְׁחוּ ***ḥašḥû*** [NEED (noun)] 1x

<2820> חָשַׂךְ ***ḥāśaḵ*** [WITHHOLD] 28x

<2821> חָשַׁךְ ***ḥāšaḵ*** [DARKEN] 19x

<2822> חֹשֶׁךְ ***ḥōšeḵ*** [DARKNESS] 80x

<2823> חָשֹׁךְ ***ḥāšōḵ*** [OBSCURE] 1x

<2824> חֶשְׁכַת ***ḥeškaṯ*** [DARKNESS] 1x

<2825> חֲשֵׁיכָה ***ḥᵃšêyḵāh,*** חֲשֵׁכָה ***ḥᵃšêḵāh*** [DARKNESS] 7x

<2826> חָשַׁל ***ḥāšal*** [FEEBLE (BE)] 1x

<2827> חֲשַׁל ***ḥᵃšal*** [SHATTER] 1x

<2828> חָשֻׁם ***ḥāšum*** [HASHUM] 5x

<2829> חֶשְׁמוֹן ***ḥešmôn*** [HESHMON] 1x

<2830> חַשְׁמַל ***ḥašmal,*** חַשְׁמַלָה ***ḥašmalāh*** [AMBER] 3x

<2831> חַשְׁמַן ***ḥašman*** [ENVOY] 1x

<2832> חַשְׁמֹנָה ***ḥašmōnāh*** [HASHMONAH] 2x

<2833> חֹשֶׁן ***ḥōšen*** [BREASTPIECE] 25x

<2834> חָשַׂף ***ḥāśap̱*** [STRIP] 11x

<2835> חָשִׂף ***ḥāśip̱*** [FLOCK (LITTLE, SMALL)] 1x

<2836> חָשַׁק ***ḥāšaq*** [DESIRE (verb)] 11x

<2837> חֵשֶׁק ***ḥêšeq*** [DESIRE (noun)] 4x

<2838> חָשׁוּק ***ḥāšûq*** [FILLET] 8x

<2839> חִשֻּׁק ***ḥiššuq*** [SPOKE] 1x

<2840> חִשּׁוּר ***ḥiššûr*** [HUB] 1x

<2841> חַשְׁרָה ***ḥašrāh*** [MASS] 1x

<2842> חֲשַׁשׁ ***ḥᵃšaš*** [GRASS (DRY)] 2x

<2843> חֻשָׁתִי ***ḥušāṯiy*** [HUSHATHITE] 5x

<2844> חַת ***ḥaṯ*** [DREAD (noun and adj.)] 4x

<2845> חֵת ***ḥêṯ*** [HETH] 14x

<2846> חָתָה ***ḥāṯāh*** [TAKE] 4x

<2847> חִתָּה ***ḥittāh*** [TERROR] 1x

<2848> חִתּוּל ***ḥittûl*** [BANDAGE] 1x

<2849> חַתְחַת ***ḥaṯḥaṯ*** [TERROR] 1x

<2850> חִתִּי ***ḥittiy*** [HITTITE] 48x

<2851> חִתִּית ***ḥittiyṯ*** [TERROR] 8x

<2852> חָתַךְ ***ḥāṯaḵ*** [DECREED (BE)] 1x

<2853> חָתַל ***ḥāṯal*** [SWADDLE] 1x

<2854> חֲתֻלָּה ***ḥᵃṯullāh*** [SWADDLING BAND] 1x

<2855> חֶתְלֹן ***ḥeṯlōn*** [HETHLON] 2x

<2856> חָתַם ***ḥāṯam*** [SEAL (verb)] 27x

<2857> חֲתַם ***ḥᵃṯam*** [SEAL (verb)] 1x

<2858> חֹתֶמֶת ***ḥōṯemeṯ*** [SEAL (noun)] 1x

<2859> חָתַן ***ḥāṯan,*** חֹתֵן ***ḥōṯên,*** חֹתֶנֶת ***ḥōṯeneṯ*** [MARRIAGE] 33x

<2860> חָתָן ***ḥāṯān*** [SON-IN-LAW] 20x

<2861> חֲתֻנָּה ***ḥᵃṯunnāh*** [WEDDING] 1x

<2862> חָתַף ***ḥāṯap̱*** [SNATCH AWAY] 1x

<2863> חֶתֶף ***ḥeṯep̱*** [ROBBER] 1x

<2864> חָתַר ***ḥāṯar*** [DIG] 8x

<2865> חָתַת ***ḥāṯaṯ*** [DISMAYED (BE)] 54x

<2866> חֲתַת ***ḥᵃṯaṯ*** [TERROR] 1x

<2867> חֲתַת ***ḥᵃṯaṯ*** [HATHATH] 1x

ט Teth

<2868> טְאֵב ***ṭᵉ'ēḇ*** [GLAD (BE)] 1x

<2869> טָב ***ṭāḇ*** [FINE (adj.)] 2x

<2870> טָבְאֵל ***ṭāḇᵉ'ēl,*** טָבְאַל ***ṭāḇᵉ'al*** [TABEEL, TABEAL] 2x

<2871> טְבוּל ***ṭᵉḇûl*** [FLOWING TURBAN] 1x

<2872> טַבּוּר ***ṭabbûr*** [CENTER] 2x

<2873> טָבַח ***ṭāḇaḥ*** [SLAUGHTER (verb)] 11x

<2874> טֶבַח ***ṭeḇaḥ*** [SLAUGHTER (noun)] 12x

<2875> טֶבַח ***ṭeḇaḥ*** [TEBAH] 1x

<2876> טַבָּח ***ṭabbāḥ*** [GUARD, IMPERIAL GUARD] 32x

<2877> טַבָּח ***ṭabbāḥ*** [GUARD] 1x

<2878> טִבְחָה ***ṭiḇḥāh*** [SLAUGHTER (noun)] 3x

<2879> טַבָּחָה ***ṭabbāḥah*** [COOK (noun)] 1x

<2880> טִבְחַת ***ṭiḇḥaṯ*** [TIBHATH] 1x

<2881> טָבַל ***ṭāḇal*** [DIP] 16x

<2882> טְבַלְיָהוּ ***ṭᵉḇalyāhû*** [TEBALIAH] 1x

<2883> טָבַע ***ṭāḇa‘*** [DROWN] 10x

<2884> טַבָּעוֹת ***ṭabbā‘ôṯ*** [TABBAOTH] 2x

<2885> טַבַּעַת ***ṭabba‘aṯ*** [RING] 49x

<2886> טַבְרִמֹּן ***ṭaḇrimmōn*** [TABRIMMON] 1x

<2887> טֵבֵת ***ṭēḇēṯ*** [TEBETH] 1x

<2888> טַבָּת ***ṭabbāṯ*** [TABBATH] 1x

<2889> טָהוֹר ***ṭāhôr,*** טָהֹר ***ṭāhōr*** [PURE] 94x

<2890> טְהָר ***ṭᵉhār,*** טֳהָר ***ṭᵒhār*** [PURENESS] 1x

<2891> טָהֵר ***ṭāhēr*** [PURE (BE, MAKE)] 94x

<2892> טֹהַר ***ṭōhar,*** טֳהָר ***ṭᵒhār*** [CLEARNESS] 4x

<2893> טָהֳרָה ***ṭāhᵒrāh*** [CLEANSING] 13x

<2894> טֵאטֵא ***ṭē'ṭē'*** [SWEEP] 1x

<2895> טוֹב ***ṭôḇ*** [HAPPY (BE)] 33x

<2896> טוֹב ***ṭôḇ,*** טוֹבָה ***ṭôḇāh,*** טֹבָה ***ṭōḇāh*** [GOOD] 559x

<2897> טוֹב ***ṭôḇ*** [TOB] 4x

<2898> טוּב ***ṭûḇ*** [GOODNESS] 32x

<2899> טוֹב אֲדוֹנִיָּה ***ṭôḇ ᵃḏôniyyāh*** [TOB-ADONIJAH] 1x

<2900> טוֹבִיָּה ***ṭôḇiyyāh,*** טוֹבִיָּהוּ ***ṭôḇiyyāhû*** [TOBIJAH] 18x

<2901> טָוָה ***ṭāwāh*** [SPIN] 2x

<2902> טוּחַ ***ṭûaḥ,*** טָחַח ***ṭāḥaḥ*** [OVERLAY] 12x

<2903> טוֹטָפוֹת ***ṭôṭāp̱ôṯ*** [FRONTLETS] 3x

<2904> טוּל ***ṭûl*** [CAST (verb)] 14x

<2905> טוּר ***ṭûr*** [ROW (noun)] 26x

<2906> טוּר ***ṭûr*** [MOUNTAIN] 2x

<2907> טוּשׂ ***ṭûś*** [SWOOP] 1x

<2908> טְוָת ***ṭᵉwāṯ*** [FAST (verb)] 1x

<2909> טָחָה ***ṭāḥāh*** [BOWSHOT] 1x

<2910> טֻחוֹת ***ṭuḥôṯ*** [INWARD PART] 2x

<2911> טְחוֹן ***ṭᵉḥôn*** [MILL] 1x

<2912> טָחַן ***ṭāḥan,*** טֹחֲנָה ***ṭōḥᵃnāh*** [GRIND, GRINDER (verb and fem. noun)] 8x

<2913> טַחֲנָה ***ṭaḥᵃnāh*** [GRINDING] 1x

<2914> טְחוֹר ***ṭᵉḥôr*** [TUMORS] 8x

<2915> טִיחַ ***ṭiyaḥ*** [COATING] 1x

<2916> טִיט ***ṭiyṭ*** [MUD] 13x

<2917> טִין ***ṭiyn*** [MIRY] 2x

<2918> טִירָה ***ṭiyrāh*** [CAMP] 7x

<2919> טַל ***ṭal*** [DEW] 31x

<2920> טַל ***ṭal*** [DEW] 5x

<2921> טָלָא ***ṭālā’*** [SPOTTED (BE)] 8x

<2922> טְלָה ***ṭᵉlāh*** [LAMB] 1x

<2923> טְלָאִים ***ṭᵉlā’iym*** [TELAIM] 1x

<2924> טָלֶה ***ṭāleh*** [LAMB] 3x

<2925> טַלְטֵלָה ***ṭalṭêlāh*** [CAPTIVITY] 1x

<2926> טָלַל ***ṭālal*** [COVER (verb)] 1x

<2927> טְלַל ***ṭᵉlal*** [SHADE (FIND)] 1x

<2928> טֶלֶם ***ṭelem*** [TELEM] 2x

<2929> טַלְמוֹן ***ṭalmôn,*** טַלְמֹן ***ṭalmōn*** [TALMON] 5x

<2930> טָמֵא ***ṭāmê’,*** טָמְאָה ***ṭām’āh*** [UNCLEAN (BE)] 161x

<2931> טָמֵא ***ṭāmê’*** [UNCLEAN] 87x

<2932> טֻמְאָה ***ṭum’āh*** [UNCLEANNESS] 37x

<2933> טָמָה ***ṭāmāh*** [STUPID] 1x

<2934> טָמַן ***ṭāman*** [HIDE] 31x

<2935> טֶנֶא ***ṭene’*** [BASKET] 4x

<2936> טָנַף ***ṭānap̱*** [SOIL] 1x

<2937> טָעָה ***ṭā‘āh*** [SEDUCE] 1x

<2938> טָעַם ***ṭā‘am*** [TASTE (verb)] 11x

<2939> טְעֵם ***ṭᵉ‘êm*** [EAT] 3x

<2940> טַעַם ***ṭa‘am*** [TASTE (noun)] 12x

<2941> טַעַם ***ṭa‘am*** [COMMAND (noun)] 5x

<2942> טְעֵם ***ṭᵉ‘êm*** [DECREE (noun)] 25x

<2943> טָעַן ***ṭā‘an*** [LOAD (verb)] 1x

<2944> טָעַן ***ṭā‘an*** [PIERCE] 1x

<2945> טַף ***ṭap̱*** [CHILD] 42x

<2946> טָפַח ***ṭāp̱aḥ*** [CARE FOR], [SPREAD OUT] 2x

<2947> טֶפַח ***ṭep̱aḥ,*** טַפְחָה ***ṭap̱ḥāh*** [HANDBREATH] 4x

<2948> טֹפַח ***ṭōp̱aḥ*** [HANDBREATH] 5x

<2949> טִפֻּחִים ***ṭippuḥiym*** [CARED FOR (ONES)] 1x

<2950> טָפַל ***ṭāp̱al*** [SMEAR] 3x

<2951> טִפְסָר ***ṭip̱sār*** [MARSHAL] 2x

<2952> טָפַף ***ṭāp̱ap̱*** [MINCE] 1x

<2953> טְפַר ***ṭᵉp̱ar*** [NAIL] 2x

<2954> טָפַשׁ ***ṭāp̱aš*** [FAT (BE)] 1x

<2955> טָפַת ***ṭāp̱aṯ*** [TAPHATH] 1x

<2956> טָרַד ***ṭāraḏ*** [CONTINUAL (BE)] 2x

<2957> טְרַד ***ṭᵉraḏ*** [DRIVE, DRIVE AWAY] 4x

<2958> טְרוֹם ***ṭᵉrôm*** [BEFORE] 1x

<2959> טָרַח ***ṭāraḥ*** [LOAD (verb)] 1x

<2960> טֹרַח ***ṭōraḥ*** [LOAD (noun)] 2x

<2961> טָרִי ***ṭāriy*** [FRESH] 2x
<2962> טֶרֶם ***ṭerem*** [BEFORE] 56x
<2963> טָרַף ***ṭārap̱*** [TEAR] 25x
<2964> טֶרֶף ***ṭerep̱*** [PREY] 23x
<2965> טָרָף ***ṭārāp̱*** [PLUCKED] 2x
<2966> טְרֵפָה ***ṭᵉrēp̱āh*** [TORN (WHAT IS)] 9x
<2967> טַרְפְּלַי ***ṭarpᵉlāy*** [TARPELITES] 1x

י Yodh

<2968> יָאַב ***yā'aḇ*** [LONG FOR] 1x
<2969> יָאָה ***yā'āh*** [DUE (BE THE)] 1x
<2970> יַאֲזַנְיָהוּ ***yaᵃzanyāhû,*** יַאֲזַנְיָה ***yaᵃzanyāh*** [JAAZANIAH] 4x
<2971> יָאִיר ***yā'iyr*** [JAIR] 10x
<2972> יָאִרִי ***yā'iriy*** [JAIRITE] 1x
<2973> יָאַל ***yā'al*** [FOOLISHLY (BE, DO, ACT)] 4x
<2974> יָאַל ***yā'al*** [CONTENT (BE)] 19x
<2975> יְאֹר ***yᵉ'ōr,*** יְאוֹר ***yᵉ'ôr*** [RIVER] 64x
<2976> יָאַשׁ ***yā'aš*** [DESPAIR (verb)] 6x
<2977> יֹאשִׁיָּהוּ ***yō'šiyyāhû,*** יוֹאשִׁיָּהוּ ***yô'šiyyāhû,*** יֹאשִׁיָּה ***yō'šiyyāh*** [JOSIAH] 53x
<2978> יִאתוֹן ***yi'tôn,*** אִיתוֹן ***'iyṯôn*** [ENTRANCE] 1x
<2979> יְאָתְרַי ***yᵉ'āṯray*** [JEATERAI] 1x
<2980> יָבַב ***yāḇaḇ*** [CRY, CRY OUT] 1x
<2981> יְבוּל ***yᵉḇûl*** [INCREASE (noun)] 13x
<2982> יְבוּס ***yᵉḇûs*** [JEBUS] 4x
<2983> יְבוּסִי ***yᵉḇûsiy,*** יְבֻסִי ***yᵉḇusiy*** [JEBUSITE] 41x
<2984> יִבְחָר ***yiḇḥār*** [IBHAR] 3x
<2985> יָבִין ***yāḇiyn*** [JABIN] 8x
<2986> יָבַל ***yāḇal*** [BRING] 18x
<2987> יְבַל ***yᵉḇal*** [BRING] 3x
<2988> יָבָל ***yāḇāl*** [STREAM (noun)] 2x
<2989> יָבָל ***yāḇāl,*** יַבֶּלֶת ***yabbeleṯ*** [JABAL] 1x
<2990> יַבֶּלֶת ***yabbeleṯ*** [DISCHARGE] 1x
<2991> יִבְלְעָם ***yiḇlᵉ'ām*** [IBLEAM] 3x
<2992> יָבַם ***yāḇam*** [MARRY] 3x
<2993> יָבָם ***yāḇām*** [HUSBAND'S BROTHER] 2x
<2994> יְבָמָה ***yᵉḇāmāh*** [BROTHER'S WIFE] 5x
<2995> יַבְנְאֵל ***yaḇnᵉ'ēl*** [JABNEEL] 2x
<2996> יַבְנֶה ***yaḇneh*** [JABNEH] 1x
<2997> יִבְנְיָה ***yiḇnᵉyāh*** [IBNEIAH] 1x
<2998> יִבְנִיָּה ***yiḇniyyāh*** [IBNIJAH] 1x
<2999> יַבֹּק ***yabbōq*** [JABBOK] 7x
<3000> יְבֶרֶכְיָהוּ ***yᵉḇereḵyāhû*** [JEBERECHIAH] 1x
<3001> יָבַשׁ ***yāḇaš,*** יָבֵשׁ ***yāḇêš*** [DRY UP] 78x
<3002> יָבֵשׁ ***yāḇêš*** [DRIED, DRY] 9x
<3003> יָבֵשׁ ***yāḇêš*** [JABESH] 24x
<3004> יַבָּשָׁה ***yabbāšāh*** [DRY GROUND, DRY LAND] 14x
<3005> יִבְשָׂם ***yiḇśām*** [IBSAM] 1x
<3006> יַבֶּשֶׁת ***yabbešeṯ*** [DRY GROUND, DRY LAND] 2x

<3007> יַבֶּשֶׁת ***yabbešeṯ*** [EARTH] 1x
<3008> יִגְאָל ***yig'āl*** [IGAL] 3x
<3009> יָגַב ***yāg̱aḇ*** [PLOWMAN (BE)] 2x
<3010> יָגֵב ***yag̱êḇ*** [FIELD] 1x
<3011> יָגְבְּהָה ***yog̱beh̄āh*** [JOGBEHA] 2x
<3012> יִגְדַּלְיָהוּ ***yig̱dalyāhû*** [IGDALIAH] 1x
<3013> יָגָה ***yāg̱āh,*** נוּג ***nûg*** [AFFLICT] 8x
<3014> יָגָה ***yāg̱āh*** [REMOVE] 1x
<3015> יָגוֹן ***yāg̱ôn*** [SORROW (noun)] 14x
<3016> יָגוֹר ***yāg̱ôr*** [AFRAID] 2x
<3017> יָגוּר ***yāg̱ûr*** [JAGUR] 1x
<3018> יְגִיעַ ***yᵉg̱iya'*** [LABOR (noun)] 16x
<3019> יָגִיעַ ***yāg̱iya'*** [WEARY (adj.)] 1x
<3020> יָגְלִי ***yogliy*** [JOGLI] 1x
<3021> יָגַע ***yāg̱a'*** [WEARY (verb)] 26x
<3022> יָגָע ***yāg̱ā'*** [FRUIT OF ONE'S TOIL] 1x
<3023> יָגֵעַ ***yāg̱êa'*** [WEARY (adj.)] 3x
<3024> יְגִיעָה ***yᵉg̱iy'āh*** [WEARINESS] 1x
<3025> יָגֹר ***yāg̱ōr*** [AFRAID (BE)] 5x
<3026> יְגַר שָׂהֲדוּתָא ***yᵉg̱ar śāhᵃḏûṯā'*** [JEGAR SAHADUTHA] 1x
<3027> יָד ***yāḏ,*** יַד אַבְשָׁלוֹם ***yaḏ 'aḇšālôm*** [HAND] 1,615x
<3028> יַד ***yaḏ*** [HAND] 17x
<3029> יְדָא ***yᵉḏā'*** [THANKS (GIVE)] 2x
<3030> יִדְאֲלָה ***yiḏᵃlāh*** [IDALAH] 1x
<3031> יִדְבָּשׁ ***yiḏbāš*** [IDBASH] 1x
<3032> יָדַד ***yāḏaḏ*** [CAST LOTS] 3x
<3033> יְדִדוּת ***yᵉḏiḏûṯ*** [BELOVED, DEARLY BELOVED] 1x
<3034> יָדָה ***yāḏāh*** [THANKS (GIVE)] 114x
<3035> יִדּוֹ ***yiddô*** [IDDO] 2x
<3036> יָדוֹן ***yāḏôn*** [JADON] 1x
<3037> יַדּוּעַ ***yaddûa'*** [JADDUA] 3x
<3038> יְדוּתוּן ***yᵉḏûṯûn,*** יְדֻתוּן ***yᵉḏûṯûn*** [JEDUTHUN] 17x
<3039> יָדִיד ***yāḏiyḏ,*** יְדִידוֹת ***yᵉḏiyḏôṯ*** [BELOVED] 9x
<3040> יְדִידָה ***yᵉḏiyḏāh*** [JEDIDAH] 1x
<3041> יְדִידְיָה ***yᵉḏiyḏyāh*** [JEDIDIAH] 1x
<3042> יְדָיָה ***yᵉḏāyāh*** [JEDAIAH] 2x
<3043> יְדִיעֲאֵל ***yᵉḏiyᵃ'êl*** [JEDIAEL] 6x
<3044> יִדְלָף ***yiḏlāp̱*** [JIDLAPH] 1x
<3045> יָדַע ***yāḏa'*** [KNOW] 947x
<3046> יְדַע ***yᵉḏa'*** [KNOW] 47x
<3047> יָדָע ***yāḏā'*** [JADA] 2x
<3048> יְדַעְיָה ***yᵉḏa'yāh*** [JEDAIAH] 11x
<3049> יִדְּעֹנִי ***yiddᵉ'ōniy*** [SPIRITIST] 11x
<3050> יָהּ ***yāh*** [LORD] 49x
<3051> יָהַב ***yāhaḇ,*** הַב ***haḇ*** [GIVE] 34x
<3052> יְהַב ***yᵉhaḇ*** [GIVE] 28x
<3053> יְהָב ***yᵉhāḇ*** [BURDEN] 1x
<3054> יָהַד ***yāhaḏ*** [JEWS (BECOME, DECLARE THEMSELVES)] 1x
<3055> יְהֻד ***yᵉhuḏ*** [JEHUD] 1x
<3056> יַהְדַּי ***yāhday*** [JAHDAI] 1x
<3057> יְהֻדִיָּה ***yᵉhuḏiyyāh*** [JEHUDIJAH] 1x

<3058> יֵהוּא ***yêhû'*** [JEHU] 58x
<3059> יְהוֹאָחָז ***yᵉhô'āḥāz*** [JEHOAHAZ] 20x
<3060> יְהוֹאָשׁ ***yᵉhô'āš*** [JEHOASH] 16x
<3061> יְהוּד ***yᵉhûḏ*** [JUDAH] 7x
<3062> יְהוּדַי ***yᵉhûḏay*** [JEW] 10x
<3063> יְהוּדָה ***yᵉhûḏāh*** [JUDAH] 818x
<3064> יְהוּדִי ***yᵉhûḏiy*** [JEW] 3,064x
<3065> יְהוּדִי ***yᵉhûḏiy*** [JEHUDI] 4x
<3066> יְהוּדִית ***yᵉhûḏiyṯ*** [HEBREW (IN)] 6x
<3067> יְהוּדִית ***yᵉhûḏiyṯ*** [JUDITH] 1x
<3068> יְהוָֹה ***yᵉhōwāh*** [LORD] 6,519x
<3069> יֱהוִֹה ***yᵉhōwih*** [GOD] 305x
<3070> יְהוָֹה יִרְאֶה ***yᵉhōwāh yir'eh*** [JEHOVAH JIREH] 1x
<3071> יְהוָֹה נִסִּי ***yᵉhōwāh nissiy*** [JEHOVAH NISSI] 1x
<3072> יְהוָֹה צִדְקֵנוּ ***yᵉhōwāh ṣiḏqênû*** [JEHOVAH TSIDKENU] 2x
<3073> יְהוָֹה שָׁלוֹם ***yᵉhōwāh šālôm*** [JEHOVAH SHALOM] 1x
<3074> יְהוָֹה שָׁמָּה ***yᵉhōwāh šāmmāh*** [JEHOVAH SHAMMAH] 1x
<3075> יְהוֹזָבָד ***yᵉhôzāḇāḏ*** [JEHOZABAD] 4x
<3076> יְהוֹחָנָן ***yᵉhôḥānān*** [JEHOHANAN] 9x
<3077> יְהוֹיָדָע ***yᵉhôyāḏā'*** [JEHOIADA] 51x
<3078> יְהוֹיָכִין ***yᵉhôyāḵiyn*** [JEHOIACHIN] 10x
<3079> יְהוֹיָקִים ***yᵉhôyāqiym*** [JEHOIACHIM] 37x
<3080> יְהוֹיָרִיב ***yᵉhôyāriyḇ*** [JEHOIARIB] 2x
<3081> יְהוּכַל ***yᵉhûḵal*** [JEHUCAL] 1x
<3082> יְהוֹנָדָב ***yᵉhônāḏāḇ*** [JEHONADAB] 8x
<3083> יהוֹנָתָן ***yᵉhônāṯān*** [JONATHAN] 82x
<3084> יְהוֹסֵף ***yᵉhôsêp̄*** [JOSEPH] 1x
<3085> יְהוֹעַדָּה ***yᵉhô'addāh*** [JEHOADAH] 2x
<3086> יְהוֹעַדָּן ***yᵉhô'addān*** [JEHOADDAN] 2x
<3087> יְהוֹצָדָק ***yᵉhôṣāḏāq*** [JEHOZADAK] 8x
<3088> יְהוֹרָם ***yᵉhôrām*** [JEHORAM] 29x
<3089> יְהוֹשֶׁבַע ***yᵉhôšeḇa'*** [JEHOSHEBA] 1x
<3090> יְהוֹשַׁבְעַת ***yᵉhôšaḇ'aṯ*** [JEHOSHABEATH] 1x
<3091> יְהוֹשׁוּעַ ***yᵉhôšûa',*** יְהוֹשֻׁעַ ***yᵉhôšua'*** [JOSHUA] 218x
<3092> יְהוֹשָׁפָט ***yᵉhôšāp̄āṭ*** [JEHOSHAPHAT] 84x
<3093> יָהִיר ***yāhiyr*** [HAUGHTY] 2x
<3094> יְהַלֶּלְאֵל ***yᵉhallel'êl*** [JEHALLELEL] 2x
<3095> יַהֲלֹם ***yahᵃlōm,*** יָהֲלֹם ***yāhᵃlōm*** [DIAMOND] 3x
<3096> יַהַץ ***yahaṣ,*** יַהְצָה ***yahṣāh*** [JAHAZ] 9x
<3097> יוֹאָב ***yô'āḇ*** [JOAB] 145x
<3098> יוֹאָח ***yô'āḥ*** [JOAH] 11x
<3099> יוֹאָחָז ***yô'āḥāz*** [JEHOAHAZ, JOAHAZ] 4x
<3100> יוֹאֵל ***yô'êl*** [JOEL] 19x
<3101> יוֹאָשׁ ***yô'āš*** [JOASH] 47x
<3102> יוֹב ***yôḇ*** [JOB] 1x
<3103> יוֹבָב ***yôḇāḇ*** [JOBAB] 9x
<3104> יוֹבֵל ***yôḇêl*** [RAM] 27x
<3105> יוּבַל ***yûḇal*** [STREAM (noun)] 1x
<3106> יוּבָל ***yûḇāl*** [JUBAL] 1x
<3107> יוֹזָבָד ***yôzāḇāḏ*** [JOZABAD] 10x
<3108> יוֹזָכָר ***yôzāḵār*** [JOZACHAR] 1x

<3109> יוֹחָא ***yôḥā'*** [JOHA] 2x
<3110> יוֹחָנָן ***yôḥānān*** [JOHANAN] 24x
<3111> יוֹיָדָע ***yôyāḏā'*** [JEHOIADA] 5x
<3112> יוֹיָכִין ***yôyaḵiyn*** [JEHOIACHIN] 1x
<3113> יוֹיָקִים ***yôyāqiym*** [JOIAKIM] 3x
<3114> יוֹיָרִיב ***yôyāriyḇ*** [JOIARIB] 5x
<3115> יוֹכֶבֶד ***yôḵeḇeḏ*** [JOCHEBED] 2x
<3116> יוֹכֶבֶד ***yôḵeḇeḏ*** [JUCAL] 1x
<3117> יוֹם ***yôm*** [DAY] 2,279x
<3118> יוֹם ***yôm*** [DAY] 16x
<3119> יוֹמָם ***yômām*** [DAY (BY)] 51x
<3120> יָוָן ***yāwān*** [JAVAN] 11x
<3121> יָוֵן ***yāwên*** [MIRY] 2x
<3122> יוֹנָדָב ***yônāḏāḇ*** [JONADAB] 7x
<3123> יוֹנָה ***yônāh*** [DOVE] 32x
<3124> יוֹנָה ***yônāh*** [JONAH] 19x
<3125> יְוָנִי ***yᵉwāniy*** [GRECIAN] 1x
<3126> יֹנֵק ***yōnêq,*** יוֹנֵק ***yônêq*** [INFANT] 11x
<3127> יוֹנֶקֶת ***yôneqeṯ*** [SHOOT (noun)] 6x
<3128> יוֹנַת אֵלֶם רְחֹקִים ***yônaṯ 'êlem rᵉḥōqiym*** [JONATH ELEM REHOKIM] 1x
<3129> יוֹנָתָן ***yônāṯān*** [JONATHAN] 42x
<3130> יוֹסֵף ***yôsêp̱*** [JOSEPH] 213x
<3131> יוֹסִפְיָה ***yôsip̱yāh*** [JOSIPHIAH] 1x
<3132> יוֹעֵאלָה ***yô'ê'lāh*** [JOELAH] 1x
<3133> יוֹעֵד ***yô'êḏ*** [JOED] 1x
<3134> יוֹעֶזֶר ***yô'ezer*** [JOEZER] 1x
<3135> יוֹעָשׁ ***yô'āš*** [JOASH] 2x
<3136> יוֹצָדָק ***yôṣāḏāq*** [JOZADAK] 5x
<3137> יוֹקִים ***yôqiym*** [JOKIM] 1x
<3138> יוֹרֶה ***yôreh*** [RAIN (AUTUMN, EARLY, FIRST, FORMER)] 3x
<3139> יוֹרָה ***yôrāh*** [JORAH] 1x
<3140> יוֹרַי ***yôray*** [JORAI] 1x
<3141> יֹרָם ***yôrām*** [JORAM] 20x
<3142> יוּשַׁב חֶסֶד ***yûšaḇ ḥeseḏ*** [JUSHAB-HESED] 1x
<3143> יוֹשִׁבְיָה ***yôšiḇyāh*** [JOSHIBIAH] 1x
<3144> יוֹשָׁה ***yôšāh*** [JOSHAH] 1x
<3145> יוֹשַׁוְיָה ***yôšawyāh*** [JOSHAVIAH] 1x
<3146> יוֹשָׁפָט ***yôšāp̱āṭ*** [JOSHAPHAT] 2x
<3147> יוֹתָם ***yôṯām*** [JOTHAM] 24x
<3148> יוֹתֵר ***yôṯêr,*** יֹתֵר ***yōṯêr*** [MORE, MORE THAN] 8x
<3149> יְזוּאֵל ***yᵉzû'êl*** [JEZIEL] 1x
<3150> יִזִּיָּה ***yizziyyāh*** [IZZIAH] 1x
<3151> יָזִיז ***yāziyz*** [JAZIZ] 1x
<3152> יִזְלִיאָה ***yizliy'āh*** [IZLIAH] 1x
<3153> יְזַנְיָהוּ ***yᵉzanyāhû,*** יְזַנְיָה ***yᵉzanyāh*** [JEZANIAH] 2x
<3154> יֶזַע ***yeza'*** [SWEAT] 1x
<3155> יִזְרָח ***yizrāḥ*** [IZRAHITE] 1x
<3156> יִזְרַחְיָה ***yizraḥyāh*** [IZRAHIAH] 2x
<3157> יִזְרְעֶאל ***yizrᵉ'e'l*** [JEZREEL] 36x
<3158> יִזְרְעֵאלִי ***yizrᵉ'ê'liy*** [JEZREELITE] 8x
<3159> יִזְרְעֵאלִית ***yizrᵉ'ê'liyṯ,*** יִזְרְעֵאלִת ***yizrᵉ'ê'liṯ*** [JEZREELITESS] 5x

<3160> יְחֻבָּה ***y^{e}ḥubbāh*** [JEHUBBAH] 1x

<3161> יָחַד ***yāḥaḏ*** [UNITE] 3x

<3162> יַחַד ***yaḥaḏ,*** יַחְדָּו ***yaḥdāw,*** יַחְדָּיו ***yaḥdāyw*** [TOGETHER] 142x

<3163> יַחְדּוֹ ***yaḥdô*** [JAHDO] 1x

<3164> יַחְדִּיאֵל ***yaḥdiy'ēl*** [JAHDIEL] 1x

<3165> יֶחְדְּיָהוּ ***yeḥd^{e}yāhû*** [JEHDEIAH] 2x

<3166> יַחֲזִיאֵל ***yaḥ^{a}ziy'ēl*** [JAHAZIEL] 6x

<3167> יַחְזְיָה ***yaḥz^{e}yāh*** [JAHAZIAH] 1x

<3168> יְחֶזְקֵאל ***y^{e}ḥezqē'l*** [EZEKIEL] 3x

<3169> יְחִזְקִיָּה ***y^{e}ḥizqiyyāh,*** יְחִזְקִיָּהוּ ***y^{e}ḥizqiyyāhû*** [HEZEKIAH] 44x

<3170> יַחְזֵרָה ***yaḥzērāh*** [JAHZERAH] 1x

<3171> יְחִיאֵל ***y^{e}ḥiy'ēl,*** יְחוֹאֵל ***y^{e}ḥô'ēl*** [JEHIEL] 14x

<3172> יְחִיאֵלִי ***y^{e}ḥiy'ēliy*** [JEHIELI] 2x

<3173> יָחִיד ***yāḥiyḏ*** [ONLY] 12x

<3174> יְחִיָּה ***y^{e}ḥiyyāh*** [JEHIAH] 1x

<3175> יָחִיל ***yāḥiyl*** [HOPE (verb)] 1x

<3176> יָחַל ***yāḥal*** [WAIT] 42x

<3177> יַחְלְאֵל ***yaḥl^{e}'ēl*** [JAHLEEL] 2x

<3178> יַחְלְאֵלִי ***yaḥl^{e}'ēliy*** [JAHLEELITE] 1x

<3179> יָחַם ***yāḥam*** [CONCEIVE] 8x

<3180> יַחְמוּר ***yaḥmûr*** [ROEBUCK] 2x

<3181> יַחְמַי ***yaḥmay*** [JAHMAI] 1x

<3182> יָחֵף ***yāḥēp̱*** [BAREFOOT] 5x

<3183> יַחְצְאֵל ***yaḥṣ^{e}'ēl*** [JAHZEEL] 2x

<3184> יַחְצְאֵלִי ***yaḥṣ^{e}'ēliy*** [JAHZEELITE] 1x

<3185> יַחְצִיאֵל ***yaḥṣiy'ēl*** [JAHZIEL] 1x

<3186> יָחַר ***yāḥar*** [DELAY (verb)] 1x

<3187> יָחַשׂ ***yāḥaś*** [GENEALOGY] 20x

<3188> יַחַשׂ ***yaḥaś*** [GENEALOGY] 1x

<3189> יַחַת ***yaḥaṯ*** [JAHATH] 8x

<3190> יָטַב ***yāṭaḇ*** [GOOD (BE, DO)] 107x

<3191> יְטַב ***y^{e}ṭaḇ*** [GOOD (SEEM)] 1x

<3192> יָטְבָה ***yoṭḇāh*** [JOTBAH] 1x

<3193> יָטְבָתָה ***yoṭḇāṯāh*** [JOTBATHAH] 3x

<3194> יוּטָּה ***yûṭṭāh,*** יֻטָּה ***yuṭṭāh*** [JUTTAH] 2x

<3195> יְטוּר ***y^{e}ṭûr*** [JETUR] 3x

<3196> יַיִן ***yayin*** [WINE] 140x

<3197> יַךְ ***yaḵ*** [WAYSIDE] 1x

<3198> יָכַח ***yāḵaḥ*** [JUDGE (verb)] 58x

<3199> יָכִין ***yāḵiyn*** [JAKIN] 8x

<3200> יָכִינִי ***yāḵiyniy*** [JACHINITE] 1x

<3201> יָכֹל ***yāḵōl*** [ABLE (BE)] 195x

<3202> יְכִל ***y^{e}ḵil*** [ABLE (BE)] 12x

<3203> יְכָלְיָה ***y^{e}ḵolyāh,*** יְכָלְיָהוּ ***y^{e}ḵolyāhû*** [JECOLIAH] 2x

<3204> יְכוֹנְיָה ***y^{e}ḵônyāh,*** יְכָנְיָה ***y^{e}ḵonyāh,*** יְכָנְיָהוּ ***y^{e}ḵonyāhû*** [JECONIAH] 7x

<3205> יָלַד ***yālaḏ,*** לֵדָה ***lēḏāh*** [BIRTH (GIVE)] 498x

<3206> יֶלֶד ***yeleḏ*** [CHILD] 89x

<3207> יַלְדָּה ***yaldāh*** [GIRL] 3x

<3208> יַלְדוּת ***yalḏûṯ*** [YOUTH] 3x

<3209> יִלּוֹד ***yillôḏ*** [BORN] 5x

<3210> יָלוֹן ***yālôn*** [JALON] 1x

<3211> יָלִיד ***yāliyḏ*** [DESCENDANT] 13x
<3212> יָלַךְ ***yālaḵ*** [GO] 1,043x (KJV)
<3213> יָלַל ***yālal*** [WAIL (verb)] 31x
<3214> יְלֵל ***y^{e}lêl*** [HOWLING] 1x
<3215> יְלָלָה ***y^{e}lālāh*** [WAIL (noun)] 5x
<3216> יָלַע ***yāla'*** [DEVOUR] 1x
<3217> יַלֶּפֶת ***yallepeṯ*** [SCAB] 11x
<3218> יֶלֶק ***yeleq*** [LOCUST (YOUNG, CRAWLING)] 9x
<3219> יַלְקוּט ***yalqûṭ*** [POUCH] 1x
<3220> יָם ***yām*** [SEA] 396x
<3221> יַם ***yam*** [SEA] 2x
<3222> יֵם ***yêm*** [MULE] 1x
<3223> יְמוּאֵל ***y^{e}mû'êl*** [JEMUEL] 2x
<3224> יְמִימָה ***y^{e}miymāh*** [JEMIMAH] 1x
<3225> יָמִין ***yāmiyn*** [RIGHT HAND] 139x
<3226> יָמִין ***yāmiyn*** [JAMIN] 6x
<3227> יְמִינִי ***y^{e}miyniy*** [RIGHT HAND] 2x
<3228> יָמִינִי ***yāmiyniy***, יְמִינִי ***y^{e}miy-niy*** [JAMINITE] 5x
<3229> יִמְלָא ***yimlā'***, יִמְלָה ***yimlāh*** [IMLAH] 4x
<3230> יַמְלֵךְ ***yamlêḵ*** [JAMLECH] 1x
<3231> יָמַן ***yāman*** [RIGHT (GO TO THE, TURN TO THE)] 5x
<3232> יִמְנָה ***yimnāh*** [IMNAH] 5x
<3233> יְמָנִי ***y^{e}māniy*** [RIGHT, RIGHT HAND] 33x
<3234> יִמְנָע ***yimnā'*** [IMNA] 1x
<3235> יָמַר ***yāmar*** [BOAST (verb)] 2x
<3236> יִמְרָה ***yimrāh*** [IMRAH] 1x
<3237> יָמַשׁ ***yāmaš*** [FEEL] 1x
<3238> יָנָה ***yānāh*** [OPPRESS] 21x
<3239> יָנוֹחַ ***yānôaḥ***, יָנוֹחָה ***yānôḥāh*** [JANOAH] 3x
<3240> יָנַח ***yānaḥ*** [REST (verb)] 75x (KJV)
<3241> יָנִים ***yāniym*** [JANUM] 1x
<3242> יְנִיקָה ***y^{e}niyqāh*** [TWIG] 1x
<3243> יָנַק ***yānaq*** [NURSE (verb and noun)] 32x
<3244> יַנְשׁוּף ***yanšûp̄***, יַנְשׁוֹף ***yanšôp̄*** [OWL (GREAT, SCREECH, SHORT-EARED)] 3x
<3245> יָסַד ***yāsaḏ*** [FOUNDATION (LAY A)] 42x
<3246> יְסֻד ***y^{e}suḏ*** [BEGIN] 1x
<3247> יְסוֹד ***y^{e}sôḏ*** [FOUNDATION] 20x
<3248> יְסוּדָה ***y^{e}sûḏāh*** [FOUNDATION] 1x
<3249> יָסוּר ***yāsûr*** [TURN AWAY (THOSE WHO)] 1x
<3250> יִסּוֹר ***yissôr*** [CONTENDS (ONE WHO)] 1x
<3251> יָסַךְ ***yāsaḵ*** [POUR] 1x
<3252> יִסְכָּה ***yiskāh*** [ISCAH] 1x
<3253> יִסְמַכְיָהוּ ***yismaḵyāhû*** [ISMACHIAH] 1x
<3254> יָסַף ***yāsap̄*** [CONTINUE] 213x
<3255> יְסַף ***y^{e}sap̄*** [ADD] 1x
<3256> יָסַר ***yāsar***, סָרַר ***sārar*** [ADMONISH] 22x
<3257> יָע ***yā'*** [SHOVEL] 9x
<3258> יַעְבֵּץ ***ya'bêṣ*** [JABEZ] 4x
<3259> יָעַד ***yā'aḏ*** [APPOINT] 29x
<3260> יֶעְדּוֹ ***ye'dô*** [IDDO] 1x
<3261> יָעָה ***yā'āh*** [SWEEP AWAY] 1x

<3262> יְעוּאֵל ***y^{e}ʻûʼêl*** [JEUEL] 1x
<3263> יְעוּץ ***y^{e}ʻûṣ*** [JEUZ] 1x
<3264> יְעוֹרִים ***y^{e}ʻôriym*** [WOODS] 1x
<3265> יָעוּר ***yāʻûr*** [JAIR] 1x
<3266> יְעוּשׁ ***y^{e}ʻûš*** [JEUSH] 9x
<3267> יָעַז ***yāʻaz*** [FIERCE] 1x
<3268> יַעֲזִיאֵל ***ya^{a}ziyʼêl*** [JAAZIEL] 1x
<3269> יַעֲזִיָּהוּ ***ya^{a}ziyyāhû*** [JAAZIAH] 2x
<3270> יַעֲזֵיר ***ya^{a}zêyr,*** יַעְזֵר ***yaʻzêr*** [JAZER] 13x
<3271> יָעַט ***yāʻat*** [COVER (verb)] 1x
<3272> יְעַט ***y^{e}ʻaṭ*** [CONSULT TOGETHER] 3x
<3273> יְעִיאֵל ***y^{e}ʻiyʼêl,*** יְעוּאֵל ***y^{e}ʻûʼêl*** [JEIEL] 13x
<3274> יְעִישׁ ***y^{e}ʻiyš*** [JEISH] 3x
<3275> יַעְכָּן ***yaʻkān*** [JACAN] 1x
<3276> יָעַל ***yāʻal*** [PROFIT (verb)] 23x
<3277> יָעֵל ***yāʻêl*** [GOAT (WILD, MOUNTAIN)] 3x
<3278> יָעֵל ***yāʻêl*** [JAEL] 6x
<3279> יַעֲלָא ***ya^{a}laʼ,*** יַעֲלָה ***ya^{a}lāh*** [JAALA] 2x
<3280> יַעֲלָה ***ya^{a}lāh*** [DOE] 1x
<3281> יַעְלָם ***yaʻlām*** [JAALAM] 4x
<3282> יַעַן ***yaʻan*** [BECAUSE] 17x
<3283> יָעֵן ***yāʻên*** [OSTRICH] 1x
<3284> יַעֲנָה ***ya^{a}nāh*** [OWL] 8x
<3285> יַעְנַי ***yaʻnay*** [JAANAI] 1x
<3286> יָעֵף ***yāʻêp̱*** [FAINT (verb)] 9x
<3287> יָעֵף ***yāʻêp̱*** [WEARY (adj.)] 4x
<3288> יְעָף ***y^{e}ʻāp̱*** [WEARINESS] 1x
<3289> יָעַץ ***yāʻaṣ*** [COUNSEL (verb)] 80x
<3290> יַעֲקֹב ***ya^{a}qōḇ*** [JACOB] 349x
<3291> יַעֲקֹבָה ***ya^{a}qōḇāh*** [JAAKOBAH] 1x
<3292> יַעֲקָן ***ya^{a}qān*** [JAAKAN] 1x
<3293> יַעַר ***yaʻar*** [FOREST] 58x
<3294> יַעְרָה ***yaʻrāh*** [JARAH] 1x
<3295> יַעֲרָה ***ya^{a}rāh*** [HONEYCOMB] 2x
<3296> יַעֲרֵי אֹרְגִים ***ya^{a}rêy ʼōr^{e}g̱iym*** [JAARE-OREGIM] 1x
<3297> יְעָרִים ***y^{e}ʻāriym*** [JEARIM] 1x
<3298> יַעֲרֶשְׁיָה ***ya^{a}rešyāh*** [JARESIAH] 1x
<3299> יַעֲשָׂו ***ya^{a}śāw*** [JAASU] 1x
<3300> יַעֲשִׂיאֵל ***ya^{a}śiyʼêl*** [JAASIEL] 2x
<3301> יִפְדְיָה ***yip̱d^{e}yāh*** [IPHDEIAH] 1x
<3302> יָפָה ***yāp̱āh*** [BEAUTIFUL (BE, MAKE ONESELF)] 8x
<3303> יָפֶה ***yāp̱eh*** [BEAUTIFUL] 41x
<3304> יְפֵיפִיָּה ***y^{e}p̱êyp̱iyyah*** [BEAUTIFUL] 1x
<3305> יָפוֹא ***yāp̱ôʼ,*** יָפוֹ ***yāp̱ô*** [JOPPA] 4x
<3306> יָפַח ***yāp̱aḥ*** [BREATH (GASP FOR)] 1x
<3307> יָפֵחַ ***yāp̱êaḥ*** [BREATH OUT] 1x
<3308> יֳפִי ***y^{o}p̱iy*** [BEAUTY] 19x
<3309> יָפִיעַ ***yāp̱iyaʻ*** [JAPHIA] 5x
<3310> יַפְלֵט ***yap̱lêṭ*** [JAPHLET] 3x
<3311> יַפְלֵטִי ***yap̱lêṭiy*** [JAPHLETITE] 1x
<3312> יְפֻנֶּה ***y^{e}p̱unneh*** [JEPHUNNEH] 16x

<3313> יָפַע **yāp̱a‘** [SHINE, SHINE FORTH] 8x
<3314> יִפְעָה **yip̱‘āh** [SPLENDOR] 2x
<3315> יֶפֶת **yep̱eṯ** [JAPHETH] 11x
<3316> יִפְתָּח **yip̱tāḥ** [JEPHTHAH] 30x
<3317> יִפְתַּח־אֵל **yip̱taḥ ’ēl** [IPHTAHEL] 2x
<3318> יוֹצֵאת **yôṣē’ṯ,** יָצָא **yāṣā’** [GO OUT] 1,069x
<3319> יְצָא **y^{e}ṣa’** [FINISH] 1x
<3320> יָצַב **yāṣaḇ** [STAND (TAKE A, MAKE A)] 48x
<3321> יְצַב **y^{e}ṣaḇ** [TRUTH] 1x
<3322> יָצַג **yāṣag** [SET] 16x
<3323> יִצְהָר **yiṣhār** [OIL] 23x
<3324> יִצְהָר **yiṣhār** [IZHAR] 9x
<3325> יִצְהָרִי **yiṣhāriy** [IZHARITE] 4x
<3326> יָצוּעַ **yāṣûa‘** [BED] 11x
<3327> יִצְחָק **yiṣḥāq** [ISAAC] 108x
<3328> יִצְחַר **yiṣḥar** [IZHAR] 1x
<3329> יָצִיא **yāṣiy’** [COMING FORTH] 1x
<3330> יַצִּיב **yaṣṣiyḇ** [CERTAIN] 5x
<3331> יָצַע **yāṣa‘** [SPREAD (verb)] 4x
<3332> יָצַק **yāṣaq** [POUR, POUR OUT] 53x
<3333> יְצֻקָה **y^{e}ṣuqāh** [CASTING] 1x
<3334> יָצַר **yāṣar** [DISTRESSED (BE)] 9x
<3335> יָצַר **yāṣar** [FORM (verb)] 62x
<3336> יֵצֶר **yêṣer** [FORMED] 9x
<3337> יֵצֶר **yêṣer** [JEZER] 3x
<3338> יְצֻרִים **y^{e}ṣuriym** [MEMBERS] 1x
<3339> יִצְרִי **yiṣriy** [IZRI] 1x
<3340> יִצְרִי **yiṣriy** [JEZERITE] 1x
<3341> יָצַת **yāṣaṯ** [BURN (verb)] 29x
<3342> יֶקֶב **yeqeḇ** [WINEPRESS, WINE VAT] 16x
<3343> יְקַבְצְאֵל **y^{e}qaḇṣ^{e}’êl** [JEKABZEEL] 1x
<3344> יָקַד **yāqaḏ** [BURN (verb)] 9x
<3345> יְקַד **y^{e}qaḏ** [BURNING (verb)] 8x
<3346> יְקֵדָה **y^{e}qêḏāh** [BURNING (noun)] 1x
<3347> יָקְדְעָם **yoqḏ^{e}‘ām** [JOKDEAM] 1x
<3348> יָקֶה **yāqeh** [JAKEH] 1x
<3349> יְקָהָה **y^{e}qāhāh** [OBEDIENCE] 2x
<3350> יְקוֹד **y^{e}qôḏ,** יְקֹד **y^{e}qōḏ** [BURNING (noun)] 1x
<3351> יְקוּם **y^{e}qûm** [LIVING (noun)] 3x
<3352> יָקוֹשׁ **yāqôš** [FOWLER] 1x
<3353> יָקוּשׁ **yaqûš** [FOWLER] 3x
<3354> יְקוּתִיאֵל **y^{e}qûṯiy’êl** [JEKUTHIEL] 1x
<3355> יָקְטָן **yoqṭān** [JOKTAN] 6x
<3356> יָקִים **yāqiym** [JAKIM] 2x
<3357> יַקִּיר **yaqqiyr** [DEAR] 1x
<3358> יַקִּיר **yaqqiyr** [NOBLE] 2x
<3359> יְקַמְיָה **y^{e}qamyāh** [JEKAMIAH] 3x
<3360> יְקַמְעָם **y^{e}qam‘ām** [JEKAMEAM] 2x
<3361> יָקְמְעָם **yoqm^{e}‘ām** [JOKMEAM] 2x
<3362> יָקְנְעָם **yoqn^{e}‘ām** [JOKNEAM] 3x
<3363> יָקַע **yāqa‘** [ALIENATED (BE)] 8x

<3364> יָקַץ ***yāqaṣ*** [AWAKEN] 10x
<3365> יָקַר ***yāqar*** [PRECIOUS (BE)] 11x
<3366> יְקָר ***y^{e}qār*** [HONOR (noun)] 17x
<3367> יְקָר ***y^{e}qār*** [HONOR (noun)] 7x
<3368> יָקָר ***yāqār*** [PRECIOUS] 36x
<3369> יָקֹשׁ ***yāqōš*** [SNARE, BE SNARED] 8x
<3370> יָקְשָׁן ***yoqšān*** [JOKSHAN] 4x
<3371> יָקְתְאֵל ***yoqṯ^{e}'ēl*** [JOKTHEEL] 2x
<3372> יָרֵא ***yārê'*** [FEAR (verb)] 314x
<3373> יָרֵא ***yārê'*** [FEARING] 64x
<3374> יִרְאָה ***yir'āh*** [FEAR (noun)] 45x
<3375> יִרְאוֹן ***yir'ôn*** [IRON] 1x
<3376> יִרְאִיָּיה ***yir'iyyāyh*** [IRIJAH] 2x
<3377> יָרֵב ***yārêḇ*** [JAREB] 2x
<3378> יְרֻבַּעַל ***y^{e}rubba'al*** [JERUBBAAL] 14x
<3379> יָרָבְעָם ***yāroḇ'ām*** [JEROBOAM] 104x
<3380> יְרֻבֶּשֶׁת ***y^{e}rubbešeṯ*** [JERUBBESHETH] 1x
<3381> יָרַד ***yāraḏ*** [GO DOWN] 372x
<3382> יֶרֶד ***yereḏ*** [JARED] 7x
<3383> יַרְדֵּן ***yardên*** [JORDAN] 182x
<3384> יָרָה ***yārāh,*** יוֹרֶה ***yôreh,*** מוֹרֶה ***môreh,*** יָרָהּ ***yārah*** [SHOOT (verb)] 84x
<3385> יְרוּאֵל ***y^{e}rû'êl*** [JERUEL] 1x
<3386> יָרוֹחַ ***yārôaḥ*** [JAROAH] 1x
<3387> יָרוֹק ***yārôq*** [GREEN THING] 1x
<3388> יְרוּשָׁה ***y^{e}rûšāh,*** יְרוּשָׁא ***y^{e}rûšā'*** [JERUSHA] 2x
<3389> יְרוּשָׁלַם ***y^{e}rûšālam,*** יְרוּשָׁלַיִם ***y^{e}rûšālayim*** [JERUSALEM] 643x
<3390> יְרוּשְׁלֶם ***y^{e}rûš^{e}lem*** [JERUSALEM] 26x
<3391> יֶרַח ***yeraḥ*** [MONTH] 13x
<3392> יֶרַח ***yeraḥ*** [JERAH] 2x
<3393> יְרַח ***y^{e}raḥ*** [MONTH] 2x
<3394> יָרֵחַ ***yārêaḥ*** [MOON] 26x
<3395> יְרֹחָם ***y^{e}rōḥām*** [JEROHAM] 10x
<3396> יְרַחְמְאֵל ***y^{e}raḥm^{e}'êl*** [JERAHMEEL] 8x
<3397> יְרַחְמְאֵלִי ***y^{e}raḥm^{e}'êliy*** [JERAHMEELITE] 2x
<3398> יַרְחָע ***yarḥā'*** [JARHA] 2x
<3399> יָרַט ***yāraṭ*** [TURN OVER] 2x
<3400> יְרִיאֵל ***y^{e}riy'ēl*** [JERIEL] 1x
<3401> יָרִיב ***yāriyḇ*** [CONTENDS (ONE WHO)] 3x
<3402> יָרִיב ***yāriyḇ*** [JARIB] 3x
<3403> יְרִיבַי ***y^{e}riyḇay*** [JERIBAI] 1x
<3404> יְרִיָּה ***y^{e}riyyāh,*** יְרִיָּהוּ ***y^{e}riyyāhû*** [JERIAH] 3x
<3405> יְרֵחוֹ ***y^{e}rêḥô,*** יְרִיחוֹ ***y^{e}riyḥô*** [JERICHO] 57x
<3406> יְרֵמוֹת ***y^{e}rêmôṯ,*** יְרִימוֹת ***y^{e}riymôṯ*** [JERIMOTH] 15x
<3407> יְרִיעָה ***y^{e}riy'āh*** [CURTAIN] 54x
<3408> יְרִיעוֹת ***y^{e}riy'ôṯ*** [JERIOTH] 1x
<3409> יָרֵךְ ***yārêḵ*** [THIGH] 34x
<3410> יַרְכָה ***yarḵāh*** [THIGH] 1x
<3411> יַרְכָה ***yarḵāh,*** יְרֵכָה ***y^{e}rêḵāh*** [BORDER] 28x
<3412> יַרְמוּת ***yarmûṯ*** [JARMUTH] 7x
<3413> יְרֵמַי ***y^{e}rêmay*** [JEREMAI] 1x
<3414> יִרְמְיָה ***yirm^{e}yāh,*** יִרְמְיָהוּ ***yirm^{e}yāhû*** [JEREMIAH] 147x

<3415> יָרַע ***yāra‘*** [TREMBLE] 1x

<3416> יִרְפְּאֵל ***yirp^{e}’êl*** [IRPEEL] 1x

<3417> יָרַק ***yāraq*** [SPIT (verb)] 3x

<3418> יֶרֶק ***yereq*** [GRASS] 8x

<3419> יָרָק ***yārāq*** [GRASS] 5x

<3420> יֵרָקוֹן ***yêrāqôn*** [MILDEW] 6x

<3421> יָרְקְעָם ***yorq^{e}‘ām*** [JORKOAM] 1x

<3422> יְרַקְרַק ***y^{e}raqraq*** [GREENISH] 3x

<3423> יָרַשׁ ***yāraš*** [HEIR (BE)] 232x

<3424> יְרֵשָׁה ***y^{e}rêšāh*** [POSSESSION] 2x

<3425> יְרֻשָּׁה ***y^{e}ruššāh*** [POSSESSION] 14x

<3426> יֵשׁ ***yêš*** [BE] 133x

<3427> יָשַׁב ***yāšaḇ*** [DWELL] 1,088x

<3428> יֶשֶׁבְאָב ***yešeḇ’āḇ*** [JESHEBEAB] 1x

<3429> יֹשֵׁב בַּשֶּׁבֶת ***yōšêḇ baššeḇeṯ*** [SEAT (WHO SAT IN THE)] 1x

<3430> יִשְׁבִּי בְּנֹב ***yišbiy b^{e}nōḇ*** [ISHBI-BENOB] 1x

<3431> יִשְׁבָּח ***yišbāḥ*** [ISHBAH] 1x

<3432> יָשׁוּבִי ***yāšûḇiy*** [JASHUBITE] 1x

<3433> יָשֻׁבִי לָחֶם ***yāšuḇiy lāḥem*** [JASHUBI LEHEM] 1x

<3434> יָשָׁבְעָם ***yāšoḇ‘ām*** [JASHOBEAM] 3x

<3435> יִשְׁבָּק ***yišbāq*** [ISHBAK] 2x

<3436> יָשְׁבְּקָשָׁה ***yošb^{e}qāšāh*** [JOSHBEKASHAH] 2x

<3437> יָשׁוּב ***yāšûḇ*** [JASHUB] 4x

<3438> יִשְׁוָה ***yišwāh*** [ISHUAH, ISHVAH] 2x

<3439> יְשׁוֹחָיָה ***y^{e}šôḥāyāh*** [JESHOHAIAH] 1x

<3440> יִשְׁוִי ***yišwiy*** [ISHVI] 4x

<3441> יִשְׁוִי ***yišwiy*** [ISHVITE] 1x

<3442> יֵשׁוּעַ ***yêšûa‘*** [JESHUA] 29x

<3443> יֵשׁוּעַ ***yêšûa‘*** [JESHUA] 1x

<3444> יְשׁוּעָה ***y^{e}šû‘āh*** [SALVATION] 78x

<3445> יֶשַׁח ***yešaḥ*** [CASTING DOWN] 1x

<3446> יִשְׂחָק ***yiśḥāq*** [ISAAC] 4x

<3447> יָשַׁט ***yāšaṭ*** [HOLD OUT] 3x

<3448> יִשַׁי, ***yišay,*** אִישַׁי ***’iyšay*** [JESSE] 42x

<3449> יִשִּׁיָּהוּ ***yiššiyyāhû,*** יִשִּׁיָּה ***yiššiyyāh*** [ISSHIAH] 7x

<3450> יְשִׂימִאֵל ***y^{e}śiymi’êl*** [JESIMIEL] 1x

<3451> יְשִׁימָה ***y^{e}šiymāh*** [DESOLATION] 1x

<3452> יְשִׁימוֹן ***y^{e}šiymôn,*** יְשִׁמוֹן ***y^{e}šimôn*** [JESHIMON] 13x

<3453> יָשִׁישׁ ***yāšiyš*** [AGED] 4x

<3454> יְשִׁישַׁי ***y^{e}šiyšay*** [JESHISHAI] 1x

<3455> יָשַׂם ***yāśam*** [PUT] 1x

<3456> יָשַׁם ***yāšam*** [DESOLATE (BE, BECOME)] 4x

<3457> יִשְׁמָא ***yišmā’*** [ISHMA] 1x

<3458> יִשְׁמָעֵאל ***yišmā‘ê’l*** [ISHMAEL] 48x

<3459> יִשְׁמְעֵאלִי ***yišm^{e}‘ê’liy*** [ISHMAELITE] 8x

<3460> יִשְׁמַעְיָה ***yišma‘yāh,*** יִשְׁמַעְיָהוּ ***yišma‘yāhû*** [ISHMAIAH] 2x

<3461> יִשְׁמְרַי ***yišm^{e}ray*** [ISHMERAI] 1x

<3462> יָשֵׁן ***yāšên*** [SLEEP (verb)] 19x

<3463> יָשֵׁן ***yāšên*** [SLEEPING] 9x

<3464> יָשֵׁן ***yāšên*** [JASHEN] 1x

<3465> יָשָׁן ***yāšān*** [OLD] 7x

<3466> יְשָׁנָה ***yešānāh*** [JESHANAH] 1x
<3467> יָשַׁע ***yāša‘*** [SAVE] 205x
<3468> יֵשַׁע ***yêša‘***, יֶשַׁע ***yeša‘*** [SALVATION] 36x
<3469> יִשְׁעִי ***yiš‘iy*** [ISHI] 5x
<3470> יְשַׁעְיָה ***yeša‘yāh***, יְשַׁעְיָהוּ ***yeša‘yāhû*** [ISAIAH] 39x
<3471> יָשְׁפֵה ***yāšepêh*** [JASPER] 3x
<3472> יִשְׁפָּה ***yišpāh*** [ISHPAH] 1x
<3473> יִשְׁפָּן ***yišpān*** [ISHPAN] 1x
<3474> יָשַׁר ***yāšar*** [STRAIGHT (BE)] 26x
<3475> יֵשֶׁר ***yêšer*** [JESHER] 1x
<3476> יֹשֶׁר ***yōšer*** [UPRIGHTNESS] 13x
<3477> יָשָׁר ***yāšār*** [RIGHT] 119x
<3478> יִשְׂרָאֵל ***yiśrā’êl*** [ISRAEL] 2,505x
<3479> יִשְׂרָאֵל ***yiśra’êl*** [ISRAEL] 7x
<3480> יְשַׂרְאֵלָה ***yeśar’êlāh*** [JESHARELAH] 1x
<3481> יִשְׂרְאֵלִי ***yiśre’êliy*** [ISRAELITE] 2x
<3482> יִשְׂרְאֵלִית ***yiśre’êliyṯ*** [ISRAELITESS] 2x
<3483> יִשְׁרָה ***yišrāh*** [UPRIGHTNESS] 1x
<3484> יְשֻׁרוּן ***yešurûn*** [JESHURUN] 4x
<3485> יִשָּׂשכָר ***yiśśaśḵār*** [ISSACHAR] 43x
<3486> יָשֵׁשׁ ***yāšêš*** [AGED] 1x
<3487> יָת ***yāṯ*** [____] 1x
<3488> יְתִב ***yeṯiḇ*** [SIT] 5x
<3489> יָתֵד ***yaṯêḏ*** [PEG] 24x
<3490> יָתוֹם ***yāṯôm*** [ORPHAN] 42x
<3491> יְתוּר ***yeṯûr*** [RANGE (noun)] 1x
<3492> יַתִּיר ***yattiyr***, יַתִּר ***yattir*** [JATTIR] 4x
<3493> יַתִּיר ***yattiyr*** [EXCELLENT] 8x
<3494> יִתְלָה ***yiṯlāh*** [ITHLAH] 1x
<3495> יִתְמָה ***yiṯmāh*** [ITHMAH] 1x
<3496> יַתְנִיאֵל ***yaṯniy’êl*** [JATHNIEL] 1x
<3497> יִתְנָן ***yiṯnān*** [ITHNAN] 1x
<3498> יָתַר ***yāṯar*** [REMAIN] 107x
<3499> יֶתֶר ***yeṯer*** [REMAINDER] 101x
<3500> יֶתֶר ***yeṯer*** [JETHRO, JETHER] 9x
<3501> יִתְרָא ***yiṯrā’*** [ITHRA, JETHER] 1x
<3502> יִתְרָה ***yiṯrāh*** [ABUNDANCE] 2x
<3503> יִתְרוֹ ***yiṯrô*** [JETHRO] 9x
<3504> יִתְרוֹן ***yiṯrôn*** [PROFIT (noun)] 10x
<3505> יִתְרִי ***yiṯriy*** [ITHRITE] 3x
<3506> יִתְרָן ***yiṯrān*** [ITHRAN] 3x
<3507> יִתְרְעָם ***yiṯre‘ām*** [ITHREAM] 2x
<3508> יֹתֶרֶת ***yōṯereṯ*** [LOBE (LONG, FATTY)] 11x
<3509> יְתֵת ***yeṯêṯ*** [JETHETH] 2x

כ Kaph

<3510> כָּאַב ***kā’aḇ*** [PAIN (BE IN)] 8x
<3511> כְּאֵב ***ke’êḇ*** [PAIN (noun)] 6x

<3512> כָּאָה ***kā'āh*** [GRIEVED (BE)] 3x
<3513> כָּבֵד ***kāḇêḏ*** [HEAVY (BE)] 113x
<3514> כֹּבֶד ***kōḇeḏ*** [HEAVINESS] 4x
<3515> כָּבֵד ***kāḇêḏ*** [HEAVY] 38x
<3516> כָּבֵד ***kāḇêḏ*** [LIVER] 14x
<3517> כְּבֵדֻת ***kᵉḇêḏuṯ*** [DIFFICULTY] 1x
<3518> כָּבָה ***kāḇāh*** [QUENCH] 24x
<3519> כָּבוֹד ***kāḇôḏ,*** כָּבֹד ***kāḇōḏ*** [GLORY] 200x
<3520> כָּבוֹד ***kāḇôḏ,*** כְּבוּדָּה ***kᵉḇûddāh*** [GLORIOUS] 3x
<3521> כָּבוּל ***kāḇûl*** [CABUL] 2x
<3522> כַּבּוֹן ***kabbôn*** [CABBON] 1x
<3523> כָּבִיר ***kāḇiyr*** [PILLOW] 2x
<3524> כַּבִּיר ***kabbiyr*** [MIGHTY] 11x
<3525> כֶּבֶל ***keḇel*** [FETTERS] 2x
<3526> כָּבַס ***kāḇas*** [WASH] 51x
<3527> כָּבַר ***kāḇar*** [MULTIPLY] 2x
<3528> כְּבָר ***kᵉḇār*** [ALREADY] 9x
<3529> כְּבָר ***kᵉḇār*** [CHEBAR] 8x
<3530> כִּבְרָה ***kiḇrāh*** [DISTANCE (SOME, LITTLE)] 3x
<3531> כְּבָרָה ***kᵉḇārāh*** [SIEVE] 1x
<3532> כֶּבֶשׂ ***keḇeś*** [SHEEP] 107x
<3533> כָּבַשׁ ***kāḇaš*** [SUBDUE] 13x
<3534> כֶּבֶשׁ ***keḇeš*** [FOOTSTOOL] 1x
<3535> כִּבְשָׂה ***kiḇśāh,*** כַּבְשָׂה ***kaḇśāh*** [LAMB (EWE, FEMALE)] 8x
<3536> כִּבְשָׁן ***kiḇšān*** [FURNACE] 4x
<3537> כַּד ***kaḏ*** [JAR] 18x
<3538> כְּדַב ***kᵉḏaḇ*** [LYING] 1x
<3539> כַּדְכֹּד ***kaḏkōḏ*** [AGATE] 2x
<3540> כְּדָרְלָעֹמֶר ***kᵉḏārlā'ōmer*** [CHEDORLAOMER] 5x
<3541> כֹּה ***kōh*** [THIS, IN THIS WAY, THIS IS WHAT] 25x
<3542> כָּה ***kāh*** [POINT (AT THIS)] 1x
<3543> כָּהָה ***kāhāh*** [DIM (BE)] 8x
<3544> כֵּהֶה ***kêheh*** [DARK] 9x
<3545> כֵּהָה ***kêhāh*** [HEALING] 1x
<3546> כְּהַל ***kᵉhal*** [ABLE (BE)] 4x
<3547> כָּהַן ***kāhan*** [PRIEST (MINISTER AS, SERVE AS)] 23x
<3548> כֹּהֵן ***kōhên*** [PRIEST] 750x
<3549> כָּהֵן ***kāhên*** [PRIEST] 8x
<3550> כְּהֻנָּה ***kᵉhunnāh*** [PRIESTHOOD] 14x
<3551> כַּוָּה ***kawwāh*** [WINDOW] 1x
<3552> כּוּב ***kûḇ*** [CHUB] 1x
<3553> כּוֹבַע ***kôḇa'*** [HELMET] 6x
<3554> כָּוָה ***kāwāh*** [BURN (verb)] 2x
<3555> כְּוִיָּה ***kᵉwiyyāh*** [BURN (noun)] 1x
<3556> כּוֹכָב ***kôḵāḇ*** [STAR] 37x
<3557> כּוּל ***kûl*** [CONTAIN] 37x
<3558> כּוּמָז ***kûmāz*** [NECKLACE] 2x
<3559> כּוּן ***kûn*** [SET UP] 219x
<3560> כּוּן ***kûn*** [CHUN] 1x
<3561> כַּוָּן ***kawwān*** [CAKE] 2x
<3562> כּוֹנַנְיָהוּ ***kônanyāhû*** [CONANIAH] 3x

<3563> כּוֹס ***kôs*** [CUP] 31x, [OWL, LITTLE OWL] 3x
<3564> כּוּר ***ḵûr*** [FURNACE] 9x, [PIERCE] 1x
<3565> כּוֹר עָשָׁן ***kôr 'āšān*** [CORASHAN] 1x
<3566> כּוֹרֶשׁ ***kôreš,*** כֹּרֶשׁ ***kōreš*** [CYRUS] 15x
<3567> כּוֹרֶשׁ ***kôreš*** [CYRUS] 8x
<3568> כּוּשׁ ***Kûš*** [CUSH] 30x
<3569> כּוּשִׁי ***kûšiy*** [CUSHITE, CUSHI] 23x
<3570> כּוּשִׁי ***kûšiy*** [CUSHI] 2x
<3571> כּוּשִׁית ***kûšiyṯ*** [CUSHITE] 1x
<3572> כּוּשָׁן ***kûšān*** [CUSHAN] 1x
<3573> כּוּשַׁן רִשְׁעָתַיִם ***kûšan riš'ā-ṯayim*** [CUSHAN-RISHATHAIM] 2x
<3574> כּוֹשָׁרָה ***kōshārāh*** [PROSPERITY] 1x
<3575> כּוּת ***kûṯ,*** כּוּתָה ***kûṯāh*** [CUTHAH] 2x
<3576> כָּזַב ***kāzaḇ*** [LIAR (BE A, DECLARE A, MAKE A)] 16x
<3577> כָּזָב ***kāzāḇ*** [LIE (noun)] 31x
<3578> כֹּזֵבָא ***kōzêḇa'*** [COZEBA] 1x
<3579> כָּזְבִּי ***kozbiy*** [COZBI] 2x
<3580> כְּזִיב ***k^eziyḇ*** [CHEZIB] 1x
<3581> כֹּחַ ***kōaḥ,*** כּוֹחַ ***kôaḥ*** [LIZARD (MONITOR)] 1x, [STRENGTH] 125x
<3582> כָּחַד ***kāḥaḏ*** [CUT OFF] 32x
<3583> כָּחַל ***kāḥal*** [PAINT] 1x
<3584> כָּחַשׁ ***kāḥaš*** [DENY] 22x
<3585> כַּחַשׁ ***kaḥaš*** [LIE (noun)] 6x
<3586> כֶּחָשׁ ***keḥāš*** [LYING] 1x
<3587> כִּי ***kiy*** [BRANDING] 1x
<3588> כִּי ***kiy*** [BECAUSE] 46x
<3589> כִּיד ***kiyḏ*** [DESTRUCTION] 1x
<3590> כִּידוֹד ***kiyḏôḏ*** [SPARK] 1x
<3591> כִּידוֹן ***kiyḏôn*** [SPEAR] 9x
<3592> כִּידֹן ***kiyḏōn*** [CHIDON] 1x
<3593> כִּידוֹר ***kiyḏôr*** [BATTLE] 1x
<3594> כִּיּוּן ***kiyyûn*** [CHIUN] 1x
<3595> כִּיּוֹר ***kiyyôr*** [BASIN] 23x
<3596> כִּילַי ***kiylay,*** כֵּלַי ***kêlay*** [SCOUNDREL] 2x
<3597> כֵּילַף ***kêylap̱*** [HAMMER (noun)] 1x
<3598> כִּימָה ***kiymāh*** [PLEIADES] 3x
<3599> כִּיס ***kiys*** [BAG] 6x
<3600> כִּיר ***kiyr*** [STOVE, COOKING STOVE] 1x
<3601> כִּישׁוֹר ***kiyšôr*** [DISTAFF] 1x
<3602> כָּכָה ***kāḵāh*** [THUS] 34x
<3603> כִּכָּר ***kikkār*** [ROUND (SOMETHING)] 68x
<3604> כַּכַּר ***kakkar*** [TALENT] 1x
<3605> כֹּל ***kōl*** [ALL] 5,159x
<3606> כֹּל ***kōl*** [ALL] 75x
<3607> כָּלָא ***kālā'*** [RESTRAIN] 18x
<3608> כֶּלֶא ***kele'*** [PRISON] 10x
<3609> כִּלְאָב ***kil'āḇ*** [CHILEAB] 1x
<3610> כִּלְאַיִם ***kil'ayim*** [KIND (DIFFERENT, DIVERSE, ANOTHER] 4x
<3611> כֶּלֶב ***keleḇ*** [DOG] 32x
<3612> כָּלֵב ***kālêḇ*** [CALEB] 35x
<3613> כָּלֵב אֶפְרָתָה ***kālêḇ 'ep̱rāṯāh*** [CALEB-EPHRATAH] 1x

<3614> כָּלִבִּי ***kālibbiy*** [CALEBITE] 1x
<3615> כָּלָה ***kālāh*** [FINISH] 206x
<3616> כָּלֶה ***kāleh*** [LONGING] 1x
<3617> כָּלָה ***kālāh*** [DESTRUCTION] 22x
<3618> כַּלָּה ***kallāh*** [BRIDE] 34x
<3619> כְּלוּב ***k^{e}lûḇ*** [BASKET] 3x
<3620> כְּלוּב ***k^{e}lûḇ*** [CHELUB] 2x
<3621> כְּלוּבָי ***k^{e}lûḇāy*** [CHELUBAI] 1x
<3622> כְּלוּהוּ ***k^{e}lûhû*** [CHELLUH] 1x
<3623> כְּלוּלָה ***k^{e}lûlāh*** [BETROTHAL] 1x
<3624> כֶּלַח ***kelaḥ*** [VIGOR] 2x
<3625> כֶּלַח ***kelaḥ*** [CALAH] 2x
<3626> כָּל־חֹזֶה ***kol-ḥōzeh*** [COL-HOZEH] 2x
<3627> כְּלִי ***k^{e}liy*** [ARTICLE] 325x
<3628> כְּלִיא ***k^{e}liy',*** כְּלוּא ***k^{e}lû'*** [PRISON] 2x
<3629> כִּלְיָה ***kilyāh*** [KIDNEY] 31x
<3630> כִּלְיוֹן ***kilyôn*** [CHILION] 3x
<3631> כִּלָּיוֹן ***killāyôn*** [FAILING] 2x
<3632> כָּלִיל ***kāliyl*** [WHOLE] 15x
<3633> כַּלְכֹּל ***kalkōl*** [CALCOL] 2x
<3634> כָּלַל ***kālal*** [PERFECT (MAKE)] 2x
<3635> כְּלַל ***k^{e}lal*** [FINISH] 7x
<3636> כְּלָל ***k^{e}lāl*** [CHELAL] 1x
<3637> כָּלַם ***kālam*** [ASHAMED (BE)] 38x
<3638> כִּלְמַד ***kilmaḏ*** [CHILMAD] 1x
<3639> כְּלִמָּה ***k^{e}limmāh*** [SHAME] 30x
<3640> כְּלִמּוּת ***k^{e}limmûṯ*** [SHAME] 1x
<3641> כַּלְנֶה ***kalneh,*** כַּלְנֵה ***kalnêh,*** כַּלְנוֹ ***kalnô*** [CALNEH, CALNO] 3x
<3642> כָּמַהּ ***kāmah*** [FAINT FOR] 1x
<3643> כִּמְהָם ***kimhām,*** כִּמְהָן ***kimhān*** [CHIMHAM] 4x
<3644> כְּמוֹ ***k^{e}mô*** [LIKE] 20x
<3645> כְּמוֹשׁ ***k^{e}môš*** [CHEMOSH] 8x
<3646> כַּמֹּן ***kammōn*** [CUMIN, CUMMIN] 2x
<3647> כָּמַס ***kāmas*** [STORE (LAY IN)] 1x
<3648> כָּמַר ***kāmar*** [YEARN] 4x
<3649> כֹּמֶר ***kōmer*** [PRIEST] 3x
<3650> כִּמְרִיר ***kimriyr*** [BLACKNESS] 1x
<3651> כֵּן ***kên*** [THEREFORE] 42x
<3652> כֵּן ***kên*** [THUS] 8x
<3653> כֵּן ***kên*** [STAND (noun)] 17x
<3654> כֵּן ***kên*** [GNAT] 7x
<3655> כָּנָה ***kānāh*** [FLATTER] 4x
<3656> כַּנֶּה ***kanneh*** [CANNEH] 1x
<3657> כַּנָּה ***kannāh*** [ROOT (noun)] 1x
<3658> כִּנּוֹר ***kinnôr*** [LYRE] 42x
<3659> כָּנְיָהוּ ***konyāhû*** [CONIAH] 3x
<3660> כְּנֵמָא ***k^{e}nêmā'*** [THUS] 5x
<3661> כָּנַן ***kānan*** [SHOOT UP] 1x
<3662> כְּנָנִי ***k^{e}nāniy*** [CHENANI] 1x
<3663> כְּנַנְיָהוּ ***k^{e}nanyāhû,*** כְּנַנְיָה ***k^{e}nanyāh*** [CHENANIAH] 3x
<3664> כָּנַס ***kānas*** [GATHER] 11x

<3665> כָּנַע ***kāna'*** [SUBDUE] 36x
<3666> כִּנְעָה ***kin'āh*** [BUNDLE] 1x
<3667> כְּנַעַן ***k^{e}na'an*** [CANAAN] 94x
<3668> כְּנַעֲנָה ***k^{e}na^{a}nāh*** [CHENAANAH] 5x
<3669> כְּנַעֲנִי ***k^{e}na^{a}niy*** [CANAANITE] 70x, [MERCHANT] 3x
<3670> כָּנַף ***kānap̱*** [HIDE (verb)] 1x
<3671> כָּנָף ***kānāp̱*** [WING] 108x
<3672> כִּנְּרוֹת ***kinn^{e}rôṯ,*** כִּנֶּרֶת ***kinnereṯ*** [CHINNERETH] 7x
<3673> כְּנַשׁ ***k^{e}naš*** [GATHER] 3x
<3674> כְּנָת ***k^{e}nāṭ*** [COMPANION] 1x
<3675> כְּנָת ***k^{e}nāṯ*** [COMPANION] 7x
<3676> כֵּס ***kês*** [THRONE] 1x
<3677> כֶּסֶא ***kese',*** כֶּסֶה ***keseh*** [FULL MOON] 2x
<3678> כִּסֵּא ***kissê',*** כִּסֵּה ***kissêh*** [THRONE] 135x
<3679> כַּסְדָּי ***kasdāy*** [CHALDEAN] 1x
<3680> כָּסָה ***kāsāh*** [COVER (verb)] 152x
<3681> כָּסוּי ***kāsûy*** [COVERING] 2x
<3682> כְּסוּת ***k^{e}sûṯ*** [COVERING] 8x
<3683> כָּסַח ***kāsaḥ*** [CUT, CUT DOWN, CUT UP] 2x
<3684> כְּסִיל ***k^{e}siyl*** [FOOL, FOOLISH] 70x
<3685> כְּסִיל ***k^{e}siyl*** [CONSTELLATION] 4x
<3686> כְּסִיל ***k^{e}siyl*** [CHESIL] 1x
<3687> כְּסִילוּת ***k^{e}siylûṯ*** [FOLLY] 1x
<3688> כָּסַל ***kāsal*** [FOOLISH (BE)] 1x
<3689> כֶּסֶל ***kesel*** [LOINS] 13x
<3690> כִּסְלָה ***kislāh*** [CONFIDENCE] 2x
<3691> כִּסְלֵו ***kislêw*** [CHISLEV] 2x
<3692> כִּסְלוֹן ***kislôn*** [CHISLON] 1x
<3693> כְּסָלוֹן ***k^{e}sālôn*** [CHESALON] 1x
<3694> כְּסוּלּוֹת ***k^{e}sûllôṯ*** [CHESULLOTH] 1x
<3695> כַּסְלֻחִים ***kasluḥiym*** [CASLUHIM] 2x
<3696> כִּסְלֹת תָּבֹר ***kislōṯ tāḇōr*** [CHISLOTH TABOR] 1x
<3697> כָּסַם ***kāsam*** [TRIM] 2x
<3698> כֻּסֶּמֶת ***kussemeṯ*** [SPELT] 3x
<3699> כָּסַס ***kāsas*** [COUNT (MAKE ONE'S)] 1x
<3700> כָּסַף ***kāsap̱*** [LONG FOR] 5x
<3701> כֶּסֶף ***kesep̱*** [SILVER] 403x
<3702> כְּסַף ***k^{e}sap̱*** [SILVER] 13x
<3703> כָּסִפְיָא ***kāsip̱yā'*** [CASIPHIA] 1x
<3704> כֶּסֶת ***keseṯ*** [MAGIC BAND] 2x
<3705> כְּעַן ***k^e'an*** [NOW] 13x
<3706> כְּעֶנֶת ***k^e'eneṯ,*** כְּעֶת ***k^e'eṯ*** [NOW, AND NOW] 4x
<3707> כָּעַס ***kā'as*** [ANGER (PROVOKE TO)] 54x
<3708> כַּעַס ***ka'as,*** כַּעַשׂ ***ka'aś*** [PROVOCATION] 25x
<3709> כַּף ***kap̱*** [HAND] 192x
<3710> כֵּף ***kêp̱*** [ROCK] 2x
<3711> כָּפָה ***kāp̱āh*** [PACIFY] 1x
<3712> כִּפָּה ***kippāh*** [BRANCH] 3x
<3713> כְּפוֹר ***k^{e}p̱ôr*** [BOWL] 3x, [FROST] 3x
<3714> כָּפִיס ***kāp̱iys*** [BEAM] 1x
<3715> כְּפִיר ***k^{e}p̱iyr*** [LION (YOUNG)] 32x

<3716> כְּפִירָה ***k***^{e}***p̱iyrāh*** [CHEPHIRAH] 4x

<3717> כָּפַל ***kāp̱al*** [DOUBLE (verb)] 4x

<3718> כֶּפֶל ***kep̱el*** [DOUBLE, DOUBLED] 3x

<3719> כָּפַן ***kāp̱an*** [BEND] 1x

<3720> כָּפָן ***kāp̱ān*** [FAMINE] 2x

<3721> כָּפַף ***kāp̱ap̱*** [BOW, BOW DOWN] 5x

<3722> כָּפַר ***kāp̱ar*** [COVER (verb)] 102x

<3723> כָּפָר ***kāp̱ār*** [VILLAGE] 2x

<3724> כֹּפֶר ***kōp̱er*** [RANSOM (noun)] 17x

<3725> כִּפֻּרִים ***kippuriym*** [ATONEMENT] 8x

<3726> כְּפַר הָעַמּוֹנִי ***k***^{e}***p̱ar haʿam-môniy*** [CHEPHAR-AMMONI] 1x

<3727> כַּפֹּרֶת ***kappōreṯ*** [MERCY SEAT] 27x

<3728> כָּפַשׁ ***kāp̱aš*** [COWER (MAKE)] 1x

<3729> כְּפַת ***k***^{e}***p̱aṯ*** [BIND] 4x

<3730> כַּפְתּוֹר ***kaptôr,*** כַּפְתֹּר ***kap̱tōr*** [BULB] 18x

<3731> כַּפְתּוֹר ***kaptôr,*** כַּפְתֹּר ***kap̱tōr*** [CAPHTOR] 3x

<3732> כַּפְתֹּרִי ***kap̱tōriy*** [CAPHTORITE] 3x

<3733> כַּר ***kar*** [LAMB] 16x

<3734> כֹּר ***kōr*** [COR] 9x

<3735> כְּרָה ***k***^{e}***rāh*** [GRIEVED (BE)] 1x

<3736> כִּרְבֵּל ***kirbêl*** [CLOTHED WITH, CLOTHED IN (BE)] 1x

<3737> כַּרְבְּלָה ***karb***^{e}***lāh*** [HAT] 1x

<3738> כָּרָה ***kārāh*** [DIG] 16x

<3739> כָּרָה ***kārāh*** [BUY] 5x

<3740> כֵּרָה ***kêrāh*** [BANQUET] 1x

<3741> כָּרָה ***kārāh*** [CAVE] 1x

<3742> כְּרוּב ***k***^{e}***rûḇ*** [CHERUB, CHERUBIM] 91x

<3743> כְּרוּב ***k***^{e}***rûḇ*** [CHERUB] 2x

<3744> כָּרוֹז ***kārôz*** [HERALD] 1x

<3745> כְּרַז ***k***^{e}***raz*** [PROCLAMATION] 1x

<3746> כָּרִי ***kāriy*** [CAPTAIN] 3x

<3747> כְּרִית ***k***^{e}***riyṯ*** [CHERITH] 2x

<3748> כְּרִיתוּת ***k***^{e}***riyṯûṯ*** [DIVORCE] 4x

<3749> כַּרְכֹּב ***karkōḇ*** [LEDGE] 2x

<3750> כַּרְכֹּם ***karkōm*** [SAFFRON] 1x

<3751> כַּרְכְּמִישׁ ***kark***^{e}***miyš*** [CARCHEMISH] 3x

<3752> כַּרְכַּס ***karkas*** [CARCAS] 1x

<3753> כִּרְכָּרָה ***kirkārāh*** [CAMEL] 1x

<3754> כֶּרֶם ***kerem*** [VINEYARD] 93x

<3755> כֹּרֵם ***kōrêm*** [VINEDRESSER] 5x

<3756> כַּרְמִי ***karmiy*** [CARMI] 8x

<3757> כַּרְמִי ***karmiy*** [CARMITE] 1x

<3758> כַּרְמִיל ***karmiyl*** [CRIMSON] 3x

<3759> כַּרְמֶל ***karmel*** [FIELD (FERTILE, FRUITFUL, PLENTIFUL)] 13x

<3760> כַּרְמֶל ***karmel*** [CARMEL] 26x

<3761> כַּרְמְלִי ***karm***^{e}***liy*** [CARMELITE] 5x

<3762> כַּרְמְלִית ***karm***^{e}***liyṯ*** [CARMELITESS] 2x

<3763> כְּרָן ***k***^{e}***rān*** [CHERAN] 2x

<3764> כָּרְסֵא ***korsê'*** [THRONE] 2x

<3765> כִּרְסֵם ***kirsêm*** [RAVAGE (verb)] 1x

<3766> כָּרַע ***kāraʿ*** [BOW (verb)] 35x

<3767> כְּרַע ***kᵉra‘*** [LEG] 9x
<3768> כַּרְפַּס ***karpas*** [LINEN] 1x
<3769> כָּרַר ***kārar*** [DANCE (verb)] 2x
<3770> כָּרֵשׂ ***kārēś*** [STOMACH] 1x
<3771> כַּרְשְׁנָא ***karšᵉnā’*** [CARSHENA] 1x
<3772> כָּרַת ***kāraṯ*** [CUT (verb)] 288x
<3773> כְּרֻתוֹת ***kᵉruṯôṯ*** [BEAM] 3x
<3774> כְּרֵתִי ***kᵉrēṯiy*** [KERETHITES] 10x
<3775> כֶּשֶׂב ***keśeḇ*** [SHEEP] 13x
<3776> כִּשְׂבָּה ***kiśbāh*** [LAMB] 1x
<3777> כֶּשֶׂד ***keśeḏ*** [CHESED] 1x
<3778> כַּשְׂדִּים ***kaśdiym*** [CHALDEAN] 80x
<3779> כַּשְׂדָּי ***kaśdāy*** [CHALDEAN] 8x
<3780> כָּשָׂה ***kāśāh*** [OBESE (BE)] 1x
<3781> כַּשִּׁיל ***kaššiyl*** [AX] 1x
<3782> כָּשַׁל ***kāšal*** [FALL (verb)] 65x
<3783> כִּשָּׁלוֹן ***kiššālôn*** [FALL (noun)] 1x
<3784> כָּשַׁף ***kāšap̱*** [WITCHCRAFT (USE, PRACTICE)] 3x
<3785> כֶּשֶׁף ***kešep̱*** [SORCERY] 6x
<3786> כַּשָּׁף ***kaššāp̱*** [SORCERER] 1x
<3787> כָּשֵׁר ***kāšêr*** [SUCCESS (BRING, GIVE)] 3x
<3788> כִּשְׁרוֹן ***kišrôn*** [SKILL] 3x
<3789> כָּתַב ***kāṯaḇ*** [WRITE] 223x
<3790> כְּתַב ***kᵉṯaḇ*** [WRITE] 8x
<3791> כְּתָב ***kᵉṯāḇ*** [WRITING] 17x
<3792> כְּתָב ***kᵉṯāḇ*** [WRITING] 12x
<3793> כְּתֹבֶת ***kᵉṯōḇeṯ*** [MARK (noun)] 1x
<3794> כִּתִּי ***kittiy*** [KITTIM] 8x
<3795> כָּתִית ***kāṯiyṯ*** [BEATEN] 5x
<3796> כֹּתֶל ***kōṯel*** [WALL] 1x
<3797> כְּתַל ***kᵉṯal*** [WALL] 2x
<3798> כִּתְלִישׁ ***kiṯliyš*** [KITHLISH] 1x
<3799> כָּתַם ***kāṯam*** [MARKED (BE)] 1x
<3800> כֶּתֶם ***keṯem*** [GOLD, FINE GOLD, PURE GOLD] 9x
<3801> כֻּתֹּנֶת ***kuttōneṯ*** [COAT (noun)] 29x
<3802> כָּתֵף ***kāṯêp̱*** [SHOULDER] 67x
<3803> כָּתַר ***kāṯar*** [SURROUND] 7x
<3804> כֶּתֶר ***keṯer*** [CROWN (noun)] 3x
<3805> כֹּתֶרֶת ***kōṯereṯ*** [CAPITAL] 24x
<3806> כָּתַשׁ ***kāṯaš*** [GRIND] 1x
<3807> כָּתַת ***kāṯaṯ*** [CRUSH] 17x

ל Lamedh

<3808> לֹא ***lō’,*** לוֹא ***lô’,*** לֹה ***lōh*** [NO, NOT, NEVER] 76x
<3809> לָא ***lā’*** [NO, NOT, NEVER] 82x
<3810> לֹא דְבָר ***lō’ ḏᵉḇār,*** לוֹ דְבָר ***lô ḏᵉḇār*** [LO DEBAR] 3x
<3811> לָאָה ***lā’āh*** [WEARY (BE, BECOME)] 19x
<3812> לֵאָה ***lê’āh*** [LEAH] 34x

<3813> לָאַט ***lā'aṭ*** [COVER (verb)] 1x
<3814> לָאט ***lā'ṭ*** [SOFTLY] 1x
<3815> לָאֵל ***lā'êl*** [LAEL] 1x
<3816> לְאוֹם ***lᵉ'ôm,*** לְאֹם ***lᵉ'ōm*** [PEOPLE] 35x
<3817> לְאֻמִּים ***lᵉ'ummiym*** [LEUMMIM] 1x
<3818> לֹא עַמִּי ***lō' 'ammiy*** [LO-AMMI] 2x
<3819> לֹא רֻחָמָה ***lō' ruḥāmāh*** [LO-RUHAMAH] 3x
<3820> לֵב ***lêḇ*** [HEART] 593x
<3821> לֵב ***lêḇ*** [HEART] 1x
<3822> לְבָאוֹת ***lᵉḇā'ôṯ*** [LEBAOTH] 1x
<3823> לָבַב ***lāḇaḇ*** [HEART (RAVISH THE)] 5x
<3824> לֵבָב ***lêḇāḇ*** [HEART] 252x
<3825> לְבַב ***lêḇaḇ*** [HEART] 7x
<3826> לִבָּה ***libbāh*** [HEART] 8x
<3827> לַבָּה ***labbāh*** [FLAME] 1x
<3828> לְבוֹנָה ***lᵉḇônah,*** לְבֹנָה ***lᵉḇōnāh*** [INCENSE] 21x
<3829> לְבוֹנָה ***lᵉḇônāh*** [LEBONAH] 1x
<3830> לְבוּשׁ ***lᵉḇûš,*** לְבֻשׁ ***lᵉḇuš,*** לָבוּשׁ ***lāḇûš,*** לָבֻשׁ ***lāḇuš*** [CLOTHING] 32x
<3831> לְבוּשׁ ***lᵉḇûš*** [CLOTHING] 2x
<3832> לָבַט ***lāḇaṭ*** [RUIN (COME TO)] 3x
<3833> לָבֶא ***leḇe',*** לְבָאָה ***liḇ'āh,*** לְבִיָּא ***lᵉḇiyyā',*** לָבִיא ***lāḇiy'*** [LION, LIONESS] 14x
<3834> לְבִבָה ***lᵉḇiḇāh*** [CAKE] 3x
<3835> לָבֵן ***lāḇên*** [BRICK (MAKE)] 3x
<3836> לָבָן ***lāḇān*** [WHITE] 29x
<3837> לָבָן ***lāḇān*** [LABAN] 55x
<3838> לְבָנָה ***lᵉḇānāh*** [LEBANAH] 2x
<3839> לִבְנֶה ***liḇneh*** [POPLAR] 2x
<3840> לִבְנָה ***liḇnāh*** [PAVEMENT] 1x
<3841> לִבְנָה ***liḇnāh*** [LIBNAH] 18x
<3842> לְבָנָה ***lᵉḇānāh*** [MOON] 3x
<3843> לְבֵנָה ***lᵉḇênāh*** [BRICK] 11x
<3844> לְבָנוֹן ***lᵉḇānôn*** [LEBANON] 71x
<3845> לִבְנִי ***liḇniy*** [LIBNI] 5x
<3846> לִבְנִי ***liḇniy,*** לֵב קָמָי ***lêḇ qāmāy*** [LIBNITE] 3x
<3847> לָבַשׁ ***lāḇaš,*** לָבֵשׁ ***lāḇêš*** [CLOTHE] 112x
<3848> לְבַשׁ ***lᵉḇaš*** [CLOTHE] 3x
<3849> לֹג ***lōg̱*** [LOG] 5x
<3850> לֹד ***lōḏ*** [LOD] 4x
<3851> לַהַב ***lahaḇ*** [FLAME] 12x
<3852> לֶהָבָה ***lehāḇāh*** [FLAME] 19x
<3853> לְהָבִים ***lᵉhāḇiym*** [LEHABITES] 2x
<3854> לַהַג ***lahag̱*** [STUDY (noun)] 1x
<3855> לָהַד ***lāhaḏ*** [LAHAD] 1x
<3856> לָהַהּ ***lāhah,*** לָהָה ***lāhāh*** [MADMAN] 1x, [LANGUISH] 1x
<3857> לָהַט ***lāhaṭ*** [BURN (verb)] 11x
<3858> לַהַט ***lahaṭ,*** לְהָטִים ***lᵉhāṭiym*** [FLAMING] 2x
<3859> לָהַם ***lāham*** [MORSEL (DAINTY, DELICIOUS, CHOICE)] 2x
<3860> לָהֵן ***lāhên*** [THEREFORE] 1x
<3861> לָהֵן ***lāhên*** [THEREFORE] 10x
<3862> לַהֲקָה ***lahᵃqāh*** [COMPANY] 1x

<3863> לֻא ***lu'***, לוּ ***lû***, לוּא ***lû'*** [OH THAT] 22x
<3864> לוּבִי ***lûḇiy*** [LUBIM] 4x
<3865> לוּד ***lûḏ*** [LUD, LYDIA] 5x
<3866> לוּדִים ***lûḏiym*** [LUDITES, LYDIANS] 3x
<3867> לָוָה ***lāwāh*** [BORROW] 10x, [JOIN] 16x
<3868> לוּז ***lûz*** [PERVERSE] 6x
<3869> לוּז ***lûz*** [ALMOND TREE] 1x
<3870> לוּז ***lûz*** [LUZ] 8x
<3871> לוּחַ ***lûaḥ*** [BOARD] 43x
<3872> לוּחִית ***lûḥiyṯ*** [LUHITH] 2x
<3873> הַלּוֹחֵשׁ ***hallôḥêš*** [HALLOHESH] 2x
<3874> לוּט ***lûṭ*** [WRAP] 3x
<3875> לוֹט ***lôṭ*** [COVERING] 1x
<3876> לוֹט ***lôṭ*** [LOT (proper noun)] 33x
<3877> לוֹטָן ***lôṭān*** [LOTAN] 7x
<3878> לֵוִי ***lêwiy*** [LEVI] 64x
<3879> לֵוָי ***lêwāy*** [LEVITE] 4x
<3880> לִוְיָה ***liwyāh*** [GARLAND] 2x
<3881> לֵוִי ***lêwiy*** [LEVITE] 286x
<3882> לִוְיָתָן ***liwyāṯān*** [LEVIATHAN] 6x
<3883> לוּל ***lûl*** [STAIRWAY] 1x
<3884> לוּלֵא ***lûlê'***, לוּלֵי ***lûlêy*** [IF NOT] 14x
<3885> לִין ***liyn***, לוּן ***lûn*** [LODGE (verb)] 73x, [MURMUR] 14x
<3886> לָעַע ***lā'a'*** [SWALLOW (verb)] 3x
<3887> לוּץ ***lûṣ***, לִיץ ***liyṣ***, לֵץ ***lêṣ*** [MOCK] 27x
<3888> לוּשׁ ***lûš*** [KNEAD] 5x
<3889> לָוִשׁ ***lāwiš*** [LAISH] 1x
<3890> לְוָת ***l***^{e}***wāṯ*** [FROM] 1x
<3891> לָזוּת ***lāzûṯ*** [PERVERSITY] 1x
<3892> לַח ***laḥ*** [GREEN] 6x
<3893> לֵחַ ***lêaḥ*** [VIGOR] 1x
<3894> לְחוּם ***l***^{e}***ḥûm*** [ENTRAILS] 2x
<3895> לְחִי ***l***^{e}***ḥiy*** [JAW] 21x
<3896> לֶחִי ***leḥiy*** [LEHI] 3x
<3897> לָחַךְ ***lāḥaḵ*** [LICK, LICK UP] 6x
<3898> לָחַם ***lāḥam*** [EAT] 6x, [FIGHT] 171x
<3899> לֶחֶם ***leḥem*** [BREAD] 297x
<3900> לְחֶם ***l***^{e}***ḥem*** [FEAST] 1x
<3901> לָחֶם ***lāḥem*** [WAR] 1x
<3902> לַחְמִי ***laḥmiy*** [LAHMI] 1x
<3903> לַחְמָס ***laḥmās*** [LAHMAS] 1x
<3904> לְחֵנָה ***l***^{e}***ḥênāh*** [CONCUBINE] 3x
<3905> לָחַץ ***lāḥaṣ*** [OPPRESS] 19x
<3906> לַחַץ ***laḥaṣ*** [OPPRESSION] 12x
<3907> לָחַשׁ ***lāḥaš*** [WHISPER (verb)] 3x
<3908> לַחַשׁ ***laḥaš*** [CHARM] 5x
<3909> לָט ***lāṭ*** [ENCHANTMENT] 6x
<3910> לֹט ***lōṭ*** [MYRRH] 2x
<3911> לְטָאָה ***l***^{e}***ṭā'āh*** [LIZARD] 1x
<3912> לְטוּשִׁם ***l***^{e}***ṭûšiym*** [LETUSHITES] 1x
<3913> לָטַשׁ ***lāṭaš*** [SHARPEN] 5x

<3914> לֹיָה ***lōyāh*** [WREATH] 3x

<3915> לַיְלָה ***laylāh,*** לָיִל ***lāyilā,*** לַיִל ***layil*** [NIGHT, MIDNIGHT] 233x

<3916> לֵילְיָא ***lêyl^{e}yā'*** [NIGHT] 5x

<3917> לִילִית ***liyliyṯ*** [NIGHT BIRD, NIGHT CREATURE, NIGHT MONSTER] 1x

<3918> לַיִשׁ ***layiš*** [LION] 3x

<3919> לַיִשׁ ***layiš,*** לַיְשָׁה ***lay^{e}šāh*** [LAISH] 7x

<3920> לָכַד ***lāḵaḏ*** [CAPTURE (verb)] 121x

<3921> לֶכֶד ***leḵeḏ*** [CAPTURE (noun)] 1x

<3922> לֵכָה ***lêḵāh*** [LECAH] 1x

<3923> לָכִישׁ ***lāḵiyš*** [LACHISH] 24x

<3924> לֻלָאוֹת ***lulā'ôṯ*** [LOOPS] 13x

<3925> לָמַד ***lāmaḏ*** [LEARN] 86x

<3926> לְמוֹ ***l^{e}mô*** [FOR] 4x

<3927> לְמוּאֵל ***l^{e}mû'ēl,*** לְמוֹאֵל ***l^{e}mô'ēl*** [LEMUEL] 2x

<3928> לִמּוּד ***limmûḏ,*** לִמֻּד ***limmuḏ*** [ACCUSTOMED] 6x

<3929> לֶמֶךְ ***lemeḵ*** [LAMECH] 11x

<3930> לֹעַ ***lōa'*** [THROAT] 1x

<3931> לָעַב ***lā'aḇ*** [MOCK] 1x

<3932> לָעַג ***lā'ag̱*** [MOCK] 18x

<3933> לַעַג ***la'ag̱*** [SCORN (noun)] 7x

<3934> לָעֵג ***lā'ēg̱*** [STAMMERING] 2x

<3935> לַעְדָּה ***la'dāh*** [LAADAH] 1x

<3936> לַעְדָּן ***la'dān*** [LADAN] 7x

<3937> לָעַז ***lā'az*** [LANGUAGE (OF STRANGE)] 1x

<3938> לָעַט ***lā'aṭ*** [FEED (verb)] 1x

<3939> לַעֲנָה ***la^{a}nāh*** [WORMWOOD] 8x

<3940> לַפִּיד ***lappiyḏ*** [TORCH] 14x

<3941> לַפִּידוֹת ***lappiyḏôṯ*** [LAPPIDOTH] 1x

<3942> לִפְנֵי ***lip̱nāy*** [FRONT OF (IN)] 1x

<3943> לָפַת ***lāp̱aṯ*** [HOLD OF (TAKE)] 3x

<3944> לָצוֹן ***laṣôn*** [MOCKER] 3x

<3945> לְצָצִים ***l^{e}ṣaṣiym,*** לָצַץ ***lāṣaṣ*** [MOCKER] 1x

<3946> לַקּוּם ***laqqûm*** [LAKKUM] 1x

<3947> לָקַח ***lāqaḥ*** [TAKE] 965x

<3948> לֶקַח ***leqaḥ*** [LEARNING] 9x

<3949> לִקְחִי ***liqḥiy*** [LIKHI] 1x

<3950> לָקַט ***lāqaṭ*** [GATHER] 37x

<3951> לֶקֶט ***leqeṭ*** [GLEANING] 2x

<3952> לָקַק ***lāqaq*** [LAP (verb)] 7x

<3953> לָקַשׁ ***lāqaš*** [GLEAN] 1x

<3954> לֶקֶשׁ ***leqeš*** [CROP] 2x

<3955> לָשָׁד ***lāšāḏ*** [CAKE BAKED] 2x

<3956> לָשׁוֹן ***lāšôn,*** לָשֹׁן ***lāšōn*** [TONGUE] 117x

<3957> לִשְׁכָּה ***liškāh*** [ROOM] 47x

<3958> לֶשֶׁם ***lešem*** [JACINTH] 2x

<3959> לֶשֶׁם ***lešem*** [LESHEM] 2x

<3960> לָשַׁן ***lāšan*** [SLANDER] 3x

<3961> לִשָּׁן ***liššān*** [LANGUAGE] 7x

<3962> לֶשַׁע ***leša'*** [LASHA] 1x

<3963> לֶתֶךְ ***leṯeḵ*** [LETHECH] 1x

מ Mem

<3964> מָא ***mā'*** [WHAT] 1x
<3965> מַאֲבוּס ***maᵃḇûs*** [GRANARY] 1x
<3966> מְאֹד ***mᵉ'ōḏ*** [VERY] 299x
<3967> מֵאָה ***mê'āh*** [HUNDRED] 581x
<3968> מֵאָה ***mê'āh*** [MEAH] 2x
<3969> מְאָה ***mᵉ'āh*** [HUNDRED] 8x
<3970> מַאְוַי ***ma'way*** [DESIRE (noun)] 1x
<3971> מוּם ***mûm,*** מאוּם ***m'ûm,*** מֻאום ***mu'wm*** [DEFECT] 22x
<3972> מְאוּמָה ***mᵉ'ûmāh,*** מוּמָה ***mûmāh*** [ANYTHING] 32x
<3973> מָאוֹס ***mā'ôs*** [REFUSE (noun)] 1x
<3974> מָאוֹר ***mā'ôr,*** מָאֹר ***mā'ōr*** [LIGHT (noun)] 19x
<3975> מְאוּרָה ***mᵉ'ûrāh*** [DEN] 1x
<3976> מֹאזְנַיִם ***mō'zᵉnayim*** [SCALES] 15x
<3977> מֹאזְנֵא ***mō'zᵉnê'*** [SCALES] 1x
<3978> מַאֲכָל ***maᵃḵāl*** [FOOD] 30x
<3979> מַאֲכֶלֶת ***maᵃḵeleṯ*** [KNIFE] 4x
<3980> מַאֲכֹלֶת ***maᵃḵōleṯ*** [FUEL] 2x
<3981> מַאֲמָץ ***maᵃmāṣ*** [FORCES] 1x
<3982> מַאֲמַר ***maᵃmar*** [COMMAND (noun)] 3x
<3983> מֵאמַר ***mê'mar*** [REQUEST] 2x
<3984> מָאן ***mā'n*** [VESSEL] 7x
<3985> מָאַן ***mā'an*** [REFUSE (verb)] 41x
<3986> מָאֵן ***mā'ên*** [REFUSE (verb)] 4x
<3987> מֵאֵן ***mê'ên*** [REFUSE (verb)] 1x
<3988> מָאַס ***mā'as*** [REJECT] 76x
<3989> מַאֲפֶה ***maᵃp̱eh*** [BAKED] 1x
<3990> מַאֲפֵל ***maᵃp̱êl*** [DARKNESS] 1x
<3991> מַאְפֵלְיָה ***ma'pêlyāh*** [DARKNESS] 1x
<3992> מָאַר ***mā'ar*** [PAINFUL (BE)] 4x
<3993> מַאֲרָב ***maᵃrāḇ*** [AMBUSH] 5x
<3994> מְאֵרָה ***mᵉ'êrāh*** [CURSE (noun)] 5x
<3995> מִבְדָּלָה ***miḇdālāh*** [SEPARATE (adj.)] 1x
<3996> מָבוֹא ***māḇô'*** [ENTRANCE] 24x
<3997> מְבוֹאָה ***mᵉḇô'āh*** [ENTRANCE] 1x
<3998> מְבוּכָה ***mᵉḇûḵāh*** [PERPLEXITY] 2x
<3999> מַבּוּל ***mabbûl*** [FLOOD] 13x
<4000> מְבוּנִים ***mᵉḇûniym*** [TAUGHT (WHO)] 1x
<4001> מְבוּסָה ***mᵉḇûsāh*** [TREADING DOWN] 3x
<4002> מַבּוּעַ ***mabbûaʿ*** [SPRING] 3x
<4003> מְבוּקָה ***mᵉḇûqāh*** [DESOLATE] 1x
<4004> מָבְחוֹר ***māḇḥôr*** [CHOICE, CHOICEST] 2x
<4005> מִבְחָר ***miḇḥār*** [CHOICE, CHOICEST] 12x
<4006> מִבְחָר ***miḇḥār*** [MIBHAR] 1x
<4007> מַבָּט ***mabbāṭ*** [HOPE (noun)] 3x
<4008> מִבְטָא ***miḇṭā'*** [RASH] 2x
<4009> מִבְטָח ***miḇṭāḥ*** [TRUST (noun)] 15x
<4010> מַבְלִיגִית ***maḇliygiyṯ*** [COMFORTER] 1x
<4011> מִבְנֶה ***miḇneh*** [STRUCTURE] 1x

<4012> מְבֻנַּי ***mᵉḇunnay*** [MEBUNNAI] 1x
<4013> מִבְצָר ***miḇṣār*** [FORTIFICATION] 37x
<4014> מִבְצָר ***miḇṣār*** [MIBZAR] 2x
<4015> מִבְרָח ***miḇrāḥ*** [FUGITIVE] 1x
<4016> מְבוּשִׁים ***mᵉḇûšiym*** [PRIVATE PARTS] 1x
<4017> מִבְשָׂם ***miḇśām*** [MIBSAM] 3x
<4018> מְבַשְּׁלוֹת ***mᵉḇaššᵉlôṯ*** [HEARTHS] 1x
<4019> מַגְבִּישׁ ***magḇiyš*** [MAGBISH] 1x
<4020> מִגְבָּלוֹת ***migḇālôṯ*** [BRAIDED] 1x
<4021> מִגְבָּעָה ***migḇāʿāh*** [CAP] 4x
<4022> מֶגֶד ***meg̱eḏ*** [PRECIOUS THING] 8x
<4023> מְגִדּוֹ ***mᵉg̱iddô,*** מְגִדּוֹן ***mᵉg̱iddôn*** [MEGIDDO] 12x
<4024> מִגְדּוֹל ***migdôl,*** מִגְדֹּל ***migḏōl*** [TOWER] 7x
<4025> מַגְדִּיאֵל ***mag̱diyʾēl*** [MAGDIEL] 2x
<4026> מִגְדָּל ***mig̱dāl*** [TOWER] 50x
<4027> מִגְדַּל־אֵל ***mig̱dal ʾēl*** [MIGDAL EL] 1x
<4028> מִגְדַּל־גָּד ***mig̱dal gāḏ*** [MIGDAL GAD] 1x
<4029> מִגְדַּל־עֵדֶר ***mig̱dal-ʿēḏer*** [MIGDAL EDER] 1x
<4030> מִגְדָּנָה ***mig̱dānāh*** [PRECIOUS THING] 4x
<4031> מָגוֹג ***māg̱ôg*** [MAGOG] 4x
<4032> מָגוֹר ***māg̱ôr*** [TERROR] 8x
<4033> מָגוּר ***māg̱ûr,*** מָגוֹר ***mag̱ôr*** [SOJOURNING] 11x
<4034> מְגוֹרָה ***mᵉg̱ôrāh*** [FEAR (noun)] 1x
<4035> מְגוּרָה ***mᵉg̱ûrāh*** [FEAR (noun)] 3x
<4036> מָגוֹר מִסָּבִיב ***māg̱ôr mis-sāḇiyḇ*** [MAGOR-MISSABIB] 1x
<4037> מַגְזֵרָה ***mag̱zērāh*** [AX] 1x
<4038> מַגָּל ***maggāl*** [SICKLE] 2x
<4039> מְגִלָּה ***mᵉg̱illāh*** [SCROLL] 21x
<4040> מְגִלָּה ***mᵉg̱illāh*** [SCROLL] 1x
<4041> מְגַמָּה ***mᵉg̱ammāh*** [HORDE] 1x
<4042> מָגַן ***māg̱an*** [DELIVER] 3x
<4043> מָגֵן ***māg̱ēn*** [SHIELD (noun)] 63x
<4044> מְגִנָּה ***mᵉg̱innāh*** [SORROW (noun)] 1x
<4045> מִגְעֶרֶת ***mig̱ʿereṯ*** [REBUKE (noun)] 1x
<4046> מַגֵּפָה ***maggēp̄āh*** [PLAGUE (noun)] 21x
<4047> מַגְפִּיעָשׁ ***mag̱piyʿāš*** [MAGPIASH] 1x
<4048> מָגַר ***māg̱ar*** [DELIVER OVER] 2x
<4049> מְגַר ***mᵉg̱ar*** [OVERTHROW (verb)] 1x
<4050> מְגֵרָה ***mᵉg̱ērāh*** [SAW (noun)] 4x
<4051> מִגְרוֹן ***mig̱rôn*** [MIGRON] 2x
<4052> מִגְרָעָה ***mig̱rāʿāh*** [LEDGE (NARROW, NARROWED, OFFSET)] 1x
<4053> מֶגְרָפָה ***meg̱rāp̄āh*** [CLOD] 1x
<4054> מִגְרָשׁ ***mig̱rāš*** [PASTURELAND] 111x
<4055> מַד ***maḏ*** [CLOTHES] 12x
<4056> מַדְבַּח ***maḏbaḥ*** [ALTAR] 1x
<4057> מִדְבָּר ***miḏbār*** [DESERT (noun)] 270x, [MOUTH] 1x
<4058> מָדַד ***māḏaḏ*** [MEASURE (verb)] 51x
<4059> מִדַּד ***middaḏ*** [GONE] 1x
<4060> מִדָּה ***middāh*** [MEASURE (noun)] 54x, [TAX (noun)] 1x
<4061> מִדָּה ***middāh,*** מִנְדָּה ***mindāh*** [TRIBUTE] 4x
<4062> מַדְהֵבָה ***maḏhēḇāh*** [FURY] 1x

<4063> מַדְוֶה **maḏweh** [GARMENT] 2x

<4064> מַדְוֶה **maḏweh** [DISEASE] 2x

<4065> מַדּוּחַ **maddûaḥ** [MISLEADING] 1x

<4066> מָדוֹן **māḏôn** [STRIFE] 18x

<4067> מָדוֹן **māḏôn** [STATURE] 1x

<4068> מָדוֹן **māḏôn** [MADON] 2x

<4069> מַדּוּעַ **maddûa’,** מַדֻּעַ **maddûa’** [WHEREFORE] 72x

<4070> מְדוֹר **m**^{e}**ḏôr,** מְדָר **m**^{e}**ḏār** [DWELLING, DWELLING PLACE] 4x

<4071> מְדוּרָה **m**^{e}**ḏûrāh** [PILE] 2x

<4072> מִדְחֶה **miḏḥeh** [RUIN (noun)] 1x

<4073> מַדְחֵפָה **maḏḥêp̱āh** [OVERTHROW (verb)] 1x

<4074> מָדַי **māḏay** [MADAI] 16x

<4075> מָדִי **māḏiy** [MEDE] 1x

<4076> מָדַי **māḏay** [MEDES] 5x

<4077> מָדָיָא **māḏāy’ā** [MEDE] 1x

<4078> מַדַּי **madday** [SUFFICIENTLY] 1x

<4079> מִדְיָנִים **miḏyāniym** [CONTENTIONS] 9x

<4080> מִדְיָן **miḏyān** [MIDIAN] 59x

<4081> מִדִּין **middiyn** [MIDDIN] 1x

<4082> מְדִינָה **m**^{e}**ḏiynāh** [PROVINCE] 44x

<4083> מְדִינָה **m**^{e}**ḏiynāh** [PROVINCE] 11x

<4084> מִדְיָנִי **miḏyāniy** [MIDIANITE] 7x

<4085> מְדֹכָה **m**^{e}**ḏōḵāh** [MORTAR] 1x

<4086> מַדְמֵן **maḏmên** [MADMEN] 1x

<4087> מַדְמֵנָה **maḏmênāh** [DUNGHILL] 1x

<4088> מַדְמֵנָה **maḏmênāh** [MADMENAH] 1x

<4089> מַדְמַנָּה **maḏmannāh** [MADMANNAH] 2x

<4090> מְדָנִים **m**^{e}**ḏāniym** [STRIFES] 3x

<4091> מְדָן **m**^{e}**ḏan** [MEDAN] 2x

<4092> מְדָנִי **m**^{e}**ḏāniy** [MIDIANITE] 1x

<4093> מַדָּע **maddā’** [KNOWLEDGE] 6x

<4094> מַדְקֵרָה **maḏqêrāh** [THRUST] 1x

<4095> מַדְרֵגָה **maḏrêg̱āh** [CLIFF] 2x

<4096> מִדְרָךְ **miḏrāḵ** [FOOTSTEP] 1x

<4097> מִדְרָשׁ **miḏrāš** [STORY] 2x

<4098> מְדֻשָׁה **m**^{e}**ḏušāh** [THRESHING (noun)] 1x

<4099> הַמְּדָתָא **hamm**^{e}**ḏāṯā’** [HAMMEDATHA] 5x

<4100> מָה **māh,** מֶה **meh** [WHAT?] 725x

<4101> מָה **māh** [WHAT?] 13x

<4102> מָהַהּ **māhah** [LINGER] 9x

<4103> מְהוּמָה **m**^{e}**hûmāh** [CONFUSION] 12x

<4104> מְהוּמָן **m**^{e}**hûmān** [MEHUMAN] 1x

<4105> מְהֵיטַבְאֵל **m**^{e}**hêyṭaḇ’êl** [MEHETABEL] 3x

<4106> מָהִיר **māhiyr** [SKILLED] 4x

<4107> מָהַל **māhal** [MIX] 1x

<4108> מַהְלְכִים **mahl**^{e}**ḵiym** [ACCESS] 1x

<4109> מַהֲלָךְ **mah**^{a}**lāḵ** [JOURNEY (noun)] 4x

<4110> מַהֲלָל **mah**^{a}**lāl** [PRAISE (noun)] 1x

<4111> מַהֲלַלְאֵל **mah**^{a}**lal’êl** [MAHALALEL] 7x

<4112> מַהֲלֻמוֹת **mah**^{a}**lumôṯ** [BEATINGS] 2x

<4113> מַהֲמֹר **mah**^{a}**mōr** [PIT (MIRY, DEEP)] 1x

<4114> מַהְפֵּכָה ***mahpêḵāh*** [OVERTHROW (noun and verb)] 6x
<4115> מַהְפֶּכֶת ***mahpeḵeṯ*** [STOCKS] 4x
<4116> מָהַר ***māhar*** [HURRY] 64x
<4117> מָהַר ***māhar*** [ENDOW] 2x
<4118> מַהֵר ***mahêr*** [QUICK, QUICKLY] 18x
<4119> מֹהַר ***mōhar*** [DOWRY] 3x
<4120> מְהֵרָה ***mᵉhêrāh*** [QUICKLY] 20x
<4121> מַהֲרַי ***mahᵃray*** [MAHARAI] 3x
<4122> מַהֵר שָׁלָל חָשׁ בַּז ***mahêr šālāl ḥāš baz*** [Maher-Shalel-Hash-BaZ] 2x
<4123> מַהֲתַלָּה ***mahᵃṯallāh*** [ILLUSION] 1x
<4124> מוֹאָב ***mô’āḇ*** [MOAB] 181x
<4125> מוֹאָבִי ***mô’āḇiy*** [MOABITE] 16x
<4126> מוֹבָא ***môḇā’*** [COMING IN] 2x
<4127> מוּג ***mûḡ*** [MELT AWAY] 17x
<4128> מוֹד ***môḏ*** [MEASURE (verb)] 1x
<4129> מֹדָע ***mōḏā‘,*** מוֹדַע ***môda‘*** [RELATIVE] 2x
<4130> מוֹדַעַת ***môḏa‘aṯ*** [RELATIVE] 1x
<4131> מוֹט ***môṭ*** [REMOVED (BE)] 39x
<4132> מוֹט ***môṭ*** [POLE] 6x
<4133> מוֹטָה ***môṭāh*** [YOKE] 12x
<4134> מוּךְ ***mûḵ*** [POOR (BECOME, BE)] 5x
<4135> מוּל ***mûl*** [CIRCUMCISE] 36x
<4136> מוּל ***mûl,*** מוֹאל ***mô’l,*** מוֹל ***môl*** [AGAINST] 36x
<4137> מוֹלָדָה ***môlāḏāh*** [MOLADAH] 4x
<4138> מוֹלֶדֶת ***môleḏeṯ*** [KINDRED] 22x
<4139> מוּלָה ***mûlāh*** [CIRCUMCISION] 1x
<4140> מוֹלִיד ***môliyḏ*** [MOLID] 1x
<4141> מוּסַב ***mûsaḇ*** [STRUCTURE] 1x
<4142> מוּסַבּוֹת ***mûsabbôṯ*** [ENCLOSED] 5x
<4143> מוּסָד ***mûsāḏ*** [FOUNDATION] 2x
<4144> מוֹסָד ***môsāḏ*** [FOUNDATION] 13x
<4145> מוּסָדָה ***mûsāḏāh*** [FOUNDATION] 2x
<4146> מוֹסָדָה ***môsāḏāh*** [FOUNDATION] 10x
<4147> מוֹסֵר ***môsêr,*** מוֹסֵרָה ***môsêrāh*** [BOND] 11x
<4148> מוּסָר ***mûsār*** [INSTRUCTION] 50x
<4149> מוֹסֵרָה ***môsêrāh,*** מֹסֵרוֹת ***mōsêrôṯ*** [MOSERAH, MOSEROTH] 3x
<4150> מוֹעֵד ***mô‘êḏ*** [APPOINTED TIME, APPOINTED PLACE] 223x
<4151> מוֹעָד ***mô‘āḏ*** [APPOINTED TIMES] 1x
<4152> מוּעָדָה ***mû‘āḏāh*** [DESIGNATED] 1x
<4153> מוֹעַדְיָה ***mô‘aḏyāh*** [MOADIAH] 1x
<4154> מוּעֶדֶת ***mû‘eḏeṯ*** [UNSTEADY] 1x
<4155> מוּעָף ***mû‘āp̱*** [GLOOM] 1x
<4156> מוֹעֵצָה ***mô‘êṣāh*** [COUNSEL (noun)] 7x
<4157> מוּעָקָה ***mû‘āqāh*** [AFFLICTION] 1x
<4158> מֵיפַעַת ***mêyp̱a‘aṯ,*** מוֹפַעַת ***môp̱a‘aṯ*** [MEPHAATH] 4x
<4159> מוֹפֵת ***môp̱êṯ*** [WONDER] 36x
<4160> מֵץ ***mêṣ*** [OPPRESSOR] 1x
<4161> מוֹצָא ***môṣā’*** [GOING OUT, GOING FORTH] 27x
<4162> מוֹצָא ***môṣā’*** [MOZA] 5x
<4163> מוֹצָאָה ***môṣā’āh*** [GOING FORTH] 2x
<4164> מוּצָק ***mûṣāq,*** מוּצַק ***muṣaq*** [CONSTRAINT] 3x

<4165> מוּצָק ***mûṣāq*** [CAST (noun)] 7x
<4166> מוּצָקָה ***mûṣāqāh*** [PIPE] 2x
<4167> מוּק ***mûq*** [SCOFF] 7x
<4168> מוֹקֵד ***môqêḏ*** [HEARTH] 2x
<4169> מוֹקְדָה ***môqᵉḏāh*** [HEARTH] 1x
<4170> מוֹקֵשׁ ***môqêš*** [SNARE (noun)] 27x
<4171> מוּר ***mûr*** [EXCHANGE (verb)] 14x
<4172> מֹרָא ***mōrā'*** [FEAR (noun)] 13x
<4173> מוֹרַג ***môraḡ*** [THRESHING (adj.)] 3x
<4174> מוֹרָד ***môrāḏ*** [DESCENT] 5x
<4175> מוֹרֶה ***môreh*** [RAIN (noun)] 3x
<4176> מוֹרֶה ***môreh*** [MOREH] 3x
<4177> מוֹרָה ***môrāh*** [RAZOR] 3x
<4178> מוֹרָט ***môrāṭ*** [SMOOTH] 2x
<4179> מוֹרִיָּה ***môriyyāh,*** מֹרִיָּה ***mōriyyāh*** [MORIAH] 2x
<4180> מוֹרָשׁ ***môrāš*** [DESIRE (noun)] 1x, [POSSESSION] 2x
<4181> מוֹרָשָׁה ***môrāšāh*** [POSSESSION] 9x
<4182> מוֹרֶשֶׁת גַּת ***môrešeṯ gaṯ*** [MORESHETH GATH] 1x
<4183> מוֹרַשְׁתִּי ***môraštiy,*** מֹרַשְׁתִּי ***mōraštiy*** [MORASTHITE] 2x
<4184> מוּשׁ ***mûš*** [FEEL] 3x
<4185> מוּשׁ ***mûš*** [DEPART] 21x
<4186> מוֹשָׁב ***môšāḇ*** [SEAT] 4x
<4187> מוּשִׁי ***mûšiy*** [MUSHI] 8x
<4188> מוּשִׁי ***mûšiy*** [MUSHITE] 2x
<4189> מוֹשְׁכָה ***môšᵉḵāh*** [CORD] 1x
<4190> מוֹשָׁעָה ***môšā'āh*** [SALVATION] 1x
<4191> מוּת ***mûṯ*** [DIE] 809x
<4192> מוּת לַבֵּן ***mûṯ labbên*** [MUTH-LABBEN] 1x
<4193> מוֹת ***môṯ*** [DEATH] 1x
<4194> מָוֶת ***māweṯ*** [DEATH] 160x
<4195> מוֹתָר ***môṯār*** [PROFIT (noun)] 3x
<4196> מִזְבֵּחַ ***mizbêaḥ*** [ALTAR] 402x
<4197> מֶזֶג ***mezeḡ*** [WINE (MIXED, BLENDED)] 1x
<4198> מָזֶה ***māzeh*** [WASTED] 1x
<4199> מִזָּה ***mizzāh*** [MIZZAH] 3x
<4200> מָזוּ ***māzû*** [BARN] 1x
<4201> מְזוּזָה ***mᵉzûzāh*** [DOORPOST] 19x
<4202> מָזוֹן ***māzôn*** [FOOD] 2x
<4203> מָזוֹן ***māzôn*** [FOOD] 2x
<4204> מָזוֹר ***māzôr*** [TRAP] 1x
<4205> מָזוֹר ***māzôr*** [WOUND (noun)] 2x
<4206> מֵזַח ***mêzaḥ*** [BELT] 3x
<4207> מַזְלֵג ***mazlêḡ,*** מִזְלָגָה ***mizlāḡāh*** [FORK] 7x
<4208> מַזָּל ***mazzāl*** [CONSTELLATION] 1x
<4209> מְזִמָּה ***mᵉzimmāh*** [PLAN (noun)] 19x
<4210> מִזְמוֹר ***mizmôr*** [PSALM] 57x
<4211> מַזְמֵרָה ***mazmêrāh*** [PRUNING HOOK] 4x
<4212> מְזַמֶּרֶת ***mᵉzammereṯ*** [SNUFFERS] 5x
<4213> מִזְעָר ***miz'ār*** [VERY] 4x
<4214> מִזְרֶה ***mizreh*** [FAN, WINNOWING FAN] 2x
<4215> מְזָרֶה ***mᵉzāreh*** [NORTH] 1x

<4216> מַזָּרוֹת ***mazzārôṯ*** [MAZZAROTH] 1x
<4217> מִזְרָח ***mizrāḥ*** [EAST] 74x
<4218> מִזְרָע ***mizrā'*** [SOWN] 1x
<4219> מִזְרָק ***mizrāq*** [BASIN] 32x
<4220> מֵחַ ***mêaḥ*** [FAT ANIMAL, FAT BEAST, FAT ONE] 2x
<4221> מֹחַ ***mōaḥ*** [MARROW] 1x
<4222> מָחָא ***māḥā'*** [CLAP] 3x
<4223> מְחָא ***m^{e}ḥā'*** [STRIKE] 4x
<4224> מַחֲבֵא ***maḥ^{a}ḇê'***, מַחֲבֹא ***maḥ^{a}ḇō'*** [HIDING PLACE] 2x
<4225> מַחְבֶּרֶת ***maḥbereṯ*** [LOOP] 8x
<4226> מְחַבְּרָה ***m^{e}ḥabb^{e}rāh*** [FITTING] 2x
<4227> מַחֲבַת ***maḥ^{a}ḇaṯ*** [GRIDDLE] 5x
<4228> מַחֲגֹרֶת ***maḥ^{a}gōreṯ*** [GIRDING] 1x
<4229> מָחָה ***māḥāh*** [WIPE, WIPE OUT] 36x
<4230> מְחוּגָה ***m^{e}ḥûḡāh*** [COMPASS (noun)] 1x
<4231> מָחוֹז ***maḥōz*** [HAVEN] 1x
<4232> מְחוּיָאֵל ***m^{e}ḥûyā'êl***, מְחִיָּיאֵל ***m^{e}ḥiyyāy'êl*** [MEHUJAEL] 2x
<4233> מַחֲוִים ***maḥ^{a}wiym*** [MAHAVITE] 1x
<4234> מָחוֹל ***māḥôl*** [DANCING] 6x
<4235> מָחוֹל ***māḥôl*** [MAHOL] 1x
<4236> מַחֲזֶה ***maḥ^{a}zeh*** [VISION] 4x
<4237> מֶחֱזָה ***meḥ^{e}zāh*** [WINDOW] 4x
<4238> מַחֲזִיאוֹת ***maḥ^{a}ziy'ôṯ*** [MAHAZIOTH] 2x
<4239> מְחִי ***m^{e}ḥiy*** [BLOW (noun)] 1x
<4240> מְחִידָא ***m^{e}ḥiyḏā'*** [MEHIDA] 2x
<4241> מִחְיָה ***miḥ^{e}yāh*** [PRESERVATION OF LIFE] 8x
<4242> מְחִיר ***m^{e}ḥiyr*** [PRICE] 15x
<4243> מְחִיר ***m^{e}ḥiyr*** [MEHIR] 1x
<4244> מַחְלָה ***maḥlāh*** [MAHLAH] 5x
<4245> מַחֲלֶה ***maḥ^{a}leh***, מַחֲלָה ***maḥ^{a}lāh*** [DISEASE] 6x
<4246> מְחֹלָה ***m^{e}ḥōlāh*** [DANCING] 8x
<4247> מְחִלָּה ***m^{e}ḥillāh*** [CAVE] 1x
<4248> מַחְלוֹן ***maḥlôn*** [MAHLON] 4x
<4249> מַחְלִי ***maḥliy*** [MAHLI] 12x
<4250> מַחְלִי ***maḥliy*** [MAHLITE] 2x
<4251> מַחֲלוּ ***maḥ^{a}lû*** [DISEASE] 1x
<4252> מַחֲלָף ***maḥ^{a}lāp̱*** [KNIFE] 1x
<4253> מַחְלָפָה ***maḥlāp̱āh*** [LOCK (noun)] 2x
<4254> מַחֲלָצָה ***maḥ^{a}lāṣāh*** [FESTAL APPAREL] 2x
<4255> מַחְלְקָה ***maḥl^{e}qāh*** [GROUP] 1x
<4256> מַחֲלֹקֶת ***maḥ^{a}lōqeṯ*** [ESCAPE (noun)] 43x
<4257> מָחֲלַת ***māḥ^{a}laṯ*** [MAHALATH] 2x
<4258> מָחֲלַת ***māḥ^{a}laṯ*** [MAHALATH] 2x
<4259> מְחֹלָתִי ***m^{e}ḥōlāṯiy*** [MEHOLATHITE] 2x
<4260> מַחֲמָאֹת ***maḥ^{a}mā'ōṯ*** [BUTTER] 1x
<4261> מַחְמָד ***maḥmāḏ*** [PRECIOUS] 13x
<4262> מַחֲמֹד ***maḥ^{a}mōḏ*** [PLEASANT THING] 2x
<4263> מַחְמָל ***maḥmāl*** [DELIGHT (noun)] 1x
<4264> מַחֲנֶה ***maḥ^{a}neh*** [CAMP] 216x
<4265> מַחֲנֵה־דָן ***maḥ^{a}nêh-ḏān*** [MAHANEH DAN] 1x
<4266> מַחֲנַיִם ***maḥ^{a}nayim*** [MAHANAIM] 13x

<4267> מַחֲנָק ***maḥ^{a}naq*** [STRANGLING] 1x

<4268> מַחְסֶה ***maḥseh*** [REFUGE] 20x

<4269> מַחְסוֹם ***maḥsôm*** [MUZZLE (noun)] 1x

<4270> מַחְסוֹר ***maḥsôr,*** מַחְסֹר ***maḥsōr*** [NEED] 13x

<4271> מַחְסֵיָה ***maḥsêyāh*** [MAHSEIAH] 2x

<4272> מָחַץ ***māḥaṣ*** [PIERCE] 14x

<4273> מַחַץ ***maḥaṣ*** [STROKE] 1x

<4274> מַחְצֵב ***maḥṣêḇ*** [HEWN] 3x

<4275> מֶחֱצָה ***meḥ^{e}ṣāh*** [HALF] 2x

<4276> מַחֲצִית ***maḥ^{a}ṣiyṯ*** [HALF] 17x

<4277> מָחַק ***māḥaq*** [CRUSH] 1x

<4278> מֶחְקָר ***meḥqār*** [DEPTH] 1x

<4279> מָחָר ***māḥār*** [TOMORROW] 52x

<4280> מַחֲרָאָה ***maḥ^{a}rā'āh*** [LATRINE] 1x

<4281> מַחֲרֵשָׁה ***maḥ^{a}rêšāh*** [MATTOCK] 2x

<4282> מַחֲרֶשֶׁת ***maḥ^{a}rešeṯ*** [PLOWSHARE] 1x

<4283> מָחֳרָת ***moḥ^{o}rāṯ*** [NEXT DAY] 32x

<4284> מַחֲשָׁבָה ***maḥ^{a}šāḇāh,*** מַחֲשֶׁבֶת ***maḥ^{a}šeḇeṯ*** [THOUGHT] 56x

<4285> מַחְשָׁךְ ***maḥšāḵ*** [DARKNESS] 7x

<4286> מַחְשֹׂף ***maḥśōp̱*** [EXPOSING] 1x

<4287> מַחַת ***maḥaṯ*** [MAHATH] 3x

<4288> מְחִתָּה ***m^{e}ḥittāh*** [RUIN (noun)] 11x

<4289> מַחְתָּה ***maḥtāh*** [CENSER] 22x

<4290> מַחְתֶּרֶת ***maḥtereṯ*** [BREAKING IN] 2x

<4291> מְטָא ***m^{e}ṭā',*** מְטָה ***m^{e}ṭāh*** [REACH] 8x

<4292> מַטְאֲטֵא ***maṭ^{a}ṭê'*** [BROOM] 1x

<4293> מַטְבֵּחַ ***maṭbêaḥ*** [SLAUGHTER, PLACE OF SLAUGHTER] 1x

<4294> מַטֶּה ***maṭṭeh,*** מַטָּה ***maṭṭāh*** [STAFF] 251x

<4295> מַטָּה ***maṭṭāh*** [BELOW] 19x

<4296> מִטָּה ***miṭṭāh*** [BED] 29x

<4297> מֻטֶּה ***muṭṭeh*** [INJUSTICE] 1x

<4298> מֻטָּה ***muṭṭāh*** [SPREAD (noun)] 1x

<4299> מַטְוֶה ***maṭweh*** [SPUN (THAT WHICH IS)] 1x

<4300> מָטִיל ***māṭiyl*** [BAR] 1x

<4301> מַטְמוֹן ***maṭmôn,*** מַטְמֻן ***maṭmun*** [TREASURE] 5x

<4302> מַטָּע ***maṭṭā‘*** [PLANTING] 6x

<4303> מַטְעָם ***maṭ‘ām*** [DELICIOUS FOOD] 8x

<4304> מִטְפַּחַת ***miṭpaḥaṯ*** [CLOAK] 2x

<4305> מָטַר ***māṭar*** [RAIN (verb)] 17x

<4306> מָטָר ***māṭār*** [RAIN (noun)] 38x

<4307> מַטָּרָה ***maṭṭārāh,*** מַטָּרָא ***maṭṭārā'*** [GUARD] 16x

<4308> מַטְרֵד ***maṭrêḏ*** [MATRED] 2x

<4309> מַטְרִי ***maṭriy*** [MATRI] 1x

<4310> מִי ***miy*** [WHO, WHOSE, WHOM] 12x

<4311> מֵידְבָא ***mêyḏ^{e}ḇā'*** [MEDEBA] 5x

<4312> מֵידָד ***mêyḏāḏ*** [MEDAD] 2x

<4313> מֵי הַיַּרְקוֹן ***mêy hayyarqôn*** [ME JARKON] 1x

<4314> מֵי זָהָב ***mêy zāhāḇ*** [MEZAHAB] 2x

<4315> מֵיטָב ***mêyṭāḇ*** [BEST] 5x

<4316> מִיכָא ***miyḵā'*** [MICA] 5x

<4317> מִיכָאֵל ***miyḵā'êl*** [MICHAEL] 13x

<4318> מִיכָה ***miyḵāh*** [MICAH] 31x

<4319> מִיכָהוּ ***miyḵāhû*** [MICAIAH] 1x

<4320> מִיכָיָה ***miyḵāyāh*** [MICAIAH] 4x

<4321> מִיכָיְהוּ ***miyḵāyᵉhû,*** מִכָיְהוּ ***miḵāyᵉhû*** [MICAH] 20x

<4322> מִיכָיָהוּ ***miyḵāyāhû*** [MICAIAH] 2x

<4323> מִיכָל ***miyḵāl*** [BROOK] 1x

<4324> מִיכַל ***miyḵal*** [MICHAL] 18x

<4325> מַיִם ***mayim*** [WATER (noun)] 582x

<4326> מִיָּמִן ***miyyāmin*** [MIJAMIN] 4x

<4327> מִין ***miyn*** [KIND] 31x

<4328> מְיֻסָּדָה ***mᵉyussāḏāh*** [FOUNDATION] 1x

<4329> מוּסַךְ ***mûsaḵ*** [COVERED WAY] 1x

<4330> מִיץ ***miyṣ*** [CHURNING] 3x

<4331> מֵישָׁא ***mêyšā’*** [MESHA] 1x

<4332> מִישָׁאֵל ***miyšā’êl*** [MISHAEL] 7x

<4333> מִישָׁאֵל ***miyšā’êl*** [MISHAEL] 1x

<4334> מִישׁוֹר ***miyšôr*** [STRAIGHT] 23x

<4335> מֵישַׁךְ ***mêyšaḵ*** [MESHACH] 2x

<4336> מֵישַׁךְ ***mêyšaḵ*** [MESHACH] 14x

<4337> מֵישָׁע ***mêyšā‘*** [MESHA] 1x

<4338> מֵישַׁע ***mêyša‘*** [MESHA] 1x

<4339> מֵישָׁר ***mêyšār*** [LEVEL (noun)] 19x

<4340> מֵיתָר ***mêyṯār*** [STRING] 9x

<4341> מַכְאוֹב ***maḵ’ôḇ*** [SUFFERING] 16x

<4342> מַכְבִּיר ***maḵbiyr*** [ABUNDANCE] 1x

<4343> מַכְבֵּנָה ***maḵbênāh*** [MACHBENAH] 1x

<4344> מַכְבַּנַּי ***maḵbannay*** [MACHBANNAI] 1x

<4345> מִכְבָּר ***miḵbār*** [GRATING] 6x

<4346> מַכְבֵּר ***maḵbêr*** [CLOTH, TICK CLOTH] 1x

<4347> מַכָּה ***makkāh*** [BLOW (noun)] 48x

<4348> מִכְוָה ***miḵwāh*** [BURN (noun)] 3x

<4349> מָכוֹן ***māḵôn*** [DWELLING] 17x

<4350> מְכוֹנָה ***mᵉḵônāh,*** מְכֹנָה ***mᵉḵōnāh*** [STAND (noun)] 23x

<4351> מְכוּרָה ***mᵉḵûrāh,*** מְכֹרָה ***mᵉḵōrāh*** [ORIGIN] 3x

<4352> מָכִי ***māḵiy*** [MACHI] 1x

<4353> מָכִיר ***maḵiyr*** [MACHIR] 22x

<4354> מָכִירִי ***māḵiyriy*** [MACHIRITE] 1x

<4355> מָכַךְ ***māḵaḵ*** [BRING LOW] 3x

<4356> מִכְלָאָה ***miḵlā’āh,*** מִכְלָה ***miḵlāh*** [FOLD (noun)] 3x

<4357> מִכְלָה ***miḵlāh*** [PUREST] 1x

<4358> מִכְלוֹל ***miḵlôl*** [SPLENDIDLY] 2x

<4359> מִכְלָל ***miḵlāl*** [PERFECTION] 1x

<4360> מַכְלוּל ***maḵlûl*** [CHOICE GARMENT] 1x

<4361> מַכֹּלֶת ***makkōleṯ*** [FOOD] 1x

<4362> מִכְמָן ***miḵmān*** [TREASURE] 1x

<4363> מִכְמָס ***miḵmās,*** מִכְמָשׂ ***miḵmāś*** [MICHMASH] 11x

<4364> מַכְמֹר ***maḵmōr,*** מִכְמָר ***miḵmār*** [NET] 2x

<4365> מִכְמֶרֶת ***miḵmereṯ,*** מִכְמֹרֶת ***miḵmōreṯ*** [NET] 3x

<4366> מִכְמְתָת ***miḵmᵉṯāṯ*** [MICHMETHAH] 2x

<4367> מַכְנַדְבַי ***maḵnaḏbay*** [MACHNADEBAI] 1x

<4368> מְכֹנָה ***mᵉḵōnāh*** [MECONAH] 1x

<4369> מְכֻנָה ***m^{e}ḵunāh*** [BASE (noun)] 1x
<4370> מִכְנָס ***miḵnās*** [UNDERGARMENT] 5x
<4371> מֶכֶס ***meḵes*** [TRIBUTE] 6x
<4372> מִכְסֶה ***miḵseh*** [COVERING] 16x
<4373> מִכְסָה ***miḵsāh*** [NUMBER (noun)] 2x
<4374> מְכַסֶּה ***m^{e}ḵasseh*** [COVERING] 4x
<4375> מַכְפֵּלָה ***maḵpêlāh*** [MACHPELAH] 6x
<4376> מָכַר ***māḵar*** [SELL] 80x
<4377> מֶכֶר ***meḵer*** [MERCHANDISE] 3x
<4378> מַכָּר ***makkār*** [ACQUAINTANCE] 2x
<4379> מִכְרֶה ***miḵreh*** [PIT] 1x
<4380> מְכֵרָה ***m^{e}ḵêrāh*** [SWORD] 1x
<4381> מִכְרִי ***miḵriy*** [MICHRI] 1x
<4382> מְכֵרָתִי ***m^{e}ḵêrāṯiy*** [MECHERATHITE] 1x
<4383> מִכְשׁוֹל ***miḵšôl*** [STUMBLING BLOCK] 14x
<4384> מַכְשֵׁלָה ***maḵšêlāh*** [RUIN, HEAP OF RUINS] 2x
<4385> מִכְתָּב ***miḵtāḇ*** [WRITING] 9x
<4386> מְכִתָּה ***m^{e}ḵittāh*** [FRAGMENT] 1x
<4387> מִכְתָּם ***miḵtām*** [MICHTAM] 6x
<4388> מַכְתֵּשׁ ***maḵtêš*** [HOLLOW PLACE] 2x
<4389> מַכְתֵּשׁ ***maḵtêš*** [MAKTESH] 1x
<4390> מָלֵא ***mālê'*** [FULL (BE)] 251x
<4391> מְלָא ***m^{e}lā'*** [FILL, FILLED (BE)] 2x
<4392> מָלֵא ***mālê'*** [FULL (adj.)] 65x
<4393> מְלֹא ***m^{e}lō',*** מְלוֹא ***m^{e}lô',*** מְלוֹ ***m^{e}lô*** [FULL (noun)] 37x
<4394> מִלֻּא ***millu',*** מִלּוּא ***millû'*** [SETTING] 15x
<4395> מְלֵאָה ***m^{e}lê'āh*** [HARVEST] 3x
<4396> מִלֻּאָה ***millu'āh*** [SETTING] 3x
<4397> מַלְאָךְ ***mal'āḵ*** [MESSENGER] 214x
<4398> מַלְאַךְ ***mal'aḵ*** [ANGEL] 2x
<4399> מְלָאכָה ***m^{e}lā'ḵāh*** [WORK] 167x
<4400> מַלְאָכוּת ***mal'āḵûṯ*** [MESSAGE] 1x
<4401> מַלְאָכִי ***mal'āḵiy*** [MALACHI] 1x
<4402> מִלֵּאת ***millê'ṯ*** [FITLY] 1x
<4403> מַלְבּוּשׁ ***malbûš*** [CLOTHING] 8x
<4404> מַלְבֵּן ***malbên*** [BRICK KILN] 3x
<4405> מִלָּה ***millāh*** [WORD] 38x
<4406> מִלָּה ***millāh*** [WORD] 24x
<4407> מִלּוֹא ***millô'*** [MILLO] 10x
<4408> מַלּוּחַ ***mallûaḥ*** [MALLOW] 1x
<4409> מַלּוּךְ ***mallûḵ,*** מַלּוּכִי ***mallûḵiy*** [MALLUCH] 7x
<4410> מְלוּכָה ***m^{e}lûḵāh*** [KINGDOM] 24x
<4411> מָלוֹן ***mālôn*** [LODGING] 8x
<4412> מְלוּנָה ***m^{e}lûnāh*** [HUT] 2x
<4413> מַלּוֹתִי ***mallôṯiy*** [MALLOTHI] 2x
<4414> מָלַח ***mālaḥ*** [SEASON (verb)] 4x, [VANISH] 1x
<4415> מְלַח ***m^{e}laḥ*** [SALT (EAT THE)] 1x
<4416> מְלַח ***m^{e}laḥ*** [SALT (noun)] 3x
<4417> מֶלַח ***melaḥ*** [SALT (noun)] 28x
<4418> מֶלַח ***melaḥ*** [WORN-OUT CLOTHES] 2x
<4419> מַלָּח ***mallāḥ*** [MARINER] 4x

<4420> מְלֵחָה ***mᵉlêḥāh*** [BARRENNESS] 3x
<4421> מִלְחָמָה ***milḥāmāh*** [WAR] 319x
<4422> מָלַט ***mālaṭ*** [ESCAPE (verb)] 95x
<4423> מֶלֶט ***meleṭ*** [MORTAR] 1x
<4424> מְלַטְיָה ***mᵉlaṭyāh*** [MELATIAH] 1x
<4425> מְלִילָה ***mᵉliylāh*** [KERNEL] 1x
<4426> מְלִיצָה ***mᵉliyṣāh*** [SAYING] 2x
<4427> מָלַךְ ***mālak̲*** [KING (BE, MAKE)] 348x
<4428> מֶלֶךְ ***melek̲*** [KING] 2,523x
<4429> מֶלֶךְ ***melek̲,*** הַמֶּלֶךְ ***hammelek̲*** [MELECH, HAMMELECH] 4x
<4430> מֶלֶךְ ***melek̲*** [KING] 180x
<4431> מְלַךְ ***mᵉlak̲*** [ADVICE] 1x
<4432> מֹלֶךְ ***mōlek̲*** [MOLECH] 8x
<4433> מַלְכָּה ***malkāh*** [QUEEN] 2x
<4434> מַלְכֹּדֶת ***malkōd̲eṯ*** [TRAP] 1x
<4435> מִלְכָּה ***milkāh*** [MILCAH] 11x
<4436> מַלְכָּה ***malkāh*** [QUEEN] 35x
<4437> מַלְכוּ ***malk̲û*** [KINGDOM] 57x
<4438> מַלְכוּת ***malk̲ûṯ*** [KINGDOM] 91x
<4439> מַלְכִּיאֵל ***malkiy'êl*** [MALCHIEL] 3x
<4440> מַלְכִּיאֵלִי ***malkiy'êliy*** [MALCHIELITES] 1x
<4441> מַלְכִּיָּה ***malkiyyāh,*** מַלְכִּיָּהוּ ***malkiyyahû*** [MALCHIJAH] 16x
<4442> מַלְכִּי־צֶדֶק ***malkiy-ṣed̲eq*** [MELCHIZEDEK] 2x
<4443> מַלְכִּירָם ***malkiyrām*** [MALCHIRAM] 1x
<4444> מַלְכִּישׁוּעַ ***malkiyšûa',*** מַלְכִּי שׁוּעַ ***malkiy šûa'*** [MALCHI-SHUA] 5x
<4445> מִלְכֹּם ***milkōm,*** מַלְכָּם ***malkām*** [MALCHAM] 7x
<4446> מְלֶכֶת ***mᵉlek̲eṯ*** [QUEEN] 5x
<4447> הַמֹּלֶכֶת ***hammōlek̲eṯ*** [HAMMOLECHETH, HAMMOLEKETH] 1x
<4448> מָלַל ***mālal*** [SPEAK] 5x
<4449> מְלַל ***mᵉlal*** [SPEAK] 5x
<4450> מִלֲלַי ***milᵃlay*** [MILALAI] 1x
<4451> מַלְמָד ***malmād̲*** [GOAD] 1x
<4452> מָלַץ ***mālaṣ*** [SWEET] 1x
<4453> מֶלְצַר ***melṣar*** [STEWARD] 2x
<4454> מָלַק ***mālaq*** [WRING OFF] 2x
<4455> מַלְקוֹחַ ***malqôaḥ*** [JAW] 1x, [PREY] 7x
<4456> מַלְקוֹשׁ ***malqôš*** [RAIN (LATER, LATTER, SPRING)] 8x
<4457> מֶלְקָחַיִם ***melqāḥayim,*** מַלְקָחַיִם ***malqāḥayim*** [WICK TRIMMERS] 6x
<4458> מֶלְתָּחָה ***meltāḥāh*** [WARDROBE] 1x
<4459> מַלְתָּעוֹת ***maltā'ôṯ*** [FANGS] 1x
<4460> מַמְּגוּרָה ***mammᵉg̲ûrāh*** [GRANARY] 1x
<4461> מֵמַד ***mêmad̲*** [MEASUREMENT] 1x
<4462> מְמוּכָן ***mᵉmûk̲ān*** [MEMUCAN] 3x
<4463> מָמוֹת ***māmôṯ*** [DEATH] 2x
<4464> מַמְזֵר ***mamzêr*** [FORBIDDEN UNION (ONE BORN OF)] 2x
<4465> מִמְכָּר ***mimkār*** [SALE] 10x
<4466> מִמְכֶּרֶת ***mimkereṯ*** [SALE] 1x
<4467> מַמְלָכָה ***mamlāk̲āh*** [KINGDOM] 117x
<4468> מַמְלָכוּת ***mamlāk̲ûṯ*** [KINGDOM] 9x
<4469> מִמְסָךְ ***mimsāk̲*** [MIXED WINE] 2x
<4470> מֶמֶר ***memer*** [BITTERNESS] 1x

<4471> מַמְרֵא ***mamrê'*** [MAMRE] 10x
<4472> מַמְרֹר ***mamrōr*** [BITTERNESS] 1x
<4473> מִמְשַׁח ***mimšaḥ*** [ANOINTED] 1x
<4474> מִמְשָׁל ***mimšāl*** [DOMINION] 3x
<4475> מֶמְשָׁלָה ***memšālāh*** [DOMINION] 17x
<4476> מִמְשָׁק ***mimšāq*** [POSSESSED] 1x
<4477> מַמְתַּקִּים ***mamtaqqiym*** [SWEETNESS] 2x
<4478> מָן ***mān*** [MANNA] 14x
<4479> מַן ***man*** [WHO, WHOEVER, WHAT] 10x
<4480> מִן ***min,*** מִנִּי ***minniy,*** מִנֵּי ***minnêy*** [FROM] 6,493x
<4481> מִן ***min*** [FROM] 109x
<4482> מֵן ***mên*** [PORTION] 1x, [STRINGED INSTRUMENT] 2x
<4483> מְנָא ***m^{e}nā',*** מְנָה ***m^{e}nāh*** [APPOINT] 5x
<4484> מְנֵא ***m^{e}nê'*** [MENE] 2x
<4485> מַנְגִּינָה ***mangiynāh*** [MOCKING SONG] 1x
<4486> מַנְדַּע ***manda'*** [KNOWLEDGE] 4x
<4487> מָנָה ***mānāh*** [COUNT] 28x
<4488> מָנֶה ***māneh*** [MINA] 5x
<4489> מֹנֶה ***mōneh*** [TIME] 2x
<4490> מָנָה ***mānāh*** [PORTION] 14x
<4491> מִנְהָג ***minhāg̱*** [DRIVING] 2x
<4492> מִנְהָרָה ***minhārāh*** [DEN] 1x
<4493> מָנוֹד ***mānôḏ*** [SHAKING OF THE HEAD] 1x
<4494> מָנוֹחַ ***mānôaḥ*** [RESTING PLACE] 7x
<4495> מָנוֹחַ ***mānôaḥ*** [MANOAH] 18x
<4496> מְנוּחָה ***m^{e}nûḥāh,*** מְנֻחָה ***m^{e}nuḥāh*** [RESTING PLACE] 21x
<4497> מָנוֹן ***mānôn*** [SON] 1x
<4498> מָנוֹס ***mānôs*** [REFUGE] 8x
<4499> מְנוּסָה ***m^{e}nûsāh,*** מְנֻסָה ***m^{e}nusāh*** [FLIGHT] 2x
<4500> מָנוֹר ***mānôr*** [BEAM] 4x
<4501> מְנוֹרָה ***m^{e}nôrāh,*** מְנֹרָה ***m^{e}nōrāh*** [LAMPSTAND] 40x
<4502> מִנְּזָר ***minn^{e}zār*** [CROWNED ONE] 1x
<4503> מִנְחָה ***minḥāh*** [GIFT] 211x
<4504> מִנְחָה ***minḥāh*** [OFFERING] 2x
<4505> מְנַחֵם ***m^{e}naḥêm*** [MENAHEM] 8x
<4506> מָנַחַת ***mānaḥaṯ,*** מָנַחְתִּי ***mānaḥtiy*** [MANAHATH] 5x
<4507> מְנִי ***m^{e}niy*** [NUMBER (noun)] 1x
<4508> מִנִּי ***minniy*** [MINNI] 1x
<4509> מִנְיָמִין ***minyāmiyn*** [MINIAMIN] 3x
<4510> מִנְיָן ***minyān*** [NUMBER (noun)] 1x
<4511> מִנִּית ***minniyṯ*** [MINNITH] 2x
<4512> מִנְלֶה ***minleh*** [PERFECTION] 1x
<4513> מָנַע ***māna'*** [HOLD, WITHHOLD] 29x
<4514> מַנְעוּל ***man'ûl,*** מַנְעֻל ***man'ul*** [BOLT] 6x
<4515> מִנְעָל ***min'āl*** [LOCK (noun)] 1x
<4516> מַנְעַמִּים ***man'ammiym*** [DELICACIES] 1x
<4517> מְנַעַנְעִים ***m^{e}na'an'iym*** [CASTANETS] 1x
<4518> מְנַקִּית ***m^{e}naqqiyṯ*** [BOWL] 4x
<4519> מְנַשֶּׁה ***m^{e}naššeh*** [MANASSEH] 146x
<4520> מְנַשִּׁי ***m^{e}naššiy*** [MANASSITE] 4x
<4521> מְנָת ***m^{e}nāṯ*** [PORTION] 9x

<4522> מַס ***mas*** [FORCED LABOR] 23x
<4523> מָס ***mās*** [AFFLICTED] 1x
<4524> מֵסַב ***mêsaḇ,*** מְסִבָּה ***misbāh*** [AROUND] 5x
<4525> מַסְגֵּר ***masgêr*** [PRISON] 3x, [SMITH] 4x
<4526> מִסְגֶּרֶת ***misgereṯ*** [RIM] 17x
<4527> מַסַּד ***massaḏ*** [FOUNDATION] 1x
<4528> מִסְדְּרוֹן ***misdᵉrôn*** [PORCH] 1x
<4529> מָסָה ***māsāh*** [MELT] 4x
<4530> מִסָּה ***missāh*** [TRIBUTE] 1x
<4531> מַסָּה ***massāh*** [TRIAL] 9x
<4532> מַסָּה ***massāh*** [MASSAH] 4x
<4533> מַסְוֶה ***masweh*** [VEIL] 3x
<4534> מְסוּכָה ***mᵉsûḵāh*** [THORN EDGE] 1x
<4535> מַסָּח ***massāḥ*** [DEFENSE] 1x
<4536> מִסְחָר ***misḥār*** [WARES] 1x
<4537> מָסַךְ ***māsaḵ*** [MIX] 5x
<4538> מֶסֶךְ ***meseḵ*** [MIXTURE] 1x
<4539> מָסָךְ ***māsāḵ*** [CURTAIN] 25x
<4540> מְסֻכָּה ***mᵉsuḵāh*** [COVERING] 1x
<4541> מַסֵּכָה ***massêḵāh*** [COVERING] 28x
<4542> מִסְכֵּן ***miskên*** [POOR] 4x
<4543> מִסְכְּנוֹת ***miskᵉnôṯ*** [STORAGE] 7x
<4544> מִסְכֵּנֻת ***misḵênuṯ*** [SCARCITY] 1x
<4545> מַסֶּכֶת ***masseḵeṯ*** [WEB] 2x
<4546> מְסִלָּה ***mᵉsillāh*** [HIGHWAY] 27x
<4547> מַסְלוּל ***maslûl*** [HIGHWAY] 1x
<4548> מַסְמֵר ***masmêr,*** מִסְמֵר ***mismêr,*** מַשְׂמֵר ***maśmêr*** [NAIL] 5x
<4549> מָסַס ***māsas*** [MELT] 21x
<4550> מַסַּע ***massa'*** [JOURNEY (verb)] 12x
<4551> מַסָּע ***massā'*** [DART] 1x, [QUARRY] 1x
<4552> מִסְעָד ***mis'āḏ*** [SUPPORT (noun)] 1x
<4553> מִסְפֵּד ***mispêḏ*** [LAMENTATION] 16x
<4554> מִסְפּוֹא ***mispô'*** [FODDER] 5x
<4555> מִסְפָּחָה ***mispāḥāh*** [VEIL] 2x
<4556> מִסְפַּחַת ***mispaḥaṯ*** [RASH] 3x
<4557> מִסְפָּר ***mispār*** [NUMBER (noun)] 134x
<4558> מִסְפָּר ***mispār*** [MISPAR] 1x
<4559> מִסְפֶּרֶת ***mispereṯ*** [MISPERETH] 1x
<4560> מָסַר ***māsar*** [PROVIDE] 2x
<4561> מֹסָר ***mōsār*** [INSTRUCTION] 1x
<4562> מָסֹרֶת ***māsōreṯ*** [BOND] 1x
<4563> מִסְתּוֹר ***mistôr*** [SHELTER] 1x
<4564> מַסְתֵּר ***mastêr*** [HIDE] 1x
<4565> מִסְתָּר ***mistār*** [HIDING PLACE] 10x
<4566> מַעֲבָד ***maᵃḇāḏ*** [WORK] 1x
<4567> מַעֲבָד ***maᵃḇāḏ*** [WORK] 1x
<4568> מַעֲבֶה ***maᵃḇeh*** [CLAY] 1x
<4569> מַעֲבָר ***maᵃḇar,*** מַעְבָּרָה ***ma'bārāh*** [FORD] 11x
<4570> מַעְגָּל ***ma'gāl*** [ENCAMPMENT] 16x
<4571> מָעַד ***mā'aḏ*** [SLIP] 8x
<4572> מַעֲדַי ***maᵃḏay*** [MAADAI] 1x

<4573> מַעַדְיָה ***maʿaḏyāh*** [MAADIAH] 1x
<4574> מַעֲדָן ***ma^{a}ḏān,*** מַעֲדַנָּה ***ma^{a}ḏanāh,*** מַעֲדַנִּים ***ma^{a}ḏanniym*** [CHAIN] 5x
<4575> מַעֲדַנּוֹת ***ma^{a}ḏannôṯ*** [CHAINS] 1x
<4576> מַעְדֵּר ***maʿdêr*** [HOE] 1x
<4577> מְעֵה ***m^{e}ʿêh*** [BELLY] 1x
<4578> מֵעֶה ***mêʿeh*** [BOWELS] 32x
<4579> מָעָה ***māʿāh*** [GRAIN] 1x
<4580> מָעוֹג ***māʿôg̱*** [BREAD] 2x
<4581> מָעוֹז ***māʿôz,*** מָעוֹזֶן ***māʿôzen*** [STRONGHOLD] 37x
<4582> מָעוֹךְ ***māʿôḵ*** [MAOCH] 1x
<4583> מָעוֹן ***māʿôn,*** מָעִין ***māʿiyn*** [HABITATION] 19x
<4584> מָעוֹן ***māʿôn*** [MAON] 8x
<4585> מְעוֹנָה ***m^{e}ʿônāh,*** מְעֹנָה ***m^{e}ʿōnāh*** [DWELLING PLACE] 9x
<4586> מְעוּנִים ***m^{e}ʿûniym*** [MEUNIM, MEUNITES] 4x
<4587> מְעוֹנֹתַי ***m^{e}ʿônōṯay*** [MEONOTHAI] 1x
<4588> מָעוּף ***māʿûp̱*** [DIMNESS] 1x
<4589> מָעוֹר ***māʿôr*** [NAKEDNESS] 1x
<4590> מַעַזְיָה ***maʿazyāh,*** מַעַזְיָהוּ ***maʿazyāhû*** [MAAZIAH] 2x
<4591> מָעַט ***māʿaṭ*** [DECREASE] 22x
<4592> מְעַט ***m^{e}ʿaṭ*** [LITTLE (noun)] 102x
<4593> מְעֻטָּה ***m^{e}ʿuṭṭāh*** [WRAPPED UP] 1x
<4594> מַעֲטֶה ***ma^{a}ṭeh*** [GARMENT] 1x
<4595> מַעֲטֶפֶת ***ma^{a}ṭep̱eṯ*** [MANTLE] 1x
<4596> מְעִי ***m^{e}ʿiy*** [RUIN (noun)] 1x
<4597> מָעַי ***māʿay*** [MAAI] 1x
<4598> מְעִיל ***m^{e}ʿiyl*** [ROBE] 28x
<4599> מַעְיָן ***maʿyān*** [FOUNTAIN] 23x
<4600> מָעַךְ ***māʿaḵ*** [CRUSH] 4x
<4601> מַעֲכָה ***ma^{a}ḵāh*** [MAACAH] 23x
<4602> מַעֲכָתִי ***ma^{a}ḵāṯiy*** [MAACATHITE] 8x
<4603> מָעַל ***māʿal*** [TRANSGRESS] 35x
<4604> מַעַל ***maʿal*** [TRANSGRESSION] 29x
<4605> מַעַל ***maʿal*** [ABOVE] 138x
<4606> מֵעָל ***meʿāl*** [GOING DOWN] 1x
<4607> מֹעַל ***mōʿal*** [LIFTING UP] 1x
<4608> מַעֲלֶה ***ma^{a}leh*** [ASCENT] 12x
<4609> מַעֲלָה ***ma^{a}lāh*** [ASCENT] 47x
<4610> מַעֲלֵה עַקְרַבִּים ***ma^{a}lêh ʿaqrabbiym*** [SCORPION PASS] 3x
<4611> מַעֲלָל ***ma^{a}lāl*** [ACTION] 41x
<4612> מַעֲמָד ***ma^{a}māḏ*** [ATTENDANCE] 5x
<4613> מָעֳמָד ***mo^{o}māḏ*** [FOOTHOLD] 1x
<4614> מַעֲמָסָה ***ma^{a}māsāh*** [HEAVY, VERY HEAVY] 1x
<4615> מַעֲמַקִּים ***ma^{a}maqqiym*** [DEPTHS] 5x
<4616> מַעַן ***maʿan*** [SO THAT] 250x
<4617> מַעֲנֶה ***ma^{a}neh*** [ANSWER (noun)] 8x
<4618> מַעֲנָה ***ma^{a}nāh*** [FURROW] 2x
<4619> מַעַץ ***maʿaṣ*** [MAAZ] 1x
<4620> מַעֲצֵבָה ***ma^{a}ṣêḇāh*** [TORMENT (noun)] 1x
<4621> מַעֲצָד ***ma^{a}ṣāḏ*** [CUTTING TOOL] 2x
<4622> מַעְצוֹר ***maʿṣôr*** [RESTRAINT] 1x
<4623> מַעְצָר ***maʿṣār*** [SELF-CONTROL] 1x

<4624> מַעֲקֶה ***maᵃqeh*** [PARAPET] 1x
<4625> מַעֲקַשִּׁים ***maᵃqaššiym*** [ROUGH PLACES] 1x
<4626> מַעַר ***ma'ar*** [NAKEDNESS] 2x
<4627> מַעֲרָב ***maᵃrāḇ*** [MERCHANDISE] 9x
<4628> מַעֲרָב ***maᵃrāḇ*** [WEST, WEST SIDE] 14x
<4629> מַעֲרֶה ***maᵃreh,*** מַעֲרֵה־גָבַע ***maᵃrêh gāḇa'*** [MEADOW] 1x
<4630> מַעֲרָה ***maᵃrāh*** [ARMY] 1x
<4631> מְעָרָה ***mᵉ'ārāh*** [CAVE] 39x
<4632> מְעָרָה ***mᵉ'ārāh,*** עָרָה ***'ārāh*** [MEARAH, ARAH] 1x
<4633> מַעֲרָךְ ***maᵃrāḵ*** [PLAN (verb)] 1x
<4634> מַעֲרָכָה ***maᵃrāḵāh*** [ARRAY (noun)] 20x
<4635> מַעֲרֶכֶת ***maᵃreḵeṯ*** [ROW (noun)] 9x
<4636> מַעֲרֹם ***maᵃrōm*** [NAKED (ONE WHO IS)] 1x
<4637> מַעֲרָצָה ***maᵃraṣāh*** [TERROR] 1x
<4638> מַעֲרָת ***maᵃrāṯ*** [MAARATH] 1x
<4639> מַעֲשֶׂה ***maᵃśeh*** [WORK] 235x
<4640> מַעְשַׂי ***ma'śay*** [MAASAI] 1x
<4641> מַעֲשֵׂיָה ***maᵃśêyāh,*** מַעֲשֵׂיָהוּ ***maᵃśêyāhû*** [MAASEIAH] 23x
<4642> מַעֲשַׁקּוֹת ***ma'šaqqôṯ*** [OPPRESSIONS] 2x
<4643> מַעֲשֵׂר ***maᵃśêr*** [TENTH] 32x
<4644> מֹף ***mōp̱*** [MEMPHIS] 1x
<4645> מִפְגָּע ***mip̱gā'*** [TARGET] 1x
<4646> מַפָּח ***mappāḥ*** [BREATHING OUT] 1x
<4647> מַפֻּחַ ***mappuaḥ*** [BELLOWS] 1x
<4648> מְפִיבֹשֶׁת ***mᵉp̱iyḇōšeṯ*** [MEPHIBOSHETH] 13x
<4649> מֻפִּים ***muppiym*** [MUPPIM] 1x
<4650> מֵפִיץ ***mep̱iyṣ*** [CLUB, WAR CLUB] 1x
<4651> מַפָּל ***mappāl*** [CHAFF] 2x
<4652> מִפְלָאָה ***mip̱lā'āh*** [WONDROUS WORK] 1x
<4653> מִפְלַגָּה ***mip̱laggāh*** [DIVISION] 1x
<4654> מַפָּלָה ***mappālāh*** [RUIN (noun)] 3x
<4655> מִפְלָט ***mip̱lāṭ*** [SHELTER] 1x
<4656> מִפְלֶצֶת ***mip̱leṣeṯ*** [IMAGE] 4x
<4657> מִפְלָשׂ ***mip̱laś*** [BALANCING] 1x
<4658> מַפֶּלֶת ***mappeleṯ*** [FALL (noun)] 8x
<4659> מִפְעָל ***mip̱'āl,*** מִפְעָלָה ***mip̱'ālāh*** [WORK] 3x
<4660> מַפָּץ ***mappāṣ*** [SLAUGHTER (noun)] 1x
<4661> מַפֵּץ ***mappêṣ*** [WAR CLUB] 1x
<4662> מִפְקָד ***mip̱qāḏ*** [APPOINTMENT] 4x
<4663> מִפְקָד ***mip̱qāḏ*** [INSPECTION] 1x
<4664> מִפְרָץ ***mip̱raṣ*** [LANDING] 1x
<4665> מַפְרֶקֶת ***map̱reqeṯ*** [NECK] 1x
<4666> מִפְרָשׂ ***mip̱rāś*** [SPREADING] 2x
<4667> מִפְשָׂעָה ***mip̱śā'āh*** [HIP] 1x
<4668> מַפְתֵּחַ ***map̱têaḥ*** [KEY] 3x
<4669> מִפְתָּח ***mip̱tāḥ*** [OPENING] 1x
<4670> מִפְתָּן ***mip̱tān*** [THRESHOLD] 8x
<4671> מֹץ ***mōts*** [CHAFF] 8x
<4672> מָצָא ***māṣā'*** [FIND] 456x
<4673> מַצָּב ***maṣṣāḇ*** [GARRISON] 10x
<4674> מֻצָּב ***muṣṣāḇ*** [TOWER] 1x

<4675> מַצָּבָה ***maṣṣāḇāh,*** מִצָּבָה ***miṣṣāḇāh*** [GARRISON] 2x
<4676> מַצֵּבָה ***maṣṣêḇāh*** [PILLAR] 32x
<4677> מְצֹבָיָה ***m^{e}ṣōḇyāh*** [MESOBAITE, MEZOBAITE] 1x
<4678> מַצֶּבֶת ***maṣṣeḇeṯ*** [PILLAR] 6x
<4679> מְצָד ***m^{e}ṣāḏ,*** מְצַד ***m^{e}ṣaḏ*** [STRONGHOLD] 11x
<4680> מָצָה ***māṣāh*** [DRAIN] 7x
<4681> מֹצָה ***mōṣāh*** [MOZAH] 1x
<4682> מַצָּה ***maṣṣāh*** [UNLEAVENED BREAD] 53x
<4683> מַצָּה ***maṣṣāh*** [STRIFE] 3x
<4684> מִצְהָלוֹת ***miṣhālôṯ*** [NEIGHING] 2x
<4685> מָצוֹד ***māṣôḏ,*** מְצוֹדָה ***m^{e}ṣôḏāh*** [NET] 4x
<4686> מְצוּדָה ***m^{e}ṣûḏāh*** [NET] 4x, [STRONGHOLD] 16x
<4687> מִצְוָה ***miṣwāh*** [COMMAND (noun)] 185x
<4688> מְצוֹלָה ***m^{e}ṣôlāh,*** מְצוּלָה ***m^{e}ṣûlāh,*** מְצֻלָה ***m^{e}ṣulāh*** [DEPTH] 12x
<4689> מָצוֹק ***māṣôq*** [DISTRESS (noun)] 6x
<4690> מָצוּק ***māṣûq*** [PILLAR] 2x
<4691> מְצוּקָה ***m^{e}ṣûqāh*** [DISTRESS (noun)] 7x
<4692> מָצוֹר ***māṣôr*** [SIEGE] 25x
<4693> מָצוֹר ***māṣôr*** [MATSOR] 4x
<4694> מְצוּרָה ***m^{e}ṣûrāh,*** מְצֻרָה ***m^{e}ṣurāh*** [FORTIFIED PLACE] 8x
<4695> מַצּוּת ***maṣṣûṯ*** [CONTEND] 1x
<4696> מֵצַח ***mēṣaḥ*** [FOREHEAD] 13x
<4697> מִצְחָה ***miṣḥāh*** [GREAVES] 1x
<4698> מְצִלָּה ***m^{e}ṣillāh*** [BELL] 1x
<4699> מְצֻלָה ***m^{e}ṣulāh*** [RAVINE] 1x
<4700> מְצִלְתַּיִם ***m^{e}ṣiltayim*** [CYMBALS] 13x
<4701> מִצְנֶפֶת ***miṣnepeṯ*** [TURBAN] 2x
<4702> מַצָּע ***maṣṣā'*** [BED] 1x
<4703> מִצְעָד ***miṣ'āḏ*** [STEP (noun)] 3x
<4704> מִצְעִירָה ***miṣ'iyrāh*** [SMALL] 1x
<4705> מִצְעָר ***miṣ'ār*** [LITTLE ONE] 5x
<4706> מִצְעָר ***miṣār*** [MIZAR] 1x
<4707> מִצְפֶּה ***miṣpeh*** [WATCHTOWER] 2x
<4708> מִצְפֶּה ***miṣpeh*** [MIZPEH] 14x
<4709> מִצְפָּה ***miṣpāh*** [MIZPAH] 32x
<4710> מַצְפּוֹן ***maṣpôn*** [HIDDEN TREASURE] 1x
<4711> מָצַץ ***māṣaṣ*** [DRINK DEEPLY] 1x
<4712> מֵצַר ***mêṣar*** [DISTRESS (noun)] 3x
<4713> מִצְרִי ***miṣriy*** [EGYPTIAN] 30x
<4714> מִצְרַיִם ***miṣrayim*** [MIZRAIM] 681x
<4715> מַצְרֵף ***maṣrêp̄*** [CRUCIBLE] 2x
<4716> מַק ***maq*** [STENCH] 2x
<4717> מַקֶּבֶת ***maqqeḇeṯ*** [HAMMER (noun)] 4x
<4718> מַקֶּבֶת ***maqqeḇeṯ*** [QUARRY (noun)] 1x
<4719> מַקֵּדָה ***maqqêḏah*** [MAKKEDAH] 9x
<4720> מִקְדָּשׁ ***miqdāš*** [SANCTUARY] 74x
<4721> מַקְהֵל ***maqhêl*** [CONGREGATION] 2x
<4722> מַקְהֵלֹת ***maqhêlōṯ*** [MAKHELOTH] 2x
<4723> מִקְוֵא ***miqwê',*** מִקְוֶה ***miqweh,*** קְוֵא ***q^{e}wê',*** קְוֶה ***q^{e}weh*** [HOPE (noun)] 5x
<4724> מִקְוָה ***miqwāh*** [RESERVOIR] 1x
<4725> מָקוֹם ***māqôm,*** מָקֹם ***māqōm*** [PLACE (noun)] 402x

<4726> מָקוֹר ***māqôr*** [FOUNTAIN] 18x
<4727> מִקָּח ***miqqaḥ*** [TAKING] 1x
<4728> מַקָּחוֹת ***maqqāḥôṯ*** [MERCHANDISE] 1x
<4729> מִקְטָר ***miqṭār*** [BURNING (PLACE FOR)] 1x
<4730> מִקְטֶרֶת ***miqṭereṯ*** [CENSER] 2x
<4731> מַקֵּל ***maqqêl*** [STICK] 18x
<4732> מִקְלוֹת ***miqlôṯ*** [MIKLOTH] 4x
<4733> מִקְלָט ***miqlāṭ*** [REFUGE] 20x
<4734> מִקְלַעַת ***miqla'aṯ*** [CARVING] 4x
<4735> מִקְנֶה ***miqneh*** [LIVESTOCK] 75x
<4736> מִקְנָה ***miqnāh*** [PURCHASE (noun)] 15x
<4737> מִקְנֵיָהוּ ***miqnêyāhû*** [MIKNEIAH] 2x
<4738> מִקְסָם ***miqsām*** [DIVINATION] 2x
<4739> מָקַץ ***māqaṣ*** [MAKAZ] 1x
<4740> מִקְצוֹעַ ***miqṣôa'***, מִקְצֹעַ ***miqṣōa'*** [CORNER (noun)] 12x
<4741> מַקְצֻעָה ***maqṣu'āh*** [PLANE] 1x
<4742> מְקֻצְעָת ***mequṣ'āt*** [CORNER (noun)] 2x
<4743> מָקַק ***māqaq*** [WASTE AWAY] 10x
<4744> מִקְרָא ***miqrā'*** [ASSEMBLY] 23x
<4745> מִקְרֶה ***miqreh*** [CHANCE] 10x
<4746> מְקָרֶה ***meqāreh*** [RAFTER] 1x
<4747> מְקֵרָה ***meqêrāh*** [ROOF CHAMBER] 2x
<4748> מִקְשֶׁה ***miqšeh*** [HAIR] 1x
<4749> מִקְשָׁה ***miqšāh*** [HAMMERED, HAMMERED WORK] 10x
<4750> מִקְשָׁה ***miqšāh*** [CUCUMBER FIELD] 2x
<4751> מַר ***mar***, מָר ***mār*** [BITTER, BITTERLY, BITTERNESS] 38x
<4752> מַר ***mar*** [DROP (noun)] 1x
<4753> מֹר ***mōr***, מוֹר ***môr*** [MYRRH] 12x
<4754> מָרָא ***mārā'*** [FILTHY (BE)] 1x, [LIFT ONESELF] 1x
<4755> מָרָא ***mārā'*** [MARA] 1x
<4756> מָרֵא ***mārê'*** [LORD] 4x
<4757> מְרֹאדַךְ בַּלְאֲדָן ***merō'ḏaḵ balaḏān*** [MERODACH-BALADAN] 1x
<4758> מַרְאֶה ***mar'eh*** [SIGHT] 103x
<4759> מַרְאָה ***mar'āh*** [VISION] 12x
<4760> מֻרְאָה ***mur'āh*** [CROP] 1x
<4761> מַרְאָשׁוֹת ***mar'āšôṯ*** [PRINCIPALITIES] 1x
<4762> מָרֵשָׁה ***mārêšāh***, מָרֵאשָׁה ***mārê'šāh*** [MARESHAH] 8x
<4763> מְרַאֲשׁוֹת ***mera'šôṯ*** [HEAD (noun)] 10x
<4764> מֵרַב ***mêraḇ*** [MERAB] 3x
<4765> מַרְבַד ***marḇāḏ*** [COVERING] 2x
<4766> מַרְבֶּה ***marbeh*** [INCREASE (noun)] 2x
<4767> מִרְבָּה ***mirbāh*** [MUCH] 1x
<4768> מַרְבִּית ***marbiyṯ*** [INCREASE (noun)] 5x
<4769> מַרְבֵּץ ***marbêṣ*** [RESTING PLACE] 2x
<4770> מַרְבֵּק ***marbêq*** [FAT, FATTED, FATTENED] 4x
<4771> מַרְגּוֹעַ ***margôa'*** [REST (noun)] 1x
<4772> מַרְגְּלוֹת ***margelôṯ*** [FEET] 5x
<4773> מַרְגֵּמָה ***margêmāh*** [SLING (noun)] 1x
<4774> מַרְגֵּעָה ***margê'āh*** [REPOSE] 1x
<4775> מָרַד ***māraḏ*** [REBEL (verb)] 25x
<4776> מְרַד ***meraḏ*** [REBELLION] 1x

<4777> מֶרֶד ***mereḏ*** [REBELLION] 1x

<4778> מֶרֶד ***mereḏ*** [MERED] 2x

<4779> מָרָד ***mārāḏ*** [REBELLIOUS] 2x

<4780> מַרְדּוּת ***mardûṯ*** [REBELLIOUS] 1x

<4781> מְרֹדַךְ ***m^{e}rōḏāḵ*** [MERODACH] 1x

<4782> מָרְדֳּכַי ***mord^{e}ḵay*** [MORDECAI] 58x

<4783> מֻרְדָּף ***murdāp̱*** [PERSECUTION] 1x

<4784> מָרָה ***mārāh*** [REBELLIOUS (BE)] 44x

<4785> מָרָה ***mārāh*** [MARAH] 5x

<4786> מֹרָה ***mōrāh*** [GRIEF] 2x

<4787> מָרַּה ***morrah*** [BITTERNESS] 1x

<4788> מָרוּד ***mārûḏ*** [WANDERING] 3x

<4789> מֵרוֹז ***mêrôz*** [MEROZ] 1x

<4790> מָרוֹחַ ***mārôaḥ*** [CRUSHED] 1x

<4791> מָרוֹם ***mārôm*** [HEIGHT] 54x

<4792> מֵרוֹם ***mêrôm*** [MEROM] 2x

<4793> מֵרוֹץ ***mêrôṣ*** [RACE] 1x

<4794> מְרוּצָה ***m^{e}rûṣāh*** [RUNNING] 4x

<4795> מָרוּק ***mārûq*** [BEAUTIFICATION] 1x

<4796> מָרוֹת ***mārôṯ*** [MAROTH] 1x

<4797> מִרְזַח ***mirzaḥ*** [BANQUETING] 1x

<4798> מַרְזֵחַ ***marzêaḥ*** [MOURNING] 2x

<4799> מָרַח ***māraḥ*** [APPLY] 1x

<4800> מֶרְחָב ***merḥāḇ*** [BREADTH] 6x

<4801> מֶרְחָק ***merḥāq*** [FAR] 18x

<4802> מַרְחֶשֶׁת ***marḥešeṯ*** [PAN] 2x

<4803> מָרַט ***māraṭ*** [PULL, PULL OUT] 14x

<4804> מְרַט ***m^{e}raṭ*** [PLUCK, PLUCK OFF] 1x

<4805> מְרִי ***m^{e}riy*** [REBELLIOUSNESS] 23x

<4806> מְרִיא ***m^{e}riy'*** [FAT, FATLING, FATTENED] 8x

<4807> מְרִיב בַּעַל ***m^{e}riyḇ ba'al*** [MERIB-BAAL] 3x

<4808> מְרִיבָה ***m^{e}riyḇāh*** [STRIFE] 7x

<4809> מְרִיבָה ***m^{e}riyḇāh,*** מְרִיבה קָדֵשׁ ***m^{e}riyḇaṯ qāḏêš*** [MERIBAH] 8x

<4810> מְרִי בַעַל ***m^{e}riy ḇa'al*** [MERIB-BAAL] 1x

<4811> מְרָיָה ***m^{e}rāyāh*** [MERAIAH] 1x

<4812> מְרָיוֹת ***m^{e}rāyôṯ*** [MERAIOTH] 7x

<4813> מִרְיָם ***miryām*** [MIRIAM] 15x

<4814> מְרִירוּת ***m^{e}riyrûṯ*** [BITTER GRIEF] 1x

<4815> מְרִירִי ***m^{e}riyriy*** [BITTER] 1x

<4816> מֹרֶךְ ***mōreḵ*** [FAINTNESS] 1x

<4817> מֶרְכָּב ***merkāḇ*** [SADDLE] 3x

<4818> מֶרְכָּבָה ***merkāḇāh*** [CHARIOT] 44x

<4819> מַרְכֹּלֶת ***markōleṯ*** [MERCHANDISE] 1x

<4820> מִרְמָה ***mirmāh*** [DECEIT] 39x

<4821> מִרְמָה ***mirmāh*** [MIRMAH] 1x

<4822> מְרֵמוֹת ***m^{e}rêmôṯ*** [MEREMOTH] 7x

<4823> מִרְמָס ***mirmās*** [TRAMPLED, TRAMPLED DOWN] 7x

<4824> מֵרֹנֹתִי ***mêrōnōṯiy*** [MERONOTHITE] 2x

<4825> מֶרֶס ***meres*** [MERES] 1x

<4826> מַרְסְנָא ***mars^{e}nā'*** [MARSENA] 1x

<4827> מֵרַע ***mêra'*** [EVIL] 1x

<4828> מֵרֵעַ ***mêrêa'*** [FRIEND] 8x
<4829> מִרְעֶה ***mir'eh*** [PASTURE] 13x
<4830> מַרְעִית ***mar'iyṯ*** [PASTURE] 10x
<4831> מַרְעֲלָה ***marᵃlāh*** [MARALAH] 1x
<4832> מַרְפֵּא ***marpê'*** [CALMNESS] 2x, [REMEDY] 14x
<4833> מִרְפַּשׂ ***mirpaś*** [MUDDY] 1x
<4834> מָרַץ ***māraṣ*** [GRIEVOUS] 4x
<4835> מְרוּצָה ***mᵉrûṣāh*** [VIOLENCE] 1x
<4836> מַרְצֵעַ ***marṣêa'*** [AWL] 2x
<4837> מַרְצֶפֶת ***marṣepeṯ*** [PAVEMENT] 1x
<4838> מָרַק ***māraq*** [POLISH] 4x
<4839> מָרָק ***māraq*** [BROTH] 3x
<4840> מֶרְקָח ***merqāḥ*** [SCENTED, SWEET-SCENTED] 1x
<4841> מֶרְקָחָה ***merqāḥāh*** [OINTMENT (POT OF, JAR OF)] 2x
<4842> מִרְקַחַת ***mirqaḥaṯ*** [MIXTURE] 3x
<4843> מָרַר ***mārar*** [BITTER (BE, MAKE)] 15x
<4844> מָרֹר ***mārōr*** [BITTER, BITTER HERB] 5x
<4845> מְרֵרָה ***mᵉrêrāh*** [GALL] 2x
<4846> מְרֹרָה ***mᵉrōrāh*** [GALL] 4x
<4847> מְרָרִי ***mᵉrāriy*** [MERARI] 39x
<4848> מְרָרִי ***mᵉrāriy*** [MERARITE] 1x
<4849> מִרְשַׁעַת ***mirša'aṯ*** [WICKED WOMAN] 1x
<4850> מְרָתַיִם ***mᵉrāṯayim*** [MERATHAIM] 1x
<4851> מַשׁ ***maš*** [MASH] 1x
<4852> מֵשָׁא ***mêšā'*** [MESHA] 1x
<4853> מַשָּׂא ***maśśā'*** [BURDEN] 66x
<4854> מַשָּׂא ***maśśā'*** [MASSA] 2x
<4855> מַשָּׁא ***maššā'*** [USURY] 4x
<4856> מַשֹּׂא ***maśśō'*** [PARTIALITY] 1x
<4857> מַשְׁאָב ***maš'āḇ*** [WATERING PLACE] 1x
<4858> מַשָּׂאָה ***maśśā'āh*** [SMOKE (noun)] 1x
<4859> מַשָּׁאָה ***maššā'āh*** [LOAN] 2x
<4860> מַשָּׁאוֹן ***maššā'ôn*** [DECEPTION] 1x
<4861> מִשְׁאָל ***miš'āl*** [MISHAL] 2x
<4862> מִשְׁאָלָה ***miš'ālāh*** [DESIRE (noun)] 2x
<4863> מִשְׁאֶרֶת ***miš'ereṯ*** [KNEADING BOWL, KNEADING TROUGH] 4x
<4864> מַשְׂאֵת ***maś'êṯ*** [GIFT] 15x
<4865> מִשְׁבְּצוֹת ***mišbᵉṣôṯ*** [FILIGREE] 9x
<4866> מַשְׁבֵּר ***mašbêr*** [BIRTH] 3x
<4867> מִשְׁבָּר ***mišbār*** [WAVE] 5x
<4868> מִשְׁבָּת ***mišbāṯ*** [DOWNFALL] 1x
<4869> מִשְׂגָּב ***miśgāḇ*** [STRONGHOLD] 17x
<4870> מִשְׁגֶּה ***mišgeh*** [MISTAKE] 1x
<4871> מָשָׁה ***māšāh*** [DRAW] 3x
<4872> מֹשֶׁה ***mōšeh*** [MOSES] 766x
<4873> מֹשֶׁה ***mōšeh*** [MOSES] 1x
<4874> מַשֶּׁה ***maššeh*** [LOAN] 1x
<4875> מְשׁוֹאָה ***mᵉšô'āh,*** מְשֹׁאָה ***mᵉšō'āh*** [WASTE (noun)] 3x
<4876> מַשּׁוּאָה ***maššû'āh*** [RUINS] 2x
<4877> מְשׁוֹבָב ***mᵉšôḇāḇ*** [MESHOBAB] 1x
<4878> מְשׁוּבָה ***mᵉšûḇāh*** [TURNING AWAY] 13x

<4879> מְשׁוּגָה ***mᵉšûg̱āh*** [ERROR] 1x
<4880> מָשׁוֹט ***māšôṭ,*** מִשּׁוֹט ***miššôṭ*** [OAR] 2x
<4881> מְשׂוּכָה ***mᵉśûkāh,*** מְשֻׂכָה ***mᵉśukāh*** [HEDGE] 2x
<4882> מְשׁוּסָה ***mᵉšûsāh*** [SPOIL (noun)] 1x
<4883> מַשּׂוֹר ***maśśôr*** [SAW (noun)] 1x
<4884> מְשׂוּרָה ***mᵉśûrāh*** [MEASURE (noun)] 4x
<4885> מָשׂוֹשׂ ***māśôś*** [JOY] 17x
<4886> מָשַׁח ***māšaḥ*** [ANOINT] 70x
<4887> מְשַׁח ***mᵉšaḥ*** [OIL, OLIVE OIL] 2x
<4888> מִשְׁחָה ***mišḥāh,*** מָשְׁחָה ***mošḥāh*** [ANOINTING] 26x
<4889> מַשְׁחִית ***mašḥiyṯ*** [DESTRUCTION] 14x
<4890> מִשְׂחָק ***miśḥāq*** [SCORN (noun)] 1x
<4891> מִשְׁחָר ***mišḥār*** [MORNING] 1x
<4892> מַשְׁחֵת ***mašḥêṯ*** [DESTROYING] 1x
<4893> מִשְׁחַת ***mišḥaṯ,*** מָשְׁחָת ***mošḥāṯ*** [MARRED] 2x
<4894> מִשְׁטוֹחַ ***mišṭôaḥ*** [SPREADING] 3x
<4895> מַשְׂטֵמָה ***maśṭêmāh*** [HOSTILITY] 2x
<4896> מִשְׁטָר ***mišṭār*** [RULE (noun)] 1x
<4897> מֶשִׁי ***mešiy*** [SILK] 2x
<4898> מְשֵׁיזַבְאֵל ***mᵉšêyzaḇʼēl*** [MESHEZABEL] 3x
<4899> מָשִׁיחַ ***māšiyaḥ*** [ANOINTED] 39x
<4900> מָשַׁךְ ***māšaḵ*** [PULL] 36x
<4901> מֶשֶׁךְ ***mešeḵ*** [BAG] 2x
<4902> מֶשֶׁךְ ***mešeḵ*** [MESHEC] 10x
<4903> מִשְׁכַּב ***miškaḇ*** [BED] 6x
<4904> מִשְׁכָּב ***miškāḇ*** [BED] 46x
<4905> מַשְׂכִּיל ***maśkiyl*** [MASKIL] 13x
<4906> מַשְׂכִּית ***maśkiyṯ*** [PICTURE] 6x
<4907> מִשְׁכַּן ***miškan*** [DWELLING] 1x
<4908> מִשְׁכָּן ***miškān*** [TABERNACLE] 139x
<4909> מַשְׂכֹּרֶת ***maśkōreṯ*** [WAGES] 4x
<4910> מָשַׁל ***māšal*** [RULE (verb)] 81x
<4911> מָשַׁל ***māšal*** [PROVERB] 16x
<4912> מָשָׁל ***māšāl*** [PROVERB] 39x
<4913> מָשָׁל ***māšāl*** [MASHAL] 1x
<4914> מְשֹׁל ***mᵉšōl*** [BYWORD] 1x
<4915> מֹשֶׁל ***mōšel*** [AUTHORITY] 3x
<4916> מִשְׁלוֹחַ ***mišlôaḥ,*** מִשְׁלָח ***mišlāḥ*** [HAND ON (PUT, LAY)] 10x
<4917> מִשְׁלַחַת ***mišlaḥaṯ*** [DISCHARGE] 2x
<4918> מְשֻׁלָּם ***mᵉšullām*** [MESHULLAM] 25x
<4919> מְשִׁלֵּמוֹת ***mᵉšillêmôṯ*** [MESHILLEMOTH] 2x
<4920> מְשֶׁלֶמְיָה ***mᵉšelemyāh,*** מְשֶׁלֶמְיָהוּ ***mᵉšelemyāhû*** [MESHELEMIAH] 4x
<4921> מְשִׁלֵּמִית ***mᵉšillêmiyṯ*** [MESHILLEMITH] 1x
<4922> מְשֻׁלֶּמֶת ***mᵉšullemeṯ*** [MESHULLEMETH] 1x
<4923> מְשַׁמָּה ***mᵉšammāh*** [DESOLATION] 7x
<4924> מִשְׁמָן ***mišmān,*** מַשְׁמַנִּים ***mašmanniym*** [FATNESS] 7x
<4925> מִשְׁמַנָּה ***mišmannāh*** [MISHMANNAH] 1x
<4926> מִשְׁמָע ***mišmāʻ*** [HEARING] 1x
<4927> מִשְׁמָע ***mišmāʻ*** [MISHMA] 4x
<4928> מִשְׁמַעַת ***mišmaʻaṯ*** [GUARD] 4x
<4929> מִשְׁמָר ***mišmār*** [CUSTODY] 22x

<4930> מַשְׂמֵרָה ***maśmêrāh*** [NAIL] 1x
<4931> מִשְׁמֶרֶת ***mišmereṯ*** [GUARD] 78x
<4932> מִשְׁנֶה ***mišneh*** [DOUBLE] 35x
<4933> מְשִׁסָּה ***m^{e}šissāh*** [SPOIL (noun)] 6x
<4934> מִשְׁעוֹל ***miš‘ôl*** [PATH] 1x
<4935> מִשְׁעִי ***miš‘iy*** [CLEANSING] 1x
<4936> מִשְׁעָם ***miš‘ām*** [MISHAM] 1x
<4937> מִשְׁעָן ***miš‘ān,*** מַשְׁעֵן ***maš‘ên*** [SUPPORT (noun)] 3x
<4938> מַשְׁעֵנָה ***maš‘ênāh,*** מִשְׁעֶנֶת ***miš‘eneṯ*** [SUPPORT (noun)] 12x
<4939> מִשְׂפָּח ***miśpāḥ*** [BLOODSHED] 1x
<4940> מִשְׁפָּחָה ***mišpāḥāh*** [CLAN] 301x
<4941> מִשְׁפָּט ***mišpāṭ*** [JUSTICE] 421x
<4942> מִשְׁפְּתַיִם ***mišp^{e}ṯayim*** [BURDEN] 2x
<4943> מֶשֶׁק ***mešeq*** [HEIR] 1x
<4944> מַשָּׁק ***maššāq*** [RUSHING] 1x
<4945> מַשְׁקֶה ***mašqeh*** [CUPBEARER] 12x, [DRINK (noun)] 6x
<4946> מִשְׁקוֹל ***mišqôl*** [WEIGHT] 1x
<4947> מַשְׁקוֹף ***mašqôp̱*** [LINTEL] 3x
<4948> מִשְׁקָל ***mišqāl*** [WEIGHT] 49x
<4949> מִשְׁקֶלֶת ***mišqeleṯ,*** מִשְׁקֹלֶת ***mišqōleṯ*** [PLUMB LINE] 2x
<4950> מִשְׁקָע ***mišqā‘*** [CLEAR] 1x
<4951> מִשְׂרָה ***miśrāh*** [GOVERNMENT] 2x
<4952> מִשְׁרָה ***mišrāh*** [JUICE] 1x
<4953> מַשְׁרוֹקִי ***mašrôqiy*** [FLUTE] 4x
<4954> מִשְׁרָעִי ***mišrā‘iy*** [MISHRAITE] 1x
<4955> מִשְׂרָפָה ***miśrāp̱āh*** [BURNING (noun)] 2x
<4956> מִשְׂרְפוֹת מַיִם ***miśr^{e}p̱ôṯ mayim*** [MISREPHOTH MAIM] 2x
<4957> מַשְׂרֵקָה ***maśrêqāh*** [MASREKAH] 2x
<4958> מַשְׂרֵת ***maśrêṯ*** [PAN] 1x
<4959> מָשַׁשׁ ***māšaš*** [FEEL] 9x
<4960> מִשְׁתֶּה ***mišteh*** [FEAST] 46x
<4961> מִשְׁתֵּא ***mištê’*** [BANQUET] 1x
<4962> מַת ***maṯ*** [FEW IN NUMBER] 22x
<4963> מַתְבֵּן ***maṯbên*** [STRAW] 1x
<4964> מֶתֶג ***meṯeḡ*** [BRIDLE] 4x
<4965> מֶתֶג הָאַמָּה ***meṯeḡ hā’ammāh*** [METHEG AMMAH] 1x
<4966> מָתוֹק ***māṯôq*** [SWEET] 12x
<4967> מְתוּשָׁאֵל ***m^{e}ṯûšā’êl*** [METHUSAEL] 1x
<4968> מְתוּשֶׁלַח ***m^{e}ṯûšelaḥ*** [METHUSELAH] 6x
<4969> מָתַח ***māṯaḥ*** [SPREAD, SPREAD OUT] 1x
<4970> מָתַי ***māṯay*** [WHEN] 43x
<4971> מַתְכֹּנֶת ***maṯkōneṯ*** [PROPORTION] 5x
<4972> מַתְּלָאָה ***matt^{e}lā’āh*** [WEARINESS] 1x
<4973> מְתַלְּעוֹת ***m^{e}ṯall^{e}‘ôṯ*** [JAWS] 4x
<4974> מְתֹם ***m^{e}ṯōm*** [SOUNDNESS] 4x
<4975> מָתְנַיִם ***moṯnayim*** [LOINS] 47x
<4976> מַתָּן ***mattān*** [GIFT] 5x
<4977> מַתָּן ***mattān*** [MATTAN] 3x
<4978> מַתְּנָה ***matt^{e}nāh*** [GIFT] 3x
<4979> מַתָּנָה ***mattānāh*** [GIFT] 17x
<4980> מַתָּנָה ***mattānāh*** [MATTANAH] 2x

<4981> מִתְנִי ***miṯniy*** [MITHNITE] 1x

<4982> מַתְּנַי ***mattᵉnay*** [MATTENAI] 3x

<4983> מַתַּנְיָה ***mattanyāh,*** מַתַּנְיָהוּ ***mattanyāhû*** [MATTANIAH] 16x

<4984> מִתְנַשֵּׂא ***miṯnaśē'*** [EXALT ONESELF] 2x

<4985> מָתַק ***māṯaq*** [SWEETNESS] 6x

<4986> מָתֵק ***māṯēq*** [SWEETNESS] 2x

<4987> מֹתֶק ***mōṯeq*** [SWEETNESS] 1x

<4988> מָתָק ***māṯāq*** [SWEETLY (FEED)] 1x

<4989> מִתְקָה ***miṯqāh*** [MITHCAH] 2x

<4990> מִתְרְדָת ***miṯrᵉḏāṯ*** [MITHREDATH] 2x

<4991> מַתַּת ***mattaṯ,*** מַתָּת ***mattāṯ*** [GIFT] 6x

<4992> מַתַּתָּה ***mattattāh*** [MATTATTAH] 1x

<4993> מַתִּתְיָה ***mattiṯyāh,*** מַתִּתְיָהוּ ***mattiṯyāhû*** [MATTITHIAH] 8x

נ Nun

<4994> נָא ***nā'*** [PLEASE] 158x

<4995> נָא ***nā'*** [RAW] 1x

<4996> נֹא ***nō'*** [NO (proper noun)] 5x

<4997> נֹאד ***nō'ḏ,*** נְאוֹד ***nᵉ'ôḏ*** [BOTTLE] 6x

<4998> נָאָה ***nā'āh*** [BEAUTIFUL (BE)] 3x

<4999> נָאָה ***nā'āh*** [DWELLING] 12x

<5000> נָאוֶה ***nā'weh*** [BEAUTIFUL] 9x

<5001> נָאַם ***nā'am*** [DECLARE] 1x

<5002> נְאֻם ***nᵉ'um*** [DECLARE] 376x

<5003> נָאַף ***nā'ap̱*** [ADULTERY (COMMIT)] 31x

<5004> נִאֻף ***ni'up̱*** [ADULTERY] 2x

<5005> נַאֲפוּף ***naᵃpûp̱*** [ADULTERY] 1x

<5006> נָאַץ ***nā'aṣ*** [SPURN] 25x

<5007> נֶאָצָה ***ne'āṣāh*** [DISGRACE (noun)] 5x

<5008> נָאַק ***nā'aq*** [GROAN (verb)] 2x

<5009> נְאָקָה ***nᵉ'āqāh*** [GROANING] 4x

<5010> נָאַר ***nā'ar*** [RENOUNCE] 2x

<5011> נֹב ***nōḇ*** [NOB] 6x

<5012> נָבָא ***nāḇā'*** [PROPHESY] 115x

<5013> נְבָא ***nᵉḇā'*** [PROPHESY] 1x

<5014> נָבַב ***nāḇaḇ,*** נָבוּב ***nāḇûḇ*** [HOLLOW (noun)] 4x, [HOLLOW (verb)] 3x

<5015> נְבוֹ ***nᵉḇô,*** נְבוּ שַׂר־סְכִים ***nᵉḇû śar-sᵉkiym*** [NEBO] 13x

<5016> נְבוּאָה ***nᵉḇû'āh*** [PROPHECY] 3x

<5017> נְבוּאָה ***nᵉḇû'āh*** [PROPHESYING] 1x

<5018> נְבוּזַרְאֲדָן ***nᵉḇûzarᵃḏān*** [NEBUZARADAN] 15x

<5019> נְבוּכַדְנֶאצַּר ***nᵉḇûḵaḏne'ṣṣar,*** נְבוּכַדְרֶאצַּר ***nᵉḇûḵaḏre'ṣṣar*** [NEBUCHADNEZZAR] 60x

<5020> נְבוּכַדְנֶצַּר ***nᵉḇûḵaḏneṣṣar*** [NEBUCHADNEZZAR] 29x

<5021> נְבוּשַׁזְבָּן ***nᵉḇûšazbān*** [Nebushazban] 1x

<5022> נָבוֹת ***nāḇôṯ*** [NABOTH] 22x

<5023> נְבִזְבָּה ***nᵉḇizbāh*** [REWARD (noun)] 2x

<5024> נָבַח ***nāḇaḥ*** [BARK] 1x

<5025> נֹבַח ***nōḇaḥ*** [NOBAH] 3x

<5026> נִבְחַז ***niḇḥaz*** [NIBHAZ] 1x

<5027> נָבַט ***naḇaṭ*** [LOOK (verb)] 69x

<5028> נְבָט ***nᵉḇāṭ*** [NEBAT] 25x

<5029> נְבִיא ***nᵉḇiy'*** [PROPHET] 4x

<5030> נָבִיא ***nāḇiy'*** [PROPHET] 316x

<5031> נְבִיאָה ***nᵉḇiy'āh*** [PROPHETESS] 6x

<5032> נְבָיוֹת ***nᵉḇāyôṯ,*** נְבָיֹת ***nᵉḇāyōṯ*** [NEBAIOTH] 5x

<5033> נֵבֶךְ ***nêḇeḵ*** [SPRING] 1x

<5034> נָבֵל ***nāḇêl*** [FOOLISH (be)] 5x, [WITHER] 19x

<5035> נֵבֶל ***nêḇel,*** נֶבֶל ***neḇel*** [HARP] 28x, [SKIN BOTTLE] 10x

<5036> נָבָל ***nāḇāl*** [FOOLISH] 18x

<5037> נָבָל ***nāḇāl*** [NABAL] 22x

<5038> נְבֵלָה ***nᵉḇêlāh*** [CORPSE] 49x

<5039> נְבָלָה ***nᵉḇālāh*** [FOLLY] 13x

<5040> נַבְלוּת ***naḇlûṯ*** [LEWDNESS] 1x

<5041> נְבַלָּט ***nᵉḇallaṭ*** [NEBALLAT] 1x

<5042> נָבַע ***nāḇaʻ*** [UTTER] 11x

<5043> נֶבְרְשָׁה ***neḇrᵉšāh*** [LAMPSTAND] 1x

<5044> נִבְשָׁן ***niḇšān*** [NIBSHAN] 1x

<5045> נֶגֶב ***neg̱eḇ*** [SOUTH] 112x

<5046> נָגַד ***nāg̱aḏ*** [TELL] 5,046x

<5047> נְגַד ***nᵉg̱aḏ*** [FLOW (verb)] 1x

<5048> נֶגֶד ***neg̱eḏ*** [BEFORE] 141x

<5049> נֶגֶד ***neg̱eḏ*** [TOWARD] 1x

<5050> נָגַהּ ***nāg̱ah*** [LIGHTEN] 6x

<5051> נֹגַהּ ***nōg̱ah*** [BRIGHTNESS] 19x

<5052> נֹגַהּ ***nōg̱ah*** [NOGAH] 2x

<5053> נֹגַהּ ***nōg̱ah*** [MORNING] 1x

<5054> נְגֹהָה ***nᵉg̱ōhāh*** [BRIGHTNESS] 1x

<5055> נָגַח ***nāg̱aḥ*** [GORE] 11x

<5056> נַגָּח ***naggāḥ*** [GORING] 2x

<5057> נָגִיד ***nāg̱iyḏ*** [LEADER] 44x

<5058> נְגִינָה ***nᵉg̱iynāh,*** נְגִינַת ***nᵉg̱iynaṯ*** [SONG] 14x

<5059> נָגַן ***nāg̱an*** [PLAY] 15x

<5060> נָגַע ***nāg̱aʻ*** [TOUCH] 150x

<5061> נֶגַע ***neg̱aʻ*** [SORE (noun)] 78x

<5062> נָגַף ***nāg̱ap̱*** [SMITE] 49x

<5063> נֶגֶף ***neg̱ep̱*** [PLAGUE (noun)] 7x

<5064> נָגַר ***nāg̱ar*** [SPILL] 10x

<5065> נָגַשׂ ***nāg̱aś*** [OPPRESS] 23x

<5066> נָגַשׁ ***nāg̱aš*** [COME NEAR] 125x

<5067> נֵד ***nêḏ*** [HEAP (noun)] 6x

<5068> נָדַב ***nāḏaḇ*** [GIVE WILLINGLY] 15x

<5069> נְדַב ***nᵉḏaḇ*** [OFFER FREELY] 4x

<5070> נָדָב ***nāḏāḇ*** [NADAB] 20x

<5071> נְדָבָה ***nᵉḏāḇāh*** [FREEWILL OFFERING] 35x

<5072> נְדַבְיָה ***nᵉḏaḇyāh*** [NEDABIAH] 1x

<5073> נִדְבָּךְ ***niḏbāḵ*** [LAYER, LYING] 2x

<5074> נָדַד ***nāḏaḏ*** [FLEE] 28x

<5075> נְדַד ***nᵉḏaḏ*** [FLEE] 1x

<5076> נְדֻדִים ***nᵉḏuḏiym*** [TOSSING] 1x

<5077> נָדָא ***nāḏā',*** נָדָה ***nāḏāh*** [DRIVE] 3x

<5078> נֵדֶה ***nêḏeh*** [GIFT] 1x
<5079> נִדָּה ***niddāh*** [IMPURITY] 29x
<5080> נָדַח ***nāḏaḥ*** [DRIVE] 52x
<5081> נָדִיב ***nāḏiyḇ*** [WILLING] 28x
<5082> נְדִיבָה ***nᵉḏiyḇāh*** [DIGNITY] 4x
<5083> נָדָן ***nāḏān*** [GIFT] 1x
<5084> נָדָן ***nāḏān*** [SHEATH] 1x
<5085> נִדְנֶה ***niḏneh*** [BODY] 1x
<5086> נָדַף ***nāḏap̱*** [DRIVE AWAY] 9x
<5087> נָדַר ***nāḏar*** [VOW, MAKE A VOW (verb)] 31x
<5088> נֵדֶר ***nêḏer,*** נֶדֶר ***neḏer*** [VOW (noun)] 60x
<5089> נֹהַּ ***nōah*** [PREEMINENCE] 1x
<5090> נָהַג ***nāhaḡ*** [DRIVE] 31x
<5091> נָהָה ***nāhāh*** [LAMENT] 3x
<5092> נְהִי ***nᵉhiy*** [WAILING] 7x
<5093> נִהְיָה ***nihyāh*** [BITTER, BITTERLY] 1x
<5094> נְהִיר ***nᵉhiyr,*** נַהִירוּ ***nahiyrû*** [LIGHT (noun)] 3x
<5095> נָהַל ***nāhal*** [LEAD] 10x
<5096> נַהֲלֹל ***nahᵃlōl,*** נַהֲלָל ***nahᵃlāl*** [NAHALAL, NAHALOL] 3x
<5097> נַהֲלֹל ***nahᵃlōl*** [PASTURE] 1x
<5098> נָהַם ***nāham*** [ROAR (verb)] 5x
<5099> נַהַם ***naham*** [ROAR (noun)] 2x
<5100> נְהָמָה ***nᵉhāmāh*** [ROARING] 2x
<5101> נָהַק ***nāhaq*** [BRAY] 2x
<5102> נָהַר ***nāhar*** [FLOW (verb)] 6x
<5103> נְהַר ***nᵉhar*** [RIVER] 15x
<5104> נָהָר ***nāhār*** [RIVER] 120x
<5105> נְהָרָה ***nᵉhārāh*** [LIGHT (noun)] 1x
<5106> נוּא ***nû'*** [FORBID] 9x
<5107> נוּב ***nûḇ*** [INCREASE (verb)] 4x
<5108> נוֹב ***nôḇ,*** נִיב ***niyḇ*** [FRUIT] 2x
<5109> נֵיבָי ***nêḇāy*** [NEBAI] 1x
<5110> נוּד ***nûḏ*** [FLEE] 24x
<5111> נוּד ***nûḏ*** [FLEE] 1x
<5112> נוֹד ***nôḏ*** [WANDERING] 1x
<5113> נוֹד ***nôḏ*** [NOD] 1x
<5114> נוֹדָב ***nôḏāḇ*** [NODAB] 1x
<5115> נָוָה ***nāwāh*** [PRAISE (verb)] 2x
<5116> נָוֶה ***nāweh,*** נָוָה ***nāwāh*** [HABITATION] 36x
<5117> נוּחַ ***nûaḥ,*** מֻנָּח ***munnāḥ*** [FREE SPACE] 2x, [REST (verb)] 62x
<5118> נוּחַ ***nûaḥ*** נוֹחַ ***nôaḥ*** [RESTING PLACE] 4x
<5119> נוֹחָה ***nôḥāh*** [NOAH] 1x
<5120> נוּט ***nûṭ*** [SHAKE] 1x
<5121> נָיוֹת ***nāyôṯ*** [NAIOTH] 5x
<5122> נְוָלוּ ***nᵉwālû,*** נְוָלִי ***nᵉwāliy*** [DUNGHILL] 3x
<5123> נוּם ***nûm*** [SLUMBER (verb)] 6x
<5124> נוּמָה ***nûmāh*** [DROWSINESS] 1x
<5125> נוּן ***nûn*** [CONTINUE] 1x
<5126> נוּן ***nun,*** נוֹן ***nôn*** [NUN, NON] 30x
<5127> נוּס ***nûs*** [FLEE] 161x
<5128> נוּעַ ***nûaʻ*** [WANDER] 42x

<5129> נוֹעַדְיָה ***nô'aḏyāh*** [NOADIAH] 2x
<5130> נוּף ***nûp̱*** [SPRINKLE] 37x
<5131> נוֹף ***nôp̱*** [ELEVATION] 1x
<5132> נוּץ ***nûṣ*** [BUD (verb)] 2x, [FLEE, FLEE AWAY] 1x
<5133> נוֹצָה ***nôṣāh,*** נֹצָה ***nōṣāh*** [FEATHER] 4x
<5134> נוּק ***nûq*** [NURSE (verb)] 1x
<5135> נוּר ***nûr*** [FIRE] 17x
<5136> נוּשׁ ***nûš*** [SICK (BE)] 1x
<5137> נָזָה ***nāzāh*** [SPRINKLE] 25x
<5138> נָזִיד ***nāziyḏ*** [STEW] 6x
<5139> נָזִיר ***nāziyr*** [NAZIRITE] 16x
<5140> נָזַל ***nāzal,*** נֹזֵל ***nōzêl*** [FLOW (verb and noun)] 16x
<5141> נֶזֶם ***nezem*** [RING] 17x
<5142> נְזַק ***nᵉzaq*** [DAMAGE (verb)] 4x
<5143> נֵזֶק ***nêzeq*** [LOSS] 1x
<5144> נָזַר ***nāzar*** [SEPARATE] 10x
<5145> נֵזֶר ***nêzer*** [CONSECRATION] 25x
<5146> נֹחַ ***nōaḥ*** [NOAH] 46x
<5147> נַחְבִּי ***naḥbiy*** [NAHBI] 1x
<5148> נָחָה ***nāḥāh*** [LEAD] 39x
<5149> נְחוּם ***nᵉḥûm*** [NEHUM] 1x
<5150> נִחוּם ***niḥûm,*** נִחֻם ***niḥum*** [COMFORT (verb)] 3x
<5151> נַחוּם ***naḥûm*** [NAHUM] 1x
<5152> נָחוֹר ***nāḥôr*** [NAHOR] 18x
<5153> נָחוּשׁ ***nāḥûš*** [BRONZE] 1x
<5154> נְחוּשָׁה ***nᵉḥûšāh*** [BRONZE] 10x
<5155> נְחִילָה ***nᵉḥiylāh*** [NEHILOTH] 1x
<5156> נָחִיר ***nāḥiyr*** [NOSTRIL] 1x
<5157> נָחַל ***nāḥal*** [POSSESSION (TAKE)] 59x
<5158> נַחֲלָה ***naḥᵃlāh,*** נַחַל ***naḥal*** [WADI] 141x
<5159> נַחֲלָה ***naḥᵃlāh*** [POSSESSION] 222x
<5160> נַחֲלִיאֵל ***naḥᵃliy'êl*** [NAHALIEL] 1x
<5161> נֶחֱלָמִי ***neḥᵉlāmiy*** [NEHELAMITE] 3x
<5162> נָחַם ***nāḥam*** [SORRY (BE)] 108x
<5163> נַחַם ***naḥam*** [NAHAM] 1x
<5164> נֹחַם ***nōḥam*** [COMPASSION] 1x
<5165> נֶחָמָה ***neḥāmāh*** [COMFORT (noun)] 2x
<5166> נְחֶמְיָה ***nᵉḥemyāh*** [NEHEMIAH] 8x
<5167> נַחֲמָנִי ***naḥᵃmāniy*** [NAHAMANI] 1x
<5168> נַחְנוּ ***naḥnû*** [WE] 6x
<5169> נָחַץ ***nāḥaṣ*** [HASTE (REQUIRE)] 1x
<5170> נַחַר ***naḥar,*** נַחֲרָה ***naḥᵃrāh*** [SNORTING] 2x
<5171> נַחֲרַי ***naḥᵃray,*** נַחְרַי ***naḥray*** [NAHARAI] 2x
<5172> נָחַשׁ ***naḥaš*** [DIVINATION (PRACTICE)] 11x
<5173> נַחַשׁ ***naḥaš*** [ENCHANTMENT] 2x
<5174> נְחָשׁ ***nᵉḥāš*** [BRONZE] 9x
<5175> נָחָשׁ ***nāḥāš*** [SERPENT] 31x
<5176> נָחָשׁ ***nāḥāš*** [NAHASH] 9x
<5177> נַחְשׁוֹן ***naḥšôn*** [NAHSON] 10x
<5178> נְחֹשֶׁת ***nᵉḥōšeṯ*** [COPPER] 140x, [LUST (noun)] 1x
<5179> נְחֻשְׁתָּא ***nᵉḥuštā'*** [NEHUSHTA] 1x

<5180> נְחֻשְׁתָּן ***nᵉḥuštān*** [NEHUSHTAN] 1x
<5181> נָחַת ***nāḥaṯ*** [BEND] 8x
<5182> נְחֵת ***nᵉḥêṯ*** [BRING DOWN] 6x
<5183> נַחַת ***naḥaṯ*** [DESCENT] 1x, [REST (noun)] 7x
<5184> נַחַת ***naḥaṯ*** [NAHATH] 5x
<5185> נָחֵת ***nāḥêṯ*** [GOING DOWN] 1x
<5186> נָטָה ***nāṭāh*** [STRETCH OUT] 214x
<5187> נָטִיל ***naṭiyl*** [WEIGH OUT] 1x
<5188> נְטִיפָה ***nᵉṭiyp̱āh,*** נְטִפָה ***nᵉṭip̱āh*** [PENDANT] 2x
<5189> נְטִישׁוֹת ***nᵉṭiyšôṯ*** [BRANCHES] 3x
<5190> נָטַל ***nāṭal*** [OFFER] 4x
<5191> נְטַל ***nᵉṭal*** [LIFT, LIFT UP] 2x
<5192> נֵטֶל ***nêṭel*** [BURDEN] 1x
<5193> נָטַע ***nāṭaʿ*** [PLANT (verb)] 58x
<5194> נֶטַע ***neṭaʿ*** [PLANT (noun)] 4x
<5195> נָטִיעַ ***nāṭiyaʿ*** [PLANT (noun)] 1x
<5196> נְטָעִים ***nᵉṭāʿiym*** [NETAIM] 1x
<5197> נָטַף ***nāṭap̱*** [DROP (verb)] 18x
<5198> נָטָף ***nāṭāp̱,*** נֶטֶף ***neṭep̱*** [STACTE] 2x
<5199> נְטֹפָה ***nᵉṭōp̱āh*** [NETOPHAH] 2x
<5200> נְטוֹפָתִי ***nᵉṭôp̱āṯiy*** [NETOPHATHITE] 11x
<5201> נָטַר ***nāṭar*** [KEEP] 9x
<5202> נְטַר ***nᵉṭar*** [KEEP] 1x
<5203> נָטַשׁ ***nāṭaš*** [FORSAKE] 40x
<5204> נִי ***niy*** [WAILING] 1x
<5205> נִיד ***niyḏ*** [COMFORT (noun)] 1x
<5206> נִידָה ***niyḏāh*** [UNCLEAN] 1x
<5207> נִיחוֹחַ ***niyḥôaḥ,*** נִיחֹחַ ***niyḥōaḥ*** [PLEASING] 43x
<5208> נִיחוֹחַ ***niyḥôaḥ,*** נִיחֹחַ ***niyḥōaḥ*** [PLEASING] 2x
<5209> נִין ***niyn*** [OFFSPRING] 3x
<5210> נִינְוֵה ***niynᵉwêh*** [NINEVEH] 17x
<5211> נִיס ***niys*** [FLEES (ONE WHO)] 1x
<5212> נִיסָן ***niysān*** [NISAN] 2x
<5213> נִיצוֹץ ***niyṣôṣ*** [SPARK] 1x
<5214> נִיר ***niyr*** [BREAK UP] 2x
<5215> נִיר ***niyr*** [FALLOW GROUND] 4x
<5216> נִיר ***niyr,*** נֵר ***nêr,*** נֵיר ***neyr*** [LAMP] 48x
<5217> נָכָא ***nāḵā'*** [DRIVE OUT] 1x
<5218> נָכֵא ***nāḵê',*** נָכָא ***nāḵā'*** [CRUSHED] 4x
<5219> נְכֹאת ***nᵉḵō'ṯ*** [SPICE] 2x
<5220> נֶכֶד ***neḵeḏ*** [POSTERITY] 3x
<5221> נָכָה ***nāḵāh*** [STRIKE] 500x
<5222> נֵכֶה ***nêḵeh*** [ATTACKER] 1x
<5223> נָכֶה ***nāḵeh*** [CRIPPLED] 3x
<5224> נְכוֹ ***nᵉḵô*** [NECHO] 3x
<5225> נָכוֹן ***nāḵôn*** [NACHON] 1x
<5226> נֵכַח ***nêḵaḥ*** [OPPOSITE (adv.)] 2x
<5227> נֹכַח ***nōḵaḥ*** [OPPOSITE (adv.)] 23x
<5228> נָכֹחַ ***naḵōaḥ*** [RIGHT] 4x
<5229> נְכֹחָה ***nᵉḵōḥāh*** [RIGHT] 4x
<5230> נָכַל ***nāḵal*** [DECEIVE] 4x

<5231> נֵכֶל ***nêḵel*** [TRICK] 1x
<5232> נְכַס ***nᵉḵas*** [GOODS] 2x
<5233> נֶכֶס ***neḵes*** [WEALTH] 5x
<5234> נָכַר ***nāḵar*** [DETERMINE] 50x
<5235> נֶכֶר ***neḵer,*** נֹכֶר ***nōḵer*** [DISASTER] 2x
<5236> נֵכָר ***nêḵār*** [FOREIGN] 35x
<5237> נָכְרִי ***noḵriy*** [STRANGE] 46x
<5238> נְכֹת ***nᵉḵōṯ*** [TREASURE] 2x
<5239> נָלָה ***nālāh*** [END (MAKE AN)] 1x
<5240> נְמִבְזָה ***nᵉmiḇzāh*** [DESPISED] 1x
<5241> נְמוּאֵל ***nᵉmû'êl*** [NEMUEL] 3x
<5242> נְמוּאֵלִי ***nᵉmû'êliy*** [NEMUELITE] 1x
<5243> נָמַל ***nāmal*** [CUT DOWN] 5x
<5244> נְמָלָה ***nᵉmālāh*** [ANT] 2x
<5245> נְמַר ***nᵉmar*** [LEOPARD] 1x
<5246> נָמֵר ***nāmêr*** [LEOPARD] 6x
<5247> נִמְרָה ***nimrāh*** [NIMRAH] 1x
<5248> נִמְרֹד ***nimrōḏ*** [NIMROD] 4x
<5249> נִמְרִים ***nimriym*** [NIMRIM] 2x
<5250> נִמְשִׁי ***nimšiy*** [NIMSHI] 5x
<5251> נֵס ***nês*** [BANNER] 20x
<5252> נְסִבָּה ***nᵉsibbāh*** [EVENTS (TURN OF)] 1x
<5253> נָסַג ***nāsag*** [MOVE] 9x
<5254> נָסָה ***nāsāh*** [TEST] 36x
<5255> נָסַח ***nāsaḥ*** [TEAR] 4x
<5256> נְסַח ***nᵉsaḥ*** [PULL] 1x
<5257> נָסִיךְ ***nāsiyḵ*** [DRINK OFFERING] 1x, [METAL IMAGE] 1x, [PRINCE] 5x
<5258> נָסַךְ ***nāsaḵ*** [POUR OUT] 25x
<5259> נָסַךְ ***nāsaḵ*** [SPREAD (verb)] 2x
<5260> נְסַךְ ***nᵉsaḵ*** [OFFER] 1x
<5261> נְסַךְ ***nᵉsaḵ*** [DRINK OFFERING] 1x
<5262> נֵסֶךְ ***nêseḵ,*** נֶסֶךְ ***nêseḵ*** [DRINK OFFERING] 64x
<5263> נָסַס ***nāsas*** [SICK MAN] 1x
<5264> נָסַס ***nāsas*** [SPARKLE] 1x
<5265> נָסַע ***nāsa'*** [SET OUT] 146x
<5266> נָסַק ***nāsaq*** [ASCEND] 1x
<5267> נְסַק ***nᵉsaq*** [TAKE UP] 2x
<5268> נִסְרֹךְ ***nisrōḵ*** [NISROCK] 2x
<5269> נֵעָה ***nê'āh*** [NEAH] 1x
<5270> נֹעָה ***nō'āh*** [NOAH] 4x
<5271> נְעוּרִים ***nᵉ'ûriym,*** נְעוּרוֹת ***nᵉ'ûrôṯ*** [YOUTH] 47x
<5272> נְעִיאֵל ***nᵉ'iy'êl*** [NEIEL] 1x
<5273> נָעִים ***nā'iym*** [PLEASANT] 13x
<5274> נָעַל ***nā'al*** [LOCK (verb)] 6x, [SHOD] 2x
<5275> נַעַל ***na'al*** [SANDAL] 22x
<5276> נָעֵם ***nā'êm*** [PLEASANT] 8x
<5277> נַעַם ***na'am*** [NAAM] 1x
<5278> נֹעַם ***nō'am*** [BEAUTY] 7x
<5279> נַעֲמָה ***na'ᵃmāh*** [NAAMAH] 5x
<5280> נַעֲמִי ***na'ᵃmiy*** [NAAMITE] 1x
<5281> נָעֳמִי ***nā'ᵒmiy*** [NAOMI] 21x

<5282> נַעֲמָן ***na^{a}mān*** [PLEASANT] 1x
<5283> נַעֲמָן ***na^{a}mān*** [NAAMAN] 16x
<5284> נַעֲמָתִי ***na^{a}māṯiy*** [NAAMATHITE] 4x
<5285> נַעֲצוּץ ***na^{a}ṣûṣ*** [THORN BUSH] 2x
<5286> נָעַר ***nāʿar*** [GROWL] 1x
<5287> נָעַר ***nāʿar*** [SHAKE] 11x
<5288> נַעַר ***naʿar*** [BOY] 223x
<5289> נַעַר ***naʿar*** [YOUNG, YOUNG ONE] 1x
<5290> נֹעַר ***nōʿar*** [YOUTH] 4x
<5291> נַעֲרָה ***na^{a}rāh*** [GIRL] 62x
<5292> נַעֲרָה ***na^{a}rāh,*** נַעֲרָתָה ***na^{a}rāṯāh*** [NAARAH] 3x
<5293> נַעֲרַי ***na^{a}ray*** [NAARAI] 1x
<5294> נְעַרְיָה ***n^{e}ʿaryāh*** [NEARIAH] 3x
<5295> נַעֲרָן ***na^{a}rān*** [NAARAN] 1x
<5296> נְעֹרֶת ***n^{e}ʿōreṯ*** [TOW] 2x
<5297> נֹף ***nōp̄*** [MEMPHIS] 7x
<5298> נֶפֶג ***nep̄eg*** [NEPHEG] 4x
<5299> נָפָה ***nāphāh,*** נָפוֹת ***nāp̄ôṯ*** [SIEVE] 5x
<5300> נְפוּשְׁסִים ***n^{e}p̄ûš^{e}siym*** [NEPHUSHESIM, NEPHUSSIM] 2x
<5301> נָפַח ***nāp̄aḥ*** [BREATHE] 12x
<5302> נֹפַח ***nōp̄aḥ*** [NOPHAH] 1x
<5303> נְפִילִים ***n^{e}p̄iyliym*** [NEPHILIM] 3x
<5304> נְפִישְׁסִים ***n^{e}p̄iyš^{e}siym*** [NEPHISHESIM, NEPHUSSIM] 2x
<5305> נָפִישׁ ***nāp̄iyš*** [NAPHISH] 3x
<5306> נֹפֶךְ ***nōp̄eḵ*** [TURQUOISE] 4x
<5307> נָפַל ***nāp̄al*** [FALL (verb)] 428x
<5308> נְפַל ***n^{e}p̄al*** [FALL (verb)] 11x
<5309> נֵפֶל ***nêpel,*** נֶפֶל ***nep̄el*** [STILLBORN] 3x
<5310> נָפַץ ***nāp̄aṣ*** [BREAK] 22x
<5311> נֶפֶץ ***nep̄eṣ*** [CLOUDBURST] 1x
<5312> נְפַק ***n^{e}p̄aq*** [TAKE OUT] 11x
<5313> נִפְקָה ***nip̄qāh*** [COST] 2x
<5314> נָפַשׁ ***nāp̄aš*** [REST (verb)] 3x
<5315> נֶפֶשׁ ***nep̄eš*** [BREATH] 753x
<5316> נֶפֶת ***nep̄eṯ,*** נָפוֹת ***nāp̄ôṯ*** [NAPHOTH] 1x
<5317> נֹפֶת ***nōp̄eṯ*** [HONEYCOMB] 5x
<5318> נֶפְתּוֹחַ ***nep̄tôaḥ*** [NEPHTOAH] 2x
<5319> נַפְתּוּלִים ***nap̄tûliym*** [WRESTLINGS] 1x
<5320> נַפְתֻּחִים ***nap̄tuḥiym*** [NAPHTUHITES, NAPHTUHIM] 2x
<5321> נַפְתָּלִי ***nap̄tāliy*** [NAPHTALI] 50x
<5322> נֵץ ***nêṣ*** [FLOWER] 2x, [HAWK] 2x
<5323> נָצָא ***nāṣāʾ*** [FLY (verb)] 1x
<5324> נָצַב ***nāṣaḇ*** [STAND (verb)] 75x
<5325> נִצָּב ***niṣṣāḇ*** [HILT] 1x
<5326> נִצְבָּה ***niṣbāh*** [STRENGTH] 1x
<5327> נָצָה ***nāṣāh*** [FIGHT] 7x, [RUINS (BE, LIE IN)] 3x
<5328> נִצָּה ***niṣṣāh*** [FLOWER] 2x
<5329> נָצַח ***nāṣaḥ*** [OVERSEE] 65x
<5330> נְצַח ***n^{e}ṣaḥ*** [DISTINGUISH ONESELF] 1x
<5331> נֵצַח ***nêṣaḥ,*** נֶצַח ***neṣaḥ*** [FOREVER] 43x
<5332> נֵצַח ***nêṣaḥ*** [BLOOD] 2x

<5333> נְצִיב ***n***^{e}***ṣiyḇ*** [GARRISON] 12x
<5334> נְצִיב ***n***^{e}***ṣiyḇ*** [NEZIB] 1x
<5335> נְצִיחַ ***n***^{e}***ṣiyaḥ*** [NEZIAH] 2x
<5336> נָצִיר ***nāṣiyr*** [PRESERVED] 1x
<5337> נָצַל ***nāṣal*** [DELIVER] 213x
<5338> נְצַל ***n***^{e}***ṣal*** [DELIVER] 3x
<5339> נִצָּן ***niṣṣān*** [FLOWER] 1x
<5340> נָצַץ ***nāṣaṣ*** [SPARKLE] 4x
<5341> נָצַר ***nāṣar*** [KEEP] 63x
<5342> נֵצֶר ***nêṣer*** [BRANCH] 4x
<5343> נְקֵא ***n***^{e}***qê'*** [PURE] 1x
<5344> נָקַב ***nāqaḇ*** [PIERCE] 25x
<5345> נֶקֶב ***neqeḇ*** [SETTING] 1x
<5346> נֶקֶב ***neqeḇ*** [NEKEB] 1x
<5347> נְקֵבָה ***n***^{e}***qêḇāh*** [FEMALE] 22x
<5348> נָקֹד ***nāqōḏ*** [SPECKLED] 9x
<5349> נֹקֵד ***nōqêḏ*** [SHEEP BREEDER] 2x
<5350> נִקֻּדִים ***niqqûḏiym*** [MOLDY] 3x
<5351> נְקֻדָּה ***n***^{e}***quddāh*** [STUD] 1x
<5352> נָקָה ***nāqāh*** [FREE (BE)] 44x
<5353> נְקוֹדָא ***n***^{e}***qôḏā'*** [NEKODA] 4x
<5354> נָקַט ***nāqaṯ*** [WEARY (BE)] 1x
<5355> נָקִי ***nāqiy,*** נָקִיא ***nāqiy'*** [INNOCENT] 44x
<5356> נִקָּיוֹן ***niqqāyôn,*** נִקָּיֹן ***niqqāyōn*** [INNOCENCE] 5x
<5357> נָקִיק ***nāqiyq*** [CLEFT] 3x
<5358> נָקַם ***nāqam*** [VENGEANCE (TAKE)] 35x
<5359> נָקָם ***nāqām*** [VENGEANCE] 17x
<5360> נְקָמָה ***n***^{e}***qāmāh*** [VENGEANCE] 27x
<5361> נָקַע ***nāqa'*** [DISGUSTED (BECOME)] 3x
<5362> נָקַף ***nāqap̱*** [CUT DOWN] 2x, [SURROUND] 17x
<5363> נֹקֶף ***nōqep̱*** [SHAKING] 2x
<5364> נִקְפָּה ***niqpāh*** [ROPE] 1x
<5365> נָקַר ***nāqar*** [GOUGE] 8x
<5366> נְקָרָה ***n***^{e}***qārāh*** [CLEFT] 2x
<5367> נָקַשׁ ***nāqaš*** [ENSNARE] 5x
<5368> נְקַשׁ ***n***^{e}***qaš*** [KNOCK] 1x
<5369> נֵר ***nêr*** [NER] 16x
<5370> נֵרְגַל ***nêrgal*** [NERGAL] 1x
<5371> נֵרְגַל שַׂר־אֶצֶר ***nêrgal śar-'eṣer*** [NERGAL-SHAREZER] 3x
<5372> נִרְגָּן ***nirgān*** [WHISPERER] 4x
<5373> נֵרְדְּ ***nêrd*** [NARD] 3x
<5374> נֵרִיָּה ***nêriyyāh,*** נֵרִיָּהוּ ***nêriyyāhû*** [NERIAH] 10x
<5375> נָשָׂא ***nāśā'*** [CARRY] 640x
<5376> נְשָׂא ***n***^{e}***śā'*** [INSURRECTION (MAKE)] 3x
<5377> נָשָׁא ***nāšā'*** [DECEIVE] 16x
<5378> נָשָׁא ***nāšā'*** [DEBT (BE IN)] 5x
<5379> נִשֵּׂאת ***niśśê'ṯ*** [GIFT] 1x
<5380> נָשַׁב ***nāšaḇ*** [DRIVE] 3x
<5381> נָשַׂג ***nāśag*** [OVERTAKE] 50x
<5382> נָשָׁה ***nāšāh*** [FORGET] 6x
<5383> נָשָׁה ***nāšāh,*** נָשָׁא ***nāšā'*** [LEND] 13x

<5384> נָשֶׁה ***nāšeh*** [SHRANK (WHICH, THAT)] 1x
<5385> נְשׂוּאָה ***n^{e}śû'āh*** [CARRIAGE] 1x
<5386> נְשִׁי ***n^{e}šiy*** [DEBT] 1x
<5387> נָשִׂיא ***nāśiy'*** [RULER] 132x
<5388> נְשִׁיָּה ***n^{e}šiyyāh*** [FORGETFULNESS] 1x
<5389> נְשִׁין ***n^{e}šiyn*** [WIVES] 1x
<5390> נְשִׁיקָה ***n^{e}šiyqāh*** [KISS (noun)] 2x
<5391> נָשַׁךְ ***nāšak̲*** [BITE] 16x
<5392> נֶשֶׁךְ ***nešek̲*** [INTEREST] 12x
<5393> נִשְׁכָּה ***niškāh*** [CHAMBER] 3x
<5394> נָשַׁל ***nāšal*** [REMOVE] 7x
<5395> נָשַׁם ***nāšam*** [GASP] 1x
<5396> נִשְׁמָה ***nišmāh*** [BREATH] 1x
<5397> נְשָׁמָה ***n^{e}šāmāh*** [BREATH] 24x
<5398> נָשַׁף ***nāšap̲*** [BLOW (verb)] 2x
<5399> נֶשֶׁף ***nešep̲*** [TWILIGHT] 12x
<5400> נָשַׂק ***nāśaq*** [KINDLE] 3x
<5401> נָשַׁק ***nāšaq*** [KISS (verb)] 35x
<5402> נֵשֶׁק ***nêšeq***, נֶשֶׁק ***nešeq*** [WEAPONS] 10x
<5403> נְשַׁר ***n^{e}šar*** [EAGLE] 2x
<5404> נֶשֶׁר ***nešer*** [EAGLE] 26x
<5405> נָשַׁת ***našat̲*** [DRY UP] 4x
<5406> נִשְׁתְּוָן ***ništ^{e}wān*** [LETTER] 2x
<5407> נִשְׁתְּוָן ***ništ^{e}wān*** [LETTER] 3x
<5408> נָתַח ***nāt̲aḥ*** [CUT (verb)] 9x
<5409> נֵתַח ***nêt̲aḥ*** [PIECES] 13x
<5410> נָתִיב ***nat̲iyb̲***, נְתִיבָה ***n^{e}t̲iyb̲āh*** [PATH] 26x
<5411> נְתִינִים ***n^{e}t̲iyniym*** [NETHINIM] 16x
<5412> נְתִינִין ***n^{e}t̲iyniyn*** [NETHINIM] 1x
<5413> נָתַךְ ***nāt̲ak̲*** [POUR OUT] 21x
<5414> נָתַן ***nāthan*** [GIVE] 2,008x
<5415> נְתַן ***n^{e}t̲an*** [GIVE] 7x
<5416> נָתָן ***nāt̲ān*** [NATHAN] 42x
<5417> נְתַנְאֵל ***n^{e}t̲an'ēl*** [NETHANEL] 14x
<5418> נְתַנְיָה ***n^{e}t̲anyāh***, נְתַנְיָהוּ ***n^{e}t̲anyāhû*** [NETHANIAH] 20x
<5419> נְתַן־מֶלֶךְ ***n^{e}t̲an-melek̲*** [NATHAN-MELECH] 1x
<5420> נָתַס ***nāt̲as*** [BREAK] 1x
<5421> נָתַע ***nāt̲a'*** [BREAK] 1x
<5422> נָתַץ ***nāt̲aṣ*** [DESTROY] 42x
<5423> נָתַק ***nāt̲aq*** [BREAK] 27x
<5424> נֶתֶק ***net̲eq*** [SKIN DISEASE] 9x
<5425> נָתַר ***nāt̲ar*** [LEAP] 3x, [LOOSE (LET)] 5x
<5426> נְתַר ***n^{e}t̲ar*** [STRIP OFF] 1x
<5427> נֶתֶר ***net̲er*** [SODA] 2x
<5428> נָתַשׁ ***nāt̲aš*** [UPROOT] 21x

ס Samekh

<5429> סְאָה ***s^{e}'āh*** [SEAH] 9x
<5430> סְאוֹן ***s^{e}'ôn*** [BOOT] 1x

<5431> סָאַן ***sā'an*** [WARRIOR] 1x
<5432> סַאסְּאָה ***sa'ssᵉ'āh*** [WARFARE] 1x
<5433> סָבָא ***sāḇā'*** [DRUNKARD] 6x
<5434> סְבָא ***sᵉḇā'*** [SEBA] 4x
<5435> סֹבֶא ***sōḇe'*** [WINE] 3x
<5436> סְבָאִים ***sᵉḇā'iym,*** סָבָאִים ***sāḇā'iym*** [SABEANS] 2x
<5437> סָבַב ***sāḇaḇ*** [AROUND (GO, TURN)] 160x
<5438> סִבָּה ***sibbāh*** [TURN OF EVENTS] 1x
<5439> סָבִיב ***sāḇiyḇ*** [ALL AROUND] 284x
<5440> סָבַךְ ***sāḇaḵ*** [ENTWINE] 2x
<5441> סְבֹךְ ***sᵉḇōḵ*** [THICKET] 1x
<5442> סְבַךְ ***sᵉḇaḵ*** [THICKET] 3x
<5443> סַבְּכָא ***sabbᵉḵā',*** שַׂבְּכָא ***śabbᵉḵā'*** [TRIGON] 4x
<5444> סִבְּכַי ***sibbᵉḵai*** [SIBBECAI] 4x
<5445> סָבַל ***sāḇal*** [BEAR (verb)] 9x
<5446> סְבַל ***sᵉḇal*** [RETAIN] 1x
<5447> סֵבֶל ***sêḇel*** [BURDEN] 3x
<5448> סֹבֶל ***sōḇel*** [BURDEN] 3x
<5449> סַבָּל ***sabbāl*** [BURDEN-BEARER] 5x
<5450> סְבָלָה ***sᵉḇālāh*** [BURDEN] 6x
<5451> סִבֹּלֶת ***sibbōleṯ*** [SIBBOLETH] 1x
<5452> סְבַר ***sᵉḇar*** [THINK] 1x
<5453> סִבְרַיִם ***siḇrayim*** [SIBRAIM] 1x
<5454> סַבְתָּא ***saḇtā',*** סַבְתָּה ***saḇtāh*** [SABTA, SABTAH] 2x
<5455> סַבְתְּכָא ***saḇtᵉḵā'*** [SABTECHA] 2x
<5456> סָגַד ***sāg̱aḏ*** [FALL DOWN] 4x
<5457> סְגִד ***sᵉg̱hiḏ*** [FALL, FALL DOWN] 12x
<5458> סְגוֹר ***sᵉg̱ôr*** [CAUL] 1x, [GOLD] 1x
<5459> סְגֻלָּה ***sᵉg̱ullāh*** [TREASURED POSSESSION] 8x
<5460> סְגַן ***sᵉg̱an*** [PREFECT] 5x
<5461> סֶגֶן ***seg̱en,*** סָגָן ***sāg̱ān*** [RULER] 17x
<5462> סָגַר ***sāg̱ar*** [CLOSE] 86x, [PURE] 5x
<5463> סְגַר ***sᵉg̱ar*** [SHUT] 1x
<5464> סַגְרִיר ***sag̱riyr*** [CONTINUAL] 1x
<5465> סַד ***saḏ*** [STOCKS] 2x
<5466> סָדִין ***sāḏiyn*** [LINEN GARMENT] 4x
<5467> סְדֹם ***sᵉḏōm*** [SODOM] 39x
<5468> סֵדֶר ***sêḏer*** [ORDER] 1x
<5469> סַהַר ***sahar*** [ROUNDED] 1x
<5470> סֹהַר ***sōhar*** [PRISON] 6x
<5471> סוֹא ***sô'*** [SO] 1x
<5472> סוּג ***sûg̱*** [TURN BACK] 14x
<5473> סוּג ***sûg̱*** [ENCIRCLE] 1x
<5474> סוּגַר ***sûg̱ar*** [CAGE] 1x
<5475> סוֹד ***sôḏ*** [COUNSEL (noun)] 21x
<5476> סוֹדִי ***sôḏiy*** [SODI] 1x
<5477> סוּחַ ***sûaḥ*** [SUAH] 1x
<5478> סוּחָה ***sûḥāh*** [REFUSE (noun)] 1x
<5479> סוֹטַי ***sôṭay*** [SOTAI] 2x
<5480> סוּךְ ***sûk*** [ANOINT] 9x
<5481> סוּמְפּוֹנְיָה ***sûmpônyāh*** [BAGPIPE] 4x

<5482> סְוֵנֵה **s^{e}wênêh** [SYENE] 2x

<5483> סוּס **sûs,** סֻס **sus** [HORSE] 140x

<5484> סוּסָה **sûsāh** [MARE] 1x

<5485> סוּסִי **sûsiy** [SUSI] 1x

<5486> סוּף **sûp̱** [CONSUME, BE CONSUMED] 8x

<5487> סוּף **sûp̱** [CONSUME] 2x

<5488> סוּף **sûp̱** [REED] 28x

<5489> סוּף **sûp̱** [SUPH] 1x

<5490> סוֹף **sôp̱** [END] 5x

<5491> סוֹף **s̱ōph** [END] 5x

<5492> סוּפָה **sûp̱āh** [STORM (noun)] 16x

<5493> סוּר **sûr,** סָר **sār** [TURN ASIDE] 301x

<5494> סוּר **sûr** [DEGENERATE] 1x

<5495> סוּר **sûr** [SUR] 1x

<5496> סוּת **sûṯ** [ENTICE] 18x

<5497> סוּת **sûṯ** [CLOTHES] 1x

<5498> סָחַב **sāḥaḇ** [DRAG (verb)] 5x

<5499> סְחָבָה **s^{e}ḥāḇāh** [RAG] 2x

<5500> סָחָה **sāḥāh** [SCRAPE] 1x

<5501> סְחִי **s^{e}ḥiy** [SCUM] 1x

<5502> סָחַף **sāḥap̱** [SWEEP] 2x

<5503> סָחַר **sāḥar** [MERCHANT] 20x

<5504> סַחַר **saḥar** [MERCHANDISE] 5x

<5505> סָחָר **sāḥār** [MERCHANDISE] 3x

<5506> סְחֹרָה **s^{e}ḥōrāh** [MARKET] 1x

<5507> סֹחֵרָה **sōḥêrāh** [BUCKLER] 1x

<5508> סֹחֶרֶת **sōḥereṯ** [PRECIOUS STONE] 1x

<5509> סִיג **siyg,** סוּג **sûg̱** [DROSS] 8x

<5510> סִיוָן **siywān** [SIVAN] 1x

<5511> סִיחוֹן **siyḥôn** [SIHON] 37x

<5512> סִין **siyn** [SIN (proper noun)] 6x

<5513> סִינִי **siyniy** [SINITE] 2x

<5514> סִינַי **siynay** [SINAI] 35x

<5515> סִינִים **siyniym** [SINIM] 1x

<5516> סִיסְרָא **siys^{e}rā'** [SISERA] 21x

<5517> סִיעָא **siy'ā',** סִיעֲהָא **siy^{a}hā'** [SIAHA] 2x

<5518> סִיר **siyr** [POT] 29x, [THORN] 5x

<5519> סָךְ **sāḵ** [THRONG] 1x

<5520> סֹךְ **sōḵ** [ABODE] 4x

<5521> סֻכָּה **sukkāh** [BOOTH] 31x

<5522> סִכּוּת **sikkûṯ** [SIKKUTH] 1x

<5523> סֻכּוֹת **sukkôṯ** [SIKKUTH] 18x

<5524> סֻכּוֹת בְּנוֹת **sukkôṯ b^{e}nôṯ** [SUCCOTH BENOTH] 1x

<5525> סֻכִּיִּים **sukkiyyiym** [SUKKITES] 1x

<5526> סָכַךְ **sāḵaḵ,** שָׂכַךְ **śāḵaḵ** [COVER (verb)] 23x

<5527> סְכָכָה **s^{e}ḵāḵāh** [SECACAH] 1x

<5528> סָכַל **sāḵal** [FOOLISHLY (ACT, DO)] 8x

<5529> סֶכֶל **seḵel** [FOLLY] 1x

<5530> סָכָל **sāḵāl** [FOOL] 7x

<5531> סִכְלוּת **siḵlûṯ,** שִׂכְלוּת **śiḵlûṯ** [FOOLISHNESS] 7x

<5532> סָכַן **sāḵan,** סֹכֵן **sōḵên** [PROFITABLE (BE)] 12x

<5533> סָכַן ***sāḵan*** [IMPOVERISHED] 2x
<5534> סָכַר ***sāḵar*** [CLOSE] 2x, [GIVE OVER] 1x
<5535> סָכַת ***sāḵaṯ*** [SILENT (BE)] 1x
<5536> סַל ***sal*** [BASKET] 15x
<5537> סָלָא ***sālā'*** [WORTH THEIR WEIGHT] 1x
<5538> סִלָּא ***sillā'*** [SILLA] 1x
<5539> סָלַד ***sālaḏ*** [REJOICE] 1x
<5540> סֶלֶד ***seleḏ*** [SELED] 1x
<5541> סָלָה ***sālāh*** [REJECT] 2x, [VALUE (verb)] 2x
<5542> סֶלָה ***selāh*** [SELAH!] 74x
<5543> סַלּוּ ***sallû,*** סַלַּי ***sallay,*** סָלוּא ***sālû',*** סַלּוּא ***sallû',*** סַלֻא ***salu'***
[SALLU, SALU] 6x
<5544> סַלּוֹן ***sallôn*** [THORN] 2x
<5545> סָלַח ***sālaḥ*** [FORGIVE] 46x
<5546> סַלָּח ***sallāḥ*** [FORGIVING] 1x
<5547> סְלִיחָה ***s^{e}liyḥāh*** [FORGIVENESS] 3x
<5548> סַלְכָה ***salḵāh*** [SALECAH] 4x
<5549> סָלַל ***sālal*** [EXALT] 12x
<5550> סֹלְלָה ***sōl^{e}lāh,*** סוֹלְלָה ***sôl^{e}lāh*** [SIEGE MOUND, SIEGE RAMP] 11x
<5551> סֻלָּם ***sullām*** [LADDER] 1x
<5552> סַלְסִלָּה ***salsillāh*** [BRANCH] 1x
<5553> סֶלַע ***sela'*** [ROCK] 60x
<5554> סֶלַע ***sela'*** [SELA] 4x
<5555> סֶלַע הַמַּחְלְקוֹת ***sela' hammaḥl^{e}qôṯ*** [SELA-HAMMAHLEKOTH] 1x
<5556> סָלְעָם ***sol'ām*** [LOCUST (BALD, DEVASTATING)] 1x
<5557> סָלַף ***sālap̱*** [OVERTHROW (verb)] 7x
<5558> סֶלֶף ***selep̱*** [CROOKEDNESS] 2x
<5559> סָלַק ***sālaq,*** סְלֵק ***s^{e}lêq*** [GO UP] 9x
<5560> סֹלֶת ***sōleṯ*** [FINE FLOUR] 53x
<5561> סַם ***sam*** [SWEET] 17x
<5562> סַמְגַּר נְבוֹ ***samgar-n^{e}ḇô,*** סַמְגַּר ***samgar*** [SAMGAR-NEBU, SAMGAR] 1x
<5563> סְמָדַר ***s^{e}māḏar*** [GRAPE (TENDER)] 3x
<5564> סָמַךְ ***sāmaḵ*** [LAY ON] 48x
<5565> סְמַכְיָהוּ ***s^{e}maḵyāhû*** [SHEMAIAH] 1x
<5566> סֵמֶל ***sêmel,*** סֶמֶל ***semel*** [IDOL] 5x
<5567> סָמַן ***sāman*** [APPOINT] 1x
<5568> סָמַר ***sāmar*** [STAND UP] 2x
<5569> סָמָר ***sāmār*** [BRISTLING] 1x
<5570> סְנָאָה ***s^{e}nā'āh,*** הַסְּנָאָה ***hass^{e}nā'āh*** [SENAAH, HASSENAAH] 3x
<5571> סַנְבַלַּט ***sanḇallaṭ*** [SANBALLAT] 10x
<5572> סְנֶה ***s^{e}neh*** [BUSH] 6x
<5573> סֶנֶּה ***senneh*** [SENEH] 1x
<5574> סְנוּאָה ***s^{e}nû'āh,*** הַסְּנֻאָה ***hass^{e}u'āh*** [SENUAH, HASSENUAH] 2x
<5575> סַנְוֵרִים ***sanwêriym*** [BLINDNESS] 3x
<5576> סַנְחֵרִיב ***sanḥêriyḇ*** [SENNACHERIB] 13x
<5577> סַנְסִנָּה ***sansinnāh*** [FRUIT] 1x
<5578> סַנְסַנָּה ***sansannāh*** [SANSANNAH] 1x
<5579> סְנַפִּיר ***s^{e}nappiyr*** [FIN] 5x
<5580> סָס ***sās*** [WORM] 1x
<5581> סִסְמָי ***sismāy*** [SISMAI] 2x
<5582> סָעַד ***sā'aḏ*** [REFRESH] 12x

<5583> סְעַד ***s^e'aḏ*** [SUPPORT (verb)] 1x
<5584> סָעָה ***sā'āh*** [WIND] 1x
<5585> סָעִיף ***sa'iyp̱*** [BRANCH] 2x, [CLEFT] 4x
<5586> סָעַף ***sā'ap̱*** [LOP, LOP OFF] 1x
<5587> שְׂעִפִּים ***s^e'ippiym*** [OPINION] 3x
<5588> סֵעֵף ***sê'êp̱*** [DOUBLE-MINDED] 1x
<5589> סְעַפָּה ***s^e'appāh*** [BOUGH] 2x
<5590> סָעַר ***sā'ar*** [TEMPESTUOUS (BE, GROW)] 7x
<5591> סַעַר ***sa'ar,*** סְעָרָה ***s^e'ārāh*** [TEMPEST] 24x
<5592> סַף ***sap̱*** [BASIN] 6x, [THRESHOLD] 26x
<5593> סַף ***sap̱*** [SAPH] 1x
<5594> סָפַד ***sāp̱aḏ*** [MOURN] 30x
<5595> סָפָה ***sāp̱āh*** [DESTROY] 20x
<5596> סָפַח ***sāp̱aḥ,*** שָׂפַח ***śāp̱aḥ*** [JOIN] 6x
<5597> סַפַּחַת ***sappaḥaṯ*** [SCAB] 2x
<5598> סִפַּי ***sippay*** [SIPPAI] 1x
<5599> סָפִיחַ ***sāp̱iyaḥ*** [GROWS OF ITSELF (WHAT)] 4x, [TORRENT] 1x
<5600> סְפִינָה ***s^{e}p̱iynāh*** [SHIP] 1x
<5601> סַפִּיר ***sappiyr*** [SAPPHIRE] 11x
<5602> סֵפֶל ***sêp̱el*** [BOWL] 2x
<5603> סָפַן ***sāp̱an*** [COVER (verb)] 7x
<5604> סִפֻּן ***sippun*** [CEILING] 1x
<5605> סָפַף ***sāp̱ap̱*** [DOORKEEPER (BE A)] 1x
<5606> סָפַק ***sāp̱aq,*** שָׂפַק ***śāp̱aq*** [STRIKE] 9x
<5607> סֵפֶק ***sêp̱eq,*** שֶׂפֶק ***śep̱eq,*** שֶׂפֶק ***sep̱eq*** [SUFFICIENCY] 2x
<5608> סָפַר ***sāp̱ar,*** סֹפֵר ***sōp̱êr,*** סוֹפֵר ***sôp̱êr*** [NUMBER (verb)] 161x
<5609> סְפַר ***s^{e}p̱ar*** [BOOK] 5x
<5610> סְפָר ***s̱^{e}p̱ār*** [CENSUS] 1x
<5611> סְפָר ***s^{e}p̱ār*** [SEPHAR] 1x
<5612> סֵפֶר ***sêp̱er,*** סִפְרָה ***siprāh*** [BOOK] 184x
<5613> סָפַר ***sāp̱ar*** [SCRIBE] 6x
<5614> סְפָרַד ***s^{e}p̱āraḏ*** [SEPHARAD] 1x
<5615> סְפֹרָה ***s^{e}p̱ōrāh*** [NUMBER (noun)] 1x
<5616> סְפַרְוִי ***s^{e}p̱arwiy*** [SEPHARVITE] 1x
<5617> סְפַרְוַיִם ***s^{e}p̱arwayim*** [SEPHARVAIM] 6x
<5618> סֹפֶרֶת ***sōp̱ereṯ,*** הַסֹּפֶרֶת ***hassōp̱ereṯ*** [SOPHERETH, HASSOPHERETH] 2x
<5619> סָקַל ***sāqal*** [STONE (verb)] 22x
<5620> סַר ***sar*** [SULLEN] 3x
<5621> סָרָב ***sārāḇ*** [BRIER] 1x
<5622> סַרְבָּל ***sarbāl*** [COAT (noun)] 2x
<5623> סַרְגּוֹן ***sargôn*** [SARGON] 1x
<5624> סֶרֶד ***sereḏ*** [SERED] 2x
<5625> סַרְדִּי ***sardiy*** [SEREDITE] 1x
<5626> סִרָה ***sirāh*** [SIRAH] 1x
<5627> סָרָה ***sārāh*** [REBELLION] 8x
<5628> סָרַח ***sāraḥ*** [HANG] 6x, [VANISH] 1x
<5629> סֶרַח ***seraḥ*** [REMNANT] 1x
<5630> סִרְיֹן ***siryôn*** [ARMOR] 2x
<5631> סָרִיס ***sariys*** [EUNUCH] 42x
<5632> סָרַךְ ***sāraḵ*** [COMMISSIONER] 5x
<5633> סֶרֶן ***seren*** [LORD] 22x

<5634> סַרְעַפָּה ***sarʿappāh*** [BOUGH] 1x
<5635> סָרַף ***sārap̱*** [BURN (verb)] 1x
<5636> סִרְפָּד ***sirpaḏ*** [BRIER] 1x
<5637> סָרַר ***sārar*** [REBELLIOUS] 17x
<5638> סְתָו ***sᵉṯāw*** [WINTER (noun)] 1x
<5639> סְתוּר ***sᵉṯûr*** [SETHUR] 1x
<5640> סָתַם ***sāṯam,*** שָׂתַם ***śāṯam*** [STOP, STOP UP] 14x
<5641> סָתַר ***sāṯar*** [HIDE] 82x
<5642> סְתַר ***sᵉṯar*** [HIDE] 2x
<5643> סֵתֶר ***sêṯer,*** סִתְרָה ***siṯrāh*** [COVERING] 36x
<5644> סִתְרִי ***siṯriy*** [SITHRI] 1x

ע Ayin

<5645> עָב ***ʿāḇ*** [CLAY] 1x [THICK CLOUD] 30x, [THICKET] 1x
<5646> עָב ***ʿāḇ,*** עֹב ***ʿōḇ*** [CANOPY] 3x
<5647> עָבַד ***ʿāḇaḏ*** [SERVE] 290x
<5648> עֲבַד ***ʿᵃḇaḏ*** [MAKE] 28x
<5649> עֲבַד ***ʿᵃḇaḏ*** [SERVANT] 7x
<5650> עֶבֶד ***ʿeḇeḏ*** [SERVANT] 800x
<5651> עֶבֶד ***ʿeḇeḏ*** [EBED] 6x
<5652> עֲבָד ***ʿᵃḇāḏ*** [DEED] 1x
<5653> עַבְדָּא ***ʿaḇdāʾ*** [ABDA] 2x
<5654> עֹבֵד אֱדוֹם ***ʿōḇêḏ ʾᵉḏôm*** [OBED-EDOM] 20x
<5655> עַבְדְּאֵל ***ʿaḇdᵉʾêl*** [ABDEEL] 1x
<5656> עֲבוֹדָה ***ʿᵃḇôḏāh,*** עֲבֹדָה ***ʿᵃḇōḏāh*** [WORK] 141x
<5657> עֲבֻדָּה ***ʿᵃḇuddāh*** [SERVANTS] 2x
<5658> עַבְדּוֹן ***ʿaḇdôn*** [ABDON] 8x
<5659> עַבְדֻת ***ʿaḇduṯ*** [BONDAGE] 3x
<5660> עַבְדִּי ***ʿaḇdiy*** [ABDI] 3x
<5661> עַבְדִּיאֵל ***ʿaḇdiyʾêl*** [ABDIEL] 1x
<5662> עֹבַדְיָה ***ʿōḇaḏyāh,*** עֹבַדְיָהוּ ***ʿōḇaḏyāhû*** [OBADIAH] 20x
<5663> עֶבֶד מֶלֶךְ ***ʿeḇeḏ meleḵ*** [EBED-MELECH] 6x
<5664> עֲבֵד נְגוֹ ***ʿᵃḇeḏ nᵉgô*** [ABED-NEGO] 1x
<5665> עֲבֵד נְגוֹא ***ʿᵃḇêḏ nᵉg̱ôʾ*** [ABED-NEGO] 14x
<5666> עָבָה ***ʿāḇāh*** [THICK (BE, GROW)] 3x
<5667> עֲבוֹט ***ʿᵃḇôṭ*** [PLEDGE (noun)] 4x
<5668> עֲבוּר ***ʿᵃḇûr*** [BECAUSE] 48x
<5669> עֲבוּר ***ʿᵃḇûr*** [PRODUCE (noun)] 2x
<5670> עָבַט ***ʿāḇaṭ*** [LEND] 4x, [SWERVE] 1x
<5671> עַבְטִיט ***ʿaḇṭiyṭ*** [PLEDGE (noun)] 1x
<5672> עֲבִי ***ʿᵃḇiy,*** עֳבִי ***ʿᵒḇiy*** [THICKNESS] 4x
<5673> עֲבִידָה ***ʿᵃḇiyḏāh*** [WORK] 6x
<5674> עָבַר ***ʿāḇar*** [PASS THROUGH, PASS OVER] 599x
<5675> עֲבַר ***ʿᵃḇar*** [SIDE] 14x
<5676> עֵבֶר ***ʿêḇer*** [SIDE] 90x
<5677> עֵבֶר ***ʿêḇer*** [EBER] 15x
<5678> עֶבְרָה ***ʿeḇrāh*** [WRATH] 34x
<5679> עֲבָרָה ***ʿᵃḇārāh*** [FORD] 3x

<5680> עִבְרִי ***ʿiḇriy*** [HEBREW] 34x
<5681> עִבְרִי ***ʿiḇriy*** [IBRI] 1x
<5682> עֲבָרִים ***ʿᵃḇāriym*** [ABARIM] 5x
<5683> עֶבְרֹן ***ʿeḇrōn*** [EBRON] 1x
<5684> עַבְרֹנָה ***ʿaḇrōnāh*** [ABRONAH] 2x
<5685> עָבַשׁ ***ʿāḇaš*** [SHRIVEL] 1x
<5686> עָבַת ***ʿāḇaṯ*** [WEAVE] 1x
<5687> עָבֹת ***ʿāḇōṯ*** [LEAFY] 4x
<5688> עֲבוֹת ***ʿᵃḇōṯ*** [BOUGH (THICK)] 5x, [ROPE] 20x
<5689> עָגַב ***ʿāg̱aḇ*** [LUST (verb)] 7x
<5690> עָגָב ***ʿāg̱āḇ*** [LOVE (noun)] 2x
<5691> עֲגָבָה ***ʿᵃg̱āḇāh*** [LUST (noun)] 1x
<5692> עֻגָה ***ʿug̱āh*** [CAKE] 7x
<5693> עָגוּר ***ʿāg̱ûr*** [CRANE] 2x
<5694> עָגִיל ***ʿāg̱iyl*** [EARRINGS] 2x
<5695> עֵגֶל ***ʿêg̱el*** [CALF] 35x
<5696> עָגֹל ***ʿāg̱ōl,*** עָגוֹל ***ʿāg̱ôl*** [CIRCULAR] 6x
<5697> עֶגְלָה ***ʿeg̱lāh,*** עֶגְלַת שְׁלִשִׁיָּה ***ʿeg̱laṯ šᵉlišiyyāh*** [EGLATH SHELISHIYAH] 2x, [HEIFER] 12x
<5698> עֶגְלָה ***ʿeg̱lāh*** [EGLAH] 2x
<5699> עֲגָלָה ***ʿᵃg̱ālāh*** [WAGON] 25x
<5700> עֶגְלוֹן ***ʿeg̱lôn*** [EGLON] 12x
<5701> עָגַם ***ʿāg̱am*** [GRIEVED (BE)] 1x
<5702> עָגַן ***ʿāg̱an*** [REFRAIN] 1x
<5703> עַד ***ʿaḏ*** [ETERNITY] 49x
<5704> עַד ***ʿaḏ*** [UNTIL] 99x
<5705> עַד ***ʿaḏ*** [UNTIL] 32x
<5706> עַד ***ʿaḏ*** [PREY] 3x
<5707> עֵד ***ʿêḏ*** [WITNESS] 69x
<5708> עֵד ***ʿêḏ,*** עִדָּה ***ʿiddāh*** [FILTHY] 1x
<5709> עֲדָה ***ʿᵃḏāh*** [CHANGE (verb)] 9x
<5710> עָדָה ***ʿāḏāh*** [ADORN] 8x, [PASS OVER] 2x
<5711> עָדָה ***ʿāḏāh*** [ADAH] 8x
<5712> עֵדָה ***ʿêḏāh*** [CONGREGATION] 149x
<5713> עֵדָה ***ʿêḏāh*** [WITNESS] 5x
<5714> עִדֹּא ***ʿiddōʾ,*** עִדּוֹ ***ʿiddô,*** עִדּוֹא ***ʿiddôʾ,*** עִדּוֹ ***ʿiddō*** [IDDO] 10x
<5715> עֵדוּת ***ʿêḏûṯ*** [TESTIMONY] 59x
<5716> עֲדִי ***ʿᵃḏiy*** [ORNAMENT] 13x
<5717> עֲדִיאֵל ***ʿᵃḏiyʾêl*** [ADIEL] 3x
<5718> עֲדָיָהוּ ***ʿᵃḏāyāhû,*** עֲדָיָה ***ʿᵃḏāyāh*** [ADAIAH] 9x
<5719> עָדִין ***ʿāḏiyn*** [PLEASURES (GIVEN TO, LOVER OF)] 1x
<5720> עָדִין ***ʿāḏiyn*** [ADIN] 4x
<5721> עֲדִינָא ***ʿᵃḏiynāʾ*** [ADINA] 1x
<5722> עֲדִינוֹ הָעֶצְנִי ***ʿᵃḏiynô hāʿeṣniy*** [ADINO THE EZNITE] 1x
<5723> עֲדִיתַיִם ***ʿᵃḏiyṯayim*** [ADITHAIM] 1x
<5724> עַדְלַי ***ʿaḏlay*** [ADLAI] 1x
<5725> עֲדֻלָּם ***ʿᵃḏullām*** [ADULLAM] 8x
<5726> עֲדֻלָּמִי ***ʿᵃḏullāmiy*** [ADULLAMITE] 3x
<5727> עָדַן ***ʿāḏan*** [DELIGHT ONESELF] 1x
<5728> עֲדֶן ***ʿᵃḏen,*** עֲדֶנָה ***ʿᵃḏenāh*** [YET] 2x
<5729> עֶדֶן ***ʿeḏen*** [EDEN] 3x

<5730> עֵדֶן **'êḏen,** עֶדְנָה **'eḏnāh** [DELIGHT (noun)] 4x
<5731> עֵדֶן **'êḏen** [EDEN] 17x
<5732> עִדָּן **'iddān** [TIME] 13x
<5733> עַדְנָא **'aḏnā'** [ADNA] 2x
<5734> עַדְנָח **'aḏnāh** [ADNAH] 2x
<5735> עַדְעָדָה **'aḏ'āḏāh** [ADADAH] 1x
<5736> עָדַף **'āḏap̱** [LEFT, LEFT OVER] 9x
<5737> עָדַר **'āḏar** [CULTIVATE] 2x, [LACK, LACKING (BE)] 7x, [RANK (KEEP)] 1x
<5738> עֶדֶר **'eḏer** [EDER] 1x
<5739> עֵדֶר **'êḏer** [FLOCK] 38x
<5740> עֵדֶר **'êḏer** [EDER] 3x
<5741> עַדְרִיאֵל **'aḏriy'êl** [ADRIEL] 2x
<5742> עֲדָשִׁים **'ᵃḏāšiym** [LENTILS] 4x
<5743> עוּב **'ûḇ** [CLOUD (COVER WITH A)] 1x
<5744> עוֹבֵד **'ôḇêḏ,** עֹבֵד **'ōḇêḏ** [OBED] 10x
<5745> עוֹבָל **'ôḇāl** [OBAL] 1x
<5746> עוּג **'ûg** [BAKE] 1x
<5747> עוֹג **'ôg,** עֹג **'ōg** [OG] 22x
<5748> עוּגָב **'ûgāḇ,** עֻגָב **'ugāḇ** [FLUTE] 4x
<5749> עוּד **'ûḏ** [WITNESS (BEAR)] 45x
<5750> עוֹד **'ôḏ** [AGAIN] 244x (NAS)
<5751> עוֹד **'ôḏ** [WHILE] 1x
<5752> עֹדֵד **'ōḏeḏ,** עוֹדֵד **ōḏeḏ** [ODED] 3x
<5753> עָוָה **'āwāh** [INIQUITY (COMMIT)] 17x
<5754> עַוָּה **'awwāh** [RUIN (noun)] 1x
<5755> עַוָּא **'awwā',** עִוָּה **'iwwāh** [AVVA] 4x
<5756> עוּז **'ûz** [SAFETY (FLEE FOR)] 4x
<5757> עַוִּי **'awwiy** [AVITE] 3x
<5758> עֲוָיָה **'ᵃwāyāh** [INIQUITY] 1x
<5759> עֲוִיל **'ᵃwiyl** [LITTLE BOY] 2x
<5760> עֲוִיל **'ᵃwiyl** [UNGODLY] 1x
<5761> עַוִּים **'awwiym** [AVVIM] 1x
<5762> עֲוִית **'ᵃwiyṯ** [AVITH] 2x
<5763> עוּל **'ûl** [NURSE (verb)] 5x
<5764> עוּל **'ûl** [NURSING CHILD] 2x
<5765> עָוַל **'āwal** [UNJUSTLY (DEAL)] 2x
<5766> עָוֶל **'āwel,** עֶוֶל **'ewel,** עַוְלָה **'awlāh,** עֹלָתָה **'ōlāṯāh** [INJUSTICE] 55x
<5767> עַוָּל **'awwāl** [WICKED] 5x
<5768> עוֹלֵל **'ôlêl,** עוֹלָל **'ôlāl** [CHILD] 20x
<5769> עוֹלָם **'ôlām** [FOREVER] 439x
<5770> עָוַן **'āwan** [EYE (verb)] 1x
<5771> עָוֹן **'āwōn** [INIQUITY] 230x
<5772> עֹנָה **'ōnāh,** עוֹנָה **'ônāh** [MARITAL RIGHTS] 2x
<5773> עִוְעִים **'iw'iym** [CONFUSION] 1x
<5774> עוּף **'ûp̱** [FLY (verb)] 32x
<5775> עוֹף **'ôp̱** [BIRD] 71x
<5776> עוֹף **'ôp̱** [BIRD] 2x
<5777> עוֹפֶרֶת **'ôpereṯ,** עֹפֶרֶת **'ōpereṯ** [LEAD (noun)] 9x
<5778> עֵיפַי **'êyp̱ay** [EPHAI] 1x
<5779> עוּץ **'ûṣ** [COUNSEL (TAKE)] 2x
<5780> עוּץ **'ûṣ** [UZ] 8x

<5781> עוּק ***‘ûq*** [WEIGHTED DOWN (BE)] 1x
<5782> עוּר ***‘ûr*** [AWAKE] 81x
<5783> עוּר ***‘ûr*** [UNCOVER] 1x
<5784> עוּר ***‘ûr*** [CHAFF] 1x
<5785> עוֹר ***‘ôr*** [SKIN] 99x
<5786> עָוַר ***‘āwar*** [EYES (PUT OUT THE)] 5x
<5787> עִוֵּר ***‘iwwêr*** [BLIND (adj.)] 26x
<5788> עִוָּרוֹן ***‘iwwārôn,*** עַוֶּרֶת ***‘awwereṯ*** [BLINDNESS] 3x
<5789> עוּשׁ ***‘ûš*** [HASTEN] 1x
<5790> עוּת ***‘ûṯ*** [SUSTAIN] 1x
<5791> עָוַת ***‘āwaṯ*** [BEND] 11x
<5792> עַוָּתָה ***‘awwāṯāh*** [WRONG (noun)] 1x
<5793> עוּתַי ***‘ûṯay*** [UTHAI] 2x
<5794> עַז ***‘az*** [STRONG] 23x
<5795> עֵז ***‘êz*** [FEMALE GOAT] 74x
<5796> עֵז ***‘êz*** [GOAT] 1x
<5797> עֹז ***‘ōz,*** עוֹז ***‘ôz*** [STRONG] 93x
<5798> עֻזָּא ***‘uzzā’,*** עֻזָּה ***‘uzzāh*** [UZZAH, UZZA] 14x
<5799> עֲזָאזֵל ***‘ᵃzā’zêl*** [SCAPEGOAT] 3x
<5800> עָזַב ***‘āzaḇ*** [LEAVE] 215x
<5801> עִזָּבוֹן ***‘izzāḇôn*** [WARES] 7x
<5802> עַזְבּוּק ***‘azbûq*** [AZBUK] 1x
<5803> עַזְגָּד ***‘azgāḏ*** [AZGAD] 4x
<5804> עַזָּה ***‘azzāh*** [GAZA] 21x
<5805> עֲזוּבָה ***‘ᵃzûḇāh*** [FORSAKEN PLACE] 1x
<5806> עֲזוּבָה ***‘ᵃzûḇāh*** [AZUBAH] 4x
<5807> עֱזוּז ***‘ᵉzûz*** [STRENGTH] 3x
<5808> עִזּוּז ***‘izzûz*** [STRONG] 2x
<5809> עַזּוּר ***‘azzûr*** [AZZUR] 3x
<5810> עָזַז ***‘āzaz*** [STRENGTHEN] 12x
<5811> עָזָז ***‘āzāz*** [AZAZ] 1x
<5812> עֲזַזְיָהוּ ***‘ᵃzazyāhû*** [AZAZIAH] 3x
<5813> עֻזִּי ***‘uzziy*** [UZZI] 11x
<5814> עֻזִּיָּא ***‘uziyyā’*** [UZZIA] 1x
<5815> עֲזִיאֵל ***‘Aziy’êl*** [AZIEL] 1x
<5816> עֻזִּיאֵל ***‘uzziy’êl*** [UZZIEL] 16x
<5817> עָזִּיאֵלִי ***‘ozziy’êliy*** [UZZIELITE] 2x
<5818> עֻזִּיָּהוּ ***‘uzziyyāhû,*** עֻזִּיָּה ***‘uzziyyāh*** [UZZIAH] 27x
<5819> עֲזִיזָא ***‘ᵃziyzā’*** [AZIZA] 1x
<5820> עַזְמָוֶת ***‘azmāweṯ*** [AZMAVETH] 8x
<5821> עַזָּן ***‘azzān*** [AZZAN] 1x
<5822> עָזְנִיָּה ***‘ozniyyāh*** [VULTURE (BLACK)] 2x
<5823> עָזַק ***‘āzaq*** [DIG] 1x
<5824> עִזְקָה ***‘izqāh*** [SIGNET, SIGNET RING] 1x
<5825> עֲזֵקָה ***‘ᵃzêqāh*** [AZEKAH] 7x
<5826> עָזַר ***‘āzar*** [HELP (verb)] 82x
<5827> עֶזֶר ***‘ezer*** [EZER] 2x
<5828> עֵזֶר ***‘êzer*** [HELP (noun)] 21x
<5829> עֵזֶר ***‘êzer*** [EZER] 4x
<5830> עֶזְרָא ***‘ezrā’*** [EZRA] 22x
<5831> עֶזְרָא ***‘ezrā’*** [EZRA] 3x

<5832> עֲזַרְאֵל **‘^{a}zar’ēl** [AZAREL, AZAREEL] 6x
<5833> עֶזְרָה **‘ezrāh,** עֶזְרָת **‘ezrāth** [HELP (noun)] 26x
<5834> עֶזְרָה **‘ezrāh** [EZRA] 1x
<5835> עֲזָרָה **‘^{a}zārāh** [LEDGE] 9x
<5836> עֶזְרִי **‘ezriy** [EZRI] 1x
<5837> עַזְרִיאֵל **‘azriy’ēl** [AZRIEL] 3x
<5838> עֲזַרְיָה **‘^{a}zaryāh,** עֲזַרְיָהוּ **‘^{a}zaryāhû** [AZARIAH] 48x
<5839> עֲזַרְיָה **‘^{a}zaryāh** [AZARIAH] 1x
<5840> עַזְרִיקָם **‘azriyqām** [AZRIKAM] 6x
<5841> עַזָּתִי **‘azzāṯiy** [GAZITE, GAZATHITE] 2x
<5842> עֵט **‘ēṭ** [PEN] 4x
<5843> עֵטָה **‘ēṭāh** [PRUDENCE] 1x
<5844> עָטָה **‘āṭāh** [WRAP AROUND] 17x
<5845> עֲטִין **‘^{a}ṭiyn** [BODY] 1x
<5846> עֲטִישָׁה **‘^{a}ṭiyšāh** [SNEEZING] 1x
<5847> עֲטַלֵּף **‘^{a}ṭallēp̱** [BAT] 3x
<5848> עָטַף **‘āṭap̱** [TURN (verb)] 16x
<5849> עָטַר **‘āṭar** [CROWN (noun and verb)] 7x
<5850> עֲטָרָה **‘^{a}ṭārāh** [CROWN (noun)] 23x
<5851> עֲטָרָה **‘^{a}ṭārāh** [ATARAH] 1x
<5852> עֲטָרוֹת **‘^{a}ṭārôṯ,** עֲטָרֹת **‘^{a}ṭārōṯ** [ATAROTH] 5x
<5853> עַטְרוֹת אַדָּר **‘aṭrôṯ ’addār** [ATAROTH-ADDAR] 2x
<5854> עַטְרוֹת בֵּית יוֹאָב **‘aṭrôṯ-bêṯ-yô’āḇ** [ATROTH-BETH-JOAB] 1x
<5855> עַטְרוֹת שׁוֹפָן **‘aṭrôṯ šôp̱ān** [ATROTH-SHOPHAN] 1x
<5856> עִי **‘iy** [RUINS] 5x
<5857> עַי **‘ay,** עַיָּא **‘ayya’,** עַיָּת **‘ayyāṯ** [AI] 40x
<5858> עֵיבָל **‘êyḇāl** [EBAL] 8x
<5859> עִיּוֹן **‘iyyôn** [IJON] 3x
<5860> עִיט **‘iyṭ** [RUSH GREEDILY] 3x
<5861> עַיִט **‘ayiṭ** [BIRD OF PREY] 7x
<5862> עֵיטָם **‘êyṭām** [ETAM] 5x
<5863> עִיֵּי הָעֲבָרִים **‘iyyêy hā‘^{a}-ḇāriym** [IYE-ABARIM] 2x
<5864> עִיִּים **‘iyyiym** [IYIM] 2x
<5865> עֵילוֹם **‘êylôm** [FOREVER] 1x
<5866> עִילַי **‘iylay** [ILAI] 1x
<5867> עֵילָם **‘êylām** [ELAM] 28x
<5868> עֲיָם **‘^{a}yām** [SCORCHING] 1x
<5869> עַיִן **‘ayin,** עֵינַיִם **‘êynayim** [EYE (noun)] 886x
<5870> עַיִן **‘ayin** [EYE (noun)] 5x
<5871> עַיִן **‘ayin** [AIN] 5x
<5872> עֵין גֶּדִי **‘êyn geḏiy** [ENGEDI] 6x
<5873> עֵין גַּנִּים **‘êyn ganniym** [EN-GANNIM] 3x
<5874> עֵין דֹּאר **‘êyn dō’r** [EN-DOR] 3x
<5875> עֵין הַקּוֹרֵא **‘êyn haqqôrê’** [EN-HAKKORE] 1x
<5876> עֵין חַדָּה **‘êyn ḥaddāh** [EN-HADDAH] 1x
<5877> עֵין חָצוֹר **‘êyn ḥāṣôr** [EN-HAZOR] 1x
<5878> עֵין חֲרֹד **‘êyn ḥ^{a}rōḏ** [HAROD (WELL OF, SPRING OF)] 1x
<5879> עֵינָם **‘ênām** [ENAM] 1x
<5880> עֵין מִשְׁפָּט **‘êyn mišpāṭ** [EN-MISHPAT] 1x
<5881> עֵינָן **‘êynān** [ENAN] 5x
<5882> עֵין עֶגְלַיִם **‘êyn ‘eḡlayim** [ENEGLAIM] 1x

<5883> עֵין רֹגֵל ***‘êyn rōḡêl*** [EN-ROGEL] 4x
<5884> עֵין רִמּוֹן ***‘êyn rimmôn*** [EN-RIMMON] 1x
<5885> עֵין שֶׁמֶשׁ ***‘êyn šemeš*** [EN-SHEMESH] 2x
<5886> עֵין הַתַּנִּין ***‘êyn hattanniyn*** [DRAGON’S SPRING] 1x
<5887> עֵין תַּפּוּחַ ***‘êyn tappûaḥ*** [EN-TAPPUAH] 1x
<5888> עִיף ***‘iyp̱*** [WEARY (BE)] 5x
<5889> עָיֵף ***‘āyêp̱*** [WEARY (adj.)] 17x
<5890> עֵיפָה ***‘êyp̱āh*** [DARKNESS] 2x
<5891> עֵיפָה ***‘êyp̱āh*** [EPHAH] 5x
<5892> עִיר ***‘iyr*** [CITY] 1,089x
<5893> עִיר ***‘iyr*** [IR] 1x
<5894> עִיר ***‘iyr*** [WATCHER] 3x
<5895> עַיִר ***‘ayir,*** עִיר ***‘iyr*** [DONKEY] 8x
<5896> עִירָא ***‘iyrā’*** [IRA] 6x
<5897> עִירָד ***‘iyrāḏ*** [IRAD] 1x
<5898> עִיר הַמֶּלַח ***‘iyr hammelaḥ*** [CITY OF SALT] 1x
<5899> עִיר הַתְּמָרִים ***‘iyr hat-tᵉmāriym*** [CITY OF PALMS] 4x
<5900> עִירוּ ***‘iyrû*** [IRU] 1x
<5901> עִירִי ***‘iyriy*** [IRI] 1x
<5902> עִירָם ***‘iyrām*** [IRAM] 2x
<5903> עֵירֹם ***‘êyrōm,*** עֵרֹם ***‘êrōm*** [NAKED] 10x
<5904> עִיר נָחָשׁ ***‘iyr nāḥāš*** [IR-NAHASH] 1x
<5905> עִיר שֶׁמֶשׁ ***‘iyr šemeš*** [IR-SHEMESH] 1x
<5906> עַיִשׁ ***‘ayiš,*** עָשׁ ***‘āš*** [BEAR (noun)] 2x
<5907> עַכְבּוֹר ***‘aḵbôr*** [ACHBOR] 7x
<5908> עַכָּבִישׁ ***‘akkāḇiyš*** [SPIDER] 2x
<5909> עַכְבָּר ***‘aḵbār*** [MOUSE] 6x
<5910> עַכּוֹ ***‘akkô*** [ACCO] 1x
<5911> עָכוֹר ***’aḵôr*** [ACHOR] 5x
<5912> עָכָן ***‘āḵān*** [ACHAN] 6x
<5913> עָכַס ***‘āḵas*** [TINKLE] 1x
<5914> עֶכֶס ***‘eḵes*** [ANKLET] 1x, [FETTER] 1x
<5915> עַכְסָה ***‘aḵsāh*** [ACHSAH] 5x
<5916> עָכַר ***‘āḵar*** [TROUBLE (BRING)] 14x
<5917> עָכָר ***‘āḵār*** [ACHAR] 1x
<5918> עָכְרָן ***‘oḵrān*** [OCRAN] 5x
<5919> עַכְשׁוּב ***‘aḵšûḇ*** [VIPER] 1x
<5920> עַל ***‘al*** [ABOVE] 6x
<5921> עַל ***‘al*** [UPON] 48x
<5922> עַל ***‘al*** [UPON] 99x
<5923> עֹל ***‘ōl*** [YOKE] 40x
<5924> עֵלָּא ***‘êllā’*** [OVER] 1x
<5925> עֻלָּא ***‘ullā’*** [ULLA] 1x
<5926> עִלֵּג ***‘illêg*** [STAMMERING] 1x
<5927> עָלָה ***‘ālāh*** [OFFER] 889x
<5928> עֲלָה ***ᵃlāh*** [BURNT OFFERING] 1x
<5929> עָלֶה ***‘āleh*** [LEAF] 18x
<5930> עֹלָה ***‘ōlāh*** [BURNT OFFERING] 287x
<5931> עִלָּה ***‘illāh*** [COMPLAINT (GROUND FOR)] 2x
<5932> עַלְוָה ***‘alwāh*** [INIQUITY] 1x
<5933> עַלְוָה ***‘alwāh,*** עַלְיָה ***‘alyāh*** [ALVAH] 2x

<5934> עֲלוּמִים ***ʻ^{e}lûmiym*** [YOUTH] 4x

<5935> עַלְוָן ***ʻalwān,*** עַלְיָן ***ʻalyān*** [ALVAN] 2x

<5936> עֲלוּקָה ***ʻ^{e}lûqāh*** [LEECH] 1x

<5937> עָלַז ***ʻālaz*** [REJOICE] 16x

<5938> עָלֵז ***ʻālêz*** [JUBILANT] 1x

<5939> עֲלָטָה ***ʻ^{a}lāṭāh*** [DARKNESS] 4x

<5940> עֱלִי ***ʻ^{e}liy*** [PESTLE] 1x

<5941> עֵלִי ***ʻêliy*** [ELI] 33x

<5942> עִלִּי ***ʻilliy*** [UPPER] 2x

<5943> עִלָּי ***ʻillāy*** [MOST HIGH] 10x

<5944> עֲלִיָּה ***ʻ^{a}liyyāh*** [UPPER ROOM] 20x

<5945> עֶלְיוֹן ***ʻelyôn*** [MOST HIGH] 31x

<5946> עֶלְיוֹן ***ʻelyôn*** [MOST HIGH] 4x

<5947> עַלִּיז ***ʻalliyz*** [REJOICING] 7x

<5948> עֲלִיל ***ʻ^{a}liyl*** [FURNACE] 1x

<5949> עֲלִילָה ***ʻ^{a}liylāh*** [DEED] 24x

<5950> עֲלִילִיָּה ***ʻ^{a}liyliyyāh*** [DEED] 1x

<5951> עֲלִיצֻת ***ʻ^{a}liyṣuṯ*** [REJOICING] 1x

<5952> עִלִּי ***ʻilliy*** [CHAMBER] 1x

<5953> עָלַל ***ʻālal*** [DO] 20x

<5954> עֲלַל ***ʻ^{a}lal*** [ENTER] 12x

<5955> עֹלֵלוֹת ***ʻōlêlôṯ*** [GLEANING] 6x

<5956> עָלַם ***ʻālam*** [HIDE] 28x

<5957> עָלַם ***ʻālam*** [EVERLASTING] 15x

<5958> עֶלֶם ***ʻelem*** [YOUNG MAN] 2x

<5959> עַלְמָה ***ʻalmāh*** [YOUNG WOMAN] 7x

<5960> עַלְמוֹן ***ʻalmôn*** [ALMON] 1x

<5961> עֲלָמוֹת ***ʻ^{a}lāmôṯ*** [ALAMOTH] 2x

<5962> עֵלְמָי ***ʻêlmāy*** [ELAMITE] 1x

<5963> עַלְמֹן דִּבְלָתָיְמָה ***ʻalmon diḇlaṯāy^{e}māh*** [ALMON-DIBLATHAIM] 2x

<5964> עָלֶמֶת ***ʻālemeṯ*** [ALEMETH] 4x

<5965> עָלַס ***ʻālas,*** נֶעֱלָסָה ***ne^{e}lāsāh*** [ENJOY] 3x

<5966> עָלַע ***ʻālaʻ*** [SUCK UP] 1x

<5967> עֲלַע ***ʻ^{a}laʻ*** [RIB] 1x

<5968> עָלַף ***ʻālap̱*** [COVER (verb)] 2x, [FAINT (verb)] 3x

<5969> עֻלְפֶּה ***ʻulpeh*** [FAINTED] 1x

<5970> עָלַץ ***ʻālaṣ*** [REJOICE] 8x

<5971> עַם ***ʻam,*** עָם ***ʻām*** [PEOPLE] 1,862x

<5972> עַם ***ʻam*** [PEOPLE] 14x

<5973> עִם ***ʻim*** [WITH] 124x (NAS)

<5974> עִם ***ʻim*** [WITH] 20x

<5975> עָמַד ***ʻāmaḏ*** [STAND (verb)] 521x

<5976> עָמַד ***ʻāmaḏ*** [SHAKE] 1x

<5977> עֹמֶד ***ʻōmeḏ*** [PLACE (noun)] 10x

<5978> עִמָּד ***ʻimmāḏ*** [WITH] 12x

<5979> עֶמְדָּה ***ʻemdāh*** [STANDING PLACE] 1x

<5980> עֻמָּה ***ʻummāh*** [NEXT TO] 32x

<5981> עֻמָּה ***ʻummāh*** [UMMAH] 1x

<5982> עַמּוּד ***ʻammûḏ*** [PILLAR] 110x

<5983> עַמּוֹן ***ʻammôn*** [AMMON] 105x

<5984> עַמּוֹנִי ***ʻammôniy*** [AMMONITE] 18x

<5985> עַמֹּנִית ***ʿammōniyṯ*** [AMMONITESS] 4x
<5986> עָמוֹס ***ʿāmôs*** [AMOS] 7x
<5987> עָמוֹק ***ʿāmôq*** [AMOK] 2x
<5988> עַמִּיאֵל ***ʿammiyʾel*** [AMMIEL] 6x
<5989> עַמִּיהוּד ***ʿammiyhûḏ*** [AMMIHUD] 10x
<5990> עַמִּיזָבָד ***ʿammiyzaḇaḏ*** [AMMIZABAD] 1x
<5991> עַמִּיחוּר ***ʿammiyḥûr*** [AMMICHUR] 1x
<5992> עַמִּינָדָב ***ʿammiynāḏaḇ*** [AMMINADAB] 13x
<5993> עַמִּי נָדִיב ***ʿammiy nāḏiyḇ*** [AMMINADIB] 1x
<5994> עֲמִיק ***ʿᵃmiyq*** [PROFOUND] 1x
<5995> עָמִיר ***ʿāmiyr*** [GRAIN (SHEAF OF, FALLEN)] 4x
<5996> עַמִּישַׁדָּי ***ʿammiyšaddāy*** [AMMISHADDAI] 5x
<5997> עָמִית ***ʿāmiyṯ*** [NEIGHBOR] 12x
<5998> עָמַל ***ʿāmal*** [LABOR (verb)] 11x
<5999> עָמָל ***ʿāmāl*** [LABOR (noun)] 55x
<6000> עָמָל ***ʿāmāl*** [AMAL] 1x
<6001> עָמֵל ***ʿāmêl*** [TOIL (noun and verb)] 9x
<6002> עֲמָלֵק ***ʿᵃmālêq*** [AMALEK] 39x
<6003> עֲמָלֵקִי ***ʿᵃmālêqiy*** [AMALEK, AMALEKITE] 12x
<6004> עָמַם ***ʿāmam*** [DIM (BECOME, GROW)] 3x
<6005> עִמָּנוּאֵל ***ʿimmānûʾêl*** [IMMANUEL] 2x
<6006> עָמַס ***ʿāmas,*** עָמַשׂ ***ʿāmaś*** [LOAD (verb)] 9x
<6007> עֲמַסְיָה ***ʿᵃmasyāh*** [AMASIAH] 1x
<6008> עַמְעָד ***ʿamʿāḏ*** [AMAD] 1x
<6009> עָמַק ***ʿāmaq*** [DEEP, DEEP (BE)] 9x
<6010> עֵמֶק ***ʿêmeq*** [VALLEY] 69x
<6011> עֹמֶק ***ʿōmeq*** [DEPTH] 1x
<6012> עָמֵק ***ʿāmêq*** [UNINTELLIGIBLE] 3x
<6013> עָמֹק ***ʿāmōq*** [DEEP (adj.)] 16x
<6014> עָמַר ***ʿāmar*** [SLAVE (TREAT AS A)] 3x
<6015> עֲמַר ***ʿᵃmar*** [WOOL] 1x
<6016> עֹמֶר ***ʿōmer*** [OMER] 6x, [SHEAF] 8x
<6017> עֲמֹרָה ***ʿᵃmōrāh*** [GOMORRAH] 19x
<6018> עָמְרִי ***ʿomriy*** [OMRI] 18x
<6019> עַמְרָם ***ʿamrām*** [AMRAM] 14x
<6020> עַמְרָמִי ***ʿamrāmiy*** [AMRAMITE] 2x
<6021> עֲמָשָׂא ***ʿᵃmāśāʾ*** [AMASA] 16x
<6022> עֲמָשַׂי ***ʿᵃmāśay*** [AMASAI] 5x
<6023> עֲמַשְׁסַי ***ʿᵃmašsay*** [AMASHAI] 1x
<6024> עֲנָב ***ʿᵃnāb*** [ANAB] 2x
<6025> עֵנָב ***ʿênāḇ*** [GRAPE] 19x
<6026> עָנַג ***ʿānag̱*** [DELIGHT (HAVE, FIND, TAKE)] 10x
<6027> עֹנֶג ***ʿōneg̱*** [DELIGHT (noun)] 2x
<6028> עָנֹג ***ʿānōg̱*** [DELICATE] 3x
<6029> עָנַד ***ʿānaḏ*** [BIND] 2x
<6030> עָנָה ***ʿānāh,*** לְעַנּוֹת ***lᵉʿannôṯ*** [ANSWER (verb)] 329x
<6031> עָנָה ***ʿānāh*** [AFFLICTED (BE)] 84x
<6032> עֲנָה ***ʿᵃnāh*** [ANSWER (verb)] 30x
<6033> עֲנָה ***ʿᵃnāh*** [OPPRESSED] 1x
<6034> עֲנָה ***ʿᵃnāh*** [ANAH] 12x
<6035> עָנָו ***ʿānāw*** [HUMBLE] 25x

<6036> עָנוּב ***‘ānûḇ*** [ANUB] 1x
<6037> עַנְוָה ***‘anwāh*** [HUMILITY] 1x
<6038> עֲנָוָה ***‘anāwāh*** [HUMILITY] 7x
<6039> עֱנוּת ***‘enûṯ*** [AFFLICTION] 1x
<6040> עֳנִי ***‘oniy*** [AFFLICTION] 37x
<6041> עָנִי ***‘āniy*** [POOR] 78x
<6042> עֻנִּי ***‘unniy*** [UNNI] 3x
<6043> עֲנָיָה ***‘anāyāh*** [ANAIAH] 2x
<6044> עָנִים ***‘āniym*** [ANIM] 1x
<6045> עִנְיָן ***‘inyān*** [TASK] 8x
<6046> עָנֵם ***‘ānêm*** [ANEM] 1x
<6047> עֲנָמִים ***‘anāmiym*** [ANAMIM] 2x
<6048> עֲנַמֶּלֶךְ ***‘anammeleḵ*** [ANAMMELECH] 1x
<6049> עָנַן ***‘ānan*** [WITCHCRAFT (PRACTICE)] 11x
<6050> עֲנַן ***‘anan*** [CLOUD] 1x
<6051> עָנָן ***‘ānān*** [CLOUD] 87x
<6052> עָנָן ***‘ānān*** [ANAN] 1x
<6053> עֲנָנָה ***‘anānāh*** [CLOUD] 1x
<6054> עֲנָנִי ***‘anāniy*** [ANANI] 1x
<6055> עֲנָנְיָה ***‘anāneyāh*** [ANANIAH] 2x
<6056> עֲנַף ***‘anap̱*** [BRANCH] 3x
<6057> עָנָף ***‘ānāp̱*** [BRANCH] 7x
<6058> עָנֵף ***‘ānêp̱*** [BRANCHES (FULL OF)] 1x
<6059> עָנַק ***‘ānaq*** [LIBERALLY (FURNISH, SUPPLY)] 2x
<6060> עֲנָק ***‘anāq*** [CHAIN] 3x
<6061> עֲנָק ***‘anāq*** [ANAK] 9x
<6062> עֲנָקִי ***‘anaqiy*** [ANAKITE] 9x
<6063> עָנֵר ***‘ānêr*** [ANER] 3x
<6064> עָנַשׁ ***‘ānaš*** [FINE (verb)] 9x
<6065> עֲנָשׁ ***‘anāš*** [CONFISCATION] 1x
<6066> עֹנֶשׁ ***‘ōneš*** [FINE (noun)] 2x
<6067> עֲנָת ***‘anāṯ*** [ANATH] 2x
<6068> עֲנָתוֹת ***‘anāṯôṯ*** [ANATHOTH] 15x
<6069> עַנְּתוֹתִי ***‘anneṯôṯiy*** [ANATHOTHITE] 5x
<6070> עַנְתֹתִיָּה ***‘anṯōṯiyyāh*** [ANTOTHIJAH] 1x
<6071> עָסִיס ***‘āsiys*** [WINE] 5x
<6072> עָסַס ***‘āsas*** [TREAD DOWN] 1x
<6073> עֳפָאִים ***‘op̱a’yim*** [BRANCHES] 1x
<6074> עֳפִי ***‘op̱iy*** [LEAF] 3x
<6075> עָפַל ***‘āp̱al*** [PRESUME] 2x
<6076> עֹפֶל ***‘ōp̱el*** [HILL] 3x, [TUMOR] 6x
<6077> עֹפֶל ***‘ōp̱el*** [OPHEL] 5x
<6078> עָפְנִי ***‘op̱niy*** [OPHNI] 1x
<6079> עַפְעַף ***‘ap̱‘ap̱*** [EYELID] 10x
<6080> עָפַר ***‘āp̱ar*** [FLING] 1x
<6081> עֵפֶר ***‘êp̱er*** [EPHER] 4x
<6082> עֹפֶר ***‘ōp̱er*** [YOUNG] 5x
<6083> עָפָר ***‘āp̱ār*** [DUST] 110x
<6084> עָפְרָה ***‘op̱rāh*** [OPHRAH] 8x
<6085> עֶפְרוֹן ***‘ep̱rôn*** [OPHRAH] 14x
<6086> עֵץ ***‘êṣ*** [TREE] 328x

<6087> עָצַב ***ʿāṣaḇ*** [HURT] 17x
<6088> עֲצִיב ***ʿᵃṣiyḇ*** [TROUBLED] 1x
<6089> עֶצֶב ***ʿeṣeḇ*** [PAIN (noun)] 7x
<6090> עֹצֶב ***ʿōṣeḇ*** [PAIN (noun)] 4x
<6091> עָצָב ***ʿāṣāḇ*** [IDOL] 17x
<6092> עָצֵב ***ʿāṣêḇ*** [WORKER] 1x
<6093> עִצָּבוֹן ***ʿiṣṣāḇôn*** [PAIN (noun)] 3x
<6094> עַצֶּבֶת ***ʿaṣṣeḇeṯ*** [SORROW (noun)] 5x
<6095> עָצָה ***ʿāṣāh*** [WINK] 1x
<6096> עָצֶה ***ʿāṣeh*** [BACKBONE] 1x
<6097> עֵצָה ***ʿêṣāh*** [TREES] 1x
<6098> עֵצָה ***ʿêṣāh*** [PLAN (noun)] 88x
<6099> עָצוּם ***ʿāṣûm*** [MIGHTY] 31x
<6100> עֶצְיוֹן גֶּבֶר ***ʿeṣyôn geḇer*** [EZION GEBER] 7x
<6101> עָצַל ***ʿāṣal*** [HESITATE] 1x
<6102> עָצֵל ***ʿāṣêl*** [SLUGGARD] 14x
<6103> עַצְלָה ***ʿaṣlāh*** [LAZINESS] 2x
<6104> עַצְלוּת ***ʿaṣlûṯ*** [IDLENESS] 1x
<6105> עָצַם ***ʿāṣam*** [CLOSE] 2x, [MIGHTY (BE)] 18x
<6106> עֶצֶם ***ʿeṣem*** [BONE] 126x
<6107> עֶצֶם ***ʿeṣem*** [EZEM] 3x
<6108> עֹצֶם ***ʿōṣem*** [STRENGTH] 4x
<6109> עָצְמָה ***ʿoṣmāh*** [STRENGTH] 2x
<6110> עַצֻמוֹת ***ʿaṣumôṯ*** [ARGUMENTS (STRONG)] 1x
<6111> עַצְמוֹן ***ʿaṣmôn*** [AZMON] 3x
<6112> עֵצֶן ***ʿêṣen*** [EZNITE] 1x
<6113> עָצַר ***ʿāṣar*** [RESTRAIN] 46x
<6114> עֶצֶר ***ʿeṣer*** [RESTRAINT] 1x
<6115> עֹצֶר ***ʿōṣer*** [OPPRESSION] 3x
<6116> עֲצָרָה ***ʿaṣārāh,*** עֲצֶרֶת ***ʿᵃṣereṯ*** [ASSEMBLY] 11x
<6117> עָקַב ***ʿāqaḇ*** [SUPPLANT] 5x
<6118> עֵקֶב ***ʿêqeḇ*** [BECAUSE] 15x
<6119> עָקֵב ***ʿāqêḇ*** [HEEL] 13x
<6120> עָקֵב ***ʿāqêḇ*** [HEEL] 1x
<6121> עָקֹב ***ʿāqōḇ*** [DECEITFUL] 3x
<6122> עָקְבָּה ***ʿoqbāh*** [CUNNING] 1x
<6123> עָקַד ***ʿāqaḏ*** [BIND] 1x
<6124> עָקֹד ***ʿāqōḏ*** [STRIPED] 6x
<6125> עָקָה ***ʿāqāh*** [OPPRESSION] 1x
<6126> עַקּוּב ***ʿaqqûḇ*** [AKKUB] 8x
<6127> עָקַל ***ʿāqal*** [PERVERTED] 1x
<6128> עֲקַלְקַל ***ʿᵃqalqal*** [CROOKED] 2x
<6129> עֲקַלָּתוֹן ***ʿᵃqallāṯôn*** [TWISTING] 1x
<6130> עֲקָן ***ʿᵃqān*** [AKAN] 1x
<6131> עָקַר ***ʿāqar*** [HAMSTRING] 7x
<6132> עֲקַר ***ʿᵃqar*** [ROOTS (PLUCK UP, PLUCK OUT, PULL OUT BY THE)] 1x
<6133> עֵקֶר ***ʿêqer*** [MEMBER] 1x
<6134> עֵקֶר ***ʿêqer*** [EKER] 1x
<6135> עָקָר ***ʿāqār*** [BARREN] 12x
<6136> עִקַּר ***ʿiqqar*** [STUMP] 3x
<6137> עַקְרָב ***ʿaqrāḇ,*** עַקְרַבִּים ***ʿaqraḇḇiym*** [SCORPION] 9x

<6138> עֶקְרוֹן ***‘eqrôn*** [EKRON] 22x

<6139> עֶקְרוֹנִי ***‘eqrôniy*** [EKRONITE] 2x

<6140> עָקַשׁ ***‘āqaš*** [CROOKED (MAKE, BE)] 5x

<6141> עִקֵּשׁ ***‘iqqêš*** [PERVERSE] 11x

<6142> עִקֵּשׁ ***‘iqqêš*** [IKKESH] 3x

<6143> עִקְּשׁוּת ***‘iqqᵉšûṯ*** [CROOKED] 2x

<6144> עָר ***‘ār*** [AR] 6x

<6145> עָר ***‘ār*** [ENEMY] 2x

<6146> עָר ***‘ār*** [ENEMY] 1x

<6147> עֵר ***‘êr*** [ER] 7x

<6148> עָרַב ***‘āraḇ*** [PLEDGE (BE A)] 22x

<6149> עָרֵב ***‘āraḇ*** [PLEASING (BE)] 8x

<6150> עָרַב ***‘āraḇ*** [EVENING (BECOME)] 3x

<6151> עֲרַב ***‘ᵃraḇ*** [MIX] 2x

<6152> עֲרָב ***‘ᵃrāḇ,*** עֲרַב ***‘ᵃraḇ*** [ARABIA] 5x

<6153> עֶרֶב ***‘ereḇ*** [EVENING] 137x

<6154> עֵרֶב ***‘êreḇ*** [MIXED] 14x

<6155> עֶרֶב ***‘ereḇ*** [WILLOW] 5x

<6156> עָרֵב ***‘ārêḇ*** [SWEET] 2x

<6157> עָרֹב ***‘ārōḇ*** [SWARM OF FLIES] 9x

<6158> עֹרֵב ***‘orêḇ*** [RAVEN] 10x

<6159> עוֹרֵב ***‘ôrêḇ*** [OREB] 7x

<6160> עֲרָבָה ***‘ᵃrāḇāh*** [DESERT (noun)] 61x

<6161> עֲרֻבָּה ***‘ᵃrubbāh*** [PLEDGE (noun)] 2x

<6162> עֵרָבוֹן ***‘êraḇôn*** [PLEDGE (noun)] 3x

<6163> עַרְבִי ***‘arḇiy,*** עֲרָבִי ***‘ᵃrāḇiy*** [ARABIAN] 9x

<6164> עַרְבָתִי ***‘arḇāṯiy*** [ARBATHITE] 2x

<6165> עָרַג ***‘ārag*** [PANT] 2x

<6166> עֲרָד ***‘ᵃrād*** [ARAD] 3x

<6167> עֲרָד ***‘ᵃrāḏ*** [WILD DONKEY] 1x

<6168> עָרָה ***‘ārāh*** [EMPTY (verb)] 15x

<6169> עָרוֹת ***‘ārôṯ*** [BULRUSHES] 1x

<6170> עֲרוּגָה ***‘ᵃrûḡāh*** [BED] 4x

<6171> עָרוֹד ***‘ārôḏ*** [WILD DONKEY] 1x

<6172> עֶרְוָה ***‘erwāh*** [NAKEDNESS] 54x

<6173> עַרְוָה ***‘arwāh*** [DISHONOR (noun)] 1x

<6174> עָרוֹם ***‘ārôm*** [NAKED] 16x

<6175> עָרוּם ***‘ārûm*** [PRUDENT] 11x

<6176> עֲרוֹעֵר ***‘ᵃrô‘êr*** [SHRUB] 2x

<6177> עֲרוֹעֵר ***‘ᵃrô‘êr,*** עֲרֹעֵר ***‘ᵃrō‘êr,*** עַרְעוֹר ***‘ar‘ôr*** [AROER] 16x

<6178> עָרוּץ ***‘ārûṣ*** [CLIFF] 1x

<6179> עֵרִי ***‘êriy*** [ERI] 2x

<6180> עֵרִי ***‘êriy*** [ERITE] 1x

<6181> עֶרְיָה ***‘eryāh*** [NAKEDNESS] 6x

<6182> עֲרִיסָה ***‘ᵃriysāh*** [DOUGH] 4x

<6183> עֲרִיפִים ***‘ᵃriyp̄iym*** [CLOUD] 1x

<6184> עָרִיץ ***‘āriyṣ*** [RUTHLESS] 20x

<6185> עֲרִירִי ***‘āriyriy*** [CHILDLESS] 4x

<6186> עָרַךְ ***‘āraḵ*** [ARRANGE] 70x, [VALUE (verb)] 4x

<6187> עֵרֶךְ ***‘êreḵ*** [EVALUATION] 33x

<6188> עָרֵל ***‘ārêl*** [NAKEDNESS (EXPOSE ONE’S)] 2x

<6189> עָרֵל ***'ārêl*** [UNCIRCUMCISED] 35x
<6190> עָרְלָה ***'orlāh*** [FORESKIN] 16x
<6191> עָרַם ***'āram*** [CRAFTY (BE)] 4x
<6192> עָרַם ***'āram*** [PILED UP] 1x
<6193> עֹרֶם ***'ōrem*** [CRAFTINESS] 1x
<6194> עֲרֵמָה ***ªrêmāh*** [HEAP (noun)] 11x
<6195> עָרְמָה ***'ormāh*** [PRUDENCE] 5x
<6196> עַרְמוֹן ***'armôn*** [PLANE TREE] 2x
<6197> עֵרָן ***'êrān*** [ERAN] 1x
<6198> עֵרָנִי ***'êrāniy*** [ERANITE] 1x
<6199> עַרְעָר ***'ar'ār*** [DESTITUTE] 1x, [SHRUB] 1x
<6200> עֲרֹעֵרִי ***ªrō'êriy*** [AROERITE] 1x
<6201> עָרַף ***'āraḇ*** [DROP, DROP DOWN] 2x
<6202> עָרַף ***'āraḇ*** [NECK (BREAK THE)] 6x
<6203> עֹרֶף ***'ōreḇ*** [NECK] 33x
<6204> עָרְפָּה ***'orpāh*** [ORPAH] 2x
<6205> עֲרָפֶל ***ªrāḇel*** [CLOUD] 15x
<6206> עָרַץ ***'āraṣ*** [TREMBLE] 15x
<6207> עָרַק ***'āraq*** [GNAW, GNAWING] 2x
<6208> עַרְקִי ***'arqiy*** [ARKITE] 2x
<6209> עָרַר ***'ārar*** [STRIP] 3x
<6210> עֶרֶשׂ ***'ereś*** [BED] 10x
<6211> עָשׁ ***'āš*** [MOTH] 7x
<6212> עֵשֶׂב ***'êśeḇ,*** עֲשַׂב ***ªśaḇ*** [GRASS] 33x
<6213> עָשָׂה ***'āśāh*** [DO] 2,601x (NAS)
<6214> עֲשָׂהאֵל ***ªśāh'êl*** [ASAHEL] 18x
<6215> עֵשָׂו ***'êśāw*** [ESAU] 97x
<6216> עָשׁוֹק ***'āšôq*** [OPPRESSOR] 1x
<6217> עֲשׁוּקִים ***ªšûqiym*** [OPPRESSIONS] 3x
<6218> עָשׂוֹר ***'āśôr*** [TEN] 16x
<6219> עָשׁוֹת ***'āšôṯ*** [WROUGHT] 1x
<6220> עַשְׁוָת ***'ašwāṯ*** [ASHVATH] 1x
<6221> עֲשִׂיאֵל ***ªśiy'êl*** [ASIEL] 1x
<6222> עֲשָׂיָה ***ªśāyāh*** [ASAIAH] 8x
<6223> עָשִׁיר ***'āšiyr*** [RICH (noun)] 23x
<6224> עֲשִׂירִי ***ªśiyriy*** [TENTH] 29x
<6225> עָשַׁן ***'āšan*** [SMOKE (noun and verb)] 6x
<6226> עָשֵׁן ***'āšên*** [SMOKING] 2x
<6227> עָשָׁן ***'āšān*** [SMOKE (noun)] 25x
<6228> עָשָׁן ***'āšān*** [ASHAN] 4x
<6229> עָשַׂק ***'āśaq*** [CONTEND] 1x
<6230> עֵשֶׂק ***'êśeq*** [ESEK] 1x
<6231> עָשַׁק ***'āšaq*** [OPPRESS] 37x
<6232> עֵשֶׁק ***'êšeq*** [ESHEK] 1x
<6233> עֹשֶׁק ***'ōšeq*** [OPPRESSION] 15x
<6234> עָשְׁקָה ***'ošqāh*** [OPPRESSED (BE)] 1x
<6235> עֶשֶׂר ***'eśer,*** עֲשָׂרָה ***ªśārāh*** [TEN] 175x
<6236> עֲשַׂר ***ªśar,*** עַשְׂרָה ***'aśrāh*** [TEN] 6x
<6237> עָשַׂר ***'āśar*** [TITHE (GIVE, RECEIVE)] 9x
<6238> עָשַׁר ***'āšar*** [RICH (BE, BECOME, GROW, MAKE)] 18x
<6239> עֹשֶׁר ***'ōšer*** [RICHES] 37x

<6240> עָשָׂר ***‘āśār*** [TEN] 335x
<6241> עִשָּׂרוֹן ***‘iśśārôn*** [TEN] 28x
<6242> עֶשְׂרִים ***‘eśriym*** [TWENTY] 315x
<6243> עֶשְׂרִין ***‘eśriyn*** [TWENTY] 1x
<6244> עָשֵׁשׁ ***‘āšēš*** [WASTE AWAY] 3x
<6245> עָשַׁת ***‘āšaṯ*** [CONCERNED (BE)] 1x, [SLEEK (BE)] 1x
<6246> עֲשִׁת ***‘ašiṯ,*** עֲשִׁית ***‘ašiyṯ*** [PLAN (verb)] 1x
<6247> עֶשֶׁת ***‘ešeṯ*** [POLISHED] 1x
<6248> עַשְׁתּוֹת ***‘aštôṯ*** [THOUGHT] 1x
<6249> עַשְׁתֵּי ***‘aštê*** [ELEVEN] 19x
<6250> עֶשְׁתֹּנָה ***‘eštōnāh*** [THOUGHT] 1x
<6251> עַשְׁתְּרוֹת ***‘ašterôṯ*** [FLOCKS] 4x
<6252> עַשְׁתָּרוֹת ***‘aštārôṯ*** [ASHTAROTH] 12x
<6253> עַשְׁתֹּרֶת ***‘aštōreṯ*** [ASHTORETH] 3x
<6254> עַשְׁתְּרָתִי ***‘ašterāṯiy*** [ASHTERATHITE] 1x
<6255> עַשְׁתְּרֹת קַרְנַיִם ***‘ašterōṯ qarnayim*** [ASHTEROTH KARNAIM] 1x
<6256> עֵת ***‘ēṯ*** [TIME] 296x
<6257> עָתַד ***‘āṯaḏ*** [READY (BE, MAKE, GET)] 2x
<6258> עַתָּה ***‘attāh*** [NOW] 431x (NAS)
<6259> עָתוּד ***‘āṯûḏ*** [TREASURE] 1x
<6260> עַתּוּד ***‘attûḏ*** [GOAT] 29x
<6261> עִתִּי ***‘ittiy*** [READINESS (IN)] 1x
<6262> עַתַּי ***‘attay*** [ATTAI] 4x
<6263> עֲתִיד ***‘aṯiyḏ*** [READY] 1x
<6264> עָתִיד ***‘āṯiyḏ*** [READY] 6x
<6265> עֲתָיָה ***‘aṯāyāh*** [ATHAIAH] 1x
<6266> עָתִיק ***‘āṯiyq*** [FINE (adj.)] 1x
<6267> עַתִּיק ***‘attiyq*** [ANCIENT] 2x
<6268> עַתִּיק ***‘attiyq*** [ANCIENT] 3x
<6269> עֲתָךְ ***‘aṯāḵ*** [ATHACH] 1x
<6270> עַתְלָי ***‘aṯlāy*** [ATHLAI] 1x
<6271> עֲתַלְיָה ***‘aṯalyāh,*** עֲתַלְיָהוּ ***‘aṯalyāhû*** [ATHALIAH] 17x
<6272> עָתַם ***‘āṯam*** [SCORCH] 1x
<6273> עָתְנִי ***‘oṯniy*** [OTHNI] 1x
<6274> עָתְנִיאֵל ***‘oṯniy’ēl*** [OTHNIEL] 7x
<6275> עָתַק ***‘āṯaq*** [MOVE] 9x
<6276> עָתֵק ***‘āṯēq*** [ENDURING] 1x
<6277> עָתָק ***‘āṯāq*** [ARROGANCE] 4x
<6278> עִתָּה קָצִין ***‘ittāh qaṣiyn,*** עֵת קָצִין ***‘ēṯ qāṣiyn*** [ETH-KAZIN] 1x
<6279> עָתַר ***‘āṯar*** [PRAY] 20x
<6280> עָתַר ***‘āthar*** [MULTIPLY] 2x
<6281> עֶתֶר ***‘ēṯer*** [ETHER] 2x
<6282> עָתָר ***‘āṯār*** [WORSHIPPER] 2x
<6283> עֲתֶרֶת ***‘aṯereṯ*** [ABUNDANCE] 1x

פ Pê

<6284> פָּאָה ***pā’āh*** [PIECES (CUT TO, DASH IN)] 1x
<6285> פֵּאָה ***pê’āh*** [CORNER (noun)] 86x

<6286> פָּאַר ***pā’ar*** [GLORIFY] 14x

<6287> פְּאֵר ***pᵉ’êr*** [TURBAN] 7x

<6288> פֹּארָה ***pō’rāh,*** פֻּארָה ***pu’rāh*** [BRANCH] 7x

<6289> פָּארוּר ***pā’rûr*** [BLACKNESS] 2x

<6290> פָּארָן ***pā’rān*** [PARAN] 11x

<6291> פַּג ***pag̱*** [FIG, GREEN FIG] 1x

<6292> פִּגּוּל ***piggûl*** [OFFENSIVE THING] 4x

<6293> פָּגַע ***pāg̱a‘*** [MEET] 46x

<6294> פֶּגַע ***peg̱a‘*** [OCCURRENCE] 2x

<6295> פַּגְעִיאֵל ***pag̱‘iy’êl*** [PAGIEL] 5x

<6296> פָּגַר ***pāg̱ar*** [EXHAUSTED (BE)] 2x

<6297> פֶּגֶר ***peg̱er*** [CORPSE] 22x

<6298> פָּגַשׁ ***pāg̱aš*** [MEET] 14x

<6299> פָּדָה ***pāḏāh*** [REDEEM] 59x

<6300> פְּדַהְאֵל ***pᵉḏah’êl*** [PEDAHEL] 1x

<6301> פְּדָהצוּר ***pᵉḏāhṣûr*** [PEDAHZUR] 5x

<6302> פְּדוּיִים ***pᵉḏûyiym*** [REDEMPTION] 3x

<6303> פָּדוֹן ***pāḏôn*** [PADON] 2x

<6304> פְּדוּת ***pᵉḏûṯ*** [REDEMPTION] 4x

<6305> פְּדָיָה ***pᵉḏāyāh,*** פְּדָיָהוּ ***pᵉḏāyāhû*** [PEDAIAH] 8x

<6306> פִּדְיוֹם ***piḏyôm,*** פִּדְיוֹן ***piḏyôn*** [REDEMPTION] 4x

<6307> פַּדָּן ***paddān,*** פַּדַּן אֲרָם ***paddan ᵃrām*** [PADDAN, PADDAN ARAM] 11x

<6308> פָּדַע ***pāḏa‘*** [DELIVER] 1x

<6309> פֶּדֶר ***peḏer*** [SUET] 3x

<6310> פֶּה ***peh*** [MOUTH] 498x

<6311> פֹּא ***pō’,*** פֹּה ***pōh,*** פּוֹ ***pô*** [HERE] 65x

<6312> פּוּאָה ***pû’āh,*** פֻּוָּה ***puwwāh*** [PUAH] 4x

<6313> פּוּג ***pûg̱*** [STUNNED (BECOME)] 4x

<6314> פּוּגָה ***pûg̱āh*** [REST (noun)] 1x

<6315> פּוּחַ ***pûaḥ*** [BREATHE] 13x

<6316> פּוּט ***pûṭ*** [PUT] 7x

<6317> פּוּטִיאֵל ***pûṭiy’êl*** [PUTIEL] 1x

<6318> פּוֹטִיפַר ***pôṭiyp̱ar*** [POTIPHAR] 2x

<6319> פּוֹטִי פֶרַע ***pôṭiy p̱era‘*** [POTIPHERAH] 3x

<6320> פּוּךְ ***pûḵ*** [ANTIMONY] 2x, [MAKEUP] 2x

<6321> פּוֹל ***pôl*** [BEANS] 2x

<6322> פּוּל ***pûl*** [PUL] 4x

<6323> פּוּן ***pûn*** [DESPAIR (BE IN)] 1x

<6324> פּוּנִי ***pûniy*** [PUNITES] 1x

<6325> פּוּנֹן ***pûnōn*** [PUNON] 2x

<6326> פּוּעָה ***pû‘āh*** [PUAH] 1x

<6327> פּוּץ ***pûṣ*** [SCATTER] 66x

<6328> פּוּק ***pûq*** [STUMBLE] 2x

<6329> פּוּק ***pûq*** [OBTAIN] 7x

<6330> פּוּקָה ***pûqāh*** [GRIEF] 1x

<6331> פּוּר ***pûr*** [NOTHING (BRING TO)] 3x

<6332> פּוּר ***pûr*** [PUR, PURIM] 8x

<6333> פּוּרָה ***pûrāh*** [WINEPRESS] 2x

<6334> פּוֹרָתָה ***pôrāṯah*** [PORATHA] 1x

<6335> פּוּשׁ ***pûš*** [FROLIC] 4x

<6336> פּוּתִי ***pûṯiy*** [PUTHITES] 1x

<6337> פַּז ***paz*** [GOLD] 9x
<6338> פָּזַז ***pāzaz*** [REFINED (BE)] 1x
<6339> פָּזַז ***pāzaz*** [AGILE (MAKE)] 2x
<6340> פָּזַר ***pāzar*** [SCATTER, SCATTERED (BE)] 10x
<6341> פַּח ***paḥ*** [SNARE (noun)] 27x
<6342> פָּחַד ***pāḥaḏ*** [DREAD (verb)] 25x
<6343> פַּחַד ***paḥaḏ*** [DREAD (noun)] 49x
<6344> פַּחַד ***paḥaḏ*** [THIGH] 1x
<6345> פַּחְדָּה ***paḥdāh*** [DREAD (noun)] 1x
<6346> פֶּחָה ***peḥāh*** [GOVERNOR] 28x
<6347> פֶּחָה ***peḥāh*** [GOVERNOR] 10x
<6348> פָּחַז ***pāḥaz*** [RECKLESS (BE)] 2x
<6349> פַּחַז ***paḥaz*** [RECKLESSNESS] 1x
<6350> פַּחֲזוּת ***paḥ^azûṯ*** [RECKLESSNESS] 1x
<6351> פָּחַח ***pāḥaḥ*** [TRAPPED (BE)] 1x
<6352> פֶּחָם ***peḥām*** [COAL] 3x
<6353> פֶּחָר ***peḥār*** [POTTER] 1x
<6354> פַּחַת ***paḥaṯ*** [PIT] 10x
<6355> פַּחַת מוֹאָב ***paḥaṯ mô'āḇ*** [PAHATH-MOAB] 6x
<6356> פְּחֶתֶת ***p^eḥeṯeṯ*** [EATING AWAY] 1x
<6357> פִּטְדָה ***piṭḏāh*** [TOPAZ] 4x
<6358> פָּטוּר ***pāṭûr*** [OPEN] 4x
<6359> פָּטִיר ***pāṭiyr*** [FREE] 1x
<6360> פַּטִּישׁ ***pattiyš*** [HAMMER (noun)] 3x
<6361> פַּטִּישׁ ***pattiyš*** [TROUSERS] 1x
<6362> פָּטַר ***pāṯar*** [OPEN] 9x
<6363> פֶּטֶר ***peṭer,*** פִּטְרָה ***piṭrāh*** [OPEN] 12x
<6364> פִּי בֶסֶת ***piy ḇeseṯ*** [PI-BESETH] 1x
<6365> פִּיד ***piyḏ*** [DISASTER] 3x
<6366> פֵּיָה ***pêyāh*** [EDGE] 1x
<6367> פִּי הַחִירֹת ***piy haḥiyrōṯ*** [PI-HAHIROTH] 4x
<6368> פִּיחַ ***piyaḥ*** [ASHES] 2x
<6369> פִּיכֹל ***piyḵōl*** [PHICOL] 3x
<6370> פִּילֶגֶשׁ ***piylegeš*** [CONCUBINE] 37x
<6371> פִּימָה ***piymāh*** [FAT (noun)] 1x
<6372> פִּינְחָס ***piyn^eḥās*** [PHINEAS] 25x
<6373> פִּינֹן ***piynōn*** [PINON] 2x
<6374> פִּיפִיּוֹת ***piyp̄iyyôṯ*** [TWO-EDGED] 2x
<6375> פִּיק ***piyq*** [SMITE TOGETHER] 1x
<6376> פִּישׁוֹן ***piyšôn*** [PISHON] 1x
<6377> פִּיתוֹן ***piyṯôn*** [PITHON] 2x
<6378> פַּךְ ***paḵ*** [FLASK] 3x
<6379> פָּכָה ***pāḵāh*** [TRICKLE] 1x
<6380> פֹּכֶרֶת הַצְּבָיִים ***pōḵereṯ haṣṣ^eḇāyiym*** [POKERETH-HAZZEBAIM] 2x
<6381> פָּלָא ***pālā'*** [WONDERFUL (DO SOMETHING)] 71x
<6382> פֶּלֶא ***pele'*** [WONDER] 13x
<6383> פִּלְאִי ***pil'iy,*** פֶּלִיא ***peliy'*** [WONDERFUL] 2x
<6384> פַּלֻּאִי ***pallu'iy*** [PALLUITES] 1x
<6385> פָּלַג ***pālag*** [DIVIDE] 4x
<6386> פְּלַג ***p^elag*** [DIVIDE] 1x
<6387> פְּלַג ***p^elag*** [HALF] 1x

<6388> פֶּלֶג ***peleg̱*** [STREAM (noun)] 10x
<6389> פֶּלֶג ***peleg̱*** [PELEG] 7x
<6390> פְּלַגָּה ***p^{e}laggāh*** [DIVISION] 3x
<6391> פְּלֻגָּה ***p^{e}luggāh*** [DIVISION] 1x
<6392> פְּלֻגָּה ***p^{e}luggāh*** [DIVISION] 1x
<6393> פְּלָדָה ***p^{e}lāḏāh*** [STEEL] 1x
<6394> פִּלְדָּשׁ ***pildāš*** [PILDASH] 1x
<6395> פָּלָה ***pālāh*** [DISTINCTION (MAKE)] 7x
<6396> פַּלּוּא ***pallû'*** [PALLU] 5x
<6397> פְּלוֹנִי ***p^{e}lôniy*** [PELONITE] 3x
<6398> פָּלַח ***pālaḥ*** [CUT (verb)] 5x
<6399> פְּלַח ***p^{e}laḥ*** [SERVE] 10x
<6400> פֶּלַח ***pelaḥ*** [PIECE] 6x
<6401> פִּלְחָא ***pilḥā'*** [PILHA] 1x
<6402> פָּלְחַן ***polḥan*** [SERVICE] 1x
<6403> פָּלַט ***pālaṯ*** [DELIVER] 25x
<6404> פֶּלֶט ***peleṯ*** [PELET] 2x
<6405> פָּלֵט ***pālêṯ,*** פַּלֵּט ***pallêṯ*** [ESCAPE (noun)] 5x
<6406> פַּלְטִי ***palṭiy*** [PALTI] 2x
<6407> פַּלְטִי ***palṭiy*** [PALTITE] 1x
<6408> פִּלְטָי ***pilṭāy*** [PILTAI] 1x
<6409> פַּלְטִיאֵל ***palṭiy'ēl*** [PALTIEL] 2x
<6410> פְּלַטְיָה ***p^{e}laṭyāh,*** פְּלַטְיָהוּ ***p^{e}laṭyāhû*** [PELATIAH] 5x
<6411> פְּלָאיָה ***p^{e}lā'yāh,*** פְּלָיָה ***p^{e}lāyāh*** [PELAIAH] 3x
<6412> פָּלִיט ***pāliyṯ,*** פָּלֵיט ***pālêṯ*** [REFUGEE] 21x
<6413> פְּלֵיטָה ***p^{e}lêyṭāh*** [DELIVERANCE] 5x
<6414> פָּלִיל ***pāliyl*** [JUDGE (noun)] 3x
<6415> פְּלִילָה ***p^{e}liylāh*** [JUDGMENT] 1x
<6416> פְּלִילִי ***p^{e}liyliy*** [JUDGES (PUNISHABLE BY)] 1x
<6417> פְּלִילִיָּה ***p^{e}liyliyyah*** [JUDGMENT] 1x
<6418> פֶּלֶךְ ***peleḵ*** [DISTRICT] 8x, [SPINDLE] 2x
<6419> פָּלַל ***pālal*** [PRAY] 84x
<6420> פָּלָל ***pālāl*** [PALAL] 1x
<6421> פְּלַלְיָה ***p^{e}lalyāh*** [PELALIAH] 1x
<6422> פַּלְמוֹנִי ***palmôniy*** [CERTAIN ONE] 1x
<6423> פְּלֹנִי ***p^{e}lōniy*** [CERTAIN ONE] 3x
<6424> פָּלַס ***pālas*** [WEIGH, WEIGH OUT] 6x
<6425> פֶּלֶס ***peles*** [BALANCE] 2x
<6426> פָּלַץ ***pālaṣ*** [SHAKE] 1x
<6427> פַּלָּצוּת ***pallāṣûṯ*** [TREMBLING] 4x
<6428> פָּלַשׁ ***pālaš*** [ROLL IN] 4x
<6429> פְּלֶשֶׁת ***p^{e}lešeṯ*** [PHILISTIA] 8x
<6430> פְּלִשְׁתִּי ***p^{e}lištiy*** [PHILISTINE] 288x
<6431> פֶּלֶת ***peleṯ*** [PELETH] 2x
<6432> פְּלֵתִי ***p^{e}lêṯiy*** [PELETHITES] 7x
<6433> פֻּם ***pum*** [MOUTH] 6x
<6434> פֵּן ***pên*** [CORNER (noun)] 1x
<6435> פֶּן ***pen*** [SO THAT] 82x
<6436> פַּנַּג ***pannag̱*** [CAKE] 1x
<6437> פָּנָה ***pānāh*** [TURN (verb)] 133x
<6438> פִּנָּה ***pinnāh*** [CORNER (noun)] 28x

<6439> פְּנוּאֵל ***p^{e}nû'êl,*** פְּנִיאֵל ***p^{e}niy'êl*** [PENUEL] 9x

<6440> פָּנֶה ***pāneh,*** פָּנִים ***pāniym*** [FACE (noun)] 2,109x (KJV)

<6441> פְּנִימָה ***p^{e}niymāh*** [WITHIN] 14x

<6442> פְּנִימִי ***p^{e}niymiy*** [INNER] 32x

<6443> פְּנִינִים ***p^{e}niyniym*** [JEWELS] 6x

<6444> פְּנִנָּה ***p^{e}ninnāh*** [PENINNAH] 3x

<6445> פָּנַק ***pānaq*** [PAMPER] 1x

<6446> פַּס ***pas*** [COLORS (OF MANY)] 5x

<6447> פַּס ***pas*** [PART (noun)] 2x

<6448> פָּסַג ***pāsag̱*** [CONSIDER] 1x

<6449> פִּסְגָּה ***pisgāh*** [PISGAH] 8x

<6450> פַּס דַּמִּים ***pas dammiym*** [PAS DAMMIM] 1x

<6451> פִּסָּה ***pissāh*** [ABUNDANCE] 1x

<6452> פָּסַח ***pasaḥ*** [PASS OVER] 7x

<6453> פֶּסַח ***pesaḥ*** [PASSOVER] 49x

<6454> פָּסֵחַ ***pāsêaḥ*** [PASEAH] 4x

<6455> פִּסֵּחַ ***pissêaḥ*** [LAME] 14x

<6456> פָּסִיל ***pāsiyl*** [IDOL] 23x

<6457> פָּסַךְ ***pāsaḵ*** [PASACH] 1x

<6458> פָּסַל ***pāsal*** [CUT (verb)] 6x

<6459> פֶּסֶל ***pesel*** [IDOL] 31x

<6460> פְּסַנְטֵרִין ***p^{e}sanṭêriyn,*** פְּסַנְתֵּרִין ***p^{e}santêriyn*** [PSALTERY] 4x

<6461> פָּסַס ***pāsas*** [VANISH] 1x

<6462> פִּסְפָּה ***pispāh*** [PISPAH] 1x

<6463> פָּעָה ***pā'āh*** [CRY (verb)] 1x

<6464> פָּעוּ ***pā'û,*** פָּעִי ***pā'iy*** [PAU] 2x

<6465> פְּעוֹר ***p^{e}'ôr*** [PEOR] 5x

<6466> פָּעַל ***pā'al*** [MAKE] 56x

<6467> פֹּעַל ***pō'al*** [WORK] 38x

<6468> פְּעֻלָּה ***p^{e}'ullāh*** [WORK] 14x

<6469> פְּעֻלְּתַי ***p^{e}'ull^{e}ṯay*** [PEULLETHAI] 1x

<6470> פָּעַם ***pā'am*** [TROUBLED (BE)] 5x

<6471> פַּעַם ***pa'am*** [TIME] 112x

<6472> פַּעֲמוֹן ***pa'$^{\breve{a}}$môn*** [BELL] 7x

<6473> פָּעַר ***pā'ar*** [OPEN] 4x

<6474> פַּעֲרַי ***pa'$^{\breve{a}}$ray*** [PAARAI] 1x

<6475> פָּצָה ***pāṣāh*** [OPEN] 15x

<6476> פָּצַח ***pāṣaḥ*** [BREAK FORTH] 8x

<6477> פְּצִירָה ***p^{e}ṣiyrāh*** [CHARGE (noun)] 1x

<6478> פָּצַל ***pāṣal*** [PEEL] 2x

<6479> פְּצָלָה ***p^{e}ṣālāh*** [STRIPE] 1x

<6480> פָּצַם ***pāṣam*** [TEAR OPEN] 1x

<6481> פָּצַע ***pāṣa'*** [WOUND (verb)] 3x

<6482> פֶּצַע ***peṣa'*** [WOUND (noun)] 8x

<6483> פִּצֵּץ ***piṣṣêṣ*** [HAPPIZZEZ] 1x

<6484> פָּצַר ***pāṣar*** [PRESS] 7x

<6485> פָּקַד ***pāqaḏ*** [ATTEND] 305x

<6486> פְּקֻדָּה ***p^{e}quddāh*** [ARRANGEMENT] 32x

<6487> פִּקָּדוֹן ***piqqāḏôn*** [DEPOSIT] 3x

<6488> פְּקִדֻת ***p^{e}qiḏuṯ*** [GUARD] 1x

<6489> פְּקוֹד ***p^{e}qôḏ*** [PEKOD] 2x

<6490> פִּקּוּד ***piqqûḏ***, פְּקוּדִים ***p^{e}qûḏiym*** [PRECEPT] 24x
<6491> פָּקַח ***pāqaḥ*** [OPEN] 20x
<6492> פֶּקַח ***peqaḥ*** [PEKAH] 11x
<6493> פִּקֵּחַ ***piqqêaḥ*** [SEEING] 2x
<6494> פְּקַחְיָה ***p^{e}qaḥyāh*** [PEKAHIAH] 3x
<6495> פְּקַח־קוֹחַ ***p^{e}qaḥ-qôaḥ*** [OPENING OF THE PRISON] 1x
<6496> פָּקִיד ***pāqiyḏ*** [OVERSEER] 13x
<6497> פְּקָעִים ***p^{e}qā'iym*** [GOURDS] 2x
<6498> פַּקֻּעֹת ***paqqu'ōṯ*** [GOURDS] 1x
<6499> פַּר ***par***, פָּר ***pār*** [BULL, YOUNG BULL] 133x
<6500> פָּרָא ***pārā'*** [FRUITFUL (BE)] 1x
<6501> פֶּרֶא ***pere'*** [DONKEY (WILD)] 10x
<6502> פִּרְאָם ***pir'ām*** [PIRAM] 1x
<6503> פַּרְבָּר ***parbār*** [PRECINCTS] 3x
<6504> פָּרַד ***pāraḏ*** [DIVIDE] 26x
<6505> פֶּרֶד ***pereḏ*** [MULE] 15x
<6506> פִּרְדָּה ***pirdāh*** [MULE] 3x
<6507> פְּרֻדֹת ***p^{e}ruḏōṯ*** [SEED] 1x
<6508> פַּרְדֵּס ***pardês*** [FOREST] 3x
<6509> פָּרָה ***pārāh*** [FRUITFUL (BE)] 28x
<6510> פָּרָה ***pārāh*** [COW] 26x
<6511> פָּרָה ***pārāh*** [PARAH] 1x
<6512> פֵּרָה ***pêrāh*** [MOLE] 1x
<6513> פֻּרָה ***purāh*** [PURAH] 2x
<6514> פְּרוּדָא ***p^{e}rûḏā'***, פְּרִידָא ***p^{e}riyḏā'*** [PERUDA, PERIDA] 2x
<6515> פָּרוּחַ ***pārûaḥ*** [PARUAH] 1x
<6516> פַּרְוַיִם ***parwayim*** [PARVAIM] 1x
<6517> פָּרוּר ***pārûr*** [POT] 3x
<6518> פָּרָז ***pārāz*** [WARRIOR] 1x
<6519> פְּרָזָה ***p^{e}rāzāh*** [TOWN (UNWALLED, RURAL)] 3x
<6520> פְּרָזוֹן ***p^{e}rāzôn*** [VILLAGER] 2x
<6521> פְּרָזִי ***p^{e}rāziy*** [UNWALLED] 3x
<6522> פְּרִזִּי ***p^{e}rizziy*** [PERIZZITE] 23x
<6523> פַּרְזֶל ***parzel*** [IRON] 20x
<6524> פָּרַח ***pāraḥ*** [BREAK OUT] 36x
<6525> פֶּרַח ***peraḥ*** [FLOWER] 17x
<6526> פִּרְחָח ***pirḥāḥ*** [BROOD] 1x
<6527> פָּרַט ***pāraṭ*** [IMPROVISE] 1x
<6528> פֶּרֶט ***pereṭ*** [FALLEN GRAPES] 1x
<6529> פְּרִי ***p^{e}riy*** [FRUIT] 119x
<6530> פָּרִיץ ***pariyṣ*** [VIOLENT] 6x
<6531> פֶּרֶךְ ***pereḵ*** [SEVERITY] 6x
<6532> פָּרֹכֶת ***pārōḵeṯ*** [VEIL] 25x
<6533> פָּרַם ***pāram*** [TEAR] 3x
<6534> פַּרְמַשְׁתָּא ***parmaštā'*** [PARMASHTA] 1x
<6535> פַּרְנָךְ ***parnāḵ*** [PARNACH] 1x
<6536> פָּרַס ***pāras*** [DIVIDE] 14x
<6537> פְּרַס ***pāras***, פְּרֵס ***p^{e}rês***, וּפַרְסִין ***ûp̱arsiyn***, פַּרְסִין ***parsiyn*** [DIVIDE] 2x
<6538> פֶּרֶס ***peres*** [VULTURE] 2x
<6539> פָּרַס ***pāras*** [PERSIA] 28x
<6540> פָּרַס ***pāras*** [PERSIA] 6x

<6541> פַּרְסָה ***parsāh*** [HOOF] 19x
<6542> פַּרְסִי ***parsiy*** [PERSIAN] 1x
<6543> פַּרְסָיָא ***parsāyā'*** [PERSIAN] 1x
<6544> פָּרַע ***pāra'*** [GO (LET)] 16x
<6545> פֶּרַע ***pera'*** [LOCK OF HAIR] 2x
<6546> פֶּרַע ***pera'*** [LEADER] 2x
<6547> פַּרְעֹה ***par'ōh*** [PHARAOH] 268x
<6548> פַּרְעֹה חָפְרַע ***par'ōh ḥop̱ra'*** [PHARAOH HOPHRA] 1x
<6549> פַּרְעֹה נְכֹה ***par'ōh n^{e}ḵōh*** [PHARAOH NECO] 6x
<6550> פַּרְעֹשׁ ***par'ōš*** [FLEA] 2x
<6551> פַּרְעֹשׁ ***par'ōš*** [PAROSH] 6x
<6552> פִּרְעָתוֹן ***pir'āṯôn*** [PIRATHON] 1x
<6553> פִּרְעָתוֹנִי ***pir'āṯôniy*** [PIRATHONITE] 5x
<6554> פַּרְפַּר ***parpar*** [PHARPAR] 1x
<6555> פָּרַץ ***pāraṣ*** [BREAK OUT, BREAK DOWN] 49x
<6556> פֶּרֶץ ***pereṣ*** [BREACH] 19x
<6557> פֶּרֶץ ***pereṣ*** [BREACH] 15x
<6558> פַּרְצִי ***parṣiy*** [PEREZITE] 1x
<6559> פְּרָצִים ***p^{e}rāṣiym*** [PERAZIM] 1x
<6560> פֶּרֶץ עֻזָּא ***pereṣ 'uzzā'*** [PEREZ UZZAH] 2x
<6561> פָּרַק ***pāraq*** [BREAK OFF] 10x
<6562> פְּרַק ***p^{e}raq*** [BREAK AWAY, BREAK OFF] 1x
<6563> פֶּרֶק ***pereq*** [CROSSROAD] 1x, [PLUNDER (noun)] 1x
<6564> פָּרָק ***pārāq*** [BROTH] 1x
<6565> פָּרַר ***pārar*** [BREAK] 50x
<6566> פָּרַשׂ ***pāraś*** [SPREAD, SPREAD OUT] 67x
<6567> פָּרַשׁ ***pāraš*** [CLEAR (BE, MAKE)] 3x, [SCATTER] 1x, [STING (verb)] 1x
<6568> פְּרַשׁ ***p^{e}raš*** [CLEAR (MAKE)] 1x
<6569> פֶּרֶשׁ ***pereš*** [DUNG] 7x
<6570> פֶּרֶשׁ ***pereš*** [PERESH] 1x
<6571> פָּרָשׁ ***pārāš*** [HORSEMEN] 57x
<6572> פַּרְשֶׁגֶן ***paršeg̱en,*** פַּתְשֶׁגֶן ***paṯšeg̱en*** [COPY (noun)] 4x
<6573> פַּרְשֶׁגֶן ***paršeg̱en*** [COPY (noun)] 3x
<6574> פַּרְשְׁדֹנָה ***parš^{e}ḏōnāh*** [DUNG] 1x
<6575> פָּרָשָׁה ***pārāšāh*** [SUM, EXACT SUM] 2x
<6576> פַּרְשֵׁז ***paršêz*** [SPREAD (verb)] 1x
<6577> פַּרְשַׁנְדָּתָא ***paršandāṯā'*** [PARSHANDATHA] 1x
<6578> פְּרָת ***p^{e}raṯ*** [EUPHRATES] 19x
<6579> פַּרְתְּמִים ***part^{e}miym*** [NOBLE] 3x
<6580> פַּשׁ ***paš*** [TRANSGRESSION] 1x
<6581> פָּשָׂה ***pāśāh*** [SPREAD (verb)] 22x
<6582> פָּשַׁח ***pāšaḥ*** [PIECES (TEAR IN, TEAR TO, PULL IN)] 1x
<6583> פַּשְׁחוּר ***pašḥûr*** [PASHUR] 14x
<6584> פָּשַׁט ***pāšaṭ*** [STRIP OFF] 43x
<6585> פָּשַׂע ***pāśa'*** [MARCH (verb)] 1x
<6586> פָּשַׁע ***pāša'*** [REBEL (verb)] 41x
<6587> פֶּשַׂע ***peśa'*** [STEP (noun)] 1x
<6588> פֶּשַׁע ***peša'*** [TRANSGRESSION] 93x
<6589> פָּשַׂק ***pāśaq*** [OPEN, OPEN WIDE] 2x
<6590> פְּשַׁר ***p^{e}šar*** [INTERPRET] 2x
<6591> פְּשַׁר ***p^{e}šar*** [INTERPRETATION] 31x

<6592> פֵּשֶׁר ***pêšer*** [INTERPRETATION] 1x
<6593> פֵּשֶׁת ***pêšeṯ*** [LINEN] 16x
<6594> פִּשְׁתָּה ***pištāh*** [FLAX] 3x
<6595> פַּת ***paṯ,*** פְּתוֹת ***pᵉṯôṯ*** [PIECE] 15x
<6596> פֹּת ***pōṯ*** [FOREHEAD] 1x, [HINGE] 1x, [SECRET PARTS] 1x
<6597> פִּתְאוֹם ***piṯ'ôm*** [SUDDENLY] 25x
<6598> פַּתְבַּג ***paṯbaḡ*** [FOOD, CHOICE FOOD] 6x
<6599> פִּתְגָם ***piṯgām*** [EDICT] 2x
<6600> פִּתְגָם ***piṯgām*** [ANSWER (noun)] 6x
<6601> פָּתָה ***pāṯāh*** [ENLARGE] 1x, [ENTICE] 27x
<6602> פְּתוּאֵל ***pᵉṯû'êl*** [PETHUEL] 1x
<6603> פִּתּוּחַ ***pittûaḥ*** [ENGRAVING] 11x
<6604> פְּתוֹר ***pᵉṯôr*** [PETHOR] 2x
<6605> פָּתַח ***pāṯaḥ*** [OPEN] 144x
<6606> פְּתַח ***pᵉṯaḥ*** [OPEN] 2x
<6607> פֶּתַח ***peṯaḥ*** [DOOR] 163x
<6608> פֵּתַח ***pêṯaḥ*** [UNFOLDING] 1x
<6609> פְּתִיחָה ***pᵉṯiyḥāh*** [SWORD (DRAWN)] 1x
<6610> פִּתְחוֹן ***piṯḥôn*** [OPEN] 2x
<6611> פְּתַחְיָה ***pᵉṯaḥyāh*** [PETHAHIAH] 4x
<6612> פֶּתִי ***peṯiy*** [SIMPLE] 19x
<6613> פְּתָי ***pᵉṯāy*** [WIDTH] 2x
<6614> פְּתִיגִיל ***pᵉṯiyḡiyl*** [RICH ROBE] 1x
<6615> פְּתַיּוּת ***pᵉṯayyûṯ*** [SIMPLE] 1x
<6616> פָּתִיל ***pāṯiyl*** [CORD] 11x
<6617> פָּתַל ***pāṯal*** [WRESTLE] 5x
<6618> פְּתַלְתֹּל ***pᵉṯaltōl*** [CROOKED] 1x
<6619> פִּתֹם ***piṯōm*** [PITHOM] 1x
<6620> פֶּתֶן ***peṯen*** [ASP] 6x
<6621> פֶּתַע ***peṯa'*** [SUDDENLY] 7x
<6622> פָּתַר ***pāṯar*** [INTERPRET] 7x
<6623> פִּתְרוֹן ***piṯrôn*** [INTERPRETATION] 5x
<6624> פַּתְרוֹס ***paṯrôs*** [PATHROS] 5x
<6625> פַּתְרֻסִים ***paṯrusiym*** [PATHRUSITE] 2x
<6626> פָּתַת ***pāṯaṯ*** [BREAK] 1x

צ Tsadde

<6627> צֵאָה ***tṣê'āh*** [EXCREMENT] 2x
<6628> צֶאֱלִים ***ṣeᵉliym*** [LOTUS PLANTS, LOTUS TREES] 2x
<6629> צֹאן ***ṣō'n*** [SHEEP] 272x
<6630> צַאֲנָן ***ṣa'ănan*** [ZAANAN] 1x
<6631> צֶאֱצָא ***ṣeᵉṣā'*** [OFFSPRING] 7x
<6632> צָב ***ṣāḇ*** [COVERED] 3x
<6633> צָבָא ***ṣāḇā'*** [SERVE] 13x
<6634> צְבָא ***ṣᵉḇā'*** [WISH] 7x
<6635> צָבָא ***ṣāḇā'*** [SERVICE] 485x
<6636> צְבֹאִים ***ṣᵉḇō'iym,*** צְבֹיִים ***ṣᵉḇōyiym*** [ZEBOIIM] 5x
<6637> צֹבֵבָה ***ṣōḇêḇāh,*** הַצֹּבֵבָה ***haṣṣōḇêḇāh*** [ZOBEBAH] 1x

<6638> צָבָה ***ṣāḇāh*** [SWELL] 2x
<6639> צָבֶה ***ṣāḇeh*** [SWELL] 1x
<6640> צְבוּ ***ṣᵉḇû*** [SITUATION] 1x
<6641> צָבוּעַ ***ṣāḇûaʻ*** [SPECKLED] 1x
<6642> צָבַט ***ṣāḇaṭ*** [SERVE] 1x
<6643> צְבִי ***ṣᵉḇiy*** [GLORY] 32x
<6644> צִבְיָא ***ṣiḇyā'*** [ZIBIA] 1x
<6645> צִבְיָה ***ṣiḇyāh*** [ZIBIAH] 2x
<6646> צְבִיָּה ***ṣᵉḇiyyāh*** [GAZELLE] 2x
<6647> צְבַע ***ṣᵉḇaʻ*** [WET (BE)] 5x
<6648> צֶבַע ***ṣeḇaʻ*** [DYED WORK, DYED MATERIALS] 3x
<6649> צִבְעוֹן ***ṣiḇʻôn*** [ZIBEON] 8x
<6650> צְבֹעִים ***ṣᵉḇōʻiym*** [ZEBOIM] 2x
<6651> צָבַר ***ṣāḇar*** [STORE UP] 7x
<6652> צִבֻּר ***ṣibbur,*** צִבּוּר ***ṣibbûr*** [HEAP (noun)] 1x
<6653> צֶבֶת ***ṣeḇeṯ*** [BUNDLE] 1x
<6654> צַד ***ṣaḏ*** [SIDE] 33x
<6655> צַד ***ṣaḏ*** [CONCERNING] 2x
<6656> צְדָא ***ṣᵉḏā'*** [TRUE] 1x
<6657> צְדָד ***ṣᵉḏāḏ*** [ZEDAD] 2x
<6658> צָדָה ***ṣāḏāh*** [LIE IN WAIT] 2x
<6659> צָדוֹק ***ṣāḏôq*** [ZADOK] 53x
<6660> צְדִיָּה ***ṣᵉḏiyyāh*** [LYING IN WAIT] 2x
<6661> צִדִּים ***ṣiddiym*** [ZIDDIM] 1x
<6662> צַדִּיק ***ṣaddiyq*** [JUST] 206x
<6663> צָדַק ***ṣāḏaq*** [JUST (BE)] 41x
<6664> צֶדֶק ***ṣeḏeq*** [RIGHTEOUSNESS] 116x
<6665> צִדְקָה ***ṣiḏqāh*** [RIGHTEOUSNESS] 1x
<6666> צְדָקָה ***ṣᵉḏāqāh*** [RIGHTEOUSNESS] 157x
<6667> צִדְקִיָּה ***ṣiḏqiyyāh,*** צִדְקִיָּהוּ ***ṣiḏqiyyāhû*** [ZEDEKIAH] 63x
<6668> צָהַב ***ṣāhaḇ*** [SHINY] 1x
<6669> צָהֹב ***ṣāhoḇ*** [YELLOW, YELLOWISH] 3x
<6670> צָהַל ***ṣāhal*** [CRY OUT] 8x, [SHINE) 1x
<6671> צָהַר ***ṣāhar*** [OIL] 1x
<6672> צֹהַר ***ṣōhar*** [NOON] 23x, [WINDOW] 1x
<6673> צַו ***ṣaw,*** צָו ***ṣāw*** [PRECEPT] 9x
<6674> צוֹא ***ṣô',*** צוֹאִי ***ṣô'iy*** [FILTHY] 2x
<6675> צוֹאָה ***ṣô'āh*** [FILTHINESS] 3x
<6676> צַוַּאר ***ṣawwa'r*** [NECK] 3x
<6677> צַוָּאר ***ṣawwā'r,*** צַוְּרֹנִים ***ṣawwārōniym*** [NECK] 42x
<6678> צוֹבָא ***ṣôḇā',*** צוֹבָה ***ṣôḇāh*** [ZOBAH] 13x
<6679> צוּד ***ṣûḏ,*** צִיד ***ṣiyḏ*** [HUNT] 15x
<6680> צָוָה ***ṣāwāh*** [COMMAND (verb)] 578x
<6681> צָוַח ***ṣāwaḥ*** [SHOUT (verb)] 1x
<6682> צְוָחָה ***ṣᵉwāḥāh*** [CRY (noun)] 4x
<6683> צוּלָה ***ṣûlāh*** [DEEP (noun)] 1x
<6684> צוּם ***ṣûm*** [FAST (verb)] 21x
<6685> צוֹם ***ṣôm*** [FASTING] 26x
<6686> צוּעָר ***ṣûʻār*** [ZUAR] 5x
<6687> צוּף ***ṣûp̱*** [FLOW OVER] 3x
<6688> צוּף ***ṣûp̱*** [HONEYCOMB] 2x

<6689> צוּף ***ṣûp̱***, צוֹפַי ***ṣôp̱ay*** [ZUPH] 4x
<6690> צוֹפַח ***ṣôp̱aḥ*** [ZOPHAH] 2x
<6691> צוֹפַר ***ṣôp̱ar*** [ZOPHAR] 4x
<6692> צוּץ ***ṣûṣ*** [BLOSSOM (verb)] 9x
<6693> צוּק ***ṣûq*** [OPPRESS] 10x
<6694> צוּק ***ṣûq*** [SMELT] 3x
<6695> צוֹק ***ṣôq***, צוּקָה ***ṣûqāh*** [DISTRESS (noun)] 4x
<6696> צוּר ***ṣûr*** [BESIEGE] 38x
<6697> צוּר ***ṣûr*** [ROCK] 78x
<6698> צוּר ***ṣûr*** [ZUR] 5x
<6699> צוּרָה ***ṣûrāh*** [DESIGN] 3x
<6700> צוּרִיאֵל ***ṣûriy'ēl*** [ZURIEL] 1x
<6701> צוּרִישַׁדָּי ***ṣûriyšadday*** [ZURISHADDAI] 5x
<6702> צוּת ***ṣûṯ*** [BURN (verb)] 1x
<6703> צַח ***ṣaḥ*** [DAZZLING] 4x
<6704> צִחֶה ***ṣiḥeh*** [PARCHED] 1x
<6705> צָחַח ***ṣāḥaḥ*** [WHITER] 1x
<6706> צְחִיחַ ***ṣ*ᵉ*ḥiyaḥ*** [BARE (noun)] 5x
<6707> צְחִיחָה ***ṣ*ᵉ*ḥiyḥāh*** [PARCHED LAND] 1x
<6708> צְחִיחִי ***ṣ*ᵉ*ḥiyḥiy*** [PLACE (HIGHER, OPENED, EXPOSED)] 1x
<6709> צַחֲנָה ***ṣaḥ*ᵃ*nāh*** [FOUL SMELL, FOUL ODOR] 1x
<6710> צַחְצָחָה ***ṣaḥṣāḥāh*** [SCORCHED PLACE] 1x
<6711> צָחַק ***ṣāḥaq*** [LAUGH] 13x
<6712> צְחֹק ***ṣ*ᵉ*ḥōq*** [LAUGHTER] 2x
<6713> צַחַר ***ṣaḥar*** [WHITE] 1x
<6714> צֹחַר ***ṣōḥar*** [ZOAR] 5x
<6715> צָחֹר ***ṣāḥōr*** [WHITE] 1x
<6716> צִי ***ṣiy*** [SHIP] 4x
<6717> צִיבָא ***ṣiyḇā'*** [ZIBA] 13x
<6718> צַיִד ***ṣayiḏ*** [FOOD] 18x
<6719> צַיָּד ***ṣayyāḏ*** [HUNTER] 1x
<6720> צֵידָה ***ṣêyḏāh*** [FOOD] 10x
<6721> צִידוֹן ***ṣiyḏôn***, צִידֹן ***ṣiyḏōn*** [SIDON] 22x
<6722> צִידֹנִי ***ṣiyḏōniy*** [SIDONIAN] 15x
<6723> צִיָּה ***ṣiyyāh*** [DRYNESS] 16x
<6724> צָיוֹן ***ṣāyôn*** [DRY PLACE] 2x
<6725> צִיּוּן ***ṣiyyûn*** [MONUMENT] 3x
<6726> צִיּוֹן ***ṣiyyôn*** [ZION] 154x
<6727> צִיחָא ***ṣiyḥā'*** [ZIHA] 3x
<6728> צִיִּים ***ṣiyyiym*** [WILDERNESS] 6x
<6729> צִינֹק ***ṣiynōq*** [NECK IRON] 1x
<6730> צִיעֹר ***ṣiy'ōr*** [ZIOR] 1x
<6731> צִיץ ***ṣiyṣ*** [FLOWER] 15x
<6732> צִיץ ***ṣiyṣ*** [ZIZ] 1x
<6733> צִיצָה ***ṣiyṣāh*** [FLOWER] 1x
<6734> צִיצִת ***ṣiyṣiṯ*** [TASSEL] 4x
<6735> צִיר ***ṣiyr*** [HINGE] 1x, [MESSENGER] 6x, [PAIN, LABOR PAINS] 5x
<6736> צִיר ***ṣiyr*** [FORM (noun)] 2x
<6737> צָיַר ***ṣāyar*** [AMBASSADOR (BE)] 1x
<6738> צֵל ***ṣēl*** [SHADOW] 49x
<6739> צְלָא ***ṣ*ᵉ*lā'*** [PRAY] 2x

<6740> צָלָה ***ṣālāh*** [ROAST] 3x
<6741> צִלָּה ***ṣillāh*** [ZILLAH] 3x
<6742> צְלוּל ***ṣᵉlûl,*** צְלִיל ***ṣᵉliyl*** [CAKE] 1x
<6743> צָלַח ***ṣālaḥ,*** צָלֵחַ ***ṣālêaḥ*** [RUSH (verb)] 65x
<6744> צְלַח ***ṣᵉlaḥ*** [PROSPER] 4x
<6745> צֵלָחָה ***ṣêlāḥāh*** [PAN] 1x
<6746> צְלֹחִית ***ṣᵉlōḥiyṯ*** [BOWL] 1x
<6747> צַלַּחַת ***ṣallaḥaṯ*** [BOSOM] 2x, [DISH] 3x
<6748> צָלִי ***ṣāliy*** [ROASTED] 3x
<6749> צָלַל ***ṣālal*** [SINK] 1x
<6750> צָלַל ***ṣālal*** [TINGLE] 4x
<6751> צָלַל ***ṣālal*** [DARK (BE, GROW)] 2x
<6752> צֵלֶל ***ṣêlel*** [SHADOW] 4x
<6753> צְלֶלְפּוֹנִי ***ṣᵉlelpôniy,*** הַצְלֶלְפּוֹנִי ***haṣṣᵉlelpôniy*** [HAZZELELPONI] 1x
<6754> צֶלֶם ***ṣelem*** [IMAGE] 17x
<6755> צֶלֶם ***ṣelem,*** צְלֵם ***ṣᵉlêm*** [IMAGE] 17x
<6756> צַלְמוֹן ***ṣalmôn*** [ZALMON] 3x
<6757> צַלְמָוֶת ***ṣalmāweṯ*** [SHADOW OF DEATH] 18x
<6758> צַלְמֹנָה ***ṣalmōnāh*** [ZALMONAH] 2x
<6759> צַלְמֻנָּע ***ṣalmunnā'*** [ZALMMUNNA] 12x
<6760> צָלַע ***ṣāla'*** [LIMP] 4x
<6761> צֶלַע ***ṣela'*** [STUMBLING] 4x
<6762> צֵלַע ***ṣêla'*** [ZELAH] 2x
<6763> צֵלָע ***ṣêlā'*** [SIDE] 41x
<6764> צָלָף ***ṣālāp̱*** [ZALAPH] 1x
<6765> צְלָפְחָד ***ṣᵉlāp̱ᵉḥāḏ*** [ZELOPHEHAD] 11x
<6766> צֶלְצַח ***ṣelṣaḥ*** [ZELZAH] 1x
<6767> צִלְצָל ***ṣilṣāl,*** צְלָצַל ***ṣᵉlāṣal,*** צֶלְצְלִים ***ṣelṣᵉliym*** [WHIRRING] 6x
<6768> צֶלֶק ***ṣeleq*** [ZELEK] 2x
<6769> צִלְּתַי ***ṣillᵉṯay*** [ZILLETHAI] 2x
<6770> צָמֵא ***ṣāmê'*** [THIRSTY (BE)] 9x
<6771> צָמֵא ***ṣāmê'*** [THIRSTY] 9x
<6772> צָמָא ***ṣāmā'*** [THIRST] 17x
<6773> צִמְאָה ***ṣim'āh*** [THIRST] 1x
<6774> צִמָּאוֹן ***ṣimmā'ôn*** [THIRSTY GROUND] 3x
<6775> צָמַד ***ṣāmaḏ*** [JOIN] 5x
<6776> צֶמֶד ***ṣemeḏ*** [PAIR] 15x
<6777> צַמָּה ***ṣammāh*** [VEIL] 4x
<6778> צִמּוּק ***simmûq*** [RAISINS (CLUSTER OF, CAKE OF)] 4x
<6779> צָמַח ***ṣāmaḥ*** [GROW] 33x
<6780> צֶמַח ***ṣemaḥ*** [BRANCH] 12x
<6781> צָמִיד ***ṣāmiyḏ*** [BRACELET] 7x
<6782> צַמִּים ***ṣammiym*** [SNARE (noun)] 2x
<6783> צְמִיתֻת ***ṣᵉmiyṯuṯ*** [PERMANENTLY] 2x
<6784> צָמַק ***ṣāmaq*** [DRY (verb)] 1x
<6785> צֶמֶר ***ṣemer*** [WOOL] 16x
<6786> צְמָרִי ***ṣᵉmāriy*** [ZEMARITE] 2x
<6787> צְמָרַיִם ***ṣᵉmārayim*** [ZEMARAIM] 2x
<6788> צַמֶּרֶת ***ṣammereṯ*** [TOP (noun)] 5x
<6789> צָמַת ***ṣāmaṯ*** [END (PUT TO AN)] 15x
<6790> צִן ***ṣin*** [ZIN] 10x

<6791> צֵן ***ṣên*** [THORN] 3x
<6792> צֹנֵא ***ṣōnê'***, צֹנֶה ***ṣōneh*** [SHEEP] 2x
<6793> צִנָּה ***ṣinnāh*** [HOOK] 22x
<6794> צִנּוֹר ***ṣinnôr*** [WATER SHAFT] 2x
<6795> צָנַח ***ṣānaḥ*** [GET OFF] 2x, [GO THROUGH] 1x
<6796> צָנִין ***ṣāniyn*** [THORN] 2x
<6797> צָנִיף ***ṣāniyp̱*** [TURBAN] 5x
<6798> צָנַם ***ṣānam*** [WITHERED] 1x
<6799> צְנָן ***ṣᵉnān*** [ZENAN] 1x
<6800> צָנַע ***ṣāna'***, צָנוּעַ ***ṣānûa'*** [HUMBLE (BE)] 2x
<6801> צָנַף ***ṣānap̱*** [WEAR] 2x
<6802> צְנֵפָה ***ṣᵉnêp̱āh*** [TOSS (noun)] 1x
<6803> צִנְצֶנֶת ***ṣinṣeneṯ*** [JAR] 1x
<6804> צַנְתָּרוֹת ***ṣantārôṯ*** [PIPES] 1x
<6805> צָעַד ***ṣā'aḏ*** [WALK (verb)] 8x
<6806> צַעַד ***ṣa'aḏ*** [STEP (noun)] 14x
<6807> צְעָדָה ***ṣᵉ'āḏāh*** [MARCHING] 3x
<6808> צָעָה ***ṣā'āh*** [CAPTIVE EXILE] 1x, [LIE DOWN] 1x, [MARCH (verb)] 3x, [STRIDE] 1x, [TIP OVER] 1x
<6809> צָעִיף ***ṣa'iyp̱*** [VEIL] 3x
<6810> צָעִיר ***ṣā'iyr*** [YOUNG] 22x
<6811> צָעִירָה ***ṣā'iyrāh*** [ZAIR] 1x
<6812> צְעִירָה ***ṣᵉ'iyrāh*** [YOUTH] 1x
<6813> צָעַן ***ṣā'an*** [FOLD (verb)] 1x
<6814> צֹעַן ***ṣō'an*** [ZOAN] 7x
<6815> צַעֲנַנִּים ***ṣa'ᵃnanniym*** [ZAANANNIM] 2x
<6816> צַעֲצֻעִים ***ṣa'ᵃṣu'iym*** [SCULPTED] 1x
<6817> צָעַק ***ṣā'aq*** [CRY OUT] 55x
<6818> צְעָקָה ***ṣᵉ'āqāh*** [CRY (noun)] 21x
<6819> צָעַר ***ṣā'ar*** [BRING LOW] 3x
<6820> צוֹעַר ***ṣô'ar*** [ZOAR] 10x
<6821> צָפַד ***ṣāp̱aḏ*** [SHRIVELED UP (BE)] 1x
<6822> צָפָה ***ṣāp̱āh*** [WATCH (verb)] 37x
<6823> צָפָה ***ṣāp̱āh*** [OVERLAY] 46x
<6824> צָפָה ***ṣāp̱āh*** [DISCHARGE] 1x
<6825> צְפוֹ ***ṣᵉp̱ô***, צְפִי ***ṣᵉp̱iy*** [ZEPHO] 3x
<6826> צִפּוּי ***ṣippûy*** [OVERLAYING] 5x
<6827> צְפוֹן ***ṣᵉp̱ôn*** [ZEPHON] 1x
<6828> צָפוֹן ***ṣāp̱ôn*** [NORTH] 153x
<6829> צָפוֹן ***ṣāp̱ôn*** [ZAPHON] 3x
<6830> צְפוֹנִי ***ṣᵉp̱ôniy*** [NORTHERN ARMY] 1x
<6831> צְפוֹנִי ***ṣᵉp̱ôniy*** [ZEPHONITE] 1x
<6832> צְפִיעַ ***ṣᵉp̱iya'*** [DUNG] 1x
<6833> צִפּוֹר ***ṣippôr*** [BIRD] 40x
<6834> צִפּוֹר ***ṣippôr*** [ZIPPOR] 7x
<6835> צַפַּחַת ***ṣappaḥaṯ*** [JAR] 7x
<6836> צְפִיָּה ***ṣᵉp̱iyyāh*** [WATCHING] 1x
<6837> צִפְיוֹן ***ṣip̱yôn*** [ZIPHON] 1x
<6838> צַפִּיחִת ***ṣap̱iyḥiṯ*** [WAFER] 1x
<6839> צֹפִים ***ṣōp̱iym*** [ZOPHIM] 1x
<6840> צָפִין ***ṣāp̱iyn*** [TREASURE, HIDDEN TREASURE] 1x

<6841> צְפִיר ***ṣᵉp̱iyr*** [MALE GOAT] 1x
<6842> צָפִיר ***ṣāp̱iyr*** [MALE GOAT] 6x
<6843> צְפִירָה ***ṣᵉp̱iyrāh*** [CROWN (noun)] 3x
<6844> צָפִית ***ṣāp̱iyṯ*** [RUG] 1x
<6845> צָפַן ***ṣāp̱an*** [HIDE] 33x
<6846> צְפַנְיָה ***ṣᵉp̱anyāh,*** צְפַנְיָהוּ ***ṣᵉp̱anyāhû*** [ZEPHANIAH] 10x
<6847> צָפְנַת פַּעְנֵחַ ***ṣāp̱naṯ paʿnêaḥ*** [ZAPHENATH-PANEAH] 1x
<6848> צֶפַע ***ṣepaʿ,*** צִפְעוֹנִי ***ṣip̱ʿôniy*** [VIPER] 5x
<6849> צְפִיעָה ***ṣᵉp̱iyʿāh*** [ISSUE] 1x
<6850> צָפַף ***ṣāpap̱*** [CHIRP] 4x
<6851> צַפְצָפָה ***ṣapṣāp̱āh*** [WILLOW] 1x
<6852> צָפַר ***ṣāp̱ar*** [DEPART] 1x
<6853> צִפַּר ***ṣippar*** [BIRD] 4x
<6854> צְפַרְדֵּעַ ***ṣᵉp̱ardêaʿ*** [FROG] 13x
<6855> צִפֹּרָה ***ṣippōrāh*** [ZIPPORAH] 3x
<6856> צִפֹּרֶן ***ṣippōren*** [NAIL] 2x
<6857> צְפַת ***ṣᵉp̱aṯ*** [ZEPHATH] 1x
<6858> צֶפֶת ***ṣep̱eṯ*** [CAPITAL] 1x
<6859> צְפָתָה ***ṣᵉp̱āṯāh*** [ZEPHATHAH] 1x
<6860> צִיקְלַג ***ṣiyqlag*** [ZIKLAG] 15x
<6861> צִקְלוֹן ***ṣiqlôn*** [SACK] 1x
<6862> צַר ***ṣar*** [NARROWNESS] 105x
<6863> צֵר ***ṣêr*** [ZER] 1x
<6864> צֹר ***ṣōr*** [FLINT] 5x
<6865> צֹר ***ṣōr,*** צוֹר ***ṣôr*** [TYRE] 42x
<6866> צָרַב ***ṣāraḇ*** [BURN (verb)] 1x
<6867> צָרָב ***ṣārāḇ,*** צָרֶבֶת ***ṣāreḇeṯ*** [BURNING (adj. and noun)] 2x
<6868> צְרֵדָה ***ṣᵉrêḏāh,*** צְרֵדָתָה ***ṣᵉrêḏaṯah*** [ZEREDA] 2x
<6869> צָרָה ***ṣārāh*** [TROUBLE (noun)] 73x
<6870> צְרוּיָה ***ṣᵉrûyāh*** [ZERUIAH] 26x
<6871> צְרוּעָה ***ṣᵉrûʿāh*** [ZERUAH] 1x
<6872> צְרוֹר ***ṣᵉrôr*** [BAG] 11x
<6873> צָרַח ***ṣāraḥ*** [CRY (verb)] 2x
<6874> צְרִי ***ṣᵉriy*** [ZERI] 1x
<6875> צֳרִי ***ṣᵒriy,*** צְרִי ***ṣᵉriy*** [BALM] 6x
<6876> צֹרִי ***ṣōriy*** [TYRIAN] 5x
<6877> צְרִיחַ ***ṣᵉriyaḥ*** [STRONGHOLD] 3x
<6878> צֹרֶךְ ***ṣōreḵ*** [NEED] 1x
<6879> צָרַע ***ṣāraʿ*** [LEPER (BE A)] 20x
<6880> צִרְעָה ***ṣirʿāh*** [HORNETS] 3x
<6881> צָרְעָה ***ṣorʿāh*** [ZORAH] 10x
<6882> צָרְעִי ***ṣorʿiy,*** צָרְעָתִי ***ṣorʿāṯiy*** [ZORITE, ZORATHITE] 3x
<6883> צַרַעַת ***ṣarʿaṯ*** [LEPROSY] 35x
<6884> צָרַף ***ṣārap̱*** [REFINE] 33x
<6885> צֹרְפִי ***ṣōrp̱iy*** [GOLDSMITH] 1x
<6886> צָרְפַת ***ṣārᵉp̱aṯ*** [ZAREPHATH] 3x
<6887> צָרַר ***ṣārar*** [TROUBLED (BE)] 58x
<6888> צְרֵרָה ***ṣᵉrêrāh*** [ZERERAH] 1x
<6889> צֶרֶת ***ṣereṯ*** [ZERETH] 1x
<6890> צֶרֶת הַשַּׁחַר ***ṣereṯ haššaḥar*** [ZERETH SHAHAR] 1x
<6891> צָרְתָן ***ṣārᵉṯān*** [ZARETHAN, ZARETAN] 4x

ק Qoph

<6892> קֵא ***qê’***, קֵיא ***qêy’*** [VOMIT (noun)] 4x
<6893> קָאַת ***qā’aṯ*** [PELICAN] 5x
<6894> קַב ***qaḇ*** [KAB] 1x
<6895> קָבַב ***qāḇaḇ*** [CURSE (verb)] 14x
<6896> קֵבָה ***qêḇāh*** [STOMACH] 2x
<6897> קֹבָה ***qōḇāh*** [BODY] 1x
<6898> קֻבָּה ***qubbāh*** [TENT] 1x
<6899> קִבּוּץ ***qibbûṣ*** [COLLECTION] 1x
<6900> קְבוּרָה ***q^{e}ḇûrāh***, קְבֻרָה ***q^{e}burāh*** [BURIAL PLACE] 14x
<6901> קָבַל ***qāḇal*** [ACCEPT] 13x
<6902> קְבַל ***qāḇal*** [RECEIVE] 3x
<6903> קְבֵל ***q^{e}ḇêl*** [BEFORE] 29x
<6904> קֹבֶל ***qōḇel***, קְבֹל ***q^{e}ḇōl*** [BATTERING RAM] 2x
<6905> קָבָל ***qāḇāl*** [BEFORE] 1x
<6906> קָבַע ***qāḇa‘*** [ROB] 6x
<6907> קֻבַּעַת ***qubba‘aṯ*** [DREGS] 2x
<6908> קָבַץ ***qāḇaṣ*** [GATHER] 127x
<6909> קַבְצְאֵל ***qaḇṣ^{e}’êl*** [KABZEEL] 3x
<6910> קְבֻצָה ***q^{e}ḇuṣāh*** [GATHERING] 1x
<6911> קִבְצַיִם ***qiḇṣayim*** [KIBZAIM] 1x
<6912> קָבַר ***qāḇar*** [BURY] 133x
<6913> קֶבֶר ***qeḇer*** [GRAVE] 67x
<6914> קִבְרוֹת הַתַּאֲוָה ***qiḇrôṯ hatta^{a}wāh*** [KIBROTH HATTAAVAH] 5x
<6915> קָדַד ***qāḏaḏ*** [BOW DOWN] 15x
<6916> קִדָּה ***qiddāh*** [CASSIA] 2x
<6917> קְדוּמִים ***q^{e}ḏûmiym*** [ANCIENT] 1x
<6918> קָדוֹשׁ ***qāḏôš*** [HOLY] 116x
<6919> קָדַח ***qāḏaḥ*** [KINDLE] 5x
<6920> קַדַּחַת ***qaddaḥaṯ*** [FEVER] 2x
<6921> קָדִים ***qāḏiym*** [EAST, EAST WIND] 69x
<6922> קַדִּישׁ ***qaddiš*** [HOLY] 13x
<6923> קָדַם ***qādam*** [MEET] 26x
<6924> קֶדֶם ***qeḏem*** [EAST] 87x
<6925> קֳדָם ***q^{o}ḏām*** [BEFORE] 42x
<6926> קִדְמָה ***qiḏmāh*** [EAST] 4x
<6927> קַדְמָה ***qaḏmāh*** [FORMER TIME] 6x
<6928> קַדְמָה ***qaḏmāh*** [FORMER TIME] 2x
<6929> קֵדְמָה ***qêḏ^{e}māh*** [KEDEMAH] 2x
<6930> קַדְמוֹן ***qaḏmôn*** [EASTERN] 1x
<6931> קַדְמוֹנִי ***qaḏmôniy***, קַדְמֹנִי ***qaḏmōniy*** [EASTERN] 10x
<6932> קְדֵמוֹת ***q^{e}ḏêmôṯ*** [KEDEMOTH] 4x
<6933> קַדְמָי ***qaḏmāy*** [FIRST] 3x
<6934> קַדְמִיאֵל ***qaḏmiy’êl*** [KADMIEL] 8x
<6935> קַדְמֹנִי ***qaḏmōniy*** [KADMONITE] 1x
<6936> קָדְקֹד ***qoḏqōḏ*** [HEAD (CROWN OF, TOP OF)] 11x
<6937> קָדַר ***qāḏar*** [DARK (BE)] 17x
<6938> קֵדָר ***qêḏār*** [KEDAR] 12x
<6939> קִדְרוֹן ***qiḏrôn*** [KIDRON] 11x

<6940> קַדְרוּת ***qaḏrûṯ*** [BLACKNESS] 1x
<6941> קְדֹרַנִּית ***qᵉḏōranniyṯ*** [MOURNFULLY] 1x
<6942> קָדַשׁ ***qāḏaš*** [HOLY (BE)] 172x
<6943> קֶדֶשׁ ***qeḏeš*** [KEDESH] 12x
<6944> קֹדֶשׁ ***qōḏeš*** [HOLY THING] 468x
<6945> קָדֵשׁ ***qāḏêš*** [PROSTITUTE (MALE TEMPLE, CULT, SHRINE)] 6x
<6946> קָדֵשׁ ***qāḏêš*** [KADESH] 18x
<6947> קָדֵשׁ בַּרְנֵעַ ***qāḏêš barnêa‘*** [KADESH BARNEA] 14x
<6948> קְדֵשָׁה ***qᵉḏêšāh*** [PROSTITUTE (FEMALE TEMPLE)] 5x
<6949> קָהָה ***qāhāh*** [BLUNT (BE)] 4x
<6950> קָהַל ***qāhal*** [ASSEMBLE] 39x
<6951> קָהָל ***qāhāl*** [ASSEMBLY] 123x
<6952> קְהִלָּה ***qᵉhillāh*** [ASSEMBLY] 2x
<6953> קֹהֶלֶת ***qōheleṯ*** [PREACHER] 7x
<6954> קְהֵלָתָה ***qᵉhêlāṯāh*** [KEHELATHAH] 2x
<6955> קְהָת ***qᵉhāṯ*** [KOHATH] 32x
<6956> קְהָתִי ***qᵉhāṯiy*** [KOHATHITE] 15x
<6957> קַו ***qaw,*** קָו ***qāw*** [LINE, MEASURING LINE] 21x
<6958> קוֹה ***qôh,*** קָיָה ***qāyāh*** [VOMIT (verb)] 8x
<6959> קוֹבַע ***qôḇa‘*** [HELMET] 2x
<6960> קָוָה ***qāwāh*** [WAIT FOR] 49x
<6961> קָוֶה ***qāweh*** [LINE, MEASURING LINE] 1x
<6962> קוּט ***qûṭ*** [LOATHE] 7x
<6963> קוֹל ***qôl*** [VOICE] 506x
<6964> קוֹלָיָה ***qôlāyāh*** [KOLAIAH] 2x
<6965> קוּם ***qûm*** [STAND, STAND UP] 628x
<6966> קוּם ***qûm*** [STAND, STAND UP] 35x
<6967> קוֹמָה ***qômāh*** [HEIGHT] 45x
<6968> קוֹמְמִיּוּת ***qômᵉmiyyûṯ*** [UPRIGHT] 1x
<6969> קוּן ***qûn,*** קִין ***qiyn,*** קוֹנֵן ***qônên*** [LAMENT] 8x
<6970> קוֹעַ ***qôa‘*** [KOA] 1x
<6971> קוֹף ***qôp̱*** [APE] 2x
<6972> קוּץ ***qûṣ,*** קִיץ ***qiyṣ*** [SUMMER (verb)] 1x
<6973> קוּץ ***qûṣ*** [LOATHE] 9x
<6974> קוּץ ***qûṣ,*** קִיץ ***qiyṣ*** [AWAKE] 22x
<6975> קוֹץ ***qôṣ*** [THORN, THORNBUSH] 12x
<6976> קוֹץ ***qôṣ,*** הַקּוֹץ ***haqqôṣ*** [KOZ] 6x
<6977> קְוֻצָּה ***qᵉwuṣṣāh*** [LOCK, LOCK OF HAIR] 2x
<6978> קו ***qaw,*** קַו קַו ***qaw-qaw,*** קָו ***qāw*** [POWERFUL] 2x
<6979> קוּר ***qûr*** [DIG] 6x
<6980> קוּר ***qûr*** [WEB] 2x
<6981> קוֹרֵא ***qôrê’,*** קֹרֵא ***qōrê’*** [KORE] 3x
<6982> קוֹרָה ***qôrāh*** [BEAM] 5x
<6983> קוֹשׁ ***qôš*** [SNARE (LAY A)] 1x
<6984> קוּשָׁיָהוּ ***qûšāyāhû*** [KUSHAIAH] 1x
<6985> קָט ***qāṭ*** [VERY] 1x
<6986> קֶטֶב ***qeṭeḇ*** [DESTRUCTION] 3x
<6987> קֹטֶב ***qōṭeḇ*** [DESTRUCTION] 1x
<6988> קְטוֹרָה ***qᵉṭôrāh*** [INCENSE] 1x
<6989> קְטוּרָה ***qᵉṭûrāh*** [KETURAH] 4x
<6990> קָטַט ***qāṭaṭ*** [CUT OFF (BE)] 1x

<6991> קָטַל ***qāṭal*** [SLAY] 3x
<6992> קְטַל ***qᵉṭal*** [SLAY] 7x
<6993> קֶטֶל ***qeṭel*** [SLAUGHTER (noun)] 1x
<6994> קָטַן ***qāṭan*** [WORTHY (BE NOT)] 4x
<6995> קֹטֶן ***qōṭen*** [LITTLE FINGER] 2x
<6996> קָטָן ***qāṭān,*** קָטֹן ***qāṭōn*** [SMALL] 101x
<6997> קָטָן ***qāṭān,*** הַקָּטָן ***haqqāṭan*** [HAKKATAN] 1x
<6998> קָטַף ***qāṭap̱*** [PLUCK] 5x
<6999> קָטַר ***qāṭar*** [BURN (verb)] 117x
<7000> קָטַר ***qāṭar*** [JOINED (BE)] 1x
<7001> קְטַר ***qᵉṭar*** [HIP JOINT] 1x, [PROBLEM] 2x
<7002> קִטֵּר ***qiṭṭêr*** [INCENSE] 1x
<7003> קִטְרוֹן ***qiṭrôn*** [KITRON] 1x
<7004> קְטֹרֶת ***qᵉṭōreṯ*** [INCENSE] 60x
<7005> קַטָּת ***qaṭṭāṯ*** [KATTAH] 1x
<7006> קִיא ***qiy'*** [VOMIT (verb and noun)] 12x
<7007> קַיִט ***qayiṭ*** [SUMMER (noun)] 1x
<7008> קִיטוֹר ***qiyṭôr,*** קִיטֹר ***qiyṭōr*** [SMOKE (noun)] 4x
<7009> קִים ***qiym*** [ADVERSARY] 1x
<7010> קְיָם ***qᵉyām*** [STATUTE] 2x
<7011> קַיָּם ***qayyām*** [ENDURING] 2x
<7012> קִימָה ***qiymāh*** [RISING, RISING UP] 1x
<7013> קַיִן ***qayin*** [SPEAR, SPEARHEAD] 1x
<7014> קַיִן ***qayin*** [CAIN] 19x
<7015> קִינָה ***qiynāh*** [LAMENTATION] 18x
<7016> קִינָה ***qiynāh*** [KINAH] 1x
<7017> קֵינִי ***qêyniy*** [KENITE] 13x
<7018> קֵינָן ***qêynān*** [KENAN] 6x
<7019> קַיִץ ***qayiṣ*** [SUMMER, SUMMER FRUIT] 20x
<7020> קִיצוֹן ***qiyṣôn*** [OUTERMOST] 4x
<7021> קִיקָיוֹן ***qiyqāy>ôn*** [PLANT (noun)] 4x
<7022> קִיקָלוֹן ***qiyqāl>ôn*** [DISGRACE (noun)] 1x
<7023> קִיר ***qiyr,*** קִר ***qir,*** קִירָה ***qiyrāh*** [WALL] 74x
<7024> קִיר ***qiyr*** [KIR] 5x
<7025> קִיר חֲרֶשֶׂת ***qiyr ḥᵃreśeṯ,*** קִיר חֶרֶשׂ ***qiyr ḥereś*** [KIR HARESETH, KIR HERES] 5x
<7026> קֵירֹס ***qêyrōs,*** קֵרֹס ***qêrōs*** [KEROS] 2x
<7027> קִישׁ ***qiyš*** [KISH] 21x
<7028> קִישׁוֹן ***qiyšôn*** [KISHON] 6x
<7029> קִישִׁי ***qiyšiy*** [KISHI] 1x
<7030> קִיתָרֹס ***qiyṯārōs*** [LYRE] 8x
<7031> קַל ***qal*** [SWIFT] 13x
<7032> קָל ***qāl*** [SOUND] 7x
<7033> קָלָה ***qālāh*** [ROAST] 4x
<7034> קָלָה ***qālāh*** [DESPISED (BE)] 6x
<7035> קָלָה ***qālāh*** [ASSEMBLE] 1x
<7036> קָלוֹן ***qālôn*** [SHAME] 17x
<7037> קַלַּחַת ***qallaḥaṯ*** [CAULDRON] 2x
<7038> קָלַט ***qālaṭ*** [STUNTED (BE)] 1x
<7039> קָלִי ***qāliy,*** קָלִיא ***qāliy'*** [PARCHED GRAIN] 6x
<7040> קַלָּי ***qāllāy*** [KALLAI] 1x
<7041> קֵלָיָה ***qêlāyāh*** [KELAIAH] 1x

<7042> קְלִיטָא ***qeliyṭā’*** [KELITA] 3x
<7043> קָלַל ***qālal*** [SLIGHT (BE)] 82x
<7044> קָלָל ***qālal*** [BURNISHED (adj.)] 2x
<7045> קְלָלָה ***q***^{e}***lālāh*** [BURNISHED (noun)] 33x
<7046> קָלַס ***qālas*** [MOCK] 4x
<7047> קֶלֶס ***qeles*** [DERISION] 3x
<7048> קַלָּסָה ***qallāsāh*** [MOCKERY] 1x
<7049> קָלַע ***qāla‘*** [CARVE] 3x, [SLING (verb)] 4x
<7050> קֶלַע ***qela‘*** [CURTAIN] 16x, [SLING (noun)] 6x
<7051> קַלָּע ***qallā‘*** [SLINGER] 1x
<7052> קְלֹקֵל ***q***^{e}***lōqêl*** [WORTHLESS] 1x
<7053> קִלְּשׁוֹן ***qill***^{e}***šôn*** [FORK] 1x
<7054> קָמָה ***qāmāh*** [STANDING GRAIN, STANDING CORN] 10x
<7055> קְמוּאֵל ***q***^{e}***mû’ēl*** [KEMUEL] 3x
<7056> קָמוֹן ***qāmôn*** [KAMON] 1x
<7057> קִמּוֹשׂ ***qimmôś*** [NETTLES] 3x
<7058> קֶמַח ***qemaḥ*** [FLOUR] 14x
<7059> קָמַט ***qāmaṭ*** [SHRIVEL] 2x
<7060> קָמַל ***qāmal*** [WITHER] 2x
<7061> קָמַץ ***qāmaṣ*** [TAKE A HANDFUL] 3x
<7062> קֹמֶץ ***qōmeṣ*** [HANDFUL] 4x
<7063> קִמָּשׁוֹן ***qimmaśôn*** [THORNS] 1x
<7064> קֵן ***qên*** [NEST] 13x
<7065> קָנָא ***qānā’*** [JEALOUS (BE)] 33x
<7066> קְנָא ***q***^{e}***nā’*** [BUY] 1x
<7067> קַנָּא ***qannā’*** [JEALOUS] 6x
<7068> קִנְאָה ***qin’āh*** [JEALOUSY] 43x
<7069> קָנָה ***qānāh*** [ACQUIRE] 84x
<7070> קָנֶה ***qāneh*** [STALK] 62x
<7071> קָנָה ***qānāh*** [KANAH] 3x
<7072> קַנּוֹא ***qannô’*** [JEALOUS] 2x
<7073> קְנַז ***q***^{e}***naz*** [KENAZ] 11x
<7074> קְנִזִּי ***q***^{e}***nizziy*** [KENIZZITE] 4x
<7075> קִנְיָן ***qinyān*** [GOODS] 10x
<7076> קִנָּמוֹן ***qinnāmôn*** [CINNAMON] 3x
<7077> קָנַן ***qānan*** [NEST (MAKE, BUILD A)] 5x
<7078> קֶנֶץ ***qeneṣ*** [SNARE (noun)] 1x
<7079> קְנָת ***q***^{e}***nāṯ*** [KENATH] 2x
<7080> קָסַם ***qāsam*** [DIVINATION (PRACTICE)] 20x
<7081> קֶסֶם ***qesem*** [DIVINATION] 11x
<7082> קָסַס ***qāsas*** [CUT OFF] 1x
<7083> קֶסֶת ***qeseṯ*** [INKHORN] 3x
<7084> קְעִילָה ***q***^{e}***‘iylāh*** [KEILAH] 18x
<7085> קַעֲקַע ***qa***^{a}***qa‘*** [TATTOO] 1x
<7086> קְעָרָה ***q***^{e}***‘ārāh*** [DISH] 17x
<7087> קָפָא ***qāp̱ā’*** [CONGEAL] 4x
<7088> קָפַד ***qāp̱aḏ*** [ROLL UP] 1x
<7089> קְפָדָה ***q***^{e}***p̱āḏāh*** [TERROR] 1x
<7090> קִפּוֹד ***qippôḏ,*** קִפֹּד ***qippōḏ*** [PORCUPINE] 3x
<7091> קִפּוֹז ***qippôz*** [OWL] 1x
<7092> קָפַץ ***qāp̱aṣ*** [SHUT] 7x

<7093> קֵץ ***qêṣ*** [END] 67x
<7094> קָצַב ***qāṣaḇ*** [CUT, CUT OFF, CUT DOWN] 2x
<7095> קֶצֶב ***qeṣeḇ*** [FORM (noun)] 3x
<7096> קָצָה ***qāṣāh*** [CUT OFF] 5x
<7097> קָצֶה ***qāṣeh,*** קֵצֶה ***qêṣeh*** [END] 96x
<7098> קָצָה ***qāṣāh*** [END] 35x
<7099> קָצוּ ***qāṣû,*** קִצְוָה ***qiṣwāh*** [END] 6x
<7100> קֶצַח ***qeṣaḥ*** [DILL] 3x
<7101> קָצִין ***qāṣiyn*** [CAPTAIN] 12x
<7102> קְצִיעָה ***qᵉṣiyʿāh*** [CASSIA] 1x
<7103> קְצִיעָה ***qᵉṣiyʿāh*** [KEZIA] 1x
<7104> קְצִיץ ***qᵉṣiyṣ*** [KEZIZ] 1x
<7105> קָצִיר ***qāṣiyr*** [HARVEST] 54x
<7106> קָצַע ***qāṣaʿ*** [CORNER (verb)] 3x, [SCRAPE] 1x
<7107> קָצַף ***qāṣap̱*** [ANGRY (BE)] 34x
<7108> קְצַף ***qᵉṣap̱*** [ANGRY (BE)] 1x
<7109> קְצַף ***qᵉṣap̱*** [WRATH] 1x
<7110> קֶצֶף ***qeṣep̱*** [WRATH] 29x
<7111> קְצָפָה ***qᵉṣāp̱āh*** [SPLINTER] 1x
<7112> קָצַץ ***qāṣaṣ,*** קָצוּץ ***qāṣûṣ*** [CUT OFF] 14x
<7113> קְצַץ ***qᵉṣaṣ*** [CUT OFF] 1x
<7114> קָצַר ***qāṣar*** [REAP], [SHORTEN] 49x
<7115> קוֹצֶר ***qôṣer*** [ANGUISH] 1x
<7116> קָצֵר ***qāṣār*** [SHORT] 5x
<7117> קְצָת ***qᵉṣāṯ*** [END] 8x
<7118> קְצָת ***qᵉṣāṯ*** [END] 3x
<7119> קַר ***q>ar*** [COLD (adj.)] 3x
<7120> קֹר ***q>ōr*** [COLD (noun)] 1x
<7121> קָרָא ***q>ārā'*** [CALL] 735x
<7122> קָרָא ***q>ārā'*** [MEET] 16x
<7123> קְרָא ***q>ᵉrā'*** [READ] 11x
<7124> קֹרֵא ***qōrê'*** [PARTRIDGE] 2x
<7125> קִרְאָה ***qir'āh*** [MEETING] 121x
<7126> קָרַב ***qāraḇ*** [COME NEAR] 270x
<7127> קְרֵב ***qᵉrêḇ*** [COME NEAR] 9x
<7128> קְרָב ***qᵉrāḇ*** [BATTLE] 9x
<7129> קְרָב ***qᵉrāḇ*** [WAR] 3x
<7130> קֶרֶב ***qereḇ*** [MIDDLE] 222x
<7131> קָרֵב ***qārêḇ*** [DRAWING NEAR] 11x
<7132> קִרְבָה ***qirḇāh*** [NEARNESS] 2x
<7133> קָרְבָּן ***qorbān,*** קֻרְבָּן ***qurbān*** [OFFERING] 82x
<7134> קַרְדֹּם ***qardōm*** [AX] 5x
<7135> קָרָה ***qārāh*** [COLD (noun)] 5x
<7136> קָרָה ***qārāh*** [HAPPEN] 27x
<7137> קָרֶה ***qāreh*** [NOCTURNAL EMISSION] 1x
<7138> קָרוֹב ***qārôḇ,*** קָרֹב ***qārōḇ*** [NEAR] 78x
<7139> קָרַח ***qāraḥ*** [SHAVE THE HEAD] 5x
<7140> קֶרַח ***qeraḥ*** [ICE] 7x
<7141> קֹרַח ***qōraḥ*** [KORAH] 37x
<7142> קֵרֵחַ ***qêrêaḥ*** [BALD] 3x
<7143> קָרֵחַ ***qārêaḥ*** [KAREAH] 14x

<7144> קָרְחָה ***qorḥāh,*** קָרְחָא ***qorḥā'*** [BALDNESS] 11x
<7145> קָרְחִי ***qorḥiy*** [KORAHITE] 8x
<7146> קָרַחַת ***qārḥaṯ*** [BALD HEAD] 4x
<7147> קְרִי ***qeriy*** [HOSTILITY] 7x
<7148> קָרִיא ***qāriy'*** [CHOSEN] 3x
<7149> קִרְיָא ***qiryā',*** קִרְיָה ***qiryāh*** [CITY] 9x
<7150> קְרִיאָה ***qᵉriy'āh*** [MESSAGE] 1x
<7151> קִרְיָה ***qiryāh*** [CITY] 31x
<7152> קְרִיּוֹת ***qᵉriyyôṯ,*** קְרִיּוֹת חֶצְרוֹן ***qᵉriyyôṯ ḥeṣrôn*** [KERIOTH, KERIOTH HEZBON] 4x
<7153> קִרְיַת אַרְבַּע ***qiryaṯ 'arba',*** קִרְיַת הָאַרְבַּע ***qiryaṯ hā'arba'*** [KIRIATH ARBA] 9x
<7154> קִרְיַת בַּעַל ***qiryaṯ ba'al*** [KIRIATH BAAL] 2x
<7155> קִרְיַת חֻצוֹת ***qiryaṯ ḥuṣôṯ*** [KIRIATH HUZOTH] 1x
<7156> קִרְיָתַיִם ***qiryāṯayim*** [KIRIATHAIM] 6x
<7157> קִרְיַת יְעָרִים ***qiryaṯ yᵉ'āriym,*** קִרְיַת עָרִים ***qiryaṯ 'āriym,*** קִרְיַת ***qiryaṯ*** [KIRIATH JEARIM] 20x
<7158> קִרְיַת סֵפֶר ***qiryaṯ sēp̄er,*** קִרְיַת סַנָּה ***qiryath sannāh*** [KIRIATH SEPHER, KIRIATH SANNAH] 5x
<7159> קָרַם ***qāram*** [COVER (verb)] 2x
<7160> קָרַן ***qāran*** [HORNES (HAVE)] 1x, [SHINE] 3x
<7161> קֶרֶן ***qeren,*** קַרְנַיִם ***qarnayim*** [HORN] 75x
<7162> קֶרֶן ***qeren*** [HORN] 10x
<7163> קֶרֶן הַפּוּךְ ***qeren happûḵ*** [KEREN-HAPPUCH] 1x
<7164> קָרַס ***qāras*** [STOOP] 2x
<7165> קֶרֶס ***qeres*** [CLASP] 10x
<7166> קַרְסֹל ***qarsōl*** [FOOT] 2x
<7167> קָרַע ***qāra'*** [TEAR] 63x
<7168> קֶרַע ***qera'*** [PIECE] 4x
<7169> קָרַץ ***qāraṣ*** [WINK] 5x
<7170> קְרַץ ***qᵉraṣ*** [ACCUSE] 2x
<7171> קֶרֶץ ***qereṣ*** [DESTRUCTION] 1x
<7172> קַרְקַע ***qarqa'*** [FLOOR] 8x
<7173> קַרְקַע ***qarqa'*** [KARKA] 1x
<7174> קַרְקֹר ***qarqōr*** [KARKOR] 1x
<7175> קֶרֶשׁ ***qereš*** [BOARD] 51x
<7176> קֶרֶת ***qereṯ*** [CITY] 5x
<7177> קַרְתָּה ***qartāh*** [KARTAH] 2x
<7178> קַרְתָּן ***qartān*** [KARTAN] 1x
<7179> קַשׁ ***qaš*** [STUBBLE] 16x
<7180> קִשֻּׁאָה ***qiššu'āh*** [CUCUMBER] 1x
<7181> קָשַׁב ***qāšaḇ*** [LISTEN] 46x
<7182> קֶשֶׁב ***qešeḇ*** [ATTENTION] 4x
<7183> קַשָּׁב ***qaššāḇ,*** קַשֻּׁב ***qaššuḇ*** [ATTENTIVE] 5x
<7184> קַשָׂה ***qaśāh,*** קַשְׂוָה ***qaśwāh*** [JAR] 4x
<7185> קָשָׁה ***qāšāh*** [HARD (BE)] 28x
<7186> קָשֶׁה ***qāšeh*** [HARD (BE)] 36x
<7187> קְשׁוֹט ***qāšôṭ,*** קְשֹׁט ***qᵉšōṭ*** [TRUTH] 2x
<7188> קָשַׁח ***qāšaḥ*** [HARDEN] 2x
<7189> קֹשֶׁט ***qōšeṭ,*** קֹשְׁטְ ***qōšᵉṭ*** [TRUTH] 2x
<7190> קְשִׁי ***qᵉšiy*** [STUBBORNNESS] 1x
<7191> קִשְׁיוֹן ***qišyôn*** [KISHION] 2x
<7192> קְשִׂיטָה ***qᵉśiyṭāh*** [PIECE OF MONEY] 3x

<7193> קַשְׂקֶשֶׂת ***qaśqeśeṯ*** [SCALE (noun)] 8x
<7194> קָשַׁר ***qāšar*** [BIND] 44x
<7195> קֶשֶׁר ***qešer*** [CONSPIRACY] 16x
<7196> קִשֻּׁרִים ***qiššuriym*** [ATTIRE] 2x
<7197> קָשַׁשׁ ***qāšaš*** [GATHER] 8x
<7198> קֶשֶׁת ***qešeṯ*** [BOW (noun)] 77x
<7199> קַשָּׁת ***qaššāṯ*** [ARCHER] 1x

ר Resh

<7200> רָאָה ***rā'āh,*** רֹאֶה ***rō'eh*** [SEE] 1,290x (NAS)
<7201> רָאָה ***rā'āh*** [RED KITE] 1x
<7202> רָאֶה ***rā'eh*** [CONSCIOUS] 1x
<7203> רֹאֶה ***rō'eh*** [VISION] 1x
<7204> רֹאֶה ***rō'eh,*** הָרֹאֶה ***hārō'eh*** [HAROEH] 1x
<7205> רְאוּבֵן ***rᵉ'ûḇên*** [REUBEN] 72x
<7206> רְאוּבֵנִי ***rᵉ'ûḇêniy*** [REUBENITE] 18x
<7207> רַאֲוָה ***raᵃwāh*** [BEHOLD (verb)] 1x
<7208> רְאוּמָה ***rᵉ'ûmāh*** [REUMAH] 1x
<7209> רְאִי ***rᵉ'iy*** [MIRROR] 1x
<7210> רֳאִי ***rᵒ'iy*** [SIGHT] 6x
<7211> רְאָיָה ***rᵉ'āyāh*** [REAIA, REAIAH] 4x
<7212> רְאִית ***rᵉ'iyṯ,*** רְאוּת ***rᵉ'ûṯ*** [BEHOLDING] 1x
<7213> רָאַם ***rā'am*** [RISE] 1x
<7214> רְאֵם ***rᵉ'êm,*** רְאֵים ***rᵉ'êym,*** רֵים ***rêym,*** רֵם ***rêm*** [WILD OX] 9x
<7215> רָאמוֹת ***rā'môṯ*** [CORAL] 2x
<7216> רָאמוֹת ***rā'môṯ,*** רָאמֹת ***rā'mōṯ*** [RAMOTH] 5x
<7217> רְאֵשׁ ***rᵉ'êš*** [HEAD (noun)] 14x
<7218> רֹאשׁ ***rō'š*** [HEAD (noun)] 598x
<7219> רֹאשׁ ***rō'š,*** רוֹשׁ ***rôš*** [POISON (noun)] 12x
<7220> רֹאשׁ ***rō'š*** [ROSH] 5x
<7221> רִאשָׁה ***ri'šāh*** [BEGINNING] 1x
<7222> רֹאשָׁה ***rō'šāh*** [TOP] 1x
<7223> רִאשׁוֹן ***ri'šôn,*** רִאשֹׁן ***ri'šōn*** [FIRST] 182x
<7224> רִאשֹׁנִי ***ri'šôniy*** [FIRST] 1x
<7225> רֵאשִׁית ***rê'šiyṯ*** [BEGINNING] 51x
<7226> רַאֲשֹׁת ***raᵃšōṯ*** [HEAD (noun)] 1x
<7227> רַב ***raḇ*** [MANY] 458x
<7228> רַב ***raḇ*** [ARCHER] 2x
<7229> רַב ***raḇ*** [GREAT] 14x
<7230> רֹב ***rōḇ*** [NUMBER (LARGE, GREAT)] 155x
<7231> רָבַב ***rāḇaḇ*** [MANY (BE, BECOME)] 17x
<7232> רָבַב ***rāḇaḇ*** [SHOOT, SHOOT OUT] 2x
<7233> רְבָבָה ***rᵉḇāḇāh*** [MYRIAD] 16x
<7234> רָבַד ***rāḇaḏ*** [SPREAD (verb)] 1x
<7235> רָבָה ***rāḇāh,*** הַרְבֵּה ***harbêh*** [MANY (BE, BECOME)] 266x
<7236> רְבָה ***rᵉḇāh*** [GREAT (BECOME)] 6x
<7237> רַבָּה ***rabbāh*** [RABBAH] 15x
<7238> רְבוּ ***rᵉḇû*** [GREATNESS] 5x

<7239> רִבּוֹ ***ribbô*** [MYRIAD] 11x
<7240> רִבּוֹ ***ribbô*** [MYRIAD] 2x
<7241> רָבִיב ***rāḇiyḇ*** [SHOWER] 6x
<7242> רָבִיד ***rāḇiyḏ*** [NECKLACE] 4x
<7243> רְבִיעִי ***rᵉḇiyʿiy,*** רְבִעִי ***rᵉḇiʿiy*** [FOURTH] 56x
<7244> רְבִיעִי ***rᵉḇiyʿiy,*** רְבִעִי ***rᵉḇiʿiy*** [FOURTH] 5x
<7245> רַבִּית ***rabbiyṯ*** [RABBITH] 1x
<7246> רָבַךְ ***rāḇaḵ*** [STIRRED] 3x
<7247> רִבְלָה ***riḇlāh*** [RIBLAH] 11x
<7248> רַב־מָג ***raḇ-māg̱*** [RAB-MAG] 2x
<7249> רַב־סָרִיס ***raḇ-sāriys*** [RAB-SARIS] 3x
<7250> רָבַע ***rāḇaʿ*** [LIE DOWN] 4x
<7251> רָבַע ***rāḇaʿ*** [SQUARE (BE)] 12x
<7252> רֶבַע ***reḇaʿ*** [LYING DOWN] 1x
<7253> רֶבַע ***reḇaʿ*** [FOURTH] 7x
<7254> רֶבַע ***reḇaʿ*** [REBA] 2x
<7255> רֹבַע ***rōḇaʿ*** [FOURTH, FOURTH PART] 2x
<7256> רִבֵּעַ ***ribbêaʿ*** [FOURTH] 4x
<7257> רָבַץ ***rāḇaṣ*** [LIE DOWN] 30x
<7258> רֵבֶץ ***rêḇeṣ*** [RESTING PLACE] 4x
<7259> רִבְקָה ***riḇqāh*** [REBEKAH] 30x
<7260> רַבְרַב ***raḇraḇ*** [GREAT, GREAT THINGS] 8x
<7261> רַבְרְבָן ***raḇrᵉḇān*** [NOBLE] 8x
<7262> רַב־שָׁקֵה ***raḇ-šāqêh*** [RABSHAKEH] 16x
<7263> רֶגֶב ***regeḇ*** [CLOD] 2x
<7264> רָגַז ***rāg̱az*** [SHAKE] 41x
<7265> רְגַז ***rᵉg̱az*** [ANGER (verb)] 1x
<7266> רֹגֶז ***rᵉg̱az*** [RAGE (noun)] 1x
<7267> רֹגֶז ***rōg̱ez*** [TURMOIL] 7x
<7268> רַגָּז ***raggāz*** [TREMBLING] 1x
<7269> רָגְזָה ***rog̱zāh*** [TREMBLING] 1x
<7270> רָגַל ***rāg̱al*** [SLANDER], [SPY OUT], [WALK (TEACH TO)] 25x
<7271> רְגַל ***rᵉg̱al*** [FOOT] 7x
<7272> רֶגֶל ***reg̱el*** [FOOT] 247x
<7273> רַגְלִי ***rag̱liy*** [FOOT (ON)] 12x
<7274> רֹגְלִים ***rōg̱liym*** [ROGELIM] 2x
<7275> רָגַם ***rāg̱am*** [STONE (verb)] 16x
<7276> רֶגֶם ***regem*** [REGEM] 1x
<7277> רִגְמָה ***rig̱māh*** [THRONG] 1x
<7278> רֶגֶם מֶלֶךְ ***regem meleḵ*** [REGEM-MELECH] 1x
<7279> רָגַן ***rāg̱an*** [MURMUR] 7x
<7280> רָגַע ***rāg̱aʿ*** [MOMENT (BE FOR A)] 13x
<7281> רֶגַע ***reg̱aʿ*** [MOMENT] 22x
<7282> רָגֵעַ ***rāg̱êaʿ*** [QUIET (adj.)] 1x
<7283> רָגַשׁ ***rāg̱aš*** [RAGE (verb)] 1x
<7284> רְגַשׁ ***rᵉg̱aš*** [ASSEMBLE TOGETHER] 3x
<7285> רֶגֶשׁ ***reg̱eš*** [THRONG (noun)] 2x
<7286> רָדַד ***rāḏaḏ*** [SUBDUE] 4x
<7287> רָדָה ***rāḏāh*** [RULE (verb)] 27x
<7288> רַדַּי ***radday*** [RADDAI] 1x
<7289> רְדִיד ***rᵉḏiyḏ*** [VEIL] 2x

<7290> רָדַם ***rāḏam*** [ASLEEP (BE, FALL)] 7x

<7291> רָדַף ***rāḏap̱*** [PURSUE] 143x

<7292> רָהַב ***rāhaḇ*** [BOLD (BE, MAKE)] 4x

<7293> רַהַב ***rahaḇ*** [PROUD] 3x

<7294> רַהַב ***rahaḇ*** [RAHAB] 5x

<7295> רָהָב ***rāhāḇ*** [PROUD] 1x

<7296> רֹהַב ***rōhaḇ*** [STRENGTH] 1x

<7297> רָהָה ***rāhāh*** [AFRAID (BE)] 1x

<7298> רַהַט ***rahaṭ*** [TROUGH] 4x

<7299> רֵו ***rêw*** [APPEARANCE] 2x

<7300> רוּד ***rûḏ*** [RESTLESS (BE, BECOME, GROW)] 4x

<7301> רָוָה ***rāwāh*** [DRINK ONE'S FILL] 14x

<7302> רָוֶה ***rāweh*** [WATERED] 4x

<7303> רוֹהֲגָה ***rôh^{a}gāh,*** רָהְגָּה ***rohgāh*** [ROHGAH] 1x

<7304> רָוַח ***rāwaḥ*** [REFRESHED (BE)] 3x

<7305> רֶוַח ***rewaḥ*** [SPACE] 2x

<7306> רוּחַ ***rûaḥ,*** רִיחַ ***riyaḥ*** [REFRESHED (BE)] 11x

<7307> רוּחַ ***rûaḥ*** [SPIRIT] 375x (NAS)

<7308> רוּחַ ***rûaḥ*** [SPIRIT] 11x

<7309> רְוָחָה ***r^{e}wāḥāh*** [RELIEF] 2x

<7310> רְוָיָה ***r^{e}wāyāh*** [OVERFLOW (noun)] 2x

<7311> רוּם ***rûm*** [EXALT] 194x

<7312> רוּם ***rûm,*** רֻם ***rum*** [HEIGHT] 6x

<7313> רוּם ***rûm*** [EXALT] 4x

<7314> רוּם ***rûm*** [HEIGHT] 5x

<7315> רוֹם ***rôm*** [HIGH, ON HIGH] 1x

<7316> רוּמָה ***rûmāh*** [RUMAH] 1x

<7317> רוֹמָה ***rômāh*** [HAUGHTILY] 1x

<7318> רוֹמַם ***rômam*** [PRAISE, HIGH PRAISE] 2x

<7319> רוֹמְמָה ***rôm^{e}māh*** [PRAISE, HIGH PRAISE] 1x

<7320> רוֹמַמְתִּי עֶזֶר ***rômamtiy ʿezer,*** רֹמַמְתִּי עֶזֶר ***rōmamtiy ʿezer*** [ROMAMTI-EZER] 2x

<7321> רוּעַ ***rûaʿ*** [SHOUT (verb)] 46x

<7322> רוּף ***rûp̱,*** רָפַף ***rāp̱ap̱*** [TREMBLE] 1x

<7323> רוּץ ***rûṣ*** [RUN] 104x

<7324> רוּק ***rûq,*** רִיק ***riyq*** [EMPTY (verb)] 19x

<7325> רוּק ***rûq,*** רִיק ***riyq*** [FLOW (verb)] 1x

<7326> רוּשׁ ***rûš*** [POOR (BE)] 24x

<7327> רוּת ***rûṯ*** [RUTH] 12x

<7328> רַז ***raz*** [MYSTERY] 9x

<7329> רָזָה ***rāzāh*** [LEAN (GROW, BECOME, WAX)] 2x

<7330> רָזֶה ***rāzeh*** [LEAN (adj.)] 2x

<7331> רְזוֹן ***r^{e}zôn*** [REZON] 1x

<7332> רָזוֹן ***rāzôn*** [LEANNESS] 3x

<7333> רָזוֹן ***rāzôn*** [PRINCE] 1x

<7334> רָזִי ***rāziy*** [LEANNESS] 2x

<7335> רָזַם ***rāzam*** [FLASH (verb)] 1x

<7336> רָזַן ***rāzan*** [HEAVY (BE)] 6x

<7337> רָחַב ***rāḥaḇ*** [ENLARGE] 25x

<7338> רַחַב ***rāḥaḇ*** [BROAD PLACE] 2x

<7339> רְחֹב ***r^{e}ḥōḇ,*** רְחוֹב ***r^{e}ḥôḇ*** [STREET] 43x

<7340> רְחוֹב ***r^{e}ḥôḇ*** [REHOB] 10x

<7341> רֹחַב ***rōḥaḇ*** [BREADTH] 101x
<7342> רָחָב ***rāḥāḇ*** [BROAD] 21x
<7343> רָחָב ***rāḥaḇ*** [RAHAB] 5x
<7344> רְחֹבוֹת ***r^{e}ḥōḇôṯ***, רְחֹבוֹת עִיר ***r^{e}ḥōḇôṯ ʻiyr*** [REHOBOTH] 4x
<7345> רְחַבְיָה ***r^{e}ḥaḇyāh***, רְחַבְיָהוּ ***r^{e}ḥaḇyāhû*** [REHABIAH] 5x
<7346> רְחַבְעָם ***r^{e}ḥaḇʻām*** [REHOBOAM] 50x
<7347> רֵחֶה ***rêḥeh***, רֵחַיִם ***rêḥayim*** [MILLSTONE] 5x
<7348> רְחוּם ***r^{e}ḥûm*** [REHUM] 8x
<7349> רַחוּם ***raḥûm*** [COMPASSIONATE] 13x
<7350> רָחוֹק ***rāḥôq***, רָחֹק ***rāḥōq*** [FAR OFF, FAR AWAY] 84x
<7351> רָחִיט ***rāḥiyṭ***, רָהִיט ***rāhiyṭ*** [RAFTERS] 1x
<7352> רַחִיק ***rāḥiyq*** [FAR] 1x
<7353> רָחֵל ***rāḥêl*** [EWE] 4x
<7354> רָחֵל ***rāḥêl*** [RACHEL] 47x
<7355> רָחַם ***rāḥam***, רֻחָמָה ***ruḥāmāh*** [COMPASSION (HAVE)] 47x
<7356> רַחַם ***raḥam*** [WOMB] 44x
<7357> רַחַם ***raḥam*** [RAHAM] 1x
<7358> רֶחֶם ***reḥem*** [WOMB] 26x
<7359> רַחֲמִין ***raḥ^{a}miyn*** [COMPASSION] 1x
<7360> רָחָם ***rāḥām***, רָחָמָה ***rāḥāmāh*** [CARRION VULTURE] 2x
<7361> רַחֲמָה ***raḥ^{a}māh*** [WOMB] 1x
<7362> רַחֲמָנִי ***raḥ^{a}māniy*** [COMPASSIONATE] 1x
<7363> רָחַף ***rāḥap̱*** [HOVER] 3x
<7364> רָחַץ ***rāḥaṣ*** [WASH AWAY, WASH OFF] 72x
<7365> רְחַץ ***r^{e}ḥaṣ*** [TRUST (verb)] 1x
<7366> רַחַץ ***raḥaṣ*** [WASHBASIN] 2x
<7367> רַחְצָה ***raḥṣāh*** [WASHING] 2x
<7368> רָחַק ***rāḥaq*** [FAR AWAY (BE, BECOME)] 58x
<7369> רָחֵק ***rāḥêq*** [FAR] 1x
<7370> רָחַשׁ ***rāḥaš*** [OVERFLOW (verb)] 1x
<7371> רַחַת ***raḥaṯ*** [SHOVEL] 1x
<7372> רָטַב ***rāṭaḇ*** [WET (BE)] 1x
<7373> רָטֹב ***rāṭōḇ*** [LUSH] 1x
<7374> רֶטֶט ***reṭeṭ*** [PANIC] 1x
<7375> רֻטֲפַשׁ ***ruṭ^{a}p̱aš*** [FRESH (BE, BECOME)] 1x
<7376> רָטַשׁ ***rāṭaš*** [DASH IN PIECES] 6x
<7377> רִי ***riy*** [MOISTURE] 1x
<7378> רִיב ***riyḇ***, רוּב ***rûḇ*** [STRIVE] 67x
<7379> רִיב ***riyḇ***, רִב ***riḇ***, רִיבָה ***riyḇāh*** [STRIFE] 62x
<7380> רִיבַי ***riyḇay*** [RIBAI] 2x
<7381> רֵיחַ ***rêyaḥ*** [ODOR] 58x
<7382> רֵיחַ ***rêyaḥ*** [SMELL (noun)] 1x
<7383> רִיפָה ***riyp̱āh***, רִפָה ***rip̱āh*** [GRAIN] 2x
<7384> רִיפַת ***riyp̱aṯ***, דִּיפַת ***diyp̱aṯ*** [RIPHATH] 2x
<7385> רִיק ***riyq*** [EMPTINESS] 12x
<7386> רֵיק ***rêyq***, רֵק ***rêq*** [EMPTY (adj.)] 14x
<7387> רֵיקָם ***rêyqām*** [EMPTY-HANDED] 16x
<7388> רִיר ***riyr*** [SALIVA] 1x, [WHITE] 1x,
<7389> רֵישׁ ***rêyš***, רֵאשׁ ***rê'š***, רִישׁ ***riyš*** [POVERTY] 7x
<7390> רַךְ ***raḵ*** [GENTLE] 16x
<7391> רֹךְ ***rōḵ*** [REFINEMENT] 1x

<7392> רָכַב ***rāḵaḇ*** [RIDE] 78x
<7393> רֶכֶב ***reḵeḇ*** [CHARIOT] 117x, [MILLSTONE (UPPER)] 3x
<7394> רֵכָב ***rêḵāḇ*** [RECHAB] 13x
<7395> רַכָּב ***rakkāḇ*** [DRIVER OF A CHARIOT] 3x
<7396> רִכְבָּה ***riḵbāh*** [SADDLE] 1x
<7397> רֵכָה ***rêḵāh,*** רֵכָבִי ***rêḵāḇiy*** [RECAH, RECHAH, RECHABITE] 5x
<7398> רְכוּב ***rᵉḵûḇ*** [CHARIOT] 1x
<7399> רְכוּשׁ ***rᵉḵûš,*** רְכֻשׁ ***rᵉḵuš*** [POSSESSIONS] 28x
<7400> רָכִיל ***rāḵiyl*** [SLANDER, SLANDERER] 6x
<7401> רָכַךְ ***rākak*** [FAINT (BE, MAKE)] 9x
<7402> רָכַל ***rāḵal*** [MERCHANDISE (SELL)] 17x
<7403> רָכָל ***rāḵāl*** [RACAL, RACHAL] 1x
<7404> רְכֻלָּה ***rᵉḵullāh*** [MERCHANDISE] 4x
<7405> רָכַס ***rāḵas*** [BIND] 2x
<7406> רֶכֶס ***reḵes*** [ROUGH PLACE] 1x
<7407> רֹכֶס ***rōḵes*** [CONSPIRACY] 1x
<7408> רָכַשׁ ***rāḵaš*** [ACCUMULATE] 4x
<7409> רֶכֶשׁ ***reḵeš*** [HORSE] 4x
<7410> רָם ***rām*** [RAM] 7x
<7411> רָמָה ***rāmāh*** [DECEIVE] 8x, [THROW] 4x
<7412> רְמָה ***rᵉmāh*** [THROW] 12x
<7413> רָמָה ***rāmāh*** [HIGH PLACE] 5x
<7414> רָמָה ***rāmāh*** [RAMAH] 37x
<7415> רִמָּה ***rimmāh*** [WORM] 7x
<7416> רִמּוֹן ***rimmôn,*** רִמֹּן ***rimmōn*** [POMEGRANATE] 32x
<7417> רִמּוֹן ***rimmôn,*** רִמּוֹנוֹ ***rimmônô,*** רִמּוֹן הַמְּתֹאָר ***rimmôn hammᵉtō'ār*** [RIMMON] 16x
<7418> רָמוֹת נֶגֶב ***rāmôṯ negeḇ*** [RAMOTH NEGEV] 1x
<7419> רָמוּת ***rāmûṯ*** [CARCASS] 1x
<7420> רֹמַח ***rōmaḥ*** [SPEAR] 15x
<7421> רַמִּי ***rammiy*** [SYRIAN] 1x
<7422> רַמְיָה ***ramyāh*** [RAMIAH] 1x
<7423> רְמִיָּה ***rᵉmiyyāh*** [DECEIT] 15x
<7424> רַמָּךְ ***rammāḵ*** [ROYAL STUD] 1x
<7425> רְמַלְיָהוּ ***rᵉmalyāhû*** [REMALIAH] 13x
<7426> רָמַם ***rāmam*** [EXALTED] 7x
<7427> רֹמֵמֻת ***rōmêmuṯ,*** רוֹמֵמֻת ***rômêmuṯ*** [LIFTING UP] 1x
<7428> רִמּוֹן פֶּרֶץ ***rimmôn pereṣ*** [RIMMON PEREZ] 2x
<7429> רָמַס ***rāmas*** [TRAMPLE] 19x
<7430> רָמַשׂ ***rāmaś*** [CREEP] 17x
<7431> רֶמֶשׂ ***remeś*** [CREEPING THING] 17x
<7432> רֶמֶת ***remeṯ*** [REMETH] 1x
<7433> רָמוֹת ***rāmôṯ,*** רָמוֹת גִּלְעָד ***rāmôṯ gil'āḏ*** [RAMOTH, RAMOTH GILEAD] 22x
<7434> רָמַת הַמִּצְפֶּה ***rāmaṯ hammiṣpeh*** [RAMATH MITZPEH] 1x
<7435> רָמָתִי ***rāmāṯiy*** [RAMATHITE] 1x
<7436> רָמָתַיִם צוֹפִים ***rāmāṯayim ṣôp̄iym,*** רָמָתַיִם ***rāmāṯayim*** [RAMATHAIM-ZOPHIM] 1x
<7437> רָמַת לְחִי ***rāmāṯ lᵉḥiy*** [RAMATH LEHI] 1x
<7438> רֹן ***rōn*** [SONG] 1x
<7439> רָנָה ***rānāh*** [RATTLE] 1x
<7440> רִנָּה ***rinnāh*** [CRY (noun)] 33x
<7441> רִנָּה ***rinnāh*** [RINNAH] 1x
<7442> רָנַן ***rānan,*** רוּן ***rûn*** [SHOUT (verb)] 52x

<7443> רֶנֶן ***renen*** [OSTRICH] 1x
<7444> רַנֵּן ***rannên*** [SINGING] 1x
<7445> רְנָנָה ***rᵉnānāh*** [JOYFUL SHOUT] 4x
<7446> רִסָּה ***rissāh*** [RISSAH] 2x
<7447> רָסִיס ***rāsiys*** [DEW] 2x
<7448> רֶסֶן ***resen*** [BRIDLE] 4x
<7449> רֶסֶן ***resen*** [RESEN] 1x
<7450> רָסַס ***rāsas*** [MOISTEN] 1x
<7451> רַע ***ra‘,*** רָעָה ***rā‘āh*** [BAD] 359x (NAS)
<7452> רֵעַ ***rêa‘*** [NOISE] 3x
<7453> רֵעַ ***rêa‘,*** רֵיעַ ***rêya‘*** [PERSON (ANOTHER)] 188x
<7454> רֵעַ ***rêa‘*** [THOUGHT] 2x
<7455> רֹעַ ***rōa‘*** [EVIL] 18x
<7456> רָעֵב ***rā‘êḇ*** [HUNGRY (BE)] 11x
<7457> רָעֵב ***rā‘êḇ*** [HUNGRY] 22x
<7458> רָעָב ***rā‘āḇ*** [HUNGER] 101x
<7459> רְעָבוֹן ***rᵉ‘āḇôn*** [FAMINE] 3x
<7460> רָעַד ***rā‘aḏ*** [TREMBLE] 3x
<7461> רַעַד ***ra‘aḏ,*** רְעָדָה ***rᵉ‘āḏāh*** [TREMBLING] 6x
<7462> רָעָה ***rā‘āh*** [FEED (verb)] 173x
<7463> רֵעֶה ***rê‘eh*** [FRIEND] 3x
<7464> רֵעָה ***rê‘āh*** [FRIEND] 3x
<7465> רֹעָה ***rō‘āh*** [BROKEN] 1x
<7466> רְעוּ ***rᵉ‘û*** [REU] 5x
<7467> רְעוּאֵל ***rᵉ‘û’êl*** [REUEL] 11x
<7468> רְעוּת ***rᵉ‘ûṯ*** [NEIGHBOR] 6x
<7469> רְעוּת ***rᵉ‘ûṯ*** [STRIVING] 7x
<7470> רְעוּ ***rᵉ‘û,*** רְעוּת ***rᵉ‘ûṯ*** [DECISION] 2x
<7471> רְעִי ***rᵉ‘iy*** [PASTURE] 1x
<7472> רֵעִי ***rê‘iy*** [REI] 1x
<7473> רֹעִי ***rō‘iy*** [SHEPHERD] 1x
<7474> רַעְיָה ***ra‘yāh*** [LOVE (noun)] 9x
<7475> רַעְיוֹן ***ra‘yôn*** [STRIVING] 3x
<7476> רַעְיוֹן ***ra‘yôn*** [THOUGHT] 6x
<7477> רָעַל ***rā‘al*** [BRANDISH] 1x
<7478> רַעַל ***ra‘al*** [REELING] 1x
<7479> רְעָלָה ***rᵉ‘ālāh*** [VEIL] 1x
<7480> רְעֵלָיָה ***rᵉ‘êlāyāh*** [REELAIAH] 1x
<7481> רָעַם ***rā‘am*** [IRRITATE] 2x, [THUNDER (verb)] 11x
<7482> רַעַם ***ra‘am*** [THUNDER (noun)] 6x
<7483> רַעְמָה ***ra‘māh*** [THUNDER (noun)] 1x
<7484> רַעְמָה ***ra‘māh,*** רַעְמָא ***ra‘mā’*** [RAAMAH] 5x
<7485> רַעַמְיָה ***ra‘amyāh*** [RAAMIAH] 1x
<7486> רַעַמְסֵס ***ra‘amsês,*** רַעְמְסֵס ***ra‘mᵉsês*** [RAAMSES, RAMESES] 5x
<7487> רָעַן ***rā‘an,*** רַעֲנַן ***ra‘ᵃnan*** [GREEN (BE)] 2x
<7488> רַעֲנָן ***ra‘ᵃnān*** [GREEN] 20x
<7489> רָעַע ***rā‘a‘*** [BAD (BE)] 83x
<7490> רְעַע ***rᵉ‘a‘*** [BREAK IN PIECES] 2x
<7491> רָעַף ***rā‘ap̱*** [DRIP (verb)] 5x
<7492> רָעַץ ***rā‘aṣ*** [SHATTER] 2x
<7493> רָעַשׁ ***rā‘aš*** [SHAKE] 30x

<7494> רַעַשׁ ***ra'aš*** [SHAKING] 17x
<7495> רָפָא ***rāp̱a'*** [HEAL] 67x
<7496> רָפָא ***rāp̱ā'*** [DEAD (noun)] 8x
<7497> רְפָאִים ***rᵉp̱ā'iym,*** רָפָא ***rāp̱a',*** רָפָה ***rāp̱ah*** [REPHAIM] 25x
<7498> רָפָא ***rāp̱a',*** רָפָה ***rāp̱āh*** [RAPHA] 8x
<7499> רְפוּאָה ***rᵉp̱û'āh*** [MEDICINE] 3x
<7500> רִפְאוּת ***rip̱'ûṯ*** [HEALING] 1x
<7501> רְפָאֵל ***rᵉp̱ā'êl*** [REPHAEL] 1x
<7502> רָפַד ***rāp̱aḏ*** [REFRESH] 1x, [SPREAD, SPREAD OUT] 2x
<7503> רָפָה ***rāp̱āh*** [CEASE] 45x
<7504> רָפֶה ***rāp̱eh*** [WEAK (adj.)] 4x
<7505> רָפוּא ***rāp̱û'*** [RAPHU] 1x
<7506> רֶפַח ***rep̱āḥ*** [REPHAH] 1x
<7507> רְפִידָה ***rᵉp̱iyḏāh*** [SUPPORT (noun)] 1x
<7508> רְפִידִים ***rᵉp̱iyḏiym*** [REPHIDIM] 5x
<7509> רְפָיָה ***rᵉp̱āyāh*** [REPHAIAH] 5x
<7510> רִפְיוֹן ***rip̱yôn*** [LIMPNESS] 1x
<7511> רָפַס ***rāp̱as*** [SUBMIT] 2x
<7512> רָפַס ***rāp̱as*** [TRAMPLE] 2x
<7513> רַפְסֹדָה ***rap̱sôḏāh*** [RAFT] 1x
<7514> רָפַק ***rāp̱āq*** [LEAN (verb)] 1x
<7515> רָפַשׂ ***rāp̱aś*** [FOUL] 3x
<7516> רֶפֶשׁ ***rep̱eś*** [MIRE] 1x
<7517> רֶפֶת ***rep̱eṯ*** [STALL] 1x
<7518> רַץ ***raṣ*** [PIECE] 1x
<7519> רָצָא ***rāṣā'*** [RUN] 1x
<7520> רָצַד ***rāṣaḏ*** [ENVY (LOOK WITH, GAZE IN, FUME WITH)] 1x
<7521> רָצָה ***rāṣāh*** [PLEASURE (TAKE)] 57x
<7522> רָצוֹן ***rāṣôn,*** רָצֹן ***raṣōn*** [PLEASURE] 56x
<7523> רָצַח ***rāṣaḥ*** [KILL] 47x
<7524> רֶצַח ***reṣaḥ*** [BREAKING] 2x
<7525> רִצְיָא ***riṣyā'*** [REZIA] 1x
<7526> רְצִין ***rᵉṣiyn*** [REZIN] 11x
<7527> רָצַע ***rāṣā'*** [PIERCE] 1x
<7528> רָצַף ***rāṣap̱*** [INLAY] 1x
<7529> רֶצֶף ***reṣep̱*** [BAKED ON COALS, HOT COALS, HOT STONES] 1x
<7530> רֶצֶף ***reṣep̱*** [REZEPH] 2x
<7531> רִצְפָּה ***riṣpāh*** [HOT COAL] 2x, [PAVEMENT] 7x
<7532> רִצְפָּה ***riṣpāh*** [RIZPAH] 4x
<7533> רָצַץ ***rāṣāṣ*** [BREAK] 19x
<7534> רַק ***raq*** [LEAN (adj.)] 3x
<7535> רַק ***raq*** [ONLY] 16x
<7536> רֹק ***rōq*** [SPIT (noun and verb)] 3x
<7537> רָקֵב ***rāqaḇ*** [ROT (verb)] 2x
<7538> רָקָב ***rāqāḇ*** [ROTTENNESS] 5x
<7539> רִקָּבוֹן ***riqqāḇôn*** [ROTTEN] 1x
<7540> רָקַד ***rāqaḏ*** [DANCE (verb)] 9x
<7541> רַקָּה ***raqqāh*** [TEMPLE (of the head)] 5x
<7542> רַקּוֹן ***raqqôn*** [RAKKON] 1x
<7543> רָקַח ***rāqaḥ*** [COMPOUND] 8x
<7544> רֶקַח ***reqaḥ*** [SPICED] 1x

<7545> רֹקַח ***rōqaḥ*** [PERFUME] 2x
<7546> רַקָּח ***raqqāḥ*** [PERFUMER] 1x
<7547> רִקֻּחַ ***riquaḥ,*** רִקּוּחַ ***riqûaḥ*** [PERFUME] 1x
<7548> רַקָּחָה ***raqqāḥāh*** [PERFUMER] 1x
<7549> רָקִיעַ ***rāqiya'*** [EXPANSE] 17x
<7550> רָקִיק ***rāqiyq*** [WAFER] 8x
<7551> רָקַם ***rāqam*** [WEAVER] 9x
<7552> רֶקֶם ***reqem*** [REKEM] 6x
<7553> רִקְמָה ***riqmāh*** [EMBROIDERED WORK] 12x
<7554> רָקַע ***rāqa'*** [BEAT] 11x
<7555> רִקּוּעַ ***riqqûa',*** רִקֻּעַ ***riqqua'*** [HAMMERED] 1x
<7556> רָקַק ***rāqaq*** [SPIT (verb)] 1x
<7557> רַקַּת ***rāqqat̲*** [RAKKATH] 1x
<7558> רִשְׁיוֹן ***rišyôn*** [PERMISSION] 1x
<7559> רָשַׁם ***rāšam*** [INSCRIBE] 1x
<7560> רְשַׁם ***r^e^šam*** [INSCRIBE] 7x
<7561> רָשַׁע ***rāša'*** [WICKEDLY (ACT)] 34x
<7562> רֶשַׁע ***reša'*** [WICKEDNESS] 30x
<7563> רָשָׁע ***rāšā'*** [WICKED] 263x
<7564> רִשְׁעָה ***riš'āh*** [WICKED] 1x
<7565> רֶשֶׁף ***rešep̲*** [FLASH (noun)] 7x
<7566> רֶשֶׁף ***rešep̲*** [RESHEPH] 1x
<7567> רָשַׁשׁ ***rāšaš*** [DEMOLISH] 2x
<7568> רֶשֶׁת ***rešet̲*** [NET] 21x
<7569> רַתּוֹק ***rattôq*** [CHAIN] 2x
<7570> רָתַח ***rāt̲aḥ*** [BOIL (verb)] 3x
<7571> רֶתַח ***ret̲aḥ*** [BOILING] 1x
<7572> רַתִּיקָה ***rattiyqāh*** [CHAIN] 1x
<7573> רָתַם ***rāt̲am*** [HARNESS] 1x
<7574> רֶתֶם ***ret̲em,*** רֹתֶם ***rōt̲em*** [BROOM TREE, BROOM BUSH] 4x
<7575> רִתְמָה ***rit̲māh*** [RITMAH] 2x
<7576> רָתַק ***rāt̲aq*** [BIND] 2x
<7577> רְתוּקָה ***r^e^t̲ûqāh*** [CHAIN] 1x
<7578> רְתֵת ***r^e^t̲êt̲*** [TREMBLING] 1x

שׂ, שׁ Sin, Shin

<7579> שָׁאַב ***šā'ab̲*** [DRAW] 19x
<7580> שָׁאַג ***šā'ag*** [ROAR (verb)] 20x
<7581> שְׁאָגָה ***š^e^'āgāh*** [ROARING] 7x
<7582> שָׁאָה ***šā'āh*** [ROAR (verb)] 2x, [WASTE (LAY, LIE)] 4x
<7583> שָׁאָה ***šā'āh*** [GAZE] 1x
<7584> שַׁאֲוָה ***ša^a^wāh*** [STORM (noun)] 1x
<7585> שְׁאוֹל ***š^e^'ôl,*** שְׁאֹל ***š^e^'ōl*** [SHEOL] 65x
<7586> שָׁאוּל ***šā'ûl*** [SAUL] 400x
<7587> שָׁאוּלִי ***šā'ûliy*** [SHAULITE] 1x
<7588> שָׁאוֹן ***šā'ôn*** [TUMULT] 17x
<7589> שְׁאָט ***š^e^'āṭ*** [MALICE] 3x
<7590> שָׁאט ***šā'ṭ,*** שׁוּט ***šûṭ*** [DESPISE] 3x

<7591> שְׁאִיָּה ***šᵉ'iyyāh*** [RUIN (noun)] 1x
<7592> שָׁאַל ***šā'al*** [ASK] 173x
<7593> שְׁאֵל ***šᵉ'êl*** [ASK] 6x
<7594> שְׁאָל ***šᵉ'āl*** [SHEAL] 1x
<7595> שְׁאֵלָה ***šᵉ'êlāh*** [DECISION] 1x
<7596> שְׁאֵלָה ***šᵉ'êlāh,*** שֵׁלָה ***šêlāh*** [REQUEST] 14x
<7597> שְׁאַלְתִּיאֵל ***šᵉ'altiy'êl,*** שַׁלְתִּיאֵל ***šaltiy'êl*** [SHEALTIEL] 9x
<7598> שְׁאַלְתִּיאֵל ***šᵉ'altiy'êl*** [SHEALTIEL] 1x
<7599> שָׁאַן ***šā'an*** [EASE (BE AT)] 5x
<7600> שַׁאֲנָן ***ša'ᵃnān*** [EASE (AT)] 11x
<7601> שָׁאַס ***šā'as*** [PLUNDER (verb)] 1x
<7602> שָׁאַף ***šā'ap̱*** [LONG FOR] 14x
<7603> שְׂאֹר ***šᵉ'ōr*** [LEAVEN] 5x
<7604> שָׁאַר ***šā'ar*** [REMAIN] 133x
<7605> שְׁאָר ***šᵉ'ār*** [REMNANT] 26x
<7606> שְׁאָר ***šᵉ'ār*** [REMAINDER] 10x
<7607> שְׁאֵר ***šᵉ'êr*** [FLESH] 16x
<7608> שַׁאֲרָה ***šaᵃrāh*** [KINSWOMAN] 6x
<7609> שֶׁאֱרָה ***šeᵉrāh*** [SHEERAH] 1x
<7610> שְׁאָר יָשׁוּב ***šᵉ'ār yāšûḇ*** [SHEAR-JASHUB] 1x
<7611> שְׁאֵרִית ***šᵉ'êriyṯ*** [REMNANT] 66x
<7612> שֵׁאת ***šê'ṯ*** [DEVASTATION] 1x
<7613> שְׂאֵת ***šᵉ'êṯ*** [DIGNITY] 14x
<7614> שְׁבָא ***šᵉḇā'*** [SHEBA] 23x
<7615> שְׁבָאִי ***šᵉḇā'iy*** [SABEAN] 1x
<7616> שְׁבָבִים ***šᵉḇaḇiym*** [BROKEN IN PIECES] 1x
<7617> שָׁבָה ***šāḇāh*** [CAPTIVE (TAKE)] 47x
<7618> שְׁבוֹ ***šᵉḇô*** [AGATE] 2x
<7619> שְׁבוּאֵל ***šᵉḇû'êl,*** שׁוּבָאֵל ***šûḇā'êl*** [SHEBUEL, SHUBAEL] 6x
<7620> שָׁבוּעַ ***šāḇûa'*** [SEVEN] 20x
<7621> שְׁבוּעָה ***šᵉḇû'āh*** [OATH] 30x
<7622> שְׁבוּת ***šᵉḇûṯ,*** שְׁבִית ***šᵉḇiyṯ*** [CAPTIVITY, CAPTIVES] 43x
<7623> שָׁבַח ***šāḇaḥ*** [SOOTHE] 11x
<7624> שְׁבַח ***šᵉḇaḥ*** [PRAISE (verb)] 5x
<7625> שְׁבַט ***šᵉḇaṭ*** [TRIBE] 1x
<7626> שֵׁבֶט ***šêḇeṭ*** [ROD] 190x
<7627> שְׁבָט ***šᵉḇāṭ*** [SHEBAT] 1x
<7628> שְׁבִי ***šᵉḇiy*** [CAPTIVITY, CAPTIVES] 49x
<7629> שֹׁבִי ***šōḇiy*** [SHOBI] 1x
<7630> שֹׁבָי ***šōḇāy*** [SHOBAI] 2x
<7631> שְׁבִיב ***šᵉḇiyḇ*** [FLAME] 2x
<7632> שָׁבִיב ***šāḇiyḇ*** [FLAME] 1x
<7633> שִׁבְיָה ***šiḇyāh*** [CAPTIVES] 9x
<7634> שָׁבְיָה ***šoḇyāh*** [SACHIA, SACHIAH] 1x
<7635> שָׁבִיל ***šāḇiyl,*** שָׁבוּל ***šāḇûl*** [PATH] 2x
<7636> שָׁבִיס ***šaḇiys*** [HEADBAND] 1x
<7637> שְׁבִיעִי ***šᵉḇiy'iy,*** שְׁבִיעִית ***šᵉḇiy'iṯ*** [SEVENTH] 98x
<7638> שָׂבָךְ ***šāḇāḵ*** [NET] 1x
<7639> שְׂבָכָה ***šᵉḇāḵāh*** [NET] 15x
<7640> שֹׁבֶל ***šōḇel*** [SKIRT] 1x
<7641> שִׁבֹּלֶת ***šibbōleṯ*** [GRAIN (HEAD OF, EAR OF)] 16x, [STREAM (noun)] 3x

<7642> שַׁבְּלוּל ***šablûl*** [SNAIL] 1x
<7643> שְׂבָם ***śeḇām,*** שִׂבְמָה ***śiḇmāh*** [SEBAM, SIBMAH] 6x
<7644> שֶׁבְנָא ***šeḇnā',*** שֶׁבְנָה ***šeḇnāh*** [SHEBNA, SHEBNAH] 9x
<7645> שְׁבַנְיָהוּ ***šeḇanyāhû,*** שְׁבַנְיָה ***šeḇanyāh*** [SHEBANIAH] 7x
<7646> שָׂבַע ***śāḇa',*** שָׂבֵעַ ***śāḇêa'*** [SATISFIED] 95x
<7647> שָׂבָע ***śāḇā'*** [PLENTY] 8x
<7648> שֹׂבַע ***śōḇa'*** [FULL (noun)] 8x
<7649> שָׂבֵעַ ***śaḇêa'*** [FULL (adj.)] 9x
<7650> שָׁבַע ***šaḇa'*** [SWEAR] 187x
<7651> שֶׁבַע ***šeḇa',*** שִׁבְעָה ***šiḇ'āh*** [SEVEN] 399x
<7652> שֶׁבַע ***šeḇa'*** [SHEBA] 10x
<7653> שִׂבְעָה ***śiḇ'āh*** [FULLNESS] 1x
<7654> שָׂבְעָה ***śoḇ'āh*** [ABUNDANCE] 6x
<7655> שִׁבְעָה ***šiḇ'āh,*** שְׁבַע ***šeba'*** [SEVEN] 6x
<7656> שִׁבְעָה ***šiḇ'āh*** [SHIBAH] 1x
<7657> שִׁבְעִים ***šiḇ'iym*** [SEVENTY] 91x
<7658> שִׁבְעָנָה ***šiḇ'ānāh*** [SEVEN] 1x
<7659> שִׁבְעָתַיִם ***šiḇ'āṯayim*** [SEVENFOLD] 6x
<7660> שָׁבַץ ***šāḇaṣ*** [WEAVE] 2x
<7661> שָׁבָץ ***šāḇaṣ*** [ANGUISH] 1x
<7662> שְׁבַק ***šeḇaq*** [LEAVE, LEAVE ALONE] 5x
<7663> שָׂבַר ***śāḇar*** [INSPECT] 2x, [WAIT] 6x
<7664> שֵׂבֶר ***śêḇer*** [HOPE (verb)] 2x
<7665> שָׁבַר ***šāḇar*** [BREAK] 150x
<7666> שָׁבַר ***šāḇar*** [BUY] 21x
<7667> שֶׁבֶר ***šêḇer*** [DESTRUCTION] 44x
<7668> שֶׁבֶר ***šeḇer*** [GRAIN] 9x
<7669> שֶׁבֶר ***šeḇer*** [SHEBER] 1x
<7670> שִׁבְרוֹן ***šiḇrôn*** [DESTRUCTION] 2x
<7671> שְׁבָרִים ***šeḇāriym*** [SHEBARIM] 1x
<7672> שְׁבַשׁ ***šeḇaš*** [PERPLEXED (BE)] 1x
<7673> שָׁבַת ***šaḇaṯ*** [REST (verb)] 71x
<7674> שֶׁבֶת ***šeḇeṯ*** [LOSS OF TIME] 3x
<7675> שֶׁבֶת ***šeḇeṯ*** [SEAT] 7x
<7676> שַׁבָּת ***šabbāṯ*** [SABBATH] 108x
<7677> שַׁבָּתוֹן ***šabbāṯôn*** [REST (noun)] 22x
<7678> שַׁבְּתַי ***šabbeṯay*** [SHABBETHAI] 3x
<7679> שָׂגָא ***śāḡā'*** [GREAT (MAKE)] 2x
<7680> שְׂגָא ***śeḡā'*** [GROW] 3x
<7681> שָׁגֵה ***šāḡêh*** [SHAGEE] 1x
<7682> שָׂגַב ***śagaḇ*** [EXALTED (BE)] 20x
<7683> שָׁגַג ***šāḡag*** [ERR] 4x
<7684> שְׁגָגָה ***šeḡāḡāh*** [ERROR] 19x
<7685> שָׂגָה ***śāḡāh*** [GROW] 4x
<7686> שָׁגָה ***šaḡāh*** [ERR] 21x
<7687> שְׂגוּב ***śeḡûḇ*** [SEGUB] 3x
<7688> שָׁגַח ***šāḡāḥ*** [LOOK (verb)] 3x
<7689> שַׂגִּיא ***śaggiy'*** [EXALTED] 2x
<7690> שַׂגִּיא ***śaggiy'*** [GREAT] 13x
<7691> שְׁגִיאָה ***šeḡiy'āh*** [ERROR] 1x
<7692> שִׁגָּיוֹן ***šiggāyôn,*** שִׁגְיֹנָה ***šiggāyōnāh*** [SHIGGAION] 2x

<7693> שָׁגַל ***šāg̱al*** [RAPE] 4x
<7694> שֵׁגַל ***šêg̱al*** [QUEEN] 2x
<7695> שֵׁגַל ***šêg̱al*** [WIFE] 3x
<7696> שָׁגַע ***šag̱a'*** [MAD (BE, DRIVE)] 7x
<7697> שִׁגָּעוֹן ***šiggā'ôn*** [MADNESS] 3x
<7698> שֶׁגֶר ***šeg̱er*** [OFFSPRING] 5x
<7699> שַׁד ***šad̠,*** שֹׁד ***šōd̠*** [BREAST] 24x
<7700> שֵׁד ***šêd̠*** [DEMON] 2x
<7701> שֹׁד ***šōd̠,*** שׁוֹד ***šôd̠*** [DESTRUCTION] 25x
<7702> שָׂדַד ***śād̠ad̠*** [HARROW] 3x
<7703> שָׁדַד ***šād̠ad̠*** [DESTROY] 58x
<7704> שָׂדַי ***śad̠ay,*** שָׂדֶה ***śād̠eh*** [FIELD] 333x
<7705> שִׁדָּה ***šiddāh*** [CONCUBINE] 1x
<7706> שַׁדַּי ***šadday*** [ALMIGHTY] 48x
<7707> שְׁדֵיאוּר ***š^ed̠êy'ûr*** [SHEDEUR] 5x
<7708> שִׂדִּים ***śiddiym*** [SIDDIM] 3x
<7709> שְׁדֵמָה ***š^ed̠êmāh*** [FIELD] 5x, [SCORCHED] 1x
<7710> שָׁדַף ***šād̠ap̱*** [SCORCHED] 3x
<7711> שְׁדֵפָה ***š^ed̠êp̱āh,*** שִׁדָּפוֹן ***šiddāp̱ôn*** [SCORCHED] 6x
<7712> שְׁדַר ***š^ed̠ar*** [LABOR (verb)] 1x
<7713> שְׂדֵרָה ***ś^ed̠êrāh*** [RANK] 4x
<7714> שַׁדְרַךְ ***šad̠rak̠*** [SHADRACH] 1x
<7715> שַׁדְרַךְ ***šad̠rak̠*** [SHADRACH] 13x
<7716> שֶׂה ***śeh*** [SHEEP] 46x
<7717> שָׂהֵד ***śāhêd̠*** [ADVOCATE] 1x
<7718> שֹׁהַם ***šōham*** [ONYX] 11x
<7719> שֹׁהַם ***šōham*** [SHOHAM] 1x
<7720> שַׂהֲרוֹן ***śah^arôn*** [ORNAMENT] 3x
<7721> שׂוֹא ***śô',*** שׂוֹאָה ***śô'āh,*** שֹׁאָה ***šō'āh*** [ARISE] 1x
<7722> שׁוֹאָה ***šô'*** [RAVAGE (noun)] 13x
<7723> שָׁוְא ***šāw'*** [EMPTINESS] 53x
<7724> שְׁוָא ***š^ewā'*** [SHEVA] 2x
<7725> שׁוּב ***šûḇ*** [TURN (verb)] 1,066x (KJV)
<7726> שׁוֹבָב ***šôḇāḇ*** [BACKSLIDING] 3x
<7727> שׁוֹבָב ***šôḇāḇ*** [SHOBAB] 4x
<7728> שׁוֹבֵב ***šôḇêḇ*** [BACKSLIDING] 3x
<7729> שׁוּבָה ***šûḇāh*** [RETURNING] 1x
<7730> שׂוֹבֶךְ ***śôḇek̠*** [THICK BRANCH] 1x
<7731> שׁוֹבָךְ ***šôḇāk̠*** [SHOBACH] 2x
<7732> שׁוֹבָל ***šôḇal*** [SHOBAL] 9x
<7733> שׁוֹבֵק ***šôḇêq*** [SHOBEK] 1x
<7734> שׂוּג ***śûg*** [TURN (verb)] 1x
<7735> שׂוּג ***śûg*** [GROW] 1x
<7736> שׁוּד ***šûd̠*** [WASTE, LAY WASTE] 1x
<7737> שָׁוָה ***šāwāh*** [LIKE (BE, BECOME)] 21x
<7738> שָׁוָה ***šāwāh*** [SUBSTANCE] 1x
<7739> שְׁוָה ***š^ewāh*** [MAKE, MAKE LIKE] 2x
<7740> שָׁוֵה ***šāwêh*** [SHAVEH] 1x
<7741> שָׁוֵה קִרְיָתַיִם ***šāwêh qiryāt̠ayim*** [SHAVEH-KIRIATHAIM] 1x
<7742> שׂוּחַ ***śûaḥ*** [MEDITATE] 1x
<7743> שׁוּחַ ***šûaḥ,*** שִׁיחַ ***šiyaḥ*** [BOW DOWN] 6x

<7744> שׁוּחַ ***šûaḥ*** [SHUAH] 2x
<7745> שׁוּחָה ***šûḥāh*** [PIT] 5x
<7746> שׁוּחָה ***šûḥāh*** [SHUHAH] 1x
<7747> שׁוּחִי ***šûḥiy*** [SHUHITE] 5x
<7748> שׁוּחָם ***šûḥām*** [SHUHAM] 1x
<7749> שׁוּחָמִי ***šûḥāmiy*** [SHUHAMITE] 2x
<7750> שׂוּט ***śûṭ,*** סוּט ***sûṭ*** [TURN ASIDE] 2x
<7751> שׁוּט ***šûṭ*** [GO ABOUT] 13x
<7752> שׁוֹט ***šôṭ*** [WHIP] 11x
<7753> שׂוּךְ ***śûḵ*** [HEDGE (MAKE A, PUT A)] 3x
<7754> שׂוֹךְ ***śôḵ,*** שׂוֹכָה ***śôḵāh*** [BRANCH] 2x
<7755> שׂוֹכוֹ ***śôḵô,*** שׂוֹכֹה ***śôḵōh,*** שׂוֹכֹה ***śôkōh,*** שׂוֹכוֹ ***śôḵô*** [SOCO, SOCOH] 8x
<7756> שׂוּכָתִים ***śûḵāṯiym*** [SUCATHITES] 1x
<7757> שׁוּל ***šûl*** [HEM] 11x
<7758> שׁוֹלָל ***šôlāl*** [STRIPPED] 3x
<7759> שׁוּלַמִּית ***šûlammiyṯ*** [SHUNAMMITE] 2x
<7760> שׂוּם ***śûm,*** שִׂים ***śiym*** [PUT] 585x
<7761> שׂוּם ***śûm,*** שִׂים ***śiym*** [PUT] 26x
<7762> שׁוּם ***šûm*** [GARLIC] 1x
<7763> שׁוֹמֵר ***šômêr,*** שֹׁמֵר ***šōmêr*** [SHOMER] 3x
<7764> שׁוּנִי ***šûniy*** [SHUNI] 2x
<7765> שׁוּנִי ***šûniy*** [SHUNITE] 1x
<7766> שׁוּנֵם ***šûnêm*** [SHUNEM] 3x
<7767> שׁוּנַמִּית ***šûnammiyṯ*** [SHUNAMMITE] 8x
<7768> שָׁוַע ***šāwa‘*** [CRY (verb)] 21x
<7769> שׁוּעַ ***šûa‘,*** שׁוּעַ ***shûa‘*** [CRY (noun)] 3x
<7770> שׁוּעַ ***šûa‘*** [SHUA] 3x
<7771> שׁוֹעַ ***šôa‘*** [RICH (noun)] 3x
<7772> שׁוֹעַ ***šôa‘*** [SHOA] 1x
<7773> שֶׁוַע ***šewa‘*** [CRY (noun)] 1x
<7774> שׁוּעָא ***šû‘ā’*** [SHUA] 1x
<7775> שַׁוְעָה ***šaw***^{e}***‘āh*** [CRY (noun)] 11x
<7776> שׁוּעָל ***šû‘āl*** [FOX] 7x
<7777> שׁוּעָל ***šû‘āl*** [SHUAL] 2x
<7778> שׁוֹעֵר ***šô‘êr,*** שֹׁעֵר ***šō‘êr*** [GATEKEEPER] 37x
<7779> שׁוּף ***šûp̱*** [BRUISE (verb] 3x
<7780> שׁוֹפָךְ ***šôp̱āḵ*** [SHOPHACH] 2x
<7781> שׁוּפָמִי ***šûp̱āmiy*** [SHUPHAMITE] 1x
<7782> שׁוֹפָר ***šôp̱ār,*** שֹׁפָר ***šōp̱ār*** [TRUMPET] 72x
<7783> שׁוּק ***šûq*** [OVERFLOW (verb)] 3x
<7784> שׁוּק ***šûq*** [STREET] 4x
<7785> שׁוֹק ***šôq*** [LEG] 19x
<7786> שׂוּר ***śûr*** [RULE (verb)] 2x
<7787> שׂוּר ***śûr*** [SAW (verb)] 1x
<7788> שׁוּר ***šûr*** [JOURNEY (verb)] 3x
<7789> שׁוּר ***šûr*** [LOOK (verb)] 16x
<7790> שׁוּר ***šûr*** [ENEMY] 1x
<7791> שׁוּר ***šûr,*** שׁוּרָה ***šûrāh*** [WALL] 4x
<7792> שׁוּר ***šûr*** [WALL] 3x
<7793> שׁוּר ***šûr*** [SHUR] 6x
<7794> שׁוֹר ***šôr*** [OX] 78x

<7795> שׁוּרָה ***šôrah*** [ROW (noun)] 1x
<7796> שׂוֹרֵק ***śôrêq,*** שֹׂרֵק ***śōrêq*** [SOREK] 1x
<7797> שׂוּשׂ ***śûś,*** שִׂישׂ ***śiyś*** [REJOICE] 27x
<7798> שַׁוְשָׁא ***šawšā'*** [SHAVSHA] 1x
<7799> שׁוּשַׁן ***šûšan,*** שׁוֹשָׁן ***šôšān,*** שׁוֹשַׁנָּה ***šôšannāh,*** שׁוֹשַׁנִּים ***šôšanniym*** [LILY] 15x
<7800> שׁוּשַׁן ***šûšan*** [SHUSHAN] 21x
<7801> שׁוּשַׁנְכִי ***šûšanḵiy*** [SUSANCHITES] 1x
<7802> שׁוּשַׁן עֵדוּת ***šûšan 'êḏûṯ,*** שׁוֹשַׁנִּים עֵדוּת ***šôšanniym 'êḏûṯ*** [SHUSHAN EDUTH] 2x
<7803> שׁוּתֶלַח ***šûṯelaḥ*** [SHUTHELAH] 4x
<7804> שְׁזַב ***š^{e}zaḇ,*** שֵׁיזִב ***šêyziḇ*** [DELIVER] 7x
<7805> שָׁזַף ***šāzap̱*** [SEE] 3x
<7806> שָׁזַר ***šāzar*** [TWIST] 21x
<7807> שַׁח ***šaḥ*** [HUMBLE] 1x
<7808> שֵׂחַ ***śêaḥ*** [THOUGHT] 1x
<7809> שָׁחַד ***šāḥaḏ*** [REWARD (GIVE A)] 2x
<7810> שֹׁחַד ***šōḥaḏ*** [BRIBE (noun)] 23x
<7811> שָׂחָה ***śāḥāh*** [SWIM] 3x
<7812> שָׁחָה ***shāchāh*** [BOW DOWN] 23x
<7813> שָׂחוּ ***śāḥû*** [SWIMMING] 1x
<7814> שְׂחוֹק ***ś^{e}ḥôq,*** שְׂחֹק ***ś^{e}ḥōq*** [LAUGHTER] 15x
<7815> שְׁחוֹר ***š^{e}ḥôr*** [SOOT] 1x
<7816> שְׁחוּת ***š^{e}ḥûṯ*** [PIT] 1x
<7817> שָׁחַח ***šāḥaḥ*** [BOW DOWN] 21x
<7818> שָׂחַט ***śāḥaṭ*** [PRESS] 1x
<7819> שָׁחַט ***šāḥaṭ*** [KILL] 81x
<7820> שָׁחַט ***šāḥaṭ*** [BEAT] 4x
<7821> שְׁחִיטָה ***š^{e}ḥiyṭāh,*** שַׁחֲטָה ***šaḥ^{a}ṭāh*** [SLAUGHTER (noun)] 2x
<7822> שְׁחִין ***š^{e}ḥiyn*** [BOIL (noun)] 13x
<7823> שָׁחִיס ***šāḥiys,*** סָחִישׁ ***sāḥiyš*** [SPRINGS FROM THE SAME (WHAT)] 2x
<7824> שָׂחִיף ***śaḥiyp̱*** [PANELED] 1x
<7825> שְׁחִית ***š^{e}ḥiyṯ*** [PIT] 2x
<7826> שַׁחַל ***šaḥal*** [LION] 7x
<7827> שְׁחֵלֶת ***š^{e}ḥêleṯ*** [ONYCHA] 1x
<7828> שַׁחַף ***šaḥap̱*** [SEA GULL] 2x
<7829> שַׁחֶפֶת ***šaḥepeṯ*** [CONSUMPTION] 2x
<7830> שַׁחַץ ***šaḥaṣ*** [PRIDE] 2x
<7831> שַׁחֲצוּם ***šaḥ^{a}ṣûm,*** שַׁחֲצִים ***šaḥ^{a}ṣiym*** [SHAHAZUMAH] 1x
<7832> שָׂחַק ***śāḥaq*** [LAUGH] 36x
<7833> שָׁחַק ***šāḥaq*** [BEAT] 4x
<7834> שַׁחַק ***šaḥaq*** [CLOUD] 21x
<7835> שָׁחַר ***šāḥar*** [BLACK (BE, GROW, TURN)] 1x
<7836> שָׁחַר ***šāḥar*** [SEEK DILIGENTLY] 12x
<7837> שַׁחַר ***šaḥar*** [DAWN (noun)] 24x
<7838> שָׁחֹר ***šāḥōr*** [BLACK] 6x
<7839> שַׁחֲרוּת ***šaḥ^{a}rûṯ*** [YOUTH] 1x
<7840> שְׁחַרְחֹר ***š^{e}ḥarḥōr*** [DARK] 1x
<7841> שְׁחַרְיָה ***š^{e}ḥaryāh*** [SHEHARIAH] 1x
<7842> שַׁחֲרַיִם ***šaḥ^{a}rayim*** [SHAHARAIM] 1x
<7843> שָׁחַת ***šāḥaṯ*** [DESTROY] 147x
<7844> שְׁחַת ***š^{e}ḥaṯ*** [CORRUPT (verb)] 2x
<7845> שַׁחַת ***šaḥaṯ*** [PIT] 23x

<7846> שֵׂט ***śêṭ,*** סֵט ***sêṭ*** [REVOLTER] 2x
<7847> שָׂטָה ***śāṭāh*** [ASIDE (GO, TURN)] 6x
<7848> שִׁטָּה ***šiṭṭāh*** [ACACIA] 28x
<7849> שָׁטַח ***šāṭaḥ*** [SPREAD OUT] 6x
<7850> שֹׁטֵט ***šōṭêṭ*** [WHIP] 1x
<7851> שִׁטִּים ***šiṭṭiym*** [SHITTIM] 5x
<7852> שָׂטַם ***śāṭam*** [HATE] 6x
<7853> שָׂטַן ***śāṭan*** [ACCUSE] 6x
<7854> שָׂטָן ***śāṭān*** [ACCUSER] 27x
<7855> שִׂטְנָה ***śiṭnāh*** [ACCUSATION] 1x
<7856> שִׂטְנָה ***śiṭnāh*** [SITNAH] 1x
<7857> שָׁטַף ***šāṭap̱*** [WASH] 31x
<7858> שֶׁטֶף ***šeṭep̱*** [FLOOD] 6x
<7859> שְׂטַר ***śᵉṭar*** [SIDE] 1x
<7860> שֹׁטֵר ***šōṭêr*** [SCRIBE] 25x
<7861> שִׁטְרַי ***šiṭray*** [SHITRAI] 1x
<7862> שַׁי ***šay*** [GIFT] 3x
<7863> שִׂיא ***śiy'*** [LOFTINESS] 1x
<7864> שְׁיָא ***šᵉyā'*** [SHEJA] 1x
<7865> שִׂיאֹן ***śiy'ōn*** [SION] 1x
<7866> שִׁיאֹן ***šiy'ōn*** [SHION] 1x
<7867> שִׂיב ***śiyḇ*** [GRAY, GRAY-HAIRED, GRAYHEADED (BE)] 2x
<7868> שִׂיב ***śiyḇ,*** שָׂב ***śāḇ*** [ELDER] 5x
<7869> שֵׂיב ***śeyḇ*** [AGE] 1x
<7870> שִׁיבָה ***šiyḇāh*** [CAPTIVITY] 1x
<7871> שִׁיבָה ***šiyḇāh*** [STAY (noun)] 1x
<7872> שֵׂיבָה ***śeyḇāh*** [OLD AGE] 19x
<7873> שִׂיג ***śiyg*** [RELIEVE ONESELF] 1x
<7874> שִׂיד ***śiyḏ*** [PLASTER (verb)] 2x
<7875> שִׂיד ***śiyḏ*** [PLASTER (noun)] 4x
<7876> שָׁיָה ***šāyāh*** [UNMINDFUL (BE)] 1x
<7877> שִׁיזָא ***šiyzā'*** [SHIZA] 1x
<7878> שִׂיחַ ***śiyaḥ*** [TELL] 20x
<7879> שִׂיחַ ***śiyaḥ*** [COMPLAINT] 14x
<7880> שִׂיחַ ***śiyaḥ*** [BUSH] 4x
<7881> שִׂיחָה ***śiyḥāh*** [MEDITATION] 3x
<7882> שִׁיחָה ***šiyḥāh*** [PIT] 3x
<7883> שִׁיחוֹר ***šiyḥôr*** [SHIHOR] 4x
<7884> שִׁיחוֹר לִבְנָת ***šiyḥôr liḇnaṯ*** [SHIHOR LIBNATH] 1x
<7885> שַׁיִט ***šayiṭ*** [OAR] 1x
<7886> שִׁילֹה ***šiylōh*** [SHILOH] 1x
<7887> שִׁילֹה ***šiylōh,*** שִׁלֹה ***šilōh,*** שִׁילוֹ ***šiylô,*** שִׁלוֹ ***šilô*** [SHILOH] 32x
<7888> שִׁילֹנִי ***šiylōniy,*** שִׁילוֹנִי ***šiylôniy,*** שִׁלֹנִי ***šilōniy*** [SHILONITE] 7x
<7889> שִׁימוֹן ***šiymôn*** [SHIMON] 1x
<7890> שַׁיִן ***šayin*** [URINE] 2x
<7891> שִׁיר ***šiyr*** [SING] 87x
<7892> שִׁירָה ***šiyrāh,*** שִׁיר ***šiyr*** [SONG] 90x
<7893> שַׁיִשׁ ***šayiš*** [MARBLE] 1x
<7894> שִׁישָׁא ***šiyšā'*** [SHISHA] 1x
<7895> שִׁישַׁק ***šiyšaq*** [SHISHAK] 7x
<7896> שִׁית ***šiyṯ*** [PUT] 85x

<7897> שִׁית ***šiyṯ*** [GARMENT] 2x

<7898> שַׁיִת ***šayiṯ*** [THORN] 7x

<7899> שֵׂךְ ***śêḵ*** [BARB] 1x

<7900> שֹׂךְ ***śōḵ*** [TABERNACLE] 1x

<7901> שָׁכַב ***šāḵaḇ*** [LIE DOWN] 208x

<7902> שְׁכָבָה ***šᵉḵāḇāh*** [LAYER] 9x

<7903> שְׁכֹבֶת ***šᵉḵōḇeṯ*** [INTERCOURSE] 4x

<7904> שָׁכָה ***šāḵāh*** [LUSTY] 1x

<7905> שֻׂכָּה ***śukkāh*** [HARPOON] 1x

<7906> שֵׂכוּ ***śêḵû*** [SECU, SECHU] 1x

<7907> שֶׂכְוִי ***śeḵwiy*** [MIND] 1x

<7908> שְׁכוֹל ***šᵉḵôl*** [LOSS OF CHILDREN] 3x

<7909> שַׁכּוּל ***šakkûl,*** שְׁכוּלָה ***šᵉḵûlāh*** [BEREAVED] 6x

<7910> שִׁכּוֹר ***šikkôr,*** שִׁכֹּר ***šikkor*** [DRUNK, DRUNKEN, DRUNKARD] 13x

<7911> שָׁכַח ***šāḵaḥ*** [FORGET] 102x

<7912> שְׁכַח ***šᵉḵaḥ*** [FORGET] 18x

<7913> שָׁכֵחַ ***šāḵêaḥ*** [FORGET] 2x

<7914> שְׂכִיָּה ***śᵉḵiyyāh,*** שָׂכְיָה ***śāḵᵉyāh*** [VESSEL] 2x

<7915> שַׂכִּין ***śakkiyn*** [KNIFE] 1x

<7916> שָׂכִיר ***śaḵiyr*** [HIRED] 17x

<7917> שְׂכִירָה ***śᵉḵiyrāh*** [HIRED] 1x

<7918> שָׁכַךְ ***šāḵaḵ*** [SUBSIDE] 5x

<7919> שָׂכַל ***sāḵal,*** שָׂכַל ***sākhal*** [CONSIDER] 63x

<7920> שְׂכַל ***śᵉḵal*** [CONSIDER] 1x

<7921> שָׁכֹל ***šāḵōl*** [DEPRIVED OF CHILDREN] 25x

<7922> שֶׂכֶל ***śeḵel,*** שֵׂכֶל ***śêḵel*** [INTELLIGENCE] 16x

<7923> שִׁכֻּלִים ***šikkuliym*** [BEREAVEMENT] 1x

<7924> שָׂכְלְתָנוּ ***śoḵlᵉṯānû*** [UNDERSTANDING] 3x

<7925> שָׁכַם ***šāḵam*** [RISE EARLY] 65x

<7926> שְׁכֶם ***šᵉḵem*** [SHOULDER] 22x

<7927> שְׁכֶם ***šeḵem*** [SHECHEM] 62x

<7928> שֶׁכֶם ***šeḵem*** [SHECHEM] 14x

<7929> שִׁכְמָה ***šiḵmāh*** [SHOULDER] 1x

<7930> שִׁכְמִי ***šiḵmiy*** [SHECHEMITE] 1x

<7931> שָׁכַן ***šāḵan*** [SETTLE DOWN] 129x

<7932> שְׁכַן ***šᵉḵan*** [DWELL] 2x

<7933> שֵׁכֶן ***šêḵen*** [DWELLING] 1x

<7934> שָׁכֵן ***šāḵên*** [INHABITANT] 20x

<7935> שְׁכַנְיָהוּ ***šᵉḵanyāhû,*** שְׁכַנְיָה ***šᵉḵanyāh*** [SHECHANIAH] 11x

<7936> שָׂכַר ***śāḵar,*** סָכַר ***sāḵar*** [HIRE] 21x

<7937> שָׁכֻר ***šāḵur,*** שָׁכַר ***šāḵar*** [DRUNK, DRUNKEN] 19x

<7938> שֶׂכֶר ***śeḵer*** [REWARD (noun)] 2x

<7939> שָׂכָר ***śāḵār*** [WAGES] 28x

<7940> שָׂכָר ***śāḵār*** [SACAR] 2x

<7941> שֵׁכָר ***šêḵār*** [STRONG DRINK] 23x

<7942> שִׁכְּרוֹן ***šikkᵉrôn*** [SHIKKERON, SHICRON] 1x

<7943> שִׁכָּרוֹן ***šikkārôn*** [DRUNKENNESS] 3x

<7944> שַׁל ***šal*** [ERROR] 1x

<7945> שַׁ ***ša,*** שֶׁ ***še,*** שְׁ ***šᵉ*** [WHO, WHICH WHAT] 44x

<7946> שַׁלְאֲנַן ***šalᵃnan*** [EASE (AT)] 1x

<7947> שָׁלַב ***šālaḇ*** [PARALLEL (SET)] 2x

<7948> שָׁלָב ***šālāḇ*** [FRAME] 2x
<7949> שָׁלַג ***šālag̱*** [SNOW (BE AS WHITE AS)] 1x
<7950> שֶׁלֶג ***šeleg̱*** [SNOW] 20x
<7951> שָׁלָה ***šālāh,*** שָׁלַו ***šālaw*** [EASE (BE AT)] 7x
<7952> שָׁלָה ***šālāh*** [NEGLIGENT (BE)] 2x
<7953> שָׁלָה ***šālāh*** [TAKE AWAY] 1x
<7954> שְׁלֵה ***šᵉlêh*** [EASE (BE AT)] 1x
<7955> שָׁלֶה ***šālûh*** [AMISS] 1x
<7956> שֵׁלָה ***šēlāh*** [SHELAH] 8x
<7957> שַׁלְהֶבֶת ***šalheḇeṯ,*** שַׁלְהֶבֶתְיָה ***šalheḇeṯyāh*** [FLAME] 3x
<7958> שְׂלָו ***śᵉlāw*** [QUAIL] 4x
<7959> שָׁלוּ ***šālû*** [PROSPERITY] 1x
<7960> שָׁלוּ ***šālû*** [NEGLECT (noun)] 4x
<7961> שָׁלֵו ***šālêw,*** שָׁלֵיו ***šālêyw,*** שְׁלֵיו ***šᵉlêyw*** [EASE (AT)] 8x
<7962> שַׁלְוָה ***šalwāh*** [PROSPERITY] 8x
<7963> שְׁלֵוָה ***šᵉlêwāh*** [PROSPERITY] 1x
<7964> שִׁלּוּחִים ***šillûḥiym*** [PARTING GIFT] 3x
<7965> שָׁלוֹם ***šālôm*** [PEACE] 237x
<7966> שִׁלּוּם ***šillûm,*** שִׁלֻּם ***šillum*** [RECOMPENSE (noun)] 3x
<7967> שַׁלּוּם ***šallûm,*** שַׁלֻּם ***šallum*** [SHALLUM] 27x
<7968> שַׁלּוּן ***šallûn*** [SHALLUM, SHALLUN] 1x
<7969> שָׁלוֹשׁ ***šālôš,*** שָׁלֹשׁ ***šālōš,*** שְׁלֹשָׁה ***šᵉlōšāh*** [THREE] 430x
<7970> שְׁלוֹשִׁים ***šᵉlôšiym,*** שְׁלֹשִׁים ***šᵉlōšiym*** [THIRTY] 175x
<7971> שָׁלַח ***šālaḥ*** [SEND FORTH, SEND AWAY] 842x
<7972> שְׁלַח ***šᵉlaḥ*** [SEND, BE SENT] 14x
<7973> שֶׁלַח ***šelaḥ*** [PLANTS] 1x, [WEAPON] 7x
<7974> שֶׁלַח ***šelaḥ*** [SHELAH] 9x
<7975> שִׁלֹחַ ***šilōaḥ,*** שֶׁלַח ***šelaḥ*** [SHILOAH] 2x
<7976> שִׁלֻּחָה ***šilluḥāh*** [SHOOT (noun)] 1x
<7977> שִׁלְחִי ***šilḥiy*** [SHILHI] 2x
<7978> שִׁלְחִים ***šilḥiym*** [SHILHIM] 1x
<7979> שֻׁלְחָן ***šulḥān*** [TABLE] 70x
<7980> שָׁלַט ***šālaṭ*** [RULE OVER] 8x
<7981> שְׁלַט ***šᵉlaṭ*** [RULE OVER] 7x
<7982> שֶׁלֶט ***šeleṭ*** [SHIELD (noun)] 7x
<7983> שִׁלְטוֹן ***šilṭôn*** [POWER] 2x
<7984> שִׁלְטוֹן ***šilṭôn*** [OFFICIAL] 2x
<7985> שָׁלְטָן ***šolṭān*** [DOMINION] 14x
<7986> שַׁלֶּטֶת ***šalleṭeṯ*** [BRAZEN] 1x
<7987> שְׁלִי ***šᵉliy*** [PRIVATELY] 1x
<7988> שִׁלְיָה ***šilyāh*** [AFTERBIRTH] 1x
<7989> שַׁלִּיט ***šalliyṭ*** [POWER] 4x
<7990> שַׁלִּיט ***šalliyṭ*** [MASTERY] 10x
<7991> שָׁלִישׁ ***šāliyš*** [THIRD] 20x
<7992> שְׁלִישִׁי ***šᵉliyšiy,*** שָׁלִשִׁי ***šālišiy*** [THIRD] 108x
<7993> שָׁלַךְ ***šālaḵ*** [THROW] 125x
<7994> שָׁלָךְ ***šālaḵ*** [CORMORANT] 2x
<7995> שַׁלֶּכֶת ***šalleḵeṯ*** [FELLING] 1x
<7996> שַׁלֶּכֶת ***šalleḵeṯ*** [SHALLECHETH] 1x
<7997> שָׁלַל ***šālal*** [PLUNDER (verb)] 16x
<7998> שָׁלָל ***šālāl*** [PLUNDER (noun)] 73x

<7999> שָׁלַם ***šālam*** [COMPLETED (BE)] 116x
<8000> שְׁלֵם ***šᵉlêm*** [COMPLETE (verb)] 3x
<8001> שְׁלָם ***šᵉlām*** [PEACE] 4x
<8002> שֶׁלֶם ***šelem*** [PEACE OFFERINGS] 87x
<8003> שָׁלֵם ***šālêm*** [SAFE] 27x
<8004> שָׁלֵם ***šālêm*** [SALEM] 2x
<8005> שִׁלֵּם ***šillêm*** [RECOMPENSE (noun)] 1x
<8006> שִׁלֵּם ***šillêm*** [SHILLEM] 3x
<8007> שַׂלְמָא ***śalmā'*** [SALMA] 4x
<8008> שַׂלְמָה ***śalmāh*** [CLOTHING] 16x
<8009> שַׂלְמָה ***śalmāh*** [SALMON] 1x
<8010> שְׁלֹמֹה ***šᵉlōmōh*** [SOLOMON] 293x
<8011> שִׁלֻּמָה ***šillumāh*** [RECOMPENSE (noun)] 1x
<8012> שַׂלְמוֹן ***śalmôn*** [SALMON] 1x
<8013> שְׁלֹמוֹת ***šᵉlōmôṯ*** [SHELOMOTH, SHELOMITH] 5x
<8014> שַׂלְמַי ***śalmay,*** שַׁלְמַי ***šalmay*** [SHALMAI] 2x
<8015> שְׁלֹמִי ***šᵉlōmiy*** [SHELOMI] 1x
<8016> שִׁלֵּמִי ***šillêmiy*** [SHILLEMITE] 1x
<8017> שְׁלֻמִיאֵל ***šᵉlumiy'êl*** [SHELUMIEL] 5x
<8018> שֶׁלֶמְיָה ***šelemyāh,*** שֶׁלֶמְיָהוּ ***šelemyāhû*** [SHELEMIAH] 10x
<8019> שְׁלוֹמִית ***šᵉlōmiyṯ*** [SHELOMITH] 8x
<8020> שַׁלְמַן ***šalman*** [SHALMAN] 1x
<8021> שַׁלְמֹן ***šalmon*** [GIFT] 1x
<8022> שַׁלְמַנְאֶסֶר ***šalman'eser*** [SHALMANESER] 2x
<8023> שִׁלֹנִי ***šilōniy*** [SHILONI] 1x
<8024> שֵׁלָנִי ***šêlāniy*** [SHELANITE] 2x
<8025> שָׁלַף ***šālap̱*** [DRAW OUT] 25x
<8026> שֶׁלֶף ***šelep̱*** [SHELEPH] 2x
<8027> שָׁלַשׁ ***šālaš*** [DIVIDE INTO THREE PARTS] 9x
<8028> שֵׁלֶשׁ ***šêleš*** [SHELESH] 1x
<8029> שִׁלֵּשׁ ***šillêš*** [THIRD] 5x
<8030> שִׁלְשָׁה ***šilšāh*** [SHILSHAH] 1x
<8031> שָׁלִשָׁה ***šālišāh*** [SHALISHAH] 1x
<8032> שִׁלְשׁוֹם ***šilšôm,*** שִׁלְשֹׁם ***šilšōm*** [BEFORE] 25x
<8033> שָׁם ***šām*** [BEFORE] 152x (NAS)
<8034> שֵׁם ***šêm*** [NAME (noun)] 864x (KJV)
<8035> שֵׁם ***šêm*** [SHEM] 17x
<8036> שֻׁם ***šum*** [NAME (noun)] 10x
<8037> שַׁמָּא ***šammā'*** [SHAMMA] 1x
<8038> שֶׁמְאֵבֶר ***šem'êḇer*** [SHEMEBER] 1x
<8039> שִׁמְאָה ***šim'āh*** [SHIMEAH] 1x
<8040> שְׂמֹאול ***śᵉmō'wl,*** שְׂמֹאל ***śᵉmō'l*** [LEFT] 54x
<8041> שִׂמְאֵל ***śim'êl*** [LEFT (GO TO THE)] 5x
<8042> שְׂמָאלִי ***śᵉmā'liy*** [LEFT, ON THE LEFT] 9x
<8043> שִׁמְאָם ***šim'ām*** [SHIMEAM] 1x
<8044> שַׁמְגַּר ***šamgar*** [SHAMGAR] 2x
<8045> שָׁמַד ***šāmaḏ*** [DESTROYED (BE)] 90x
<8046> שְׁמַד ***šᵉmaḏ*** [CONSUME] 1x
<8047> שַׁמָּה ***šāmmāh*** [RUIN (noun)] 39x
<8048> שַׁמָּה ***šammāh*** [SHAMMAH] 8x
<8049> שַׁמְהוּת ***šamhûṯ*** [SHAMHUTH] 1x

<8050> שְׁמוּאֵל ***šᵉmû'ēl*** [SAMUEL] 140x

<8051> שַׁמּוּעַ ***šammûa'*** [SHAMMUA] 5x

<8052> שְׁמוּעָה ***šᵉmû'āh*** [REPORT] 27x

<8053> שָׁמוּר ***šāmûr*** [SHAMUR] 1x

<8054> שַׁמּוֹת ***šammôṯ*** [SHAMMOTH] 1x

<8055> שָׂמַח ***śāmaḥ*** [REJOICE] 152x

<8056> שָׂמֵחַ ***śāmêaḥ*** [JOYFUL] 23x

<8057> שִׂמְחָה ***śimḥāh*** [JOY] 94x

<8058> שָׁמַט ***šāmaṭ*** [RELEASE (verb)] 9x

<8059> שְׁמִטָּה ***šᵉmiṭṭāh*** [REMISSION] 4x

<8060> שַׁמַּי ***šammay*** [SHAMMAI] 5x

<8061> שְׁמִידָע ***šᵉmiyḏā'*** [SHEMIDA] 3x

<8062> שְׁמִידָעִי ***šᵉmiyḏā'iy*** [SHEMIDAITE] 1x

<8063> שְׂמִיכָה ***śᵉmiyḵāh*** [BLANKET] 1x

<8064> שָׁמַיִם ***šāmayim*** [HEAVEN] 420x

<8065> שְׁמַיִן ***šemayin*** [HEAVEN] 38x

<8066> שְׁמִינִי ***šᵉmiyniy*** [EIGHTH] 28x

<8067> שְׁמִינִית ***šᵉmiyniyṯ*** [SHEMINITH] 3x

<8068> שָׁמִיר ***šāmiyr*** [BRIER] 8x, [DIAMOND] 3x

<8069> שָׁמִיר ***šāmiyr*** [SHAMIR] 4x

<8070> שְׁמִירָמוֹת ***šᵉmiyrāmôṯ*** [SHEMIRAMOTH] 4x

<8071> שִׂמְלָה ***śimlāh*** [CLOTHING] 29x

<8072> שַׂמְלָה ***śamlāh*** [SAMLAH] 4x

<8073> שַׁמְלַי ***šamlay*** [SHAMLAI] 1x

<8074> שָׁמֵם ***šāmêm*** [DESTROYED (BE)] 92x

<8075> שְׁמַם ***šᵉmam*** [ASTONISHED (BE)] 1x

<8076> שָׁמֵם ***šāmêm*** [DESOLATE] 2x

<8077> שִׁמְמָה ***šimmāh***, שְׁמָמָה ***šᵉmāmāh*** [DESOLATION] 58x

<8078> שִׁמָּמוֹן ***šimmāmôn*** [HORROR] 2x

<8079> שְׂמָמִית ***śᵉmāmiyṯ*** [LIZARD] 1x

<8080> שָׁמַן ***šāman***, שָׁמֵן ***šāmên*** [FAT (BE, BECOME)] 5x

<8081> שֶׁמֶן ***šemen*** [OIL] 193x

<8082> שָׁמֵן ***šāmên***, שָׁמָן ***šāmān*** [FAT, FATNESS] 10x

<8083> שְׁמֹנֶה ***šᵉmōneh***, שְׁמֹנָה ***šᵉmōnāh*** [EIGHT, EIGHTH] 109x

<8084> שְׁמֹנִים ***šᵉmōniym***, שְׁמוֹנִים ***šᵉmôniym*** [EIGHTY, EIGHTIETH] 38x

<8085> שָׁמַע ***šāma'*** [HEAR] 1,159x

<8086> שְׁמַע ***šᵉma'*** [HEAR] 9x

<8087> שֶׁמַע ***šema'*** [SHEMA] 5x

<8088> שֵׁמַע ***šêma'*** [HEARING] 18x

<8089> שֹׁמַע ***šōma'*** [FAME] 4x

<8090> שְׁמַע ***šᵉma'*** [SHEMA] 1x

<8091> שָׁמָע ***šāmā'*** [SHAMA] 1x

<8092> שִׁמְעָא ***šim'ā'*** [SHIMEA] 5x

<8093> שִׁמְעָה ***šim'āh*** [SHIMEAH] 3x

<8094> שְׁמָעָה ***šᵉmā'āh*** [SHEMAAH] 1x

<8095> שִׁמְעוֹן ***šim'ôn*** [SIMEON] 44x

<8096> שִׁמְעִי ***šim'iy*** [SHIMEI] 43x

<8097> שִׁמְעִי ***šim'iy*** [SHIMEITES] 2x

<8098> שְׁמַעְיָה ***šᵉma'yāh***, שְׁמַעְיָהוּ ***šᵉmāyāhû*** [SHEMAIAH] 41x

<8099> שִׁמְעֹנִי ***šim'ōniy*** [SIMEONITES] 4x

<8100> שִׁמְעַת ***šim'aṯ*** [SHIMEATH] 2x

<8101> שִׁמְעָתִים ***šimʿāṯiym*** [SHIMEATHITES] 1x
<8102> שֶׁמֶץ ***šēmeṣ*** [WHISPER (noun)] 2x
<8103> שִׁמְצָה ***šimṣāh*** [DERISION] 1x
<8104> שָׁמַר ***šāmar*** [KEEP] 468x
<8105> שֶׁמֶר ***šemer*** [DREGS] 5x
<8106> שֶׁמֶר ***šemer,*** שָׁמֶד ***šāmed*** [SHEMER, SHAMER] 4x
<8107> שִׁמֻּר ***šimmur*** [WATCHING] 2x
<8108> שָׁמְרָה ***šāmrāh*** [GUARD] 1x
<8109> שְׁמֻרָה ***šᵉmurāh*** [OPEN] 1x
<8110> שִׁמְרוֹן ***šimrôn*** [SHIMRON] 5x
<8111> שֹׁמְרוֹן ***šōmᵉrôn*** [SAMARIA] 109x
<8112> שִׁמְרוֹן מְרוֹן ***šimrôn mᵉrôn*** [SHIMRON MERON] 1x
<8113> שִׁמְרִי ***šimriy*** [SHIMRI] 4x
<8114> שְׁמַרְיָהוּ ***šᵉmaryāhû,*** שְׁמַרְיָה ***šᵉmaryāh*** [SHEMARIAH] 4x
<8115> שָׁמְרַיִן ***šāmᵉrayin*** [SAMARIA] 2x
<8116> שִׁמְרִית ***šimriyṯ*** [SHIMRITH] 1x
<8117> שִׁמְרֹנִי ***šimrōniy*** [SHIMRONITE] 1x
<8118> שֹׁמְרֹנִי ***šōmᵉrōniy*** [SAMARITAN] 1x
<8119> שִׁמְרָת ***šimrāṯ*** [SHIMRATH] 1x
<8120> שְׁמַשׁ ***šᵉmaš*** [SERVE] 1x
<8121> שֶׁמֶשׁ ***šemeš*** [SUN] 134x
<8122> שֶׁמֶשׁ ***šemeš*** [SUN] 1x
<8123> שִׁמְשׁוֹן ***šimšôn*** [SAMSON] 38x
<8124> שִׁמְשַׁי ***šimšay*** [SHIMSHAI] 4x
<8125> שַׁמְשְׁרַי ***šamšᵉray*** [SHAMSHERAI] 1x
<8126> שֻׁמָתִי ***šumāṯiy*** [SHUMATHITE] 1x
<8127> שֵׁן ***šēn*** [TOOTH] 55x
<8128> שֵׁן ***šēn*** [TOOTH] 3x
<8129> שֵׁן ***šēn*** [SHEN] 1x
<8130> שָׂנֵא ***śānê'*** [HATE] 146x
<8131> שְׂנֵא ***śᵉnê'*** [HATE] 1x
<8132> שָׁנָא ***šānā'*** [CHANGE (verb)] 3x
<8133> שְׁנָא ***šᵉnā'*** [CHANGE (verb)] 21x
<8134> שִׁנְאָב ***šin'āḇ*** [SHINAB] 1x
<8135> שִׂנְאָה ***śin'āh*** [HATRED] 16x
<8136> שִׁנְאָן ***šin'ān*** [THOUSANDS (UPON, OF)] 1x
<8137> שֶׁנְאַצַּר ***šen'aṣṣar*** [SHENAZZAR] 1x
<8138> שָׁנָה ***šānāh*** [CHANGE (verb)] 22x
<8139> שְׁנָה ***šᵉnāh*** [SLEEP (noun)] 1x
<8140> שְׁנָה ***šᵉnāh*** [YEAR] 7x
<8141> שָׁנָה ***šānāh*** [YEAR] 864x
<8142> שֵׁנָא ***šēnā',*** שֵׁנָה ***šēnāh*** [SLEEP (noun)] 23x
<8143> שֶׁנְהַבִּים ***šenhabbiym*** [IVORY] 2x
<8144> שָׁנִי ***šāniy*** [SCARLET] 42x
<8145> שֵׁנִי ***šēniy*** [SECOND] 156x
<8146> שָׂנִיא ***śāniy'*** [UNLOVED] 1x
<8147> שְׁנַיִם ***šᵉnayim,*** שְׁתַּיִם ***šᵉttayim*** [TWO] 768x
<8148> שְׁנִינָה ***šᵉniynāh*** [BYWORD] 4x
<8149> שְׂנִיר ***śᵉniyr,*** שְׁנִיר ***šᵉniyr*** [SENIR, SHENIR] 4x
<8150> שָׁנַן ***šānan*** [SHARPEN] 9x
<8151> שָׁנַס ***šānas*** [GIRD UP] 1x

<8152> שִׁנְעָר ***šin'ār*** [SHINAR] 8x
<8153> שְׁנַת ***šᵉnaṯ*** [SLEEP (noun)] 1x
<8154> שָׁסָה ***šāsāh,*** שָׁשָׂה ***šāśāh*** [PLUNDER (verb)] 12x
<8155> שָׁסַס ***šāsas*** [PLUNDER (verb)] 5x
<8156> שָׁסַע ***šāsa'*** [SPLIT] 9x
<8157> שֶׁסַע ***šesa'*** [CLEFT] 4x
<8158> שָׁסַף ***šāsap̱*** [HEW TO PIECES] 1x
<8159> שָׁעָה ***šā'āh,*** שָׁתַע ***šāṯa'*** [LOOK WITH FAVOR OR IN DISMAY] 15x
<8160> שָׁעָה ***šā'āh*** [IMMEDIATELY] 5x
<8161> שַׁעֲטָה ***šaᵃṭāh*** [STAMPING] 1x
<8162> שַׁעַטְנֵז ***ša'aṭnêz*** [MATERIAL (TWO KINDS OF)] 2x
<8163> שָׂעִיר ***śā'iyr,*** שָׂעִר ***śā'ir*** [GOAT] 59x
<8164> שָׂעִיר ***śā'iyr*** [DROPLET] 1x
<8165> שֵׂעִיר ***śê'iyr*** [SEIR] 39x
<8166> שְׂעִירָה ***śᵉ'iyrāh*** [GOAT] 2x
<8167> שְׂעִירָה ***śᵉ'iyrāh*** [SEIRAH] 1x
<8168> שֹׁעַל ***šō'al*** [HANDFUL] 3x
<8169> שַׁעַלְבִים ***ša'alḇiym,*** שַׁעֲלַבִּין ***šaᵃlabbiyn*** [SHAALBIM, SHAALABBIN] 3x
<8170> שַׁעַלְבֹנִי ***ša'alḇōniy*** [SHAALBONITE] 2x
<8171> שַׁעֲלִים ***ša'aliym*** [SHALIM, SHAALIM] 1x
<8172> שָׁעַן ***šā'an*** [LEAN (verb)] 22x
<8173> שָׁעַע ***šā'a'*** [BLINDED (BE)] 9x
<8174> שַׁעַף ***šā'ap̱*** [SHAAPH] 2x
<8175> שָׂעַר ***śā'ar*** [SWEEP AWAY] 4x
<8176> שָׁעַר ***šā'ar*** [THINK] 1x
<8177> שְׂעַר ***śᵉ'ar*** [HAIR] 3x
<8178> שַׂעַר ***śa'ar*** [HORROR] 4x
<8179> שַׁעַר ***ša'ar*** [GATE] 371x
<8180> שַׁעַר ***ša'ar*** [HUNDREDFOLD] 1x
<8181> שֵׂעָר ***śê'ār*** [HAIR] 28x
<8182> שֹׁעָר ***šō'ār*** [VILE] 1x
<8183> שְׂעָרָה ***śᵉ'ārāh*** [TEMPEST] 2x
<8184> שְׂעֹרָה ***śᵉ'ōrāh*** [BARLEY] 34x
<8185> שַׂעֲרָה ***śaᵃrāh*** [HAIR] 7x
<8186> שַׁעֲרוּר ***šaᵃrûr,*** שַׁעֲרוּרָה ***šaᵃrûrāh,*** שַׁעֲרוּרִי ***šaᵃrûriy,*** שַׁעֲרוּרִיָּה ***šaᵃrûriyyāh***
[HORRIBLE THING] 4x
<8187> שְׁעַרְיָה ***šᵉ'aryāh*** [SHEARIAH] 2x
<8188> שְׂעֹרִים ***śᵉ'ōriym*** [SEORIM] 1x
<8189> שַׁעֲרַיִם ***šaᵃrayim*** [SHAARAIM] 3x
<8190> שַׁעַשְׁגַּז ***ša'ašgaz*** [SHAASHGAZ] 1x
<8191> שַׁעֲשֻׁעִים ***šaᵃšu'iym*** [DELIGHT (noun)] 9x
<8192> שָׁפָה ***šāp̄āh*** [STICK OUT] 2x
<8193> שָׂפָה ***śap̄āh*** [LIP] 176x
<8194> שָׁפָה ***šāp̄āh,*** שְׁפוֹת ***šᵉp̄ôṯ*** [CHEESE] 1x
<8195> שְׁפוֹ ***šᵉp̄ô,*** שְׁפִי ***šᵉp̄iy*** [SHEPHO, SHEPHI] 2x
<8196> שְׁפוֹט ***šᵉp̄ôṭ*** [JUDGMENT] 2x
<8197> שְׁפוּפָם ***šᵉp̄ûp̄am,*** שְׁפוּפָן ***šᵉp̄ûp̄ān*** [SHEPHUPHAM, SHEPHUPHAN] 2x
<8198> שִׁפְחָה ***šip̄ḥāh*** [MAIDSERVANT] 63x
<8199> שָׁפַט ***šāp̄aṭ*** [JUDGE (verb)] 203x
<8200> שְׁפַט ***šᵉp̄aṭ*** [JUDGE (verb)] 1x
<8201> שֶׁפֶט ***šep̄eṭ*** [JUDGMENT] 16x

<8202> שָׁפָט ***šāp̱āṭ*** [SHAPHAT] 8x
<8203> שְׁפַטְיָהוּ ***šᵉp̱aṭyāhû,*** שְׁפַטְיָה ***šᵉp̱aṭyāh*** [SHAPHAT] 13x
<8204> שִׁפְטָן ***šip̱ṭān*** [SHIPHTAN] 1x
<8205> שְׁפִי ***šᵉpiy*** [BARE (noun)] 9x
<8206> שֻׁפִּים ***šuppiym*** [SHUPPIM] 3x
<8207> שְׁפִיפֹן ***šᵉpiyp̱ōn*** [VIPER] 1x
<8208> שָׁפִיר ***šāp̱iyr*** [SAPHIR] 1x
<8209> שַׁפִּיר ***šapiyr*** [BEAUTIFUL] 2x
<8210> שָׁפַךְ ***šāp̱aḵ*** [POUR OUT] 115x
<8211> שֶׁפֶךְ ***šep̱eḵ*** [HEAP (noun)] 2x
<8212> שָׁפְכָה ***šop̱kāh*** [MALE ORGAN] 1x
<8213> שָׁפֵל ***šāp̱al*** [HUMBLE, HUMBLE (MAKE)] 29x
<8214> שְׁפַל ***šᵉpal*** [HUMBLE, HUMBLE (MAKE)] 4x
<8215> שְׁפַל ***šᵉpal*** [LOWLIEST] 1x
<8216> שֵׁפֶל ***šêp̱el*** [LOW PLACE] 2x
<8217> שָׁפָל ***šāp̱āl*** [HUMBLE] 19x
<8218> שִׁפְלָה ***šip̱lāh*** [LOW PLACE] 1x
<8219> שְׁפֵלָה ***šᵉpêlāh*** [LOWLAND] 20x
<8220> שִׁפְלוּת ***šip̱lûṯ*** [IDLENESS] 1x
<8221> שְׁפָם ***šᵉpām*** [SHEPHAM] 2x
<8222> שָׂפָם ***śāp̱ām*** [BEARD] 5x
<8223> שָׁפָם ***šāp̱ām*** [SHAPHAM] 1x
<8224> שִׂפְמוֹת ***śip̱môṯ*** [SIPHMOTH] 1x
<8225> שִׁפְמִי ***šip̱miy*** [SIPHMITE] 1x
<8226> שָׂפַן ***śāpan*** [TREASURE] 1x
<8227> שָׁפָן ***šāp̱ān*** [BADGER] 4x, [SHAPHAN] 30x
<8228> שֶׁפַע ***šepaʻ*** [ABUNDANCE] 1x
<8229> שִׁפְעָה ***šip̱ʻāh*** [ABUNDANCE] 6x
<8230> שִׁפְעִי ***šip̱ʻiy*** [SHIPHI] 1x
<8231> שָׁפַר ***šāp̱ar*** [BEAUTIFUL (BE)] 1x
<8232> שְׁפַר ***šᵉpar*** [GOOD (BE, SEEM, THINK)] 3x
<8233> שֶׁפֶר ***šep̱er*** [BEAUTIFUL] 1x
<8234> שֶׁפֶר ***šep̱er*** [SHEPHER] 2x
<8235> שִׁפְרָה ***šip̱rāh*** [FAIR] 1x
<8236> שִׁפְרָה ***šip̱rāh*** [SHIPHRAH] 1x
<8237> שַׁפְרִיר ***šap̱riyr*** [CANOPY] 1x
<8238> שְׁפַרְפָּר ***šᵉp̱arpār*** [DAWN (noun)] 1x
<8239> שָׁפַת ***šāp̱aṯ*** [ESTABLISH] 5x
<8240> שְׁפַתַּיִם ***šᵉpattayim*** [HOOK] 2x
<8241> שֶׁצֶף ***šeṣep*** [SURGE] 1x
<8242> שַׂק ***śaq*** [SACKCLOTH] 48x
<8243> שָׁק ***šāq*** [LEG] 1x
<8244> שָׂקַד ***śāqaḏ*** [BIND] 1x
<8245> שָׁקַד ***šāqaḏ*** [WATCH (verb)] 12x
<8246> שָׁקַד ***šāqaḏ*** [ALMOND (MADE LIKE, SHAPED LIKE)] 6x
<8247> שָׁקֵד ***šāqêḏ*** [ALMOND, ALMOND TREE] 4x
<8248> שָׁקָה ***šāqāh*** [WATER (GIVE)] 73x
<8249> שִׁקֻּו ***šiqquw*** [DRINK (noun)] 1x
<8250> שִׁקּוּי ***šiqqûy*** [DRINK (noun)] 3x
<8251> שִׁקּוּץ ***šiqqûṣ,*** שִׁקֻּץ ***šiqquṣ*** [ABOMINATION] 28x
<8252> שָׁקַט ***šāqaṭ*** [STILL (BE)] 41x

<8253> שֶׁקֶט ***šeqeṭ*** [QUIET (noun)] 1x
<8254> שָׁקַל ***šāqal*** [WEIGH] 2x
<8255> שֶׁקֶל ***šeqel*** [SHEKEL] 88x
<8256> שִׁקְמָה ***šiqmāh*** [SYCAMORE] 7x
<8257> שָׁקַע ***šāqa'*** [DIE DOWN, DIE OUT] 6x
<8258> שְׁקַעֲרוּרָה ***šᵉqaʿᵃrûrāh*** [DEPRESSION] 1x
<8259> שָׁקַף ***šāqap̱*** [LOOK DOWN] 22x
<8260> שֶׁקֶף ***šeqep̱*** [FRAME] 1x
<8261> שָׁקוּף ***šāqûp̱***, שָׁקֻף ***šāqup̱*** [FRAME] 2x
<8262> שָׁקַץ ***šāqaṣ*** [DETEST] 6x
<8263> שֶׁקֶץ ***šeqeṣ*** [ABOMINABLE THING] 11x
<8264> שָׁקַק ***šāqaq***, שׁוֹקֵק ***šôqêq*** [RUSH (verb)] 6x
<8265> שָׂקַר ***śāqar*** [WANTONLY (GLANCE)] 1x
<8266> שָׁקַר ***šāqar*** [FALSELY (DEAL)] 6x
<8267> שֶׁקֶר ***šeqer*** [LIE (noun)] 113x
<8268> שֹׁקֶת ***šōqeṯ*** [TROUGH] 2x
<8269> שַׂר ***śar*** [PRINCE] 421x
<8270> שֹׁר ***šōr*** [NAVEL] 3x
<8271> שְׁרֵא ***šᵉrê'*** [LOOSEN] 6x
<8272> שַׂרְאֶצֶר ***śar'eṣer***, שַׁרְאֶצֶר ***šar'eṣer*** [SHAREZER] 3x
<8273> שָׁרָב ***šārāḇ*** [BURNING SAND] 2x
<8274> שֵׁרֵבְיָה ***šērêḇyāh*** [SHEREBIAH] 8x
<8275> שַׁרְבִיט ***šarḇiyṭ*** [SCEPTER] 3x
<8276> שָׂרַג ***śārag̱*** [KNIT TOGETHER (BE)] 2x
<8277> שָׂרַד ***śāraḏ*** [REMAIN] 1x
<8278> שְׂרָד ***śᵉrāḏ*** [WOVEN] 4x
<8279> שֶׂרֶד ***śereḏ*** [MARKER] 1x
<8280> שָׂרָה ***śārāh*** [STRUGGLE (verb)] 2x
<8281> שָׁרָה ***šārāh*** [LOOSE (LET)] 1x
<8282> שָׂרָה ***sārāh*** [PRINCESS] 5x
<8283> שָׂרָה ***śārāh*** [SARAH] 38x
<8284> שָׂרָה ***śārāh***, שׂוּרָה ***śûrāh*** [VINEYARD] 1x
<8285> שֵׁרָה ***šêrāh*** [BRACELET] 1x
<8286> שְׂרוּג ***śᵉrûg̱*** [SERUG] 5x
<8287> שָׁרוּחֶן ***šārûḥen*** [SHARUHEN] 1x
<8288> שְׂרוֹךְ ***śᵉrûḵ*** [STRAP] 2x
<8289> שָׁרוֹן ***šārôn***, לַשָּׁרוֹן ***laššārôn*** [SHARON, LASHARON] 7x
<8290> שָׁרוֹנִי ***šarôniy*** [SHARONITE] 1x
<8291> שָׂרֹק ***śārōq*** [PLANT (CHOICE, PRINCIPAL)] 1x
<8292> שְׁרוּקָה ***šᵉriyqāh***, שְׁרִקָה ***šᵉriqāh*** [PIPING] 2x
<8293> שֵׁרוּת ***šᵉrûṯ*** [SET FREE] 1x
<8294> שֶׂרַח ***śeraḥ*** [SERAH] 3x
<8295> שָׂרַט ***śāraṭ*** [CUT (verb)] 2x
<8296> שֶׂרֶט ***śereṭ***, שָׂרֶטֶת ***śāreṭeṯ*** [CUT (noun)] 2x
<8297> שָׂרַי ***śāray*** [SARAI] 13x
<8298> שָׁרַי ***šāray*** [SHARAI] 1x
<8299> שָׂרִיג ***śāriyg̱*** [BRANCH] 3x
<8300> שָׂרִיד ***śāriyḏ*** [REMNANT] 28x
<8301> שָׂרִיד ***śāriyḏ*** [SARID] 2x
<8302> שִׁרְיוֹן ***širyôn***, שִׁרְיָן ***širyān***, שִׁרְיָה ***širyāh*** [ARMOR] 8x
<8303> שִׂרְיֹן ***śiryōn*** [SIRION] 2x

<8304> שְׂרָיָה ***śᵉrāyāh,*** שְׂרָיָהוּ ***śᵉrāyāhû*** [SERAIAH] 18x
<8305> שָׂרִיק ***śāriyq*** [COMBED] 1x
<8306> שָׁרִיר ***šāriyr*** [MUSCLE] 1x
<8307> שְׁרִירוּת ***šᵉriyrût,*** שְׁרִרוּת ***šᵉrirût*** [STUBBORNESS] 10x
<8308> שָׂרַךְ ***śārak*** [TRAVERSE] 1x
<8309> שְׁרֵמָה ***šᵉrêmāh*** [FIELD] 1x
<8310> שַׂרְסְכִים ***śarsᵉkiym*** [SAR-SEKIM] 1x
<8311> שָׂרַע ***śāraʻ*** [DEFORMED (BE)] 2x, [STRETCH] 1x
<8312> שַׂרְעַפִּים ***śarʻappiym*** [ANXIETY] 2x
<8313> שָׂרַף ***śārap*** [BURN (verb)] 117x
<8314> שָׂרָף ***śārāp*** [SERPENT] 7x
<8315> שָׂרָף ***śārāp*** [SARAPH] 1x
<8316> שְׂרֵפָה ***śᵉrêpāh*** [BURNING (noun)] 13x
<8317> שָׁרַץ ***šāraṣ*** [MULTIPLY] 134x
<8318> שֶׁרֶץ ***šereṣ*** [CREATURE (LIVING, MOVING)] 15x
<8319> שָׁרַק ***šāraq*** [HISS] 12x
<8320> שָׂרֹק ***śārōq*** [SORREL] 1x
<8321> שֹׂרֵק ***śōrêq,*** שֹׂרֵקָה ***śōrêqāh*** [VINE (CHOICE, CHOICEST, NOBLE)] 3x
<8322> שְׁרֵקָה ***šᵉrêqāh*** [HISSING] 7x
<8323> שָׂרַר ***śārar*** [RULE (verb)] 4x
<8324> שֹׁרֵר ***šôrêr,*** שׁוֹרֵר ***šôrêr*** [ENEMY] 5x
<8325> שָׁרָר ***šārār*** [SHARAR] 1x
<8326> שֹׁרֶר ***šōrer*** [NAVEL] 1x
<8327> שָׁרַשׁ ***šāraš*** [ROOT (TAKE)] 8x
<8328> שֶׁרֶשׁ ***šereš*** [ROOT (noun)] 33x
<8329> שֶׁרֶשׁ ***šereš*** [SHERESH] 1x
<8330> שֹׁרֶשׁ ***šōreš*** [ROOT (noun)] 3x
<8331> שַׁרְשָׁה ***šaršāh*** [CHAIN] 1x
<8332> שְׁרֹשׁוּ ***šᵉrōšû*** [BANISHMENT] 1x
<8333> שַׁרְשְׁרָה ***šaršᵉrāh*** [CHAIN] 5x
<8334> שָׁרַת ***šārat*** [SERVE] 97x
<8335> שָׁרֵת ***šārêt*** [SERVICE] 2x
<8336> שֵׁשׁ ***šêš*** [LINEN, FINE LINEN] 25x
<8337> שֵׁשׁ ***šêš,*** שִׁשָּׁה ***šiššāh*** [SIX, SIXTH] 215x
<8338> שָׁשָׁא ***šāšā'*** [DRIVE] 1x
<8339> שֶׁשְׁבַּצַּר ***šešbaṣṣar*** [SHESHBAZZAR] 2x
<8340> שֵׁשְׁבַּצַּר ***šêšbaṣṣār*** [SHESHBAZZAR] 2x
<8341> שָׁשָׁה ***šāšāh*** [SIXTH PART (GIVE A)] 1x
<8342> שָׂשׂוֹן ***śāśôn*** [JOY] 22x
<8343> שָׁשַׁי ***šāšay*** [SHASHAI] 1x
<8344> שֵׁשַׁי ***šêšai*** [SHESHAI] 3x
<8345> שִׁשִּׁי ***šiššiy*** [SIXTH] 28x
<8346> שִׁשִּׁים ***šiššiym*** [SIXTY] 59x
<8347> שֵׁשַׁךְ ***šêšak*** [SHESHACH] 2x
<8348> שֵׁשָׁן ***šêšān*** [SHESHAN] 5x
<8349> שָׁשָׁק ***šāšāq*** [SHASHAK] 2x
<8350> שָׁשֵׁר ***šāšêr*** [VERMILION] 2x
<8351> שֵׁת ***šêt*** [BUTTOCKS] 2x
<8352> שֵׁת ***šêt*** [SETH] 9x
<8353> שֵׁת ***šêt,*** שִׁת ***šit*** [SIX, SIXTH] 2x
<8354> שָׁתָה ***šātāh*** [DRINK (verb)] 217x

<8355> שְׁתָה ***š^{e}ṯāh*** [DRINK (verb)] 5x
<8356> שָׁתָה ***šāṯāh*** [FOUNDATION] 2x
<8357> שֵׁתָה ***šēṯāh*** [BUTTOCKS] 1x
<8358> שְׁתִי ***š^{e}ṯiy*** [DRUNKENNESS] 1x
<8359> שְׁתִי ***š^{e}ṯiy*** [WARP] 1x
<8360> שְׁתִיָּה ***š^{e}ṯiyyāh*** [DRINKING] 1x
<8361> שִׁתִּין ***šittiyn*** [SIXTY] 4x
<8362> שָׁתַל ***šāṯal*** [PLANT (verb)] 10x
<8363> שְׁתִל ***š^{e}ṯil,*** שָׁתִיל ***šāṯiyl*** [PLANT (noun)] 1x
<8364> שֻׁתַלְחִי ***šuṯalḥiy*** [SHUTHELAHITE] 1x
<8365> שָׁתַם ***šāṯam*** [OPEN, BE OPEN] 2x
<8366> שָׁתַן ***šaṯan*** [URINATE AGAINST THE WALL] 6x
<8367> שָׁתַק ***šāṯaq*** [QUIET (BE)] 4x
<8368> שָׁתַר ***šāṯar*** [BREAK OUT] 1x
<8369> שֵׁתָר ***šēṯar*** [SHETHAR] 1x
<8370> שְׁתַר בּוֹזְנַי ***š^{e}ṯar bôz^{e}nay*** [SHETHAR-BOZENAI] 4x
<8371> שָׁתַת ***šāṯaṯ*** [LAY, LAY CLAIM] 2x

ת Tau

<8372> תָּא ***tā'*** [ROOM] 13x
<8373> תָּאַב ***tā'aḇ*** [LONG FOR] 2x
<8374> תָּאַב ***tā'aḇ*** [ABHOR] 1x
<8375> תַּאֲבָה ***ta^{ă}ḇāh*** [LONGING] 1x
<8376> תָּאָה ***tā'āh*** [DRAW A LINE] 2x
<8377> תְּאוֹ ***t^{e}'ô*** [ANTELOPE] 2x
<8378> תַּאֲוָה ***ta^{ă}wāh*** [DESIRE (noun)] 20x
<8379> תַּאֲוָה ***ta^{ă}wāh*** [UTMOST BOUND] 1x
<8380> תָּאוֹם ***tā'ôm,*** תּוֹאָם ***tô'ām*** [TWIN] 4x
<8381> תַּאֲלָה ***ta^{ă}lāh*** [CURSE (noun)] 1x
<8382> תָּאַם ***tā'am*** [DOUBLE (BE)] 4x
<8383> תְּאֻן ***t^{e}'un*** [TOIL (noun)] 1x
<8384> תְּאֵנָה ***t^{e}'ēnāh*** [FIG, FIG TREE] 39x
<8385> תַּאֲנָה ***ta^{ă}nāh*** [HEAT (noun)] 1x, [OCCASION] 1x
<8386> תַּאֲנִיָּה ***ta^{ă}niyyāh*** [MOURNING] 2x
<8387> תַּאֲנַת שִׁלֹה ***ta^{ă}naṯ šilōh*** [TAANATH-SHILOH] 1x
<8388> תָּאַר ***tā'ar*** [OUTLINE (MAKE AN)] 2x [TURN (verb)] 7x
<8389> תֹּאַר ***tō'ar*** [FORM (noun)] 15x
<8390> תַּאֲרֵעַ ***ta^{ă}rēa'*** [TAREA] 1x
<8391> תְּאַשּׁוּר ***t^{e}^{ă}ššûr*** [BOX TREE] 2x
<8392> תֵּבָה ***tēḇāh*** [ARK] 28x
<8393> תְּבוּאָה ***t^{e}ḇû'āh*** [HARVEST] 42x
<8394> תְּבוּנָה ***t^{e}ḇûnāh*** [UNDERSTANDING] 43x
<8395> תְּבוּסָה ***t^{e}ḇûsāh*** [DOWNFALL] 1x
<8396> תָּבוֹר ***tāḇôr*** [TABOR] 10x
<8397> תֶּבֶל ***teḇel*** [PERVERSION] 2x
<8398> תֵּבֵל ***tēḇēl*** [WORLD] 36x
<8399> תַּבְלִית ***taḇliyṯ*** [DESTRUCTION] 1x
<8400> תְּבַלֻּל ***t^{e}ḇallul*** [DEFECT] 1x

<8401> תֶּבֶן ***teḇen*** [STRAW] 17x
<8402> תִּבְנִי ***tiḇniy*** [TIBNI] 2x
<8403> תַּבְנִית ***taḇniyṯ*** [PLAN (noun)] 20x
<8404> תַּבְעֵרָה ***taḇʻērāh*** [TABERAH] 2x
<8405> תֵּבֵץ ***têḇêṣ*** [THEBEZ] 3x
<8406> תְּבַר ***tᵉḇar*** [BRITTLE (BE)] 1x
<8407> תִּגְלַת פִּלְאֶסֶר ***tiglaṯ pil'eser,*** תִּלְגַת פִּלְנֶסֶר ***tilgaṯ pilneser,*** תִּלְגַת פִּלְנְאֶסֶר ***tilgaṯ pilnᵉ'eser*** [TIGLATH-PILESER] 6x
<8408> תַּגְמוּל ***tagmûl*** [BENEFIT] 1x
<8409> תִּגְרָה ***tigrāh*** [OPPOSITION] 1x
<8410> תִּדְהָר ***tiḏhār*** [PINE] 2x
<8411> תְּדִיר ***tᵉḏiyr,*** תְּדִירָא ***tᵉḏiyrā'*** [CONTINUALLY] 2x
<8412> תַּדְמֹר ***taḏmōr*** [TADMOR] 2x
<8413> תִּדְעָל ***tiḏʻāl*** [TIDAL] 2x
<8414> תֹּהוּ ***tōhû*** [FORMLESS] 20x
<8415> תְּהוֹם ***tᵉhôm,*** תְּהֹם ***tᵉhōm*** [DEEP (noun)] 36x
<8416> תְּהִלָּה ***tᵉhillāh*** [PRAISE (noun)] 57x
<8417> תָּהֳלָה ***tāhᵒlāh*** [ERROR] 1x
<8418> תַּהֲלֻכָה ***tahᵃluḵāh*** [PROCEEDING] 1x
<8419> תַּהְפֻּכָה ***tahpuḵāh*** [PERVERSE] 10x
<8420> תָּו ***tāw*** [MARK (noun)] 3x
<8421> תּוּב ***tûḇ*** [RETURN (verb)] 8x
<8422> תּוּבַל ***tûḇal,*** תֻּבַל ***tuḇal*** [TUBAL] 8x
<8423> תּוּבַל קַיִן ***tûḇal qayin*** [TUBAL-CAIN] 1x
<8424> תּוּגָה ***tûḡāh*** [SORROW (noun)] 4x
<8425> תּוֹגַרְמָה ***tôḡarmāh,*** תֹּגַרְמָה ***tōḡarmāh,*** בֵּית תּוֹגַרְמָה ***bêyṯ tôḡarmāh*** [TOGARMAH] 4x
<8426> תּוֹדָה ***tôḏāh*** [THANKSGIVING] 32x
<8427> תָּוָה ***tāwāh*** [SCRIBBLE] 2x
<8428> תָּוָה ***tāwāh*** [VEX] 1x
<8429> תְּוַהּ ***tᵉwah*** [ASTONISHED (BE)] 1x
<8430> תּוֹחַ ***tôaḥ*** [TOAH] 1x
<8431> תּוֹחֶלֶת ***tôḥeleṯ*** [HOPE (noun)] 6x
<8432> תָּוֶךְ ***tāweḵ*** [MIDST (IN THE)] 415x
<8433> תּוֹכֵחָה ***tôḵêḥāh,*** תּוֹכַחַת ***tôḵaḥaṯ*** [REBUKE (noun)] 28x
<8434> תּוֹלָד ***tôlāḏ*** [TOLAD] 1x
<8435> תּוֹלֵדוֹת ***tôlêḏôṯ*** [GENERATION] 39x
<8436> תִּילוֹן ***tiylôn*** [TILON] 1x
<8437> תּוֹלָל ***tôlāl*** [TORMENTOR] 1x
<8438> תּוֹלָע ***tôlāʻ,*** תּוֹלֵעָה ***tôlêʻāh,*** תּוֹלַעַת ***tôlaʻaṯ*** [CRIMSON] 43x
<8439> תּוֹלָע ***tôlāʻ*** [TOLA] 6x
<8440> תּוֹלָעִי ***tôlāʻiy*** [TOLAITE] 1x
<8441> תּוֹעֵבָה ***tôʻêḇāh,*** תֹּעֵבָה ***tōʻêḇāh*** [ABOMINATION] 117x
<8442> תּוֹעָה ***tôʻāh*** [ERROR] 2x
<8443> תּוֹעָפָה ***tôʻāpāh*** [STRENGTH] 4x
<8444> תּוֹצָאָה ***tôṣā'āh,*** תֹּצָאָה ***tōṣā'āh*** [BORDER] 23x
<8445> תּוֹקְהַת ***towqᵉhaṯ,*** תָּקְהַת ***toqhaṯ*** [TOKHATH] 1x
<8446> תּוּר ***tûr*** [SEEK OUT] 23x
<8447> תּוֹר ***tôr,*** תֹּר ***tōr*** [TURN (noun)] 5x
<8448> תּוֹר ***tôr*** [ESTATE] 1x
<8449> תּוֹר ***tôr,*** תֹּר ***tōr*** [TURTLEDOVE] 14x
<8450> תּוֹר ***tôr*** [BULL] 7x

<8451> תּוֹרָה ***tôrâh,*** תֹּרָה ***tōrâh*** [LAW] 219x

<8452> תּוֹרָה ***tôrâh*** [CUSTOM] 1x

<8453> תּוֹשָׁב ***tôšāḇ,*** תֹּשָׁב ***tōšāḇ,*** תִּשְׁבֵּי ***tišbêy*** [SOJOURNER] 14x

<8454> תּוּשִׁיָּה ***tûšiyyâh*** [WISDOM] 12x

<8455> תּוֹתָח ***tôṯāḥ*** [CLUB] 1x

<8456> תָּזַז ***tāzaz*** [CUT DOWN] 1x

<8457> תַּזְנוּת ***taznûṯ*** [PROSTITUTION] 20x

<8458> תַּחְבֻּלָה ***taḥbulâh*** [COUNSEL (noun)] 6x

<8459> תֹּחוּ ***tōḥû*** [TOHU] 1x

<8460> תְּחוֹת ***t^{e}ḥôṯ*** [UNDER] 4x

<8461> תַּחְכְּמֹנִי ***taḥk^{e}mōniy*** [TAHKEMONITE] 1x

<8462> תְּחִלָּה ***t^{e}ḥillâh*** [BEGINNING] 22x

<8463> תַּחֲלוּא ***taḥ^{a}lû',*** תַּחֲלֻא ***taḥ^{a}lu'*** [SICKNESS] 5x

<8464> תַּחְמָס ***taḥmās*** [OWL] 2x

<8465> תַּחַן ***taḥan*** [TAHAN] 2x

<8466> תַּחֲנָה ***taḥ^{a}nâh*** [CAMP] 1x

<8467> תְּחִנָּה ***t^{e}ḥinnâh*** [SUPPLICATION] 25x

<8468> תְּחִנָּה ***t^{e}ḥinnâh*** [TEHINNAH] 1x

<8469> תַּחֲנוּן ***taḥ^{a}nûn*** [SUPPLICATION] 18x

<8470> תַּחֲנִי ***taḥ^{a}niy*** [TAHANITE] 1x

<8471> תַּחְפַּנְחֵס ***taḥpanḥês,*** תְּחַפְנְחֵס ***t^{e}ḥap̱n^{e}ḥês*** [TAHPANHES] 7x

<8472> תַּחְפְּנֵיס ***taḥp^{e}nêys*** [TAHPENES] 2x

<8473> תַּחְרָא ***taḥrā'*** [COAT OF MAIL] 2x

<8474> תַּחֲרָה ***taḥ^{a}râh*** [COMPETE] 2x

<8475> תַּחְרֵעַ ***taḥrêa'*** [TAHREA] 1x

<8476> תָּחַשׁ ***tāḥaš*** [BADGER] 14x

<8477> תַּחַשׁ ***taḥaš*** [TAHASH, THAHASH] 1x

<8478> תַּחַת ***taḥaṯ*** [UNDER] 313x

<8479> תַּחַת ***taḥaṯ*** [UNDER] 1x

<8480> תַּחַת ***taḥaṯ*** [TAHATH] 6x

<8481> תַּחְתּוֹן ***taḥtôn*** [LOWER, LOWEST] 13x

<8482> תַּחְתִּי ***taḥtiy*** [LOWER, LOWEST] 14x

<8483> תַּחְתִּים חָדְשִׁי ***taḥtiym ḥoḏšiy*** [TAHTIM-HODSHI] 1x

<8484> תִּיכוֹן ***tiyḵôn,*** תִּיכֹן ***tiyḵōn*** [MIDDLE] 11x

<8485> תֵּימָא ***têymā'*** [TEMA] 5x

<8486> תֵּימָן ***têymān*** [SOUTH] 23x

<8487> תֵּימָן ***têymān*** [TEMAN] 12x

<8488> תֵּימְנִי ***têym^{e}niy*** [TEMENI] 1x

<8489> תֵּימָנִי ***têymāniy*** [TEMANITE] 8x

<8490> תִּימָרָה ***tiymārâh*** [COLUMN] 2x

<8491> תִּיצִי ***tiyṣiy*** [TIZITE] 1x

<8492> תִּירוֹשׁ ***tiyrôš*** [NEW WINE] 38x

<8493> תִּירְיָא ***tiyryā'*** [TIRIA] 1x

<8494> תִּירָס ***tiyrās*** [TIRAS] 2x

<8495> תַּיִשׁ ***tayiš*** [GOAT] 4x

<8496> תֹּךְ ***tōḵ,*** תּוֹךְ ***tôḵ*** [OPPRESSION] 4x

<8497> תָּכָה ***tāḵâh*** [SIT DOWN] 1x

<8498> תְּכוּנָה ***t^{e}ḵûnâh*** [ARRANGEMENT] 3x

<8499> תְּכוּנָה ***t^{e}khûnâh*** [SEAT] 1x

<8500> תֻּכִּיִּים ***tukkiyyiym*** [PEACOCK] 2x

<8501> תָּכָךְ ***tāḵaḵ*** [OPPRESSOR] 1x

<8502> תִּכְלָה ***tiḵlāh*** [PERFECTION] 1x
<8503> תַּכְלִית ***taḵliyṯ*** [END] 5x
<8504> תְּכֵלֶת ***t***^{e}***ḵêleṯ*** [BLUE] 50x
<8505> תָּכַן ***tāḵan*** [WEIGH] 18x
<8506> תֹּכֶן ***tōḵen*** [QUOTA] 2x
<8507> תֹּכֶן ***tōḵen*** [TOKEN] 1x
<8508> תָּכְנִית ***toḵniyṯ*** [PERFECTION] 2x
<8509> תַּכְרִיךְ ***taḵriyḵ*** [ROBE] 1x
<8510> תֵּל ***têl*** [HEAP (noun)] 5x
<8511> תָּלָא ***tālā'*** [HANG] 3x
<8512> תֵּל אָבִיב ***têl 'āḇiyḇ*** [TEL-ABIB] 1x
<8513> תְּלָאָה ***t***^{e}***lā'āh*** [HARDSHIP] 5x
<8514> תַּלְאוּבָה ***tal'ûḇāh*** [DROUGHT] 1x
<8515> תְּלַאשָּׂר ***t***^{e}***la'śśār*** [TEL ASSAR] 2x
<8516> תִּלְבֹּשֶׁת ***tilbōšeṯ*** [CLOTHING] 1x
<8517> תְּלַג ***t***^{e}***lag*** [SNOW] 1x
<8518> תָּלָה ***tālāh*** [HANG] 28x
<8519> תְּלֻנָּה ***t***^{e}***lunāh*** [GRUMBLING] 8x
<8520> תֶּלַח ***telaḥ*** [TELAH] 1x
<8521> תֵּל חַרְשָׁא ***tel ḥarša'*** [TEL HARSHA] 2x
<8522> תְּלִי ***t***^{e}***liy*** [QUIVER] 1x
<8523> תְּלִיתָי ***t***^{e}***liyṯāy,*** תַּלְתַּי ***taltay*** [THIRD] 2x
<8524> תָּלוּל ***tālûl*** [LOFTY] 1x
<8525> תֶּלֶם ***telem*** [FURROW] 5x
<8526> תַּלְמַי ***talmay*** [TALMAI] 6x
<8527> תַּלְמִיד ***talmiyḏ*** [PUPIL] 1x
<8528> תֵּל מְלַח ***têl m***^{e}***laḥ*** [TEL MELAH] 2x
<8529> תָּלַע ***tāla'*** [SCARLET] 1x
<8530> תַּלְפִּיּוֹת ***talpiyyôṯ*** [ROWS OF STONES] 1x
<8531> תְּלַת ***t***^{e}***laṯ,*** תַּלְתָּא ***taltā'*** [THIRD] 1x
<8532> תְּלָת ***t***^{e}***lāṯ,*** תְּלָתָה ***t***^{e}***lāṯāh*** [THREE, THIRD] 11x
<8533> תְּלָתִין ***t***^{e}***lāṯiyn*** [THIRTY] 2x
<8534> תַּלְתַּל ***taltal*** [WAVY] 1x
<8535> תָּם ***tām*** [PERFECT (adj.)] 13x
<8536> תָּם ***tām,*** תַּמָּה ***tammāh*** [THERE] 4x
<8537> תֹּם ***tōm*** [COMPLETENESS] 27x
<8538> תֻּמָּה ***tummāh*** [INTEGRITY] 5x
<8539> תָּמַהּ ***tāmah*** [ASTONISHED (BE)] 8x
<8540> תְּמַהּ ***t***^{e}***mah*** [WONDER] 3x
<8541> תִּמָּהוֹן ***timmāhôn*** [CONFUSION] 2x
<8542> תַּמּוּז ***tāmmûz*** [TAMMUZ] 1x
<8543> תְּמוֹל ***t***^{e}***môl,*** תְּמֹל ***t***^{e}***mōl*** [BEFORE] 23x
<8544> תְּמוּנָה ***t***^{e}***mûnāh*** [LIKENESS] 10x
<8545> תְּמוּרָה ***t***^{e}***mûrāh*** [EXCHANGE (noun)] 6x
<8546> תְּמוּתָה ***t***^{e}***mûṯāh*** [DEATH] 2x
<8547> תֶּמַח ***temaḥ*** [TEMAH] 2x
<8548> תָּמִיד ***tāmiyḏ*** [CONTINUITY] 104x
<8549> תָּמִים ***tāmiym*** [COMPLETE (adj.)] 91x
<8550> תֻּמִּים ***tummiym*** [THUMMIN] 5x
<8551> תָּמַךְ ***tāmaḵ*** [GRASP] 21x
<8552> תָּמַם ***tāmam*** [COMPLETE (BE)] 64x

<8553> תִּמְנָה ***timnāh*** [TIMNAH] 12x
<8554> תִּמְנִי ***timniy*** [TIMNITE] 1x
<8555> תִּמְנָע ***timnā‘*** [TIMNA] 6x
<8556> תִּמְנַת חֶרֶס ***timnat̲ ḥeres,*** תִּמְנַת סֶרַח ***timnat̲ seraḥ*** [TIMNATH HERES, TIMNATH SERAH] 3x
<8557> תֶּמֶס ***temes*** [MELT AWAY] 1x
<8558> תָּמָר ***tāmār*** [PALM TREE] 12x
<8559> תָּמָר ***tāmār*** [TAMAR] 24x
<8560> תֹּמֶר ***tōmer*** [PALM TREE] 2x
<8561> תִּמֹרָה ***timōrāh*** [PALM TREE] 19x
<8562> תַּמְרוּק ***tamrûq*** [COSMETICS] 4x
<8563> תַּמְרוּר ***tamrûr*** [BITTER, BITTERLY] 3x
<8564> תַּמְרוּר ***tamrûr*** [GUIDEPOST] 1x
<8565> תַּן ***tān*** [JACKAL] 14x
<8566> תָּנָה ***tānāh*** [HIRE] 2x
<8567> תָּנָה ***tānāh*** [RECOUNT] 2x
<8568> תָּנָּה ***tānnāh*** [DRAGON] 1x
<8569> תְּנוּאָה ***tᵉnû’āh*** [OPPOSITION] 2x
<8570> תְּנוּבָה ***tᵉnûḇāh*** [FRUIT] 5x
<8571> תְּנוּךְ ***tᵉnûḵ*** [LOBE] 8x
<8572> תְּנוּמָה ***tᵉnûmāh*** [SLUMBER (noun)] 5x
<8573> תְּנוּפָה ***tᵉnûp̄āh*** [WAVE OFFERING, WAVING OFFERING] 30x
<8574> תַּנּוּר ***tannûr*** [FURNACE] 15x
<8575> תַּנְחוּם ***tanḥûm*** [CONSOLATION] 5x
<8576> תַּנְחֻמֶת ***tanḥumet̲*** [TANHUMETH] 2x
<8577> תַּנִּין ***tanniyn*** [SERPENT] 28x
<8578> תִּנְיָן ***tinyān*** [SECOND] 1x
<8579> תִּנְיָנוּת ***tinyānût̲*** [SECOND TIME] 1x
<8580> תִּנְשֶׁמֶת ***tinšemet̲*** [WHITE OWL] 3x
<8581> תָּעַב ***ta‘aḇ*** [ABHOR] 22x
<8582> תָּעָה ***tā‘āh*** [WANDER] 50x
<8583> תֹּעוּ ***tō‘û,*** תֹּעִי ***tō‘iy*** [TOU] 5x
<8584> תְּעוּדָה ***tᵉ‘ûḏāh*** [TESTIMONY] 3x
<8585> תְּעָלָה ***tᵉ‘ālāh*** [HEALING] 2x, [TRENCH] 9x
<8586> תַּעֲלוּלִים ***taᵃlûliym*** [CAPRICIOUS CHILDREN] 2x
<8587> תַּעֲלֻמָה ***taᵃlumāh*** [SECRET] 3x
<8588> תַּעֲנוּג ***taᵃnûḡ*** [DELIGHT (noun)] 5x
<8589> תַּעֲנִית ***taᵃniyt̲*** [FASTING] 1x
<8590> תַּעְנָךְ ***ta‘nāḵ,*** תַּעְנַךְ ***ta‘naḵ*** [TAANACH] 7x
<8591> תָּעַע ***tā‘a‘,*** תְּעוּפָה ***tᵉ‘ûp̄āh*** [DECEIVE] 3x
<8592> תַּעֲצֻמָה ***taᵃṣumāh*** [POWER] 1x
<8593> תַּעַר ***ta‘ar***[RAZOR] 13x
<8594> תַּעֲרוּבָה ***taᵃrûḇāh*** [HOSTAGE] 2x
<8595> תַּעְתֻּעִים ***ta‘tu‘iym*** [MOCKERY] 2x
<8596> תֹּף ***tōp̄*** [TAMBOURINE] 17x
<8597> תִּפְאָרָה ***tiph’ārāh*** [BEAUTY] 51x
<8598> תַּפּוּחַ ***tappûaḥ*** [APPLE, APPLE TREE] 6x
<8599> תַּפּוּחַ ***tappûaḥ*** [TAPPUAH] 5x
<8600> תְּפוֹצָה ***tᵉpôṣāh*** [DISPERSION] 1x
<8601> תֻּפִּינִים ***tuppiyniym*** [BAKED] 1x
<8602> תָּפֵל ***tāp̄êl*** [FOOLISH] 7x

<8603> תֹּפֶל ***tōp̱el*** [TOPHEL] 1x
<8604> תִּפְלָה ***tip̱lāh*** [WRONGDOING] 3x
<8605> תְּפִלָּה ***tᵉp̱illāh*** [PRAYER] 77x
<8606> תִּפְלֶצֶת ***tip̱leṣeṯ*** [TERROR] 1x
<8607> תִּפְסַח ***tip̱saḥ*** [TIPHSAH] 2x
<8608> תָּפַף ***tāp̱ap̱*** [TAMBOURINES (PLAYING, BEATING)] 2x
<8609> תָּפַר ***tāp̱ar*** [SEW] 4x
<8610> תָּפַשׂ ***tāp̱aś*** [CATCH (verb)] 65x
<8611> תֹּפֶת ***tōp̱eṯ*** [SPIT (noun)] 1x
<8612> תֹּפֶת ***tōp̱eṯ*** [TOPHETH] 9x
<8613> תָּפְתֶּה ***top̱teh*** [TOPHET, TOPHETH] 1x
<8614> תִּפְתָּי ***tip̱tāy*** [MAGISTRATE] 2x
<8615> תִּקְוָה ***tiqwāh*** [CORD] 2x, [HOPE (noun)] 32x
<8616> תִּקְוָה ***tiqwāh*** [TIKVAH] 3x
<8617> תְּקוּמָה ***tᵉqûmāh*** [STAND (verb)] 1x
<8618> תְּקוֹמֵם ***tᵉqômêm*** [RISES UP (ONE WHO)] 1x
<8619> תָּקוֹעַ ***tāqôaʻ*** [TRUMPET] 1x
<8620> תְּקוֹעַ ***tᵉqôaʻ*** [TEKOA] 7x
<8621> תְּקוֹעִי ***tᵉqôʻiy,*** תְּקֹעִי ***tᵉqōʻiy*** [TEKOITE] 7x
<8622> תְּקוּפָה ***tᵉqûp̱āh*** [TURN (noun)] 4x
<8623> תַּקִּיף ***taqqiyp̱*** [MIGHTY] 4x
<8624> תַּקִּיף ***taqqiyp̱*** [MIGHTY] 5x
<8625> תְּקַל ***tᵉqal,*** תְּקֵל ***tᵉqêl*** [WEIGH] 3x
<8626> תָּקַן ***tāqan*** [STRAIGHT (MAKE)] 3x
<8627> תְּקַן ***tᵉqan*** [ESTABLISHED (BE)] 1x
<8628> תָּקַע ***tāqaʻ*** [BLOW (verb)] 69x
<8629> תֵּקַע ***têqaʻ*** [SOUND] 1x
<8630> תָּקֵף ***tāqêp̱*** [PREVAIL] 3x
<8631> תְּקֵף ***tᵉqêp̱*** [STRONG (BE, BECOME, GROW)] 5x
<8632> תְּקָף ***tᵉqāp̱,*** תְּקֹף ***tᵉqōp̱*** [MIGHT] 2x
<8633> תֹּקֶף ***tōqep̱*** [AUTHORITY] 3x
<8634> תַּרְאֲלָה ***tarʼᵃlāh*** [TARALAH] 1x
<8635> תַּרְבּוּת ***tarbûṯ*** [BROOD] 1x
<8636> תַּרְבִּית ***tarbiyṯ*** [PROFIT (noun)] 6x
<8637> תִּרְגַּל ***tirgal*** [WALK (TEACH TO)] 1x
<8638> תִּרְגַּם ***tirgam*** [TRANSLATE] 1x
<8639> תַּרְדֵּמָה ***tardêmāh*** [DEEP SLEEP] 7x
<8640> תִּרְהָקָה ***tirhāqāh*** [TIRHAKAH] 2x
<8641> תְּרוּמָה ***tᵉrûmāh*** [OFFERING] 76x
<8642> תְּרוּמִיָּה ***tᵉrûmiyyāh*** [ALLOTMENT] 1x
<8643> תְּרוּעָה ***tᵉrûʻāh*** [SHOUT (noun)] 36x
<8644> תְּרוּפָה ***tᵉrûp̱āh*** [HEALING] 1x
<8645> תִּרְזָה ***tirzāh*** [CYPRESS] 1x
<8646> תֶּרַח ***teraḥ*** [TERAH] 13x
<8647> תִּרְחֲנָה ***tirḥᵃnāh*** [TIRHANAH] 1x
<8648> תְּרֵין ***tᵉrêyn*** [TWO] 4x
<8649> תָּרְמָה ***tarmāh,*** תַּרְמִית ***tarmiyṯ*** [DECETFULNESS] 6x
<8650> תֹּרֶן ***tōren*** [FLAG] 3x
<8651> תְּרַע ***tᵉraʻ*** [COURT] 2x
<8652> תָּרָע ***tārāʻ*** [DOORKEEPER] 1x
<8653> תַּרְעֵלָה ***tarʻêlāh*** [STAGGER (THAT MAKES)] [3] x

<8654> תִּרְעָתִים ***tir'āṯiym*** [TIRAHITES] 1x
<8655> תְּרָפִים ***t***^{e}***rāp̱iym*** [HOUSEHOLD IDOL] 15x
<8656> תִּרְצָה ***tirṣāh*** [TIRZAH] 18x
<8657> תֶּרֶשׁ ***tereš*** [TERESH] 2x
<8658> תַּרְשִׁישׁ ***taršiyš*** [BERYL] 7x
<8659> תַּרְשִׁישׁ ***taršiyš*** [TARSHISH (proper noun)] 4x
<8660> תִּרְשָׁתָא ***tiršāṯā'*** [GOVERNOR] 4x
<8661> תַּרְתָּן ***tartān*** [TARTAN] 2x
<8662> תַּרְתָּק ***tartāq*** [TARTAK] 1x
<8663> תְּשֻׁאָה ***t***^{e}***shu'āh,*** תְּשֻׁוָה ***t***^{e}***shûwāh*** [STORM (noun)] 5x
<8664> תִּשְׁבִּי ***tišbey*** [TISHBITE] 6x
<8665> תַּשְׁבֵּץ ***tašbêṣ*** [WOVEN] 1x
<8666> תְּשׁוּבָה ***t***^{e}***šûḇāh*** [RETURN (noun)] 8x
<8667> תְּשׂוּמֶת ***t***^{e}***śûmeṯ*** [SECURITY] 1x
<8668> תְּשׁוּעָה ***t***^{e}***šû'āh*** [DELIVERANCE] 34x
<8669> תְּשׁוּקָה ***t***^{e}***šûqāh*** [DESIRE (noun)] 3x
<8670> תְּשׁוּרָה ***t***^{e}***šûrāh*** [PRESENT (noun)] 1x
<8671> תְּשִׁיעִי ***t***^{e}***šiy'iy*** [NINTH] 18x
<8672> תֵּשַׁע ***têša'*** [NINE] 68x
<8673> תִּשְׁעִים ***tiš'iym*** [NINETY] 20x
<8674> תַּתְּנַי ***tatt***^{e}***nay*** [TATNAI, TATTENAI] 4x

Bibliography

The Complete Word Study Dictionary: Old Testament

Abbreviated Bibliography

Abegg, Martin, Jr., Peter Flint and Eugene Ulrich. *The Dead Sea Scrolls Bible.* San Francisco: Harper Collins Publishers, 1999.

Botterweck, G. and H. Ringgren. *Theological Dictionary of the Old Testament.* Translated by John T. Willis. Grand Rapids: Eerdmans, 1974.

Bromiley, Geoffrey W. *The International Standard Bible Encyclopedia.* 4 vols. William B. Eerdmans Publishing Company, 1970–1988.

Brown, F., S. R. Driver, and C. Briggs, eds. *A Hebrew and English Lexicon of the Old Testament.* Oxford: Clarendon Press, 1907.

Carpenter, Eugene E. and Philip Comfort. *Treasury of Key Bible Words.* Nashville, TN: Broadman, 2000.

Harris, R. Laird, Gleason L. Archer, Jr., and Bruce K. Waltke. *Theological Wordbook of the Old Testament.* 2 vols. Chicago: Moody Press, 1980.

Holladay, William L., ed. *A Concise Hebrew and Aramaic Lexicon of the Old Testament.* Leiden: E. J. Brill, 1971.

Jenni, E. and C. Westermann. *Theologisches Handworterbuch zum Alten Testament.* Munchen: Chr. Kaise, 1979.

Jones, Alfred. *Jones' Dictionary of Old Testament Proper Names.* 1856. Reprint edition. Grand Rapids: Kregel, 1990.

Koehler, L., W. Baumgartner, and J. Stamm, eds. *The Hebrew and Aramaic Lexicon of the Old Testament.* Leiden: E. J. Brill, 1996.

Owens, J., ed. *Analytical Key to the Old Testament.* Grand Rapids: Baker, 1990.

Rasmussen, Carl G. *Zondervan NIV Atlas of the Bible.* Grand Rapids, MI: Zondervan Publishing House, 1989.

VanGemeren, W., ed. *New International Dictionary of Old Testament Theology and Exegesis.* Grand Rapids: Zondervan, 1997.

Wood, Leon J. *A Survey of Israel's History.* Rev. ed., David O'Brien. Grand Rapids, MI: Zondervan Publishing House, 1986.

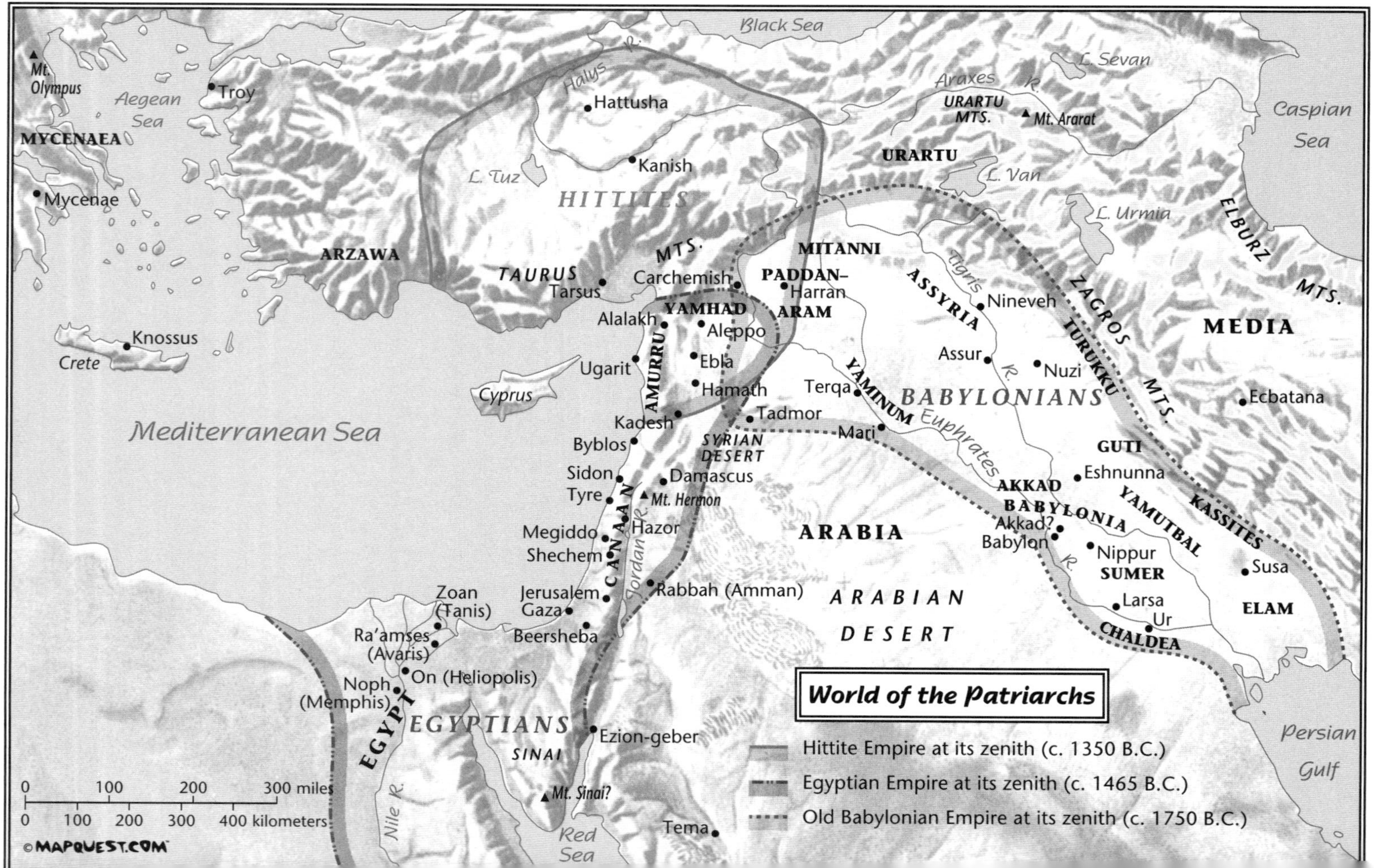
World of the Patriarchs
Hittite Empire at its zenith (c. 1350 B.C.)
Egyptian Empire at its zenith (c. 1465 B.C.)
Old Babylonian Empire at its zenith (c. 1750 B.C.)
Black Sea
Caspian Sea
Aegean Sea
Mediterranean Sea
Persian Gulf
Red Sea
Mt. Olympus
MYCENAEA
Mycenae
Troy
Crete
Knossus
ARZAWA
Cyprus
Hattusha
Halys R.
L. Tuz
Kanish
HITTITES
TAURUS MTS.
Tarsus
Carchemish
MITANNI
PADDAN–ARAM
Harran
YAMHAD
Alalakh
Aleppo
Ebla
Ugarit
AMURRU
Hamath
Kadesh
Byblos
Sidon
Tyre
Mt. Hermon
Damascus
SYRIAN DESERT
Tadmor
Terqa
YAMINUM
Mari
CANAAN
Hazor
Megiddo
Shechem
Jordan R.
Jerusalem
Gaza
Beersheba
Rabbah (Amman)
Zoan (Tanis)
Ra'amses (Avaris)
On (Heliopolis)
Noph (Memphis)
EGYPT
EGYPTIANS
Nile R.
SINAI
Mt. Sinai?
Ezion-geber
Tema
ARABIA
ARABIAN DESERT
URARTU MTS.
Araxes R.
Mt. Ararat
L. Sevan
URARTU
L. Van
L. Urmia
ASSYRIA
Tigris R.
Nineveh
Assur
Nuzi
BABYLONIANS
Euphrates
ZAGROS MTS.
TURUKKU
ELBURZ MTS.
MEDIA
Ecbatana
GUTI
Eshnunna
AKKAD
BABYLONIA
Akkad?
Babylon
YAMUTBAL
KASSITES
Nippur
SUMER
Susa
ELAM
Larsa
Ur
CHALDEA
0 100 200 300 miles
0 100 200 300 400 kilometers
©MAPQUEST.COM

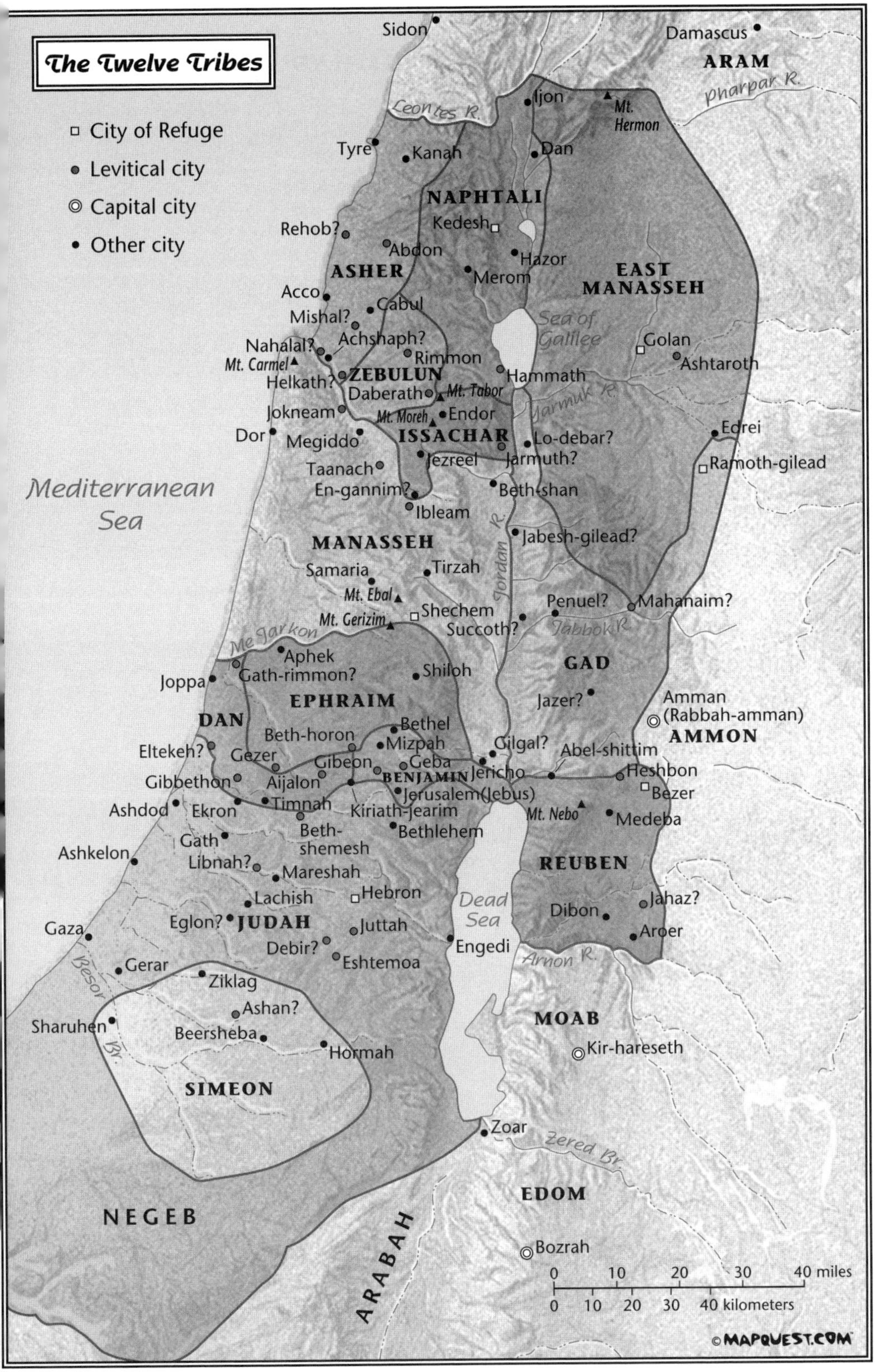
The Twelve Tribes
City of Refuge
Levitical city
Capital city
Other city
Sidon
Damascus
ARAM
Pharpar R.
Leontes R.
Ijon
Mt. Hermon
Tyre
Kanah
Dan
NAPHTALI
Kedesh
Rehob?
Abdon
Hazor
ASHER
Merom
EAST MANASSEH
Acco
Cabul
Mishal?
Sea of Galilee
Nahalal?
Achshaph?
Golan
Mt. Carmel
Rimmon
Ashtaroth
Helkath?
ZEBULUN
Hammath
Daberath
Mt. Tabor
Yarmuk R.
Jokneam
Mt. Moreh
Endor
Edrei
Dor
Megiddo
ISSACHAR
Lo-debar?
Jezreel
Jarmuth?
Taanach
Ramoth-gilead
Mediterranean Sea
En-gannim?
Beth-shan
Ibleam
Jordan R.
Jabesh-gilead?
MANASSEH
Samaria
Tirzah
Mt. Ebal
Penuel?
Mahanaim?
Shechem
Mt. Gerizim
Succoth?
Jabbok R.
Me Jarkon
Aphek
GAD
Shiloh
Joppa
Gath-rimmon?
EPHRAIM
Amman (Rabbah-amman)
Jazer?
DAN
Bethel
AMMON
Beth-horon
Mizpah
Gilgal?
Elteketh?
Gezer
Abel-shittim
Gibeon
Geba
Heshbon
Gibbethon
Aijalon
BENJAMIN
Jericho
Bezer
Timnah
Jerusalem (Jebus)
Ashdod
Ekron
Kiriath-jearim
Mt. Nebo
Medeba
Beth-shemesh
Bethlehem
Gath
Ashkelon
Libnah?
Mareshah
REUBEN
Lachish
Hebron
Dead Sea
Jahaz?
Dibon
Eglon?
JUDAH
Juttah
Gaza
Aroer
Debir?
Engedi
Eshtemoa
Arnon R.
Gerar
Besor Br.
Ziklag
Ashan?
MOAB
Sharuhen
Beersheba
Hormah
Kir-hareseth
SIMEON
Zoar
Zered Br.
EDOM
NEGEB
ARABAH
Bozrah
0 10 20 30 40 miles
0 10 20 30 40 kilometers
©MAPQUEST.COM

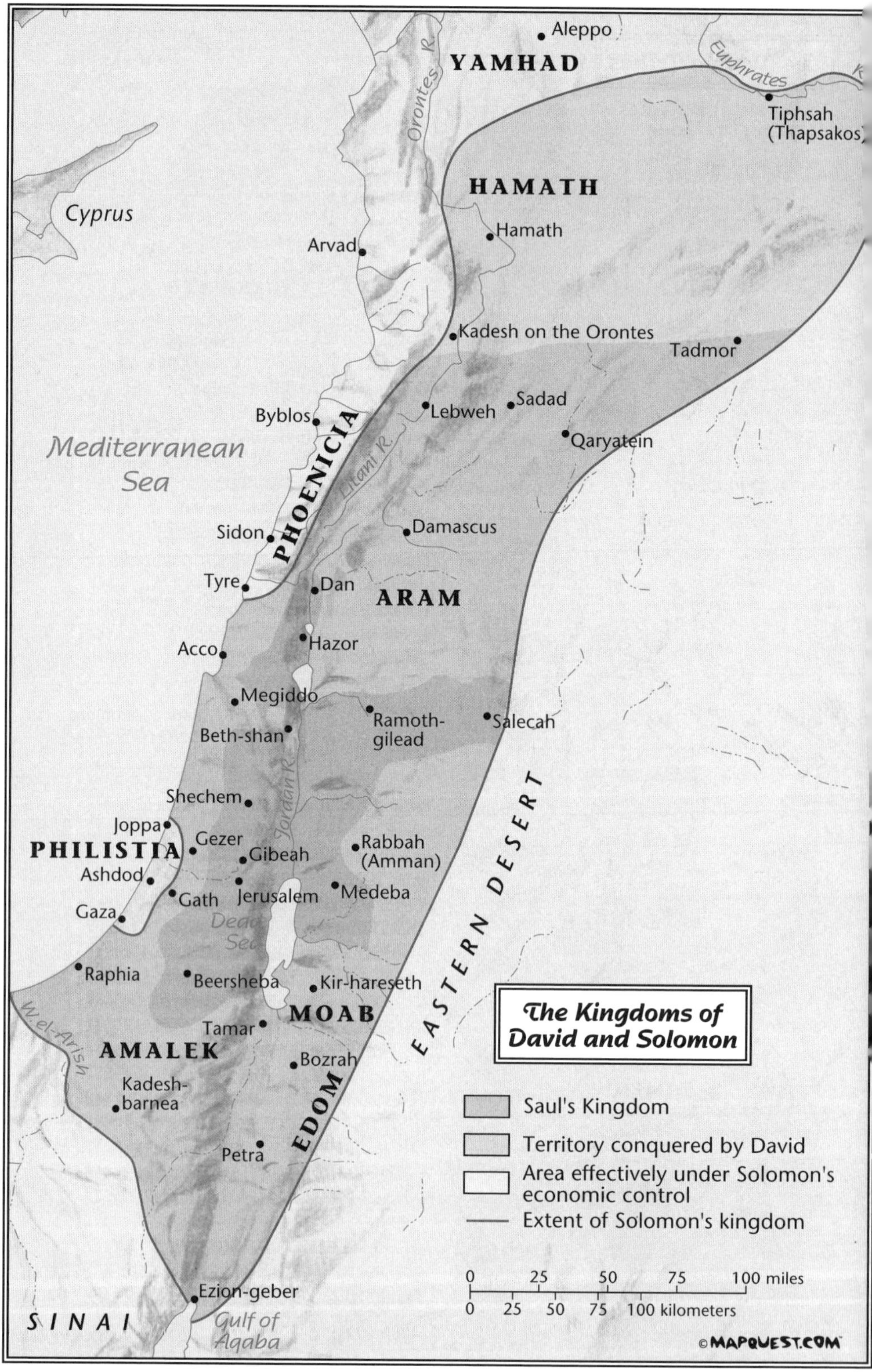
The Kingdoms of David and Solomon
Saul's Kingdom
Territory conquered by David
Area effectively under Solomon's economic control
Extent of Solomon's kingdom
0 25 50 75 100 miles
0 25 50 75 100 kilometers
©MAPQUEST.COM
Aleppo
YAMHAD
Euphrates R.
Orontes R.
Tiphsah (Thapsakos)
Cyprus
HAMATH
Hamath
Arvad
Kadesh on the Orontes
Tadmor
Byblos
Lebweh
Sadad
PHOENICIA
Litani R.
Qaryatein
Mediterranean Sea
Sidon
Damascus
Tyre
Dan
ARAM
Acco
Hazor
Megiddo
Ramoth-gilead
Salecah
Beth-shan
Shechem
Jordan R.
Joppa
Gezer
PHILISTIA
Gibeah
Rabbah (Amman)
Ashdod
Jerusalem
Medeba
Gath
Gaza
Dead Sea
EASTERN DESERT
Raphia
Beersheba
Kir-hareseth
W. el-Arish
MOAB
Tamar
AMALEK
Bozrah
Kadesh-barnea
EDOM
Petra
Ezion-geber
SINAI
Gulf of Aqaba

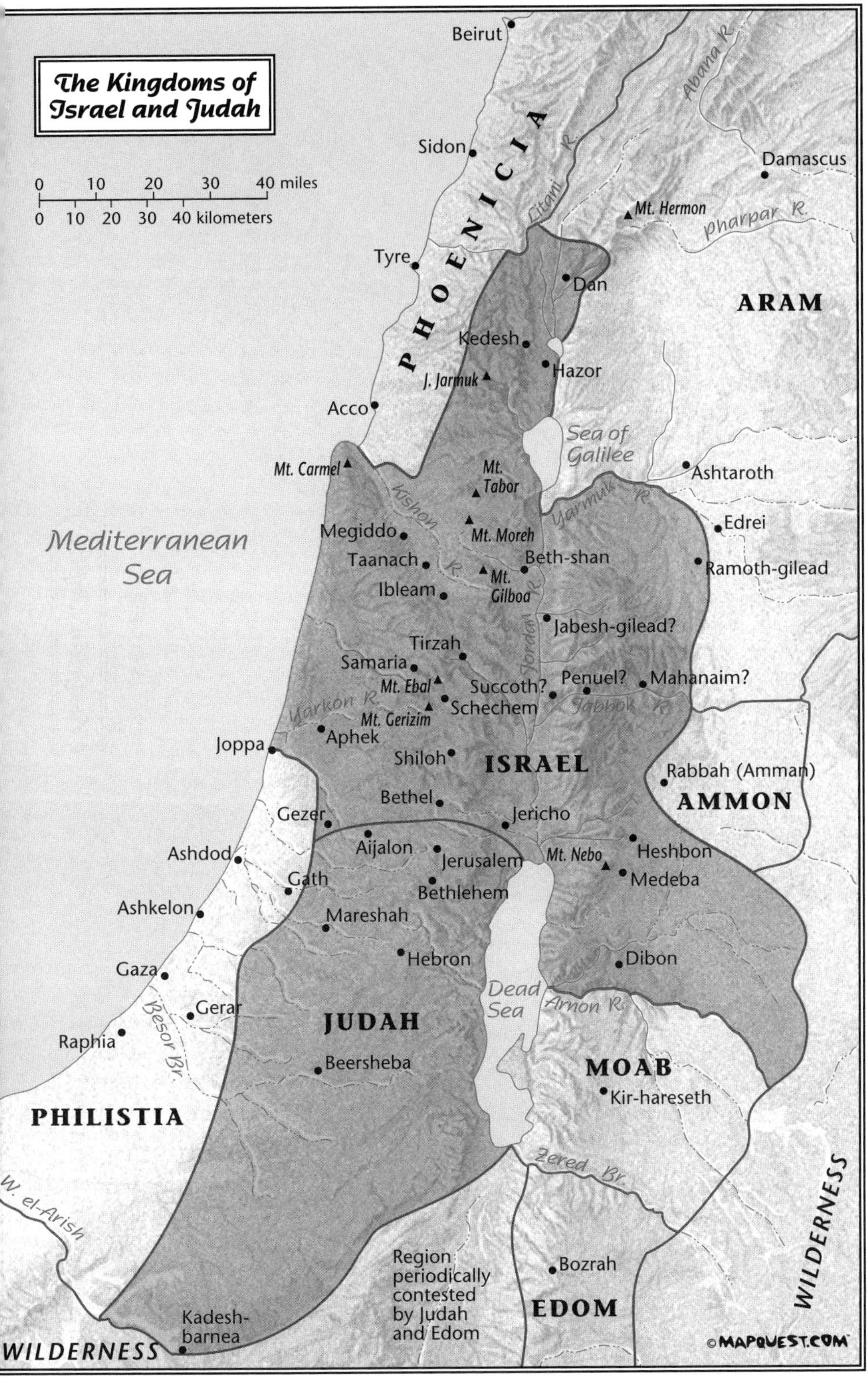

The Kingdoms of Israel and Judah
0 10 20 30 40 miles
0 10 20 30 40 kilometers
Beirut
Abana R.
Sidon
PHOENICIA
Litani R.
Damascus
Mt. Hermon
Pharpar R.
Tyre
Dan
ARAM
Kedesh
Hazor
J. Jarmuk
Acco
Sea of Galilee
Mt. Carmel
Mt. Tabor
Ashtaroth
Kishon R.
Yarmuk R.
Edrei
Mediterranean Sea
Megiddo
Mt. Moreh
Taanach
Beth-shan
Ramoth-gilead
Mt. Gilboa
Ibleam
Jordan R.
Jabesh-gilead?
Tirzah
Samaria
Mt. Ebal
Succoth?
Penuel?
Mahanaim?
Schechem
Jabbok R.
Yarkon R.
Mt. Gerizim
Aphek
Joppa
Shiloh
ISRAEL
Rabbah (Amman)
Bethel
AMMON
Gezer
Jericho
Aijalon
Heshbon
Ashdod
Jerusalem
Mt. Nebo
Medeba
Gath
Bethlehem
Ashkelon
Mareshah
Hebron
Dibon
Gaza
Dead Sea
Arnon R.
Gerar
Besor Br.
JUDAH
Raphia
Beersheba
MOAB
Kir-hareseth
PHILISTIA
Zered Br.
W. el-Arish
WILDERNESS
Region periodically contested by Judah and Edom
Bozrah
EDOM
Kadesh-barnea
WILDERNESS
©MAPQUEST.COM

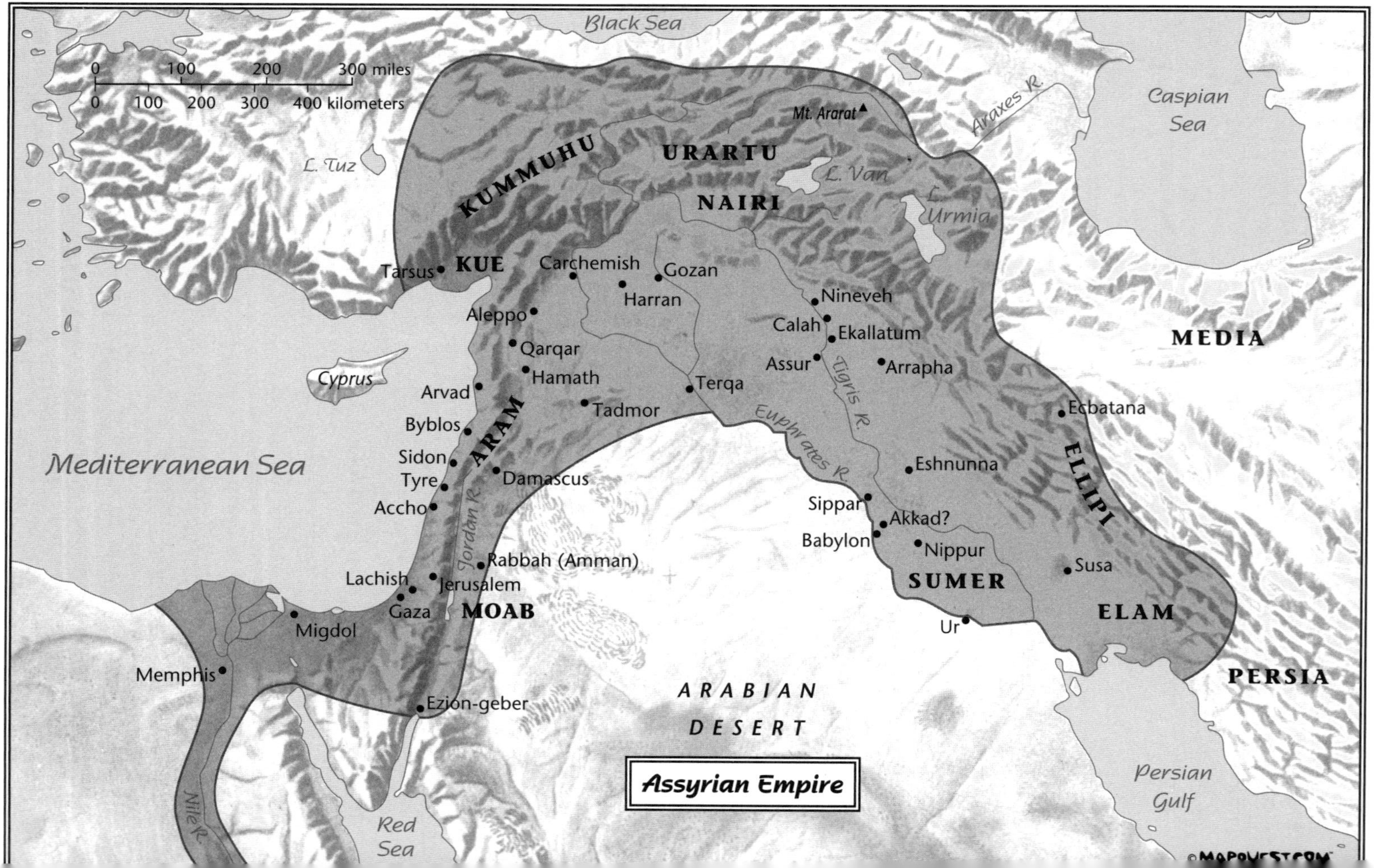
Assyrian Empire
Black Sea
Caspian Sea
Mediterranean Sea
Red Sea
Persian Gulf
0 100 200 300 miles
0 100 200 300 400 kilometers
L. Tuz
Cyprus
KUMMUHU
URARTU
NAIRI
KUE
ARAM
MOAB
MEDIA
ELLIPI
SUMER
ELAM
PERSIA
ARABIAN DESERT
Mt. Ararat
L. Van
L. Urmia
Araxes R.
Tigris R.
Euphrates R.
Jordan R.
Nile R.
Tarsus
Carchemish
Gozan
Harran
Aleppo
Qarqar
Hamath
Arvad
Tadmor
Byblos
Sidon
Tyre
Accho
Damascus
Rabbah (Amman)
Lachish
Jerusalem
Gaza
Migdol
Memphis
Ezion-geber
Terqa
Nineveh
Calah
Ekallatum
Assur
Arrapha
Ecbatana
Eshnunna
Sippar
Akkad?
Babylon
Nippur
Susa
Ur
©MAPQUEST.COM